The National Hockey League

Official Guide & Record Book

1990-91

Published by the National Hockey League.
Compiled by the NHL Communications Department
and the 21 NHL club Public Relations Directors.
Copyright © 1990 by the National Hockey League

THE NATIONAL HOCKEY LEAGUE
Official Guide & Record Book/1990-91

Copyright © 1990 by The National Hockey League. Compiled by the NHL Communications Department and the 21 NHL Club Public Relations Directors.

Printed in Canada. All rights reserved under the Pan-American and International Copyright Conventions.

Staff:
Senior editors: Stu Hackel, Gerry Helper, Gary Meagher; Statisticians: Benny Ercolani, Greg Inglis; Player Register Editor: Glenn Cole; Editorial Staff: Brian Albert, Michael Berger, Jordan Berman, Jane Freer, Suzanne Greenwald, Shannon Shay, Ed Sonkin, Mike Stein, Italo Zanzi.

Managing Editor: Ralph Dinger

Proofreader: Patty Curmi

European Editor: Tom Ratschunas

Contributors:
Bill Benswanger, Richard H. Bland, Hal Bock, Happy Charron, John Damon, Luca Del-Vita, Joe Dary, Greg Drinnan, Norm Dueck (WHL), Mike Emrick (NHLBA), Mel Foster, Jay M. Grossman, Pierre Hebert, Alan Jeddry, Cindy Kiernan, Sam Malkin, Carol McLaughlin, Kevin P. McMullen, Mike Meyers (IHL), Marc Nathan, Keith Perreault, Stephen Podonyi, Robert J. Reid, Renato Rossi, Hellen M. Schroeder (AHL), Howie Stalwick, Steven Steinsaltz, Mike Stojakovic, Robert A. Styer, Ed Sweeney, Pete Tingley, Patrick E. Tobin, David I. Young.

Consulting Publisher: Dan Diamond

Photo Credits:
Special thanks to the Hockey Hall of Fame and Museum, Toronto and to the New York Rangers.

Historical and special event photos: Bruce Bennett, David Bier, Rice Studio, Robert Shaver, Imperial Oil Turofsky Collection, Hockey Hall of Fame.

Current photos: Graig Abel, Toronto; Joe Angeles, St. Louis; Steve Babineau, Boston; Sol Benjamin, Chicago, Bruce Bennett, NY Islanders, Tony Biegun, Winnipeg, Denis Brodeur, Montreal; Mark Buckner, St. Louis; Denny Cavanaugh, Pittsburgh; Steve Crandall, New Jersey; Bill Cunningham, Vancouver; Willie Dagenais, Montreal; Bob Fisher, Montreal; Frank Howard, Minnesota; George Kalinsky, NY Rangers; Deborah King, Washington; Jim Mackey, Detroit; Doug MacLellan, Hockey Hall of Fame; Bill McKeown, Edmonton; Photography Ink, Los Angeles; Andre Pichette, Quebec; Richard Pilling, New Jersey; Photography, Minnesota; Wen Roberts, Los Angeles, Al Ruelle, Boston; Harry Scull, Jr., Buffalo; Diane Sobolewski, Hartford; Jim Turner, New Jersey; Brad Watson, Calgary; Westfile, Edmonton; Bill Wippert, Bufffalo.

Canadian representatives: Cannon Book Distribution Ltd., Toronto 416/252-5207

International representatives: Worldwide Media Services, Inc., 115 East Twenty-third Street, New York, NY 10010.

Typesetting: Q Composition Inc., Toronto
Printing: The Alger Press Limited, Oshawa and Toronto

9 8 7 6 5 4 3 2 1
Digit on the right indicates the number of this printing.

ISBN 0-920445-12-8

The National Hockey League
1155 Metcalfe Street, suite 960, Montreal, Quebec H3B 2W2
650 Fifth Avenue, 33rd floor, New York, New York 10019-6108
75 International Boulevard, suite 300, Toronto, Ontario M9W 6L9

Table of Contents

Table of Contents *continued*

 Introduction

New features for 1990-91

Welcome to the 1990-91 edition of the *NHL Official Guide & Record Book*. At 392 pages, this is the biggest-ever edition of hockey's best-selling statistical annual. The information in this book and the manner in which it is presented is now in its sixth decade of refinement, making the *NHL Official Guide & Record Book* the patriarch of regularly published sports books in North America.

Having a lengthy history is no substitute for the detailed work necessary to keep this book fresh and relevant each year. This is where the *NHL Guide* excels. Because it is issued to reporters, broadcasters, scouts and general managers throughout the League, this book is used by some of the most knowledgeable people in the game every day. Their comments are invaluable. As well, correspondence from readers like yourself has provided many valuable suggestions that have led to changes that improve the book.

New features in this edition include:

1. **Additional 1989-90 team statistics**: records when leading, trailing or tied; plus/minus differentials; records when scoring first goal; and five-year point totals (page 99).

2. **Assists added to scoring leaders from 1919 to 1926** (page 103).

3. **Full rosters and scores for early Stanley Cup challenges** including games played from 1893 to 1900 (page 188).

4. **Leading playoff scorers and overtime game lists** extended to cover the years 1918 to 1926 (page 203).

5. **The post-war dynasty teams** are examined in a detailed look at the NHL's modern-era powerhouses from 1947 Leafs to 1990 Oilers (page 190).

6. **More players and goaltenders** profiled in an expanded player register that now tops 2,000 skaters and includes more Soviets, Czechs and Scandinavians as well as North Americans playing in Europe.

Our thanks to those readers and members of the media who took the time to give us their comments. They are listed as contributors on page 2. As well, the efforts of the public relations directors of the NHL's 21 member clubs are vital in keeping the *NHL Official Guide & Record Book* accurate and up to date.

ACCURACY remains the *Guide & Record Book's* top priority. We appreciate comments and clarifications from our readers. Please direct these to editors Stu Hackel and Gerry Helper (33rd floor, 650 Fifth Ave., New York, N.Y. 10019-6108) or Gary Meagher (Suite 960, 1155 Metcalfe St., Montreal, Quebec H3B 2W2). Your involvement makes a better book.

Best wishes for an enjoyable NHL season in 1990-91.

National Hockey League

Organized November 22, 1917

Board of Governors

BOARD OF GOVERNORS — Officers
Chairman — William W. Wirtz
Vice-Chairman — Ronald Corey
Secretary — Robert O. Swados

Boston Bruins
(Boston Professional Hockey Association, Inc.)
Jeremy Jacobs — Governor
Harry Sinden — Alternate Governor
Louis Jacobs — Alternate Governor

Buffalo Sabres
(Niagara Frontier Limited Partnership)
Seymour H. Knox III — Governor
Robert O. Swados — Alternate Governor
Gerry Meehan — Alternate Governor
Seymour Knox IV — Alternate Governor

Calgary Flames
(Calgary Flames Hockey Club)
Cliff Fletcher — Governor
Harley Hotchkiss — Alternate Governor

Chicago Blackhawks
(Chicago Blackhawk Hockey Team, Inc.)
William W. Wirtz — Governor
Arthur M. Wirtz, Jr. — Alternate Governor
Thomas N. Ivan — Alternate Governor
Robert Pulford — Alternate Governor
W. Rockwell Wirtz — Alternate Governor

Detroit Red Wings
(Detroit Red Wings, Inc.)
Michael Ilitch — Governor
James Devellano — Alternate Governor
James Lites — Alternate Governor

Edmonton Oilers
(Edmonton Oilers Hockey, Limited)
Peter Pocklington — Governor
Glen Sather — Alternate Governor
Robert Lloyd — Alternate Governor

Hartford Whalers
(Hartford Whalers Hockey Club Limited Partnership)
Richard Gordon — Governor
Emile Francis — Alternate Governor
Don Conrad — Alternate Governor
Ben Sisti — Alternate Governor

Los Angeles Kings
(L.A. Kings, Ltd.)
Bruce McNall — Governor
Rogatien Vachon — Alternate Governor
Roy Mlakar — Alternate Governor

Minnesota North Stars
(Northstar Hockey Partnership)
Norman N. Green — Governor
Bob Clarke — Alternate Governor
Morris Belzberg — Alternate Governor
Lou Nanne — Alternate Governor
Howard Baldwin — Alternate Governor

Montreal Canadiens
(Le Club de Hockey Canadien, Inc.)
Ronald Corey — Governor
Ron Bowman — Alternate Governor
Serge Savard — Alternate Governor

New Jersey Devils
(Meadowlanders, Inc.)
John J. McMullen — Governor
Louis A. Lamoriello — Alternate Governor
Max McNab — Alternate Governor
John C. Whitehead — Alternate Governor

New York Islanders
(Nassau Sports)
John O. Pickett — Governor
William Torrey — Alternate Governor
William Skehan — Alternate Governor
John H. Krumpe — Alternate Governor

New York Rangers
(New York Rangers Hockey Club — a division of
Madison Square Garden Center, Inc.)
Richard Evans — Governor
Michael D. Walker — Alternate Governor
John Diller — Alternate Governor
Ken Munoz — Alternate Governor
Thomas A. Conway — Alternate Governor
Neil Smith — Alternate Governor

Philadelphia Flyers
(Philadelphia Flyers Limited Partnership)
Jay T. Snider — Governor
Edward M. Snider — Alternate Governor
Ronald Rutenberg — Alternate Governor
Ron Ryan — Alternate Governor
Russ Farwell — Alternate Governor

Pittsburgh Penguins
(Pittsburgh Penguins, Inc.)
Marie Denise DeBartolo York — Governor
Craig Patrick — Alternate Governor
J. Paul Martha — Alternate Governor

Quebec Nordiques
(Club de Hockey Les Nordiques de Québec)
Société en commandite)
Marcel Aubut — Governor
Maurice Filion — Alternate Governor
Gilles Leger — Alternate Governor

St. Louis Blues
(St. Louis Blues Hockey Club, L.P.)
Michael F. Shanahan — Governor
Jack Quinn — Alternate Governor
Ronald Caron — Alternate Governor

Toronto Maple Leafs
(Maple Leafs Gardens Limited)
Donald P. Giffin — Governor
Rosanne Rocchi — Alternate Governor
Floyd Smith — Alternate Governor

Vancouver Canucks
(Vancouver Hockey Club, Limited)
Arthur R. Griffiths — Governor
Pat Quinn — Alternate Governor
Frank A. Griffiths — Alternate Governor
Frank W. Griffiths — Alternate Governor

Washington Capitals
(Washington Hockey Limited Partnership)
Abe Pollin — Governor
Richard M. Patrick — Alternate Governor
David Poile — Alternate Governor

Winnipeg Jets
(8 Hockey Ventures, Inc.)
Barry L. Shenkarow — Governor
Bill Davis — Alternate Governor
Michael A. Smith — Alternate Governor

League Offices

MONTREAL
960 Sun Life Building,
1155 Metcalfe Street,
Montreal, Que. H3B 2W2
Phone: 514/871-9220
Executive TWX: 610-421-3260
Central Registry TWX: 610-421-3188

ENVOY ID	
Accounting	NHLMTL.ACTG
Auto-delivery station	NHLMTL.AUTO
Central Registry	BON
Computer Operations	NHLMTL.MIS
General	NHLMTL.GNRL
Public Relations	NHLMTL.PR

Telex via CCI NY 7601297
FAX 514/871-1663

NEW YORK
33rd Floor, 650 Fifth Avenue,
New York, N.Y., 10019-6108
Phone: 212/398-1100

ENVOY ID	
Accounting	NHLNY.ACTG
Auto-delivery station	NHLNY.AUTO
Broadcasting	NHLNY.TV
General	NHLNY.GNRL
Marketing	NHLNY.MKTG
Public Relations	NHLNY.PR

Telex via CCI NY 7601278
FAX 212/245-8221

TORONTO
75 International Blvd., Suite 300
Rexdale, Ont., M9W 6L9
Phone: 416/798-0809
TWX: 610-492-2703

ENVOY ID	
Auto-delivery station	NHLTOR.AUTO
Central Scouting	NHLTOR.SCTG
General	NHLTOR.GNRL
Jim Gregory	HOCKEY.OPERATIONS
Officiating	OFFICIATING.TOR

Telex via CCI NY 7601296
FAX 416/798-0819

OFFICERS
President — John A. Ziegler, Jr.
Executive Vice-President — Brian F. O'Neill
Vice-President/General Counsel — Gilbert Stein
Vice-President of Finance and Treasurer — Kenneth G. Sawyer
Vice-President, Hockey Operations — Jim Gregory
Vice-President, NHL Project Development — Ian Morrison
Vice-President, Broadcasting — Joel Nixon
Vice-President, Marketing/Public Relations — Steve Ryan

League Departments

MONTREAL
Administration
Brian O'Neill — Executive Vice President
Madeleine Supino — Secretary
Phil Scheuer — Director of Administration
Michael Humes — Assistant Director of Administration
Nancy Starnino — Secretary
Robert Bouchard — Administrative Assistant
Central Registry
Garry Lovegrove — Director of Central Registry
Madeleine Supino — Assistant Director
Audrey Harari — Assistant
Communications
Gary Meagher — Executive Director of Communications
Benny Ercolani — Associate Director of Information/
Statistician
Jane Freer — Assistant Director of Information
Greg Inglis — Assistant Director of Information
Computer Operations
Mario Carangi — Director of Management Information
Systems
Miranda Ishak — Assistant Director — MIS
Luc Coulombe — Project Leader
Sharon Jardine — Programmer
Johanne Hinds — Operations

Finance
Kenneth G. Sawyer — Vice-President of Finance and
   Treasurer
Donald P. Grinton — Director of Accounting
Joseph DeSousa — Controller
Mary Skiadopoulos — Assistant Controller
Steve Hatzepetros — Manager, Finance
Lynne Blagrave — Manager, Pension Administration
Donna Gillman — Accountant
Doris Long — Secretary
Vivianne Chen — Secretary
Jocelyne Comeau — Accounting Clerk
Vicki Sciortino — Accountant

Office Services
Jean Huard — Printer
Darrin Burke — Office Assistant
Marcia Golding — Receptionist

NEW YORK

Broadcasting
Joel Nixon — Vice-President, Broadcasting
Stu Hackel — Director of Broadcasting
Suzanne Greenwald — Project Coordinator
Lois Cutler — Administrative Assistant

Finance
Patricia Cassell-Cooper — Controller
Evelyn Torres — Accounts Payable
Ivonne Merchant — Secretary

Legal Department
Gilbert Stein — Vice-President/General Counsel
Pat Honig — Assistant

Marketing and Communications
Steve Ryan — Vice-President, Marketing and Public Relations
Lucia Ripi — Secretary
Steve Flatow — Director of Marketing/General Manager,
   Promotional Licensing Division
Kathleen Dober — Secretary
Maureen Brady — Director, Events & Services Division
Maria Pace — Manager, Client and Team Services
Fred Scalera — General Manager, Retail Licensing Division
Ann Kiely — Secretary
Stu Hackel — General Manager, Publishing & Video Division
Gerry Helper — Director of Public Relations
Michael A. Berger — Editor, Goal Magazine
Karen Hovsepian — Manager of Special Events
Krista Lizzi — Special Events Coordinator
Karen Lechner — Executive Director, On-Site Management,
   NHL All-Star Weekend 312/201-1055

Office Administration
Janet Meyers — Office Services Manager
Lola Skaro — Receptionist
Scott Shanes — Administrative Assistant

President's Staff
Susan Rudin — Assistant to the President
Joanne Blute — Administrative Assistant

Security
Frank Torpey — Director of Security

TORONTO

Jim Gregory — Vice-President of Hockey Operations
Bryan Lewis — Director of Officiating
Wally Harris — Assistant Director of Officiating
Will Norris — Coordinator of Development
Dave Newell — Officiating Coach
Frank Bonello — Director of Central Scouting
John Andersen — Central Scouting Administration
Al Wiseman — Assistant Director of Security

Secretarial Staff
Dorothy Reaves, Mary Keenan, Kelley Bright

Officiating Supervisory Staff
John Ashley, Matt Pavelich, Lou Maschio, Jim Christison,
John D'Amico, Bob Nadin, Sam Sisco

Central Scouting Staff
Mike Abbamont, Jack Birch, Mike Donaldson, Gary
Eggleston, Laurence Ferguson, Paul Goulet, Ron Harris,
Tom Martin, Kevin Penny, David Prior, Richard Rose, Jack
Timmins, Barry Trapp

Hockey Hall of Fame
Exhibition Place
Toronto, Ont. M6K 3C3
Phone: 416/595-1345
FAX 416/971-5828
Ian Morrison — President
Esther Richards — Executive Secretary
Jeff Denomme — Director of Administration
Ray Paquet — Exhibit Coordinator
Philip Pritchard — Marketing Services Manager
Joseph Romain — Librarian/Associate Curator
James Duplacey — Associate Curator
M.H. (Lefty) Reid — Historical Consultant
Marilyn Robbins — Receptionist
Raymond Bruce — Security Coordinator

National Hockey League
Players' Association
37 Maitland St.
Toronto, Ont. M4Y 1C8
Phone: 416/924-7800
FAX 416/924-3004
Envoy ID NHLPA.TOR
Alan Eagleson — Executive Director
Bob Goodenow — Deputy Executive Director
Sam Simpson — Director of Operations

Referees and Linesmen

RON ASSELSTINE . . . Linesman . . . Born: Nov. 6, 1946 in Toronto, Ont. . . . First NHL Game: Oct. 10, 1979 . . . Total NHL Games: 884 . . . In 1989, was selected to work in three NHL-Soviet Super Series games and the 40th NHL All-Star Game in Edmonton. Ron is very active in his community as chairman of the "Make-A-Wish" Foundation and as an Ontario Provincial Police "Auxiliary" Officer. He is married and has two children.

WAYNE BONNEY . . . Linesman . . . Born: May 27, 1953 in Ottawa, Ont. . . . First NHL Game: Oct. 10, 1979 . . . Total NHL Games: 842 . . . Joined the NHL in 1979. In 1988-89, Bonney was selected to work in the 40th NHL All-Star Game in Edmonton. He currently resides in Kirkland, Que., with his wife and daughter and is an avid baseball player.

RYAN BOZAK . . . Linesman . . . Born: Jan. 3, 1947 in Swift Current, Sask. . . . First NHL Game: 1972 . . . Total NHL Games: 1,321 . . . Joined the NHL in 1972 and worked his 1,300th NHL game in 1989-90. He was selected to officiate in the 1983 NHL All-Star Game on Long Island. During the off-season he enjoys golf and tennis and resides in San Diego, CA. Bozak has two children.

GORD BROSEKER . . . Linesman . . . Born: July 8, 1950 in Baltimore, MD . . . First NHL Game: Jan 14, 1975 . . . Total NHL Games: 1,137 . . . Joined the NHL in 1973 and officiated in his 1,100th NHL game in 1989-90. Before beginning his officiating career, he played baseball in the Texas Rangers' organization. Broseker was selected to officiate in the 1986 NHL All-Star Game in Hartford. He currently resides in Richmond, VA, with his wife and daughter.

KEVIN COLLINS . . . Linesman . . . Born: Dec. 15,1950 in Springfield, MA . . . First NHL Game: Oct. 13, 1977 . . . Total NHL Games: 1,051 . . . Joined the NHL in 1971. He was selected to officiate in the 1988 NHL All-Star Game in St. Louis and officiated in his 1,000th NHL game in 1989-90. Currently residing in Springfield, MA, Collins is married and has three children.

PIERRE CHAMPOUX . . . Linesman . . . Born: Apr. 18, 1963 in Ville St. Pierre, Que. . . . First NHL Game: Oct. 8, 1988 . . . Total NHL Games: 91 . . . Began officiating minor league games at the age of 12 in the Quebec pee wee league. Since then he has worked in two international competitions, having officiated in an exhibition game between the United States and Canada at the Forum and in Canada Cup 1987. During the off-season, Champoux is a part-time firefighter in Ville St. Pierre, Quebec and enjoys playing golf, softball and volleyball. Champoux is single.

MICHAEL CVIK . . . Linesman . . . Born: July 6, 1962 in Calgary, Alta. . . . First NHL Game: Oct. 8, 1987 . . . Total NHL Games: 208 . . . The tallest of the officials at 6'9", began his officiating career in the AAHA in 1978. After working his way through the WHL, he joined the NHL in 1987. During the off-season, Mike participates in the Annual Child Find Bike Ride for Child Find Alberta. He is an avid cyclist and enjoys reading and golf. He is single.

PAT DAPUZZO . . . Linesman . . . Born: Dec. 29, 1958 in Hoboken, NJ . . . First NHL Game: Dec. 5, 1984 . . . Total NHL Games: 420 . . . Officiated in his first NHL game on Dec. 5, 1984, in Madison Square Garden. In 1989, he was selected to officiate in the 88-89 Super Series when the New Jersey Devils faced the Central Red Army on January 2. Pat resides in Bergen, NJ and is single. He is an avid weightlifter and karate enthusiast.

PAUL DEVORSKI . . . Referee . . . Born: Aug. 18, 1958 in Guelph, Ont. . . . Joined the NHL in 1987. In 1989-90 he worked 23 NHL games. Devorski is a part owner of Gold's Gym in Guelph and plays fastball. He is married.

MARK FAUCETTE . . . Referee . . . Born: June 9, 1958 in Springfield, MA . . . First NHL Game: 1985 . . . Total NHL Games: 62 . . . Joined the NHL in 1985. He resided in Agawam, MA. During the off-season, he organizes softball tournaments to raise funds for Boston Children Hospital's "Jimmy Fund". He is married.

RON FINN . . . Linesman . . . Born: Dec. 1, 1940 in Toronto, Ont. . . . First NHL Game: October 11, 1969 . . . Total NHL Games: 1,634 . . . Has worked in more games than any other active official. . . . A resident of Brampton, Ont. He has worked in two All-Star Games including 1977 (Vancouver) and 1982 (Washington, D.C.). He also worked during Rendez-Vous '87 in Quebec City. Finn was selected to work in the Stanley Cup Finals for the 12th consecutive year in 1989-90, bringing his career total to 33 games (seventh on the all-time list). He is active in his community during the off-season, working with the Canadian Special Olympics and is an instructor at various officiating schools in Ontario and New Brunswick. Ron is married and has four children.

KERRY FRASER . . . Referee . . . Born: June 30, 1952 in Sarnia, Ont. . . . Total NHL Games: 607 . . . After playing minor league hockey as a youngster, attended the NHL training camp for officials in 1972. Fraser has become one of the League's most experienced and respected referees, as proven by his selection to referee four Stanley Cup Final series (1985, 1986 and 1989). He worked the 1990 All-Star Game in Pittsburgh. During the off-season, Fraser instructs at the WHL School of Officiating in Calgary and represents drug awareness programs with the RCMP and local police agencies. He is Co-Chairman of a celebrity dinner benefitting the Children's Center and also a golf tournament to aid the Cancer Society. Fraser enjoys sailing and golf. He is married and has six children.

GERARD GAUTHIER . . . Linesman . . . Born: Sept. 5, 1948 in Montreal, Que. . . . First NHL Game: Oct. 16, 1971 . . . Total NHL Games: 1,456 . . . Attended his first NHL training camp in 1971 after two years in junior hockey. He has been selected to work at two NHL All-Star Games in his career; Los Angeles (1981) and Calgary (1985). In addition, he worked in the 1984 Canada Cup. Gauthier has worked in two Stanley Cup Final series in 1982 and 1983. During the off-season, Gauthier enjoys golfing and tennis. He is married and has two children.

TERRY GREGSON . . . Referee . . . Born: Nov. 7 1953 in Guelph, Ont. . . . First NHL Game: Dec. 19, 1981 . . . Total NHL Games: 485 . . . Joined the NHL in 1979. In 1988, Gregson was selected to officiate at the NHL All-Star Game in St. Louis as well as the Boston vs. Central Red Army Game in Super Series '88-89. Gregson is a Co-Chairman of the Officials' "Make A Wish" Foundation and is an avid traveller and photographer. Gregson is married.

SHANE HEYER . . . Referee . . . Born: Feb. 7,1964 in Summerland, B.C. . . . First NHL Game: Oct. 5, 1988 . . . Total NHL Games: 157 . . . Began officiating in Penticton, B.C., at the age of 10 and was invited to join the NHL program in 1988. In his first year of service, Heyer was selected to work in the December 31 game between the Los Angeles Kings and the Dynamo Riga club during Super Series '88-89. Heyer is single.

BOB HODGES . . . Linesman . . . Born: Aug. 16, 1944 in Galt, Ont. . . . First NHL Game: Oct. 14, 1972 . . . Total NHL Games: 1,371 . . . Hired by the NHL in 1972-73 season at the age of 28, Hodges is one of the NHL's senior officials. He has been chosen to work in the Stanley Cup Finals three times (1982, 1986 and 1987) and officiated at the All-Star Game in Calgary (1985) and Pittsburgh (1990). During the off-season he works with the Royal Canadian Legion and enjoys hunting, fishing and baseball. Hodges is married and has two children.

RON HOGGARTH . . . Referee . . . Born: Apr. 12, 1948 in Barrie, Ont. . . . First NHL Game: Oct. 16, 1971 . . . Total NHL Games: 898 . . . Began officiating while still a student at McMaster University. He joined the NHL in 1971. In addition to officiating in several Soviet-NHL matches, Hoggarth was selected to referee the 1989 NHL All-Star Game in Edmonton. During the summer, Hoggarth owns and operates KoHo pools in Barrie and is active in golf and tennis. He is married and has two daughters.

DAVE JACKSON . . . Referee . . . Born: Nov. 28, 1964 in Montreal, Que. . . . One of two officials to join the NHL in 1989. He became an NHL trainee at the age of 21 after having attended Ron Fournier's Referee School. In 1989-90 he worked in the AHL. During the off-season, he works in lawn equipment sales. He is active in softball tournaments and is an avid golfer.

Referees and Linesmen continued

SWEDE KNOX . . . Linesman . . . Born: Mar. 2, 1948 in Edmonton, Alta. . . . First NHL Game: Oct. 14, 1972 . . . Total NHL Games: 1,418 . . . Joined the NHL in 1971. In 1982, he was selected to work in the NHL All-Star Game in Washington, D.C. He has been selected to officiate in the Stanley Cup Finals for the last three years. A full-time resident of Edmonton, Swede is married and has two children. He enjoys carpentry during the off-season.

DENNIS LARUE . . . Referee . . . Born: July 14, 1959 in Savannah, GA . . . Attended the USA Hockey Referee Development Camp in 1983 and joined the NHL in 1988. Last season, LaRue worked in the AHL. During the off-season he is involved in summer camp programs for children and in the Referee Development Program. He is an avid water-skiier and golfer. Dennis is married and has two children.

BRAD LAZAROWICH . . . Linesman . . . Born: Aug. 4, 1962 in Vancouver, B.C. . . . First NHL Game: Oct. 9, 1986 . . . Total NHL Games: 315 . . . Joined the NHL in 1986. In 1988, he was chosen to officiate in Super Series '88-89 (Dynamo Riga vs. Vancouver). During the off-season, Brad is employed by the Delta Corporation in the Water Works division and is an avid bicyclist, golfer and weightlifter. He is married and has a daughter.

DON KOHARSKI . . . Referee . . . Born: Dec. 2, 1955 in Halifax, N.S. . . . First NHL Game: Oct. 14, 1977 . . . Total NHL Games: 608 (163 as a linesman) . . . Hired as an official in the WHA at the age of 18. He joined the NHL in 1977 as a linesman, becoming a referee after 163 games. Koharski gained international experience in Canada Cup 1987 and has worked in four Stanley Cup Finals (1986, 1987, 1988 and 1990). During the off-season, Koharski is active in the Make-A-Wish Foundation of Burlington, Ont. He is married and has two sons.

DAN MAROUELLI . . . Referee . . . Born: July 16, 1955 in Edmonton, Alta. . . . First NHL Game: Nov. 2, 1984 . . . Total NHL Games: 338 . . . Began his officiating career at the age of 13 with the Knights of Columbus. He joined the NHL in 1982. He was selected to officiate the game between Dynamo Riga and Chicago during Super Series '88-89. During the summer, Marouelli works at a number of refereeing schools and owns a small construction business. He is an avid golfer. Dan is married and has three children.

BILL McCREARY . . . Referee . . . Born: Nov. 17, 1955 in Guelph, Ont. . . . First NHL Game: Nov. 3, 1984 . . . Total NHL Games: 350 . . . Joined the NHL in 1982. He was selected to referee the Red Army vs. Buffalo Sabres game on January 9 in Super Series '88-89. During the off-season, McCreary is active in golf tournaments and coaching baseball. He also enjoys hunting and fishing. He is married and has two sons and a daughter.

DAN McCOURT . . . Linesman . . . Born: Aug. 14, 1954 . . . First NHL Game: Dec. 27, 1980 . . . Total NHL Games: 666 . . . Joined the NHL in 1979. . . . Worked the 1990 All-Star game in Pittsburgh. During the off-season, he instructs at various officiating schools and is involved with local charities. He enjoys golf, baseball and raquetball. McCourt is married.

MIKE McGEOUGH . . . Referee . . . Born: June 20, 1957 in Regina, Sask. . . . Total NHL Games: 31 . . . Began his NHL career in 1987. During the off-season, McGeough enjoys golf and bicycling. He instructs at various refereeing schools. He is married and has three children.

RANDY MITTON . . . Linesman . . . Born: Sept. 22, 1950 in Fredericton, N.B. . . . First NHL Game: Dec. 26, 1973 . . . Total NHL Games: 1,217 . . . Became involved in NHL officiating in 1972 after working in the WHL and AHL for two years. He gained international experience as a linesman for the 1987 Canada Cup and was selected to officiate in the 1988 NHL All-Star Game in St. Louis. During the off-season, Mitton is active with the Elks Club and teaches at a number of officiating schools in Western Canada. He is married and has two children.

DENIS MOREL . . . Referee . . . Born: Dec. 13, 1948 in Quebec City, Que. . . . First NHL Game: Jan. 18, 1976 . . . Total NHL Games: 867 . . . Began officiating in Quebec minor leagues before joining the NHL in 1976. He was selected to be the standby referee at the 1983 NHL All-Star Game in Washington D.C. and the 1988 All-Star Game in St. Louis. Morel has also been an official in the Stanley Cup Finals (1988 and 1989). During the summer, he is active in the Trois-Rivieres Special Olympics Program and is an instructor at two hockey schools in the area. He enjoys swimming and golf and is an avid reader. He is married and has two children.

BRIAN MURPHY . . . Linesman . . . Born: Dec. 13, 1964 in Dover, NH . . . First NHL Game: Oct. 7, 1988 . . . Total NHL Games: 97 . . . The youngest NHL official. Joined the League in 1988-89 after graduating from the University of New Hampshire with a degree in Business Administration. During his years at University, he worked in the NCAA officiating ranks, including the 1988 NCAA Division I National Championship Game in Lake Placid. During the off-season, Murphy works as a part-time accountant and is an instructor at AHAUS Officiating Development Camps.

DAVE NEWELL . . . Officiating Coach . . . Born: Feb. 25, 1945 in Sudbury, Ont. . . . First NHL Game: Mar. 5, 1968 Total NHL Games: 1,172 . . . Joined the NHL in 1967 and worked 23 NHL seasons. Will work as an officiating coach in 1990-91. He was selected to officiate in the 1980 NHL All-Star Game in Detroit as well as Rendez-Vous '87 in Quebec City. He has served as president of the Officials' Association for nine years. During the off-season, he enjoys fishing, hunting and golf and is active in many local charities. Newell is married and has three children.

MARK PARE . . . Linesman . . . Born: July 26, 1957 in Windsor, Ont. . . . First NHL Game: Oct. 11, 1979 . . . Total NHL Games: 868 . . . Joined the NHL in 1979 after working minor leagues in Windsor. During the off-season, he is a salesman for a food products company. He enjoys golfing. Pare is married and has two children.

JERRY PATEMAN . . . Linesman . . . Born: Jan. 12, 1958 in The Hague, Netherlands . . . First NHL Game: Nov. 10, 1982 . . . Total NHL Games: 284 . . . The only NHL official not born in North America, Pateman started refereeing minor hockey in Chatham, Ont. at the age of 14. He joined the NHL in 1982. During the summer, Pateman works part-time at a food products company and instructs at officiating schools in the area. Pateman now resides in Tecumseh, Ont. with his wife and two children.

LANCE ROBERTS . . . Referee . . . Born: May 28, 1957 in Edmonton, Alta. . . . Joined the NHL in 1987, working eight games in 1989-90 . . . Began his career at the age of 15 in the minor leagues of Alberta. Roberts instructs at the AAHA Development Camp during the summer as well as playing golf and reading. He is married and has two daughters.

RAY SCAPINELLO . . . Linesman . . . Born: Nov. 5, 1946 in Guelph, Ont. . . . First NHL Game in 1971 in Buffalo . . . Total NHL Games: 1,539. . . . Joined NHL in 1971 . . . Has worked three All-Star Games, nine consecutive Stanley Cup Finals plus the Canada Cup, Challenge Cup and Rendez-Vous 87 . . . In the off-season, Ray is a two-handicap golfter and works with the "Make-A-Wish" chapter in Guelph . . . He is married and has a son.

DAN SCHACHTE . . . Linesman . . . Born: July 13, 1958 in Madison, WI . . . First NHL Game: October 8, 1982 . . . Total NHL Games: 535 . . . Joined the NHL in 1982. He was chosen to officiate in Super Series '88-89 in the Dynamo Riga vs. Chicago game. During the off-season, Schachte owns and operates a construction business in Madison, WI where he lives with his wife and son. He enjoys hunting, fishing and boating.

JAY SHARRERS . . . Linesman . . . Born: July 3, 1967 in New Westminster, B.C. . . . New to NHL staff in 1990 . . . Worked WHL and BCJHL games in 1989-90 . . . Has also worked Canadian college games and, in 1985-86, a tournament involving college teams from the U.S., Canada and Japan . . . Enjoys weightlifting, cycling, baseball and golf.

ROB SHICK . . . Referee . . . Born: Dec. 4, 1957, in Port Alberni, B.C. . . . First NHL Game: Apr. 6, 1986 . . . Total NHL Games: 175 . . . Joined the NHL in 1985. He is married. During the off-season, he is an avid fastball player and runs a landscaping business in Lethbridge, Alta.

PAUL STEWART . . . Referee . . . Born: Mar. 21, 1955 in Boston, MA . . . First NHL Game: Mar. 27, 1987 . . . Total NHL Games: 171 . . . Joined the NHL in 1986. Shortly after joining the League, he was asked to officiate in the 1987 Canada Cup. Stewart joins Joh Ashley as the only ex-NHL players to become NHL officials. During the off-season, Stewart continues his graduate studies at Northeastern University and is employed in estate planning. He enjoys landscaping, gardening and golf.

LEON STICKLE . . . Linesman . . . Born: Apr. 20, 1948 in Toronto, Ont. . . . First NHL Game: Oct. 17, 1970 . . . Total NHL Games: 1,533 . . . Joined the NHL in 1969 after four years in the minor leagues. In his career, he has worked in three NHL All-Star Games (Montreal, 1975; Buffalo, 1978 and Long Island, 1983). He also was selected as an official for the Canada Cup tournament in 1981 and 1984. He has worked in the Stanley Cup Finals six times (1977, 1978, 1980, 1981, 1984 and 1985). During the off-season, Stickle is active with the Ontario and Canadian Special Olympics and coaches minor league baseball. He also enjoys golf. He is married and has three children.

RICHARD TROTTIER . . . Referee . . . Born: Feb. 28, 1957 in Laval, Que. . . . One of two new officials to join the NHL in 1989. He worked in the AHL last season as well as working five NHL games. During his career, he has served as the executive vice-president for the Quebec Esso Cup in 1987-88 and 1988-89 and has been the referee-in-chief for the Quebec Ice Hockey Federation since 1986. During the off-season, he instructs at Ron Fournier's Officiating School and is an avid golfer and raquetball player.

ANDY vanHELLEMOND . . . Referee . . . Born: Feb. 16, 1948 in Winnipeg, Man. . . . First NHL Game: Nov. 22, 1972 . . . Total NHL Games: 1,131 . . . Joined the NHL in 1971 and has become one of the senior NHL officials. He worked in the NHL All-Star contest in Calgary (1985) and Rendez-Vous '87 in Quebec City. He has been selected to work in the Stanley Cup Final series 14 consecutive years since 1977. During the off-season, vanHellemond enjoys golfing, gardening and baseball.

MARK VINES . . . Linesman . . . Born: Dec. 3, 1960 in Elmira, Ont. . . . First NHL Game: Oct. 13, 1984 . . . Total NHL Games: 488 . . . Joined the NHL in 1984. He attends university during the off-season and is single.

STEPHEN WALKOM . . . Referee . . . Born: Aug. 8, 1963 in North Bay, Ontario. . . . NHL officiating trainee in 1989-90, working OHL and minor pro games . . . Has also worked Canadian college, Northern OHA, senior and junior B . . . Honors degree in Commerce from Laurentian U . . . Lives in Kitchener, Ont. . . . Enjoys running, cycling, racquet sports . . . Power-skating instructor.

League Presidents

Top: The NHL's first president, Frank Calder, at left, presents the Calder trophy to Boston goaltender Frank Brimsek as the outstanding rookie of 1938-39. Middle: Mervyn "Red" Dutton, president from 1943-46, at right, congratulates Clarence S. Campbell who served as NHL president from 1946 to 1977. Bottom: John A. Ziegler, Jr., president from 1977 to date.

Frank Calder
President, 1917-1943

After an illustrious tenure as secretary of the National Hockey Association, Frank Calder was elected as the first president of the National Hockey League when the League was formed in 1917. He served in this capacity until his death on February 4, 1943.

Born in England in 1877, Calder came to Canada at the turn of the century as a school teacher, but turned to sports writing in 1909. His forthright writing style won him the attention and respect of Montreal Canadiens' owner George Kennedy whose support helped Calder to the position of NHL president.

For nearly 26 years, Calder worked hard to change the League from a small-time circuit to a grand international sports organization. Among his many achievements, Calder guided the NHL through its first expansion into the U.S., including the addition of the Boston Bruins in 1924 and the Chicago Blackhawks, Detroit Cougars and New York Rangers in 1926.

To commemorate his years of service, the League established the Calder Memorial Trophy to honor the rookie of the year at the conclusion of each season. Additionally, Calder was elected to the Hockey Hall of Fame in 1945 as one of its first inductees.

Mervyn "Red" Dutton
President, 1943-46

Born on July 23, 1898 in Russell, Manitoba, Mervyn "Red" Dutton succeeded Frank Calder as the second president of the NHL. For two seasons, 1943-44 and 1944-45, Dutton remained at the head of the League before resuming his career in private business. Most remembered for his rugged playing style, Dutton overcame severe war injuries to skate as a professional for over a decade. After anchoring the defense for Calgary in the Western Hockey League from 1921 to 1925, Dutton signed with the NHL's Montreal Maroons. He stayed with the Maroons through 1930 when he joined the New York Americans. In 1936, he took over coaching and managing that club and remained there until 1942 when the team disbanded.

Upon Frank Calder's death in 1943, Dutton became president of the NHL, a position he maintained until Clarence Campbell assumed the role in 1946. Dutton was elected to the Hockey Hall of Fame in 1958.

Clarence Campbell
President, 1946-77

Clarence Campbell was a Rhodes Scholar who was born July 9, 1905 in Fleming, Saskatchewan. In 1926, a 20-year-old Campbell graduated from the University of Alberta with bachelor of arts and bachelor of law degrees.

Following his studies at Oxford, England, Campbell returned to Canada to begin his law practice. Forever active in sports, he also became an NHL referee, working 155 regular-season games and twelve Stanley Cup playoff contests through 1939 when he joined the Canadian Armed Forces for the duration of World War II.

On September 5, 1946, Campbell became the NHL's third president succeeding Mervyn "Red" Dutton. Within a year of his appointment, he established the NHL Players' Pension Plan which has since become the prototype for other professional sports leagues.

Campbell led the League through its greatest era of expansion in 1967 when the NHL doubled in size from six to twelve teams. In 1972, he also succeeded in breaking ground in a new era of international competition, when, for the first time in hockey history, Canada's finest NHL talent faced-off against the Soviet Union's elite in an eight-game challenge series.

Elected to the Hockey Hall of Fame in 1966, Campbell also received the Lester Patrick Trophy for "outstanding service to hockey in the United States" in 1972. He retired from the NHL in 1977, but continued to stay close to the League until his death in 1984.

John A. Ziegler, Jr.
President, 1977 to date

John A. Ziegler, Jr., President and Chief Executive Officer of the National Hockey League, was born in Grosse Pointe, Michigan, on February 9, 1934.

He graduated from the University of Michigan in 1957, earning a bachelor of arts and *juris* doctor degrees. Upon graduation he joined the Detroit law firm of Dickinson, Wright, McKean and Cudlip and became a partner in the firm in 1964. In 1969 he left the firm and in September of 1970 he set up his own firm, Ziegler, Dykhouse & Wise. He continued as senior partner in the firm until assuming his present position in September, 1977.

In 1959 he began to do legal work for Olympia Stadium, the Detroit Red Wings and Mr. Bruce Norris. He continued to serve these clients in various capacities until his election as president of the National Hockey League. In 1966 he joined the NHL Board of Governors as an alternate governor for the Detroit Red Wings and, as such, worked on many of the NHL's committees and was involved in various aspects of the League's litigation as well as relations and negotiations with the Players' Association.

In June of 1976, he succeeded William Wirtz as Chairman of the National Hockey League Board of Governors. He was inducted into the Hockey Hall of Fame as a Builder in June, 1987.

An ardent sports fan, Ziegler played amateur hockey in the Detroit area from 1949 to 1969. He has continued to make his home in the Detroit area (Ortonville, Michigan) while maintaining offices in Montreal and New York.

Edmonton's Esa Tikkanen was a 1990 finalist for the Frank Selke Trophy awarded to the NHL's top defensive forward.

NHL Attendance

| Season | Regular Season | | Playoffs | | Total |
	Games	Attendance	Games	Attendance	Attendance
1960-61	210	2,317,142	17	242,000	2,559,142
1961-62	210	2,435,424	18	277,000	2,712,424
1962-63	210	2,590,574	16	220,906	2,811,480
1963-64	210	2,732,642	21	309,149	3,041,791
1964-65	210	2,822,635	20	303,859	3,126,494
1965-66	210	2,941,164	16	249,000	3,190,184
1966-67	210	3,084,759	16	248,336	3,333,095
1967-68[1]	444	4,938,043	40	495,089	5,433,132
1968-69	456	5,550,613	33	431,739	5,982,352
1969-70	456	5,992,065	34	461,694	6,453,759
1970-71[2]	546	7,257,677	43	707,633	7,965,310
1971-72	546	7,609,368	36	582,666	8,192,034
1972-73[3]	624	8,575,651	38	624,637	9,200,288
1973-74	624	8,640,978	38	600,442	9,241,420
1974-75[4]	720	9,521,536	51	784,181	10,305,717
1975-76	720	9,103,761	48	726,279	9,830,040
1976-77	720	8,563,890	44	646,279	9,210,169
1977-78	720	8,526,564	45	686,634	9,213,198
1978-79	680	7,758,053	45	694,521	8,452,574
1979-80[5]	840	10,533,623	63	976,699	11,510,322
1980-81	840	10,726,198	68	966,390	11,692,588
1981-82	840	10,710,894	71	1,058,948	11,769,842
1982-83	840	11,020,610	66	1,088,222	12,028,832
1983-84	840	11,359,386	70	1,107,400	12,466,786
1984-85	840	11,633,730	70	1,107,500	12,741,230
1985-86	840	11,621,000	72	1,152,503	12,773,503
1986-87	840	11,855,880	87	1,383,967	13,239,847
1987-88	840	12,117,512	83	1,336,901	13,454,413
1988-89	840	12,417,969	83	1,327,214	13,745,183
1989-90	840	12,579,651	85	1,355,593	13,935,244

[1] First expansion: Los Angeles, Pittsburgh, California, Philadelphia, St. Louis and Minnesota
[2] Second expansion: Buffalo and Vancouver
[3] Third expansion: Atlanta and New York Islanders
[4] Fourth expansion: Kansas City (Colorado, New Jersey) and Washington
[5] Fifth expansion: Edmonton, Hartford, Quebec and Winnipeg

Boston's Don Sweeney tries to move Rick Vaive of the Sabres from in front of the Bruins' net. Vaive became the NHL's 29th 400-goal scorer on December 22, 1989.

Boston Bruins

1989-90 Results: 46w-25l-9t 101pts. First, Adams Division

Craig Janney registered 62 points in 55 games for Boston in 1989-90.

Schedule

Home		Away	
Oct. Thur. 4 Philadelphia		**Oct.** Sun. 7 Quebec	
Sat. 6 Quebec		Wed. 10 Winnipeg	
Thur. 25 Vancouver		Thur. 11 Minnesota	
Sat. 27 Chicago		Sat. 13 Los Angeles	
Nov. Thur. 1 St Louis		Wed. 17 Vancouver	
Sat. 3 Buffalo		Fri. 19 Edmonton	
Sat. 10 Pittsburgh		Sat. 20 Calgary	
Thur. 15 Quebec		Wed. 31 Buffalo	
Sat. 17 Montreal		**Nov.** Mon. 5 NY Rangers	
Fri. 23 Hartford*		Wed. 7 Montreal	
Thur. 29 Edmonton		Sun. 11 Washington	
Dec. Sat. 1 NY Rangers		Wed. 14 Hartford	
Thur. 6 Montreal		Mon. 19 Toronto	
Sat. 13 Hartford		Sat. 24 Hartford	
Sat. 15 New Jersey		**Dec.** Tues. 4 Detroit	
Thur. 20 Buffalo		Sat. 8 Montreal	
Sat. 22 Minnesota		Sun. 9 Buffalo	
Jan. Thur. 3 Vancouver		Wed. 12 Hartford	
Sat. 5 Washington		Tues. 23 New Jersey	
Mon. 7 Winnipeg		Sun. 23 NY Rangers	
Thur. 10 Quebec		Wed. 26 Buffalo	
Sat. 12 Philadelphia		Fri. 28 Winnipeg	
Mon. 14 Detroit		Sat. 29 Minnesota	
Thur. 17 Los Angeles		**Jan.** Tues. 8 Quebec	
Thur. 24 Hartford		Tues. 15 NY Islanders	
Sat. 26 Calgary*		Tues. 22 Buffalo	
Thur. 31 Montreal		Sun. 27 Montreal*	
Feb. Sun. 3 Pittsburgh		**Feb.** Sat. 2 Pittsburgh*	
Tues. 5 Edmonton		Sun. 10 Quebec*	
Thur. 7 Calgary		Wed. 13 Montreal	
Sat. 9 Chicago*		Sat. 16 Los Angeles	
Thur. 28 NY Islanders		Thur. 21 Chicago	
Mar. Sat. 2 Buffalo*		Sat. 23 St Louis	
Thur. 7 St Louis		**Mar.** Sun. 3 New Jersey	
Sat. 9 Toronto*		Tues. 5 Toronto	
Thur. 14 Montreal		Sun. 17 Philadelphia	
Sat. 16 Detroit*		Tues. 19 Hartford	
Thur. 21 Quebec		Sun. 24 Washington*	
Sat. 23 Buffalo*		Tues. 26 Quebec	
Sun. 31 Hartford		Sat. 30 NY Islanders	

* Denotes afternoon game.

Home Starting Times:

Weeknights	7:35 p.m.
Saturdays and Sundays	7:05 p.m.
Matinees	1:35 p.m.
Except Nov. 17	8:05 p.m.
Mar. 9	12:35 p.m.

Franchise date: November 1, 1924

Prince of WALES CONFERENCE

67th NHL Season

Year-by-Year Record

Season	GP	Home W	L	T	Road W	L	T	Overall W	L	T	GF	GA	Pts.	Finished	Playoff Result
1989-90	80	23	13	4	23	12	5	46	25	9	289	232	101	1st, Adams Div.	Lost Final
1988-89	80	17	15	8	20	14	6	37	29	14	289	256	88	2nd, Adams Div.	Lost Div. Final
1987-88	80	24	13	3	20	17	3	44	30	6	300	251	94	2nd, Adams Div.	Lost Final
1986-87	80	25	11	4	14	23	3	39	34	7	301	276	85	3rd, Adams Div.	Lost Div. Semi-Final
1985-86	80	24	9	7	13	22	5	37	31	12	311	288	86	3rd, Adams Div.	Lost Div. Semi-Final
1984-85	80	21	15	4	15	19	6	36	34	10	303	287	82	4th, Adams Div.	Lost Div. Semi-Final
1983-84	80	25	12	3	24	13	3	49	25	6	336	261	104	1st, Adams Div.	Lost Div. Semi-Final
1982-83	80	28	6	6	22	14	4	50	20	10	327	228	110	1st, Adams Div.	Lost Conf. Championship
1981-82	80	24	12	4	19	15	6	43	27	10	323	285	96	2nd, Adams Div.	Lost Div. Final
1980-81	80	26	10	4	11	20	9	37	30	13	316	272	87	2nd, Adams Div.	Lost Prelim. Round
1979-80	80	27	9	4	19	12	9	46	21	13	310	234	105	2nd, Adams Div.	Lost Quarter-Final
1978-79	80	25	10	5	18	13	9	43	23	14	316	270	100	1st, Adams Div.	Lost Semi-Final
1977-78	80	29	6	5	22	12	6	51	18	11	333	218	113	1st, Adams Div.	Lost Final
1976-77	80	27	7	6	22	16	2	49	23	8	312	240	106	1st, Adams Div.	Lost Final
1975-76	80	27	5	8	21	10	9	48	15	17	313	237	113	1st, Adams Div.	Lost Semi-Final
1974-75	80	29	5	6	11	21	8	40	26	14	345	245	94	2nd, Adams Div.	Lost Prelim. Round
1973-74	78	33	4	2	19	13	7	52	17	9	349	221	113	1st, East Div.	Lost Final
1972-73	78	27	10	2	24	12	3	51	22	5	330	235	107	2nd, East Div.	Lost Quarter-Final
1971-72	78	28	4	7	26	9	4	54	13	11	330	204	119	1st, East Div.	**Won Stanley Cup**
1970-71	78	33	4	2	24	10	5	57	14	7	399	207	121	1st, East Div.	Lost Quarter-Final
1969-70	76	27	3	8	13	14	11	40	17	19	277	216	99	2nd, East Div.	**Won Stanley Cup**
1968-69	76	29	3	6	13	15	10	42	18	16	303	221	100	2nd, East Div.	Lost Semi-Final
1967-68	74	22	9	6	15	18	4	37	27	10	259	216	84	3rd, East Div.	Lost Quarter-Final
1966-67	70	10	21	4	7	22	6	17	43	10	182	253	44	6th,	Out of Playoffs
1965-66	70	15	17	3	6	26	3	21	43	6	174	275	48	5th,	Out of Playoffs
1964-65	70	12	17	6	9	26	0	21	43	6	166	253	48	6th,	Out of Playoffs
1963-64	70	13	15	7	5	25	5	18	40	12	170	212	48	6th,	Out of Playoffs
1962-63	70	7	18	10	7	21	7	14	39	17	198	281	45	6th,	Out of Playoffs
1961-62	70	9	22	4	6	25	4	15	47	8	177	306	38	6th,	Out of Playoffs
1960-61	70	13	17	5	2	25	8	15	42	13	176	254	43	6th,	Out of Playoffs
1959-60	70	21	11	3	7	23	5	28	34	8	220	241	64	5th,	Out of Playoffs
1958-59	70	21	11	3	11	18	6	32	29	9	205	215	73	2nd,	Lost Semi-Final
1957-58	70	15	14	6	12	14	9	27	28	15	199	194	69	4th,	Lost Final
1956-57	70	20	9	6	14	15	6	34	24	12	195	174	80	3rd,	Lost Final
1955-56	70	14	14	7	9	20	6	23	34	13	147	185	59	5th,	Out of Playoffs
1954-55	70	16	10	9	7	16	12	23	26	21	169	188	67	4th,	Lost Semi-Final
1953-54	70	22	8	5	10	20	5	32	28	10	177	181	74	4th,	Lost Semi-Final
1952-53	70	19	10	6	9	19	7	28	29	13	152	172	69	3rd,	Lost Final
1951-52	70	15	12	8	10	17	8	25	29	16	162	176	66	4th,	Lost Semi-Final
1950-51	70	13	12	10	9	18	8	22	30	18	178	197	62	4th,	Lost Semi-Final
1949-50	70	15	12	8	7	20	8	22	32	16	198	228	60	5th,	Out of Playoffs
1948-49	60	18	10	2	11	13	6	29	23	8	178	163	66	2nd,	Lost Semi-Final
1947-48	60	12	8	10	11	16	3	23	24	13	167	168	59	3rd,	Lost Semi-Final
1946-47	60	18	7	5	8	16	6	26	23	11	190	175	63	3rd,	Lost Semi-Final
1945-46	50	11	5	4	13	13	4	24	18	8	167	156	56	2nd,	Lost Final
1944-45	50	11	12	2	5	18	2	16	30	4	179	219	36	4th,	Lost Semi-Final
1943-44	50	15	8	2	4	18	3	19	26	5	223	268	43	5th,	Out of Playoffs
1942-43	50	17	3	5	7	14	4	24	17	9	195	176	57	2nd,	Lost Final
1941-42	48	17	4	3	8	13	3	25	17	6	160	118	56	3rd,	Lost Semi-Final
1940-41	48	15	4	5	12	4	8	27	8	13	168	102	67	1st,	**Won Stanley Cup**
1939-40	48	20	3	1	11	9	4	31	12	5	170	98	67	1st,	Lost Semi-Final
1938-39	48	20	2	2	16	8	0	36	10	2	156	76	74	1st,	**Won Stanley Cup**
1937-38	48	18	3	3	12	8	4	30	11	7	142	89	67	1st, Amn. Div.	Lost Semi-Final
1936-37	48	9	11	4	14	7	3	23	18	7	120	110	53	2nd, Amn. Div.	Lost Quarter-Final
1935-36	48	15	8	1	7	12	5	22	20	6	92	83	50	2nd, Amn. Div.	Lost Quarter-Final
1934-35	48	17	7	0	9	9	6	26	16	6	129	112	58	1st, Amn. Div.	Lost Semi-Final
1933-34	48	11	11	2	7	14	3	18	25	5	111	130	41	4th, Amn. Div.	Out of Playoffs
1932-33	48	20	3	1	5	13	5	25	15	8	124	88	58	1st, Amn. Div.	Lost Semi-Final
1931-32	48	11	10	3	4	11	9	15	21	12	122	117	42	4th, Amn. Div.	Out of Playoffs
1930-31	44	17	1	5	11	9	1	28	10	6	143	90	62	1st, Amn. Div.	Lost Semi-Final
1929-30	44	23	1	0	15	4	1	38	5	1	179	98	77	1st, Amn. Div.	Lost Final
1928-29	44	16	6	1	10	7	4	26	13	5	89	52	57	1st, Amn. Div.	**Won Stanley Cup**
1927-28	44	13	4	5	7	9	6	20	13	11	77	70	51	1st, Amn. Div.	Lost Semi-Final
1926-27	44	15	7	0	6	13	3	21	20	3	97	89	45	2nd, Amn. Div.	Lost Final
1925-26	36	10	7	1	7	8	3	17	15	4	92	85	38	4th,	Out of Playoffs
1924-25	30	3	12	0	3	12	0	6	24	0	49	119	12	6th,	Out of Playoffs

1990-91 Player Personnel

FORWARDS	HT	WT	S	Place of Birth	Date	1989-90 Club
BRICKLEY, Andy	5-11	200	L	Melrose, MA	8/9/61	Boston
BUDA, Dave	6-4	190	L	Mississauga, Ont.	3/14/66	Maine
BURRIDGE, Randy	5-9	180	L	Fort Erie, Ont.	1/7/66	Boston
BYCE, John	6-1	180	L	Madison, WI	8/9/67	U. Wisconsin-Boston
BYERS, Lyndon	6-1	200	R	Nipawin, Sask.	2/29/64	Boston
CARPENTER, Bob	6-0	190	L	Beverly, MA	7/13/63	Boston
CARTER, John	5-10	180	L	Winchester, MA	5/3/63	Boston-Maine
CHRISTIAN, Dave	6-0	175	R	Warroad, MN	5/12/59	Washington-Boston
CIMETTA, Robert	6-0	190	L	Toronto, Ont.	2/15/70	Boston-Maine
CRAWFORD, Lou	6-0	185	L	Belleville, Ont.	11/5/62	Boston-Maine
CRUICKSHANK, Gord	5-11	185	R	Mississauga, Ont.	5/4/65	Maine
DOURIS, Peter	6-1	195	R	Toronto, Ont.	2/19/66	Boston-Maine
FERREIRA, Brian	6-0	175	R	Falmouth, MA	1/2/68	R.P.I.
FLAHERTY, Jeff	6-3	210	R	Boston, MA	7/16/68	U. of Lowell
GARDNER, Joel	6-0	175	L	Petrolia, Ont.	9/16/67	Colgate
GOULD, Bobby	6-0	195	R	Petrolia, Ont.	9/2/57	Boston
HOOVER, Ron	6-1	185	L	Oakville, Ont.	10/28/66	Boston-Maine
JANNEY, Craig	6-1	190	L	Hartford, CT	9/26/67	Boston
JONES, Casey	5-11	170	L	Temiscaming, Que.	5/30/68	Cornell
KEKALAINEN, Jarmo	6-0	190	R	Kuopio, Finland	7/3/66	Boston-Maine
LALONDE, Todd	6-0	190	L	Sudbury, Ont.	8/4/69	Maine
LeMARQUE, Eric	5-10	185	R	Canoga Park, CA	7/1/69	U. of N. Michigan
MARKWART, Nevin	5-10	180	L	Toronto, Ont.	12/9/64	Boston
MONTANARI, Mark	5-9	185	L	Toronto, Ont.	6/3/69	Kitchener-Maine
NEELY, Cam	6-1	210	R	Comox, B.C.	6/6/65	Boston
NILAN, Chris	6-0	205	R	Boston, MA	2/9/58	NY Rangers
PENNEY, Jackson	5-10	180	L	Edmonton, Alta.	2/5/69	Victoria
PESKLEWIS, Matt	6-2	185	L	Edmonton, Alta.	5/21/68	Did Not Play
POULIN, Dave	5-11	190	L	Timmins, Ont.	12/17/58	Philadelphia-Boston
STEVENSON, Shayne	6-1	190	R	London, Ont.	10/26/70	Kitchener
SWEENEY, Bob	6-3	200	R	Concord, MA	1/25/64	Boston
TOWNSHEND, Graeme	6-2	225	R	Kingston, Jamaica	10/23/65	Boston-Maine
WALZ, Wes	5-10	180	R	Calgary, Alta.	5/15/70	Lethbridge-Boston

DEFENSEMEN:	HT	WT	S	Place of Birth	Date	1989-90 Club
ALLAIN, Rick	6-0	190	L	Guelph, Ont.	5/20/69	Kitchener
BEERS, Bob	6-2	200	R	Cheektowaga, NY	5/20/67	Boston-Maine
BLUM, John	6-3	205	R	Detroit, MI	10/8/59	Boston-Maine
BOURQUE, Ray	5-11	210	L	Montreal, Que.	12/28/60	Boston
GALLEY, Garry	6-0	190	L	Montreal, Que.	4/16/63	Boston
KLUZAK, Gord	6-4	215	L	Climax, Sask.	3/4/64	Boston
MOKOSAK, John	5-11	200	L	Edmonton, Alta.	9/7/63	Detroit-Adirondack
PEDERSEN, Allen	6-3	210	L	Ft. Saskatchewan, Alta.	1/13/65	Boston
QUINTAL, Stephane	6-3	215	R	Boucherville, Que.	10/22/68	Boston-Maine
SHOEBOTTOM, Bruce	6-2	200	L	Windsor, Ont.	8/20/65	Boston-Maine
SWEENEY, Don	5-11	170	L	St. Stephen, N.B.	8/17/66	Boston-Maine
THELVEN, Michael	5-11	185	R	Stockholm, Sweden	1/7/61	Boston
WESLEY, Glen	6-1	195	L	Red Deer, Alta.	10/2/68	Boston
WIEMER, Jim	6-4	210	L	Sudbury, Ont.	1/9/61	Boston-Maine

GOALTENDERS	HT	WT	C	Place of Birth	Date	1989-90 Club
FOSTER, Norm	5-9	175	L	Vancouver, B.C.	2/10/65	Maine
HARVEY, Chris	6-1	180	L	Cambridge, MA	12/8/67	Brown
LEMELIN, Reggie	5-11	170	L	Quebec City, Que.	11/19/54	Boston
MOOG, Andy	5-8	170	L	Penticton, B.C.	2/18/60	Boston
PARSON, Mike	6-0	170	L	Listowel, Ont.	3/12/70	Owen Sound

Coaching History

Arthur H. Ross, 1924-25 to 1927-28; Cy Denneny, 1928-29; Arthur H. Ross, 1929-30 to 1933-34; Frank Patrick, 1934-35 to 1935-36; Arthur H. Ross, 1936-37 to 1938-39; Ralph (Cooney) Weiland, 1939-40 to 1940-41; Arthur H. Ross, 1941-42 to 1944-45; Aubrey V. (Dit) Clapper, 1945-46 to 1948-49; George (Buck) Boucher, 1949-50; Lynn Patrick, 1950-51 to 1953-54; Lynn Patrick and Milt Schmidt, 1954-55; Milt Schmidt, 1955-56 to 1960-61; Phil Watson, 1961-62; Phil Watson and Milt Schmidt, 1962-63; Milt Schmidt, 1963-64 to 1965-66; Harry Sinden, 1966-67 to 1969-70; Tom Johnson, 1970-71 to 1971-72; Tom Johnson and Bep Guidolin, 1972-73; Bep Guidolin, 1973-74; Don Cherry, 1974-75 to 1978-79; Fred Creighton and Harry Sinden, 1979-80; Gerry Cheevers, 1980-81 to 1983-84; Gerry Cheevers and Harry Sinden, 1984-85; Butch Goring, 1985-86; Butch Goring and Terry O'Reilly, 1986-87; Terry O'Reilly, 1987-88 to 1988-89; Mike Milbury, 1989-90 to date.

Captains' History

No Captain, 1924-25 to 1926-27; Lionel Hitchman, 1927-28 to 1930-31; George Owen, 1931-32; Dit Clapper, 1932-33 to 1937-38; Cooney Weiland, 1938-39; Dit Clapper, 1939-40 to 1945-46; Dit Clapper, John Crawford, 1946-47; John Crawford 1947-48 to 1949-50; Milt Schmidt, 1950-51 to 1953-54; Milt Schmidt, Ed Sanford, 1954-55; Fern Flaman, 1955-56 to 1960-61; Don McKenney, 1961-62, 1962-63; Leo Boivin, 1963-64 to 1965-66; John Bucyk, 1966-67; no captain, 1967-68 to 1972-73; John Bucyk, 1973-74 to 1976-77; Wayne Cashman, 1977-78 to 1982-83; Terry O'Reilly, 1983-84, 1984-85; Ray Bourque, Rick Middleton (co-captains) 1985-86 to 1987-88; Ray Bourque, 1988-89 to date.

1989-90 Scoring

Regular Season

* rookie

Pos	#	Player	Team	GP	G	A	Pts	+/-	PIM	PP	SH	GW	GT	S	%
R	8	Cam Neely	BOS	76	55	37	92	10	117	25	0	12	0	271	20.3
D	77	Ray Bourque	BOS	76	19	65	84	31	50	8	0	3	0	310	6.1
C	23	Craig Janney	BOS	55	24	38	62	3	4	11	0	5	2	105	22.9
L	11	Bob Carpenter	BOS	80	25	31	56	3–	97	5	0	5	0	220	11.4
C	20	Bob Sweeney	BOS	70	22	24	46	2	93	5	2	6	0	147	15.0
C	19	Dave Poulin	PHI	28	9	8	17	5	12	0	0	1	1	46	19.6
			BOS	32	6	19	25	11	12	0	1	0	0	42	14.3
			TOTAL	60	15	27	42	16	24	0	1	1	1	88	17.0
L	36	Brian Propp	PHI	40	13	15	28	3	31	5	0	0	0	108	12.0
			BOS	14	3	9	12	2	10	0	1	0	0	45	6.7
			TOTAL	54	16	24	40	5	41	5	1	0	0	153	10.5
R	27	Dave Christian	WSH	28	3	8	11	12–	4	0	0	1	0	54	5.6
			BOS	50	12	17	29	4	8	2	0	3	0	99	12.1
			TOTAL	78	15	25	40	8–	12	2	0	4	0	153	9.8
L	25	Andy Brickley	BOS	43	12	28	40	11	8	6	0	1	0	69	17.4
L	31	John Carter	BOS	76	17	22	39	17	26	2	1	1	0	142	12.0
C	38	Greg Hawgood	BOS	77	11	27	38	12	76	2	0	1	0	127	8.7
D	26	Glen Wesley	BOS	78	9	27	36	6	48	5	0	4	0	166	5.4
D	28	Garry Galley	BOS	71	8	27	35	2	75	1	0	0	0	142	5.6
L	12	Randy Burridge	BOS	63	17	15	32	9	47	7	0	1	0	118	14.4
R	18	Bob Gould	BOS	77	8	17	25	3–	92	0	0	2	0	92	8.7
D	30	Jim Wiemer	BOS	61	5	14	19	11	63	0	0	1	0	90	5.6
L	14	*Rob Cimetta	BOS	47	8	9	17	4	33	0	0	0	0	28	28.6
L	29	Brian Lawton	HFD	13	2	1	3	2–	6	1	0	0	0	17	11.8
			QUE	14	5	6	11	9–	10	3	0	0	0	25	20.0
			BOS	8	0	0	0	4–	14	0	0	0	0	10	.0
			TOTAL	35	7	7	14	15–	30	4	0	0	0	52	13.5
R	16	Peter Douris	BOS	36	5	6	11	8	15	1	0	0	0	63	7.9
R	34	Lyndon Byers	BOS	43	4	4	8	0	159	0	0	0	1	43	9.3
D	32	Don Sweeney	BOS	58	3	5	8	11	58	0	0	0	0	49	6.1
R	42	Mike Millar	BOS	15	1	4	5	2–	0	0	0	0	0	18	5.6
L	29	*Jarmo Kekalainen	BOS	11	2	2	4	2	8	0	0	1	1	7	28.6
D	21	Stephane Quintal	BOS	38	2	2	4	11–	22	0	0	0	0	43	4.7
L	17	Nevin Markwart	BOS	8	1	2	3	2–	15	1	0	0	0	6	16.7
D	41	Allen Pedersen	BOS	68	1	2	3	5–	71	0	0	0	0	32	3.1
G	35	Andy Moog	BOS	46	0	3	3	0	18	0	0	0	0	0	.0
C	37	*Wes Walz	BOS	2	1	1	2	1–	0	1	0	0	0	1	100.0
R	39	Greg Johnston	BOS	9	1	1	2	1–	6	0	0	0	0	9	11.1
D	22	Michael Thelven	BOS	6	0	2	2	3	23	0	0	0	0	8	.0
D	6	Gord Kluzak	BOS	8	0	2	2	4	11	0	0	0	0	8	.0
L	43	*Bob Beers	BOS	3	0	1	1	2	6	0	0	0	0	0	.0
C	10	Bill O'Dwyer	BOS	6	0	1	1	2–	2	0	0	0	0	7	.0
R	19	Ray Neufeld	BOS	1	0	0	0	0	0	0	0	0	0	1	.0
D	33	John Blum	BOS	2	0	0	0	1–	0	0	0	0	0	0	.0
C	44	*Ron Hoover	BOS	2	0	0	0	2–	0	0	0	0	0	2	.0
D	40	Bruce Shoebottom	BOS	2	0	0	0	0	4	0	0	0	0	3	.0
R	48	*Graeme Townshend	BOS	4	0	0	0	1–	7	0	0	0	0	3	.0
L	37	*Lou Crawford	BOS	7	0	0	0	1	20	0	0	0	0	6	.0
G	1	Rejean Lemelin	BOS	43	0	0	0	0	32	0	0	0	0	0	.0

Goaltending

No.	Goaltender	GPI	Mins	Avg	W	L	T	EN	SO	GA	SA	S%
1	Rejean Lemelin	43	2310	2.81	22	15	2	2	2	108	1002	.892
35	Andy Moog	46	2536	2.89	24	10	7	0	3	122	1145	.893
	Totals	**80**	**4856**	**2.87**	**46**	**25**	**9**	**2**	**5**	**232**	**2147**	**.892**

Playoffs

Pos	#	Player	Team	GP	G	A	Pts	+/-	PIM	PP	SH	GW	OT	S	%
R	8	Cam Neely	BOS	21	12	16	28	7	51	4	1	2	0	65	18.5
C	23	Craig Janney	BOS	18	3	19	22	3	2	1	0	2	0	27	11.1
D	77	Ray Bourque	BOS	17	5	12	17	11	16	1	0	0	0	64	7.8
L	12	Randy Burridge	BOS	21	4	11	15	2	14	0	1	0	0	39	10.3
C	19	Dave Poulin	BOS	18	8	5	13	1	8	2	0	2	0	36	22.2
L	36	Brian Propp	BOS	20	4	9	13	5	2	1	0	2	0	39	10.3
L	11	Bob Carpenter	BOS	21	4	6	10	3–	39	2	0	1	0	41	9.8
L	31	John Carter	BOS	21	6	3	9	0	45	0	1	0	0	47	12.8
D	26	Glen Wesley	BOS	21	2	6	8	6	36	0	0	1	0	30	6.7
D	28	Garry Galley	BOS	21	3	3	6	8–	34	1	0	2	1	35	8.6
D	32	Don Sweeney	BOS	21	1	5	6	10–	18	1	0	0	0	27	3.7
R	27	Dave Christian	BOS	21	4	1	5	6–	4	1	0	0	0	37	10.8
C	38	Greg Hawgood	BOS	15	1	3	4	9–	12	1	0	0	0	18	5.6
C	42	*John Byce	BOS	8	2	0	2	2	2	0	0	0	0	7	28.6
L	43	*Bob Beers	BOS	14	1	1	2	1	18	0	0	0	0	11	9.1
C	20	Bob Sweeney	BOS	20	0	2	2	7–	30	0	0	0	0	19	.0
R	39	Greg Johnston	BOS	5	1	0	1	1–	4	0	0	1	0	7	14.3
R	34	Lyndon Byers	BOS	17	1	0	1	4–	12	0	0	0	0	11	9.1
R	16	Peter Douris	BOS	8	0	1	1	0	5	0	0	0	0	1	0.0
D	30	Jim Wiemer	BOS	8	0	1	1	4–	4	0	0	0	0	8	.0
L	37	*Lou Crawford	BOS	1	0	0	0	1–	0	0	0	0	0	1	.0
C	10	Bill O'Dwyer	BOS	1	0	0	0	0	2	0	0	0	0	0	.0
L	25	Andy Brickley	BOS	2	0	0	0	0	0	0	0	0	0	0	.0
G	1	Rejean Lemelin	BOS	3	0	0	0	0	0	0	0	0	0	0	.0
R	18	Bob Gould	BOS	17	0	0	0	3–	4	0	0	0	0	14	.0
G	35	Andy Moog	BOS	20	0	0	0	0	6	0	0	0	0	0	.0
D	41	Allen Pedersen	BOS	21	0	0	0	1–	41	0	0	0	0	4	.0

Goaltending

No.	Goaltender	GPI	Mins	Avg	W	L	EN	SO	GA	SA	S%
35	Andy Moog	20	1195	2.21	13	7	2	2	44	486	.909
1	Rejean Lemelin	3	135	5.78	0	1	0	0	13	57	.772
	Totals	21	1331	2.66	13	8	2	2	59	543	.891

Club Records

Team

(Figures in brackets for season records are games played; records for fewest points, wins, ties, losses, goals, goals against are for 70 or more games)

Most Points	121	1970-71 (78)
Most Wins	57	1970-71 (78)
Most Ties	21	1954-55 (70)
Most Losses	47	1961-62 (70)
Most Goals	399	1970-71 (78)
Most Goals Against	306	1961-62 (70)
Fewest Points	38	1961-62 (70)
Fewest Wins	14	1962-63 (70)
Fewest Ties	5	1972-73 (78)
Fewest Losses	13	1971-72 (78)
Fewest Goals	147	1955-56 (70)
Fewest Goals Against	172	1952-53 (70)

Longest Winning Streak

Over-all	14	Dec. 3/29-Jan. 9/30
Home	*20	Dec. 3/29-Mar. 18/30
Away	8	Feb. 17-Mar. 8/72

Longest Undefeated Streak

Over-all	23	Dec. 22/40-Feb. 23/41 (15 wins, 8 ties)
Home	27	Nov. 22/70-Mar. 20/71 (26 wins, 1 tie)
Away	15	Dec. 22/40-Mar. 16/41 (9 wins, 6 ties)

Longest Losing Streak

Over-all	11	Dec. 3/24-Jan. 5/25
Home	*11	Dec. 8/24-Feb. 17/25
Away	14	Dec. 27/64-Feb. 21/65

Longest Winless Streak

Over-all	20	Jan. 28-Mar. 11/62 (16 losses, 4 ties)
Home	11	Dec. 8/24-Feb. 17/25 (11 losses)

Away	14	Three times
Most Shutouts, Season	15	1927-28 (44)
Most PIM, Season	2,443	1987-88 (80)
Most Goals, Game	14	Jan. 21/45 (NYR 3 at Bos. 14)

Individual

Most Seasons	21	John Bucyk
Most Games	1,436	John Bucyk
Most Goals, Career	545	John Bucyk
Most Assists, Career	794	John Bucyk
Most Points, Career	1,339	John Bucyk (545 goals, 794 assists)
Most PIM, Career	2,095	Terry O'Reilly
Most Shutouts, Career	74	Tiny Thompson

Longest Consecutive Games Streak	418	John Bucyk (Jan. 23/69-Mar. 2/75)
Most Goals, Season	76	Phil Esposito (1970-71)
Most Assists, Season	102	Bobby Orr (1970-71)
Most Points, Season	152	Phil Esposito (1970-71) (76 goals, 76 assists)
Most PIM, Season	304	Jay Miller (1987-88)
Most Points, Defenseman Season	*139	Bobby Orr (1970-71) (37 goals, 102 assists)
Most Points, Center Season	152	Phil Esposito (1970-71) (76 goals, 76 assists)
Most Points, Right Wing Season	105	Ken Hodge (1970-71) (43 goals, 62 assists) Ken Hodge (1973-74) (50 goals, 55 assists) Rick Middleton (1983-84) (47 goals, 58 assists)

Most Points, Left Wing Season	116	John Bucyk (1970-71) (51 goals, 65 assists)
Most Points, Rookie Season	92	Barry Pederson (1981-82) (44 goals, 48 assists)
Most Shutouts, Season	15	Hal Winkler (1927-28)
Most Goals, Game	4	Several players
Most Assists, Game	6	Ken Hodge (Feb. 9/71) Bobby Orr (Jan. 1/73)
Most Points, Game	7	Bobby Orr (Nov. 15/73) Phil Esposito (Dec. 19/74) Barry Pederson (Apr. 4/82) Cam Neely (Oct. 16/88)

* NHL Record.

General Managers' History

Arthur H. Ross, 1924-25 to 1953-54; Lynn Patrick, 1954-55 to 1964-65; Leighton "Hap" Emms, 1965-66 to 1966-67; Milt Schmidt, 1967-68 to 1971-72; Harry Sinden, 1972-73 to date.

Retired Numbers

2	Eddie Shore	1926-1940
3	Lionel Hitchman	1925-1934
4	Bobby Orr	1966-1976
5	Dit Clapper	1927-1947
7	Phil Esposito	1967-1975
9	John Bucyk	1957-1978
15	Milt Schmidt	1936-1955

All-time Record vs. Other Clubs

Regular Season

	At Home							On Road							Total						
	GP	W	L	T	GF	GA	PTS	GP	W	L	T	GF	GA	PTS	GP	W	L	T	GF	GA	PTS
Buffalo	68	40	20	8	288	210	88	67	23	33	11	219	252	57	135	63	53	19	507	462	145
Calgary	33	20	9	4	114	90	44	34	19	13	2	128	125	40	67	39	22	6	242	215	84
Chicago	271	157	82	32	986	761	346	273	91	138	44	731	879	226	544	248	220	76	1717	1640	572
Detroit	274	149	82	43	967	722	341	274	74	148	52	687	911	200	548	223	230	95	1654	1633	541
Edmonton	17	13	2	2	80	44	28	18	8	7	3	61	61	19	35	21	9	5	141	105	47
Hartford	40	26	10	4	162	105	56	40	15	20	5	147	153	35	80	41	30	9	309	258	91
Los Angeles	49	37	9	3	235	134	77	48	28	15	5	185	158	61	97	65	24	8	420	292	138
Minnesota	49	36	6	7	225	116	79	48	28	11	9	185	129	65	97	64	17	16	410	245	144
Montreal	294	134	109	51	866	788	319	293	79	171	43	666	1001	201	587	213	280	94	1532	1789	520
New Jersey	28	19	7	2	130	88	40	27	16	3	8	106	69	40	55	35	10	10	236	157	80
NY Islanders	34	18	8	8	132	99	44	33	17	13	3	111	103	37	67	35	21	11	243	202	81
NY Rangers	273	149	86	38	996	759	336	274	102	119	53	765	831	257	547	251	205	91	1761	1590	593
Philadelphia	47	32	9	6	200	138	70	47	21	20	6	142	158	48	94	53	29	12	342	296	118
Pittsburgh	48	37	6	5	225	133	79	49	20	13	10	199	149	62	97	63	19	15	424	282	141
Quebec	40	20	15	5	161	135	45	40	22	14	4	179	155	48	80	42	29	9	340	290	93
St. Louis	46	31	9	6	211	122	68	47	21	17	9	167	140	51	93	52	26	15	378	262	119
Toronto	275	148	80	47	913	737	343	275	84	145	46	709	935	214	550	232	225	93	1622	1672	557
Vancouver	38	32	3	3	174	83	67	39	21	11	7	173	133	49	77	50	14	10	347	216	116
Washington	30	19	8	3	125	81	41	29	15	7	7	114	86	37	59	34	15	10	239	167	78
Winnipeg	18	13	2	3	88	59	29	17	9	7	1	62	58	19	35	22	9	4	150	117	48
Defunct Club	164	112	39	13	525	306	237	164	79	67	18	496	440	176	328	191	106	31	1021	746	413

Totals 2136 1242 601 293 7803 5710 2777 2136 798 992 346 6232 6926 1942 4272 2040 1593 639 14035 12636 4719

Playoffs

	Series	W	L	GP	W	L	T	GF	GA	Last Mtg.	Round	Result
Buffalo	4	4	0	22	15	7	0	94	70	1989	DSF	W 4-1
Chicago	6	5	1	22	16	5	1	97	63	1978	QF	W 4-0
Detroit	7	4	3	33	19	14	0	96	98	1957	SF	W 4-1
Edmonton	2	0	2	9	1	8	0	20	41	1990	F	L 1-4
Hartford	1	1	0	7	4	3	0	23	21	1990	DSF	W 4-3
Los Angeles	2	2	0	13	8	5	0	56	38	1977	QF	W 4-2
Minnesota	1	0	1	3	0	3	0	13	20	1981	PR	L 0-3
Montreal	25	4	21	121	40	81	0	285	384	1990	DF	W 4-1
New Jersey	1	1	0	7	4	3	0	30	19	1988	CF	W 4-3
NY Islanders	2	0	2	11	3	8	0	35	49	1983	CF	L 2-4
NY Rangers	9	6	3	42	22	18	2	114	104	1973	QF	L 1-4
Philadelphia	4	2	2	20	11	9	0	60	57	1978	SF	W 4-1
Pittsburgh	2	2	0	9	7	2	0	37	21	1980	PR	W 3-2
Quebec	2	1	1	11	6	5	0	37	36	1983	DSF	W 3-1
St. Louis	2	2	0	8	8	0	0	48	15	1972	SF	W 4-0
Toronto	13	5	8	62	30	31	1	153	150	1974	QF	W 4-0
Washington	1	1	0	4	4	0	0	15	6	1990	CF	W 4-0
Defunct Clubs	3	1	2	11	4	5	2	20	20			
Totals	87	41	46	415	202	207	6	1233	1212			

Playoff Results 1990-86

Year	Round	Opponent	Result	GF	GA
1990	F	Edmonton	L 1-4	8	20
	CF	Washington	W 4-0	15	6
	DF	Montreal	W 4-1	16	12
	DSF	Hartford	W 4-3	23	21
1989	DF	Montreal	L 1-4	13	16
	DSF	Buffalo	W 4-1	16	14
1988	F	Edmonton	L 0-4	12	21
	CF	New Jersey	W 4-3	30	19
	DF	Montreal	W 4-1	15	10
	DSF	Buffalo	W 4-2	28	22
1987	DSF	Montreal	L 1-4	13	16
1986	DSF	Montreal	L 0-3	6	10

Abbreviations: Round: F – Final; **CF** – conference final; **DF** – division final; **DSF** – division semi-final; **SF** – semi-final; **QF** – quarter-final; **PR** – preliminary round. **GA** – goals against; **GF** – goals for.

1989-90 Results

		Home				Away	
Oct.	5	Pittsburgh	5-4	Oct	7	Quebec	1-4
	9	Montreal	2-0		11	Montreal	2-4
	26	Quebec	4-2		13	Edmonton	3-3
	28	Hartford	0-1		15	Vancouver*	6-7
Nov.	2	Los Angeles	5-4		17	Los Angeles	3-2
	4	Buffalo	3-3		20	Edmonton	3-0
	9	Edmonton	6-2		21	Calgary	2-5
	16	Montreal	3-2		29	Montreal	3-4
	18	New Jersey	6-4	Nov.	10	Washington	5-3
	23	Toronto	6-0		15	Hartford	5-2
	30	Buffalo	5-1		21	Detroit	2-1
Dec.	2	St Louis	1-2		25	Montreal	3-5
	7	Hartford	3-4		28	St Louis	5-1
	9	Washington*	3-7	Dec.	3	Philadelphia	2-1
	16	Buffalo*	1-3		5	Quebec	3-3
	21	Minnesota	2-2		12	Pittsburgh	5-7
	23	Detroit*	6-5		13	Buffalo	4-2
	26	Toronto	6-4		17	New Jersey	1-3
Jan.	4	Winnipeg	4-2		20	Hartford	3-4
	6	Washington	5-3		26	Buffalo	4-3
	11	Quebec	3-1		30	Toronto	6-7
	13	NY Rangers*	2-3	Jan.	2	Pittsburgh	5-2
	15	Hartford	4-1		7	Buffalo	2-1
	18	Calgary	2-2		17	Hartford	5-5
	25	NY Islanders	5-3		23	Quebec	9-2
	27	Philadelphia*	2-1		29	Montreal	2-1
Feb.	1	Montreal	2-4	Feb.	4	Quebec*	3-2
	3	NY Rangers	1-2		6	Detroit	2-0
	8	Quebec	5-1		14	Winnipeg	2-3
	10	NY Islanders*	3-4		18	Vancouver	7-2
	11	Vancouver*	2-4		20	Calgary	5-3
Mar.	1	Montreal	5-3		22	Chicago	6-3
	3	Chicago*	3-1		24	Minnesota	3-2
	8	Buffalo	4-10		26	NY Rangers	1-6
	15	Winnipeg	3-3	Mar.	4	Chicago*	4-1
	17	Los Angeles*	4-5		6	Philadelphia	2-1
	22	Quebec	7-3		10	NY Islanders	3-3
	24	Minnesota	6-7		11	Hartford	4-3
	29	Hartford	3-2		27	St Louis	3-0
Apr.	1	New Jersey	3-3		31	Montreal	2-2

* Denotes afternoon game.

Entry Draft
Selections 1990-76

1990
Pick
21	Bryan Smolinski
63	Cameron Stewart
84	Jerome Buckley
105	Mike Bales
126	Mark Woolf
147	Jim Mackey
168	John Gruden
189	Darren Wetherill
210	Dean Capuano
231	Andy Bezeau
252	Ted Miskolczi

1989
Pick
17	Shayne Stevenson
38	Mike Parson
57	Wes Walz
80	Jackson Penney
101	Mark Montanari
122	Stephen Foster
143	Otto Hascak
164	Rick Allain
185	James Lavish
206	Geoff Simpson
227	David Franzosa

1988
Pick
18	Robert Cimetta
60	Stephen Heinze
81	Joe Juneau
102	Daniel Murphy
123	Derek Geary
165	Mark Krys
186	Jon Rohloff
228	Eric Reisman
249	Doug Jones

1987
Pick
3	Glen Wesley
14	Stephane Quintal
56	Todd Lalonde
67	Darwin McPherson
77	Matt Delguidice
98	Ted Donato
119	Matt Glennon
140	Rob Cheevers
161	Chris Winnes
182	Paul Ohman
203	Casey Jones
224	Eric Lemarque
245	Sean Gorman

1986
Pick
13	Craig Janney
34	Pekka Tirkkonen
76	Dean Hall
97	Matt Pesklewis
118	Garth Premak
139	Paul Beraldo
160	Brian Ferreira
181	Jeff Flaherty
202	Greg Hawgood
223	Steffan Malmquist
244	Joel Gardner

1985
Pick
31	Alain Cote
52	Bill Ranford
73	Jaime Kelly
94	Steve Moore
115	Gord Hynes
136	Per Martinele
157	Randy Burridge
178	Gord Cruickshank
199	Dave Buda
210	Bob Beers
220	John Byce
241	Marc West

1984
Pick
19	Dave Pasin
40	Ray Podloski
61	Jeff Cornelius
82	Robert Joyce
103	Mike Bishop
124	Randy Oswald
145	Mark Thietke
166	Don Sweeney
186	Kevin Heffernan
207	J.D. Urbanic
227	Bill Kopecky
248	Jim Newhouse

1983
Pick
21	Nevin Markwart
42	Greg Johnston
62	Greg Puhalski
82	Alain Larochelle
102	Allen Pederson
122	Terry Taillefor
142	Ian Armstrong
162	Francois Olivier
182	Harri Laurilla
202	Paul Fitzsimmons
222	Norm Foster
242	Greg Murphy

1982
Pick
1	Gord Kluzak
22	Brian Curran
39	Lyndon Byers
60	Dave Reid
102	Bob Nicholson
123	Bob Sweeney
144	John Meulenbrooks
165	Tony Fiore
186	Doug Kostynski
207	Tony Gilliard
228	Tommy Lehmann
249	Bruno Campese

1981
Pick
14	Normand Leveille
35	Luc Dufour
77	Scott McLellan
98	Joe Mantione
119	Bruce Milton
140	Mats Thelin
161	Armel Parisee
182	Don Sylvester
203	Richard Bourque

1980
Pick
18	Barry Pederson
60	Tom Fergus
81	Steve Kasper
102	Randy Hillier
123	Steve Lyons
144	Tony McMurchy
165	Mike Moffat
186	Michael Thelven
207	Jens Ohling

1979
Pick
8	Ray Bourque
15	Brad McCrimmon
36	Doug Morrison
57	Keith Crowder
78	Larry Melnyk
99	Marco Baron
120	Mike Krushelnyski

1978
Pick
16	Al Secord
35	Graeme Nicolson
52	Brad Knelson
68	George Buat
85	Darryl MacLeod
102	Jeff Brubaker
119	Murray Skinner
136	Robert Hehir
153	Craig MacTavish

1977
Pick
16	Dwight Foster
34	Dave Parro
52	Mike Forbes
70	Brian McGregor
88	Doug Butler
106	Keith Johnson
122	Ralph Cox
138	Mario Claude

1976
Pick
16	Clayton Pachal
34	Larry Gloeckner
70	Bob Miller
88	Peter Vandermark
106	Ted Olson

General Manager

SINDEN, HARRY JAMES
President and General Manager, Boston Bruins.
Born in Collins Bay, Ont., September 14, 1932.

Harry Sinden never played a game in the NHL but stepped into the Bruins' organization with an impressive coaching background in minor professional hockey and his continued excellence has earned him a place in the Hockey Hall of Fame as one of the true builders in hockey history. In 1965-66 as playing-coach of Oklahoma City Blazers in the CPHL, Sinden led the club to second place in the regular standings and then to eight straight playoff victories for the Jack Adams Trophy. After five years in OHA Senior hockey — including 1958 with the World Amateur Champion Whitby Dunlops — Sinden was named playing-coach in the old Eastern Professional League and its successor, the Central Professional League. Under his guidance, the Bruins of 1967-68 made the playoffs for the first time in nine seasons, finishing third in the East Division, and were nosed out of first place in 1968-69 by Montreal. In 1969-70, Sinden led the Bruins to their first Stanley Cup win since 1940-41. The following season he went into private business but returned to the hockey scene in the summer of 1972 when he was appointed coach of Team Canada. He moulded that group of NHL stars into a powerful unit and led them into an exciting eight-game series against the Soviet national team in September of 1972. Team Canada emerged the winner by a narrow margin with a record of four wins, three losses and one tie. Sinden then returned to the Bruins organization early in the 1972-73 season. Sinden took over as the Bruins' coach in February 1985, after replacing Gerry Cheevers. Boston finished 11-10-3 with Sinden behind the bench before being defeated by Montreal in five games in the Adams Division semi-finals.

NHL Coaching Record

Season	Team		Regular Season				Playoffs			
		Games	W	L	T	%	Games	W	L	%
1966-67	Boston	70	17	43	10	.314				
1967-68	Boston	74	37	27	10	.568	4	0	4	.000
1968-69	Boston	76	42	18	16	.658	10	6	4	.600
1969-70	Boston	76	40	17	19	.651	14	12	2	.857*
1979-80	Boston	7	6	1	0	.857	9	4	5	.444
1984-85	Boston	24	11	10	3	.521	5	2	3	.400
	NHL Totals	327	153	116	58	.557	42	24	18	.571

* Stanley Cup win.

Club Directory

Boston Garden
150 Causeway Street
Boston, Massachusetts 02114
Phone **617/227-3206**
FAX 617/523-7184
ENVOY ID
  Front Office: BRUINS. GM
  Public
  Relations: BRUINS. PR
Capacity: 14,448

Executive
Owner and Governor	Jeremy M. Jacobs
Alternative Governor	Louis Jacobs
Alternative Governor, President and General Manager	Harry Sinden
Vice President	Tom Johnson
Assistant to the President	Nate Greenberg
Director of Administration	Dale Hamilton
Administrative Assistant	Carol Gould

Coaching Staff
Assistant General Manager and Coach	Mike Milbury
Assistant Coaches	Gordie Clark, Ted Sator
Goaltending Coach	Joe Bertagna
Coach, Maine Mariners (AHL)	Rick Bowness

Scouting Staff
Coordinator of Minor League Player Personnel/Scouting	Bob Tindall
Director of Player Evaluation	Bart Bradley
Scouting Staff	Jim Morrison (Ontario), Andre Lachapelle (Quebec), Joe Lyons (New England), Don Saatzer (Minnesota), Lars Waldner (Europe), Marcel Pelletier (Pro Consultant), Jean Ratelle (College & High School)

Communications Staff
Director of Media Relations	Heidi Holland
Director of Community Relations, Marketing Services	Sue Byrne
Director of Player & Alumni Community Relations	John Bucyk
Administrative Assistant	Marilyn Viola
Video Production	Joe Curnane

Medical and Training Staff
Athletic Trainer	Jim Narrigan
Athletic Therapist	Don Worden
Equipment Manager	Ken Fleger
Assistant Equipment Manager	Eric Anderson
Team Physicians	Dr. Bertram Zarins, Dr. John J. Boyle, Dr. Ashby Moncure
Team Dentists	Dr. Robert Thomas and Dr. Richard Miner
Team Psychologist	Dr. Fred Neff

Ticketing and Finance Staff
Director of Ticket Operations	Matt Brennan
Assistant Director of Ticket Operations	Jim Foley
Receptionist	Linda Bartlett
Controller	John J. Dionne
Accounting Manager	Richard McGlinchey
Accounts Payable	Barbara Johnson

Television and Radio
Broadcasters (TV-38)	Fred Cusick and Derek Sanderson
Broadcasters (NESN)	Fred Cusick, Derek Sanderson and Dave Shea
Broadcasters (Radio)	Bob Wilson and John Bucyk
TV Channels	New England Sports Network (Home Games) and WSBK TV-38 (Road Games)
Radio Station	WEEI (590 AM) and Bruins Radio Network
Dimensions of Rink	191 feet by 83 feet
Club Colors	Gold, Black and White
Training Camp Site	Wilmington, MA.

Coach

MILBURY, MIKE
Coach, Boston Bruins. Born in Brighton, Mass., June 17, 1952.

Milbury was named the 18th head coach of the Bruins on May 16, 1989 after spending two seasons as general manager and coach of the Bruins' AHL affiliate — the Maine Mariners. In his first year with the Mariners (1987-88), he led them to the Northern Division championship and was named the Hockey News' Minor League Coach of the Year and co-winner of the AHL Coach of the Year.

Milbury has spent his entire professional career in the Bruins' organization since signing as a free agent out of Colgate University on November 5, 1974. He first retired as a player on May 6, 1985 and was named the Bruins' assistant coach under Butch Goring, but injuries late in the season saw his return to the Boston blueline. He won his first game as an NHL co-coach with Terry O'Reilly on November 8, 1986 and assumed the title of player-assistant coach on November 14, 1986 when O'Reilly took the head coaching job. His 14-year playing career came to a conclusion on July 16, 1987 when he was named to the Maine position. He finished his playing career with 49-189-238 totals in 754 games, ranking tenth on the Bruins' all-time games played list.

Coaching Record

Season	Team		Regular Season				Playoffs			
		Games	W	L	T	%	Games	W	L	%
1987-88	Maine (AHL)	80	44	29	7	.594	10	5	5	.500
1988-89	Maine (AHL)	80	32	40	8	.450	....	....	....	....
1989-90	Boston (NHL)	80	46	25	9	.631	21	13	8	.619
	NHL Totals	80	46	25	9	.631	21	13	8	.619

Buffalo Sabres

1989-90 Results: 45w-27L-8T 98PTS. Second, Adams Division

Year-by-Year Record

Season	GP	Home W	Home L	Home T	Road W	Road L	Road T	Overall W	Overall L	Overall T	GF	GA	Pts.	Finished	Playoff Result
1989-90	80	27	11	2	18	16	6	45	27	8	286	248	98	2nd, Adams Div.	Lost Div. Semi-Final
1988-89	80	25	12	3	13	23	4	38	35	7	291	299	83	3rd, Adams Div.	Lost Div. Semi-Final
1987-88	80	19	14	7	18	18	4	37	32	11	283	305	85	3rd, Adams Div.	Lost Div. Semi-Final
1986-87	80	18	18	4	10	26	4	28	44	8	280	308	64	5th, Adams Div.	Out of Playoffs
1985-86	80	23	16	1	14	21	5	37	37	6	296	291	80	5th, Adams Div.	Out of Playoffs
1984-85	80	23	10	7	15	18	7	38	28	14	290	237	90	3rd, Adams Div.	Lost Div. Semi-Final
1983-84	80	25	9	6	23	16	1	48	25	7	315	257	103	2nd, Adams Div.	Lost Div. Semi-Final
1982-83	80	25	7	8	13	22	5	38	29	13	318	285	89	3rd, Adams Div.	Lost Div. Final
1981-82	80	23	8	9	16	18	6	39	26	15	307	273	93	3rd, Adams Div.	Lost Div. Semi-Final
1980-81	80	21	7	12	18	13	9	39	20	21	327	250	99	1st, Adams Div.	Lost Quarter-Final
1979-80	80	27	5	8	20	12	8	47	17	16	318	201	110	1st, Adams Div.	Lost Semi-Final
1978-79	80	19	13	8	17	15	8	36	28	16	280	263	88	2nd, Adams Div.	Lost Prelim. Round
1977-78	80	25	7	8	19	12	9	44	19	17	288	215	105	2nd, Adams Div.	Lost Quarter-Final
1976-77	80	27	8	5	21	16	3	48	24	8	301	220	104	2nd, Adams Div.	Lost Quarter-Final
1975-76	80	28	7	5	18	14	8	46	21	13	339	240	105	2nd, Adams Div.	Lost Quarter-Final
1974-75	80	28	6	6	21	10	9	49	16	15	354	240	113	1st, Adams Div.	Lost Final
1973-74	78	23	10	6	9	24	6	32	34	12	242	250	76	5th, East Div.	Out of Playoffs
1972-73	78	30	6	3	7	21	11	37	27	14	257	219	88	4th, East Div.	Lost Quarter-Final
1971-72	78	11	19	9	5	24	10	16	43	19	203	289	51	6th, East Div.	Out of Playoffs
1970-71	78	16	13	10	8	26	5	24	39	15	217	291	63	5th, East Div.	Out of Playoffs

Schedule

Home			Away		
Oct.	Thur. 4	Montreal	**Oct.**	Sat. 6	Montreal
	Fri. 12	Quebec		Wed. 10	Hartford
	Wed. 17	Montreal		Sat. 13	Quebec
	Fri. 19	Pittsburgh		Sat. 20	NY Islanders
	Sun. 28	Hartford		Thur. 25	New Jersey
	Wed. 31	Boston		Sat. 27	Toronto
Nov.	Sun. 4	Calgary	**Nov.**	Sat. 3	Boston
	Fri. 9	Vancouver		Wed. 7	NY Rangers
	Wed. 21	NY Rangers		Sat. 10	Washington
	Fri. 23	Edmonton		Wed. 14	Los Angeles
Dec.	Sun. 2	Detroit		Fri. 16	Edmonton
	Fri. 7	Hartford		Sat. 17	Calgary
	Sun. 9	Boston		Mon. 26	NY Rangers
	Fri. 14	Pittsburgh		Wed. 28	Montreal
	Sun. 16	St Louis	**Dec.**	Sat. 1	Quebec
	Sun. 23	Quebec		Thur. 6	Philadelphia
	Wed. 26	Boston		Tues. 11	Detroit
	Fri. 28	Chicago		Tues. 18	Hartford
	Mon. 31	Philadelphia		Thur. 20	Boston
Jan.	Wed. 2	NY Islanders		Sat. 29	New Jersey
	Fri. 4	Winnipeg	**Jan.**	Tues. 8	Vancouver
	Wed. 16	Detroit		Thur. 10	Los Angeles
	Tues. 22	Boston		Sat. 12	Minnesota
	Sun. 27	Calgary*		Mon. 14	Toronto
	Thur. 31	Quebec		Thur. 24	Chicago
Feb.	Sun. 3	Edmonton		Sat. 26	Montreal^
	Wed. 6	St Louis		Tues. 29	St Louis
	Fri. 8	Los Angeles	**Feb.**	Sun. 10	Winnipeg*
	Wed. 13	Minnesota		Tues. 12	Quebec
	Fri. 15	Montreal		Tues. 19	Pittsburgh
	Sun. 17	Toronto		Sat. 23	Hartford
	Sun. 24	Hartford		Tues. 26	NY Islanders
Mar.	Wed. 6	New Jersey		Thur. 28	Quebec
	Fri. 8	Chicago	**Mar.**	Sat. 2	Boston*
	Sun. 10	Vancouver		Tues. 12	Minnesota
	Sun. 17	Hartford		Wed. 13	Winnipeg
	Wed. 20	Montreal		Sat. 16	Montreal
	Sun. 24	Philadelphia*		Sat. 23	Boston*
	Thur. 28	Quebec		Tues. 26	Washington
	Sun. 31	Washington		Sat. 30	Hartford

* Denotes afternoon game.

Home Starting Times:
Weeknights .... 7:35 p.m.
Sundays .... 7:05 p.m.
Matinees .... 2:05 p.m.

Franchise date: May 22, 1970

21st NHL Season

Dave Andreychuk, here being checked by former Hab Chris Chelios, led the Sabres with 18 powerplay goals.

1990-91 Player Personnel

FORWARDS

	HT	WT	S	Place of Birth	Date	1989-90 Club
ANDREYCHUK, Dave	6-3	220	R	Hamilton, Ont.	9/29/63	Buffalo
AUDETTE, Donald	5-8	177	R	Laval, Que.	9/23/69	Rochester-Buffalo
BOYCE, Ian	5-8	177	R	St. Laurent, Que.	1/24/68	
CORKUM, Bob	6-2	215	R	Salisbury, MA	12/18/67	Rochester-Buffalo
DONNELLY, Mike	5-11	185	L	Detroit, MI	10/10/63	Rochester
FOLIGNO, Mike	6-2	195	R	Sudbury, Ont.	1/29/59	Buffalo
GAGE, Jody	6-0	190	R	Toronto, Ont.	11/29/59	Rochester
GUAY, Francois	6-0	190	L	Gatineau, Que.	6/8/68	Rochester
HARTMAN, Mike	6-0	183	L	Detroit, MI	2/7/67	Buffalo
HAWERCHUK, Dale	5-11	185	L	Toronto, Ont.	4/4/63	Winnipeg
HOGUE, Benoit	5-10	190	L	Repentigny, Que.	10/28/66	Buffalo
HUTTON, Dwaine	5-11	175	L	Edmonton, Alta.	4/18/65	
JACKSON, Jim	5-8	185	R	Oshawa, Ont.	2/1/60	Rochester
KERR, Kevin	5-10	190	R	North Bay, Ont.	9/18/67	Rochester
LOEWEN, Darcy	5-10	185	L	Calgary, Alta.	2/26/69	Rochester
LUDZIK, Steve	5-11	185	L	Toronto, Ont.	4/3/62	Rochester
MacVICAR, Andrew	6-1	195	L	Dartmouth, N.S.	3/12/69	Sudbury
MAY, Brad	6-0	200	L	Toronto, Ont.	11/29/71	Niagara Falls
McCRORY, Scott	5-10	185	R	Sudbury, Ont.	2/27/67	Rochester
METCALFE, Scott	6-0	200	L	Toronto, Ont.	1/6/67	Rochester
MOGILNY, Alexander	5-11	195	L	Khabarovsk, USSR	2/18/69	Buffalo
MOLLOY, Mitch	6-3	212	L	Red Lake, Ont.	10/10/66	Roch.-Johnstown
NAUD, Sylvain	5-10	188	R	Lachine, Que.	3/29/70	Laval
NELSON, John	5-10	174	L	Scarborough, Ont.	7/9/69	Kingston
PRIESTLAY, Ken	5-10	190	L	Vancouver, B.C.	8/24/67	Buffalo
RAY, Robert	6-0	210	L	Stirling, Ont.	6/8/68	Rochester-Buffalo
RUHACHUK, Brad	5-11	173	L	Winnipeg, Man.	6/11/70	Lethbridge
RUUTTU, Christian	5-11	190	L	Lappeen, Finland	2/20/64	Buffalo
SAVAGE, Joel	5-11	205	R	Surrey, B.C.	12/25/69	Rochester
SHANNON, Darrin	6-2	200	L	Barrie, Ont.	12/8/69	Rochester-Buffalo
SNUGGERUD, Dave	6-0	190	L	Minnetonka, MN	6/20/66	Buffalo
TKACHUK, Grant	5-10	180	L	Lake La Biche, Alta.	9/24/68	Phoenix
TUCKER, John	6-0	200	R	Windsor, Ont.	9/29/64	Buf.-Washington
TURGEON, Pierre	6-1	203	L	Rouyn, Que.	8/29/69	Buffalo
VAIVE, Rick	6-1	192	R	Ottawa, Ont.	5/14/59	Buffalo
WINCH, Jason	6-1	203	L	Listowel, Ont.	5/23/71	Niagara Falls

DEFENSEMEN

	HT	WT	S	Place of Birth	Date	1989-90 Club
ANDERSON, Shawn	6-1	200	L	Montreal, Que.	2/7/68	Buffalo-Rochester
BASSEGIO, Dave	6-3	186	L	Niagara Falls, Ont.	10/28/67	Rochester
BODGER, Doug	6-2	210	L	Chemainua, B.C.	6/18/66	Buffalo
BROWN, Greg	5-11	180	R	Hartford, CT	3/7/68	Boston College
DeGRAY, Dale	6-0	200	R	Oshawa, Ont.	9/1/63	Roch.-N.Haven-Buf.
HALLER, Kevin	6-2	183	L	Trochu, Alta.	12/5/70	Regina
HOFFORD, Jim	6-0	205	R	Sudbury, Ont.	10/4/64	Rochester
KENNEDY, Dean	6-2	190	R	Redver, Sask.	1/18/63	Buffalo
KRUPP, Uwe	6-6	235	R	Cologne, W. Germ.	6/24/65	Buffalo
LEDYARD, Grant	6-2	200	L	Winnipeg, Man.	11/19/61	Buffalo
McSWEEN, Don	5-11	195	L	Detroit, MI	6/9/64	Rochester
MILLER, Brad	6-4	220	L	Edmonton, Alta.	7/23/69	Rochester
PLAYFAIR, Larry	6-4	205	L	Ft. St. James, B.C.	6/23/58	Buffalo
RAMSEY, Mike	6-3	195	L	Minneapolis, MN	12/3/60	Buffalo
SMITH, Steve	5-9	215	L	Trenton, Ont.	4/4/63	Rochester
SUTTON, Ken	6-0	195	L	Edmonton, Alta.	5/11/69	Rochester
WELLS, Jay	6-1	210	L	Paris, Ont.	5/18/59	Philadelphia-Buffalo

GOALTENDERS

	HT	WT	C	Place of Birth	Date	1989-90 Club
BOJCUN, Todd	5-9	151	L	Toronto, Ont.	4/13/70	Peterborough
LITTMAN, David	6-0	172	L	Cranston, RI	6/13/67	Rochester
MALARCHUK, Clint	6-0	187	L	Grande Prairie, Alta.	5/1/61	Buffalo
PUPPA, Daren	6-3	205	R	Kirkland Lake, Ont.	3/23/65	Buffalo
WAKALUK, Darcy	5-11	180	L	Pincher Creek, Alta.	3/14/66	Rochester

General Managers' History

George "Punch" Imlach, 1970-71 to 1977-78; John Anderson (acting), 1978-79; Scott Bowman, 1979-80 to 1985-86; Scott Bowman and Gerry Meehan, 1986-87; Gerry Meehan, 1987-88 to date.

Coaching History

"Punch" Imlach, 1970-71; "Punch" Imlach, Floyd Smith and Joe Crozier, 1971-72; Joe Crozier, 1972-73 to 1973-74; Floyd Smith, 1974-75 to 1976-77; Marcel Pronovost, 1977-78; Marcel Pronovost and Bill Inglis, 1978-79; Scott Bowman, 1979-80; Roger Neilson, 1980-81; Jim Roberts and Scott Bowman, 1981-82; Scott Bowman 1982-83 to 1984-85; Jim Schoenfeld and Scott Bowman, 1985-86; Scott Bowman, Craig Ramsay and Ted Sator, 1986-87; Ted Sator, 1987-88 to 1988-89; Rick Dudley, 1989-90 to date.

Captains' History

Floyd Smith, 1970-71; Gerry Meehan, 1971-72 to 1973-74; Jim Schoenfeld, 1974-75 to 1976-77; Danny Gare, 1977-78 to 1980-81; Gil Perreault, 1981-82 to 1985-86; Gil Perreault and Lindy Ruff, 1986-87; Lindy Ruff, 1987-88; Lindy Ruff and Mike Foligno, 1988-89; Mike Foligno, 1989-90 to date.

1989-90 Scoring

Regular Season

* rookie

Pos	#	Player	Team	GP	G	A	Pts	+/−	PIM	PP	SH	GW	GT	S	%
C	77	Pierre Turgeon	BUF	80	40	66	106	10	29	17	1	10	1	193	20.7
L	25	Dave Andreychuk	BUF	73	40	42	82	6	42	18	0	3	0	206	19.4
D	6	Phil Housley	BUF	80	21	60	81	11	32	8	1	4	0	201	10.4
C	21	Christian Ruuttu	BUF	75	19	41	60	9	66	4	1	2	1	160	11.9
R	22	Rick Vaive	BUF	70	29	19	48	9	74	8	0	4	0	195	14.9
D	8	Doug Bodger	BUF	71	12	36	48	0	64	8	0	1	0	167	7.2
L	89	*Alexander Mogilny	BUF	65	15	28	43	8	16	4	0	2	1	130	11.5
R	17	Mike Foligno	BUF	61	15	25	40	13	99	3	0	1	0	107	14.0
L	9	Scott Arniel	BUF	79	18	14	32	4	77	1	1	4	0	123	14.6
R	18	*Dave Snuggerud	BUF	80	14	16	30	8	41	1	2	2	0	120	11.7
D	5	Mike Ramsey	BUF	73	4	21	25	21	47	1	0	2	0	91	4.4
D	4	Uwe Krupp	BUF	74	3	20	23	15	85	0	1	1	0	69	4.3
L	20	Mike Hartman	BUF	60	11	10	21	10	211	2	0	3	0	97	11.3
D	24	Jay Wells	PHI	59	3	16	19	4	129	0	0	0	0	76	3.9
			BUF	1	0	1	1	1	0	0	0	0	0	0	.0
			TOTAL	60	3	17	20	5	129	0	0	0	0	76	3.9
C	33	Benoit Hogue	BUF	45	11	7	18	0	79	1	0	1	0	73	15.1
D	3	Grant Ledyard	BUF	67	2	13	15	2	37	0	0	1	0	91	2.2
C	56	Ken Priestlay	BUF	35	7	7	14	1	14	1	0	1	0	66	10.6
D	26	Dean Kennedy	BUF	80	2	12	14	12−	53	0	0	0	0	51	3.9
C	29	Jeff Parker	BUF	61	4	5	9	9−	70	0	0	0	0	61	6.6
L	16	*Darrin Shannon	BUF	17	2	7	9	6	4	0	0	0	0	20	10.0
R	23	Ray Sheppard	BUF	18	4	2	6	3	0	1	0	1	0	31	12.9
D	37	Shawn Anderson	BUF	16	1	3	4	2	8	0	0	0	0	16	6.3
G	31	Daren Puppa	BUF	56	0	4	4	0	4	0	0	0	0	0	.0
L	32	*Robert Ray	BUF	27	2	1	3	2−	99	0	0	0	0	20	10.0
L	7	Mike Donnelly	BUF	12	1	2	3	4−	8	0	0	0	0	20	5.0
D	42	*Bob Corkum	BUF	8	2	2	2	4	4	0	0	0	0	6	33.3
G	30	Clint Malarchuk	BUF	29	0	2	2	0	14	0	0	0	0	0	.0
D	27	Larry Playfair	BUF	4	0	1	1	2−	2	0	0	0	0	0	.0
C	14	Steve Ludzik	BUF	11	0	1	1	6−	6	0	0	0	0	15	.0
L	43	*Francois Guay	BUF	1	0	0	0	0	0	0	0	0	0	1	.0
D	55	Reed Larson	BUF	1	0	0	0	1	0	0	0	0	0	1	.0
D	44	*Brad Miller	BUF	1	0	0	0	1	0	0	0	0	0	1	.0
D	15	*Kevin Haller	BUF	2	0	0	0	0	0	0	0	0	0	0	.0
L	40	*Mitch Molloy	BUF	2	0	0	0	0	10	0	0	0	0	0	.0
L	36	*Darcy Loewen	BUF	4	0	0	0	3−	4	0	0	0	0	1	.0
D	39	*Don McSween	BUF	4	0	0	0	3−	4	0	0	0	0	4	.0
D	28	Dale DeGray	BUF	6	0	0	0	4−	6	0	0	0	0	5	.0
L	12	*Scott Metcalfe	BUF	7	0	0	0	5	0	0	0	0	0	5	.0

Goaltending

No.	Goaltender	GPI	Mins	Avg	W	L	T	EN	SO	GA	SA	S%
31	Daren Puppa	56	3241	2.89	31	16	6	2	1	156	1610	.903
30	Clint Malarchuk	29	1596	3.35	14	11	2	1	0	89	914	.903
	Totals	80	4850	3.07	45	27	8	3	1	248	2524	.902

Playoffs

Pos	#	Player	Team	GP	G	A	Pts	+/−	PIM	PP	SH	GW	OT	S	%
L	25	Dave Andreychuk	BUF	6	2	5	7	2	2	1	0	0	0	20	10.0
R	22	Rick Vaive	BUF	6	4	2	6	2	6	4	0	1	0	21	19.0
C	77	Pierre Turgeon	BUF	6	2	4	6	2	2	0	0	1	0	13	15.4
D	8	Doug Bodger	BUF	6	1	5	6	4	6	0	0	0	0	11	9.1
D	6	Phil Housley	BUF	6	1	4	5	0	4	1	0	0	0	16	6.3
D	26	Dean Kennedy	BUF	6	1	1	2	3−	12	0	0	0	0	9	11.1
L	9	Scott Arniel	BUF	5	1	0	1	4	0	0	0	0	0	9	11.1
D	19	*Bob Corkum	BUF	5	1	0	1	0	4	0	0	0	0	4	25.0
L	89	*Alexander Mogilny	BUF	4	0	1	1	2−	2	0	0	0	0	8	.0
R	17	Mike Foligno	BUF	6	0	1	1	0	12	0	0	0	0	4	.0
D	5	Mike Ramsey	BUF	6	0	1	1	7−	8	0	0	0	0	4	.0
L	16	*Darrin Shannon	BUF	6	0	1	1	7−	4	0	0	0	0	4	.0
R	45	*Donald Audette	BUF	2	0	0	0	0	0	0	0	0	0	2	.0
C	33	Benoit Hogue	BUF	3	0	0	0	0	10	0	0	0	0	7	.0
C	56	Ken Priestlay	BUF	6	0	0	0	2−	4	0	0	0	0	7	.0
L	20	Mike Hartman	BUF	6	0	0	0	2	18	0	0	0	0	5	.0
D	4	Uwe Krupp	BUF	6	0	0	0	4−	4	0	0	0	0	8	.0
G	31	Daren Puppa	BUF	6	0	0	0	0	0	0	0	0	0	0	.0
C	21	Christian Ruuttu	BUF	6	0	0	0	4−	4	0	0	0	0	12	.0
R	18	*Dave Snuggerud	BUF	6	0	0	0	6−	2	0	0	0	0	6	.0
D	24	Jay Wells	BUF	6	0	0	0	3	12	0	0	0	0	2	.0

Goaltending

No.	Goaltender	GPI	Mins	Avg	W	L	EN	SO	GA	SA	S%
31	Daren Puppa	6	370	2.43	2	4	2	0	15	192	.922
	Totals	6	373	2.73	2	4	2	0	17	192	.911

Retired Numbers

2	Tim Horton	1972-1974

Club Records

Team

(Figures in brackets for season records are games played; records for fewest points, wins, ties, losses, goals, goals against are for 70 or more games)

Most Points 113 1974-75 (80)
Most Wins 49 1974-75 (80)
Most Ties 21 1980-81 (80)
Most Losses 44 1986-87 (80)
Most Goals 354 1974-75 (80)
Most Goals Against 308 1986-87 (80)
Fewest Points 51 1971-72 (78)
Fewest Wins 16 1971-72 (78)
Fewest Ties 6 1985-86 (80)
Fewest Losses 16 1974-75 (80)
Fewest Goals 203 1971-72 (78)
Fewest Goals Against 201 1979-80 (80)

Longest Winning Streak
Over-all ....10 Jan. 4-23/84
Home ....12 Nov. 12/72-
　　　　　　　　　　Jan. 7/73
　　　　　　　　　　Oct. 13-
　　　　　　　　　　Dec. 10/89
Away ....10 Dec. 10/83-
　　　　　　　　　　Jan. 23/84

Longest Undefeated Streak
Over-all ....14 March 6-
　　　　　　　　　　April 6/80
　　　　　　　　　　(8 wins, 6 ties)
Home ....21 Oct. 8/72-
　　　　　　　　　　Jan. 7/73
　　　　　　　　　　(18 wins, 3 ties)
Away ....10 Dec. 10/83-
　　　　　　　　　　Jan. 23/84
　　　　　　　　　　(10 wins)

Longest Losing Streak
Over-all ....7 Oct. 25-
　　　　　　　　　　Nov. 8/70
Home ....5 Feb. 15-Mar. 3/85
　　　　　　　　　　Dec. 29/89-
　　　　　　　　　　Jan. 26/90
Away ....7 Oct. 14-
　　　　　　　　　　Nov. 7/70
　　　　　　　　　　Feb. 6-27/71

Longest Winless Streak
Over-all ....10 Nov. 7-
　　　　　　　　　　Dec. 1/71
　　　　　　　　　　(8 losses, 2 ties)

Home ....6 Feb. 27-
　　　　　　　　　　Mar. 26/72
　　　　　　　　　　(3 losses, 3 ties)
　　　　　　　　　　Nov. 23-
　　　　　　　　　　Dec. 16/84
　　　　　　　　　　(1 loss, 5 ties)
Away ....23 Oct. 30/71-
　　　　　　　　　　Feb. 19/72
　　　　　　　　　　(15 losses, 8 ties)

Most Shutouts, Season 7 1974-75 (80)
Most PIM, Season 2,277 1987-88 (80)
Most Goals, Game ....14 Jan. 21/75
　　　　　　　　　　(Wsh. 2 at Buf. 14)
　　　　　　　　　　Mar. 19/81
　　　　　　　　　　(Tor. 4 at Buf. 14)

Individual

Most Seasons ....17 Gilbert Perreault
Most Games ....1,191 Gilbert Perreault
Most Goals, Career .....512 Gilbert Perreault
Most Assists, Career ....814 Gilbert Perreault
Most Points, Career ...1,326 Gilbert Perreault
Most PIM, Career ......1,390 Larry Playfair
Most Shutouts, Career ...14 Don Edwards

Longest Consecutive
Games Streak ....776 Craig Ramsay
　　　　　　　　　　(Mar. 27/73-Feb. 10/83)
Most Goals, Season ....56 Danny Gare
　　　　　　　　　　(1979-80)
Most Assists, Season......69 Gilbert Perreault
　　　　　　　　　　(1975-76)
Most Points, Season .....113 Gilbert Perreault
　　　　　　　　　　(1975-76)
　　　　　　　　　　(44 goals, 69 assists)
Most PIM, Season ....316 Mike Hartman
　　　　　　　　　　(1988-89)

Most Points, Defenseman
Season ....81 Phil Housley
　　　　　　　　　　(1989-90)
　　　　　　　　　　(21 goals, 60 assists)

Most Points, Center
Season ....113 Gilbert Perreault
　　　　　　　　　　(1975-76)
　　　　　　　　　　(44 goals, 69 assists)

Most Points, Right Wing
Season ....100 Rene Robert
　　　　　　　　　　(1974-75)
　　　　　　　　　　(40 goals, 60 assists)

Most Points, Left Wing
Season ....95 Richard Martin
　　　　　　　　　　(1974-75)
　　　　　　　　　　(52 goals, 43 assists)

Most Points, Rookie
Season ....74 Richard Martin
　　　　　　　　　　(1971-72)
　　　　　　　　　　(44 goals, 30 assists)

Most Shutouts, Season .....5 Don Edwards
　　　　　　　　　　(1977-78)
　　　　　　　　　　Tom Barrasso
　　　　　　　　　　(1984-85)

Most Goals, Game ....5 Dave Andreychuk
　　　　　　　　　　(Feb. 6/86)

Most Assists, Game ....5 Gilbert Perreault
　　　　　　　　　　(Feb. 1/76;
　　　　　　　　　　Mar. 9/80;
　　　　　　　　　　Jan. 4/84)

Most Points, Game ....7 Gilbert Perreault
　　　　　　　　　　(Feb. 1/76)

All-time Record vs. Other Clubs

Regular Season

			At Home							On Road							Total					
	GP	W	L	T	GF	GA	PTS	GP	W	L	T	GF	GA	PTS	GP	W	L	T	GF	GA	PTS
Boston	67	33	23	11	252	219	77	68	20	40	8	210	288	48	135	53	63	19	462	507	125
Calgary	33	19	10	4	141	100	42	33	11	13	9	112	122	31	66	30	23	13	253	222	73
Chicago	39	25	8	6	158	104	56	39	11	22	6	98	126	28	78	36	30	12	256	230	84
Detroit	40	29	5	6	183	96	64	42	17	21	4	129	153	38	82	46	26	10	312	249	102
Edmonton	17	7	7	3	73	73	17	18	3	13	2	47	82	8	35	10	20	5	120	155	25
Hartford	40	21	14	5	164	135	47	40	21	15	4	123	117	46	80	42	29	9	287	252	93
Los Angeles	41	21	13	7	171	128	49	40	19	14	7	141	137	45	81	40	27	14	312	265	94
Minnesota	41	23	9	9	156	107	55	40	18	16	6	128	123	42	81	41	25	15	284	230	97
Montreal	63	28	19	16	196	188	72	63	17	38	8	189	262	42	126	45	57	24	385	450	114
New Jersey	28	22	3	3	139	78	47	27	19	4	4	117	78	42	55	41	7	7	256	156	89
NY Islanders	34	18	12	4	118	95	40	34	16	13	5	103	100	37	68	34	25	9	219	195	77
NY Rangers	41	26	10	5	185	131	57	39	14	15	10	115	133	38	80	40	25	15	300	264	95
Philadelphia	38	18	14	6	133	115	42	40	8	26	6	99	148	22	78	26	40	12	232	263	64
Pittsburgh	40	22	5	13	185	104	57	41	14	15	12	148	154	40	81	36	20	25	333	258	97
Quebec	40	25	10	5	166	130	55	40	14	21	5	120	153	33	80	39	31	10	286	283	88
St. Louis	38	26	8	4	161	111	56	39	11	23	5	101	148	27	77	37	31	9	262	259	83
Toronto	46	29	15	2	199	133	60	44	19	18	7	160	143	45	90	48	33	9	359	276	105
Vancouver	39	21	10	8	143	108	50	40	12	19	9	131	152	33	79	33	29	17	274	260	83
Washington	30	22	5	3	134	82	47	29	19	4	6	126	78	44	59	41	9	9	260	160	91
Winnipeg	18	15	1	2	87	49	32	17	8	7	2	62	59	18	35	23	8	4	149	108	50
Defunct Club	23	13	5	5	94	63	31	23	12	8	3	97	76	27	46	25	13	8	191	139	58
Totals	796	463	206	127	3236	2349	1053	796	303	365	128	2556	2832	734	1592	766	571	255	5792	5181	1787

Playoffs

	Series	W	L	GP	W	L	T	GF	GA	Last Mtg.	Round	Result
Boston	4	0	4	22	7	15	0	70	94	1989	DSF	L 1-4
Chicago	2	2	0	9	8	1	0	36	17	1980	QF	W 4-0
Minnesota	2	1	1	7	3	4	0	28	26	1981	QF	L 1-4
Montreal	4	2	2	21	11	10	0	58	69	1990	DSF	L 2-4
NY Islanders	3	0	3	16	4	12	0	45	59	1980	SF	L 2-4
NY Rangers	1	1	0	3	2	1	0	11	6	1978	PR	W 2-1
Philadelphia	2	0	2	11	3	8	0	23	35	1978	QF	L 1-4
Pittsburgh	1	0	1	3	1	2	0	9	9	1979	PR	L 1-2
Quebec	2	0	2	8	2	6	0	27	35	1985	DSF	L 2-3
St. Louis	1	1	0	3	2	1	0	7	8	1976	PR	W 2-1
Vancouver	2	2	0	7	6	1	0	28	14	1981	PR	W 3-0
Totals	24	9	15	110	49	61	0	342	372			

Playoff Results 1990-86

Year	Round	Opponent	Result	GF	GA
1990	DSF	Montreal	L 2-4	13	17
1989	DSF	Boston	L 1-4	14	16
1988	DSF	Boston	L 2-4	22	28

Abbreviations: Round: F – Final; **CF** – conference final; **DF** – division final; **DSF** – division semi-final; **PR** – preliminary round. **GA** – goals against; **GF** – goals for.

1989-90 Results

		Home					Away	
Oct.	5	Quebec	4-3	Oct.	7	Montreal	1-5
	8	Minnesota	2-2		11	Toronto	7-1
	13	Hartford	4-1		14	Detroit	2-6
	20	Montreal	6-2		18	Hartford	1-2
	27	Toronto	6-5		21	Pittsburgh	4-2
	29	Boston	4-3		25	Minnesota	2-4
Nov.	5	Los Angeles	5-3	Nov.	2	Montreal	4-3
	10	Vancouver	4-2		4	Boston	3-3
	12	Edmonton	6-5		8	Hartford	6-3
	22	NY Rangers	4-1		16	Calgary	4-4
	26	Boston	4-2		17	Edmonton	0-3
Dec.	1	New Jersey	6-4		19	Vancouver	2-2
	3	St Louis	4-3		25	Quebec	3-2
	10	Washington	4-3		28	Hartford	4-2
	13	Boston	2-4		30	Boston	1-5
	17	Philadelphia	4-3	Dec.	5	NY Islanders	0-3
	22	Montreal	2-2		7	Philadelphia	3-4
	26	Detroit	6-3		16	Boston*	3-1
	29	Boston	3-4		20	NY Rangers	2-2
	31	NY Islanders	2-4		23	Quebec	6-5
Jan.	7	Boston	1-2	Jan.	2	New Jersey	3-5
	19	Washington	3-6		6	Montreal	3-6
	26	Chicago	2-4		11	Calgary	3-5
	28	Pittsburgh*	7-2		13	Vancouver	5-3
	31	Quebec	6-3		16	Los Angeles	4-2
Feb.	4	NY Islanders	0-1		23	Philadelphia	3-2
	7	Montreal	3-1		24	Chicago	3-2
	9	NY Rangers	3-2		30	Quebec	5-2
	16	Montreal	5-3	Feb.	3	Montreal	0-1
	18	Hartford	4-6		11	St Louis	2-4
	23	Hartford	7-3		13	Chicago	1-4
	25	Winnipeg	3-1		20	Winnipeg	4-3
Mar.	4	Quebec	5-3		21	Edmonton	3-7
	14	Los Angeles	5-6		27	St Louis	1-4
	16	Toronto	3-4	Mar.	3	Quebec	3-3
	18	Winnipeg	4-3		6	Washington	1-1
	21	Calgary	5-4		8	Boston	10-4
	25	New Jersey*	3-4		10	Hartford	5-0
	29	Minnesota	4-2		27	Detroit	6-5
Apr.	1	Quebec	5-2		31	Pittsburgh	3-2

* Denotes afternoon game.

Entry Draft Selections 1990-76

1990
Pick
14 Brad May
82 Brian McCarthy
97 Richard Smehlik
100 Todd Bojcun
103 Brad Pascall
142 Viktor Gordijuk
166 Milan Nedoma
187 Jason Winch
208 Sylvain Naud
229 Kenneth Martin
250 Brad Rubachuk

1989
Pick
14 Kevin Haller
56 John (Scott) Thomas
77 Doug MacDonald
98 Ken Sutton
107 Bill Pye
119 Mike Barkley
161 Derek Plante
183 Donald Audette
194 Mark Astley
203 John Nelson
224 Todd Henderson
245 Michael Bavis

1988
Pick
13 Joel Savage
55 Darcy Loewen
76 Keith E. Carney
89 Alexander Mogilny
97 Robert Ray
106 David DiVita
118 Mike McLaughlin
139 Mike Griffith
160 Daniel Ruoho
181 Wade Flaherty
223 Thomas Nieman
244 Robert Wallwork

1987
Pick
1 Pierre Turgeon
22 Brad Miller
53 Andrew MacVicar
84 John Bradley
85 David Pergola
106 Chris Marshall
127 Paul Flanagan
148 Sean Dooley
153 Tim Roberts
169 Grant Tkachuk
190 Ian Herbers
211 David Littman
232 Allan MacIsaac

1986
Pick
5 Shawn Anderson
26 Greg Brown
47 Bob Corkum
56 Kevin Kerr
68 David Baseggio
89 Larry Rooney
110 Miguel Baldris
131 Mike Hartman
152 Francois Guay
173 Shawn Whitham
194 Kenton Rein
215 Troy Arndt

1985
Pick
14 Calle Johansson
35 Benoit Hogue
56 Keith Gretzky
77 Dave Moylan
98 Ken Priestlay
119 Joe Reekie
140 Petri Matikainen
161 Trent Kaese
182 Jiri Sejba
203 Boyd Sutton
224 Guy Larose
245 Ken Baumgartner

1984
Pick
18 Mikael Andersson
39 Doug Trapp
60 Ray Sheppard
81 Bob Halkidis
102 Joey Rampton
123 James Gasseau
144 Darcy Wakaluk
165 Orwar Stambert
207 Brian McKinnon
228 Grant Delcourt
249 Sean Baker

1983
Pick
5 Tom Barrasso
10 Normand Lacombe
11 Adam Creighton
31 John Tucker
34 Richard Hajdu
74 Daren Puppa
94 Jayson Meyer
114 Jim Hofford
134 Christian Ruuttu
154 Don McSween
174 Tim Hoover
194 Mark Ferner
214 Uwe Krupp
234 Marc Hamelin
235 Kermit Salfi

1982
Pick
6 Phil Housley
9 Paul Cyr
16 Dave Andreychuk
26 Mike Anderson
30 Jens Johansson
68 Timo Jutila
79 Jeff Hamilton
100 Bob Logan
111 Jeff Parker
121 Jacob Gustavsson
142 Allen Bishop
163 Claude Verrett
184 Rob Norman
205 Mike Craig
226 Jim Plankers

1981
Pick
17 Jiri Dudacek
38 Hannu Virta
59 Jim Aldred
60 Colin Chisholm
80 Jeff Eatough
83 Anders Wikberg
101 Mauri Eivola
122 Ali Butorac
143 Haikki Leime
164 Gates Orlando
185 Venci Sebeck
206 Warren Harper

1980
Pick
20 Steve Patrick
41 Mike Moller
56 Sean McKenna
62 Jay North
83 Jim Wiemer
104 Dirk Reuter
125 Daniel Naud
146 Jari Paavola
167 Randy Cunneyworth
188 Dave Beckon
209 John Bader

1979
Pick
11 Mike Ramsey
32 Lindy Ruff
53 Mark Robinson
55 Jacques Cloutier
74 Gilles Hamel
95 Alan Haworth
116 Rick Knickle

1978
Pick
13 Larry Playfair
32 Tony McKegney
49 Rob McClanahan
66 Mike Gazdic
82 Randy Ireland
99 Cam MacGregor
116 Dan Eastman
133 Eric Strobel
150 Eugene O'Sullivan

1977
Pick
14 Ric Seiling
32 Ron Areshenkoff
68 Bill Stewart
86 Richard Sirois
104 Wayne Ramsey

1976
Pick
33 Joe Kowal
69 Henry Maze
87 Ron Roscoe
105 Don Lemieux

Coach

DUDLEY, RICK
Coach, Buffalo Sabres. Born in Toronto, Ont., January 31, 1949.

Rick Dudley was named head coach of the Sabres on June 16, 1989, marking his return to a club for which he played 279 games between 1972-73 and 1980-81. Dudley's NHL playing career included stints in Buffalo and Winnipeg. He tallied 174 points (75-99-174) in 309 NHL games before ending his playing career in 1981-82.

Dudley's coaching career began in 1982-83 when he assumed the head coaching duties for the Carolina Thunderbirds of the ACHL. He met with instant success as he led his club to the title in his first season. In 1983-84 and 1984-85, Dudley led his team to a first-place finish during the regular-season, before winning another title in 1985-86. Dudley joined the Flint Generals (IHL) in 1986-87 and led them to the Turner Cup Finals in 1987-88. In 1988-89, he was the head coach for the New Haven Nighthawks (AHL) where he again led his club to the Final series. In seven years, Dudley compiled a minor league coaching record of 315-157-38 for a .655 winning percentage.

Coaching Record

| Season | Team | Games | Regular Season | | | | Playoffs | | | |
			W	L	T	%	Games	W	L	%
1982-83	Carolina (ACHL)	68	51	10	7	.619	8	8	0	1.000
1983-84	Carolina (ACHL)	72	43	24	5	.632	10	5	5	.500
1984-85	Carolina (ACHL)	64	53	11	0	.828	10	8	2	.800
1985-86	Carolina (ACHL)	63	49	14	0	.778	11	8	3	.727
1986-87	Flint (IHL)	82	42	33	7	.555	6	2	4	.333
1987-88	Flint (IHL)	82	42	31	9	.567	16	10	6	.625
1988-89	New Haven (AHL)	80	35	35	10	.500	17	9	8	.529
1989-90	Buffalo (NHL)	80	45	27	8	.613	6	2	4	.333
	NHL Totals	80	45	27	8	.613	6	2	4	.333

Club Directory

Memorial Auditorium
Buffalo, N.Y. 14202
Phone 716/856-7300
Outside Buffalo: **800/333-PUCK**
GM FAX 716/856-7350
FAX 716/856-7351
ENVOY ID
Front Office: SABRES. GM
Public
Relations: SABRES. PR
Capacity: 16,433

Board of Directors

Chairman of the Board and President	Seymour H. Knox, III
Vice-Chairman of the Board and Counsel	Robert O. Swados
Vice-Chairman of the Board	Robert E. Rich, Jr.
Treasurer	Joseph T.J. Stewart
Board of Directors	Edwin C. Andrews
Niagara Frontier Hockey L.P. (includes above listed officers)	Peter C. Andrews
	George L. Collins, Jr. M.D.
	John B. Fisher
	John Houghton
	Richard W. Rupp
	Howard T. Saperston, Jr.
	Paul A. Schoellkopf
	George Strawbridge, Jr., Arthur Victor, Jr.
Consultant	Northrup R. Knox
Assistant to the President	Seymour H. Knox, IV
Senior Vice-President/Administration	Mitchell Owen
Senior Vice-President/Finance	Robert Pickel
Vice-President/Marketing	George Bergantz
General Manager	Gerry Meehan
Head Coach	Rick Dudley
Associate Head Coach	John Van Boxmeer
Assistant Coach	John Tortorella
Assistant to the General Manager	Craig Ramsay
Director of Player Personnel	Don Luce
Director of Scouting	Rudy Migay
Coordinator of Minor League Pro. Development	Joe Crozier
Assistant to the General Manager	Debbie Bonner
Scouting Staff	Don Barrie, Jack Bowman, Larry Carriere, Dennis McIvor, Paul Merritt, Mike Racicot, Frank Zywiec
Information Manager – Hockey Dept.	Ken Bass
Head Athletic Trainer	Jim Pizzutelli
Trainer	Rip Simonick
Equipment Supervisor	John Allaway
Administrative Assistants	Carol McHugh, Verna Wojcik
Controller	Dan DiPofi
Director of Amateur Hockey Development	John Mickler
Director of Communications	Paul Wieland
Director of Community Relations and Promotions	Stan Makowski
Director of Event Sales	Jeffrey Pickel
Director of Information	Budd Bailey
Director of Media Relations	Steve Rossi
Director of Public Relations	John Gurtler
Director of Sales	Steve Donner
Director of Sales & NFSN	Don Angelo
Marketing Associates	John Livsey, Bob Russell
Assistant Ticket Manager	John Sinclair
Manager – Sabreland	Shirley Curry
Voice of the Sabres	Ted Darling
Club Doctor	John L. Butsch, M.D.
Orthopedic Consultant	Peter James, M.D.
Club Dentist	Donald DeRose, D.D.S.
Club Staff: Olive Anticola, Evelyn Battleson, Barbara Blendowski, Robert M. Dahar, Cyndi Dyll, Birgid Haensel, Chris Ivansitz, Mary Jones, Mike Kaminska, Sally Lippert, Gerry Magill, Jennifer Nappo, Melissa Nitkowski, Mary Onofrio, Cheryl Schoenthaler, Ann Marie Seaman, Carm Tramont, Bruce Wawrzyniak	
Dimensions of Rink	196 feet by 83.5 feet
Location of Press Box	Suspended from ceiling on west side
Club Colors	Blue, White, Gold
Off-Ice Officials. Hank Olejniczak (Supervisor and Offical Scorer), Tony Caggiano, Sam Costello, Richard Costolnick, Dale Guynn, Robert Kalenik, Don Kwak, Walter Mendel, Duke Morettin, Jim Murdoch, Clifford Smith, Bill Truman	
Photographer	Bill Wippert
Anthem Singers	Sue Brittain, John Putnam
Music	Dave Perry
Public Address Announcer	Milt Ellis

General Manager

MEEHAN, GERARD MARCUS (GERRY)
General Manager, Buffalo Sabres. Born in Toronto, Ont., September 3, 1946.

Gerry Meehan became general manager of the Sabres midway through the 1986-87 season. He retired as a player in 1979 after ten NHL seasons as a center with six different clubs. He played in Buffalo from 1970 to 1974 and, after his playing career, remained in the Buffalo area, earning an undergraduate degree from Canisius College and a law degree from the University of Buffalo. He practiced law in Buffalo before accepting the post of assistant GM for the Sabres in 1984-85 when he became the first former Buffalo player to move into the club's front office.

Calgary Flames

1989-90 Results: 42W-23L-15T 99PTS. First, Smythe Division

Year-by-Year Record

Season	GP	Home W	L	T	Road W	L	T	Overall W	L	T	GF	GA	Pts.	Finished	Playoff Result
1989-90	80	28	7	5	14	16	10	42	23	15	348	265	99	1st, Smythe Div.	Lost Div. Semi-Final
1988-89	80	32	4	4	22	13	5	54	17	9	354	226	117	1st, Smythe Div.	Won Stanley Cup
1987-88	80	26	11	3	22	12	6	48	23	9	397	305	105	1st, Smythe Div.	Lost Div. Final
1986-87	80	25	13	2	21	18	1	46	31	3	318	289	95	2nd, Smythe Div.	Lost Div. Semi-Final
1985-86	80	23	11	6	17	20	3	40	31	9	354	315	89	2nd, Smythe Div.	Lost Final
1984-85	80	23	11	6	18	16	6	41	27	12	363	302	94	3rd, Smythe Div.	Lost Div. Final
1983-84	80	22	11	7	12	21	7	34	32	14	311	314	82	2nd, Smythe Div.	Lost Div. Final
1982-83	80	21	12	7	11	22	7	32	34	14	321	317	78	2nd, Smythe Div.	Lost Div. Final
1981-82	80	20	11	9	9	23	8	29	34	17	334	345	75	3rd, Smythe Div.	Lost Div. Semi-Final
1980-81	80	25	5	10	14	22	4	39	27	14	329	298	92	3rd, Patrick Div.	Lost Semi-Final
1979-80	80	18	15	7	17	17	6	35	32	13	282	269	83	4th, Patrick Div.	Lost Prelim. Round
1978-79	80	25	11	4	16	20	4	41	31	8	327	280	90	4th, Patrick Div.	Lost Prelim. Round
1977-78	80	20	13	7	14	14	12	34	27	19	274	252	87	3rd, Patrick Div.	Lost Prelim. Round
1976-77	80	22	11	7	12	23	5	34	34	12	264	265	80	3rd, Patrick Div.	Lost Prelim. Round
1975-76	80	19	14	7	16	19	5	35	33	12	262	237	82	3rd, Patrick Div.	Lost Prelim. Round
1974-75	80	24	9	7	10	22	8	34	31	15	243	233	83	4th, Patrick Div.	Out of Playoffs
1973-74	78	17	15	7	13	19	7	30	34	14	214	238	74	4th, West Div.	Lost Quarter-Final
1972-73	78	16	16	7	9	22	8	25	38	15	191	239	65	7th, West Div.	Out of Playoffs

Schedule

Home

Oct. Thur. 4 Vancouver
Sat. 6 Toronto
Thur. 18 St Louis
Sat. 20 Boston
Thur. 25 Edmonton
Sat. 27 Washington
Tues. 30 New Jersey
Nov. Thur. 1 Winnipeg
Thur. 15 NY Islanders
Sat. 17 Buffalo
Thur. 22 Los Angeles
Sat. 24 Chicago
Dec. Wed. 5 NY Rangers
Fri. 7 Quebec
Tues. 18 Vancouver
Thur. 20 Los Angeles
Sat. 22 Edmonton
Sat. 29 Hartford
Mon. 31 Montreal
Jan. Sat. 5 Detroit
Tues. 15 Winnipeg
Wed. 30 NY Rangers
Feb. Sat. 2 Chicago
Fri. 15 Washington
Sun 17 St Louis
Tues. 19 Detroit
Thur. 21 Vancouver
Sat. 23 Quebec
Wed. 27 Edmonton
Mar. Fri. 1 Pittsburgh
Sat. 2 Minnesota
Mon. 4 Montreal
Thur. 7 Philadelphia
Tues. 12 Winnipeg
Thur. 14 NY Islanders
Sat. 16 Los Angeles
Mon. 18 Winnipeg
Tues. 26 Vancouver
Thur. 28 Edmonton
Sun. 31 Los Angeles*

Away

Oct. Mon. 8 Winnipeg
Wed. 10 Detroit
Sat. 13 New Jersey
Sun. 14 Chicago*
Sun. 21 Edmonton
Tues. 23 Los Angeles
Nov. Sat. 3 Toronto
Sun. 4 Buffalo
Tues. 6 Pittsburgh
Thur. 8 Philadelphia
Sat. 10 NY Islanders
Sun. 11 NY Rangers
Mon. 19 Vancouver
Wed. 28 Winnipeg
Dec. Sat. 1 Montreal
Sun. 2 Quebec
Sun. 9 Edmonton
Tues. 11 Minnesota
Thur. 13 Los Angeles
Sun. 16 Vancouver*
Thur. 27 Edmonton
Jan. Wed. 2 Winnipeg
Tues. 8 Toronto
Thur. 10 Pittsburgh
Fri. 11 Washington
Sun. 13 Winnipeg
Tues. 22 Philadelphia
Wed. 23 Hartford
Sat. 26 Boston*
Sun. 27 Buffalo*
Feb. Tues. 5 New Jersey
Thur. 7 Boston
Sat. 9 Hartford
Tues. 12 Los Angeles
Mon. 25 Vancouver
Mar. Sat. 9 St Louis
Sun. 10 Minnesota
Wed. 20 Vancouver
Sat. 23 Los Angeles*
Fri. 29 Edmonton

* Denotes afternoon game.

Home Starting Times:

Weeknights .... 7:35 p.m.
Except Dec. 31 .... 6:05 p.m.
Saturdays and Sundays .... 6:05 p.m.
Except Mar. 31 .... 1:35 p.m.

Franchise date: June 24, 1980.
Transferred from Atlanta

19th NHL Season

Theoren Fleury led the Flames with six game-winning goals in 1989-90.

1990-91 Player Personnel

FORWARDS	HT	WT	S	Place of Birth	Date	1989-90 Club
BANKS, Darren	6-2	215	L	Toronto, Ont.	3/18/66	Salt Lake
BUCYK, Randy	5-11	185	L	Edmonton, Alta.	11/9/62	Salt Lake
BUREAU, Marc	6-0	190	R	Trois Rivieres, Que.	5/19/66	Salt Lake-Calgary
CHERNOMAZ, Rick	5-8	185	R	Selkirk, Man.	9/1/63	Salt Lake
CLARK, Kerry	6-1	190	R	Kelvington, Sask.	8/21/68	Springfield-Phoenix
DEASLEY, Bryan	6-3	205	L	Toronto, Ont.	11/26/68	Salt Lake
FLEURY, Theoren	5-6	160	R	Oxbow, Sask.	6/29/68	Calgary
GILMOUR, Doug	5-11	170	L	Kingston, Ont.	6/25/63	Calgary
GRIMSON, Stu	6-5	220	L	Kamloops, B.C.	5/20/65	Salt Lake-Calgary
HARKINS, Todd	6-3	210	R	Cleveland, OH	10/8/68	U. of Miami of Ohio
HOLMES, Mark	6-2	200	R	Kingston, Jamaica	6/7/64	Salt Lake
HRDINA, Jiri	6-0	195	R	Prague, Czech.	1/5/58	Calgary
HUNTER, Mark	6.0	200	R	Petrolia, Ont.	11/12/62	Calgary
HUNTER, Tim	6-2	202	R	Calgary, Alta.	9/10/60	Calgary
KRUSE, Paul	6-0	202	L	Merritt, B.C.	3/15/70	Kamloops
LYONS, Corey	5-10	186	L	Calgary, Alta.	6/13/70	Lethbridge
MacLELLAN, Brian	6-3	215	L	Guelph, Ont.	10/27/58	Calgary
MAKAROV, Sergei	5-11	185	R	Chelyabinsk, USSR	6/19/58	Calgary
MATTEAU, Stephane	6-3	190	L	Rouyn-Noranda, Que.	9/2/69	Salt Lake
NIEUWENDYK, Joe	6-1	195	L	Oshawa, Ont.	9/10/66	Calgary
OLSEN, Darryl	6-0	180	L	Calgary, Alta.	10/7/66	Salt Lake
OTTO, Joel	6-4	220	R	Elk River, MN	10/29/61	Calgary
PATTERSON, Colin	6-2	195	R	Rexdale, Ont.	5/11/60	Calgary
PICKELL, Doug	5-11	190	L	Sherwood Park, Alta.	5/7/68	Salt Lake
PRIAKIN, Sergei	6-3	210	L	Moscow, USSR	12/7/63	Calgary-Salt Lake
RANHEIM, Paul	6-0	195	R	St. Louis, MO	1/25/66	Calgary
REICHEL, Robert	5-10	185	L	Litvinov, Czech.	6/25/71	Litvinov, Czech.
ROBERTS, Gary	6-1	190	L	North York, Ont.	5/23/66	Calgary
SIMARD, Martin	6-3	215	R	Montreal, Que.	6/25/66	Salt Lake
SWEENEY, Tim	5-11	180	L	Boston, MA	4/12/67	Salt Lake

DEFENSEMEN						
GLYNN, Brian	6-4	215	L	Iserlohn, W. Ger.	11/23/67	Calgary
GRANT, Kevin	6-3	210	R	Toronto, Ont.	1/9/69	Sudbury-Salt Lake
KAUTOMEN, Veli-P.	6-2	195	L	Helsinki, Finland	5/9/70	IFK Helsinki (Fin.)
JOHANSSON, Roger	6-1	185	L	Ljungby, Sweden	4/17/67	Calgary
LESSARD, Rick	6-2	200	L	Timmins, Ont.	1/9/68	Salt Lake
MacINNIS, Al	6-2	196	R	Inverness, N.S.	7/11/63	Calgary
MACOUN, Jamie	6-2	197	L	Newmarket, Ont.	8/17/61	Calgary
McCRADY, Scott	6-1	195	R	Calgary, Alta.	10/30/68	Kalamazoo
MELROSE, Kevan	5-10	185	L	Calgary, Alta.	3/28/66	Harvard
MURZYN, Dana	6-2	200	L	Calgary, Alta.	12/9/66	Calgary
NATTRESS, Ric	6-2	210	R	Hamilton, Ont.	5/25/62	Calgary
OSIECKI, Mark	6-2	200	R	St. Paul, MN	7/23/68	U. Wisconsin
SABOURIN, Ken	6-3	205	L	Scarborough, Ont.	4/28/66	Salt Lake-Calgary
SUMNER, Rob	6-1	210	L	N. Vancouver, B.C.	9/28/70	Victoria
SUTER, Gary	6-0	190	L	Madison, WI	6/24/64	Calgary

GOALTENDERS	HT	WT	C	Place of Birth	Date	1989-90 Club
COWLEY, Wayne	6-0	185	L	Scarborough, Ont.	12/4/64	Salt Lake
GUENETTE, Steve	5-10	175	L	Gloucester, Ont.	11/13/65	Salt Lake-Calgary
KIDD, Trevor	6-2	180	L	Dugald, Man.	3/29/72	Brandon
SHARPLES, Warren	6-0	180	L	Calgary, Alta.	3/1/68	U. of Michigan
VERNON, Mike	5-9	170	L	Calgary, Alta.	2/24/63	Calgary
WAMSLEY, Rick	5-11	185	L	Simcoe, Ont.	5/25/59	Calgary

Lanny McDonald's #9 is the first number retired by the Flames.

1989-90 Scoring

Regular Season

* rookie

Pos	#	Player	Team	GP	G	A	Pts	+/-	PIM	PP	SH	GW	GT	S	%
C	25	Joe Nieuwendyk	CGY	79	45	50	95	32	40	18	0	3	0	226	19.9
C	39	Doug Gilmour	CGY	78	24	67	91	20	54	12	1	3	0	152	15.8
D	2	Al MacInnis	CGY	79	28	62	90	20	82	14	1	3	0	304	9.2
R	42	*Sergei Makarov	CGY	80	24	62	86	33	55	6	0	4	0	118	20.3
D	20	Gary Suter	CGY	76	16	60	76	4	97	5	0	1	0	211	7.6
L	10	Gary Roberts	CGY	78	39	33	72	31	222	5	0	5	0	175	22.3
R	7	Joe Mullen	CGY	78	36	33	69	6	24	8	3	5	0	236	15.3
C	14	Theo Fleury	CGY	80	31	35	66	22	157	9	3	6	3	200	15.5
L	28	*Paul Ranheim	CGY	80	26	28	54	27	23	1	3	4	2	197	13.2
L	27	Brian MacLellan	CGY	65	20	18	38	3-	26	10	0	3	1	127	15.7
D	34	Jamie Macoun	CGY	78	8	27	35	34	70	1	0	1	0	120	6.7
C	29	Joel Otto	CGY	75	13	20	33	4	116	7	0	0	0	96	13.5
R	17	Jiri Hrdina	CGY	64	12	18	30	10	31	0	0	3	0	96	12.5
D	5	Dana Murzyn	CGY	78	7	13	20	19	140	1	0	0	0	97	7.2
D	4	Brad McCrimmon	CGY	79	4	15	19	18	78	0	0	0	0	97	4.1
D	6	Ric Nattress	CGY	49	1	14	15	14	26	0	0	0	0	65	1.5
L	11	Colin Patterson	CGY	61	5	3	8	4-	20	0	0	0	0	56	8.9
R	18	*Jonas Bergqvist	CGY	22	2	5	7	10	10	0	0	0	0	30	6.7
L	26	Jim Korn	N.J.	37	2	3	5	1-	99	0	0	0	0	18	11.1
			CGY	9	0	2	2	1	26	0	0	0	0	3	.0
			TOTAL	46	2	5	7	0	125	0	0	0	0	21	9.5
R	22	Mark Hunter	CGY	10	2	3	5	0	39	2	0	0	0	15	13.3
R	19	Tim Hunter	CGY	67	2	3	5	9-	279	0	0	0	0	69	2.9
D	21	*Roger Johansson	CGY	35	0	5	5	9	48	0	0	0	0	23	.0
R	16	*Sergei Priakin	CGY	20	2	2	4	7-	0	0	0	1	0	17	11.8
G	30	Mike Vernon	CGY	47	0	3	3	0	21	0	0	0	0	0	.0
L	24	Jim Peplinski	CGY	6	1	0	1	1-	4	0	0	0	0	12	8.3
D	32	Brian Glynn	CGY	1	0	0	0	1-	0	0	0	0	0	0	.0
G	1	Steve Guenette	CGY	2	0	0	0	0	2	0	0	0	0	0	.0
L	35	*Stu Grimson	CGY	3	0	0	0	1-	17	0	0	0	0	0	.0
R	33	*Marc Bureau	CGY	5	0	0	0	1-	4	0	0	0	0	3	.0
D	55	*Ken Sabourin	CGY	5	0	0	0	1	10	0	0	0	0	0	.0
G	31	Rick Wamsley	CGY	36	0	0	0	0	4	0	0	0	0	0	.0

Goaltending

No.	Goaltender	GPI	Mins	Avg	W	L	T	EN	SO	GA	SA	S%
30	Mike Vernon	47	2795	3.13	23	14	9	2	0	146	1122	.870
31	Rick Wamsley	36	1969	3.26	18	8	6	2	2	107	855	.875
1	Steve Guenette	2	119	4.03	1	1	0	0	0	8	50	.840
	Totals	**80**	**4895**	**3.25**	**42**	**23**	**15**	**4**	**2**	**265**	**2027**	**.869**

Playoffs

Pos	#	Player	Team	GP	G	A	Pts	+/-	PIM	PP	SH	GW	OT	S	%
C	25	Joe Nieuwendyk	CGY	6	4	6	10	6	4	1	0	1	0	19	21.1
L	10	Gary Roberts	CGY	6	2	5	7	5	41	0	0	0	0	10	20.0
R	42	*Sergei Makarov	CGY	6	0	6	6	3	0	0	0	0	0	5	.0
C	14	Theo Fleury	CGY	6	2	3	5	4	10	0	0	0	0	19	10.5
D	2	Al MacInnis	CGY	6	2	3	5	1	8	1	0	0	0	19	10.5
C	39	Doug Gilmour	CGY	6	3	1	4	6-	8	0	0	1	0	12	25.0
D	5	Dana Murzyn	CGY	6	2	2	4	2	2	0	0	0	0	14	14.3
C	29	Joel Otto	CGY	6	2	2	4	2	2	0	0	0	0	9	22.2
L	28	*Paul Ranheim	CGY	6	1	3	4	2	0	0	0	0	0	11	9.1
R	7	Joe Mullen	CGY	6	3	0	3	4-	0	1	0	0	0	12	25.0
D	34	Jamie Macoun	CGY	6	0	3	3	2	10	0	0	0	0	5	.0
D	6	Ric Nattress	CGY	6	0	2	2	2	8	0	0	0	0	11	18.2
L	27	Brian MacLellan	CGY	6	0	2	2	7-	8	0	0	0	0	13	.0
D	4	Brad McCrimmon	CGY	6	0	2	2	0	8	0	0	0	0	1	.0
L	26	Jim Korn	CGY	4	1	0	1	0	12	0	0	0	2	50.0
R	17	Jiri Hrdina	CGY	6	0	1	1	0	2	0	0	0	0	10	.0
D	20	Gary Suter	CGY	6	0	1	1	0	14	0	0	0	0	20	.0
G	31	Rick Wamsley	CGY	1	0	0	0	0	0	0	0	0	0	0	.0
R	16	*Sergei Priakin	CGY	2	0	0	0	0	0	0	0	0	0	1	.0
R	19	Tim Hunter	CGY	6	0	0	0	0	4	0	0	0	0	2	.0
G	30	Mike Vernon	CGY	6	0	0	0	0	0	0	0	0	0	0	.0

Goaltending

No.	Goaltender	GPI	Mins	Avg	W	L	EN	SO	GA	SA	S%
30	Mike Vernon	6	342	3.33	2	3	1	0	19	150	.873
31	Rick Wamsley	1	49	11.02	0	1	0	0	9	23	.609
	Totals	**6**	**392**	**4.44**	**2**	**4**	**1**	**0**	**29**	**173**	**.832**

General Manager's History
Cliff Fletcher, 1972-73 to date.

Coaching History
Bernie Geoffrion, 1972-73 to 1973-74; Bernie Geoffrion and Fred Creighton, 1974-75; Fred Creighton, 1975-76 to 1978-79 (Atlanta); 1980-81 to 1981-82 (Calgary); Al MacNeil, 1979-80 (Atlanta); 1980-81 to 1981-82 (Calgary); Bob Johnson, 1982-83 to 1986-87; Terry Crisp, 1987-88 to 1989-90; Doug Risebrough, 1990-91.

Captains' History
Keith McCreary, 1972-73 to 1974-75; Pat Quinn, 1975-76, 1976-77; Tom Lysiak, 1977-78, 1978-79; Jean Pronovost, 1979-80; Brad Marsh, 1980-81; Phil Russell, 1981-82, 1982-83; Lanny McDonald, Doug Risebrough (co-captains), 1983-84; Lanny McDonald, Doug Risebrough, Jim Peplinski (tri-captains) to 1986-87; Lanny McDonald, Jim Peplinski (co-captains), 1987-88; Lanny McDonald, Jim Peplinski, Tim Hunter (tri-captains), 1988-89; Brad McCrimmon, 1989-90.

Retired Numbers
9	Lanny McDonald	1981-1989

Club Records

Team

(Figures in brackets for season records are games played; records for fewest points, wins, ties, losses, goals, goals against are for 70 or more games)

Most Points	117	1988-89 (80)	
Most Wins	54	1988-89 (80)	
Most Ties	19	1977-78 (80)	
Most Losses	38	1972-73 (78)	
Most Goals	397	1987-88 (80)	
Most Goals Against	345	1981-82 (80)	
Fewest Points	65	1972-73 (78)	
Fewest Wins	25	1972-73 (78)	
Fewest Ties	3	1986-87 (80)	
Fewest Losses	17	1988-89 (80)	
Fewest Goals	191	1972-73 (78)	
Fewest Goals Against	226	1988-89 (80)	

Longest Winning Streak
- Overall ... 10 Oct. 14-Nov. 3/78
- Home ... 9 Oct. 17-Nov. 15/78 Jan. 3-Feb. 5/89 Mar. 3-Apr. 1/90
- Away ... 7 Nov. 10-Dec. 4/88

Longest Undefeated Streak
- Over-all ... 13 Nov. 10-Dec. 8/88 (12 wins, 1 tie)
- Home ... 17 Oct. 6-Dec. 15/88 (14 wins, 3 ties)
- Away ... 9 Feb. 20-Mar. 21/88 (6 wins, 3 ties)

Longest Losing Streak
- Over-all ... 11 Dec. 14/85-Jan. 7/86
- Home ... 4 Four times
- Away ... 9 Dec. 1/85-Jan. 12/86

Longest Winless Streak
- Over-all ... 11 Dec. 14/85-Jan. 7/86 (11 losses)

- Home ... 6 Nov. 25-Dec. 18/82 (5 losses, 1 tie)
- Away ... 13 Feb. 3-Mar. 29/73 (10 losses, 3 ties)

Most Shutouts, Season	8	1974-75 (80)
Most PIM, Season	2,431	1987-88 (80)
Most Goals, Game	12	Mar. 21/75 (Van. 4 at Atl. 12) Feb. 22/90 (Tor. 2 at Cgy. 12)

Individual

Most Seasons	10	Jim Peplinski
Most Games	705	Jim Peplinski
Most Goals, Career	229	Kent Nilsson
Most Assists, Career	398	Al MacInnis
Most Points, Career	562	Kent Nilsson (229 goals, 333 assists)
Most PIM, Career	2,095	Tim Hunter
Most Shutouts, Career	20	Dan Bouchard
Longest Consecutive Games Streak	257	Brad Marsh (Oct. 11/78-Nov. 10/81)
Most Goals, Season	66	Lanny McDonald (1982-83)
Most Assists, Season	82	Kent Nilsson (1980-81)
Most Points, Season	131	Kent Nilsson (1980-81) (49 goals, 82 assists)
Most PIM, Season	375	Tim Hunter (1988-89)
Most Points, Defenseman Season	91	Gary Suter (1987-88) (21 goals, 70 assists)
Most Points, Center Season	131	Kent Nilsson (1980-81) (49 goals, 82 assists)
Most Points, Right Wing Season	110	Joe Mullen (1988-89) (51 goals, 59 assists)
Most Points, Left Wing Season	83	Eric Vail (1978-79) (35 goals, 48 assists)
Most Points, Rookie Season	92	Joe Nieuwendyk (1987-88) (51 goals, 41 assists)
Most Shutouts, Season	5	Dan Bouchard (1973-74) Phil Myre (1974-75)
Most Goals, Game	5	Joe Nieuwendyk (Jan. 11/89)
Most Assists, Game	6	Guy Chouinard (Feb. 25/81) Gary Suter (Apr. 4/86)
Most Points, Game	7	Sergei Makarov (Feb. 25/90)

All-time Record vs. Other Clubs

Regular Season

	At Home						On Road						Total					
	GP	W	L	T	GF	GA	PTS	GP	W	L	T	GF	GA	PTS	GP	W	L	T	GF	GA	PTS
Boston	34	13	19	2	125	128	28	33	9	20	4	90	114	22	67	22	39	6	215	242	50
Buffalo	33	13	11	9	122	112	35	33	10	19	4	100	141	24	66	23	30	13	222	253	59
Chicago	36	19	10	7	126	107	45	35	10	17	8	105	131	28	71	29	27	15	231	238	73
Detroit	02	21	7	4	140	97	40	00	11	17	5	110	131	27	05	32	24	9	258	228	73
Edmonton	40	19	17	4	189	161	42	40	10	22	8	149	189	28	80	29	39	12	338	350	70
Hartford	18	14	3	1	99	65	29	17	8	6	3	68	60	19	35	22	9	4	167	125	48
Los Angeles	56	34	14	8	268	189	76	55	22	29	4	210	222	48	111	56	43	12	478	411	124
Minnesota	35	21	4	10	144	94	52	35	13	17	5	113	130	31	70	34	21	15	257	224	83
Montreal	32	7	20	5	100	121	19	33	9	19	5	80	117	23	65	16	39	10	180	238	42
New Jersey	32	25	3	4	158	80	54	32	22	7	3	129	86	47	64	47	10	7	287	166	101
NY Islanders	38	17	10	11	141	120	45	39	10	20	9	106	153	29	77	27	30	20	247	273	74
NY Rangers	38	22	10	6	175	120	50	39	18	17	4	145	141	40	77	40	27	10	320	261	90
Philadelphia	39	19	12	8	162	135	46	39	10	28	1	97	164	21	78	29	40	9	259	299	67
Pittsburgh	33	19	7	7	139	94	45	33	10	14	9	113	118	29	66	29	21	16	252	212	74
Quebec	17	10	3	4	75	47	24	18	8	7	3	71	76	19	35	18	10	7	146	123	43
St. Louis	35	18	14	3	123	100	39	36	17	14	5	117	127	39	71	35	28	8	240	227	78
Toronto	35	21	11	3	183	119	45	33	12	14	7	127	137	31	68	33	25	10	290	256	76
Vancouver	57	40	9	8	262	158	88	57	25	20	12	193	197	62	114	65	29	20	455	355	150
Washington	27	19	5	3	115	62	41	28	12	12	4	106	106	28	55	31	17	7	221	168	69
Winnipeg	38	27	7	4	191	117	58	37	14	17	6	138	156	34	75	41	24	10	329	273	92
Defunct Club	13	8	4	1	51	34	17	13	7	3	3	43	33	17	26	15	7	4	94	67	34
Totals	**718**	**406**	**200**	**112**	**3076**	**2260**	**924**	**718**	**267**	**339**	**112**	**2410**	**2729**	**646**	**1436**	**673**	**539**	**224**	**5486**	**4989**	**1570**

Playoffs

	Series	W	L	GP	W	L	T	GF	GA	Last Mtg.	Round	Result
Chicago	2	2	0	8	7	1	0	30	17	1989	CF	W 4-1
Detroit	1	0	1	2	0	2	0	5	8	1978	PR	L 0-2
Edmonton	4	1	3	23	8	15	0	76	110	1978	DF	L 0-4
Los Angeles	5	2	3	20	11	9	0	74	72	1990	DSF	L 2-4
Minnesota	1	0	1	6	2	4	0	18	25	1981	SF	L 2-4
Montreal	2	1	1	11	5	6	0	32	31	1989	F	W 4-2
NY Rangers	1	0	1	4	1	3	0	8	14	1980	PR	L 1-3
Philadelphia	2	1	1	11	4	7	0	28	43	1981	QF	W 4-3
St. Louis	1	1	0	7	4	3	0	28	22	1986	CF	W 4-3
Toronto	1	0	1	2	0	2	0	5	9	1979	PR	L 0-2
Vancouver	4	3	1	18	10	8	0	62	57	1989	DSF	W 4-3
Winnipeg	3	1	2	13	6	7	0	43	45	1987	DSF	L 2-4
Totals	**27**	**12**	**15**	**125**	**58**	**67**	**0**	**419**	**453**			

Playoff Results 1990-86

Year	Round	Opponent	Result	GF	GA
1990	DSF	Los Angeles	L 2-4	24	29
1989	F	Montreal	W 4-2	19	16
	CF	Chicago	W 4-1	15	8
	DF	Los Angeles	W 4-0	22	11
	DSF	Vancouver	W 4-3	26	20
1988	DF	Edmonton	L 0-4	11	18
	DSF	Los Angeles	W 4-1	30	18
1987	DSF	Winnipeg	L 2-4	15	22
1986	F	Montreal	L 1-4	13	15
	CF	St. Louis	W 4-3	28	22
	DF	Edmonton	W 4-3	25	24
	DSF	Winnipeg	W 3-0	15	8

Abbreviations: Round: F Final; **CF** conference final; **DF** division final; **DSF** division semi-final; **SF** semi-final; **QF** quarter-final. **PR** preliminary round. **GA** goals against; **GF** goals for.

1989-90 Results

		Home					Away	
Oct.	5	Detroit	10-7	Oct.	10	New Jersey	4-2
	7	NY Islanders	6-3		11	NY Rangers	4-5
	21	Boston	5-2		14	Washington	4-4
	23	Washington	3-3		15	Philadelphia	3-2
	27	Vancouver	5-5		17	Quebec	8-8
Nov.	1	Winnipeg	5-3		18	Montreal	1-2
	4	New Jersey	7-3		25	Los Angeles	5-0
	6	Edmonton	5-1		28	Vancouver	3-4
	14	Los Angeles	6-8	Nov.	3	Edmonton	2-5
	16	Buffalo	4-4		8	Los Angeles	5-4
	16	Chicago	4-4		11	Minnesota	2-3
	30	Minnesota	5-2		12	Winnipeg	2-3
Dec.	2	Toronto	7-4		20	Montreal	2-3
	6	Winnipeg	3-4		21	Quebec	4-4
	14	Quebec	8-2		24	Detroit	2-3
	16	Pittsburgh	4-3		25	St. Louis	3-3
	20	Vancouver	2-1	Dec.	10	Winnipeg*	1-4
	29	Winnipeg	1-2		11	Edmonton	3-3
	30	Montreal	5-3		19	Vancouver	2-1
Jan.	2	Philadelphia	4-4		23	Edmonton	1-2
	5	Hartford	6-4		27	Los Angeles	5-5
	9	Edmonton	2-3	Jan.	7	Edmonton	3-1
	11	Buffalo	5-3		13	Toronto	5-6
	25	NY Rangers	8-5		14	Chicago	6-5
	27	Minnesota	3-1		16	St. Louis	5-2
Feb.	1	Vancouver	4-3		18	Boston	2-2
	6	Los Angeles	3-5		19	Hartford	3-3
	20	Boston	3-5		30	Vancouver	7-2
	22	Toronto	12-2	Feb.	3	Los Angeles	3-4
	25	Edmonton	10-4		10	Detroit*	5-7
Mar.	1	Philadelphia	2-4		11	NY Rangers*	5-2
	3	Vancouver	5-1		13	NY Islanders	4-2
	5	Los Angeles	5-0		15	Chicago	3-2
	7	Pittsburgh	6-3		18	Winnipeg*	1-5
	12	Winnipeg	5-4	Mar.	9	Vancouver	4-4
	15	New Jersey	5-4		11	Winnipeg*	6-4
	17	Hartford	5-4		21	Buffalo	3-3
	19	St Louis	5-2		24	Pittsburgh*	3-3
	30	Edmonton	6-2		25	Washington*	1-4
Apr.	1	Los Angeles	8-4		27	NY Islanders	4-2

* Denotes afternoon game.

Entry Draft
Selections 1990-76

1990
Pick
11	Trevor Kidd
26	Nicolas P. Perreault
32	Vesa Viitakoski
41	Etienne Belzile
62	Glen Mears
83	Paul Kruse
125	Chris Tschupp
146	Dimitri Frolov
167	Shawn Murray
188	Mike Murray
209	Rob Sumner
230	invalid claim
251	Leo Gudas

1989
Pick
24	Kent Manderville
42	Ted Drury
50	Veli-Pekka Kautonen
63	Corey Lyons
70	Robert Reichel
84	Ryan O'Leary
105	Francis (Toby) Kearney
147	Alex Nikolic
168	Kevin Wortman
189	Sergei Gomolyakov
210	Dan Sawyer
231	Alexander Yudin
252	Kenneth Kennholt

1988
Pick
21	Jason Muzzatti
42	Todd Harkins
84	Gary Socha
85	Thomas Forslund
90	Scott Matusovich
126	Jonas Bergqvist
147	Stefan Nilsson
168	Troy Kennedy
189	Brett Peterson
210	Guy Darveau
231	Dave Tretowicz
252	Sergei Priakin

1987
Pick
19	Bryan Deasley
25	Stephane Matteau
40	Kevin Grant
61	Scott Mahoney
70	Tim Harris
103	Tim Corkery
124	Joe Aloi
145	Peter Ciavaglia
166	Theoren Fleury
187	Mark Osiecki
208	William Sedergren
229	Peter Hasselblad
250	Magnus Svensson

1986
Pick
16	George Pelawa
37	Brian Glynn
79	Tom Quinlan
100	Scott Bloom
121	John Parker
142	Rick Lessard
163	Mark Olsen
184	Warren Sharples
205	Doug Pickell
226	Anders Lindstrom
247	Antonin Stavjana

1985
Pick
17	Chris Biotti
27	Joe Nieuwendyk
38	Jeff Wenaas
59	Lane MacDonald
80	Roger Johansson
101	Esa Keskinen
122	Tim Sweeney
143	Stu Grimson
164	Nate Smith
185	Darryl Olsen
206	Peter Romberg
227	Alexandr Koznevnikov
248	Bill Gregoire

1984
Pick
12	Gary Roberts
33	Ken Sabourin
38	Paul Ranheim
75	Peter Rosol
96	Joel Paunio
117	Brett Hull
138	Kevan Melrose
159	Jiri Hrdina
180	Gary Suter
200	Peter Rucka
221	Stefan Jonsson
241	Rudolf Suchanek

1983
Pick
13	Dan Quinn
51	Brian Bradley
55	Perry Berezan
66	John Bekkers
71	Kevan Guy
77	Bill Claviter
91	Igor Liba
111	Grant Blair
131	Jeff Hogg
151	Chris MacDonald
171	Rob Kivell
191	Tom Pratt
211	Jaroslav Benak
231	Sergei Makarov

1982
Pick
29	Dave Reierson
37	Richard Kromm
51	Jim Laing
65	Dave Meszaros
72	Mark Lamb
93	Lou Kiriakou
114	Jeff Vaive
118	Mats Kihlstrom
135	Brad Ramsden
156	Roy Myllari
177	Ted Pearson
198	Jim Uens
219	Rick Erdall
240	Dale Thompson

1981
Pick
15	Allan MacInnis
56	Mike Vernon
78	Peter Madach
99	Mario Simioni
120	Todd Hooey
141	Rick Heppner
162	Dale Degray
183	George Boudreau
204	Bruce Eakin

1980
Pick
13	Denis Cyr
31	Tony Curtale
32	Kevin LaVallee
39	Steve Konroyd
76	Marc Roy
97	Randy Turnbull
118	John Multan
139	Dave Newsom
160	Claude Drouin
181	Hakan Loob
202	Steve Fletcher

1979
Pick
12	Paul Reinhart
23	Mike Perovich
33	Pat Riggin
54	Tim Hunter
75	Jim Peplinski
96	Brad Kempthorne
117	Glenn Johnson

1978
Pick
11	Brad Marsh
47	Tim Bernhardt
64	Jim MacRae
80	Gord Wappel
97	Greg Meredith
114	Dave Hindmarch
131	Dave Morrison
148	Doug Todd
165	Mark Green
180	Robert Sullivan
196	Berhn Engelbeckt

1977
Pick
20	Miles Zaharko
28	Red Laurence
31	Brian Hill
72	Jim Craig
82	Curt Christofferson
100	Bernard Harbec
118	Bob Gould
133	Jim Bennett
148	Tim Harrer

1976
Pick
8	David Shand
10	Harold Phillipoff
28	Bob Simpson
46	Richard Hodgson
64	Kent Nilsson
82	Mark Earp

Club Directory

Olympic Saddledome
P.O. Box 1540 Station M
Calgary, Alberta T2P 3B9
Phone **403/261-0475**
FAX 403/261-0470
ENVOY ID
Public
Relations: FLAMES. PR
Capacity: 20,130

Owners
Harley N. Hotchkiss	Byron J. Seaman
Norman L. Kwong	Daryl K. Seaman
Sonia Scurfield	

President, General Manager, Governor	Cliff Fletcher
Vice-President, Business and Finance	Clare Rhyasen
Vice-President, Hockey Operations	Al MacNeil
Vice-President, Sales & Broadcasting	Leo Ornest
Vice-President, Corporate & Community Relations	Lanny McDonald
Director of Hockey Administration	Al Coates
Assistant General Manager/Head Coach	Doug Risebrough
Controller	Lynne Tosh
Director of Public Relations	Rick Skaggs
Assistant Coaches	Paul Baxter, Guy Charron
Goaltending Consultant	Glenn Hall
Director of Professional Development	Terry Crisp
Salt Lake City Head Coach	Bobby Francis
Salt Lake City Assistant Coach	Jamie Hislop
Chief Scout	Gerry Blair
Co-ordinator of Scouting	Ian McKenzie
Scouts	Ray Clearwater, Al Godfrey, Gerry McNamara, Larry Popein, Lou Reycroft
Scouting Staff	Garth Malarchuk, David Mayville, Lars Norrman, Pekka Rautakallio, Tom Thompson
Executive Secretaries	Brenda Koyich, Bernie Doenz, June Yeates
Ticket Manager	Ann-Marie Malarchuk
Assistant Ticket Manager	Linda Forrest
Secretary	Lynn Horton
Assistant Public Relations Director	Mike Burke
Assistant Controller	Dorothy Stuart
Assistant to Vice-President, Sales	Judy Shupe
Marketing and Advertising	Pat Halls
Manager, Retail Operations	Mark Mason
Receptionist	Anita Cranston
Trainer	Jim ''Bearcat'' Murray
Equipment Manager	Bobby Stewart
Assistant Trainer	Al Murray
Director of Medicine	Dr. Terry Groves
Orthopedic Surgeon	Dr. Lowell Van Zuiden
Team Dentist	Dr. Bill Blair
Consulting Psychologists	Hap Davis, Ph.D. and Robert Offenberger, Ph.D.
Location of Press Boxes	Print/TV—North side; Radio—South Side
Dimensions of Rink	200 feet by 85 feet
Ends of Rink	Tempered Glass
Club Colours	White, Red and Gold
Club Trains at	Olympic Saddledome
TV Channels	CFAC-TV (Channels 2 & 7) CBC-TV (Channels 6 & 9)
Radio	CFR Radio (660 AM)

General Manager

FLETCHER, GEORGE CLIFFORD (CLIFF)
General Manager, Calgary Flames. Born in Montreal, Que., August 16, 1935.

Cliff Fletcher's career in professional hockey began in 1956 when he joined the Montreal Canadiens' organization as manager of the Junior ''B'' Verdun Blues. For the next 10 years, working closely with former Canadien manager Sam Pollock, Fletcher carried out a variety of functions, including coaching and managing the Junior Canadiens and scouting for the parent team. In May, 1966, he joined the St. Louis Blues as chief scout for eastern Canada and remained in that post until June, 1969, when he was appointed assistant general manager, a position he held until the end of the 1970-71 season. During his four full seasons with St. Louis, the Blues never failed to reach the playoffs; were Stanley Cup finalists three years in a row and captured two West Division titles. He was named general manager of the Atlanta Flames, January 10, 1972, and retained the position when the franchise was transferred to Calgary in 1980.

Coach

RISEBROUGH, DOUG
Coach, Calgary Flames. Born in Guelph, Ont., January 29, 1954

Doug Risebrough was appointed head coach of the Calgary Flames on May 18, 1990. After ending his 14-year NHL playing career with the Flames in 1987, Risebrough was named an assistant coach, joining Terry Crisp behind the bench. On June 27, 1989 he was appointed assistant general manager. He retains that title in addition to his coaching duties.

Risebrough was Montreal's first selection, seventh overall, in the 1974 Amateur Draft. During his nine years with the Canadiens, he helped his club to four consecutive Stanley Cup championships between 1976 and 1979. He joined the Flames just prior to the start of the club's 1982 training camp. During his NHL career, his clubs have won five Stanley Cups (1976-1979 and 1989 with Calgary) and two Presidents' Trophies (1987-88 and 1988-89).

Chicago Blackhawks

1989-90 Results: 41W-33L-6T 88PTS. First, Norris Division

Year-by-Year Record

Season	Home GP	Home W	Home L	Home T	Road W	Road L	Road T	Overall W	Overall L	Overall T	GF	GA	Pts.	Finished		Playoff Result
1989-90	80	25	13	2	16	20	4	41	33	6	316	294	88	1st,	Norris Div.	Lost Conf. Championship
1988-89	80	16	14	10	11	27	2	27	41	12	297	335	66	4th,	Norris Div.	Lost Conf. Championship
1987-88	80	21	17	2	9	24	7	30	41	9	284	326	69	3rd,	Norris Div.	Lost Div. Semi-Final
1986-87	80	18	13	9	11	24	5	29	37	14	290	310	72	3rd,	Norris Div.	Lost Div. Semi-Final
1985-86	80	23	12	5	16	21	3	39	33	8	351	349	86	1st,	Norris Div.	Lost Div. Semi-Final
1984-85	80	22	16	2	16	19	5	38	35	7	309	299	83	2nd,	Norris Div.	Lost Conf. Championship
1983-84	80	25	13	2	5	29	6	30	42	8	277	311	68	4th,	Norris Div.	Lost Div. Semi-Final
1982-83	80	29	8	3	18	15	7	47	23	10	338	268	104	1st,	Norris Div.	Lost Conf. Championship
1981-82	80	20	13	7	10	25	5	30	38	12	332	363	72	4th,	Norris Div.	Lost Conf. Championship
1980-81	80	21	11	8	10	22	8	31	33	16	304	315	78	2nd,	Smythe Div.	Lost Prelim. Round
1979-80	80	21	12	7	13	15	12	34	27	19	241	250	87	1st,	Smythe Div.	Lost Quarter-Final
1978-79	80	18	12	10	11	24	5	29	36	15	244	277	73	1st,	Smythe Div.	Lost Quarter-Final
1977-78	80	20	9	11	12	20	8	32	29	19	230	220	83	1st,	Smythe Div.	Lost Quarter-Final
1976-77	80	19	16	5	7	27	6	26	43	11	240	298	63	3rd,	Smythe Div.	Lost Prelim. Round
1975-76	80	17	15	8	15	15	10	32	30	18	254	261	82	1st,	Smythe Div.	Lost Quarter-Final
1974-75	80	24	12	4	13	23	4	37	35	8	268	241	82	3rd,	Smythe Div.	Lost Quarter-Final
1973-74	78	20	6	13	21	8	10	41	14	23	272	164	105	2nd,	West Div.	Lost Semi-Final
1972-73	78	26	9	4	16	18	5	42	27	9	284	225	93	1st,	West Div.	Lost Final
1971-72	78	28	3	8	18	14	7	46	17	15	256	166	107	1st,	West Div.	Lost Semi-Final
1970-71	78	30	6	3	19	14	6	49	20	9	277	184	107	1st,	West Div.	Lost Final
1969-70	76	26	7	5	19	15	4	45	22	9	250	170	99	1st,	East Div.	Lost Semi-Final
1968-69	76	20	14	4	14	19	5	34	33	9	280	246	77	6th,	East Div.	Out of Playoffs
1967-68	74	20	13	4	12	13	12	32	26	16	212	222	80	4th,	East Div.	Lost Semi-Final
1966-67	70	24	5	6	17	12	6	41	17	12	264	170	94	1st,		Lost Semi-Final
1965-66	70	21	8	6	16	17	2	37	25	8	240	187	82	2nd,		Lost Semi-Final
1964-65	70	20	13	2	14	15	6	34	28	8	224	176	76	3rd,		Lost Final
1963-64	70	26	4	5	10	18	7	36	22	12	218	169	84	2nd,		Lost Semi-Final
1962-63	70	17	9	9	15	12	8	32	21	17	194	178	81	2nd,		Lost Semi-Final
1961-62	70	20	10	5	11	16	8	31	26	13	217	186	75	3rd,		Lost Final
1960-61	**70**	20	6	9	9	18	8	**29**	**24**	**17**	**198**	**180**	**75**	**3rd,**		**Won Stanley Cup**
1959-60	70	18	11	6	10	18	7	28	29	13	191	180	69	3rd,		Lost Semi-Final
1958-59	70	14	12	9	14	17	4	28	29	13	197	208	69	3rd,		Lost Semi-Final
1957-58	70	15	17	3	9	22	4	24	39	7	163	202	55	5th,		Out of Playoffs
1956-57	70	12	15	8	4	24	7	16	39	15	169	225	47	6th,		Out of Playoffs
1955-56	70	9	19	7	10	20	5	19	39	12	155	216	50	6th,		Out of Playoffs
1954-55	70	6	21	8	7	19	9	13	40	17	161	235	43	6th,		Out of Playoffs
1953-54	70	8	21	6	4	30	1	12	51	7	133	242	31	6th,		Out of Playoffs
1952-53	70	14	11	10	13	17	5	27	28	15	169	175	69	4th,		Lost Semi-Final
1951-52	70	9	19	7	8	25	2	17	44	9	158	241	43	6th,		Out of Playoffs
1950-51	70	8	22	5	5	25	5	13	47	10	171	280	36	6th,		Out of Playoffs
1949-50	70	13	18	4	9	20	6	22	38	10	203	244	54	6th,		Out of Playoffs
1948-49	60	13	12	5	8	19	3	21	31	8	173	211	50	5th,		Out of Playoffs
1947-48	60	10	17	3	10	17	3	20	34	6	195	225	46	6th,		Out of Playoffs
1946-47	60	10	17	3	9	20	1	19	37	4	193	274	42	6th,		Out of Playoffs
1945-46	50	15	5	5	8	15	2	23	20	7	200	178	53	3rd,		Lost Semi-Final
1944-45	50	9	14	2	4	16	5	13	30	7	141	194	33	5th,		Out of Playoffs
1943-44	50	15	6	4	7	17	1	22	23	5	178	187	49	4th,		Lost Final
1942-43	50	14	3	8	3	15	7	17	18	15	179	180	49	5th,		Out of Playoffs
1941-42	48	15	8	1	7	15	2	22	23	3	145	155	47	4th,		Lost Quarter-Final
1940-41	48	11	10	3	5	15	4	16	25	7	112	139	39	5th,		Lost Semi-Final
1939-40	48	15	7	2	8	12	4	23	19	6	112	120	52	4th,		Lost Quarter-Final
1938-39	48	5	13	6	7	15	2	12	28	8	91	132	32	7th,		Out of Playoffs
1937-38	**48**	10	10	4	4	15	5	**14**	**25**	**9**	**97**	**139**	**37**	**3rd,**	**Amn. Div.**	**Won Stanley Cup**
1936-37	48	8	13	3	6	14	4	14	27	7	99	131	35	4th,	Amn. Div.	Out of Playoffs
1935-36	48	15	7	2	6	12	6	21	19	8	93	92	50	3rd,	Amn. Div.	Lost Quarter-Final
1934-35	48	12	9	3	14	8	2	26	17	5	118	88	57	2nd,	Amn. Div.	Lost Quarter-Final
1933-34	**48**	13	4	7	7	13	4	**20**	**17**	**11**	**88**	**83**	**51**	**2nd,**	**Amn. Div.**	**Won Stanley Cup**
1932-33	48	12	7	5	4	13	7	16	20	12	88	101	44	4th,	Amn. Div.	Out of Playoffs
1931-32	48	13	5	6	5	14	5	18	19	11	86	101	47	2nd,	Amn. Div.	Lost Quarter-Final
1930-31	44	14	7	1	10	10	2	24	17	3	108	78	51	2nd,	Amn. Div.	Lost Final
1929-30	44	12	9	1	9	9	4	21	18	5	117	111	47	2nd,	Amn. Div.	Lost Quarter-Final
1928-29	44	3	13	6	4	16	2	7	29	8	33	85	22	5th,	Amn. Div.	Out of Playoffs
1927-28	44	2	18	2	5	16	1	7	34	3	68	134	17	5th,	Amn. Div.	Out of Playoffs
1926-27	44	12	8	2	7	14	1	19	22	3	115	116	41	3rd,	Amn. Div.	Lost Quarter-Final

Schedule

Home				Away			
Oct.	Thur.	4	NY Rangers	Oct.	Sat.	6	St Louis
	Sun.	7	NY Islanders		Sat.	13	Minnesota
	Thur.	11	Pittsburgh		Tues.	16	Detroit
	Sun.	14	Calgary*		Sat.	20	Toronto
	Thur.	18	Toronto		Sat.	27	Boston
	Sun.	21	Minnesota	Nov.	Sat.	3	Philadelphia*
	Thur.	25	Washington		Tues.	6	Hartford
	Sun.	28	Montreal		Sat.	10	Toronto
Nov.	Thur.	1	Quebec		Wed.	14	Detroit
	Sun.	4	Los Angeles		Fri.	16	Washington
	Thur.	8	Edmonton		Sat.	17	Quebec
	Sun.	11	Winnipeg		Tues.	20	Edmonton
	Thur.	29	Detroit		Wed.	21	Vancouver
Dec.	Sun.	2	St Louis		Sat.	24	Calgary
	Thur.	6	NY Islanders	Dec.	Sat.	1	Detroit*
	Sun.	9	Philadelphia		Sat.	8	Toronto
	Thur.	13	Winnipeg		Tues.	11	Pittsburgh
	Sun.	16	Minnesota*		Sat.	15	Minnesota*
	Wed.	19	Washington		Sat.	22	St Louis
	Sun.	23	Detroit		Fri.	28	Buffalo
	Wed.	26	St Louis		Sat.	29	NY Islanders
Jan.	Thur.	3	New Jersey		Mon.	31	Detroit
	Sun.	6	Los Angeles	Jan.	Fri.	11	Winnipeg
	Thur.	10	Toronto		Wed.	16	New Jersey
	Sun.	13	Minnesota		Thur.	17	NY Rangers
	Thur.	24	Buffalo		Mon.	28	Vancouver
	Sat.	26	Toronto	Feb.	Fri.	1	Edmonton
Feb.	Thur.	14	Quebec		Sat.	2	Calgary
	Sun.	17	Detroit*		Wed.	6	Montreal
	Thur.	21	Boston		Sat.	9	Boston*
	Sun.	24	St Louis		Sun.	10	Hartford
	Thur.	28	Hartford		Mon.	18	Philadelphia*
Mar.	Sun.	3	Vancouver		Sat.	23	Minnesota
	Wed.	6	Montreal		Tues.	26	St Louis
	Sun.	10	NY Rangers	Mar.	Fri.	8	Buffalo
	Sun.	17	St Louis		Thur.	14	Los Angeles
	Thur.	21	New Jersey		Sat.	16	St Louis
	Sun.	24	Minnesota*		Sat.	23	Pittsburgh*
	Thur.	28	Toronto		Tues.	26	Toronto
	Sun.	31	Detroit		Sat.	30	Minnesota

* Denotes afternoon game.

Home Starting Times:
All Games .... 7:35 p.m.
Except Matinees .... 1:35 p.m.
Jan. 26 .... 7:05 p.m.

Franchise date: September 25, 1926

65th NHL Season

Coaching History

Pete Muldoon, 1926-27; Barney Stanley and Hugh Lehman, 1927-28; Herb Gardiner, 1928-29; Tom Shaughnessy and Bill Tobin, 1929-30; Dick Irvin, 1930-31; Dick Irvin and Bill Tobin, 1931-32; Godfrey Matheson, Emil Iverson and Tommy Gorman, 1932-33; Tommy Gorman, 1933-34; Clem Loughlin, 1934-35 to 1936-37; Bill Stewart, 1937-38; Bill Stewart and Paul Thompson, 1938-39; Paul Thompson, 1939-40 to 1943-44; Paul Thompson and Johnny Gottselig, 1944-45; Johnny Gottselig, 1945-46 to 1946-47; Johnny Gottselig and Charlie Conacher, 1947-48; Charlie Conacher, 1948-49 to 1949-50; Ebbie Goodfellow, 1950-51 to 1951-52; Sid Abel, 1952-53 to 1953-54; Frank Eddolls, 1954-55; Dick Irvin, 1955-56; Tommy Ivan, 1956-57; Tommy Ivan and Rudy Pilous, 1957-58; Rudy Pilous, 1958-59 to 1962-63; Billy Reay, 1963-64 to 1975-76; Billy Reay and Bill White, 1976-77; Bob Pulford, 1977-78 to 1978-79; Eddie Johnston, 1979-80; Keith Magnuson, 1980-81; Keith Magnuson and Bob Pulford, 1981-82; Orval Tessier, 1982-83 to 1983-84; Orval Tessier and Bob Pulford, 1984-85; Bob Pulford, 1985-86 to 1986-87; Bob Murdoch, 1987-88; Mike Keenan, 1988-89 to date.

Captains' History

Dick Irvin, 1926-27 to 1928-29; Duke Dutkowski, 1929-30; Ty Arbour, 1930-31; Cy Wentworth, 1931-32; Helge Bostrom, 1932-33; Chuck Gardiner, 1933-34; no captain, 1934-35; Johnny Gottselig, 1935-36 to 1939-40; Earl Seibert, 1940-41, 1941-42; Doug Bentley, 1942-43, 1943-44; Clint Smith 1944-45; John Mariucci, 1945-46; Red Hamill, 1946-47; John Mariucci, 1947-48; Gaye Stewart, 1948-49; Doug Bentley, 1949-50; Jack Stewart, 1950-51, 1951-52; Bill Gadsby, 1952-53, 1953-54; Gus Mortson, 1954-55 to 1956-57; no captain, 1957-58; Eddie Litzenberger, 1958-59 to 1960-61; Pierre Pilote, 1961-62 to 1967-68, no captain, 1968-69; Pat Stapleton, 1969-70; no captain, 1970-71 to 1974-75; Stan Mikita, Pit Martin, 1975-76; Stan Mikita, Pit Martin, Keith Magnuson, 1976-77; Keith Magnuson, 1977-78, 1978-79; Keith Magnuson, Terry Ruskowski, 1979-80; Terry Ruskowski, 1980-81, 1981-82; Darryl Sutter, 1982-83 to 1986-87; Keith Brown, Troy Murray, Denis Savard, 1987-88; Dirk Graham, 1988-89 to date.

1990-91 Player Personnel

FORWARDS	HT	WT	S	Place of Birth	Date	1989-90 Club
BASSEN, Bob	5-10	180	L	Calgary, Alta.	5/6/65	Indianapolis-Chicago
BELANGER, Hugo	6-1	190	L	St. Herbert, Que.	5/28/70	Clarkson
BRACCIA, Rick	6-0	195	L	Revere, MA	9/5/67	Boston College
CREIGHTON, Adam	6-5	214	L	Burlington, Ont.	6/2/65	Chicago
DAM, Trevor	5-10	208	R	Scarborough, Ont.	4/20/70	London
DUBINSKY, Steve	6-0	180	L	Montreal, Que.	7/9/70	Clarkson
EAGLES, Mike	5-10	180	L	Sussex, N.B.	3/7/63	Indianapolis-Chicago
EDGERLY, Derek	6-1	190	L	Malden, MA	4/3/71	Stoneham H.S.
EGELAND, Tracy	6-1	180		Lethbridge, Alta.	8/20/70	Prince Albert
ELVENAS, Stefan	6-1	183	L	Lund, Sweden	3/30/70	Rogle (Sweden)
ERIKSSON, Tom	5-11	183	R	Umea, Sweden	5/3/66	Husum (Sweden)
GILBERT, Greg	6-1	192	L	Mississauga, Ont.	1/22/62	NY Islanders-Chicago
GOULET, Michel	6-1	195	L	Peribonka, Que.	4/21/60	Quebec-Chicago
GRAHAM, Dirk	5-11	190	R	Regina, Sask.	7/29/59	Chicago
GREYERBIEHL, Jason	6-0	175	L	Bramalea, Ont.	3/24/70	Colgate
GROSSI, Dino	6-0	190	R	Toronto, Ont.	6/25/70	Northeastern
HUDSON, Mike	6-1	185	L	Guelph, Ont.	2/6/67	Chicago
JOHANNSON, Jim	6-2	200	L	Rochester, MN	3/10/64	Indianapolis
KOZAK, Mike	6-2	195		Toronto, Ont.	3/14/69	Clarkson
LACOUTURE, Bill	6-2	192	R	Framingham, MA	5/28/68	U. N. Hampshire
LAFAYETTE, Justin	6-6	200	L	Vancouver, B.C.	1/23/70	Ferris State
LAPPIN, Mike	5-10	175	L	Chicago, IL	1/1/69	Boston U.
LARMER, Steve	5-10	189	L	Peterborough, Ont.	6/16/61	Chicago
LEMIEUX, Jocelyn	5-10	200	L	Mont-Laurier, Que.	11/18/67	Montreal-Chicago
LESSARD, Owen	6-1	196	L	Sudbury, Ont.	1/11/70	Owen Sound
LOACH, Lonnie	5-10	181	L	New Liskeard, Ont.	4/14/68	Indy-Ft. Wayne
LUPZIG, Andreas	6-2	185	L	West Germany	8/5/68	Koln (W. Ger.)
MARQUETTE, Dale	5-11	187	L	Prince George, B.C.	3/8/68	Indianapolis
McCORMICK, Mike	6-2	220	L	St. Boniface, Man.	5/14/68	U. N. Dakota
McNEILL, Mike	6-0	195	L	Winona, MN	7/22/66	Indianapolis
MURRAY, Troy	6-1	195	R	Calgary, Alta.	7/31/62	Chicago
NANNE, Marty	6-0	180	R	Edina, MN	7/21/67	Indianapolis
NOONAN, Brian	6-1	180	R	Boston, MA	5/29/65	Indianapolis-Chicago
PERSSON, Joakim	5-8	163		Gavle, Sweden	5/15/66	Brynas (Swe.)
PETERSON, Erik	6-0	185	L	Boston, MA	4/31/72	Brockton H.S.
PHILLIPS, Guy	6-0	178	R	Brooks, Alta.	2/13/66	Indianapolis
POJAR, Jon	6-0	179	L	St. Paul, MN	5/5/70	Colorado College
PRESLEY, Wayne	5-11	172	R	Detroit, MI	3/23/65	Chicago
PULLOLA, Tommi	6-5	202		Vaasa, Finland	5/18/71	Lukko (Fin.)
REILLY, John	6-3	188	L	Lawrence, MA	1/5/68	Boston College
ROENICK, Jeremy	5-11	170	R	Boston, MA	1/17/70	Chicago
RUCINSKI, Mike	5-11	190	L	Chicago, IL	12/12/63	Indianapolis
RYCHEL, Warren	6-0	190	L	Tecumseh, Ont.	5/12/67	Indianapolis
SANDSTROM, Ulf	5-10	180	R	Fagerstad, Sweden	4/24/67	Modo (Sweden)
SAUNDERS, Matt	6-0	180		Ottawa, Ont.	7/17/70	Northeastern
STICKNEY, Brett	6-5	205	L	Hanover, N.H.	5/26/72	St. Paul's Prep.
TEPPER, Stephen	6-4	205	R	Santa Ana, Calif.	3/10/69	U. of Maine
THAYER, Chris	6-2	190	R	Exeter, N.H	11/9/67	U. N. Hampshire
THOMAS, Steve	5-10	185	L	Stockport, England	7/15/63	Chicago
TORKKI, Jari	6-0	163	L	Finland	8/11/65	Indianapolis
TUCKER, Chris	5-11	183	L	White Plains, NY	2/9/72	Jefferson H.S.
VAN DORP, Wayne	6-4	225	L	Vancouver, B.C.	5/19/61	Chicago
WERNESS, Lance	6-0	175	R	Burnsville, MN	3/28/69	U. of Minnesota
WILLIAMS, Sean	6-1	182	L	Oshawa, Ont.	1/28/68	Indianapolis
WOODCROFT, Craig	6-1	185	L	Toronto, Ont.	12/3/69	Colgate
DEFENSEMEN						
BENNETT, Adam	6-4	206	R	Georgetown, Ont.	3/30/71	Sudbury
BROWN, Keith	6-1	191	R	Cornerbrook, Nfld.	5/6/60	Chicago
CASSIDY, Bruce	5-11	176	L	Ottawa, Ont.	5/20/65	Indianapolis-Chicago
CHELIOS, Chris	6-1	186	R	Chicago, IL	1/25/62	Montreal
CLEARY, Joe	5-11	186	R	Buffalo, NY	1/17/70	Boston College
DAGENAIS, Mike	6-3	198	L	Gloucester, Ont.	7/22/69	Peterborough
DROPPA, Ivan	6-2	209	L	Czechoslovakia	2/1/72	Mikulas (Czech.)
DYKHUIS, Karl	6-2	184	L	Sept-Iles, Que.	7/8/72	Hull
HEED, Jonas	6-0	174	L	Sodertalje, Sweden	1/3/67	Sodertalje (Sweden)
HENTGES, Mathew	6-5	197	L	St. Paul, MN	12/19/69	Merrimack
KELLOG, Bob	6-4	200	L	Springfield, MA	2/16/71	Northeastern
KONROYD, Steve	6-1	195	L	Scarborough, Ont.	2/10/61	Chicago
LANZ, Rick	6-2	195	R	Karlouyvary, Czech.	9/16/61	Ambri (Switz.)
MANSON, Dave	6-2	190	L	Prince Albert, Sask.	1/27/67	Chicago
McGILL, Bob	6-1	190	R	Edmonton, Alta.	4/27/62	Chicago
McGILL, Ryan	6-2	197	R	Sherwood Park, Alta.	2/28/69	Indianapolis
MOSCALUK, Gary	6-0	195	L	Waskatenau, Alta.	5/23/67	Indianapolis
MURRAY, Bob	5-10	186	R	Kingston, Ont.	11/26/54	Chicago
PELUSO, Mike	6-4	225	L	Pengilly, MN	11/8/65	Indianapolis-Chicago
PLAYFAIR, Jim	6-4	200	L	Ft. St. James, B.C.	5/22/64	Indianapolis
RUSSELL, Cam	6-4	175	L	Halifax, N.S.	1/12/69	Indianapolis-Chicago
SPEER, Michael	6-2	202	L	Toronto, Ont.	3/26/71	Owen Sound
TENZER, Dirk	6-2	193	R	New York, NY	7/26/70	St. Paul's H.S.
TICHY, Milan	6-3	194		Czechoslovakia	9/22/69	Trencin (Czech)
WILSON, Doug	6-1	187	L	Ottawa, Ont.	7/5/57	Chicago
YAWNEY, Trent	6-3	183	L	Hudson Bay, Sask.	9/29/65	Chicago

GOALTENDERS	HT	WT	C	Place of Birth	Date	1989-90 Club
BELFOUR, Ed	5-11	170	L	Carman, Man.	4/21/65	Cdn. Nationals
CLOUTIER, Jacques	5-7	169	L	Noranda, Que.	1/3/60	Chicago
DONEGHEY, Michael	6-0	165	L	Boston, MA	7/28/70	Catholic Memorial
HASEK, Dominik	5-11	165	L	Pardubice, Czech.	1/29/65	Dukla Jihlava (Czech.)
LeBLANC, Ray	5-10	170		Fitchburg, MA	10/24/64	Indy-Ft. Wayne
MILLEN, Greg	5-9	175	R	Toronto, Ont.	6/25/57	St. L.-Que.-Chi.
PANG, Darren	5-5	155	L	Medford, Ont.	2/17/64	Saginaw-Chicago
WAITE, Jim	6-0	163	R	Sherbrooke, Que.	4/15/69	Saginaw-Chicago

1989-90 Scoring

Regular Season

* rookie

Pos	#	Player	Team	GP	G	A	Pts	+/−	PIM	PP	SH	GW	GT	S	%
R	28	Steve Larmer	CHI	80	31	59	90	25	40	8	2	4	0	265	11.7
C	18	Denis Savard	CHI	60	27	53	80	8	56	10	2	4	1	181	14.9
D	24	Doug Wilson	CHI	70	23	50	73	13	40	13	1	2	0	242	9.5
L	32	Steve Thomas	CHI	76	40	30	70	3−	91	13	0	7	0	235	17.0
C	22	Adam Creighton	CHI	80	34	36	70	4	224	12	0	3	0	156	21.8
C	27	*Jeremy Roenick	CHI	78	26	40	66	2	54	6	0	4	0	173	15.0
C	19	Troy Murray	CHI	68	17	38	55	2−	86	3	1	4	0	111	15.3
R	33	Dirk Graham	CHI	73	22	32	54	1	102	2	3	1	0	180	12.2
L	16	Michel Goulet	QUE	57	16	29	45	33−	42	8	0	0	0	144	11.1
			CHI	8	4	1	5	1	9	1	1	0	0	10	40.0
			TOTAL	65	20	30	50	32−	51	9	1	0	0	154	13.0
L	14	Greg Gilbert	CHI	70	12	25	37	27	54	0	0	3	1	108	11.1
D	3	Dave Manson	CHI	59	5	23	28	4	301	1	0	1	0	126	4.0
R	26	Jocelyn Lemieux	MTL	34	4	2	6	1−	61	0	0	1	0	34	11.8
			CHI	39	10	11	21	0	47	1	0	1	0	78	12.8
			TOTAL	73	14	13	27	1−	108	1	0	2	0	112	12.5
D	4	Keith Brown	CHI	67	5	20	25	26	87	2	0	0	0	111	4.5
D	6	Bob Murray	CHI	49	5	19	24	3	45	3	0	1	0	84	6.0
L	20	Al Secord	CHI	43	14	7	21	5	131	1	0	0	0	68	20.6
C	43	Mike Hudson	CHI	49	9	12	21	3−	56	0	0	3	0	51	17.6
D	8	Trent Yawney	CHI	70	5	15	20	6−	82	1	0	1	0	58	8.6
R	12	Duane Sutter	CHI	72	4	14	18	2−	156	0	0	1	0	70	5.7
D	5	Steve Konroyd	CHI	75	3	14	17	6	34	1	0	0	0	93	3.2
R	17	Wayne Presley	CHI	49	6	7	13	19−	69	1	0	0	0	75	8.0
D	25	Bob McGill	CHI	69	2	10	12	7−	204	0	1	0	0	53	3.8
L	23	Wayne Van Dorp	CHI	61	7	4	11	3−	303	0	0	1	0	38	18.4
L	11	Mike Eagles	CHI	23	1	2	3	4−	34	0	0	0	0	23	4.3
D	37	Bruce Cassidy	CHI	2	1	1	2	1−	0	1	0	0	0	3	33.3
C	15	Bob Bassen	CHI	6	1	1	2	1	8	0	0	0	0	7	14.3
C	10	Brian Noonan	CHI	8	0	2	2	0	6	0	0	0	0	13	.0
D	52	*Cam Russell	CHI	19	0	1	1	3−	27	0	0	0	0	10	.0
G	29	Greg Millen	STL	21	0	0	0	0	0	0	0	0	0	0	.0
			QUE	18	0	0	0	0	0	0	0	0	0	0	.0
			CHI	10	0	1	1	0	0	0	0	0	0	0	.0
			TOTAL	49	0	1	1	0	0	0	0	0	0	0	.0
D	26	*Mike Peluso	CHI	2	0	0	0	0	15	0	0	0	0	0	.0
G	29	*Jim Waite	CHI	4	0	0	0	0	0	0	0	0	0	0	.0
G	31	Jacques Cloutier	CHI	43	0	0	0	0	8	0	0	0	0	0	.0

Goaltending

No.	Goaltender	GPI	Mins	Avg	W	L	T	EN	SO	GA	SA	S%
31	Jacques Cloutier	43	2178	3.09	18	15	2	2	2	112	931	.880
29	Greg Millen	10	575	3.34	5	4	1	1	0	32	267	.880
30	Alain Chevrier	39	1894	4.18	16	14	3	1	0	132	898	.853
60	*Jim Waite	4	183	4.59	2	0	0	0	0	14	92	.848
	Totals	**80**	**4835**	**3.65**	**41**	**33**	**6**	**4**	**2**	**294**	**2188**	**.866**

Playoffs

Pos	#	Player	Team	GP	G	A	Pts	+/−	PIM	PP	SH	GW	OT	S	%
R	28	Steve Larmer	CHI	20	7	15	22	2	8	2	2	2	0	67	10.4
C	18	Denis Savard	CHI	20	7	15	22	0	41	4	0	1	0	69	10.1
C	27	*Jeremy Roenick	CHI	20	11	7	18	1−	8	4	0	1	0	47	23.4
R	17	Wayne Presley	CHI	19	9	6	15	8	29	1	1	1	0	44	20.5
D	24	Doug Wilson	CHI	20	3	12	15	5	18	1	0	1	0	64	4.7
L	32	Steve Thomas	CHI	20	7	6	13	2	33	1	0	3	0	60	11.7
L	14	Greg Gilbert	CHI	19	5	8	13	10	34	0	0	0	0	24	20.8
C	22	Adam Creighton	CHI	20	3	6	9	1	59	0	1	0	0	24	12.5
R	26	Jocelyn Lemieux	CHI	18	1	8	9	1	28	0	0	0	0	23	4.3
C	19	Troy Murray	CHI	20	4	4	8	2	22	1	0	0	0	23	17.4
D	8	Trent Yawney	CHI	20	3	5	8	1−	27	3	0	1	0	27	11.1
L	16	Michel Goulet	CHI	14	2	4	6	2	6	0	0	0	0	18	11.1
D	6	Bob Murray	CHI	16	2	4	6	8	8	0	0	0	0	30	6.7
D	3	Dave Manson	CHI	20	2	4	6	5−	46	1	0	0	0	36	5.6
R	33	Dirk Graham	CHI	5	1	5	6	0	2	0	1	0	0	10	10.0
D	5	Steve Konroyd	CHI	20	1	3	4	6	19	0	0	0	0	19	5.3
D	4	Keith Brown	CHI	18	0	4	4	2	43	0	0	0	0	18	.0
R	12	Duane Sutter	CHI	20	1	1	2	1−	48	0	0	0	0	12	8.3
G	30	*Ed Belfour	CHI	9	0	1	1	0	6	0	0	0	0	0	.0
C	15	Bob Bassen	CHI	1	0	0	0	1−	2	0	0	0	0	0	.0
D	52	*Cam Russell	CHI	1	0	0	0	1−	0	0	0	0	0	0	.0
G	31	Jacques Cloutier	CHI	4	0	0	0	0	0	0	0	0	0	0	.0
C	43	Mike Hudson	CHI	4	0	0	0	2−	2	0	0	0	0	1	.0
D	25	Bob McGill	CHI	5	0	0	0	1	2	0	0	0	0	0	.0
L	23	Wayne Van Dorp	CHI	8	0	0	0	1−	23	0	0	0	0	2	.0
L	20	Al Secord	CHI	12	0	0	0	2−	8	0	0	0	0	6	.0
G	29	Greg Millen	CHI	14	0	0	0	0	4	0	0	0	0	0	.0

Goaltending

No.	Goaltender	GPI	Mins	Avg	W	L	EN	SO	GA	SA	S%
30	*Ed Belfour	9	409	2.49	4	2	0	0	17	200	.915
31	Jacques Cloutier	4	175	2.74	0	2	0	0	8	75	.893
29	Greg Millen	14	613	3.92	6	6	0	0	40	300	.867
	Totals	20	1200	3.25	10	10	0	0	65	575	.887

Retired Numbers

1	Glenn Hall	1957-1967
9	Bobby Hull	1957-1972
21	Stan Mikita	1958-1980
35	Tony Esposito	1969-1984

Club Records

Team

(Figures in brackets for season records are games
played; records for fewest points, wins, ties, losses,
goals, goals against are for 70 or more games)

Most Points	107	1970-71 (78) 1971-72 (78)
Most Wins	49	1970-71 (78)
Most Ties	23	1973-74 (78)
Most Losses	51	1953-54 (70)
Most Goals	351	1985-86 (80)
Most Goals Against	363	1981-82 (80)
Fewest Points	31	1953-54 (70)
Fewest Wins	12	1953-54 (70)
Fewest Ties	6	1989-90 (80)
Fewest Losses	14	1973-74 (78)
Fewest Goals	*133	1953-54 (70)
Fewest Goals Against	164	1973-74 (78)

Longest Winning Streak
Over-all .... 8 Dec. 9-26/71
                         Jan. 4-21/81
Home .... 13 Nov. 11-
                         Dec. 20/70
Away .... 7 Dec. 9-29/64

Longest Undefeated Streak
Over-all .... 15 Jan. 14-
                         Feb. 16/67
                         (12 wins, 3 ties)
Home .... 18 Oct. 11-
                         Dec. 20/70
                         (16 wins, 2 ties)
Away .... 12 Oct. 29-
                         Dec. 3/75
                         (6 wins, 9 ties)

Longest Losing Streak
Over-all .... 13 Feb. 25-
                         Oct. 11/51
Home .... 11 Feb. 8-
                         Nov. 22/28
Away .... 17 Jan. 2-
                         Oct. 7/54

Longest Winless Streak
Over-all .... 21 Dec. 17/50-
                         Jan. 28/51
                         (18 losses, 3 ties)

Home .... *15 Dec. 16/28-
                         Feb. 28/29
                         (11 losses, 4 ties)
Away .... 23 Dec. 19/50-
                         Oct. 11/51
                         (15 losses, 8 ties)
Most Shutouts, Season 15 1969-70 (76)
Most PIM, Season 2,496 1988-89 (80)
Most Goals, Game .... 12 Jan. 30/69
                         (Chi. 12 at Phil. 0)

Individual

Most Seasons	22	Stan Mikita
Most Games	1,394	Stan Mikita
Most Goals, Career	604	Bobby Hull
Most Assists, Career	926	Stan Mikita
Most Points, Career	1,467	Stan Mikita (541 goals, 926 assists)
Most PIM, Career	1,442	Keith Magnuson
Most Shutouts, Career	74	Tony Esposito

Longest Consecutive
Games Streak .... 640 Steve Larmer
                         (1982-83 to present)
Most Goals, Season .... 58 Bobby Hull
                         (1968-69)
Most Assists, Season ..... 87 Denis Savard (81-82, 87-88)
Most Points, Season ..... 131 Denis Savard
                         (1987-88)
                         (44 goals, 87 assists)
Most PIM, Season ...... 352 Dave Manson
                         (1988-89)
Most Points, Defenseman
  Season .... 85 Doug Wilson
                         (1981-82)
                         (39 goals, 46 assists)
Most Points, Center,
  Season .... 131 Denis Savard
                         (1987-88)
                         (44 goals, 87 assists)

Most Points, Right Wing,
  Season .... 92 Jim Pappin
                         (1972-73)
                         (41 goals, 51 assists)
Most Points, Left Wing,
  Season .... 107 Bobby Hull
                         (1968-69)
                         (58 goals, 49 assists)
Most Points, Rookie,
  Season .... 90 Steve Larmer
                         (1982-83)
                         (43 goals, 47 assists)
Most Shutouts, Season ....15 Tony Esposito
                         (1969-70)
Most Goals, Game .... 5 Grant Mulvey
                         (Feb. 3/82)
Most Assists, Game .... 6 Pat Stapleton
                         (Mar. 30/69)
Most Points, Game .... 7 Max Bentley
                         (Jan. 28/43)
                         Grant Mulvey
                         (Feb. 3/82)

* NHL Record.

All-time Record vs. Other Clubs

Regular Season

	At Home							On Road							Total						
	GP	W	L	T	GF	GA	PTS	GP	W	L	T	GF	GA	PTS	GP	W	L	T	GF	GA	PTS
Boston	273	138	91	44	879	731	320	271	82	157	32	761	986	196	544	220	248	76	1640	1717	516
Buffalo	39	22	11	6	126	98	50	39	8	25	6	104	158	22	78	30	36	12	230	256	72
Calgary	35	17	10	8	131	105	42	36	10	19	7	107	126	27	71	27	29	15	238	231	69
Detroit	294	139	109	46	891	806	324	293	85	181	27	720	1015	197	587	224	290	73	1611	1821	521
Edmonton	18	9	7	2	81	85	20	17	4	12	1	62	91	9	35	13	19	3	143	176	29
Hartford	18	10	5	3	85	55	23	17	8	8	1	63	68	17	35	18	13	4	148	123	40
Los Angeles	46	25	15	6	186	142	56	48	22	21	5	168	170	49	94	47	36	11	354	312	105
Minnesota	73	46	18	9	302	196	101	73	31	32	10	257	265	72	146	77	50	19	559	461	173
Montreal	262	88	120	54	704	732	230	263	50	165	48	614	1019	148	525	138	285	102	1318	1751	378
New Jersey	33	22	7	4	144	92	48	34	14	15	5	109	108	33	67	36	22	9	253	200	81
NY Islanders	35	16	15	4	111	125	36	35	8	16	11	102	132	27	70	24	31	15	213	257	63
NY Rangers	273	123	108	42	834	759	288	274	105	115	54	775	810	264	547	228	223	96	1609	1569	552
Philadelphia	49	24	9	16	172	127	64	48	14	26	8	134	165	36	97	38	35	24	306	292	100
Pittsburgh	48	32	7	9	203	136	73	46	20	22	4	151	163	44	94	52	29	13	354	299	117
Quebec	17	9	7	1	72	62	19	18	6	8	4	69	79	16	35	15	15	5	141	141	35
St. Louis	76	45	21	10	307	236	100	74	24	36	14	239	264	62	150	69	57	24	546	500	162
Toronto	284	139	106	39	869	752	317	285	82	155	48	726	991	212	569	221	261	87	1595	1743	529
Vancouver	45	28	12	5	161	106	61	44	14	19	11	132	133	39	89	42	31	16	293	239	100
Washington	27	16	6	5	115	83	37	28	8	17	3	87	112	19	55	24	23	8	202	195	56
Winnipeg	19	14	4	1	103	61	29	20	8	9	3	80	86	19	39	22	13	4	183	147	48
Defunct Club	139	79	40	20	408	267	178	140	52	67	21	316	345	125	279	131	107	41	724	612	303
Totals	**2103**	**1041**	**728**	**334**	**6884**	**5756**	**2416**	**2103**	**655**	**1125**	**323**	**5776**	**7286**	**1633**	**4206**	**1696**	**1853**	**657**	**12660**	**13042**	**4049**

Playoffs

	Series	W	L	GP	W	L	T	GF	GA	Last Mtg.	Round	Result
Boston	6	1	5	22	5	16	1	63	97	1978	QF	L 0-4
Buffalo	2	0	2	9	1	8	0	17	36	1980	QF	L 0-4
Calgary	2	0	2	8	1	7	0	17	30	1989	DF	L 1-4
Detroit	12	7	5	60	33	27	0	187	171	1989	DSF	W 4-2
Edmonton	3	0	3	16	4	12	0	56	94	1990	CF	L 2-4
Los Angeles	1	1	0	5	4	1	0	10	7	1974	QF	W 4-1
Minnesota	5	4	1	27	17	10	0	103	96	1990	DSF	W 4-3
Montreal	17	5	12	81	29	50	2	185	261	1976	QF	L 0-4
NY Islanders	2	0	2	6	0	6	0	6	21	1979	QF	L 0-4
NY Rangers	5	4	1	24	14	10	0	66	54	1973	SF	W 4-1
Philadelphia	1	1	0	4	4	0	0	20	8	1971	QF	W 4-0
Pittsburgh	1	1	0	4	4	0	0	14	8	1972	QF	W 4-0
St. Louis	7	6	1	35	23	12	0	137	97	1990	DF	W 4-3
Toronto	5	2	5	25	9	15	1	57	76	1986	DSF	L 0-3
Vancouver	1	0	1	5	1	4	0	13	18	1982	CF	L 1-4
Defunct Clubs	4	2	2	9	5	3	1	16	15			
Totals	**76**	**34**	**42**	**340**	**154**	**181**	**5**	**967**	**1089**			

Playoff Results 1990-86

Year	Round	Opponent	Result	GF	GA
1990	CF	Edmonton	L 2-4	20	25
	DF	St. Louis	W 4-3	28	22
	DSF	Minnesota	W 4-3	21	18
1989	CF	Calgary	L 1-4	8	15
	DF	St. Louis	W 4-1	19	12
	DSF	Detroit	W 4-2	25	18
1988	DSF	St. Louis	L 4-1	17	21
1987	DSF	Detroit	L 0-4	6	15
1986	DSF	Toronto	L 0-3	9	18

Abbreviations: Round: F Final; CF conference final; DF division final; DSF division semi-final;
SF semi-final; QF quarter-final. GA goals against; GF goals for.

1989-90 Results

	Home				Away		
Oct.	5	St Louis	3-8	**Oct.**	7	Washington	3-2
	8	NY Rangers	3-5		14	St Louis	1-2
	12	Toronto	9-6		17	NY Rangers	3-3
	15	Detroit	3-0		20	Winnipeg	4-2
	19	Quebec	3-5		24	Detroit	5-3
	22	Los Angeles	7-4		28	New Jersey	2-3
	26	Montreal	5-3		31	Quebec	5-3
	29	Washington	1-0	**Nov.**	4	Minnesota	0-3
Nov.	2	Minnesota	4-3		11	NY Islanders	5-3
	5	Winnipeg	4-3		16	Vancouver	3-4
	9	Pittsburgh	4-3		18	Calgary	4-4
	12	Hartford	4-2		19	Edmonton	4-5
	30	NY Islanders	0-2		22	Los Angeles	3-6
Dec.	3	Detroit	3-4		26	Minnesota	3-5
	6	Toronto	6-4	**Dec.**	9	Pittsburgh	6-4
	10	Vancouver	7-1		13	Montreal	3-1
	17	Edmonton	6-5		15	Detroit	4-8
	20	St Louis	9-6		23	Toronto	7-5
	22	Toronto	3-5		26	St Louis	3-8
	28	Minnesota	1-1	**Jan.**	10	NY Rangers	2-2
	30	Hartford	7-3		11	Philadelphia	5-4
Jan.	3	Edmonton	3-2		15	Toronto	6-7
	6	Philadelphia	8-5		26	Buffalo	4-2
	14	Calgary	5-6		27	Hartford	4-6
	17	Minnesota	3-1	**Feb.**	1	Los Angeles	7-4
	19	Vancouver	5-2		4	Winnipeg	3-7
	24	Buffalo	2-3		8	Detroit	4-6
Feb.	13	Buffalo	4-1		10	Minnesota*	4-6
	15	Calgary	1-4		17	NY Islanders*	3-1
	18	Pittsburgh*	6-4		20	St Louis	8-3
	22	Boston	3-5		24	New Jersey*	2-3
	25	Philadelphia*	4-1		27	Washington	0-4
Mar.	1	St Louis	4-6	**Mar.**	3	Boston*	3-4
	4	Boston*	1-4		7	Minnesota	4-5
	11	St Louis	4-6		10	St Louis	2-2
	13	Detroit	3-3		15	Quebec	6-3
	22	New Jersey	6-3		17	Montreal	2-3
	25	Detroit*	3-2		19	Toronto	3-2
	29	Toronto	4-2		24	Detroit*	3-5
Apr.	1	Minnesota	4-1		31	Toronto	4-6

* Denotes afternoon game.

Entry Draft Selections 1990-76

1990
Pick
16 Karl Dykhuis
37 Ivan Droppa
79 Chris Tucker
121 Brett Stickney
124 Derek Edgerly
163 Hugo Belanger
184 Owen Lessard
205 Erik Peterson
226 Steve Dubinsky
247 Dino Grossi

1989
Pick
6 Adam Bennett
27 Michael Speer
48 Bob Kellogg
111 Tommi Pullola
132 Tracy Egeland
153 Milan Tichy
174 Jason Greyerbiehl
195 Matt Saunders
216 Mike Kozak
237 Michael Doneghey

1988
Pick
8 Jeremy Roenick
50 Trevor Dam
71 Stefan Elvenas
92 Joe Cleary
113 Justin Lafayette
134 Craig Woodcroft
155 Jon Pojar
176 Mathew Hentges
197 Daniel Maurice
218 Dirk Tenzer
239 Lupzig Andreas

1987
Pick
8 Jimmy Waite
29 Ryan McGill
50 Cam Russell
60 Mike Dagenais
92 Ulf Sandstrom
113 Mike McCormick
134 Stephen Tepper
155 John Reilly
176 Lance Werness
197 Dale Marquette
218 Bill Lacouture
239 Mike Lappin

1986
Pick
14 Everett Sanipass
35 Mark Kurzawski
77 Kucera Frantisek
98 Lonnie Loach
119 Mario Doyon
140 Mike Hudson
161 Marty Nanne
182 Geoff Benic
203 Glen Lowes
224 Chris Thayer
245 Sean Williams

1985
Pick
11 Dave Manson
53 Andy Helmuth
74 Dan Vincellette
87 Rick Herbert
95 Brad Belland
116 Jonas Heed
137 Victor Posa
158 John Reid
179 Richard LaPlante
200 Brad Hamilton
221 Ian Pound
237 Rick Braccia

1984
Pick
3 Ed Olczyk
45 Trent Yawney
66 Tommy Eriksson
90 Timo Lehkonen
101 Darin Sceviour
111 Chris Clifford
132 Mike Stapleton
153 Glen Greenough
174 Ralph Di Fiorie
195 Joakim Persson
216 Bill Brown
224 David Mackey
237 Dan Williams

1983
Pick
18 Bruce Cassidy
39 Wayne Presley
59 Marc Bergevin
79 Tarek Howard
99 Kevin Robinson
115 Jari Torkki
119 Mark Lavarre
139 Scott Birnie
159 Kevin Paynter
179 Brian Noonan
199 Domenic Hasek
219 Steve Pepin

1982
Pick
7 Ken Yaremchuk
28 Rene Badeau
49 Tom McMurchy
70 Bill Watson
91 Brad Beck
112 Mark Hatcher
133 Jay Ness
154 Jeff Smith
175 Phil Patterson
196 Jim Camazzola
217 Mike James
238 Bob Andrea

1981
Pick
12 Tony Tanti
25 Kevin Griffin
54 Darrell Anholt
75 Perry Pelensky
96 Doug Chessell
117 Bill Schafhauser
138 Marc Centrone
159 Johan Mellstrom
180 John Benns
201 Sylvain Roy

1980
Pick
3 Denis Savard
15 Jerome Dupont
28 Steve Ludzik
30 Ken Solheim
36 Len Dawes
57 Troy Murray
58 Marcel Frere
67 Carey Wilson
78 Brian Shaw
99 Kevin Ginnell
120 Steve Larmer
141 Sean Simpson
162 Jim Ralph
183 Don Dietrich
204 Dan Frawley

1979
Pick
7 Keith Brown
28 Tim Trimper
49 Bill Gardner
70 Louis Begin
91 Lowell Loveday
112 Doug Crossman

1978
Pick
10 Tim Higgins
29 Doug Lecuyer
46 Rick Paterson
63 Brian Young
79 Mark Murphy
96 Dave Feamster
113 Dave Mancuso
130 Sandy Ross
147 Mark Locken
164 Glenn Van
179 Darryl Sutter

1977
Pick
6 Doug Wilson
19 Jean Savard
60 Randy Ireland
78 Gary Platt
96 Jack O'Callahan
114 Floyd Lahache
129 Jeff Geiger
144 Stephen Ough

1976
Pick
9 Real Cloutier
27 Jeff McDill
45 Thomas Gradin
63 Dave Debol
81 Terry McDonald
99 John Peterson
115 John Rothstein

Club Directory

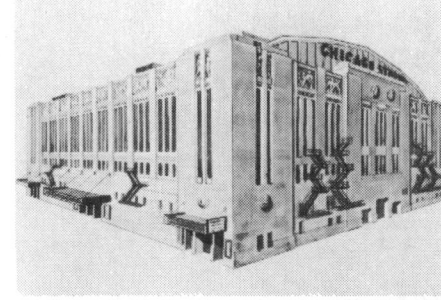

Chicago Stadium
1800 W. Madison St.
Chicago, Ill. 60612
Phone **312/733-5300**
FAX 312/733-5356
ENVOY ID
Front Office: HAWKS. GM
Public
Relations: HAWKS. PR
Capacity: 17,317

President . . . . William W. Wirtz
Vice-President . . . . Arthur Michael Wirtz, Jr.
Vice-President & Assistant to the President . . . . Thomas N. Ivan
Senior Vice President . . . . Robert Pulford
General Manager/Head Coach . . . . Mike Keenan
Assistant G.M. & Director of Player Personnel . . Jack Davison
Associate Coach . . . . Darryl Sutter
Assistant Coach . . . . E.J. McGuire
Scouts . . . . Kerry Davison, Michel Dumas, Dave Lucas, Jim Pappin, Jan Spieczny, Jim Walker, Russ Houston, Steve Lyons, Duane Sutter, Brian DeBruyn
Secretary to the General Manager . . . . Cindy Bodnarchuk
Public Relations Director . . . . Jim DeMaria
Asst. PR & Director of Community Relations . . . . Tom Finks
Director of Team Services . . . . Steve Williams
Receptionist . . . . Vicki Stokes
Season Tickets . . . . Mildred Hornik
Club Doctors . . . . Dr. Louis W. Kolb
Dr. Howard Baim
Club Dentist . . . . Dr. Robert Duresa
Trainers . . . . Lou Varga, Randy Lacey, Mike Gapski
Executive Offices . . . . Chicago Stadium
Largest Hockey Crowd . . . . 20,960 on April 10, 1982 vs Minnesota
Location of Press Box . . . . West side of the Stadium
Dimensions of Rink . . . . 185 feet by 85 feet
Ends of Rink . . . . Plexi-glass extends above boards around rink
Club Colors . . . . Red, Black and White
Radio Station . . . . WBBM (AM 780)
Television Station . . . . SportsChannel
Broadcasters . . . . Pat Foley, Dale Tallon
Organist . . . . Frank Pellico
Soloist . . . . Wayne Messmer
Public Address Announcer . . . . Harvey Wittenberg

Rookie sensation Jeremy Roenick had 11 goals in the 1990 playoffs, the second-highest total ever recorded by a rookie in one playoff year.

Coach and General Manager

KEENAN, MICHAEL (MIKE)
Coach and General Manager, Chicago Blackhawks.
Born in Toronto, Ont., October 21, 1949.

In his second season as coach of the Blackhawks, Mike Keenan led his club to its best regular-season finish in seven years and second consecutive Campbell Conference Championship berth. The Blackhawks were the League's most improved team in 1989-90, posting a 22-point improvement over their 1988-89 record. After defeating Minnesota and St. Louis in divisional post-season play, the Blackhawks lost a six-game series to the Stanley Cup champion Edmonton Oilers in the Campbell Conference Championship. He assumed the post of general manager on June 5, 1990.

Keenan spent four years as head coach of the Philadelphia Flyers (1984-85 to 1987-88) before being hired by the Blackhawks on June 9, 1988. While with the Flyers, he led his team to the Stanley Cup Final twice in four years and distinguished himself as the first coach in League history to register 40-or-more wins in each of his first three seasons. Keenan was the head coach for Team Canada in the 1987 Canada Cup and led his club to a 2-1 series victory over the Soviet Union in the final.

A former team captain of the St. Lawrence University Saints, Keenan began coaching at the Junior B level, winning back-to-back championships in the Metro Toronto League. After leading the OHL's Peterborough Petes to the 1979-80 Memorial Cup Finals, he joined the AHL's Rochester Americans, carrying that team to the 1982-83 Calder Cup title. The following season, 1983-84, immediately preceding his tenure with the Flyers, Keenan posted yet another championship, this time taking the CIAU Canadian college title with the University of Toronto Blues.

Coaching Record

			Regular Season				Playoffs			
Season	Team	Games	W	L	T	%	Games	W	L	%
1979-80	Peterborough (OHL)	68	47	20	1	.699	18	15	3	.833
1980-81	Rochester (AHL)	80	30	42	8	.425	...	...	...	...
1981-82	Rochester (AHL)	80	40	31	9	.556	9	4	5	.444
1982-83	Rochester (AHL)	80	46	25	9	.631	16	12	4	.750
1983-84	U. of Toronto (CIAU)	49	41	5	3	.867	...	...	...	...
1984-85	Philadelphia (NHL)	80	53	20	7	.706	19	12	7	.632
1985-86	Philadelphia (NHL)	80	53	23	4	.688	5	2	3	.400
1986-87	Philadelphia (NHL)	80	46	26	8	.625	26	15	11	.577
1987-88	Philadelphia (NHL)	80	38	33	9	.531	7	3	4	.429
1988-89	Chicago (NHL)	80	27	41	12	.413	16	9	7	.563
1989-90	Chicago (NHL)	80	41	33	6	.550	20	10	10	.500
	NHL Totals	**480**	**258**	**176**	**46**	**.585**	**93**	**51**	**42**	**.548**

General Managers' History

Major Frederic McLaughlin, 1926-27 to 1941-42; Bill Tobin, 1942-43 to 1953-54; Tommy Ivan, 1954-55 to 1976-77; Bob Pulford, 1977-78 to 1989-90; Mike Keenan, 1990-91.

Detroit Red Wings

1989-90 Results: 28W-38L-14T 70PTS. Fifth, Norris Division

Shawn Burr had his best year offensively in 1989-90 with 24 goals and 32 assists in 76 games.

Schedule

Home		Away	
Oct. Wed. 10 Calgary		**Oct.** Thur. 4 New Jersey	
Fri. 12 Hartford		Sat. 6 Washington	
Tues. 16 Chicago		Sun. 7 Philadelphia	
Thur. 18 Montreal		Sat. 13 Toronto	
Tues. 23 Vancouver		Sat. 20 Quebec*	
Fri. 26 Minnesota		Sat. 27 Minnesota	
Tues. 30 St Louis		**Nov.** Sat. 3 Montreal	
Nov. Thur. 1 Toronto		Tues. 6 Vancouver	
Wed. 14 Chicago		Thur. 8 Los Angeles	
Thur. 15 Toronto		Sat. 10 St Louis	
Mon. 19 Washington		Sat. 17 Toronto	
Wed. 21 Minnesota		Thur. 29 Chicago	
Fri. 23 St Louis		**Dec.** Sun. 2 Buffalo	
Tues. 27 Los Angeles		Sat. 8 St Louis	
Dec. Sat. 1 Chicago*		Sat. 15 Philadelphia*	
Tues. 4 Boston		Sun. 16 Pittsburgh	
Fri. 7 St Louis		Sat. 22 Winnipeg	
Tues. 11 Buffalo		Sun. 23 Chicago	
Thur. 13 Quebec		Fri. 28 Pittsburgh	
Tues. 18 Philadelphia		**Jan.** Fri. 4 Edmonton	
Thur. 20 Winnipeg		Sat. 5 Calgary	
Mon. 31 Chicago		Sat. 12 NY Islanders	
Jan. Wed. 2 Minnesota		Mon. 14 Boston	
Wed. 9 Edmonton		Wed. 16 Buffalo	
Fri. 11 NY Rangers		Sat. 26 St Louis	
Tues. 22 Washington		Wed. 30 Minnesota	
Fri. 25 St Louis		**Feb.** Sat. 2 Toronto	
Mon. 28 New Jersey		Sat. 9 Minnesota	
Feb. Fri. 1 Toronto		Wed. 13 Hartford	
Mon. 4 Los Angeles		Sun. 17 Chicago*	
Fri. 8 NY Islanders		Tues. 19 Calgary	
Tues. 12 Winnipeg		Fri. 22 Edmonton	
Sat. 16 Minnesota*		Sat. 23 Vancouver	
Wed. 27 Montreal		**Mar.** Sat. 9 Minnesota*	
Mar. Fri. 1 New Jersey		Sun. 10 St Louis	
Tues. 5 Quebec		Wed. 13 NY Rangers	
Thur. 7 NY Islanders		Thur. 14 Hartford	
Fri. 22 Toronto		Sat. 16 Boston*	
Wed. 27 Pittsburgh		Sat. 23 Toronto	
Sat. 30 NY Rangers*		Sun. 31 Chicago	

* Denotes afternoon game.

Home Starting Times:
All games .... 7:35 p.m.
Except Matinees .... 1:05 p.m.

Franchise date: September 25, 1926

65th NHL Season

Year-by-Year Record

Season	GP	Home			Road			Overall						Finished		Playoff Result
		W	L	T	W	L	T	W	L	T	GF	GA	Pts.			
1989-90	80	20	14	6	8	24	8	28	38	14	288	323	70	5th,	Norris Div.	Out of Playoffs
1900-09	80	20	14	6	14	20	6	34	34	12	313	316	80	1st,	Norris Div.	Lost Div. Semi-Final
1987-88	80	24	10	6	17	18	5	41	28	11	322	269	93	1st,	Norris Div.	Lost Conf. Championship
1986-87	80	20	14	6	14	22	4	34	36	10	260	274	78	2nd,	Norris Div.	Lost Conf. Championship
1985-86	80	10	26	4	7	31	2	17	57	6	266	415	40	5th,	Norris Div.	Out of Playoffs
1984-85	80	19	14	7	8	27	5	27	41	12	313	357	66	3rd,	Norris Div.	Lost Div. Semi-Final
1983-84	80	18	20	2	13	22	5	31	42	7	298	323	69	3rd,	Norris Div.	Lost Div. Semi-Final
1982-83	80	14	19	7	7	25	8	21	44	15	263	344	57	5th,	Norris Div.	Out of Playoffs
1981-82	80	15	19	6	6	28	6	21	47	12	270	351	54	6th,	Norris Div.	Out of Playoffs
1980-81	80	16	15	9	3	28	9	19	43	18	252	339	56	5th,	Norris Div.	Out of Playoffs
1979-80	80	14	21	5	12	22	6	26	43	11	268	306	63	5th,	Norris Div.	Out of Playoffs
1978-79	80	15	17	8	8	24	8	23	41	16	252	295	62	5th,	Norris Div.	Out of Playoffs
1977-78	80	22	11	7	10	23	7	32	34	14	252	266	78	2nd,	Norris Div.	Lost Quarter-Final
1976-77	80	12	22	6	4	33	3	16	55	9	183	309	41	5th,	Norris Div.	Out of Playoffs
1975-76	80	17	15	8	9	29	2	26	44	10	226	300	62	4th,	Norris Div.	Out of Playoffs
1974-75	80	17	17	6	6	28	6	23	45	12	259	335	58	4th,	Norris Div.	Out of Playoffs
1973-74	78	21	12	6	8	27	4	29	39	10	255	319	68	6th,	East Div.	Out of Playoffs
1972-73	78	22	12	5	15	17	7	37	29	12	265	243	86	5th,	East Div.	Out of Playoffs
1971-72	78	25	11	3	8	24	7	33	35	10	261	262	76	5th,	East Div.	Out of Playoffs
1970-71	78	17	15	7	5	30	4	22	45	11	209	308	55	7th,	East Div.	Out of Playoffs
1969-70	76	20	11	7	20	10	8	40	21	15	246	199	95	3rd,	East Div.	Lost Quarter-Final
1968-69	76	23	8	7	10	23	5	33	31	12	239	221	78	5th,	East Div.	Out of Playoffs
1967-68	74	18	15	4	9	20	0	27	35	12	245	257	66	6th,	East Div.	Out of Playoffs
1966-67	70	21	11	3	6	28	1	27	39	4	212	241	58	5th,		Out of Playoffs
1965-66	70	20	8	7	11	19	5	31	27	12	221	194	74	4th,		Lost Final
1964-65	70	25	7	3	15	16	4	40	23	7	224	175	87	1st,		Lost Semi-Final
1963-64	70	23	9	3	7	20	8	30	29	11	191	204	71	4th,		Lost Final
1962-63	70	19	10	6	13	15	7	32	25	13	200	194	77	4th,		Lost Final
1961-62	70	17	11	7	6	22	7	23	33	14	184	219	60	5th,		Out of Playoffs
1960-61	70	15	13	7	10	16	9	25	29	16	195	215	66	4th,		Lost Final
1959-60	70	18	14	3	8	15	12	26	29	15	186	197	67	4th,		Lost Semi-Final
1958-59	70	13	17	5	12	20	3	25	37	8	167	218	58	6th,		Out of Playoffs
1957-58	70	16	11	8	13	18	4	29	29	12	176	207	70	3rd,		Lost Semi-Final
1956-57	70	23	7	5	15	13	7	38	20	12	198	157	88	1st,		Lost Semi-Final
1955-56	70	21	6	8	9	18	8	30	24	16	183	148	76	2nd,		Lost Final
1954-55	70	25	5	5	17	12	6	42	17	11	204	134	95	1st,		**Won Stanley Cup**
1953-54	70	24	4	7	13	15	7	37	19	14	191	132	88	1st,		**Won Stanley Cup**
1952-53	70	20	5	10	16	11	8	36	16	18	222	133	90	1st,		Lost Semi-Final
1951-52	70	24	7	4	20	7	8	44	14	12	215	133	100	1st,		**Won Stanley Cup**
1950-51	70	25	3	7	19	10	6	44	13	13	236	139	101	1st,		Lost Semi-Final
1949-50	70	19	9	7	18	10	7	37	19	14	229	164	88	1st,		**Won Stanley Cup**
1948-49	60	21	6	3	13	13	4	34	19	7	195	145	75	1st,		Lost Final
1947-48	60	16	9	5	14	9	7	30	18	12	187	148	72	2nd,		Lost Final
1946-47	60	14	10	6	8	17	5	22	27	11	190	193	55	4th,		Lost Semi-Final
1945-46	50	16	5	4	4	15	6	20	20	10	146	159	50	4th,		Lost Semi-Final
1944-45	50	19	5	1	12	9	4	31	14	5	218	161	67	2nd,		Lost Final
1943-44	50	18	5	2	8	13	4	26	18	6	214	177	58	2nd,		Lost Semi-Final
1942-43	50	16	4	5	9	10	6	25	14	11	169	124	61	1st,		**Won Stanley Cup**
1941-42	48	14	7	3	5	18	1	19	25	4	140	147	42	5th,		Lost Final
1940-41	48	14	5	5	7	11	6	21	16	11	112	102	53	3rd,		Lost Final
1939-40	48	11	10	3	5	16	3	16	26	6	90	126	38	5th,		Lost Semi-Final
1938-39	48	14	8	2	4	16	4	18	24	6	107	128	42	5th,		Lost Semi-Final
1937-38	48	8	10	6	4	15	5	12	25	11	99	133	35	4th,	Amn. Div.	Out of Playoffs
1936-37	48	14	5	5	11	9	4	25	14	9	128	102	59	1st,	Amn. Div.	**Won Stanley Cup**
1935-36	48	14	5	5	10	11	3	24	16	8	124	103	56	1st,	Amn. Div.	**Won Stanley Cup**
1934-35	48	11	8	5	8	14	2	19	22	7	127	114	45	4th,	Amn. Div.	Out of Playoffs
1933-34*	48	15	5	4	10	9	5	25	14	10	113	98	58	1st,	Amn. Div.	Lost Final
1932-33	48	17	3	4	8	12	4	25	15	8	111	93	58	2nd,	Amn. Div.	Lost Semi-Final
1931-32	48	13	8	3	5	12	7	18	20	10	95	108	46	3rd,	Amn. Div.	Lost Quarter-Final
1930-31**	44	10	7	5	6	14	2	16	21	7	102	105	39	4th,	Amn. Div.	Out of Playoffs
1929-30	44	9	10	3	5	14	2	14	24	6	117	133	34	4th,	Amn. Div.	Out of Playoffs
1928-29	44	11	6	5	8	10	4	19	16	9	72	63	47	3rd,	Amn. Div.	Lost Quarter-Final
1927-28	44	9	10	3	10	9	3	19	19	6	88	79	44	4th,	Amn. Div.	Out of Playoffs
1926-27***	44	6	15	1	6	13	3	12	28	4	76	105	28	5th,	Amn. Div.	Out of Playoffs

* Team name changed to Red Wings. ** Team name changed to Falcons. *** Team named Cougars.

1990-91 Player Personnel

FORWARDS	HT	WT	S	Place of Birth	Date	1989-90 Club
BARR, David	6-1	190	R	Toronto, Ont.	11/30/60	Detroit-Adirondack
BURR, Shawn	6-1	195	L	Sarnia, Ont.	7/1/66	Detroit-Adirondack
CARSON, Jimmy	6-0	200	R	Southfield, MI	7/20/68	Edmonton-Detroit
CHABOT, John	6-2	200	L	Summerside, P.E.I.	5/18/62	Detroit
FEDEROV, Sergei	6-1	191	R	Pskow, USSR	12/13/69	CSKA (USSR)
FEDYK, Brent	6-0	195	R	Yorkton, Sask.	3/8/67	Adirondack-Detroit
GALLANT, Gerard	5-10	185	L	Summerside, P.E.I.	9/2/63	Detroit
GARPENLOV, Johan	5-11	185	L	Stockholm, Sweden	3/21/68	Djurgarden (Swe.)
HABSCHIED, Marc	6-0	185	R	Swift Current, Sask.	3/1/63	Detroit
HOLLAND, Dennis	5-10	165	L	Vernon, B.C.	1/30/69	Adirondack
KENNEDY, Sheldon	5-10	170	R	Brandon, Man.	6/15/69	Adirondack-Detroit
KOCUR, Joe	6-0	195	R	Calgary, Alta.	12/21/64	Detroit
KOCUR, Kory	5-11	188	R	Kelvington, Sask.	3/6/69	Adirondack
McCLELLAND, Kevin	6-2	205	R	Oshawa, Ont.	7/4/62	Edmonton-Detroit
McKAY, Randy	6-1	185	R	Montreal, Que.	1/25/67	Adirondack-Detroit
McRAE, Chris	6-0	200	L	Beaverton, Ont.	8/26/65	Adirondack-Detroit
MERKOSKY, Glenn	5-10	175	L	Edmonton, Alta.	4/8/59	Adirondack-Detroit
PROBERT, Bob	6-3	215	L	Windsor, Ont.	6/5/65	Detroit
SHANK, Daniel	5-10	190	R	Montreal, Que.	5/12/67	Adirondack-Detroit
SILLINGER, Mike	5-10	191	R	Regina, Sask.	6/29/71	Regina-Adirondack
YZERMAN, Steve	5-11	185	R	Cranbrook, B.C.	5/9/65	Detroit

DEFENSEMEN	HT	WT	S	Place of Birth	Date	1989-90 Club
CHIASSON, Steve	6-1	205	L	Barrie, Ont.	4/14/67	Detroit
DJOOS, Per	5-11	175	L	Mora, Sweden	5/11/68	Brynas (Swe.)
HOUDA, Doug	6-2	200	L	Blairmore, Alta.	6/3/66	Detroit
GREEN, Rick	6-3	220	L	Belleville, Ont.	2/20/56	Merano (Italy)
KRUPPKE, Gord	6-1	200	R	Slave Lake, Alta.	4/2/69	Adirondack
LUONGO, Chris	6-0	190	R	Detroit, MI	3/17/67	Adirondack-Phoenix
MAYER, Derek	6-0	185	R	Rossland, B.C.	5/21/67	Adirondack
McCRIMMON, Brad	5-11	197	L	Dodsland, Sask.	3/29/59	Calgary
MORTON, Dean	6-1	196	R	Peterborough, Ont.	2/27/68	Adirondack-Detroit
NORWOOD, Lee	6-1	198	L	Oakland, CA	2/2/60	Detroit
PAZNIK, Jody	6-1	180	L	Winnipeg, Man.	6/28/69	Adirondack-Detroit
PICARD, Robert	6-2	207	R	Montreal, Que.	5/25/67	Quebec-Detroit
RACINE, Yves	6-0	185	L	Matane, Que.	2/7/69	Adirondack-Detroit
SCHENA, Rob	6/1	190	L	Saugess, MA	2/5/67	Phoenix-Hampton-Adir.
WILKIE, Bob	6-2	200	R	Calgary, Alta.	2/11/69	Adirondack
ZOMBO, Rick	6-1	195	R	DesPlaines, IL	5/8/63	Detroit

GOALTENDERS	HT	WT	C	Place of Birth	Date	1989-90 Club
CHEVELDAE, Tim	5-10	175	L	Melville, Sask.	2/15/68	Adirondack-Detroit
CHEVRIER, Alain	5-8	180	L	Cornwall, Ont.	4/23/61	Chicago-Pittsburgh
GAGNON, Dave	6-0	185		Windsor, Ont.	10/31/67	Colgate
GLICKMAN, Jason	5-9	179	L	Chicago, IL	3/25/69	Regina
HANLON, Glen	6-0	185	R	Brandon, Man.	2/20/57	Detroit
HANSCH, Randy	5-10	165	R	Edmonton, Alta.	2/8/66	Hampton
KING, Scott	6-1	185		Thunder Bay, Ont.	6/25/67	U. of Maine
REIMER, Mark	5-11	170	L	Calgary, Alta.	3/23/67	Adirondack
STEFAN, Greg	5-11	180	L	Brantford, Ont.	2/11/61	Detroit-Adirondack

1989-90 Scoring

Regular Season

*rookie

Pos	#	Player	Team	GP	G	A	Pts	+/−	PIM	PP	SH	GW	GT	S	%
C	19	Steve Yzerman	DET	79	65	62	127	6−	79	16	7	8	2	332	18.7
L	17	Gerard Gallant	DET	69	36	44	80	6−	254	12	3	5	1	219	16.4
C	42	Bernie Federko	DET	73	17	40	57	8−	24	3	0	0	0	108	15.7
L	11	Shawn Burr	DET	76	24	32	56	14	82	4	3	2	0	173	13.9
C	16	John Chabot	DET	69	9	40	49	5	24	0	2	0	0	91	9.9
D	3	Steve Chiasson	DET	67	14	28	42	16−	114	4	0	2	0	190	7.4
C	10	Jimmy Carson	EDM	4	1	2	3	2−	0	1	0	0	0	11	9.1
			DET	44	20	16	36	6−	8	10	0	1	1	127	15.7
			TOTAL	48	21	18	39	8−	8	11	0	1	1	138	15.2
R	26	Joey Kocur	DET	71	16	20	36	4−	268	1	0	5	0	128	12.5
R	22	Dave Barr	DET	62	10	25	35	5	45	2	3	0	1	96	10.4
R	25	Marc Habscheid	DET	66	15	11	26	1	33	0	0	0	0	114	13.2
D	4	Rick Zombo	DET	77	5	20	25	13	95	0	0	0	0	62	8.1
R	34	*Daniel Shank	DET	57	11	13	24	1	143	0	0	1	0	61	18.0
D	23	Lee Norwood	DET	64	8	14	22	14	95	1	0	1	0	60	13.3
D	21	Borje Salming	DET	49	2	17	19	20	52	2	0	0	0	52	3.8
D	2	Mike O'Connell	DET	66	4	14	18	12−	22	0	0	0	0	57	7.0
L	20	Greg C. Adams	QUE	7	1	3	4	2−	17	0	0	0	0	8	12.5
			DET	28	3	7	10	0	16	0	0	0	0	19	15.8
			TOTAL	35	4	10	14	2−	33	0	0	0	0	27	14.8
D	33	*Yves Racine	DET	28	4	9	13	3−	23	1	0	0	0	49	8.2
R	18	Kevin McClelland	EDM	10	1	1	2	1−	13	0	0	0	0	7	14.3
			DET	61	4	5	9	5−	183	0	0	0	0	24	16.7
			TOTAL	71	5	6	11	6−	196	0	0	0	0	31	16.1
D	27	Doug Houda	DET	73	2	9	11	5−	127	0	0	0	0	59	3.4
R	29	*Randy McKay	DET	33	3	6	9	1	51	0	0	0	0	33	9.1
R	12	*Sheldon Kennedy	DET	20	2	7	9	0	10	0	0	1	0	23	8.7
D	7	Robert Picard	QUE	24	0	5	5	5−	28	0	0	0	0	25	.0
			DET	20	0	3	3	2	20	0	0	0	0	14	.0
			TOTAL	44	0	8	8	3−	48	0	0	0	0	39	.0
L	14	Torrie Robertson	DET	42	1	5	6	3−	112	0	0	0	0	20	5.0
R	15	*Brent Fedyk	DET	27	1	4	5	1−	6	0	0	0	0	28	3.6
L	24	Bob Probert	DET	4	3	0	3	0	21	0	0	0	0	12	25.0
G	1	Glen Hanlon	DET	45	0	3	3	0	24	0	0	0	0	0	.0
R	8	Jim Nill	DET	15	0	2	2	3−	18	0	0	0	0	10	.0
D	5	*Dean Morton	DET	1	1	0	1	1−	2	0	0	0	0	2	50.0
R	5	*Chris McRae	DET	7	1	0	1	0	45	0	0	0	1	1	100.0
G	30	Greg Stefan	DET	7	0	1	1	0	4	0	0	0	0	0	.0
G	32	*Tim Cheveldae	DET	28	0	1	1	0	2	0	0	0	0	0	.0
D	37	*John Mokosak	DET	33	0	1	1	9−	82	0	0	0	0	15	.0
C	43	Murray Eaves	DET	1	0	0	0	0	2	0	0	0	0	2	.0
D	5	*Peter Dineen	DET	2	0	0	0	0	5	0	0	0	0	4	.0
D	29	Chris Kotsopoulos	DET	2	0	0	0	1−	10	0	0	0	0	4	.0
C	44	Glenn Merkosky	DET	3	0	0	0	0	0	0	0	0	0	3	.0
G	35	Sam St. Laurent	DET	14	0	0	0	0	2	0	0	0	0	0	.0

Goaltending

No.	Goaltender	GPI	Mins	Avg	W	L	T	EN	SO	GA	SA	S%
35	Sam St. Laurent	14	607	3.76	2	6	1	2	0	38	325	.883
32	*Tim Cheveldae	28	1600	3.79	10	9	8	1	0	101	854	.882
30	Greg Stefan	7	359	4.01	1	5	0	0	0	24	147	.837
1	Glen Hanlon	45	2290	4.03	15	18	5	3	1	154	1159	.867
	Totals	80	4880	3.97	28	38	14	6	1	323	2485	.870

Retired Numbers

6	Larry Aurie	1927-1939
9	Gordie Howe	1946-1971

Captains' History

Art Duncan, 1926-27; Reg Noble, 1927-28 to 1929-30; George Hay, 1930-31; Carson Cooper, 1931-32; Larry Aurie, 1932-33; Herbie Lewis, 1933-34; Ebbie Goodfellow, 1934-35; Doug Young, 1935-36 to 1937-38; Ebbie Goodfellow, 1938-39 to 1941-42; Sid Abel, 1942-43; Mud Bruneteau, Bill Hollett (co-captains), 1943-44; Bill Hollett, 1944-45; Bill Hollett, Sid Abel, 1945-46; Sid Abel, 1946-47 to 1951-52; Ted Lindsay, 1952-53 to 1955-56; Red Kelly, 1956-57, 1957-58; Gordie Howe, 1958-59 to 1961-62; Alex Delvecchio, 1962-63 to 1973-74; Marcel Dionne, 1974-75; Danny Grant, Terry Harper, 1975-76; Danny Grant, Dennis Polonich, 1976-77; Dan Maloney, Dennis Hextall, 1977-78; Dennis Hextall, Nick Libett, Paul Woods, 1978-79; Dale McCourt, 1979-80; Errol Thompson, Reed Larson, 1980-81; Reed Larson, 1981-82; Danny Gare, 1982-83 to 1985-86; Steve Yzerman, 1986-87 to date.

General Managers' History

Art Duncan, 1926-27; Jack Adams, 1927-28 to 1962-63; Sidney Abel, 1963-64 to 1969-70; Sidney Abel and Ned Harkness, 1970-71; Ned Harkness, 1971-72 to 1973-74; Alex Delvecchio, 1974-75 to 1975-76; Alex Delvecchio and Ted Lindsay, 1976-77; Ted Lindsay, 1977-78 to 1979-80; Jimmy Skinner, 1980-81 to 1981-82; Jim Devellano, 1982-83 to 1989-90; Bryan Murray, 1990-91.

Coaching History

Art Duncan, 1926-27; Jack Adams, 1927-28 to 1946-47; Tommy Ivan, 1947-48 to 1953-54; Jimmy Skinner, 1954-55 to 1956-57; Jimmy Skinner and Sid Abel, 1957-58; Sid Abel, 1958-59 to 1967-68; Bill Gadsby, 1968-69; Bill Gadsby and Sid Abel, 1969-70; Ned Harkness and Doug Barkley, 1970-71; Doug Barkley and John Wilson, 1971-72; John Wilson, 1972-73; Ted Garvin and Alex Delvecchio, 1973-74; Alex Delvecchio, 1974-75; Doug Barkley and Alex Delvecchio, 1975-76; Alex Delvecchio and Larry Wilson, 1976-77; Bobby Kromm, 1977-78 to 1978-79; Bobby Kromm and Ted Lindsay, 1979-80; Ted Lindsay and Wayne Maxner, 1980-81; Wayne Maxner and Billy Dea, 1981-82; Nick Polano, 1982-83 to 1984-85; Harry Neale and Brad Park, 1985-86; Jacques Demers, 1986-87 to 1989-90; Bryan Murray, 1990-91.

Club Records

Team

(Figures in brackets for season records are games played; records for fewest points, wins, ties, losses, goals, goals against are for 70 or more games)

Record		
Most Points	**101**	1950-51 (70)
Most Wins	**44**	1950-51 (70) 1951-52 (70)
Most Ties	**18**	1952-53 (70) 1980-81 (80)
Most Losses	**57**	1985-86 (80)
Most Goals	**322**	1987-88 (80)
Most Goals Against	**415**	1985-86 (80)
Fewest Points	**40**	1985-86 (80)
Fewest Wins	**16**	1976-77 (80)
Fewest Ties	**4**	1966-67 (70)
Fewest Losses	**13**	1950-51 (70)
Fewest Goals	**167**	1958-59 (70)
Fewest Goals Against	**132**	1953-54 (70)
Longest Winning Streak		
Over-all	**9**	Mar. 3-21/51; Feb. 27- Mar. 20/55
Home	**14**	Jan. 21- Mar. 25/65
Away	**5**	Four times
Longest Undefeated Streak		
Over-all	**15**	Nov. 27- Dec. 28/52 (8 wins, 7 ties)
Home	**18**	Dec. 26/54- Mar. 20/55 (13 wins, 5 ties)
Away	**15**	Oct. 18- Dec. 20/51 (10 wins, 5 ties)
Longest Losing Streak		
Over-all	**14**	Feb. 24- Mar. 25/82
Home	**7**	Feb. 20- Mar. 25/82
Away	**14**	Oct. 19- Dec. 21/66
Longest Winless Streak		
Over-all	**19**	Feb. 26- Apr. 3/77 (18 losses, 1 tie)
Home	**10**	Dec. 11/85- Jan. 18/86 (9 losses, 1 tie)
Away	**26**	Dec. 15/76- Apr. 3/77 (23 losses, 3 ties)
Most Shutouts, Season	**13**	1953-54 (70)
Most. PIM, Season	**2,393**	1985-86 (80)
Most Goals, Game	**15**	Jan. 23/44 (NYR at Det. 15)

Individual

Record		
Most Seasons	**25**	Gordie Howe
Most Games	**1,687**	Gordie Howe
Most Goals, Career	**786**	Gordie Howe
Most Assists, Career	**1,023**	Gordie Howe
Most Points, Career	**1,809**	Gordie Howe (786 goals, 1,023 assists)
Most PIM, Career	**1,643**	Gordie Howe
Most Shutouts, Career	**85**	Terry Sawchuk
Longest Consecutive Games Streak	**548**	Alex Delvecchio (Dec. 13/56- Nov. 11/64)
Most Goals, Season	**65**	Steve Yzerman (1988-89)
Most Assists, Season	**90**	Steve Yzerman (1988-89)
Most Points, Season	**155**	Steve Yzerman (1988-89) (65 goals, 90 assists)
Most PIM, Season	**398**	Bob Probert (1987-88)
Most Points, Defenseman Season	**74**	Reed Larson (1982-83) (22 goals, 52 assists)
Most Points, Center, Season	**155**	Steve Yzerman (1988-89) (65 goals, 90 assists)
Most Points, Right Wing, Season	**103**	Gordie Howe (1968-69) (44 goals, 59 assists)
Most Points, Left Wing, Season	**105**	John Ogrodnick (1984-85) (55 goals, 50 assists)
Most Points, Rookie, Season	**87**	Steve Yzerman (1983-84) (39 goals, 48 assists)
Most Shutouts, Season	**12**	Terry Sawchuk (1951-52; 1953-54; 1954-55) Glenn Hall (1955-56)
Most Goals, Game	**6**	Syd Howe (Feb. 3/44)
Most Assists, Game	***7**	Billy Taylor (Mar. 16/47)
Most Points, Game	**7**	Carl Liscombe (Nov. 5/42) Don Grosso (Feb. 3/44) Billy Taylor (Mar. 16/47)

* NHL Record

All-time Record vs. Other Clubs

Regular Season

	At Home							On Road							Total						
	GP	W	L	T	GF	GA	PTS	GP	W	L	T	GF	GA	PTS	GP	W	L	T	GF	GA	PTS
Boston	274	148	74	52	911	687	348	274	82	149	43	722	967	207	548	230	223	95	1633	1654	555
Buffalo	42	21	17	4	153	129	46	40	5	29	6	96	183	16	82	26	46	10	249	312	62
Calgary	33	17	11	5	131	110	39	32	7	21	4	97	148	18	65	24	32	9	228	258	57
Chicago	293	181	85	27	1015	720	389	294	109	139	46	806	891	264	587	290	224	73	1821	1611	653
Edmonton	18	5	12	1	68	91	11	17	5	10	2	74	98	12	35	10	22	3	142	189	23
Hartford	18	5	7	6	62	57	16	17	5	11	1	47	70	11	35	10	18	7	109	127	27
Los Angeles	52	22	23	7	209	191	51	53	12	31	10	156	228	34	105	34	54	17	365	419	85
Minnesota	68	31	25	12	265	234	74	69	20	38	11	198	271	51	137	51	63	23	463	505	125
Montreal	269	122	94	53	759	690	297	269	62	164	43	600	952	167	538	184	258	96	1359	1642	464
New Jersey	27	17	8	2	122	84	36	28	8	14	6	76	104	22	55	25	22	8	198	188	58
NY Islanders	32	16	14	2	115	109	34	33	12	20	1	93	134	25	65	28	34	3	208	243	59
NY Rangers	272	154	74	44	950	666	352	272	85	130	57	692	838	227	544	239	204	101	1642	1504	579
Philadelphia	47	20	18	9	164	159	49	46	9	27	10	133	188	28	93	29	45	19	297	347	77
Pittsburgh	53	34	9	10	210	145	78	52	13	36	3	151	229	29	105	47	45	13	361	374	107
Quebec	17	9	7	1	69	63	19	18	5	11	2	61	81	12	35	14	18	3	130	144	31
St. Louis	69	27	31	11	239	218	65	68	17	41	10	179	258	44	137	44	72	21	418	476	109
Toronto	287	149	95	43	842	695	341	287	91	153	43	745	949	225	574	240	248	86	1587	1644	566
Vancouver	39	22	11	6	166	121	50	39	12	21	6	122	162	30	78	34	32	12	288	283	80
Washington	33	14	9	10	125	98	38	34	12	18	4	101	131	28	67	26	27	14	226	229	66
Winnipeg	19	9	7	3	77	79	21	20	6	7	7	64	71	19	39	15	14	10	141	150	40
Defunct	141	76	40	25	429	307	177	141	49	63	29	363	375	127	282	125	103	54	792	682	304
Totals	**2103**	**1099**	**671**	**333**	**7081**	**5653**	**2531**	**2103**	**626**	**1133**	**344**	**5576**	**7328**	**1596**	**4206**	**1725**	**1804**	**677**	**12657**	**12981**	**4127**

Playoffs

	Series	W	L	GP	W	L	T	GF	GA	Last Mtg.	Round	Result
Boston	7	3	4	33	14	19	0	98	96	1957	SF	L 1-4
Calgary	1	1	0	2	2	0	0	8	5	1978	PR	W 2-0
Chicago	12	5	7	60	27	33	0	171	187	1989	DSF	L 2-4
Edmonton	2	0	2	10	2	8	0	26	39	1988	CF	L 1-4
Montreal	12	7	5	62	29	33	0	149	161	1978	QF	L 1-4
NY Rangers	5	4	1	23	13	10	0	57	49	1950	F	W 4-3
St. Louis	2	1	1	9	5	4	0	33	27	1988	DF	W 4-1
Toronto	22	11	11	110	56	54	0	291	287	1988	DSF	W 4-2
Defunct Clubs	4	3	1	10	7	2	1	21	13			
Totals	**67**	**35**	**32**	**319**	**155**	**163**	**1**	**854**	**864**			

Playoff Results 1990-86

Year	Round	Opponent	Result	GF	GA
1989	DSF	Chicago	L 2-4	18	25
1988	CF	Edmonton	L 1-4	16	23
	DF	St. Louis	W 4-1	21	14
	DSF	Toronto	W 4-2	32	20
1987	CF	Edmonton	L 1-4	10	16
	DF	Toronto	W 4-3	20	18
	DSF	Chicago	W 4-0	15	6

Abbreviations: Round: F Final; **CF** conference final; **DF** division final; **DSF** division semi-final; **SF** semi-final; **QF** quarter-final. **PR** preliminary round. **GA** goals against; **GF** goals for.

1989-90 Results

Home				Away			
Oct.	12	Winnipeg	5-4	**Oct.**	5	Calgary	7-10
	14	Buffalo	6-2		7	Vancouver	3-5
	18	Minnesota	4-3		8	Los Angeles	0-5
	24	Chicago	3-5		15	Chicago	0-3
	26	Pittsburgh	3-3		19	St Louis	4-3
Nov.	1	Philadelphia	5-5		21	Hartford	3-3
	3	Hartford	3-4		28	Toronto	4-6
	14	Hartford	0-3	**Nov.**	4	NY Islanders	2-3
	16	St Louis	2-7		6	NY Rangers	1-6
	21	Boston	1-2		9	Minnesota	1-5
	24	Calgary	3-2		11	Toronto	2-4
	27	Edmonton	2-6		18	Quebec	8-1
	29	Washington	3-5	**Dec.**	1	Winnipeg	3-3
Dec.	5	St Louis	2-2		3	Chicago	4-3
	8	Minnesota	2-1		9	Minnesota	3-1
	13	Toronto	2-4		16	Montreal	1-3
	15	Chicago	8-4		23	Boston*	5-6
	20	Toronto	4-2		26	Buffalo	3-6
	31	New Jersey	6-4		27	Toronto	7-7
Jan.	2	Vancouver	4-1		29	Washington	1-2
	4	Quebec	4-1	**Jan.**	6	Minnesota	3-4
	9	Minnesota	9-0		12	Winnipeg	5-7
	23	St Louis	3-6		13	Minnesota	4-6
	25	Pittsburgh	3-5		16	Edmonton	6-4
	31	Edmonton	7-5		18	Los Angeles	4-9
Feb.	2	Toronto	5-2		27	Quebec	8-6
	6	Boston	0-2	**Feb.**	3	St Louis	2-4
	8	Chicago	6-8		12	New Jersey	1-1
	10	Calgary*	7-5		17	St Louis	1-6
	14	Los Angeles	6-5		24	NY Islanders*	3-3
	16	Philadelphia	9-6		25	Washington*	4-9
	19	Montreal	5-5	**Mar.**	3	Toronto	5-2
	21	NY Rangers	4-4		5	NY Rangers	2-3
	28	NY Islanders	4-3		10	Montreal	3-3
Mar.	2	Toronto	3-2		13	Chicago	3-3
	8	St Louis	3-2		15	Pittsburgh	1-6
	20	Vancouver	4-4		17	St Louis	4-3
	22	Minnesota	1-5		25	Chicago*	2-3
	24	Chicago*	5-3		31	New Jersey*	1-5
	27	Buffalo	5-6	**Apr.**	1	Philadelphia	3-3

* Denotes afternoon game.

Entry Draft Selections 1990-76

1990
Pick
3	Keith Primeau
45	Viacheslav Kozlov
66	Stewart Malgunas
87	Tony Burns
108	Claude Barthe
129	Jason York
150	Wes McCauley
171	Anthony Gruba
192	Travis Tucker
213	Brett Larson
234	John Hendry

1989
Pick
11	Mike Sillinger
32	Bob Boughner
53	Niklas Lidstrom
74	Sergei Fedorov
95	Shawn McCosh
116	Dallas Drake
137	Scott Zygulski
158	Andy Suhy
179	Bob Jones
200	Greg Bignell
204	Rick Judson
221	Vladimir Konstantivov
242	Joseph Frederick
246	Jason Glickman

1988
Pick
17	Kory Kocur
38	Serge Anglehart
47	Guy Dupuis
59	Petr Hrbek
80	Sheldon Kennedy
143	Kelly Hurd
164	Brian McCormack
185	Jody Praznik
206	Glen Goodall
227	Darren Colbourne
248	Donald Stone

1987
Pick
11	Yves Racine
32	Gordon Kruppke
41	Bob Wilkie
52	Dennis Holland
74	Mark Reimer
95	Radomir Brazda
116	Sean Clifford
137	Mike Gober
158	Kevin Scott
179	Mikko Haapakoski
200	Darin Bannister
221	Craig Quinlan
242	Tomas Jansson

1986
Pick
1	Joe Murphy
22	Adam Graves
43	Derek Mayer
64	Tim Cheveldae
85	Johan Garpenlov
106	Jay Stark
127	Per Djoos
148	Dean Morton
169	Marc Potvin
190	Scott King
211	Tom Bissett
232	Peter Ekroth

1985
Pick
8	Brent Fedyk
29	Jeff Sharples
50	Steve Chiasson
71	Mark Gowans
92	Chris Luongo
113	Randy McKay
134	Thomas Bjur
155	Mike Luckraft
176	Rob Schenna
197	Eerik Hamalainen
218	Bo Svanberg
239	Mikael Lindman

1984
Pick
7	Shawn Burr
28	Doug Houda
49	Milan Chalupa
91	Mats Lundstrom
112	Randy Hansch
133	Stefan Larsson
152	Lars Karlsson
154	Urban Nordin
175	Bill Shibicky
195	Jay Rose
216	Tim Kaiser
236	Tom Nickolau

1983
Pick
4	Steve Yzerman
25	Lane Lambert
46	Bob Probert
68	David Korol
86	Petr Klima
88	Joey Kocur
106	Chris Pusey
126	Bob Pierson
146	Craig Butz
166	Dave Sikorski
186	Stuart Grimson
206	Jeff Frank
226	Charles Chiatto

1982
Pick
17	Murray Craven
23	Yves Courteau
44	Carmine Vani
66	Craig Coxe
86	Brad Shaw
107	Claude Vilgrain
128	Greg Hudas
149	Pat Lahey
170	Gary Cullen
191	Brent Meckling
212	Mike Stern
233	Shaun Reagan

1981
Pick
23	Claude Loiselle
44	Corrado Micalef
86	Larry Trader
107	Gerard Gallant
128	Greg Stefan
149	Rick Zombo
170	Don Leblanc
191	Robert Nordmark

1980
Pick
11	Mike Blaisdell
46	Mark Osborne
88	Mike Corrigan
109	Wayne Crawford
130	Mike Braun
151	John Beukeboom
172	Dave Miles
193	Brian Rorabeck

1979
Pick
3	Mike Foligno
45	Jody Gage
46	Boris Fistric
66	John Ogrodnick
87	Joe Paterson
108	Carmen Cirella

1978
Pick
9	Willie Huber
12	Brent Peterson
28	Glenn Hicks
31	Al Jensen
53	Doug Derkson
62	Bjorn Skaare
78	Ted Nolan
95	Sylvain Locas
112	Wes George
129	John Barrett
146	Jim Malazdrewicz
163	Goeff Shaw
178	Carl Van Harrewyn
194	Ladislav Svozil
208	Tom Bailey
219	Larry Lozinski
224	Randy Betty
226	Brian Crawley
228	Doug Feasby

1977
Pick
1	Dale McCourt
37	Rick Vasko
55	John Hilworth
73	Jim Korn
91	Jim Baxter
109	Randy Wilson
125	Raymond Roy
141	Kip Churchill
155	Lance Gatoni
163	Robert Plumb
170	Alain Belanger
175	Dean Willers
178	Roland Cloutier
181	Edward Hill
184	Val James
185	Grant Morin

1976
Pick
4	Fred Williams
22	Reed Larson
40	Fred Berry
58	Kevin Schamehorn
76	Dwight Schofield
94	Tony Horvath
111	Fernand Leblanc
120	Claude Legris

Club Directory

Joe Louis Sports Arena
600 Civic Center Drive
Detroit, Michigan 48226
Phone **(313) 567-7333**
FAX 313/567-0296
ENVOY ID
Front Office: DRW. GM
Public
Relations: DRW. PR
Capacity: 19,275

Owner and President	Michael Ilitch
Owner and Secretary-Treasurer	Marian Ilitch
Executive Vice-President	James Lites
General Counsel	Denise Ilitch-Lites
Sr. Vice-President	Jim Devellano
Asst. General Manager	Nick Polano
General Manager and Head Coach	Bryan Murray
Assistant Coaches	Dave Lewis, Doug McLean
Goaltending Consultant	Phil Myre
Director of Amateur Scouting	Ken Holland
Director of Pro Scouting	Dan Belisle
Ontario Scout	Wayne Meier
Quebec and Eastern U.S. College Scout	Bill Dineen
Director of U.S. Scouting	Billy Dea
Western U.S. Scout	Chris Coury
Eastern U.S. Scout	Jerry Moschella
Northern Ontario Scout	Dave Polano
European Scout	Hakan Andersson
Alberta Scout	Lionel Matichuk
Saskatchewan Scout	Ian McDonnell
Manitoba Scout	Doug Overton Jr.
Director of Public Relations	Bill Jamieson
Director of Finance	Scott Fisher
Director of Advertising Sales	Terry Murphy
Director of Corporate Sales	Gary Vitto
Director of Broadcast Sales	Tony Nagorsen
Director of Marketing	Jeff Cogen
Director of Community Relations	Dave Strader
Director of Season Ticket Sales	Greg Strausser
Director of Arena Operations	John Pettit
Director of Merchandising Sales	Jules Goldman
Director of Business Administration	Nancy Beard
Office Manager	Dave Agius
Box Office Manager	Bob Kerlin
Associate Director of Public Relations	Kathy Best
Public Relations Coordinator	Howard Berlin
Print Advertising Coordinator	Amy Goan
Assistant Director of Arena Operations	Jay Cooper
Building Manager	Albert Sobotka
Athletic Therapist	Kirk Vickers
Athletic Trainer	Mark Brennan
Assistant Trainer	Larry Wasylon
Team Physicians	Dr. John Finley, D.O., Dr. David Collon, M.D.
Team Dentist	Dr. C.J. Regula, D.M.D.
Team Psychologist	Dr. Hugh Bray, Ph.D.
Team Opthamologist	Dr. Charles Slater, M.D.
Assistant to Executive Vice-President	Donna Gregory
Administrative Ass't./Finance	Cathy Witzke
Creative Director	Beverly Ostrom
P.R. Assistant	Marilyn Rowe
Marketing Assistant	Nancy King
Administrative Coordinator/Sales & Promotion	Lori Sbroglia
Largest crowd	21,019* Nov. 25, 1983; Detroit 5, Pittsburgh 2
Location of Press Box, Radio-TV Booths	Jefferson Ave. side of Arena, top of seats (Row 42)
Location of Media Hospitality Lounge	First floor, in hallway, near Red Wings' dressing room, Atwater St. side of Arena.
Dimensions of Rink	200 feet by 85 feet; S.A.R. Plastic extends above boards all around rink
Club Colors	Red and White
Radio Flagship Station	WJR-AM, 760
TV Stations	Pro-Am Sports System (PASS-Cable) WKBD-TV (Channel 50)
Radio Announcer	Bruce Martyn, Paul Woods
TV Announcers	Dave Strader, Mickey Redmond

*NHL Record

Coach and General Manager

MURRAY, BRYAN CLARENCE
Coach and General Manager, Detroit Red Wings.
Born in Shawville, Que., December 5, 1942.

Appointed coach and G.M. of the Red Wings in the summer of 1990, Bryan Murray came to Detroit after nine seasons behind the bench in Washington.

A graduate of McGill, his first major coaching experience came in junior hockey when he took over the last-place Regina Pats and carried the team to the WHL championship in 1979-80. His one-year success in Regina translated into a professional coaching job in 1980-81 with the Capitals' AHL farm team, the Hershey Bears, whom he guided to their best season in over 40 years. That first-year effort netted him the Hockey News Minor League Coach-of-the-Year honors. Although he began the 1981-82 campaign in Hershey, Murray was promoted to Washington and the NHL on November 11, 1981.

Coaching Record

Season	Team	Games	Regular Season W	L	T	%	Playoffs Games	W	L	%
1979-80	Regina (WHL)	72	47	24	1	.660	22	16	6	.727
1980-81	Hershey (AHL)	80	47	24	9	.644	10	6	4	.600
1981-82	Washington (NHL)	76	25	28	13	.477	....	....	....	....
1982-83	Washington (NHL)	80	39	25	16	.588	4	1	3	.250
1983-84	Washington (NHL)	80	48	27	5	.631	8	4	4	.500
1984-85	Washington (NHL)	80	46	25	9	.631	5	2	3	.400
1985-86	Washington (NHL)	80	50	23	7	.669	9	5	4	.556
1986-87	Washington (NHL)	80	38	32	10	.538	7	3	4	.429
1987-88	Washington (NHL)	80	38	33	9	.531	14	7	7	.500
1988-89	Washington (NHL)	80	41	29	10	.575	6	2	4	.333
1989-90	Washington (NHL)	46	18	24	4	.435	....	....	....	....
	NHL Totals	672	343	246	83	.572	53	24	29	.453

Edmonton Oilers
1989-90 Results: 38w-28L-14T 90PTS. Second, Smythe Division

Year-by-Year Record

		Home			Road			Overall							
Season	GP	W	L	T	W	L	T	W	L	T	GF	GA	Pts.	Finished	Playoff Result
1989-90	80	23	11	6	15	17	8	38	28	14	315	283	90	2nd, Smythe Div.	Won Stanley Cup
1988-89	80	21	16	3	17	18	5	38	34	8	325	306	84	3rd, Smythe Div.	Lost Div. Semi-Final
1987-88	80	28	8	4	16	17	7	44	25	11	363	288	99	2nd, Smythe Div.	Won Stanley Cup
1986-87	80	29	6	5	21	18	1	50	24	6	372	284	106	1st, Smythe Div.	Won Stanley Cup
1985-86	80	32	6	2	24	11	5	56	17	7	426	310	119	1st, Smythe Div.	Lost Div. Final
1984-85	80	26	7	7	23	13	4	49	20	11	401	298	109	1st, Smythe Div.	Won Stanley Cup
1983-84	80	31	5	4	26	13	1	57	18	5	446	314	119	1st, Smythe Div.	Won Stanley Cup
1982-83	80	25	9	6	22	12	6	47	21	12	424	315	106	1st, Smythe Div.	Lost Final
1981-82	80	31	5	4	17	12	11	48	17	15	417	295	111	1st, Smythe Div.	Lost Div. Semi-Final
1980-81	80	17	13	10	12	22	6	29	35	16	328	327	74	4th, Smythe Div.	Lost Quarter-Final
1979-80	80	17	14	9	11	25	4	28	39	13	301	322	69	4th, Smythe Div.	Lost Prelim. Round

Schedule

Home				Away			
Oct.	Sat.	6	Winnipeg	**Oct.**	Thur.	11	Los Angeles
	Sun.	7	Toronto		Sun.	14	Vancouver*
	Tues.	16	St Louis		Wed.	24	Winnipeg
	Fri.	19	Boston		Thur.	25	Calgary
	Sun.	21	Calgary	**Nov.**	Tues.	6	St Louis
	Sun.	28	Washington		Thur.	8	Chicago
	Wed.	31	Winnipeg		Sat.	10	Los Angeles
Nov.	Sat.	3	New Jersey		Fri.	23	Buffalo
	Wed.	14	Vancouver		Sat.	24	Toronto
	Fri.	16	Buffalo		Tues.	27	Pittsburgh
	Sun.	18	NY Islanders		Thur.	29	Boston
	Tues.	20	Chicago	**Dec.**	Sat.	1	Hartford
Dec.	Wed.	5	Quebec		Sun.	2	Philadelphia
	Fri.	7	NY Rangers		Sat.	15	Los Angeles
	Sun.	9	Calgary		Thur.	20	Vancouver
	Wed.	12	Vancouver		Sat.	22	Calgary
	Tues.	18	Los Angeles		Fri.	28	Vancouver
	Sun.	23	Vancouver	**Jan.**	Tues.	8	Pittsburgh
	Thur.	27	Calgary		Wed.	9	Detroit
	Sun.	30	Hartford		Sat.	12	New Jersey*
Jan.	Wed.	2	Montreal		Sun.	13	Philadelphia
	Fri.	4	Detroit		Tues.	15	NY Rangers
	Tues.	22	Los Angeles		Thur.	17	NY Islanders
	Fri.	25	NY Rangers		Wed.	23	Vancouver
	Wed.	30	Vancouver		Sun.	27	Winnipeg*
Feb.	Fri.	1	Chicago	**Feb.**	Sun.	3	Buffalo
	Mon.	11	Pittsburgh		Tues.	5	Boston
	Tues.	12	St Louis		Wed.	6	Hartford
	Thur.	14	Los Angeles		Fri.	8	Washington
	Fri.	22	Detroit		Sat.	16	Toronto
	Sun.	24	Quebec		Mon.	18	New Jersey
Mar.	Fri.	1	Minnesota		Wed.	20	Minnesota
	Sat.	2	Montreal		Wed.	27	Calgary
	Fri.	8	Philadelphia	**Mar.**	Tues.	5	Winnipeg
	Sun.	10	Washington		Wed.	6	Minnesota
	Wed.	13	NY Islanders		Fri.	15	Winnipeg
	Sat.	23	Winnipeg		Sun.	17	Montreal
	Sun.	24	Los Angeles		Tues.	19	Quebec
	Fri.	29	Calgary		Tues.	26	Los Angeles
	Sun.	31	Winnipeg		Thur.	28	Calgary

* Denotes afternoon game.

Home Starting Times:
Weeknights .... 7:35 p.m.
Saturdays and Sundays .... 6:05 p.m.

Franchise date: June 22, 1979

12th NHL Season

Bill Ranford—1990 Conn Smythe Trophy winner.

1990-91 Player Personnel

FORWARDS

	HT	WT	S	Place of Birth	Date	1989-90 Club
ANDERSON, Glenn	6-1	190	L	Vancouver, B.C.	10/2/60	Edmonton
BEAULIEU, Nicolas	6-2	200	L	Rimouski, Que.	8/19/68	Phoenix
BORGO, Richard	5-11	190	R	Thunder Bay, Ont.	9/25/70	Kitchener
BROWN, Dave	6-5	205	R	Saskatoon, Sask.	11/12/62	Phoenix-Edmonton
BUCHBERGER, Kelly	6-2	210	L	Langenburg, Sask.	12/2/66	Edmonton
CURRIE, Dan	6-2	195	L	Burlington, Ont.	3/15/68	Cape Breton
DRULIA, Stan	5-11	190	R	Elmira, NY	1/5/68	Phoenix-Cape Breton
GELINAS, Martin	5-11	195	L	Shawinigan, Que.	6/5/70	Edmonton
GRAVES, Adam	5-11	185	L	Toronto, Ont.	4/12/68	Detroit-Edmonton
HAAS, David	6-2	196	L	Toronto, Ont.	6/23/68	Cape Breton
ISSEL, Kim	6-4	196	R	Regina, Sask.	9/25/67	Cape Breton
JOSEPH, Fabian	5-8	170	L	Sydney, N.S.	12/5/65	Cape Breton
KAPUSTA, Tomas	6-0	187	L	Zlin, Czech.	2/23/67	Zlin (Czech.)-Cape Breton
KLIMA, Petr	6-0	190	L	Chaomutov, Czech.	12/23/64	Detroit-Edmonton
LAFORGE, Marc	6-2	210	L	Sudbury, Ont.	1/3/68	Hfd.-Bing'ton-Cape Breton
LAMB, Mark	5-9	180	L	Ponteix, Sask.	8/3/64	Edmonton
LeBLANC, John	6-1	190	L	Campbellton, N.B.	1/21/64	Cape Breton
MacTAVISH, Craig	6-1	195	L	London, Ont.	8/15/58	Edmonton
MATULIK, Ivan	6-1	200	L	Nitra, Czech.	6/17/68	Cape Breton-Phoenix
MESSIER, Mark	6-1	210	L	Edmonton, Alta.	1/18/61	Edmonton
MURPHY, Joe	6-1	190	L	London, Ont.	10/16/67	Detroit-Edmonton
RUZICKA, Vladimir	6-3	212	L	Most, Czech.	6/6/63	Litvinov (Czech.)-Edm.
SEMENOV, Anatoli	6-2	190	L	Moscow, USSR	3/5/62	Moscow Dynamo (USSR)-Edm.
SIM, Trevor	6-2	192	L	Calgary, Alta.	6/9/70	Swift Current-Kamloops-Edm.
SIMPSON, Craig	6-2	195	R	London, Ont.	2/15/67	Edmonton
SOBERLAK, Peter	6-2	195	L	Kamloops, B.C.	5/12/69	Cape Breton
TIKKANEN, Esa	6-1	200	L	Helsinki, Finland	1/25/65	Edmonton
TISDALE, Tim	6-1	186	L	Swift Current, Sask.	5/28/68	Cape Breton
VAN ALLEN, Shaun	6-1	200	L	Shaunavon, Sask.	8/29/67	Cape Breton
WARE, Mike	6-5	208	R	York, Ont.	3/22/67	Cape Breton-Edm.

DEFENSEMEN

	HT	WT	S	Place of Birth	Date	1989-90 Club
BARBE, Mario	6-0	204	L	Cadillac, Que.	3/17/67	Cape Breton
BAUER, Collin	6-1	180	L	Edmonton, Alta.	9/6/70	Saskatoon
BELL, Bruce	6-1	190	L	Toronto, Ont.	2/15/65	Cape Breton-Edm.
BEUKEBOOM, Jeff	6-4	215	R	Ajax, Ont.	3/28/65	Edmonton
FOSTER, Corey	6-3	200	L	Ottawa, Ont.	10/27/69	Cape Breton
GREGG, Randy	6-4	215	L	Edmonton, Alta.	2/19/56	Edmonton
HUDDY, Charlie	6-0	210	L	Oshawa, Ont.	6/2/59	Edmonton
JOSEPH, Chris	6-2	210	R	Burnaby, B.C.	9/10/69	Cape Breton-Edm.
LEROUX, Francois	6-6	221	L	Ste-Adele, Que.	4/18/70	Edm.-St. Jean-Vict'ville
LOWE, Kevin	6-2	195	L	Lachute, Que.	4/15/59	Edmonton
MACIVER, Norm	5-11	180	L	Thunder Bay, Ont.	9/8/64	Bing.-Cape Breton-Edm.
MUNI, Craig	6-3	200	L	Toronto, Ont.	7/19/62	Edmonton
SMITH, Geoff	6-3	200	L	Edmonton, Alta.	3/7/69	Edmonton
SMITH, Steve	6-4	215	L	Glasgow, Scotland	4/30/63	Edmonton

GOALTENDERS

	HT	WT	C	Place of Birth	Date	1989-90 Club
FUHR, Grant	5-10	186	R	Spruce Grove, Alta.	9/28/62	Edm.-Cape Breton
GREENLAY, Mike	6-3	200	L	Vitoria, Brazil	9/15/68	Cape Breton
RANFORD, Bill	5-10	170	L	Brandon, Man.	12/14/66	Edmonton
REDDICK, Eldon	5-8	170	L	Halifax, N.S.	10/6/64	Edm.-Cape Breton-Phoenix

Retired Numbers

3	Al Hamilton	1972-1980

General Manager's History

Glen Sather, 1979-80 to date.

Coaching History

Glen Sather, 1979-80; Bryan Watson and Glen Sather, 1980-81; Glen Sather, 1981-82 to 1988-89; John Muckler, 1989-90 to date.

1989-90 Scoring

Regular Season

* rookie

Pos	#	Player	Team	GP	G	A	Pts	+/−	PIM	PP	SH	GW	GT	S	%
C	11	Mark Messier	EDM	79	45	84	129	19	79	13	6	3	2	211	21.3
R	17	Jari Kurri	EDM	78	33	60	93	18	48	10	2	2	1	201	16.4
R	9	Glenn Anderson	EDM	73	34	38	72	1−	107	17	1	7	1	204	16.7
L	85	Petr Klima	DET	13	5	5	10	8−	6	2	0	0	0	37	13.5
			EDM	63	25	28	53	1−	66	7	0	3	0	149	16.8
			TOTAL	76	30	33	63	9−	72	9	0	3	0	186	16.1
L	10	Esa Tikkanen	EDM	79	30	33	63	17	161	6	4	6	0	199	15.1
L	18	Craig Simpson	EDM	80	29	32	61	2−	180	7	0	2	1	129	22.5
C	14	Craig MacTavish	EDM	80	21	22	43	13	89	1	6	5	0	109	19.3
D	5	Steve Smith	EDM	75	7	34	41	6	171	3	0	1	0	125	5.6
D	4	Kevin Lowe	EDM	78	7	26	33	18	140	2	1	0	0	74	9.5
C	8	Joe Murphy	DET	9	3	1	4	4	4	0	0	1	0	16	18.8
			EDM	62	7	18	25	1	56	2	0	0	0	101	6.9
			TOTAL	71	10	19	29	5	60	2	0	1	0	117	8.5
C	7	Mark Lamb	EDM	58	12	16	28	10	42	2	0	2	0	81	14.8
L	20	*Martin Gelinas	EDM	46	17	8	25	0	30	5	0	2	2	71	23.9
D	21	Randy Gregg	EDM	48	4	20	24	24	42	0	0	0	0	41	9.8
D	22	Charlie Huddy	EDM	70	1	23	24	13−	56	1	0	1	0	119	.8
L	12	Adam Graves	DET	13	0	1	1	5−	13	0	0	0	0	10	.0
			EDM	63	9	12	21	5	123	1	0	1	0	84	10.7
			TOTAL	76	9	13	22	0	136	1	0	1	0	94	9.6
C	29	*Vladimir Ruzicka	EDM	25	11	6	17	21−	10	4	0	1	0	52	21.2
D	28	Craig Muni	EDM	71	5	12	17	22	81	0	2	0	0	42	11.9
D	25	*Geoff Smith	EDM	74	4	11	15	13	52	1	0	0	0	66	6.1
D	26	Reijo Ruotsalainen	N.J.	31	2	5	7	4	14	1	0	0	0	52	3.8
			EDM	10	1	7	8	1−	6	0	0	0	0	28	3.6
			TOTAL	41	3	12	15	5−	20	1	0	0	0	80	3.8
D	6	Jeff Beukeboom	EDM	46	1	12	13	5	86	0	0	0	0	36	2.8
L	16	Kelly Buchberger	EDM	55	2	6	8	8−	168	0	0	0	0	35	5.7
L	26	*Peter Eriksson	EDM	20	3	3	6	1−	24	1	0	0	0	23	13.0
R	32	Dave Brown	EDM	60	0	6	6	3−	145	0	0	0	0	32	.0
D	2	Chris Joseph	EDM	4	2	2	4	2	2	0	0	0	0	5	.0
G	30	Bill Ranford	EDM	56	0	2	2	0	18	0	0	0	0	0	.0
G	35	*Mike Greenlay	EDM	2	0	1	1	0	0	0	0	0	0	0	.0
D	35	*Francois Leroux	EDM	3	0	1	1	2−	0	0	0	0	0	0	.0
R	15	*Trevor Sim	EDM	3	0	1	1	2	0	0	0	0	0	1	.0
D	36	Bruce Bell	EDM	1	0	1	1	0	0	0	0	0	0	1	.0
G	35	*Randy Exelby	EDM	1	0	0	0	0	0	0	0	0	0	0	.0
C	23	Tom Lehmann	EDM	1	0	0	0	1	0	0	0	0	0	0	.0
D	36	Norm Maciver	EDM	1	0	0	0	1−	4	0	0	0	0	0	.0
R	34	*Mike Ware	EDM	3	0	0	0	1−	4	0	0	0	0	1	.0
G	33	Eldon Reddick	EDM	11	0	0	0	0	0	0	0	0	0	0	.0
G	31	Grant Fuhr	EDM	21	0	0	0	0	2	0	0	0	0	0	.0

Goaltending

No.	Goaltender	GPI	Mins	Avg	W	L	T	EN	SO	GA	SA	S%
33	Eldon Reddick	11	604	3.08	5	4	2	2	0	31	283	.890
30	Bill Ranford	56	3107	3.19	24	16	9	5	1	165	1463	.887
31	Grant Fuhr	21	1081	3.89	9	7	3	0	1	70	532	.868
35	*Randy Exelby	1	60	5.00	0	1	0	1	0	5	30	.833
35	*Mike Greenlay	2	20	12.00	0	0	0	0	0	4	17	.765
	Totals	80	4882	3.48	38	28	14	8	2	283	2325	.878

Playoffs

Pos	#	Player	Team	GP	G	A	Pts	+/−	PIM	PP	SH	GW	OT	S	%
L	18	Craig Simpson	EDM	22	16	15	31	11	8	6	0	3	0	42	38.1
C	11	Mark Messier	EDM	22	9	22	31	5	20	1	1	1	0	47	19.1
R	17	Jari Kurri	EDM	22	10	15	25	13	18	6	0	3	0	58	17.2
L	10	Esa Tikkanen	EDM	22	13	11	24	12	26	2	2	0	0	54	24.1
R	9	Glenn Anderson	EDM	22	10	12	22	12	20	2	0	2	0	46	21.7
C	7	Mark Lamb	EDM	22	6	11	17	12	2	1	0	2	1	34	17.6
D	5	Steve Smith	EDM	22	5	10	15	15	37	1	0	1	0	35	14.3
C	8	Joe Murphy	EDM	22	6	8	14	1	16	0	0	2	1	29	20.7
D	26	Reijo Ruotsalainen	EDM	22	2	11	13	13	12	1	0	0	0	55	3.6
L	12	Adam Graves	EDM	22	5	6	11	1	17	0	0	1	0	46	10.9
D	21	Randy Gregg	EDM	20	2	6	8	1	16	1	0	0	0	17	11.8
C	14	Craig MacTavish	EDM	22	2	6	8	6	29	0	0	0	0	21	9.5
D	22	Charlie Huddy	EDM	22	0	6	6	11	10	0	0	0	0	35	.0
L	85	Petr Klima	EDM	21	5	0	5	2−	8	1	0	1	1	25	20.0
L	20	*Martin Gelinas	EDM	20	2	3	5	0	6	0	0	0	0	24	8.3
L	16	Kelly Buchberger	EDM	19	0	5	5	2	13	0	0	0	0	15	.0
D	28	Craig Muni	EDM	22	0	3	3	7	16	0	0	0	0	13	.0
D	4	Kevin Lowe	EDM	20	0	2	2	3	14	0	0	0	0	11	.0
G	30	Bill Ranford	EDM	22	0	2	2	0	4	0	0	0	0	0	.0
G	33	Eldon Reddick	EDM	1	0	0	0	0	0	0	0	0	0	0	.0
D	6	Jeff Beukeboom	EDM	2	0	0	0	1	4	0	0	0	0	0	.0
	19	Anatoli Semenov	EDM	2	0	0	0	1−	0	0	0	0	0	1	.0
R	32	Dave Brown	EDM	2	0	0	0	0	2	0	0	0	0	2	.0
D	25	Geoff Smith	EDM	2	0	0	0	0	0	0	0	0	0	0	.0
Pos	#	Player	Team	GP	G	A	Pts	+/−	PIM	PP	SH	GW	OT	S	%

Goaltending

No.	Goaltender	GPI	Mins	Avg	W	L	EN	SO	GA	SA	S%
33	Eldon Reddick	1	2	.00	0	0	0	0	0	1	1.000
30	Bill Ranford	22	1401	2.53	16	6	1	1	59	672	.912
	Totals	22	1405	2.56	16	6	1	1	60	673	.911

Captains' History

Ron Chipperfield, 1979-80; Lee Fogolin, 1980-81 to 1982-83; Wayne Gretzky, 1983-84 to 1987-88; Mark Messier, 1988-89 to date.

Club Records

Team

(Figures in brackets for season record are games played; records for fewest points, wins, ties, losses, goals, goals against are for 70 or more)

Most Points	119	1983-84 (80)
		1985-86 (80)
Most Wins	57	1983-84 (80)
Most Ties	16	1980-81 (80)
Most Losses	39	1979-80 (80)
Most Goals	*446	1983-84 (80)
Most Goals Against	327	1980-81 (80)
Fewest Points	69	1979-80 (80)
Fewest Wins	28	1979-80 (80)
Fewest Ties	5	1983-84 (80)
Fewest Losses	17	1981-82 (80)
		1985-86 (80)
Fewest Goals	301	1979-80 (80)
Fewest Goals Against	283	1989-90 (80)

Longest Winning Streak
Over-all ... 8 Five times
Home ... 8 Jan. 19/85-Feb. 22/85
Feb. 24-Apr. 2/86
Away ... 8 Dec. 9/86-Jan. 17/87

Longest Undefeated Streak
Over-all ... 15 Oct. 11/84-Nov. 9/84 (12 wins, 3 ties)
Home ... 12 Oct. 5-Dec. 3/83 (10 wins, 2 ties)
Away ... 9 Jan. 17-Mar. 2/82 (6 wins, 3 ties)
Nov. 23/82-Jan. 18/83 (7 wins, 2 ties)

Longest Losing Streak
Over-all ... 6 Feb. 29-Mar. 9/80
Home ... 3 Four times
Away ... 9 Nov. 25-Dec. 30/80

Longest Winless Streak
Over-all ... 6 Five times
Home ... 7 Oct. 24-Nov. 19/80 (3 losses, 4 ties)
Away ... 9 Nov. 25-Dec. 30/80 (9 losses)

Most Shutouts, Season ... 4 1987-88 (80)
Most PIM, Season ... 2,173 1987-88 (80)
Most Goals, Game ... 13 Nov. 19/83 (NJ 4 at Edm. 13)
Nov. 8/85 (Van. 0 at Edm. 13)

Individual

Most Seasons	11	Kevin Lowe
		Mark Messier
Most Games	838	Kevin Lowe
Most Goals, Career	583	Wayne Gretzky
Most Assists, Career	1,086	Wayne Gretzky
Most Points, Career	1,669	Wayne Gretzky (583 goals, 1,086 assists)
Most PIM, Career	1,278	Kevin McClelland
Most Shutouts, Career	8	Grant Fuhr

Longest Consecutive Games Streak ... 362 Wayne Gretzky (Nov. 2/79-Feb. 3/84)

Most Goals, Season ... *92 Wayne Gretzky (1981-82)
Most Assists, Season ... *163 Wayne Gretzky (1985-86)
Most Points, Season ... *215 Wayne Gretzky (1985-86) (52 goals, 163 assists)
Most PIM, Season ... 286 Steve Smith (1987-88)

Most Points, Defenseman, Season ... 138 Paul Coffey (1985-86) (48 goals, 90 assists)

Most Points, Center, Season ... *215 Wayne Gretzky (1985-86) (52 goals, 163 assists)

Most Points, Right Wing, Season ... 135 Jari Kurri (1984-85) (71 goals, 64 assists)

Most Points, Left Wing, Season ... 106 Mark Messier (1982-83) (48 goals, 58 assists)

Most Points, Rookie, Season ... 75 Jari Kurri (1980-81) (32 goals, 43 assists)

Most Shutouts, Season ... 4 Grant Fuhr (1987-88)

Most Goals, Game ... 5 Wayne Gretzky (Feb. 18/81, Dec. 30/81, Dec. 15/84, Dec. 6/87)
Jari Kurri (Nov. 19/83)
Pat Hughes (Feb. 3/84)

Most Assists, Game ... *7 Wayne Gretzky (Feb. 15/80; Dec. 11/85; Feb. 14/86)

Most Points, Game ... 8 Wayne Gretzky (Nov. 19/83)
Paul Coffey (Mar. 14/86)
Wayne Gretzky (Jan. 4/84)

* NHL Record.

All-time Record vs. Other Clubs

Regular Season

	At Home							On Road							Total					
	GP	W	L	T	GF	GA	PTS	GP	W	L	T	GF	GA	PTS	GP	W	L	T	GF	GA	PTS
Boston	18	7	8	3	61	61	17	17	2	13	2	44	80	6	35	9	21	5	105	141	23
Buffalo	18	13	3	2	82	47	28	17	7	7	3	73	73	17	35	20	10	5	155	120	45
Calgary	40	22	10	8	189	149	52	40	17	19	4	161	189	38	80	39	29	12	350	338	90
Chicago	17	12	4	1	91	62	25	18	7	9	2	85	81	16	35	19	13	3	176	143	41
Detroit	17	10	5	2	98	74	22	18	12	5	1	91	68	25	35	22	10	3	189	142	47
Hartford	18	13	2	3	86	56	29	17	7	7	3	68	75	17	35	20	9	6	154	131	46
Los Angeles	40	24	7	9	232	161	57	40	20	13	7	199	167	47	80	44	20	16	431	328	104
Minnesota	18	12	1	5	98	60	29	17	9	4	4	67	60	22	35	21	5	9	165	120	51
Montreal	17	11	6	0	69	52	22	18	5	10	3	59	69	13	35	16	16	3	128	121	35
New Jersey	20	12	5	3	110	80	27	20	9	9	2	71	71	20	40	21	14	5	181	151	47
NY Islanders	17	9	5	3	69	57	21	18	3	8	7	75	81	13	35	12	13	10	144	138	34
NY Rangers	17	9	7	1	75	61	19	18	10	6	2	79	78	22	35	19	13	3	154	139	41
Philadelphia	18	10	5	3	69	54	23	17	3	13	1	48	80	7	35	13	18	4	117	134	30
Pittsburgh	18	14	3	1	102	62	29	17	10	6	1	85	62	21	35	24	9	2	187	124	50
Quebec	17	13	4	0	100	52	26	18	10	6	2	86	71	22	35	23	10	2	186	123	48
St. Louis	17	12	3	2	90	67	26	18	10	5	3	87	72	23	35	22	8	5	177	139	49
Toronto	18	12	2	4	105	59	28	17	10	6	1	91	71	21	35	22	8	5	196	130	49
Vancouver	40	29	7	4	214	125	62	40	23	11	6	179	137	52	80	52	18	10	393	262	114
Washington	17	8	5	4	74	61	20	18	8	9	1	71	78	17	35	16	14	5	145	139	37
Winnipeg	38	28	8	2	194	124	58	37	22	12	3	191	155	47	75	50	20	5	385	279	105
Totals	**440**	**280**	**100**	**60**	**2208**	**1524**	**620**	**440**	**204**	**178**	**58**	**1910**	**1818**	**466**	**880**	**484**	**278**	**118**	**4118**	**3342**	**1086**

Playoffs

	Series	W	L	GP	W	L	T	GF	GA	Last Mtg.	Round	Result
Boston	2	2	0	9	8	1	0	41	20	1990	F	W 4-1
Calgary	4	3	1	23	15	8	0	110	76	1988	DF	W 4-0
Chicago	3	3	0	16	12	4	0	94	56	1990	CF	W 4-2
Detroit	2	2	0	10	8	2	0	39	26	1988	CF	W 4-1
Los Angeles	5	3	2	24	16	8	0	110	89	1990	DF	W 4-0
Minnesota	1	1	0	4	4	0	0	22	10	1984	CF	W 4-0
Montreal	1	1	0	3	3	0	0	15	6	1981	PR	W 3-0
NY Islanders	3	1	2	15	6	9	0	47	58	1984	F	W 4-1
Philadelphia	3	2	1	15	8	7	0	49	44	1987	F	W 4-3
Vancouver	1	1	0	3	3	0	0	17	5	1986	DSF	W 3-0
Winnipeg	6	6	0	26	22	4	0	120	75	1990	DSF	W 4-3
Totals	**31**	**25**	**6**	**146**	**103**	**43**	**0**	**664**	**465**			

Playoff Results 1990-86

Year	Round	Opponent	Result	GF	GA
1990	F	**Boston**	W 4-1	20	8
	CF	Chicago	W 4-2	25	20
	DF	Los Angeles	W 4-0	24	10
	DSF	Winnipeg	W 4-3	24	22
1989	DSF	Los Angeles	L 3-4	20	25
1988	F	**Boston**	W 4-0	21	12
	CF	Detroit	W 4-1	23	16
	DF	Calgary	W 4-0	18	11
	DSF	Winnipeg	W 4-1	25	17
1987	F	**Philadelphia**	W 4-3	22	18
	CF	Detroit	W 4-1	16	10
	DF	Winnipeg	W 4-0	17	9
	DSF	Los Angeles	W 4-1	32	20
1986	DF	Calgary	L 3-4	24	25
	DSF	Vancouver	W 3-0	17	5

Abbreviations: Round: F Final; **CF** conference final; **DF** division final; **DSF** division semi-final; **PR** preliminary round. **GA** goals against; **GF** goals for.

1989-90 Results

		Home				Away	
Oct.	11	Vancouver	2-5	Oct.	5	Vancouver	4-1
	13	Boston	3-3		7	Los Angeles	6-5
	15	Los Angeles	4-5		22	Winnipeg	4-5
	18	Winnipeg	7-2		24	NY Islanders	3-3
	20	Boston	0-3		25	NY Rangers	3-3
Nov.	1	New Jersey	6-6		28	Quebec	6-3
	3	Calgary	5-2		29	Montreal	4-5
	4	Pittsburgh	1-3	Nov.	6	Calgary	1-5
	15	Los Angeles	2-2		9	Boston	2-6
	17	Buffalo	3-0		11	Washington	5-3
	19	Chicago	5-4		12	Buffalo	5-6
	21	Vancouver	4-3		24	Philadelphia*	1-5
Dec.	2	Minnesota	6-1		25	NY Islanders	7-2
	3	Toronto	5-3		27	Detroit	6-2
	8	Los Angeles	5-4		30	Los Angeles	7-6
	11	Calgary	3-3	Dec.	16	St Louis	3-3
	13	Quebec	5-1		17	Chicago	5-6
	21	Winnipeg	3-2		19	Minnesota	5-0
	23	Calgary	2-1		31	Winnipeg*	2-3
	27	Philadelphia	2-1	Jan.	2	St Louis	6-4
	29	Montreal	6-2		3	Chicago	2-3
Jan.	6	Hartford	4-4		9	Calgary	3-2
	7	Calgary	1-3		11	Los Angeles	3-3
	16	Detroit	4-6		30	Hartford	4-4
	17	Winnipeg	6-3		31	Detroit	5-7
	23	NY Rangers	4-3	Feb.	4	Pittsburgh	5-4
	25	Los Angeles	7-6		4	Washington*	5-4
	27	Vancouver	6-2		6	New Jersey	2-2
Feb.	11	Winnipeg	7-4		7	NY Rangers	2-5
	14	Washington	3-4		16	Vancouver	2-2
	18	Minnesota	3-2		20	Vancouver	4-2
	21	Buffalo	7-3		25	Calgary	4-10
	23	Toronto	5-6		28	Los Angeles	2-4
Mar.	3	Philadelphia	5-3	Mar.	9	Winnipeg	5-7
	4	Vancouver	6-3		10	Toronto	2-3
	6	Pittsburgh	4-3		13	Quebec	4-1
	17	New Jersey	1-4		14	Montreal	3-3
	18	Hartford	1-3		27	Vancouver	4-1
	21	St Louis	8-6		30	Calgary	2-6
	24	NY Islanders	5-5	Apr.	1	Winnipeg*	4-2

* Denotes afternoon game.

Entry Draft
Selections 1990-79

1990
Pick
- 17 Scott Allison
- 38 Alexandre Legault
- 59 Joe Crowley
- 67 Joel Blain
- 101 Greg Louder
- 122 Keijo Sailynoja
- 143 Mike Power
- 164 Roman Mejzlik
- 185 Richard Zemlicka
- 206 Petr Korinek
- 227 invalid claim
- 248 Sami Nuutiinen

1989
Pick
- 15 Jason Soules
- 36 Richard Borgo
- 78 Josef Beranek
- 92 Peter White
- 120 Anatoli Semenov
- 140 Davis Payne
- 141 Sergei Yashin
- 162 Darcy Martini
- 225 Roman Bozek

1988
Pick
- 19 Francois Leroux
- 39 Petro Koivunen
- 53 Trevor Sim
- 61 Collin Bauer
- 82 Cam Brauer
- 103 Don Martin
- 124 Len Barrie
- 145 Mike Glover
- 166 Shjon Podein
- 187 Tom Cole
- 208 Vladimir Zubkov
- 229 Darin MacDonald
- 250 Tim Tisdale

1987
Pick
- 21 Peter Soberlak
- 42 Brad Werenka
- 63 Geoff Smith
- 64 Peter Eriksson
- 105 Shaun Van Allen
- 126 Radek Toupal
- 147 Tomas Srsen
- 168 Age Ellingsen
- 189 Gavin Armstrong
- 210 Mike Tinkham
- 231 Jeff Pauletti
- 241 Jesper Duus
- 252 Igor Viazmikin

1986
Pick
- 21 Kim Issel
- 42 Jamie Nichols
- 63 Ron Shudra
- 84 Dan Currie
- 105 David Haas
- 126 Jim Ennis
- 147 Ivan Matulik
- 168 Nicolas Beaulieu
- 189 Mike Greenlay
- 210 Matt Lanza
- 231 Mojmir Bozik
- 252 Tony Hand

1985
Pick
- 20 Scott Metcalfe
- 41 Todd Carnelley
- 62 Mike Ware
- 104 Thomas Kapusta
- 125 Brian Tessier
- 146 Shawn Tyers
- 167 Tony Fairfield
- 188 Kelly Buchberger
- 209 Mario Barbe
- 230 Peter Headon
- 251 John Haley

1984
Pick
- 21 Selmar Odelein
- 42 Daryl Reaugh
- 63 Todd Norman
- 84 Rich Novak
- 105 Richard Lambert
- 106 Emanuel Viveiros
- 126 Ivan Dornic
- 147 Heikki Riihijarvi
- 168 Todd Ewen
- 209 Joel Curtis
- 229 Simon Wheeldon
- 250 Darren Gani

1983
Pick
- 19 Jeff Beukeboom
- 40 Mike Golden
- 60 Mike Flanagan
- 80 Esa Tikkanen
- 120 Don Barber
- 140 Dale Derkatch
- 160 Ralph Vos
- 180 Dave Roach
- 200 Warren Yadlowski
- 220 John Miner
- 240 Steve Woodburn

1982
Pick
- 20 Jim Playfair
- 41 Steve Graves
- 62 Brent Loney
- 83 Jaroslav Pouzar
- 104 Dwayne Boettger
- 125 Raimo Summanen
- 146 Brian Small
- 167 Dean Clark
- 188 Ian Wood
- 209 Grant Dion
- 230 Chris Smith
- 251 Jeff Crawford

1981
Pick
- 8 Grant Fuhr
- 29 Todd Strueby
- 71 Paul Houck
- 92 Phil Drouillard
- 111 Steve Smith
- 113 Marc Habscheid
- 155 Mike Sturgeon
- 176 Miloslav Horava
- 197 Gord Sherven

1980
Pick
- 6 Paul Coffey
- 48 Shawn Babcock
- 69 Jari Kurri
- 90 Walt Poddubny
- 111 Mike Winther
- 132 Andy Moog
- 153 Rob Polmantuin
- 174 Lars-Gunnar Petersson

1979
Pick
- 21 Kevin Lowe
- 48 Mark Messier
- 69 Glenn Anderson
- 84 Max Kostovich
- 105 Mike Toal
- 126 Blair Barnes

Club Directory

Northlands Coliseum
Edmonton, Alberta T5B 4M9
Phone **403/474-8561**
Ticketing 403/471-2191
FAX 403/471-2171
ENVOY ID   OILERS.GM
                OILERS.PR

Capacity: 17,313 (standing 190)

Owner/Governor . . . . Peter Pocklington
Alternate Governor . . . . Glen Sather
General Counsel . . . . Bob Lloyd, Gary Frohlich
President/General Manager . . . . Glen Sather
Exec. Vice-President, Assistant G.M. . . . . Bruce MacGregor
Coach . . . . John Muckler
Co-Coach . . . . Ted Green
Assistant Coach . . . . Ron Low
Director of Player Personnel/Chief Scout . . . . . . Barry Fraser
Scouting Staff . . . . Ace Bailey, Ed Chadwick, Lorne Davis,
                                                          Bob Freeman, Harry Howell, Matti Vaisanen
Executive Secretary . . . . Lana Anderson
Receptionist/Secretary . . . . Lori Willoughby

Medical and Training Staff
Athletic Trainer/Therapist . . . . Ken Lowe
Athletic Trainer . . . . Barrie Stafford
Assistant Trainer . . . . Lyle Kulchisky
Massage Therapist . . . . Stewart Poirier
Team Physician . . . . Dr. Gordon Cameron
Fitness Consultant . . . . Dr. Art Quinney

Finance
Vice-President, Finance . . . . Werner Baum
Accountants . . . . Lori Bandola, Ellie Merrick
Systems Administrator . . . . Maureen West

Public Relations
Director of Public Relations . . . . Bill Tuele
Co-ordinator of Publications and Statistics . . . . . . Steve Knowles
Director of Community Relations/Special Events . . Trish Kerr
Public Relations Secretary . . . . Fiona Liew

Marketing
Director of Marketing . . . . Stew MacDonald
Marketing Representative/Merchandising Mgr. . . . Darrell Holowaychuk
Marketing Representative . . . . Brad MacGregor
Sales Representative . . . . Dave Semenko
Marketing Secretary . . . . Heather Hansch
Merchandising Clerk . . . . Julia Sharman
Warehouse Supervisor . . . . Raymond MacDonald

Ticketing
Director of Ticketing Operations . . . . Sheila Stock
Ticketing Operations . . . . Marcia Godwin, Marcella Kinsman, Sheila
                                                          McCaskill

Location of Press Boxes . . . . East Side at top (Radio/TV)
                                                          West Side at top (Media)
Dimensions of Rink . . . . 200 feet by 85 feet
Ends of Rink . . . . Herculite extends above boards around rink
Club Colors . . . . Blue, Orange and White
Training Camp Site . . . . Northlands Coliseum, Edmonton, Alberta
Television Channel . . . . CITV (Channel 13) (Cable 8)
                                                          CBXT TV (Channel 5) (Cable 4)
Radio Station . . . . CFRN (1260 AM)
Official Photographer . . . . Bob Mummery

General Manager

SATHER, GLEN CAMERON
President and General Manager, Edmonton Oilers. Born in High River, Alta., Sept. 2, 1943.

A journeyman left-winger who played for six different teams during his nine-year NHL career, 47-year-old Glen Sather was one of the League's most successful coaches ever before relinquishing his coaching duties on June 12, 1989. He was the 1985-86 Jack Adams Award winner, led his club to four Stanley Cup championships and had a ten-year winning percentage of .629 (442-241-99). His 442 wins place him sixth on the all-time list in regular season wins. In addition, Sather led his team to 89 play-off victories, fourth on the all-time list. His .706 winning percentage in the playoffs ranks him first.

After closing out his NHL playing career in 1975-76 with an 80-113-193 scoring mark in 660 games, Sather jumped to the Oilers in the World Hockey Association, where he enjoyed his best and last season as a player with totals of 19-34-53 in 81 games. Midway through that 1976-77 campaign, on January 27, 1977, he also assumed the Oilers coaching duties and led his team to the first of its 11 straight WHA and NHL playoff appearances. Three years later, when the club entered the NHL, Sather took on the added responsibilities of Oilers' president and general manager, which he currently maintains.

NHL Coaching Record

			Regular Season				Playoffs			
Season	Team	Games	W	L	T	%	Games	W	L	%
1979-80	Edmonton (NHL)	80	28	39	13	.431	3	0	3	.000
1980-81	Edmonton (NHL)	62	25	26	11	.492	9	5	4	.555
1981-82	Edmonton (NHL)	80	48	17	15	.694	5	2	3	.400
1982-83	Edmonton (NHL)	80	47	21	12	.663	16	11	5	.687
1983-84	Edmonton (NHL)	80	57	18	5	.744	19	15	4	.789*
1984-85	Edmonton (NHL)	80	49	20	11	.681	18	15	3	.833*
1985-86	Edmonton (NHL)	80	56	17	7	.744	10	6	4	.600
1986-87	Edmonton (NHL)	80	50	24	6	.663	21	16	5	.762*
1987-88	Edmonton (NHL)	80	44	25	11	.619	18	16	2	.889*
1988-89	Edmonton (NHL)	80	38	34	8	.538	7	3	4	.429
	NHL Totals	782	442	241	99	.629	126	89	37	.706

* Stanley Cup win

Coach

MUCKLER, JOHN
Coach, Edmonton Oilers. Born in Paris, Ont. on April 13, 1934.

John Muckler was named head coach of the Oilers on June 12, 1989 after seven years as an assistant and co-coach with Glen Sather. A Stanley Cup winner in his first season as head coach, Muckler first joined the Oilers' organization in 1981 when he coached the Oilers' affiliate in the Central Hockey League, the Wichita Wind. Muckler was named an assistant coach with Edmonton in 1982 and was elevated to the position of co-coach in 1985-86.

Muckler started his coaching career in 1959 as the head coach of the Long Island Ducks in the Eastern Hockey League. In 1966, Muckler became director of player personnel with the New York Rangers, followed by a six-year stint as general manager with various clubs within the Minnesota North Stars system. In 1974-75, he coached the Providence Reds of the AHL before joining Dallas of the CHL in 1978-79. Muckler has been named Coach of the Year in three leagues (EHL, 1963-64; AHL 1974-75; CHL, 1978-79) and has led three teams to league championships (Long Island, 1963-64; Providence, 1974-75 and Dallas 1978-79).

Coaching Record

			Regular Season				Playoffs			
Season	Team	Games	W	L	T	%	Games	W	L	%
1964-65	Long Island (EHL)	72	42	29	1	.590	15	11	4	.733
1965-66	Long Island (EHL)	72	46	23	3	.660	12	7	5	.583
1968-69	**Minnesota (NHL)**	**35**	**6**	**23**	**6**	**.257**	....	....	....	....
1971-72	Cleveland (AHL)	76	32	34	10	.487	6	2	4	.333
1972-73	*Cleveland (AHL)	76	23	44	9	.362	....	....	....	....
1973-74	Providence (AHL)	76	38	26	12	.579	15	9	6	.600
1974-75	Providence (AHL)	76	43	21	12	.645	6	2	4	.333
1975-76	Providence (AHL)	76	34	34	8	.500	3	0	3	.000
1976-77	Providence (AHL)	53	21	30	2	.415	....	....	....	....
1978-79	Dallas (CHL)	76	45	28	3	.612	9	8	1	.889
1981-82	Wichita (CHL)	80	44	33	3	.569	7	3	4	.423
1989-90	**Edmonton (NHL)**	**80**	**38**	**28**	**14**	**.563**	**22**	**16**	**6**	**.727****
	NHL Totals	115	44	51	20	.470	22	16	6	.727

* Club moved to Jacksonville during regular season. ** Stanley Cup Win.

Hartford Whalers

1989-90 Results: 38W-33L-9T 85PTS. Fourth, Adams Division

Year-by-Year Record

Season	GP	Home W	Home L	Home T	Road W	Road L	Road T	Overall W	Overall L	Overall T	GF	GA	Pts.	Finished	Playoff Result
1989-90	80	17	18	5	21	15	4	38	33	9	275	268	85	4th, Adams Div.	Lost Div. Semi-Final
1988-89	80	21	17	2	16	21	3	37	38	5	299	290	79	4th, Adams Div.	Lost Div. Semi-Final
1987-88	80	21	14	5	14	24	2	35	38	7	249	267	77	4th, Adams Div.	Lost Div. Semi-Final
1986-87	80	26	9	5	17	21	2	43	30	7	287	270	93	1st, Adams Div.	Lost Div. Semi-Final
1985-86	80	21	17	2	19	19	2	40	36	4	332	302	84	4th, Adams Div.	Lost Div. Final
1984-85	80	17	18	5	13	23	4	30	41	9	268	318	69	5th, Adams Div.	Out of Playoffs
1983-84	80	19	16	5	9	26	5	28	42	10	288	320	66	5th, Adams Div.	Out of Playoffs
1982-83	80	13	22	5	6	32	2	19	54	7	261	403	45	5th, Adams Div.	Out of Playoffs
1981-82	80	13	17	10	8	24	8	21	41	18	264	351	60	5th, Adams Div.	Out of Playoffs
1980-81	80	14	17	9	7	24	9	21	41	18	292	372	60	4th, Norris Div.	Out of Playoffs
1979-80	80	22	12	6	5	22	13	27	34	19	303	312	73	4th, Norris Div.	Lost Prelim. Round

Schedule

Home			Away		
Oct.	Thur. 4	Quebec	**Oct.**	Mon. 8	Montreal
	Sat. 6	NY Rangers		Fri. 12	Detroit
	Wed. 10	Buffalo		Tues. 16	Quebec
	Sat. 13	Montreal		Wed. 17	Toronto
	Sat. 27	Vancouver		Fri. 19	Los Angeles
	Wed. 31	Montreal		Wed. 24	Minnesota
Nov.	Sat. 3	St Louis		Sun. 28	Buffalo
	Tues. 6	Chicago	**Nov.**	Fri. 9	Winnipeg
	Wed. 14	Boston		Sat. 10	Minnesota
	Sat. 17	Washington		Thur. 15	New Jersey
	Wed. 21	Quebec		Fri. 23	Boston*
	Sat. 24	Boston		Thur. 29	Pittsburgh
	Wed. 28	Quebec	**Dec.**	Mon. 3	Montreal
Dec.	Sat. 1	Edmonton		Fri. 7	Buffalo
	Wed. 5	Montreal		Thur. 13	Boston
	Sat. 8	Pittsburgh		Sat. 15	Washington
	Wed. 12	Boston		Thur. 20	NY Islanders
	Tues. 18	Buffalo		Wed. 26	Quebec
	Sat. 22	Philadelphia		Sat. 29	Calgary
	Sun. 23	Minnesota		Sun. 30	Edmonton
Jan.	Wed. 2	Vancouver	**Jan.**	Tues. 8	Los Angeles
	Sat. 5	Winnipeg		Thur. 10	Vancouver
	Wed. 16	Los Angeles		Sat. 12	Toronto
	Wed. 23	Calgary		Sun. 13	NY Rangers
	Sat. 26	Philadelphia		Thur. 24	Boston
	Tues. 29	NY Islanders		Thur. 31	St Louis
Feb.	Wed. 6	Edmonton	**Feb.**	Sat. 2	Philadelphia*
	Sat. 9	Calgary		Sun. 3	NY Islanders
	Sun. 10	Chicago		Fri. 15	NY Rangers
	Wed. 13	Detroit		Sat. 16	Montreal
	Wed. 20	Montreal		Sun. 24	Buffalo
	Sat. 23	Buffalo		Tues. 26	Winnipeg
Mar.	Sun. 3	Toronto		Thur. 28	Chicago
	Tues. 5	St Louis	**Mar.**	Sat. 2	Quebec
	Sat. 9	Pittsburgh		Tues. 12	Washington
	Sun. 10	Quebec		Sun. 17	Buffalo
	Thur. 14	Detroit		Sat. 23	Quebec
	Sat. 16	New Jersey		Mon. 25	Montreal
	Tues. 19	Boston		Wed. 27	New Jersey
	Sat. 30	Buffalo		Sun. 31	Boston

* Denotes afternoon game.

Home Starting Times:

Weeknights and Saturdays	7:35 p.m.
Sundays	7:05 p.m.
Except Oct. 13	8:05 p.m.
Dec. 23	7:35 p.m.

Franchise date: June 22, 1979

12th NHL Season

In his first year with the Whalers, Pat Verbeek led the team with 44 goals.

1990-91 Player Personnel

FORWARDS

	HT	WT	S	Place of Birth	Date	1989-90 Club
ANDERSSON, Mikael	5-11	185	L	Malmo, Sweden	5/10/66	Hartford
ATCHEYNUM, Blair	6-2	190	R	Estevan, Sask.	4/20/69	Hartford-Binghamton
BLACK, James	5-11	185	L	Regina, Sask.	8/15/69	Binghamton-Hartford
BODAK, Bob	6-2	190	L	Thunder Bay, Ont.	5/28/61	Binghamton-Hartford
CORRIVEAU, Yvon	6-1	195	L	Welland, Ont.	2/8/67	Washington-Hartford
CUNNEYWORTH, Randy	6-0	180	L	Etobicoke, Ont.	5/10/61	Winnipeg-Hartford
DANIELS, Scott	6-3	200	L	Prince Albert, B.C.	9/19/69	Regina
DAY, Joe	5-11	180	L	Chicago, IL	5/11/68	St. Lawrence Univ.
DINEEN, Kevin	5-11	190	R	Quebec City, Que.	10/28/63	Hartford
EVASON, Dean	5-10	180	R	Flin Flon, Man.	8/22/64	Hartford
FERRARO, Ray	5-10	185	L	Trail, B.C.	8/23/64	Hartford
FRANCIS, Ron	6-2	200	L	Sault Ste. Marie, Ont.	3/1/63	Hartford
GOVEDARIS, Chris	6-0	200	L	Toronto, Ont.	2/2/70	Hartford-Binghamton
GREIG, Mark	5-11	190	R	High River, Atla.	1/25/70	Lethbridge
HOLIK, Robert	6-3	210	L	Jihlava, Czech.	1/1/71	Dukla Jihlava (Czech)
KASTELIC, Ed	6-4	215	R	Toronto, Ont.	1/29/64	Hartford
KRYGIER, Todd	5-11	180	L	Northville, MI	10/12/65	Hartford-Binghamton
LINDBERG, Chris	6-1	190	L	Fort Francis, Ont.	4/16/67	Binghamton
McKENZIE, Jim	6-3	205	L	Gull Lake, Sask.	11/3/69	Binghamton-Hartford
PICARD, Michel	5-11	190	L	Beauport, Que.	11/7/69	Binghamton
SANDERSON, Geoff	6-0	185		St. Albert, Alta.	2/1/72	Swift Current
SAUMIER, Raymond	6-0	195	R	Hull, Que.	2/27/69	Binghamton
TANCILL, Chris	5-10	185		Livonia, MI	2/7/68	Wisconsin
TIPPETT, Dave	5-10	180	L	Moosomin, Sask.	8/25/61	Hartford
TOMLAK, Mike	6-3	205	L	Thunder Bay, Ont.	10/17/64	Hartford
VERBEEK, Pat	5-9	190	R	Sarnia, Ont.	5/24/64	Hartford
WILSON, Carey	6-2	205	R	Winnipeg, Man.	5/19/62	NY Rangers
YAKE, Terry	5-11	185	R	N. Westmin'r, B.C.	10/22/68	Binghamton-Hartford
YOUNG, Scott	6-0	190	R	Clinton, MA	10/1/67	Hartford

DEFENSEMEN

	HT	WT	S	Place of Birth	Date	1989-90 Club
BABYCH, Dave	6-2	215	L	Edmonton, Alta.	5/23/61	Hartford
BACA, Jergus	6-2	211	L	Kosice, Czech.	4/1/65	Kosice (Czech.)
BEAULIEU, Corey	6-2	210	L	Winnipeg, Man.	9/10/69	Binghamton
BRAUER, Cam	6-3	200	L	Calgary, Alta.	1/4/70	Regina-Seattle
BURKE, Jim	6-2	200	L	Newtown, Mass.	1/3/68	U. Maine-Binghamton
BURT, Adam	6-0	190	L	Detroit, MI	1/15/69	Hartford
CHAPMAN, Brian	6-0	195	L	Brockville, Ont.	2/10/68	Binghamton
COTE, Sylvain	5-11	185	R	Duberger, Que.	1/19/66	Hartford
HUMENIUK, Scott	6-0	190	R	Saskatoon, Sask.	10/10/69	Moose Jaw-Bing.
JENNINGS, Grant	6-3	200	L	Hudson Bay, Sask.	5/5/65	Hartford
KENNAN, Corey	6-1	182	L	St. Louis, MO	3/19/70	Kitchener
LADOUCEUR, Randy	6-2	220	L	Brockville, Ont.	6/30/60	Hartford
QUENNEVILLE, Joel	6-1	200	L	Windsor, Ont.	9/15/58	Hartford
SAMUELSSON, Ulf	6-1	195	L	Fagersta, Sweden	3/26/64	Hartford
SHAW, Brad	6-0	190	R	Cambridge, Ont.	4/28/64	Hartford
VIVEIROS, Emanuel	6-0	170	L	St. Albert, Alta.	1/8/66	Did Not Play
WHITE, Rob	6-0	190	R	Brockville, Ont.	3/9/68	St. Lawrence U.

GOALTENDERS

	HT	WT	C	Place of Birth	Date	1989-90 Club
LENARDUZZI, Mike	6-0	175	L	Mississauga, Ont.	9/14//72	Oshawa-S.S. Marie
REAUGH, Daryl	5-8	175	L	Prince George, B.C.	2/13/65	Binghamton
SIDORKIEWICZ, Peter	5-9	180	L	D. Bialostocka, Pol.	6/29/63	Hartford
WHITMORE, Kay	5-11	175	L	Sudbury, Ont.	4/10/67	Hartford-Binghamton

Retired Numbers

2	Rick Ley	1979-1981
9	Gordie Howe	1979-1980
19	John McKenzie	1976-1979

1989-90 Scoring

Regular Season

* rookie

Pos	#	Player	Team	GP	G	A	Pts	+/−	PIM	PP	SH	GW	GT	S	%
C	10	Ron Francis	HFD	80	32	69	101	13	73	15	1	5	1	170	18.8
R	16	Pat Verbeek	HFD	80	44	45	89	1	228	14	0	5	1	219	20.1
R	11	Kevin Dineen	HFD	67	25	41	66	7	164	8	2	2	2	214	11.7
R	27	Scott Young	HFD	80	24	40	64	24−	47	10	2	5	0	239	10.0
C	26	Ray Ferraro	HFD	79	25	29	54	15−	109	7	0	4	1	138	18.1
C	12	Dean Evason	HFD	78	18	25	43	7	138	2	2	2	0	150	12.0
D	44	Dave Babych	HFD	72	6	37	43	16−	62	4	0	1	0	164	3.7
L	34	Mikael Andersson	HFD	50	13	24	37	0	6	1	2	2	0	86	15.1
D	32	*Brad Shaw	HFD	64	3	32	35	2	30	3	0	0	0	65	4.6
C	17	*Todd Krygier	HFD	58	18	12	30	4	52	5	1	3	1	103	17.5
L	7	Randy Cunneyworth	WPG	28	5	6	11	7−	34	2	0	1	0	51	9.8
			HFD	43	9	9	18	4−	41	2	0	1	0	70	12.9
			TOTAL	71	14	15	29	11−	75	4	0	2	0	121	11.6
L	15	Dave Tippett	HFD	66	8	19	27	0	32	0	1	3	0	91	8.8
C	28	*Mike Tomlak	HFD	70	7	14	21	5	48	1	1	2	0	64	10.9
L	20	Yvon Corriveau	WSH	50	9	6	15	1−	50	1	0	0	0	76	11.8
			HFD	13	4	1	5	3	22	0	0	0	0	14	28.6
			TOTAL	63	13	7	20	2	72	1	0	1	0	90	14.4
R	8	Jody Hull	HFD	38	7	10	17	6−	21	2	0	0	0	46	15.2
D	29	Randy Ladouceur	HFD	71	3	12	15	6−	126	0	0	0	0	45	6.7
D	5	Ulf Samuelsson	HFD	55	2	11	13	15	177	0	0	0	0	57	3.5
D	6	*Adam Burt	HFD	63	4	8	12	3	105	1	0	0	0	83	4.8
D	25	Grant Jennings	HFD	64	3	6	9	4−	171	0	0	0	0	45	6.7
R	22	Ed Kastelic	HFD	67	6	2	8	3−	198	0	0	0	0	35	17.1
D	21	Sylvain Cote	HFD	28	4	2	6	2	14	1	0	1	1	50	8.0
D	3	Joel Quenneville	HFD	44	1	4	5	9	34	0	0	0	0	17	5.9
L	24	Tom Martin	HFD	21	1	2	3	0	37	0	0	0	0	13	7.7
C	38	*Terry Yake	HFD	2	0	1	1	1−	0	0	0	0	0	2	.0
D	41	*Jim Culhane	HFD	6	0	1	1	3	4	0	0	0	0	6	.0
G	35	*Kay Whitmore	HFD	9	0	1	1	0	4	0	0	0	0	0	.0
L	14	*Chris Govedaris	HFD	12	0	1	1	0	6	0	0	0	0	13	.0
G	30	Peter Sidorkiewicz	HFD	46	0	1	1	0	4	0	0	0	0	0	.0
C	23	*James Black	HFD	1	0	0	0	0	0	0	0	0	0	1	.0
L	31	*Bob Bodak	HFD	1	0	0	0	0	7	0	0	0	0	1	.0
D	40	Allan Tuer	HFD	2	0	0	0	1−	6	0	0	0	0	0	.0
L	31	*Jim McKenzie	HFD	5	0	0	0	0	4	0	0	0	0	0	.0
D	4	Steve Dykstra	HFD	9	0	0	0	2	20	0	0	0	0	10	.0
L	42	*Marc Laforge	HFD	9	0	0	0	1−	43	0	0	0	0	0	.0

Goaltending

No.	Goaltender	GPI	Mins	Avg	W	L	T	EN	SO	GA	SA	S%
1	Mike Liut	29	1683	2.64	15	12	1	3	3	74	745	.901
35	*Kay Whitmore	9	442	3.53	4	2	1	0	0	26	183	.858
30	Peter Sidorkiewicz	46	2703	3.57	19	19	7	4	1	161	1203	.866
	Totals	**80**	**4843**	**3.32**	**38**	**33**	**9**	**7**	**4**	**268**	**2131**	**.874**

Playoffs

Pos	#	Player	Team	GP	G	A	Pts	+/−	PIM	PP	SH	GW	OT	S	%
D	32	*Brad Shaw	HFD	7	2	5	7	1	0	1	0	0	0	7	28.6
C	10	Ron Francis	HFD	7	3	3	6	2	8	1	0	0	0	21	14.3
R	11	Kevin Dineen	HFD	6	3	2	5	4	18	0	1	0	1	15	20.0
C	12	Dean Evason	HFD	7	2	2	4	3	22	0	0	0	0	9	22.2
R	16	Pat Verbeek	HFD	7	2	2	4	1	26	1	0	1	0	19	10.5
L	15	Dave Tippett	HFD	7	1	3	4	1	2	0	0	0	0	5	20.0
C	17	*Todd Krygier	HFD	7	2	1	3	2	4	0	0	0	0	12	16.7
D	44	Dave Babych	HFD	7	1	2	3	5	0	0	0	0	0	14	7.1
L	34	Mikael Andersson	HFD	5	0	3	3	0	2	0	0	0	0	5	.0
C	26	Ray Ferraro	HFD	7	0	3	3	1	2	0	0	0	0	5	.0
R	27	Scott Young	HFD	7	2	0	2	2	0	0	0	0	0	15	13.3
L	20	Yvon Corriveau	HFD	4	1	0	1	0	0	0	0	0	0	4	25.0
D	29	Randy Ladouceur	HFD	7	1	0	1	4−	10	0	0	0	0	7	14.3
D	5	Ulf Samuelsson	HFD	7	1	0	1	2	18	0	0	0	0	5	20.0
R	8	Jody Hull	HFD	5	0	1	1	1	2	0	0	0	0	5	.0
C	28	*Mike Tomlak	HFD	7	0	1	1	2−	2	0	0	0	0	7	.0
D	6	*Adam Burt	HFD	7	0	1	1	2−	0	0	0	0	0	7	.0
L	14	*Chris Govedaris	HFD	2	0	0	0	2	0	0	0	0	0	1	.0
R	22	Ed Kastelic	HFD	2	0	0	0	0	2	0	0	0	0	0	.0
L	7	Randy Cunneyworth	HFD	1	0	0	0	1−	0	0	0	0	0	4	.0
D	21	Sylvain Cote	HFD	5	0	0	0	2	0	0	0	0	0	10	.0
D	25	Grant Jennings	HFD	7	0	0	0	3	17	0	0	0	0	6	.0
G	30	Peter Sidorkiewicz	HFD	7	0	0	0	0	0	0	0	0	0	0	.0

Goaltending

No.	Goaltender	GPI	Mins	Avg	W	L	EN	SO	GA	SA	S%
30	Peter Sidorkiewicz	7	429	3.22	3	4	0	0	23	193	.881
	Totals	**7**	**433**	**3.19**	**3**	**4**	**0**	**0**	**23**	**193**	**.881**

General Managers' History

Jack Kelly, 1979-80 to 1981-82; Emile Francis, 1982-83 to 1988-89; Ed Johnston, 1989-90 to date.

Coaching History

Don Blackburn, 1979-80; Don Blackburn and Larry Pleau, 1980-81; Larry Pleau, 1981-82; Larry Kish and Larry Pleau, 1982-83; Jack "Tex" Evans, 1983-84 to 1986-87; Jack "Tex" Evans and Larry Pleau, 1987-88; Larry Pleau, 1988-89; Rick Ley, 1989-90 to date.

Captains' History

Rick Ley, 1979-80; Rick Ley and Mike Rogers, 1980-81. Dave Keon, 1981-82; Russ Anderson, 1982-83; Mark Johnson, 1983-84; Mark Johnson and Ron Francis, 1984-85; Ron Francis, 1985-86 to date.

Club Records

Team

(Figures in brackets for season records are games played; records for fewest points, wins, ties, losses, goals, goals against are for 70 or more games)

Most Points	93	1986-87 (80)
Most Wins	43	1986-87 (80)
Most Ties	19	1979-80 (80)
Most Losses	54	1982-83 (80)
Most Goals	332	1985-86 (80)
Most Goals Against	403	1982-83 (80)
Fewest Points	45	1982-83 (80)
Fewest Wins	19	1982-83 (80)
Fewest Ties	4	1985-86 (80)
Fewest Losses	30	1986-87 (80)
Fewest Goals	249	1987-88 (80)
Fewest Goals Against	267	1987-88 (80)

Longest Winning Streak
Over-all 7   Mar. 16-29/85
Home 5   Mar. 17-29/85
Away 5   Nov. 30-
Dec. 19/89

Longest Undefeated Streak
Over-all 10   Jan. 20-
Feb. 10/82
(6 wins, 4 ties)
Home 7   Mar. 15-
Apr. 5/86
(5 wins, 2 ties)
Away 6   Jan. 23-Feb. 10/82
(3 wins, 3 ties)
Nov. 30-
Dec. 26/89
(5 wins, 1 tie)

Longest Losing Streak
Over-all 9   Feb. 19/83-
Mar. 8/83
Home 6   Feb. 19/83-
Mar. 12/83
Feb. 10-
Mar. 3/85
Away 13   Dec. 18/82-
Feb. 5/83

Longest Winless Streak
Over-all 12   Dec. 18/82-
Jan. 11/83
(11 losses, 1 tie)
Home 13   Jan. 15-
Mar. 10/85
(11 losses, 2 ties)
Away 15   Nov. 11/79-
Jan. 9/80
(11 losses, 4 ties)

Most Shutouts, Season 5   1986-87 (80)
1989-90 (80)
Most PIM, Season   2,102   1989-90 (80)
Most Goals, Game 11   Feb. 12/84
(Edm. 0 at Hfd. 11)
Oct. 19/85
(Mtl. 6 at Hfd. 11)
Jan. 17/86
(Que. 6 at Hfd. 11)
Mar. 15/86
(Chi. 4 at Hfd. 11)

Individual

Most Seasons 9   Ron Francis,
Paul MacDermid
Most Games 647   Ron Francis
Most Goals, Career 243   Ron Francis
Most Assists, Career 502   Ron Francis
Most Points, Career 745   Ron Francis
(243 goals, 502 assists)
Most PIM, Career 1,368   Torrie Robertson
Most Shutouts, Career 13   Mike Liut
Longest Consecutive Games Streak 419   Dave Tippett
(Mar. 3/84-Oct. 7/89)
Most Goals, Season 56   Blaine Stoughton
(1979-80)
Most Assists, Season 69   Ron Francis
(1989-90)
Most Points, Season 105   Mike Rogers
(1979-80)
(44 goals, 61 assists)
(1980-81)
(40 goals, 65 assists)
Most PIM, Season 358   Torrie Robertson
(1985-86)
Most Points, Defenseman
Season 69   Dave Babych
(1985-86)
(14 goals, 55 assists)
Most Points, Center,
Season 105   Mike Rogers
(1979-80)
(44 goals, 61 assists)
Mike Rogers
(1980-81)
(40 goals, 65 assists)

Most Points, Right Wing,
Season 100   Blaine Stoughton
(1979-80)
(56 goals, 44 assists)
Most Points, Left Wing,
Season 80   Pat Boutette
(1980-81)
(28 goals, 52 assists)
Most Points, Rookie,
Season 72   Sylvain Turgeon
(1983-84)
(40 goals, 32 assists)
Most Shutouts, Season 4   Mike Liut
(1986-87)
Peter Sidorkiewicz
(1988-89)
Most Goals, Game 4   Jordy Douglas
(Feb. 3/80)
Ron Francis
(Feb. 12/84)
Most Assists, Game 6   Ron Francis
(Mar. 5/87)
Most Points, Game 6   Paul Lawless
(Jan. 4/87)
Ron Francis
(Mar. 5/87,
Oct. 8/89)

All-time Record vs. Other Clubs

Regular Season

			At Home							On Road							Total				
	GP	W	L	T	GF	GA	PTS	GP	W	L	T	GF	GA	PTS	GP	W	L	T	GF	GA	PTS
Boston	40	20	15	5	153	147	45	40	10	26	4	105	162	24	80	30	41	9	258	309	69
Buffalo	40	15	21	4	117	123	34	40	14	21	5	135	164	33	80	29	42	9	252	287	67
Calgary	17	6	8	3	60	68	15	18	3	14	1	65	99	7	35	9	22	4	125	167	22
Chicago	17	8	8	1	68	63	17	18	5	10	3	55	85	13	35	13	18	4	123	148	30
Detroit	17	11	5	1	70	47	23	18	7	5	6	57	62	20	35	18	10	7	127	109	43
Edmonton	17	7	7	3	75	68	17	18	2	13	3	56	86	7	35	9	20	6	131	154	24
Los Angeles	18	10	6	2	76	76	22	17	6	9	2	70	73	14	35	16	15	4	146	149	36
Minnesota	18	0	0	0	67	66	4	18	17	6	10	1	61	78	13	35	1	19	1	128	144	31
Montreal	40	14	21	5	127	156	33	40	5	29	6	119	198	16	80	19	50	11	246	354	49
New Jersey	18	10	4	4	69	54	24	17	8	7	2	77	62	18	35	18	11	6	146	116	42
NY Islanders	18	7	8	3	61	67	17	17	6	10	1	47	71	13	35	13	18	4	108	138	30
NY Rangers	18	10	6	2	73	64	22	17	6	9	2	52	72	14	35	16	15	4	125	136	36
Philadelphia	17	6	7	4	75	77	16	18	3	14	1	46	81	7	35	9	21	5	121	158	23
Pittsburgh	17	11	6	0	85	70	22	18	6	9	3	71	79	15	35	17	15	3	156	149	37
Quebec	40	18	14	8	144	142	44	40	12	23	5	136	183	29	80	30	37	13	280	325	73
St. Louis	17	8	7	2	61	52	18	18	7	9	2	63	67	16	35	15	16	4	124	119	34
Toronto	18	12	4	2	93	60	26	17	10	6	1	77	66	21	35	22	10	3	170	126	47
Vancouver	17	7	6	4	59	63	18	18	6	7	5	48	61	17	35	13	13	9	107	124	35
Washington	18	6	10	2	59	76	14	17	5	11	1	47	64	11	35	11	21	3	106	140	25
Winnipeg	18	9	5	4	78	59	22	17	8	9	0	61	62	16	35	17	14	4	139	121	38
Totals	**440**	**204**	**177**	**59**	**1670**	**1598**	**467**	**440**	**135**	**251**	**54**	**1448**	**1875**	**324**	**880**	**339**	**428**	**113**	**3118**	**3473**	**791**

Playoffs

	Series	W	L	GP	W	L	T	GF	GA	Last Mtg.	Round	Result
Boston	1	0	1	7	3	4	0	21	23	1990	DSF	L 3-4
Montreal	4	0	4	20	5	15	0	52	75	1989	DSF	L 0-4
Quebec	2	1	1	9	5	4	0	35	34	1987	DSF	L 2-4
Totals	**7**	**1**	**6**	**36**	**13**	**23**	**0**	**108**	**132**			

Playoff Results 1990-86

Year	Round	Opponent	Result	GF	GA
1990	DSF	Boston	L 3-4	21	23
1989	DSF	Montreal	L 0-4	11	18
1988	DSF	Montreal	L 2-4	20	23
1987	DSF	Quebec	L 2-4	19	27
1986	DF	Montreal	L 3-4	13	16
	DSF	Quebec	W 3-0	16	7

Abbreviations: Round: F Final; **CF** conference final; **DF** division final; **DSF** division semi-final; **GA** goals against; **GF** goals for.

1989-90 Results

		Home				Away	
Oct.	5	Montreal	1-4	Oct.	8	Quebec	9-6
	7	Minnesota	4-6		13	Buffalo	1-4
	11	Washington	4-1		19	NY Rangers	3-7
	14	New Jersey	2-3		23	Montreal	2-3
	18	Buffalo	2-1		26	New Jersey	7-3
	21	Detroit	3-3		28	Boston	1-0
	26	Quebec	2-0	Nov.	3	Detroit	4-3
Nov.	1	St Louis	3-5		10	Winnipeg	4-2
	4	Los Angeles	6-3		12	Chicago	2-4
	8	Buffalo	3-6		14	Detroit	3-0
	15	Boston	2-5		26	Buffalo	2-4
	18	NY Rangers	2-3		30	St Louis	5-3
	22	Quebec	2-4	Dec.	2	Montreal	4-3
	25	Philadelphia	5-2		7	Boston	4-3
	28	Buffalo	2-4		14	Philadelphia	3-2
Dec.	6	NY Islanders	3-4		19	Pittsburgh	8-4
	9	New Jersey	7-3		26	Quebec	3-3
	13	Los Angeles	2-5		30	Chicago	3-7
	16	Washington	2-5	Jan.	5	Calgary	4-6
	20	Boston	4-3		6	Edmonton	4-4
	23	Minnesota	4-3		10	Vancouver	3-1
Jan.	3	Winnipeg	2-4		13	Los Angeles	6-3
	17	Boston	5-5		15	Boston	1-4
	19	Calgary	3-3		25	St Louis	2-3
	23	NY Islanders	4-2	Feb.	1	Philadelphia	1-2
	27	Chicago	6-4		3	Quebec*	5-1
	30	Edmonton	4-4		4	Montreal	0-2
Feb.	9	Vancouver	1-4		7	Minnesota	5-3
	10	Toronto	6-2		14	Toronto	6-6
	21	Quebec	3-2		17	Montreal	3-7
	24	Winnipeg	1-3		18	Buffalo	6-4
	28	Montreal	3-1		23	Buffalo	3-7
Mar.	3	NY Rangers	6-4	Mar.	2	Washington	4-3
	8	Toronto	6-7		6	NY Islanders	4-2
	10	Buffalo	0-5		13	Vancouver	1-0
	11	Boston	3-4		17	Calgary	4-5
	21	Quebec	4-1		18	Edmonton	3-1
	24	Montreal	7-4		27	Pittsburgh	3-3
	25	Pittsburgh	4-2		29	Boston	2-3
Apr.	1	Montreal	1-1		31	Quebec	3-2

* Denotes afternoon game.

Entry Draft Selections 1990-79

1990
Pick
- 15 Mark Greig
- 36 Geoff Sanderson
- 57 Mike Lenarduzzi
- 78 Chris Bright
- 120 Cory Keenan
- 141 Jergus Baca
- 162 Martin D'Orsonnens
- 183 Corey Osmak
- 204 Espen Knutsen
- 225 Tommie Eriksen
- 246 Denis Chalifoux

1989
Pick
- 10 Robert Holik
- 52 Blair Atcheynum
- 73 Jim McKenzie
- 94 James Black
- 115 Jerome Bechard
- 136 Scott Daniels
- 157 Raymond Saumier
- 178 Michel Picard
- 199 Trevor Buchanan
- 220 John Battice
- 241 Peter Kasowski

1988
Pick
- 11 Chris Govedaris
- 32 Barry Richter
- 74 Dean Dyer
- 95 Scott Morrow
- 116 Corey Beaulieu
- 137 Kerry Russell
- 158 Jim Burke
- 179 Mark Hirth
- 200 Wayde Bucsis
- 221 Rob White
- 242 Dan Slatalla

1987
Pick
- 18 Jody Hull
- 39 Adam Burt
- 81 Terry Yake
- 102 Marc Rousseau
- 123 Jeff St. Cyr
- 144 Greg Wolf
- 165 John Moore
- 186 Joe Day
- 228 Kevin Sullivan
- 249 Steve Laurin

1986
Pick
- 11 Scott Young
- 32 Marc Laforge
- 74 Brian Chapman
- 95 Bill Horn
- 116 Joe Quinn
- 137 Steve Torrel
- 158 Ron Hoover
- 179 Robert Glasgow
- 200 Sean Evoy
- 221 Cal Brown
- 242 Brian Verbeek

1985
Pick
- 5 Dana Murzyn
- 26 Kay Whitmore
- 68 Gary Callaghan
- 110 Shane Churla
- 131 Chris Brant
- 152 Brian Puhalsky
- 173 Greg Dornbach
- 194 Paul Tory
- 215 Jerry Pawlowski
- 236 Bruce Hill

1984
Pick
- 11 Sylvain Cote
- 110 Mike Millar
- 131 Mike Vellucci
- 173 John Devereaux
- 194 Brent Regan
- 215 Jim Culhane
- 236 Pete Abric

1983
Pick
- 2 Sylvain Turgeon
- 20 David Jensen
- 23 Ville Siren
- 61 Leif Karlsson
- 64 Dave MacLean
- 72 Ron Chyzowski
- 104 Brian Johnson
- 124 Joe Reekie
- 143 Chris Duperron
- 144 James Falle
- 164 Bill Fordy
- 193 Reine Karlsson
- 204 Allan Acton
- 224 Darcy Kaminski

1982
Pick
- 14 Paul Lawless
- 35 Mark Paterson
- 56 Kevin Dineen
- 67 Ulf Samuelsson
- 88 Ray Ferraro
- 109 Randy Gilhen
- 130 Jim Johannson
- 151 Mickey Kramptoich
- 172 Kevin Skilliter
- 214 Martin Linse
- 235 Randy Cameron

1981
Pick
- 4 Ron Francis
- 61 Paul MacDermid
- 67 Michael Hoffman
- 93 Bill Maguire
- 103 Dan Bourbonnais
- 130 John Mokosak
- 151 Denis Dore
- 172 Jeff Poeschl
- 193 Larry Power

1980
Pick
- 8 Fred Arthur
- 29 Michel Galarneau
- 50 Mickey Volcan
- 71 Kevin McClelland
- 100 Darren Jensen
- 113 Mario Cerri
- 134 Mike Martin
- 155 Brent Denat
- 176 Paul Fricker
- 197 Lorne Bokshowan

1979
Pick
- 18 Ray Allison
- 39 Stuart Smith
- 60 Don Nachbaur
- 81 Ray Neufeld
- 102 Mark Renaud
- 123 Dave McDonald

Club Directory

Hartford Civic Center Coliseum
One Civic Center Plaza
Hartford, Connecticut 06103
Phone **203/728-3366**
GM FAX 203/247-1274
FAX 203/522-7707
TWX 710-425-8732
ENVOY ID

Front Office: WHALERS. GM
Public
Relations: WHALERS. PR
Capacity: 15,635

Managing General Partner/Governor	Richard Gordon
General Partner/Alternate Governor	Ben J. Sisti
President/Alternate Governor	Emile Francis
Special Assistant to the MGP	Gordie Howe
Vice President/General Manager	Ed Johnston
Assistant General Manager	Robert W. Crocker
Head Coach	Rick Ley
Assistant Coaches	Jay Leach and Brent Peterson
Director of Player Personnel and Scouting	Ken Schinkel
Scouting Staff	Leo Boivin, Steve Brklacich, Bruce Haralson, Fred Gore, Claude Larose, Jiri Chra
Head Trainer	Bud Gouveia
Strength and Conditioning Coach	Doug McKenney
Assistant Trainer & Equipment Manager	Skip Cunningham
Club Doctor	Dr. John Falkerson
Club Dentist	Dr. Walter Kunisch
Executive Vice-President of Finance & Administration	W. David Andrews III
Vice-President of Marketing & Public Relations	William E. Barnes
Treasurer	Michael J. Amendola
Director of Public Relations	Phil Langan
Assistant Director of Public Relations	Mark Willand
Chief Statistician	Frank Polnaszek
Advertising Sales Manager	Rick Francis
Merchandise Manager	Mike Reddy
Director of Properties/Development	Don Cox
Ticket Sales Manager	Jeff Morander
Ticket Office Supervisor	Steve Ross
Radio Play-By-Play	Chuck Kaiton
TV/Cable Play-By-Play	Rick Peckham
Dimensions of Rink	200 feet by 85 feet
Location of Press Box	Center ice, Upper Level, Asylum Street
Location of Broadcast Booth	Center ice, Upper Level, Asylum Street
Location of Press Room	Adjacent to press box, Upper Level, Asylum Street
TV Outlet	WTXX (Channel 20)
Cable TV Outlet	SportsChannel
Radio Outlet	WTIC-AM (1080) Flagship station of the Whalers 13-Station Radio Network
Team Colors	Green, Blue and White

Selected fourth overall in the 1981 Entry Draft, Ron Francis had the first 100-point season of his nine-year NHL career in 1989-90.

General Manager

JOHNSTON, ED
Vice-President and General Manager, Hartford Whalers.
Born in Montreal, Que., November 24, 1935.

Ed Johnston was named vice-president and general manager of the Whalers on May 11, 1989 after serving in the Pittsburgh Penguins' organization for six years. He was the general manager of the Penguins from 1982-83 to 1987-88 before being named assistant general manager in 1988-89.

Johnston's coaching career began with the Chicago Blackhawks organization. He coached Moncton of the AHL in 1978-79 before taking over as Blackhawks head coach for the 1979-80 campaign. He was head coach of the Penguins for three years (1980-81 to 1982-83). His NHL coaching record is 113-156-54.

Johnston played 11 years with the Boston Bruins and was a member of two NHL Stanley Cup championship teams. He also played with Toronto, St. Louis and Chicago during his 16-year NHL career and had a 3.25 career goals-against-average and 32 shutouts. Johnston owns the distinction of being the last goaltender to play an entire NHL regular season—having played all 70 games during the 1963-64 season.

NHL Coaching Record

Season	Team	Games	Regular Season				Playoffs			
			W	L	T	%	Games	W	L	%
1979-80	Chicago	80	34	27	19	.544	4	0	4	.000
1980-81	Pittsburgh	80	30	37	13	.456	5	2	3	.400
1981-82	Pittsburgh	80	31	36	13	.469	5	2	3	.400
1982-83	Pittsburgh	80	18	53	9	.281	....	....	....	....
	NHL Totals	**320**	**113**	**156**	**54**	**.438**	**14**	**4**	**10**	**.286**

Coach

LEY, RICK
Coach, Hartford Whalers. Born in Orillia, Ont., November 2, 1948.

Rick Ley was named head coach of the Whalers on June 7, 1989 after a seven-year coaching career in the minor leagues. After knee injuries ended his playing career in 1981-82, Ley was named the assistant coach of the Whalers. Mid way through the 1982-83 season, he was named the head coach of the Binghamton Whalers (AHL). In 1983, Ley left the Whalers' organization to coach the Mohawk Valley Stars of the Atlantic Coast Hockey League. A year later, he was hired by Ed Johnston to coach the Pittsburgh Penguins' IHL affiliate—the Muskegon Lumberjacks. Ley coached Muskegon to first-place finishes each year from 1984-85 to 1987-88. He was the IHL Co-Coach of the Year in 1984-85, led his club to the Turner Cup in 1985-86 and won the regular-season championship in 1987-88. In July of 1988, Ley was hired by the Vancouver Canucks to coach the Milwaukee Admirals (IHL).

Ley was one of the first players to join the New England Whalers of the WHA in 1972-73 after four seasons with the Toronto Maple Leafs. He played 559 career games with the Whalers from 1972-73 to 1980-81, serving as captain for his final six seasons. Ley played in each of the nine WHA All-Star Games and was named the League's top defenseman in 1978-79.

Coaching Record

Season	Team	Games	Regular Season				Playoffs			
			W	L	T	%	Games	W	L	%
1982-83	Binghamton (AHL)	44	22	17	5	.534	5	1	4	.200
1983-84	Mohawk Valley (ACHL)	75	29	39	7	.433	5	1	4	.200
1984-85	Muskegon (IHL)	82	50	29	3	.628	17	11	6	.647
1985-86	Muskegon (IHL)	82	50	32	0	.610	14	12	2	.857
1986-87	Muskegon (IHL)	82	47	30	5	.604	15	10	5	.667
1987-88	Muskegon (IHL)	82	58	14	10	.768	6	2	4	.333
1988-89	Milwaukee (IHL)	82	54	23	5	.689	11	5	6	.455
1989-90	Hartford (NHL)	80	38	33	9	.531	7	3	4	.429
	NHL Totals	**80**	**38**	**33**	**9**	**.531**	**7**	**3**	**4**	**.429**

Los Angeles Kings

1989-90 Results: 34W-39L-7T 75PTS. Fourth, Smythe Division

Year-by-Year Record

Season	GP	Home W	L	T	Road W	L	T	Overall W	L	T	GF	GA	Pts.	Finished	Playoff Result
1989-90	80	21	16	3	13	23	4	34	39	7	338	337	75	4th, Smythe Div.	Lost Div. Final
1988-89	80	25	12	3	17	19	4	42	31	7	376	335	91	2nd, Smythe Div.	Lost Div. Final
1987-88	80	19	18	3	11	24	5	30	42	8	318	359	68	4th, Smythe Div.	Lost Div. Semi-Final
1986-87	80	20	17	3	11	24	5	31	41	8	318	341	70	4th, Smythe Div.	Lost Div. Semi-Final
1985-86	80	9	27	4	14	22	4	23	49	8	284	389	54	5th, Smythe Div.	Out of Playoffs
1984-85	80	20	14	6	14	18	8	34	32	14	339	326	82	4th, Smythe Div.	Lost Div. Semi-Final
1983-84	80	13	19	8	10	25	5	23	44	13	309	376	59	5th, Smythe Div.	Out of Playoffs
1982-83	80	20	13	7	7	28	5	27	41	12	308	365	66	5th, Smythe Div.	Out of Playoffs
1981-82	80	19	15	6	5	26	9	24	41	15	314	369	63	4th, Smythe Div.	Lost Div. Final
1980-81	80	22	11	7	21	13	6	43	24	13	337	290	99	2nd, Norris Div.	Lost Prelim. Round
1979-80	80	18	13	9	12	23	5	30	36	14	290	313	74	2nd, Norris Div.	Lost Prelim. Round
1978-79	80	20	13	7	14	21	5	34	34	12	292	286	80	3rd, Norris Div.	Lost Prelim. Round
1977-78	80	18	16	6	13	18	9	31	34	15	243	245	77	3rd, Norris Div.	Lost Prelim. Round
1976-77	80	20	13	7	14	18	8	34	31	15	271	241	83	2nd, Norris Div.	Lost Quarter-Final
1975-76	80	22	13	5	16	20	4	38	33	9	263	265	85	2nd, Norris Div.	Lost Quarter-Final
1974-75	80	22	7	11	20	10	10	42	17	21	269	185	105	2nd, Norris Div.	Lost Prelim. Round
1973-74	78	22	13	4	11	20	8	33	33	12	233	231	78	3rd, West Div.	Lost Quarter-Final
1972-73	78	21	11	7	10	25	4	31	36	11	232	245	73	6th, West Div.	Out of Playoffs
1971-72	78	14	23	2	6	26	7	20	49	9	206	305	49	7th, West Div.	Out of Playoffs
1970-71	78	17	14	8	8	26	5	25	40	13	239	303	63	5th, West Div.	Out of Playoffs
1969-70	76	12	22	4	2	30	6	14	52	10	168	290	38	6th, West Div.	Out of Playoffs
1968-69	76	19	14	5	5	28	5	24	42	10	185	260	58	4th, West Div.	Lost Semi-Final
1967-68	74	20	13	4	11	20	6	31	33	10	200	224	72	2nd, West Div.	Lost Quarter-Final

Schedule

	Home		Away
Oct.	Thur. 4 NY Islanders	**Oct.**	Tues. 9 Vancouver
	Sat. 6 Vancouver		Fri. 26 Winnipeg
	Thur. 11 Edmonton		Sun. 28 Winnipeg
	Sat. 13 Boston		Tues. 30 NY Islanders
	Sun. 14 St Louis		Wed. 31 NY Rangers
	Wed. 17 Minnesota	**Nov.**	Fri. 2 Washington
	Fri. 19 Hartford		Sun. 4 Chicago
	Tues. 23 Calgary		Thur. 22 Calgary
Nov.	Thur. 8 Detroit		Sat. 24 Montreal
	Sat. 10 Edmonton		Sun. 25 Quebec
	Wed. 14 Buffalo		Tues. 27 Detroit
	Sat. 17 Pittsburgh		Thur. 29 St Louis
	Tues. 20 New Jersey	**Dec.**	Tues. 18 Edmonton
Dec.	Sat. 1 Toronto		Thur. 20 Calgary
	Wed. 5 Winnipeg		Sat. 22 Vancouver
	Sat. 8 Winnipeg		Mon. 31 Minnesota
	Tues. 11 NY Rangers	**Jan.**	Wed. 2 NY Rangers
	Thur. 13 Calgary		Thur. 3 NY Islanders
	Sat. 15 Edmonton		Sat. 5 Toronto
	Thur. 27 Philadelphia		Sun. 6 Chicago
	Sat. 29 Montreal		Mon. 14 New Jersey
Jan.	Tues. 8 Hartford		Wed. 16 Hartford
	Thur. 10 Buffalo		Thur. 17 Boston
	Sat. 12 Vancouver		Tues. 22 Edmonton
	Sat. 26 Vancouver		Fri. 25 Vancouver
	Wed. 30 New Jersey	**Feb.**	Mon. 4 Detroit
Feb.	Sat. 2 Vancouver		Tues. 5 Philadelphia
	Tues. 12 Calgary		Fri. 8 Buffalo
	Sat. 16 Boston		Sat. 9 St Louis
	Mon. 18 Washington*		Thur. 14 Edmonton
	Wed. 20 Quebec		Fri. 22 Winnipeg
	Tues. 26 Pittsburgh		Sun. 24 Winnipeg*
	Thur. 28 Winnipeg	**Mar.**	Tues. 5 Washington
Mar.	Sat. 2 Winnipeg		Thur. 7 Pittsburgh
	Tues. 12 Philadelphia		Sat. 9 Quebec
	Thur. 14 Chicago		Sun. 10 Montreal
	Wed. 20 Toronto		Sat. 16 Calgary
	Sat. 23 Calgary*		Sun. 17 Vancouver
	Tues. 26 Edmonton		Sun. 24 Edmonton
	Thur. 28 Minnesota		Sun. 31 Calgary*

* Denotes afternoon game.

Home Starting Times:
All Games .... 7:35 p.m.
Except Matinees .... 1:05 p.m.

Franchise date: June 5, 1967

24th
NHL
Season

At age 33, John Tonelli had his second consecutive 31-goal season with the Kings in 1989-90.

1990-91 Player Personnel

LEFT WINGS	HT	WT	S	Place of Birth	Date	1989-90 Club
BECHARD, Jerome	5-11	187	L	Regina, Sask.	3/30/69	Moose Jaw
BELANGER, Francois	6-3	201	L	Beauport, Que.	1/9/70	Chicoutimi
BERG, Bob	6-2	190	L	Beamsville, Ont.	7/2/70	Belleville
BUCHANEN, Trevor	6-0	182	L	Ft. McMurray, Alta.	6/7/69	Kamloops-Victoria
DUNCANSON, Craig	6-0	190	L	Naughton, Ont.	3/17/67	Los Angeles-New Haven
GAWLICKI, Jeff	6-2	200	L	Edmonton, Alta.	4/15/68	U.N.-Michigan
GRANATO, Tony	5-10	185	R	Downers Grove, IL	7/25/64	L.A.-NY Rangers
GRAVES, Steve	5-10	175	L	Trenton, Ont.	4/7/64	Team Canada
GUDEN, Dave	6-1	175	L	Brighton, Mass.	4/26/68	Providence
JONES, Brad	6-0	195	L	Sterling Hts, Mich.	6/26/65	Wpg.-Moncton-New Haven
LAWTON, Brian	6-0	190	L	New Brunswick, N.J.	6/29/65	Hfd.-Que.-Bos.-Maine
MARTIN, Tom	6-2	200	L	Kelowna, B.C.	5/11/65	Hartford
MAKELA, Mikko	6-2	193	L	Tampere, Finland	2/28/65	L.A.-NY Islanders
MILLER, Jay	6-2	210	L	Wellesley, Mass.	7/16/60	Los Angeles
ROBITAILLE, Luc	6-1	190	L	Montreal, Que.	2/17/66	Los Angeles
TONELLI, John	6-1	200	L	Milton, Ont.	3/23/57	Los Angeles
WILLIAMS, Darryl	5-11	185	L	Mt. Pearl, Nfld.	2/9/68	New Haven
CENTERS						
AIVAZOFF, Micah	6-0	192	L	Powell River, B.C.	5/4/69	New Haven
ALLISON, Mike	6-0	200	R	Fort Francis, Ont.	3/28/61	Los Angeles-New Haven
BERGERON, Yvan	5-11	178	L	Warwick, Que.	6/9/70	Shawinigan
BOKENFOHR, Murray	6-0	190	L	Morinville, Alta.	6/7/69	Red Deer College
COUTURIER, Sylvain	6-2	205	L	Greenfield Pk. Que.	4/23/68	New Haven
DEMERS, Normand	6-0	198	R	Montreal, Que.	5/6/70	Laval
ELIK, Todd	6-2	190	L	Brampton, Ont.	4/15/66	Los Angeles-New Haven
GRETZKY, Wayne	6-0	170	L	Brantford, Ont.	1/26/61	Los Angeles
KASPER, Steve	5-8	175	L	Montreal, Que.	9/28/61	Los Angeles
KONTOS, Chris	6-1	195	L	Toronto, Ont.	12/10/63	Los Angeles-New Haven
KRUSHELNYSKI, Mike	6-2	200	L	Montreal, Que.	4/27/60	Los Angeles
LeBLANC, Denis	6-1	207	L	Montreal, Que.	1/18/70	St. Hyacinthe
LINDHOLM, Mikael	6-0	190	L	Brynas, Sweden	12/19/64	Los Angeles
McCOSH, Shawn	6-0	188	R	Oshawa, Ont.	6/5/69	Niagara Falls
O'DWYER, Bill	6-0	190	L	Boston, Mass.	1/25/60	Maine-Boston
RYDMARK, Daniel	5-10	176	L	Vasteras, Sweden	2/23/70	Farjestad (Swe.)
WHITE, Kevin	6-1	197	R	Charlottetown, P.E.I.	6/22/70	Windsor
RIGHT WINGS						
BJUGSTAD, Scott	6-1	185	L	St. Paul, MN	6/2/61	Los Angeles-New Haven
BREAULT, Francois	5-11	185	L	Acton Vale, Que.	5/11/67	New Haven
CHASSE, Denis	6-0	194	R	Montreal, Que.	2/7/70	Chicoutimi
CROWDER, Keith	6-0	190	R	Windsor, Ont.	1/6/59	Los Angeles
KARJALAINEN, Kyosti	6-1	190	L	Gavle, Sweden	6/19/67	Brynas
KUDELSKI, Bob	6-1	200	R	Springfield, Mass.	3/3/64	Los Angeles
SANDSTROM, Tomas	6-2	200	L	Jakobstad, Finland	9/4/64	L.A.-NY Rangers
SEMCHUK, Brandy	6-1	185	R	Calgary, Alta.	9/22/71	Canadian Nat'l
SIMON, Joey	6-1	190	R	Toronto, Ont.	7/11/70	Kingston-Hamilton
TAYLOR, Dave	6-0	195	R	Levack, Ont.	12/4/55	Los Angeles
THOMSON, Jim	6-1	205	R	Edmonton, Alta.	10/30/65	N.J.-Bing.-Utica
VAN KESSEL, John	6-4	193	R	Bridgewater, Ont.	12/19/69	North Bay-New Haven
WHYTE, Sean	6-0	198	R	Sudbury, Ont.	5/4/70	Owen Sound
WILSON, Ross	6-3	197	R	The Pas, Man.	6/26/69	New Haven
DEFENSEMEN						
BENNING, Brian	6-0	195	L	Edmonton, Alta.	6/10/66	St. Louis-Los Angeles
BLAKE, Rob	6-3	200	R	Simcoe, Ont.	12/10/69	Bowling Green-L.A.
BRUMWELL, Murray	6-2	190	L	Calgary, Alta.	3/31/60	New Haven
CHAPDELAINE, Rene	6-1	195	R	Weyburn, Sask.	9/27/66	New Haven
DUCHESNE, Steve	5-11	190	L	Sept-Iles, Que.	6/30/65	Los Angeles
HALKIDIS, Bob	5-11	200	L	Toronto, Ont.	3/5/66	L.A.-New Haven-Roch.
HAYWARD, Rick	6-0	180	L	Toledo, OH	2/25/66	Salt Lake
HOLDEN, Paul	6-3	210	L	Kitchener, Ont.	3/15/70	London-New Haven
JAQUES, Steve	5-11	180	L	Burnaby, B.C.	2/21/69	Tri-Cities
LAIDLAW, Tom	6-2	205	L	Brampton, Ont.	4/15/58	Los Angeles
MacDONALD, Kevin	6-0	195		Prescott, Ont.	2/24/66	New Haven-Phoenix
McSORLEY, Marty	6-1	225	R	Hamilton, Ont.	5/18/63	Los Angeles
PRAJSLER, Petr	6-2	200	L	Hradec Kralove, Czech.	9/21/65	New Haven-Los Angeles
RICARD, Eric	6-4	220	R	St. Cesaire, Que.	2/16/69	New Haven
RICHER, Stephane	5-11	200	R	Hull, Quebec	4/28/66	Sherbrooke
ROBINSON, Larry	6-4	220	L	Winchester, Ont.	6/2/51	Los Angeles
SMITH, Dennis	5-11	190	L	Detroit, MI	7/27/64	Baltimore
SYDOR, Darryl	6-0	200	L	Edmonton, Alta.	5/13/72	Kamloops
THOMPSON, Brent	6-2	175	L	Calgary, Alta.	1/9/71	Medicine Hat
WATTERS, Tim	5-11	185	L	Kamloops, B.C.	7/25/59	Los Angeles
YOUNG, Scott	6-1	195	R	Burlington, Ont.	5/26/65	New Haven

GOALTENDERS	HT	WT	C	Place of Birth	Date	1989-90 Club
GILMOUR, Darryl	6-0	171	L	Winnipeg, Man.	2/13/67	New Haven-Nashville
GOSSELIN, Mario	5-8	160	L	Thetford Mines, Que.	6/15/63	Los Angeles
GOVERDE, Dave	6-1	205	L	Toronto, Ont.	4/9/70	Sudbury
HRUDEY, Kelly	5-10	180	L	Edmonton, Alta.	1/13/61	Los Angeles
SCOTT, Ron	5-8	155	L	Guelph, Ontario	7/21/60	New Haven-L.A.
STAUBER, Robb	6-0	170	L	Duluth, MN	11/25/67	New Haven-L.A.
WILSON, Jeff	5-7	182	L	Gloucester, Ont.	3/20/70	Kingston

Captains' History

Bob Wall, 1967-68, 1968-69; Larry Cahan, 1969-70, 1970-71; Bob Pulford, 1971-72, 1972-73; Terry Harper, 1973-74, 1974-75; Mike Murphy, 1975-76 to 1980-81; Dave Lewis, 1981-82, 1982-83; Terry Ruskowski, 1983-84, 1984-85; Dave Taylor, 1985-86 to 1988-89; Wayne Gretzky, 1989-90 to date.

1989-90 Scoring

Regular Season

* rookie

Pos	#	Player	Team	GP	G	A	Pts	+/−	PIM	PP	SH	GW	GT	S	%
C	99	Wayne Gretzky	L.A.	73	40	102	142	8	42	10	4	4	1	236	16.9
L	20	Luc Robitaille	L.A.	80	52	49	101	8	38	20	0	7	0	210	24.8
R	7	Tomas Sandstrom	NYR	48	19	19	38	10−	100	6	0	3	0	166	11.4
			L.A.	28	13	20	33	1−	28	1	1	0	1	83	15.7
			TOTAL	76	32	39	71	11−	128	7	1	3	1	249	12.9
L	27	John Tonelli	L.A.	73	31	37	68	8−	62	15	0	4	0	163	19.0
D	28	Steve Duchesne	L.A.	79	20	42	62	3−	36	6	0	1	1	224	8.9
C	11	Steve Kasper	L.A.	77	17	28	45	4	27	1	1	4	0	72	23.6
L	26	Mike Krushelnyski	L.A.	63	16	25	41	7	50	2	2	2	1	101	15.8
R	18	Dave Taylor	L.A.	58	15	26	41	17	96	2	0	1	0	100	15.0
D	19	Larry Robinson	L.A.	64	7	32	39	7	34	1	0	1	1	80	8.8
R	37	Robert Kudelski	L.A.	62	23	13	36	7−	49	2	2	3	0	135	17.0
D	33	Marty McSorley	L.A.	75	15	21	36	2	322	2	1	0	1	127	11.8
R	14	Tony Granato	NYR	37	7	18	25	1	77	1	0	0	0	79	8.9
			L.A.	19	5	6	11	2−	45	1	0	0	0	41	12.2
			TOTAL	56	12	24	36	1−	122	2	0	0	0	120	10.0
C	6	*Todd Elik	L.A.	48	10	23	33	4	41	1	0	0	0	86	11.6
R	24	Mikko Makela	NYI	20	2	3	5	10−	2	1	0	0	0	24	8.3
			L.A.	45	7	14	21	4−	16	0	0	0	1	58	12.1
			TOTAL	65	9	17	26	14−	18	1	0	0	1	82	11.0
D	2	Brian Benning	STL	7	1	1	2	3−	2	0	0	0	0	8	12.5
			L.A.	48	5	18	23	1	104	3	0	0	0	114	4.4
			TOTAL	55	6	19	25	2−	106	3	0	0	0	122	4.9
R	23	Keith Crowder	L.A.	55	4	13	17	2	93	0	0	1	0	48	8.3
R	10	Mike Allison	L.A.	55	2	11	13	6−	78	0	0	1	0	25	8.0
L	29	Jay Miller	L.A.	68	10	2	12	6−	224	0	0	1	0	44	22.7
D	5	Tim Watters	L.A.	62	1	10	11	23	92	0	0	0	0	50	2.0
D	25	*Petr Prajsler	L.A.	34	3	7	10	9−	47	1	0	0	0	49	6.1
D	3	Tom Laidlaw	L.A.	57	1	8	9	4	42	0	0	0	0	27	3.7
D	21	Barry Beck	L.A.	52	1	7	8	3	53	0	0	0	0	36	2.8
R	36	*Craig Duncanson	L.A.	10	3	2	5	1	9	0	0	0	0	12	25.0
L	15	Chris Kontos	L.A.	6	2	2	4	3	4	0	0	0	0	9	22.2
C	51	*Mikael Lindholm	L.A.	18	2	2	4	2	2	0	0	0	0	10	20.0
D	22	Bob Halkidis	L.A.	20	0	4	4	4	56	0	0	0	0	19	.0
C	8	Scott Bjugstad	L.A.	11	1	2	3	2	2	0	0	1	0	10	10.0
R	4	Jim Fox	L.A.	11	1	1	2	1−	0	0	0	1	0	7	14.3
L	14	Gord Walker	L.A.	1	0	0	0	0	0	0	0	0	0	0	.0
G	35	*Robb Stauber	L.A.	2	0	0	0	0	0	0	0	0	0	0	.0
D	4	*Rob Blake	L.A.	4	0	0	0	0	4	0	0	0	0	3	.0
G	1	*Ron Scott	L.A.	12	0	0	0	0	2	0	0	0	0	0	.0
G	31	Mario Gosselin	L.A.	26	0	0	0	0	0	0	0	0	0	0	.0
G	32	Kelly Hrudey	L.A.	52	0	0	0	0	18	0	0	0	0	1	.0

Goaltending

No.	Goaltender	GPI	Mins	Avg	W	L	T	EN	SO	GA	SA	S%
1	*Ron Scott	12	654	3.67	5	6	0	2	0	40	321	.875
31	Mario Gosselin	26	1226	3.87	7	11	1	4	0	79	587	.865
32	Kelly Hrudey	52	2860	4.07	22	21	6	7	2	194	1532	.873
35	*Robb Stauber	2	83	7.95	0	1	0	0	0	11	43	.744
	Totals	**80**	**4846**	**4.17**	**34**	**39**	**7**	**13**	**2**	**337**	**2483**	**.864**

Playoffs

Pos	#	Player	Team	GP	G	A	Pts	+/−	PIM	PP	SH	GW	OT	S	%
C	6	*Todd Elik	LA	10	3	9	12	1	10	1	0	0	0	30	10.0
D	28	Steve Duchesne	LA	10	2	9	11	2−	6	1	0	0	0	32	6.3
L	20	Luc Robitaille	LA	10	5	5	10	5−	12	1	0	1	0	28	17.9
C	99	Wayne Gretzky	LA	7	3	7	10	4−	0	1	0	0	0	13	23.1
R	14	Tony Granato	LA	10	5	4	9	2−	12	2	1	2	1	26	19.2
R	7	Tomas Sandstrom	LA	10	5	4	9	5−	19	0	0	0	0	26	19.2
R	18	Dave Taylor	LA	6	4	4	8	2	6	2	0	0	0	11	36.4
D	19	Larry Robinson	LA	10	2	3	5	2	10	0	0	0	0	12	16.7
D	4	*Rob Blake	LA	8	1	3	4	4−	4	1	0	0	0	11	9.1
L	26	Mike Krushelnyski	LA	10	1	3	4	0	12	0	0	1	1	16	6.3
D	33	Marty McSorley	LA	10	1	3	4	8−	18	1	0	0	0	26	3.8
R	37	Robert Kudelski	LA	8	1	2	3	5−	2	0	0	0	0	9	11.1
L	27	John Tonelli	LA	10	1	2	3	6−	6	0	0	0	0	14	7.1
C	11	Steve Kasper	LA	10	1	1	2	4−	2	0	0	0	0	13	7.7
L	29	Jay Miller	LA	10	1	1	2	6−	10	0	0	0	0	1	100.0
D	2	Brian Benning	LA	7	0	2	2	9−	6	0	0	0	0	12	.0
R	10	Mike Allison	LA	4	1	0	1	2−	2	0	1	0	0	5	20.0
L	15	Chris Kontos	LA	5	1	0	1	6−	0	1	0	0	0	8	12.5
R	23	Keith Crowder	LA	7	1	0	1	1−	9	0	0	0	0	8	12.5
D	22	Bob Halkidis	LA	8	0	1	1	7−	8	0	0	0	0	10	.0
G	32	Kelly Hrudey	LA	9	0	1	1	0	0	0	0	0	0	0	.0
R	24	Mikko Makela	LA	1	0	0	0	0	0	0	0	0	0	0	.0
G	1	*Ron Scott	LA	1	0	0	0	0	0	0	0	0	0	0	.0
C	8	Scott Bjugstad	LA	2	0	0	0	1−	2	0	0	0	0	0	.0
G	31	Mario Gosselin	LA	3	0	0	0	0	0	0	0	0	0	0	.0
D	25	*Petr Prajsler	LA	3	0	0	0	1−	0	0	0	0	0	0	.0
D	5	Tim Watters	LA	4	0	0	0	4	6	0	0	0	0	0	.0

Goaltending

No.	Goaltender	GPI	Mins	Avg	W	L	EN	SO	GA	SA	S%
31	Mario Gosselin	3	62	2.90	0	2	1	0	3	23	.870
32	Kelly Hrudey	9	539	4.34	4	4	1	0	39	265	.853
1	*Ron Scott	1	32	7.50	0	0	0	0	4	10	.600
	Totals	10	637	4.52	4	6	2	0	48	298	.839

Retired Numbers

30 Rogatien Vachon 1971-1978

Club Records

Team

(Figures in brackets for season records are games played; records for fewest points, wins, ties, losses, goals, goals against are for 70 or more games)

Most Points	105	1974-75 (80)
Most Wins	43	1980-81 (80)
Most Ties	21	1974-75 (80)
Most Losses	52	1969-70 (76)
Most Goals	376	1988-89 (80)
Most Goals Against	389	1985-86 (80)
Fewest Points	38	1969-70 (76)
Fewest Wins	14	1969-70 (76)
Fewest Ties	7	1988-89 (80)
		1989-90 (80)
Fewest Losses	17	1974-75 (80)
Fewest Goals	168	1969-70 (76)
Fewest Goals Against	185	1974-75 (80)

Longest Winning Streak

Over-all	8	Oct. 21-Nov. 7/72
Home	7	Four times
Away	8	Dec. 18/74-Jan. 16/75

Longest Undefeated Streak

Over-all	11	Feb. 28-Mar. 24/74 (9 wins, 2 ties)
Home	10	Oct. 21-Nov. 18/72 (8 wins, 2 ties) Mar. 2-28/74 (8 wins, 2 ties)
Away	11	Oct. 10-Dec. 11/74 (6 wins, 5 ties)

Longest Losing Streak

Over-all	10	Feb. 22-Mar. 9/84
Home	9	Feb. 8-Mar. 12/86
Away	12	Jan. 11-Feb. 15/70

Longest Winless Streak

Over-all	17	Jan. 29-Mar. 5/70 (13 losses, 4 ties)
Home	9	Jan. 29-Mar. 5/70 (8 losses, 1 tie) Feb. 8-Mar. 12/86 (9 losses)
Away	21	Jan. 11-Apr. 3/70 (17 losses, 4 ties)

Most Shutouts, Season	9	1974-75 (80)
Most PIM, Season	2,215	1989-90 (80)
Most Goals, Game	12	Nov. 28/84 (Van. 1 at L.A. 12)

Individual

Most Seasons	13	Dave Taylor
Most Games	921	Marcel Dionne
Most Goals, Career	550	Marcel Dionne
Most Assists, Career	757	Marcel Dionne
Most Points Career	1,307	Marcel Dionne
Most PIM, Career	1,446	Jay Wells
Most Shutouts, Career	32	Rogie Vachon
Longest Consecutive Games Streak	324	Marcel Dionne (Jan. 7/78-Jan. 9/82)
Most Goals, Season	70	Bernie Nicholls (1988-89)
Most Assists, Season	114	Wayne Gretzky (1988-89)
Most Points, Season	168	Wayne Gretzky (1988-89) (54 goals, 114 assists)
Most PIM, Season	358	Dave Williams (1986-87)
Most Points, Defenseman Season	76	Larry Murphy (1980-81) (16 goals, 60 assists)
Most Points, Center, Season	168	Wayne Gretzky (1988-89) (54 goal, 114 assists)

Most Points, Right Wing, Season	112	Dave Taylor (1980-81) (47 goals, 65 assists)
Most Points, Left Wing, Season	111	Luc Robitaille (1987-88) (53 goals, 58 assists)
Most Points, Rookie, Season	84	Luc Robitaille (1986-87) (45 goals, 39 assists)
Most Shutouts, Season	8	Rogie Vachon (1976-77)
Most Goals, Game	4	Several players
Most Assists, Game	6	Bernie Nicholls (Dec. 1/88)
Most Points, Game	8	Bernie Nicholls (Dec. 1/88)

Coaching History

Leonard "Red" Kelly, 1967-68 to 1968-69; Hal Laycoe and John Wilson, 1969-70; Larry Regan, 1970-71; Larry Regan and Fred Glover, 1971-72; Bob Pulford, 1972-73 to 1976-77; Ron Stewart, 1977-78; Bob Berry, 1978-79 to 1980-81; Parker MacDonald and Don Perry, 1981-82; Don Perry, 1982-83; Don Perry, Rogatien Vachon and Roger Neilson, 1983-84; Pat Quinn, 1984-85 to 1985-86; Pat Quinn and Mike Murphy 1986-87; Mike Murphy and Robbie Ftorek, 1987-88; Robbie Ftorek, 1988-89; Tom Webster, 1989-90 to date.

All-time Record vs. Other Clubs

Regular Season

			At Home								On Road								Total				
	GP	W	L	T	GF	GA	PTS	GP	W	L	T	GF	GA	PTS	GP	W	L	T	GF	GA	PTS
Boston	48	15	28	5	158	185	35	49	9	37	3	134	235	21	97	24	65	8	292	420	56
Buffalo	40	14	19	7	137	141	35	41	13	21	7	128	1/1	33	81	27	40	14	265	312	08
Calgary	55	29	22	4	222	210	62	56	14	34	8	189	268	36	111	43	56	12	411	478	98
Chicago	48	21	22	5	170	168	47	46	15	25	6	142	186	36	94	36	47	11	312	354	83
Detroit	53	31	12	10	228	156	72	52	23	22	7	191	209	53	105	54	34	17	419	365	125
Edmonton	40	13	20	7	167	199	33	40	7	24	9	161	232	23	80	20	44	16	328	431	56
Hartford	17	9	6	2	73	70	20	18	6	10	2	76	76	14	35	15	16	4	149	146	34
Minnesota	51	23	14	14	193	158	60	53	13	33	7	139	216	33	104	36	47	21	332	374	93
Montreal	53	14	33	6	158	215	34	52	6	36	10	135	243	22	105	20	69	16	293	458	56
New Jersey	30	23	1	6	173	91	52	30	13	12	5	114	100	31	60	36	13	11	287	191	83
NY Islanders	33	13	13	7	113	113	33	32	9	19	4	90	124	22	65	22	32	11	203	237	55
NY Rangers	47	19	19	9	156	163	47	46	15	26	5	138	180	35	93	34	45	14	294	343	82
Philadelphia	52	14	31	7	144	179	35	52	13	32	7	135	204	33	104	27	63	14	279	383	68
Pittsburgh	57	35	14	8	217	149	78	59	17	34	8	187	227	42	116	52	48	16	404	376	120
Quebec	18	10	7	1	83	68	21	17	8	7	2	71	72	18	35	18	14	3	154	140	39
St. Louis	52	26	19	7	187	154	59	51	13	33	5	134	195	31	103	39	52	12	321	349	90
Toronto	48	29	14	5	174	130	63	49	12	28	9	160	211	33	97	41	42	14	334	341	96
Vancouver	61	35	17	9	253	185	79	61	21	28	12	211	240	54	122	56	45	21	464	425	133
Washington	34	21	10	3	142	100	45	33	15	13	5	124	139	35	67	36	23	8	266	239	80
Winnipeg	37	12	20	5	154	162	29	38	12	19	7	139	171	31	75	24	39	12	293	333	60
Defunct Club	35	27	6	2	141	76	56	34	11	14	9	91	109	31	69	38	20	11	232	185	87
Totals	**909**	**433**	**347**	**129**	**3443**	**3072**	**995**	**909**	**265**	**507**	**137**	**2889**	**3808**	**667**	**1818**	**698**	**854**	**266**	**6332**	**6880**	**1662**

Playoffs

	Series	W	L	GP	W	L	T	GF	GA	Last Mtg.	Round	Result
Boston	2	0	2	13	5	8	0	38	56	1977	QF	L 2-4
**Calgary	5	3	2	20	9	11	0	72	84	1990	DSF	W 4-2
Chicago	1	0	1	5	1	4	0	7	10	1974	QF	L 1-4
Edmonton	5	2	3	24	8	16	0	89	110	1990	DF	L 0-4
Minnesota	1	0	1	7	3	4	0	21	26	1968	QF	L 3-4
NY Islanders	1	0	1	4	1	3	0	10	21	1980	PR	L 1-3
NY Rangers	2	0	2	6	1	5	0	14	32	1981	PR	L 1-3
St. Louis	1	0	1	4	0	4	0	5	16	1969	SF	L 0-4
Toronto	2	0	2	5	1	4	0	9	18	1978	PR	L 0-2
Vancouver	1	0	1	5	1	4	0	14	19	1982	DF	L 1-4
Defunct Clubs	1	1	0	7	4	3	0	23	25			
Totals	**22**	**6**	**16**	**100**	**34**	**66**	**0**	**302**	**417**			

Playoff Results 1990-86

Year	Round	Opponent	Result	GF	GA
1990	DF	Edmonton	L 0-4	10	24
	DSF	Calgary	W 4-2	29	24
1989	DF	Calgary	L 0-4	11	22
	DSF	Edmonton	W 4-3	25	20
1988	DSF	Calgary	L 4-1	18	30
1987	DSF	Edmonton	L 1-4	20	32

Abbreviations: Round: F Final; **CF** conference final; **DF** division final; **DSF** division semi-final; **SF** semi-final; **QF** quarter-final. **PR** preliminary round. **GA** goals against; **GF** goals for.

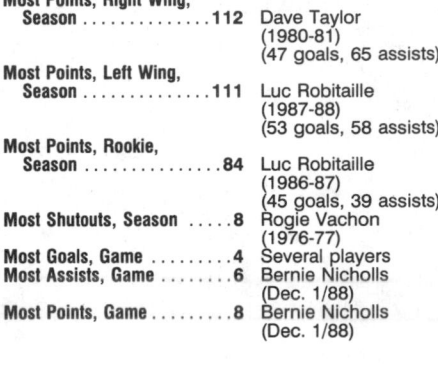

1989-90 Results

		Home				Away	
Oct.	5	Toronto	4-2	Oct.	13	Vancouver	6-5
	7	Edmonton	5-6		15	Edmonton	5-4
	8	Detroit	5-0		21	St Louis	6-4
	11	NY Islanders	4-7		22	Chicago	4-7
	17	Boston	2-3		27	Winnipeg	3-1
	25	Calgary	0-5		29	Winnipeg	1-6
Nov.	8	Calgary	4-5		31	Pittsburgh	8-4
	11	Montreal	5-4	Nov.	2	Boston	4-5
	18	Washington	5-3		4	Hartford	3-6
	22	Chicago	6-3		5	Buffalo	3-5
	25	Vancouver	7-4		14	Calgary	8-6
	30	Edmonton	6-7		15	Edmonton	2-2
Dec.	2	NY Rangers	6-0		26	Vancouver	3-3
	6	Vancouver	5-4	Dec.	8	Edmonton	4-5
	19	Winnipeg	9-5		10	Quebec*	8-4
	21	Quebec	6-1		11	Montreal	2-2
	23	Vancouver	4-1		13	Hartford	5-2
	27	Calgary	5-5		15	New Jersey	5-7
	30	Philadelphia	3-6		16	Philadelphia	2-5
Jan.	9	St Louis	3-4	Jan.	1	Washington*	7-4
	11	Edmonton	3-3		2	NY Islanders	3-5
	13	Hartford	3-6		4	New Jersey	2-4
	16	Buffalo	2-4		23	Toronto	4-7
	18	Detroit	9-4		23	Vancouver	3-3
	27	NY Rangers	1-3		25	Edmonton	6-7
	30	New Jersey	5-2	Feb.	6	Calgary	5-3
Feb.	1	Chicago	4-7		10	Pittsburgh	6-7
	3	Calgary	4-3		12	Toronto	3-3
	8	Winnipeg	1-5		14	Detroit	5-6
	17	Quebec	7-1		15	Minnesota	3-6
	19	Washington*	3-2	Mar.	2	Winnipeg	3-9
	21	Minnesota	4-2		4	Winnipeg*	2-5
	24	Vancouver	4-6		5	Calgary	0-5
	28	Edmonton	4-2		12	NY Rangers	6-2
Mar.	7	Montreal	2-5		14	Buffalo	6-5
	10	Pittsburgh*	2-5		17	Boston*	5-4
	22	NY Islanders	3-1		18	Philadelphia	4-7
	24	St Louis	9-3		20	Minnesota	2-5
	27	Winnipeg	4-4		31	Vancouver	3-6
	29	Winnipeg	0-1	Apr.	1	Calgary	4-8

* Denotes afternoon game.

Entry Draft
Selections 1990-76

1990
Pick
7 Daryl Sydor
28 Brandy Semchuk
49 Bob Berg
91 David Goverde
112 Erik Andersson
133 Robert Lang
154 Dean Hulett
175 Denis Leblanc
196 Patrik Ross
217 K.J. (Kevin) White
238 Troy Mohns

1989
Pick
39 Brent Thompson
81 Jim Maher
102 Eric Ricard
103 Thomas Newman
123 Daniel Rydmark
144 Ted Kramer
165 Sean Whyte
182 Jim Giacin
186 Martin Maskarinec
207 Jim Hiller
228 Steve Jaques
249 Kevin Sneddon

1988
Pick
7 Martin Gelinas
28 Paul Holden
49 John Van Kessel
70 Rob Blake
91 Jeff Robison
109 Micah Aivazoff
112 Robert Larsson
133 Jeff Kruesel
154 Timo Peltomaa
175 Jim Larkin
196 Brad Hyatt
217 Doug Laprade
238 Joe Flanagan

1987
Pick
4 Wayne McBean
27 Mark Fitzpatrick
43 Ross Wilson
90 Mike Vukonich
111 Greg Batters
132 Kyosti Karjalainen
174 Jeff Gawlicki
195 John Preston
216 Rostislav Vlach
237 Mikael Lindholm

1986
Pick
2 Jimmy Carson
44 Denis Larocque
65 Sylvain Couturier
86 Dave Guden
107 Robb Stauber
128 Sean Krakiwsky
149 Rene Chapdelaine
170 Trevor Pochipinski
191 Paul Kelly
212 Russ Mann
233 Brian Hayton

1985
Pick
9 Craig Duncanson
10 Dan Gratton
30 Par Edlund
72 Perry Florio
93 Petr Prajzler
135 Tim Flannigan
156 John Hyduke
177 Steve Horner
219 Trent Ciprick
240 Marion Howarth

1984
Pick
6 Craig Redmond
24 Brian Wilks
48 John English
69 Tom Glavine
87 Dave Grannis
108 Greg Strome
129 Tim Hanley
150 Shannon Deegan
171 Luc Robitaille
192 Jeff Crossman
213 Paul Kenny
234 Brian Martin

1983
Pick
47 Bruce Shoebottom
67 Guy Benoit
87 Bob LaForest
100 Garry Galley
107 Dave Lundmark
108 Kevin Stevens
127 Tim Burgess
147 Ken Hammond
167 Bruce Fishback
187 Thomas Ahlen
207 Jan Blaha
227 Chad Johnson

1982
Pick
27 Mike Heidt
48 Steve Seguin
64 Dave Gans
82 Dave Ross
90 Darcy Roy
95 Ulf Issakson
132 Victor Nechaev
153 Peter Helander
174 Dave Chartier
195 John Franzosa
216 Ray Shero
237 Mats Ulander

1981
Pick
2 Doug Smith
39 Dean Kennedy
81 Marty Dallman
123 Brad Thompson
134 Craig Hurley
144 Peter Sawkins
165 Dan Brennan
186 Allan Tuer
207 Jeff Baikie

1980
Pick
4 Larry Murphy
10 Jim Fox
33 Greg Terrion
34 Dave Morrison
52 Steve Bozek
73 Bernie Nicholls
94 Alan Graves
115 Darren Eliot
136 Mike O'Connor
157 Bill O'Dwyer
178 Daryl Evans
199 Kim Collins

1979
Pick
16 Jay Wells
29 Dean Hopkins
30 Mark Hardy
50 J.P. Kelly
71 John Gibson
92 Jim Brown
113 Jay MacFarlane

1978
Pick
77 Paul Mancini
94 Doug Keans
111 Don Waddell
128 Rob Mierkains
145 Ric Scully
162 Brad Thiessen
177 Jim Armstrong
193 Claude Larochelle

1977
Pick
84 Julian Baretta
85 Warren Holmes
103 Randy Rudnyk
121 Bob Suter

1976
Pick
21 Steve Clippingdale
49 Don Moores
67 Bob Mears
85 Rob Palmer
103 Larry McRae

Club Directory

The Great Western Forum
3900 West Manchester Blvd.
P.O. Box 17013
Inglewood, California 90308
Phone 213/419-3160
FAX 213/673-8927
ENVOY ID
  Front Office: KINGS.GM
  Public Relations: KINGS.PR
Capacity: 16,005

Executive
Governor/President . . . . Bruce McNall
Alternate Governors . . . . Roy A. Mlakar, Rogatien Vachon
Executive Vice-President . . . . Roy A. Mlakar
Executive Secretary to Vice-President . . . . Susie Pulkkila
Vice-President . . . . Steven H. Nesenblatt
Vice-President . . . . Nora J. Rothrock
Vice-President . . . . Susan A. Waks
Vice-President, Adminstration/Marketing . . . . Robert Moor
Vice President, Finance . . . . Bruce Bargmann
Executive Director, Communications and Public
Relations . . . . Scott Carmichael

Hockey Operations
General Manager . . . . Rogatien Vachon
Assistant General Manager . . . . Nick Beverley
Administrative Assistant to General Manager . . . . John Wolf
Executive Secretary to General Manager . . . . Marcia Galloway
Head Coach . . . . Tom Webster
Assistant Coaches . . . . Rick Wilson, Cap Raeder
Director of Scouting and Development . . . . Bob Owen
Scouting Staff . . . . Jim Anderson, Ron Ansell, Serge Blanchard,
John Bymark, Gary Harker, Jan Lindgren,
Mark Miller, Al Murray, Vaclav Nedomansky,
Ted O'Connor, Don Perry, Alex Smart

Medical Staff
Head Trainer . . . . Peter Demers
Assistant Trainer . . . . Mark O'Neill
Equipment Manager . . . . Peter Millar
Team Physicians . . . . Dr. Steve Lombardo, Dr. Ron Kvitne
Internist . . . . Dr. Michael Mellman
Team Dentist . . . . Dr. Gordon Knuth
Team Opthalmologist . . . . Dr. Howard Lazerson
Team Hospital . . . . Centinela Hospital Medical Centre

Communications/Marketing/Finance
Media Relations . . . . Susan Carpenter
Director of Team Services . . . . Ron Muniz
Director of Publications . . . . Nick Salata
Director of Community and Player Relations . . . . Jim Fox
Director of Promotions . . . . Michel Gilbert
Director of Merchandising . . . . Harvey Boles
Director of Sales . . . . Dennis Metz
Director of Accounting . . . . Martin Greenspun
Advertising Coordinator . . . . Tricia Webb
Administrative Assistants . . . . Kelley Clark, Angela Ladd
Play-by-Play Announcer . . . . Bob Miller
Color Commentator . . . . Nick Nickson
Video Coordinator . . . . Bob Borgen
Radio Station . . . . XTRA (690 AM)
Television . . . . Prime Ticket Cable Network

Home ice . . . . The Great Western Forum
Dimensions of Rink . . . . 200 feet by 85 feet
Supervisor of Off-Ice Officials . . . . Bill Meuris
Public Address Announcer . . . . David Courtney
Colors . . . . Black, White and Silver
Training Camp . . . . Hull, Quebec
Location of Press Box . . . . Westside Colonade, Sec. 28, Row 1-10

General Managers' History
Larry Regan, 1967-68 to 1972-73; Larry Regan and
Jake Milford, 1973-74; Jake Milford, 1974-75 to
1976-77; George Maguire, 1977-78 to 1982-83;
George Maguire and Rogatien Vachon, 1983-84;
Rogatien Vachon, 1984-85 to date.

General Manager
VACHON, ROGATIEN
General Manager, Los Angeles Kings. Born in Palmorelle, Que., September 8, 1945.
Rogie Vachon was named general manager of the Kings on Jan. 30, 1984 after
spending the first half of the 1983-84 season as an assistant coach to Don Perry.
In his first year as GM of the club, Los Angeles improved from 59 points in 1983-
84 to 82 points in 1984-85. A veteran of 16 NHL seasons, Vachon spent seven
years in a Los Angeles uniform, in addition to Montreal, Detroit and Boston.
While with the Canadiens in 1967-68, Vachon shared the Vezina Trophy with
Lorne "Gump" Worsley. During his seven-year stint in Los Angeles from 1971 to
1978, Vachon helped the club emerge as one of the NHL's top defensive teams.
In 1974-75, his finest season, Vachon was named *Hockey News'* Player of the
Year after compiling a 2.24 average and a 27-14-13 record while leading the
Kings to their highest point total in team history (105). Following his retirement in
1982, he returned to Los Angeles to instruct the Kings' young goaltenders.

Coach
WEBSTER, TOM
Coach, Los Angeles Kings. Born in Kirkland Lake, Ont., October 4, 1948.
Tom Webster was named the 16th head coach of the Los Angeles Kings on May
31, 1989 after a two-year stint with the Windsor Spitfires of the OHL. While with
Windsor he led his club to the OHL Championship in 1988.
In 1981, Webster led the Adirondack Red Wings of the AHL to a Calder Cup
Championship and in 1984 he coached the Tulsa Oilers to the CHL
Championship. Webster was the head coach of the New York Rangers for 14
games in 1986-87 before stepping down due to an ear ailment. Webster coached
Canada's national junior team to a fourth-place finish at the 1989 World
Championships in Alaska.
Drafted by the Boston Bruins in 1967, Webster spent two seasons in the NHL with
the Detroit Red Wings (1970-71) and Oakland Seals (1971-72) before joining the
New England Whalers of the WHA for seven seasons (1972-79). He completed
his NHL career with the Red Wings in 1979-80.

Coaching Record

| Season | Team | | Regular Season | | | | | Playoffs | | | |
		Games	W	L	T	%	Games	W	L	%
1979-80	Adirondack (AHL)	80	32	37	11	.469	5	1	4	.200
1980-81	Adirondack (AHL)	80	35	40	5	.469	18	12	6	.667
1981-82	Springfield (AHL)	80	32	43	5	.431	....	....	....	....
1982-83	Tulsa (CHL)	80	32	47	1	.406	....	....	....	....
1983-84	Tulsa (CHL)	68	36	27	5	.566	9	8	1	.889
1984-85	Salt lake (IHL)	82	35	39	8	.476	7	3	4	.429
1986-87	NY Rangers (NHL)	14	5	7	2	.429	....	....	....	....
1987-88	Windsor (OHL)	66	50	14	2	.773	12	12	0	1.000
1988-89	Windsor (OHL)	66	25	37	4	.409	4	0	4	.000
1989-90	Los Angeles (NHL)	80	34	39	7	.469	10	4	6	.400
	NHL Totals	94	39	46	9	.463	10	4	6	.400

Minnesota North Stars

1989-90 Results: 36w-40L-4T 76PTS. Fourth, Norris Division

Schedule

Home				Away		
Oct.	Thur.	4	St Louis	Oct.	Mon.	8	NY Rangers

Oct. Thur. 4 St Louis — Oct. Mon. 8 NY Rangers
Sat. 6 NY Islanders — Tues. 9 New Jersey
Thur. 11 Boston — Wed. 17 Los Angeles
Sat. 13 Chicago — Sat. 20 St Louis
Wed. 24 Hartford — Sun. 21 Chicago
Sat. 27 Detroit — Fri. 26 Detroit
Nov. Thur. 8 Quebec — Tues. 30 Toronto
Sat. 10 Hartford — Nov. Thur. 1 Philadelphia
Tues. 13 Pittsburgh — Sat. 3 Quebec
Thur. 15 NY Rangers — Sun. 4 Montreal
Sat. 17 St Louis — Mon. 19 NY Rangers
Fri. 23 Vancouver — Wed. 21 Detroit
Sat. 24 New Jersey — Tues. 27 Vancouver
Dec. Sat. 1 Pittsburgh — Fri. 30 Winnipeg
Thur. 6 Toronto — Dec. Wed. 5 Toronto
Sat. 8 Philadelphia — Thur. 13 St Louis
Tues. 11 Calgary — Sun. 16 Chicago*
Sat. 15 Chicago* — Thur. 20 Pittsburgh
Wed. 26 Winnipeg — Sat. 22 Boston
Sat. 29 Boston — Sun. 23 Hartford
Mon. 31 Los Angeles — Jan. Wed. 2 Detroit
Jan. Thur. 3 Toronto — Tues. 8 NY Islanders
Sat. 5 Vancouver — Sun. 13 Chicago
Sat. 12 Buffalo — Mon. 21 Winnipeg
Tues. 15 Montreal — Fri. 25 Washington
Thur. 17 Washington — Sat. 26 New Jersey
Tues. 22 St Louis — Mon. 28 Toronto
Wed. 30 Detroit — Feb. Sat. 2 Quebec
Feb. Thur. 7 Toronto — Mon. 4 Montreal
Sat. 9 Detroit — Tues. 12 NY Islanders
Wed. 20 Edmonton — Wed. 13 Buffalo
Sat. 23 Chicago — Sat. 16 Detroit*
Tues. 26 Philadelphia — Mar. Fri. 1 Edmonton
Mar. Wed. 6 Edmonton — Sat. 2 Calgary
Sat. 9 Detroit* — Thur. 14 St Louis
Sun. 10 Calgary — Sat. 16 Toronto
Tues. 12 Buffalo — Fri. 22 Washington
Sun. 17 Toronto — Sun. 24 Chicago*
Mon. 25 St Louis — Thur. 28 Los Angeles
Sat. 30 Chicago — Sun. 31 St Louis

* Denotes afternoon game.

Home Starting Times:
All Games .... 7:35 p.m.
Except Sundays .... 7:05 p.m.
Except Matinees .... 1:35 p.m.

Franchise date: June 5, 1967

24th NHL Season

Larry Murphy had 68 points in the 1989-90 season to rank seventh among NHL defencemen.

Year-by-Year Record

Season	GP	Home W	L	T	Road W	L	T	Overall W	L	T	GF	GA	Pts.	Finished		Playoff Result
1989-90	80	26	12	2	10	28	2	36	40	4	284	291	76	4th,	Norris Div.	Lost Div. Semi-Final
1988-89	80	17	15	8	10	22	8	27	37	16	258	278	70	3rd,	Norris Div.	Lost Div. Semi-Final
1987-88	80	10	24	6	9	24	7	19	48	13	242	349	51	5th,	Norris Div.	Out of Playoffs
1986-87	80	17	20	3	13	20	7	30	40	10	296	314	70	5th,	Norris Div.	Out of Playoffs
1985-86	80	21	15	4	17	18	5	38	33	9	327	305	85	2nd,	Norris Div.	Lost Div. Semi-Final
1984-85	80	14	19	7	11	24	5	25	43	12	268	321	62	4th,	Norris Div.	Lost Div. Final
1983-84	80	22	14	4	17	17	6	39	31	10	345	344	88	1st,	Norris Div.	Lost Conf. Championship
1982-83	80	23	6	11	17	18	5	40	24	16	321	290	96	2nd,	Norris Div.	Lost Div. Final
1981-82	80	21	7	12	16	16	8	37	23	20	346	288	94	1st,	Norris Div.	Lost Div. Semi-Final
1980-81	80	23	10	7	12	18	10	35	28	17	291	263	87	3rd,	Adams Div.	Lost Final
1979-80	80	25	8	7	11	20	9	36	28	16	311	253	88	3rd,	Adams Div.	Lost Semi-Final
1978-79	80	19	15	6	9	25	6	28	40	12	257	289	68	4th,	Adams Div.	Out Of Playoffs
1977-78	80	12	24	4	6	29	5	18	53	9	218	325	45	5th,	Smythe Div.	Out of Playoffs
1976-77	80	17	14	9	6	25	9	23	39	18	240	310	64	2nd,	Smythe Div.	Lost Prelim. Round
1975-76	80	15	22	3	5	31	4	20	53	7	195	303	47	4th,	Smythe Div.	Out of Playoffs
1974-75	80	17	20	3	6	30	4	23	50	7	221	341	53	4th,	Smythe Div.	Out of Playoffs
1973-74	78	18	15	6	5	23	11	23	38	17	235	275	63	7th,	West Div.	Out of Playoffs
1972-73	78	26	8	5	11	22	6	37	30	11	254	230	85	3rd,	West Div.	Lost Quarter-Final
1971-72	78	22	11	6	15	18	6	37	29	12	212	191	86	2nd,	West Div.	Lost Quarter-Final
1970-71	78	16	15	8	12	19	8	28	34	16	191	223	72	4th,	West Div.	Lost Semi-Final
1969-70	76	11	16	11	8	19	11	19	35	22	224	257	60	3rd,	West Div.	Lost Quarter-Final
1968-69	76	11	21	6	7	22	9	18	43	15	189	270	51	6th,	West Div.	Out of Playoffs
1967-68	74	17	12	8	10	20	7	27	32	15	191	226	69	4th,	West Div.	Lost Semi-Final

1990-91 Player Personnel

FORWARDS	HT	WT	S	Place of Birth	Date	1989-90 Club
BABE, Warren	6-3	200	L	Medicine Hat, Alta.	9/7/68	Kalamazoo
BALDERIS, Helmut	5-11	195	R	Riga, Latvia	6/31/52	Minnesota
BARBER, Don	6-2	205	L	Victoria, B.C.	12/2/64	Minnesota-Kalamazoo
BARNETT, Brett	6-3	185	L	Toronto, Ont.	10/12/67	Kalamazoo
BARRAULT, Doug	6-2	205	R	Golden, B.C.	4/21/70	Lethbridge
BELLOWS, Brian	5-11	195	R	St. Catharines, Ont.	9/1/64	Minnesota
BEREZAN, Perry	6-2	190	R	Edmonton, Alta.	12/5/64	Minnesota
BINNIE, Troy	6-1	200	L	Ottawa, Ont.	9/22/70	Ottawa
BROTEN, Aaron	5-10	180	L	Roseau, MN	11/14/60	N.J.-Minnesota
BROTEN, Neal	5-9	170	L	Roseau, MN	11/29/59	Minnesota
CHURLA, Shane	6-1	200	R	Fernie, B.C.	6/24/65	Minnesota
CRAIG, Mike	6-1	180	R	St. Mary's, Ont.	6/6/71	Oshawa
DAHLEN, Ulf	6-2	195	L	Ostersund, Sweden	1/12/67	NYR-Minnesota
DePALMA, Larry	6-0	200	L	Trenton, MI	10/27/65	Kalamazoo
DONATELLI, Clark	5-10	180	L	Providence, RI	11/22/67	Kalamazoo-Minnesota
DUCHESNE, Gaetan	5-11	200	L	Les Saulles, Que.	7/11/62	Minnesota
EVANS, Kevin	5-9	185	L	Peterborough, Ont.	7/10/65	Kalamazoo
GAGNER, Dave	5-10	180	L	Chatham, Ont.	12/11/64	Minnesota
GARBUTT, Murray	6-1	205	L	Hanna, Alta.	6/29/71	Medicine Hat
GAUDREAU, Rob	5-11	185	R	Lincoln, RI	1/20/70	Providence
GAVIN, Stewart	6-0	190	L	Ottawa, Ont.	3/15/60	Minnesota
GOTAAS, Steve	5-10	180	R	Camrose, Alta.	5/10/67	Kalamazoo
JERRARD, Paul	5-10	185	R	Winnipeg, Man.	4/20/65	Kalamazoo
KOVACS, Frank	6-2	205	L	Regina, Sask.	6/6/71	Regina
LAPPIN, Peter	5-11	180	R	St. Charles, IL	12/31/65	Kalamazoo-Minnesota
McHUGH, MIke	5-10	190	L	Bowdoin, MA	8/16/65	Kalamazoo-Minnesota
McRAE, Basil	6-2	205	L	Beaverton, Ont.	1/5/61	Minnesota
McGOWAN, Cal	6-1	185	L	Sydny, Nebraska	6/19/70	Kamloops
MERCIER, Mitch	6-2	200	R	Regina, Sask.	8/21/65	Kalamazoo-Minnesota
MODANO, Mike	6-3	190	L	Livonia, MI	6/7/70	Minnesota
NORTON, Darcy	6-1	190	L	Camrose, Alta.	5/2/67	Kalamazoo
PROPP, Brian	5-10	195	L	Lanigan, Sask.	2/15/59	Philadelphia-Boston
QUINTIN, J.F.	6-1	180	L	St. Jean, Que.	5/28/69	Kalamazoo
ROBINSON, Scott	6-3	180	L	100 Mile House, B.C.	3/29/64	Kalamazoo-Minnesota
SINISALO, Ilkka	6-0	200	L	Valeakoski, Fin.	7/10/58	Philadelphia
SMITH, Bobby	6-4	214	L	North Sydney, N.S.	2/12/58	Montreal
SULLIVAN, Mike	6-2	200	L	Marshfield, MA	2/27/68	Boston U.
SULLIVAN, Kevin	6-2	180	L	S. Windsor, CT	5/16/68	Princeton
THYER, Mario	5-11	170	L	Montreal, Que.	9/29/66	Kalamazoo-Minnesota
DEFENSEMEN						
BILLECK, Laurie	6-3	210	R	Dauphin, Man.	2/2/71	Prince Albert
CHAMBERS, Shawn	6-2	200	L	Sterling Hts., MI	10/11/66	Minnesota
CICCONE, Enrico	6-4	200	L	Montreal, Que.	4/10/70	Trois-Rivieres
GAETZ, Link	6-4	210	L	Vancouver, B.C.	10/2/68	Kalamazoo-Minnesota
GILES, Curt	5-8	175	L	The Pas, Man.	11/30/58	Minnesota
HATCHER, Derian	6-5	205	L	Sterling Hts., MI	6/4/72	North Bay
KECZMER, Dan	6-1	190	L	Mt. Clemens, MI	5/25/68	Lake Superior St.
KOLSTAD, Dean	6-6	210	L	Edmonton, Alta.	6/16/68	Kalamazoo
MACKEY, Dave	6-4	200	L	Richmond, B.C.	7/24/66	Minnesota
MacLEOD, Pat	5-11	190	L	Melfort, Sask.	6/15/69	Kalamazoo
MOORE, Jayson	6-1	190	R	Souris, Man.	1/12/69	Flint-Kalamazoo-Min.
MURPHY, Larry	6-2	210	R	Scarborough, Ont.	3/8/61	Minnesota
MUSIL, Frantisek	6-3	215	L	Pardubice, Czech.	12/17/64	Minnesota
PEDERSON, Tom	5-9	165	R	Bloomington, MN	1/14/70	U. of Minnesota
PITLICK, Lance	6-0	185	R	New Hope, MN	11/5/67	U. of Minnesota
SCREMIN, Claudio	6-2	205	R	Burnaby, B.C.	5/28/68	Maine
TINORDI, Mark	6-4	205	L	Red Deer, Alta.	5/9/66	Minnesota
WILKINSON, Neil	6-3	190	R	Selkirk, Man.	10/16/67	Kalamazoo-Minnesota
ZETTLER, Rob	6-3	190	L	Sept. Iles, Que.	3/8/68	Kalamazoo-Minnesota

GOALTENDERS	HT	WT	C	Place of Birth	Date	1989-90 Club
BERTHIAUME, Daniel	5-9	150	L	Longueil, Que.	1/26/66	Winnipeg-Minnesota
BLUE, John	5-10	190	L	Huntington Beach, CA	2/19/66	Kalamazoo-Knoxville-Phoenix
CASEY, John	5-10	155	L	Grand Rapids, MN	3/29/62	Minnesota
MYLLYS, Jarno	5-8	160	L	Sovanlinna, Fin.	5/29/65	Kalamazoo-Minnesota
TAKKO, Kari	6-2	185	L	Uusikaupunki, Fin.	6/23/62	Kalamazoo-Minnesota
TUREK, Roman	6-3	190	L	Pisek, Czech.	5/21/70	Plzen (Czech.)

General Managers' History

Wren A. Blair, 1967-68 to 1973-74; Jack Gordon, 1974-75 to 1976-77; Lou Nanne, 1977-78 to 1987-88; Jack Ferreira, 1988-89 to 1989-90; Bob Clarke 1990-91.

Coaching History

Wren Blair, 1967-68; John Muckler and Wren Blair, 1968-69; Wren Blair and Charlie Bruns, 1969-70; Jackie Gordon, 1970-71 to 1972-73; Jackie Gordon and Parker MacDonald, 1973-74; Jackie Gordon and Charlie Burns, 1974-75; Ted Harris, 1975-76 to 1976-77; Ted Harris, Andre Beaulieu, Lou Nanne, 1977-78; Harry Howell and Glen Sonmor, 1978-79; Glen Sonmor, 1979-80 to 1981-82; Glen Sonmor and Murray Oliver, 1982-83; Bill Mahoney, 1983-84 to 1984-85; Lorne Henning, 1985-86; Lorne Henning and Glen Sonmor, 1986-87; Herb Brooks, 1987-88; Pierre Page, 1988-89 to 1989-90; Bob Gainey, 1990-91.

1989-90 Scoring

Regular Season

* rookie

Pos	#	Player	Team	GP	G	A	Pts	+/–	PIM	PP	SH	GW	GT	S	%
L	23	Brian Bellows	MIN	80	55	44	99	3–	72	21	1	9	0	300	18.3
C	7	Neal Broten	MIN	80	23	62	85	16–	45	9	1	4	0	212	10.8
C	15	Dave Gagner	MIN	79	40	38	78	1–	54	10	0	3	0	238	16.8
C	9	*Mike Modano	MIN	80	29	46	75	7–	63	12	0	2	0	172	16.9
D	8	Larry Murphy	MIN	77	10	58	68	13–	44	4	0	1	1	173	5.8
R	22	Ulf Dahlen	NYR	63	18	18	36	4–	30	13	0	4	0	111	16.2
			MIN	13	2	4	6	1	0	0	0	0	0	24	8.3
			TOTAL	76	20	22	42	3–	30	13	0	4	0	135	14.8
C	14	Aaron Broten	N.J.	42	10	8	18	15–	36	1	2	0	0	83	12.0
			MIN	35	9	9	18	8–	22	0	0	2	0	65	13.8
			TOTAL	77	19	17	36	23–	58	1	2	2	0	148	12.8
R	37	*Don Barber	MIN	44	15	19	34	4	32	4	0	2	0	100	15.0
L	17	Basil McRae	MIN	66	9	17	26	5–	351	2	0	2	0	95	9.5
D	26	Shawn Chambers	MIN	78	8	18	26	2–	81	0	1	2	0	116	6.9
L	12	Stewart Gavin	MIN	80	12	13	25	9	76	0	3	1	0	146	8.2
L	10	Gaetan Duchesne	MIN	72	12	8	20	5	33	0	1	1	0	93	12.9
C	21	Perry Berezan	MIN	64	3	12	15	4–	31	0	0	0	0	75	4.0
D	5	Ville Siren	MIN	53	1	13	14	1	60	0	0	0	0	53	1.9
D	2	Curt Giles	MIN	74	1	12	13	3	48	0	0	0	0	55	1.8
D	24	Mark Tinordi	MIN	66	3	7	10	0	240	1	0	0	0	50	6.0
D	6	Frantisek Musil	MIN	56	2	8	10	0	109	0	0	1	0	78	2.6
R	43	*Helmut Balderis	MIN	26	3	6	9	0	2	2	0	0	0	30	10.0
D	41	*Rob Zettler	MIN	31	0	8	8	7–	45	0	0	0	0	21	.0
L	16	*Clark Donatelli	MIN	25	3	3	6	11–	17	0	0	1	0	25	12.0
R	27	Shane Churla	MIN	53	2	3	5	4–	292	0	0	1	0	40	5.0
D	39	*Neil Wilkinson	MIN	36	0	5	5	1–	100	0	0	0	0	36	.0
G	30	Jon Casey	MIN	61	0	3	3	0	18	0	0	0	0	0	.0
L	28	Dave Mackey	MIN	16	2	0	2	3–	28	0	0	1	0	8	25.0
L	18	Curt Fraser	MIN	8	1	0	1	5–	22	0	0	0	0	7	14.3
G	1	Kari Takko	MIN	21	0	1	1	0	2	0	0	0	0	0	.0
G	33	Daniel Berthiaume	WPG	24	0	1	1	0	6	0	0	0	0	0	.0
			MIN	5	0	0	0	0	2	0	0	0	0	0	.0
			TOTAL	29	0	1	1	0	8	0	0	0	0	0	.0
R	48	*Scott Robinson	MIN	1	0	0	0	0	2	0	0	0	0	0	.0
C	22	*Mitch Messier	MIN	2	0	0	0	2–	0	0	0	0	0	1	.0
L	45	*Mike McHugh	MIN	3	0	0	0	1–	0	0	0	0	0	2	.0
D	3	Ken Leiter	MIN	4	0	0	0	2–	0	0	0	0	0	5	.0
G	35	*Jarmo Myllys	MIN	4	0	0	0	0	0	0	0	0	0	0	.0
D	36	*Link Gaetz	MIN	5	0	0	0	5–	33	0	0	0	0	4	.0
D	38	*Jay More	MIN	5	0	0	0	1	16	0	0	0	0	4	.0
C	47	*Mario Thyer	MIN	5	0	0	0	3–	0	0	0	0	0	4	.0
C	20	*Peter Lappin	MIN	6	0	0	0	5–	2	0	0	0	0	8	.0

Goaltending

No.	Goaltender	GPI	Mins	Avg	W	L	T	EN	SO	GA	SA	S%
30	Jon Casey	61	3407	3.22	31	22	4	5	3	183	1757	.896
33	Daniel Berthiaume	5	240	3.50	1	3	0	0	0	14	104	.865
1	Kari Takko	21	1012	4.03	4	12	0	4	0	68	482	.859
35	*Jarmo Myllys	4	156	6.15	0	3	0	1	0	16	83	.807
	Totals	**80**	**4833**	**3.61**	**36**	**40**	**4**	**10**	**3**	**291**	**2426**	**.880**

Playoffs

Pos	#	Player	Team	GP	G	A	Pts	+/–	PIM	PP	SH	GW	OT	S	%
L	23	Brian Bellows	MIN	7	4	3	7	4–	10	3	0	1	0	28	14.3
R	37	*Don Barber	MIN	7	3	3	6	2–	8	2	0	1	0	14	21.4
C	15	Dave Gagner	MIN	7	2	3	5	3–	16	1	0	0	0	28	7.1
R	22	Ulf Dahlen	MIN	7	1	4	5	2–	2	0	0	0	0	19	5.3
C	14	Aaron Broten	MIN	7	0	5	5	2–	8	0	0	0	0	18	.0
C	7	Neal Broten	MIN	7	2	2	4	2	18	1	0	0	0	13	15.4
D	26	Shawn Chambers	MIN	7	2	1	3	5–	10	1	0	0	0	13	15.4
D	8	Larry Murphy	MIN	7	1	2	3	4–	31	0	0	1	0	16	6.3
C	9	*Mike Modano	MIN	7	1	1	2	3–	12	0	0	0	0	17	5.9
L	12	Stewart Gavin	MIN	7	0	2	2	3–	12	0	0	0	0	4	.0
D	39	*Neil Wilkinson	MIN	7	0	2	2	1	11	0	0	0	0	8	.0
C	21	Perry Berezan	MIN	5	1	0	1	2–	0	0	0	0	0	7	14.3
L	17	Basil McRae	MIN	7	1	0	1	1	24	0	0	0	0	5	20.0
D	2	Curt Giles	MIN	7	0	1	1	2–	6	0	0	0	0	6	.0
D	24	Mark Tinordi	MIN	7	0	1	1	1	16	0	0	0	0	5	.0
G	1	Kari Takko	MIN	1	0	0	0	0	0	0	0	0	0	0	.0
C	47	*Mario Thyer	MIN	1	0	0	0	0	2	0	0	0	0	0	.0
D	5	Ville Siren	MIN	3	0	0	0	1–	2	0	0	0	0	3	.0
D	6	Frantisek Musil	MIN	4	0	0	0	2–	14	0	0	0	0	5	.0
G	30	Jon Casey	MIN	7	0	0	0	0	8	0	0	0	0	0	.0
R	27	Shane Churla	MIN	7	0	0	0	1	44	0	0	0	0	3	.0
L	10	Gaetan Duchesne	MIN	7	0	0	0	0	6	0	0	0	0	8	.0

Goaltending

No.	Goaltender	GPI	Mins	Avg	W	L	EN	SO	GA	SA	S%
1	Kari Takko	1	4	.00	0	0	0	0	0	0	.000
30	Jon Casey	7	415	3.04	3	4	0	1	21	219	.904
	Totals	**7**	**420**	**3.00**	**3**	**4**	**0**	**1**	**21**	**219**	**.904**

Captains' History

Bob Woytowich, 1967-68; Elmer Vasko, 1968-69; Claude Larose, 1969-70; Ted Harris, 1970-71 to 1973-74; Bill Goldsworthy, 1974-75, 1975-76; Bill Hogaboam, 1976-77; Nick Beverly, 1977-78; J.P. Parise, 1978-79; Paul Shmyr, 1979-80, 1980-81; Tim Young, 1981-82; Craig Hartsburg, 1982-83; Brian Bellows, Craig Hartsburg, 1983-84; Craig Hartsburg, 1984-85 to 1987-88; Curt Fraser, Bob Rouse and Curt Giles, 1988-89; Curt Giles, 1989-90 to date.

Club Records

Team

(Figures in brackets for season records are games played; records for fewest points, wins, ties, losses, goals, goals against are for 70 or more games)

Most Points	96	1982-83 (80)
Most Wins	40	1982-83 (80)
Most Ties	22	1969-70 (76)
Most Losses	53	1975-76, 1977-78 (80)
Most Goals	346	1981-82 (80)
Most Goals Against	349	1987-88 (80)
Fewest Points	45	1977-78 (80)
Fewest Wins	18	1968-69 (76)
		1977-78 (80)
Fewest Ties	4	1989-90 (80)
Fewest Losses	23	1981-82 (80)
Fewest Goals	189	1968-69 (76)
Fewest Goals Against	191	1971-72 (78)

Longest Winning Streak
Over-all .... 7 Mar. 16-28/80
Home .... 11 Nov. 4-
               Dec. 27/72
Away .... 5 Dec. 2-16/67
               Feb. 5-
               Mar. 5/83

Longest Undefeated Streak
Over-all .... 12 Feb. 18-
               Mar. 15/82
               (9 wins, 3 ties)
Home .... 13 Oct. 28-
               Dec. 27/72
               (12 wins, 1 tie)
               Nov. 21-
               Jan. 9/80
               (10 wins, 3 ties)
Away .... 6 Nov. 30-
               Dec. 16/67
               (5 wins, 1 tie)
               Nov. 7-27/71
               (5 wins, 1 tie)
               Nov. 9-Dec. 3/83
               (5 wins, 1 tie)

Longest Losing Streak
Over-all .... 10 Feb. 1-20/70
Home .... 6 Jan. 17-
               Feb. 4/70
Away .... 8 Oct. 19-
               Nov. 13/75; Jan. 28-
               Mar. 3/88

Longest Winless Streak
Over-all .... 20 Jan. 15-
               Feb. 28/70
               (15 losses, 5 ties)
Home .... 12 Jan. 17-
               Feb. 25/70
               (8 losses, 4 ties)
Away .... 23 Oct. 25/74-
               Jan. 28/75
               (19 losses, 4 ties)

Most Shutouts, Season 7 1972-73 (78)
Most PIM, Season 2,313 1987-88 (80)
Most Goals, Game .... 15 Nov. 11/81
               (Wpg. 2 at Minn. 15)

Individual

Most Seasons .... 12 Fred Barrett
Most Games .... 730 Fred Barrett
Most Goals, Career ..... 332 Dino Ciccarelli
Most Assists, Career ..... 444 Neal Broten
Most Points Career ..... 660 Neal Broten
               (216 goals, 444 assists)
Most PIM, Career ..... 1,000 Brad Maxwell
Most Shutouts, Career ..... 26 Cesare Maniago
Longest Consecutive
   Games Streak .... 442 Danny Grant
               (Dec. 4/68-Apr. 7/74)
Most Goals, Season ...... 55 Dino Ciccarelli
               (1981-82)
               Brian Bellows
               (1989-90)
Most Assists, Season ..... 76 Neal Broten
               (1985-86)
Most Point, Season ..... 114 Bobby Smith
               (1981-82)
               (43 goals, 71 assists)
Most PIM, Season ...... 382 Basil McRae
               (1987-88)
Most Points, Defenseman
   Season .... 77 Craig Hartsburg
               (1981-82)
               (17 goals, 60 assists)
Most Points, Center,
   Season .... 114 Bobby Smith
               (1981-82)
               (43 goals, 71 assists)

Most Points, Right Wing,
   Season .... 107 Dino Ciccarelli
               (1981-82)
               (55 goals, 52 assists)
Most Point, Left Wing,
   Season .... 99 Brian Bellows
               (1989-90)
               (55 goals, 44 assists)
Most Points, Rookie,
   Season .... 98 Neal Broten
               (1981-82)
               (38 goals, 60 assists)
Most Shutouts, Season ..... 6 Cesare Maniago
               (1967-68)
Most Goals, Game .... 5 Tim Young
               (Jan. 15/79)
Most Assists, Game .... 5 Murray Oliver
               (Oct. 24/71)
               Larry Murphy
               (Oct. 17/89)
Most Points, Game .... 7 Bobby Smith
               (Nov. 11/81)

All-time Record vs. Other Clubs

Regular Season

		At Home						On Road						Total					
	GP	W	L	T	GF	GA	PTS	GP	W	L	T	GF	GA	PTS	GP	W	L	T	GF	GA	PTS
Boston	48	11	28	9	129	185	31	49	6	36	7	116	225	19	97	17	64	16	245	410	50
Buffalo	40	16	18	6	123	128	38	41	9	23	9	107	156	27	81	25	41	15	230	284	65
Calgary	35	17	13	5	130	113	39	35	4	21	10	94	144	18	70	21	34	15	224	257	57
Chicago	73	32	31	10	265	257	74	73	18	46	9	196	302	45	146	50	77	19	461	559	119
Detroit	69	38	20	11	271	198	87	68	25	31	12	234	265	62	137	63	51	23	505	463	149
Edmonton	17	4	9	4	60	67	12	18	1	12	5	60	98	7	35	5	21	9	120	165	19
Hartford	17	10	6	1	78	61	21	18	9	9	0	66	67	18	35	19	15	1	144	128	39
Los Angeles	53	33	13	7	216	139	73	51	14	23	14	158	193	42	104	47	36	21	374	332	115
Montreal	47	12	25	10	122	170	34	46	9	31	6	117	202	24	93	21	56	16	239	372	58
New Jersey	33	20	7	6	137	84	46	32	14	15	3	106	107	31	65	34	22	9	243	191	77
NY Islanders	35	12	18	5	101	137	29	34	8	18	8	100	139	24	69	20	36	13	201	276	53
NY Rangers	49	15	27	7	152	194	37	48	10	29	9	133	173	29	97	25	56	16	285	367	66
Philadelphia	53	21	20	12	173	184	54	55	8	37	10	123	217	26	108	29	57	22	296	401	80
Pittsburgh	51	29	17	5	200	174	63	52	15	32	5	139	198	35	103	44	49	10	339	372	98
Quebec	18	10	6	2	73	60	22	17	2	13	2	43	88	6	35	12	19	4	116	148	28
St. Louis	77	34	28	15	265	232	83	79	24	40	15	231	284	63	156	58	68	30	496	516	146
Toronto	70	36	26	8	277	239	80	71	25	32	14	240	261	64	141	61	58	22	517	500	144
Vancouver	43	27	9	7	182	119	61	44	14	23	7	139	181	35	87	41	32	14	321	300	96
Washington	28	12	8	8	107	83	32	27	9	12	6	83	90	24	55	21	20	14	190	173	56
Winnipeg	20	12	6	2	94	61	26	19	9	9	1	69	70	19	39	21	15	3	163	131	45
Defunct Club	33	19	8	6	123	86	44	32	10	16	6	84	105	26	65	29	24	12	207	191	70
Totals	909	420	343	146	3278	2971	986	909	243	508	158	2638	3565	644	1818	663	851	304	5916	6536	1630

Playoffs

	Series	W	L	GP	W	L	T	GF	GA	Last Mtg.	Round	Result
Boston	1	1	0	3	3	0	0	20	13	1981	PR	W 3-0
Buffalo	2	1	1	7	4	3	0	26	28	1981	QF	W 4-1
Calgary	1	1	0	6	4	2	0	25	18	1981	SF	W 4-2
Chicago	5	1	4	27	10	17	0	96	103	1990	DSF	L 3-4
Edmonton	1	0	1	4	0	4	0	10	22	1984	CF	L 0-4
Los Angeles	1	1	0	7	4	3	0	26	21	1968	QF	W 4-3
Montreal	2	1	1	13	6	7	0	37	48	1980	QF	W 4-3
NY Islanders	1	0	1	5	1	4	0	16	26	1981	F	L 1-4
Philadelphia	2	0	2	11	3	8	0	26	41	1980	SF	L 1-4
St. Louis	8	3	5	46	22	24	0	136	135	1989	DSF	L 1-4
Toronto	2	2	0	7	6	1	0	35	26	1983	DSF	W 3-1
Totals	26	11	15	136	63	73	0	453	481			

Abbreviations: Round: F Final; **CF** conference final; **DF** division final; **DSF** division semi-final; **SF** semi-final; **QF** quarter-final. **PR** preliminary round. **GA** goals against; **GF** goals for.

Playoff Results 1990-86

Year	Round	Opponent	Result	GF	GA
1990	DSF	Chicago	L 3-4	18	21
1989	DSF	St. Louis	L 1-4	15	23
1986	DSF	St. Louis	L 2-3	20	18

1989-90 Results

		Home					Away	
Oct.	5	NY Islanders	6-5	Oct.	7	Hartford	6-4
	12	St Louis	3-0		8	Buffalo	2-2
	14	Quebec	3-2		17	NY Islanders	6-3
	25	Buffalo	4-2		18	Detroit	3-4
	28	Philadelphia	6-5		21	Quebec	2-7
	31	Toronto	4-6		26	St Louis	1-4
Nov.	4	Chicago	3-0	Nov.	2	Chicago	3-4
	9	Detroit	5-1		6	Toronto	1-2
	11	Calgary	3-2		15	New Jersey	2-1
	12	Toronto	6-3		16	Philadelphia	3-6
	18	St Louis	3-0		21	St Louis	4-7
	22	Toronto	6-3		30	Calgary	2-5
	24	New Jersey	7-6	Dec.	2	Edmonton	1-6
	26	Chicago	5-3		3	Vancouver	5-6
Dec.	6	Montreal	1-4		8	Detroit	1-2
	9	Detroit	1-3		16	Toronto	4-3
	12	Vancouver	2-4		21	Boston	2-4
	14	Pittsburgh	4-4		23	Hartford	3-4
	19	Edmonton	0-5		26	Winnipeg	3-5
	31	St Louis	2-1		28	Chicago	1-1
Jan.	4	NY Rangers	8-2		30	St Louis	2-3
	6	Detroit	4-3	Jan.	9	Detroit	0-9
	11	NY Islanders	4-8		15	Montreal	3-4
	13	Detroit	6-4		17	Chicago	1-3
	18	Quebec	7-4		24	Toronto	3-7
	29	Winnipeg	4-2		26	Vancouver	6-3
	31	Washington	3-4		27	Calgary	2-5
Feb.	7	Hartford	3-5	Feb.	3	Philadelphia*	6-7
	10	Chicago*	6-4		4	NY Rangers*	3-4
	13	St Louis	1-2		11	Washington*	3-5
	15	Los Angeles	6-3		18	Edmonton	2-3
	24	Boston	2-3		21	Los Angeles	2-4
	27	Winnipeg	8-3	Mar.	4	Pittsburgh*	6-8
Mar.	3	Montreal	3-2		12	Toronto	4-1
	7	Chicago	3-0		17	Pittsburgh	6-2
	10	NY Rangers*	2-2		22	Detroit	5-1
	13	New Jersey	1-3		24	Boston*	7-6
	18	Washington	3-4		29	Buffalo	2-4
	20	Los Angeles	5-2		31	St Louis	6-3
	26	Toronto	5-4	Apr.	1	Chicago	1-4

* Denotes afternoon game.

Entry Draft Selections 1990-76

1990
Pick
8	Derian Hatcher
50	Laurie Billeck
70	Cal McGowan
71	Frank Kovacs
92	Enrico Ciccone
113	Roman Turek
134	Jeff Levy
155	Doug Barrault
176	Joe Biondi
197	Troy Binnie
218	Ole Dahlstrom
239	John McKersie

1989
Pick
7	Doug Zmolek
28	Mike Craig
60	Murray Garbutt
75	Jean-François Quintin
87	Pat MacLeod
91	Bryan Schoen
97	Rhys Hollyman
112	Scott Cashman
154	Jonathan Pratt
175	Kenneth Blum
196	Artur Irbe
217	Tom Pederson
238	Helmut Balderis

1988
Pick
1	Mike Modano
40	Link Gaetz
43	Shaun Kane
64	Jeffrey Stolp
148	Ken MacArthur
169	Travis Richards
190	Ari Matilainen
211	Grant Bischoff
232	Trent Andison

1987
Pick
6	David Archibald
35	Scott McCrady
48	Kevin Kaminski
73	John Weisbrod
88	Teppo Kivela
109	D'Arcy Norton
130	Timo Kulonen
151	Don Schmidt
172	Jarmo Myllys
193	Larry Olimb
214	Mark Felicio
235	Dave Shields

1986
Pick
12	Warren Babe
30	Neil Wilkinson
33	Dean Kolstad
54	Eric Bennett
55	Rob Zettler
58	Brad Turner
75	Kirk Tomlinson
96	Jari Gronstand
159	Scott Mathias
180	Lance Pitlick
201	Dan Keczmer
222	Garth Joy
243	Kurt Stahura

1985
Pick
51	Stephane Roy
69	Mike Berger
90	Dwight Mullins
111	Mike Mullowney
132	Mike Kelfer
153	Ross Johnson
174	Tim Helmer
195	Gordon Ernst
216	Ladislav Lubina
237	Tommy Sjodin

1984
Pick
13	David Quinn
46	Ken Hodge
76	Miroslav Maly
89	Jiri Poner
97	Kari Takko
118	Gary McColgan
139	Vladimir Kyhos
160	Darin MacInnis
181	Duane Wahlin
201	Mike Orn
222	Tom Terwilliger
242	Mike Nightengale

1983
Pick
1	Brian Lawton
36	Malcolm Parks
38	Frantisek Musil
56	Mitch Messier
76	Brian Durand
96	Rich Geist
116	Tom McComb
136	Sean Toomey
156	Don Biggs
176	Paul Pulis
196	Milos Riha
212	Oldrich Valek
236	Paul Roff

1982
Pick
2	Brian Bellows
59	Wally Chapman
80	Rob Rouse
81	Dusan Pasek
101	Marty Wiitala
122	Todd Carlile
143	Victor Zhluktov
164	Paul Miller
185	Pat Micheletti
206	Arnold Kadlec
227	Scott Knutson

1981
Pick
13	Ron Meighan
27	Dave Donnelly
31	Mike Sands
33	Tom Hirsch
34	Dave Preuss
41	Jali Wahlsten
69	Terry Tait
76	Jim Malwitz
97	Kelly Hubbard
118	Paul Guay
139	Jim Archibald
160	Kari Kanervo
181	Scott Bjugstad
202	Steve Kudebeh

1980
Pick
16	Brad Palmer
32	Don Beaupre
53	Randy Velischek
79	Mark Huglen
100	Dave Jensen
121	Dan Zavarise
142	Bill Stewart
163	Jeff Walters
184	Bob Lakso
205	Dave Richter

1979
Pick
6	Craig Hartsburg
10	Tom McCarthy
42	Neal Broten
63	Kevin Maxwell
90	Jim Dobson
111	Brian Gualazzi

1978
Pick
1	Bobby Smith
19	Steve Payne
24	Steve Christoff
54	Curt Giles
70	Roy Kerling
87	Bob Bergloff
104	Kim Spencer
121	Mike Cotter
138	Brent Gogol
155	Mike Seide

1977
Pick
7	Brad Maxwell
25	Dave Semenko
61	Kevin McCloskey
79	Bob Parent
97	Jamie Gallimore
115	J.P. Sanvido
133	Greg Tebbutt
151	Keith Hanson

1976
Pick
3	Glen Sharpley
31	Jim Roberts
39	Don Jackson
51	Ron Zanussi
75	Mike Federko
93	Phil Verchota
111	Dave Delich
129	Jeff Barr

Club Directory

Metropolitan Sports Center
7901 Cedar Avenue South
Bloomington, Minnesota
55425
Phone 612/853-9333
FAX 612/853-9432
GM FAX 612/853-9408
TWX 910-576-2853
ENVOY ID
Front Office: STARS. GM
Public
Relations: STARS. PR
Capacity: 15,093

Governor	Norman N. Green
Alternate Governors	Morris Belzberg, Bob Clarke, Lou Nanne, Howard Baldwin

Owner
Norman N. Green

Executive
President & CEO	Norman N. Green
Vice-President/General Manager	Bob Clarke
Vice-President of Administration	Dick Arneson
Vice President of Marketing & P.R.	Lou Nanne
Vice-President of Finance	George Wettstaedt

Hockey
Head Coach	Bob Gainey
Assistant Coaches	Doug Jarvis, Andy Murray
Director of Player Personnel	Les Jackson
Team Services	Doug Armstrong
Secretary	Jane Marostica
Chief Scout	Dennis Patterson
Scouts	Craig Button, Doug Overton, Wayne Simpson
Head Athletic Trainer	Dave Surprenant
Assistant Trainer	Dave Smith
Equipment Manager	Mark Baribeau
Team Physicians	Dr. William Simonet, Dr. George Nagabods, Dr. John Schaefer, Dr. Jim Schaffausen
Team Dentists	Dr. Paul Belvedere, Dr. Doug Lambert
Team Physical Therapist	Tom Coplin

Administration
Director of Merchandise Sales	Peter Jocketty
Director of Ticket Sales	Bill Cox
Director of Public Relations and Advertising	Elaine Waddell
Director of Met Center	Jack Larson
Director of Operations	Eric Kruse
Communications Manager	Joan Preston
Legal Counsel	Jim Erickson

Team and Building Information
Location of Press Boxes	North Side — Press and Radio South Side — Television
Dimensions of Rink	200 feet by 85 feet
Ends of Rink	Unbreakable glass extends above boards around rink
Uniforms	White base at home, Green base on the road
Radio	KSTP-AM 1500; Al Shaver
Television	KMSP-TV, Channel 9; Doug McLeod, Lou Nanne

Retired Numbers
19	Bill Masterton	1967-1968

General Manager

CLARKE, ROBERT EARLE (BOB)
General Manager, Minnesota North Stars. Born in Flin Flon, Man., August 13, 1949.

After 21 seasons with the Philadelphia Flyers, Bob Clarke joined the Minnesota North Stars on June 8, 1990. Clarke, 41, spent the previous six seasons as general manager of the Flyers, for whom he played 15 seasons (1969-84). During his tenure as Flyers' general manager, Clarke's team compiled a record of 256-177-47.

As a player, the former Philadelphia captain led his club to Stanley Cup championships in 1974 and 1975 and captured numerous individual awards, including the Hart Trophy as the League's most valuable player in 1973, 1975 and 1976. The four-time All-Star also received the Masterton Memorial Trophy (perserverance and dedication) in 1972 and the Frank J. Selke Trophy (top defensive forward) in 1983. He appeared in nine All-Star Games and was elected to the Hockey Hall of Fame in 1987. He was awarded the Lester Patrick Trophy in 1979-80 in recognition of his contribution to hockey in the United States. Clarke appeared in 1,144 regular-season games, recording 358 goals and 852 assists for 1,210 points. He also added 119 points in 136 playoff games.

Coach

GAINEY, BOB
Coach, Minnesota North Stars. Born in Peterborough, Ont., December 13, 1953.

Gainey, 36, was appointed head coach of the Minnesota North Stars on June 19, 1990, following a 16-year NHL playing career and a one-year coaching stint in Epinal, France.

Gainey was Montreal's first choice, eighth overall, in the 1973 Amateur Draft. During his 16-year career with the Canadiens, Gainey was a member of five Stanley Cup-winning teams and was named the Conn Smythe Trophy winner in 1979. He was a four-time recipient of the Frank Selke Trophy (1978-81), awarded to the League's top defensive forward, and participated in four NHL All-Star Games (1977, 1978, 1980 and 1981). He served as team captain for eight seasons (1981-89). During his career, he played in 1,160 regular-season games, registering 239 goals and 262 assists for 501 points. In addition, he tallied 73 points (25-48-73) in 182 post-season games. He retired in July of 1989 and served as player/coach for Epinal, a second division French team.

Montreal Canadiens

1989-90 Results: 41W-28L-11T 93PTS. Third, Adams Division

Defensive forwards Mike McPhee (far left) and Brian Skrudland.

Schedule

Home		Away	
Oct. Sat. 6 Buffalo		**Oct.** Thur. 4 Buffalo	
Mon. 8 Hartford		Fri. 12 NY Rangers	
Mon. 15 Washington		Sat. 13 Hartford	
Sat. 20 Philadelphia		Wed. 17 Buffalo	
Wed. 24 NY Islanders		Thur. 18 Detroit	
Nov. Sat. 3 Detroit		Tues. 23 Pittsburgh	
Sun. 4 Minnesota		Sat. 27 St Louis	
Wed. 7 Boston		Sun. 28 Chicago	
Sat. 10 New Jersey		Wed. 31 Hartford	
Sun. 11 Quebec		**Nov.** Tues. 13 New Jersey	
Sat. 24 Los Angeles		Thur. 15 Philadelphia	
Sun. 25 Winnipeg		Sat. 17 Boston	
Wed. 28 Buffalo		Mon. 19 Quebec	
Dec. Sat. 1 Calgary		Fri. 30 Washington	
Mon. 3 Hartford		**Dec.** Wed. 5 Hartford	
Sat. 8 Boston		Thur. 6 Boston	
Wed. 19 Quebec		Wed. 12 Toronto	
Sat. 22 NY Rangers		Sat. 15 Winnipeg	
Jan. Sat. 5 Quebec		Tues. 18 Quebec	
Sun. 6 Pittsburgh		Sun. 23 Philadelphia	
Wed. 9 NY Islanders		Thur. 27 Vancouver	
Sat. 12 Washington		Sat. 29 Los Angeles	
Sun. 13 St Louis		Mon. 31 Calgary	
Wed. 23 Toronto		**Jan.** Wed. 2 Edmonton	
Sat. 26 Buffalo*		Tues. 15 Minnesota	
Sun. 27 Boston*		Thur. 17 St Louis	
Wed. 30 Winnipeg		Thur. 31 Boston	
Feb. Mon. 4 Minnesota		**Feb.** Sat. 2 NY Islanders	
Wed. 6 Chicago		Thur. 7 Quebec	
Sat. 9 NY Rangers		Fri. 15 Buffalo	
Wed. 13 Boston		Wed. 20 Hartford	
Sat. 16 Hartford		Wed. 27 Detroit	
Sat. 23 Toronto		**Mar.** Fri. 1 Vancouver	
Mar. Sat. 9 Vancouver		Sat. 2 Edmonton	
Sun. 10 Los Angeles		Mon. 4 Calgary	
Sat. 16 Buffalo		Wed. 6 Chicago	
Sun. 17 Edmonton		Tues. 12 Pittsburgh	
Sat. 23 New Jersey		Thur. 14 Boston	
Mon. 25 Hartford		Wed. 20 Buffalo	
Sat. 30 Quebec		Sun. 31 Quebec	

* Denotes afternoon game.

Home Starting Times:
Weeknights .... 7:35 p.m.
Saturdays .... 8:05 p.m.
Sundays .... 7:05 p.m.
Matinees .... 1.05 p.m.

Franchise date: November 22, 1917

Prince of WALES CONFERENCE

74th NHL Season

Year-by-Year Record

Season	GP	Home W	L	T	Road W	L	T	Overall W	L	T	GF	GA	Pts.	Finished	Playoff Result
1989-90	80	26	8	6	15	20	5	41	28	11	288	234	93	3rd, Adams Div.	Lost Div. Final
1988-89	80	30	6	4	23	12	5	53	18	9	315	218	115	1st, Adams Div.	Lost Final
1987-88	80	26	8	6	19	14	7	45	22	13	298	238	103	1st, Adams Div.	Lost Div. Final
1986-87	80	27	9	4	14	20	6	41	29	10	277	241	92	2nd, Adams Div.	Lost Conf. Championship
1985-86	80	25	11	4	15	22	3	40	33	7	330	280	87	**2nd, Adams Div.**	**Won Stanley Cup**
1984-85	80	24	10	6	17	17	6	41	27	12	309	262	94	1st, Adams Div.	Lost Div. Final
1983-84	80	19	19	2	16	21	3	35	40	5	286	295	75	4th, Adams Div.	Lost Conf. Championship
1982-83	80	25	6	9	17	18	5	42	24	14	350	286	98	2nd, Adams Div.	Lost Div. Semi-Final
1981-82	80	25	6	9	21	11	8	46	17	17	360	223	109	1st, Adams Div.	Lost Div. Semi-Final
1980-81	80	31	7	2	14	15	11	45	22	13	332	232	103	1st, Norris Div.	Lost Prelim. Round
1979-80	80	30	7	3	17	13	10	47	20	13	328	240	107	1st, Norris Div.	Lost Quarter-Final
1978-79	80	29	6	5	23	11	6	52	17	11	337	204	115	**1st, Norris Div.**	**Won Stanley Cup**
1977-78	80	32	4	4	27	6	7	59	10	11	359	183	129	**1st, Norris Div.**	**Won Stanley Cup**
1976-77	80	33	1	6	27	7	6	60	8	12	387	171	132	**1st, Norris Div.**	**Won Stanley Cup**
1975-76	80	32	3	5	26	8	6	58	11	11	337	174	127	**1st, Norris Div.**	**Won Stanley Cup**
1974-75	80	27	8	5	20	6	14	47	14	19	374	225	113	1st, Norris Div.	Lost Semi-Final
1973-74	78	24	12	3	21	12	6	45	24	9	293	240	99	2nd, East Div.	Lost Quarter-Final
1972-73	78	29	4	6	23	6	10	52	10	16	329	184	120	**1st, East Div.**	**Won Stanley Cup**
1971-72	78	29	3	7	17	13	9	46	16	16	307	205	108	3rd, East Div.	Lost Quarter-Final
1970-71	78	29	7	3	13	16	10	42	23	13	291	216	97	**3rd, East Div.**	**Won Stanley Cup**
1969-70	76	21	9	8	17	13	8	38	22	16	244	201	92	5th, East Div.	Out of Playoffs
1968-69	76	26	7	5	20	12	6	46	19	11	271	202	103	**1st, East Div.**	**Won Stanley Cup**
1967-68	74	26	5	6	16	17	4	42	22	10	236	167	94	**1st, East Div.**	**Won Stanley Cup**
1966-67	70	19	9	7	13	16	6	32	25	13	202	188	77	2nd,	Lost Final
1965-66	70	23	11	1	18	10	7	41	21	8	239	173	90	**1st,**	**Won Stanley Cup**
1964-65	70	20	8	7	16	15	4	36	23	11	211	185	83	**2nd,**	**Won Stanley Cup**
1963-64	70	22	7	6	14	14	7	36	21	13	209	167	85	1st,	Lost Semi-Final
1962-63	70	15	10	10	13	9	13	28	19	23	225	183	79	3rd,	Lost Semi-Final
1961-62	70	26	2	7	16	12	7	42	14	14	259	166	98	1st,	Lost Semi-Final
1960-61	70	24	6	5	17	13	5	41	19	10	254	188	92	1st,	Lost Semi-Final
1959-60	70	23	4	8	17	14	4	40	18	12	255	178	92	**1st,**	**Won Stanley Cup**
1958-59	70	21	8	6	18	10	7	39	18	13	258	158	91	**1st,**	**Won Stanley Cup**
1957-58	70	23	8	4	20	9	6	43	17	10	250	158	96	**1st,**	**Won Stanley Cup**
1956-57	70	23	6	6	12	17	6	35	23	12	210	155	82	**2nd,**	**Won Stanley Cup**
1955-56	70	29	5	1	16	10	9	45	15	10	222	131	100	**1st,**	**Won Stanley Cup**
1954-55	70	26	5	4	15	13	7	41	18	11	228	157	93	2nd,	Lost Final
1953-54	70	27	5	3	8	19	8	35	24	11	195	141	81	2nd,	Lost Final
1952-53	70	18	12	5	10	11	14	28	23	19	155	148	75	**2nd,**	**Won Stanley Cup**
1951-52	70	22	8	5	12	18	5	34	26	10	195	164	78	2nd,	Lost Final
1950-51	70	17	10	8	8	20	7	25	30	15	173	184	65	3rd,	Lost Final
1949-50	70	17	8	10	12	14	9	29	22	19	172	150	77	2nd,	Lost Semi-Final
1948-49	60	19	8	3	9	15	6	28	23	9	152	126	65	3rd,	Lost Semi-Final
1947-48	60	13	13	4	7	16	7	20	29	11	147	169	51	5th,	Out of Playoffs
1946-47	60	19	6	5	15	10	5	34	16	10	189	138	78	1st,	Lost Final
1945-46	50	16	6	3	12	11	2	28	17	5	172	134	61	**1st,**	**Won Stanley Cup**
1944-45	50	21	2	2	17	6	2	38	8	4	228	121	80	1st,	Lost Semi-Final
1943-44	50	22	0	3	16	5	4	38	5	7	234	109	83	**1st,**	**Won Stanley Cup**
1942-43	50	14	4	7	5	15	5	19	19	12	181	191	50	4th,	Lost Semi-Final
1941-42	48	12	10	2	6	17	1	18	27	3	134	173	39	6th,	Lost Quarter-Final
1940-41	48	11	9	4	5	17	2	16	26	6	121	147	38	6th,	Lost Quarter-Final
1939-40	48	5	14	5	5	19	0	10	33	5	90	167	25	7th,	Out of Playoffs
1938-39	48	8	11	5	7	13	4	15	24	9	115	146	39	6th,	Lost Quarter-Final
1937-38	48	13	4	7	5	13	6	18	17	13	123	128	49	3rd, Cdn. Div.	Lost Quarter-Final
1936-37	48	16	8	0	8	10	6	24	18	6	115	111	54	1st, Cdn. Div.	Lost Semi-Final
1935-36	48	5	11	8	6	15	3	11	26	11	82	123	33	4th, Cdn. Div.	Out of Playoffs
1934-35	48	11	11	2	8	12	4	19	23	6	110	145	44	3rd, Cdn. Div.	Lost Quarter-Final
1933-34	48	16	6	2	6	14	4	22	20	6	99	101	50	2nd, Cdn. Div.	Lost Quarter-Final
1932-33	48	15	5	4	3	20	1	18	25	5	92	115	41	3rd, Cdn. Div.	Lost Quarter-Final
1931-32	48	18	3	3	7	13	4	25	16	7	128	111	57	1st, Cdn. Div.	Lost Semi-Final
1930-31	44	15	3	4	11	7	4	26	10	8	129	89	60	**1st, Cdn. Div.**	**Won Stanley Cup**
1929-30	44	13	5	4	8	9	5	21	14	9	142	114	51	**2nd, Cdn. Div.**	**Won Stanley Cup**
1928-29	44	12	4	6	10	3	9	22	7	15	71	43	59	1st, Cdn. Div.	Lost Semi-Final
1927-28	44	12	7	3	14	4	4	26	11	7	116	48	59	1st, Cdn. Div.	Lost Semi-Final
1926-27	44	15	5	2	13	9	0	28	14	2	99	67	58	2nd, Cdn. Div.	Lost Final
1925-26	36	5	12	1	6	12	0	11	24	1	79	108	23	7th,	Out of Playoffs
1924-25	30	10	5	0	7	6	2	17	11	2	93	56	36	3rd,	Lost Final
1923-24	24	10	2	0	3	9	0	13	11	0	59	48	26	**2nd,**	**Won Stanley Cup**
1922-23	24	10	2	0	3	9	2	13	9	2	73	61	28	2nd,	Lost NHL Final
1921-22	24	9	3	1	4	8	1	12	11	1	88	94	25	3rd,	Out of Playoffs
1920-21	24	8	4	0	5	7	0	13	11	0	112	99	26	3rd and 2nd*	Out of Playoffs
1919-20	24	8	4	0	5	7	0	13	11	0	129	113	26	2nd and 3rd*	Out of Playoffs
1918-19	18	7	2	0	3	6	0	10	8	0	88	78	20	1st and 2nd*	Cup Final but no Decision
1917-18	22	8	3	0	5	6	0	13	9	0	115	84	26	1st and 3rd*	Lost NHL Final

* Season played in two halves with no combined standing at end.
From 1917-18 through 1925-26, NHL champions played against PCHL champions for Stanley Cup.

1990-91 Player Personnel

FORWARDS	HT	WT	S	Place of Birth	Date	1989-90 Club
BOBYCK, Brent	5-10	174	L	Regina, Sask.	4/26/68	North Dakota
BRUNET, Benoit	5-11	184	L	Ste-Anne de Bellevue, Qué.	8/24/68	Sherbrooke
CADIEUX, Steve	6-0	176	L	Ste-Thérèse, Qué.	6/17/69	Shawinigan
CARBONNEAU, Guy	5-11	184	R	Sept-Iles, Qué.	3/18/60	Montréal
CARNBACK, Patrik	6-0	187	L	Goteborg, Sweden	2/1/68	Frolunda (Sweden)
CASSELS, Andrew	6-0	192	L	Bramalea, Ont.	7/23/69	Montréal-Sherbrooke
CHORSKE, Tom	6-1	204	L	Minneapolis, MN	9/18/66	Montréal-Sherbrooke
CORSON, Shayne	6-0	201	L	Barrie, Ont.	8/13/66	Montréal
COURTNALL, Russ	5-11	183	R	Duncan, B.C.	6/2/65	Montréal
CRISTOFOLI, Ed	6-2	203	L	Trail, B.C.	5/14/67	Montréal-Sherbrooke
DESJARDINS, Martin	5-11	165	L	Ste-Rose, Qué.	1/28/67	Montréal-Sherbrooke
DESJARDINS, Norman	5-10	184	R	Montréal, Qué.	3/25/68	Sherbrooke
DIONNE, Gilbert	6-0	194	L	Niagara Falls, Ont.	9/19/70	Kitchener
EWEN,Todd	6-2	220	R	Saskatoon, Sask.	3/22/66	Mtl.-St. L.-Peoria
FERGUSON, John Jr.	6-0	192	L	Winnipeg, Man.	7/7/67	Sherbrooke-Peoria
FLEETWOOD, Brent	6-1	180	L	Edmonton, Alta.	6/4/70	Portland
GILCHRIST, Brent	5-11	181	L	Moose Jaw, Sask.	4/3/67	Montréal
KEANE, Mike	5-10	178	R	Winnipeg, Man.	5/28/67	Montréal
KJELLBERG, Patrik	6-2	196	L	Falun, Sweden	6/17/69	AIK (Sweden)
LEBEAU, Patrick	5-10	172	L	St-Jérôme, Qué.	3/17/70	Victoriaville
LEBEAU, Stéphan	5-10	172	R	St-Jérôme, Qué.	2/28/68	Montreal
LeCLAIR, John	6-1	185	L	St. Albans, VT	7/5/69	U. of Vermont
LEMIEUX, Claude	6-1	213	R	Buckingham, Qué.	7/16/65	Montréal
McPHEE, Mike	6-1	203	L	Sydney, N.S.	7/14/60	Montréal
NESICH, Jim	5-11	183	R	Dearborn, MI	2/22/66	Sherbrooke
PEDERSON, Mark	6-2	196	L	Prelate, Sask.	1/14/68	Montréal-Sherbrooke
RICHER, Stéphane J.J.	6-2	212	R	Ripon, Qué.	6/7/66	Montréal
ROBERGE, Mario	5-11	185	L	Québec, Qué.	1/23/64	Sherbrooke
SAGISSOR, Tom	5-11	202	R	Hastings, MN	9/12/67	U. Wisconsin
SAVARD, Denis	5-10	175	R	Pt. Gatineau, Qué.	2/4/61	Chicago
SKRUDLAND, Brian	6-0	196	L	Peace River, Alta.	7/31/63	Montréal
St. AMOUR, Martin	6-3	194	L	Montréal, Qué.	1/30/70	Trois-Rivières
WALTER, Ryan	6-0	200	L	N. Westmin'r, B.C.	4/23/58	Montréal
WOODLEY, Dan	5-11	188	R	Oklahoma City, OK	12/29/67	Sherbrooke

DEFENSEMEN	HT	WT	S	Place of Birth	Date	1989-90 Club
BISHOP, Mike	6-2	212	L	Sarnia, Ont.	6/15/66	Ft. Wayne-Knoxville
CHARRON, Eric	6-3	191	L	Verdun, Qué.	1/14/70	St Hyacinthe-Sher.
COTE, Alain	6-0	200	R	Montmagny, Qué.	4/14/67	Washington-Baltimore
DAIGNEAULT, J.J.	5-11	185	L	Montréal, Que.	10/12/65	Montréal-Sherbrooke
DARVEAU, Guy	6-1	203	L	Montréal, Qué.	4/7/68	Sherbrooke
DESJARDINS, Eric	6-1	200	R	Rouyn, Qué.	6/14/69	Montréal
DUFRESNE, Donald	6-1	206	R	Québec, Qué.	4/10/67	Montréal-Sherbrooke
GAUTHIER, Luc	5-9	195	R	Longueuil, Qué.	4/19/64	Sherbrooke
HOHENBERGER, H.	5-11	184	R	Villach, Austria	2/8/69	Hull-Sherbrooke
LEFEBVRE, Sylvain	6-2	204	L	Richmond, Qué.	10/14/67	Montréal
LUDWIG, Craig	6-3	222	L	Rhinelander, WI	3/15/61	Montréal
MITCHELL, Roy	6-0	196	R	Edmonton, Alta.	3/14/69	Sherbrooke
ODELEIN, Lyle	5-10	206	L	Quill Lake, Sask.	7/21/68	Montréal-Sherbrooke
RICHARDS, Todd	6-0	180	R	Robindale, MN	10/20/66	Sherbrooke
SCHNEIDER, Mathieu	5-11	189	L	New York, NY	6/12/69	Montréal-Sherbrooke
SVOBODA, Petr	6-1	174	L	Most, Czech.	2/14/66	Montréal

GOALTENDERS	HT	WT	C	Place of Birth	Date	1989-90 Club
BERGERON, J.C.	6-2	192	L	Hauterive, Qué.	10/14/68	Sherbrooke
CHABOT, Frederic	5-11	175	L	Hebertville-Stn., Qué.	2/12/68	Sherbrooke-Ft. Wayne
HAYWARD, Brian	5-10	180	L	Weston, Ont.	6/25/60	Montréal
RACICOT, Andre	5-11	165	L	Rouyn-Noranda, Qué.	6/9/69	Montréal-Sherbrooke
ROY, Patrick	6-0	182	L	Québec, Qué.	10/5/65	Montréal

1989-90 Scoring

Regular Season

* rookie

Pos	#	Player	Team	GP	G	A	Pts	+/-	PIM	PP	SH	GW	GT	S	%
R	44	Stephane Richer	MTL	75	51	40	91	35	46	9	0	8	0	269	19.0
C	27	Shayne Corson	MTL	76	31	44	75	33	144	7	0	6	1	192	16.1
R	6	Russ Courtnall	MTL	80	27	32	59	14	27	3	0	2	2	294	9.2
C	21	Guy Carbonneau	MTL	68	19	36	55	21	37	1	1	3	0	125	15.2
C	39	Brian Skrudland	MTL	59	11	31	42	21	56	4	0	1	0	70	15.7
L	35	Mike McPhee	MTL	56	23	18	41	28	47	0	1	1	2	118	19.5
L	26	Mats Naslund	MTL	72	21	20	41	3	19	6	0	3	0	136	15.4
D	25	Petr Svoboda	MTL	60	5	31	36	20	98	2	0	2	0	90	5.6
C	47	*Stephan Lebeau	MTL	57	15	20	35	13	11	5	0	3	0	79	19.0
D	24	Chris Chelios	MTL	53	9	22	31	20	136	1	2	1	0	123	7.3
C	15	Bobby Smith	MTL	53	12	14	26	4–	35	4	0	2	1	102	11.8
C	41	Brent Gilchrist	MTL	57	9	15	24	3	28	1	0	0	0	80	11.3
R	12	Mike Keane	MTL	74	9	15	24	0	78	1	0	1	0	92	9.8
L	11	Ryan Walter	MTL	70	8	16	24	4	59	1	0	1	0	109	7.3
D	18	*Mathieu Schneider	MTL	44	7	14	21	2	25	5	0	1	0	84	8.3
R	32	Claude Lemieux	MTL	39	8	10	18	8–	106	3	0	1	0	104	7.7
D	28	Eric Desjardins	MTL	55	3	13	16	1	51	1	0	0	0	48	6.3
D	17	Craig Ludwig	MTL	73	1	15	16	24	108	0	0	0	0	49	2.0
D	3	*Sylvain Lefebvre	MTL	68	3	10	13	18	61	0	0	0	0	89	3.4
D	48	J.J. Daigneault	MTL	36	2	10	12	11	14	0	0	1	0	40	5.0
R	36	Todd Ewen	STL	3	0	0	0	2–	11	0	0	0	0	3	.0
			MTL	41	4	6	10	1	158	0	0	2	0	26	15.4
			TOTAL	44	4	6	10	1–	169	0	0	2	0	29	13.8
G	33	Patrick Roy	MTL	54	0	5	5	0	0	0	0	0	0	0	.0
L	31	*Tom Chorske	MTL	14	3	1	4	2	2	0	0	0	0	19	15.8
D	34	*Donald Dufresne	MTL	18	0	4	4	1	23	0	0	0	0	6	.0
C	43	*Andrew Cassels	MTL	6	2	0	2	1	2	0	0	1	0	5	40.0
C	36	*Martin Desjardins	MTL	8	0	2	2	4–	2	0	0	0	0	7	.0
D	38	*Lyle Odelein	MTL	8	0	2	2	1–	33	0	0	0	0	1	.0
L	14	*Mark Pederson	MTL	9	0	2	2	0	2	0	0	0	0	10	.0
L	46	*Ed Cristofoli	MTL	9	0	1	1	1–	4	0	0	0	0	6	.0
G	53	*Andre Racicot	MTL	1	0	0	0	0	0	0	0	0	0	0	.0
L	8	Steve Martinson	MTL	13	0	0	0	2–	64	0	0	0	0	2	.0
G	1	Brian Hayward	MTL	29	0	0	0	0	4	0	0	0	0	0	.0

Goaltending

No.	Goaltender	GPI	Mins	Avg	W	L	T	EN	SO	GA	SA	S%
33	Patrick Roy	54	3173	2.53	31	16	5	2	3	134	1524	.912
1	Brian Hayward	29	1674	3.37	10	12	6	1	1	94	770	.878
53	*Andre Racicot	1	13	13.85	0	0	0	0	0	3	6	.500
	Totals	**80**	**4870**	**2.88**	**41**	**28**	**11**	**3**	**4**	**234**	**2300**	**.898**

Playoffs

Pos	#	Player	Team	GP	G	A	Pts	+/-	PIM	PP	SH	GW	OT	S	%
R	44	Stephane Richer	MTL	9	7	3	10	8	2	1	0	1	0	22	31.8
C	27	Shayne Corson	MTL	11	2	8	10	8	20	0	0	0	0	29	6.9
C	39	Brian Skrudland	MTL	11	3	5	8	5	30	0	0	1	1	18	16.7
R	6	Russ Courtnall	MTL	11	5	1	6	1	10	0	0	0	0	38	13.2
C	21	Guy Carbonneau	MTL	11	2	3	5	4–	6	0	0	0	0	23	8.7
C	15	Bobby Smith	MTL	11	1	4	5	3	6	0	0	0	0	17	5.9
D	25	Petr Svoboda	MTL	10	0	5	5	7	2	0	0	0	0	12	.0
D	18	*Matt Schneider	MTL	9	1	3	4	3–	31	1	0	0	0	14	7.1
R	32	Claude Lemieux	MTL	11	1	3	4	2	38	0	0	1	0	24	4.2
C	47	*Stephan Lebeau	MTL	2	3	0	3	1	0	0	0	1	0	9	33.3
C	41	Brent Gilchrist	MTL	8	2	0	2	2	2	0	0	0	0	9	22.2
L	26	Mats Naslund	MTL	3	1	1	2	0	0	0	0	1	0	3	33.3
L	35	Mike McPhee	MTL	9	1	1	2	4–	16	0	0	0	0	24	4.2
L	11	Ryan Walter	MTL	11	0	2	2	2	0	0	0	0	0	10	.0
D	24	Chris Chelios	MTL	5	0	1	1	4–	8	0	0	0	0	6	.0
D	34	*Donald Dufresne	MTL	10	0	1	1	6	18	0	0	0	0	11	.0
R	12	Mike Keane	MTL	11	0	1	1	3–	8	0	0	0	0	13	.0
D	17	Craig Ludwig	MTL	11	0	1	1	5	16	0	0	0	0	9	.0
G	33	Patrick Roy	MTL	11	0	1	1	0	0	0	0	0	0	0	.0
G	1	Brian Hayward	MTL	1	0	0	0	0	0	0	0	0	0	0	.0
L	14	*Mark Pederson	MTL	2	0	0	0	1–	0	0	0	0	0	4	.0
D	28	Eric Desjardins	MTL	6	0	0	0	0	10	0	0	0	0	15	.0
D	3	*Sylvain Lefebvre	MTL	6	0	0	0	1–	2	0	0	0	0	6	.0
D	48	J.J. Daigneault	MTL	9	0	0	0	4	2	0	0	0	0	13	.0
R	36	Todd Ewen	MTL	10	0	0	0	0	4	0	0	0	0	0	.0

Goaltending

No.	Goaltender	GPI	Mins	Avg	W	L	EN	SO	GA	SA	S%
33	Patrick Roy	11	641	2.43	5	6	1	1	26	292	.911
1	Brian Hayward	1	33	3.64	0	0	0	0	2	18	.889
	Totals	11	676	2.57	5	6	1	1	29	310	.906

General Managers' History

Joseph Cattarinich, 1909-1910; George Kennedy, 1910-11 to 1919-20; Leo Dandurand, 1920-21 to 1934-35; Ernest Savard, 1935-36; Cecil Hart, 1936-37 to 1938-39; Jules Dugal, 1939-40; Tom P. Gorman, 1941-42 to 1945-46; Frank J. Selke, 1946-47 to 1963-64; Sam Pollock, 1964-65 to 1977-78; Irving Grundman, 1978-79 to 1982-83; Serge Savard, 1983-84 to date.

Coaching History

George Kennedy, 1917-18 to 1919-20; Leo Dandurand, 1920-21 to 1924-25; Cecil Hart, 1925-26 to 1931-32; Newsy Lalonde, 1932-33 to 1933-34; Newsy Lalonde and Leo Dandurand, 1934-35; Sylvio Mantha, 1935-36; Cecil Hart, 1936-37 to 1937-38; Cecil Hart and Jules Dugal, 1938-39; "Babe" Siebert, 1939*; Pit Lepine, 1939-40; Dick Irvin 1940-41 to 1954-55; Toe Blake, 1955-56 to 1967-68; Claude Ruel, 1968-69 to 1969-70; Claude Ruel and Al MacNeil, 1970-71; Scott Bowman, 1971-72 to 1978-79; Bernie Geoffrion and Claude Ruel, 1979-80; Claude Ruel, 1980-81; Bob Berry, 1981-82 to 1982-83; Bob Berry and Jacques Lemaire, 1983-84; Jacques Lemaire, 1984-85; Jean Perron, 1985-86 to 1987-88; Pat Burns, 1988-89 to date.

* Named coach in summer but died before 1939-40 season began.

Captains' History

Newsy Lalonde, 1917-18 to 1920-21; Sprague Cleghorn, 1921-22 to 1924-25; Bill Couture, 1925-26; Sylvio Mantha, 1926-27 to 1931-32; George Hainsworth, 1932-33; Sylvio Mantha, 1933-34 to 1935-36; Babe Seibert, 1936-37 to 1938-39; Walter Buswell, 1939-40; Toe Blake, 1940-41 to 1946-47; Toe Blake, Bill Durnan (co-captains) 1947-48; Emile Bouchard, 1948-49 to 1955-56; Maurice Richard, 1956-57 to 1959-60; Doug Harvey, 1960-61; Jean Beliveau, 1961-62 to 1970-71; Henri Richard, 1971-72 to 1974-75; Yvan Cournoyer, 1975-76 to 1978-79; Serge Savard, 1979-80, 1980-81; Bob Gainey, 1981-82 to 1988-89, Guy Carbonneau and Chris Chelios (co-captains), 1989-90; Guy Carbonneau, 1990-91.

Retired Numbers

2	Doug Harvey	1947-1961
4	Jean Béliveau	1950-1971
7	Howie Morenz	1923-1937
9	Maurice Richard	1942-1960
10	Guy Lafleur	1971-1984
16	Henri Richard	1955-1975

Club Records

Team

(Figures in brackets for season records are games played; records for fewest points, wins, ties, losses, goals, goals against are for 70 or more games)

Most Points	*132	1976-77 (80)
Most Wins	*60	1976-77 (80)
Most Ties	23	1962-63 (70)
Most Losses	40	1983-84 (80)
Most Goals	387	1976-77 (80)
Most Goals Against	295	1983-84 (80)
Fewest Points	65	1950-51 (70)
Fewest Wins	25	1950-51 (70)
Fewest Ties	5	1983-84 (80)
Fewest Losses	*8	1976-77 (80)
Fewest Goals	155	1952-53 (70)
Fewest Goals Against	*131	1955-56 (70)

Longest Winning Streak

Over-all	12	Jan. 6- Feb. 3/68
Home	13	Nov. 2/43- Jan. 8/44 Jan. 30- Mar. 26/77
Away	8	Dec. 18/77- Jan. 18/78 Jan. 21- Feb. 21/82

Longest Undefeated Streak

Over-all	28	Dec. 12/77- Feb. 23/78 (23 wins, 5 ties)
Home	*34	Nov. 1/76- Apr. 2/77 (28 wins, 6 ties)
Away	*23	Nov. 27/74- Mar. 12/75 (14 wins, 9 ties)

Longest Losing Streak

Over-all	12	Feb. 13/26- Mar. 13/26
Home	7	Dec. 16/39- Jan. 18/40
Away	10	Dec. 1/25- Feb. 2/26

Longest Winless Streak

Over-all	12	Feb. 13- Mar. 13/26 (12 losses) Nov. 28- Dec. 29/35 (8 losses, 4 ties)
Home	*15	Dec. 16/39- Mar. 7/40 (12 losses, 3 ties)
Away	12	Oct. 20- Dec. 13/51 (8 losses, 4 ties)

Most Shutouts, Season	*22	1928-29 (44)
Most PIM, Season	1,840	1987-88 (80)
Most Goals, Game	*16	Mar. 3/20 (Mtl. 16 at Que. 3)

Individual

Most Seasons	20	Henri Richard
Most Games	1,256	Henri Richard
Most Goals Career	544	Maurice Richard
Most Assists, Career	728	Guy Lafleur
Most Points Career	1,246	Guy Lafleur (518 goals, 728 assists)
Most PIM, Career	2,174	Chris Nilan
Most Shutouts, Career	75	George Hainsworth

Longest Consecutive Games Streak	560	Doug Jarvis (Oct. 8/75-Apr. 4/82)
Most Goals, Season	60	Steve Shutt (1976-77) Guy Lafleur (1977-78)
Most Assists, Season	82	Peter Mahovlich (1974-75)

Most Points, Season	136	Guy Lafleur (1976-77) (56 goals, 80 assists)
Most PIM, Season	358	Chris Nilan (1984-85)
Most Points, Defenseman Season	85	Larry Robinson (1976-77) (19 goals, 66 assists)
Most Points, Center, Season	117	Peter Mahovlich (1974-75) (35 goals, 82 assists)
Most Points, Right Wing, Season	136	Guy Lafleur (1976-77) (56 goals, 80 assists)
Most Points, Left Wing, Season	110	Mats Naslund (1985-86) (43 goals, 67 assists)
Most Points, Rookie, Season	71	Mats Naslund (1982-83) (26 goals, 45 assists) Kjell Dahlin (1985-86) (32 goals, 39 assists)
Most Shutouts, Season	*22	George Hainsworth (1928-29)
Most Goals, Game	6	Newsy Lalonde (Jan. 10/20)
Most Assists, Game	6	Elmer Lach (Feb. 6/43)
Most Points, Game	8	Maurice Richard 5G-3A (Dec. 28/44) Bert Olmstead 4G-4A (Jan. 9/54)

* NHL Record.

All-time Record vs. Other Clubs

Regular Season

			At Home							On Road							Total				
	GP	W	L	T	GF	GA	PTS	GP	W	L	T	GF	GA	PTS	GP	W	L	T	GF	GA	PTS
Boston	293	171	79	43	1001	666	385	294	109	134	51	788	866	269	587	280	213	94	1789	1532	654
Buffalo	63	38	17	8	262	189	84	63	19	28	16	188	196	54	126	57	45	24	450	385	138
Calgary	33	19	9	5	117	80	43	32	20	7	5	121	100	45	65	39	16	10	238	180	88
Chicago	263	165	50	48	1019	614	378	262	120	88	54	732	704	294	525	285	138	102	1751	1318	672
Detroit	269	164	62	43	952	600	371	269	94	122	53	690	759	241	538	258	184	96	1642	1359	612
Edmonton	18	10	5	3	69	59	23	17	6	11	0	52	69	12	35	16	16	3	121	128	35
Hartford	40	29	5	6	198	119	64	40	21	14	5	156	127	47	80	50	19	11	354	246	111
Los Angeles	52	36	6	10	243	135	82	53	33	14	6	215	158	72	105	69	20	16	458	293	154
Minnesota	46	31	9	6	202	117	68	47	25	12	10	170	122	60	93	56	21	16	372	239	128
New Jersey	27	20	4	3	121	70	43	28	22	6	0	140	71	44	55	42	10	3	261	141	87
NY Islanders	32	18	8	6	121	99	42	34	15	16	3	103	114	33	66	33	24	9	224	213	75
NY Rangers	263	175	54	34	1042	608	384	263	108	105	50	769	753	266	526	283	159	84	1811	1361	650
Philadelphia	47	27	10	10	184	131	64	46	19	16	11	140	123	49	93	46	26	21	324	254	113
Pittsburgh	53	44	4	5	277	130	93	52	28	16	8	195	151	64	105	72	20	13	472	281	157
Quebec	40	27	8	5	186	122	59	40	17	21	2	141	145	36	80	44	29	7	327	267	95
St. Louis	47	35	7	5	214	122	75	46	24	9	13	163	115	61	93	59	16	18	377	237	136
Toronto	309	188	82	39	1096	758	415	310	109	157	44	812	938	262	619	297	239	83	1908	1696	677
Vancouver	40	32	6	2	205	103	66	36	25	5	8	150	89	58	78	57	11	10	355	192	124
Washington	33	24	4	5	163	67	53	34	16	12	6	122	88	38	67	40	16	11	285	155	91
Winnipeg	17	15	2	0	95	40	30	18	8	9	1	76	60	20	35	23	0	4	171	100	50
Defunct Club	231	148	58	25	779	469	321	230	98	97	35	586	606	231	461	246	155	60	1365	1075	552
Totals	**2216**	**1416**	**489**	**311**	**8546**	**5298**	**3143**	**2216**	**936**	**896**	**384**	**6509**	**6354**	**2256**	**4432**	**2352**	**1385**	**695**	**15055**	**11652**	**5399**

Playoffs

	Series	W	L	GP	W	L	T	GF	GA	Last Mtg.	Round	Result
Boston	25	21	4	121	81	40	0	384	285	1990	DF	L 1-4
Buffalo	4	2	2	21	10	11	0	69	58	1990	DSF	W 4-2
Calgary	2	1	1	11	6	5	0	31	32	1989	F	L 2-4
Chicago	17	12	5	81	50	29	2	261	185	1976	QF	W 4-0
Detroit	12	5	7	62	33	29	0	161	149	1978	QF	W 4-1
Edmonton	1	0	1	3	0	3	0	6	15	1981	PR	L 0-3
Hartford	4	4	0	20	15	5	0	75	52	1989	DSF	W 4-0
Minnesota	2	1	1	13	7	6	0	48	37	1980	QF	L 3-4
NY Islanders	3	2	1	17	10	7	0	48	44	1984	CF	L 2-4
NY Rangers	13	7	6	55	32	21	2	171	139	1986	CF	W 4-1
Philadelphia	4	3	1	21	14	7	0	72	52	1989	CF	W 4-2
Quebec	4	2	2	25	13	12	0	86	69	1987	DF	W 4-3
St. Louis	3	3	0	12	12	0	0	42	14	1977	QF	W 4-0
Toronto	13	7	6	67	39	28	0	203	148	1979	QF	W 4-0
Vancouver	1	1	0	5	4	1	0	20	9	1975	QF	W 4-1
Defunct Clubs	12	7	5	32	18	10	4	82	83			
Totals	**121***	**78**	**42**	**566**	**344**	**208**	**8**	**1759**	**1371**			

* 1919 Final incomplete due to influenza epidemic.

Abbreviations: Round: F – Final; **CF** – conference final; **DF** – division final; **DSF** – division semi-final; **PR** – preliminary round. **QF** – quarter-final; **GF** – goals for; **GA** – goals against; **GF** – goals for.

Playoff Results 1990-86

Year	Round	Opponent	Result	GF	GA
1990	DF	Boston	L 1-4	12	16
	DSF	Buffalo	W 4-2	17	13
1989	F	Calgary	L 2-4	16	19
	CF	Philadelphia	W 4-2	17	8
	DF	Boston	W 4-1	16	13
	DSF	Hartford	W 4-0	18	11
1988	DF	Boston	L 1-4	10	15
	DSF	Hartford	W 4-2	23	20
1987	CF	Philadelphia	L 2-4	22	22
	DF	Quebec	W 4-3	26	21
	DSF	Boston	W 4-0	19	11
1986	F	Calgary	W 4-1	15	13
	CF	NY Rangers	W 4-1	15	9
	DF	Hartford	W 4-3	16	13
	DSF	Boston	W 3-0	10	6

1989-90 Results

		Home				Away	
Oct.	7	Buffalo	5-1	Oct.	5	Hartford	4-1
	11	Boston	4-2		9	Boston	0-2
	16	Washington	3-4		13	New Jersey	4-3
	18	Calgary	2-1		14	Pittsburgh	1-2
	22	New Jersey	4-5		20	Buffalo	2-6
	23	Hartford	3-2		26	Chicago	3-5
	28	Pittsburgh	5-1		31	NY Islanders	3-0
	29	Edmonton	5-4	Nov.	8	NY Rangers	3-2
Nov.	2	Buffalo	3-4		9	St Louis	1-1
	4	NY Rangers	3-2		11	Los Angeles	4-5
	6	St Louis	3-3		16	Boston	2-3
	15	Winnipeg	5-1		22	Philadelphia	1-5
	18	Toronto	4-3		30	Quebec	6-2
	20	Calgary	3-2	Dec.	6	Minnesota	4-1
	25	Boston	5-3		8	Winnipeg	6-6
	29	Quebec	5-2		9	Toronto	4-7
Dec.	2	Hartford	3-4		17	NY Rangers	2-0
	11	Los Angeles	2-2		22	Buffalo	2-2
	13	Chicago	1-3		27	Vancouver	1-2
	16	Detroit	3-1		28	Edmonton	2-6
	23	Philadelphia	3-5		30	Calgary	3-5
Jan.	6	Buffalo	6-3	Jan.	9	Quebec	2-5
	7	Vancouver	5-3		12	New Jersey	5-2
	13	Philadelphia	2-2		26	Washington	3-6
	15	Minnesota	4-3		27	Toronto	5-3
	17	NY Islanders	3-6	Feb.	1	Boston	4-2
	24	Quebec	7-3		7	Buffalo	1-3
	29	Boston	1-2		16	Buffalo	3-5
Feb.	3	Buffalo	1-0		19	Detroit	5-5
	4	Hartford	2-0		22	Quebec	6-5
	10	Quebec	7-2		28	Hartford	1-3
	14	Vancouver	10-1	Mar.	1	Boston	3-5
	17	Hartford	7-3		3	Minnesota	2-3
	24	Pittsburgh	11-1		7	Los Angeles	5-2
	25	St Louis	6-5		13	NY Islanders	4-2
Mar.	10	Detroit	3-3		21	Winnipeg	2-3
	14	Edmonton	3-3		23	Washington	4-2
	17	Chicago	3-2		24	Hartford	4-7
	18	Quebec	8-3		29	Quebec	5-2
	31	Boston	2-2	Apr.	1	Hartford	1-1

* Denotes afternoon game.

Coach

BURNS, PAT
Coach, Montreal Canadiens. Born in St-Henri, Que., April 4, 1952.

Since becoming head coach in 1988-89 Pat Burns has led the Montreal Canadiens to 115 and 93-point seasons. In 1988-89, after leading his club to the Stanley Cup Finals, Burns was named recipient of the Jack Adams Award, only the third rookie coach in League history to receive that honor. Following 17 years of service with the Gatineau (Quebec) and Ottawa Police Departments, Burns began his rise to the NHL coaching ranks by assuming the head coaching position with the Hull Olympiques of the Quebec Major Hockey League in 1983-84. In 1985-86, his best year at Hull, he led the Olympiques to the Memorial Cup Final after finishing the regular-season with a 54-18-0 record. Later that year he served as an assistant coach to Bert Templeton for Team Canada at the 1986 World Junior Hockey Championships in Czechoslovkia. Burns' pro coaching career began in 1987-88 when he guided the Canadiens' top minor league affiliate, the AHL Sherbrooke Canadiens, to a 42-34-4 regular-season record.

Coaching Record

Season	Team	Games	Regular Season				Playoffs			
			W	L	T	%	Games	W	L	%
1983-84	Hull (QMJHL)	70	25	45	0	.357	....	....	....	....
1984-85	Hull (QMJHL)	68	33	34	1	.493	5	1	4	.200
1985-86	Hull (QMJHL)	72	54	18	0	.750	15	15	0	1.000
1986-87	Hull (QMJHL)	70	26	39	5	.407	8	4	4	.500
1987-88	Sherbrooke (AHL)	80	42	34	4	.550	6	2	4	.333
1988-89	Montreal (NHL)	80	53	18	9	.719	21	14	7	.667
1989-90	Montreal (NHL)	80	41	28	11	.581	11	5	6	.455
	NHL Totals	**160**	**94**	**46**	**20**	**.650**	**32**	**19**	**13**	**.594**

General Manager

SAVARD, SERGE A.
Managing Director, Montreal Canadiens. Born in Montreal, Que., January 22, 1946.

When Serge Savard was named managing director of the Montreal Canadiens on April 28, 1983, he took over a club that finished in fourth place with 75 points. In 1984-85, the Canadiens were vastly improved, finishing first with 94 points. Evidence of Savard's front office efforts were visible throughout the organization where he spent 14 of his 16 NHL seasons as a standout defenseman and an important part of eight Stanley Cup winning teams. As a player, Savard captured the Conn Smythe Trophy as the most valuable player in the 1969 Stanley Cup playoffs and was recipient of the Bill Masterton Trophy in 1978-79 for his dedication, perserverance and sportsmanship to the game of hockey. He was acquired by the Winnipeg Jets in the 1981 Waiver Draft and closed out his playing career with two seasons as a leader and teacher to the young Jets' team which showed remarkable improvement during Savard's term. In the 1960's, Savard twice suffered multiple leg fractures and most experts doubted he would ever play again. He was named to the NHL's Second All-Star Team in 1978-79.

Entry Draft
Selections 1990-76

1990
Pick
- 12 Turner Stevenson
- 39 Ryan Kuwabara
- 58 Charles Poulin
- 60 Robert Guillet
- 81 Gilbert Dionne
- 102 Paul Dipietro
- 123 Craig Conroy
- 144 Stephen Rohr
- 165 Brent Fleetwood
- 186 Derek Maguire
- 207 Mark Kettelhut
- 228 John Uniac
- 249 Sergei Martinyuk

1989
Pick
- 13 Lindsay Vallis
- 30 Patrice Brisebois
- 41 Steve Larouche
- 51 Pierre Sevigny
- 83 Andre Racicot
- 104 Marc Deschamps
- 146 Craig Ferguson
- 167 Patrick Lebeau
- 188 Roy Mitchell
- 209 Ed Henrich
- 230 Justin Duberman
- 251 Steve Cadieux

1988
Pick
- 20 Eric Charron
- 34 Martin St. Amour
- 46 Neil Carnes
- 83 Patrik Kjellberg
- 92 Peter Popovic
- 104 Jean-Claude Bergeron
- 125 Patrik Carnback
- 146 Tim Chase
- 167 Sean Hill
- 188 Haris Vitolinis
- 209 Juri Krivohija
- 230 Kevin Dahl
- 251 Dave Kunda

1987
Pick
- 17 Andrew Cassels
- 33 John Leclair
- 38 Eric Desjardins
- 44 Mathieu Schneider
- 58 Francois Gravel
- 80 Kris Miller
- 101 Steve McCool
- 122 Les Kuntar
- 143 Rob Kelley
- 164 Will Geist
- 185 Eric Tremblay
- 206 Barry McKinlay
- 227 Ed Ronan
- 248 Bryan Herring

1986
Pick
- 15 Mark Pederson
- 27 Benoit Brunet
- 57 Jyrkki Lumme
- 78 Brent Bobyck
- 94 Eric Aubertin
- 99 Mario Milani
- 120 Steve Bisson
- 141 Lyle Odelin
- 162 Rick Hayward
- 183 Antonin Routa
- 204 Eric Bohemier
- 225 Charlie Moore
- 246 Karel Svoboda

1985
Pick
- 12 Jose Charbonneau
- 16 Tom Chorske
- 33 Todd Richards
- 47 Rockey Dundas
- 75 Martin Desjardins
- 79 Brent Gilchrist
- 96 Tom Sagissor
- 117 Donald Dufresne
- 142 Ed Cristofoli
- 163 Mike Claringbull
- 184 Roger Beedon
- 198 Maurice Mansi
- 205 Chad Arthur
- 226 Mike Bishop
- 247 John Ferguson Jr.

1984
Pick
- 5 Petr Svoboda
- 9 Shayne Corson
- 29 Stephane Richer
- 51 Patrick Roy
- 54 Graeme Bonar
- 65 Lee Brodeur
- 95 Gerald Johannson
- 116 Jim Nesich
- 137 Scott MacTavish
- 158 Brad McCaughey
- 179 Eric Demers
- 199 Ron Annear
- 220 Dave Tanner
- 240 Troy Crosby

1983
Pick
- 17 Alfie Turcotte
- 26 Claude Lemieux
- 27 Sergio Momesso
- 35 Todd Francis
- 45 Daniel Letendre
- 78 John Kordic
- 98 Dan Wurst
- 118 Arto Javanainen
- 138 Vladislav Tretiak
- 158 Rob Bryden
- 178 Grant MacKay
- 198 Thomas Rundquist
- 218 Jeff Perpich
- 238 Jean Guy Bergeron

1982
Pick
- 19 Alain Heroux
- 31 Jocelyn Gauvreau
- 32 Kent Carlson
- 33 David Maley
- 40 Scott Sandelin
- 61 Scott Harlow
- 69 John Devoe
- 103 Kevin Houle
- 117 Ernie Vargas
- 124 Michael Dark
- 145 Hannu Jarvenpaa
- 150 Steve Smith
- 166 Tom Kolioupoulos
- 187 Brian Williams

1981
Pick
- 7 Mark Hunter
- 18 Gilbert Delorme
- 19 Jan Ingman
- 32 Lars Eriksson
- 40 Chris Chelios
- 46 Dieter Hegen
- 82 Kjell Dahlin
- 88 Steve Rooney
- 124 Tom Anastos
- 145 Tom Kurvers
- 166 Paul Gess
- 187 Scott Ferguson
- 208 Danny Burrows

1980
Pick
- 1 Doug Wickenheiser
- 27 Ric Nattress
- 40 John Chabot
- 45 John Newberry
- 61 Craig Ludwig
- 82 Jeff Teal
- 103 Remi Gagne
- 124 Mike McPhee
- 145 Bill Norton
- 166 Steve Penney
- 187 John Schmidt
- 208 Scott Robinson

1979
Pick
- 27 Gaston Gingras
- 37 Mats Naslund
- 43 Craig Levie
- 44 Guy Carbonneau
- 58 Rick Wamsley
- 79 Dave Orleski
- 100 Yvon Joly
- 121 Greg Moffatt

1978
Pick
- 8 Dan Geoffrion
- 17 Dave Hunter
- 30 Dale Yakiwchuk

- 208 Bob Emery
- 229 Darren Acheson
- 250 Bill Brauer

- 36 Ron Carter
- 42 Richard David
- 69 Kevin Reeves
- 86 Kevin Boyd
- 103 Keith Acton
- 120 Jim Lawson
- 137 Larry Landon
- 154 Kevin Constantine
- 171 John Swan
- 186 Daniel Metivier
- 201 Vjacselev Fetisov
- 212 Jeff Mars
- 222 Greg Tignanelli
- 225 George Goulakos
- 227 Ken Moodie
- 229 Serge Leblanc
- 230 Bob Magnuson

- 231 Chris Nilan
- 232 Rick Wilson
- 233 Louis Sleigher
- 234 Doug Robb

1977
Pick
- 10 Mark Napier
- 18 Normand Dupont
- 36 Rod Langway
- 43 Alain Cote
- 46 Pierre Lagace
- 49 Moe Robinson
- 54 Gord Roberts
- 64 Bob Holland
- 90 Gaetan Royer
- 108 Bill Himmelright
- 124 Richard Sevigny

- 137 Keith Hendrickson
- 140 Mike Reilly
- 152 Barry Barrett
- 154 Sid Tanchak
- 160 Mark Holden
- 162 Craig Laughlin
- 167 Daniel Poulin
- 169 Tom McDonnell
- 173 Cary Farelli
- 174 Carey Walker
- 176 Mark Wells
- 177 Stan Palmer
- 179 Jean Belisle
- 180 Bob Daly
- 183 Bob Boileau
- 183 John Costello

1976
Pick
- 12 Peter Lee
- 13 Rod Schutt
- 18 Bruce Baker
- 36 Barry Melrose
- 54 Bill Baker
- 72 Ed Clarey
- 90 Maurice Barrette
- 108 Pierre Brassard
- 118 Rich Gosselin
- 123 John Gregory
- 125 Bruce Horsch
- 127 John Tavella
- 129 Mark Davidson
- 131 Bill Wells
- 133 Ron Wilson

Club Directory

Montreal Forum
2313 St. Catherine Street West
Montreal, Quebec H3H 1N2
Phone 514/932-2582
FAX (Hockey) 514/932-8736
P.R. 514/932-8285
ENVOY ID
Front Office: CANADIEN.
GM
Public
Relations: CANADIEN. PR
Capacity: 16,197

Owner: The Molson Companies Limited

Chairman of the Board, President and Governor	Ronald Corey
Vice-President, Hockey, Managing Director and Alternate Governor	Serge Savard
Senior Vice-President, Corporate Affairs	Jean Béliveau
Vice-President, Forum Operations	Aldo Giampaolo
Vice-President, Finance and Administration	Fred Steer
Vice-President, Planning and Development	Louis-Joseph Regimbal
Assistant to the Managing Director	Jacques Lemaire
Assistant to the Managing Director, Director of Recruitment and Managing Director of Fredericton Canadiens	André Boudrias
Head Coach	Pat Burns
Assistant Coaches	Jacques Laperrière, Charles Thiffault
Goaltending Instructor	François Allaire
Director of Player Development and Scout	Claude Ruel
Chief Scout	Doug Robinson
Scouting Staff	Neil Armstrong, Scott Baker, Pat Flannery, Pierre Mondou, Gerry O'Flaherty, Richard Scammell, Eric Taylor, Jean-Claude Tremblay, Del Wilson
Farm Team (AHL)	Fredericton Canadiens
Head Coach	Paulin Bordeleau
Director of Operations	Wayne Gamble

Medical and Training Staff

Club Physician	Dr. D.G. Kinnear
Athletic Trainer	Gaetan Lefebvre
Assistant to the Athletic Trainer	John Shipman
Equipment Manager	Eddy Palchak
Assistants to the Equipment Manager	Pierre Gervais, Sylvain Toupin

Marketing

EFFIX Inc.	François-Xavier Seigneur
Director of Advertising Sales	Floyd Curry
Director of Boutiques Souvenirs	Maurice Corey

Communications

Director of Public Relations	Claude Mouton
Director of Press Relations	Michele Lapointe
Director of Special Events	Camil Desroches
Computer Supervisor	Sylvain Roy

Finance

Controller	Dennis McKinley
Administrative Supervisor	Dave Poulton
Accountants	Françoise Brault, Gilles Viens

Forum

Director of Concessions	Yvon Gosselin
Director of Purchasing	Robert Loiseau
Forum Superintendent	Alain Gauthier

Ticketing

Box Office Supervisor	René St-Jacques
Box Office Manager	Doug Foster

Executive Secretaries
President (Lise Beaudry)/Managing Director (Donna Stuart)/Senior V.P., C.A. (Louise Richer)/ V.P. Forum Operations (Vicky Mercuri)/V.P. Finance (Susan Cryans)/Public Rel. (Normande Herget)/Press Rel. (Frédérique Cardinal)

Location of Press Box	suspended above ice — west side
Location of Radio and TV booth	suspended above ice — east side
Dimensions of rink	200 feet by 85 feet
Ends of rink	Herculite extends above boards all around rink
Club colors	Red, White and Blue
Club trains at	Montreal Forum
Play-by-Play — Radio/TV	Dick Irvin (English) Richard Garneau, Claude Quennville, Michel Bergeron (French)
TV Channels	CBMT (6), CFTM (10), CBFT (2)
Radio Stations	CBF (690), CFCF (600)

New Jersey Devils

1989-90 Results: 37W-34L-9T 83PTS. Second, Patrick Division

Year-by-Year Record

		Home			Road			Overall							
Season	GP	W	L	T	W	L	T	W	L	T	GF	GA	Pts.	Finished	Playoff Result
1989-90	80	22	15	3	15	19	6	37	34	9	295	288	83	2nd, Patrick Div.	Lost Div. Semi-Final
1988-89	80	17	18	5	10	23	7	27	41	12	281	325	66	5th, Patrick Div.	Out of Playoffs
1987-88	80	23	16	1	15	20	5	38	36	6	295	296	82	4th, Patrick Div.	Lost Conf. Championship
1986-87	80	20	17	3	9	28	3	29	45	6	293	368	64	6th, Patrick Div.	Out of Playoffs
1985-86	80	17	21	2	11	28	1	28	49	3	300	374	59	6th, Patrick Div.	Out of Playoffs
1984-85	80	13	21	6	9	27	4	22	48	10	264	346	54	5th, Patrick Div.	Out of Playoffs
1983-84	80	10	28	2	7	28	5	17	56	7	231	350	41	5th, Patrick Div.	Out of Playoffs
1982-83	80	11	20	9	6	29	5	17	49	14	230	338	48	5th, Patrick Div.	Out of Playoffs
1981-82	80	14	21	5	4	28	8	18	49	13	241	362	49	5th, Smythe Div.	Out of Playoffs
1980-81	80	15	16	9	7	29	4	22	45	13	258	344	57	5th, Smythe Div.	Out of Playoffs
1979-80	80	12	20	8	7	28	5	19	48	13	234	308	51	6th, Smythe Div.	Out of Playoffs
1978-79	80	8	24	8	7	29	4	15	53	12	210	331	42	4th, Smythe Div.	Out of Playoffs
1977-78	80	17	14	9	2	26	12	19	40	21	257	305	59	2nd, Smythe Div.	Lost Prelim. Round
1976-77	80	12	20	8	8	26	6	20	46	14	226	307	54	5th, Smythe Div.	Out of Playoffs
1975-76	80	8	24	8	4	32	4	12	56	12	190	351	36	5th, Smythe Div.	Out of Playoffs
1974-75	80	12	20	8	3	34	3	15	54	11	184	328	41	5th, Smythe Div.	Out of Playoffs

Schedule

	Home			Away	
Oct.	Thur. 4 Detroit		**Oct.**	Sun. 7 Pittsburgh	
	Sat. 6 Philadelphia			Thur. 11 Philadelphia	
	Tues. 9 Minnesota			Sat. 20 Washington	
	Sat. 13 Calgary			Tues. 23 NY Islanders	
	Wed. 17 Washington			Tues. 30 Calgary	
	Fri. 19 NY Rangers		**Nov.**	Thur. 1 Vancouver	
	Thur. 25 Buffalo			Sat. 3 Edmonton	
	Sat. 27 Pittsburgh			Sat. 10 Montreal	
Nov.	Wed. 7 NY Islanders			Sun. 18 Philadelphia	
	Fri. 9 NY Rangers			Tues. 20 Los Angeles	
	Tues. 13 Montreal			Sat. 24 Minnesota	
	Thur. 15 Hartford		**Dec.**	Sat. 1 St Louis	
	Sat. 17 Philadelphia*			Mon. 3 Winnipeg	
	Wed. 28 Philadelphia			Fri. 7 Washington	
	Fri. 30 NY Islanders			Tues. 11 NY Islanders	
Dec.	Wed. 5 Vancouver			Thur. 13 Pittsburgh	
	Sat. 8 Washington			Sat. 15 Boston	
	Tues. 18 Boston			Thur. 20 Philadelphia	
	Sun. 23 Toronto			Sat. 22 Quebec	
	Thur. 27 NY Islanders			Sun. 30 NY Rangers	
	Sat. 29 Buffalo		**Jan.**	Tues. 1 Washington*	
Jan.	Tues. 8 St Louis			Thur. 3 Chicago	
	Sat. 12 Edmonton*			Sat. 5 Pittsburgh*	
	Mon. 14 Los Angeles			Tues. 22 Pittsburgh	
	Wed. 16 Chicago			Mon. 28 Detroit	
	Thur. 24 Quebec			Wed. 30 Los Angeles	
	Sat. 26 Minnesota		**Feb.**	Sat. 2 St Louis	
Feb.	Tues. 5 Calgary			Sat. 9 Quebec*	
	Sun. 10 Vancouver*			Wed. 13 NY Rangers	
	Thur. 14 Winnipeg			Sun. 24 NY Rangers*	
	Sat. 16 Philadelphia*			Wed. 27 Toronto	
	Mon. 18 Edmonton		**Mar.**	Fri. 1 Detroit	
	Fri. 22 Pittsburgh			Tues. 5 NY Islanders	
	Mon. 25 Washington			Wed. 6 Buffalo	
Mar.	Sun. 3 Boston			Sun. 10 Winnipeg*	
	Wed. 13 Toronto			Sat. 16 Hartford	
	Fri. 15 NY Rangers			Thur. 21 Chicago	
	Tues. 19 Pittsburgh			Sat. 23 Montreal	
	Wed. 27 Hartford			Tues. 26 NY Rangers	
	Sun. 31 NY Islanders			Sat. 30 Washington	

* Denotes afternoon game.

Home Starting Times:
All Games . . . . 7:45 p.m.
Except Nov. 17, Jan. 12, Feb. 16 . . . . . 1:35 p.m.
Feb. 10 . . . . 5:05 p.m.

Franchise date: June 30, 1982. Transferred from Denver to New Jersey, Previously transferred from Kansas City to Denver, Colorado.

17th NHL Season

Patrik Sundstrom

1990-91 Player Personnel

FORWARDS	HT	WT	S	Place of Birth	Date	1989-90 Club
ANDERSON, Perry	6-1	225	L	Barrie, Ont.	10/14/61	Utica
BODNARCHUK, Mike	6-1	175	R	Bramalea, Ont.	3/26/70	Kingston
BRADY, Neil	6-2	200	L	Montreal, Que.	4/12/68	New Jersey-Utica
BROOKE, Bob	5-11	195	R	Acton, MA	12/16/60	Minnesota-N.J.
BROWN, Doug	5-10	180	R	Southborough, MA	6/12/64	New Jersey
CHRISTIAN, Jeff	6-1	195	L	Burlington, Ont.	7/30/70	London-Owen Sound
CIGER, Zdeno	6-2	190	L	Martin, Czech.	10/19/69	Trencin (Czech.)
CONACHER, Pat	5-8	190	L	Edmonton, Alt.	5/1/59	New Jersey-Utica
CROWDER, Troy	6-4	215	R	Sudbury, Ont.	5/3/68	New Jersey-Nashville
HAVILAND, Mike	6-2	215	L	New York, NY	7/24/67	Elmira
HUARD, Bill	6-1	200	L	Welland, Ont.	6/24/67	Utica-Nashville
HUSCROFT, Jamie	6-2	200	L	Creston, B.C.	1/9/67	New Jersey-Utica
KIRTON, Doug	6-2	190	R	Penetang'ene, Ont.	3/21/66	Colorado College
LUIK, Scott	6-1	210	L	Scarborough, Ont.	1/15/70	Miami Ohio-Oshawa
MacLEAN, John	6-0	200	R	Oshawa, Ont.	11/20/64	New Jersey
MADILL, Jeff	5-11	195	L	Oshawa, Ont.	6/21/67	Utica
MALEY, David	6-2	195	L	Beaver Dam, WI	4/24/63	New Jersey
MILLER, Jason	6-1	190	L	Edmonton, Alta.	3/1/71	Medicine Hat
MORRIS, Jon	6-0	175	R	Lowell, MA	5/6/66	New Jersey-Utica
MULLER, Kirk	6-0	205	L	Kingston, Ont.	2/8/66	New Jersey
NEZIOL, Tom	6-1	190	L	Burlington, Ont.	8/7/67	U. of Miami of Ohio
OJANEN, Janne	6-2	200	L	Tampere, Finland	4/9/68	New Jersey
PODDUBNY, Walt	6-1	210	L	Thunder Bay, Ont.	2/14/60	New Jersey-Utica
ROONEY, Steve	6-2	205	L	Canton, MA	6/28/62	Utica
SHANAHAN, Brendan	6-3	210	R	Mimico, Ont.	1/23/69	New Jersey
SIMON, Jason	6-1	190	L	Sarnia, Ont.	3/21/69	Utica
SKALDE, Jarrod	6-0	170	L	Niagara Falls, Ont.	2/26/71	Oshawa
STASTNY, Peter	6-1	200	L	Bratislava, Czech.	9/18/56	Quebec-New Jersey
STEWART, Al	6-0	195	L	Fort St. John, B.C.	1/31/64	Utica
SUNDSTROM, Patrik	6-1	200	L	Skelleftea, Sweden	12/14/61	New Jersey
TODD, Kevin	5-10	175	L	Winnipeg, Man.	5/4/63	Utica
TURGEON, Sylvain	6-0	200	L	Noranda, Que.	1/17/65	New Jersey
VILGRAIN, Claude	6-1	205	R	Port-au-Prince, Haiti	3/1/63	New Jersey-Utica
YOUNG, C.J.	5-10	180	R	Waban, MA	1/1/68	Harvard
YSEBAERT, Paul	6-1	190	L	Sarnia, Ont.	5/15/66	New Jersey-Utica
DEFENSEMEN						
ALBELIN, Tommy	6-1	190	L	Stockholm, Sweden	5/21/64	New Jersey
COPELAND, Todd	6-2	210	L	Ridgewood, N.J.	5/18/67	U. of Michigan
DANEYKO, Ken	6-0	210	L	Windsor, Ont.	4/17/64	New Jersey
DRIVER, Bruce	6-0	185	L	Toronto, Ont.	4/29/62	New Jersey
FETISOV, Viacheslav	6-1	220	L	Moscow, USSR	5/20/58	New Jersey
KASATONOV, Alexei	6-1	215	L	Leningrad, USSR	10/14/59	CSKA (USSR)-Utica-New Jersey
KIENE, Chris	6-5	220	L	S. Windsor, CT	3/16/66	Utica
LANIEL, Marc	6-1	195	L	Oshawa, Ont.	1/16/68	Utica-Phoenix
MALKOC, Dean	6-3	200	L	Vancouver, B.C.	1/26/70	Kamloops
MARCINYSHYN, Dave	6-3	210	L	Edmonton, Alta.	2/4/67	Utica
O'CONNOR, Myles	5-11	185	L	Calgary, Alta.	4/2/67	Utica
PERSSON, Lars	6-2	205	L	Ostersund, Sweden	8/24/69	Leksands (Swe.)
SHARPLES, Jeff	6-1	195	L	Terrace, B.C.	7/28/67	Utica-Adirondack-Cape Breton
STARIKOV, Sergei	5-10	225	L	Chelyabinsk, USSR	12/4/58	New Jersey-Utica
WEINRICH, Eric	6-1	210	L	Roanoke, VA	12/19/66	New Jersey-Utica
WOODS, Bob	6-1	195	L	Leroy, Sask.	1/24/68	Utica

GOALTENDERS	HT	WT	C	Place of Birth	Date	1989-90 Club
BILLINGTON, Craig	5-10	170	L	London, Ont.	9/11/66	Utica
BRODEUR, Martin	6-1	190	L	Montreal, Que.	5/6/72	St. Hyacinthe
BURKE, Sean	6-4	210	L	Windsor, Ont.	1/29/67	New Jersey
MELANSON, Roland	5-10	185	L	Moncton, N.B.	6/28/60	Utica
ROMAINE, Mark	5-9	160	L	Sharon, MA	10/25/68	Providence
SCHWAB, Corey	6-0	180	L	N. Battleford, Sask.	11/4/70	Seattle
TERRERI, Chris	5-8	160	L	Providence, RI	11/15/64	New Jersey

1989-90 Scoring

Regular Season

* rookie

Pos	#	Player	Team	GP	G	A	Pts	+/−	PIM	PP	SH	GW	GT	S	%
C	9	Kirk Muller	N.J.	80	30	56	86	1−	74	9	0	6	1	200	15.0
R	15	John MacLean	N.J.	80	41	38	79	17	80	10	3	11	0	322	12.7
L	17	Patrik Sundstrom	N.J.	74	27	49	76	15	34	8	1	0	2	142	19.0
C	29	Peter Stastny	QUE	62	24	38	62	45−	24	10	0	0	1	131	18.3
			N.J.	12	5	6	11	1−	16	2	0	1	0	25	20.0
			TOTAL	74	29	44	73	46−	40	12	0	1	1	156	18.6
R	11	Brendan Shanahan	N.J.	73	30	42	72	15	137	8	0	5	0	196	15.3
D	23	Bruce Driver	N.J.	75	7	46	53	6	63	1	0	0	1	185	3.8
C	16	Sylvain Turgeon	N.J.	72	30	17	47	8−	81	7	0	3	0	218	13.8
C	12	Mark Johnson	N.J.	63	16	29	45	8−	12	4	0	1	0	82	19.5
D	2	*Viacheslav Fetisov	N.J.	72	8	34	42	9	52	2	0	0	0	108	7.4
R	24	Doug Brown	N.J.	69	14	20	34	7	16	1	3	3	0	135	10.4
C	22	*Janne Ojanen	N.J.	64	17	13	30	5−	12	1	0	1	1	76	22.4
D	26	Tommy Albelin	N.J.	68	6	23	29	1−	63	4	0	0	0	125	4.8
C	10	Bob Brooke	MIN	38	4	4	8	5−	33	0	3	0	0	65	6.2
			N.J.	35	8	10	18	3	30	0	0	1	0	44	18.2
			TOTAL	73	12	14	26	2−	63	0	3	1	0	109	11.0
L	8	David Maley	N.J.	67	8	17	25	2−	160	0	0	2	0	82	9.8
D	7	*Alexei Kasatonov	N.J.	39	6	15	21	15	16	1	0	0	0	60	10.0
D	3	Ken Daneyko	N.J.	74	6	15	21	15	216	0	1	1	0	64	9.4
L	21	Walt Poddubny	N.J.	33	4	10	14	4−	28	1	0	0	1	50	8.0
C	20	*Jon Morris	N.J.	20	6	7	13	12	8	2	0	1	0	17	35.3
D	5	*Eric Weinrich	N.J.	19	2	7	9	1	11	1	0	1	0	16	12.5
C	32	Pat Conacher	N.J.	19	3	3	6	2	4	0	0	0	0	18	16.7
D	27	Randy Velischek	N.J.	62	0	6	6	4	72	0	0	0	0	34	.0
D	18	*Jamie Huscroft	N.J.	42	2	3	5	2−	149	0	0	0	0	19	10.5
C	19	*Neil Brady	N.J.	19	1	4	5	1−	13	0	0	0	0	10	10.0
C	19	*Paul Ysebaert	N.J.	5	1	2	3	0	0	0	0	0	0	6	16.7
C	19	*Claude Vilgrain	N.J.	6	1	2	3	1−	4	0	0	0	0	13	7.7
L	20	Peter Sundstrom	N.J.	21	1	2	3	1	4	0	0	0	0	16	6.3
D	4	*Sergei Starikov	N.J.	16	0	1	1	8−	8	0	0	0	0	6	.0
G	1	Sean Burke	N.J.	52	0	1	1	0	38	0	0	0	0	0	.0
R	25	Jim Thomson	N.J.	3	0	0	0	3−	31	0	0	0	0	3	.0
R	25	*Troy Crowder	N.J.	10	0	0	0	0	23	0	0	0	0	4	.0
G	31	Chris Terreri	N.J.	35	0	0	0	0	0	0	0	0	0	0	.0

Goaltending

No.	Goaltender	GPI	Mins	Avg	W	L	T	EN	SO	GA	SA	S%
31	Chris Terreri	35	1931	3.42	15	12	3	3	0	110	1004	.890
1	Sean Burke	52	2914	3.60	22	22	6	0	0	175	1453	.880
	Totals	**80**	**4864**	**3.55**	**37**	**34**	**9**	**3**	**0**	**288**	**2457**	**.883**

Playoffs

Pos	#	Player	Team	GP	G	A	Pts	+/−	PIM	PP	SH	GW	OT	S	%
R	11	Brendan Shanahan	NJ	6	3	3	6	0	20	1	0	1	0	16	18.8
D	23	Bruce Driver	NJ	6	1	5	6	3	6	0	0	0	0	21	4.8
R	15	John MacLean	NJ	6	4	1	5	1−	12	2	1	0	0	22	18.2
C	29	Peter Stastny	NJ	6	3	2	5	1−	4	1	0	1	0	9	33.3
C	20	*Jon Morris	NJ	6	1	3	4	0	23	1	0	0	0	8	12.5
C	9	Kirk Muller	NJ	6	1	3	4	2−	11	0	0	0	0	12	8.3
L	17	Patrik Sundstrom	NJ	6	1	3	4	1	2	0	0	0	0	14	7.1
D	5	*Eric Weinrich	NJ	6	1	3	4	3	17	0	0	0	0	11	9.1
D	7	*Alex Kasatonov	NJ	6	0	3	3	2−	14	0	0	0	0	7	.0
D	3	Ken Daneyko	NJ	6	2	0	2	4−	21	0	0	0	0	3	66.7
D	2	*Viacheslav Fetisov	NJ	6	0	2	2	5−	10	0	0	0	0	11	.0
C	32	Pat Conacher	NJ	5	1	0	1	0	10	0	0	0	0	4	25.0
R	24	Doug Brown	NJ	6	0	1	1	1−	2	0	0	0	0	5	.0
C	16	Sylvain Turgeon	NJ	1	0	0	0	1−	0	0	0	0	0	3	.0
G	1	Sean Burke	NJ	2	0	0	0	0	2	0	0	0	0	0	.0
R	25	*Troy Crowder	NJ	2	0	0	0	0	10	0	0	0	0	0	.0
C	12	Mark Johnson	NJ	2	0	0	0	1−	0	0	0	0	0	1	.0
G	31	Chris Terreri	NJ	4	0	0	0	0	0	0	0	0	0	0	.0
C	19	*Claude Vilgrain	NJ	4	0	0	0	2−	0	0	0	0	0	3	.0
C	10	Bob Brooke	NJ	5	0	0	0	0	14	0	0	0	0	2	.0
D	18	*Jamie Huscroft	NJ	5	0	0	0	0	16	0	0	0	0	1	.0
L	8	David Maley	NJ	6	0	0	0	2−	25	0	0	0	0	2	.0
D	27	Randy Velischek	NJ	6	0	0	0	5−	4	0	0	0	0	2	.0

Goaltending

No.	Goaltender	GPI	Mins	Avg	W	L	EN	SO	GA	SA	S%
31	Chris Terreri	4	238	3.28	2	2	0	0	13	103	.874
1	Sean Burke	2	125	3.84	0	2	0	0	8	57	.860
	Totals	6	366	3.44	2	4	0	0	21	160	.869

General Managers' History

(Kansas City) Sidney Abel, 1974-75 to 1975-76; (Colorado) Ray Miron, 1976-77 to 1981-82; Billy MacMillan, 1982-83; Billy MacMillan and Max McNab, 1983-84; Max McNab 1984-85 to 1986-87; Lou Lamoriello, 1987-88 to date.

Coaching History

(Kansas City) Bep Guidolin, 1974-75; Bep Guidolin, Sid Abel, and Eddie Bush, 1975-76; (Colorado) John Wilson, 1976-77; Pat Kelly, 1977-78; Pat Kelly, Aldo Guidolin, 1978-79; Don Cherry, 1979-80; Bill MacMillan, 1980-81; Bert Marshall and Marshall Johnston, 1981-82; (New Jersey) Bill MacMillan, 1982-83; Bill MacMillan and Tom McVie, 1983-84; Doug Carpenter, 1984-85 to 1986-87; Doug Carpenter and Jim Schoenfeld, 1987-88; Jim Schoenfeld, 1988-89; Jim Schoenfeld and John Cunniff, 1989-90; John Cunniff, 1990-91.

Captains' History

Simon Nolet, 1974-75 to 1976-77; Wilf Paiement, 1977-78; Gary Croteau, 1978-79; Mike Christie, Rene Robert, Lanny McDonald, 1979-80; Lanny McDonald, 1980-81, Lanny McDonald, Rob Ramage, 1981-82; Don Lever, 1982-83; Don Lever, Mel Bridgman, 1983-84; Mel Bridgman, 1984-85, 1985-86; Kirk Muller, 1987-88 to date.

Club Records

Team

(Figures in brackets for season records are games played; records for fewest points, wins, ties, losses, goals, goals against are for 70 or more games)

Most Points	83	1989-90 (80)
Most Wins	38	1987-88 (80)
Most Ties	21	1977-78 (80)
Most Losses	56	1983-84 (80)
		1975-76 (80)
Most Goals	300	1985-86 (80)
Most Goals Against	374	1985-86
Fewest Points	*36	1975-76 (80)
	41	1983-84 (80)
Fewest Wins	*12	1975-76 (80)
	17	1982-83 (80)
		1983-84 (80)
Fewest Ties	3	1985-86 (80)
Fewest Losses	34	1989-90 (80)
Fewest Goals	*184	1974-75 (80)
	230	1982-83 (80)
Fewest Goals Against	288	1989-90 (80)

Longest Winning Streak
Over-all .... 5 Mar. 27-
Apr. 3/88
Home .... 8 Oct. 9-
Nov. 7/87
Away .... 4 Oct. 5-23/89

Longest Undefeated Streak
Over-all .... 8 Mar. 20-
Apr. 3/88
(7 wins, 1 tie)
Home .... 9 Oct. 9-
Nov. 12/87
(8 wins, 1 tie)
Away .... 6 Jan. 20-
Feb. 9/89
(3 wins, 3 ties)
Mar. 12-
Apr. 3/88
(5 wins, 1 tie)

Longest Losing Streak
Over-all .... *14 Dec. 30/75-
Jan. 29/76
10 Oct. 14-
Nov. 4/83
Home .... 9 Dec. 22/85-
Feb. 6/86
Away .... 12 Oct. 19/83-
Dec. 1/83

Longest Winless Streak
Over-all .... *27 Feb. 12-
Apr. 4/76
(21 losses, 6 ties)
18 Oct. 20-
Nov. 26/82
(14 losses 4 ties)
Home .... *14 Feb. 12-
Mar. 30/76
(10 losses, 4 ties)
Feb. 4-
Mar. 31/79
(12 losses, 2 ties)
9 Dec. 22/85-
Feb. 6/86
(9 losses)
Away .... *32 Nov. 12/77-
Mar. 15/78
(22 losses, 10 ties)
14 Dec. 26/82-
Mar. 5/83
(13 losses, 1 tie)

Most Shutouts, Season	3	1988-89 (80)
Most PIM, Season	2,494	1988-89 (80)
Most Goals, Game	9	Apr. 1/79

(St.L. 5 at Col. 9)
Feb. 12/82
(Que. 2 at Col. 9)
Apr. 6/86
(NYI 7 at N.J. 9)
Mar. 10/90
(Que. 3 at N.J. 9)

Individual

Most Seasons .... 8 Mike Kitchen
Aaron Broten
Most Games .... 641 Aaron Broten
Most Goals, Career .... 172 John MacLean
Most Assists, Career .... 307 Aaron Broten
Most Points, Career .... 469 Aaron Broten
(162 goals, 307 assists)
Most PIM, Career .... 1,048 Ken Daneyko
Most Shutouts, Career .... 4 Sean Burke
Longest Consecutive
Games Streak .... 308 Aaron Broten
(Dec. 6/82-Jan. 4/90)
Most Goals, Season .... 47 Pat Verbeek
(1987-88)
Most Assists, Season .... 57 Aaron Broten,
Kirk Muller
(1987-88)
Most Points, Season .... 94 Kirk Muller
(1987-88)
(37 goals, 57 assists)
Most PIM, Season ...... 283 Ken Daneyko
(1988-89)

Most Points, Defenseman
Season .... 66 Tom Kurvers
(1988-89)
(16 goals, 50 assists)
Most Points, Center
Season .... 94 Kirk Muller
(1987-88)
(37 goals, 57 assists)
Most Points, Right Wing,
Season .... *87 Wilf Paiement
(1977-78)
(31 goals, 56 assists)
87 John MacLean
(1988-89)
(42 goals, 45 assists)
Most Points, Left Wing,
Season .... 83 Aaron Broten
(1987-88)
(26 goals, 57 assists)
Most Points, Rookie,
Season .... *60 Barry Beck
(1977-78)
(22 goals, 38 assists)
54 Kirk Muller
(1984-85)
(17 goals, 37 assists)
Most Shutouts, Season .... 3 Sean Burke
(1988-89)
Most Goals, Game .... 4 Bob MacMillan
(Jan. 8/82)
Pat Verbeek
(Feb. 28/88)
Most Assists, Game ...... 5 Kirk Muller
(Mar. 25/87)
Greg Adams
(Oct. 10/86)
Tom Kurvers
(Feb. 13/89)
Most Points, Game .... 6 Kirk Muller
(Nov. 29/86)
(3 goals, 3 assists)

* – Record includes Kansas City Scouts and Colorado Rockies from 1974-75 through 1981-82

All-time Record vs. Other Clubs

Regular Season

		At Home							On Road							Total					
	GP	W	L	T	GF	GA	PTS	GP	W	L	T	GF	GA	PTS	GP	W	L	T	GF	GA	PTS
Boston	27	3	16	8	69	106	14	28	7	19	2	88	130	16	55	10	35	10	157	236	30
Buffalo	27	4	19	4	78	117	12	28	3	22	3	78	139	9	55	7	41	7	156	256	21
Calgary	32	7	22	3	86	129	17	32	3	25	4	80	158	10	64	10	47	7	166	287	27
Chicago	34	15	14	5	108	109	35	33	7	22	4	92	144	18	67	22	36	9	200	253	53
Detroit	28	14	8	6	104	76	34	27	8	17	2	84	122	18	55	22	25	8	188	198	52
Edmonton	20	9	9	2	71	71	20	20	5	12	3	80	110	13	40	14	21	5	151	181	33
Hartford	17	7	8	2	62	77	16	18	4	10	4	54	69	12	35	11	18	6	116	146	28
Los Angeles	30	12	13	5	100	114	29	30	1	23	6	91	173	8	60	13	36	11	191	287	37
Minnesota	32	15	14	3	107	106	33	33	7	20	6	84	137	20	65	22	34	9	191	243	53
Montreal	28	6	22	0	71	140	12	27	4	20	3	70	121	11	55	10	42	3	141	261	23
NY Islanders	46	16	24	6	153	193	38	46	2	38	6	121	230	10	92	18	62	12	274	423	48
NY Rangers	47	18	25	4	167	192	40	45	13	27	5	151	203	31	92	31	52	9	318	395	71
Philadelphia	45	17	25	3	159	194	37	46	7	35	4	98	205	18	91	24	60	7	257	399	55
Pittsburgh	43	20	15	8	165	156	48	44	16	25	3	160	184	35	87	36	40	11	325	340	83
Quebec	18	8	9	1	79	70	17	17	5	10	2	59	83	12	35	13	19	3	138	153	29
St. Louis	34	13	14	7	105	100	33	33	7	23	3	101	154	17	67	20	37	10	206	254	50
Toronto	27	9	9	9	99	90	27	28	6	20	2	94	130	14	55	15	29	11	193	220	41
Vancouver	36	13	17	6	104	114	32	36	6	19	11	108	130	23	72	10	36	17	212	264	55
Washington	44	16	22	6	140	143	38	43	8	32	3	128	202	19	87	24	54	9	268	345	57
Winnipeg	17	5	8	4	54	60	14	18	3	13	2	43	74	8	35	8	21	6	97	134	22
Defunct Club	8	4	2	2	25	19	10	8	2	3	3	19	27	7	16	6	5	5	44	46	17
Totals	**640**	**231**	**315**	**94**	**2106**	**2387**	**556**	**640**	**124**	**435**	**81**	**1883**	**2934**	**329**	**1280**	**355**	**750**	**175**	**3989**	**5321**	**885**

Playoffs

	Series	W	L	GP	W	L	T	GF	GA	Last Mtg.	Round	Result
Boston	1	0	1	7	3	4	0	19	30	1988	CF	L 3-4
NY Islanders	1	1	0	6	4	2	0	23	18	1988	DSF	W 4-2
Philadelphia	1	0	1	2	0	2	0	3	6	1978	PR	L 0-2
Washington	2	1	1	13	6	7	0	43	44	1990	DSF	L 2-4
Totals	**5**	**2**	**3**	**28**	**13**	**15**	**0**	**88**	**98**			

Abbreviations: Round: F – Final; **CF** – conference final; **DF** – division final; **DSF** – division semi-final; **PR** – preliminary round. **GA** – goals against; **GF** – goals for.

Playoff Results 1990-86

Year	Round	Opponent	Result	GF	GA
1990	DSF	Washington	L 2-4	18	21
1988	CF	Boston	L 3-4	19	30
	DF	Washington	W 4-3	25	23
	DSF	NY Islanders	W 4-2	23	18

Entry Draft Selections 1990-76

1990
Pick
20 Martin Brodeur
24 David Harlock
29 Chris Gotziaman
53 Michael Dunham
56 Brad Bombardir
64 Mike Bodnarchuk
95 Dean Malkoc
104 Peter Kuchyna
116 Lubomir Kolnik
137 Chris McAlpine
179 Jaroslav Modry
200 Corey Schwab
221 Valeri Zelepukin
242 Todd Reirden

1989
Pick
5 Bill Guerin
18 Jason Miller
26 Jarrod Skalde
47 Scott Pellerin
89 Mike Heinke
110 David Emma
152 Sergei Starikov
173 Andre Faust
215 Jason Simon
236 Peter Larsson

1988
Pick
12 Corey Foster
23 Jeff Christian
54 Zdenek Ciger
65 Matt Ruchty
75 Scott Luik
96 Chris Nelson
117 Chad Johnson
138 Chad Erickson
159 Bryan Lafort
180 Sergei Svetlov
201 Bob Woods
207 Alexander Semak
222 Charles Hughes
243 Michael Pohl

1987
Pick
2 Brendan Shanahan
23 Rickard Persson
65 Brian Sullivan
86 Kevin Dean
107 Ben Hankinson
128 Tom Neziol
149 Jim Dowd
170 John Blessman
191 Peter Fry
212 Alain Charland

1986
Pick
3 Neil Brady
24 Todd Copeland
45 Janne Ojanen
62 Marc Laniel
66 Anders Carlsson
108 Troy Crowder
129 Kevin Todd
150 Ryan Pardoski
171 Scott McCormack
192 Frederic Chabot
213 John Andersen
236 Doug Kirton

1985
Pick
3 Craig Wolanin
24 Sean Burke
32 Eric Weinrich
45 Myles O'Connor
66 Gregg Polak
108 Bill McMillan
129 Kevin Schrader
150 Ed Krayer
171 Jamie Huscroft
192 Terry Shold
213 Jamie McKinley
234 David Williams

1984
Pick
2 Kirk Muller
23 Craig Billington
44 Neil Davey
74 Paul Ysebaert
86 Jon Morris
107 Kirk McLean
128 Ian Ferguson
149 Vladimir Kames
170 Mike Roth
190 Mike Peluso
211 Jarkko Piiparinen
231 Chris Kiene

1983
Pick
6 John MacLean
24 Shawn Evans
87 Chris Terreri
108 Gordon Mark
129 Greg Evtushevski
150 Viacheslav Fetisov
171 Jay Octeau
192 Alexi Chernykh
213 Allan Stewart
234 Alexei Kasatonov

1982
Pick
8 Rocky Trottier
18 Ken Daneyko
43 Pat Verbeek
54 Dave Kasper
85 Scott Brydges
106 Mike Moher
127 Paul Fulcher
148 John Hutchings
169 Alan Hepple
190 Brent Shaw
207 Tony Gilliard
211 Scott Fusco
232 Dan Dorian

1981
Pick
5 Joe Cirella
26 Rich Chernomaz
48 Ullie Hiemer
66 Gus Greco
87 Doug Speck
108 Bruce Driver
129 Jeff Larmer
150 Tony Arima
171 Tim Army
192 John Johannson

1980
Pick
19 Paul Gagne
22 Joe Ward
64 Rick LaFerriere
85 Ed Cooper
106 Aaron Broten
127 Dan Fascinato
148 Andre Hidi
169 Shawn MacKenzie
190 Bob Jansch

1979
Pick
1 Rob Ramage
64 Steve Peters
85 Gary Dillon
106 Bob Attwell

1978
Pick
4 Mike Gillis
27 Merlin Malinowski
41 Paul Messier
58 Dave Watson
73 Tim Thomlison
74 Rod Guimont
91 John Hynes
108 Andy Clark
125 John Oliver
142 Kevin Krook
159 Jeff Jensen
174 Bo Ericsson
190 Jari Viitala
204 Ulf Zetterstrom

1977
Pick
2 Barry Beck
38 Doug Berry
47 Randy Pierce
92 Daniel Lempe
110 Rick Doyle
126 Joe Contini
142 Jack Hughes

1976
Pick
11 Paul Gardner
38 Mike Kitchen
74 Rick McIntyre
92 Larry Skinner

Club Directory

Byrne Meadowlands Arena
P.O. Box 504
East Rutherford, N.J. 07073
Phone **201/935-6050**
GM FAX 201/507-0711
FAX 201/935-2127
ENVOY ID
Front Office: DEVILS. GM
Public
Relations: DEVILS. PR
Capacity: 19,040

Chairman	John J. McMullen
President & General Manager	Louis A. Lamoriello
Executive Vice-President	Max McNab
Vice-President, Community Development	Jerry Dailey
Vice-President, Operations/Human Resources	Peter McMullen
Vice-President, Finance	Chris Modrzynski
Vice-President, Marketing	Brian Petrovek

Hockey Club Personnel

Director of Player Personnel	Marshall Johnston
Head Coach	John Cunniff
Assistant Coach	Tim Burke
Assistant Director of Player Personnel	David Conte
Scouting Staff	Bob Bellemore, Claude Carrier, Glen Dirk, Milt Fisher, Frank Jay, Dan Labraaten, Ed Thomlinson, Les Widdifield
Special Assignment Scout	Bob Sauve
Athletic Trainer	Ted Schuch
Equipment Specialists	Jeff Croop, Dave Baglio
Strength Coach	Dimitri Lopuchin
Team Orthopedists	Dr. Barry Fisher, Dr. Len Jaffe
Team Internist	Dr. Richard Commentucci
Team Cardiologist	Dr. Joseph Niznik
Team Dentist	Dr. H. Hugh Gardy
Exercise Physiologist	Dr. Garret Caffrey
Massage Therapist	Bob Huddleston
Administrative Assistants to the President/GM	Marie Carnevale, Charlotte Smaldone
Staff Assistant	Angela Gorgone

Communications Department

Director, Public & Media Relations	David Freed
Director of Broadcast Operations	Chris Moore
Assistant Director, Media Relations	Mike Levine
Public & Media Relations Assistant	Nelson Rodriguez
Receptionist	Jelsa Belotta

Finance Department

Assistant Controller	Scott Struble
Staff Accountants	Eric Mandelbaum, Frank Vumbaca
Secretary	Eileen Musikant

Marketing Department

Director of Promotional Marketing	Ken Ferriter
Group Sales Manager	Don Gleeson
Sales Managers	Neil Desormeaux, Holly Meyer, Matt Zanelli
Secretary	Karen Lynch

Ticketing Department

Director, Ticket Operations	Terry Farmer
Assistant Director, Ticket Operations	Scott Tanfield
Team Photographers	Steve Crandall, Jim Turner
Video Consultant	Mitch Kaufman
Location of Press Box	Section 108, center ice
Location of Broadcast Booth	Front, Section 234
Dimensions of Rink	200 feet by 85 feet
Club Colors	Red, Green and White
Television Outlet	SportsChannel
Television Announcers	Gary Thorne (play-by-play); Peter McNab (color)
Flagship Radio Station	WABC (770 AM)
Radio Announcers	Chris Moore (play-by-play); Larry Brooks (color)

General Manager

LAMORIELLO, LOU
President and General Manager, New Jersey Devils.
Born in Providence, Rhode Island, October 21, 1942.

Lou Lamoriello is entering his third season as president and general manager of the Devils following a more than 20-year association with Providence College as a player, coach and administrator. A member of the varsity hockey Friars during his undergraduate days, he became an assistant coach with the college club after graduating in 1963. Lamoriello was later named head coach and in the ensuing 15 years, led his teams to a 248-179-13 record, a .578 winning percentage and appearances in 10 post-season tournaments, including the 1983 NCAA Final Four. Lamoriello also served a five-year term as athletic director at Providence and was a co-founder of Hockey East, one of the strongest collegiate hockey conferences in the U.S. He remained as athletic director until he was hired as president of the Devils on April 30, 1987. He assumed the dual responsibility of general manager on September 10, 1987.

Coach

CUNNIFF, JOHN
Coach, New Jersey Devils. Born in South Boston, Ma, July 9, 1943.

John Cunniff took over head coaching duties for the Devils on November 6, 1989. In his first season as head coach, the Devils posted a 37-34-9 record, a 17-point improvement over their 1988-89 record.

The 45-year-old Cunniff joined the Devils on May 31, 1989 as an assistant coach after spending three years in that capacity for the Boston Bruins. Cunniff joined the Bruins' organization in November, 1986 after five years as a member of the Hartford Whalers' hockey operations staff. A native of South Boston, Cunniff earned All-American honors at Boston College before playing for the U.S. National Team in 1966-67 and the Olympic Team in 1968. Thereafter, Cunniff enjoyed a seven-year playing career in the AHL, CHL and WHA. Cunniff served as coach of the Binghamton Whalers (AHL) in 1982-83, but joined the NHL Whalers' staff on January 4, 1983.

Coaching Record

| Season | Team | Games | Regular Season | | | | Playoffs | | | |
			W	L	T	%	Games	W	L	%
1982-83	Binghamton (AHL)									
1989-90	New Jersey (NHL)	66	31	28	7	.523	6	2	4	.333
	NHL Totals	66	31	28	7	.523	6	2	4	.333

New York Islanders
1989-90 Results: 31w-38L-11T 73PTS. Fourth, Patrick Division

Year-by-Year Record

Season	GP	Home W	L	T	Road W	L	T	Overall W	L	T	GF	GA	Pts.	Finished	Playoff Result
1989-90	80	15	17	8	16	21	3	31	38	11	281	288	73	4th, Patrick Div.	Lost Div. Semi-Final
1988-89	80	19	18	3	9	29	2	28	47	5	265	325	61	6th, Patrick Div.	Out of Playoffs
1987-88	80	24	10	6	15	21	4	39	31	10	308	267	88	1st, Patrick Div.	Lost Div. Semi-Final
1986-87	80	20	15	5	15	18	7	35	33	12	279	281	82	3rd, Patrick Div.	Lost Div. Final
1985-86	80	22	11	7	17	18	5	39	29	12	327	284	90	3rd, Patrick Div.	Lost Div. Semi-Final
1984-85	80	26	11	3	14	23	3	40	34	6	345	312	86	3rd, Patrick Div.	Lost Div. Final
1983-84	80	28	11	1	22	15	3	50	26	4	357	269	104	1st, Patrick Div.	Lost Final
1982-83	**80**	**26**	**11**	**3**	**16**	**15**	**9**	**42**	**26**	**12**	**302**	**226**	**96**	**2nd, Patrick Div.**	**Won Stanley Cup**
1981-82	**80**	**33**	**3**	**4**	**21**	**13**	**6**	**54**	**16**	**10**	**385**	**250**	**118**	**1st, Patrick Div.**	**Won Stanley Cup**
1980-81	**80**	**23**	**6**	**11**	**25**	**12**	**3**	**48**	**18**	**14**	**355**	**260**	**110**	**1st, Patrick Div.**	**Won Stanley Cup**
1979-80	**80**	**26**	**9**	**5**	**13**	**19**	**8**	**39**	**28**	**13**	**281**	**247**	**91**	**2nd, Patrick Div.**	**Won Stanley Cup**
1978-79	80	31	3	6	20	12	8	51	15	14	358	214	116	1st, Patrick Div.	Lost Semi-Final
1977-78	80	29	3	8	19	14	7	48	17	15	334	210	111	1st, Patrick Div.	Lost Quarter-Final
1976-77	80	24	11	5	23	10	7	47	21	12	288	193	106	2nd, Patrick Div.	Lost Semi-Final
1975-76	80	24	8	8	18	13	9	42	21	17	297	190	101	2nd, Patrick Div.	Lost Semi-Final
1974-75	80	22	6	12	11	19	10	33	25	22	264	221	88	3rd, Patrick Div.	Lost Semi-Final
1973-74	78	13	17	9	6	24	9	19	41	18	182	247	56	8th, East Div.	Out of Playoffs
1972-73	78	10	25	4	2	35	2	12	60	6	170	347	30	8th, East Div.	Out of Playoffs

Schedule

Home				Away			
Oct.	Sat.	13	Pittsburgh	Oct.	Thur.	4	Los Angeles
	Tues.	16	Winnipeg		Sat.	6	Minnesota
	Sat.	20	Buffalo		Sun.	7	Chicago
	Tues.	23	New Jersey		Fri.	19	Washington
	Sat.	27	Philadelphia		Wed.	24	Montreal
	Tues.	30	Los Angeles		Sun.	28	Pittsburgh
Nov.	Sat.	3	Washington	Nov.	Fri.	2	NY Rangers
	Tues.	6	Toronto		Wed.	7	New Jersey
	Sat.	10	Calgary		Thur.	15	Calgary
	Thur.	22	Winnipeg		Fri.	16	Vancouver
	Sat.	24	NY Rangers*		Sun.	18	Edmonton
	Tues.	27	Philadelphia		Sun.	25	Philadelphia
Dec.	Sat.	1	Washington		Fri.	30	New Jersey
	Tues.	4	Vancouver	Dec.	Thur.	6	Chicago
	Tues.	11	New Jersey		Thur.	13	Philadelphia
	Tues.	18	Toronto		Sat.	15	Quebec
	Thur.	20	Hartford		Sun.	23	Pittsburgh
	Sat.	22	Pittsburgh		Thur.	27	New Jersey
	Sat.	29	Chicago	Jan.	Wed.	2	Buffalo
	Mon.	31	Quebec*		Wed.	9	Montreal
Jan.	Thur.	3	Los Angeles		Sun.	13	Quebec
	Sat.	5	Philadelphia		Fri.	25	Winnipeg
	Tues.	8	Minnesota		Sun.	27	Washington*
	Sat.	12	Detroit		Tues.	29	Hartford
	Tues.	15	Boston	Feb.	Wed.	6	NY Rangers
	Thur.	17	Edmonton		Fri.	8	Detroit
	Tues.	22	NY Rangers		Sat.	9	Toronto
	Thur.	31	Washington		Thur.	14	Pittsburgh
Feb.	Sat.	2	Montreal		Mon.	18	NY Rangers*
	Sun.	3	Hartford		Thur.	21	St Louis
	Tues.	12	Minnesota		Sun.	24	Philadelphia
	Sat.	16	Pittsburgh		Thur.	28	Boston
	Sat.	23	Philadelphia	Mar.	Sat.	2	Washington
	Tues.	26	Buffalo		Thur.	7	Detroit
Mar.	Tues.	5	New Jersey		Wed.	13	Edmonton
	Sat.	9	NY Rangers		Thur.	14	Calgary
	Sun.	10	Pittsburgh		Sat.	16	Vancouver
	Thur.	21	Washington		Sun.	24	NY Rangers
	Sat.	23	St Louis		Thur.	28	St Louis
	Sat.	30	Boston		Sun.	31	New Jersey

* Denotes afternoon game.

Home Starting Times:
All Games .... 7:35 p.m.
Except Nov. 24, Dec. 31 .... 2:05 p.m.
Feb. 2, Feb. 3,
Mar. 9, Mar. 10 .... 5:05 p.m.

Franchise date: June 6, 1972

 19th NHL Season

Mark Fitzpatrick had three shutouts in 1989-90.

1990-91 Player Personnel

FORWARDS	HT	WT	Place of Birth	Date	1989-90 Club
BERG, Bill	6-1	190	St. Catharines, Ont.	10/21/67	Springfield
BYRAM, Shawn	6-2	204	Neepawa, Man.	9/12/68	Springfield
CHYZOWSKI, David	6-1	190	Edmonton, Alta.	7/11/71	NYI-Springfield-Kamloops
DALGARNO, Brad	6-3	215	Vancouver, B.C.	8/11/67	Did Not Play
DIMAIO, Rob	5-8	175	Calgary, Alta.	2/19/68	NYI-Springfield
DOUCET, Wayne	6-2	203	Etobicoke, Ont.	6/19/70	Kingston
ENS, Kelly	6-2	194	Saskatoon, Sask.	6/15/69	Lethbridge
EWEN, Dean	6-1	185	St. Albert, Alta.	2/28/69	Springfield
FITZGERALD, Tom	6-1	193	Melrose, MA	8/28/68	NYI-Springfield
FLATLEY, Patrick	6-2	197	Toronto, Ont.	10/3/63	NY Islanders
FLEURY, Sylvain	5-11	189	Drum'ville, Que.	4/30/70	Longueil
FRASER, Iain	5-10	175	Scarborough, Ont.	8/10/69	Oshawa
GREEN, Travis	6-0	196	Creston, B.C.	12/20/70	Medicine Hat-Spokane
GRIEVE, Brent	6-1	205	Oshawa, Ont.	5/9/69	Oshawa
GUAY, Paul	5-11	185	Providence, R.I.	9/2/63	Utica
HUBER, Phil	5-11	196	Calgary, Alta.	1/10/69	Kamloops
JABLONSKI, Jeff	6-1	185	Toledo, OH	6/20/67	Lake Superior
KELFER, Mike	5-10	180	Peabody, MA	1/2/67	Springfield
KERR, Alan	5-11	195	Hazelton, B.C.	3/28/64	NY Islanders
KING, Derek	6-1	210	Hamilton, Ont.	2/11/67	NYI-Springfield
KROMM, Rich	5-11	180	Trail, B.C.	3/29/64	Europe
LaFONTAINE, Pat	5-10	177	St. Louis, MO	2/22/65	NY Islanders
LAUER, Brad	6-0	195	Humboldt, Sask.	10/27/66	NYI-Springfield
LAXDAL, Derek	6-1	175	St. Boniface, Man.	2/21/66	NYI-Springfield-Newmarket
LeBRUN, Sean	6-2	200	Prince George, B.C.	5/2/69	Springfield
MALONEY, Don	6-1	190	Lindsay, Ont.	9/5/58	NY Islanders
McDONOUGH, Hubie	5-9	180	Manchester, NH	7/8/63	Los Angeles-NYI
PARKS, Greg	5-9	180	Edmonton, Alta.	3/25/67	Springfield
ROHLICEK, Jeff	6-0	180	Park Ridge, IL	1/27/66	Springfield-Milwaukee
SCISSONS, Scott	6-1	195	Saskatoon, Sask.	10/29/71	Saskatoon
SUTTER, Brent	5-11	180	Viking, Alta.	6/10/62	NY Islanders
TAYLOR, Chris	6-0	185	Stratford, Ont.	3/6/72	London
VOLEK, David	6-0	185	Prague, Czech.	6/18/66	NY Islanders
VUKOTA, Mick	6-2	195	Saskatoon, Sask.	9/14/66	NY Islanders
WOOD, Randy	6-0	195	Princeton, NJ	10/12/63	NY Islanders
YOUNG, Steve	6-4	210	Calgary, Atla.	5/17/69	Portland-Pr. Albert-Moose Jaw

DEFENSEMEN					
BAUMGARTNER, Ken	6-1	200	Flin Flon, Man.	3/11/66	Los Angeles-NYI
BERGEVIN, Marc	6-0	185	Montreal, Que.	8/11/65	NYI-Springfield
CHEVELDAYOFF, Kevin	6-0	202	Saskatoon, Sask.	2/4/70	Springfield-Brandon
CHYNOWETH, Dean	6-2	190	Calgary, Alta.	10/30/68	NY Islanders-Springfield
CROSSMAN, Doug	6-2	190	Peterborough, Ont.	6/30/60	NY Islanders
DIDUCK, Gerald	6-2	207	Edmonton, Alta.	4/6/65	NY Islanders
FINLEY, Jeff	6-2	185	Edmonton, Alta.	4/14/67	NYI-Springfield
GRONSTRAND, Jari	6-3	195	Tampere, Finland	11/14/62	Quebec-NYI
LAMMENS, Hank	6-2	210	Brockville, Ont.	2/21/66	Springfield
LEHTO, Joni	6-0	195	Turku, Finland	7/15/70	Ottawa
McBEAN, Wayne	6-2	185	Calgary, Alta.	2/21/69	NYI-Springfield
NORTON, Jeff	6-2	190	Acton, MA	11/25/65	NY Islanders
NYLUND, Gary	6-4	210	Surrey, B.C.	10/28/63	NY Islanders
PILON, Richard	6-0	202	Saskatoon, Sask.	4/30/68	NY Islanders
PRYOR, Chris	5-11	210	St. Paul, MN	1/31/61	NYI-Springfield
REEKIE, Joe	6-3	215	Petawawa, Ont.	2/22/65	NY Islanders
VASKE, Dennis	6-2	210	Rockford, IL	10/11/67	Minn.-Duluth

GOALTENDERS	HT	WT	Place of Birth	Date	1989-90 Club
COHEN, Paul	5-11	185	Toronto, Ont.	1/31/65	Springfield
FITZPATRICK, Mark	6-2	190	Toronto, Ont.	11/13/68	NY Islanders
HACKETT, Jeff	6-1	175	London, Ont.	6/1/68	Springfield
HEALY, Glenn	5-10	175	Pickering, Ont.	8/23/62	NY Islanders
LORENZ, Danny	5-10	170	Murrayeville, B.C.	12/12/69	Seattle
MANELUK, George	5-11	185	Winnipeg, Man.	7/25/67	Springfield

General Managers' History
William A. Torrey, 1972-73 to date.

Coaching History
Phil Goyette and Earl Ingarfield, 1972-73; Al Arbour, 1973-74 to 1985-86; Terry Simpson, 1986-87 to 1987-88; Terry Simpson and Al Arbour, 1988-89; Al Arbour, 1989-90 to date.

Captains' History
Ed Westfall, 1972-73 to 1975-76; Ed Westfall, Clark Gillies, 1976-77; Clark Gillies, 1977-78, 1978-79; Denis Potvin, 1979-80 to 1986-87; Brent Sutter, 1987-88 to date.

1989-90 Scoring

Regular Season
*rookie

Pos	#	Player	Team	GP	G	A	Pts	+/-	PIM	PP	SH	GW	GT	S	%
C	16	Pat LaFontaine	NYI	74	54	51	105	13−	38	13	2	8	1	286	18.9
C	21	Brent Sutter	NYI	67	33	35	68	9	65	17	3	3	0	198	16.7
D	3	Doug Crossman	NYI	80	15	44	59	3	54	8	0	1	2	159	9.4
D	4	Jeff Norton	NYI	60	4	49	53	9−	65	4	0	0	0	104	3.8
R	26	Patrick Flatley	NYI	62	17	32	49	10	101	4	0	2	0	136	12.5
L	11	Randy Wood	NYI	74	24	24	48	10−	39	6	1	3	0	185	13.0
L	28	Don Maloney	NYI	79	16	27	43	6	47	0	1	2	0	113	14.2
L	27	Derek King	NYI	46	13	27	40	2	20	5	0	1	0	91	14.3
L	25	David Volek	NYI	80	17	22	39	2−	41	6	0	0	0	181	9.4
C	39	*Hubie McDonough	L.A.	22	3	4	7	4	10	0	0	1	0	13	23.1
			NYI	54	18	11	29	10	26	0	3	3	0	92	19.6
			TOTAL	76	21	15	36	14	36	0	3	4	0	105	20.0
R	10	Alan Kerr	NYI	75	15	21	36	1−	129	3	0	1	0	127	11.8
D	36	Gary Nylund	NYI	64	4	21	25	8	144	2	0	0	2	65	6.2
C	19	Bryan Trottier	NYI	59	13	11	24	11−	29	4	0	0	0	84	15.5
L	32	Brad Lauer	NYI	63	6	18	24	5	19	0	0	2	0	86	7.0
D	4	Gerald Diduck	NYI	76	3	17	20	2	163	1	0	0	0	102	2.9
L	9	*Dave Chyzowski	NYI	34	8	6	14	4−	45	3	0	1	0	59	13.6
R	12	Mick Vukota	NYI	76	4	8	12	10	290	0	0	0	0	55	7.3
D	29	Joe Reekie	NYI	31	1	8	9	13	43	0	0	1	0	22	4.5
D	44	Jari Gronstrand	QUE	7	0	1	1	1−	2	0	0	0	0	3	.0
			NYI	41	3	4	7	0	27	0	0	2	0	23	13.0
			TOTAL	48	3	5	8	1−	29	0	0	2	0	26	11.5
C	7	*Tom Fitzgerald	NYI	19	2	5	7	3−	4	0	0	1	0	24	8.3
D	24	Ken Baumgartner	L.A.	12	1	0	1	10−	28	0	0	0	0	7	14.3
			NYI	53	0	5	5	6	194	0	0	0	0	41	.0
			TOTAL	65	1	5	6	4−	222	0	0	0	0	48	2.1
R	38	Derek Laxdal	NYI	12	3	1	4	4−	4	0	0	0	0	20	15.0
D	33	Marc Bergevin	NYI	18	0	4	4	8−	30	0	0	0	0	12	.0
D	47	Richard Pilon	NYI	14	0	2	2	2	31	0	0	0	0	5	.0
D	2	*Dean Chynoweth	NYI	20	0	2	2	0	39	0	0	0	0	8	.0
L	20	Dale Henry	NYI	20	0	2	2	4−	2	0	0	0	0	6	.0
G	30	Mark Fitzpatrick	NYI	47	0	2	2	0	18	0	0	0	0	0	.0
D	57	*Shawn Evans	NYI	2	0	1	1	1−	0	1	0	0	0	4	25.0
L	17	Paul Gagne	NYI	9	1	0	1	1−	4	0	0	0	0	10	10.0
D	6	Wayne McBean	NYI	5	0	1	1	1−	2	0	0	0	0	3	.0
D	37	*Jeff Finley	NYI	11	0	1	1	0	0	0	0	0	0	7	.0
G	35	Glenn Healy	NYI	39	0	1	1	0	7	0	0	0	0	0	.0
L	46	*Dale Kushner	NYI	2	0	0	0	2	2	0	0	0	0	1	.0
C	34	*Rob DiMaio	NYI	7	0	0	0	2−	2	0	0	0	0	2	.0
D	17	Chris Pryor	NYI	10	0	0	0	7−	24	0	0	0	0	2	.0

Goaltending

No.	Goaltender	GPI	Mins	Avg	W	L	T	EN	SO	GA	SA	S%
30	Mark Fitzpatrick	47	2653	3.39	19	19	4	3	1	150	1472	.898
35	Glenn Healy	39	2197	3.50	12	19	6	6	2	128	1210	.894
	Totals	**80**	**4872**	**3.55**	**31**	**38**	**11**	**10**	**5**	**288**	**2682**	**.893**

Playoffs

Pos	#	Player	Team	GP	G	A	Pts	+/-	PIM	PP	SH	GW	OT	S	%
C	21	Brent Sutter	NYI	5	2	3	5	0	2	2	0	1	1	17	11.8
L	25	Dave Volek	NYI	5	1	4	5	3−	0	0	0	0	0	19	5.3
D	8	Jeff Norton	NYI	4	1	3	4	0	17	0	0	0	0	7	14.3
R	26	Patrick Flatley	NYI	5	3	0	3	1	2	0	0	0	0	12	25.0
D	6	Wayne McBean	NYI	5	1	2	3	0	0	0	0	0	0	7	14.3
L	11	Randy Wood	NYI	5	1	1	2	2−	4	0	0	0	0	15	6.7
R	38	Derek Laxdal	NYI	1	0	2	2	2	2	0	0	0	0	0	.0
L	32	Brad Lauer	NYI	4	0	2	2	4	10	0	0	0	0	9	.0
D	37	*Jeff Finley	NYI	5	0	2	2	3−	2	0	0	0	0	2	.0
D	36	Gary Nylund	NYI	5	0	2	2	1	17	0	0	0	0	8	.0
C	34	*Rob Dimaio	NYI	1	1	0	1	2	4	0	0	0	0	4	25.0
C	7	*Tom Fitzgerald	NYI	4	1	0	1	0	4	0	0	0	0	3	33.3
C	19	Bryan Trottier	NYI	4	1	0	1	4−	0	0	0	0	0	7	14.3
C	39	*Hubie McDonough	NYI	5	1	0	1	2−	4	0	0	0	0	7	14.3
L	17	*Rod Dallman	NYI	1	0	1	1	1	0	0	0	0	0	5	.0
C	16	Pat LaFontaine	NYI	2	0	1	1	1	0	0	0	0	0	6	.0
G	35	Glenn Healy	NYI	4	0	1	1	0	0	0	0	0	0	0	.0
D	3	Doug Crossman	NYI	5	0	1	1	1	6	0	0	0	0	6	.0
D	33	Marc Bergevin	NYI	1	0	0	0	0	0	0	0	0	0	1	.0
R	12	Mick Vukota	NYI	4	0	0	0	0	17	0	0	0	0	3	.0
D	44	Jari Gronstrand	NYI	3	0	0	0	1−	0	0	0	0	0	1	.0
D	24	Ken Baumgartner	NYI	4	0	0	0	1	27	0	0	0	0	2	.0
G	30	Mark Fitzpatrick	NYI	4	0	0	0	0	19	0	0	0	0	0	.0
R	10	Alan Kerr	NYI	4	0	0	0	3−	10	0	0	0	0	7	.0
L	27	Derek King	NYI	4	0	0	0	2−	0	0	0	0	0	6	.0
D	4	Gerald Diduck	NYI	5	0	0	0	5−	12	0	0	0	0	12	.0
L	28	Don Maloney	NYI	1	0	0	0	2−	0	0	0	0	0	4	.0

Goaltending

No.	Goaltender	GPI	Mins	Avg	W	L	EN	SO	GA	SA	S%
35	Glenn Healy	4	166	3.25	1	2	0	0	9	79	.886
30	Mark Fitzpatrick	4	152	5.13	0	2	0	0	13	71	.817
	Totals	**5**	**321**	**4.11**	**1**	**4**	**0**	**0**	**22**	**150**	**.853**

Club Records

Team

(Figures in brackets for season records are games played; records for fewest points, wins, ties, losses, goals, goals against are for 70 or more games)

Most Points	118	1981-82 (80)
Most Wins	54	1981-82 (80)
Most Ties	22	1974-75 (80)
Most Losses	60	1972-73 (78)
Most Goals	385	1981-82 (80)
Most Goals Against	347	1972-73 (78)
Fewest Points	30	1972-73 (78)
Fewest Wins	12	1972-73 (78)
Fewest Ties	4	1983-84 (80)
Fewest Losses	15	1978-79 (80)
Fewest Goals	170	1972-73 (78)
Fewest Goals Against	190	1975-76 (80)

Longest Winning Streak
Over-all .... *15 Jan. 21/82-Feb. 20/82
Home .... 14 Jan. 2/82-Feb. 27/82
Away .... 8 Feb. 27/81-Mar. 31/81

Longest Undefeated Streak
Over-all .... 15 Jan. 21-Feb. 21/82 (15 wins)
Nov. 4-Dec. 4/80 (13 wins, 2 ties)
Home .... 23 Oct. 17/78-Jan. 27/79 (19 wins, 4 ties)
Jan. 2/82-Apr. 3/82 (21 wins, 2 ties)
Away .... 8 Four times

Longest Losing Streak
Over-all .... 12 Dec. 27/72-Jan. 18/73
Nov. 22-Dec. 17/88

Home .... 5 Jan. 2-23/73
Feb. 28-
Mar. 19/74
Nov. 22-
Dec. 17/88
Away .... 15 Jan. 20-
Apr. 1/73

Longest Winless Streak
Over-all .... 15 Nov. 22-Dec. 23/72 (12 losses, 3 ties)
Home .... 7 Oct. 14-Nov. 21/72 (6 losses, 1 tie)
Nov. 28-Dec. 23/72 (5 losses, 2 ties)
Feb. 13-Mar. 13/90 (4 losses, 3 ties)
Away .... 20 Nov. 3/72-Jan. 13/73 (19 losses, 1 tie)

Most Shutouts, Season 10 1975-76 (80)
Most PIM, Season 1,857 1986-87 (80)
Most Goals, Game .... 11 Dec. 20/83 (Pit. 3 at NYI 11)
Mar. 3/84 (NYI 11 at Tor. 6)

Individual

Most Seasons	17	Billy Smith
Most Games	1,123	Bryan Trottier
Most Goals, Career	573	Mike Bossy
Most Assists, Career	853	Bryan Trottier
Most Points, Career	1,353	Bryan Trottier (500 goals, 853 assists)
Most PIM, Career	1,466	Garry Howatt
Most Shutouts, Career	25	Glenn Resch
Longest Consecutive Games Streak	576	Bill Harris (Oct. 7/72-Nov. 30/79)

Most Goals, Season	69	Mike Bossy (1978-79)
Most Assists, Season	87	Bryan Trottier (1978-79)
Most Points, Season	147	Mike Bossy (1981-82) (64 goals, 83 assists)
Most PIM, Season	356	Brian Curran (1986-87)
Most Points, Defenseman, Season	101	Denis Potvin (1978-79) (31 goals, 70 assists)
Most Points, Center, Season	134	Bryan Trottier (1978-79) (47 goals, 87 assists)
Most Points, Right Wing, Season	*147	Mike Bossy (1981-82) (64 goals, 83 assists)
Mot Points, Left Wing, Season	100	John Tonelli (1984-85) (42 goals, 58 assists)
Most Points, Rookie, Season	95	Bryan Trottier (1975-76) (32 goals, 63 assists)
Most Shutouts, Season	7	Glenn Resch (1975-76)
Most Goals, Game	5	Bryan Trottier (Dec. 23/78; Feb. 13/82) John Tonelli (Jan. 6/81)
Most Assists, Game	6	Mike Bossy (Jan. 6/81)
Most Points, Game	8	Bryan Trottier (Dec. 23/78)

* NHL Record.

All-time Record vs. Other Clubs

Regular Season

	At Home						On Road						Total					
	GP	W	L	T	GF	GA	PTS	GP	W	L	T	GF	GA	PTS	GP	W	L	T	GF	GA	PTS
Boston	33	13	17	3	103	111	29	34	8	18	8	99	132	24	67	21	35	11	202	243	53
Buffalo	34	13	16	5	100	103	31	34	12	18	4	95	116	28	68	25	34	9	195	219	59
Calgary	39	20	10	9	153	106	49	38	10	17	11	120	141	31	77	30	27	20	273	247	80
Chicago	35	16	8	11	132	102	43	35	15	16	4	125	111	34	70	31	24	15	257	213	77
Detroit	33	20	12	1	134	93	41	32	14	16	2	109	115	30	65	34	28	3	243	208	71
Edmonton	18	8	3	7	81	75	23	17	5	9	3	57	69	13	35	13	12	10	138	144	36
Hartford	17	10	6	1	71	47	21	18	8	7	3	67	61	19	35	18	13	4	138	108	40
Los Angeles	32	19	9	4	124	90	42	33	13	13	7	113	113	33	65	32	22	11	237	203	75
Minnesota	34	18	8	8	139	100	44	35	18	12	5	137	101	41	69	36	20	13	276	201	85
Montreal	34	16	15	3	114	103	35	32	8	18	6	99	121	22	66	24	33	9	213	224	57
New Jersey	46	38	2	6	230	121	82	46	24	16	6	193	153	54	92	62	18	12	423	274	136
NY Rangers	57	37	16	4	245	177	78	58	16	37	5	178	235	37	115	53	53	9	423	412	115
Philadelphia	57	28	19	10	225	168	66	57	17	33	7	175	214	41	114	45	52	17	400	382	107
Pittsburgh	51	32	11	8	227	153	72	51	18	23	10	175	190	46	102	50	34	18	402	343	118
Quebec	18	11	6	1	82	66	23	17	7	9	1	56	69	15	35	18	15	2	138	135	38
St. Louis	36	22	5	9	143	76	53	34	16	12	6	120	117	38	70	38	17	15	263	193	91
Toronto	33	20	11	2	149	103	42	35	17	15	3	130	120	37	68	37	26	5	279	223	79
Vancouver	35	21	6	8	140	90	50	35	18	15	2	116	111	38	70	39	21	10	256	201	88
Washington	46	34	11	1	207	133	69	46	22	17	7	161	142	51	92	56	28	8	368	275	120
Winnipeg	17	8	4	5	69	55	21	18	12	5	1	75	54	25	35	20	9	6	144	109	46
Defunct Club	13	11	0	2	75	33	24	13	4	5	4	35	41	12	26	15	5	6	110	74	36
Totals	718	415	195	108	2943	2105	938	718	282	331	105	2435	2526	669	1436	697	526	213	5378	4631	1607

Playoffs

	Series	W	L	GP	W	L	T	GF	GA	Last Mtg.	Round	Result
Boston	2	2	0	11	8	3	0	49	35	1983	CF	W 4-2
Buffalo	3	3	0	16	12	4	0	59	45	1980	SF	W 4-2
Chicago	2	2	0	6	6	0	0	21	6	1979	QF	W 4-0
Edmonton	3	2	1	15	9	6	0	58	47	1984	F	L 1-4
Los Angeles	1	1	0	4	3	1	0	21	10	1980	PR	W 3-1
Minnesota	1	1	0	5	4	1	0	26	16	1981	F	W 4-1
Montreal	3	1	2	17	7	10	0	44	48	1984	CF	W 4-2
New Jersey	1	0	1	6	2	4	0	18	23	1988	DSF	L 2-4
NY Rangers	7	5	2	35	20	15	0	126	110	1990	DSF	L 1-4
Philadelphia	4	1	3	25	11	14	0	69	83	1987	DF	L 3-4
Pittsburgh	2	2	0	12	7	5	0	43	31	1982	DSF	W 3-2
Quebec	1	1	0	4	4	0	0	18	9	1982	CF	W 4-0
Toronto	2	1	1	10	6	4	0	33	20	1981	PR	W 3-0
Vancouver	2	2	0	6	6	0	0	26	14	1982	F	W 4-0
Washington	5	4	1	24	14	10	0	76	66	1987	DSF	W 4-3
Totals	39	28	11	196	119	77	0	687	563			

Abbreviations: Round: F – Final; **CF** – conference final; **DF** – division final; **DSF** – division semi-final; **SF** – semi-final; **QF** – quarter-final; **PR** – preliminary round; **GA** – goals against; **GF** – goals for.

Playoff Results 1990-86

Year	Round	Opponent	Result	GF	GA
1990	DSF	NY Rangers	L 1-4	13	22
1988	DSF	New Jersey	L 2-4	18	23
1987	DF	Philadelphia	L 3-4	16	23
	DSF	Washington	W 4-3	19	19
1986	DSF	Washington	L 0-3	4	11

1989-90 Results

		Home				Away	
Oct.	14	Philadelphia	3-3	Oct.	5	Minnesota	5-6
	17	Minnesota	3-6		7	Calgary	3-6
	21	Vancouver	1-2		9	Vancouver*	5-2
	24	Edmonton	3-3		11	Los Angeles	7-4
	28	NY Rangers	1-4		20	Washington	5-3
	31	Montreal	0-3		27	NY Rangers	5-5
Nov.	4	Detroit	3-2	Nov.	2	Pittsburgh	2-5
	7	Washington	3-5		5	Philadelphia	2-3
	9	Quebec	5-7		12	NY Rangers	2-4
	11	Chicago	3-5		18	Pittsburgh	3-5
	14	Philadelphia	4-5		22	Washington	3-5
	16	Toronto	6-2		28	New Jersey	2-3
	21	Winnipeg	3-4		30	Chicago	2-0
	25	Edmonton	2-7	Dec.	2	Winnipeg	6-3
Dec.	5	Buffalo	3-0		6	Hartford	4-3
	9	NY Rangers	0-0		13	New Jersey	2-5
	12	New Jersey	2-7		15	Washington	5-3
	16	NY Rangers	4-3		30	Quebec	3-6
	19	New Jersey	5-4		31	Buffalo	4-2
	23	Pittsburgh*	0-0	Jan.	10	Toronto	3-1
	28	St Louis	3-2		11	Minnesota	8-4
Jan.	2	Los Angeles	5-3		17	Montreal	6-3
	6	Quebec	5-2		19	Winnipeg	6-4
	13	Washington	4-2		23	Hartford	2-4
	16	Vancouver	3-0		25	Boston	2-5
	27	Pittsburgh*	9-3	Feb.	4	Buffalo	1-0
	28	New Jersey*	4-5		6	Pittsburgh	8-7
	30	St Louis	1-2		8	Philadelphia	5-5
Feb.	2	Washington	5-3		10	Boston*	4-3
	13	Calgary	2-4		18	Philadelphia*	2-3
	17	Chicago	1-3		22	Pittsburgh	3-4
	24	Detroit*	3-3		28	Detroit	3-4
	25	New Jersey*	3-3	Mar.	2	NY Rangers	3-6
Mar.	6	Hartford	2-4		3	St Louis	4-5
	10	Boston	3-3		8	New Jersey	2-4
	13	Montreal	2-4		15	Philadelphia	4-5
	17	NY Rangers*	6-3		20	Washington	0-3
	18	Pittsburgh*	2-2		22	Los Angeles	1-3
	27	Calgary	2-4		24	Edmonton	5-5
	31	Philadelphia	6-2		28	Toronto	6-3

* Denotes afternoon game.

Entry Draft
Selections 1990-76

1990
Pick
6 Scott Scissons
27 Chris Taylor
48 Dan Plante
90 Chris Marinucci
111 Joni Lehto
132 Michael Guilbert
153 Sylvain Fleury
174 John Joyce
195 Richard Enga
216 Martin Lacroix
237 Andy Shier

1989
Pick
2 Dave Chyzowski
23 Travis Green
44 Jason Zent
65 Brent Grieve
86 Jace Reed
90 Steve Young
99 Kevin O'Sullivan
128 Jon Larson
133 Brett Harkins
149 Phil Huber
170 Matthew Robbins
191 Vladimir Malakhov
212 Kelly Ens
233 Iain Fraser

1988
Pick
16 Kevin Cheveldayoff
29 Wayne Doucet
37 Sean Le Brun
58 Danny Lorenz
79 Andre Brassard
100 Paul Rutherford
111 Pavel Gross
121 Jason Rathbone
142 Yves Gaucher
163 Marty McInnis
184 Jeff Blumer
205 Jeff Kampersal
226 Phillip Neururer
247 Joe Capprini

1987
Pick
13 Dean Chynoweth
34 Jeff Hackett
55 Dean Ewen
76 George Maneluk
97 Petr Vlk
118 Rob Dimaio
139 Knut Walbye
160 Jeff Saterdalen
181 Shawn Howard
202 John Herlihy
223 Michael Erickson
244 Will Averill

1986
Pick
17 Tom Fitzgerald
38 Dennis Vaske
59 Bill Berg
80 Shawn Byram
101 Dean Sexsmith
104 Todd McLellan
122 Tony Schmalzbauer
138 Will Anderson
143 Richard Pilon
164 Peter Harris
185 Jeff Jablonski
206 Kerry Clark
227 Dan Beaudette
248 Paul Thompson

1985
Pick
6 Brad Dalgarno
13 Derek King
34 Brad Lauer
55 Jeff Finley
76 Kevin Herom
89 Tommy Hedlund
97 Jeff Sveen
118 Rod Dallman
139 Kurt Lackten
160 Hank Lammens
181 Rich Wiest
202 Real Arsenault
223 Mike Volpe
244 Tony Grenier

1984
Pick
20 Duncan MacPherson
41 Bruce Melanson
62 Jeff Norton
70 Doug Wieck
83 Ari Eerik Haanpaa
104 Mike Murray
125 Jim Wilharm
146 Kelly Murphy
167 Franco Desantis
187 Tom Warden
208 David Volek
228 Russ Becker
249 Allister Brown

1983
Pick
3 Pat LaFontaine
16 Gerald Diduck
37 Garnet McKechney
57 Mike Neill
65 Mikko Makela
84 Bob Caulfield
97 Ron Viglasi
117 Darin Illikainen
137 Jim Sprenger
157 Dale Henry
177 Kevin Vescio
197 Dave Shellington
217 John Bjorkman
237 Peter McGeough

1982
Pick
21 Patrick Flatley
42 Vern Smith
63 Garry Lacey
84 Alan Kerr
105 Rene Breton
126 Roger Kortko
147 John Tiano
168 Todd Okerlund
189 Gord Paddock
210 Eric Faust
231 Pat Goff
252 Jim Koudys

1981
Pick
21 Paul Boutilier
42 Gord Dineen
57 Ron Handy
63 Neal Coulter
84 Todd Lumbard
94 Jacques Sylvestre
126 Chuck Brimmer
147 Teppo Virta
168 Bill Dowd
189 Scott MacLellan
210 Dave Randerson

1980
Pick
17 Brent Sutter
38 Kelly Hrudey
59 Dave Simpson
68 Monty Trottier
80 Greg Gilbert
101 Ken Leiter
122 Dan Revell
143 Mark Hamway
164 Morrison Gare
185 Peter Steblyk
206 Glen Johannesen

1979
Pick
17 Duane Sutter
25 Tomas Jonsson
38 Bill Carroll
59 Roland Melanson
80 Tom Lockridge
101 Glen Duncan
122 John Gibb

1978
Pick
15 Steve Tambellini
34 Randy Johnston
51 Dwayne Lowdermilk
84 Greg Hay
101 Kelly Davis
118 Richard Pepin
135 David Cameron
152 Paul Joswiak
169 Scott Cameron
184 Chris Lowdall
199 Gunnar Persson

1977
Pick
15 Mike Bossy
33 John Tonelli
50 Hector Marini
51 Bruce Andres
69 Steve Stoyanovich
87 Markus Mattsson
105 Steve Letzgus
121 Harold Luckner

1976
Pick
14 Alex McKendry
32 Mike Kaszycki
50 Garth McGuigan
68 Ken Morrow
86 Mike Hordy
104 Yvon Vautour

Club Directory

Nassau Veterans'
Memorial Coliseum
Uniondale, N.Y. 11553
Phone **516/794-4100**
GM FAX 516/542-9350
FAX 516/542-9348
ENVOY ID
Front Office: ISLANDERS. GM
Public
Relations: ISLANDERS. PR
Capacity: 16,297

Owner	John O. Pickett, Jr.
Chairman of the Board and General Manager	William A. Torrey
President	John H. Krumpe
General Counsel	William M. Skehan
Vice-President/Administration	Joseph H. Dreyer
Vice-President/Finance	Arthur J. McCarthy
Vice-President/Media Sales	Arthur Adler
Head Coach	Al Arbour
Assistant Coaches	Lorne Henning, Darcy Regier
Assistant General Manager/Director of Scouting	Gerry Ehman
Scouting Staff	Harry Boyd, Richard Green, Earl Ingarfield, Hal Laycoe, Bert Marshall, Mario Saraceno, Jack Vivian, Anders Kallur
Publicity Director	Greg Bouris
Assistant Publicity Director	Catherine Schutte
Publicity Assistant	Kevin Dessart
Editor, Islander News	Chris Botta
Controller	Ralph Sellitti
Director of Public Affairs	Jill Knee
Director of Sales	Jim Johnson
Director of Special Projects	Bob Nystrom
Administrative Assistants:	
Owner	Rosemarie LaNasa, Grace Hare
Chairman of the Board and General Manager	Joanne Holewa, Jill Murphy
Athletic Trainer	Ed Tyburski
Assistant Trainers	John Doolan, Terry Murphy
Team Orthopedists	Jeffrey Minkoff, M.D., Barry Fisher, M.D.
Team Internist	Gerald Cordani, M.D.
Team Dentist	Bruce Michnick, D.D.S., Jan Sherman, D.D.S.
Photographer	Bruce Bennett
Location of Press Box	East Side of Building
Dimensions of Rink	200 feet by 85 feet
Ends of Rink	Herculite extends above boards around rink
Club Colors	Blue, Orange and White
Training Camp Site/Practice Facilities	Cantiague Park, Hicksville, NY, Hidden Pond Park, Islip, NY
Television Announcers	Jiggs McDonald, Ed Westfall, Stan Fischler
Television Station	SportsChannel
Radio Station	WEVD (1050 AM), WBAB (1240 AM)
Radio Announcers	Barry Landers, Bob Nystrom

General Manager

TORREY, WILLIAM ARTHUR (BILL)
President and General Manager, New York Islanders.
Born in Montreal, Que., June 23, 1934.

Although he never played professionally, Bill Torrey has been a valuable addition to professional hockey and was named winner of the 1983 Lester Patrick Trophy for his contribution to hockey in the United States. He attended St. Lawrence University in Canton, N.Y. where he played for the varsity team and graduated in 1957 with a Bachelor of Science degree. He joined the Pittsburgh Hornets of the American Hockey League in 1960 and served with that club until 1965, first as director of public relations and later as business manager. In September 1968, Torrey moved to the California Seals of the NHL as executive vice-president and during his tenure, the Seals went from last place in the West Division to playoff berths the following two seasons. On February 15, 1972, he was appointed general manager of the New York Islanders and has moulded the franchise into one of the greatest in the history of professional sports. His most satisfying season was 1979-80 when the Islanders won their first of four consecutive Stanley Cup titles.

Coach

ARBOUR, AL
Coach, New York Islanders. Born in Sudbury, Ont., November 1, 1932.

Al Arbour was named head coach of the Islanders on June 26, 1989 after serving as the vice-president in charge of player development for three years. In 1989-90, his first full season since returning to coaching, Arbour's Islanders enjoyed a 12-point single-season improvement.

Arbour, 57, began his coaching career with the St. Louis Blues in 1970 and coached parts of three seasons there before joining the Islanders at the start of the 1973-74 season.

Coaching Record

Season	Team	Games	Regular Season				Playoffs			
			W	L	T	%	Games	W	L	%
1970-71	St. Louis (NHL)	50	21	15	14	.560	.....	.....	.....	.....
1971-72	St. Louis (NHL)	44	19	19	6	.500	11	4	7	.364
1972-73	St. Louis (NHL)	13	2	6	5	.346	.....	.....	.....	.....
1973-74	NY Islanders (NHL)	78	19	41	18	.358	.....	.....	.....	.....
1974-75	NY Islanders (NHL)	80	33	25	22	.550	.....	.....	.....	.....
1975-76	NY Islanders (NHL)	80	42	21	17	.631	13	7	6	.538
1976-77	NY Islanders (NHL)	80	47	21	12	.663	12	8	4	.666
1977-78	NY Islanders (NHL)	80	48	17	15	.694	7	3	4	.429
1978-79	NY Islanders (NHL)	80	51	15	14	.725	10	6	4	.600
1979-80	NY Islanders (NHL)	80	39	28	13	.589	21	15	6	.714*
1980-81	NY Islanders (NHL)	80	48	18	14	.600	18	15	3	.833*
1981-82	NY Islanders (NHL)	80	54	16	10	.738	19	15	4	.789*
1982-83	NY Islanders (NHL)	80	42	26	12	.600	20	15	5	.750*
1983-84	NY Islanders (NHL)	80	50	26	4	.650	21	12	9	.571
1984-85	NY Islanders (NHL)	80	40	34	6	.538	10	4	6	.400
1985-86	NY Islanders (NHL)	80	39	29	12	.563	3	0	3	.000
1988-89	NY Islanders (NHL)	53	21	29	3	.425	.....	.....	.....	.....
1989-90	NY Islanders (NHL)	80	31	38	11	.456	5	1	4	.200
	NHL Totals	1269	646	424	208	.591	187	114	73	.610

* Stanley Cup win

New York Rangers

1989-90 Results: 36w-31L-13T 85PTS. First, Patrick Division

Mike Gartner had 11 goals in 12 games with the Rangers after a late-season trade from Minnesota.

Schedule

	Home			Away
Oct.	Mon. 8 Minnesota	**Oct.**	Thur. 4 Chicago
	Wed. 10 Washington		Sat. 6 Hartford
	Fri. 12 Montreal		Sat. 13 Washington
	Wed. 17 Winnipeg		Fri. 19 New Jersey
	Mon. 22 Toronto		Sat. 20 Pittsburgh
	Thur. 25 Philadelphia		Sat. 27 Quebec
	Mon. 29 Quebec	**Nov.**	Sat. 3 Pittsburgh
	Wed. 31 Los Angeles		Fri. 9 New Jersey
Nov.	Fri. 2 NY Islanders		Tues. 13 Philadelphia
	Mon. 5 Boston		Thur. 15 Minnesota
	Wed. 7 Buffalo		Fri. 16 Winnipeg
	Sun. 11 Calgary		Wed. 21 Buffalo
	Mon. 19 Minnesota		Sat. 24 NY Islanders*
	Mon. 26 Buffalo		Fri. 30 Philadelphia
	Wed. 28 Washington	**Dec.**	Sat. 1 Boston
Dec.	Mon. 3 Pittsburgh		Wed. 5 Calgary
	Mon. 17 Washington		Fri. 7 Edmonton
	Wed. 19 Toronto		Tues. 11 Los Angeles
	Sun. 23 Boston		Fri. 14 Vancouver
	Sun. 30 New Jersey		Sat. 22 Montreal
Jan.	Wed. 2 Los Angeles		Fri. 28 Washington
	Mon. 7 Philadelphia	**Jan.**	Thur. 3 Pittsburgh
	Wed. 9 St Louis		Sat. 5 St Louis
	Sun. 13 Hartford		Fri. 11 Detroit
	Tues. 15 Edmonton		Tues. 22 NY Islanders
	Thur. 17 Chicago		Fri. 25 Edmonton
Feb.	Sun. 3 Winnipeg		Wed. 30 Calgary
	Wed. 6 NY Islanders		Thur. 31 Vancouver
	Fri. 8 Vancouver	**Feb.**	Sat. 9 Montreal
	Wed. 13 New Jersey		Thur. 21 Philadelphia
	Fri. 15 Hartford		Fri. 22 Washington
	Mon. 18 NY Islanders*		Thur. 28 St Louis
	Sun. 24 New Jersey*	**Mar.**	Sat. 2 Toronto
	Wed. 27 Washington		Thur. 7 Quebec
Mar.	Mon. 4 Philadelphia		Sat. 9 NY Islanders
	Wed. 13 Detroit		Sun. 10 Chicago
	Sun. 17 Pittsburgh*		Fri. 15 New Jersey
	Sun. 24 NY Islanders		Thur. 21 Philadelphia*
	Tues. 26 New Jersey		Sat. 23 Philadelphia*
	Sun. 31 Pittsburgh		Sat. 30 Detroit*

* Denotes afternoon game.

Home Starting Times:
All Games .... 7:35 p.m.
Matinees .... 1:35 p.m.

Franchise date: May 15, 1926

65th NHL Season

Year-by-Year Record

		Home			Road			Overall							
Season	GP	W	L	T	W	L	T	W	L	T	GF	GA	Pts.	Finished	Playoff Result
1989-90	80	20	11	9	16	20	4	36	31	13	279	267	85	1st, Patrick Div.	Lost Div. Final
1988-89	80	21	17	2	16	18	6	37	35	8	310	307	82	3rd, Patrick Div.	Lost Div. Semi-Final
1987-88	80	22	13	5	14	21	5	36	34	10	300	283	82	5th, Patrick Div.	Out of Playoffs
1986-87	80	18	18	4	16	20	4	34	38	8	307	323	76	4th, Patrick Div.	Lost Div. Semi-Final
1985-86	80	20	18	2	16	20	4	36	38	6	280	276	78	4th, Patrick Div.	Lost Conf. Championship
1984-85	80	16	18	6	10	26	4	26	44	10	295	345	62	4th, Patrick Div.	Lost Div. Semi-Final
1983-84	80	27	12	1	15	17	8	42	29	9	314	304	93	4th, Patrick Div.	Lost Div. Semi-Final
1082-03	80	24	13	3	11	22	7	35	35	10	306	287	80	4th, Patrick Div.	Lost Div. Final
1981-82	80	19	15	6	20	12	8	39	27	14	316	306	92	2nd, Patrick Div.	Lost Div. Final
1980-81	80	17	13	10	13	23	4	30	36	14	312	317	74	4th, Patrick Div.	Lost Semi-Final
1979-80	80	22	10	8	16	22	2	38	32	10	308	284	86	3rd, Patrick Div.	Lost Quarter-Final
1978-79	80	19	13	8	21	16	3	40	29	11	316	292	91	3rd, Patrick Div.	Lost Final
1977-78	80	18	15	7	12	22	6	30	37	13	279	280	73	4th, Patrick Div.	Lost Prelim. Round
1976-77	80	17	18	5	12	19	9	29	37	14	272	310	72	4th, Patrick Div.	Out of Playoffs
1975-76	80	16	16	8	13	26	1	29	42	9	262	333	67	4th, Patrick Div.	Out of Playoffs
1974-75	80	21	11	8	16	18	6	37	29	14	319	276	88	2nd, Patrick Div.	Lost Prelim. Round
1973-74	78	26	7	6	14	17	8	40	24	14	300	251	94	3rd, East Div.	Lost Semi-Final
1972-73	78	26	8	5	21	15	3	47	23	8	297	208	102	3rd, East Div.	Lost Semi-Final
1971-72	78	26	6	7	22	11	6	48	17	13	317	192	109	2nd, East Div.	Lost Final
1970-71	78	30	2	7	19	16	4	49	18	11	259	177	109	2nd, East Div.	Lost Semi-Final
1969-70	76	22	8	8	16	14	8	38	22	16	246	189	92	4th, East Div.	Lost Quarter-Final
1968-69	76	27	7	4	14	19	5	41	26	9	231	196	91	3rd, East Div.	Lost Quarter-Final
1967-68	74	22	8	7	17	15	5	39	23	12	226	183	90	2nd, East Div.	Lost Quarter-Final
1966-67	70	18	12	5	12	16	7	30	28	12	188	189	72	4th,	Lost Semi-Final
1965-66	70	12	16	7	6	25	4	18	41	11	195	261	47	6th,	Out of Playoffs
1964-65	70	8	19	8	12	19	4	20	38	12	179	246	52	5th,	Out of Playoffs
1963-64	70	14	13	8	8	25	2	22	38	10	186	242	54	5th,	Out of Playoffs
1962-63	70	12	17	6	10	19	6	22	36	12	211	233	56	5th,	Out of Playoffs
1961-62	70	16	11	8	10	21	4	26	32	12	195	207	64	4th,	Lost Semi-Final
1960-61	70	15	15	5	7	23	5	22	38	10	204	248	54	5th,	Out of Playoffs
1959-60	70	10	15	10	7	23	5	17	38	15	187	247	49	6th,	Out of Playoffs
1958-59	70	14	16	5	12	16	7	26	32	12	201	217	64	5th,	Out of Playoffs
1957-58	70	14	15	6	18	10	7	32	25	13	195	188	77	2nd,	Lost Semi-Final
1956-57	70	15	12	8	11	18	6	26	30	14	184	227	66	4th,	Lost Semi-Final
1955-56	70	20	7	8	12	21	2	32	28	10	204	203	74	3rd,	Lost Semi-Final
1954-55	70	10	12	13	7	23	5	17	35	18	150	210	52	5th,	Out of Playoffs
1953-54	70	18	12	5	11	19	5	29	31	10	161	182	68	5th,	Out of Playoffs
1952-53	70	11	14	10	6	23	6	17	37	16	152	211	50	6th,	Out of Playoffs
1951-52	70	16	13	6	7	21	7	23	34	13	192	219	59	5th,	Out of Playoffs
1950-51	70	14	11	10	6	18	11	20	29	21	169	201	61	5th,	Out of Playoffs
1949-50	70	19	12	4	9	19	7	28	31	11	170	189	67	4th,	Lost Final
1948-49	60	13	12	5	5	19	6	18	31	11	133	172	47	6th,	Out of Playoffs
1947-48	60	11	12	7	10	14	6	21	26	13	176	201	55	4th,	Lost Semi-Final
1946-47	60	11	14	5	11	18	1	22	32	6	167	186	50	5th,	Out of Playoffs
1945-46	50	8	12	5	5	16	4	13	28	9	144	191	35	6th,	Out of Playoffs
1944-45	50	7	11	7	4	18	3	11	29	10	154	247	32	6th,	Out of Playoffs
1943-44	50	4	17	4	2	22	1	6	39	5	162	310	17	6th,	Out of Playoffs
1942-43	50	7	13	5	4	18	3	11	31	8	161	253	30	6th,	Out of Playoffs
1941-42	48	15	8	1	14	9	1	29	17	2	177	143	60	1st,	Lost Semi-Final
1940-41	48	13	7	4	8	12	4	21	19	8	143	125	50	4th,	Lost Quarter-Final
1939-40	**48**	**17**	**4**	**3**	**10**	**7**	**7**	**27**	**11**	**10**	**136**	**77**	**64**	**2nd,**	**Won Stanley Cup**
1938-39	48	13	8	3	13	8	3	26	16	6	149	105	58	2nd,	Lost Semi-Final
1937-38	48	15	5	4	12	10	2	27	15	6	149	96	60	2nd, Amn. Div.	Lost Quarter-Final
1936-37	48	9	7	8	10	13	1	19	20	9	117	106	47	3rd, Amn. Div.	Lost Final
1935-36	48	11	6	7	8	11	5	19	17	12	91	96	50	4th, Amn. Div.	Out of Playoffs
1934-35	48	11	8	5	11	12	1	22	20	6	137	139	50	3rd, Amn. Div.	Lost Semi-Final
1933-34	48	11	7	6	10	12	2	21	19	8	120	113	50	3rd, Amn. Div.	Lost Quarter-Final
1932-33	**48**	**12**	**7**	**5**	**11**	**10**	**3**	**23**	**17**	**8**	**135**	**107**	**54**	**3rd, Amn. Div.**	**Won Stanley Cup**
1931-32	48	13	7	4	10	10	4	23	17	8	134	112	54	1st, Amn. Div.	Lost Final
1930-31	44	10	9	3	9	7	6	19	16	9	106	87	47	3rd, Amn. Div.	Lost Semi-Final
1929-30	44	11	5	6	6	12	4	17	17	10	136	143	44	3rd, Amn. Div.	Lost Semi-Final
1928-29	44	12	6	4	9	7	6	21	13	10	72	65	52	2nd, Amn. Div.	Lost Final
1927-28	**44**	**10**	**8**	**4**	**9**	**8**	**5**	**19**	**16**	**9**	**94**	**79**	**47**	**2nd, Amn. Div.**	**Won Stanley Cup**
1926-27	44	13	5	4	12	8	2	25	13	6	95	72	56	1st, Amn. Div.	Lost Quarter-Final

1990-91 Player Personnel

FORWARDS	HT	WT	S	Place of Birth	Date	1989-90 Club
ARCHIBALD, David	6-1	190	L	Chilliwack, B.C.	4/14/69	Min-NYR-Flint
BENNETT, Rick	6-3	215	L	Springfield, MA	7/24/67	Providence-NYR
BERGERON, Martin	6-0	180	L	Verdun, Que.	1/20/68	Erie
BROTEN, Paul	5-11	175	R	Roseau, MN	10/27/65	Flint-NYR
DeBRUSK, Louie	6-1	200	L	Cambridge, Ont.	3/19/71	London
DOMI, Tahir	5-10	200	R	Windsor, Ont.	11/1/69	Newmarket-Toronto
ERIXON, Jan	6-0	196	L	Skelleftea, Sweden	7/8/62	NY Rangers
FITZPATRICK, Ross	6-0	195	L	Penticton, B.C.	10/7/60	Hershey
GARTNER, Mike	6-0	190	R	Ottawa, Ont.	10/29/59	Minnesota-NYR
GOLDEN, Mike	6-1	195	R	Boston, MA	6/14/65	Flint
HULL, Jody	6-2	200	R	Cambridge, Ont.	2/2/69	Hartford-Binghamton
JANSSENS, Mark	6-3	195	L	Surrey, B.C.	5/19/68	NY Rangers
KING, Kris	5-11	210	L	Bracebridge, Ont.	2/18/66	NY Rangers
KISIO, Kelly	5-9	180	R	Peace River, Alta.	9/18/59	NY Rangers
LACROIX, Daniel	6-2	185	L	Montreal, Que	3/11/69	Flint
MALLETTE, Troy	6-2	190	L	Sudbury, Ont.	2/25/70	NY Rangers
McREYNOLDS, Brian	6-1	180	L	Penetang'ene, Ont.	1/5/65	Winnipeg-Moncton
MILLEN, Corey	5-7	165	R	Cloquet, MN	4/29/64	NY Rangers-Flint
MILLER, Kevin	5-10	180	R	Lansing, MI	8/9/65	Flint-NY Rangers
MULLEN, Brian	5-10	180	L	New York, NY	3/16/62	NY Rangers
NICHOLLS, Bernie	6-0	185	R	Haliburton, Ont.	6/24/61	L.A.-NY Rangers
OGRODNICK, John	6-0	205	L	Ottawa, Ont.	6/20/59	NY Rangers
PATERSON, Joe	6-2	207	L	Toronto, Ont.	6/25/60	Flint
POESCHEK, Rudy	6-1	210	R	Kamloops, B.C.	9/29/66	NY Rangers-Flint
RICE, Steven	6-0	210	R	Kitchener, Ont.	5/26/71	Kitchener
RUFF, Lindy	6-2	200	L	Warburg, Alta.	2/17/60	NY Rangers
SHEPPARD, Ray	6-1	180	R	Pembroke, Ont.	5/27/66	Buffalo-Rochester
TRUE, Soren	6-1	185	L	Aarhus, Denmark	2/9/68	Flint
TURCOTTE, Darren	6-0	185	L	Boston, MA	3/2/68	NY Rangers
ZAMUNER, Rob	6-2	202	L	Oakville, Ont.	9/17/69	Flint

DEFENSEMEN	HT	WT	S	Place of Birth	Date	1989-90 Club
BLOEMBERG, Jeff	6-2	200	R	Listowel, Ont.	1/31/68	Flint-NY Rangers
CERNICH, Kord	5-11	195	L	Anchorage, AK	10/20/66	Lake Superior State
CHARLESWORTH, Todd	6-1	190	L	Calgary, Alta.	3/22/65	Cape Breton-Flint-NY Rangers
DUVAL, Murray	6-1	195	L	Thompson, Man.	1/22/70	Tri-City-Kamloops
FIORENTINO, Peter	6-1	200	R	Niagara Falls, Ont.	12/22/68	Flint
GERMAIN, Eric	6-1	195	L	Quebec City, Que.	6/26/66	New Haven
HARDY, Mark	5-11	195	L	Semaden, Switz.	2/1/59	NY Rangers
HORAVA, Miloslav	6-0	190	L	Kladno, Czech.	9/14/61	NY Rangers
HURLBUT, Mike	6-2	195	L	Massena, NY	10/7/66	Flint
LAVIOLETTE, Peter	6-2	200	L	Norwood, MA	12/7/64	Flint
LEETCH, Brian	5-11	185	L	Corpus Christi, TX	3/3/68	NY Rangers
MOLLER, Randy	6-2	207	R	Red Deer, Alta.	8/23/63	NY Rangers
PATRICK, James	6-2	192	R	Winnipeg, Man.	6/14/63	NY Rangers
ROCHEFORT, Normand	6-1	200	L	Trois Rivieres, Que.	1/28/61	NY Rangers
SHAW, David	6-2	204	R	St. Thomas, Ont.	5/25/64	NY Rangers
VIAL, Dennis	6-1	190	L	Sault Ste. Marie, Ont.	4/10/69	Flint

GOALTENDERS	HT	WT	C	Place of Birth	Date	1989-90 Club
BROWER, Scott	6-0	185	L	Viking, Alta.	9/26/64	Phoenix-Flint
FROESE, Bob	5-11	178	L	St. Catharines, Ont.	6/30/58	NY Rangers
LaFOREST, Mark	5-11	190	L	Welland, Ont.	7/10/62	Toronto-Newmarket
RICHTER, Mike	5-10	185	L	Abington, PA	9/22/66	Flint-NY Rangers
ST. LAURENT, Sam	5-10	190	L	Arvida, Que.	2/16/59	Adirondack-Detroit
VANBIESBROUCK, John	5-8	179	L	Detroit, MI	9/4/63	NY Rangers

Coaching History

Lester Patrick, 1926-27 to 1938-39; Frank Boucher, 1939-40 to 1947-48; Frank Boucher and Lynn Patrick, 1948-49; Lynn Patrick, 1949-50; Neil Colville, 1950-51; Neil Colville and Bill Cook, 1951-52; Bill Cook, 1952-53; Frank Boucher and Murray Patrick, 1953-54; Murray Patrick, 1954-55; Phil Watson, 1955-56 to 1958-59; Phil Watson and Alf Pike, 1959-60; Alf Pike, 1960-61; Doug Harvey, 1961-62; Murray Patrick and George Sullivan, 1962-63; George Sullivan, 1963-64 to 1964-65; George Sullivan and Emile Francis, 1965-66; Emile Francis, 1966-67 to 1967-68; Bernie Geoffrion and Emile Francis, 1968-69; Emile Francis, 1969-70 to 1972-73; Larry Popein and Emile Francis, 1973-74; Emile Francis, 1974-75; Ron Stewart and John Ferguson, 1975-76; John Ferguson, 1976-77; Jean-Guy Talbot, 1977-78; Fred Shero, 1978-79 to 1979-80; Fred Shero and Craig Patrick, 1980-81; Herb Brooks, 1981-82 to 1983-84; Herb Brooks and Craig Patrick, 1984-85; Ted Sator, 1985-86; Ted Sator, Tom Webster, Phil Esposito 1986-87; Michel Bergeron, 1987-88; Michel Bergeron and Phil Esposito, 1988-89; Roger Neilson, 1989-90 to date.

General Managers' History

Lester Patrick, 1927-28 to 1945-46; Frank Boucher, 1946-47 to 1954-55; Murray "Muzz" Patrick, 1955-56 to 1963-64; Emile Francis, 1964-65 to 1974-75; Emile Francis and John Ferguson, 1975-76; John Ferguson, 1976-77 to 1977-78; John Ferguson and Fred Shero, 1978-79; Fred Shero, 1979-80; Fred Shero and Craig Patrick, 1980-81; Craig Patrick, 1981-82 to 1985-86; Phil Esposito, 1986-87 to 1988-89; Neil Smith, 1989-90 to date.

1989-90 Scoring

Regular Season

* rookie

Pos	#	Player	Team	GP	G	A	Pts	+/-	PIM	PP	SH	GW	GT	S	%
C	9	Bernie Nicholls	L.A.	47	27	48	75	6–	66	8	0	1	0	172	15.7
			NYR	32	12	25	37	3–	20	7	0	0	0	115	10.4
			TOTAL	79	39	73	112	9–	86	15	0	1	0	287	13.6
R	22	Mike Gartner	MIN	67	34	36	70	8–	32	15	4	2	0	240	14.2
			NYR	12	11	5	16	4	6	6	0	3	0	48	22.9
			TOTAL	79	45	41	86	4–	38	21	4	5	0	288	15.6
L	25	John Ogrodnick	NYR	80	43	31	74	11	44	19	0	8	0	215	20.0
R	19	Brian Mullen	NYR	76	27	41	68	7	42	7	3	3	1	186	14.5
R	8	*Darren Turcotte	NYR	76	32	34	66	3	32	10	1	4	0	205	15.6
C	11	Kelly Kisio	NYR	68	22	44	66	11	105	7	2	1	0	128	17.2
D	3	James Patrick	NYR	73	14	43	57	4	50	9	0	0	0	136	10.3
D	2	Brian Leetch	NYR	72	11	45	56	18–	26	5	0	2	1	222	5.0
L	26	*Troy Mallette	NYR	79	13	16	29	8–	305	4	0	1	0	107	12.1
C	17	Carey Wilson	NYR	41	9	17	26	4	57	4	0	1	0	64	14.1
D	14	Mark Hardy	NYR	54	0	15	15	4	94	0	0	0	0	55	.0
D	6	*Miloslav Horava	NYR	45	4	10	14	10	26	1	0	1	1	50	8.0
L	12	Kris King	NYR	68	6	7	13	2	286	0	0	0	0	49	12.2
C	15	*Mark Janssens	NYR	80	5	8	13	26–	161	0	0	0	0	61	8.2
L	20	Jan Erixon	NYR	58	4	9	13	17–	8	0	0	1	0	61	6.6
D	24	Randy Moller	NYR	60	1	12	13	1–	139	0	0	0	0	47	2.1
D	21	David Shaw	NYR	22	2	10	12	3–	22	1	1	0	0	24	8.3
L	10	David Archibald	MIN	12	1	5	6	1	6	1	0	1	0	26	3.8
			NYR	19	2	3	5	0	6	1	0	0	0	30	6.7
			TOTAL	31	3	8	11	1	12	2	0	1	0	56	5.4
D	4	Ron Greschner	NYR	55	1	9	10	7–	53	0	0	0	0	26	3.8
L	44	Lindy Ruff	NYR	56	3	6	9	10–	80	0	0	2	0	59	5.1
R	37	*Paul Broten	NYR	32	5	3	8	4–	26	0	0	0	0	43	11.6
D	38	*Jeff Bloemberg	NYR	28	3	3	6	8–	25	2	0	1	0	20	15.0
C	32	*Kevin Miller	NYR	16	0	5	5	1–	2	0	0	0	0	9	.0
D	5	Normand Rochefort	NYR	31	3	1	4	2	24	0	0	1	0	30	10.0
R	30	Chris Nilan	NYR	25	1	2	3	8–	59	0	0	0	0	24	4.2
G	35	*Mike Richter	NYR	23	0	3	3	0	0	0	0	0	0	0	.0
G	34	John Vanbiesbrouck	NYR	47	0	2	2	0	24	0	0	0	0	0	.0
L	27	*Eric Bennett	NYR	6	1	0	1	4–	5	0	0	0	0	6	16.7
C	23	*Corey Millen	NYR	4	0	0	0	2–	2	0	0	0	0	4	.0
D	36	Todd Charlesworth	NYR	7	0	0	0	3–	6	0	0	0	0	4	.0
G	33	Bob Froese	NYR	15	0	0	0	0	0	0	0	0	0	0	.0
R	29	Rudy Poeschek	NYR	15	0	0	0	1–	55	0	0	0	0	1	.0

Goaltending

No.	Goaltender	GPI	Mins	Avg	W	L	T	EN	SO	GA	SA	S%
35	*Mike Richter	23	1320	3.00	12	5	5	0	0	66	686	.904
33	Bob Froese	15	812	3.33	5	7	1	1	0	45	355	.873
34	John Vanbiesbrouck	47	2734	3.38	19	19	7	1	1	154	1362	.887
	Totals	**80**	**4878**	**3.28**	**36**	**31**	**13**	**2**	**1**	**267**	**2403**	**.889**

Playoffs

Pos	#	Player	Team	GP	G	A	Pts	+/-	PIM	PP	SH	GW	OT	S	%
C	9	Bernie Nicholls	NYR	10	7	5	12	1	16	3	0	0	0	30	23.3
D	3	James Patrick	NYR	10	3	8	11	2–	0	2	0	1	0	25	12.0
C	11	Kelly Kisio	NYR	10	2	8	10	1	8	0	1	0	0	17	11.8
L	25	John Ogrodnick	NYR	10	6	3	9	4–	0	3	0	1	0	31	19.4
R	22	Mike Gartner	NYR	10	5	3	8	0	12	4	0	1	0	26	19.2
D	24	Randy Moller	NYR	10	1	6	7	1	32	0	0	0	0	16	6.3
R	8	*Darren Turcotte	NYR	10	1	6	7	3–	4	0	0	1	0	25	4.0
L	26	*Troy Mallette	NYR	10	2	2	4	4–	81	0	0	0	0	18	11.1
R	19	Brian Mullen	NYR	10	2	2	4	2	8	2	0	0	0	27	7.4
C	15	*Mark Janssens	NYR	9	2	1	3	0	10	0	0	1	0	6	33.3
D	5	Normand Rochefort	NYR	10	2	1	3	1–	26	0	1	0	0	11	18.2
C	17	Carey Wilson	NYR	10	2	1	3	5–	0	1	0	0	0	12	16.7
D	38	*Jeff Bloemberg	NYR	7	0	3	3	0	5	0	0	0	0	8	.0
L	44	Lindy Ruff	NYR	8	0	3	3	3–	12	0	0	0	0	4	.0
R	37	*Paul Broten	NYR	6	1	1	2	2–	2	0	1	0	0	16	6.3
L	20	Jan Erixon	NYR	10	1	0	1	2	2	0	1	0	0	11	9.1
D	6	*Miloslav Horava	NYR	2	0	1	1	1	0	0	0	0	0	1	.0
D	14	Mark Hardy	NYR	3	0	1	1	1–	2	0	0	0	0	1	.0
R	30	Chris Nilan	NYR	4	0	1	1	1	19	0	0	0	0	5	.0
L	12	Kris King	NYR	10	0	1	1	1	30	0	0	0	0	4	.0
C	32	*Kevin Miller	NYR	1	0	0	0	1–	0	0	0	0	0	0	.0
G	35	*Mike Richter	NYR	6	0	0	0	0	0	0	0	0	0	0	.0
G	34	John Vanbiesbrouck	NYR	6	0	0	0	0	4	0	0	0	0	0	.0
D	4	Ron Greschner	NYR	10	0	0	0	0	16	0	0	0	0	3	.0

Goaltending

No.	Goaltender	GPI	Mins	Avg	W	L	EN	SO	GA	SA	S%
34	John Vanbiesbrouck	6	298	3.02	2	3	0	0	15	153	.902
35	*Mike Richter	6	330	3.45	3	2	1	0	19	182	.896
	Totals	**10**	**628**	**3.34**	**5**	**5**	**1**	**0**	**35**	**335**	**.896**

Captains' History

Bill Cook, 1926-27 to 1936-37; Art Coulter, 1937-38 to 1941-42; Ott Heller, 1942-43 to 1944-45; Neil Colville 1945-46 to 1948-49; Buddy O'Connor, 1949-50; Frank Eddolls, 1950-51; Frank Eddolls, Allan Stanley, 1951-52; Allan Stanley, 1952-53; Allan Stanley, Don Raleigh, 1953-54; Don Raleigh, 1954-55; Harry Howell, 1955-56, 1956-57; George Sullivan, 1957-58 to 1960-61; Andy Bathgate, 1961-61, 1962-63; Andy Bathgate, Camille Henry, 1963-64; Camille Henry, Bob Nevin, 1964-65; Bob Nevin 1965-66 to 1970-71; Vic Hadfield, 1971-72 to 1973-74; Brad Park, 1974-75; Brad Park, Phil Esposito, 1975-76; Phil Esposito, 1976-77, 1977-78; Dave Maloney, 1978-79, 1979-80; Dave Maloney, Walt Tkaczuk, Barry Beck, 1980-81; Barry Beck, 1981-82 to 1985-86; Ron Greschner, 1986-87; Ron Greschner and Kelly Kisio, 1987-88; Kelly Kisio, 1988-89 to date.

Retired Numbers

1	Eddie Giacomin	1965-1976
7	Rod Gilbert	1960-1978

Club Records

Team

(Figures in brackets for season records are games played; records for fewest points, wins, ties, losses, goals, goals against are for 70 or more games)

Most Points	109	1970-71 (78)
		1971-72 (78)
Most Wins	49	1970-71 (78)
Most Ties	21	1950-51 (70)
Most Losses	44	1984-85 (80)
Most Goals	319	1974-75 (80)
Most Goals Against	345	1984-85 (80)
Fewest Points	47	1965-66 (70)
Fewest Wins	17	1952-53; 54-55; 59-60 (70)
Fewest Ties	6	1985-86 (80)
Fewest Losses	17	1971-72 (78)
Fewest Goals	150	1954-55 (70)
Fewest Goals Against	177	1970-71 (78)

Longest Winning Streak
Over-all .... 10 Dec. 19/39-
Jan. 13/40
Jan. 19-
Feb. 10/73
Home .... 14 Dec. 19/39-
Feb. 25/40
Away .... 7 Jan. 12-
Feb. 12/35
Oct. 28-
Nov. 29/78

Longest Undefeated Streak
Over-all .... 19 Nov. 23/39-
Jan. 13/40
(14 wins, 5 ties)
Home .... 26 Mar. 29/70-
Feb. 2/71
(19 wins, 7 ties)
Away .... 11 Nov. 5/39-
Jan. 13/40
(6 wins, 5 ties)

Longest Losing Streak
Over-all .... 11 Oct. 30-
Nov. 27/43
Home .... 7 Oct. 20-
Nov. 14/76
Away .... 10 Oct. 30-
Dec. 23/43

Longest Winless Streak
Over-all .... 21 Jan. 23-
Mar. 19/44
(17 losses, 4 ties)
Home .... 10 Jan. 30-
Mar. 19/44
(7 losses, 3 ties)
Away .... 16 Oct. 9-
Dec. 20/52
(12 losses, 4 ties)

Most Shutouts, Season	13	1928-29 (44)
Most PIM, Season	2,018	1989-90 (80)
Most Goals, Game	12	Nov. 21/71 (Cal. 1 at NYR 12)

Individual

Most Seasons	17	Harry Howell
Most Games	1,160	Harry Howell
Most Goals, Career	406	Rod Gilbert
Most Assists, Career	615	Rod Gilbert
Most Points, Career	1,021	Rod Gilbert (406 goals, 615 assists)
Most PIM, Career	1,226	Ron Greschner
Most Shutouts, Career	49	Ed Giacomin

Longest Consecutive Games Streak ...... 560 Andy Hebenton
(Oct. 7/55-Mar. 24/63)

Most Goals, Season ...... 50 Vic Hadfield (1971-72)

Most Assists, Season ...... 65 Mike Rogers (1981-82)

Most Points, Season ...... 109 Jean Ratelle (1971-72) (46 goals, 63 assists)

Most PIM, Season ...... 305 Troy Mallette (1989-90)

Most Points, Defenseman
Season .... 82 Brad Park (1973-74) (25 goals, 57 assists)

Most Points, Center,
Season .... 109 Jean Ratelle (1971-72) (46 goals, 63 assists)

Most Points, Right Wing,
Season .... 97 Rod Gilbert (1971-72) (43 goals, 54 assists) Rod Gilbert (1974-75) (36 goals, 61 assists)

Most Points, Left Wing,
Season .... 106 Vic Hadfield (1971-72) (50 goals, 56 assists)

Most Points, Rookie,
Season .... 76 Mark Pavelich (1981-82) (33 goals, 43 assists)

Most Shutouts, Season ...... 13 John Ross Roach (1928-29)

Most Goals, Game ...... 5 Don Murdoch (Oct. 12/76) Mark Pavelich (Feb. 23/83)

Most Assists, Game ...... 5 Walt Tkaczuk (Feb. 12/72) Rod Gilbert (Mar. 2/75; Mar. 30/75; Oct. 8/76) Don Maloney (Jan. 3/87)

Most Points, Game ...... 7 Steve Vickers (Feb. 18/76)

All-time Record vs. Other Clubs

Regular Season

			At Home							On Road							Total					
	GP	W	L	T	GF	GA	PTS	GP	W	L	T	GF	GA	PTS	GP	W	L	T	GF	GA	PTS
Boston	274	119	102	53	831	765	291	273	86	149	38	759	996	210	547	205	251	91	1590	1761	501
Buffalo	39	15	14	10	133	115	40	41	10	26	5	131	185	25	80	25	40	15	264	300	65
Calgary	39	17	18	4	141	145	38	38	10	22	6	120	175	26	77	27	40	10	261	320	64
Chicago	274	115	105	54	810	775	284	273	108	123	42	759	834	258	547	223	228	96	1569	1609	542
Detroit	272	130	85	57	838	692	317	272	74	154	44	666	950	192	544	204	239	101	1504	1642	509
Edmonton	18	6	10	2	78	79	14	17	7	9	1	61	75	15	35	13	19	3	139	154	29
Hartford	17	9	6	2	72	62	20	10	0	10	0	64	73	14	35	15	16	4	136	125	34
Los Angeles	46	26	15	5	180	138	57	47	19	19	9	163	156	47	93	45	34	14	343	294	104
Minnesota	48	29	10	9	173	133	67	49	27	15	7	194	152	61	97	56	25	16	367	285	128
Montreal	263	105	108	50	753	769	260	263	54	175	34	608	1042	142	526	159	283	84	1361	1811	402
New Jersey	45	27	13	5	203	151	59	47	25	18	4	192	167	54	92	52	31	9	395	318	113
NY Islanders	58	37	16	5	235	178	79	57	16	37	4	177	245	36	115	53	53	9	412	423	115
Philadelphia	71	28	25	18	227	215	74	71	26	34	11	208	245	63	142	54	59	29	435	460	137
Pittsburgh	65	34	24	7	273	221	75	65	31	23	11	239	227	73	130	65	47	18	512	448	148
Quebec	18	12	3	3	77	47	27	17	5	9	3	75	80	13	35	17	12	6	152	127	40
St. Louis	49	40	4	5	215	110	85	49	21	21	7	160	151	49	98	61	25	12	374	261	134
Toronto	263	108	100	55	801	774	271	263	76	149	38	680	908	190	526	184	249	93	1481	1682	461
Vancouver	42	32	7	3	190	105	67	40	28	10	2	166	128	58	82	60	17	5	356	233	125
Washington	46	24	17	5	202	166	53	46	15	23	8	155	186	38	92	39	40	13	357	352	91
Winnipeg	17	8	7	2	85	77	18	18	9	7	2	68	68	20	35	17	14	4	153	145	38
Defunct Club	139	87	30	22	460	290	196	139	82	34	23	441	291	187	278	169	64	45	901	581	383
Totals	2103	1008	719	376	6977	5997	2392	2103	735	1067	301	6085	7334	1771	4206	1743	1786	677	13062	13331	4163

Playoffs

	Series	W	L	GP	W	L	T	GF	GA	Last Mtg.	Round	Result
Boston	9	3	6	42	18	22	2	104	114	1973	QF	W 4-1
Buffalo	1	0	1	3	1	2	0	6	11	1978	PR	L 1-2
Calgary	1	1	0	4	3	1	0	14	8	1980	PR	W 3-1
Chicago	5	1	4	24	10	14	0	54	66	1973	SF	L 1-4
Detroit	5	1	4	23	10	13	0	49	57	1950	F	L 3-4
Los Angeles	2	2	0	6	5	1	0	32	14	1981	PR	W 3-1
Montreal	13	6	7	55	21	32	2	139	171	1986	CF	L 1-4
NY Islanders	7	2	5	35	15	20	0	110	126	1990	DSF	W 4-1
Philadelphia	8	4	4	38	19	19	0	130	119	1987	DSF	L 2-4
Pittsburgh	1	0	1	4	0	4	0	11	19	1989	DSF	L 0-4
St. Louis	1	1	0	6	4	2	0	29	22	1981	QF	W 4-2
Toronto	8	5	3	35	19	16	0	86	86	1971	QF	W 4-2
Washington	2	1	1	11	5	6	0	35	47	1990	DF	L 1-4
Defunct Clubs	9	6	3	22	11	7	4	43	29			
Totals	72	33	39	308	141	159	8	842	889			

Playoff Results 1990-86

Year	Round	Opponent	Result	GF	GA
1990	DF	Washington	L 1-4	15	22
	DSF	NY Islanders	W 4-1	22	13
1989	DSF	Pittsburgh	L 0-4	11	19
1987	DSF	Philadelphia	L 2-4	13	22
1986	CF	Montreal	L 1-4	9	15
	DF	Washington	W 4-2	20	25
	DSF	Philadelphia	W 3-2	18	15

Abbreviations: Round: F Final; **CF** conference final; **DF** division final; **DSF** division semi-final; **SF** semi-final; **QF** quarter-final. **PR** preliminary round. **GA** goals against; **GF** goals for.

1989-90 Results

		Home					Away	
Oct.	11	Calgary	5-4	Oct.	6	Winnipeg	4-1
	15	Pittsburgh	4-2		8	Chicago	5-3
	17	Chicago	3-3		13	Washington	4-7
	19	Hartford	7-3		21	Philadelphia	3-1
	23	Vancouver	5-3		28	NY Islanders	4-1
	25	Edmonton	3-3	Nov.	4	Montreal	2-3
	27	NY Islanders	5-5		14	Pittsburgh	0-6
	30	Philadelphia	1-3		17	New Jersey	4-5
Nov.	2	Quebec	6-1		18	Hartford	3-2
	6	Detroit	6-1		22	Buffalo	1-4
	8	Montreal	2-3		25	Toronto	4-7
	12	NY Islanders	4-2		29	Winnipeg	4-5
	20	Winnipeg	3-3	Dec.	1	Vancouver	4-3
	26	Quebec	3-1		2	Los Angeles	0-6
Dec.	6	New Jersey	5-3		9	NY Islanders	0-0
	10	Philadelphia	2-4		16	NY Islanders	3-4
	13	St Louis	1-3		23	Washington	2-3
	17	Montreal	0-2		27	Pittsburgh	4-7
	20	Buffalo	2-2		29	New Jersey	2-3
	26	New Jersey	4-4	Jan.	4	Minnesota	2-3
	31	Pittsburgh*	4-5		6	St Louis	3-4
Jan.	3	Washington	2-1		13	Boston*	3-2
	8	Pittsburgh	5-7		18	Pittsburgh	3-3
	10	Chicago	2-2		23	Edmonton	4-3
	14	Philadelphia	4-3		25	Calgary	5-8
	31	St Louis	2-2		27	Los Angeles	3-1
Feb.	4	Minnesota*	4-3	Feb.	3	Boston*	2-1
	7	Edmonton	5-2		9	Buffalo	2-3
	11	Calgary*	2-5		13	Philadelphia	4-3
	14	Pittsburgh	3-4		16	New Jersey	2-1
	19	New Jersey*	4-3		21	Detroit	4-4
	26	Boston	6-1		23	Washington	6-3
	28	Washington	3-2	Mar.	3	Hartford	4-6
Mar.	2	NY Islanders	6-3		8	Philadelphia	7-5
	5	Detroit	3-2		10	Minnesota*	2-2
	12	Los Angeles	2-6		14	Toronto	8-2
	18	Vancouver	5-2		17	NY Islanders*	3-6
	21	Toronto	7-3		27	Quebec	7-4
	25	Philadelphia*	7-3		29	New Jersey	4-6
Apr.	1	Washington	2-3		31	Washington	1-2

* Denotes afternoon game.

Entry Draft
Selections 1990-76

1990
Pick
13 Michael Stewart
34 Doug Weight
55 John Vary
69 Jeff Nielsen
76 Rick Willis
85 Sergei Zubov
99 Lubos Rob
118 Jason Weinrich
139 Bryan Lonsinger
160 Todd Hedlund
181 Andrew Silverman
202 Jon Hillebrandt
223 Brett Lievers
244 Sergei Nemchinov

1989
Pick
20 Steven Rice
40 Jason Prosofsky
45 Rob Zamuner
49 Louie Debrusk
67 Jim Cummins
88 Aaron Miller
118 Joby Messier
139 Greg Leahy
160 Greg Spenrath
181 Mark Bavis
202 Roman Oksyuta
223 Steve Locke
244 Ken MacDermid

1988
Pick
22 Troy Mallette
26 Murray Duval
68 Tony Amonte
99 Martin Bergeron
110 Dennis Vial
131 Mike Rosati
152 Eric Couvrette
173 Shorty Forrest
194 Paul Cain
202 Eric Fenton
215 Peter Fiorentino
236 Keith Slifstien

1987
Pick
10 Jayson More
31 Daniel Lacroix
46 Simon Gagne
69 Michael Sullivan
94 Eric O'Borsky
115 Ludek Cajka
136 Clint Thomas
157 Charles Wiegand
178 Eric Burrill
199 David Porter

205 Brett Barnett
220 Lance Marciano

1986
Pick
9 Brian Leetch
51 Bret Walter
53 Shawn Clouston
72 Mark Janssens
93 Jeff Bloemberg
114 Darren Turcotte
135 Robb Graham
156 Barry Chyzowski
177 Pat Scanlon
198 Joe Ranger
219 Russell Parent
240 Soren True

1985
Pick
7 Ulf Dahlen
28 Mike Richter
49 Sam Lindstahl
70 Pat Janostin
91 Brad Stephan
112 Brian McReynolds
133 Neil Pilon
154 Lary Bernard
175 Stephane Brochu
196 Steve Nemeth
217 Robert Burakovski
238 Rudy Poeschek

1984
Pick
14 Terry Carkner
35 Raimo Helminen
77 Paul Broten
98 Clark Donatelli
119 Kjell Samuelsson
140 Thomas Hussey
161 Brian Nelson
182 Ville Kentala
188 Heinz Ehlers
202 Kevin Miller
223 Tom Lorentz
243 Scott Brower

1983
Pick
12 Dave Gagner
33 Randy Heath
49 Vesa Salo
53 Gordie Walker
73 Peter Andersson
93 Jim Andonoff
113 Bob Alexander
133 Steve Orth
153 Peter Marcov
173 Paul Jerrard
213 Bryan Walker
233 Ulf Nilsson

1982
Pick
15 Chris Kontos
36 Tomas Sandstrom
57 Corey Millen
78 Chris Jensen
120 Tony Granato
141 Sergei Kapustin
160 Brian Glynn
162 Jan Karlsson
183 Kelly Miller
193 Simo Saarinen
204 Bob Lowes
225 Andy Otto
246 Dwayne Robinson

1981
Pick
9 James Patrick
30 Jan Erixon
50 Peter Sundstrom
51 Mark Morrison
72 John Vanbiesbrouck
114 Eric Magnuson
135 Mike Guentzel
156 Ari Lahtenmaki
177 Paul Reifenberger
198 Mario Proulx

1980
Pick
14 Jim Malone
35 Mike Allison
77 Kurt Kleinendorst
98 Scot Kleinendorst
119 Reijo Ruotsalainen
140 Bob Scurfield
161 Bart Wilson
182 Chris Wray
203 Anders Backstrom

1979
Pick
13 Doug Sulliman
34 Ed Hospodar
76 Pat Conacher
97 Dan Makuch
118 Stan Adams

1978
Pick
26 Don Maloney
43 Ray Markham
44 Dean Turner
59 Dave Silk
60 Andre Dore
76 Mike McDougall
93 Tom Laidlaw
110 Dan Clark
127 Greg Kostenko
144 Brian McDavid
161 Mark Rodrigues
176 Steve Weeks
192 Pierre Daigneault
206 Chris McLaughlin
217 Todd Johnson
223 Dan McCarthy

1977
Pick
8 Lucien DeBlois
13 Ron Duguay
26 Mike Keating
44 Steve Baker
62 Mario Marois
80 Benoit Gosselin
98 John Bethel
116 Robert Sullivan
131 Lance Nethery
146 Alex Jeans
157 Peter Raps
164 Mike Brown
171 Mark Miller

1976
Pick
6 Don Murdoch
24 Dave Farrish
42 Mike McEwen
60 Claude Periard
78 Doug Gaines
96 Barry Scully
112 Remi Levesque

General Manager

SMITH, NEIL
General Manager, New York Rangers. Born in Toronto, Ont., January 9, 1954.

Smith, 36-years-old, joined the Rangers on July 17, 1989 after seven seasons with the Detroit Red Wings and two with the New York Islanders. After serving as a scout for the Islanders in 1980-81 and 1981-82, Smith joined the Red Wings. While with the Red Wings, Smith held several positions including director of scouting and player development. He also served as general manager of the Adirondack Red Wings (AHL), leading that club to two Calder Cups (1985-86 and 1988-89).

A former All-American defenseman from Western Michigan University, Smith was drafted in 1974 by the New York Islanders. After receiving his degree in communications and business, Smith played two seasons in the IHL–1978-79 with the Kalamazoo Wings and Saginaw Gears and 1979-80 with the Dayton Gems, Milwaukee Admirals and Muskegon Mohawks.

Coach

NEILSON, ROGER PAUL
Coach, New York Rangers. Born in Toronto, Ont., June 16, 1934.

Roger Neilson began his coaching career as a 17-year-old with a neighborhood baseball team in his native Toronto. He began scouting Ontario prospects for the Montreal Canadiens before becoming coach of the Peterborough Petes of the OHA in 1966. He remained in Peterborough for ten seasons, winning one OHA championship while finishing lower than third in regular-season play only twice. He made his pro coaching debut with the Dallas Black Hawks of the CHL in 1976-77 and moved up to the NHL with the Toronto Maple Leafs in 1977-78. He joined the Buffalo Sabres in 1979-80 as associate coach under Scotty Bowman. He acted as Sabres' bench coach for part of this campaign and for all of 1980-81. He became associate coach of the Vancouver Canucks under Harry Neale in 1981-82 and coached five games late in the season when Neale was serving a suspension. He also guided the Canucks in the 1982 playoffs and in 1982-83. In 1983-84, he coached the Los Angeles Kings for the last 28 games of the regular season. He served as co-coach of the Chicago Blackhawks from 1984-85 through 1986-87 before taking on special scouting assignments for the Blackhawks. He also has provided television commentary on Canadian NHL telecasts.

Club Directory

Madison Square Garden
4 Pennsylvania Plaza
New York, New York 10001
Phone 212/465-6000
PR FAX 212/465-6494
ENVOY ID
  Front Office: RANGERS. GM
  Public
  Relations: RANGERS. PR
Capacity: 17,520

Executive Management
Chief Executive Officer & Governor	Richard H. Evans
President	John C. Diller
Vice-President & General Manager	Neil Smith
Vice-President, Business Affairs & Administration	David Peterson
Vice-President, Legal Affairs	Kevin Billet
Director of Communications	Barry Watkins
Director of Marketing	Kevin Kennedy
Alternate NHL Governors	John C. Diller, Neil Smith, Kenneth W. Munoz, Michael D. Walker, Thomas A. Conway

Team Management
Assistant General Manager/Player Development	Larry Pleau
Director of Administration	Mark Piazza
Coach	Roger Neilson
Assistant Coaches	Wayne Cashman, Ron Smith
Development Coach	John Paddock
Scouting Staff	John Chapman, Tony Feltrin, Herb Hammond, Lou Jankowski, David McNab, Christer Rockstrom
Manager of Team Services	Matthew Loughran
Scouting Assistant	Bill Short
Administrative Assistant to the V.P. and G.M.	Linda Olmstead

Medical/Training Staff
Team Physician/Ortho Surgeon	Barton Nisonson, M.D.
Medical Consultants	Howard Chester, Anthony Maddalo, Irwin Miller, James A. Nicholas, Ronald Weissman,
Trainer/Medical	Dave Smith
Trainer/Equipment	Joe Murphy
Assistant Trainers	Larry Nastasi, Tim Paris
Locker-room Assistant	Benny Petrizzi

Communications Staff
Assistant to the Director of Communications	Kevin McDonald
Communications Assistant	Tina Pietroluongo
Statistician	Arthur Friedman

MSG Sports Group Staff
Executive Administrative Assistant	Maggie McLoughlin
Administrative Assistant	Janet Ungarten
Manager of Community Relations	Rod Gilbert
Marketing Assistant	Caroline Calabrese
Community Relations Assistant	Jim Pfeiffer
Senior Secretary	Dawn Owens

Home Ice	Madison Square Garden
Press Facilities	33rd Street
Television Facilities	31st Street
Radio Facilities	33rd Street
Rink Dimensions	200 feet by 85 feet
Ends and Sides of Rink	Plexiglass (8 feet)
Club Colors	Blue, Red and White
Training Camp	Rye, New York
TV Announcers	Bruce Beck, John Davidson, Sam Rosen
Radio Announcers	Marv Albert, Sal Messina, Howie Rose
Television Outlets	Madison Square Garden Cable Network
Radio Outlet	WFAN (66 AM)

The New York Rangers Hockey Club is part of the
MSG Sports Group of Madison Sqaure Garden Corporation
A Paramount Communications Company

Coaching Record

Season	Team	Games	Regular Season W	L	T	%	Playoffs Games	W	L	%
1966-67	Peterborough (OHA)					UNAVAILABLE				
1967-68	Peterborough (OHA)	54	27	18	9	.583	....	....	....	....
1968-69	Peterborough (OHA)	54	29	13	12	.648	....	....	....	....
1969-70	Peterborough (OHA)	54	29	13	12	.648	....	....	....	....
1970-71	Peterborough (OHA)	62	41	13	8	.726	....	....	....	....
1971-72	Peterborough (OHA)	63	34	20	9	.611	....	....	....	....
1972-73	Peterborough (OHA)	63	42	13	8	.730	....	....	....	....
1973-74	Peterborough (OHA)	70	35	21	14	.600	....	....	....	....
1974-75	Peterborough (OHA)	70	37	20	13	.621	....	....	....	....
1975-76	Peterborough (OHA)	66	18	37	11	.356	....	....	....	....
1976-77	Dallas (CHL)	76	35	25	16	.566	....	....	....	....
1977-78	Toronto (NHL)	80	41	29	10	.575	13	6	7	.462
1978-79	Toronto (NHL)	80	34	33	13	.506	6	2	4	.333
1979-80	Buffalo (NHL)	26	14	6	6	.654	....	....	....	....
1980-81	Buffalo (NHL)	80	39	20	21	.619	8	4	4	.500
1981-82	Vancouver (NHL)	5	4	0	1	.900	17	11	6	.647
1982-83	Vancouver (NHL)	80	30	35	15	.469	4	1	3	.250
1983-84	Los Angeles (NHL)	28	8	17	3	.339	....	....	....	....
1989-90	Los Angeles (NHL)	80	36	31	13	.531	10	5	5	.500
	NHL Totals	**507**	**223**	**197**	**87**	**.526**	**58**	**29**	**29**	**.500**

Philadelphia Flyers

1989-90 Results: 30w-39L-11T 71PTS. Sixth, Patrick Division

Year-by-Year Record

		Home			Road			Overall						
Season	GP	W	L	T	W	L	T	W	L	T	GF	GA	Pts.	Finished	Playoff Result
1989-90	80	17	19	4	13	20	7	30	39	11	290	297	71	6th, Patrick Div.	Out of Playoffs
1988-89	80	22	15	3	14	21	5	36	36	8	307	285	80	4th, Patrick Div.	Lost Conf. Championship
1987-88	80	20	14	6	18	19	3	38	33	9	292	292	85	3rd, Patrick Div.	Lost Div. Semi-Final
1986-87	80	29	9	2	17	17	6	46	26	8	310	245	100	1st, Patrick Div.	Lost Final
1985-86	80	33	6	1	20	17	3	53	23	4	335	241	110	1st, Patrick Div.	Lost Div. Semi-Final
1984-85	80	32	4	4	21	16	3	53	20	7	348	241	113	1st, Patrick Div.	Lost Final
1983-84	80	25	10	5	19	16	5	44	26	10	350	290	98	3rd, Patrick Div.	Lost Div. Semi-Final
1982-83	80	29	8	3	20	15	5	49	23	8	326	240	106	1st, Patrick Div.	Lost Div. Semi-Final
1981-82	80	25	10	5	13	21	6	38	31	11	325	313	87	3rd, Patrick Div.	Lost Div. Semi-Final
1980-81	80	23	9	8	18	15	7	41	24	15	313	249	97	2nd, Patrick Div.	Lost Quarter-Final
1979-80	80	27	5	8	21	7	12	48	12	20	327	254	116	1st, Patrick Div.	Lost Final
1978-79	80	26	10	4	14	15	11	40	25	15	281	248	95	2nd, Patrick Div.	Lost Quarter-Final
1977-78	80	29	6	5	16	14	10	45	20	15	296	200	105	2nd, Patrick Div.	Lost Semi-Final
1976-77	80	33	6	1	15	10	15	48	16	16	323	213	112	1st, Patrick Div.	Lost Semi-Final
1975-76	80	36	2	2	15	11	14	51	13	16	348	209	118	1st, Patrick Div.	Lost Final
1974-75	**80**	**32**	**6**	**2**	**19**	**12**	**9**	**51**	**18**	**11**	**293**	**181**	**113**	**1st, Patrick Div.**	**Won Stanley Cup**
1973-74	**78**	**28**	**6**	**5**	**22**	**10**	**7**	**50**	**16**	**12**	**273**	**164**	**112**	**1st, West Div.**	**Won Stanley Cup**
1972-73	78	27	8	4	10	22	7	37	30	11	296	256	85	2nd, West Div.	Lost Semi-Final
1971-72	78	19	13	7	7	25	7	26	38	14	200	236	66	5th, West Div.	Out of Playoffs
1970-71	78	20	10	9	8	23	8	28	33	17	207	225	73	3rd, West Div.	Lost Quarter-Final
1969-70	76	11	14	13	6	21	11	17	35	24	197	225	58	5th, West Div.	Out of Playoffs
1968-69	76	14	16	8	6	19	13	20	35	21	174	225	61	3rd, West Div.	Lost Quarter-Final
1967-68	74	17	13	7	14	19	4	31	32	11	173	179	73	1st, West Div.	Lost Quarter-Final

Schedule

Home	Away
Oct. Sun. 7 Detroit	**Oct.** Thur. 4 Boston
Thur. 11 New Jersey	Sat. 6 New Jersey
Sat. 13 Winnipeg	Tues. 16 Pittsburgh
Thur. 18 Quebec	Sat. 20 Montreal
Tues. 23 Washington	Thur. 25 NY Rangers
Tues. 30 Pittsburgh	Sat. 27 NY Islanders
Nov. Thur. 1 Minnesota	**Nov.** Sun. 4 Toronto
Sat. 3 Chicago*	Tues. 6 Winnipeg
Thur. 8 Calgary	Sat. 10 Quebec
Sun. 11 Vancouver	Sat. 17 New Jersey*
Tues. 13 NY Rangers	Wed. 21 Pittsburgh
Thur. 15 Montreal	Tues. 27 NY Islanders
Sun. 18 New Jersey	Wed. 28 New Jersey
Fri. 23 Toronto*	**Dec.** Sat. 8 Minnesota
Sun. 25 NY Islanders	Sun. 9 Chicago
Fri. 30 NY Rangers	Tues. 11 Washington
Dec. Sun. 2 Edmonton	Sun. 16 Winnipeg
Thur. 6 Buffalo	Tues. 18 Detroit
Thur. 13 NY Islanders	Sat. 22 Hartford
Sat. 15 Detroit*	Thur. 27 Los Angeles
Thur. 20 New Jersey	Sat. 29 St Louis
Sun. 23 Montreal	Mon. 31 Buffalo
Jan. Sun. 13 Edmonton	**Jan.** Fri. 4 Washington
Tues. 15 Pittsburgh	Sat. 5 NY Islanders
Thur. 17 Quebec	Mon. 7 NY Rangers
Tues. 22 Calgary	Sat. 12 Boston
Thur. 24 Washington	Sat. 26 Hartford
Thur. 31 Pittsburgh	**Feb.** Sun. 10 Washington*
Feb. Sat. 2 Hartford*	Wed. 13 Toronto
Tues. 5 Los Angeles	Sat. 16 New Jersey*
Thur. 7 Vancouver	Sat. 23 NY Islanders
Mon. 18 Chicago*	Tues. 26 Minnesota
Thur. 21 NY Rangers	**Mar.** Mon. 4 NY Rangers
Sun. 24 NY Islanders	Thur. 7 Calgary
Mar. Sat. 2 St Louis	Fri. 8 Edmonton
Sun. 17 Boston	Tues. 12 Los Angeles
Thur. 21 St Louis	Wed. 13 Vancouver
Sat. 23 NY Rangers*	Sat. 16 Washington
Tues. 26 Pittsburgh	Sun. 24 Buffalo*
Thur. 28 Washington	Sat. 30 Pittsburgh*

* Denotes afternoon game.

Home Starting Times:
Weeknights & Saturdays .... 7:35 p.m.
Sundays .... 7:05 p.m.
Matinees .... 1:05 p.m.
Except Sat. Feb. 2, ... 11:05 a.m.

Franchise date: June 5, 1967

24th
NHL
Season

Gord Murphy led all Flyers' defensemen in points with 41 in 1989-90.

1990-91 Player Personnel

FORWARDS	HT	WT	S	Place of Birth	Date	1989-90 Club
ACTON, Keith	5-8	170	L	Stouffville, Ont.	4/15/58	Flyers
ARMSTRONG, Bill	6-2	195	L	London, Ont.	6/25/66	Hershey
BARRIE, Len	6-0	200	R	Kimberly, B.C.	6/4/69	Kamloops-Flyers
BASSEN, Mark	5-10	170	R	Calgary, Alta.	5/9/69	Hershey
BERUBE, Craig	6-1	205	L	Calahoo, Alta.	11/17/65	Flyers
BOIVIN, Claude	6-2	200	L	St. Foy, Que.	3/1/70	Laval
CRAVEN, Murray	6-2	185	L	Medicine Hat, Alta.	7/20/64	Flyers
DALLMAN, Rod	5-11	185	L	Prince Albert, Sask.	1/26/67	Springfield
DANIELS, Kimbi	5-10	175	R	Brandon, Man.	1/19/72	Swift Current
DOBBIN, Brian	5-11	205	R	Petrolia, Ont.	8/18/66	Flyers-Hershey
EKLUND, Pelle	5-10	175	L	Stockholm, Sweden	3/22/63	Flyers
FISHER, Craig	6-1	170	L	Oshawa, Ont.	6/30/70	Miami of Ohio-Flyers
FREER, Mark	5-10	180	L	Peterborough, Ont.	7/14/68	Hershey-Flyers
HARDING, Jeff	6-3	220	R	Toronto, Ont.	4/6/69	Hershey-Flyers-Cdn. Nationals
HAWLEY, Kent	6-3	215	L	Kingston, Ont.	2/20/68	Hershey
HORACEK, Tony	6-4	210	L	Vancouver, B.C.	2/3/67	Flyers-Hershey
JENSEN, Chris	5-10	170	R	Fort St. John, B.C.	10/28/63	Flyers-Hershey
KERR, Tim	6-3	230	R	Windsor, Ont.	1/5/60	Flyers
KINISKY, Al	6-4	220	L	Pt. Coquitlam, B.C.	5/31/72	Seattle
KUSHNER, Dale	6-1	195	L	Terrace, B.C.	6/13/66	Springfield
LACOMBE, Normand	6-0	205	R	Pierrefonds, Que.	10/18/64	Edmonton-Flyers
MELLANBY, Scott	6-1	205	R	Montreal, Que.	6/11/66	Flyers
RICCI, Mike	6-0	190	L	Scarborough, Ont.	11/27/71	Peterborough
SCHIEFELE, Steve	6-0	190	R	Alexandria, VA	4/18/68	Boston Col.-Hershey
SANDWITH, Terran	6-4	210	L	Stoney Plain, Alta.	4/17/72	Tri-City
SIMPSON, Reid	6-1	211	L	Flin Flon, Man.	5/21/69	Pr. Albert-Hershey
SIMON, Chris	6-3	220	L	Wawa, Ont.	1/30/72	Ottawa
SMITH, Derrick	6-2	215	L	Scarborough, Ont.	1/22/65	Flyers
SUTTER, Ron	6-0	180	R	Viking, Alta.	12/2/63	Flyers
TOCCHET, Rick	6-0	205	R	Scarborough, Ont.	4/9/64	Flyers
TOOKEY, Tim	5-11	190	L	Edmonton, Alta.	8/29/60	Hershey

DEFENSEMEN						
ARMSTRONG, Bill	6-4	215	L	Richmond Hill, Ont.	5/18/70	Oshawa
BARON, Murray	6-3	210	L	Prince George, B.C.	6/1/67	Hershey-Flyers
BEADLE, Steve	5-11	190	L	Lansing, MI	5/30/68	Michigan State
CARKNER, Terry	6-3	212	L	Smiths Falls, Ont.	3/7/66	Flyers
CHYCHRUN, Jeff	6-4	212	R	LaSalle, Que.	5/3/66	Flyers
FENYVES, Dave	5-11	192	L	Dunnville, Ont.	4/29/60	Hershey-Flyers
HOWE, Mark	5-11	185	L	Detroit, MI	5/28/55	Flyers
HUFFMAN, Kerry	6-2	200	L	Peterborough, Ont.	1/3/68	Flyers
KORDIC, Daniel	6-5	220	L	Edmonton, Alta.	4/18/71	Medicine Hat
LATAL, Jiri	6-0	190	L	Olomouc, Czech.	2/2/67	Hershey-Flyers
MURPHY, Gord	6-2	190	R	Willowdale, Ont.	2/23/67	Flyers
RUMBLE, Darren	6-1	200	L	Barrie, Ont.	1/23/69	Hershey
SABOL, Shaun	6-2	215	L	Minneapolis, MN	7/13/66	Hershey-Flyers
SAMUELSSON, Kjell	6-6	235	R	Tyringe, Sweden	10/18/58	Flyers
SANDELIN, Scott	6-0	180	R	Hibbing, MN	8/8/64	Hershey
STOTHERS, Mike	6-4	212	L	Toronto, Ont.	2/22/62	Hershey

GOALTENDERS	HT	WT	C	Place of Birth	Date	1989-90 Club
HEXTALL, Ron	6-3	192	L	Brandon, Man.	5/3/64	Flyers-Hershey
HOFFORT, Bruce	5-10	185	L	N. Battleford, Sask.	7/30/66	Hershey-Flyers
PEETERS, Pete	6-1	195	L	Edmonton, Alta.	8/17/57	Flyers
ROUSSEL, Dominic	6-1	185	L	Hull, Que.	2/22/70	Shawinigan
WREGGET, Ken	6-1	195	L	Brandon, Man.	3/25/64	Flyers

1989-90 Scoring

Regular Season

* rookie

Pos	#	Player	Team	GP	G	A	Pts	+/-	PIM	PP	SH	GW	GT	S	%
R	22	Rick Tocchet	PHI	75	37	59	96	4	196	15	1	0	0	269	13.8
L	32	Murray Craven	PHI	76	25	50	75	2	42	7	2	3	0	175	14.3
C	10	Mike Bullard	PHI	70	27	37	64	0	67	6	0	4	0	181	14.9
C	9	Pelle Eklund	PHI	70	23	39	62	7	16	5	3	2	0	126	18.3
R	12	Tim Kerr	PHI	40	24	24	48	3 —	34	9	0	2	2	162	14.8
C	14	Ron Sutter	PHI	75	22	26	48	2	104	0	2	6	0	157	14.0
R	23	Ilkka Sinisalo	PHI	59	23	23	46	6	26	4	3	4	0	102	22.5
D	3	Gordon Murphy	PHI	75	14	27	41	7 —	95	4	0	1	0	160	8.8
C	18	Ken Linseman	BOS	32	6	16	22	12	66	1	0	0	0	47	12.8
			PHI	29	5	9	14	7 —	30	1	0	0	0	32	15.6
			TOTAL	61	11	25	36	5	96	2	0	0	0	79	13.9
D	2	Mark Howe	PHI	40	7	21	28	22	24	3	1	1	0	63	11.1
C	25	Keith Acton	PHI	69	13	14	27	2 —	80	0	2	0	0	94	13.8
R	19	Scott Mellanby	PHI	57	6	17	23	4 —	77	0	0	1	0	104	5.8
D	28	Kjell Samuelsson	PHI	66	5	17	22	20	91	0	0	0	0	88	5.7
D	29	Terry Carkner	PHI	63	4	18	22	8 —	169	1	0	1	0	60	6.7
D	11	*Jiri Latal	PHI	32	6	13	19	4	6	3	0	0	0	59	10.2
L	17	Craig Berube	PHI	74	4	14	18	7 —	291	0	0	0	0	52	7.7
R	20	Kevin Maguire	BUF	61	6	9	15	3 —	115	0	0	1	0	62	9.7
			PHI	5	1	0	1	1 —	6	0	0	0	0	7	14.3
			TOTAL	66	7	9	16	4 —	121	0	0	1	0	69	10.1
D	5	Kerry Huffman	PHI	43	1	12	13	3 —	34	0	0	0	0	70	1.4
L	21	*Tony Horacek	PHI	48	5	5	10	6	117	0	0	1	0	31	16.1
R	36	Normand Lacombe	EDM	15	5	2	7	4	21	0	0	0	0	15	33.3
			PHI	18	0	2	2	0	7	0	0	0	0	21	.0
			TOTAL	33	5	4	9	4	28	0	0	0	0	36	13.9
L	24	Derrick Smith	PHI	55	3	6	9	15 —	32	0	0	0	0	72	4.2
D	6	Jeff Chychrun	PHI	79	2	7	9	12 —	248	0	0	1	0	52	3.8
L	15	Doug Sulliman	PHI	28	3	4	7	4	0	0	0	0	0	28	10.7
D	8	*Murray Baron	PHI	16	2	2	4	1 —	12	0	0	0	0	18	11.1
C	46	*Don Biggs	PHI	11	2	0	2	4 —	8	1	0	0	0	14	14.3
R	18	Brian Dobbin	PHI	9	1	1	2	1	11	1	0	0	0	11	9.1
C	35	Ken Wregget	PHI	51	0	2	2	0	12	0	0	0	0	0	.0
C	42	Don Nachbaur	PHI	2	0	1	1	0	0	0	0	0	0	0	.0
G	33	Pete Peeters	PHI	24	0	1	1	0	2	0	0	0	0	0	.0
C	20	*Len Barrie	PHI	1	0	0	0	2 —	0	0	0	0	0	0	.0
C	45	Chris Jensen	PHI	1	0	0	0	1 —	2	0	0	0	0	0	.0
C	7	*Craig Fisher	PHI	2	0	0	0	0	0	0	0	0	0	5	.0
C	37	*Mark Freer	PHI	2	0	0	0	0	0	0	0	0	0	2	.0
D	47	*Shaun Sabol	PHI	2	0	0	0	0	0	0	0	0	0	2	.0
G	30	*Bruce Hoffort	PHI	7	0	0	0	0	2	0	0	0	0	0	.0
G	27	Ron Hextall	PHI	8	0	0	0	0	14	0	0	0	0	0	.0
R	34	*Jeff Harding	PHI	9	0	0	0	1 —	18	0	0	0	0	11	.0
D	26	Dave Fenyves	PHI	12	0	0	0	6 —	4	0	0	0	0	10	.0

Goaltending

No.	Goaltender	GPI	Mins	Avg	W	L	T	EN	SO	GA	SA	S%
35	Ken Wregget	51	2961	3.42	22	24	3	3	0	169	1560	.892
30	*Bruce Hoffort	7	329	3.65	3	0	2	0	0	20	159	.874
33	Pete Peeters	24	1140	3.74	1	13	5	5	1	71	606	.883
27	Ron Hextall	8	419	4.15	4	2	1	0	0	29	219	.868
	Totals	80	4870	3.66	30	39	11	8	1	297	2544	.883

Murray Craven had 50 assists in 1989-90, the highest total of his eight-year NHL career.

General Managers' History

Normand Robert Poile, 1967-68 to 1969-70; Keith Allen, 1970-71 to 1982-83; Bob McCammon, 1983-84; Bobby Clarke, 1984-85 to 1989-90; Russ Farwell, 1990-91.

Coaching History

Keith Allen, 1967-68 to 1968-69; Vic Stasiuk, 1969-70 to 1970-71; Fred Shero, 1971-72 to 1977-78; Bob McCammon and Pat Quinn, 1978-79; Pat Quinn, 1979-80 to 1980-81; Pat Quinn and Bob McCammon, 1981-82; Bob McCammon, 1982-83 to 1983-84; Mike Keenan, 1984-85 to 1987-88; Paul Holmgren, 1988-89 to date.

Captains' History

Lou Angotti, 1967-68; Ed Van Impe, 1968-69 to 1971-72; Ed Van Impe, Bob Clarke, 1972-73; Bob Clarke, 1973-74 to 1978-79; Mel Bridgman, 1979-80, 1980-81; Bill Barber, 1981-82; Bill Barber, Bob Clarke, 1982-83; Bob Clarke, 1983-84; Dave Poulin, 1984-85 to 1989-90.

Retired Numbers

1	Bernie Parent	1967-1971 and 1973-1979
4	Barry Ashbee	1970-1974
16	Bobby Clarke	1969-1984

Club Records

Team

(Figures in brackets for season records are games played; records for fewest points, wins, ties, losses, goals, goals against are for 70 or more games)

Most Points	118	1975-76 (80)
Most Wins	53	1984-85 (80)
		1985-86 (80)
Most Ties	.........*24	1969-70 (76)
Most Losses	38	1971-72 (78)
Most Goals	350	1983-84 (80)
Most Goals Against	...313	1981-82 (80)
Fewest Points	58	1969-70 (76)
Fewest Wins	17	1969-70 (76)
Fewest Ties	4	1985-86 (80)
Fewest Losses	12	1979-80 (80)
Fewest Goals	173	1967-68 (74)
Fewest Goals Against	...164	1973-74 (78)

Longest Winning Streak

Over-all ....13 Oct. 19-Nov. 17/85
Home ....*20 Jan. 4-
Apr. 3/76
Away .... 8 Dec. 22/82-
Jan. 16/83

Longest Undefeated Streak

Over-all ....*35 Oct. 14/79-
Jan. 6/80
(25 wins, 10 ties)
Home ....26 Oct. 11/79-
Feb. 3/80
(19 wins, 7 ties)
Away ....16 Oct. 20/79-
Jan. 6/80
(11 wins, 5 ties)

Longest Losing Streak

Over-all .... 6 Mar. 25-
Apr. 4/70
Home .... 5 Jan. 30-
Feb. 15/69
Away .... 8 Oct. 25-
Nov. 26/72

Longest Winless Streak

Over-all ....11 Nov. 21-
Dec. 14/69
(9 losses, 2 ties)
Dec. 10/70-
Jan. 3/71
(9 losses, 2 ties)
Home .... 8 Dec. 19/68-
Jan. 18/69
(4 losses, 4 ties)
Away ....19 Oct. 23/71-
Jan. 27/72
(15 losses, 4 ties)

Most Shutouts, Season ...13 1974-75 (80)
Most PIM, Season 2,621 1980-81 (80)
Most Goals, Game ....13 Mar. 22/84
(Pit. 4 at Phi. 13)
Oct. 18/84
(Van. 2 at Phil. 13)

Individual

Most Seasons ....15 Bobby Clarke
Most Games ....1,144 Bobby Clarke
Most Goals, Career ......420 Bill Barber
Most Assists, Career ....852 Bobby Clarke
Most Points, Career ....1,210 Bobby Clarke
(358 goals, 852 assists)
Most PIM, Career ......1,600 Paul Holmgren
Most Shutouts, Career .....50 Bernie Parent
Longest Consecutive
Game Streak ....287 Rick MacLeish
(Oct. 6/72-Feb. 5/76)
Most Goals, Season ....61 Reggie Leach
(1975-76)
Most Assists, Season .....89 Bobby Clarke
(1974-75; 1975-76)
Most Points, Season .....119 Bobby Clarke
(1975-76)
(30 goals, 89 assists)
Most PIM, Season ......*472 Dave Schultz
(1974-75)

Most Points, Defenseman,
Season ....82 Mark Howe
(1985-86)
(24 goals, 58 assists)
Most Points, Center,
Season ....119 Bobby Clarke
(1975-76)
(30 goals, 89 assists)
Most Points, Right Wing,
Season ....98 Tim Kerr
(1984-85)
(54 goals, 44 assists)
Most Points, Left Wing,
Season ....112 Bill Barber
(1975-76)
(50 goals, 62 assists)
Most Points, Rookie,
Season ....76 Dave Poulin
(1983-84)
(31 goals, 45 assists)
Most Shutouts, Season ....12 Bernie Parent
(1973-74; 1974-75)
Most Goals, Game .... 4 Rick MacLeish
(Feb. 13/73; Mar. 4/73)
Tom Bladon
(Dec. 11/77)
Tim Kerr
(Oct. 25/84, Jan. 17/85,
Feb. 9/85, Nov. 20/86)
Brian Propp
(Dec. 2/86)
Rick Tocchet
(Feb. 27/88;
Jan. 25/90)
Most Assists, Game ....5 Bobby Clarke
(Apr. 1/76)
Most Points, Game ....8 Tom Bladon
(Dec. 11/77)

* NHL Record.

All-time Record vs. Other Clubs

Regular Season

	At Home						On Road						Total					
	GP	W	L	T	GF	GA	PTS	GP	W	L	T	GF	GA	PTS	GP	W	L	T	GF	GA	PTS
Boston	47	20	21	6	158	142	46	47	9	32	6	138	200	24	94	29	53	12	296	342	70
Buffalo	40	26	8	6	148	99	58	38	14	18	6	115	133	34	78	40	26	12	263	232	92
Calgary	39	28	10	1	164	97	57	39	12	19	8	135	162	32	78	40	29	9	299	259	89
Chicago	48	26	14	8	165	134	60	49	9	24	16	127	172	34	97	35	38	24	292	306	94
Detroit	46	27	9	10	188	133	64	47	18	20	9	159	164	45	93	45	29	19	347	297	109
Edmonton	17	13	3	1	80	48	27	18	5	10	3	54	69	13	35	18	13	4	134	117	40
Hartford	18	14	3	1	81	46	29	17	7	6	4	77	75	18	35	21	9	5	158	121	47
Los Angeles	52	32	13	7	204	135	71	52	31	14	7	170	144	69	104	63	27	14	383	279	140
Minnesota	55	37	8	10	217	123	84	53	20	21	12	184	173	52	108	57	29	22	401	296	136
Montreal	46	16	19	11	123	140	43	47	10	27	10	131	184	30	93	26	46	21	254	324	73
New Jersey	46	35	7	4	205	98	74	45	25	17	3	194	159	53	91	60	24	7	399	257	127
NY Islanders	57	33	17	7	214	175	73	57	19	28	10	168	225	48	114	52	45	17	382	400	121
NY Rangers	71	34	26	11	245	208	79	71	25	28	18	215	227	68	142	59	54	29	460	435	147
Pittsburgh	71	57	8	6	326	162	120	70	29	28	13	225	222	71	141	86	36	19	551	384	191
Quebec	17	13	2	2	72	43	28	18	6	5	7	67	64	19	35	19	7	9	139	107	47
St. Louis	54	37	9	8	215	121	82	55	26	22	7	166	160	59	109	63	31	15	381	281	141
Toronto	47	30	10	7	192	114	67	47	17	17	13	153	165	47	94	47	27	20	345	279	114
Vancouver	40	29	11	0	190	117	58	41	21	10	10	159	121	52	81	50	21	10	349	238	110
Washington	46	28	14	4	185	124	60	46	22	17	7	172	162	51	92	50	31	11	357	286	111
Winnipeg	18	15	3	0	91	50	30	17	8	8	1	64	62	17	35	23	11	1	155	112	47
Defunct Club	34	24	4	6	137	67	54	05	10	14	0	102	09	34	09	37	18	14	239	156	88
Totals	**909**	**574**	**219**	**116**	**3600**	**2376**	**1264**	**909**	**346**	**385**	**178**	**2984**	**3132**	**870**	**1818**	**920**	**604**	**294**	**6584**	**5508**	**2134**

Playoffs

	Series	W	L	GP	W	L	T	GF	GA	Last Mtg.	Round	Result
Boston	4	2	2	20	9	11	0	57	60	1978	QF	L 1-4
Buffalo	2	2	0	11	8	3	0	35	23	1978	QF	W 4-1
**Calgary	2	1	1	11	7	4	0	43	28	1981	QF	L 3-4
Chicago	1	0	1	4	0	4	0	8	20	1971	QF	L 0-4
Edmonton	3	1	2	15	7	8	0	44	49	1987	F	L 3-4
Minnesota	2	2	0	11	8	3	0	41	26	1980	SF	W 4-1
Montreal	4	1	3	21	6	15	0	52	72	1989	CF	L 2-4
*New Jersey	1	1	0	2	2	0	0	6	3	1978	PR	W 2-0
NY Islanders	4	3	1	25	14	11	0	83	69	1987	DF	W 4-3
NY Rangers	8	4	4	38	19	19	0	119	130	1987	DSF	W 4-2
Pittsburgh	1	1	0	7	4	3	0	31	24	1989	DF	W 4-3
Quebec	2	2	0	11	7	4	0	39	29	1985	CF	W 4-2
St. Louis	2	0	2	11	3	8	0	20	34	1969	QF	L 0-4
Toronto	3	3	0	17	12	5	0	67	47	1977	QF	W 4-2
Vancouver	1	1	0	3	2	1	0	15	9	1979	PR	W 2-1
Washington	3	1	2	16	7	9	0	55	65	1989	DSF	W 4-2
Totals	**43**	**25**	**18**	**223**	**116**	**107**	**0**	**715**	**688**			

Playoff Results 1990-86

Year	Round	Opponent	Result	GF	GA
1989	CF	Montreal	L 2-4	8	17
	DF	Pittsburgh	W 4-3	31	24
	DSF	Washington	W 4-2	25	19
1988	DSF	Washington	L 3-4	25	31
1987	F	Edmonton	L 3-4	18	22
	CF	Montreal	W 4-2	22	22
	DF	NY Islanders	W 4-3	23	16
	DSF	NY Rangers	W 4-2	22	13
1986	DSF	NY Rangers	L 2-3	15	18

Abbreviations: Round: F Final; **CF** conference final; **DF** division final; **DSF** division semi-final; **SF** semi-final; **QF** quarter-final. **PR** preliminary round. **GA** goals against; **GF** goals for.

Entry Draft Selections 1990-76

1990
Pick
4 Mike Ricci
25 Chris Simon
40 Mikael Renberg
42 Terran Sandwith
44 Kimbi Daniels
46 Bill Armstrong
47 Chris Therien
52 Al Kinisky
88 Dan Kordic
109 Vjateslav Butsayev
151 Patrik Englund
172 Toni Porkka
193 Greg Hanson
214 Tommy Soderstrom
235 William Lund

1989
Pick
33 Greg Johnson
34 Patrik Juhlin
72 Reid Simpson
117 Niklas Eriksson
138 John Callahan Jr.
159 Sverre Sears
180 Glen Wisser
201 Al Kummu
222 Matt Brait
243 James Pollio

1988
Pick
14 Claude Boinvin
35 Pat Murray
56 Craig Fisher
63 Dominic Roussel
77 Scott Lagrand
98 Edward O'Brien
119 Gordie Frantti
140 Jamie Cooke
161 Johan Salle
182 Brian Arthur
203 Jeff Dandreta
224 Scott Billey
245 Drahomir Kadlec

1987
Pick
20 Darren Rumble
30 Jeff Harding
62 Martin Hostak
83 Tomaz Eriksson
104 Bill Gall
125 Tony Link
146 Mark Strapon
167 Darryl Ingham
188 Bruce McDonald
209 Steve Morrow
230 Darius Rusnak
251 Dale Roehl

1986
Pick
20 Kerry Huffman
23 Jukka Seppo
28 Kent Hawley
83 Mark Bar
125 Steve Scheifele
146 Sami Wahlsten
167 Murray Baron
188 Blaine Rude
209 Shawn Sabol
230 Brett Lawrence
251 Daniel Stephano

1985
Pick
21 Glen Seabrooke
42 Bruce Rendall
48 Darryl Gilmour
63 Shane Whelan
84 Paul Marshall
105 Daril Holmes
126 Ken Alexander
147 Tony Horacek
168 Mike Cusack
189 Gordon Murphy
231 Rod Williams
252 Paul Maurice

1984
Pick
22 Greg Smyth
27 Scott Mellanby
37 Jeff Chychrun
43 Dave McLay
47 John Stevens
79 Dave Hanson
100 Brian Dobbin
121 John Dzikowski
142 Tom Allen
163 Luke Vitale
184 Bill Powers
205 Daryn Fersovitch
247 Juraj Bakos

1983
Pick
41 Peter Zezel
44 Derrick Smith
81 Alan Bourbeau
101 Jerome Carrier
121 Rick Tocchet
141 Bobby Mormina
161 Per-Erik Eklund
181 Rob Nichols
201 William McCormick
221 Brian Jopling
241 Harold Duvall

1982
Pick
4 Ron Sutter
46 Miroslav Dvorak
47 Bill Campbell
77 Mikael Hjalm
98 Todd Bergen
119 Ron Hextall
140 Dave Brown
161 Alain Lavigne
182 Magnus Roupe
203 Tom Allen
224 Rick Gal
245 Mark Vichorek

1981
Pick
16 Steve Smith
37 Rich Costello
47 Barry Tobobondung
58 Ken Strong
65 David Michayluk
79 Ken Latta
100 Justin Hanley
121 Andre Villeneuve
137 Vladimir Svitek
142 Gil Hudon
163 Steve Taylor
184 Len Hachborn
205 Steve Tsujiura

1980
Pick
21 Mike Stothers
42 Jay Fraser
63 Paul Mercier
84 Taras Zytynsky
105 Dan Held
126 Brian Tutt
147 Ross Fitzpatrick
168 Mark Botell
189 Peter Dineen
195 Bob O'Brien
210 Andy Brickley

1979
Pick
14 Brian Propp
22 Blake Wesley
35 Pelle Lindbergh
56 Lindsay Carson
77 Don Gillen
98 Thomas Eriksson
119 Gord Williams

1978
Pick
6 Behn Wilson
7 Ken Linseman
14 Dan Lucas
33 Mike Simurda
37 Gord Salt
50 Glen Cochrane
67 Russ Wilderman
83 Brad Tamblyn
100 Mark Taylor
117 Mike Ewanouski
126 Jerry Price
134 Darren Switzer
151 Greg Francis
167 Rick Berard
168 Don Lucia
182 Mark Berge
183 Ken Moore
195 Jim Olson
198 Anton Stastny

1977
Pick
17 Kevin McCarthy
35 Tom Gorence
53 Dave Hoyda
67 Yves Guillemette
71 Rene Hamelin
89 Dan Clark
107 Alain Chaput
123 Richard Dalpe
135 Pete Peeters
136 Clint Eccles
139 Mike Greeder
150 Tom Bauer
151 Mike Bauman
153 Bruce Crowder
158 Bob Nicholson
159 Dave Isherwood
161 Steve Jones
165 Jim Trainor
166 Barry Duench
168 Rob McNais
172 Mike Laycock

1976
Pick
17 Mark Suzor
35 Drew Callander
53 Craig Hammer
71 Dave Hynek
89 Robin Lang
107 Paul Klasinski
117 Ray Kurpis

Club Directory

The Spectrum
Pattison Place
Philadelphia, PA 19148
Phone 215/465-4500
PR FAX 215/389-9403
Pres. & GM FAX 215/389-9409
TWX 910-997-2239
ENVOY ID
Front Office: FLYERS. GM
Public
Relations: FLYERS. PR
Capacity: 17,423

Board of Directors
Ed Snider, Jay Snider, Joe Scott, Keith Allen, Fred Shabel, Sylvan Tobin

Majority Ownership	Ed Snider and family
Limited Partners	Sylvan and Fran Tobin
Chairman of the Board Emeritus	Joe Scott
President	Jay Snider
Executive Vice-President, Hockey Operations	Keith Allen
General Manager	Russ Farwell
Assistant General Manager	John Blackwell
Head Coach	Paul Holmgren
Assistant Coaches	Craig Hartsburg, Ken Hitchcock
Goaltending Instructor	Bernie Parent
Head Coach, Hershey Bears (AHL)	Murray Eaves
Physical Conditioning Coach	Pat Croce, LPT, ATC
Director of Pro Scouting	Bill Barber
Pro Scout & Player Development Coordinator	Kevin McCarthy
Chief Scout	Jerry Melnyk
Scouts	Walt Atanas, Inge Hammarstrom, Kevin Maxwell, Simon Nolet, Glen Sonmor, Red Sullivan
Executive Vice-President, Administration	Ron Ryan
Vice-President, Sales	Jack Betson
Marketing Assistant	Lynn McGoldrick
Vice-President, Communications	John Brogan
Director of Public Relations	Rodger Gottlieb
Assistant Director of Public Relations	Jill Vogel
Public Relations Assistant	Suzann Waters
Director of Community Relations	Linda Panasci
Vice-President, Finance	Bob Baer
Accounting Manager	Jeff Niessen
Accountant	Susann Schaffer
Accounting Clerk	Karen Rehm
Accounts Payable Clerk	Michelle Stanek
Director of Team Services	Joe Kadlec
Computer Analyst, Hockey Dept.	Michael Blair
Video Coordinator, Hockey Dept.	Leon Friedrich
Executive Assistants/Secretaries	Ileen Forcine, Dianna Taylor, Robin Walther
Ticket Manager	Ceil Baker
Ticket Office Assistant	Carmen Moses
Product Development and Sales Manager	Jeff Landis
Merchandising Assistant	Marci Sorkin
Archivist	Mott Linn
Receptionist	Dolores McDermott
P.A. Announcer	Lou Nolan
Team Physician	Jeff Hartzell, M.D.
Orthopedic Surgeon	Arthur Bartolozzi, M.D.
Oral Surgeon	Everett Borghesani, D.D.S.
Team Dentist	Jim Larson, D.D.S.
Trainer	Dave Settlemyre
Assistant Trainer	Jim Evers
Manager, Practice Facility	Anthony Tomasco
Dimensions of rink	200 feet by 85 feet
Location of Press Box	Mid-ice, North side, concourse level
Club colors	Orange, Black and White
Training camp site and Practice Facility	The Coliseum, Voorhees, NJ
TV Announcers	Mike Emrick, Bill Clement
Radio Announcers	Gene Hart, Bobby Taylor
WGBS-TV Host	Steve Coates
TV Stations	WGBS-TV (Ch. 57), PRISM
Radio Station	610 WIP All Sports Radio

General Manager

FARWELL, RUSS
General Manager, Philadelphia Flyers. Born in Peace River, Alta., April 20, 1956.

Before being appointed to his position on June 6, 1990, Russ Farwell, 34, spent eight seasons in the Western Hockey League. He served as general manager of the Seattle Thunderbirds from 1988-90 and was named the WHL and CHL Executive of the Year in 1990. In two seasons under Farwell's leadership, the Thunderbirds were 85-52-7, including a 52-17-3 mark last year. Prior to his position with Seattle, Farwell spent six seasons as general manager of the Medicine Hat Tigers. During that time, the Tigers were 281-135-16, participated in the WHL's Eastern Division Finals five times and won consecutive Memorial Cup titles in 1986-87 and 1987-88.

Farwell is the first individual to be named an NHL general manager directly from junior hockey since Wren Blair went from Oshawa to Minnesota in 1967-68. The only other man to do so was Leighton "Hap" Emms, who went from Barrie to Boston in 1965-66.

Coach

HOLMGREN, PAUL
Coach, Philadelphia Flyers. Born in St. Paul, MN., December 2, 1955.

After serving as an assistant coach for the Flyers for three years, Holmgren assumed the head coaching duties on June 1, 1988. In his first NHL season, he led the Flyers to a 36-36-8 record (80 points) and the Wales Conference Championship series where they lost to Montreal.

Always a Philadelphia fan favorite, the St. Paul native played 500 of his 527 career NHL games in a Flyers' uniform, accumulating 138-171-309 scoring totals and setting an all-time club record with 1,600 penalty minutes. Holmgren was traded to the North Stars on February 23, 1984, where he played a total of 27 games over two years before retiring following the 1984-85 season. On July 22, 1985, he rejoined the Flyers as an assistant coach.

Coaching Record

			Regular Season					Playoffs			
Season	Team	Games	W	L	T	%		Games	W	L	%
1988-89	Philadelphia (NHL)	80	36	36	8	.500		19	10	9	.526
1989-90	Philadelphia (NHL)	80	30	39	11	.444		.....	.....	.....	.....
	NHL Totals	160	66	75	19	.472		19	10	9	.526

Pittsburgh Penguins

1989-90 Results: 32w-40L-8T 72PTS. Fifth, Patrick Division

Year-by-Year Record

Season	GP	Home			Road			Overall					Pts.	Finished	Playoff Result
		W	L	T	W	L	T	W	L	T	GF	GA			
1989-90	80	22	15	3	10	25	5	32	40	8	318	359	72	5th, Patrick Div.	Out of Playoffs
1988-89	80	24	13	3	16	20	4	40	33	7	347	349	87	2nd, Patrick Div.	Lost Div. Final
1987-88	80	22	12	6	14	23	3	36	35	9	319	316	81	6th, Patrick Div.	Out of Playoffs
1986-87	80	19	15	6	11	23	6	30	38	12	297	290	72	5th, Patrick Div.	Out of Playoffs
1985-86	80	20	15	5	14	23	3	34	38	8	313	305	76	5th, Patrick Div.	Out of Playoffs
1984-85	80	17	20	3	7	31	2	24	51	5	276	385	53	6th, Patrick Div.	Out of Playoffs
1983-84	80	7	29	4	9	29	2	16	58	6	254	390	38	6th, Patrick Div.	Out of Playoffs
1982-83	80	14	22	4	4	31	5	18	53	9	257	394	45	6th, Patrick Div.	Out of Playoffs
1981-82	80	21	11	8	10	25	5	31	36	13	310	337	75	4th, Patrick Div.	Lost Div. Semi-Final
1980-81	80	21	16	3	9	21	10	30	37	13	302	345	73	3rd, Norris Div.	Lost Prelim. Round
1979-80	80	20	13	7	10	24	6	30	37	13	251	303	73	3rd, Norris Div.	Lost Prelim. Round
1978-79	80	23	12	5	13	19	8	36	31	13	281	279	85	2nd, Norris Div.	Lost Quarter-Final
1977-78	80	16	15	9	9	22	9	25	37	18	254	321	68	4th, Norris Div.	Out of Playoffs
1976-77	80	22	12	6	12	21	7	34	33	13	240	252	81	3rd, Norris Div.	Lost Prelim. Round
1975-76	80	23	11	6	12	22	6	35	33	12	339	303	82	3rd, Norris Div.	Lost Prelim. Round
1974-75	80	25	5	10	12	23	5	37	28	15	326	289	89	3rd, Norris Div.	Lost Quarter-Final
1973-74	78	15	18	6	13	23	3	28	41	9	242	273	65	5th, West Div.	Out of Playoffs
1972-73	78	24	11	4	8	26	5	32	37	9	257	265	73	5th, West Div.	Out of Playoffs
1971-72	78	18	15	6	8	23	8	26	38	14	220	258	66	4th, West Div.	Lost Quarter-Final
1970-71	78	18	12	9	3	25	11	21	37	20	221	240	62	6th, West Div.	Out of Playoffs
1969-70	76	17	13	8	9	25	4	26	38	12	182	238	64	2nd, West Div.	Lost Semi-Final
1968-69	76	12	20	6	8	25	5	20	45	11	189	252	51	5th, West Div.	Out of Playoffs
1967-68	74	15	12	10	12	22	3	27	34	13	195	216	67	5th, West Div.	Out of Playoffs

Schedule

Home				Away			
Oct.	Sun.	7	New Jersey	**Oct.**	Fri.	5	Washington
	Tues.	16	Philadelphia		Tues.	9	St Louis
	Sat.	20	NY Rangers		Thur.	11	Chicago
	Tues.	23	Montreal		Sat.	13	NY Islanders
	Thur.	25	Quebec		Fri.	19	Buffalo
	Sun.	28	NY Islanders		Sat.	27	New Jersey
Nov.	Sat.	3	NY Rangers		Tues.	30	Philadelphia
	Tues.	6	Calgary	**Nov.**	Sat.	10	Boston
	Thur.	8	St Louis		Tues.	13	Minnesota
	Wed.	21	Philadelphia		Wed.	14	Winnipeg
	Sat.	24	Washington		Sat.	17	Los Angeles
	Tues.	27	Edmonton		Fri.	23	Washington
	Thur.	29	Hartford	**Dec.**	Sat.	1	Minnesota
Dec.	Wed.	5	Washington		Mon.	3	NY Rangers
	Fri.	7	Vancouver		Sat.	8	Hartford
	Tues.	11	Chicago		Fri.	14	Buffalo
	Thur.	13	New Jersey		Sat.	22	NY Islanders
	Sun.	16	Detroit		Wed.	26	Washington
	Tues.	18	Winnipeg		Sat.	29	Toronto
	Thur.	20	Minnesota	**Jan.**	Sun.	6	Montreal
	Sun.	23	NY Islanders		Tues.	15	Philadelphia
	Fri.	28	Detroit		Thur.	17	Toronto
	Mon.	31	St Louis		Sat.	26	Quebec
Jan.	Thur.	3	NY Rangers		Thur.	31	Philadelphia
	Sat.	5	New Jersey*	**Feb.**	Sun.	3	Boston
	Tues.	8	Edmonton		Fri.	8	Winnipeg
	Thur.	10	Calgary		Mon.	11	Edmonton
	Tues.	22	New Jersey		Sat.	16	NY Islanders
	Tues.	29	Washington		Fri.	22	New Jersey
Feb.	Sat.	2	Boston*		Sun.	24	Washington*
	Thur.	14	NY Islanders		Tues.	26	Los Angeles
	Tues.	19	Buffalo		Wed.	27	Vancouver
	Thur.	21	Toronto	**Mar.**	Fri.	1	Calgary
Mar.	Tues.	5	Vancouver		Sat.	9	Hartford
	Thur.	7	Los Angeles		Sun.	10	NY Islanders
	Tues.	12	Montreal		Sun.	17	NY Rangers*
	Sat.	16	Quebec*		Tues.	19	New Jersey
	Thur.	21	NY Rangers		Tues.	26	Philadelphia
	Sat.	23	Chicago*		Wed.	27	Detroit
	Sat.	30	Philadelphia*		Sun.	31	NY Rangers

* Denotes afternoon game.

Home Starting Times:

All Games	7:35 p.m.
Except Matinees	1:35 p.m.
Nov. 24	8:05 p.m.
Dec. 31	6:05 p.m.

Franchise date: June 5, 1967

24th NHL Season

Mario Lemieux's 46-game scoring streak during the 1989-90 season was the second longest in NHL history.

1990-91 Player Personnel

FORWARDS	HT	WT	Place of Birth	Date	1989-90 Club
BOURQUE, Phil	6-1	196	Chelmsford, MA	6/8/62	Pittsburgh
BROWN, Rob	5-11	185	Kingston, Ont.	4/10/68	Pittsburgh
CALLANDER, Jock	6-1	187	Regina, Sask.	4/23/61	Pittsburgh-Muskegon
CAUFIELD, Jay	6-4	237	Philadelphia, PA	7/17/60	Pittsburgh
CULLEN, John	5-10	187	Puslinch, Ont.	8/2/64	Pittsburgh
DANIELS, Jeff	6-1	197	Oshawa, Ont.	6/24/68	Muskegon
ERREY, Bob	5-10	183	Montreal, Que.	9/21/64	Pittsburgh
GAUTHIER, Daniel	6-1	186	Charlemagne, Que.	5/17/70	Victoriaville
GILHEN, Randy	5-10	190	Zweibrucken, W. Ger.	6/13/63	Winnipeg
HEWARD, Jamie	6-2	183	Regina, Sask.	3/30/71	Regina
JAGR, Jaromir	6-2	208	Kladno, Czech.	2/12/72	Kladno (Czech.)
KACHOWSKI, Mark	5-10	196	Edmonton, Alta.	2/20/65	Pittsburgh-Muskegon
LEACH, Jamie	6-1	197	Winnipeg, Man.	8/25/69	Pittsburgh-Muskegon
LEMIEUX, Mario	6-4	210	Montreal, Que.	10/5/65	Pittsburgh
LONEY, Troy	6-3	209	Bow Island, Alta.	9/21/63	Pittsburgh
MAJOR, Mark	6-3	217	Toronto, Ont.	3/20/70	Kingston
MICHAYLUK, Dave	5-10	189	Wakaw, Sask.	5/18/62	Muskegon
MICK, Troy	5-11	183	Barnaby, B.C.	3/30/69	Regina
MULLEN, Joe	5-9	180	New York, NY	2/26/57	Calgary
PEDERSON, Barry	5-11	185	Big River, Sask.	3/13/61	Vancouver-Pittsburgh
RECCHI, Mark	5-10	185	Kamloops, B.C.	2/1/68	Muskegon-Pittsburgh
SMART, Jason	6-4	212	Prince George, B.C.	1/23/70	Saskatoon
STEVENS, Kevin	6-3	217	Brockton, MA	4/15/65	Pittsburgh
TANTI, Tony	5-9	185	Toronto, Ont.	10/9/63	Vancouver-Pittsburgh
TROTTIER, Bryan	5-11	195	Val Marie, Sask.	7/17/56	NY Islanders

DEFENSEMEN	HT	WT	Place of Birth	Date	1989-90 Club
BUSKAS, Rod	6-1	205	Wetaskiwin, Alta.	1/7/61	Pittsburgh-Vancouver
COFFEY, Paul	6-1	205	Weston, Ont.	6/1/61	Pittsburgh
DAHLQUIST, Chris	6-1	191	Fridley, MN	12/14/62	Pittsburgh-Muskegon
DELORME, Gilbert	6-1	199	Boucherville, Que.	11/25/62	Pittsburgh
DINEEN, Gord	6-0	191	Quebec City, Que.	9/21/62	Pittsburgh
HILLIER, Randy	6-1	188	Toronto, Ont.	3/30/60	Pittsburgh
JOHNSON, Jim	6-1	193	New Hope, MN	8/9/62	Pittsburgh
KYTE, Jim	6-5	220	Ottawa, Ont.	3/21/64	Pittsburgh
LAUS, Paul	6-1	200	Beamsville, Ont.	9/26/70	Niagara Falls
PAEK, Jim	6-1	200	Seoul, Korea	4/7/67	Muskegon
STANTON, Paul	6-0	190	Boston, MA	6/22/67	Muskegon
STOLK, Darren	6-4	208	Taber, Alta.	7/22/68	Muskegon
ZALAPSKI, Zarley	6-1	211	Edmonton, Alta.	4/22/68	Pittsburgh

GOALTENDERS	HT	WT	Place of Birth	Date	1989-90 Club
BARRASSO, Tom	6-3	211	Boston, MA	3/31/65	Pittsburgh
CLIFFORD, Chris	5-9	167	Kingston, Ont.	5/26/66	Muskegon
PIETRANGELO, Frank	5-9	182	Niagara Falls, Ont.	12/17/64	Pittsburgh-Muskegon
RACINE, Bruce	6-0	178	Cornwall, Ont.	8/9/66	Muskegon
YOUNG, Wendell	5-9	181	Halifax, N.S.	8/1/63	Pittsburgh

1989-90 Scoring

Regular Season
rookie

Pos	#	Player	Team	GP	G	A	Pts	+/−	PIM	PP	SH	GW	GT	S	%
C	66	Mario Lemieux	PIT	59	45	78	123	18−	78	14	3	4	1	226	19.9
D	77	Paul Coffey	PIT	80	29	74	103	25−	95	10	0	3	1	324	9.0
C	11	John Cullen	PIT	72	32	60	92	13−	138	9	0	4	0	197	16.2
R	44	Rob Brown	PIT	80	33	47	80	10−	102	12	0	3	0	157	21.0
L	25	Kevin Stevens	PIT	76	29	41	70	13−	171	12	0	1	0	179	16.2
R	8	*Mark Recchi	PIT	74	30	37	67	6	44	6	2	4	1	143	21.0
R	9	Tony Tanti	VAN	41	14	18	32	1	50	5	0	0	1	103	13.6
			PIT	37	14	18	32	11−	22	7	0	0	0	89	15.7
			TOTAL	78	28	36	64	10−	72	12	0	0	1	192	14.6
L	29	Phil Bourque	PIT	76	22	17	39	7−	108	2	1	3	1	110	20.0
L	12	Bob Errey	PIT	78	20	19	39	3	109	0	1	1	0	127	15.7
D	33	Zarley Zalapski	PIT	51	6	25	31	14−	37	5	0	2	0	85	7.1
C	10	Barry Pederson	VAN	16	2	7	9	3−	10	0	0	0	0	22	9.1
			PIT	38	4	18	22	10−	29	1	0	1	0	58	6.9
			TOTAL	54	6	25	31	13−	39	1	0	1	0	80	7.5
L	24	Troy Loney	PIT	67	11	16	27	9−	168	0	0	1	0	78	14.1
C	19	Randy Gilhen	PIT	61	5	11	16	8−	54	0	0	1	0	67	7.5
D	6	Jim Johnson	PIT	75	3	13	16	20−	154	1	0	0	0	72	4.2
D	23	Randy Hillier	PIT	61	3	12	15	11	71	0	0	1	0	45	6.7
D	4	Chris Dahlquist	PIT	62	4	10	14	2−	56	0	0	1	0	57	7.0
R	14	Jock Callander	PIT	30	4	7	11	0	49	0	0	1	0	22	18.2
R	27	Gilbert Delorme	PIT	54	3	7	10	3	44	0	0	0	0	37	8.1
C	15	Doug Smith	VAN	30	3	4	7	1	72	0	1	0	0	40	7.5
			PIT	10	1	1	2	2−	25	0	0	0	0	11	9.1
			TOTAL	40	4	5	9	1−	97	0	1	0	0	51	7.8
D	5	Gord Dineen	PIT	69	1	8	9	6	125	0	0	0	0	38	2.6
C	18	Richard Zemlak	PIT	19	1	5	6	6−	43	1	0	0	0	11	9.1
D	3	Jim Kyte	PIT	56	3	1	4	10−	125	0	0	0	0	23	13.0
G	1	Wendell Young	PIT	43	0	4	4	0	8	0	0	0	0	0	.0
R	16	Jay Caufield	PIT	37	1	2	3	0	123	0	0	0	6	16.7
R	20	*Jamie Leach	PIT	10	0	3	3	3	0	0	0	0	0	10	.0
D	7	Rod Buskas	VAN	17	0	3	3	1	36	0	0	0	0	11	.0
			PIT	6	0	0	0	4−	13	0	0	0	0	1	.0
			TOTAL	23	0	3	3	3−	49	0	0	0	0	12	.0
G	30	Alain Chevrier	CHI	39	0	2	2	0	6	0	0	0	0	0	.0
			PIT	3	0	1	1	0	2	0	0	0	0	0	.0
			TOTAL	42	0	3	3	0	8	0	0	0	0	0	.0
L	26	Mark Kachowski	PIT	14	0	1	1	1	40	0	0	0	0	4	.0
G	40	Frank Pietrangelo	PIT	21	0	0	0	0	2	0	0	0	0	0	.0
G	35	Tom Barrasso	PIT	24	0	0	0	0	8	0	0	0	0	0	.0

Goaltending

No.	Goaltender	GPI	Mins	Avg	W	L	T	EN	SO	GA	SA	S%
1	Wendell Young	43	2318	4.17	16	20	3	4	1	161	1267	.873
40	Frank Pietrangelo	21	1066	4.33	8	6	2	0	0	77	580	.867
35	Tom Barrasso	24	1294	4.68	7	12	3	2	0	101	748	.865
30	Alain Chevrier	3	166	5.06	1	2	0	0	0	14	89	.843
	Totals	80	4856	4.44	32	40	8	6	1	359	2684	.866

Pittsburgh defensemen Randy Hillier (near right) and Jim Johnson.

Retired Numbers
21 Michel Briere 1969-1970

General Managers' History
Jack Riley, 1967-68 to 1969-70; Leonard "Red" Kelly, 1970-71 to 1971-72; Jack Riley, 1972-73 to 1973-74; Jack Button, 1974-75; Wren A. Blair, 1975-76 to 1976-77; Baz Bastien, 1977-78 to 1982-83; Ed Johnston, 1983-84 to 1987-88; Tony Esposito, 1988-89; Tony Esposito and Craig Patrick, 1989-90; Craig Patrick, 1990-91.

Coaching History
George Sullivan, 1967-68 to 1968-69; Red Kelly, 1969-70 to 1971-72; Red Kelly and Ken Schinkel, 1972-73; Ken Schinkel and Marc Boileau, 1973-74; Marc Boileau, 1974-75; Marc Boileau and Ken Schinkel, 1975-76; Ken Schinkel, 1976-77; John Wilson, 1977-78 to 1979-80; Eddie Johnston, 1980-81 to 1982-83; Lou Angotti, 1983-84; Bob Berry, 1984-85 to 1986-87; Pierre Creamer, 1987-88; Gene Ubriaco, 1988-89; Gene Ubriaco and Craig Patrick, 1989-90. Bob Johnson, 1990-91.

Captains' History
Ab McDonald, 1967-68; no captain, 1968-69 to 1972-73; Ron Schock, 1973-74 to 1976-77; Jean Pronovost, 1977-78; Orest Kindrachuk, 1978-79 to 1980-81; Randy Carlyle, 1981-82 to 1983-84; Mike Bullard, 1984-85, 1985-86; Mike Bullard and Terry Ruskowski, 1986-87; Dan Frawley and Mario Lemieux, 1987-88; Mario Lemieux, 1988-89 to date.

Club Records

Team

(Figures in brackets for season records are games played; records for fewest points, wins, ties, losses, goals, goals against are for 70 or more games)

Most Points	89	1974-75 (80)
Most Wins	40	1988-89 (80)
Most Ties	20	1970-71 (78)
Most Losses	58	1983-84 (80)
Most Goals	347	1988-89 (80)
Most Goals Against	394	1982-83 (80)
Fewest Points	38	1983-84 (80)
Fewest Wins	16	1983-84 (80)
Fewest Ties	5	1984-85 (80)
Fewest Losses	28	1974-75 (80)
Fewest Goals	182	1969-70 (76)
Fewest Goals Against	216	1967-68 (74)

Longest Winning Streak
Over-all ... 7 Oct. 9-
Oct. 22/86
Home ... 9 Feb. 26-
Apr. 5/75
Away ... 4 Oct. 14-
Nov. 2/83;
Jan. 16-
Jan. 23/88

Longest Undefeated Streak
Over-all ... 11 Feb. 7-28/76
(7 wins, 4 ties)
Home ... 20 Nov. 30/74-
Feb. 22/75
(12 wins, 8 ties)
Away ... 7 Mar. 13-27/79
(5 wins, 2 ties)

Longest Losing Streak
Over-all ... 11 Jan. 22/83-
Feb. 10/83
Home ... 7 Oct. 8-29/83
Away ... 18 Dec. 23/82-
Mar. 4/83

Longest Winless Streak
Over-all ... 18 Jan. 2/83-
Feb. 10/83
(17 losses, 1 tie)
Home ... 11 Oct. 8-
Nov. 19/83
(9 losses, 2 ties)

Away ... 18 Oct. 25/70-
Jan. 14/71
(11 losses, 7 ties)
Dec. 23/82-
Mar. 4/83
(18 losses)
Most Shutouts, Season ... 6 1967-68 (74)
1976-77 (80)
Most PIM, Season ... *2,670 1988-89 (80)
Most Goals, Game ... 12 Mar. 15/75
(Wash. 1 at Pit. 12)

Individual

Most Seasons ... 11 Rick Kehoe
Most Games ... 753 Jean Pronovost
Most Goals, Career ... 345 Mario Lemieux
Most Assists, Career ... 493 Mario Lemieux
Most Points, Career ... 838 Mario Lemieux
(345 goals, 493 assists)
Most PIM, Career ... 959 Rod Buskas
Most Shutouts, Career ... 11 Les Binkley
Longest Consecutive
Games Streak ... 320 Ron Schock
(Oct. 24/73-Apr. 3/77)
Most Goals, Season ... 85 Mario Lemieux
(1988-89)
Most Assists, Season ... 114 Mario Lemieux
(1988-89)
Most Points, Season ... 199 Mario Lemieux
(1988-89)
Most PIM, Season ... 409 Paul Baxter
(1981-82)
Most Points, Defenseman,
Season ... 113 Paul Coffey
(1988-89)
(30 goals, 83 assists)
Most Points, Center,
Season ... 199 Mario Lemieux
(1988-89)
(85 goals, 114 assists)
Most Points, Right Wing,
Season ... 115 Rob Brown
(1988-89)
(49 goals, 66 assists)

Most Points, Left Wing,
Season ... 82 Lowell MacDonald
(1973-74)
(43 goals, 39 assists)
Most Points, Rookie,
Season ... 100 Mario Lemieux
(1984-85)
(43 goals, 57 assists)
Most Shutouts, Season ... 6 Les Binkley
(1967-68)
Most Goals, Game ... 5 Mario Lemieux
(Dec. 31/88)
Most Assists, Game ... 6 Ron Stackhouse
(Mar. 8/75)
Greg Malone
(Nov. 28/79)
Mario Lemieux
(Oct. 15/88)
Most Points, Game ... 8 Mario Lemieux
(Oct. 15/88,
Dec. 31/88)

* NHL Record.

All-time Record vs. Other Clubs

Regular Season

			At Home							On Road							Total				
	GP	W	L	T	GF	GA	PTS	GP	W	L	T	GF	GA	PTS	GP	W	L	T	GF	GA	PTS
Boston	49	13	26	10	149	199	36	48	6	37	5	133	225	17	97	19	63	15	282	424	53
Buffalo	41	15	14	12	154	148	42	40	5	22	13	104	185	23	81	20	36	25	258	333	65
Calgary	33	14	10	9	118	113	37	33	7	19	7	94	139	21	66	21	29	16	212	252	58
Chicago	46	22	20	4	163	151	48	48	7	32	9	136	203	23	94	29	52	13	299	354	71
Detroit	52	36	13	3	229	151	75	53	9	34	10	145	210	28	105	45	47	13	374	361	103
Edmonton	17	6	10	1	62	85	13	18	3	14	1	62	102	7	35	9	24	2	124	187	20
Hartford	18	9	6	3	79	71	21	17	6	11	0	70	85	12	35	15	17	3	149	156	33
Los Angeles	59	34	17	8	227	187	76	57	14	35	8	149	217	36	116	48	52	16	376	404	112
Minnesota	52	32	15	5	198	139	69	51	17	29	5	174	200	39	103	49	44	10	372	339	108
Montreal	52	16	28	8	151	195	40	53	4	44	5	130	277	13	105	20	72	13	281	472	53
New Jersey	44	25	16	3	184	160	53	43	15	20	8	156	165	38	87	40	36	11	340	325	91
NY Islanders	51	23	18	10	190	175	56	51	11	32	8	153	227	30	102	34	50	18	343	402	86
NY Rangers	65	23	31	11	227	239	57	65	24	34	7	221	273	55	130	47	65	18	448	512	112
Philadelphia	70	28	29	13	222	225	69	71	8	57	6	162	326	22	141	36	86	19	384	551	91
Quebec	17	9	6	2	73	72	20	18	8	10	0	67	82	16	35	17	16	2	140	154	36
St. Louis	51	22	18	11	188	158	55	53	13	35	5	143	209	31	104	35	53	16	331	367	86
Toronto	49	25	19	5	188	163	55	48	16	22	10	160	195	42	97	41	41	15	348	358	97
Vancouver	38	24	8	6	171	133	54	39	17	19	3	150	149	37	77	41	27	9	321	282	91
Washington	52	25	21	6	219	179	56	52	21	28	3	194	231	45	104	46	49	9	413	410	101
Winnipeg	18	12	6	0	74	56	24	17	9	7	1	65	66	19	35	21	13	1	139	122	43
Defunct Club	35	22	6	7	148	93	51	34	13	10	11	108	101	37	69	35	16	18	256	194	88
Totals	**909**	**435**	**337**	**137**	**3414**	**3092**	**1007**	**909**	**233**	**551**	**125**	**2776**	**3867**	**591**	**1818**	**668**	**888**	**262**	**6190**	**6959**	**1598**

Playoffs

	Series	W	L	GP	W	L	T	GF	GA	Last Mtg.	Round	Result
Boston	2	0	2	9	2	7	0	21	37	1980	PR	L 2-3
Buffalo	1	1	0	3	2	1	0	9	9	1979	PR	W 2-1
Chicago	1	0	1	4	0	4	0	8	14	1972	QF	L 0-4
NY Islanders	2	0	2	12	5	7	0	31	43	1982	DSF	L 2-3
NY Rangers	1	1	0	4	4	0	0	19	11	1989	DSF	W 4-0
Philadelphia	1	0	1	7	3	4	0	24	31	1989	DF	L 3-4
St. Louis	3	1	2	13	6	7	0	40	45	1981	PR	L 2-3
Toronto	2	0	2	6	2	4	0	13	21	1977	PR	L 1-2
Defunct Clubs	1	1	0	4	4	0	0	13	6			
Totals	**14**	**4**	**10**	**62**	**28**	**34**	**0**	**178**	**217**			

Playoff Results 1990-86

Year	Round	Opponent	Result	GF	GA
1989	DF	Philadelphia	L 3-4	24	31
	DSF	NY Rangers	W 4-0	19	11

Abbreviations: Round: F Final; **CF** conference final; **DF** division final; **DSF** division semi-final; **QF** quarter-final. **PR** preliminary round. **GA** goals against; **GF** goals for.

1989-90 Results

		Home					Away	
Oct.	10	Winnipeg	5-1	Oct.	5	Boston	4-5
	14	Montreal	2-1		7	New Jersey	4-4
	17	Toronto	7-5		15	NY Rangers	2-4
	18	St Louis	3-9		26	Detroit	3-3
	21	Buffalo	2-4		28	Montreal	1-5
	25	Toronto	6-8	Nov.	4	Edmonton	3-1
	31	Los Angeles	4-8		5	Vancouver	3-5
Nov.	2	NY Islanders	5-2		9	Chicago	3-4
	14	NY Rangers	6-0		11	St Louis	3-8
	16	Quebec	8-2		24	Washington	7-4
	18	NY Islanders	5-3		30	Philadelphia	1-4
	22	New Jersey	3-6	Dec.	2	Quebec	7-4
	25	Washington	1-4		8	New Jersey	3-2
	28	Philadelphia	3-6		14	Minnesota	4-4
Dec.	6	Washington	5-3		16	Calgary	3-4
	9	Chicago	4-6		23	NY Islanders*	6-8
	12	Boston	7-5		26	Washington	3-6
	19	Hartford	4-8		31	NY Rangers*	5-4
	21	Washington	5-8	Jan.	8	NY Rangers	7-5
	27	NY Rangers	7-4		10	New Jersey	3-6
Jan.	2	Boston	2-5		12	Washington	6-4
	4	Vancouver	4-3		25	Detroit	5-3
	6	Winnipeg	5-3		27	NY Islanders*	3-9
	16	Philadelphia	4-3		28	Buffalo*	2-7
	18	NY Rangers	3-3	Feb.	3	Toronto	4-8
	23	New Jersey	2-4		11	Philadelphia	4-1
	30	Philadelphia	3-6		14	NY Rangers	4-3
Feb.	2	Edmonton	6-3		16	Winnipeg	3-3
	6	NY Islanders	7-8		18	Chicago*	4-6
	8	Washington	7-5		24	Montreal	1-11
	10	Los Angeles	6-4		26	Quebec	2-3
	20	Philadelphia	6-4	Mar.	2	New Jersey	5-6
	22	NY Islanders	4-3		6	Edmonton	3-4
	28	New Jersey	2-1		7	Calgary	3-6
Mar.	4	Minnesota	8-6		10	Los Angeles*	2-8
	15	Detroit	6-1		11	Vancouver	3-5
	17	Minnesota*	2-6		18	NY Islanders*	2-2
	24	Calgary*	3-3		22	Philadelphia	3-5
	27	Hartford	3-3		25	Hartford	2-4
	31	Buffalo	2-3		29	St Louis	4-5

* Denotes afternoon game.

Entry Draft Selections 1990-76

1990
Pick
5 Jaromir Jagr
61 Joe Dziedzic
68 Chris Tamer
89 Brian Farrell
107 Ian Moran
110 Denis Casey
130 Mika Valila
131 Ken Plaquin
145 Pat Neaton
152 Petteri Koskimaki
173 Ladislav Karabin
194 Timothy Fingerhut
215 Michael Thompson
236 Brian Bruininks

1989
Pick
16 Jamie Heward
37 Paul Laus
58 John Brill
79 Todd Nelson
100 Tom Nevers
121 Mike Markovich
126 Mike Needham
142 Patrick Schafhauser
163 Dave Shute
184 Andrew Wolf
205 Greg Hagen
226 Scott Farrell
247 Jason Smart

1988
Pick
4 Darrin Shannon
25 Mark Major
62 Daniel Gauthier
67 Mark Recchi
88 Greg Andrusak
130 Troy Mick
151 Jeff Blaeser
172 Rob Gaudreau
193 Donald Pancoe
214 Cory Laylin
235 Darren Stolk

1987
Pick
5 Chris Joseph
26 Richard Tabaracci
47 Jamie Leach
68 Risto Kurkinen
89 Jeff Waver
110 Shawn McEachern
131 Jim Bodden
152 Jiri Kucera
173 Jack MacDougall
194 Daryn McBride
215 Mark Carlson
236 Ake Lilljebjorn

1986
Pick
4 Zarley Zalapski
25 Dave Capuano
46 Brad Aitken
67 Rob Brown
88 Sandy Smith
109 Jeff Daniels
130 Doug Hobson
151 Steve Rohlik
172 Dave McLlwain
193 Kelly Cain
214 Stan Drulia
235 Rob Wilson

1985
Pick
2 Craig Simpson
23 Lee Giffin
58 Bruce Racine
86 Steve Gotaas
107 Kevin Clemens
114 Stuart Marston
128 Steve Titus
149 Paul Stanton
170 Jim Paek
191 Steve Shaunessy
212 Doug Greschuk
233 Gregory Choules

1984
Pick
1 Mario Lemieux
9 Doug Bodger
16 Roger Belanger
64 Mark Teevens
85 Arto Javanainen
127 Tom Ryan
169 John Del Col
189 Steve Hurt
210 Jim Steen
250 Mark Ziliotto

1983
Pick
15 Bob Errey
22 Todd Charlesworth
58 Mike Rowe
63 Frank Pietrangelo
103 Patrick Emond
123 Paul Ames
163 Marty Ketola
183 Alec Haidy
203 Garth Hildebrand
223 Dave Goertz

1982
Pick
10 Rich Sutter
38 Tim Hrynewich
52 Troy Loney
94 Grant Sasser
136 Grant Couture
157 Peter Derkson
178 Greg Gravel
199 Stu Wenaas
220 Chris McCauley
241 Stan Bautch

1981
Pick
28 Steve Gatzos
49 Tom Thornbury
70 Norm Schmidt
109 Paul Edwards
112 Rod Buskas
133 Geoff Wilson
154 Mitch Lamoureaux
175 Dean Defazio
196 David Hannan

1980
Pick
9 Mike Bullard
51 Randy Boyd
72 Tony Feltrin
93 Doug Shedden
114 Pat Graham
156 Robert Geale
177 Brian Lundberg
198 Steve McKenzie

1979
Pick
31 Paul Marshall
52 Bennett Wolf
73 Brian Cross
94 Nick Ricci
115 Marc Chorney

1978
Pick
25 Mike Meeker
61 Shane Pearsall
75 Rob Garner

1977
Pick
30 Jim Hamilton
48 Kim Davis
66 Mark Johnson
102 Greg Millen

1976
Pick
2 Blair Chapman
19 Greg Malone
29 Peter Marsh
47 Morris Lukowich
65 Greg Redquist
83 Brendan Lowe
101 Vic Sirko

Club Directory

Civic Arena
Pittsburgh, PA 15219
Phone **412/642-1800**
FAX 412/261-0382
ENVOY ID
Front Office: PENS. GM.
Public
Relations   PENS. PR

Capacity: 16,236

Chairman of the Board	Edward J. DeBartolo, Sr.
President	Marie Denise DeBartolo York
Secretary & Treasurer	Anthony W. Liberati
Vice-President & General Counsel	Paul Martha
General Manager	Craig Patrick
Director of Player Development & Recruitment	Scott Bowman
Head Coach	Bob Johnson
Assistant Coaches	Rick Kehoe, Rick Paterson, Barry Smith
Trainer	Skip Thayer
Conditioning Coach	John Welday
Equipment Manager	Steve Latin
Scouts	Greg Malone, Les Binkley, John Gill, Charlie Hodge, Doug McCauley, Ralph Cox, Pierre Maguire, Gilles Meloche
Vice President, Communications & Sales	Bill Strong
Vice President, Marketing	Tinsy Labrie
Controller	Rick McLaughlin
Purchasing Agent	Dana Backstrom
Director of Press Relations	Cindy Himes
Assistant Director of Press Relations	Harry Sanders
Director of Ticket Sales	Jeff Mercer
Ticket Manager	Carol Coulson
Team Physician	Dr. Charles Burke
Team Dentists	Dr. Ronald Linaburg, Dr. Raymond Rainka, Dr. David Donatelli
Executive Office	Civic Arena, Gate 2
Location of Press Box	East Side of Building
Dimensions of Rink	200 feet by 85 feet
Club Colors	Black, Gold and White
Club Trains at	Pittsburgh, PA
Radio Station	KDKA (1020 AM)
Television Station	KDKA-TV
Play-by-Play Announcer	Mike Lange
Color Commentator	Paul Steigerwald

General Manager

PATRICK, CRAIG
General Manger, Pittsburgh Penguins. Born in Detroit, MI, May 20, 1946.
Craig Patrick was appointed general manager on December 5, 1989. In his first season with the Penguins, they compiled a 32-40-8 record. Patrick formerly served as vice-president and general manager for the New York Rangers from 1980-86.

A 1969 graduate of the University of Denver, Patrick was captain of the Pioneers' NCAA Championship hockey team that year. He returned to his alma mater in 1986 where he served as director of athletics and recreation for two years. Patrick served as administrative assistant to the president of the Amateur Hockey Association of the United States in 1980 and as an assistant coach/assistant general manager for the 1980 gold-medal winning U.S. Olympic hockey team. Before pursuing a coaching career, Patrick played professional hockey with Washington, Kansas City, St. Louis, Minnesota and California from 1971-79. In eight seasons, Patrick tallied 163 points (72-91-163) in 401 games.

NHL Coaching Record

Season	Team	Games	Regular Season				Games	Playoffs		
			W	L	T	%		W	L	%
1980-81	NY Rangers (NHL)	59	26	23	10	.525	14	7	7	.500
1984-85	NY Rangers (NHL)	35	11	22	2	.343	3	0	3	.000
1989-90	Pittsburgh (NHL)	54	22	26	6	.463	....	....	....	....
	NHL Totals	148	59	71	18	.459	17	10	7	.412

Coach

JOHNSON, BOB
Coach, Pittsburgh Penguins. Born in Minneapolis, MN, March 4, 1931.
Bob Johnson took over head coaching duties for the Penguins on June 12, 1990 after spending the past three years as Executive Director of USA Hockey in Colorado. Johnson began his coaching career in 1956 at Warroad High School in Minnesota before advancing to the college level with Colorado College in 1963. He was appointed the first hockey coach at the University of Wisconsin where he compiled a 367-175-23 record through 15 seasons. He led the Badgers to three NCAA Championships in 1973, 1977 and 1981 and earned NCAA Coach of the Year honors in 1977. Johnson coached the U.S. National Team in 1973, 1974, 1975 and 1981. He moved to the NHL ranks in 1982 where he served as the head coach of the Calgary Flames for five seasons, leading that team to its first Campbell Conference Championship in 1986 and a berth in the Stanley Cup Finals.

Coaching Record

Season	Team	Games	Regular Season				Games	Playoffs		
			W	L	T	%		W	L	%
1966-67	U. Wisconsin (WCHA)	26	16	10	0	.615	....	....	....	....
1967-68	U. Wisconsin (WCHA)	31	21	10	0	.677	....	....	....	....
1968-69	U. Wisconsin (WCHA)	34	22	10	2	.676	....	....	....	....
1969-70	U. Wisconsin (WCHA)	34	23	11	0	.676	....	....	....	....
1970-71	U. Wisconsin (WCHA)	34	20	13	1	.603	....	....	....	....
1971-72	U. Wisconsin (WCHA)	38	27	10	1	.724	....	....	....	....
1972-73	U. Wisconsin (WCHA)	40	29	9	2	.750	....	....	....	....
1973-74	U. Wisconsin (WCHA)	36	18	13	5	.569	....	....	....	....
1974-75	U. Wisconsin (WCHA)	38	24	12	2	.658	....	....	....	....
1976-77	U. Wisconsin (WCHA)	45	37	7	1	.833	....	....	....	....
1977-78	U. Wisconsin (WCHA)	43	28	12	3	.686	....	....	....	....
1978-79	U. Wisconsin (WCHA)	40	24	13	3	.638	....	....	....	....
1979-80	U. Wisconsin (WCHA)	36	15	20	1	.431	....	....	....	....
1980-81	U. Wisconsin (WCHA)	42	27	14	1	.655	....	....	....	....
1981-82	U. Wisconsin (WCHA)	47	35	11	1	.755	....	....	....	....
1982-83	Calgary (NHL)	80	32	34	14	.487	9	4	5	.444
1983-84	Calgary (NHL)	80	34	32	14	.512	11	6	5	.545
1984-85	Calgary (NHL)	80	41	27	12	.587	6	2	4	.333
1985-86	Calgary (NHL)	80	40	31	9	.556	22	12	10	.545
1986-87	Calgary (NHL)	80	46	31	3	.594	6	2	4	.333
	NHL Totals	400	193	155	52	.547	54	26	28	.481

Quebec Nordiques

1989-90 Results: 12w-61L-7T 31PTS. Fifth, Adams Division

Year-by-Year Record

		Home			Road			Overall						
Season	GP	W	L	T	W	L	T	W	L	T	GF	GA	Pts.	Finished	Playoff Result
1989-90	80	8	26	6	4	35	1	12	61	7	240	407	31	5th, Adams Div.	Out of Playoffs
1988-89	80	16	20	4	11	26	3	27	46	7	269	342	61	5th, Adams Div.	Out of Playoffs
1987-88	80	15	23	2	17	20	3	32	43	5	271	306	69	5th, Adams Div.	Out of Playoffs
1986-87	80	20	13	7	11	26	3	31	39	10	267	276	72	4th, Adams Div.	Lost Div. Final
1985-86	80	23	13	4	20	18	2	43	31	6	330	289	92	1st, Adams Div.	Lost Div. Semi-Final
1984-85	80	24	12	4	17	18	5	41	30	9	323	275	91	2nd, Adams Div.	Lost Conf. Championship
1983-84	80	24	11	5	18	17	5	42	28	10	360	278	94	3th, Adams Div.	Lost Div. Final
1982-83	80	23	10	7	11	24	5	34	34	12	343	336	80	4th, Adams Div.	Lost Div. Semi-Final
1981-82	80	24	13	3	9	18	13	33	31	16	356	345	82	4th, Adams Div.	Lost Conf. Championship
1980-81	80	18	11	11	12	21	7	30	32	18	314	318	78	4th, Adams Div.	Lost Prelim. Round
1979-80	80	17	16	7	8	28	4	25	44	11	248	313	61	5th, Adams Div.	Out of Playoffs

Schedule

Home		Away	
Oct. Sun. 7 Boston		**Oct.** Thur. 4 Hartford	
Sat. 13 Buffalo		Sat. 6 Boston	
Tues. 16 Hartford		Wed. 10 Toronto	
Sat. 20 Detroit*		Fri. 12 Buffalo	
Sun. 21 Vancouver*		Thur. 18 Philadelphia	
Sat. 27 NY Rangers		Thur. 25 Pittsburgh	
Nov. Sat. 3 Minnesota		Mon. 29 NY Rangers	
Tues. 6 Washington		**Nov.** Thur. 1 Chicago	
Sat. 10 Philadelphia		Thur. 8 Minnesota	
Sat. 17 Chicago		Sun. 11 Montreal	
Mon. 19 Montreal		Tues. 13 St Louis	
Sat. 24 Winnipeg		Thur. 15 Boston	
Sun. 25 Los Angeles		Wed. 21 Hartford	
Dec. Sat. 1 Buffalo		Wed. 28 Hartford	
Sun 2 Calgary		**Dec.** Wed. 5 Edmonton	
Sat. 15 NY Islanders		Fri. 7 Calgary	
Tues. 18 Montreal		Mon. 10 Vancouver	
Sat. 22 New Jersey		Thur. 13 Detroit	
Wed. 26 Hartford		Wed. 19 Montreal	
Sat. 29 Washington		Sun. 23 Buffalo	
Jan. Tues. 8 Boston		Mon. 31 NY Islanders*	
Sat. 12 St Louis		**Jan.** Thur. 3 St Louis	
Sun. 13 NY Islanders		Sat. 5 Montreal	
Tues. 22 Toronto		Thur. 10 Boston	
Sat. 26 Pittsburgh		Thur. 17 Philadelphia	
Tues. 29 Winnipeg		Thur. 24 New Jersey	
Feb. Sat. 2 Minnesota		Thur. 31 Buffalo	
Thur. 7 Montreal		**Feb.** Thur. 14 Chicago	
Sat. 9 New Jersey*		Sun. 17 Winnipeg*	
Sun. 10 Boston*		Mon. 18 Vancouver	
Tues. 12 Buffalo		Wed. 20 Los Angeles	
Thur. 28 Buffalo		Sat. 23 Calgary	
Mar. Sat. 2 Hartford		Sun. 24 Edmonton	
Thur. 7 NY Rangers		**Mar.** Tues. 5 Detroit	
Sat. 9 Los Angeles		Sun. 10 Hartford	
Tues. 12 Toronto		Thur. 14 Washington	
Tues. 19 Edmonton		Sat. 16 Pittsburgh*	
Sat. 23 Hartford		Thur. 21 Boston	
Tues. 26 Boston		Thur. 28 Buffalo	
Sun. 31 Montreal		Sat. 30 Montreal	

* Denotes afternoon game.

Home Starting Times:
All Games .... 7:35 p.m.
Except Matinees .... 2:05 p.m.

Franchise date: June 22, 1979

12th NHL Season

Twenty year-old Joe Sakic finished in the top 10 in scoring in 1989-90.

1990-91 Player Personnel

FORWARDS	HT	WT	Place of Birth	Date	1989-90 Club
BAKER, Jamie	6-0	190	Ottawa, Ont.	8/31/66	Québec-Halifax
BERGER, Phil	6-0	190	Dearborn, MI	12/3/66	Greensboro
DEBLOIS, Lucien	5-11	200	Joliette, Qué.	6/21/57	Québec
DORE, Daniel	6-3	202	Ferme-Neuve, Qué.	4/9/70	Québec-Chicoutimi
FORTIER, Marc	6-0	192	Windsor, Qué.	2/26/66	Québec-Halifax
GILLIS, Paul	5-11	198	Toronto, Ont.	12/31/63	Québec
HOUGH, Mike	6-1	192	Montréal, Qué.	2/6/63	Québec
HRKAC, Tony	5-11	170	Thunder Bay, Ont.	7/7/66	St.L.-Qué.-Halifax
IHNACAK, Miroslav	5-11	175	Poprad, Czech.	11/19/62	Halifax
JACKSON, Jeff	6-1	195	Dresden, Ont.	4/24/65	Québec
JARVI, Iiro	6-1	198	Helsinki, Finland	3/23/65	Québec-Halifax
KAMINSKI, Kevin	5-9	170	Churchbridge, Sask.	3/13/69	Québec-Halifax
KIMBLE, Darin	6-2	205	Lucky Lake, Sask.	11/22/68	Québec-Halifax
LAFLEUR, Guy	6-0	185	Thurso, Qué.	9/20/51	Québec
LAPOINTE, Claude	5-9	173	Lachine, Qué.	10/11/68	Halifax
LATTA, David	6-1	190	Thunder Bay, Ont.	1/3/67	Halifax
LOISELLE, Claude	5-11	195	Ottawa, Ont.	5/29/63	Québec
McKEGNEY, Tony	6-1	200	Montréal, Qué.	2/15/58	Québec-Detroit
McRAE, Ken	6-1	195	Winchester, Ont.	4/23/68	Québec
MAJOR, Bruce	6-3	180	Vernon, B.C.	1/3/67	Halifax-Greensboro
MIDDENDORF, Max	6-4	210	Syracuse, NY	12/18/67	Québec-Halifax
MILLER, Kip	5-10	160	Lansing, MI	6/11/69	Michigan State U.
MORIN, Stephane	6-0	174	Montréal, Qué.	3/27/69	Québec-Halifax
NOLAN, Owen	6-1	194	Belfast, Ireland	2/12/72	Cornwall
NOREN, Darryl	5-10	180	Livonia, Mich	8/7/68	U. of Ill.-Chicago
QUINNEY, Ken	5-10	186	New Westmin'r, B.C.	5/23/65	Halifax
SAKIC, Joe	5-11	185	Burnaby, B.C.	7/7/69	Québec
SANIPASS, Everett	6-2	204	Big Cove, N.B.	2/13/68	Québec-Chicago
SASSO, Tom	6-1	190	Maiden, MA	11/20/66	Greensboro-Knoxville
SEVCIK, Jaroslav	5-9	170	Brno, Czech.	5/15/65	Québec-Halifax
SEVERYN, Brent	6-2	210	Vegreville, Alta.	2/22/66	Québec-Halifax
STIENBURG, Trevor	6-1	200	Kingston, Ont.	5/13/66	Halifax
VERMETTE, Mark	6-1	203	Cochenour, Ont.	10/3/67	Québec-Halifax
VINCELETTE, Daniel	6-2	202	Verdun, Qué.	8/1/67	Québec-Chicago-Indianapolis

DEFENSEMEN	HT	WT	Place of Birth	Date	1989-90 Club
BZDEL, Gérald	6-1	196	Wynyard, Sask.	3/13/68	Halifax
CIRELLA, Joe	6-3	210	Hamilton, Ont.	5/9/63	Québec
DOYON, Mario	6-0	174	Québec, Qué.	8/27/68	Québec-Indianapolis
DUBOIS, Eric	6-0	193	Montréal, Qué.	5/9/70	Laval
ESPE, David	6-0	185	St. Paul, MI	11/3/66	Halifax
FINN, Steven	6-0	198	Laval, Qué.	8/20/66	Québec
FOGARTY, Brian	6-2	198	Brantford, Ont.	6/11/69	Québec-Halifax
FOOTE, Adam	6-1	180	Toronto, Ont.	7/10/71	Sault Ste. Marie
GUERARD, Stephane	6-2	198	Ste-Elizabeth, Qué	4/12/68	Québec-Halifax
LAMBERT, Dan	5-8	177	St. Boniface, Man.	1/12/70	Swift Current
LESCHYSHYN, Curtis	6-1	205	Thompson, Man.	9/21/69	Québec
MAROIS, Mario	5-11	190	Québec, Qué.	12/15/57	Québec
PETIT, Michel	6-1	205	Québec, Qué.	2/12/64	Québec
RICHARD, Jean-Marc	5-11	178	St. Raymond, Qué.	10/8/66	Québec-Halifax
SMYTH, Greg	6-3	212	Oakville, Ont.	4/23/66	Québec-Halifax
SPROTT, Jim	6-1	200	Oakville, Ont.	4/11/69	Halifax
VELISCHER, Randy	6-0	200	Montréal, Qué.	2/10/62	New Jersey
WOLANIN, Craig	6-3	205	Grosse Pointe, MI	7/27/67	Québec-New Jersey

GOALTENDERS	HT	WT	Place of Birth	Date	1989-90 Club
FISET, Stephane	6-0	175	Montréal, Qué.	6/17/70	Québec-Victoriaville
GORDON, Scott	5-10	175	Brockton, MA	2/6/63	Québec-Halifax
TANNER, John	6-3	182	Cambridge, Ont.	3/17/71	Québec-Peterborough-London
TUGNUTT, Ron	5-11	155	Scarborough, Ont.	10/22/67	Québec-Halifax

1989-90 Scoring

Regular Season

* rookie

Pos	#	Player	Team	GP	G	A	Pts	+/–	PIM	PP	SH	GW	GT	S	%
C	19	Joe Sakic	QUE	80	39	63	102	40–	27	8	1	2	1	234	16.7
D	24	Michel Petit	QUE	63	12	24	36	38–	215	5	0	0	0	137	8.8
R	10	Guy Lafleur	QUE	39	12	22	34	15–	4	6	0	2	0	100	12.0
L	14	Tony McKegney	DET	14	2	1	3	2	8	0	0	0	0	18	11.1
			QUE	48	16	11	27	31–	45	5	0	0	0	89	18.0
			TOTAL	62	18	12	30	29–	53	5	0	0	0	107	16.8
C	9	Marc Fortier	QUE	59	13	17	30	16–	28	3	1	1	0	89	14.6
C	28	Tony Hrkac	STL	28	5	12	17	1	8	1	0	0	1	41	12.2
			QUE	22	4	8	12	5–	2	2	0	0	0	29	13.8
			TOTAL	50	9	20	29	4–	10	3	0	0	1	70	12.9
L	18	Mike Hough	QUE	43	13	13	26	24–	84	3	1	0	0	93	14.0
C	20	Claude Loiselle	QUE	72	11	14	25	27–	104	0	3	0	0	128	8.6
C	23	Paul Gillis	QUE	71	8	14	22	24–	234	0	1	0	0	68	11.8
L	25	Jeff Jackson	QUE	65	8	12	20	21–	71	0	1	0	0	73	11.0
L	11	Iiro Jarvi	QUE	41	7	13	20	11–	18	1	0	1	0	52	13.5
D	2	Joe Cirella	QUE	56	4	14	18	27–	67	1	0	0	0	76	5.3
D	44	Mario Marois	QUE	67	3	15	18	45–	104	2	0	0	0	108	2.8
C	32	Lucien Deblois	QUE	70	9	8	17	29–	45	1	0	1	1	83	10.8
C	12	Ken McRae	QUE	66	7	8	15	38–	191	0	0	1	0	83	8.4
D	43	*Bryan Fogarty	QUE	45	4	10	14	47–	31	2	0	0	0	93	4.3
D	29	Steven Finn	QUE	64	3	9	12	33–	208	1	0	0	0	74	4.1
D	6	Craig Wolanin	N.J.	37	1	7	8	13–	47	0	0	0	0	35	2.9
			QUE	13	0	3	3	2	10	0	0	0	0	25	.0
			TOTAL	50	1	10	11	11–	57	0	0	0	0	60	1.7
L	21	Everett Sanipass	CHI	12	2	2	4	0	17	0	0	0	0	16	12.5
			QUE	9	3	3	6	4–	8	2	0	0	0	16	18.8
			TOTAL	21	5	5	10	4–	25	2	0	0	0	32	15.6
R	15	Darin Kimble	QUE	44	5	5	10	20–	185	2	0	1	0	40	12.5
D	7	Curtis Leschyshyn	QUE	68	2	6	8	41–	44	1	0	0	0	42	4.8
R	27	*Mark Vermette	QUE	11	1	5	6	3–	8	0	0	0	0	16	6.3
D	28	*Mario Doyon	QUE	9	2	3	5	1–	6	1	0	0	0	19	10.5
R	33	*Daniel Dore	QUE	16	2	3	5	8–	59	1	0	0	0	5	40.0
C	22	*Stephane Morin	QUE	6	2	2	4	1	2	0	0	0	0	11	.0
L	27	*Jaroslav Sevcik	QUE	13	0	2	2	5–	2	0	0	0	0	9	.0
L	5	*Brent Severyn	QUE	35	0	2	2	19–	42	0	0	0	0	28	.0
L	17	Dan Vincelette	CHI	2	0	0	0	1–	4	0	0	0	0	2	.0
			QUE	11	0	1	1	6–	25	0	0	0	0	15	.0
			TOTAL	13	0	1	1	7–	29	0	0	0	0	17	.0
C	21	*Jamie Baker	QUE	1	0	0	0	1–	0	0	0	0	0	0	.0
C	17	*Kevin Kaminski	QUE	1	0	0	0	1–	0	0	0	0	0	0	.0
D	41	*Jean-Marc Richard	QUE	1	0	0	0	1–	0	0	0	0	0	0	.0
G	31	*John Tanner	QUE	1	0	0	0	0	0	0	0	0	0	0	.0
R	48	*Max Middendorf	QUE	3	0	0	0	9–	0	0	0	0	0	5	.0
D	6	Stephane Guerard	QUE	4	0	0	0	5–	6	0	0	0	0	9	.0
G	30	Mario Brunetta	QUE	6	0	0	0	0	0	0	0	0	0	0	.0
G	30	*Stephane Fiset	QUE	6	0	0	0	0	0	0	0	0	0	0	.0
R	14	*Jean-Marc Routhier	QUE	8	0	0	0	3–	9	0	0	0	0	8	.0
G	30	*Scott Gordon	QUE	10	0	0	0	0	0	0	0	0	0	0	.0
G	34	*Sergei Mylnikov	QUE	10	0	0	0	0	0	0	0	0	0	0	.0
D	4	Greg Smyth	QUE	13	0	0	0	8–	57	0	0	0	0	4	.0
G	1	Ron Tugnutt	QUE	35	0	0	0	0	2	0	0	0	0	0	.0

Goaltending

No.	Goaltender	GPI	Mins	Avg	W	L	T	EN	SO	GA	SA	S%
31	*John Tanner	1	60	3.00	0	1	0	0	0	3	30	.900
30	Mario Brunetta	6	191	4.08	1	2	0	0	0	13	99	.869
1	Ron Tugnutt	35	1978	4.61	5	24	3	4	0	152	1080	.859
34	*Sergei Mylnikov	10	568	4.96	1	7	2	1	0	47	330	.858
31	Greg Millen	18	1080	5.28	3	14	1	3	0	95	648	.853
30	*Scott Gordon	10	597	5.33	2	8	0	1	0	53	368	.856
31	*Stephane Fiset	6	342	5.96	0	5	1	1	0	34	199	.829
	Totals	**80**	**4836**	**5.05**	**12**	**61**	**7**	**10**	**0**	**407**	**2754**	**.852**

Guy Lafleur enters his 17th NHL season in 1990-91.

Retired Numbers

3	J.C. Tremblay	1972-1979
8	Marc Tardif	1979-1983

General Managers' History

Maurice Filion, 1979-80 to 1987-88; Martin Madden 1988-89; Martin Madden and Maurice Filion, 1989-90; Pierre Page, 1990-91.

Coaching History

Jacques Demers, 1979-80; Maurice Filion and Michel Bergeron, 1980-81; Michel Bergeron, 1981-82 to 1986-87; André Savard and Ron Lapointe, 1987-88; Ron Lapointe, and Jean Perron, 1988-89; Michel Bergeron, 1989-90; Dave Chambers, 1990-91.

Captains' History

Marc Tardif, 1979-80, 1980-81; Robbie Ftorek, Andre Dupont, 1981-82; Mario Marois, 1982-83 to 1984-85; Mario Marois, Peter Stastny, 1985-86; Peter Stastny, 1986-87 to 1989-90.

Club Records

Team

(Figures in brackets for season records are games played; records for fewest points, wins, ties, losses, goals, goals against are for 70 or more games)

Most Points	94	1983-84 (80)
Most Wins	43	1985-86 (80)
Most Ties	18	1980-81 (80)
Most Losses	61	1989-90 (80)
Most Goals	360	1983-84 (80)
Most Goals Against	407	1989-90 (80)
Fewest Points	31	1989-90 (80)
Fewest Wins	12	1989-90 (80)
Fewest Ties	5	1987-88 (80)
Fewest Losses	28	1983-84 (80)
Fewest Goals	240	1989-90 (80)
Fewest Goals Against	275	1984-85 (80)

Longest Winning Streak
Over-all .... 7 Nov. 24-
Dec. 10/83
Oct. 10-21/85
Dec. 31/85-
Jan. 11/86
Home .... 10 Nov. 26/83-
Jan. 10/84
Away .... 5 Feb. 28-
Mar. 24, 1986

Longest Undefeated Streak
Over-all .... 11 Mar. 10-31/81
(7 wins, 4 ties)
Home .... 14 Nov. 19/83
Jan. 21/84
(11 wins, 3 ties)
Away .... 8 Feb. 17/81-
Mar. 22/81
(6 wins, 2 ties)

Longest Losing Streak
Over-all .... 11 Jan. 18-
Feb. 10/90
Home .... 6 Jan. 13-
Feb. 4/90
Away .... 18 Jan. 18-
Apr. 1/90

Longest Winless Streak
Over-all .... 14 Nov. 25-
Dec. 26/89
(10 losses, 4 ties)
Home .... 11 Nov. 14-
Dec. 26/89
(7 losses, 4 ties)

Away .... 18 Jan. 18-
Apr. 1/90
(18 losses)
Most Shutouts, Season ... 6 1985-86 (80)
Most PIM, Season ... 2,104 1989-90 (80)
Most Goals, Game .... 12 Feb. 1/83
(Hfd. 3 at Que. 12)
Oct. 20/84
(Que. 12 at Tor. 3)

Individual

Most Seasons	11	Michel Goulet
Most Games	813	Michel Goulet
Most Goals, Career	456	Michel Goulet
Most Assists, Career	668	Peter Stastny
Most Points, Career	1,048	Peter Stastny

(380 goals, 668 assists)
Most PIM, Career ..... 1,545 Dale Hunter
Most Shutouts, Career ...... 6 Mario Gosselin

Longest Consecutive
Games Streak .... 312 Dale Hunter
(Oct. 9/80-Mar. 13/84)
Most Goals, Season ...... 57 Michel Goulet
(1982-83)
Most Assists, Season ..... 93 Peter Stastny
(1981-82)
Most Points, Season .... 139 Peter Stastny
(1981-82)
(46 goals, 93 assists)
Most PIM, Season ...... 301 Gord Donnelly
(1987-88)

Most Points, Defenseman,
Season .... 68 Jeff Brown
(1988-89)
(21 goals, 47 assists)

Most Points, Center,
Season .... 139 Peter Stastny
(1981-82)
(46 goals, 93 assists)

Most Points, Right Wing,
Season .... 103 Jacques Richard
(1980-81)
(52 goals, 51 assists)

Most Points, Left Wing,
Season .... *121 Michel Goulet
(1983-84)
(56 goals, 65 assists)

Most Points, Rookie,
Season .... *109 Peter Stastny
(1980-81)
(39 goals, 70 assists)
Most Shutouts, Season ..... 4 Clint Malarchuk
(1985-86)
Most Goals, Game .... 4 Michel Goulet
(Dec. 14/85;
Mar. 17/86)
Peter Stastny
(Feb. 22/81;
Feb. 11/89)
Most Assists, Game .... 5 Anton Stastny
(Feb. 22/81)
Michel Goulet
(Jan. 3/84)
Most Points, Game .... 8 Peter Stastny
(Feb. 22/81)
Anton Stastny
(Feb. 22/81)

* NHL Record.

All-time Record vs. Other Clubs

Regular Season

	At Home						On Road						Total						
	GP	W	L	T	GF	GA	PTS	GP	W	L	T	GF	GA	PTS	GP	W	L	T	GF	GA	PTS
Boston	40	14	22	4	155	179	32	40	15	20	5	135	161	35	80	29	42	9	290	340	67
Buffalo	40	21	14	5	153	120	47	40	10	25	5	130	166	25	80	31	39	10	283	286	72
Calgary	18	7	8	3	76	71	17	17	3	10	4	47	75	10	35	10	18	7	123	146	27
Chicago	18	8	6	4	79	69	20	17	7	9	1	62	72	15	35	15	15	5	141	141	35
Detroit	18	11	5	2	81	61	24	17	7	9	1	63	69	15	35	18	14	3	144	130	39
Edmonton	18	6	10	2	71	86	14	17	4	13	0	52	100	8	35	10	23	2	123	100	22
Hartford	40	23	12	5	183	136	51	40	14	18	8	142	144	36	80	37	30	13	325	280	87
Los Angeles	17	7	8	2	72	71	16	18	7	10	1	68	83	15	35	14	18	3	140	154	31
Minnesota	17	13	2	2	88	43	28	18	6	10	2	60	73	14	35	19	12	4	148	116	42
Montreal	40	21	17	2	145	141	44	40	8	27	5	122	186	21	80	29	44	7	267	327	65
New Jersey	17	10	5	2	83	59	22	18	9	8	1	70	79	19	35	19	13	3	153	138	41
NY Islanders	17	9	7	1	69	56	19	18	6	11	1	66	82	13	35	15	18	2	135	138	32
NY Rangers	17	9	5	3	80	75	21	18	3	12	3	47	77	9	35	12	17	6	127	152	30
Philadelphia	18	5	6	7	64	67	17	17	2	13	2	43	72	6	35	7	19	9	107	139	23
Pittsburgh	18	10	8	0	82	67	20	17	6	9	2	72	73	14	35	16	17	2	154	140	34
St. Louis	18	9	7	2	65	60	20	17	3	13	1	54	80	7	35	12	20	3	119	140	27
Toronto	17	9	4	4	71	59	22	18	8	8	2	78	60	18	35	17	12	6	149	119	40
Vancouver	18	7	7	4	55	54	18	17	6	10	1	70	75	13	35	13	17	5	125	129	31
Washington	17	6	7	4	57	64	16	18	8	8	2	67	76	18	35	14	15	6	124	140	34
Winnipeg	17	7	8	2	70	69	16	18	6	8	4	74	75	16	35	13	16	6	144	144	32
Totals	**440**	**212**	**168**	**60**	**1799**	**1607**	**484**	**440**	**138**	**251**	**51**	**1522**	**1878**	**327**	**880**	**350**	**419**	**111**	**3321**	**3485**	**811**

Playoffs

	Series	W	L	GP	W	L	T	GF	GA	Last Mtg.	Round	Result
Boston	2	1	1	11	5	6	0	36	37	1983	DSF	L 1-3
Buffalo	2	2	0	8	6	2	0	35	27	1985	DSF	W 3-2
Hartford	2	1	1	9	4	5	0	34	35	1987	DSF	W 4-2
Montreal	4	2	2	25	12	13	0	69	86	1987	DF	L 3-4
NY Islanders	1	0	1	4	0	4	0	9	18	1982	CF	L 0-4
Philadelphia	2	0	2	11	4	7	0	29	39	1985	CF	L 2-4
Totals	**13**	**6**	**7**	**68**	**31**	**37**	**0**	**212**	**242**			

Playoff Results 1990-86

Year	Round	Opponent	Result	GF	GA
1987	DF	Montreal	L 3-4	21	26
	DSF	Hartford	W 4-2	27	19
1986	DSF	Hartford	L 0-3	7	16
1985	CF	Philadelphia	L 2-4	12	17
	DF	Montreal	W 4-3	24	24
	DSF	Buffalo	W 3-2	22	22

Abbreviations: Round: F Final; **CF** conference final; **DF** division final; **DSF** division semi-final; **GA** goals against; **GF** goals for.

1989-90 Results

	Home				Away	
Oct.	7	Boston	4-1	Oct. 5	Buffalo	3-4
	8	Hartford	6-9	12	Philadelphia	2-4
	17	Calgary	8-8	14	Minnesota	2-3
	21	Minnesota	7-2	19	Chicago	5-3
	28	Edmonton	3-6	25	Hartford	0-2
	31	Chicago	3-5	26	Boston	2-4
Nov.	4	St Louis*	2-5	Nov. 2	NY Rangers	1-6
	5	Washington*	0-3	8	New Jersey	3-6
	11	Vancouver	3-2	9	NY Islanders	7-5
	14	Winnipeg	3-5	16	Pittsburgh	2-8
	18	Detroit	1-8	22	Hartford	4-2
	21	Calgary	4-4	26	NY Rangers	1-3
	25	Buffalo	2-3	29	Montreal	2-5
	30	Montreal	2-6	Dec. 13	Edmonton	1-5
Dec.	2	Pittsburgh	4-7	14	Calgary	2-8
	5	Boston	3-3	17	Vancouver	2-2
	9	Philadelphia*	6-6	21	Los Angeles	1-6
	10	Los Angeles*	4-8	Jan. 3	Toronto	4-5
	23	Buffalo	5-6	4	Detroit	1-4
	26	Hartford	3-3	6	NY Islanders	2-5
	30	NY Islanders	6-3	11	Boston	1-3
Jan.	9	Montreal	5-2	16	Winnipeg	8-6
	13	New Jersey	4-5	18	Minnesota	4-7
	23	Boston	2-9	24	Montreal	3-7
	27	Detroit	6-8	31	Buffalo	3-6
	30	Buffalo	2-5	Feb. 6	Washington	2-12
Feb.	3	Hartford*	1-5	8	Boston	1-5
	4	Boston*	2-3	10	Montreal	2-7
	13	Vancouver	5-3	15	St Louis	2-9
	22	Montreal	5-6	17	Los Angeles	1-7
	24	St Louis	1-6	21	Hartford	2-3
	26	Pittsburgh	3-2	28	Toronto	4-5
Mar.	3	Buffalo	3-3	Mar. 4	Buffalo	3-5
	13	Edmonton	1-4	7	Winnipeg	3-6
	15	Chicago	3-6	9	Washington	3-4
	17	Philadelphia	6-3	10	New Jersey	3-9
	24	Toronto	3-4	18	Montreal	3-8
	27	NY Rangers	4-7	21	Hartford	1-4
	29	Montreal	2-5	22	Boston	3-7
	31	Hartford	2-3	Apr. 12	Buffalo	2-5

* Denotes afternoon game.

Entry Draft Selections 1990-79

1990
Pick
1	Owen Nolan
22	Ryan Hughes
43	Bradley Zavisha
106	Jeff Parrott
127	Dwayne Norris
148	Andrei Kovalenko
158	Alexander Karpovtsev
169	Pat Mazzoli
190	Scott Davis
211	Mika Stromberg
232	Wade Klippenstein

1989
Pick
1	Mats Sundin
22	Adam Foote
43	Stephane Morin
54	John Tanner
68	Niclas Andersson
76	Eric Dubois
85	Kevin Kaiser
106	Dan Lambert
127	Sergei Mylnikov
148	Paul Krake
169	Viacheslav Bykov
190	Andrei Khumutov
211	Byron Witkowski
232	Noel Rahn

1988
Pick
3	Curtis Leschyshyn
5	Daniel Dore
24	Stephane Fiset
45	Petri Aaltonen
66	Darin Kimble
87	Stephane Venne
108	Ed Ward
129	Valeri Kamensky
150	Sakari Lindfors
171	Dan Wiebe
213	Alexei Gusarov
234	Claude Lapointe

1987
Pick
9	Bryan Fogarty
15	Joe Sakic
51	Jim Sprott
72	Kip Miller
93	Rob Mendel
114	Garth Snow
135	Tim Hanus
156	Jake Enebak
177	Jaroslav Sevcik
183	Ladislav Tresl
198	Darren Nauss
219	Mike Williams

1986
Pick
18	Ken McRae
39	Jean-M Routhier
41	Stephane Guerard
81	Ron Tugnutt
102	Gerald Bzdel
117	Scott White
123	Morgan Samuelsson
134	Mark Vermette
144	Jean-Francois Nault
165	Keith Miller
186	Pierre Millier
207	Chris Lappin
228	Martin Latreille
249	Sean Boudreault

1985
Pick
15	David Latta
36	Jason Lafreniere
57	Max Middendorf
65	Peter Massey
78	David Espe
99	Bruce Major
120	Andy Akervik
141	Mike Oliverio
162	Mario Brunetta
183	Brit Peer
204	Tom Sasso
225	Gary Murphy
246	Jean Bois

1984
Pick
15	Trevor Stienburg
36	Jeff Brown
57	Steve Finn
78	Terry Perkins
120	Darren Cota
141	Henrik Cedegren
162	Jyrki Maki
183	Guy Ouellette
203	Ken Quinney
244	Peter Loob

1983
Pick
32	Yves Heroux
52	Bruce Bell
54	Iiro Jarvi
92	Luc Guenette
112	Brad Walcott
132	Craig Mack
152	Tommy Albelin
172	Wayne Groulx
192	Scott Shaunessy
232	Bo Berglund
239	Dinorich Kokrement

1982
Pick
13	David Shaw
34	Paul Gillis
55	Mario Gosselin
76	Jiri Lala
97	Phil Stanger
131	Daniel Poudrier
181	Mike Hough
202	Vincent Lukac
223	Andre Martin
244	Jozef Lukac
248	Jan Jasko

1981
Pick
11	Randy Moller
53	Jean-Marc Gaulin
74	Clint Malarchuk
95	Ed Lee
116	Mike Eagles
158	Andre Cote
179	Marc Brisebois
200	Kari Takko

1980
Pick
24	Normand Rochefort
66	Jay Miller
108	Mark Kumpel
129	Gaston Therrien
150	Michel Bolduc
171	Christian Tanguay
192	William Robinson

1979
Pick
20	Michel Goulet
41	Dale Hunter
62	Lee Norwood
83	Anton Stastny
104	Pierre Lacroix
125	Scott McGeown

Club Directory

Colisée de Québec
2205 Ave du Colisée
Québec City, Quebec
G1L 4W7
Phone **418/529-8441**
FAX 418/529-1052
ENVOY ID
Front Office: NORDIQUES. GM
Public
Relations: NORDIQUES. PR
NORDIQUES.
Marketing: MKTG
Capacity: 15,399

President and Governor	Marcel Aubut
Alternate Governors	Pierre Pagé, Gilles Léger
Executive Secretaries to the President	Louise Marois, Nicole Vandal

Hockey Club Personnel
Vice-President/Hockey Operations	Maurice Filon
General Manager	Pierre Pagé
Assistant to the General Manager	Gilles Léger
Head Coach	Dave Chambers
Associate Coach	Jacques Martin
Assistant Coach	Robbie Ftorek
Director of Player Personnel	TBA
Scouts – Professional hockey and special assignments	André Savard, TBA
Chief Scout	Pierre Gauthier
Assistant to the Chief Scout	Darwin Bennett
Scouts	Don Boyd, Michel Georges, Mark Kelley, Bob Mancini, Frank Moberg, Don Paarup
Physiotherapist	Jacques Lavergne
Trainers	René Lacasse, René Lavigueur, Brian Turpin
Team Physician	Dr. Pierre Beauchemin
Executive Secretary – hockey department and Travel Coordinator	Suzanne Lussier
Executive Secretary	Liza Boivin

Administration and Finance
Vice President/Administration and Finance	Jean Laflamme
Director of Finance	TBA
Assistant to the Director of Finance	TBA
General Counsel	Jean Pelletier
Executive Secretary	Josette Gagne

Marketing and Communications
Vice-President/Marketing and Communications	Jean-D. Legault
Supervisor of Public Relations	Marius Fortier
Supervisor of Press Relations	Jean Martineau
Coordinator – Public Relations	Nicole Bouchard
Coordinator – Promotions	Diane Thivierge
Marketing Coordinator	Bernard Thiboutot
Graphic Communications Coordinator	Daniel Gagné
Director of Sales & Promotions	André Lestourneau
Supervisor of Novelties & Souvenirs	André Pelletier
Executive Secretaries – Marketing	Marie Godin, Linda Boisselle
Executive Secretary – Sales and Promotions	Marie-Josée Aubin
Team Photographer	Jean-Yves Michaud

Location of Press Boxes	East & West side of building, upper level
Dimensions of Rink	200 feet by 85 feet
Club Colors	Blue, White and Red
Training Camp Site	Québec City
Radio Station	CJRP 1060
Radio Announcers	Alain Crête
TV Station	CFAP (2) Quatre-Saisons
TV Announcers	André Côté, Claude Bédard

General Manager

PAGE, PIERRE
General Manager, Quebec Nordiques. Born in St. Hermas, Que., April 30, 1948.

Pierre Page was named general manager of the Nordiques on May 4, 1990 after two seasons as head coach of the Minnesota North Stars. In his rookie season with Minnesota, the club posted a 27-37-16 record for 70 points, a 19-point improvement over the previous year and earned its first playoff berth since 1985-86. In 1989-90, the North Stars continued improving, finishing the season with 76 points (36-40-4).

Page, 42, joined the Calgary Flames in 1980-81 as an assistant coach to Al MacNeil. He served in that capacity through the 1981-82 season before accepting a position as coach and general manager of the Flames' top minor league affiliate in Denver (two seasons) and, later, Moncton (one season). In 1985-86, Page returned to Calgary as an assistant to head coach Bob Johnson and remained in that capacity through the 1987-88 season under Terry Crisp.

Before joining the Flames, Page was head coach of the Dalhousie University Tigers of the CIAU where in 1978-79, he guided his club to a second place finish in the national final. He also served as an assistant coach with the 1980 Canadian Olympic Team and the 1981 Team Canada entry in the Canada Cup.

NHL Coaching Record

			Regular Season				Playoffs			
Season	Team	Games	W	L	T	%	Games	W	L	%
1988-89	Minnesota (NHL)	80	27	37	16	.438	5	1	4	.200
1989-90	Minnesota (NHL)	80	36	40	4	.475	7	3	4	.429
	NHL Totals	160	63	77	20	.456	12	4	8	.333

Coach

CHAMBERS, DAVE
Coach, Quebec Nordiques. Born in Leaside, Ont., May 7, 1940.

Dave Chambers was named head coach of the Quebec Nordiques on June 5, 1990 after serving as an assistant coach for the Minnesota North Stars in 1989-90. Prior to joining the North Stars, Chambers' coaching career spanned 20 seasons in the amateur ranks.

He began his collegiate coaching career in 1967 at the University of Saskatchewan. He coached three more seasons at the University of Guelph and Ohio State University before landing at York University in Toronto. During a five-year stay at York, he led his club to three division titles and earned coach of the year honors twice — 1975 and 1977. Chambers coached the Toronto Marlboros of the OHL from 1978-79 until 1979-80 and earned Emms Division coach of the year honors in 1980. After serving as a coaching consultant for the Oshawa Generals in 1983-84, Chambers returned to York where he led his team to the OUAA and CIAU Championship in 1984-85 and the regional championship in 1985-86. Chambers was involved with the Canadian national junior team and Team Canada for five years, leading the Canadian junior team to the national title at the World Junior Championships in Moscow in 1987-88.

Coaching Record

			Regular Season					Playoffs		
Season	Team	Games	W	L	T	%	Games	W	L	%
1967-68	U. Sask. (CIAU)						....	....	....	....
1968-69	U. Sask. (CIAU)						....	....	....	....
1969-70	U. Guelph (CIAU)	29	14	14	1	.500	....	....	....	....
1970-71	Ohio State (CCHA)	29	20	9	0	.690	....	....	....	....
1971-72	Ohio State (CCHA)	29	24	5	0	.828	....	....	....	....
1972-73	York Univ. (CIAU)						....	....	....	....
1973-74	York Univ. (CIAU)						....	....	....	....
1974-75	York Univ. (CIAU)						....	....	....	....
1975-76	York Univ. (CIAU)						....	....	....	....
1976-77	York Univ. (CIAU)						....	....	....	....
1977-78	Italy	43	29	11	3	.709	....	....	....	....
1978-79	Toronto (OHL)	68	32	31	5	.507	....	....	....	....

St. Louis Blues
1989-90 Results: 37w-34L-9T 83PTS. Second, Norris Division

Year-by-Year Record

Season	GP	Home W	L	T	Road W	L	T	Overall W	L	T	GF	GA	Pts.	Finished	Playoff Result
1989-90	80	20	15	5	17	19	4	37	34	9	295	279	83	2nd, Norris Div.	Lost Div. Final
1988-89	80	22	11	7	11	24	5	33	35	12	275	285	78	2nd, Norris Div.	Lost Div. Final
1987-88	80	18	17	5	16	21	3	34	38	8	278	294	76	2nd, Norris Div.	Lost Div. Final
1986-87	80	21	12	7	11	21	8	32	33	15	281	293	79	1st, Norris Div.	Lost Div. Semi-Final
1985-86	80	23	11	6	14	23	3	37	34	9	302	291	83	3rd, Norris Div.	Lost Conf. Championship
1984-85	80	21	12	7	16	19	5	37	31	12	299	288	86	1st, Norris Div.	Lost Div. Semi-Final
1983-84	80	23	14	3	9	27	4	32	41	7	293	316	71	2nd, Norris Div.	Lost Div. Final
1982-83	80	16	16	8	9	24	7	25	40	15	285	316	65	4th, Norris Div.	Lost Div. Semi-Final
1981-82	80	22	14	4	10	26	4	32	40	8	315	349	72	3rd, Norris Div.	Lost Div. Final
1980-81	80	29	7	4	16	11	13	45	18	17	352	281	107	1st, Smythe Div.	Lost Quarter-Final
1979-80	80	20	13	7	14	21	5	34	34	12	266	278	80	2nd, Smythe Div.	Lost Prelim. Round
1978-79	80	14	20	6	4	30	6	18	50	12	249	348	48	3rd, Smythe Div.	Out of Playoffs
1977-78	80	12	20	8	8	27	5	20	47	13	195	304	53	4th, Smythe Div.	Out of Playoffs
1976-77	80	22	13	5	10	26	4	32	39	9	239	276	73	1st, Smythe Div.	Lost Quarter-Final
1975-76	80	20	12	8	9	25	6	29	37	14	249	290	72	3rd, Smythe Div.	Lost Prelim. Round
1974-75	80	23	13	4	12	18	10	35	31	14	269	267	84	2nd, Smythe Div.	Lost Prelim. Round
1973-74	78	16	16	7	10	24	5	26	40	12	206	248	64	6th, West Div.	Out of Playoffs
1972-73	78	21	11	7	11	23	5	32	34	12	233	251	76	4th, West Div.	Lost Quarter-Final
1971-72	78	17	17	5	11	22	6	28	39	11	208	247	67	3rd, West Div.	Lost Semi-Final
1970-71	78	23	7	9	11	18	10	34	25	19	223	208	87	2nd, West Div.	Lost Quarter-Final
1969-70	76	24	9	5	13	18	7	37	27	12	224	179	86	1st, West Div.	Lost Final
1968-69	76	21	8	9	16	17	5	37	25	14	204	157	88	1st, West Div.	Lost Final
1967-68	74	18	12	7	9	19	9	27	31	16	177	191	70	3rd, West Div.	Lost Final

Schedule

Home	Away
Oct. Sat. 6 Chicago	**Oct.** Thur. 4 Minnesota
Tues. 9 Pittsburgh	Fri. 12 Vancouver
Sat. 20 Minnesota	Sun. 14 Los Angeles
Thur. 25 Toronto	Tues. 16 Edmonton
Sat. 27 Montreal	Thur. 18 Calgary
Nov. Tues. 6 Edmonton	Wed. 24 Toronto
Sat. 10 Detroit	Tues. 30 Detroit
Tues. 13 Quebec	**Nov.** Thur. 1 Boston
Tues. 20 Winnipeg	Sat. 3 Hartford
Sat. 24 Vancouver	Thur. 8 Pittsburgh
Tues. 27 Toronto	Sat. 17 Minnesota
Thur. 29 Los Angeles	Sun. 18 Winnipeg
Dec. Sat. 1 New Jersey	Fri. 23 Detroit
Sat. 8 Detroit	**Dec.** Sun. 2 Chicago
Tues. 11 Winnipeg	Fri. 7 Detroit
Thur. 13 Minnesota	Sat. 15 Toronto
Thur. 20 Washington	Sun. 16 Buffalo
Sat. 22 Chicago	Wed. 26 Chicago
Sat. 29 Philadelphia	Thur. 27 Toronto
Jan. Thur. 3 Quebec	Mon. 31 Pittsburgh
Sat. 5 NY Rangers	**Jan.** Tues. 8 New Jersey
Tues. 15 Washington	Wed. 9 NY Rangers
Thur. 17 Montreal	Sat. 12 Quebec
Sat. 26 Detroit	Sun. 13 Montreal
Tues. 29 Buffalo	Tues. 22 Minnesota
Thur. 31 Hartford	Fri. 25 Detroit
Feb. Sat. 2 New Jersey	**Feb.** Mon. 4 Toronto
Sat. 9 Los Angeles	Wed. 6 Buffalo
Tues. 19 Toronto	Tues. 12 Edmonton
Thur. 21 NY Islanders	Thur. 14 Vancouver
Sat. 23 Boston	Sun. 17 Calgary
Tues. 26 Chicago	Sun. 24 Chicago
Thur. 28 NY Rangers	**Mar.** Sat. 2 Philadelphia
Mar. Sat. 9 Calgary	Tues. 5 Hartford
Sun. 10 Detroit	Thur. 7 Boston
Thur. 14 Minnesota	Sun. 17 Chicago
Sat. 16 Chicago	Tues. 19 Washington
Thur. 28 NY Islanders	Thur. 21 Philadelphia
Sat. 30 Toronto	Sat. 23 NY Islanders
Sun. 31 Minnesota	Mon. 25 Minnesota

* Denotes afternoon game.

Home Starting Times:
Weeknights & Saturdays .... 7:35 p.m.
Sundays .... 6:05 p.m.

Franchise date: June 5, 1967.

 **24th NHL Season**

Brett Hull had 72 goals in 1989-90 to lead the NHL.

1990-91 Player Personnel

FORWARDS	HT	WT	S	Place of Birth	Date	1989-90 Club
BRIND'AMOUR, Rod	6-1	202	L	Ottawa, Ont.	8/9/70	St. Louis
BRUCE, David	5-11	190	R	Thunder Bay, Ont.	10/7/64	Milwaukee
CAVALLINI, Gino	6-1	218	L	Toronto, Ont.	11/24/62	St. Louis
CHASE, Kelly	5-11	195	R	Porcupine, Sask.	10/25/67	St. Louis-Peoria
COURTNALL, Geoff	6-1	190	L	Victoria, B.C.	8/18/62	Washington
EMERSON, Nelson	5-11	178	R	Hamilton, Ont.	8/17/67	Peoria-Bowling Green
HEJNA, Tony	6-0	190	L	Buffalo, NY	1/8/68	RPI
HEROUX, Yves	5-11	185	R	Terrebonne, Que.	4/27/65	Peoria
HULL, Brett	5-10	201	R	Belleville, Ont.	8/9/64	St. Louis
LAMB, Jeff	6-1	190	L	Waterloo, IA	7/14/65	Phoenix
LOWRY, Dave	6-1	195	L	Sudbury, Ont.	2/14/65	St. Louis
MacLEAN, Paul	6-2	218	R	Grotenquin, France	3/9/58	St. Louis
MacLEAN, Terry	6-1	178	L	Montreal, Que.	1/14/68	Peoria
MEAGHER, Rick	5-8	172	L	Belleville, Ont.	11/2/53	St. Louis
McPHERSON, Darwin	6-2	210	L	Flin Flon, Man.	5/16/68	Peoria
MIEHM, Kevin	6-2	197	L	Kitchener, Ont.	9/10/69	Peoria
MOMESSO, Sergio	6-3	218	L	Montreal, Que	9/4/65	St. Louis
MONGEAU, Michel	5-9	190	L	Nun's Island, Que.	2/9/65	St. Louis-Peoria
OATES, Adam	5-11	189	R	Weston, Ont.	8/27/62	St. Louis
O'BRIEN, David	6-1	188	R	Brighton, MA	9/13/66	Peoria
OSBORNE, Keith	6-1	188	R	Toronto, Ont.	4/2/69	St. Louis-Peoria
PION, Richard	5-10	165	R	Montreal, Que.	7/20/65	Peoria
RAGLAN, Herb	6-0	205	R	Peterborough, Ont.	8/5/67	St. Louis
RONNING, Cliff	5-8	175	L	Vancouver, B.C.	10/1/65	Italy
RYMSHA, Andy	6-1	203	L	St. Catharines, Ont.	12/10/68	W. Michigan
SUTTER, Rich	5-11	188	R	Viking, Alta.	12/2/63	Vancouver-St. Louis
THOMLINSON, Dave	6-1	196	L	Edmonton, Alta.	10/22/66	St. Louis-Peoria
TUTTLE, Steve	6-1	197	R	Vancouver, BC.	1/5/66	St. Louis
VESEY, Jim	6-1	202	R	Columbus, MA	10/29/65	St. Louis-Peoria
WILSON, Ron	5-9	180	L	Toronto, Ont.	5/13/56	St. Louis
WOLAK, Mike	5-10	170	L	Utica, NY	4/29/68	Peoria

DEFENSEMEN						
BROOKS, Dan	6-3	205	R	St. Paul, MN	4/26/67	U. of Denver
BROWN, Jeff	6-1	204	R	Ottawa, Ont.	4/30/66	Quebec-St. Louis
CAVALLINI, Paul	6-1	210	L	Toronto, Ont.	10/13/65	St. Louis
DIRK, Robert	6-4	218	L	Regina, Sask.	8/20/66	St. Louis-Peoria
FEATHERSTONE, Glen	6-4	216	L	Toronto, Ont.	7/8/68	St. Louis
LAVOIE, Dominic	6-2	205	R	Montreal, Que.	11/21/67	St. Louis-Peoria
PALUCH, Scott	6-3	205	L	Chicago, IL	3/9/66	Peoria
ROBERTS, Gordie	6-0	190	L	Detroit, MI	10/2/57	St. Louis
ROBINSON, Rob	6-1	214	L	St. Catharines, Ont.	4/19/67	Peoria
SKARDA, Randy	6-1	205	R	St. Paul, MN	5/5/68	St. Louis-Peoria
SNEPSTS, Harold	6-3	210	L	Edmonton, Alta.	10/24/54	Vancouver-St. Louis
STEVENS, Scott	6-2	215	L	Kitchener, Ontario	4/1/64	Washington
TILLEY, Tom	6-0	189	R	Trenton, Ont.	3/28/65	St. Louis-Peoria
TWIST, Tony	6-1	212	L	Sherwood Park, Alta.	5/9/68	St. Louis-Peoria

GOALTENDERS	HT	WT	C	Place of Birth	Date	1989-90 Club
HEBERT, Guy	5-11	180	L	Troy, NY	1/7/67	Peoria
JABLONSKI, Pat	6-0	178	L	Toledo, OH	6/20/67	St. Louis-Peoria
JOSEPH, Curtis	5-10	182	L	Keswick, Ont.	4/29/67	St. Louis-Peoria
RIENDEAU, Vincent	5-10	181	L	St. Hyacinthe, Que.	4/20/66	St. Louis

General Managers' History

Lynn Patrick, 1967-68 to 1968-69; Scotty Bowman, 1969-70 to 1970-71; Lynn Patrick, 1971-72; Sid Abel, 1972-73; Charles Catto, 1973-74; Gerry Ehman, 1974-75; Dennis Ball, 1975-76; Emile Francis, 1976-77 to 1982-83; Ron Caron, 1983-84 to date.

Coaching History

Lynn Patrick and Scott Bowman, 1967-68; Scott Bowman, 1968-69 to 1969-70; Al Arbour and Scott Bowman, 1970-71; Sid Abel, Bill McCreary, Al Arbour, 1971-72; Al Arbour and Jean-Guy Talbot, 1972-73; Jean-Guy Talbot and Lou Angotti, 1973-74; Lou Angotti, Lynn Patrick and Garry Young, 1974-75; Garry Young, Lynn Patrick and Leo Boivin, 1975-76; Emile Francis, 1976-77; Leo Boivin and Barclay Plager, 1977-78; Barclay Plager, 1978-79; Barclay Plager and Red Berenson, 1979-80; Red Berenson, 1980-81; Red Berenson and Emile Francis, 1981-82; Barclay Plager and Emile Francis, 1982-83; Jacques Demers, 1983-84 to 1985-86; Jacques Martin, 1986-87 to 1987-88. Brian Sutter, 1988-89 to date.

Captains' History

Al Arbour, 1967-68 to 1969-70; Red Berenson, Barclay Plager, 1970-71; Barclay Plager, 1971-72 to 1975-76; no captain, 1976-77; Red Berenson, 1977-78; Barry Gibbs, 1978-79; Brian Sutter, 1979-80 to 1987-88; Bernie Federko, 1988-89; Rick Meagher, 1989-90 to date.

1989-90 Scoring

Regular Season

* rookie

Pos	#	Player	Team	GP	G	A	Pts	+/-	PIM	PP	SH	GW	GT	S	%
R	16	Brett Hull	STL	80	72	41	113	1 −	24	27	0	12	0	385	18.7
C	12	Adam Oates	STL	80	23	79	102	9	30	6	2	3	1	168	13.7
C	9	Peter Zezel	STL	73	25	47	72	9 −	30	7	0	3	0	158	15.8
R	15	Paul MacLean	STL	78	34	33	67	2	100	12	0	6	1	141	24.1
C	19	*Rod Brind'Amour	STL	79	26	35	61	23	46	10	0	1	1	160	16.3
L	27	Sergio Momesso	STL	79	24	32	56	15 −	199	4	0	4	1	182	13.2
D	21	Jeff Brown	QUE	29	6	10	16	14 −	18	2	0	3	0	104	5.8
			STL	48	10	28	38	12 −	37	6	1	0	0	180	5.6
			TOTAL	77	16	38	54	26 −	55	8	1	3	0	284	5.6
D	14	Paul Cavallini	STL	80	8	39	47	38	106	2	1	0	0	135	5.9
L	17	Gino Cavallini	STL	80	15	15	30	8 −	77	1	0	4	0	134	11.2
L	10	Dave Lowry	STL	78	19	6	25	1	75	0	2	1	1	98	19.4
C	22	Rick Meagher	STL	76	8	17	25	4	47	0	2	1	0	99	8.1
R	35	Steve Tuttle	STL	71	12	10	22	6 −	4	1	1	1	0	92	13.0
R	23	Rich Sutter	VAN	62	9	9	18	1 −	133	0	1	1	0	100	9.0
			STL	12	0	2	2	2 −	22	0	0	0	0	22	9.1
			TOTAL	74	11	9	20	3 −	155	0	1	1	0	122	9.0
L	18	Ron Wilson	STL	33	3	17	20	5	23	1	0	1	0	40	7.5
D	4	Gordie Roberts	STL	75	3	14	17	12 −	140	0	0	0	0	56	5.4
D	26	Mike Lalor	STL	78	0	16	16	6 −	81	0	0	0	0	79	.0
D	36	*Glen Featherstone	STL	58	0	12	12	1 −	145	0	0	0	0	34	.0
C	41	*Michel Mongeau	STL	7	1	5	6	4	2	0	0	0	0	2	50.0
D	5	Harold Snepsts	VAN	39	1	3	4	3	26	1	0	1	0	13	7.7
			STL	7	0	1	1	4 −	10	0	0	0	0	2	.0
			TOTAL	46	1	4	5	1 −	36	1	0	1	0	15	6.7
D	34	*Randy Skarda	STL	25	0	5	5	2	11	0	0	0	0	8	.0
D	20	Tom Tilley	STL	34	0	5	5	10	6	0	0	0	0	19	.0
R	39	*Kelly Chase	STL	43	1	3	4	1 −	244	0	0	0	0	9	11.1
L	40	*Dave Thomlinson	STL	19	1	2	3	4 −	12	0	0	0	0	17	5.9
D	38	*Dominic Lavoie	STL	13	1	2	5	1 −	16	1	0	0	0	20	5.0
D	37	Robert Dirk	STL	37	1	1	2	9	128	0	0	0	0	14	7.1
L	28	*Keith Osborne	STL	5	0	2	2	2 −	8	0	0	0	0	4	.0
C	33	*Jim Vesey	STL	6	0	1	1	3 −	0	0	0	0	0	2	.0
R	25	Herb Raglan	STL	11	0	1	1	5 −	21	0	0	0	0	13	.0
G	31	*Curtis Joseph	STL	15	0	1	1	0	0	0	0	0	0	0	.0
D	5	Dave Richter	STL	2	0	0	0	0	0	0	0	0	0	3	.0
G	1	*Pat Jablonski	STL	4	0	0	0	0	0	0	0	0	0	0	.0
D	6	*Tony Twist	STL	28	0	0	0	2 −	124	0	0	0	0	2	.0
G	30	Vincent Riendeau	STL	43	0	0	0	0	6	0	0	0	0	0	.0

Goaltending

No.	Goaltender	GPI	Mins	Avg	W	L	T	EN	SO	GA	SA	S%
29	Greg Millen	21	1245	2.94	11	7	3	2	1	61	556	.890
31	*Curtis Joseph	15	852	3.38	9	5	1	0	0	48	435	.890
30	Vincent Riendeau	43	2551	3.50	17	19	5	2	1	149	1271	.883
1	*Pat Jablonski	4	208	4.90	0	3	0	0	0	17	98	.827
	Totals	80	4861	3.44	37	34	9	4	2	279	2360	.882

Playoffs

Pos	#	Player	Team	GP	G	A	Pts	+/-	PIM	PP	SH	GW	OT	S	%
R	16	Brett Hull	STL	12	13	8	21	1	17	7	0	3	0	68	19.1
C	12	Adam Oates	STL	12	2	12	14	10 −	4	1	0	0	0	27	7.4
C	19	*Rod Brind'Amour	STL	12	5	8	13	0	6	1	0	0	0	29	17.2
D	21	Jeff Brown	STL	12	2	10	12	6 −	4	1	0	1	0	42	4.8
L	18	Ron Wilson	STL	12	3	5	8	1	18	2	0	0	0	23	13.0
C	9	Peter Zezel	STL	12	1	7	8	3	4	1	0	0	0	28	3.6
R	15	Paul MacLean	STL	12	4	3	7	5 −	20	3	0	0	0	14	28.6
L	27	Sergio Momesso	STL	12	3	2	5	3	63	0	0	1	1	12	25.0
D	14	Paul Cavallini	STL	12	2	3	5	4	20	0	0	0	0	13	15.4
L	17	Gino Cavallini	STL	12	1	3	4	4 −	2	0	0	1	0	15	6.7
L	10	Dave Lowry	STL	12	2	1	3	7 −	39	0	0	0	0	20	10.0
R	23	Rich Sutter	STL	12	2	1	3	3 −	39	0	1	1	0	18	11.1
D	5	Harold Snepsts	STL	11	0	3	3	4 −	38	0	0	0	0	8	.0
D	4	Gordie Roberts	STL	10	0	2	2	6	26	0	0	0	0	6	.0
D	36	*Glen Featherstone	STL	12	0	2	2	4 −	47	0	0	0	0	7	.0
D	26	Mike Lalor	STL	12	0	2	2	3 −	31	0	0	0	0	6	.0
C	22	Rick Meagher	STL	8	1	0	1	2 −	2	0	0	0	0	10	10.0
R	39	*Kelly Chase	STL	9	1	0	1	1 −	46	0	0	0	0	4	25.0
C	41	*Michel Mongeau	STL	2	0	1	1	1 −	0	0	0	0	0	2	.0
R	35	Steve Tuttle	STL	5	0	1	1	1 −	2	0	0	0	0	5	.0
D	37	Robert Dirk	STL	3	0	0	0	1 −	0	0	0	0	0	0	.0
G	31	*Curtis Joseph	STL	6	0	0	0	0	2	0	0	0	0	0	.0
G	30	Vincent Riendeau	STL	8	0	0	0	0	0	0	0	0	0	0	.0

Goaltending

No.	Goaltender	GPI	Mins	Avg	W	L	EN	SO	GA	SA	S%
31	*Curtis Joseph	6	327	3.30	4	1	0	0	18	167	.892
30	Vincent Riendeau	8	397	3.63	3	4	1	0	24	223	.892
	Totals	12	726	3.64	7	5	2	0	44	390	.887

Retired Numbers

3	Bob Gassoff	1973-1977
8	Barclay Plager	1967-1977
11	Brian Sutter	1976-1988

Club Records

Team

(Figures in brackets for season records are games played; records for fewest points, wins, ties, losses, goals, goals against are for 70 or more games)

Most Points	107	1980-81 (80)
Most Wins	45	1980-81 (80)
Most Ties	19	1970-71 (78)
Most Losses	50	1978-79 (80)
Most Goals	352	1980-81 (80)
Most Goals Against	349	1981-82 (80)
Fewest Points	48	1978-79 (80)
Fewest Wins	18	1978-79 (80)
Fewest Ties	7	1983-84 (80)
Fewest Losses	18	1980-81 (80)
Fewest Goals	177	1967-68 (74)
Fewest Goals Against	157	1968-69 (76)

Longest Winning Streak
Over-all .... 7 Jan. 21-Feb. 3/88
Home .... 7 Nov. 28-Dec. 29/81
Away .... 4 Dec. 16/73-Jan. 8/74; Jan. 21-Feb. 3/88

Longest Undefeated Streak
Over-all .... 12 Nov. 10-Dec. 8/68 (5 wins, 7 ties)
Home .... 11 Feb. 12-Mar. 19/69 (5 wins, 6 ties) Feb. 7-Mar. 29/75 (9 wins, 2 ties)
Away .... 7 Dec. 9-26/87 (4 wins, 3 ties)

Longest Losing Streak
Over-all .... 7 Nov. 12-26/67 and Feb. 12-25/89
Home .... 5 Nov. 19-Dec. 6/77
Away .... 10 Jan. 20/82-Mar. 8/82

Longest Winless Streak
Over-all .... 12 Jan. 17-Feb. 15/78 (10 losses, 2 ties)

Home .... 7 Dec. 28/82-Jan. 25/83 (5 losses, 2 ties)
Away .... 17 Jan. 23-Apr. 7/74 (14 losses, 3 ties)

Most Shutouts, Season ... 13 1968-69 (76)
Most PIM, Season ... 1,919 1987-88 (80)
Most Goals, Game ... 10 Feb. 2/82 (Wpg. 6 at St. L. 10) Dec. 1/84 (Det. 5 at St. L. 10) Jan. 15/86 (Tor. 1 at St. L. 10)

Individual

Most Seasons ... 13 Bernie Federko
Most Games ... 927 Bernie Federko
Most Goals, Career ... 352 Bernie Federko
Most Assists, Career ... 721 Bernie Federko
Most Points, Career ... 1,073 Bernie Federko
Most PIM, Career ... 1,786 Brian Sutter
Most Shutouts, Career ... 16 Glenn Hall

Longest Consecutive Games Streak ... 662 Garry Unger (Feb. 7/71-Apr. 8/79)

Most Goals, Season ... 72 Brett Hull (1989-90)
Most Assists, Season ... 79 Adam Oates (1989-90)
Most Points, Season ... 113 Brett Hull (1989-90) (72 goals, 41 assists)
Most PIM, Season ... 306 Bob Gassoff (1975-76)

Most Points, Defenseman
Season ... 66 Rob Ramage (1985-86) (10 goals, 56 assists)

Most Points, Center,
Season ... 107 Bernie Federko (1983-84) (41 goals, 66 assists)

Most Points, Right Wing,
Season ... 113 Brett Hull (1989-90) (72 goals, 41 assists)

Most Points, Left Wing,
Season ... 85 Chuck Lefley (1975-76) (43 goals, 42 assists)

Most Points, Rookie,
Season ... 73 Jorgen Pettersson (1980-81) (37 goals, 36 assists)

Most Shutouts, Season ... 8 Glenn Hall (1968-69)
Most Goals, Game ... 6 Red Berenson (Nov. 7/68)
Most Assists, Game ... 4 Several players
Most Points, Game ... 7 Red Berenson (Nov. 7/68) Garry Unger (Mar. 13/71)

All-time Record vs. Other Clubs

Regular Season

		At Home							On Road							Total					
	GP	W	L	T	GF	GA	PTS	GP	W	L	T	GF	GA	PTS	GP	W	L	T	GF	GA	PTS
Boston	47	17	21	9	140	167	43	46	9	31	6	122	211	24	93	26	52	15	262	378	67
Buffalo	39	23	11	5	148	101	51	38	8	26	4	111	161	20	77	31	37	9	259	262	71
Calgary	36	14	17	5	127	117	33	35	14	18	3	100	123	31	71	28	35	8	227	240	64
Chicago	74	36	24	14	264	239	86	76	21	45	10	236	307	52	150	57	69	24	500	546	138
Detroit	68	41	17	10	258	179	92	69	31	27	11	218	239	73	137	72	44	21	476	418	165
Edmonton	18	5	10	3	72	87	13	17	3	12	2	67	90	8	35	8	22	5	139	177	21
Hartford	18	9	7	2	67	63	20	17	7	8	2	52	61	16	35	16	15	4	119	124	36
Los Angeles	51	33	13	5	195	134	71	52	19	26	7	154	187	45	103	52	39	12	349	321	116
Minnesota	79	40	24	15	284	231	95	77	28	34	15	232	265	71	156	68	58	30	516	496	166
Montreal	46	9	24	13	115	163	31	47	7	35	5	122	214	19	93	16	59	18	237	377	50
New Jersey	33	23	7	3	154	101	49	34	14	13	7	100	105	35	67	37	20	10	254	206	84
NY Islanders	34	12	16	6	117	120	30	36	5	22	9	76	143	19	70	17	38	15	193	263	49
NY Rangers	49	21	21	7	151	159	49	49	4	40	5	110	215	13	98	25	61	12	261	374	62
Philadelphia	55	22	26	7	160	166	51	54	9	37	8	121	215	26	109	31	63	15	281	381	77
Pittsburgh	53	35	13	5	209	143	75	51	18	22	11	158	188	47	104	53	35	16	367	331	122
Quebec	17	13	3	1	80	54	27	18	7	9	2	60	65	16	35	20	12	3	140	119	43
Toronto	69	41	18	10	242	195	92	68	18	43	7	200	275	43	137	59	61	17	442	470	135
Vancouver	45	27	12	6	182	134	60	44	19	20	5	140	142	43	89	46	32	11	322	276	103
Washington	27	12	8	7	112	82	31	28	11	14	3	88	101	25	55	23	22	10	200	183	56
Winnipeg	19	8	4	7	84	64	23	20	4	11	5	63	75	13	39	12	15	12	147	139	36
Defunct Club	32	25	4	3	131	55	53	33	11	10	12	95	100	34	65	36	14	15	226	155	87
Totals	909	466	300	143	3292	2754	1075	909	267	503	139	2625	3482	673	1818	733	803	282	5917	6236	1748

Playoffs

	Series	W	L	GP	W	L	T	GF	GA	Last Mtg.	Round	Result
Boston	2	0	2	8	0	8	0	15	48	1972	SF	L 0-4
Buffalo	1	0	1	3	1	2	0	8	7	1976	PR	L 1-2
Calgary	1	0	1	7	3	4	0	22	28	1986	CF	L 3-4
Chicago	7	1	6	35	12	23	0	97	137	1990	DF	L 3-4
Detroit	2	1	1	9	4	5	0	27	33	1988	DF	L 1-4
Los Angeles	1	1	0	4	4	0	0	16	5	1969	SF	W 4-0
Minnesota	8	5	3	46	24	22	0	135	136	1989	DSF	W 4-1
Montreal	3	0	3	12	0	12	0	14	42	1977	QF	L 0-4
NY Rangers	1	0	1	6	2	4	0	22	29	1981	QF	L 2-4
Philadelphia	2	2	0	11	8	3	0	34	20	1969	QF	W 4-0
Pittsburgh	3	2	1	13	7	6	0	45	40	1981	PR	W 3-2
Toronto	3	2	1	18	10	8	0	56	53	1990	DSF	W 4-1
Winnipeg	1	1	0	4	3	1	0	20	13	1982	DSF	W 3-1
Totals	35	15	20	176	78	98	0	511	591			

Abbreviations: Round: F Final; **CF** conference final; **DF** division final; **DSF** division semi-final; **SF** semi-final; **QF** quarter-final. **PR** preliminary round. **GA** goals against; **GF** goals for.

Playoff Results 1990-86

Year	Round	Opponent	Result	GF	GA
1990	DF	Chicago	L 3-4	22	28
	DSF	Toronto	W 4-1	20	16
1989	DF	Chicago	L 1-4	12	19
	DSF	Minnesota	W 4-1	23	15
1988	DF	Detroit	L 1-4	14	21
	DSF	Chicago	W 4-1	21	17
1987	DSF	Toronto	L 2-4	12	15
1986	CF	Calgary	L 3-4	22	28
	DF	Toronto	W 4-3	24	22
	DSF	Minnesota	W 3-2	18	20

Entry Draft Selections 1990-76

1990
Pick
33 Craig Johnson
54 Patrice Tardif
96 Jason Ruff
117 Kurtis Miller
138 Wayne Conlan
180 Parris Duffus
201 Steve Widmeyer
222 Joe Hawley
243 Joe Fleming

1989
Pick
9 Jason Marshall
31 Rick Corriveau
55 Denny Felsner
93 Daniel Laperriere
114 David Roberts
124 Derek Frenette
135 Jeff Batters
156 Kevin Plager
177 John Roderick
198 John Valo
219 Brian Lukowski

1988
Pick
9 Rod Brind' Amour
30 Adrien Plavsic
51 Rob Fournier
72 Jaan Luik
105 Dave Lacouture
114 Dan Fowler
135 Matt Hayes
156 John McCoy
177 Tony Twist
198 Bret Hedican
219 Heath Deboer
240 Michael Francis

1987
Pick
12 Keith Osborne
54 Kevin Miehm
59 Robert Nordmark
75 Darin Smith
82 Andy Rymsha
117 Rob Robinson
138 Tobb Crabtree
159 Guy Hebert
180 Robert Dumas
201 David Marvin
207 Andy Cesarski
222 Dan Rolfe
243 Ray Savard

1986
Pick
10 Jocelyn Lemieux
31 Mike Posma
52 Tony Hejna
73 Glen Featherstone
87 Michael Wolak
115 Mike O'Toole
136 Andy May
157 Randy Skarda
178 Martyn Ball
199 Rod Thacker
220 Terry MacLean
234 Bill Butler
241 David Obrien

1985
Pick
37 Herb Raglan
44 Nelson Emerson
54 Ned Osmond
100 Dan Brooks
121 Rick Burchill
138 Pat Jablonski
159 Scott Brickey
180 Jeff Urban
201 Vince Guidotti
222 Ron Saatzer
243 Dave Jecha

1984
Pick
26 Brian Benning
32 Tony Hrkac
50 Toby Ducolon
53 Robert Dirk
56 Alan Perry
71 Graham Herring
92 Scott Paluch
113 Steve Tuttle
134 Cliff Ronning
148 Don Porter
155 Jim Vesey
176 Daniel Jomphe
196 Tom Tilley
217 Mark Cupolo
237 Mark Lanigan

1983
DID NOT DRAFT

1982
Pick
50 Mike Posavad
92 Scott Machej
113 Perry Ganchar
134 Doug Gilmour
155 Chris Delaney
176 Matt Christensen
197 John Shumski
218 Brian Ahern
239 Peter Smith

1981
Pick
20 Marty Ruff
36 Hakin Nordin
62 Gordon Donnelly
104 Mike Hickey
125 Peter Aslin
146 Erik Holmberg
167 Alain Vigneault
188 Dan Wood
209 Richard Zemlak

1980
Pick
12 Rik Wilson
54 Jim Pavese
75 Bob Brooke
96 Alain Lemieux
117 Perry Anderson
138 Roger Hagglund
159 Par Rabbitt
180 Peter Lindberg
201 John Smyth

1979
Pick
2 Perry Turnbull
65 Bob Crawford
86 Mark Reeds
107 Gilles Leduc

1978
Pick
3 Wayne Babych
39 Steve Harrison
72 Kevin Willison
89 Jim Nill
106 Steve Stockman
109 Paul MacLean
123 Denis Houle
140 Tony Meagher
143 Rick Simpson
157 Jim Lockhurst
160 Bob Froese
170 Dan Lerg
173 Risto Siltanen
175 Dan Hermansson
181 Jean-Francois Boutin
185 John Sullivan
188 Serge Menard
191 Don Boyd
197 Paul Stasiuk
200 Gerhard Truntschka
203 Victor Shkurdjuk
205 Carl Bloomberg
207 Terry Kitching
209 Brian O'Connor
210 Brian Crombeen
211 Mike Pidgeon
214 John Cochrane
216 Joe Casey
218 Jim Farrell
221 Blair Wheeler

1977
Pick
9 Scott Campbell
27 Neil Labatte
45 Tom Roulston
63 Tony Currie
81 Bruce Hamilton
99 Gary McMonagle
117 Matti Forss
132 Raimo Hirvonen
147 Bjorn Olsson

1976
Pick
7 Bernie Federko
20 Brian Sutter
25 John Smrke
43 Jim Kirkpatrick
56 Mike Liut
61 Paul Skidmore
97 Nels Goddard
113 Mike Eaves
121 Jacques Soquel
124 Dave Dornself
126 Brad Wilson
128 Dan Hoene
130 Goran Lindblom
132 Jim Bales
134 Anders Hakansson
135 Johani Wallenius

Club Directory

St. Louis Arena
5700 Oakland Avenue
St. Louis, MO 63110
Phone **314/781-1397**
Night line 314/781-5352
GM FAX 314/645-1573
FAX 314/645-1340
ENVOY ID
Front Office: BLUES. GM
Public
Relations: BLUES. PR
Capacity: 17,188

Board of Directors
Michael F. Shanahan, Jerome V. LaBarbera, Phil McCarty, Bob Mohrman, Jack Quinn

Advisor to Board
Lewis N. Wolff

Management

Chairman of the Board	Michael F. Shanahan
Vice-Chairman	Jerome V. LaBarbera
President	Jack J. Quinn
Vice-President/General Manager	Ronald Caron
Vice-President/Director of Sales	Bruce Affleck
Vice-President/Director of Player Personnel and Scouting	Ted Hampson
Vice-President/Director of Broadcast Sales	Matt Hyland
Vice-President/Director of Finance and Administration	Jerry Jasiek
Vice-President/Director of Marketing and Public Relations	Susie Mathieu
Vice-President/Director of Player Development	Bob Plager
Secretary and General Counsel	Timothy R. Wolf
Head Coach	Brian Sutter
Assistant Coach	Joe Micheletti
Assistant Coach	Bob Berry
Coach, Peoria Rivermen	Wayne Thomas
Assistant Director of Scouting	Jack Evans
Western Canada/U.S. Scout	Pat Ginnell
Director of Alumni Services	Norm Mackie
Promotions/Community Relations	Tracy Lovasz
Assistant Director of Public Relations	Jeff Trammel
Assistant Director of Public Relations	Michael Caruso
Controller	Margaret Steinmeyer
Accountant	Rita Russell
Accountant	Steve Froemming
Sales Staff	John Casson, Wes Edwards, Tammy Iuli, Jill Mann
Merchandise Manager	George Pavlik
Head Trainer	Mike Folga
Equipment Manager	Frank Burns
Conditioning Consultant	Mackie Shilstone
Executive Secretary	Lynn Diederichsen
Hockey Secretary	Sue Profeta
Marketing/Public Relations Secretary	Donna Quirk
Receptionist	Pam Barrett
Orthopedic Surgeon	Dr. Jerome Gilden
Internist	Dr. Aaron Birenbaum
Dentist	Dr. Les Rich
Sports Psychologist	Dr. Jim Jarvis
Photographer	Mark Buckner
Largest Hockey Attendance	20,009 (March 31/73)
Location of Press Box	East side of building, upper level
Club Colors	Blue, Gold, Red and White
Training Camp	Brentwood Ice Rink, St. Louis Mo.
Radio Station	KMOX Radio
Television Station	KPLR-TV (Channel 11)
Broadcasters	Bruce Affleck, John Kelly, Ken Wilson

General Manager

CARON, RON
Vice-President General Manager and Alternate Governor, St. Louis Blues.
Born in Hull, Que., December 19, 1929

Ron Caron joined the St. Louis Blues on August 13, 1983 after a 26-year association with the Montreal Canadiens' organization. He joined the Canadiens in 1957 on a part-time scouting basis after coaching in the amateur ranks. In 1966, Caron was promoted to a full-time position as chief scout of the Montreal Junior Canadiens and was instrumental in assembling two Memorial Cup championship teams. In 1968, he was named chief scout of the parent club and served as an assistant to former manager Sam Pollock. In 1969 he added the responsibilities of general manager of the Montreal Voyageurs of the AHL and maintained that role until 1978 when he was named director of scouting and player personnel for the Canadiens. Caron remained with the Montreal organization until the conclusion of the 1982-83 campaign.

Coach

SUTTER, BRIAN
Coach, St. Louis Blues. Born in Viking, Alta., October 7, 1956.

Brian Sutter, 34, became the youngest head coach in the NHL on June 20, 1988 when he was named to that position with the Blues. In two seasons behind the bench, Sutter has led the Blues to consecutive second-place finishes.

The Blues' second choice, 20th overall, in the 1976 Amateur Draft, Brian was the first of a record six brothers to play in the NHL. After a junior career with Lethbridge of the Western Junior League, Sutter turned pro in 1976 and played in only 38 games in the minor leagues (Kansas City, CHL) before making his NHL debut with the Blues. From 1979-80 until his retirement last season, Sutter served as captain of the St. Louis club. He also appeared in three NHL All-Star Games (1982, 1983 and 1985) and ranks second on the Blues' all-time list in games played (779), goals (303), assists (333) and points (636).

Coaching Record

Team			Regular Season				Playoffs			
	Seasons	Games	W	L	T	%	Games	W	L	%
1988-89	St. Louis (NHL)	80	33	35	12	.488	10	5	5	.500
1989-90	St. Louis (NHL)	80	37	34	9	.519	12	7	5	.583
	NHL Totals	160	70	69	21	.503	22	12	10	.545

Toronto Maple Leafs

1989-90 Results: 38W-38L-4T 80PTS. Third, Norris Division

Gary Leeman became just the second Leafs' player in team history to score more than 50 goals in a season, firing 51 in 1989-90.

Schedule

Home

Oct.	Wed.	10	Quebec
	Sat.	13	Detroit
	Wed.	17	Hartford
	Sat.	20	Chicago
	Wed.	24	St Louis
	Sat.	27	Buffalo
	Tues.	30	Minnesota
Nov.	Sat.	3	Calgary
	Sun.	4	Philadelphia
	Thur.	8	Vancouver
	Sat.	10	Chicago
	Mon.	12	Winnipeg
	Wed.	14	Washington
	Sat.	17	Detroit
	Mon.	19	Boston
	Sat.	24	Edmonton
Dec.	Wed.	5	Minnesota
	Sat.	8	Chicago
	Wed.	12	Montreal
	Sat.	15	St Louis
	Thur.	27	St Louis
	Sat.	29	Pittsburgh
Jan.	Sat.	5	Los Angeles
	Tues.	8	Calgary
	Sat.	12	Hartford
	Mon.	14	Buffalo
	Thur.	17	Pittsburgh
	Mon.	28	Minnesota
Feb.	Sat.	2	Detroit
	Mon.	4	St Louis
	Sat.	9	NY Islanders
	Wed.	13	Philadelphia
	Sat.	16	Edmonton
	Wed.	27	New Jersey
Mar.	Sat.	2	NY Rangers
	Tues.	5	Boston
	Thur.	7	Vancouver
	Sat.	16	Minnesota
	Sat.	23	Detroit
	Tues.	26	Chicago

Away

Oct.	Thur.	4	Winnipeg
	Sat.	6	Calgary
	Sun.	7	Edmonton
	Thur.	18	Chicago
	Mon.	22	NY Rangers
	Thur.	25	St Louis
Nov.	Thur.	1	Detroit
	Tues.	6	NY Islanders
	Thur.	15	Detroit
	Wed.	21	Washington
	Fri.	23	Philadelphia*
	Tues.	27	St Louis
	Thur.	29	Vancouver
Dec.	Sat.	1	Los Angeles
	Thur.	6	Minnesota
	Tues.	18	NY Islanders
	Wed.	19	NY Rangers
	Sat.	22	Washington*
	Sun.	23	New Jersey
Jan.	Thur.	3	Minnesota
	Thur.	10	Chicago
	Tues.	22	Quebec
	Wed.	23	Montreal
	Sat.	26	Chicago
Feb.	Fri.	1	Detroit
	Wed.	6	Winnipeg
	Thur.	7	Minnesota
	Sun.	17	Buffalo
	Tues.	19	St Louis
	Thur.	21	Pittsburgh
	Sat.	23	Montreal
Mar.	Sun.	3	Hartford
	Sat.	9	Boston*
	Tues.	12	Quebec
	Wed.	13	New Jersey
	Sun.	17	Minnesota
	Wed.	20	Los Angeles
	Fri.	22	Detroit
	Thur.	28	Chicago
	Sat.	30	St Louis

* Denotes afternoon game.

Home Starting Times:

Weeknights	7:35 p.m.
Saturdays	8:05 p.m.
Sundays	7:05 p.m.

Franchise date: November 22, 1917

74th NHL Season

Year-by-Year Record

Season	GP	Home W	Home L	Home T	Road W	Road L	Road T	Overall W	Overall L	Overall T	GF	GA	Pts.	Finished		Playoff Result
1989-90	80	24	14	2	14	24	2	38	38	4	337	358	80	3rd,	Norris Div.	Lost Div. Semi-Final
1988-89	80	15	20	5	13	26	1	28	46	6	259	342	62	5th,	Norris Div.	Out of Playoffs
1987-88	80	14	20	6	7	29	4	21	49	10	273	345	52	4th,	Norris Div.	Lost Div. Semi-Final
1986-87	80	22	14	4	10	28	2	32	42	6	286	319	70	4th,	Norris Div.	Lost Div. Final
1985-86	80	16	21	3	9	27	4	25	48	7	311	386	57	4th,	Norris Div.	Lost Div. Final
1984-85	80	10	28	2	10	24	6	20	52	8	253	358	48	5th,	Norris Div.	Out of Playoffs
1983-84	80	17	16	7	9	29	2	26	45	9	303	287	61	5th,	Norris Div.	Out of Playoffs
1982-83	80	20	15	5	8	25	7	28	40	12	293	330	68	3rd,	Norris Div.	Lost Div. Semi-Final
1981-82	80	12	20	8	8	24	8	20	44	16	298	380	56	5th,	Norris Div.	Out of Playoffs
1980-81	80	14	21	5	14	16	10	28	37	15	322	367	71	5th,	Adams Div.	Lost Prelim. Round
1979-80	80	17	19	4	18	21	1	35	40	5	304	327	75	4th,	Adams Div.	Lost Prelim. Round
1978-79	80	20	12	8	14	21	5	34	33	13	267	252	81	3rd,	Adams Div.	Lost Quarter-Final
1977-78	80	21	13	6	20	16	4	41	29	10	271	237	92	3rd,	Adams Div.	Lost Semi-Final
1976-77	80	18	13	9	15	19	6	33	32	15	301	285	81	3rd,	Adams Div.	Lost Quarter-Final
1975-76	80	23	12	5	11	19	10	34	31	15	294	276	83	3rd,	Adams Div.	Lost Quarter-Final
1974-75	80	19	12	9	12	21	7	31	33	16	280	309	78	3rd,	Adams Div.	Lost Quarter-Final
1973-74	78	21	11	7	14	16	9	35	27	16	274	230	86	4th,	East Div.	Lost Quarter-Final
1972-73	78	20	12	7	7	29	3	27	41	10	247	279	64	6th,	East Div.	Out of Playoffs
1971-72	78	21	11	7	12	20	7	33	31	14	209	208	80	4th,	East Div.	Lost Quarter-Final
1970-71	78	24	9	6	13	24	2	37	33	8	248	211	82	4th,	East Div.	Lost Quarter-Final
1969-70	76	18	13	7	11	21	6	29	34	13	222	242	71	6th,	East Div.	Out of Playoffs
1968-69	76	20	8	10	15	18	5	35	26	15	234	217	85	4th,	East Div.	Lost Quarter-Final
1967-68	74	24	9	4	9	22	6	33	31	10	209	176	76	5th,	East Div.	Out of Playoffs
1966-67	70	21	8	6	11	19	5	32	27	11	204	211	75	3rd,		Won Stanley Cup
1965-66	70	22	9	4	12	16	7	34	25	11	208	187	79	3rd,		Lost Semi-Final
1964-65	70	17	15	3	13	11	11	30	26	14	204	173	74	4th,		Lost Semi-Final
1963-64	70	22	7	6	11	18	6	33	25	12	192	172	78	3rd,		Won Stanley Cup
1962-63	70	21	8	6	14	15	6	35	23	12	221	180	82	1st,		Won Stanley Cup
1961-62	70	25	5	5	12	17	6	37	22	11	232	180	85	2nd,		Won Stanley Cup
1960-61	70	21	6	8	18	13	4	39	19	12	234	176	90	2nd,		Lost Semi-Final
1959-60	70	20	9	6	15	17	3	35	26	9	199	195	79	2nd,		Lost Final
1958-59	70	17	13	5	10	19	6	27	32	11	189	201	65	4th,		Lost Final
1957-58	70	12	16	7	9	22	4	21	38	11	192	226	53	6th,		Out of Playoffs
1956-57	70	12	16	7	9	18	8	21	34	15	174	192	57	5th,		Out of Playoffs
1955-56	70	19	10	6	5	23	7	24	33	13	153	181	61	4th,		Lost Semi-Final
1954-55	70	14	10	11	10	14	11	24	24	22	147	135	70	3rd,		Lost Semi-Final
1953-54	70	22	6	7	10	18	7	32	24	14	152	131	78	3rd,		Lost Semi-Final
1952-53	70	17	12	6	10	18	7	27	30	13	156	167	67	5th,		Out of Playoffs
1951-52	70	17	10	8	12	15	8	29	25	16	168	157	74	3rd,		Lost Semi-Final
1950-51	70	22	8	5	19	8	8	41	16	13	212	138	95	2nd,		Won Stanley Cup
1949-50	70	18	9	8	13	18	4	31	27	12	176	173	74	3rd,		Lost Semi-Final
1948-49	60	12	8	10	10	17	3	22	25	13	147	161	57	4th,		Won Stanley Cup
1947-48	60	22	3	5	10	12	8	32	15	13	182	143	77	1st,		Won Stanley Cup
1946-47	60	20	8	2	11	11	8	31	19	10	209	172	72	2nd,		Won Stanley Cup
1945-46	50	10	13	2	9	11	5	19	24	7	174	185	45	5th,		Out of Playoffs
1944-45	50	13	9	3	11	13	1	24	22	4	183	161	52	3rd,		Won Stanley Cup
1943-44	50	13	11	1	10	12	3	23	23	4	214	174	50	3rd,		Lost Semi-Final
1942-43	50	17	6	2	5	13	7	22	19	9	198	159	53	3rd,		Lost Semi-Final
1941-42	48	18	6	0	9	12	3	27	18	3	158	136	57	2nd,		Won Stanley Cup
1940-41	48	16	5	3	12	9	3	28	14	6	145	99	62	2nd,		Lost Semi-Final
1939-40	48	15	3	6	10	14	0	25	17	6	134	110	56	3rd,		Lost Final
1938-39	48	13	8	3	6	12	6	19	20	9	114	107	47	3rd,		Lost Final
1937-38	48	13	6	5	11	9	4	24	15	9	151	127	57	1st,	Cdn. Div.	Lost Final
1936-37	48	14	9	1	8	12	4	22	21	5	119	115	49	3rd,	Cdn. Div.	Lost Quarter-Final
1935-36	48	15	4	5	8	15	1	23	19	6	126	106	52	2nd,	Cdn. Div.	Lost Final
1934-35	48	16	6	2	14	8	2	30	14	4	157	111	64	1st,	Cdn. Div.	Lost Final
1933-34	48	19	2	3	7	11	6	26	13	9	174	119	61	1st,	Cdn. Div.	Lost Semi-Final
1932-33	48	16	4	4	8	14	2	24	18	6	119	111	54	1st,	Cdn. Div.	Lost Final
1931-32	48	17	4	3	6	14	4	23	18	7	155	127	53	2nd,	Cdn. Div.	Won Stanley Cup
1930-31	44	15	4	3	7	9	6	22	13	9	118	99	53	2nd,	Cdn. Div.	Lost Quarter-Final
1929-30	44	10	8	4	7	13	2	17	21	6	116	124	40	4th,	Cdn. Div.	Out of Playoffs
1928-29	44	15	5	2	6	13	3	21	18	5	85	69	47	3rd,	Cdn. Div.	Lost Semi-Final
1927-28	44	9	8	5	9	10	3	18	18	8	89	88	44	4th,	Cdn. Div.	Out of Playoffs
1926-27*	44	10	10	2	5	14	3	15	24	5	79	94	35	5th,	Cdn. Div.	Out of Playoffs
1925-26	36	11	5	2	1	16	1	12	21	3	92	114	27	6th,		Out of Playoffs
1924-25	30	10	5	0	9	6	0	19	11	0	90	84	38	2nd,		Lost NHL S-Final
1923-24	24	7	5	0	3	9	0	10	14	0	59	85	20	3rd,		Out of Playoffs
1922-23	24	10	1	1	3	9	0	13	10	1	82	88	27	3rd,		Out of Playoffs
1921-22	24	8	4	0	5	6	1	13	10	1	98	97	27	2nd,		Won Stanley Cup
1920-21	24	9	3	0	6	6	0	15	9	0	105	100	30	2nd and 1st***		Lost NHL Final
1919-20**	24	8	4	0	4	8	0	12	12	0	119	106	24	3rd and 2nd***		Lost NHL Final
1918-19	18	5	4	0	0	9	0	5	13	0	64	92	10	3rd and 3rd***		Out of Playoffs
1917-18	22	10	1	0	3	9	0	13	9	0	108	109	26	2nd and 1st***		Won Stanley Cup

* Name changed from St. Patricks to Maple Leafs. ** Name changed from Arenas to St. Patricks.
*** Season played in two halves with no combined standing at end.

1990-91 Player Personnel

FORWARDS	HT	WT	S	Place of Birth	Date	1989-90 Club
BEAN, Tim	6-1	200	L	Saulte Ste. Marie, Ont.	3/9/67	Newmarket
BELLEFEUILLE, Brian	6-2	185	L	Natick, MA	3/21/67	U. of Maine
BRENNAN, Stephen	6-1	190	R	Winchester, MA	3/22/67	Clarkson
CHARTRAND, Steve	5-9	158	L	Verdun, Que.	1/8/69	Drum'ville-Newmarket
CLARK, Wendel	5-11	194	L	Kelvington, Sask.	10/25/66	Toronto
DAMPHOUSSE, Vince	6-1	190	L	Montreal, Que.	12/17/67	Toronto
DOERS, Michael	6-0	175	R	Madison, WI	6/17/71	U. of Vermont
EASTWOOD, Michael	6-2	190	R	Ottawa, Ont.	7/1/67	Western Michigan
ELVENAS, Roger	6-1	183	L	Lund, Sweden	5/29/68	Rogle (Sweden)
FERGUS, Tom	6-3	210	L	Chicago, IL	6/16/62	Toronto
FRANCESCHETTI, Lou	6-0	190	L	Toronto, Ont.	3/28/58	Toronto
HANNAN, David	5-10	185	L	Sudbury, Ont.	11/26/61	Toronto
HENDRICKSON, Darby	6-0	175	L	Richfield, MN	8/28/72	Richfield H.S.
HULST, Kent	6-0	180	L	St. Thomas, Ont.	4/8/68	Newmarket
JACKSON, Mike	6-0	192	R	Mississauga, Ont.	2/4/69	Cornwall
JOBE, Trevor	6-1	200	L	Lethbridge, Alta.	5/14/67	Hampton Roads
JOHNSTON, Greg	6-1	190	R	Barrie, Ont.	1/14/65	Boston-Maine
KORDIC, John	6-1	190	R	Edmonton, Alta.	3/22/65	Toronto
LACROIX, Eric	6-1	200	L	Montreal, Que.	7/15/71	Gov. Dummer H.S.
LEEMAN, Gary	5-11	180	R	Toronto, Ont.	2/19/64	Toronto
MAGUIRE, Kevin	6-2	200	R	Toronto, Ont.	1/5/63	Buffalo-Philadelphia
MALLGRAVE, Matt	6-0	180	R	Washington, D.C.	5/3/70	Harvard
MAROIS, Daniel	6-1	190	R	Montreal, Que.	10/3/68	Toronto
McINTYRE, John	6-1	175	L	Ravenswood, Ont.	4/29/69	Newmarket-Toronto
MERKLER, Keith	6-2	205	L	Syosset, NY	4/23/71	Princeton
MILLAR, Mike	5-10	170	L	St. Catharines, Ont.	4/28/65	Boston-Maine
MOES, Mike	5-11	185	L	Burlington, Ont.	3/30/67	U. of Michigan
OLCZYK, Ed	6-1	200	L	Chicago, IL	8/16/66	Toronto
OSBORNE, Mark	6-2	205	L	Toronto, Ont.	8/13/61	Toronto
PEARSON, Rob	6-1	173	R	Oshawa, Ont.	8/3/71	Belleville
PEARSON, Scott	6-1	203	L	Cornwall, Ont.	12/19/69	Newmarket-Toronto
REID, Dave	6-0	205	L	Toronto, Ont.	5/15/64	Toronto
REYNOLDS, Bobby	5-11	175	L	Flint, MI	7/14/67	Newmarket-Toronto
ROBITAILLE, Martin	5-10	165	R	Medford, MA	7/31/70	U. of Maine
SACCO, Joe	6-1	180	R	Medford, MA	2/4/69	Boston U.
SHEDDEN, Doug	6-0	185	R	Wallaceburg, Ont.	4/29/61	Newmarket
STEVENS, Mike	5-11	195	R	Kitchener, Ont.	12/30/65	Newmkt.-Springfield
STIVER, Dan	6-0	185	R	Chicoutimi, Que.	9/14/71	U. of Michigan
ST. LAURENT, Jeffrey	6-2	175	R	Sanford, MA	5/16/71	U. of New Hampshire
THIBAUDEAU, Gilles	5-10	170	L	Montreal, Que.	3/4/63	NY Islanders-Toronto
THORNTON, Scott	6-2	200	L	London, Ont.	1/9/71	Belleville
TOMBERLIN, Justin	6-0	191	L	Grand Rapids, MN	11/15/70	U. of Maine
TOMLINSON, David	5-11	177	L	N. Vancouver, B.C.	5/8/68	Boston U.
VACHON, Nick	5-10	190	L	Montreal, Que.	9/20/72	Gov. Dummer H.S.
WALTERS, Greg	6-1	195	R	Calgary, Alta.	8/12/70	Ottawa
WHITTEMORE, Todd	6-1	175	R	Taunton, MA	6/20/67	Providence
DEFENSEMEN						
BEREHOWSKY, Drake	6-1	211	R	Toronto, Ont.	1/3/72	Kingston
BANCROFT, Steve	6-1	214	L	Toronto, Ont.	10/6/70	Belleville
BLAD, Brian	6-2	202	L	Brockville, Ont.	7/22/67	Newmarket
BUCKLEY, David	6-4	195	L	Newton, MA	1/27/66	Hampton Roads
BURKE, David	6-1	182	L	Detroit, MI	10/15/70	Cornell
CARNEY, Keith	6-1	175	L	Cumberland, RI	2/7/71	U. of Lowell
CHEBATOR, Rob	6-0	170	L	Arlington, MA	12/1/70	Arlington H.S.
CROWLEY, Edward	6-2	188	R	Concord, MA	5/3/70	Boston College
CURRAN, Brian	6-5	215	L	Toronto, Ont.	11/5/63	Toronto
DELAY, Mike	6-0	190	L	Boston, MA	8/31/69	Boston College
ESAU, Leonard	6-3	190	R	Meadow Lake, Sask.	3/16/68	St. Cloud College
GODYNUK, Alexander	6-0	207	L	Soviet Union	1/27/70	Sokol Kiev (USSR)
GILL, Todd	6-1	185	L	Brockville, Ont.	11/9/65	Toronto
HAMMOND, Ken	6-1	190	L	Port Credit, Ont.	8/22/63	Newmarket
HEPPLE, Alan	5-9	200	L	Blaydon-on-Tyne, U.K.	8/16/63	Newmarket
HOARD, Brian	6-4	218	R	Oshawa, Ont.	3/10/68	Newmarket
IAFRATE, Al	6-3	215	L	Dearborn, MI	3/21/66	Toronto
JENSEN, Chris	6-2	190	R	Wilmette, IL	6/29/68	U. of New Hampshire
KURVERS, Tom	6-2	195	L	Minneapolis, MN	9/14/62	New Jersey-Toronto
LANGILLE, Derek	6-0	184	L	Toronto, Ont.	6/25/69	Newmarket
MALONE, Scott	6-0	180	L	Boston, MA	1/16/71	Northfield-Mt. Hermon
MARSH, Brad	6-3	220	L	London, Ont.	3/31/58	Toronto
MARTIN, Matt	6-3	190	L	Hamden, CT	4/30/71	Avon Old Farms H.S.
RAMAGE, Rob	6-2	195	R	Byron, Ont.	1/11/59	Toronto
RICHARDSON, Luke	6-4	210	L	Ottawa, Ont.	3/26/69	Toronto
ROOT, Bill	6-0	210	R	Toronto, Ont.	9/6/59	Newmarket
SACCO, David	6-1	190	R	Malden, MA	7/31/70	Boston U.
SEROWIK, Jeff	6-0	190	R	Manchester, NH	10/1/67	Providence College
SHANNON, Darryl	6-2	190	L	Barrie, Ont.	6/21/68	Newmarket-Toronto
SLANINA, Peter	6-2	185	R	Czechoslovakia	12/16/59	USZ Kosice (Czech.)
SPANGLER, Ken	5-11	190	R	Edmonton, Alta.	5/2/67	Phoenix
UVIRA, Edourd			R	Opava, Czech.	7/12/61	Bratislava (Czech.)
VEITCH, Darren	6-0	190	R	Saskatoon, Sask.	4/24/60	Newmarket
WEINRICH, Alex	6-0	178		Lewiston, MA	3/12/69	Merrimack

GOALTENDERS	HT	WT	C	Place of Birth	Date	1989-90 Club
ANDERSON, Dean	5-10	175	L	Oshawa, Ont.	7/14/66	Knoxville
BESTER, Allan	5-7	150	L	Hamilton, Ont.	3/26/64	Toronto-Newmarket
GREGORIO, Mike	6-3	195	L	Reading, MA	8/17/69	Kent State
HORYNA, Robert	5-11	183	L		9/10/70	Dukla Jihlava (Czech.)
ING, Peter	6-2	165	L	Toronto, Ont.	4/28/69	Newmarket-Toronto
POTVIN, Felix	6-0	183	L	Montreal, Que.	6/23/71	Chicoutimi
REESE, Jeff	5-9	170	L	Brantford, Ont.	3/24/66	Toronto-Newmarket
RHODES, Damian	6-0	165	L	St. Paul, MN	5/28/69	Michigan Tech.

Retired Numbers

5	Bill Barilko	1946-1951
6	Irwin "Ace" Bailey	1927-1934

1989-90 Scoring

Regular Season

* rookie

Pos	#	Player	Team	GP	G	A	Pts	+/−	PIM	PP	SH	GW	GT	S	%
R	11	Gary Leeman	TOR	80	51	44	95	4	63	14	1	5	0	256	19.9
L	10	Vince Damphousse	TOR	80	33	61	94	2	56	9	0	5	1	229	14.4
C	16	Ed Olczyk	TOR	79	32	56	88	0	78	6	0	4	0	208	15.4
R	32	Dan Marois	TOR	68	39	37	76	1	82	14	0	3	1	183	21.3
L	12	Mark Osborne	TOR	78	23	50	73	2	91	3	1	6	0	137	16.8
D	33	Al Iafrate	TOR	75	21	42	63	4−	135	6	1	0	0	153	13.7
D	25	Tom Kurvers	N.J.	1	0	0	0	1−	0	0	0	0	0	0	.0
			TOR	70	15	37	52	8−	29	9	1	1	0	156	9.6
			TOTAL	71	15	37	52	9−	29	9	1	1	0	156	9.6
D	8	Rob Ramage	TOR	80	8	41	49	1−	202	3	0	1	0	196	4.1
C	19	Tom Fergus	TOR	54	19	26	45	18−	62	4	0	2	0	120	15.8
R	15	Lou Franceschetti	TOR	80	21	15	36	12−	127	0	2	4	0	76	27.6
L	14	Dave Reid	TOR	70	9	19	28	8−	9	0	4	1	0	97	9.3
L	17	Wendel Clark	TOR	38	18	8	26	2	116	7	0	2	0	85	21.2
C	7	Gilles Thibaudeau	NYI	20	4	4	8	2	17	0	0	0	0	23	17.4
			TOR	21	7	11	18	6	13	3	0	2	0	44	15.9
			TOTAL	41	11	15	26	8	30	3	0	2	0	67	16.4
C	24	Dan Daoust	TOR	65	7	11	18	1	89	0	4	0	0	53	13.2
D	2	Luke Richardson	TOR	67	4	14	18	1−	122	0	0	0	0	80	5.0
C	44	*John McIntyre	TOR	59	5	12	17	12−	117	0	1	1	0	44	11.4
C	9	Dave Hannan	TOR	39	6	9	15	12−	55	0	1	0	0	39	15.4
L	22	*Scott Pearson	TOR	41	5	10	15	7−	90	0	0	1	0	66	7.6
D	23	Todd Gill	TOR	48	1	14	15	8−	92	0	0	0	0	44	2.3
D	3	Brad Marsh	TOR	79	1	13	14	14	95	0	0	0	0	50	2.0
R	27	John Kordic	TOR	55	9	4	13	8−	252	3	0	0	0	48	18.8
D	28	Brian Curran	TOR	72	2	9	11	2−	301	0	0	0	0	21	9.5
L	20	*Bobby Reynolds	TOR	7	1	1	2	3−	0	0	0	0	0	13	7.7
C	18	Peter Ihnacak	TOR	5	0	2	2	3	0	0	0	0	0	5	.0
G	30	Allan Bester	TOR	42	0	2	2	0	4	0	0	0	0	0	.0
L	20	Paul Lawless	TOR	6	0	1	1	4−	0	0	0	0	0	6	.0
D	4	*Darryl Shannon	TOR	10	0	1	1	10−	12	0	0	0	0	16	.0
G	35	*Jeff Reese	TOR	21	0	1	1	0	10	0	0	0	0	0	.0
G	1	Mark LaForest	TOR	27	0	1	1	0	23	0	0	0	0	0	.0
D	26	*Jack Capuano	TOR	1	0	0	0	1−	0	0	0	0	0	1	.0
C	26	Mike Stevens	TOR	1	0	0	0	0	0	0	0	0	0	2	.0
R	40	*Tie Domi	TOR	2	0	0	0	0	42	0	0	0	0	0	.0
G	31	*Peter Ing	TOR	3	0	0	0	0	0	0	0	0	0	0	.0
R	34	*Rocky Dundas	TOR	5	0	0	0	1−	14	0	0	0	0	1	.0
R	21	Sean McKenna	TOR	5	0	0	0	3−	20	0	0	0	0	6	.0

Goaltending

No.	Goaltender	GPI	Mins	Avg	W	L	T	EN	SO	GA	SA	S%
1	Mark LaForest	27	1343	3.89	9	14	0	2	0	87	765	.886
35	*Jeff Reese	21	1101	4.41	9	6	3	0	0	81	630	.871
30	Allan Bester	42	2206	4.49	20	16	0	4	0	165	1296	.873
31	*Peter Ing	3	182	5.93	0	2	1	1	0	18	107	.832
	Totals	**80**	**4842**	**4.44**	**38**	**38**	**4**	**7**	**0**	**358**	**2798**	**.872**

Playoffs

Pos	#	Player	Team	GP	G	A	Pts	+/−	PIM	PP	SH	GW	OT	S	%
R	11	Gary Leeman	TOR	5	3	3	6	3	16	2	0	0	0	11	27.3
L	12	Mark Osborne	TOR	5	2	3	5	1	12	0	1	0	0	6	33.3
R	32	Dan Marois	TOR	5	2	2	4	1	12	2	0	0	0	10	20.0
C	19	Tom Fergus	TOR	5	2	1	3	1	4	0	0	0	0	9	22.2
C	16	Ed Olczyk	TOR	5	1	2	3	3	14	0	0	0	0	15	6.7
D	8	Rob Ramage	TOR	5	1	2	3	1	20	0	0	0	0	21	4.8
D	23	Todd Gill	TOR	5	0	3	3	0	16	0	0	0	0	7	.0
D	25	Tom Kurvers	TOR	5	0	3	3	1−	4	0	0	0	0	22	.0
L	22	*Scott Pearson	TOR	2	2	0	2	1	10	0	0	0	0	2	100.0
L	17	Wendel Clark	TOR	5	1	1	2	2−	19	0	0	0	0	14	7.1
L	10	Vincent Damphousse	TOR	5	0	2	2	1	2	0	0	0	0	10	.0
C	9	Dave Hannan	TOR	3	1	0	1	2−	4	0	0	1	0	6	16.7
D	3	Brad Marsh	TOR	5	1	0	1	1	2	0	0	0	0	3	33.3
D	28	Brian Curran	TOR	5	0	1	1	1−	19	0	0	0	0	2	.0
C	24	Dan Daoust	TOR	5	0	1	1	1	20	0	0	0	0	5	.0
R	15	Lou Franceschetti	TOR	5	0	1	1	3−	26	0	0	0	0	5	.0
R	27	John Kordic	TOR	5	0	1	1	1−	33	0	0	0	0	2	.0
C	44	*John McIntyre	TOR	2	0	0	0	0	2	0	0	0	0	0	.0
G	35	*Jeff Reese	TOR	2	0	0	0	0	0	0	0	0	0	0	.0
L	14	Dave Reid	TOR	3	0	0	0	2−	0	0	0	0	0	1	.0
G	30	Allan Bester	TOR	4	0	0	0	0	0	0	0	0	0	0	.0
D	2	Luke Richardson	TOR	5	0	0	0	1−	22	0	0	0	0	5	.0

Goaltending

No.	Goaltender	GPI	Mins	Avg	W	L	EN	SO	GA	SA	S%
35	*Jeff Reese	2	108	3.33	1	1	0	0	6	50	.880
30	Allan Bester	4	196	4.29	0	3	0	0	14	120	.883
	Totals	**5**	**306**	**3.92**	**1**	**4**	**0**	**0**	**20**	**170**	**.882**

Captains' History

Hap Day, 1927-28 to 1936-37; Charlie Conacher, 1937-38; Red Horner, 1938-39, 1939-40; Syl Apps, 1940-41 to 1942-43; Bob Davidson, 1943-44, 1944-45; Syl Apps, 1945-46 to 1947-48; Ted Kennedy, 1948-49 to 1954-55; Sid Smith, 1955-56; Ted Kennedy, Jim Thomson, 1956-57; George Armstrong, 1957-58 to 1968-69; Dave Keon, 1969-70 to 1974-75; Darryl Sittler, 1975-76 to 1980-81; Rick Vaive, 1981-82 to 1985-86; no captain, 1986-87 to 1988-89; Rob Ramage, 1989-90 to date.

Club Records

Team

(Figures in brackets for season records are games played; records for fewest points, wins, ties, losses, goals, goals against are for 70 or more games)

Most Points 95 1950-51 (70)
Most Wins 41 1950-51 (70)
1977-78 (80)
Most Ties 22 1954-55 (70)
Most Losses 52 1984-85 (80)
Most Goals 337 1989-90 (80)
Most Goals Against 387 1983-84 (80)
Fewest Points 48 1984-85 (80)
Fewest Wins 20 1981-82, 1984-85 (80)
Fewest Ties 4 1989-90 (80)
Fewest Losses 16 1950-51 (70)
Fewest Goals 147 1954-55 (70)
Fewest Goals Against ...*131 1953-54 (70)

Longest Winning Streak
Over-all .... 9 Jan. 30-Feb. 28/25
Home .... 9 Nov. 11-Dec. 26/53
Away .... 7 Nov. 14-Dec. 15/40
Dec. 4/60-Jan. 5/61

Longest Undefeated Streak
Over-all ....11 Oct. 15-Nov. 8/50 (8 wins, 3 ties)
Home ....18 Nov. 28/33-Mar. 10/34 (15 wins, 3 ties)
Oct. 31/53-Jan. 23/54 (16 wins, 2 ties)
Away .... 9 Nov. 30/47-Jan. 11/48 (4 wins, 5 ties)

Longest Losing Streak
Over-all ....10 Jan. 15-Feb. 8/67
Home .... 7 Nov. 10-Dec. 5/84
Jan. 26-Feb. 25/85
Away ....11 Feb. 20/-Apr. 1/88

Longest Winless Streak
Over-all ....15 Dec. 26/87-Jan. 25/88 (11 losses, 4 ties)
Home ....11 Dec. 19/87-Jan. 25/88 (7 losses, 4 ties)
Away ....18 Oct. 6/82-Jan. 5/83 (13 losses, 5 ties)

Most Shutouts, Season 13 1953-54 (70)
Most PIM, Season 2,419 1989-90 (80)
Most Goals, Game ....14 Mar. 16/57 (NYR 1 at Tor. 14)

Individual

Most Seasons ....21 George Armstrong
Most Games ....1,187 George Armstrong
Most Goals, Career ......389 Darryl Sittler
Most Assists, Career .....620 Borje Salming
Most Points, Career ......916 Darryl Sittler (389 goals, 527 assists)
Most PIM, Career ......1,670 Dave Williams
Most Shutouts, Career .....62 Turk Broda
Longest Consecutive Games Streak ....486 Tim Horton (Feb. 11/61-Feb. 4/68)
Most Goals, Season ....54 Rick Vaive (1981-82)
Most Assists, Season ......72 Darryl Sittler (1977-78)
Most Points, Season .....117 Darryl Sittler (1977-78) (45 goals, 72 assists)
Most PIM, Season ....351 Dave Williams (1977-78)
Most Points, Defenseman Season ....79 Ian Turnbull (1976-77) (22 goals, 57 assists)
Most Points, Center Season ....117 Darryl Sittler (1977-78) (45 goals, 72 assists)
Most Points, Right Wing, Season ....97 Wilf Paiement (1980-81) (40 goals, 57 assists)
Most Points, Left Wing, Season ....94 Vince Damphousse (1989-90) (33 goals, 61 assists)
Most Points, Rookie, Season ....66 Peter Ihnacak (1982-83) (28 goals, 38 assists)
Most Shutouts, Season ....13 Harry Lumley (1953-54)
Most Goals, Game ....6 Corb Denneny (Jan. 26/21)
Darryl Sittler (Feb. 7/76)
Most Assists,Game ....6 Babe Pratt (Jan. 8/44)
Most Points, Game ....*10 Darryl Sittler (Feb. 7/76)

* NHL Record.

Coaching History

Conn Smythe, 1927-28 to 1929-30; Conn Smythe and Art Duncan, 1930-31; Art Duncan and Dick Irvin, 1931-32; Dick Irvin, 1932-33 to 1939-40; Hap Day, 1940-41 to 1949-50; Joe Primeau, 1950-51 to 1952-53; "King" Clancy, 1953-54 to 1955-56; Howie Meeker, 1956-57; Billy Reay, 1957-58; Billy Reay and "Punch" Imlach, 1958-59; "Punch" Imlach, 1959-60 to 1968-69; John McLellan, 1969-70 to 1970-71; John McLellan and "King" Clancy, 1971-72; John McLellan, 1972-73; Red Kelly, 1973-74 to 1976-77; Roger Neilson, 1977-78 to 1978-79; Floyd Smith, Dick Duff and "Punch" Imlach, 1979-80; "Punch" Imlach, Joe Crozier and Mike Nykoluk, 1980-81; Mike Nykoluk, 1981-82 to 1983-84; Dan Maloney, 1984-85 to 1985-86; John Brophy, 1986-87 to 1987-88; John Brophy and George Armstrong, 1988-89; Doug Carpenter, 1989-90 to date.

1989-90 Results

Home				Away			
Oct.	11	Buffalo	1-7	Oct.	5	Los Angeles	2-4
	14	Winnipeg	1-5		7	St Louis	8-5
	18	Vancouver	4-3		12	Chicago	6-9
	21	Washington	8-4		17	Pittsburgh	5-7
	23	New Jersey	4-5		25	Pittsburgh	8-6
	28	Detroit	6-4		27	Buffalo	5-6
Nov.	4	Philadelphia	4-7		31	Minnesota	6-4
	6	Minnesota	2-1	Nov.	3	Washington	1-2
	11	Detroit	4-2		9	Philadelphia	4-1
	15	St Louis	5-2		12	Minnesota	3-6
	25	NY Rangers	7-4		16	NY Islanders	2-6
Dec.	9	Montreal	7-4		18	Montreal	3-4
	11	St Louis	3-1		22	Minnesota	3-6
	16	Minnesota	3-4		23	Boston	0-6
	18	St Louis	6-3		29	Vancouver	3-2
	23	Chicago	5-7	Dec.	2	Calgary	4-7
	27	Detroit	7-7		3	Edmonton	3-5
	30	Boston	7-6		6	Chicago	4-6
Jan.	3	Quebec	5-4		7	St Louis	5-2
	6	Los Angeles	7-4		13	Detroit	4-2
	8	Washington	8-6		20	Detroit	2-4
	10	NY Islanders	1-3		22	Chicago	5-3
	13	Calgary	6-5		26	Boston	4-6
	15	Chicago	7-6	Jan.	18	St Louis	4-1
	24	Minnesota	7-3		26	New Jersey	5-1
	27	Montreal	3-5		31	Winnipeg	5-5
Feb.	3	Pittsburgh	8-4	Feb.	2	Detroit	2-5
	7	St Louis	7-1		6	St Louis	4-6
	12	Los Angeles	5-3		10	Hartford	2-6
	14	Hartford	6-6		15	Philadelphia	0-3
	17	New Jersey	5-4		22	Calgary	2-12
	28	Quebec	5-4		23	Edmonton	6-5
Mar.	3	Detroit	2-5		26	Vancouver	2-5
	10	Edmonton	3-2	Mar.	2	Detroit	2-3
	12	Minnesota	1-4		8	Hartford	7-6
	14	NY Rangers	2-8		16	Buffalo	4-3
	17	Winnipeg	4-5		21	NY Rangers	5-5
	19	Chicago	2-3		24	Quebec	4-3
	28	NY Islanders	3-6		26	Minnesota	4-5
	31	Chicago	6-4		29	Chicago	2-4

* Denotes afternoon game.

All-time Record vs. Other Clubs

Regular Season

	At Home							On Road							Total						
	GP	W	L	T	GF	GA	PTS	GP	W	L	T	GF	GA	PTS	GP	W	L	T	GF	GA	PTS
Boston	275	145	84	46	935	709	336	275	80	148	47	737	913	207	550	225	232	93	1672	1622	543
Buffalo	44	18	19	7	143	160	43	46	15	29	2	133	199	32	90	33	48	9	276	359	75
Calgary	33	14	12	7	137	127	35	35	11	21	3	119	163	25	68	25	33	10	256	290	60
Chicago	285	155	82	48	991	726	358	284	106	139	39	752	869	251	569	261	221	87	1743	1595	609
Detroit	287	153	91	43	949	745	349	287	95	149	43	695	842	233	574	248	240	86	1644	1587	582
Edmonton	17	6	10	1	71	91	13	18	2	12	4	59	105	8	35	8	22	5	130	196	21
Hartford	17	6	10	1	66	77	13	18	4	12	2	60	93	10	35	10	22	3	126	170	23
Los Angeles	49	28	12	9	211	160	65	48	14	29	5	130	174	33	97	42	41	14	341	334	98
Minnesota	71	32	25	14	261	240	78	70	26	36	8	239	277	60	141	58	61	22	500	517	138
Montreal	310	157	109	44	938	812	358	309	82	188	39	758	1096	203	619	239	297	83	1696	1908	561
New Jersey	28	20	6	2	130	94	42	27	9	9	9	90	99	27	55	29	15	11	220	193	69
NY Islanders	35	15	17	3	120	130	33	33	11	20	2	103	149	24	68	26	37	5	223	279	57
NY Rangers	263	149	76	38	908	680	336	263	100	108	55	774	801	255	526	249	184	93	1682	1481	591
Philadelphia	47	17	17	13	165	153	47	47	10	30	7	114	192	27	94	27	47	20	279	345	74
Pittsburgh	48	22	16	10	195	160	54	49	19	25	5	163	188	43	97	41	41	15	358	348	97
Quebec	18	8	8	2	60	78	18	17	4	9	4	59	71	12	35	12	17	6	119	149	30
St. Louis	68	43	18	7	275	200	93	69	18	41	10	195	242	46	137	61	59	17	470	442	139
Vancouver	39	17	14	8	151	138	42	40	12	21	7	130	142	31	79	29	35	15	281	280	73
Washington	30	17	9	4	143	107	38	29	10	17	2	82	113	22	59	27	26	6	225	220	60
Winnipeg	20	5	14	1	77	101	11	19	7	10	2	86	92	16	39	12	24	3	163	193	27
Defunct Club	232	158	53	21	860	515	337	233	84	120	29	607	745	197	465	242	173	50	1467	1260	534
Totals	**2216**	**1185**	**702**	**329**	**7786**	**6203**	**2699**	**2216**	**719**	**1173**	**324**	**6085**	**7565**	**1762**	**4432**	**1904**	**1875**	**653**	**13871**	**13768**	**4461**

Playoffs

	Series	W	L	GP	W	L	T	GF	GA	Last Mtg.	Round	Result
Boston	13	8	5	62	31	30	1	150	153	1974	QF	L 0-4
Calgary	1	1	0	2	2	0	0	9	5	1979	PR	W 2-0
Chicago	7	5	2	25	15	9	1	76	57	1986	DSF	W 3-0
Detroit	22	11	11	110	54	56	0	287	291	1988	DSF	L 2-4
Los Angeles	2	2	0	5	4	1	0	18	9	1978	PR	W 2-0
Minnesota	2	0	2	7	1	6	0	26	35	1983	DSF	L 1-3
Montreal	13	6	7	67	28	39	0	148	203	1979	QF	L 0-4
NY Islanders	2	1	1	10	4	6	0	20	33	1981	PR	L 0-3
NY Rangers	8	3	5	35	16	19	0	86	86	1971	QF	L 2-4
Philadelphia	3	0	3	17	5	12	0	47	67	1977	QF	L 2-4
Pittsburgh	2	2	0	6	4	2	0	21	13	1977	PR	W 2-1
St. Louis	3	1	2	18	8	10	0	53	56	1990	DSF	L 1-4
Defunct Clubs	4	3	1	10	5	4	1	20	16			
Totals	**82**	**43**	**39**	**374**	**177**	**194**	**3**	**961**	**1024**			

Playoff Results 1990-86

Year	Round	Opponent	Result	GF	GA
1990	DSF	St. Louis	L 1-4	16	20
1988	DSF	Detroit	L 2-4	20	32
1987	DF	Detroit	L 3-4	18	20
	DSF	St. Louis	W 4-2	15	12
1986	DF	St. Louis	L 3-4	22	24
	DSF	Chicago	W 3-0	18	9

Abbreviations: Round: F Final; **CF** conference final; **DF** division final; **DSF** division semi-final; **QF** quarter-final. **PR** preliminary round. **GA** goals against; **GF** goals for.

Entry Draft Selections 1990-76

1990
Pick
10	Drake Berehowsky
31	Felix Potvin
73	Darby Hendrickson
80	Greg Walters
115	Alexander Godynyuk
136	Eric Lacroix
157	Dan Stiver
178	Robert Horyna
199	Rob Chebator
220	Scott Malone
241	Nick Vachon

1989
Pick
3	Scott Thornton
12	Rob Pearson
21	Steve Bancroft
66	Matt Martin
96	Keith Carney
108	David Burke
125	Michael Doers
129	Keith Merkler
150	Derek Langille
171	Jeffrey St. Laurent
192	Justin Tomberlin
213	Mike Jackson
234	Steve Chartrand

1988
Pick
6	Scott Pearson
27	Tie Domi
48	Peter Ing
69	Ted Crowley
87	Leonard Esau
132	Matt Mallgrave
153	Roger Elvenas
174	Mike Delay
195	David Sacco
216	Mike Gregorio
237	Peter Deboer

1987
Pick
7	Luke Richardson
28	Daniel Marois
49	John McIntyre
71	Joe Sacco
91	Mike Eastwood
112	Damian Rhodes
133	Trevor Jobe
154	Chris Jensen
175	Brian Blad
196	Ron Bernacci
217	Ken Alexander
238	Alex Weinrich

1986
Pick
6	Vincent Damphousse
36	Darryl Shannon
48	Sean Boland
69	Kent Hulst
90	Scott Taylor
111	Stephane Giguere
132	Danny Hie
153	Stephen Brennan
174	Brian Bellefeuille
195	Sean Davidson
216	Mark Holick
237	Brian Hoard

1985
Pick
1	Wendel Clark
22	Ken Spangler
43	Dave Thomlinson
64	Greg Vey
85	Jeff Serowik
106	Jiri Latal
127	Tim Bean
148	Andy Donahue
169	Todd Whittemore
190	Bob Reynolds
211	Tim Armstrong
232	Mitch Murphy

1984
Pick
4	Al Iafrate
25	Todd Gill
67	Jeff Reese
88	Jack Capuano
109	Joe Fabian
130	Joe McInnis
151	Derek Laxdal
172	Dan Turner
192	David Buckley
213	Mikael Wurst
233	Peter Slanina

1983
Pick
7	Russ Courtnall
28	Jeff Jackson
48	Allan Bester
83	Dan Hodgson
128	Cam Plante
148	Paul Bifano
168	Cliff Albrecht
188	Brian Ross
208	Mike Tomlak
228	Ron Choules

1982
Pick
3	Gary Nylund
24	Gary Leeman
25	Peter Ihnacak
45	Ken Wregget
73	Vaclav Ruzicka
87	Eduard Uvara
99	Sylvain Charland
108	Ron Dreger
115	Craig Kales
129	Dom Campedelli
139	Jeff Triano
171	Miroslav Ihnacak
192	Leigh Verstraete
213	Tim Loven
234	Jim Appleby

1981
Pick
6	Jim Benning
24	Gary Yaremchuk
55	Ernie Godden
90	Normand LeFrancois
102	Barry Brigley
132	Andrew Wright
153	Richard Turmel
174	Greg Barber
195	Marc Magnan

1980
Pick
25	Craig Muni
26	Bob McGill
43	Fred Boimistruck
74	Stewart Gavin
95	Hugh Larkin
116	Ron Dennis
137	Russ Adam
158	Fred Perlini
179	Darwin McCutcheon
200	Paul Higgins

1979
Pick
9	Laurie Boschman
51	Normand Aubin
72	Vincent Tremblay
93	Frank Nigro
114	Bill McCreary

1978
Pick
21	Joel Quenneville
48	Mark Kirton
65	Bob Parent
81	Jordy Douglas
92	Mel Hewitt
98	Normand Lefebvre
115	John Scammell
132	Kevin Reinhart
149	Mike Waghorne
166	Laurie Cuvelier

1977
Pick
11	John Anderson
12	Trevor Johansen
24	Bob Gladney
29	Rockey Saganiuk
65	Dan Eastman
83	John Wilson
101	Roy Sommer
119	Lynn Jorgenson

1976
Pick
30	Randy Carlyle
48	Alain Belanger
52	Gary McFayden
66	Tim Williams
84	Greg Hotham
102	Dan Dkjakalovic

Club Directory

Maple Leaf Gardens
60 Carlton Street
Toronto, Ontario M5B 1L1
Phone **416/977-1641**
FAX 416/977-5364
ENVOY ID
  Front Office: LEAFS. GM
  Public
  Relations: LEAFS. PR
Capacity: 16,182 (standing 200)

Board of Directors

Thor Eaton	Edward McDowell	Douglas H. Roxborough
Donald P. Giffin	Edward Rogers	Steve Stavro
Edward Lawrence		

President, Managing Director and Governor	Donald P. Giffin
Vice President, Marketing	Steve Stavro
Vice President	Donald Crump
Alternate Governors	Floyd Smith, Rosanne Rocchi
General Manager	Floyd Smith
Director of Business Operations and Communications	Bob Stellick
Head Coach	Doug Carpenter
Assistant Coaches	Mike Kitchen, Tom Watt
Director of Scouting	Pierre Dorion
Scouts	George Armstrong, Jim Bzdell, Dick Duff, Jack Gardiner, Bob Johnson, Dan Marr, Doug Woods
Public Relations Coordinator	Pat Park
Public Relations Assistant	Mark Hillier
Administrative Assistants	Ellen Salnek, Mary Speck
Athletic Therapist	Chris Broadhurst
Trainers	Dan Lemelin, Brian Papineau, Brent Smith
Director of Attractions & Advertising	Bill Cluff
Controller	Ian Clarke
Box Office Manager	I.M. (Patty) Patoff
Building Superintendent	Wayne Gillespie
Dimensions of rink	200 feet by 85 feet
Club Colors	Home - Blue and White
Press Box	East Side
TV Broadcasters	Bob Cole, Harry Neale, Joe Bowen (CBC-TV 5 and Global TV)
Radio Network	TBS
Radio Play-by-Play Broadcasters	Joe Bowen, Ken Daniels

General Manager

SMITH, FLOYD
General Manager, Toronto Maple Leafs. Born in Perth, Ont., May 16, 1935.

Floyd Smith assumed the role of general manager on August 15, 1989. Originally hired as a coach by the Leafs in 1979, Smith joined the Toronto scouting staff the following season.

After a 12-year NHL playing career with Boston, the New York Rangers, Detroit, Toronto and Buffalo, Smith began his coaching career. He coached Cincinnati (both in the AHL and WHA) and the Buffalo Sabres, prior to joining the Leafs. In 1975, he led the Sabres to a berth in the Stanley Cup Finals.

NHL Coaching Record

Season	Team	Games	Regular Season W	L	T	%	Playoffs Games	W	L	%
1971-72	Buffalo (NHL)	1	0	1	0	.000	....	....	....	....
1974-75	Buffalo (NHL)	80	49	16	15	.706	17	10	7	.588
1975-76	Buffalo (NHL)	80	46	21	13	.656	9	4	5	.444
1976-77	Buffalo (NHL)	80	48	24	8	.650	6	2	4	.333
1979-80	Toronto (NHL)	68	30	33	5	.478	....	....	....	....
	NHL Totals	309	173	95	41	.626	32	16	16	.500

General Managers' History

Conn Smythe, 1927-28 to 1956-57; Hap Day, 1957-58; George "Punch" Imlach, 1958-59 to 1968-69; Jim Gregory, 1969-70 to 1978-79; Punch Imlach, 1979-80 to 1980-81; Punch Imlach and Gerry McNamara, 1981-82; Gerry McNamara, 1982-83 to 1987-88; Gord Stellick, 1988-89; Floyd Smith, 1989-90 to date.

Coach

CARPENTER, DOUG
Coach, Toronto Maple Leafs. Born in Cornwall, Ont., July 1, 1942.

48-year-old Doug Carpenter was named coach of the Maple Leafs on August 16, 1989, returning to the organization that saw him launch his career as a coach in professional hockey. A graduate of Montreal's McGill University in 1962 and Loyola College in 1967, Carpenter spent eight seasons as a minor league defenseman/left-winger in the Eastern and International Leagues (1966-74) before becoming head coach of the Cornwall Royals of the Quebec Junior League in 1978-79. After leading Cornwall to the Memorial Cup in 1979-80, he was hired by the Toronto Maple Leafs as coach of their top minor league affiliates. These included New Brunswick (AHL) in 1980-81, Cincinnati (CHL) in 1981-82 and St. Catharines (AHL) in 1982-83 and 1983-84.

He moved up to the NHL as coach of the New Jersey Devils in 1984-85. After his rookie season with New Jersey, Carpenter was named head coach of Team Canada at the 1985 World Championships in Czechoslovakia, where his squad defeated the Soviet Union 3-1 for Canada's first win against the Soviets in an IIHF championship since 1961. Carpenter's Canadian team went on to win a silver medal. Carpenter coached the improving young Devils club for 3 1/2 seasons until January of 1988. He coached Halifax of the AHL in 1988-89.

Coaching Record

Season	Team	Games	Regular Season W	L	T	%	Playoffs Games	W	L	%
1978-79	Cornwall (QJHL)	72	29	36	7	.451	7	3	4	.429
1979-80	Cornwall (QJHL)	72	41	25	6	.611	17	12	5	.706
1980-81	New Brunswick (AHL)	80	37	33	10	.525	13	7	6	.538
1981-82	Cincinnati (CHL)	80	46	30	4	.600	4	1	3	.250
1982-83	St. Catharines (AHL)	80	33	41	6	.450	....	....	....	....
1983-84	St. Catharines (AHL)	79	43	30	6	.583	7	3	4	.429
1984-85	New Jersey (NHL)	80	22	48	10	.338	....	....	....	....
1985-86	New Jersey (NHL)	80	28	49	3	.369	....	....	....	....
1986-87	New Jersey (NHL)	80	29	45	6	.400	....	....	....	....
1987-88	New Jersey (NHL)	50	21	24	5	.470	....	....	....	....
1988-89	Halifax (AHL)	80	42	30	8	.575	4	0	4	.000
1989-90	Toronto (NHL)	80	38	38	4	.500	5	1	4	.200
	NHL Totals	370	138	204	28	.411	5	1	4	.200

Vancouver Canucks

1989-90 Results: 25w-41L-14T 64PTS. Fifth, Smythe Division

Year-by-Year Record

Season	GP	Home W	L	T	Road W	L	T	Overall W	L	T	GF	GA	Pts.	Finished		Playoff Result
1989-90	80	13	16	11	12	25	3	25	41	14	245	306	64	5th,	Smythe Div.	Out of Playoffs
1988-89	80	19	15	6	14	24	2	33	39	8	251	253	74	4th,	Smythe Div.	Lost Div. Semi-Final
1987-88	80	15	20	5	10	26	4	25	46	9	272	320	59	5th,	Smythe Div.	Out of Playoffs
1986-87	80	17	19	4	12	24	4	29	43	8	282	314	66	5th,	Smythe Div.	Out of Playoffs
1985-86	80	17	18	5	6	26	8	23	44	13	282	333	59	4th,	Smythe Div.	Lost Div. Semi-Final
1984-85	80	15	21	4	10	25	5	25	46	9	284	401	59	5th,	Smythe Div.	Out of Playoffs
1983-84	80	20	16	4	12	23	5	32	39	9	306	328	73	3rd,	Smythe Div.	Lost Div. Semi-Final
1982-83	80	20	12	8	10	23	7	30	35	15	303	309	75	3rd,	Smythe Div.	Lost Div. Semi-Final
1981-82	80	20	8	12	10	25	5	30	33	17	290	286	77	2nd,	Smythe Div.	Lost Final
1980-81	80	17	12	11	11	20	9	28	32	20	289	301	76	3rd,	Smythe Div.	Lost Prelim. Round
1979-80	80	14	17	9	13	20	7	27	37	16	256	281	70	3rd,	Smythe Div.	Lost Prelim. Round
1978-79	80	15	18	7	10	24	6	25	42	13	217	291	63	2nd,	Smythe Div.	Lost Prelim. Round
1977-78	80	13	15	12	7	28	5	20	43	17	239	320	57	3rd,	Smythe Div.	Out of Playoffs
1976-77	80	13	21	6	12	21	7	25	42	13	235	294	63	4th,	Smythe Div.	Out of Playoffs
1975-76	80	22	11	7	11	21	8	33	32	15	271	272	81	2nd,	Smythe Div.	Lost Prelim. Round
1974-75	80	23	12	5	15	20	5	38	32	10	271	254	86	1st,	Smythe Div.	Lost Quarter-Final
1973-74	78	14	18	7	10	25	4	24	43	11	224	296	59	7th,	East Div.	Out of Playoffs
1972-73	78	17	18	4	5	29	5	22	47	9	233	339	53	7th,	East Div.	Out of Playoffs
1971-72	78	14	20	5	6	30	3	20	50	8	203	297	48	7th,	East Div.	Out of Playoffs
1970-71	78	17	18	4	7	28	4	24	46	8	229	296	56	6th,	East Div.	Out of Playoffs

Schedule

Home			Away		
Oct.	Tues. 9	Los Angeles	**Oct.**	Thur. 4	Calgary
	Fri. 12	St Louis		Sat. 6	Los Angeles
	Sun. 14	Edmonton*		Fri. 19	Winnipeg
	Wed. 17	Boston		Sun. 21	Quebec*
	Tues. 30	Washington		Tues. 23	Detroit
Nov.	Thur. 1	New Jersey		Thur. 25	Boston
	Sat. 3	Winnipeg		Sat. 27	Hartford
	Tues. 6	Detroit	**Nov.**	Thur. 8	Toronto
	Fri. 16	NY Islanders		Fri. 9	Buffalo
	Mon. 19	Calgary		Sun. 11	Philadelphia
	Wed. 21	Chicago		Wed. 14	Edmonton
	Tues. 27	Minnesota		Fri. 23	Minnesota
	Thur. 29	Toronto		Sat. 24	St Louis
Dec.	Mon. 10	Quebec	**Dec.**	Sun. 2	Winnipeg
	Fri. 14	NY Rangers		Tues. 4	NY Islanders
	Sun. 16	Calgary*		Wed. 5	New Jersey
	Thur. 20	Edmonton		Fri. 7	Pittsburgh
	Sat. 22	Los Angeles		Wed. 12	Edmonton
	Thur. 27	Montreal		Tues. 18	Calgary
	Fri. 28	Edmonton		Sun. 23	Edmonton
Jan.	Tues. 8	Buffalo		Mon. 31	Winnipeg
	Thur. 10	Hartford	**Jan.**	Wed. 2	Hartford
	Wed. 16	Winnipeg		Thur. 3	Boston
	Wed. 23	Edmonton		Sat. 5	Minnesota
	Fri. 25	Los Angeles		Sat. 12	Los Angeles
	Mon. 28	Chicago		Sat. 26	Los Angeles
	Thur. 31	NY Rangers		Wed. 30	Edmonton
Feb.	Thur. 14	St Louis	**Feb.**	Sat. 2	Los Angeles
	Sat. 16	Washington		Tues. 5	Washington
	Mon. 18	Quebec		Thur. 7	Philadelphia
	Sat. 23	Detroit		Fri. 8	NY Rangers
	Mon. 25	Calgary		Sun. 10	New Jersey*
	Wed. 27	Pittsburgh		Wed. 20	Winnipeg
Mar.	Fri. 1	Montreal		Thur. 21	Calgary
	Wed. 13	Philadelphia	**Mar.**	Sun. 3	Chicago
	Sat. 16	NY Islanders		Tues. 5	Pittsburgh
	Sun. 17	Los Angeles		Thur. 7	Toronto
	Wed. 20	Calgary		Sat. 9	Montreal
	Fri. 22	Winnipeg		Sun. 10	Buffalo
	Thur. 28	Winnipeg		Tues. 26	Calgary

* Denotes afternoon game.

Home Starting Times:

Weeknights	7:35 p.m.
Saturdays	5:05 p.m.
Sundays and Holidays	7:05 p.m.
Matinees	2:05 p.m.

Franchise date: May 22, 1970.

21st NHL Season

A 12-year veteran with the Canucks, Stan Smyl battles here with the Kings' Marty McSorley.

1990-91 Player Personnel

FORWARDS	HT	WT	S	Place of Birth	Date	1989-90 Club
ADAMS, Greg	6-3	190	L	Nelson, B.C.	8/1/63	Vancouver
ANTOSKI, Shawn	6-4	234	L	Brantford, Ont.	3/25/70	North Bay
BAKOVIC, Peter	6-2	200	R	Thunder Bay, Ont.	1/31/65	Milwaukee
BOZEK, Steve	5-11	180	L	Kelowna, B.C.	11/26/60	Vancouver
BRADLEY, Brian	5-10	180	R	Kitchener, Ont.	1/21/65	Vancouver
BROWN, Cam	6-1	205	L	Saskatoon, Sask.	5/15/69	Brandon
BRUCE, Dave	5-11	185	R	Thunder Bay, Ont.	10/7/64	Milwaukee
CAPUANO, Dave	6-2	190	L	Warwick, R.I.	7/27/68	Musk.-Mil'w.-Pit.-Van.
CHARBONNEAU, Jose	6-0	195	R	Ferme-Neuve, Que.	11/21/66	Milwaukee
CLOUSTON, Shaun	6-1	205	L	Viking, Alta.	2/21/68	Milwaukee
COXE, Craig	6-4	220	L	Chula Vista, CA	1/21/64	Vancouver-Milwaukee
DeBOER, Peter	6-0	195	R	Windsor, Ont.	6/13/68	Milwaukee
HAWKINS, Todd	6-1	195	R	Kingston, Ont.	8/2/66	Vancouver-Milwaukee
JOHNSON, Steve	6-1	190	R	Grand Forks, ND	3/3/66	Milwaukee-Phoenix
KRON, Robert	5-10	174	R	Brno, Czech.	2/27/67	Zetor Brno (Czech.)
KRUTOV, Vladimir	5-9	200	L	Moscow, USSR	6/1/60	Vancouver
LARIONOV, Igor	5-9	165	L	Voskresensk, USSR	12/3/60	Vancouver
LENARDON, Tim	6-2	185	L	Trail, B.C.	5/11/62	Milwaukee-Vancouver
LINDEN, Trevor	6-4	205	R	Medicine Hat, Alta.	4/11/70	Vancouver
MAZUR, Jay	6-2	195	R	Hamilton, Ont.	1/22/65	Vancouver
McBAIN, Andrew	6-1	205	R	Scarborough, Ont.	1/18/65	Pittsburgh-Vancouver
MURANO, Eric	6-0	190	R	LaSalle, Que.	5/4/67	U. of Denver
MURPHY, Rob	6-3	205	L	Hull, Que.	4/7/69	Vancouver-Milwaukee
NEDVED, Petr	6-2	178	L	Liberec, Czech.	12/9/71	Seattle
REVENBERG, Jim	6-1	199	R	Windsor, Ont.	7/23/69	Milwaukee
QUINN, Dan	5-10	175	L	Ottawa, Ont.	6/1/65	Pittsburgh-Vancouver
SANDLAK, Jim	6-3	219	R	Kitchener, Ont.	12/12/66	Vancouver
SKRIKO, Petri	5-10	180	L	Lapeenranta, Finland	3/12/62	Vancouver
SMYL, Stan	5-8	195	R	Glendon, Alta.	1/28/58	Vancouver
STANLEY, Daryl	6-2	200	L	Winnipeg, Man.	12/2/62	Vancouver
STERN, Ronnie	6-0	195	R	St. Agathe, Que.	1/11/67	Vancouver-Milwaukee
STREET, Keith	6-0	170	L	Moose Jaw, Sask.	3/18/65	Milwaukee
VARGAS, Ernie	6-1	180	L	St. Paul, MN	3/1/64	Milwaukee

DEFENSEMEN						
AGNEW, Jim	6-1	190	L	Hartney, Man.	3/21/66	Milwaukee-Vancouver
BENNING, Jim	6-0	185	L	Edmonton, Alta.	4/29/63	Vancouver
BUTCHER, Garth	6-0	200	R	Regina, Sask.	1/8/63	Vancouver
CAPUANO, Jack	6-2	210	L	Cranston, R.I.	7/7/66	Newmkt.-Sprgfld.-Milw.
GIBSON, Don	6-1	210	R	Deloriane, Man.	12/29/67	Michigan State-Milw.
GUY, Kevan	6-3	202	R	Edmonton, Alta.	7/16/65	Vancouver-Milwaukee
HERNIMAN, Steve	6-4	210	L	Windsor, Ont.	6/9/68	Milwaukee-Virginia
HUNT, Curtis	6-0	195	L	North Battleford, Sask.	1/28/67	Milwaukee
KIDD, Ian	5-11	195	R	Gresham, OR	5/11/64	Milwaukee
LIDSTER, Doug	6-1	200	R	Kamloops, B.C.	10/18/60	Vancouver
LUMME, Jyrki	6-1	207	L	Tampere, Finland	7/16/66	Montreal-Vancouver
MELNYK, Larry	6-0	195	L	Saskatoon, Sask.	2/21/60	Vancouver
NORDMARK, Robert	6-1	200	R	Lulea, Sweden	8/20/62	Vancouver
PLAVSIC, Adrien	6-1	190	L	Montreal, Que.	1/13/70	Peoria-St.L.-Van.-Milw.
REINHART, Paul	5-11	200	L	Kitchener, Ont.	1/8/60	Vancouver
VALIMONT, Carl	6-1	200	L	Southington, CT	3/1/66	Milwaukee
VEILLEUX, Steve	6-0	198	R	Lachenaie, Que.	3/9/69	Milwaukee

GOALTENDERS	HT	WT	C	Place of Birth	Date	1989-90 Club
GAMBLE, Troy	5-11	195	L	New Glasgow, N.S.	4/7/67	Milwaukee
McKICHAN, Steve	5-11	180	L	Strathroy, Ont.	9/29/67	Milwaukee-Virginia
McLEAN, Kirk	6-0	185	L	Willowdale, Ont.	6/26/66	Vancouver
WEEKS, Steve	5-11	170	L	Scarborough, Ont.	6/30/58	Vancouver

1989-90 Scoring

Regular Season

* rookie

Pos	#	Player	Team	GP	G	A	Pts	+/−	PIM	PP	SH	GW	GT	S	%
C	7	Dan Quinn	PIT	41	9	20	29	15 −	22	5	0	2	0	86	10.5
			VAN	37	16	18	34	2 −	27	6	0	3	0	95	16.8
			TOTAL	78	25	38	63	17 −	49	11	0	5	0	181	13.8
D	23	Paul Reinhart	VAN	67	17	40	57	2	30	9	1	1	2	139	12.2
R	16	Trevor Linden	VAN	73	21	30	51	17 −	43	6	2	3	0	171	12.3
L	8	Greg Adams	VAN	65	30	20	50	8 −	18	13	0	1	1	181	16.6
C	10	Brian Bradley	VAN	67	19	29	48	5	65	2	0	1	1	121	15.7
L	26	Petri Skriko	VAN	77	15	33	48	21 −	36	3	1	2	0	172	8.7
C	18	*Igor Larionov	VAN	74	17	27	44	5 −	20	8	0	2	1	118	14.4
D	3	Doug Lidster	VAN	80	8	28	36	16 −	36	1	0	0	1	143	5.6
L	17	*Vladimir Krutov	VAN	61	11	23	34	5 −	20	2	0	1	0	81	13.6
D	21	*Jyrki Lumme	MTL	54	1	19	20	17	41	0	0	0	0	79	1.3
			VAN	11	3	7	10	0	8	0	0	1	0	30	10.0
			TOTAL	65	4	26	30	17	49	0	0	1	0	109	3.7
R	19	Jim Sandlak	VAN	70	15	8	23	15 −	104	1	0	2	1	135	11.1
L	14	Steve Bozek	VAN	58	14	9	23	3 −	32	0	1	2	0	105	13.3
R	9	Andrew McBain	PIT	41	5	9	14	8 −	51	1	0	0	0	56	8.9
			VAN	26	4	5	9	3 −	22	3	0	0	0	50	8.0
			TOTAL	67	9	14	23	11 −	73	4	0	0	0	106	8.5
D	5	Garth Butcher	VAN	80	6	14	20	10 −	205	1	0	1	0	87	6.9
R	12	Stan Smyl	VAN	47	1	15	16	14 −	71	0	0	0	0	58	1.7
D	6	Robert Nordmark	VAN	44	2	11	13	16 −	34	1	0	0	0	86	2.3
D	4	Jim Benning	VAN	45	3	9	12	4	26	0	1	0	0	49	6.1
C	28	*Dave Capuano	PIT	6	0	0	0	0	2	0	0	0	0	1	.0
			VAN	27	3	5	8	7 −	10	0	0	1	0	25	12.0
			TOTAL	33	3	5	8	7 −	12	0	0	1	0	26	11.5
D	2	Kevan Guy	VAN	30	2	5	7	12 −	32	0	0	0	0	44	4.5
D	15	*Adrien Plavsic	STL	4	0	1	1	3	2	0	0	0	0	0	.0
			VAN	11	3	2	5	2 −	8	2	0	0	0	13	23.1
			TOTAL	15	3	3	6	1	10	2	0	0	0	14	21.4
R	20	Ronnie Stern	VAN	34	2	3	5	17 −	208	0	0	0	0	27	7.4
L	22	Craig Coxe	VAN	25	1	4	5	4 −	66	0	0	1	0	11	9.1
G	1	Kirk McLean	VAN	63	0	3	3	0	6	0	0	0	0	0	.0
C	44	*Rob Murphy	VAN	12	1	1	2	13 −	0	0	0	1	0	6	16.7
L	29	Daryl Stanley	VAN	23	1	1	2	2 −	27	0	0	1	0	7	14.3
D	24	Larry Melnyk	VAN	67	0	2	2	27 −	91	0	0	0	0	45	.0
C	33	*Tim Lenardon	VAN	8	1	0	1	2 −	4	0	0	0	0	9	11.1
R	38	*Todd Hawkins	VAN	4	0	0	0	1 −	6	0	0	0	0	3	.0
R	33	*Jay Mazur	VAN	5	0	0	0	2 −	4	0	0	0	0	4	.0
D	36	*Jim Agnew	VAN	7	0	0	0	1 −	36	0	0	0	0	0	.0
G	31	Steve Weeks	VAN	21	0	0	0	0	0	0	0	0	0	0	.0

Goaltending

No.	Goaltender	GPI	Mins	Avg	W	L	T	EN	SO	GA	SA	S%
1	Kirk McLean	63	3739	3.47	21	30	10	7	0	216	1804	.880
31	Steve Weeks	21	1142	4.15	4	11	4	4	0	79	623	.873
	Totals	80	4892	3.75	25	41	14	11	0	306	2427	.874

A trade brought centerman Dan Quinn to the Canucks midway through the 1989-90 season.

General Managers' History

Normand Robert Poile, 1970-71 to 1972-73; Hal Laycoe, 1973-74; Phil Maloney, 1974-75 to 1976-77; Jake Milford, 1977-78 to 1981-82; Harry Neale, 1982-83 to 1984-85; Jack Gordon, 1985-86 to 1986-87; Pat Quinn, 1987-88 to date.

Coaching History

Hal Laycoe, 1970-71 to 1971-72; Vic Stasiuk, 1972-73; Bill McCreary and Phil Maloney, 1973-74; Phil Maloney, 1974-75 to 1975-76; Phil Maloney and Orland Kurtenbach, 1976-77; Orland Kurtenbach, 1977-78; Harry Neale, 1978-79 to 1981-82; Harry Neale and Roger Neilson, 1981-82; Roger Neilson 1982-83, 1983-84; Harry Neale, 1983-84; Bill Laforge, 1984-85; Tom Watt, 1985-86, 1986-87; Bob McCammon, 1987-88 to date.

Captains' History

Orland Kurtenbach, 1970-71 to 1973-74; no captain, 1974-75; Andre Boudrias, 1975-76; Chris Oddleifson, 1976-77; Don Lever, 1977-78; Don Lever, Kevin McCarthy, 1978-79; Kevin McCarthy, 1979-80 to 1981-82; Stan Smyl, 1982-83 to date.

Retired Numbers

11	Wayne Maki	1971-1973

Club Records

Team

(Figures in brackets for season records are games played; records for fewest points, wins, ties, losses, goals, goals against are for 70 or more games)

Most Points	86	1974-75 (80)
Most Wins	38	1974-75 (80)
Most Ties	20	1980-81 (80)
Most Losses	50	1971-72 (78)
Most Goals	306	1983-84 (80)
Most Goals Against	401	1984-85 (80)
Fewest Points	48	1971-72 (78)
Fewest Wins	20	1971-72 (78)
		1977-78 (80)
Fewest Ties	8	1970-71 (78)
		1971-72 (78)
		1986-87 (80)
		1988-89 (80)
Fewest Losses	32	1974-75 (80)
		1975-76 (80)
		1980-81 (80)
Fewest Goals	203	1971-72 (78)
Fewest Goals Against	253	1988-89 (80)

Longest Winning Streak

Over-all	7	Feb. 10-23/89
Home	8	Feb. 27/83- Mar. 21/83 Jan. 31- Mar. 10/89
Away	3	Ten times

Longest Undefeated Streak

Over-all	10	Mar. 5-25/77 (5 wins, 5 ties)
Home	12	Oct. 29- Dec. 17/74 (11 wins, 1 tie) Jan. 29- Mar. 18/89 (10 wins, 2 ties)
Away	5	Three times

Longest Losing Streak

Over-all	9	Four times
Home	6	Dec. 18/70- Jan. 20/71 Nov. 3-18/78
Away	12	Nov. 28/81- Feb. 6/82

Longest Winless Streak

Over-all	13	Nov. 9- Dec. 7/73 (10 losses, 3 ties)
Home	11	Dec. 18/70- Feb. 6/71 (10 losses, 1 tie)
Away	20	Jan. 2/86- Apr. 2/86 (14 losses, 6 ties)

Most Shutouts, Season	8	1974-75 (80)
Most PIM, Season	2,196	1987-88 (80)
Most Goals, Game	11	Mar. 28/71 (Cal. 5 at Van. 11) Nov. 25/86 (L.A. 5 at Van. 11)

Individual

Most Seasons	12	Stan Smyl, Harold Snepsts
Most Games	851	Stan Smyl
Most Goals, Career	260	Stan Smyl
Most Assists, Career	399	Stan Smyl
Most Points, Career	659	Stan Smyl (260 goals, 399 assists)
Most PIM, Career	1,469	Stan Smyl
Most Shutouts, Career	11	Gary Smith
Longest Consecutive Games Streak	437	Don Lever (Oct. 7/72-Jan. 14/78)
Most Goals, Season	45	Tony Tanti (1983-84)
Most Assists, Season	62	Andre Boudrias (1974-75)
Most Points, Season	91	Patrik Sundstrom (1983-84) (38 goals, 53 assists)
Most PIM, Season	343	Dave Williams (1980-81)
Most Points, Defenseman, Season	63	Doug Lidster (1986-87) (12 goals, 51 assists)

Most Points, Center, Season	91	Patrik Sundstrom (1983-84) (38 goals, 53 assists)
Most Points, Right Wing, Season	88	Stan Smyl (1982-83) (38 goals, 50 assists)
Most Points, Left Wing, Season	81	Darcy Rota (1982-83) (42 goals, 39 assists)
Most Points, Rookie, Season	60	Ivan Hlinka (1981-82) (23 goals, 37 assists)
Most Shutouts, Season	6	Gary Smith (1974-75)
Most Goals, Game	4	Several players
Most Assists, Game	6	Patrik Sundstrom (Feb. 29/84)
Most Points, Game	7	Patrik Sundstrom (Feb. 29/84)

All-time Record vs. Other Clubs

Regular Season

			At Home							On Road							Total				
	GP	W	L	T	GF	GA	PTS	GP	W	L	T	GF	GA	PTS	GP	W	L	T	GF	GA	PTS
Boston	39	11	21	7	133	173	29	38	3	32	3	83	174	9	77	14	53	10	216	347	38
Buffalo	40	19	12	9	152	131	47	39	10	21	8	108	143	28	79	29	33	17	260	274	75
Calgary	57	20	25	12	197	193	52	57	9	40	8	158	262	26	114	29	65	20	355	455	78
Chicago	44	19	14	11	133	132	40	45	12	28	5	106	161	29	80	31	42	16	239	293	78
Detroit	39	21	12	6	162	122	48	39	11	22	6	121	166	28	78	32	34	12	283	288	76
Edmonton	40	11	23	6	137	179	28	40	7	29	4	125	214	18	80	18	52	10	262	393	46
Hartford	18	7	6	5	61	48	19	17	6	7	4	63	59	16	35	13	13	9	124	107	35
Los Angeles	61	28	21	12	240	211	68	61	17	35	9	185	253	43	122	45	56	21	425	464	111
Minnesota	44	23	14	7	181	139	53	43	9	27	7	119	182	25	87	32	41	14	300	321	78
Montreal	38	5	25	8	89	150	18	40	6	32	2	103	205	14	78	11	57	10	192	355	32
New Jersey	36	19	6	11	139	108	49	36	17	13	6	125	104	40	72	36	19	17	264	212	89
NY Islanders	35	15	18	2	111	116	32	35	6	21	8	90	140	20	70	21	39	10	201	256	52
NY Rangers	40	10	28	2	128	166	22	42	7	32	3	105	190	17	82	17	60	5	233	356	39
Philadelphia	41	10	21	10	121	159	30	40	11	29	0	117	190	22	81	21	50	10	238	349	52
Pittsburgh	39	19	17	3	149	150	41	38	9	24	5	133	171	22	77	27	41	9	282	321	63
Quebec	17	10	6	1	75	70	21	18	7	7	4	54	55	18	35	17	13	5	129	125	39
St. Louis	44	20	19	5	142	140	45	45	12	27	6	134	102	30	89	32	46	11	276	242	75
Toronto	40	21	12	7	142	130	49	39	14	17	8	138	151	36	79	35	29	15	280	281	85
Washington	27	12	11	4	95	91	28	28	11	15	2	88	90	24	55	23	26	6	183	181	52
Winnipeg	38	21	11	6	152	122	48	37	10	21	6	135	153	26	75	31	32	12	287	275	74
Defunct Club	19	14	3	2	82	48	30	19	10	8	1	71	68	21	38	24	11	3	153	116	51
Totals	**796**	**335**	**325**	**136**	**2821**	**2778**	**806**	**796**	**203**	**487**	**106**	**2361**	**3313**	**512**	**1592**	**538**	**812**	**242**	**5182**	**6091**	**1318**

Playoffs

	Series	W	L	GP	W	L	T	GF	GA	Last Mtg.	Round	Result
Buffalo	2	0	2	7	1	6	0	14	28	1981	PR	L 0-3
Calgary	4	1	3	18	8	10	0	57	62	1989	DSF	L 3-4
Chicago	1	1	0	5	4	1	0	18	13	1982	CF	W 4-1
Edmonton	1	0	1	3	0	3	0	5	17	1986	DSF	L 0-3
Los Angeles	1	1	0	5	4	1	0	19	14	1982	DF	W 4-1
Montreal	1	0	1	5	1	4	0	9	20	1975	QF	L 1-4
NY Islanders	2	0	2	6	0	6	0	14	26	1982	F	L 0-4
Philadelphia	1	0	1	3	1	2	0	9	15	1979	PR	L 1-2
Totals	**13**	**3**	**10**	**52**	**19**	**33**	**0**	**145**	**195**			

Abbreviations: Round: F – Final; **CF** – conference final; **DF** – division final; **DSF** – division semi-final; **PR** – preliminary round. **QF** – quarter-final. **GA** – goals against; **GF** – goals for.

Playoff Results 1990-86

Year	Round	Opponent	Result	GF	GA
1989	DSF	Calgary	L 3-4	20	26
1986	DSF	Edmonton	L 0-3	5	17

1989-90 Results

		Home				Away	
Oct.	5	Edmonton	1-4	Oct.	11	Edmonton	5-2
	7	Detroit	5-3		18	Toronto	3-4
	9	NY Islanders*	2-5		20	New Jersey	3-2
	13	Los Angeles	5-6		21	NY Islanders	2-1
	15	Boston*	7-6		23	NY Rangers	3-5
	28	Calgary	4-3		27	Calgary	5-5
	31	New Jersey	4-3	Nov.	8	Winnipeg	2-3
Nov.	3	Winnipeg	2-3		10	Buffalo	2-4
	5	Pittsburgh	5-3		11	Quebec	2-3
	14	Washington	4-4		21	Edmonton	3-4
	16	Chicago	4-3		25	Los Angeles	4-7
	19	Buffalo	2-2	Dec.	6	Los Angeles	4-5
	26	Los Angeles	3-3		9	St Louis	4-6
	29	Toronto	2-3		10	Chicago	1-7
Dec.	1	NY Rangers	3-4		12	Minnesota	4-2
	3	Minnesota	6-5		13	Winnipeg	3-3
	15	Winnipeg	3-3		20	Calgary	1-2
	19	Quebec	2-2		23	Los Angeles	1-4
	19	Calgary	1-2	Jan.	2	Detroit	1-4
	27	Montreal	2-1		4	Pittsburgh	3-4
	31	Philadelphia	2-2		5	Washington	5-2
Jan.	10	Hartford	1-3		7	Montreal	3-5
	12	St Louis	2-5		16	NY Islanders	0-3
	13	Buffalo	3-5		18	Philadelphia	3-2
	23	Los Angeles	3-3		19	Chicago	2-5
	26	Minnesota	3-6		27	Edmonton	2-6
	30	Calgary	2-7	Feb.	1	Calgary	3-4
Feb.	4	New Jersey	4-2		2	Winnipeg	1-8
	6	Winnipeg	5-3		9	Hartford	4-1
	16	Edmonton	2-2		11	Boston*	4-2
	18	Boston	2-7		13	Quebec	3-5
	20	Edmonton	2-4		14	Montreal	1-10
	26	Toronto	5-2		24	Los Angeles	6-4
	28	Philadelphia	7-7	Mar.	3	Calgary	1-5
Mar.	9	Calgary	4-4		4	Edmonton	3-6
	11	Pittsburgh*	5-3		15	St Louis	6-5
	13	Hartford	0-1		17	Washington	3-1
	25	Winnipeg	3-3		18	NY Rangers	2-5
	27	Edmonton	1-4		20	Detroit	4-4
	31	Los Angeles	6-3		23	Winnipeg	4-2

* Denotes afternoon game.

Entry Draft Selections 1990-76

1990
Pick
2	Petr Nedved
18	Shawn Antoski
23	Jiri Slegr
65	Darin Bader
86	Gino Odjick
128	Daryl Filipek
149	Paul O'Hagan
170	Mark Cipriano
191	Troy Neumier
212	Tyler Ertel
233	Karri Kivi

1989
Pick
8	Jason Herter
29	Robert Woodward
71	Brett Hauer
113	Pavel Bure
134	James Revenberg
155	Rob Sangster
176	Sandy Moger
197	Gus Morschauser
218	Hayden O'Rear
239	Darcy Cahill
248	Jan Bergman

1988
Pick
2	Trevor Linden
33	Leif Rohlin
44	Dane Jackson
107	Corrie D'Alessio
122	Phil Von Stefenelli
128	Dixon Ward
149	Greg Geldart
170	Roger Akerstorm
191	Paul Constantin
212	Chris Wolanin
233	Steffan Nilsson

1987
Pick
24	Rob Murphy
45	Steve Veilleux
66	Doug Torrel
87	Sean Fabian
108	Gary Valk
129	Todd Fanning

1986
Pick
7	Dan Woodley
49	Don Gibson
70	Ronnie Stern
91	Eric Murano
112	Steve Herniman
133	Jon Helgeson
154	Jeff Noble
175	Matt Merton
196	Marc Lyons
217	Todd Hawkins
238	Vladimir Krutov

1985
Pick
4	Jim Sandlak
25	Troy Gamble
46	Shane Doyle
67	Randy Siska
88	Robert Kron
109	Martin Hrstka
130	Brian McFarlane
151	Hakan Ahlund
172	Curtis Hunt
193	Carl Valimont
214	Igor Larionov
235	Darren Taylor

1984
Pick
10	J.J. Daigneault
31	Jeff Rolicek
52	Dave Saunders
55	Landis Chaulk
58	Mike Stevens
73	Brian Bertuzzi
94	Brett MacDonald
115	Jeff Korchinski
136	Blaine Chrest
157	Jim Agnew
178	Rex Grant
198	Ed Lowney
219	Doug Clarke
239	Ed Kister

1983
Pick
9	Cam Neely
30	Dave Bruce
50	Scott Tottle
70	Tim Lorentz
90	Doug Quinn
110	Dave Lowry
130	Terry Maki
150	John Labatt
170	Allan Measures
190	Roger Grillo
210	Steve Kayser
230	Jay Mazur

1982
Pick
11	Michel Petit
53	Yves Lapointe
71	Shawn Kilroy
116	Taylor Hall
137	Parie Proft
158	Newell Brown
179	Don McLaren
200	Al Raymond
221	Steve Driscoll
242	Shawn Green

1981
Pick
10	Garth Butcher
52	Jean-Marc Lanthier
73	Wendell Young
105	Moe Lemay
115	Stu Kulak
136	Bruce Holloway
157	Petri Skriko
178	Frank Caprice
199	Rejean Vignola

1980
Pick
7	Rick Lanz
49	Andy Schliebener
70	Marc Crawford
91	Darrel May
112	Ken Berry
133	Doug Lidster
154	John O'Connor
175	Patrik Sundstrom
196	Grant Martin

1979
Pick
5	Rick Vaive
26	Brent Ashton
47	Ken Ellacott
68	Art Rutland
89	Dirk Graham
110	Shane Swan

1978
Pick
4	Bill Derlago
22	Curt Fraser
40	Stan Smyl
56	Harold Luckner
57	Brad Smith
90	Gerry Minor
107	Dave Ross
124	Steve O'Neill
141	Charlie Antetomaso
158	Richard Martens

1977
Pick
4	Jere Gillis
22	Jeff Bandura
40	Glen Hanlon
56	Dave Morrow
58	Murray Bannerman
76	Steve Hazlett
94	Brian Drumm
112	Ray Creasey

1976
Pick
26	Bob Manno
44	Rob Flockhart
62	Elmer Ray
80	Rick Durston
98	Rob Tudor
114	Brad Rhiness
122	Stu Ostlund

1983 (additional)
150	Viktor Tuminev
171	Craig Daly
192	John Fletcher
213	Roger Hansson
233	Neil Eisenhut
234	Matt Evo

Club Directory

Pacific Coliseum
100 North Renfrew Street
Vancouver, B.C. V5K 3N7
Phone **604/254-5141**
FAX 604/251-5123
GM FAX 604/251-5514
ENVOY ID
Front Office: CANUCKS. GM
Public
Relations: CANUCKS. PR
Capacity: 16,123

Northwest Sports Enterprises Ltd.
Board of Directors

J. Lawrence Dampier	W.L. McEwen	Andrew E. Saxton
Arthur R. Griffiths	David S. Owen	Peter W. Webster
Frank A. Griffiths, C.A.	Senator Ray Perrault	Sydney W. Welsh
F.W. Griffiths	J. Raymond Peters	D.A. Williams, C.A.
Coleman E. Hall	Peter Paul Saunders	D. Alexander Farac (Sec.)
Senator E.M. Lawson		

Chairman	Frank A. Griffiths, C.A.
Vice-Chairman and Governor	Arthur R. Griffiths
President and General Manager	Pat Quinn
Vice-President and Director of Hockey Operations	Brian Burke
Vice-President and Director of Marketing and Communications	Glen Ringdal
Vice-President of Finance/Administration	Carlos Mascarenhas
Senior Advisor	Jack Gordon
Head Coach	Bob McCammon
Assistant Coaches	Ron Wilson, Jack McIlhargey
Trainers	Larry Ashley, Pat O'Neill, Ed Georgica
Strength Coach	Wayne Wilson
Massage Therapist	Richard Wong
Director of Public and Media Relations	Darcy Rota
Director of Scouting	Mike Penny
Director of Pro Scouting	Murray Oliver
Scouting Staff	Scott Carter, Ron Delorme, Ron Lapointe, Paul MacIntosh, Jack McCartan, Ed McColgan, Noel Price, Ken Slater, Ernie Vargas
Director of Publishing	Norm Jewison
Director of Special Events	TBA
Director of Ticket Sales	Lynn Harrison
Director of Sales	Duke Dickson
Sales Coordinator	Gail Nishi
Box Office Manager	Fiona Hayes
Executive Secretary, Pres. & GM	Jette Sandeford
Executive Secretary, Vice-President and Director of Hockey Operations	Patti Timms
Executive Secretary, Vice-President and Director of Marketing and Communications	Dena Pelkey
Manager of Food and Beverage Operations	Terreeia Rauffman
Director of Retail Sales	Larry Donen
Travel Coordinator	Dave Nonis
General Manager Farm Team (Milwaukee Admirals)	Phil Wittliff
Milwaukee Head Coach	Mike Murphy
Club Doctors	Dr. Gord Matheson, Dr. Ross Davidson
Club Dentist	Dr. David Lawson
Club Colors	White, Black, Red and Gold
Press Box	West Side, Renfrew St. Entrance
Dimensions of rink	200 feet by 85 feet
Club Trains at:	Victoria, B.C.
Play-by-Play Broadcaster	Jim Robson (radio and TV)
Radio Station	CKNW (980)
TV Channel	CBC (2), BCTV (8)

Coach

McCAMMON, BOB
Coach, Vancouver Canucks. Born in Kenora, Ont., April 14, 1941.

Bob McCammon was named head coach of the Canucks on June 22, 1987. In 1988-89, his second year with Vancouver, McCammon led the Canucks to a 33-39-8 record marking a 15-point improvement in their performance. They earned their first playoff berth since 1985-86 and McCammon was the runner-up for the Jack Adams Award.

After retiring from his 11-year minor league playing career with the Port Huron Flags in 1972-73, McCammon remained with the IHL club as coach through 1976-77. The following season, he joined the Philadelphia Flyers' organization as coach of the Maine Mariners, their top farm club in the AHL, leading them to the AHL's Calder Cup championship and earning Coach-of-the-Year honors.

In 1978-79, the Flyers named McCammon to their head coaching position and then guided the NHL team to a 22-17-11 record in 50 games before returning to Maine in mid-season. In each of the next three years, he piloted the Mariners to 40 or more wins and again won AHL Coach-of-the-Year honors in 1980-81.

Late in the 1981-82 season, McCammon worked his way back to the Flyers as head coach and was promoted to general manager/head coach in 1983-84. In 218 NHL games with Philadelphia, he compiled a record of 119-68-31 for a .617 winning percentage.

In 1985-86, McCammon was named to an assistant coaching position with the Edmonton Oilers and later became that club's head of player development.

Coaching Record

Season	Team	Games	Regular Season W	L	T	%	Playoffs Games	W	L	%
1973-74	Port Huron (IHL)	76	29	44	3	.401	....	....	....	....
1974-75	Port Huron (IHL)	76	35	38	3	.480	5	1	4	.200
1975-76	Port Huron (IHL)	78	36	31	11	.532	15	8	7	.533
1976-77	Port Huron (IHL)	78	27	43	8	.397	....	....	....	....
1977-78	Maine (AHL)	80	43	28	9	.594	12	8	4	.667
1978-79	**Philadelphia (NHL)**	50	22	17	11	.550	....	....	....	....
1978-79	Maine (AHL)	30	17	8	5	.650	11	8	3	.727
1979-80	Maine (AHL)	80	41	28	11	.581	12	6	6	.500
1980-81	Maine (AHL)	80	45	28	7	.606	20	10	10	.500
1981-82	Maine (AHL)	79	40	23	6	.544	....	....	....	....
	Philadelphia (NHL)	8	4	2	2	.625	4	1	3	.250
1982-83	**Philadelphia (NHL)**	80	49	23	8	.663	3	0	3	.000
1983-84	**Philadelphia (NHL)**	80	44	26	10	.613	3	0	3	.000
1987-88	**Vancouver (NHL)**	80	25	46	9	.369	....	....	....	....
1988-89	**Vancouver (NHL)**	80	33	39	8	.463	7	3	4	.429
1989-90	**Vancouver (NHL)**	80	25	41	14	.400	....	....	....	....
	NHL Totals	458	202	194	62	.509	17	4	13	.235

General Manager

QUINN, PAT
President and General Manager, Vancouver Canucks.
Born in Hamilton, Ont., January 29, 1943.

Pat Quinn took up management responsibilities with the Vancouver Canucks in 1987-88 after coaching in Los Angeles from 1984 to 1987 and in Philadelphia from 1978 to 1982. In Philadelphia, Quinn was awarded the Jack Adams award for leading the Flyers to the Stanley Cup finals in 1979-80. He started his coaching career with the Maine Mariners of the AHL and eventually was promoted to the head coaching job with Philadelphia. An NHL defenseman himself, Quinn played in more than 600 games over nine years.

NHL Coaching Record

Season	Team	Games	Regular Season W	L	T	%	Playoffs Games	W	L	%
1978-79	Philadelphia	30	18	8	4	.667	8	3	5	.375
1979-80	Philadelphia	80	48	12	20	.725	19	13	6	.684
1980-81	Philadelphia	80	41	24	15	.606	12	6	6	.500
1981-82	Philadelphia	72	34	29	9	.535	....	....	....	....
1984-85	Los Angeles	80	34	32	14	.513	3	0	3	.000
1985-86	Los Angeles	80	23	49	8	.338	....	....	....	....
1986-87	Los Angeles	42	18	20	4	.476	....	....	....	....
	NHL Totals	464	216	174	74	.545	42	22	20	.524

Washington Capitals

1989-90 Results: 36w-38L-6T 78PTS. Third, Patrick Division

Year-by-Year Record

Season	GP	Home W	Home L	Home T	Road W	Road L	Road T	Overall W	Overall L	Overall T	GF	GA	Pts.	Finished	Playoff Result
1989-90	80	19	18	3	17	20	3	36	38	6	284	275	78	3rd, Patrick Div.	Lost Conf. Championship
1988-89	80	25	12	3	16	17	7	41	29	10	305	259	92	1st, Patrick Div.	Lost Div. Semi-Final
1987-88	80	22	14	4	16	19	5	38	33	9	281	249	85	2nd, Patrick Div.	Lost Div. Final
1986-87	80	22	15	3	16	17	7	38	32	10	285	278	86	2nd, Patrick Div.	Lost Div. Semi-Final
1985-86	80	30	8	2	20	15	5	50	23	7	315	272	107	2nd, Patrick Div.	Lost Div. Final
1984-85	80	27	11	2	19	14	7	46	25	9	322	240	101	2nd, Patrick Div.	Lost Div. Semi-Final
1983-84	80	26	11	3	22	16	2	48	27	5	308	226	101	2nd, Patrick Div.	Lost Div. Final
1982-83	80	22	12	6	17	13	10	39	25	16	306	283	94	3rd, Patrick Div.	Lost Div. Semi-Final
1981-82	80	16	16	8	10	25	5	26	41	13	319	338	65	5th, Patrick Div.	Out of Playoffs
1980-81	80	16	17	7	10	19	11	26	36	18	286	317	70	5th, Patrick Div.	Out of Playoffs
1979-80	80	20	14	6	7	26	7	27	40	13	261	293	67	5th, Patrick Div.	Out of Playoffs
1978-79	80	15	19	6	9	22	9	24	41	15	273	338	63	4th, Norris Div.	Out of Playoffs
1977-78	80	10	23	7	7	26	7	17	49	14	195	321	48	5th, Norris Div.	Out of Playoffs
1976-77	80	17	15	8	7	27	6	24	42	14	221	307	62	4th, Norris Div.	Out of Playoffs
1975-76	80	6	26	8	5	33	2	11	59	10	224	394	32	5th, Norris Div.	Out of Playoffs
1974-75	80	7	28	5	1	39	0	8	67	5	181	446	21	5th, Norris Div.	Out of Playoffs

Schedule

		Home			Away
Oct.	Fri.	5 Pittsburgh	**Oct.**	Wed.	10 NY Rangers
	Sat.	6 Detroit		Mon.	15 Montreal
	Fri.	12 Winnipeg		Wed.	17 New Jersey
	Sat.	13 NY Rangers		Tues.	23 Philadelphia
	Fri.	19 NY Islanders		Thur.	25 Chicago
	Sat.	20 New Jersey		Sat.	27 Calgary
Nov.	Fri.	2 Los Angeles		Sun.	28 Edmonton
	Sat.	10 Buffalo		Tues.	30 Vancouver
	Sun.	11 Boston	**Nov.**	Sat.	3 NY Islanders
	Fri.	16 Chicago		Tues.	6 Quebec
	Wed.	21 Toronto		Wed.	14 Toronto
	Fri.	23 Pittsburgh		Sat.	17 Hartford
	Fri	30 Montreal		Mon	19 Detroit
Dec.	Fri.	7 New Jersey		Sat.	24 Pittsburgh
	Tues.	11 Philadelphia		Wed.	28 NY Rangers
	Sat.	15 Hartford	**Dec.**	Sat.	1 NY Islanders
	Sat.	22 Toronto*		Wed.	5 Pittsburgh
	Wed.	26 Pittsburgh		Sat.	8 New Jersey
	Fri.	28 NY Rangers		Mon.	17 NY Rangers
Jan.	Tues.	1 New Jersey*		Wed.	19 Chicago
	Fri.	4 Philadelphia		Thur.	20 St Louis
	Fri.	11 Calgary		Sat.	29 Quebec
	Fri.	25 Minnesota	**Jan.**	Sat.	5 Boston
	Sun.	27 NY Islanders*		Sat.	12 Montreal
Feb.	Sat.	2 Winnipeg		Tues.	15 St Louis
	Tues.	5 Vancouver		Thur.	17 Minnesota
	Fri.	8 Edmonton		Tues.	22 Detroit
	Sun.	10 Philadelphia*		Thur.	24 Philadelphia
	Fri.	22 NY Rangers		Tues.	29 Pittsburgh
	Sun.	24 Pittsburgh*		Thur.	31 NY Islanders
Mar.	Sat.	2 NY Islanders	**Feb.**	Fri.	15 Calgary
	Tues.	5 Los Angeles		Sat.	16 Vancouver
	Tues.	12 Hartford		Mon.	18 Los Angeles*
	Thur.	14 Quebec		Mon.	25 New Jersey
	Sat.	16 Philadelphia		Wed.	27 NY Rangers
	Tues.	19 St Louis	**Mar.**	Fri.	8 Winnipeg
	Fri.	22 Minnesota		Sun.	10 Edmonton
	Sun.	24 Boston*		Thur.	21 NY Islanders
	Tues.	26 Buffalo		Thur.	28 Philadelphia
	Sat.	30 New Jersey		Sun.	31 Buffalo

* Denotes afternoon game.

Home Starting Times:

Saturdays and Mondays through Thursdays	7:35 p.m.
Fridays	8:05 p.m.
Sundays	7:05 p.m.
Matinees	1:35 p.m.
Except Nov. 21	8:05 p.m.
Jan. 27	12:05 p.m.

Franchise date: June 11, 1974

17th NHL Season

Kevin Hatcher

1990-91 Player Personnel

FORWARDS	HT	WT	S	Place of Birth	Date	1989-90 Club
BAWA, Robin	6-2	214	R	Chemainos, B.C.	3/26/66	Wsh.-Balt.
BERGLAND, Tim	6-2	194	R	Crookston, MN	1/11/65	Wsh.-Balt.
CICCARELLI, Dino	5-10	175	R	Sarnia, Ont.	2/8/60	Washington
DRUCE, John	6-1	200	L	Peterborough, Ont.	2/23/66	Wsh.-Balt.
GERVAIS, Victor	5-9	172	L	Prince George, B.C.	3/13/69	Seattle
GREENLAW, Jeff	6-1	230	L	Toronto, Ont.	2/28/68	Baltimore
HLUSHKO, Todd	5-11	180	L	Toronto, Ont.	2/7/70	London
HUNTER, Dale	5-10	198	L	Petrolia, Ont.	7/31/60	Washington
JOYCE, Bob	6-1	195	L	St. John's, N.B.	7/11/66	Boston-Wsh.
KYPREOS, Nick	6-0	195	L	Toronto, Ont.	6/4/66	Wsh.-Balt.
LARTER, Tyler	5-10	190	L	Charlottetown, P.E.I.	3/12/68	Wsh.-Balt.
LEACH, Steve	5-11	198	R	Cambridge, MA	1/16/66	Washington
LONGO, Chris	5-10	180	R	Belleville, Ont.	1/5/72	Peterborough
LORENTZ, Dave	5-9	182	L	Kitchener, Ont.	3/16/69	Peterborough
MALTAIS, Steve	6-2	210	L	Arvida, Que.	1/25/69	Wsh.-Balt.
MARTELL, Steve	5-10	185	R	Sydney, N.S.	3/3/70	London
MAY, Alan	6-1	200	R	Barrhead, Alta.	1/14/65	Washington
MEWS, Harry	5-10	175	L	Nepean, Ont.	2/9/67	Northeastern
MILLER, Kelly	5-11	196	L	Detroit, MI.	3/3/63	Washington
MURRAY, Rob	6-0	185	R	Toronto, Ont.	4/4/67	Washington
PEARCE, Randy	5-11	203	L	Kitchener, Ont.	2/23/70	Kitchener
PIVONKA, Michal	6-2	198	L	Kladno, Czech.	1/28/66	Washington
PURVES, John	6-0	201	R	Toronto, Ont.	2/12/68	Baltimore
RIDLEY, Mike	6-1	200	L	Winnipeg, Man.	7/8/63	Washington
SAKIC, Brian	5-10	179	L	Burnaby, B.C.	4/9/71	Swift Cur't-Tri Cit.
SAVAGE, Reggie	5-10	187	L	Montreal, Que.	5/1/70	Victoriaville
SEFTEL, Steve	6-2	210	L	Kitchener, Ont.	5/14/68	Baltimore
SJOGREN, Thomas	5-9	185	R	Unea, Sweden	6/8/68	Sodertalje (Sweden)
TAYLOR, Tim	6-0	180	L	Stratford, Ont.	2/6/69	London
TURCOTTE, Alfie	5-11	185	L	Gary, Indiana	6/5/65	Wsh.-Balt.
ZEZEL, Peter	5-11	200	L	Toronto, Ont.	4/22/65	St. Louis

DEFENCEMEN						
BABCOCK, Bobby	6-1	222	L	Toronto, Ont.	8/3/68	Baltimore
BALLANTYNE, Jeff	6-1	203	L	Elmira, Ont.	1/7/69	Ottawa-Owen Sound
BARTLEY, Wade	6-0	190	R	Killarney, Man.	5/16/70	Sudbury
FELIX, Chris	5-10	191	R	Bramalea, Ont.	5/27/64	Balt.-Wsh.
FERNER, Mark	6-0	193	L	Regina, Sask.	9/5/65	Wsh.-Balt.
HATCHER, Kevin	6-4	225	R	Detroit, MI	9/9/66	Washington
HOULDER, Bill	6-2	212	L	Thunder Bay, Ont.	3/11/67	Wsh.-Balt.
JOHANSSON, Calle	5-11	205	L	Goteberg, Sweden	2/14/67	Washington
LALOR, Mike	6-0	200	L	Buffalo, NY	3/8/65	St. Louis
LANGWAY, Rod	6-3	224	L	Formosa	5/3/57	Washington
LOVSIN, Ken	6-0	195	R	Peace River, Alta.	12/3/68	Canadian Nat'l
MATHIESON, Jim	6-1	209	R	Kindersley, Sask.	1/24/70	Wsh.-Regina
MENDEL, Rob	6-1	195	L	Los Angeles, CA	9/19/68	U. Wisconsin
PASMA, Rod	6-4	207	L	Brampton, Ont.	2/26/72	Cornwall
PAYNTER, Kent	6-0	186	L	Summerside, P.E.I.	4/27/65	Wsh.-Balt.
ROUSE, Bob	6-1	210	R	Surrey, B.C.	6/18/64	Washington
SHEEHY, Neil	6-2	214	R	Internat'l Falls, MN	2/9/60	Washington
SLANEY, John	6-0	186	L	St. John's, Nfld.	2/7/72	Cornwall

GOALTENDERS	HT	WT	C	Place of Birth	Date	1989-90 Club
BEAUPRE, Don	5-9	165	L	Waterloo, Ont.	9/19/61	Washington
DAFOE, Byron	5-11	175	L	Duncan, B.C.	2/25/71	Portland
HRIVNAK, Jim	6-2	185	L	Montreal, Que.	5/28/68	Wsh.-Balt.
KOLZIG, Olaf	6-3	207	L	Jo'burg, S. Africa	4/9/70	Wsh.-Tri-Cities
LIUT, Mike	6-2	195	L	Weston, Ont.	1/7/56	Hartford-Wsh.
SIMPSON, Shawn	5-11	183	R	Gloucester, Ont.	8/10/68	Baltimore

Retired Numbers

7	Yvon Labre	1973-1981

General Managers' History

Milt Schmidt, 1974-75 to 1975-76; Max McNab, 1976-77 to 1980-81; Roger Crozier, 1981-82; David Poile, 1982-83 to date.

Coaching History

Jim Anderson, George Sullivan, Milt Schmidt, 1974-75; Milt Schmidt and Tom McVie, 1975-76; Tom McVie, 1976-77 to 1977-78; Danny Belisle, 1978-79; Danny Belisle and Gary Green, 1979-80; Gary Green, 1980-81; Gary Green and Bryan Murray, 1981-82; Bryan Murray, 1982-83 to 1988-89; Bryan Murray and Terry Murray, 1989-90; Terry Murray, 1990-91.

Captains' History

Doug Mohns, 1974-75; Bill Clement, Yvon Labre, 1975-76; Yvon Labre, 1976-77, 1977-78; Guy Charron, 1978-79; Ryan Walter, 1979-80 to 1981-82; Rod Langway, 1982-83 to date.

1989-90 Scoring

Regular Season

* rookie

Pos	#	Player	Team	GP	G	A	Pts	+/−	PIM	PP	SH	GW	GT	S	%
R	22	Dino Ciccarelli	WSH	80	41	38	79	5−	122	10	0	6	0	267	15.4
L	14	Geoff Courtnall	WSH	80	35	39	74	27	104	9	0	2	1	307	11.4
C	17	Mike Ridley	WSH	74	30	43	73	0	27	8	3	3	0	124	24.2
C	20	Michal Pivonka	WSH	77	25	39	64	7−	54	10	3	0	0	149	16.8
C	32	Dale Hunter	WSH	80	23	39	62	17	233	9	1	6	0	123	18.7
D	4	Kevin Hatcher	WSH	80	13	41	54	4	102	4	0	2	0	240	5.4
L	10	Kelly Miller	WSH	80	18	22	40	2−	49	3	2	2	0	107	16.8
D	3	Scott Stevens	WSH	56	11	29	40	1	154	7	0	0	0	143	7.7
D	6	Calle Johansson	WSH	70	8	31	39	7	25	4	0	2	0	103	7.8
R	21	Stephen Leach	WSH	70	18	14	32	10	104	0	0	2	0	122	14.8
C	12	John Tucker	BUF	8	1	2	3	3−	2	1	0	0	0	8	12.5
			WSH	38	9	19	28	11	10	1	0	1	0	61	14.8
			TOTAL	46	10	21	31	8	12	2	0	1	0	69	14.5
D	8	Bob Rouse	WSH	70	4	16	20	2−	123	0	0	2	0	72	5.6
R	16	*Alan May	WSH	77	7	10	17	1−	339	1	0	2	0	67	10.4
L	27	Bob Joyce	BOS	23	1	2	3	8−	22	0	0	0	0	32	3.1
			WSH	24	5	8	13	2	4	1	0	1	0	30	16.7
			TOTAL	47	6	10	16	6−	26	1	0	1	0	62	9.7
D	2	Bill Houlder	WSH	41	1	11	12	8	28	0	0	0	1	49	2.0
R	19	John Druce	WSH	45	8	3	11	3−	52	1	0	1	0	66	12.1
L	9	*Nick Kypreos	WSH	31	5	4	9	2	82	0	0	2	0	27	18.5
C	23	*Rob Murray	WSH	41	2	7	9	10−	58	0	0	0	0	29	6.9
C	18	Doug Wickenheiser	WSH	27	1	8	9	1	20	0	0	0	0	44	2.3
D	5	Rod Langway	WSH	58	0	8	8	7	39	0	0	0	0	46	.0
R	11	*Tim Bergland	WSH	32	2	5	7	2	31	0	0	0	0	20	10.0
D	15	Neil Sheehy	WSH	59	1	5	6	8	291	0	0	0	0	32	3.1
D	29	Scot Kleinendorst	WSH	15	1	3	4	4	16	0	0	0	0	13	7.7
D	36	*Kent Paynter	WSH	13	1	2	3	7−	18	0	0	0	0	15	6.7
C	34	*Mike Richard	WSH	3	0	2	2	0	2	0	0	0	0	5	.0
C	39	Alfie Turcotte	WSH	4	0	2	2	0	0	0	0	0	0	4	.0
R	25	*Robin Bawa	WSH	5	1	0	1	3−	6	0	0	0	0	1	100.0
D	28	*Chris Felix	WSH	6	1	0	1	6−	2	1	0	0	0	3	33.3
D	37	*Brian Tutt	WSH	7	1	0	1	4−	2	0	0	0	0	5	20.0
G	35	*Jim Hrivnak	WSH	11	0	1	1	0	0	0	0	0	0	0	.0
G	33	Don Beaupre	WSH	48	0	1	1	0	24	0	0	0	0	0	.0
C	39	*Tyler Larter	WSH	1	0	0	0	1−	0	0	0	0	0	2	.0
D	39	Alain Cote	WSH	2	0	0	0	2−	7	0	0	0	0	2	.0
D	40	*Mark Ferner	WSH	2	0	0	0	1−	0	0	0	0	0	2	.0
G	35	*Olaf Kolzig	WSH	2	0	0	0	0	0	0	0	0	0	0	.0
D	36	*Jim Mathieson	WSH	2	0	0	0	0	4	0	0	0	0	0	.0
D	38	*Dennis Smith	WSH	4	0	0	0	0	0	0	0	0	0	0	.0
L	26	*Steve Maltais	WSH	8	0	0	0	2−	2	0	0	0	0	11	.0
G	31	Bob Mason	WSH	16	0	0	0	0	4	0	0	0	0	0	.0
G	1	Mike Liut	HFD	29	0	0	0	0	0	0	0	0	0	0	.0
			WSH	8	0	0	0	0	0	0	0	0	0	0	.0
			TOTAL	37	0	0	0	0	0	0	0	0	0	0	.0

Goaltending

No.	Goaltender	GPI	Mins	Avg	W	L	T	EN	SO	GA	SA	S%
1	Mike Liut	8	478	2.13	4	4	0	3	1	17	217	.922
33	Don Beaupre	48	2793	3.22	23	18	5	3	2	150	1362	.890
31	Bob Mason	16	822	3.50	4	9	1	4	0	48	389	.877
35	*Jim Hrivnak	11	609	3.55	5	5	0	2	0	36	293	.877
35	*Olaf Kolzig	2	120	6.00	0	2	0	0	0	12	63	.810
	Totals	**80**	**4837**	**3.41**	**36**	**38**	**6**	**12**	**3**	**275**	**2324**	**.882**

Playoffs

Pos	#	Player	Team	GP	G	A	Pts	+/−	PIM	PP	SH	GW	OT	S	%
R	19	John Druce	WSH	15	14	3	17	2−	23	8	1	4	1	44	31.8
L	14	Geoff Courtnall	WSH	15	4	9	13	3−	32	1	0	2	0	49	8.2
C	32	Dale Hunter	WSH	15	4	8	12	1−	61	1	0	0	0	13	30.8
R	22	Dino Ciccarelli	WSH	8	8	3	11	0	6	1	0	1	1	28	28.6
D	3	Scott Stevens	WSH	15	2	7	9	1−	25	1	0	0	0	35	5.7
L	10	Kelly Miller	WSH	15	3	5	8	3	23	0	1	0	0	26	11.5
C	12	John Tucker	WSH	12	1	7	8	4	0	0	0	0	0	12	8.3
D	4	Kevin Hatcher	WSH	11	0	8	8	4	32	0	0	0	0	37	.0
C	17	Mike Ridley	WSH	14	3	4	7	0	8	0	1	0	0	16	18.8
D	6	Calle Johansson	WSH	15	1	6	7	2	4	0	0	0	0	17	5.9
D	8	Bob Rouse	WSH	15	2	3	5	4−	47	1	0	0	0	18	11.1
D	5	Rod Langway	WSH	15	1	4	5	0	12	0	0	1	1	17	5.9
R	21	Stephen Leach	WSH	14	2	2	4	4	8	0	0	0	0	22	9.1
L	27	Bob Joyce	WSH	14	2	1	3	0	9	0	0	0	0	26	7.7
R	11	*Tim Bergland	WSH	15	1	1	2	1−	10	0	0	0	0	17	5.9
C	20	Michal Pivonka	WSH	11	0	2	2	1	6	0	0	0	0	16	.0
L	9	*Nick Kypreos	WSH	7	1	0	1	1−	15	0	0	0	0	10	10.0
D	15	Neil Sheehy	WSH	13	0	1	1	4	92	0	0	0	0	3	.0
L	26	*Steve Maltais	WSH	1	0	0	0	1−	0	0	0	0	0	0	.0
D	29	Scot Kleinendorst	WSH	3	0	0	0	3−	0	0	0	0	0	3	.0
D	34	*Kent Paynter	WSH	3	0	0	0	1−	10	0	0	0	0	2	.0
G	33	Don Beaupre	WSH	8	0	0	0	0	2	0	0	0	0	0	.0
G	1	Mike Liut	WSH	9	0	0	0	0	0	0	0	0	0	0	.0
C	23	*Rob Murray	WSH	9	0	0	0	1−	18	0	0	0	0	4	.0
R	16	*Alan May	WSH	15	0	0	0	1−	37	0	0	0	0	7	.0

Goaltending

No.	Goaltender	GPI	Mins	Avg	W	L	EN	SO	GA	SA	S%
33	Don Beaupre	8	401	2.69	4	3	1	0	18	187	.904
1	Mike Liut	9	507	3.31	4	4	1	0	28	223	.874
	Totals	15	913	3.15	8	7	2	0	48	410	.883

Club Records

Team

(Figures in brackets for season records are games played; records for fewest points, wins, ties, losses, goals, goals against are for 70 or more games)

Most Points	107	1985-86 (80)
Most Wins	50	1985-86 (80)
Most Ties	18	1980-81 (80)
Most Losses	..........*67	1974-75 (80)
Most Goals	322	1984-85 (80)
Most Goals Against	....*446	1974-75 (80)
Fewest Points	..........*21	1974-75 (80)
Fewest Wins	............*8	1974-75 (80)
Fewest Ties	5	1974-75 (80)
		1983-84 (80)
Fewest Losses	23	1985-86 (80)
Fewest Goals	181	1974-75 (80)
Fewest Goals Against	...226	1983-84 (80)

Longest Winning Streak
Over-all ....10 Jan. 27-
Feb. 18/84
Home ....8 Feb. 1-
Mar. 11/86
Mar. 3-
April 1/89
Away ....6 Feb. 26-
Apr. 1/84

Longest Undefeated Streak
Over-all ....14 Nov. 24-
Dec. 23/82
(9 wins, 5 ties)
Home ....12 Nov. 7/82-
Dec. 14/82
(9 wins, 3 ties)
Away ....10 Nov. 24/82-
Jan. 8/83
(6 wins, 4 ties)

Longest Losing Streak
Over-all ....*17 Feb. 18-
Mar. 26/75
Home ....*11 Feb. 18-
Mar. 30/75
Away ....*37 Oct. 9/74-
Mar. 26/75

Longest Winless Streak
Over-all ....25 Nov. 29/75-
Jan. 21/76
(22 losses, 3 ties)
Home ....14 Dec. 3/75-
Jan. 21/76
(11 losses, 3 ties)

Away ....*37 Oct. 9/74-
Mar. 26/75
(37 losses)
Most Shutouts, Season 8 1983-84 (80)
Most PIM, Season 2,204 1989-90 (80)
Most Goals, Game ....11 Dec. 11/81
(Tor. 2 at Wash. 11)

Individual

Most Seasons ....10 Mike Gartner
Most Games ....756 Mike Gartner
Most Goals, Career .....397 Mike Gartner
Most Assists, Career .....392 Mike Gartner
Most Points, Career .....789 Mike Gartner
(397 goals, 392 assists)
Most PIM, Career ......1,630 Scott Stevens
Most Shutouts, Career ......8 Al Jensen
Longest Consecutive
Games Streak ....422 Bob Carpenter
Most Goals, Season ....60 Dennis Maruk
(1981-82)
Most Assists, Season .....76 Dennis Maruk
(1981-82)
Most Points, Season .....136 Dennis Maruk
(1981-82)
(60 goals, 76 assists)
Most PIM, Season ....339 Alan May
(1989-90)
Most Points, Defenseman,
Season ....81 Larry Murphy
(1986-87)
(23 goals, 58 assists)
Most Points, Center,
Season ....136 Dennis Maruk
(1981-82)
(60 goals, 76 assists)
Most Points, Right Wing,
Season ....102 Mike Gartner
(1984-85)
(50 goals, 52 assists)
Most Points, Left Wing,
Season ....87 Ryan Walter
(1981-82)
(38 goals, 49 assists)

Most Points, Rookie,
Season ....67 Bobby Carpenter
(1981-82)
(32 goals, 35 assists)
Chris Valentine
(1981-82)
(30 goals, 37 assists)
Most Shutouts, Season .....4 Al Jensen, Pat Riggin
(1983-84)
Clint Malarchuk
(1987-88)
Pete Peeters
(1988-89)
Most Goals, Game ....5 Bengt Gustafsson
(Jan. 8/84)
Most Assists, Game ....6 Mike Ridley
(Jan. 7/89)
Most Points, Game ....7 Dino Ciccarelli
(Mar. 18/89)

* NHL Record.

All-time Record vs. Other Clubs

Regular Season

			At Home							On Road							Total				
	GP	W	L	T	GF	GA	PTS	GP	W	L	T	GF	GA	PTS	GP	W	L	T	GF	GA	PTS
Boston	29	7	15	7	86	114	21	30	8	19	3	81	125	19	59	15	34	10	167	239	40
Buffalo	29	4	19	6	78	126	14	30	5	22	3	82	134	13	59	9	41	9	160	260	27
Calgary	28	12	12	4	106	106	28	27	5	19	3	62	115	13	55	17	31	7	168	221	41
Chicago	28	17	8	3	112	87	37	27	6	16	5	83	115	17	55	23	24	8	195	202	54
Detroit	34	18	12	4	131	101	40	33	9	14	10	98	125	28	67	27	26	14	229	226	68
Edmonton	18	9	8	1	78	71	19	17	5	8	4	61	74	14	35	14	16	5	139	145	33
Hartford	17	11	5	1	64	47	23	18	10	6	2	76	59	22	35	21	11	3	140	106	45
Los Angeles	33	13	15	5	139	124	31	34	10	21	3	100	142	23	67	23	36	8	239	266	54
Minnesota	27	12	9	6	90	83	30	28	8	12	8	83	107	24	55	20	21	14	173	190	54
Montreal	34	12	16	6	88	122	30	33	4	24	5	67	163	13	67	16	40	11	155	285	43
New Jersey	43	32	8	3	202	128	67	44	22	16	6	143	140	50	87	54	24	9	345	268	117
NY Islanders	46	17	22	7	142	161	41	46	11	34	1	133	207	23	92	28	56	8	275	368	64
NY Rangers	46	23	15	8	186	155	54	46	17	24	5	166	202	39	92	40	39	13	352	357	93
Philadelphia	46	17	22	7	162	172	41	46	14	28	4	124	185	32	92	31	50	11	286	357	73
Pittsburgh	52	28	21	3	231	194	59	52	21	25	6	179	219	48	104	49	46	9	410	413	107
Quebec	18	8	8	2	76	67	18	17	7	6	4	64	57	18	35	15	14	6	140	124	36
St. Louis	28	14	11	3	101	88	31	27	8	12	7	82	112	23	55	22	23	10	183	200	54
Toronto	29	17	10	2	113	82	36	30	9	17	4	107	143	22	59	26	27	6	220	225	58
Vancouver	28	15	11	2	90	88	32	27	11	12	4	91	95	26	55	26	23	6	181	183	58
Winnipeg	17	12	4	1	84	53	25	18	5	8	5	67	67	15	35	17	12	6	151	120	40
Defunct Club	10	2	8	0	28	42	4	10	4	5	1	30	39	9	20	6	13	1	58	81	13
Totals	**640**	**300**	**259**	**81**	**2387**	**2211**	**681**	**640**	**199**	**348**	**93**	**1979**	**2625**	**491**	**1280**	**499**	**607**	**174**	**4366**	**4836**	**1172**

Playoffs

	Series	W	L	GP	W	L	T	GF	GA	Last Mtg.	Round	Result
Boston	1	0	1	4	0	4	0	6	15	1990	CF	L 0-4
New Jersey	2	1	1	13	7	6	0	44	43	1990	DSF	W 4-2
NY Islanders	5	1	4	24	10	14	0	66	76	1987	DSF	L 3-4
NY Rangers	2	1	1	11	6	5	0	47	35	1990	DF	W 4-1
Philadelphia	3	2	1	16	9	7	0	65	55	1989	DSF	L 2-4
Totals	**13**	**5**	**8**	**68**	**32**	**36**	**0**	**228**	**224**			

Playoff Results 1990-86

Year	Round	Opponent	Result	GF	GA
1990	CF	Boston	L 0-4	6	15
	DF	NY Rangers	W 4-1	22	15
	DSF	New Jersey	W 4-2	21	18
1989	DSF	Philadelphia	L 2-4	19	25
1988	DF	New Jersey	L 3-4	23	25
	DSF	Philadelphia	W 4-3	31	25
1987	DSF	NY Islanders	L 3-4	19	19
1986	DF	NY Rangers	L 2-4	25	20
	DSF	NY Islanders	W 3-0	11	4

Abbreviations: Round: F Final; **CF** conference final; **DF** division final; **DSF** division semi-final; **GA** goals against; **GF** goals for.

1989-90 Results

		Home				Away	
Oct.	6	Philadelphia	5-3	Oct.	11	Hartford	1-4
	7	Chicago	2-3		16	Montreal	4-3
	13	NY Rangers	7-4		21	Toronto	4-8
	14	Calgary	4-4		23	Calgary	3-3
	20	NY Islanders	3-5		25	Winnipeg	4-6
	31	St Louis	1-1		28	St Louis	0-1
Nov.	3	Toronto	2-1		29	Chicago	0-1
	10	Boston	3-5	Nov.	5	Quebec*	3-0
	11	Edmonton	3-5		7	NY Islanders	5-3
	22	NY Islanders	5-3		14	Vancouver	4-4
	24	Pittsburgh	4-7		18	Los Angeles	3-5
Dec.	1	Philadelphia	2-3		25	Pittsburgh	4-1
	15	NY Islanders	3-5		29	Detroit	5-3
	23	NY Rangers	3-2	Dec.	2	New Jersey	5-3
	26	Pittsburgh	6-3		5	Philadelphia	4-3
	29	Detroit	2-1		6	Pittsburgh	3-5
Jan.	1	Los Angeles*	4-7		9	Boston*	7-3
	5	Vancouver	2-5		10	Buffalo	3-4
	12	Pittsburgh	4-6		16	Hartford	5-2
	16	New Jersey	9-6		19	Philadelphia	2-1
	23	Winnipeg	3-4		21	Pittsburgh	2-5
	26	Montreal	6-3		27	New Jersey	3-1
	28	Philadelphia*	7-2	Jan.	3	NY Rangers	1-2
Feb.	4	Edmonton*	4-5		6	Boston	3-5
	6	Quebec	12-2		8	Toronto	6-8
	9	New Jersey	3-5		10	Winnipeg	1-6
	11	Minnesota*	5-3		13	NY Islanders	2-4
	23	NY Rangers	3-6		19	Buffalo	6-3
	25	Detroit*	9-4		24	New Jersey	2-3
	27	Chicago	4-0		31	Minnesota	4-3
Mar.	2	Hartford	3-4	Feb.	2	NY Islanders	3-5
	4	New Jersey*	4-3		3	Pittsburgh	5-7
	6	Buffalo	1-1		14	Edmonton	4-3
	9	Quebec	4-3		19	Los Angeles*	2-3
	13	St Louis	1-4		28	NY Rangers	2-3
	17	Vancouver	1-3	Mar.	10	Philadelphia	4-3
	20	NY Islanders	3-0		18	Minnesota	4-3
	23	Montreal	2-4		27	New Jersey	1-4
	25	Calgary*	4-1		29	Philadelphia	2-2
	31	NY Rangers	2-1	Apr.	1	NY Rangers	3-2

* Denotes afternoon game.

General Manager

POILE, DAVID
Vice-President and General Manager, Washington Capitals.
Born in Toronto, Ont., February 14, 1949.

David Poile was named to the position of general manager of the Capitals on August 30, 1982 and quickly built the franchise into a solid Stanley Cup contender. During his inaugural campaign (1982-83), he led the Caps' to their first winning season (39-25-16) and a first-time berth in the Stanley Cup playoffs. He received *The Sporting News* "Executive of the Year" award in 1982-83 for his efforts and duplicated the feat in 1983-84 following the Capitals' 48-27-5 season. Poile, a graduate of Northeastern University with a degree in business administration, began his professional hockey management career in 1972 as an administrative assistant for the Atlanta Flames organization where he served until joining the Washington franchise. A former collegiate hockey star at Northeastern, he won MVP and scoring honors during his senior year.

Coach

MURRAY, TERRY RODNEY
Coach, Washington Capitals. Born in Shawville, Que., July 20, 1950.

With nearly 20 years of professional hockey experience, Terry Murray was named head coach of the Washington Capitals on January 15, 1990. Murray spent six seasons as an assistant coach with the Capitals. He was then named head coach of the Baltimore Skipjacks in June, 1988 where he led his club to a 64-point season in 1988-89 and was 26-17-1 during his 1989-90 tenure.

Murray was selected 88th overall by California in the 1970 Amateur Draft. He enjoyed a successful playing career with the Maine Mariners, leading that club to two Calder Cup championships in 1977-78 and 1978-79. He was awarded the Eddie Shore Trophy as the AHL's outstanding defenseman in 1978 and 1979. In addition he was an AHL First Team All-Star in 1975-76, 1977-78 and 1978-79. While serving as an assistant coach with the Capitals, they compiled a 259-165-66 record. His AHL coaching record stands at 56-63-5.

Coaching Record

Team		Games	W	L	T	%	Games	W	L	%
1988-89	Baltimore (AHL)	80	30	46	4	.400	....	....	....	....
1989-90	Baltimore (AHL)	44	26	17	1	.603	....	....	....	....
1989-90	Washington (NHL)	34	18	14	2	.559	15	8	7	.533
	NHL Totals	34	18	14	2	.559	15	8	7	.533

Entry Draft Selections 1990-76

1990
Pick
9 John Slaney
30 Rod Pasma
51 Chris Longo
72 Randy Pearce
93 Brian Sakic
94 Mark Ouimet
114 Andrei Kovalev
135 Roman Kontsek
156 Peter Bondra
159 Steve Martell
177 Ken Klee
198 Michael Boback
219 Alan Brown
240 Todd Hlushko

1989
Pick
19 Olaf Kolzig
35 Byron Dafoe
59 Jim Mathieson
61 Jason Woolley
82 Trent Klatt
145 Dave Lorentz
166 Dean Holoien
187 Victor Gervais
208 Jiri Vykoukal
229 Andri Sidorov
250 Ken House

1988
Pick
15 Reginald Savage
36 Tim Taylor
41 Wade Bartley
57 Duane Derksen
78 Rob Krauss
120 Dimitri Hristich
141 Keith Jones
144 Brad Schlegal
162 Todd Hilditch
183 Petr Pavlas
192 Mark Sorensen
204 Claudio Scremin
225 Chris Venkus
246 Ron Pascucci

1987
Pick
36 Jeff Ballantyne
57 Steve Maltais
78 Tyler Larter
99 Pat Beauchesne
120 Rich Defreitas
141 Devon Oleniuk
162 Thomas Sjogren
204 Chris Clarke
225 Milos Vanik
240 Dan Brettschneider
246 Ryan Kummu

1986
Pick
19 Jeff Greenlaw
40 Steve Seftel
60 Shawn Simpson
61 Jimmy Hrivnak
82 Erin Ginnell
103 John Purves
124 Stefan Nilsson
145 Peter Choma
166 Lee Davidson
187 Tero Toivola
208 Bobby Bobcock
229 John Schratz
250 Scott McCrory

1985
Pick
19 Yvon Corriveau
40 John Druce
61 Robert Murray
82 Bill Houlder
83 Larry Shaw
103 Claude Dumas
124 Doug Stromback
145 Jamie Nadjiwan
166 Mark Haarmann
187 Steve Hollett
208 Dallas Eakins
229 Steve Hrynewich
250 Frank DiMuzio

1984
Pick
17 Kevin Hatcher
34 Steve Leach
59 Michal Pivonka
80 Kris King
122 Vito Cramarossa
143 Timo Iijima
164 Frank Joo
185 Jim Thomson
205 Paul Cavallini
225 Mikhail Tatarinov
246 Per Schedrin

1983
Pick
75 Tim Bergland
95 Martin Bouliane
135 Dwaine Hutton
155 Marty Abrams
175 David Cowan
195 Yves Beaudoin
215 Alain Raymond
216 Anders Huss

1982
Pick
5 Scott Stevens
58 Milan Novy
89 Dean Evason
110 Ed Kastelic
152 Wally Schreiber
173 Jamie Reeves
194 Juha Nurmi
215 Wayne Prestage
236 John Holden
247 Marco Kallas

1981
Pick
3 Bob Carpenter
45 Eric Calder
68 Tony Kellin
89 Mike Siltala
91 Peter Sidorkiewicz
110 Jim McGeough
131 Risto Jalo
152 Gaetan Duchesne
173 George White
194 Chris Valentine

1980
Pick
5 Darren Veitch
47 Dan Miele
55 Torrie Robertson
89 Timo Blomqvist
110 Todd Bidner
131 Frank Perkins
152 Bruce Raboin
173 Peter Andersson
194 Tony Camazzola

1979
Pick
4 Mike Gartner
24 Errol Rausse
67 Harvie Pocza
88 Tim Tookey
109 Greg Theberge

1978
Pick
2 Ryan Walter
18 Tim Coulis
20 Paul Mulvey
23 Paul MacKinnon
38 Glen Currie
45 Jay Johnston
55 Bengt Gustafsson
71 Lou Franceschetti
88 Vince Magnan
105 Mats Hallin
122 Rick Sirois
139 Denis Pomerleau
156 Barry Heard
172 Mark Toffolo
187 Paul Hogan
189 Steve Barger
202 Rod Pacholsuk
213 Wes Jarvis
215 Ray Irwin

1977
Pick
3 Robert Picard
21 Mark Lofthouse
39 Eddy Godin
57 Nelson Burton
75 Denis Turcotte
93 Perry Schnarr
111 Rollie Bouton
127 Brent Tremblay
143 Don Micheletti
165 Archie Henderson

1976
Pick
1 Rick Green
15 Greg Carroll
37 Tom Rowe
55 Al Glendinning
73 Doug Patey
91 Jim Bedard
109 Dale Rideout
119 Allan Dumba

Club Directory

Capital Centre
Landover, Maryland 20785
Phone 301/386-7000
TWX 710/600-7017
PR FAX 301/386-7012
GM FAX 301/386-7082
ENVOY ID
  Front Office: CAPS. GM
  Public
  Relations: CAPS. PR
Capacity: 18,130

Board of Directors
Abe Pollin — Chairman	Albert Cohen	Arthur K. Mason
David P. Bindeman	J. Martin Irving	Dr. Jack Meshel
Stewart L. Bindeman	James T. Lewis	David M. Osnos
James E. Cafritz	R. Robert Linowes	Richard M. Patrick
A. James Clark		

Management
Chairman & Governor .... Abe Pollin
President & Alternate Governor .... Richard M. Patrick
Vice-President and General Manager .... David Poile
Legal Counsel and Alternate Governors .... David M. Osnos, Peter F. O'Malley
Vice-President and Comptroller .... Edmund Stelzer

Coaching Staff
Head Coach .... Terry Murray
Assistant Coach .... John Perpich
Head Coach, Baltimore (AHL) .... Rob Laird
Assistant Coach, Baltimore (AHL) .... Barry Trotz

Scouting Staff
Director of Player Personnel and Recruitment .. Jack Button
Chief U.S. Scout .... Jack Barzee
Chief Eastern Scout .... Jack Ferguson
Chief Western Scout .... Bruce Hamilton
Coordinator of Scouting .... Hugh Rogers
Scouts .... Gilles Cote, Fred Devereaux, Eje Johansson, Richard Rothermel, Bob Schmidt, Dan Sylvester, Darrell Young

Training Staff
Head Trainer .... Stan Wong
Assistant Trainer/Head Equipment Mgr. ...... Doug Shearer
Assistant Equipment Mgr. .... Craig Leydig
Strength and Conditioning Coach .... Frank Costello
Team Nutritionist .... Dr. Pat Mann

Front Office Staff
Vice-President/Marketing .... Lew Strudler
Director of Public Relations .... Lou Corletto
Assistant Director of Marketing .... Debi Angus
Director of Community Relations .... Yvon Labre
Director of Team Services .... Tod Button
Director of Promotions .... Charles Copeland
Director of Season Subscriptions .... Joanne Kowalski
Assistant Comptroller .... Aggie Ballard
Assistant Director of Public Relations ..... David Ferry
Administrative Assistant to the
  General Manager .... Pat Young
Administrative Assistant to the
  V.P./Marketing .... Karen Merewitz
Administrative Assistant to the PR Director .... Julie Hensley
Administrative Assistant to the Comptroller ... Sharon Baxter
Administrative Assistant to the Sales Dept. ... Janice Toepper
Partial Plans Administrator .... Stephanie Rhine
Corporate Sales Manager .... Kerry Gregg
Regional Sales Managers .... Jerry Murphy, Ron Potter, Paul Van
Sales Coordinator .... John Oakes
Accounting Assistants .... David Berman, Crystal Coffren, Melanie Sakacs
Secretary to the Marketing Dept. .... Kim Fagnilli
Receptionist .... Nancy Woodall
Assistant to the Hockey Dept. .... Todd Warren

Operations Staff
Director of Telescreen .... Brad Froman
Director of Television .... Ernie Fingers
Director of Production .... Bill Harpole
Manager of Production .... Mike Long

Medical Team
Team Physicians .... Dr. Stephen S. Haas, Dr. Carl C. MacCartee, Jr. Dr. Frank S. Melograna, Dr. Richard Grossman
Team Dentist .... Dr. Howard Salob
Organist .... Chris Mitchell
Public Address Announcer .... Marv Brooks
Dimensions of Rink .... 200 feet by 85 feet
Team Nickname .... Capitals
Club Colors .... Red, White and Blue
Training Camp .... Alexandria, Virginia
Radio Station .... WMAL (630 AM), WCAO (600 AM)
TV Stations .... WDCA-TV (Channel 20), Home Team Sports (Cable)

Winnipeg Jets

1989-90 Results: 37W-32L-11T 85PTS. Third, Smythe Division

Year-by-Year Record

Season	GP	Home W	L	T	Road W	L	T	Overall W	L	T	GF	GA	Pts.	Finished		Playoff Result
1989-90	80	22	13	5	15	19	6	37	32	11	298	290	85	3rd,	Smythe Div.	Lost Div. Semi-Final
1988-89	80	17	18	5	9	24	7	26	42	12	300	355	64	5th,	Smythe Div.	Out of Playoffs
1987-88	80	20	14	6	13	22	5	33	36	11	292	310	77	3rd,	Smythe Div.	Lost Div. Semi-Final
1986-87	80	25	12	3	15	20	5	40	32	8	279	271	88	3rd,	Smythe Div.	Lost Div. Final
1985-86	80	18	19	3	8	28	4	26	47	7	295	372	59	3rd,	Smythe Div.	Lost Div. Semi-Final
1984-85	80	21	13	6	22	14	4	43	27	10	358	332	96	2nd,	Smythe Div.	Lost Div. Final
1983-84	80	17	15	8	14	23	3	31	38	11	340	374	73	4th,	Smythe Div.	Lost Div. Semi-Final
1982-83	80	22	16	2	11	23	6	33	39	8	311	333	74	4th,	Smythe Div.	Lost Div. Semi-Final
1981-82	80	18	13	9	15	20	5	33	33	14	319	332	80	2nd,	Norris Div.	Lost Div. Semi-Final
1980-81	80	7	25	8	2	32	6	9	57	14	246	400	32	6th,	Smythe Div.	Out of Playoffs
1979-80	80	13	19	8	7	30	3	20	49	11	214	314	51	5th,	Smythe Div.	Out of Playoffs

Schedule

	Home			**Away**	
Oct.	Thur.	4 Toronto	**Oct.**	Sat.	6 Edmonton
	Mon.	8 Calgary		Fri.	12 Washington
	Wed.	10 Boston		Sat.	13 Philadelphia
	Fri.	19 Vancouver		Tues.	16 NY Islanders
	Wed.	24 Edmonton		Wed.	17 NY Rangers
	Fri.	26 Los Angeles		Wed.	31 Edmonton
	Sun.	28 Los Angeles	**Nov.**	Thur.	1 Calgary
Nov.	Tues.	6 Philadelphia		Sat.	3 Vancouver
	Fri.	9 Hartford		Sun.	5 Chicago
	Wed.	14 Pittsburgh		Mon.	12 Toronto
	Fri.	16 NY Rangers		Tues.	20 St Louis
	Sun.	18 St Louis		Thur.	22 NY Islanders
	Wed.	28 Calgary		Sat.	24 Quebec
	Fri.	30 Minnesota		Sun.	25 Montreal
Dec.	Sun.	2 Vancouver	**Dec.**	Wed.	5 Los Angeles
	Mon.	3 New Jersey		Sat.	8 Los Angeles
	Sat.	15 Montreal		Tues.	11 St Louis
	Sun.	16 Philadelphia		Thur.	13 Chicago
	Sat.	22 Detroit		Tues.	18 Pittsburgh
	Fri.	28 Boston		Thur.	20 Detroit
	Mon.	31 Vancouver		Wed.	26 Minnesota
Jan.	Wed.	2 Calgary	**Jan.**	Fri.	4 Buffalo
	Fri.	11 Chicago		Sat.	5 Hartford
	Sun.	13 Calgary		Mon.	7 Boston
	Mon.	21 Minnesota		Tues.	15 Calgary
	Fri.	25 NY Islanders		Wed.	16 Vancouver
	Sun.	27 Edmonton*		Tues.	29 Quebec
Feb.	Wed.	6 Toronto		Wed.	30 Montreal
	Fri.	8 Pittsburgh	**Feb.**	Sat.	2 Washington
	Sun.	10 Buffalo*		Sun.	3 NY Rangers
	Sun.	17 Quebec*		Tues.	12 Detroit
	Wed.	20 Vancouver		Thur.	14 New Jersey
	Fri.	22 Los Angeles		Thur.	28 Los Angeles
	Sun.	24 Los Angeles*	**Mar.**	Sat.	2 Los Angeles
	Tues.	26 Hartford		Tues.	12 Calgary
Mar.	Tues.	5 Edmonton		Mon.	18 Calgary
	Fri.	8 Washington		Fri.	22 Vancouver
	Sun.	10 New Jersey*		Sat.	23 Edmonton
	Wed.	13 Buffalo		Thur.	28 Vancouver
	Fri.	15 Edmonton		Sun.	31 Edmonton

* Denotes afternoon game.

Home Starting Times:
Weeknights	7:35 p.m.
Saturdays & Sundays	7:05 p.m.
Matinees	2:35 p.m.
Except Dec 31	4:05 p.m.
Jan. 27	1:05 p.m.

Franchise date: June 22, 1979

12th NHL Season

Fredrik Olausson led all Jets' defensemen with 55 points in 1989-90.

1990-91 Player Personnel

FORWARDS	HT	WT	S	Place of Birth	Date	1989-90 Club
ARNIEL, Scott	6-1	188	L	Kingston, Ont.	7/17/62	Buffalo
ASHTON, Brent	6-1	210	L	Saskatoon, Sask.	5/18/60	Winnipeg
BARNES, Stu	5-10	175	R	Edmonton, Alta.	12/25/70	Tri-Cities
BERNARD, Larry	6-2	195	L	Crookston, MN	4/16/67	Moncton
BORSATO, Luciano	5-10	165	R	Richmond Hill, Ont.	1/7/66	Moncton
BOSCHMAN, Laurie	6-0	185	L	Major, Sask.	6/4/60	Winnipeg
CIRONE, Jason	5-9	184	L	Toronto, Ont.	2/21/71	Cornwall
COLE, Danton	5-11	189	C	Lansing, MI	1/10/67	Moncton-Winnipeg
DRAPER, Kris	5-11	188	L	Toronto, Ont.	5/24/71	Cdn. National
ELYNUIK, Pat	6-0	185	L	Foam Lake, Sask.	10/30/67	Winnipeg
ERIKSSON, Bryan	5-9	175	R	Roseau, MN	7/3/60	Moncton
EVANS, Doug	5-9	185	L	Peterborough, Ont.	6/2/63	St. Louis-Winnipeg
FENTON, Paul	5-11	180	L	Springfield, MA	12/22/64	Los Angeles-Winnipeg
HANKINSON, Peter	5-9	175	R	Edina, MN	11/24/67	U. of Minnesota
HUGHES, Brent	5-11	190	L	New Westmin'r, B.C.	4/5/66	Moncton-Winnipeg
HUNT, Brian	6-1	184	L	Toronto, Ont.	2/12/69	Moncton
JOSEPH, Tony	6-4	203	R	Cornwall, Ont.	3/1/69	Moncton
KUMPEL, Mark	6-0	190	R	Wakefield, MA	3/7/61	Winnipeg
LAROSE, Guy	5-10	175	L	Hull, Que.	7/31/67	Moncton
LEVINS, Scott	6-3	200	R	Portland, OR	1/30/70	Tri-City
MacDERMID, Paul	6-1	205	R	Chesley, Ont.	4/14/63	Hartford-Winnipeg
MARTIN, Craig	6-2	219	R	Amherst, N.S.	1/21/71	Hull
McLLWAIN, Dave	6-0	190	L	Seaforth, Ont.	1/9/67	Winnipeg
OTTENBREIT, Grant	6-2	210	L	Weyburn, Sask.	11/26/66	Erie
PARKER, Jeff	6-3	194	L	St. Paul, MN	9/7/64	Buffalo
PASLAWSKI, Greg	5-11	190	R	Kindersley, Sask.	8/25/61	Winnipeg
PELTOLA, Pekka	6-2	196	R	Helsinki, Finland	6/24/65	HPK (Finland)
SCHNEIDER, Scott	6-1	180	R	Rochester, MN	5/18/65	Winnipeg
SMAIL, Doug	5-9	175	L	Moose Jaw, Sask.	9/2/57	Winnipeg
STEEN, Thomas	5-10	195	L	Tockmark, Sweden	6/8/60	Winnipeg
SYKES, Phil	6-0	175	L	Dawson Creek, B.C.	3/18/59	Winnipeg
WHEELDON, Simon	5-11	180	L	Vancouver, B.C.	8/30/66	Flint

DEFENSEMEN						
BATEMAN, Rob	6-0	175	R	LaSalle, Que.	1/2/68	U. of Vermont
CARLYLE, Randy	5-10	200	L	Sudbury, Ont.	4/19/56	Winnipeg
CRONIN, Shawn	6-2	210	R	Flushing, MI	8/20/63	Winnipeg
DONNELLY, Gord	6-1	202	R	Montreal, Que.	2/2/62	Winnipeg
EAKINS, Dallas	6-2	195	L	Dade City, FL	2/27/67	Moncton
ELLETT, Dave	6-1	200	L	Cleveland, OH	3/30/64	Winnipeg
FLICHEL, Todd	6-3	195	R	Osgoode, Ont.	9/14/64	Moncton-Winnipeg
GALLOWAY, Kyle	5-11	170	L	Winnipeg, Man.	11/10/69	U. of Manitoba
HERVEY, Matt	5-11	205	R	Whittier CA	5/16/66	Moncton
HOUSLEY, Phil	5-10	179	L	St. Paul, MN	3/9/64	Buffalo
MANTHA, Moe	6-2	210	R	Lakewood, OH	1/21/61	Winnipeg
MARCHMENT, Bryan	6-1	198	L	Scarborough, Ont.	5/1/69	Moncton-Winnipeg
MARTILLA, Jukka	6-0	185	L	Tampere, Finland	4/15/60	Tappara (Fin.)
McLENNAN, Don	6-3	210	L	Winnipeg, Man.	10/4/68	U. of Denver
NORTON, Chris	6-2	200	R	Oakville, Ont.	3/11/65	Moncton
NUMMINEN, Teppo	6-1	190	R	Tampere, Finland	7/3/68	Winnipeg
OLAUSSON, Fredrik	6-2	200	R	Vaxsjo, Sweden	10/5/66	Winnipeg
RICHISON, Grant	6-2	205	L	Detroit, MI	5/5/67	Moncton
TAGLIANETTI, Peter	6-2	200	L	Framingham, MA	9/16/63	Winnipeg

GOALTENDERS	HT	WT	C	Place of Birth	Date	1989-90 Club
BEAUREGARD, Stephane	5-11	182	R	Cowansville, Que.	1/10/68	Ft. Wayne-Winnipeg
DRAPER, Tom	5-11	180	L	Outrement, Que.	11/20/66	Moncton-Winnipeg
ESSENSA, Bob	6-0	160	L	Toronto, Ont.	1/14/65	Moncton-Winnipeg
O'NEILL, Mike	5-7	160	L	Montreal, Que.	11/3/67	Tappara (Finland)
TABARACCI, Rich	5-10	185	L	Toronto, Ont.	1/2/69	Moncton-Ft. Wayne

General Managers' History

John Ferguson, 1979-80 to 1987-88; John Ferguson and Mike Smith, 1988-89; Mike Smith, 1989-90 to date.

Coaching History

Tom McVie, 1979-80; Tom McVie and Bill Sutherland, 1980-81; Tom Watt, 1981-82 to 1982-83; Tom Watt, John Ferguson and Barry Long, 1983-84; Barry Long, 1984-85; Barry Long and John Ferguson, 1985-86. Dan Maloney, 1986-87 to 1987-88; Dan Maloney and Rick Bowness 1988-89; Bob Murdoch, 1989-90 to date.

Captains' History

Lars-Erik Sjoberg, 1979-80; Morris Lukowich, 1980-81; Dave Christian, 1981-82; Dave Christian, Lucien DeBlois, 1982-83; Lucien DeBlois, 1983-84; Dale Hawerchuk, 1984-85 to 1988-89; Randy Carlyle, Dale Hawerchuk and Thomas Steen, 1989-90; Thomas Steen, 1990-91.

1989-90 Scoring

Regular Season

* rookie

Pos	#	Player	Team	GP	G	A	Pts	+/−	PIM	PP	SH	GW	GT	S	%
C	10	Dale Hawerchuk	WPG	79	26	55	81	11−	70	8	0	2	0	211	12.3
R	15	Pat Elynuik	WPG	80	32	42	74	2	83	14	0	3	1	132	24.2
C	25	Thomas Steen	WPG	53	18	48	66	2	35	5	0	3	1	129	14.0
L	7	Brent Ashton	WPG	79	22	34	56	4	37	3	0	5	0	167	13.2
D	4	Fredrik Olausson	WPG	77	9	46	55	1−	32	3	0	0	0	147	6.1
C	20	Dave McLlwain	WPG	80	25	26	51	1−	60	1	7	2	0	180	13.9
L	11	Paul Fenton	WPG	80	32	18	50	2	40	4	1	1	1	152	21.1
L	12	Doug Smail	WPG	79	25	24	49	15	63	1	1	6	0	165	15.2
R	28	Greg Paslawski	WPG	71	18	30	48	4−	14	7	0	6	2	122	14.8
D	2	Dave Ellett	WPG	77	17	29	46	15−	96	8	0	1	0	205	8.3
D	27	Teppo Numminen	WPG	79	11	32	43	4−	20	1	0	1	0	105	10.5
R	23	Paul MacDermid	HFD	29	6	12	18	1	69	3	0	2	0	37	16.2
			WPG	44	7	10	17	4	100	1	0	1	0	48	14.6
			TOTAL	73	13	22	35	5	169	4	0	3	0	85	15.3
D	22	Moe Mantha	WPG	73	2	26	28	8	28	0	1	0	0	114	1.8
C	16	Laurie Boschman	WPG	66	10	17	27	11−	103	3	1	1	0	87	11.5
L	39	Doug Evans	STL	3	0	0	0	0	0	0	0	0	0	1	.0
			WPG	27	10	8	18	7	33	2	1	1	0	36	27.8
			TOTAL	30	10	8	18	7	33	2	1	1	0	37	27.0
D	8	Randy Carlyle	WPG	53	3	15	18	8	50	2	0	0	0	92	3.3
R	21	Mark Kumpel	WPG	56	8	9	17	5−	21	0	1	1	0	74	10.8
L	17	Phil Sykes	WPG	48	9	6	15	8−	26	0	1	0	0	50	18.0
D	32	Peter Taglianetti	WPG	49	3	6	9	20	136	0	0	1	0	57	5.3
R	34	Gord Donnelly	WPG	55	3	3	6	3	222	0	0	0	0	43	7.0
D	44	*Shawn Cronin	WPG	61	0	4	4	16−	243	0	0	0	0	30	.0
L	46	Brent Hughes	WPG	11	1	2	3	4−	33	0	0	1	0	7	14.3
D	29	Brad Berry	WPG	12	1	2	3	2−	6	0	0	0	0	7	14.3
C	36	*Danton Cole	WPG	2	1	1	2	1−	0	0	0	0	0	2	50.0
D	3	*Bryan Marchment	WPG	7	0	2	2	0	28	0	0	0	0	5	.0
C	26	*Brian McReynolds	WPG	9	0	2	2	4−	4	0	0	0	0	11	.0
G	35	*Bob Essensa	WPG	36	0	2	2	0	0	0	0	0	0	0	.0
D	5	*Todd Flichel	WPG	3	0	1	1	0	2	0	0	0	0	1	.0
L	38	Brad Jones	WPG	2	0	0	0	2−	0	0	0	0	0	0	.0
G	37	*Tom Draper	WPG	6	0	0	0	0	0	0	0	0	0	0	.0
G	30	*Steph Beauregard	WPG	19	0	0	0	0	4	0	0	0	0	0	.0

Goaltending

No.	Goaltender	GPI	Mins	Avg	W	L	T	EN	SO	GA	SA	S%
35	*Bob Essensa	36	2035	3.15	18	9	5	5	1	107	988	.892
30	*Steph Beauregard	19	1079	3.28	7	8	3	4	0	59	570	.896
30	Daniel Berthiaume	24	1387	3.72	10	11	3	2	1	86	667	.871
37	*Tom Draper	6	359	4.35	2	4	0	1	0	26	153	.830
	Totals	80	4873	3.57	37	32	11	12	2	290	2378	.878

Playoffs

Pos	#	Player	Team	GP	G	A	Pts	+/−	PIM	PP	SH	GW	OT	S	%
C	10	Dale Hawerchuk	WPG	7	3	5	8	5	2	0	0	1	0	21	14.3
C	25	Thomas Steen	WPG	7	2	5	7	5−	16	1	0	0	0	20	10.0
R	15	Pat Elynuik	WPG	7	2	4	6	4−	2	0	0	0	0	11	18.2
D	22	Moe Mantha	WPG	7	1	5	6	0	2	0	0	0	0	15	6.7
L	7	Brent Ashton	WPG	7	3	1	4	1−	2	2	0	1	0	21	14.3
L	39	Doug Evans	WPG	7	2	2	4	0	10	0	0	0	0	14	14.3
R	28	Greg Paslawski	WPG	7	1	3	4	2	0	0	0	0	0	10	10.0
D	27	Teppo Numminen	WPG	7	1	2	3	1	10	0	0	0	0	10	10.0
D	2	Dave Ellett	WPG	7	2	0	2	6−	6	2	0	1	1	22	9.1
L	11	Paul Fenton	WPG	7	2	0	2	2−	23	2	0	0	0	11	18.2
R	21	Mark Kumpel	WPG	7	2	0	2	0	2	0	0	0	0	9	22.2
R	23	Paul MacDermid	WPG	7	0	2	2	2−	8	0	0	0	0	3	.0
D	4	Fredrik Olausson	WPG	7	0	2	2	5−	2	0	0	0	0	9	.0
L	12	Doug Smail	WPG	5	1	0	1	0	0	0	0	0	0	10	10.0
R	34	Gord Donnelly	WPG	6	0	1	1	3	8	0	0	0	0	4	.0
C	20	Dave McLlwain	WPG	7	0	1	1	3−	2	0	0	0	0	8	.0
D	29	Brad Berry	WPG	1	0	0	0	1−	0	0	0	0	0	1	.0
C	16	Laurie Boschman	WPG	2	0	0	0	0	2	0	0	0	0	1	.0
G	30	*Stephane Beauregard	WPG	4	0	0	0	0	0	0	0	0	0	0	.0
G	35	*Bob Essensa	WPG	4	0	0	0	0	0	0	0	0	0	0	.0
L	17	Phil Sykes	WPG	4	0	0	0	1	0	0	0	0	0	0	.0
D	44	*Shawn Cronin	WPG	7	0	0	0	2−	2	0	0	0	0	2	.0
D	32	Peter Taglianetti	WPG	5	0	0	0	4−	6	0	0	0	0	6	.0

Goaltending

No.	Goaltender	GPI	Mins	Avg	W	L	EN	SO	GA	SA	S%
30	*Stephane Beauregard	4	238	3.03	1	3	0	0	12	105	.886
35	*Bob Essensa	4	206	3.50	2	1	0	0	12	100	.880
	Totals	7	445	3.24	3	4	0	0	24	205	.883

Retired Numbers

9	Bobby Hull	1972-1980

Club Records

Team

(Figures in brackets for season records are games played; records for fewest points, wins, ties, losses, goals, goals against are for 70 or more games)

Most Points 96	1984-85 (80)	
Most Wins 43	1984-85 (80)	
Most Ties 14	1980-81 (80)	
	1981-82 (80)	
Most Losses 57	1980-81 (80)	
Most Goals 358	1984-85 (80)	
Most Goals Against 400	1980-81 (80)	
Fewest Points 32	1980-81 (80)	
Fewest Wins 9	1980-81 (80)	
Fewest Ties 7	1985-86 (80)	
Fewest Losses 27	1984-85 (80)	
Fewest Goals 214	1979-80 (80)	
Fewest Goals Against ...271	1986-87 (80)	

Longest Winning Streak
- Over-all 9   Mar. 8-27/85
- Home 7   Jan. 23-Mar. 1/87
- Away 8   Feb. 25-Apr. 6/85

Longest Undefeated Streak
- Over-all 13   Mar. 8-Apr. 7/85 (10 wins, 3 ties)
- Home 11   Dec. 23/83 Feb. 5/84 (6 wins, 5 ties)
- Away 9   Feb. 25-Apr. 7/85 (8 wins, 1 tie)

Longest Losing Streak
- Over-all 10   Nov. 30-Dec. 20/80
- Home 4   Four times
- Away 9   Dec. 26/79-Jan. 22/80

Longest Winless Streak
- Over-all ....*30   Oct. 19-Dec. 20/80 (23 losses, 7 ties)
- Home 14   Oct. 19-Dec. 14/80 (9 losses, 5 ties)
- Away 18   Oct. 10-Dec. 20/80 (16 losses, 2 ties)

Most Shutouts, Season 3	1981-82 (80)	
Most PIM, Season 2,278	1987-88 (80)	
Most Goals, Game 12	Feb. 25/85 (Wpg. 12 at NYR. 5)	

Individual

Most Seasons 10	Doug Smail	
Most Games 713	Dale Hawerchuk	
Most Goals, Career 379	Dale Hawerchuk	
Most Assists, Career 550	Dale Hawerchuk	
Most Points, Career 929	Dale Hawerchuk (379 goals, 550 assists)	
Most PIM, Career 1,338	Laurie Boschman	
Most Shutouts, Career 3	Markus Mattsson	

Longest Consecutive Games Streak 475   Dale Hawerchuk (Dec. 19/82-Dec. 10/89)

Most Goals, Season 53   Dale Hawerchuk (1984-85)

Most Assists, Season 77   Dale Hawerchuk (1984-85, 1987-88)

Most Points, Season 130   Dale Hawerchuk (1984-85) (53 goals, 77 assists)

Most PIM, Season 287   Jimmy Mann (1979-80)

Most Points, Defenseman Season 74   David Babych (1982-83) (13 goals, 61 assists)

Most Points, Center, Season 130   Dale Hawerchuk (1984-85) (53 goals, 77 assists)

Most Points, Right Wing, Season 101   Paul Maclean (1984-85) (41 goals, 60 assists)

Most Points, Left Wing, Season 92   Morris Lukowich (1981-82) (43 goals, 49 assists)

Most Points, Rookie, Season 103   Dale Hawerchuk (1981-82) (45 goals, 58 assists)

Most Shutouts, Season 2	Markus Mattsson (1979-80)	
	Doug Soetaert (1981-82)	
	Dan Bouchard (1985-86)	
	Daniel Berthiaume (1987-88)	
Most Goals, Game 5	Willy Lindstrom (Mar. 2/82)	
Most Assists, Game 5	Dale Hawerchuk (Mar. 6/84, Mar. 18/89, Mar. 4/90)	
Most Points, Game 6	Willy Lindstrom (Mar. 2/82)	
	Dale Hawerchuk (Dec. 14/83, Mar. 18/89)	
	Thomas Steen (Oct. 24/84)	

* NHL Record.

All-time Record vs. Other Clubs

Regular Season

		At Home							On Road							Total					
	GP	W	L	T	GF	GA	PTS	GP	W	L	T	GF	GA	PTS	GP	W	L	T	GF	GA	PTS
Boston	17	7	9	1	58	62	15	18	2	13	3	59	88	7	35	9	22	4	117	150	22
Buffalo	17	7	8	2	59	62	16	18	1	15	2	49	87	4	35	8	23	4	108	149	20
Calgary	37	17	14	6	156	138	40	38	7	27	4	117	191	18	75	24	41	10	273	329	58
Chicago	20	9	8	3	86	80	21	19	4	14	1	61	103	9	39	13	22	4	147	183	30
Detroit	20	7	6	7	71	64	21	19	7	9	3	79	77	17	39	14	15	10	150	141	38
Edmonton	37	12	22	3	155	191	27	38	8	28	2	124	194	18	75	20	50	5	279	385	45
Hartford	17	9	8	0	62	61	18	18	5	9	4	59	78	14	35	14	17	4	121	130	32
Los Angeles	38	19	12	7	171	139	45	37	20	12	5	162	154	45	75	39	24	12	333	293	90
Minnesota	19	9	9	1	70	69	19	20	6	12	2	61	94	14	39	15	21	3	131	163	33
Montreal	18	6	8	4	60	76	16	17	2	15	0	40	95	4	35	8	23	4	100	171	20
New Jersey	18	13	3	2	74	43	28	17	8	5	4	60	54	20	35	21	8	6	134	97	48
NY Islanders	18	5	12	1	54	75	11	17	4	8	5	55	69	13	35	9	20	6	109	144	24
NY Rangers	18	7	9	2	68	68	16	17	7	8	2	77	85	16	35	14	17	4	145	153	32
Philadelphia	17	8	8	1	62	64	17	18	3	15	0	50	91	6	35	11	23	1	112	155	23
Pittsburgh	17	7	9	1	66	65	15	18	6	12	0	56	74	12	35	13	21	1	122	139	27
Quebec	18	8	6	4	75	74	20	17	8	7	2	69	70	18	35	16	13	6	144	144	38
St. Louis	20	11	4	5	75	63	27	19	4	8	7	64	84	15	39	15	12	12	139	147	42
Toronto	19	10	7	2	92	86	22	20	14	5	1	101	77	29	39	24	12	3	193	163	51
Vancouver	37	21	10	6	153	135	48	38	11	21	6	122	152	28	75	32	31	12	275	287	76
Washington	18	8	5	5	67	67	21	17	4	12	1	53	84	9	35	12	17	6	120	151	30
Totals	**440**	**200**	**177**	**63**	**1734**	**1682**	**463**	**440**	**131**	**255**	**54**	**1518**	**2001**	**316**	**880**	**331**	**432**	**117**	**3252**	**3683**	**779**

Playoffs

	Series	W	L	GP	W	L	T	GF	GA	Last Mtg.	Round	Result
Calgary	3	2	1	13	7	6	0	45	43	1987	DSF	W 4-2
Edmonton	6	0	6	26	4	22	0	75	120	1990	DSF	L 3-4
St. Louis	1	0	1	4	1	3	0	13	20	1982	DSF	L 1-3
Totals	**10**	**2**	**8**	**43**	**12**	**31**	**0**	**133**	**183**			

Abbreviations: Round: F – Final; **CF** – conference final; **DF** – division final; **DSF** – division semi-final; **GA** – goals against; **GF** – goals for.

Playoff Results 1990-86

Year	Round	Opponent	Result	GF	GA
1990	DSF	Edmonton	L 3-4	22	24
1988	DSF	Edmonton	L 1-4	17	25
1987	DF	Edmonton	L 0-4	9	17
	DSF	Calgary	W 4-2	22	15
1986	DSF	Calgary	L 0-3	8	15

1989-90 Results

	Home				Away	
Oct.	6	NY Rangers	1-4	Oct. 10	Pittsburgh	1-5
	8	Philadelphia	5-3	12	Detroit	4-5
	20	Chicago	2-4	14	Toronto	5-1
	22	Edmonton	5-4	18	Edmonton	2-7
	25	Washington	6-4	Nov. 1	Calgary	3-5
	27	Los Angeles	1-3	3	Vancouver	3-2
	29	Los Angeles	6-1	5	Chicago	3-4
Nov.	8	Vancouver	3-2	14	Quebec	5-3
	10	Hartford	2-4	15	Montreal	1-5
	12	Calgary	3-2	18	Philadelphia*	1-0
	23	St Louis	2-5	20	NY Rangers	3-3
	25	New Jersey	1-3	21	NY Islanders	4-3
	29	NY Rangers	5-4	Dec. 6	Calgary	4-3
Dec.	1	Detroit	3-3	15	Vancouver	3-3
	2	NY Islanders	3-6	19	Los Angeles	5-9
	8	Montreal	6-6	21	Edmonton	2-3
	10	Calgary*	4-1	29	Calgary	2-1
	13	Vancouver	3-3	Jan. 3	Hartford	4-2
	26	Minnesota	5-3	4	Boston	2-4
	31	Edmonton*	3-2	6	Pittsburgh	3-5
Jan.	10	Washington	6-1	8	New Jersey	4-3
	12	Detroit	7-5	17	Edmonton	3-6
	14	St Louis	6-5	23	Washington	4-3
	16	Quebec	6-8	25	Philadelphia	6-8
	19	NY Islanders	4-6	27	St Louis	3-3
	31	Toronto	5-5	29	Minnesota	2-4
Feb.	2	Vancouver	8-1	Feb. 6	Vancouver	3-5
	4	Chicago	7-3	8	Los Angeles	5-1
	14	Boston	3-2	11	Edmonton	4-7
	16	Pittsburgh	3-3	22	New Jersey	4-2
	18	Calgary*	5-1	24	Hartford	3-1
	20	Buffalo	3-4	25	Buffalo	1-3
Mar.	2	Los Angeles	9-3	27	Minnesota	3-8
	4	Los Angeles*	5-2	Mar. 12	Calgary	4-5
	7	Quebec	6-3	15	Boston	3-3
	9	Edmonton	7-5	17	Toronto	5-4
	11	Calgary*	4-6	18	Buffalo	3-4
	21	Montreal	3-2	25	Vancouver	3-3
	23	Vancouver	2-4	27	Los Angeles	4-4
Apr.	1	Edmonton*	2-4	29	Los Angeles	1-0

^ Denotes afternoon game.

Entry Draft Selections 1990-79

1990
Pick
19	Keith Tkachuk
35	Mike Muller
74	Roman Meluzin
75	Scott Levins
77	Alexei Zhamnov
98	Craig Martin
119	Daniel Jardemyr
140	John Lilley
161	Henrik Andersson
182	Rauli Raitanen
203	Mika Alatalo
224	Sergei Selyanin
245	Keith Morris

1989
Pick
4	Stu Barnes
25	Dan Ratushny
46	Jason Cirone
62	Kris Draper
64	Mark Brownschidle
69	Allain Roy
109	Dan Bylsma
130	Pekka Peltola
131	Doug Evans
151	Jim Solly
172	Stephane Gauvin
193	Joe Larson
214	Bradley Podiak
235	Genneyna Davydov
240	Sergei Kharin

1988
Pick
10	Teemu Selanne
31	Russell Romaniuk
52	Stephane Beauregard
73	Brian Hunt
94	Anthony Joseph
101	Benoit Lebeau
115	Ronald Jones
127	Markus Akerblom
136	Jukka Marttila
157	Mark Smith
178	Mike Helber
199	Pavei Kostichkin
220	Kevin Heise
241	Kyle Galloway

1987
Pick
16	Bryan Marchment
37	Patrik Eriksson
79	Don McLennan
96	Ken Gernander
100	Darrin Amundson
121	Joe Harwell
142	Todd Hartje
163	Markku Kyllonen
184	Jim Fernholz
226	Roger Rougelot
247	Hans Goran Elo

1986
Pick
8	Pat Elynuik
29	Teppo Numminen
50	Esa Palosaari
71	Hannu Jarvenpaa
92	Craig Endean
113	Robertson Bateman
155	Frank Furlan
176	Mark Green
197	John Blue
218	Matt Cote
239	Arto Blomsten

1985
Pick
18	Ryan Stewart
39	Roger Ohman
60	Dan Berthiaume
81	Fredrik Olausson
102	John Borrell
123	Danton Cole
144	Brent Mowery
165	Tom Draper
186	Nevin Kardum
207	Dave Quigley
228	Chris Norton
249	Anssi Melametsa

1984
Pick
30	Peter Douris
68	Chris Mills
72	Sean Clement
93	Scott Schneider
114	Gary Lorden
135	Luciano Borsato
156	Brad Jones
177	Gord Whitaker
197	Rick Forst
218	Mike Warus
238	Jim Edmonds

1983
Pick
8	Andrew McBain
14	Bobby Dollas
29	Brad Berry
43	Peter Taglianetti
69	Bob Essensa
89	Harry Armstrong
109	Joel Baillargeon
129	Iain Duncan
149	Ron Pessetti
169	Todd Flichel
189	Cory Wright
209	Eric Cormier
229	Jamie Husgen

1982
Pick
12	Jim Kyte
74	Tom Martin
75	Dave Ellett
96	Tim Mishler
138	Derek Ray
159	Guy Gosselin
180	Tom Ward
201	Mike Savage
222	Bob Shaw
243	Jan Urban Ericson

1981
Pick
1	Dale Hawerchuk
22	Scott Arniel
43	Jyrki Seppa
64	Kirk McCaskill
85	Marc Behrend
106	Bob O'Connor
127	Peter Nilsson
148	Dan McFaul
169	Greg Dick
190	Vladimir Kadlec
211	Dave Kirwin

1980
Pick
2	David Babych
23	Moe Mantha
44	Murray Eaves
65	Guy Fournier
86	Glen Ostir
107	Ron Loustel
128	Brian Mullen
135	Mike Lauen
149	Sandy Beadle
170	Ed Christian
191	Dave Chartier

1979
Pick
19	Jimmy Mann
40	Dave Christian
61	Bill Whelton
82	Pat Daley
103	Thomas Steen
124	Tim Watters

Bob Murdoch won the Jack Adams Award as NHL coach of the year in 1989-90.

Coach

MURDOCH, ROBERT JOHN (BOB)
Head Coach, Winnipeg Jets. Born in Kirkland Lake, Ont., November 20, 1946.

Murdoch joined the Jets on May 25, 1989 after eight years in the Calgary Flames organization, including three as a player and five as an assistant coach. A former NHL defenseman, Murdoch began his head coaching career with the Chicago Blackhawks in 1987-88.

An alumnus of the University of Waterloo in Ontario, Murdoch opened his 12-year NHL playing career with the 1970-71 Stanley Cup champion Montreal Canadiens. After earning another championship ring in 1972-73, he was dealt by Montreal to the Los Angeles Kings, with whom he played until 1978-79, when the Flames acquired his services. At the conclusion of his playing days, Murdoch had registered scoring totals of 60-218-278 in 757 games.

Bob Murdoch led the Winnipeg Jets to an 85-point season and a 21-point single-season improvement in 1989-90, earning him the Jack Adams Award as NHL coach of the year.

Coaching Record

			Regular Season					Playoffs			
Season	Team	Games	W	L	T	%	Games	W	L	%
1987-88	Chicago (NHL)	80	30	41	9	.431	5	1	4	.200
1989-90	Winnipeg (NHL)	80	37	32	11	.531	7	3	4	.429
	NHL Totals	160	67	73	20	.481	12	4	8	.333

Club Directory

Winnipeg Arena
15-1430 Maroons Road
Winnipeg, Manitoba R3G 0L5
Phone **204/783-5387**
Mktg, PR FAX 204/788-4668
ENVOY ID
General
Manager: JETS. GM
Public
Relations: JETS. PR
Marketing: JETS. MAR
Capacity: 15,393

Board of Directors

Barry L. Shenkarow	Marvin Shenkarow	Harvey Secter
Jerry Kruk	Don Binda	Bill Davis
Bob Chapman	Steve Bannatyne	

President & Governor .... Barry L. Shenkarow
Alternate Governors.......................... Michael Smith, Bill Davis

Hockey Operations

Vice-President & General Manager .... Michael Smith
Assistant General Manager/Director of Hockey
Operations .... Dennis McDonald
Coach.................................... Bob Murdoch
Assistant Coaches .... Clare Drake, Terry Simpson
GM/Head Coach, Moncton (AHL)............. Dave Farrish
Assistant Coach, Moncton (AHL) .... TBA
Director of Scouting .... Bill Lesuk
Assistant Director of Scouting .... Joe Yannetti
Scouts .... Connie Broden, Mike Antonovitch, Paul Henry, Tom Savage
Executive Ass't. to Vice-President & G.M. ..... Pat MacDonald
Administrative Ass't - Hockey Operations....... Loris Enns

Finance and Administration

Director of Finance & Administration .... Don Binda
Director of Team Services .... Murray Harding
Controller .... Glenda Leiske
Ticket Manager............................ Dianne Gabbs
Accounting/Ticketing Assistants .... Trish Benson
Accounting Assistants .... Bryan Braun, Allan Kinnaird
Administrative Assistant/Team Services/
Communications .... Heather Reynolds
Administrative Assistant/Novelty Operations .... Lynda Sweetland
Receptionist .... Sherry Larson
Jets' All Sports Store Manager .... Sherri Wilson

Public Relations

Director of Communications .... Mike O'Hearn
Director of Community Relations .... Lori Summers
Statistician/Communications Assistant .... Bruce Barton
Administrative Ass't., Community Relations .... Anne-Marie Blake
Administrative Ass't., Goals for Kids .... Lisa Winslow
Communications Assistant.................. Bryn Griffiths

Marketing

Vice-President of Marketing.................. Madeline Hanson
Director of Sales........................... Val Overwater
Marketing Assistant .... Val Kuhn
Senior Account Executive .... Gord Dmytriw
Merchandising Manager..................... Chris Newman
Administrative Assistant/Sales .... Debbie Mavins
Account Executive .... Hartley Miller

Dressing Room

Athletic Therapists .... Jim Ramsay, Phil Walker
Equipment Manager .... Craig Heisinger
Assistant Equipment Manager .... Stan Wilson
Team Physician .... Dr. Wayne Hildahl
Team Dentist............................. Dr. Gene Solmundson
Team Colors .... Blue, Red and White
Training Camp .... Saskatoon, Sask. and Winnipeg
Press Box Location .... East Side
TV Channel .... CKY-TV
Radio Station .... CKY AM 580
Play-by-Play............................. Curt Keilback (TV and Radio)
Color Commentary .... Bryn Griffiths (Radio)
Gary Green (TV)

General Manager

MIKE SMITH
General Manager, Winnipeg Jets. Born on August 31, 1945 in Potsdam, New York.

Mike Smith was appointed general manager of the club on December 3, 1988 after ten years of service within the Jets organization. He had held the position of assistant general manager and director of scouting since 1984.

Smith began his NHL career in 1976-77 when he was an assistant coach with the New York Rangers under John Ferguson. After two seasons in New York, he assumed the same coaching duties with the Colorado Rockies. When the Jets entered the League in 1979-80, Smith was hired as general manager of their CHL franchise in Tulsa. In 1980-81, midway through the season, Smith was asked to come to Winnipeg to be head coach. In 1981-82 he became the team's director of recruiting.

1989-90 Final Statistics

Standings

Abbreviations: GA – goals against; **GF** – goals for; **GP** – games played; **L** – losses; **PTS** – points; **T** – ties; **W** – wins; **%** – percentage of games won.

CLARENCE CAMPBELL CONFERENCE

Norris Division

	GP	W	L	T	GF	GA	PTS	%
Chicago	80	41	33	6	316	294	88	.550
St. Louis	80	37	34	9	295	279	83	.519
Toronto	80	38	38	4	337	358	80	.500
Minnesota	80	36	40	4	284	291	76	.475
Detroit	80	28	38	14	288	323	70	.438

Smythe Division

	GP	W	L	T	GF	GA	PTS	%
Calgary	80	42	23	15	348	265	99	.619
Edmonton	80	38	28	14	315	283	90	.563
Winnipeg	80	37	32	11	298	290	85	.531
Los Angeles	80	34	39	7	338	337	75	.469
Vancouver	80	25	41	14	245	306	64	.400

PRINCE OF WALES CONFERENCE

Adams Division

	GP	W	L	T	GF	GA	PTS	%
Boston	80	46	25	9	289	232	101	.631
Buffalo	80	45	27	8	286	248	98	.613
Montreal	80	41	28	11	288	234	93	.581
Hartford	80	38	33	9	275	268	85	.531
Quebec	80	12	61	7	240	407	31	.194

Patrick Division

	GP	W	L	T	GF	GA	PTS	%
NY Rangers	80	36	31	13	279	267	85	.531
New Jersey	80	37	34	9	295	288	83	.519
Washington	80	36	38	6	284	275	78	.488
NY Islanders	80	31	38	11	281	288	73	.456
Pittsburgh	80	32	40	8	318	359	72	.450
Philadelphia	80	30	39	11	290	297	71	.444

Steve Yzerman's 62 goals in 1989-90 made him the only player to score 60 or more goals in each of the past two seasons.

INDIVIDUAL LEADERS

Goal Scoring

Player	Team	GP	G
Brett Hull	St. L.	80	72
Steve Yzerman	Det.	79	62
Cam Neely	Bos.	76	55
Brian Bellows	Min.	80	55
Pat LaFontaine	NYI	74	54
Luc Robitaille	L.A.	80	52
Stephane Richer	Mtl.	75	51
Gary Leeman	Tor.	80	51

Assists

Player	Team	GP	A
Wayne Gretzky	L.A.	73	102
Mark Messier	Edm.	79	84
Adam Oates	St. L.	80	79
Mario Lemieux	Pit.	59	78
Paul Coffey	Pit.	80	74
Bernie Nicholls	L.A.–NYR	79	73

Power-Play Goals

Player	Team	GP	PP
Brett Hull	St. L.	80	27
Cam Neely	Bos.	76	25
Mike Gartner	Min.–NYR	79	21
Brian Bellows	Min.	80	21
Luc Robitaille	L.A.	80	20

Short-Hand Goals

Player	Team	GP	SH
Steve Yzerman	Det.	79	7
Dave McLlwain	Wpg.	80	7
Mark Messier	Edm.	79	6
Craig MacTavish	Edm.	80	6
Dan Daoust	Tor.	65	4
Dave Reid	Tor.	70	4
Wayne Gretzky	L.A.	73	4
Mike Gartner	Min.–NYR	79	4
Esa Tikkanen	Edm.	79	4

Game-Winning Goals

Player	Team	GP	GW
Cam Neely	Bos.	76	12
Brett Hull	St. L.	80	12
John MacLean	N.J.	80	11
Pierre Turgeon	Buf.	80	10
Brian Bellows	Min.	80	9

Game-Tying Goals

Player	Team	GP	GT
Theo Fleury	Cgy.	80	3

Fourteen players with two each.

Shots

Player	Team	GP	S
Brett Hull	St. L.	80	385
Steve Yzerman	Det.	79	332
Paul Coffey	Pit.	80	324
John MacLean	N.J.	80	322
Ray Bourque	Bos.	76	310
Geoff Courtnall	Wsh.	80	307
Al MacInnis	Cgy.	79	304
Brian Bellows	Min.	80	300

First Goals

Player	Team	GP	FG
Cam Neely	Bos.	76	12
Mark Messier	Edm.	79	12
Dave Andreychuk	Buf.	73	10
Dave Gagner	Min.	79	9

Eight players with eight each.

Shooting Percentage
(minimum 80 shots)

Player	Team	GP	G	S	%
Luc Robitaille	L.A.	80	52	210	24.8
Pat Elynuik	Wpg.	80	32	132	24.2
Mike Ridley	Wsh.	74	30	124	24.2
Paul MacLean	St. L.	78	34	141	24.1
Craig Janney	Bos.	55	24	105	22.9

Plus/Minus

Player	Team	GP	+/–
Paul Cavallini	St. L.	80	38
Stephane Richer	Mtl.	75	35
Jamie Macoun	Cgy.	78	34
Shayne Corson	Mtl.	76	33
*Sergei Makarov	Cgy.	80	33
Joe Nieuwendyk	Cgy.	79	32
Ray Bourque	Bos.	76	31
Gary Roberts	Cgy.	78	31

Individual Leaders

Abbreviations: * – rookie eligible for Calder Trophy; **A** – assists; **G** – goals; **GP** – games played; **GT** – game-tying goals; **GW** – game-winning goals; **PIM** – penalties in minutes; **PP** – power play goals; **Pts** – points; **S** – shots on goal; **SH** – short-handed goals; **%** – percentage of shots resulting in goals; +/– – difference between Goals For (**GF**) scored when a player is on the ice with his team at even strength or short-handed and Goals Against (**GA**) scored when the same player is on the ice with his team at even strength or on a power play.

Individual Scoring Leaders for Art Ross Trophy

Player	Team	GP	G	A	Pts	+/–	PIM	PP	SH	GW	GT	S	%
Wayne Gretzky	Los Angeles	73	40	102	142	8	42	10	4	4	1	236	16.9
Mark Messier	Edmonton	79	45	84	129	19	79	13	6	3	2	211	21.3
Steve Yzerman	Detroit	79	62	65	127	6–	79	16	7	8	2	332	18.7
Mario Lemieux	Pittsburgh	59	45	78	123	18–	78	14	3	4	1	226	19.9
Brett Hull	St. Louis	80	72	41	113	1–	24	27	0	12	0	385	18.7
Bernie Nicholls	L.A.–Rangers	79	39	73	112	9–	86	15	0	1	0	287	13.6
Pierre Turgeon	Buffalo	80	40	66	106	10	29	17	1	10	1	193	20.7
Pat LaFontaine	NY Islanders	74	54	51	105	13–	38	13	2	8	1	286	18.9
Paul Coffey	Pittsburgh	80	29	74	103	25–	95	10	0	3	1	324	9.0
Joe Sakic	Quebec	80	39	63	102	40–	27	8	1	2	1	234	16.7
Adam Oates	St. Louis	80	23	79	102	9	30	6	2	3	1	168	13.7
Luc Robitaille	Los Angeles	80	52	49	101	8	38	20	0	7	0	210	24.8
Ron Francis	Hartford	80	32	69	101	13	73	15	1	5	1	170	18.8
Brian Bellows	Minnesota	80	55	44	99	3–	72	21	1	9	0	300	18.3
Rick Tocchet	Philadelphia	75	37	59	96	4	196	15	1	0	0	269	13.8
Gary Leeman	Toronto	80	51	44	95	4	63	14	1	5	0	256	19.9
Joe Nieuwendyk	Calgary	79	45	50	95	32	40	18	0	3	0	226	19.9
Vince Damphousse	Toronto	80	33	61	94	2	56	9	0	5	1	229	14.4
Jari Kurri	Edmonton	78	33	60	93	18	48	10	2	2	1	201	16.4
Cam Neely	Boston	76	55	37	92	10	117	25	0	12	0	271	20.3
John Cullen	Pittsburgh	72	32	60	92	13–	138	6	0	4	0	197	16.2
Stephane Richer	Montreal	75	51	40	91	35	46	9	0	8	0	269	19.0
Doug Gilmour	Calgary	78	24	67	91	20	54	12	1	3	1	152	15.8
Steve Larmer	Chicago	80	31	59	90	25	40	8	2	4	0	265	11.7
Al MacInnis	Calgary	79	28	62	90	20	82	14	1	3	0	304	9.2
Pat Verbeek	Hartford	80	44	45	89	1	228	14	0	5	1	219	20.1

Defensemen Scoring Leaders

Player	Team	GP	G	A	Pts	+/–	PIM	PP	SH	GW	GT	S	%
Paul Coffey	Pittsburgh	80	29	74	103	25–	95	10	0	3	1	324	9.0
Al MacInnis	Calgary	79	28	62	90	20	82	14	1	3	0	304	9.2
Ray Bourque	Boston	76	19	65	84	31	50	8	0	3	0	310	6.1
Phil Housley	Buffalo	80	21	60	81	11	32	8	1	4	0	201	10.4
Gary Suter	Calgary	76	16	60	76	4	97	5	0	1	0	211	7.6
Doug Wilson	Chicago	70	23	50	73	13	40	13	1	2	0	242	9.5
Larry Murphy	Minnesota	77	10	58	68	13–	44	4	0	1	1	173	5.8
Al Iafrate	Toronto	75	21	42	63	4–	135	6	1	0	0	153	13.7
Steve Duchesne	Los Angeles	79	20	42	62	3–	36	6	0	1	1	224	8.9
Doug Crossman	NY Islanders	80	15	44	59	3	54	8	0	1	2	159	9.4
Paul Reinhart	Vancouver	67	17	40	57	2	30	9	1	1	2	139	12.2
James Patrick	NY Rangers	73	14	43	57	4	50	9	0	0	0	136	10.3
Brian Leetch	NY Rangers	72	11	45	56	18–	26	5	0	2	1	222	5.0
Fredrik Olausson	Winnipeg	77	9	46	55	1–	32	3	0	0	0	147	6.1
Jeff Brown	Que–St. L.	77	16	38	54	26–	55	8	1	3	0	284	5.6
Kevin Hatcher	Washington	80	13	41	54	4	102	4	0	2	0	240	5.4
Bruce Driver	New Jersey	75	7	46	53	6	63	1	0	0	1	185	3.8
Jeff Norton	NY Islanders	60	4	49	53	9–	65	4	0	0	0	104	3.8
Tom Kurvers	N.J.–Tor.	71	15	37	52	9–	29	9	1	1	0	156	9.6
Rob Ramage	Toronto	80	8	41	49	1–	202	3	0	1	0	196	4.1
Doug Bodger	Buffalo	71	12	36	48	0	64	8	0	1	0	167	7.2
Paul Cavallini	St. Louis	80	8	39	47	38	106	2	1	0	0	135	5.9
Dave Ellett	Winnipeg	77	17	29	46	15–	96	8	0	1	0	205	8.3
Teppo Numminen	Winnipeg	79	11	32	43	4–	20	1	0	1	0	105	10.5
Dave Babych	Hartford	72	6	37	43	16–	62	4	0	1	0	164	3.7
Steve Chiasson	Detroit	67	14	28	42	16–	114	4	0	2	0	190	7.4

CONSECUTIVE SCORING STREAKS

Goals

Games	Player	Team	G
11	Pat LaFontaine	NY Islanders	18
10	Brian Bellows	Minnesota	12
8	Cam Neely	Boston	9
8	Luc Robitaille	Los Angeles	8
7	Mike Gartner	Min.–NYR	8
6	*Darren Turcotte	NY Rangers	9
6	Adam Creighton	Chicago	8
6	Cam Neely	Boston	8
6	Kirk Muller	New Jersey	7
6	Joe Sakic	Quebec	7
6	Thomas Steen	Winnipeg	7
6	*Mark Recchi	Pittsburgh	6

Assists

Games	Player	Team	A
17	Wayne Gretzky	Los Angeles	35
11	Doug Gilmour	Calgary	12
9	Paul Coffey	Pittsburgh	18
9	Wayne Gretzky	Los Angeles	14
9	Steve Larmer	Chicago	14
8	Mark Messier	Edmonton	14
8	Shayne Corson	Montreal	13
8	Vincent Damphousse	Toronto	11
8	Al MacInnis	Calgary	10
8	Phil Housley	Buffalo	9

Points

Games	Player	Team	G	A	Pts
46	Mario Lemieux	Pittsburgh	39	64	103
20	Brett Hull	St. Louis	21	14	35
18	Wayne Gretzky	Los Angeles	6	35	41
18	Ed Olczyk	Toronto	11	17	28
15	Brian Bellows	Minnesota	17	10	27
15	Joe Nieuwendyk	Calgary	8	14	22
14	Wayne Gretzky	Los Angeles	12	19	31
14	Adam Creighton	Chicago	12	13	25
14	Phil Housley	Buffalo	4	15	19
13	Pat LaFontaine	NY Islanders	18	13	31
13	Paul Coffey	Pittsburgh	6	22	28
13	Pat LaFontaine	NY Islanders	8	14	22

Al MacInnis (right) had 90 points in 1989-90 to rank second among defensemen while Brian Leetch (far right) helped the New York Rangers to their first Patrick Division title.

After 13 seasons with Central Red Army in Moscow, Viacheslav Fetisov made a successful transition to the NHL in 1989-90 as a member of the New Jersey Devils.

Individual Rookie Scoring Leaders

Scoring Leaders

Rookie	Team	GP	G	A	Pts	+/−	PIM	PP	SH	GW	GT	S	%
Sergei Makarov	Calgary	80	24	62	86	33	55	6	0	4	0	118	20.3
Mike Modano	Minnesota	80	29	46	75	7−	63	12	0	2	0	172	16.9
Mark Recchi	Pittsburgh	74	30	37	67	6	44	6	2	4	1	143	21.0
Darren Turcotte	NY Rangers	76	32	34	66	3	32	10	1	4	0	205	15.6
Jeremy Roenick	Chicago	78	26	40	66	2	54	6	0	4	0	173	15.0
Rod Brind'Amour	St. Louis	79	26	35	61	23	46	10	0	1	1	160	16.3
Paul Ranheim	Calgary	80	26	28	54	27	23	1	3	4	2	197	13.2
Igor Larionov	Vancouver	74	17	27	44	5−	20	8	0	2	1	118	14.4
Alexander Mogilny	Buffalo	65	15	28	43	8	16	4	0	2	1	130	11.5
Viacheslav Fetisov	New Jersey	72	8	34	42	9	52	2	0	0	0	108	7.4

Goal Scoring

Rookie	Team	GP	G
Darren Turcotte	NYR	76	32
Mark Recchi	Pit.	74	30
Mike Modano	Min.	80	29
Jeremy Roenick	Chi.	78	26
Rod Brind'Amour	St. L.	79	26
Paul Ranheim	Cgy.	80	26

Assists

Rookie	Team	GP	A
Sergei Makarov	Cgy.	80	62
Mike Modano	Min.	80	46
Jeremy Roenick	Chi.	78	40
Mark Recchi	Pit.	74	37
Rod Brind'Amour	St. L.	79	35

Power-Play Goals

Rookie	Team	GP	PP
Mike Modano	Min.	80	12
Darren Turcotte	NYR	76	10
Rod Brind'Amour	St. L.	79	10
Igor Larionov	Van.	74	8

Short-Hand Goals

Rookie	Team	GP	SH
Hubie McDonough	L.A.–NYI	76	3
Paul Ranheim	Cgy.	80	3
Mark Recchi	Pit.	74	2
Dave Snuggerud	Buf.	80	2

Game-Winning Goals

Rookie	Team	GP	GW
Mark Recchi	Pit.	74	4
Hubie McDonough	L.A.–NYI	76	4
Darren Turcotte	NYR	76	4
Jeremy Roenick	Chi.	78	4
Sergei Makarov	Cgy.	80	4
Paul Ranheim	Cgy.	80	4

Game-Tying Goals

Rookie	Team	GP	GT
Martin Gelinas	Edm.	46	2
Paul Ranheim	Cgy.	80	2

Shots

Rookie	Team	GP	S
Darren Turcotte	NYR	76	205
Paul Ranheim	Cgy.	80	197
Jeremy Roenick	Chi.	78	173
Mike Modano	Min.	80	172
Rod Brind'Amour	St. L.	79	160

First Goals

Rookie	Team	GP	FG
Todd Krygier	Hfd	58	8
Darren Turcotte	NYR	76	7
Rod Brind'Amour	St. L.	79	6

Shooting Percentage
(minimum 80 shots)

Rookie	Team	GP	G	S	%
Mark Recchi	Pit.	74	30	143	21.0
Sergei Makarov	Cgy.	80	24	118	20.3
Hubie McDonough	L.A.–NYI	76	21	105	20.0
Todd Krygier	Hfd.	58	18	103	17.5
Mike Modano	Min.	80	29	172	16.9

Plus/Minus

Rookie	Team	GP	+/−
Sergei Makarov	Cgy.	80	33
Paul Ranheim	Cgy.	80	27
Rod Brind'Amour	St. L.	79	23
Sylvain Lefebvre	Mtl.	68	18
Jyrki Lumme	Mtl.–Van.	65	17

CONSECUTIVE ROOKIE SCORING STREAKS

Goals

Games	Rookie	Team	G
6	Darren Turcotte	NY Rangers	9
6	Mark Recchi	Pittsburgh	6
5	Jeremy Roenick	Chicago	6
5	Don Barber	Minnesota	5

Assists

Games	Rookie	Team	A
7	Sergei Makarov	Calgary	14
6	Brad Shaw	Hartford	9
6	Todd Elik	Los Angeles	6

Points

Games	Rookie	Team	G	A	Pts
10	Mark Recchi	Pittsburgh	8	8	16
10	Mike Modano	Minnesota	8	4	12
9	Jeremy Roenick	Chicago	9	7	16
9	Stephan Lebeau	Montreal	6	5	11
8	Todd Elik	Los Angeles	2	8	10
7	Sergei Makarov	Calgary	2	14	16
7	Darren Turcotte	NY Rangers	9	3	12
7	Mike Modano	Minnesota	4	7	11

Three-or-More-Goal Games

Player	Team	Date	Final Score				G
Glenn Anderson	Edmonton	Dec. 02	MIN	1	EDM	6	3
Dave Andreychuk	Buffalo	Mar. 27	BUF	6	DET	5	3
Brian Bellows	Minnesota	Jan. 04	NYR	2	MIN	8	3
Andy Brickley	Boston	Nov. 18	N.J.	4	BOS	6	3
Neal Broten	Minnesota	Mar. 24	MIN	7	BOS	6	3
Rob Brown	Pittsburgh	Dec. 12	BOS	5	PIT	7	3
Rob Brown	Pittsburgh	Feb. 10	L.A.	6	PIT	7	3
Rob Brown	Pittsburgh	Mar. 04	MIN	6	PIT	8	3
Shawn Burr	Detroit	Jan. 09	MIN	0	DET	9	3
Bob Carpenter	Boston	Jan. 23	BOS	9	QUE	2	3
Jimmy Carson	Detroit	Dec. 27	DET	7	TOR	7	3
Gino Cavallini	St Louis	Feb. 10	N.J.	0	STL	7	3
Dino Ciccarelli	Washington	Feb. 06	QUE	2	WSH	12	4
Wendel Clark	Toronto	Oct. 12	TOR	6	CHI	9	3
Geoff Courtnall	Washington	Jan. 28	PHI	2	WSH	7	3
Russ Courtnall	Montreal	Feb. 19	MTL	5	DET	5	3
John Cullen	Pittsburgh	Feb. 20	PHI	4	PIT	6	3
Vincent Damphousse	Toronto	Feb. 23	TOR	6	EDM	5	3
Vincent Damphousse	Toronto	Mar. 16	TOR	4	BUF	3	3
Kevin Dineen	Hartford	Nov. 04	L.A.	3	HFD	6	3
Kevin Dineen	Hartford	Mar. 06	HFD	4	NYI	2	3
Ray Ferraro	Hartford	Dec. 09	N.J.	3	HFD	7	3
Ron Francis	Hartford	Oct. 08	HFD	9	QUE	6	3
Mike Gartner	Minnesota	Dec. 03	MIN	5	VAN	6	3
Mike Gartner	Minnesota	Dec. 15	L.A.	3	MIN	6	3
*Martin Gelinas	Edmonton	Mar. 04	VAN	3	EDM	6	3
Dirk Graham	Chicago	Feb. 08	CHI	8	DET	6	3
Adam Graves	Edmonton	Dec. 17	EDM	6	CHI	6	3
Wayne Gretzky	Los Angeles	Oct. 31	L.A.	8	PIT	4	3
*Tony Horacek	Philadelphia	Dec. 30	PHI	6	L.A.	3	3
Brett Hull	St Louis	Oct. 18	STL	9	PIT	3	3
Brett Hull	St Louis	Dec. 20	STL	6	CHI	9	3
Brett Hull	St Louis	Jan. 14	STL	5	WPG	6	3
Brett Hull	St Louis	Feb. 15	QUE	2	STL	9	3
Brett Hull	St Louis	Feb. 25	STL	5	MTL	3	3
Derek King	NY Islanders	Feb. 06	NYI	8	PIT	7	3
Normand Lacombe	Edmonton	Nov. 25	EDM	7	NYI	2	3
Pat LaFontaine	NY Islanders	Dec. 31	NYI	4	BUF	2	3
Pat LaFontaine	NY Islanders	Feb. 06	NYI	8	PIT	7	3
Gary Leeman	Toronto	Jan. 08	WSH	6	TOR	8	3
Gary Leeman	Toronto	Mar. 08	TOR	7	HFD	5	3
Jocelyn Lemieux	Chicago	Feb. 20	CHI	8	STL	3	3
Mario Lemieux	Pittsburgh	Oct. 17	TOR	5	PIT	7	3
Mario Lemieux	Pittsburgh	Dec. 02	PIT	7	QUE	4	3
Mario Lemieux	Pittsburgh	Jan. 08	PIT	7	NYR	5	4
Mario Lemieux	Pittsburgh	Feb. 02	EDM	3	PIT	6	3
Paul MacLean	St Louis	Mar. 24	STL	3	L.A.	9	3
Brian MacLellan	Calgary	Jan. 14	CGY	6	CHI	5	4
Dan Marois	Toronto	Jan. 06	L.A.	4	TOR	7	3
Mark Messier	Edmonton	Nov. 21	VAN	3	EDM	4	3
Mark Messier	Edmonton	Jan. 17	WPG	3	EDM	6	3
Mark Messier	Edmonton	Mar. 03	PHI	3	EDM	5	4
*Mike Modano	Minnesota	Mar. 17	MIN	6	PIT	2	3
Joe Mullen	Calgary	Feb. 22	TOR	2	CGY	12	3
Troy Murray	Chicago	Oct. 24	CHI	5	DET	3	3
Dana Murzyn	Calgary	Feb. 22	TOR	2	CGY	12	3
Cam Neely	Boston	Mar. 22	QUE	3	BOS	7	3
Joe Nieuwendyk	Calgary	Dec. 14	QUE	2	CGY	8	3
Ed Olczyk	Toronto	Dec. 09	MTL	4	TOR	7	3
Dan Quinn	Vancouver	Feb. 24	VAN	6	L.A.	4	3
Stephane Richer	Montreal	Feb. 10	QUE	2	MTL	7	3
Stephane Richer	Montreal	Mar. 24	MTL	4	HFD	1	3
Gary Roberts	Calgary	Mar. 30	EDM	2	CGY	6	3
Luc Robitaille	Los Angeles	Nov. 25	VAN	4	L.A.	7	3
Luc Robitaille	Los Angeles	Mar. 10	PIT	2	L.A.	8	3
*Jeremy Roenick	Chicago	Dec. 23	CHI	7	TOR	5	3
Joe Sakic	Quebec	Oct. 08	HFD	9	QUE	6	3
Denis Savard	Chicago	Dec. 30	HFD	3	CHI	7	3
Al Secord	Chicago	Jan. 11	CHI	5	PHI	4	3
Peter Stastny	Quebec	Nov. 09	QUE	7	NYI	5	3
Kevin Stevens	Pittsburgh	Oct. 31	L.A.	8	PIT	4	3
Brent Sutter	NY Islanders	Mar. 17	NYR	3	NYI	6	3
Rich Sutter	Vancouver	Oct. 20	VAN	3	N.J.	2	3
Bob Sweeney	Boston	Nov. 09	EDM	2	BOS	6	3
Tony Tanti	Pittsburgh	Jan. 30	PHI	6	PIT	3	3
Dave Taylor	Los Angeles	Jan. 25	L.A.	6	EDM	4	3
Steve Thomas	Chicago	Jan. 14	CGY	6	CHI	5	3
Steve Thomas	Chicago	Mar. 22	N.J.	3	CHI	6	4
Rick Tocchet	Philadelphia	Oct. 08	PHI	3	WPG	5	3
Rick Tocchet	Philadelphia	Jan. 25	WPG	6	PHI	8	3
*Darren Turcotte	NY Rangers	Feb. 26	BOS	1	NYR	6	3
Pierre Turgeon	Buffalo	Dec. 01	N.J.	4	BUF	6	3
Sylvain Turgeon	New Jersey	Oct. 05	N.J.	6	PHI	2	3
Mick Vukota	NY Islanders	Oct. 20	NYI	5	WSH	3	3
Randy Wood	NY Islanders	Jan. 19	NYI	6	WPG	4	3
Steve Yzerman	Detroit	Dec. 15	CHI	4	DET	8	3
Steve Yzerman	Detroit	Jan. 31	EDM	5	DET	7	4
Steve Yzerman	Detroit	Feb. 14	L.A.	5	DET	6	3

NOTE: 88 Three-or-more-goal games recorded in 1989-90.

Rick Tocchet was one of seven players to score four goals in a game during the 1989-90 campaign.

Goaltending Leaders

Minimum 25 games

Goals Against Average

Goaltender	Team	GPI	MINS	GA	AVG
Patrick Roy	Montreal	54	3173	134	**2.53**
Mike Liut	Hfd.–Wsh.	37	2161	91	**2.53**
Rejean Lemelin	Boston	43	2310	108	**2.81**
Daren Puppa	Buffalo	56	3241	156	**2.89**
Andy Moog	Boston	46	2536	122	**2.89**

Save Percentage

Goaltender	Team	GPI	MINS	GA	SA	S%	W	L	T
Patrick Roy	Montreal	54	3173	134	1524	**.912**	31	16	5
Mike Liut	Hfd.–Wsh.	37	2161	91	962	**.905**	19	16	1
Daren Puppa	Buffalo	56	3241	156	1610	**.903**	31	16	6
Clint Malarchuk	Buffalo	29	1596	89	914	**.903**	14	11	2
Mark Fitzpatrick	NY Islanders	47	2653	150	1472	**.898**	19	19	5

Wins

Goaltender	Team	GPI	MINS	W	L	T
Patrick Roy	Montreal	54	3173	**31**	16	5
Daren Puppa	Buffalo	56	3241	**31**	16	6
Jon Casey	Minnesota	61	3407	**31**	22	4
Andy Moog	Boston	46	2536	**24**	10	7
Bill Ranford	Edmonton	56	3107	**24**	16	9

Shutouts

Goaltender	Team	GPI	MINS	SO	W	L	T
Mike Liut	Hfd.–Wsh.	37	2161	**4**	19	16	1
Andy Moog	Boston	46	2536	**3**	24	10	7
Mark Fitzpatrick	NY Islanders	47	2653	**3**	19	19	5
Patrick Roy	Montreal	54	3173	**3**	31	16	5
Jon Casey	Minnesota	61	3407	**3**	31	22	4

Team-by-Team Point Totals

1984-85 to 1989-90

(Ranked by five-year average)

	89-90	88-89	87-88	86-87	85-86	Average
Edmonton	90	84	99	106	119	99.6
Calgary	88	117	105	95	89	98.8
Montreal	93	115	103	92	87	98.0
Boston	101	88	94	85	86	90.8
Washington	78	92	85	86	72	89.6
Philadelphia	71	80	85	100	110	89.2
Hartford	85	79	77	93	84	83.6
Buffalo	98	83	85	64	80	82.0
NY Rangers	85	82	82	76	78	80.6
St. Louis	83	78	76	79	83	79.8
NY Islanders	73	61	88	82	90	78.8
Chicago	99	66	69	72	86	78.4
Pittsburgh	72	87	81	72	76	77.6
Winnipeg	85	64	77	88	59	74.6
Detroit	70	80	93	78	40	72.2
Los Angeles	75	91	68	70	54	71.6
New Jersey	83	66	82	64	59	70.8
Minnesota	76	70	51	70	85	70.4
Quebec	31	61	69	72	92	65.0
Vancouver	64	74	59	66	59	64.4
Toronto	80	62	62	70	57	64.2

Team Records When Scoring First Goal of a Game

(Ranked by winning percentage)

Team	First Goal	W	L	T	%
Buffalo	37	26	8	3	.743
Montreal	44	31	10	3	.739
Boston	44	30	10	4	.727
Los Angeles	37	26	10	1	.716
Chicago	36	24	9	3	.708
Calgary	41	25	8	8	.707
Washington	42	27	10	5	.702
Edmonton	48	30	12	6	.688
NY Rangers	42	25	10	7	.679
Hartford	45	29	14	2	.667
Pittsburgh	40	24	11	5	.663
Toronto	40	25	13	2	.650
St. Louis	41	25	13	3	.646
Winnipeg	45	25	12	8	.644
Minnesota	39	23	13	3	.628
Philadelphia	42	22	13	7	.607
Detroit	33	16	9	8	.606
Vancouver	37	19	12	6	.595
New Jersey	46	24	18	4	.565
NY Islanders	33	14	12	7	.530
Quebec	27	7	16	4	.333

Team Plus/Minus Differential

Team	Goals For	per game	Goals Against	per game	Goal Differential
Calgary	348	4.35	265	3.31	+ 1.04
Boston	289	3.61	232	2.90	+ 0.71
Montreal	288	3.60	234	2.93	+ 0.68
Buffalo	286	3.58	248	3.10	+ 0.48
Edmonton	315	3.94	283	3.54	+ 0.40
Chicago	316	3.95	294	3.68	+ 0.28
St. Louis	295	3.69	279	3.49	+ 0.20
NY Rangers	279	3.49	267	3.34	+ 0.15
Washington	284	3.55	275	3.44	+ 0.11
Winnipeg	298	3.73	290	3.63	+ 0.10
Hartford	275	3.44	268	3.35	+ 0.09
New Jersey	295	3.69	288	3.60	+ 0.09
Los Angeles	338	4.23	337	4.21	+ 0.02
Philadelphia	290	3.63	297	3.71	− 0.09
Minnesota	284	3.55	291	3.64	− 0.09
NY Islanders	281	3.51	288	3.60	− 0.09
Detroit	288	3.60	323	4.04	− 0.44
Pittsburgh	318	3.98	359	4.49	− 0.51
Toronto	337	4.21	358	4.48	− 0.26
Vancouver	245	3.06	306	3.83	− 0.76
Quebec	240	3.00	407	5.09	− 2.09

Team Records when Leading, Trailing, Tied

Team	Leading after 1 period W	L	T	Leading after 2 periods W	L	T	Trailing after 1 period W	L	T	Trailing after 2 periods W	L	T	Tied after 1 period W	L	T	Tied after 2 periods W	L	T
Boston	20	5	2	30	5	4	9	9	4	4	16	3	17	11	3	12	4	2
Buffalo	19	4	2	31	5	3	6	16	3	6	21	4	20	7	3	8	4	1
Calgary	24	3	8	31	4	7	6	11	4	4	11	4	12	9	3	7	8	4
Chicago	25	6	3	33	1	2	11	15	2	3	25	1	5	12	1	5	7	3
Detroit	13	3	4	16	2	5	8	23	5	7	34	5	7	12	5	5	2	4
Edmonton	26	3	6	31	3	4	2	17	4	2	20	4	10	8	4	5	5	6
Hartford	23	4	3	26	1	1	4	15	3	1	27	4	11	14	3	11	5	4
Los Angeles	22	8	1	22	5	1	4	21	5	5	26	4	8	10	1	7	8	2
Minnesota	19	9	3	31	4	2	3	23	1	3	26	1	14	8	0	2	10	1
Montreal	19	4	2	34	4	3	6	14	8	2	18	6	16	10	1	5	6	2
New Jersey	21	9	2	28	5	3	8	14	4	4	24	4	8	11	5	5	4	2
NY Islanders	10	7	7	22	2	4	7	18	1	4	26	5	14	13	3	5	10	2
NY Rangers	17	6	4	25	5	3	4	15	6	3	22	3	14	13	3	5	10	2
Philadelphia	16	4	5	23	4	5	5	18	2	7	26	2	9	17	4	6	9	4
Pittsburgh	19	4	3	20	1	3	5	25	2	4	31	1	8	11	3	8	8	4
Quebec	3	4	1	8	4	1	2	43	3	0	59	2	5	14	3	4	7	4
St. Louis	22	7	2	30	4	2	5	10	4	3	27	2	10	17	3	4	3	5
Toronto	15	8	1	25	4	1	8	22	2	5	31	1	15	8	1	8	3	2
Vancouver	12	4	3	17	2	2	4	22	6	3	31	7	9	15	5	5	8	5
Washington	21	7	1	27	5	4	6	20	1	4	22	1	9	11	4	5	11	1
Winnipeg	19	11	7	28	4	8	5	14	2	3	23	0	13	7	2	6	5	7

Team Statistics

TEAMS' HOME-AND-ROAD RECORD

Norris Division

			Home									Road					
	GP	W	L	T	GF	GA	PTS	%	GP	W	L	T	GF	GA	PTS	%
CHI	40	25	13	2	165	135	52	.650	40	16	20	4	151	159	36	.450
ST.L.	40	20	15	5	156	141	45	.563	40	17	19	4	139	138	38	.475
TOR	40	24	14	2	187	171	50	.625	40	14	24	2	150	187	30	.375
MIN	40	26	12	2	160	127	54	.675	40	10	28	2	124	164	22	.275
DET	40	20	14	6	161	148	46	.575	40	8	24	8	127	175	24	.300
Total	200	115	68	17	829	722	247	.618	200	65	115	20	691	823	150	.375

Smythe Division

	GP	W	L	T	GF	GA	PTS	%	GP	W	L	T	GF	GA	PTS	%
CGY	40	28	7	5	207	131	61	.763	40	14	16	10	141	134	38	.475
EDM	40	23	11	6	165	130	52	.650	40	15	17	8	150	153	38	.475
WPG	40	22	13	5	170	140	49	.613	40	15	19	6	128	150	36	.450
L.A.	40	21	16	3	174	141	45	.563	40	12	23	4	164	196	30	.375
VAN	40	13	16	11	129	144	37	.463	40	12	25	3	116	162	27	.338
Total	200	107	63	30	845	686	244	.610	200	69	100	31	699	795	169	.423

Adams Division

	GP	W	L	T	GF	GA	PTS	%	GP	W	L	T	GF	GA	PTS	%
BOS	40	23	13	4	148	119	50	.625	40	23	12	5	141	113	51	.638
BUF	40	27	11	2	160	121	56	.700	40	18	16	6	126	127	42	.525
MTL	40	26	8	6	165	102	58	.725	40	15	20	5	123	132	35	.438
HFD	40	17	18	5	134	135	39	.488	40	21	15	4	141	133	46	.575
QUE	40	8	26	6	139	192	22	.275	40	4	35	1	101	215	9	.113
Total	200	101	76	23	746	669	225	.563	200	81	98	21	632	720	183	.458

Patrick Division

	GP	W	L	T	GF	GA	PTS	%	GP	W	L	T	GF	GA	PTS	%
NYR	40	20	11	9	147	119	49	.613	40	16	20	4	132	148	36	.450
N.J.	40	22	15	3	140	123	47	.588	40	15	19	6	155	155	36	.450
WSH	40	19	18	3	155	137	41	.513	40	17	20	3	129	138	37	.463
NYI	40	15	17	8	133	134	38	.475	40	16	21	3	148	154	35	.438
PIT	40	22	15	3	178	166	47	.588	40	10	25	5	140	193	25	.313
PHI	40	17	19	4	135	125	38	.475	40	13	20	7	155	172	33	.413
Total	240	115	95	30	888	804	260	.542	240	87	125	28	859	970	202	.421
Total	840	438	302	100	3308	2881	976	.581	840	302	438	100	2881	3308	704	.419

TEAMS' DIVISIONAL RECORD

Norris Division

			Against Own Division								Against Other Divisions					
	GP	W	L	T	GF	GA	PTS	%	GP	W	L	T	GF	GA	PTS	%
CHI	32	14	15	3	131	134	31	.484	48	27	18	3	185	160	57	.594
ST.L.	32	14	16	2	115	119	30	.469	48	23	18	7	180	160	53	.552
TOR	32	16	15	1	137	128	33	.516	48	22	23	3	200	230	47	.490
MIN	32	17	14	1	105	99	35	.547	48	19	26	3	179	192	41	.427
DET	32	14	15	3	111	119	31	.484	48	14	23	11	177	204	39	.406
Total	160	75	75	10	599	599	160	.500	240	105	108	27	921	946	237	.494

Smythe Division

	GP	W	L	T	GF	GA	PTS	%	GP	W	L	T	GF	GA	PTS	%
CGY	32	16	12	4	128	101	36	.563	48	26	11	11	220	164	63	.656
EDM	32	18	10	4	127	114	40	.625	48	20	18	10	188	169	50	.521
WPG	32	16	12	4	121	108	36	.563	48	21	20	7	177	182	49	.510
L.A.	32	11	15	6	123	144	28	.438	48	23	24	1	215	193	47	.490
VAN	32	6	18	8	95	127	20	.313	48	19	23	6	150	179	44	.458
Total	160	67	67	26	594	594	160	.500	240	109	96	35	950	887	253	.527

Adams Division

	GP	W	L	T	GF	GA	PTS	%	GP	W	L	T	GF	GA	PTS	%
BOS	32	18	10	4	109	88	40	.625	48	28	15	5	180	144	61	.635
BUF	32	20	9	3	123	91	43	.672	48	25	18	5	163	157	55	.573
MTL	32	17	12	3	115	90	37	.578	48	24	16	8	173	144	56	.583
HFD	32	14	15	3	93	106	31	.484	48	24	18	6	182	162	54	.563
QUE	32	3	26	3	84	149	9	.141	48	9	35	4	156	258	22	.229
Total	160	72	72	16	524	524	160	.500	240	110	102	28	854	865	248	.517

Patrick Division

	GP	W	L	T	GF	GA	PTS	%	GP	W	L	T	GF	GA	PTS	%
NYR	35	15	16	4	121	123	34	.486	45	21	15	9	158	144	51	.567
N.J.	35	18	12	5	140	118	41	.586	45	19	22	4	155	170	42	.467
WSH	35	18	16	1	126	121	37	.529	45	18	22	5	158	154	41	.456
NYI	35	11	17	7	127	137	29	.414	45	20	21	4	154	151	44	.489
PIT	35	18	14	3	146	144	39	.557	45	14	26	5	172	215	33	.367
PHI	35	13	18	4	118	135	30	.429	45	17	21	7	172	162	41	.456
Total	210	93	93	24	778	778	210	.500	270	109	127	34	969	996	252	.467

TEAM STREAKS

Consecutive Wins

Games	Team	From	To
9	NY Islanders	Dec. 31	Jan. 19
7	Boston	Nov. 9	Nov. 23
6	Edmonton	Nov. 25	Dec. 8
5	NY Islanders	Dec. 15	Dec. 28
5	Edmonton	Dec. 19	Dec. 29
5	Boston	Jan. 2	Jan. 11
5	Toronto	Jan. 13	Jan. 26
5	St Louis	Feb. 10	Feb. 17
5	Calgary	Mar. 11	Mar. 19
5	New Jersey	Mar. 24	Mar. 31

Consecutive Home Wins

Games	Team	From	To
12	Buffalo	Oct. 13	Dec. 10
9	NY Islanders	Dec. 16	Jan. 27
9	Calgary	Mar. 3	Apr. 1
8	Minnesota	Nov. 4	Nov. 26
7	Chicago	Oct. 22	Nov. 12
7	Montreal	Feb. 3	Feb. 25
7	Pittsburgh	Feb. 8	Mar. 15
6	Toronto	Nov. 6	Dec. 11
6	Edmonton	Nov. 17	Dec. 8
6	Detroit	Dec. 15	Jan. 9
6	Boston	Dec. 21	Jan. 11
6	St Louis	Feb. 3	Feb. 17

Consecutive Road Wins

Games	Team	From	To
5	Hartford	Nov. 30	Dec. 19
5	NY Islanders	Dec. 31	Jan. 19
5	Buffalo	Jan. 13	Jan. 30
4	New Jersey	Oct. 5	Oct. 23
4	Hartford	Oct. 26	Nov. 10
4	Washington	Nov. 25	Dec. 5
4	Boston	Jan. 23	Feb. 6
4	Boston	Feb. 18	Feb. 24
4	Buffalo	Mar. 8	Mar. 31
4	Minnesota	Mar. 12	Mar. 24

Consecutive Undefeated

Games	Team	W	T	From	To
9	Buffalo	7	2	Oct. 27	Nov. 16
9	Boston	8	1	Nov. 2	Nov. 23
9	Edmonton	7	2	Nov. 25	Dec. 16
9	NY Islanders	9	0	Dec. 31	Jan. 19
9	Calgary	8	1	Mar. 3	Mar. 19
8	NY Rangers	5	3	Oct. 15	Oct. 28
8	St Louis	5	3	Oct. 26	Nov. 11
8	Calgary	6	2	Jan. 14	Feb. 1
7	Los Angeles	5	2	Nov. 11	Nov. 26
7	Boston	5	2	Jan. 15	Jan. 29
7	St Louis	5	2	Jan. 23	Feb. 6
7	NY Rangers	6	1	Feb. 16	Mar. 2

Consecutive Home Undefeated

Games	Team	W	T	From	To
14	Buffalo	13	1	Oct. 5	Dec. 10
14	Edmonton	11	3	Nov. 15	Jan. 6
12	Montreal	9	3	Feb. 3	Mar. 31
10	NY Islanders	9	1	Dec. 16	Jan. 28
9	Detroit	6	3	Feb. 10	Mar. 20
9	Calgary	9	0	Mar. 3	Apr. 1
8	Calgary	6	2	Oct. 5	Nov. 6
8	Minnesota	8	0	Nov. 4	Nov. 26
8	Winnipeg	6	2	Dec. 8	Jan. 14
8	St Louis	7	1	Jan. 25	Feb. 17
7	NY Rangers	4	3	Oct. 11	Oct. 27
7	Chicago	7	0	Oct. 22	Nov. 12
7	Boston	6	1	Nov. 2	Nov. 30
7	Montreal	6	1	Nov. 4	Nov. 29
7	Pittsburgh	7	0	Feb. 8	Mar. 15

Consecutive Road Undefeated

Games	Team	W	T	From	To
7	Boston	6	1	Jan. 2	Feb. 6
6	Hartford	5	1	Nov. 30	Dec. 26
6	Buffalo	4	2	Mar. 3	Mar. 31
6	Boston	4	2	Mar. 4	Mar. 31
5	Philadelphia	4	1	Oct. 30	Nov. 14
5	Winnipeg	3	2	Nov. 18	Dec. 15
5	NY Islanders	5	0	Dec. 31	Jan. 19
5	Buffalo	5	0	Jan. 13	Jan. 30
5	Calgary	3	2	Jan. 14	Jan. 30

John MacLean had ten power-play goals and three shorthanded goals for the New Jersey Devils in 1989-90.

Team Penalties

Abbreviations: GP - games played; **PEN** - total penalty minutes, including bench penalties; **BMI** - total bench minor minutes; **AVG** - average penalty minutes per game calculated by dividing total penalty minutes by games played.

Team	GP	PEN	BMI	AVG
BUF	80	1449	16	18.1
BOS	80	1458	20	18.2
MTL	80	1590	8	19.9
WPG	80	1639	10	20.5
VAN	80	1644	22	20.6
N.J.	80	1659	8	20.7
CGY	80	1751	26	21.9
NYI	80	1777	10	22.2
STL	80	1809	12	22.6
L.A.	80	1844	24	23.1
NYR	80	2021	24	25.3
MIN	80	2041	28	25.5
EDM	80	2046	22	25.6
PHI	80	2067	18	25.8
HFD	80	2102	12	26.3
QUE	80	2104	20	26.3
PIT	80	2132	14	26.7
DET	80	2140	8	26.8
WSH	80	2204	12	27.6
TOR	80	2419	18	30.2
CHI	80	2426	30	30.3
TOTAL	**840**	**40322**	**362**	**48.0**

TEAMS' POWER-PLAY RECORD

Abbreviations: ADV – total advantages; **PPGF** – power-play goals for; **%** – calculated by dividing number of power-play goals by total advantages.

	Home Team	GP	ADV	PPGF	%	Road Team	GP	ADV	PPGF	%	Overall Team	GP	ADV	PPGF	%
1	CGY	40	181	57	31.5	NYI	40	158	42	26.6	CGY	80	357	99	27.7
2	TOR	40	188	49	26.1	NYR	40	209	55	26.3	BOS	80	352	83	23.6
3	MIN	40	196	51	26.0	CGY	40	176	42	23.9	NYI	80	330	78	23.6
4	QUE	40	197	49	24.9	BOS	40	170	40	23.5	TOR	80	348	81	23.3
5	CHI	40	184	45	24.5	STL	40	179	40	22.3	NYR	80	442	103	23.3
6	BOS	40	182	43	23.6	CHI	40	165	35	21.2	CHI	80	349	80	22.9
7	L.A.	40	180	42	23.3	PHI	40	166	35	21.1	STL	80	351	79	22.5
8	BUF	40	192	44	22.9	BUF	40	166	35	21.1	L.A.	80	343	76	22.2
9	STL	40	172	39	22.7	L.A.	40	163	34	20.9	BUF	80	358	79	22.1
10	WPG	40	183	41	22.4	PIT	40	189	39	20.6	PIT	80	403	86	21.3
11	HFD	40	218	48	22.0	EDM	40	194	39	20.1	MIN	80	386	81	21.0
12	PIT	40	214	47	22.0	TOR	40	160	32	20.0	EDM	80	407	84	20.6
13	EDM	40	213	45	21.1	N.J.	40	153	30	19.6	HFD	80	398	80	20.1
14	NYI	40	172	36	20.9	VAN	40	171	33	19.3	PHI	80	338	65	19.2
15	NYR	40	233	48	20.6	HFD	40	180	32	17.8	N.J.	80	337	64	19.0
16	DET	40	191	39	20.4	WSH	40	195	32	16.4	QUE	80	371	70	18.9
17	N.J.	40	184	34	18.5	MIN	40	190	30	15.8	WPG	80	347	65	18.7
18	MTL	40	181	32	17.7	WPG	40	164	24	14.6	VAN	80	374	64	17.1
19	WSH	40	217	38	17.5	MTL	40	159	22	13.8	WSH	80	412	70	17.0
20	PHI	40	172	30	17.4	QUE	40	174	21	12.1	DET	80	354	58	16.4
21	VAN	40	203	31	15.3	DET	40	163	19	11.7	MTL	80	340	54	15.9
	TOTAL	**840**	**4053**	**888**	**21.9**		**840**	**3644**	**711**	**19.5**		**840**	**7697**	**1599**	**20.8**

SHORT HAND GOALS FOR

	Home Team	GP	SHGF	Road Team	GP	SHGF	Overall Team	GP	SHGF
1	EDM	40	13	PHI	40	10	EDM	80	22
2	TOR	40	11	EDM	40	9	DET	80	18
3	DET	40	10	DET	40	8	TOR	80	16
4	L.A.	40	8	MIN	40	8	MIN	80	14
5	WPG	40	8	CGY	40	7	PHI	80	14
6	HFD	40	7	CHI	40	6	WPG	80	14
7	NYI	40	7	WPG	40	6	HFD	80	12
8	MIN	40	6	PIT	40	5	L.A.	80	11
9	VAN	40	6	N.J.	40	5	CGY	80	11
10	CHI	40	5	TOR	40	5	CHI	80	11
11	WSH	40	5	STL	40	5	NYI	80	10
12	QUE	40	5	HFD	40	5	N.J.	80	10
13	N.J.	40	5	WSH	40	4	STL	80	9
14	NYR	40	5	QUE	40	3	WSH	80	9
15	BOS	40	4	NYI	40	3	QUE	80	8
16	BUF	40	4	BUF	40	3	VAN	80	8
17	PHI	40	4	L.A.	40	3	PIT	80	7
18	CGY	40	4	MTL	40	2	BUF	80	7
19	STL	40	4	NYR	40	2	NYR	80	7
20	MTL	40	2	VAN	40	2	BOS	80	5
21	PIT	40	2	BOS	40	1	MTL	80	4
	TOTAL	**840**	**125**		**840**	**102**		**840**	**227**

TEAMS' PENALTY KILLING RECORD

Abbreviations: TSH – times short-handed; **PPGA** – power-play goals against; **%** – calculated by dividing times short minus power-play goals against by times short.

	Home Team	GP	TSH	PPGA	%	Road Team	GP	TSH	PPGA	%	Overall Team	GP	TSH	PPGA	%
1	MIN	40	190	23	87.9	WPG	40	173	27	84.4	BUF	80	351	58	83.5
2	BUF	40	171	27	84.2	BOS	40	170	28	83.5	BOS	80	316	53	83.2
3	MTL	40	150	24	84.0	BUF	40	180	31	82.8	WPG	80	333	57	82.9
4	CHI	40	200	34	83.0	HFD	40	213	38	82.2	HFD	80	401	74	81.5
5	STL	40	159	27	83.0	WSH	40	206	40	80.6	MIN	80	397	74	81.4
6	BOS	40	146	25	82.9	CGY	40	202	40	80.2	PHI	80	406	77	81.0
7	PHI	40	166	29	82.5	PHI	40	240	48	80.0	STL	80	351	67	80.9
8	WPG	40	160	30	81.3	N.J.	40	184	37	79.9	WSH	80	370	71	80.8
9	EDM	40	197	37	81.2	EDM	40	220	45	79.5	MTL	80	295	57	80.7
10	WSH	40	164	31	81.1	TOR	40	209	43	79.4	N.J.	80	340	67	80.3
11	HFD	40	188	36	80.9	STL	40	192	40	79.2	EDM	80	417	82	80.3
12	N.J.	40	156	30	80.8	NYR	40	187	41	78.1	CHI	80	379	75	80.2
13	L.A.	40	176	34	80.7	VAN	40	176	40	77.3	CGY	80	366	76	79.2
14	NYI	40	176	36	79.5	MTL	40	145	33	77.2	NYR	80	362	77	78.7
15	NYR	40	175	36	79.4	CHI	40	179	41	77.1	TOR	80	408	89	78.2
16	CGY	40	164	36	78.0	MIN	40	207	51	75.4	NYI	80	371	87	76.5
17	PIT	40	174	39	77.6	NYI	40	195	51	73.8	L.A.	80	366	88	76.0
18	DET	40	183	42	77.0	DET	40	189	50	73.5	DET	80	372	92	75.3
19	TOR	40	199	46	76.9	PIT	40	198	55	72.2	VAN	80	342	86	74.9
20	QUE	40	184	43	76.6	QUE	40	198	55	72.2	PIT	80	372	94	74.7
21	VAN	40	166	46	72.3	L.A.	40	190	54	71.6	QUE	80	382	98	74.3
	TOTAL	**840**	**3644**	**711**	**80.5**		**840**	**4053**	**888**	**78.1**		**840**	**7697**	**1599**	**79.2**

SHORT HAND GOALS AGAINST

	Home Team	GP	SHGA	Road Team	GP	SHGA	Overall Team	GP	SHGA
1	BOS	40	1	NYR	40	1	BOS	80	3
2	EDM	40	2	BOS	40	2	CGY	80	6
3	NYI	40	2	CGY	40	2	EDM	80	6
4	BUF	40	3	VAN	40	3	MTL	80	7
5	PHI	40	3	MTL	40	4	BUF	80	7
6	WPG	40	3	EDM	40	4	WPG	80	7
7	MTL	40	3	BUF	40	4	NYI	80	8
8	CGY	40	4	CHI	40	4	VAN	80	8
9	MIN	40	5	HFD	40	4	NYR	80	8
10	CHI	40	5	WPG	40	4	CHI	80	9
11	VAN	40	5	N.J.	40	5	HFD	80	10
12	DET	40	5	NYI	40	6	N.J.	80	12
13	HFD	40	5	STL	40	6	STL	80	12
14	WSH	40	6	QUE	40	7	PHI	80	13
15	STL	40	6	L.A.	40	7	DET	80	13
16	PIT	40	6	DET	40	8	L.A.	80	14
17	L.A.	40	7	TOR	40	9	QUE	80	15
18	N.J.	40	7	WSH	40	9	WSH	80	15
19	NYR	40	7	PHI	40	10	MIN	80	16
20	QUE	40	8	MIN	40	11	TOR	80	17
21	TOR	40	8	PIT	40	15	PIT	80	21
	TOTAL	**840**	**102**		**840**	**125**		**840**	**227**

Overtime Results

Team	1989-90 GP	W	L	T	1988-89 GP	W	L	T	1987-88 GP	W	L	T	1986-87 GP	W	L	T	1985-86 GP	W	L	T	1984-85 GP	W	L	T	1983-84 GP	W	L	T
Boston	14	3	2	9	19	3	2	14	14	4	4	6	12	2	3	7	17	2	3	12	18	4	4	10	7	1	0	6
Buffalo	15	4	3	8	13	2	4	7	12	0	1	11	13	1	4	8	9	1	2	6	17	0	3	14	13	5	1	7
Calgary	21	3	3	15	17	5	3	9	15	2	4	9	4	1	0	3	12	1	2	9	14	1	1	12	18	4	0	14
Chicago	10	2	2	6	17	2	3	12	15	4	2	9	15	1	0	14	12	3	1	8	12	2	3	7	9	0	1	8
Detroit	17	2	1	14	16	3	1	12	16	2	3	11	17	2	5	10	13	2	5	6	14	0	2	12	11	3	1	7
Edmonton	20	5	1	14	15	4	3	8	16	3	2	11	14	5	3	6	14	5	2	7	12	0	1	11	9	4	0	5
Hartford	9	0	0	9	10	1	4	5	12	3	2	7	9	2	0	7	7	1	2	4	17	4	4	9	15	2	3	10
Los Angeles	12	3	2	7	14	6	1	7	12	1	3	8	12	2	2	8	14	3	3	8	19	3	2	14	17	1	3	13
Minnesota	11	3	4	4	17	0	1	16	16	1	2	13	14	2	2	10	15	4	2	9	15	1	2	12	18	5	3	10
Montreal	17	4	2	11	11	2	0	9	16	1	2	13	16	2	4	10	14	1	6	7	18	3	3	12	7	1	1	5
New Jersey	16	3	4	9	17	1	4	12	12	4	2	6	13	3	4	6	10	4	3	3	12	0	2	10	15	1	7	7
NY Islanders	16	3	2	11	11	3	3	5	13	3	0	10	20	5	3	12	17	4	1	12	15	1	8	6	10	3	3	4
NY Rangers	17	2	2	13	10	1	1	8	11	0	1	10	19	5	6	8	13	0	7	6	17	2	5	10	17	5	3	9
Philadelphia	18	2	5	11	14	1	5	8	13	1	3	9	10	1	1	8	9	4	1	4	9	1	1	7	14	3	1	10
Pittsburgh	14	3	3	8	10	2	1	7	16	5	2	9	21	5	4	12	14	3	3	8	8	3	0	5	12	1	5	6
Quebec	8	0	1	7	10	2	1	7	9	2	2	5	14	0	4	10	11	4	1	6	14	3	2	9	15	0	5	10
St. Louis	15	2	4	9	16	3	1	12	13	1	2	10	21	4	2	15	17	5	3	9	15	2	1	12	11	3	1	7
Toronto	11	3	4	4	11	1	4	6	13	1	2	10	13	3	4	6	17	4	6	7	15	5	2	8	13	1	3	9
Vancouver	21	2	5	14	14	2	4	8	11	0	2	9	10	2	0	8	16	1	2	13	17	7	1	9	16	3	4	9
Washington	9	2	1	6	16	2	4	10	15	2	4	9	17	5	2	10	11	4	0	7	12	3	0	9	9	1	3	5
Winnipeg	19	4	4	11	20	6	2	12	21	8	2	11	11	2	1	8	8	0	1	7	14	3	1	10	24	7	6	11
Totals	**155**	**55**		**100**	**149**	**52**		**97**	**146**	**49**		**97**	**148**	**55**		**93**	**135**	**56**		**79**	**152**	**48**		**104**	**140**	**54**		**86**

1989-90
Home Team Wins: 30
Visiting Team Wins: 25

1989-90 Penalty Shots

Scored

Mario Lemieux (Pittsburgh) scored against Bob Mason (Washington), November 24. Final score: Pittsburgh 7 at Washington 4.

Lindy Ruff (NY Rangers) scored against Mario Brunetta (Quebec), November 26. Final score: Quebec 1 at NY Rangers 3.

Joe Sakic (Quebec) scored against Ken Wregget (Philadelphia), December 9. Final score: Philadelphia 6 at Quebec 6.

Tomas Sandstrom (Los Angeles) scored against Wendell Young (Pittsburgh), February 10. Final score: Los Angeles 6 at Pittsburgh 7.

Russ Courtnall (Montreal) scored against Tim Chevaldae (Detroit), February 19. Final score: Montreal 5 at Detroit 5.

Keith Acton (Philadelphia) scored against John Vanbiesbrouck (NY Rangers), March 25. Final score: Philadelphia 3 at NY Rangers 7.

Stopped

Mark Fitzpatrick (NY Islanders) stopped Doug Gilmour (Calgary), October 7. Final score: NY Islanders 3 at Calgary 6.

Tom Barrasso (Pittsburgh) stopped Doug Smail (Winnipeg), October 10. Final score: Winnipeg 1 at Pittsburgh 5.

Mike Richter (NY Rangers) stopped Kevin Dineen (Hartford), October 19. Final score: Hartford 3 at NY Rangers 7.

Bill Ranford (Edmonton) stopped Claude Loiselle (Quebec), October 28. Final score: Edmonton 6 at Quebec 3.

Mike Liut (Hartford) stopped Jimmy Carson (Detroit), November 3. Final score: Hartford 4 at Detroit 3.

Wendell Young (Pittsburgh) stopped Dale Hunter (Washington), December 6. Final score: Washington 3 at Pittsburgh 5.

Jacques Cloutier (Chicago) stopped Greg Adams (Vancouver), December 10. Final score: Vancouver 1 at Chicago 7.

Mike Richter (NY Rangers) stopped Per-Erik Eklund, January 14. Final score: Philadelphia 3 at NY Rangers 4.

Summary
14 penalty shots resulted in 6 goals.

Mike Richter was the only NHL goaltender to stop two penalty shots in 1989-90.

NHL Record Book

All-Time Standings of NHL Teams
(ranked by percentage)

Team	Games	Won	Lost	Tied	Goals For	Goals Against	Points	%
Edmonton	880	484	278	118	4118	3342	1086	.617
Montreal	4432	2352	1385	695	15055	11652	5399	.609
Philadelphia	1818	920	604	294	6584	5508	2134	.587
Buffalo	1592	766	571	255	5792	5181	1787	.561
NY Islanders	1436	697	526	213	5380	4629	1607	.560
Boston	4272	2040	1593	639	14035	12636	4719	.552
**Calgary	1436	673	539	224	5486	4989	1570	.547
Toronto	4432	1904	1875	653	13871	13768	4461	.503
NY Rangers	4206	1743	1786	677	13062	13331	4163	.495
Detroit	4206	1725	1804	677	12657	12981	4127	.491
Chicago	4206	1696	1853	657	12660	13033	4049	.481
St. Louis	1818	733	803	282	5917	6236	1748	.481
Quebec	880	350	419	111	3321	3485	811	.461
Washington	1280	499	607	174	4366	4836	1172	.458
Los Angeles	1818	698	854	266	6332	6880	1662	.457
Hartford	880	339	428	113	3118	3473	791	.449
Minnesota	1818	663	851	304	5907	6536	1630	.448
Winnipeg	880	331	432	117	3252	3683	779	.443
Pittsburgh	1818	668	888	262	6190	6959	1598	.439
Vancouver	1592	538	812	242	5182	6093	1318	.414
*New Jersey	1280	355	750	175	3987	5321	885	.346

* Totals included those of Kansas City (1974-75, 1975-76) and Colorado (1976-77 through 1981-82)
** Totals include those of Atlanta (1972-73 through 1979-80)

Year-By-Year Final Standings & Leading Scorers

Note: Assists not tabulated until 1918-19.
*Stanley Cup winner.

1917-18

Team	GP	W	L	T	GF	GA	PTS
Montreal	22	13	9	0	115	84	26
*Toronto	22	13	9	0	108	109	26
Ottawa	22	9	13	0	102	114	18
**Mtl. Wanderers	6	1	5	0	17	35	2

**Montreal Arena burned down and Wanderers forced to withdraw from League. Canadiens and Toronto each counted a win for defaulted games with Wanderers.

Leading Scorers

Player	Club	GP	G	A	PTS
Malone, Joe	Montreal	20	44	—	44
Denneny, Cy	Ottawa	22	36	—	36
Noble, Reg	Toronto	20	28	—	28
Lalonde, Newsy	Montreal	14	23	—	23
Denneny, Corbett	Toronto	21	20	—	20
Pitre, Didier	Montreal	19	17	—	17
Cameron, Harry	Toronto	20	17	—	17
Darragh, Jack	Ottawa	18	14	—	14
Hyland, Harry	Mtl.W., Ott.	16	14	—	14
Skinner, Alf	Toronto	19	13	—	13
Gerard, Eddie	Ottawa	21	13	—	13

1918-19

Team	GP	W	L	T	GF	GA	PTS
Ottawa	18	12	6	0	71	53	24
Montreal	18	10	8	0	88	78	20
Toronto	18	5	13	0	64	92	10

Leading Scorers

Player	Club	GP	G	A	PTS	PIM
Lalonde, Newsy	Montreal	17	21	9	30	40
Cleghorn, Odie	Montreal	17	23	6	29	33
Denneny, Cy	Ottawa	18	18	4	22	43
Nighbor, Frank	Ottawa	18	18	4	22	27
Pitre, Didier	Montreal	17	14	4	18	9
Skinner, Alf	Toronto	17	12	3	15	26
Cameron, Harry	Tor., Ott.	14	11	3	14	35
Noble, Reg	Toronto	17	11	3	14	35
Darragh, Jack	Ottawa	14	12	1	13	27
Randall, Ken	Toronto	14	7	6	13	27

Montreal's Joe Malone was the NHL's first scoring champion.

1919-20

Team	GP	W	L	T	GF	GA	PTS
*Ottawa	24	19	5	0	121	64	38
Montreal	24	13	11	0	129	113	26
Toronto	24	12	12	0	119	106	24
Quebec	24	4	20	0	91	177	8

Leading Scorers

Player	Club	GP	G	A	PTS	PIM
Malone, Joe	Quebec	24	39	9	48	12
Lalonde, Newsy	Montreal	23	36	6	42	33
Denneny, Corbett	Toronto	23	23	12	35	18
Nighbor, Frank	Ottawa	23	26	7	33	18
Noble, Reg	Toronto	24	24	7	31	51
Darragh, Jack	Ottawa	22	22	5	27	22
Arbour, Amos	Montreal	20	22	4	26	10
Wilson, Cully	Toronto	23	21	5	26	79
Broadbent, Punch	Ottawa	20	19	4	23	39
Pitre, Didier	Montreal	22	15	7	22	6

1920-21

Team	GP	W	L	T	GF	GA	PTS
Toronto	24	15	9	0	105	100	30
*Ottawa	24	14	10	0	97	75	28
Montreal	24	13	11	0	112	99	26
Hamilton	24	6	18	0	92	132	12

Leading Scorers

Player	Club	GP	G	A	PTS	PIM
Lalonde, Newsy	Montreal	24	33	8	41	36
Denneny, Cy	Ottawa	24	34	5	39	0
Dye, Babe	Ham., Tor.	24	35	2	37	32
Malone, Joe	Hamilton	20	30	4	34	2
Cameron, Harry	Toronto	24	18	9	27	35
Noble, Reg	Toronto	24	20	6	26	54
Prodgers, Goldie	Hamilton	23	18	8	26	8
Denneny, Corbett	Toronto	20	17	6	23	27
Nighbor, Frank	Ottawa	24	18	3	21	10
Berlinquette, Louis	Montreal	24	12	9	21	24

1921-22

Team	GP	W	L	T	GF	GA	PTS
Ottawa	24	14	8	2	106	84	30
*Toronto	24	13	10	1	98	97	27
Montreal	24	12	11	1	88	94	25
Hamilton	24	7	17	0	88	105	14

Leading Scorers

Player	Club	GP	G	A	PTS	PIM
Broadbent, Punch	Ottawa	24	32	14	46	24
Denneny, Cy	Ottawa	22	27	12	39	18
Dye, Babe	Toronto	24	30	7	37	18
Malone, Joe	Hamilton	24	25	7	32	4
Cameron, Harry	Toronto	24	19	8	27	18
Denneny, Corbett	Toronto	24	19	7	26	28
Noble, Reg	Toronto	24	17	8	25	10
Cleghorn, Odie	Montreal	23	21	3	24	26
Cleghorn, Sprague	Montreal	24	17	7	24	63
Reise, Leo	Hamilton	24	9	14	23	8

1922-23

Team	GP	W	L	T	GF	GA	PTS
*Ottawa	24	14	9	1	77	54	29
Montreal	24	13	9	2	73	61	28
Toronto	24	13	10	1	82	88	27
Hamilton	24	6	18	0	81	110	12

Leading Scorers

Player	Club	GP	G	A	PTS	PIM
Dye, Babe	Toronto	22	26	11	37	19
Denneny, Cy	Ottawa	24	21	10	31	20
Adams, Jack	Toronto	23	19	9	28	42
Boucher, Billy	Montreal	24	23	4	27	52
Cleghorn, Odie	Montreal	24	19	7	26	14
Roach, Mickey	Hamilton	23	17	8	25	8
Boucher, George	Ottawa	23	15	9	24	44
Joliat, Aurel	Montreal	24	13	9	22	31
Noble, Reg	Toronto	24	12	10	22	41
Wilson, Cully	Hamilton	23	16	3	19	46

1923-24

Team	GP	W	L	T	GF	GA	PTS
Ottawa	24	16	8	0	74	54	32
*Montreal	24	13	11	0	59	48	26
Toronto	24	10	14	0	59	85	20
Hamilton	24	9	15	0	63	68	18

Leading Scorers

Player	Club	GP	G	A	PTS	PIM
Denneny, Cy	Ottawa	21	22	1	23	10
Boucher, Billy	Montreal	23	16	6	22	33
Joliat, Aurel	Montreal	24	15	5	20	19
Dye, Babe	Toronto	19	17	2	19	23
Boucher, George	Ottawa	21	14	5	19	28
Burch, Billy	Hamilton	24	16	2	18	4
Clancy, King	Ottawa	24	9	8	17	18
Adams, Jack	Toronto	22	13	4	17	49
Morenz, Howie	Montreal	24	13	3	16	20
Noble, Reg	Toronto	23	12	3	15	23

1924-25

Team	GP	W	L	T	GF	GA	PTS
Hamilton	30	19	10	1	90	60	39
Toronto	30	19	11	0	90	84	38
Montreal	30	17	11	2	93	56	36
Ottawa	30	17	12	1	83	66	35
Mtl. Maroons	30	9	19	2	45	65	20
Boston	30	6	24	0	49	119	12

Leading Scorers

Player	Club	GP	G	A	PTS	PIM
Dye, Babe	Toronto	29	38	6	44	41
Denneny, Cy	Ottawa	28	27	15	42	16
Joliat, Aurel	Montreal	24	29	11	40	85
Morenz, Howie	Montreal	30	27	7	34	31
Boucher, Billy	Montreal	30	18	13	31	92
Adams, Jack	Toronto	27	21	8	29	66
Burch, Billy	Hamilton	27	20	4	24	10
Green, Red	Hamilton	30	19	4	23	63
Herberts, Jimmy	Boston	30	17	5	22	50
Day, Hap	Toronto	26	10	12	22	27

1925-26

Team	GP	W	L	T	GF	GA	PTS
Ottawa	36	24	8	4	77	42	52
*Mtl. Maroons	36	20	11	5	91	73	45
Pittsburgh	36	19	16	1	82	70	39
Boston	36	17	15	4	92	85	38
NY Americans	36	12	20	4	68	89	28
Toronto	36	12	21	3	92	114	27
Montreal	36	11	24	1	79	108	23

Leading Scorers

Player	Club	GP	G	A	PTS	PIM
Stewart, Nels	Mtl. Maroons	36	34	8	42	119
Denneny, Cy	Ottawa	36	24	12	36	18
Cooper, Carson	Boston	36	28	3	31	10
Herberts, Jimmy	Boston	36	26	5	31	47
Morenz, Howie	Montreal	31	23	3	26	39
Adams, Jack	Toronto	36	21	5	26	52
Joliat, Aurel	Montreal	35	17	9	26	52
Burch, Billy	NY Americans	36	22	3	25	33
Smith, Hooley	Ottawa	28	16	9	25	53
Nighbor, Frank	Ottawa	35	12	13	25	40

1926-27

Canadian Division

Team	GP	W	L	T	GF	GA	PTS
*Ottawa	44	30	10	4	86	69	64
Montreal	44	28	14	2	99	67	58
Mtl. Maroons	44	20	20	4	71	68	44
NY Americans	44	17	25	2	82	91	36
Toronto	44	15	24	5	79	94	35

American Division

Team	GP	W	L	T	GF	GA	PTS
New York	44	25	13	6	95	72	56
Boston	44	21	20	3	97	89	45
Chicago	44	19	22	3	115	116	41
Pittsburgh	44	15	26	3	79	108	33
Detroit	44	12	28	4	76	105	28

Leading Scorers

Player	Club	GP	G	A	PTS	PIM
Cook, Bill	New York	44	33	4	37	58
Irvin, Dick	Chicago	43	18	18	36	34
Morenz, Howie	Montreal	44	25	7	32	49
Fredrickson, Frank	Det., Bos.	41	18	13	31	46
Dye, Cecil	Chicago	41	25	5	30	14
Bailey, Ace	Toronto	42	15	13	28	82
Boucher, Frank	New York	44	13	15	28	17
Burch, Billy	NY Americans	43	19	8	27	40
Oliver, Harry	Boston	42	18	6	24	17
Keats, Gordon	Bos., Det.	42	16	8	24	52

Frank Nighbor finished in the top ten in NHL scoring on four occasions.

1927-28

Canadian Division

Team	GP	W	L	T	GF	GA	PTS
Montreal	44	26	11	7	116	48	59
Mtl. Maroons	44	24	14	6	96	77	54
Ottawa	44	20	14	10	78	57	50
Toronto	44	18	18	8	89	88	44
NY Americans	44	11	27	6	63	128	28

American Division

Team	GP	W	L	T	GF	GA	PTS
Boston	44	20	13	11	77	70	51
*New York	44	19	16	9	94	79	47
Pittsburgh	44	19	17	8	67	76	46
Detroit	44	19	19	6	88	79	44
Chicago	44	7	34	3	68	134	17

Leading Scorers

Player	Club	GP	G	A	PTS	PIM
Morenz, Howie	Montreal	43	33	18	51	66
Joliat, Aurel	Montreal	44	28	11	39	105
Boucher, Frank	New York	44	23	12	35	15
Hay, George	Detroit	42	22	13	35	20
Stewart, Nels	Mtl. Maroons	41	27	7	34	104
Gagne, Art	Montreal	44	20	10	30	75
Cook, Fred	New York	44	14	14	28	45
Carson, Bill	Toronto	32	20	6	26	36
Finnigan, Frank	Ottawa	38	20	5	25	34
Cook, Bill	New York	43	18	6	24	42
Keats, Gordon	Chi., Det.	38	14	10	24	60

1928-29

Canadian Division

Team	GP	W	L	T	GF	GA	PTS
Montreal	44	22	7	15	71	43	59
NY Americans	44	19	13	12	53	53	50
Toronto	44	21	18	5	85	69	47
Ottawa	44	14	17	13	54	67	41
Mtl. Maroons	44	15	20	9	67	65	39

American Division

Team	GP	W	L	T	GF	GA	PTS
*Boston	44	26	13	5	89	52	57
New York	44	21	13	10	72	65	52
Detroit	44	19	16	9	72	63	47
Pittsburgh	44	9	27	8	46	80	26
Chicago	44	7	29	8	33	85	22

Leading Scorers

Player	Club	GP	G	A	PTS	PIM
Bailey, Ace	Toronto	44	22	10	32	78
Stewart, Nels	Mtl. Maroons	44	21	8	29	74
Cooper, Carson	Detroit	43	18	9	27	14
Morenz, Howie	Montreal	42	17	10	27	47
Blair, Andy	Toronto	44	12	15	27	41
Boucher, Frank	New York	44	10	16	26	8
Oliver, Harry	Boston	43	17	6	23	24
Cook, Bill	New York	43	15	8	23	41
Ward, Jimmy	Mtl. Maroons	43	14	8	22	46

Seven players tied with 19 points

1929-30

Canadian Division

Team	GP	W	L	T	GF	GA	PTS
Mtl. Maroons	44	23	16	5	141	114	51
*Montreal	44	21	14	9	142	114	51
Ottawa	44	21	15	8	138	118	50
Toronto	44	17	21	6	116	124	40
NY Americans	44	14	25	5	113	161	33

American Division

Team	GP	W	L	T	GF	GA	PTS
Boston	44	38	5	1	179	98	77
Chicago	44	21	18	5	117	111	47
New York	44	17	17	10	136	143	44
Detroit	44	14	24	6	117	133	34
Pittsburgh	44	5	36	3	102	185	13

Leading Scorers

Name	Club	GP	G	A	PTS	PIM
Weiland, Cooney	Boston	44	43	30	73	27
Boucher, Frank	New York	42	26	36	62	16
Clapper, Dit	Boston	44	41	20	61	48
Cook, Bill	New York	44	29	30	59	56
Kilrea, Hec	Ottawa	44	36	22	58	72
Stewart, Nels	Mtl. Maroons	44	39	16	55	81
Morenz, Howie	Montreal	44	40	10	50	72
Himes, Norm	NY Americans	44	28	22	50	15
Lamb, Joe	Ottawa	44	29	20	49	119
Gainor, Norm	Boston	42	18	31	49	39

1930-31

Canadian Division

Team	GP	W	L	T	GF	GA	PTS
*Montreal	44	26	10	8	129	89	60
Toronto	44	22	13	9	118	99	53
Mtl. Maroons	44	20	18	6	105	106	46
NY Americans	44	18	16	10	76	74	46
Ottawa	44	10	30	4	91	142	24

American Division

Team	GP	W	L	T	GF	GA	PTS
Boston	44	28	10	6	143	90	62
Chicago	44	24	17	3	108	78	51
New York	44	19	16	9	106	87	47
Detroit	44	16	21	7	102	105	39
Philadelphia	44	4	36	4	76	184	12

Leading Scorers

Player	Club	GP	G	A	PTS	PIM
Morenz, Howie	Montreal	39	28	23	51	49
Goodfellow, Ebbie	Detroit	44	25	23	48	32
Conacher, Charlie	Toronto	37	31	12	43	78
Cook, Bill	New York	43	30	12	42	39
Bailey, Ace	Toronto	40	23	19	42	46
Primeau, Joe	Toronto	38	9	32	41	18
Stewart, Nels	Mtl. Maroons	42	25	14	39	75
Boucher, Frank	New York	44	12	27	39	20
Weiland, Cooney	Boston	44	25	13	38	14
Cook, Fred	New York	44	18	17	35	72
Joliat, Aurel	Montreal	43	13	22	35	73

1931-32

Canadian Division

Team	GP	W	L	T	GF	GA	PTS
Montreal	48	25	16	7	128	111	57
*Toronto	48	23	18	7	155	127	53
Mtl. Maroons	48	19	22	7	142	139	45
NY Americans	48	16	24	8	95	142	40

American Division

Team	GP	W	L	T	GF	GA	PTS
New York	48	23	17	8	134	112	54
Chicago	48	18	19	11	86	101	47
Detroit	48	18	20	10	95	108	46
Boston	48	15	21	12	122	117	42

Leading Scorers

Player	Club	GP	G	A	PTS	PIM
Jackson, Harvey	Toronto	48	28	25	53	63
Primeau, Joe	Toronto	46	13	37	50	25
Morenz, Howie	Montreal	48	24	25	49	46
Conacher, Charlie	Toronto	44	34	14	48	66
Cook, Bill	New York	48	34	14	48	33
Trottier, Dave	Mtl. Maroons	48	26	18	44	94
Smith, Reg	Mtl. Maroons	43	11	33	44	49
Siebert, Albert	Mtl. Maroons	48	21	18	39	64
Clapper, Dit	Boston	48	17	22	39	21
Joliat, Aurel	Montreal	48	15	24	39	46

Defenseman "Bullet" Joe Simpson played for the New York Americans from 1925 to 1931.

1932-33

Canadian Division

Team	GP	W	L	T	GF	GA	PTS
Toronto	48	24	18	6	119	111	54
Mtl. Maroons	48	22	20	6	135	119	50
Montreal	48	18	25	5	92	115	41
NY Americans	48	15	22	11	91	118	41
Ottawa	48	11	27	10	88	131	32

American Division

Team	GP	W	L	T	GF	GA	PTS
Boston	48	25	15	8	124	88	58
Detroit	48	25	15	8	111	93	58
*New York	48	23	17	8	135	107	54
Chicago	48	16	20	12	88	101	44

Leading Scorers

Player	Club	GP	G	A	PTS	PIM
Cook, Bill	New York	48	28	22	50	51
Jackson, Harvey	Toronto	48	27	17	44	43
Northcott, Lawrence	Mtl. Maroons	48	22	21	43	30
Smith, Reg	Mtl. Maroons	48	20	21	41	66
Haynes, Paul	Mtl. Maroons	48	16	25	41	18
Joliat, Aurel	Montreal	48	18	21	39	53
Barry, Marty	Boston	48	24	13	37	40
Cook, Fred	New York	48	22	15	37	35
Stewart, Nels	Boston	47	18	18	36	62
Morenz, Howie	Montreal	46	14	21	35	32
Gagnon, Johnny	Montreal	48	12	23	35	64
Shore, Eddie	Boston	48	8	27	35	102
Boucher, Frank	New York	47	7	28	35	4

1933-34

Canadian Division

Team	GP	W	L	T	GF	GA	PTS
Toronto	48	26	13	9	174	119	61
Montreal	48	22	20	6	99	101	50
Mtl. Maroons	48	19	18	11	117	122	49
NY Americans	48	15	23	10	104	132	40
Ottawa	48	13	29	6	115	143	32

American Division

Team	GP	W	L	T	GF	GA	PTS
Detroit	48	24	14	10	113	98	58
*Chicago	48	20	17	11	88	83	51
New York	48	21	19	8	120	113	50
Boston	48	18	25	5	111	130	41

Leading Scorers

Player	Club	GP	G	A	PTS	PIM
Conacher, Charlie	Toronto	42	32	20	52	38
Primeau, Joe	Toronto	45	14	32	46	8
Boucher, Frank	New York	48	14	30	44	4
Barry, Marty	Boston	48	27	12	39	12
Dillon, Cecil	New York	48	13	26	39	10
Stewart, Nels	Boston	48	21	17	38	68
Jackson, Harvey	Toronto	38	20	18	38	38
Joliat, Aurel	Montreal	48	22	15	37	27
Smith, Reg	Mtl. Maroons	47	18	19	37	58
Thompson, Paul	Chicago	48	20	16	36	17

1934-35

Canadian Division

Team	GP	W	L	T	GF	GA	PTS
Toronto	48	30	14	4	157	111	64
*Mtl. Maroons	48	24	19	5	123	92	53
Montreal	48	19	23	6	110	145	44
NY Americans	48	12	27	9	100	142	33
St. Louis	48	11	31	6	86	144	28

American Division

Team	GP	W	L	T	GF	GA	PTS
Boston	48	26	16	6	129	112	58
Chicago	48	26	17	5	118	88	57
New York	48	22	20	6	137	139	50
Detroit	48	19	22	7	127	114	45

Leading Scorers

Player	Club	GP	G	A	PTS	PIM
Conacher, Charlie	Toronto	47	36	21	57	24
Howe, Syd	St.L., Det.	50	22	25	47	34
Aurie, Larry	Detroit	48	17	29	46	24
Boucher, Frank	New York	48	13	32	45	2
Jackson, Harvey	Toronto	42	22	22	44	27
Lewis, Herb	Detroit	47	16	27	43	26
Chapman, Art	NY Americans	47	9	34	43	4
Barry, Marty	Boston	48	20	20	40	33
Schriner, Sweeney	NY Americans	48	18	22	40	6
Stewart, Nels	Boston	47	21	18	39	45
Thompson, Paul	Chicago	48	16	23	39	20

CHARLIE CONACHER
ALL-STAR RIGHT WING
1933-34, 1934-35, 1935-36

Charlie Conacher won consecutive scoring titles in the 1930's.

1935-36

Canadian Division

Team	GP	W	L	T	GF	GA	PTS
Mtl. Maroons	48	22	16	10	114	106	54
Toronto	48	23	19	6	126	106	52
NY Americans	48	16	25	7	109	122	39
Montreal	48	11	26	11	82	123	33

American Division

Team	GP	W	L	T	GF	GA	PTS
*Detroit	48	24	16	8	124	103	56
Boston	48	22	20	6	92	83	50
Chicago	48	21	19	8	93	92	50
New York	48	19	17	12	91	96	50

Leading Scorers

Player	Club	GP	G	A	PTS	PIM
Schriner, Sweeney	NY Americans	48	19	26	45	8
Barry, Marty	Detroit	48	21	19	40	16
Thompson, Paul	Chicago	45	17	23	40	19
Thoms, Bill	Toronto	48	23	15	38	29
Conacher, Charlie	Toronto	44	23	15	38	74
Smith, Reg	Mtl. Maroons	47	19	19	38	75
Romnes, Doc	Chicago	48	13	25	38	6
Chapman, Art	NY Americans	47	10	28	38	14
Lewis, Herb	Detroit	45	14	23	37	25
Northcott, Lawrence	Mtl. Maroons	48	15	21	36	41

1936-37

Canadian Division

Team	GP	W	L	T	GF	GA	PTS
Montreal	48	24	18	6	115	111	54
Mtl. Maroons	48	22	17	9	126	110	53
Toronto	48	22	21	5	119	115	49
NY Americans	48	15	29	4	122	161	34

American Division

Team	GP	W	L	T	GF	GA	PTS
*Detroit	48	25	14	9	128	102	59
Boston	48	23	18	7	120	110	53
New York	48	19	20	9	117	106	47
Chicago	48	14	27	7	99	131	35

Leading Scorers

Player	Club	GP	G	A	PTS	PIM
Schriner, Sweeney	NY Americans	48	21	25	46	17
Apps, Syl	Toronto	48	16	29	45	10
Barry, Marty	Detroit	48	17	27	44	6
Aurie, Larry	Detroit	45	23	20	43	20
Jackson, Harvey	Toronto	46	21	19	40	12
Gagnon, Johnny	Montreal	48	20	16	36	38
Gracie, Bob	Mtl. Maroons	47	11	25	36	18
Stewart, Nels	Bos., NYA	43	23	12	35	37
Thompson, Paul	Chicago	47	17	18	35	28
Cowley, Bill	Boston	46	13	22	35	4

1937-38

Canadian Division

Team	GP	W	L	T	GF	GA	PTS
Toronto	48	24	15	9	151	127	57
NY Americans	48	19	18	11	110	111	49
Montreal	48	18	17	13	123	128	49
Mtl. Maroons	48	12	30	6	101	149	30

American Division

Team	GP	W	L	T	GF	GA	PTS
Boston	48	30	11	7	142	89	67
New York	48	27	15	6	149	96	60
*Chicago	48	14	25	9	97	139	37
Detroit	48	12	25	11	99	133	35

Leading Scorers

Player	Club	GP	G	A	PTS	PIM
Drillon, Gord	Toronto	48	26	26	52	4
Apps, Syl	Toronto	47	21	29	50	9
Thompson, Paul	Chicago	48	22	22	44	14
Mantha, Georges	Montreal	47	23	19	42	12
Dillon, Cecil	New York	48	21	18	39	6
Cowley, Bill	Boston	48	17	22	39	8
Schriner, Sweeney	NY Americans	49	21	17	38	22
Thoms, Bill	Toronto	48	14	24	38	14
Smith, Clint	New York	48	14	23	37	0
Stewart, Nels	NY Americans	48	19	17	36	29
Colville, Neil	New York	45	17	19	36	11

1938-39

Team	GP	W	L	T	GF	GA	PTS
*Boston	48	36	10	2	156	76	74
New York	48	26	16	6	149	105	58
Toronto	48	19	20	9	114	107	47
NY Americans	48	17	21	10	119	157	44
Detroit	48	18	24	6	107	128	42
Montreal	48	15	24	9	115	146	39
Chicago	48	12	28	8	91	132	32

Leading Scorers

Player	Club	GP	G	A	PTS	PIM
Blake, Hector	Montreal	48	24	23	47	10
Schriner, Sweeney	NY Americans	48	13	31	44	20
Cowley, Bill	Boston	34	8	34	42	2
Smith, Clint	New York	48	21	20	41	2
Barry, Marty	Detroit	48	13	28	41	4
Apps, Syl	Toronto	44	15	25	40	4
Anderson, Tom	NY Americans	48	13	27	40	14
Gottselig, Johnny	Chicago	48	16	23	39	15
Haynes, Paul	Montreal	47	5	33	38	27
Conacher, Roy	Boston	47	26	11	37	12
Carr, Lorne	NY Americans	46	19	18	37	16
Colville, Neil	New York	48	18	19	37	12
Watson, Phil	New York	48	15	22	37	42

1939-40

Team	GP	W	L	T	GF	GA	PTS
Boston	48	31	12	5	170	98	67
*New York	48	27	11	10	136	77	64
Toronto	48	25	17	6	134	110	56
Chicago	48	23	19	6	112	120	52
Detroit	48	16	26	6	90	126	38
NY Americans	48	15	29	4	106	140	34
Montreal	48	10	33	5	90	167	25

Leading Scorers

Player	Club	GP	G	A	PTS	PIM
Schmidt, Milt	Boston	48	22	30	52	37
Dumart, Woody	Boston	48	22	21	43	16
Bauer, Bob	Boston	48	17	26	43	2
Drillon, Gord	Toronto	43	21	19	40	13
Cowley, Bill	Boston	48	13	27	40	24
Hextall, Bryan	New York	48	24	15	39	52
Colville, Neil	New York	48	19	19	38	22
Howe, Syd	Detroit	46	14	23	37	17
Blake, Hector	Montreal	48	17	19	36	48
Armstrong, Murray	NY Americans	48	16	20	36	12

1940-41

Team	GP	W	L	T	GF	GA	PTS
*Boston	48	27	8	13	168	102	67
Toronto	48	28	14	6	145	99	62
Detroit	48	21	16	11	112	102	53
New York	48	21	19	8	143	125	50
Chicago	48	16	25	7	112	139	39
Montreal	48	16	26	6	121	147	38
NY Americans	48	8	29	11	99	186	27

Leading Scorers

Player	Club	GP	G	A	PTS	PIM
Cowley, Bill	Boston	46	17	45	62	16
Hextall, Bryan	New York	48	26	18	44	16
Drillon, Gord	Toronto	42	23	21	44	2
Apps, Syl	Toronto	41	20	24	44	6
Patrick, Lynn	New York	48	20	24	44	12
Howe, Syd	Detroit	48	20	24	44	8
Colville, Neil	New York	48	14	28	42	28
Wiseman, Eddie	Boston	48	16	24	40	10
Bauer, Bobby	Boston	48	17	22	39	2
Schriner, Sweeney	Toronto	48	24	14	38	6
Conacher, Roy	Boston	40	24	14	38	7
Schmidt, Milt	Boston	44	13	25	38	23

1941-42

Team	GP	W	L	T	GF	GA	PTS
New York	48	29	17	2	177	143	60
*Toronto	48	27	18	3	158	136	57
Boston	48	25	17	6	160	118	56
Chicago	48	22	23	3	145	155	47
Detroit	48	19	25	4	140	147	42
Montreal	48	18	27	3	134	173	39
Brooklyn	48	16	29	3	133	175	35

Leading Scorers

Player	Club	GP	G	A	PTS	PIM
Hextall, Bryan	New York	48	24	32	56	30
Patrick, Lynn	New York	47	32	22	54	18
Grosso, Don	Detroit	48	23	30	53	13
Watson, Phil	New York	48	15	37	52	48
Abel, Sid	Detroit	48	18	31	49	45
Blake, Hector	Montreal	47	17	28	45	19
Thoms, Bill	Chicago	47	15	30	45	8
Drillon, Gord	Toronto	48	23	18	41	6
Apps, Syl	Toronto	38	18	23	41	0
Anderson, Tom	Brooklyn	48	12	29	41	54

1942-43

Team	GP	W	L	T	GF	GA	PTS
*Detroit	50	25	14	11	169	124	61
Boston	50	24	17	9	195	176	57
Toronto	50	22	19	9	198	159	53
Montreal	50	19	19	12	181	191	50
Chicago	50	17	18	15	179	180	49
New York	50	11	31	8	161	253	30

Leading Scorers

Player	Club	GP	G	A	PTS	PIM
Bentley, Doug	Chicago	50	33	40	73	18
Cowley, Bill	Boston	48	27	45	72	10
Bentley, Max	Chicago	47	26	44	70	2
Patrick, Lynn	New York	50	22	39	61	28
Carr, Lorne	Toronto	50	27	33	60	15
Taylor, Billy	Toronto	50	18	42	60	2
Hextall, Bryan	New York	50	27	32	59	28
Blake, Hector	Montreal	48	23	36	59	28
Lach, Elmer	Montreal	45	18	40	58	14
O'Connor, Herb	Montreal	50	15	43	58	2

1943-44

Team	GP	W	L	T	GF	GA	PTS
*Montreal	50	38	5	7	234	109	83
Detroit	50	26	18	6	214	177	58
Toronto	50	23	23	4	214	174	50
Chicago	50	22	23	5	178	187	49
Boston	50	19	26	5	223	268	43
New York	50	6	39	5	162	310	17

Leading Scorers

Player	Club	GP	G	A	PTS	PIM
Cain, Herb	Boston	48	36	46	82	4
Bentley, Doug	Chicago	50	38	39	77	22
Carr, Lorne	Toronto	50	36	38	74	9
Liscombe, Carl	Detroit	50	36	37	73	17
Lach, Elmer	Montreal	48	24	48	72	23
Smith, Clint	Chicago	50	23	49	72	4
Cowley, Bill	Boston	36	30	41	71	12
Mosienko, Bill	Chicago	50	32	38	70	10
Jackson, Art	Boston	49	28	41	69	8
Bodnar, Gus	Toronto	50	22	40	62	18

1944-45

Team	GP	W	L	T	GF	GA	PTS
Montreal	50	38	8	4	228	121	80
Detroit	50	31	14	5	218	161	67
*Toronto	50	24	22	4	183	161	52
Boston	50	16	30	4	179	219	36
Chicago	50	13	30	7	141	194	33
New York	50	11	29	10	154	247	32

Leading Scorers

Player	Club	GP	G	A	PTS	PIM
Lach, Elmer	Montreal	50	26	54	80	37
Richard, Maurice	Montreal	50	50	23	73	36
Blake, Hector	Montreal	49	29	38	67	15
Cowley, Bill	Boston	49	25	40	65	2
Kennedy, Ted	Toronto	49	29	25	54	14
Mosienko, Bill	Chicago	50	28	26	54	0
Carveth, Joe	Detroit	50	26	28	54	6
DeMarco, Albert	New York	50	24	30	54	10
Smith, Clint	Chicago	50	23	31	54	6
Howe, Syd	Detroit	46	17	36	53	6

Bill Mosienko finished in the top 10 in NHL scoring five times during his 14-year career.

Though he never won a scoring title, Maurice "Rocket" Richard's intensity on the ice translated into a knack for scoring crucial goals. He is the League's leading scorer in Stanley Cup playoff overtime.

1945-46

Team	GP	W	L	T	GF	GA	PTS
*Montreal	50	28	17	5	172	134	61
Boston	50	24	18	8	167	156	56
Chicago	50	23	20	7	200	178	53
Detroit	50	20	20	10	146	159	50
Toronto	50	19	24	7	174	185	45
New York	50	13	28	9	144	191	35

Leading Scorers

Player	Club	GP	G	A	PTS	PIM
Bentley, Max	Chicago	47	31	30	61	6
Stewart, Gaye	Toronto	50	37	15	52	8
Blake, Hector	Montreal	50	29	21	50	2
Smith, Clint	Chicago	50	26	24	50	2
Richard, Maurice	Montreal	50	27	21	48	50
Mosienko, Bill	Chicago	40	18	30	48	12
DeMarco, Albert	New York	50	20	27	47	20
Lach, Elmer	Montreal	50	13	34	47	34
Kaleta, Alex	Chicago	49	19	27	46	17
Taylor, Billy	Toronto	48	23	18	41	14
Horeck, Pete	Chicago	50	20	21	41	34

1946-47

Team	GP	W	L	T	GF	GA	PTS
Montreal	60	34	16	10	189	138	78
*Toronto	60	31	19	10	209	172	72
Boston	60	26	23	11	190	175	63
Detroit	60	22	27	11	190	193	55
New York	60	22	32	6	167	186	50
Chicago	60	19	37	4	193	274	42

Leading Scorers

Player	Club	GP	G	A	PTS	PIM
Bentley, Max	Chicago	60	29	43	72	12
Richard, Maurice	Montreal	60	45	26	71	69
Taylor, Billy	Detroit	60	17	46	63	35
Schmidt, Milt	Boston	59	27	35	62	40
Kennedy, Ted	Toronto	60	28	32	60	27
Bentley, Doug	Chicago	52	21	34	55	18
Bauer, Bob	Boston	58	30	24	54	4
Conacher, Roy	Detroit	60	30	24	54	6
Mosienko, Bill	Chicago	59	25	27	52	2
Dumart, Woody	Boston	60	24	28	52	12

1947-48

Team	GP	W	L	T	GF	GA	PTS
*Toronto	60	32	15	13	182	143	77
Detroit	60	30	18	12	187	148	72
Boston	60	23	24	13	167	168	59
New York	60	21	26	13	176	201	55
Montreal	60	20	29	11	147	169	51
Chicago	60	20	34	6	195	225	46

Leading Scorers

Player	Club	GP	G	A	PTS	PIM
Lach, Elmer	Montreal	60	30	31	61	72
O'Connor, Buddy	New York	60	24	36	60	8
Bentley, Doug	Chicago	60	20	37	57	16
Stewart, Gaye	Tor., Chi.	61	27	29	56	83
Bentley, Max	Chi., Tor.	59	26	28	54	14
Poile, Bud	Tor., Chi.	58	25	29	54	17
Richard, Maurice	Montreal	53	28	25	53	89
Apps, Syl	Toronto	55	26	27	53	12
Lindsay, Ted	Detroit	60	33	19	52	95
Conacher, Roy	Chicago	52	22	27	49	4

1948-49

Team	GP	W	L	T	GF	GA	PTS
Detroit	60	34	19	7	195	145	75
Boston	60	29	23	8	178	163	66
Montreal	60	28	23	9	152	126	65
*Toronto	60	22	25	13	147	161	57
Chicago	60	21	31	8	173	211	50
New York	60	18	31	11	133	172	47

Leading Scorers

Player	Club	GP	G	A	PTS	PIM
Conacher, Roy	Chicago	60	26	42	68	8
Bentley, Doug	Chicago	58	23	43	66	38
Abel, Sid	Detroit	60	28	26	54	49
Lindsay, Ted	Detroit	50	26	28	54	97
Conacher, Jim	Det., Chi.	59	26	23	49	43
Ronty, Paul	Boston	60	20	29	49	11
Watson, Harry	Toronto	60	26	19	45	0
Reay, Billy	Montreal	60	22	23	45	33
Bodnar, Gus	Chicago	59	19	26	45	14
Peirson, John	Boston	59	22	21	43	45

1949-50

Team	GP	W	L	T	GF	GA	PTS
*Detroit	70	37	19	14	229	164	88
Montreal	70	29	22	19	172	150	77
Toronto	70	31	27	12	176	173	74
New York	70	28	31	11	170	189	67
Boston	70	22	32	16	198	228	60
Chicago	70	22	38	10	203	244	54

Leading Scorers

Player	Club	GP	G	A	PTS	PIM
Lindsay, Ted	Detroit	69	23	55	78	141
Abel, Sid	Detroit	69	34	35	69	46
Howe, Gordie	Detroit	70	35	33	68	69
Richard, Maurice	Montreal	70	43	22	65	114
Ronty, Paul	Boston	70	23	36	59	8
Conacher, Roy	Chicago	70	25	31	56	16
Bentley, Doug	Chicago	64	20	33	53	28
Peirson, John	Boston	57	27	25	52	49
Prystai, Metro	Chicago	65	29	22	51	31
Guidolin, Bep	Chicago	70	17	34	51	42

1950-51

Team	GP	W	L	T	GF	GA	PTS
Detroit	70	44	13	13	236	139	101
*Toronto	70	41	16	13	212	138	95
Montreal	70	25	30	15	173	184	65
Boston	70	22	30	18	178	197	62
New York	70	20	29	21	169	201	62
Chicago	70	13	47	10	171	280	36

Leading Scorers

Player	Club	GP	G	A	PTS	PIM
Howe, Gordie	Detroit	70	43	43	86	74
Richard, Maurice	Montreal	65	42	24	66	97
Bentley, Max	Toronto	67	21	41	62	34
Abel, Sid	Detroit	69	23	38	61	30
Schmidt, Milt	Boston	62	22	39	61	33
Kennedy, Ted	Toronto	63	18	43	61	32
Lindsay, Ted	Detroit	67	24	35	59	110
Sloan, Tod	Toronto	70	31	25	56	105
Kelly, Red	Detroit	70	17	37	54	24
Smith, Sid	Toronto	70	30	21	51	10
Gardner, Cal	Toronto	66	23	28	51	42

1951-52

Team	GP	W	L	T	GF	GA	PTS
*Detroit	70	44	14	12	215	133	100
Montreal	70	34	26	10	195	164	78
Toronto	70	29	25	16	168	157	74
Boston	70	25	29	16	162	176	66
New York	70	23	34	13	192	219	59
Chicago	70	17	44	9	158	241	43

Leading Scorers

Player	Club	GP	G	A	PTS	PIM
Howe, Gordie	Detroit	70	47	39	86	78
Lindsay, Ted	Detroit	70	30	39	69	123
Lach, Elmer	Montreal	70	15	50	65	36
Raleigh, Don	New York	70	19	42	61	14
Smith, Sid	Toronto	70	27	30	57	6
Geoffrion, Bernie	Montreal	67	30	24	54	66
Mosienko, Bill	Chicago	70	31	22	53	10
Abel, Sid	Detroit	62	17	36	53	32
Kennedy, Ted	Toronto	70	19	33	52	33
Schmidt, Milt	Boston	69	21	29	50	57
Peirson, John	Boston	68	20	30	50	30

1952-53

Team	GP	W	L	T	GF	GA	PTS
Detroit	70	36	16	18	222	133	90
*Montreal	70	28	23	19	155	148	75
Boston	70	28	29	13	152	172	69
Chicago	70	27	28	15	169	175	69
Toronto	70	27	30	13	156	167	67
New York	70	17	37	16	152	211	50

Leading Scorers

Player	Club	GP	G	A	PTS	PIM
Howe, Gordie	Detroit	70	49	46	95	57
Lindsay, Ted	Detroit	70	32	39	71	111
Richard, Maurice	Montreal	70	28	33	61	112
Hergesheimer, Wally	New York	70	30	29	59	10
Delvecchio, Alex	Detroit	70	16	43	59	28
Ronty, Paul	New York	70	16	38	54	20
Prystai, Metro	Detroit	70	16	34	50	12
Kelly, Red	Detroit	70	19	27	46	8
Olmstead, Bert	Montreal	69	17	28	45	83
Mackell, Fleming	Boston	65	27	17	44	63
McFadden, Jim	Chicago	70	23	21	44	29

1953-54

Team	GP	W	L	T	GF	GA	PTS
*Detroit	70	37	19	14	191	132	88
Montreal	70	35	24	11	195	141	81
Toronto	70	32	24	14	152	131	78
Boston	70	32	28	10	177	181	74
New York	70	29	31	10	161	182	68
Chicago	70	12	51	7	133	242	31

Leading Scorers

Player	Club	GP	G	A	PTS	PIM
Howe, Gordie	Detroit	70	33	48	81	109
Richard, Maurice	Montreal	70	37	30	67	112
Lindsay, Ted	Detroit	70	26	36	62	110
Geoffrion, Bernie	Montreal	54	29	25	54	87
Olmstead, Bert	Montreal	70	15	37	52	85
Kelly, Red	Detroit	62	16	33	49	18
Reibel, Earl	Detroit	69	15	33	48	18
Sandford, Ed	Boston	70	16	31	47	42
Mackell, Fleming	Boston	67	15	32	47	60
Mosdell, Ken	Montreal	67	22	24	46	64
Ronty, Paul	New York	70	13	33	46	18

1954-55

Team	GP	W	L	T	GF	GA	PTS
*Detroit	70	42	17	11	204	134	95
Montreal	70	41	18	11	228	157	93
Toronto	70	24	24	22	147	135	70
Boston	70	23	26	21	169	188	67
New York	70	17	35	18	150	210	52
Chicago	70	13	40	17	161	235	43

Leading Scorers

Player	Club	GP	G	A	PTS	PIM
Geoffrion, Bernie	Montreal	70	38	37	75	57
Richard, Maurice	Montreal	67	38	36	74	125
Beliveau, Jean	Montreal	70	37	36	73	58
Reibel, Earl	Detroit	70	25	41	66	15
Howe, Gordie	Detroit	64	29	33	62	68
Sullivan, George	Chicago	69	19	42	61	51
Olmstead, Bert	Montreal	70	10	48	58	103
Smith, Sid	Toronto	70	33	21	54	14
Mosdell, Ken	Montreal	70	22	32	54	82
Lewicki, Danny	New York	70	29	24	53	8

1955-56

Team	GP	W	L	T	GF	GA	PTS
*Montreal	70	45	15	10	222	131	100
Detroit	70	30	24	16	183	148	76
New York	70	32	28	10	204	203	74
Toronto	70	24	33	13	153	181	61
Boston	70	23	34	13	147	185	59
Chicago	70	19	39	12	155	216	50

Leading Scorers

Player	Club	GP	G	A	PTS	PIM
Beliveau, Jean	Montreal	70	47	41	88	143
Howe, Gordie	Detroit	70	38	41	79	100
Richard, Maurice	Montreal	70	38	33	71	89
Olmstead, Bert	Montreal	70	14	56	70	94
Sloan, Tod	Toronto	70	37	29	66	100
Bathgate, Andy	New York	70	19	47	66	59
Geoffrion, Bernie	Montreal	59	29	33	62	66
Reibel, Earl	Detroit	68	17	39	56	10
Delvecchio, Alex	Detroit	70	25	26	51	24
Creighton, Dave	New York	70	20	31	51	43
Gadsby, Bill	New York	70	9	42	51	84

1956-57

Team	GP	W	L	T	GF	GA	PTS
Detroit	70	38	20	12	198	157	88
*Montreal	70	35	23	12	210	155	82
Boston	70	34	24	12	195	174	80
New York	70	26	30	14	184	227	66
Toronto	70	21	34	15	174	192	57
Chicago	70	16	39	15	169	225	47

Leading Scorers

Player	Club	GP	G	A	PTS	PIM
Howe, Gordie	Detroit	70	44	45	89	72
Lindsay, Ted	Detroit	70	30	55	85	103
Beliveau, Jean	Montreal	69	33	51	84	105
Bathgate, Andy	New York	70	27	50	77	60
Litzenberger, Ed	Chicago	70	32	32	64	48
Richard, Maurice	Montreal	63	33	29	62	74
McKenney, Don	Boston	69	21	39	60	31
Moore, Dickie	Montreal	70	29	29	58	56
Richard, Henri	Montreal	63	18	36	54	71
Ullman, Norm	Detroit	64	16	36	52	47

1957-58

Team	GP	W	L	T	GF	GA	PTS
*Montreal	70	43	17	10	250	158	96
New York	70	32	25	13	195	188	77
Detroit	70	29	29	12	176	207	70
Boston	70	27	28	15	199	194	69
Chicago	70	24	39	7	163	202	55
Toronto	70	21	38	11	192	226	53

Leading Scorers

Player	Club	GP	G	A	PTS	PIM
Moore, Dickie	Montreal	70	36	48	84	65
Richard, Henri	Montreal	67	28	52	80	56
Bathgate, Andy	New York	65	30	48	78	42
Howe, Gordie	Detroit	64	33	44	77	40
Horvath, Bronco	Boston	67	30	36	66	71
Litzenberger, Ed	Chicago	70	32	30	62	63
Mackell, Fleming	Boston	70	20	40	60	72
Beliveau, Jean	Montreal	55	27	32	59	93
Delvecchio, Alex	Detroit	70	21	38	59	22
McKenney, Don	Boston	70	28	30	58	22

1958-59

Team	GP	W	L	T	GF	GA	PTS
*Montreal	70	39	18	13	258	158	91
Boston	70	32	29	9	205	215	73
Chicago	70	28	29	13	197	208	69
Toronto	70	27	32	11	189	201	65
New York	70	26	32	12	201	217	64
Detroit	70	25	37	8	167	218	58

Leading Scorers

Player	Club	GP	G	A	PTS	PIM
Moore, Dickie	Montreal	70	41	55	96	61
Beliveau, Jean	Montreal	64	45	46	91	67
Bathgate, Andy	New York	70	40	48	88	48
Howe, Gordie	Detroit	70	32	46	78	57
Litzenberger, Ed	Chicago	70	33	44	77	37
Geoffrion, Bernie	Montreal	59	22	44	66	30
Sullivan, George	New York	70	21	42	63	56
Hebenton, Andy	New York	70	33	29	62	8
McKenney, Don	Boston	70	32	30	62	20
Sloan, Tod	Chicago	59	27	35	62	79

1959-60

Team	GP	W	L	T	GF	GA	PTS
*Montreal	70	40	18	12	255	178	92
Toronto	70	35	26	9	199	195	79
Chicago	70	28	29	13	191	180	69
Detroit	70	26	29	15	186	197	67
Boston	70	28	34	8	220	241	64
New York	70	17	38	15	187	247	49

Leading Scorers

Player	Club	GP	G	A	PTS	PIM
Hull, Bobby	Chicago	70	39	42	81	68
Horvath, Bronco	Boston	68	39	41	80	60
Beliveau, Jean	Montreal	60	34	40	74	57
Bathgate, Andy	New York	70	26	48	74	28
Richard, Henri	Montreal	70	30	43	73	66
Howe, Gordie	Detroit	70	28	45	73	46
Geoffrion, Bernie	Montreal	59	30	41	71	36
McKenney, Don	Boston	70	20	49	69	28
Stasiuk, Vic	Boston	69	29	39	68	121
Prentice, Dean	New York	70	32	34	66	43

1960-61

Team	GP	W	L	T	GF	GA	PTS
Montreal	70	41	19	10	254	188	92
Toronto	70	39	19	12	234	176	90
*Chicago	70	29	24	17	198	180	75
Detroit	70	25	29	16	195	215	66
New York	70	22	38	10	204	248	54
Boston	70	15	42	13	176	254	43

Leading Scorers

Player	Club	GP	G	A	PTS	PIM
Geoffrion, Bernie	Montreal	64	50	45	95	29
Beliveau, Jean	Montreal	69	32	58	90	57
Mahovlich, Frank	Toronto	70	48	36	84	131
Bathgate, Andy	New York	70	29	48	77	22
Howe, Gordie	Detroit	64	23	49	72	30
Ullman, Norm	Detroit	70	28	42	70	34
Kelly, Red	Toronto	64	20	50	70	12
Moore, Dickie	Montreal	57	35	34	69	62
Richard, Henri	Montreal	70	24	44	68	91
Delvecchio, Alex	Detroit	70	27	35	62	26

1961-62

Team	GP	W	L	T	GF	GA	PTS
Montreal	70	42	14	14	259	166	98
*Toronto	70	37	22	11	232	180	85
Chicago	70	31	26	13	217	186	75
New York	70	26	32	12	195	207	64
Detroit	70	23	33	14	184	219	60
Boston	70	15	47	8	177	306	38

Leading Scorers

Player	Club	GP	G	A	PTS	PIM
Hull, Bobby	Chicago	70	50	34	84	35
Bathgate, Andy	New York	70	28	56	84	44
Howe, Gordie	Detroit	70	33	44	77	54
Mikita, Stan	Chicago	70	25	52	77	97
Mahovlich, Frank	Toronto	70	33	38	71	87
Delvecchio, Alex	Detroit	70	26	43	69	18
Backstrom, Ralph	Montreal	66	27	38	65	29
Ullman, Norm	Detroit	70	26	38	64	54
Hay, Bill	Chicago	60	11	52	63	34
Provost, Claude	Montreal	70	33	29	62	22

1962-63

Team	GP	W	L	T	GF	GA	PTS
*Toronto	70	35	23	12	221	180	82
Chicago	70	32	21	17	194	178	81
Montreal	70	28	19	23	225	183	79
Detroit	70	32	25	13	200	194	77
New York	70	22	36	12	211	233	56
Boston	70	14	39	17	198	281	45

Leading Scorers

Player	Club	GP	G	A	PTS	PIM
Howe, Gordie	Detroit	70	38	48	86	100
Bathgate, Andy	New York	70	35	46	81	54
Mikita, Stan	Chicago	65	31	45	76	69
Mahovlich, Frank	Toronto	67	36	37	73	56
Richard, Henri	Montreal	67	23	50	73	57
Beliveau, Jean	Montreal	69	18	49	67	68
Bucyk, John	Boston	69	27	39	66	36
Delvecchio, Alex	Detroit	70	20	44	64	8
Hull, Bobby	Chicago	65	31	31	62	27
Oliver, Murray	Boston	65	22	40	62	38

1963-64

Team	GP	W	L	T	GF	GA	PTS
Montreal	70	36	21	13	209	167	85
Chicago	70	36	22	12	218	169	84
*Toronto	70	33	25	12	192	172	78
Detroit	70	30	29	11	191	204	71
New York	70	22	38	10	186	242	54
Boston	70	18	40	12	170	212	48

Leading Scorers

Player	Club	GP	G	A	PTS	PIM
Mikita, Stan	Chicago	70	39	50	89	146
Hull, Bobby	Chicago	70	43	44	87	50
Beliveau, Jean	Montreal	68	28	50	78	42
Bathgate, Andy	NYR, Tor.	71	19	58	77	34
Howe, Gordie	Detroit	69	26	47	73	70
Wharram, Ken	Chicago	70	39	32	71	18
Oliver, Murray	Boston	70	24	44	68	41
Goyette, Phil	New York	67	24	41	65	15
Gilbert, Rod	New York	70	24	40	64	62
Keon, Dave	Toronto	70	23	37	60	6

1964-65

Team	GP	W	L	T	GF	GA	PTS
Detroit	70	40	23	7	224	175	87
*Montreal	70	36	23	11	211	185	83
Chicago	70	34	28	8	224	176	76
Toronto	70	30	26	14	204	173	74
New York	70	20	38	12	179	246	52
Boston	70	21	43	6	166	253	48

Leading Scorers

Player	Club	GP	G	A	PTS	PIM
Mikita, Stan	Chicago	70	28	59	87	154
Ullman, Norm	Detroit	70	42	41	83	70
Howe, Gordie	Detroit	70	29	47	76	104
Hull, Bobby	Chicago	61	39	32	71	32
Delvecchio, Alex	Detroit	68	25	42	67	16
Provost, Claude	Montreal	70	27	37	64	28
Gilbert, Rod	New York	70	25	36	61	52
Pilote, Pierre	Chicago	68	14	45	59	162
Bucyk, John	Boston	68	26	29	55	24
Backstrom, Ralph	Montreal	70	25	30	55	41
Esposito, Phil	Chicago	70	23	32	55	44

1965-66

Team	GP	W	L	T	GF	GA	PTS
*Montreal	70	41	21	8	239	173	90
Chicago	70	37	25	8	240	187	82
Toronto	70	34	25	11	208	187	79
Detroit	70	31	27	12	221	194	74
Boston	70	21	43	6	174	275	48
New York	70	18	41	11	195	261	47

Leading Scorers

Player	Club	GP	G	A	PTS	PIM
Hull, Bobby	Chicago	65	54	43	97	70
Mikita, Stan	Chicago	68	30	48	78	58
Rousseau, Bobby	Montreal	70	30	48	78	20
Beliveau, Jean	Montreal	67	29	48	77	50
Howe, Gordie	Detroit	70	29	46	75	83
Ullman, Norm	Detroit	70	31	41	72	35
Delvecchio, Alex	Detroit	70	31	38	69	16
Nevin, Bob	New York	69	29	33	62	10
Richard, Henri	Montreal	62	22	39	61	47
Oliver, Murray	Boston	70	18	42	60	30

1966-67

Team	GP	W	L	T	GF	GA	PTS
Chicago	70	41	17	12	264	170	94
Montreal	70	32	25	13	202	188	77
*Toronto	70	32	27	11	204	211	75
New York	70	30	28	12	188	189	72
Detroit	70	27	39	4	212	241	58
Boston	70	17	43	10	182	253	44

Leading Scorers

Player	Club	GP	G	A	PTS	PIM
Mikita, Stan	Chicago	70	35	62	97	12
Hull, Bobby	Chicago	66	52	28	80	52
Ullman, Norm	Detroit	68	26	44	70	26
Wharram, Ken	Chicago	70	31	34	65	21
Howe, Gordie	Detroit	69	25	40	65	53
Rousseau, Bobby	Montreal	68	19	44	63	58
Esposito, Phil	Chicago	69	21	40	61	40
Goyette, Phil	New York	70	12	49	61	6
Mohns, Doug	Chicago	61	25	35	60	58
Richard, Henri	Montreal	65	21	34	55	28
Delvecchio, Alex	Detroit	70	17	38	55	10

1967-68

East Division

Team	GP	W	L	T	GF	GA	PTS
*Montreal	74	42	22	10	236	167	94
New York	74	39	23	12	226	183	90
Boston	74	37	27	10	259	216	84
Chicago	74	32	26	16	212	222	80
Toronto	74	33	31	10	209	176	76
Detroit	74	27	35	12	245	257	66

West Division

Team	GP	W	L	T	GF	GA	PTS
Philadelphia	74	31	32	11	173	179	73
Los Angeles	74	31	33	10	200	224	72
St. Louis	74	27	31	16	177	191	70
Minnesota	74	27	32	15	191	226	69
Pittsburgh	74	27	34	13	195	216	67
Oakland	74	15	42	17	153	219	47

Leading Scorers

Player	Club	GP	G	A	PTS	PIM
Mikita, Stan	Chicago	72	40	47	87	14
Esposito, Phil	Boston	74	35	49	84	21
Howe, Gordie	Detroit	74	39	43	82	53
Ratelle, Jean	New York	74	32	46	78	18
Gilbert, Rod	New York	73	29	48	77	12
Hull, Bobby	Chicago	71	44	31	75	39
Ullman, Norm	Det., Tor.	71	35	37	72	28
Delvecchio, Alex	Detroit	74	22	48	70	14
Bucyk, John	Boston	72	30	39	69	8
Wharram, Ken	Chicago	74	27	42	69	18

1968-69

East Division

Team	GP	W	L	T	GF	GA	PTS
*Montreal	76	46	19	11	271	202	103
Boston	76	42	18	16	303	221	100
New York	76	41	26	9	231	196	91
Toronto	76	35	26	15	234	217	85
Detroit	76	33	31	12	239	221	78
Chicago	76	34	33	9	280	246	77

West Division

Team	GP	W	L	T	GF	GA	PTS
St. Louis	76	37	25	14	204	157	88
Oakland	76	29	36	11	219	251	69
Philadelphia	76	20	35	21	174	225	61
Los Angeles	76	24	42	10	185	260	58
Pittsburgh	76	20	45	11	189	252	51
Minnesota	76	18	43	15	189	270	51

Leading Scorers

Player	Club	GP	G	A	PTS	PIM
Esposito, Phil	Boston	74	49	77	126	79
Hull, Bobby	Chicago	74	58	49	107	48
Howe, Gordie	Detroit	76	44	59	103	58
Mikita, Stan	Chicago	74	30	67	97	52
Hodge, Ken	Boston	75	45	45	90	75
Cournoyer, Yvan	Montreal	76	43	44	87	31
Delvecchio, Alex	Detroit	72	25	58	83	8
Berenson, Red	St. Louis	76	35	47	82	43
Beliveau, Jean	Montreal	69	33	49	82	55
Mahovlich, Frank	Detroit	76	49	29	78	38
Ratelle, Jean	New York	75	32	46	78	26

*Claude Provost and coach "Toe"
Blake were part of the great Montreal teams
of the 1950's and 1960's.*

1969-70

East Division

Team	GP	W	L	T	GF	GA	PTS
Chicago	76	45	22	9	250	170	99
*Boston	76	40	17	19	277	216	99
Detroit	76	40	21	15	246	199	95
New York	76	38	22	16	246	189	92
Montreal	76	38	22	16	244	201	92
Toronto	76	29	34	13	222	242	71

West Division

Team	GP	W	L	T	GF	GA	PTS
St. Louis	76	37	27	12	224	179	86
Pittsburgh	76	26	38	12	182	238	64
Minnesota	76	19	35	22	224	257	60
Oakland	76	22	40	14	169	243	58
Philadelphia	76	17	35	24	197	225	58
Los Angeles	76	14	52	10	168	290	38

Leading Scorers

Player	Club	GP	G	A	PTS	PIM
Orr, Bobby	Boston	76	33	87	120	125
Esposito, Phil	Boston	76	43	56	99	50
Mikita, Stan	Chicago	76	39	47	86	50
Goyette, Phil	St. Louis	72	29	49	78	16
Tkaczuk, Walt	New York	76	27	50	77	38
Ratelle, Jean	New York	75	32	42	74	28
Berenson, Red	St. Louis	67	33	39	72	38
Parise, Jean-Paul	Minnesota	74	24	48	72	72
Howe, Gordie	Detroit	76	31	40	71	58
Mahovlich, Frank	Detroit	74	38	32	70	59
Balon, Dave	New York	76	33	37	70	100
McKenzie, John	Boston	72	29	41	70	114

1970-71

East Division

Team	GP	W	L	T	GF	GA	PTS
Boston	78	57	14	7	399	207	121
New York	78	49	18	11	259	177	109
*Montreal	78	42	23	13	291	216	97
Toronto	78	37	33	8	248	211	82
Buffalo	78	24	39	15	217	291	63
Vancouver	78	24	46	8	229	296	56
Detroit	78	22	45	11	209	308	55

West Division

Team	GP	W	L	T	GF	GA	PTS
Chicago	78	49	20	9	277	184	107
St. Louis	78	34	25	19	223	208	87
Philadelphia	78	28	33	17	207	225	73
Minnesota	78	28	34	16	191	223	72
Los Angeles	78	25	40	13	239	303	63
Pittsburgh	78	21	37	20	221	240	62
California	78	20	53	5	199	320	45

Leading Scorers

Player	Club	GP	G	A	PTS	PIM
Esposito, Phil	Boston	78	76	76	152	71
Orr, Bobby	Boston	78	37	102	139	91
Bucyk, John	Boston	78	51	65	116	8
Hodge, Ken	Boston	78	43	62	105	113
Hull, Bobby	Chicago	78	44	52	96	32
Ullman, Norm	Toronto	73	34	51	85	24
Cashman, Wayne	Boston	77	21	58	79	100
McKenzie, John	Boston	65	31	46	77	120
Keon, Dave	Toronto	76	38	38	76	4
Beliveau, Jean	Montreal	70	25	51	76	40
Stanfield, Fred	Boston	75	24	52	76	12

1971-72

East Division

Team	GP	W	L	T	GF	GA	PTS
*Boston	78	54	13	11	330	204	119
New York	78	48	17	13	317	192	109
Montreal	78	46	16	16	307	205	108
Toronto	78	33	31	14	209	208	80
Detroit	78	33	35	10	261	262	76
Buffalo	78	16	43	19	203	289	51
Vancouver	78	20	50	8	203	297	48

West Division

Team	GP	W	L	T	GF	GA	PTS
Chicago	78	46	17	15	256	166	107
Minnesota	78	37	29	12	212	191	86
St. Louis	78	28	39	11	208	247	67
Pittsburgh	78	26	38	14	220	258	66
Philadelphia	78	26	38	14	200	236	66
California	78	21	39	18	216	288	60
Los Angeles	78	20	49	9	206	305	49

Leading Scorers

Player	Club	GP	G	A	PTS	PIM
Esposito, Phil	Boston	76	66	67	133	76
Orr, Bobby	Boston	76	37	80	117	106
Ratelle, Jean	New York	63	46	63	109	4
Hadfield, Vic	New York	78	50	56	106	142
Gilbert, Rod	New York	73	43	54	97	64
Mahovlich, Frank	Montreal	76	43	53	96	36
Hull, Bobby	Chicago	78	50	43	93	24
Cournoyer, Yvan	Montreal	73	47	36	83	15
Bucyk, John	Boston	78	32	51	83	4
Clarke, Bobby	Philadelphia	78	35	46	81	87
Lemaire, Jacques	Montreal	77	32	49	81	26

Bobby Orr and Gerry Cheevers were two of the key reasons behind the Bruins' Stanley Cup wins in 1970 and 1972.

In 1977-78, Terry O'Reilly became the first player with more than 200 penalty minutes to finish in the top 10 in scoring.

1972-73

East Division

Team	GP	W	L	T	GF	GA	PTS
*Montreal	78	52	10	16	329	184	120
Boston	78	51	22	5	330	235	107
NY Rangers	78	47	23	8	297	208	102
Buffalo	78	37	27	14	257	219	88
Detroit	78	37	29	12	265	243	86
Toronto	78	27	41	10	247	279	64
Vancouver	78	22	47	9	233	339	53
NY Islanders	78	12	60	6	170	347	30

West Division

Team	GP	W	L	T	GF	GA	PTS
Chicago	78	42	27	9	284	225	93
Philadelphia	78	37	30	11	296	256	85
Minnesota	78	37	30	11	254	230	85
St. Louis	78	32	34	12	233	251	76
Pittsburgh	78	32	37	9	257	265	73
Los Angeles	78	31	36	11	232	245	73
Atlanta	78	25	38	15	191	239	65
California	78	16	46	16	213	323	48

Leading Scorers

Player	Club	GP	G	A	PTS	PIM
Esposito, Phil	Boston	78	55	75	130	87
Clarke, Bobby	Philadelphia	78	37	67	104	80
Orr, Bobby	Boston	63	29	72	101	99
MacLeish, Rick	Philadelphia	78	50	50	100	69
Lemaire, Jacques	Montreal	77	44	51	95	16
Ratelle, Jean	NY Rangers	78	41	53	94	12
Redmond, Mickey	Detroit	76	52	41	93	24
Bucyk, John	Boston	78	40	53	93	12
Mahovlich, Frank	Montreal	78	38	55	93	51
Pappin, Jim	Chicago	76	41	51	92	82

1973-74

East Division

Team	GP	W	L	T	GF	GA	PTS
Boston	78	52	17	9	349	221	113
Montreal	78	45	24	9	293	240	99
NY Rangers	78	40	24	14	300	251	94
Toronto	78	35	27	16	274	230	86
Buffalo	78	32	34	12	242	250	76
Detroit	78	29	39	10	255	319	68
Vancouver	78	24	43	11	224	296	59
NY Islanders	78	19	41	18	182	247	56

West Division

Team	GP	W	L	T	GF	GA	PTS
*Philadelphia	78	50	16	12	273	164	112
Chicago	78	41	14	23	272	164	105
Los Angeles	78	33	33	12	233	231	78
Atlanta	78	30	34	14	214	238	74
Pittsburgh	78	28	41	9	242	273	65
St. Louis	78	26	40	12	206	248	64
Minnesota	78	23	38	17	235	275	63
California	78	13	55	10	195	342	36

Leading Scorers

Player	Club	GP	G	A	PTS	PIM
Esposito, Phil	Boston	78	68	77	145	58
Orr, Bobby	Boston	74	32	90	122	82
Hodge, Ken	Boston	76	50	55	105	43
Cashman, Wayne	Boston	78	30	59	89	111
Clarke, Bobby	Philadelphia	77	35	52	87	113
Martin, Rick	Buffalo	78	52	34	86	38
Apps, Syl	Pittsburgh	75	24	61	85	37
Sittler, Darryl	Toronto	78	38	46	84	55
MacDonald, Lowell	Pittsburgh	78	43	39	82	14
Park, Brad	NY Rangers	78	25	57	82	148
Hextall, Dennis	Minnesota	78	20	62	82	138

1974-75

PRINCE OF WALES CONFERENCE

Norris Division

Team	GP	W	L	T	GF	GA	PTS
Montreal	80	47	14	19	374	225	113
Los Angeles	80	42	17	21	269	185	105
Pittsburgh	80	37	28	15	326	289	89
Detroit	80	23	45	12	259	335	58
Washington	80	8	67	5	181	446	21

Adams Division

Team	GP	W	L	T	GF	GA	PTS
Buffalo	80	49	16	15	354	240	113
Boston	80	40	26	14	345	245	94
Toronto	80	31	33	16	280	309	78
California	80	19	48	13	212	316	51

CLARENCE CAMPBELL CONFERENCE

Patrick Division

Team	GP	W	L	T	GF	GA	PTS
*Philadelphia	80	51	18	11	293	181	113
NY Rangers	80	37	29	14	319	276	88
NY Islanders	80	33	25	22	264	221	88
Atlanta	80	34	31	15	243	233	83

Smythe Division

Team	GP	W	L	T	GF	GA	PTS
Vancouver	80	38	32	10	271	254	86
St. Louis	80	35	31	14	269	267	84
Chicago	80	37	35	8	268	241	82
Minnesota	80	23	50	7	221	341	53
Kansas City	80	15	54	11	184	328	41

Leading Scorers

Player	Club	GP	G	A	PTS	PIM
Orr, Bobby	Boston	80	46	89	135	101
Esposito, Phil	Boston	79	61	66	127	62
Dionne, Marcel	Detroit	80	47	74	121	14
Lafleur, Guy	Montreal	70	53	66	119	37
Mahovlich, Pete	Montreal	80	35	82	117	64
Clarke, Bobby	Philadelphia	80	27	89	116	125
Robert, Rene	Buffalo	74	40	60	100	75
Gilbert, Rod	NY Rangers	76	36	61	97	22
Perreault, Gilbert	Buffalo	68	39	57	96	36
Martin, Rick	Buffalo	68	52	43	95	72

1975-76

PRINCE OF WALES CONFERENCE

Norris Division

Team	GP	W	L	T	GF	GA	PTS
*Montreal	80	58	11	11	337	174	127
Los Angeles	80	38	33	9	263	265	85
Pittsburgh	80	35	33	12	339	303	82
Detroit	80	26	44	10	226	300	62
Washington	80	11	59	10	224	394	32

Adams Division

Boston	80	48	15	17	313	237	113
Buffalo	80	46	21	13	339	240	105
Toronto	80	34	31	15	294	276	83
California	80	27	42	11	250	278	65

CLARENCE CAMPBELL CONFERENCE

Patrick Division

Philadelphia	80	51	13	16	348	209	118
NY Islanders	80	42	21	17	297	190	101
Atlanta	80	35	33	12	262	237	82
NY Rangers	80	29	42	9	262	333	67

Smythe Division

Chicago	80	32	30	18	254	261	82
Vancouver	80	33	32	15	271	272	81
St. Louis	80	29	37	14	249	290	72
Minnesota	80	20	53	7	195	303	47
Kansas City	80	12	56	12	190	351	36

Leading Scorers

Player	Club	GP	G	A	PTS	PIM
Lafleur, Guy	Montreal	80	56	69	125	36
Clarke, Bobby	Philadelphia	76	30	89	119	136
Perreault, Gilbert	Buffalo	80	44	69	113	36
Barber, Bill	Philadelphia	80	50	62	112	104
Larouche, Pierre	Pittsburgh	76	53	58	111	33
Ratelle, Jean	Bos., NYR	80	36	69	105	18
Mahovlich, Pete	Montreal	80	34	71	105	76
Pronovost, Jean	Pittsburgh	80	52	52	104	24
Sittler, Darryl	Toronto	79	41	59	100	90
Apps, Syl	Pittsburgh	80	32	67	99	24

1976-77

PRINCE OF WALES CONFERENCE

Norris Division

Team	GP	W	L	T	GF	GA	PTS
*Montreal	80	60	8	12	387	171	132
Los Angeles	80	34	31	15	271	241	83
Pittsburgh	80	34	33	13	240	252	81
Washington	80	24	42	14	221	307	62
Detroit	80	16	55	9	183	309	41

Adams Division

Boston	80	49	23	8	312	240	106
Buffalo	80	48	24	8	301	220	104
Toronto	80	33	32	15	301	285	81
Cleveland	80	25	42	13	240	292	63

CLARENCE CAMPBELL CONFERENCE

Patrick Division

Philadelphia	80	48	16	16	323	213	112
NY Islanders	80	47	21	12	288	193	106
Atlanta	80	34	34	12	264	265	80
NY Rangers	88	29	37	14	272	310	72

Smythe Division

St. Louis	80	32	39	9	239	276	73
Minnesota	80	23	39	18	240	310	64
Chicago	80	26	43	11	240	298	63
Vancouver	80	25	42	13	235	294	63
Colorado	80	20	46	14	226	307	54

Leading Scorers

Player	Club	GP	G	A	PTS	PIM
Lafleur, Guy	Montreal	80	56	80	136	20
Dionne, Marcel	Los Angeles	80	53	69	122	12
Shutt, Steve	Montreal	80	60	45	105	28
MacLeish, Rick	Philadelphia	79	49	48	97	42
Perreault, Gilbert	Buffalo	80	39	56	95	30
Young, Tim	Minnesota	80	29	66	95	58
Ratelle, Jean	Boston	78	33	61	94	22
McDonald, Lanny	Toronto	80	46	44	90	77
Sittler, Darryl	Toronto	73	38	52	90	89
Clarke, Bobby	Philadelphia	80	27	63	90	71

1977-78

PRINCE OF WALES CONFERENCE

Norris Division

Team	GP	W	L	T	GF	GA	PTS
*Montreal	80	59	10	11	359	183	129
Detroit	80	32	34	14	252	266	78
Los Angeles	80	31	34	15	243	245	77
Pittsburgh	80	25	37	18	254	321	68
Washington	80	17	49	14	195	321	48

Adams Division

Boston	80	51	18	11	333	218	113
Buffalo	80	44	19	17	288	215	105
Toronto	80	41	29	10	271	237	92
Cleveland	80	22	45	13	230	325	57

CLARENCE CAMPBELL CONFERENCE

Patrick Division

NY Islanders	80	48	17	15	334	210	111
Philadelphia	80	45	20	15	296	200	105
Atlanta	80	34	27	19	274	252	87
NY Rangers	80	30	37	13	279	280	73

Smythe Division

Chicago	80	32	29	19	230	220	83
Colorado	80	19	40	21	257	305	59
Vancouver	80	20	43	17	239	320	57
St. Louis	80	20	47	13	195	304	53
Minnesota	80	18	53	9	218	325	45

Leading Scorers

Player	Club	GP	G	A	PTS	PIM
Lafleur, Guy	Montreal	79	60	72	132	26
Trottier, Bryan	NY Islanders	77	46	77	123	46
Sittler, Darryl	Toronto	80	45	72	117	100
Lemaire, Jacques	Montreal	76	36	61	97	14
Potvin, Denis	NY Islanders	80	30	64	94	81
Bossy, Mike	NY Islanders	73	53	38	91	6
O'Reilly, Terry	Boston	77	29	61	90	211
Perreault, Gilbert	Buffalo	79	41	48	89	20
Clarke, Bobby	Philadelphia	71	21	68	89	83
McDonald, Lanny	Toronto	74	47	40	87	54
Paiement, Wilf	Colorado	80	31	56	87	114

1978-79

PRINCE OF WALES CONFERENCE

Norris Division

Team	GP	W	L	T	GF	GA	PTS
*Montreal	80	52	17	11	337	204	115
Pittsburgh	80	36	31	13	281	279	85
Los Angeles	80	34	34	12	292	286	80
Washington	80	24	41	15	273	338	63
Detroit	80	23	41	16	252	295	62

Adams Division

Boston	80	43	23	14	316	270	100
Buffalo	80	36	28	16	280	263	88
Toronto	80	34	33	13	267	252	81
Minnesota	80	28	40	12	257	289	68

CLARENCE CAMPBELL CONFERENCE

Patrick Division

NY Islanders	80	51	15	14	358	214	116
Philadelphia	80	40	25	15	281	248	95
NY Rangers	80	40	29	11	316	292	91
Atlanta	80	41	31	8	327	280	90

Smythe Division

Chicago	80	29	36	15	244	277	73
Vancouver	80	25	42	13	217	291	63
St. Louis	80	18	50	12	249	348	48
Colorado	80	15	53	12	210	331	42

Leading Scorers

Player	Club	GP	G	A	PTS	PIM
Trottier, Bryan	NY Islanders	76	47	87	134	50
Dionne, Marcel	Los Angeles	80	59	71	130	30
Lafleur, Guy	Montreal	80	52	77	129	28
Bossy, Mike	NY Islanders	80	69	57	126	25
MacMillan, Bob	Atlanta	79	37	71	108	14
Chouinard, Guy	Atlanta	80	50	57	107	14
Potvin, Denis	NY Islanders	73	31	70	101	58
Federko, Bernie	St. Louis	74	31	64	95	14
Taylor, Dave	Los Angeles	78	43	48	91	124
Gillies, Clark	NY Islanders	75	35	56	91	68

Pierre Larouche was one of three Pittsburgh Penguins to finish in the top ten in scoring during the 1975-76 season.

1979-80

PRINCE OF WALES CONFERENCE

Norris Division

Team	GP	W	L	T	GF	GA	PTS
Montreal	80	47	20	13	328	240	107
Los Angeles	80	30	36	14	290	313	74
Pittsburgh	80	30	37	13	251	303	73
Hartford	80	27	34	19	303	312	73
Detroit	80	26	43	11	268	306	63

Adams Division

Buffalo	80	47	17	16	318	201	110
Boston	80	46	21	13	310	234	105
Minnesota	80	36	28	16	311	253	88
Toronto	80	35	40	5	304	327	75
Quebec	80	25	44	11	248	313	61

CLARENCE CAMPBELL CONFERENCE

Patrick Division

Philadelphia	80	48	12	20	327	254	116
*NY Islanders	80	39	28	13	281	247	91
NY Rangers	80	38	32	10	308	284	86
Atlanta	80	35	32	13	282	269	83
Washington	80	27	40	13	261	293	67

Smythe Division

Chicago	80	34	27	19	241	250	87
St. Louis	80	34	34	12	266	278	80
Vancouver	80	27	37	16	256	281	70
Edmonton	80	28	39	13	301	322	69
Winnipeg	80	20	49	11	214	314	51
Colorado	80	19	48	13	234	308	51

Leading Scorers

Player	Club	GP	G	A	PTS	PIM
Dionne, Marcel	Los Angeles	80	53	84	137	32
Gretzky, Wayne	Edmonton	79	51	86	137	21
Lafleur, Guy	Montreal	74	50	75	125	12
Perreault, Gilbert	Buffalo	80	40	66	106	57
Rogers, Mike	Hartford	80	44	61	105	10
Trottier, Bryan	NY Islanders	78	42	62	104	68
Simmer, Charlie	Los Angeles	64	56	45	101	65
Stoughton, Blaine	Hartford	80	56	44	100	16
Sittler, Darryl	Toronto	73	40	57	97	62
MacDonald, Blair	Edmonton	80	46	48	94	6
Federko, Bernie	St. Louis	79	38	56	94	24

1980-81

PRINCE OF WALES CONFERENCE

Norris Division

Team	GP	W	L	T	GF	GA	PTS
Montreal	80	45	22	13	332	232	103
Los Angeles	80	43	24	13	337	290	99
Pittsburgh	80	30	37	13	302	345	73
Hartford	80	21	41	18	292	372	60
Detroit	80	19	43	18	252	339	56

Adams Division

Buffalo	80	39	20	21	327	250	99
Boston	80	37	30	13	316	272	87
Minnesota	80	35	28	17	291	263	87
Quebec	80	30	32	18	314	318	78
Toronto	80	28	37	15	322	367	71

CLARENCE CAMPBELL CONFERENCE

Patrick Division

*NY Islanders	80	48	18	14	355	260	110
Philadelphia	80	41	24	15	313	249	97
Calgary	80	39	27	14	329	298	92
NY Rangers	80	30	36	14	312	317	74
Washington	80	26	36	18	286	317	70

Smythe Division

St. Louis	80	45	18	17	352	281	107
Chicago	80	31	33	16	304	315	78
Vancouver	80	28	32	20	289	301	76
Edmonton	80	29	35	16	328	327	74
Colorado	80	22	45	13	258	344	57
Winnipeg	80	9	57	14	246	400	32

Leading Scorers

Player	Club	GP	G	A	PTS	PIM
Gretzky, Wayne	Edmonton	80	55	109	164	28
Dionne, Marcel	Los Angeles	80	58	77	135	70
Nilsson, Kent	Calgary	80	49	82	131	26
Bossy, Mike	NY Islanders	79	68	51	119	32
Taylor, Dave	Los Angeles	72	47	65	112	130
Stastny, Peter	Quebec	77	39	70	109	37
Simmer, Charlie	Los Angeles	65	56	49	105	62
Rogers, Mike	Hartford	80	40	65	105	32
Federko, Bernie	St. Louis	78	31	73	104	47
Richard, Jacques	Quebec	78	52	51	103	39
Middleton, Rick	Boston	80	44	59	103	16
Trottier, Bryan	NY Islanders	73	31	72	103	74

1981-82

CLARENCE CAMPBELL CONFERENCE

Norris Division

Team	GP	W	L	T	GF	GA	PTS
Minnesota	80	37	23	20	346	288	94
Winnipeg	80	33	33	14	319	332	80
St. Louis	80	32	40	8	315	349	72
Chicago	80	30	38	12	332	363	72
Toronto	80	20	44	16	298	380	56
Detroit	80	21	47	12	270	351	54

Smythe Division

Edmonton	80	48	17	15	417	295	111
Vancouver	80	30	33	17	290	286	77
Calgary	80	29	34	17	334	345	75
Los Angeles	80	24	41	15	314	369	63
Colorado	80	18	49	13	241	362	49

PRINCE OF WALES CONFERENCE

Adams Division

Montreal	80	46	17	17	360	223	109
Boston	80	43	27	10	323	285	96
Buffalo	80	39	26	15	307	273	93
Quebec	80	33	31	16	356	345	82
Hartford	80	21	41	18	264	351	60

Patrick Division

*NY Islanders	80	54	16	10	385	250	118
NY Rangers	80	39	27	14	316	306	92
Philadelphia	80	38	31	11	325	313	87
Pittsburgh	80	31	36	13	310	337	75
Washington	80	26	41	13	319	338	65

Leading Scorers

Player	Club	GP	G	A	PTS	PIM
Gretzky, Wayne	Edmonton	80	92	120	212	26
Bossy, Mike	NY Islanders	80	64	83	147	22
Stastny, Peter	Quebec	80	46	93	139	91
Maruk, Dennis	Washington	80	60	76	136	128
Trottier, Bryan	NY Islanders	80	50	79	129	88
Savard, Denis	Chicago	80	32	87	119	82
Dionne, Marcel	Los Angeles	78	50	67	117	50
Smith, Bobby	Minnesota	80	43	71	114	82
Ciccarelli, Dino	Minnesota	76	55	51	106	138
Taylor, Dave	Los Angeles	78	39	67	106	130

1982-83

CLARENCE CAMPBELL CONFERENCE

Norris Division

Team	GP	W	L	T	GF	GA	PTS
Chicago	80	47	23	10	338	268	104
Minnesota	80	40	24	16	321	290	96
Toronto	80	28	40	12	293	330	68
St. Louis	80	25	40	15	285	316	65
Detroit	80	21	44	15	263	344	57

Smythe Division

Edmonton	80	47	21	12	424	315	106
Calgary	80	32	34	14	321	317	78
Vancouver	80	30	35	15	303	309	75
Winnipeg	80	33	39	8	311	333	74
Los Angeles	80	27	41	12	308	365	66

PRINCE OF WALES CONFERENCE

Adams Division

Boston	80	50	20	10	327	228	110
Montreal	80	42	24	14	350	286	98
Buffalo	80	38	29	13	318	285	89
Quebec	80	34	34	12	343	336	80
Hartford	80	19	54	7	261	403	45

Patrick Division

Philadelphia	80	49	23	8	326	240	106
*NY Islanders	80	42	26	12	302	226	96
Washington	80	39	25	16	306	283	94
NY Rangers	80	35	35	10	306	287	80
New Jersey	80	17	49	14	230	338	48
Pittsburgh	80	18	53	9	257	394	45

Leading Scorers

Player	Club	GP	G	A	PTS	PIM
Gretzky, Wayne	Edmonton	80	71	125	196	59
Stastny, Peter	Quebec	75	47	77	124	78
Savard, Denis	Chicago	78	35	86	121	99
Bossy, Mike	NY Islanders	79	60	58	118	20
Dionne, Marcel	Los Angeles	80	56	51	107	22
Pederson, Barry	Boston	77	46	61	107	47
Messier, Mark	Edmonton	77	48	58	106	72
Goulet, Michel	Quebec	80	57	48	105	51
Anderson, Glenn	Edmonton	72	48	56	104	70
Nilsson, Kent	Calgary	80	46	58	104	10
Kurri, Jari	Edmonton	80	45	59	104	22

In 1980-81—his second NHL season—Kent Nilsson finished third in scoring with 131 points.

1983-84

CLARENCE CAMPBELL CONFERENCE

Norris Division

Team	GP	W	L	T	GF	GA	PTS
Minnesota	80	39	31	10	345	344	88
St. Louis	80	32	41	7	293	316	71
Detroit	80	31	42	7	298	323	69
Chicago	80	30	42	8	277	311	68
Toronto	80	26	45	9	303	387	61

Smythe Division

Team	GP	W	L	T	GF	GA	PTS
*Edmonton	80	57	18	5	446	314	119
Calgary	80	34	32	14	311	314	82
Vancouver	80	32	39	9	306	328	73
Winnipeg	80	31	38	11	340	374	73
Los Angeles	80	23	44	13	309	376	59

PRINCE OF WALES CONFERENCE

Adams Division

Team	GP	W	L	T	GF	GA	PTS
Boston	80	49	25	6	336	261	104
Buffalo	80	48	25	7	315	257	103
Quebec	80	42	28	10	360	278	94
Montreal	80	35	40	5	286	295	75
Hartford	80	28	42	10	288	320	66

Patrick Division

Team	GP	W	L	T	GF	GA	PTS
NY Islanders	80	50	26	4	357	269	104
Washington	80	48	27	5	308	226	101
Philadelphia	80	44	26	10	350	290	98
NY Rangers	80	42	29	9	314	304	93
New Jersey	80	17	56	7	231	350	41
Pittsburgh	80	16	58	6	254	390	38

Leading Scorers

Player	Club	GP	G	A	PTS	PIM
Gretzky, Wayne	Edmonton	74	87	118	205	39
Coffey, Paul	Edmonton	80	40	86	126	104
Goulet, Michel	Quebec	75	56	65	121	76
Stastny, Peter	Quebec	80	46	73	119	73
Bossy, Mike	NY Islanders	67	51	67	118	8
Pederson, Barry	Boston	80	39	77	116	64
Kurri, Jari	Edmonton	64	52	61	113	14
Trottier, Bryan	NY Islanders	68	40	71	111	59
Federko, Bernie	St. Louis	79	41	66	107	43
Middleton, Rick	Boston	80	47	58	105	14

1984-85

CLARENCE CAMPBELL CONFERENCE

Norris Division

Team	GP	W	L	T	GF	GA	PTS
St. Louis	80	37	31	12	299	288	86
Chicago	80	38	35	7	309	299	83
Detroit	80	27	41	12	313	357	66
Minnesota	80	25	43	12	268	321	62
Toronto	80	20	52	8	253	358	48

Smythe Division

Team	GP	W	L	T	GF	GA	PTS
*Edmonton	80	49	20	11	401	298	109
Winnipeg	80	43	27	10	358	332	96
Calgary	80	41	27	12	363	302	94
Los Angeles	80	34	32	14	339	326	82
Vancouver	80	25	46	9	284	401	59

PRINCE OF WALES CONFERENCE

Adams Division

Team	GP	W	L	T	GF	GA	PTS
Montreal	80	41	27	12	309	262	94
Quebec	80	41	30	9	323	275	91
Buffalo	80	38	28	14	290	237	90
Boston	80	36	34	10	303	287	82
Hartford	80	30	41	9	268	318	69

Patrick Division

Team	GP	W	L	T	GF	GA	PTS
Philadelphia	80	53	20	7	348	241	113
Washington	80	46	25	9	322	240	101
NY Islanders	80	40	34	6	345	312	86
NY Rangers	80	26	44	10	295	345	62
New Jersey	80	22	48	10	264	346	54
Pittsburgh	80	24	51	5	276	385	53

Leading Scorers

Player	Club	GP	G	A	PTS	PIM
Gretzky, Wayne	Edmonton	80	73	135	208	52
Kurri, Jari	Edmonton	73	71	64	135	30
Hawerchuk, Dale	Winnipeg	80	53	77	130	74
Dionne, Marcel	Los Angeles	80	46	80	126	46
Coffey, Paul	Edmonton	80	37	84	121	97
Bossy, Mike	NY Islanders	76	58	59	117	38
Ogrodnick, John	Detroit	79	55	50	105	30
Savard, Denis	Chicago	79	38	67	105	56
Federko, Bernie	St. Louis	76	30	73	103	27
Gartner, Mike	Washington	80	50	52	102	71

1985-86

CLARENCE CAMPBELL CONFERENCE

Norris Division

Team	GP	W	L	T	GF	GA	PTS
Chicago	80	39	33	8	351	349	86
Minnesota	80	38	33	9	327	305	85
St. Louis	80	37	34	9	302	291	83
Toronto	80	25	48	7	311	386	57
Detroit	80	17	57	6	266	415	40

Smythe Division

Team	GP	W	L	T	GF	GA	PTS
Edmonton	80	56	17	7	426	310	119
Calgary	80	40	31	9	354	315	89
Winnipeg	80	26	47	7	295	372	59
Vancouver	80	23	44	13	282	333	59
Los Angeles	80	23	49	8	284	389	54

PRINCE OF WALES CONFERENCE

Adams Division

Team	GP	W	L	T	GF	GA	PTS
Quebec	80	43	31	6	330	289	92
*Montreal	80	40	33	7	330	280	87
Boston	80	37	31	12	311	288	86
Hartford	80	40	36	4	332	302	84
Buffalo	80	37	37	6	296	291	80

Patrick Division

Team	GP	W	L	T	GF	GA	PTS
Philadelphia	80	53	23	4	335	241	110
Washington	80	50	23	7	315	272	107
NY Islanders	80	39	29	12	327	284	90
NY Rangers	80	36	38	6	280	276	78
Pittsburgh	80	34	38	8	313	305	76
New Jersey	80	28	49	3	300	374	59

Leading Scorers

Player	Club	GP	G	A	PTS	PIM
Gretzky, Wayne	Edmonton	80	52	163	215	52
Lemieux, Mario	Pittsburgh	79	48	93	141	43
Coffey, Paul	Edmonton	79	48	90	138	120
Kurri, Jari	Edmonton	78	68	63	131	22
Bossy, Mike	NY Islanders	80	61	62	123	14
Stastny, Peter	Quebec	76	41	81	122	60
Savard, Denis	Chicago	80	47	69	116	111
Naslund, Mats	Montreal	80	43	67	110	16
Hawerchuk, Dale	Winnipeg	80	46	59	105	44
Broten, Neal	Minnesota	80	29	76	105	47

1986-87

CLARENCE CAMPBELL CONFERENCE

Norris Division

Team	GP	W	L	T	GF	GA	PTS
St. Louis	80	32	33	15	281	293	79
Detroit	80	34	36	10	260	274	78
Chicago	80	29	37	14	290	310	72
Toronto	80	32	42	6	286	319	70
Minnesota	80	30	40	10	296	314	70

Smythe Division

Team	GP	W	L	T	GF	GA	PTS
*Edmonton	80	50	24	6	372	284	106
Calgary	80	46	31	3	318	289	95
Winnipeg	80	40	32	8	279	271	88
Los Angeles	80	31	41	8	318	341	70
Vancouver	80	29	43	8	282	314	66

PRINCE OF WALES CONFERENCE

Adams Division

Team	GP	W	L	T	GF	GA	PTS
Hartford	80	43	30	7	287	270	93
Montreal	80	41	29	10	277	241	92
Boston	80	39	34	7	301	276	85
Quebec	80	31	39	10	267	276	72
Buffalo	80	28	44	8	280	308	64

Patrick Division

Team	GP	W	L	T	GF	GA	PTS
Philadelphia	80	46	26	8	310	245	100
Washington	80	38	32	10	285	278	86
NY Islanders	80	35	33	12	279	281	82
NY Rangers	80	34	38	8	307	323	76
Pittsburgh	80	30	38	12	297	290	72
New Jersey	80	29	45	6	293	368	64

Leading Scorers

Player	Club	GP	G	A	PTS	PIM
Gretzky, Wayne	Edmonton	79	62	121	183	28
Kurri, Jari	Edmonton	79	54	54	108	41
Lemieux, Mario	Pittsburgh	63	54	53	107	57
Messier, Mark	Edmonton	77	37	70	107	73
Gilmour, Doug	St. Louis	80	42	63	105	58
Ciccarelli, Dino	Minnesota	80	52	51	103	92
Hawerchuk, Dale	Winnipeg	80	47	53	100	54
Goulet, Michel	Quebec	75	49	47	96	61
Kerr, Tim	Philadelphia	75	58	37	95	57
Bourque, Ray	Boston	78	23	72	95	36

Denis Savard finished in the top ten in scoring on five occasions during his years with the Chicago Blackhawks.

Peter Stastny had six 100-or-more point seasons for the Quebec Nordiques during the 1980's.

1987-88

CLARENCE CAMPBELL CONFERENCE

Norris Division

Team	GP	W	L	T	GF	GA	PTS
Detroit	80	41	28	11	322	269	93
St. Louis	80	34	38	8	278	294	76
Chicago	80	30	41	9	284	326	69
Toronto	80	21	49	10	273	345	52
Minnesota	80	19	48	13	242	349	51

Smythe Division

Team	GP	W	L	T	GF	GA	PTS
Calgary	80	48	23	9	397	305	105
*Edmonton	80	44	25	11	363	288	99
Winnipeg	80	33	36	11	292	310	77
Los Angeles	80	30	42	8	318	359	68
Vancouver	80	25	46	9	272	320	59

PRINCE OF WALES CONFERENCE

Adams Division

Team	GP	W	L	T	GF	GA	PTS
Montreal	80	45	22	13	298	238	103
Boston	80	44	30	6	300	251	94
Buffalo	80	37	32	11	283	305	85
Hartford	80	35	38	7	249	267	77
Quebec	80	32	43	5	271	306	69

Patrick Division

Team	GP	W	L	T	GF	GA	PTS
NY Islanders	80	39	31	10	308	267	88
Washington	80	38	33	9	281	249	85
Philadelphia	80	38	33	9	292	282	85
New Jersey	80	38	36	6	295	296	82
NY Rangers	80	36	34	10	300	283	82
Pittsburgh	80	36	35	9	319	316	81

Leading Scorers

Player	Club	GP	G	A	PTS	PIM
Lemieux, Mario	Pittsburgh	76	70	98	168	92
Gretzky, Wayne	Edmonton	64	40	109	149	24
Savard, Denis	Chicago	80	44	87	131	95
Hawerchuk, Dale	Winnipeg	80	44	77	121	59
Robitaille, Luc	Los Angeles	80	53	58	111	82
Stastny, Peter	Quebec	76	46	65	111	69
Messier, Mark	Edmonton	77	37	74	111	103
Carson, Jimmy	Los Angeles	80	55	52	107	45
Loob, Hakan	Calgary	80	50	56	106	47
Goulet, Michel	Quebec	80	48	58	106	56

1988-89

CLARENCE CAMPBELL CONFERENCE

Norris Division

Team	GP	W	L	T	GF	GA	PTS
Detroit	80	34	34	12	313	316	80
St. Louis	80	33	35	12	275	285	78
Minnesota	80	27	37	16	258	278	70
Chicago	80	27	41	12	297	335	66
Toronto	80	28	46	6	259	342	62

Smythe Division

Team	GP	W	L	T	GF	GA	PTS
*Calgary	80	54	17	9	354	226	117
Los Angeles	80	42	31	7	376	335	91
Edmonton	80	38	34	8	325	306	84
Vancouver	80	33	39	8	251	253	74
Winnipeg	80	26	42	12	300	355	64

PRINCE OF WALES CONFERENCE

Adams Division

Team	GP	W	L	T	GF	GA	PTS
Montreal	80	53	18	9	315	218	115
Boston	80	37	29	14	289	256	88
Buffalo	80	38	35	7	291	299	83
Hartford	80	37	38	5	299	290	79
Quebec	80	27	46	7	269	342	61

Patrick Division

Team	GP	W	L	T	GF	GA	PTS
Washington	80	41	29	10	305	259	92
Pittsburgh	80	40	33	7	347	349	87
NY Rangers	80	37	35	8	310	307	82
Philadelphia	80	36	36	8	307	285	80
New Jersey	80	27	41	12	281	325	66
NY Islanders	80	28	47	5	265	325	61

Leading Scorers

Player	Club	GP	G	A	PTS	PIM
Lemieux, Mario	Pittsburgh	76	85	114	199	100
Gretzky, Wayne	Los Angeles	78	54	114	168	26
Yzerman, Steve	Detroit	80	65	90	155	61
Nicholls, Bernie	Los Angeles	79	70	80	150	96
Brown, Rob	Pittsburgh	68	49	66	115	118
Coffey, Paul	Pittsburgh	75	30	83	113	193
Mullen, Joe	Calgary	79	51	59	110	16
Kurri, Jari	Edmonton	76	44	58	102	69
Carson, Jimmy	Edmonton	80	49	51	100	36
Robitaille, Luc	Los Angeles	78	46	52	98	65

1989-90

CLARENCE CAMPBELL CONFERENCE

Norris Division

Team	GP	W	L	T	GF	GA	PTS
Chicago	80	41	33	6	316	294	88
St. Louis	80	37	34	9	295	279	83
Toronto	80	38	38	4	337	358	80
Minnesota	80	36	40	4	284	291	76
Detroit	80	28	38	14	288	323	70

Smythe Division

Team	GP	W	L	T	GF	GA	PTS
Calgary	80	42	23	15	348	265	99
*Edmonton	80	38	28	14	315	283	90
Winnipeg	80	37	32	11	298	290	85
Los Angeles	80	34	39	7	338	337	75
Vancouver	80	25	41	14	245	306	64

PRINCE OF WALES CONFERENCE

Adams Division

Team	GP	W	L	T	GF	GA	PTS
Boston	80	46	25	9	289	232	101
Buffalo	80	45	27	8	286	248	98
Montreal	80	41	28	11	288	234	93
Hartford	80	38	33	9	275	268	85
Quebec	80	12	61	7	240	407	31

Patrick Division

Team	GP	W	L	T	GF	GA	PTS
NY Rangers	80	36	31	13	279	267	85
New Jersey	80	37	34	9	295	288	83
Washington	80	36	38	6	284	275	78
NY Islanders	80	31	38	11	281	288	73
Pittsburgh	80	32	40	8	318	359	72
Philadelphia	80	30	39	11	290	297	71

Leading Scorers

Player	Club	GP	G	A	PTS	PIM
Gretzky, Wayne	Los Angeles	73	40	102	142	42
Messier, Mark	Edmonton	79	45	84	129	79
Yzerman, Steve	Detroit	79	62	65	127	79
Lemieux, Mario	Pittsburgh	59	45	78	123	78
Hull, Brett	St. Louis	80	72	41	113	24
Nicholls, Bernie	L.A., NYR	79	39	73	112	86
Turgeon, Pierre	Buffalo	80	40	66	106	29
LaFontaine, Pat	NY Islanders	74	54	51	105	38
Coffey, Paul	Pittsburgh	80	29	74	103	95
Sakic, Joe	Quebec	80	39	63	102	27
Oates, Adam	St. Louis	80	23	79	102	30

Note: Detailed statistics for 1989-90 are listed in the Final Statistics, 1989-90 section of the **NHL Guide & Record Book.**

NHL History

1917 — National Hockey League organized November 22 in Montreal following suspension of operations by the National Hockey Association of Canada Limited (NHA). Montreal Canadiens, Montreal Wanderers, Ottawa Senators and Quebec Bulldogs attended founding meeting. Delegates decided to use NHA rules.

Toronto Arenas were later admitted as fifth team; Quebec decided not to operate during the first season. Quebec players allocated to remaining four teams.

Frank Calder elected president and secretary-treasurer.

First NHL games played December 19, with Toronto only arena with artificial ice. Clubs played 22-game split schedule.

1918 — Emergency meeting held January 3 due to destruction by fire of Montreal Arena which was home ice for both Canadiens and Wanderers.

Wanderers withdrew, reducing the NHL to three teams; Canadiens played remaining home games at 3,250-seat Jubilee rink.

Quebec franchise sold to P.J. Quinn of Toronto on October 18 on the condition that the team operate in Quebec City for 1918-19 season. Quinn did not attend the November League meeting and Quebec did not play in 1918-19.

1919-20 — NHL reactivated Quebec Bulldogs franchise. Former Quebec players returned to the club. New Mount Royal Arena became home of Canadiens. Toronto Arenas changed name to St. Patricks. Clubs played 24-game split schedule.

1920-21 — H.P. Thompson of Hamilton, Ontario made application for the purchase of an NHL franchise. Quebec franchise shifted to Hamilton with other NHL teams providing players to strengthen the club.

1921-22 — Split schedule abandoned. First and second place teams at the end of full schedule to play for championship.

1922-23 — Clubs agreed that players could not be sold or traded to clubs in any other league without first being offered to all other clubs in the NHL. In March, Foster Hewitt broadcast radio's first hockey game.

1923-24 — Ottawa's new 10,000-seat arena opened. First U.S. franchise granted to Boston for following season.

Dr. Cecil Hart Trophy donated to NHL to be awarded to the player judged most useful to his team.

1924-25 — Canadian Arena Company of Montreal granted a franchise to operate Montreal Maroons. NHL now six team league with two clubs in Montreal. Inaugural game in new Montreal Forum played November 29, 1924 as Canadiens defeated Toronto 7-1. Forum was home rink for the Maroons, but no ice was available in the Canadiens arena November 29, resulting in shift to Forum.

Hamilton finished first in the standings, receiving a bye into the finals. But Hamilton players, demanding $200 each for additional games in the playoffs, went on strike. The NHL suspended all players, fining them $200 each. Stanley Cup finalist to be the winner of NHL semi-final between Toronto and Canadiens.

Prince of Wales and Lady Byng trophies donated to NHL.

Clubs played 30-game schedule.

1925-26 — Hamilton club dropped from NHL. Players signed by new New York Americans franchise. Franchise granted to Pittsburgh.

Clubs played 36-game schedule.

1926-27 — New York Rangers granted franchise April 17, 1926. Chicago Black Hawks and Detroit Cougars granted franchises May 15, 1926. NHL now ten-team league with an American and a Canadian Division.

Stanley Cup came under the control of NHL. In previous seasons, winners of the now-defunct Western or Pacific Coast leagues would play NHL champion in Cup finals.

Toronto franchise sold to a new company controlled by Hugh Aird and Conn Smythe. Name changed from St. Patricks to Maple Leafs.

Clubs played 44-game schedule.

The Montreal Canadiens donated the Vezina Trophy to be awarded to the team allowing the fewest goals-against in regular season play. The winning team would, in turn, present the trophy to the goaltender playing in the greatest number of games during the season.

1929-30 — Detroit franchise changed name from Cougars to Falcons.

1930-31 — Pittsburgh transferred to Philadelphia for one season. Pirates changed name to Philadelphia Quakers. Trading deadline for teams set at February 15 of each year. NHL approved operation of farm teams by Rangers, Americans, Falcons and Bruins. Four-sided electric arena clock first demonstrated.

1931-32 — Philadelphia dropped out. Ottawa withdrew for one season. New Maple Leaf Gardens completed.

Clubs played 48-game schedule.

1932-33 — Franchise application received from St. Louis but refused because of additional travel costs. Ottawa team resumed play.

1933-34 — Detroit franchise changed name from Falcons to Red Wings. First All-Star Game played as a benefit for injured player Ace Bailey. Stanley Cup champion Leafs defeated All-Stars 7-3 in Toronto.

1934-35 — Ottawa franchise transferred to St. Louis. Team called St. Louis Eagles and consisted largely of Ottawa's players.

1935-36 — Ottawa-St. Louis franchise terminated. Montreal Canadiens finished season with very poor record. To strengthen the club, NHL gave Canadiens first call on the services of all French-Canadian players for three seasons.

1937-38 — Second benefit all-star game staged November 2 in Montreal in aid of the family of the late Canadiens star Howie Morenz.

Montreal Maroons withdrew from the NHL on June 22, 1938, leaving seven clubs in the League.

1938-39 — Expenses for each club regulated at $5 per man per day for meals and $2.50 per man per day for accommodation.

1939-40 — Benefit All-Star Game played October 29, 1939 in Montreal for the children of the late Albert (Babe) Siebert.

1940-41 — Ross-Tyer puck adopted as the official puck of the NHL. Early in the season it was apparent that this puck was too soft. The Spalding puck was adopted in its place.

After the playoffs, Arthur Ross, NHL governor from Boston, donated a perpetual trophy to be awarded annually to the player voted outstanding in the league.

1941-42 — New York Americans changed name to Brooklyn Americans.

1942-43 — Brooklyn Americans withdrew from NHL, leaving six teams: Boston, Chicago, Detroit, Montreal, New York and Toronto. Playoff format saw first place team play third-place team and second play fourth.

Clubs played 50-game schedule.

Frank Calder, president of the NHL since its inception, died in Montreal. Mervyn "Red" Dutton, former manager of the New York Americans, became president. The NHL commissioned the Calder Memorial Trophy to be awarded to the League's outstanding rookie each year.

1945-46 — Philadelphia, Los Angeles and San Francisco applied for NHL franchises.

The Philadelphia Arena Company of the American Hockey League applied for an injunction to prevent the possible operation of an NHL franchise in that city.

1946-47 — Mervyn Dutton retired as president of the NHL prior to the start of the season. He was succeeded by Clarence S. Campbell.

Individual trophy winners and all-star team members to receive $1,000 awards.

Playoff guarantees for players introduced.

Clubs played 60-game schedule.

1947-48 — The first annual All-Star Game for the benefit of the players' pension fund was played when the All-Stars defeated the Stanley Cup Champion Toronto Maple Leafs 4-3 in Toronto on October 13, 1947.

Ross Trophy, awarded to the NHL's outstanding player since 1941, to be awarded annually to the League's scoring leader.

Philadelphia and Los Angeles franchise applications refused.

National Hockey League Pension Society formed.

1949-50 — Clubs played 70-game schedule.

First intra-league draft held April 30, 1950. Clubs allowed to protect 30 players. Remaining players available for $25,000 each.

1951-52 — Referees included in the League's pension plan.

1952-53 — In May of 1952, City of Cleveland applied for NHL franchise. Application denied. In March of 1953, the Cleveland Barons of the AHL challenged the NHL champions for the Stanley Cup. The NHL governors did not accept this challenge.

1953-54 — The James Norris Memorial Trophy presented to the NHL for annual presentation to the League's best defenseman.

Intra-league draft rules amended to allow teams to protect 18 skaters and two goaltenders, claiming price reduced to $15,000.

1954-55 — Each arena to operate an "out-of-town" scoreboard. Referees and linesmen to wear shirts of black and white vertical stripes. Teams agree to wear white uniforms at home and colored uniforms on the road.

1956-57 — Standardized signals for referees and linesmen introduced.

1960-61 — Canadian National Exhibition, City of Toronto and NHL reach agreement for the construction of a Hockey Hall of Fame on the CNE grounds. Hall opens on August 26, 1961.

1963-64 — Player development league established with clubs operated by NHL franchises located in Minneapolis, St. Paul, Indianapolis, Omaha and, beginning in 1964-65, Tulsa. First universal amateur draft took place. All players of qualifying age (17) unaffected by sponsorship of junior teams available to be drafted.

1964-65 — Conn Smythe Trophy presented to the NHL to be awarded annually to the outstanding player in the Stanley Cup playoffs.

Minimum age of players subject to amateur draft changed to 18.

1965-66 — NHL announced expansion plans for a second six-team division to begin play in 1967-68.

1966-67 — Fourteen applications for NHL franchises received.

Lester Patrick Trophy presented to the NHL to be awarded annually for outstanding service to hockey in the United States.

NHL sponsorship of junior teams ceased, making all players of qualifying age not already on NHL-sponsored lists eligible for the amateur draft.

1967-68 — Six new teams added: California Seals, Los Angeles Kings, Minnesota North Stars, Philadelphia Flyers, Pittsburgh Penguins, St. Louis Blues. New teams to play in West Division. Remaining six teams to play in East Division.

Minimum age of players subject to amateur draft changed to 20.

Clubs played 74-game schedule.

Clarence S. Campbell Trophy awarded to team finishing the regular season in first place in West Division.

California Seals changed name to Oakland Seals on December 8, 1967.

1968-69 — Clubs played 76-game schedule.

Amateur draft expanded to cover any amateur player of qualifying age throughout the world.

1970-71 — Two new teams added: Buffalo Sabres and Vancouver Canucks. These teams joined East Division: Chicago switched to West Division.

Clubs played 78-game schedule.

1971-72 — Playoff format amended. In each division, first to play fourth; second to play third.

1972-73 — Soviet Nationals and Canadian NHL stars play eight-game pre-season series. Canadians win 4-3-1.

Two new teams added. Atlanta Flames join West Division; New York Islanders join East Division.

1974-75 — Two new teams added: Kansas City Scouts and Washington Capitals. Teams realigned into two nine-team conferences, the Prince of Wales made up of the Norris and Adams Divisions, and the Clarence Campbell made up of the Smythe and Patrick Divisions.

Clubs played 80-game schedule.

1976-77 — California franchise transferred to Cleveland. Team named Cleveland Barons. Kansas City franchise transferred to Denver. Team named Colorado Rockies.

1977-78 — Clarence S. Campbell retires as NHL president. Succeeded by John A. Ziegler, Jr.

1978-79 — Cleveland and Minnesota franchises merge, leaving NHL with 17 teams. Merged team placed in Adams Division, playing home games in Minnesota.

Minimum age of players subject to amateur draft changed to 19.

1979-80 — Four new teams added: Edmonton Oilers, Hartford Whalers, Quebec Nordiques and Winnipeg Jets.

Minimum age of players subject to entry draft changed to 18.

1980-81 — Atlanta franchise shifted to Calgary, retaining "Flames" name.

1981-82 — Unbalanced schedule adopted.

1982-83 — Colorado Rockies franchise shifted to East Rutherford, New Jersey. Team named New Jersey Devils.

Major Rule Changes

1910-11 — Game changed from two 30-minute periods to three 20-minute periods.

1911-12 — National Hockey Association (forerunner of the NHL) originated six-man hockey, replacing seven-man game.

1917-18 — Goalies permitted to fall to the ice to make saves. Previously a goaltender was penalized for dropping to the ice.

1918-19 — Penalty rules amended. For minor fouls, substitutes not allowed until penalized player had served three minutes. For major fouls, no substitutes for five minutes. For match fouls, no substitutes allowed for the remainder of the game.

With the addition of two lines painted on the ice twenty feet from center, three playing zones were created, producing a forty-foot neutral center ice area in which forward passing was permitted. Kicking the puck was permitted in this neutral zone.

Tabulation of assists began.

1921-22 — Goaltenders allowed to pass the puck forward up to their own blue line.

Overtime limited to twenty minutes.

Minor penalties changed from three minutes to two minutes.

1923-24 — Match foul defined as actions deliberately injuring or disabling an opponent. For such actions, a player was fined not less than $50 and ruled off the ice for the balance of the game. A player assessed a match penalty may be replaced by a substitute at the end of 20 minutes. Match penalty recipients must meet with the League president who can assess additional punishment.

1925-26 — Delayed penalty rules introduced. Each team must have a minimum of four players on the ice at all times.

Two rules were amended to encourage offense: No more than two defensemen permitted to remain inside a team's own blue line when the puck has left the defensive zone. A faceoff to be called for ragging the puck unless short-handed.

Team captains only players allowed to talk to referees.

Goaltender's leg pads limited to 12-inch width.

Timekeeper's gong to mark end of periods rather than referee's whistle. Teams to dress a maximum of 12 players for each game from a roster of no more than 14 players.

1926-27 — Blue lines repositioned to sixty feet from each goal-line, thereby enlarging the neutral zone and standardizing distance from blueline to goal.

Uniform goal nets adopted throughout NHL with goal posts securely fastened to the ice.

1927-28 — To further encourage offense, forward passes allowed in defending and neutral zones and goaltender's pads reduced in width from 12 to 10 inches.

Game standardized at three twenty-minute periods of stop-time separated by ten-minute intermissions.

Teams to change ends after each period.

Ten minutes of sudden-death overtime to be played if the score is tied after regulation time.

Minor penalty to be assessed to any player other than a goaltender for deliberately picking up the puck while it is in play. Minor penalty to be assessed for deliberately shooting the puck out of play.

The Art Ross goal net adopted as the official net of the NHL.

Maximum length of hockey sticks limited to 53 inches measured from heel of blade to end of handle. No minimum length stipulated.

Home teams given choice of goals to defend at start of game.

1928-29 — Forward passing permitted in defensive and neutral zones and into attacking zone if pass receiver is in neutral zone when pass is made. No forward passing allowed inside attacking zone.

Minor penalty to be assessed to any player who delays the game by passing the puck back into his defensive zone.

Ten-minute overtime without sudden-death provision to be played in games tied after regulation time. Games tied after this overtime period declared a draw.

Exclusive of goaltenders, team to dress at least 8 and no more than 12 skaters.

1929-30 — Forward passing permitted inside all three zones but not permitted across either blue line.

Kicking the puck allowed, but a goal cannot be scored by kicking the puck in.

No more than three players including the goaltender may remain in their defensive zone when the puck has gone up ice. Minor penalties to be assessed for the first two violations of this rule in a game; major penalties thereafter.

Goaltenders forbidden to hold the puck. Pucks caught must be cleared immediately. For infringement of this rule, a faceoff to be taken ten feet in front of the goal with no player except the goaltender standing between the faceoff spot and the goal-line.

Highsticking penalties introduced.

Maximum number of players in uniform increased from 12 to 15.

December 21, 1929 — Forward passing rules instituted at the beginning of the 1929-30 season more than doubled number of goals scored. Partway through the season, these rules were further amended to read, "No attacking player allowed to precede the play when entering the opposing defensive zone." This is similar to modern offside rule.

1930-31 — A player without a complete stick ruled out of play and forbidden from taking part in further action until a new stick is obtained. A player who has broken his stick must obtain a replacement at his bench.

A further refinement of the offside rule stated that the puck must first be propelled into the attacking zone before any player of the attacking side can enter that zone; for infringement of this rule a faceoff to take place at the spot where the infraction took place.

1931-32 — Though there is no record of a team attempting to play with two goaltenders on the ice, a rule was instituted which stated that each team was allowed only one goaltender on the ice at one time. Attacking players forbidden to impede the movement or obstruct the vision of opposing goaltenders.

Defending players with the exception of the goaltender forbidden from falling on the puck within 10 feet of the net.

1932-33 — Each team to have captain on the ice at all times.

If the goaltender is removed from the ice to serve a penalty, the manager of the club to appoint a substitute.

Match penalty with substitution after five minutes instituted for kicking another player.

1933-34 — Number of players permitted to stand in defensive zone restricted to three including goaltender.

Visible time clocks required in each rink.

Two referees replace one referee and one linesman.

1934-35 — Penalty shot awarded when a player is tripped and thus prevented from having a clear shot on goal, having no player to pass to other than the offending player. Shot taken from inside a 10-foot circle located 38 feet from the goal. The goaltender must not advance more than one foot from his goal-line when the shot is taken.

1937-38 — Rules introduced governing icing the puck.

Penalty shot awarded when a player other than a goaltender falls on the puck within 10 feet of the goal.

1938-39 — Penalty shot modified to allow puck carrier to skate in before shooting.

One referee and one linesman replace two referee system.

Blue line widened to 12 inches.

Maximum number of players in uniform increased from 14 to 15.

1939-40 — A substitute replacing a goaltender removed from ice to serve a penalty may use a goaltender's stick and gloves but no other goaltending equipment.

1940-41 — Flooding ice surface between periods made obligatory.

1941-42 — Penalty shots classified as minor and major. Minor shot to be taken from a line 28 feet from the goal. Major shot, awarded when a player is tripped with only the goaltender to beat, permits the player taking the penalty shot to skate right into the goalkeeper and shoot from point-blank range.

One referee and two linesmen employed to officiate games.

For playoffs, standby minor league goaltenders employed by NHL as emergency substitutes.

1942-43 — Because of wartime restrictions on train scheduling, regular-season overtime was discontinued on November 21, 1942.

Player limit reduced from 15 to 14. Minimum of 12 men in uniform abolished.

1943-44 — Red line at center ice introduced to speed up the game and reduce offside calls. This rule is considered to mark the beginning of the modern era in the NHL.

Delayed penalty rules introduced.

1945-46 — Goal indicator lights synchronized with official time clock required at all rinks.

1946-47 — System of signals by officials to indicate infractions introduced.

Linesmen from neutral cities employed for all games.

1947-48 — Goal awarded when a player with the puck has an open net to shoot at and a thrown stick prevents the shot on goal. Major penalty to any player who throws his stick in any zone other than defending zone. If a stick is thrown by a player in his defending zone but the thrown stick is not considered to have prevented a goal, a penalty shot is awarded.

All playoff games played until a winner determined, with 20-minute sudden-death overtime periods separated by 10-minute intermissions.

1949-50 — Ice surface painted white.

Clubs allowed to dress 17 players exclusive of goaltenders.

Major penalties incurred by goaltenders served by a member of the goaltender's team instead of resulting in a penalty shot.

1950-51 — Each team required to provide an emergency goaltender in attendance with full equipment at each game for use by either team in the event of illness or injury to a regular goaltender.

1951-52 — Visiting teams to wear basic white uniforms; home teams basic colored uniforms.

Goal crease enlarged from 3 × 7 feet to 4 × 8 feet.

Number of players in uniform reduced to 15 plus goaltenders.

Faceoff circles enlarged from 10-foot to 15-foot radius.

1952-53 — Teams permitted to dress 15 skaters on the road and 16 at home.

1953-54 — Number of players in uniform set at 16 plus goaltenders.

1954-55 — Number of players in uniform set at 18 plus goaltenders up to December 1 and 16 plus goaltenders thereafter.

1956-57 — Player serving a minor penalty allowed to return to ice when a goal is scored by opposing team.

1959-60 — Players prevented from leaving their benches to enter into an altercation. Substitutions permitted providing substitutes do not enter into altercation.

1960-61 — Number of players in uniform set at 16 plus goaltenders.

1961-62 — Penalty shots to be taken by the player against whom the foul was committed. In the event of a penalty shot called in a situation where a particular player hasn't been fouled, the penalty shot to be taken by any player on the ice when the foul was committed.

1964-65 — No bodily contact on faceoffs.

In playoff games, each team to have its substitute goaltender dressed in his regular uniform except for leg pads and body protector. All previous rules governing standby goaltenders terminated.

1965-66 — Teams required to dress two goaltenders for each regular-season game.

1966-67 — Substitution allowed on coincidental major penalties.

Between-periods intermissions fixed at 15 minutes.

1967-68 — If a penalty incurred by a goaltender is a co-incident major, the penalty to be served by a player of the goaltender's team on the ice at the time the penalty was called.

1970-71 — Home teams to wear basic white uniforms; visiting teams basic colored uniforms.

Limit of curvature of hockey stick blade set at $^1/_2$ inch.

Minor penalty for deliberately shooting the puck out of the playing area.

1971-72 — Number of players in uniform set at 17 plus 2 goaltenders.

Third man to enter an altercation assessed an automatic game misconduct penalty.

1972-73 — Minimum width of stick blade reduced to 2 inches from 2-$^1/_2$ inches.

1974-75 — Bench minor penalty imposed if a penalized player does not proceed directly and immediately to the penalty box.

1976-77 — Rule dealing with fighting amended to provide a major and game misconduct penalty for any player who is clearly the instigator of a fight.

1977-78 — Teams requesting a stick measurement to be assessed a minor penalty in the event that the measured stick does not violate the rules.

1981-82 — If both of a team's listed goaltenders are incapacitated, the team can dress and play any eligible goaltender who is available.

1982-83 — Number of players in uniform set 18 plus 2 goaltenders.

1983-84 — Five-minute sudden-death overtime to be played in regular-season games that are tied at the end of regulation time.

1985-86 — Substitutions allowed in the event of co-incidental minor penalties.

1986-87 — Delayed off-side is no longer in effect once the players of the offending team have cleared the opponents' defensive zone.

Team Records

BEST WINNING PERCENTAGE, ONE SEASON:
.875 — **Boston Bruins,** 1929-30. 38W-5L-1T. 77PTS in 44GP
.830 — Montreal Canadiens, 1943-44. 38W-5L-7T. 83PTS in 50GP
.825 — Montreal Canadiens, 1976-77. 60W-8L-12T. 132PTS in 80GP
.806 — Montreal Canadiens, 1977-78. 59W-10L-11T. 129PTS in 80GP
.800 — Montreal Canadiens, 1944-45. 38W-8L-4T. 80PTS in 50GP

MOST POINTS, ONE SEASON:
132 — **Montreal Canadiens,** 1976-77. 60W-8L-12T. 80GP
129 — Montreal Canadiens, 1977-78. 59W-10L-11T. 80GP
127 — Montreal Canadiens, 1975-76. 58W-11L-11T. 80GP

FEWEST POINTS, ONE SEASON:
8 — **Quebec Bulldogs,** 1919-20. 4W-20L-0T. 24GP
10 — Toronto Arenas, 1918-19. 5W-13L-0T. 18GP
12 — Hamilton Tigers, 1920-21. 6W-18L-0T. 24GP
— Hamilton Tigers, 1922-23. 6W-18L-0T. 24GP
— Boston Bruins, 1924-25. 6W-24L-0T. 30GP
— Philadelphia Quakers, 1930-31. 4W-36L-4T. 44GP

FEWEST POINTS, ONE SEASON (MINIMUM 70-GAME SCHEDULE):
21 — **Washington Capitals,** 8W-67L-5T. 80GP
30 — NY Islanders, 1972-73. 12W-60L-6T. 78GP
31 — Chicago Blackhawks, 1953-54. 12W-51L-7T. 70GP
— Quebec Nordiques, 1989-90. 12W-61L-7T. 80GP

MOST WINS, ONE SEASON:
60 — **Montreal Canadiens,** 1976-77. 80GP
59 — Montreal Canadiens, 1977-78. 80GP
58 — Montreal Canadiens, 1975-76. 80GP

FEWEST WINS, ONE SEASON:
4 — **Quebec Bulldogs,** 1919-20. 24GP
— **Philadelphia Quakers,** 1930-31. 44GP
5 — Toronto Arenas, 1918-19. 18GP
— Pittsburgh Pirates, 1929-30. 44GP

FEWEST WINS, ONE SEASON (MINIMUM 70-GAME SCHEDULE):
8 — **Washington Capitals,** 1974-75. 80GP
9 — Winnipeg Jets, 1980-81 80GP
11 — Washington Capitals, 1975-76. 80GP

MOST LOSSES, ONE SEASON:
67 — **Washington Capitals,** 1974-75. 80GP
61 — Quebec Nordiques, 1989-90. 80GP
60 — NY Islanders, 1972-73. 78GP
59 — Washington Capitals, 1975-76. 80GP

FEWEST LOSSES, ONE SEASON:
5 — **Ottawa Senators,** 1919-20. 24GP
— **Boston Bruins,** 1929-30. 44GP
— **Montreal Canadiens,** 1943-44. 50GP

FEWEST LOSSES, ONE SEASON (MINIMUM 70-GAME SCHEDULE):
8 — **Montreal Canadiens,** 1976-77. 80GP
10 — Montreal Canadiens, 1972-73. 78GP
— Montreal Canadiens, 1977-78. 80GP
11 — Montreal Canadiens, 1975-76. 80GP

MOST TIES, ONE SEASON:
24 — **Philadelphia Flyers,** 1969-70. 76GP
23 — Montreal Canadiens, 1962-63. 70GP
— Chicago Blackhawks, 1973-74. 78GP

FEWEST TIES, ONE SEASON (Since 1926-27):
1 — **Boston Bruins,** 1929-30. 44GP
2 — NY Americans, 1926-27. 44GP
— Montreal Canadiens, 1926-27. 44GP
— Boston Bruins, 1938-39. 48GP
— NY Rangers, 1941-42. 48GP

FEWEST TIES, ONE SEASON (MINIMUM 70-GAME SCHEDULE):
3 — **New Jersey Devils,** 1985-86. 80GP
— **Calgary Flames,** 1986-87. 80GP
4 — Detroit Red Wings, 1966-67. 70GP
— NY Islanders, 1983-84. 80GP
— Hartford Whalers, 1985-86. 80GP
— Philadelphia Flyers, 1985-86. 80GP
— Minnesota North Stars, 1989-90. 80GP
— Toronto Maple Leafs, 1989-90. 80GP

MOST HOME WINS, ONE SEASON:
36 — **Philadelphia Flyers,** 1975-76. 40GP
33 — Boston Bruins, 1970-71. 39GP
— Boston Bruins, 1973-74. 39GP
— Montreal Canadiens, 1976-77. 40GP
— Philadelphia Flyers, 1976-77. 40GP
— NY Islanders, 1981-82. 40GP
— Philadelphia Flyers, 1985-86. 40GP

MOST ROAD WINS, ONE SEASON:
27 — **Montreal Canadiens,** 1976-77. 40GP
— **Montreal Canadiens,** 1977-78. 40GP
26 — Boston Bruins, 1971-72. 39GP
— Montreal Canadiens, 1975-76. 40GP
— Edmonton Oilers, 1983-84. 40GP

MOST HOME LOSSES, ONE SEASON:
29 — **Pittsburgh Penguins,** 1983-84. 40GP
28 — Washington Capitals, 1974-75. 40GP
— New Jersey Devils, 1983-84. 40GP
— Toronto Maple Leafs, 1984-85. 40GP
27 — Los Angeles Kings, 1985-86. 40GP

Goaltender Ken Dryden was the last NHL goaltender to reach double figures in shutouts, recording a career-high 10 in 1976-77.

MOST ROAD LOSSES, ONE SEASON:
39 — Washington Capitals, 1974-75. 40GP
37 — California Seals, 1973-74. 39GP
35 — NY Islanders, 1972-73. 39GP
— Quebec Nordiques, 1989-90. 40GP

MOST HOME TIES, ONE SEASON:
13 — NY Rangers, 1954-55. 35GP
— **Philadelphia Flyers,** 1969-70. 38GP
— **California Seals,** 1971-72. 39GP
— **California Seals,** 1972-73. 39GP
— **Chicago Blackhawks,** 1973-74. 39GP
12 — NY Islanders, 1974-75. 40GP
— Vancouver Canucks, 1977-78. 40GP
— Buffalo Sabres, 1980-81. 40GP
— Minnesota North Stars, 1981-82. 40GP
— Vancouver Canucks, 1981-82. 40GP

MOST ROAD TIES, ONE SEASON:
15 — Philadelphia Flyers, 1976-77. 40GP
14 — Montreal Canadiens, 1952-53. 35GP
— Montreal Canadiens, 1974-75. 40GP
— Philadelphia Flyers, 1975-76. 40GP

FEWEST HOME WINS, ONE SEASON:
2 — Chicago Blackhawks, 1927-28. 22GP
3 — Boston Bruins, 1924-25. 15GP
— Chicago Blackhawks, 1928-29. 22GP
— Philadelphia Quakers, 1930-31. 22GP

FEWEST HOME WINS, ONE SEASON (MINIMUM 70-GAME SCHEDULE):
6 — Chicago Blackhawks, 1954-55. 35GP
— **Washington Capitals,** 1975-76. 40GP
7 — Boston Bruins, 1962-63. 35GP
— Washington Capitals, 1974-75. 40GP
— Winnipeg Jets, 1980-81. 40GP
— Pittsburgh Penguins, 1983-84. 40GP

FEWEST ROAD WINS, ONE SEASON:
0 — Toronto Arenas, 1918-19. 9GP
— **Quebec Bulldogs,** 1919-20. 12GP
— **Pittsburgh Pirates,** 1929-30. 22GP
1 — Hamilton Tigers, 1921-22. 12GP
— Toronto St. Patricks, 1925-26. 18GP
— Philadelphia Quakers, 1930-31. 22GP
— NY Americans, 1940-41. 24GP
— Washington Capitals, 1974-75. 40GP

FEWEST ROAD WINS, ONE SEASON (MINIMUM 70-GAME SCHEDULE):
1 — Washington Capitals, 1974-75. 40GP
2 — Boston Bruins, 1960-61. 35GP
— Los Angeles Kings, 1969-70. 38GP
— NY Islanders, 1972-73. 39GP
— California Seals, 1973-74. 39GP
— Colorado Rockies, 1977-78. 40GP
— Winnipeg Jets, 1980-81. 40GP

FEWEST HOME LOSSES, ONE SEASON:
0 — Ottawa Senators, 1922-23. 12GP
— **Montreal Canadiens,** 1943-44. 25GP
1 — Toronto Arenas, 1917-18. 11GP
— Ottawa Senators, 19. 9GP
— Ottawa Senators, 1919-20. 12GP
— Toronto St. Patricks, 1922-23. 12GP
— Boston Bruins, 1929-30 and 1930-31. 22GP
— Montreal Canadiens, 1976-77. 40GP

FEWEST HOME LOSSES, ONE SEASON (MINIMUM 70-GAME SCHEDULE):
1 — Montreal Canadiens, 1976-77. 40GP
2 — Montreal Canadiens, 1961-62. 35GP
— NY Rangers, 1970-71. 39GP
— Philadelphia Flyers, 1975-76. 40GP

FEWEST ROAD LOSSES, ONE SEASON:
3 — Montreal Canadiens, 1928-29. 22GP
4 — Ottawa Senators, 1919-20. 12GP
— Montreal Canadiens, 1927-28. 22GP
— Boston Bruins, 1929-30. 20GP
— Boston Bruins, 1940-41. 24GP

FEWEST ROAD LOSSES, ONE SEASON (MINIMUM 70-GAME SCHEDULE):
6 — Montreal Canadiens, 1972-73. 39GP
— **Montreal Canadiens,** 1974-75. 40GP
— **Montreal Canadiens,** 1977-78. 40GP
7 — Detroit Red Wings, 1951-52. 35GP
— Montreal Canadiens, 1976-77. 40GP
— Philadelphia Flyers, 1979-80. 40GP

LONGEST WINNING STREAK:
15 Games — NY Islanders, Jan. 21, 1982 - Feb. 20, 1982.
14 Games — Boston Bruins, Dec. 3, 1929 - Jan. 9, 1930.
13 Games — Boston Bruins, Feb. 23, 1971 - March 20, 1971.
— Philadelphia Flyers, Oct. 19, 1985 - Nov. 17, 1985.

LONGEST WINNING STREAK FROM START OF SEASON:
8 Games — Toronto Maple Leafs, 1934-35.
— **Buffalo Sabres,** 1975-76.
7 Games — Edmonton Oilers, 1983-84.
— Quebec Nordiques, 1985-86.
— Pittsburgh Penguins, 1986-87.

LONGEST HOME WINNING STREAK FROM START OF SEASON:
11 Games — Chicago Blackhawks, 1963-64.
10 Games — Ottawa Senators, 1925-26
9 Games — Montreal Canadiens, 1953-54.
— Chicago Blackhawks, 1971-72.
8 Games — Boston Bruins, 1983-84.
— Philadelphia Flyers, 1986-87.
— New Jersey Devils, 1987-88.

LONGEST WINNING STREAK, INCLUDING PLAYOFFS:
15 Games — Detroit Red Wings, Feb. 27, 1955 - April 5, 1955. Nine regular-season games, six playoff games.

LONGEST HOME WINNING STREAK (ONE SEASON):
20 Games — Boston Bruins, Dec. 3, 1929 - Mar. 18, 1930.
— **Philadelphia Flyers,** Jan. 4, 1976 - April 3, 1976.

LONGEST HOME WINNING STREAK, INCLUDING PLAYOFFS:
24 Games — Philadelphia Flyers, Jan. 4, 1976 - April 25, 1976. 20 regular-season games, 4 playoff games.

LONGEST ROAD WINNING STREAK (ONE SEASON):
10 Games — Buffalo Sabres, Dec. 10, 1983 - Jan. 23, 1984.
8 Games — Boston Bruins, Feb. 17, 1972 - Mar. 8, 972.
— Los Angeles Kings, Dec. 18, 1974 - Jan. 16, 1975.
— Montreal Canadiens, Dec. 18, 1977 - Jan. 18, 1978.
— NY Islanders, Feb. 27, 1981 - March 29, 1981.
— Montreal Canadiens, Jan. 21, 1982 - Feb. 21, 1982.
— Philadelphia Flyers, Dec. 22, 1982 - Jan. 16, 1983.
— Winnipeg Jets, Feb. 25, 1985 - Apr. 6, 1985.
— Edmonton Oilers, Dec. 9, 1986 - Jan. 17, 1987.

LONGEST UNDEFEATED STREAK (ONE SEASON):
35 Games — Philadelphia Flyers, Oct. 14, 1979 - Jan. 6, 1980. 25W-10T.
28 Games — Montreal Canadiens, Dec. 18, 1977 - Feb. 23, 1978. 23W-5T.
23 Games — Boston Bruins, Dec. 22, 1940 - Feb. 23, 1941. 15W-8T.
— Philadelphia Flyers, Jan. 29, 1976 - Mar. 18, 1976. 17W-6T.

LONGEST UNDEFEATED STREAK FROM START OF SEASON:
15 Games — Edmonton Oilers, 1984-85. 12W-3T
14 Games — Montreal Canadiens, 1943-44. 11W-3T
13 Games — Montreal Canadiens, 1972-73. 9W-4T

LONGEST HOME UNDEFEATED STREAK (ONE SEASON):
34 Games — Montreal Canadiens, Nov. 1, 1976 - Apr. 2, 1977. 28W-6T.
27 Games — Boston Bruins, Nov. 22, 1970 - Mar. 20, 1971. 26W-1T.

LONGEST HOME UNDEFEATED STREAK, INCLUDING PLAYOFFS:
38 Games — Montreal Canadiens, Nov. 1, 1976 - April 26, 1977. 28W-6T in regular season and 4W in playoffs).

LONGEST ROAD UNDEFEATED STREAK (ONE SEASON):
23 Games — Montreal Canadiens, Nov. 27, 1974 - Mar. 12, 1975. 14W-9T.
17 Games — Montreal Canadiens, Dec. 18, 1977 - March 1, 1978. 14W-3T.
16 Games — Philadelphia Flyers, Oct. 20, 1979 - Jan. 6, 1980. 11W-5T.

LONGEST LOSING STREAK (ONE SEASON):
17 Games — Washington Capitals, Feb. 18, 1975 - Mar. 26, 1975.
15 Games — Philadelphia Quakers, Nov. 29, 1930 - Jan. 8, 1931.

LONGEST LOSING STREAK FROM START OF SEASON:
11 Games — NY Rangers, 1943-44.
7 Games — Montreal Canadiens, 1938-39.
— Chicago Blackhawks, 1947-48.
— Washington Capitals, 1983-84.

LONGEST HOME LOSING STREAK (ONE SEASON):
11 Games — Boston Bruins, Dec. 8, 1924 - Feb. 17, 1925.
— **Washington Capitals,** Feb. 18, 1975 - Mar. 30, 1975.

LONGEST ROAD LOSING STREAK (ONE SEASON):
37 Games — Washington Capitals, Oct. 9, 1974 - Mar. 26, 1975.

LONGEST WINLESS STREAK (ONE SEASON):
30 Games — Winnipeg Jets, Oct. 19, 1980 - Dec. 20, 1980. 23L-7T.
27 Games — Kansas City Scouts, Feb. 12, 1976 - April 4, 1976. 21L-6T.
25 Games — Washington Capitals, Nov. 29, 1975 - Jan. 21, 1976. 22L-3T.

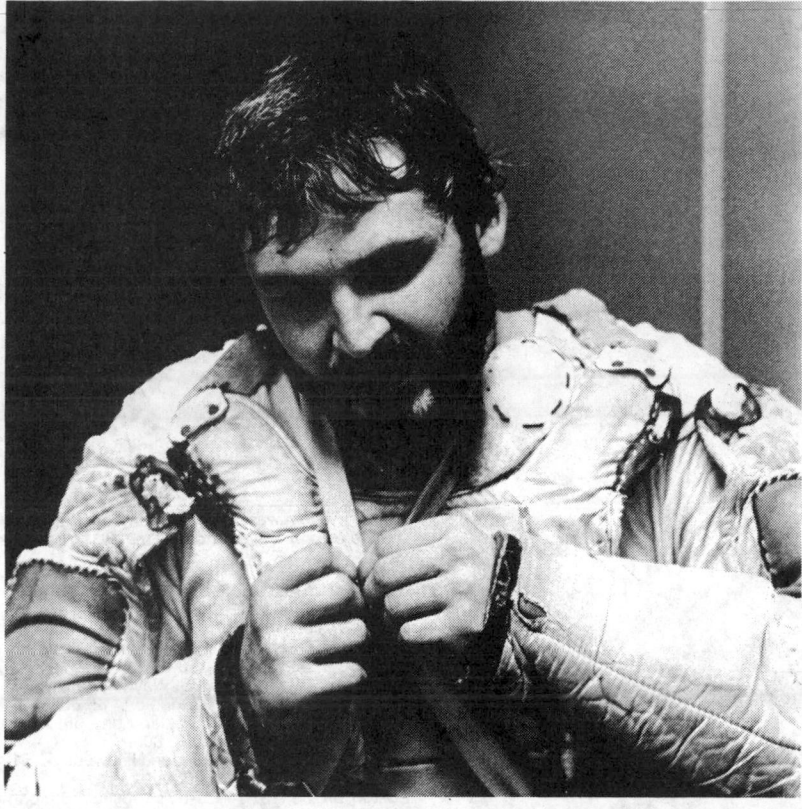

Bernie Parent was a key member of the Philadelphia Flyers' team which won 20 consecutive games at home during the 1975-76 season, tying an NHL record that had stood for 46 years.

LONGEST WINLESS STREAK FROM START OF SEASON:
15 Games — NY Rangers, 1943-44. 14L-1T
12 Games — Pittsburgh Pirates, 1927-28. 9L-3T
11 Games — Minnesota North Stars, 1973-74. 5L-6T

LONGEST HOME WINLESS STREAK (ONE SEASON):
15 Games — Chicago Blackhawks, Dec. 16, 1928 - Feb. 28, 1929. 11L-4T.
— Montreal Canadiens, Dec. 16, 1939 - Mar. 7, 1940. 12L-3T.

LONGEST ROAD WINLESS STREAK (ONE SEASON):
37 Games — Washington Capitals, Oct. 9, 1974 - Mar. 26, 1975. 37L-0T.

LONGEST NON-SHUTOUT STREAK:
264 Games — Calgary Flames, Nov. 12, 1981 - Jan. 9, 1985.
262 Games — Los Angeles Kings, Mar. 15, 1986 - Oct. 25, 1989.
230 Games — Quebec Nordiques, Feb. 10, 1980 - Jan. 13, 1983.
229 Games — Edmonton Oilers, Mar. 15, 1981 - Feb. 11, 1984.
228 Games — Chicago Blackhawks, Mar. 14, 1970 - Feb. 21, 1973.

LONGEST NON-SHUTOUT STREAK INCLUDING PLAYOFFS:
264 Games — Los Angeles Kings, Mar. 15 1986 - Apr. 6, 1989.
(5 playoff games in 1987; 5 in 1988; 2 in 1989)
262 Games — Chicago Blackhawks, Mar. 14, 1970 - Feb. 21, 1973. (8 playoff games in 1970; 18 in 1971; 8 in 1972).
251 Games — Quebec Nordiques, Feb. 10, 1980 - Jan. 13, 1983. (5 playoff games in 1981; 16 in 1982).
235 Games — Boston Bruins, Oct. 26, 1977 - Feb. 20, 1980. (15 playoff games In 1978; 11 in 1979).

MOST CONSECUTIVE GAMES SHUT OUT:
8 — Chicago Blackhawks, 1928-29.

MOST SHUTOUTS, ONE SEASON:
22 — Montreal Canadiens, 1928-29. All by George Hainsworth. 44GP
16 — NY Americans, 1928-29. Roy Worters had 13; Flat Walsh 3. 44GP
15 — Ottawa Senators, 1925-26. All by Alex Connell. 36GP
— Ottawa Senators, 1927-28. All by Alex Connell. 44GP
— Boston Bruins, 1927-28. All by Hal Winkler. 44GP
— Chicago Blackhawks, 1969-70. All by Tony Esposito. 76GP

MOST GOALS, ONE SEASON:
446 — Edmonton Oilers, 1983-84. 80GP
426 — Edmonton Oilers, 1985-86. 80GP
424 — Edmonton Oilers, 1982-83. 80GP
417 — Edmonton Oilers, 1981-82. 80GP
401 — Edmonton Oilers, 1984-85. 80GP

HIGHEST GOALS-PER-GAME AVERAGE, ONE SEASON:
5.58 — Edmonton Oilers, 1983-84. 446G in 80GP.
5.38 — Montreal Canadiens, 1919-20. 129G in 24GP.
5.33 — Edmonton Oilers, 1985-86. 426G in 80GP.
5.30 — Edmonton Oilers, 1982-83. 424G in 80GP.
5.23 — Montreal Canadiens, 1917-18. 115G in 22GP.

FEWEST GOALS, ONE SEASON:
33 — Chicago Blackhawks, 1928-29. 44GP
45 — Montreal Maroons, 1924-25. 30GP
46 — Pittsburgh Pirates, 1928-29. 44GP

FEWEST GOALS, ONE SEASON (MINIMUM 70-GAME SCHEDULE):
133 — Chicago Blackhawks, 1953-54. 70GP
147 — Toronto Maple Leafs, 1954-55. 70GP
— Boston Bruins, 1955-56. 70GP
150 — NY Rangers, 1954-55. 70GP

LOWEST GOALS-PER-GAME AVERAGE, ONE SEASON:
.75 — Chicago Blackhawks, 1928-29, 33G in 44GP.
1.05 — Pittsburgh Pirates, 1928-29. 46G in 44GP.
1.20 — NY Americans, 1928-29. 53G in 44GP.

MOST GOALS AGAINST, ONE SEASON:
446 — Washington Capitals, 1974-75. 80GP
415 — Detroit Red Wings, 1985-86. 80GP
407 — Quebec Nordiques, 1989-90. 80GP
403 — Hartford Whalers, 1982-83. 80GP
401 — Vancouver Canucks, 1984-85. 80GP

HIGHEST GOALS-AGAINST-PER-GAME AVERAGE, ONE SEASON:
7.38 — Quebec Bulldogs, 1919-20, 177GA vs. in 24GP.
6.20 — NY Rangers, 1943-44, 310GA vs. in 50GP.
5.58 — Washington Capitals, 1974-75, 446GA vs. in 80GP.

FEWEST GOALS AGAINST, ONE SEASON:
42 — Ottawa Senators, 1925-26. 36GP
43 — Montreal Canadiens, 1928-29. 44GP
40 — Montreal Canadiens, 1923-24. 24GP
— Montreal Canadiens, 1927-28. 44GP

FEWEST GOALS AGAINST, ONE SEASON (MINIMUM 70-GAME SCHEDULE):
131 — Toronto Maple Leafs, 1953-54. 70GP
— **Montreal Canadiens,** 1955-56. 70GP
132 — Detroit Red Wings, 1953-54. 70GP
133 — Detroit Red Wings, 1951-52. 70GP
— Detroit Red Wings, 1952-53. 70GP

LOWEST GOALS-AGAINST-PER-GAME AVERAGE, ONE SEASON:
.98 — Montreal Canadiens, 1928-29. 43GA vs. in 44GP.
1.09 — Montreal Canadiens, 1927-28. 48GA vs. in 44GP.
1.17 — Ottawa Senators, 1925-26. 42GA vs. in 36GP.

MOST POWER-PLAY GOALS, ONE SEASON:
120 — Pittsburgh Penguins, 1988-89. 80GP
111 — NY Rangers, 1987-88. 80GP
110 — Pittsburgh Penguins, 1987-88. 80GP
— Winnipeg Jets, 1987-88, 80GP
109 — Calgary Flames, 1987-88. 80GP

Bernie Nicholls scored 327 goals for Los Angeles from 1981-82 to 1989-90.

MOST POWER-PLAY GOALS AGAINST, ONE SEASON:
122 — Chicago Blackhawks, 1988-89. 80GP
120 — Pittsburgh Penguins, 1987-88. 80GP
115 — New Jersey Devils, 1988-89. 80GP
111 — Detroit Red Wings, 1985-86. 80GP
— Pittsburgh Penguins, 1988-89. 80GP
110 — Pittsburgh Penguins, 1982-83. 80GP

MOST SHORTHAND GOALS, ONE SEASON:
36 — Edmonton Oilers, 1983-84. 80GP
28 — Edmonton Oilers, 1986-87. 80GP
27 — Edmonton Oilers, 1985-86. 80GP
— Edmonton Oilers, 1988-89. 80GP

MOST SHORTHAND GOALS AGAINST, ONE SEASON:
22 — Pittsburgh Penguins, 1984-85. 80GP
21 — Calgary Flames, 1984-85. 80GP
— Pittsburgh Penguins, 1989-90. 80GP
20 — Minnesota North Stars, 1982-83. 80GP
— Quebec Nordiques, 1985-86. 80GP

MOST ASSISTS, ONE SEASON:
737 — Edmonton Oilers, 1985-86. 80GP
736 — Edmonton Oilers, 1983-84. 80GP
706 — Edmonton Oilers, 1981-82. 80GP

FEWEST ASSISTS, ONE SEASON:
45 — NY Rangers, 1926-27. 44GP

FEWEST ASSISTS, ONE SEASON (MINIMUM 70-GAME SCHEDULE):
206 — Chicago Blackhawks, 1953-54. 70GP

MOST SCORING POINTS, ONE SEASON:
1,182 — Edmonton Oilers, 1983-84. 80GP
1,163 — Edmonton Oilers, 1985-86. 80GP
1,123 — Edmonton Oilers, 1981-82. 80GP

MOST 50-OR-MORE-GOAL SCORERS, ONE SEASON:
3 — Edmonton Oilers, 1983-84. Wayne Gretzky, 87; Glenn Anderson, 54; Jari Kurri, 52. 80GP.
— Edmonton Oilers, 1985-86. Jari Kurri, 68; Glenn Anderson, 54; Wayne Gretzky, 52. 80GP.
2 — Boston Bruins, 1970-71. Phil Esposito, 76; John Bucyk, 51. 78GP
— Boston Bruins, 1973-74. Phil Esposito, 68; Ken Hodge, 50. 78GP
— Philadelphia Flyers, 1975-76. Reggie Leach, 61; Bill Barber, 50. 80GP
— Pittsburgh Penguins, 1975-76. Pierre Larouche, 53; Jean Pronovost, 52. 80GP
— Montreal Canadiens, 1976-77. Steve Shutt, 60; Guy Lafleur, 56. 80GP
— Los Angeles Kings, 1979-80. Charlie Simmer, 56; Marcel Dionne, 53. 80GP
— Montreal Canadiens, 1979-80. Pierre Larouche, 50; Guy Lafleur, 50. 80GP
— Los Angeles Kings, 1980-81. Marcel Dionne, 58; Charlie Simmer, 56. 80GP
— Edmonton Oilers, 1981-82. Wayne Gretzky, 92; Mark Messier, 50. 80GP
— NY Islanders, 1981-82. Mike Bossy, 64; Bryan Trottier, 50. 80GP
— Edmonton Oilers, 1984-85. Wayne Gretzky, 73; Jari Kurri, 71. 80GP
— Washington Capitals, 1984-85. Bob Carpenter, 53; Mike Gartner, 50. 80GP
— Edmonton Oilers, 1986-87. Wayne Gretzky, 62; Jari Kurri, 54. 80GP
— Calgary Flames, 1987-88. Joe Nieuwendyk, 51; Hakan Loob, 50. 80GP
— Los Angeles Kings, 1987-88. Jimmy Carson, 55; Luc Robitaille, 53. 80GP
— Los Angeles Kings, 1988-89. Bernie Nicholls, 70; Wayne Gretzky, 54. 80GP
— Calgary Flames, 1988-89. Joe Nieuwendyk, 51; Joe Mullen, 51. 80GP

Bob Nystrom was one of six New York Islanders to score 30-or-more goals during the 1977-78 season.

MOST 40-OR-MORE-GOAL SCORERS, ONE SEASON:
4 — Edmonton Oilers, 1982-83. Wayne Gretzky, 71; Glenn Anderson, 48; Mark Messier, 48; Jari Kurri, 45. 80GP
— Edmonton Oilers, 1983-84. Wayne Gretzky, 87; Glenn Anderson, 54; Jari Kurri, 52; Paul Coffey, 40. 80GP
— Edmonton Oilers, 1984-85. Wayne Gretzky, 73; Jari Kurri, 71; Mike Krushelnyski, 43; Glenn Anderson, 42. 80GP
— Edmonton Oilers, 1985-86. Jari Kurri, 68; Glenn Anderson, 54; Wayne Gretzky, 52; Paul Coffey, 48. 80GP
— Calgary Flames, 1987-88. Joe Nieuwendyk, 51; Hakan Loob, 50; Mike Bullard, 48; Joe Mullen, 40. 80GP
3 — Boston Bruins, 1970-71. Phil Esposito, 76; John Bucyk, 51; Ken Hodge, 43. 78GP
— NY Rangers, 1971-72. Vic Hadfield, 50; Jean Ratelle, 46; Rod Gilbert, 43. 78GP
— Buffalo Sabres, 1975-76. Danny Gare, 50; Rick Martin, 49; Gilbert Perreault, 44. 80GP
— Montreal Canadiens, 1979-80. Guy Lafleur, 50; Pierre Larouche, 50; Steve Shutt, 47. 80GP
— Buffalo Sabres, 1979-80. Danny Gare, 56; Rick Martin, 45; Gilbert Perreault, 40. 80GP
— Los Angeles Kings, 1980-81. Marcel Dionne, 58; Charlie Simmer, 56; Dave Taylor, 47. 80GP
— Los Angeles Kings, 1984-85. Marcel Dionne, 46; Bernie Nicholls, 46; Dave Taylor, 41. 80GP
— NY Islanders, 1984-85. Mike Bossy, 58; Brent Sutter, 42; John Tonelli, 42. 80GP
— Chicago Blackhawks, 1985-86. Denis Savard, 47; Troy Murray, 45; Al Secord, 40. 80GP
— Chicago Blackhawks, 1987-88. Denis Savard, 44; Rick Vaive, 43; Steve Larmer, 41. 80GP
— Edmonton Oilers, 1987-88. Craig Simpson, 43; Jari Kurri, 43; Wayne Gretzky, 40. 80GP
— Los Angeles Kings, 1988-89. Bernie Nicholls, 70; Wayne Gretzky 54; Luc Robitaille, 46. 80GP

MOST 30-OR-MORE GOAL SCORERS, ONE SEASON:
6 — Buffalo Sabres, 1974-75. Rick Martin, 52; Rene Robert, 40; Gilbert Perreault, 39; Don Luce, 33; Rick Dudley, Danny Gare, 31 each. 80GP
— NY Islanders, 1977-78. Mike Bossy, 53; Bryan Trottier, 46; Clark Gillies, 35; Denis Potvin, Bob Nystrom, Bob Bourne, 30 each. 80GP
— Winnipeg Jets, 1984-85. Dale Hawerchuk, 53; Paul MacLean, 41; Laurie Boschman, 32; Brian Mullen, 32; Doug Smail, 31; Thomas Steen, 30. 80GP
5 — Chicago Blackhawks, 1968-69. 76GP
— Boston Bruins, 1970-71. 78GP
— Montreal Canadiens, 1971-72. 78GP
— Philadelphia Flyers, 1972-73. 78GP
— Boston Bruins, 1973-74. 78GP
— Montreal Canadiens, 1974-75. 80GP
— Montreal Canadiens, 1975-76. 80GP
— Pittsburgh Penguins, 1975-76. 80GP
— NY Islanders, 1978-79. 80GP
— Detroit Red Wings, 1979-80. 80GP
— Philadelphia Flyers, 1979-80. 80GP
— NY Islanders, 1980-81. 80GP
— St. Louis Blues, 1980-81. 80GP
— Chicago Blackhawks, 1981-82. 80GP
— Edmonton Oilers, 1981-82. 80GP
— Montreal Canadiens, 1981-82. 80GP
— Quebec Nordiques, 1981-82. 80GP
— Washington Capitals, 1981-82. 80GP
— Edmonton Oilers, 1982-83. 80GP
— Edmonton Oilers, 1983-84. 80GP
— Edmonton Oilers, 1984-85. 80GP
— Los Angeles Kings, 1984-85. 80GP
— Edmonton Oilers, 1985-86. 80GP
— Edmonton Oilers, 1986-87. 80GP
— Edmonton Oilers, 1987-88. 80GP
— Edmonton Oilers, 1988-89. 80GP

MOST 20-OR-MORE GOAL SCORERS, ONE SEASON:
11 — **Boston Bruins,** 1977-78; Peter McNab, 41; Terry O'Reilly, 29; Bobby Schmautz, Stan Jonathan, 27 each; Jean Ratelle, Rick Middleton, 25 each; Wayne Cashman, 24; Gregg Sheppard, 23; Brad Park, 22; Don Marcotte, Bob Miller, 20 each. 80GP
10 — Boston Bruins, 1970-71. 78GP
— Montreal Canadiens, 1974-75. 80GP
— St. Louis Blues, 1980-81. 80GP

MOST 100 OR-MORE-POINT SCORERS, ONE SEASON:
4 — **Boston Bruins,** 1970-71, Phil Esposito, 76G-76A-152PTS; Bobby Orr, 37G-102A-139PTS; John Bucyk, 51G-65A-116PTS; Ken Hodge, 43G-62A-105PTS. 78GP
— **Edmonton Oilers,** 1982-83, Wayne Gretzky, 71G-125A-196PTS; Mark Messier, 48G-58A-106PTS; Glenn Anderson, 48G-56A-104PTS; Jari Kurri, 45G-59A-104PTS. 80GP
— **Edmonton Oilers,** 1983-84, Wayne Gretzky, 87G-118A-205PTS; Paul Coffey, 40G-86A-126PTS; Jari Kurri, 52G-61A-113PTS; Mark Messier, 37G-64A-101PTS. 80GP
— **Edmonton Oilers,**1985-86, Wayne Gretzky, 52G-163A-215PTS; Paul Coffey, 48G-90A-138PTS; Jari Kurri, 68G-63A-131PTS; Glenn Anderson, 54G-48A-102PTS. 80GP
3 — Boston Bruins, 1973-74, Phil Esposito, 68G-77A-145PTS; Bobby Orr, 32G-90A-122PTS; Ken Hodge, 50G-55A-105PTS. 78GP
— NY Islanders, 1978-79, Bryan Trottier, 47G-87A-134PTS; Mike Bossy, 69G-57A-126PTS; Denis Potvin, 31G-70A-101PTS. 80GP
— Los Angeles Kings, 1980-81, Marcel Dionne, 58G-77A-135PTS; Dave Taylor, 47 G-65A-112PTS; Charlie Simmer, 56G-49A-105PTS. 80GP
— Edmonton Oilers, 1984-85, Wayne Gretzky, 73G-135A-208PTS; Jari Kurri, 71G-64A-135PTS; Paul Coffey, 37G-84A-121PTS. 80GP
— NY Islanders, 1984-85, Mike Bossy, 58G-59A-117PTS; Brent Sutter, 42G-60A-102PTS; John Tonelli, 42G-58A-100PTS. 80GP
— Edmonton Oilers, 1986-87, Wayne Gretzky, 62G-121A-183PTS; Jari Kurri, 54G-54A-108PTS; Mark Messier, 37G-70A-107PTS. 80GP
— Pittsburgh Penguins, 1988-89, Mario Lemieux, 85G-114A-199PTS; Rob Brown, 49G-66A-115PTS; Paul Coffey, 30G-83A-113PTS. 80GP

MOST PENALTY MINUTES, ONE SEASON:
2,670 – Pittsburgh Penguins, 1988-89. 80GP
2,621 – Philadelphia Flyers, 1980-81. 80GP
2,499 – New Jersey Devils, 1988-89. 80GP
2,496 – Chicago Blackhawks, 1988-89. 80GP

MOST GOALS, BOTH TEAMS, ONE GAME:
21 — **Montreal Canadiens, Toronto St. Patricks,** at Montreal, Jan. 10, 1920. Montreal won 14-7.
— **Edmonton Oilers, Chicago Blackhawks,** at Chicago, Dec. 11, 1985. Edmonton won 12-9.
20 — Edmonton Oilers, Minnesota North Stars, at Edmonton, Jan. 4, 1984. Edmonton won 12-8.
— Toronto Maple Leafs, Edmonton Oilers, at Toronto, Jan. 8, 1986. Toronto won 11-9.
19 — Montreal Wanderers, Toronto Arenas, at Montreal, Dec. 19, 1917. Montreal won 10-9.
— Montreal Canadiens, Quebec Bulldogs, at Quebec, March 3, 1920, Montreal won 16-3.
— Montreal Canadiens, Hamilton Tigers, at Montreal, Feb. 26, 1921. Canadiens won 13-6.
— Boston Bruins, NY Rangers, at Boston, March 4, 1944, Boston won 10-9.
— Boston Bruins, Detroit Red Wings, at Detroit, March 16, 1944. Detroit won 10-9.
— Vancouver Canucks, Minnesota North Stars, at Vancouver, Oct. 7, 1983. Vancouver won 10-9.

MOST GOALS, ONE TEAM, ONE GAME:
16 — **Montreal Canadiens,** March 3, 1920, at Quebec. Defeated Quebec Bulldogs 16-3.

MOST CONSECUTIVE GOALS, ONE TEAM, ONE GAME:
15 — **Detroit Red Wings,** Jan. 23, 1944, at Detroit. Defeated NY Rangers 15-0.

MOST POINTS, BOTH TEAMS, ONE GAME:
62 — **Edmonton Oilers, Chicago Blackhawks,** at Chicago, Dec. 11, 1985. Edmonton won 12-9. Edmonton had 24A, Chicago, 17.
53 — Quebec Nordiques, Washington Capitals, at Washington, Feb. 22, 1981. Quebec won 11-7. Quebec had 22A, Washington, 13.
— Edmonton Oilers, Minnesota North Stars, at Edmonton, Jan. 4, 1984. Edmonton won 12-8. Edmonton had 20A, Minnesota 13.
— Minnesota North Stars, St. Louis Blues, at St. Louis, Jan. 27, 1984. Minnesota won 10-8. Minnesota had 19A, St. Louis 16.
52 — Mtl. Maroons, NY Americans, at New York, Feb. 18, 1936. 8-8 tie. New York had 20A, Montreal 16. (3A allowed for each goal.)
— Vancouver Canucks, Minnesota North Stars, at Vancouver, Oct. 7, 1983. Vancouver won 10-9. Vancouver had 16A, Minnesota 17.

MOST POINTS, ONE TEAM, ONE GAME:
40 — **Buffalo Sabres,** Dec. 21, 1975, at Buffalo. Buffalo defeated Washington 14-2, receiving 26A.
39 — Minnesota North Stars, Nov. 11, 1981, at Minnesota. Minnesota defeated Winnipeg 15-2, receiving 24A.
37 — Detroit Red Wings, Jan. 23, 1944, at Detroit. Detroit defeated NY Rangers 15-0, receiving 22A.
— Toronto Maple Leafs, March 16, 1957, at Toronto. Toronto defeated NY Rangers 14-1, receiving 23A.
— Buffalo Sabres, Feb. 25, 1978, at Cleveland. Buffalo defeated Cleveland 13-3, receiving 24A.
36 — Edmonton Oilers, Dec. 11, 1985, at Chicago. Edmonton defeated Chicago 12-9, receiving 24A.

MOST SHOTS, BOTH TEAMS, ONE GAME:
141—**NY Americans, Pittsburgh Pirates,** Dec. 26, 1925, at New York. NY Americans, who won game 3-1, had 73 shots; Pit. Pirates, 68 shots.

MOST SHOTS, ONE TEAM, ONE GAME:
83—**Boston Bruins,** March 4, 1941, at Boston. Bruins defeated Chicago 3-2.
73—NY Americans, Dec. 26, 1925, at New York. Americans defeated Pit. Pirates 3-1.
72—Boston Bruins, Dec. 10, 1970, at Boston. Bruins defeated Buffalo 8-2.

MOST PENALTIES, BOTH TEAMS, ONE GAME: (AND)
MOST PENALTY MINUTES, BOTH TEAMS, ONE GAME:
84 Penalties; 406 Minutes — **Minnesota North Stars, Boston Bruins** at Boston, Feb. 26, 1981. Minnesota received 18 minors, 13 majors, 4 10-minute misconducts and 7 game misconducts; a total 42 penalties and 211PIM. Boston received 20 minors, 13 majors, 3 10-minute misconducts and 6 game misconducts; a total 42 penalties and 195PIM.

MOST PENALTIES, ONE TEAM, ONE GAME:
42 — **Minnesota North Stars,** Feb. 26, 1981, at Boston. Minnesota received 18 minors, 13 majors, 4 10-minute misconducts and 7 game misconducts.
— **Boston Bruins,** Feb. 26, 1981, at Boston vs. Minnesota. Boston received 20 minors, 13 majors, 3 10-minute misconducts and 7 game misconducts.

MOST PENALTY MINUTES, ONE TEAM, ONE GAME:
211—**Minnesota North Stars,** Feb. 26, 1981, at Boston. Minnesota received 18 minors, 13 majors, 4 10-minute misconducts and 7 game misconducts.

MOST GOALS, BOTH TEAMS, ONE PERIOD:
12 — **Buffalo Sabres, Toronto Maple Leafs,** at Buffalo, March 19, 1981, second period. Buffalo scored 9 goals, Toronto 3. Buffalo won 14-4.
— **Edmonton Oilers, Chicago Blackhawks,** at Chicago, Dec. 11, 1985, second period. Edmonton scored 6 goals, Chicago 6. Edmonton won 12-9.
10 — NY Rangers, NY Americans, at NY Americans, March 16, 1939, third period. NY Rangers scored 7 goals, NY Americans 3. NY Rangers won 11-5.
— Toronto Maple Leafs, Detroit Red Wings, at Detroit, March 17, 1946, third period. Toronto scored 6 goals, Detroit 4. Toronto won 11-7.
— Vancouver Canucks, Buffalo Sabres, at Buffalo, Jan. 8, 1976, third period. Buffalo scored 6 goals, Vancouver 4. Buffalo won game 8-5.
— Buffalo Sabres, Montreal Canadiens, at Montreal, Oct. 26, 1982, first period. Montreal scored 5 goals, Buffalo 5. 7-7 tie.
— Boston Bruins, Quebec Nordiques, at Quebec, Dec. 7, 1982, second period. Quebec scored 6 goals, Boston 4. Quebec won 10-5.
— Calgary Flames, Vancouver Canucks, at Vancouver, Jan. 16, 1987, first period. Vancouver scored 6 goals, Calgary 4. Vancouver won 9-5.
— Winnipeg Jets, Detroit Red Wings, at Detroit, Nov. 25, 1987, third period. Detroit scored 7 goals, Winnipeg 3. Detroit won game 10-8.
— Chicago Blackhawks, St. Louis Blues, at St. Louis, Mar. 15, 1988, third period. Chicago scored 5 goals, St. Louis 5. 7-7 tie.

MOST GOALS, ONE TEAM, ONE PERIOD:
9 — **Buffalo Sabres,** March 19, 1981, at Buffalo, second period during 14-4 win over Toronto.
8 — Detroit Red Wings, Jan. 23, 1944, at Detroit, third period during 15-0 win over NY Rangers.
— Boston Bruins, March 16, 1969, at Boston, second period during 11-3 win over Toronto.
— NY Rangers, Nov. 21, 1971, at New York, third period during 12-1 win over California.
— Philadelphia Flyers, March 31, 1973, at Philadelphia, second period during 10-2 win over NY Islanders.
— Buffalo Sabres, Dec. 21, 1975, at Buffalo, third period during 14-2 win over Washington.
— Minnesota North Stars, Nov. 11, 1981, at Minnesota, second period during 15-2 win over Winnipeg.

MOST POINTS, BOTH TEAMS, ONE PERIOD:
35 — **Edmonton, Oilers, Chicago Blackhawks,** at Chicago, Dec. 11, 1985, second period. Edmonton had 6G, 12A; Chicago, 6G, 11A. Edmonton won 12-9.
31 — Buffalo Sabres, Toronto Maple Leafs, at Buffalo, March 19, 1981, second period. Buffalo had 9G, 14A; Toronto, 3G, 5A. Buffalo won 14-4.
29 — Winnipeg Jets, Detroit Red Wings, at Detroit, Nov. 25, 1987, third period. Detroit had 7G, 13A; Winnipeg had 3G, 6A. Detroit won 10-8.
— Chicago Blackhawks, St. Louis Blues, at St. Louis, Mar. 15, 1988, third period. St. Louis had 5G, 10A; Chicago had 5G, 9A. 7-7 tie.

MOST POINTS, ONE TEAM, ONE PERIOD:
23 — **NY Rangers,** Nov. 21, 1971, at New York, third period during 12-1 win over California. NY Rangers scored 8G and 15A.
— **Buffalo Sabres,** Dec. 21, 1975, at Buffalo, third period during 14-2 win over Washington. Buffalo scored 8G and 15A.
— **Buffalo Sabres,** March 19, 1981, at Buffalo, second period, during 14-4 win over Toronto. Buffalo scored 9G and 14A.
22 — Detroit Red Wings, Jan. 23, 1944, at Detroit, third period during 15-0 win over NY Rangers. Detroit scored 8G and 14A.
— Boston Bruins, March 16, 1969, at Boston, second period during 11-3 win over Toronto Maple Leafs. Boston scored 8G and 14A.
— Minnesota North Stars, Nov. 11, 1981, at Minnesota, second period during 15-2 win over Winnipeg. Minnesota scored 8G and 14A.

MOST SHOTS, ONE TEAM, ONE PERIOD:
33 — **Boston Bruins,** March 4, 1941, at Boston, second period. Boston defeated Chicago 3-2.

MOST PENALTIES, BOTH TEAMS, ONE PERIOD:
67 — **Minnesota North Stars, Boston Bruins,** at Boston, Feb. 26, 1981, first period. Minnesota received 15 minors, 8 majors, 4 10-minute misconducts and 7 game misconducts, a total 34 penalties. Boston had 16 minors, 8 majors, 3 10-minute misconducts and 6 game misconducts, a total 33 penalties.

MOST PENALTY MINUTES, BOTH TEAMS, ONE PERIOD:
372 — **Los Angeles Kings, Philadelphia Flyers** at Philadelphia, March 11, 1979, first period. Philadelphia received 4 minors, 8 majors, 6 10-minute misconducts and 8 game misconducts for 188 minutes. Los Angeles received 2 minors, 8 majors, 6 10-minute misconducts and 8 game misconducts for 184 minutes.

MOST PENALTIES, ONE TEAM, ONE PERIOD:
34 — **Minnesota North Stars,** Feb. 26, 1981, at Boston, first period. 15 minors, 8 majors, 4 10-minute misconducts, 7 game misconducts.

MOST PENALTY MINUTES, ONE TEAM, ONE PERIOD:
188 — **Philadelphia Flyers,** March 11, 1979, at Philadelphia vs. Los Angeles, first period. Flyers received 4 minors, 8 majors, 6 10-minute misconducts and 8 game misconducts.

FASTEST SIX GOALS, BOTH TEAMS
3 Minutes, 15 Seconds — **Montreal Canadiens, Toronto Maple Leafs,** at Montreal, Jan. 4, 1944, first period. Montreal scored 4G, Toronto 2. Montreal won 6-3.

FASTEST FIVE GOALS, BOTH TEAMS:
1 Minute, 24 Seconds — **Chicago Blackhawks, Toronto Maple Leafs,** at Toronto, Oct. 15, 1983, second period. Scorers were: Gaston Gingras, Toronto, 16:49; Denis Savard, Chicago, 17:12; Steve Larmer, Chicago, 17:27; Savard, 17:42; and John Anderson, Toronto, 18:13. Toronto won 10-8.
1 Minute, 39 Seconds — Detroit Red Wings, Toronto Maple Leafs, at Toronto, Nov. 15, 1944, third period. Scorers were: Ted Kennedy, Toronto, 10:36 and 10:55; Hal Jackson, Detroit, 11:48; Steve Wochy, Detroit, 12:02; Don Grosso, Detroit, 12:15. Detroit won 8-4.

FASTEST FIVE GOALS, ONE TEAM:
2 Minutes, 7 Seconds — **Pittsburgh Penguins,** at Pittsburgh, Nov. 22, 1972, third period. Scorers: Bryan Hextall, 12:00; Jean Pronovost, 12:18; Al McDonough, 13:40; Ken Schinkel, 13:49; Ron Schock, 14:07. Pittsburgh defeated St. Louis 10-4.
2 Minutes, 37 seconds — NY Islanders, at New York, Jan. 26, 1982, first period. Scorers: Duane Sutter, 1:31; John Tonelli, 2:30; Bryan Trottier, 2:46; Bryan Trottier, 3:31; Duane Sutter, 4:08. NY Islanders defeated Pittsburgh 9-2.
2 Minutes, 55 Seconds — Boston Bruins, at Boston, Dec. 19, 1974. Scorers: Bobby Schmautz, 19:13 (first period); Ken Hodge, 0:18; Phil Esposito, 0:43; Don Marcotte, 0:58; John Bucyk, 2:08 (second period). Boston defeated NY Rangers 11-3.

FASTEST FOUR GOALS, BOTH TEAMS:
53 Seconds — **Chicago Blackhawks, Toronto Maple Leafs,** at Toronto, Oct. 15, 1983, second period. Scorers were: Gaston Gingras, Toronto, 16:49; Denis Savard, Chicago, 17:12; Steve Larmer, Chicago, 17:27; and Savard at 17:42. Toronto won 10-8.
57 Seconds — Quebec Nordiques, Detroit Red Wings, at Quebec, Jan. 27, 1990, first period. Scorers were: Paul Gillis, Quebec, 18:01; Claude Loiselle, Quebec, 18:12; Joe Sakic, Quebec, 18:27; and Jimmy Carson, Detroit, 18:58. Detroit won 8-6.
1 Minute, 1 Second — Colorado Rockies, NY Rangers, at New York, Jan. 15, 1980, first period. Scorers were: Doug Sulliman, NY Rangers, 7:52; Ed Johnstone, NY Rangers, 7:57; Warren Miller, NY Rangers, 8:20; Rob Ramage, Colorado, 8:53. 6-6 tie.
— Chicago Blackhawks, Toronto Maple Leafs, at Toronto, Oct. 15, 1983, second period. Scorers were: Denis Savard, Chicago, 17:12; Steve Larmer, Chicago, 17:27; Savard, 17:42; John Anderson, Toronto, 18:13. Toronto won game 10-8.

FASTEST FOUR GOALS, ONE TEAM:
1 Minute, 20 Seconds — **Boston Bruins,** at Boston, Jan. 21, 1945, second period. Scorers were: Bill Thoms at 6:34; Frank Mario at 7:08 and 7:27; and Ken Smith at 7:54. Boston defeated NY Rangers 14-3.

FASTEST THREE GOALS, BOTH TEAMS:
15 Seconds — **Minnesota North Stars, NY Rangers,** at Minnesota, Feb. 10, 1983, second period. Scorers were: Mark Pavelich, NY Rangers, 19:18; Ron Greschner, NY Rangers, 19:27; Willi Plett, Minnesota, 19:33. Minnesota won 7-5.
18 Seconds — Montreal Canadiens, NY Rangers, at Montreal, Dec. 12, 1963, first period. Scorers were: Dave Balon, Montreal, 0:58; Gilles Tremblay, Montreal, 1:04; Camille Henry, NY Rangers, 1:16. Montreal won 6-4.
18 Seconds — California Golden Seals, Buffalo Sabres, at California, Feb. 1, 1976, third period. Scorers were: Jim Moxey, California, 19:38; Wayne Merrick, California, 19:45; Danny Gare, Buffalo, 19:56. Buffalo won 9-5.

FASTEST THREE GOALS, ONE TEAM:
20 Seconds — **Boston Bruins,** at Boston, Feb. 25, 1971, third period. John Bucyk scored at 4:50, Ed Westfall at 5:02 and Ted Green at 5:10. Boston defeated Vancouver 8-3.
21 Seconds — Chicago Blackhawks, at New York, Mar. 23, 1952, third period. Bill Mosienko scored all three goals, at 6:09, 6:20 and 6:30. Chicago defeated NY Rangers 7-6.

FASTEST THREE GOALS FROM START OF PERIOD, BOTH TEAMS:
1 Minute, 5 seconds — **Hartford Whalers, Montreal Canadiens,** at Montreal, March 11, 1989, second period. Scorers were: Kevin Dineen, Hartford, 0:11; Guy Carbonneau, Montreal, 0:36; Petr Svoboda, Montreal, 1:05. Montreal won 5-3.

FASTEST TWO GOALS, BOTH TEAMS:
2 Seconds — **St. Louis Blues, Boston Bruins,** at Boston, Dec. 19, 1987, third period. Scorers were: Ken Linseman, Boston, at 19:50; Doug Gilmour, St. Louis, at 19:52. St. Louis won 7-5.
3 Seconds — Chicago Blackhawks, Minnesota North Stars, at Minnesota, November 5, 1988, third period. Scorers were: Steve Thomas, Chicago, at 6:03; Dave Gagner, Minnesota, at 6:06. 5-5 tie.

FASTEST TWO GOALS, ONE TEAM:
4 Seconds — **Montreal Maroons,** at Montreal, Jan. 3, 1931, third period. Nels Stewart scored both goals, at 8:24 and 8:28. Mtl. Maroons defeated Boston 5-3.
— **Buffalo Sabres,** at Buffalo, Oct. 17, 1974, third period. Scorers were: Lee Fogolin at 14:55 and Don Luce at 14:59. Buffalo defeated California 6-1.
— **Toronto Maple Leafs,** at Quebec, December 29, 1988, third period. Scorers were: Ed Olczyk at 5:24 and Gary Leeman at 5:28. Toronto defeated Quebec 6-5.
— **Calgary Flames,** at Quebec, October 17, 1989, third period. Scorers were: Doug Gilmour at 19:45 and Paul Ranheim at 19:49. Calgary and Quebec tied 8-8.

FASTEST TWO GOALS FROM START OF PERIOD, BOTH TEAMS:
14 Seconds — **NY Rangers, Quebec Nordiques,** at Quebec, Nov. 5, 1983, third period. Scorers: Andre Savard, Quebec, 0:08; Pierre Larouche, NY Rangers, 0:14. 4-4 tie.
28 Seconds — Boston Bruins, Montreal Canadiens, at Montreal, Oct. 11, 1989, third period. Scorers: Jim Wiemer, Boston 0:10, Tom Chorske, Montreal 0:28. Montreal won 4-2.
35 Seconds — Boston Bruins, Pittsburgh Penguins, at Boston, Feb. 10, 1973, second period. Scorers: Lowell MacDonald, Pittsburgh, 0:07; Phil Esposito, Boston, 0:35. Boston won 6-3.

FASTEST TWO GOALS FROM START OF GAME, ONE TEAM:
24 Seconds — **Edmonton Oilers,** March 28, 1982, at Los Angeles. Mark Messier, at 0:14 and Dave Lumley, at 0:24, scored in first period. Edmonton defeated Los Angeles 6-2.
29 Seconds — Pittsburgh Penguins, Dec. 6, 1981, at Pittsburgh. George Ferguson, at 0:17, and Greg Malone, at 0:29, scored in first period. Pittsburgh defeated Chicago 6-4.
32 Seconds — Calgary Flames, Mar. 11, 1987, at Hartford. Doug Risebrough scored at 0:09 and Colin Patterson, at 0:32, in first period. Calgary defeated Hartford 6-1.

FASTEST TWO GOALS FROM START OF PERIOD, ONE TEAM:
21 Seconds — **Chicago Blackhawks,** Nov. 5, 1983, at Minnesota, second period. Ken Yaremchuk scored at 0:12 and Darryl Sutter at 0:21. Minnesota defeated Chicago 10-5.
30 Seconds — Washington Capitals, Jan. 27, 1980, at Washington, second period. Mike Gartner scored at 0:08 and Bengt Gustafsson at 0:30. Washington defeated NY Islanders 7-1.
31 Seconds — Buffalo Sabres, Jan. 10, 1974, at Buffalo, third period. Rene Robert scored at 0:21 and Rick Martin at 0:30. Buffalo defeated NY Rangers 7-2.
— NY Islanders, Feb. 22, 1986, at New York, third period. Roger Kortko scored at 0:10 and Bob Bourne at 0:31. NY Islanders defeated Detroit 5-2.

Ron Greschner registered the second of three goals to be scored in 15 seconds during a game between the New York Rangers and Minnesota on February 10, 1983.

Individual Records
Career

MOST SEASONS:
26 — Gordie Howe, Detroit, 1946-47 – 1970-71; Hartford, 1979-80.
24 — Alex Delvecchio, Detroit, 1950-51 – 1973-74.
— Tim Horton, Toronto, NY Rangers, Pittsburgh, Buffalo, 1949-50, 1951-52 – 1973-74.
23 — John Bucyk, Detroit, Boston, 1955-56 – 1977-78.
22 — Dean Prentice, NY Rangers, Boston, Detroit, Pittsburgh, Minnesota, 1952-53 – 1973-74.
— Doug Mohns, Boston, Chicago, Minnesota, Atlanta, Washington, 1953-54 – 1974-75.
— Stan Mikita, Chicago, 1958-59 – 1979-80.

MOST GAMES:
1,767 — Gordie Howe, Detroit, 1946-47 – 1970-71; Hartford, 1979-80.
1,549 — Alex Delvecchio, Detroit, 1950-51 – 1973-74.
1,540 — John Bucyk, Boston, 1955-56 – 1977-78.

MOST GOALS:
801 — Gordie Howe, Detroit, Hartford, in 26 seasons, 1,767GP.
731 — Marcel Dionne, Detroit, Los Angeles, NY Rangers, in 18 seasons, 1,348GP.
717 — Phil Esposito, Chicago, Boston, NY Rangers, in 18 seasons, 1,282GP.
677 — Wayne Gretzky, Edmonton, Los Angeles, in 11 seasons, 874GP.
610 — Bobby Hull, Chicago, Winnipeg, Hartford, in 16 seasons, 1,063GP.

HIGHEST GOALS-PER-GAME AVERAGE, CAREER
(AMONG PLAYERS WITH 200 OR MORE GOALS):
.808 — Mario Lemieux, Pittsburgh, 345G, 427GP, from 1984-85 – 1989-90.
.799 — Wayne Gretzky, Edmonton, Los Angeles, 677, 847GP from 1979-80 – 1989-90.
.767 — Cy Denneny, Ottawa, Boston, 250G, 326GP from 1917-18 – 1928-29.
.762 — Mike Bossy, NY Islanders, 573G, 752GP from 1977-78 – 1986-87.
.738 — Babe Dye, Toronto, Chicago, NY Americans, 200G, 271GP from 1919-20 – 1930-31.

MOST ASSISTS:
1,302 — Wayne Gretzky, Edmonton, Los Angeles, in 11 seasons, 847GP.
1,049 — Gordie Howe, Detroit, Hartford in 26 seasons, 1,767GP.
1,040 — Marcel Dionne, Detroit, Los Angeles, NY Rangers, in 18 seasons, 1,348GP.
926 — Stan Mikita, Chicago, in 22 seasons, 1,394GP.
873 — Phil Esposito, Chicago, Boston, NY Rangers in 18 seasons, 1,282GP.

HIGHEST ASSIST-PER-GAME AVERAGE, CAREER
(AMONG PLAYERS WITH 300 OR MORE ASSISTS):
1.537 — Wayne Gretzky, Edmonton, Los Angeles, 1,302A, 847GP from 1979-80 – 1989-90.
1.155 — Mario Lemieux, Pittsburgh, 493A, 427GP from 1984-85 – 1989-90.
.982 — Bobby Orr, Boston, Chicago, 645A, 657GP from 1966-67 – 1978-79.
.913 — Paul Coffey, Edmonton, Pittsburgh, 669A, 733GP from 1980-81 – 1989-90.
.900 — Peter Stastny, Quebec, New Jersey, 674A, 749GP from 1980-81 – 1989-90.
.899 — Denis Savard, Chicago, 662A, 736GP from 1980-81 – 1989-90.

MOST POINTS:
1,979 — Wayne Gretzky, Edmonton, Los Angeles, in 11 seasons, 847GP (677G-1302A).
1,850 — Gordie Howe, Detroit, Hartford, in 26 seasons, 1,767GP (801G-1049A).
1,771 — Marcel Dionne, Detroit, Los Angeles, NY Rangers, in 18 seasons, 1,348GP (731G-1,040A).
1,590 — Phil Esposito, Chicago, Boston, NY Rangers in 18 seasons, 1,282GP (717G-873A).
1,467 — Stan Mikita, Chicago in 22 seasons, 1,394GP (541G-926A).

MOST GOALS BY A CENTER, CAREER
731 — Marcel Dionne, Detroit, Los Angeles, NY Rangers, in 18 seasons
717 — Phil Esposito, Chicago, Boston, NY Rangers, in 18 seasons.
677 — Wayne Gretzky, Edmonton, Los Angeles, in 11 seasons.
541 — Stan Mikita, Chicago, in 22 seasons.
512 — Gilbert Perreault, Buffalo, in 17 seasons.
507 — Jean Beliveau, Montreal, in 20 seasons.

MOST ASSISTS BY A CENTER, CAREER;
1,302 — Wayne Gretzky, Edmonton, Los Angeles, in 11 seasons.
1,040 — Marcel Dionne, Detroit, Los Angeles, NY Rangers, in 18 seasons.
926 — Stan Mikita, Chicago, in 22 seasons.
873 — Phil Esposito, Chicago, Boston, NY Rangers, in 18 seasons.
853 — Bryan Trottier, NY Islanders, in 15 seasons.

MOST POINTS BY A CENTER, CAREER:
1,979 — Wayne Gretzky, Edmonton, Los Angeles, in 11 seasons.
1,771 — Marcel Dionne, Detroit, Los Angeles, NY Rangers, in 18 seasons.
1,590 — Phil Esposito, Chicago, Boston, NY Rangers, in 18 seasons.
1,467 — Stan Mikita, Chicago, in 22 seasons
1,353 — Bryan Trottier, NY Islanders, in 15 seasons.
1,326 — Gilbert Perreault, Buffalo, in 17 seasons.

MOST GOALS BY A LEFT WING, CAREER:
610 — Bobby Hull, Chicago, Winnipeg, Hartford, in 16 seasons.
556 — John Bucyk, Detroit, Boston, in 23 seasons.
533 — Frank Mahovlich, Toronto, Detroit, Montreal, in 18 seasons.
460 — Michel Goulet, Quebec, Chicago, in 11 seasons.
424 — Steve Shutt, Montreal, Los Angeles, in 13 seasons.
420 — Bill Barber, Philadelphia, in 12 seasons.

MOST ASSISTS BY A LEFT WING, CAREER:
813 — John Bucyk, Detroit, Boston, in 23 seasons.
570 — Frank Mahovlich, Toronto, Detroit, Montreal, in 18 seasons.
560 — Bobby Hull, Chicago, Winnipeg, Hartford, in 16 seasons.
516 — Wayne Cashman, Boston, in 17 seasons.
490 — Michel Goulet, Quebec, Chicago, in 11 seasons.
488 — Brian Propp, Philadelphia, Boston, in 11 seasons.
484 — John Tonelli, NY Islanders, Calgary, Los Angeles, in 12 seasons.

MOST POINTS BY A LEFT WING, CAREER:
1,369 — John Bucyk, Detroit, Boston, in 23 seasons.
1,170 — Bobby Hull, Chicago, Winnipeg, Hartford, in 16 seasons.
1,103 — Frank Mahovlich, Toronto, Detroit, Montreal, in 18 seasons.
950 — Michel Goulet, Quebec, Chicago, in 11 seasons.
883 — Bill Barber, Philadelphia, in 12 seasons.
860 — Dean Prentice, NY Rangers, Boston, Detroit, Pittsburgh, Minnesota, in 22 seasons.
— Brian Propp, Philadelphia, Boston, in 11 seasons.

MOST GOALS BY A RIGHT WING, CAREER:
801 — Gordie Howe, Detroit, Hartford, in 26 seasons.
573 — Mike Bossy, NY Islanders, in 10 seasons.
548 — Guy Lafleur, Montreal, NY Rangers, Quebec, in 16 seasons.
544 — Maurice Richard, Montreal, in 18 seasons.

MOST ASSISTS BY A RIGHT WING, CAREER:
1,049 — Gordie Howe, Detroit, Hartford, in 26 seasons.
777 — Guy Lafleur, Montreal, NY Rangers, Quebec, in 16 seasons.
024 — Andy Bathgate, NY Rangers, Toronto, Detroit, Pittsburgh in 17 seasons.
615 — Rod Gilbert, NY Rangers, in 18 seasons.

MOST POINTS BY A RIGHT WING, CAREER:
1,850 — Gordie Howe, Detroit, Hartford, in 26 seasons.
1,325 — Guy Lafleur, Montreal, NY Rangers, Quebec, in 16 seasons.
1,126 — Mike Bossy, NY Islanders, in 10 seasons.
1,043 — Jari Kurri, Edmonton In 10 seasons.
1,021 — Rod Gilbert, NY Rangers, in 18 seasons.

Wayne Gretzky surpassed Gordie Howe as the NHL's all-time assist leader when he recorded his 1,050th assist on March 1, 1988.

Jari Kurri has seven regular-season overtime goals and is tied with Mario Lemieux for the all-time NHL lead.

Frank Mahovlich ranks in the top three in career goals, assists and points by a leftwinger.

MOST GOALS BY A DEFENSEMAN, CAREER:
310 — **Denis Potvin,** NY Islanders, in 15 seasons.
283 — Paul Coffey, Edmonton, Pittsburgh in 10 seasons.
270 — Bobby Orr, Boston, Chicago, in 12 seasons.
248 — Doug Mohns, Boston, Chicago, Minnesota, Atlanta, Washington, in 22 seasons.
230 — Ray Bourque, Boston, in 11 seasons.

MOST ASSISTS BY A DEFENSEMAN, CAREER:
742 — **Denis Potvin,** NY Islanders, in 15 seasons.
718 — Larry Robinson, Montreal, Los Angeles, in 18 seasons.
683 — Brad Park, NY Rangers, Boston, Detroit, in 17 seasons.
669 — Paul Coffey, Edmonton, Pittsburgh, in 10 seasons.
645 — Bobby Orr, Boston, Chicago, in 12 seasons.

MOST POINTS BY A DEFENSEMAN, CAREER:
1,052 — **Denis Potvin,** NY Islanders, in 15 seasons.
952 — Paul Coffey, Edmonton, Pittsburgh, in 10 seasons.
922 — Larry Robinson, Montreal, Los Angeles, in 18 seasons.
915 — Bobby Orr, Boston, Chicago, in 12 seasons.
896 — Brad Park, NY Rangers, Boston, Detroit, in 17 seasons.

MOST OVERTIME GOALS, CAREER:
7 — **Mario Lemieux**, Pittsburgh.
— **Jari Kurri**, Edmonton.
6 — Paul MacLean, Winnipeg, Detroit, St. Louis.
5 — Greg Paslawski, St. Louis, Winnipeg.

MOST OVERTIME ASSISTS, CAREER:
9 — **Bernie Federko**, St. Louis.
8 — Wayne Gretzky, Edmonton, Los Angeles.
— Dale Hawerchuk, Winnipeg.
7 — Mario Lemieux, Pittsburgh.
— Paul MacLean, Winnipeg, Detroit, St. Louis.

MOST OVERTIME POINTS, CAREER:
14 — **Mario Lemieux**, Pittsburgh, 7G-7A
13 — Paul MacLean, Winnipeg, Detroit, St. Louis. 6G-7A
12 — Dale Hawerchuk, Winnipeg. 4G-8A
11 — Jari Kurri, Edmonton. 7G-4A
10 — Wayne Gretzky, Edmonton, Los Angeles. 2G-8A

HIGHEST POINTS-PER-GAME AVERAGE, CAREER:
(AMONG PLAYERS WITH 500 OR MORE POINTS):
2.336 — **Wayne Gretzky**, Edmonton, Los Angeles, 1,979PTS (637G-1,302A), 847GP from 1979-80 – 1989-90.
1.963 — Mario Lemieux, Pittsburgh, 838PTS (345G-493A), 427GP from 1984-85 – 1989-90.
1.497 — Mike Bossy, NY Islanders, 1,126PTS (573G-553A), 752GP from 1978-79 – 1986-87.
1.414 — Peter Stastny, Quebec, New Jersey, 1,059PTS (385G-674A), 749GP from 1980-81 – 1989-90.
1.393 — Bobby Orr, Boston, Chicago, 915PTS (270G-645A), 657GP from 1966-67 – 1978-79.

MOST PENALTY MINUTES:
3,966 — **Dave Williams,** Toronto, Vancouver, Detroit, Los Angeles, Hartford, in 14 seasons, 962GP.
2,572 — Willi Plett, Atlanta, Calgary, Minnesota, Boston, in 12 seasons, 834GP.
2,506 — Chris Nilan, Monteal, NY Rangers, in 11 seasons, 591GP.
2,294 — Dave Schultz, Philadelphia, Los Angeles, Pittsburgh, Buffalo, in 9 seasons, 535GP.
2,237 — Dale Hunter, Quebec, Washington, in 9 seasons, 762GP.

MOST GAMES, INCLUDING PLAYOFFS:
1,924 — **Gordie Howe,** Detroit, Hartford, 1,767 regular-season and 157 playoff games.
1,670 — Alex Delvecchio, Detroit, 1,549 regular-season and 121 playoff games.
1,664 — John Bucyk, Detroit, Boston, 1,540 regular-season and 124 playoff games.

MOST GOALS, INCLUDING PLAYOFFS:
869 — **Gordie Howe,** Detroit, Hartford, 801 regular-season goals and 68 playoff goals.
778 — Phil Esposito, Chicago, Boston, NY Rangers, 717 regular-season and 61 playoff goals.
766 — Wayne Gretzky, Edmonton, Los Angeles, 677 regular-season and 89 playoff goals.
752 — Marcel Dionne, Detroit, Los Angeles, NY Rangers, 731 regular-season and 21 playoff goals.

MOST ASSISTS, INCLUDING PLAYOFFS:
1,497 — **Wayne Gretzky,** Edmonton, Los Angeles, 1,302 regular-season and 195 playoff assists.
1,141 — Gordie Howe, Detroit, Hartford, 1,049 regular-season and 92 playoff assists.
1,064 — Marcel Dionne, Detroit, Los Angeles, NY Rangers, 1,040 regular-season and 24 playoff assists.
1,017 — Stan Mikita, Chicago, 926 regular-season and 91 playoff assists.
959 — Bryan Trottier, NY Islanders, 853 regular-season and 284 playoff assists.

MOST POINTS, INCLUDING PLAYOFFS:
2,263 — **Wayne Gretzky,** Edmonton, Los Angeles, 1,979 regular-season and 284 playoff points.
2,010 — Gordie Howe, Detroit, Hartford, 1,850 regular-season and 160 playoff assists.
1,816 — Marcel Dionne, Detroit, Los Angeles, NY Rangers, 1,771 regular-season and 45 playoff points.
1,727 — Phil Esposito, Chicago, Boston, NY Rangers, 1,590 regular-season and 137 playoff points.
1,617 — Stan Mikita, Chicago, 1,467 regular-season and 150 playoff points.

Phil Esposito had 717 regular season and 61 playoff goals during his 18-year NHL career.

Goaltender Glenn Hall played 502 consecutive complete games from 1955 to 1962.

MOST PENALTY MINUTES, INCLUDING PLAYOFFS:
4,421 — **Dave Williams,** Toronto, Vancouver, Los Angeles, 3,966 in regular season; 455 in playoffs.
3,038 — Willi Plett, Atlanta, Calgary, Minnesota, Boston, 2,572 in regular-season; 466 in playoffs.
2,980 — Chris Nilan, Montreal, NY Rangers, 2,506 in regular-season; 464 in playoffs.
2,744 — Dale Hunter, Quebec, Washington, 2,237 in regular-season; 507 in playoffs.
2,706 — Dave Schultz, Philadelphia, Los Angeles, Pittsburgh, Buffalo, 2,294 regular-season; 412 in playoffs.

MOST CONSECUTIVE GAMES:
962 — **Doug Jarvis,** Montreal, Washington, Hartford, from Oct. 8, 1975 – Apr. 5, 1987.
914 — Garry Unger, Toronto, Detroit, St. Louis, Atlanta from Feb. 24, 1968, – Dec. 21, 1979.
776 — Craig Ramsay, Buffalo, from March 27, 1973, – Feb. 10, 1983.
640 — Steve Larmer, Chicago, from Oct. 6, 1982 to April 1, 1990.
630 — Andy Hebenton, NY Rangers, Boston, nine complete 70-game seasons from 1955-56 – 1963-64.

MOST GAMES APPEARED IN BY A GOALTENDER, CAREER:
971 — **Terry Sawchuk,** Detroit, Boston, Toronto, Los Angeles, NY Rangers from 1949-50 – 1969-70.
906 — Glenn Hall, Detroit, Chicago, St. Louis from 1952-53 – 1970-71.
886 — Tony Esposito, Montreal, Chicago from 1968-69 – 1983-84.
860 — Lorne "Gump" Worsley, NY Rangers, Montreal, Minnesota from 1952-53 – 1973-74.

MOST CONSECUTIVE COMPLETE GAMES BY A GOALTENDER:
502 — **Glenn Hall,** Detroit, Chicago. Played 502 games from beginning of 1955-56 season - first 12 games of 1962-63. In his 503rd straight game, Nov. 7, 1962, at Chicago, Hall was removed from the game against Boston with a back injury in the first period.

MOST SHUTOUTS BY A GOALTENDER, CAREER:
103 — **Terry Sawchuk,** Detroit, Boston, Toronto, Los Angeles, NY Rangers in 20 seasons.
94 — George Hainsworth, Montreal Canadiens, Toronto in 10 seasons.
84 — Glenn Hall, Detroit, Chicago, St. Louis in 16 seasons.

MOST GAMES SCORING THREE-OR-MORE GOALS:
46 — **Wayne Gretzky,** Edmonton, Los Angeles, in 11 seasons, 33 three-goal games, 9 four-goal games, 4 five-goal games.
39 — Mike Bossy, NY Islanders, in 10 seasons, 30 three-goal games, 9 four-goal games.
32 — Phil Esposito, Chicago, Boston, NY Rangers, in 18 seasons, 27 three-goal games, 5 four-goal games.
28 — Bobby Hull, Chicago, Winnipeg, Hartford, in 16 seasons, 24 three-goal games, 4 four-goal games.
— Marcel Dionne, Detroit, Los Angeles, NY Rangers, in 18 seasons, 25 three-goal games, 3 four-goal games.
26 — Cy Denneny, Ottawa in 12 seasons. 20 three-goal games, 5 four-goal games, 1 six-goal game.
— Maurice Richard, Montreal, in 18 seasons, 23 three-goal games, 2 four-goal games, 1 five-goal game.

MOST 20-OR-MORE GOAL SEASONS:
22 — **Gordie Howe,** Detroit, Hartford in 26 seasons.
17 — Marcel Dionne, Detroit, Los Angeles, NY Rangers, in 18 seasons.
16 — Phil Esposito, Chicago, Boston, NY Rangers, in 18 seasons.
— Norm Ullman, Detroit, Toronto, in 19 seasons.
— John Bucyk, Detroit, Boston, in 22 seasons.
15 — Frank Mahovlich, Toronto, Detroit, Montreal in 17 seasons.
— Gilbert Perreault, Buffalo, in 17 seasons.

MOST CONSECUTIVE 20-OR-MORE GOAL SEASONS:
22 — **Gordie Howe,** Detroit, 1949-50 – 1970-71.
17 — Marcel Dionne, Detroit, Los Angeles, NY Rangers, 1971-72 – 1987-88.
16 — Phil Esposito, Chicago, Boston, NY Rangers, 1964-65 – 1979-80.
14 — Maurice Richard, Montreal, 1943-44 – 1956-57.
— Stan Mikita, Chicago, 1961-62 — 1974-75.
— Bobby Hull, Chicago, 1959-60 – 1971-72.
13 — Guy Lafleur, Montreal, 1971-72 – 1983-84.
— Bryan Trottier, NY Islanders, 1975-76 – 1987-88.

MOST 30-OR-MORE GOAL SEASONS:
14 — **Gordie Howe,** Detroit, Hartford in 26 seasons.
— **Marcel Dionne,** Detroit, Los Angeles, NY Rangers, in 18 seasons.
13 — Bobby Hull, Chicago, Winnipeg, Hartford in 16 seasons.
— Phil Esposito, Chicago, Boston, NY Rangers, in 18 seasons.

MOST CONSECUTIVE 30-OR-MORE GOAL SEASONS:
13 — **Bobby Hull,** Chicago, 1959-60 – 1971-72.
— **Phil Esposito,** Boston, NY Rangers, 1967-68 – 1979-80.
12 — Marcel Dionne, Detroit, Los Angeles, 1974-75 – 1985-86.
11 — Mike Gartner, Washington, Minnesota, NY Rangers, 1979-80 – 1989-90.
— Wayne Gretzky, Edmonton, Los Angeles, 1979-80 – 1989-90.
10 — Darryl Sittler, Toronto, Philadelphia, 1973-74 – 1982-83.
— Mike Bossy, NY Islanders, 1977-78 – 1986-87.

MOST 40-OR-MORE GOAL SEASONS:
11 — **Wayne Gretzky,** Edmonton, Los Angeles, in 11 seasons.
10 — Marcel Dionne, Detroit, Los Angeles, NY Rangers, in 18 seasons.
9 — Mike Bossy, NY Islanders, in 10 seasons.
8 — Bobby Hull, Chicago, Winnipeg, Hartford, in 16 seasons.
— Phil Esposito, Chicago, Boston, NY Rangers, in 18 seasons.
7 — Michel Goulet, Quebec, in 10 seasons.
— Jari Kurri, Edmonton, in 10 seasons.
— Dale Hawerchuk, Winnipeg, in 9 seasons.

MOST CONSECUTIVE 40-OR-MORE GOAL SEASONS:
11 — **Wayne Gretzky,** Edmonton, Los Angeles, 1979-80 – 1989-90.
9 — Mike Bossy, NY Islanders, 1977-78 – 1985-86.
7 — Phil Esposito, Boston, 1968-69 – 1974-75.
— Michel Goulet, Quebec, 1981-82 – 1987-88.
— Jari Kurri, Edmonton, 1982-83 – 1988-89.
6 — Guy Lafleur, Montreal, 1974-75 – 1979-80.
— Joe Mullen, St. Louis, Calgary, 1983-84 – 1988-89.
— Mario Lemieux, Pittsburgh, 1984-85 – 1989-90.

MOST 50-OR-MORE GOAL SEASONS:
9 — **Mike Bossy,** NY Islanders, in 11 seasons.
— **Wayne Gretzky,** Edmonton, Los Angeles, in 11 seasons.
6 — Guy Lafleur, Montreal, NY Rangers, Quebec, in 16 seasons.
— Marcel Dionne, Detroit, Los Angeles, NY Rangers, in 18 seasons.
5 — Bobby Hull, Chicago, Winnipeg, Hartford, in 16 seasons.
— Phil Esposito, Chicago, Boston, NY Rangers, in 18 seasons.

MOST CONSECUTIVE 50-OR-MORE GOAL SEASONS:
9 — **Mike Bossy,** NY Islanders, 1977-78 – 1985-86.
8 — Wayne Gretzky, Edmonton, 1979-80 – 1986-87.
6 — Guy Lafleur, Montreal, 1974-75 – 1979-80.
5 — Phil Esposito, Boston, 1970-71 – 1974-75.
— Marcel Dionne, Los Angeles, 1978-79 – 1982-83.

MOST 60-OR-MORE GOAL SEASONS:
5 — **Mike Bossy,** NY Islanders, in 10 seasons.
— **Wayne Gretzky,** Edmonton, Los Angeles, in 11 seasons.
4 — Phil Esposito, Chicago, Boston, NY Rangers, in 18 seasons.

MOST CONSECUTIVE 60-OR-MORE GOAL SEASONS:
4 — **Wayne Gretzky,** Edmonton, 1981-82 – 1984-85.
3 — Mike Bossy, NY Islanders, 1980-81 – 1982-83.
2 — Phil Esposito, Boston, 1970-71 – 1971-72, 1973-74 – 1974-75.
— Jari Kurri, Edmonton, 1984-85 – 1985-86.
— Mario Lemieux, Pittsburgh, 1987-88 – 1988-89.
— Steve Yzerman, Detroit, 1988-89 – 1989-90.

Single Season

MOST GOALS, ONE SEASON:
92 — **Wayne Gretzky,** Edmonton, 1981-82. 80 game schedule.
87 — Wayne Gretzky, Edmonton, 1983-84. 80 game schedule.
85 — Mario Lemieux, Pittsburgh, 1988-89. 80 game schedule.
76 — Phil Esposito, Boston, 1970-71. 78 game schedule.
73 — Wayne Gretzky, Edmonton, 1984-85. 80 game schedule.
72 — Brett Hull, St. Louis, 1989-90. 80 game schedule.
71 — Jari Kurri, Edmonton, 1984-85 80 game schedule.
— Wayne Gretzky, Edmonton, 1982-83. 80 game schedule.
70 — Mario Lemieux, Pittsburgh, 1987-1988. 80 game schedule.
— Bernie Nicholls, Los Angeles, 1988-89. 80 game schedule.
69 — Mike Bossy, NY Islanders, 1978-79. 80 game schedule.
68 — Phil Esposito, Boston, 1973-74. 78 game schedule.
— Mike Bossy, NY Islanders, 1980-81. 80 game schedule.
— Jari Kurri, Edmonton, 1985-86. 80 game schedule.

MOST ASSISTS, ONE SEASON:
163 — **Wayne Gretzky,** Edmonton , 1985-86. 80 game schedule.
135 — Wayne Gretzky, Edmonton, 1984-85. 80 game schedule.
125 — Wayne Gretzky, Edmonton, 1982-83. 80 game schedule.
121 — Wayne Gretzky, Edmonton, 1986-87. 80 game schedule.
120 — Wayne Gretzky, Edmonton, 1981-82. 80 game schedule.
118 — Wayne Gretzky, Edmonton, 1983-84. 80 game schedule.
114 — Wayne Gretzky, Los Angeles, 1988-89. 80 game schedule.
— Mario Lemieux, Pittsburgh, 1988-89. 80 game schedule.
109 — Wayne Gretzky, Edmonton, 1980-81. 80 game schedule.
— Wayne Gretzky, Edmonton, 1987-88. 80 game schedule.
102 — Bobby Orr, Boston, 1970-71. 78 game schedule.
— Wayne Gretzky, Los Angeles, 1989-90. 80 game schedule.

MOST POINTS, ONE SEASON:
215 — **Wayne Gretzky,** Edmonton, 1985-86. 80 game schedule.
212 — Wayne Gretzky, Edmonton, 1981-82. 80 game schedule.
208 — Wayne Gretzky, Edmonton, 1984-85. 80 game schedule.
205 — Wayne Gretzky, Edmonton, 1983-84. 80 game schedule.
199 — Mario Lemieux, Pittsburgh, 1988-89. 80 game schedule.
196 — Wayne Gretzky, Edmonton, 1982-83. 80 game schedule.
183 — Wayne Gretzky, Edmonton, 1986-87. 80 game schedule.
168 — Mario Lemieux, Pittsburgh, 1987-88. 80 game schedule.
— Wayne Gretzky, Los Angeles, 1988-89. 80 game schedule.
164 — Wayne Gretzky, Edmonton, 1980-81. 80 game schedule.
155 — Steve Yzerman, Detroit, 1988-89. 80 game schedule.
152 — Phil Esposito, Boston, 1970-71. 78 game schedule.
150 — Bernie Nicholls, Los Angeles, 1988-89. 80 game schedule.

MOST GAMES SCORING AT LEAST THREE GOALS, ONE SEASON:
10 — **Wayne Gretzky,** Edmonton, 1981-82. 6 three-goal games, 3 four-goal games, 1 five-goal game.
— **Wayne Gretzky,** Edmonton, 1983-84. 6 three-goal games, 4 four-goal games.
9 — Mike Bossy, NY Islanders, 1980-81. 6 three-goal games, 3 four-goal games.
— Mario Lemieux, Pittsburgh, 1988-89. 7 three-goal games, 1 four-goal game, 1 five-goal game.
7 — Joe Malone, Montreal, 1917-18. 2 three-goal games, 2 four-goal games, 3 five-goal games.
— Phil Esposito, Boston, 1970-71. 7 three-goal games.
— Rick Martin, Buffalo, 1975-76. 6 three-goal games, 1 four-goal game.

HIGHEST GOALS-PER-GAME AVERAGE, ONE SEASON
(AMONG PLAYERS WITH 20-OR-MORE GOALS):
2.20 — **Joe Malone,** Montreal, 1917-18, with 44G in 20GP.
1.64 — Cy Denneny, Ottawa, 1917-18, with 36G in 22GP.
— Newsy Lalonde, Montreal, 1917-18, with 23G in 14GP.
1.63 — Joe Malone, Quebec, 1919-20, with 39G in 24GP.
1.57 — Newsy Lalonde, Montreal, 1919-20, with 36G in 23GP.
1.50 — Joe Malone, Hamilton, 1920-21, with 30G in 20GP.

MOST 100-OR-MORE POINT SEASONS:
11 — **Wayne Gretzky,** Edmonton, Los Angeles, 1979-80 – 1989-90.
8 — Marcel Dionne, Detroit, 1974-75; Los Angeles, 1976-77; 1978-79 – 1982-83; 1984-85.
7 — Mike Bossy, NY Islanders, 1978-79; 1980-81 – 1985-86.
— Peter Stastny, Quebec, 1980-81 – 1985-86; 1987-88.
6 — Phil Esposito, Boston, 1968-69; 1970-71 – 1974-75.
— Bobby Orr, Boston, 1969-70 – 1974-75.
— Guy Lafleur, Montreal, 1974-75 – 1979-80.
— Bryan Trottier, NY Islanders, 1977-78 – 1981-82; 1983-84.
— Dale Hawerchuk, Winnipeg, 1981-82; 1983-84 – 1987-88.
— Jari Kurri, Edmonton, 1982-83 – 1986-87; 1988-89.
— Mario Lemieux, Pittsburgh, 1984-85 – 1989-90.

MOST CONSECUTIVE 100-OR-MORE POINT SEASONS:
11 — **Wayne Gretzky,** Edmonton, Los Angeles, 1979-80 – 1989-90.
6 — Bobby Orr, Boston, 1969-70 – 1974-75.
— Guy Lafleur, Montreal, 1974-75 – 1979-80.
— Mike Bossy, NY Islanders, 1980-81 – 1985-86.
— Peter Stastny, Quebec, 1980-81 – 1985-86.
— Mario Lemieux, Pittsburgh, 1984-85 – 1989-90.

HIGHEST GOALS-PER-GAME AVERAGE, ONE SEASON
(AMONG PLAYERS WITH 50-OR-MORE GOALS):
1.18 — **Wayne Gretzky,** Edmonton, 1983-84, with 87G in 74GP.
1.15 — Wayne Gretzky, Edmonton, 1981-82, with 92G in 80GP.
1.12 — Mario Lemieux, Pittsburgh, 1988-89, with 85G in 76GP.
1.00 — Maurice Richard, Montreal, 1944-45, with 50G in 50GP.
.97 — Phil Esposito, Boston, 1970-71, with 76G in 78GP.
— Jari Kurri, Edmonton, 1984-85, with 71G in 73GP.
.91 — Wayne Gretzky, Edmonton, 1984-85, with 73G in 80GP.
— Mario Lemieux, Pittsburgh, 1987-88, with 70G in 77GP.
.90 — Brett Hull, St. Louis, 1989-90, with 72G in 80GP.

Michel Goulet had seven consecutive 40-goal seasons for the Nordiques from 1981-82 to 1987-88.

HIGHEST ASSISTS-PER-GAME AVERAGE, ONE SEASON
(AMONG PLAYERS WITH 35-OR-MORE ASSISTS):
2.04 — **Wayne Gretzky,** Edmonton, 1985-86, with 163A in 80GP.
1.70 — Wayne Grezky, Edmonton, 1987-88, with 109A in 64GP.
1.69 — Wayne Gretzky, Edmonton, 1984-85, with 135A in 80GP.
1.59 — Wayne Gretzky, Edmonton, 1983-84, with 118A in 74GP.
1.56 — Wayne Gretzky, Edmonton, 1982-83, with 125A in 80GP.
1.53 — Wayne Gretzky, Edmonton, 1986-87, with 121A in 79GP.
1.50 — Wayne Gretzky, Edmonton, 1981-82, with 120A in 80GP.
1.50 — Mario Lemieux, Pittsburgh, 1988-89, with 114A in 76GP.
1.46 — Wayne Gretzky, Los Angeles, 1988-89, with 114A in 78GP.
1.40 — Wayne Gretzky, Los Angeles, 1989-90, with 102A in 73GP.
1.36 — Wayne Gretzky, Edmonton, 1980-81, with 109A in 80GP.
1.32 — Mario Lemieux, Pittsburgh, 1989-90, with 78A in 59GP.
1.31 — Bobby Orr, Boston, 1970-71, with 102A in 78GP.
1.27 — Mario Lemieux, Pittsburgh, 1987-88, with 98A in 77GP.
1.22 — Bobby Orr, Boston, 1973-74, with 90A in 74GP.
1.17 — Bobby Clarke, Philadelphia, 1975-76, with 89A in 76GP.

HIGHEST POINTS-PER-GAME AVERAGE, ONE SEASON
(AMONG PLAYERS WITH 50-OR-MORE POINTS):
2.77 — **Wayne Gretzky,** Edmonton, 1983-84, with 205PTS in 74GP.
2.69 — Wayne Gretzky, Edmonton, 1985-86, with 215PTS in 80GP.
2.65 — Wayne Gretzky, Edmonton, 1981-82, with 212PTS in 80GP.
2.62 — Mario Lemieux, Pittsburgh, 1988-89, with 199PTS in 78GP.
2.60 — Wayne Gretzky, Edmonton, 1984-85, with 208PTS in 80GP.
2.45 — Wayne Gretzky, Edmonton, 1982-83, with 196PTS in 80GP.
2.33 — Wayne Gretzky, Edmonton, 1987-88, with 149PTS in 64GP.
2.32 — Wayne Gretzky, Edmonton, 1986-87, with 183PTS in 79GP.
2.18 — Mario Lemieux, Pittsburgh, 1987-88 with 168PTS in 77GP.
2.15 — Wayne Gretzky, Los Angeles, 1988-89, with 168PTS in 78GP.
2.08 — Mario Lemieux, Pittsburgh, 1989-90, with 123 PTS in 59GP.
2.05 — Wayne Gretzky, Edmonton, 1980-81, with 164PTS in 80GP.
1.97 — Bill Cowley, Boston, 1943-44, with 71PTS in 36GP.
1.95 — Phil Esposito, Boston, 1970-71, with 152PTS in 78GP.
— Wayne Gretzky, Los Angeles, 1989-90, with 142PTS in 73GP.

MOST GOALS, ONE SEASON, INCLUDING PLAYOFFS:
100 — **Wayne Gretzky,** Edmonton, 1983-84, 87G in 74 regular-season games and 13G in 19 playoff games.
97 — Wayne Gretzky, Edmonton, 1981-82, 92G in 80 regular-season games and 5G in 5 playoff games.
— Mario Lemieux, Pittsburgh, 1988-89, 85G in 76 regular-season games and 12G in 11 playoff games.
90 — Wayne Gretzky, Edmonton, 1984-85, 73G in 80 regular season games and 17G in 18 playoff games.
— Jari Kurri, Edmonton, 1984-85, 71G in 80 regular season games and 19G in 18 playoff games.
85 — Mike Bossy, NY Islanders, 1980-81, 68G in 79 regular-season games and 17G in 18 playoff games.
— Brett Hull, St. Louis, 1989-90, 72G in 80 regular season games and 13G in 12 playoff games.
83 — Wayne Gretzky, Edmonton, 1982-83, 71G in 73 regular-season games and 12G in 16 playoff games.
81 — Mike Bossy, NY Islanders, 1981-82, 64G in 80 regular-season games and 17G in 19 playoff games.
80 — Reggie Leach, Philadelphia, 1975-76, 61G in 80 regular-season games and 19G in 16 playoff games.

MOST ASSISTS, ONE SEASON, INCLUDING PLAYOFFS:
174 — **Wayne Gretzky,** Edmonton, 1985-86, 163A in 80 regular-season games and 11A in 10 playoff games.
165 — Wayne Gretzky, Edmonton, 1984-85, 135A in 80 regular-season games and 30A in 18 playoff games.
151 — Wayne Gretzky, Edmonton, 1982-83, 125A in 80 regular-season games and 26A in 16 playoff games.
150 — Wayne Gretzky, Edmonton, 1986-87, 121A in 79 regular-season games and 29A in 21 playoff games.
140 — Wayne Gretzky, Edmonton, 1983-84, 118A in 74 regular-season games and 22A in 19 playoff games.
— Wayne Gretzky, Edmonton, 1987-88, 109A in 64 regular-season games and 31A in 19 playoff games.
131 — Wayne Gretzky, Los Angeles, 1988-89, 114A in 78 regular-season games and 17A in 11 playoff games.
127 — Wayne Gretzky, Edmonton, 1981-82, 120A in 80 regular-season games and 7A in 5 playoff games.
123 — Wayne Gretzky, Edmonton, 1980-81, 109A in 80 regular-season games and 14A in 9 playoff games.
121 — Mario Lemieux, Pittsburgh, 1988-89, 114A in 76 regular-season games and 7A in 11 playoff games.
109 — Bobby Orr, Boston, 1970-71, 102A in 78 regular-season games and 7A in 7 playoff games.
— Paul Coffey, Edmonton, 1984-85, 84A in 80 regular-season games and 25A in 18 playoff games.
— Wayne Gretzky, Los Angeles, 1989-90, 102A in 73 regular season games and 7A in 7 playoff games.

MOST POINTS, ONE SEASON, INCLUDING PLAYOFFS:
255 — **Wayne Gretzky,** Edmonton, 1984-85, 208PTS in 80 regular-season games and 47PTS in 18 playoff games.
240 — Wayne Gretzky, Edmonton, 1983-84, 205PTS in 74 regular-season games and 35PTS in 19 playoff games.
234 — Wayne Gretzky, Edmonton, 1982-83, 196PTS in 80 regular-season games and 38PTS in 16 playoff games.
— Wayne Gretzky, Edmonton, 1985-86, 215PTS in 80 regular-season games and 19PTS in 10 playoff games.
224 — Wayne Gretzky, Edmonton, 1981-82, 212PTS in 80 regular-season games and 12PTS in 5 playoff games.
218 — Mario Lemieux, Pittsburgh, 1988-89, 199PTS in 76 regular-season games and 19PTS in 11 playoff games.
217 — Wayne Gretzky, Edmonton, 1986-87, 183PTS in 79 regular-season games and 34PTS in 21 playoff games.
192 — Wayne Gretzky, Edmonton, 1987-88, 149PTS in 64 regular-season games and 43PTS in 19 playoff games.
190 — Wayne Gretzky, Los Angeles, 1988-89, 168PTS in 78 regular-season games and 22PTS in 11 playoff games.
185 — Wayne Gretzky, Edmonton, 1980-81, 164PTS in 80 regular-season games and 21PTS in 9 playoff games.

Shown here accepting the Calder Trophy as the NHL's top rookie in 1985-86, Mario Lemieux had a career-high 85 goals during the 1988-89 season.

MOST GOALS, ONE SEASON, BY A DEFENSEMAN:
48 — **Paul Coffey,** Edmonton, 1985-86. 80 game schedule.
46 — Bobby Orr, Boston, 1974-75. 80 game schedule.
40 — Paul Coffey, Edmonton, 1983-84. 80 game schedule.
39 — Doug Wilson, Chicago, 1981-82. 80 game schedule.
37 — Bobby Orr, Boston, 1970-71. 78 game schedule.
   — Bobby Orr, Boston, 1971-72. 78 game schedule.
   — Paul Coffey, Edmonton, 1984-85 80 game schedule..
33 — Bobby Orr, Boston, 1969-70. 76 game schedule.
32 — Bobby Orr, Boston, 1973-74. 78 game schedule.
31 — Denis Potvin, NY Islanders, 1975-76. 80 game schedule.
   — Denis Potvin, NY Islanders, 1978-79. 80 game schedule.
   — Raymond Bourque, Boston, 1983-84. 80 game schedule.
   — Phil Housley, Buffalo, 1983-84. 80 game schedule.
30 — Denis Potvin, NY Islanders, 1979-80. 80 game schedule.
   — Paul Coffey, Pittsburgh, 1988-89. 80 game schedule.

MOST GOALS, ONE SEASON, BY A CENTER:
92 — **Wayne Gretzky,** Edmonton, 1981-82. 80 game schedule.
87 — Wayne Gretzky, Edmonton, 1983-84. 80 game schedule.
85 — Mario Lemieux, Pittsburgh, 1988-89. 80 game schedule.
76 — Phil Esposito, Boston, 1970-71. 78 game schedule.
73 — Wayne Gretzky, Edmonton, 1984-85. 80 game schedule.
71 — Wayne Gretzky, Edmonton, 1982-83. 80 game schedule.
70 — Mario Lemieux, Pittsburgh, 1987-88. 80 game schedule.
   — Bernie Nicholls, Los Angeles, 1988-89. 80 game schedule.

MOST GOALS, ONE SEASON, BY A RIGHT WINGER:
72 — **Brett Hull,** St. Louis, 1989-90. 80 game schedule.
71 — Jari Kurri, Edmonton, 1984-85. 80 game schedule.
69 — Mike Bossy, NY Islanders, 1978-79. 80 game schedule.
68 — Jari Kurri, Edmonton, 1985-86. 80 game schedule..
   — Mike Bossy, NY Islanders, 1980-81. 80 game schedule.
66 — Lanny McDonald, Calgary, 1982-83. 80 game schedule.
64 — Mike Bossy, NY Islanders, 1981-82. 80 game schedule.
61 — Reggie Leach, Philadelphia, 1975-76. 80 game schedule.
   — Mike Bossy, NY Islanders, 1985-86. 80 game schedule.
60 — Guy Lafleur, Montreal, 1977-78. 80 game schedule.
   — Mike Bossy, NY Islanders, 1982-83. 80 game schedule.
58 — Mike Bossy, NY Islanders, 1984-85. 80 game schedule.
   — Tim Kerr, Philadelphia, 1985-86. 80 game schedule.
   — Tim Kerr, Philadelphia, 1986-87. 80 game schedule.

MOST GOALS, ONE SEASON, BY A LEFT WINGER:
60 — **Steve Shutt,** Montreal, 1976-77. 80 game schedule.
58 — Bobby Hull, Chicago, 1968-69. 76 game schedule.
57 — Michel Goulet, Quebec, 1982-83. 80 game schedule.
56 — Charlie Simmer, Los Angeles, 1979-80. 80 game schedule.
   — Charlie Simmer, Los Angeles, 1980-81. 80 game schedule.
   — Michel Goulet, Quebec, 1983-84. 80 game schedule.
55 — Michel Goulet, Quebec, 1984-85. 80 game schedule.
   — John Ogrodnick, Detroit, 1984-85. 80 game schedule.
54 — Bobby Hull, Chicago, 1965-66. 70 game schedule.
   — Al Secord, Chicago, 1982-83. 80 game schedule.

MOST GOALS, ONE SEASON, BY A ROOKIE:
53 — **Mike Bossy,** NY Islanders, 1977-78. 80 game schedule.
51 — Joe Nieuwendyk, Calgary, 1987-88. 80 game schedule.
45 — Dale Hawerchuk, Winnipeg, 1981-82. 80 game schedule.
   — Luc Robitaille, Los Angeles, 1986-87. 80 game schedule.
44 — Richard Martin, Buffalo, 1971-72. 80 game schedule.
   — Barry Pederson, Boston, 1981-82. 80 game schedule.
43 — Steve Larmer, Chicago, 1982-83. 80 game schedule.
   — Mario Lemieux, Pittsburgh, 1984-85. 80 game schedule.
40 — Darryl Sutter, Chicago, 1980-81. 80 game schedule.
   — Sylvain Turgeon, Hartford, 1983-84. 80 game schedule.
   — Warren Young, Pittsburgh, 1984-85. 80 game schedule.

MOST GOALS, ONE SEASON, BY A ROOKIE DEFENSEMAN:
23 — **Brian Leetch,** NY Rangers, 1988-89. 80 game schedule.
22 — Barry Beck, Colorado, 1977-78. 80 game schedule.
19 — Reed Larson, Detroit, 1977-78. 80 game schedule.
   — Phil Housley, Buffalo, 1982-83. 80 game schedule.

MOST ASSISTS, ONE SEASON, BY A DEFENSEMAN:
102 — **Bobby Orr,** Boston, 1970-71. 78 game schedule.
90 — Paul Coffey, Edmonton, 1985-86. 80 game schedule.
90 — Bobby Orr, Boston, 1973-74. 78 game schedule.
89 — Bobby Orr, Boston, 1974-75. 80 game schedule.

MOST ASSISTS, ONE SEASON, BY A CENTER:
163 — **Wayne Gretzky,** Edmonton, 1985-86. 80 game schedule.
135 — Wayne Gretzky, Edmonton, 1984-85. 80 game schedule.
125 — Wayne Gretzky, Edmonton, 1982-83. 80 game schedule.
121 — Wayne Gretzky, Edmonton, 1986-87. 80 game schedule.
120 — Wayne Gretzky, Edmonton, 1981-82. 80 game schedule.
118 — Wayne Gretzky, Edmonton, 1983-84. 80 game schedule.
114 — Wayne Gretzky, Edmonton, 1988-89. 80 game schedule.
   — Mario Lemieux, Pittsburgh, 1988-89. 80 game schedule.
109 — Wayne Gretzky, Edmonton, 1980-81. 80 game schedule.
   — Wayne Gretzky, Edmonton, 1987-88. 80 game schedule.

MOST ASSISTS, ONE SEASON, BY A RIGHT WINGER:
83 — **Mike Bossy,** NY Islanders, 1981-82. 80 game schedule.
80 — Guy Lafleur, Montreal, 1976-77. 80 game schedule.
77 — Guy Lafleur, Montreal, 1978-79. 80 game schedule.

MOST ASSISTS, ONE SEASON, BY A LEFT WINGER:
67 — **Mats Naslund,** Montreal, 1985-86. 80 game schedule.
65 — John Bucyk, Boston, 1970-71. 78 game schedule.
   — Michel Goulet, Quebec, 1983-84. 80 game schedule.
64 — Mark Messier, Edmonton, 1983-84. 80 game schedule.
62 — Bill Barber, Philadelphia, 1975-76. 80 game schedule.
61 — Vincent Damphousse, Toronto, 1989-90. 80 game schedule.
60 — Anton Stastny, Quebec, 1982-83. 80 game schedule.

MOST ASSISTS, ONE SEASON, BY A ROOKIE:
70 — **Peter Stastny,** Quebec, 1980-81. 80 game schedule.
63 — Bryan Trottier, NY Islanders, 1975-76. 80 game schedule.
62 — Sergei Makarov, Calgary, 1989-90. 80 game schedule.
60 — Larry Murphy, Los Angeles, 1980-81. 80 game schedule.

MOST ASSISTS, ONE SEASON, BY A ROOKIE DEFENSEMAN:
60 — **Larry Murphy,** Los Angeles, 1980-81. 80 game schedule.
55 — Chris Chelios, Montreal, 1984-85. 80 game schedule.
50 — Stefan Persson, NY Islanders, 1977-78. 80 game schedule.
   — Gary Suter, Calgary, 1985-86, 80 game schedule..
48 — Raymond Bourque, Boston, 1979-80. 80 game schedule.
   — Brian Leetch, NY Rangers, 1988-89. 80 game schedule.

Dale Hawerchuk had 45 goals in his rookie year.

MOST POINTS, ONE SEASON, BY A DEFENSEMAN:
139 — **Bobby Orr,** Boston, 1970-71. 78 game schedule.
138 — Paul Coffey, Edmonton,1985-86. 80 game schedule.
135 — Bobby Orr, Boston, 1974-75. 80 game schedule.
126 — Paul Coffey, Edmonton, 1983-84. 80 game schedule.
122 — Bobby Orr, Boston, 1973-74. 78 game schedule.

MOST POINTS, ONE SEASON, BY A CENTER:
215 — **Wayne Gretzky,** Edmonton, 1985-86. 80 game schedule.
212 — Wayne Gretzky, Edmonton, 1981-82. 80 game schedule.
208 — Wayne Gretzky, Edmonton, 1984-85. 80 game schedule.
205 — Wayne Gretzky, Edmonton, 1983-84. 80 game schedule.
199 — Mario Lemieux, Pittsburgh, 1988-89. 80 game schedule.
196 — Wayne Gretzky, Edmonton, 1982-83. 80 game schedule.
183 — Wayne Gretzky, Edmonton, 1986-87. 80 game schedule.
168 — Mario Lemieux, Pittsburgh, 1987-88. 80 game schedule.
— Wayne Gretzky, Los Angeles, 1988-89. 80 game schedule.
164 — Wayne Gretzky, Edmonton, 1980-81. 80 game schedule.
155 — Steve Yzerman, Detroit, 1988-89. 80 game schedule.

MOST POINTS, ONE SEASON, BY A RIGHT WINGER:
147 — **Mike Bossy,** NY Islanders, 1981-82. 80 game schedule.
136 — Guy Lafleur, Montreal, 1976-77. 80 game schedule.
135 — Jari Kurri, Edmonton, 1984-85. 80 game schedule.
132 — Guy Lafleur, Montreal, 1977-78. 80 game schedule.

MOST POINTS, ONE SEASON, BY A LEFT WINGER:
121 — **Michel Goulet,** Quebec, 1983-84. 80 game schedule.
116 — John Bucyk, Boston, 1970-71. 78 game schedule.
112 — Bill Barber, Philadelphia, 1975-76. 80 game schedule.
111 — Luc Robitaille, Los Angeles, 1987-88. 80 game schedule.
110 — Mats Naslund, Montreal, 1985-86. 80 game schedule.
107 — Bobby Hull, Chicago, 1968-69. 76 game schedule.

MOST POINTS, ONE SEASON, BY A ROOKIE:
109 — **Peter Stastny,** Quebec, 1980-81. 80 game schedule.
103 — Dale Hawerchuk, Winnipeg, 1981-82. 80 game schedule.
100 — Mario Lemieux, Pittsburgh, 1984-85. 80 game schedule.
98 — Neal Broten, Minnesota, 1981-82. 80 game schedule.

MOST POINTS, ONE SEASON, BY A ROOKIE DEFENSEMAN:
76 — **Larry Murphy,** Los Angeles, 1980-81. 80 game schedule.
71 — Brian Leetch, NY Rangers, 1988-89. 80 game schedule.
68 — Gary Suter, Calgary, 1985-86. 80 game schedule.
66 — Phil Housley, Buffalo, 1982-83. 80 game schedule.
65 — Raymond Bourque, Boston, 1979-80. 80 game schedule.
64 — Chris Chelios, Montreal, 1984-85. 80 game schedule.

MOST POINTS, ONE SEASON, BY A GOALTENDER:
14 — **Grant Fuhr,** Edmonton, 1983-84. (14A)
8 — Mike Palmateer, Washington, 1980-81. (8A)
— Grant Fuhr, Edmonton, 1987-88. (8A)
— Ron Hextall, Philadelphia, 1988-89. (8A)
7 — Ron Hextall, Philadelphia, 1987-88. (1G-6A)
— Mike Vernon, Calgary, 1987-88. (7A)
6 — Gilles Meloche, California, 1974-75. (6A)
— Grant Fuhr, Edmonton, 1981-82. (6A)
— Tom Barraso, Buffalo, 1985-86. (6A)
— Ron Hextall, Philadelphia, 1986-87. (6A)
— Roland Melanson, Los Angeles, 1986-87. (6A)
— Patrick Roy, Montreal, 1988-89. (6A)

MOST POWER-PLAY GOALS, ONE SEASON:
34 — **Tim Kerr,** Philadelphia, 1985-86. 80 game schedule.
31 — Joe Nieuwendyk, Calgary, 1987-88. 80 game schedule.
— Mario Lemieux, Pittsburgh, 1988-89. 80 game schedule.
29 — Michel Goulet, Quebec, 1987-88. 80 game schedule.
28 — Phil Esposito, Boston, 1971-72. 78 game schedule.
— Mike Bossy, NY Islanders, 1980-81. 80 game schedule.
— Michel Goulet, Quebec, 1985-86. 80 game schedule.

MOST SHORTHAND GOALS, ONE SEASON:
13 — **Mario Lemieux,** Pittsburgh, 1988-89. 80 game schedule.
12 — Wayne Gretzky, Edmonton, 1983-84. 80 game schedule.
11 — Wayne Gretzky, Edmonton, 1984-85. 80 game schedule.
10 — Marcel Dionne, Detroit, 1974-75. 80 game schedule.
— Mario Lemieux, Pittsburgh, 1987-88. 80 game schedule.
— Dirk Graham, Chicago, 1988-89. 80 game schedule.

MOST SHOTS ON GOAL, ONE SEASON:
550 — **Phil Esposito,** Boston, 1970-71. 78 game schedule.
426 — Phil Esposito, Boston, 1971-72. 78 game schedule.
414 — Bobby Hull, Chicago, 1968-69. 76 game schedule.

MOST PENALTY MINUTES, ONE SEASON:
472 — **Dave Schultz,** Philadelphia, 1974-75.
409 — Paul Baxter, Pittsburgh, 1981-82.
405 — Dave Schultz, Los Angeles, Pittsburgh, 1977-78.

MOST SHUTOUTS, ONE SEASON:
22 — **George Hainsworth,** Montreal, 1928-29. 44GP
15 — Alex Connell, Ottawa, 1925-26. 36GP
— Alex Connell, Ottawa, 1927-28. 44GP
— Hal Winkler, Boston, 1927-28. 44GP
— Tony Esposito, Chicago, 1969-70. 63GP
14 — George Hainsworth, Montreal, 1926-27. 44GP

LONGEST UNDEFEATED STREAK BY A GOALTENDER:
32 Games — **Gerry Cheevers,** Boston, 1971-72. 24w-8T.
31 Games — Pete Peeters, Boston, 1982-83. 26w-5T.
27 Games — Pete Peeters, Philadelphia, 1979-80. 22w-5T.
23 Games — Frank Brimsek, Boston, 1940-41. 15w-8T.
— Glenn Resch, NY Islanders, 1978-79. 15w-8T.
— Grant Fuhr, Edmonton, 1981-82. 15w-8T.

MOST GAMES, ONE SEASON, BY A GOALTENDER:
75 — **Grant Fuhr,** Edmonton, 1987-88.
73 — Bernie Parent, Philadelphia, 1973-74.
72 — Gary Smith, Vancouver, 1974-75.
— Don Edwards, Buffalo, 1977-78.
71 — Gary Smith, California, 1970-71.
— Tony Esposito, Chicago, 1974-75.

MOST WINS, ONE SEASON, BY A GOALTENDER:
47 — **Bernie Parent,** Philadelphia, 1973-74.
44 — Bernie Parent, Philadelphia, 1974-75.
— Terry Sawchuk, Detroit, 1950-51.
— Terry Sawchuk, Detroit, 1951-52.

LONGEST WINNING STREAK, ONE SEASON, BY A GOALTENDER:
17 — **Gilles Gilbert,** Boston, 1975-76.
14 — Don Beaupre, Minnesota, 1985-86.
— Ross Brooks, Boston, 1973-74.
— Tiny Thompson, Boston, 1929-30.

Stefan Persson had 50 assists as a
rookie defenseman in 1977-78.

MOST GOALS, 50 GAMES FROM START OF SEASON:
61 — **Wayne Gretzky**, Edmonton, 1981-82. Oct. 7, 1981 - Jan. 22, 1982. (80-game schedule)
— **Wayne Gretzky**, Edmonton, 1983-84. Oct. 5, 1983 - Jan. 25, 1984. (80-game schedule)
54 — Mario Lemieux, Pittsburgh, 1988-89. Oct. 7, 1988 - Jan. 31, 1989. (80-game schedule)
53 — Wayne Gretzky, Edmonton, 1984-85. Oct. 11, 1984 - Jan. 28, 1985. (80-game schedule)
50 — Maurice Richard, Montreal, 1944-45. Oct. 28, 1944 - March 18, 1945. (50-game schedule)
— Mike Bossy, NY Islanders, 1980-81. Oct. 11, 1980 - Jan. 24, 1981. (80-game schedule)

LONGEST CONSECUTIVE POINT-SCORING STREAK FROM START OF SEASON:
51 Games — **Wayne Gretzky**, Edmonton, 1983-84. 61G-92A-153PTS during streak which was stopped by goaltender Markus Mattsson and the Los Angeles on Jan. 28, 1984.

LONGEST CONSECUTIVE POINT SCORING STREAK:
51 Games — **Wayne Gretzky**, Edmonton, 1983-84. 61G-92A-153PTS during streak.
46 Games — Mario Lemieux, Pittsburgh, 1989-90. 39G-64A-103PTS during streak.
39 Games — Wayne Gretzky, Edmonton, 1985-86. 33G-75A-108PTS during streak.
30 Games — Wayne Gretzky, Edmonton, 1982-83. 24G52A76PTS during streak.
28 Games — Guy Lafleur, Montreal, 1976-77. 19G-42A-61PTS during streak.
— Wayne Gretzky, Edmonton, 1984-85. 20G-43A-63PTS during streak.
— Mario Lemieux, Pittsburgh, 1985-86. 21G-38A-59PTS during streak.
— Paul Coffey, Edmonton, 1985-86. 16G-39A-55PTS during a streak.
— Steve Yzerman, Detroit, 1988-89. 29G-36A-65PTS during streak.

LONGEST CONSECUTIVE POINT-SCORING STREAK BY A DEFENSEMAN:
28 Games — **Paul Coffey**, Edmonton, 1985-86. 16G-39A-55PTS during streak.
19 Games — Ray Bourque, Boston, 1987-88. 6G-21A-27PTS during streak.
17 Games — Ray Bourque, Boston, 1984-85. 4G-24A-28PTS during streak.
16 Games — Gary Suter, Calgary, 1987-88. 8G-17A-25PTS during streak.
15 Games — Bobby Orr, Boston, 1973-74. 8G-15A-23PTS during streak.
15 Games — Bobby Orr, Boston, 1970-71. 10G-23A-33PTS during streak.

LONGEST CONSECUTIVE GOAL-SCORING STREAK:
16 Games — **Harry (Punch) Broadbent**, Ottawa, 1921-22. 25 goals during streak.
14 Games — Joe Malone, Montreal, 1917-18. 35 goals during streak.
13 Games — Newsy Lalonde, Montreal, 1920-21. 24 goals during streak.
— Charlie Simmer, Los Angeles, 1979-80. 17 goals during streak.
12 Games — Cy Denneny, Ottawa, 1917-18. 23 goals during streak.
— Dave Lumley, Edmonton, 1981-82. 15 goals during streak.
11 Games — Babe Dye, Toronto, Hamilton, 1920-21. 22 goals during streak.
— Babe Dye, Toronto, 1921-22. 15 goals during streak.
— Marcel Dionne, Los Angeles, 1982-83. 14 goals during streak.
— Pat LaFontaine, NY Islanders, 1989-90. 18 goals during streak.

LONGEST CONSECUTIVE ASSIST-SCORING STREAK:
17 Games — **Wayne Gretzky**, Edmonton, 1983-84. 38A during streak.
— **Paul Coffey**, Edmonton, 1985-86. 27A during streak.
— **Wayne Gretzky**, Los Angeles, 1989-90. 35A during streak.
15 Games — Jari Kurri, Edmonton, 1983-84. 21A during streak.
14 Games — Stan Mikita, Chicago, 1967-68. 18A during streak.
— Bobby Orr, Boston, 1970-71. 23A during streak.
— Jude Drouin, Minnesota, 1971-72. 21A during streak.
— Wayne Gretzky, Edmonton, 1981-82. 26A during streak.
— Wayne Gretzky, Edmonton, 1985-86. 39A during streak.
— Mario Lemieux, Pittsburgh, 1985-86. 23A during streak.
12 Games — Norm Ullman, Toronto, 1970-71. 15A during streak.
— Pete Mahovlich, Montreal, 1974-75. 18A during streak.
— Bobby Clarke, Philadelphia, 1975-76. 20A during streak.
— Bobby Clarke, Philadelphia, 1977-78. 16A during streak.
— Guy Lafleur, Montreal, 1979-80. 15A during streak.
— Wayne Gretzky, Edmonton, 1982-83. 20A during streak.
— Barry Pederson, Boston, 1982-83. 15A during streak.
— Wayne Gretzky, Edmonton, 1985-86. 24A during streak.
— Ken Linseman, Boston, 1985-86. 19A during streak.

LONGEST SHUTOUT SEQUENCE BY A GOALTENDER:
461 Minutes, 29 Seconds — **Alex Connell**, Ottawa, 1927-28, six consecutive shutouts. (Forward passing not permitted in attacking zones in 1927-1928.)
343 Minutes, 5 Seconds — George Hainsworth, Montreal, 1928-29, four consecutive shutouts.
324 Minutes, 40 Seconds — Roy Worters, NY Americans, 1930-31, four consecutive shutouts.
309 Minutes, 21 Seconds — Bill Durnan, Montreal, 1948-49, four consecutive shutouts.

Single Game

MOST GOALS, ONE GAME:
7 — **Joe Malone**, Quebec Bulldogs, Jan. 31, 1920, at Quebec. Quebec 10, Toronto 6.
6 — Newsy Lalonde, Montreal, Jan. 10, 1920, at Montreal. Montreal 14, Toronto 7.
— Joe Malone, Quebec Bulldogs, March 10, 1920, at Quebec. Quebec 10, Ottawa 4.
— Corb Denneny, Toronto, Jan. 26, 1921, at Toronto. Toronto 10, Hamilton 3.
— Cy Denneny, Ottawa, March 7, 1921, at Ottawa. Ottawa 12, Hamilton 5.
— Syd Howe, Detroit, Feb. 3, 1944, at Detroit. Detroit 12, NY Rangers 2.
— Red Berenson, St. Louis, Nov. 7, 1968, at Philadelphia. St. Louis 8, Philadelphia 0.
— Darryl Sittler, Toronto, Feb. 7, 1976, at Toronto. Toronto 11, Boston 4.

Don Grosso of the Red Wings had one goal and six assists against the New York Rangers on November 5, 1944.

MOST GOALS, ONE ROAD GAME:
6 — **Red Berenson**, St. Louis, Nov. 7, 1968, at Philadelphia. St. Louis 8, Philadelphia 0.
5 — Joe Malone, Montreal, Dec. 19, 1917, at Ottawa. Montreal 9, Ottawa 4.
— Redvers Green, Hamilton, Dec. 5, 1924, at Toronto. Hamilton 10, Toronto 3.
— Babe Dye, Toronto, Dec. 22, 1924, at Boston. Toronto 10, Boston 2.
— Harry Broadbent, Mtl. Maroons, Jan. 7, 1925, at Hamilton. Mtl. Maroons 6, Hamilton 2.
— Don Murdoch, NY Rangers, Oct. 12, 1976, at Minnesota. NY Rangers 10, Minnesota 4.
— Tim Young, Minnesota, Jan. 15, 1979, at NY Rangers. Minnesota 8, NY Rangers 1.
— Willy Lindstrom, Winnipeg, March 2, 1982, at Philadelphia. Winnipeg 7, Philadelphia 6.
— Bengt Gustafsson, Washington, Jan. 8, 1984, at Philadelphia. Washington 7, Philadelphia 1.
— Wayne Gretzky, Edmonton, Dec. 15, 1984, at St. Louis. Edmonton 8, St. Louis 2.
— Dave Andreychuk, Buffalo, Feb. 6, 1986, at Boston. Buffalo 8, Boston 6.

MOST ASSISTS, ONE GAME:

- 7 — **Billy Taylor,** Detroit, March 16, 1947, at Chicago. Detroit 10, Chicago 6.
- — **Wayne Gretzky,** Edmonton, Feb. 15, 1980, at Edmonton. Edmonton 8, Washington 2.
- — **Wayne Gretzky,** Edmonton, Dec. 11, 1985, at Chicago. Edmonton 12, Chicago 9.
- — **Wayne Gretzky,** Edmonton, Feb. 14, 1986, at Edmonton. Edmonton 8, Quebec 2.
- 6 — Elmer Lach, Montreal, Feb. 6, 1943, at Montreal. Montreal 8, Boston 3.
- — Walter (Babe) Pratt, Toronto, Jan. 8, 1944, at Toronto. Toronto 12, Boston 3.
- — Don Grosso, Detroit, Feb. 3, 1944, at Detroit. Detroit 12, NY Rangers 2.
- — Pat Stapleton, Chicago, March 30, 1969, at Chicago. Chicago 9, Detroit 5.
- — Ken Hodge, Boston, Feb. 9, 1971, at Boston. Boston 6, NY Rangers 3.
- — Bobby Orr, Boston, Jan. 1, 1973, at Vancouver. Boston 8, Vancouver 2.
- — Ron Stackhouse, Pittsburgh, March 8, 1975, at Pittsburgh. Pittsburgh 8, Philadelphia 2.
- — Greg Malone, Pittsburgh, Nov. 28, 1979, at Pittsburgh. Pittsburgh 7, Quebec 2.
- — Mike Bossy, NY Islanders, Jan. 6, 1981, at New York. NY Islanders 6, Toronto 3.
- — Guy Chouinard, Calgary, Feb. 25, 1981, at Calgary. Calgary 11, NY Islanders 4.
- — Mark Messier, Edmonton, Jan. 4, 1984, at Edmonton. Edmonton 12, Minnesota 8.
- — Patrik Sundstrom, Vancouver, Feb 29, 1984, at Pittsburgh. Vancouver 9, Pittsburgh 5.
- — Wayne Gretzky, Edmonton, Dec. 20, 1985, at Edmonton. Edmonton 9, Los Angeles 4.
- — Paul Coffey, Edmonton, March 14, 1986 at Edmonton. Edmonton 12, Detroit 3.
- — Gary Suter, Calgary, Apr. 4, 1986 at Calgary. Calgary 9, Edmonton 3.
- — Ron Francis, Hartford, March 5, 1987 at Hartford. Hartford 10, Boston 2.
- — Mario Lemieux, Pittsburgh, Oct. 15, 1988, at Pittsburgh. Pittsburgh 9, St. Louis 2.
- — Bernie Nicholls, Los Angeles, Dec. 1, 1988, at Los Angeles. Los Angeles 9, Toronto 3.
- — Mario Lemieux, Pittsburgh, Dec. 31, 1988 at Pittsburgh. Pittsburgh 8, New Jersey 6.

MOST ASSISTS, ONE ROAD GAME:

- 7 — **Billy Taylor,** Detroit, March 16, 1947, at Chicago. Detroit 10, Chicago 6.
- — **Wayne Gretzky,** Edmonton, Dec. 11, 1985, at Chicago. Edmonton 12, Chicago 9.
- 6 — Bobby Orr, Boston, Jan. 1, 1973, at Vancouver. Boston 8, Vancouver 2.
- — Patrik Sundstrom, Vancouver, Feb. 29, 1984, at Pittsburgh. Vancouver 9, Pittsburgh 5.

MOST POINTS, ONE GAME:

- 10 — **Darryl Sittler,** Toronto, Feb. 7, 1976, at Toronto, 6G-4A. Toronto 11, Boston 4.
- 8 — Maurice Richard, Montreal, Dec. 28, 1944, at Montreal, 5G-3A. Montreal 9, Detroit 1.
- — Bert Olmstead, Montreal, Jan. 9, 1954, at Montreal, 4G-4A. Montreal 12, Chicago 1.
- — Tom Bladon, Philadelphia, Dec. 11, 1977, at Philadelphia, 4G-4A. Philadelphia 11, Cleveland 1.
- — Bryan Trottier, NY Islanders, Dec. 23, 1978, at New York, 5G-3A. NY Islanders 9, NY Rangers 4.
- — Peter Stastny, Quebec, Feb. 22, 1981, at Washington, 4G-4A. Quebec 11, Washington 7.
- — Anton Stastny, Quebec, Feb. 22, 1981, at Washington, 3G-5A. Quebec 11, Washington 7.
- — Wayne Gretzky, Edmonton, Nov. 19, 1983, at Edmonton, 3G-5A. Edmonton 13, New Jersey 4.
- — Wayne Gretzky, Edmonton, Jan. 4, 1984, at Edmonton, 4G 4A. Edmonton 12 Minnesota 8.
- — Paul Coffey, Edmonton, March 14, 1986, at Edmonton, 2G-6A. Edmonton 12, Detroit 3.
- — Mario Lemieux, Pittsburgh, Oct. 15, 1988, at Pittsburgh, 2G-6A. Pittsburgh 9, St. Louis 2.
- — Mario Lemieux, Pittsburgh, Dec. 31, 1988, at Pittsburgh, 5G-3A. Pittsburgh 8, New Jersey 6.
- — Bernie Nicholls, Los Angeles, Dec. 1, 1988, at Los Angeles, 2G-6A. Los Angeles 9, Toronto 3.
- 7 Seven points have been scored by one player in one game on 33 occasions. Most recently, Sergei Makarov of Calgary (Feb 28, 1990 vs. Edmonton) and Stephane Richer of Montreal (Feb 14, 1990 vs. Vancouver) had 7-point games.
   Joe Malone had the first 7-point game in the NHL on Jan. 31, 1920 when his Quebec Bulldogs defeated Toronto St. Patrick's 10-6 in Quebec. All of Malone's 7 points were goals.
   Wayne Gretzky recorded seven 7-point games in the 1980s.

MOST POINTS, ONE ROAD GAME:

- 8 — **Peter Stastny,** Quebec, Feb. 22, 1981, at Washington, 4G-4A. Quebec 11, Washington 7.
- — **Anton Stastny,** Quebec, Feb. 22, 1981, at Washington, 3G-5A. Quebec 11, Washington 7.
- 7 — Billy Taylor, Detroit, March 16, 1947, at Chicago, 7A. Detroit 10, Chicago. 6.
- — Red Berenson, St. Louis, Nov. 7, 1968, at Philadelphia, 6G-1A. St. Louis 8, Philadelphia 0.
- — Gilbert Perreault, Buffalo, Feb. 1, 1976, at California, 2G-5A. Buffalo 9, California 5.
- — Peter Stastny, Quebec, April 1, 1982, at Boston, 3G-4A. Quebec 8, Boston 5.
- — Wayne Gretzky, Edmonton, Nov. 6, 1983, at Winnipeg, 4G-3A. Edmonton 8, Winnipeg 5.
- — Patrik Sundstrom, Vancouver, Feb. 29, 1984, at Pittsburgh, 1G-6A. Vancouver 9, Pittsburgh 5.
- — Wayne Gretzky, Edmonton, Dec. 11, 1985, at Chicago, 7A. Edmonton 12, Chicago 9.
- — Mario Lemieux, Pittsburgh, Jan. 21, 1989, at Edmonton, 2G, 5A. Pittsburgh 7, Edmonton 4.
- — Cam Neely, Boston, Oct. 16, 1988, at Chicago, 3G, 4A. Boston 10, Chicago 3.
- — Dino Ciccarelli, Washington, March 18, 1989, at Hartford, 4G, 3A. Washington 8, Hartford 2.

MOST GOALS, ONE GAME, BY A DEFENSEMAN:

- 5 — **Ian Turnbull,** Toronto, Feb. 2, 1977, at Toronto. Toronto 9, Detroit 1.
- 4 — Harry Cameron, Toronto, Dec. 26, 1917, at Toronto. Toronto 7, Montreal 5.
- — Harry Cameron, Montreal, March 3, 1920, at Quebec City. Montreal 16, Que. Bulldogs 3.
- — Sprague Cleghorn, Montreal, Jan. 14, 1922, at Montreal. Montreal 10, Hamilton 5.
- — Johnny McKinnon, Pit. Pirates, Nov. 19, 1929, at Pittsburgh. Pit. Pirates 10, Toronto 5.
- — Hap Day, Toronto, Nov. 19, 1929, at Pittsburgh. Pit. Pirates 10, Toronto 5.
- — Tom Bladon, Philadelphia, Dec. 11, 1977, at Philadelphia. Philadelphia 11, Cleveland 1.
- — Ian Turnbull, Los Angeles, Dec. 12, 1981, at Los Angeles. Los Angeles 7, Vancouver 5.
- — Paul Coffey, Edmonton, Oct. 26, 1984, at Calgary. Edmonton 6, Calgary 5.

MOST GOALS BY ONE PLAYER IN HIS FIRST NHL GAME:

- 3 — **Alex Smart,** Montreal, Jan. 14, 1943, at Montreal. Montreal 5, Chicago 1.
- — **Real Cloutier,** Quebec, Oct. 10, 1979, at Quebec. Atlanta 5, Quebec 3.

MOST GOALS, ONE GAME, BY A PLAYER IN HIS FIRST NHL SEASON:

- 5 — **Howie Meeker,** Toronto, Jan. 8, 1947, at Toronto. Toronto 10, Chicago 4.
- — **Don Murdoch,** NY Rangers, Oct. 12, 1976, at Minnesota. NY Rangers 10, Minnesota 4.

MOST ASSISTS, ONE GAME, BY A DEFENSEMAN:

- 6 — **Babe Pratt,** Toronto, Jan. 8, 1944, at Toronto. Toronto 12, Boston 3.
- — **Pat Stapleton,** Chicago, March 30, 1969, at Chicago. Chicago 9, Detroit 5.
- — **Bobby Orr,** Boston, Jan. 1, 1973, at Vancouver, Boston 8, Vancouver 2.
- — **Ron Stackhouse,** Pittsburgh, March 8, 1975, at Pittsburgh. Pittsburgh 8, Philadelphia 2.
- — **Paul Coffey,** Edmonton, Mar. 14, 1986, at Edmonton. Edmonton 12, Detroit 3.
- — **Gary Suter,** Calgary, Apr. 4, 1986, at Calgary. Calgary 9, Edmonton 3.

MOST ASSISTS BY ONE PLAYER IN HIS FIRST NHL GAME:

- 4 — **Earl (Dutch) Reibel,** Detroit, Oct. 8, 1953, at Detroit. Detroit 4, NY Rangers 1.
- — **Roland Eriksson,** Minnesota, Oct. 6, 1976, at New York. NY Rangers 6, Minnesota 5.
- 3 — Al Hill, Philadelphia, Feb. 14, 1977, at Philadelphia. Philadelphia 6, St. Louis 4.

MOST ASSISTS, ONE GAME, BY A PLAYER IN HIS FIRST NHL SEASON:

- 7 — **Wayne Gretzky,** Edmonton, Feb. 15, 1980, at Edmonton. Edmonton 8, Washington 2.
- 6 — Gary Suter, Calgary, Apr. 4, 1986, at Calgary. Calgary 9, Edmonton 3.
- 5 — Jim McFadden, Detroit, Nov. 23, 1947, at Chicago. Detroit 9, Chicago 3.
- — Mark Howe, Hartford, Jan. 30, 1980, at Hartford. Hartford 8, Boston 2.
- — Anton Stastny, Quebec, Feb. 22, 1981, at Washington. Quebec 11, Washington 7.
- — Mark Osborne, Detroit, Feb. 7, 1982, at Detroit. Detroit 8, St. Louis 5.
- — Sergei Makarov, Calgary, Feb. 25, 1990, at Calgary. Calgary 10, Edmonton 4.

MOST POINTS, ONE GAME, BY A DEFENSEMAN:

- 8 — **Tom Bladon,** Philadelphia, Dec. 11, 1977, at Philadelphia. 4G-4A. Philadelphia 11, Cleveland 1.
- — **Paul Coffey,** Edmonton, Mar. 14, 1986, at Edmonton. 2G-6A. Edmonton 12, Detroit 3.
- 7 — Bobby Orr, Boston, Nov. 15, 1973, at Boston, 3G-4A. Boston 10, NY Rangers 2.

MOST POINTS BY ONE PLAYER IN HIS FIRST NHL GAME:

- 5 — **Al Hill,** Philadelphia, Feb. 14, 1977, at Philadelphia. 2G-3A. Philadelphia 6, St. Louis 4.
- 4 — Alex Smart, Montreal, Jan. 14, 1943, at Montreal, 3G-1A. Montreal 5, Chicago 1.
- — Earl (Dutch) Reibel, Detroit, Oct. 8, 1953, at Detroit. 4A. Detroit 4, NY Rangers 1.
- — Roland Eriksson, Minnesota, Oct. 6, 1976 at New York. 4A. NY Rangers 6, Minnesota 5.

MOST POINTS, ONE GAME, BY A PLAYER IN HIS FIRST NHL SEASON:
8 — **Peter Stastny,** Quebec, Feb. 22, 1981, at Washington. 4G-4A. Quebec 11, Washington 7.
— **Anton Stastny,** Quebec, Feb. 22, 1981, at Washington. 3G-5A. Quebec 11, Washington 7.
7 — **Wayne Gretzky,** Edmonton, Feb. 15, 1980, at Edmonton. 7A. Edmonton 8, Washington 2.
— **Sergei Makarov,** Calgary, Feb. 25, 1990, at Calgary. 2G-5A. Calgary 10, Edmonton 4.
6 — **Wayne Gretzky,** Edmonton, March 29, 1980, at Toronto. 2G-4A. Edmonton 8, Toronto 5.
— **Gary Suter,** Calgary, Apr. 4, 1986, at Calgary. 6A. Calgary 9, Edmonton 3.

MOST PENALTIES, ONE GAME:
9 — **Jim Dorey,** Toronto, Oct. 16, 1968, at Toronto against Pittsburgh. 4 minors, 2 majors, 2 10-minute misconducts, 1 game misconduct.
— **Dave Schultz,** Pittsburgh, Apr. 6, 1978, at Detroit. 5 minors, 2 majors, 2 10-minute misconducts.
— **Randy Holt,** Los Angeles, Mar. 11, 1979, at Philadelphia. 1 minor, 3 majors, 2 10-minute misconducts, 3 game misconducts.
— **Russ Anderson,** Pittsburgh, Jan. 19, 1980, at Pittsburgh. 3 minors, 3 majors, 3 game misconducts.
— **Kim Clackson,** Quebec, March 8, 1981, at Quebec. 4 minors, 3 majors, 2 game misconducts.
— **Terry O'Reilly,** Boston, Dec. 19, 1984 at Hartford. 5 minors, 3 majors, 1 game misconduct.
— **Larry Playfair,** Los Angeles, Dec. 9, 1986, at NY Islanders. 6 minors, 2 majors, 1 10-minute misconduct.

MOST PENALTY MINUTES, ONE GAME:
67 — **Randy Holt,** Los Angeles, Mar. 11, 1979, at Philadelphia. 1 minor, 3 majors, 2 10-minute misconducts, 3 game misconducts.
55 — **Frank Bathe,** Philadelphia, March 11, 1979, at Philadelphia. 3 majors, 2 10-minute misconducts, 2 game misconducts.
51 — **Russ Anderson,** Pittsburgh, Jan. 19, 1980, at Pittsburgh. 3 minors, 3 majors, 3 game misconducts.

MOST GOALS, ONE PERIOD:
4 — **Harvey (Busher) Jackson,** Toronto, Nov. 20, 1934, at St. Louis, third period. Toronto 5, St. Louis Eagles 2.
— **Max Bentley,** Chicago, Jan. 28, 1943, at Chicago, third period. Chicago 10, NY Rangers 1.
— **Clint Smith,** Chicago, March 4, 1945, at Chicago, third period. Chicago 6, Montreal 4.
— **Red Berenson,** St. Louis, Nov. 7, 1968, at Philadelphia, second period. St. Louis 8, Philadelphia 0.
— **Wayne Gretzky,** Edmonton, Feb. 18, 1981, at Edmonton, third period. Edmonton 9, St. Louis 2.
— **Grant Mulvey,** Chicago, Feb. 3, 1982, at Chicago, first period. Chicago 9, St. Louis 5.
— **Bryan Trottier,** NY Islanders, Feb 13, 1982, at New York, second period. NY Islanders 8, Philadelphia 2.
— **Al Secord,** Chicago, Jan. 7, 1987 at Chicago, second period. Chicago 6, Toronto 4.
— **Joe Nieuwendyk,** Calgary, Jan. 11, 1989, at Calgary, second period. Calgary 8, Winnipeg 3.

MOST ASSISTS, ONE PERIOD:
5 — **Dale Hawerchuk,** Winnipeg, Mar. 6, 1984, at Los Angeles, second period. Winnipeg 7, Los Angeles 3.
4 — Four assists have been recorded in one period on 39 occasions since Buddy O'Connor of Montreal first accomplished the feat vs. NY Rangers on Nov. 8, 1942. Wayne Gretzky (Edmonton, Los Angeles) has recorded four assists in one period on 10 occasions including the NHL's most recent equalling of this mark on Mar. 4, 1989 vs. Philadelphia at Los Angeles.

MOST POINTS, ONE PERIOD:
6 — **Bryan Trottier,** NY Islanders, Dec. 23, 1978, at NY Islanders, second period. 3G, 3A. NY Islanders 9, NY Rangers 4.
5 — **Les Cunningham,** Chicago, Jan. 28, 1940, at Chicago, third period. 2G, 3A. Chicago 8, Montreal 1.
— **Max Bentley,** Chicago, Jan. 28, 1943, at Chicago, third period. 4G, 1A. Chicago 10, NY Rangers 1.
— **Leo Labine,** Boston, Nov. 28, 1954, at Boston, second period, 3G, 2A. Boston 6, Detroit 2.
— **Darryl Sittler,** Toronto, Feb. 7, 1976, at Toronto, second period. 3G, 2A. Toronto 11, Boston 4.
— **Dale Hawerchuk,** Winnipeg, Mar. 6, 1984, at Los Angeles, second period. 5A. Winnipeg 7 Los Angeles 3.
— **Jari Kurri,** Edmonton, October 26, 1984 at Edmonton, second period. Edmonton 8, Los Angeles 2.
— **Pat Elynuik,** Winnipeg, Jan. 20, 1989, at Winnipeg, second period. 2G, 3A. Winnipeg 7, Pittsburgh 3.
— **Ray Ferraro,** Hartford, Dec. 9, 1989, at Hartford, first period. 3G, 2A. Hartford 7, New Jersey 3.
— **Stephane Richer,** Montreal, Feb. 14, 1990, at Montreal, first period. 2G, 3A. Montreal 10, Vancouver 1.

MOST PENALTIES, ONE PERIOD:
9 — **Randy Holt,** Los Angeles, Mar. 11, 1979, at Philadelphia, first period. 1 minor, 3 majors, 2 10-minute misconducts, 3 game misconducts.

MOST PENALTY MINUTES, ONE PERIOD:
67 — **Randy Holt,** Los Angeles, Mar. 11, 1979, at Philadelphia, first period. 1 minor, 3 majors, 2 10-minute misconducts, 3 game misconducts.

FASTEST GOAL BY A ROOKIE IN HIS FIRST NHL GAME:
15 Seconds — **Gus Bodnar,** Toronto, Oct. 30, 1943. Toronto 5, NY Rangers 2.
18 Seconds — Danny Gare, Buffalo, Oct. 10, 1974. Buffalo 9, Boston 5.
36 Seconds — Al Hill, Philadelphia, Feb. 14, 1977. Philadelphia 6, St. Louis 4.

FASTEST GOAL FROM START OF GAME:
5 Seconds — **Doug Small,** Winnipeg, Dec. 20, 1981, at Winnipeg. Winnipeg 5, St. Louis 4.
— **Bryan Trottier,** NY Islanders, Mar. 22, 1984, at Boston. NY Islanders 3, Boston 3
6 Seconds — Henry Boucha, Detroit, Jan. 28, 1973, at Montreal. Detroit 4, Montreal 2
— Jean Pronovost, Pittsburgh, March 25, 1976, at St. Louis. St. Louis 5, Pittsburgh 2
7 Seconds — Charlie Conacher, Toronto, Feb. 6, 1932, at Toronto. Toronto 6, Boston 0
— Danny Gare, Buffalo, Dec. 17, 1978, at Buffalo. Buffalo 6, Vancouver 3
— Dave Williams, Los Angeles, Feb. 14, 1987 at Los Angeles. Los Angeles 5, Harford 2.
8 Seconds — Ron Martin, NY Americans, Dec. 4, 1932, at New York. NY Americans 4, Montreal 2
— Chuck Arnason, Colorado, Jan. 28, 1977, at Atlanta. Colorado 3, Atlanta 3
— Wayne Gretzky, Edmonton, Dec. 14, 1983, at New York. Edmonton 9, NY Rangers 4
— Gaetan Duchesne, Washington, Mar. 14, 1987, at St. Louis. Washington 3, St. Louis 3.
— Tim Kerr, Philadelphia, March 7, 1989, at Philadelphia. Philadelphia 4, Edmonton 4.

FASTEST GOAL FROM START OF A PERIOD:
4 Seconds — **Claude Provost,** Montreal, Nov. 9, 1957, at Montreal, second period. Montreal 4, Boston 2.
— **Denis Savard,** Chicago, Jan. 12, 1986, at Chicago, third period. Chicago 4, Hartford 2.

FASTEST TWO GOALS:
4 Seconds — **Nels Stewart,** Mtl. Maroons, Jan. 3, 1931, at Montreal at 8:24 and 8:28, third period. Mtl. Maroons 5, Boston 3.
5 Seconds — Pete Mahovlich, Montreal, Feb. 20, 1971, at Montreal at 12:16 and 12:21, third period. Montreal 7, Chicago 1.
6 Seconds — Jim Pappin, Chicago, Feb. 16, 1972, at Chicago at 2:57 and 3:03, third period. Chicago 3, Philadelphia 3.
— Ralph Backstrom, Los Angeles, Nov. 2, 1972, at Los Angeles at 8:30 and 8:36, third period. Los Angeles 5, Boston 2.
— Lanny McDonald, Calgary, Mar. 22, 1984, at Calgary at 16:23 and 16:29, first period. Detroit 6, Calgary 4.
— Sylvain Turgeon, Hartford, Mar. 28, 1987, at Hartford at 13:59 and 14:05, second period. Hartford 5, Pittsburgh 4.

FASTEST THREE GOALS:
21 Seconds — **Bill Mosienko,** Chicago, March 23, 1952, at New York, against goaltender Lorne Anderson. Mosienko scored at 6:09, 6:20 and 6:30, third period, all with both teams as full strength. Chicago 7, NY Rangers 6.
44 Seconds — Jean Béliveau, Montreal, Nov. 5, 1955 at Montreal against goaltender Terry Sawchuk. Béliveau scored at :42, 1:08 and 1:26 of second period, all with Montreal holding a 6-4 man advantage. Montreal 4, Boston 2.

FASTEST THREE ASSISTS:
21 Seconds — **Gus Bodnar,** Chicago, March 23, 1952, at New York, Bodnar assisted on Bill Mosienko's three goals at 6:09, 6:20, 6:30 of third period. Chicago 7, NY Rangers 6.
44 Seconds — Bert Olmstead, Montreal, Nov. 5, 1955, at Montreal against Boston. Olmstead assisted on Jean Béliveau's three goals at :42, 1:08 and 1:26 of second period. Montreal 4, Boston 2.

Top 100 All-Time Goal-Scoring Leaders

* active player

(figures in parentheses indicate ranking of top 10 by goals per game)

Player	Seasons	Games	Goals	Goals per game
1. Gordie Howe, Det., Hfd.	26	1,767	801	.453
2. Marcel Dionne, Det., L.A., NYR	18	1,348	731	.542
3. Phil Esposito, Chi., Bos., NYR	18	1,282	717	.559(10)
*4. Wayne Gretzky, Edm., L.A.	11	847	677	.799 (2)
5. Bobby Hull, Chi., Wpg., Hfd.	16	1,063	610	.574 (6)
6. Mike Bossy, NYI	10	752	573	.762 (3)
7. John Bucyk, Det., Bos.	23	1,540	556	.361
*8. Guy Lafleur, Mtl., NYR, Que.	16	1,067	548	.514
9. Maurice Richard, Mtl.	18	978	544	.556
10. Stan Mikita, Chi.	22	1,394	541	.388
11. Frank Mahovlich, Tor., Det., Mtl., ...	18	1,181	533	.451
12. Gilbert Perreault, Buf.	17	1,191	512	.430
13. Jean Beliveau, Mtl.	20	1,125	507	.451
14. Lanny McDonald, Tor., Col., Cgy. ...	16	1,111	500	.450
*15. Bryan Trottier, NYI	15	1,123	500	.445
16. Jean Ratelle, NYR, Bos.	21	1,281	491	.383
17. Norm Ullman, Det., Tor.	20	1,410	490	.348
18. Darryl Sittler, Tor., Phi., Det.	15	1,096	484	.442
*19. Jari Kurri, Edm.	10	754	474	.629 (4)
*20. Michel Goulet, Que., Chi.	11	821	460	.560 (9)
21. Alex Delvecchio, Det.	24	1,549	456	.294
*22. Mike Gartner, Wsh., Min., NYR	11	850	449	.528
23. Rick Middleton, NYR, Bos.	14	1,005	448	.446
24. Yvan Cournoyer, Mtl.	16	968	428	.442
25. Steve Shutt, Mtl., L.A.	13	930	424	.456
26. Bill Barber, Phi.	12	903	420	.465
*27. Rick Vaive, Van., Tor., Chi., Buf.	11	785	415	.529
28. Garry Unger, Tor., Det., St. L., Atl., L.A., Edm.	16	1,105	413	.374
29. Rod Gilbert, NYR	18	1,065	406	.381
30. Dave Keon, Tor., Hfd.	18	1,296	396	.306
31. Pierre Larouche, Pit., Mtl., Hfd., NYR	14	812	395	.486
32. Bernie Geoffrion, Mtl., NYR	16	883	393	.445
33. Jean Pronovost, Pit., Atl., Wsh.	14	998	391	.392
34. Dean Prentice, NYR, Bos., Det., Pit., Min.	22	1,378	391	.284
*35. Glenn Anderson, Edm.	10	754	389	.516
*36. Dave Taylor, L.A.	13	880	388	.441
*37. Dino Ciccarelli, Min., Wsh.	10	693	385	.556
*38. Peter Stastny, Que., N.J.	10	749	385	.514
39. Richard Martin, Buf., L.A.	11	685	384	.561 (8)
40. Reggie Leach, Bos., Cal., Phi., Det. .	13	934	381	.408
*41. Mark Messier, Edm.	11	798	380	.476
*42. Dale Hawerchuk, Wpg.	9	713	379	.532
43. Ted Lindsay, Det., Chi.	17	1,068	379	.355
44. Butch Goring, L.A., NYI, Bos.	16	1,107	375	.339
*45. Brian Propp, Phi., Bos.	11	804	372	.463
46. Rick Kehoe, Tor., Pit.	14	906	371	.409
*47. Bernie Federko, St. L., Det.	14	1,000	369	.369
48. Jacques Lemaire, Mtl.	12	853	366	.429
49. Peter McNab, Buf., Bos., Van., N.J. ...	14	954	363	.381
50. Ivan Boldirev, Bos., Cal., Chi., Atl., Van., Det.	15	1,052	361	.343
51. Bobby Clarke, Phi.	15	1,144	358	.313
52. Henri Richard, Mtl.	20	1,256	358	.285
53. Dennis Maruk, Cal., Cle., Wsh., Min.	13	882	356	.404
54. Wilf Paiement, K.C., Col., Tor., Que., NYR, Buf., Pit.	14	946	356	.376
55. Danny Gare, Buf., Det., Edm.	13	827	354	.428
*56. Denis Savard, Chi.	10	736	351	.477
57. Rick MacLeish, Phi., Hfd., Pit., Det. . .	14	846	349	.413
58. Andy Bathgate, NYR, Tor., Det., Pit. ..	17	1,069	349	.326
*59. Tim Kerr, Phi.	10	574	348	.606 (5)
^60. John Ogrodnick, Det., Que., NYR ...	11	775	348	.449
*61. Mario Lemieux, Pit.	6	427	345	.808 (1)
62. Charlie Simmer, Cal., Cle., L.A., Bos., Pit.	14	712	342	.480
*63. Joey Mullen, St. L., Cgy.	9	646	341	.528
*64. Bernie Nicholls, L.A., NYR	9	634	339	.535
65. Ron Ellis, Tor.	16	1,034	332	.321
66. Ken Hodge, Chi., Bos., NYR	13	881	328	.372
*67. Bobby Smith, Min., Mtl.	12	891	328	.368
68. Nels Stewart, Mtl. M., Bos., NYA ...	15	654	324	.495
69. Pit Martin, Det., Bos., Chi., Van.	17	1,101	324	.294
70. Vic Hadfield, NYR, Pit.	16	1,002	323	.322
*71. Mike Foligno, Det., Buf.	11	819	320	.391
72. Clark Gillies, NYI, Buf.	14	958	319	.333
*73. Paul MacLean, St. L., Wpg., Det.	9	677	318	.470
*74. Mike Bullard, Pit., Cgy., St. L., Phi. ..	10	662	315	.476
75. Don Lever, Van., Atl., Cgy., Col., N.J., Buf.	15	1,020	313	.307

Bernie "Boom Boom" Geoffrion

Player	Seasons	Games	Goals	Goals per game
76. Denis Potvin, NYI	15	1,060	310	.292
*77. John Tonelli, NYI, Cgy., L.A.	12	905	308	.340
78. Bob Nevin, Tor., NYR, Min., L.A.	18	1,128	307	.272
79. Brian Sutter, St. L.	12	779	303	.389
*80. Tony McKegney, Buf., Que., Min., St. L., Det.	13	853	303	.355
81. Dennis Hull, Chi., Det.	14	959	303	.316
*82. Steve Larmer, Chi.	10	647	298	.461
83. George Armstrong, Tor.	21	1,187	296	.249
84. Tom Lysiak, Atl., Chi.	13	919	292	.318
*85. Steve Yzerman, Det.	7	514	291	.566 (7)
86. Peter Mahovlich, Det., Mtl., Pit.	16	884	288	.326
87. Rene Robert, Pit., Buf., Col., Tor.	12	744	284	.382
*88. Dave Christian, Wsh., Bos.	11	784	284	.362
*89. Paul Coffey, Edm., Pit.	10	733	283	.386
90. Bill Goldsworthy, Bos., Min., NYR ...	14	771	283	.367
91. Dick Duff, Tor., NYR, Mtl., L.A., Buf. .	18	1,030	283	.275
92. John Anderson, Tor., Que., Hfd.	12	814	282	.346
93. Bob Pulford, Tor., L.A.	16	1,079	281	.260
94. Red Kelly, Det., Tor.	20	1,316	281	.214
95. Camille Henry, NYR, Chi., St. L.	12	727	279	.384
96. Jim Pappin, Tor., Chi., Cal., Cle.	14	767	278	.362
97. Ralph Backstrom, Mtl., L.A., Chi.	17	1,032	278	.269
*98. Brian Bellows, Min.	8	593	277	.467
99. Wayne Cashman, Bos.	17	1,027	277	.270
100. Ron Stewart, Tor., Bos., St. L., NYR, Van., NYI	21	1,353	276	.204

Top 100 All-Time Assist Leaders

* active player
(figures in parentheses indicate ranking of top 10 in order of assists per game)

Player	Seasons	Games	Assists	Assists per game
*1. Wayne Gretzky, Edm., L.A.	11	847	**1,302**	1.537 (1)
2. Gordie Howe, Det., Hfd.	26	1,767	**1,049**	.594
3. Marcel Dionne, Det., L.A., NYR	18	1,348	**1,040**	.772 (8)
4. Stan Mikita, Chi.	22	1,394	**926**	.664
5. Phil Esposito, Chi., Bos., NYR	18	1,282	**873**	.681
*6. Bryan Trottier, NYI	15	1,123	**853**	.760
7. Bobby Clarke, Phi.	15	1,144	**852**	.745
8 Alex Delvecchio, Det.	24	1,549	**825**	.533
9. Gilbert Perreault, Buf.	17	1,191	**814**	.683
10. John Bucyk, Det., Bos	23	1,540	**813**	.528
*11. Guy Lafleur, Mtl., NYR, Que.	16	1,067	**777**	.728
12. Jean Ratelle, NYR, Bos.	21	1,281	**776**	.606
*13. Bernie Federko, St. L., Det.	14	1,000	**761**	.761
14. Denis Potvin, NYI	15	1,060	**742**	.700
15. Norm Ullman, Det., Tor.	20	1,410	**739**	.524
*16. Larry Robinson, Mtl., L.A.	17	1,266	**718**	.567
17. Jean Beliveau, Mtl.	20	1,125	**712**	.633
18. Henri Richard, Mtl.	20	1,256	**688**	.548
19. Brad Park, NYR, Bos., Det.	17	1,113	**683**	.614
*20. Peter Stastny, Que. N.J.	10	749	**674**	.900 (5)
*21. Paul Coffey, Edm., Pit.	10	733	**669**	.913 (4)
*22. Denis Savard, Chi.	10	736	**662**	.899 (6)
23. Bobby Orr, Bos., Chi.	12	657	**645**	.982 (3)
24. Darryl Sittler, Tor., Phi., Det.	15	1,096	**637**	.581
*25. Borje Salming, Tor., Det.	17	1,148	**637**	.555
26. Andy Bathgate, NYR, Tor., Det., Pit.	17	1,069	**624**	.584
27. Rod Gilbert, NYR	18	1,065	**615**	.577
*28. Ray Bourque, Bos.	11	794	**610**	.768
*29. Bobby Smith, Min., Mtl.	12	891	**604**	.678
*30. Mark Messier, Edm.	11	798	**590**	.739
31. Dave Keon, Tor., Hfd.	18	1,296	**590**	.455
*32. Dave Taylor, L.A.	13	880	**577**	.656
33. Frank Mahovlich, Tor., Det., Mtl.	18	1,181	**570**	.483
*34. Jari Kurri, Edm.	10	754	**569**	.755
35. Bobby Hull, Chi., Wpg., Hfd.	16	1,063	**560**	.527
36. Mike Bossy, NYI	10	752	**553**	.735
37. Tom Lysiak, Atl., Chi.	13	919	**551**	.600
*38. Dale Hawerchuk, Wpg.	9	713	**550**	.771(10)
39. Red Kelly, Det., Tor.	20	1,316	**542**	.412
40. Rick Middleton, NYR, Bos.	14	1,005	**540**	.537
*41. Doug Wilson, Chi.	12	887	**525**	.592
*42. Ken Linseman, Phi., Edm., Bos.	12	802	**522**	.651
43. Dennis Maruk, Cal., Cle., Wsh., Min.	13	882	**521**	.591
44. Wayne Cashman, Bos.	17	1,027	**516**	.502
45. Butch Goring, L.A., NYI, Bos.	16	1,107	**513**	.463
46. Lanny McDonald, Tor., Col., Cgy.	16	1,111	**506**	.455
47. Ivan Boldirev, Bos., Cal., Chi., Atl., Van., Det.	15	1,052	**505**	.480
*48. Ron Francis, Hfd.	9	647	**502**	.776 (7)
*49. Mario Lemieux, Pit.	6	427	**493**	1.155 (2)
*50. Michel Goulet, Que., Chi.	11	821	**490**	.597
*51. Brian Propp, Phi., Bos.	11	804	**488**	.607
52. Peter Mahovlich, Det., Mtl., Pit.	16	884	**485**	.549
53. Pit Martin, Det., Bos., Chi., Van.	17	1,101	**485**	.441
*54. John Tonelli, NYI, Cgy., L.A.	12	905	**484**	.535
*55. Larry Murphy, L.A., Wsh., Min.	10	785	**478**	.609
56. Ken Hodge, Chi., Bos., NYR	13	881	**472**	.536
57. Ted Lindsay, Det., Chi.	17	1,068	**472**	.442
*58. Randy Carlyle, Tor., Pit., Wpg.	14	915	**470**	.514
59. Jacques Lemaire, Mtl.	12	853	**469**	.550
60. Dean Prentice, NYR, Bos., Det., Pit., Min.	22	1,378	**469**	.340
61. Phil Goyette, Mtl., NYR, St. L., Buf.	16	941	**467**	.496
62. Bill Barber, Phi.	12	903	**463**	.513
*63. Reed Larson, Det., Bos., Edm., NYI, Min., Buf.	14	904	**463**	.512
64. Doug Mohns, Bos., Chi., Min., Atl., Wsh.	22	1,390	**462**	.332
*65. Mark Howe, Hfd., Phi.	11	746	**461**	.618
66. Bobby Rousseau, Mtl., Min., NYR	15	942	**458**	.486
67. Wilf Paiement, K.C., Col., Tor., Que., NYR, Buf. Pit.	14	946	**458**	.484
*68. Bernie Nicholls, L.A., NYR	9	634	**456**	.719
69. Murray Oliver, Det., Bos., Tor., Min.	17	1,127	**454**	.403
*70. Glenn Anderson, Edm.	10	754	**452**	.599
71. Doug Harvey, Mtl., NYR, Det., St. L.	19	1,113	**452**	.406
72. Guy Lapointe, Mtl., St. L., Bos.	16	884	**451**	.510
73. Walt Tkachuk, NYR	14	945	**451**	.477
74. Peter McNab, Buf., Bos., Van., N.J.	14	954	**450**	.472
75. Mel Bridgman, Phi., Cgy., N.J., Van.	14	977	**449**	.460
*76. Neal Broten, Min.	10	639	**444**	.695
*77. Mike Gartner, Wsh., Min., NYR	11	850	**440**	.518
*78. Dave Babych, Wpg., Hfd.	10	731	**438**	.599
79. Bill Gadsby, Chi., NYR, Det.	20	1248	**437**	.350
80. Yvan Cournoyer, Mtl.	16	968	**435**	.449
*81. Dale Hunter, Que., Wsh.	10	762	**431**	.566
*82. Ron Greschner, NYR	16	982	**431**	.439
83. Bernie Geoffrion, Mtl., NYR	16	883	**429**	.486

Doug Wilson ranks 41st on the all-time assist leader board.

Player	Seasons	Games	Assists	Assists per game
84. Pierre Larouche, Pit., Mtl., Hfd., NYR	14	812	**427**	.526
*85. Paul Reinhart, Atl., Cgy., Van.	11	648	**426**	.657
86. Syl Apps, Jr., NYR, Pit., L.A.	10	727	**423**	.582
87. Kent Nilsson, Atl., Cgy., Min., Edm.	8	547	**422**	.771 (9)
88. Bert Olmstead, Chi., Mtl., Tor.	14	848	**421**	.496
89. Maurice Richard, Mtl.	18	978	**421**	.430
90. Craig Ramsay, Buf.	14	1,070	**420**	.393
91. Bob Nevin, Tor., NYR, Min., L.A.	18	1,128	**419**	.371
92. Rene Robert, Pit., Buf., Col., Tor.	12	744	**418**	.562
93. Pierre Pilote, Chi., Tor.	14	890	**418**	.470
94. Carol Vadnais, Mtl., Oak., Cal., Bos., NYR, N.J.	17	1,087	**418**	.385
95. George Armstrong, Tor.	21	1,187	**417**	.351
96. Rick MacLeish, Phi., Hfd., Pit., Det.	14	846	**410**	.485
97. Elmer Lach, Mtl.	14	664	**408**	.614
98. Fred Stanfield, Chi., Bos., Min., Buf.	14	914	**405**	.443
99. Tim Horton, Tor., NYR, Pit., Buf.	24	1,446	**403**	.279
100. Terry O'Reilly, Bos.	14	891	**402**	.451

Wayne Gretzky celebrates the 1,851st point of his career against Edmonton on October 15, 1989 to surpass Gordie Howe as the NHL's all-time point leader.

Top 100 All-Time Point Leaders

* active player

(figures in parentheses indicate ranking of top 10 by points per game)

Player	Seasons	Games	Goals	Assists	Points	Points per game
*1. **Wayne Gretzky**, Edm., L.A. .	11	847	677	1,302	**1,979**	2.336 (1)
2. **Gordie Howe**, Det., Hfd.	26	1,767	801	1,049	**1,850**	1.047
3. **Marcel Dionne**, Det., L.A., NYR	18	1,348	731	1,040	**1,771**	1.314 (9)
4. **Phil Esposito**, Chi., Bos., NYR	18	1,282	717	873	**1,590**	1.240
5. **Stan Mikita**, Chi.	22	1,394	541	926	**1,467**	1.052
6. **John Bucyk**, Det., Bos.	23	1,540	556	813	**1,369**	.889
*7. **Bryan Trottier**, NYI	15	1.123	500	853	**1,353**	1.205
8. **Gilbert Perreault**, Buf.	17	1,191	512	814	**1,326**	1.113
*9. **Guy Lafleur**, Mtl., NYR, Que.	16	1,067	548	777	**1,325**	1.242
10. **Alex Delvecchio**, Det.	24	1,549	456	825	**1,281**	.827
11. **Jean Ratelle**, NYR, Bos.	21	1,281	491	776	**1,267**	.989
12. **Norm Ullman**, Det., Tor.	20	1,410	490	739	**1,229**	.872
13. **Jean Beliveau**, Mtl.	20	1,125	507	712	**1,219**	1.084
14. **Bobby Clarke**, Phi.	15	1,144	358	852	**1,210**	1.058
15. **Bobby Hull**, Chi., Wpg., Hfd.	16	1,063	610	560	**1,170**	1.101
*19. **Bernie Federko**, St. L., Det. .	14	1,000	369	761	**1,130**	1.130
17. **Mike Bossy**, NYI	10	752	573	553	**1,126**	1.497 (3)
18. **Darryl Sittler**, Tor., Phi., Det.	15	1,096	484	637	**1,121**	1.023
19. **Frank Mahovlich**, Tor., Det., Mtl.	18	1,181	533	570	**1,103**	.934
*20. **Peter Stastny**, Que., N.J.	10	749	385	674	**1,059**	1.414 (4)
21. **Denis Potvin**, NYI	15	1,060	310	742	**1,052**	.992
22. **Henri Richard**, Mtl.	20	1,256	358	688	**1,046**	.833
*23. **Jari Kurri**, Edm.	10	754	474	569	**1,043**	1.383 (6)
24. **Rod Gilbert**, NYR	18	1,065	406	615	**1,021**	.959
*25. **Denis Savard**, Chi.	10	736	351	662	**1,013**	1.376 (7)
26. **Lanny McDonald**, Tor., Col., Cgy.	16	1,111	500	506	**1,006**	.905
27. **Rick Middleton**, NYR, Bos. .	14	1,005	448	540	**988**	.983
28. **Dave Keon**, Tor., Hfd.	18	1,296	396	590	**986**	.761
29. **Andy Bathgate**, NYR, Tor., Det., Pit.	17	1,069	349	624	**973**	.910
*30. **Mark Messier**, Edm.	11	798	380	590	**970**	1.216
*31. **Dave Taylor**, L.A.	13	880	388	577	**965**	1.097
32. **Maurice Richard**, Mtl.	18	978	544	421	**965**	.987
*33. **Paul Coffey**, Edm., Pit.	10	733	283	669	**952**	1.299
*34. **Michel Goulet**, Que., Chi. ...	11	821	460	490	**950**	1.157
*35. **Bobby Smith**, Min., Mtl.	12	891	328	604	**932**	1.046
*36. **Dale Hawerchuk**, Wpg. ..	9	713	379	550	**929**	1.303 (10)
*37. **Larry Robinson**, Mtl., L.A. ..	17	1,266	204	718	**922**	.728
38. **Bobby Orr**, Bos., Chi.	12	657	270	645	**915**	1.393 (5)
39. **Brad Park**, NYR, Bos., Det. .	17	1,113	213	683	**896**	.805
*40. **Mike Gartner**, Wsh., Min., NYR	11	850	449	440	**889**	1.046
41. **Butch Goring**, L.A., NYI, Bos.	16	1,107	375	513	**888**	.802
42. **Bill Barber**, Phi.	12	903	420	463	**883**	.978
43. **Dennis Maruk**, Cal., Cle., Wsh., Mln.	13	882	356	521	**877**	.994
44. **Ivan Boldirev**, Bos., Cal., Chi., Atl., Van., Det.	15	1,052	361	505	**866**	.823
45. **Yvan Cournoyer**, Mtl.	16	968	428	435	**863**	.892
*46. **Brian Propp**, Phi., Bos.	11	804	372	488	**860**	1.070
47. **Dean Prentice**, NYR, Bos., Det., Pit., Min.	22	1,378	391	469	**860**	.624
48. **Ted Lindsay**, Det., Chi.	17	1,068	379	472	**851**	.797
49. **Tom Lysiak**, Atl., Chi.	13	919	292	551	**843**	.917
*50. **Glenn Anderson**, Edm.	10	754	389	452	**841**	1.115
*51. **Ray Bourque**, Bos.	11	794	230	610	**840**	1.058
*52. **Mario Lemieux**, Pit.	6	427	345	493	**838**	1.963 (2)
53. **Jacques Lemaire**, Mtl.	12	853	366	469	**835**	.979
54. **Red Kelly**, Det., Tor.	20	1,316	281	542	**823**	.625
55. **Pierre Larouche**, Pit., Mtl., Hfd., NYR	14	812	395	427	**822**	1.012
56. **Bernie Geoffrion**, Mtl., NYR .	16	883	393	429	**822**	.931

Player	Seasons	Games	Goals	Assists	Points	Points per game
57. **Steve Shutt**, Mtl., L.A.	13	930	424	393	**817**	.878
58. **Wilf Paiement**, K.C., Col., Tor., Que., NYR, Buf., Pit. .	14	946	356	458	**814**	.860
59. **Peter McNab**, Buf., Bos., Van., N.J.	14	954	363	450	**813**	.852
60. **Pit Martin**, Det., Bos., Chi., Van.	17	1,101	324	485	**809**	.735
61. **Garry Unger**, Tor., Det., St. L., Atl., L.A., Edm. .	16	1,105	413	391	**804**	.728
62. **Ken Hodge**, Chi., Bos., NYR	13	881	328	472	**800**	.908
*63. **Bernie Nicholls**, L.A., NYR ..	9	634	339	456	**795**	1.254
64. **Wayne Cashman**, Bos.	17	1,027	277	516	**793**	.772
*65. **John Tonelli**, NYI, Cgy., L.A.	12	905	308	484	**792**	.875
*66. **Borje Salming**, Tor., Det. ...	17	1,140	150	637	**787**	.686
67. **Jean Pronovost**, Pit., Atl., Wsh.	14	998	391	383	**774**	.776
68. **Peter Mahovlich**, Det., Mtl., Pit.	16	884	288	485	**773**	.874
*69. **Ken Linseman**, Edm., Bos. .	11	802	249	522	**771**	.961
70. **Rick Kehoe**, Tor., Pit.	14	906	371	396	**767**	.847
71. **Rick MacLeish**, Phi., Hfd., Pit., Det.	14	846	349	410	**759**	.897
*72. **Ron Francis**, Hfd.	9	647	243	502	**745**	1.151
*73. **Dino Ciccarelli**, Min., Wsh. .	10	693	385	360	**745**	1.075
*74. **Doug Wilson**, Chi.	13	887	214	525	**739**	.833
*75. **Rick Vaive**, Van., Tor., Chi., Buf.	11	785	415	317	**732**	.932
*76. **John Ogrodnick**, Det., Que., NYR	11	775	348	383	**731**	.943
77. **Murray Oliver**, Det., Bos., Tor., Min.	17	1,127	274	454	**728**	.646
78. **Bob Nevin**, Tor., NYR, Min., L.A.	18	1,128	307	419	**726**	.644
*79. **Joey Mullen**, St. L., Cgy. ..	9	646	341	382	**723**	1.119
80. **George Armstrong**, Tor.	21	1,187	296	417	**713**	.601
81. **Vic Hadfield**, NYR, Pit.	16	1,002	323	389	**712**	.711
82. **Charlie Simmer**, Cal., Cle., L.A., Bos., Pit.	14	712	342	369	**711**	.999
83. **Doug Mohns**, Bos., Chi., Min., Atl., Wsh.	22	1,390	248	462	**710**	.511
84. **Bobby Rousseau**, Mtl., Min., NYR	15	942	245	458	**703**	.746
85. **Rene Robert**, Pit., Buf., Col., Tor.	12	744	284	418	**702**	.944
86. **Richard Martin**, Buf., L.A. ..	11	685	384	317	**701**	1.023
87. **Mel Bridgman**, Phi., Chi., N.J., Det., Van.	14	977	252	449	**701**	.718
88. **Clark Gillies**, NYI, Buf.	14	958	319	378	**697**	.728
*89. **Steve Yzerman**, Det.	7	514	291	401	**692**	1.346 (8)
90. **Kent Nilsson**, Atl., Cgy., Min., Edm.	8	547	263	422	**685**	1.252
91. **Danny Gare**, Buf., Det., Edm.	13	827	354	331	**685**	.828
*92. **Reed Larson**, Det., Bos., Edm., NYI, Min., Buf.	14	904	222	463	**685**	.758
93. **Don Lever**, Van., Atl., Cgy., Col., N.J., Buf.	15	1,020	313	367	**680**	.667
*94. **Steve Larmer**, Chi.	10	647	298	380	**678**	1.048
95. **Walt Tkaczuk**, NYR	14	945	227	451	**678**	.717
96. **Phil Goyette**, Mtl., NYR, St. L., Buf.	16	941	207	467	**674**	.716
97. **Craig Ramsay**, Buf.	14	1,070	252	420	**672**	.628
98. **Reggie Leach**, Bos., Cal., Phi., Det.	13	934	381	285	**666**	.713
*99. **Mike Foligno**, Det., Buf.	11	819	320	342	**662**	.808
*100. **Neal Broten**, Min.	10	639	216	444	**660**	1.033

All-Time Games Played Leaders

Regular Season

* active player

	Player	Team	Seasons	GP
1.	Gordie Howe	Detroit	25	1,687
		Hartford	1	80
		Total	**26**	**1,767**
2.	Alex Delvecchio	**Detroit**	**24**	**1,549**
3.	John Bucyk	Detroit	2	104
		Boston	21	1,436
		Total	**23**	**1,540**
4.	Tim Horton	Toronto	$19\frac{3}{4}$	1,185
		NY Rangers	$1\frac{1}{4}$	93
		Pittsburgh	1	44
		Buffalo	2	124
		Total	**24**	**1,446**
5.	Harry Howell	NY Rangers	17	1,160
		California	$1\frac{1}{2}$	83
		Los Angeles	$2\frac{1}{2}$	168
		Total	**21**	**1,411**
6.	Norm Ullman	Detroit	$12\frac{1}{2}$	875
		Toronto	$7\frac{1}{2}$	535
		Total	**20**	**1,410**
7.	Stan Mikita	**Chicago**	**22**	**1,394**
8.	Doug Mohns	Boston	11	710
		Chicago	$6\frac{1}{2}$	415
		Minnesota	$2\frac{1}{2}$	162
		Atlanta	1	28
		Washington	1	75
		Total	**22**	**1,390**
9.	Dean Prentice	NY Rangers	$10\frac{1}{2}$	666
		Boston	3	170
		Detroit	$3\frac{1}{2}$	230
		Pittsburgh	2	144
		Minnesota	3	168
		Total	**22**	**1,378**
10.	Ron Stewart	Toronto	13	838
		Boston	2	126
		St. Louis	$\frac{1}{2}$	19
		NY Rangers	4	306
		Vancouver	1	42
		NY Islanders	$\frac{1}{2}$	22
		Total	**21**	**1,353**
11.	Marcel Dionne	Detroit	4	309
		Los Angeles	$11\frac{3}{4}$	921
		NY Rangers	$2\frac{1}{4}$	118
		Total	**18**	**1,348**
12.	Red Kelly	Detroit	$12\frac{1}{2}$	846
		Toronto	$7\frac{1}{2}$	470
		Total	**20**	**1,316**
13.	Dave Keon	Toronto	15	1,062
		Hartford	3	234
		Total	**18**	**1,296**
14.	Phil Esposito	Chicago	4	235
		Boston	$8\frac{1}{4}$	625
		NY Rangers	$5\frac{3}{4}$	422
		Total	**18**	**1,282**
15.	Jean Ratelle	NY Rangers	$15\frac{1}{4}$	862
		Boston	$5\frac{3}{4}$	419
		Total	**21**	**1,281**
* 16.	Larry Robinson	Montreal	17	1,202
		Los Angeles	1	64
		Total	**18**	**1,266**
17.	Henri Richard	**Montreal**	**20**	**1,256**
18.	Bill Gadsby	Chicago	$8\frac{1}{2}$	468
		NY Rangers	$6\frac{1}{2}$	457
		Detroit	5	323
		Total	**20**	**1,248**
19.	Allan Stanley	NY Rangers	$6\frac{1}{4}$	307
		Chicago	$1\frac{3}{4}$	111
		Boston	2	129
		Toronto	9	633
		Philadelphia	1	64
		Total	**21**	**1,244**
20.	Eddie Westfall	Boston	11	734
		NY Islanders	7	493
		Total	**18**	**1,227**
21.	Eric Nesterenko	Toronto	5	206
		Chicago	16	1,013
		Total	**21**	**1,219**
22.	Marcel Pronovost	Detroit	16	983
		Toronto	5	223
		Total	**21**	**1,206**
23.	Gilbert Perreault	**Buffalo**	**17**	**1,191**
24.	George Armstrong	**Toronto**	**21**	**1,187**
25.	Frank Mahovlich	Toronto	$11\frac{3}{4}$	720
		Detroit	$2\frac{3}{4}$	198
		Montreal	$3\frac{1}{2}$	263
		Total	**18**	**1,181**
26.	Don Marshall	Montreal	10	585
		NY Rangers	7	479
		Buffalo	1	62
		Toronto	1	50
		Total	**19**	**1,176**
27.	Bob Gainey	**Montreal**	**16**	**1,160**
28.	Leo Boivin	Toronto	$3\frac{1}{4}$	137
		Boston	$11\frac{1}{2}$	717
		Detroit	$1\frac{1}{4}$	85
		Pittsburgh	$1\frac{1}{2}$	114
		Minnesota	$1\frac{1}{2}$	97
		Total	**19**	**1,150**
* 29.	Borje Salming	Toronto	16	1,099
		Detroit	1	49
		Total	**17**	**1,148**
30.	Bobby Clarke	**Philadelphia**	**15**	**1,144**
31.	Bob Nevin	Toronto	$5\frac{3}{4}$	250
		NY Rangers	$7\frac{1}{4}$	505
		Minnesota	2	138
		Los Angeles	3	235
		Total	**18**	**1,128**
32.	Murray Oliver	Detroit	$2\frac{1}{2}$	101
		Boston	$6\frac{1}{2}$	429
		Toronto	3	226
		Minnesota	5	371
		Total	**17**	**1,127**
33.	Jean Beliveau	**Montreal**	**20**	**1,125**
* 34.	Bryan Trottier	**NY Islanders**	**15**	**1,123**
35.	Doug Harvey	Montreal	14	890
		NY Rangers	3	151
		Detroit	1	2
		St. Louis	1	70
		Total	**19**	**1,113**
36.	Brad Park	NY Rangers	$7\frac{1}{2}$	465
		Boston	$7\frac{1}{2}$	501
		Detroit	2	147
		Total	**17**	**1,113**
37.	Lanny McDonald	Toronto	$6\frac{1}{2}$	477
		Colorado	$1\frac{3}{4}$	142
		Calgary	$7\frac{3}{4}$	441
		Total	**16**	**1,111**
38.	Butch Goring	Los Angeles	$10\frac{3}{4}$	736
		NY Islanders	$4\frac{3}{4}$	332
		Boston	$\frac{1}{2}$	39
		Total	**16**	**1,107**
39.	Garry Unger	Toronto	$\frac{1}{2}$	15
		Detroit	3	216
		St. Louis	$8\frac{1}{2}$	662
		Atlanta	1	79
		Los Angeles	$\frac{3}{4}$	58
		Edmonton	$2\frac{1}{4}$	75
		Total	**16**	**1,105**
40.	Pit Martin	Detroit	$3\frac{1}{4}$	119
		Boston	$1\frac{3}{4}$	111
		Chicago	$10\frac{1}{4}$	740
		Vancouver	$1\frac{3}{4}$	131
		Total	**17**	**1,101**
41.	Darryl Sittler	Toronto	$11\frac{1}{2}$	844
		Philadelphia	$2\frac{1}{2}$	191
		Detroit	1	61
		Total	**15**	**1,096**
42.	Carol Vadnais	Montreal	2	42
		Oakland	2	152
		California	$1\frac{3}{4}$	94
		Boston	$3\frac{1}{2}$	263
		NY Rangers	$6\frac{3}{4}$	485
		New Jersey	1	51
		Total	**17**	**1,087**
43.	Bob Pulford	Toronto	14	947
		Los Angeles	2	132
		Total	**16**	**1,079**
44.	Craig Ramsay	**Buffalo**	**14**	**1,070**
45.	Andy Bathgate	NY Rangers	$11\frac{3}{4}$	719
		Toronto	$1\frac{1}{4}$	70
		Detroit	2	130
		Pittsburgh	2	150
		Total	**17**	**1,069**
46.	Ted Lindsay	Detroit	14	862
		Chicago	3	206
		Total	**17**	**1,068**
* 47.	Guy Lafleur	Montreal	14	961
		NY Rangers	1	67
		Quebec	1	39
		Total	**16**	**1,067**
48.	Terry Harper	Montreal	10	554
		Los Angeles	3	234
		Detroit	4	252
		St. Louis	1	11
		Colorado	1	15
		Total	**19**	**1,066**
49.	Rod Gilbert	**NY Rangers**	**18**	**1,065**
50.	Bobby Hull	Chicago	15	1,036
		Winnipeg	$\frac{2}{3}$	18
		Hartford	$\frac{1}{3}$	9
		Total	**16**	**1,063**
51.	Denis Potvin	**NY Islanders**	**15**	**1,060**
52.	Jean Guy Talbot	Montreal	13	791
		Minnesota	$\frac{1}{4}$	4
		Detroit	$\frac{1}{2}$	32
		St. Louis	$2\frac{1}{2}$	172
		Buffalo	$\frac{3}{4}$	57
		Total	**17**	**1,056**
53.	Ivan Boldirev	Boston	$1\frac{1}{4}$	13
		California	$2\frac{3}{4}$	191
		Chicago	$4\frac{3}{4}$	384
		Atlanta	1	65
		Vancouver	$2\frac{3}{4}$	216
		Detroit	$2\frac{1}{2}$	183
		Total	**15**	**1,052**
54.	Eddie Shack	NY Rangers	$2\frac{1}{4}$	141
		Toronto	$8\frac{3}{4}$	504
		Boston	2	120
		Los Angeles	$1\frac{1}{4}$	84
		Buffalo	$1\frac{1}{2}$	111
		Pittsburgh	$1\frac{1}{4}$	87
		Total	**17**	**1,047**
55.	Serge Savard	Montreal	15	917
		Winnipeg	2	123
		Total	**17**	**1,040**
56.	Ron Ellis	**Toronto**	**16**	**1,034**
57.	Ralph Backstrom	Montreal	$14\frac{1}{2}$	844
		Los Angeles	$2\frac{1}{4}$	172
		Chicago	$\frac{1}{4}$	16
		Total	**17**	**1,032**
58.	Dick Duff	Toronto	$9\frac{3}{4}$	582
		NY Rangers	$\frac{3}{4}$	43
		Montreal	5	305
		Los Angeles	$\frac{3}{4}$	39
		Buffalo	$1\frac{3}{4}$	61
		Total	**18**	**1,030**
59.	Wayne Cashman	**Boston**	**17**	**1,027**
60.	Jim Neilson	NY Rangers	12	810
		California	2	98
		Cleveland	2	115
		Total	**16**	**1,023**
61.	Don Lever	Vancouver	$7\frac{2}{3}$	593
		Atlanta	$\frac{1}{3}$	28
		Calgary	$1\frac{1}{4}$	85
		Colorado	$\frac{3}{4}$	59
		New Jersey	3	216
		Buffalo	2	39
		Total	**15**	**1,020**
62.	Phil Russell	Chicago	$6\frac{3}{4}$	504
		Atlanta	$1\frac{1}{4}$	93
		Calgary	3	229
		New Jersey	$2\frac{3}{4}$	172
		Buffalo	$1\frac{1}{4}$	18
		Total	**15**	**1,016**
63.	Dave Lewis	NY Islanders	$6\frac{3}{4}$	514
		Los Angeles	$3\frac{1}{4}$	221
		New Jersey	3	209
		Detroit	2	64
		Total	**15**	**1,008**
* 64.	Bob Murray	**Chicago**	**15**	**1,008**
65.	Jim Roberts	Montreal	$9\frac{2}{3}$	611
		St. Louis	$5\frac{1}{3}$	395
		Total	**15**	**1,006**
66.	Claude Provost	**Montreal**	**15**	**1,005**
67.	Rick Middleton	NY Rangers	2	124
		Boston	12	881
		Total	**14**	**1,005**
68.	Vic Hadfield	NY Rangers	13	839
		Pittsburgh	3	163
		Total	**16**	**1,002**
* 69.	Bernie Federko	St. Louis	14	927
		Detroit	1	73
		Total	**15**	**1,000**

Goaltending Records

* active player

All-Time Shutout Leaders

Goaltender	Team	Seasons	Games	Shutouts
Terry Sawchuk	Detroit	14	734	85
(1949-1970)	Boston	2	102	11
	Toronto	3	91	4
	Los Angeles	1	36	2
	NY Rangers	1	8	1
	Total	21	971	**103**
George Hainsworth	Montreal	7$\frac{1}{2}$	318	75
(1926-1937)	Toronto	3$\frac{1}{2}$	146	19
	Total	11	464	**94**
Glenn Hall	Detroit	4	148	17
(1952-1971)	Chicago	10	618	51
	St. Louis	4	140	16
	Total	18	906	**84**
Jacques Plante	Montreal	11	556	58
(1952-1973)	NY Rangers	2	98	5
	St. Louis	2	69	10
	Toronto	2$\frac{3}{4}$	106	7
	Boston	$\frac{1}{4}$	8	2
	Total	18	837	**82**
Tiny Thompson	Boston	10$\frac{1}{4}$	468	74
(1928-1940)	Detroit	1$\frac{3}{4}$	85	7
	Total	12	553	**81**
Alex Connell	Ottawa	8	293	64
(1925-1937)	Detroit	1	48	6
	NY Americans	1	1	0
	Mtl. Maroons	2	75	11
	Total	12	417	**81**
Tony Esposito	Montreal	1	13	2
(1968-1984)	Chicago	15	873	74
	Total	16	886	**76**
Lorne Chabot	NY Rangers	2	80	21
(1926-1937)	Toronto	5	214	33
	Montreal	1	47	8
	Chicago	1	48	8
	Mtl. Maroons	1	16	2
	NY Americans	1	6	1
	Total	11	411	**73**
Harry Lumley	Detroit	6$\frac{1}{2}$	324	26
(1943-1960)	NY Rangers	$\frac{1}{2}$	1	0
	Chicago	2	134	5
	Toronto	4	267	34
	Boston	3	78	6
	Total	16	804	**71**
Roy Worters	Pittsburgh Pirates	3	123	22
(1925-1937)	NY Americans	9	360	44
	*Montreal		1	0
	Total	12	484	**66**
Turk Broda	Toronto	14	629	**62**
(1936-1952)				
John Roach	Toronto	7	223	13
(1921-1935)	NY Rangers	4	89	30
	Detroit	3	180	15
	Total	14	492	**58**

Goaltender	Team	Seasons	Games	Shutouts
Clint Benedict	Ottawa	7	158	19
(1917-1930)	Mtl. Maroons	6	204	38
	Total	13	362	**57**
Bernie Parent	Boston	2	57	1
(1965-1979)	Philadelphia	9$\frac{1}{2}$	486	50
	Toronto	1$\frac{1}{2}$	65	4
	Total	13	608	**55**
Ed Giacomin	NY Rangers	10$\frac{1}{4}$	539	49
(1965-1978)	Detroit	2$\frac{3}{4}$	71	5
	Total	13	610	**54**
David Kerr	Mtl. Maroons	3	101	11
(1930-1941)	NY Americans	1	1	0
	NY Rangers	7	324	40
	Total	11	426	**51**
Rogie Vachon	Montreal	5$\frac{1}{4}$	206	13
(1966-1982)	Los Angeles	6$\frac{3}{4}$	389	32
	Detroit	2	109	4
	Boston	2	91	2
	Total	16	795	**51**
Ken Dryden	Montreal	8	397	**46**
(1970-1979)				
Gump Worsley	NY Rangers	10	583	24
(1952-1974)	Montreal	6$\frac{1}{2}$	172	16
	Minnesota	4$\frac{1}{2}$	107	3
	Total	21	862	**43**
Chuck Gardiner	Chicago	7	316	**42**
(1927-1934)				
Frank Brimsek	Boston	9	444	35
(1938-1950)	Chicago	1	70	5
	Total	10	514	**40**
Johnny Bower	NY Rangers	3	77	5
(1953-1970)	Toronto	12	475	32
	Total	15	552	**37**
Bill Durnan	Montreal	7	383	**34**
(1943-1950)				
Eddie Johnston	Boston	11	444	27
(1962-1978)	Toronto	1	26	1
	St. Louis	3$\frac{2}{3}$	118	4
	Chicago	$\frac{1}{3}$	4	0
	Total	16	592	**32**
Roger Crozier	Detroit	7	313	20
(1963-1977)	Buffalo	6	202	10
	Washington	1	3	0
	Total	14	518	**30**
Cesare Maniago	Toronto	1	7	0
(1960-1978)	Montreal	1	14	0
	NY Rangers	2	34	2
	Minnesota	9	420	26
	Vancouver	2	93	2
	Total	15	568	**30**

*Played 1 game for Canadiens in 1929-30.

Ten or More Shutouts, One Season

Number of Shutouts	Goaltender	Team	Season	Length of Schedule
22	George Hainsworth	Montreal	1928-29	44
15	Alex Connell	Ottawa	1925-26	36
	Alex Connell	Ottawa	1927-28	44
	Hal Winkler	Boston	1927-28	44
	Tony Esposito	Chicago	1969-70	76
14	George Hainsworth	Montreal	1926-27	44
13	Clint Benedict	Mtl. Maroons	1926-27	44
	Alex Connell	Ottawa	1926-27	44
	George Hainsworth	Montreal	1927-28	44
	Roy Worters	NY Americans	1927-28	44
	John Roach	NY Rangers	1928-29	44
	Roy Worters	NY Americans	1928-29	44
	Harry Lumley	Toronto	1953-54	70
12	Tiny Thompson	Boston	1928-29	44
	Lorne Chabot	Toronto	1928-29	44
	Chuck Gardiner	Chicago	1930-31	44
	Terry Sawchuk	Detroit	1951-52	70
	Terry Sawchuk	Detroit	1953-54	70
	Terry Sawchuk	Detroit	1954-55	70
	Glenn Hall	Detroit	1955-56	70
	Bernie Parent	Philadelphia	1973-74	78
	Bernie Parent	Philadelphia	1974-75	80
11	Lorne Chabot	NY Rangers	1927-28	44
	Harry Holmes	Detroit	1927-28	44
	Clint Benedict	Mtl. Maroons	1928-29	44
	Joe Miller	Pittsburgh Pirates	1928-29	44
	Tiny Thompson	Boston	1932-33	48
	Terry Sawchuk	Detroit	1950-51	70
10	Lorne Chabot	NY Rangers	1926-27	44
	Roy Worters	Pittsburgh Pirates	1927-28	44
	Clarence Dolson	Detroit	1928-29	44
	John Roach	Detroit	1932-33	48
	Chuck Gardiner	Chicago	1933-34	48
	Tiny Thompson	Boston	1935-36	48
	Frank Brimsek	Boston	1938-39	48
	Bill Durnan	Montreal	1948-49	60
	Gerry McNeil	Montreal	1952-53	70
	Harry Lumley	Toronto	1952-53	70
	Tony Esposito	Chicago	1973-74	78
	Ken Dryden	Montreal	1976-77	80

All-Time Win Leaders

(Minimum 200 Wins)

Wins	Goaltender	GP	Decisions	Mins.	Losses	Ties	%
435	Terry Sawchuk	971	960	57,154	337	188	.551
434	Jacques Plante	837	817	49,553	246	137	.615
423	Tony Esposito	886	881	52,585	307	151	.566
407	Glenn Hall	906	899	53,484	327	165	.544
355	Rogie Vachon	795	761	46,298	291	115	.542
335	Gump Worsley	862	838	50,232	353	150	.489
332	Harry Lumley	804	799	48,097	324	143	.505
305	Billy Smith	680	643	38,431	233	105	.556
302	Turk Broda	629	627	38,173	224	101	.562
289	Ed Giacomin	610	592	35,693	206	97	.570
286	Dan Bouchard	655	631	37,919	232	113	.543
284	Tiny Thompson	553	553	34,174	194	75	.581
270	Bernie Parent	608	588	35,136	197	121	.562
270	*Mike Liut	607	587	35,198	248	69	.519
270	Gilles Meloche	788	752	45,401	351	131	.446
258	Ken Dryden	397	389	23,352	57	74	.758
252	Frank Brimsek	514	514	31,210	182	80	.568
251	Johnny Bower	549	537	32,016	196	90	.551
247	George Hainsworth	464	467	29,415	146	74	.608
237	*Pete Peeters	463	435	26,429	148	50	.602
236	Eddie Johnston	592	579	34,209	256	87	.483
231	Glenn Resch	571	537	32,279	224	82	.507
230	Gerry Cheevers	418	398	24,394	94	74	.671
220	*Grant Fuhr	410	384	23,132	113	51	.639
218	John Roach	491	491	30,423	204	69	.514
212	*Greg Millen	591	579	34,832	281	86	.440
209	*Rejean Lemelin	456	406	25,228	137	60	.589
208	Bill Durnan	383	382	22,945	112	62	.626
208	Don Edwards	459	440	26,181	155	77	.560
206	Lorne Chabot	411	411	25,309	140	65	.580
206	Roger Crozier	518	477	28,566	197	74	.509
203	David Kerr	426	426	26,519	148	75	.565

* Active player

Active Shutout Leaders

Goaltender	Teams	Seasons	Games	Shutouts
Mike Liut	St. L., Hfd., Wsh.	11	607	24
Pete Peeters	Phi., Bos., Wsh.	12	463	20
Greg Millen	Pit., Hfd., St. L., Que., Chi.	12	591	17
Bob Froese	Philadelphia, NY Rangers	8	242	13
Tom Barrasso	Buffalo, Pittsburgh	7	334	13
Glen Hanlon	Van., St. L., NYR, Det.	13	458	13
Patrick Roy	Montreal	5	241	12
Rick Wamsley	Mtl., St. L., Cgy.	10	358	12
Clint Malarchuk	Que., Wsh., Buf.	8	272	11
Rejean Lemelin	Atl., Cgy., Bos.	12	456	11
Kelly Hrudey	NY Islanders, Los Angeles	7	309	9
Andy Moog	Edmonton, Boston	10	328	9
Grant Fuhr	Edmonton	9	410	8

Active Goaltending Leaders

(Ranked by winning percentage; minimum 250 games played)

Goaltender	Teams	Seasons	GP	Decisions	W	L	T	Winning %
Andy Moog	Edmonton, Boston	10	328	304	189	79	36	.681
Grant Fuhr	Edmonton	9	410	384	220	113	51	.639
Pete Peeters	Phi., Bos., Wsh.	12	463	435	237	148	50	.602
Rick Wamsley	Mtl., St. L., Cgy.	10	358	338	183	114	41	.602
Rejean Lemelin	Atl., Cgy., Bos.	12	456	406	209	137	60	.589
Rollie Melanson	NYI, L.A.	9	281	260	124	103	33	.540
Kelly Hrudey	NY Islanders, Los Angeles	7	309	287	138	115	34	.540
Tom Barrasso	Buffalo, Pittsburgh	7	334	316	149	129	38	.532
Clint Malarchuk	Que., Wsh., Buf.	8	272	254	119	103	32	.531
Brian Hayward	Winnipeg, Montreal	8	306	290	134	123	33	.519
Mike Liut	St. L., Hfd., Wsh.	11	607	587	270	248	69	.519
J. Vanbiesbrouck	NY Rangers	8	316	297	138	128	31	.517
Don Beaupre	Minnesota, Washington	10	375	351	154	147	50	.510
Steve Weeks	NYR, Hfd., Van.	10	253	239	102	106	31	.492
Greg Stefan	Detroit	9	299	272	115	127	30	.478
Glen Hanlon	Van., St. L., NYR, Det.	13	458	417	163	196	58	.460
Greg Millen	Pit., Hfd., St. L., Que., Chi.	12	591	579	212	281	86	.440
Ken Wregget	Philadelphia, Toronto	7	254	235	78	137	20	.374

Goals Against Average Leaders

(minimum 25 games played, 1926–27 to date; 15 games, 1917–18 to 1925–26)

Season	Goaltender and Club	GP	Mins.	GA	SO	AVG.
1989-90	Patrick Roy, Montreal	54	3,173	134	3	2.53
	Mike Liut, Hartford, Washington	37	2,161	91	4	2.53
1988-89	Patrick Roy, Montreal	48	2,744	113	4	2.47
1987-88	Pete Peeters, Washington	35	1,896	88	2	2.78
1986-87	Brian Hayward, Montreal	37	2,178	102	1	2.81
1985-86	Bob Froese, Philadelphia	51	2,728	116	5	2.55
1984-85	Tom Barrasso, Buffalo	54	3,248	144	5	2.66
1983-84	Pat Riggin, Washington	41	2,299	102	4	2.66
1982-83	Pete Peeters, Boston	62	3,611	142	8	2.36
1981-82	Denis Herron, Montreal	27	1,547	68	3	2.64
1980-81	Richard Sevigny, Montreal	33	1,777	71	2	2.40
1979-80	Bob Sauve, Buffalo	32	1,880	74	4	2.36
1978-79	Ken Dryden, Montreal	47	2,814	108	5	2.30
1977-78	Ken Dryden, Montreal	52	3,071	105	5	2.05
1976-77	Michel Larocque, Montreal	26	1,525	53	4	2.09
1975-76	Ken Dryden, Montreal	62	3,580	121	8	2.03
1974-75	Bernie Parent, Philadelphia	68	4,041	137	12	2.03
1973-74	Bernie Parent, Philadelphia	73	4,314	136	12	1.89
1972-73	Ken Dryden, Montreal	54	3,165	119	6	2.26
1971-72	Tony Esposito, Chicago	48	2,780	82	9	1.77
1970-71	Jacques Plante, Toronto	40	2,329	73	4	1.88
1969-70	Ernie Wakely, St. Louis	30	1,651	58	4	2.11
1968-69	Jacques Plante, St. Louis	37	2,139	70	5	1.96
1967-68	Lorne Worsley, Montreal	40	2,213	73	6	1.98
1966-67	Glenn Hall, Chicago	32	1,664	66	2	2.38
1965-66	Johnny Bower, Toronto	35	1,998	75	3	2.25
1964-65	Johnny Bower, Toronto	34	2,040	81	3	2.38
1963-64	Johnny Bower, Toronto	51	3,009	106	5	2.11
1962-63	Jacques Plante, Montreal	56	3,320	138	5	2.49
1961-62	Jacques Plante, Montreal	70	4,200	166	4	2.37
1960-61	Johnny Bower, Toronto	58	3,480	145	2	2.50
1959-60	Jacques Plante, Montreal	69	4,140	175	3	2.54
1958-59	Jacques Plante, Montreal	67	4,000	144	9	2.16
1957-58	Jacques Plante, Montreal	57	3,386	119	9	2.11
1956-57	Jacques Plante, Montreal	61	3,660	123	9	2.02
1955-56	Jacques Plante, Montreal	64	3,840	119	7	1.86
1954-55	Harry Lumley, Toronto	69	4,140	134	8	1.94
	Terry Sawchuk, Detroit	68	4,080	132	12	1.94

Season	Goaltender and Club	GP	Mins.	GA	SO	AVG.
1953-54	Harry Lumley, Toronto	69	4,140	128	13	1.86
1952-53	Terry Sawchuk, Detroit	63	3,780	120	9	1.90
1951-52	Terry Sawchuk, Detroit	70	4,200	133	12	1.90
1950-51	Al Rollins, Toronto	40	2,367	70	5	1.77
1949-50	Bill Durnan, Montreal	64	3,840	141	8	2.20
1948-49	Bill Durnan, Montreal	60	3,600	126	10	2.10
1947-48	Turk Broda, Toronto	60	3,600	143	5	2.38
1946-47	Bill Durnan, Montreal	60	3,600	138	4	2.30
1945-46	Bill Durnan, Montreal	40	2,400	104	4	2.60
1944-45	Bill Durnan, Montreal	50	3,000	121	1	2.42
1943-44	Bill Durnan, Montreal	50	3,000	109	2	2.18
1942-43	Johnny Mowers, Detroit	50	3,010	124	6	2.47
1941-42	Frank Brimsek, Boston	47	2,930	115	3	2.35
1940-41	Turk Broda, Toronto	48	2,970	99	5	2.00
1939-40	Dave Kerr, NY Rangers	48	3,000	77	8	1.54
1938-39	Frank Brimsek, Boston	43	2,610	68	10	1.56
1937-38	Tiny Thompson, Boston	48	2,970	89	7	1.80
1936-37	Normie Smith, Detroit	48	2,980	102	6	2.05
1935-36	Tiny Thompson, Boston	48	2,930	82	10	1.68
1934-35	Lorne Chabot, Chicago	48	2,940	88	8	1.80
1933-34	Wilf Cude, Detroit, Montreal	30	1,920	47	5	1.47
1932-33	Tiny Thompson, Boston	48	3,000	88	11	1.76
1931-32	Chuck Gardiner, Chicago	48	2,989	92	4	1.85
1930-31	Roy Worters, NY Americans	44	2,760	74	8	1.61
1929-30	Tiny Thompson, Boston	44	2,680	98	3	2.19
1928-29	George Hainsworth, Montreal	44	2,800	43	22	0.92
1927-28	George Hainsworth, Montreal	44	2,730	48	13	1.05
1926-27	Clint Benedict, Mtl. Maroons	43	2,748	65	13	1.42
1925-26	Alex Connell, Ottawa	36	2,231	42	15	1.13
1924-25	Georges Vezina, Montreal	30	1,860	56	5	1.81
1923-24	Georges Vezina, Montreal	24	1,459	48	3	1.97
1922-23	Clint Benedict, Ottawa	24	1,486	54	4	2.18
1921-22	Clint Benedict, Ottawa	24	1,508	84	2	3.34
1920-21	Clint Benedict, Ottawa	24	1,457	75	2	3.09
1919-20	Clint Benedict, Ottawa	24	1,443	64	5	2.66
1918-19	Clint Benedict, Ottawa	18	1,113	53	2	2.86
1917-18	Georges Vezina, Montreal	22	1,282	84	1	3.93

Coaching Records

(Minimum 600 regular-season games. Ranked by number of games coached.)

Coach	Team	Seasons	Games	Wins	Losses	Ties	%*
Dick Irvin	Chicago	1930-31; 55-56	114	43	56	15	.443
	Toronto	1931-40	427	216	152	59	.575
	Montreal	1940-55	896	431	313	152	.566
	Total		**1,437**	**690**	**521**	**226**	**.559**
Al Arbour	St. Louis	1970-73	107	42	40	25	.509
	NY Islanders	1973-86; 88-90	1,171	604	384	183	.594
	Total		**1,278**	**646**	**424**	**208**	**.587**
Scott Bowman	St. Louis	1967-71	238	110	83	45	.557
	Montreal	1971-79	634	419	110	105	.744
	Buffalo	1979-87	404	210	134	60	.594
	Total		**1,276**	**739**	**327**	**210**	**.661**
Billy Reay	Toronto	1957-59	90	26	50	14	.367
	Chicago	1963-77	1,012	516	335	161	.589
	Total		**1,102**	**542**	**385**	**175**	**.571**
Jack Adams	Detroit	1927-44	**964**	**413**	**390**	**161**	**.512**
Sid Abel	Chicago	1952-54	140	39	79	22	.357
	Detroit	1957-68; 69-70	810	340	338	132	.501
	St. Louis	1971-72	10	3	6	1	.350
	Kansas City	1975-76	3	0	3	0	.000
	Total		**963**	**382**	**426**	**155**	**.477**
Punch Imlach	Toronto	1958-69; 79-81	840	391	311	138	.548
	Buffalo	1970-72	119	32	62	25	.374
	Total		**959**	**423**	**373**	**163**	**.526**
Toe Blake	Montreal	1955-68	**914**	**500**	**255**	**159**	**.634**
Michel Bergeron	Quebec	1980-87; 89-90	634	265	283	86	.486
	NY Rangers	1987-89	158	73	67	18	.519
	Total		**792**	**338**	**350**	**104**	**.492**
Glen Sather	Edmonton	1979-89	**782**	**442**	**241**	**99**	**.629**
Emile Francis	NY Rangers	1965-75	654	347	209	98	.606
	St. Louis	1976-77, 81-83	124	46	64	14	.427
	Total		**778**	**393**	**273**	**112**	**.577**
Bob Pulford	Los Angeles	1972-77	396	178	150	68	.535
	Chicago	1977-79 1981-82; 84-87	375	158	155	62	.504
	Total		**771**	**336**	**305**	**130**	**.520**
Milt Schmidt	Boston	1954-61; 62-66	726	245	360	121	.421
	Washington	1974-76	43	5	33	5	.174
	Total		**769**	**250**	**393**	**126**	**.407**
Red Kelly	Los Angeles	1967-69	150	55	75	20	.433
	Pittsburgh	1969-73	274	90	132	52	.423
	Toronto	1973-77	318	133	123	62	.516
	Total		**742**	**278**	**330**	**134**	**465**
Fred Shero	Philadelphia	1971-78	554	308	151	95	.642
	NY Rangers	1978-81	180	82	74	24	.522
	Total		**734**	**390**	**225**	**119**	**.612**
Art Ross	Boston	1924-45	**728**	**361**	**277**	**90**	**.558**
Bob Berry	Los Angeles	1978-81	240	107	94	39	.527
	Montreal	1981-84	223	116	71	36	.601
	Pittsburgh	1984-87	240	88	127	25	.419
	Total		**703**	**311**	**292**	**100**	**.514**
Bryan Murray	Washington	1981-90	**672**	**343**	**246**	**83**	**.572**
Jacques Demers	Quebec	1979-80	80	25	44	11	.381
	St. Louis	1983-86	240	106	106	28	.500
	Detroit	1986-90	320	137	136	47	.502
	Total		**640**	**268**	**286**	**86**	**.486**
Jack Evans	California	1975-76	80	27	42	11	.406
	Cleveland	1976-78	160	47	87	26	.375
	Hartford	1983-88	374	163	174	37	.485
	Total		**614**	**237**	**303**	**74**	**.446**
Tommy Ivan	Detroit	1947-54	470	262	118	90	.653
	Chicago	1956-58	140	40	78	22	.364
	Total		**610**	**302**	**196**	**112**	**.587**
Lester Patrick	NY Rangers	1926-39	**604**	**281**	**216**	**107**	**.554**

* % arrived at by dividing possible points into actual points.

Emile Francis registered 393 wins as coach of the Rangers and St. Louis.

All-Time Penalty-Minute Leaders

* active player

(Regular season. Minimum 1,500 minutes)

Player	Teams	Seasons	Games	Penalty Minutes	Mins. per game
Dave Williams,	Tor., Van., Det., L.A., Hfd.	14	962	**3,966**	4.12
Willi Plett,	Atl., Cgy., Minn., Bos.	12	834	**2,572**	3.08
***Chris Nilan,**	Mtl., NYR	11	591	**2,506**	4.24
Dave Schultz,	Phi., L.A., Pit., Buf.	9	535	**2,294**	4.29
***Dale Hunter,**	Que., Wsh.	9	762	**2,237**	2.94
Bryan Watson,	Mtl., Det., Cal., Pit., St. L., Wsh.	16	878	**2,212**	2.52
***Tim Hunter,**	Calgary	8	481	**2,095**	4.36
Terry O'Reilly,	Boston	14	891	**2,095**	2.35
***Al Secord,**	Chi., Tor., Phi.	11	766	**2,093**	2.73
Phil Russell,	Chi., Atl., Cgy., N.J., Buf.	15	1,016	**2,038**	2.01
Andre Dupont,	NYR, St. L., Phi., Que.	13	810	**1,986**	2.45
***Laurie Boschman,**	Tor., Edm., Wpg.	11	786	**1,964**	2.50
***Harold Snepsts,**	Van., Min., Det., St. L.	16	979	**1,959**	2.00
Garry Howatt,	NYI, Hfd., N.J.	12	720	**1,836**	2.55
***Rob Ramage,**	Col., St. L., Cgy., Tor.	11	835	**1,822**	2.18
Carol Vadnais,	Mtl., Oak., Cal., Bos., NYR, N.J.	17	1,087	**1,813**	1.67
***Larry Playfair,**	Buf., L.A.	11	688	**1,812**	2.63
Ted Lindsay,	Det., Chi.	17	1,068	**1,808**	1.69
***Jim Korn,**	Det., Tor., Buf., N.J., Cgy.	10	597	**1,801**	3.02
Brian Sutter,	St. L.	12	779	**1,786**	2.29
***Jay Wells,**	L.A., Phi., Buf.	11	731	**1,759**	2.41
Wilf Paiment,	K.C., Col., Tor., Que., NYR, Buf., Pit.	14	946	**1,757**	1.86
***Mike Foligno,**	Det., Buf.	11	819	**1,755**	2.14
***Torrie Robertson,**	Wsh., Hfd., Det.	9	442	**1,751**	3.96
Gordie Howe,	Det., Hfd.	26	1,767	**1,685**	0.95
Paul Holmgren,	Phi., Min.	9	527	**1,684**	3.20
***Ken Linseman,**	Phi., Edm., Bos.	12	802	**1,631**	2.03
Jerry Korab,	Chi., Van., Buf., L.A.	15	975	**1,629**	1.67
***Scott Stevens,**	Wsh.	8	601	**1,628**	2.71
***Mel Bridgman,**	Phi., Cgy., N.J., Det., Van.	14	977	**1,625**	1.66
***Kevin McClelland,**	Pit., Edm., Det.	9	561	**1,613**	2.88
Tim Horton,	Tor., NYR, Pit., Buf.	24	1,446	**1,611**	1.11
***Mario Marois,**	NYR, Van., Que., Win.	13	840	**1,593**	1.90
***Basil McRae,**	Que., Tor., Det., Min.	9	343	**1,592**	4.64
Paul Baxter,	Que., Pit., Cgy.	8	472	**1,564**	3.31
***Marty McSorley,**	Pit., Edm., L.A.	7	388	**1,558**	4.02
***Glen Cochrane,**	Phi., Van., Chi., Edm.	9	411	**1,556**	3.79
Mike Milbury,	Boston	12	754	**1,552**	2.06
Dave Hutchison,	L.A., Tor., Chi., N.J.	10	584	**1,550**	2.65
Doug Risebrough,	Mtl., Cal.	13	740	**1,542**	2.08
Bill Gadsby,	Chi., NYR, Det.	20	1,248	**1,539**	1.23

One Season Scoring Records

Goals-Per-Game Leaders, One Season

(Among players with 20 goals or more in one season)

Player	Team	Season	Games	Goals	Average
Joe Malone	Montreal	1917-18	20	44	2.20
Cy Denneny	Ottawa	1917-18	22	36	1.64
Newsy Lalonde	Montreal	1917-18	14	23	1.64
Joe Malone	Quebec	1919-20	24	39	1.63
Newsy Lalonde	Montreal	1919-20	23	36	1.57
Joe Malone	Hamilton	1920-21	20	30	1.50
Babe Dye	Ham., Tor.	1920-21	24	35	1.46
Cy Denneny	Ottawa	1920-21	24	34	1.42
Reg Noble	Toronto	1917-18	20	28	1.40
Newsy Lalonde	Montreal	1920-21	24	33	1.38
Odie Cleghorn	Montreal	1918-19	17	23	1.35
Harry Broadbent	Ottawa	1921-22	24	32	1.33
Babe Dye	Toronto	1924-25	29	38	1.31
Babe Dye	Toronto	1921-22	24	30	1.25
Newsy Lalonde	Montreal	1918-19	17	21	1.24
Cy Denneny	Ottawa	1921-22	22	27	1.23
Aurel Joliat	Montreal	1924-25	24	29	1.21
Wayne Gretzky	Edmonton	1983-84	74	87	1.18
Babe Dye	Toronto	1922-23	22	26	1.18
Wayne Gretzky	Edmonton	1981-82	80	92	1.15
Frank Nighbor	Ottawa	1919-20	23	26	1.13
Mario Lemieux	Pittsburgh	1988-89	76	85	1.12
Amos Arbour	Montreal	1919-20	20	22	1.10
Cy Denneny	Ottawa	1923-24	21	22	1.05
Joe Malone	Hamilton	1921-22	24	25	1.04
Billy Boucher	Montreal	1922-23	24	25	1.04
Maurice Richard	Montreal	1944-45	50	50	1.00
Howie Morenz	Montreal	1924-25	30	30	1.00
Reg Noble	Toronto	1919-20	24	24	1.00
Corbett Denneny	Toronto	1919-20	23	23	1.00
Jack Darragh	Ottawa	1919-20	22	22	1.00
Cooney Weiland	Boston	1929-30	44	43	.98
Phil Esposito	Boston	1970-71	78	76	.97
Jari Kurri	Edmonton	1984-85	73	71	.97

Assists-Per-Game Leaders, One Season

(Among players with 35 assists or more in one season)

Player	Team	Season	Games	Assists	Average
Wayne Gretzky	Edmonton	1985-86	80	163	2.04
Wayne Gretzky	Edmonton	1987-88	64	109	1.70
Wayne Gretzky	Edmonton	1984-85	80	135	1.69
Wayne Gretzky	Edmonton	1983-84	74	118	1.59
Wayne Gretzky	Edmonton	1982-83	80	125	1.56
Wayne Gretzky	Edmonton	1986-87	79	121	1.53
Wayne Gretzky	Edmonton	1981-82	80	120	1.50
Mario Lemieux	Pittsburgh	1988-89	76	114	1.50
Wayne Gretzky	Los Angeles	1988-89	78	114	1.46
Wayne Gretzky	Los Angeles	1989-90	73	102	1.40
Wayne Gretzky	Edmonton	1980-81	80	109	1.36
Mario Lemieux	Pittsburgh	1989-90	59	78	1.32
Bobby Orr	Boston	1970-71	78	102	1.31
Mario Lemieux	Pittsburgh	1987-88	77	98	1.27
Bobby Orr	Boston	1973-74	74	90	1.22
Mario Lemieux	Pittsburgh	1985-86	79	93	1.18
Bobby Clarke	Philadelphia	1975-76	76	89	1.17
Peter Stastny	Quebec	1981-82	80	93	1.16
Paul Coffey	Edmonton	1985-86	79	90	1.14
Bobby Orr	Boston	1969-70	76	87	1.14
Bryan Trottier	NY Islanders	1978-79	76	87	1.14
Bobby Orr	Boston	1972-73	63	72	1.14
Bill Cowley	Boston	1943-44	36	41	1.14
Steve Yzerman	Detroit	1988-89	80	90	1.13
Paul Coffey	Pittsburgh	1987-88	46	52	1.13
Bobby Orr	Boston	1974-75	80	89	1.11
Bobby Clarke	Philadelphia	1974-75	80	89	1.11
Paul Coffey	Pittsburgh	1988-89	75	83	1.11
Denis Savard	Chicago	1982-83	78	86	1.10
Denis Savard	Chicago	1981-82	80	87	1.09
Denis Savard	Chicago	1987-88	80	87	1.09
Wayne Gretzky	Edmonton	1979-80	79	86	1.09
Paul Coffey	Edmonton	1983-84	80	86	1.08
Elmer Lach	Montreal	1944-45	50	54	1.08
Peter Stastny	Quebec	1985-86	76	81	1.07
Mark Messier	Edmonton	1989-90	79	84	1.06
Paul Coffey	Edmonton	1984-85	80	84	1.05
Marcel Dionne	Los Angeles	1979-80	80	84	1.05
Bobby Orr	Boston	1971-72	76	80	1.05
Mike Bossy	NY Islanders	1981-82	80	83	1.04
Phil Esposito	Boston	1968-69	74	77	1.04
Bryan Trottier	NY Islanders	1983-84	68	71	1.04
Pete Mahovlich	Montreal	1974-75	80	82	1.03
Kent Nilsson	Calgary	1980-81	80	82	1.03
Peter Stastny	Quebec	1982-83	75	77	1.03
Bernie Nicholls	Los Angeles	1988-89	79	80	1.01
Guy Lafleur	Montreal	1979-80	74	75	1.01
Guy Lafleur	Montreal	1976-77	80	80	1.00
Marcel Dionne	Los Angeles	1984-85	80	80	1.00
Bryan Trottier	NY Islanders	1977-78	77	77	1.00
Mike Bossy	NY Islanders	1983-84	67	67	1.00
Jean Ratelle	NY Rangers	1971-72	63	63	1.00
Ron Francis	Hartford	1985-86	53	53	1.00
Guy Chouinard	Calgary	1980-81	52	52	1.00
Elmer Lach	Montreal	1943-44	48	48	1.00

Penalty Leaders

* Match Misconduct penalty not included in total penalty minutes.
** Three Match Misconduct penalties not included in total penalty minutes.

1946-47 was the first season that a Match penalty was automatically written into the player's total penalty minutes as 20 minutes. Now all penalties, Match, Game Misconduct, and Misconduct, are written as 10 minutes. Penalty minutes not calculated in 1917-18.

Season	Player and Club	GP	PIM	Season	Player and Club	GP	PIM	Season	Player and Club	GP	PIM
1989-90	Basil McRae, Minnesota	66	351	1965-66	Reg Fleming, Bos., NYR	69	166	1941-42	Jimmy Orlando, Detroit	48	81**
1988-89	Tim Hunter, Calgary	75	375	1964-65	Carl Brewer, Toronto	70	177	1940-41	Jimmy Orlando, Detroit	48	99
1987-88	Bob Probert, Detroit	74	398	1963-64	Vic Hadfield, NY Rangers	69	151	1939-40	Red Horner, Toronto	30	87
1986-87	Tim Hunter, Calgary	73	361	1962-63	Howie Young, Detroit	64	273	1938-39	Red Horner, Toronto	48	85
1985-86	Joey Kocur, Detroit	59	377	1961-62	Lou Fontinato, Montreal	54	167	1937-38	Red Horner, Toronto	47	82*
1984-85	Chris Nilan, Montreal	77	358	1960-61	Pierre Pilote, Chicago	70	165	1936-37	Red Horner, Toronto	48	124
1983-84	Chris Nilan, Montreal	76	338	1959-60	Carl Brewer, Toronto	67	150	1935-36	Red Horner, Toronto	43	167
1982-83	Randy Holt, Washington	70	275	1958-59	Ted Lindsay, Chicago	70	184	1934-35	Red Horner, Toronto	46	125
1981-82	Paul Baxter, Pittsburgh	76	409	1957-58	Lou Fontinato, NY Rangers	70	152	1933-34	Red Horner, Toronto	42	126*
1980-81	Dave Williams, Vancouver	77	343	1956-57	Gus Mortson, Chicago	70	147	1932-33	Red Horner, Toronto	48	144
1979-80	Jimmy Mann, Winnipeg	72	287	1955-56	Lou Fontinato, NY Rangers	70	202	1931-32	Red Dutton, NY Americans	47	107
1978-79	Dave Williams, Toronto	77	298	1954-55	Fern Flaman, Boston	70	150	1930-31	Harvey Rockburn, Detroit	42	118
1977-78	Dave Schultz, L.A., Pit.	74	405	1953-54	Gus Mortson, Chicago	68	132	1929-30	Joe Lamb, Ottawa	44	119
1976-77	Dave Williams, Toronto	77	338	1952-53	Maurice Richard, Montreal	70	112	1928-29	Red Dutton, Mtl. Maroons	44	139
1975-76	Steve Durbano, Pit., K.C.	69	370	1951-52	Gus Kyle, Boston	69	127	1927-28	Eddie Shore, Boston	44	165
1974-75	Dave Schultz, Philadelphia	76	472	1950-51	Gus Mortson, Toronto	60	142	1926-27	Nels Stewart, Mtl. Maroons	44	133
1973-74	Dave Schultz, Philadelphia	73	348	1949-50	Bill Ezinicki, Toronto	67	144	1925-26	Bert Corbeau, Toronto	36	121
1972-73	Dave Schultz, Philadelphia	76	259	1948-49	Bill Ezinicki, Toronto	52	145	1924-25	Billy Boucher, Montreal	30	92
1971-72	Bryan Watson, Pittsburgh	75	212	1947-48	Bill Barilko, Toronto	57	147	1923-24	Bert Corbeau, Toronto	24	55
1970-71	Keith Magnuson, Chicago	76	291	1946-47	Gus Mortson, Toronto	60	133	1922-23	Billy Boucher, Montreal	24	52
1969-70	Keith Magnuson, Chicago	76	213	1945-46	Jack Stewart, Detroit	47	73	1921-22	Sprague Cleghorn, Montreal	24	63
1968-69	Forbes Kennedy, Phi., Tor.	77	219	1944-45	Pat Egan, Boston	48	86	1920-21	Bert Corbeau, Montreal	24	86
1967-68	Barclay Plager, St. Louis	49	153	1943-44	Mike McMahon, Montreal	42	98	1919-20	Cully Wilson, Toronto	23	79
1966-67	John Ferguson, Montreal	67	177	1942-43	Jimmy Orlando, Detroit	40	89*	1918-19	Joe Hall, Montreal,	17	85

Points-Per-Game Leaders, One Season

(Among players with 50 points or more in one season)

Player	Team	Season	Games	Points	Average	Player	Team	Season	Games	Points	Average
Wayne Gretzky	Edmonton	1983-84	74	205	2.77	Guy Lafleur	Montreal	1977-78	78	132	1.69
Wayne Gretzky	Edmonton	1985-86	80	215	2.69	Guy Lafleur	Montreal	1979-80	74	125	1.69
Wayne Gretzky	Edmonton	1981-82	80	212	2.65	Rob Brown	Pittsburgh	1988-89	68	115	1.69
Mario Lemieux	Pittsburgh	1988-89	76	199	2.62	Jari Kurri	Edmonton	1985-86	78	131	1.68
Wayne Gretzky	Edmonton	1984-85	80	208	2.60	Phil Esposito	Boston	1972-73	78	130	1.67
Wayne Gretzky	Edmonton	1982-83	80	196	2.45	Cooney Weiland	Boston	1929-30	44	73	1.66
Wayne Gretzky	Edmonton	1987-88	64	149	2.33	Peter Stastny	Quebec	1982-83	75	124	1.65
Wayne Gretzky	Edmonton	1986-87	79	183	2.32	Bobby Orr	Boston	1973-74	74	122	1.65
Mario Lemieux	Pittsburgh	1987-88	77	168	2.18	Kent Nilsson	Calgary	1980-81	80	131	1.64
Wayne Gretzky	Los Angeles	1988-89	78	168	2.15	Marcel Dionne	Los Angeles	1978-79	80	130	1.63
Mario Lemieux	Pittsburgh	1989-90	59	123	2.08	Dale Hawerchuk	Winnipeg	1984-85	80	130	1.63
Wayne Gretzky	Edmonton	1980-81	80	164	2.05	Mark Messier	Edmonton	1989-90	79	129	1.63
Bill Cowley	Boston	1943-44	36	71	1.97	Bryan Trottier	NY Islanders	1983-84	68	111	1.63
Phil Esposito	Boston	1970-71	78	152	1.95	Charlie Simmer	Los Angeles	1980-81	65	105	1.62
Wayne Gretzky	Los Angeles	1989-90	73	142	1.95	Guy Lafleur	Montreal	1978-79	80	129	1.61
Steve Yzerman	Detroit	1988-89	80	155	1.94	Bryan Trottier	NY Islanders	1981-82	80	129	1.61
Bernie Nicholls	Los Angeles	1988-89	79	150	1.90	Phil Esposito	Boston	1974-75	79	127	1.61
Phil Esposito	Boston	1973-74	78	145	1.86	Steve Yzerman	Detroit	1989-90	79	127	1.61
Jari Kurri	Edmonton	1984-85	73	135	1.85	Peter Stastny	Quebec	1985-86	76	122	1.61
Mike Bossy	NY Islanders	1981-82	80	147	1.84	Michel Goulet	Quebec	1983-84	75	121	1.61
Mario Lemieux	Pittsburgh	1985-86	79	141	1.78	Bryan Trottier	NY Islanders	1977-78	77	123	1.60
Bobby Orr	Boston	1970-71	78	139	1.78	Bobby Orr	Boston	1972-73	63	101	1.60
Jari Kurri	Edmonton	1983-84	64	113	1.77	Guy Chouinard	Calgary	1980-81	52	83	1.60
Bryan Trottier	NY Islanders	1978-79	76	134	1.76	Elmer Lach	Montreal	1944-45	50	80	1.60
Mike Bossy	NY Islanders	1983-84	67	118	1.76	Steve Yzerman	Detroit	1987-88	64	102	1.59
Paul Coffey	Edmonton	1985-86	79	138	1.75	Mike Bossy	NY Islanders	1978-79	80	126	1.58
Phil Esposito	Boston	1971-72	76	133	1.75	Paul Coffey	Edmonton	1983-84	80	126	1.58
Peter Stastny	Quebec	1981-82	80	139	1.74	Marcel Dionne	Los Angeles	1984-85	80	126	1.58
Wayne Gretzky	Edmonton	1979-80	79	137	1.73	Bobby Orr	Boston	1969-70	76	120	1.58
Jean Ratelle	NY Rangers	1971-72	63	109	1.73	Charlie Simmer	Los Angeles	1979-80	64	101	1.58
Marcel Dionne	Los Angeles	1979-80	80	137	1.71	Bobby Clarke	Philadelphia	1975-76	76	119	1.57
Herb Cain	Boston	1943-44	48	82	1.71	Guy Lafleur	Montreal	1975-76	80	125	1.56
Guy Lafleur	Montreal	1976-77	80	136	1.70	Dave Taylor	Los Angeles	1980-81	72	112	1.56
Dennis Maruk	Washington	1981-82	80	136	1.70	Denis Savard	Chicago	1982-83	78	121	1.55
Phil Esposito	Boston	1968-69	74	126	1.70	Mike Bossy	NY Islanders	1985-86	80	123	1.54
Guy Lafleur	Montreal	1974-75	70	119	1.70	Bobby Orr	Boston	1971-72	76	117	1.54
Mario Lemieux	Pittsburgh	1986-87	63	107	1.70	Mike Bossy	NY Islanders	1984-85	76	117	1.54
Bobby Orr	Boston	1974-75	80	135	1.69	Doug Bentley	Chicago	1943-44	50	77	1.54
Marcel Dionne	Los Angeles	1980-81	80	135	1.69	Marcel Dionne	Los Angeles	1976-77	80	122	1.53
						Paul Coffey	Pittsburgh	1988-89	75	113	1.51

Mark Messier had a points-per-game average of 1.63 during the 1989-90 season.

Active NHL Players' Three-or-More-Goal Games

Regular Season

Teams named are the ones the players were with at the time of their multiple-scoring games. Players listed alphabetically.

Bryan Trottier had 16 three-or-more-goal games during his 15 years with the New York Islanders.

Player	Team	3-Goals	4-Goals	5-Goals
Acton, Keith	Mtl., Min.	3	—	—
Adams, Greg	Washington	1	1	—
Adams, Gregory C.	Vancouver	1	—	—
Allison, Mike	NY Rangers	1	—	—
Anderson, Glenn	Edmonton	17	3	—
Anderson, Perry	New Jersey	1	—	—
Andreychuk, Dave	Buffalo	5	—	1
Arniel, Scott	Winnipeg	1	—	—
Ashton, Brent	Que., Wpg.	6	—	—
Barber, Don	Minnesota	1	—	—
Barr, Dave	St. L., Det.	2	—	—
Bellows, Brian	Minnesota	3	1	—
Bjugstad, Scott	Minnesota	3	—	—
Boschman, Laurie	Winnipeg	2	—	—
Bourque, Raymond	Boston	2	—	—
Bozek, Steve	Los Angeles	1	—	—
Brickley, Andy	Pit., Bos.	2	—	—
Brooke, Bob	NY Rangers	1	—	—
Broten, Aaron	New Jersey	1	—	—
Broten, Neal	Minnesota	6	—	—
Brown, Rob	Pittsburgh	7	—	—
Bullard, Mike	Pittsburgh	7	—	—
Burr, Shawn	Detroit	2	—	—
Burridge, Randy	Boston	2	—	—
Carbonneau, Guy	Montreal	—	1	—
Carpenter, Bob	Wsh., Bos.	2	1	—
Carson, Jimmy	L.A., Edm., Det.	6	1	—
Cavallini, Gino	St. Louis	1	—	—
Chabot, John	Pittsburgh	1	—	—
Christian, Dave	Wpg., Wsh.	2	—	—
Ciccarelli, Dino	Min., Wsh.	13	3	1
Clark, Wendel	Toronto	2	1	—
Coffey, Paul	Edmonton	4	1	—
Carson, Shayne	Montreal	2	—	—
Cote, Alain	Quebec	1	—	—
Courtnall, Geoff	Bos., Wsh.	2	—	—
Courtnall, Russ	Tor., Mtl.	2	—	—
Craven, Murray	Philadelphia	2	—	—
Creighton, Adam	Buf., Chi.	2	—	—
Crowder, Keith	Boston	2	—	—
Cullen, John	Pittsburgh	1	—	—
Cunneyworth, R.	Pittsburgh	1	1	—
Cyr, Paul	Buffalo	1	—	—
Dahlen, Ulf	NY Rangers	1	—	—
Damphousse, V.	Toronto	3	—	—
Daoust, Dan	Toronto	1	—	—
DeBlois, Lucien	Winnipeg	1	—	—
Dineen, Kevin	Hartford	5	—	—
Duchesne, Steve	Los Angeles	1	—	—
Duncan, Iain	Winnipeg	1	—	—
Evason, Dean	Hartford	1	—	—
Federko, Bernie	St. Louis	11	—	—
Fergus, Tom	Toronto	4	—	—
Ferraro, Ray	Hartford	5	—	—
Flatley, Patrick	NY Islanders	—	1	—
Foligno, Mike	Det., Buf.	8	—	—
Francis, Ron	Hartford	7	1	—
Fraser, Curt	Chicago	1	—	—
Gagne, Dave	Minnesota	2	—	—
Gagne, Paul	New Jersey	1	—	—
Gallant, Gerard	Detroit	4	—	—
Gartner, Mike	Wsh., Min.	12	2	—
Gelinas, Martin	Edmonton	1	—	—
Gilbert, Greg	NY Islanders	2	—	—
Gillis, Paul	Quebec	1	—	—
Gilmour, Doug	St. Louis	2	—	—
Gould, Bobby	Calgary	1	—	—
Goulet, Michel	Quebec	11	2	—
Graham, Dirk	Minnesota	1	—	—
Granato, Tony	NY Rangers	2	1	—
Graves, Adam	Edmonton	1	—	—
Greschner, Ron	NY Rangers	1	—	—
Gretzky, Wayne	Edm., L.A.	33	9	4
Gustafsson, Bengt	Washington	1	—	1
Hamel, Gilles	Buffalo	1	—	—
Hannan, Dave	Edmonton	1	—	—
Hawerchuk, Dale	Winnipeg	11	—	—
Horacek, Tony	Philadelphia	1	—	—
Housley, Phil	Buffalo	2	—	—
Howe, Mark	Hartford	1	—	—
Hrdina, Jiri	Calgary	1	1	—
Hull, Brett	Cgy., St. L.	6	—	—
Hull, Jody	Hartford	1	—	—
Hunter, Dale	Quebec	3	—	—
Hunter, Mark	St. L., Cgy.	5	1	—
Ihnacak, Peter	Toronto	1	—	—
Janney, Craig	Boston	1	—	—
Johnson, Mark	Hfd., NJ	5	—	—
Kasper, Steve	Boston	3	—	—
Kerr, Tim	Philadelphia	13	4	—
King, Derek	NY Islanders	1	—	—
Klima, Petr	Detroit	3	—	—
Korn, Jim	Toronto	1	—	—
Krushelnyski, Mike	Edmonton	1	—	—
Kurri, Jari	Edmonton	18	1	1
Lacombe, Normand	Edmonton	1	—	—
Lafleur, Guy	Mtl., NYR	16	1	—
LaFontaine, Pat	NY Islanders	6	—	—
Lambert, Lane	Detroit	2	—	—
Larmer, Steve	Chicago	4	—	—
Larson, Reed	Detroit	3	—	—
Lawless, Paul	Hartford	1	—	—
Lawton, Brian	Minnesota	2	—	—
Leeman, Gary	Toronto	4	—	—
Lemieux, Claude	Montreal	1	—	—
Lemieux, Jocelyn	Chicago	1	—	—
Lemieux, Mario	Pittsburgh	18	6	1
Linden, Trevor	Vancouver	2	—	—
Linseman, Ken	Phi., Edm., Bos.	3	—	—
Loob, Hakan	Calgary	5	1	—
Ludzik, Steve	Chicago	1	—	—
MacLean, John	New Jersey	4	—	—
MacLean, Paul	Wpg., St. L.	7	1	—
MacLellan, Brian	L.A., NYR, Min., Cgy.	2	2	—
MacTavish, Craig	Edmonton	1	—	—
Makela, Mikko	NY Islanders	1	—	—
Maloney, Don	NY Rangers	4	—	—
Marois, Daniel	Toronto	3	—	—
McBain, Andrew	Winnipeg	1	—	—
McKegney, Tony	Buf., Que., Min., St. L.	7	1	—
McKenna, Sean	Buffalo	1	—	—
McPhee, Mike	Montreal	2	—	—
Meagher, Rick	Hartford	2	—	—
Messier, Mark	Edmonton	10	3	—
Modano, Mike	Minnesota	1	—	—
Momesso, Sergio	Montreal	1	—	—
Mullen, Brian	Wpg., NYR	1	—	—
Mullen, Joe	St. L., Cgy.	5	2	—
Muller, Kirk	New Jersey	3	—	—
Murray, Troy	Chicago	1	—	—
Murzyn, Dana	Calgary	1	—	—
Naslund, Mats	Montreal	4	1	—
Neely, Cam	Boston	6	—	—
Neufeld, Ray	Winnipeg	4	—	—
Nicholls, Bernie	Los Angeles	12	2	—
Nieuwendyk, Joe	Calgary	4	2	1
Ogrodnick, John	Detroit	6	—	—
Olczyk, Ed	Toronto	2	—	—
Osborne, Mark	Detroit	1	—	—
Otto, Joel	Calgary	1	—	—
Paslawski, Greg	St. Louis	2	—	—
Pederson, Barry	Boston	6	1	—
Poddubny, Walt	Tor., Que.	4	1	—
Poulin, Dave	Philadelphia	5	—	—
Presley, Wayne	Chicago	1	—	—
Probert, Bob	Detroit	1	—	—
Propp, Brian	Philadelphia	3	1	—
Quinn, Dan	Pit., Van.	4	—	—
Reeds, Mark	St. Louis	1	—	—
Reinhart, Paul	Calgary	1	—	—
Richer, Stephane	Montreal	4	1	—
Ridley, Mike	NYR, Wsh.	2	1	—
Roberts, Gary	Calgary	1	—	—
Robertson, Torrie	Hartford	1	—	—
Robinson, Larry	Montreal	1	—	—
Robitaille, Luc	Los Angeles	7	—	—
Roenick, Jeremy	Chicago	1	—	—
Ronning, Cliff	St. Louis	1	—	—
Ruff, Lindy	Buffalo	1	1	—
Sakic, Joe	Quebec	3	—	—
Salming, Borje	Toronto	1	—	—
Sandlak, Jim	Vancouver	1	—	—
Sandstrom, Tomas	NY Rangers	3	1	—
Savard, Denis	Chicago	11	—	—
Secord, Al	Chicago	4	2	—
Shanahan, Brendan	New Jersey	1	—	—
Shedden, Doug	Pittsburgh	2	—	—
Sheppard, Ray	Buffalo	3	—	—
Sinisalo, Ilkka	Philadelphia	3	—	—
Simpson, Craig	Pit., Edm.	3	—	—
Skriko, Petri	Vancouver	4	1	—
Smail, Doug	Winnipeg	2	—	—
Smith, Derrick	Philadelphia	1	—	—
Smith, Bobby	Minnesota	5	1	—
Smyl, Stan	Vancouver	7	—	—
Stastny, Peter	Quebec	14	2	—
Steen, Thomas	Winnipeg	3	—	—
Stevens, Kevin	Pittsburgh	1	—	—
Sulliman, Doug	Hartford	2	—	—
Sundstrom, Patrik	Vancouver	2	—	—
Sundstrom, Peter	NY Rangers	2	—	—
Sutter, Brent	NY Islanders	6	—	—
Sutter, Rich	Vancouver	1	—	—
Sweeney, Bob	Boston	1	—	—
Tanti, Tony	Van., Pit.	10	1	—
Taylor, Dave	Los Angeles	7	1	—
Thomas, Steve	Chicago	2	1	—
Tikkanen, Esa	Edmonton	2	—	—
Tocchet, Rick	Philadelphia	5	2	—
Tonelli, John	NYI, L.A.	4	—	1
Trottier, Bryan	NY Islanders	13	1	2
Tucker, John	Buffalo	1	—	—
Turcotte, Darren	NY Rangers	2	—	—
Turgeon, Pierre	Buffalo	1	—	—
Turgeon, Sylvain	Hfd., N.J.	4	—	—
Vaive, Rick	Tor., Chi.	10	3	—
Verbeek, Pat	New Jersey	4	1	—
Vukota, Mick	NY Islanders	1	—	—
Walter, Ryan	Montreal	1	—	—
Wickenheiser, Doug	Mtl., St. L.	2	—	—
Wilson, Carey	Calgary	2	—	—
Wood, Randy	NY Islanders	1	—	—
Yzerman, Steve	Detroit	8	1	—
Zezel, Peter	Philadelphia	1	—	—

As a rookie, Ron Francis had 68 points in 59 games in 1981-82.

Rookie Scoring Records

All-Time Top 50 Goal-Scoring Rookies

	Rookie	Team	Position	Season	GP	G	A	PTS
1.	*Mike Bossy	NY Islanders	Right wing	1977-78	73	53	38	91
2.	*Joe Niewendyk	Calgary	Center	1987-88	75	51	41	92
3.	*Dale Hawerchuk	Winnipeg	Center	1981-82	80	45	58	103
4.	*Luc Robitaille	Los Angeles	Left wing	1986-87	79	45	39	84
5.	Barry Pederson	Boston	Center	1981-82	80	44	48	92
	Rick Martin	Buffalo	Left wing	1971-72	73	44	30	74
7.	*Steve Larmer	Chicago	Right wing	1982-83	80	43	47	90
	*Mario Lemieux	Pittsburgh	Center	1984-85	73	43	57	100
9.	Darryl Sutter	Chicago	Left wing	1980-81	76	40	22	62
	Sylvain Turgeon	Hartford	Left wing	1983-84	76	40	32	72
	Warren Young	Pittsburgh	Left wing	1984-85	80	40	32	72
12.	Anton Stastny	Quebec	Left wing	1980-81	80	39	46	85
	Steve Yzerman	Detroit	Center	1983-84	80	39	48	87
	*Peter Stastny	Quebec	Center	1980-81	77	39	70	109
	*Eric Vail	Atlanta	Left wing	1974-75	72	39	21	60
16.	Neal Broten	Minnesota	Center	1981-82	73	38	60	98
	*Gilbert Perreault	Buffalo	Center	1970-71	78	38	34	72
	Ray Sheppard	Buffalo	Right wing	1987-88	74	38	27	65
19.	Jimmy Carson	Los Angeles	Centre	1986-87	80	37	42	79
	Jorgen Pettersson	St. Louis	Left wing	1980-81	62	37	36	73
	Mike Bullard	Pittsburgh	Center	1981-82	75	36	27	63
22.	Mike Foligno	Detroit	Right wing	1979-80	80	36	35	71
	Tony Granato	NY Rangers	Right wing	1988-89	78	36	27	63
	Paul MacLean	Winnipeg	Right wing	1981-82	74	36	25	61
25.	Marian Stastny	Quebec	Right wing	1981-82	74	35	54	89
	Bobby Carpenter	Washington	Center	1981-82	80	32	35	67
	Brian Bellows	Minnesota	Right wing	1982-83	78	35	30	65
28.	Nels Stewart	Mtl. Maroons	Center	1925-26	36	34	8	42
	*Danny Grant	Minnesota	Left wing	1968-69	75	34	31	65
	Norm Ferguson	Oakland	Right wing	1968-69	76	34	20	54
	Brian Propp	Philadelphia	Left wing	1979-80	80	34	41	75
	Wendel Clark	Toronto	Left wing	1985-86	66	34	11	45
	Darren Turcotte	NY Rangers	Right wing	1989-90	76	32	34	66
34.	Mark Pavelich	NY Rangers	Center	1981-82	79	33	43	76
	*Willi Plett	Atlanta	Right wing	1976-77	64	33	23	56
	Dale McCourt	Detroit	Center	1977-78	76	33	39	72
	Ron Flockhart	Philadelphia	Center	1981-82	72	33	39	72
	Steve Bozek	Los Angeles	Center	1981-82	71	33	23	56
39.	Jari Kurri	Edmonton	Left wing	1980-81	75	32	43	75
	Bill Mosienko	Chicago	Right wing	1943-44	50	32	38	70
	Don Murdoch	NY Rangers	Right wing	1976-77	59	32	24	56
	Michel Bergeron	Detroit	Right wing	1975-76	72	32	27	59
	*Bryan Trottier	NY Islanders	Center	1975-76	80	32	63	95
	Bobby Carpenter	Washington	Center	1981-82	80	32	35	67
	Kjell Dahlin	Montreal	Right wing	1985-86	77	32	39	71
	Petr Klima	Detroit	Left wing	1985-86	74	32	24	56
47.	Danny Gare	Buffalo	Right wing	1974-75	78	31	31	62
	Pierre Larouche	Pittsburgh	Center	1974-75	79	31	37	68
	Dave Poulin	Philadelphia	Center	1983-84	73	31	45	76
	Daniel Marois	Toronto	Right wing	1988-89	76	31	23	54

* Calder Trophy Winner.

All-Time Top 50 Point-Scoring Rookies

	Rookie	Team	Position	Season	GP	G	A	PTS
1.	*Peter Stastny	Quebec	Center	1980-81	77	39	70	109
2.	*Dale Hawerchuk	Winnipeg	Center	1981-82	80	45	58	103
3.	*Mario Lemieux	Pittsburgh	Center	1984-85	73	43	57	100
4.	Neal Broten	Minnesota	Center	1981-82	73	38	60	98
5.	*Bryan Trottier	NY Islanders	Center	1975-76	80	32	63	95
6.	*Joe Niewendyk	Calgary	Center	1987-88	75	51	41	92
	Barry Pederson	Boston	Center	1981-82	80	44	48	92
8.	*Mike Bossy	NY Islanders	Right wing	1977-78	73	53	38	91
9.	*Steve Larmer	Chicago	Right wing	1982-83	80	43	47	90
10.	Marian Stastny	Quebec	Right wing	1981-82	74	35	54	89
11.	Steve Yzerman	Detroit	Center	1983-84	80	39	48	87
12.	*Sergei Makarov	Calgary	Right wing	1989-90	80	24	62	86
13.	Anton Stastny	Quebec	Left wing	1980-81	80	39	46	85
14.	*Luc Robitaille	Los Angeles	Left wing	1986-87	79	45	39	84
15.	Jimmy Carson	Los Angeles	Center	1986-87	80	37	42	79
16.	Marcel Dionne	Detroit	Center	1971-72	78	28	49	77
17.	Mark Pavelich	NY Rangers	Center	1981-82	79	33	43	76
	Larry Murphy	Los Angeles	Defense	1980-81	80	16	60	76
	Dave Poulin	Philadelphia	Center	1983-84	73	31	45	76
20.	Brian Propp	Philadelphia	Left wing	1979-80	80	34	41	75
	Jari Kurri	Edmonton	Left wing	1980-81	75	32	43	75
	Mike Modano	Minnesota	Center	1989-90	80	29	46	75
	Denis Savard	Chicago	Center	1980-81	76	28	47	75
24.	Rick Martin	Buffalo	Left wing	1971-72	73	44	30	74
	*Bobby Smith	Minnesota	Center	1978-79	80	30	44	74
26.	Jorgen Pettersson	St. Louis	Left wing	1980-81	62	37	36	73
27.	Sylvain Turgeon	Hartford	Left wing	1983-84	76	40	32	72
	Warren Young	Pittsburgh	Left wing	1984-85	80	40	32	72
	*Gilbert Perreault	Buffalo	Center	1970-71	78	38	34	72
	Ron Flockhart	Philadelphia	Center	1981-82	72	33	39	72
	Dale McCourt	Detroit	Center	1977-78	76	33	39	72
	Carey Wilson	Calgary	Center	1984-85	74	24	48	72
33.	Mike Foligno	Detroit	Right wing	1979-80	80	36	35	71
	Kjell Dahlin	Montreal	Right wing	1985-86	77	32	39	71
	Dave Christian	Winnipeg	Center	1980-81	80	28	43	71
	Mats Naslund	Montreal	Left wing	1982-83	74	26	45	71
	*Brian Leetch	NY Rangers	Defense	1988-89	68	23	48	71
38.	Bill Mosienko	Chicago	Right wing	1943-44	50	32	38	70
39.	Roland Eriksson	Minnesota	Center	1976-77	80	25	44	69
40.	Pierre Larouche	Pittsburgh	Center	1974-75	79	31	37	68
	Ron Francis	Hartford	Center	1981-82	59	25	43	68
	*Gary Suter	Calgary	Defense	1985-86	80	18	50	68
	Jude Drouin	Minnesota	Center	1970-71	75	16	52	68
44.	Bobby Carpenter	Washington	Center	1981-82	80	32	35	67
	Chris Valentine	Washington	Center	1981-82	60	30	37	67
	Mark Recchi	Pittsburgh	Right wing	1989-90	74	30	37	67
	Tom Webster	Detroit	Right wing	1970-71	78	30	37	67
	Mark Osborne	Detroit	Left wing	1981-82	80	26	41	67
49.	Darren Turcotte	NY Rangers	Center	1989-90	76	32	34	66
	Peter Ihnacak	Toronto	Center	1982-83	80	28	38	66
	Jeremy Roenick	Chicago	Center	1989-90	78	26	40	66
	Phil Housley	Buffalo	Defense	1982-83	77	19	47	66
	Per-Erik Eklund	Philadelphia	Center	1985-86	70	15	51	66

* Calder Trophy Winner.

50-Goal Seasons

Bobby Hull

Bill Barber

Dennis Maruk

Player	Team	Date of 50th Goal	Score		Goaltender	Player's Game No.	Team Game No.	Total Goals	Total Games	Age When First 50th Scored (Yrs. & Mos.)
Maurice Richard	Mtl.	18-3-45	Mtl. 4	at Bos. 2	Harvey Bennett	50	50	50	50	23.7
Bernie Geoffrion	Mtl.	16-3-61	Tor. 2	at Mtl. 5	Cesare Maniago	62	68	50	64	30.1
Bobby Hull	Chi.	25-3-62	Chi. 1	at NYR 4	Gump Worsley	70	70	50	70	23.2
Bobby Hull	Chi.	2-3-66	Det. 4	at Chi. 5	Hank Bassen	52	57	54	65	
Bobby Hull	Chi.	18-3-67	Chi. 5	at Tor. 9	Bruce Gamble	63	66	52	66	
Bobby Hull	Chi.	5-3-69	NYR 4	at Chi. 4	Ed Giacomin	64	66	58	74	
Phil Esposito	Bos.	20-2-71	Bos. 4	at L.A. 5	Denis DeJordy	58	58	76	78	29.0
John Bucyk	Bos.	16-3-71	Bos. 11	at Det. 4	Roy Edwards	69	69	51	78	35.1
Phil Esposito	Bos.	20-2-72	Bos. 3	at Chi. 1	Tony Esposito	60	60	66	76	
Bobby Hull	Chi.	2-4-72	Det. 1	at Chi. 6	Andy Brown	78	78	50	78	
Vic Hadfield	NYR	2-4-72	Mtl. 6	at NYR 5	Denis DeJordy	78	78	50	78	31.6
Phil Esposito	Bos.	25-3-73	Buf. 1	at Bos. 6	Roger Crozier	75	75	55	78	
Mickey Redmond	Det.	27-3-73	Det. 8	at Tor. 1	Ron Low	73	75	52	76	25.3
Rick MacLeish	Phi.	1-4-73	Phi. 4	at Pit. 5	Cam Newton	78	78	50	78	23.2
Phil Esposito	Bos.	20-2-74	Bos. 5	at Min. 5	Cesare Maniago	56	56	68	78	
Mickey Redmond	Det.	23-3-74	NYR 3	at Det. 5	Ed Giacomin	69	71	51	76	
Ken Hodge	Bos.	6-4-74	Bos. 2	at Mtl. 6	Michel Larocque	75	77	50	76	29.10
Rick Martin	Buf.	7-4-74	St.L. 2	at Buf. 5	Wayne Stephenson	78	78	52	78	22.9
Phil Esposito	Bos.	8-2-75	Bos. 8	at Det. 5	Jim Rutherford	54	54	61	79	
Guy Lafleur	Mtl.	29-3-75	K.C. 1	at Mtl. 4	Denis Herron	66	76	53	70	23.6
Danny Grant	Det.	2-4-75	Wsh. 3	at Det. 8	John Adams	78	78	50	80	29.2
Rick Martin	Buf.	3-4-75	Bos. 2	at Buf. 4	Ken Broderick	67	79	52	68	
Reggie Leach	Phi.	14-3-76	Atl. 1	at Phi. 6	Daniel Bouchard	69	69	61	80	25.11
Jean Pronovost	Pit.	24-3-76	Bos. 5	at Pit. 5	Gilles Gilbert	74	74	52	80	31.3
Guy Lafleur	Mtl.	27-3-76	K.C. 2	at Mtl. 8	Denis Herron	76	76	56	80	
Bill Barber	Phi.	3-4-76	Buf. 2	at Phi. 5	Al Smith	79	79	50	80	23.9
Pierre Larouche	Pit.	3-4-76	Wash. 5	at Pit. 4	Ron Low	75	79	53	76	20.5
Danny Gare	Buf.	4-4-76	Tor. 2	at Buf. 5	Gord McRae	79	80	50	79	21.11
Steve Shutt	Mtl.	1-3-77	Mtl. 5	at NYI 4	Glenn Resch	65	65	60	80	24.8
Guy Lafleur	Mtl.	6-3-77	Mtl. 1	at Buf. 4	Don Edwards	68	68	56	80	
Marcel Dionne	L.A.	2-4-77	Min. 2	at L.A. 7	Pete LoPresti	79	79	53	80	25.8
Guy Lafleur	Mtl.	8-3-78	Wsh. 3	at Mtl. 4	Jim Bedard	63	65	60	78	
Mike Bossy	NYI	1-4-78	Wsh. 2	at NYI 3	Bernie Wolfe	69	76	53	73	21.2
Mike Bossy	NYI	24-2-79	Det. 1	at NYI 3	Rogie Vachon	58	58	69	80	
Marcel Dionne	L.A.	11-3-79	L.A. 3	at Phi. 6	Wayne Stephenson	68	68	59	80	
Guy Lafleur	Mtl.	31-3-79	Pit. 3	at Mtl. 5	Denis Herron	76	76	52	80	
Guy Chouinard	Atl.	6-4-79	NYR 2	at Atl. 9	John Davidson	79	79	50	80	22.5
Marcel Dionne	L.A.	12-3-80	L.A. 2	at Pit. 4	Nick Ricci	70	70	53	80	
Mike Bossy	NYI	16-3-80	NYI 6	at Chi. 1	Tony Esposito	68	71	51	75	
Charlie Simmer	L.A.	19-3-80	Det. 3	at L.A. 4	Jim Rutherford	57	73	56	64	26.0
Pierre Larouche	Mtl.	25-3-80	Chi. 4	at Mtl. 8	Tony Esposito	72	75	50	73	
Danny Gare	Buf.	27-3-80	Det. 1	at Buf. 10	Jim Rutherford	71	75	56	76	
Blaine Stoughton	Hfd.	28-3-80	Hfd. 4	at Van. 4	Glen Hanlon	75	75	56	80	27.0
Guy Lafleur	Mtl.	2-4-80	Mtl. 7	at Det. 2	Rogie Vachon	72	78	50	74	
Wayne Gretzky	Edm.	2-4-80	Min. 1	at Edm. 1	Gary Edwards	78	79	51	79	19.2
Reggie Leach	Phi.	3-4-80	Wsh. 2	at Phi. 4	(empty net)	75	79	50	76	
Mike Bossy	NYI	24-1-81	Que. 3	at NYI 7	Ron Grahame	50	50	68	79	
Charlie Simmer	L.A.	26-1-81	L.A. 7	at Que. 5	Michel Dion	51	51	56	65	
Marcel Dionne	L.A.	8-3-81	L.A. 4	at Wpg. 1	Markus Mattsson	68	68	58	80	
Wayne Babych	St.L.	12-3-81	St.L. 3	at Mtl. 4	Richard Sevigny	70	68	54	78	22.9
Wayne Gretzky	Edm.	15-3-81	Edm. 3	at Cgy. 3	Pat Riggin	69	69	55	80	
Rick Kehoe	Pit.	16-3-81	Pit. 7	at Edm. 6	Eddie Mio	70	70	55	80	29.7
Jacques Richard	Que.	29-3-81	Mtl. 0	at Que. 4	Richard Sevigny	76	75	52	78	28.6
Dennis Maruk	Wsh.	5-4-81	Det. 2	at Wsh. 7	Larry Lozinski	80	80	50	80	25.3
Wayne Gretzky	Edm.	30-12-81	Phi. 5	at Edm. 7	(empty net)	39	39	92	80	
Dennis Maruk	Wsh.	21-2-82	Wpg. 3	at Wsh. 6	Doug Soetaert	61	61	60	80	
Mike Bossy	NYI	4-3-82	Tor. 1	at NYI 10	Michel Larocque	66	66	64	80	
Dino Ciccarelli	Min.	8-3-82	St.L. 1	at Min. 8	Mike Liut	67	68	55	76	21.7
Rick Vaive	Tor.	24-3-82	St.L. 3	at Tor. 4	Mike Liut	72	75	54	77	22.10
Rick Middleton	Bos.	28-3-82	Bos. 5	at Buf. 9	Paul Harrison	72	77	51	75	
Blaine Stoughton	Hfd.	28-3-82	Min. 5	at Hfd. 2	Gilles Meloche	76	76	52	80	28.3
Marcel Dionne	L.A.	30-3-82	Cgy. 7	at L.A. 5	Pat Riggin	75	77	50	78	
Mark Messier	Edm.	31-3-82	L.A. 3	at Edm. 7	Mario Lessard	78	79	50	78	21.3
Bryan Trottier	NYI	3-4-82	Phi. 3	at NYI 6	Pete Peeters	79	79	50	80	25.9
Lanny McDonald	Cgy.	18-2-83	Cgy. 1	at Buf. 5	Bob Sauve	60	60	66	80	30.0
Wayne Gretzky	Edm.	19-2-83	Edm. 10	at Pit. 7	Nick Ricci	60	60	71	80	
Michel Goulet	Que.	5-3-83	Que. 7	at Hfd. 3	Mike Veisor	67	67	57	80	22.11
Mike Bossy	NYI	12-3-83	Wsh. 2	at NYI 6	Al Jensen	70	71	60	79	
Marcel Dionne	L.A.	17-3-83	Que. 3	at L.A. 4	Daniel Bouchard	71	71	56	80	
Al Secord	Chi.	20-3-83	Tor. 3	at Chi. 7	Mike Palmateer	73	73	54	80	25.0
Rick Vaive	Tor.	30-3-83	Tor. 4	at Det. 2	Gilles Gilbert	76	78	51	78	

Player	Team	Date of 50th Goal	Score	Goaltender	Player's Game No.	Team Game No.	Total Goals	Total Games	Age When First 50th Scored (Yrs. & Mos.)
Wayne Gretzky	Edm.	7-1-84	Hfd. 3 at Edm. 5	Greg Millen	42	42	87	74	
Michel Goulet	Que.	8-3-84	Que. 8 at Pit. 6	Denis Herron	63	69	56	75	
Rick Vaive	Tor.	14-3-84	Min. 3 at Tor. 3	Gilles Meloche	69	72	52	76	
Mike Bullard	Pit.	14-3-84	Pit. 6 at L.A. 7	Markus Mattsson	71	72	51	76	23.0
Jari Kurri	Edm.	15-3-84	Edm. 2 at Mtl. 3	Rick Wamsley	57	73	52	64	23.10
Glenn Anderson	Edm.	21-3-84	Hfd. 3 at Edm. 5	Greg Millen	76	76	54	80	23.6
Tim Kerr	Phi.	22-3-84	Pit. 4 at Phi. 13	Denis Herron	74	75	54	79	24.3
Mike Bossy	NYI	31-3-84	NYI 3 at Wsh. 1	Pat Riggin	67	79	51	67	
Wayne Gretzky	Edm.	26-1-85	Pit. 3 at Edm. 6	Denis Herron	49	49	73	80	
Jari Kurri	Edm.	3-2-85	Hfd. 3 at Edm. 6	Greg Millen	50	53	71	73	
Mike Bossy	NYI	5-3-85	Phi. 5 at NYI 4	Bob Froese	61	65	58	76	
Tim Kerr	Phi.	7-3-85	Wsh. 6 at Phi. 9	Pat Riggin	63	65	54	74	
John Ogrodnick	Det.	13-3-85	Det. 6 at Edm. 7	Grant Fuhr	69	69	55	79	25.9
Bob Carpenter	Wsh.	21-3-85	Wsh. 2 at Mtl. 3	Steve Penney	72	72	53	80	21.9
Michel Goulet	Que.	26-3-85	Buf. 3 at Que. 4	Tom Barrasso	62	73	55	69	
Dale Hawerchuk	Wpg.	29-4-85	Chi. 5 at Wpg. 5	W. Skorodenski	77	77	53	80	21.1
Mike Gartner	Wsh.	7-4-85	Pit. 3 at Wsh. 7	Brian Ford	80	80	50	80	25.5
Jari Kurri	Edm.	4-3-86	Edm. 6 at Van. 2	Richard Brodeur	63	65	68	78	
Mike Bossy	NYI	11-3-86	Cgy. 4 at NYI 8	Rejean Lemelin	67	67	61	80	
Glenn Anderson	Edm.	14-3-86	Det. 3 at Edm. 12	Greg Stefan	63	71	54	72	
Michel Goulet	Que.	17-3-86	Que. 8 at Mtl. 6	Patrick Roy	67	72	53	75	
Wayne Gretzky	Edm.	18-3-86	Wpg. 2 at Edm. 6	Brian Hayward	72	72	52	80	
Tim Kerr	Phi.	20-3-86	Pit. 1 at Phi. 5	Roberto Romano	68	72	58	76	
Wayne Gretzky	Edm.	2-4-87	Edm. 6 at Min. 5	Don Beaupre	55	55	62	79	
Tim Kerr	Phi.	3-17-87	NYR 1 at Phi. 4	J. Vanbiesbrouck	67	71	58	75	
Jari Kurri	Edm.	3-17-87	N.J. 4 at Edm. 7	Craig Billington	69	70	54	79	
Mario Lemieux	Pit.	3-12-87	Que. 3 at Pit. 6	Mario Gosselin	53	70	54	63	21.5
Dino Ciccarelli	Min.	3-7-87	Pit. 7 at Min. 3	Gilles Meloche	66	66	52	80	
Mario Lemieux	Pit.	2-2-88	Wsh. 2 at Pit. 3	Pete Peeters	51	54	70	77	
Steve Yzerman	Det.	1-3-88	Buf. 0 at Det. 4	Tom Barrasso	64	64	50	64	22.10
Joe Nieuwendyk	Cgy.	12-3-88	Buf. 4 at Cgy. 10	Tom Barrasso	66	70	51	75	21.5
Craig Simpson	Edm.	15-3-88	Buf. 4 at Edm. 6	Jacques Cloutier	71	71	56	80	21.1
Jimmy Carson	L.A.	26-3-88	Chi. 5 at L.A. 9	Darren Pang	77	77	55	88	19.7
Luc Robitaille	L.A.	1-4-88	L.A. 6 at Cgy. 3	Mike Vernon	79	79	53	80	21.10
Hakan Loob	Cgy.	3-4-88	Min. 1 at Cgy. 4	Don Beaupre	80	80	50	80	27.9
Stephane Richer	Mtl.	3-4-88	Mtl. 4 at Buf. 4	Tom Barrasso	72	80	50	72	21.10
Mario Lemieux	Pit.	20-1-89	Pit. 3 at Wpg. 7	Eldon Reddick	44	46	85	76	
Bernie Nicholls	L.A.	28-1-89	Edm. 7 at L.A. 6	Grant Fuhr	51	51	70	79	27.7
Steve Yzerman	Det.	5-2-89	Det. 6 at Wpg. 2	Eldon Reddick	55	55	65	80	
Wayne Gretzky	L.A.	4-3-89	Phi. 2 at L.A. 6	Ron Hextall	66	67	54	78	
Joe Nieuwendyk	Cgy.	21-3-89	NYI 1 at Cgy. 4	Mark Fitzpatrick	72	74	51	77	
Joe Mullen	Cgy.	31-3-89	Wpg. 1 at Cgy. 4	Bob Essensa	78	79	51	79	32.1
Brett Hull	St.L.	6-2-90	Tor. 4 at St.L. 6	Jeff Reese	54	54	72	80	25.6
Steve Yzerman	Det.	24-2-90	Det. 3 at NYI 3	Glenn Healy	63	63	79	62	
Cam Neely	Bos.	10-3-90	Bos. 3 at NYI 3	Mark Fitzpatrick	69	71	76	55	24.9
Brian Bellows	Min.	22-3-90	Min. 5 at Det. 1	Tim Cheveldae	75	75	80	55	25.6
Pat LaFontaine	NYI	24-3-90	NYI 5 at Edm. 6	Bill Ranford	71	77	74	54	25.1
Stephane Richer	Mtl.	24-3-90	Mtl. 4 at Hfd. 7	Peter Sidorkiewicz	75	77	75	51	
Gary Leeman	Tor.	28-3-90	NYI 6 at Tor. 3	Mark Fitzpatrick	78	78	80	51	26.1
Luc Robitaille	L.A.	21-3-90	L.A. 3 at Van. 6	Kirk McLean	79	79	80	52	

John Ogrodnick

Dino Ciccarelli

Players' 1,000th Points

Player	Team	Date	Game No.	G or A	Score	Total Points (G A PTS)	Total Games
Gordie Howe	Detroit	Nov. 27/60	938	(A)	Tor. 0 at Det. 2	801-1,049-1,850	1,767
Jean Beliveau	Montreal	Mar. 3/68	911	(G)	Mtl. 2 at Det. 5	507-712-1,219	1,125
Alex Delvecchio	Detroit	Feb. 16/69	1,143	(A)	LA 3 at Det. 0	450-825-1,281	1,540
Norm Ullman	Toronto	Oct. 16/71	1,113	(A)	NYR 5 at Tor. 3	490-739-1,229	1,410
Bobby Hull	Chicago	Dec. 12/71	909	(A)	Minn. 3 at Chi. 5	610-560-1,170	1,063
Stan Mikita	Chicago	Oct. 15/72	924	(A)	St.L. 3 at Chi. 1	541-926-1,467	1,394
John Bucyk	Boston	Nov. 9/72	1,144	(G)	Det. 3 at Bos. 8	556-813-1,369	1,540
Frank Mahovlich	Montreal	Feb. 13/73	1,090	(A)	Phi. 7 at Mtl. 6	533-570-1,103	1,181
Henri Richard	Montreal	Dec. 20/73	1,194	(G)	Mtl. 2 at Buf. 2	358-688-1,046	1,256
Phil Esposito	Boston	Feb. 15/74	745	(A)	Bos. 4 at Van. 2	717-873-1,590	1,282
Rod Gilbert	NY Rangers	Feb. 19/77	1,027	(G)	NYR 2 at NYI 5	406-615-1,021	1,065
Jean Ratelle	Boston	Apr. 3/77	1,007	(A)	Tor. 4 at Bos. 7	491-776-1,267	1,281
Bobby Clarke	Philadelphia	Mar. 19/81	922	(G)	Bos. 3 at Phi. 5	358-852-1,210	1,144
Marcel Dionne	Los Angeles	Jan. 7/81	740	(G)	L.A. 5 at Hfd. 3	731-1,040-1,771	1,348
*Guy Lafleur	Montreal	Mar. 4/81	720	(G)	Mtl. 9 at Wpg. 3	548-777-1,325	1,067
Gilbert Perreault	Buffalo	Apr. 3/82	871	(A)	Buf. 5 at Mtl. 4	512-814-1,326	1,191
Darryl Sittler	Philadelphia	Jan. 20/83	927	(A)	Buf. 5 at Phi. 5	484-637-1,121	1,096
*Wayne Gretzky	Edmonton	Dec. 19/84	424	(A)	L.A. 3 at Edm. 7	677-1,302-1,979	847
*Bryan Trottier	NY Islanders	Jan. 29/85	726	(G)	Min. 4 at NYI 4	500-853-1,353	1,123
Mike Bossy	NY Islanders	Jan. 24/86	656	(G)	NYI 7 at Tor. 5	573-553-1,126	752
Denis Potvin	NY Islanders	Apr. 4/87	987	(G)	Buf. 6 at NYI 6	310-742-1,052	1,060
*Bernie Federko	St. Louis	Mar. 19/88	855	(A)	Hfd. 5 at St.L. 3	369-761-1,130	1,000
Lanny McDonald	Calgary	Mar. 7/89	1,101	(G)	Wpg. 5 at Cgy. 9	500-506-1,006	1,111
*Peter Stastny	Quebec	Oct. 19/89	682	(A)	Que. 5 at Chi. 3	385-674-1,059	749
*Jari Kurri	Edmonton	Jan. 2/90	716	(A)	Edm. 6 at St.L. 4	474-569-1,043	754
*Denis Savard	Chicago	Mar. 11/90	727	(A)	St.L. 6 at Chi. 4	351-662-1,013	736

* Active

Bernie Federko

100-Point Seasons

Bobby Clarke

Jacques Richard

Blaine Stoughton

Player	Team	Date of 100th Point	G or A	Score			Player's Game No.	Team Game No.	Points G - A	PTS	Total Games	Age when first 100th point scored (Yrs. & Mos.)
Phil Esposito	Bos.	2-3-69	(G)	Pit. 0	at	Bos. 4	60	62	49-77 —	126	74	27.1
Bobby Hull	Chi.	20-3-69	(G)	Chi. 5	at	Bos. 5	71	71	58-49 —	107	76	30.2
Gordie Howe	Det.	30-3-69	(G)	Det. 5	at	Chi. 9	76	76	44-59 —	103	76	41.0
Bobby Orr	Bos.	15-3-70	(G)	Det. 5	at	Bos. 5	67	67	33-87 —	120	76	22.11
Phil Esposito	Bos.	6-2-71	(A)	Buf. 3	at	Bos. 4	51	51	76-76 —	152	78	
Bobby Orr	Bos.	22-2-71	(A)	Bos. 4	at	L.A. 5	58	58	37-102 —	139	78	
John Bucyk	Bos.	13-3-71	(G)	Bos. 6	at	Van. 3	68	68	51-65 —	116	78	35.10
Ken Hodge	Bos.	21-3-71	(A)	Buf. 7	at	Bos. 5	72	72	43-62 —	105	78	26.9
Jean Ratelle	NYR	18-2-72	(A)	NYR 2	at	Cal. 2	58	58	46-63 —	109	63	31.4
Phil Esposito	Bos.	19-2-72	(A)	Bos. 6	at	Min. 4	59	59	66-67 —	133	76	
Bobby Orr	Bos.	2-3-72	(A)	Van. 3	at	Bos. 7	64	64	37-80 —	117	76	
Vic Hadfield	NYR	25-3-72	(A)	NYR 3	at	Mtl. 3	74	74	50-56 —	106	78	31.5
Phil Esposito	Bos.	3-3-73	(A)	Bos. 1	at	Mtl. 5	64	64	55-75 —	130	78	
Bobby Clarke	Phi.	29-3-73	(G)	Atl. 2	at	Phi. 4	76	76	37-67 —	104	78	23.7
Bobby Orr	Bos.	31-3-73	(A)	Bos. 3	at	Tor. 7	62	77	29-72 —	101	63	
Rick MacLeish	Phi.	1-4-73	(G)	Phi. 4	at	Pit. 5	78	78	50-50 —	100	78	23.3
Phil Esposito	Bos.	13-2-74	(A)	Bos. 9	at	Cal. 2	53	53	68-77 —	145	78	
Bobby Orr	Bos.	12-3-74	(A)	Buf. 0	at	Bos. 4	62	66	32-90 —	122	74	
Ken Hodge	Bos.	24-3-74	(A)	Mtl. 3	at	Bos. 6	72	72	50-55 —	105	76	
Phil Esposito	Bos.	8-2-75	(A)	Bos. 8	at	Det. 5	54	54	61-66 —	127	79	
Bobby Orr	Bos.	13-2-75	(A)	Bos. 1	at	Buf. 3	57	57	46-89 —	135	80	
Guy Lafleur	Mtl.	7-3-75	(G)	Wsh. 4	at	Mtl. 8	56	66	53-66 —	119	70	24.6
Pete Mahovlich	Mtl.	9-3-75	(G)	Mtl. 8	at	NYR 3	67	67	35-82 —	117	80	29.5
Marcel Dionne	Det.	9-3-75	(A)	Det. 5	at	Phi. 8	67	67	47-74 —	121	80	23.7
Bobby Clarke	Phi.	22-3-75	(A)	Min. 0	at	Phi. 4	72	72	27-89 —	116	80	
Reńe Robert	Buf.	5-4-75	(A)	Buf. 4	at	Tor. 2	74	80	40-60 —	100	74	26.4
Guy Lafleur	Mtl.	10-3-76	(G)	Mtl. 5	at	Chi. 1	69	69	56-69 —	125	80	
Bobby Clarke	Phi.	11-3-76	(A)	Buf. 1	at	Phi. 6	64	68	30-89 —	119	76	
Bill Barber	Phi.	18-3-76	(A)	Van. 2	at	Phi. 3	71	71	50-62 —	112	80	23.8
Gilbert Perreault	Buf.	21-3-76	(A)	K.C. 1	at	Buf. 3	73	73	44-69 —	113	80	25.4
Pierre Larouche	Pit.	24-3-76	(G)	Bos. 5	at	Pit. 5	70	74	53-58 —	111	76	20.4
Pete Mahovlich	Mtl.	28-3-76	(A)	Mtl. 2	at	Bos. 2	77	77	34-71 —	105	80	
Jean Ratelle	Bos.	30-3-76	(G)	Buf. 4	at	Bos. 4	77	77	36-69 —	105	80	
Jean Pronovost	Pit.	3-4-76	(A)	Wsh. 5	at	Pit. 4	79	79	52-52 —	104	80	30.4
Darryl Sittler	Tor.	3-4-76	(A)	Bos. 4	at	Tor. 2	78	79	41-59 —	100	79	26.7
Guy Lafleur	Mtl.	26-2-77	(A)	Clev. 3	at	Mtl. 5	63	63	56-80 —	136	80	
Marcel Dionne	L.A.	5-3-77	(G)	Pit. 3	at	L.A. 3	67	67	53-69 —	122	80	
Steve Shutt	Mtl.	27-3-77	(A)	Mtl. 6	at	Det. 0	77	77	60-45 —	105	80	24.9
Bryan Trottier	NYI	25-2-78	(A)	Chi. 1	at	NYI 7	59	60	46-77 —	123	77	21.7
Guy Lafleur	Mtl.	28-2-78	(G)	Det. 3	at	Mtl. 9	59	61	60-72 —	132	78	
Darryl Sittler	Tor.	12-3-78	(A)	Tor. 7	at	Pit. 1	67	67	45-72 —	117	80	
Guy Lafleur	Mtl.	27-2-79	(A)	Mtl. 3	at	NYI 7	61	61	52-77 —	129	30	
Bryan Trottier	NYI	6-3-79	(A)	Buf. 3	at	NYI 2	59	63	47-87 —	134	76	
Marcel Dionne	L.A.	8-3-79	(G)	L.A. 4	at	Buf. 6	66	66	59-71 —	130	80	
Mike Bossy	NYI	11-3-79	(G)	NYI 4	at	Bos. 4	66	66	69-57 —	126	80	22.2
Bob MacMillan	Atl.	15-3-79	(A)	Atl. 4	at	Phi. 5	68	69	37-71 —	108	79	26.6
Guy Chouinard	Atl.	30-3-79	(G)	L.A. 3	at	Atl. 5	75	75	50-57 —	107	80	22.5
Denis Potvin	NYI	8-4-79	(A)	NYI 5	at	NYR 2	73	80	31-70 —	101	73	25.5
Marcel Dionne	L.A.	6-2-80	(A)	L.A. 3	at	Hfd. 7	53	53	53-84 —	137	80	
Guy Lafleur	Mtl.	10-2-80	(A)	Mtl. 3	at	Bos. 2	55	55	50-75 —	125	74	
Wayne Gretzky	Edm.	24-2-80	(A)	Bos. 4	at	Edm. 2	61	62	51-86 —	137	79	19.2
Bryan Trottier	NYI	30-3-80	(A)	NYI 9	at	Que. 6	75	77	42-62 —	104	78	
Gilbert Perreault	Buf.	1-4-80	(A)	Buf. 5	at	Atl. 2	77	77	40-66 —	106	80	
Mike Rogers	Hfd.	4-4-80	(A)	Que. 2	at	Hfd. 9	79	79	44-61 —	105	80	25.5
Charlie Simmer	L.A.	5-4-80	(G)	Van. 5	at	L.A. 3	64	80	56-45 —	101	64	26.0
Blaine Stoughton	Hfd.	6-4-80	(A)	Det. 3	at	Hfd. 5	80	80	56-44 —	100	80	27.0
Wayne Gretzky	Edm.	6-2-81	(G)	Wpg. 4	at	Edm. 10	53	53	55-109 —	164	80	
Marcel Dionne	L.A.	12-2-81	(A)	L.A. 5	at	Chi. 5	58	58	58-77 —	135	80	
Charlie Simmer	L.A.	14-2-81	(A)	Bos. 5	at	L.A. 4	59	59	56-49 —	105	65	
Kent Nilsson	Cgy.	27-2-81	(G)	Hfd. 1	at	Cgy. 5	64	64	49-82 —	131	80	24.6
Mike Bossy	NYI	3-3-81	(G)	Edm. 8	at	NYI 8	65	66	68-51 —	119	79	
Dave Taylor	L.A.	14-3-81	(G)	Min. 4	at	L.A. 10	63	70	47-65 —	112	72	25.3
Mike Rogers	Hfd.	22-3-81	(G)	Tor. 3	at	Hfd. 3	74	74	40-65 —	105	80	
Bernie Federko	St.L.	28-3-81	(A)	Buf. 4	at	St.L. 7	74	76	31-73 —	104	78	24.10
Rick Middleton	Bos.	28-3-81	(A)	Chi. 2	at	Bos. 5	76	76	44-59 —	103	80	27.4
Jacques Richard	Que.	29-3-81	(G)	Mtl. 0	at	Que. 4	75	76	52-51 —	103	78	28.6
Bryan Trottier	NYI	29-3-81	(G)	NYI 5	at	Wsh. 4	69	76	31-72 —	103	73	
Peter Stastny	Que.	29-3-81	(A)	Mtl. 0	at	Que. 4	73	76	39-70 —	109	77	24.6
Wayne Gretzky	Edm.	27-12-81	(G)	L.A. 3	at	Edm. 10	38	38	92-120 —	212	80	
Mike Bossy	NYI	13-2-82	(A)	Phi. 2	at	NYI 8	55	55	64-83 —	147	80	
Peter Stastny	Que.	16-2-82	(A)	Wpg. 3	at	Que. 7	60	60	46-93 —	139	80	
Dennis Maruk	Wsh.	20-2-82	(A)	Wsh. 3	at	Min. 7	60	60	60-76 —	136	80	26.3
Bryan Trottier	NYI	23-2-82	(G)	Chi. 1	at	NYI 5	61	61	50-79 —	129	80	
Denis Savard	Chi.	27-2-82	(A)	Chi. 5	at	L.A. 3	64	64	32-87 —	119	80	21.1
Bobby Smith	Min.	3-3-82	(A)	Det. 4	at	Min. 6	66	66	43-71 —	114	80	24.1
Marcel Dionne	L.A.	6-3-82	(G)	L.A. 6	at	Hfd. 7	64	66	50-67 —	117	78	
Dave Taylor	L.A.	20-3-82	(G)	Pit. 5	at	L.A. 7	71	72	39-67 —	106	78	
Dale Hawerchuk	Wpg.	24-3-82	(A)	L.A. 3	at	Wpg. 5	74	74	45-58 —	103	80	18.11
Dino Ciccarelli	Min.	27-3-82	(A)	Min. 6	at	Bos. 5	72	76	55-52 —	107	76	21.8
Glenn Anderson	Edm.	28-3-82	(G)	Edm. 6	at	L.A. 2	78	78	38-67 —	105	80	21.7
Mike Rogers	NYR	2-4-82	(G)	Pit. 7	at	NYR 5	79	79	38-65 —	103	80	

Player	Team	Date of 100th Point	G or A	Score			Player's Game No.	Team Game No.	Points G - A PTS	Total Games	Age when first 100th point scored (Yrs. & Mos.)
Wayne Gretzky	Edm.	5-1-83	(A)	Edm. 8	at	Wpg. 3	42	42	71-125 - 196	80	
Mike Bossy	NYI	3-3-83	(A)	Tor. 1	at	NYI. 5	66	67	60-58 — 118	79	
Peter Stastny	Que.	5-3-83	(A)	Hfd. 3	at	Que. 10	62	67	47-77 — 124	75	
Denis Savard	Chi.	6-3-83	(A)	Mtl. 4	at	Chi. 5	65	67	35-86 — 121	78	
Mark Messier	Edm.	23-3-83	(G)	Edm. 4	at	Wpg. 7	73	76	48-58 — 106	77	22.2
Barry Pederson	Bos.	26-3-83	(A)	Hfd. 4	at	Bos. 7	73	76	46-61 — 107	77	22.0
Marcel Dionne	L.A.	26-3-83	(A)	Edm. 9	at	L.A. 3	75	75	56-51 — 107	80	
Michel Goulet	Que.	27-3-83	(A)	Que. 6	at	Buf. 6	77	77	57-48 — 105	80	
Glenn Anderson	Edm.	29-3-83	(A)	Edm. 7	at	Van. 4	70	78	48-56 — 104	72	22.11
Jari Kurri	Edm.	29-3-83	(A)	Edm. 7	at	Van. 4	78	78	45-59 — 104	80	22.10
Kent Nilsson	Cgy.	29-3-83	(G)	L.A. 3	at	Cgy. 5	78	78	46-58 — 104	80	
Wayne Gretzky	Edm.	18-12-83	(G)	Edm. 7	at	Wpg. 5	34	34	87-118 — 205	74	
Paul Coffey	Edm.	4-3-84	(A)	Mtl. 1	at	Edm. 6	68	68	40-86 — 126	80	22.9
Michel Goulet	Que.	4-3-84	(A)	Que. 1	at	Buf. 1	62	67	56-65 — 121	75	
Jari Kurri	Edm.	7-3-84	(G)	Chi. 4	at	Edm. 7	53	69	52-61 — 113	64	
Peter Stastny	Que.	8-3-84	(A)	Que. 8	at	Pit. 6	69	69	46-73 — 119	80	
Mike Bossy	NYI	8-3-84	(G)	Tor. 5	at	NYI 9	56	68	51-67 — 118	67	
Barry Pederson	Bos.	14-3-84	(A)	Bos. 4	at	Det. 2	71	71	39-77 — 116	80	
Bryan Trottier	NYI	18-3-84	(G)	NYI 4	at	Hfd. 5	62	73	40-71 — 111	68	
Bernie Federko	St.L.	20-3-84	(A)	Wpg. 3	at	St.L. 9	75	76	41-66 — 107	79	
Rick Middleton	Bos.	27-3-84	(A)	Bos. 6	at	Que. 4	77	77	47-58 — 105	80	
Dale Hawerchuk	Wpg.	27-3-84	(A)	Wpg. 3	at	L.A. 3	77	77	37-65 — 102	80	
Mark Messier	Edm.	27-3-84	(G)	Edm. 9	at	Cgy. 2	72	79	37-64 — 101	73	
Wayne Gretzky	Edm.	29-12-84	(A)	Det. 3	at	Edm. 6	35	35	73-135 — 208	80	
Jari Kurri	Edm.	29-1-85	(G)	Edm. 4	at	Cgy. 2	48	51	71-64 — 135	73	
Mike Bossy	NYI	23-2-85	(G)	Bos. 1	at	NYI 7	56	60	58-59 — 117	76	
Dale Hawerchuk	Wpg.	25-2-85	(A)	Wpg. 12	at	NYR 5	64	64	53-77 — 130	80	
Marcel Dionne	L.A.	5-3-85	(A)	Pit. 0	at	L.A. 6	66	66	46-80 — 126	80	
Brent Sutter	NYI	12-3-85	(A)	NYI 6	at	St. L. 5	68	68	42-60 — 102	72	22.10
John Ogrodnick	Det.	22-3-85	(A)	NYR 3	at	Det. 5	73	73	55-50 — 105	79	25.9
Paul Coffey	Edm.	26-3-85	(G)	Edm. 7	at	NYI 5	74	74	37-84 — 121	80	
Denis Savard	Chi.	29-3-85	(A)	Chi. 5	at	Wpg. 5	75	76	38-67 — 105	79	
Peter Stastny	Que.	2-4-85	(A)	Bos. 4	at	Que. 6	74	77	32-68 — 100	75	
Bernie Federko	St.L.	4-4-85	(A)	NYR 5	at	St.L. 4	74	78	30-73 — 103	76	
John Tonelli	NYI	6-4-85	(G)	NJ 5	at	NYI 5	80	80	42-58 — 100	80	28.1
Paul MacLean	Wpg.	6-4-85	(A)	Wpg. 6	at	Edm. 5	78	79	41-60 — 101	79	27.1
Mike Gartner	Wsh.	7-4-85	(G)	Pit. 3	at	Wsh. 7	80	80	50-52 — 102	80	25.6
Bernie Nicholls	L.A.	6-4-85	(A)	Van. 4	at	L.A. 4	80	80	46-54 — 100	80	22.9
Mario Lemieux	Pit.	7-4-85	(G)	Pit. 3	at	Wsh. 7	73	80	43-57 — 100	73	19.6
Wayne Gretzky	Edm.	4-1-86	(A)	Hfd. 3	at	Edm. 4	39	39	52-163 — 215	80	
Mario Lemieux	Pit.	15-2-86	(G)	Van. 4	at	Pit. 9	55	56	48-93 — 141	79	
Paul Coffey	Edm.	19-2-86	(A)	Tor. 5	at	Edm. 9	59	60	48-90 — 138	79	
Jari Kurri	Edm.	2-3-86	(A)	Phi. 1	at	Edm. 2	62	64	68-63 — 131	78	
Peter Stastny	Que.	1-3-86	(A)	Buf. 8	at	Que. 4	66	68	41-81 — 122	76	
Mike Bossy	NYI	8-3-86	(G)	Wsh. 6	at	NYI 2	65	65	61-62 — 123	80	
Denis Savard	Chi.	12-3-86	(A)	Buf. 7	at	Chi. 6	69	69	47-69 — 116	80	
Mats Naslund	Mtl.	13-3-86	(A)	Mtl. 2	at	Bos. 3	70	70	43-67 — 110	80	26.4
Michel Goulet	Que.	24-3-86	(A)	Que. 1	at	Min. 0	70	75	53-50 — 103	75	
Glenn Anderson	Edm.	25-3-86	(A)	Edm. 7	at	Det. 2	66	74	54-48 — 102	72	
Neal Broten	Min.	26-3-86	(A)	Min. 6	at	Tor. 1	76	76	29-76 — 105	80	26.4
Dale Hawerchuk	Wpg.	31-3-86	(A)	Wpg. 5	at	L.A. 2	78	78	46-59 — 105	80	
Bernie Federko	St.L.	5-4-86	(A)	Chi. 5	at	St.L. 7	79	79	34-68 — 102	80	
Wayne Gretzky	Edm.	1-11-87	(A)	Cgy. 3	at	Edm. 5	42	42	62-121 — 183	79	
Jari Kurri	Edm.	3-14-87	(A)	Buf. 3	at	Edm. 5	67	68	54-54 — 108	79	
Mario Lemieux	Pit.	3-18-87	(A)	St.L. 4	at	Pit. 5	55	72	54-53 — 107	63	
Mark Messier	Edm.	3-19-87	(A)	Edm. 4	at	Cgy. 5	71	71	37-70 — 107	77	
Doug Gilmour	St.L.	4-2-87	(A)	Buf. 3	at	St.L. 5	78	78	42-63 — 105	80	23.10
Dino Ciccarelli	Min.	3-30-87	(A)	NYR 6	at	Min. 5	78	78	52-51 — 103	80	
Dale Hawerchuk	Wpg.	4-5-87	(A)	Wpg. 3	at	Cgy. 1	80	80	47-53 — 100	80	
Mario Lemieux	Pit.	20-1-88	(G)	Plt. 8	at	Chi. 3	45	48	70-98 — 168	77	
Wayne Gretzky	Edm.	11-2-88	(A)	Edm. 7	at	Van. 2	43	56	40-109 — 149	64	
Denis Savard	Chi.	12-2-88	(A)	St.L. 4	at	Chi. 4	57	57	44-87 — 131	80	
Dale Hawerchuk	Wpg.	23-2-88	(G)	Wpg. 4	at	Pit. 3	61	61	44-77 — 121	80	
Steve Yzerman	Det.	27-2-88	(A)	Det. 4	at	Que. 5	63	63	50-52 — 102	64	22.10
Peter Stastny	Que.	8-3-88	(A)	Hfd. 4	at	Que. 6	67	67	46-65 — 111	76	
Mark Messier	Edm.	15-3-88	(A)	Buf. 4	at	Edm. 6	68	71	37-74 — 111	77	
Jimmy Carson	L.A.	26-3-88	(A)	Chi. 5	at	L.A. 9	77	77	55-52 — 107	80	19.8
Hakan Loob	Cgy.	26-3-88	(A)	Van. 1	at	Cgy. 6	76	76	50-56 — 106	80	27.9
Mike Bullard	Cgy.	26-3-88	(A)	Van. 1	at	Cgy. 6	76	76	48-55 — 103	79	27.1
Michel Goulet	Que.	27-3-88	(A)	Pit. 6	at	Que. 3	76	76	48-58 — 106	80	
Luc Robitaille	L.A.	30-3-88	(G)	Cgy. 7	at	L.A. 9	78	78	53-58 — 111	80	22.1
Mario Lemieux	Pit.	31-12-88	(G)	N.J. 6	at	Pit. 8	36	38	85-114-199	76	
Wayne Gretzky	L.A.	21-1-89	(A)	L.A. 4	at	Hfd. 5	47	48	54-114-168	78	
Steve Yzerman	Det.	27-1-89	(G)	Tor. 1	at	Det. 8	50	50	65-90-155	80	
Bernie Nicholls	L.A.	21-1-89	(A)	L.A. 4	at	Hfd. 5	48	48	70-80-150	79	
Rob Brown	Pit.	16-3-89	(A)	Pit. 2	at	N.J. 1	60	72	49-66-115	68	20.11
Paul Coffey	Pit.	20-3-89	(A)	Plt. 2	at	Min. 7	69	74	30-83-113	75	
Joe Mullen	Cgy.	23-3-89	(A)	L.A. 2	at	Cgy. 4	74	75	51-59-110	79	32.1
Jari Kurri	Edm.	29-3-89	(A)	Edm. 5	at	Van. 2	75	79	44-58-102	76	
Jimmy Carson	Edm.	2-4-89	(A)	Edm. 2	at	Cgy. 4	80	80	49-51-100	80	
Mario Lemieux	Pit.	28-1-90	(G)	Pit. 2	at	Buf. 7	50	50	45-78-123	59	
Wayne Gretzky	L.A.	30-1-90	(A)	N.J. 4	at	L.A. 5	51	51	40-102-142	73	
Steve Yzerman	Det.	19-2-90	(A)	Mtl. 5	at	Det. 5	61	61	62-65-127	79	
Mark Messier	Edm.	20-2-90	(A)	Edm. 4	at	Van. 2	62	62	45-84-129	79	
Brett Hull	St.L.	3-3-90	(A)	NYI 4	at	St.L. 5	67	67	72-41-113	80	25.7
Bernie Nicholls	NYR	12-3-90	(A)	L.A. 6	at	NYR 2	70	71	39-73-112	79	
Pierre Turgeon	Buf.	25-3-90	(G)	N.J. 4	at	Buf. 3	76	76	40-66-106	80	20.7
Paul Coffey	Pit.	25-3-90	(A)	Pit. 2	at	Hfd. 4	77	77	29-74-103	80	
Pat LaFontaine	NYI	27-3-90	(G)	Cgy. 4	at	NYI 2	72	78	54-51-105	74	25.1
Adam Oates	St.L.	29-3-90	(G)	Pit. 4	at	St.L. 5	79	79	23-79-102	80	27.7
Joe Sakic	Que.	31-3-90	(G)	Hfd. 3	at	Que. 2	79	79	39-63-102	80	20.8
Ron Francis	Hfd.	31-3-90	(G)	Hfd. 3	at	Que. 2	79	79	32-69-101	80	27.0
Luc Robitaille	L.A.	1-4-90	(A)	L.A. 4	at	Cgy. 8	80	80	52-49-101	80	

Rick Middleton

Paul Coffey

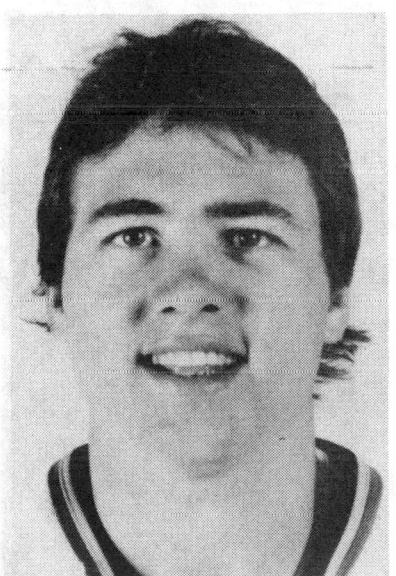

Neal Broten

Five-or-more-Goal Games

Player	Team	Date	Score			Opposing Goaltender
SEVEN GOALS						
Joe Malone	Quebec Bulldogs	Jan. 31/20	Tor. 6	at Que. 10		Ivan Mitchell
SIX GOALS						
Newsy Lalonde	Montreal	Jan. 10/20	Tor. 7	at Mtl. 14		Ivan Mitchell
Joe Malone	Quebec Bulldogs	Mar. 10/20	Ott. 4	at Que. 10		Clint Benedict
Corb Denneny	Toronto St. Pats	Jan. 26/21	Ham. 3	at Tor. 10		Howard Lockhart
Cy Denneny	Ottawa Senators	Mar. 7/21	Ham. 5	at Ott. 12		Howard Lockhart
Syd Howe	Detroit	Feb. 3/44	NYR 2	at Det. 12		Ken McAuley
Red Berenson	St. Louis	Nov. 7/68	St. L. 8	at Phil 0		Doug Favell
Darryl Sittler	Toronto	Feb. 7/76	Bos. 4	at Tor. 11		Dave Reece
FIVE GOALS						
Joe Malone	Montreal	Dec. 19/17	Mtl. 9	at Ott. 4		Clint Benedict
Harry Hyland	Mtl. Wanderers	Dec. 19/17	Tor. 9	at Mtl. 10		Arthur Brooks
Joe Malone	Montreal	Jan. 12/18	Ott. 4	at Mtl. 9		Clint Benedict
Joe Malone	Montreal	Feb. 2/18	Tor. 2	at Mtl. 11		Harry Holmes
Mickey Roach	Toronto St. Pats	Mar. 6/20	Que. 2	at Tor. 11		Frank Brophy
Newsy Lalonde	Montreal	Feb. 16/21	Ham. 5	at Mtl. 10		Howard Lockhart
Babe Dye	Toronto St. Pats	Dec. 16/22	Mtl. 2	at Tor. 7		Georges Vezina
Redvers Green	Hamilton Tigers	Dec. 5/24	Ham. 10	at Tor. 3		John Roach
Babe Dye	Toronto St. Pats	Dec. 22/24	Tor. 10	at Bos. 2		Charlie Stewart
Harry Broadbent	Mtl. Maroons	Jan. 7/25	Mtl. 6	at Ham. 2		Vernon Forbes
Pit Lepine	Montreal	Dec. 14/29	Ott. 4	at Mtl. 6		Alex Connell
Howie Morenz	Montreal	Mar. 18/30	NYA 3	at Mtl. 8		Roy Worters
Charlie Conacher	Toronto	Jan. 19/32	NYA 3	at Tor. 11		Roy Worters
Ray Getliffe	Montreal	Feb. 6/43	Bos. 3	at Mtl. 8		Frank Brimsek
Maurice Richard	Montreal	Dec. 28/44	Det. 1	at Mtl. 9		Harry Lumley
Howie Meeker	Toronto	Jan. 8/47	Chi. 4	at Tor. 10		Paul Bibeault
Bernie Geoffrion	Montreal	Feb. 19/55	NYR 2	at Mtl. 10		Gump Worsley
Bobby Rousseau	Montreal	Feb. 1/64	Det. 3	at Mtl. 9		Roger Crozier
Yvan Cournoyer	Montreal	Feb. 15/75	Chi. 3	at Mtl. 12		Mike Veisor
Don Murdoch	NY Rangers	Oct. 12/76	NYR 10	at Min. 4		Gary Smith
Ian Turnbull	Toronto	Feb. 2/77	Det. 1	at Tor. 9		Ed Giacomin (2) Jim Rutherford (3)
*Bryan Trottier	NY Islanders	Dec. 23/78	NYR 4	at NYI 9		Wayne Thomas (4) John Davidson (1)
Tim Young	Minnesota	Jan. 15/79	Min. 8	at NYR 1		Doug Soetaert (3) Wayne Thomas (2)
*John Tonelli	NY Islanders	Jan. 6/81	Tor. 3	at NYI 6		Jiri Crha (5)
*Wayne Gretzky	Edmonton	Feb. 18/81	St.L. 2	at Edm. 9		Mike Liut (3) Ed Staniowski (2)
*Wayne Gretzky	Edmonton	Dec. 30/81	Phi. 5	at Edm. 7		Pete Peeters (4) Empty Net (1)
Grant Mulvey	Chicago	Feb. 3/82	St.L. 5	at Chi. 9		Mike Liut (4) Gary Edwards (1)
*Bryan Trottier	NY Islanders	Feb. 13/82	Phi. 2	at NYI 8		Pete Peeters
Willy Lindstrom	Winnipeg	Mar. 2/82	Wpg. 7	at Phi. 6		Pete Peeters
Mark Pavelich	NY Rangers	Feb. 23/83	Hfd. 3	at NYR 11		Greg Millen
*Jari Kurri	Edmonton	Nov. 19/83	N.J. 4	at Edm. 13		Glenn Resch (3) Ron Low (2)
Bengt Gustafsson	Washington	Jan. 8/84	Wsh. 7	at Phi. 1		Pelle Lindbergh
Pat Hughes	Edmonton	Feb. 3/84	Cgy. 5	at Edm. 10		Don Edwards (3) Rejean Lemelin (2)
*Wayne Gretzky	Edmonton	Dec. 15/84	Edm. 8	at St. L. 2		Rick Wamsley (4) Mike Liut (1)
*Dave Andreychuk	Buffalo	Feb. 6/86	Buf. 8	at Bos. 6		Pat Riggin (1) Doug Keans (4)
*Wayne Gretzky	Edmonton	Dec. 6/87	Min. 4	at Edm. 10		Don Beaupre (4) Kari Takko (1)
*Mario Lemieux	Pittsburgh	Dec. 31/88	N.J. 6	at Pit. 8		Bob Sauve (3) Chris Terreri (2)
*Joe Nieuwendyk	Calgary	Jan. 11/89	Wpg. 3	at Cgy. 8		Daniel Berthiaume (5)

* Active.

Bengt Gustafsson had a five-goal night against the Philadelphia Flyers on January 8, 1984.

In 1975, John Bucyk became the seventh player in NHL history to score 500 goals.

Players' 500th Goals

Player	Team	Date	Game No.	Score			Opposing Goaltender	Total Goals	Total Games
Maurice Richard	Montreal	Oct. 19/57	863	Chi. 1	at Mtl. 3		Glenn Hall	544	978
Gordie Howe	Detroit	Mar. 14/62	1,045	Det. 2	at NYR 3		Gump Worsley	801	1,767
Bobby Hull	Chicago	Feb. 21/70	861	NYR. 2	at Chi. 4		Ed Giacomin	610	1,063
Jean Beliveau	Montreal	Feb. 11/71	1,101	Min. 2	at Mtl. 6		Gilles Gilbert	507	1,125
Frank Mahovlich	Montreal	Mar. 21/73	1,105	Van. 2	at Mtl. 3		Dunc Wilson	533	1,181
Phil Esposito	Boston	Dec. 22/74	803	Det. 4	at Bos. 5		Jim Rutherford	717	1,282
John Bucyk	Boston	Oct. 30/75	1,370	St. L. 2	at Bos. 3		Yves Belanger	556	1,540
Stan Mikita	Chicago	Feb. 27/77	1,221	Van. 4	at Chi. 3		Cesare Maniago	541	1,394
Marcel Dionne	Los Angeles	Dec. 14/82	887	L.A. 2	at Wsh. 7		Al Jensen	731	1,348
*Guy Lafleur	Montreal	Dec. 20/83	918	Mtl. 6	at N.J. 0		Glenn Resch	548	1,067
Mike Bossy	NY Islanders	Jan. 2/86	647	Bos. 5	at NYI 7		empty net	573	752
Gilbert Perreault	Buffalo	Mar. 9/86	1,159	NJ 3	at Buf. 4		Alain Chevrier	512	1,191
*Wayne Gretzky	Edmonton	Nov. 22/86	575	Van. 2	at Edm. 5		empty net	677	847
Lanny McDonald	Calgary	Mar. 21/89	1,107	NYI 1	at Cgy. 4		Mark Fitzpatrick	500	1,111
*Bryan Trottier	NY Islanders	Feb. 13/90	1,104	Cgy. 4	at NYI 2		Rick Wamsley	500	1,123

* Active

Individual Awards

Hart Memorial Trophy

Art Ross Trophy

Calder Memorial Trophy

James Norris Memorial Trophy

HART MEMORIAL TROPHY

An annual award "to the player adjudged to be the most valuable to his team". Winner selected in poll by Professional Hockey Writers' Association in the 21 NHL cities at the end of the regular schedule. The winner receives $3,000 and the runner-up $1,000.

History: The Hart Memorial Trophy was presented by the National Hockey League in 1960 after the original Hart Trophy was retired to the Hockey Hall of Fame. The original Hart Trophy was donated to the NHL in 1923 by Dr. David A. Hart, father of Cecil Hart, former manager-coach of the Montreal Canadiens.

1989-90 Winner: Mark Messier, Edmonton Oilers
Runners-up: Raymond Bourque, Boston Bruins
Brett Hull, St. Louis Blues

Edmonton Oilers captain Mark Messier edged Boston defenseman Raymond Bourque by two votes to capture the Hart Memorial Trophy, awarded to "the player adjudged to be the most valuable to his team."

Messier, who became the second Edmonton player to win the award, had 227 of a maximum 315 points compared with 225 for Bourque. Both players received 29 first-place votes of a possible 63 while Bourque had 26 second-place votes compared with 24 for Messier. However the Edmonton centre, who was the only player named on all 63 Hart Trophy ballots, had 10 third-place votes compared with two for Bourque. Brett Hull of the St. Louis Blues placed third in the voting with 80 votes.

The previous closest voting for the Hart Trophy was in 1981 when Wayne Gretzky, then with Edmonton, won his second Hart, collecting 242 votes compared with 237 for goaltender Mike Liut, who was playing for the St. Louis Blues. Prior to that, the previous narrowest margin was six points in 1953-54 when Chicago netminder Al Rollins edged defenseman Red Kelly of Detroit for the award.

Messier finished second in the NHL scoring race during the 1989-90 season with 45 goals and 84 assists for 129 points, just 13 points behind Los Angeles captain Gretzky, who won the Hart Trophy for a League record ninth time last season.

This is the first time that Messier has won an NHL trophy during the regular season. The 11-year NHL veteran won the Conn Smythe Trophy, as the most valuable performer in the playoffs, in 1984.

ART ROSS TROPHY

An annual award "to the player who leads the league in scoring points at the end of the regular season." Overall winner receives $3,000 and the overall runner-up $1,000.

History: Arthur Howie Ross, former manager-coach of Boston Bruins, presented the trophy to the National Hockey League in 1947. If two players finish the schedule with the same number of points, the trophy is awarded in the following manner: 1. Player with most goals. 2. Player with fewer games played. 3. Player scoring first goal of the season.

1989-90 Winner: Wayne Gretzky, Los Angeles Kings
Runners-up: Mark Messier, Edmonton Oilers
Steve Yzerman, Detroit Red Wings

Wayne Gretzky of the Los Angeles Kings won the Art Ross Trophy in 1989-90, ending Mario Lemieux's two-year hold on the award. Gretzky had 40 goals and 102 assists for 142 points in 73 games en route to the eighth Art Ross Trophy of his 11 year NHL career.

CALDER MEMORIAL TROPHY

An annual award "to the player selected as the most proficient in his first year of competition in the National Hockey League". Winner selected in poll by Professional Hockey Writers' Association at the end of the regular schedule. The winner receives $3,000 and the runner-up $1,000.

History: From 1936-37 until his death in 1943, Frank Calder, NHL President, bought a trophy each year to be given permanently to the outstanding rookie. After Calder's death, the NHL presented the Calder Memorial Trophy in his memory and the trophy is to be kept in perpetuity. To be eligible for the award, a player cannot have played more than 25 games in any single preceding season nor in six or more games in each of any two preceding seasons in any major professional league. Beginning in 1990-91, to be eligible for this award a player must not have attained his twenty-sixth birthday by September 15th of the season in which he is eligible.

1989-90 Winner: Sergei Makarov, Calgary Flames
Runners-up: Mike Modano, Minnesota North Stars
Jeremy Roenick, Chicago Blackhawks

Sergei Makarov of the Calgary Flames became the first player from the Soviet Union to win an award in the National Hockey League as he captured the Calder Memorial Trophy given to "the player selected as the most proficient in his first season."

Makarov, who had 37 of a possible 63 first-place votes, finished with 204 points compared with 120 for center Mike Modano of the Minnesota North Stars. Third place went to Jeremy Roenick of the Chicago Blackhawks who garnered 71 points.

Makarov, a right winger, is the third member of the Flames to win the Calder Trophy in the past five years. Defenseman Gary Suter won in 1986 and centre Joe Nieuwendyk was the 1988 winner.

During his initial NHL campaign, Makarov, who joined the Flames from the Soviet Central Army team this fall, finished with 24 goals and 62 assists for 86 points and a plus 33. His assists and points totals were tops among first-year players in the NHL and his plus-minus mark tied him for fourth over-all in the League.

JAMES NORRIS MEMORIAL TROPHY

An annual award "to the defense player who demonstrates throughout the season the greatest all-round ability in the position." Winner selected in poll by Professional Hockey Writers' Association at the end of the regular schedule. The winner receives $3,000 and the runner-up $1,000.

History: The James Norris Memorial Trophy was presented in 1953 by the four children of the late James Norris in memory of the former owner-president of the Detroit Red Wings.

1989-90 Winner: Raymond Bourque, Boston Bruins
Runners-up: Al MacInnis, Calgary Flames
Doug Wilson, Chicago Blackhawks

Veteran Boston defenseman Raymond Bourque received all 63 first-place votes en route to his third James Norris Memorial Trophy as the defenseman demonstrating "the greatest all-around ability in the position."

Bourque finished with a maximum 315 points compared with 127 for runner-up Al MacInnis of the Calgary Flames, who was third in the voting last season. Doug Wilson, who won the Norris Trophy in 1982, was third in the balloting with 40 points.

A native of Montreal, Bourque was second on the Bruins in scoring with 19 goals and 65 assists for 84 points, also good enough for third spot among NHL defensemen. Of his 19 goals, eight were power-play efforts and six were game-winners and Bourque also maintained a team-high plus 31 in the 76 games in which he participated.

Vezina Trophy

Lady Byng Memorial Trophy

Frank J. Selke Trophy

Conn Smythe Trophy

VEZINA TROPHY

An annual award "to the goalkeeper adjudged to be the best at his position" as voted by the general managers of each of the 21 clubs. Over-all winner receives $3,000, runner-up $1,000.

History: Leo Dandurand, Louis Letourneau and Joe Cattarinich, former owners of the Montreal Canadiens, presented the trophy to the National Hockey League in 1926-27 in memory of Georges Vezina, outstanding goalkeeper of the Canadiens who collapsed during an NHL game November 28, 1925, and died of tuberculosis a few months later. Until the 1981-82 season, the goalkeeper(s) of the team allowing the fewest number of goals during the regular-season were awarded the Vezina Trophy.

1989-90 Winner: Patrick Roy, Montreal Canadiens
Runners-up: Daren Puppa, Buffalo Sabres
Andy Moog, Boston Bruins

Montreal Canadiens goaltender Patrick Roy obtained 91 of a possible 105 points, including 15 first-place votes en route to his second consecutive Vezina Trophy awarded annually to the "goaltender adjudged to be the best in his position."

Roy, who also had 15 first-place votes last season, finished ahead of Buffalo netminder Daren Puppa, who had 59 points for second spot with Boston Bruins goaltender Andy Moog finishing third.

Appearing in 54 games during the past season, Roy tied with Washington's Mike Liut for the best individual goals-against mark – 2.53. Roy, who had three shutouts, tied with Puppa and Minnesota's Jon Casey for the most victories – 31 and led the NHL with a .912 save percentage. Roy and teammate Brian Hayward finished second in the Jennings Trophy competition for the best goals-against average after winning the Jennings in the three previous years.

LADY BYNG MEMORIAL TROPHY

An annual award "to the player adjudged to have exhibited the best type of sportsmanship and gentlemanly conduct combined with a high standard of playing ability." Winner selected in poll by Professional Hockey Writers' Association at the end of the regular schedule. The winner receives $3,000 and the runner-up $1,000.

History: Lady Byng, wife of Canada's Governor-General at the time, presented the Lady Byng Trophy in 1925. After Frank Boucher of New York Rangers won the award seven times in eight seasons, he was given the trophy to keep and Lady Byng donated another trophy in 1936. After Lady Byng's death in 1949, the National Hockey League presented a new trophy, changing the name to Lady Byng Memorial Trophy.

1989-90 Winner: Brett Hull, St. Louis Blues
Runners-up: Wayne Gretzky, Los Angeles Kings
Pat Lafontaine, NY Islanders

Brett Hull of the St. Louis Blues joined his father, Bobby, on the NHL honor roll as a trophy winner by taking the Lady Byng Memorial Trophy awarded annually "to the player adjudged to have exhibited the best type of sportsmanship and gentlemanly conduct combined with a high standard of playing ability." The Hulls are the first father-son combination to both win League awards.

While scoring 72 goals and 113 points for the Blues this season, the younger Hull spent just 24 minutes in the penalty box. He received 42 of a possible 63 first-place votes and finished with 238 points compared with 79 for Wayne Gretzky of the Los Angeles Kings, who finished second. Pat LaFontaine of the New York Islanders placed third with 72 points.

Hull's father won the Hart Memorial Trophy as the player adjudged to be most valuable to his team in 1965 and 1966 while playing for the Chicago Blackhawks and also won the Art Ross Trophy as the NHL's scoring champion thrice.

FRANK J. SELKE TROPHY

An annual award "to the forward who best excels in the defensive aspects of the game." Winner selected in poll by Professional Hockey Writers' Association at the end of the regular schedule. The winner receives $3,000 and the runner-up $1,000.

History: Presented to the National Hockey League in 1977 by the Board of Governors of the NHL in honour of Frank J. Selke, one of the great architects of NHL championship teams.

1989-90 Winner: Rick Meagher, St. Louis Blues
Runners-up: Guy Carbonneau, Montreal Canadiens
Esa Tikkanen, Edmonton Oilers

St. Louis Blues captain Rick Meagher edged two-time winner Guy Carbonneau of the Montreal Canadiens and captured the Frank J. Selke Trophy, presented to the "forward who best excels in the defensive aspects of the game."

Meagher, 36, finished with 105 points, including 16 first-place votes, to finish five points ahead of Carbonneau, who had won the award in each of the two previous seasons. Esa Tikkanen of the Edmonton Oilers finished third with 81 points.

A native of Belleville, Ontario, Meagher was originally signed as a free agent by the Canadiens June 27, 1977 following the completion of his college career with Boston University. He played with Hartford and New Jersey before joining the Blues prior to the 1985-86 season.

This season, Meagher had eight goals and 17 assists in 76 games for the Blues and finished with a plus 4.

CONN SMYTHE TROPHY

An annual award "to the most valuable player for his team in the playoffs." Winner selected by the Professional Hockey Writers' Association at the conclusion of the final game in the Stanley Cup Finals. The winner receives $3,000.

History: Presented by Maple Leaf Gardens Limited in 1964 to honor Conn Smythe, the former coach, manager, president and owner-governor of the Toronto Maple Leafs.

1989-90 Winner: Bill Ranford, Edmonton Oilers

Bill Ranford became the eighth goaltender in league history to capture the Conn Smythe Trophy. He helped lead his team to series victories over Winnipeg, Los Angeles, Chicago and Boston. A late season injury to teammate Grant Fuhr allowed Ranford the opportunity to step in and supply the Oilers with the goaltending (2.53 goals-against-average in 22 games) they required to win the Stanley Cup.

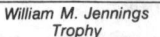

William M. Jennings
Trophy

Jack Adams
Award

Bill Masterton
Trophy

Lester Patrick
Trophy

Alka-Seltzer
Plus Award

WILLIAM M. JENNINGS TROPHY

An annual award "to the goalkeeper(s) having played a minimum of 25 games for the team with the fewest goals scored against it." Winners selected on regular-season play. Overall winner receives $3,000, runner-up $1,000. Leader at end of first half of season and leader in second half each receive $250.

History: The Jennings Trophy was presented in 1981-82 by the National Hockey League's Board of Governors to honor the late William M. Jennings, longtime governor and president of the New York Rangers and one of the great builders of hockey in the United States.

1989-90 Winners: Andy Moog and Rejean Lemelin, Boston Bruins
Runners-up: Patrick Roy and Brian Hayward, Montreal Canadiens

Combining for a league-leading 2.87 goals-against-average, Moog and Lemelin's efforts marked the first time that the Bruins' led the League in goals-against-average since 1941-42. Lemelin had 2 shutouts and was third in goals-against-average (2.81). Moog registered 3 shutouts and was fifth in goals-against-average (2.89).

JACK ADAMS AWARD

An annual award presented by the National Hockey League Broadcasters' Association to "the NHL coach adjudged to have contributed the most to his team's success." Winner selected by poll among members of the NHL Broadcasters' Association at the end of the regular season. The winner receives $1,000 from the NHLBA.

History: The award was presented by the NHL Broadcasters' Association in 1974 to commemorate the late Jack Adams, coach and general manager of Detroit Red Wings, whose lifetime dedication to hockey serves as an inspiration to all who aspire to further the game.

1989-90 Winner: Bob Murdoch, Winnipeg Jets
Runners-up: Mike Milbury, Boston Bruins
Roger Neilson, NY Rangers

Winnipeg head coach Bob Murdoch became the second Jets coach to win the Jack Adams Trophy presented to the "NHL coach adjudged to have contributed the most to his team's success." Murdoch finished ahead of Boston rookie head coach Mike Milbury and veteran mentor Roger Neilson of the New York Rangers to win the award.

Murdoch, who assumed the reins in Winnipeg this season, led the Jets to a solid 37–32–11 record for 85 points and a third-place finish in the Smythe Division.

The other Jets coach to win the Adams Trophy was Tom Watt in 1982.

BILL MASTERTON MEMORIAL TROPHY

An annual award under the trusteeship of the Professional Hockey Writers' Association to "the National Hockey League player who best exemplifies the qualities of perseverance, sportsmanship and dedication to hockey." Winner selected by poll among the 21 chapters of the PHWA at the end of the regular season. A $2,500 grant from the PHWA is awarded annually to the Bill Masterton Scholarship Fund, based in Bloomington, MN, in the name of the Masterton Trophy winner.

History: The trophy was presented by the NHL Writers' Association in 1968 to commemorate the late William Masterton, a player of the Minnesota North Stars, who exhibited to a high degree the qualities of perseverance, sportsmanship and dedication to hockey, and who died January 15, 1968.

1989-90 Winner: Gord Kluzak, Boston Bruins

Boston defenseman Gord Kluzak is the winner of the Bill Masterton Memorial Trophy, an annual award under the trusteeship of the Professional Hockey Writers Association which is given to "the National Hockey League player who best exemplifies the qualities of perseverance, sportsmanship and dedication to hockey."

Each PHWA chapter nominated a player for consideration and Kluzak, who has now undergone 11 operations on his left knee, was selected as the winner.

Kluzak missed the 1984-85 and 1986-87 seasons because of problems with his knee but returned in each of the following years. This season, Kluzak appeared in eight games with the Bruins after surgery on his knee.

LESTER PATRICK TROPHY

An annual award "for outstanding service to hockey in the United States." Eligible recipients are players, officials, coaches, executives and referees. Winner selected by an award committee consisting of the President of the NHL, an NHL Governor, a representative of the New York Rangers, a member of the Hockey Hall of Fame Builder's section, a member of the Hockey Hall of Fame Player's section, a member of the U.S. Hockey Hall of Fame, a member of the NHL Broadcasters' Association and a member of the Professional Hockey Writers' Association. Each except the League President is rotated annually. The winner receives a miniature of the trophy.

History: Presented by the New York Rangers in 1966 to honor the late Lester Patrick, longtime general manager and coach of the New York Rangers, whose teams finished out of the playoffs only once in his first 16 years with the club.

1989-90 Winner: Len Ceglarski

Len Ceglarski, the winningest coach in American college hockey history, is the 1990 recipient of the Lester Patrick Trophy.

Ceglarski's longevity and winning consistency is unmatched in the hockey coaching ranks, as Ceglarski-coached teams have sported winning records in 29 of his 32 years and earned four trips to the NCAA Tournament finals. He has fashioned a career coaching record of 632-309-35 and is the only collegiate coach to ever win 250 or more games at two different institutions (254 in 14 years at Clarkson, 378 in 18 years at Boston College).

He has had sixteen 20-victory seasons and his teams have appeared in 12 NCAA Tournaments and 18 ECAC Tournaments. Ceglarski has earned three Spencer Penrose Awards as National Coach of the Year (1965-66, 1972-73, and 1984-85).

A native of Walpole, Massachusetts, Ceglarski was a triple-letter winner in both hockey and baseball at Boston College. He earned All-America recognition as a junior in 1950 and captained the hockey team as a senior in 1951.

Ceglarski continued his hockey career as a member of the 1952 Silver Medal United States Olympic Team before joining the Marine Corps. After his tour of duty, he returned to the Boston area to coach at Norwood High School, then at Walpole High.

In 1958, Ceglarski began his coaching career at Clarkson College where, in 14 seasons, he compiled a 254-97-11 record, including 11 consecutive trips to the ECAC Tournament, one ECAC Championship and four NCAA Tournament berths.

After the 1971-72 season, Ceglarski returned to BC, replacing his own collegiate mentor, John "Snooks" Kelley. Ceglarski's record at BC is 378-212-24 and his 1989-90 team captured the Hockey East title (fifth time in six years) and advanced to the NCAA Final Four in Detroit. Ceglarski has coached nine first team All-Americans and eight U.S. Olympians at BC. Current NHL players coached by Ceglarski at BC include 1989 Calder Trophy winner Brian Leetch of the New York Rangers and 1989 Lady Byng Trophy winner Joe Mullen, now with Pittsburgh.

ALKA-SELTZER PLUS AWARD

An annual award "to the player, having played a minimum of 60 games, who leads the League in plus/minus statistics" at the end of the regular season. Miles, Inc. will contribute $5,000 on behalf of the winner to the charity of his choice and $1000 on behalf of each individual team winner.

History: The award was presented to the NHL in 1989-90 by Miles, Inc., to recognize the League leader in plus-minus statistics. Plus-minus statistics are calculated by giving a player a "plus" when on-ice for an even-strength or shorthand goal scored by his team. He receives a "minus" when on-ice for an even-strength or shorthand goal scored by the opposing team. A plus-minus award has been presented since the 1982-83 season.

1989-90 Winner: Paul Cavallini, St. Louis Blues

In compiling the best plus-minus in the NHL at +38, Cavallini was on the ice for 134 of St. Louis' 295 goals scored including 26 powerplay goals for an offensive net of 108. Defensively, he was on for 112 of the 279 goals the Blues surrendered including 42 opposition powerplay goals for a defensive net of 70. Individual team leaders include: Ray Bourque, Boston; Mike Ramsay, Buffalo; Jamie Macoun, Calgary; Greg Gilbert, Chicago; Lee Norwood, Detroit; Craig Muni, Edmonton; Ron Francis, Hartford; Tim Watters, Los Angeles; Stewart Gavin, Minnesota; Stephane Richer, Montreal; John MacLean, New Jersey; Mick Vukota and Pat Flatley, NY Islanders; John Ogrodnick and Kelly Kisio, NY Rangers; Kjell Samuelsson, Philadelphia; Randy Hillier, Pittsburgh; Jeff Jackson, Quebec; Brad Marsh, Toronto; Brian Bradley, Vancouver; Geoff Courtnall, Washington; Doug Smail, Winnipeg.

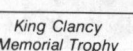

King Clancy
Memorial Trophy

Lester B. Pearson
Award

Budweiser/NHL
Man of The Year

Trico Goaltender
Award

Presidents'
Trophy

KING CLANCY MEMORIAL TROPHY

An annual award "to the player who best exemplifies leadership qualities on and off the ice and has made a noteworthy humanitarian contribution in his community". The winner receives $3,000 and the runner-up $1,000.

History: The King Clancy Memorial Trophy was presented to the National Hockey League by the Board of Governors in 1988 to honor the late Frank "King" Clancy.

1989-90 Winner: Kevin Lowe, Edmonton Oilers

Veteran defenseman Kevin Lowe of the Edmonton Oilers is the winner of the King Clancy Memorial Trophy, awarded to the "player who best exemplifies leadership qualities on and off the ice and has made a noteworthy humanitarian contribution in his community." Lowe was selected by his teammates to represent the Oilers and was chosen the winner by a special panel of judges appointed by the President.

Lowe, who was the Oilers first-ever NHL draft choice in 1979 and has been on Edmonton's roster since, has played on five Stanley Cup championship teams in Edmonton. Lowe, an assistant captain in Edmonton, has been actively involved in the NHL Players Association in recent seasons.

Off the ice, Lowe is honorary chairman of Edmonton's City Christmas Bureau and is considered instrumental in assuring the campaign meets its goal to feed all of Edmonton's needy families at Christmas. Lowe is also heavily involved in the "Shining Lights" campaign, an RCMP initiative to prevent child abuse.

In addition, Lowe is the host of an annual golf tournament in his hometown of Lachute, Que., to raise money for charitable causes.

LESTER B. PEARSON AWARD

An annual award presented to the NHL's outstanding player as selected by the members of the National Hockey League Players' Association. The winner receives $3,000 and the runner-up $1,500.

History: The award was presented in 1970-71 by the NHLPA in honor of the late Lester B. Pearson, former Prime Minister of Canada.

1989-90 Winner: Mark Messier, Edmonton Oilers
Runners-up: Ray Bourque, Boston Bruins
Brett Hull, St. Louis Blues

Messier finished the regular season with the highest career point total of his 11 year NHL career. The Oilers' captain tied for the League lead in first goals scored (12), tied for second place with six shorthanded goals and ranked second in points (129) and assists (84).

NHL AWARD MONEY BREAKDOWN

(All team awards are based on units of 21 per team except Presidents' Trophy which is based on 20 units.)

Stanley Cup Playoffs

		Individual	Total Shares
Division Semi-Final Losers	(8 teams)	$ 3,000	$ 504,000
Division Final Losers	(4 teams)	6,000	504,000
Conference Championship Losers	(2 teams)	11,000	462,000
Stanley Cup Championship Losers		18,000	378,000
Stanley Cup Winners		25,000	525,000
TOTAL PLAYOFF AWARD MONEY			$2,373,000

Final Standings, Regular Season

Presidents' Trophy (Team's share $100,000)		$5,000	$200,000
Division Winners	(4 teams)	5,000	420,000
Second Place	(4 teams)	2,500	210,000
TOTAL CHAMPIONSHIP POOL			$830,000

Individual Awards

First Team All-Stars		$5,000	$30,000
Second Team All-Stars		2,000	12,000
All-Star Game winners' share		1,000	20,000
All-Star Game losers' share		750	15,000
Individual Award Winners		3,000	30,000
Individual Award Runners-up		1,000	9,000
TOTAL INDIVIDUAL AWARD MONEY			$116,000

BUDWEISER/NHL MAN OF THE YEAR

An annual award to the player recognized in the local community as a positive role model through his conduct on and off the ice. This includes involvement with local youth groups, charities and causes, as well as recognition among his peers and fans as a player who extols sportsmanlike qualities while maximizing his efforts toward improving his play and that of the team. The winner is selected by a special committee of distinguished NHL officials and management executives. The Bud/NHL Man of the Year recognizes one player from each of the local media representatives. Each nominated player receives a check for $1,000 to be given to his favorite charity. The winner receives $21,000 to be distributed to his favorite charities.

1989-90 Winner: Kevin Lowe, Edmonton Oilers
Runners-up: Kevin Dineen, Hartford Whalers
Doug Wilson, Chicago Blackhawks

A native of Lachute, Quebec, the 6-foot-2, 195-pound Lowe has recorded 343 points (68 goals, 275 assists) in 838 NHL games. The six-time All-Star ranks second among defensemen in career scoring for Edmonton and is sixth overall on the Oilers' all-time list.

Lowe, who finished second in last year's Budweiser/NHL Man of the Year balloting, is very active in several charities. He is the honorary chairman for Edmonton's Christmas Bureau, an umbrella organization which coordinates the collection of money and delivery of services to people in need at Christmas time. Lowe spends many hours and makes hundreds of appearances throughout the year to further the campaign effort. He is heavily involved in many other children-oriented charities.

TRICO GOALTENDER AWARD

An annual award to the goaltender with the best save percentage during the regular schedule. The winner receives $10,000 to benefit the charitable organization of his choice. The runners-up each receive $1,000 to be presented in their names to the charity of their choice.

History: The award was presented to the National Hockey League in 1988-89 by Trico to recognize the goaltender with the best save percentage during the regular schedule.

1989-90 Winner: Patrick Roy, Montreal Canadiens
Runners-up: Mike Liut, Washington Capitals
Daren Puppa, Buffalo Sabres

Patrick Roy won his second consecutive Trico Goaltender Award with a .912 save percentage, bettering his 1988-89 mark of .908.

Roy, who led the Trico Award rankings (minimum 35 games played) at three of the statistical update intervals in 1989-90: December (.910), January (.906) and March (.911), stopped 1390 of the 1524 shots he faced (.912) to edge Washington netminder Mike Liut (.905) and Buffalo Sabres' Daren Puppa (.903). Trico will contribute $1,000 on behalf of Liut and Puppa to the charity of their choice. This season marks the second year of Trico's NHL sponsorship.

Team Award
PRESIDENTS' TROPHY

An annual award to the club finishing the regular-season with the best overall record. The winner receives $200,000, to be split evenly between the team and its players. Based on 20 players in each game during the regular-season, a player who appears in all 80 games receives $5,000. Players appearing in less than 80 games receive pro-rated amounts.

History: Presented to the National Hockey League in 1985-86 by the NHL Board of Governors to recognize the team compiling the top regular-season record.

1989-90 Winner: Boston Bruins
Runners-up: Calgary Flames
Buffalo Sabres

The Boston Bruins won the 1989-90 Presidents' Trophy with the NHL's best regular-season record of 46–25–9 for 101 points. The Calgary Flames finished second at 42–23–15 for 99 points, while the Buffalo Sabres had the third best regular-season mark of 45–27–8 for 98 points.

DODGE PERFORMER OF THE YEAR AWARD

An annual award presented by Dodge to the National Hockey League's most outstanding performer in the regular-season. The winner receives the Dodge vehicle of his choice and is awarded $7,500 to benefit youth hockey.

History: The award was first presented in 1984-85 to recognize the NHL's top player. Dodge also sponsors the Performer of the Week and Performer of the Month awards, donating $500 and $1,000, respectively, to youth hockey organizations across North America in the recipients' honor.

1989-90 Winner: Pat LaFontaine, NY Islanders

LaFontaine captured the Dodge/NHL Performer of the Week Award two times (January 14 and February 11) during the 1989-90 campaign. He was also a runner-up on two occasions for both Dodge Performer of the Week and Month honors. He led the New York Islanders in scoring for the third straight season, and recorded both his first 50-goal and 100-point season since joining the Islanders in 1984, and he became just the second player in Islanders' history to top the 50-goal plateau. He put together an eleven-game goal-scoring streak, the fifth longest in NHL history, to lead the Islanders from last place to the top spot in the Patrick Division during a 23-6-3 stretch.

The 25-year-old native of Michigan represented the Islanders at the NHL All-Star Game in Pittsburgh on January 21, his third consecutive appearance with the Wales Conference squad.

LaFontaine joins Wayne Gretzky (three times) and Mario Lemieux (two times) as just the third player to receive the NHL/Dodge Performer of the Year honors in the award's six-year history.

DODGE RAM TOUGH AWARD

An annual award presented to the player who wins the overall Ram Tough statistical category (combined total of power play, shorthanded, game-winning and game-tying goals). Dodge Truck presents each individual team winner $1,000 to be donated to the youth hockey association of his choice.

History: The award was presented to the NHL in 1987-88 by Dodge to recognize the League leader in Ram Tough statistics.

1989-90 Winner: Brett Hull, St. Louis Blues
Runner-up: Cam Neely, Boston Bruins

Right wing Brett Hull of the St. Louis Blues, who led the National Hockey League with 72 regular-season goals, was presented the 1989-90 Dodge Ram Tough Award and a 1990 Dodge Dakota Sport Truck, for his League-leading 39 Dodge Ram Tough Ranking.

Hull, a 25-year-old native of Belleville, Ontario, led the League in goals (72), power play goals (27) and shots (385) and shared the lead with Neely for game-winning goals (12) during the regular season. Hull became only the sixth player in League history to record 70-or-more goals in a season while helping his club to a 37-34-9 record. The Blues scored a total of 79 power play goals, of which Hull recorded a point on 44 (27-17-44), for a 51.9% efficiency rating. Hull added 13 playoff goals to total 85 goals in regular-season and playoff competition, tying Mike Bossy for the fourth highest total in NHL history.

1989-90 Dodge/NHL Award Winners

Performer of the Week

Week Ending	Player	Club	Youth Hockey/Charitable Recipient
October 16	**Wayne Gretzky**	Los Angeles	Red Cross Earthquake Relief (CA)
October 22	**Peter Stastny**	Quebec	Hockey Mineur Bernieres (Que.)
October 29	**Mike Liut**	Hartford	Simsbury Youth Hockey (CT)
November 5	**Don Beaupre**	Washington	Waterloo Minor Hockey (Ont.)
November 12	**Jon Casey**	Minnesota	Eagan Youth Hockey (MN)
November 19	**Wendell Young**	Pittsburgh	Halifax Hawks (N.S.)
November 26	**Mike Gartner**	Minnesota	Edina Youth Hockey (MN)
December 3	**Andy Moog**	Boston	Penticton Minor Hockey (B.C.)
December 10	**Mark Fitzpatrick**	NY Islanders	Kitimat Youth Hockey (B.C.)
December 17	**Patrik Sundstrom**	New Jersey	IF Bjorkloven (Sweden
December 24	**Bill Ranford**	Edmonton	Red Deer Minor Hockey (Alta.)
	Ron Francis	Hartford	Avon Canton Farmington Minor Hockey (CT)
January 1	**Bob Essensa**	Winnipeg	Goals for Kids (Man.)
January 7	**Rejean Lemelin**	Boston	Lynnfield Knights "A" (MA)
January 14	**Pat LaFontaine**	NY Islanders	Suffolk County PAL League (NY)
			Nassau County Hockey (NY)
January 21	**Steve Larmer**	Chicago	Chicago Blackhawks Alumni Scholarship Foundation (IL)
January 28	**Mark Messier**	Edmonton	St. Albert Minor Hockey (Alta.)
February 4	**Patrick Roy**	Montreal	Hockey Mineur de Ste-Foy (Que.)
February 11	**Pat LaFontaine**	NY Islanders	Suffolk County PAL League (NY)
			Nassau County Hockey (NY)
February 18	**Curtis Joseph**	St. Louis	Notre Dame T-II (Sask.)
February 25	**Sergei Makarov**	Calgary	Parkdale Elementary (Alta.)
March 4	**Pat Verbeek**	Hartford	Kirkland Lake Minor Hockey (Ont.)
March 11	**Daren Puppa**	Buffalo	Sports Legend (Que.)
March 18	**Patrick Roy**	Montreal	Marlucci Youth Hockey (MN)
March 25	**Brian Bellows**	Minnesota	NJ Devils Youth Hockey (NJ)

Performer of the Month

Month	Player	Club	Youth Hockey/Charitable Recipient
October	**Wayne Gretzky**	Los Angeles	So. Cal. Youth Hockey (CA)
November	**Andy Moog**	Boston	Lynnfield Youth Hockey (MA)
December	**Bill Ranford**	Edmonton	Red Deer Minor Hockey (Alta.)
January	**Brett Hull**	St. Louis	Missouri Amateur Hockey (MO)
February	**Paul Coffey**	Pittsburgh	Chinquacousy Minor Hockey (Ont.)
March	**Viacheslav Fetisov**	New Jersey	St. Catharines' Minor Hockey (Ont.)

Performer of the Year

Year	Player	Club	Youth Hockey/Charitable Recipient
1989-90	**Pat LaFontaine**	NY Islanders	Lakeland Minor Hockey (MI)
			Suffolk County PAL League (NY)
			Nassau County Hockey (NY)

Dodge Ram Tough Award

Dodge Performer of The Year Award

NATIONAL HOCKEY LEAGUE INDIVIDUAL AWARD WINNERS

ART ROSS TROPHY

	Winner	Runner-up
1990	Wayne Gretzky, L.A.	Mark Messier, Edm.
1989	Mario Lemieux, Pit.	Wayne Gretzky, L.A.
1988	Mario Lemieux, Pit.	Wayne Gretzky, Edm.
1987	Wayne Gretzky, Edm.	Jari Kurri, Edm.
1986	Wayne Gretzky, Edm.	Mario Lemieux, Pit.
1985	Wayne Gretzky, Edm.	Jari Kurri, Edm.
1984	Wayne Gretzky, Edm.	Paul Coffey, Edm.
1983	Wayne Gretzky, Edm.	Peter Stastny, Que.
1982	Wayne Gretzky, Edm.	Mike Bossy, NYI
1981	Wayne Gretzky, Edm.	Marcel Dionne, L.A.
1980	Marcel Dionne, L.A.	Wayne Gretzky, Edm.
1979	Bryan Trottier, NYI	Marcel Dionne, L.A.
1978	Guy Lafleur, Mtl.	Bryan Trottier, NYI
1977	Guy Lafleur, Mtl.	Marcel Dionne, L.A.
1976	Guy Lafleur, Mtl.	Bobby Clarke, Phi.
1975	Bobby Orr, Bos.	Phil Esposito, Bos.
1974	Phil Esposito, Bos.	Bobby Orr, Bos.
1973	Phil Esposito, Bos.	Bobby Clarke, Phi.
1972	Phil Esposito, Bos.	Bobby Orr, Bos.
1971	Phil Esposito, Bos.	Bobby Orr, Bos.
1970	Bobby Orr, Bos.	Phil Esposito, Bos.
1969	Phil Esposito, Bos.	Bobby Hull, Chi.
1968	Stan Mikita, Chi.	Phil Esposito, Bos.
1967	Stan Mikita, Chi.	Bobby Hull, Chi.
1966	Bobby Hull, Chi.	Stan Mikita, Chi.
1965	Stan Mikita, Chi.	Norm Ullman, Det.
1964	Stan Mikita, Chi.	Bobby Hull, Chi.
1963	Gordie Howe, Det.	Andy Bathgate, NYR
1962	Bobby Hull, Chi.	Andy Bathgate, NYR
1961	Bernie Geoffrion, Mtl.	Jean Beliveau, Mtl.
1960	Bobby Hull, Chi.	Bronco Horvath, Bos.
1959	Dickie Moore, Mtl.	Jean Beliveau, Mtl.
1958	Dickie Moore, Mtl.	Henri Richard, Mtl.
1957	Gordie Howe, Det.	Ted Lindsay, Det.
1956	Jean Beliveau, Mtl.	Gordie Howe, Det.
1955	Bernie Geoffrion, Mtl.	Maurice Richard, Mtl.
1954	Gordie Howe, Det.	Maurice Richard, Mtl.
1953	Gordie Howe, Det.	Ted Lindsay, Det.
1952	Gordie Howe, Det.	Ted Lindsay, Det.
1951	Gordie Howe, Det.	Maurice Richard, Mtl.
1950	Ted Lindsay, Det.	Sid Abel, Det.
1949	Roy Conacher, Chi.	Doug Bentley, Chi.
1948	Elmer Lach, Mtl.	Buddy O'Connor, NYR
1947*	Max Bentley, Chi.	Maurice Richard, Mtl.
1946	Max Bentley, Chi.	Gaye Stewart, Tor.
1945	Elmer Lach, Mtl.	Maurice Richard, Mtl.
1944	Herbie Cain, Bos.	Doug Bentley, Chi.
1943	Doug Bentley, Chi.	Bill Cowley, Bos.
1942	Bryan Hextall, NYR	Lynn Patrick, NYR
1941	Bill Cowley, Bos.	Bryan Hextall, NYR
1940	Milt Schmidt, Bos.	Woody Dumart, Bos.
1939	Toe Blake, Mtl.	Dave Schriner, NYA
1938	Gordie Drillon, Tor.	Syl Apps, Tor.
1937	Dave Schriner, NYA	Syl Apps, Tor.
1936	Dave Schriner, NYA	Marty Barry, Det.
1935	Charlie Conacher, Tor.	Syd Howe, St.L-Det.
1934	Charlie Conacher, Tor.	Joe Primeau, Tor
1933	Bill Cook, NYR	Harvey Jackson, Tor.
1932	Harvey Jackson, Tor.	Joe Primeau, Tor.
1931	Howie Morenz, Mtl.	Ebbie Goodfellow, Det.
1930	Cooney Weiland, Bos.	Frank Boucher, NYR
1929	Ace Bailey, Tor.	Nels Stewart, Mtl.M
1928	Howie Morenz, Mtl.	Aurel Joliat, Mtl.
1927	Bill Cook, NYR	Dick Irvin, Chi.
1926	Nels Stewart, Mtl.M.	Cy Denneny, Ott.
1925	Babe Dye, Tor.	Cy Denneny, Ott.
1924	Cy Denneny, Ott.	Billy Boucher, Mtl.
1923	Babe Dye, Tor.	Cy Denneny, Ott.
1922	Punch Broadbent, Ott.	Cy Denneny, Ott.
1921	Newsy Lalonde, Mtl.	Cy Denneny, Ott.
1920	Joe Malone, Que.	Newsy Lalonde, Mtl.
1919	Newsy Lalonde, Mtl.	Odie Cleghorn, Mtl.
1918	Joe Malone, Mtl.	Cy Denneny, Ott.

* Scoring leader prior to inception of Art Ross Trophy in 1947-48

HART TROPHY

	Winner	Runner-up
1990	Mark Messier, Edm.	Raymond Bourque, Bos.
1989	Wayne Gretzky, L.A.	Mario Lemieux, Pit.
1988	Mario Lemieux, Pit.	Grant Fuhr, Edm.
1987	Wayne Gretzky, Edm.	Raymond Bourque, Bos.
1986	Wayne Gretzky, Edm.	Mario Lemieux, Pit.
1985	Wayne Gretzky, Edm.	Dale Hawerchuk, Wpg.
1984	Wayne Gretzky, Edm.	Rod Langway, Wash.
1983	Wayne Gretzky, Edm.	Pete Peeters, Bos.
1982	Wayne Gretzky, Edm.	Bryan Trottier, NYI
1981	Wayne Gretzky, Edm.	Mike Liut, St.L.
1980	Wayne Gretzky, Edm.	Marcel Dionne, L.A.
1979	Bryan Trottier, NYI	Guy Lafleur, Mtl
1978	Guy Lafleur, Mtl.	Bryan Trottier, NYI
1977	Guy Lafleur, Mtl.	Bobby Clarke, Phi.
1976	Bobby Clarke, Phi.	Denis Potvin, NYI
1975	Bobby Clarke, Phi.	Rogatien Vachon, L.A.
1974	Phil Esposito, Bos.	Bernie Parent, Phi.
1973	Bobby Clarke, Phi.	Phil Esposito, Bos.
1972	Bobby Orr, Bos.	Ken Dryden, Mtl.
1971	Bobby Orr, Bos.	Phil Esposito, Bos.
1970	Bobby Orr, Bos.	Tony Esposito, Chi.
1969	Phil Esposito, Bos.	Jean Beliveau, Mtl.
1968	Stan Mikita, Chi.	Jean Beliveau, Mtl.
1967	Stan Mikita, Chi.	Ed Giacomin, NYR
1966	Bobby Hull, Chi.	Jean Beliveau, Mtl.
1965	Bobby Hull, Chi.	Norm Ullman, Det.
1964	Jean Beliveau, Mtl.	Bobby Hull, Chi.
1963	Gordie Howe, Det.	Stan Mikita, Chi.
1962	Jacques Plante, Mtl.	Doug Harvey, NYR
1961	Bernie Geoffrion, Mtl.	Johnny Bower, Tor.
1960	Gordie Howe, Det.	Bobby Hull, Chi.
1959	Andy Bathgate, NYR	Gordie Howe, Det.
1958	Gordie Howe, Det.	Andy Bathgate, NYR
1957	Gordie Howe, Det.	Jean Beliveau, Mtl.
1956	Jean Beliveau, Mtl.	Tod Sloan, Tor.
1955	Ted Kennedy, Tor.	Harry Lumley, Tor.
1954	Al Rollins, Chi.	Red Kelly, Det.
1953	Gordie Howe, Det.	Al Rollins, Chi.
1952	Gordie Howe, Det.	Elmer Lach, Mtl.
1951	Milt Schmidt, Bos.	Maurice Richard, Mtl.
1950	Charlie Rayner, NYR	Ted Kennedy, Tor.
1949	Sid Abel, Det.	Bill Durnan, Mtl.
1948	Buddy O'Connor, NYR	Frank Brimsek, Bos.
1947	Maurice Richard, Mtl.	Milt Schmidt, Bos.
1946	Max Bentley, Chi.	Gaye Stewart, Tor.
1945	Elmer Lach, Mtl.	Maurice Richard, Mtl.
1944	Babe Pratt, Tor.	Bill Cowley, Bos.
1943	Bill Cowley, Bos.	Doug Bentley, Chi.
1942	Tom Anderson, Bro.	Syl Apps, Tor.
1941	Bill Cowley, Bos.	Dit Clapper, Bos.
1940	Ebbie Goodfellow, Det.	Syl Apps, Tor.
1939	Toe Blake, Mtl.	Syl Apps, Tor.
1938	Eddie Shore, Bos.	Paul Thompson, Chi.
1937	Babe Siebert, Mtl.	Lionel Conacher, Mtl.M
1936	Eddie Shore, Bos.	Hooley Smith, Mtl.M
1935	Eddie Shore, Bos.	Charlie Conacher, Tor.
1934	Aurel Joliat, Mtl.	Lionel Conacher, Chi.
1933	Eddie Shore, Bos.	Bill Cook, NYR
1932	Howie Morenz, Mtl.	Ching Johnson, NYR
1931	Howie Morenz, Mtl.	Eddie Shore, Bos.
1930	Nels Stewart, Mtl.M.	Lionel Hitchman, Bos.
1929	Roy Worters, NYA	Ace Bailey, Tor.
1928	Howie Morenz, Mtl.	Roy Worters, Pit.
1927	Herb Gardiner, Mtl.	Bill Cook, NYR
1926	Nels Stewart, Mtl.M.	Sprague Cleghorn, Bos.
1925	Billy Burch, Ham.	Howie Morenz, Mtl.
1924	Frank Nighbor, Ott.	Sprague Cleghorn, Mtl.

LADY BYNG TROPHY

	Winner	Runner-up
1990	Brett Hull, St.L.	Wayne Gretzky, L.A.
1989	Joe Mullen, Cgy.	Wayne Gretzky, L.A.
1988	Mats Naslund, Mtl.	Wayne Gretzky, Edm.
1987	Joe Mullen, Cgy.	Wayne Gretzky, Edm.
1986	Mike Bossy, NYI	Jari Kurri, Edm.
1985	Jari Kurri, Edm.	Joe Mullen, St.L.
1984	Mike Bossy, NYI	Rick Middleton, Bos.
1983	Mike Bossy, NYI	Rick Middleton, Bos.
1982	Rick Middleton, Bos.	Mike Bossy, NYI
1981	Rick Kehoe, Pit.	Wayne Gretzky, Edm.
1980	Wayne Gretzky, Edm.	Marcel Dionne, L.A.
1979	Bob MacMillan, Atl.	Marcel Dionne, L.A.
1978	Butch Goring, L.A.	Peter McNab, Bos.
1977	Marcel Dionne, L.A.	Jean Ratelle, Bos.
1976	Jean Ratelle, NYR-Bos.	Jean Pronovost, Pit.
1975	Marcel Dionne, Det.	John Bucyk, Bos.
1974	John Bucyk, Bos.	Lowell MacDonald, Pit.
1973	Gilbert Perreault, Buf.	Jean Ratelle, NYR
1972	Jean Ratelle, NYR	John Bucyk, Bos.
1971	John Bucyk, Bos.	Dave Keon, Tor.
1970	Phil Goyette, St.L.	John Bucyk, Bos.
1969	Alex Delvecchio, Det.	Ted Hampson, Oak.
1968	Stan Mikita, Chi.	John Bucyk, Bos.
1967	Stan Mikita, Chi.	Dave Keon, Tor.
1966	Alex Delvecchio, Det.	Bobby Rousseau, Mtl.
1965	Bobby Hull, Chi.	Alex Delvecchio, Det.
1964	Ken Wharram, Chi.	Dave Keon, Tor.
1963	Dave Keon, Tor.	Camille Henry, NYR
1962	Dave Keon, Tor.	Claude Provost, Mtl.
1961	Red Kelly, Tor.	Norm Ullman, Det.
1960	Don McKenney, Bos.	Andy Hebenton, NYR
1959	Alex Delvecchio, Det.	Andy Hebenton, NYR
1958	Camille Henry, NYR	Don Marshall, Mtl.
1957	Andy Hebenton, NYR	Earl Reibel, Det.
1956	Earl Reibel, Det.	Floyd Curry, Mtl.
1955	Sid Smith, Tor.	Danny Lewicki, NYR
1954	Red Kelly, Det.	Don Raleigh, NYR
1953	Red Kelly, Det.	Wally Hergesheimer, NYR
1952	Sid Smith, Tor.	Red Kelly, Det.
1951	Red Kelly, Det.	Woody Dumart, Bos.
1950	Edgar Laprade, NYR	Red Kelly, Det.
1949	Bill Quackenbush, Det.	Harry Watson, Tor.
1948	Buddy O'Connor, NYR	Syl Aps, Tor.
1947	Bobby Bauer, Bos.	Syl Apps, Tor.
1946	Toe Blake, Mtl.	Clint Smith, Chi.
1945	Bill Mosienko, Chi.	Syd Howe, Det.
1944	Clint Smith, Chi.	Herb Cain, Bos.
1943	Max Bentley, Chi.	Buddy O'Connor, Mtl.
1942	Syl Apps, Tor.	Gordie Drillon, Tor.
1941	Bobby Bauer, Bos.	Gordie Drillon, Tor.
1940	Bobby Bauer, Bos.	Clint Smith, NYR
1939	Clint Smith, NYR	Marty Barry, Det.
1938	Gordie Drillon, Tor.	Clint Smith, NYR
1937	Marty Barry, Det.	Gordie Drillon, Tor.
1936	Doc Romnes, Chi.	Dave Schriner, NYA
1935	Frank Boucher, NYR	Russ Blinco, Mtl.M
1934	Frank Boucher, NYR	Joe Primeau, Tor.
1933	Frank Boucher, NYR	Joe Primeau, Tor.
1932	Joe Primeau, Tor.	Frank Boucher, NYR
1931	Frank Boucher, NYR	Normie Himes, NYA
1930	Frank Boucher, NYR	Normie Himes, NYA
1929	Frank Boucher, NYR	Harry Darragh, Pit.
1928	Frank Boucher, NYR	George Hay, Det.
1927	Billy Burch, NYA	Dick Irvin, Chi.
1926	Frank Nighbor, Ott.	Billy Burch, NYA
1925	Frank Nighbor, Ott.	none

FRANK J. SELKE TROPHY WINNERS

	Winner	Runner-up
1990	Rick Meagher, St.L.	Guy Carbonneau, Mtl.
1989	Guy Carbonneau, Mtl.	Esa Tikkanen, Edm.
1988	Guy Carbonneau, Mtl.	Steve Kasper, Bos.
1987	Dave Poulin, Phi.	Guy Carbonneau, Mtl.
1986	Troy Murray, Chi.	Ron Sutter, Phi.
1985	Craig Ramsay, Buf.	Doug Jarvis, Wsh.
1984	Doug Jarvis, Wsh.	Bryan Trottier, NYI
1983	Bobby Clarke, Phi.	Jari Kurri, Edm.
1982	Steve Kasper, Bos.	Bob Gainey, Mtl.
1981	Bob Gainey, Mtl.	Craig Ramsay, Buf.
1980	Bob Gainey, Mtl.	Craig Ramsay, Buf.
1979	Bob Gainey, Mtl.	Don Marcotte, Bos.
1978	Bob Gainey, Mtl.	Craig Ramsay, Buf.

LESTER B. PEARSON AWARD WINNERS

1990	Mark Messier	Edmonton
1989	Steve Yzerman	Detroit
1988	Mario Lemieux	Pittsburgh
1987	Wayne Gretzky	Edmonton
1986	Mario Lemieux	Pittsburgh
1985	Wayne Gretzky	Edmonton
1984	Wayne Gretzky	Edmonton
1983	Wayne Gretzky	Edmonton
1982	Wayne Gretzky	Edmonton
1981	Mike Liut	St. Louis
1980	Marcel Dionne	Los Angeles
1979	Marcel Dionne	Los Angeles
1978	Guy Lafleur	Montreal
1977	Guy Lafleur	Montreal
1976	Guy Lafleur	Montreal
1975	Bobby Orr	Boston
1974	Bobby Clarke	Philadelphia
1973	Phil Esposito	Boston
1972	Jean Ratelle	NY Rangers
1971	Phil Esposito	Boston

WILLIAM M. JENNINGS TROPHY WINNERS

	Winner	Runner-up
1990	Andy Moog, Bos. Rejean Lemelin	Patrick Roy, Mtl. Brian Hayward
1989	Patrick Roy, Mtl. Brian Hayward	Mike Vernon, Cgy. Rick Wamsley
1988	Patrick Roy, Mtl. Brian Hayward	Clint Malarchuk, Wsh. Pete Peeters
1987	Patrick Roy, Mtl. Brian Hayward	Ron Hextall, Phi.
1986	Bob Froese, Phi. Darren Jensen	Al Jensen, Wsh. Pete Peeters
1985	Tom Barrasso, Buf. Bob Sauve	Pat Riggin, Wsh.
1984	Al Jensen, Wsh. Pat Riggin	Tom Barrasso, Buf. Bob Sauve
1983	Roland Melanson, NYI Bill Smith	Pete Peeters, Bos.
1982	Rick Wamsley, Mtl. Denis Herron	Billy Smith, NYI Roland Melanson

VEZINA TROPHY

	Winner	Runner-up
1990	Patrick Roy, Mtl.	Daren Puppa, Buf.
1989	Patrick Roy, Mtl.	Mike Vernon, Cgy.
1988	Grant Fuhr, Edm.	Tom Barrasso, Buf.
1987	Ron Hextall, Phi.	Mike Liut, Hfd.
1986	John Vanbiesbrouck, NYR	Bob Froese, Phi.
1985	Pelle Lindbergh, Phi.	Tom Barrasso, Buf.
1984	Tom Barrasso, Buf.	Rejean Lemelin, Cgy.
1983	Pete Peeters, Bos.	Roland Melanson, NYI
1982	Bill Smith, NYI	Grant Fuhr, Edm.
1981	Richard Sevigny, Mtl.	Pete Peeters, Phi.
	Denis Herron, Mtl.	Rick St. Croix, Phi.
	Michel Larocque, Mtl.	
1980	Bob Sauve, Buf.	Gerry Cheevers, Bos.
	Don Edwards, Buf.	Gilles Gilbert, Bos.
1979	Ken Dryden, Mtl.	Glenn Resch, NYI
	Michel Larocque, Mtl.	Bill Smith, NYI
1978	Ken Dryden, Mtl.	Bernie Parent, Phi.
	Michel Larocque	Wayne Stephenson, Phi.
1977	Ken Dryden, Mtl.	Glenn Resch, NYI
	Michel Larocque, Mtl.	Bill Smith, NYI
1976	Ken Dryden, Mtl.	Glenn Resch, NYI
		Bill Smith, NYI
1975	Bernie Parent, Phi.	Rogie Vachon, L.A.
		Gary Edwards, L.A.
1974	Bernie Parent, Phi. (tie)	Gilles Gilbert, Bos.
	Tony Esposito, Chi. (tie)	
1973	Ken Dryden, Mtl.	Ed Giacomin, NYR
		Gilles Villemure, NYR
1972	Tony Esposito, Chi.	Cesare Maniago, Min.
	Gary Smith, Chi.	Lorne Worsley, Min.
1971	Ed Giacomin, NYR	Tony Esposito, Chi.
	Gilles Villemure, NYR	
1970	Tony Esposito, Chi.	Jacques Plante, St.L.
		Ernie Wakely, St.L.
1969	Jacques Plante, St.L.	Ed Giacomin, NYR
	Glenn Hall, St.L.	
1968	Lorne Worsley, Mtl.	Johnny Bower, Tor.
	Rogatien Vachon, Mtl.	Bruce Gamble, Tor.
1967	Glenn Hall, Chi.	Charlie Hodge, Mtl.
	Denis Dejordy, Chi.	
1966	Lorne Worsley, Mtl.	Glenn Hall, Chi.
	Charlie Hodge, Mtl.	
1965	Terry Sawchuk, Tor.	Roger Crozier, Det.
	Johnny Bower, Tor.	
1964	Charlie Hodge, Mtl.	Glenn Hall, Chi.
1963	Glenn Hall, Chi.	Johnny Bower, Tor.
		Don Simmons, Tor.
1962	Jacques Plante, Mtl.	Johnny Bower, Tor.
1961	Johnny Bower, Tor.	Glenn Hall, Chi.
1960	Jacques Plante, Mtl.	Glenn Hall, Chi.
1959	Jacques Plante, Mtl.	Johnny Bower, Tor.
		Ed Chadwick, Tor.
1958	Jacques Plante, Mtl.	Lorne Worsley, NYR
		Marcel Paille, NYR
1957	Jacques Plante, Mtl.	Glenn Hall, Det.
1956	Jacques Plante, Mtl.	Glenn Hall, Det.
1955	Terry Sawchuk, Det.	Harry Lumley, Tor.
1954	Harry Lumley, Tor.	Terry Sawchuk, Det.
1953	Terry Sawchuk, Det.	Gerry McNeil, Mtl.
1952	Terry Sawchuk, Det.	Al Rollins, Tor.
1951	Al Rollins, Tor.	Terry Sawchuk, Det.
1950	Bill Durnan, Mtl.	Harry Lumley, Det.
1949	Bill Durnan, Mtl.	Harry Lumley, Det.
1948	Turk Broda, Tor.	Harry Lumley, Det.
1947	Bill Durnan, Mtl.	Turk Broda, Tor.
1946	Bill Durnan, Mtl.	Frank Brimsek, Bos.
1945	Bill Durnan, Mtl.	Frank McCool, Tor. (tie)
		Harry Lumley, Det. (tie)
1944	Bill Durnan, Mtl.	Paul Bibeault, Tor.
1943	Johnny Mowers, Det.	Turk Broda, Tor.
1942	Frank Brimsek, Bos.	Turk Broda, Tor.
1941	Turk Broda, Tor.	Frank Brimsek, Bos. (tie)
		Johnny Mowers, Det. (tie)
1940	Dave Kerr, NYR	Frank Brimsek, Bos.
1939	Frank Brimsek, Bos.	Dave Kerr, NYR
1938	Tiny Thompson, Bos.	Dave Kerr, NYR
1937	Normie Smith, Det.	Dave Kerr, NYR
1936	Tiny Thompson, Bos.	Mike Karakas, Chi.
1935	Lorne Chabot, Chi.	Alex Connell, Mtl.M
1934	Charlie Gardiner, Chi.	Wilf Cude, Det.
1933	Tiny Thompson, Bos.	John Roach, Det.
1932	Charlie Gardiner, Chi.	Alex Connell, Det.
1931	Roy Worters, NYA	Charlie Gardiner, Chi.
1930	Tiny Thompson, Bos.	Charlie Gardiner, Chi.
1929	George Hainsworth, Mtl.	Tiny Thompson, Bos.
1928	George Hainsworth, Mtl.	Alex Connell, Ott.
1927	George Hainsworth, Mtl.	Clint Benedict, Mtl.M

CALDER MEMORIAL TROPHY WINNERS

	Winner	Runner-up
1990	Sergei Makarov, Cgy.	Mike Modano, Min.
1989	Brian Leetch, NYR	Trevor Linden, Van.
1988	Joe Nieuwendyk, Cgy.	Ray Sheppard, Buf.
1987	Luc Robitaille, L.A.	Ron Hextall, Phi.
1986	Gary Suter, Cgy.	Wendel Clark, Tor.
1985	Mario Lemieux, Pit.	Chris Chelios, Mtl.
1984	Tom Barrasso, Buf.	Steve Yzerman, Det.
1983	Steve Larmer, Chi.	Phil Housley, Buf.
1982	Dale Hawerchuk, Wpg.	Barry Pederson, Bos.
1981	Peter Stastny, Que.	Larry Murphy, L.A.
1980	Ray Bourque, Bos.	Mike Foligno, Det.
1979	Bobby Smith, Min	Ryan Walter, Wsh.
1978	Mike Bossy, NYI	Barry Beck, Col.
1977	Willi Plett, Atl.	Don Murdoch, NYR
1976	Bryan Trottier, NYI	Glenn Resch, NYI
1975	Eric Vail, Atl.	Pierre Larouche, Pit.
1974	Denis Potvin, NYI	Tom Lysiak, Atl.
1973	Steve Vickers, NYR	Bill Barber, Phi.
1972	Ken Dryden, Mtl.	Rick Martin, Buf.
1971	Gilbert Perreault, Buf.	Jude Drouin, Min.
1970	Tony Esposito, Chi.	Bill Fairbairn, NYR
1969	Danny Grant, Min.	Norm Ferguson, Oak.
1968	Derek Sanderson, Bos.	Jacques Lemaire, Mtl.
1967	Bobby Orr, Bos.	Ed Van Impe, Chi.
1966	Brit Selby, Tor.	Bert Marshall, Det.
1965	Roger Crozier, Det.	Ron Ellis, Tor.
1964	Jacques Laperriere, Mtl.	John Ferguson, Mtl.
1963	Kent Douglas, Tor.	Doug Barkley, Det.
1962	Bobby Rousseau, Mtl.	Cliff Pennington, Bos.
1961	Dave Keon, Tor.	Bob Nevin, Tor.
1960	Bill Hay, Chi.	Murray Oliver, Det.
1959	Ralph Backstrom, Mtl.	Carl Brewer, Tor.
1958	Frank Mahovlich, Tor.	Bobby Hull, Chi.
1957	Larry Regan, Bos.	Ed Chadwick, Tor.
1956	Glenn Hall, Det.	Andy Hebenton, NYR
1955	Ed Litzenberger, Chi.	Don McKenney, Bos.
1954	Camille Henry, NYR	Earl Reibel, Det.
1953	Lorne Worsley, NYR	Gordie Hannigan, Tor.
1952	Bernie Geoffrion, Mtl.	Hy Buller, NYR
1951	Terry Sawchuk, Det.	Al Rollins, Tor.
1950	Jack Gelineau, Bos.	Phil Maloney, Bos.
1949	Pentti Lund, NYR	Allan Stanley, NYR
1948	Jim McFadden, Det.	Pete Babando, Bos.
1947	Howie Meeker, Tor.	Jimmy Conacher, Det.
1946	Edgar Laprade, NYR	George Gee, Chi.
1945	Frank McCool, Tor.	Ken Smith, Bos.
1944	Gus Bodnar, Tor.	Bill Durnan, Mtl.
1943	Gaye Stewart, Tor.	Glen Harmon, Mtl.
1942	Grant Warwick, NYR	Buddy O'Connor, Mtl.
1941	Johnny Quilty, Mtl.	Johnny Mowers, Det.
1940	Kilby MacDonald, NYR	Wally Stanowski, Tor.
1939	Frank Brimsek, Bos.	Roy Conacher, Bos.
1938	Cully Dahlstrom, Chi.	Murph Chamberlain, Tor.
1937	Syl Apps, Tor.	Gordie Drillon, Tor.
1936	Mike Karakas, Chi.	Bucko McDonald, Det.
1935	Dave Schriner, NYA	Bert Connolly, NYR
1934	Russ Blinko, Mtl.M	
1933	Carl Voss, Det.	

JAMES NORRIS TROPHY WINNERS

	Winner	Runner-up
1990	Ray Bourque, Bos.	Al MacInnis, Cgy.
1989	Chris Chelios, Mtl	Paul Coffey, Pit.
1988	Ray Bourque, Bos.	Scott Stevens, Wsh.
1987	Ray Bourque, Bos.	Mark Howe, Phi.
1986	Paul Coffey, Edm.	Mark Howe, Phi.
1985	Paul Coffey, Edm.	Ray Bourque, Bos.
1984	Rod Langway, Wsh.	Paul Coffey, Edm.
1983	Rod Langway, Wsh.	Mark Howe, Phi.
1982	Doug Wilson, Chi.	Ray Bourque, Bos.
1981	Randy Carlyle, Pit.	Denis Potvin, NYI
1980	Larry Robinson, Mtl.	Borje Salming, Tor.
1979	Denis Potvin, NYI	Larry Robinson, Mtl.
1978	Denis Potvin, NYI	Brad Park, Bos.
1977	Larry Robinson, Mtl.	Borje Salming, Tor.
1976	Denis Potvin, NYI	Brad Park, NYR-Bos.
1975	Bobby Orr, Bos.	Denis Potvin, NYI
1974	Bobby Orr, Bos.	Brad Park, NYR
1973	Bobby Orr, Bos.	Guy Lapointe, Mtl.
1972	Bobby Orr, Bos.	Brad Park, NYR
1971	Bobby Orr, Bos.	Brad Park, NYR
1970	Bobby Orr, Bos.	Brad Park, NYR
1969	Bobby Orr, Bos.	Tim Horton, Tor.
1968	Bobby Orr, Bos.	J.C. Tremblay, Mtl
1967	Harry Howell, NYR	Pierre Pilote, Chi.
1966	Jacques Laperriere, Mtl.	Pierre Pilote, Chi.
1965	Pierre Pilote, Chi.	Jacques Laperriere, Mtl.
1964	Pierre Pilote, Chi.	Tim Horton, Tor.
1963	Pierre Pilote, Chi.	Carl Brewer, Tor.
1962	Doug Harvey, NYR	Pierre Pilote, Chi.
1961	Doug Harvey, Mtl.	Marcel Pronovost, Det.
1960	Doug Harvey, Mtl.	Allan Stanley, Tor.
1959	Tom Johnson, Mtl.	Bill Gadsby, NYR
1958	Doug Harvey, Mtl.	Bill Gadsby, NYR
1957	Doug Harvey, Mtl.	Red Kelly, Det.
1956	Doug Harvey, Mtl.	Bill Gadsby, NYR
1955	Doug Harvey, Mtl.	Red Kelly, Det.
1954	Red Kelly, Det.	Doug Harvey, Mtl.

JACK ADAMS AWARD WINNERS

	Winner	Runner-up
1990	Bob Murdoch, Wpg.	Mike Milbury, Bos.
1989	Pat Burns, Mtl.	Bob McCammon, Van.
1988	Jacques Demers, Det.	Terry Crisp, Cgy.
1987	Jacques Demers, Det.	Jack Evans, Hfd.
1986	Glen Sather, Edm.	Jacques Demers, St.L.
1985	Mike Keenan, Phi.	Barry Long, Wpg.
1984	Bryan Murray, Wsh.	Scott Bowman, Buf.
1983	Orval Tessier, Chi.	
1982	Tom Watt, Wpg.	
1981	Red Berenson, St.L.	Bob Berry, L.A.
1980	Pat Quinn, Phi.	
1979	Al Arbour, NYI	Fred Shero, NYR
1978	Bobby Kromm, Det.	Don Cherry, Bos.
1977	Scott Bowman, Mtl.	Tom McVie, Wsh.
1976	Don Cherry, Bos.	
1975	Bob Pulford, L.A.	
1974	Fred Shero, Phi.	

Roger Crozier—1964-65 Calder Memorial Trophy winner.

LESTER PATRICK TROPHY WINNERS

1990	Len Ceglarski
1989	Dan Kelly
	Lou Nanne
	*Lynn Patrick
	Bud Poile
1988	Keith Allen
	Fred Cusick
	Bob Johnson
1987	*Hobey Baker
	Frank Mathers
1986	John MacInnes
	Jack Riley
1985	Jack Butterfield
	Arthur M. Wirtz
1984	John A. Ziegler Jr.
	*Arthur Howie Ross
1983	Bill Torrey
1982	Emile P. Francis
1981	Charles M. Schulz
1980	Bobby Clarke
	Edward M. Snider
	Frederick A. Shero
	1980 U.S. Olympic Hockey Team
1979	Bobby Orr
1978	Philip A. Esposito
	Tom Fitzgerald
	William T. Tutt
	William W. Wirtz
1977	John P. Bucyk
	Murray A. Armstrong
	John Mariucci
1976	Stanley Mikita
	George A. Leader
	Bruce A. Norris
1975	Donald M. Clark
	William L. Chadwick
	Thomas N. Ivan
1974	Alex Delvecchio
	Murray Murdoch
	*Weston W. Adams, Sr.
	*Charles L. Crovat
1973	Walter L. Bush, Jr.
1972	Clarence S. Campbell
	John Kelly
	Ralph "Cooney" Weiland
	*James D. Norris
1971	William M. Jennings
	*John B. Sollenberger
	*Terrance G. Sawchuk
1970	Edward W. Shore
	*James C. V. Hendy
1969	Robert M. Hull
	*Edward J. Jeremiah
1968	Thomas F. Lockhart
	*Walter A. Brown
	*Gen. John R. Kilpatrick
1967	Gordon Howe
	*Charles F. Adams
	*James Norris, Sr.
1966	J.J. "Jack" Adams

* awarded posthumously

CONN SMYTHE TROPHY WINNERS

1990	Bill Ranford	Edmonton
1989	Al MacInnis	Calgary
1988	Wayne Gretzky	Edmonton
1987	Ron Hextall	Philadelphia
1986	Patrick Roy	Montreal
1985	Wayne Gretzky	Edmonton
1984	Mark Messier	Edmonton
1983	Bill Smith	NY Islanders
1982	Mike Bossy	NY Islanders
1981	Butch Goring	NY Islanders
1980	Bryan Trottier	NY Islanders
1979	Bob Gainey	Montreal
1978	Larry Robinson	Montreal
1977	Guy Lafleur	Montreal
1976	Reggie Leach	Philadelphia
1975	Bernie Parent	Philadelphia
1974	Bernie Parent	Philadelphia
1973	Yvan Cournoyer	Montreal
1972	Bobby Orr	Boston
1971	Ken Dryden	Montreal
1970	Bobby Orr	Boston
1969	Serge Savard	Montreal
1968	Glenn Hall	St. Louis
1967	Dave Keon	Toronto
1966	Roger Crozier	Detroit
1965	Jean Beliveau	Montreal

KING CLANCY MEMORIAL TROPHY WINNERS

1990	Kevin Lowe	Edmonton
1989	Bryan Trottier	NY Islanders
1988	Lanny McDonald	Calgary

BILL MASTERTON TROPHY WINNERS

1990	Gord Kluzak	Boston
1989	Tim Kerr	Philadelphia
1988	Bob Bourne	Los Angeles
1987	Doug Jarvis	Hartford
1986	Charlie Simmer	Boston
1985	Anders Hedberg	NY Rangers
1984	Brad Park	Detroit
1983	Lanny McDonald	Calgary
1982	Glenn Resch	Colorado
1981	Blake Dunlop	St. Louis
1980	Al MacAdam	Minnesota
1979	Serge Savard	Montreal
1978	Butch Goring	Los Angeles
1977	Ed Westfall	NY Islanders
1976	Rod Gilbert	NY Rangers
1975	Don Luce	Buffalo
1974	Henri Richard	Montreal
1973	Lowell MacDonald	Pittsburgh
1972	Bobby Clarke	Philladelphia
1971	Jean Ratelle	NY Rangers
1970	Pit Martin	Chicago
1969	Ted Hampson	Oakland
1968	Claude Provost	Montreal

DODGE PERFORMER OF THE YEAR AWARD WINNERS

1990	Pat LaFontaine	NY Islanders
1989	Mario Lemieux	Pittsburgh
1988	Mario Lemieux	Pittsburgh
1987	Wayne Gretzky	Edmonton
1986	Wayne Gretzky	Edmonton
1985	Wayne Gretzky	Edmonton

DODGE RAM TOUGH AWARD WINNERS

1990	Brett Hull	St. Louis
1989	Mario Lemieux	Pittsburgh
1988	Joe Nieuwendyk	Calgary

BUD MAN OF THE YEAR AWARD WINNERS

1990	Kevin Lowe	Edmonton
1989	Lanny McDonald	Calgary
1988	Bryan Trottier	NY Islanders

TRICO GOALTENDER AWARD WINNERS

1990	Patrick Roy	Montreal
1989	Patrick Roy	Montreal

ALKA-SELTZER PLUS AWARD WINNER

1990	Paul Cavallini	St. Louis

Butch Goring—1981 Conn Smythe Trophy winner.

NHL Amateur and Entry Draft
History

Owen Nolan, first overall pick in the 1990 Entry Draft.

Year	Site	Date	Total Players Drafted
1963	Queen Elizabeth Hotel	June 5	21
1964	Queen Elizabeth Hotel	June 11	24
1965	Queen Elizabeth Hotel	April 27	11
1966	Mount Royal Hotel	April 25	24
1967	Queen Elizabeth Hotel	June 7	18
1968	Queen Elizabeth Hotel	June 13	24
1969	Queen Elizabeth Hotel	June 12	84
1970	Queen Elizabeth Hotel	June 11	115
1971	Queen Elizabeth Hotel	June 10	117
1972	Queen Elizabeth Hotel	June 8	152
1973	Mount Royal Hotel	May 15	168
1974	NHL Montreal Office	May 28	247
1975	NHL Montreal Office	June 3	217
1976	NHL Montreal Office	June 1	135
1977	NHL Montreal Office	June 14	185
1978	Queen Elizabeth Hotel	June 15	234
1979	Queen Elizabeth Hotel	August 9	126
1980	Montreal Forum	June 11	210
1981	Montreal Forum	June 10	211
1982	Montreal Forum	June 9	252
1983	Montreal Forum	June 8	242
1984	Montreal Forum	June 9	250
1985	Toronto Convention Centre	June 15	252
1986	Montreal Forum	June 21	252
1987	Joe Louis Sports Arena	June 13	252
1988	Montreal Forum	June 11	252
1989	Metropolitan Sports Center	June 17	252
1990	B. C. Place	June 16	250

* The NHL Amateur Draft became the NHL Entry Draft in 1979

Draft Summary

Following is a summary of the number of players drafted from the Ontario Hockey League (OHL), Western Hockey League (WHL), Quebec Major Junior Hockey League (QMJHL), United States Colleges, United States High Schools, European Leagues and other Leagues throughout North America since 1969:

	OHL	WHL	QMJHL	US Coll.	US HS	International	Other
1969	36	20	11	7	0	1	9
1970	51	22	13	16	0	0	13
1971	41	28	13	22	0	0	13
1972	46	44	30	21	0	0	11
1973	56	49	24	25	0	0	14
1974	69	66	40	41	0	6	25
1975	45	54	28	59	0	6	25
1976	47	33	18	26	0	8	3
1977	42	44	40	49	0	5	5
1978	59	48	22	73	0	15	17
1979	48	37	19	15	0	6	1
1980	73	41	24	42	7	13	10
1981	59	37	28	21	17	32	17
1982	60	55	17	20	47	35	18
1983	57	41	24	14	35	34	37
1984	55	37	16	22	44	40	36
1985	59	48	15	20	48	30	32
1986	66	32	22	22	40	28	42
1987	32	36	17	40	69	38	20
1988	32	30	22	48	56	39	25
1989	39	44	16	48	47	38	20
1990	39	33	14	38	57	53	16
Total	1111	879	473	689	466	427	412

First Selections

Year	Player	Pos	Drafted By	Drafted From	Age
1969	Rejean Houle	LW	Montreal	Jr. Canadiens	19.8
1970	Gilbert Perreault	C	Buffalo	Jr. Canadiens	19.7
1971	Guy Lafleur	RW	Montreal	Quebec Remparts	19.9
1972	Billy Harris	RW	NY Islanders	Toronto Marlboros	20.4
1973	Denis Potvin	D	NY Islanders	Ottawa 67's	19.7
1974	Greg Joly	D	Washington	Regina Pats	20.0
1975	Mel Bridgman	C	Philadelphia	Victoria Cougars	20.1
1976	Rick Green	D	Washington	London Knights	20.3
1977	Dale McCourt	C	Detroit	St. Catharines Fincups	20.4
1978	Bobby Smith	C	Minnesota	Ottawa 67's	20.4
1979	Bob Ramage	D	Colorado	London Knights	20.5
1980	Doug Wickenheiser	C	Montreal	Regina Pats	19.2
1981	Dale Hawerchuk	C	Winnipeg	Cornwall Royals	18.2
1982	Gord Kluzak	D	Boston	Nanaimo Islanders	18.3
1983	Brian Lawton	C	Minnesota	Mount St. Charles HS	18.11
1984	Mario Lemieux	C	Pittsburgh	Laval Voisins	18.8
1985	Wendel Clark	LW/D	Toronto	Saskatoon Blades	18.7
1986	Joe Murphy	C	Detroit	Michigan State	18.8
1987	Pierre Turgeon	C	Buffalo	Granby Bisons	17.10
1988	Mike Modano	C	Minnesota	Prince Albert Raiders	18.0
1989	Mats Sundin	RW	Quebec	Nacka (Sweden)	18.4
1990	Owen Nolan	RW	Quebec	Cornwall Royals	18.4

Ontario Hockey League

Club	'69	'70	'71	'72	'73	'74	'75	'76	'77	'78	'79	'80	'81	'82	'83	'84	'85	'86	'87	'88	'89	'90	Total
Peterborough	5	5	4	5	9	4	3	1	4	6	9	10	3	5	7	3	9	2	5	2	2	4	107
Kitchener	1	6	2	8	4	13	3	1	3	4	4	4	5	5	8	4	6	3	2	1	7	5	99
Oshawa	5	4	3	5	5	7	6	6	1	3	3	2	9	5	5	6	6	6	3	2	4	2	98
Toronto	3	7	6	5	6	8	4	4	7	5	4	10	2	6	4	4	3	4	1	2	2	–	97
London	4	9	1	5	6	6	3	5	4	3	6	2	5	5	3	7	1	3	2	6	3	3	92
Ottawa	2	4	3	4	6	5	6	5	5	5	3	8	4	9	2	2	3	3	2	1	–	5	87
S.S. Marie	–	–	–	4	5	2	5	1	5	3	3	8	1	6	4	5	7	1	2	3	1		66
Hamilton	2	3	5	4	6	4	7	3	–	8	1	–	–	–	–	3	6	4	4	–	–		60
Kingston	–	–	–	–	4	4	6	4	9	2	8	5	2	1	3	3	4	1	1	–	2		59
Sudbury	–	–	–	6	6	4	5	4	4	3	7	2	4	–	2	5	3	1	–	1	2		59
Niagara Falls	4	2	1	4	–	–	–	2	3	5	8	6	6	–	–	–	–	–	–	–	4	4	49
St. Catharines	5	5	8	5	4	7	3	4	6	–													47
Windsor	–	–	–	–	2	1	4	2	3	5	3	2	2	3	7	–	5	2	1				42
Cornwall	–	–	–	–	–	–	–	–	7	4	3	2	2	3	3	2	3						29
Brantford	–	–	–	–	–	3	8	5	2	7	2	–	–										27
North Bay	–	–	–	–	–	–	–	–	4	4	3	3	3	3	1	4							25
Belleville	–	–	–	–	–	–	–	–	3	4	4	5	2	–	4	2							24
Guelph	–	–	–	–	–	–	–	–	1	5	3	8	2	–	4	–							23
Montreal	5	6	8	1	–	–	–	–	–	–	–	–	–	–	–	–	–	–	–	–	–	–	20
Owen Sound	–	–	–	–	–	–	–	–	–	–	–	–	–	–	–	–	–	–	–	–	1		1

Year	Total Ontario Drafted	Total Players Drafted	Ontario %
1969	36	84	42.9
1970	51	115	44.3
1971	41	117	35.0
1972	46	152	30.3
1973	56	168	33.3
1974	69	247	27.9
1975	45	217	20.7
1976	47	135	34.8
1977	42	185	22.7
1978	59	234	25.2
1979	48	126	38.1
1980	73	210	34.8
1981	59	211	28.0
1982	60	252	23.8
1983	57	242	23.6
1984	55	250	22.0
1985	59	252	23.4
1986	66	252	26.2
1987	32	252	12.7
1988	32	252	12.7
1989	39	252	15.5
1990	39	250	15.6
Total	1111	4455	24.9

Western Hockey League

Club	'69	'70	'71	'72	'73	'74	'75	'76	'77	'78	'79	'80	'81	'82	'83	'84	'85	'86	'87	'88	'89	'90	Total
Regina	–	–	5	5	1	8	5	3	1	4	1	3	5	6	8	4	4	3	2	–	5	1	74
Saskatoon	1	–	1	3	8	4	5	3	4	1	2	3	5	5	3	1	5	4	4	3	2		69
Portland	–	–	–	–	–	–	4	1	8	7	8	6	7	7	5	2	4	3	1				67
Calgary	3	5	2	7	4	8	4	4	3	–	2	5	4	3	3	3	2	–	–	–	–		66
Victoria	–	–	2	2	5	7	4	3	3	1	8	6	2	3	4	2	1	2	4	4	2		65
New Westm'r	–	–	6	8	7	9	5	8	6	5	1	–	–	–	–	–	–	–	–	–	–		62
Medicine Hat	–	–	4	6	4	5	3	5	4	–	4	2	1	2	1	6	2	5	1	4	1		60
Brandon	–	3	1	5	2	7	4	3	1	10	5	2	2	1	3	2	1	3	3	–	1		59
Kamloops	–	–	–	–	4	4	4	–	1	–	–	2	4	4	4	4	3	1	5	4			47
Lethbridge	–	–	–	–	–	2	3	5	4	1	4	7	2	1	5	1	–	3	3	4			45
Flin Flon	4	4	5	3	4	7	4	3	1	5	–	–	–	–	–	–	–	–	–				39
Winnipeg	3	2	4	2	5	4	4	–	4	–	1	4	1	–	–	–	–	–	–				34
Edmonton	4	4	5	6	6	2	3	2	–	2	–	–	–	–	–	–	–	–	–				34
Seattle	–	–	–	–	–	–	–	4	2	3	6	–	1	3	1	2	4	2	6				34
Prince Albert	–	–	–	–	–	–	–	–	4	2	2	6	6	1	3	3	4						31
Swift Current	1	–	1	–	3	6	–	–	–	–	–	–	–	–	–	5	2	2	2				22
Billings	–	–	–	–	–	–	–	4	3	4	2	–	–	–	–	–	–						13
Moose Jaw	–	–	–	–	–	–	–	–	–	–	–	–	4	1	3	–	3	1					12
Estevan	4	4	4	–	–	–	–	–	–	–	–	–	–	–	–	–	–						12
Kelowna	–	–	–	–	–	–	–	–	–	2	4	5	–	–	–	–							11
Spokane	–	–	–	–	–	–	–	–	–	–	–	–	–	1	3	2	1						7
Tri-Cities	–	–	–	–	–	–	–	–	–	–	–	–	–	4	3								7
Nanaimo	–	–	–	–	–	–	–	–	5	1	–	–	–	–									6
Vancouver	–	–	–	2	–	–	–	–	–	–	–												2

Year	Total Western Drafted	Total Players Drafted	Western %
1969	20	84	23.8
1970	22	115	19.1
1971	28	117	23.9
1972	44	152	28.9
1973	49	168	29.2
1974	66	247	26.7
1975	54	217	24.9
1976	33	135	24.4
1977	44	185	23.8
1978	48	234	20.5
1979	37	126	29.4
1980	41	210	19.5
1981	37	211	17.5
1982	55	252	21.8
1983	41	242	16.9
1984	37	250	14.8
1985	48	252	19.0
1986	32	252	12.7
1987	36	252	14.3
1988	30	252	11.9
1989	44	252	17.5
1990	33	250	13.2
Total	879	4455	19.7

Quebec Major Junior Hockey League

Club	'69	'70	'71	'72	'73	'74	'75	'76	'77	'78	'79	'80	'81	'82	'83	'84	'85	'86	'87	'88	'89	'90	Total
Quebec	1	1	2	4	6	1	3	7	1	3	2	2	1	2	2	3	–	–	–	–	–		47
Cornwall	2	1	2	6	4	8	1	3	1	6	1	5	5	–	–								45
Shawinigan	3	2	1	6	1	5	3	–	3	–	2	2	5	5	2	–	2	1	–	2	–		45
Trois Rivieres	–	1	2	2	2	2	3	2	6	3	2	2	2	1	3	–	3	–	1	3	3	1	44
Sherbrooke	–	–	2	2	4	3	7	5	6	3	4	1	5	2	–	–	–	–					44
Montreal	–	–	–	–	4	4	8	1	3	2	4	3	–	3	–	–	–	–					32
Hull	–	–	–	–	–	3	2	2	3	–	3	1	–	3	1	–	4	3	2	2	3		32
Laval	–	–	–	1	–	2	1	1	4	2	1	–	2	1	2	–	5	3	1	3	3		32
Chicoutimi	–	–	–	–	1	–	5	1	1	3	6	1	3	–	3	1	2	2	1	1			31
Sorel	2	3	1	3	1	8	1	1	3	–	–	–	5	–	–	–	–						28
Drummondville	2	4	1	4	2	1	–	–	–	–	1	2	2	2	4	1	–						26
Verdun	–	1	1	2	–	–	–	1	3	3	–	3	3	–	3	0	3	1	–				24
Granby	–	–	–	–	–	–	–	2	1	3	2	2	–	–	–	–							16
Longueuil	–	–	–	–	–	–	–	1	2	1	2	1	–	–	2								9
St. Jean	–	–	–	–	–	–	–	–	2	–	1	1	0	3	1	–							8
Victoriaville	–	–	–	–	–	–	–	–	–	–	–	4	–	1									5
St. Hyacinthe	–	–	–	–	–	–	–	–	–	–	–	–	3										3
St. Jerome	1	–	1	–	–	–	–	–	–	–	–	–											2

Year	Total Quebec Drafted	Total Players Drafted	Quebec %
1969	11	84	13.1
1970	13	115	11.3
1971	13	117	11.1
1972	30	152	19.7
1973	24	168	14.3
1974	40	247	16.2
1975	28	217	12.9
1976	18	135	13.3
1977	40	185	21.6
1978	22	234	9.4
1979	19	126	15.1
1980	24	210	11.4
1981	28	211	13.3
1982	17	252	6.7
1983	24	242	9.9
1984	16	250	6.4
1985	15	252	5.9
1986	22	252	8.7
1987	17	252	6.7
1988	22	252	8.7
1989	16	252	6.3
1990	14	250	5.6
Total	473	4455	10.6

International

Country	'69	'70	'71	'72	'73	'74	'75	'76	'77	'78	'79	'80	'81	'82	'83	'84	'85	'86	'87	'88	'89	'90	Total
Sweden	–	–	–	–	–	5	2	5	2	8	5	9	13	14	10	14	15	9	15	14	9	8	157
Czechoslovakia	–	–	–	–	–	–	–	1	1	–	4	13	9	13	8	6	11	5	8	21			100
Finland	1	–	–	1	3	2	3	2	–	4	13	5	9	10	4	10	6	7	3	8			91
Soviet Union	–	–	–	–	–	–	1	–	2	–	–	3	5	1	2	1	2	11	18	14			60
West Germany	–	–	–	–	–	–	–	2	–	2	–	1	2	1	–	2	–	–					11
Norway	–	–	–	–	–	–	–	–	–	–	–	2	–	–	2								4
Denmark	–	–	–	–	–	–	–	–	–	–	1	1	–	–									2
Switzerland	–	–	–	–	–	1	–	–	–	–	–	1											1
Scotland	–	–	–	–	–	–	–	–	–	–	1	–	–										1

Year	Total International Drafted	Total Players Drafted	International %
1969	1	84	1.2
1970	0	115	0
1971	0	117	0
1972	0	152	0
1973	0	168	0
1974	6	247	2.4
1975	6	217	2.8
1976	8	135	5.9
1977	5	185	2.7
1978	15	234	6.4
1979	6	126	4.8
1980	13	210	6.2
1981	32	211	15.2
1982	35	252	13.9
1983	34	242	14.0
1984	40	250	17.6
1985	30	252	12.0
1986	28	252	11.1
1987	38	252	15.1
1988	39	252	15.5
1989	38	252	15.1
1990	53	250	21.2
Total	428	4455	9.6

United States Colleges

Club	'69	'70	'71	'72	'73	'74	'75	'76	'77	'78	'79	'80	'81	'82	'83	'84	'85	'86	'87	'88	'89	'90	Total
Minnesota	1	3	2	–	–	9	4	4	5	5	2	3	1	1	1	–	2	1	1	1	–		46
Michigan Tech	–	–	3	1	2	5	4	4	1	2	1	4	–	1	–	2	2	2	1	1	2	1	39
Wisconsin	–	1	2	4	5	4	4	2	2	–	3	–	1	1	–	1	1	–	1	1	–	–	35
Denver	1	3	2	4	2	3	1	2	2	2	2	1	–	1	–	–	1	2	4	1	1	–	35
Michigan	1	–	–	–	2	2	3	3	1	6	–	4	–	–	1	1	–	1	2	3	5		35
Boston U.	–	4	–	1	1	1	1	4	5	1	–	1	–	–	1	1	2	2	3	1	2		31
North Dakota	2	3	3	1	4	2	1	–	1	2	3	3	1	–	–	1	–	–	–	2	1		30
Providence	–	–	–	–	–	3	2	3	4	–	5	4	1	2	–	1	1	–	–	–	1		27
Michigan State	–	–	1	–	1	1	1	1	–	–	–	2	–	2	–	2	–	1	1	4	4	5	26
New Hampshire	–	–	–	1	1	3	6	–	4	1	1	2	1	1	1	2	–	–	1	–	–		25
Clarkson	–	2	2	1	–	2	–	2	2	1	1	1	1	1	–	–	–	1	1	1	3		23
Cornell	–	–	2	1	1	–	1	1	1	–	1	1	1	–	1	2	–	1	2	5	2		23
Colorado	2	1	–	–	–	1	3	1	2	2	–	–	–	3	–	1	–	1	–	–	2		20
Notre Dame	–	2	3	–	7	2	–	3	1	1	–	–	–	–	–	–	–	–	–	–	–		19
Lake Superior	–	–	–	1	1	1	–	3	–	–	–	–	1	–	3	–	3	2	3				18
Boston College	–	1	–	–	–	1	1	–	5	–	2	1	1	–	–	1	2	–	2	–			17
Bowling Green	–	–	–	–	1	3	2	1	1	–	1	–	–	–	–	–	3	2	1				17
Harvard	–	2	–	–	2	–	2	2	–	–	1	1	–	2	–	1	–	2	1				16
St. Lawrence	–	–	–	–	1	–	1	4	–	–	3	–	1	1	1	1	1	1	1				16
RPI	–	–	–	–	–	1	–	3	–	1	2	1	1	–	1	–	2	2	–	–			15
Northern Mich.	–	–	–	–	–	–	–	4	–	1	2	1	–	–	–	4	1	2	–				15
Vermont	–	–	–	–	1	4	–	1	1	–	1	1	–	1	1	2	–	1	–				14
W. Michigan	–	–	–	–	–	–	2	–	2	–	2	2	2	–	2	1	1	1	1				14
Minn.-Duluth	–	2	1	–	–	–	–	–	1	–	–	1	–	–	–	–	2	1	2				11
Brown	–	–	–	1	2	1	–	3	2	–	1	–	–	–	–	–	–	–					10
Yale	–	–	1	–	1	–	2	1	–	–	–	1	2	–	1	–							9
Ohio State	–	–	–	–	–	2	1	–	–	1	–	2	2	–	1								9
Maine	–	–	–	–	–	–	1	1	–	1	–	3	2	1									9
Miami of Ohio	–	–	–	–	–	–	–	–	1	2	4	2	–										9
Colgate	–	–	–	1	–	–	2	1	–	–	1	1	2										8
Northeastern	–	–	–	1	–	1	–	1	–	1	1	–	1	1									8
Princeton	–	–	–	1	–	1	1	–	–	1	1	–											7
St. Louis	–	–	–	1	2	1	2	–	–	–	–	–											6
U. of Ill.-Chi.	–	–	–	–	–	–	1	2	1	2	–												6
Pennsylvania	–	1	2	1	–	–	–	–	–	–													5
Ferris State	–	–	–	–	–	–	2	1	1	1													5
Union College	–	–	–	–	4	–	–	–	–														4
Dartmouth	–	–	1	–	1	–	–	–	–														4
Lowell	–	–	–	1	1	1	–	1	–														4
Merrimack	–	–	–	1	–	1	–	1															3
Babson College	–	–	–	–	1	1	1																3
Alaska-Anchorage	–	–	–	–	–	–	2	1															3
Salem State	–	1	–	–	–	–	2																2
Bemidji State	1	–	–	–	1																		1
San Diego U.	–	1	–	1																			1
Greenway	–	1	1																				1
St. Anselen College	–	1	1																				1
Hamilton College	–	1	1																				1
St. Thomas	–	1	1																				1
St. Cloud State	–	1	1																				1
Amer. Int'l College	1	1																					1
Alaska-Fairbanks	1	1																					1

Year	Total College Drafted	Total Players Drafted	College %
1969	7	84	8.3
1970	16	115	13.9
1971	22	117	18.8
1972	21	152	13.8
1973	25	168	14.9
1974	41	247	16.6
1975	59	217	26.7
1976	26	135	19.3
1977	49	185	26.5
1978	73	234	31.2
1979	15	126	11.9
1980	42	210	20.0
1981	21	211	10.0
1982	20	252	7.9
1983	14	242	5.8
1984	22	250	8.8
1985	20	252	7.9
1986	22	252	8.7
1987	40	252	15.9
1988	48	252	19.0
1989	48	252	19.0
1990	38	250	15.2
Total	**689**	**4455**	**15.5**

1990 Entry Draft

Transferred draft choice notation:
Example: L.A.-Phi. represents a draft choice transferred **from** Los Angeles **to** Philadelphia.

Pick	Player	Claimed By	Amateur Club	Position
ROUND # 1				
1	NOLAN, Owen	Que.	Cornwall	RW
2	NEDVED, Petr	Van.	Seattle	C
3	PRIMEAU, Keith	Det.	Niagara Falls	C
4	RICCI, Mike	Phi.	Peterborough	C
5	JAGR, Jaromir	Pit.	Poldi Kladno	LW
6	SCISSONS, Scott	NYI	Saskatoon	C
7	SYDOR, Daryl	L.A.	Kamloops	D
8	HATCHER, Derian	Min.	North Bay	D
9	SLANEY, John	Wsh.	Cornwall	D
10	BEREHOWSKY, Drake	Tor.	Kingston	D
11	KIDD, Trevor	N.J.-Cgy.	Brandon	G
12	STEVENSON, Turner	St. L.-Mtl.	Seattle	RW
13	STEWART, Michael	NYR	Michigan State	D
14	MAY, Brad	Wpg.-Buf.	Niagara Falls	LW
15	GREIG, Mark	Hfd.	Lethbridge	RW
16	DYKHUIS, Karl	Chi.	Hull	D
17	ALLISON, Scott	Edm.	Prince Albert	C
18	ANTOSKI, Shawn	Mtl.-St.L.-Van.	North Bay	LW
19	TKACHUK, Keith	Buf.-Wpg.	Malden Catholic	LW
20	BRODEUR, Martin	Cgy.-N.J.	St. Hyacinthe	G
21	SMOLINSKI, Bryan	Bos.	Michigan State	C
ROUND # 2				
22	HUGHES, Ryan	Que.	Cornell	C
23	SLEGR, Jiri	Van.	Litvinov	D
24	HARLOCK, David	Det.-Cgy.-N.J.	Michigan	D
25	SIMON, Chris	Phi.	Ottawa	LW
26	PERREAULT, Nicolas P.	Pit.-Cgy.	Hawkesbury T-II Jr. A	D
27	TAYLOR, Chris	NYI	London	C
28	SEMCHUK, Brandy	L.A.	Canadian Olympic	RW
29	GOTZIAMAN, Chris	Min.-Cgy.-N.J.	Roseau	RW
30	PASMA, Rod	Wsh.	Cornwall	D
31	POTVIN, Felix	Tor.	Chicoutimi	G
32	VIITAKOSKI, Vesa	N.J.-Cgy.	Saipa	LW
33	JOHNSON, Craig	St. L.	Hill-Murray H.S.	C
34	WEIGHT, Doug	NYR	Lake Superior	C
35	MULLER, Mike	Wpg.	Wayzata	D
36	SANDERSON, Geoff	Hfd.	Swift Current	C
37	DROPPA, Ivan	Chi.	L. Mikulas	D
38	LEGAULT, Alexandre	Edm.	Boston University	RW
39	KUWABARA, Ryan	Mtl.	Ottawa	RW
40	RENBERG, Mikael	Buf.-Phi.	Pitea	LW
41	BELZILE, Etienne	Cgy.	Cornell	D
42	SANDWITH, Terran	Bos.-Phi.	Tri-Cities	D
ROUND # 3				
43	ZAVISHA, Bradley	Que.	Seattle	LW
44	DANIELS, Kimbi	Van.-Phi.	Swift Current	C
45	KOZLOV, Viacheslav	Det.	Khimik	C
46	ARMSTRONG, Bill	Phi.	Oshawa	D
47	THERIEN, Chris	Pit.-Phi.	Northwood Prep	D
48	PLANTE, Dan	NYI	Edina	RW
49	BERG, Bob	L.A.	Belleville	LW
50	BILLECK, Laurie	Min.	Prince Albert	D
51	LONGO, Chris	Wsh.	Peterborough	RW
52	KINISKY, Al	Tor.-Phi.	Seattle	LW
53	DUNHAM, Michael	N.J.	Canterbury	G
54	TARDIF, Patrice	St. L.	Lennoxville	C
55	VARY, John	NYR	North Bay	D
56	BOMBARDIR, Brad	Wpg.-N.J.	Powell River T-II Jr. A	D
57	LENARDUZZI, Mike	Hfd.	Sault-Ste-Marie	G
58	POULIN, Charles	Chi.-Mtl.	St. Hyacinthe	C
59	CROWLEY, Joe	Edm.	Lawrence Academy	LW
60	GUILLET, Robert	Mtl.	Longueuil	RW
61	DZIEDZIC, Joe	Buf.-Pit.	Edison	LW
62	MEARS, Glen	Cgy.	Rochester Jr. A	D
63	STEWART, Cameron	Bos.	Elmira Jr. B	C
ROUND # 4				
64	BODNARCHUK, Mike	Que.-N.J.	Kingston	RW
65	BADER, Darin	Van.	Saskatoon	LW
66	MALGUNAS, Stewart	Det.	Seattle	D
67	BLAIN, Joel	Phi.-Edm.	Hull	LW
68	TAMER, Mike	Pit.	Michigan	D
69	NIELSEN, Jeff	NYI-L.A.-NYR	Grand Rapids	RW
70	McGOWAN, Cal	L.A.-NYR-Min.	Kamloops	C
71	KOVACS, Frank	Min.	Regina	LW
72	PEARCE, Randy	Wsh.	Kitchener	LW
73	HENDRICKSON, Darby	Tor.	Richfield	C
74	MELUZIN, Roman	N.J.-Wpg.	Zetor Brno	RW
75	LEVINS, Scott	St. L.-Wpg.	Tri-Cities	RW
76	WILLIS, Rick	NYR	Pingree	LW
77	ZHAMNOV, Alexei	Wpg.	Dynamo Moscow	C
78	BRIGHT, Chris	Hfd.	Moose Jaw	C
79	TUCKER, Chris	Chi.	Jefferson	C
80	WALTERS, Greg	Edm.-Tor.	Ottawa	C
81	DIONNE, Gilbert	Mtl.	Kitchener	LW
82	McCARTHY, Brian	Buf.	Pingree	C
83	KRUSE, Paul	Cgy.	Kamloops	LW
84	BUCKLEY, Jerome	Bos.	Northwood Prep	RW

1990 Entry Draft (continued)

Pick	Player	Claimed By	Amateur Club	Position
ROUND # 5				
85	ZUBOV, Sergei	Que.-NYR	CSKA	D
86	ODJICK, Gino	Van.	Laval	LW
87	BURNS, Tony	Det.-NYR- Det.	Duluth-Denfeld	D
88	KORDIC, Dan	Phi.	Medicine Hat	D
89	FARRELL, Brian	Pit.	Avon Old Farms	C
90	MARINUCCI, Chris	NYI	Grand Rapids	C
91	GOVERDE, David	L.A.	Sudbury	G
92	CICCONE, Enrico	Min.	Trois Rivieres	D
93	SAKIC, Brian	Wsh.	Tri-Cities	C
94	OUIMET, Mark	Tor-Wsh.	Michigan	C
95	MALKOC, Dean	N.J.	Kamloops	D
96	RUFF, Jason	St. L.	Lethbridge	LW
97	SMEHLIK, Richard	NYR-Buf.	Vitkovice	D
98	MARTIN, Craig	Wpg.	Hull	RW
99	ROB, Lubos	Hfd. NYR	Budejovice	C
100	BOJCUN, Todd	Chi.-Buf.	Peterborough	G
101	LOUDER, Greg	Edm.-Wpg.- Edm.	Cushing Academy	G
102	DIPIETRO, Paul	Mtl.	Sudbury	C
103	PASCALL, Brad	Buf.	North Dakota	D
104	KUCHYUNA, Peter	Cgy.-N.J.	Dukla Jihlava	D
105	BALES, Mike	Bos.	Ohio State	G
ROUND # 6				
106	PARROTT, Jeff	Que.	Minnesota-Duluth	D
107	MORAN, Ian	Van.-Pit.	Belmont Hill	D
108	BARTHE, Claude	Det.	Victoriaville	D
109	BUTSAYEV, Vjateslav	Phi.	CSKA	C
110	CASEY, Denis	Pit.	Colorado College	G
111	LEHTO, Joni	NYI	Ottawa	D
112	ANDERSSON, Erik	L.A.	Danderyd	LW
113	TUREK, Roman	Min.	Plzen	G
114	KOVALEV, Andrei	Wsh.	Dynamo Moscow	RW
115	GODYNYUK, Alexander	Tor.	Sokol Kiev	D
116	KOLNIK, Lubomir	N.J.	Dukla Trencin	RW
117	MILLER, Kurtis	St. L.	Rochester Jr. A	LW
118	WEINRICH, Jason	NYR	Springfield Jr. B	D
119	JARDEMYR, Daniel	Wpg.	Uppsala	D
120	KEENAN, Cory	Hfd.	Kitchener	D
121	STICKNEY, Brett	Chi.	St. Paul's	C
122	SAILYNOJA, Keijo	Edm.	Jokerit	LW
123	CONROY, Craig	Mtl.	Northwood Prep	C
124	EDGERLY, Derek	Buf.-Chi.	Stoneham	C
125	TSCHUPP, Chris	Cgy.	Trinity-Pawling	C
126	WOOLF, Mark	Bos.	Spokane	RW
ROUND # 7				
127	NORRIS, Dwayne	Que.	Michigan State	RW
128	FILIPEK, Daryl	Van.	Ferris State	D
129	YORK, Jason	Det.	Kitchener	D
130	VALILA, Mika	Phi.-Pit.	Tappara	C
131	PLAQUIN, Ken	Pit.	Michigan Tech	D
132	GUILBERT, Michael	NYI	Governor Dummer	D
133	LANG, Robert	L.A.	Litvinov	C
134	LEVY, Jeff	Min.	Rochester Jr. A	G
135	KONTSEK, Roman	Wsh.	Dukla Trencin	RW
136	LACROIX, Eric	Tor.	Governor Dummer	LW
137	MCALPINE, Chris	N.J.	Roseville	D
138	CONLAN, Wayne	St. L.	Trinity-Pawling	C
139	LONSINGER, Bryan	NYR	Choate	D
140	LILLEY, John	Wpg.	Cushing Academy	C
141	BACA, Jergus	Hfd.	Kosice	D
142	GORDIJUK, Viktor	Chi.-Buf.	Krylja Sovetov	RW
143	POWER, Mike	Edm.	Western Michigan	G
144	ROHR, Stephen	Mtl.	Culver Academy	RW
145	NEATON, Pat	Buf.-Pit.	Michigan	D
146	FROLOV, Dimitri	Cgy.	Dynamo Moscow	D
147	MACKEY, Jim	Bos.	Hotchkiss	D
ROUND # 8				
148	KOVALENKO, Andrei	Que.	CSKA	RW
149	O'HAGAN, Paul	Van.	Oshawa	D
150	McCAULEY, Wes	Det.	Michigan State	D
151	ENGLUND, Patrik	Phi.	AIK	LW
152	KOSKIMAKI, Petteri	Pit.	Boston University	C
153	FLEURY, Sylvain	NYI	Longueuil	LW
154	HULETT, Dean	L.A.	Lake Superior	RW
155	BARRAULT, Doug	Min.	Lethbridge	RW
156	BONDRA, Peter	Wsh.	Kosice	C
157	STIVER, Dan	Tor.	Michigan	RW
158	KARPOVTSEV, Alex	N.J.-Que.	Dynamo Moscow	D
159	MARTELL, Steve	St. L.-Wsh.	London	RW
160	HEDLUND, Todd	NYR	Roseau	RW
161	ANDERSSON, Henrik	Wpg.	Vasteras	D
162	D'ORSONNENS, Martin	Hfd.	Clarkson	D
163	BELANGER, Hugo	Chi.	Clarkson	LW
164	MEJZLIK, Roman	Edm.	Dukla Jihlava	
165	FLEETWOOD, Brent	Mtl.	Portland	LW
166	NEDOMA, Milan	Buf.	Zetor Brno	D
167	MURRAY, Shawn	Cgy.	Hill-Murray	G
168	GRUDEN, John	Bos.	Waterloo Jr. A	D

Pick	Player	Claimed By	Amateur Club	Position
ROUND # 9				
169	MAZZOLI, Pat	Que.	Humboldt T-II Jr. A	G
170	CIPRIANO, Mark	Van.	Victoria	RW
171	GRUBA, Anthony	Det.	Hill-Murray	RW
172	PORKKA, Toni	Phi.	Lukko	D
173	KARABIN, Ladislav	Pit.	Bratislava	LW
174	JOYCE, John	NYI	Avon Old Farms	C
175	LEBLANC, Denis	L.A.	St. Hyacinthe	C
176	BIONDI, Joe	Min.	Minnesota-Duluth	C
177	KLEE, Ken	Wsh.	Bowling Green	D
178	HORYNA, Robert	Tor.	Dukla Jihlava	G
179	MODRY, Jaroslav	N.J.	Budejovice	D
180	DUFFUS, Parris	St. L.	Melfort	G
181	SILVERMAN, Andrew	NYR	Beverly	D
182	RAITANEN, Rauli	Wpg.	ASSAT	C
183	OSMAK, Corey	Hfd.	Nipiwan T-II Jr. A	C
184	LESSARD, Owen	Chi.	Owen Sound	LW
185	ZEMLICKA, Richard	Edm.	Sparta Praha	
186	MAGUIRE, Derek	Mtl.	Delbarton	D
187	WINCH, Jason	Buf.	Niagara Falls	LW
188	MURRAY, Mike	Cgy.	Cushing Academy	RW
189	WETHERILL, Darren	Bos.	Minot T-II Jr. A	D
ROUND # 10				
190	DAVIS, Scott	Que.	U. of Manitoba	D
191	NEUMIER, Troy	Van.	Prince Albert	D
192	TUCKER, Travis	Det.	Avon Old Farms	D
193	HANSON, Greg	Phi.	Bloomington-Kennedy	D
194	FINGERHUT, Timothy	Pit.	Canterbury	LW
195	ENGA, Richard	NYI	Culver Academy	C
196	ROSS, Patrick	L.A.	HV 71	RW
197	BINNIE, Troy	Min.	Ottawa	RW
198	BOBACK, Michael	Wsh.	Providence College	C
199	CHEBATOR, Rob	Tor.	Arlington	D
200	SCHWAB, Corey	N.J.	Seattle	G
201	WIDMEYER, Steve	St. L.	U. of Maine	D
202	HILLEBRANDT, Jon	NYR	Monona Grove H.S.	G
203	ALATALO, Mika	Wpg.	KooKoo	LW
204	KNUTSEN, Espen	Hfd.	Valerengen	C
205	PETERSON, Erik	Chi.	Brockton	C
206	KORINEK, Petr	Edm.	Skoda Plzen	C
207	KETTELHUT, Mark	Mtl.	Duluth East	D
208	NAUD, Sylvain	Buf.	Laval	RW
209	SUMNER, Rob	Cgy.	Victoria	D
210	CAPUANO, Dean	Bos.	Mount St. Charles	D
ROUND # 11				
211	STROMBERG, Mika	Que.	Jokerit	D
212	ERTEL, Tyler	Van.	North Bay	C
213	LARSON, Brett	Det.	Duluth-Denfeld	D
214	SODERSTROM, Tommy	Phi.	Djurgarden	G
215	THOMPSON, Michael	Pit.	Michigan State	RW
216	LACROIX, Martin	NYI	St. Lawrence U.	RW
217	WHITE, K.J. (Kevin)	L.A.	Windsor	C
218	DAHLSTROM, Ole	Min.	Furuset	C
219	BROWN, Alan	Wsh.	Colgate	D
220	MALONE, Scott	Tor.	Northfield-Mt. Hermon	D
221	ZELEPUKIN, Valeri	N.J.	Khimik	RW
222	HAWLEY, Joe	St. L.	Peterborough	RW
223	LIEVERS, Brett	NYR	Wayzata	C
224	SELYANIN, Sergei	Wpg.	Khimik	D
225	ERIKSEN, Tommie	Hfd.	Prince Albert	D
226	DUBINSKY, Steve	Chi.	Clarkson	C
227	Invalid Claim	Edm.		
228	UNIAC, John	Mtl.	Kitchener	D
229	MARTIN, Kenneth	Buf.	Belmont Hill	LW
230	Invalid Claim	Cgy.		
231	BEZEAU, Andy	Bos.	Niagara Falls	LW
ROUND # 12				
232	KLIPPENSTEIN, Wade	Que.	Alaska-Fairbanks	LW
233	KIVI, Karri	Van.	Ilves	D
234	HENDRY, John	Det.	Lake Superior	LW
235	LUND, William	Phi.	Roseau	C
236	BRUININKS, Brian	Pit.	Colorado College	C
237	SHIER, Andy	NYI	Detroit Comp. Jr. A	C
238	MOHNS, Troy	L.A.	Colgate	D
239	McKERSIE, John	Min.	West High	G
240	HLUSHKO, Todd	Wsh.	London	LW
241	VACHON, Nick	Tor.	Governor Dummer	D
242	REIRDEN, Todd	N.J.	Tabor Academy	D
243	FLEMING, Joe	St. L.	Xaverian	D
244	NEMCHINOV, Sergei	NYR	Krlja Sovetov	C
245	MORRIS, Keith	Wpg.	Alaska-Anchorage	C
246	CHALIFOUX, Denis	Hfd.	Laval	C
247	GROSSI, David	Chi.	Northeastern	RW
248	NUUTINEN, Sami	Edm.	K-Espoo	D
249	MARTINYUK, Sergei	Mtl.	Torpedo Jaroslav	LW
250	RUBACHUK, Brad	Buf.	Lethbridge	C
251	GUDAS, Leo	Cgy.	Sparta Praha	D
252	MISKOLCZI, Ted	Bos.	Belleville	RW

Draft Choices, 1989-69

1989

FIRST ROUND

Selection	Claimed By	Amateur Club
1. SUNDIN, Mats	Que.	Nacka (Sweden)
2. CHYZOWSKI, Dave	NYI	Kamloops
3. THORNTON, Scott	Tor.	Belleville
4. BARNES, Stu	Wpg.	Tri-Cities
5. GUERIN, Bill	N.J.	Springfield Jr. B
6. BENNETT, Adam	Chi.	Sudbury
7. ZMOLEK, Doug	Min.	John Marshall
8. HERTER, Jason	Van.	U. of North Dakota
9. MARSHALL, Jason	St. L.	Vernon T-II Jr. A
10. HOLIK, Robert	Hfd.	Jihlava (Czech.)
11. SILLINGER, Mike	Det.	Regina
12. PEARSON, Rob	Tor.	Belleville
13. VALLIS, Lindsay	Mtl.	Seattle
14. HALLER, Kevin	Buf.	Regina
15. SOULES, Jason	Edm.	Niagara Falls
16. HEWARD, Jamie	Pit.	Regina
17. STEVENSON, Shayne	Bos.	Kitchener
18. MILLER, Jason	N.J.	Medicine Hat
19. KOLZIG, Olaf	Wsh.	Tri-Cities
20. RICE, Steven	NYR	Kitchener
21. BANCROFT, Steve	Tor.	Belleville

SECOND ROUND

Selection	Claimed By	Amateur Club
22. FOOTE, Adam	Que.	Sault Ste. Marie
23. GREEN, Travis	NYI	Spokane
24. MANDERVILLE, Kent	Cgy.	Notre Dame T-II Jr. A
25. RATUSHNY, Dan	Wpg.	Cornell
26. SKALDE, Jarrod	N.J.	Oshawa
27. SPEER, Michael	Chi.	Guelph
28. CRAIG, Mike	Min.	Oshawa
29. WOODWARD, Robert	Van.	Deerfield
30. BRISEBOIS, Patrice	Mtl.	Laval
31. CORRIVEAU, Rick	St. L.	London
32. BOUGHNER, Bob	Det.	Sault-Ste. Marie
33. JOHNSON, Greg	Phi.	Thunder Bay Jr. A
34. JUHLIN, Patrik	Phi.	Vasteras (Sweden)
35. DAFOE, Byron	Wsh.	Portland
36. BORGO, Richard	Edm.	Kitchener
37. LAUS, Paul	Pit.	Niagara Falls
38. PARSON, Mike	Bos.	Guelph
39. THOMPSON, Brent	L.A.	Medicine Hat
40. PROSOFSKY, Jason	NYR	Medicine Hat
41. LAROUCHE, Steve	Mtl.	Trois-Rivieres
42. DRURY, Ted	Cgy.	Fairfield Prep

Pierre Turgeon was selected first overall by the Buffalo Sabres in the 1987 Entry Draft.

1988

FIRST ROUND

Selection	Claimed By	Amateur Club
1. MODANO, Mike	Min.	Prince Albert
2. LINDEN, Trevor	Van.	Medicine Hat
3. LESCHYSHYN, Curtis	Que.	Saskatoon
4. SHANNON, Darrin	Pit.	Windsor
5. DORE, Daniel	Que.	Drummondville
6. PEARSON, Scott	Tor.	Kingston
7. GELINAS, Martin	L.A.	Hull
8. ROENICK, Jeremy	Chi.	Thayer Academy
9. BRIND'AMOUR, Rod	St.L.	Notre Dame Jr.A
10. SELANNE, Teemu	Wpg.	Jokerit (Finland)
11. GOVEDARIS, Chris	Hfd.	Toronto
12. FOSTER, Corey	N.J.	Peterborough
13. SAVAGE, Joel	Buf.	Victoria
14. BOIVIN, Claude	Phi.	Drummondville
15. SAVAGE, Reginald	Wsh.	Victoriaville
16. CHEVELDAYOFF, Kevin	NYI	Brandon
17. KOCUR, Kory	Det.	Saskatoon
18. CIMETTA, Robert	Bos.	Toronto
19. LEROUX, Francois	Edm.	St. Jean
20. CHARRON, Eric	Mtl.	Trois-Rivieres
21. MUZZATTI, Jason	Cgy.	Michigan State

SECOND ROUND

Selection	Claimed By	Amateur Club
22. MALLETTE, Troy	NYR	Sault Ste. Marie
23. CHRISTIAN, Jeff	N.J.	London
24. FISET, Stephane	Que.	Victoriaville
25. MAJOR, Mark	Pit.	North Bay
26. DUVAL, Murray	NYR	Spokane
27. DOMI, Tie	Tor.	Peterborough
28. HOLDEN, Paul	L.A.	London
29. DOUCET, Wayne	NYI	Hamilton
30. PLAVSIC, Adrien	St.L.	U. of New Hampshire
31. ROMANIUK, Russell	Wpg.	St. Boniface Jr. A
32. RICHTER, Barry	Hfd.	Culver Academy
33. ROHLIN, Leif	Van.	VIK (Sweden)
34. ST. AMOUR, Martin	Mtl.	Verdun
35. MURRAY, Pat	Phi.	Michigan State
36. TAYLOR, Tim	Wsh.	London
37. LE BRUN, Sean	NYI	New Westminster
38. ANGLEHART, Serge	Det.	Drummondville
39. KOIVUNEN, Petro	Edm.	K-Espoo (Finland)
40. GAETZ, Link	Min.	Spokane
41. BARTLEY, Wade	Wsh.	Dauphin Jr. A
42. HARKINS, Todd	Cgy.	Miami-Ohio

1987

FIRST ROUND

Selection	Claimed By	Amateur Club
1. TURGEON, Pierre	Buf.	Granby
2. SHANAHAN, Brendan	N.J.	London
3. WESLEY, Glen	Bos.	Portland
4. McBEAN, Wayne	L.A.	Medicine Hat
5. JOSEPH, Chris	Pit.	Seattle
6. ARCHIBALD, David	Min.	Portland
7. RICHARDSON, Luke	Tor.	Peterborough
8. WAITE, Jimmy	Chi.	Chicoutimi
9. FOGARTY, Bryan	Que.	Kingston
10. MORE, Jayson	NYR	New Westminster
11. RACINE, Yves	Det.	Longueuil
12. OSBORNE, Keith	St.L.	North Bay
13. CHYNOWETH, Dean	NYI	Medicine Hat
14. QUINTAL, Stephane	Bos.	Granby
15. SAKIC, Joe	Que.	Swift Current
16. MARCHMENT, Bryan	Wpg.	Belleville
17. CASSELS, Andrew	Mtl.	Ottawa
18. HULL, Jody	Hfd.	Peterborough
19. DEASLEY, Bryan	Cgy.	U. of Michigan
20. RUMBLE, Darren	Phi.	Kitchener
21. SOBERLAK, Peter	Edm.	Swift Current

SECOND ROUND

Selection	Claimed By	Amateur Club
22. MILLER, Brad	Buf.	Regina
23. PERSSON, Rickard	N.J.	Ostersund, Sweden
24. MURPHY, Rob	Van.	Laval
25. MATTEAU, Stephane	Cgy.	Hull
26. TABARACCI, Richard	Pit.	Cornwall
27. FITZPATRICK, Mark	L.A.	Medicine Hat
28. MAROIS, Daniel	Tor.	Chicoutimi
29. McGILL, Ryan	Chi.	Swift Current
30. HARDING, Jeff	Phi.	St. Michael's Jr. B
31. LACROIX, Daniel	NYR	Granby
32. KRUPPKE, Gordon	Det.	Prince Albert
33. LECLAIR, John	Mtl.	Bellows Academy
34. HACKETT, Jeff	NYI	Oshawa
35. McCRADY, Scott	Min.	Medicine Hat
36. BALLANTYNE, Jeff	Wsh.	Ottawa
37. ERIKSSON, Patrik	Wpg.	Brynas, Sweden
38. DESJARDINS, Eric	Mtl.	Granby
39. BURT, Adam	Hfd.	North Bay
40. GRANT, Kevin	Cgy.	Kitchener
41. WILKIE, Bob	Det.	Swift Current
42. WERENKA, Brad	Edm.	N. Michigan

1986

FIRST ROUND

Selection	Claimed By	Amateur Club
1. MURPHY, Joe	Det.	Michigan State
2. CARSON, Jimmy	L.A.	Verdun Juniors
3. BRADY, Neil	N.J.	Medicine Hat Tigers
4. ZALAPSKI, Zarley	Pit.	Team Canada
5. ANDERSON, Shawn	Buf.	Team Canada
6. DAMPHOUSSE, Vincent	Tor.	Laval Olympiques
7. WOODLEY, Dan	Van.	Portland Winterhawks
8. ELYNUIK, Pat	Wpg.	Prince Albert Raiders
9. LEETCH, Brian	NYR	Avon Old Farms HS
10. LEMIEUX, Jocelyn	St.L.	Laval Olympiques
11. YOUNG, Scott	Hfd.	Boston University
12. BABE, Warren	Min.	Lethbridge Broncos
13. JANNEY, Craig	Bos.	Boston College
14. SANIPASS, Everett	Chi.	Verdun Juniors
15. PEDERSON, Mark	Mtl.	Medicine Hat Tigers
16. PELAWA, George	Cgy.	Bemidji HS
17. FITZGERALD, Tom	NYI	Austin Prep
18. McRAE, Ken	Que.	Sudbury Wolves
19. GREENLAW, Jeff	Wsh.	Team Canada
20. HUFFMAN, Kerry	Phi.	Guelph Platers
21. ISSEL, Kim	Edm.	Prince Albert Raiders

SECOND ROUND

Selection	Claimed By	Amateur Club
22. GRAVES, Adam	Det.	Windsor Spitfires
23. SEPPO, Jukka	Phi.	Vasa Sport, (Finland)
24. COPELAND, Todd	N.J.	Bolmont Hill HS
25. CAPUANO, Dave	Pit.	Mt. St. Charles HS
26. BROWN, Greg	Buf.	St. Mark's
27. BRUNET, Benoit	Mtl.	Hull Olympiques
28. HAWLEY, Kent	Phi.	Ottawa 67's
29. NUMMINEN, Teppo	Wpg.	Tappara, (Finland)
30. WILKINSON, Neil	Min.	Selkirk Settlers
31. POSMA, Mike	St.L.	Buffalo Jr. Sabres
32. LaFORGE, Marc	Hfd.	Kingston Canadians
33. KOLSTAD, Dean	Min.	Prince Albert Raiders
34. TIRKKONEN, Pekka	Bos.	Sapko, (Finland)
35. KURZAWSKI, Mark	Chi.	Windsor Spitfires
36. SHANNON, Darryl	Tor.	Windsor Spitfires
37. GLYNN, Brian	Cgy.	Saskatoon Blades
38. VASKE, Dennis	NYI	Armstrong HS
39. ROUTHIER, Jean-M	Que.	Hull Olympiques
40. SEFTEL, Steve	Wsh.	Kingston Canadians
41. GUERARD, Stephane	Que.	Shawinigan Cataractes
42. NICHOLS, Jamie	Edm.	Portland Winter Hawks

1985

FIRST ROUND

Selection	Claimed By	Amateur Club
1. CLARK, Wendel	Tor.	Saskatoon Blades
2. SIMPSON, Craig	Pit.	Michigan State
3. WOLANIN, Craig	N.J.	Kitchener Rangers
4. SANDLAK, Jim	Van.	London Knights
5. MURZYN, Dana	Hfd.	Cgy. Wranglers
6. DALGARNO, Brad	NYI	Hamilton Steelhawks
7. DAHLEN, Ulf	NYR	Ostersund (Sweden)
8. FEDYK, Brent	Det.	Regina Pats
9. DUNCANSON, Craig	L.A.	Sudbury Wolves
10. GRATTON, Dan	L.A.	Oshawa Generals
11. MANSON, David	Chi.	Prince Albert Raiders
12. CHARBONNEAU, Jose	Mtl.	Drummondville
13. KING, Derek	NYI	Sault Greyhounds
14. JOHANSSON, Carl	Buf.	V. Frolunda (Sweden)
15. LATTA, Dave	Que.	Kitchener Rangers
16. CHORSKE, Tom	Mtl.	Minneapolis HS
17. BIOTTI, Chris	Cgy.	Belmont Hill HS
18. STEWART, Ryan	Wpg.	Kamloops Blazers
19. CORRIVEAU, Yvon	Wsh.	Tor. Marlboros
20. METCALFE, Scott	Edm.	Kingston Canadians
21. SEABROOKE, Glen	Phi.	Peterborough Petes

SECOND ROUND

Selection	Claimed By	Amateur Club
22. SPANGLER, Ken	Tor.	Cgy. Wranglers
23. GIFFIN, Lee	Pit.	Oshawa Generals
24. BURKE, Sean	N.J.	Tor. Marlboros
25. GAMBLE, Troy	Van.	Medicine Hat Tigers
26. WHITMORE, Kay	Hfd.	Peterborough Petes
27. NIEUWENDYK, Joe	Cgy.	Cornell Big Red
28. RICHTER, Mike	NYR	Northwood Prep
29. SHARPLES, Jeff	Det.	Kelowna Wings
30. EDLUND, Par	L.A.	Bjorkloven (Sweden)
31. COTE, Alain	Bos.	Que. Remparts
32. WEINRICH, Eric	N.J.	North Yarmouth
33. RICHARD, Todd	Mtl.	Armstrong HS
34. LAUER, Brad	NYI	Regina Pats
35. HOGUE, Benoit	Buf.	St Jean Castors
36. LAFRENIERE, Jason	Que.	Hamilton Steelhawks
37. RAGLAN, Herb	St.L.	Kingston Canadians
38. WENAAS, Jeff	Cgy.	Medicine Hat Tigers
39. OHMAN, Roger	Wpg.	Leksand Jr. (Sweden)
40. DRUCE, John	Wsh.	Peterborough Petes
41. CARNELLEY, Todd	Edm.	Kamloops Blazers
42. RENDALL, Bruce	Phi.	Chatham Maroons

1984

FIRST ROUND

Selection	Claimed By	Amateur Club
1. LEMIEUX, Mario	Pit.	Laval Voisins
2. MULLER, Kirk	N.J.	Team Canada-Guelph
3. OLCZYK, Ed	Chi.	Team USA
4. IAFRATE, Al	Tor.	Team USA-Belleville
5. SVOBODA, Petr	Mtl.	Czechoslovakia Jr.
6. REDMOND, Craig	L.A.	Team Canada
7. BURR, Shawn	Det.	Kitchener Rangers
8. CORSON, Shayne	Mtl.	Brantford Alexanders
9. BODGER, Doug	Pit.	Kamloops Jr. Oilers
10. DAIGNEAULT, J.J.	Van.	Canada-Longueuil
11. COTE, Sylvain	Hfd.	Que. Remparts
12. ROBERTS, Gary	Cgy.	Ottawa 67's
13. QUINN, David	Min.	Kent High School
14. CARKNER, Terry	NYR	Peterborough Petes
15. STIENBURG, Trevor	Que.	Guelph Platers
16. BELANGER, Roger	Pit.	Kingston Canadians
17. HATCHER, Kevin	Wsh.	North Bay Centennials
18. ANDERSSON, Bo Mikael	Buf.	V. Frolunda (Sweden)
19. PASIN, Dave	Bos.	Prince Albert Raiders
20. MACPHERSON, Duncan	NYI	Saskatoon Blades
21. ODELEIN, Selmar	Edm.	Regina Pats

SECOND ROUND

Selection	Claimed By	Amateur Club
22. SMYTH, Greg	Phi.	London Knights
23. BILLINGTON, Craig	N.J.	Belleville Bulls
24. WILKS, Brian	L.A.	Kitchener Rangers
25. GILL, Todd	Tor.	Windsor Spitfires
26. BENNING, Brian	St.L.	Portland Winter Hawks
27. MELLANBY, Scott	Phi.	Henry Carr Jr. B
28. HOUDA, Doug	Det.	Cgy. Wranglers
29. RICHER, Stephane	Mtl.	Granby Bisons
30. DOURIS, Peter	Wpg.	U. of N. Hampshire
31. ROHLICEK, Jeff	Van.	Portland Winter Hawks
32. HRKAC, Anthony	St.L.	Orillia Jr. A
33. SABOURIN, Ken	Cgy.	Sault Greyhounds
34. LEACH, Stephen	Wsh.	Matignon High School
35. HELMINEN, Raimo Ilmari	NYR	Ilves (Finland)
36. BROWN, Jeff	Que.	Sudbury Wolves
37. CHYCHRUN, Jeff	Phi.	Kingston Canadians
38. RANHEIM, Paul	Cgy.	Edina Hornets HS
39. TRAPP, Doug	Buf.	Regina Pats
40. PODLOSKI, Ray	Bos.	Portland Winter Hawks
41. MELANSON, Bruce	NYI	Oshawa Generals
42. REAUGH, Daryl	Edm.	Kamloops Jr. Oilers

1983

FIRST ROUND

Selection	Claimed By	Amateur Club
1. LAWTON, Brian	Min.	Mount St. Charles HS
2. TURGEON, Sylvain	Hfd.	Hull Olympiques
3. LAFONTAINE, Pat	NYI	Verdun Juniors
4. YZERMAN, Steve	Det.	Peterborough Petes
5. BARRASSO, Tom	Buf.	Acton-Boxboro HS
6. MacLEAN, John	N.J.	Oshawa Generals
7. COURTNALL, Russ	Tor.	Victoria Cougars
8. McBAIN, Andrew	Wpg.	North Bay Centennials
9. NEELY, Cam	Van.	Portland Winter Hawks
10. LACOMBE, Normand	Buf.	University of New Hampshire
11. CREIGHTON, Adam	Buf.	Ottawa 67's
12. GAGNER, Dave	NYR	Brantford Alexanders
13. QUINN, Dan	Cgy.	Belleville Bulls
14. DOLLAS, Bobby	Wpg.	Laval Voisins
15. ERREY, Bob	Pit.	Peterborough Petes
16. DIDUCK, Gerald	NYI	Lethbridge Broncos
17. TURCOTTE, Alfie	Mtl.	Portland Winter Hawks
18. CASSIDY, Bruce	Chi.	Ottawa 67's
19. BEUKEBOOM, Jeff	Edm.	Sault Greyhounds
20. JENSEN, David	Hfd.	Lawrence Academy
21. MARKWART, Nevin	Bos.	Regina Pats

SECOND ROUND

Selection	Claimed By	Amateur Club
22. CHARLESWORTH, Todd	Pit.	Oshawa Generals
23. SIREN, Ville	Hfd.	Ilves (Finland)
24. EVANS, Shawn	N.J.	Peterborough Petes
25. LAMBERT, Lane	Det.	Saskatoon Blades
26. LEMIEUX, Claude	Mtl.	Trois Rivieres Draveurs
27. MOMESSO, Sergio	Mtl.	Shawinigan Cataractes
28. JACKSON, Jeff	Tor.	Brantford Alexanders
29. BERRY, Brad	Wpg.	St. Albert Saints
30. BRUCE, Dave	Van.	Kitchener Rangers
31. TUCKER, John	Buf.	Kitchener Rangers
32. HEROUX, Yves	Que.	Chicoutimi Sagueneens
33. HEATH, Randy	NYR	Portland Winter Hawks
34. HAJDU, Richard	Buf.	Kamloops Jr. Oilers
35. FRANCIS, Todd	Mtl.	Brantford Alexanders
36. PARKS, Malcolm	Min.	St. Albert Saints
37. McKECHNEY, Grant	NYI	Kitchener Rangers
38. MUSIL, Frantisek	Min.	Czech. National Team
39. PRESLEY, Wayne	Chi.	Kitchener Rangers
40. GOLDEN, Mike	Edm.	Reading High School
41. ZEZEL, Peter	Phi.	Tor. Malboros
42. JOHNSTON, Greg	Bos.	Tor. Malboros

1982

FIRST ROUND

Selection	Claimed By	Amateur Club
1. KLUZAK, Gord	Bos.	Nanaimo Islanders
2. BELLOWS, Brian	Min.	Kitchener Rangers
3. NYLUND, Gary	Tor.	Portland Winter Hawks
4. SUTTER, Ron	Phi.	Lethbridge Broncos
5. STEVENS, Scott	Wsh.	Kitchener Rangers
6. HOUSLEY, Phil	Buf.	S. St. Paul High School
7. YAREMCHUK, Ken	Chi.	Portland Winter Hawks
8. TROTTIER, Rocky	N.J.	Nanaimo Islanders
9. CYR, Paul	Buf.	Victoria Cougars
10. SUTTER, Rich	Pit.	Lethbridge Broncos
11. PETIT, Michel	Van.	Sherbrooke Castors
12. KYTE, Jim	Wpg.	Cornwall Royals
13. SHAW, David	Que.	Kitchener Rangers
14. LAWLESS, Paul	Hfd.	Windsor Spitfires
15. KONTOS, Chris	NYR	Tor. Marlboros
16. ANDREYCHUK, Dave	Buf.	Oshawa Generals
17. CRAVEN, Murray	Det.	Medicine Hat Tigers
18. DANEYKO, Ken	N.J.	Seattle Breakers
19. HEROUX, Alain	Mtl.	Chicoutimi Sagueneens
20. PLAYFAIR, Jim	Edm.	Portland Winter Hawks
21. FLATLEY, Pat	NYI	University of Wisconsin

SECOND ROUND

Selection	Claimed By	Amateur Club
22. CURRAN, Brian	Bos.	Portland Winter Hawks
23. COURTEAU, Yves	Det.	Laval Voisins
24. LEEMAN, Gary	Tor.	Regina Pats
25. IHNACAK, Peter	Tor.	Czech National Team
26. ANDERSON, Mike	Buf.	N. St. Paul High School
27. HEIDT, Mike	L.A.	Cgy. Wranglers
28. BADEAU, Rene	Chi.	Que. Remparts
29. REIERSON, Dave	Cgy.	Prince Albert Raiders
30. JOHANSSON, Jens	Buf.	Pitea (Sweden)
31. GAUVREAU, Jocelyn	Mtl.	Granby Bisons
32. CARLSON, Kent	Mtl.	St. Lawrence University
33. MALEY, David	Mtl.	Edina High School
34. GILLIS, Paul	Que.	Niagara Falls Flyers
35. PATERSON, Mark	Hfd.	Ottawa 67's
36. SANDSTROM, Tomas	NYR	Farjestads (Sweden)
37. KROMM, Richard	Cgy.	Portland Winter Hawks
38. HRYNEWICH, Tim	Pit.	Sudbury Wolves
39. BYERS, Lyndon	Bos.	Regina Pats
40. SANDELIN, Scott	Mtl.	Hibbing High School
41. GRAVES, Steve	Edm.	Sault Greyhounds
42. SMITH, Vern	NYI	Lethbridge Broncos

1981

FIRST ROUND

Selection	Claimed By	Amateur Club
1. HAWERCHUK, Dale	Wpg.	Cornwall Royals
2. SMITH, Doug	L.A.	Ottawa 67's
3. CARPENTER, Bobby	Wsh.	St. John's High School
4. FRANCIS, Ron	Hfd.	Sault Greyhounds
5. CIRELLA, Joe	Col.	Oshawa Generals
6. BENNING, Jim	Tor.	Portland Winter Hawks
7. HUNTER, Mark	Mtl.	Brantford Alexanders
8. FUHR, Grant	Edm.	Victoria Cougars
9. PATRICK, James	NYR	U. of North Dakota
10. BUTCHER, Garth	Van.	Regina Pats
11. MOLLER, Randy	Que.	Lethbridge Broncos
12. TANTI, Tony	Chi.	Oshawa Generals
13. MEIGHAN, Ron	Min.	Niagara Falls Flyers
14. LEVEILLE, Normand	Bos.	Chicoutimi Sagueneens
15. MacINNIS, Allan	Cgy.	Kitchener Rangers
16. SMITH, Steve	Phi.	Sault Greyhounds
17. DUDACEK, Jiri	Buf.	Kladno (Czech.)
18. DELORME, Gilbert	Mtl.	Chicoutimi Sagueneens
19. INGMAN, Jan	Mtl.	Sweden
20. RUFF, Marty	St.L.	Lethbridge Broncos
21. BOUTILIER, Paul	NYI	Sherbrooke Castors

SECOND ROUND

Selection	Claimed By	Amateur Club
22. ARNIEL, Scott	Wpg.	Cornwall Royals
23. LOISELLE, Claude	Det.	Windsor Spitfires
24. YAREMCHUK, Gary	Tor.	Portland Winter Hawks
25. GRIFFIN, Kevin	Chi.	Portland Winter Hawks
26. CHERNOMAZ, Rich	Col.	Victoria Cougars
27. DONNELLY, Dave	Min.	St. Albert Saints
28. GATZOS, Steve	Pit.	Sault Greyhounds
29. STRUEBY, Todd	Edm.	Regina Pats
30. ERIXON, Jan	NYR	Skelleftea (Sweden)
31. SANDS, Mike	Min.	Sudbury Wolves
32. ERIKSSON, Lars	Mtl.	Brynas (Sweden)
33. HIRSCH, Tom	Min.	Patrick Henry HS
34. PREUSS, Dave	Min.	St. Thomas Academy
35. DUFOUR, Luc	Bos.	Chicoutimi Sagueneens
36. NORDIN, Hakan	St.L.	Farjestads (Sweden)
37. COSTELLO, Rich	Phi.	Natick High School
38. VIRTA, Hannu	Buf.	TPS Finland
39. KENNEDY, Dean	L.A.	Brandon Wheat Kings
40. CHELIOS, Chris	Mtl.	Moose Jaw Canucks
41. WAHLSTEN, Jali	Min.	TPS Finland
42. DINEEN, Gord	NYI	Sault Greyhounds

1980

FIRST ROUND

Selection	Claimed By	Amateur Club
1. WICKENHEISER, Doug	Mtl.	Regina Pats
2. BABYCH, Dave	Wpg.	Portland Winter Hawks
3. SAVARD, Denis	Chi.	Mtl. Juniors
4. MURPHY, Larry	L.A.	Peterborough Petes
5. VEITCH, Darren	Wsh.	Regina Pats
6. COFFEY, Paul	Edm.	Kitchener Rangers
7. LANZ, Rick	Van.	Oshawa Generals
8. ARTHUR, Fred	Hfd.	Cornwall Royals
9. BULLARD, Mike	Pit.	Brantford Alexanders
10. FOX, Jimmy	L.A.	Ottawa 67's
11. BLAISDELL, Mike	Det.	Regina Pats
12. WILSON, Rik	St.L.	Kingston Canadians
13. CYR, Denis	Cgy.	Mtl. Juniors
14. MALONE, Jim	NYR	Tor. Marlboros
15. DUPONT, Jerome	Chi.	Tor. Marlboros
16. PALMER, Brad	Min.	Victoria Cougars
17. SUTTER, Brent	NYI	Red Deer Rustlers
18. PEDERSON, Barry	Bos.	Victoria Cougars
19. GAGNE, Paul	Col.	Windsor Spitfires
20. PATRICK, Steve	Buf.	Brandon Wheat Kings
21. STOTHERS, Mike	Phi.	Kingston Canadians

SECOND ROUND

Selection	Claimed By	Amateur Club
22. WARD, Joe	Col.	Seattle Breakers
23. MANTHA, Moe	Wpg.	Tor. Marlboros
24. ROCHEFORT, Normand	Que.	Que. Remparts
25. MUNI, Craig	Tor.	Kingston Canadians
26. McGILL, Bob	Tor.	Victoria Cougars
27. NATTRESS, Ric	Mtl.	Brantford Alexanders
28. LUDZIK, Steve	Chi.	Niagara Falls Flyers
29. GALARNEAU, Michel	Hfd.	Hull Olympiques
30. SOLHEIM, Ken	Chi.	Medicine Hat Tigers
31. CURTALE, Tony	Cgy.	Brantford Alexanders
32. LaVALLEE, Kevin	Cgy.	Brantford Alexanders
33. TERRION, Greg	L.A.	Brantford Alexanders
34. MORRISON, Dave	L.A.	Peterborough Petes
35. ALLISON, Mike	NYR	Sudbury Wolves
36. DAWES, Len	Chi.	Victoria Cougars
37. BEAUPRE, Don	Min.	Sudbury Wolves
38. HRUDEY, Kelly	NYI	Medicine Hat Tigers
39. KONROYD, Steve	Cgy.	Oshawa Generals
40. CHABOT, John	Mtl.	Hull Olympiques
41. MOLLER, Mike	Buf.	Lethbridge Broncos
42. FRASER, Jay	Phi.	Ottawa 67's

All-Star Teams
1930 - 90

Voting for the NHL All-Star Team is conducted among the representatives of the Professional Hockey Writers' Association at the end of the season.

Following is a list of the First and Second All-Star Teams since their inception in 1930-31.

First Team		Second Team
1989-90		
Roy, Patrick, Mtl.	G	Puppa, Daren, Buf.
Bourque, Raymond, Bos.	D	Coffey, Paul, Pit.
MacInnis, Al, Cgy.	D	Wilson, Doug, Chi.
Messier, Mark, Edm.	C	Gretzky, Wayne, L.A.
Hull, Brett, St. L.	RW	Neely, Cam, Bos.
Robitaille, Luc, L.A.	LW	Bellows, Brian, Min.
1988-89		
Roy, Patrick, Mtl.	G	Vernon, Mike, Cgy.
Chelios, Chris, Mtl.	D	MacInnis, Al, Cgy.
Coffey, Paul, Pit.	D	Bourque, Ray, Bos.
Lemieux, Mario, Pit.	C	Gretzky, Wayne, L.A.
Mullen, Joe, Cgy.	RW	Kurri, Jari, Edm.
Robitaille, Luc, L.A.	LW	Gallant, Gerard, Det.
1987-88		
Fuhr, Grant, Edm.	G	Roy, Patrick, Mtl.
Bourque, Raymond, Bos.	D	Suter, Gary, Cgy.
Stevens, Scott, Wsh.	D	McCrimmon, Brad, Cgy.
Lemieux, Mario, Pit.	C	Gretzky, Wayne, Edm.
Loob, Hakan, Cgy.	RW	Neely, Cam, Bos.
Robitaille, Luc, L.A.	LW	Goulet, Michel, Que.
1986-87		
Hextall, Ron, Phi.	G	Liut, Mike, Hfd.
Bourque, Raymond, Bos.	D	Murphy, Larry, Wsh.
Howe, Mark, Phi.	D	MacInnis, Al, Cgy.
Gretzky, Wayne, Edm.	C	Lemieux, Mario, Pit.
Kurri, Jari, Edm.	RW	Kerr, Tim, Phi.
Goulet, Michel, Que.	LW	Robitaille, Luc, L.A.
1985-86		
Vanbiesbrouck, J., NYR	G	Froese, Bob Phi.
Coffey, Paul, Edm.	D	Robinson, Larry, Mtl.
Howe, Mark, Phi.	D	Bourque, Raymond, Bos.
Gretzky, Wayne, Edm.	C	Lemieux, Mario, Pit.
Bossy, Mike, NYI	RW	Kurri, Jari, Edm.
Goulet, Michel, Que.	LW	Naslund, Mats, Mtl.
1984-85		
Lindbergh, Pelle, Phi.	G	Barrasso, Tom Buf.
Coffey, Paul, Edm.	D	Langway, Rod, Wsh.
Bourque, Raymond, Bos.	D	Wilson, Doug, Chi.
Gretzky, Wayne, Edm.	C	Hawerchuk, Dale, Wpg.
Kurri, Jari, Edm.	RW	Bossy, Mike, NYI
Ogrodnick, John, Det.	LW	Tonelli, John, NYI
1983-84		
Barrasso, Tom, Buf.	G	Riggin, Pat Wsh.
Langway, Rod, Wsh.	D	Coffey, Paul, Edm
Bourque, Raymond, Bos.	D	Potvin, Denis, NYI
Gretzky, Wayne, Edm.	C	Trottier, Bryan, NYI
Bossy, Mike, NYI	RW	Kurri, Jari, Edm.
Goulet, Michel, Que.	LW	Messier, Mark, Edm.
1982-83		
Peeters, Pete, Bos.	G	Melanson, Roland, NYI
Howe, Mark, Phi.	D	Bourque, Raymond, Bos.
Langway, Rod, Wsh.	D	Coffey, Paul, Edm.
Gretzky, Wayne, Edm.	C	Savard, Denis, Chi.
Bossy, Mike, NYI	RW	McDonald, Lanny, Cgy.
Messier, Mark, Edm.	LW	Goulet, Michel, Que.

First Team		Second Team
1981-82		
Smith, Bill, NYI	G	Fuhr, Grant, Edm.
Wilson, Doug, Chi.	D	Coffey, Paul, Edm.
Bourque, Raymond, Bos.	D	Engblom, Brian, Mtl.
Gretzky, Wayne, Edm.	C	Trottier, Bryan, NYI
Bossy, Mike, NYI	RW	Middleton, Rick, Bos.
Messier, Mark, Edm.	LW	Tonelli, John, NYI
1980-81		
Liut, Mike, St.L.	G	Lessard, Mario, L.A.
Potvin, Denis, NYI	D	Robinson, Larry, Mtl.
Carlyle, Randy, Pit.	D	Bourque, Raymond, Bos.
Gretzky, Wayne, Edm.	C	Dionne, Marcel, L.A.
Bossy, Mike, NYI	RW	Taylor, Dave, L.A.
Simmer, Charlie, L.A.	LW	Barber, Bill, Phi.
1979-80		
Esposito, Tony, Chi.	G	Edwards, Don, Buf.
Robinson, Larry, Mtl.	D	Salming, Borje, Tor.
Bourque, Raymond, Bos.	D	Schoenfeld, Jim, Buf.
Dionne, Marcel, L.A.	C	Gretzky, Wayne, Edm.
Lafleur, Guy, Mtl.	RW	Gare, Danny, Buf.
Simmer, Charlie, L.A.	LW	Shutt, Steve, Mtl.
1978-79		
Dryden, Ken, Mtl.	G	Resch, Glenn, NYI
Potvin, Denis, NYI	D	Salming, Borje, Tor.
Robinson, Larry, Mtl.	D	Savard, Serge, Mtl.
Trottier, Bryan, NYI	C	Dionne, Marcel, L.A.
Lafleur, Guy, Mtl.	RW	Bossy, Mike, NYI
Gillies, Clark, NYI	LW	Barber, Bill, Phi.

First Team		Second Team
1977-78		
Dryden, Ken, Mtl.	G	Edwards, Don, Buf.
Potvin, Denis, NYI	D	Robinson, Larry, Mtl.
Park, Brad, Bos.	D	Salming, Borje, Tor.
Trottier, Bryan, NYI	C	Sittler, Darryl, Tor.
Lafleur, Guy, Mtl.	RW	Bossy, Mike, NYI
Gillies, Clark, NYI	LW	Shutt, Steve, Mtl.
1976-77		
Dryden, Ken, Mtl.	G	Vachon, Rogatien, L.A.
Robinson, Larry, Mtl.	D	Potvin, Denis, NYI
Salming, Borje, Tor.	D	Lapointe, Guy, Mtl.
Dionne, Marcel, L.A.	C	Perreault, Gilbert, Buf.
Lafleur, Guy, Mtl.	RW	McDonald, Lanny, Tor.
Shutt, Steve, Mtl.	LW	Martin, Richard, Buf.
1975-76		
Dryden, Ken, Mtl.	G	Resch, Glenn, NYI
Potvin, Denis, NYI	D	Salming, Borje, Tor.
Park, Brad, Bos.	D	Lapointe, Guy, Mtl.
Clarke, Bobby, Phi.	C	Perreault, Gilbert, Buf.
Lafleur, Guy, Mtl.	RW	Leach, Reggie, Phi.
Barber, Bill, Phi.	LW	Martin, Richard, Buf.
1974-75		
Parent, Bernie, Phi.	G	Vachon, Rogie, L.A.
Orr, Bobby, Bos.	D	Lapointe, Guy, Mtl.
Potvin, Denis, NYI	D	Salming, Borje, Tor.
Clarke, Bobby, Phi.	C	Esposito, Phil, Bos.
Lafleur, Guy, Mtl.	RW	Robert, Rene, Buf.
Martin, Richard, Buf.	LW	Vickers, Steve, NYR

Bobby Clarke was chosen to the Second All-Star Team in 1973 and 1974 and to the first All-Star Team in 1975 and 1976.

1979

FIRST ROUND

Selection	Claimed By	Amateur Club
1. RAMAGE, Rob	Col.	London Knights
2. TURNBULL, Perry	St.L.	Portland Winter Hawks
3. FOLIGNO, Mike	Det.	Sudbury Wolves
4. GARTNER, Mike	Wsh.	Niagara Falls Flyers
5. VAIVE, Rick	Van.	Sherbrooke Castors
6. HARTSBURG, Craig	Min.	Sault Greyhounds
7. BROWN, Keith	Chi.	Portland Winter Hawks
8. BOURQUE, Raymond	Bos.	Verdun Black Hawks
9. BOSCHMAN, Laurie	Tor.	Brandon Wheat Kings
10. McCARTHY, Tom	Min.	Oshawa Generals
11. RAMSEY, Mike	Buf.	University of Min.
12. REINHART, Paul	Atlanta	Kitchener Rangers
13. SULLIVAN, Doug	NYR	Kitchener Rangers
14. PROPP, Brian	Phi.	Brandon Wheat Kings
15. McCRIMMON, Brad	Bos.	Brandon Wheat Kings
16. WELLS, Jay	L.A.	Kingston Canadians
17. SUTTER, Duane	NYI	Lethbridge Broncos
18. ALLISON, Ray	Hfd.	Brandon Wheat Kings
19. MANN, Jimmy	Wpg.	Sherbrooke Beavers
20. GOULET, Michel	Que.	Que. Remparts
21. LOWE, Kevin	Edm.	Que. Remparts

SECOND ROUND

Selection	Claimed By	Amateur Club
22. WESLEY, Blake	Phi.	Portland Winter Hawks
23. PEROVICH, Mike	Atlanta	Brandon Wheat Kings
24. RAUSSE, Errol	Wsh.	Seattle Breakers
25. JONSSON, Tomas	NYI	MoDo AIK (Sweden)
26. ASHTON, Brent	Van.	Saskatoon Blades
27. GINGRAS, Gaston	Mtl.	Hamilton Fincups
28. TRIMPER, Tim	Chi.	Peterborough Petes
29. HOPKINS, Dean	L.A.	London Knights
30. HARDY, Mark	L.A.	Mtl. Juniors
31. MARSHALL, Paul	Pit.	Brantford Alexanders
32. RUFF, Lindy	Buf.	Lethbridge Broncos
33. RIGGIN, Pat	Atlanta	London Knights
34. HOSPODAR, Ed	NYR	Ottawa 67's
35. LINDBERGH, Pelle	Phi.	Solna (Sweden)
36. MORRISON, Doug	Bos.	Lethbridge Broncos
37. NASLUND, Mats	Mtl.	Brynas IFK (Sweden)
38. CARROLL, Billy	NYI	London Knights
39. SMITH, Stuart	Hfd.	Peterborough Petes
40. CHRISTIAN, Dave	Wpg.	U. of North Dakota
41. HUNTER, Dale	Que.	Sudbury Wolves
42. BROTEN, Neal	Min.	University of Min.

1978

FIRST ROUND

Selection	Claimed By	Amateur Club
1. SMITH, Bobby	Min.	Ottawa 67's
2. WALTER, Ryan	Wsh.	Seattle Breakers
3. BABYCH, Wayne	St.L.	Portland Winter Hawks
4. DERLAGO, Bill	Van.	Brandon Wheat Kings
5. GILLIS, Mike	Col.	Kingston Canadians
6. WILSON, Behn	Phi.	Kingston Canadians
7. LINSEMAN, Ken	Phi.	Kingston Canadians
8. GEOFFRION, Danny	Mtl.	Cornwall Royals
9. HUBER, Willie	Det.	Hamilton Fincups
10. HIGGINS, Tim	Chi.	Ottawa 67's
11. MARSH, Brad	Atl.	London Knights
12. PETERSON, Brent	Det.	Portland Winter Hawks
13. PLAYFAIR, Larry	Buf.	Portland Winter Hawks
14. LUCAS, Danny	Phi.	Sault Greyhounds
15. TAMBELLINI, Steve	NYI	Lethbridge Broncos
16. SECORD, Al	Bos.	Hamilton Fincups
17. HUNTER, Dave	Mtl.	Sudbury Wolves
18. COULIS, Tim	Wsh.	Hamilton Fincups

SECOND ROUND

Selection	Claimed By	Amateur Club
19. PAYNE, Steve	Min.	Ottawa 67's
20. MULVEY, Paul	Wsh.	Portland Winter Hawks
21. QUENNEVILLE, Joel	Tor.	Windsor Spitfires
22. FRASER, Curt	Van.	Victoria Cougars
23. MacKINNON, Paul	Wsh.	Peterborough Petes
24. CHRISTOFF, Steve	Min.	University of Min.
25. MEEKER, Mike	Pit.	Peterborough Petes
26. MALONEY, Don	NYR	Kitchener Rangers
27. MALINOWSKI, Merlin	Col.	Medicine Hat Tigers
28. HICKS, Glenn	Det.	Flin Flon Bombers
29. LECUYER, Doug	Chi.	Portland Winter Hawks
30. YAKIWCHUK, Dale	Mtl.	Portland Winter Hawks
31. JENSEN, Al	Det.	Hamilton Fincups
32. McKEGNEY, Tony	Buf.	Kingston Canadians
33. SIMURDA, Mike	Phi.	Kingston Canadians
34. JOHNSTON, Randy	NYI	Peterborough Petes
35. NICOLSON, Graeme	Bos.	Cornwall Royals
36. CARTER, Ron	Mtl.	Sherbrooke Castors

1977

FIRST ROUND

Selection	Claimed By	Amateur Club
1. McCOURT, Dale	Det.	St. Catharines Fincups
2. BECK, Barry	Col.	New Westminster
3. PICARD, Robert	Wsh.	Mtl. Jrs.
4. GILLIS, Jere	Van.	Sherbrooke Castors
5. CROMBEEN, Mike	Cle.	Kingston Canadians
6. WILSON, Doug	Chi.	Ottawa 67's
7. MAXWELL, Brad	Min.	New Westminster
8. DEBLOIS, Lucien	NYR	Sorel Black Hawks
9. CAMPBELL, Scott	St.L.	London Knights
10. NAPIER, Mark	Mtl.	Tor. Marlboros
11. ANDERSON, John	Tor.	Tor. Marlboros
12. JOHANSON, Trevor	Tor.	Tor. Marlboros
13. DUGUAY, Ron	NYR	Sudbury Wolves
14. SEILING, Ric	Buf.	St. Catharines Fincups
15. BOSSY, Mike	NYI	Laval Nationales
16. FOSTER, Dwight	Bos.	Kitchener Rangers
17. McCARTHY, Kevin	Phi.	Wpg. Monarchs
18. DUPONT, Norm	Mtl.	Montreal Jrs.

SECOND ROUND

Selection	Claimed By	Amateur Club
19. SAVARD, Jean	Chi.	Que. Remparts
20. ZAHARKO, Miles	Atl.	New Westminster
21. LOFTHOUSE, Mark	Wsh.	New Westminster
22. BANDURA, Jeff	Van.	Portland Winter Hawks
23. CHICOINE, Daniel	Cle.	Sherbrooke Castors
24. GLADNEY, Bob	Tor.	Oshawa Generals
25. SEMENKO, Dave	Min.	Brandon Wheat Kings
26. KEATING, Mike	NYR	St. Catherines Fincups
27. LABATTE, Neil	St.L.	Tor. Marlboros
28. LAURENCE, Don	Atl.	Kitchener Rangers
29. SAGANIUK, Rocky	Tor.	Lethbridge Broncos
30. HAMILTON, Jim	Pit.	London Knights
31. HILL, Brian	Atl.	Medicine Hat Tigers
32. ARESHENKOFF, Ron	Buf.	Medicine Hat Tigers
33. TONELLI, John	NYI	Tor. Marlboros
34. PARRO, Dave	Bos.	Saskatoon Blades
35. GORENCE, Tom	Phi.	U. of Minnesota
36. LANGWAY, Rod	Mtl.	U. of N. Hampshire

1976

FIRST ROUND

Selection	Claimed By	Amateur Club
1. GREEN, Rick	Wsh.	London Knights
2. CHAPMAN, Blair	Pit.	Saskatoon Blades
3. SHARPLEY, Glen	Min.	Hull Festivals
4. WILLIAMS, Fred	Det.	Saskatoon Blades
5. JOHANSSON, Bjorn	Cal.	Sweden
6. MURDOCH, Don	NYR	Medicine Hat Tigers
7. FEDERKO, Bernie	St.L.	Saskatoon Blades
8. SHAND, Dave	Atl.	Peterborough Petes
9. CLOUTIER, Real	Chi.	Que. Remparts
10. PHILLIPOFF, Harold	Atl.	New Westminster
11. GARDNER, Paul	K.C.	Oshawa Generals
12. LEE, Peter	Mtl.	Ottawa 67's
13. SCHUTT, Rod	Mtl.	Sudbury Wolves
14. McKENDRY, Alex	NYI	Sudbury Wolves
15. CARROLL, Greg	Wsh.	Medicine Hat Tigers
16. PACHAL, Clayton	Bos.	New Westminster
17. SUZOR, Mark	Phi.	Kingston Canadians
18. BAKER, Bruce	Mtl.	Ottawa 67's

SECOND ROUND

Selection	Claimed By	Amateur Club
19. MALONE, Greg	Pit.	Oshawa Generals
20. SUTTER, Brian	St.L.	Lethbridge Broncos
21. CLIPPINGDALE, Steve	L.A.	New Westminster
22. LARSON, Reed	Det.	University of Min.
23. STENLUND, Vern	Cal.	London Knights
24. FARRISH, Dave	NYR	Sudbury Wolves
25. SMRKE, John	St.L.	Tor. Marlboros
26. MANNO, Bob	Van.	St. Catharines Hawks
27. McDILL, Jeff	Chi.	Victoria Cougars
28. SIMPSON, Bobby	Atl.	Sherbrooke Castors
29. MARSH, Peter	Pit.	Sherbrooke Castors
30. CARLYLE, Randy	Tor.	Sudbury Wolves
31. ROBERTS, Jim	Min.	Ottawa 67's
32. KASZYCKI, Mike	NYI	Sault Greyhounds
33. KOWAL, Joe	Buf.	Hamilton Fincups
34. GLOECKNER, Larry	Bos.	Victoria Cougars
35. CALLANDER, Drew	Phi.	Regina Pats
36. MELROSE, Barry	Mtl.	Kamloops Chiefs

Dale McCourt (right) and Barry Beck (left) were selected one-two in the 1977 Entry Draft.

1975

FIRST ROUND

Selection	Claimed By	Amateur Club
1. BRIDGMAN, Mel	Phi.	Victoria Cougars
2. DEAN, Barry	K.C.	Medicine Hat Tigers
3. KLASSEN, Ralph	Cal.	Saskatoon Blades
4. MAXWELL, Brian	Min.	Medicine Hat Tigers
5. LAPOINTE, Rick	Det.	Victoria Cougars
6. ASHBY, Don	Tor.	Cgy. Centennials
7. VAYDIK, Greg	Chi.	Medicine Hat Tigers
8. MULHERN, Richard	Atl.	Sherbrooke Beavers
9. SADLER, Robin	Mtl.	Edm. Oil Kings
10. BLIGHT, Rick	Van.	Brandon Wheat Kings
11. PRICE, Pat	NYI	Saskatoon Blades
12. DILLON, Wayne	NYR	Tor. Marlboros
13. LAXTON, Gord	Pit.	New Westminster
14. HALWARD, Doug	Bos.	Peterborough Petes
15. MONDOU, Pierre	Mtl.	Montreal Juniors
16. YOUNG, Tim	L.A.	Ottawa 67's
17. SAUVE, Bob	Buf.	Laval Nationales
18. FORSYTH, Alex	Wsh.	Kingston Canadians

SECOND ROUND

Selection	Claimed By	Amateur Club
19. SCAMURRA, Peter	Wsh.	Peterborough Petes
20. CAIRNS, Don	K.C.	Victoria Cougars
21. MARUK, Dennis	Cal.	London Knights
22. ENGBLOM, Brian	Mtl.	University of Wisconsin
23. ROLLINS, Jerry	Det.	Wpg. Jr. Jets
24. JARVIS, Doug	Tor.	Peterborough Petes
25. ARNDT, Daniel	Chi.	Saskatoon Blades
26. BOWNASS, Rick	Atl.	Montreal Juniors
27. STANIOWSKI, Ed	St.L.	Regina Pats
28. GASSOFF, Brad	Van.	Kamloops Chiefs
29. SALVIAN, David	NYI	St. Catharines Hawks
30. SOETAERT, Doug	NYR	Edm. Oil Kings
31. ANDERSON, Russ	Pit.	U. of Minnesota
32. SMITH, Barry	Bos.	New Westminster
33. BUCYK, Terry	L.A.	Lethbridge Broncos
34. GREENBANK, Kelvin	Mtl.	Wpg. Jr. Jets
35. BREITENBACH, Ken	Buf.	St. Catharines Hawks
36. MASTERS, Jamie	St.L.	Ottawa 67's

1973-74
First Team	Pos	Second Team
Parent, Bernie, Phi.	G	Esposito, Tony, Chi.
Orr, Bobby, Bos.	D	White, Bill, Chi.
Park, Brad, NYR	D	Ashbee, Barry, Phi.
Esposito, Phil, Bos.	C	Clarke, Bobby, Phi.
Hodge, Ken, Bos.	RW	Redmond, Mickey, Det.
Martin, Richard, Buf.	LW	Cashman, Wayne, Bos.

1972-73
First Team	Pos	Second Team
Dryden, Ken, Mtl.	G	Esposito, Tony, Chi.
Orr, Bobby, Bos.	D	Park, Brad, NYR
Lapointe, Guy, Mtl.	D	White, Bill, Chi.
Esposito, Phil, Bos.	C	Clarke, Bobby, Phi.
Redmond, Mickey, Det.	RW	Cournoyer, Yvan, Mtl.
Mahovlich, Frank, Mtl.	LW	Hull, Dennis, Chi.

1971-72
First Team	Pos	Second Team
Esposito, Tony, Chi.	G	Dryden, Ken, Mtl.
Orr, Bobby, Bos.	D	White, Bill, Chi.
Park, Brad, NYR	D	Stapleton, Pat, Chi.
Esposito, Phil, Bos.	C	Ratelle, Jean, NYR
Gilbert, Rod, NYR	RW	Cournoyer, Yvan, Mtl.
Hull, Bobby, Chi.	LW	Hadfield, Vic, NYR

1970-71
First Team	Pos	Second Team
Giacomin, Ed, NYR	G	Plante, Jacques, Tor.
Orr, Bobby, Bos.	D	Park, Brad, NYR
Tremblay, J.C., Mtl.	D	Stapleton, Pat, Chi.
Esposito, Phil, Bos.	C	Keon, Dave, Tor.
Hodge, Ken, Bos.	RW	Cournoyer, Yvan, Mtl.
Bucyk, John, Bos.	LW	Hull, Bobby, Chi.

1969-70
First Team	Pos	Second Team
Esposito, Tony, Chi.	G	Giacomin, Ed, NYR
Orr, Bobby, Bos.	D	Brewer, Carl, Det.
Park, Brad, NYR	D	Laperriere, Jacques, Mtl.
Esposito, Phil, Bos.	C	Mikita, Stan, Chi.
Howe, Gordie, Det.	RW	McKenzie, John, Bos.
Hull, Bobby, Chi.	LW	Mahovlich, Frank, Det.

1968-69
First Team	Pos	Second Team
Hall, Glenn, St.L.	G	Giacomin, Ed, NYR
Orr, Bobby, Bos.	D	Green, Ted, Bos.
Horton, Tim, Tor.	D	Harris, Ted, Mtl.
Esposito, Phil, Bos.	C	Beliveau, Jean, Mtl.
Howe, Gordie, Det.	RW	Cournoyer, Yvan, Mtl
Hull, Bobby, Chi.	LW	Mahovlich, Frank, Det.

1967-68
First Team	Pos	Second Team
Worsley, Lorne, Mtl.	G	Giacomin, Ed, NYR
Orr, Bobby, Bos.	D	Tremblay, J.C., Mtl.
Horton, Tim, Tor.	D	Neilson, Jim, NYR
Mikita, Stan, Chi.	C	Esposito, Phil, Bos.
Howe, Gordie, Det.	RW	Gilbert, Rod, NYR
Hull, Bobby, Chi.	LW	Bucyk, John, Bos.

1966-67
First Team	Pos	Second Team
Giacomin, Ed, NYR	G	Hall, Glenn, Chi.
Pilote, Pierre, Chi.	D	Horton, Tim, Tor.
Howell, Harry, NYR	D	Orr, Bobby, Bos.
Mikita, Stan, Chi.	C	Ullman, Norm, Det.
Wharram, Ken, Chi.	RW	Howe, Gordie, Det.
Hull, Bobby, Chi.	LW	Marshall, Don, NYR

1965-66
First Team	Pos	Second Team
Hall, Glenn, Chi.	G	Worsley, Lorne, Mtl.
Laperriere, Jacques, Mtl.	D	Stanley, Allan, Tor.
Pilote, Pierre, Chi.	D	Stapleton, Pat, Chi.
Mikita, Stan, Chi.	C	Beliveau, Jean, Mtl.
Howe, Gordie, Det.	RW	Rousseau, Bobby, Mtl.
Hull, Bobby, Chi.	LW	Mahovlich, Frank, Tor.

1964-65
First Team	Pos	Second Team
Crozier, Roger, Det.	G	Hodge, Charlie, Mtl.
Pilote, Pierre, Chi.	D	Gadsby, Bill, Det.
Laperriere, Jacques, Mtl.	D	Brewer, Carl, Tor.
Ullman, Norm, Det.	C	Mikita, Stan, Chi.
Provost, Claude, Mtl.	RW	Howe, Gordie, Det.
Hull, Bobby, Chi.	LW	Mahovlich, Frank, Tor.

1963-64
First Team	Pos	Second Team
Hall, Glenn, Chi.	G	Hodge, Charlie, Mtl.
Pilote, Pierre, Chi.	D	Vasko, Elmer, Chi.
Horton, Tim, Tor.	D	Laperriere, Jacques, Mtl.
Mikita, Stan, Chi.	C	Beliveau, Jean, Mtl.
Wharram, Ken, Chi.	RW	Howe, Gordie, Det.
Hull, Bobby, Chi.	LW	Mahovlich, Frank, Tor.

1962-63
First Team	Pos	Second Team
Hall, Glenn, Chi.	G	Sawchuk, Terry, Det.
Pilote, Pierre, Chi.	D	Horton, Tim, Tor.
Brewer, Carl, Tor.	D	Vasko, Elmer, Chi.
Mikita, Stan, Chi.	C	Richard, Henri, Mtl.
Howe, Gordie, Det.	RW	Bathgate, Andy, NYR
Mahovlich, Frank, Tor.	LW	Hull, Bobby, Chi.

1961-62
First Team	Pos	Second Team
Plante, Jacques, Mtl.	G	Hall, Glenn, Chi.
Harvey, Doug, NYR	D	Brewer, Carl, Tor.
Talbot, Jean-Guy, Mtl.	D	Pilote, Pierre, Chi.
Mikita, Stan, Chi.	C	Keon, Dave, Tor.
Bathgate, Andy, NYR	RW	Howe, Gordie, Det.
Hull, Bobby, Chi.	LW	Mahovlich, Frank, Tor.

1960-61
First Team	Pos	Second Team
Bower, Johnny, Tor.	G	Hall, Glenn, Chi.
Harvey, Doug, Mtl.	D	Stanley, Allan, Tor.
Pronovost, Marcel, Det.	D	Pilote, Pierre, Chi.
Beliveau, Jean, Mtl.	C	Richard, Henri, Mtl.
Geoffrion, Bernie, Mtl.	RW	Howe, Gordie, Det.
Mahovlich, Frank, Tor.	LW	Moore, Dickie, Mtl.

1959-60
First Team	Pos	Second Team
Hall, Glenn, Chi.	G	Plante, Jacques, Mtl.
Harvey, Doug, Mtl.	D	Stanley, Allan, Tor.
Pronovost, Marcel, Det.	D	Pilote, Pierre, Chi.
Beliveau, Jean, Mtl.	C	Horvath, Bronco, Bos.
Howe, Gordie, Det.	RW	Geoffrion, Bernie, Mtl.
Hull, Bobby, Chi.	LW	Prentice, Dean, NYR

1958-59
First Team	Pos	Second Team
Plante, Jacques, Mtl.	G	Sawchuk, Terry, Det.
Johnson, Tom, Mtl.	D	Pronovost, Marcel, Det.
Gadsby, Bill, NYR	D	Harvey, Doug, Mtl.
Beliveau, Jean, Mtl.	C	Richard, Henri, Mtl.
Bathgate, Andy, NYR	RW	Howe, Gordie, Det.
Moore, Dickie, Mtl	LW	Delvecchio, Alex, Det.

1957-58
First Team	Pos	Second Team
Hall, Glenn, Chi.	G	Plante, Jacques, Mtl.
Harvey, Doug, Mtl.	D	Flaman, Fern, Bos.
Gadsby, Bill, NYR	D	Pronovost, Marcel, Det.
Richard, Henri, Mtl.	C	Beliveau, Jean, Mtl.
Howe, Gordie, Det.	RW	Bathgate, Andy, NYR
Moore, Dickie, Mtl.	LW	Henry, Camille, NYR

1956-57
First Team	Pos	Second Team
Hall, Glenn, Det.	G	Plante, Jacques, Mtl.
Harvey, Doug, Mtl.	D	Flaman, Fern, Bos.
Kelly, Red, Det.	D	Gadsby, Bill, NYR
Beliveau, Jean, Mtl.	C	Litzenberger, Eddie, Chi.
Howe, Gordie, Det.	RW	Richard, Maurice, Mtl.
Lindsay, Ted, Det.	LW	Chevrefils, Real, Bos.

1955-56
First Team	Pos	Second Team
Plante, Jacques, Mtl.	G	Hall, Glenn, Det.
Harvey, Doug, Mtl.	D	Kelly, Red, Det.
Gadsby, Bill, NYR	D	Johnson, Tom, Mtl.
Beliveau, Jean, Mtl.	C	Sloan, Tod, Tor.
Richard, Maurice, Mtl.	RW	Howe, Gordie, Det.
Lindsay, Ted, Det.	LW	Olmstead, Bert, Mtl.

1954-55
First Team	Pos	Second Team
Lumley, Harry, Tor.	G	Sawchuk, Terry, Det.
Harvey, Doug, Mtl.	D	Goldham, Bob, Det.
Kelly, Red, Det.	D	Flaman, Fern, Bos.
Beliveau, Jean, Mtl.	C	Mosdell, Ken, Mtl.
Richard, Maurice, Mtl.	RW	Geoffrion, Bernie, Mtl.
Smith, Sid, Tor.	LW	Lewicki, Danny, NYR

1953-54
First Team	Pos	Second Team
Lumley, Harry, Tor.	G	Sawchuk, Terry, Det.
Kelly, Red, Det.	D	Gadsby, Bill, Chi.
Harvey, Doug, Mtl.	D	Horton, Tim, Tor.
Mosdell, Ken, Mtl.	C	Kennedy, Ted, Tor.
Howe, Gordie, Det.	RW	Richard, Maurice, Mtl.
Lindsay, Ted, Det.	LW	Sandford, Ed, Bos.

1952-53
First Team	Pos	Second Team
Sawchuk, Terry, Det.	G	McNeil, Gerry, Mtl.
Kelly, Red, Det.	D	Quackenbush, Bill, Bos.
Harvey, Doug, Mtl.	D	Gadsby, Bill, Chi.
Mackell, Fleming, Bos.	C	Delvecchio, Alex, Det.
Howe, Gordie, Det.	RW	Richard, Maurice, Mtl.
Lindsay, Ted, Det.	LW	Olmstead, Bert, Mtl.

1951-52
First Team	Pos	Second Team
Sawchuk, Terry, Det.	G	Henry, Jim, Bos.
Kelly, Red, Det.	D	Buller, Hy, NYR
Harvey, Doug, Mtl.	D	Thomson, Jim, Tor.
Lach, Elmer, Mtl.	C	Schmidt, Milt, Bos.
Howe, Gordie, Det.	RW	Richard, Maurice, Mtl.
Lindsay, Ted, Det.	LW	Smith, Sid, Tor.

1950-51
First Team	Pos	Second Team
Sawchuk, Terry, Det.	G	Rayner, Chuck, NYR
Kelly, Red, Det.	D	Thomson, Jim, Tor.
Quackenbush, Bill, Bos.	D	Reise, Leo, Det.
Schmidt, Milt, Bos.	C	Abel, Sid, Det.
	(tied)	Kennedy, Ted, Tor.
Howe, Gordie, Det.	RW	Richard, Maurice, Mtl.
Lindsay, Ted, Det.	LW	Smith, Sid, Tor.

1949-50
First Team	Pos	Second Team
Durnan, Bill, Mtl.	G	Rayner, Chuck, NYR
Mortson, Gus, Tor.	D	Reise, Leo, Det.
Reardon, Kenny, Mtl.	D	Kelly, Red, Det.
Abel, Sid, Det.	C	Kennedy, Ted, Tor.
Richard, Maurice, Mtl.	RW	Howe, Gordie, Det.
Lindsay, Ted, Det.	LW	Leswick, Tony, NYR

1948-49
First Team	Pos	Second Team
Durnan, Bill, Mtl.	G	Rayner, Chuck, NYR
Quackenbush, Bill, Det.	D	Harmon, Glen, Mtl.
Stewart, Jack, Det.	D	Reardon, Kenny, Mtl.
Abel, Sid, Det.	C	Bentley, Doug, Chi.
Richard, Maurice, Mtl.	RW	Howe, Gordie, Det.
Conacher, Roy, Chi.	LW	Lindsay, Ted, Det.

1947-48
First Team	Pos	Second Team
Broda, W. "Turk", Tor.	G	Brimsek, Frank, Bos.
Quackenbush, Bill, Det.	D	Reardon, Kenny, Mtl.
Stewart, Jack, Det.	D	Colville, Neil, NYR
Lach, Elmer, Mtl.	C	O'Connor, "Buddy", NYR
Richard, Maurice, Mtl.	RW	Poile, "Bud", Chi.
Lindsay, Ted, Det.	LW	Stewart, Gaye, Chi.

First Team		Second Team

1946-47

Durnan, Bill, Mtl.	G	Brimsek, Frank, Bos.
Reardon, Kenny, Mtl.	D	Stewart, Jack, Det.
Bouchard, Emile, Mtl.	D	Quackenbush, Bill, Det.
Schmidt, Milt, Bos.	C	Bentley, Max, Chi.
Richard, Maurice, Mtl.	RW	Bauer, Bobby, Bos.
Bentley, Doug, Chi.	LW	Dumart, Woody, Bos.

1945-46

Durnan, Bill, Mtl.	G	Brimsek, Frank, Bos.
Crawford, Jack, Bos.	D	Reardon, Kenny, Mtl.
Bouchard, Emile, Mtl.	D	Stewart, Jack, Det.
Bentley, Max, Chi.	C	Lach, Elmer, Mtl.
Richard, Maurice, Mtl.	RW	Mosienko, Bill, Chi.
Stewart, Gaye, Tor.	LW	Blake, "Toe", Mtl.
Irvin, Dick, Mtl.	Coach	Gottselig, John, Chi.

1944-45

Durnan, Bill, Mtl.	G	Karakas, Mike, Chi.
Bouchard, Emile, Mtl.	D	Harmon, Glen, Mtl.
Hollett, Bill, Det.	D	Pratt, "Babe", Tor.
Lach, Elmer, Mtl.	C	Cowley, Bill, Bos.
Richard, Maurice, Mtl.	RW	Mosienko, Bill, Chi.
Blake, "Toe", Mtl.	LW	Howe, Syd, Det.
Irvin, Dick, Mtl.	Coach	Adams, Jack, Det.

1943-44

Durnan, Bill, Mtl.	G	Bibeault, Paul, Tor.
Seibert, Earl, Chi.	D	Bouchard, Emile, Mtl.
Pratt, "Babe", Tor.	D	Clapper, "Dit", Bos.
Cowley, Bill, Bos.	C	Lach, Elmer, Mtl.
Carr, Lorne, Tor.	RW	Richard, Maurice, Mtl.
Bentley, Doug, Chi.	LW	Cain, Herb, Bos.
Irvin, Dick, Mtl.	Coach	Day, C.H., "Hap", Tor.

1942-43

Mowers, Johnny, Det.	G	Brimsek, Frank, Bos.
Seibert, Earl, Chi.	D	Crawford, Johnny, Bos.
Stewart, Jack, Det.	D	Hollett, Bill, Bos.
Cowley, Bill, Bos.	C	Apps, Syl, Tor.
Carr, Lorne, Tor.	RW	Hextall, Bryan, NYR
Bentley, Doug, Chi.	LW	Patrick, Lynn, NYR
Adams, Jack, Det.	Coach	Ross, Art, Bos.

1941-42

Brimsek, Frank, Bos.	G	Broda, W. "Turk", Tor.
Seibert, Earl, Chi.	D	Egan, Pat, NYA
Anderson, Tommy, NYA	D	McDonald, Bucko, Tor.
Apps, Syl, Tor.	C	Watson, Phil, NYR
Hextall, Bryan, NYR	RW	Drillon, Gord, Tor.
Patrick, Lynn, NYR	LW	Abel, Sid, Det.
Boucher, Frank, NYR	Coach	Thompson, Paul, Chi.

1940-41

Broda, W. "Turk", Tor.	G	Brimsek, Frank, Bos.
Clapper, "Dit", Bos.	D	Seibert, Earl, Chi.
Stanowski, Wally, Tor.	D	Heller, Ott, NYR
Cowley, Bill, Bos.	C	Apps, Syl, Tor.
Hextall, Bryan, NYR	RW	Bauer, Bobby, Bos.
Schriner, Dave, Tor.	LW	Dumart, Woody, Bos.
Weiland, "Cooney", Bos.	Coach	Irvin, Dick, Mtl.

1939-40

Kerr, Dave, NYR	G	Brimsek, Frank, Bos.
Clapper, "Dit", Bos.	D	Coulter, Art, NYR
Goodfellow, Ebbie, Det.	D	Seibert, Earl, Chi.
Schmidt, Milt, Bos.	C	Colville, Neil, NYR
Hextall, Bryan, NYR	RW	Bauer, Bobby, Bos.
Blake, "Toe", Mtl.	LW	Dumart, Woody, Bos.
Thompson, Paul, Chi.	Coach	Boucher, Frank, NYR

First Team		Second Team

1938-39

Brimsek, Frank, Bos.	G	Robertson, Earl, NYA
Shore, Eddie, Bos.	D	Seibert, Earl, Chi.
Clapper, "Dit", Bos.	D	Coulter, Art, NYR
Apps, Syl, Tor.	C	Colville, Neil, NYR
Drillon, Gord, Tor.	RW	Bauer, Bobby, Bos.
Blake, "Toe", Mtl.	LW	Gottselig, Johnny, Chi.
Ross, Art, Bos.	Coach	Dutton, "Red", NYA

1937-38

Thompson, "Tiny", Bos.	G	Kerr, Dave, NYR
Shore, Eddie, Bos.	D	Coulter, Art, NYR
Seibert, "Babe", Mtl.	D	Seibert, Earl, Chi.
Cowley, Bill, Bos.	C	Apps, Syl, Tor.
Dillon, Cecil, NYR	RW	Dillon, Cecil, NYR
Drillon, Gord, Tor.	(tied)	Drillon, Gord, Tor.
Thompson, Paul, Chi.	LW	Blake, Toe, Mtl.
Patrick, Lester, NYR	Coach	Ross, Art, Bos.

1936-37

Smith, Norm, Det.	G	Cude, Wilf, Mtl.
Siebert, "Babe", Mtl.	D	Seibert, Earl, Chi.
Goodfellow, Ebbie, Det.	D	Conacher, Lionel, Mtl. M.
Barry, Marty, Det.	C	Chapman, Art, NYA
Aurie, Larry, Det.	RW	Dillon, Cecil, NYR
Jackson, Harvey, Tor.	LW	Schriner, Dave, NYA
Adams, Jack, Det.	Coach	Hart, Cecil, Mtl.

1935-36

Thompson, "Tiny", Bos.	G	Cude, Wilf, Mtl.
Shore, Eddie, Bos.	D	Seibert, Earl, Chi.
Seibert, "Babe", Bos.	D	Goodfellow, Ebbie, Det.
Smith, "Hooley", Mtl. M.	C	Thoms, Bill, Tor.
Conacher, Charlie, Tor.	RW	Dillon, Cecil, NYR
Schriner, Dave, NYA	LW	Thompson, Paul, Chi.
Patrick, Lester, NYR	Coach	Gorman, T.P., Mtl. M.

1934-35

Chabot, Lorne, Chi.	G	Thompson, "Tiny", Bos.
Shore, Eddie, Bos.	D	Wentworth, Cy, Mtl. M.
Seibert, Earl, NYR	D	Coulter, Art, Chi.
Boucher, Frank, NYR	C	Weiland, "Cooney", Det.
Conacher, Charlie, Tor.	RW	Clapper, "Dit", Bos.
Jackson, Harvey, Tor.	LW	Joliat, Aurel, Mtl.
Patrick, Lester, NYR	Coach	Irvin, Dick, Tor.

First Team		Second Team

1933-34

Gardiner, Charlie, Chi.	G	Worters, Roy, NYA
Clancy, "King", Tor.	D	Shore, Eddie, Bos.
Conacher, Lionel, Chi.	D	Johnson, "Ching", NYR
Boucher, Frank, NYR	C	Primeau, Joe, Tor.
Conacher, Charlie, Tor.	RW	Cook, Bill, NYR
Jackson, Harvey, Tor.	LW	Joliat, Aurel, Mtl.
Patrick, Lester, NYR	Coach	Irvin, Dick, Tor.

1932-33

Roach, John Ross, Det.	G	Gardiner, Charlie, Chi.
Shore, Eddie, Bos.	D	Clancy, "King", Tor.
Johnson, "Ching", NYR	D	Conacher, Lionel, Mtl. M.
Boucher, Frank, NYR	C	Morenz, Howie, Mtl.
Cook, Bill, NYR	RW	Conacher, Charlie, Tor.
Northcott, "Baldy", Mtl M.	LW	Jackson, Harvey, Tor.
Patrick, Lester, NYR	Coach	Irvin, Dick, Tor.

1931-32

Gardiner, Charlie, Chi.	G	Worters, Roy, NYA
Shore, Eddie, Bos.	D	Mantha, Sylvio, Mtl.
Johnson, "Ching", NYR	D	Clancy, "King", Tor.
Morenz, Howie, Mtl.	C	Smith, "Hooley", Mtl. M.
Cook, Bill, NYR	RW	Conacher, Charlie, Tor.
Jackson, Harvey, Tor.	LW	Joliat, Aurel, Mtl.
Patrick, Lester, NYR	Coach	Irvin, Dick, Tor.

1930-31

Gardiner, Charlie, Chi.	G	Thompson, "Tiny", Bos.
Shore, Eddie, Bos.	D	Mantha, Sylvio, Mtl.
Clancy, "King", Tor.	D	Johnson, "Ching", NYR
Morenz, Howie, Mtl.	C	Boucher, Frank, NYR
Cook, Bill, NYR	RW	Clapper, "Dit", Bos.
Joliet, Aurel, Mtl.	LW	Cook, "Bun", NYR
Patrick, Lester, NYR	Coach	Irvin, Dick, Chi.

Frank Brimsek was a First or Second Team All-Star on eight occasions.

NHL ALL-ROOKIE TEAM

Voting for the NHL's All-Rookie Team is conducted among the representatives of the Professional Hockey Writers' Association at the end of the season. The rookie all-star team was first selected for the 1982-83 season.

1989-90

Bob Essensa, Winnipeg	Goal
Brad Shaw, Hartford	Defense
Geoff Smith, Edmonton	Defense
Mike Modano, Minnesota	Center
Sergei Makarov, Calgary	Right Wing
Rod Brind'Amour, St. Louis	Left Wing

1987-88

Darren Pang, Chicago	Goal
Glen Wesley, Boston	Defense
Calle Johansson, Buffalo	Defense
Joe Nieuwendyk, Calgary	Center
Ray Sheppard, Buffalo	Right Wing
Iain Duncan, Winnipeg	Left Wing

1985-86

Patrick Roy, Montreal	Goal
Gary Suter, Calgary	Defense
Dana Murzyn, Hartford	Defense
Mike Ridley, NY Rangers	Center
Kjell Dahlin, Montreal	Right Wing
Wendel Clark, Toronto	Left Wing

1983-84

Tom Barrasso, Buffalo	Goal
Thomas Eriksson, Philadelphia	Defense
Jamie Macoun, Calgary	Defense
Steve Yzerman, Detroit	Center
Hakan Loob, Calgary	Right Wing
Sylvain Turgeon, Hartford	Left Wing

1988-89

Peter Sidorkiewicz, Hartford	
Brian Leetch, NY Rangers	
Zarley Zalapski, Pittsburgh	
Trevor Linden, Vancouver	
Tony Granato, NY Rangers	
David Volek, NY Islanders	

1986-87

Ron Hextall, Philadelphia	
Steve Duchesne, Los Angeles	
Brian Benning, St. Louis	
Jimmy Carson, Los Angeles	
Jim Sandlak, Vancouver	
Luc Robitaille, Los Angeles	

1984-85

Steve Penney, Montreal	
Chris Chelios, Montreal	
Bruce Bell, Quebec	
Mario Lemieux, Pittsburgh	
Tomas Sandstrom, NYR	
Warren Young, Pittsburgh	

1982-83

Pelle Lindbergh, Philadelphia	
Scott Stevens, Washington	
Phil Housley, Buffalo	
Dan Daoust, Montreal/Toronto	
Steve Larmer, Chicago	
Mats Naslund, Montreal	

Defenseman Brad Shaw shows the form that resulted in his selection to the NHL All-Rookie Team in 1989-90.

All-Star Game Results

Year	Venue	Score	Coaches	Attendance
1990	Pittsburgh	Wales 12, Campbell 7	Pat Burns, Terry Crisp	16,236
1989	Edmonton	Campbell 9, Wales 5	Glen Sather, Terry O'Reilly	17,503
1988	St. Louis	Wales 6, Campbell 5 OT	Mike Keenan, Glen Sather	17,878
1986	Hartford	Wales 4, Campbell 3 OT	Mike Keenan, Glen Sather	15,100
1985	Calgary	Wales 6, Campbell 4	Al Arbour, Glen Sather	16,825
1984	New Jersey	Wales 7, Campbell 6	Al Arbour, Glen Sather	18,939
1983	NY Islanders	Campbell 9, Wales 3	Roger Neilson, Al Arbour	15,230
1982	Washington	Wales 4, Campbell 2	Al Arbour, Glen Sonmor	18,130
1981	Los Angeles	Campbell 4, Wales 1	Pat Quinn, Scott Bowman	15,761
1980	Detroit	Wales 6, Campbell 3	Scott Bowman, Al Arbour	21,002
1978	Buffalo	Wales 3, Campbell 2 OT	Scott Bowman, Fred Shero	16,433
1977	Vancouver	Wales 4, Campbell 3	Scott Bowman, Fred Shero	15,607
1976	Philadelphia	Wales 7, Campbell 5	Floyd Smith, Fred Shero	16,436
1975	Montreal	Wales 7, Campbell 1	Bep Guidolin, Fred Shero	16,080
1974	Chicago	West 6, East 4	Billy Reay, Scott Bowman	16,426
1973	New York	East 5, West 4	Tom Johnson, Billy Reay	16,986
1972	Minnesota	East 3, West 2	Al MacNeil, Billy Reay	15,423
1971	Boston	West 2, East 1	Scott Bowman, Harry Sinden	14,790
1970	St. Louis	East 4, West 1	Claude Ruel, Scott Bowman	16,587
1969	Montreal	East 3, West 3	Toe Blake, Scott Bowman	16,260
1968	Toronto	Toronto 4, All-Stars 3	Punch Imlach, Toe Blake	15,753
1967	Montreal	Montreal 3, All-Stars 0	Toe Blake, Sid Abel	14,284
1965	Montreal	All-Stars 5, Montreal 2	Billy Reay, Toe Blake	13,529
1964	Toronto	All-Stars 3, Toronto 2	Sid Abel, Punch Imlach	14,232
1963	Toronto	All-Stars 3, Toronto 3	Sid Abel, Punch Imlach	14,034
1962	Toronto	Toronto 4, All-Stars 1	Punch Imlach, Rudy Pilous	14,236
1961	Chicago	All-Stars 3, Chicago 1	Sid Abel, Rudy Pilous	14,534
1960	Montreal	All-Stars 2, Montreal 1	Punch Imlach, Toe Blake	13,949
1959	Montreal	Montreal 6, All-Stars 1	Toe Blake, Punch Imlach	13,818
1958	Montreal	Montreal 6, All-Stars 3	Toe Blake, Milt Schmidt	13,989
1957	Montreal	All-Stars 5, Montreal 3	Milt Schmidt, Toe Blake	13,003
1956	Montreal	All-Stars 1, Montreal 1	Jim Skinner, Toe Blake	13,095
1955	Detroit	Detroit 3, All-Stars 1	Jim Skinner, Dick Irvin	10,111
1954	Detroit	All-Stars 2, Detroit 2	King Clancy, Jim Skinner	10,689
1953	Montreal	All-Stars 3, Montreal 1	Lynn Patrick, Dick Irvin	14,153
1952	Detroit	1st team 1, 2nd team 1	Tommy Ivan, Dick Irvin	10,680
1951	Toronto	1st team 2, 2nd team 2	Joe Primeau, Hap Day	11,469
1950	Detroit	Detroit 7, All-Stars 1	Tommy Ivan, Lynn Patrick	9,166
1949	Toronto	All-Stars 3, Toronto 1	Tommy Ivan, Hap Day	13,541
1948	Chicago	All-Stars 3, Toronto 1	Tommy Ivan, Hap Day	12,794
1947	Toronto	All-Stars 4, Toronto 3	Dick Irvin, Hap Day	14,169

There was no All-Star contest during the calendar year of 1966 since the game was moved from the start of season to mid-season. In 1979, the Challenge Cup series between the Soviet Union and Team NHL replaced the All-Star Game. In 1987, Rendez-Vous '87, two games between the Soviet Union and Team NHL replaced the All-Star Game.

1989-90 All-Star Game Summary

January 21, 1990 at Pittsburgh   Wales 12, Campbell 7

PLAYERS ON ICE: **Campbell Conference** — McLean, *Vernon, *MacInnis, *Lowe, Cavallini, Wilson, Duchesne, Iafrate, Mullen, Nicholls, Smail, Messier, Gartner, *Hull, Kurri, Yzerman, *Robitaille, Nieuwendyk, Larmer, *Gretzky.
Wales Conference — Puppa, *Roy, Leetch, Hatcher, Housley, *Coffey, Chelios, *Bourque, *Neely, Muller, Francis, LaFontaine, Turgeon, Sakic, Tocchet, Andreychuk, *Propp, Corson, Richer, *Lemieux.

* Indicates voted to respective All-Star Team by fans.

GOALTENDERS				
	Campbell:	Vernon	29 minutes	8 goals against
		McLean	31 minutes	4 goals against
	Wales:	Roy	29 minutes	3 goals against
		Puppa	31 minutes	4 goals against

SUMMARY
First Period

1.	Wales	Lemieux	(Propp, Neely)	0.21
2.	Wales	Andreychuk		5:13
3.	Wales	Turgeon	(Francis)	9:22
4.	Campbell	Messier	(Hull, Smail)	11:01
5.	Wales	Lemieux	(Housley)	13:00
6.	Campbell	Yzerman		14:31
7.	Wales	Tocchet	(Bourque, Muller)	16:55
8.	Wales	Lemieux	(Coffey)	17:37
9.	Wales	Turgeon	(Francis, Andreychuk)	10:52

PENALTIES: None.

Second Period

10.	Wales	Muller	(Coffey, Sakic)	8:47
11.	Campbell	MacInnis	(Lowe)	9:03 PPG
12.	Campbell	Mullen	(Nicholls)	13:00
13.	Wales	Corson	(LaFontaine)	16:43

PENALTIES: Roy (W) 7:05, Iafrate (C) 17:28.

Third Period

14.	Wales	Lemieux	(Neely)	1:07
15.	Wales	Neely	(Sakic, Hatcher)	11:20
16.	Campbell	Robitaille	(Yzerman, Hull)	15:09
17.	Campbell	Robitaille	(Hull, Yzerman)	16:11
18.	Wales	Muller	(Tocchet)	17:50
19.	Campbell	Smail	(Mullen, Nieuwendyk)	19:35

PENALTIES: Neely (W) 6:17, Smail (C) 7:33.

SHOTS ON GOAL BY:				
Wales Conference	16	15	14	**45**
Campbell Conference	9	11	22	**42**

Attendance: 16, 236

All-Star Game Records
1947 through 1990

TEAM RECORDS

MOST GOALS, BOTH TEAMS, ONE GAME:
19 Wales 12, Campbell 7, 1990 at Pittsburgh
14 — Campbell 9, Wales 5, 1989 at Edmonton
13 — Wales 7, Campbell 6, 1984 at New Jersey
12 — Campbell 9, Wales 3, 1983 at NY Islanders
— Wales 7, Campbell 5, 1976 at Philadelphia
11 — Wales 6, Campbell 5, 1988 at St. Louis
10 — West 6, East 4, 1974 at Chicago
— Wales 6, Campbell 4, 1985 at Calgary

FEWEST GOALS, BOTH TEAMS, ONE GAME:
2 NHL All-Stars 1, Montreal Canadiens 1, 1956 at Montreal
— First Team All-Stars 1, Second Team All-Stars 1, 1952 at Detroit
3 — West 2, East 1, 1971 at Boston
— Montreal Canadiens 3, NHL All-Stars 0, 1967 at Montreal
— NHL All-Stars 2, Montreal Canadiens 1, 1960 at Montreal

MOST GOALS, ONE TEAM, ONE GAME:
12 Wales 12, Campbell 7, 1990 at Pittsburgh
9 Campbell 9, Wales 3, 1983 at NY Islanders
Campbell 9, Wales 5, 1989 at Edmonton
7 — Wales 7, Campbell 5, 1976 at Philadelphia
— Wales 7, Campbell 1, 1975 at Montreal
— Detroit Red Wings 7, NHL All-Stars 1, 1950 at Detroit
— Wales 7, Campbell 6, 1984 at New Jersey
— Campbell 7, Wales 12, 1990 at Pittsburgh

FEWEST GOALS, ONE TEAM, ONE GAME:
0 — NHL All-Stars 0, Montreal Canadiens 3, 1967 at Montreal
1 — 17 times (1981, 1975, 1971, 1970, 1962, 1961, 1960, 1959, both teams 1956, 1955, 1953, both teams 1952, 1950, 1949, 1948)

MOST SHOTS, BOTH TEAMS, ONE GAME (SINCE 1955):
87 — 1990 at Pittsburgh — Wales 12 (45 shots), Campbell 7 (42 shots)
81 — 1968 at Toronto — NHL All-Stars 4 (40 shots), Toronto Maple Leafs 4 (41 shots)
75 — 1955 at Detroit — NHL All-Stars 1 (31 shots), Detroit Red Wings 3 (44 shots)
— 1989 at Edmonton — Campbell 9 (37 shots), Wales 5 (38 shots)
74 — 1963 at Toronto — NHL All-Stars 3 (38 shots), Toronto Maple Leafs 3 (36 shots)

FEWEST SHOTS, BOTH TEAMS, ONE GAME (SINCE 1955):
52 — 1978 at Buffalo — Campbell 2 (12 shots), Wales 3 (40 shots)
53 — 1960 at Montreal — NHL All-Stars 2 (27 shots), Montreal Canadiens 1 (26 shots)
55 — 1956 at Montreal — NHL All-Stars 1 (28 shots), Montreal Canadiens 1 (27 shots)
55 — 1971 at Boston — West 2 (28 shots), East 1 (27 shots)

MOST SHOTS, ONE TEAM, ONE GAME (SINCE 1955):
45 — 1990 at Pittsburgh — Wales (12-7 vs. Campbell)
44 — 1955 at Detroit — Detroit Red Wings (3-1 vs. NHL All-Stars)
44 — 1970 at St. Louis — East (4-1 vs. West)
43 — 1981 at Los Angeles — Campbell (4-1 vs. Wales)
42 — 1976 at Philadelphia — Wales (7-5 vs. Campbell)
42 — 1990 at Pittsburgh — Campbell (7-12 vs. Wales)

FEWEST SHOTS, ONE TEAM, ONE GAME (SINCE 1955):
12 — 1978 at Buffalo — Campbell (2-3 vs. Wales)
17 — 1970 at St. Louis — West (1-4 vs. East)
23 — 1961 at Chicago — Chicago Black Hawks (1-3 vs. NHL All-Stars)
24 — 1976 at Philadelphia — Campbell (5-7 vs. Wales)

MOST POWER-PLAY GOALS, BOTH TEAMS, ONE GAME (SINCE 1950):
3 — 1953 at Montreal — NHL All-Stars 3 (2 power-play goals), Montreal Canadiens 1 (1 power-play goal)
3 — 1954 at Detroit — NHL All-Stars 2 (1 power-play goal), Detroit Red Wings 2 (2 power-play goals)
3 — 1958 at Montreal — NHL All-Stars 3 (1 power-play goal), Montreal Canadiens 6 (2 power-play goals)

FEWEST POWER-PLAY GOALS, BOTH TEAMS, ONE GAME (SINCE 1950):
0 — 13 times (1952, 1959, 1960, 1967, 1968, 1969, 1972, 1973, 1976, 1980, 1981, 1984, 1985)

FASTEST TWO GOALS, BOTH TEAMS, FROM START OF GAME:
37 seconds — 1970 at St. Louis — Jacques Laperriere of East scored at 20 seconds and Dean Prentice of West scored at 37 seconds. Final score: East 4, West 1.
4:08 — 1963 at Toronto — Frank Mahovlich scored for Toronto Maple Leafs at 2:22 of first period and Henri Richard scored at 4:08 for NHL All-Stars. Final score: NHL All-Stars 3, Toronto Maple Leafs 3.
4:19 — 1980 at Detroit — Larry Robinson scored at 3:58 for Wales and Steve Payne scored at 4:19 for Wales. Final score: Wales 6, Campbell 3.

FASTEST TWO GOALS, BOTH TEAMS:
10 seconds — 1976 at Philadelphia — Dennis Ververgaert scored at 4:33 and at 4:43 of third period for Campbell. Final score: Wales 7, Campbell 5.
14 seconds — 1989 at Edmonton. Steve Yzerman and Gary Leeman scored at 17:21 and 17:35 of second period for Campbell. Final score: Campbell 9, Wales 5.
16 seconds — 1990 at Pittsburgh. Kirk Muller of Wales scored at 8:47 of second period and Al MacInnis of Campbell scored at 9:03. Final score: Wales 12, Campbell 7.

FASTEST THREE GOALS, BOTH TEAMS:
1:32 — 1980 at Detroit — all by Wales — Ron Stackhouse scored at 11:40 of third period, Craig Hartsburg scored at 12:40; and Reed Larson scored at 13:12. Final score: Wales 6, Campbell 3.
1:57 — 1990 at Pittsburgh — all by Wales – Rick Tocchet scored at 16:55 of first period, Mario Lemieux scored at 17:37; Pierre Turgeon scored at 18:52. Final score: Wales 12, Campbell 7.
2:01 — 1976 at Philadelphia — Curt Bennett scored at 16:59 of first period for Campbell; Pete Mahovlich scored at 18:31 for Wales; Brad Park scored at 19:00 for Wales. Final score: Wales 7, Campbell 5.

FASTEST FOUR GOALS, BOTH TEAMS:
4:21 — 1990 at Pittsbrugh — Steve Yzerman scored at 14:31 of first period for Campbell; Rick Tocchet scored at 16:55 for Wales; Mario Lemieux scored at 17:37 for Wales. Final score: Wales 12, Campbell 7.
4:26 — 1990 at Pittsbrugh — Luc Robitaille scored at 15:09 and 16:11 of third period for Campbell; Kirk Muller scored at 17:50 for Wales; Doug Smail scored at 19:35 Campbell. Final score: Wales 12, Campbell 7.
4:26 — 1980 at Detroit — all by Wales; Ron Stackhouse scored at 11:40 of third period; Craig Hartsburg scored at 12:40; Reed Larson scored at 13:12; Real Cloutier scored at 16:06. Final score: Wales 6, Campbell 3.

Curt Bennett had the first of three goals to be scored in just over two minutes at the 1976 All-Star Game.

FASTEST TWO GOALS, ONE TEAM, FROM START OF GAME:
4:19 — 1980 at Detroit — Wales — Larry Robinson scored at 3:58 and Steve Payne scored at 4:19. Final score: Wales 6, Campbell 3.

4:38 — 1971 at Boston — West — Chico Maki scored at 36 seconds and Bobby Hull scored at 4:38. Final score: West 2, East 1.

5:25 — 1953 at Montreal — NHL All-Stars — Wally Hergesheimer scored at 4:06 and 5:25. Final score: NHL All-Stars 3, Montreal Canadiens 1.

5:13 — 1990 at Pittsburgh — Wales — Mario Lemieux scored at :21 and Dave Andreychuk scored at 5:13. Final score: Wales 12, Campbell 7.

FASTEST TWO GOALS, ONE TEAM:
10 seconds — 1976 at Philadelphia — Campbell — Dennis Ververgaert scored at 4:33 and at 4:43 of third period. Final score: Wales 7, Campbell 5.

14 seconds — 1989 at Edmonton — Campbell — Steve Yzerman and Gary Leeman scored at 17:21 and 17:35 of second period. Final score: Campbell 9, Wales 5.

21 seconds — 1980 at Detroit — Wales — Larry Robinson scored at 3:58 of first period and Steve Payne scored at 4:19. Final score: Wales 6, Campbell 3.

29 seconds — 1976 at Philadelphia — Campbell — Denis Potvin scored at 14:17 of third period and Steve Vickers scored at 14:46. Final score: Wales 7, Campbell 5.

29 seconds — 1976 at Philadelphia — Wales — Pete Mahovlich scored at 18:31 of first period and Brad Park scored at 19:00. Final score: Wales 7, Campbell 5.

FASTEST THREE GOALS, ONE TEAM:
1:32 — 1980 at Detroit — Wales — Ron Stackhouse scored at 11:40 of third period; Craig Hartsburg scored at 12:40; Reed Larson scored at 13:12. Final score: Wales 6, Campbell 3.

1:57 — 1990 at Pittsburgh — Wales — Rick Tocchett scored at 16:55 of first period; Mario Lemieux scored at 17:37; Pierre Turgeon scored at 18:52. Final score: Wales 12, Campbell 7.

2:25 — 1984 at New Jersey — Wales — Rick Middleton scored at 14:49 of first period; Mats Naslund scored at 16:40; Pierre Larouche at 17:14. Final score: Wales 7, Campbell 6.

3:26 — 1980 at Detroit — Wales — Craig Hartsburg scored at 12:40 of third period, Reed Larson scored at 13:12; Real Cloutier scored at 16:06. Final score: Wales 6, Campbell 3.

FASTEST FOUR GOALS, ONE TEAM:
4:26 — 1980 at Detroit — Wales — Ron Stackhouse scored at 11:40 of third period; Craig Hartsburg scored at 12:40; Reed Larson scored at 13:12; Real Cloutier scored at 16:06. Final score: Wales 6, Campbell 3.

5:52 — 1990 at Pittsburgh — Wales — Mario Lemieux scored at 13:00 of first period; Rick Tocchett scored at 16:55; Mario Lemieux scored at 17:37; Pierre Turgeon scored at 18:52. Final score: Wales 12, Campbell 7.

7:25 — 1976 at Philadelphia — Wales — Al MacAdam scored at 9:34 of second period; Guy Lafleur scored at 11:54; Marcel Dionne scored at 13:51; Dan Maloney scored at 16:59. Final score: Wales 7, Campbell 5.

MOST GOALS, BOTH TEAMS, ONE PERIOD:
9 — 1990 at Pittsburgh — First Period — Wales (7), Campbell (2). Final score: Wales 12, Campbell 7.

7 — 1983 at NY Islanders — Third period — Campbell (6), Wales (1) Final score: Campbell 9, Wales 3.

6 — 1989 at Edmonton — Third period — Campbell (4), Wales (2). Final score: Campbell 9, Wales 5.

6 — 1990 at Pittsburgh — Third period — Wales (3), Campbell (3). Final score: Wales 12, Campbell 7.

MOST GOALS, ONE TEAM, ONE PERIOD:
7 — 1990 at Pittsburgh — First period — Wales. Final score: Wales 12, Campbell 7.

6 — 1983 at NY Islanders — Third period — Campbell. Final score: Campbell 9, Wales 3.

5 — 1984 at New Jersey — First period — Wales. Final score: Wales 7, Campbell 6.

MOST SHOTS, BOTH TEAMS, ONE PERIOD:
36 — 1990 at Pittsburgh — Third period — Campbell (22), Wales (14). Final score: Wales 12, Campbell 7.

30 — 1959 at Montreal — Second period — NHL All-Stars (16), Montreal (14). Final score: Montreal Canadiens 6, NHL All-Stars 1.

29 — 1955 at Detroit — Third period — Detroit Red Wings (18), NHL All-Stars (11). Final score: Detroit Red Wings 3, NHL All-Stars 1.

29 — 1968 at Toronto — Second period — Toronto Maple Leafs (18), NHL All-Stars (11). Final score: Toronto Maple Leafs 4, NHL All-Stars 3.

29 — 1980 at Detroit — Third period — Wales (17), Campbell (12). Final score: Wales 6, Campbell 3.

29 — 1989 at Edmonton — Third period — Wales (15). Campbell (14). Final score: Campbell 9, Wales 5.

Larry Robinson (pictured here) and Steve Payne combined to score two goals for the Wales Conference in the first four minutes and 19 seconds of the 1980 All-Star game, a record which still stands.

MOST SHOTS, ONE TEAM, ONE PERIOD:
22 — 1990 at Pittsburgh — Third period — Campbell. Final score: Wales 12, Campbell 7.

20 — 1970 at St. Louis — Third period — East. Final score: East 4, West 1.

18 — 1955 at Detroit — Third period — Detroit Red Wings. Final score: Detroit Red Wings 3, NHL All-Stars 1.

18 — 1968 at Toronto — Second period — Toronto Maple Leafs. Final score: Toronto Maple Leafs 4, NHL All-Stars 3.

18 — 1981 at Los Angeles — First period — Campbell. Final score: Campbell 4, Wales 1.

FEWEST SHOTS, BOTH TEAMS, ONE PERIOD:
9 — 1971 at Boston — Third period — East (2), West (7). Final score: West 2, East 1.

9 — 1980 at Detroit — Second period — Campbell (4), Wales (5). Final score: Wales 6, Campbell 3.

13 — 1982 at Washington — Third period — Campbell (6), Wales (7). Final score: Wales 4, Campbell 2.

14 — 1978 at Buffalo — First period — Campbell (7), Wales (7). Final score: Wales 3, Campbell 2.

14 — 1986 at Hartford — First period — Campbell (6), Wales (8). Final score: Wales 4, Campbell 3.

FEWEST SHOTS, ONE TEAM, ONE PERIOD:
2 — 1971 at Boston — Third period — East. Final score: West 2, East 1.

2 — 1978 at Buffalo — Second period — Campbell. Final score: Wales 3, Campbell 2.

3 — 1978 at Buffalo — Third period — Campbell. Final score: Wales 3, Campbell 2.

4 — 1955 at Detroit — First period — NHL All-Stars. Final score: Detroit Red Wings 3, NHL All-Stars 1.

4 — 1980 at Detroit — Second period — Campbell. Final score: Wales 6, Campbell 3.

INDIVIDUAL RECORDS
Career

MOST GAMES PLAYED:
23 — Gordie Howe from 1948 through 1980
15 — Frank Mahovlich from 1959 through 1974
13 — Jean Beliveau from 1953 through 1969
— Alex Delvecchio from 1953 through 1967
— Doug Harvey from 1951 through 1969
— Maurice Richard from 1947 through 1959

MOST GOALS:
10 — Gordie Howe in 23GP
9 — Wayne Gretzky in 10GP
— Mario Lemieux in 5 GP
8 — Frank Mahovlich in 15GP
7 — Maurice Richard in 13GP
5 — Bobby Hull in 12GP
— Ted Lindsay in 11GP
— Denis Potvin in 8GP
— Luc Robitaille in 3GP

MOST ASSISTS:
9 — Gordie Howe in 23GP
7 — Doug Harvey in 13GP
— Guy Lafleur in 5GP
— Raymond Bourque in 9GP
6 — Red Kelly in 11GP
— Norm Ullman in 11GP
— Mats Naslund in 3GP
— Paul Coffey in 8GP

MOST POINTS:
19 — Gordie Howe (10G-9A in 23GP)
14 — Mario Lemieux (9G-5A in 5GP)
13 — Frank Mahovlich (8G-5A in 15GP)
— Wayne Gretzky (10G-3A in 10GP)
10 — Bobby Hull (5G-5A in 12GP)
— Ted Lindsay (5G-5A in 11GP)
9 — Maurice Richard (7G-2A in 13GP)
— Henri Richard (4G-5A in 10GP)
— Denis Potvin (5G-4A in 8GP)
— Raymond Bourque (2G-7A in 9GP)

MOST PENALTY MINUTES:
27 — Gordie Howe in 23GP
21 — Gus Mortson in 9GP
16 — Harry Howell in 7GP

MOST POWER-PLAY GOALS:
6 — Gordie Howe in 23GP
3 — Bobby Hull in 12GP
2 — Maurice Richard in 13GP

Game

MOST GOALS, ONE GAME:
4 — Wayne Gretzky, Campbell, 1983
— **Mario Lemieux**, Wales, 1990
3 — Ted Lindsay, Detroit Red Wings, 1950
— Mario Lemieux, Wales, 1988
2 — Wally Hergesheimer, NHL All-Stars, 1953
— Earl Reibel, Detroit Red Wings, 1955
— Andy Bathgate, NHL All-Stars, 1958
— Maurice Richard, Montreal Canadiens, 1958
— Frank Mahovlich, Toronto Maple Leafs, 1963
— Gordie Howe, NHL All-Stars, 1965
— John Ferguson, Montreal Canadiens, 1967
— Frank Mahovlich, East All-Stars, 1969
— Greg Polis, West All-Stars, 1973
— Syl Apps, Wales, 1975
— Dennis Ververgaert, Campbell, 1976
— Richard Martin, Wales, 1977
— Lanny McDonald, Wales, 1977
— Mike Bossy, Wales, 1982
— Pierre Larouche, Wales, 1984
— Mario Lemieux, Wales 1985
— Brian Propp, Wales, 1986
— Luc Robitaille, Campbell, 1988
— Joe Mullen, Campbell, 1989
— Pierre Turgeon, Wales, 1990
— Kirk Muller, Wales, 1990
— Luc Robitaille, Campbell, 1990

MOST ASSISTS, ONE GAME:
5 — Mats Naslund, Wales, 1988
4 — Raymond Bourque, Wales, 1985
3 — Dickie Moore, Montreal Canadiens, 1958
— Doug Harvey, Montreal Canadiens, 1959
— Guy Lafleur, Wales, 1975
— Pete Mahovlich, Wales, 1976
— Mark Messier, Campbell, 1983
— Rick Vaive, Campbell, 1984
— Mark Johnson, Wales, 1984
— Don Maloney, Wales, 1984
— Mike Krushelnyski, Campbell, 1985
— Brett Hull, Campbell, 1990

MOST POINTS, ONE GAME:
6 — Mario Lemieux, Wales, 1988 (3G-3A)
5 — Mats Naslund, Wales, 1988 (5A)
4 — Ted Lindsay, Detroit Red Wings, 1950 (3G-1A)
— Gordie Howe, NHL All-Stars, 1965 (2G-2A)
— Pete Mahovlich, Wales, 1976 (1G-3A)
— Wayne Gretzky, Campbell, 1983 (4G)
— Don Maloney, Wales, 1984 (1G-3A)
— Raymond Bourque, Wales, 1985 (4A)
— Mario Lemieux, Wales, 1990 (4G)

MOST GOALS, ONE PERIOD:
4 — Wayne Gretzky, Campbell, Third period, 1983
3 — Mario Lemieux, Wales, First period, 1990
2 — Ted Lindsay, Detroit Red Wings, First period, 1950
— Wally Hergesheimer, NHL All-Stars, First period, 1953
— Andy Bathgate, NHL All-Stars, Third period, 1958
— Frank Mahovlich, Toronto Maple Leafs, First period, 1963
— Dennis Ververgaert, Campbell, Third period, 1976
— Richard Martin, Wales, Third period, 1977
— Pierre Turgeon, Wales, First period, 1990
— Luc Robitaille, Campbell, Third period, 1990

MOST ASSISTS, ONE PERIOD:
3 — Mark Messier, Clarence Campbell, Third period, 1983
2 — By several players

MOST POINTS, ONE PERIOD:
4 — Wayne Gretzky, Campbell, Third period, 1983 (4G)
3 — Gordie Howe, NHL All-Stars, Second period, 1965 (1G-2A)
— Pete Mahovlich, Wales, First period, 1976 (1G-2A)
— Mark Messier, Campbell, Third period, 1983 (3A)
— Mario Lemieux, Wales, Second period, 1988 (1G-2A)
— Mario Lemieux, Wales, First period, 1990 (3G)

FASTEST GOAL FROM START OF GAME:
19 seconds — Ted Lindsay, Detroit Red Wings, 1950
20 seconds — Jacques Laperriere, East All-Stars, 1970
21 seconds — Mario Lemieux, Wales, 1990
36 seconds — Chico Maki, West All-Stars, 1971
37 seconds — Dean Prentice, West All-Star, 1970

FASTEST GOAL FROM START OF A PERIOD:
19 seconds — Ted Lindsay, Detroit Red Wings, 1950 (first period)
20 seconds — Jacques Laperriere, East, 1970 (first period)
21 seconds — Mario Lemieux, Wales, 1990 (first period)
26 seconds — Wayne Gretzky, Campbell, 1982 (second period)
28 seconds — Maurice Richard, NHL All-Stars, 1947 (third period)
33 seconds — Bert Olmstead, Montreal Canadiens, 1957 (second period)

FASTEST TWO GOALS FROM START OF GAME:
5:25 — Wally Hergesheimer, NHL All-Stars, 1953, at 4:06 and 5:25 of first period.
12:11 — Frank Mahovlich, Toronto, 1963, at 2:22 and 12:11 of first period.
12:39 — Mario Lemieux, Wales, 1990, at :21 and 13:00 of first period.

FASTEST TWO GOALS FROM START OF A PERIOD:
4:43 — Dennis Ververgaert, Campbell, 1976, at 4:33 and 4:43 of third period.
5:25 — Wally Hergesheimer, NHL All-Stars, 1953, at 4:06 and 5:25 of first period.
12:11 — Frank Mahovlich, Toronto, 1963. Scored at 2:22 and 12:11 of first period.
12:39 — Mario Lemieux, Wales, 1990, Scored at :21 and 13:00 of first period.

FASTEST TWO GOALS:
10 seconds — Dennis Ververgaert, Campbell, 1976. Scored at 4:33 and 4:43 of third period.
1:02 — Luc Robitaille, Campbell, 1990. Scored at 15:09 and 16:11 of third period.
1:19 — Wally Hergesheimer, NHL All-Stars, 1953. Scored at 4:06 and 5:25 of first period.
4:09 — Mike Bossy, Wales, 1982. Scored at 17:10 of second period and 1:19 of third period.

Goaltenders

MOST GAMES PLAYED:
13 — Glenn Hall from 1955-1969
11 — Terry Sawchuk from 1950-1968
8 — Jacques Plante from 1956-1970
6 — Tony Esposito from 1970-1980
— Ed Giacomin from 1967-1973

MOST GOALS AGAINST:
22 — Glenn Hall in 13GP
19 — Terry Sawchuk in 11GP
18 — Jacques Plante in 8GP
14 — Turk Broda in 4GP

BEST GOALS-AGAINST-AVERAGE AMONG THOSE WITH AT LEAST TWO GAMES PLAYED:
0.68 — Gilles Villemure in 3GP
1.02 — Frank Brimsek in 2GP
1.59 — Johnny Bower in 4GP
1.64 — Lorne "Gump" Worsley in 4GP
1.98 — Gerry McNeil in 3GP
2.03 — Don Edwards in 2GP
2.44 — Terry Sawchuk in 11GP

MOST MINUTES PLAYED:
467 — Terry Sawchuk in 11GP
421 — Glenn Hall in 13GP
370 — Jacques Plante in 8GP
209 — Turk Broda in 4GP
182 — Ed Giacomin in 6GP
165 — Tony Esposito in 6GP

NHL-Soviet Game Record, 1972-1990

Date	Venue	Score	Goaltenders
9/2/72	Montreal	Soviet Union 7, Team Canada 3	Tretiak – Dryden
9/4/72	Toronto	Team Canada 4, Soviet Union 1	Esposito – Tretiak
9/6/72	Winnipeg	Soviet Union 4, Team Canada 4	Tretiak – Esposito
9/8/72	Vancouver	Soviet Union 5, Team Canada 3	Tretiak – Dryden
9/22/72	Moscow	Soviet Union 5, Team Canada 4	Tretiak – Esposito
9/24/72	Moscow	Team Canada 3, Soviet Union 2	Dryden – Tretiak
9/26/72	Moscow	Team Canada 4, Soviet Union 3	Esposito – Tretiak
9/28/72	Moscow	Team Canada 6, Soviet Union 5	Dryden – Tretiak
12/28/75	New York	Red Army 7, NY Rangers 3	Tretiak – Davidson
12/29/75	Pittsburgh	Soviet Wings 7, Pittsburgh 4	Sidelnikov – Plasse
12/31/75	Montreal	Montreal 3, Red Army 3	Dryden – Tretiak
1/4/76	Buffalo	Buffalo 12, Soviet Wings 6	Desjardins – Kylikov, Sidelnikov
1/7/76	Chicago	Soviet Wings 4, Chicago 2	Sidelnikov – Esposito
1/8/76	Boston	Red Army 5, Boston 2	Tretiak – Gilbert
1/10/76	New York	Soviet Wings 2, NY Islanders 1	Sidelnikov – Resch
1/11/76	Philadelphia	Philadelphia 4, Red Army 1	Stephenson – Tretiak
9/9/76	Philadelphia	Soviet Union 5, Team U.S.A. 0	Tretiak – Curran
9/11/76	Toronto	Team Canada 3, Soviet Union 1	Vachon – Tretiak
12/28/77	Vancouver	Vancouver 2, Spartak 0	Ridley – Pashkov
1/3/78	Denver	Spartak 8, Colorado 3	Pashkov – Favell, McKenzie
1/5/78	St. Louis	Spartak 2, St. Louis 1	Doroshenko – Johnston, Myre
1/6/78	Montreal	Montreal 5, Spartak 2	Dryden, Larocque – Pashkov
1/8/78	Atlanta	Spartak 2, Atlanta 1	Doroshenko – Belanger
12/31/78	Minnesota	Soviet Wings 8, Minnesota 5	Myshkin – Edwards, LoPresti
1/2/79	Philadelphia	Philadelphia 4, Soviet Wings 4	Parent – Myshkin
1/4/79	Detroit	Detroit 6, Soviet Wings 5	Rutherford, Vachon – Myshkin
1/9/79	Boston	Soviet Wings 4, Boston 1	Sidelnikov – Cheevers, Pettie
2/8/79	New York	Team NHL 4, Soviet Union 2	Dryden – Tretiak
2/10/79	New York	Soviet Union 5, Team NHL 4	Tretiak – Dryden
2/11/79	New York	Soviet Union 6, Team NHL 0	Myshkin – Cheevers
12/26/79	Vancouver	Vancouver 6, Dynamo 2	Ridley – Myshkin
12/27/79	New York	Red Army 5, NY Rangers 2	Tretiak – Baker, Davidson
12/29/79	New York	Red Army 3, NY Islanders 2	Tretiak – Smith
12/31/79	Montreal	Montreal 4, Red Army 2	Sevigny – Tretiak
1/2/80	Winnipeg	Dynamo 7, Winnipeg 0	Myshkin – Hamel, Middlebrook
1/3/80	Buffalo	Buffalo 6, Red Army 1	Edwards – Tretiak
1/4/80	Edmonton	Dynamo 4, Edmonton 1	Myshkin – Mio
1/6/80	Quebec	Red Army 6, Quebec 4	Tretiak – Dion
1/8/80	Washington	Washington 5, Dynamo 5	Inness – Myshkin
9/5/81	Edmonton	Soviet Union 4, Team U.S.A. 1	Tretiak – Esposito
9/9/81	Montreal	Team Canada 7, Soviet Union 3	Liut – Myshkin
9/13/81	Montreal	Soviet Union 8, Team Canada 1	Tretiak – Liut
12/28/82	Edmonton	Edmonton 4, Soviet Union 3	Moog – Myshkin
12/30/82	Quebec	Soviet Union 3, Quebec 0	Tretiak – Bouchard
12/31/82	Montreal	Soviet Union 5, Montreal 0	Tretiak – Sevigny
1/2/83	Calgary	Calgary 3, Soviet Union 2	Edwards, Lemelin – Myshkin
1/4/83	Minnesota	Soviet Union 6, Minnesota 3	Tretiak – Mattson, Beaupre
1/6/83	Philadelphia	Soviet Union 5, Philadelphia 1	Tretiak – Lindbergh
9/8/84	Edmonton	Soviet Union 2, Team U.S.A. 1	Myshkin – Barrasso
9/10/84	Edmonton	Soviet Union 6, Team Canada 3	Tyzhnykh – Lemelin
9/13/84	Calgary	Team Canada 3, Soviet Union 2	Peeters – Myshkin
12/26/85	Los Angeles	Red Army 5, Los Angeles 2	Mylnikov – Janecyk
12/27/85	Edmonton	Red Army 6, Edmonton 3	Mylnikov – Moog
12/29/85	Quebec	Quebec 5, Red Army 1	Malarchuk – Mylnikov
12/29/85	Calgary	Calgary 4, Dynamo 3	Vernon – Myshkin
12/31/85	Montreal	Red Army 6, Montreal 1	Mylnikov – Soetaert, Roy
1/2/86	St. Louis	Red Army 4, St. Louis 2	Mylnikov – Millen, Wamsley
1/4/86	Minnesota	Red Army 4, Minnesota 3	Mylnikov – Casey
1/4/86	Pittsburgh	Dynamo 3, Pittsburgh 3	Myshkin – Herron
1/6/86	Boston	Dynamo 6, Boston 4	Myshkin – Keans
1/8/86	Buffalo	Dynamo 7, Buffalo 4	Myshkin – Cloutier
2/11/87	Quebec	NHL All-Stars 3, Soviet Union 2	Fuhr – Belosheykin
2/13/87	Quebec	Soviet Union 5, NHL All-Stars 3	Belosheykin – Fuhr
9/4/87	Hartford	Soviet Union 5, Team USA 1	Mylnikov – Barrasso
9/6/87	Hamilton, Ont.	Team Canada 3, Soviet Union 3	Fuhr – Belosheykin
9/11/87	Montreal	Soviet Union 6, Team Canada 5	Mylnikov – Fuhr
9/13/87	Hamilton, Ont.	Team Canada 6, Soviet Union 5	Fuhr – Belosheykin
9/15/87	Hamilton, Ont.	Team Canada 6, Soviet Union 5	Fuhr – Mylnikov
12/26/88	Quebec	Red Army 5, Quebec 5	Mylnikov – Mason
12/27/88	Calgary	Dynamo Riga 2, Calgary 2	Irbe – Wamsley
12/28/88	Edmonton	Edmonton 2, Dynamo Riga 1	Irbe – Fuhr
12/29/88	NY Islanders	Red Army 3, NY Islanders 1	Mylnikov – Smith, Hrudey
12/30/88	Vancouver	Vancouver 6, Dynamo Riga 1	Irbe – McLean
12/31/88	Boston	Red Army 5, Boston 4	Mylnikov – Lemelin
12/31/88	Los Angeles	Dynamo Riga 5, Los Angeles 2	Irbe – Fitzpatrick
1/2/89	New Jersey	Red Army 5, New Jersey 0	Mylnikov – Terreri
1/4/89	Pittsburgh	Pittsburgh 4, Red Army 2	Mylnikov, Goloshumov – Pietrangelo, Young
1/4/89	Chicago	Chicago 4, Dynamo Riga 1	Irbe – Belfour
1/5/89	St. Louis	St. Louis 5, Dynamo Riga 0	Irbe – Jablonski
1/7/89	Minnesota	Dynamo Riga 2, Minnesota 1	Irbe – Myllys
1/7/89	Hartford	Red Army 6, Hartford 3	Goloshumov – Liut
1/9/89	Buffalo	Buffalo 6, Red Army 5	Goloshumov, Mylnikov – Cloutier, Puppa
12/4/89	Los Angeles	Khimik 6, Los Angeles 3	Chervyakov – Gosselin
12/6/89	Edmonton	Edmonton 6, Khimik 2	Fuhr – Chervyakov
12/8/89	Calgary	Calgary 4, Khimik 3	Wamsley – Chervyakov
12/11/89	Detroit	Khimik 4, Detroit 2	Chervyakov – Cheveldae
12/12/89	Washington	Washington 5, Khimik 2	Mason – Chervyakov
12/14/89	St. Louis	Khimik 6, St. Louis 3	Chervyakov – Hebert

Khimik, Dynamo & Red Army to Each Play 7 Games vs. NHL in 1990-91

Beginning on December 3, 1990, Soviet club teams will begin a 21-game exhibition tour against NHL opponents. This tour will be the eighth occasion one or more Soviet clubs have played NHL teams in North America. This season's Super Series features three Soviet teams, and will see one game played by each NHL club.

USSR-Khimik, third-place finisher in Soviet play last season, is appearing in North America for the second time. Last season USSR-Khimik split its six-game series 3-3 in the club's inaugural tour.

USSR-Central Red Army, second-place finisher in the Soviet National League last season, is making its sixth NHL tour, the club compiling an impressive 18-7-2 career record in Super Series play to date.

USSR-Dynamo, which captured the Soviet National League championship in 1989-90, will be making its fourth appearance here and has a 7-5-2 record.

Results from the 21-game challenge, as well as the eight games involving the Montreal Canadiens and Minnesota North Stars to be played in the Soviet Union during September's Friendship Tour '90, will be totalled and the winner will be honored.

Super Series 1990-91 Schedule

USSR-KHIMIK

Monday	Dec. 3	at	Los Angeles
Wednesday	Dec. 5	at	St Louis
Saturday	Dec. 8	at	NY Islanders
Monday	Dec. 10	at	Montreal
Wednesday	Dec. 12	at	Buffalo
Sunday	Dec. 16	at	Boston
Tuesday	Dec. 18	at	Minnesota

USSR-DYNAMO MOSCOW

Tuesday	Jan. 1	at	Toronto
Thursday	Jan. 3	at	Hartford
Sunday	Jan. 6	at	New Jersey
Tuesday	Jan. 8	at	Washington
Thursday	Jan. 10	at	Philadelphia
Saturday	Jan. 12	at	Pittsburgh
Tuesday	Jan. 15	at	Quebec

USSR-CENTRAL RED ARMY

Wednesday	Dec. 26	at	Detroit
Monday	Dec. 31	at	NY Rangers*
Wednesday	Jan. 2	at	Chicago*
Friday	Jan. 4	at	Calgary
Sunday	Jan. 6	at	Edmonton*
Wednesday	Jan. 9	at	Winnipeg
Sunday	Jan. 13	at	Vancouver

*afternoon game

Date	Venue	Score	Goaltenders
12/26/89	NY Islanders	NY Islanders 5, Soviet Wings 4	Fitzpatrick, Healy – Bratash
12/27/89	Hartford	Hartford 4, Soviet Wings 3	Whitmore – Drozdov
12/27/89	Winnipeg	Winnipeg 4, Red Army 1	Beauregard – Irbe
12/29/89	Pittsburgh	Dynamo Moscow 5, Pittsburgh 2	Karpin – Young
12/29/89	Vancouver	Red Army 6, Vancouver 0	Irbe – Weeks
12/31/89	Quebec	Soviet Wings 4, Quebec 4	Bratash – Tugnutt, Millen
12/31/89	Toronto	Dynamo Moscow 7, Toronto 4	Karpin – Laforest
1/1/90	NY Rangers	Soviet Wings 3, NY Rangers 1	Drozdov – Richter
1/2/90	Minnesota	Red Army 4, Minnesota 2	Irbe – Myllys
1/3/90	Montreal	Montreal 2, Soviet Wings 1	Hayward – Drozdov
1/3/90	Buffalo	Buffalo 4, Dynamo Moscow 2	Malarchuk – Karpin
1/5/90	New Jersey	New Jersey 7, Dynamo Moscow 1	Terreri – Karpin, Myshkin
1/7/90	Chicago	Red Army 6, Chicago 4	Irbe – Waite
1/9/90	Philadelphia	Red Army 5, Philadelphia 4	Mikhailovsky – Peeters
1/9/90	Boston	Dynamo Moscow 3, Boston 1	Myshkin – Foster

Hockey Hall of Fame

Location: Toronto's Exhibition Park, on the shore of Lake Ontario, adjacent to Ontario Place and Exhibition Stadium. The Hockey Hall of Fame building is in the middle of Exhibition Place, directly north of the stadium.

Telephone: (416) 595-1345.

Hours: Mid-May to mid-August - 10 am to 7 pm Tuesday through Sunday; Mondays 10 am to 5 pm. Mid-August to Labor Day - Hours vary during annual Exhibition. September after Labor Day to mid-May - 10 am to 4:30 pm. Also closed Christmas day, New Year's Day and the day prior to the annual Exhibition.

Admission: Adults $3, Seniors & Students $2. Group rates, and reduced rate during Exhibition.

History: The Hockey Hall of Fame building was completed May 1, 1961, and officially opened August 26, 1961, by the Prime Minister of Canada, John G. Diefenbaker, and U.S. ambassador to Canada, Livingston T. Merchant. The six member clubs of the NHL operating at the time provided the funds required for construction. The City of Toronto, owner of the grounds, provided an ideal site, and the Canadian National Exhibition Association, as administrator of the park area, agreed to service and maintain the building in perpetuity for the purposes of the Hockey Hall of Fame. Hockey exhibits are provided and financed by the NHL with co-operative support of the Canadian Amateur Hockey Association. Staff and most administration costs are underwritten by the NHL.

Eligibility Requirements: Any person who is, or has been distinguished in hockey as a player, executive or referee/linesman, shall be eligible for election. Player and referee/linesman candidates will normally have completed their active participating careers three years prior to election, but in exceptional cases this period may be shortened by the Hockey Hall of Fame Board of Directors. Veteran player candidates must have concluded their careers as active players in the sport of hockey for at least 25 years. Candidates for election as executives and referees/linesmen shall be nominated only by the Board of Directors and upon election shall be known as Builders or referees/linesmen. Candidates for election as players shall be chosen on the basis of "playing ability, integrity, character and their contribution to their team and the game of hockey in general."

Honor Roll: There are 276 Honored Members of the Hockey Hall of Fame. Of the total, 192 are listed as players, 73 as Builders and 11 as Referees/Linesmen. Ian (Scotty) Morrison is President of the Hall.

(Year of election to the Hall is indicated in brackets after the Members' names).

1990 Hall of Fame Inductee—"Fern" Flaman.

PLAYERS

Abel, Sidney Gerald (1969)
*Adams, John James "Jack" (1959)
Apps, Charles Joseph Sylvanus "Syl" (1961)
Armstrong, George Edward (1975)
Bailey, Irvine Wallace "Ace" (1975)
*Bain, Donald H. "Dan" (1945)
*Baker, Hobart "Hobey" (1945)
Barber, William Charles "Bill" (1990)
*Barry, Martin J. "Marty" (1965)
Bathgate, Andrew James "Andy" (1978)
Beliveau, Jean Arthur (1972)
*Benedict, Clinton S. (1965)
*Bentley, Douglas Wagner (1964)
*Bentley, Maxwell H. L. (1966)
Blake, Hector "Toe" (1966)
Boivin, Leo Joseph (1986)
*Boon, Richard R. "Dickie" (1952)
Bouchard, Emile Joseph "Butch" (1966)
*Boucher, Frank (1958)
*Boucher, George "Buck" (1960)
Bower, John William (1976)
*Bowie, Russell (1945)
Brimsek, Francis Charles (1966)
*Broadbent, Harry L. "Punch" (1962)
*Broda, Walter Edward "Turk" (1967)
Bucyk, John Paul (1981)
*Burch, Billy (1974)
*Cameron, Harold Hugh "Harry" (1962)
Cheevers, Gerald Michael "Gerry" (1985)
*Clancy, Francis Michael "King" (1958)
*Clapper, Aubrey "Dit" (1947)
Clarke, Robert "Bobby" (1987)
*Cleghorn, Sprague (1958)
Colville, Neil MacNeil (1967)
*Conacher, Charles W. (1961)
*Connell, Alex (1958)
*Cook, William Osser (1952)
Coulter, Arthur Edmund (1974)
Cournoyer, Yvan Serge (1982)
Cowley, William Mailes (1968)
*Crawford, Samuel Russell "Rusty" (1962)
*Darragh, John Proctor "Jack" (1962)
*Davidson, Allan M. "Scotty" (1950)
*Day, Clarence Henry "Hap" (1961)
Delvecchio, Alex (1977)
*Denneny, Cyril "Cy" (1959)
*Drillon, Gordon Arthur (1975)
*Drinkwater, Charles Graham (1950)

Dryden, Kenneth Wayne (1983)
*Dunderdale, Thomas (1974)
*Durnan, William Ronald (1964)
*Dutton, Mervyn A. "Red" (1958)
*Dye, Cecil Henry "Babe" (1970)
Esposito, Anthony James "Tony" (1988)
Esposito, Philip Anthony (1984)
*Farrell, Arthur F. (1965)
Flaman, Ferdinand Charles "Fern" (1990)
*Foyston, Frank (1958)
*Frederickson, Frank (1958)
Gadsby, William Alexander (1970)
*Gardiner, Charles Robert "Chuck" (1945)
*Gardiner, Herbert Martin "Herb" (1958)
*Gardner, James Henry "Jimmy" (1962)
Geoffrion, Jos. A. Bernard "Boom Boom" (1972)
*Gerard, Eddie (1945)
Giacomin, Edward "Eddie" (1987)
Gilbert, Rodrigue Gabriel "Rod" (1982)
*Gilmour, Hamilton Livingstone "Billy" (1962)
*Goheen, Frank Xavier "Moose" (1952)
*Goodfellow, Ebenezer R. "Ebbie" (1963)
*Grant, Michael "Mike" (1950)
*Green, Wilfred "Shorty" (1962)
*Griffis, Silas Seth "Si" (1950)
*Hainsworth, George (1961)
Hall, Glenn Henry (1975)
*Hall, Joseph Henry (1961)
*Harvey, Douglas Norman (1973)
*Hay, George (1958)
*Hern, William Milton "Riley" (1962)
Hextall, Bryan Aldwyn (1969)
*Holmes, Harry "Hap" (1972)
*Hooper, Charles Thomas "Tom" (1962)
Horner, George Reginald "Red" (1965)
*Horton, Miles Gilbert "Tim" (1977)
Howe, Gordon (1972)
*Howe, Sydney Harris (1965)
Howell, Henry Vernon "Harry" (1979)
Hull, Robert Marvin (1983)
*Hutton, John Bower "Bouse" (1962)
*Hyland, Harry M. (1962)
*Irvin, James Dickenson "Dick" (1958)
*Jackson, Harvey "Busher" (1971)
*Johnson, Ernest "Moose" (1952)
*Johnson, Ivan "Ching" (1958)
Johnson, Thomas Christian (1970)
*Joliat, Aurel (1947)

*Keats, Gordon "Duke" (1958)
Kelly, Leonard Patrick "Red" (1969)
Kennedy, Theodore Samuel "Teeder" (1966)
Keon, David Michael (1986)
Lach, Elmer James (1966)
Lafleur, Guy Damien (1988)
*Lalonde, Edouard Charles "Newsy" (1950)
Laperriere, Jacques (1987)
*Laviolette, Jean Baptiste "Jack" (1962)
*Lehman, Hugh (1958)
Lemaire, Jacques Gerard (1984)
*LeSueur, Percy (1961)
Lewis, Herbert A. (1989)
Lindsay, Robert Blake Theodore "Ted" (1966)
Lumley, Harry (1980)
*MacKay, Duncan "Mickey" (1952)
Mahovlich, Frank William (1981)
*Malone, Joseph "Joe" (1950)
*Mantha, Sylvio (1960)
*Marshall, John "Jack" (1965)
*Maxwell, Fred G. "Steamer" (1962)
*McGee, Frank (1945)
*McGimsie, William George "Billy" (1962)
*McNamara, George (1958)
Mikita, Stanley (1983)
Moore, Richard Winston (1974)
*Moran, Patrick Joseph "Paddy" (1958)
*Morenz, Howie (1945)
*Mosienko, William "Billy" (1965)
*Nighbor, Frank (1947)
*Noble, Edward Reginald "Reg" (1962)
*O'Connor, Herbert William "Buddy" (1988)
*Oliver, Harry (1967)
Olmstead, Murray Bert "Bert" (1985)
Orr, Robert Gordon (1979)
Parent, Bernard Marcel (1984)
Park, Douglas Bradford "Brad" (1988)
*Patrick, Joseph Lynn (1980)
*Patrick, Lester (1947)
Perreault, Gilbert (1990)
Phillips, Tommy (1945)
Pilote, Joseph Albert Pierre Paul (1975)
*Pitre, Didier "Pit" (1962)
*Plante, Joseph Jacques Omer (1978)
*Pratt, Walter "Babe" (1966)
*Primeau, A. Joseph (1963)
Pronovost, Joseph Reńe Marcel (1978)
*Pulford, Harvey (1945)

HOCKEY HALL OF FAME AND MUSEUM

Quackenbush, Hubert George "Bill" (1976)
*Rankin, Frank (1961)
Ratelle, Joseph Gilbert Yvan Jean "Jean" (1985)
Rayner, Claude Earl "Chuck" (1973)
Reardon, Kenneth Joseph (1966)
Richard, Joseph Henri (1979)
Richard, Joseph Henri Maurice "Rocket" (1961)
*Richardson, George Taylor (1950)
*Roberts, Gordon (1971)
*Ross, Arthur Howie (1945)
*Russel, Blair (1965)
*Russell, Ernest (1965)
*Ruttan, J.D. "Jack" (1962)
Savard, Serge A. (1986)
*Sawchuk, Terrance Gordon "Terry" (1971)
*Scanlan, Fred (1965)
Schmidt, Milton Conrad "Milt" (1961)
*Schriner, David "Sweeney" (1962)
*Seibert, Earl Walter (1963)
*Seibert, Oliver Levi (1961)
*Shore, Edward W. "Eddie" (1947)
*Siebert, Albert C. "Babe" (1964)
*Simpson, Harold Edward "Bullet Joe" (1962)
Sittler, Daryl Glen (1989)
*Smith, Alfred E. (1962)
*Smith, Reginald "Hooley" (1972)
*Smith, Thomas James (1973)
Stanley, Allan Herbert (1981)
*Stanley, Russell "Barney" (1962)
*Stewart, John Sherratt "Black Jack" (1964)
*Stewart, Nelson "Nels" (1962)
*Stuart, Bruce (1961)
*Stuart, Hod (1945)
*Taylor, Frederic "Cyclone" (O.B.E.) (1947)
*Thompson, Cecil R. "Tiny" (1959)
Tretiak, Vladislav (1989)
*Trihey, Col. Harry J. (1950)
Ullman, Norman Victor Alexander "Norm" (1982)
*Vezina, Georges (1945)
*Walker, John Phillip "Jack" (1960)
*Walsh, Martin "Marty" (1962)
*Watson, Harry E. (1962)
*Weiland, Ralph "Cooney" (1971)
*Westwick, Harry (1962)
*Whitcroft, Fred (1962)
*Wilson, Gordon Allan "Phat" (1962)
Worsley, Lorne John "Gump" (1980)
*Worters, Roy (1969)

BUILDERS

*Adams, Charles Francis (1960)
*Adams, Weston W. (1972)
*Ahearn, Thomas Franklin "Frank" (1962)
*Ahearne, John Francis "Bunny" (1977)
*Allan, Sir Montagu (C.V.O.) (1945)
*Ballard, Harold Edwin (1977)
*Bauer, Father David (1989)
*Bickell, John Paris (1978)
*Brown, George V. (1961)
*Brown, Walter A. (1962)
Buckland, Frank (1975)
Butterfield, Jack Arlington (1980)
*Calder, Frank (1947)
*Campbell, Angus D. (1964)
*Campbell, Clarence Sutherland (1966)
*Cattarinich, Joseph (1977)
*Dandurand, Joseph Viateur "Leo" (1963)
Dilio, Francis Paul (1964)
*Dudley, George S. (1958)
*Dunn, James A. (1968)
Eagleson, Robert Alan (1989)
Francis, Emile (1982)
*Gibson, Dr. John L. "Jack" (1976)
*Gorman, Thomas Patrick "Tommy" (1963)
Hanley, William (1986)
*Hay, Charles (1974)
*Hendy, James C. (1968)
*Hewitt, Foster (1965)
*Hewitt, William Abraham (1947)
*Hume, Fred J. (1962)
*Imlach, George "Punch" (1984)
Ivan, Thomas N. (1974)
*Jennings, William M. (1975)
Juckes, Gordon W. (1979)
*Kilpatrick, Gen. John Reed (1960)
*Leader, George Alfred (1969)
LeBel, Robert (1970)
*Lockhart, Thomas F. (1965)
*Loicq, Paul (1961)
*Mariucci, John (1985)
*McLaughlin, Major Frederic (1963)
*Milford, John "Jake" (1984)
Molson, Hon. Hartland de Montarville (1973)
*Nelson, Francis (1947)
*Norris, Bruce A. (1969)
*Norris, Sr., James (1958)
*Norris, James Dougan (1962)
*Northey, William M. (1947)
*O'Brien, John Ambrose (1962)
*Patrick, Frank (1958)
*Pickard, Allan W. (1958)
Pilous, Rudy (1985)
Poile, Norman "Bud" (1990)
Pollock, Samuel Patterson Smyth (1978)
*Raymond, Sen. Donat (1958)
*Robertson, John Ross (1947)
*Robinson, Claude C. (1947)
*Ross, Philip D. (1976)
*Selke, Frank J. (1960)
Sinden, Harry James (1983)
*Smith, Frank D. (1962)
^Smythe, Conn (1958)
Snider, Edward M. (1988)
*Stanley of Preston, Lord (G.C.B.) (1945)
*Sutherland, Cap. James T. (1947)
Tarasov, Anatoli V. (1974)
*Turner, Lloyd (1958)
*Tutt, William Thayer (1978)
Voss, Carl Potter (1974)
*Waghorn, Fred C. (1961)
*Wirtz, Arthur Michael (1971)
Wirtz, William W. "Bill" (1976)
Ziegler, John A. Jr. (1987)

REFEREES/LINESMEN

Ashley, John George (1981)
Chadwick, William L. (1964)
*Elliott, Chaucer (1961)
*Hayes, George William (1988)
*Hewitson, Robert W. (1963)
*Ion, Fred J. "Mickey" (1961)
Pavelich, Matt (1987)
*Rodden, Michael J. "Mike" (1962)
*Smeaton, J. Cooper (1961)
Storey, Roy Alvin "Red" (1967)
Udvari, Frank Joseph (1973)

*Deceased

United States Hockey Hall of Fame

The United States Hockey Hall of Fame is located in Eveleth, Minnesota, 60 miles north of Duluth, on Highway 53. The facility is open Monday to Saturday 9 a.m. to 5 p.m. and Sundays noon to 5 p.m. from the day after Labor Day until June 14. During the remaining summer period the Monday to Saturday hours are 9 a.m. to 8 p.m. and Sundays 10 a.m. to 8 p.m.; Adult $2.50; Seniors $2.25; Juniors $1.50; and Children 7-12 $1.25; Children under 6 free. Group rates available.

The Hall was dedicated and opened on June 21, 1973, largely as the result of the work of D. Kelly Campbell, Chairman of the Eveleth Civic Association's Project H Committee. The National Hockey League contributed $100,000 towards the construction of the building. There are now 70 enshrinees consisting of 45 players, 10 coaches, 14 administrators, and one referee. New members are inducted annually in October and must have made a significant contribution toward hockey in the United States through the vehicle of their careers.

PLAYERS
*Abel, Clarence "Taffy"
*Baker, Hobart "Hobey"
Bartholome, Earl
Bessone, Peter
Blake, Robert
Brimsek, Frank
*Chaisson, Ray
Chase, John P.
Christian, Roger
Christian, William "Bill"
Cleary, Robert
Cleary, William
*Conroy, Anthony
Dahlstrom, Carl "Cully"
DesJardins, Victor
Desmond, Richard
Dill, Robert
Everett, Doug
*Garrison, John B.
Garrity, Jack
*Goheen, Frank "Moose"
Harding, Austin "Austie"
Iglehart, Stewart
Johnson, Virgil
Karakas, Mike
Kirrane, Jack
Lane, Myles J.
*Linder, Joseph
*LoPresti, Sam L.
*Mariucci, John
Mayasich, John
McCartan, Jack
Moe, William
Moseley, Fred
*Murray, Hugh "Muzz" Sr.
*Nelson, Hubert "Hub"
Olson , Eddie
*Owen, Jr., George
*Palmer, Winthrop
Paradise, Robert
Purpur, Clifford "Fido"
Riley, William
*Romnes, Elwin "Doc"
Rondeau, Richard
Williams, Thomas
*Winters, Frank "Coddy"
Yackel, Ken

COACHES
*Almquist, Oscar
*Gordon, Malcolm K.
Heyliger, Victor
*Jeremiah, Edward J.
*Kelley, John "Snooks"
Riley, Jack
Ross, Larry
*Thompson, Clifford, R.
*Stewart, William
*Winsor, Alfred "Ralph"

ADMINISTRATORS
*Brown, George V.
*Brown, Walter A.
Bush, Walter
Clark, Donald
*Gibson, J.C. "Doc"
*Jennings, William M.
*Kahler, Nick
*Lockhart, Thomas F.
Marvin, Cal
Ridder, Robert
Trumble, Harold
*Tutt, William Thayer
Wirtz, William W. "Bill"
*Wright, Lyle Z.

REFEREE
Chadwick, William

*Deceased

William Jennings is an honored member of both the U.S. Hockey Hall of Fame in Eveleth, MN and the Hockey Hall of Fame in Toronto, Ontario. He began his association with hockey in 1959, becoming president of the New York Rangers in 1962. Jennings worked for recognition of American participation in the game and established the Lester Patrick Award for service to hockey in the U.S. in 1966. He was a recipient of this award in 1971 in part for his efforts to facilitate the expansion of the NHL. After his death in 1981, the William Jennings Trophy was established to honor the goaltender(s) on the NHL team allowing the fewest goals-against.

1990 Stanley Cup Playoffs

Craig Simpson led all scorers in the 1990 playoffs with 16 goals in 22 games.

Results

Prince of Wales Conference

DIVISION SEMI-FINALS
(Best of seven series)

Series 'A'
Thu. Apr. 5	Hartford 4	at Boston 3
Sat. Apr. 7	Hartford 1	at Boston 3
Mon. Apr. 9	Boston 3	at Hartford 5
Wed. Apr. 11	Boston 6	at Hartford 5
Fri. Apr. 13	Hartford 2	at Boston 3
Sun. Apr. 15	Boston 2	at Hartford 3*
Tue. Apr. 17	Hartford 1	at Boston 3

* Kevin Dineen scored at 12:30 of overtime
Boston won series 4-3

Series 'B'
Thu. Apr. 5	Montreal 1	at Buffalo 4
Sat. Apr. 7	Montreal 3	at Buffalo 0
Mon. Apr. 9	Buffalo 1	at Montreal 2*
Wed. Apr. 11	Buffalo 4	at Montreal 2
Fri. Apr. 13	Montreal 4	at Buffalo 2
Sun. Apr. 15	Buffalo 2	at Montreal 5

* Brian Skrudland scored at 12:35 of overtime
Montreal won series 4-2

Series 'C'
Thu. Apr. 5	NY Islanders 1	at NY Rangers 2
Sat. Apr. 7	NY Islanders 2	at NY Rangers 5
Mon. Apr. 9	NY Rangers 3	at NY Islanders 4*
Wed. Apr. 11	NY Rangers 6	at NY Islanders 1
Fri. Apr. 13	NY Islanders 5	at NY Rangers 6

* Brent Sutter scored at 20:59 of overtime
NY Rangers won series 4-1

Series 'D'
Thu. Apr. 5	Washington 5	at New Jersey 4*
Sat. Apr. 7	Washington 5	at New Jersey 6
Mon. Apr. 9	New Jersey 2	at Washington 1
Wed. Apr. 11	New Jersey 1	at Washington 3
Fri. Apr. 13	Washington 4	at New Jersey 3
Sun. Apr. 15	New Jersey 2	at Washington 3

* Dino Ciccarelli scored at 5:34 of overtime
Washington won series 4-2

DIVISION FINALS
(Best-of-seven series)

Series 'I'
Thu. Apr. 19	Montreal 0	at Boston 1
Sat. Apr. 21	Montreal 4	at Boston 5*
Mon. Apr. 23	Boston 6	at Montreal 3
Wed. Apr. 25	Boston 1	at Montreal 4
Fri. Apr. 27	Montreal 1	at Boston 3

* Garry Galley scored at 3:42 of overtime
Boston won series 4-1

Series 'J'
Thu. Apr. 19	Washington 3	at NY Rangers 7
Sat. Apr. 21	Washington 6	at NY Rangers 3
Mon. Apr. 23	NY Rangers 1	at Washington 7
Wed. Apr. 25	NY Rangers 3	at Washington 4*
Fri. Apr. 27	Washington 2	at NY Rangers 1**

* Rod Langway scored at 0:34 of overtime
** John Druce scored at 6:48 of overtime
Washington won series 4-1

CONFERENCE CHAMPIONSHIPS
(Best-of-seven series)

Series 'M'
Thu. May 3	Washington 3	at Boston 5
Sat. May 5	Washington 0	at Boston 3
Mon. May 7	Boston 4	at Washington 1
Wed. May 9	Boston 3	at Washington 2

Boston won series 4-0

Clarence Campbell Conference

Series 'E'
Wed. Apr. 4	Minnesota 2	at Chicago 1
Fri. Apr. 6	Minnesota 3	at Chicago 5
Sun. Apr. 8	Chicago 2	at Minnesota 1
Tue. Apr. 10	Chicago 0	at Minnesota 4
Thu. Apr. 12	Minnesota 1	at Chicago 5
Sat. Apr. 14	Chicago 3	at Minnesota 5
Mon. Apr. 16	Minnesota 2	at Chicago 5

Chicago won series 4-3

Series 'F'
Wed. Apr. 4	Toronto 2	at St. Louis 4
Fri. Apr. 6	Toronto 2	at St. Louis 4
Sun. Apr. 8	St. Louis 6	at Toronto 5*
Tue. Apr. 10	St. Louis 2	at Toronto 4
Thu. Apr. 12	Toronto 3	at St. Louis 4

* Sergio Momesso scored at 6:04 of overtime
St. Louis won series 4-1

Series 'G'
Wed. Apr. 4	Los Angeles 5	at Calgary 3
Fri. Apr. 6	Los Angeles 5	at Calgary 8
Sun. Apr. 8	Calgary 1	at Los Angeles 2*
Tue. Apr. 10	Calgary 4	at Los Angeles 12
Thu. Apr. 12	Los Angeles 1	at Calgary 5
Sat. Apr. 14	Calgary 3	at Los Angeles 4**

* Tony Granato scored at 8:37 of overtime
** Mike Krushelnyski scored at 23:14 of overtime
Los Angeles won series 4-2

Series 'H'
Wed. Apr. 4	Winnipeg 7	at Edmonton 5
Fri. Apr. 6	Winnipeg 2	at Edmonton 3*
Sun. Apr. 8	Edmonton 1	at Winnipeg 2
Tue. Apr. 10	Edmonton 3	at Winnipeg 4**
Thu. Apr. 12	Winnipeg 3	at Edmonton 4
Sat. Apr. 14	Edmonton 4	at Winnipeg 3
Mon. Apr. 16	Winnipeg 1	at Edmonton 4

* Mark Lamb scored at 4:21 of overtime
** Dave Ellett scored at 21:08 of overtime
Edmonton won series 4-3

Series 'K'
Wed. Apr. 18	St Louis 4	at Chicago 3
Fri. Apr. 20	St Louis 3	at Chicago 5
Sun. Apr. 22	Chicago 4	at St Louis 5
Tue. Apr. 24	Chicago 3	at St Louis 2
Thu. Apr. 26	St Louis 2	at Chicago 3
Sat. Apr. 28	Chicago 2	at St Louis 4
Mon. Apr. 30	St Louis 2	at Chicago 8

Chicago won series 4-3

Series 'L'
Wed. Apr. 18	Los Angeles 0	at Edmonton 7
Fri. Apr. 20	Los Angeles 1	at Edmonton 6
Sun. Apr. 22	Edmonton 5	at Los Angeles 4
Tue. Apr. 24	Edmonton 6	at Los Angeles 5*

* Joe Murphy scored at 4:42 of overtime
Edmonton won series 4-0

Series 'N'
Wed. May 2	Chicago 2	at Edmonton 5
Fri. May 4	Chicago 4	at Edmonton 3
Sun. May 6	Edmonton 1	at Chicago 5
Tue. May 8	Edmonton 4	at Chicago 2
Thu. May 10	Chicago 3	at Edmonton 4
Sat. May 12	Edmonton 8	at Chicago 4

Edmonton won series 4-2

STANLEY CUP CHAMPIONSHIP
(Best-of-seven series)

Series 'O'
Tue. May 15	Edmonton 3	at Boston 2*
Fri. May 18	Edmonton 7	at Boston 2
Sun. May 20	Boston 2	at Edmonton 1
Tue. May 22	Boston 1	at Edmonton 5
Thu. May 24	Edmonton 4	at Boston 1

* Petr Klima scored at 55:13 of overtime
Edmonton won series 4-1

Team Playoff Records

	GP	W	L	GF	GA	%
Edmonton	22	16	6	93	60	.727
Boston	21	13	8	62	59	.619
Chicago	20	10	10	69	65	.500
Washington	15	8	7	49	48	.533
St Louis	12	7	5	42	44	.583
NY Rangers	10	5	5	37	35	.500
Montreal	11	5	6	29	29	.455
Los Angeles	10	4	6	39	48	.400
Winnipeg	7	3	4	22	24	.429
Hartford	7	3	4	21	23	.429
Minnesota	7	3	4	18	21	.429
Calgary	6	2	4	24	29	.333
New Jersey	6	2	4	18	21	.333
Buffalo	6	2	4	13	17	.333
Toronto	5	1	4	16	20	.200
NY Islanders	5	1	4	13	22	.200

Individual Leaders

Abbreviations: * – rookie eligible for Calder Trophy; **A** – assists; **G** – goals; **GP** – games played; **GW** – game-winning goals; **OT** – overtime goals; **PIM** – penalties in minutes; **PP** – power play goals; **PTS** – points; **S** – shots on goal; **SH** – short-handed goals; **%** – percentage of shots resulting in goals; +/– – difference between Goals For (**GF**) scored when a player is on the ice with his team at even strength or short-handed and Goals Against (**GA**) scored when the same player is on the ice with his team at even strength or on a power play.

Playoff Scoring Leaders

Player	Team	GP	G	A	Pts	+/−	PIM	PP	SH	GW	OT	S	%
Craig Simpson	Edmonton	22	16	15	31	11	8	6	0	3	0	42	38.1
Mark Messier	Edmonton	22	9	22	31	5	20	1	1	1	0	47	19.1
Cam Neely	Boston	21	12	16	28	7	51	4	1	2	0	65	18.5
Jari Kurri	Edmonton	22	10	15	25	13	18	6	0	3	0	58	17.2
Esa Tikkanen	Edmonton	22	13	11	24	12	26	2	2	0	0	54	24.1
Glenn Anderson	Edmonton	22	10	12	22	12	20	2	0	2	0	46	21.7
Steve Larmer	Chicago	20	7	15	22	8	8	2	2	2	0	67	10.4
Denis Savard	Chicago	20	7	15	22	0	41	4	0	1	0	69	10.1
Craig Janney	Boston	18	3	19	22	3	2	1	0	2	0	27	11.1
Brett Hull	St Louis	12	13	8	21	1	17	7	0	3	0	68	19.1
*Jeremy Roenick	Chicago	20	11	7	18	1−	8	4	0	1	0	47	23.4
John Druce	Washington	15	14	3	17	2−	23	8	0	4	1	44	31.8
Mark Lamb	Edmonton	22	6	11	17	12	2	1	0	2	1	34	17.6
Ray Bourque	Boston	17	5	12	17	11	16	1	0	0	0	64	7.8
Wayne Presley	Chicago	19	9	6	15	8	29	1	1	1	0	44	20.5
Steve Smith	Edmonton	22	5	10	15	15	37	0	1	1	0	35	14.3
Randy Burridge	Boston	21	4	11	15	2	14	0	1	0	0	39	10.3
Doug Wilson	Chicago	20	3	12	15	5	18	1	0	1	0	64	4.7
Joe Murphy	Edmonton	22	6	8	14	1	16	0	0	2	1	29	20.7
Adam Oates	St Louis	12	2	12	14	10−	4	1	0	0	0	27	7.4

Playoff Defensemen Scoring Leaders

Player	Team	GP	G	A	Pts	+/−	PIM	PP	SH	GW	OT	S	%
Ray Bourque	Boston	17	5	12	17	11	16	1	0	0	0	64	7.8
Steve Smith	Edmonton	22	5	10	15	15	37	0	1	1	0	35	14.3
Doug Wilson	Chicago	20	3	12	15	5	18	1	0	1	0	64	4.7
Reijo Ruotsalainen	Edmonton	22	2	11	13	13	12	1	0	0	0	55	3.6
Jeff Brown	St Louis	12	2	10	12	6−	4	1	0	1	0	42	4.8
James Patrick	NY Rangers	10	3	8	11	2−	0	2	0	1	0	25	12.0
Steve Duchesne	Los Angeles	10	2	9	11	2−	6	1	0	0	0	32	6.3
Scott Stevens	Washington	15	2	7	9	1−	25	1	0	0	0	35	5.7
Trent Yawney	Chicago	20	3	5	8	1−	27	3	0	1	0	27	11.1
Randy Gregg	Edmonton	20	2	6	8	1	16	1	0	0	0	17	11.8
Glen Wesley	Boston	21	2	6	8	6	36	0	0	1	0	30	6.7
Kevin Hatcher	Washington	11	0	8	8	4	32	0	0	0	0	37	.0

GOALTENDING LEADERS

(Minimum 240 Minutes)

Goals Against Average

Goaltender	Team	GPI	Mins.	GA	AVG
Andy Moog	Boston	20	1195	44	2.21
Patrick Roy	Montreal	11	641	26	2.43
Daren Puppa	Buffalo	6	370	15	2.43
*Ed Belfour	Chicago	9	409	17	2.49
Bill Ranford	Edmonton	22	1401	59	2.53

Wins

Goaltender	Team	GPI	Mins.	W	L
Bill Ranford	Edmonton	22	1401	16	6
Andy Moog	Boston	20	1195	13	7
Greg Millen	Chicago	14	613	6	6
Patrick Roy	Montreal	11	641	5	6

Save Percentage

Goaltender	Team	GPI	Mins.	GA	SA	S%	W	L
Daren Puppa	Buffalo	6	370	15	192	.921	2	4
*Ed Belfour	Chicago	9	409	17	200	.915	4	2
Bill Ranford	Edmonton	22	1401	59	672	.912	16	6
Patrick Roy	Montreal	11	641	26	292	.911	5	6
Andy Moog	Boston	20	1195	44	486	.909	13	7

Shutouts

Goaltender	Team	GPI	Mins.	SO	W	L
Andy Moog	Boston	20	1195	2	13	7
Jon Casey	Minnesota	7	415	1	3	4
Patrick Roy	Montreal	11	641	1	5	6
Bill Ranford	Edmonton	22	1401	1	16	6

Goal Scoring

Name	Team	GP	G
Craig Simpson	Edmonton	22	16
John Druce	Washington	15	14
Brett Hull	St Louis	12	13
Esa Tikkanen	Edmonton	22	13
Cam Neely	Boston	21	12

Assists

Name	Team	GP	A
Mark Messier	Edmonton	22	22
Craig Janney	Boston	18	19
Cam Neely	Boston	21	16
Steve Larmer	Chicago	20	15
Denis Savard	Chicago	20	15
Jari Kurri	Edmonton	22	15
Craig Simpson	Edmonton	22	15

Power-Play Goals

Name	Team	GP	PP
John Druce	Washington	15	8
Brett Hull	St Louis	12	7
Jari Kurri	Edmonton	22	6
Craig Simpson	Edmonton	22	6
Rick Vaive	Buffalo	6	4
Mike Gartner	NY Rangers	10	4
*Jeremy Roenick	Chicago	20	4
Denis Savard	Chicago	20	4
Cam Neely	Boston	21	4

Short-Hand Goals

Name	Team	GP	SH
Steve Larmer	Chicago	20	2
Esa Tikkanen	Edmonton	22	2

22 Players with one

Game-Winning Goals

Name	Team	GP	GW
John Druce	Washington	15	4
Brett Hull	St Louis	12	3
Steve Thomas	Chicago	20	3
Jari Kurri	Edmonton	22	3
Craig Simpson	Edmonton	22	3

Overtime Goals

Name	Team	GP	OT
Brent Sutter	NY Islanders	5	1
Kevin Dineen	Hartford	6	1
Dave Ellett	Winnipeg	7	1
Dino Ciccarelli	Washington	8	1
Tony Granato	Los Angeles	10	1
Mike Krushelnyski	Los Angeles	10	1
Brian Skrudland	Montreal	11	1
Sergio Momesso	St Louis	12	1
John Druce	Washington	15	1
Rod Langway	Washington	15	1
Garry Galley	Boston	21	1
Petr Klima	Edmonton	21	1
Mark Lamb	Edmonton	22	1
Joe Murphy	Edmonton	22	1

Shots

Name	Team	GP	S
Denis Savard	Chicago	20	69
Brett Hull	St Louis	12	68
Steve Larmer	Chicago	20	67
Cam Neely	Boston	21	65
Ray Bourque	Boston	17	64
Doug Wilson	Chicago	20	64

First Goals

Name	Team	GP	FG
Glenn Anderson	Edmonton	22	5
Brett Hull	St Louis	12	3
Esa Tikkanen	Edmonton	22	3

12 Players with two

Plus/Minus

Name	Team	GP	+/−
Steve Smith	Edmonton	22	15
Jari Kurri	Edmonton	22	13
R. Ruotsalainen	Edmonton	22	13
Glenn Anderson	Edmonton	22	12
Mark Lamb	Edmonton	22	12
Esa Tikkanen	Edmonton	22	12

Team Statistics

TEAMS' HOME-AND-ROAD RECORD

			Home							Road			
	GP	W	L	GF	GA	%	GP	W	L	GF	GA	%
EDM	11	8	3	47	26	.727	11	8	3	46	34	.727
BOS	12	8	4	34	30	.667	9	5	4	28	29	.556
CHI	11	7	4	46	32	.636	9	3	6	23	33	.333
WSH	7	4	3	21	16	.571	8	4	4	28	32	.500
STL	6	5	1	23	16	.833	6	2	4	19	28	.333
NYR	6	4	2	24	19	.667	4	1	3	13	16	.250
MTL	5	3	2	16	14	.600	6	2	4	13	15	.333
L.A.	5	3	2	27	19	.600	5	1	4	12	29	.200
WPG	3	2	1	9	8	.667	4	1	3	13	16	.250
HFD	3	2	1	13	11	.667	4	1	3	8	12	.250
MIN	3	2	1	10	5	.667	4	1	3	8	16	.250
CGY	3	2	1	16	11	.667	3	0	3	8	18	.000
N.J.	3	1	2	13	14	.333	3	1	2	5	7	.333
BUF	3	1	2	6	8	.333	3	1	2	7	9	.333
TOR	2	1	1	9	8	.500	3	0	3	7	12	.000
NYI	2	1	1	5	9	.500	3	0	3	8	13	.000
TOTAL	85	54	31	319	246	.635	85	31	54	246	319	.365

TEAMS' POWER PLAY RECORD

Abbreviations: ADV-total advantages; **PPGF**-power play goals for; **%** arrived by dividing number of power-play goals by total advantages.

		Home						Road						Overall		
	Team	GP	ADV	PPGF	%	Team	GP	ADV	PPGF	%	Team	GP	ADV	PPGF	%
1	NYI	2	12	4	33.3	BUF	3	14	4	28.6	STL	12	62	16	25.8
2	STL	6	33	9	27.3	MIN	4	24	6	25.0	NYR	10	63	15	23.8
3	NYR	6	37	10	27.0	WPG	4	20	5	25.0	EDM	22	99	21	21.2
4	EDM	11	57	13	22.8	STL	6	29	7	24.1	BUF	6	30	6	20.0
5	N.J.	3	19	4	21.1	L.A.	5	32	7	21.9	WPG	7	36	7	19.4
6	WSH	7	39	8	20.5	NYR	4	26	5	19.2	MIN	7	43	8	18.6
7	BOS	12	58	11	19.0	EDM	11	42	8	19.0	WSH	15	71	13	18.3
8	CHI	11	65	12	18.5	WSH	8	32	5	15.6	L.A.	10	65	11	16.9
9	HFD	3	11	2	18.2	CHI	9	44	6	13.6	CHI	20	109	18	16.5
10	TOR	2	12	2	16.7	TOR	3	16	2	12.5	N.J.	6	31	5	16.1
11	BUF	3	16	2	12.5	BOS	9	35	4	11.4	BOS	21	93	15	16.1
12	WPG	3	16	2	12.5	N.J.	3	12	1	8.3	NYI	5	26	4	15.4
13	L.A.	5	33	4	12.1	HFD	4	23	1	4.3	TOR	5	28	4	14.3
14	CGY	3	17	2	11.8	MTL	6	28	1	3.6	HFD	7	34	3	8.8
15	MIN	3	19	2	10.5	NYI	3	14	0	.0	CGY	6	33	2	6.1
16	MTL	5	23	1	4.3	CGY	3	16	0	.0	MTL	11	51	2	3.9
	TOTAL	85	467	88	18.8		85	407	62	15.2		85	874	150	17.2

TEAMS' PENALTY KILLING RECORD

Abbreviations: TSH-Total times short-handed; **PPGA**-power play goals against; **%** arrived by dividing-times short minus power-play goals against-by times short.

		Home						Road						Overall		
	Team	GP	TSH	PPGA	%	Team	GP	TSH	PPGA	%	Team	GP	TSH	PPGA	%
1	MIN	3	15	0	100.0	BUF	3	16	1	93.8	BUF	6	29	2	93.1
2	L.A.	5	22	1	95.5	EDM	11	50	6	88.0	BOS	21	88	9	89.8
3	BOS	12	53	4	92.5	MTL	6	33	4	87.9	MIN	7	43	5	88.4
4	BUF	3	13	1	92.3	N.J.	3	16	2	87.5	N.J.	6	29	4	86.2
5	NYR	6	26	2	92.3	BOS	9	35	5	85.7	L.A.	10	49	7	85.7
6	HFD	3	9	1	88.9	CGY	3	24	4	83.3	EDM	22	98	14	85.7
7	WSH	7	35	4	88.6	CHI	9	52	9	82.7	MTL	11	56	9	83.9
8	N.J.	3	13	2	84.6	STL	6	34	6	82.4	WSH	15	79	13	83.5
9	WPG	3	13	2	84.6	MIN	4	28	5	82.1	STL	12	70	12	82.9
10	STL	6	36	6	83.3	WPG	4	20	4	80.0	WPG	7	33	6	81.8
11	EDM	11	48	8	83.3	WSH	8	44	9	79.5	CHI	20	109	22	79.8
12	MTL	5	23	5	78.3	L.A.	5	27	6	77.8	NYR	10	54	11	79.6
13	CHI	11	57	13	77.2	TOR	3	17	5	70.6	CGY	6	46	10	78.3
14	TOR	2	11	3	72.7	NYI	3	20	6	70.0	HFD	7	32	8	75.0
15	CGY	3	22	6	72.7	HFD	4	23	7	69.6	TOR	5	28	8	71.4
16	NYI	2	11	4	63.6	NYR	4	28	9	67.9	NYI	5	31	10	67.7
	TOTAL	85	407	62	84.8		85	467	88	81.2		85	874	150	82.8

SHORT-HANDED GOALS

	For			Against	
Team	Games	Goals	Team	Games	Goals
CHI	20	5	BUF	6	0
NYR	10	4	N.J.	6	0
EDM	22	4	BOS	21	1
WSH	15	3	CHI	20	1
BOS	21	3	HFD	7	1
CGY	6	2	CGY	6	1
L.A.	10	2	TOR	5	1
TOR	5	1	EDM	22	2
N.J.	6	1	MTL	11	2
STL	12	1	NYR	10	2
NYI	5	0	MIN	7	2
BUF	6	0	WPG	7	2
HFD	7	0	NYI	5	2
MIN	7	0	WSH	15	3
WPG	7	0	STL	12	3
MTL	11	0	L.A.	10	3
TOTAL	85	26	**TOTAL**	85	26

Team Penalties

Abbreviations: GP – games played; **PEN** – total penalty minutes, including bench penalites; **BMI** – total bench penalty minutes; **AVG** – average penalty minutes per game.

Team	Games	PEN	BMI	AVG
EDM	22	288	0	13.1
WPG	7	110	0	15.7
L.A.	10	164	2	16.4
BOS	21	421	12	20.0
HFD	7	143	2	20.4
BUF.	6	126	2	21.0
MTL	11	235	4	21.4
CGY	6	149	2	24.8
CHI	20	532	6	26.6
NYR	10	291	2	29.1
WSH	15	480	0	32.0
NYI	5	175	0	35.0
STL	12	432	2	36.0
N.J.	6	225	2	37.5
MIN	7	274	14	39.1
TOR	5	257	0	51.4
TOTAL	85	4302	54	50.6

During the 1990 playoffs, John Druce (top) of Washington had four game-winning goals while Steve Larmer (bottom) of Chicago had 22 points in 20 games.

Stanley Cup Record Book

THE STANLEY CUP

Awarded annually to the team winning the National Hockey League's best-of-seven final playoff round. It is symbolic of the World's Professional Hockey Championship.

The first four teams in each division at the end of the regular schedule advance to the playoffs. In each division, the first-place team opposes the fourth-place club while the second and third-place teams meet, all in best-of-seven Division Semi-Finals. The winners oppose the other winners in each division in best-of-seven Division Final Series. The division winners then play the opposite winners in each of the two conferences in best-of-seven Conference Championships. The Prince of Wales Conference champions then meet the Clarence Campbell Conference champions in the best-of-seven Stanley Cup Championship Series.

History: The Stanley Cup, the oldest trophy competed for by professional athletes in North America, was donated by Frederick Arthur, Lord Stanley of Preston and son of the Earl of Derby, in 1893. Lord Stanley purchased the trophy for 10 guineas ($50 at that time) for presentation to the amateur hockey champions of Canada. Since 1910, when the National Hockey Association took possession of the Stanley Cup, the trophy has been the symbol of professional hockey supremacy. It has been competed for only by NHL teams since 1926 and has been under the exclusive control of the NHL since 1946.

1989-90 Winner: Edmonton Oilers

The Edmonton Oilers won their fifth Stanley Cup championship since 1984 by defeating the Boston Bruins in five games.

The Oilers won game one in Boston after 55 minutes of overtime and went on to take a 2-0 lead in games with a 7-2 victory in game two. Boston won game three 2-1 in Edmonton before the Oilers clinched the Cup with 5-1 and 4-1 wins in games four and five.

STANLEY CUP WINNERS PRIOR TO FORMATION OF NHL IN 1917

Season	Champion	Challenger
1916-17	Seattle Metropolitans	Montreal Canadiens
1915-16	Montreal Canadiens	Portland Rosebuds
1914-15	Vancouver Millionaires	Ottawa Senators
1913-14	Toronto Blueshirts	Victoria Cougars
		Montreal Canadiens
1912-13**	Quebec Bulldogs	Sydney Miners
1911-12	Quebec Bulldogs	Moncton Victorias
1910-11	Ottawa Senators	Port Arthur Bearcats
		Galt
1909-10	Montreal Wanderers	Berlin Union Jacks
		Edmonton Eskimos
		Galt
1908-09	Ottawa Senators	(no challenger)
1907-08	Montreal Wanderers	Edmonton Eskimos
		Toronto Trolley Leaguers
		Winnipeg Maple Leafs
		Ottawa Victorias
1906-07	Montreal Wanderers (Mar.)	Kenora Thistles
1906-07	Kenora Thistles (Jan.)	Montreal Wanderers
1905-06	Montreal Wanderers (Mar.)	New Glasgow Cubs
		Ottawa Silver Seven
1905-06	Ottawa Silver Seven (Feb.)	Montreal Wanderers
		Smith's Falls
		Queen's University
1904-05	Ottawa Silver Seven	Rat Portage Thistles
		Dawson City Nuggets
1903-04	Ottawa Silver Seven	Brandon Wheat Kings
		Montreal Wanderers
		Toronto Marlboros
		Winnipeg Rowing Club
1902-03	Ottawa Silver Seven (Mar.)	Rat Portage Thistles
		Montreal Victorias
1902-03	Montreal A.A.A. (Feb.)	Winnipeg Victorias
1901-02	Montreal A.A.A. (Mar.)	Winnipeg Victorias
1901-02	Winnipeg Victorias (Jan.)	Toronto Wellingtons
1900-01	Winnipeg Victorias	Montreal Shamrocks
1899-1900	Montreal Shamrocks	Halifax Crescents
		Winnipeg Victorias
1898-99	Montreal Shamrocks (Mar.)	Queen's University
1898-99	Montreal Victorias (Feb.)	Winnipeg Victorias
1897-98	Montreal Victorias	(no challenger)
1896-97	Montreal Victorias	Ottawa Capitals
1895-96	Montreal Victorias (Dec.)	Winnipeg Victorias
1895-96	Winnipeg Victorias (Feb.)	Montreal Victorias
1894-95	Montreal Victorias	(no challenger)
1893-94	Montreal A.A.A.	Ottawa Generals
1892-93	Montreal A.A.A.	(no challenger)

**Victoria defeated Quebec in unofficial challenge series.

STANLEY CUP WINNERS AND FINALISTS

Season	Champion	Finalist	GP in Final
1989-90	Edmonton Oilers	Boston Bruins	5
1988-89	Calgary Flames	Montreal Canadiens	6
1987-88	Edmonton Oilers	Boston Bruins	4
1986-87	Edmonton Oilers	Philadelphia Flyers	7
1985-86	Montreal Canadiens	Calgary Flames	5
1984-85	Edmonton Oilers	Philadelphia Flyers	5
1983-84	Edmonton Oilers	New York Islanders	5
1982-83	New York Islanders	Edmonton Oilers	4
1981-82	New York Islanders	Vancouver Canucks	4
1980-81	New York Islanders	Minnesota North Stars	5
1979-80	New York Islanders	Philadelphia Flyers	6
1978-79	Montreal Canadiens	New York Rangers	5
1977-78	Montreal Canadiens	Boston Bruins	6
1976-77	Montreal Canadiens	Boston Bruins	4
1975-76	Montreal Canadiens	Philadelphia Flyers	4
1974-75	Philadelphia Flyers	Buffalo Sabres	6
1973-74	Philadelphia Flyers	Boston Bruins	6
1972-73	Montreal Canadiens	Chicago Blackhawks	6
1971-72	Boston Bruins	New York Rangers	6
1970-71	Montreal Canadiens	Chicago Blackhawks	7
1969-70	Boston Bruins	St. Louis Blues	4
1968-69	Montreal Canadiens	St. Louis Blues	4
1967-68	Montreal Canadiens	St. Louis Blues	4
1966-67	Toronto Maple Leafs	Montreal Canadiens	6
1965-66	Montreal Canadiens	Detroit Red Wings	6
1964-65	Montreal Canadiens	Chicago Blackhawks	7
1963-64	Toronto Maple Leafs	Detroit Red Wings	7
1962-63	Toronto Maple Leafs	Detroit Red Wings	5
1961-62	Toronto Maple Leafs	Chicago Blackhawks	6
1960-61	Chicago Blackhawks	Detroit Red Wings	6
1959-60	Montreal Canadiens	Toronto Maple Leafs	4
1958-59	Montreal Canadiens	Toronto Maple Leafs	5
1957-58	Montreal Canadiens	Boston Bruins	6
1956-57	Montreal Canadiens	Boston Bruins	5
1955-56	Montreal Canadiens	Detroit Red Wings	5
1954-55	Detroit Red Wings	Montreal Canadiens	7
1953-54	Detroit Red Wings	Montreal Canadiens	7
1952-53	Montreal Canadiens	Boston Bruins	5
1951-52	Detroit Red Wings	Montreal Canadiens	4

Season	Champion	Finalist	GP in Final
1950-51	Toronto Maple Leafs	Montreal Canadiens	5
1949-50	Detroit Red Wings	New York Rangers	7
1948-49	Toronto Maple Leafs	Detroit Red Wings	4
1947-48	Toronto Maple Leafs	Detroit Red Wings	4
1946-47	Toronto Maple Leafs	Montreal Canadiens	6
1945-46	Montreal Canadiens	Boston Bruins	5
1944-45	Toronto Maple Leafs	Detroit Red Wings	7
1943-44	Montreal Canadiens	Chicago Blackhawks	4
1942-43	Detroit Red Wings	Boston Bruins	4
1941-42	Toronto Maple Leafs	Detroit Red Wings	7
1940-41	Boston Bruins	Detroit Red Wings	4
1939-40	New York Rangers	Toronto Maple Leafs	6
1938-39	Boston Bruins	Toronto Maple Leafs	5
1937-38	Chicago Blackhawks	Toronto Maple Leafs	4
1936-37	Detroit Red Wings	New York Rangers	5
1935-36	Detroit Red Wings	Toronto Maple Leafs	4
1934-35	Montreal Maroons	Toronto Maple Leafs	3
1933-34	Chicago Blackhawks	Detroit Red Wings	4
1932-33	New York Rangers	Toronto Maple Leafs	4
1931-32	Toronto Maple Leafs	New York Rangers	3
1930-31	Montreal Canadiens	Chicago Blackhawks	5
1929-30	Montreal Canadiens	Boston Bruins	2
1928-29	Boston Bruins	New York Rangers	2
1927-28	New York Rangers	Montreal Maroons	5
1926-27	Ottawa Senators	Boston Bruins	4
1925-26	Montreal Maroons	Victoria Cougars	4
1924-25	Victoria Cougars	Montreal Canadiens	4
1923-24	Montreal Canadiens	Vancouver, Calgary	2,2
1922-23	Ottawa Senators	Vancouver, Edmonton	3,2
1921-22	Toronto St. Pats	Vancouver Millionaires	5
1920-21	Ottawa Senators	Vancouver Millionaires	5
1919-20	Ottawa Senators	Seattle Metropolitans	5
1918-19	No decision*	No decision*	5
1917-18	Toronto Arenas	Vancouver Millionaires	5

* In the spring of 1919 the Montreal Canadiens travelled to Seattle to meet Seattle, PCHL champions. After five games had been played — teams were tied at 2 wins and 1 tie — the series was called off by the local Department of Health because of the influenza epidemic and the death of Joe Hall from influenza.

Championship Trophies

PRINCE OF WALES TROPHY

Beginning with the 1981-82 season, the club which advances to the Stanley Cup Finals as the winner of the Wales Conference Championship is presented with the Prince of Wales Trophy.

History: His Royal Highnesss, the Prince of Wales, donated the trophy to the National Hockey League in 1924. From 1927-28 through 1937-38, the award was presented to the team finishing first in the American Division of the NHL. From 1938-39, when the NHL reverted to one section, to 1966-67, it was presented to the team winning the NHL championship. With expansion in 1967-68, it again became a divisional trophy, awarded to the champions of the East Division through to the end of the 1973-74 season. Beginning in 1974-75, it was awarded to the regular-season winner of the conference bearing the name of the trophy. Starting with the 1981-82 season, the trophy has been presented to the playoff champion in the Wales Conference.

1989-90 Winner: Boston Bruins

The Boston Bruins captured their second Prince of Wales Trophy in the past three years on May 9, 1990, with a 4-0 series sweep over the Washington Capitals in the Prince of Wales Conference Championship. After series wins over Hartford and Montreal, the Bruins prevailed over the Capitals by scores of 5-3, 3-0, 4-1 and 3-2.

PRINCE OF WALES TROPHY WINNERS

1989-90	**Boston Bruins**	1956-57	Detroit Red Wings
1988-89	Montreal Canadiens	1955-56	Montreal Canadiens
1987-88	Boston Bruins	1954-55	Detroit Red Wings
1986-87	Philadelphia Flyers	1953-54	Detroit Red Wings
1985-86	Montreal Canadiens	1952-53	Detroit Red Wings
1984-85	Philadelphia Flyers	1951-52	Detroit Red Wings
1983-84	New York Islanders	1950-51	Detroit Red Wings
1982-83	New York Islanders	1949-50	Detroit Red Wings
1981-82	New York Islanders	1948-49	Detroit Red Wings
1980-81	Montreal Canadiens	1947-48	Toronto Maple Leafs
1979-80	Buffalo Sabres	1946-47	Montreal Canadiens
1978-79	Montreal Canadiens	1945-46	Montreal Canadiens
1977-78	Montreal Canadiens	1944-45	Montreal Canadiens
1976-77	Montreal Canadiens	1943-44	Montreal Canadiens
1975-76	Montreal Canadiens	1942-43	Detroit Red Wings
1974-75	Buffalo Sabres	1941-42	New York Rangers
1973-74	Boston Bruins	1940-41	Boston Bruins
1972-73	Montreal Canadiens	1939-40	Boston Bruins
1971-72	Boston Bruins	1938-39	Boston Bruins
1970-71	Boston Bruins	1937-38	Boston Bruins
1969-70	Chicago Blackhawks	1936-37	Detroit Red Wings
1968-69	Montreal Canadiens	1935-36	Detroit Red Wings
1967-68	Montreal Canadiens	1934-35	Boston Bruins
1966-67	Chicago Blackhawks	1933-34	Detroit Red Wings
1965-66	Montreal Canadiens	1932-33	Boston Bruins
1964-65	Detroit Red Wings	1931-32	New York Rangers
1963-64	Montreal Canadiens	1930-31	Boston Bruins
1962-63	Toronto Maple Leafs	1929-30	Boston Bruins
1961-62	Montreal Canadiens	1928-29	Boston Bruins
1960-61	Montreal Canadiens	1927-28	Boston Bruins
1959-60	Montreal Canadiens	1926-27	Ottawa Senators
1958-59	Montreal Canadiens	1925-26	Montreal Maroons
1957-58	Montreal Canadiens	1924-25	Montreal Canadiens

Prince of Wales Trophy

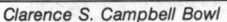

Clarence S. Campbell Bowl

Stanley Cup

CLARENCE S. CAMPBELL BOWL

Beginning with the 1981-82 season, the club which advances to the Stanley Cup Finals as the winner of the Campbell Conference championship is presented with the Clarence S. Campbell Bowl.

History: Presented by the member clubs in 1968 for perpetual competition by the National Hockey League in recognition of the services of Clarence S. Campbell, President of the NHL from 1946 to 1977. From 1967-68 through 1973-74, the trophy was awarded to the champions of the West Division. Beginning in 1974-75, it was awarded to the regular-season winner of the conference bearing the name of the trophy. Starting with the 1981-82 season, the trophy has been presented to the playoff champion in the Campbell Conference. The trophy itself is a hallmark piece made of sterling silver and was crafted by a British silversmith in 1878.

1989-90 Winner: Edmonton Oilers

The Edmonton Oilers won their sixth Clarence S. Campbell Bowl during the club's 11-year history with a 4-2 series win over the Chicago Blackhawks in the Campbell Conference Championship. Before defeating the Blackhawks, the Oilers had series' wins over Winnipeg and Los Angeles.

CLARENCE S. CAMPBELL BOWL WINNERS

1989-90	**Edmonton Oilers**		
1988-89	Calgary Flames	1977-78	New York Islanders
1987-88	Edmonton Oilers	1976-77	Philadelphia Flyers
1986-87	Edmonton Oilers	1975-76	Philadelphia Flyers
1985-86	Calgary Flames	1974-75	Philadelphia Flyers
1984-85	Edmonton Oilers	1973-74	Philadelphia Flyers
1983-84	Edmonton Oilers	1972-73	Chicago Blackhawks
1982-83	Edmonton Oilers	1971-72	Chicago Blackhawks
1981-82	Vancouver Canucks	1970-71	Chicago Blackhawks
1980-81	New York Islanders	1969-70	St. Louis Blues
1979-80	Philadelphia Flyers	1968-69	St. Louis Blues
1978-79	New York Islanders	1967-68	Philadelphia Flyers

Stanley Cup Winners:

Rosters and Final Series Scores

1989-90 — Edmonton Oilers — Kevin Lowe, Steve Smith, Jeff Beukeboom, Mark Lamb, Joe Murphy, Glenn Anderson, Mark Messier, Adam Graves, Craig MacTavish, Kelly Buchberger, Jari Kurri, Craig Simpson, Martin Gelinas, Randy Gregg, Charlie Huddy, Geoff Smith, Reijo Ruotsalainen, Craig Muni, Bill Ranford, Dave Brown, Eldon Reddick, Petr Klima, Esa Tikkanen, Grant Fuhr, Peter Pocklington (Owner), Glen Sather (President/General Manager), John Muckler (Coach), Ted Green (Co-Coach), Ron Low (Ass't Coach), Bruce MacGregor (Ass't General Manager), Barry Fraser (Director of Player Personnel), John Blackwell (Director of Operations, AHL), Ace Bailey, Ed Chadwick, Lorne Davis, Harry Howell, Matti Vaisanen and Albert Reeves (Scouts), Bill Tuele (Director of Public Relations), Werner Baum (Controller), Dr. Gordon Cameron (Medical Chief of Staff), Dr. David Reid (Team Physician), Barrie Stafford (Athletic Trainer), Ken Lowe (Athletic Therapist), Stuart Poirier (Massage Therapist), Lyle Kulchisky (Ass't Trainer).

Scores: May 15 at Boston — Edmonton 3, Boston 2; May 18 at Boston — Edmonton 7, Boston 2; May 20 at Edmonton — Boston 2, Edmonton 1; May 22 at Edmonton — Edmonton 5, Boston 1; May 24 at Boston — Edmonton 4, Boston 1.

1988-89 — Calgary Flames — Mike Vernon, Rick Wamsley, Al MacInnis, Brad McCrimmon, Dana Murzyn, Ric Nattress, Joe Mullen, Lanny McDonald (Co-captain), Gary Roberts, Colin Patterson, Hakan Loob, Theoren Fleury, Tim Hunter (Ass't. captain), Gary Suter, Mark Hunter, Jim Peplinski (Co-captain), Joe Nieuwendyk, Brian MacLellan, Joel Otto, Jamie Macoun, Doug Gilmour, Rob Ramage. Norman Green, Harley Hotchkiss, Norman Kwong, Sonia Scurfield, B.J. Seaman, D.K. Seaman (Owners), Cliff Fletcher (President and General Manager), Al MacNeil (Ass't General Manager), Al Coates (Ass't to the President), Terry Crisp (Head Coach), Doug Risebrough, Tom Watt (Ass't Coaches), Glenn Hall (Goaltending Consultant), Jim Murray (Trainer), Bob Stewart (Equipment Manager), Al Murray (Ass't Trainer).

Scores: May 14 at Calgary — Calgary 3, Montreal 2; May 17 at Calgary — Montreal 4, Calgary 2; May 19 at Montreal — Montreal 4, Calgary 3; May 21 at Montreal — Calgary 4, Montreal 2; May 23 at Calgary — Calgary 3, Montreal 2; May 25 at Montreal — Calgary 4, Montreal 2.

1987-88 — Edmonton Oilers — Keith Acton, Glenn Anderson, Jeff Beukeboom, Geoff Courtnall, Grant Fuhr, Randy Gregg, Wayne Gretzky, Dave Hannan, Charlie Huddy, Mike Krushelnyski, Jari Kurri, Normand Lacombe, Kevin Lowe, Craig MacTavish, Kevin McClelland, Marty McSorley, Mark Messier, Craig Muni, Bill Ranford, Craig Simpson, Steve Smith, Esa Tikkanen, Peter Pocklington (Owner), Glen Sather (General Manager/Coach), John Muckler (Co-Coach), Ted Green (Ass't Coach), Barry Fraser (Director of Player Personnel), Bill Tuele (Director of Public Relations), Dr. Gordon Cameron (Team Physician), Peter Millar (Athletic Therapist), Barrie Stafford (Trainer), Juergen Mers (Massage Therapist), Lyle Kulchisky (Ass't Trainer).

Scores: May 18 at Edmonton — Edmonton 2, Boston 1; May 20 at Edmonton — Edmonton 4, Boston 2; May 22 at Boston — Edmonton 6, Boston 3; May 24 at Boston — Boston 3, Edmonton 3 (suspended due to power failure); May 26 at Edmonton — Edmonton 6, Boston 3.

1986-87 — Edmonton Oilers — Glenn Anderson, Jeff Beukeboom, Kelly Buchberger, Paul Coffey, Grant Fuhr, Randy Gregg, Wayne Gretzky, Charlie Huddy, Dave Hunter, Mike Krushelnyski, Jari Kurri, Moe Lemay, Kevin Lowe, Craig MacTavish, Kevin McClelland, Marty McSorley, Mark Messier, Andy Moog, Craig Muni, Kent Nilsson, Jaroslav Pouzar, Reijo Ruotsalainen, Steve Smith, Esa Tikkanen, Peter Pocklington (Owner), Glen Sather (General Manager/Coach), John Muckler (Co-Coach), Ted Green (Ass't Coach), Ron Low (Ass't Coach), Bruce MacGregor (Ass't. General Manager), Barry Fraser (Director of Player Personnel), Peter Millar (Athletic Therapist), Barrie Stafford (Trainer), Lyle Kulchisky (Ass't Trainer).

Scores: May 17 at Edmonton — Edmonton 4, Philadelphia 3; May 20 at Edmonton — Edmonton 3, Philadelphia 2; May 22 at Philadelphia — Philadelphia 5, Edmonton 3; May 24 at Philadelphia — Edmonton 4, Philadelphia 1; May 26 at Edmonton — Philadelphia 4, Edmonton 3; May 28 at Philadelphia — Philadelphia 3, Edmonton 2; May 31 at Edmonton — Edmonton 3, Philadelphia 1.

1985-86 — Montreal Canadiens — Bob Gainey, Doug Soetaert, Patrick Roy, Rick Green, David Maley, Ryan Walter, Serge Boisvert, Mario Tremblay, Bobby Smith, Craig Ludwig, Tom Kurvers, Kjell Dahlin, Larry Robinson, Guy Carbonneau, Chris Chelios, Petr Svoboda, Mats Naslund, Lucien DeBlois, Steve Rooney, Gaston Gingras, Mike Lalor, Chris Nilan, John Kordic, Claude Lemieux, Mike McPhee, Brian Skrudland, Stephane Richer, Ronald Corey (President), Serge Savard (General Manager), Jean Perron (Coach), Jacques Laperriere (Ass't. Coach), Jean Beliveau (Vice President), Francois-Xavier Seigneur (Vice President), Fred Steer (Vice President), Jacques Lemaire (Ass't. General Manager), Andre Boudrias (Ass't. General Manager), Claude Ruel (Ass't. General Manager), Yves Belanger (Athletic Therapist), Gaetan Lefebvre (Ass't Athletic Therapist), Eddy Palchek (Trainer), Sylvain Toupin (Ass't. Trainer).

Scores: May 16 at Calgary — Calgary 5, Montreal 3; May 18 at Calgary — Montreal 3, Calgary 2; May 20 at Montreal — Montreal 5, Calgary 3; May 22 at Montreal — Montreal 1, Calgary 0; May 24 at Calgary — Montreal 4, Calgary 3.

1984-85 — Edmonton Oilers — Glenn Anderson, Bill Carroll, Paul Coffey, Lee Fogolin, Grant Fuhr, Randy Gregg, Wayne Gretzky, Charlie Huddy, Pat Hughes, Dave Hunter, Don Jackson, Mike Krushelnyski, Jari Kurri, Willy Lindstrom, Kevin Lowe, Dave Lumley, Kevin McClelland, Larry Melnyk, Mark Messier, Andy Moog, Mark Napier, Jaroslav Pouzar, Dave Semenko, Esa Tikkanen, Peter Pocklington (Owner), Glen Sather (General Manager/Coach), John Muckler (Ass't. Coach), Ted Green (Ass't. Coach), Bruce MacGregor (Ass't. General Manager), Barry Fraser (Director of Player Personnel/Chief Scout), Peter Millar (Athletic Therapist), Barrie Stafford, Lyle Kulchisky (Trainers).

Scores: May 21 at Philadelphia — Philadelphia 4, Edmonton 1; May 23 at Philadelphia — Edmonton 3, Philadelphia 1; May 25 at Edmonton — Edmonton 4, Philadelphia 3; May 28 at Edmonton — Edmonton 5, Philadelphia 3; May 30 at Edmonton — Edmonton 8, Philadelphia 3.

1983-84 — Edmonton Oilers — Glenn Anderson, Paul Coffey, Pat Conacher, Lee Fogolin, Grant Fuhr, Randy Gregg, Wayne Gretzky, Charlie Huddy, Pat Hughes, Dave Hunter, Don Jackson, Jari Kurri, Willy Lindstrom, Ken Linseman, Kevin Lowe, Dave Lumley, Kevin McClelland, Mark Messier, Andy Moog, Jaroslav Pouzar, Dave Semenko, Peter Pocklington (Owner), Glen Sather (General Manager/Coach), John Muckler (Ass't. Coach), Ted Green (Ass't. Coach), Bruce MacGregor (Ass't. General Manager), Barry Fraser (Director of Player Personnel/Chief Scout), Peter Millar (Athletic Therapist), Barrie Stafford (Trainer)

Scores: May 10 at New York — Edmonton 1, NY Islanders 0; May 12 at New York — NY Islanders 6, Edmonton 1; May 15 at Edmonton — Edmonton 7, NY Islanders 2; May 17 at Edmonton — Edmonton 7, NY Islanders 2; May 19 at Edmonton — Edmonton 5, NY Islanders 2.

1982-83 — New York Islanders — Mike Bossy, Bob Bourne, Paul Boutilier, Bill Carroll, Greg Gilbert, Clark Gillies, Butch Goring, Mats Hallin, Tomas Jonsson, Anders Kallur, Gord Lane, Dave Langevin, Mike McEwen, Roland Melanson, Wayne Merrick, Ken Morrow, Bob Nystrom, Stefan Persson, Denis Potvin, Bill Smith, Brent Sutter, Duane Sutter, John Tonelli, Bryan Trottier, Al Arbour (coach), Lorne Henning (ass't coach), Bill Torrey (general manager), Ron Waske, Jim Pickard (trainers)

Scores: May 10 at Edmonton — NY Islanders 2, Edmonton 0; May 12 at Edmonton — NY Islanders 6, Edmonton 3; May 14 at New York — NY Islanders 5, Edmonton 1; May 17 at New York — NY Islanders 4, Edmonton 2

1981-82 — New York Islanders — Mike Bossy, Bob Bourne, Bill Carroll, Butch Goring, Greg Gilbert, Clark Gillies, Tomas Jonsson, Anders Kallur, Gord Lane, Dave Langevin, Hector Marini, Mike McEwen, Roland Melanson, Wayne Merrick, Ken Morrow, Bob Nystrom, Stefan Persson, Denis Potvin, Bill Smith, Brent Sutter, Duane Sutter, John Tonelli, Bryan Trottier, Al Arbour (coach), Lorne Henning (ass't coach), Bill Torrey (general manager), Ron Waske, Jim Pickard (trainers)

Scores: May 8 at New York — NY Islanders 6, Vancouver 5; May 11 at New York — NY Islanders 6, Vancouver 4; May 13 at Vancouver — NY Islanders 3, Vancouver 0; May 16 at Vancouver — NY Islanders 3, Vancouver 1

1980-81 — New York Islanders — Denis Potvin, Mike McEwen, Ken Morrow, Gord Lane, Bob Lorimer, Stefan Persson, Dave Langevin, Mike Bossy, Bryan Trottier, Butch Goring, Wayne Merrick, Clark Gillies, John Tonelli, Bob Nystrom, Bill Carroll, Bob Bourne, Hector Marini, Anders Kallur, Duane Sutter, Garry Howatt, Lorne Henning, Bill Smith, Roland Melanson, Al Arbour (coach), Bill Torrey (general manager), Ron Waske, Jim Pickard (trainers).

Scores: May 12 at New York — NY Islanders 6, Minnesota 3; May 14 at New York — NY Islanders 6, Minnesota 3; May 17 at Minnesota — NY Islanders 7, Minnesota 5; May 19 at Minnesota— Minnesota 4, NY Islanders 2; May 21 at New York — NY Islanders 5, Minnesota 1.

Ken Morrow was on all four of the New York Islanders' Stanley Cup winning teams of the 1980's.

1979-80 — New York Islanders — Gord Lane, Jean Potvin, Bob Lorimer, Denis Potvin, Stefan Persson, Ken Morrow, Dave Langevin, Duane Sutter, Garry Howatt, Clark Gillies, Lorne Henning, Wayne Merrick, Bob Bourne, Steve Tambellini, Bryan Trottier, Mike Bossy, Bob Nystrom, John Tonelli, Anders Kallur, Butch Goring, Alex McKendry, Glenn Resch, Billy Smith, Al Arbour (coach), Bill Torrey (general manager), Ron Waske, Jim Pickard (trainers).

Scores: May 13 at Philadelphia — NY Islanders 4, Philadelphia 3; May 15 at Philadelphia — Philadelphia 8, NY Islanders 3; May 17 at Long Island — NY Islanders 6, Philadelphia 2; May 19 at Long Island — NY Islanders 5, Philadelphia 2; May 22 at Philadelphia — Philadelphia 6, NY Islanders 3; May 24 at Long Island — NY Islanders 5, Philadelphia 4.

1978-79 — Montreal Canadiens — Ken Dryden, Larry Robinson, Serge Savard, Guy Lapointe, Brian Engblom, Gilles Lupien, Rick Chartraw, Guy Lafleur, Steve Shutt, Jacques Lemaire, Yvan Cournoyer, Rejean Houle, Pierre Mondou, Bob Gainey, Doug Jarvis, Yvon Lambert, Doug Risebrough, Mario Tremblay, Cam Connor, Pat Hughes, Rod Langway, Mark Napier, Michel Larocque, Richard Sevigny, Scotty Bowman (coach), Irving Grundman (managing director), Eddy Palchak, Pierre Meilleur (trainers).

Scores: May 13 at Montreal — NY Rangers 4, Montreal 1; May 15 at Montreal — Montreal 6, NY Rangers 2; May 17 at New York — Montreal 4, NY Rangers 1; May 19 at New York — Montreal 4, NY Rangers 3; May 21 at Montreal — Montreal 4, NY Rangers 1.

1977-78 — Montreal Canadiens — Ken Dryden, Larry Robinson, Serge Savard, Guy Lapointe, Bill Nyrop, Pierre Bouchard, Brian Engblom, Gilles Lupien, Rick Chartraw, Guy Lafleur, Steve Shutt, Jacques Lemaire, Yvan Cournoyer, Rejean Houle, Pierre Mondou, Bob Gainey, Doug Jarvis, Yvon Lambert, Doug Risebrough, Pierre Larouche, Mario Tremblay, Michel Larocque, Scotty Bowman (coach), Sam Pollock (general manager), Eddy Palchak, Pierre Meilleur (trainers).

Scores: May 13 at Montreal — Montreal 4, Boston 1; May 16 at Montreal — Montreal 3, Boston 2; May 18 at Boston — Boston 4, Montreal 0; May 21 at Boston — Boston 4, Montreal 3; May 23 at Montreal — Montreal 4, Boston 1; May 25 at Boston — Montreal 4, Boston 1.

1976-77 — Montreal Canadiens — Ken Dryden, Guy Lapointe, Larry Robinson, Serge Savard, Jimmy Roberts, Rick Chartraw, Bill Nyrop, Pierre Bouchard, Brian Engblom, Yvan Cournoyer, Guy Lafleur, Jacques Lemaire, Steve Shutt, Pete Mahovlich, Murray Wilson, Doug Jarvis, Yvon Lambert, Bob Gainey, Doug Risebrough, Mario Tremblay, Rejean Houle, Pierre Mondou, Mike Polich, Michel Larocque, Scotty Bowman (coach), Sam Pollock (general manager), Eddy Palchak, Pierre Meilleur (trainers).

Scores: May 7 at Montreal — Montreal 7, Boston 3; May 10 at Montreal — Montreal 3, Boston 0; May 12 at Boston — Montreal 4, Boston 2; May 14 at Boston — Montreal 2, Boston 1.

1975-76 — Montreal Canadiens — Ken Dryden, Serge Savard, Guy Lapointe, Larry Robinson, Bill Nyrop, Pierre Bouchard, Jim Roberts, Guy Lafleur, Steve Shutt, Pete Mahovlich, Yvan Cournoyer, Jacques Lemaire, Yvon Lambert, Bob Gainey, Doug Jarvis, Doug Risebrough, Murray Wilson, Mario Tremblay, Rick Chartraw, Michel Larocque, Scotty Bowman (coach), Sam Pollock (general manager), Eddy Palchak, Pierre Meilleur (trainers).

Scores: May 9 at Montreal — Montreal 4, Philadelphia 3; May 11 at Montreal — Montreal 2, Philadelphia 1; May 13 at Philadelphia — Montreal 3, Philadelphia 2; May 16 at Philadelphia — Montreal 5, Philadelphia 3.

1974-75 — Philadelphia Flyers — Bernie Parent, Wayne Stephenson, Ed Van Impe, Tom Bladon, Andfe Dupont, Joe Watson, Jim Watson, Ted Harris, Larry Goodenough, Rick MacLeish, Bobby Clarke, Bill Barber, Reggie Leach, Gary Dornhoefer, Ross Lonsberry, Bob Kelly, Terry Crisp, Don Saleski, Dave Schultz, Orest Kindrachuk, Bill Clement, Fred Shero (coach), Keith Allen (general manager), Frank Lewis, Jim McKenzie (trainers).

Scores: May 15 at Philadelphia — Philadelphia 4, Buffalo 1; May 18 at Philadelphia — Philadelphia 2, Buffalo 1; May 20 at Buffalo — Buffalo 5, Philadelphia 4; May 22 at Buffalo — Buffalo 4, Philadelphia 2; May 25 at Philadelphia — Philadelphia 5, Buffalo 1; May 27 at Buffalo — Philadelphia 2, Buffalo 0.

1973-74 — Philadelphia Flyers — Bernie Parent, Ed Van Impe, Tom Bladon, Andre Dupont, Joe Watson, Jim Watson, Barry Ashbee, Bill Barber, Dave Schultz, Don Saleski, Gary Dornhoefer, Terry Crisp, Bobby Clarke, Simon Nolet, Ross Lonsberry, Rick MacLeish, Bill Flett, Orest Kindrachuk, Bill Clement, Bob Kelly, Bruce Cowick, Al MacAdam, Bobby Taylor, Fred Shero (coach), Keith Allen (general manager), Frank Lewis, Jim McKenzie (trainers).
Scores: May 7 at Boston — Boston 3, Philadelphia 2; May 9 at Boston — Philadelphia 3, Boston 2; May 12 at Philadelphia — Philadelphia 4, Boston 1; May 14 at Philadelphia — Philadelphia 4, Boston 2; May 16 at Boston — Boston 5, Philadelphia 1; May 19 at Philadelphia — Philadelphia 1, Boston 0.

1972-73 — Montreal Canadiens — Ken Dryden, Guy Lapointe, Serge Savard, Larry Robinson, Jacques Laperriere, Bob Murdoch, Pierre Bouchard, Jim Roberts, Yvan Cournoyer, Frank Mahovlich, Jacques Lemaire, Pete Mahovlich, Marc Tardif, Henri Richard, Rejean Houle, Guy Lafleur, Chuck Lefley, Claude Larose, Murray Wilson, Steve Shutt, Michel Plasse, Scotty Bowman (coach), Sam Pollock (general manager), Ed Palchak, Bob Williams (trainers).
Scores: April 29 at Montreal — Montreal 8, Chicago 3; May 1 at Montreal — Montreal 4, Chicago 1; May 3 at Chicago — Chicago 7, Montreal 4; May 6 at Chicago — Montreal 4, Chicago 0; May 8 at Montreal — Chicago 8, Montreal 7; May 10 at Chicago — Montreal 6, Chicago 4.

1971-72 — Boston Bruins — Gerry Cheevers, Ed Johnston, Bobby Orr, Ted Green, Carol Vadnais, Dallas Smith, Don Awrey, Phil Esposito, Ken Hodge, John Bucyk, Mike Walton, Wayne Cashman, Garnet Bailey, Derek Sanderson, Fred Stanfield, Ed Westfall, John McKenzie, Don Marcotte, Garry Peters, Chris Hayes, Tom Johnson (coach), Milt Schmidt (general manager), Dan Canney, John Forristall (trainers).
Scores: April 30 at Boston — Boston 6, NY Rangers 5; May 2 at Boston — Boston 2, NY Rangers 1; May 4 at New York — NY Rangers 5, Boston 2; May 7 at New York — Boston 3, NY Rangers 2; May 9 at Boston — NY Rangers 3, Boston 2; May 11 at New York — Boston 3, NY Rangers 0.

1970-71 — Montreal Canadiens — Ken Dryden, Rogatien Vachon, Jacques Laperriere, Jean-Claude Tremblay, Guy Lapointe, Terry Harper, Pierre Bouchard, Jean Beliveau, Marc Tardif, Yvan Cournoyer, Rejean Houle, Claude Larose, Henri Richard, Phil Roberto, Pete Mahovlich, Leon Rochefort, John Ferguson, Bobby Sheehan, Jacques Lemaire, Frank Mahovlich, Bob Murdoch, Chuck Lefley, Al MacNeil (coach), Sam Pollock (general manager), Yvon Belanger, Ed Palchak (trainers).
Scores: May 4 at Chicago — Chicago 2, Montreal 1; May 6 at Chicago — Chicago 5, Montreal 3; May 9 at Montreal — Montreal 4, Chicago 2; May 11 at Montreal — Montreal 5, Chicago 2; May 13 at Chicago — Chicago 2, Montreal 0; May 16 at Montreal — Montreal 4, Chicago 3; May 18 at Chicago — Montreal 3, Chicago 2.

1969-70 — Boston Bruins — Gerry Cheevers, Ed Johnston, Bobby Orr, Rick Smith, Dallas Smith, Bill Speer, Gary Doak, Don Awrey, Phil Esposito, Ken Hodge, John Bucyk, Wayne Carleton, Wayne Cashman, Derek Sanderson, Fred Stanfield, Ed Westfall, John McKenzie, Jim Lorentz, Don Marcotte, Bill Lesuk, Dan Schock, Harry Sinden (coach), Milt Schmidt (general manager), Dan Canney, John Forristall (trainers).
Scores: May 3 at St. Louis — Boston 6, St. Louis 1; May 5 at St. Louis — Boston 6, St. Louis 2; May 7 at Boston — Boston 4, St. Louis 1; May 10 at Boston — Boston 4, St. Louis 3.

1968-69 — Montreal Canadiens — Lorne Worsley, Rogatien Vachon, Jacques Laperriere, Jean-Claude Tremblay, Ted Harris, Serge Savard, Terry Harper, Larry Hillman, Jean Beliveau, Ralph Backstrom, Dick Duff, Yvan Cournoyer, Claude Provost, Bobby Rousseau, Henri Richard, John Ferguson, Christian Bordeleau, Mickey Redmond, Jacques Lemaire, Lucien Grenier, Tony Esposito, Claude Ruel (coach), Sam Pollock (general manager), Larry Aubut, Eddy Palchak (trainers).
Scores: April 27 at Montreal — Montreal 3, St. Louis 1; April 29 at Montreal — Montreal 3, St. Louis 1; May 1 at St. Louis — Montreal 4, St. Louis 0; May 4 at St. Louis — Montreal 2, St. Louis 1.

1967-68 — Montreal Canadiens — Lorne Worsley, Rogatien Vachon, Jacques Laperriere, Jean-Claude Tremblay, Ted Harris, Serge Savard, Terry Harper, Carol Vadnais, Jean Beliveau, Gilles Tremblay, Ralph Backstrom, Dick Duff, Claude Larose, Yvan Cournoyer, Claude Provost, Bobby Rousseau, Henri Richard, John Ferguson, Danny Grant, Jacques Lemaire, Mickey Redmond, Toe Blake (coach), Sam Pollock (general manager), Larry Aubut, Eddy Palchak (trainers).
Scores: May 5 at St. Louis — Montreal 3, St. Louis 2; May 7 at St. Louis — Montreal 1, St. Louis 0; May 9 at Montreal — Montreal 4, St. Louis 3; May 11 at Montreal — Montreal 3, St. Louis 2.

1966-67 — Toronto Maple Leafs — Johnny Bower, Terry Sawchuk, Larry Hillman, Marcel Pronovost, Tim Horton, Bob Baun, Aut Erickson, Allan Stanley, Red Kelly, Ron Ellis, George Armstrong, Pete Stemkowski, Dave Keon, Mike Walton, Jim Pappin, Bob Pulford, Brian Conacher, Eddie Shack, Frank Mahovlich, Milan Marcetta, Larry Jeffrey, Bruce Gamble, Punch Imlach (manager-coach), Bob Haggart (trainer).
Scores: April 20 at Montreal — Toronto 2, Montreal 6; April 22 at Montreal — Toronto 3, Montreal 0; April 25 at Toronto — Toronto 3, Montreal 2; April 27 at Toronto — Toronto 2, Montreal 6; April 29 at Montreal — Toronto 4, Montreal 1; May 2 at Toronto — Toronto 3, Montreal 1.

1965-66 — Montreal Canadiens — Lorne Worsley, Charlie Hodge, Jean-Claude Tremblay, Ted Harris, Jean-Guy Talbot, Terry Harper, Jacques Laperriere, Noel Price, Jean Beliveau, Ralph Backstrom, Dick Duff, Gilles Tremblay, Claude Larose, Yvan Cournoyer, Claude Provost, Bobby Rousseau, Henri Richard, Dave Balon, John Ferguson, Leon Rochefort, Jim Roberts, Toe Blake (coach), Sam Pollock (general manager), Larry Aubut, Andy Galley (trainers).
Scores: April 24 at Montreal — Detroit 3, Montreal 2; April 26 at Montreal — Detroit 5, Montreal 2; April 28 at Detroit — Montreal 4, Detroit 2; May 1 at Detroit — Montreal 2, Detroit 1; May 3 at Montreal — Montreal 5, Detroit 1; May 5 at Detroit — Montreal 3, Detroit 2.

1964-65 — Montreal Canadiens — Lorne Worsley, Charlie Hodge, Jean-Claude Tremblay, Ted Harris, Jean-Guy Talbot, Terry Harper, Jacques Laperriere, Jean Gauthier, Noel Picard, Jean Beliveau, Ralph Backstrom, Dick Duff, Claude Larose, Yvan Cournoyer, Claude Provost, Bobby Rousseau, Henri Richard, Dave Balon, John Ferguson, Red Berenson, Jim Roberts, Toe Blake (coach), Sam Pollock (general manager), Larry Aubut, Andy Galley (trainers).
Scores: April 17 at Montreal — Montreal 3, Chicago 2; April 20 at Montreal — Montreal 2, Chicago 0; April 22 at Chicago — Montreal 1, Chicago 3; April 25 at Chicago — Montreal 1, Chicago 5; April 27 at Montreal — Montreal 6, Chicago 0; April 29 at Chicago — Montreal 1, Chicago 2; May 1 at Montreal — Montreal 4, Chicago 0.

1963-64 — Toronto Maple Leafs — Johnny Bower, Carl Brewer, Tim Horton, Bob Baun, Allan Stanley, Larry Hillman, Al Arbour, Red Kelly, Gerry Ehman, Andy Bathgate, George Armstrong, Ron Stewart, Dave Keon, Billy Harris, Don McKenney, Jim Pappin, Bob Pulford, Eddie Shack, Frank Mahovlich, Eddie Litzenberger, Punch Imlach (manager-coach), Bob Haggert (trainer).
Scores: April 11 at Toronto — Toronto 3, Detroit 2; April 14 at Toronto — Toronto 3, Detroit 4; April 16 at Detroit — Toronto 3, Detroit 4; April 18 at Detroit — Toronto 4, Detroit 2; April 21 at Toronto — Toronto 1, Detroit 2; April 23 at Detroit — Toronto 4, Detroit 3; April 25 at Toronto — Toronto 4, Detroit 0.

1962-63 — Toronto Maple Leafs — Johnny Bower, Don Simmons, Carl Brewer, Tim Horton, Kent Douglas, Allan Stanley, Bob Baun, Larry Hillman, Red Kelly, Dick Duff, George Armstrong, Bob Nevin, Ron Stewart, Dave Keon, Billy Harris, Bob Pulford, Eddie Shack, Ed Litzenberger, Frank Mahovlich, John MacMillan, Punch Imlach (manager-coach), Bob Haggert (trainer).
Scores: April 9 at Toronto — Toronto 4, Detroit 2; April 11 at Toronto — Toronto 4, Detroit 2; April 14 at Detroit — Toronto 2, Detroit 3; April 16 at Detroit — Toronto 4, Detroit 2; April 18 at Toronto — Toronto 3, Detroit 1.

1961-62 — Toronto Maple Leafs — Johnny Bower, Don Simmons, Carl Brewer, Tim Horton, Bob Baun, Allan Stanley, Al Arbour, Larry Hillman, Red Kelly, Dick Duff, George Armstrong, Frank Mahovlich, Bob Nevin, Ron Stewart, Bill Harris, Bert Olmstead, Bob Pulford, Eddie Shack, Dave Keon, Ed Litzenberger, John MacMillan, Punch Imlach (manager-coach), Bob Haggert (trainer).
Scores: April 10 at Toronto — Toronto 4, Chicago 1; April 12 at Toronto — Toronto 3, Chicago 2; April 15 at Chicago — Toronto 0, Chicago 3; April 17 at Chicago — Toronto 1, Chicago 4; April 19 at Toronto — Toronto 8, Chicago 4; April 22 at Chicago — Toronto 2, Chicago 1.

1960-61 — Chicago Blackhawks — Glenn Hall, Al Arbour, Pierre Pilote, Elmer Vasko, Jack Evans, Dollard St. Laurent, Reg Fleming, Tod Sloan, Ron Murphy, Eddie Litzenberger, Bill Hay, Bobby Hull, Ab McDonald, Eric Nesterenko, Ken Wharram, Earl Balfour, Stan Mikita, Murray Balfour, Chico Maki, Wayne Hicks, Tommy Ivan (manager), Rudy Pilous (coach), Nick Garen (trainer).
Scores: April 6 at Chicago — Chicago 3, Detroit 2; April 8 at Detroit — Detroit 3, Chicago 1; April 10 at Chicago — Chicago 3, Detroit 1; April 12 at Detroit — Detroit 2, Chicago 1; April 14 at Chicago — Chicago 6, Detroit 3; April 16 at Detroit — Chicago 5, Detroit 1.

1959-60 — Montreal Canadiens — Jacques Plante, Charlie Hodge, Doug Harvey, Tom Johnson, Bob Turner, Jean-Guy Talbot, Albert Langlois, Ralph Backstrom, Jean Beliveau, Marcel Bonin, Bernie Geoffrion, Phil Goyette, Bill Hicke, Don Marshall, Ab McDonald, Dickie Moore, Andre Pronovost, Claude Provost, Henri Richard, Maurice Richard, Frank Selke (manager), Toe Blake (coach), Hector Dubois, Larry Aubut (trainers).
Scores: April 7 at Montreal — Montreal 4, Toronto 2; April 9 at Montreal — Montreal 2, Toronto 1; April 12 at Toronto — Montreal 5, Toronto 2; April 14 at Toronto — Montreal 4, Toronto 0.

1958-59 — Montreal Canadiens — Jacques Plante, Charlie Hodge, Doug Harvey, Tom Johnson, Bob Turner, Jean-Guy Talbot, Albert Langlois, Bernie Geoffrion, Ralph Backstrom, Bill Hicke, Maurice Richard, Dickie Moore, Claude Provost, Ab McDonald, Henri Richard, Marcel Bonin, Phil Goyette, Don Marshall, Andre Pronovost, Jean Beliveau, Frank Selke (manager), Toe Blake (coach), Hector Dubois, Larry Aubut (trainers).
Scores: April 9 at Montreal — Montreal 5, Toronto 3; April 11 at Montreal — Montreal 3, Toronto 1; April 14 at Toronto — Toronto 3, Montreal 2; April 16 at Toronto — Montreal 3, Toronto 2; April 18 at Montreal — Montreal 5, Toronto 3.

1957-58 — Montreal Canadiens — Jacques Plante, Gerry McNeil, Doug Harvey, Tom Johnson, Bob Turner, Dollard St-Laurent, Jean-Guy Talbot, Albert Langlois, Jean Beliveau, Bernie Geoffrion, Maurice Richard, Dickie Moore, Claude Provost, Floyd Curry, Bert Olmstead, Henri Richard, Marcel Bonin, Phil Goyette, Don Marshall, Andre Pronovost, Connie Broden, Frank Selke (manager), Toe Blake (coach), Hector Dubois, Larry Aubut (trainers).
Scores: April 8 at Montreal — Montreal 2, Boston 1; April 10 at Montreal — Boston 5, Montreal 2; April 13 at Boston — Montreal 3, Boston 0; April 15 at Boston — Boston 3, Montreal 1; April 17 at Montreal — Montreal 3, Boston 2; April 20 at Boston — Montreal 5, Boston 3.

1956-57 — Montreal Canadiens — Jacques Plante, Gerry McNeil, Doug Harvey, Tom Johnson, Bob Turner, Dollard St. Laurent, Jean-Guy Talbot, Jean Beliveau, Bernie Geoffrion, Floyd Curry, Dickie Moore, Maurice Richard, Claude Provost, Bert Olmstead, Henri Richard, Phil Goyette, Don Marshall, Andre Pronovost, Connie Broden, Frank Selke (manager), Toe Blake (coach), Hector Dubois, Larry Aubut (trainers).
Scores: April 6, at Montreal — Montreal 5, Boston 1; April 9, at Montreal — Montreal 1, Boston 0; April 11, at Boston — Montreal 4, Boston 2; April 14, at Boston — Boston 2, Montreal 0; April 16, at Montreal — Montreal 5, Boston 1.

1955-56 — Montreal Canadiens — Jacques Plante, Doug Harvey, Emile Bouchard, Bob Turner, Tom Johnson, Jean-Guy Talbot, Dollard St. Laurent, Jean Beliveau, Bernie Geoffrion, Bert Olmstead, Floyd Curry, Jackie Leclair, Maurice Richard, Dickie Moore, Henri Richard, Ken Mosdell, Don Marshall, Claude Provost, Frank Selke (manager), Toe Blake (coach), Hector Dubois (trainer).
Scores: March 31, at Montreal — Montreal 6, Detroit 4; April 3, at Montreal — Montreal 5, Detroit 1; April 5, at Detroit — Detroit 3, Montreal 1; April 8, at Detroit — Montreal 3, Detroit 0; April 10, at Montreal — Montreal 3, Detroit 1.

1954-55 — Detroit Red Wings — Terry Sawchuk, Red Kelly, Bob Goldham, Marcel Pronovost, Ben Woit, Jim Hay, Larry Hillman, Ted Lindsay, Tony Leswick, Gordie Howe, Alex Delvecchio, Marty Pavelich, Glen Skov, Earl Reibel, John Wilson, Bill Dineen, Vic Stasiuk, Marcel Bonin, Jack Adams (manager), Jimmy Skinner (coach), Carl Mattson (trainer).
Scores: April 3, at Detroit — Detroit 4, Montreal 2; April 5, at Detroit — Detroit 7, Montreal 1, April 7 at Montreal — Montreal 4, Detroit 2; April 9, at Montreal — Montreal 5, Detroit 3; April 10, at Detroit — Detroit 5, Montreal 1; April 12, at Montreal — Montreal 6, Detroit 3; April 14, at Detroit — Detroit 3, Montreal 1

1953-54 — Detroit Red Wings — Terry Sawchuk, Red Kelly, Bob Goldham, Ben Woit, Marcel Pronovost, Al Arbour, Keith Allen, Ted Lindsay, Tony Leswick, Gordie Howe, Marty Pavelich, Alex Delvecchio, Metro Prystai, Glen Skov, John Wilson, Bill Dineen, Jim Peters, Earl Reibel, Vic Stasiuk, Jack Adams (manager), Tommy Ivan (coach), Carl Mattson (trainer).
Scores: April 4, at Detroit — Detroit 3, Montreal 1; April 6, at Detroit — Montreal 3, Detroit 1; April 8, at Montreal — Detroit 5, Montreal 2; April 10, at Montreal — Detroit 2, Montreal 0; April 11, at Detroit — Montreal 1, Detroit 0; April 13, at Montreal — Montreal 4, Detroit 1; April 16, at Detroit — Detroit 2, Montreal 1.

1952-53 — Montreal Canadiens — Gerry McNeil, Jacques Plante, Doug Harvey, Emile Bouchard, Tom Johnson, Dollard St. Laurent, Bud MacPherson, Maurice Richard, Elmer Lach, Bert Olmstead, Bernie Geoffrion, Floyd Curry, Paul Masnick, Billy Reay, Dickie Moore, Ken Mosdell, Dick Gamble, Johnny McCormack, Lorne Davis, Calum McKay, Eddie Mazur, Frank Selke (manager), Dick Irvin (coach), Hector Dubois (trainer).
Scores: April 9, at Montreal — Montreal 4, Boston 2; April 11, at Montreal — Boston 4, Montreal 1; April 12, at Boston — Montreal 3, Boston 0; April 14, at Boston — Montreal 7, Boston 3; April 16, at Montreal — Montreal 1, Boston 0.

1951-52 — Detroit Red Wings — Terry Sawchuk, Bob Goldham, Ben Woit, Red Kelly, Leo Reise, Marcel Pronovost, Ted Lindsay, Tony Leswick, Gordie Howe, Metro Prystai, Marty Pavelich, Sid Abel, Glen Skov, Alex Delvecchio, John Wilson, Vic Stasiuk, Larry Zeidel, Jack Adams (manager) Tommy Ivan (coach), Carl Mattson (trainer).
Scores: April 10, at Montreal — Detroit 3, Montreal 1; April 12 at Montreal — Detroit 2, Montreal 1; April 13, at Detroit — Detroit 3, Montreal 0; April 15, at Detroit — Detroit 3, Montreal 0.

1950-51 — Toronto Maple Leafs — Turk Broda, Al Rollins, Jim Thomson, Gus Mortson, Bill Barilko, Bill Juzda, Fern Flaman, Hugh Bolton, Ted Kennedy, Sid Smith, Tod Sloan, Cal Gardner, Howie Meeker, Harry Watson, Max Bentley, Joe Klukay, Danny Lewicki, Ray Timgren, Fleming Mackell, Johnny McCormack, Bob Hassard, Conn Smythe (manager), Joe Primeau (coach), Tim Daly (trainer).
Scores: April 11, at Toronto — Toronto 3, Montreal 2; April 14, at Toronto — Montreal 3, Toronto 2; April 17, at Montreal — Toronto 2, Montreal 1; April 19, at Montreal — Toronto 3, Montreal 2; April 21, at Toronto — Toronto 3, Montreal 2.

1949-50 — Detroit Red Wings — Harry Lumley, Jack Stewart, Leo Reise, Clare Martin, Al Dewsbury, Lee Fogolin, Marcel Pronovost, Red Kelly, Ted Lindsay, Sid Abel, Gordie Howe, George Gee, Jimmy Peters, Marty Pavelich, Jim McFadden, Pete Babando, Max McNab, Gerry Couture, Joe Carveth, Steve Black, John Wilson, Larry Wilson, Jack Adams (manager), Tommy Ivan (coach), Carl Mattson (trainer).
Scores: April 11, at Detroit — Detroit 4, NY Rangers 1; April 13, at Toronto* — NY Rangers 3, Detroit 1; April 15, at Toronto — Detroit 4, NY Rangers 0; April 18, at Detroit — NY Rangers 4, Detroit 3; April 20, at Detroit — NY Rangers 2, Detroit 1; April 22, at Detroit — Detroit 5, NY Rangers 4; April 23, at Detroit — Detroit 4, NY Rangers 3.

* Ice was unavailable in Madison Square Garden and Rangers elected to play second and third games on Toronto ice.

1948-49 — Toronto Maple Leafs — Turk Broda, Jim Thomson, Gus Mortson, Bill Barilko, Garth Boesch, Bill Juzda, Ted Kennedy, Howie Meeker, Vic Lynn, Harry Watson, Bill Ezinicki, Cal Gardner, Max Bentley, Joe Klukay, Sid Smith, Don Metz, Ray Timgren, Fleming Mackell, Harry Taylor, Bob Dawes, Tod Sloan, Conn Smythe (manager), Hap Day (coach), Tim Daly (trainer).
Scores: April 8, at Detroit — Toronto 3, Detroit 2; April 10, at Detroit — Toronto 3, Detroit 1; April 13, at Toronto — Toronto 3, Detroit 1; April 16, at Toronto — Toronto 3, Detroit 1.

1947-48 — Toronto Maple Leafs — Turk Broda, Jim Thomson, Wally Stanowski, Garth Boesch, Bill Barilko. Gus Mortson, Phil Samis, Syl Apps, Bill Ezinicki, Harry Watson, Ted Kennedy, Howie Meeker, Vic Lynn, Nick Metz, Max Bentley, Joe Klukay, Les Costello, Don Metz, Sid Smith, Conn Smythe (manager), Hap Day (coach), Tim Daly (trainer).
Scores: April 7, at Toronto — Toronto 5, Detroit 3; April 10, at Toronto — Toronto 4, Detroit 2; April 11, at Detroit — Toronto 2, Detroit 0; April 14, at Detroit — Toronto 7, Detroit 2.

1946-47 — Toronto Maple Leafs — Turk Broda, Garth Boesch, Gus Mortson, Jim Thomson, Wally Stanowski, Bill Barilko, Harry Watson, Bud Poile, Ted Kennedy, Syl Apps, Don Metz, Nick Metz, Bill Ezinicki, Vic Lynn, Howie Meeker, Gaye Stewart, Joe Klukay, Gus Bodnar, Bob Goldham, Conn Smythe (manager), Hap Day (coach), Tim Daly (trainer).
Scores: April 8, at Montreal — Montreal 6, Toronto 0; April 10, at Montreal — Toronto 4, Montreal 0; April 12, at Toronto — Toronto 4, Montreal 2; April 15, at Toronto — Toronto 2, Montreal 1; April 17, at Montreal — Montreal 3, Toronto 1; April 19, at Toronto — Toronto 2, Montreal 1.

1945-46 — Montreal Canadiens — Elmer Lach, Toe Blake, Maurice Richard, Bob Fillion, Dutch Hiller, Murph Chamberlain, Ken Mosdell, Buddy O'Connor, Glen Harmon, Jim Peters, Emile Bouchard, Bill Reay, Ken Reardon, Leo Lamoureux, Frank Eddolls, Gerry Plamondon, Bill Durnan, Tommy Gorman (manager), Dick Irvin (coach), Ernie Cook (trainer).
Scores: March 30, at Montreal — Montreal 4, Boston 3; April 2, at Montreal — Montreal 3, Boston 2; April 4, at Boston — Montreal 4, Boston 2; April 7, at Boston — Boston 3, Montreal 2; April 9, at Montreal — Montreal 6, Boston 3.

1944-45 — Toronto Maple Leafs — Don Metz, Frank McCool, Wally Stanowski, Reg Hamilton, Elwyn Morris, Johnny McCreedy, Tommy O'Neill, Ted Kennedy, Babe Pratt, Gus Bodnar, Art Jackson, Jack McLean, Mel Hill, Nick Metz, Bob Davidson, Dave Schriner, Lorne Carr, Conn Smythe (manager), Frank Selke (business manager), Hap Day (coach), Tim Daly (trainer).
Scores: April 6, at Detroit — Toronto 1, Detroit 0; April 8, at Detroit — Toronto 2, Detroit 0; April 12, at Toronto — Toronto 1, Detroit 0; April 14, at Toronto — Detroit 5, Toronto 3; April 19, at Detroit — Detroit 2, Toronto 0; April 21, at Toronto — Detroit 1, Toronto 0; April 22, at Detroit — Toronto 2, Detroit 1.

1943-44 — Montreal Canadiens — Toe Blake, Maurice Richard, Elmer Lach, Ray Getliffe, Murph Chamberlain, Phil Watson, Emile Bouchard, Glen Harmon, Buddy O'Connor, Jerry Heffernan, Mike McMahon, Leo Lamoureux, Fernand Majeau, Bob Fillion, Bill Durnan, Tommy Gorman (manager), Dick Irvin (coach), Ernie Cook (trainer).
Scores: April 4, at Montreal — Montreal 5, Chicago 1; April 6, at Chicago — Montreal 3, Chicago 1; April 9, at Chicago — Montreal 3, Chicago 2; April 13, at Montreal — Montreal 5, Chicago 4.

1942-43 — Detroit Red Wings — Jack Stewart, Jimmy Orlando, Sid Abel, Alex Motter, Harry Watson, Joe Carveth, Mud Bruneteau, Eddie Wares, Johnny Mowers, Cully Simon, Don Grosso, Carl Liscombe, Connie Brown, Syd Howe, Les Douglas, Hal Jackson, Joe Fisher, Jack Adams (manager), Ebbie Goodfellow (playing-coach), Honey Walker (trainer).
Scores: April 1, at Detroit — Detroit 6, Boston 2; April 4, at Detroit — Detroit 4, Boston 3; April 7, at Boston — Detroit 4, Boston 0; April 8, at Boston — Detroit 2, Boston 0.

1941-42 — Toronto Maple Leafs — Wally Stanowski, Syl Apps, Bob Goldham, Gord Drillon, Hank Goldup, Ernie Dickens, Dave Schriner, Bucko McDonald, Bob Davidson, Nick Metz, Bingo Kampman, Don Metz, Gaye Stewart, Turk Broda, Johnny McCreedy, Lorne Carr, Pete Langelle, Billy Taylor, Conn Smythe (manager), Hap Day (coach), Frank Selke (business manager), Tim Daly (trainer).
Scores: April 4, at Toronto — Detroit 3, Toronto 2; April 7, at Toronto — Detroit 4, Toronto 2; April 9, at Detroit — Detroit 5, Toronto 2; April 12, at Detroit — Toronto 4, Detroit 3; April 14, at Toronto — Toronto 9, Detroit 3; April 16, at Detroit — Toronto 3, Detroit 0; April 18, at Toronto — Toronto 3, Detroit 1.

1940-41 — Boston Bruins — Bill Cowley, Des Smith, Dit Clapper, Frank Brimsek, Flash Hollett, John Crawford, Bobby Bauer, Pat McCreavy, Herb Cain, Mel Hill, Milt Schmidt, Woody Dumart, Roy Conacher, Terry Reardon, Art Jackson, Eddie Wiseman, Art Ross (manager), Cooney Weiland (coach), Win Green (trainer).
Scores: April 6, at Boston — Detroit 2, Boston 3; April 8, at Boston — Detroit 1, Boston 2; April 10, at Detroit — Boston 4, Detroit 2; April 12, at Detroit — Boston 3, Detroit 1.

1939-40 — New York Rangers — Dave Kerr, Art Coulter, Ott Heller, Alex Shibicky, Mac Colville, Neil Colville, Phil Watson, Lynn Patrick, Clint Smith, Muzz Patrick, Babe Pratt, Bryan Hextall, Kilby Macdonald, Dutch Hiller, Alf Pike, Sanford Smith, Lester Patrick (manager), Frank Boucher (coach), Harry Westerby (trainer).
Scores: April 2, at New York — NY Rangers 2, Toronto 1; April 3, at New York — NY Rangers 6, Toronto 2; April 6, at Toronto — NY Rangers 1, Toronto 2; April 9, at Toronto — NY Rangers 0, Toronto 3; April 11, at Toronto — NY Rangers 2, Toronto 1; April 13, at Toronto — NY Rangers 3, Toronto 2.

1938-39 — Boston Bruins — Bobby Bauer, Mel Hill, Flash Hollett, Roy Conacher, Gord Pettinger, Milt Schmidt, Woody Dumart, Jack Crawford, Ray Getliffe, Frank Brimsek, Eddie Shore, Dit Clapper, Bill Cowley, Jack Portland, Red Hamill, Cooney Weiland, Art Ross (manager-coach), Win Green (trainer).
Scores: April 6, at Boston — Toronto 1, Boston 2; April 9, at Boston — Toronto 3, Boston 2; April 11, at Toronto — Toronto 1, Boston 3; April 13 at Toronto — Toronto 0, Boston 3; April 16, at Boston — Toronto 1, Boston 3.

1937-38 — Chicago Blackhawks — Art Wiebe, Carl Voss, Hal Jackson, Mike Karakas, Mush March, Jack Shill, Earl Seibert, Cully Dahlstrom, Alex Levinsky, Johnny Gottselig, Lou Trudel, Pete Palangio, Bill MacKenzie, Doc Romnes, Paul Thompson, Roger Jenkins, Alf Moore, Bert Connolly, Virgil Johnson, Paul Goodman, Bill Stewart (manager-coach), Eddie Froelich (trainer).
Scores: April 5, at Toronto — Chicago 3, Toronto 1; April 7, at Toronto — Chicago 1, Toronto 5; April 10 at Chicago — Chicago 2, Toronto 1; April 12, at Chicago — Chicago 4, Toronto 1.

Eddie Shore (left) and Jack Portland (right) were both members of the Bruins' Stanley Cup championship team in 1939.

1936-37 — Detroit Red Wings — Normie Smith, Pete Kelly, Larry Aurie, Herbie Lewis, Hec Kilrea, Mud Bruneteau, Syd Howe, Wally Kilrea, Jimmy Franks, Bucko McDonald, Gordon Pettinger, Ebbie Goodfellow, Johnny Gallagher, Scotty Bowman, Johnny Sorrell, Marty Barry, Earl Robertson, Johnny Sherf, Howard Mackie, Jack Adams (manager-coach), Honey Walker (trainer).
Scores: April 6, at New York — Detroit 1, NY Rangers 5; April 8, at Detroit — Detroit 4, NY Rangers 2; April 11, at Detroit — Detroit 0, NY Rangers 1; April 13, at Detroit — Detroit 1, NY Rangers 0; April 15, at Detroit — Detroit 3, NY Rangers 0.

1935-36 — Detroit Red Wings — Johnny Sorrell, Syd Howe, Marty Barry, Herbie Lewis, Mud Bruneteau, Wally Kilrea, Hec Kilrea, Gordon Pettinger, Bucko McDonald, Scotty Bowman, Pete Kelly, Doug Young, Ebbie Goodfellow, Normie Smith, Jack Adams (manager-coach), Honey Walker (trainer).
Scores: April 5, at Detroit — Detroit 3, Toronto 1; April 7, at Detroit — Detroit 9, Toronto 4; April 9, at Toronto — Detroit 3, Toronto 4; April 11, at Toronto — Detroit 3, Toronto 1.

1934-35 — Montreal Maroons — Marvin (Cy) Wentworth, Alex Connell, Toe Blake, Stew Evans, Earl Robinson, Bill Miller, Dave Trottier, Jimmy Ward, Larry Northcott, Hooley Smith, Russ Blinco, Allan Shields, Sammy McManus, Gus Marker, Bob Gracie, Herb Cain, Tommy Gorman (manager), Lionel Conacher (coach), Bill O'Brien (trainer).
Scores: April 4, at Toronto — Mtl. Maroons 3, Toronto 2; April 6, at Toronto — Mtl. Maroons 3, Toronto 1; April 9, at Montreal — Mtl. Maroons 4, Toronto 1.

1933-34 — Chicago Blackhawks — Taffy Abel, Lolo Couture, Lou Trudel, Lionel Conacher, Paul Thompson, Leroy Goldsworthy, Art Coulter, Roger Jenkins, Don McFayden, Tommy Cook, Doc Romnes, Johnny Gottselig, Mush March, Johny Sheppard, Chuck Gardiner (captain), Bill Kendall, Tommy Gorman (manager-coach), Eddie Froelich (trainer).
Scores: April 3, at Detroit — Chicago 1, Detroit 2; April 5, at Detroit — Chicago 4, Detroit 1; April 8, at Chicago — Detroit 5, Chicago 2; April 10, at Chicago — Chicago 1, Detroit 0.

1932-33 — New York Rangers — Ching Johnson, Butch Keeling, Frank Boucher, Art Somers, Babe Siebert, Bun Cook, Andy Aitkinhead, Ott Heller, Ozzie Asmundson, Gord Pettinger, Doug Brennan, Cecil Dillon, Bill Cook (captain), Murray Murdock, Earl Seibert, Lester Patrick (manager-coach), Harry Westerby (trainer).
Scores: April 4, at New York — NY Rangers 5, Toronto 1; April 8, at Toronto — NY Rangers 3, Toronto 1; April 11, at Toronto — Toronto 3, NY Rangers 2; April 13, at Toronto — NY Rangers 1, Toronto 0.

1931-32 — Toronto Maple Leafs — Charlie Conacher, Harvey Jackson, King Clancy, Andy Blair, Red Horner, Lorne Chabot, Alex Levinsky, Joe Primeau, Hal Darragh, Hal Cotton, Frank Finnigan, Hap Day, Ace Bailey, Bob Gracie, Fred Robertson, Earl Miller, Conn Smythe (manager), Dick Irvin (coach), Tim Daly (trainer).
Scores: April 5 at New York — Toronto 6, NY Rangers 4; April 7, at Boston* — Toronto 6, NY Rangers 2; April 9, at Toronto — Toronto 6, NY Rangers 4.
* Ice was unavailable in Madison Square Garden and Rangers elected to play the second game on neutral ice.

1930-31 — Montreal Canadiens — George Hainsworth, Wildor Larochelle, Marty Burke, Sylvio Mantha, Howie Morenz, Johnny Gagnon, Aurel Joliat, Armand Mondou, Pit Lepine, Albert Leduc, Georges Mantha, Art Lesieur, Nick Wasnie, Bert McCaffrey, Gus Rivers, Jean Pusie, Leo Dandurand (manager), Cecil Hart (coach), Ed Dufour (trainer).
Scores: April 3, at Chicago — Montreal 2, Chicago 1; April 5, at Chicago — Chicago 2, Montreal 1; April 9, at Montreal — Chicago 3, Montreal 2; April 11, at Montreal — Montreal 4, Chicago 2; April 14, at Montreal — Montreal 2, Chicago 0.

1929-30 — Montreal Canadiens — George Hainsworth, Marty Burke, Sylvio Mantha, Howie Morenz, Bert McCaffrey, Aurel Joliat, Albert Leduc, Pit Lepine, Wildor Larochelle, Nick Wasnie, Gerald Carson, Armand Mondou, Georges Mantha, Gus Rivers, Leo Dandurand (manager), Cecil Hart (coach), Ed Dufour (trainer).
Scores: April 1 at Boston — Montreal 3, Boston 0; April 3 at Montreal — Montreal 4, Boston 3.

1928-29 — Boston Bruins — Cecil (Tiny) Thompson, Eddie Shore, Lionel Hitchman, Perk Galbraith, Eric Pettinger, Frank Fredrickson, Mickey Mackay, Red Green, Dutch Gainor, Harry Oliver, Eddie Rodden, Dit Clapper, Cooney Weiland, Lloyd Klein, Cy Denneny, Bill Carson, George Owen, Myles Lane, Art Ross (manager-coach), Win Green (trainer).
Scores: March 28 at Boston — Boston 2, NY Rangers 0; March 29 at New York — Boston 2, NY Rangers 1.

1927-28 — New York Rangers — Lorne Chabot, Taffy Abel, Leon Bourgault, Ching Johnson, Bill Cook, Bun Cook, Frank Boucher, Billy Boyd, Murray Murdoch, Paul Thompson, Alex Gray, Joe Miller, Patsy Callighen, Lester Patrick (manager-coach), Harry Westerby (trainer).
Scores: April 5 at Montreal — Mtl. Maroons 2, NY Rangers 0; April 7 at Montreal — NY Rangers 2, Mtl. Maroons 1; April 10 at Montreal — Mtl. Maroons 2, NY Rangers 1; April 12 at Montreal — NY Rangers 1, Mtl. Maroons 0; April 14 at Montreal — NY Rangers 2, Mtl. Maroons 1.

1926-27 — Ottawa Senators — Alex Connell, King Clancy, George (Buck) Boucher, Ed Gorman, Frank Finnigan, Alex Smith, Hec Kilrea, Hooley Smith, Cy Denneny, Frank Nighbor, Jack Adams, Milt Halliday, Dave Gil (manager-coach).
Scores: April 7 at Boston — Ottawa 0, Boston 0; April 9 at Boston — Ottawa 3, Boston 1; April 11 at Ottawa — Boston 1, Ottawa 1; April 13 at Ottawa — Ottawa 3, Boston 1.

1925-26 — Montreal Maroons — Clint Benedict, Reg Noble, Frank Carson, Dunc Munro, Nels Stewart, Harry Broadbent, Babe Siebert, Dinny Dinsmore, Bill Phillips, Hobart (Hobie) Kitchen, Sammy Rothschiel, Albert (Toots) Holway, Shorty Horne, Bern Brophy, Eddie Gerard (manager-coach), Bill O'Brien (trainer).
Scores: March 30 at Montreal — Mtl. Maroons 3, Victoria 0; April 1 at Montreal — Mtl. Maroons 3, Victoria 0; April 3 at Montreal — Victoria 3, Mtl. Maroons 2; April 6 at Montreal — Mtl. Maroons 2, Victoria 0.

The series in the spring of 1926 ended the annual playoffs between the champions of the east and the champions of the west. The west coast league disbanded, selling its players to Chicago, Detroit and New York Rangers. Since 1926-27 the annual playoffs in the National Hockey League have decided the Stanley Cup champions.

1924-25 — Victoria Cougars — Harry (Happy) Holmes, Clem Loughlin, Gordie Fraser, Frank Fredrickson, Jack Walker, Harold (Gizzy) Hart, Harold (Slim) Halderson, Frank Foyston, Wally Elmer, Harry Meeking, Jocko Anderson, Lester Patrick (manager-coach).
Scores: March 21 at Victoria — Victoria 5, Montreal 2; March 23 at Vancouver — Victoria 3, Montreal 1; March 27 at Victoria — Montreal 4, Victoria 2; March 30 at Victoria — Victoria 6, Montreal 1.

1923-24 — Montreal Canadiens — Georges Vezina, Sprague Cleghorn, Billy Couture, Howie Morenz, Aurel Joliat, Billy Boucher, Odie Cleghorn, Sylvio Mantha, Bobby Boucher, Billy Bell, Billy Cameron, Joe Malone, Fortier, Leo Dandurand (manager-coach).
Scores: March 18 at Montreal — Montreal 3, Van. Maroons 2; March 20 at Montreal — Montreal 2, Van. Maroons 1. March 22 at Montreal — Montreal 6, Cgy. Tigers 1; March 25 at Ottawa* — Montreal 3, Cgy. Tigers 0. (Because of an agreement between the NHL and the two western leagues WCHL and PCHA, Montreal had to play the champions of each league during the Stanley Cup series of 1924.)
*Game transferred to Ottawa to benefit from an artificial ice surface.

1922-23 — Ottawa Senators — George (Buck) Boucher, Lionel Hitchman, Frank Nighbor, King Clancy, Harry Helman, Clint Benedict, Jack Darragh, Eddie Gerard, Cy Denneny, Harry Broadbent, Tommy Gorman (manager), Pete Green (coach), F. Dolan (trainer).
Scores: March 16 at Vancouver — Ottawa 1, Van. Maroons 0; March 19 at Vancouver — Van. Maroons 4, Ottawa 1; March 23 at Vancouver — Ottawa 3, Van. Maroons 2; March 26 at Vancouver — Ottawa 5, Van. Maroons 1; March 29 at Vancouver — Ottawa 2, Edm. Eskimos 1; March 31 at Vancouver — Ottawa 1, Edm. Eskimos 0. (Because of an agreement between the NHL and the two western leagues, WCHL and PCHA, Ottawa had to play the champions of each league during the Stanley Cup series of 1923.)

1921-22 — Toronto St. Pats — Ted Stackhouse, Corb Denneny, Rod Smylie, Lloyd Andrews, John Ross Roach, Harry Cameron, Bill (Red) Stuart, Cecil (Babe) Dye, Ken Randall, Reg Noble, Eddie Gerard (borrowed for one game from Ottawa), Stan Jackson, Nolan Mitchell, Charlie Querrie (manager), Eddie Powers (coach).
Scores: March 17 at Toronto — Van. Millionaires 4, Toronto 3; March 20 at Toronto — Toronto 2, Van. Millionaires 1; March 23 at Toronto — Van. Millionaires 3, Toronto 0; March 25 at Toronto — Toronto 6, Van. Millionaires 0; March 28 at Toronto — Toronto 5, Van. Millionaires 1.

1920-21 — Ottawa Senators — Jack McKell, Jack Darragh, Morley Bruce, George (Buck) Boucher, Eddie Gerard, Clint Benedict, Sprague Cleghorn, Frank Nighbor, Harry Broadbent, Cy Denneny, Leth Graham, Tommy Gorman (manager), Pete Green (coach), F. Dolan (trainer).
Scores: March 21 at Vancouver — Van. Millionaires 2, Ottawa 1; March 24 at Vancouver — Ottawa 4, Van. Millionaires 3; March 28 at Vancouver — Ottawa 3, Van. Millionaires 2; March 31 at Vancouver — Van. Millionaires 3, Ottawa 2; April 4 at Vancouver — Ottawa 2, Van. Millionaires 1

1919-20 — Ottawa Senators — Jack McKell, Jack Darragh, Morley Bruce, Horrace Merrill, George (Buck) Boucher, Eddie Gerard, Clint Benedict, Sprague Cleghorn, Frank Nighbor, Harry Broadbent, Cy Denneny, Price, Tommy Gorman (manager), Pete Green (coach).
Scores: March 22 at Ottawa — Ottawa 3, Seattle 2; March 24 at Ottawa — Ottawa 3, Seattle 0; March 27 at Ottawa — Seattle 3, Ottawa 1; March 30 at Toronto* — Seattle 5, Ottawa 2; April 1 at Toronto* — Ottawa 6, Seattle 1.
*Games transferred to Toronto to benefit from artificial ice surface.

1918-19 — No decision, Series halted by Spanish influenza epidemic, illness of several players and death of Joe Hall of Montreal Canadiens from flu. Five games had been played when the series was halted, each team having won two and tied one. The results are shown:
Scores: March 19 at Seattle — Seattle 7, Montreal 0; March 22 at Seattle — Montreal 4, Seattle 2; March 24 at Seattle — Seattle 7, Montreal 2; March 26 at Seattle — Montreal 0, Seattle 0; March 30 at Seattle — Montreal 4, Seattle 3.

1917-18 — Toronto Arenas — Rusty Crawford, Harry Meeking, Ken Randall, Corb Dennony, Harry Cameron, Jack Adams, Alf Skinner, Harry Mummery, Harry (Happy) Holmes, Reg Noble, Sammy Hebert, Jack Marks, Jack Coughlin, Neville, Charlie Querrie (manager), Dick Carroll (coach), Frank Carroll (trainer).
Scores: March 20 at Toronto — Toronto 5, Van. Millionaires 3; March 23 at Toronto — Van. Millionaires 6, Toronto 4; March 26 at Toronto — Toronto 6, Van. Millionaires 3; March 28 at Toronto — Van. Millionaires 8, Toronto 1; March 30 at Toronto — Toronto 2, Van. Millionaires 1.

1916-17 — Seattle Metropolitans — Harry (Happy) Holmes, Ed Carpenter, Cully Wilson, Jack Walker, Bernie Morris, Frank Foyston, Roy Rickey, Jim Riley, Bobby Rowe (captain), Peter Muldoon (manager).
Scores: March 17 at Seattle — Montreal 8, Seattle 4; March 20 at Seattle — Seattle 6, Montreal 1, March 23 at Seattle — Seattle 4, Montreal 1; March 25 at Seattle — Seattle 9, Montreal 1.

1915-16 — Montreal Canadiens — Georges Vezina, Bert Corbeau, Jack Laviolette, Newsy Lalonde, Louis Berlinguette, Goldie Prodgers, Howard McNamara, Didier Pitre, Skene Ronan, Amos Arbour, Skinner Poulin, Jack Fournier, George Kennedy (manager).
Scores: March 20 at Montreal — Portland 2, Montreal 0; March 22 at Montreal — Montreal 2, Portland 1; March 25 at Montreal — Montreal 6, Portland 3; March 28 at Montreal — Portland 6, Montreal 5; March 30 at Montreal — Montreal 2, Portland 1.

1914-15 — Vancouver Millionaires — Kenny Mallen, Frank Nighbor, Fred (Cyclone) Taylor, Hughie Lehman, Lloyd Cook, Mickey MacKay, Barney Stanley, Jim Seaborn, Si Griffis (captain), Jean Matz, Frank Patrick (playing manager).
Scores: March 22 at Vancouver — Van. Millionaires 6, Ottawa 2; March 24 at Vancouver — Van. Millionaires 8, Ottawa 3; March 26 at Vancouver — Van. Millionaires 12, Ottawa 3.

1913-14 — Toronto Blueshirts — Con Corbeau, F. Roy McGiffen, Jack Walker, George McNamara, Cully Wilson, Frank Foyston, Harry Cameron, Harry (Happy) Holmes, Alan M. Davidson (captain), Harriston, Jack Marshall (playing-manager), Frank and Dick Carroll (trainers).
Scores: March 7 at Montreal — Montreal 2, Toronto 0; March 11 at Toronto — Toronto 6, Montreal 0; Total goals: Toronto 6, Montreal 2. March 14 at Toronto — Toronto 5, Victoria 2; March 17 at Toronto — Toronto 6, Victoria 5; March 19 at Toronto — Toronto 2, Victoria 1.

1912-13 — Quebec Bulldogs — Joe Malone, Joe Hall, Paddy Moran, Harry Mummery, Tommy Smith, Jack Marks, Russell Crawford, Billy Creighton, Jeff Malone, Rocket Power, M.J. Quinn (manager), D. Beland (trainer).
Scores: March 8 at Quebec — Que. Bulldogs 14, Sydney 3; March 10 at Quebec — Que. Bulldogs 6, Sydney 2.

Victoria challenged Quebec but the Bulldogs refused to put the Stanley Cup in competition so the two teams played an exhibition series with Victoria winning two games to one by scores of 7-5, 3-6, 6-1. It was the first meeting between the Eastern champions and the Western champions. The following year, and until the Western Hockey League disbanded after the 1926 playoffs, the Cup went to the winner of the series between East and West.

1911-12 — Quebec Bulldogs — Goldie Prodgers, Joe Hall, Walter Rooney, Paddy Moran, Jack Marks, Jack MacDonald, Eddie Oatman, Leonard, Joe Malone (captain), C. Nolan (coach), M.J. Quinn (manager), D. Beland (trainer).
Scores: March 11 at Quebec — Que. Bulldogs 9, Moncton 3; March 13 at Quebec — Que. Bulldogs 8, Moncton 0.

Prior to 1912, teams could challenge the Stanley Cup champions for the title, thus there was more than one Championship Series played in most of the seasons between 1894 and 1911.

1910-11 — Ottawa Senators — Hamby Shore, Percy LeSueur, Jack Darragh, Bruce Stuart, Marty Walsh, Bruce Ridpath, Fred Lake, Albert (Dubby) Kerr, Alex Currie, Horace Gaul.
Scores: March 13 at Ottawa — Ottawa 7, Galt 4; March 16 at Ottawa — Ottawa 13, Port Arthur 4.

1909-10 — Montreal Wanderers — Cecil W. Blackford, Ernie (Moose) Johnson, Ernie Russell, Riley Hern, Harry Hyland, Jack Marshall, Frank (Pud) Glass (captain), Jimmy Gardner, R. R. Boon (manager).
Scores: March 12 at Montreal — Mtl. Wanderers 7, Berlin (Kitchener) 3.

1908-09 — Ottawa Senators — Fred Lake, Percy LeSueur, Fred (Cyclone) Taylor, H.L. (Billy) Gilmour, Albert Kerr, Edgar Dey, Marty Walsh, Bruce Stuart (captain).
Scores: Ottawa, as champions of the Eastern Canada Hockey Association took over the Stanley Cup in 1909 and, although a challenge was accepted by the Cup trustees from Winnipeg Shamrocks but could not be arranged because of the lateness of the season, no other challenges were made in 1909. The following season — 1909-10 — however, the Senators accepted two challenges as defending Cup Champions. The first was against Galt in a two-game, total-point series, and the second against Edmonton, also a two-game, total-point series. Results: January 5 at Ottawa — Ottawa 12, Galt 3; January 7 at Ottawa — Ottawa 3, Galt 1. January 18 at Ottawa — Ottawa 8, Edm. Eskimos 4; January 20 at Ottawa — Ottawa 13, Edm. Eskimos 7.

1907-08 — Montreal Wanderers — Riley Hern, Art Ross, Walter Small, Frank (Pud) Glass, Bruce Stuart, Ernie Russell, Ernie (Moose) Johnson, Cecil Blachford (captain), Tom Hooper, Larry Gilmour, Ernie Liffiton, R.R. Boon (manager).
Scores: Wanderers accepted four challenges for the Cup: January 9 at Montreal — Mtl. Wanderers 9, Ott. Victorias 3; January 13 at Montreal — Mtl. Wanderers 13, Ott. Victorias 1; March 10 at Montreal — Mtl. Wanderers 11, Wpg. Maple Leafs 5; March 12 at Montreal — Mtl. Wanderers 9, Wpg. Maple Leafs 3; March 14 at Montreal — Mtl. Wanderers 6, Tor. Maple Leafs 4. Note: Toronto played in the Ontario Professional Hockey League (1908, 1909). This club was not associated with the current NHL franchise. At start of following season, 1908-09, Wanderers were challenged by Edmonton. Results: December 28 at Montreal — Mtl. Wanderers 7, Edm. Eskimos 3; December 30 at Montreal — Edm. Eskimos 7, Mtl. Wanderers 6. Total goals: Mtl. Wanderers 13, Edm. Eskimos 10.

1906-07 — (March) — Montreal Wanderers — W. S. (Billy) Strachan, Riley Hern, Lester Patrick, Hod Stuart, Frank (Pud) Glass, Ernie Russell, Cecil Blachford (captain), Ernie (Moose) Johnson, Rod Kennedy, Jack Marshall, R. R. Boon (manager).
Scores: March 23 at Winnipeg — Mtl. Wanderers 7, Kenora 2; March 25 at Winnipeg — Kenora 6, Mtl. Wanderers 5. Total goals: Mtl. Wanderers 12, Kenora 8.

1906-07 — (January) — Kenora Thistles — Eddie Geroux, Art Ross, Si Griffis, Tom Hooper, Billy McGimsie, Roxy Beaudro, Tom Phillips.
Scores: January 17 at Montreal — Kenora 4, Mtl. Wanderers 2; Jan. 21 at Montreal — Kenora 8, Mtl. Wanderers 6.

1905-06 — (March) — (Montreal Wanderers — H. Menard, Billy Strachan, Rod Kennedy, Lester Patrick, Frank (Pud) Glass, Ernie Russell, Ernie (Moose) Johnson, Cecil Blachford (captain), Josh Arnold, R. R. Boon (manager).
Scores: March 14 at Montreal — Mtl. Wanderers 9, Ottawa 1; March 17 at Ottawa — Ottawa 9, Mtl. Wanderers 3. Total goals: Mtl. Wanderers 12, Ottawa 10. Wanderers accepted a challenge from New Glasgow, N.S., prior to the start of the 1906-07 season. Results: December 27 at Montreal — Mtl. Wanderers 10, New Glasgow 3; December 29 at Montreal — Mtl. Wanderers 7, New Glasgow 2.

1905-06 — (February) — Ottawa Silver Seven — Harvey Pulford (captain), Arthur Moore, Harry Westwick, Frank McGee, Alf Smith (playing coach), Billy Gilmour, Billy Hague, Percy LeSueur, Harry Smith, Tommy Smith, Dion, Ebbs.
Scores: February 27 at Ottawa — Ottawa 16, Queen's University 7; February 28 at Ottawa — Ottawa 12, Queen's University 7; March 6 at Ottawa — Ottawa 6, Smith's Falls 5; March 8 at Ottawa — Ottawa 8, Smith's Falls 2.

1904-05 — Ottawa Silver Seven — Dave Finnie, Harvey Pulford (captain), Arthur Moore, Harry Westwick, Frank McGee, Alf Smith (playing coach), Billy Gilmour, Frank White, Horace Gaul, Hamby Shore, Allen.
Scores: January 13 at Ottawa — Ottawa 9, Dawson City 2; January 16 at Ottawa — Ottawa 23, Dawson City 2; March 7 at Ottawa — Rat Portage 9, Ottawa 3; March 9 at Ottawa — Ottawa 4, Rat Portage 2; March 11 at Ottawa — Ottawa 5, Rat Portage 4.

1903-04 — Ottawa Silver Seven — S. C. (Suddy) Gilmour, Arthur Moore, Frank McGee, J.B. (Bouse) Hutton, H.L. (Billy) Gilmour, Jim McGee, Harry Westwick, E. H. (Harvey) Pulford (captain), Scott, A. T. (Alf) Smith (playing coach).
Scores: December 30 at Ottawa — Ottawa 9, Wpg. Rowing Club 1; January 1 at Ottawa — Wpg. Rowing Club 6, Ottawa 2; January 4 at Ottawa — Ottawa 2, Wpg. Rowing Club 0. February 23 at Ottawa — Ottawa 6, Tor. Malboros 3; February 25 at Ottawa — Ottawa 11, Tor. Marlboros 2; March 2 at Montreal — Ottawa 5, Mtl. Wanderers 5. Following the tie game, a new two-game series was ordered to be played in Ottawa but Wanderers refused unless the tie-game was replayed in Montreal. When no settlement could be reached, the series was abandoned and Ottawa retained the Cup and accepted a two-game challenge from Brandon. Results: (both games at Ottawa), March 9, Ottawa 6, Brandon 3; March 11, Ottawa 9, Brandon 3.

1902-03 — (March) — Ottawa Silver Seven — S. C. (Suddy) Gilmour, P.T. (Percy) Sims, J. B. (Bouse) Hutton, D. J. (Dave) Gilmour, H. L. (Billy) Gilmour, Harry Westwick, Frank McGee, F. H. Wood, A. A. Fraser, Charles D. Spittal, E. H. (Harvey) Pulford (captain), Arthur Moore, A. T. (Alf) Smith (coach.)
Scores: March 7 at Montreal — Ottawa 1, Mtl. Victorias 1; March 10 at Ottawa — Ottawa 8, Mtl. Victorias 0. Total goals: Ottawa 9, Mtl. Victorias 1; March 12 at Ottawa — Ottawa 6, Rat Portage 2; March 14 at Ottawa — Ottawa 4, Rat Portage 2.

1902-03 — (February) — Montreal AAA — Tom Hodge, R.R. (Dickie) Boon, W.C. (Billy) Nicholson, Art Hooper, W.J. (Billy) Bellingham, Charles A. Liffiton, Jack Marshall, Jim Gardner, Cecil Blachford, George Smith.
Scores: January 29 at Montreal — Mtl. AAA 8, Wpg. Victorias 1; January 31 at Montreal — Wpg. Victorias 2, Mtl. AAA 2; February 2 at Montreal — Wpg. Victorias 4, Mtl. AAA 2; February 4 at Montreal — Mtl. AAA 5, Wpg. Victorias 1.

1901-02 — (March) — Montreal AAA — Tom Hodge, R. R. (Dickie) Boon, W.C. (Billy) Nicholson, Art Hooper, W. J. (Billy) Bellingham, Charles A. Liffiton, Jack Marshall, Roland Elliott, Jim Gardner.
Scores: March 13 at Winnipeg — Wpg. Victorias 1, Mtl. AAA 0; March 15 at Winnipeg — Mtl. AAA 5, Wpg. Victorias 0; March 17 at Winnipeg — Mtl. AAA 2, Wpg. Victorias 1.

1901-02 — (January) — Winnipeg Victorias — Burke Wood, A.B. (Tony) Gingras, Charles W. Johnstone, R.M. (Rod) Flett, Nagnus L. Flett, Dan Bain (captain), Fred Scanlon, F. Cadham, G. Brown.
Scores: January 21 at Winnipeg — Wpg. Victorias 5, Tor Wellingtons 3; January 23 at Winnipeg — Wpg. Victorias 5, Tor. Wellingtons 3.

1900-01 — Winnipeg Victorias — Burke Wood, Jack Marshall, A.B. (Tony) Gingras, Charles W. Johnstone, R. M. (Rod) Flett, Magnus L. Flett, Dan Bain (captain), G. Brown.
Scores: January 29 at Montreal — Wpg. Victorias 4, Mtl. Shamrocks 3; January 31 at Montreal — Wpg. Victorias 2, Mtl. Shamrocks 1.

1899-1900 — Montreal Shamrocks — Joe McKenna, Frank Tansey, Frank Wall, Art Farrell, Fred Scanlon, Harry Trihey (captain), Jack Brannen.
Scores: February 12 at Montreal — Mtl. Shamrocks 4, Wpg. Victorias 3; February at Montreal — Wpg. Victorias 3, Mtl. Shamrocks 2; February 16 at Montreal — Mtl. Shamrocks 5, Wpg. Victorias 4; March 5 at Montreal — Mtl. Shamrocks 10, Halifax 2; March 7 at Montreal — Mtl. Shamrocks 11, Halifax 0.

1898-99 — (March) — Montreal Shamrocks — Joe McKenna, Frank Tansey, Frank Wall, Harry Trihey (captain), Art Farrell, Fred Scanlon, Jack Brannen, Dalby, Hoerner.
Scores: March 14 at Montreal — Mtl. Shamrocks 6, Queen's University 2.

1898-99 — (February) — Montreal Victorias — Gordon Lewis, Mike Grant, Graham Drinkwater, Cam Davidson, Bob McDougall, Ernie McLea, Frank Richardson, Jack Ewing, Russell Bowie, Douglas Acer, Fred McRobie.
Scores: February 15 at Montreal — Mtl. Victorias 2, Wpg. Victorias 1; February 18 at Montreal — Mtl. Victorias 3, Wpg. Victorias 2.

1897-98 — Montreal Victorias — Gordon Lewis, Hartland McDougall, Mike Grant, Graham Drinkwater, Cam Davidson, Bob McDougall, Ernie McLea, Frank Richardson (captain), Jack Ewing.
The Victorias as champions of the Amateur Hockey Association, retained the Cup and were not called upon to defend it.

1896-97 — Montreal Victorias — Gordon Lewis, Harold Henderson, Mike Grant (captain), Cam Davidson, Graham Drinkwater, Robert McDougall, Ernie McLea, Shirley Davidson, Hartland McDougall, Jack Ewing, Percy Molson, David Gillilan, McLellan.
Scores: December 27 at Montreal — Mtl. Victorias 15, Ott. Capitals 2.

1895-96 — (December) — Montreal Victorias — Gordon Lewis, Harold Henderson, Mike Grant (captain), Robert McDougall, Graham Drinkwater, Shirley Davidson, Ernie McLea, Robert Jones, Cam Davidson, Hartland McDougall, David Gillilan, Reg Wallace, Stanley Willett.
Scores: December 30 at Winnipeg — Mtl. Victorias 6, Wpg. Victorias 5.

1895-96 — (February) — Winnipeg Victorias — G.H. Merritt, Rod Flett, Fred Higginbotham, Jack Armitage (captain), C.J. (Tote) Campbell, Dan Bain, Charles Johnstone, H. Howard.
Scores: February 14 at Montreal — Wpg. Victorias 2, Mtl. Victorias 0.

1894-95 — Montreal Victorias — Robert Jones, Harold Henderson, Mike Grant (captain), Shirley Davidson, Bob McDougall, Norman Rankin, Graham Drinkwater, Roland Elliot, William Pullan, Hartland McDougall, Arthur Fenwick, A. McDougall.
Montreal Victorias as champions of the Amateur Hockey Association were prepared to defend the Stanley Cup. However, the Stanley Cup trustees had already accepted a challenge match between the 1894 champion Montreal AAA and Queen's University. It was declared that if Montreal AAA defeated Queen's University, Montreal Victorias would be declared Stanley Cup champions. If Queen's University won, the Cup would go to the university club. In a game played March 9, 1895, Montreal AAA defeated Queen's University 5-1. As a result, Montreal Victorias were awarded the Stanley Cup.

1893-94 — Montreal AAA — Herbert Collins, Allan Cameron, George James, Billy Barlow, Clare Mussen, Archie Hodgson, Haviland Routh, Alex Irving, James Stewart, A.C. (Toad) Waud, A. Kingan, E. O'Brien.
Scores: March 17 at Mtl. Victorias — Mtl. AAA 3, Mtl. Victorias 2; March 22 at Montreal — Mtl. AAA 3, Ott. Generals 1.

1892-93 — Montreal AAA — Tom Paton, James Stewart, Allan Cameron, Alex Irving, Haviland Routh, Archie Hodgson, Billy Barlow, A.B. Kingan, J. Lowe.
In accordance with the terms governing the presentation of the Stanley Cup, it was awarded for the first time to the Montreal AAA as champions of the Amateur Hockey Association in 1893. Once Montreal AAA had been declared holders of the Stanley Cup, any Canadian hockey team could challenge for the trophy.

All-Time NHL Playoff Formats

1917-18 — The regular-season was split into two halves. The winners of both halves faced each other in a two-game, total-goals series for the NHL championship and the right to meet the PCHA champion in the best-of-five Stanley Cup Finals.

1918-19 — Same as 1917-18, except that the Stanley Cup Finals was extended to a best-of-seven series.

1919-20 — Same as 1917-1918, except that Ottawa won both halves of the split regular-season schedule to earn an automatic berth into the best-of-five Stanley Cup Finals against the PCHA champions.

1921-22 — The top two teams at the conclusion of the regular-season faced each other in a two-game, total-goals series for the NHL championship. The NHL champion then moved on to play the winner of the PCHA-WCHL playoff series in the best-of-five Stanley Cup Finals.

1922-23 — The top two teams at the conclusion of the regular-season faced each other in a two-game, total-goals series for the NHL championship. The NHL champion then moved on to play the PCHA champion in the best-of-three Stanley Cup Semi-Finals, and the winner of the Semi-Finals played the WCHL champion, which had been given a bye, in the best-of-three Stanley Cup Finals.

1923-24 — The top two teams at the conclusion of the regular-season faced each other in a two-game, total-goals series for the NHL championship. The NHL champion then moved to play the loser of the PCHA-WCHL playoff (the winner of the PCHA-WCHL playoff earned a bye into the Stanley Cup Finals) in the best-of-three Stanley Cup Semi-Finals. The winner of this series met the PCHA-WCHL playoff winner in the best-of-three Stanley Cup Finals.

1924-25 — The first place team (Hamilton) at the conclusion of the regular-season was supposed to play the winner of a two-game, total goals series between the second (Toronto) and third (Montreal) place clubs. However, Hamilton refused to abide by this new format, demanding greater compensation than offered by the League. Thus, Toronto and Montreal played their two-game, total-goals series, and the winner (Montreal) earned the NHL title and then played the WCHL champion (Victoria) in the best-of-five Stanley Cup Finals.

1925-26 — The format which was intended for 1924-25 went into effect. The winner of the two-game, total-goals series between the second and third place teams squared off against the first place team in the two-game, total-goals NHL championship series. The NHL champion then moved on to play the WHL champion in the best-of-five Stanley Cup Finals.

After the 1925 season, the NHL was the only major professional hockey league still in existence and consequently took over sole control of the Stanley Cup competition.

1926-27 — The 10-team league was divided into two divisions — Canadian and American — of five teams apiece. In each division, the winner of the two-game, total-goals series between the second and third place teams faced the first place team in a two-game, total-goals series for the division title. The two division title winners then met in the best-of-five Stanley Cup Finals.

1928-29 — Both first place teams in the two divisions played each other in a best-of-five series. Both second place teams in the two divisions played each other in a two-game, total-goals series as did the two third place teams. The winners of these latter two series then played each other in a best-of-three series for the right to meet the winner of the series between the two first place clubs. This Stanley Cup Finals was a best-of-three.

    Series A: First in Canadian Division versus first in American (best-of-five)
    Series B: Second in Canadian Division versus second in American (two-game, total-goals)
    Series C: Third in Canadian Division versus third in American (two-game, total-goals)
    Series D: Winner of Series B versus winner of Series C (best-of-three)
    Series E: Winner of Series A versus winner of Series D (best of three) for Stanley Cup

1931-32 — Same as 1928-29, except that Series D was changed to a two-game, total-goals series.

1936-37 — Same as 1928-29, except that Series A and E were both best-of-five and Series B, C, and D were each best-of-three.

Stanley Cup Standings
1918-90

Team	Yrs.	Series	Won	Lost	Games	Won	Lost	Tied	GF	GA	Cup Wins	Winning %
Montreal	64	119*	77	41	539	340	212	8	1681	1317	22**	.612
Toronto	53	87	47	40	391	184	203	4	935	974	13	.476
Boston	50	83	38	44	384	189	199	6	1159	1132	5	.487
Chicago	44	73	32	40	304	144	171	5	882	1003	3	.452
NY Rangers	40	70	32	37	294	136	154	8	805	854	3	.476
Detroit	39	67	35	31	313	155	163	1	854	866	7	.490
Philadelphia	20	43	25	17	204	116	107	0	714	685	2	.520
St. Louis	19	33	14	18	154	71	93	0	468	547	0	.429
Calgary***	15	26	12	14	97	59	60	0	395	424	1	.443
Los Angeles	15	20	5	14	79	30	60	0	263	369	0	.329
NY Islanders	14	38	28	10	191	118	73	0	674	540	4	.618
Minnesota	14	25	11	13	124	60	69	0	435	461	0	.476
Buffalo	14	23	9	13	99	47	57	0	329	355	0	.465
Edmonton	10	27	21	5	119	89	37	0	527	377	5	.723
Pittsburgh	10	14	4	9	51	28	34	0	178	217	0	.412
Vancouver	10	13	3	9	45	19	33	0	145	195	0	.356
Quebec	7	13	6	7	68	31	37	0	217	238	0	.456
Washington	7	11	4	6	47	24	29	0	178	176	0	.468
Winnipeg	7	9	2	7	36	9	27	0	111	159	0	.250
Hartford	5	6	1	4	25	10	19	0	86	109	0	.400
New Jersey****	2	4	2	2	22	11	11	0	70	77	0	.500

* 1919 final incomplete due to influenza epidemic.   *** Includes totals of Atlanta 1974-80.
** Canadiens also won the Stanley Cup in 1916.   **** Includes totals of Colorado 1976-82.

1938-39 — With the NHL reduced to seven teams, the two-division system was replaced by one seven-team league. Based on final regular-season standings, the following playoff format was adopted:

    Series A: First versus Second (best-of-seven)
    Series B: Third versus Fourth (best-of-three)
    Series C: Fifth versus Sixth (best-of-three)
    Series D: Winner of Series B versus winner of Series C (best-of-three)
    Series E: Winner of Series A versus winner of Series D (best-of-seven)

1942-43 — With the NHL reduced to six teams (the "original six"), only the top four finishers qualified for playoff action. The best-of-seven Semi-Finals pitted Team #1 vs Team #3 and Team #2 vs Team #4. The winners of each Semi-Final series met in the best-of-seven Stanley Cup Finals.

1967-68 — When it doubled in size from 6 to 12 teams, the NHL once again was divided into two divisions — East and West — of six teams apiece. The top four clubs in each division qualified for the playoffs (all series were best-of-seven):

    Series A: Team #1 (East) vs Team #3 (East)
    Series B: Team #2 (East) vs Team #4 (East)
    Series C: Team #1 (West) vs Team #3 (West)
    Series D: Team #2 (West) vs Team #4 (West)

    Series E: Winner of Series A vs winner of Series B
    Series F: Winner of Series C vs winner of Series D
    Series G: Winner of Series E vs Winner of Series F

1970-71 — Same as 1967-68 except that Series E matched the winners of Series A and D, and Series F matched the winners of Series B and C.

1971-72 — Same as 1970-71, except that Series A and C matched Team #1 vs Team #4, and Series B and D matched Team #2 vs Team #3.

1974-75 — With the League now expanded to 18 teams in four divisions, a completely new playoff format was introduced. First, the #2 and #3 teams in each of the four divisions were pooled together in the Preliminary round. Those eight (#2 and #3) clubs were ranked #1 to #8 based on regular-season record:

    Series A: Team #1 vs Team #8 (best-of-three)
    Series B: Team #2 vs Team #7 (best-of-three)
    Series C: Team #3 vs Team #6 (best-of-three)
    Series D: Team #4 vs Team #5 (best-of-three)
The winners of this Preliminary round then pooled together with the four division winners, which had received byes into this Quarter-Final round. These eight teams were again ranked #1 to #8 based on regular-season record:
    Series E: Team #1 vs Team #8 (best-of-seven)
    Series F: Team #2 vs Team #7 (best-of-seven)
    Series G: Team #3 vs Team #6 (best-of-seven)
    Series H: Team #4 vs Team #5 (best-of-seven)
The four Quarter-Finals winners, which moved on to the Semi-Finals, were then ranked #1 to #4 based on regular season record:
    Series I: Team #1 vs Team #4 (best-of-seven)
    Series J: Team #2 vs Team #3 (best-of-seven)
    Series K: Winner of Series I vs winner of Series J (best-of-seven)

1977-78 — Same as 1974-75, except that the Preliminary round consisted of the #2 teams in the four divisions and the next four teams based on regular-season record (not their standings within their divisions).

1979-80 — With the addition of four WHA franchises, the League expanded its playoff structure to include 16 of its 21 teams. The four first place teams in the four divisions automatically earned playoff berths. Among the 17 other clubs, the top 12, according to regular-season record, also earned berths. All 16 teams were then pooled together and ranked #1 to #16 based on regular-season record:

    Series A: Team #1 vs Team #16 (best-of-five)
    Series B: Team #2 vs Team #15 (best-of-five)
    Series C: Team #3 vs Team #14 (best-of-five)
    Series D: Team #4 vs Team #13 (best-of-five)
    Series E: Team #5 vs Team #12 (best-of-five)
    Series F: Team #6 vs Team #11 (best-of-five)
    Series G: Team #7 vs Team #10 (best-of-five)
    Series H: Team #8 vs Team # 9 (best-of-five)
The eight Preliminary round winners, ranked #1 to #8 based on regular-season record, moved on to the Quarter-Finals:
    Series I: Team #1 vs Team #8 (best-of-seven)
    Series J: Team #2 vs Team #7 (best-of-seven)
    Series K: Team #3 vs Team #6 (best-of-seven)
    Series L: Team #4 vs Team #5 (best-of-seven)
The eight Quarter-Finals winners, ranked #1 to #4 based on regular-season record, moved on to the semi-finals:
    Series M: Team #1 vs Team #4 (best-of-seven)
    Series N: Team #2 vs Team #3 (best-of-seven)
    Series O: Winner of Series M vs winner of Series N (best-of-seven)

1981-82 — The first four teams in each division earn playoff berths. In each division, the first-place team opposes the fourth-place team and the second-place team opposes the third-place team in a best-of-five Division Semi-Final series (DSF). In each division, the two winners of the DSF meet in a best-of-seven Division Final series (DF). The two winners in each conference meet in a best-of-seven Conference Final series (CF). In the Prince of Wales Conference, the Adams Division winner opposes the Patrick Division winner; in the Clarence Campbell Conference, the Smythe Division winner opposes the Norris Division winner. The two CF winners meet in a best-of-seven Stanley Cup Final (F) series.

1986-87 — Division Semi-Final series changed from best-of-five to best-of-seven.

SPECIAL FEATURE

The Post-War Dynasties

The Edmonton Oilers' 1990 Stanley Cup triumph established the club as one of the great teams in NHL history. Since the end of World War II, the NHL has almost always had one or two powerhouse clubs that are a threat to win the Cup every season. These dynasty teams include legendary clubs like the Detroit Red Wings of the early 1950s, the Montreal Canadiens of the late 1950s and, more recently, the Canadiens of the late 1970s and the NY Islanders of the early 1980s.

Although the definition of a "dynasty" can be debated, the following criteria have been used here:

a) Three-or-more consecutive Stanley Cup wins;
b) Five or six consecutive playoff appearances including four Stanley Cup wins.
c) Seven consecutive playoff appearances including five Stanley Cup wins.

Eight teams fit this definition of a dynasty:

1)	Toronto	1947-51
2)	Detroit	1950-55
3)	Montreal	1956-60
4)	Toronto	1962-64
5)	Montreal	1965-69
6)	Montreal	1976-79
7)	NY Islanders	1980-83
8)	Edmonton	1984-90

Gordie Howe (above) was the offensive leader of the Detroit Red Wings during the club's dynasty years in the 1950's. Jean Beliveau (below, left) was a member of the great Montreal teams of the 1950's and 1960's. Bob Nystrom (below, right) celebrates his Stanley Cup winning goal in overtime against the Philadelphia Flyers in 1980. Nystrom's goal clinched the first of four consecutive Stanley Cup triumphs for the New York Islanders.

DYNASTY TEAM	Standings											Players on all Stanley Cup teams	All-Star Team Selections			Individual Awards

Toronto 1947-51

	Regular Season					Playoffs					Players on all Stanley Cup teams	All-Star Team Selections			Individual Awards
	GP	W	L	T	%	GP	W	L	%		Bill Barilko, Turk Broda, Ted Kennedy,	Turk Broda	G	1st (1948)	Howie Meeker, Calder, 1947
* 1946-47	60	31	19	10	.600	11	8	3	.727		Joe Klukay, Howie Meeker, Gus Mortson,	Gus Mortson	D	1st (1950)	Turk Broda, Vezina, 1948
* 1947-48	60	32	15	13	.642	9	8	1	.889		Jim Thomson, Harry Watson	Ted Kennedy	C	2nd (1950, 1951)	Al Rollins, Vezina, 1951
* 1948-49	60	22	25	13	.475	9	8	1	.889			Jim Thomson	D	2nd (1951)	
1949-50	70	31	27	12	.529	7	3	4	.429			Sid Smith	LW	2nd (1951)	
* 1950-51	70	41	16	13	.679	**11	8	2	**.773						
Total	320	157	102	61	.586	47	35	11	.755						

** Suspended game vs. Boston counted as a tie

Detroit 1950-55

	Regular Season					Playoffs					Players on all Stanley Cup teams	All-Star Team Selections			Individual Awards
	GP	W	L	T	%	GP	W	L	%		Gordie Howe, Red Kelly, Ted Lindsay,	Sid Abel	C	1st (1950), 2nd (1951)	Ted Lindsay, Art Ross, 1950
* 1949-50	70	37	19	14	.629	14	8	6	.571		Marty Pavelich, Marcel Pronovost,	Ted Lindsay	LW	1st (1950, 1951, 1952, 1953, 1954)	Gordie Howe, Art Ross, 1951, 1952, 1953, 1954
1950-51	70	44	13	13	.721	6	2	4	.333		Johnny Wilson	Leo Reise	D	2nd (1950, 1951)	Gordie Howe, Hart, 1952, 1953
* 1951-52	70	44	14	12	.714	8	8	0	1.000			Red Kelly	D	1st (1951, 1952, 1953, 1954, 1955), 2nd (1950)	Red Kelly, Norris, 1954; Lady Byng, 1951, 1953, 1954
1952-53	70	36	16	18	.643	6	2	4	.333			Gordie Howe	RW	1st (1951, 1952, 1953, 1954), 2nd (1950)	Terry Sawchuk, Calder, 1951; Vezina, 1952, 1953, 1955
* 1953-54	70	37	19	14	.629	12	8	4	.667			Terry Sawchuk	G	1st (1951, 1952, 1953), 2nd (1954, 1955)	
* 1954-55	70	42	17	11	.679	11	8	3	.727			Alex Delvecchio	C	2nd (1953)	
Total	420	240	98	82	.669	57	36	21	.632			Bob Goldham	D	2nd (1955)	

Montreal 1956-60

	Regular Season					Playoffs					Players on all Stanley Cup teams	All-Star Team Selections			Individual Awards
	GP	W	L	T	%	GP	W	L	%		Jean Beliveau, Bernie Geoffrion, Doug	Jacques Plante	G	1st (1956, 1959), 2nd (1957, 1958, 1960)	Jean Beliveau, Art Ross, 1956; Hart, 1956
* 1955-56	70	45	15	10	.714	10	8	2	.800		Harvey, Tom Johnson, Don Marshall,	Doug Harvey	D	1st (1956, 1957, 1958, 1960), 2nd (1959)	Dickie Moore, Art Ross, 1958, 1959
* 1956-57	70	35	23	12	.586	10	8	2	.800		Dickie Moore, Jacques Plante, Claude	Jean Beliveau	C	1st (1956, 1957, 1959, 1960), 2nd (1958)	Doug Harvey, Norris, 1956, 1957, 1958, 1960
* 1957-58	70	43	17	10	.686	10	8	2	.800		Provost, Henri Richard, Maurice	Maurice Richard	RW	1st (1956), 2nd (1957)	Tom Johnson, Norris, 1959
* 1958-59	70	39	18	13	.650	11	8	3	.727		Richard, Jean-Guy Talbot	Tom Johnson	D	1st (1959), 2nd (1956)	Ralph Backstrom, Calder, 1959
* 1959-60	70	40	18	12	.657	8	8	0	1.000			Bert Olmstead	LW	2nd (1956)	Jacques Plante, Vezina, 1956, 1957, 1958, 1959, 1960
Total	350	202	91	57	.659	49	40	9	.816			Dickie Moore	LW	1st (1958, 1959)	
												Bernie Geoffrion	RW	2nd (1960)	

Toronto 1962-64

	Regular Season					Playoffs					Players on all Stanley Cup teams	All-Star Team Selections			Individual Awards
	GP	W	L	T	%	GP	W	L	%		George Armstrong, Bob Baun, Johnny	Carl Brewer	D	1st (1963), 2nd (1962)	Dave Keon, Lady Byng, 1962, 1963
* 1961-62	70	37	22	11	.607	12	8	4	.667		Bower, Carl Brewer, Billy Harris, Tim	Frank Mahovlich	LW	1st (1963), 2nd (1962, 1964)	Kent Douglas, Calder, 1963
* 1962-63	70	35	23	12	.586	10	8	2	.800		Horton, Red Kelly, Dave Keon, Frank	Dave Keon	C	2nd (1962)	
* 1963-64	70	33	25	12	.557	14	8	6	.571		Mahovlich, Bob Pulford, Ed Shack, Allan	Tim Horton	D	1st (1964), 2nd (1963)	
Total	210	105	70	35	.583	36	24	12	.667		Stanley, Ron Stewart				

Montreal 1965-69

	Regular Season					Playoffs					Players on all Stanley Cup teams	All-Star Team Selections			Individual Awards
	GP	W	L	T	%	GP	W	L	%		Ralph Backstrom, Jean Beliveau, Yvan	Jacques Laperriere	D	1st (1965, 1966)	Jacques Laperriere, Norris, 1966
* 1964-65	70	36	23	11	.593	13	8	5	.615		Cournoyer, Dick Duff, John Ferguson,	Claude Provost	RW	1st (1965)	Lorne Worsley, Vezina, 1966, 1968
* 1965-66	70	41	21	8	.643	10	8	2	.800		Terry Harper, Ted Harris, Jacques	Charlie Hodge	G	2nd (1965)	Charlie Hodge, Vezina, 1966
1966-67	70	32	25	13	.550	10	6	4	.600		Laperriere, Claude Provost, Henri	Gump Worsley	G	1st (1968), 2nd (1966)	Rogatien Vachon, Vezina, 1968
* 1967-68	70	42	22	10	.671	13	12	1	.923		Richard, Bobby Rousseau, J.C.	Jean Beliveau	C	2nd (1966, 1969)	Claude Provost, Masterton, 1968
* 1968-69	70	46	19	11	.736	14	12	2	.857		Tremblay, Gump Worsley	Bobby Rousseau	RW	2nd (1966)	Jean Beliveau, Conn Smythe, 1965
Total	350	197	110	53	.639	60	46	14	.767			J.C. Tremblay	D	2nd (1968)	Serge Savard, Conn Smythe, 1969
												Ted Harris	D	2nd (1969)	
												Yvan Cournoyer	RW	2nd (1969)	

Montreal 1976-79

	Regular Season					Playoffs					Players on all Stanley Cup teams	All-Star Team Selections			Individual Awards
	GP	W	L	T	%	GP	W	L	%		Rick Chartraw, Yvan Cournoyer, Ken	Ken Dryden	G	1st (1976, 1977, 1978, 1979)	Guy Lafleur, Art Ross, 1976, 1977, 1978
* 1975-76	80	58	11	11	.794	13	12	1	.923		Dryden, Bob Gainey, Doug Jarvis, Guy	Guy Lafleur	RW	1st (1976, 1977, 1978, 1979)	Guy Lafleur, Hart, 1977, 1978; Conn Smythe, 1977
* 1976-77	80	60	8	12	.825	14	12	2	.857		Lafleur, Yvon Lambert, Michel Larocque,	Guy Lapointe	D	2nd (1976, 1977)	Larry Robinson, Norris, 1977; Conn Smythe, 1978
* 1977-78	80	59	10	11	.806	15	12	3	.800		Jacques Lemaire, Doug Risebrough, Steve	Larry Robinson	D	1st (1977, 1979), 2nd (1978)	Serge Savard, Masterton, 1979
* 1978-79	80	52	17	11	.719	16	12	4	.750		Shutt, Mario Tremblay	Steve Shutt	LW	1st (1977), 2nd (1978)	Bob Gainey, Selke, 1978, 1979; Conn Smythe, 1979
Total	320	229	46	45	.786	58	48	10	.828			Serge Savard	D	2nd (1979)	Serge Savard, Masterton, 1979
															Ken Dryden, Vezina, 1976, 1977, 1978, 1979
															Michel Larocque, Vezina, 1977, 1978, 1979

NY Islanders 1980-83

	Regular Season					Playoffs					Players on all Stanley Cup teams	All-Star Team Selections			Individual Awards
	GP	W	L	T	%	GP	W	L	%		Mike Bossy, Bob Bourne, Clark Gillies,	Denis Potvin	D	1st (1981)	Mike Bossy, Lady Byng, 1983, Conn Smythe, 1982
* 1979-80	80	39	28	13	.569	21	15	6	.714		Butch Goring, Anders Kallur, Gord Lane,	Mike Bossy	RW	1st (1981, 1982, 1983, 1984)	Billy Smith, Vezina, 1982; Jennings, 1983
* 1980-81	80	48	18	14	.688	18	15	3	.833		Dave Langevin, Wayne Merrick, Ken	Billy Smith	G	1st (1982)	Billy Smith, Conn Smythe, 1983
* 1981-82	80	54	16	10	.738	19	15	4	.789		Morrow, Bob Nystrom, Stefan Persson,	Bryan Trottier	C	2nd (1982)	Roland Melanson, Jennings, 1983
* 1982-83	80	42	26	12	.600	20	15	5	.750		Denis Potvin, Billy Smith, Duane	John Tonelli	LW	2nd (1982)	Bryan Trottier, Conn Smythe, 1980
Total	320	183	88	49	.648	78	60	18	.769		Sutter, John Tonelli, Bryan Trottier	Roland Melanson	G	2nd (1983)	Butch Goring, Conn Smythe, 1981

Edmonton 1984-90

	Regular Season					Playoffs					Players on all Stanley Cup teams	All-Star Team Selections			Individual Awards
	GP	W	L	T	%	GP	W	L	%		Glenn Anderson, Grant Fuhr, Randy	Wayne Gretzky	C	1st (1984, 1985, 1986, 1987), 2nd (1988)	Wayne Gretzky, Art Ross, 1984, 1985, 1986, 1987
* 1983-84	80	57	18	5	.744	19	15	4	.789		Gregg, Charlie Huddy, Jari Kurri, Kevin	Paul Coffey	D	1st (1985, 1986), 2nd (1984)	Wayne Gretzky, Hart, 1984, 1985, 1986, 1987
* 1984-85	80	49	20	11	.681	18	15	3	.833		Lowe, Mark Messier	Jari Kurri	RW	1st (1985, 1987), 2nd (1984, 1986, 1989)	Wayne Gretzky, Conn Smythe, 1985, 1988
* 1985-86	80	56	17	7	.744	10	6	4	.600			Mark Messier	C	1st (1990), LW 2nd (1984)	Mark Messier, Hart, 1990, Conn Smythe, 1984
* 1986-87	80	50	24	6	.663	21	16	5	.762			Grant Fuhr	G	1st (1988)	Jari Kurri, Lady Byng, 1985
* 1987-88	80	44	25	11	.619	18	16	2	.889						Paul Coffey, Norris, 1985, 1986
1988-89	80	38	34	8	.525	7	3	4	.429						Grant Fuhr, Vezina, 1988
* 1989-90	80	38	28	14	.563	22	16	6	.727						Bill Ranford, Conn Smythe, 1990
Total	560	332	166	62	.648	115	87	28	.757						

* Stanley Cup Winning Team

Team Records

1918-1990

MOST STANLEY CUP CHAMPIONSHIPS:
22 — **Montreal Canadiens** 1924-30-31-44-46-53-56-57-58-59-60-65-66-68-69-71-73-76-77-78-79-86
13 — Toronto Maple Leafs 1918-22-32-42-45-47-48-49-51-62-63-64-67
7 — Detroit Red Wings 1936-37-43-50-52-54-55

MOST FINAL SERIES APPEARANCES:
32 — **Montreal Canadiens** in 73-year history.
21 — Toronto Maple Leafs in 73-year history.
18 — Detroit Red Wings in 64-year history.

MOST YEARS IN PLAYOFFS:
65 — **Montreal Canadiens in 73-year history.**
54 — Toronto Maple Leafs in 73-year history.
51 — Boston Bruins in 66-year history.

MOST CONSECUTIVE STANLEY CUP CHAMPIONSHIPS:
5 — **Montreal Canadiens** (1956-57-58-59-60)
4 — NY Islanders (1980-81-82-83)
— Montreal Canadiens (1976-77-78-79)

MOST CONSECUTIVE FINAL SERIES APPEARANCES:
10 — **Montreal Canadiens** (1951-60, inclusive)

MOST CONSECUTIVE PLAYOFF APPEARANCES:
23 — **Boston Bruins** (1968-90, inclusive)
21 — Montreal Canadiens (1949-69, inclusive)
20 — Detroit Red Wings (1939-58, inclusive)
— Montreal Canadiens (1971-90, inclusive)

MOST GOALS BOTH TEAMS, ONE PLAYOFF SERIES:
69 — **Edmonton Oilers, Chicago Blackhawks** in 1985 CF. Edmonton won best-of-seven series 4-2, outscoring Chicago 44-25.
62 — Chicago Blackhawks, Minnesota North Stars in 1985 DF. Chicago won best-of-seven series 4-2, outscoring Minnesota 33-29.
60 — Edmonton Oilers, Calgary Flames in 1984 DF. Edmonton won best-of-seven series 4-3, outscoring Calgary 33-27.

MOST GOALS ONE TEAM, ONE PLAYOFF SERIES:
44 — **Edmonton Oilers** in 1985 CF. Edmonton won best-of-seven series 4-2, outscoring Chicago 44-25.
35 — Edmonton Oilers in 1983 DF. Edmonton won best-of-seven series 4-1, outscoring Calgary 35-13.

MOST GOALS, BOTH TEAMS, TWO-GAME SERIES:
17 — **Toronto St. Patricks, Montreal Canadiens** in 1918 NHL F. Toronto won two-game total goal series 10-7.
15 — Boston Bruins, Chicago Blackhawks in 1927 QF. Boston won two-game total goal series 10-5.
— Pittsburgh Penguins, St. Louis Blues in 1975 PR. Pittsburgh won best-of-three series 2-0, outscoring St. Louis 9-6.

MOST GOALS, ONE TEAM, TWO-GAME SERIES:
11 — **Buffalo Sabres** in 1977 PR. Buffalo won best-of-three series 2-0, outscoring Minnesota 11-3.
— **Toronto Maple Leafs** in 1978 PR. Toronto won best-of-three series 2-0, outscoring Los Angeles 11-3.
10 — Boston Bruins in 1927 QF. Boston won two-game total goal series 10-5.

MOST GOALS, BOTH TEAMS, THREE-GAME SERIES:
33 — **Minnesota North Stars, Boston Bruins** in 1981 PR. Minnesota won best-of-five series 3-0, outscoring Boston 20-13.
31 — Chicago Blackhawks, Detroit Red Wings in 1985 DSF. Chicago won best-of-five series 3-0, outscoring Detroit 23-8.
28 — Toronto Maple Leafs, NY Rangers in 1932 F. Toronto won best-of-five series 3-0, outscoring New York 18-10.

MOST GOALS, ONE TEAM, THREE-GAME SERIES:
23 — **Chicago Blackhawks** in 1985 DSF. Chicago won best-of-five series 3-0, outscoring Detroit 23-8.
20 — Minnesota North Stars in 1981 PR. Minnesota won best-of-five series 3-0, outscoring Boston 20-13.
— NY Islanders in 1981 PR. New York won best-of-five series 3-0, outscoring Toronto 20-4.

MOST GOALS, BOTH TEAMS, FOUR-GAME SERIES:
36 — **Boston Bruins, St. Louis Blues** in 1972 SF. Boston won best-of-seven series 4-0, outscoring St. Louis 28-8.
— **Edmonton Oilers, Chicago Blackhawks** in 1983 CF. Edmonton won best-of-seven series 4-0, outscoring Chicago 25-11.
— **Minnesota North Stars, Toronto Maple Leafs** in 1983 DSF. Minnesota won best-of-five series 3-1; teams tied in scoring 18-18.
35 — NY Rangers, Los Angeles Kings in 1981 PR. NY Rangers won best-of-five series 3-1, outscoring Los Angeles 23-12.

MOST GOALS, ONE TEAM, FOUR-GAME SERIES:
28 — **Boston Bruins** in 1972 SF. Boston won best-of-seven series 4-0, outscoring St. Louis 28-8.

MOST GOALS, BOTH TEAMS, FIVE-GAME SERIES:
52 — **Edmonton Oilers, Los Angeles Kings** in 1987 DSF. Edmonton won best-of-seven series 4-1, outscoring Los Angeles 32-20.
50 — Los Angeles Kings, Edmonton Oilers in 1982 DSF. Los Angeles won best-of-five series 3-2, outscoring Edmonton 27-23.
48 — Edmonton Oilers, Calgary Flames in 1983 DF. Edmonton won best-of-seven series 4-1, outscoring Calgary 35-13.
— Calgary Flames, Los Angeles Kings in 1988 DSF. Calgary won best-of-seven series 4-1, outscoring Los Angeles 30-18.

MOST GOALS, ONE TEAM, FIVE-GAME SERIES:
35 — **Edmonton Oilers** in 1983 DF. Edmonton won best-of-seven series 4-1, outscoring Calgary 35-13.
32 — Edmonton Oilers in 1987 DSF. Edmonton won best-of-seven series 4-1, outscoring Los Angeles 32-20.
28 — NY Rangers in 1979 QF. NY Rangers won best-of-seven series 4-1, outscoring Philadelphia 28-8.
27 — Philadelphia Flyers in 1980 SF. Philadelphia won best-of-seven series 4-1, outscoring Minnesota 27-14.
— Los Angeles Kings, in 1982 DSF. Los Angeles won best-of-five series 3-2, outscoring Edmonton 27-23.

MOST GOALS, BOTH TEAMS, SIX-GAME SERIES:
69 — **Edmonton Oilers, Chicago Blackhawks** in 1985 CF. Edmonton won best-of-seven series 4-2, outscoring Chicago 44-25.
62 — Chicago Blackhawks, Minnesota North Stars in 1985 DF. Chicago won best-of-seven series 4-2, outscoring Minnesota 33-29.
56 — Montreal Canadiens, Chicago Blackhawks in 1973 F. Montreal won best-of-seven series 4-2, outscoring Chicago 33-23.

MOST GOALS, ONE TEAM, SIX-GAME SERIES:
44 — **Edmonton Oilers** in 1985 CF. Edmonton won best-of-seven series 4-2, outscoring Chicago 44-25.
33 — Chicago Blackhawks in 1985 DF. Chicago won best-of-seven series 4-2, outscoring Minnesota 33-29.
— Montreal Canadiens in 1973 F. Montreal won best-of-seven series 4-2, outscoring Chicago 33-23.

MOST GOALS, BOTH TEAMS, SEVEN-GAME SERIES:
60 — **Edmonton Oilers, Calgary Flames** in 1984 DF. Edmonton won best-of-seven series 4-3, outscoring Calgary 33-27.

MOST GOALS, ONE TEAM, SEVEN-GAME SERIES:
33 — **Philadelphia Flyers** in 1976 QF. Philadelphia won best-of-seven series 4-3, outscoring Toronto 33-23.
— **Boston Bruins** in 1983 DF. Boston won best-of-seven series 4-3, outscoring Buffalo 33-23.
— **Edmonton Oilers** in 1984 DF. Edmonton won best-of-seven series 4-3, outscoring Calgary 33-27.

FEWEST GOALS, BOTH TEAMS, TWO-GAME SERIES:
1 — **NY Rangers, NY Americans,** in 1929 SF. NY Rangers defeated NY Americans 1-0 in two-game, total-goal series.
— **Mtl. Maroons, Chicago Blackhawks** in 1935 SF. Mtl. Maroons defeated Chicago 1-0 in two-game, total-goal series.

FEWEST GOALS, ONE TEAM, TWO-GAME SERIES:
0 — **Mtl. Maroons** in 1937 SF. Lost best-of-three series 2-0 to NY Rangers while being outscored 5-0.
— **NY Americans** in 1939 QF. Lost best-of-three series 2-0 to Toronto while being outscored 6-0.
— **NY Americans** in 1929 SF. Lost two-game total-goal series 1-0 against NY Rangers.
— **Chicago Blackhawks** in 1935 SF. Lost two-game total-goal series 1-0 against Mtl. Maroons.

FEWEST GOALS, BOTH TEAMS, THREE-GAME SERIES:
7 — **Boston Bruins, Montreal Canadiens** in 1929 SF. Boston won best-of-five series 3-0, outscoring Montreal 5-2.
— **Detroit Red Wings, Mtl. Maroons** in 1936 SF. Detroit won best-of-five series 3-0, outscoring Mtl. Maroons 6-1.

FEWEST GOALS, ONE TEAM, THREE-GAME SERIES:
1 — **Mtl. Maroons** in 1936 SF. Lost best-of-five series 3-0 to Detroit and were outscored 6-1.

FEWEST GOALS, BOTH TEAMS, FOUR-GAME SERIES:
9 — **Toronto Maple Leafs, Boston Bruins** in 1935 SF. Toronto won best-of-five series 3-1, outscoring Boston 7-2.

FEWEST GOALS, ONE TEAM, FOUR-GAME SERIES:
2 — **Boston Bruins** in 1935 SF. Toronto won best-of-five series 3-1, outscoring Boston 7-2.
— **Montreal Canadiens** in 1952 F. Detroit won best-of-seven series 4-0, outscoring Montreal 11-2.

FEWEST GOALS, BOTH TEAMS, FIVE-GAME SERIES:
11 — **NY Rangers, Mtl. Maroons** in 1928 F. NY Rangers won best-of-five series 3-2, while outscored by Mtl. Maroons 6-5.

FEWEST GOALS, ONE TEAM, FIVE-GAME SERIES:
5 — **NY Rangers** in 1928 F. NY Rangers won best-of-five series 3-2, while outscored by Mtl. Maroons 6-5.

FEWEST GOALS, BOTH TEAMS, SIX-GAME SERIES:
22 — **Toronto Maple Leafs, Boston Bruins** in 1951 SF. Toronto won best-of-seven series 4-1 with 1 tie, outscoring Boston 17-5.

FEWEST GOALS, ONE TEAM, SIX-GAME SERIES:
5 — Boston Bruins in 1951 SF. Toronto won best-of-seven series 4-1 with 1 tie, outscoring Boston 17-5.

FEWEST GOALS, BOTH TEAMS, SEVEN-GAME SERIES:
18 — Toronto Maple Leafs, Detroit Red Wings in 1945 F. Toronto won best-of-seven series 4-3; teams tied in scoring 9-9.

FEWEST GOALS, ONE TEAM, SEVEN-GAME SERIES:
9 — Toronto Maple Leafs, in 1945 F. Toronto won best-of- seven series 4-3; teams tied in scoring 9-9.
  — Detroit Red Wings, in 1945 F. Toronto won best-of-seven series 4-3; teams tied in scoring 9-9.

MOST GOALS, BOTH TEAMS, ONE GAME:
18 — Los Angeles Kings, Edmonton Oilers at Edmonton, April 7, 1982. Los Angeles 10, Edmonton 8. Los Angeles won best-of-five DSF 3-2.
17 — Pittsburgh Penguins, Philadelphia Flyers at Pittsburgh, April 25, 1989. Pittsburgh 10, Philadelphia 7. Philadelphia won best-of-seven DF 4-3.
16 — Edmonton Oilers, Los Angeles Kings at Edmonton, April 9, 1987. Edmonton 13, Los Angeles 3. Edmonton won best-of-seven DSF 4-1.
  — Los Angeles Kings, Calgary Flames at Los Angeles, April 10, 1990. Los Angeles 12, Calgary 4. Los Angeles won best-of-seven DF 4-2.

MOST GOALS, ONE TEAM, ONE GAME:
13 — Edmonton Oilers at Edmonton, April 9, 1987. Edmonton 13, Los Angeles 3. Edmonton won best-of-seven DSF 4-1.
12 — Los Angeles Kings at Los Angeles, April 10, 1990. Los Angeles 12, Calgary 4. Los Angeles won best-of-seven DSF 4-2.
11 — Montreal Canadiens at Montreal, March 30, 1944. Montreal 11, Toronto 0. Canadiens won best-of-seven SF 4-1.
  — Edmonton Oilers at Edmonton May 4, 1985. Edmonton 11, Chicago 2. Edmonton won best-of-seven CF 4-2.

MOST GOALS, BOTH TEAMS, ONE PERIOD:
9 — NY Rangers, Philadelphia Flyers, April 24, 1979, at Philadelphia, third period. NY Rangers won 8-3 scoring six of nine third-period goals.
  — Los Angeles Kings, Calgary Flames at Los Angeles, April 10, 1990, second period. Los Angeles won game 12-4, scoring five of nine second-period goals.
8 — Chicago Blackhawks, Montreal Canadiens at Montreal, May 8, 1973, in the second period. Chicago won 8-7 scoring five of eight second-period goals.
  — Chicago Blackhawks, Edmonton Oilers at Chicago, May 12, 1985 in the first period. Chicago won 8-6, scoring five of eight first-period goals.
  — Edmonton Oilers, Winnipeg Jets at Edmonton, April 6, 1988 in the third period. Edmonton won 7-4, scoring six of eight third period goals.
  — Hartford Whalers, Montreal Canadiens at Hartford, April 10, 1988 in the third period. Hartford won 7-5, scoring five of eight third period goals.

MOST GOALS, ONE TEAM, ONE PERIOD:
7 — Montreal Canadiens, March 30, 1944, at Montreal in third period, during 11-0 win against Toronto.

LONGEST OVERTIME:
116 Minutes, 30 Seconds — Detroit Red Wings, Mtl. Maroons at Montreal, March 24, 25, 1936. Detroit 1, Mtl. Maroons 0. Mud Bruneteau scored, assisted by Hec Kilrea, at 16:30 of sixth overtime period, or after 176 minutes, 30 seconds from start of game, which ended at 2:25 a.m. Detroit won best-of-five SF 3-0.

SHORTEST OVERTIME:
9 Seconds — Montreal Canadiens, Calgary Flames, at Calgary, May 18, 1986. Montreal won 3-2 on Brian Skrudland's goal and captured the best-of-seven F 4-1.
11 Seconds — NY Islanders, NY Rangers, at NY Rangers, April 11, 1975. NY Islanders won 4-3 on Jean-Paul Parise's goal and captured the best-of-three PR 2-1.

MOST OVERTIME GAMES, ONE PLAYOFF YEAR:
16 — 1982. Of 71 games played, 16 went into overtime.

FEWEST OVERTIME GAMES, ONE PLAYOFF YEAR:
0 — 1963. None of the 16 games went into overtime, the only year since 1926 that no overtime was required in any playoff series.

MOST OVERTIME-GAME VICTORIES, ONE TEAM, ONE PLAYOFF YEAR:
6 — NY Islanders, 1980. One against Los Angeles in the PR; two against Boston in the QF; one against Buffalo in the SF; and two against Philadelphia in the F. Islanders played 21 games.

MOST OVERTIME GAMES, FINAL SERIES:
5 — Toronto Maple Leafs,, Montreal Canadiens in 1951. Toronto defeated Montreal 4-1 in best-of-seven series.

MOST OVERTIME GAMES, SEMI-FINAL SERIES:
4 — Toronto Maple Leafs, Boston Bruins in 1933. Toronto won best-of-five series 3-2.
  — Boston Bruins, NY Rangers in 1939. Boston won best-of-seven series 4-3.
  — St. Louis Blues, Minnesota North Stars in 1968. St. Louis won best-of-seven series 4-3.

MOST GAMES PLAYED BY ALL TEAMS, ONE PLAYOFF YEAR:
87 — 1987. There were 44 DSF, 25 DF, 11 CF and 7 F games.
85 — 1990. There were 49 DSF, 21 DF, 10 CF and 5 F games.
83 — 1988. There were 46 DSF, 27 DF, 12 CF and 4 F games.
82 — 1989. There were 44 DSF, 21 DF, 11 CF and 6 F games.
72 — 1986. There were 28 DSF, 27 DF, 12 CF and 5 F games.

MOST GAMES PLAYED, ONE TEAM, ONE PLAYOFF YEAR:
26 — Philadelphia Flyers, 1987. Won DSF 4-2 against NY Rangers, DF 4-3 against NY Islanders, CF 4-2 against Montreal, and lost F 4-3 against Edmonton.
22 — Calgary Flames,1986. Won DSF 3-0 against Winnipeg, DF 4-3 against Edmonton, CF 4-3 against St. Louis and lost F 4-1 against Montreal.
  — Boston Bruins, 1988. Won DSF 4-2 against Buffalo, DF 4-1 against Montreal, CF 4-3 against New Jersey and lost F 4-0 against Edmonton.
  — Calgary Flames, 1989. Won DSF 4-3 against Vancouver, DF 4-0 against Los Angeles, CF 4-1 against Chicago and F 4-2 against Montreal.
  — Edmonton Oilers, 1990. Won DSF 4-3 against Winnipeg, DF 4-0 against Los Angeles, CF 4-2 against Chicago and F 4-1 against Boston.

MOST ROAD VICTORIES, ONE TEAM, ONE PLAYOFF YEAR:
8 — NY Islanders, 1980. Won two at Los Angeles in PR; three at Boston in QF; two at Buffalo in SF; and one at Philadelphia in F series.
  Philadelphia Flyers, 1987. Won two at NY Rangers in DSF; two at NY Islanders in DF; three at Montreal in CF; and one at Edmonton in F series.
  — Edmonton Oilers, 1990. Won one at Winnipeg in DSF; two at Los Angeles in DF; two at Chicago in CF and three at Boston in F series.

MOST HOME VICTORIES, ONE TEAM, ONE PLAYOFF YEAR:
11 — Edmonton Oilers, 1988
10 — Edmonton Oilers, 1985 in 10 home-ice games.
  — Montreal Canadiens, 1986
9 — Philadelphia Flyers, 1974
  — Philadelphia Flyers, 1980
  — NY Islanders, 1981
  — NY Islanders, 1983
  — Edmonton Oilers, 1984
  — Edmonton Oilers, 1987
  — Calgary Flames, 1989

MOST ROAD VICTORIES, ALL TEAMS, ONE PLAYOFF YEAR:
46 — 1987. Of 87 games played, road teams won 46 (22 DSF, 14 DF, 8 CF and 2 Stanley Cup).

MOST CONSECUTIVE PLAYOFF GAME VICTORIES:
12 — Edmonton Oilers. Streak began May 15, 1984 at Edmonton with a 7-2 win over NY Islanders in third game of F series, and ended May 9, 1985 when Chicago defeated Edmonton 5-2 at Chicago. Included in the streak were three wins over the NY Islanders, in 1984, three over Los Angeles, four over Winnipeg and two over Chicago, all in 1985.
11 — Montreal Canadiens. Streak began April 16, 1959, at Toronto with 3-2 win in fourth game of F series, won by Montreal 4-1, and ended March 23, 1961, when Chicago defeated Montreal 4-3 in second game of SF series. Included in streak were eight straight victories in 1960.
  — Montreal Canadiens. Streak began April 28, 1968, at Montreal with 4-3 win in fifth game of SF series, won by Montreal 4-1, and ended April 17, 1969, at Boston when Boston defeated them 5-0 in third game of SF series. Included in the streak were four straight wins over St. Louis in the 1968 F and four straight wins over NY Rangers in a 1969 QF series.
  — Boston Bruins. Streak began April 14, 1970, at Boston with 3-2 victory over NY Rangers in fifth game of a QF series, won by Boston 4-2. It continued with a four-game victory over Chicago in the 1970 SF and a four-game win over St. Louis in the 1970 F. Boston then won the first game of a 1971 QF series against Montreal. Montreal ended the streak April 8, 1971, at Boston with a 7-5 victory.
  — Montreal Canadiens. Streak started May 6, 1976, at Montreal with 5-2 win in fifth game of a SF series against NY Islanders, won by Montreal 4-1. Continued with a four-game sweep over Philadelphia in the 1976 F and a four-game win against St. Louis in the 1977 QF. Montreal won the first two games of a 1977 SF series against the NY Islanders before NY Islanders ended the streak, April 2, 1977 at New York with a 5-3 victory.

MOST CONSECUTIVE VICTORIES, ONE PLAYOFF YEAR:
10 — Boston Bruins in 1970. Boston won last two games of best-of-seven QF against NY Rangers to win series 4-2 and then defeated Chicago 4-0 in best-of-seven SF and St. Louis 4-0 in best-of-seven F.

LONGEST PLAYOFF LOSING STREAK:
16 Games — Chicago Blackhawks. Streak started in 1975 QF against Buffalo when Chicago lost last two games. Then Chicago lost four games to Montreal in 1976 QF; two games to NY Islanders in 1977 PR; four games to Boston in 1978 QF and four games to NY Islanders in 1979 QF. Streak ended on April 8, 1980 when Chicago defeated St. Louis 3-2 in the opening game of their 1980 PR series.
12 Games — Toronto Maple Leafs. Streak started on April 16, 1979 as Toronto lost four straight games in a QF series against Montreal. Continued with three-game PR defeats versus Philadelphia and NY Islanders in 1980 and 1981 respectively. Toronto failed to qualify for the 1982 playoffs and lost the first two games of a 1983 DSF against Minnesota. Toronto ended the streak with a 6-3 win against the North Stars on April 9, 1983.
10 Games — NY Rangers. Streak started in 1968 QF against Chicago when NY Rangers lost last four games and continued through 1969 (four straight losses to Montreal in QF) and 1970 (two straight losses to Boston in QF) before ending with a 4-3 win against Boston, at New York, April 11, 1970.
  — Philadelphia Flyers. Streak started on April 18, 1968, the last game in the 1968 QF series against St. Louis, and continued through 1969 (four straight losses to St. Louis in QF), 1971 (four straight losses to Chicago in QF) and 1973 (opening game loss to Minnesota in QF) before ending with a 4-1 win against Minnesota, at Philadelphia, April 5, 1973.

MOST SHUTOUTS, ONE PLAYOFF YEAR, ALL TEAMS:
8 — **1937.** Of 17 games played, NY Rangers had 4. Detroit 3, Boston 1.
 — **1975.** Of 51 games played, Philadelphia had 5, Montreal 2, NY Islanders 1.
 — **1980.** Of 67 games played, Buffalo had 3, Philadelphia 2, Montreal, NY Islanders and Minnesota 1 each.
 — **1984.** Of 70 games played, Montreal had 3, Edmonton, Minnesota, NY Rangers, St. Louis and Vancouver 1 each.

FEWEST SHUTOUTS, ONE PLAYOFF YEAR, ALL TEAMS:
0 — **1959.** 18 games played.

MOST SHUTOUTS, BOTH TEAMS, ONE SERIES:
5 — **1945 F, Toronto Maple Leafs, Detroit Red Wings.** Toronto had 3 shutouts, Detroit 2. Toronto won best-of-seven series 4-3.
 — **1950 SF, Toronto Maple Leafs, Detroit Red Wings.** Toronto had 3 shutouts, Detroit 2. Detroit won best-of-seven series 4-3.

MOST PENALTIES, BOTH TEAMS, ONE SERIES:
219 — **New Jersey Devils, Washington Capitals** in 1988 DF won by New Jersey 4-3. New Jersey received 98 minors, 11 majors, 9 misconducts and 1 match penalty. Washington received 80 minors, 11 majors, 8 misconducts and 1 match penalty.

MOST PENALTY MINUTES, BOTH TEAMS, ONE SERIES:
656 — **New Jersey Devils, Washington Capitals** in 1988 DF won by New Jersey 4-3. New Jersey had 351 minutes; Washington 305.

MOST PENALTIES, ONE TEAM, ONE SERIES:
119 — **New Jersey Devils** in 1988 DF versus Washington. New Jersey received 98 minors, 11 majors, 9 misconducts and 1 match penalty.

MOST PENALTY MINUTES, ONE TEAM, ONE SERIES:
351 — **New Jersey Devils** in 1988 DF versus Washington. Series won by New Jersey 4-3.

MOST PENALTY MINUTES, BOTH TEAMS, ONE GAME:
267 Minutes — **NY Rangers, Los Angeles Kings,** at Los Angeles, April 9, 1981. NY Rangers received 31 penalties for 142 minutes; Los Angeles 28 penalties for 125 minutes. Los Angeles won 5-4.

MOST PENALTIES, BOTH TEAMS, ONE GAME:
62 — **New Jersey Devils, Washington Capitals,** at New Jersey, April 22, 1988. New Jersey received 32 penalties; Washington 30. New Jersey won 10-4.

MOST PENALTIES, ONE TEAM, ONE GAME:
32 — **New Jersey Devils,** at Washington, April 22,1988. New Jersey won 10-4.
31 — NY Rangers, at Los Angeles, April 9, 1981. Los Angeles won 5-4.
30 — Philadelphia Flyers, at Toronto, April 15, 1976. Toronto won 5-4.

MOST PENALTY MINUTES, ONE TEAM, ONE GAME:
142 — **NY Rangers,** at Los Angeles, April 9, 1981. Los Angeles won 5-4.

MOST PENALTIES, BOTH TEAMS, ONE PERIOD:
43 — **NY Rangers, Los Angeles Kings,** April 9, 1981, at Los Angeles, first period. NY Rangers had 24 penalties; Los Angeles 19. Los Angeles won 5-4.

MOST PENALTY MINUTES, BOTH TEAMS, ONE PERIOD:
248 — **NY Islanders, Boston Bruins,** April 17, 1980, first period, at Boston. Each team received 124 minutes. Islanders won 5-4.

MOST PENALTIES, ONE TEAM, ONE PERIOD: (AND) MOST PENALTY MINUTES, ONE TEAM, ONE PERIOD:
24 Penalties; 125 Minutes — **NY Rangers,** April 9, 1981, at Los Angeles, first period. Los Angeles won 5-4.

FEWEST PENALTIES, BOTH TEAMS, BEST-OF-SEVEN SERIES:
19 — **Detroit Red Wings, Toronto Maple Leafs** in 1945 F, won by Toronto 4-3. Detroit received 10 minors. Toronto 9 minors.

FEWEST PENALTIES, ONE TEAM, BEST-OF-SEVEN SERIES:
9 — **Toronto Maple Leafs** in 1945 F, won by Toronto 4-3 against Detroit.

MOST POWER-PLAY GOALS BY ALL TEAMS, ONE PLAYOFF YEAR:
199 — **1988** in 83 games.

MOST POWER-PLAY GOALS, ONE TEAM, ONE PLAYOFF YEAR:
32 — **Edmonton Oilers,** 1988 in 18 games.
31 — NY Islanders, 1981, in 18 games.

MOST POWER-PLAY GOALS, BOTH TEAMS, ONE SERIES:
21 — **NY Islanders, Philadelphia Flyers** in 1980 F, won by NY Islanders 4-2. NY Islanders had 15 and Flyers 6.
 — **NY Islanders, Edmonton Oilers** in 1981 QF, won by NY Islanders 4-2. NY Islanders had 13 and Edmonton 8.
 — **Philadelphia Flyers, Pittsburgh Penguins** in 1989 DF, won by Philadelphia 4-3. Philadelphia had 11 and Pittsburgh 10.
20 — Toronto Maple Leafs, Philadelphia Flyers in 1976 QF series won by Philadelphia 4-3. Toronto had 12 power-play goals; Philadelphia 8.

MOST POWER-PLAY GOALS, ONE TEAM, ONE SERIES:
15 — **NY Islanders** in 1980 F against Philadelphia. NY Islanders won series 4-2.
13 — NY Islanders in 1981 QF against Edmonton. NY Islanders won series 4-2.
 — Calgary Flames in 1986 CF against St. Louis. Calgary won series 4-3.
12 — Toronto Maple Leafs in 1976 QF series won by Philadelphia 4-3.

MOST POWER-PLAY GOALS, BOTH TEAMS, ONE GAME:
7 — **Minnesota North Stars, Edmonton Oilers,** April 28, 1984 at Minnesota. Minnesota had 4, Edmonton 3. Edmonton won 8-5.
 — **Philadelphia Flyers, NY Rangers,** April 13, 1985 at New York. Philadelphia had 4, NY Rangers 3. Philadelphia won 6-5.
 — **Edmonton Oilers, Chicago Blackhawks,** May 14, 1985 at Edmonton. Chicago had 5, Edmonton 2. Edmonton won 10-5.
 — **Edmonton Oilers, Los Angeles Kings,** April 9, 1987 at Edmonton. Edmonton had 5, Los Angeles 2. Edmonton won game 13-3.
 — **Vancouver Canucks, Calgary Flames,** April 9, 1989 at Vancouver. Vancouver had 4, Calgary 3. Vancouver won 5-3.
6 — Detroit Red Wings, Montreal Canadiens, March 23, 1939, at Detroit. Detroit had 4, Montreal 2. Detroit won 7-3.
 — Boston Bruins, April 2, 1969, at Boston against Toronto. Boston won 10-0, scoring 6 power-play goals.
 — Boston Bruins, Chicago Blackhawks, April 21, 1974, at Boston. Each had 3. Boston won 8-6.
 — Toronto Maple Leafs, Philadelphia Flyers April 15, 1976, at Toronto. Toronto had 5, Philadelphia 1. Toronto won 5-4.
 — NY Islanders, Edmonton Oilers, April 17, 1981, at New York. NY Islanders had 4. Edmonton 2. NY Islanders won 6-3.
 — NY Rangers, Philadelphia Flyers, April 8, 1982, at New York. NY Rangers had 4, Philadelphia 2. NY Rangers won 7-3.
 — Minnesota North Stars, Chicago Blackhawks, Apr. 6, 1990 at Chicago. Minnesota had 3, Chicago 3. Chicago won game 5-3.

MOST POWER-PLAY GOALS, ONE TEAM, ONE GAME:
6 — **Boston Bruins,** April 2, 1969, at Boston against Toronto. Boston won 10-0.

MOST POWER-PLAY GOALS, BOTH TEAMS, ONE PERIOD:
5 — **Minnesota North Stars, Edmonton Oilers,** April 28, 1984, second period, at Minnesota. Minnesota had 4 and Edmonton 1. Edmonton won 8-5.
 — **Vancouver Canucks, Calgary Flames,** April 9, 1989, third period at Vancouver. Vancouver had 3 and Calgary 2. Vancouver won 5-3.

MOST POWER-PLAY GOALS, ONE TEAM, ONE PERIOD:
4 — **Toronto Maple Leafs,** March 26, 1936, second period against Boston at Toronto. Toronto won 8-3.
 — **Minnesota North Stars,** April 28, 1984, second period against Edmonton at Minnesota. Edmonton won 8-5.

MOST SHORTHAND GOALS BY ALL TEAMS, ONE PLAYOFF YEAR:
33 — **1988,** in 83 games.

MOST SHORTHAND GOALS, ONE TEAM, ONE PLAYOFF YEAR:
10 — **Edmonton Oilers 1983, in 16 games.**
9 — NY Islanders, 1981, in 19 games.
8 — Philadelphia Flyers, 1989, in 19 games.
7 — NY Islanders, 1980, in 21 games.
7 — Chicago Blackhawks, 1989, in 16 games.

MOST SHORTHAND GOALS, BOTH TEAMS, ONE SERIES:
7 — **Boston Bruins (4), NY Rangers (3),** in 1958 SF, won by Boston 4-2.
 — **Edmonton Oilers (5), Calgary Flames (2),** in 1983 DF won by Edmonton 4-1.

MOST SHORTHAND GOALS, ONE TEAM, ONE SERIES:
5 — **Edmonton Oilers** in 1983 against Calgary in best-of-seven DF won by Edmonton 4-1.
 — **NY Rangers** in 1979 against Philadelphia in best-of-seven QF, won by NY Rangers 4-1.
4 — Boston Bruins in 1958 against NY Rangers in best-of-seven SF series, won by Boston 4-2.
 — Minnesota North Stars in 1981 against Calgary in best-of-seven SF, won by Minnesota 4-2.
 — Chicago Blackhawks in 1989 against Detroit in best-of-seven DSF won by Chicago 4-2.
 — Philadelphia Flyers in 1989 against Pittsburgh in best-of-seven DF won by Philadelphia 4-3.

MOST SHORTHAND GOALS, BOTH TEAMS, ONE GAME:
4 — **NY Islanders, NY Rangers,** April 17, 1983 at NY Rangers. NY Islanders had 3 shorthand goals, NY Rangers 1. NY Rangers won 7-6.
 — **Boston Bruins, Minnesota North Stars,** April 11, 1981, at Minnesota. Boston had 3 shorthand goals, Minnesota 1. Minnesota won 6-3.
3 — Toronto Maple Leafs, Detroit Red Wings, April 5, 1947, at Toronto. Toronto had 2 shorthand goals, Detroit 1. Toronto won 6-1.
 — NY Rangers, Boston Bruins, April 1, 1958, at Boston. NY Rangers had 2 shorthand goals, Boston 1. NY Rangers won 5-2.
 — Minnesota North Stars, Philadelphia Flyers, May 4, 1980, at Minnesota. Minnesota had 2 shorthand goals, Philadelphia 1. Philadelphia won 5-3.
 — Edmonton Oilers, Winnipeg Jets, April 9, 1988 at Winnipeg. Winnipeg had 2 shorthand goals, Edmonton 1. Winnipeg won 6-4.
 — New Jersey Devils, NY Islanders, April 14, 1988 at New Jersey. NY Islanders had 2 shorthand goals, New Jersey 1. New Jersey won 6-5.

MOST SHORTHAND GOALS, ONE TEAM, ONE GAME:
3 — **Boston Bruins,** April 11, 1981, at Minnesota. Minnesota won 6-3.
 — **NY Islanders,** April 17, 1983, at NY Rangers. NY Rangers won 7-6.

MOST SHORTHAND GOALS, BOTH TEAMS, ONE PERIOD:
3 — **Toronto Maple Leafs, Detroit Red Wings,** April 5, 1947, at Toronto, first period. Toronto scored two short-hand goals; Detroit one. Toronto won 6-1.

MOST SHORTHAND GOALS ONE TEAM, ONE PERIOD:
2 — **Toronto Maple Leafs,** April 5, 1947, at Toronto against Detroit, first period. Toronto won 6-1.
  — **Toronto Maple Leafs,** April 13, 1965, at Toronto against Montreal, first period. Montreal won 4-3.
  — **Boston Bruins,** April 20, 1969, at Boston against Montreal, first period. Boston won 3-2.
  — **Boston Bruins,** April 8, 1970, at Boston against NY Rangers, second period. Boston won 8-2.
  — **Boston Bruins,** April 30, 1972, at Boston against NY Rangers, first period. Boston won 6-5.
  — **Chicago Blackhawks,** May 3, 1973, at Chicago against Montreal, first period. Chicago won 7-4.
  — **Montreal Canadiens,** April 23, 1978, at Detroit, first period. Montreal won 8-0.
  — **NY Islanders,** April 8, 1980, at New York against Los Angeles, second period. NY Islanders won 8-1.
  — **Los Angeles Kings,** April 9, 1980, at NY Islanders, first period. Los Angeles won 6-3.
  — **Boston Bruins,** April 13, 1980, at Pittsburgh, second period. Boston won 8-3.
  — **Minnesota North Stars,** May 4, 1980, at Minnesota against Philadelphia, second period. Philadelphia won 5-3.
  — **Boston Bruins,** April 11, 1981, at Minnesota, third period. Minnesota won 6-3.
  — **NY Islanders,** May 12, 1981, at New York against Minnesota, first period. NY Islanders won 6-3.
  — **Montreal Canadiens,** April 7, 1982, at Montreal against Quebec, third period. Montreal won 5-1.
  — **Edmonton Oilers,** April 24, 1983, at Edmonton against Chicago, third period. Edmonton won 8-4.
  — **Winnipeg Jets,** April 14, 1985, at Calgary, second period. Winnipeg won 5-3.
  — **Boston Bruins,** April 6, 1988 at Boston against Buffalo, first period. Boston won 7-3.
  — **NY Islanders,** April 14, 1988 at New Jersey, third period. New Jersey won 6-5.

FASTEST TWO GOALS, BOTH TEAMS:
5 Seconds — Pittsburgh Penguins, Buffalo Sabres at Buffalo, April 14, 1979. Gilbert Perreault scored for Buffalo at 12:59 and Jim Hamilton for Pittsburgh at 13:04 of first period. Pittsburgh won 4-3 and best-of-three PR 2-1.
8 seconds — Minnesota North Stars, St. Louis Blues at Minnesota, April 9, 1989. Bernie Federko scored for St. Louis at 2:28 of third period and Perry Berezan at 2:36 for Minnesota. Minnesota won 5-4. St. Louis won best-of-seven DSF 4-1.
9 seconds — NY Islanders, Washington Capitals at Washington, April 10, 1986. Bryan Trottier scored for New York at 18:26 of second period and Scott Stevens at 18:35 for Washington. Washington won 5-2, and won best-of-five DSF 3-0.
10 Seconds — Washington Capitals, New Jersey Devils at New Jersey, April 5, 1990. Pat Conacher scored for New Jersey at 8:02 of second period and Dale Hunter at 8:12 for Washington. Washington won 5-4, and won best-of-seven DSF 4-2.

FASTEST TWO GOALS, ONE TEAM:
5 Seconds — Detroit Red Wings at Detroit, April 11, 1965, against Chicago. Norm Ullman scored at 17:35 and 17:40, 2nd period. Detroit won 4-2. Chicago won best-of-seven SF 4-3.

FASTEST THREE GOALS, BOTH TEAMS:
21 Seconds — Edmonton Oilers, Chicago Blackhawks at Edmonton, May 7, 1985. Behn Wilson scored for Chicago at 19:22 of third period, Jari Kurri at 19:36 and Glenn Anderson at 19:43 for Edmonton. Edmonton won 7-3 and best-of-seven CF 4-2.
31 Seconds — Edmonton Oilers, Philadelphia Flyers at Edmonton, May 25, 1985. Wayne Gretzky scored for Edmonton at 1:10 and 1:25 of first period, Derrick Smith scored for Philadelphia at 1:41. Edmonton won 4-3 and best-of-seven F 4-1.
36 Seconds — Los Angeles Kings, Edmonton Oilers at Edmonton, April 7, 1982. Steve Bozek of Los Angeles scored at 6:00 of first period, Tom Roulston of Edmonton scored at 6:16 and Risto Siltanen of Edmonton scored at 6:36. Los Angeles won 10-8 and best-of-five DSF 3-2.

FASTEST THREE GOALS, ONE TEAM:
23 Seconds — Toronto Maple Leafs at Toronto, April 12, 1979, against Atlanta Flames. Darryl Sittler scored at 4:04 of first period and again at 4:16 and Ron Ellis at 4:27. Leafs won 7-4 and best-of-seven PR 2-0.
38 Seconds — NY Rangers at New York, April 12, 1986. Jim Wiemer scored at 12:29 of third period, Bob Brooke at 12:43 and Ron Greschner at 13:07. NY Rangers won 5-2 and best-of-seven DSF 3-2.
56 Seconds — Montreal Canadiens at Detroit, April 6, 1954. Dickie Moore scored at 15:03 of first period, Maurice Richard at 15:28 and again at 15:59. Montreal won 3-1. Detroit won best-of-seven F 4-3.

FASTEST FOUR GOALS, BOTH TEAMS:
1 Minute, 33 Seconds — Philadelphia Flyers, Toronto Maple Leafs at Philadelphia, April 20, 1976. Don Saleski of Philadelphia scored at 10:04 of second period; Bob Neely, Toronto, 10:42; Gary Dornhoefer, Philadelphia, 11:24; and Don Saleski, 11:37. Philadelphia won 7-1 and best-of-seven QF series 4-3.
1 minute, 34 seconds — Montreal Canadiens, Calgary Flames at Montreal, May 20, 1986. Joel Otto of Calgary scored at 17:59 of first period; Bobby Smith, Montreal, 18:25; Mats Naslund, Montreal, 19:17; and Bob Gainey, Montreal, 19:33. Montreal won 5-3 and best-of-seven F series 4-1.
1 Minute, 38 Seconds — Boston Bruins, Philadelphia Flyers at Philadelphia, April 26, 1977. Gregg Sheppard of Boston scored at 14:01 of second period; Mike Milbury, Boston, 15:01; Gary Dornhoefer, Philadelphia, 15:16; and Jean Ratelle, Boston, 15:39. Boston won 5-4 and best-of-seven SF series 4-0.

Mats Naslund had the third of four goals scored in just over a minute and a half in the third game of the 1986 Stanley Cup finals.

FASTEST FOUR GOALS, ONE TEAM:
2 Minutes, 35 Seconds — Montreal Canadiens at Montreal, March 30, 1944, against Toronto. Toe Blake scored at 7:58 of third period and again at 8:37; Maurice Richard, 9:17; Ray Getliffe, 10:33. Montreal won 11-0 and best-of-seven SF 4-0.

FASTEST FIVE GOALS, BOTH TEAMS:
3 Minutes, 6 Seconds — Chicago Blackhawks, Minnesota North Stars, at Chicago April 21, 1985. Keith Brown scored for Chicago at 1:12, second period; Ken Yaremchuk, Chicago, 1:27; Dino Ciccarelli, Minnesota, 2:48; Tony McKegney, Minnesota, 4:07; and Curt Fraser, Chicago, 4:18. Chicago won 6-2 and best-of-seven DF 4-2.
3 Minutes, 20 Seconds — Minnesota North Stars, Philadelphia Flyers, at Philadelphia, April 29, 1980. Paul Shmyr scored for Minnesota at 13:20, first period; Steve Christoff, Minnesota, 13:59; Ken Linseman, Philadelphia, 14:54; Tom Gorence, Philadelphia, 15:36; and Linseman, 16:40. Minnesota won 6-5. Philadelphia won best-of-seven SF 4-1.
4 Minutes, 19 Seconds — Toronto Maple Leafs, NY Rangers at Toronto, April 9, 1932. Ace Bailey scored for Toronto at 15:07, third period; Fred Cook, NY Rangers, 16:32; Bob Gracie, Toronto, 17:36; Frank Boucher, NY Rangers, 18:26 and again at 19:26. Toronto won 6-4 and best-of-five F 3-0.

FASTEST FIVE GOALS, ONE TEAM:
3 Minutes, 36 Seconds — Montreal Canadiens at Montreal, March 30, 1944, against Toronto. Toe Blake scored at 7:58 of third period and again at 8:37; Maurice Richard, 9:17; Ray Getliffe, 10:33; and Buddy O'Connor, 11:34. Canadiens won 11-0 and best-of-seven SF 4-0.

MOST THREE-OR-MORE GOAL GAMES BY ALL TEAMS, ONE PLAYOFF YEAR:
12 — 1983 in 66 games.
 — 1988 in 83 games.
11 — 1985 in 70 games.

MOST THREE-OR-MORE GOAL GAMES, ONE TEAM, ONE PLAYOFF YEAR:
6 — Edmonton Oilers in 16 games, 1983.
 — Edmonton Oilers in 18 games, 1985.

Individual Records

Career

MOST YEARS IN PLAYOFFS:
20 — Gordie Howe, Detroit, Hartford (1947-58 incl.; 60-61; 63-66 incl.; 70 & 80)
19 — Red Kelly, Detroit, Toronto
18 — Stan Mikita, Chicago
— Larry Robinson, Montreal, Los Angeles

MOST CONSECUTIVE YEARS IN PLAYOFFS:
18 — Larry Robinson, Montreal, Los Angeles (1973-1990, inclusive).
17 — Brad Park, NY Rangers, Boston, Detroit (1969-1985, inclusive).
16 — Jean Beliveau, Montreal (1954-69, inclusive).

MOST PLAYOFF GAMES:
213 — Larry Robinson, Montreal, Los Angeles
185 — Denis Potvin, NY Islanders
182 — Bob Gainey, Montreal
180 — Henri Richard, Montreal
175 — Bryan Trottier, NY Islanders

MOST POINTS IN PLAYOFFS (CAREER):
284 — Wayne Gretzky, Edmonton, Los Angeles, 89G, 195A
202 — Jari Kurri, Edmonton, 92G, 110A
200 — Mark Messier, Edmonton, 76G, 124A
176 — Jean Beliveau, Montreal, 79G, 97A
170 — Glenn Anderson, Edmonton, 75G, 95A
— Bryan Trottier, NY Islanders, 64G, 106A

MOST GOALS IN PLAYOFFS (CAREER):
92 — Jari Kurri, Edmonton
89 — Wayne Gretzky, Edmonton, Los Angeles
85 — Mike Bossy, NY Islanders
82 — Maurice Richard, Montreal
76 — Mark Messier, Edmonton

MOST GAME-WINNING GOALS IN PLAYOFFS (CAREER):
18 — Maurice Richard, Montreal
17 — Mike Bossy, NY Islanders
16 — Wayne Gretzky, Edmonton, Los Angeles
15 — Jean Beliveau, Montreal
— Yvan Cournoyer, Montreal

MOST OVERTIME GOALS IN PLAYOFFS (CAREER):
6 — Maurice Richard, Montreal (1 in 1946; 3 in 1951; 1 in 1957; 1 in 1958.)
4 — Bob Nystrom, NY Islanders
— Dale Hunter, Quebec, Washington
3 — Mel Hill, Boston
— Rene Robert, Buffalo
— Danny Gare, Buffalo
— Jacques Lemaire, Montreal
— Bobby Clarke, Philadelphia
— Terry O'Reilly, Boston
— Mike Bossy, NY Islanders
— Steve Payne, Minnesota
— Ken Morrow, NY Islanders
— Lanny McDonald, Toronto, Calgary
— Glenn Anderson, Edmonton
— Peter Stastny, Quebec

MOST POWER-PLAY GOALS IN PLAYOFFS (CAREER):
35 — Mike Bossy, NY Islanders
27 — Denis Potvin, NY Islanders
26 — Jean Beliveau, Montreal
24 — Wayne Gretzky, Edmonton, Los Angeles
22 — Bobby Hull, Chicago
— Phil Esposito, Chicago, Boston, NY Rangers

MOST SHORTHAND GOALS IN PLAYOFFS (CAREER):
11 — Mark Messier, Edmonton
10 — Wayne Gretzky, Edmonton, Los Angeles
8 — Ed Westfall, Boston, NY Islanders
7 — Jari Kurri, Edmonton

MOST THREE-OR-MORE-GOAL GAMES IN PLAYOFFS (CAREER):
7 — Maurice Richard, Montreal. Four three-goal games; two four-goal games; one five-goal game.
— **Wayne Gretzky, Edmonton.** Two four-goal games; five three-goal games.
— **Jari Kurri, Edmonton.** One four-goal game; six three-goal games.
5 — Mike Bossy, NY Islanders. Four three-goal games; one four-goal game.

MOST ASSISTS IN PLAYOFFS (CAREER):
195 — Wayne Gretzky, Edmonton, Los Angeles
124 — Mark Messier, Edmonton
112 — Larry Robinson, Montreal, Los Angeles
110 — Jari Kurri, Edmonton
108 — Denis Potvin, NY Islanders

MOST PENALTY MINUTES IN PLAYOFFS (CAREER):
505 — Dale Hunter, Quebec, Washington
466 — Willi Plett, Atlanta, Calgary, Minnesota, Boston
464 — Chris Nilan, Montreal, NY Rangers
455 — Dave Williams, Toronto, Vancouver, Los Angeles
412 — Dave Schultz, Philadelphia, Los Angeles, Buffalo

MOST SHUTOUTS IN PLAYOFFS (CAREER):
15 — Clint Benedict, Ottawa, Mtl. Maroons in 9 playoff years.
14 — Jacques Plante, Montreal, St. Louis in 16 playoff years.
13 — Turk Broda, Toronto
12 — Terry Sawchuk, Detroit, Toronto, Los Angeles

MOST PLAYOFF GAMES APPEARED IN BY A GOALTENDER (CAREER):
132 — Bill Smith, NY Islanders
115 — Glenn Hall, Detroit, Chicago, St. Louis
112 — Jacques Plante, Montreal, St. Louis, Toronto, Boston
— Ken Dryden, Montreal
106 — Terry Sawchuk, Detroit, Toronto, Los Angeles, NY Rangers

MOST MINUTES PLAYED BY A GOALTENDER (CAREER):
7,645 — Billy Smith, NY Islanders
6,899 — Glenn Hall, Detroit, Chicago, St. Louis
6,841 — Ken Dryden, Montreal
6,651 — Jacques Plante, Montreal, St. Louis, Toronto, Boston

Jacques Plante played on six Stanley Cup winners in Montreal.

Single Playoff Year

MOST POINTS, ONE PLAYOFF YEAR:
47 — Wayne Gretzky, Edmonton, in 1985. 17 goals, 30 assists in 18 games.
43 — Wayne Gretzky, Edmonton, in 1988. 12 goals, 31 assists in 19 games.
38 — Wayne Gretzky, Edmonton, in 1983. 12 goals, 26 assists in 16 games.
37 — Paul Coffey, Edmonton, in 1985. 12 goals, 25 assists in 18 games.
35 — Mike Bossy, NY Islanders, in 1981. 17 goals, 18 assists in 18 games.
— Wayne Gretzky, Edmonton, in 1984. 13 goals, 22 assists in 19 games.
— Mark Messier, Edmonton, in 1988. 11 goals, 23 assists in 19 games.
34 — Wayne Gretzky, Edmonton, in 1987. 5 goals, 29 assists in 21 games.
33 — Rick Middleton Boston, in 1983. 11 goals, 22 assists in 17 games.
32 — Barry Pederson, Boston, in 1983. 14 goals, 18 assists in 17 games.

MOST POINTS BY A DEFENSEMAN, ONE PLAYOFF YEAR:
37 — Paul Coffey, Edmonton, in 1985. 12 goals, 25 assists in 18 games.
31 — Al MacInnis, Calgary, in 1989. 7 goals, 24 assists in 18 games.
25 — Denis Potvin, NY Islanders, in 1981. 8 goals, 17 assists in 18 games.
24 — Bobby Orr, Boston, in 1972. 5 goals, 19 assists in 15 games.

MOST POINTS BY A ROOKIE, ONE PLAYOFF YEAR:
21 — Dino Ciccarelli, Minnesota, in 1981. 14 goals, 7 assists in 19 games.
20 — Don Maloney, NY Rangers, in 1979. 7 goals, 13 assists in 18 games.

LONGEST CONSECUTIVE POINT-SCORING STREAK, ONE PLAYOFF YEAR:
18 games — Bryan Trottier, NY Islanders, 1981. 11 goals, 18 assists, 29 points.
17 games — Wayne Gretzky, Edmonton, 1988. 12 goals, 29 assists, 41 points.
— Al MacInnis, Calgary, 1989. 7 goals, 19 assists, 24 points.

**LONGEST CONSECUTIVE POINT-SCORING STREAK,
MORE THAN ONE PLAYOFF YEAR:**
27 games — Bryan Trottier, NY Islanders, 1980, 1981 and 1982. 7 games in 1980 (3 G, 5 A, 8 PTS), 18 games in 1981 (11 G, 18 A, 29 PTS), and two games in 1982 (2 G, 3 A, 5 PTS). Total points, 42.
19 games — Wayne Gretzky, Edmonton, Los Angeles 1988 and 1989. 17 games in 1988 (12 G, 29 A, 41 PTS with Edmonton), 2 games in 1989 (1 G, 2 A, 3 PTS with Los Angeles). Total points, 44.
18 games — Phil Esposito, Boston, 1970 and 1971. 13 G, 20 A, 33 PTS.

MOST GOALS, ONE PLAYOFF YEAR:
19 — Newsy Lalonde, Montreal, 1919. 10 games.
— **Reggie Leach, Philadelphia,** 1976. 16 games.
— **Jari Kurri, Edmonton,** 1985. 18 games.
17 — Mike Bossy, NY Islanders, 1981. 18 games.
— Steve Payne, Minnesota, 1981. 19 games.
— Mike Bossy, NY Islanders, 1982. 19 games.
— Mike Bossy, NY Islanders, 1983. 19 games
— Wayne Gretzky, Edmonton, 1985. 18 games.

MOST GOALS BY A DEFENSEMAN, ONE PLAYOFF YEAR:
12 — **Paul Coffey, Edmonton,** 1985. 18 games.
9 — Bobby Orr, Boston, 1970. 14 games.
— Brad Park, Boston, 1978. 15 games.
8 — Denis Potvin, NY Islanders, 1981. 18 games.
— Raymond Bourque, Boston, 1983. 17 games.
— Denis Potvin, NY Islanders, 1983. 20 games.
— Paul Coffey, Edmonton, 1984. 19 games

MOST GOALS BY A ROOKIE, ONE PLAYOFF YEAR:
14 — **Dino Ciccarelli, Minnesota,** 1981. 19 games.
11 — Jeremy Roenick, Chicago, 1990. 20 games.
10 — Claude Lemieux, Montreal, 1986. 20 games.
9 — Pat Flatley, NY Islanders, 1984. 21 games
8 — Steve Christoff, Minnesota, 1980. 14 games.
— Brad Palmer, Minnesota, 1981. 19 games.
— Mike Krushelnyski, Boston, 1983. 17 games.
— Bob Joyce, Boston, 1988. 23 games.

MOST GAME-WINNING GOALS, ONE PLAYOFF YEAR:
5 — Mike Bossy, NY Islanders, 1983. 19 games.
— **Jari Kurri, Edmonton,** 1987. 21 games.

MOST OVERTIME GOALS, ONE PLAYOFF YEAR:
3 — **Mel Hill, Boston,** 1939. All against NY Rangers in best-of-seven SF, won by Boston 4-3.
— **Maurice Richard, Montreal,** 1951. 2 against Detroit in best-of-seven SF, won by Montreal 4-2; 1 against Toronto best-of-seven F, won by Toronto 4-1.

MOST POWER-PLAY GOALS, ONE PLAYOFF YEAR:
9 — **Mike Bossy, NY Islanders,** 1981. 18 games against Toronto, Edmonton, NY Rangers and Minnesota.
8 — Tim Kerr, Philadelphia, 1989. 19 games.
— John Druce, Washington, 1990. 15 games
7 — Michel Goulet, Quebec, 1985. 17 games.
— Mark Messier, Edmonton, 1988. 19 games.
— Mario Lemieux, Pittsburgh, 1989. 11 games.
— Brett Hull, St. Louis, 1990. 12 games.

MOST SHORTHAND GOALS, ONE PLAYOFF YEAR:
3 — **Derek Sanderson, Boston,** 1969. 1 against Toronto in QF, won by Boston 4-0; 2 against Montreal in SF, won by Montreal, 4-2.
— **Bill Barber, Philadelphia,** 1980. All against Minnesota in SF, won by Philadelphia 4-1.
— **Lorne Henning, NY Islanders,** 1980. 1 against Boston in QF won by NY Islanders 4-1; 1 against Buffalo in SF, won by NY Islanders 4-2, 1 against Philadelphia in F, won by NY Islanders 4-2.
— **Wayne Gretzky, Edmonton,** 1983. 2 against Winnipeg in DSF won by Edmonton 3-0; 1 against Calgary in DF, won by Edmonton 4-1.
— **Wayne Presley, Chicago,** 1989. All against Detroit in DSF won by Chicago 4-2.

MOST THREE-OR-MORE GOAL GAMES, ONE PLAYOFF YEAR:
4 — **Jari Kurri, Edmonton,** 1985. 1 four-goal game, 3 three-goal games.
3 — Mark Messier, Edmonton, 1983. 3 three-goal games.
— Mike Bossy, NY Islanders, 1983. 1 four-goal game, 2 three-goal games
2 — Newsy Lalonde, Montreal, 1919. 1 five-goal game, 1 four-goal game.
— Maurice Richard, Montreal, 1944. 1 five-goal game; 1 three-goal game.
— Doug Bentley, Chicago, 1944. 2 three-goal games.
— Norm Ullman, Detroit, 1964. 2 three-goal games.
— Phil Esposito, Boston, 1970. 2 three-goal games.
— Pit Martin, Chicago, 1973. 2 three-goal games.
— Rick MacLeish, Philadelphia, 1975. 2 three-goal games.
— Lanny McDonald, Toronto, 1977. 1 three-goal game; 1 four-goal game.
— Wayne Gretzky, Edmonton, 1981. 2 three goal games.
— Wayne Gretzky, Edmonton, 1983. 2 four-goal games.
— Wayne Gretzky, Edmonton, 1985. 2 three-goal games.
— Petr Klima, Detroit, 1988. 2 three-goal games.

LONGEST CONSECUTIVE GOAL-SCORING STREAK, ONE PLAYOFF YEAR:
9 Games — **Reggie Leach, Philadelphia,** 1976. Streak started April 17 at Toronto and ended May 9 at Montreal. He scored one goal in each of seven games; two in one game; and five in another; a total of 14 goals.

MOST ASSISTS, ONE PLAYOFF YEAR:
31 — **Wayne Gretzky, Edmonton,** 1988. 19 games.
30 — Wayne Gretzky, Edmonton, 1985. 18 games.
29 — Wayne Gretzky, Edmonton, 1987. 21 games.
26 — Wayne Gretzky, Edmonton, 1983. 16 games.
25 — Paul Coffey, Edmonton, 1985. 18 games.
24 — Al MacInnis, Calgary, 1989. 22 games.

MOST ASSISTS BY A DEFENSEMAN, ONE PLAYOFF YEAR:
25 — **Paul Coffey, Edmonton,** 1985. 18 games.
24 — Al MacInnis, Calgary, 1989. 22 games.
19 — Bobby Orr, Boston, 1972. 15 games.
18 — Ray Bourque, Boston, 1988. 23 games.
17 — Larry Robinson, Montreal, 1978. 15 games.
— Denis Potvin, NY Islanders, 1981. 18 games.
— Charlie Huddy, Edmonton, 1985. 18 games.
— Larry Robinson, Montreal, 1987. 17 games.

MOST MINUTES PLAYED BY A GOALTENDER, ONE PLAYOFF YEAR:
1,540 — **Ron Hextall, Philadelphia,** 1987. 26 games.
1,401 — Bill Ranford, Edmonton, 1990. 22 games.
1,381 — Mike Vernon, Calgary, 1989. 22 games.
1,229 — Mike Vernon, Calgary, 1986. 21 games.
1,221 — Ken Dryden, Montreal, 1971. 20 games.
1,218 — Patrick Roy, Montreal, 1986. 20 games.
1,206 — Patrick Roy, Montreal, 1989. 19 games.

MOST WINS BY A GOALTENDER, ONE PLAYOFF YEAR:
16 — **Grant Fuhr, Edmonton,** 1988. 19 games.
— **Mike Vernon, Calgary,** 1989. 22 games.
— **Bill Ranford, Edmonton,** 1990. 22 games
15 — Bill Smith, NY Islanders, 1980. 20 games.
— Bill Smith, NY Islanders, 1982. 18 games.
— Grant Fuhr, Edmonton, 1985. 18 games.
— Patrick Roy, Montreal, 1986. 20 games.
— Ron Hextall, Philadelphia, 1987. 26 games.
14 — Bill Smith, NY Islanders, 1981. 17 games.
14 — Grant Fuhr, Edmonton, 1987. 19 games.

MOST CONSECUTIVE WINS BY A GOALTENDER, ONE PLAYOFF YEAR:
10 — **Gerry Cheevers, Boston,** 1970. 2 wins against NY Rangers in QF, won by Boston 4-2; 4 wins against Chicago in SF, won by Boston 4-0; and 4 wins against St. Louis in F, won by Boston 4-0.

MOST SHUTOUTS, ONE PLAYOFF YEAR:
4 — **Clint Benedict, Mtl. Maroons,** 1926. 8 games.
— **Clint Benedict, Mtl. Maroons,** 1928. 9 games.
— **Dave Kerr, NY Rangers,** 1937. 9 games.
— **Frank McCool, Toronto,** 1945. 13 games.
— **Terry Sawchuk, Detroit,** 1952. 8 games.
— **Bernie Parent, Philadelphia,** 1975. 17 games.
— **Ken Dryden, Montreal,** 1977. 14 games.

MOST CONSECUTIVE SHUTOUTS:
3 — **Clint Benedict, Mtl. Maroons,** 1926. Benedict shut out Ottawa 1-0, Mar. 27; he then shut out Victoria twice, 3-0, Mar. 30; 3-0, Apr. 1. Mtl. Maroons won NHL F vs. Ottawa 2 goals to 1 and won the best-of-five F vs. Victoria 3-1.
— **Frank McCool, Toronto,** 1945. McCool shut out Detroit 1-0, April 6; 2-0, April 8; 1-0, April 12. Toronto won the best-of-seven F 4-3.

LONGEST SHUTOUT SEQUENCE:
248 Minutes, 32 Seconds — **Norm Smith, Detroit,** 1936. In best-of-five SF, Smith shut out Mtl. Maroons 1-0, March 24, in 116:30 overtime; shut out Maroons 3-0 in second game, March 26; and was scored against at 12:02 of first period, March 29, by Gus Marker. Detroit won SF 3-0.

One-Series Records

MOST POINTS IN FINAL SERIES:
13 — **Wayne Gretzky, Edmonton,** in 1988, 4 games plus suspended game vs. Boston. 3 goals, 10 assists.
12 — Gordie Howe, Detroit, in 1955, 7 games vs. Montreal. 5 goals, 7 assists.
— Yvan Cournoyer, Montreal, in 1973, 6 games vs. Chicago. 6 goals, 6 assists.
— Jacques Lemaire, Montreal, in 1973, 6 games vs. Chicago. 3 goals, 9 assists.

MOST GOALS IN FINAL SERIES:
9 — **Babe Dye, Toronto,** in 1922, 5 games vs. Van. Millionaires.
8 — Alf Skinner, Toronto, in 1918, 5 games vs. Van. Millionaires.
7 — Jean Beliveau, Montreal, in 1956, during 5 games vs. Detroit.
— Mike Bossy, NY Islanders, in 1982, during 4 games vs. Vancouver.
— Wayne Gretzky, Edmonton, in 1985, during 5 games vs. Philadelphia.

MOST ASSISTS IN FINAL SERIES:
10 — **Wayne Gretzky, Edmonton,** in 1988, 4 games plus suspended game vs. Boston.
9 — Jacques Lemaire, Montreal, in 1973, 6 games vs. Chicago.
— Wayne Gretzky, Edmonton, in 1987, 7 games vs. Philadelphia.

MOST POINTS IN ONE SERIES (OTHER THAN FINAL):
19 — Rick Middleton, Boston, in 1983 DF, 7 games vs. Buffalo. 5 goals, 14 assists.
18 — Wayne Gretzky, Edmonton, in 1985 CF, 6 games vs. Chicago. 4 goals, 14 assists.
16 — Barry Pederson, Boston, in 1983 DF, 7 games vs. Buffalo. 7 goals, 9 assists.
15 — Jari Kurri, Edmonton, in 1985 CF, 6 games vs. Chicago. 12 goals, 3 assists.
— Wayne Gretzky, Edmonton, in 1987 DSF, 5 games vs. Los Angeles. 2 goals, 13 assists.
— Tim Kerr, Philadelphia, in 1989 DF, 7 games vs. Pittsburgh. 10 goals, 5 assists.

MOST GOALS IN ONE SERIES (OTHER THAN FINAL):
12 — Jari Kurri, Edmonton, in 1985 CF, 6 games vs. Chicago.
11 — Newsy Lalonde, Montreal, in 1919 NHL F, 5 games vs. Ottawa.
10 — Tim Kerr, Philadelphia, in 1989 DF, 7 games vs. Pittsburgh.
9 — Reggie Leach, Philadelphia, in 1976 SF, 5 games vs. Boston.
— Bill Barber, Philadelphia, in 1980 SF, 5 games vs. Minnesota.
— Mike Bossy, NY Islanders, in 1983 CF, 6 games vs. Boston.
— Mario Lemieux, Pittsburgh, in 1989 DF, 7 games vs. Philadelphia.

MOST ASSISTS IN ONE SERIES (OTHER THAN FINAL):
14 — Rick Middleton, Boston, in 1983 DF, 7 games vs. Buffalo.
— **Wayne Gretzky, Edmonton,** in 1985 CF, 6 games vs. Chicago.
13 — Wayne Gretzky, Edmonton, in 1987 DSF, 5 games vs. Los Angeles.
11 — Mark Messier, Edmonton, in 1989 DSF, 7 games vs. Los Angeles.
— Al MacInnis, Calgary, in 1984 DF, 7 games vs. Edmonton.
10 — Fleming Mackell, Boston, in 1958 SF, 6 games vs. NY Rangers.
— Stan Mikita, Chicago, in 1962 SF, 6 games vs. Montreal.
— Bob Bourne, NY Islanders, in 1983 DF, 6 games vs. NY Rangers.
— Wayne Gretzky, Edmonton, in 1988 DSF, 5 games vs. Winnipeg.

MOST OVERTIME GOALS, ONE PLAYOFF SERIES:
3 — Mel Hill, Boston, 1939, SF vs. NY Rangers, won by Boston 4-3. Hill scored at 59:25 overtime March 21 for a 2-1 win; at 8:24, March 23 for a 3-2 win; and at 48:00, April 2 for a 2-1 win.

MOST POWER-PLAY GOALS, ONE PLAYOFF SERIES:
6 — Chris Kontos, Los Angeles, 1989, DSF vs. Edmonton, won by Los Angeles 4-3.
5 — Andy Bathgate, Detroit, 1966, SF vs. Chicago, won by Detroit 4-2.
— Denis Potvin, NY Islanders, 1981, QF vs. Edmonton, won by NY Islanders 4-2.
— Ken Houston, Calgary, 1981, QF vs. Philadelphia, won by Calgary 4-3.
— Rick Vaive, Chicago, 1988, DSF vs. St. Louis, won by St. Louis 4-1.
— Tim Kerr, Philadelphia, 1989, DF vs. Pittsburgh, won by Philadelphia 4-3.
— Mario Lemieux, Pittsburgh, 1989, DF vs. Philadelphia won by Philadelphia 4-3.
— John Druce, Washington, 1990, DF vs. NY Rangers won by Washington 4-1.

MOST SHORTHAND GOALS, ONE PLAYOFF SERIES:
3 — Bill Barber, Philadelphia, 1980, SF vs. Minnesota, won by Philadelphia 4-1.
— **Wayne Presley, Chicago,** 1989, DSF vs. Detroit, won by Chicago 4-2.
2 — Mac Colville, NY Rangers, 1940, SF vs. Boston, won by NY Rangers 4-2.
— Jerry Toppazzini, Boston, 1958, SF vs. NY Rangers, won by Boston 4-2.
— Dave Keon, Toronto, 1963, F vs. Detroit, won by Toronto 4-1.
— Bob Pulford, Toronto, 1964, F vs. Detroit, won by Toronto 4-3.
— Serge Savard, Montreal, 1968, F vs. St. Louis, won by Montreal 4-0.
— Derek Sanderson, Boston, 1969, SF vs. Montreal, won by Montreal 4-2.
— Bryan Trottier, NY Islanders, 1980, PR vs. Los Angeles, won by NY Islanders 3-1.
— Bobby Lalonde, Boston, 1981, PR vs. Minnesota, won by Minnesota 3-0.
— Butch Goring, NY Islanders, 1981, SF vs. NY Rangers, won by NY Islanders 4-0.
— Wayne Gretzky, Edmonton, 1983, DSF vs. Winnipeg, won by Edmonton 3-0.
— Mark Messier, Edmonton, 1983, DF vs. Calgary, won by Edmonton 4-1.
— Jari Kurri, Edmonton, 1983, CF vs. Chicago, won by Edmonton 4-0.
— Wayne Gretzky, Edmonton, 1985, DF vs. Winnipeg, won by Edmonton 4-0.
— Kevin Lowe, Edmonton, 1987, F vs. Philadelphia, won by Edmonton 4-3.
— Bob Gould, Washington, 1988, DSF vs. Philadelphia, won by Washington 4-3.
— Dave Poulin, Philadelphia, 1989, DF vs. Pittsburgh, won by Philadelphia 4-3.

MOST THREE-OR-MORE-GOAL GAMES, ONE PLAYOFF SERIES:
3 — Jari Kurri, Edmonton 1985, CF vs. Chicago won by Edmonton 4-2. Kurri scored 3 G May 7 at Edmonton in 7-3 win, 3 G May 14 in 10-5 win and 4 G May 16 at Chicago in 8-2 win.
2 — Doug Bentley, Chicago, 1944, SF vs. Detroit, won by Chicago 4-1. Bentley scored 3 G Mar. 28 at Chicago in 7-1 win and 3 G Mar. 30 at Detroit in 5-2 win.
— Norm Ullman, Detroit, 1964, SF vs. Chicago, won by Detroit 4-3. Ullman scored 3 G Mar. 29 at Chicago in 7-1 win and 3 G April 7 at Detroit in 7-2 win.
— Mark Messier, Edmonton, 1983, DF vs. Calgary won by Edmonton 4-1. Messier scored 4 G April 14 at Edmonton in 6-3 win and 3 G April 17 at Calgary in 10-2 win.
— Mike Bossy, NY Islanders, 1983, CF vs. Boston won by NY Islanders 4-2. Bossy scored 3 G May 3 at New York in 8-3 win and 4 G on May 7 at New York in 8-4 win.

Dickie Moore (left) had six points in a 1954 playoff game against the Bruins. Tim Kerr (right) had five powerplay goals in a seven-game series against Pittsburgh in 1989.

Single Playoff Game Records

MOST POINTS, ONE GAME:
8 — Patrik Sundstrom, New Jersey, April 22, 1988 at New Jersey during 10-4 win over Washington. Sundstrom had 3 goals, 5 assists.
— **Mario Lemieux, Pittsburgh,** April 25, 1989 at Pittsburgh during 10-7 win over Philadelphia. Lemieux had 5 goals, 3 assists.
7 — Wayne Gretzky, Edmonton, April 17, 1983 at Calgary during 10-2 win. Gretzky had 4 goals, 3 assists.
— Wayne Gretzky, Edmonton, April 25,1985 at Winnipeg during 8-3 win. Gretzky had 3 goals, 4 assists.
— Wayne Gretzky, Edmonton, April 9, 1987, at Edmonton during 13-3 win over Los Angeles. Gretzky had 1 goal, 6 assists.
6 — Dickie Moore, Montreal, March 25, 1954, at Montreal during 8-1 win over Boston. Moore had 2 goals, 4 assists.
— Phil Esposito, Boston, April 2, 1969, at Boston during 10-0 win over Toronto. Esposito had 4 goals, 2 assists.
— Darryl Sittler, Toronto, April 22, 1976, at Toronto during 8-5 win over Philadelphia. Sittler had 5 goals, 1 assist.
— Guy Lafleur, Montreal, April 11, 1977, at Montreal during 7-2 victory vs. St. Louis. Lafleur had 3 goals, 3 assists.
— Mikko Leinonen, NY Rangers, April 8, 1982, at New York during 7-3 win over Philadelphia. Leinonen had 6 assists.
— Paul Coffey, Edmonton, May 14, 1985 at Edmonton during 10-5 win over Chicago. Coffey had 1 goal, 5 assists.
— John Anderson, Hartford, April 12, 1986 at Hartford during 9-4 win over Quebec. Anderson had 2 goals, 4 assists.

MOST POINTS BY A DEFENSEMAN, ONE GAME:
6 — Paul Coffey, Edmonton, May 14, 1985 at Edmonton. 1 goal, 5 assists. Edmonton won 10-5.
5 — Eddie Bush, Detroit, April 9, 1942, at Detroit. 1 goal, 4 assists. Detroit won 5-2.
— Bob Dailey, Philadelphia, May 1, 1980, at Philadelphia vs. Minnesota. 1 goal, 4 assists. Philadelphia won 7-0.
— Denis Potvin, NY Islanders, April 17, 1981, at New York vs. Edmonton. 3 goals, 2 assists. NY Islanders won 6-3.
— Risto Siltanen, Quebec, April 14, 1987 at Hartford. 5 assists. Quebec won 7-5.

MOST GOALS, ONE GAME:
5 — Newsy Lalonde, Montreal, March 1, 1919, at Montreal. Final score: Montreal 6, Ottawa 3.
— **Maurice Richard, Montreal,** March 23, 1944, at Montreal. Final score: Montreal 5, Toronto 1.
— **Darryl Sittler, Toronto,** April 22, 1976, at Toronto. Final score: Toronto 8, Philadelphia 5.
— **Reggie Leach, Philadelphia,** May 6, 1976, at Philadelphia. Final score: Philadelphia 6, Boston 3.
— **Mario Lemieux, Pittsburgh,** April 25, 1989 at Pittsburgh. Final score: Pittsburgh 10, Philadelphia 7.

MOST GOALS BY A DEFENSEMAN, ONE GAME:
3 — Bobby Orr, Boston, April 11, 1971 at Montreal. Final score: Boston 5, Montreal 2.
— **Dick Redmond, Chicago,** April 4, 1973 at Chicago. Final score: Chicago 7, St. Louis 1.
— **Denis Potvin, NY Islanders,** April 17, 1981 at New York. Final score: NY Islanders 6, Edmonton 3.
— **Paul Reinhart, Calgary,** April 14, 1983 at Edmonton. Final score: Edmonton 6, Calgary 3.
— **Paul Reinhart, Calgary,** April 8, 1984 at Vancouver. Final score: Calgary 5, Vancouver 1.
— **Doug Halward, Vancouver,** April 7, 1984 at Vancouver. Final score: Vancouver 7, Calgary 0.

MOST POWER-PLAY GOALS, ONE GAME:

3 — **Syd Howe, Detroit,** March 23, 1939, at Detroit vs. Montreal, Detroit won 7-3.
— **Sid Smith, Toronto,** April 10, 1949, at Detroit. Toronto won 3-1.
— **Phil Esposito, Boston,** April 2, 1969, at Boston vs. Toronto. Boston won 10-0.
— **John Bucyk, Boston,** April 21, 1974, at Boston vs. Chicago. Boston won 8-6.
— **Denis Potvin, NY Islanders,** April 17, 1981, at New York vs. Edmonton. NY Islanders won 6-3.
— **Tim Kerr, Philadelphia,** April 13, 1985, at Rangers. Philadelphia won 6-5.
— **Jari Kurri, Edmonton,** April 9, 1987, at Edmonton vs. Los Angeles. Edmonton won 13-3.
— **Mark Johnson, New Jersey,** April 22, 1988, at New Jersey vs. Washington. New Jersey won 10-4.

MOST SHORTHAND GOALS, ONE GAME:

2 — **Dave Keon, Toronto,** April 18, 1963, at Toronto, in 3-1 win vs. Detroit.
— **Bryan Trottier, NY Islanders,** April 8, 1980 at New York, in 8-1 win vs. Los Angeles.
— **Bobby Lalonde, Boston,** April 11, 1981 at Minnesota, in 6-3 win by Minnesota.
— **Wayne Gretzky, Edmonton,** April 6, 1983 at Edmonton, in 6-3 win vs. Winnipeg.
— **Jari Kurri, Edmonton,** April 24, 1983, at Edmonton, in 8-3 win vs. Chicago.

MOST ASSISTS, ONE GAME:

6 — **Mikko Leinonen, NY Rangers,** April 8, 1982, at New York. Final score: NY Rangers 7, Philadelphia 3.
— **Wayne Gretzky, Edmonton,** April 9, 1987, at Edmonton. Final score: Edmonton 13, Los Angeles 3.
5 — Toe Blake, Montreal, March 23, 1944, at Montreal. Final score: Montreal 5, Toronto 1.
— Maurice Richard, Montreal, March 27, 1956, at Montreal. Final score: Montreal 7, NY Rangers 0.
— Bert Olmstead, Montreal, March 30, 1957, at Montreal. Final score: Montreal 8, NY Rangers 3.
— Don McKenney, Boston, April 5, 1958, at Boston. Final score: Boston 8, NY Rangers 2.
— Stan Mikita, Chicago, April 4, 1973, at Chicago. Final score: Chicago 7, St. Louis 1.
— Wayne Gretzky, Edmonton, April 8, 1981, at Montreal. Final score: Edmonton 6, Montreal 3.
— Paul Coffey, Edmonton, May 14, 1985, at Edmonton. Final score: Edmonton 10, Chicago 5.
— Doug Gilmour, St. Louis, April 15, 1986, at Minnesota. Final score: St. Louis 6, Minnesota 3.
— Risto Siltanen, Quebec, April 14, 1987 at Hartford. Final score: Quebec 7, Hartford 5.
— Patrik Sundstrom, New Jersey, April 22, 1988, at New Jersey. Final score: New Jersey 10, Washington 4.

MOST PENALTY MINUTES, ONE GAME:

42 — **Dave Schultz, Philadelphia,** April 22, 1976, at Toronto. One minor, 2 majors, 1 10-minute misconduct and 2 game-misconducts. Final score: Toronto 8, Philadelphia 5.

MOST PENALTIES, ONE GAME:

8 — **Forbes Kennedy, Toronto,** April 2, 1969, at Boston. Four minors, 2 majors, 1 10-minute misconduct, 1 game misconduct. Final score: Boston 10, Toronto 0.
— **Kim Clackson, Pittsburgh,** April 14, 1980, at Boston. Five minors, 2 majors, 1 10-minute misconduct. Final score: Boston 6, Pittsburgh 2

MOST POINTS, ONE PERIOD:

4 — **Maurice Richard, Montreal,** March 29, 1945, at Montreal vs. Toronto. Third period, 3 goals, 1 assist. Final score: Montreal 10, Toronto 3.
— **Dickie Moore, Montreal,** March 25, 1954, at Montreal vs. Boston. First period, 2 goals, 2 assists. Final score: Montreal 8, Boston 1.
— **Barry Pederson, Boston,** April 8, 1982, at Boston vs. Buffalo. Second period, 3 goals, 1 assist. Final score: Boston 7, Buffalo 3.
— **Peter McNab, Boston,** April 11, 1982, at Buffalo. Second period, 1 goal, 3 assists. Final score: Boston 5, Buffalo 2.
— **Tim Kerr, Philadelphia,** April 13, 1985 at New York. Second period, 4 goals. Final score: Philadelphia 6, Rangers 5.
— **Ken Linseman, Boston,** April 14, 1985 at Boston vs. Montreal. Second period, 2 goals, 2 assists. Final score: Boston 7, Montreal 6.
— **Wayne Gretzky, Edmonton,** April 12, 1987, at Los Angeles. Third period, 1 goal, 3 assists. Final score: Edmonton 6, Los Angeles 3.
— **Glenn Anderson, Edmonton,** April 6, 1988, at Edmonton vs. Winnipeg. Third period, 3 goals, 1 assist. Final score: Edmonton 7, Winnipeg 4.
— **Mario Lemieux, Pittsburgh,** April 25, 1989, at Pittsburgh vs. Philadelphia. First period, 4 goals. Final score: Pittsburgh 10, Philadelphia 7.

MOST GOALS, ONE PERIOD:

4 — **Tim Kerr, Philadelphia,** April 13, 1985, at New York vs. NY Rangers, second period. Final score: Philadelphia 6, NY Rangers 5.
— **Mario Lemieux, Pittsburgh,** April 25, 1989, at Pittsburgh vs. Philadelphia, first period. Final score: Pittsburgh 10, Philadelphia 7.
3 — Harvey (Busher) Jackson, Toronto, April 5, 1932, at New York vs. NY Rangers, second period. Final score: Toronto 6, NY Rangers 4.
— Maurice Richard, Montreal, March 23, 1944, at Montreal vs. Toronto, second period. Final score: Montreal 5, Toronto 1.
— Maurice Richard, Montreal, March 29, 1945, at Montreal vs. Toronto, third period. Final score: Montreal 10, Toronto 3.
— Maurice Richard, Montreal, April 6, 1957 at Montreal vs. Boston, second period. Final score: Montreal 5, Boston 1.
— Ted Lindsay, Detroit, April 5, 1955, at Detroit vs. Montreal, second period. Final score: Detroit 7, Montreal 1.
— Red Berenson, St. Louis, April 15, 1969, at St. Louis vs. Los Angeles, second period. Final score: St. Louis 4, Los Angeles 0.
— Jacques Lemaire, Montreal, April 20, 1971, at Montreal vs. Minnesota, second period. Final score: Montreal 7, Minnesota 2.
— Rick MacLeish, Philadelphia, April 11, 1974, at Philadelphia vs. Atlanta, second period. Final score: Philadelphia 5, Atlanta 1.
— Tom Williams, Los Angeles, April 14, 1974, at Los Angeles vs. Chicago, third period. Final score: Los Angeles 5, Chicago 1.
— Darryl Sittler, Toronto, April 22, 1976, at Toronto vs. Philadelphia, second period. Final score: Toronto 8, Philadelphia 5.
— Reggie Leach, Philadelphia, May 6, 1976, at Philadelphia vs. Boston, second period. Final score: Philadelphia 6, Boston 3.
— Bobby Schmautz, Boston, April 11, 1977, at Boston vs. Los Angeles, first period. Final score: Boston 8, Los Angeles 3.
— George Ferguson, Toronto, April 11, 1978, at Toronto vs. Los Angeles, third period. Final score: Toronto 7, Los Angeles 3.
— Barry Pederson, Boston, April 8, 1982, at Boston vs. Buffalo, second period. Final score: Boston 7, Buffalo 3.
— Peter Stastny, Quebec, April 5, 1983, at Boston, first period. Final score: Boston 4, Quebec 3.
— Wayne Gretzky, Edmonton, April 6, 1983 at Edmonton, second period. Final score: Edmonton 6, Winnipeg 3.
— Mike Bossy, NY Islanders, May 7, 1983 at New York, second period. Final score: NY Islanders 8, Boston 4.
— Dave Andreychuk, Buffalo, April 14, 1985, at Buffalo vs. Quebec, third period. Final score: Buffalo 7, Quebec 4.
— Wayne Gretzky, Edmonton, May 25, 1985, at Edmonton vs. Philadelphia, first period. Final score: Edmonton 4, Philadelphia 3.
— Glenn Anderson, Edmonton, April 6, 1988, at Edmonton vs. Winnipeg, third period. Final score: Edmonton 7, Winnipeg 4.
— Tim Kerr, Philadelphia, April 19, 1989, at Pittsburgh vs. Penguins, first period. Final score: Philadelphia 4, Pittsburgh 2.

MOST POWER PLAY GOALS, ONE PERIOD:

3 — **Tim Kerr, Philadelphia,** April 13, 1985 at New York, second period in 6-5 win vs. NY Rangers.
2 — Two power play goals have been scored by one player in one period on 32 occasions. Charlie Conacher of Toronto was the first to score two power play goals in one period, setting the mark on Mar. 26, 1936. John Druce of Washington equalled the mark most recently on April 23, 1990 vs. NY Rangers.

John Bucyk of Boston, Denis Savard of Chicago and Tim Kerr of Philadelphia have each scored two power play goals in one period on two occasions.

MOST SHORTHAND GOALS, ONE PERIOD:

2 — **Bryan Trottier, NY Islanders,** April 8, 1980, second period at New York in 8-1 win vs. Los Angeles.
— **Bobby Lalonde, Boston,** April 11, 1981, third period at Minnesota in 6-3 win by Minnesota
— **Jari Kurri, Edmonton,** April 24, 1983, third period at Edmonton in 8-4 win vs. Chicago.

MOST ASSISTS, ONE PERIOD:

3 — Three assists by one player in one period of a playoff game have been recorded on **48** occasions. Dave Andreychuk of Buffalo is the most recent to equal this mark with 3 assists in the second period at Montreal, April 11, 1990. Final score: Buffalo 4, Montreal 2.

Wayne Gretzky has had 3 assists in one period 5 times; Ray Bourque, 3 times; Toe Blake, Jean Beliveau, Doug Harvey and Bobby Orr, twice.

Nick Metz of Toronto was the first player to be credited with 3 assists in one period of a playoff game Mar. 21, 1941 at Toronto vs. Boston.

MOST PENALTIES, ONE PERIOD AND MOST PENALTY MINUTES, ONE PERIOD:

6 Penalties; 39 Minutes — **Ed Hospodar, NY Rangers,** April 9, 1981, at Los Angeles, first period. Two minors, 1 major, 1 10-minute misconduct, 2 game misconducts. Final score: Los Angeles 5, NY Rangers 4.

FASTEST TWO GOALS:

5 Seconds — **Norm Ullman, Detroit,** at Detroit, April 11, 1965, vs. Chicago and goaltender Glenn Hall. Ullman scored at 17:35 and 17:40 of second period. Detroit won 4-2.

FASTEST GOAL FROM START OF GAME:

6 Seconds — **Don Kozak, Los Angeles,** April 17, 1977, at Los Angeles vs. Boston and goaltender Gerry Cheevers. Los Angeles won 7-4.
7 Seconds — Bob Gainey, Montreal, May 5, 1977, at New York vs. NY Islanders and goaltender Glenn Resch. Montreal won 2-1.
— Terry Murray, Philadelphia, April 12, 1981, at Quebec vs. goaltender Dan Bouchard. Quebec won 4-3 in overtime.
8 Seconds — Stan Smyl, Vancouver, April 7, 1982, at Vancouver vs. Calgary and goaltender Pat Riggin. Vancouver won 5-3.

Pelle Eklund scored seven seconds into the second period of a playoff game on April 25, 1989.

FASTEST GOAL FROM START OF PERIOD (OTHER THAN FIRST):
6 Seconds — Pelle Eklund, Phiadelphia, April 25, 1989, at Pittsburgh vs. goaltender Tom Barrasso, second period. Pittsburgh won 10-7.
9 Seconds — Bill Collins, Minnesota, April 9, 1968, at Minnesota vs. Los Angeles and goaltender Wayne Rutledge, third period. Minnesota won 7-5.
— Dave Balon, Minnesota, April 25, 1968, at St. Louis vs. goaltender Glenn Hall, third period. Minnesota won 5-1.
— Murray Oliver, Minnesota, April 8, 1971, at St. Louis vs. goaltender Ernie Wakely, third period. St. Louis won 4-2.
— Clark Gillies, NY Islanders, April 15, 1977, at Buffalo vs. goaltender Don Edwards, third period. NY Islanders won 4-3.
— Eric Vail, Atlanta, April 11, 1978, at Atlanta vs. Detroit and goaltender Ron Low, third period. Detroit won 5-3.
— Stan Smyl, Vancouver, April 10, 1979, at Philadelphia vs. goaltender Wayne Stephenson, third period. Vancouver won 3-2.
— Wayne Gretzky, Edmonton, April 6, 1983, at Edmonton vs. Winnipeg and goaltender Brian Hayward, second period. Edmonton won 6-3.
— Mark Messier, Edmonton, April 16, 1984, at Calgary vs. goaltender Don Edwards, third period. Edmonton won 5-3.
— Brian Skrudland, Montreal, May 18, 1986 at Calgary vs. Calgary and goaltender Mike Vernon, overtime. Montreal won 3-2.

FASTEST TWO GOALS FROM START OF GAME:
1 Minute, 8 Seconds — Dick Duff, Toronto, April 9, 1963 at Toronto vs. Detroit and goaltender Terry Sawchuk. Duff scored at 49 seconds and 1:08. Final score: Toronto 4, Detroit 2.

FASTEST TWO GOALS FROM START OF PERIOD:
35 Seconds — Pat LaFontaine, NY Islanders, May 19, 1984 at Edmonton vs. goaltender Andy Moog. LaFontaine scored at 13 and 35 seconds of third period. Final score: Edmonton 5, NY Islanders 2.

Early Playoff Records

1893-1918
Team Records

MOST GOALS, BOTH TEAMS, ONE GAME:
25 — **Ottawa Silver Seven, Dawson City** at Ottawa, Jan. 16, 1905. Ottawa 23, Dawson City 2. Ottawa won best-of-three series 2-0.

MOST GOALS, ONE TEAM, ONE GAME:
23 — **Ottawa Silver Seven** at Ottawa, Jan. 16, 1905. Ottawa defeated Dawson City 23-2.

MOST GOALS, BOTH TEAMS, BEST-OF-THREE SERIES:
42 — **Ottawa Silver Seven, Queen's University** at Ottawa, 1906. Ottawa defeated Queen's 16-7, Feb. 27, and 12-7, Feb. 28.

MOST GOALS, ONE TEAM, BEST-OF-THREE SERIES:
32 — **Ottawa Silver Seven** in 1905 at Ottawa. Defeated Dawson City 9-2, Jan. 13, and 23-2, Jan. 16.

MOST GOALS, BOTH TEAMS, BEST-OF-FIVE SERIES:
39 — **Toronto Arenas, Vancouver Millionaires** at Toronto, 1918. Toronto won 5-3, Mar. 20; 6-3, Mar. 26; 2-1, Mar. 30. Vancouver won 6-4, Mar. 23, and 8-1, Mar. 28. Toronto scored 18 goals; Vancouver 21.

MOST GOALS, ONE TEAM, BEST-OF-FIVE SERIES:
26 — **Vancouver Millionaires** in 1915 at Vancouver. Defeated Ottawa Senators 6-2, Mar. 22; 8-3, Mar. 24; and 12-3, Mar. 26.

Individual Records

MOST GOALS IN PLAYOFFS:
63 — **Frank McGee, Ottawa Silver Seven,** in 22 playoff games. Seven goals in four games, 1903; 21 goals in eight games, 1904; 18 goals in four games, 1905; 17 goals in six games, 1906.

MOST GOALS, ONE PLAYOFF SERIES:
15 — **Frank McGee, Ottawa Silver Seven,** in two games in 1905 at Ottawa. Scored one goal, Jan. 13, in 9-2 victory over Dawson City and 14 goals, Jan. 16, in 23-2 victory.

MOST GOALS, ONE PLAYOFF GAME:
14 — **Frank McGee, Ottawa Silver Seven,** Jan. 16, 1905 at Ottawa in 23-2 victory over Dawson City.

FASTEST THREE GOALS:
40 Seconds — **Marty Walsh, Ottawa Senators,** at Ottawa, March 16, 1911, at 3:00, 3:10, and 3:40 of third period. Ottawa defeated Port Arthur 13-4.

Frank McGee

Marty Walsh

Glenn Anderson ranks in the top ten in all-time playoff goals, assists and points.

All-Time Playoff Goal Leaders since 1918

(40 or more goals)

Player	Teams	Yrs.	GP	G
*Jari Kurri	Edmonton	10	146	92
*Wayne Gretzky	Edm., L.A.	11	138	89
Mike Bossy	NY Islanders	10	129	85
Maurice Richard	Montreal	15	133	82
Jean Beliveau	Montreal	17	162	79
*Mark Messier	Edmonton	11	148	76
*Glenn Anderson	Edmonton	10	146	75
Gordie Howe	Det., Hfd.	20	157	68
Yvan Cournoyer	Montreal	12	147	64
*Bryan Trottier	NY Islanders	14	175	64
Bobby Hull	Chi., Hfd.	14	119	62
Phil Esposito	Chi., Bos., NYR	15	130	61
Jacques Lemaire	Montreal	11	145	61
Stan Mikita	Chicago	18	155	59
*Guy Lafleur	Mtl., NYR	14	120	58
Bernie Geoffrion	Mtl., NYR	16	131	58
*Brian Propp	Phi., Bos.	12	136	56
Denis Potvin	NY Islanders	14	185	56
*Bobby Smith	Min., Mtl.	11	154	55
Rick MacLeish	Phi., Pit., Det.	11	114	54
*Denis Savard	Chicago	10	99	53
Bill Barber	Philadelphia	11	129	53
Frank Mahovlich	Tor., Det., Mtl.	14	137	51
Steve Shutt	Mtl., LA.	10	96	50
Henri Richard	Montreal	18	180	49
Reggie Leach	Philadelphia	8	96	47
Ted Lindsay	Det., Chi.	16	133	47
Clark Gillies	NYI, Buf.	13	164	47
Dickie Moore	Mtl., Tor., St. L.	14	135	46
Rick Middleton	NYR, Bos.	12	114	45
*Joe Mullen	St.L., Cgy.	8	81	44
Lanny McDonald	Tor., Cgy.	13	117	44
*Ken Linseman	Phi., Edm., Bos.	10	111	43
Bobby Clarke	Philadelphia	13	136	42
John Bucyk	Det., Bos.	14	124	41
Peter McNab	Bos., Van.	10	107	40
Bob Bourne	NYI, L.A.	13	139	40

* — Active player.

All-Time Playoff Assist Leaders since 1918

(60 or more assists)

Player	Teams	Yrs.	GP	A
*Wayne Gretzky	Edm., L.A.	11	138	195
*Mark Messier	Edmonton	11	148	124
*Larry Robinson	Mtl., L.A.	18	213	112
*Jari Kurri	Edmonton	10	146	110
Denis Potvin	NY Islanders	14	185	108
*Bryan Trottier	NY Islanders	14	175	106
Jean Beliveau	Montreal	17	162	97
*Glenn Anderson	Edmonton	10	146	95
Gordie Howe	Det., Hfd.	20	157	92
Stan Mikita	Chicago	18	155	91
Brad Park	NYR, Bos., Det.	16	159	90
*Bobby Smith	Min., Mtl.	11	154	84
*Paul Coffey	Edm., Pit.	8	105	80
Henri Richard	Montreal	18	180	80
Jacques Lemaire	Montreal	11	145	78
Bobby Clarke	Philadelphia	13	136	77
*Ken Linseman	Phi., Edm., Bos.	10	111	76
*Guy Lafleur	Mtl., NYR	14	128	76
Phil Esposito	Chi., Bos., NYR	15	130	76
Mike Bossy	NY Islanders	10	129	75
*Ray Bourque	Boston	11	104	71
*John Tonelli	NYI, Cgy., L.A.	12	160	71
Gilbert Perreault	Buffalo	11	85	70
*Denis Savard	Chicago	10	99	69
Alex Delvecchio	Detroit	14	121	69
*Brian Propp	Phi., Bos.	11	136	69
Bobby Hull	Chi., Hfd.	14	119	67
Frank Mahovlich	Tor., Det., Mtl.	14	137	67
Bobby Orr	Boston	8	74	66
*Bernie Federko	St. Louis	11	91	66
Jean Ratelle	NYR, Bos.	14	120	66
Dickie Moore	Mtl., Tor., St. L.	14	135	64
Doug Harvey	Mtl., NYR, St. L.	15	137	64
Yvan Cournoyer	Montreal	12	147	63
*Al MacInnis	Calgary	7	75	62
John Bucyk	Det., Bos.	14	124	62
*Doug Wilson	Chicago	11	90	60

* — Active player.

All-Time Playoff Point Leaders since 1918

(100 or more points)

Player	Teams	Yrs.	GP	G	A	Pts.
*Wayne Gretzky	Edm., L.A.	11	138	89	195	284
*Jari Kurri	Edmonton	10	146	92	110	202
*Mark Messier	Edmonton	11	148	76	124	200
Jean Beliveau	Montreal	17	162	79	97	176
*Bryan Trottier	NY Islanders	14	175	64	106	170
*Glenn Anderson	Edmonton	10	146	75	95	170
Denis Potvin	NY Islanders	14	185	56	108	164
Mike Bossy	NY Islanders	10	129	85	75	160
Gordie Howe	Det., Hfd.	20	157	68	92	160
Stan Mikita	Chicago	18	155	59	91	150
Jacques Lemaire	Montreal	11	145	61	78	139
*Larry Robinson	Mtl., L.A.	18	213	27	112	139
*Bobby Smith	Min., Mtl.	11	154	55	84	139
Phil Esposito	Chi., Bos., NYR	15	130	61	76	137
*Guy Lafleur	Mtl., NYR	14	128	58	76	134
Bobby Hull	Chi., Hfd.	14	119	62	67	129
Henri Richard	Montreal	18	180	49	80	129
Yvan Cournoyer	Montreal	12	147	64	63	127
Maurice Richard	Montreal	15	133	82	44	126
*Brian Propp	Phi., Bos.	12	136	56	69	125
Brad Park	NYR, Bos., Det.	17	162	35	90	125
*Denis Savard	Chicago	10	99	53	69	122
*Ken Linseman	Phi., Edm., Bos.	10	111	43	76	119
Bobby Clarke	Philadelphia	13	136	42	77	119
Bernie Geoffrion	Mtl., NYR	16	131	58	60	118
Frank Mahovlich	Tor., Det., Mtl.	14	137	51	67	118
*Paul Coffey	Edm., Pit.	8	105	38	80	118
Dickie Moore	Mtl., Tor., St. L.	14	135	46	64	110
*John Tonelli	NYI, Cgy., L.A.	12	160	38	71	109
Bill Barber	Philadelphia	11	129	53	55	108
Rick MacLeish	Phi., Pit., Det.	11	114	54	53	107
Alex Delvecchio	Detroit	14	121	35	69	104
John Bucyk	Det., Bos.	14	124	41	62	103
Gilbert Perreault	Buffalo	11	90	33	70	103
*Bernie Federko	St. Louis	11	91	35	66	101
Rick Middleton	NYR, Bos.	12	114	45	55	100

* — Active player.

Three-or-more-Goal Games, Playoffs 1918 – 1990

Jean Ratelle's only playoff hat-trick was scored against Montreal's Ken Dryden on May 3, 1979.

Player	Team	Date	City	Total Goals	Opposing Goaltender	Score	
Maurice Richard (7)	Mtl.	Mar.23/44	Mtl.	5	Paul Bibeault	Mtl. 5	Tor. 1
		Apr. 7/44	Chi.	3	Mike Karakas	Mtl. 3	Chi. 1
		Mar.29/45	Mtl.	4	Frank McCool	Mtl. 10	Tor. 3
		Apr. 14/53	Bos.	3	Gord Henry	Mtl. 7	Bos. 3
		Mar.20/56	Mtl.	3	Lorne Worsley	Mtl. 7	NYR 1
		Apr. 6/57	Mtl.	3	Don Simmons	Mtl. 5	Bos. 1
		Apr. 1/58	Det.	3	Terry Sawchuk	Mtl. 4	Det. 3
Wayne Gretzky (7)	Edm.	Apr. 11/81	Edm.	3	Richard Sevigny	Edm. 6	Mtl. 2
		Apr. 19/81	Edm.	3	Billy Smith	Edm. 5	NYI 2
		Apr. 6/83	Edm.	4	Brian Hayward	Edm. 6	Wpg. 3
		Apr. 17/83	Cgy.	4	Rejean Lemelin	Edm. 10	Cgy. 2
		Apr. 25/85	Wpg.	3	Bryan Hayward (2) Marc Behrend (1)	Edm. 8	Wpg. 3
		May 25/85	Edm.	3	Pelle Lindbergh	Edm. 4	Phi. 3
		Apr. 24/86	Cgy.	3	Mike Vernon	Edm. 7	Cgy. 4
		Apr. 4/84	Edm.	3	Doug Soetaert (1) Mike Veisor (2)	Edm. 9	Wpg. 2
Jari Kurri (7)	Edm.	Apr. 25/85	Wpg.	3	Bryan Hayward (2) Marc Behrend (1)	Edm. 8	Wpg. 3
		May 7/85	Edm.	3	Murray Bannerman	Edm. 7	Chi. 3
		May 14/85	Edm.	3	Murray Bannerman	Edm. 10	Chi. 5
		May 16/85	Chi.	4	Murray Bannerman	Edm. 8	Chi. 2
		Apr. 9/87	Edm.	4	Roland Melanson (2) Daren Eliot (2)	Edm. 13	L.A. 3
		May 18/90	Bos.	3	Andy Moog (2) Rejean Lemelin (1)	Edm. 7	Bos. 2
Mike Bossy (5)	NYI	Apr. 16/79	NYI	3	Tony Esposito	NYI 6	Chi. 2
		May 8/82	NYI	3	Richard Brodeur	NYI 6	Van. 5
		Apr. 10/83	Wsh.	3	Al Jensen	NYI 6	Wsh. 3
		May 3/83	NYI	3	Pete Peeters	NYI 8	Bos. 3
		May 7/83	NYI	3	Pete Peeters	NYI 8	Bos. 4
Phil Esposito (4)	Bos.	Apr. 2/69	Bos.	4	Bruce Gamble	Bos. 10	Tor. 0
		Apr. 8/70	Bos.	3	Ed Giacomin	Bos. 8	NYR 2
		Apr. 19/70	Chi.	3	Tony Esposito	Bos. 6	Chi. 3
		Apr. 8/75	Bos.	3	Tony Esposito (2) Michel Dumas (1)	Bos. 8	Chi. 2
Bernie Geoffrion (3)	Mtl.	Mar.27/52	Mtl.	3	Jim Henry	Mtl. 4	Bos. 0
		Apr. 7/55	Mtl.	3	Terry Sawchuk	Mtl. 4	Det. 2
		Mar.30/57	Mtl.	3	Lorne Worsley	Mtl. 8	NYR 3
Norm Ullman (3)	Det.	Mar.29/64	Chi.	3	Glenn Hall	Det. 5	Chi. 4
		Apr. 7/64	Det.	3	Glenn Hall (2) Denis DeJordy (1)	Det. 7	Chi. 2
		Apr. 11/65	Det.	3	Glenn Hall	Det. 4	Chi. 2
John Bucyk (3)	Bos.	May 3/70	St.L.	3	Jacques Plante (1) Ernie Wakely (2)	Bos. 6	St.L. 1
		Apr. 20/72	Bos.	3	Jacques Caron (1) Ernie Wakely (2)	Bos. 10	St.L. 2
		Apr. 21/74	Bos.	3	Tony Esposito	Bos. 8	Chi. 6
Rick MacLeish (3)	Phil	Apr. 11/74	Phil	3	Phil Myre	Phi. 5	Atl. 1
		Apr. 13/75	Phil	3	Gord McRae	Phi. 6	Tor. 3
		May 13/75	Phil	3	Glenn Resch	Phi. 4	NYI 1
Dino Ciccarelli (3)	Min.	May 5/81	Min.	3	Pat Riggin	Min. 7	Cgy. 4
		Apr. 10/82	Min.	3	Murray Bannerman	Min. 7	Chi. 1
	Wsh.	Apr. 5/90	N.J.	3	Sean Burke	Wsh. 5	N.J. 4
Denis Savard (3)	Chi.	Apr. 19/82	Chi.	3	Mike Liut	Chi. 7	StL. 4
		Apr. 10/86	Chi.	4	Ken Wregget	Tor. 6	Chi. 4
		Apr. 9/88	St.L.	3	Greg Millen	Chi. 6	St.L. 3
Mark Messier (3)	Edm.	Apr. 14/83	Edm.	3	Rejean Lemelin	Edm. 6	Cgy. 3
		Apr. 17/83	Cgy.	3	Rejean Lemelin (1) Don Edwards (2)	Edm. 10	Cgy. 2
		Apr. 26/83	Edm.	3	Murray Bannerman	Edm. 8	Chi. 2
Tim Kerr (3)	Phi.	Apr. 13/85	NYR	4	Glen Hanlon	Phi. 6	NYR 5
		Apr. 20/87	Phi.	3	Kelly Hrudey	Phi. 4	NYI 2
		Apr. 19/89	Pit.	3	Tom Barrasso	Phi. 4	Pit. 2
Newsy Lalonde (2)	Mtl.	Mar. 1/19	Mtl.	5	Clint Benedict	Mtl. 6	Ott. 3
		Mar.22/19	Sea.	4	Harry Holmes	Mtl. 4	Sea. 2
Howie Morenz (2)	Mtl.	Mar.22/24	Mtl.	3	Charles Reid	Mtl. 6	Cgy.T. 1
		Mar.27/25	Mtl.	3	Harry Holmes	Mtl. 4	Vic. 2
Toe Blake (2)	Mtl.	Mar.22/38	Mtl.	3	Mike Karakas	Mtl. 6	Chi. 4
		Mar.26/46	Chi.	3	Mike Karakas	Mtl. 7	Chi. 2
Doug Bentley (2)	Chi.	Mar.28/44	Chi.	3	Connie Dion	Chi. 7	Det. 1
		Mar.30/44	Det.	3	Connie Dion	Chi. 5	Det. 2
Ted Kennedy (2)	Tor.	Apr. 14/45	Tor.	3	Harry Lumley	Det. 5	Tor. 3
		Mar.27/48	Tor.	4	Frank Brimsek	Tor. 5	Bos. 3
Bobby Hull (2)	Chi.	Apr. 7/63	Det.	3	Terry Sawchuk	Det. 7	Chi. 4
		Apr. 9/72	Pitt	3	Jim Rutherford	Chi. 6	Pit. 5
F. St. Marseille (2)	St. L.	Apr. 28/70	St.L	3	Al Smith	St.L. 5	Pit. 0
		Apr. 6/72	Min.	3	Cesare Maniago	Min. 6	St.L. 5
Pit Martin (2)	Chi.	Apr. 4/73	Chi.	3	W. Stephenson	Chi. 7	St.L. 1
		May 10/73	Chi.	3	Ken Dryden	Mtl. 6	Chi. 4
Yvan Cournoyer (2)	Mtl.	Apr. 5/73	Mtl.	3	Dave Dryden	Mtl. 7	Buf. 3
		Apr. 11/74	Mtl.	3	Ed Giacomin	Mtl. 4	NYR 1
Guy Lafleur (2)	Mtl.	May 1/75	Mtl.	3	Roger Crozier (1) Gerry Desjardins (2)	Mtl. 7	Buf. 0
		Apr. 11/77	Mtl.	3	Ed Staniowski	Mtl. 7	St.L. 2
Lanny McDonald (2)	Tor.	Apr. 9/77	Pitt	3	Denis Herron	Tor. 5	Pit. 2
		Apr. 17/77		3	W. Stephenson	Phi. 6	Tor. 5
Butch Goring (2)	L.A.	Apr. 9/77	L.A.	3	Phil Myre	L.A. 4	Atl. 2
	NYI	May 17/81	Min.	3	Gilles Meloche	NYI 7	Min. 5
Bryan Trottier (2)	NYI	Apr. 8/80	NYI	3	Doug Keans	NYI 8	L.A. 1
		Apr. 9/81	NYI	3	Michel Larocque	NYI 5	Tor. 1

Player	Team	Date	City	Total Goals	Opposing Goaltender	Score	
Bill Barber (2)	Phil	May 4/80	Min.	4	Gilles Meloche	Phi. 5	Min. 3
		Apr. 9/81	Phil	3	Dan Bouchard	Phi. 8	Que. 5
Brian Propp (2)	Phil.	Apr. 22/81	Phi.	3	Pat Riggin	Phi. 9	Cgy. 4
		Apr. 21/85	Phi.	3	Billy Smith	Phi. 5	NYI 2
Paul Reinhart (2)	Cgy.	Apr. 14/83	Edm.	3	Andy Moog	Edm. 6	Cgy. 3
		Apr. 8/84	Van	3	Richard Brodeur	Cgy. 5	Van. 1
Peter Stastny (2)	Que.	Apr. 5/83	Bos.	3	Pete Peeters	Bos. 4	Que. 3
		Apr. 11/87	Que.	3	Mike Liut (2) Steve Weeks (1)	Que. 5	Hfd. 1
Glenn Anderson (2)	Edm.	Apr. 26/83	Edm.	4	Murray Bannerman	Edm. 8	Chi. 2
		Apr. 6/88	Wpg.	3	Daniel Berthiaume	Edm. 7	Wpg. 4
Michel Goulet (2)	Que.	Apr. 23/85	Que.	3	Steve Penney	Que. 7	Mtl. 6
		Apr. 12/87	Que.	3	Mike Liut	Que. 4	Hfd. 1
Peter Zezel (2)	Phi.	Apr. 13/86	NYR	3	J. Vanbiesbrouck	Phi. 7	NYR 1
	St. L.	Apr. 11/89	St. L.	3	Jon Casey (2) Kari Takko (1)	St. L. 6	Min. 1
Petr Klima (2)	Det.	Apr. 7/88	Tor.	3	Alan Bester (2) Ken Wregett (1)	Det. 6	Tor. 2
		Apr. 21/88	St.L.	3	Greg Millen	Det. 6	St.L. 0
Harry Meeking	Tor.	Mar.11/18	Tor.	3	Georges Vezina	Tor. 7	Mtl. 3
Alf Skinner	Tor.	Mar.23/18	Tor.	3	Hugh Lehman	Van.M. 6	Tor. 4
Joe Malone	Mtl.	Feb. 23/19	Mtl.	3	Clint Benedict	Mtl. 8	Ott. 4
Odie Cleghorn	Mtl.	Feb.27/19	Ott.	3	Clint Benedict	Mtl. 5	Ott. 3
Jack Darragh	Ott.	Apr. 1/20	Ott.	3	Harry Holmes	Ott. 6	Sea. 1
George Boucher	Ott.	Mar.10/21	Ott.	3	Jake Forbes	Ott. 5	Tor. 0
Babe Dye	Tor.	Mar.28/22	Tor.	4	Hugh Lehman	Tor. 5	Van.M. 1
Perk Galbraith	Bos.	Mar.31/27	Bos.	3	Hugh Lehman	Bos. 4	Chi. 4
Busher Jackson	Tor.	Apr. 5/32	NYR	3	John Ross Roach	Tor. 6	NYR 4
Frank Boucher	NYR	Apr. 9/32	Tor.	3	Lorne Chabot	Tor. 6	NYR 4
Charlie Conacher	Tor.	Mar.26/36	Tor.	3	Tiny Thompson	Tor. 8	Bos. 3
Syd Howe	Det.	Mar.23/39	Det.	3	Claude Bourque	Det. 7	Mtl. 3
Bryan Hextall	NYR	Apr. 3/40	NYR	3	Turk Broda	NYR 6	Tor. 2
Joe Benoit	Mtl.	Mar.22/41	Mtl.	3	Sam LoPresti	Mtl. 4	Chi. 3
Syl Apps	Tor.	Mar.25/41	Tor.	3	Frank Brimsek	Tor. 7	Bos. 2
Jack McGill	Bos.	Mar.29/42	Bos.	3	Johnny Mowers	Det. 6	Bos. 4
Don Metz	Tor.	Apr. 14/42	Tor.	3	Johnny Mowers	Tor. 9	Det. 3
Mud Bruneteau	Det.	Apr. 1/43	Det.	3	Frank Brimsek	Det. 6	Bos. 2
Don Grosso	Det.	Apr. 7/43	Det.	3	Frank Brimsek	Det. 4	Bos. 0
Carl Liscombe	Det.	Apr. 3/45	Bos.	3	Paul Bibeault	Det. 5	Bos. 3
Billy Reay	Mtl.	Apr. 1/47	Bos.	4	Frank Brimsek	Mtl. 5	Bos. 1
Gerry Plamondon	Mtl.	Mar.24/49	Bos.	3	Harry Lumley	Mtl. 4	Det. 3
Sid Smith	Tor.	Apr. 10/49	Det.	3	Harry Lumley	Tor. 3	Det. 1
Pentti Lund	NYR	Apr. 2/50	NYR	3	Bill Durnan	NYR 4	Mtl. 1
Ted Lindsay	Det.	Apr. 5/55	Det.	4	Charlie Hodge (1) Jacques Plante (3)	Det. 7	Mtl. 1
Gordie Howe	Det.	Apr. 10/55	Det.	3	Jacques Plante	Det. 5	Mtl. 1
Phil Goyette	Mtl.	Mar.25/58	Mtl.	3	Terry Sawchuk	Mtl. 8	Det. 1
Jerry Toppazzini	Bos.	Apr. 5/58	Bos.	3	Lorne Worsley	Bos. 8	NYR 2
Bob Pulford	Tor.	Apr. 19/62	Tor.	3	Glenn Hall	Tor. 8	Chi. 4
Dave Keon	Tor.	Apr. 9/64	Mtl.	3	Charlie Hodge	Tor. 3	Mtl. 1
Henri Richard	Mtl.	Apr. 20/67	Mtl.	3	Terry Sawchuk (2) Johnny Bower (1)	Mtl. 6	Tor. 2
Rosaire Paiement	Phi.	Apr. 13/68	Phi.	3	Glenn Hall (1) Seth Martin (2)	Phi. 6	St. L. 1
Jean Béliveau	Mtl.	Apr. 20/68	Mtl.	3	Denis DeJordy	Mtl. 4	Chi. 1
Red Berenson	St. L.	Apr. 15/69	St. L.	3	Gerry Desjardins	St. L. 4	L.A. 0
Ken Schinkel	Pit.	Apr. 11/70	Oak.	3	Gary Smith	Pit. 5	Oak. 2
Jim Pappin	Chi.	Apr. 11/71	Phi.	3	Bruce Gamble	Chi. 6	Phi. 2
Bobby Orr	Bos.	Apr. 11/71	Bos.	3	Ken Dryden	Bos. 5	Mtl. 2
Jacques Lemaire	Mtl.	Apr. 20/71	Mtl.	3	Lorne Worsley	Mtl. 7	Min. 2
Vic Hadfield	NYR	Apr. 22/71	NYR	3	Tony Esposito	NYR 4	Chi. 1
Fred Stanfield	Bos.	Apr. 18/72	Bos.	3	Jacques Caron	Bos. 6	St. L. 1
Ken Hodge	Bos.	Apr. 30/72	Bos.	3	Ed Giacomin	Bos. 6	NYR 5
Steve Vickers	NYR	Apr. 10/73	Bos.	3	Ross Brooks (2) Ed Johnston (1)	NYR 6	Bos. 3

Henri Richard (pictured here) and Bernie Geoffrion led all playoff scorers in 1960 with 12 points in eight games.

Leading Playoff Scorers, 1918 – 1990

Season	Player and Club	Games Played	Goals	Assists	Points
1989-90	Craig Simpson, Edmonton	22	16	15	31
	Mark Messier, Edmonton	22	9	22	31
1988-89	Al MacInnis, Calgary	22	7	24	31
1987-88	Wayne Gretzky, Edmonton	19	12	31	43
1986-87	Wayne Gretzky, Edmonton	21	5	29	34
1985-86	Doug Gilmour, St. Louis	19	9	12	21
	Bernie Federko, St. Louis	19	7	14	21
1984-85	Wayne Gretzky, Edmonton	18	17	30	47
1983-84	Wayne Gretzky, Edmonton	19	13	22	35
1982-83	Wayne Gretzky, Edmonton	16	12	26	38
1981-82	Bryan Trottier, NY Islanders	19	6	23	29
1980-81	Mike Bossy, NY Islanders	18	17	18	35
1979-80	Bryan Trottier, NY Islanders	21	12	17	29
1978-79	Jacques Lemaire, Montreal	16	11	12	23
	Guy Lafleur, Montreal	16	10	13	23
1977-78	Guy Lafleur, Montreal	15	10	11	21
	Larry Robinson, Montreal	15	4	17	21
1976-77	Guy Lafleur, Montreal	14	9	17	26
1975-76	Reggie Leach, Philadelphia	16	19	5	24
1974-75	Rick MacLeish, Philadelphia	17	11	9	20
1973-74	Rick MacLeish, Philadelphia	17	13	9	22
1972-73	Yvan Cournoyer, Montreal	17	15	10	25
1971-72	Phil Esposito, Boston	15	9	15	24
	Bobby Orr, Boston	15	5	19	24
1970-71	Frank Mahovlich, Montreal	20	14	13	27
1969-70	Phil Esposito, Boston	14	13	14	27
1968-69	Phil Esposito, Boston	10	8	10	18
1967-68	Bill Goldsworthy, Minnesota	14	8	7	15
1966-67	Jim Pappin, Toronto	12	7	8	15
1965-66	Norm Ullman, Detroit	12	6	9	15
1964-65	Bobby Hull, Chicago	14	10	7	17
1963-64	Gordie Howe, Detroit	14	9	10	19
1962-63	Gordie Howe, Detroit	11	7	9	16
	Norm Ullman, Detroit	11	4	12	16
1961-62	Stan Mikita, Chicago	12	6	15	21
1960-61	Gordie Howe, Detroit	11	4	11	15
	Pierre Pilote, Chicago	12	3	12	15
1959-60	Henri Richard, Montreal	8	3	9	12
	Bernie Geoffrion, Montreal	8	2	10	12
1958-59	Dickie Moore, Montreal	11	5	12	17
1957-58	Fleming Mackell, Boston	12	5	14	19
1956-57	Bernie Geoffrion, Montreal	11	11	7	18
1955-56	Jean Beliveau, Montreal	10	12	7	19
1954-55	Gordie Howe, Detroit	11	9	11	20
1953-54	Dickie Moore, Montreal	11	5	8	13
1952-53	Ed Sanford, Boston	11	8	3	11
1951-52	Ted Lindsay, Detroit	8	5	2	7
	Floyd Curry, Montreal	11	4	3	7
	Metro Prystai, Detroit	8	2	5	7
	Gordie Howe, Detroit	8	2	5	7
1950-51	Maurice Richard, Montreal	11	9	4	13
	Max Bentley, Toronto	11	2	11	13
1949-50	Pentti Lund, NY Rangers	12	6	5	11
1948-49	Gordie Howe, Detroit	11	8	3	11
1947-48	Ted Kennedy, Toronto	9	8	6	14
1946-47	Maurice Richard, Montreal	10	6	5	11
1945-46	Elmer Lach, Montreal	9	5	12	17
1944-45	Joe Carveth, Detroit	14	5	6	11
1943-44	Toe Blake, Montreal	9	7	11	18
1942-43	Carl Liscombe, Detroit	10	6	8	14
1941-42	Don Grosso, Detroit	12	8	6	14
1940-41	Milt Schmidt, Boston	11	5	6	11
1939-40	Phil Watson, NY Rangers	12	3	6	9
	Neil Colville, NY Rangers	12	2	7	9
1938-39	Bill Cowley, Boston	12	3	11	14
1937-38	Johnny Gottselig, Chicago	10	5	3	8
1936-37	Marty Barry, Detroit	10	4	7	11
1935-36	Buzz Boll, Toronto	9	7	3	10
1934-35	Baldy Northcott, Mtl. Maroons	7	4	1	5
	Harvey Jackson, Toronto	7	3	2	5
	Marvin Wentworth, Mtl. Maroons	7	3	2	5
1933-34	Larry Aurie, Detroit	9	3	7	10
1932-33	Cecil Dillon, NY Rangers	8	8	2	10
1931-32	Frank Boucher, NY Rangers	7	3	6	9
1930-31	Cooney Weiland, Boston	5	6	3	9
1929-30	Marty Barry, Boston	6	3	3	6
	Cooney Weiland, Boston	6	1	5	6
1928-29	Andy Blair, Toronto	4	3	0	3
	Butch Keeling, NY Rangers	6	3	0	3
	Ace Bailey, Toronto	4	1	2	3
1927-28	Frank Boucher, NY Rangers	9	7	3	10
1926-27	Harry Oliver, Boston	8	4	2	6
	Perk Galbraith, Boston	8	3	3	6
	Frank Fredrickson, Boston	8	2	4	6
1925-26	Nels Stewart, Mtl. Maroons	8	6	3	9
1924-25	Howie Morenz, Montreal	6	7	1	8
1923-24	Howie Morenz, Montreal	6	7	2	9
1922-23	Punch Broadbent, Ottawa	8	6	1	7
1921-22	Babe Dye, Toronto	7	11	2	13
1920-21	Cy Denneny, Ottawa	7	4	2	7
1919-20	Frank Nighbor, Ottawa	5	6	1	7
	Jack Darragh, Ottawa	5	5	2	7
1918-19	Newsy Lalonde, Montreal	10	17	1	18
1917-18	Alf Skinner, Toronto	7	8	1	9

Player	Team	Date	City	Total Goals	Opposing Goaltender	Score	
Dick Redmond	Chi.	Apr. 4/73	Chi.	3	Wayne Stephenson	Chi. 7	St. L. 1
Tom Williams	L.A.	Apr. 14/74	L.A.	3	Mike Veisor	L.A. 5	Chi. 1
Marcel Dionne	L.A.	Apr. 15/76	L.A.	3	Gilles Gilbert	L.A. 6	Bos. 4
Don Saleski	Phi.	Apr. 20/76	Phil.	3	Wayne Thomas	Phi. 7	Tor. 1
Darryl Sittler	Tor.	Apr. 22/76	Tor.	5	Bernie Parent	Tor. 8	Phi. 5
Reggie Leach	Phi.	May 6/76	Phi.	5	Gilles Gilbert	Phi. 6	Bos. 3
Jim Lorentz	Buf.	Apr. 7/77	Min.	3	Pete LoPresti (2) Gary Smith (1)	Buf. 7	Min. 1
Bobby Schmautz	Bos.	Apr. 11/77	Bos.	3	Rogatien Vachon	Bos. 8	L.A. 3
Billy Harris	NYI	Apr. 23/77	Mtl.	3	Ken Dryden	Mtl. 4	NYI 3
George Ferguson	Tor.	Apr. 11/78	Tor.	3	Rogatien Vachon	Tor. 7	L.A. 3
Jean Ratelle	Bos.	May 3/79	Bos.	3	Ken Dryden	Bos. 4	Mtl. 3
Stan Jonathan	Bos.	May 8/79	Bos.	3	Ken Dryden	Bos. 5	Mtl. 2
Ron Duguay	NYR	Apr. 20/80	NYR	3	Pete Peeters	NYR 4	Phi. 2
Steve Shutt	Mtl.	Apr. 22/80	Mtl.	3	Gilles Meloche	Mtl. 6	Min. 2
Gilbert Perreault	Buf.	May 6/80	NYI	3	Billy Smith (2) ENG (1)	Buf. 7	NYI 4
Paul Holmgren	Phi.	May 15/80	Phil	3	Billy Smith	Phi. 8	NYI 3
Steve Payne	Min.	Apr. 8/81	Bos.	3	Rogatien Vachon	Min. 5	Bos. 4
Denis Potvin	NYI	Apr. 17/81	NYI	3	Andy Moog	NYI 6	Edm. 3
Barry Pederson	Bos.	Apr. 8/82	Bos.	3	Don Edwards	Bos. 7	Buf. 3
Duane Sutter	NYI	Apr. 15/83	NYI	3	Glen Hanlon	NYI 5	NYR 0
Doug Halward	Van.	Apr. 7/84	Van.	3	Rejean Lemelin (2) Don Edwards (1)	Van. 7	Cgy. 0
Jorgen Pettersson	St. L.	Apr. 8/84	Det.	3	Ed Mio	St. L. 3	Det. 2
Clark Gillies	NYI	May 12/84	NYI	3	Grant Fuhr	NYI 6	Edm. 1
Ken Linseman	Bos.	Apr. 14/85	Bos.	3	Steve Penney	Bos. 7	Mtl. 6
Dave Andreychuk	Buf.	Apr. 14/85	Buf.	3	Dan Bouchard	Que. 4	Buf. 7
Greg Paslawski	StL.	Apr. 15/86	Min.	3	Don Beaupre	St. L. 6	Min. 3
Doug Risebrough	Cgy.	May 4/86	Cgy.	3	Rick Wamsley	Cgy. 8	St.L. 2
Cam Neely	Bos.	Apr. 9/87	Mtl.	3	Patrick Roy	Mtl. 4	Bos. 3
Mike McPhee	Mtl.	Apr. 11/87	Bos.	3	Doug Keans	Mtl. 5	Bos. 4
John Ogrodnick	Que.	Apr. 14/87	Hfd.	3	Mike Liut	Que. 7	Hfd. 5
Pelle-Erik Eklund	Phi.	May 10/87	Mtl.	3	Patrick Roy (1) Bryan Hayward (2)	Phi. 6	Mtl. 3
John Tucker	Buf.	Apr. 9/88	Bos.	4	Andy Moog	Buf. 6	Bos. 2
Tony Hrkac	St.L.	Apr. 10/88	St.L.	4	Darren Pang	St.L. 6	Chi. 5
Hakan Loob	Cgy.	Apr. 10/88	Cgy.	3	Glenn Healy	Cgy. 7	L.A. 3
Ed Olczyk	Tor.	Apr. 12/88	Tor.	3	Greg Stefan (2) Glen Hanlon (1)	Tor. 6	Det. 5
Aaron Broten	N.J.	Apr. 20/88	N.J.	3	Pete Peeters	N.J. 5	Wsh. 2
Mark Johnson	N.J.	Apr. 22/88	Wsh.	4	Pete Peeters	N.J. 10	Wsh. 4
Patrik Sundstrom	N.J.	Apr. 22/88	Wsh.	3	Pete Peelers (2) Clint Malarchuk (1)	N.J. 10	Wsh. 4
Esa Tikkanen	Edm.	May 22/88	Edm.	3	Rejean Lemelin	Edm. 6	Bos. 3
Bob Brooke	Min.	Apr. 5/89	St. L.	3	Greg Millen	St. L. 4	Min. 3
Chris Kontos	L.A.	Apr. 6/89	L.A.	3	Grant Fuhr	L.A. 5	Edm. 2
Mario Lemieux	Pit.	Apr. 25/89	Pit.	5	Ron Hextall	Pit. 10	Phi. 7
Wayne Presley	Chi.	Apr. 13/89	Chi.	3	Greg Stefan (1) Glen Hanlon (2)	Chi. 7	Det. 1
Steve Yzerman	Det.	Apr. 6/89	Det.	3	Alain Chevrier	Chi. 5	Det. 4
Tony Granato	L.A.	Apr. 10/90	L.A.	3	Mike Vernon (1) Rick Wamsley (2)	L.A. 12	Cgy. 4
Tomas Sandstrom	L.A.	Apr. 10/90	L.A.	3	Mike Vernon (1) Rick Wamsley (2)	L.A. 12	Cgy. 4
Dave Taylor	L.A.	Apr. 10/90	L.A.	3	Mike Vernon (1) Rick Wamsley (2)	L.A. 12	Cgy. 4
Mike Gartner	NYR	Apr. 13/90	NYR	3	Mark Fitzpatrick (2) Glenn Healy (1)	NYR 6	NYI 5
Bernie Nicholls	NYR	Apr. 19/90	NYR	3	Mike Liut	NYR 7	Wsh. 3
John Druce	Wsh.	Apr. 21/90	NYR	3	John Vanbiesbrouck	Wsh. 6	NYR 3

Overtime Games since 1918

Abbreviations: Teams/Cities: — **Atl.** - Atlanta; **Bos.** - Boston; **Buf.** - Buffalo; **Cgy.** - Calgary; **Cgy. T.** - Calgary Tigers (Western Canada Hockey League); **Chi.** - Chicago; **Col.** - Colorado; **Det.** - Detroit; **Edm.** - Edmonton; **Edm. E.** - Edmonton Eskimos (WCHL); **Hfd.** - Hartford; **L.A.** - Los Angeles; **Min.** - Minnesota; **Mtl.** - Montreal; **Mtl.M.** - Montreal Maroons; **N.J.** - New Jersey; **NY** - New York; **NYA** - NY Americans; **NYI** - New York Islanders; **NYR** - New York Rangers; **Oak.** - Oakland; **Ott.** - Ottawa; **Phi.** - Philadelphia; **Pit.** - Pittsburgh; **Que.** - Quebec; **St.L.** - St. Louis; **Sea.** - Seattle Metropolitans (Pacific Coast Hockey Association); **Tor.** - Toronto; **Van.** - Vancouver; **Van. M** - Vancouver Millionaires (PCHA); **Vic.** - Victoria Cougars (WCHL); **Wpg.** - Winnipeg; **Wsh.** - Washington.

SERIES — **CF** - conference final; **DF** - division; **DSF** - division semi-final; **F** - final; **PR** preliminary round; **QF** - quarter final; **SF** - semi-final.

Date	City	Series	Score		Scorer	Overtime	Series Winner
Mar. 26/19	Sea.	F	Mtl. 0	Sea. 0	no scorer	20:00	
Mar. 29/19	Sea.	F	Mtl. 4	Sea. 3	Odie Cleghorn	15:57	
Mar. 21/22	Tor.	F	Tor 2	Van.M. 1	Babe Dye	4:50	Tor.
Mar. 29/23	Van.	F	Ott. 2	Edm.E. 1	Cy Denneny	2:08	Ott.
Mar. 31/27	Mtl.	QF	Mtl. 1	Mtl. M. 0	Howie Morenz	12:05	Mtl.
Apr. 7/27	Bos.	F	Ott. 0	Bos. 0	no scorer	20:00	Ott.
Apr. 11/27	Ott.	F	Bos. 1	Ott. 1	no scorer	20:00	Ott.
Apr. 3/28	Mtl.	QF	Mtl. M. 1	Mtl. 0	Russ Oatman	8:20	Mtl. M.
Apr. 7/28	Mtl.	F	NYR 2	Mtl. M. 1	Frank Boucher	7:05	NYR
Mar. 21/29	NY	QF	NYR 1	NYA 0	Butch Keeling	29:50	NYR
Mar. 26/29	Tor.	SF	NYR 2	Tor. 1	Frank Boucher	2:03	NYR
Mar. 20/30	Mtl.	SF	Bos. 2	Mtl. M. 1	Harry Oliver	45:35	Bos.
Mar. 25/30	Bos.	SF	Mtl. M. 1	Bos. 0	Archie Wilcox	26:27	Bos.
Mar. 26/30	Mtl.	QF	Chi. 2	Mtl. 2	Howie Morenz (Mtl.)	51:43	Mtl.
Mar. 28/30	Mtl.	SF	Mtl. 2	NYR 1	Gus Rivers	68:52	Mtl.
Mar. 24/31	Bos.	SF	Bos. 5	Mtl. 4	Cooney Weiland	18:56	Mtl.
Mar. 26/31	Chi.	QF	Chi. 2	Tor. 1	Steward Adams	19:20	Chi.
Mar. 28/31	Mtl.	SF	Mtl. 4	Bos. 3	Georges Mantha	5:10	Mtl.
Apr. 1/31	Mtl.	SF	Mtl. 3	Bos. 2	Wildor Larochelle	19:00	Mtl.
Apr. 5/31	Chi.	F	Chi. 2	Mtl. 1	Johnny Gottselig	24:50	Mtl.
Apr. 9/31	Mtl.	F	Chi. 3	Mtl. 2	Cy Wentworth	53:50	Mtl.
Mar. 26/32	Mtl.	SF	NYR 4	Mtl. 3	Fred Cook	59:32	NYR
Apr. 2/32	Tor.	SF	Tor. 3	Mtl. M. 2	Bob Gracie	17:59	Tor.
Mar. 25/33	Bos.	SF	Bos. 2	Tor. 1	Marty Barry	14:14	Tor.
Mar. 28/33	Bos.	SF	Tor. 1	Bos. 0	Busher Jackson	15:03	Tor.
Mar. 30/33	Tor.	SF	Bos. 2	Tor. 1	Eddie Shore	4:23	Tor.
Apr. 3/33	Tor.	SF	Tor. 1	Bos. 0	Ken Doraty	104:46	Tor.
Apr. 13/33	Tor.	F	NYR 1	Tor. 0	Bill Cook	7:33	NYR
Mar. 22/34	Tor.	SF	Det. 2	Tor. 1	Herbie Lewis	1:33	Det.
Mar. 25/34	Chi.	QF	Chi. 1	Mtl. 1	Mush March (Chi)	11:05	Chi.
Apr. 3/34	Det.	F	Chi. 2	Det. 1	Paul Thompson	21:05	Chi.
Apr. 10/34	Chi.	F	Chi. 1	Det. 0	Mush March	30:05	Chi.
Mar. 23/35	Bos.	SF	Bos. 1	Tor. 0	Dit Clapper	33:26	Tor.
Mar. 26/35	Chi.	QF	Mtl. M. 1	Chi. 0	Baldy Northcott	4:02	Mtl. M.
Mar. 30/35	Tor.	SF	Tor. 2	Bos. 1	Pep Kelly	1:36	Tor.
Apr. 4/35	Tor.	F	Mtl. M. 3	Tor. 2	Dave Trottier	5:20	Mtl. M.
Mar. 24/36	Mtl.	SF	Det. 1	Mtl. M. 0	Mud Bruneteau	116:30	Det.
Apr. 9/36	Tor.	F	Tor. 4	Det. 3	Buzz Boll	0:31	Det.
Mar. 25/37	NY	QF	NYR 2	Tor. 1	Babe Pratt	13:05	NYR
Apr. 1/37	Mtl.	SF	Det. 2	Mtl. 1	Hec Kilrea	51:49	Det.
Mar. 22/38	NY	QF	NYA 2	NYR 1	Johnny Sorrell	21:25	NYA
Mar. 25/38	Tor.	SF	Tor. 1	Bos. 0	George Parsons	21:31	Tor.
Mar. 26/38	Mtl.	QF	Chi. 3	Mtl. 2	Paul Thompson	11:49	Chi.
Mar. 27/38	NY	QF	NYA 3	NYR 2	Lorne Carr	60:40	NYA
Mar. 29/38	Bos.	SF	Tor. 3	Bos. 2	Gord Drillon	10:04	Tor.
Mar. 31/38	Chi.	SF	Chi. 1	NYA 0	Cully Dahlstrom	33:01	Chi.
Mar. 21/39	NY	SF	Bos. 2	NYR 1	Mel Hill	59:25	Bos.
Mar. 23/39	Bos.	SF	Bos. 3	NYR 2	Mel Hill	8:24	Bos.
Mar. 26/39	Det.	QF	Det. 1	Mtl. 0	Marty Barry	7:47	Det.
Mar. 30/39	Bos.	SF	NYR 2	Bos. 1	Snuffy Smith	17:19	Bos.
Apr. 1/39	Tor.	SF	Tor. 5	Det. 4	Gord Drillon	5:42	Tor.
Apr. 2/39	Bos.	SF	Bos. 2	NYR 1	Mel Hill	48:00	Bos.
Apr. 9/39	Bos.	F	Tor. 3	Bos. 2	Doc Romnes	10:38	Bos.
Mar. 19/40	Det.	QF	Det. 2	NYA 1	Syd Howe	0:25	Det.
Mar. 19/40	Tor.	QF	Tor. 3	Chi. 2	Syl Apps	6:35	Tor.
Apr. 2/40	NY	F	NYR 2	Tor. 1	Alf Pike	15:30	NYR
Apr. 11/40	Tor.	F	NYR 2	Tor. 1	Muzz Patrick	31:43	NYR
Apr. 13/40	Tor.	F	NYR 3	Tor. 2	Bryan Hextall	2:07	NYR
Mar. 20/41	Det.	QF	Det. 2	NYR 1	Gus Giesebrecht	12:01	Det.
Mar. 22/41	Mtl.	QF	Mtl. 4	Chi. 3	Charlie Sands	34:04	Chi.
Mar. 29/41	Bos.	SF	Tor. 2	Bos. 1	Pete Langelle	17:31	Bos.
Mar. 30/41	Chi.	SF	Det. 2	Chi. 1	Gus Giesebrecht	9:15	Det.
Mar. 22/42	Chi.	QF	Bos. 2	Chi. 1	Des Smith	9:51	Bos.
Mar. 21/43	Bos.	SF	Bos. 5	Mtl. 4	Don Gallinger	12:30	Bos.
Mar. 23/43	Det.	SF	Tor. 3	Det. 2	Jack McLean	70:18	Det.
Mar. 25/43	Mtl.	SF	Bos. 3	Mtl. 2	Harvey Jackson	3:20	Bos.
Mar. 30/43	Tor.	SF	Det. 3	Tor. 2	Adam Brown	9:21	Det.
Mar. 30/43	Bos.	SF	Bos. 5	Mtl. 4	Ab DeMarco	3:41	Bos.
Apr. 13/44	Mtl.	F	Mtl. 5	Chi. 4	Toe Blake	9:12	Mtl.
Mar. 27/45	Tor.	SF	Tor. 4	Mtl. 3	Gus Bodnar	12:36	Tor.
Mar. 29/45	Det.	SF	Det. 3	Bos. 2	Mud Bruneteau	17:12	Det.
Apr. 21/45	Tor.	F	Det. 1	Tor. 0	Ed Bruneteau	14:16	Tor.
Mar. 28/46	Bos.	SF	Bos. 4	Det. 3	Don Gallinger	9:51	Bos.
Mar. 30/46	Mtl.	F	Mtl. 4	Bos. 3	Maurice Richard	9:08	Mtl.
Apr. 2/46	Mtl.	F	Mtl. 3	Bos. 2	Jim Peters	16:55	Mtl.
Apr. 7/46	Bos.	F	Bos. 3	Mtl. 2	Terry Reardon	15:13	Mtl.
Mar. 26/47	Tor.	SF	Tor. 3	Det. 2	Howie Meeker	3:05	Tor.
Mar. 27/47	Mtl.	SF	Mtl. 2	Bos. 1	Ken Mosdell	5:38	Mtl.
Apr. 3/47	Mtl.	SF	Mtl. 4	Bos. 3	John Quilty	36:40	Mtl.
Apr. 15/47	Tor.	F	Tor. 2	Mtl. 1	Syl Apps	16:36	Tor.
Mar. 24/48	Tor.	SF	Tor. 5	Bos. 4	Nick Metz	17:03	Tor.
Mar. 22/49	Det.	SF	Det. 2	Mtl. 1	Max McNab	44:52	Det.
Mar. 24/49	Det.	SF	Mtl. 4	Det. 3	Gerry Plamondon	2:59	Det.
Mar. 26/49	Tor.	SF	Bos. 5	Tor. 4	Woody Dumart	16:14	Tor.
Apr. 8/49	Det.	F	Tor. 3	Det. 2	Joe Klukay	17:31	Tor.
Apr. 4/50	Tor.	SF	Det. 2	Tor. 1	Leo Reise	20:38	Det.
Apr. 4/50	Mtl.	SF	Mtl. 3	NYR 2	Elmer Lach	15:19	Mtl.
Apr. 9/50	Det.	SF	Det. 1	Tor. 0	Leo Reise	8:39	Det.
Apr. 18/50	Det.	F	NYR 4	Det. 3	Don Raleigh	8:34	Det.
Apr. 20/50	Det.	F	NYR 2	Det. 1	Don Raleigh	1:38	Det.
Apr. 23/50	Det.	F	Det. 4	NYR 3	Pete Babando	28:31	Det.
Mar. 27/51	Det.	SF	Mtl. 3	Det. 2	Maurice Richard	61:09	Mtl.
Mar. 29/51	Det.	SF	Mtl. 1	Det. 0	Maurice Richard	42:20	Mtl.
Mar. 31/51	Tor.	SF	Bos. 1	Tor. 1	no scorer	20:00	Tor.
Apr. 11/51	Tor.	F	Tor. 3	Mtl. 2	Sid Smith	5:51	Tor.
Apr. 14/51	Tor.	F	Mtl. 3	Tor. 2	Maurice Richard	2:55	Tor.
Apr. 17/51	Mtl.	F	Tor. 2	Mtl. 1	Ted Kennedy	4:47	Tor.
Apr. 19/51	Mtl.	F	Tor. 3	Mtl. 2	Harry Watson	5:15	Tor.
Apr. 21/51	Tor.	F	Tor. 3	Mtl. 2	Bill Barilko	2:53	Tor.
Apr. 6/52	Bos.	SF	Mtl. 3	Bos. 2	Paul Masnick	27:49	Mtl.
Mar. 29/53	Bos.	SF	Bos. 2	Det. 1	Jack McIntyre	12:29	Bos.
Mar. 29/53	Chi.	SF	Chi. 2	Mtl. 1	Al Dewsbury	5:18	Mtl.
Apr. 16/53	Mtl.	F	Mtl. 1	Bos. 0	Elmer Lach	1:22	Mtl.
Apr. 1/54	Det.	SF	Det. 4	Tor. 3	Ted Lindsay	21:01	Det.
Apr. 11/54	Det.	F	Mtl. 1	Det. 0	Ken Mosdell	5:45	Det.
Apr. 16/54	Det.	F	Det. 2	Mtl. 1	Tony Leswick	4:29	Det.
Mar. 29/55	Bos.	SF	Mtl. 4	Bos. 3	Don Marshall	3:05	Mtl.
Mar. 24/56	Tor.	SF	Det. 5	Tor. 4	Ted Lindsay	4:22	Det.
Mar. 28/57	NY	SF	NYR 4	Mtl. 3	Andy Hebenton	13:38	Mtl.
Apr. 4/57	Mtl.	SF	Mtl. 4	NYR 3	Maurice Richard	1:11	Mtl.
Mar. 27/58	NY	SF	Bos. 4	NYR 3	Jerry Toppazzini	4:46	Bos.
Mar. 30/58	Det.	SF	Mtl. 2	Det. 1	André Pronovost	11:52	Mtl.
Apr. 17/58	Mtl.	F	Mtl. 3	Bos. 2	Maurice Richard	5:45	Mtl.
Mar. 28/59	Tor.	SF	Tor. 3	Bos. 2	Gerry Ehman	5:02	Tor.
Mar. 31/59	Tor.	SF	Tor. 3	Bos. 2	Frank Mahovlich	11:21	Tor.
Apr. 14/59	Tor.	F	Tor. 3	Mtl. 2	Dick Duff	10:06	Mtl.
Mar. 26/60	Mtl.	SF	Mtl. 4	Chi. 3	Doug Harvey	8:38	Mtl.
Mar. 27/60	Det.	SF	Tor. 5	Det. 4	Frank Mahovlich	43:00	Tor.
Mar. 29/60	Det.	SF	Det. 2	Tor. 1	Gerry Melnyk	1:54	Tor.
Mar. 22/61	Tor.	SF	Tor. 3	Det. 2	George Armstrong	24:51	Det.
Mar. 26/61	Chi.	SF	Chi. 2	Mtl. 1	Murray Balfour	52:12	Chi.
Apr. 5/62	Tor.	SF	Tor. 3	NYR 2	Red Kelly	24:23	Tor.
Apr. 2/64	Det.	SF	Chi. 3	Det. 2	Murray Balfour	8:21	Det.
Apr. 14/64	Tor.	F	Det. 3	Tor. 2	Larry Jeffrey	7:52	Tor.
Apr. 23/64	Det.	F	Tor. 4	Det. 3	Bobby Baun	1:43	Tor.
Apr. 6/65	Tor.	SF	Tor. 3	Mtl. 2	Dave Keon	4:17	Mtl.
Apr. 13/65	Tor.	SF	Mtl. 4	Tor. 3	Claude Provost	16:33	Mtl.
May 5/66	Det.	F	Mtl. 3	Det. 2	Henri Richard	2:20	Mtl.
Apr. 13/67	NY	SF	Mtl. 2	NYR 1	John Ferguson	6:28	Mtl.
Apr. 25/67	Tor.	F	Tor. 3	Mtl. 2	Bob Pulford	28:26	Tor.
Apr. 10/68	St. L.	QF	St. L. 3	Phi. 2	Larry Keenan	24:10	St. L.
Apr. 16/68	St. L.	QF	Phi. 2	St. L. 1	Don Blackburn	31:38	St. L.
Apr. 16/68	Min.	QF	Min. 4	L.A. 3	Milan Marcetta	9:11	Min.
Apr. 22/68	Min.	SF	Min. 3	St. L. 2	Parker MacDonald	3:41	St. L.
Apr. 27/68	St. L.	SF	St. L. 4	Min. 3	Gary Sabourin	1:32	St. L.
Apr. 28/68	Mtl.	SF	Mtl. 4	Chi. 3	Jacques Lemaire	2:14	Mtl.
Apr. 29/68	St. L.	SF	St. L. 3	Min. 2	Bill McCreary	17:27	St. L.
May 3/68	St. L.	SF	St. L. 2	Min. 1	Ron Schock	22:50	St. L.
May 5/68	St. L.	F	Mtl. 3	St. L. 2	Jacques Lemaire	1:41	Mtl.
May 9/68	Mtl.	F	Mtl. 4	St. L. 3	Bobby Rousseau	1:13	Mtl.
Apr. 2/69	Oak.	QF	L.A. 5	Oak. 4	Ted Irvine	0:19	L.A.
Apr. 10/69	Mtl.	SF	Mtl. 3	Bos. 2	Ralph Backstrom	0:42	Mtl.
Apr. 13/69	Mtl.	SF	Mtl. 4	Bos. 3	Mickey Redmond	4:55	Mtl.
Apr. 24/69	Bos.	SF	Mtl. 2	Bos. 1	Jean Béliveau	31:28	Mtl.
Apr. 12/70	Oak.	QF	Pit. 3	Oak. 2	Michel Briere	8:28	Pit.
May 10/70	Bos.	F	Bos. 4	St. L. 3	Bobby Orr	0:40	Bos.
Apr. 15/71	Tor.	QF	NYR 2	Tor. 1	Bob Nevin	9:07	NYR
Apr. 18/71	Chi.	SF	NYR 2	Chi. 1	Pete Stemkowski	1:37	Chi.
Apr. 27/71	Chi.	SF	Chi. 3	NYR 2	Bobby Hull	6:35	Chi.
Apr. 29/71	NY	SF	NYR 3	Chi. 2	Pete Stemkowski	41:29	Chi.
May 4/71	Chi.	F	Chi. 2	Mtl. 1	Jim Pappin	21:11	Mtl.
Apr. 6/72	Bos.	QF	Tor. 4	Bos. 3	Jim Harrison	2:58	Bos.
Apr. 6/72	Min.	QF	Min. 6	St. L. 5	Bill Goldsworthy	1:36	St. L.
Apr. 9/72	Pit.	QF	Chi. 6	Pit. 5	Pit Martin	0:12	Chi.
Apr. 16/72	Min.	QF	St. L. 2	Min. 1	Kevin O'Shea	10:07	St. L.
Apr. 01/73	Mtl.	QF	Buf. 3	Mtl. 2	René Robert	9:18	Mtl.
Apr. 10/73	Phi.	QF	Phi. 3	Min. 2	Gary Dornhoefer	8:35	Phi.
Apr. 14/73	Mtl.	SF	Phi. 5	Mtl. 4	Rick MacLeish	2:56	Mtl.
Apr. 17/73	Mtl.	SF	Mtl. 4	Phi. 3	Larry Robinson	6:45	Mtl.
Apr. 14/74	Tor.	QF	Bos. 4	Tor. 3	Ken Hodge	1:27	Bos.
Apr. 14/74	Atl.	QF	Phi. 4	Atl. 3	Dave Schultz	5:40	Phi.
Apr. 16/74	Mtl.	QF	NYR 3	Mtl. 2	Ron Harris	4:07	NYR
Apr. 23/74	Chi.	SF	Chi. 4	Bos. 3	Jim Pappin	3:48	Bos.
Apr. 28/74	NY	SF	NYR 2	Phi. 1	Rod Gilbert	4:20	Phi.
May 9/74	Bos.	F	Phi. 3	Bos. 2	Bobby Clarke	12:01	Phi.
Apr. 8/75	L.A.	PR	L.A. 3	Tor. 2	Mike Murphy	8:53	Tor.
Apr. 10/75	Tor.	PR	Tor. 3	L.A. 2	Blaine Stoughton	10:19	Tor.
Apr. 10/75	Chi.	PR	Chi. 4	Bos. 3	Ivan Boldirev	7:33	Chi.
Apr. 11/75	NY	PR	NYI 4	NYR 3	Jean-Paul Parise	0:11	NYI
Apr. 19/75	Tor.	QF	Phi. 4	Tor. 3	André Dupont	1:45	Phi.
Apr. 17/75	Chi.	QF	Chi. 5	Buf. 4	Stan Mikita	2:31	Buf.
Apr. 22/75	Mtl.	QF	Mtl. 5	Van. 4	Guy Lafleur	17:06	Mtl.
May 1/75	Phi.	SF	Phi. 5	NYI 4	Bobby Clarke	2:56	Phi.
May 7/75	NYI	SF	NYI 4	Phi. 3	Jude Drouin	1:53	Phi.
Apr. 27/75	Buf.	SF	Buf. 6	Mtl. 5	Danny Gare	4:42	Buf.
May 6/75	Buf.	SF	Buf. 5	Mtl. 4	René Robert	5:56	Buf.
May 20/75	Buf.	F	Buf. 5	Phi. 4	René Robert	18:29	Phi.
Apr. 8/76	Buf.	PR	Buf. 3	St. L. 2	Danny Gare	11:43	Buf.
Apr. 9/76	Buf.	PR	Buf. 2	St. L. 1	Don Luce	14:27	Buf.

Apr. 13/76	Bos.	QF	L.A. 3	Bos. 2	Butch Goring	0:27	Bos.
Apr. 13/76	Buf.	QF	Buf. 3	NYI 2	Danny Gare	14:04	NYI
Apr. 22/76	L.A.	QF	L.A. 4	Bos. 3	Butch Goring	18:28	Bos.
Apr. 29/76	Phi.	SF	Phi. 2	Bos. 1	Reggie Leach	13:38	Phi.
Apr. 15/77	Tor.	QF	Phi. 4	Tor. 3	Rick MacLeish	2:55	Phi.
Apr. 17/77	Tor.	QF	Phi. 6	Tor. 5	Reggie Leach	19:10	Phi.
Apr. 24/77	Phi.	SF	Bos. 4	Phi. 3	Rick Middleton	2:57	Bos.
Apr. 26/77	Phi.	SF	Bos. 5	Phi. 4	Terry O'Reilly	30:07	Bos.
May 3/77	Mtl.	SF	NYI 4	Mtl. 3	Billy Harris	3:58	Mtl.
May 14/77	Bos.	F	Mtl. 2	Bos. 1	Jacques Lemaire	4:32	Mtl.
Apr. 11/78	Phi.	PR	Phi. 3	Col. 2	Mel Bridgman	0:23	Phi.
Apr. 13/78	NY	PR	NYR 4	Buf. 3	Don Murdoch	1:37	Buf.
Apr. 19/78	Bos.	QF	Bos. 4	Chi. 3	Terry O'Reilly	1:50	Bos.
Apr. 19/78	NYI	QF	NYI 3	Tor. 2	Mike Bossy	2:50	Tor.
Apr. 21/78	Chi.	QF	Bos. 4	Chi. 3	Peter McNab	10:17	Bos.
Apr. 25/78	NYI	QF	NYI 2	Tor. 1	Bob Nystrom	8:02	Tor.
Apr. 29/78	NYI	QF	Tor. 2	NYI 1	Lanny McDonald	4:13	Tor.
May 2/78	Bos.	SF	Bos. 3	Phi. 2	Rick Middleton	1:43	Bos.
May 16/78	Mtl.	F	Mtl. 3	Bos. 2	Guy Lafleur	13:09	Mtl.
May 21/78	Bos.	F	Bos. 4	Mtl. 3	Bobby Schmautz	6:22	Mtl.
Apr. 12/79	L.A.	PR	NYR 2	L.A. 1	Phil Esposito	6:11	NYR
Apr. 14/79	Buf.	PR	Pit. 4	Buf. 3	George Ferguson	0:47	Pit.
Apr. 16/79	Phi.	QF	Phi. 3	NYR 2	Ken Linseman	0:44	NYR
Apr. 18/79	NYI	QF	NYI 1	Chi. 0	Mike Bossy	2:31	NYI
Apr. 21/79	Tor.	QF	Mtl. 4	Tor. 3	Cam Connor	25:25	Mtl.
Apr. 22/79	Tor.	QF	Mtl. 5	Tor. 4	Larry Robinson	4:14	Mtl.
Apr. 28/79	NYI	SF	NYI 4	NYR 3	Denis Potvin	8:02	NYR
May 3/79	NY	SF	NYI 3	NYR 2	Bob Nystrom	3:40	NYR
May 3/79	Bos.	SF	Bos. 4	Mtl. 3	Jean Ratelle	3:46	Mtl.
May 10/79	Mtl.	SF	Mtl. 5	Bos. 4	Yvon Lambert	9:33	Mtl.
May 19/79	NY	F	Mtl. 4	NYR 3	Serge Savard	7:25	Mtl.
Apr. 8/80	NY	PR	NYR 2	Atl. 1	Steve Vickers	0:33	NYR
Apr. 8/80	Phi.	PR	Phi. 4	Edm. 3	Bobby Clarke	8:06	Phi.
Apr. 8/80	Chi.	PR	Chi. 3	St. L. 2	Doug Lecuyer	12:34	Chi.
Apr. 11/80	Hfd.	PR	Mtl. 4	Hfd. 3	Yvon Lambert	0:29	Mtl.
Apr. 11/80	Tor.	PR	Min. 4	Tor. 3	Al MacAdam	0:32	Min.
Apr. 11/80	L.A.	PR	NYI 4	L.A. 3	Ken Morrow	6:55	NYI
Apr. 11/80	Edm.	PR	Phi. 3	Edm. 2	Ken Linseman	23:56	Phi.
Apr. 16/80	Bos.	QF	NYI 2	Bos. 1	Clark Gillies	1:02	NYI
Apr. 17/80	Bos.	QF	NYI 5	Bos. 4	Bob Bourne	1:24	NYI
Apr. 21/80	NYI	QF	Bos. 4	NYI 3	Terry O'Reilly	17:13	NYI
May 1/80	Buf.	SF	NYI 2	Buf. 1	Bob Nystrom	21:20	NYI
May 13/80	Phi.	F	NYI 4	Phi. 3	Denis Potvin	4:07	NYI
May 24/80	NYI	F	NYI 5	Phi. 4	Bob Nystrom	7:11	NYI
Apr. 8/81	Buf.	PR	Buf. 3	Van. 2	Alan Haworth	5:00	Buf.
Apr. 8/81	Bos.	PR	Min. 5	Bos. 4	Steve Payne	3:34	Min.
Apr. 11/81	Chi.	PR	Cgy. 5	Chi. 4	Willi Plett	35:17	Cgy.
Apr. 12/81	Que.	PR	Que. 4	Phi. 3	Dale Hunter	:37	Phi.
Apr. 14/81	St. L.	PR	St. L. 4	Pit. 3	Mike Crombeen	25:16	St. L.
Apr. 16/81	Buf.	QF	Min. 4	Buf. 3	Steve Payne	0:22	Min.
Apr. 20/81	Min.	QF	Buf. 5	Min. 4	Craig Ramsay	16:32	Min.
Apr. 20/81	Edm.	QF	NYI 5	Edm. 4	Ken Morrow	5:41	NYI
Apr. 7/82	Min.	DSF	Chi. 3	Min. 2	Greg Fox	3:34	Chi.
Apr. 8/82	Edm.	DSF	Edm. 3	L.A. 2	Wayne Gretzky	6:20	L.A.
Apr. 8/82	Van.	DSF	Van. 2	Cgy. 1	Dave Williams	14:20	Van.
Apr. 10/82	Pit.	DSF	Pit. 2	NYI 1	Rick Kehoe	4:14	NYI
Apr. 10/82	L.A.	DSF	L.A. 6	Edm. 5	Daryl Evans	2:35	L.A.
Apr. 13/82	Mtl.	DSF	Que. 3	Mtl. 2	Dale Hunter	0:22	Que.
Apr. 13/82	NY	DSF	NYI 4	Pit. 3	John Tonelli	6:19	NYI
Apr. 16/82	Van.	DF	L.A. 3	Van. 2	Steve Bozek	4:33	Van.
Apr. 18/82	Que.	DF	Que. 3	Bos. 2	Wilf Paiement	11:44	Que.
Apr. 18/82	NY	DF	NYI 4	NYR 3	Bryan Trottier	3:00	NYI
Apr. 18/82	L.A.	DF	Van. 4	L.A. 3	Colin Campbell	1:23	Van.
Apr. 21/82	St. L.	DF	St. L. 3	Chi. 2	Bernie Federko	3:28	Chi.
Apr. 23/82	Que.	DF	Bos. 6	Que. 5	Peter McNab	10:54	Que.
Apr. 27/82	Chi.	CF	Van. 2	Chi. 1	Jim Nill	28:58	Van.
May 1/82	Que.	CF	NYI 5	Que. 4	Wayne Merrick	16:52	NYI
May 8/82	NYI	SCF	NYI 6	Van. 5	Mike Bossy	19:58	NYI
Apr. 5/83	Bos.	DSF	Bos. 4	Que. 3	Barry Pederson	1:46	Bos.
Apr. 6/83	Cgy.	DSF	Cgy. 4	Van. 3	Eddy Beers	12:27	Cgy.
Apr. 7/83	Min.	DSF	Min. 5	Tor. 4	Bobby Smith	5:03	Min.
Apr. 10/83	Tor.	DSF	Min. 5	Tor. 4	Dino Ciccarelli	8:05	Min.
Apr. 10/83	Van.	DSF	Cgy. 4	Van. 3	Greg Meredith	1:06	Cgy.
Apr. 18/83	Min.	DF	Chi. 4	Min. 3	Rich Preston	10:34	Chi.
Apr. 24/83	Bos.	DF	Bos. 3	Buf. 2	Brad Park	1:52	Bos.
Apr. 5/84	Edm.	DSF	Edm. 5	Wpg. 4	Randy Gregg	0:21	Edm.
Apr. 7/84	Det.	DSF	St. L. 4	Det. 3	Mark Reeds	37:07	St. L.
Apr. 8/84	Det.	DSF	St. L. 3	Det. 2	Jorgen Pettersson	2:42	St. L.
Apr. 10/84	NYI	DSF	NYI 3	NYR 2	Ken Morrow	8:56	NYI
Apr. 13/84	Min.	DF	St. L. 4	Min. 3	Doug Gilmour	16:16	Min.
Apr. 13/84	Edm.	DF	Cgy. 6	Edm. 5	Carey Wilson	3:42	Edm.
Apr. 13/84	NYI	DF	NYI 5	Wsh. 4	Anders Kallur	7:35	NYI
Apr. 16/84	Mtl.	DF	Que. 4	Mtl. 3	Bo Berglund	3:00	Mtl.
Apr. 20/84	Cgy.	DF	Cgy. 5	Edm. 4	Lanny McDonald	1:04	Edm.
Apr. 22/84	Min.	DF	Min. 4	St. L. 3	Steve Payne	6:00	Min.
Apr. 10/85	Phi.	DSF	Phi. 5	NYR 4	Mark Howe	8:01	Phi.
Apr. 10/85	Wsh.	DSF	Wsh. 4	NYI 3	Alan Haworth	2:28	NYI
Apr. 10/85	Edm.	DSF	Edm. 3	L.A. 2	Lee Fogolin	3:01	Edm.
Apr. 10/85	Wpg.	DSF	Wpg. 5	Cgy. 4	Brian Mullen	7:56	Wpg.
Apr. 11/85	Wsh.	DSF	Wsh. 2	NYI 1	Mike Gartner	1:23	NYI
Apr. 13/85	L.A.	DSF	Edm. 4	L.A. 3	Glenn Anderson	0:46	Edm.
Apr. 18/85	Mtl.	DF	Que. 2	Mtl. 1	Mark Kumpel	12:23	Que.
Apr. 23/85	Que.	DF	Que. 7	Mtl. 6	Dale Hunter	18:36	Que.
May 2/85	Mtl.	DF	Que. 3	Mtl. 2	Peter Stastny	2:22	Que.
Apr. 25/85	Min.	DF	Chi. 7	Min. 6	Darryl Sutter	1:57	Chi.
Apr. 28/85	Chi.	DF	Min. 5	Chi. 4	Dennis Maruk	1:14	Chi.
Apr. 30/85	Min.	DF	Chi. 6	Min. 5	Darryl Sutter	15:41	Chi.
May 5/85	Que.	CF	Que. 2	Phi. 1	Peter Stastny	6:20	Phi.
Apr. 9/86	Que.	DSF	Hfd. 3	Que. 2	Sylvain Turgeon	2:36	Hfd.

Date	City	Series	Score		Scorer	Overtime	Series Winner
Apr. 12/86	Wpg.	DSF	Cgy. 4	Wpg. 3	Lanny McDonald	8:25	Cgy.
Apr. 17/86	Wsh.	DF	NYR 4	Wsh. 3	Brian MacLellan	1:16	NYR
Apr. 20/86	Edm.	DF	Edm. 6	Cgy. 5	Glenn Anderson	1:04	Cgy.
Apr. 23/86	Hfd.	DF	Hfd. 2	Mtl. 1	Kevin Dineen	1:07	Mtl.
Apr. 23/86	NYR	DF	NYR 6	Wsh. 5	Bob Brooke	2:40	NYR
Apr. 26/86	St L.	DF	St L. 4	Tor. 3	Mark Reeds	7:11	St L.
Apr. 29/86	Mtl.	DF	Mtl. 2	Hfd. 1	Claude Lemieux	5:55	Mtl.
May 5/86	NYR	CF	Mtl. 4	NYR 3	Claude Lemieux	9:41	Mtl.
May 12/86	St L.	CF	St L. 6	Cgy. 5	Doug Wickenheiser	7:30	Cgy.
May 18/86	Cgy.	F	Mtl. 3	Cgy. 2	Brian Skrudland	0:09	Mtl.
Apr. 8/87	Hfd.	DSF	Hfd. 3	Que. 2	Paul MacDermid	2:20	Que.
Apr. 9/87	Mtl.	DSF	Mtl. 4	Bos. 3	Mats Naslund	2:28	Mtl.
Apr. 9/87	St. L.	DSF	Tor. 3	St. L. 2	Rick Lanz	10:17	Tor.
Apr. 11/87	Wpg.	DSF	Cgy. 3	Wpg. 2	Mike Bullard	3:53	Wpg.
Apr. 11/87	Chi.	DSF	Det. 4	Chi. 3	Shawn Burr	4:51	Det.
Apr. 16/87	Que.	DSF	Que. 5	Hfd. 4	Peter Stastny	6:05	Que.
Apr. 18/87	Wsh.	DSF	NYI 3	Wsh. 2	Pat LaFontaine	68:47	NYI
Apr. 21/87	Edm.	DF	Edm. 3	Wpg. 2	Glenn Anderson	0:36	Edm.
Apr. 26/87	Que.	DF	Mtl. 3	Que. 2	Mats Naslund	5:30	Mtl.
Apr. 27/87	Tor.	DF	Tor. 3	Det. 2	Mike Allison	9:31	Det.
May 4/87	Phi.	CF	Phi. 4	Mtl. 3	Ilkka Sinislao	9:11	Phi.
May 20/87	Edm.	F	Edm. 3	Phi. 2	Jari Kurri	6:50	Edm.
Apr. 6/88	NYI	DSF	NYI 4	N.J. 3	Pat LaFontaine	6:11	N.J.
Apr. 10/88	Phi.	DSF	Phi. 5	Wsh. 4	Murray Craven	1:18	Wsh.
Apr. 10/88	N.J.	DSF	NYI 5	N.J. 4	Brent Sutter	15:07	N.J.
Apr. 10/88	Buf.	DSF	Buf. 6	Bos. 5	John Tucker	5:32	Bos.
Apr. 12/88	Det.	DSF	Tor. 6	Det. 5	Ed Olczyk	0:34	Det.
Apr. 16/88	Wsh.	DF	Wsh. 5	Phi. 4	Dale Hunter	5:57	Wsh.
Apr. 21/88	Cgy.	CF	Edm. 5	Cgy. 4	Wayne Gretzky	7:54	Edm.
May 4/88	Bos.	CF	N.J. 3	Bos. 2	Doug Brown	17:46	Bos.
May 9/88	Det.	CF	Edm. 4	Det. 3	Jari Kurri	11:02	Edm.
Apr. 5/89	St. L.	DSF	St. L. 4	Min. 3	Brett Hull	11:55	St. L.
Apr. 5/89	Cgy.	DSF	Van. 4	Cgy. 3	Paul Reinhart	2:47	Cgy.
Apr. 6/89	St. L.	DSF	St. L. 4	Min. 3	Rick Meagher	5:30	St. L.
Apr. 6/89	Det.	DSF	Chi. 5	Det. 4	Duane Sutter	14:36	Chi.
Apr. 8/89	Hfd.	DSF	Mtl. 5	Hfd. 4	Stephane Richer	5:01	Mtl.
Apr. 8/89	Phi.	DSF	Wsh. 4	Phi. 3	Kelly Miller	0:51	Phi.
Apr. 9/89	Hfd.	DSF	Mtl. 4	Hfd. 3	Russ Courtnall	15:12	Mtl.
Apr. 15/89	Cgy.	DSF	Cgy. 4	Van. 3	Joel Otto	19:21	Cgy.
Apr. 18/89	Cgy.	DF	Cgy. 4	L.A. 3	Doug Gilmour	7:47	Cgy.
Apr. 19/89	Mtl.	DF	Mtl. 3	Bos. 2	Bobby Smith	12:24	Mtl.
Apr. 20/89	St. L.	DF	St. L. 5	Chi. 4	Tony Hrkac	33:49	Chi.
Apr. 21/89	Phi.	DF	Pit. 4	Phi. 3	Phil Bourque	12:08	Phi.
May 8/89	Chi.	CF	Cgy. 2	Chi. 1	Al MacInnis	15:05	Cgy.
May 9/89	Mtl.	CF	Phi. 2	Mtl. 1	Dave Poulin	5:02	Mtl.
May 19/89	Mtl.	F	Mtl. 4	Cgy. 3	Ryan Walter	38:08	Cgy.
Apr. 5/90	N.J.	DSF	Wsh. 5	N.J. 4	Dino Ciccarelli	5:34	Wsh.
Apr. 6/90	Edm.	DSF	Edm. 3	Wpg. 2	Mark Lamb	4:21	Edm.
Apr. 8/90	Tor.	DSF	St. L. 6	Tor. 5	Sergio Momesso	6:04	St. L.
Apr. 8/90	L.A.	DSF	L.A. 2	Cgy. 1	Tony Granato	8:37	L.A.
Apr. 9/90	Mtl.	DSF	Mtl. 2	Buf. 1	Brian Skrudland	12:35	Mtl.
Apr. 9/90	NYI	DSF	NYI 4	NYR 3	Brent Sutter	20:59	NYR
Apr. 10/90	Wpg.	DSF	Wpg. 4	Edm. 3	Dave Ellett	21:08	Edm.
Apr. 14/90	L.A.	DSF	L.A. 4	Cgy. 3	Mike Krushelnyski	23:14	L.A.
Apr. 15/90	Hfd.	DSF	Hfd. 3	Bos. 2	Kevin Dineen	12:30	Bos.
Apr. 21/90	Bos.	DF	Bos. 5	Mtl. 4	Garry Galley	3:42	Bos.
Apr. 24/90	L.A.	DF	Edm. 6	L.A. 5	Joe Murphy	4:42	Edm.
Apr. 25/90	Wsh.	DF	Wsh. 4	NYR 3	Rod Langway	0:34	Wsh.
Apr. 27/90	NYR	DF	Wsh. 2	NYR 1	John Druce	6:48	Wsh.
May 15/90	Bos.	F	Edm. 3	Bos. 2	Petr Klima	55:13	Edm.

Overtime Record of Current Teams

(Listed by number of OT games played)

	Overall				Home					Road				
Team	GP	W	L	T	GP	W	L	T	Last OT Game	GP	W	L	T	Last OT Game
Montreal	97	51	44	2	45	26	16	1	Apr. 9/90	52	23	28	1	Apr. 21/90
Boston	80	31	46	3	37	18	18	1	May 15/90	43	13	28	2	Apr. 15/90
Toronto	75	36	38	1	48	22	25	1	Apr. 8/90	27	14	13	0	Apr. 12/88
NY Rangers	49	23	26	0	20	10	10	0	Apr. 27/90	29	14	15	0	Apr. 25/90
Detroit	47	20	27	0	29	10	19	0	Apr. 6/89	18	10	8	0	Apr. 27/87
Chicago	43	21	20	2	22	12	9	1	May 8/89	21	9	11	1	Apr. 20/89
Philadelphia	34	18	16	0	13	8	5	0	Apr. 21/89	21	10	11	0	May 9/89
NY Islanders	32	25	7	0	14	12	2	0	Apr. 9/90	18	13	5	0	Apr. 10/88
St. Louis	27	16	11	0	13	11	2	0	Apr. 20/89	14	5	9	0	Apr. 8/90
Minnesota	23	10	13	0	12	5	7	0	Apr. 30/85	11	5	6	0	Apr. 20/89
*Calgary	22	10	12	0	8	4	4	0	Apr. 18/89	14	6	8	0	Apr. 14/90
Edmonton	19	12	7	0	10	7	3	0	Apr. 6/90	9	5	4	0	May 15/90
Los Angeles	18	8	10	0	10	5	5	0	Apr. 24/90	8	3	5	0	Apr. 18/89
Buffalo	17	10	7	0	11	8	3	0	Apr. 10/88	6	2	4	0	Apr. 9/90
Quebec	15	9	6	0	9	5	4	0	Apr. 26/87	6	4	2	0	Apr. 8/87
Washington	12	7	5	0	6	4	2	0	Apr. 25/90	6	3	3	0	Apr. 27/90
Vancouver	11	4	7	0	3	1	2	0	Apr. 10/83	8	3	5	0	Apr. 15/89
Hartford	9	4	5	0	6	3	3	0	Apr. 15/90	3	1	2	0	Apr. 16/87
Pittsburgh	7	4	3	0	2	1	1	0	Apr. 10/82	5	3	2	0	Apr. 21/89
Winnipeg	7	3	4	0	4	2	2	0	Apr. 10/90	3	1	2	0	Apr. 6/90
**New Jersey	5	1	4	0	2	0	2	0	Apr. 5/90	3	1	2	0	May 4/88

* Totals include those of Atlanta 1974-80.
** Totals include those of Kansas City and Colorado 1975-82.

Stanley Cup Coaching Records

Coaches listed in order of total games coached in playoffs. Minimum: 65 games.

Coach	Team	Years	Series	W	L	G	W	L	T	Cups	%
Irvin, Dick	Chicago	1	3	2	1	9	5	3	1	0	.611
	Toronto	9	20	12	8	66	33	32	1	1	.508
	Montreal	14	22	11	11	115	62	53	0	3	.539
	TOTALS	24	45	25	20	190	100	88	2	4	.532
Arbour, Al	St. Louis	1	2	1	1	11	4	7	0	0	.364
	NY Islanders	13	36	27	9	176	110	66	0	4	.625
	TOTALS	14	38	28	10	187	114	73	0	4	.610
Bowman, Scott	St. Louis	4	10	6	4	52	26	26	0	0	.500
	Montreal	8	19	16	3	98	70	28	0	5	.714
	Buffalo	5	8	3	5	36	18	18	0	0	.500
	TOTALS	17	37	25	12	186	114	72	0	5	.612
Sather, Glen	Edmonton	10	27	21	6	*126	89	37	0	4	.706
Blake, Toe	Montreal	13	23	18	5	119	82	37	0	8	.689
Reay, Billy	Chicago	12	22	10	12	117	57	60	0	0	.487
Shero, Fred	Philadelphia	6	16	12	4	83	48	35	0	2	.578
	NY Rangers	2	5	3	2	25	13	12	0	0	.520
	TOTALS	8	21	15	6	108	61	47	0	2	.565
Adams, Jack	Detroit	15	27	15	12	105	52	52	1	3	.500
Francis, Emile	NY Rangers	9	14	5	9	75	34	41	0	0	.453
	St. Louis	3	4	1	3	18	6	12	0	0	.333
	TOTALS	12	18	6	12	93	40	53	0	0	.430
Keenan, Mike	Philadelphia	4	10	6	4	57	32	25	0	0	.561
	Chicago	2	6	4	2	36	19	17	0	0	.528
	TOTALS	6	16	10	6	93	51	42	0	0	.548
Imlach, Punch	Toronto	11	17	10	7	92	44	48	0	4	.478
Day, Hap	Toronto	9	14	10	4	80	49	31	0	5	.613
Abel, Sid	Chicago	1	1	0	1	7	3	4	0	0	.429
	Detroit	8	12	4	8	69	29	40	0	0	.420
	TOTALS	9	13	4	9	76	32	44	0	0	.421
Demers, Jacques	St. Louis	3	6	3	3	33	16	17	0	0	.485
	Detroit	3	7	4	3	38	20	18	0	0	.526
	TOTALS	6	13	7	6	71	36	35	0	0	.507
Ross, Art	Boston	12	19	9	10	70	32	33	5	2	.493
Bergeron, Michel	Quebec	7	13	6	7	68	31	37	0	0	.456
Ivan, Tommy	Detroit	7	12	8	4	67	36	31	0	3	.537
Pulford, Bob	Los Angeles	4	6	2	4	26	11	15	0	0	.423
	Chicago	5	9	4	5	41	17	24	0	0	.415
	TOTALS	9	15	6	9	67	28	39	0	0	.418
Patrick, Lester	NY Rangers	12	24	14	10	65	31	26	8	2	.538

* Does not include suspended game, May 24, 1988.

Ten Longest Overtime Games

Date	City	Series	Score		Scorer	Overtime	Series Winner
Mar. 24/36	Mtl.	SF	Det. 1	Mtl. M. 0	Mud Bruneteau	116:30	Det.
Apr. 3/33	Tor.	SF	Tor. 1	Bos. 0	Ken Doraty	104:46	Tor.
Mar. 23/43	Det.	SF	Tor. 3	Det. 2	Jack McLean	70:18	Det.
Mar. 28/30	Mtl.	SF	Mtl. 2	NYR 1	Gus Rivers	68:52	Mtl.
Apr. 18/87	Wsh.	DSF	NYI 3	Wsh. 2	Pat LaFontaine	68:47	NYI
Mar. 27/51	Det.	SF	Mtl. 3	Det. 2	Maurice Richard	61:09	Mtl.
Mar. 26/32	Mtl.	SF	NYR 4	Mtl. 3	Fred Cook	59:32	NYR
Mar. 21/39	NY	SF	Bos. 2	NYR 1	Mel Hill	59:25	Bos.
May 15/90	**Bos.**	**F**	**Edm. 3**	**Bos. 2**	**Petr Klima**	**55:13**	**Edm.**
Apr. 9/31	Mtl.	F	Chi. 3	Mtl. 2	Cy Wentworth	53:50	Mtl.

Punch Imlach's Leafs reached the playoffs 11 times, winning the Stanley Cup on four occasions.

Penalty Shots in Playoff Games

Date	Player	Goaltender	Scored	Final Score		Series
Mar. 25/37	Lionel Conacher, Mtl. Maroons	Tiny Thompson, Boston	No	Mtl. 0 at Bos. 4		QF
Apr. 15/37	Alex Shibicky, NY Rangers	Earl Robertson, Detroit	No	NYR 0 at Det. 3		F
Apr. 13/44	Virgil Johnson, Chicago	Bill Durnan, Montreal	No	Chi. 4 at Mtl. 5*		F
Apr. 9/68	Wayne Connelly, Minnesota	Terry Sawchuk, Los Angeles	Yes	L.A. 5 at Min. 7		QF
Apr. 27/68	Jim Roberts, St. Louis	Cesare Maniago, Minnesota	No	St. L. 4 at Min. 3		SF
May 16/71	Frank Mahovlich, Montreal	Tony Esposito, Chicago	No	Chi. 3 at Mtl. 4		F
May 7/75	Bill Barber, Philadelphia	Glenn Resch, NY Islanders	No	Phi. 3 at NYI 4		SF
Apr. 20/79	Mike Walton, Chicago	Glenn Resch, NY Islanders	No	NYI 4 at Chi. 0		QF
Apr. 9/81	Peter McNab, Boston	Don Beaupre, Minnesota	No	Min. 5 at Bos. 4*		PR
Apr. 17/81	Anders Hedberg, NY Rangers	Mike Liut, St. Louis	Yes	NYR 6 at St. L. 4		QF
Apr. 9/83	Denis Potvin, NY Islanders	Pat Riggin, Washington	No	NYI 6 at Wsh. 2		DSF
Apr. 28/84	Wayne Gretzky, Edmonton	Don Beaupre, Minnesota	Yes	Edm. 8 at Min. 5		CF
May 1/84	Mats Naslund, Montreal	Bill Smith, NY Islanders	No	Mtl. 1 at NYI 3		CF
Apr. 14/85	Bob Carpenter, Washington	Bill Smith, NY Islanders	No	Wsh. 4 at NYI. 2		DF
May 28/85	Ron Sutter, Philadelphia	Grant Fuhr, Edmonton	No	Phi. 3 at Edm. 5		F
May 30/85	Dave Poulin, Philadelphia	Grant Fuhr, Edmonton	No	Phi. 3 at Edm. 8		F
Apr. 9/88	John Tucker, Buffalo	Andy Moog, Boston	Yes	Bos. 2 at Buf 6		DSF
Apr. 9/88	Petr Klima, Detroit	Allan Bester, Toronto	Yes	Det. 6 at Tor. 3		DSF
Apr. 8/89	Neal Broten, Minnesota	Greg Millen, St. Louis	Yes	St.L. 5 at Min. 3		DSF
Apr. 4/90	Al MacInnis, Calgary	Kelly Hrudey, Los Angeles	No	L.A. 5 at Cgy. 3		DSF
Apr. 5/90	Randy Wood, NY Islanders	Mike Richter, NY Rangers	No	NYI 1 at NYR 2		DSF
May 3/90	Kelly Miller, Washington	Andy Moog, Boston	No	Wsh. 3 at Bos. 5		CF
May 18/90	Petr Klima, Edmonton	Rejean Lemelin, Boston	No	Edm. 7 at Bos. 2		F

* Game was decided in overtime, but shot taken during regulation time.

1990-91 Player Register

Note: The 1990-1991 Player Register lists forwards and defensemen only. Goaltenders are listed separately. The Player Register lists every skater who appeared in an NHL game in the 1989-90 season, every skater drafted in the first two rounds of the 1989 and 1990 Entry Drafts and other players on NHL Reserve Lists. Trades and roster changes are current as of August 15, 1990.

Abbreviations: A – assists; **G** – goals; **GP** – games played; **Lea** – league; **PIM** – penalties in minutes; **TP** – total points; ***** – league-leading total.
Pronunciations courtesy of the NHL Broadcasters' Association

Goaltender Register begins on page 369.

AALTONEN, PETRI

Center. Shoots left. 5'9", 175 lbs.   Born, Tampere, Finland, May 31, 1970.
(Quebec's 4th choice, 45th overall, in 1988 Entry Draft).

				Regular Season					Playoffs			
Season	Club	Lea	GP	G	A	TP	PIM	GP	G	A	TP	PIM
1986-87	IFK Helsinki	Fin. Jr.	30	8	5	13	24	4	0	0	0	0
1987-88	IFK Helsinki	Fin. Jr.	34	37	20	57	25	....	....	....	....	....
1988-89	IFK Helsinki	Fin.	2	0	0	0	0	....	....	....	....	....
1989-90	IFK Helsinki	Fin.	3	0	0	0	0	....	....	....	....	....

ACTON, KEITH EDWARD

Center. Shoots left. 5'8", 166 lbs.   Born, Stouffville, Ont., April 15, 1958.
(Montreal's 8th choice, 103rd overall, in 1978 Amateur Draft).

				Regular Season					Playoffs			
Season	Club	Lea	GP	G	A	TP	PIM	GP	G	A	TP	PIM
1976-77	Peterborough	OHA	65	52	69	121	93	4	1	4	5	6
1977-78	Peterborough	OHA	68	42	86	128	52	21	10	8	18	16
1978-79	Nova Scotia	AHL	79	15	26	41	22	10	4	2	6	4
1979-80	**Montreal**	**NHL**	2	0	1	1	0	....	....	....	....	....
a	Nova Scotia	AHL	75	45	53	98	38	6	1	2	3	8
1980-81	**Montreal**	**NHL**	61	15	24	39	74	2	0	0	0	6
1981-82	**Montreal**	**NHL**	78	36	52	88	88	5	0	4	4	16
1982-83	**Montreal**	**NHL**	78	24	26	50	63	3	0	0	0	0
1983-84	**Montreal**	**NHL**	9	3	7	10	4	....	....	....	....	....
	Minnesota	**NHL**	62	17	38	55	60	15	4	7	11	12
1984-85	**Minnesota**	**NHL**	78	20	38	58	90	9	4	4	8	6
1985-86	**Minnesota**	**NHL**	79	26	32	58	100	5	0	3	3	6
1986-87	**Minnesota**	**NHL**	78	16	29	45	56	....	....	....	....	....
1987-88	**Minnesota**	**NHL**	46	8	11	19	74	....	....	....	....	....
	Edmonton	**NHL**	26	3	6	9	21	7	2	0	2	16
1988-89	**Edmonton**	**NHL**	46	11	15	26	47	....	....	....	....	....
	Philadelphia	**NHL**	25	3	10	13	64	16	2	3	5	18
1989-90	**Philadelphia**	**NHL**	69	13	14	27	80	....	....	....	....	....
	NHL Totals		737	195	303	498	821	62	12	21	33	80

a   AHL Second All-Star Team (1980)
Played in NHL All-Star Game (1982)
Traded to **Minnesota** by **Montreal** with Mark Napier and Toronto's third round choice (Ken Hodge) in 1984 Entry Draft — Montreal's property via earlier transaction — for Bobby Smith, October 28, 1983. Traded to **Edmonton** by **Minnesota** for Moe Mantha, January 22, 1988. Traded to **Philadelphia** by **Edmonton** with Edmonton's fifth-round choice in 1991 Entry Draft for Dave Brown, February 7, 1989. Traded to **Winnipeg** by **Philadelphia** with Pete Peeters for future considerations, September 28, 1989. Traded to **Philadelphia** by **Winnipeg** with Pete Peeters for future considerations, October 3, 1989.

ADAMS, GREG

Center. Shoots left. 6'3", 185 lbs.   Born, Nelson, B.C., August 1, 1963.

				Regular Season					Playoffs			
Season	Club	Lea	GP	G	A	TP	PIM	GP	G	A	TP	PIM
1982-83	N. Arizona	NCAA	29	14	21	35	19	....	....	....	....	....
1983-84	N. Arizona	NCAA	26	44	29	73	24	....	....	....	....	....
1984-85	**New Jersey**	**NHL**	36	12	9	21	14	....	....	....	....	....
	Maine	AHL	41	15	20	35	12	11	3	4	7	0
1985-86	**New Jersey**	**NHL**	78	35	42	77	30	....	....	....	....	....
1986-87	**New Jersey**	**NHL**	72	20	27	47	19	....	....	....	....	....
1987-88	**Vancouver**	**NHL**	80	36	40	76	30	....	....	....	....	....
1988-89	**Vancouver**	**NHL**	61	19	14	33	24	7	2	3	5	2
1989-90	**Vancouver**	**NHL**	65	30	20	50	18	....	....	....	....	....
	NHL Totals		392	152	152	304	135	7	2	3	5	2

Played in NHL All-Star Game (1988)
Signed as a free agent by **New Jersey**, June 25, 1984. Traded to **Vancouver** by **New Jersey** with Kirk McLean for Patrik Sundstrom and Vancouver's fourth round choice (Matt Ruchty) in 1988 Entry Draft, September 10, 1987.

ADAMS, GREGORY CHARLES (GREG)

Left wing. Shoots left. 6'2", 200 lbs.   Born, Duncan, B.C., May 31, 1960.

				Regular Season					Playoffs			
Season	Club	Lea	GP	G	A	TP	PIM	GP	G	A	TP	PIM
1978-79	Victoria	WHL	71	23	31	54	151	14	5	0	5	59
1979-80	Victoria	WHL	71	62	48	110	212	16	9	11	20	71
1980-81	**Philadelphia**	**NHL**	6	3	0	3	8	....	....	....	....	....
	Maine	AHL	71	19	20	39	158	20	2	3	5	89
1981-82	**Philadelphia**	**NHL**	33	4	15	19	105	....	....	....	....	....
	Maine	AHL	45	16	21	37	241	4	0	3	3	28
1982-83	**Hartford**	**NHL**	79	10	13	23	216	....	....	....	....	....
1983-84	**Washington**	**NHL**	57	2	6	8	133	1	0	0	0	0
1984-85	**Washington**	**NHL**	51	6	12	18	72	5	0	0	0	9
	Binghamton	AHL	28	9	16	25	58	....	....	....	....	....
1985-86	**Washington**	**NHL**	78	18	38	56	152	9	1	3	4	27
1986-87	**Washington**	**NHL**	67	14	30	44	184	7	1	3	4	38
1987-88	**Washington**	**NHL**	78	15	12	27	153	14	0	5	5	58
1988-89	**Edmonton**	**NHL**	49	4	5	9	82	....	....	....	....	....
	Vancouver	**NHL**	12	4	2	6	35	7	0	0	0	21
1989-90	**Quebec**	**NHL**	7	1	3	4	17	....	....	....	....	....
	Detroit	**NHL**	28	3	7	10	16	....	....	....	....	....
	NHL Totals		545	84	143	227	1173	43	2	11	13	153

Signed as a free agent by **Philadelphia**, September 28, 1979. Traded to **Hartford** by **Philadelphia** with Ken Linseman and Philadelphia's first (David Jensen) and third (Leif Karlsson) round choices in the 1983 Entry Draft for Mark Howe and Hartford's third round (Derrick Smith) choice in the 1983 Entry Draft, August 20, 1982. Traded to **Washington** by **Hartford** for Torrie Robertson, October 3, 1983. Traded to **Edmonton** by **Washington** for the rights to Geoff Courtnall, July 22, 1988. Traded to **Vancouver** by **Edmonton** with Doug Smith for Jean LeBlanc and Vancouver's fifth-round choice (Peter White) in 1989 Entry Draft, March 7, 1989. Claimed by **Quebec** in NHL Waiver Draft, October 2, 1989. Traded to **Detroit** by **Quebec** with Robert Picard for Tony McKegney, December 4, 1989.

AGNEW, JIM

Defense. Shoots left. 6'1", 190 lbs. Born, Hartney, Man., March 21, 1966.
(Vancouver's 10th choice, 157th overall, in 1984 Entry Draft).

			Regular Season					Playoffs				
Season	Club	Lea	GP	G	A	TP	PIM	GP	G	A	TP	PIM
1982-83	Brandon	WHL	14	1	1	2	9	....	....	....	....	....
1983-84	Brandon	WHL	71	6	17	23	107	12	0	1	1	39
1984-85	Brandon	WHL	19	3	15	18	82	....	....	....	....	....
	Portland	WHL	44	5	24	29	223	6	0	2	2	44
1985-86a	Portland	WHL	70	6	30	36	286	9	0	1	1	48
1986-87	**Vancouver**	**NHL**	**4**	**0**	**0**	**0**	**0**	....	....	....	....	....
	Fredericton	AHL	67	0	5	5	261	....	....	....	....	....
1987-88	**Vancouver**	**NHL**	**10**	**0**	**1**	**1**	**16**	....	....	....	....	....
	Fredericton	AHL	63	2	8	10	188	14	0	2	2	43
1988-89	Milwaukee	IHL	47	2	10	12	181	11	0	2	2	34
1989-90	**Vancouver**	**NHL**	**7**	**0**	**0**	**0**	**36**	....	....	....	....	....
b	Milwaukee	IHL	51	4	10	14	238	....	....	....	....	....
	NHL Totals		**21**	**0**	**1**	**1**	**52**	....	....	....	....	....

a WHL First All-Star Team, West Division (1986)
b IHL Second All-Star Team (1990)

AITKEN, BRAD

Left wing. Shoots left. 6'3", 200 lbs. Born, Scarborough, Ont., October 30, 1967.
(Pittsburgh's 3rd choice, 46th overall, in 1986 Entry Draft).

			Regular Season					Playoffs				
Season	Club	Lea	GP	G	A	TP	PIM	GP	G	A	TP	PIM
1985-86	Peterborough	OHL	48	9	28	37	77	....	....	....	....	....
	S.S. Marie	OHL	20	8	19	27	11	....	....	....	....	....
1986-87	S.S. Marie	OHL	52	27	38	65	86	4	1	2	3	5
1987-88	**Pittsburgh**	**NHL**	**5**	**1**	**1**	**2**	**0**	....	....	....	....	....
	Muskegon	IHL	74	32	31	63	128	1	0	0	0	0
1988-89	Muskegon	IHL	74	35	30	65	139	13	5	5	10	75
1989-90	Muskegon	IHL	46	10	23	33	172	....	....	....	....	....
	Phoenix	IHL	8	2	1	3	18	....	....	....	....	....
	Fort Wayne	IHL	13	5	2	7	0	5	2	1	3	12
	NHL Totals		**5**	**1**	**1**	**2**	**0**	....	....	....	....	....

AITKEN, DAVID

Left wing. Shoots left. 5'11", 200 lbs. Born, St. Andrew's, N.B., September 24, 1967.
(Edmonton's 1st choice, 20th overall, in 1989 Supplemental Draft).

			Regular Season					Playoffs				
Season	Club	Lea	GP	G	A	TP	PIM	GP	G	A	TP	PIM
1986-87	N. Hampshire	H.E.	37	19	9	28	10	....	....	....	....	....
1987-88	N. Hampshire	H.E.	29	7	15	22	24	....	....	....	....	....
1988-89	N. Hampshire	H.E.	34	14	17	31	30	....	....	....	....	....
1989-90	N. Hampshire	H.E.	39	12	19	31	37	....	....	....	....	....

AIVAZOFF, MICAH

Center. Shoots left. 6', 185 lbs. Born, Powell River, B.C., May 4, 1969.
(Los Angeles' 6th choice, 109th overall, in 1988 Entry Draft).

			Regular Season					Playoffs				
Season	Club	Lea	GP	G	A	TP	PIM	GP	G	A	TP	PIM
1986-87	Victoria	WHL	72	18	39	57	112	5	1	0	1	2
1987-88	Victoria	WHL	69	26	57	83	79	8	3	4	7	14
1988-89	Victoria	WHL	70	35	65	100	136	8	5	7	12	2
1989-90	New Haven	AHL	77	20	39	59	71	....	....	....	....	....

AKERBLOM, MARKUS

Left wing. Shoots left. 5'11", 185 lbs. Born, Ostersund, Sweden, November 22, 1969.
(Winnipeg's 8th choice, 127th overall, in 1988 Entry Draft).

			Regular Season					Playoffs				
Season	Club	Lea	GP	G	A	TP	PIM	GP	G	A	TP	PIM
1986-87	Ostersund	Swe.	32	14	18	32	....	....	....	....	....	....
1987-88	Bjorkloven	Swe.	32	6	8	14	....	....	....	....	....	....
1988-89	Bjorkloven	Swe.	21	6	10	16	....	....	....	....	....	....
1989-90	Bjorkloven	Swe.	15	10	10	20	....	....	....	....	....	....

AKERSTROM, ROGER

Defense. Shoots left. 6', 185 lbs. Born, Lulea, Sweden, April 5, 1967.
(Vancouver's 5th choice, 170th overall, in 1988 Entry Draft).

			Regular Season					Playoffs				
Season	Club	Lea	GP	G	A	TP	PIM	GP	G	A	TP	PIM
1987-88	Lulea	Swe.	34	4	3	7	28	....	....	....	....	....
1988-89	Lulea	Swe.	38	6	12	18	32	....	....	....	....	....
1989-90	Lulea	Swe.	36	5	10	15	44	5	3	2	5	2

ALBELIN, TOMMY

Defense. Shoots left. 6'1", 190 lbs. Born, Stockholm, Sweden, May 21, 1964.
(Quebec's 7th choice, 152nd overall, in 1983 Entry Draft).

			Regular Season					Playoffs				
Season	Club	Lea	GP	G	A	TP	PIM	GP	G	A	TP	PIM
1982-83	Djurgarden	Swe.	19	2	5	7	4	6	1	0	1	2
1983-84	Djurgarden	Swe.	30	9	5	14	26	4	0	1	1	2
1984-85	Djurgarden	Swe.	32	9	8	17	22	8	2	1	3	4
1985-86	Djurgarden	Swe.	35	4	8	12	26	....	....	....	....	....
1986-87	Djurgarden	Swe.	33	7	5	12	49	2	0	0	0	0
1987-88	**Quebec**	**NHL**	**60**	**3**	**23**	**26**	**47**	....	....	....	....	....
1988-89	**Quebec**	**NHL**	**14**	**2**	**4**	**6**	**27**	....	....	....	....	....
	New Jersey	**NHL**	**46**	**7**	**24**	**31**	**40**	....	....	....	....	....
	Halifax	AHL	8	2	5	7	4	....	....	....	....	....
1989-90	**New Jersey**	**NHL**	**68**	**6**	**23**	**29**	**63**	....	....	....	....	....
	NHL Totals		**188**	**18**	**74**	**92**	**177**	....	....	....	....	....

Traded to **New Jersey** by **Quebec** for New Jersey's fourth-round choice (Niclas Andersson) in 1989 Entry Draft, December 12, 1988.

ALLISON, MICHAEL EARNEST (MIKE)

Center/Right wing. Shoots right. 6'1", 195 lbs. Born, Fort Frances, Ont., March 28, 1961.
(NY Rangers' 2nd choice, 35th overall, in 1980 Entry Draft).

			Regular Season					Playoffs				
Season	Club	Lea	GP	G	A	TP	PIM	GP	G	A	TP	PIM
1978-79	Sudbury	OHA	59	24	32	56	41	10	4	2	6	18
1979-80	Sudbury	OHA	67	24	71	95	74	9	8	6	14	6
1980-81	**NY Rangers**	**NHL**	**75**	**26**	**38**	**64**	**83**	**14**	**3**	**1**	**4**	**20**
1981-82	Springfield	AHL	2	0	0	0	0	....	....	....	....	....
	NY Rangers	**NHL**	**48**	**7**	**15**	**22**	**74**	**10**	**1**	**3**	**4**	**18**
1982-83	Tulsa	CHL	6	2	2	4	2	....	....	....	....	....
	NY Rangers	**NHL**	**39**	**11**	**9**	**20**	**37**	**8**	**0**	**5**	**5**	**10**
1983-84	**NY Rangers**	**NHL**	**45**	**8**	**12**	**20**	**64**	**5**	**0**	**1**	**1**	**6**
1984-85	**NY Rangers**	**NHL**	**31**	**9**	**15**	**24**	**17**	....	....	....	....	....
1985-86	**NY Rangers**	**NHL**	**28**	**2**	**13**	**15**	**22**	**16**	**0**	**2**	**2**	**38**
	New Haven	AHL	9	6	6	12	4	....	....	....	....	....
1986-87	**Toronto**	**NHL**	**71**	**7**	**16**	**23**	**66**	**13**	**3**	**5**	**8**	**15**
1987-88	**Toronto**	**NHL**	**15**	**0**	**3**	**3**	**10**	....	....	....	....	....
	Los Angeles	**NHL**	**37**	**16**	**12**	**28**	**57**	**5**	**0**	**0**	**0**	**16**
1988-89	**Los Angeles**	**NHL**	**55**	**14**	**22**	**36**	**122**	**7**	**1**	**0**	**1**	**10**
1989-90	**Los Angeles**	**NHL**	**55**	**2**	**11**	**13**	**78**	**4**	**1**	**0**	**1**	**2**
	New Haven	AHL	5	2	2	4	14	....	....	....	....	....
	NHL Totals		**499**	**102**	**166**	**268**	**630**	**82**	**9**	**17**	**26**	**135**

Traded to **Toronto** by **NY Rangers** for Walt Poddubny, August 18, 1986. Traded to **Los Angeles** by **Toronto** for Sean McKenna, December 14, 1987.

ALLISON, RAYMOND PETER (RAY)

Right wing. Shoots right. 5'10", 195 lbs. Born, Cranbrook, B.C., March 4, 1959.
(Hartford's 1st choice, 18th overall, in 1979 Entry Draft).

			Regular Season					Playoffs				
Season	Club	Lea	GP	G	A	TP	PIM	GP	G	A	TP	PIM
1975-76	Brandon	WHL	36	9	17	26	50	5	2	1	3	0
1976-77	Brandon	WHL	71	45	92	137	198	14	9	11	20	37
1977-78	Brandon	WHL	71	74	86	160	254	8	7	8	15	35
1978-79	Brandon	WHL	62	60	93	153	191	22	18	19	37	28
1979-80	Springfield	AHL	13	6	9	15	18	....	....	....	....	....
	Hartford	**NHL**	**64**	**16**	**12**	**28**	**13**	**2**	**0**	**1**	**1**	**0**
1980-81	**Hartford**	**NHL**	**6**	**1**	**0**	**1**	**0**	....	....	....	....	....
	Binghamton	AHL	74	31	39	70	81	1	0	1	1	0
1981-82	Maine	AHL	26	15	13	28	75	....	....	....	....	....
	Philadelphia	**NHL**	**51**	**17**	**37**	**54**	**104**	**3**	**2**	**0**	**2**	**2**
1982-83	**Philadelphia**	**NHL**	**67**	**21**	**30**	**51**	**57**	**3**	**0**	**1**	**1**	**12**
1983-84	**Philadelphia**	**NHL**	**37**	**8**	**13**	**21**	**47**	**3**	**0**	**1**	**1**	**4**
1984-85	**Philadelphia**	**NHL**	**11**	**1**	**1**	**2**	**2**	**1**	**0**	**0**	**0**	**2**
	Hershey	AHL	49	17	22	39	61	....	....	....	....	....
1985-86	Hershey	AHL	77	32	46	78	131	18	4	6	10	28
1986-87	**Philadelphia**	**NHL**	**2**	**0**	**0**	**0**	**0**	....	....	....	....	....
	Hershey	AHL	78	29	55	84	57	5	3	1	4	12
1987-88	Hershey	AHL	....	....	....	....	....	9	2	9	11	17
1988-89	Hershey	AHL	15	6	11	17	18	12	4	7	11	6
1989-90	Hershey	AHL	70	25	30	55	66	....	....	....	....	....
	NHL Totals		**238**	**64**	**93**	**157**	**223**	**12**	**2**	**3**	**5**	**20**

Traded to **Philadelphia** by **Hartford** with Fred Arthur and Hartford's first (Ron Sutter), second (Peter Ihnacak, which was later transferred to **Toronto**) and third-round (Miroslav Dvorak) choices in the 1982 Entry Draft for Rick MacLeish, Blake Wesley, Don Gillen and Philadelphia's first (Paul Lawless), second (Mark Paterson) and third-round (Kevin Dineen) choices in the 1982 Entry Draft, July 3, 1981.

ALLISON, SCOTT

Center. Shoots left. 6'4", 195 lbs. Born, St. Boniface, Man., April 22, 1972.
(Edmonton's 1st choice, 17th overall, in 1990 Entry Draft).

			Regular Season					Playoffs				
Season	Club	Lea	GP	G	A	TP	PIM	GP	G	A	TP	PIM
1988-89	Prince Albert	WHL	51	6	9	15	37	3	0	0	0	0
1989-90	Prince Albert	WHL	66	22	16	38	73	11	1	4	5	8

AMONTE, ANTHONY (TONY)

Right wing. Shoots right. 6', 180 lbs. Born, Hingham, MA, August 2, 1970.
(NY Rangers' 3rd choice, 68th overall, in 1988 Entry Draft).

			Regular Season					Playoffs				
Season	Club	Lea	GP	G	A	TP	PIM	GP	G	A	TP	PIM
1989-90	Boston U.	H.E.	41	25	33	58	52	....	....	....	....	....

AMUNDSON, DARRIN

Center. Shoots right. 6'2", 175 lbs. Born, Duluth, MN, November 9, 1968.
(Winnipeg's 5th choice, 100th overall, in 1987 Entry Draft).

			Regular Season					Playoffs				
Season	Club	Lea	GP	G	A	TP	PIM	GP	G	A	TP	PIM
1987-88	Minn.-Duluth	WCHA	16	0	6	6	4	....	....	....	....	....
1988-89	Minn.-Duluth	WCHA	37	5	11	16	23	....	....	....	....	....
1989-90	Minn.-Duluth	WCHA	23	5	6	11	12	....	....	....	....	....

ANDERSON, GLENN CHRIS

Right wing. Shoots left. 6'1", 190 lbs. Born, Vancouver, B.C., October 2, 1960.
(Edmonton's 3rd choice, 69th overall, in 1979 Entry Draft).

			Regular Season					Playoffs				
Season	Club	Lea	GP	G	A	TP	PIM	GP	G	A	TP	PIM
1978-79	U. of Denver	WCHA	40	26	29	55	58	....	....	....	....	....
1979-80	Seattle	WHL	7	5	5	10	4	....	....	....	....	....
	Cdn. Olympic	...	49	21	21	42	46	....	....	....	....	....
1980-81	**Edmonton**	**NHL**	**58**	**30**	**23**	**53**	**24**	**9**	**5**	**7**	**12**	**12**
1981-82	**Edmonton**	**NHL**	**80**	**38**	**67**	**105**	**71**	**5**	**2**	**5**	**7**	**8**
1982-83	**Edmonton**	**NHL**	**72**	**48**	**56**	**104**	**70**	**16**	**10**	**10**	**20**	**32**
1983-84	**Edmonton**	**NHL**	**80**	**54**	**45**	**99**	**65**	**19**	**6**	**11**	**17**	**33**
1984-85	**Edmonton**	**NHL**	**80**	**42**	**39**	**81**	**69**	**18**	**10**	**16**	**26**	**38**
1985-86	**Edmonton**	**NHL**	**72**	**54**	**48**	**102**	**90**	**10**	**8**	**3**	**11**	**14**
1986-87	**Edmonton**	**NHL**	**80**	**35**	**38**	**73**	**65**	**21**	**14**	**13**	**27**	**59**
1987-88	**Edmonton**	**NHL**	**80**	**38**	**50**	**88**	**58**	**19**	**9**	**16**	**25**	**49**
1988-89	**Edmonton**	**NHL**	**79**	**16**	**48**	**64**	**93**	**7**	**1**	**2**	**3**	**8**
1989-90	**Edmonton**	**NHL**	**73**	**34**	**38**	**72**	**107**	**22**	**10**	**12**	**22**	**20**
	NHL Totals		**754**	**389**	**452**	**841**	**712**	**146**	**75**	**95**	**170**	**273**

Played in NHL All-Star Game (1984-86, 1988)

ANDERSON, JOHN MURRAY

Right wing. Shoots left. 5'11", 200 lbs. Born, Toronto, Ont., March 28, 1957.
(Toronto's 1st choice, 11th overall, in 1977 Amateur Draft).

			Regular Season					Playoffs				
Season	Club	Lea	GP	G	A	TP	PIM	GP	G	A	TP	PIM
1973-74	Toronto	OHA	38	22	22	44	6	....	....	....	....	....
1974-75	Toronto	OHA	70	49	64	113	31	22	16	14	30	14
1975-76	Toronto	OHA	39	26	25	51	19	10	7	4	11	7
1976-77a	Toronto	OHA	64	57	62	119	42	6	3	5	8	0
1977-78	**Toronto**	**NHL**	**17**	**1**	**2**	**3**	**2**	**2**	**0**	**0**	**0**	**0**
	Dallas	CHL	55	22	23	45	6	13	*11	8	*19	2
1978-79	**Toronto**	**NHL**	**71**	**15**	**11**	**26**	**10**	**6**	**0**	**2**	**2**	**0**
1979-80	**Toronto**	**NHL**	**74**	**25**	**28**	**53**	**22**	**3**	**1**	**1**	**2**	**0**
1980-81	**Toronto**	**NHL**	**75**	**17**	**26**	**43**	**31**	**2**	**0**	**0**	**0**	**0**
1981-82	**Toronto**	**NHL**	**69**	**31**	**26**	**57**	**30**	....	....	....	....	....
1982-83	**Toronto**	**NHL**	**80**	**31**	**49**	**80**	**24**	**4**	**2**	**4**	**6**	**0**
1983-84	**Toronto**	**NHL**	**73**	**37**	**31**	**68**	**22**	....	....	....	....	....
1984-85	**Toronto**	**NHL**	**75**	**32**	**31**	**63**	**27**	....	....	....	....	....
1985-86	**Quebec**	**NHL**	**65**	**21**	**28**	**49**	**26**	....	....	....	....	....
	Hartford	**NHL**	**14**	**8**	**17**	**25**	**2**	**10**	**5**	**8**	**13**	**0**
1986-87	**Hartford**	**NHL**	**76**	**31**	**44**	**75**	**19**	**6**	**1**	**2**	**3**	**0**
1987-88	**Hartford**	**NHL**	**63**	**17**	**32**	**49**	**20**	....	....	....	....	....
1988-89	**Hartford**	**NHL**	**62**	**16**	**24**	**40**	**28**	**4**	**0**	**1**	**1**	**2**
1989-90	Binghamton	AHL	3	1	1	2	0	....	....	....	....	....
	Milano	Italy	9	7	9	16	18	....	....	....	....	....
	NHL Totals		**814**	**282**	**349**	**631**	**263**	**37**	**9**	**18**	**27**	**2**

a OHA First All-Star Team (1977)

Traded to **Quebec** by **Toronto** for Brad Maxwell, August 21, 1985. Traded to **Hartford** by **Quebec** for Risto Siltanen, March 8, 1986.

ANDERSON, JON

Forward. Shoots left. 6'2", 185 lbs. Born, White Bear Lake, MN, February 22, 1968.
(Winnipeg's 2nd choice, 8th overall, in 1989 Supplemental Draft).

			Regular Season					Playoffs				
Season	Club	Lea	GP	G	A	TP	PIM	GP	G	A	TP	PIM
1986-87	U. Minnesota	WCHA	2	0	0	0	0	....	....	....	....	....
1987-88	U. Minnesota	WCHA	10	1	2	3	8	....	....	....	....	....
1988-89	U. Minnesota	WCHA	47	20	16	36	52	....	....	....	....	....
1989-90	U. Minnesota	WCHA	42	15	14	29	41	....	....	....	....	....

ANDERSON, PERRY LYNN

Left wing. Shoots left. 6'1", 225 lbs. Born, Barrie, Ont., October 14, 1961.
(St. Louis' 5th choice, 117th overall, in 1980 Entry Draft).

			Regular Season					Playoffs				
Season	Club	Lea	GP	G	A	TP	PIM	GP	G	A	TP	PIM
1978-79	Kingston	OHA	61	6	13	19	85	5	2	1	3	6
1979-80	Kingston	OHA	63	17	16	33	52	3	0	0	0	6
1980-81	Kingston	OHA	38	9	13	22	118	....	....	....	....	....
	Brantford	OHA	31	8	27	35	43	6	4	2	6	15
1981-82	Salt Lake	CHL	71	32	32	64	117	2	1	0	1	2
	St. Louis	**NHL**	**5**	**1**	**2**	**3**	**0**	**10**	**2**	**0**	**2**	**4**
1982-83	**St. Louis**	**NHL**	**18**	**5**	**2**	**7**	**14**	....	....	....	....	....
	Salt Lake	CHL	57	23	19	42	140	....	....	....	....	....
1983-84	Montana	CHL	8	7	3	10	34	....	....	....	....	....
	St. Louis	**NHL**	**50**	**7**	**5**	**12**	**195**	**9**	**0**	**0**	**0**	**27**
1984-85	**St. Louis**	**NHL**	**71**	**9**	**9**	**18**	**146**	**3**	**0**	**0**	**0**	**7**
1985-86	**New Jersey**	**NHL**	**51**	**7**	**12**	**19**	**91**	....	....	....	....	....
1986-87	**New Jersey**	**NHL**	**57**	**10**	**9**	**19**	**107**	....	....	....	....	....
	Maine	AHL	9	5	4	9	42	....	....	....	....	....
1987-88	**New Jersey**	**NHL**	**60**	**4**	**6**	**10**	**222**	**10**	**0**	**0**	**0**	**113**
1988-89	**New Jersey**	**NHL**	**39**	**3**	**6**	**9**	**128**	....	....	....	....	....
1989-90	Utica	AHL	71	13	17	30	128	5	0	0	0	24
	NHL Totals		**351**	**46**	**51**	**97**	**903**	**32**	**2**	**0**	**2**	**151**

Traded to **New Jersey** by **St. Louis** for Rick Meagher and New Jersey's 12th round choice (Bill Butler) in 1986 Entry Draft, August 29, 1985.

ANDERSON, SHAWN

Defense. Shoots left. 6'1", 200 lbs. Born, Montreal, Que., February 7, 1968.
(Buffalo's 1st choice, 5th overall, in 1986 Entry Draft).

			Regular Season					Playoffs				
Season	Club	Lea	GP	G	A	TP	PIM	GP	G	A	TP	PIM
1985-86	Maine	H.E.	16	5	8	13	22	....	....	....	....	....
	Cdn. Olympic	....	49	4	14	18	38	....	....	....	....	....
1986-87	**Buffalo**	**NHL**	**41**	**2**	**11**	**13**	**23**	....	....	....	....	....
	Rochester	AHL	15	2	5	7	11	....	....	....	....	....
1987-88	**Buffalo**	**NHL**	**23**	**1**	**2**	**3**	**17**	....	....	....	....	....
	Rochester	AHL	22	5	16	21	19	6	0	0	0	0
1988-89	**Buffalo**	**NHL**	**33**	**2**	**10**	**12**	**18**	**5**	**0**	**1**	**1**	**4**
	Rochester	AHL	31	5	14	19	24	....	....	....	....	....
1989-90	**Buffalo**	**NHL**	**16**	**1**	**3**	**4**	**8**	....	....	....	....	....
	Rochester	AHL	39	2	16	18	41	9	1	0	1	4
	NHL Totals		**113**	**6**	**26**	**32**	**66**	**5**	**0**	**1**	**1**	**4**

ANDERSSON, BO MIKAEL

Left wing. Shoots left. 5'11", 185 lbs. Born, Malmo, Sweden, May 10, 1966.
(Buffalo's 1st choice, 18th overall, in 1984 Entry Draft).

			Regular Season					Playoffs				
Season	Club	Lea	GP	G	A	TP	PIM	GP	G	A	TP	PIM
1982-83	V. Frolunda	Swe.	1	1	0	1	0	....	....	....	....	....
1983-84	V. Frolunda	Swe.	18	0	3	6	....	....	....	....	....	....
1984-85	V. Frolunda	Swe.	30	16	11	27	18	6	3	2	5	2
1985-86	**Buffalo**	**NHL**	**32**	**1**	**9**	**10**	**4**	....	....	....	....	....
	Rochester	AHL	20	10	4	14	6	....	....	....	....	....
1986-87	**Buffalo**	**NHL**	**16**	**0**	**3**	**3**	**0**	....	....	....	....	....
1986-87	Rochester	AHL	42	6	20	26	14	9	1	2	3	2
1987-88	**Buffalo**	**NHL**	**37**	**3**	**20**	**23**	**10**	**1**	**1**	**0**	**1**	**0**
	Rochester	AHL	35	12	24	36	16	....	....	....	....	....
1988-89	**Buffalo**	**NHL**	**14**	**0**	**1**	**1**	**4**	....	....	....	....	....
	Rochester	AHL	56	18	33	51	12	....	....	....	....	....
1989-90	**Hartford**	**NHL**	**50**	**13**	**24**	**37**	**6**	**5**	**0**	**3**	**3**	**2**
	NHL Totals		**149**	**17**	**57**	**74**	**24**	**6**	**1**	**3**	**4**	**2**

Claimed by **Hartford** in NHL Waiver Draft, October 2, 1989.

ANDERSSON, NICLAS

Left wing. Shoots left. 5'9", 175 lbs. Born, Kungalv, Sweden, May 20, 1971.
(Quebec's 5th choice, 68th overall, in 1989 Entry Draft).

			Regular Season					Playoffs				
Season	Club	Lea	GP	G	A	TP	PIM	GP	G	A	TP	PIM
1987-88	V. Frolunda	Swe.	15	5	5	10	....	....	....	....	....	....
1988-89	V. Frolunda	Swe.	30	13	24	37	....	....	....	....	....	....
1989-90	V. Frolunda	Swe.	38	10	21	31	14	....	....	....	....	....

ANDISON, TRENT L.

Left wing. Shoots left. 5'10", 195 lbs. Born, Bracebridge, Ont., May 30, 1969.
(Minnesota's 9th choice, 232nd overall, in 1988 Entry Draft).

			Regular Season					Playoffs				
Season	Club	Lea	GP	G	A	TP	PIM	GP	G	A	TP	PIM
1987-88	Cornell	ECAC	27	21	17	38	22	....	....	....	....	....
1988-89	Cornell	ECAC	28	17	16	33	28	....	....	....	....	....
1989-90	Cornell	ECAC	25	8	16	24	12	....	....	....	....	....

ANDREYCHUK, DAVID (DAVE)

Left/Right wing. Shoots right. 6'3", 220 lbs. Born, Hamilton, Ont., September 29, 1963.
(Buffalo's 3rd choice, 16th overall, in 1982 Entry Draft).

			Regular Season					Playoffs				
Season	Club	Lea	GP	G	A	TP	PIM	GP	G	A	TP	PIM
1980-81	Oshawa	OHA	67	22	22	44	80	10	3	2	5	20
1981-82	Oshawa	OHL	67	57	43	100	71	3	1	4	5	16
1982-83	Oshawa	OHL	14	8	24	32	6	....	....	....	....	....
	Buffalo	**NHL**	**43**	**14**	**23**	**37**	**16**	**4**	**1**	**0**	**1**	**4**
1983-84	**Buffalo**	**NHL**	**78**	**38**	**42**	**80**	**42**	**2**	**0**	**1**	**1**	**2**
1984-85	**Buffalo**	**NHL**	**64**	**31**	**30**	**61**	**54**	**5**	**4**	**2**	**6**	**4**
1985-86	**Buffalo**	**NHL**	**80**	**36**	**51**	**87**	**61**	....	....	....	....	....
1986-87	**Buffalo**	**NHL**	**77**	**25**	**48**	**73**	**46**	....	....	....	....	....
1987-88	**Buffalo**	**NHL**	**80**	**30**	**48**	**78**	**112**	**6**	**2**	**4**	**6**	**0**
1988-89	**Buffalo**	**NHL**	**56**	**28**	**24**	**52**	**40**	**5**	**0**	**3**	**3**	**0**
1989-90	**Buffalo**	**NHL**	**73**	**40**	**42**	**82**	**42**	**6**	**2**	**5**	**7**	**2**
	NHL Totals		**551**	**242**	**308**	**550**	**413**	**28**	**9**	**15**	**24**	**12**

Played in NHL All-Star Game (1990)

ANDRUSAK, GREG

Defense. Shoots right. 6'1", 185 lbs. Born, Cranbrook, B.C., November 14, 1969.
(Pittsburgh's 5th choice, 88th overall, in 1988 Entry Draft).

			Regular Season					Playoffs				
Season	Club	Lea	GP	G	A	TP	PIM	GP	G	A	TP	PIM
1987-88	Minn.-Duluth	WCHA	37	4	5	9	42	....	....	....	....	....
1988-89	Minn.-Duluth	WCHA	35	4	8	12	74	....	....	....	....	....
1989-90	Minn.-Duluth	WCHA	35	5	29	34	74	....	....	....	....	....

ANGLEHART, SERGE

Defense. Shoots right. 6'2", 190 lbs. Born, Hull, Que., April 18, 1970.
(Detroit's 2nd choice, 38th overall, in 1988 Entry Draft).

			Regular Season					Playoffs				
Season	Club	Lea	GP	G	A	TP	PIM	GP	G	A	TP	PIM
1987-88	Drummondville	QMJHL	44	1	8	9	122	17	0	3	3	19
1988-89	Drummondville	QMJHL	39	6	15	21	89	3	0	0	0	37
	Adirondack	AHL	....	....	....	....	....	2	0	0	0	0
1989-90	Laval	QMJHL	48	2	19	21	131	10	1	6	7	69

ANTOSKI, SHAWN

Left wing. Shoots left. 6'4", 235 lbs. Born, Brantford, Ont., March 25, 1970.
(Vancouver's 2nd choice, 18th overall, in 1990 Entry Draft).

			Regular Season					Playoffs				
Season	Club	Lea	GP	G	A	TP	PIM	GP	G	A	TP	PIM
1988-89	North Bay	OHL	57	6	21	27	201	9	5	3	8	24
1989-90	North Bay	OHL	59	25	31	56	201	5	1	2	3	17

ARCHIBALD, DAVE

Center. Shoots left. 6'1", 190 lbs. Born, Chilliwack, B.C., April 14, 1969.
(Minnesota's 1st choice, 6th overall, in 1987 Entry Draft).

			Regular Season					Playoffs				
Season	Club	Lea	GP	G	A	TP	PIM	GP	G	A	TP	PIM
1984-85	Portland	WHL	47	7	11	18	10	3	0	2	2	0
1985-86	Portland	WHL	70	29	35	64	56	15	6	7	13	11
1986-87	Portland	WHL	65	50	57	107	40	20	10	18	28	11
1987-88	**Minnesota**	**NHL**	**78**	**13**	**20**	**33**	**26**	....	....	....	....	....
1988-89	**Minnesota**	**NHL**	**72**	**14**	**19**	**33**	**14**	**5**	**0**	**1**	**1**	**0**
1989-90	**Minnesota**	**NHL**	**12**	**1**	**5**	**6**	**6**	....	....	....	....	....
	NY Rangers	**NHL**	**19**	**2**	**3**	**5**	**6**	....	....	....	....	....
	Flint	IHL	41	14	38	52	16	4	3	2	5	0
	NHL Totals		**181**	**30**	**47**	**77**	**52**	**5**	**0**	**1**	**1**	**0**

Traded to **NY Rangers** by **Minnesota** for Jayson More, November 1, 1989.

ARMSTRONG, BILL

Defense. Shoots left. 6'4", 215 lbs. Born, Richmond Hill, Ont., May 18, 1970.
(Philadelphia's 6th choice, 46th overall, in 1990 Entry Draft).

			Regular Season					Playoffs				
Season	Club	Lea	GP	G	A	TP	PIM	GP	G	A	TP	PIM
1989-90	Oshawa	OHL	63	2	11	13	166	17	0	7	7	39

ARMSTRONG, TIM

Center. Shoots right. 5'11", 170 lbs. Born, Toronto, Ont., May 12, 1967
(Toronto's 11th choice, 211th overall, in 1985 Entry Draft).

			Regular Season					Playoffs				
Season	Club	Lea	GP	G	A	TP	PIM	GP	G	A	TP	PIM
1984-85	Toronto	OHL	63	17	45	62	28	5	5	2	7	0
1985-86	Toronto	OHL	64	35	69	104	36	4	1	3	4	9
1986-87	Newmarket	AHL	5	3	0	3	2	....	....	....	....	....
	Toronto	OHL	66	29	55	84	61	....	....	....	....	....
1987-88	Newmarket	AHL	78	19	40	59	26	....	....	....	....	....
1988-89	**Toronto**	**NHL**	**11**	**1**	**0**	**1**	**6**	....	....	....	....	....
	Newmarket	AHL	37	16	24	40	38	....	....	....	....	....
1989-90	Newmarket	AHL	63	25	37	62	24	....	....	....	....	....
	NHL Totals		**11**	**1**	**0**	**1**	**6**	....	....	....	....	....

ARMSTRONG, WILLIAM

Center. Shoots left. 6'2", 195 lbs. Born, London, Ont., June 25, 1966.

			Regular Season					Playoffs				
Season	Club	Lea	GP	G	A	TP	PIM	GP	G	A	TP	PIM
1986-87	W. Michigan	CCHA	43	13	20	33	86	....	....	....	....	....
1987-88	W. Michigan	CCHA	41	22	17	39	88	....	....	....	....	....
1988-89	W. Michigan	CCHA	40	23	19	42	97	....	....	....	....	....
1989-90	Hershey	AHL	58	10	6	16	99	....	....	....	....	....

Signed as a free agent by **Philadelphia**, May 16, 1989.

ARNIEL, SCOTT (ar-NEEL)

Left wing. Shoots left. 6'1", 190 lbs. Born, Kingston, Ont., September 17, 1962.
(Winnipeg's 2nd choice, 22nd overall, in 1981 Entry Draft).

			Regular Season					Playoffs				
Season	Club	Lea	GP	G	A	TP	PIM	GP	G	A	TP	PIM
1980-81	Cornwall	QJHL	68	52	71	123	102	19	14	19	33	24
1981-82	Cornwall	OHL	24	18	26	44	43	....	....	....	....	....
	Winnipeg	**NHL**	**17**	**1**	**8**	**9**	**14**	**3**	**0**	**0**	**0**	**0**
1982-83	**Winnipeg**	**NHL**	**75**	**13**	**5**	**18**	**46**	**2**	**0**	**0**	**0**	**0**
1983-84	**Winnipeg**	**NHL**	**80**	**21**	**35**	**56**	**68**	**2**	**0**	**0**	**0**	**5**
1984-85	**Winnipeg**	**NHL**	**79**	**22**	**22**	**44**	**81**	**8**	**1**	**2**	**3**	**9**
1985-86	**Winnipeg**	**NHL**	**80**	**18**	**25**	**43**	**40**	**3**	**0**	**0**	**0**	**12**
1986-87	**Buffalo**	**NHL**	**63**	**11**	**14**	**25**	**59**	....	....	....	....	....
1987-88	**Buffalo**	**NHL**	**73**	**17**	**23**	**40**	**61**	**6**	**0**	**1**	**1**	**5**
1988-89	**Buffalo**	**NHL**	**80**	**18**	**23**	**41**	**46**	**5**	**1**	**0**	**1**	**4**
1989-90	**Buffalo**	**NHL**	**79**	**18**	**14**	**32**	**77**	**5**	**1**	**0**	**1**	**4**
	NHL Totals		**626**	**139**	**169**	**308**	**492**	**34**	**3**	**3**	**6**	**39**

Traded to **Buffalo** by **Winnipeg** for Gilles Hamel, June 21, 1986. Traded to **Winnipeg** by **Buffalo** with Phil Housley, Jeff Parker and Buffalo's first round choice (Keith Tkachuk) in 1990 Entry Draft for Dale Hawerchuk, Winnipeg's first round choice (Brad May) in 1990 Entry Draft and future considerations, June 16, 1990.

ASHTON, BRENT KENNETH

Left wing. Shoots left. 6'1", 210 lbs. Born, Saskatoon, Sask., May 18, 1960.
(Vancouver's 2nd choice, 26th overall, in 1979 Entry Draft).

			Regular Season					Playoffs				
Season	Club	Lea	GP	G	A	TP	PIM	GP	G	A	TP	PIM
1977-78	Saskatoon	WHL	46	38	26	64	47	....	....	....	....	....
1978-79	Saskatoon	WHL	62	64	55	119	80	11	14	4	18	5
1979-80	**Vancouver**	**NHL**	**47**	**5**	**14**	**19**	**11**	**4**	**1**	**0**	**1**	**6**
1980-81	**Vancouver**	**NHL**	**77**	**18**	**11**	**29**	**57**	**3**	**0**	**0**	**0**	**0**
1981-82	**Colorado**	**NHL**	**80**	**24**	**36**	**60**	**26**	....	....	....	....	....
1982-83	**New Jersey**	**NHL**	**76**	**14**	**19**	**33**	**47**	....	....	....	....	....
1983-84	**Minnesota**	**NHL**	**68**	**7**	**10**	**17**	**54**	**12**	**1**	**2**	**3**	**22**
1984-85	**Minnesota**	**NHL**	**29**	**4**	**7**	**11**	**15**	....	....	....	....	....
	Quebec	**NHL**	**49**	**27**	**24**	**51**	**38**	**18**	**6**	**4**	**10**	**13**
1985-86	**Quebec**	**NHL**	**77**	**26**	**32**	**58**	**64**	**3**	**2**	**1**	**3**	**9**
1986-87	**Quebec**	**NHL**	**46**	**25**	**19**	**44**	**17**	....	....	....	....	....
	Detroit	**NHL**	**35**	**15**	**16**	**31**	**22**	**16**	**4**	**9**	**13**	**6**
1987-88	**Detroit**	**NHL**	**73**	**26**	**27**	**53**	**50**	**16**	**7**	**5**	**12**	**10**
1988-89	**Winnipeg**	**NHL**	**75**	**31**	**37**	**68**	**36**	....	....	....	....	....
1989-90	**Winnipeg**	**NHL**	**79**	**22**	**34**	**56**	**37**	**7**	**3**	**1**	**4**	**2**
	NHL Totals		**811**	**244**	**286**	**530**	**474**	**79**	**24**	**22**	**46**	**68**

Traded to **Winnipeg** by **Vancouver** with Vancouver's fourth-round choice (Tom Martin) in the 1982 Entry Draft as compensation for Vancouver's signing of Ivan Hlinka, July 15, 1981. Traded to **Colorado** by **Winnipeg** with Winnipeg's third round choice (Dave Kasper) in 1982 Entry Draft for Lucien DeBlois, July 15, 1981. Traded to **Minnesota** by **New Jersey** for Dave Lewis, October 3, 1983. Traded to **Quebec** by **Minnesota** with Brad Maxwell for Tony McKegney and Bo Berglund, December 14, 1984. Traded to **Detroit** by **Quebec** with Gilbert Delorme and Mark Kumpel for Basil McRae, John Ogrodnick and Doug Shedden, January 17, 1987. Traded to **Winnipeg** by **Detroit** for Paul MacLean, June 13, 1988.

ASTLEY, MARK

Defense. Shoots left. 5'11", 185 lbs. Born, Calgary, Alta., March 30, 1969.
(Buffalo's 9th choice, 194th overall, in 1990 Entry Draft).

			Regular Season					Playoffs				
Season	Club	Lea	GP	G	A	TP	PIM	GP	G	A	TP	PIM
1988-89	Lake Superior	CCHA	42	3	12	15	26	....	....	....	....	....
1989-90	Lake Superior	CCHA	43	7	25	32	29	....	....	....	....	....

ATCHEYNUM, BLAIR

Right wing. Shoots right. 6'2", 190 lbs. Born, Estevan, Sask., April 20, 1969.
(Hartford's 2nd choice, 52nd overall, in 1989 Entry Draft).

			Regular Season					Playoffs				
Season	Club	Lea	GP	G	A	TP	PIM	GP	G	A	TP	PIM
1985-86	Saskatoon	WHL	19	1	4	5	22	....	....	....	....	....
1986-87	Saskatoon	WHL	21	0	4	4	4	....	....	....	....	....
	Swift Current	WHL	5	2	1	3	0	....	....	....	....	....
	Moose Jaw	WHL	12	3	0	3	2	....	....	....	....	....
1987-88	Moose Jaw	WHL	60	32	16	48	52	....	....	....	....	....
1988-89a	Moose Jaw	WHL	71	70	68	138	70	7	2	5	7	13
1989-90	Binghamton	AHL	78	20	21	41	45	....	....	....	....	....

a WHL First All-Star Team (1989)

AUDETTE, DONALD

Right wing. Shoots right. 5'8", 180 lbs. Born, Laval, Que., September 23, 1969.
(Buffalo's 8th choice, 183rd overall, in 1989 Entry Draft).

			Regular Season					Playoffs				
Season	Club	Lea	GP	G	A	TP	PIM	GP	G	A	TP	PIM
1986-87	Laval	QMJHL	66	17	22	39	36	14	2	6	8	10
1987-88	Laval	QMJHL	63	48	61	109	56	14	7	12	19	20
1988-89a	Laval	QMJHL	70	76	85	161	123	17	17	12	29	43
1989-90	**Buffalo**	**NHL**	....	....	....	....	....	**2**	**0**	**0**	**0**	**0**
bc	Rochester	AHL	70	42	46	88	78	15	9	8	17	29
	NHL Totals		....	....	....	....	....	**2**	**0**	**0**	**0**	**0**

a QMJHL First All-Star Team (1989)
b AHL First All-Star Team (1990)
c Won Dudley "Red" Garret Memorial Trophy (Top Rookie-AHL) (1990)

AVERILL, WILLIAM

Defense. Shoots right. 5'11", 175 lbs. Born, Wayland, MA, December 20, 1968.
(NY Islanders' 12th choice, 244th overall, in 1987 Entry Draft).

			Regular Season					Playoffs				
Season	Club	Lea	GP	G	A	TP	PIM	GP	G	A	TP	PIM
1987-88	Northeastern	H.E.	36	2	23	25	36	....	....	....	....	....
1988-89	Northeastern	H.E.	36	4	16	20	40	....	....	....	....	....
1989-90	Northeastern	H.E.	35	6	13	19	41	....	....	....	....	....

BABCOCK, BOBBY

Defense. Shoots left. 6'1", 225 lbs. Born, Agincourt, Ont., August 3, 1968.
(Washington's 11th choice, 208th overall, in 1986 Entry Draft).

			Regular Season					Playoffs				
Season	Club	Lea	GP	G	A	TP	PIM	GP	G	A	TP	PIM
1985-86	S.S. Marie	OHL	50	1	7	8	188	....	....	....	....	....
1986-87	S.S. Marie	OHL	62	7	8	15	243	4	0	0	0	11
1987-88	S.S. Marie	OHL	8	0	2	2	30	....	....	....	....	....
	Cornwall	OHL	42	0	16	16	120	....	....	....	....	....
1988-89	Cornwall	OHL	42	0	9	9	163	18	1	3	4	29
1989-90	Baltimore	AHL	67	0	4	4	249	7	0	0	0	23

BABE, WARREN

Left wing. Shoots left. 6'3", 200 lbs. Born, Medicine Hat, Alta., September 7, 1968
(Minnesota's 1st choice, 12th overall, in 1986 Entry Draft).

			Regular Season					Playoffs				
Season	Club	Lea	GP	G	A	TP	PIM	GP	G	A	TP	PIM
1985-86	Lethbridge	WHL	63	33	24	57	125	....	....	....	....	....
1986-87	Swift Current	WHL	16	8	12	20	19	....	....	....	....	....
	Kamloops	WHL	52	28	45	73	109	11	4	6	10	8
1987-88	**Minnesota**	**NHL**	**6**	**0**	**1**	**1**	**4**	....	....	....	....	....
	Kalamazoo	IHL	6	0	0	0	7	....	....	....	....	....
	Kamloops	WHL	32	17	19	36	73	18	5	12	17	42
1988-89	**Minnesota**	**NHL**	**14**	**2**	**3**	**5**	**19**	**2**	**0**	**0**	**0**	**0**
	Kalamazoo	IHL	62	18	24	42	102	6	1	4	5	24
1989-90	DID NOT PLAY — INJURED											
	NHL Totals		**20**	**2**	**4**	**6**	**23**	**2**	**0**	**0**	**0**	**0**

BABYCH, DAVID MICHAEL (DAVE) (BAB-itch)

Defense. Shoots left. 6'2", 215 lbs. Born, Edmonton, Alta., May 23, 1961.
(Winnipeg's 1st choice, 2nd overall, in 1980 Entry Draft).

			Regular Season					Playoffs				
Season	Club	Lea	GP	G	A	TP	PIM	GP	G	A	TP	PIM
1978-79	Portland	WHL	67	20	59	79	63	25	7	22	29	22
1979-80ab	Portland	WHL	50	22	60	82	71	8	1	10	11	2
1980-81	**Winnipeg**	**NHL**	**69**	**6**	**38**	**44**	**90**	....	....	....	....	....
1981-82	**Winnipeg**	**NHL**	**79**	**19**	**49**	**68**	**92**	**4**	**1**	**2**	**3**	**29**
1982-83	**Winnipeg**	**NHL**	**79**	**13**	**61**	**74**	**56**	**3**	**0**	**0**	**0**	**0**
1983-84	**Winnipeg**	**NHL**	**66**	**18**	**39**	**57**	**62**	**3**	**1**	**1**	**2**	**0**
1984-85	**Winnipeg**	**NHL**	**78**	**13**	**49**	**62**	**78**	**8**	**2**	**7**	**9**	**6**
1985-86	**Winnipeg**	**NHL**	**19**	**4**	**12**	**16**	**14**	....	....	....	....	....
	Hartford	**NHL**	**62**	**10**	**43**	**53**	**36**	**8**	**1**	**3**	**4**	**14**
1986-87	**Hartford**	**NHL**	**66**	**8**	**33**	**41**	**44**	**6**	**1**	**1**	**2**	**14**
1987-88	**Hartford**	**NHL**	**71**	**14**	**36**	**50**	**54**	**6**	**3**	**2**	**5**	**2**
1988-89	**Hartford**	**NHL**	**70**	**6**	**41**	**47**	**54**	**4**	**1**	**5**	**6**	**2**
1989-90	**Hartford**	**NHL**	**72**	**6**	**37**	**43**	**62**	**7**	**1**	**2**	**3**	**0**
	NHL Totals		**731**	**117**	**438**	**555**	**642**	**49**	**11**	**23**	**34**	**67**

a WHL First All-Star Team (1980)
b Named WHL's Top Defenseman (1980)

Played in NHL All-Star Game (1983, 1984)

Traded to **Hartford** by **Winnipeg** for Ray Neufeld, November 21, 1985.

BAILLARGEON, JOEL (BIGH-uhr-ZHAN)

Left wing. Shoots left. 6'1", 205 lbs. Born, Quebec City, Que., October 6, 1964.
(Winnipeg's 5th choice, 109th overall, in 1983 Entry Draft).

			Regular Season					Playoffs				
Season	Club	Lea	GP	G	A	TP	PIM	GP	G	A	TP	PIM
1981-82	Trois Rivieres	QMJHL	26	1	3	4	47	22	1	1	2	58
1982-83	Trois Rivieres	QMJHL	29	4	5	9	197	....	....	....	....	....
	Hull	QMJHL	25	15	7	22	76	7	0	1	1	16
1983-84	Chicoutimi	QMJHL	60	48	35	83	184	....	....	....	....	....
	Sherbrooke	AHL	8	0	0	0	26	....	....	....	....	....
1984-85	Granby	QMJHL	32	25	24	49	160	....	....	....	....	....
1985-86	Sherbrooke	AHL	56	6	12	18	115	....	....	....	....	....
1986-87	**Winnipeg**	**NHL**	**11**	**0**	**1**	**1**	**15**	....	....	....	....	....
	Sherbrooke	AHL	44	9	18	27	137	6	2	2	4	27
	Fort Wayne	IHL	4	1	1	2	37	....	....	....	....	....
1987-88	**Winnipeg**	**NHL**	**4**	**0**	**1**	**1**	**12**	....	....	....	....	....
	Moncton	AHL	48	8	14	22	133	....	....	....	....	....
1988-89	**Quebec**	**NHL**	**5**	**0**	**0**	**0**	**4**	....	....	....	....	....
	Halifax	NHL	53	11	19	30	122	4	1	0	1	26
1989-90	Halifax	AHL	21	0	3	3	39	....	....	....	....	....
	NHL Totals		**20**	**0**	**2**	**2**	**31**	....	....	....	....	....

Traded to **Quebec** by **Winnipeg** for future considerations, July 29, 1988.

BAKER, JAMIE

Center. Shoots right. 6', 190 lbs. Born, Ottawa, Ont., August 31, 1966.
(Quebec's 2nd choice, 8th overall, in 1988 Supplemental Draft).

			Regular Season					Playoffs				
Season	**Club**	**Lea**	**GP**	**G**	**A**	**TP**	**PIM**	**GP**	**G**	**A**	**TP**	**PIM**
1985-86	St. Lawrence	ECAC	31	9	16	25	52	....	....	....	....	....
1986-87	St. Lawrence	ECAC	32	8	24	32	59	....	....	....	....	....
1987-88	St. Lawrence	ECAC	34	26	24	50	38	....	....	....	....	....
1988-89	St. Lawrence	ECAC	13	11	16	27	16	....	....	....	....	....
1989-90	**Quebec**	**NHL**	**1**	**0**	**0**	**0**	**0**	....	....	....	....	....
	Halifax	AHL	74	17	43	60	47	6	0	0	0	7
	NHL Totals		**1**	**0**	**0**	**0**	**0**	....	....	....	....	....

BAKOVIC, PETER GEORGE (BAK-oh-VIHK)

Right wing. Shoots right. 6'2", 200 lbs. Born, Thunder Bay, Ont., January 31, 1965.

			Regular Season					Playoffs				
Season	**Club**	**Lea**	**GP**	**G**	**A**	**TP**	**PIM**	**GP**	**G**	**A**	**TP**	**PIM**
1983-84	Kitchener	OHL	28	2	6	8	87	....	....	....	....	....
	Windsor	OHL	35	10	25	35	74	3	0	2	2	14
1984-85	Windsor	OHL	58	26	48	74	259	3	0	0	0	12
1985-86	Moncton	AHL	80	18	36	54	349	10	2	2	4	30
1986-87	Moncton	AHL	77	17	34	51	280	6	3	3	6	54
1987-88	**Vancouver**	**NHL**	**10**	**2**	**0**	**2**	**48**	....	....	....	....	....
	Salt Lake	IHL	39	16	27	43	221	....	....	....	....	....
1988-89	Milwaukee	IHL	40	16	14	30	211	11	4	4	8	46
1989-90	Milwaukee	IHL	56	19	30	49	230	6	4	1	5	52
	NHL Totals		**10**	**2**	**0**	**2**	**48**	....	....	....	....	....

Signed as a free agent by **Calgary**, October 10, 1985. Traded to **Vancouver** by **Calgary** with Brian Bradley and Kevin Guy for Craig Coxe, March 6, 1988.

BALDERIS, HELMUT

Right wing. Shoots right. 5'11, 190 lbs. Born, Riga, Latvia, June 30, 1952.
(Minnesota's 12th choice, 238th overall, in 1989 Entry Draft).

			Regular Season					Playoffs				
Season	**Club**	**Lea**	**GP**	**G**	**A**	**TP**	**PIM**	**GP**	**G**	**A**	**TP**	**PIM**
1973-74	Dynamo Riga	USSR	24	9	6	15	13	....	....	....	....	....
1974-75	Dynamo Riga	USSR	36	34	14	48	20	....	....	....	....	....
1975-76	Dynamo Riga	USSR	36	31	14	45	18	....	....	....	....	....
1976-77	Dynamo Riga	USSR	35	40	23	63	57	....	....	....	....	....
1977-78	CSKA	USSR	36	17	17	34	30	....	....	....	....	....
1978-79	CSKA	USSR	41	24	24	48	53	....	....	....	....	....
1979-80	CSKA	USSR	42	26	35	61	21	....	....	....	....	....
1980-81	Dynamo Riga	USSR	44	26	24	50	28	....	....	....	....	....
1981-82	Dynamo Riga	USSR	50	39	24	63	50	....	....	....	....	....
1982-83	Dynamo Riga	USSR	40	32	31	63	39	....	....	....	....	....
1983-84	Dynamo Riga	USSR	39	24	15	39	18	....	....	....	....	....
1984-85	Dynamo Riga	USSR	39	31	20	51	52	....	....	....	....	....
1985-86			DID NOT PLAY									
1986-87			DID NOT PLAY									
1987-88			DID NOT PLAY									
1988-89			DID NOT PLAY									
1989-90	**Minnesota**	**NHL**	**26**	**3**	**6**	**9**	**2**	....	....	....	....	....
	NHL Totals		**26**	**3**	**6**	**9**	**2**	....	....	....	....	....

BALL, MARTYN

Left wing. Shoots left. 6'2", 175 lbs. Born, Toronto, Ont., June 12, 1968.
(St. Louis' 9th choice, 178th overall, in 1986 Entry Draft).

			Regular Season					Playoffs				
Season	**Club**	**Lea**	**GP**	**G**	**A**	**TP**	**PIM**	**GP**	**G**	**A**	**TP**	**PIM**
1986-87	St. Lawrence	ECAC	31	11	2	13	14	....	....	....	....	....
1987-88	St. Lawrence	ECAC	33	5	15	20	18	....	....	....	....	....
1988-89	St. Lawrence	ECAC	36	11	15	26	40	....	....	....	....	....
1989-90	St. Lawrence	ECAC	31	9	11	20	40	....	....	....	....	....

BALLANTYNE, JEFF

Defense. Shoots left. 6'1", 203 lbs. Born, Elmira, Ont., January 7, 1969.
(Washington's 1st choice, 36th overall, in 1987 Entry Draft).

			Regular Season					Playoffs				
Season	**Club**	**Lea**	**GP**	**G**	**A**	**TP**	**PIM**	**GP**	**G**	**A**	**TP**	**PIM**
1986-87	Ottawa	OHL	65	2	13	15	75	5	0	0	0	9
1987-88	Ottawa	OHL	DID NOT PLAY — INJURED									
1988-89	Ottawa	OHL	61	3	21	24	155	9	0	0	0	24
1989-90	Owen Sound	OHL	58	5	14	19	136	12	1	1	2	14

BANCROFT, STEVE

Defense. Shoots left. 6'1", 215 lbs. Born, Toronto, Ont., October 6, 1970.
(Toronto's 3rd choice, 21st overall, in 1989 Entry Draft).

			Regular Season					Playoffs				
Season	**Club**	**Lea**	**GP**	**G**	**A**	**TP**	**PIM**	**GP**	**G**	**A**	**TP**	**PIM**
1988-89	Belleville	OHL	66	7	30	37	99	5	0	2	2	10
1989-90	Belleville	OHL	53	10	33	43	135	11	3	9	12	38

BANNISTER, DARIN

Defense. Shoots right. 6', 185 lbs. Born, Calgary, Alta., January 16, 1967.
(Detroit's 11th choice, 200th overall, in 1987 Entry Draft).

			Regular Season					Playoffs				
Season	**Club**	**Lea**	**GP**	**G**	**A**	**TP**	**PIM**	**GP**	**G**	**A**	**TP**	**PIM**
1986-87	Ill.-Chicago	CCHA	38	4	16	20	38	....	....	....	....	....
1987-88	Ill.-Chicago	CCHA	39	2	26	28	96	....	....	....	....	....
1988-89	Ill.-Chicago	CCHA	41	7	26	33	88	....	....	....	....	....
1989-90	Ill.-Chicago	CCHA	37	5	22	27	72	....	....	....	....	....

BARBE, MARIO (BARB)

Defense. Shoots left. 6'1", 209 lbs. Born, Cadillac, Que., March 17, 1967.
(Edmonton's 9th choice, 209th overall, in 1985 Entry Draft).

			Regular Season					Playoffs				
Season	**Club**	**Lea**	**GP**	**G**	**A**	**TP**	**PIM**	**GP**	**G**	**A**	**TP**	**PIM**
1984-85	Chicoutimi	QMJHL	64	2	13	15	211	14	0	2	2	36
1985-86	Granby	QMJHL	70	5	25	30	261	....	....	....	..	....
1986-87	Granby	QMJHL	65	7	25	32	356	7	1	5	6	38
1987-88	Granby	QMJHL	45	8	10	18	294	5	1	4	5	16
1988-89	Cape Breton	AHL	70	1	11	12	137	....	....	....	....	....
1989-90	Cape Breton	AHL	64	0	15	15	138	4	0	0	0	4

BARBER, DON

Left wing. Shoots left. 6'1", 205 lbs. Born, Victoria, B.C., December 2, 1964.
(Edmonton's 5th choice, 120th over all, in 1983 Entry Draft).

			Regular Season					Playoffs				
Season	**Club**	**Lea**	**GP**	**G**	**A**	**TP**	**PIM**	**GP**	**G**	**A**	**TP**	**PIM**
1984-85	Bowling Green	CCHA	39	15	22	37	44	....	....	....	....	....
1985-86	Bowling Green	CCHA	35	21	22	43	64	....	....	....	....	....
1986-87	Bowling Green	CCHA	43	29	34	63	107	....	....	....	....	....
1987-88	Bowling Green	CCHA	38	18	47	65	62	....	....	....	....	....
1988-89	**Minnesota**	**NHL**	**23**	**8**	**5**	**13**	**8**	**4**	**1**	**1**	**2**	**2**
	Kalamazoo	IHL	39	14	17	31	23	....	....	....	....	....
1989-90	**Minnesota**	**NHL**	**44**	**15**	**19**	**34**	**32**	**7**	**3**	**3**	**6**	**8**
	Kalamazoo	IHL	10	4	4	8	38	....	....	....	....	....
	NHL Totals		**67**	**23**	**24**	**47**	**40**	**11**	**4**	**4**	**8**	**10**

Traded to **Minnesota** by **Edmonton** with Marc Habscheid and Emanuel Viveiros for Gord Sherven and Don Biggs, December 20, 1985.

BARKLEY, MICHAEL

Right wing. Shoots right. 6', 185 lbs. Born, Port Alberni, B.C., April 7, 1970.
(Buffalo's 6th choice, 119th overall, in 1989 Entry Draft).

			Regular Season					Playoffs				
Season	**Club**	**Lea**	**GP**	**G**	**A**	**TP**	**PIM**	**GP**	**G**	**A**	**TP**	**PIM**
1988-89	U. of Maine	H.E.	41	12	13	25	16	....	....	....	....	....
1989-90	U. of Maine	H.E.	43	11	19	30	20	....	....	....	....	....

BARKOVICH, RICHARD (RICK)

Center. Shoots left. 5'10", 185 lbs. Born, Kirkland Lake, Ont., April 25, 1964.

			Regular Season					Playoffs				
Season	**Club**	**Lea**	**GP**	**G**	**A**	**TP**	**PIM**	**GP**	**G**	**A**	**TP**	**PIM**
1986-87	Brantford	Sr.	35	31	32	63	22	....	....	....	....	....
1987-88	Salt Lake	IHL	79	34	25	59	65	17	9	11	20	18
1988-89	Indianapolis	IHL	78	32	35	67	81	....	....	....	....	....
1989-90	Salt Lake	IHL	71	20	23	43	55	7	1	1	2	4

Signed as a free agent by **Calgary**, October 10, 1987.

BARNES, STU

Center. Shoots right. 5'10", 175 lbs. Born, Edmonton, Alta., December 25, 1970.
(Winnipeg's 1st choice, 4th overall, in 1989 Entry Draft).

			Regular Season					Playoffs				
Season	**Club**	**Lea**	**GP**	**G**	**A**	**TP**	**PIM**	**GP**	**G**	**A**	**TP**	**PIM**
1987-88	N. Westminster	WHL	71	37	64	101	88	5	2	3	5	6
1988-89 ab	Tri-Cities	WHL	70	59	82	141	117	7	6	5	11	10
1989-90	Tri-Cities	WHL	63	52	92	144	165	7	1	5	6	26

a WHL West Second All-Star Team (1989)
b WHL Player of the Year (1989)

BARNETT, BRETT

Left wing. Shoots left. 6'3", 185 lbs. Born, Toronto, Ont., October 12, 1967.
(NY Rangers' 11th choice, 205th overall, in 1987 Entry Draft).

			Regular Season					Playoffs				
Season	**Club**	**Lea**	**GP**	**G**	**A**	**TP**	**PIM**	**GP**	**G**	**A**	**TP**	**PIM**
1987-88	Lake Superior	CCHA	44	16	23	39	124	....	....	....	....	....
1988-89	Lake Superior	CCHA	30	15	11	26	104	....	....	....	....	....
1989-90	Kalamazoo	IHL	35	5	5	10	38	....	....	....	....	....

Rights traded to **Minnesota** by **NY Rangers** with Paul Jerrard, the rights to Mike Sullivan, and Los Angeles' third-round choice (Murray Garbutt) in 1989 Entry Draft - acquired March 10, 1987 by Minnesota - for Brian Lawton, Igor Liba and the rights to Eric Bennett, October 11, 1988.

BARON, MURRAY

Defense. Shoots left. 6'3", 215 lbs. Born, Prince George, B.C., June 1, 1967.
(Philadelphia's 7th choice, 167th overall, in 1986 Entry Draft).

			Regular Season					Playoffs				
Season	**Club**	**Lea**	**GP**	**G**	**A**	**TP**	**PIM**	**GP**	**G**	**A**	**TP**	**PIM**
1986-87	North Dakota	WCHA	41	4	10	14	62	....	....	....	....	....
1987-88	North Dakota	WCHA	41	1	10	11	95	....	....	....	....	....
1988-89	North Dakota	WCHA	40	2	6	8	92	....	....	....	....	....
	Hershey	AHL	9	0	3	3	8	....	....	....	....	....
1989-90	**Philadelphia**	**NHL**	**16**	**2**	**2**	**4**	**12**	....	....	....	....	....
	Hershey	AHL	50	0	10	10	101	....	....	....	....	....
	NHL Totals		**16**	**2**	**2**	**4**	**12**	....	....	....	....	....

BARR, DAVID (DAVE)

Right wing. Shoots right. 6'1", 195 lbs. Born, Edmonton, Alta., November 30, 1960.

			Regular Season					Playoffs				
Season	Club	Lea	GP	G	A	TP	PIM	GP	G	A	TP	PIM
1979-80	Lethbridge	WHL	60	16	38	54	47	....	....	....	....	....
1980-81	Lethbridge	WHL	72	26	62	88	106	....	....	....	....	....
1981-82	Erie	AHL	76	18	48	66	29	....	....	....	....	....
	Boston	**NHL**	**2**	**0**	**0**	**0**	**0**	**5**	**1**	**0**	**1**	**0**
1982-83	Baltimore	AHL	72	27	51	78	67	....	....	....	....	....
	Boston	**NHL**	**10**	**1**	**1**	**2**	**7**	**10**	**0**	**0**	**0**	**2**
1983-84	**NY Rangers**	**NHL**	**6**	**0**	**0**	**0**	**2**	....	....	....	....	....
	St. Louis	**NHL**	**1**	**0**	**0**	**0**	**0**	....	....	....	....	....
	Tulsa	CHL	50	28	37	65	24	....	....	....	....	....
1984-85	**St. Louis**	**NHL**	**75**	**16**	**18**	**34**	**32**	**2**	**0**	**0**	**0**	**2**
1985-86	**St. Louis**	**NHL**	**72**	**13**	**38**	**51**	**70**	**11**	**1**	**1**	**2**	**14**
1986-87	**St. Louis**	**NHL**	**2**	**0**	**0**	**0**	**0**	....	....	....	....	....
	Hartford	**NHL**	**30**	**2**	**4**	**6**	**19**	....	....	....	....	....
	Detroit	**NHL**	**37**	**13**	**13**	**26**	**49**	**13**	**1**	**0**	**1**	**14**
1987-88	**Detroit**	**NHL**	**51**	**14**	**26**	**40**	**58**	**16**	**5**	**7**	**12**	**22**
1988-89	**Detroit**	**NHL**	**73**	**27**	**32**	**59**	**69**	**6**	**3**	**1**	**4**	**6**
1989-90	**Detroit**	**NHL**	**62**	**10**	**25**	**35**	**45**	....	....	....	....	....
	Adirondack	AHL	9	1	14	15	17	....	....	....	....	....
	NHL Totals		**421**	**96**	**157**	**253**	**351**	**63**	**11**	**9**	**20**	**60**

Signed as free agent by **Boston**, September 28, 1981. Traded to **NY Rangers** by **Boston** for Dave Silk, October 5, 1983. Traded to **St. Louis** by **NY Rangers** with NY Rangers' third-round choice (Alan Perry) in the 1984 Entry Draft for Larry Patey and Bob Brooke, March 5, 1984. Traded to **Hartford** by **St. Louis** for Tim Bothwell, October 21, 1986. Traded to **Detroit** by **Hartford** for Randy Ladouceur, January 12, 1987.

BARRIE, LEN

Center. Shoots left. 5'11", 190 lbs. Born, Kelowna, B.C., June 4, 1969.
(Edmonton's 7th choice, 124th overall, in 1988 Entry Draft).

			Regular Season					Playoffs				
Season	Club	Lea	GP	G	A	TP	PIM	GP	G	A	TP	PIM
1985-86	Calgary	WHL	32	3	0	3	18	....	....	....	....	....
1986-87	Calgary	WHL	34	13	13	26	81	....	....	....	....	....
	Victoria	WHL	34	7	6	13	92	5	0	1	1	15
1987-88	Victoria	WHL	70	37	49	86	192	8	2	0	2	29
1988-89	Victoria	WHL	67	39	48	87	157	7	5	2	7	23
1989-90	**Philadelphia**	**NHL**	**1**	**0**	**0**	**0**	**0**	....	....	....	....	....
a	Kamloops	WHL	70	*85	*100	*185	108	17	*14	23	*37	24
	NHL Totals		**1**	**0**	**0**	**0**	**0**	....	....	....	....	....

a WHL West First All-Star Team (1990)

BARTEL, ROBIN DALE

Defense. Shoots left. 6', 200 lbs. Born, Drake, Sask., May 16, 1961

			Regular Season					Playoffs				
Season	Club	Lea	GP	G	A	TP	PIM	GP	G	A	TP	PIM
1982-83a	U. of Sask.	CWUAA	27	6	7	13	36	....	....	....	....	....
1983-84	Cdn. National	....	51	4	6	10	50	....	....	....	....	....
	Cdn. Olympic	....	6	0	1	1	4	....	....	....	....	....
1984-85	Moncton	AHL	41	4	11	15	54	....	....	....	....	....
1985-86	**Calgary**	**NHL**	**1**	**0**	**0**	**0**	**0**	**6**	**0**	**0**	**0**	**16**
	Moncton	AHL	74	4	21	25	100	3	0	0	0	0
1986-87	**Vancouver**	**NHL**	**40**	**0**	**1**	**1**	**14**	....	....	....	....	....
	Fredericton	AHL	10	0	2	2	15	....	....	....	....	....
1987-88	Fredericton	AHL	37	1	10	11	54	3	0	0	0	9
1988-89	Moncton	AHL	23	0	4	4	19	10	0	1	1	18
	Milwaukee	IHL	26	1	5	6	59	....	....	....	....	....
1989-90	Cdn. National	....	23	1	1	2	10	....	....	....	....	....
	NHL Totals		**41**	**0**	**1**	**1**	**14**	**6**	**0**	**0**	**0**	**16**

a CWUAA Freshman of the Year, Second All-Star Team (1983)
b IHL First All-Star Team (1990)

Signed as a free agent by **Calgary**, July 1, 1985. Signed as a free agent by **Vancouver**, June 27, 1986.

BARTLEY, WADE

Defense. Shoots right. 6', 190 lbs. Born, Killarney, Man., May 16, 1970.
(Washington's 3rd choice, 41st overall, in 1988 Entry Draft).

			Regular Season					Playoffs				
Season	Club	Lea	GP	G	A	TP	PIM	GP	G	A	TP	PIM
1988-89	North Dakota	WCHA	32	1	1	2	8	....	....	....	....	....
1989-90	Sudbury	OHL	60	23	36	59	53	7	1	4	5	10

BASSEGIO, DAVID

Defense. Shoots left. 6'3", 210 lbs. Born, Niagara Falls, Ont., October 28, 1967.
(Buffalo's 5th choice, 68th overall, in 1986 Entry Draft).

			Regular Season					Playoffs				
Season	Club	Lea	GP	G	A	TP	PIM	GP	G	A	TP	PIM
1985-86	Yale	ECAC	30	7	17	24	54	....	....	....	....	....
1986-87	Yale	ECAC	29	8	17	25	52	....	....	....	....	....
1987-88	Yale	ECAC	24	4	22	26	67	....	....	....	....	....
1988-89a	Yale	ECAC	28	10	23	33	41	....	....	....	....	....
1989-90	Indianapolis	IHL	10	1	7	8	2	10	2	4	6	6
	Rochester	AHL	41	13	15	18	41	....	....	....	....	....

a ECAC Second All-Star Team (1989)

BASSEN, BOB

Center. Shoots left. 5'10", 180 lbs. Born, Calgary, Alta., May 6, 1965.

			Regular Season					Playoffs				
Season	Club	Lea	GP	G	A	TP	PIM	GP	G	A	TP	PIM
1982-83	Medicine Hat	WHL	4	3	2	5	0	3	0	0	0	4
1983-84	Medicine Hat	WHL	72	29	29	58	93	14	5	11	16	12
1984-85a	Medicine Hat	WHL	65	32	50	82	143	10	2	8	10	39
1985-86	**NY Islanders**	**NHL**	**11**	**2**	**1**	**3**	**6**	**3**	**0**	**1**	**1**	**0**
	Springfield	AHL	54	13	21	34	111	....	....	....	....	....
1986-87	**NY Islanders**	**NHL**	**77**	**7**	**10**	**17**	**89**	**14**	**1**	**2**	**3**	**21**
1987-88	**NY Islanders**	**NHL**	**77**	**6**	**16**	**22**	**99**	**6**	**0**	**1**	**1**	**23**
1988-89	**NY Islanders**	**NHL**	**19**	**1**	**4**	**5**	**21**	....	....	....	....	....
	Chicago	**NHL**	**49**	**4**	**12**	**16**	**62**	**10**	**1**	**1**	**2**	**34**
1989-90	**Chicago**	**NHL**	**6**	**1**	**1**	**2**	**8**	**1**	**0**	**0**	**0**	**2**
b	Indianapolis	IHL	73	22	32	54	179	12	3	8	11	33
	NHL Totals		**239**	**21**	**44**	**65**	**279**	**33**	**2**	**5**	**7**	**78**

a WHL First All-Star Team (1985)
b IHL First All-Star Team (1990)

Signed as a free agent by **NY Islanders**, October 19, 1984.Traded to **Chicago** by **NY Islanders** with Steve Konroyd for Marc Bergevin and Gary Nylund, November 25, 1988.

BASSEN, MARK

Right wing. Shoots right. 5'9", 155 lbs. Born, Calgary, Alta., April 9, 1969.

			Regular Season					Playoffs				
Season	Club	Lea	GP	G	A	TP	PIM	GP	G	A	TP	PIM
1986-87	Calgary	WHL	4	1	1	2	4	....	....	....	....	....
1987-88	Lethbridge	WHL	70	19	28	47	48	....	....	....	....	....
1988-89	Lethbridge	WHL	7	1	4	5	12	....	....	....	....	....
	Brandon	WHL	65	31	65	96	74	....	....	....	....	....
1989-90	Hershey	AHL	57	5	9	14	128	....	....	....	....	....

Signed as a free agent by **Philadelphia**, October 5, 1989.

BATEMAN, ROBERTSON (ROB)

Right wing. Shoots right. 6', 175 lbs. Born, LaSalle, Que., January 2, 1968.
(Winnipeg's 6th choice, 113th overall, in 1986 Entry Draft).

			Regular Season					Playoffs				
Season	Club	Lea	GP	G	A	TP	PIM	GP	G	A	TP	PIM
1986-87	U. of Vermont	ECAC	32	2	3	5	78	....	....	....	....	....
1987-88	U. of Vermont	ECAC	34	1	3	4	64	....	....	....	....	....
1988-89	U. of Vermont	ECAC	32	1	4	5	38	....	....	....	....	....
1989-90	U. of Vermont	ECAC	31	0	4	4	62	....	....	....	....	....

BATTERS, JEFF

Defense. Shoots right. 6'2", 215 lbs. Born, Victoria, B.C., October 23, 1970.
(St. Louis' 7th choice, 135th overall, in 1989 Entry Draft).

			Regular Season					Playoffs				
Season	Club	Lea	GP	G	A	TP	PIM	GP	G	A	TP	PIM
1988-89	Alaska-Anch.	NCAA	33	8	14	22	123	....	....	....	....	....
1989-90	Alaska-Anch.	NCAA	34	6	9	15	102	....	....	....	....	....

BAUER, COLLIN

Defense. Shoots left. 6'1", 180 lbs. Born, Edmonton, Alta., September 6, 1970.
(Edmonton's 4th choice, 61st overall, in 1988 Entry Draft).

			Regular Season					Playoffs				
Season	Club	Lea	GP	G	A	TP	PIM	GP	G	A	TP	PIM
1986-87	Saskatoon	WHL	61	1	25	26	37	11	0	6	6	10
1987-88	Saskatoon	WHL	70	9	53	62	66	10	2	5	7	16
1988-89a	Saskatoon	WHL	61	17	62	79	71	8	1	8	9	8
1989-90	Saskatoon	WHL	29	4	25	29	49	10	1	8	9	14

a WHL East All-Star Team (1989)

BAUMGARTNER, KEN

Defense. Shoots left. 6'1", 200 lbs. Born, Flin, Flon, Man., March 11, 1966
(Buffalo's 12th choice, 245th overall, in 1985 Entry Draft).

			Regular Season					Playoffs				
Season	Club	Lea	GP	G	A	TP	PIM	GP	G	A	TP	PIM
1984-85	Prince Albert	WHL	60	3	9	12	252	13	1	3	4	89
1985-86	Prince Albert	WHL	70	4	23	27	277	20	3	9	12	112
1986-87	New Haven	AHL	13	0	3	3	99	6	0	0	0	60
1987-88	**Los Angeles**	**NHL**	**30**	**2**	**3**	**5**	**189**	**5**	**0**	**1**	**1**	**28**
	New Haven	AHL	48	1	5	6	181	....	....	....	....	....
1988-89	**Los Angeles**	**NHL**	**49**	**1**	**3**	**4**	**288**	**5**	**0**	**0**	**0**	**8**
	New Haven	AHL	10	1	3	4	26	....	....	....	....	....
1989-90	**Los Angeles**	**NHL**	**12**	**1**	**0**	**1**	**28**	....	....	....	....	....
	NY Islanders	**NHL**	**53**	**0**	**5**	**5**	**194**	**4**	**0**	**0**	**0**	**27**
	NHL Totals		**144**	**4**	**11**	**15**	**699**	**14**	**0**	**1**	**1**	**63**

Traded to **Los Angeles** by **Buffalo** with Sean McKenna and Larry Playfair for Brian Engblom and Doug Smith, January 29, 1986. Traded to **NY Islanders** by **Los Angeles** with Hubie McDonough for Mikko Makela, November 29, 1989.

BAVIS, MARK

Center. Shoots left. 6', 175 lbs. Born, Roslindale, MA, March 13, 1970.
(NY Rangers' 10th choice, 181st overall, in 1989 Entry Draft).

			Regular Season					Playoffs				
Season	Club	Lea	GP	G	A	TP	PIM	GP	G	A	TP	PIM
1989-90	Boston U.	H.E.	44	6	5	11	50	....	....	....	....	....

BAVIS, MICHAEL

Right wing. Shoots right. 6', 180 lbs. Born, Roslindale, MA, March 13, 1970.
(Buffalo's 12th choice, 245th overall, in 1989 Entry Draft).

			Regular Season					Playoffs				
Season	Club	Lea	GP	G	A	TP	PIM	GP	G	A	TP	PIM
1989-90	Boston U.	H.E.	44	2	11	13	28	....	....	....	....	....

BAWA, ROBIN
(BAH-wuh)

Right wing. Shoots right. 6'2", 214 lbs.   Born, Chemainus, B.C., March 26, 1966.

			Regular Season					Playoffs			
Season	Club	Lea	GP	G	A	TP	PIM	GP	G	A	TP	PIM
1982-83	Kamloops	WHL	66	10	24	34	17	7	1	2	3	0
1983-84	Kamloops	WHL	64	16	28	44	40	13	4	2	6	4
1984-85	Kamloops	WHL	52	6	19	25	45	15	4	9	13	14
1985-86	Kamloops	WHL	63	29	43	72	78	16	5	13	18	4
1986-87a	Kamloops	WHL	62	57	56	113	91	13	6	7	13	22
1987-88	Fort Wayne	IHL	55	12	27	39	239	6	1	3	4	24
1988-89	Baltimore	AHL	75	23	24	47	205	....	....	....	....	....
1989-90	**Washington**	**NHL**	**5**	**1**	**0**	**1**	**6**	....	....	....	....	....
	Baltimore	AHL	61	7	18	25	189	11	1	2	3	49
	NHL Totals		**5**	**1**	**0**	**1**	**6**	....	....	....	....	....

a WHL West All-Star Team (1987)
Signed as a free agent by **Washington**, May 22, 1987.

BEADLE, STEVE

Defense. Shoots right. 5'11", 185 lbs.   Born, Lansing, MI, May 30, 1968.
(Philadelphia's 1st choice, 4th overall, in 1990 Supplemental Draft).

			Regular Season					Playoffs			
Season	Club	Lea	GP	G	A	TP	PIM	GP	G	A	TP	PIM
1986-87	Michigan St.	CCHA	38	0	9	9	22	....	....	....	....	....
1987-88	Michigan St.	CCHA	45	7	37	44	37	....	....	....	....	....
1988-89	Michigan St.	CCHA	46	14	40	54	35	....	....	....	....	....
1989-90	Michigan St.	CCHA	45	21	36	57	50	....	....	....	....	....

BEAN, TIM

Left wing. Shoots left. 6'1", 200 lbs.   Born, Sault Ste. Marie, Ont., March 9, 1967.
(Toronto's 7th choice, 127th overall, in 1985 Entry Draft).

			Regular Season					Playoffs			
Season	Club	Lea	GP	G	A	TP	PIM	GP	G	A	TP	PIM
1983-84	Belleville	OHL	63	12	13	25	131	3	0	0	0	0
1984-85	Belleville	OHL	31	10	11	21	60	....	....	....	....	....
	North Bay	OHL	28	13	11	24	61	8	2	5	7	8
1985-86	North Bay	OHL	66	32	34	66	129	10	5	5	10	22
1986-87	North Bay	OHL	65	24	39	63	134	21	4	12	16	65
1987-88	Newmarket	AHL	76	12	16	28	118	....	....	....	....	....
1988-89	Newmarket	AHL	44	4	12	16	55	....	....	....	....	....
	Flint	IHL	3	1	3	4	4	....	....	....	....	....
1989-90	Newmarket	AHL	39	5	10	15	27	....	....	....	....	....

BEAUDETTE, DAN

Center. Shoots right. 6'3", 202 lbs.   Born, St. Paul, MN, February 18, 1968.
(NY Islanders 13th choice, 227th overall, in 1986 Entry Draft).

			Regular Season					Playoffs			
Season	Club	Lea	GP	G	A	TP	PIM	GP	G	A	TP	PIM
1986-87	Miami-Ohio	CCHA	31	5	9	14	26	....	....	....	....	....
1987-88	Miami-Ohio	CCHA	29	3	3	6	12	....	....	....	....	....
1988-89	Miami-Ohio	CCHA	34	5	13	18	32	....	....	....	....	....
1989-90	Miami-Ohio	CCHA	40	8	11	19	30	....	....	....	....	....

BEAULIEU, COREY

Defense. Shoots left. 6'2", 210 lbs.   Born, Winnipeg, Man., September 10, 1969.
(Hartford's 5th choice, 116th overall, in 1989 Entry Draft).

			Regular Season					Playoffs			
Season	Club	Lea	GP	G	A	TP	PIM	GP	G	A	TP	PIM
1985-86	Moose Jaw	WHL	68	3	1	4	111	13	1	1	2	13
1986-87	Moose Jaw	WHL	63	2	7	9	188	9	0	0	0	17
1987-88	Seattle	WHL	67	2	9	11	225	....	....	....	....	....
1988-89	Seattle	WHL	32	0	3	3	134	....	....	....	....	....
	Moose Jaw	WHL	29	3	17	20	91	7	1	2	3	16
1989-90	Binghamton	AHL	56	0	2	2	191	....	....	....	....	....

BEAULIEU, NICOLAS
(boy-YOH)

Left wing. Shoots left. 6'2", 200 lbs.   Born, Rimouski, Que., August 19, 1968.
(Edmonton's 8th choice, 168th overall, in 1986 Entry Draft).

			Regular Season					Playoffs			
Season	Club	Lea	GP	G	A	TP	PIM	GP	G	A	TP	PIM
1985-86	Drummondville	QMJHL	70	11	20	31	93	23	0	1	1	11
1986-87	Drummondville	QMJHL	69	19	34	53	198	8	0	1	1	8
1987-88	Laval	QMJHL	64	39	56	95	240	14	3	13	16	37
1988-89	Cape Breton	AHL	60	10	13	23	85	....	....	....	....	....
1989-90	Phoenix	IHL	71	28	46	72	93	....	....	....	....	....

BECK, BARRY DAVID

Defense. Shoots left. 6'3", 215 lbs.   Born, Vancouver, B.C., June 3, 1957.
(Colorado's 1st choice, 2nd overall, in 1977 Amateur Draft).

			Regular Season					Playoffs			
Season	Club	Lea	GP	G	A	TP	PIM	GP	G	A	TP	PIM
1974-75	N. Westminster	WHL	58	9	33	42	162	18	4	9	13	52
1975-76a	N. Westminster	WHL	68	19	80	99	325	17	3	9	12	58
1976-77abc	N. Westminster	WHL	61	16	46	62	167	12	4	6	10	39
1977-78	**Colorado**	**NHL**	**75**	**22**	**38**	**60**	**89**	2	0	1	1	0
1978-79	**Colorado**	**NHL**	**63**	**14**	**28**	**42**	**91**	....	....	....	....	....
1979-80	**Colorado**	**NHL**	**10**	**1**	**5**	**6**	**8**	....	....	....	....	....
	NY Rangers	**NHL**	**61**	**14**	**45**	**59**	**98**	9	1	4	5	6
1980-81	**NY Rangers**	**NHL**	**75**	**11**	**23**	**34**	**231**	14	5	8	13	32
1981-82	**NY Rangers**	**NHL**	**60**	**9**	**29**	**38**	**111**	10	1	5	6	14
1982-83	**NY Rangers**	**NHL**	**66**	**12**	**22**	**34**	**112**	9	2	4	6	8
1983-84	**NY Rangers**	**NHL**	**72**	**9**	**27**	**36**	**134**	4	1	0	1	6
1984-85	**NY Rangers**	**NHL**	**56**	**7**	**19**	**26**	**65**	3	0	1	1	11
1985-86	**NY Rangers**	**NHL**	**25**	**4**	**8**	**12**	**24**	....	....	....	....	....
1986-87			DID NOT PLAY									
1987-88			DID NOT PLAY									
1988-89			DID NOT PLAY									
1989-90	**Los Angeles**	**NHL**	**52**	**1**	**7**	**8**	**53**	....	....	....	....	....
	NHL Totals		**615**	**104**	**251**	**355**	**1016**	**51**	**10**	**23**	**33**	**77**

a WHL First All-Star Team (1976, 1977)
b Named WHL's Top Defenseman (1977)
c Named WHL's Most Valuable Player (1977)
Played in NHL All-Star Game (1978, 1982)
Traded to **NY Rangers** by **Colorado** for Pat Hickey, Lucien DeBlois, Mike McEwen, Dean Turner and future considerations (Bobby Crawford), November 2, 1979. Traded to **Los Angeles** by **NY Rangers** for NY Islanders' fourth round choice (Jeff Nielson) - previously acquired by Los Angeles - in 1990 Entry Draft, September 1, 1989.

BEERS, BOB

Defense. Shoots right. 6'2", 200 lbs.   Born, Cheektowaga, NY, May 20, 1967.
(Boston's 10th choice, 210th overall, in 1985 Entry Draft).

			Regular Season					Playoffs			
Season	Club	Lea	GP	G	A	TP	PIM	GP	G	A	TP	PIM
1985-86	N. Arizona	NCAA	28	11	39	50	96	....	....	....	....	....
1986-87	U. of Maine	H.E.	38	0	13	13	45	....	....	....	....	....
1987-88	U. of Maine	H.E.	41	3	11	14	72	....	....	....	....	....
1988-89ab	U. of Maine	H.E.	44	10	27	37	53	....	....	....	....	....
1989-90	**Boston**	**NHL**	**3**	**0**	**1**	**1**	**6**	14	1	1	2	18
	Maine	AHL	74	7	36	43	63	....	....	....	....	....
	NHL Totals		**3**	**0**	**1**	**1**	**6**	**14**	**1**	**1**	**2**	**18**

a Hockey East Second All-Star Team (1989)
b NCAA East Second All-American Team (1989)

BELL, BRUCE

Defense. Shoots left. 6', 190 lbs.   Born, Toronto, Ont., February 15, 1965.
(Quebec's 2nd choice, 52nd overall, in 1983 Entry Draft).

			Regular Season					Playoffs			
Season	Club	Lea	GP	G	A	TP	PIM	GP	G	A	TP	PIM
1981-82	S. S. Marie	OHL	67	11	18	29	63	12	0	2	2	24
1982-83	S. S. Marie	OHL	5	2	2	2	2	....	....	....	....	....
	Windsor	OHL	61	10	35	45	39	3	0	4	4	0
1983-84a	Brantford	OHL	63	7	41	48	55	6	0	3	3	6
1984-85b	**Quebec**	**NHL**	**75**	**6**	**31**	**37**	**44**	16	2	2	4	21
1985-86	**St. Louis**	**NHL**	**75**	**2**	**18**	**20**	**43**	14	0	2	2	13
1986-87	**St. Louis**	**NHL**	**45**	**3**	**13**	**16**	**18**	4	1	1	2	7
1987-88	**NY Rangers**	**NHL**	**13**	**1**	**2**	**3**	**8**	....	....	....	....	....
	Colorado	IHL	65	11	34	45	107	4	2	3	5	0
1988-89	Halifax	AHL	12	0	6	6	4	2	0	1	1	2
	Adirondack	AHL	9	1	4	5	4	....	....	....	....	....
1989-90	**Edmonton**	**NHL**	**1**	**0**	**0**	**0**	**0**	....	....	....	....	....
	Cape Breton	AHL	52	8	26	34	64	6	3	4	7	2
	NHL Totals		**209**	**12**	**64**	**76**	**113**	**34**	**3**	**5**	**8**	**41**

a OHL First All-Star Team (1984)
b NHL All-Rookie Team (1985)
Traded to **St. Louis** by **Quebec** for Gilbert Delorme, October 2, 1985. Traded to **NY Rangers** by **St. Louis** with future considerations for Tony McKegney and Rob Whistle, May 28, 1987. Traded to **Quebec** by **NY Rangers** with Jari Gronstrand, Walt Poddubny and NY Rangers' fourth round choice (Eric Dubois) in 1989 Entry Draft for Jason Lafreniere and Normand Rochefort, August 1, 1988.

BELLEFEUILLE, BRIAN

Left wing. Shoots left. 6'2", 185 lbs.   Born, Natick, MA, March 21, 1967.
(Toronto's 9th choice, 174th overall, in 1986 Entry Draft).

			Regular Season					Playoffs			
Season	Club	Lea	GP	G	A	TP	PIM	GP	G	A	TP	PIM
1986-87	Ill.-Chicago	CCHA	2	0	0	0	2	....	....	....	....	....
1987-88	U. of Maine	H.E.	15	2	2	4	30	....	....	....	....	....
1988-89	U. of Maine	H.E.	36	5	10	15	32	....	....	....	....	....
1989-90	U. of Maine	H.E.	42	13	10	23	86	....	....	....	....	....
	Newmarket	AHL	3	0	0	0	0	....	....	....	....	....

BELLOWS, BRIAN

Right wing. Shoots right. 5'11", 200 lbs. Born, St. Catharines, Ont., September 1, 1964.
(Minnesota's 1st choice, 2nd overall, in 1982 Entry Draft).

			Regular Season					Playoffs				
Season	Club	Lea	GP	G	A	TP	PIM	GP	G	A	TP	PIM
1980-81a	Kitchener	OHA	66	49	67	116	23	16	14	13	27	13
1981-82bc	Kitchener	OHL	47	45	52	97	23	15	16	13	29	11
1982-83	**Minnesota**	**NHL**	**78**	**35**	**30**	**65**	**27**	**9**	**5**	**4**	**9**	**18**
1983-84	**Minnesota**	**NHL**	**78**	**41**	**42**	**83**	**66**	**16**	**2**	**12**	**14**	**6**
1984-85	**Minnesota**	**NHL**	**78**	**26**	**36**	**62**	**72**	**9**	**2**	**4**	**6**	**9**
1985-86	**Minnesota**	**NHL**	**77**	**31**	**48**	**79**	**46**	**5**	**5**	**0**	**5**	**16**
1986-87	**Minnesota**	**NHL**	**65**	**26**	**27**	**53**	**34**	....	....	....	....	....
1987-88	**Minnesota**	**NHL**	**77**	**40**	**41**	**81**	**81**	....	....	....	....	....
1988-89	**Minnesota**	**NHL**	**60**	**23**	**27**	**50**	**55**	**5**	**2**	**3**	**5**	**8**
1989-90d	**Minnesota**	**NHL**	**80**	**55**	**44**	**99**	**72**	**7**	**4**	**3**	**7**	**10**
	NHL Totals		**593**	**277**	**295**	**572**	**453**	**51**	**20**	**26**	**46**	**67**

a OHA Third All-Star Team (1981)
b OHL First All-Star Team (1982)
c Most Sportsmanlike Player, Memorial Cup Tournament (1982)
d NHL Second All-Star Team (1990)
Played in NHL All-Star Game (1984, 1988)

BELZILE, ETIENNE

Defense. Shoots left. 6'1", 180 lbs. Born, Quebec City, Que., May 2, 1972.
(Calgary's 4th choice, 41st overall, in 1990 Entry Draft)

			Regular Season					Playoffs				
Season	Club	Lea	GP	G	A	TP	PIM	GP	G	A	TP	PIM
1989-90	Cornell	ECAC	27	1	5	6	22	....	....	....	....	....

BENAK, JAROSLAV

Defense. Shoots left. 6', 185 lbs. Born, Hrdec Brod, Czechoslovakia, April 3, 1964.
(Calgary's 13th choice, 211th overall, in 1983 Entry Draft).

			Regular Season					Playoffs				
Season	Club	Lea	GP	G	A	TP	PIM	GP	G	A	TP	PIM
1986-87	Dukla Jihlava	Czech.	34	1	6	7	....	....	....	....	....	....
1987-88	Dukla Jihlava	Czech.	26	2	8	10	....	....	....	....	....	....
1988-89	Dukla Jihlava	Czech.	28	1	6	7	....	....	....	....	....	....
1989-90	Dukla Jihlava	Czech	47	6	13	19		....	....	....	....	....

BENIC, GEOFF

Left wing. Shoots left. 6'2", 200 lbs. Born, Toronto, Ont., September 1, 1968.
(Chicago's 8th choice, 182nd overall, in 1986 Entry Draft).

			Regular Season					Playoffs				
Season	Club	Lea	GP	G	A	TP	PIM	GP	G	A	TP	PIM
1985-86	Windsor	OHL	59	3	7	10	77	14	0	1	1	10
1986-87	Windsor	OHL	63	9	7	16	169	14	2	1	3	22
1987-88	Windsor	OHL	46	2	4	6	149	12	0	0	0	16
1988-89	Indianapolis	IHL	10	1	0	1	51	....	....	....	....	....
1989-90	Virginia	ECHL	5	2	2	4	6	....	....	....	....	....

BENNETT, ADAM

Defense. Shoots right. 6'4", 205 lbs. Born, Georgetown, Ont., March 30, 1971.
(Chicago's 1st choice, 6th overall, in 1989 Entry Draft).

			Regular Season					Playoffs				
Season	Club	Lea	GP	G	A	TP	PIM	GP	G	A	TP	PIM
1988-89	Sudbury	OHL	66	7	22	29	133	....	....	....	....	....
1989-90a	Sudbury	OHL	65	18	43	61	116	7	1	2	3	23

a OHL Third All-Star Team (1990)

BENNETT, ERIC (RIC)

Left wing. Shoots left. 6'3", 200 lbs. Born, Springfield, MA, July 24, 1967.
(Minnesota's 4th choice, 54th overall, in 1986 Entry Draft).

			Regular Season					Playoffs				
Season	Club	Lea	GP	G	A	TP	PIM	GP	G	A	TP	PIM
1986-87	Providence	H.E.	32	15	12	27	34	....	....	....	....	....
1987-88	Providence	H.E.	33	9	16	25	70	....	....	....	....	....
1988-89a	Providence	H.E.	32	14	32	46	74	....	....	....	....	....
1989-90	**NY Rangers**	**NHL**	**6**	**1**	**0**	**1**	**5**	....	....	....	....	....
b	Providence	H.E.	31	12	24	36	74	....	....	....	....	....
	NHL Totals		**6**	**1**	**0**	**1**	**5**	....	....	....	....	....

a NCAA East Second All-American Team (1989)
b Hockey East All-Star Team (1990)
Rights traded to **NY Rangers** by **Minnesota** with Brian Lawton and Igor Liba for Paul Jerrard and Mark Tinordi, the rights to Bret Barnett and Mike Sullivan, and Los Angeles' third-round choice (Murray Garbutt) in 1989 Entry Draft - acquired March 10, 1987 by Minnesota - October 11, 1988.

BENNING, BRIAN

Defense. Shoots left. 6', 195 lbs. Born, Edmonton, Alta., June 10, 1966.
(St. Louis' 1st choice, 26th overall, in 1984 Entry Draft).

			Regular Season					Playoffs				
Season	Club	Lea	GP	G	A	TP	PIM	GP	G	A	TP	PIM
1983-84	Portland	WHL	38	6	41	47	108	....	....	....	....	....
1984-85	**St. Louis**	**NHL**	**4**	**0**	**2**	**2**	**0**	....	....	....	....	....
	Kamloops	WHL	17	3	18	21	26	....	....	....	....	....
1985-86	**St. Louis**	**NHL**	....	....	....	....	....	**6**	**1**	**2**	**3**	**13**
	Cdn. Olympic	....	60	6	13	19	43	....	....	....	....	....
1986-87a	**St. Louis**	**NHL**	**78**	**13**	**36**	**49**	**110**	**6**	**0**	**4**	**4**	**9**
1987-88	**St. Louis**	**NHL**	**77**	**8**	**29**	**37**	**107**	**10**	**1**	**6**	**7**	**25**
1988-89	**St. Louis**	**NHL**	**66**	**8**	**26**	**34**	**102**	**7**	**1**	**1**	**2**	**11**
1989-90	**St. Louis**	**NHL**	**7**	**1**	**1**	**2**	**2**	....	....	....	....	....
	Los Angeles	**NHL**	**48**	**5**	**18**	**23**	**104**	**7**	**0**	**2**	**2**	**10**
	NHL Totals		**280**	**35**	**112**	**147**	**425**	**36**	**3**	**15**	**18**	**68**

a NHL All-Rookie Team (1987)
Traded to **Los Angeles** by **St Louis** for Los Angeles' third round choice in 1991 Entry Draft, November 10, 1989.

BENNING, JAMES (JIM)

Defense. Shoots left. 6', 185 lbs. Born, Edmonton, Alta., April 29, 1963.
(Toronto's 1st choice, 6th overall, in 1981 Entry Draft).

			Regular Season					Playoffs				
Season	Club	Lea	GP	G	A	TP	PIM	GP	G	A	TP	PIM
1979-80	Portland	WHL	71	11	60	71	42	8	3	9	12	6
1980-81ab	Portland	WHL	72	28	*111	139	61	9	1	5	6	16
1981-82	**Toronto**	**NHL**	**74**	**7**	**24**	**31**	**46**	....	....	....	....	....
1982-83	**Toronto**	**NHL**	**74**	**5**	**17**	**22**	**47**	**4**	**1**	**1**	**2**	**2**
1983-84	**Toronto**	**NHL**	**79**	**12**	**39**	**51**	**66**	....	....	....	....	....
1984-85	**Toronto**	**NHL**	**80**	**9**	**35**	**44**	**55**	....	....	....	....	....
1985-86	**Toronto**	**NHL**	**52**	**4**	**21**	**25**	**71**	....	....	....	....	....
1986-87	**Toronto**	**NHL**	**5**	**0**	**0**	**0**	**4**	....	....	....	....	....
	Newmarket	AHL	10	1	5	6	0	....	....	....	....	....
	Vancouver	**NHL**	**54**	**2**	**11**	**13**	**40**	....	....	....	....	....
1987-88	**Vancouver**	**NHL**	**77**	**7**	**26**	**33**	**58**	....	....	....	....	....
1988-89	**Vancouver**	**NHL**	**65**	**3**	**9**	**12**	**48**	**3**	**0**	**0**	**0**	**0**
1989-90	**Vancouver**	**NHL**	**45**	**3**	**9**	**12**	**26**	....	....	....	....	....
	NHL Totals		**605**	**52**	**191**	**243**	**461**	**7**	**1**	**1**	**2**	**2**

a WHL First All-Star Team (1981)
b Named WHL's Top Defenseman (1981)
Traded to **Vancouver** by **Toronto** with Dan Hodgson for Rick Lanz, December 2, 1986

BERALDO, PAUL

Right wing. Shoots right. 5'11", 175 lbs. Born, Hamilton, Ont., October 5, 1967.
(Boston's 6th choice, 139th overall, in 1986 Entry Draft).

			Regular Season					Playoffs				
Season	Club	Lea	GP	G	A	TP	PIM	GP	G	A	TP	PIM
1985-86	S.S. Marie	OHL	61	15	13	28	48					
1986-87	S.S. Marie	OHL	63	39	51	90	117	4	3	2	5	6
1987-88	**Boston**	**NHL**	**3**	**0**	**0**	**0**	**0**	....	....	....	....	....
	Maine	AHL	62	22	15	37	112	2	0	0	0	19
1988-89	**Boston**	**NHL**	**7**	**0**	**0**	**0**	**4**	....	....	....	....	....
	Maine	AHL	73	25	28	53	134	....	....	....	....	....
1989-90	Cdn. National	....	9	2	8	10	20	....	....	....	....	....
	Maine	AHL	51	14	27	41	31	....	....	....	....	....
	NHL Totals		**10**	**0**	**0**	**0**	**4**	....	....	....	....	....

BEREHOWSKY, DRAKE

Defense. Shoots right. 6'1", 210 lbs. Born, Toronto, Ont., January 3, 1972.
(Toronto's 1st choice, 10th overall, in 1990 Entry Draft).

			Regular Season					Playoffs				
Season	Club	Lea	GP	G	A	TP	PIM	GP	G	A	TP	PIM
1988-89	Kingston	OHL	63	7	39	46	85	....	....	....	....	....
1989-90	Kingston	OHL	9	3	11	14	28	....	....	....	....	....

BERENAK, JOSEF

Center. Shoots left. 6', 180 lbs. Born, Litvinov, Czechoslovakia, October 25, 1969.
(Edmonton's 3rd choice, 78th overall, in 1989 Entry Draft).

			Regular Season					Playoffs				
Season	Club	Lea	GP	G	A	TP	PIM	GP	G	A	TP	PIM
1988-89	Litvinov	Czech.	23	14	8	22	....	....	....	....	....	....
1989-90	Trencin	Czech.	49	19	23	42	....	....	....	....	....	....

BERENS, RICK

Left wing. Shoots left. 5'11", 185 lbs. Born, Palatine, IL, August 17, 1968.
(Quebec's 2nd choice, 6th overall, in 1989 Supplemental Draft).

			Regular Season					Playoffs				
Season	Club	Lea	GP	G	A	TP	PIM	GP	G	A	TP	PIM
1987-88	U. of Denver	WCHA	39	28	20	48	52	....	....	....	....	....
1988-89	U. of Denver	WCHA	40	19	19	38	26	....	....	....	....	....
1989-90	U. of Denver	WCHA	38	27	25	52	48	....	....	....	....	....

BEREZAN, PERRY EDMUND (BAIR-ih-ZAN)

Center. Shoots right. 6'2", 190 lbs. Born, Edmonton, Alta., December 5, 1964.
(Calgary's 3rd choice, 56th overall, in 1983 Entry Draft)

			Regular Season					Playoffs				
Season	Club	Lea	GP	G	A	TP	PIM	GP	G	A	TP	PIM
1983-84	North Dakota	WCHA	44	28	24	52	29	....	....	....	....	....
1984-85a	North Dakota	WCHA	42	23	35	58	32	....	....	....	....	....
	Calgary	**NHL**	**9**	**3**	**2**	**5**	**4**	**2**	**1**	**0**	**1**	**4**
1985-86	**Calgary**	**NHL**	**55**	**12**	**21**	**33**	**39**	**8**	**1**	**1**	**2**	**6**
1986-87	**Calgary**	**NHL**	**24**	**5**	**3**	**8**	**24**	**2**	**0**	**2**	**2**	**7**
1987-88	**Calgary**	**NHL**	**29**	**7**	**12**	**19**	**66**	**8**	**0**	**2**	**2**	**13**
1988-89	**Calgary**	**NHL**	**35**	**4**	**4**	**8**	**23**	....	....	....	....	....
	Minnesota	**NHL**	**16**	**1**	**4**	**5**	**4**	**5**	**1**	**2**	**3**	**4**
1989-90	**Minnesota**	**NHL**	**64**	**3**	**12**	**15**	**31**	**5**	**1**	**0**	**1**	**0**
	NHL Totals		**232**	**35**	**58**	**93**	**191**	**30**	**4**	**7**	**11**	**34**

a WCHA Second All-Star Team (1985)
Traded to **Minnesota** by **Calgary** with Shane Churla for Brian MacLellan and Minnesota's fourth-round choice (Robert Reichel) in 1989 Entry Draft, March 4, 1989.

BERG, BILL

Defense. Shoots left. 6'1", 190 lbs. Born, St. Catharines, Ont., October 21, 1967
(NY Islanders' 3rd choice, 59th overall, in 1986 Entry Draft).

			Regular Season					Playoffs				
Season	Club	Lea	GP	G	A	TP	PIM	GP	G	A	TP	PIM
1985-86	Toronto	OHL	64	3	35	38	143	4	0	0	0	19
	Springfield	AHL	4	1	1	2	4	....	....	....	....	....
1986-87	Toronto	OHL	57	3	15	18	138	....	....	....	....	....
1987-88	Springfield	AHL	76	6	26	32	148	....	....	....	....	....
	Peoria	IHL	5	0	1	1	8	7	0	3	3	31
1988-89	**NY Islanders**	**NHL**	**7**	**1**	**2**	**3**	**10**	....	....	....	....	....
	Springfield	AHL	69	17	32	49	122	....	....	....	....	....
1989-90	Springfield	AHL	74	12	42	54	74	15	5	12	17	35
	NHL Totals		**7**	**1**	**2**	**3**	**10**	....	....	....	....	....

BERG, BOB

Left wing. Shoots left. 6'2", 190 lbs.   Born, Beamsville, Ont., July 2, 1970.
(Los Angeles' 3rd choice, 49th overall, in 1990 Entry Draft).

			Regular Season					Playoffs			
Season	Club	Lea	GP	G	A	TP	PIM	GP	G	A	TP	PIM
1988-89	Belleville	OHL	66	33	51	84	88	5	1	3	4	8
1989-90a	Belleville	OHL	66	48	49	97	124	8	2	2	4	14

a OHL First All-Star Team (1990)

BERGER, MIKE

Defense. Shoots right. 6', 200 lbs.   Born, Edmonton, Alta., June 2, 1967.
(Minnesota's 2nd choice, 69th overall, in 1985 Entry Draft).

			Regular Season					Playoffs			
Season	Club	Lea	GP	G	A	TP	PIM	GP	G	A	TP	PIM
1982-83	Lethbridge	WHL	1	0	0	0	0					
1983-84	Lethbridge	WHL	41	2	9	11	60	5	0	1	1	7
1984-85	Lethbridge	WHL	58	9	31	40	85	4	0	3	3	9
1985-86	Spokane	WHL	57	9	40	49	95	9	1	5	6	14
1986-87	Indianapolis	IHL	4	0	3	3	4	6	0	1	1	13
	Spokane	WHL	65	26	49	75	80	2	0	0	0	2
1987-88	**Minnesota**	**NHL**	**29**	**3**	**1**	**4**	**65**	....	....	....	....	....
	Kalamazoo	IHL	36	5	10	15	94	6	2	0	2	8
1988-89	**Minnesota**	**NHL**	**1**	**0**	**0**	**0**	**2**	....	....	....	....	....
	Kalamazoo	IHL	67	9	16	25	96	6	0	2	2	8
1989-90	Phoenix	IHL	51	5	12	17	75	....	....	....	....	....
	NHL Totals		**30**	**3**	**1**	**4**	**67**	....	....	....	....	....

Traded to **Hartford** by **Minnesota** for Kevin Sullivan, October 7, 1989.

BERGER, PHILIP

Left wing. Shoots left. 6', 190 lbs.   Born, Dearborn, MI, December 3, 1966.
(Quebec's 1st choice, 3rd overall, in 1988 Supplemental Draft).

			Regular Season					Playoffs			
Season	Club	Lea	GP	G	A	TP	PIM	GP	G	A	TP	PIM
1985-86	N. Michigan	WCHA	21	5	2	7	20	....	....	....	....	....
1986-87	N. Michigan	WCHA	24	11	10	21	6	....	....	....	....	....
1987-88a	N. Michigan	WCHA	38	40	32	72	22	....	....	....	....	....
1988-89b	N. Michigan	WCHA	44	30	33	63	24	....	....	....	....	....
1989-90	Fort Wayne	IHL	3	2	2	4	2	....	....	....	....	....
	Greensboro	ECHL	46	38	44	82	119	....	....	....	....	....

a WCHA First All-Star Team (1988)
b WCHA Second All-Star Team (1989)

BERGEVIN, MARC

Defense. Shoots left. 6', 185 lbs.   Born, Montreal, Que., August 11, 1965.
(Chicago's 3rd choice, 59th overall, in 1983 Entry Draft).

			Regular Season					Playoffs			
Season	Club	Lea	GP	G	A	TP	PIM	GP	G	A	TP	PIM
1982-83	Chicoutimi	QMJHL	64	3	27	30	113	....	....	....	....	....
1983-84	Chicoutimi	QMJHL	70	10	35	45	125	....	....	....	....	....
	Springfield	AHL	7	0	1	1	2	....	....	....	....	....
1984-85	Springfield	AHL	....	....	....	....	....	4	0	0	0	0
	Chicago	**NHL**	**60**	**0**	**6**	**6**	**54**	6	0	3	3	2
1985-86	**Chicago**	**NHL**	**71**	**7**	**7**	**14**	**60**	3	0	0	0	0
1986-87	**Chicago**	**NHL**	**66**	**4**	**10**	**14**	**66**	3	1	0	1	2
1987-88	**Chicago**	**NHL**	**58**	**1**	**6**	**7**	**85**	....	....	....	....	....
	Saginaw	IHL	10	2	7	9	20	....	....	....	....	....
1988-89	**Chicago**	**NHL**	**11**	**0**	**0**	**0**	**18**	....	....	....	....	....
	NY Islanders	**NHL**	**58**	**2**	**13**	**15**	**62**	....	....	....	....	....
1989-90	**NY Islanders**	**NHL**	**18**	**0**	**4**	**4**	**30**	....	....	....	....	....
	Springfield	AHL	47	7	16	23	66	17	2	11	13	16
	NHL Totals		**342**	**14**	**46**	**60**	**375**	**12**	**1**	**3**	**4**	**4**

Traded to **NY Islanders** by **Chicago** with Gary Nylund for Steve Konroyd and Bob Bassen, November 25, 1988.

BERGLAND, TIM

Right wing. Shoots right. 6'2", 195 lbs.   Born, Crookston, MN, January 11, 1965.
(Washington's 1st choice, 75th overall, in 1983 Entry Draft).

			Regular Season					Playoffs			
Season	Club	Lea	GP	G	A	TP	PIM	GP	G	A	TP	PIM
1983-84	U. Minnesota	WCHA	24	4	11	15	4	....	....	....	....	....
1984-85	U. Minnesota	WCHA	34	5	9	14	8	....	....	....	....	....
1985-86	U. Minnesota	WCHA	48	11	16	27	26	....	....	....	....	....
1986-87	U. Minnesota	WCHA	49	18	17	35	48	....	....	....	....	....
1987-88	Fort Wayne	IHL	13	2	1	3	9	....	....	....	....	....
	Binghamton	AHL	63	21	26	47	31	4	0	0	0	0
1988-89	Baltimore	AHL	78	24	29	53	39	....	....	....	....	....
1989-90	**Washington**	**NHL**	**32**	**2**	**5**	**7**	**31**	15	1	1	2	10
	Baltimore	AHL	47	12	19	31	55	....	....	....	....	....
	NHL Totals		**32**	**2**	**5**	**7**	**31**	**15**	**1**	**1**	**2**	**10**

BERGMAN, JAN

Defense. Shoots left. 5'11", 195 lbs.   Born, Sweden, July 7, 1969.
(Vancouver's 11th choice, 248th overall, in 1989 Entry Draft).

			Regular Season					Playoffs			
Season	Club	Lea	GP	G	A	TP	PIM	GP	G	A	TP	PIM
1988-89	Sodertalje	Swe.	34	2	4	6	14	....	....	....	....	....
1989-90	Sodertalje	Swe.	31	0	4	4	10	2	1	0	1	0

BERGQVIST, JONAS

Right wing. Shoots left. 6', 185 lbs.   Born, Hassleholm, Sweden, September 26, 1962.
(Calgary's 6th choice, 126th overall, in 1988 Entry Draft).

			Regular Season					Playoffs			
Season	Club	Lea	GP	G	A	TP	PIM	GP	G	A	TP	PIM
1987-88	Leksand	Swe.	37	19	12	31		....	....	....	....	....
1988-89	Leksand	Swe.	27	15	20	35	18	1	0	0	0	0
1989-90	**Calgary**	**NHL**	**22**	**2**	**5**	**6**	**10**	....	....	....	....	....
	Salt Lake	IHL	13	6	10	16	4	....	....	....	....	....
	NHL Totals		**22**	**2**	**5**	**6**	**10**	....	....	....	....	....

BERNARD, LARRY

Left wing. Shoots left. 6'2", 195 lbs.   Born, Prince George, B.C., April 16, 1967.
(NY Rangers' 8th choice, 154th overall, in 1985 Entry Draft).

			Regular Season					Playoffs			
Season	Club	Lea	GP	G	A	TP	PIM	GP	G	A	TP	PIM
1984-85	Seattle	WHL	63	18	26	44	66	....	....	....	....	....
1985-86	Seattle	WHL	54	17	25	42	64	5	1	3	4	10
1986-87	Seattle	WHL	70	40	46	86	159	....	....	....	....	....
1987-88	Colorado	IHL	64	14	13	27	68	9	0	3	3	18
1988-89	Denver	IHL	21	4	5	9	44	....	....	....	....	....
	Kalamazoo	IHL	45	9	16	25	47	1	0	0	0	5
1989-90	Moncton	AHL	66	14	17	31	93	....	....	....	....	....

Traded to **Minnesota** by **NY Rangers** with NY Ranger's fifth-round choice (Rhys Hollyman) in 1989 Entry Draft for Mark Hardy, December 9, 1988.

BERRY, BRAD

Defense. Shoots left. 6'2", 190 lbs.   Born, Bashaw, Alta., April 1, 1965.
(Winnipeg's 3rd choice, 29th overall, in 1983 Entry Draft).

			Regular Season					Playoffs			
Season	Club	Lea	GP	G	A	TP	PIM	GP	G	A	TP	PIM
1983-84	North Dakota	WCHA	32	2	7	9	8	....	....	....	....	....
1984-85	North Dakota	WCHA	40	4	26	30	26	....	....	....	....	....
1985-86	North Dakota	WCHA	40	6	29	35	26	....	....	....	....	....
	Winnipeg	**NHL**	**13**	**1**	**0**	**1**	**10**	3	0	0	0	0
1986-87	**Winnipeg**	**NHL**	**52**	**2**	**8**	**10**	**60**	7	0	1	1	14
1987-88	**Winnipeg**	**NHL**	**48**	**0**	**6**	**6**	**75**	....	....	....	....	....
	Moncton	AHL	10	1	3	4	14	....	....	....	....	....
1988-89	**Winnipeg**	**NHL**	**38**	**0**	**9**	**9**	**45**	....	....	....	....	....
	Moncton	AHL	38	3	16	19	39	....	....	....	....	....
1989-90	**Winnipeg**	**NHL**	**12**	**1**	**2**	**3**	**6**	1	0	0	0	0
	Moncton	AHL	38	1	9	10	58	....	....	....	....	....
	NHL Totals		**163**	**4**	**25**	**29**	**196**	**11**	**0**	**1**	**1**	**14**

BERRY, KENNETH E. (KEN)

Left wing. Shoots left. 5'8", 175 lbs.   Born, Burnaby, B.C., June 21, 1960.
(Vancouver's 5th choice, 112th overall, in 1980 Entry Draft).

			Regular Season					Playoffs			
Season	Club	Lea	GP	G	A	TP	PIM	GP	G	A	TP	PIM
1979-80	Cdn. National	....	57	19	20	39	48	....	....	....	....	....
	Cdn. Olympic	....	6	4	1	5	8	....	....	....	....	....
1980-81	U. of Denver	WCHA	40	22	34	56	74	....	....	....	....	....
	Wichita	CHL	9	7	6	13	13	17	2	4	6	28
1981-82	**Edmonton**	**NHL**	**15**	**2**	**3**	**5**	**9**	....	....	....	....	....
	Wichita	CHL	58	28	29	57	70	....	....	....	....	....
1982-83	Moncton	AHL	76	24	26	50	80	....	....	....	....	....
1983-84	Moncton	AHL	53	18	20	38	75	....	....	....	....	....
	Edmonton	**NHL**	**13**	**2**	**3**	**5**	**10**	....	....	....	....	....
1984-85	Nova Scotia	AHL	71	30	27	57	40	6	2	2	4	2
1985-86	Bayreuth	W.Ger.	33	27	25	52	88	....	....	....	....	....
	Cdn. National	....	8	1	2	3	20	....	....	....	....	....
1986-87	Cdn. National	....	52	17	27	44	60	....	....	....	....	....
1987-88	Cdn. National	....	59	18	15	33	47	....	....	....	....	....
	Cdn. Olympic	....	8	2	4	6	4	....	....	....	....	....
	Vancouver	**NHL**	**14**	**2**	**3**	**5**	**6**	....	....	....	....	....
1988-89	**Vancouver**	**NHL**	**13**	**2**	**1**	**3**	**5**	....	....	....	....	....
	Milwaukee	IHL	5	4	4	8	2	....	....	....	....	....
1989-90	Munich	W. Ger.	36	24	33	57	70	....	....	....	....	....
	NHL Totals		**55**	**8**	**10**	**18**	**30**	....	....	....	....	....

Traded to **Edmonton** by **Vancouver** with Garry Lariviere for Blair MacDonald and Lars-Gunnar Petersson, March 10, 1981. Signed as a free agent by **Vancouver**, March 1, 1988.

BERUBE, CRAIG   (buh-ROO-bee)

Left wing. Shoots left. 6'2", 205 lbs.   Born, Calihoo, Alta., December 17, 1965.

			Regular Season					Playoffs			
Season	Club	Lea	GP	G	A	TP	PIM	GP	G	A	TP	PIM
1982-83	Kamloops	WHL	4	0	0	0	0	....	....	....	....	....
1983-84	N. Westminster	WHL	70	11	20	31	104	8	1	2	3	5
1984-85	N. Westminster	WHL	70	25	44	69	191	10	3	2	5	4
1985-86	Kamloops	WHL	32	17	14	31	119	....	....	....	....	....
	Medicine Hat	WHL	34	14	16	30	95	25	7	8	15	102
1986-87	**Philadelphia**	**NHL**	**7**	**0**	**0**	**0**	**57**	5	0	0	0	17
	Hershey	AHL	63	7	17	24	325	....	....	....	....	....
1987-88	**Philadelphia**	**NHL**	**27**	**3**	**2**	**5**	**108**	....	....	....	....	....
	Hershey	AHL	31	5	9	14	119	....	....	....	....	....
1988-89	**Philadelphia**	**NHL**	**53**	**1**	**1**	**2**	**199**	16	0	0	0	56
	Hershey	AHL	7	0	2	2	19	....	....	....	....	....
1989-90	**Philadelphia**	**NHL**	**74**	**4**	**14**	**18**	**291**	....	....	....	....	....
	NHL Totals		**161**	**8**	**17**	**25**	**655**	**21**	**0**	**0**	**0**	**73**

Signed as a free agent by **Philadelphia**, March 19, 1986.

BEUKEBOOM, JEFF   (BOO-kuh-BOOM)

Defense. Shoots right. 6'4", 215 lbs.   Born, Ajax, Ont., March 28, 1965.
(Edmonton's 1st choice, 19th overall, in 1983 Entry Draft).

			Regular Season					Playoffs			
Season	Club	Lea	GP	G	A	TP	PIM	GP	G	A	TP	PIM
1982-83	S. S. Marie	OHL	70	0	25	25	143	16	1	4	5	46
1983-84	S. S. Marie	OHL	61	6	30	36	178	16	1	7	8	43
1984-85a	S. S. Marie	OHL	37	4	20	24	85	16	4	6	10	47
1985-86	**Edmonton**	**NHL**	....	....	....	....	....	1	0	0	0	4
	Nova Scotia	AHL	77	9	20	29	175	....	....	....	....	....
1986-87	**Edmonton**	**NHL**	**44**	**3**	**8**	**11**	**124**	....	....	....	....	....
	Nova Scotia	AHL	14	1	7	8	35	....	....	....	....	....
1987-88	**Edmonton**	**NHL**	**73**	**5**	**20**	**25**	**201**	7	0	0	0	16
1988-89	**Edmonton**	**NHL**	**36**	**0**	**5**	**5**	**94**	1	0	0	0	2
	Cape Breton	AHL	8	0	4	4	36	....	....	....	....	....
1989-90	**Edmonton**	**NHL**	**46**	**1**	**12**	**13**	**86**	2	0	0	0	0
	NHL Totals		**199**	**9**	**45**	**54**	**505**	**11**	**0**	**0**	**0**	**22**

a OHL First All-Star Team (1985)

BIGGS, DON

Center. Shoots right. 5'8", 175 lbs. Born, Mississauga, Ont., April 7, 1965.
(Minnesota's 9th choice, 156th overall, in 1983 Entry Draft).

			Regular Season					Playoffs				
Season	Club	Lea	GP	G	A	TP	PIM	GP	G	A	TP	PIM
1982-83	Oshawa	OHL	70	22	53	75	145	16	3	6	9	17
1983-84	Oshawa	OHL	58	31	60	91	149	7	4	4	8	18
1984-85	**Minnesota**	**NHL**	**1**	**0**	**0**	**0**	**0**	....	....	....	....	....
	Springfield	AHL	6	0	3	3	0	2	1	0	1	0
	Oshawa	OHL	60	48	69	117	105	5	3	4	7	6
1985-86	Springfield	AHL	28	15	16	31	46	....	....	....	....	....
	Nova Scotia	AHL	47	6	23	29	36	....	....	....	....	....
1986-87	Nova Scotia	AHL	80	22	25	47	165	5	1	2	3	4
1987-88	Hershey	AHL	77	38	41	79	151	12	5	*11	*16	22
1988-89	Hershey	AHL	76	36	67	103	158	11	5	9	14	30
1989-90	**Philadelphia**	**NHL**	**11**	**2**	**0**	**2**	**8**	....	....	....	....	....
	Hershey	AHL	66	39	53	92	125	....	....	....	....	....
	NHL Totals		**12**	**2**	**0**	**2**	**8**	....	....	....	....	....

Traded to **Edmonton** by **Minnesota** with Gord Sherven for Marc Habscheid, Don Barber and Emanuel Viveiros, December 20, 1985.

BIGNELL, GREG

Defense. Shoots left. 6', 190 lbs. Born, Kitchener, Ont., May 9, 1969.
(Detroit's 10th choice, 200th overall, in 1989 Entry Draft).

			Regular Season					Playoffs				
Season	Club	Lea	GP	G	A	TP	PIM	GP	G	A	TP	PIM
1988-89	Belleville	OHL	54	6	27	33	180	5	0	1	1	16
1989-90	Belleville	OHL	58	6	26	32	141	11	0	6	6	31

BILLECK, LAURIE

Defense. Shoots right. 6'3", 210 lbs. Born, Dauphin, Man., July 2, 1971.
(Minnesota's 2nd choice, 50th overall, in 1990 Entry Draft).

			Regular Season					Playoffs				
Season	Club	Lea	GP	G	A	TP	PIM	GP	G	A	TP	PIM
1988-89	Prince Albert	WHL	60	2	4	6	65	4	1	0	1	14
1989-90	Prince Albert	WHL	67	7	28	35	135	14	2	3	5	24

BIOTTI, CHRIS (bee-AH-tee)

Defense. Shoots left. 6'3", 200 lbs. Born, Waltham, MA., April 22, 1967.
(Calgary's 1st choice, 17th overall, in 1985 Entry Draft).

			Regular Season					Playoffs				
Season	Club	Lea	GP	G	A	TP	PIM	GP	G	A	TP	PIM
1985-86	Harvard	ECAC	15	3	5	8	18	....	....	....	....	....
1986-87	Harvard	ECAC	30	1	6	7	23	....	....	....	....	....
1987-88	Salt Lake	IHL	72	5	19	24	73	12	2	3	5	33
1988-89	Salt Lake	IHL	57	6	14	20	44	12	3	4	7	16
1989-90	Salt Lake	IHL	60	9	19	28	73	3	1	0	1	2

BISCHOFF, GRANT

Left wing. Shoots left. 5'10", 165 lbs. Born, Anoka, MN, October 26, 1968.
(Minnesota's 8th choice, 211th overall, in 1988 Entry Draft).

			Regular Season					Playoffs				
Season	Club	Lea	GP	G	A	TP	PIM	GP	G	A	TP	PIM
1987-88	U. Minnesota	WCHA	44	15	22	37	14	....	....	....	....	....
1988-89	U. Minnesota	WCHA	47	21	16	37	14	....	....	....	....	....
1989-90	U. Minnesota	WCHA	45	21	19	40	18	....	....	....	....	....

BISHOP, MICHAEL

Defense. Shoots left. 6'2", 212 lbs. Born, Sarnia, Ont., June 15, 1966.
(Montreal's 14th choice, 226th overall, in 1985 Entry Draft).

			Regular Season					Playoffs				
Season	Club	Lea	GP	G	A	TP	PIM	GP	G	A	TP	PIM
1985-86	Colgate	ECAC	17	5	6	11	47	....	....	....	....	....
1986-87	Colgate	ECAC	30	7	17	24	68	....	....	....	....	....
1987-88	Colgate	ECAC	31	8	24	32	49	....	....	....	....	....
1988-89a	Colgate	ECAC	31	8	13	21	92	....	....	....	....	....
1989-90	Fort Wayne	IHL	12	0	0	0	6	....	....	....	....	....
	Knoxville	ECHL	22	3	9	12	28	....	....	....	....	....

a ECAC Second All-Star Team (1989)

BISSETT, TOM (BIH-siht)

Center. Shoots left. 6', 180 lbs. Born, Seattle, WA, March 13, 1966.
(Detroit's 11th choice, 211th overall, in 1986 Entry Draft).

			Regular Season					Playoffs				
Season	Club	Lea	GP	G	A	TP	PIM	GP	G	A	TP	PIM
1985-86	Michigan Tech.	WCHA	40	12	21	33	18	....	....	....	....	....
1986-87	Michigan Tech.	WCHA	40	16	19	35	12	....	....	....	....	....
1987-88	Michigan Tech.	WCHA	41	18	26	44	20	....	....	....	....	....
1988-89	Adirondack	AHL	5	0	1	1	0	....	....	....	....	....
	Michigan Tech.	WCHA	42	19	28	47	16	....	....	....	....	....
1989-90	Adirondack	AHL	16	11	4	15	4	....	....	....	....	....
	Hampton-Roads	ECHL	5	7	7	14	2	....	....	....	....	....

BISSON, STEVE (BEE-sohn)

Defense. Shoots left. 6'1", 193 lbs. Born, Ottawa, Ont., May 24, 1968.
(Montreal's 7th choice, 120th overall, in 1986 Entry Draft).

			Regular Season					Playoffs				
Season	Club	Lea	GP	G	A	TP	PIM	GP	G	A	TP	PIM
1985-86	S.S. Marie	OHL	66	3	23	26	44	....	....	....	....	....
1986-87	S.S. Marie	OHL	52	5	15	20	38	4	1	1	2	4
1987-88	S.S. Marie	OHL	3	0	2	2	0	....	....	....	....	....
	Cornwall	OHL	61	10	57	67	89	10	0	7	7	10
1988-89	Sherbrooke	AHL	4	0	3	3	4	....	....	....	....	....
	North Bay	OHL	37	8	16	24	83	11	5	7	12	10
1989-90	Fort Wayne	IHL	23	1	4	5	14	....	....	....	....	....

BJUGSTAD, SCOTT (BYOOG-stad)

Right wing. Shoots left. 6'1", 185 lbs. Born, St. Paul, MN, June 2, 1961.
(Minnesota's 13th choice, 181st overall, in 1981 Entry Draft).

			Regular Season					Playoffs				
Season	Club	Lea	GP	G	A	TP	PIM	GP	G	A	TP	PIM
1979-80	U. Minnesota	WCHA	18	2	2	4	2	....	....	....	....	....
1980-81	U. Minnesota	WCHA	35	12	23	25	34	....	....	....	....	....
1981-82	U. Minnesota	WCHA	36	29	14	43	24	....	....	....	....	....
1982-83a	U. Minnesota	WCHA	26	21	35	56	12	....	....	....	....	....
1983-84	U.S. National	...	54	31	20	51	28	....	....	....	....	....
	U.S. Olympic	...	6	3	2	5	6	....	....	....	....	....
	Minnesota	**NHL**	**5**	**0**	**0**	**0**	**2**	....	....	....	....	....
	Salt Lake	CHL	15	10	8	18	6	5	3	4	7	0
1984-85	**Minnesota**	**NHL**	**72**	**11**	**4**	**15**	**32**	....	....	....	....	....
	Springfield	AHL	5	2	3	5	2	....	....	....	....	....
1985-86	**Minnesota**	**NHL**	**80**	**43**	**33**	**76**	**24**	**5**	**0**	**1**	**1**	**0**
1986-87	**Minnesota**	**NHL**	**39**	**4**	**9**	**13**	**43**	....	....	....	....	....
	Springfield	AHL	11	4	6	10	7	....	....	....	....	....
1987-88	**Minnesota**	**NHL**	**33**	**10**	**12**	**22**	**15**	....	....	....	....	....
1988-89	**Pittsburgh**	**NHL**	**24**	**3**	**0**	**3**	**4**	....	....	....	....	....
	Kalamazoo	IHL	4	5	0	5	4	....	....	....	....	....
1989-90	**Los Angeles**	**NHL**	**11**	**1**	**2**	**3**	**2**	**2**	**0**	**0**	**0**	**2**
	New Haven	AHL	47	45	21	66	40	....	....	....	....	....
	NHL Totals		**264**	**72**	**60**	**132**	**122**	**7**	**0**	**1**	**1**	**2**

a WCHA First All-Star Team (1983)

Traded to **Pittsburgh** by **Minnesota** with Gord Dineen for Ville Siren and Steve Gotaas, December 17, 1988.

BJUHR, THOMAS (BYOOR)

Right wing. Shoots left. 6'1", 205 lbs. Born, Stockholm, Sweden, August 28, 1966.
(Detroit's 7th choice, 134th overall, in 1985 Entry Draft).

			Regular Season					Playoffs				
Season	Club	Lea	GP	G	A	TP	PIM	GP	G	A	TP	PIM
1984-85	AIK	Swe. Jr.	33	38	18	56	28	....	....	....	....	....
	AIK	Swe.	3	1	0	1	0	....	....	....	....	....
1985-86	AIK	Swe.	14	0	1	1	8	....	....	....	....	....
1986-87	Portland	WHL	39	28	26	54	23	....	....	....	....	....
1987-88	Adirondack	AHL	58	4	2	6	21	....	....	....	....	....
1988-89	AIK	Swe.	34	8	9	17	40	....	....	....	....	....
1989-90	AIK	Swe.	40	19	12	31	22	....	....	....	....	....

BLACK, JAMES

Center. Shoots left. 5'11", 185 lbs. Born, Regina, Sask., August 15, 1969.
(Hartford's 4th choice, 94th overall, in 1989 Entry Draft).

			Regular Season					Playoffs				
Season	Club	Lea	GP	G	A	TP	PIM	GP	G	A	TP	PIM
1987-88	Portland	WHL	72	30	50	80	50	....	....	....	....	....
1988-89	Portland	WHL	71	45	51	96	57	19	13	6	19	28
1989-90	**Hartford**	**NHL**	**1**	**0**	**0**	**0**	**0**	....	....	....	....	....
	Binghamton	AHL	80	37	35	72	34	....	....	....	....	....
	NHL Totals		**1**	**0**	**0**	**0**	**0**	....	....	....	....	....

BLAD, BRIAN

Defense. Shoots left. 6'2", 202 lbs. Born, Brockville, Ont., July 22, 1967.
(Toronto's 9th choice, 175th overall, in 1987 Entry Draft).

			Regular Season					Playoffs				
Season	Club	Lea	GP	G	A	TP	PIM	GP	G	A	TP	PIM
1986-87	Windsor	OHL	15	1	1	2	30	....	....	....	....	....
	Belleville	OHL	20	1	5	6	43	....	....	....	....	....
1987-88	Milwaukee	IHL	28	1	6	7	45	....	....	....	....	....
	Newmarket	AHL	39	0	4	4	74	....	....	....	....	....
1988-89	Newmarket	AHL	59	2	4	6	149	5	0	1	1	5
1989-90	Newmarket	AHL	58	2	4	6	216	....	....	....	....	....

BLAESER, JEFFREY

Left wing. Shoots left. 6'3", 190 lbs. Born, Parma, OH, May 11, 1970.
(Pittsburgh's 7th choice, 151st overall, in 1988 Entry Draft).

			Regular Season					Playoffs				
Season	Club	Lea	GP	G	A	TP	PIM	GP	G	A	TP	PIM
1988-89	Yale	ECAC	31	8	19	27	12	....	....	....	....	....
1989-90	Yale	ECAC	29	17	14	31	16	....	....	....	....	....

BLAISDELL, MICHAEL WALTER (MIKE) (BLAZE-dell)

Right wing. Shoots right. 6'1", 195 lbs. Born, Moose Jaw, Sask., January 18, 1960.
(Detroit's 1st choice, 11th overall, in 1980 Entry Draft).

			Regular Season					Playoffs				
Season	Club	Lea	GP	G	A	TP	PIM	GP	G	A	TP	PIM
1977-78	Regina	WHL	6	5	5	10	2	13	4	7	11	0
1978-79	U. Wisconsin	WCHA	20	7	1	8	4	....	....	....	....	....
1979-80	Regina	WHL	63	71	38	109	62	18	*16	9	25	26
1980-81	**Detroit**	**NHL**	**32**	**3**	**6**	**9**	**10**	....	....	....	....	....
	Adirondack	AHL	41	10	4	14	8	12	2	2	4	5
1981-82	**Detroit**	**NHL**	**80**	**23**	**32**	**55**	**48**	....	....	....	....	....
1982-83	**Detroit**	**NHL**	**80**	**18**	**23**	**41**	**22**	....	....	....	....	....
1983-84	**NY Rangers**	**NHL**	**36**	**5**	**6**	**11**	**31**	....	....	....	....	....
	Tulsa	CHL	32	10	8	18	23	9	6	6	12	6
1984-85	**NY Rangers**	**NHL**	**12**	**1**	**0**	**1**	**11**	....	....	....	....	....
	New Haven	AHL	64	21	23	44	41	....	....	....	....	....
1985-86	**Pittsburgh**	**NHL**	**66**	**15**	**14**	**29**	**36**	....	....	....	....	....
1986-87	**Pittsburgh**	**NHL**	**10**	**1**	**1**	**2**	**2**	....	....	....	....	....
	Baltimore	AHL	43	12	12	24	47	....	....	....	....	....
1987-88	**Toronto**	**NHL**	**18**	**3**	**2**	**5**	**2**	**6**	**1**	**2**	**3**	**10**
	Newmarket	AHL	57	25	28	53	30	....	....	....	....	....
1988-89	**Toronto**	**NHL**	**9**	**1**	**0**	**1**	**4**	....	....	....	....	....
	Newmarket	AHL	40	16	7	23	48	....	....	....	....	....
1989-90	Cdn. National	....	50	12	18	30	40	....	....	....	....	....
	NHL Totals		**343**	**70**	**84**	**154**	**166**	**6**	**1**	**2**	**3**	**10**

Traded to **NY Rangers** by **Detroit** with Willie Huber and Mark Osborne for Ron Duguay, Eddie Mio and Eddie Johnstone, June 13, 1983. Claimed by **Pittsburgh** from **NY Rangers** in NHL Waiver Draft, October 7, 1985. Signed as a free agent by **Toronto**, July 10, 1987.

BLAKE, ROBERT

Defense. Shoots right. 6'3", 200 lbs. Born, Simcoe, Ont., December 10, 1969.
(Los Angeles' 4th choice, 70th overall, in 1988 Entry Draft).

			Regular Season					Playoffs				
Season	Club	Lea	GP	G	A	TP	PIM	GP	G	A	TP	PIM
1987-88	Bowling Green	CCHA	43	5	8	13	88	....	....	....	....	....
1988-89a	Bowling Green	CCHA	46	11	21	32	140	....	....	....	....	....
1989-90bc	Bowling Green	CCHA	42	23	36	59	140	....	....	....	....	....
	Los Angeles	**NHL**	**4**	**0**	**0**	**0**	**4**	**8**	**1**	**3**	**4**	**4**
	NHL Totals		**4**	**0**	**0**	**0**	**4**	**8**	**1**	**3**	**4**	**4**

a CCHA Second All-Star Team (1989)
b CCHA First All-Star Team (1990)
c NCAA West First All-American Team (1990)

BLESSMAN, JOHN

Defense. Shoots left. 6'3", 210 lbs. Born, Toronto, Ont., April 27, 1967.
(New Jersey's 8th choice, 170th overall, in 1987 Entry Draft).

			Regular Season					Playoffs				
Season	Club	Lea	GP	G	A	TP	PIM	GP	G	A	TP	PIM
1984-85	Toronto	OHL	25	1	3	4	42	5	0	0	0	0
1985-86	Toronto	OHL	64	2	13	15	116	4	0	0	0	11
1986-87	Toronto	OHL	61	6	24	30	130	....	....	....	....	....
1987-88	Utica	AHL	24	0	2	2	50	....	....	....	....	....
	Toronto	OHL	23	8	11	19	64	4	0	4	4	0
1988-89	Utica	AHL	26	2	3	5	46	....	....	....	....	....
	Indianapolis	IHL	31	2	5	7	60	....	....	....	....	....
1989-90	Hershey	AHL	1	0	0	0	0	....	....	....	....	....
	Greensboro	ECHL	19	0	7	7	81	....	....	....	....	....
	Winston-Salem	ECHL	17	1	6	7	108	....	....	....	....	....

BLOEMBERG, JEFF (BLOOM-buhrg)

Defense. Shoots right. 6'1", 205 lbs. Born, Listowel, Ont., January 31, 1968.
(NY Ranger's 5th choice, 93rd overall, in 1986 Entry Draft).

			Regular Season					Playoffs				
Season	Club	Lea	GP	G	A	TP	PIM	GP	G	A	TP	PIM
1985-86	North Bay	OHL	60	2	11	13	76	8	1	2	3	9
1986-87	North Bay	OHL	60	5	13	18	91	21	1	6	7	13
1987-88	Colorado	IHL	5	0	0	0	0	11	1	0	1	8
	North Bay	OHL	46	9	26	35	60	4	1	4	5	2
1988-89	**NY Rangers**	**NHL**	**9**	**0**	**0**	**0**	**0**	....	....	....	....	....
	Denver	IHL	64	7	22	29	55	1	0	0	0	0
1989-90	**NY Rangers**	**NHL**	**28**	**3**	**3**	**6**	**25**	**7**	**0**	**3**	**3**	**5**
	Flint	IHL	41	7	14	21	24	....	....	....	....	....
	NHL Totals		**37**	**3**	**3**	**6**	**25**	**7**	**0**	**3**	**3**	**5**

BLOMSTEN, ARTO

Defense. Shoots left. 6'1", 190 lbs. Born, Vasa, Finland, March 16, 1965.
(Winnipeg's 11th choice, 239th overall, in 1986 Entry Draft).

			Regular Season					Playoffs				
Season	Club	Lea	GP	G	A	TP	PIM	GP	G	A	TP	PIM
1986-87	Djurgarden	Swe.	29	2	4	6	28	....	....	....	....	....
1987-88	Djurgarden	Swe.	39	12	6	18	36	2	1	0	1	0
1988-89	Djurgarden	Swe.	40	10	9	19	38	....	....	....	....	....
1989-90	Djurgarden	Swe.	36	5	21	26	28	8	0	1	1	6

BLOOM, SCOTT

Left wing. Shoots left. 5'10", 195 lbs. Born, Edina, MN, February 8, 1968.
(Calgary's 4th choice, 100th overall, in 1986 Entry Draft).

			Regular Season					Playoffs				
Season	Club	Lea	GP	G	A	TP	PIM	GP	G	A	TP	PIM
1986-87	U. Minnesota	WCHA	44	6	11	17	28	....	....	....	....	....
1987-88	U. Minnesota	WCHA	40	10	11	21	58	....	....	....	....	....
1988-89	U. Minnesota	WCHA	19	2	5	7	22	....	....	....	....	....
1989-90	U. Minnesota	WCHA	43	24	28	52	22	....	....	....	....	....

BLUM, JOHN JOSEPH

Defense. Shoots right. 6'3", 205 lbs. Born, Detroit, MI, October 8, 1959.

			Regular Season					Playoffs				
Season	Club	Lea	GP	G	A	TP	PIM	GP	G	A	TP	PIM
1980-81	Michigan	WCHA	38	9	43	52	93	....	....	....	....	....
1981-82	Wichita	CHL	78	8	33	41	247	7	0	3	3	24
1982-83	**Edmonton**	**NHL**	**5**	**0**	**3**	**3**	**24**	....	....	....	....	....
	Moncton	AHL	76	10	30	40	219	....	....	....	....	....
1983-84	Moncton	AHL	57	3	22	25	202	....	....	....	....	....
	Edmonton	**NHL**	**4**	**0**	**1**	**1**	**2**	....	....	....	....	....
	Boston	**NHL**	**12**	**1**	**1**	**2**	**30**	**3**	**0**	**0**	**0**	**4**
1984-85	**Boston**	**NHL**	**75**	**3**	**13**	**16**	**263**	**5**	**0**	**0**	**0**	**13**
1985-86	**Boston**	**NHL**	**61**	**1**	**7**	**8**	**80**	**3**	**0**	**0**	**0**	**6**
	Moncton	AHL	12	1	5	6	37	....	....	....	....	....
1986-87	**Washington**	**NHL**	**66**	**2**	**8**	**10**	**133**	**6**	**0**	**1**	**1**	**4**
1987-88	**Boston**	**NHL**	**19**	**0**	**1**	**1**	**70**	**3**	**0**	**1**	**1**	**0**
	Maine	AHL	43	5	18	23	136	8	0	6	6	35
1988-89	**Detroit**	**NHL**	**6**	**0**	**0**	**0**	**8**	....	....	....	....	....
	Adirondack	AHL	56	1	19	20	168	12	0	1	1	18
1989-90	**Boston**	**NHL**	**2**	**0**	**0**	**0**	**0**	....	....	....	....	....
	Maine	AHL	77	1	20	21	134	....	....	....	....	....
	NHL Totals		**250**	**7**	**34**	**41**	**610**	**20**	**0**	**2**	**2**	**27**

Signed as free agent by **Edmonton**, May 5, 1981. Traded to **Boston** by **Edmonton** for Larry Melnyk, March 6, 1984. Claimed by **Washington** from **Boston** in NHL Waiver Draft, October 6, 1986. Traded to **Boston** by **Washington** for Boston's seventh round choice (Brad Schlegal) in 1988 Entry Draft, June 1, 1987. Signed as a free agent by **Detroit**, August 12, 1988. Signed as a free agent by **Boston**, July 6, 1989.

BLUM, KENNETH

Center. Shoots left. 6'1", 175 lbs. Born, Hackensack, NJ. June 8, 1971.
(Minnesota's 10th choice, 175th overall, in 1989 Entry Draft).

			Regular Season					Playoffs				
Season	Club	Lea	GP	G	A	TP	PIM	GP	G	A	TP	PIM
1988-89	St. Joseph's	HS	27	50	59	109	18	....	....	....	....	....
1989-90	Lake Superior	CCHA	19	2	1	3	14	....	....	....	....	....

BOBYCK, BRENT

Left wing. Shoots left. 5'10", 175 lbs. Born, Regina, Sask., April 26, 1968.
(Montreal's 4th choice, 78th overall, in 1986 Entry Draft).

			Regular Season					Playoffs				
Season	Club	Lea	GP	G	A	TP	PIM	GP	G	A	TP	PIM
1986-87	North Dakota	WCHA	46	8	11	19	16	....	....	....	....	....
1987-88	North Dakota	WCHA	41	10	20	30	43	....	....	....	....	....
1988-89	North Dakota	WCHA	28	11	8	19	16	....	....	....	....	....
1989-90	North Dakota	WCHA	44	16	21	37	47	....	....	....	....	....

BODAK, ROBERT PETER

Left wing. Shoots left. 6'2", 195 lbs. Born, Thunder Bay, Ont., May 28, 1961.

			Regular Season					Playoffs				
Season	Club	Lea	GP	G	A	TP	PIM	GP	G	A	TP	PIM
1983-84	Lakehead U.	GPAC	22	23	24	47	18	....	....	....	....	....
1984-85	Springfield	AHL	79	20	25	45	52	4	1	0	1	2
1985-86	Springfield	AHL	4	0	0	0	4	....	....	....	....	....
	Moncton	AHL	58	27	15	42	114	10	3	3	6	0
1986-87	Moncton	AHL	48	11	20	31	75	6	1	1	2	18
1987-88	**Calgary**	**NHL**	**3**	**0**	**0**	**0**	**22**	....	....	....	....	....
	Salt Lake	IHL	44	12	10	22	117	18	1	3	4	74
1988-89	Binghamton	AHL	44	15	25	40	135	....	....	....	....	....
	Salt Lake	IHL	4	0	0	0	2	....	....	....	....	....
1989-90	**Hartford**	**NHL**	**1**	**0**	**0**	**0**	**7**	....	....	....	....	....
	Binghamton	AHL	79	32	25	57	59	....	....	....	....	....
	NHL Totals		**4**	**0**	**0**	**0**	**29**	....	....	....	....	....

Signed as a free agent by **Calgary**, January 28, 1986. Signed as a free agent by **Hartford**, May 10, 1989.

BODDEN, JAMES (JIM)

Center. Shoots right. 5'10", 180 lbs. Born, Dundas, Ont., October 26, 1967.
(Pittsburgh's 7th choice, 131st overall, in 1987 Entry Draft).

			Regular Season					Playoffs				
Season	Club	Lea	GP	G	A	TP	PIM	GP	G	A	TP	PIM
1987-88	Miami-Ohio	CCHA	38	10	14	24	30	....	....	....	....	....
1988-89	Miami-Ohio	CCHA	33	11	10	21	15	....	....	....	....	....
1989-90	Miami-Ohio	CCHA	38	14	23	37	10	....	....	....	....	....

BODGER, DOUG

Defense. Shoots left. 6'2", 210 lbs. Born, Chemainus, B.C., June 18, 1966
(Pittsburgh's 2nd choice, 9th overall, in 1984 Entry Draft).

			Regular Season					Playoffs				
Season	Club	Lea	GP	G	A	TP	PIM	GP	G	A	TP	PIM
1982-83a	Kamloops	WHL	72	26	66	92	98	7	0	5	5	2
1983-84	Kamloops	WHL	70	21	77	98	90	17	2	15	17	12
1984-85	**Pittsburgh**	**NHL**	**65**	**5**	**26**	**31**	**67**	....	....	....	....	....
1985-86	**Pittsburgh**	**NHL**	**79**	**4**	**33**	**37**	**63**	....	....	....	....	....
1986-87	**Pittsburgh**	**NHL**	**76**	**11**	**38**	**49**	**52**	....	....	....	....	....
1987-88	**Pittsburgh**	**NHL**	**69**	**14**	**31**	**45**	**103**	....	....	....	....	....
1988-89	**Pittsburgh**	**NHL**	**10**	**1**	**4**	**5**	**7**	....	....	....	....	....
	Buffalo	**NHL**	**61**	**7**	**40**	**47**	**52**	**5**	**1**	**1**	**2**	**11**
1989-90	**Buffalo**	**NHL**	**71**	**12**	**36**	**48**	**64**	**6**	**1**	**5**	**6**	**6**
	NHL Totals		**431**	**54**	**208**	**262**	**408**	**11**	**2**	**6**	**8**	**17**

a WHL Second All-Star Team (1983)

Traded to **Buffalo** by **Pittsburgh** with Darrin Shannon for Tom Barrasso and Buffalo's third-round choice (Joe Dziedzic) in 1990 Entry Draft, November 12, 1988.

BOIVIN, CLAUDE

Left wing. Shoots left. 6'3", 200 lbs. Born, Ste. Foy, Que., March 1, 1970.
(Philadelphia's 1st choice, 14th overall, in 1988 Entry Draft).

			Regular Season					Playoffs				
Season	Club	Lea	GP	G	A	TP	PIM	GP	G	A	TP	PIM
1987-88	Drummondville	QMJHL	63	23	26	49	233	17	5	3	8	74
1988-89	Drummondville	QMJHL	63	20	36	56	218	4	0	2	2	27
1989-90	Laval	QMJHL	59	24	51	75	309	13	7	13	20	59

BOMBARDIR, BRAD

Defense. Shoots left. 6'2", 185 lbs. Born, Powell River, B.C., May 5, 1972.
(New Jersey's 5th choice, 56th overall, in 1990 Entry Draft).

			Regular Season					Playoffs				
Season	Club	Lea	GP	G	A	TP	PIM	GP	G	A	TP	PIM
1989-90	Powell River	BCJHL	60	10	35	45	93	....	....	....	....	....

BORGO, RICHARD

Right wing. Shoots right. 5'11", 190 lbs. Born, Thunder Bay, Ont., September 25, 1970.
(Edmonton's 2nd choice, 36th overall, in 1989 Entry Draft).

			Regular Season					Playoffs				
Season	Club	Lea	GP	G	A	TP	PIM	GP	G	A	TP	PIM
1987-88	Kitchener	OHL	64	24	22	46	81	4	0	4	4	0
1988-89	Kitchener	OHL	66	23	23	46	75	5	0	1	1	4
1989-90	Kitchener	OHL	32	13	22	35	43	17	5	5	10	10

BORSATO, LUCIANO

Center. Shoots right. 5'10", 165 lbs. Born, Richmond Hill, Ont., January 7, 1966.
(Winnipeg's 6th choice, 135th overall, in 1984 Entry Draft).

			Regular Season					Playoffs				
Season	Club	Lea	GP	G	A	TP	PIM	GP	G	A	TP	PIM
1984-85	Clarkson	ECAC	33	15	17	32	37	....	....	....	....	....
1985-86	Clarkson	ECAC	28	14	17	31	44	....	....	....	....	....
1986-87	Clarkson	ECAC	31	16	41	57	55	....	....	....	....	....
1987-88ab	Clarkson	ECAC	33	15	29	44	38	....	....	....	....	....
	Moncton	AHL	3	1	1	2	0	....	....	....	....	....
1988-89	Moncton	AHL	6	2	5	7	4	....	....	....	....	....
	Tappara	Fin.	44	31	36	67	69	7	0	3	3	4
1989-90	Moncton	AHL	1	1	0	1	0	....	....	....	....	....

a ECAC Second All-Star Team (1988)
b NCAA East Second All-American Team (1988)

BOSCHMAN, LAURIE JOSEPH (BOSH-man)

Center. Shoots left. 6', 185 lbs. Born, Major, Sask., June 4, 1960.
(Toronto's 1st choice, 9th overall, in 1979 Entry Draft).

			Regular Season					Playoffs				
Season	Club	Lea	GP	G	A	TP	PIM	GP	G	A	TP	PIM
1976-77	Brandon	WHL	3	0	1	1	0	12	1	1	2	17
1977-78	Brandon	WHL	72	42	57	99	227	8	2	5	7	45
1978-79a	Brandon	WHL	65	66	83	149	215	22	11	23	34	56
1979-80	**Toronto**	**NHL**	**80**	**16**	**32**	**48**	**78**	**3**	**1**	**1**	**2**	**18**
1980-81	New Brunswick	AHL	4	4	1	5	47	....	....	....	....	....
	Toronto	**NHL**	**53**	**14**	**19**	**33**	**178**	**3**	**0**	**0**	**0**	**7**
1981-82	**Toronto**	**NHL**	**54**	**9**	**19**	**28**	**150**	....	....	....	....	....
	Edmonton	**NHL**	**11**	**2**	**3**	**5**	**37**	**3**	**0**	**1**	**1**	**4**
1982-83	**Edmonton**	**NHL**	**62**	**8**	**12**	**20**	**183**	....	....	....	....	....
	Winnipeg	**NHL**	**12**	**3**	**5**	**8**	**36**	**3**	**0**	**1**	**1**	**12**
1983-84	**Winnipeg**	**NHL**	**61**	**28**	**46**	**74**	**234**	**3**	**0**	**1**	**1**	**5**
1984-85	**Winnipeg**	**NHL**	**80**	**32**	**44**	**76**	**180**	**8**	**2**	**1**	**3**	**21**
1985-86	**Winnipeg**	**NHL**	**77**	**27**	**42**	**69**	**241**	**3**	**0**	**1**	**1**	**6**
1986-87	**Winnipeg**	**NHL**	**80**	**17**	**24**	**41**	**152**	**10**	**2**	**3**	**5**	**32**
1987-88	**Winnipeg**	**NHL**	**80**	**25**	**23**	**48**	**229**	**5**	**1**	**3**	**4**	**9**
1988-89	**Winnipeg**	**NHL**	**70**	**10**	**26**	**36**	**163**	....	....	....	....	....
1989-90	**Winnipeg**	**NHL**	**66**	**10**	**17**	**27**	**103**	**2**	**0**	**0**	**0**	**2**
	NHL Totals		**786**	**201**	**312**	**513**	**1964**	**43**	**6**	**12**	**18**	**116**

a WHL First All-Star Team (1979)

Traded to **Edmonton** by **Toronto** for Walt Poddubny and Phil Drouilliard, March 8, 1982. Traded to **Winnipeg** by **Edmonton** for Willy Lindstrom, March 7, 1983.

BOTHWELL, TIMOTHY (TIM)

Defense. Shoots left. 6'3", 190 lbs. Born, Vancouver, B.C., May 6, 1955.

			Regular Season					Playoffs				
Season	Club	Lea	GP	G	A	TP	PIM	GP	G	A	TP	PIM
1976-77	Brown U.	ECAC	27	7	27	34	40	....	....	....	....	....
1977-78	Brown U.	ECAC	29	9	26	35	48	....	....	....	....	....
1978-79	**NY Rangers**	**NHL**	**1**	**0**	**0**	**0**	**2**	....	....	....	....	....
	New Haven	AHL	66	15	33	48	44	10	4	6	10	8
1979-80	New Haven	AHL	22	6	7	13	25	....	....	....	....	....
	NY Rangers	**NHL**	**45**	**4**	**6**	**10**	**20**	**9**	**0**	**0**	**0**	**8**
1980-81	**NY Rangers**	**NHL**	**3**	**0**	**1**	**1**	**0**	....	....	....	....	....
	New Haven	AHL	73	10	53	63	98	4	1	2	3	6
1981-82	**NY Rangers**	**NHL**	**13**	**0**	**3**	**3**	**10**	....	....	....	....	....
	Springfield	AHL	10	0	4	4	7	....	....	....	....	....
1982-83	**St. Louis**	**NHL**	**61**	**4**	**11**	**15**	**34**	....	....	....	....	....
1983-84	Montana	CHL	4	0	3	3	0	....	....	....	....	....
	St. Louis	**NHL**	**62**	**2**	**13**	**15**	**65**	**11**	**0**	**2**	**2**	**14**
1984-85	**St. Louis**	**NHL**	**79**	**4**	**22**	**26**	**62**	**3**	**0**	**0**	**0**	**2**
1985-86	**Hartford**	**NHL**	**62**	**2**	**8**	**10**	**53**	**10**	**0**	**0**	**0**	**8**
1986-87	**Hartford**	**NHL**	**4**	**1**	**0**	**1**	**0**	....	....	....	....	....
	St. Louis	**NHL**	**72**	**5**	**16**	**21**	**46**	**6**	**0**	**0**	**0**	**6**
1987-88	**St. Louis**	**NHL**	**78**	**6**	**13**	**19**	**76**	**10**	**0**	**1**	**1**	**18**
1988-89	**St. Louis**	**NHL**	**22**	**0**	**0**	**0**	**14**	....	....	....	....	....
	Peoria	IHL	14	0	7	7	14	....	....	....	....	....
1989-90	New Haven	IHL	75	3	26	29	56	....	....	....	....	....
	NHL Totals		**502**	**28**	**93**	**121**	**382**	**49**	**0**	**3**	**3**	**56**

Signed as free agent by **NY Rangers**, June 8, 1978. Claimed by **St. Louis** from **NY Rangers** in NHL Waiver Draft, October 4, 1982. Rights sold to **Hartford** by **St. Louis**, October 4, 1985. Traded to **St. Louis** by **Hartford** for Dave Barr, October 21, 1986.

BOUDREAU, BRUCE ALLAN (BOO-droh)

Center. Shoots left. 5'9", 175 lbs. Born, Toronto, Ont., January 9, 1955.
(Toronto's 3rd choice, 42nd overall, in 1975 Amateur Draft).

			Regular Season					Playoffs				
Season	Club	Lea	GP	G	A	TP	PIM	GP	G	A	TP	PIM
1973-74	Toronto	OHA	53	46	67	113	51	....	....	....	....	....
1974-75	Toronto	OHA	69	*68	97	*165	52	22	12	*28	40	26
1975-76	Minnesota	WHA	30	3	6	9	4	....	....	....	....	....
	Johnstown	NAHL	34	25	35	60	14	....	....	....	....	....
1976-77	Dallas	CHL	58	*37	34	71	40	1	1	1	2	0
	Toronto	**NHL**	**15**	**2**	**5**	**7**	**4**	**3**	**0**	**0**	**0**	**0**
1977-78	**Toronto**	**NHL**	**40**	**11**	**18**	**29**	**12**	....	....	....	....	....
	Dallas	CHL	22	13	9	22	11	....	....	....	....	....
1978-79	**Toronto**	**NHL**	**26**	**4**	**3**	**7**	**2**	....	....	....	....	....
	New Brunswick	AHL	49	20	38	58	20	5	1	1	2	8
1979-80	**Toronto**	**NHL**	**2**	**0**	**0**	**0**	**2**	....	....	....	....	....
	New Brunswick	AHL	75	36	54	90	47	17	6	7	13	23
1980-81	**Toronto**	**NHL**	**39**	**10**	**14**	**24**	**18**	**2**	**1**	**0**	**1**	**0**
	New Brunswick	AHL	40	17	41	58	22	8	6	5	11	14
1981-82	**Toronto**	**NHL**	**12**	**0**	**2**	**2**	**6**	....	....	....	....	....
	Cincinnati	CHL	65	42	61	103	42	4	3	1	4	8
1982-83	St. Catharines	AHL	80	50	72	122	65	....	....	....	....	....
	Toronto	**NHL**	....	....	....	....	....	**4**	**1**	**0**	**1**	**0**
1983-84	St. Catharines	AHL	80	47	62	109	44	7	0	5	5	11
1984-85	Baltimore	AHL	17	4	7	11	4	15	3	9	12	4
1985-86	**Chicago**	**NHL**	**7**	**1**	**0**	**1**	**2**	....	....	....	....	....
	Nova Scotia	AHL	65	30	36	66	36	....	....	....	....	....
1986-87	Nova Scotia	AHL	78	35	47	82	40	5	3	3	6	4
1987-88abc	Springfield	AHL	80	42	*74	*116	84	....	....	....	....	....
1988-89	Springfield	AHL	50	28	36	64	42	....	....	....	....	....
	Newmarket	AHL	20	7	16	23	12	4	0	1	1	6
1989-90	Phoenix	IHL	82	41	68	109	89	....	....	....	....	....
	NHL Totals		**141**	**28**	**42**	**70**	**46**	**9**	**2**	**0**	**2**	**0**

a AHL First All-Star Team (1988)
b Won Fred Hunt Award (Sportsmanship-AHL) (1988)
c Won John Sollenberger Trophy (Top Scorer-AHL) (1988)

Claimed by **Toronto** as fill in Expansion Draft, June 13, 1979. Signed as a free agent by **Chicago**, October 10, 1985.

BOUGHNER, BOB (BOOG-nuhr)

Defense. Shoots right. 5'11", 200 lbs. Born, Windsor, Ont., March 8, 1971.
(Detroit's 2nd choice, 32nd overall, in 1989 Entry Draft).

			Regular Season					Playoffs				
Season	Club	Lea	GP	G	A	TP	PIM	GP	G	A	TP	PIM
1987-88	St. Mary's	OHA	36	4	18	22	177	....	....	....	....	....
1988-89	S.S. Marie	OHL	64	6	15	21	182	....	....	....	....	....
1989-90	S.S. Marie	OHL	49	7	23	30	122	....	....	....	....	....

BOURQUE, PHILLIPPE RICHARD (PHIL) (BOHRK)

Left wing. Shoots left. 6'1", 200 lbs. Born, Chelmsford, MA, June 8, 1962.

			Regular Season					Playoffs				
Season	Club	Lea	GP	G	A	TP	PIM	GP	G	A	TP	PIM
1980-81	Kingston	OHL	47	4	4	8	46	6	0	0	0	10
1981-82	Kingston	OHL	67	11	40	51	111	4	0	0	0	0
1982-83	Baltimore	AHL	65	1	15	16	93	....	....	....	....	....
1983-84	**Pittsburgh**	**NHL**	**5**	**0**	**1**	**1**	**12**	....	....	....	....	....
	Baltimore	AHL	58	5	17	22	96	....	....	....	....	....
1984-85	Baltimore	AHL	79	6	15	21	164	13	2	5	7	23
1985-86	**Pittsburgh**	**NHL**	**4**	**0**	**0**	**0**	**2**	....	....	....	....	....
	Baltimore	AHL	74	8	18	26	226	....	....	....	....	....
1986-87	**Pittsburgh**	**NHL**	**22**	**2**	**3**	**5**	**32**	....	....	....	....	....
	Baltimore	AHL	49	15	16	31	183	....	....	....	....	....
1987-88	**Pittsburgh**	**NHL**	**21**	**4**	**12**	**16**	**20**	....	....	....	....	....
ab	Muskegon	IHL	52	16	36	52	66	6	1	2	3	16
1988-89	**Pittsburgh**	**NHL**	**80**	**17**	**26**	**43**	**97**	**11**	**4**	**1**	**5**	**66**
1989-90	**Pittsburgh**	**NHL**	**76**	**22**	**17**	**39**	**108**	....	....	....	....	....
	NHL Totals		**208**	**45**	**59**	**104**	**271**	**11**	**4**	**1**	**5**	**66**

a IHL First All-Star Team (1988)
b Won Governor's Trophy (Outstanding Defenseman-IHL) (1988)

Signed as free agent by **Pittsburgh**, October 4, 1982.

BOURQUE, RAYMOND JEAN (BOHRK)

Defense. Shoots left. 5'11", 210 lbs. Born, Montreal, Que., December 28, 1960.
(Boston's 1st choice, 8th overall, in 1979 Entry Draft).

			Regular Season					Playoffs				
Season	Club	Lea	GP	G	A	TP	PIM	GP	G	A	TP	PIM
1976-77	Sorel	QJHL	69	12	36	48	61	....	....	....	....	....
1977-78	Verdun	QJHL	72	22	57	79	90	4	2	1	3	0
1978-79	Verdun	QJHL	63	22	71	93	44	11	3	16	19	18
1979-80ab	**Boston**	**NHL**	**80**	**17**	**48**	**65**	**73**	**10**	**2**	**9**	**11**	**27**
1980-81c	**Boston**	**NHL**	**67**	**27**	**29**	**56**	**96**	**3**	**0**	**1**	**1**	**2**
1981-82b	**Boston**	**NHL**	**65**	**17**	**49**	**66**	**51**	**9**	**1**	**5**	**6**	**16**
1982-83c	**Boston**	**NHL**	**65**	**22**	**51**	**73**	**20**	**17**	**8**	**15**	**23**	**10**
1983-84b	**Boston**	**NHL**	**78**	**31**	**65**	**96**	**57**	**3**	**0**	**2**	**2**	**0**
1984-85b	**Boston**	**NHL**	**73**	**20**	**66**	**86**	**53**	**5**	**0**	**3**	**3**	**4**
1985-86c	**Boston**	**NHL**	**74**	**19**	**58**	**77**	**68**	**3**	**0**	**0**	**0**	**0**
1986-87bd	**Boston**	**NHL**	**78**	**23**	**72**	**95**	**36**	**4**	**1**	**2**	**3**	**0**
1987-88bd	**Boston**	**NHL**	**78**	**17**	**64**	**81**	**72**	**23**	**3**	**18**	**21**	**26**
1988-89c	**Boston**	**NHL**	**60**	**18**	**43**	**61**	**52**	**10**	**0**	**4**	**4**	**6**
1989-90bd	**Boston**	**NHL**	**76**	**19**	**65**	**84**	**84**	**17**	**5**	**12**	**17**	**16**
	NHL Totals		**794**	**230**	**610**	**840**	**652**	**104**	**20**	**71**	**91**	**107**

a Won Calder Memorial Trophy (1980)
b NHL First All-Star Team (1980, 1982, 1984, 1985, 1987, 1988, 1990)
c NHL Second All-Star Team (1981, 1983, 1986, 1989)
d Won James Norris Memorial Trophy (1987, 1988, 1990)

Played in NHL All-Star Game (1981-86, 1988-90)

BOUTILIER, PAUL ANDRE (boot-LEER)

Defense. Shoots left. 6', 200 lbs. Born, Sydney, N.S., May 3, 1963.
(NY Islanders' 1st choice, 21st overall, in 1981 Entry Draft).

			Regular Season					Playoffs				
Season	Club	Lea	GP	G	A	TP	PIM	GP	G	A	TP	PIM
1980-81	Sherbrooke	QJHL	72	10	29	39	95	14	3	7	10	10
1981-82	**NY Islanders**	**NHL**	**1**	**0**	**0**	**0**	**0**	....	....	....	....	....
ab	Sherbrooke	QJHL	57	20	60	80	62	21	7	31	38	12
1982-83	St. Jean	QJHL	22	5	14	19	30	....	....	....	....	....
	NY Islanders	**NHL**	**29**	**4**	**5**	**9**	**24**	**2**	**0**	**0**	**0**	**2**
1983-84	Indianapolis	CHL	50	6	17	23	56	....	....	....	....	....
	NY Islanders	**NHL**	**28**	**0**	**11**	**11**	**36**	**21**	**1**	**7**	**8**	**10**
1984-85	**NY Islanders**	**NHL**	**78**	**12**	**23**	**35**	**90**	**10**	**0**	**2**	**2**	**16**
1985-86	**NY Islanders**	**NHL**	**77**	**4**	**30**	**34**	**100**	**3**	**0**	**0**	**0**	**2**
1986-87	**Boston**	**NHL**	**52**	**5**	**9**	**14**	**84**	....	....	....	....	....
	Minnesota	**NHL**	**10**	**2**	**4**	**6**	**8**	....	....	....	....	....
1987-88	**NY Rangers**	**NHL**	**4**	**0**	**1**	**1**	**6**	....	....	....	....	....
	New Haven	AHL	9	0	3	3	10	....	....	....	....	....
	Colorado	IHL	9	2	6	8	4	....	....	....	....	....
	Winnipeg	**NHL**	**6**	**0**	**0**	**0**	**6**	**5**	**0**	**0**	**0**	**15**
	Moncton	AHL	41	9	29	38	40	....	....	....	....	....
1988-89	**Winnipeg**	**NHL**	**3**	**0**	**0**	**0**	**4**	....	....	....	....	....
c	Moncton	AHL	77	6	54	60	101	10	2	7	9	4
1989-90	Bern	Switz.	36	12	28	40	....	....	....	....	....	....
	Maine	AHL	12	0	4	4	21	....	....	....	....	....
	NHL Totals		**288**	**27**	**83**	**110**	**358**	**41**	**1**	**9**	**10**	**45**

a QMJHL First All-Star Team (1982)
b Named QMJHL's Top Defenseman (1982)
c AHL First All-Star Team (1989)

Acquired by **Boston** as compensation for signing of free agent Brian Curran, August 6, 1987. Traded to **Minnesota** by **Boston** for Minnesota's fourth round choice (Darwin McPherson) in 1987 Entry Draft, March 10, 1987. Traded to **NY Rangers** by **Minnesota** with Jari Gronstrand for Jay Caufield and Dave Gagne, October 8, 1987. Traded to **Winnipeg** by **NY Rangers** for future considerations, December 16, 1987. Signed as a free agent by **Boston**, February 28, 1990.

BOYKO, DARREN

Center. Shoots right. 5'9", 170 lbs. Born, Winnipeg, Man., January 16, 1964.

			Regular Season					Playoffs				
Season	Club	Lea	GP	G	A	TP	PIM	GP	G	A	TP	PIM
1981-82	Winnipeg	WHL	65	35	37	72	14	....	....	....	....	....
1982-83	Winnipeg	WHL	72	49	81	130	8	3	0	2	2	0
1983-84	U. of Toronto	OUAA	40	33	51	84	24	9	7	10	17	4
1984-85	U. of Toronto	OUAA	39	31	53	84	42	2	1	0	1	6
1985-86	IFK Helsinki	Fin.	36	18	26	44	8	....	....	....	....	....
1986-87	IFK Helsinki	Fin.	44	22	13	35	44	....	....	....	....	....
1987-88	IFK Helsinki	Fin.	44	14	40	54	16	....	....	....	....	....
1988-89	IFK Helsinki	Fin.	34	15	15	30	10	....	....	....	....	....
	Winnipeg	**NHL**	**1**	**0**	**0**	**0**	**0**	....	....	....	....	....
	Moncton	AHL	18	3	7	10	2	4	0	0	0	0
1989-90	IFK Helsinki	Fin.	42	12	20	32	36	2	1	0	1	2
	NHL Totals		**1**	**0**	**0**	**0**	**0**	....	....	....	....	....

Signed as a free agent by **Winnipeg**, May 16, 1988.

BOZEK, DARWIN L.

Defense. Shoots left. 6'1", 185 lbs. Born, Spirit River, Alta., July 17, 1966.

			Regular Season					Playoffs				
Season	Club	Lea	GP	G	A	TP	PIM	GP	G	A	TP	PIM
1988-89	U. of Alberta	CWUAA	28	4	21	25	16	....	....	....	....	....
1989-90	New Haven	AHL	36	6	7	13	20	....	....	....	....	....

Signed as a free agent by **Los Angeles**, January 12, 1990.

BOZEK, ROMAN

Right wing. Shoots left. 6', 190 lbs. Born, Czechoslovakia, November 9, 1963.
(Edmonton's 9th choice, 225th overall, in 1989 Entry Draft).

			Regular Season					Playoffs				
Season	Club	Lea	GP	G	A	TP	PIM	GP	G	A	TP	PIM
1988-89	Budejovice	Czech.	33	16	9	25	....	....	....	....	....	....
1989-90	Budejovice	Czech.	42	19	16	35	....	....	....	....	....	....

BOZEK, STEVEN MICHAEL (STEVE)

Center/Left wing. Shoots left. 5'11", 180 lbs. Born, Kelowna, B.C., November 26, 1960.
(Los Angeles' 5th choice, 52nd overall, in 1980 Entry Draft).

			Regular Season					Playoffs				
Season	Club	Lea	GP	G	A	TP	PIM	GP	G	A	TP	PIM
1979-80	N. Michigan	CCHA	41	42	47	89	32	....	....	....	....	....
1980-81	N. Michigan	CCHA	44	35	55	90	0	....	....	....	....	....
1981-82	**Los Angeles**	**NHL**	**71**	**33**	**23**	**56**	**68**	**10**	**4**	**1**	**5**	**6**
1982-83	**Los Angeles**	**NHL**	**53**	**13**	**13**	**26**	**14**	....	....	....	....	....
1983-84	**Calgary**	**NHL**	**46**	**10**	**10**	**20**	**16**	**10**	**3**	**1**	**4**	**15**
1984-85	**Calgary**	**NHL**	**54**	**13**	**22**	**35**	**6**	**3**	**1**	**0**	**1**	**4**
1985-86	**Calgary**	**NHL**	**64**	**21**	**22**	**43**	**24**	**14**	**2**	**6**	**8**	**32**
1986-87	**Calgary**	**NHL**	**71**	**17**	**18**	**35**	**22**	**4**	**1**	**0**	**1**	**2**
1987-88	**Calgary**	**NHL**	**26**	**3**	**7**	**10**	**12**	....	....	....	....	....
	St. Louis	**NHL**	**7**	**0**	**0**	**0**	**2**	**7**	**1**	**1**	**2**	**6**
1988-89	**Vancouver**	**NHL**	**71**	**17**	**18**	**35**	**64**	**7**	**0**	**2**	**2**	**4**
1989-90	**Vancouver**	**NHL**	**58**	**14**	**9**	**23**	**32**	....	....	....	....	....
	NHL Totals		**521**	**141**	**142**	**283**	**260**	**55**	**12**	**11**	**23**	**69**

Traded to **Calgary** by **Los Angeles** for Carl Mokosak and Kevin LaVallee, June 20, 1983. Traded to **St. Louis** by **Calgary** with Brett Hull for Rob Ramage and Rick Wamsley, March 7, 1988. Traded to **Calgary** by **St. Louis** with Mark Hunter, Doug Gilmour and Michael Dark for Mike Bullard, Craig Coxe and Tim Corkery, September 6, 1988. Traded to **Vancouver** by **Calgary** with Paul Reinhart for Vancouver's third-round pick (Veli-Pekka Kautonen) in 1989 Entry Draft, September 6, 1988.

BOZIK, MOJMIR

Defense. Shoots right. 5'10", 185 lbs. Born, Liptovsky Mikulas, Czech., February 26, 1952.
(Edmonton's 11th choice, 231st overall, in 1986 Entry Draft).

			Regular Season					Playoffs				
Season	Club	Lea	GP	G	A	TP	PIM	GP	G	A	TP	PIM
1980-81	VSZ Kosice	Czech.	27	1	4	5	24	....	....	....	....	....
1981-82	VSZ Kosice	Czech.	42	2	7	9	73	....	....	....	....	....
1982-83	Dukla Trencin	Czech.	DID NOT PLAY									
1983-84	Dukla Trencin	Czech.	41	1	5	6	50	....	....	....	....	....
1984-85	VSZ Kosice	Czech.	41	2	10	12	32	....	....	....	....	....
1985-86	VSZ Kosice	Czech.	47	6	20	26	22	....	....	....	....	....
1986-87	VSZ Kosice	Czech.	40	7	9	16	44	....	....	....	....	....
1987-88	VSZ Kosice	Czech.	44	5	11	16	62	....	....	....	....	....
1988-89	VSZ Kosice	Czech.	43	9	7	16	56	....	....	....	....	....
1989-90	VSZ Kosice	Czech.	49	9	14	23	....	....	....	....	....	....

BOZON, PHILIPPE

Left wing. Shoots left. 5'10", 175 lbs. Born, Charmonix, France, November 30, 1966.

			Regular Season					Playoffs				
Season	Club	Lea	GP	G	A	TP	PIM	GP	G	A	TP	PIM
1984-85	St. Jean	QMJHL	67	32	50	82	82	5	0	5	5	4
1985-86a	St. Jean	QMJHL	65	59	52	111	72	10	10	6	16	16
	Peoria	IHL	....	....	....	....	....	5	1	0	1	0
1986-87	Peoria	IHL	28	4	11	15	17	....	....	....	....	....
	St. Jean	QMJHL	25	20	21	41	75	8	5	5	10	30
1987-88	Mont-Blanc	France	18	11	15	26	34	10	15	6	21	6
1988-89			DID NOT PLAY									
1989-90	Grenoble	France	36	45	38	83	34	....	....	....	....	....

a QMJHL Second All-Star Team (1986).

Signed as a free agent by **St. Louis**, September 29, 1985.

BRADLEY, BRIAN WALTER RICHARD

Center. Shoots right. 5'10", 170 lbs. Born, Kitchener, Ont., January 21, 1965.
(Calgary's 2nd choice, 51st overall, in 1983 Entry Draft).

			Regular Season					Playoffs				
Season	Club	Lea	GP	G	A	TP	PIM	GP	G	A	TP	PIM
1982-83	London	OHL	67	37	82	119	37	3	1	0	1	0
1983-84	London	OHL	49	40	60	100	24	4	2	4	6	0
1984-85	London	OHL	32	27	49	76	22	8	5	10	15	4
1985-86	**Calgary**	**NHL**	**5**	**0**	**1**	**1**	**0**	**1**	**0**	**0**	**0**	**0**
	Moncton	AHL	59	23	42	65	40	10	6	9	15	4
1986-87	**Calgary**	**NHL**	**40**	**10**	**18**	**28**	**16**	....	....	....	....	....
	Moncton	AHL	20	12	16	28	8	....	....	....	....	....
1987-88	**Vancouver**	**NHL**	**11**	**3**	**5**	**8**	**6**	....	....	....	....	....
	Cdn. National	.....	47	8	19	37	42	....	....	....	....	....
	Cdn. Olympic	.....	7	0	4	4	0	....	....	....	....	....
1988-89	**Vancouver**	**NHL**	**71**	**18**	**27**	**45**	**42**	**7**	**3**	**4**	**7**	**10**
1989-90	**Vancouver**	**NHL**	**67**	**19**	**29**	**48**	**48**	....	....	....	....	....
	NHL Totals		**194**	**50**	**80**	**130**	**112**	**8**	**3**	**4**	**7**	**10**

Traded to **Vancouver** by **Calgary** with Peter Bakovic and Kevin Guy for Craig Coxe, March 6, 1988.

BRADY, NEIL

Center. Shoots left. 6'2", 200 lbs. Born, Montreal, Que., April 12, 1968.
(New Jersey's 1st choice, 3rd overall, in 1986 Entry Draft).

			Regular Season					Playoffs				
Season	Club	Lea	GP	G	A	TP	PIM	GP	G	A	TP	PIM
1984-85	Calgary	Midget	37	25	50	75	75	....	....	....	....	....
	Medicine Hat	WHL	....	....	....	....	....	3	0	0	0	2
1985-86a	Medicine Hat	WHL	72	21	60	81	104	21	9	11	20	23
1986-87	Medicine Hat	WHL	57	19	64	83	126	18	1	4	5	25
1987-88	Medicine Hat	WHL	61	16	35	51	110	15	0	3	3	19
1988-89	Utica	AHL	75	16	21	37	56	4	0	3	3	0
1989-90	**New Jersey**	**NHL**	**19**	**1**	**4**	**5**	**13**	....	....	....	....	....
	Utica	AHL	38	10	13	23	21	5	0	1	1	10
	NHL Totals		**19**	**1**	**4**	**5**	**13**	....	....	....	....	....

a WHL Rookie of the Year (1986)

BRAIT, MATTHEW

Defense. Shoots left. 6'2", 210 lbs. Born, Toronto, Ont., June 29, 1969.
(Philadelphia's 9th choice, 222nd overall, in 1989 Entry Draft).

			Regular Season					Playoffs				
Season	Club	Lea	GP	G	A	TP	PIM	GP	G	A	TP	PIM
1988-89	St. Michael's	Jr.B	32	5	23	28	208	....	....	....	....	....
1989-90	Kent State	NCAA	30	4	8	12	81	....	....	....	....	....

BRAUER, CAM

Defense. Shoots left. 6'3", 210 lbs. Born, Calgary, Alta., January 4, 1970.
(Edmonton's 5th choice, 82nd overall, in 1988 Entry Draft).

			Regular Season					Playoffs				
Season	Club	Lea	GP	G	A	TP	PIM	GP	G	A	TP	PIM
1987-88	RPI	ECAC	18	0	1	1	4	....	....	....	....	....
1988-89	Regina	WHL	49	0	9	9	59	....	....	....	....	....
1989-90	Regina	WHL	4	0	0	0	20	....	....	....	....	....
a	Seattle	WHL	64	1	9	10	229	10	0	0	0	27

a WHL West Second All-Star Team (1990)

Rights traded to **Hartford** by **Edmonton** for Mark Laforge, March 6, 1990.

BRAZDA, RADOMIR

Defense. Shoots right. 6'2", 175 lbs. Born, Pardubice, Czechoslovakia, October 11, 1967.
(Detroit's 6th choice, 95th overall, in 1987 Entry Draft).

			Regular Season					Playoffs				
Season	Club	Lea	GP	G	A	TP	PIM	GP	G	A	TP	PIM
1986-87	Pardubice	Czech	31	1	1	2	....	....	....	....	....	....
1987-88	Pardubice	Czech	11	1	2	3	....	....	....	....	....	....
1988-89	Dukla Trencin	Czech	35	1	1	2	....	....	....	....	....	....
1989-90	Pardubice	Czech	26	2	1	3		....	....	....	....	....

BRENNAN, STEPHEN

Right wing. Shoots right. 6'1", 190 lbs. Born, Winchester, MA, March 22, 1967.
(Toronto's 8th choice, 153rd overall, in 1986 Entry Draft).

			Regular Season					Playoffs				
Season	Club	Lea	GP	G	A	TP	PIM	GP	G	A	TP	PIM
1986-87	Clarkson	ECAC	29	3	3	6	17	....	....	....	....	....
1987-88	Clarkson	ECAC	12	4	0	4	18	....	....	....	....	....
1988-89	Clarkson	ECAC	25	3	4	7	42	....	....	....	....	....
1989-90	Clarkson	ECAC	33	7	6	13	48	....	....	....	....	....

BRICKLEY, ANDY

Left wing/Center. Shoots left. 5'11", 200 lbs. Born, Melrose, MA, August 9, 1961.
(Philadelphia's 10th choice, 210th overall, in 1980 Entry Draft).

			Regular Season					Playoffs				
Season	Club	Lea	GP	G	A	TP	PIM	GP	G	A	TP	PIM
1979-80	N. Hampshire	ECAC	27	15	17	32	8	....	....	....	....	....
1980-81	N. Hampshire	ECAC	31	27	25	52	16	....	....	....	....	....
1981-82ab	N. Hampshire	ECAC	35	26	27	53	6	....	....	....	....	....
1982-83	**Philadelphia**	**NHL**	**3**	**1**	**1**	**2**	**0**	....	....	....	....	....
c	Maine	AHL	76	29	54	83	10	17	9	5	14	0
1983-84	Springfield	AHL	7	1	5	6	2	....	....	....	....	....
	Baltimore	AHL	4	0	5	5	2	....	....	....	....	....
	Pittsburgh	**NHL**	**50**	**18**	**20**	**38**	**9**	....	....	....	....	....
1984-85	**Pittsburgh**	**NHL**	**45**	**7**	**15**	**22**	**10**	....	....	....	....	....
	Baltimore	AHL	31	13	14	27	8	15	*10	8	18	0
1985-86	Maine	AHL	60	26	34	60	20	5	0	4	4	0
1986-87	**New Jersey**	**NHL**	**51**	**11**	**12**	**23**	**8**	....	....	....	....	....
1987-88	**New Jersey**	**NHL**	**45**	**8**	**14**	**22**	**14**	**4**	**0**	**1**	**1**	**4**
	Utica	AHL	9	5	8	13	4	....	....	....	....	....
1988-89	**Boston**	**NHL**	**71**	**13**	**22**	**35**	**20**	**10**	**0**	**2**	**2**	**0**
1989-90	**Boston**	**NHL**	**43**	**12**	**28**	**40**	**8**	**2**	**0**	**0**	**0**	**0**
	NHL Totals		**308**	**70**	**112**	**182**	**69**	**16**	**0**	**3**	**3**	**4**

a ECAC First All-Star Team (1982)
b NCAA All-American Team (1982)
c AHL Second All-Star Team (1983)

Traded to **Pittsburgh** by **Philadelphia** with Mark Taylor, Ron Flockhart, Philadelphia's first round (Roger Belanger) and third round (Mike Stevens — later transferred to Vancouver) choices in 1984 Entry Draft for Rich Sutter and Pittsburgh's second round (Greg Smyth) and third round (David McLay) choices in 1984 Entry Draft, October 23, 1983. Signed as a free agent by **New Jersey**, July 8, 1986. Claimed by **Boston** in NHL Waiver Draft, October 3, 1988,

BRILL, JOHN

Right wing. Shoots right. 6'3", 180 lbs. Born, St. Paul, MN, December 3, 1970.
(Pittsburgh's 3rd choice, 58th overall, in 1989 Entry Draft).

			Regular Season					Playoffs				
Season	Club	Lea	GP	G	A	TP	PIM	GP	G	A	TP	PIM
1987-88	Grand Rapids	HS	28	15	13	28	....	....	....	....	....	....
1988-89	Grand Rapids	HS	25	23	29	52	28	....	....	....	....	....
1989-90	U. Minnesota	WCHA	34	2	8	10	22	....	....	....	....	....

BRIND'AMOUR, ROD

Left wing/Center. Shoots left. 6'1", 200 lbs. Born, Ottawa, Ont., August 9, 1970.
(St. Louis' 1st choice, 9th overall, in 1988 Entry Draft).

			Regular Season					Playoffs				
Season	Club	Lea	GP	G	A	TP	PIM	GP	G	A	TP	PIM
1987-88	Notre Dame	SJHL	56	46	61	107	136	....	....	....	....	....
1988-89a	Michigan State	CCHA	42	27	32	59	63	....	....	....	....	....
	St. Louis	**NHL**	....	....	....	....	....	**5**	**2**	**0**	**2**	**4**
1989-90b	**St. Louis**	**NHL**	**79**	**26**	**35**	**61**	**46**	**12**	**5**	**8**	**13**	**6**
	NHL Totals		**79**	**26**	**35**	**61**	**46**	**17**	**7**	**8**	**15**	**10**

a CCHA Freshman of the Year (1989)
b NHL All-Rookie Team (1990)

BRISEBOIS, PATRICE

Defense. Shoots right. 6'1", 175 lbs. Born, Montreal, Que., January 27, 1971.
(Montreal's 2nd choice, 30th overall, in 1989 Entry Draft).

			Regular Season					Playoffs				
Season	Club	Lea	GP	G	A	TP	PIM	GP	G	A	TP	PIM
1987-88	Laval	QMJHL	48	10	34	44	95	6	0	2	2	2
1988-89	Laval	QMJHL	50	20	45	65	95	17	8	14	22	45
1989-90a	Laval	QMJHL	56	18	70	88	108	13	7	9	16	26

a QMJHL Second All-Star Team (1990)

BROCHU, STEPHANE (broh-SHOO)

Defense. Shoots left. 6'1", 185 lbs. Born, Sherbrooke, Que., August 15, 1967.
(NY Rangers' 9th choice, 175th overall, in 1985 Entry Draft).

			Regular Season					Playoffs				
Season	Club	Lea	GP	G	A	TP	PIM	GP	G	A	TP	PIM
1984-85	Quebec	QMJHL	59	2	16	18	56	4	0	2	2	2
1985-86	St. Jean	QMJHL	63	14	27	41	121	3	1	0	1	2
1986-87	St. Jean	QMJHL	DID NOT PLAY - INJURED					8	0	2	2	11
1987-88	St. Jean	QMHL	29	4	35	39	88	....	....	....	....	....
	Colorado	IHL	52	4	10	14	70	12	3	3	6	13
1988-89	**NY Rangers**	**NHL**	**1**	**0**	**0**	**0**	**0**	....	....	....	....	....
	Denver	IHL	67	5	14	19	109	3	0	0	0	0
1989-90	Flint	IHL	5	0	0	0	2	....	....	....	....	....
	Fort Wayne	IHL	63	9	19	28	98	5	0	2	2	6
	NHL Totals		**1**	**0**	**0**	**0**	**0**	....	....	....	....	....

BROOKE, ROBERT W. (BOB)

Center. Shoots right. 6'1", 200 lbs. Born, Melrose, MA, December 18, 1960.
(St. Louis' 3rd choice, 75th overall, in 1980 Entry Draft).

			Regular Season					Playoffs				
Season	Club	Lea	GP	G	A	TP	PIM	GP	G	A	TP	PIM
1979-80	Yale	ECAC	24	7	22	29	38	....	....	....	....	....
1980-81	Yale	ECAC	27	12	30	42	59	....	....	....	....	....
1981-82	Yale	ECAC	25	12	30	42	60	....	....	....	....	....
1982-83ab	Yale	ECAC	21	10	27	37	48	....	....	....	....	....
1983-84	U.S. National	....	54	7	18	25	75	....	....	....	....	....
	U.S. Olympic	....	6	1	2	3	10	....	....	....	....	....
	NY Rangers	**NHL**	**9**	**1**	**2**	**3**	**4**	**5**	**0**	**0**	**0**	**7**
1984-85	**NY Rangers**	**NHL**	**72**	**7**	**9**	**16**	**79**	**3**	**0**	**0**	**0**	**8**
1985-86	**NY Rangers**	**NHL**	**79**	**24**	**20**	**44**	**111**	**16**	**6**	**9**	**15**	**28**
1986-87	**NY Rangers**	**NHL**	**15**	**3**	**5**	**8**	**20**	....	....	....	....	....
	Minnesota	**NHL**	**65**	**10**	**18**	**28**	**78**	....	....	....	....	....
1987-88	**Minnesota**	**NHL**	**77**	**5**	**20**	**25**	**108**	....	....	....	....	....
1988-89	**Minnesota**	**NHL**	**57**	**7**	**9**	**16**	**57**	**5**	**3**	**0**	**3**	**2**
1989-90	**Minnesota**	**NHL**	**38**	**4**	**4**	**8**	**33**	....	....	....	....	....
	New Jersey	**NHL**	**35**	**8**	**10**	**18**	**30**	**5**	**0**	**0**	**0**	**14**
	NHL Totals		**447**	**69**	**97**	**166**	**520**	**34**	**9**	**9**	**18**	**59**

a ECAC First All-Star Team (1983)
b NCAA All-American First Team (1983)

Rights traded to **NY Rangers** by **St. Louis** with Larry Patey for Dave Barr, NY Rangers' third round choice (Alan Perry) in 1984 Entry Draft and cash, March 5, 1984. Traded to **Minnesota** by **NY Rangers** with NY Rangers' rights to Minnesota's fourth-round choice (Jeffery Stolp) in 1988 Entry Draft previously acquired by NY Rangers in Mark Pavelich deal for Curt Giles, Tony McKegney and Minnesota's second-round choice (Troy Mallette) in 1988 Entry Draft, November 13, 1986. Traded to **New Jersey** by **Minnesota** for Aaron Broten, January 5, 1990.

BROOKS, DAN

Defense. Shoots left. 6'3", 210 lbs. Born, St. Paul, MN, April 26, 1967.
(St. Louis' 4th choice, 100th overall, in 1985 Entry Draft).

			Regular Season					Playoffs				
Season	Club	Lea	GP	G	A	TP	PIM	GP	G	A	TP	PIM
1986-87	U. of Denver	WCHA	7	0	0	0	4	....	....	....	....	....
1987-88	U. of Denver	WCHA	27	1	2	3	14	....	....	....	....	....
1988-89	U. of Denver	WCHA	41	0	6	6	36	....	....	....	....	....
1989-90	U. of Denver	WCHA	32	4	4	8	30	....	....	....	....	....

BROTEN, AARON (BRAH-tuhn)

Center. Shoots left. 5'10", 180 lbs. Born, Roseau, MN, November 14, 1960.
(Colorado's 5th choice, 106th overall, in 1980 Entry Draft).

			Regular Season					Playoffs				
Season	Club	Lea	GP	G	A	TP	PIM	GP	G	A	TP	PIM
1979-80	U. Minnesota	WCHA	41	25	47	72	8	....	....	....	....	....
1980-81	U. Minnesota	WCHA	45	*47	*59	*106	24	....	....	....	....	....
	Colorado	**NHL**	**2**	**0**	**0**	**0**	**0**	....	....	....	....	....
1981-82	Fort Worth	CHL	19	15	21	36	11	....	....	....	....	....
	Colorado	**NHL**	**58**	**15**	**24**	**39**	**6**	....	....	....	....	....
1982-83	Wichita	CHL	4	0	4	4	0	....	....	....	....	....
	New Jersey	**NHL**	**73**	**16**	**39**	**55**	**28**	....	....	....	....	....
1983-84	**New Jersey**	**NHL**	**80**	**13**	**23**	**36**	**36**	....	....	....	....	....
1984-85	**New Jersey**	**NHL**	**80**	**22**	**35**	**57**	**38**	....	....	....	....	....
1985-86	**New Jersey**	**NHL**	**66**	**18**	**25**	**43**	**26**	....	....	....	....	....
1986-87	**New Jersey**	**NHL**	**80**	**26**	**53**	**79**	**36**	....	....	....	....	....
1987-88	**New Jersey**	**NHL**	**80**	**26**	**57**	**83**	**80**	**20**	**5**	**11**	**16**	**20**
1988-89	**New Jersey**	**NHL**	**80**	**16**	**43**	**59**	**81**	....	....	....	....	....
1989-90	**New Jersey**	**NHL**	**42**	**10**	**8**	**18**	**36**	....	....	....	....	....
	Minnesota	**NHL**	**35**	**8**	**10**	**18**	**22**	**7**	**0**	**5**	**5**	**8**
	NHL Totals		**676**	**170**	**317**	**487**	**389**	**27**	**5**	**16**	**21**	**28**

Traded to **Minnesota** by **New Jersey** for Bob Brooke, January 5, 1990.

BROTEN, NEAL LaMOY (BRAH-tuhn)

Center. Shoots left. 5'9", 170 lbs. Born, Roseau, MN, November 29, 1959.
(Minnesota's 3rd choice, 42nd overall, in 1979 Entry Draft).

			Regular Season					Playoffs				
Season	Club	Lea	GP	G	A	TP	PIM	GP	G	A	TP	PIM
1978-79	U. Minnesota	WCHA	40	21	50	71	18	....	....	....	....	....
1979-80	U.S. National	...	55	25	30	55	20	....	....	....	....	....
	U.S. Olympic	...	7	2	1	3	2	....	....	....	....	....
1980-81ab	U. Minnesota	WCHA	36	17	54	71	56	....	....	....	....	....
	Minnesota	**NHL**	**3**	**2**	**0**	**2**	**12**	**19**	**1**	**7**	**8**	**9**
1981-82	**Minnesota**	**NHL**	**73**	**38**	**60**	**98**	**42**	**4**	**0**	**2**	**2**	**0**
1982-83	**Minnesota**	**NHL**	**79**	**32**	**45**	**77**	**43**	**9**	**1**	**6**	**7**	**10**
1983-84	**Minnesota**	**NHL**	**76**	**28**	**61**	**89**	**43**	**16**	**5**	**5**	**10**	**4**
1984-85	**Minnesota**	**NHL**	**80**	**19**	**37**	**56**	**39**	**9**	**2**	**5**	**7**	**10**
1985-86	**Minnesota**	**NHL**	**80**	**29**	**76**	**105**	**47**	**5**	**3**	**2**	**5**	**2**
1986-87	**Minnesota**	**NHL**	**46**	**18**	**35**	**53**	**33**	....	....	....	....	....
1987-88	**Minnesota**	**NHL**	**54**	**9**	**30**	**39**	**32**	....	....	....	....	....
1988-89	**Minnesota**	**NHL**	**68**	**18**	**38**	**56**	**57**	**5**	**2**	**2**	**4**	**4**
1989-90	**Minnesota**	**NHL**	**80**	**23**	**62**	**85**	**45**	**7**	**2**	**2**	**4**	**18**
	NHL Totals		**639**	**216**	**444**	**660**	**393**	**74**	**16**	**31**	**47**	**57**

Played in NHL All-Star Game (1983-86)
a WCHA First All-Star Team (1981)
b Won Hobey Baker Memorial Trophy (Top U.S. College Player) (1981)

BROTEN, PAUL (BRAH-tuhn)

Center. Shoots right. 5'11", 170 lbs. Born, Roseau, MN, October 27, 1965.
(NY Rangers 3rd choice, 77th overall, in 1984 Entry Draft)

			Regular Season					Playoffs				
Season	Club	Lea	GP	G	A	TP	PIM	GP	G	A	TP	PIM
1984-85	U. Minnesota	WCHA	44	8	8	16	26	....	....	....	....	....
1985-86	U. Minnesota	WCHA	38	6	16	22	24	....	....	....	....	....
1986-87	U. Minnesota	WCHA	48	17	22	39	52	....	....	....	....	....
1987-88	U. Minnesota	WCHA	38	18	21	39	42	....	....	....	....	....
1988-89	Denver	IHL	77	28	31	59	133	4	0	2	2	6
1989-90	**NY Rangers**	**NHL**	**32**	**5**	**3**	**8**	**26**	**6**	**1**	**1**	**2**	**2**
	Flint	IHL	28	17	9	26	55	....	....	....	....	....
	NHL Totals		**32**	**5**	**3**	**8**	**26**	**6**	**1**	**1**	**2**	**2**

BROWN, CAL

Defense. Shoots left. 6', 195 lbs. Born, Calgary, Alta., January 13, 1967.
(Hartford's 10th choice, 221st overall, in 1986 Entry Draft).

			Regular Season					Playoffs				
Season	Club	Lea	GP	G	A	TP	PIM	GP	G	A	TP	PIM
1986-87	Colorado	WCHA	41	7	17	24	80	....	....	....	....	....
1987-88	Colorado	WCHA	34	7	11	18	94	....	....	....	....	....
1988-89	Colorado	WCHA	37	2	27	29	63	....	....	....	....	....
1989-90	Colorado	WCHA	39	4	21	25	74	....	....	....	....	....

BROWN, DAVID

Right wing. Shoots right. 6'5", 205 lbs. Born, Saskatoon, Sask., October 12, 1962.
(Philadelphia's 7th choice, 40th overall, in 1982 Entry Draft).

			Regular Season					Playoffs				
Season	Club	Lea	GP	G	A	TP	PIM	GP	G	A	TP	PIM
1980-81	Spokane	WHL	9	2	2	4	21	....	....	....	....	....
1981-82	Saskatoon	WHL	62	11	33	44	344	5	1	0	1	4
1982-83	**Philadelphia**	**NHL**	**2**	**0**	**0**	**0**	**5**	....	....	....	....	....
	Maine	AHL	71	8	6	14	*418	16	0	0	0	*107
1983-84	Springfield	AHL	59	17	14	31	150	....	....	....	....	....
	Philadelphia	**NHL**	**19**	**1**	**5**	**6**	**98**	**2**	**0**	**0**	**0**	**12**
1984-85	**Philadelphia**	**NHL**	**57**	**3**	**6**	**9**	**165**	**11**	**0**	**0**	**0**	**59**
1985-86	**Philadelphia**	**NHL**	**76**	**10**	**7**	**17**	**277**	**5**	**0**	**0**	**0**	**16**
1986-87	**Philadelphia**	**NHL**	**62**	**7**	**3**	**10**	**274**	**26**	**1**	**2**	**3**	**59**
1987-88	**Philadelphia**	**NHL**	**47**	**12**	**5**	**17**	**114**	**7**	**1**	**0**	**1**	**27**
1988-89	**Philadelphia**	**NHL**	**50**	**0**	**3**	**3**	**100**	....	....	....	....	....
	Edmonton	**NHL**	**22**	**0**	**2**	**2**	**56**	**7**	**0**	**0**	**0**	**6**
1989-90	**Edmonton**	**NHL**	**60**	**0**	**6**	**6**	**145**	**3**	**0**	**0**	**0**	**0**
	NHL Totals		**395**	**33**	**37**	**70**	**1234**	**61**	**2**	**2**	**4**	**179**

Traded to **Edmonton** by **Philadelphia** for Keith Acton and Edmonton's fifth-round choice in 1991 Entry Draft, February 7, 1989.

BROWN, DOUG

Right wing. Shoots right. 5'10", 180 lbs. Born, Southboro, MA, July 12, 1964.

			Regular Season					Playoffs				
Season	Club	Lea	GP	G	A	TP	PIM	GP	G	A	TP	PIM
1982-83	Boston College	ECAC	22	9	8	17	0	....	....	....	....	....
1983-84	Boston College	ECAC	38	11	10	21	6	....	....	....	....	....
1984-85	Boston College	H.E.	45	37	31	68	10	....	....	....	....	....
1985-86	Boston College	H.E.	38	16	40	56	16	....	....	....	....	....
1986-87	**New Jersey**	**NHL**	**4**	**0**	**1**	**1**	**0**	....	....	....	....	....
	Maine	AHL	73	24	34	58	15	....	....	....	....	....
1987-88	**New Jersey**	**NHL**	**70**	**14**	**11**	**25**	**20**	**19**	**5**	**1**	**6**	**6**
	Utica	AHL	2	0	2	2	2	....	....	....	....	....
1988-89	**New Jersey**	**NHL**	**63**	**15**	**10**	**25**	**15**	....	....	....	....	....
	Utica	AHL	4	1	4	5	0	....	....	....	....	....
1989-90	**New Jersey**	**NHL**	**69**	**14**	**20**	**34**	**16**	**6**	**0**	**1**	**1**	**2**
	NHL Totals		**206**	**43**	**42**	**85**	**51**	**25**	**5**	**2**	**7**	**8**

Signed as a free agent by **New Jersey**, August 6, 1986.

BROWN, GREG

Defense. Shoots right. 6', 180 lbs. Born, Hartford, CT, March 7, 1968.
(Buffalo's 2nd choice, 26th overall, in 1986 Entry Draft).

			Regular Season					Playoffs				
Season	Club	Lea	GP	G	A	TP	PIM	GP	G	A	TP	PIM
1986-87	Boston College	H.E.	37	10	27	37	22	....	....	....	....	....
1987-88	U.S. National	....	55	6	29	35	22	....	....	....	....	....
	U.S. Olympic	....	6	0	4	4	2	....	....	....	....	....
1988-89abc	Boston College	H.E.	40	9	34	43	24	....	....	....	....	....
1989-90abc	Boston College	H.E.	42	5	35	40	42	....	....	....	....	....

a Hockey East First All-Star Team (1989, 1990)
b Hockey East Player of the Year (1989, 1990)
c NCAA East First All-American Team (1989, 1990)

BROWN, JEFF

Defense. Shoots right. 6'1", 202 lbs. Born, Ottawa, Ont., April 30, 1966.
(Quebec's 2nd choice, 36th overall, in 1984 Entry Draft).

			Regular Season					Playoffs				
Season	Club	Lea	GP	G	A	TP	PIM	GP	G	A	TP	PIM
1982-83	Sudbury	OHL	65	9	37	46	39	....	....	....	....	....
1983-84	Sudbury	OHL	68	17	60	77	39	....	....	....	....	....
1984-85	Sudbury	OHL	56	16	48	64	26	....	....	....	....	....
1985-86	**Quebec**	**NHL**	**8**	**3**	**2**	**5**	**6**	**1**	**0**	**0**	**0**	**0**
a	Sudbury	OHL	45	22	28	50	24	4	0	2	2	11
	Fredericton	AHL	....	....	....	....	....	1	0	1	1	0
1986-87	**Quebec**	**NHL**	**44**	**7**	**22**	**29**	**16**	**13**	**3**	**3**	**6**	**2**
	Fredericton	AHL	26	2	14	16	16	....	....	....	....	....
1987-88	**Quebec**	**NHL**	**78**	**16**	**36**	**52**	**64**	....	....	....	....	....
1988-89	**Quebec**	**NHL**	**78**	**21**	**47**	**68**	**62**	....	....	....	....	....
1989-90	**Quebec**	**NHL**	**29**	**6**	**10**	**16**	**18**	....	....	....	....	....
	St.Louis	**NHL**	**48**	**10**	**18**	**28**	**37**	**12**	**2**	**10**	**12**	**4**
	NHL Totals		**285**	**63**	**135**	**198**	**203**	**26**	**5**	**13**	**18**	**6**

a OHL First All-Star Team (1986)

Traded to **St Louis** by **Quebec** for Tony Hrkac and Greg Millen, December 13, 1989.

BROWN, KEITH JEFFREY

Defense. Shoots right. 6'1", 195 lbs. Born, Corner Brook, Nfld., May 6, 1960.
(Chicago's 1st choice, 7th overall, in 1979 Entry Draft).

			Regular Season					Playoffs				
Season	Club	Lea	GP	G	A	TP	PIM	GP	G	A	TP	PIM
1977-78a	Portland	WHL	72	11	53	64	51	8	0	3	3	2
1978-79bc	Portland	WHL	70	11	85	96	75	25	3	*30	33	21
1979-80	**Chicago**	**NHL**	**76**	**2**	**18**	**20**	**27**	**6**	**0**	**0**	**0**	**4**
1980-81	**Chicago**	**NHL**	**80**	**9**	**34**	**43**	**80**	**3**	**0**	**2**	**2**	**2**
1981-82	**Chicago**	**NHL**	**33**	**4**	**20**	**24**	**26**	**4**	**0**	**2**	**2**	**5**
1982-83	**Chicago**	**NHL**	**50**	**4**	**27**	**31**	**20**	**7**	**0**	**0**	**0**	**11**
1983-84	**Chicago**	**NHL**	**74**	**10**	**25**	**35**	**94**	**5**	**0**	**1**	**1**	**10**
1984-85	**Chicago**	**NHL**	**56**	**1**	**22**	**23**	**55**	**11**	**2**	**7**	**9**	**31**
1985-86	**Chicago**	**NHL**	**70**	**11**	**29**	**40**	**87**	**3**	**0**	**1**	**1**	**9**
1986-87	**Chicago**	**NHL**	**73**	**4**	**23**	**27**	**86**	**4**	**0**	**1**	**1**	**6**
1987-88	**Chicago**	**NHL**	**24**	**3**	**6**	**9**	**45**	**5**	**0**	**2**	**2**	**10**
1988-89	**Chicago**	**NHL**	**74**	**2**	**16**	**18**	**84**	**13**	**1**	**3**	**4**	**25**
1989-90	**Chicago**	**NHL**	**67**	**5**	**20**	**25**	**87**	**18**	**0**	**4**	**4**	**43**
	NHL Totals		**677**	**55**	**240**	**295**	**691**	**79**	**3**	**23**	**26**	**156**

a Shared WHL's Rookie of the Year with John Ogrodnick (New Westminster) (1978)
b Named WHL's Top Defenseman (1979)
c WHL First All-Star Team (1979)

BROWN, ROB

Right wing. Shoots left. 5'11", 185 lbs. Born, Kingston, Ont., April 10, 1968.
(Pittsburgh's 4th choice, 67th overall, in 1986 Entry Draft).

			Regular Season					Playoffs				
Season	Club	Lea	GP	G	A	TP	PIM	GP	G	A	TP	PIM
1984-85	Kamloops	WHL	60	29	50	79	95	15	8	8	26	28
1985-86ab	Kamloops	WHL	69	58	*115	*173	171	16	*18	*28	*46	14
1986-87abc	Kamloops	WHL	63	*76	*136	*212	101	5	6	5	11	6
1987-88	**Pittsburgh**	**NHL**	**51**	**24**	**20**	**44**	**56**	....	....	....	....	....
1988-89	**Pittsburgh**	**NHL**	**68**	**49**	**66**	**115**	**118**	**11**	**5**	**3**	**8**	**22**
1989-90	**Pittsburgh**	**NHL**	**80**	**33**	**47**	**80**	**102**	....	....	....	....	....
	NHL Totals		**199**	**106**	**133**	**239**	**276**	**11**	**5**	**3**	**8**	**22**

a WHL Player of the Year (1986, 1987)
b WHL First All-Star Team (1986, 1987)
c Canadian Major Junior Player of the Year (1987)

Played in NHL All-Star Game (1989)

BROWNSCHIDLE, MARK

Defense. Shoots right. 6'2", 185 lbs. Born, East Amherst, NY, October 26, 1970.
(Winnipeg's 5th choice, 64th overall, in 1989 Entry Draft).

			Regular Season					Playoffs				
Season	Club	Lea	GP	G	A	TP	PIM	GP	G	A	TP	PIM
1988-89	Boston U.	H.E.	35	0	7	7	12	....	....	....	....	....
1989-90	Boston U.	H.E.	38	1	4	5	12	....	....	....	....	....

BRUCE, DAVID

Right wing/Center. Shoots right. 5'11", 187 lbs. Born, Thunder Bay, Ont., October 7, 1964.
(Vancouver's 2nd choice, 30th overall, in 1983 Entry Draft).

			Regular Season					Playoffs				
Season	Club	Lea	GP	G	A	TP	PIM	GP	G	A	TP	PIM
1982-83	Kitchener	OHL	67	36	35	71	199	12	7	9	16	27
1983-84	Kitchener	OHL	62	52	40	92	203	10	5	8	13	20
1984-85	Fredericton	AHL	56	14	11	25	104	5	0	0	0	37
1985-86	**Vancouver**	**NHL**	**12**	**0**	**1**	**1**	**14**	**1**	**0**	**0**	**0**	**0**
	Fredericton	AHL	66	25	16	41	151	2	0	1	1	12
1986-87	**Vancouver**	**NHL**	**50**	**9**	**7**	**16**	**109**	....	....	....	....	....
	Fredericton	AHL	17	7	6	13	73	....	....	....	....	....
1987-88	**Vancouver**	**NHL**	**28**	**7**	**3**	**10**	**57**	....	....	....	....	....
	Fredericton	AHL	30	27	18	45	115	....	....	....	....	....
1988-89	**Vancouver**	**NHL**	**53**	**7**	**7**	**14**	**65**	....	....	....	....	....
1989-90a	Milwaukee	IHL	68	40	35	75	148	6	5	3	8	0
	NHL Totals		**143**	**23**	**18**	**41**	**245**	**1**	**0**	**0**	**0**	**0**

a IHL First All-Star Team (1990)

BRUMWELL, JAMES (MURRAY)

Defense. Shoots left. 6'2", 190 lbs. Born, Calgary, Alta., March 31, 1960.

			Regular Season					Playoffs				
Season	Club	Lea	GP	G	A	TP	PIM	GP	G	A	TP	PIM
1978-79	Billings	WHL	61	11	32	43	62	....	....	....	....	....
1979-80	Billings	WHL	67	18	54	72	50	....	....	....	....	....
1980-81	**Minnesota**	**NHL**	**1**	**0**	**0**	**0**	**0**	....	....	....	....	....
	Oklahoma City	CHL	79	12	43	55	79	3	0	0	0	4
1981-82	**Minnesota**	**NHL**	**21**	**0**	**3**	**3**	**18**	**2**	**0**	**0**	**0**	**2**
	Nashville	CHL	55	4	21	25	66	....	....	....	....	....
1982-83	Wichita	CHL	11	4	1	5	4	....	....	....	....	....
	New Jersey	**NHL**	**59**	**5**	**14**	**19**	**34**	....	....	....	....	....
1983-84	**New Jersey**	**NHL**	**42**	**7**	**13**	**20**	**14**	....	....	....	....	....
	Maine	AHL	35	4	25	29	16	17	1	5	6	15
1984-85	Maine	AHL	64	8	31	39	12	10	4	5	9	19
1985-86	**New Jersey**	**NHL**	**1**	**0**	**0**	**0**	**0**	....	....	....	....	....
	Maine	AHL	66	9	28	37	35	5	0	3	3	2
1986-87	**New Jersey**	**NHL**	**1**	**0**	**0**	**0**	**2**	....	....	....	....	....
	Maine	AHL	69	10	38	48	30	....	....	....	....	....
1987-88	**New Jersey**	**NHL**	**3**	**0**	**1**	**1**	**2**	....	....	....	....	....
a	Utica	AHL	77	13	53	66	44	....	....	....	....	....
1988-89	Utica	AHL	73	5	29	34	29	5	0	0	0	2
1989-90	New Haven	AHL	62	7	29	36	24	....	....	....	....	....
	NHL Totals		**128**	**12**	**31**	**43**	**70**	**2**	**0**	**0**	**0**	**2**

a AHL Second All-Star Team (1988)

Signed as free agent by **Minnesota**, August 7, 1980. Claimed by **New Jersey** from **Minnesota** in Waiver Draft, October 4, 1982.

BRUNET, BENOIT

Left wing. Shoots left. 5'11", 184 lbs. Born, Ste-Anne de Bellevue, Que., August 24, 1968.
(Montreal's 2nd choice, 27th overall, in 1986 Entry Draft).

			Regular Season					Playoffs				
Season	Club	Lea	GP	G	A	TP	PIM	GP	G	A	TP	PIM
1985-86	Hull	QMJHL	71	33	37	70	81	....	....	....	....	....
1986-87a	Hull	QMJHL	60	43	67	110	105	6	7	5	12	8
1987-88	Hull	QMJHL	62	54	89	143	131	10	3	10	13	11
1988-89	**Montreal**	**NHL**	**2**	**0**	**1**	**1**	**0**	....	....	....	....	....
b	Sherbrooke	AHL	73	41	76	117	95	6	2	0	2	4
1989-90	Sherbrooke	AHL	72	32	35	67	82	12	8	7	15	20
	NHL Totals		**2**	**0**	**1**	**1**	**0**	....	....	....	....	....

a QMJHL Second All-Star Team (1987)
b AHL First All-Star Team (1989)

BRYDGES, PAUL

Center. Shoots right. 5'11", 180 lbs. Born, Guelph, Ont., June 21, 1965.

			Regular Season					Playoffs				
Season	Club	Lea	GP	G	A	TP	PIM	GP	G	A	TP	PIM
1982-83	Guelph	OHL	56	13	13	26	27	....	....	....	....	....
1983-84	Guelph	OHL	68	27	23	50	37	....	....	....	....	....
1984-85	Guelph	OHL	57	22	24	46	39	....	....	....	....	....
1985-86	Guelph	OHL	62	17	40	57	88	19	10	15	25	22
1986-87	**Buffalo**	**NHL**	**15**	**2**	**2**	**4**	**6**	....	....	....	....	....
	Rochester	AHL	54	13	17	30	54	1	0	0	0	0
1987-88	Rochester	AHL	69	15	16	31	86	7	1	1	2	4
1988-89	Rochester	AHL	51	8	3	11	36	....	....	....	....	....
1989-90	New Haven	AHL	37	6	7	13	38	....	....	....	....	....
	NHL Totals		**15**	**2**	**2**	**4**	**6**	....	....	....	....	....

Signed as a free agent by **Buffalo**, June 11, 1986.

BUCHBERGER, KELLY (BUK-BUHR-GUHR)

Left wing. Shoots left. 6'2", 210 lbs. Born, Langenburg, Sask., December 2, 1966.
(Edmonton's 8th choice, 188th overall, in 1985 Entry Draft).

			Regular Season					Playoffs				
Season	Club	Lea	GP	G	A	TP	PIM	GP	G	A	TP	PIM
1984-85	Moose Jaw	WHL	51	12	17	29	114	....	....	....	....	....
1985-86	Moose Jaw	WHL	72	14	22	36	206	13	11	4	15	37
1986-87	**Edmonton**	**NHL**	....	....	....	....	....	**3**	**0**	**1**	**1**	**5**
	Nova Scotia	AHL	70	12	20	32	257	5	0	1	1	23
1987-88	**Edmonton**	**NHL**	**19**	**1**	**0**	**1**	**81**	....	....	....	....	....
	Nova Scotia	AHL	49	21	23	44	206	2	0	0	0	11
1988-89	**Edmonton**	**NHL**	**66**	**5**	**9**	**14**	**234**	....	....	....	....	....
1989-90	**Edmonton**	**NHL**	**55**	**2**	**6**	**8**	**168**	**19**	**0**	**5**	**5**	**13**
	NHL Totals		**140**	**8**	**15**	**23**	**483**	**22**	**0**	**6**	**6**	**18**

BUCKLEY, DAVID

Defense. Shoots left. 6'4", 195 lbs. Born, Newton, MA, January 27, 1966.
(Toronto's 9th choice, 192nd overall, in 1984 Entry Draft).

			Regular Season					Playoffs				
Season	Club	Lea	GP	G	A	TP	PIM	GP	G	A	TP	PIM
1985-86	Boston College	H.E.	22	0	2	2	4	....	....	....	....	....
1986-87	Boston College	H.E.	34	3	5	8	9	....	....	....	....	....
1987-88	Boston College	H.E.	33	1	8	9	40	....	....	....	....	....
1988-89	Boston College	H.E.	40	3	7	10	48	....	....	....	....	....
1989-90	Baltimore	AHL	4	0	0	0	0	....	....	....	....	....

BUCYK, RANDY (BYOO-sik)

Center. Shoots left. 5'11", 185 lbs. Born, Edmonton, Alta., November 9, 1962.

			Regular Season					Playoffs				
Season	Club	Lea	GP	G	A	TP	PIM	GP	G	A	TP	PIM
1980-81	Northeastern	ECAC	31	18	17	35	0	....	....	....	....	....
1981-82	Northeastern	ECAC	33	19	17	36	10	....	....	....	....	....
1982-83	Northeastern	ECAC	28	16	20	36	16	....	....	....	....	....
1983-84	Northeastern	ECAC	29	16	13	29	11	....	....	....	....	....
1984-85	Sherbrooke	AHL	62	21	26	47	20	8	0	0	0	20
1985-86	**Montreal**	**NHL**	**17**	**4**	**2**	**6**	**8**	**2**	**0**	**0**	**0**	**0**
	Sherbrooke	AHL	43	18	33	51	22	....	....	....	....	....
1986-87	Sherbrooke	AHL	70	24	39	63	28	17	3	11	14	2
1987-88	**Calgary**	**NHL**	**2**	**0**	**0**	**0**	**0**	....	....	....	....	....
	Salt Lake	IHL	75	37	45	82	68	19	7	8	15	12
1988-89	Salt Lake	IHL	79	28	59	87	24	14	5	5	10	4
	Cdn. National	....	4	0	0	0	2	....	....	....	....	....
1989-90	Salt Lake	IHL	67	22	41	63	16	11	2	6	8	10
	NHL Totals		**19**	**4**	**2**	**6**	**8**	**2**	**0**	**0**	**0**	**0**

Signed as a free agent by **Montreal**, January 15, 1986. Signed as a free agent by **Calgary**, June 29, 1987.

BUDA, DAVID

Center. Shoots left. 6'4", 190 lbs. Born, Mississauga, Ont., March 14, 1966.
(Boston's 9th choice, 199th overall, in 1985 Entry Draft).

			Regular Season					Playoffs				
Season	Club	Lea	GP	G	A	TP	PIM	GP	G	A	TP	PIM
1985-86	Northeastern	H.E.	39	4	4	8	39	....	....	....	....	....
1986-87	Northeastern	H.E.	37	15	15	30	32	....	....	....	....	....
1987-88	Northeastern	H.E.	37	21	16	37	66	....	....	....	....	....
1988-89a	Northeastern	H.E.	35	23	23	46	45	....	....	....	....	....
	Maine	AHL	5	3	1	4	2	....	....	....	....	....
1989-90	Maine	AHL	39	7	4	11	14	....	....	....	....	....

a Hockey East First All-Star Team (1989)

BULLARD, MICHAEL BRIAN (MIKE) (BULL-ard)

Center. Shoots left. 5'10", 185 lbs. Born, Ottawa, Ont., March 10, 1961.
(Pittsburgh's 1st choice, 9th overall, in 1980 Entry Draft).

			Regular Season					Playoffs				
Season	Club	Lea	GP	G	A	TP	PIM	GP	G	A	TP	PIM
1978-79	Brantford	OHA	66	43	56	99	66	....	....	....	....	....
1979-80a	Brantford	OHA	66	66	84	150	86	11	10	6	16	29
1980-81b	Brantford	OHA	42	47	60	107	55	6	4	5	9	10
	Pittsburgh	**NHL**	**15**	**1**	**2**	**3**	**19**	**4**	**3**	**3**	**6**	**0**
1981-82	**Pittsburgh**	**NHL**	**75**	**36**	**27**	**63**	**91**	**5**	**1**	**1**	**2**	**4**
1982-83	**Pittsburgh**	**NHL**	**57**	**22**	**22**	**44**	**60**	....	....	....	....	....
1983-84	**Pittsburgh**	**NHL**	**76**	**51**	**41**	**92**	**57**	....	....	....	....	....
1984-85	**Pittsburgh**	**NHL**	**68**	**32**	**31**	**63**	**75**	....	....	....	....	....
1985-86	**Pittsburgh**	**NHL**	**77**	**41**	**42**	**83**	**69**	....	....	....	....	....
1986-87	**Pittsburgh**	**NHL**	**14**	**2**	**10**	**12**	**17**	....	....	....	....	....
	Calgary	**NHL**	**57**	**28**	**26**	**54**	**34**	**6**	**4**	**3**	**7**	**2**
1987-88	**Calgary**	**NHL**	**79**	**48**	**55**	**103**	**68**	**6**	**0**	**2**	**2**	**6**
1988-89	**St. Louis**	**NHL**	**20**	**4**	**12**	**16**	**46**	....	....	....	....	....
	Philadelphia	**NHL**	**54**	**23**	**26**	**49**	**60**	**19**	**3**	**9**	**12**	**32**
1989-90	**Philadelphia**	**NHL**	**70**	**27**	**37**	**64**	**67**	....	....	....	....	....
	NHL Totals		**662**	**315**	**333**	**648**	**663**	**40**	**11**	**18**	**29**	**44**

a OHA Third All-Star Team (1979)
b OHA Second All-Star Team (1980)

Traded to **Calgary** by **Pittsburgh** for Dan Quinn, November 12, 1986. Traded to **St. Louis** by **Calgary** with Craig Coxe and Tim Corkery for Mark Hunter, Doug Gilmour, Steve Bozek and Michael Dark, September 6, 1988. Traded to **Philadelphia** by **St. Louis** for Peter Zezel, November 29, 1988.

BURAKOVSKI, ROBERT

Right wing. Shoots right. 5'10", 165 lbs. Born, Malmo, Sweden, November 24, 1966.
(NY Rangers' 11th choice, 217th overall, in 1985 Entry Draft).

			Regular Season					Playoffs				
Season	Club	Lea	GP	G	A	TP	PIM	GP	G	A	TP	PIM
1985-86	Leksand	Swe.	19	4	3	7	4	....	....	....	....	....
1986-87	Leksand	Swe.	36	21	15	36	26	....	....	....	....	....
1987-88	Leksand	Swe.	36	10	11	21	10	....	....	....	....	....
1988-89	Leksand	Swe.	40	23	20	43	44	10	6	7	13	4
1989-90	AIK	Swe.	37	27	29	56	32	3	0	2	2	12

BURE, PAVEL

Left wing. Shoots left. 5'10", 170 lbs. Born, Moscow, Soviet Union, March 31, 1971.
(Vancouver's 4th choice, 113th overall, in 1989 Entry Draft).

			Regular Season					Playoffs				
Season	Club	Lea	GP	G	A	TP	PIM	GP	G	A	TP	PIM
1987-88	CSKA	USSR	5	1	1	2	0	....	....	....	....	....
1988-89a	CSKA	USSR	32	17	9	26	8	....	....	....	....	....
1989-90	CSKA	USSR	46	14	11	25	22	....	....	....	....	....

a Named Soviet National League Rookie-of-the-Year (1989).

BUREAU, MARC (BEWR-oh)

Center. Shoots right. 6', 190 lbs. Born, Trois-Rivieres, Que., May 19, 1966.

			Regular Season					Playoffs				
Season	Club	Lea	GP	G	A	TP	PIM	GP	G	A	TP	PIM
1983-84	Chicoutimi	QMJHL	56	6	16	22	14	....	....	....	....	....
1984-85	Chicoutimi	QMJHL	41	30	25	55	15	....	....	....	....	....
	Granby	QMJHL	27	20	45	65	14	....	....	....	....	....
1985-86	Granby	QMJHL	19	6	17	23	36	....	....	....	....	....
	Chicoutimi	QMJHL	44	30	45	75	33	9	3	7	10	10
1986-87	Longueuil	QMJHL	66	54	58	112	68	20	17	20	37	12
1987-88	Salt Lake	IHL	69	7	20	27	86	7	0	3	3	8
1988-89	Salt Lake	IHL	76	28	36	64	119	14	7	5	12	31
1989-90	**Calgary**	**NHL**	**5**	**0**	**0**	**0**	**4**	....	....	....	....	....
a	Salt Lake	IHL	67	43	48	91	173	11	4	8	12	0
	NHL Totals		**5**	**0**	**0**	**0**	**4**	....	....	....	....	....

a IHL Second All-Star Team (1990)

Signed as a free agent by **Calgary**, May 19, 1987.

BURKE, DAVID

Defense. Shoots left. 6'1", 180 lbs. Born, Detroit, MI, October 15, 1970.
(Toronto's 6th choice, 108th overall, in 1989 Entry Draft).

			Regular Season					Playoffs				
Season	Club	Lea	GP	G	A	TP	PIM	GP	G	A	TP	PIM
1988-89	Cornell	ECAC	26	0	3	3	22	....	....	....	....	....
1989-90	Cornell	ECAC	29	0	12	12	28	....	....	....	....	....

BURKE, JAMES

Defense. Shoots left. 6'2", 200 lbs. Born, Newton, MA, January 3, 1968.
(Hartford's 7th choice, 158th overall, in 1988 Entry Draft).

			Regular Season					Playoffs				
Season	Club	Lea	GP	G	A	TP	PIM	GP	G	A	TP	PIM
1986-87	U. of Maine	H.E.	23	0	0	0	18	....	....	....	....	....
1987-88	U. of Maine	H.E.	41	2	10	12	34	....	....	....	....	....
1988-89	U. of Maine	H.E.	41	1	7	8	56	....	....	....	....	....
1989-90	U. of Maine	H.E.	45	6	23	29	60	....	....	....	....	....

BURNIE, STUART

Right wing. Shoots right. 5'11", 185 lbs. Born, Orilla, Ont., May 7, 1962.

			Regular Season					Playoffs				
Season	Club	Lea	GP	G	A	TP	PIM	GP	G	A	TP	PIM
1982-83	W. Michigan	CCHA	36	12	7	19	50	....	....	....	....	....
1983-84	W. Michigan	CCHA	42	26	13	39	73	....	....	....	....	....
1984-85	W. Michigan	CCHA	39	21	16	37	49	....	....	....	....	....
1985-86a	W. Michigan	CCHA	42	43	36	79	78	....	....	....	....	....
1986-87	Springfield	AHL	76	21	30	51	62	....	....	....	....	....
1987-88	Springfield	AHL	78	33	22	55	98	....	....	....	....	....
1988-89	Springfield	AHL	74	28	36	64	49	....	....	....	....	....
1989-90	JOKP	Fin.	37	8	1	9	36	....	....	....	....	....

a CCHA Second All-Star Team (1986)

Signed as a free agent by **NY Islanders**, September 5, 1986.

BURR, SHAWN

Left wing/Center. Shoots left. 6'1", 195 lbs. Born, Sarnia, Ont., July 1, 1966.
(Detroit's 1st choice, 7th overall, in 1984 Entry Draft).

			Regular Season					Playoffs				
Season	Club	Lea	GP	G	A	TP	PIM	GP	G	A	TP	PIM
1983-84	Kitchener	OHL	68	41	44	85	50	16	5	12	17	22
1984-85	**Detroit**	**NHL**	**9**	**0**	**0**	**0**	**2**	....	....	....	....	....
	Adirondack	AHL	4	0	0	0	2	....	....	....	....	....
	Kitchener	OHL	48	24	42	66	50	4	3	3	6	2
1985-86	**Detroit**	**NHL**	**5**	**1**	**0**	**1**	**4**	....	....	....	....	....
	Adirondack	AHL	3	2	2	4	2	17	5	7	12	32
a	Kitchener	OHL	59	60	67	127	104	5	2	3	5	8
1986-87	**Detroit**	**NHL**	**80**	**22**	**25**	**47**	**107**	**16**	**7**	**2**	**9**	**20**
1987-88	**Detroit**	**NHL**	**78**	**17**	**23**	**40**	**97**	**9**	**3**	**1**	**4**	**14**
1988-89	**Detroit**	**NHL**	**79**	**19**	**27**	**46**	**78**	**6**	**1**	**2**	**3**	**6**
1989-90	**Detroit**	**NHL**	**76**	**24**	**32**	**56**	**82**	....	....	....	....	....
	Adirondack	AHL	3	4	2	6	2	....	....	....	....	....
	NHL Totals		**327**	**83**	**107**	**190**	**370**	**31**	**11**	**5**	**16**	**40**

a OHL Second All-Star Team (1986)

BURRIDGE, RANDY

Left wing. Shoots left. 5'9", 180 lbs. Born, Fort Erie, Ont., January 7, 1966.
(Boston's 7th choice, 157th overall, in 1985 Entry Draft).

			Regular Season					Playoffs				
Season	Club	Lea	GP	G	A	TP	PIM	GP	G	A	TP	PIM
1983-84	Peterborough	OHL	55	6	7	13	44	8	3	2	5	7
1984-85	Peterborough	OHL	66	49	57	106	88	17	9	16	25	18
1985-86	Peterborough	OHL	17	15	11	26	23	3	1	3	4	2
	Boston	**NHL**	**52**	**17**	**25**	**42**	**28**	**3**	**0**	**4**	**4**	**12**
	Moncton	AHL	....	....	....	....	....	3	0	2	2	2
1986-87	**Boston**	**NHL**	**23**	**1**	**4**	**5**	**16**	**2**	**1**	**0**	**1**	**2**
	Moncton	AHL	47	26	41	67	139	3	1	2	3	30
1987-88	**Boston**	**NHL**	**79**	**27**	**28**	**55**	**105**	**23**	**2**	**10**	**12**	**16**
1988-89	**Boston**	**NHL**	**80**	**31**	**30**	**61**	**39**	**10**	**5**	**2**	**7**	**6**
1989-90	**Boston**	**NHL**	**63**	**17**	**15**	**32**	**47**	**21**	**4**	**11**	**15**	**14**
	NHL Totals		**297**	**93**	**102**	**195**	**235**	**59**	**12**	**27**	**39**	**50**

BURT, ADAM

Defense. Shoots left. 6', 195 lbs. Born, Detroit, MI, January 15, 1969.
(Hartford's 2nd choice, 39th overall, in 1987 Entry Draft).

			Regular Season					Playoffs				
Season	Club	Lea	GP	G	A	TP	PIM	GP	G	A	TP	PIM
1985-86	North Bay	OHL	49	0	11	11	81	10	0	0	0	24
1986-87	North Bay	OHL	57	4	27	31	138	24	1	6	7	68
1987-88	Binghamton	AHL	....	....	....	....	....	2	1	1	2	0
a	North Bay	OHL	66	17	53	70	176	2	0	3	3	6
1988-89	**Hartford**	**NHL**	**5**	**0**	**0**	**0**	**6**	....	....	....	....	....
	Binghamton	AHL	5	0	2	2	13	....	....	....	....	....
	North Bay	OHL	23	4	11	15	45	12	2	12	14	12
1989-90	**Hartford**	**NHL**	**63**	**4**	**8**	**12**	**105**	**2**	**0**	**0**	**0**	**0**
	NHL Totals		**68**	**4**	**8**	**12**	**111**	**2**	**0**	**0**	**0**	**0**

a OHL Second All-Star Team (1988)

BUSKAS, ROD

Defense. Shoots right. 6'1", 200 lbs. Born, Wetaskiwin, Alta., January 7, 1961.
(Pittsburgh's 5th choice, 112th overall, in 1981 Entry Draft).

			Regular Season					Playoffs				
Season	Club	Lea	GP	G	A	TP	PIM	GP	G	A	TP	PIM
1978-79	Billings	WHL	1	0	0	0	0	....	....	....	....	....
	Medicine Hat	WHL	34	1	12	13	60	....	....	....	....	....
1979-80	Medicine Hat	WHL	72	7	40	47	284	....	....	....	....	....
1980-81	Medicine Hat	WHL	72	14	46	60	164	5	1	1	2	8
1981-82	Erie	AHL	69	1	18	19	78	....	....	....	....	....
1982-83	**Pittsburgh**	**NHL**	**41**	**2**	**2**	**4**	**102**	....	....	....	....	....
	Baltimore	AHL	31	2	8	10	45	....	....	....	....	....
1983-84	**Pittsburgh**	**NHL**	**47**	**2**	**4**	**6**	**60**	....	....	....	....	....
	Baltimore	AHL	33	2	12	14	100	10	1	3	4	22
1984-85	**Pittsburgh**	**NHL**	**69**	**2**	**7**	**9**	**191**	....	....	....	....	....
1985-86	**Pittsburgh**	**NHL**	**72**	**2**	**7**	**9**	**159**	....	....	....	....	....
1986-87	**Pittsburgh**	**NHL**	**68**	**3**	**15**	**18**	**123**	....	....	....	....	....
1987-88	**Pittsburgh**	**NHL**	**76**	**4**	**8**	**12**	**206**	....	....	....	....	....
1988-89	**Pittsburgh**	**NHL**	**52**	**1**	**5**	**6**	**105**	**10**	**0**	**0**	**0**	**23**
1989-90	**Vancouver**	**NHL**	**17**	**0**	**3**	**3**	**36**	....	....	....	....	....
	Pittsburgh	**NHL**	**6**	**0**	**0**	**0**	**13**	....	....	....	....	....
	NHL Totals		**448**	**16**	**51**	**67**	**995**	**10**	**0**	**0**	**0**	**23**

Traded to **Vancouver** by **Pittsburgh** for Vancouver's sixth round choice (Ian Moran) in 1990 Entry Draft, October 24, 1989. Traded to **Pittsburgh** by **Vancouver** with Barry Pederson and Tony Tanti for Dave Capuano, Andrew McBain and Dan Quinn, January 8, 1990.

BUTCHER, GARTH

Defense. Shoots right. 6', 200 lbs. Born, Regina, Sask., January 8, 1963.
(Vancouver's 1st choice, 10th overall, in 1981 Entry Draft).

			Regular Season					Playoffs				
Season	Club	Lea	GP	G	A	TP	PIM	GP	G	A	TP	PIM
1979-80	Regina	WHL	13	0	4	4	20	....	....	....	....	....
1980-81a	Regina	WHL	69	9	77	86	230	11	5	17	22	60
1981-82a	Regina	WHL	65	24	68	92	318	19	3	17	20	95
	Vancouver	**NHL**	**5**	**0**	**0**	**0**	**9**	**1**	**0**	**0**	**0**	**0**
1982-83	**Vancouver**	**NHL**	**55**	**1**	**13**	**14**	**104**	**3**	**1**	**0**	**1**	**2**
1983-84	**Vancouver**	**NHL**	**28**	**2**	**0**	**2**	**34**	....	....	....	....	....
	Fredericton	AHL	25	4	13	17	43	6	0	2	2	19
1984-85	**Vancouver**	**NHL**	**75**	**3**	**9**	**12**	**152**	....	....	....	....	....
	Fredericton	AHL	3	1	0	1	11	....	....	....	....	....
1985-86	**Vancouver**	**NHL**	**70**	**4**	**7**	**11**	**188**	**3**	**0**	**0**	**0**	**0**
1986-87	**Vancouver**	**NHL**	**70**	**5**	**15**	**20**	**207**	....	....	....	....	....
1987-88	**Vancouver**	**NHL**	**80**	**6**	**17**	**23**	**285**	....	....	....	....	....
1988-89	**Vancouver**	**NHL**	**78**	**0**	**20**	**20**	**227**	**7**	**1**	**1**	**2**	**22**
1989-90	**Vancouver**	**NHL**	**80**	**6**	**14**	**20**	**205**	....	....	....	....	....
	NHL Totals		**541**	**27**	**95**	**122**	**1411**	**14**	**2**	**1**	**3**	**22**

a WHL First All-Star Team (1981, 1982)

BYCE, JOHN

Right wing. Shoots right. 6'1", 180 lbs. Born, Madison, WI, August 9, 1967.
(Boston's 11th choice, 220th overall, in 1985 Entry Draft).

			Regular Season					Playoffs				
Season	Club	Lea	GP	G	A	TP	PIM	GP	G	A	TP	PIM
1986-87	U. Wisconsin	WCHA	40	1	4	5	12	....	....	....	....	....
1987-88	U. Wisconsin	WCHA	41	22	12	34	18	....	....	....	....	....
1988-89a	U. Wisconsin	WCHA	42	27	28	55	16	....	....	....	....	....
1989-90ab	U. Wisconsin	WCHA	46	27	44	71	20	....	....	....	....	....
	Boston	**NHL**	....	....	....	....	....	**8**	**2**	**0**	**2**	**2**
	NHL Totals		....	....	....	....	....	**8**	**2**	**0**	**2**	**2**

a WCHA Second All-Star Team (1989, 1990)
b NCAA All-Tournament Team (1990)

BYERS, LYNDON

Right wing. Shoots right. 6'1", 200 lbs. Born, Nipawin, Sask., February 29, 1964.
(Boston's 3rd choice, 39th overall, in 1982 Entry Draft).

			Regular Season					Playoffs				
Season	Club	Lea	GP	G	A	TP	PIM	GP	G	A	TP	PIM
1981-82	Regina	WHL	57	18	25	43	169	20	5	6	11	48
1982-83	Regina	WHL	70	32	38	70	153	5	1	1	2	16
1983-84	**Boston**	**NHL**	**10**	**2**	**4**	**6**	**32**	....	....	....	....	....
	Regina	WHL	58	32	57	89	154	23	17	18	35	78
1984-85	**Boston**	**NHL**	**33**	**3**	**8**	**11**	**41**	....	....	....	..	....
	Hershey	AHL	27	4	6	10	55	....	....	....	....	....
1985-86	**Boston**	**NHL**	**5**	**0**	**2**	**2**	**9**	....	....	....	....	....
	Moncton	AHL	14	2	4	6	26	....	....	....	....	....
	Milwaukee	IHL	8	0	2	2	22	....	....	....	....	....
1986-87	**Boston**	**NHL**	**18**	**2**	**3**	**5**	**53**	**1**	**0**	**0**	**0**	**0**
	Moncton	AHL	27	5	5	10	63	....	....	....	....	....
1987-88	**Boston**	**NHL**	**53**	**10**	**14**	**24**	**236**	**11**	**1**	**2**	**3**	**62**
	Maine	AHL	2	0	1	1	18	....	....	....	....	....
1988-89	**Boston**	**NHL**	**49**	**0**	**4**	**4**	**218**	**2**	**0**	**0**	**0**	**0**
	Maine	AHL	4	1	3	4	2	....	....	....	....	....
1989-90	**Boston**	**NHL**	**43**	**4**	**4**	**8**	**159**	**17**	**1**	**0**	**1**	**12**
	NHL Totals		**211**	**21**	**39**	**60**	**159**	**31**	**2**	**2**	**4**	**74**

BYKOV, VIACHESLAV

Center. 5'8", 175 lbs. Born, Chelyabinsk, Soviet Union, July 24, 1960.
(Quebec's 11th choice, 169th overall, in 1989 Entry Draft).

			Regular Season					Playoffs				
Season	Club	Lea	GP	G	A	TP	PIM	GP	G	A	TP	PIM
1979-80	Chelyabinsk	USSR	3	2	0	2	0	....	....	....	....	....
1980-81	Chelyabinsk	USSR	48	26	16	42	4	....	....	....	....	....
1981-82	Chelyabinsk	USSR	44	20	16	36	14	....	....	....	....	....
1982-83	CSKA	USSR	44	22	22	44	10	....	....	....	....	....
1983-84	CSKA	USSR	44	22	11	33	12	....	....	....	....	....
1984-85	CSKA	USSR	36	21	14	35	4	....	....	....	....	....
1985-86	CSKA	USSR	36	10	10	20	6	....	....	....	....	....
1986-87	CSKA	USSR	40	18	15	33	10	....	....	....	....	....
1987-88	CSKA	USSR	47	17	30	47	26	....	....	....	....	....
1988-89	CSKA	USSR	40	16	20	36	10	....	....	....	....	....
1989-90	CSKA	USSR	48	21	16	37	16	....	....	....	....	....

BYLSMA, DAN

Left wing. Shoots left. 6'2", 205 lbs. Born, Grand Rapids, MI, September 19, 1970.
(Winnipeg's 7th choice, 109th overall, in 1989 Entry Draft).

			Regular Season					Playoffs				
Season	Club	Lea	GP	G	A	TP	PIM	GP	G	A	TP	PIM
1988-89	Bowling Green	CCHA	32	3	7	10	10	....	....	....	....	....
1989-90	Bowling Green	CCHA	44	13	17	30	30	....	....	....	....	....

BYRAM, SHAWN

Left wing. Shoots left. 6'2", 204 lbs. Born, Neepawa, Man., September 12, 1968.
(NY Islanders' 4th choice, 80th overall, in 1986 Entry Draft).

			Regular Season					Playoffs				
Season	Club	Lea	GP	G	A	TP	PIM	GP	G	A	TP	PIM
1985-86	Regina	WHL	46	7	6	13	45	9	0	1	1	11
1986-87	Prince Albert	WHL	67	19	21	40	147	7	1	1	2	10
1987-88	Prince Albert	WHL	61	23	28	51	178	10	5	2	7	27
1988-89	Springfield	AHL	45	5	11	16	195	....	....	....	....	....
	Indianapolis	IHL	1	0	0	0	2	....	....	....	....	....
1989-90	Springfield	AHL	31	4	4	8	30	....	....	....	....	....

BZDEL, GERALD (bayz-DEHL)

Defense. Shoots right. 6'1", 196 lbs. Born, Wynyard, Sask., March 13, 1968.
(Quebec's 5th choice, 102nd overall, in 1986 Entry Draft).

			Regular Season					Playoffs				
Season	Club	Lea	GP	G	A	TP	PIM	GP	G	A	TP	PIM
1985-86	Regina	WHL	72	2	15	17	107	10	0	3	3	14
1986-87	Regina	WHL	13	0	3	3	38	....	....	....	....	....
	Seattle	WHL	48	4	12	16	137	....	....	....	....	....
1987-88	Moose Jaw	WHL	72	4	17	21	217	....	....	....	....	....
1988-89	Halifax	AHL	36	1	3	4	46	....	....	....	....	....
1989-90	Halifax	AHL	59	2	20	22	84	6	0	1	1	24

CADIEUX, STEVE

Center. Shoots left. 6'1", 205 lbs. Born, Ste. Therese, Que., June 17, 1969.
(Montreal's 12th choice, 251st overall, in 1989 Entry Draft).

			Regular Season					Playoffs				
Season	Club	Lea	GP	G	A	TP	PIM	GP	G	A	TP	PIM
1986-87	St. Jean	QMJHL	65	28	22	50	26	8	1	7	8	4
1987-88	St. Jean	QMJHL	66	43	50	93	18	7	4	4	8	2
1988-89	St. Jean	QMJHL	17	15	24	39	8	....	....	....	....	....
	Shawinigan	QMJHL	53	65	62	127	14	10	9	12	21	12
1989-90	Shawinigan	QMJHL	67	*73	90	163	101	6	4	7	11	26

CAHILL, DARCY

Center. Shoots right. 5'11", 190 lbs. Born, Kingston, Ont., August 19, 1970.
(Vancouver's 10th choice, 239th overall, in 1989 Entry Draft).

			Regular Season					Playoffs				
Season	Club	Lea	GP	G	A	TP	PIM	GP	G	A	TP	PIM
1988-89	Cornwall	OHL	66	35	57	92	49	13	9	8	17	4
1989-90	Sudbury	OHL	58	38	71	109	73	7	1	13	14	14

CAIN, PAUL

Center. Shoots right. 5'10", 180 lbs. Born, Toronto, Ont., April 6, 1969.
(NY Rangers' 9th choice, 194th overall, in 1988 Entry Draft).

			Regular Season					Playoffs				
Season	Club	Lea	GP	G	A	TP	PIM	GP	G	A	TP	PIM
1987-88	Cornwall	OHL	21	14	9	23	41	7	0	2	2	0
1988-89	Cornwall	OHL	44	19	47	66	26	12	5	9	14	6
1989-90	Cornwall	OHL	47	28	36	64	23	6	2	4	6	2

CAJKA, LUDEK

Defense. Shoots right. 6'3", 192 lbs. Born, Cesky Tesin, Czech., November 3, 1963.
(NY Rangers' 6th choice, 115th overall, in 1987 Entry Draft).

			Regular Season					Playoffs				
Season	Club	Lea	GP	G	A	TP	PIM	GP	G	A	TP	PIM
1986-87	Dukla Jihlava	Czech.	34	4	5	9	....	....	....	....	....	....
1987-88	Gottwaldov	Czech.	33	4	5	9	....	....	....	....	....	....
1988-89	Gottwaldov	Czech.	44	6	16	22	....	....	....	....	....	....
1989-90	Gottwaldov	Czech	32	8	8	16	....	....	....	....	....	....

CALLANDER, JOHN (JOCK)

Right wing. Shoots right. 6'1", 185 lbs. Born, Regina, Sask., April 23, 1961.

			Regular Season					Playoffs				
Season	Club	Lea	GP	G	A	TP	PIM	GP	G	A	TP	PIM
1979-80	Regina	WHL	39	9	11	20	25	18	8	5	13	0
1980-81	Regina	WHL	72	67	86	153	37	11	6	7	13	14
1981-82	Regina	WHL	71	79	111	*190	59	20	13	*26	39	37
1982-83	Salt Lake	CHL	68	20	27	47	26	6	0	1	1	9
1983-84	Montana	CHL	72	27	32	59	69	....	....	....	....	....
	Toledo	IHL	2	0	0	0	0	....	....	....	....	....
1984-85	Muskegon	IHL	82	39	68	107	86	17	13	*21	*33	
1985-86a	Muskegon	IHL	82	39	72	111	121	14	*12	11	*23	12
1986-87bcd	Muskegon	IHL	82	54	82	*136	110	15	13	7	20	23
1987-88	**Pittsburgh**	**NHL**	**41**	**11**	**16**	**27**	**45**	....	....	....	....	....
	Muskegon	IHL	31	20	36	56	49	6	2	3	5	25
1988-89	**Pittsburgh**	**NHL**	**30**	**6**	**5**	**11**	**20**	**10**	**2**	**5**	**7**	**10**
	Muskegon	IHL	48	25	39	64	40	7	5	5	10	30
1989-90	**Pittsburgh**	**NHL**	**30**	**4**	**7**	**11**	**49**	....	....	....	....	....
	Muskegon	IHL	46	29	49	78	118	15	6	*14	20	54
	NHL Totals		**101**	**21**	**28**	**49**	**114**	**10**	**2**	**5**	**7**	**10**

a IHL Playoff MVP (1986)
b IHL First All-Star Team (1987)
c Shared James Gatschene Memorial Trophy (MVP-IHL) with Jeff Pyle (1987)
d Shared Leo P. Lamoureux Memorial Trophy (Top Scorer-IHL) with Jeff Pyle (1987)

Signed as free agent by **St. Louis**, September 28, 1981. Signed as a free agent by **Pittsburgh**, July 31, 1987.

CAPUANO, DAVE
(KAP-yew-AN-oh)

Center. Shoots left. 6'2", 190 lbs.   Born, Warwick, RI, July 27, 1968.
(Pittsburgh's 2nd choice, 25th overall, in 1986 Entry Draft).

			Regular Season					Playoffs				
Season	Club	Lea	GP	G	A	TP	PIM	GP	G	A	TP	PIM
1986-87	U. of Maine	H.E.	38	18	41	59	14	....	....	....	....	....
1987-88abc	U. of Maine	H.E.	42	*34	*51	*85	51	....	....	....	....	....
1988-89ac	U. of Maine	H.E.	41	37	30	67	38	....	....	....	....	....
1989-90	**Pittsburgh**	**NHL**	**6**	**0**	**0**	**0**	**2**	....	....	....	....	....
	Muskegon	IHL	27	15	15	30	22	....	....	....	....	....
	Vancouver	**NHL**	**27**	**3**	**5**	**8**	**10**	....	....	....	....	....
	Milwaukee	IHL	2	0	4	4	0	6	1	5	6	0
	NHL Totals		**33**	**3**	**5**	**8**	**12**	....	....	....	....	....

a NCAA East First All-American Team (1988, 1989)
b NCAA All-Tournament Team (1988)
c Hockey East First All-Star Team (1988, 1989)

Traded to **Vancouver** by **Pittsburgh** with Andrew McBain and Dan Quinn for Rod Buskas, Barry Pederson and Tony Tanti, January 8, 1990.

CAPUANO, JACK
(KAP-yew-AN-oh)

Defense. Shoots left. 6'2", 210 lbs.   Born, Cranston, RI, July 7, 1966.
(Toronto's 4th choice, 67th overall, in 1984 Entry Draft).

			Regular Season					Playoffs				
Season	Club	Lea	GP	G	A	TP	PIM	GP	G	A	TP	PIM
1985-86	U. of Maine	H.E.	39	9	18	27	51	....	....	....	....	....
1986-87a	U. of Maine	H.E.	42	10	34	44	20	....	....	....	....	....
1987-88bc	U. of Maine	H.E.	43	13	37	50	87	....	....	....	....	....
1988-89	Newmarket	AHL	74	5	16	21	52	1	0	0	0	0
1989-90	**Toronto**	**NHL**	**1**	**0**	**0**	**0**	**0**	....	....	....	....	....
	Newmarket	AHL	8	0	2	2	7	....	....	....	....	....
	Springfield	AHL	14	0	4	4	8	....	....	....	....	....
	Milwaukee	IHL	17	3	10	13	60	6	0	1	1	12
	NHL Totals		**1**	**0**	**0**	**0**	**0**	....	....	....	....	....

a Hockey East Second All-Star Team (1987)
b NCAA East First All-American Team (1988)
c Hockey East First All-Star Team (1988)

Traded to **NY Islanders** by **Toronto** with Paul Gagne and Derek Laxdal for Mike Stevens and Gilles Thibaudeau, December 20, 1989. Traded to **Vancouver** by **NY Islanders** for Jeff Rohlicek, March 6, 1990.

CARBONNEAU, GUY
(KAR-buhn-oh, GEE)

Center. Shoots right. 5'11", 180 lbs.   Born, Sept Iles, Que., March 18, 1960.
(Montreal's 4th choice, 44th overall, in 1979 Entry Draft).

			Regular Season					Playoffs				
Season	Club	Lea	GP	G	A	TP	PIM	GP	G	A	TP	PIM
1976-77	Chicoutimi	QJHL	59	9	20	29	8	4	1	0	1	0
1977-78	Chicoutimi	QJHL	70	28	55	83	60	....	....	....	....	....
1978-79	Chicoutimi	QJHL	72	62	79	141	47	4	2	1	3	4
1979-80	Chicoutimi	QJHL	72	72	110	182	66	12	9	15	24	28
	Nova Scotia	AHL	....	....	....	....	....	2	1	1	2	2
1980-81	**Montreal**	**NHL**	**2**	**0**	**1**	**1**	**0**	....	....	....	....	....
	Nova Scotia	AHL	78	35	53	88	87	6	1	3	4	9
1981-82	Nova Scotia	AHL	77	27	67	94	124	9	2	7	9	8
1982-83	**Montreal**	**NHL**	**77**	**18**	**29**	**47**	**68**	**3**	**0**	**0**	**0**	**2**
1983-84	**Montreal**	**NHL**	**78**	**24**	**30**	**54**	**75**	**15**	**4**	**3**	**7**	**12**
1984-85	**Montreal**	**NHL**	**79**	**23**	**34**	**57**	**43**	**12**	**4**	**3**	**7**	**8**
1985-86	**Montreal**	**NHL**	**80**	**20**	**36**	**56**	**57**	**20**	**7**	**5**	**12**	**35**
1986-87	**Montreal**	**NHL**	**79**	**18**	**27**	**45**	**68**	**17**	**3**	**8**	**11**	**20**
1987-88a	**Montreal**	**NHL**	**80**	**17**	**21**	**38**	**61**	**11**	**0**	**4**	**4**	**2**
1988-89a	**Montreal**	**NHL**	**79**	**26**	**30**	**56**	**44**	**21**	**4**	**5**	**9**	**10**
1989-90	**Montreal**	**NHL**	**68**	**19**	**36**	**55**	**37**	**11**	**2**	**3**	**5**	**6**
	NHL Totals		**622**	**165**	**244**	**409**	**453**	**110**	**24**	**31**	**55**	**95**

a Won Frank J. Selke Trophy (1988, 1989)

CARKNER, TERRY

Defense. Shoots left. 6'3", 210 lbs.   Born, Smiths Falls, Ont., March 7, 1966.
(NY Rangers' 1st choice, 14th overall, in 1984 Entry Draft).

			Regular Season					Playoffs				
Season	Club	Lea	GP	G	A	TP	PIM	GP	G	A	TP	PIM
1983-84	Peterborough	OHL	58	4	19	23	77	8	0	6	6	13
1984-85a	Peterborough	OHL	64	14	47	61	125	17	2	10	12	11
1985-86b	Peterborough	OHL	54	12	32	44	106	16	1	7	8	17
1986-87	**NY Rangers**	**NHL**	**52**	**2**	**13**	**15**	**118**	**1**	**0**	**0**	**0**	**0**
	New Haven	AHL	12	2	6	8	56	3	1	0	1	0
1987-88	**Quebec**	**NHL**	**63**	**3**	**24**	**27**	**159**	....	....	....	....	....
1988-89	**Philadelphia**	**NHL**	**78**	**11**	**32**	**43**	**149**	**19**	**1**	**5**	**6**	**28**
1989-90	**Philadelphia**	**NHL**	**63**	**4**	**18**	**22**	**169**	....	....	....	....	....
	NHL Totals		**256**	**20**	**87**	**107**	**595**	**20**	**1**	**5**	**6**	**28**

a OHL Second All-Star Team (1985)
b OHL First All-Star Team (1986)

Traded to **Quebec** by **NY Rangers** with Jeff Jackson for John Ogrodnick and David Shaw September, 30 1987. Traded to **Philadelphia** by **Quebec** for Greg Smyth and Philadelphia's third round choice (John Tanner) in the 1989 Entry Draft, July 25, 1988.

CARLSSON, ANDERS

Center. Shoots left. 5'11", 185 lbs.   Born, Gavle, Sweden, November 25, 1960.
(New Jersey's 5th choice, 66th overall, in 1986 Entry Draft).

			Regular Season					Playoffs				
Season	Club	Lea	GP	G	A	TP	PIM	GP	G	A	TP	PIM
1978-79	Brynas	Swe.	1	0	0	0	2	....	....	....	....	....
1979-80	Brynas	Swe.	17	0	1	1	2	1	0	0	0	0
1980-81	Brynas	Swe.	36	8	8	16	36	....	....	....	....	....
1981-82	Brynas	Swe.	35	5	5	10	22	....	....	....	....	....
1982-83	Brynas	Swe.	35	18	13	31	26	....	....	....	....	....
1983-84	Brynas	Swe.	35	8	26	34	34	....	....	....	....	....
1984-85	Sodertalje	Swe.	36	20	14	34	18	8	0	3	3	4
1985-86	Sodertalje	Swe.	36	12	26	38	20	7	2	4	6	0
1986-87	**New Jersey**	**NHL**	**48**	**2**	**18**	**20**	**14**	....	....	....	....	....
	Maine	AHL	6	0	6	6	2	....	....	....	....	....
1987-88	**New Jersey**	**NHL**	**9**	**1**	**0**	**1**	**0**	**3**	**1**	**0**	**1**	**2**
	Utica	AHL	33	12	22	34	16	....	....	....	....	....
1988-89	**New Jersey**	**NHL**	**47**	**4**	**8**	**12**	**20**	....	....	....	....	....
	Utica	AHL	7	2	4	6	4	....	....	....	....	....
1989-90	Brynas	Swe.	40	12	31	43	29	3	0	2	2	0
	NHL Totals		**104**	**7**	**26**	**33**	**34**	**3**	**1**	**0**	**1**	**2**

CARLSSON, LEIF

Defense. Shoots left. 6'1", 205 lbs.   Born, Ludvika, Sweden, February 18, 1965.
(Hartford's 4th choice, 61st overall, in 1983 Entry Draft).

			Regular Season					Playoffs				
Season	Club	Lea	GP	G	A	TP	PIM	GP	G	A	TP	PIM
1983-84	Farjestad	Swe.	19	3	0	3	10	....	....	....	....	....
1984-85	Farjestad	Swe.	36	4	8	12	24	3	0	0	0	0
1985-86	Farjestad	Swe.	36	7	6	13	22	7	1	3	4	4
1986-87	Farjestad	Swe.	33	9	4	13	18	7	2	2	4	10
1987-88	Farjestad	Swe.	40	10	14	24	26	9	2	1	3	4
1988-89	Farjestad	Swe.	39	6	6	12	38	....	....	....	....	....
1989-90	V. Frolunda	Swe.	37	2	10	12	24	....	....	....	....	....

CARLYLE, RANDY ROBERT

Defense. Shoots left. 5'10", 200 lbs.   Born, Sudbury, Ont., April 19, 1956.
(Toronto's 1st choice, 30th overall, in 1976 Amateur Draft).

			Regular Season					Playoffs				
Season	Club	Lea	GP	G	A	TP	PIM	GP	G	A	TP	PIM
1974-75	Sudbury	OHA	67	17	47	64	118	15	3	6	9	21
1975-76a	Sudbury	OHA	60	15	64	79	126	17	6	13	19	50
1976-77	**Dallas**	CHL	26	2	7	9	63	....	....	....	....	....
	Toronto	**NHL**	**45**	**0**	**5**	**5**	**51**	**9**	**0**	**1**	**1**	**20**
1977-78	**Dallas**	CHL	21	3	14	17	31	....	....	....	....	....
	Toronto	**NHL**	**49**	**2**	**11**	**13**	**31**	**7**	**0**	**1**	**1**	**8**
1978-79	**Pittsburgh**	**NHL**	**70**	**13**	**34**	**47**	**78**	**7**	**0**	**0**	**0**	**12**
1979-80	**Pittsburgh**	**NHL**	**67**	**8**	**28**	**36**	**45**	**5**	**1**	**0**	**1**	**4**
1980-81bc	**Pittsburgh**	**NHL**	**76**	**16**	**67**	**83**	**136**	**5**	**4**	**5**	**9**	**9**
1981-82	**Pittsburgh**	**NHL**	**73**	**11**	**64**	**75**	**131**	**5**	**1**	**3**	**4**	**16**
1982-83	**Pittsburgh**	**NHL**	**61**	**15**	**41**	**56**	**110**	....	....	....	....	....
1983-84	**Pittsburgh**	**NHL**	**50**	**3**	**23**	**26**	**82**	....	....	....	....	....
	Winnipeg	**NHL**	**5**	**0**	**3**	**3**	**2**	**3**	**0**	**2**	**2**	**4**
1984-85	**Winnipeg**	**NHL**	**71**	**13**	**38**	**51**	**98**	**8**	**1**	**5**	**6**	**13**
1985-86	**Winnipeg**	**NHL**	**68**	**16**	**33**	**49**	**93**	....	....	....	....	....
1986-87	**Winnipeg**	**NHL**	**71**	**16**	**26**	**42**	**93**	**10**	**1**	**5**	**6**	**18**
1987-88	**Winnipeg**	**NHL**	**78**	**15**	**44**	**59**	**210**	**5**	**0**	**2**	**2**	**10**
1988-89	**Winnipeg**	**NHL**	**78**	**6**	**38**	**44**	**78**	....	....	....	....	....
1989-90	**Winnipeg**	**NHL**	**53**	**3**	**15**	**18**	**50**	....	....	....	....	....
	NHL Totals		**915**	**137**	**470**	**607**	**1288**	**64**	**8**	**24**	**32**	**114**

a OHA Second All-Star Team (1976)
b Won James Norris Memorial Trophy (1981)
c NHL First All-Star Team (1981)

Played in NHL All-Star Game (1981-83, 1985)

Traded to **Pittsburgh** by **Toronto** with George Ferguson for Dave Burrows, June 14, 1978.
Traded to **Winnipeg** by **Pittsburgh** for Winnipeg's first round choice (Doug Bodger) in 1984 Entry Draft and future considerations (Moe Mantha), March 5, 1984.

CARNBACK, PATRIK

Left wing. Shoots left. 6', 187 lbs.   Born, Goteborg, Sweden, February 1, 1968.
(Montreal's 7th choice, 125th overall, in 1988 Entry Draft).

			Regular Season					Playoffs				
Season	Club	Lea	GP	G	A	TP	PIM	GP	G	A	TP	PIM
1986-87	V. Frolunda	Swe.	28	3	1	4	4	....	....	....	....	....
1987-88	V. Frolunda	Swe.	33	16	19	35	10	....	....	....	....	....
1988-89	V. Frolunda	Swe.	53	39	36	75	52	....	....	....	....	....
1989-90	V. Frolunda	Swe.	40	26	27	53	34	....	....	....	....	....

CARNEY, KEITH E.

Defense. Shoots left. 6'1", 200 lbs.   Born, Pawtucket, RI, February 3, 1970.
(Buffalo's 3rd choice, 76th overall, in 1988 Entry Draft).

			Regular Season					Playoffs				
Season	Club	Lea	GP	G	A	TP	PIM	GP	G	A	TP	PIM
1988-89	U. of Maine	H.E.	40	4	22	26	24	....	....	....	....	....
1989-90ab	U. of Maine	H.E.	41	3	41	44	43	....	....	....	....	....

a Hockey East Second All-Star Team (1990)
b NCAA East Second All-American Team (1990)

CARPENTER, ROBERT (BOB)

Center. Shoots left. 6', 190 lbs. Born, Beverly, MA, July 13, 1963.
(Washington's 1st choice, 3rd overall, in 1981 Entry Draft).

			Regular Season					Playoffs				
Season	Club	Lea	GP	G	A	TP	PIM	GP	G	A	TP	PIM
1980-81	St. John's	HS	18	14	24	38	....	....	....	....	....	....
1981-82	Washington	NHL	80	32	35	67	69	....	....	....	....	....
1982-83	Washington	NHL	80	32	37	69	64	4	1	0	1	2
1983-84	Washington	NHL	80	28	40	68	51	8	2	1	3	25
1984-85	Washington	NHL	80	53	42	95	87	5	1	4	5	8
1985-86	Washington	NHL	80	27	29	56	105	9	5	4	9	12
1986-87	Washington	NHL	22	5	7	12	21	....	....	....	....	....
	NY Rangers	NHL	28	2	8	10	20	....	....	....	....	....
	Los Angeles	NHL	10	2	3	5	6	5	1	2	3	2
1987-88	Los Angeles	NHL	71	19	33	52	84	5	1	1	2	0
1988-89	Los Angeles	NHL	39	11	15	26	16	....	....	....	....	....
	Boston	NHL	18	5	9	14	10	8	1	1	2	4
1989-90	Boston	NHL	80	25	31	56	97	21	4	6	10	39
	NHL Totals		668	241	289	530	630	65	16	19	35	92

Played in NHL All-Star Game (1985)

Traded to **NY Rangers** by **Washington** with Washington's second-round choice (Jason Prosofsky) in 1989 Entry Draft for Bob Crawford, Kelly Miller and Mike Ridley, January 1, 1987. Traded to **Los Angeles** by **NY Rangers** with Tom Laidlaw for Jeff Crossman, Marcel Dionne and Los Angeles' third-round choice in 1989 Entry Draft (Draft choice acquired by **Minnesota**, October 12, 1988. **Minnesota** selected Murray Garbutt.) Traded to **Boston** by **Los Angeles** for Steve Kasper, January 23, 1989.

CARSON, JIMMY

Center. Shoots right. 6', 200 lbs. Born, Southfield, MI, July 20, 1968.
(Los Angeles' 1st choice, 2nd overall, in 1986 Entry Draft).

			Regular Season					Playoffs				
Season	Club	Lea	GP	G	A	TP	PIM	GP	G	A	TP	PIM
1984-85	Verdun	QMJHL	68	44	72	116	12	14	9	17	26	12
1985-86a	Verdun	QMJHL	69	70	83	153	46	5	2	6	8	0
1986-87b	Los Angeles	NHL	80	37	42	79	22	5	1	2	3	6
1987-88	Los Angeles	NHL	80	55	52	107	45	5	5	3	8	4
1988-89	Edmonton	NHL	80	49	51	100	36	7	2	1	3	6
1989-90	Edmonton	NHL	4	1	2	3	0	....	....	....	....	....
	Detroit	NHL	44	20	16	36	8	....	....	....	....	....
	NHL Totals		288	162	163	325	111	17	8	6	14	16

a QMJHL Second All-Star Team (1986)
b Named to NHL All-Rookie Team (1987)

Played in NHL All-Star Game (1989)

Traded to **Edmonton** by **Los Angeles** with Martin Gelinas, Los Angeles' first round choices in 1989, (acquired by **New Jersey**, June 17, 1989. **New Jersey** selected Jason Miller), 1991 and 1993 Entry Drafts and cash for Wayne Gretzky, Mike Krushelnyski and Marty McSorley, August 9, 1988. Traded to **Detroit** by **Edmonton** with Kevin McClelland and Edmonton's fifth round choice in 1991 Entry Draft for Petr Klima, Joe Murphy, Adam Graves and Jeff Sharples, November 2, 1989.

CARTER, JOHN

Left wing. Shoots left. 5'10", 175 lbs. Born, Winchester, MA, May 3, 1963.

			Regular Season					Playoffs				
Season	Club	Lea	GP	G	A	TP	PIM	GP	G	A	TP	PIM
1982-83	RPI	ECAC	29	16	22	38	33	....	....	....	....	....
1983-84	RPI	ECAC	38	35	39	74	52	....	....	....	....	....
1984-85	RPI	ECAC	37	43	29	72	52	....	....	....	....	....
1985-86	RPI	ECAC	27	23	18	41	68	....	....	....	....	....
	Boston	NHL	3	0	0	0	0	....	....	....	....	....
1986-87	Boston	NHL	8	0	1	1	0	....	....	....	....	....
	Moncton	AHL	58	25	30	55	60	6	2	3	5	5
1987-88	Boston	NHL	4	0	1	1	2	....	....	....	....	....
	Maine	AHL	76	38	38	76	145	10	4	4	8	44
1988-89	Boston	NHL	44	12	10	22	24	10	1	2	3	6
	Maine	AHL	24	13	6	19	12	....	....	....	....	....
1989-90	Boston	NHL	76	17	22	39	26	21	6	3	9	45
	Maine	AHL	2	2	2	4	2	....	....	....	....	....
	NHL Totals		135	29	34	63	52	31	7	5	12	51

Signed as a free agent by **Boston**, May 3, 1986.

CASSELMAN, MIKE

Center. Shoots left. 5'11", 180 lbs. Born, Morrisburg, Ont., September 23, 1968.
(Detroit's 1st choice, 3rd overall, in 1990 Supplemental Draft).

			Regular Season					Playoffs				
Season	Club	Lea	GP	G	A	TP	PIM	GP	G	A	TP	PIM
1987-88	Clarkson	ECAC	24	4	1	5	....	....	....	....	....	....
1988-89	Clarkson	ECAC	31	3	14	17	....	....	....	....	....	....
1989-90	Clarkson	ECAC	34	22	21	43	69	....	....	....	....	....

CASSELS, ANDREW

Center. Shoots left. 6', 192 lbs. Born, Bramalea, Ont., July 23, 1969.
(Montreal's 1st choice, 17th overall, in 1987 Entry Draft).

			Regular Season					Playoffs				
Season	Club	Lea	GP	G	A	TP	PIM	GP	G	A	TP	PIM
1986-87a	Ottawa	OHL	66	26	66	92	28	11	5	9	14	7
1987-88bc	Ottawa	OHL	61	48	*103	*151	39	16	8	*24	*32	13
1988-89c	Ottawa	OHL	56	37	97	134	66	12	5	10	15	10
1989-90	Montreal	NHL	6	2	0	2	2	....	....	....	....	....
	Sherbrooke	AHL	55	22	45	67	25	12	2	11	13	6
	NHL Totals		6	2	0	2	0	....	....	....	....	....

a OHL Rookie of the Year (1987)
b OHL Player of the Year (1988)
c OHL First All-Star Team (1988,1989)

CASSIDY, BRUCE

Defense. Shoots left. 5'11", 175 lbs. Born, Ottawa, Ont., May 20, 1965.
(Chicago's 1st choice, 18th overall, in 1983 Entry Draft).

			Regular Season					Playoffs				
Season	Club	Lea	GP	G	A	TP	PIM	GP	G	A	TP	PIM
1982-83	Ottawa	OHL	70	25	86	111	33	9	3	9	12	10
1983-84	Chicago	NHL	1	0	0	0	0	....	....	....	....	....
a	Ottawa	OHL	67	27	68	95	58	13	6	16	22	6
1984-85	Ottawa	OHL	28	13	27	40	15	....	....	....	....	....
1985-86	Chicago	NHL	1	0	0	0	0	....	....	....	....	....
	Nova Scotia	AHL	4	0	0	0	0	....	....	....	....	....
1986-87	Chicago	NHL	2	0	0	0	0	....	....	....	....	....
	Nova Scotia	AHL	19	2	8	10	4	....	....	....	....	....
	Cdn. Olympic	....	12	3	6	9	4	....	....	....	....	....
	Saginaw	IHL	10	2	13	15	6	2	1	1	2	0
1987-88	Chicago	NHL	21	3	10	13	6	....	....	....	....	....
	Saginaw	IHL	60	9	37	46	59	10	2	3	5	19
1988-89	Chicago	NHL	9	0	2	2	4	1	0	0	0	0
b	Saginaw	IHL	72	16	64	80	80	6	0	2	2	6
1989-90	Chicago	NHL	2	1	1	2	0	....	....	....	....	....
b	Indianapolis	IHL	75	11	46	57	56	14	1	10	11	20
	NHL Totals		36	4	13	17	10	1	0	0	0	0

a OHL Second All-Star Team (1984).
b IHL First All-Star Team (1989, 1990)

CAUFIELD, JAY

Right wing. Shoots right. 6'4", 230 lbs. Born, Philadelphia, PA, July 17, 1960.

			Regular Season					Playoffs				
Season	Club	Lea	GP	G	A	TP	PIM	GP	G	A	TP	PIM
1984-85	North Dakota	WCHA	1	0	0	0	0	....	....	....	....	....
1985-86	Toledo	IHL	30	5	4	9	54	....	....	....	....	....
	New Haven	AHL	40	2	3	5	40	1	0	0	0	0
1986-87	NY Rangers	NHL	13	2	1	3	45	3	0	0	0	12
	Flint	IHL	12	4	3	7	59	....	....	....	....	....
	New Haven	AHL	13	0	0	0	43	....	....	....	....	....
1987-88	Minnesota	NHL	1	0	0	0	0	....	....	....	....	....
	Kalamazoo	IHL	65	5	10	15	273	6	0	1	1	47
1988-89	Pittsburgh	NHL	58	1	4	5	285	9	0	0	0	28
1989-90	Pittsburgh	NHL	37	1	2	3	123	....	....	....	....	....
	NHL Totals		109	4	7	11	453	12	0	0	0	40

Signed as a free agent by **NY Rangers**, October 8, 1985. Traded to **Minnesota** by **NY Rangers** with Dave Gagne for Jari Gronstrand and Paul Boutilier, October 8, 1987. Claimed by **Pittsburgh** in NHL Waiver Draft, October 3, 1988.

CAVALLINI, GINO JOHN

Left wing. Shoots left. 6'1", 215 lbs. Born, Toronto, Ont., November 24, 1962.

			Regular Season					Playoffs				
Season	Club	Lea	GP	G	A	TP	PIM	GP	G	A	TP	PIM
1982-83	Bowling Green	CCHA	40	8	16	24	52	....	....	....	....	....
1983-84	Bowling Green	CCHA	43	25	23	48	16	....	....	....	....	....
1984-85	Calgary	NHL	27	6	10	16	14	3	0	0	0	4
	Moncton	AHL	51	29	19	48	28	....	....	....	....	....
1985-86	Calgary	NHL	27	7	7	14	26	....	....	....	....	....
	Moncton	AHL	4	3	2	5	7	....	....	....	....	....
	St. Louis	NHL	30	6	5	11	36	17	4	5	9	10
1986-87	St. Louis	NHL	80	18	26	44	54	6	3	1	4	2
1987-88	St. Louis	NHL	64	15	17	32	62	10	5	5	10	19
1988-89	St. Louis	NHL	74	20	23	43	79	9	0	2	2	17
1989-90	St. Louis	NHL	80	15	15	30	77	12	1	3	4	12
	NHL Totals		382	87	103	190	348	57	13	16	29	64

Signed as a free agent by **Calgary**, May 16, 1984. Traded to **St. Louis** by **Calgary** with Eddy Beers and Charles Bourgeois for Joe Mullen, Terry Johnson and Rik Wilson, February 1, 1986.

CAVALLINI, PAUL

Defense. Shoots left. 6'1", 210 lbs. Born, Toronto, Ont., October 13, 1965.
(Washington's 10th choice, 205th overall, in 1984 Entry Draft).

			Regular Season					Playoffs				
Season	Club	Lea	GP	G	A	TP	PIM	GP	G	A	TP	PIM
1984-85	Providence	H.E.	37	4	10	14	52	....	....	....	....	....
1985-86	Binghamton	AHL	15	3	4	7	20	6	0	2	2	56
	Cdn. Olympic	....	52	1	11	12	95	....	....	....	....	....
1986-87	Washington	NHL	6	0	2	2	8	....	....	....	....	....
	Binghamton	AHL	66	12	24	36	188	13	2	7	9	35
1987-88	Washington	NHL	24	2	3	5	66	....	....	....	....	....
	St. Louis	NHL	48	4	7	11	86	10	1	6	7	26
1988-89	St. Louis	NHL	65	4	20	24	128	10	2	2	4	14
1989-90a	St. Louis	NHL	80	8	39	47	106	12	2	3	5	20
	NHL Totals		223	18	71	89	394	32	5	11	16	60

a Won Alka-Seltzer Plus Award (NHL plus/minus leader) (1990)

Played in NHL All-Star Game (1990)

Traded to **St. Louis** by **Washington** for Montreal's second round choice (Wade Bartley) in 1988 Entry Draft — St. Louis' property via earlier deal — December 11, 1987.

CERNICH, KORD

Defense, Shoots right. 5'11", 192 lbs. Born, Anchorage, AK, October 20, 1966.

			Regular Season					Playoffs				
Season	Club	Lea	GP	G	A	TP	PIM	GP	G	A	TP	PIM
1986-87	Lake Superior	CCHA	39	4	18	22	32	....	....	....	....	....
1987-88a	Lake Superior	CCHA	46	17	22	39	78	....	....	....	....	....
1988-89b	Lake Superior	CCHA	46	7	31	38	74	....	....	....	....	....
1989-90bc	Lake Superior	CCHA	46	11	25	36	59	....	....	....	....	....

a CCHA Second All-Star Team (1988)
b CCHA First All-Star Team (1989, 1990)
c NCAA West Second All-American Team (1990)

CESARSKI, ANDREW

Defense. Shoots left. 6'4", 200 lbs.   Born, Ft. Monmouth, NJ, September 21, 1968.
(St. Louis' 11th choice, 207th overall, in 1987 Entry Draft).

			Regular Season					Playoffs				
Season	Club	Lea	GP	G	A	TP	PIM	GP	G	A	TP	PIM
1987-88	Princeton	ECAC	28	2	3	5	34	.....	.....	.....	.....	.....
1988-89	Princeton	ECAC	26	6	10	16	34	.....	.....	.....	.....	.....
1989-90	Princeton	ECAC	27	1	9	10	22	.....	.....	.....	.....	.....

CHABOT, JOHN DAVID   (shah-BAHT)

Center. Shoots left. 6'2", 200 lbs.   Born, Summerside, P.E.I., May 18, 1962.
(Montreal's 3rd choice, 40th overall, in 1980 Entry Draft).

			Regular Season					Playoffs				
Season	Club	Lea	GP	G	A	TP	PIM	GP	G	A	TP	PIM
1979-80	Hull	QMJHL	68	26	57	83	28	4	1	2	3	0
1980-81	Hull	QMJHL	70	27	62	89	24	.....	.....	.....	.....	.....
	Nova Scotia	AHL	1	0	0	0	0	2	0	0	0	0
1981-82ab	Sherbrooke	QMJHL	62	34	*109	143	42	19	6	26	32	6
1982-83	Nova Scotia	AHL	76	16	73	89	19	7	1	3	4	0
1983-84	Montreal	NHL	56	18	25	43	13	11	1	4	5	0
1984-85	Montreal	NHL	10	1	6	7	2	.....	.....	.....	.....	.....
	Pittsburgh	NHL	67	8	45	53	12	.....	.....	.....	.....	.....
1985-86	Pittsburgh	NHL	77	14	31	45	6	.....	.....	.....	.....	.....
1986-87	Pittsburgh	NHL	72	14	22	36	8	.....	.....	.....	.....	.....
1987-88	Detroit	NHL	78	13	44	57	10	16	4	15	19	2
1988-89	Detroit	NHL	52	2	10	12	6	6	1	1	2	0
	Adirondack	AHL	8	3	12	15	0	.....	.....	.....	.....	.....
1989-90	Detroit	NHL	69	9	40	49	24	.....	.....	.....	.....	.....
	NHL Totals		481	79	223	302	81	33	6	20	26	2

a QMJHL First All-Star Team (1982)
b QMJHL Most Valuable Player (1982)
Traded to **Pittsburgh** by **Montreal** for Ron Flockhart, November 9, 1984. Signed as a free agent by **Detroit**, June 25, 1987.

CHAMBERS, SHAWN

Defense. Shoots left. 6'2", 210 lbs.   Born, Sterling Heights, MI, October 11, 1966.
(Minnesota's 1st choice, 4th overall, in 1987 Supplemental Draft).

			Regular Season					Playoffs				
Season	Club	Lea	GP	G	A	TP	PIM	GP	G	A	TP	PIM
1986-87	Alaska-Fair.	G.N.	28	8	29	37	84	.....	.....	.....	.....	.....
	Seattle	WHL	28	8	25	33	58	.....	.....	.....	.....	.....
	Ft. Wayne	IHL	12	2	6	8	0	10	1	4	5	5
1987-88	**Minnesota**	**NHL**	19	1	7	8	21	.....	.....	.....	.....	.....
	Kalamazoo	IHL	19	1	6	7	22	.....	.....	.....	.....	.....
1988-89	**Minnesota**	**NHL**	72	5	19	24	80	3	0	2	2	0
1989-90	**Minnesota**	**NHL**	78	8	18	26	81	7	2	1	3	10
	NHL Totals		169	14	44	58	182	10	2	3	5	10

CHANNELL, CRAIG

Defense. Shoots left. 5'11", 190 lbs.   Born, Moncton, N.B., April 24, 1962.

			Regular Season					Playoffs				
Season	Club	Lea	GP	G	A	TP	PIM	GP	G	A	TP	PIM
1979-80	Seattle	WHL	70	3	21	24	191	12	0	0	0	22
1980-81	Seattle	WHL	71	9	66	75	181	5	0	2	2	4
1981-82	Seattle	WHL	71	9	79	88	244	10	0	11	11	22
1982-83	Sherbrooke	AHL	65	0	15	15	109	.....	.....	.....	.....	.....
1983-84	Sherbrooke	AHL	80	5	18	23	112	.....	.....	.....	.....	.....
1984-85	Sherbrooke	AHL	1	0	0	0	0	.....	.....	.....	.....	.....
	Fort Wayne	IHL	78	10	35	45	110	8	0	5	5	33
1985-86	Fort Wayne	IHL	69	7	28	35	116	15	3	12	15	41
1986-87	Fort Wayne	IHL	81	12	42	54	90	11	2	1	3	29
1987-88	Fort Wayne	IHL	81	11	29	40	108	6	0	1	1	15
1988-89a	Fort Wayne	IHL	79	5	25	30	168	11	0	7	7	32
1989-90	Fort Wayne	IHL	37	6	11	17	86	.....	.....	.....	.....	.....
	Indianapolis	IHL	16	0	1	1	17	14	1	1	2	16

a IHL Second All-Star Team (1989)
Signed as a free agent by **Winnipeg**, November 9, 1981.

CHAPDELAINE, RENE   (SHAP-duh-LAYN)

Defense. Shoots right. 6'1", 195 lbs.   Born, Weyburn, Sask., September 27, 1966.
(Los Angeles' 7th choice, 149th overall, in 1986 Entry Draft).

			Regular Season					Playoffs				
Season	Club	Lea	GP	G	A	TP	PIM	GP	G	A	TP	PIM
1985-86	Lake Superior	CCHA	32	1	4	5	47	.....	.....	.....	.....	.....
1986-87	Lake Superior	CCHA	28	1	5	6	51	.....	.....	.....	.....	.....
1987-88	Lake Superior	CCHA	35	1	9	10	44	.....	.....	.....	.....	.....
1988-89	Lake Superior	CCHA	46	4	9	13	62	.....	.....	.....	.....	.....
1989-90	New Haven	AHL	41	0	1	1	35	.....	.....	.....	.....	.....

CHAPMAN, BRIAN

Defense. Shoots left. 6', 195 lbs.   Born, Brockville, Ont., February 10, 1968.
(Hartford's 3rd choice, 74th overall, in 1986 Entry Draft).

			Regular Season					Playoffs				
Season	Club	Lea	GP	G	A	TP	PIM	GP	G	A	TP	PIM
1985-86	Belleville	OHL	66	6	31	37	168	24	2	6	8	54
1986-87	Belleville	OHL	54	4	32	36	142	6	1	1	2	10
1987-88	Belleville	OHL	63	11	57	68	180	6	1	4	5	13
1988-89	Binghamton	AHL	71	5	25	30	216	.....	.....	.....	.....	.....
1989-90	Binghamton	AHL	68	2	15	17	180	.....	.....	.....	.....	.....

CHARBONNEAU, JOSE (JOE)   (SHAHR-buh-NOH)

Right wing. Shoots right. 6', 195 lbs.   Born, Ferme-Neuve, Que., November 21, 1966.
(Montreal's 1st choice, 12th overall, in 1985 Entry Draft).

			Regular Season					Playoffs				
Season	Club	Lea	GP	G	A	TP	PIM	GP	G	A	TP	PIM
1983-84	Drummondville	QMJHL	65	31	59	90	110	.....	.....	.....	.....	.....
1984-85	Drummondville	QMJHL	46	34	40	74	91	12	5	10	15	20
1985-86	Drummondville	QMJHL	57	44	45	89	158	23	16	20	36	40
1986-87	Sherbrooke	AHL	72	14	27	41	94	16	5	12	17	17
1987-88	**Montreal**	**NHL**	16	0	2	2	6	8	0	0	0	4
	Sherbrooke	AHL	55	30	35	65	108	.....	.....	.....	.....	.....
1988-89	**Montreal**	**NHL**	9	1	3	4	6	.....	.....	.....	.....	.....
	Sherbrooke	AHL	33	13	15	28	95	.....	.....	.....	.....	.....
	Vancouver	**NHL**	13	0	1	1	6	.....	.....	.....	.....	.....
	Milwaukee	IHL	13	8	5	13	46	10	3	2	5	23
1989-90	Milwaukee	IHL	65	23	38	61	137	5	0	1	1	8
	NHL Totals		38	1	6	7	18	8	0	0	0	4

Traded to **Vancouver** by **Montreal** for Dan Woodley, January 25, 1989.

CHARLESWORTH, TODD

Defense. Shoots left. 6'1", 190 lbs.   Born, Calgary, Alta., March 22, 1965.
(Pittsburgh's 2nd choice, 22nd overall, in 1983 Entry Draft).

			Regular Season					Playoffs				
Season	Club	Lea	GP	G	A	TP	PIM	GP	G	A	TP	PIM
1982-83	Oshawa	OHL	70	6	23	29	55	17	0	4	4	20
1983-84	**Pittsburgh**	**NHL**	10	0	0	0	8	.....	.....	.....	.....	.....
	Oshawa	OHL	57	11	35	46	54	7	0	4	4	4
1984-85	**Pittsburgh**	**NHL**	67	1	8	9	31	.....	.....	.....	.....	.....
1985-86	**Pittsburgh**	**NHL**	2	0	1	1	0	.....	.....	.....	.....	.....
	Baltimore	AHL	19	1	3	4	10	.....	.....	.....	.....	.....
	Muskegon	IHL	51	9	27	36	78	14	3	8	11	14
1986-87	**Pittsburgh**	**NHL**	1	0	0	0	0	.....	.....	.....	.....	.....
	Baltimore	AHL	75	5	21	26	64	.....	.....	.....	.....	.....
1987-88	**Pittsburgh**	**NHL**	6	2	0	2	2	.....	.....	.....	.....	.....
	Muskegon	IHL	64	9	31	40	49	5	0	0	0	18
1988-89a	Muskegon	IHL	74	10	53	63	85	14	2	13	15	8
1989-90	**NY Rangers**	**NHL**	7	0	0	0	6	.....	.....	.....	.....	.....
	Flint	IHL	26	3	6	9	12	.....	.....	.....	.....	.....
	NHL Totals		93	3	9	12	47	.....	.....	.....	.....	.....

a IHL Second All-Star Team (1989)
Signed as a free agent by **Edmonton**, June 21, 1989. Traded to **NY Rangers** by **Edmonton** for future considerations, January 18, 1990.

CHARRON, CRAIG M.

Center. Shoots left. 5'10", 175 lbs.   Born, North Easton, MA, November 15, 1967.
(Montreal's 1st choice, 25th overall, in 1989 Supplemental Draft).

			Regular Season					Playoffs				
Season	Club	Lea	GP	G	A	TP	PIM	GP	G	A	TP	PIM
1986-87	U. of Lowell	H.E.	36	11	16	27	48	.....	.....	.....	.....	.....
1987-88	U. of Lowell	H.E.	39	22	18	40	32	.....	.....	.....	.....	.....
1988-89	U. of Lowell	H.E.	32	14	21	35	32	.....	.....	.....	.....	.....
1989-90	U. of Lowell	H.E.	35	17	29	46	10	.....	.....	.....	.....	.....

CHARRON, ERIC

Defense. Shoots left. 6'3", 195 lbs.   Born, Verdun, Que., January 14, 1970.
(Montreal's 1st choice, 20th overall, in 1988 Entry Draft).

			Regular Season					Playoffs				
Season	Club	Lea	GP	G	A	TP	PIM	GP	G	A	TP	PIM
1987-88	Trois Rivieres	QMJHL	67	3	13	16	135	.....	.....	.....	.....	.....
1988-89	Verdun	QMJHL	67	4	31	35	177	.....	.....	.....	.....	.....
	Sherbrooke	AHL	1	0	0	0	0	.....	.....	.....	.....	.....
1989-90	Trois-Rivieres	QMJHL	68	13	38	51	152	11	3	4	7	67
	Sherbrooke	AHL	.....	.....	.....	.....	.....	2	0	0	0	0

CHARTRAND, STEVE

Left wing. Shoots left. 5'9", 160 lbs.   Born, Verdun, Que., January 8, 1969.
(Toronto's 13th choice, 234th overall, in 1989 Entry Draft).

			Regular Season					Playoffs				
Season	Club	Lea	GP	G	A	TP	PIM	GP	G	A	TP	PIM
1988-89	Drummondville	QMJHL	70	74	83	157	46	4	2	5	7	2
1989-90	Newmarket	AHL	20	4	4	8	0	.....	.....	.....	.....	.....
	Drummondville	QMJHL	44	50	41	91	34	.....	.....	.....	.....	.....

CHASE, KELLY WAYNE

Right wing. Shoots right. 5'11", 192 lbs.   Born, Porcupine Plain, Sask., October 25, 1967.

			Regular Season					Playoffs				
Season	Club	Lea	GP	G	A	TP	PIM	GP	G	A	TP	PIM
1985-86	Saskatoon	WHL	57	7	18	25	172	10	3	4	7	37
1986-87	Saskatoon	WHL	68	17	29	46	285	11	2	8	10	37
1987-88	Saskatoon	WHL	70	21	34	55	*343	9	3	5	8	32
1988-89	Peoria	IHL	38	14	7	21	278	.....	.....	.....	.....	.....
1989-90	**St. Louis**	**NHL**	43	1	3	4	244	9	1	0	1	8
	Peoria	IHL	10	1	2	3	76	.....	.....	.....	.....	.....
	NHL Totals		43	1	3	4	244	9	1	0	1	8

Signed as a free agent by **St. Louis**, February 23, 1988.

CHASE, TIMOTHY

Center. Shoots left. 6'1", 175 lbs.   Born, Gaithersburg, MD, March 23, 1970.
(Montreal's 8th choice, 146th overall, in 1988 Entry Draft).

			Regular Season					Playoffs				
Season	Club	Lea	GP	G	A	TP	PIM	GP	G	A	TP	PIM
1987-88	Tabor	HS	28	20	20	40	.....	.....	.....	.....	.....	.....
1988-89	Tabor	HS	22	21	20	41	18	.....	.....	.....	.....	.....
1989-90	Brown	ECAC	8	0	0	0	0	.....	.....	.....	.....	.....

CHELIOS, CHRIS (CHELL-EE-ohs)

Defense. Shoots right. 6'1", 186 lbs. Born, Chicago, IL, January 25, 1062.
(Montreal's 5th choice, 40th overall, in 1981 Entry Draft).

			Regular Season					Playoffs				
Season	Club	Lea	GP	G	A	TP	PIM	GP	G	A	TP	PIM
1980-81	Moose Jaw	SJHL	54	23	64	87	175	....	....	....	....	....
1981-82	U. Wisconsin	WCHA	43	6	43	49	50	....	....	....	....	....
1982-83ab	U. Wisconsin	WCHA	26	9	17	26	50	....	....	....	....	....
1983-84	U.S. National	...	60	14	35	49	58	....	....	....	....	....
	U.S. Olympic	...	6	0	4	4	8	....	....	....	....	....
	Montreal	NHL	12	0	2	2	12	15	1	9	10	17
1984-85c	Montreal	NHL	74	9	55	64	87	9	2	8	10	17
1985-86	Montreal	NHL	41	8	26	34	67	20	2	9	11	49
1986-87	Montreal	NHL	71	11	33	44	124	17	4	9	13	38
1987-88	Montreal	NHL	71	20	41	61	172	11	3	1	4	29
1988-89de	Montreal	NHL	80	15	58	73	185	21	4	15	19	28
1989-90	Montreal	NHL	53	9	22	31	136	5	0	1	1	8
	NHL Totals		402	72	237	309	783	98	16	52	68	186

a WCHA Second All-Star Team (1983)
b NCAA All-Tournament Team (1983)
c NHL All-Rookie Team (1985)
d NHL First All-Star Team (1989)
e Won Norris Trophy (1989)

Played in NHL All-Star Game (1985, 1990)

Traded to **Chicago** by **Montreal** with Montreal's second round choice in 1991 Entry Draft for Denis Savard, June 29, 1990.

CHERNOMAZ, RICHARD (RICH) (CHUR-noh-maz)

Right wing. Shoots right. 5'8", 185 lbs. Born, Selkirk, Man., September 1, 1963.
(Colorado's 2nd choice, 26th overall, in 1981 Entry Draft).

			Regular Season					Playoffs				
Season	Club	Lea	GP	G	A	TP	PIM	GP	G	A	TP	PIM
1980-81	Victoria	WHL	72	49	64	113	92	15	11	15	26	38
1981-82	Colorado	NHL	2	0	0	0	0	....	....	....	....	....
	Victoria	WHL	49	36	62	98	69	4	1	2	3	13
1982-83a	Victoria	WHL	64	71	53	124	113	12	10	5	15	18
1983-84	New Jersey	NHL	7	2	1	3	2	....	....	....	....	....
	Maine	AHL	69	17	29	46	39	2	0	1	1	0
1984-85	New Jersey	NHL	3	0	2	2	2	....	....	....	....	....
	Maine	AHL	64	17	34	51	64	10	2	2	4	4
1985-86	Maine	AHL	78	21	28	49	82	5	0	0	0	2
1986-87	New Jersey	NHL	25	6	4	10	8	....	....	....	....	....
	Maine	AHL	58	35	27	62	65	....	....	....	....	....
1987-88	Calgary	NHL	2	1	0	1	0	....	....	....	....	....
b	Salt Lake	IHL	73	48	47	95	122	18	4	14	18	30
1988-89	Calgary	NHL	1	0	0	0	0	....	....	....	....	....
	Salt Lake	IHL	81	33	68	101	122	14	7	5	12	47
1989-90	Salt Lake	IHL	65	39	35	74	170	11	6	6	12	32
	NHL Totals		40	9	7	16	12	....	....	....	....	....

a WHL First All-Star Team (1983)
b IHL Second All-Star Team (1988)

Signed as a free agent by **Calgary**, August 4, 1987.

CHERNYKH, ALEXANDER

Center. Shoots left. 6'1", 180 lbs. Born, Voskresensk, U.S.S.R., September 12, 1965.
(New Jersey's 8th choice, 192nd overall, in 1983 Entry Draft).

			Regular Season					Playoffs				
Season	Club	Lea	GP	G	A	TP	PIM	GP	G	A	TP	PIM
1981-82	Voskresensk	USSR	1	0	0	0	0	....	....	....	....	....
1982-83	Voskresensk	USSR	46	12	5	17	26	....	....	....	....	....
1983-84	Voskresensk	USSR	44	12	5	17	32	....	....	....	....	....
1984-85	Voskresensk	USSR	48	9	10	19	32	....	....	....	....	....
1985-86	CSKA	USSR	10	3	3	6	6	....	....	....	....	....
1986-87	SKA Kalanin	USSR	57	32	30	62	52	....	....	....	....	....
1987-88	Voskresensk	USSR	41	14	15	29	34	....	....	....	....	....
1988-89	Voskresensk	USSR	41	9	12	21	32	....	....	....	....	....
1989-90			DID NOT PLAY - INJURED									

CHEVELDAYOFF, KEVIN (sheh-vehl-DAY-ahf)

Defense. Shoots right. 6', 200 lbs. Born, Saskatoon, Sask., February 4, 1970.
(New York Islanders' 1st choice, 16th overall, in 1988 Entry Draft).

			Regular Season					Playoffs				
Season	Club	Lea	GP	G	A	TP	PIM	GP	G	A	TP	PIM
1986-87	Brandon	WHL	70	0	16	16	259	....	....	....	....	....
1987-88	Brandon	WHL	71	3	29	32	265	4	0	2	2	20
1988-89	Brandon	WHL	40	4	12	16	135	....	....	....	....	....
1989-90	Brandon	WHL	33	5	12	17	56	....	....	....	....	....
	Springfield	AHL	4	0	0	0	0	....	....	....	....	....

CHIASSON, STEVE (CHAY-sahn)

Defense. Shoots left. 6', 205 lbs. Born, Barrie, Ont., April 14, 1967.
(Detroit's 3rd choice, 50th over all, in 1985 Entry Draft).

			Regular Season					Playoffs				
Season	Club	Lea	GP	G	A	TP	PIM	GP	G	A	TP	PIM
1984-85	Guelph	OHL	61	8	22	30	139	....	....	....	....	....
1985-86	Guelph	OHL	54	12	30	42	126	18	10	10	20	37
1986-87	Detroit	NHL	45	1	4	5	73	2	0	0	0	19
1987-88	Detroit	NHL	29	2	9	11	57	9	2	2	4	31
	Adirondack	AHL	23	6	11	17	58	....	....	....	....	....
1988-89	Detroit	NHL	65	12	35	47	149	5	2	1	3	6
1989-90	Detroit	NHL	67	14	28	42	114	....	....	....	....	....
	NHL Totals		206	29	76	105	393	16	4	3	7	56

CHITARONI, MARIO BRIAN

Center. Shoots right. 5'8", 170 lbs. Born, Haileybury, Ont., March 11, 1966.

			Regular Season					Playoffs				
Season	Club	Lea	GP	G	A	TP	PIM	GP	G	A	TP	PIM
1987-88	Flint	IHL	80	49	47	96	156	12	9	8	17	60
1988-89	Flint	IHL	21	10	11	21	59	....	....	....	....	....
	New Haven	AHL	54	12	24	36	97	16	2	7	9	57
1989-90	Alleghe/Sile	Italy	36	39	35	74	87	10	14	11	25	29

Signed as a free agent by **Los Angeles**, July 1, 1988.

CHORSKE, TOM

Right wing. Shoots right. 6'1", 204 lbs. Born, Minneapolis, MN, September 18, 1966.
(Montreal's 2nd choice, 16th overall, in 1985 Entry Draft).

			Regular Season					Playoffs				
Season	Club	Lea	GP	G	A	TP	PIM	GP	G	A	TP	PIM
1985-86	U. Minnesota	WCHA	39	6	4	10	16	....	....	....	....	....
1986-87	U. Minnesota	WCHA	47	20	22	42	20	....	....	....	....	....
1987-88	U.S. National	....	36	9	16	25	24	....	....	....	....	....
1988-89a	U. Minnesota	WCHA	37	25	24	49	28	....	....	....	....	....
1989-90	Montreal	NHL	14	3	1	4	2	....	....	....	....	....
	Sherbrooke	AHL	59	22	24	46	54	12	4	4	8	8
	NHL Totals		14	3	1	4	2	....	....	....	....	....

a WCHA First All-Star Team (1989)

CHRISTIAN, DAVID (DAVE)

Right wing. Shoots right. 6', 175 lbs. Born, Warroad, MN, May 12, 1959.
(Winnipeg's 2nd choice, 40th overall, in 1979 Entry Draft).

			Regular Season					Playoffs				
Season	Club	Lea	GP	G	A	TP	PIM	GP	G	A	TP	PIM
1977-78	North Dakota	WCHA	38	8	16	24	14	....	....	....	....	....
1978-79	North Dakota	WCHA	40	22	24	46	22	....	....	....	....	....
1979-80	U.S. National	...	59	10	20	30	26	....	....	....	....	....
	U.S. Olympic	...	7	0	8	8	6	....	....	....	....	....
	Winnipeg	NHL	15	8	10	18	2	....	....	....	....	....
1980-81	Winnipeg	NHL	80	28	43	71	22	....	....	....	....	....
1981-82	Winnipeg	NHL	80	25	51	76	28	4	0	1	1	2
1982-83	Winnipeg	NHL	55	18	26	44	23	3	0	0	0	0
1983-84	Washington	NHL	80	29	52	81	28	8	5	4	9	5
1984-85	Washington	NHL	80	26	43	69	14	5	1	1	2	0
1985-86	Washington	NHL	80	41	42	83	15	9	4	4	8	0
1986-87	Washington	NHL	76	23	27	50	8	7	1	3	4	6
1987-88	Washington	NHL	80	37	21	58	26	14	5	6	11	6
1988-89	Washington	NHL	80	34	31	65	12	6	1	1	2	0
1989-90	Washington	NHL	28	3	8	11	4	....	....	....	....	....
	Boston	NHL	50	12	17	29	8	21	4	1	5	4
	NHL Totals		784	284	371	655	190	77	21	21	42	23

Traded to **Washington** by **Winnipeg** for Washington's first round choice (Bob Dollas) in the 1983 Entry Draft, June 8, 1983. Traded to **Boston** by **Washington** for Bob Joyce, December 13, 1989.

CHRISTIAN, JEFF

Left wing. Shoots left. 6'1", 195 lbs. Born, Burlington, Ont., July 30, 1970.
(New Jersey's 2nd choice, 23rd overall, in 1988 Entry Draft).

			Regular Season					Playoffs				
Season	Club	Lea	GP	G	A	TP	PIM	GP	G	A	TP	PIM
1987-88	London	OHL	64	15	29	44	154	9	1	5	6	27
1988-89	London	OHL	64	27	30	57	221	20	3	4	7	56
1989-90	Owen Sound	OHL	55	33	33	66	209	10	6	7	13	43

CHURLA, SHANE

Right wing. Shoots right. 6'1", 200 lbs. Born, Fernie, B.C., June 24, 1965.
(Hartford's 4th choice, 110th overall, in 1985 Entry Draft).

			Regular Season					Playoffs				
Season	Club	Lea	GP	G	A	TP	PIM	GP	G	A	TP	PIM
1983-84	Medicine Hat	WHL	48	3	7	10	115	14	1	5	6	41
1984-85	Medicine Hat	WHL	70	14	20	34	370	9	1	0	1	55
1985-86	Binghamton	AHL	52	4	10	14	306	3	0	0	0	22
1986-87	Hartford	NHL	20	0	1	1	78	2	0	0	0	42
	Binghamton	AHL	24	1	5	6	249	....	....	....	....	....
1987-88	Hartford	NHL	2	0	0	0	14	....	....	....	....	....
	Binghamton	AHL	25	5	8	13	168	....	....	....	....	....
	Calgary	NHL	29	1	5	6	132	7	0	1	1	17
1988-89	Calgary	NHL	5	0	0	0	25	....	....	....	....	....
	Salt Lake	IHL	32	3	13	16	278	....	....	....	....	....
	Minnesota	NHL	13	1	0	1	54	....	....	....	....	....
1989-90	Minnesota	NHL	53	2	3	5	292	7	0	0	0	44
	NHL Totals		122	4	9	13	595	16	0	1	1	103

Traded to **Calgary** by **Hartford** with Dana Murzyn for Neil Sheehy, Carey Wilson, and the rights to Lane MacDonald, January 3, 1988. Traded to **Minnesota** by **Calgary** with Perry Berezan for Brian MacLellan and Minnesota's fourth-round choice (Robert Reichel) in 1989 Entry Draft, March 4, 1989.

CHYCHRUN, JEFF (CHIHK-rihn)

Defense. Shoots right. 6'4", 215 lbs. Born, LaSalle, Que., May 3, 1966.
(Philadelphia's 3rd choice, 37th overall, in 1984 Entry Draft).

			Regular Season					Playoffs				
Season	Club	Lea	GP	G	A	TP	PIM	GP	G	A	TP	PIM
1983-84	Kingston	OHL	63	1	13	14	137	....	....	....	....	....
1984-85	Kingston	OHL	58	4	10	14	206	....	....	....	....	....
1985-86	Kingston	OHL	61	4	21	25	127	10	2	1	3	17
	Hershey	AHL	....	....	....	....	....	4	0	1	1	9
	Kalamazoo	IHL	....	....	....	....	....	3	1	0	1	0
1986-87	Philadelphia	NHL	1	0	0	0	4	....	....	....	....	....
	Hershey	AHL	74	1	17	18	239	4	0	0	0	10
1987-88	Philadelphia	NHL	3	0	0	0	4	....	....	....	....	....
	Hershey	AHL	55	0	5	5	210	12	0	2	2	44
1988-89	Philadelphia	NHL	80	1	4	5	245	19	0	2	2	65
1989-90	Philadelphia	NHL	79	2	7	9	248	....	....	....	....	....
	NHL Totals		163	3	11	14	501	19	0	2	2	65

CHYNOWETH, DEAN (shih-NOWTH)

Defense. Shoots right. 6'2", 190 lbs. Born, Calgary, Alta., October 30, 1968.
(NY Islanders' 1st choice, 13th overall, in 1987 Entry Draft).

			Regular Season					Playoffs				
Season	Club	Lea	GP	G	A	TP	PIM	GP	G	A	TP	PIM
1985-86	Medicine Hat	WHL	69	3	12	15	208	17	3	2	5	52
1986-87	Medicine Hat	WHL	67	3	18	21	285	13	4	2	6	28
1987-88	Medicine Hat	WHL	64	1	21	22	274	16	0	6	6	*87
1988-89	NY Islanders	NHL	6	0	0	0	48	....	....	....	....	....
1989-90	NY Islanders	NHL	20	0	2	2	39	....	....	....	....	....
	Springfield	AHL	40	0	7	7	98	17	0	4	4	36
	NHL Totals		26	0	2	2	87	....	....	....	....	....

CHYZOWSKI, BARRY (chih-ZOW-skee)

Center. Shoots right. 6', 170 lbs. Born, Edmonton, Alta., May 25, 1968.
(NY Rangers' 8th choice, 156th overall, in 1986 Entry Draft).

			Regular Season					Playoffs				
Season	Club	Lea	GP	G	A	TP	PIM	GP	G	A	TP	PIM
1986-87	Minn.-Duluth	WCHA	39	5	11	16	16	....	....	....	....	....
1987-88	Minn.-Duluth	WCHA	41	22	34	56	14	....	....	....	....	....
1988-89	Denver	IHL	69	12	21	33	48	3	0	0	0	4
1989-90	Flint	IHL	30	3	8	11	6	1	0	0	0	0
	Erie	ECHL	16	9	15	24	19	....	....	....	....	....

CHYZOWSKI, DAVE (chih-ZOW-skee)

Left wing. Shoots left. 6'2", 190 lbs. Born, Edmonton, Alta., July 11, 1971.
(NY Islanders' 1st choice, 2nd overall, in 1989 Entry Draft).

			Regular Season					Playoffs				
Season	Club	Lea	GP	G	A	TP	PIM	GP	G	A	TP	PIM
1987-88	Kamloops	WHL	66	16	17	33	117	18	2	4	6	26
1988-89a	Kamloops	WHL	68	56	48	104	139	16	15	13	28	32
1989-90	NY Islanders	NHL	34	8	6	14	45	....	....	....	....	....
	Springfield	AHL	4	0	0	0	7	....	....	....	....	....
	Kamloops	WHL	4	5	2	7	17	17	11	6	17	46
	NHL Totals		34	8	6	14	45	....	....	....	....	....

a WHL West All-Star Team (1989)

CIAVAGLIA, PETER

Center. Shoots left. 5'10", 175 lbs. Born, Albany, NY, July 15, 1969.
(Calgary's 7th choice, 145th overall, in 1987 Entry Draft).

			Regular Season					Playoffs				
Season	Club	Lea	GP	G	A	TP	PIM	GP	G	A	TP	PIM
1987-88	Harvard	ECAC	30	10	23	33	16	....	....	....	....	....
1988-89a	Harvard	ECAC	34	15	48	63	36	....	....	....	....	....
1989-90	Harvard	ECAC	28	17	18	35	22	....	....	....	....	....

a ECAC Second All-Star Team (1989)

CICCARELLI, DINO (sih-sih-REHL-ee)

Right wing. Shoots right. 5'10", 175 lbs. Born, Sarnia, Ont., February 8, 1960.

			Regular Season					Playoffs				
Season	Club	Lea	GP	G	A	TP	PIM	GP	G	A	TP	PIM
1977-78a	London	OHA	68	72	70	142	49	9	6	10	16	6
1978-79	London	OHA	30	8	11	19	35	7	3	5	8	0
1979-80	London	OHA	62	50	53	103	72	5	2	6	8	15
1980-81	Oklahoma City	CHL	48	32	25	57	45	....	....	....	....	....
	Minnesota	NHL	32	18	12	30	29	19	14	7	21	25
1981-82	Minnesota	NHL	76	55	51	106	138	4	3	1	4	2
1982-83	Minnesota	NHL	77	37	38	75	94	9	4	6	10	11
1983-84	Minnesota	NHL	79	38	33	71	58	16	4	5	9	27
1984-85	Minnesota	NHL	51	15	17	32	41	9	3	3	6	8
1985-86	Minnesota	NHL	75	44	45	89	51	5	0	1	1	6
1986-87	Minnesota	NHL	80	52	51	103	88	....	....	....	....	....
1987-88	Minnesota	NHL	67	41	45	86	79	....	....	....	....	....
1988-89	Minnesota	NHL	65	32	27	59	64	....	....	....	....	....
	Washington	NHL	11	12	3	15	12	6	3	3	6	12
1989-90	Washington	NHL	80	41	38	79	122	8	8	3	11	6
	NHL Totals		693	385	360	745	776	76	39	29	68	97

a OHA Second All-Star Team (1978)

Played in NHL All-Star Game (1982, 1983,1989)

Signed as free agent by **Minnesota**, September 28, 1979. Traded to **Washington** by **Minnesota** with Bob Rouse for Mike Gartner and Larry Murphy, March 7, 1989.

CICHOCKI, CHRIS (chih-HAH-kee)

Right wing. Shoots right. 5'11", 185 lbs. Born, Detroit, MI, September 17, 1963.

			Regular Season					Playoffs				
Season	Club	Lea	GP	G	A	TP	PIM	GP	G	A	TP	PIM
1982-83	Michigan Tech	CCHA	36	12	10	22	10	....	....	....	....	....
1983-84	Michigan Tech	CCHA	40	25	20	45	36	....	....	....	....	....
1984-85	Michigan Tech	CCHA	40	30	24	54	14	....	....	....	....	....
1985-86	Detroit	NHL	59	10	11	21	21	....	....	....	....	....
	Adirondack	AHL	9	4	4	8	6	....	....	....	....	....
1986-87	Detroit	NHL	2	0	0	0	2	....	....	....	....	....
	Adirondack	AHL	55	31	34	65	27	....	....	....	....	....
	Maine	AHL	7	2	2	4	0	....	....	....	....	....
1987-88	New Jersey	NHL	5	1	0	1	2	....	....	....	....	....
	Utica	AHL	69	36	30	66	66	....	....	....	....	....
1988-89	New Jersey	NHL	2	0	1	1	2	....	....	....	....	....
	Utica	AHL	59	32	31	63	50	5	0	1	1	2
1989-90	Utica	AHL	11	3	1	4	10	....	....	....	....	....
	Binghamton	AHL	60	21	26	47	22	....	....	....	....	....
	NHL Totals		68	11	12	23	27	....	....	....	....	....

Signed as a free agent by **Detroit**, June 28, 1985. Traded to **New Jersey** by **Detroit** with Detroit's third-round choice (later transferred to Buffalo - Andrew MacVicar) in 1987 Entry Draft for Mel Bridgman, March 9, 1987. Traded to **Hartford** by **New Jersey** for Jim Thomson, October 31, 1989.

CIGER, ZDENO

Left wing. Shoots left. 6'2", 190 lbs. Born, Martin, Czech., October 19, 1969.
(New Jersey's 3rd choice, 54th overall, in 1988 Entry Draft).

			Regular Season					Playoffs				
Season	Club	Lea	GP	G	A	TP	PIM	GP	G	A	TP	PIM
1988-89	Dukla Trencin	Czech.	32	15	21	36	18	....	....	....	....	....
1989-90	Dukla Trencin	Czech	53	18	28	46	....	....	....	....	....	....

CIMETTA, ROBERT

Left wing. Shoots left. 6', 190 lbs. Born, Toronto, Ont., February 15, 1970.
(Boston's 1st choice, 18th overall, in 1988 Entry Draft).

			Regular Season					Playoffs				
Season	Club	Lea	GP	G	A	TP	PIM	GP	G	A	TP	PIM
1986-87	Toronto	OHL	66	21	35	56	65	....	....	....	....	....
1987-88	Toronto	OHL	64	34	42	76	90	4	2	2	4	7
1988-89	Boston	NHL	7	2	0	2	0	1	0	0	0	15
a	Toronto	OHL	58	*55	47	102	89	6	3	3	6	0
1989-90	Boston	NHL	47	8	9	17	33	....	....	....	....	....
	Maine	AHL	9	3	2	5	13	....	....	....	....	....
	NHL Totals		54	10	9	19	33	1	0	0	0	15

a OHL First All-Star Team (1989)

CIRELLA, JOE (suh-REHL-uh)

Defense. Shoots right. 6'3", 210 lbs. Born, Hamilton, Ont., May 9, 1963.
(Colorado's 1st choice, 5th overall, in 1981 Entry Draft).

			Regular Season					Playoffs				
Season	Club	Lea	GP	G	A	TP	PIM	GP	G	A	TP	PIM
1980-81	Oshawa	OHA	56	5	31	36	220	11	0	2	2	41
1981-82	Colorado	NHL	65	7	12	19	52	....	....	....	....	....
	Oshawa	OHL	3	0	1	1	0	11	7	10	17	32
1982-83	New Jersey	NHL	2	0	1	1	4	....	....	....	....	....
a	Oshawa	OHL	56	13	55	68	110	17	4	16	20	37
1983-84	New Jersey	NHL	79	11	33	44	137	....	....	....	....	....
1984-85	New Jersey	NHL	66	6	18	24	141	....	....	....	....	....
1985-86	New Jersey	NHL	66	6	23	29	147	....	....	....	....	....
1986-87	New Jersey	NHL	65	9	22	31	111	....	....	....	....	....
1987-88	New Jersey	NHL	80	8	31	39	191	19	0	7	7	49
1988-89	New Jersey	NHL	80	3	19	22	155	....	....	....	....	....
1989-90	Quebec	NHL	56	4	14	18	67	....	....	....	....	....
	NHL Totals		559	54	173	227	1005	19	0	7	7	49

a OHL First All-Star Team (1983)

Played in NHL All-Star Game (1984)

Traded to **Quebec** by **New Jersey** with Claude Loiselle and New Jersey's eighth round choice (Alexander Karpovtsev) in 1990 Entry Draft for Walt Poddubny and Quebec's fourth round choice (Mike Bodnarchuk) in 1990 Entry Draft, June 17, 1989.

CIRONE, JASON

Center. Shoots left. 5'9", 185 lbs. Born, Toronto, Ont., February 21, 1971.
(Winnipeg's 3rd choice, 46th overall, in 1989 Entry Draft).

			Regular Season					Playoffs				
Season	Club	Lea	GP	G	A	TP	PIM	GP	G	A	TP	PIM
1987-88	Cornwall	OHL	53	12	11	23	41	11	1	2	3	4
1988-89	Cornwall	OHL	64	39	44	83	67	17	19	8	27	14
1989-90	Cornwall	OHL	32	22	41	63	56	6	4	2	6	14

CLARK, KERRY

Right wing. Shoots right. 6'1", 190 lbs. Born, Kelvington, Sask., August 21, 1968.
(NY Islanders' 12th choice, 206th overall, in 1986 Entry Draft).

			Regular Season					Playoffs				
Season	Club	Lea	GP	G	A	TP	PIM	GP	G	A	TP	PIM
1985-86	Regina	WHL	23	4	4	8	58	....	....	....	....	....
	Saskatoon	WHL	39	5	8	13	104	13	2	2	4	33
1986-87	Saskatoon	WHL	54	12	10	22	229	8	0	1	1	23
1987-88	Saskatoon	WHL	67	15	11	26	241	10	2	2	4	16
1988-89	Springfield	AHL	63	7	7	14	264	....	....	....	....	....
	Indianapolis	IHL	3	0	1	1	12	....	....	....	....	....
1989-90	Springfield	AHL	21	0	1	1	73	....	....	....	....	....
	Phoenix	IHL	38	4	8	12	262	....	....	....	....	....

Signed as a free agent by **Calgary**, July 23, 1990.

CLARK, WENDEL

Left wing. Shoots left. 5'11", 194 lbs. Born, Kelvington, Sask., October 25, 1966.
(Toronto's 1st choice, 1st overall, in 1985 Entry Draft).

			Regular Season					Playoffs				
Season	Club	Lea	GP	G	A	TP	PIM	GP	G	A	TP	PIM
1983-84	Saskatoon	WHL	72	23	45	68	225	....	....	....	....	....
1984-85a	Saskatoon	WHL	64	32	55	87	253	3	3	3	6	7
1985-86b	Toronto	NHL	66	34	11	45	227	10	5	1	6	47
1986-87	Toronto	NHL	80	37	23	60	271	13	6	5	11	38
1987-88	Toronto	NHL	28	12	11	23	80	....	....	....	....	....
1988-89	Toronto	NHL	15	7	4	11	66	....	....	....	....	....
1989-90	Toronto	NHL	38	18	8	26	116	5	1	1	2	19
	NHL Totals		227	108	57	165	760	28	12	7	19	104

a WHL First All-Star Team, East Division (1985)
b NHL All-Rookie Team (1986)

Played in NHL All-Star Game (1986)

CLARKE, CHRISTOPHER

Defense. Shoots left. 6', 180 lbs. Born, Arnprior, Ont., August 6, 1967.
(Washington's 8th choice, 204th overall, in 1987 Entry Draft).

			Regular Season					Playoffs				
Season	Club	Lea	GP	G	A	TP	PIM	GP	G	A	TP	PIM
1987-88	W. Michigan	CCHA	42	7	32	39	64	....	....	....	....	....
1988-89	W. Michigan	CCHA	38	3	21	24	65	....	....	....	....	....
1989-90	W. Michigan	CCHA	39	2	21	23	55	....	....	....	....	....

CLAUSS, KARL

Defense. Shoots left. 6'2", 200 lbs. Born, Williamsville, NY, May 31, 1967.
(Washington's 1st choice, 24th overall, in 1989 Supplemental Draft).

			Regular Season					Playoffs				
Season	Club	Lea	GP	G	A	TP	PIM	GP	G	A	TP	PIM
1986-87	Colgate	ECAC	12	1	1	2	0	....	....	....	....	....
1987-88	Colgate	ECAC	32	2	6	8	32	....	....	....	....	....
1988-89	Colgate	ECAC	31	1	5	6	38	....	....	....	....	....
1989-90	Colgate	ECAC	38	2	8	10	34	....	....	....	....	....

CLEARY, JOSEPH

Defense. Shoots right. 5'11", 185 lbs. Born, Buffalo, NY, January 17, 1970.
(Chicago's 5th choice, 92nd overall, in 1988 Entry Draft).

			Regular Season					Playoffs				
Season	Club	Lea	GP	G	A	TP	PIM	GP	G	A	TP	PIM
1987-88	Stratford	OPJHL	41	20	37	57	160	....	....	....	....	....
1988-89	Boston College	H.E.	38	5	7	12	36	....	....	....	....	....
1989-90	Boston College	H.E.	42	5	21	26	56	....	....	....	....	....

CLEMENT, SEAN (CLEM-ent)

Defense. Shoots left. 6'2", 185 lbs. Born, Winnipeg, Man., February 26, 1966.
(Winnipeg's 3rd choice, 72nd overall, in 1984 Entry Draft).

			Regular Season					Playoffs				
Season	Club	Lea	GP	G	A	TP	PIM	GP	G	A	TP	PIM
1984-85	Michigan State	CCHA	44	5	13	18	24	....	....	....	....	....
1985-86	Michigan State	CCHA	40	4	7	11	40	....	....	....	....	....
1986-87	Michigan State	CCHA	41	3	11	14	70	....	....	....	....	....
1987-88	Michigan State	CCHA	42	3	12	15	92	....	....	....	....	....
1988-89	Moncton	AHL	65	2	8	10	64	....	....	....	....	....
1989-90	Moncton	AHL	1	0	0	0	0	....	....	....	....	....

CLOUSTON, SHAUN

Right wing. Shoots left. 6', 210 lbs. Born, Viking, Alta., April 28, 1968.
(NY Rangers' 3rd choice, 53rd overall, in 1986 Entry Draft).

			Regular Season					Playoffs				
Season	Club	Lea	GP	G	A	TP	PIM	GP	G	A	TP	PIM
1985-86	U. of Alberta	CWUAA	53	18	21	39	75	....	....	....	....	....
1986-87	Portland	WHL	70	6	25	31	93	19	0	5	5	45
1987-88	Portland	WHL	68	29	50	79	144	....	....	....	....	....
1988-89	Portland	WHL	72	45	47	92	150	19	7	10	17	28
1989-90	Milwaukee	IHL	54	6	16	22	61	....	....	....	....	....

Signed as a free agent by **Vancouver**, May 27, 1989.

COFFEY, PAUL DOUGLAS

Defense. Shoots left. 6'1", 200 lbs. Born, Weston, Ont., June 1, 1961.
(Edmonton's 1st choice, 6th overall, in the 1980 Entry Draft).

			Regular Season					Playoffs				
Season	Club	Lea	GP	G	A	TP	PIM	GP	G	A	TP	PIM
1978-79a	S. S. Marie	OHA	68	17	72	89	103	....	....	....	....	....
1979-80b	S. S. Marie	OHA	23	10	21	31	63	....	....	....	....	....
	Kitchener	OHA	52	19	52	71	130	....	....	....	....	....
1980-81	**Edmonton**	**NHL**	**74**	**9**	**23**	**32**	**130**	**9**	**4**	**3**	**7**	**22**
1981-82c	**Edmonton**	**NHL**	**80**	**29**	**60**	**89**	**106**	**5**	**1**	**1**	**2**	**6**
1982-83c	**Edmonton**	**NHL**	**80**	**29**	**67**	**96**	**87**	**16**	**7**	**7**	**14**	**14**
1983-84c	**Edmonton**	**NHL**	**80**	**40**	**86**	**126**	**104**	**19**	**8**	**14**	**22**	**21**
1984-85de	**Edmonton**	**NHL**	**80**	**37**	**84**	**121**	**97**	**18**	**12**	**25**	**37**	**44**
1985-86de	**Edmonton**	**NHL**	**79**	**48**	**90**	**138**	**120**	**10**	**1**	**9**	**10**	**30**
1986-87	**Edmonton**	**NHL**	**59**	**17**	**50**	**67**	**49**	**17**	**3**	**8**	**11**	**30**
1987-88	**Pittsburgh**	**NHL**	**46**	**15**	**52**	**67**	**93**	....	....	....	....	....
1988-89e	**Pittsburgh**	**NHL**	**75**	**30**	**83**	**113**	**195**	**11**	**2**	**13**	**15**	**31**
1989-90c	**Pittsburgh**	**NHL**	**80**	**29**	**74**	**103**	**95**	....	....	....	....	....
	NHL Totals		**733**	**283**	**669**	**952**	**1076**	**105**	**38**	**80**	**118**	**198**

a OHA Third All-Star Team (1979)
b OHA Second All-Star Team (1980)
c NHL Second All-Star Team (1982, 1983, 1984, 1990)
d Won James Norris Memorial Trophy (1985, 1986)
e NHL First All-Star Team (1985, 1986, 1989)

Played in NHL All-Star Game (1982-86, 1988-90)

Traded to **Pittsburgh** by **Edmonton** with Dave Hunter and Wayne Van Dorp for Craig Simpson, Dave Hannan, Moe Mantha and Chris Joseph, November 24, 1987.

COLE, DANTON

Right wing. Shoots right. 5'11", 189 lbs. Born, Pontiac, MI, January 10, 1967.
(Winnipeg's 6th choice, 123rd overall, in 1985 Entry Draft).

			Regular Season					Playoffs				
Season	Club	Lea	GP	G	A	TP	PIM	GP	G	A	TP	PIM
1985-86	Michigan State	CCHA	43	11	10	21	22	....	....	....	....	....
1986-87	Michigan State	CCHA	44	9	15	24	16	....	....	....	....	....
1987-88	Michigan State	CCHA	46	20	36	56	38	....	....	....	....	....
1988-89	Michigan State	CCHA	47	29	33	62	46	....	....	....	....	....
1989-90	**Winnipeg**	**NHL**	**2**	**1**	**1**	**2**	**0**	....	....	....	....	....
	Moncton	AHL	80	31	42	73	18	....	....	....	....	....
	NHL Totals		**2**	**1**	**1**	**2**	**0**	....	....	....	....	....

COLES, BRUCE

Left wing. Shoots left. 5'9", 180 lbs. Born, Montreal, Que., January 12, 1968.
(Montreal's 1st choice, 23rd overall, in 1990 Supplemental Draft).

			Regular Season					Playoffs				
Season	Club	Lea	GP	G	A	TP	PIM	GP	G	A	TP	PIM
1987-88	RPI	ECAC	32	16	23	39	48	....	....	....	....	....
1988-89	RPI	ECAC	27	8	14	22	66	....	....	....	....	....
1989-90	RPI	ECAC	34	*28	24	52	142	....	....	....	....	....

CONACHER, PATRICK JOHN (PAT) (KAH-nuh-kuhr)

Left wing. Shoots left. 5'8", 190 lbs. Born, Edmonton, Alta., May 1, 1959.
(NY Rangers' 4th choice, 76th overall, in 1979 Entry Draft).

			Regular Season					Playoffs				
Season	Club	Lea	GP	G	A	TP	PIM	GP	G	A	TP	PIM
1977-78	Billings	WHL	72	31	44	75	105	20	15	14	29	22
1978-79	Billings	WHL	39	25	37	62	50	....	....	....	....	....
	Saskatoon	WHL	33	15	32	47	37	....	....	....	....	....
1979-80	New Haven	AHL	53	11	14	25	43	7	1	1	2	4
	NY Rangers	**NHL**	**17**	**0**	**5**	**5**	**4**	**3**	**0**	**1**	**1**	**2**
1980-81			DID NOT PLAY									
1981-82	Springfield	AHL	77	23	22	45	38	....	....	....	....	....
1982-83	**NY Rangers**	**NHL**	**5**	**0**	**1**	**1**	**4**	....	....	....	....	....
	Tulsa	CHL	63	29	28	57	44	....	....	....	....	....
1983-84	Moncton	AHL	28	7	16	23	30	....	....	....	....	....
	Edmonton	**NHL**	**45**	**2**	**8**	**10**	**31**	**3**	**1**	**0**	**1**	**2**
1984-85	Nova Scotia	AHL	68	20	45	65	44	6	3	2	5	0
1985-86	**New Jersey**	**NHL**	**2**	**0**	**2**	**2**	**2**	....	....	....	....	....
	Maine	AHL	69	15	30	45	83	5	1	1	2	11
1986-87	Maine	AHL	56	12	14	26	47	....	....	....	....	....
1987-88	**New Jersey**	**NHL**	**24**	**2**	**5**	**7**	**12**	**17**	**2**	**2**	**4**	**14**
	Utica	AHL	47	14	33	47	32	....	....	....	....	....
1988-89	**New Jersey**	**NHL**	**55**	**7**	**5**	**12**	**14**	....	....	....	....	....
1989-90	**New Jersey**	**NHL**	**19**	**3**	**3**	**6**	**4**	**5**	**1**	**0**	**1**	**10**
	Utica	AHL	57	13	36	49	53	....	....	....	....	....
	NHL Totals		**167**	**14**	**29**	**43**	**71**	**28**	**4**	**3**	**7**	**28**

Signed as free agent by **Edmonton**, October 4, 1983. Signed as a free agent by **New Jersey**, August 14, 1985.

CONSTANTIN, PAUL

Center. Shoots left. 6'2", 175 lbs. Born, Burlington, Ont., May 16, 1968.
(Vancouver's 9th choice, 191st overall, in 1988 Entry Draft).

			Regular Season					Playoffs				
Season	Club	Lea	GP	G	A	TP	PIM	GP	G	A	TP	PIM
1988-89	Lake Superior	CCHA	28	5	5	10	0	....	....	....	....	....
1989-90	Lake Superior	CCHA	29	6	2	8	10	....	....	....	....	....

COOKE, JAMES

Right wing. Shoots right. 6'2", 205 lbs. Born, Toronto, Ont., November 5, 1968.
(Philadelphia's 8th choice, 140th overall, in 1988 Entry Draft).

			Regular Season					Playoffs				
Season	Club	Lea	GP	G	A	TP	PIM	GP	G	A	TP	PIM
1988-89	Colgate	ECAC	28	13	11	24	26	....	....	....	....	....
1989-90	Colgate	ECAC	38	16	20	36	24	....	....	....	....	....

COPELAND, TODD

Defense. Shoots left. 6'2", 210 lbs. Born, Ridgewood, NJ, May 10, 1967.
(New Jersey's 2nd choice, 24th overall, in 1986 Entry Draft).

			Regular Season					Playoffs				
Season	Club	Lea	GP	G	A	TP	PIM	GP	G	A	TP	PIM
1986-87	U. of Michigan	CCHA	34	2	11	13	59	....	....	....	....	....
1987-88	U. of Michigan	CCHA	41	3	10	13	58	....	....	....	....	....
1988-89	U. of Michigan	CCHA	39	5	14	19	102	....	....	....	....	....
1989-90	U. of Michigan	CCHA	34	6	16	22	62	....	....	....	....	....

CORKERY, TIM

Defense. Shoots right. 6'4", 210 lbs. Born, Ponoka, Alta., February 17, 1967.
(Calgary's 6th choice, 103rd overall, in 1987 Entry Draft).

			Regular Season					Playoffs				
Season	Club	Lea	GP	G	A	TP	PIM	GP	G	A	TP	PIM
1986-87	Ferris State	CCHA	40	3	7	10	120	....	....	....	....	....
1987-88	Ferris State	CCHA	40	0	6	6	108	....	....	....	....	....
1988-89	Ferris State	CCHA	23	2	5	7	53	....	....	....	....	....
1989-90	Ferris State	CCHA	32	0	6	6	64	....	....	....	....	....

Traded to **St. Louis** by **Calgary** with Mike Bullard and Craig Coxe for Mark Hunter, Doug Gilmour, Steve Bozek and Michael Dark, September 6, 1988.

CORKUM, BOB

Right wing. Shoots right. 6'2", 215 lbs. Born, Salisbury, MA, December 18, 1967.
(Buffalo's 3rd choice, 57th overall, in 1986 Entry Draft).

			Regular Season					Playoffs				
Season	Club	Lea	GP	G	A	TP	PIM	GP	G	A	TP	PIM
1985-86	U. of Maine	H.E.	39	7	26	33	53	....	....	....	....	....
1986-87	U. of Maine	H.E.	35	18	11	29	24	....	....	....	....	....
1987-88	U. of Maine	H.E.	40	14	18	32	64	....	....	....	....	....
1988-89	U. of Maine	H.E.	45	17	31	48	64	....	....	....	....	....
1989-90	**Buffalo**	**NHL**	**8**	**2**	**0**	**2**	**2**	**5**	**1**	**0**	**1**	**4**
	Rochester	AHL	43	8	11	19	45	12	2	5	7	16
	NHL Totals		**8**	**2**	**0**	**2**	**2**	**5**	**1**	**0**	**1**	**4**

CORRIVEAU, RICK

Defense. Shoots left. 5'11", 205 lbs. Born, Welland, Ont., January 6, 1971.
(St. Louis' 2nd choice, 31st overall, in 1989 Entry Draft).

			Regular Season					Playoffs				
Season	Club	Lea	GP	G	A	TP	PIM	GP	G	A	TP	PIM
1987-88a	London	OHL	62	19	47	66	51	12	4	10	14	18
1988-89	London	OHL	12	4	10	14	21	1	0	0	0	0
1989-90b	London	OHL	63	22	55	77	63	6	4	3	7	12

a OHL Rookie of the Year (1988)
b OHL Third All-Star Team (1990)

CORRIVEAU, YVON

Left wing. Shoots left. 6'2", 205 lbs. Born, Welland, Ont., February 8, 1967.
(Washington's 1st choice, 19th overall, in 1985 Entry Draft).

			Regular Season					Playoffs				
Season	Club	Lea	GP	G	A	TP	PIM	GP	G	A	TP	PIM
1984-85	Toronto	OHL	59	23	28	51	65	3	0	0	0	5
1985-86	**Washington**	**NHL**	**2**	**0**	**0**	**0**	**0**	**4**	**0**	**3**	**3**	**2**
	Toronto	OHL	59	54	36	90	75	4	1	1	2	0
1986-87	**Washington**	**NHL**	**17**	**1**	**1**	**2**	**24**	....	....	....	....	....
	Toronto	OHL	23	14	19	33	23	....	....	....	....	....
	Binghamton	AHL	7	0	0	0	2	8	0	1	1	0
1987-88	**Washington**	**NHL**	**44**	**10**	**9**	**19**	**84**	**13**	**1**	**2**	**3**	**30**
	Binghamton	AHL	35	15	14	29	64	....	....	....	....	....
1988-89	**Washington**	**NHL**	**33**	**3**	**2**	**5**	**62**	**1**	**0**	**0**	**0**	**0**
	Baltimore	AHL	33	16	23	39	65	....	....	....	....	....
1989-90	**Washington**	**NHL**	**50**	**9**	**6**	**15**	**50**	....	....	....	....	....
	Hartford	**NHL**	**13**	**4**	**1**	**5**	**22**	**4**	**1**	**0**	**1**	**0**
	NHL Totals		**159**	**27**	**19**	**46**	**242**	**22**	**2**	**5**	**7**	**32**

Traded to **Hartford** by **Washington** for Mike Liut, March 6, 1990.

CORSON, SHAYNE

Center. Shoots left. 6', 201 lbs. Born, Barrie, Ont., August 13, 1966.
(Montreal's 2nd choice, 8th overall, in 1984 Entry Draft).

			Regular Season					Playoffs				
Season	Club	Lea	GP	G	A	TP	PIM	GP	G	A	TP	PIM
1983-84	Brantford	OHL	66	25	46	71	165	6	4	1	5	26
1984-85	Hamilton	OHL	54	27	63	90	154	11	3	7	10	19
1985-86	**Montreal**	**NHL**	**3**	**0**	**0**	**0**	**2**	....	....	....	....	....
	Hamilton	OHL	47	41	57	98	153	....	....	....	....	....
1986-87	**Montreal**	**NHL**	**55**	**12**	**11**	**23**	**144**	**17**	**6**	**5**	**11**	**30**
1987-88	**Montreal**	**NHL**	**71**	**12**	**27**	**39**	**152**	**3**	**1**	**0**	**1**	**12**
1988-89	**Montreal**	**NHL**	**80**	**26**	**24**	**50**	**193**	**21**	**4**	**5**	**9**	**65**
1989-90	**Montreal**	**NHL**	**76**	**31**	**44**	**75**	**144**	**11**	**2**	**8**	**10**	**20**
	NHL Totals		**285**	**81**	**106**	**187**	**635**	**52**	**13**	**18**	**31**	**127**

Played in NHL All-Star Game (1990)

COTE, ALAIN GABRIEL (koh-TAY)

Defense. Shoots right. 6', 200 lbs. Born, Montmagny, Que., April 14, 1967.
(Boston's 1st choice, 31st overall, in 1985 Entry Draft).

			Regular Season					Playoffs				
Season	Club	Lea	GP	G	A	TP	PIM	GP	G	A	TP	PIM
1983-84	Quebec	QMJHL	60	3	17	20	40	5	1	3	4	8
1984-85	Quebec	QMJHL	68	9	25	34	173	4	0	1	1	12
1985-86	Granby	QMJHL	22	4	12	16	48	....	....	....	....	....
	Boston	**NHL**	**32**	**0**	**6**	**6**	**14**	....	....	....	....	....
1986-87	**Boston**	**NHL**	**3**	**0**	**0**	**0**	**0**	....	....	....	....	....
	Granby	QMJHL	43	7	24	31	185	4	0	3	3	2
1987-88	**Boston**	**NHL**	**2**	**0**	**0**	**0**	**0**	....	....	....	....	....
	Maine	AHL	69	9	34	43	108	9	2	4	6	19
1988-89	**Boston**	**NHL**	**31**	**2**	**3**	**5**	**51**	....	....	....	....	....
	Maine	AHL	37	5	16	21	111	....	....	....	....	....
1989-90	**Washington**	**NHL**	**2**	**0**	**0**	**0**	**2**	....	....	....	....	....
	Baltimore	AHL	57	5	19	24	161	3	0	0	0	9
	NHL Totals		**70**	**2**	**9**	**11**	**67**	....	....	....	....	....

Traded to **Washington** by **Boston** for Bob Gould, September 28, 1989. Traded to **Montreal** by **Washington** for Marc Deschamps, June 22, 1990.

COTE, SYLVAIN (COH--tay)

Defense. Shoots right. 5'11", 185 lbs. Born, Quebec City, Que., January 19, 1966.
(Hartford's 1st choice, 11th overall, in 1984 Entry Draft).

			Regular Season					Playoffs				
Season	Club	Lea	GP	G	A	TP	PIM	GP	G	A	TP	PIM
1982-83	Quebec	QMJHL	66	10	24	34	50	....	....	....	....	....
1983-84	Quebec	QMJHL	66	15	50	65	89	5	1	1	2	0
1984-85	**Hartford**	**NHL**	**67**	**3**	**9**	**12**	**17**	....	....	....	....	....
1985-86	**Hartford**	**NHL**	**2**	**0**	**0**	**0**	**0**	....	....	....	....	....
a	Hull	QMJHL	26	10	33	43	14	13	6	28	34	22
	Binghamton	AHL	12	2	4	6	0	....	....	....	....	....
1986-87	**Hartford**	**NHL**	**67**	**2**	**8**	**10**	**20**	**2**	**0**	**2**	**2**	**2**
1987-88	**Hartford**	**NHL**	**67**	**7**	**21**	**28**	**30**	**6**	**1**	**1**	**2**	**4**
1988-89	**Hartford**	**NHL**	**78**	**8**	**9**	**17**	**49**	**3**	**0**	**1**	**1**	**4**
1989-90	**Hartford**	**NHL**	**28**	**4**	**2**	**6**	**14**	....	....	....	....	....
	NHL Totals		**309**	**24**	**49**	**73**	**130**	**11**	**1**	**4**	**5**	**10**

a QMJHL First All-Star Team (1986).

COURTNALL, GEOFF

Left wing. Shoots left. 6'1", 190 lbs. Born, Victoria, B.C., August 18, 1962.

			Regular Season					Playoffs				
Season	Club	Lea	GP	G	A	TP	PIM	GP	G	A	TP	PIM
1980-81	Victoria	WHL	11	3	4	7	6	15	2	1	3	7
1981-82	Victoria	WHL	72	35	57	90	100	4	1	0	1	2
1982-83	Victoria	WHL	71	41	73	114	186	12	6	7	13	42
1983-84	**Boston**	**NHL**	**4**	**0**	**0**	**0**	**0**	....	....	....	....	....
	Hershey	AHL	74	14	12	26	51	....	....	....	....	....
1984-85	**Boston**	**NHL**	**64**	**12**	**16**	**28**	**82**	**5**	**0**	**2**	**2**	**7**
	Hershey	AHL	9	8	4	12	4	....	....	....	....	....
1985-86	**Boston**	**NHL**	**64**	**21**	**16**	**37**	**61**	**3**	**0**	**0**	**0**	**2**
	Moncton	AHL	12	8	8	16	6	....	....	....	....	....
1986-87	**Boston**	**NHL**	**65**	**13**	**23**	**36**	**117**	**1**	**0**	**0**	**0**	**0**
1987-88	**Boston**	**NHL**	**62**	**32**	**26**	**58**	**108**	....	....	....	....	....
	Edmonton	**NHL**	**12**	**4**	**4**	**8**	**15**	**19**	**0**	**3**	**3**	**23**
1988-89	**Washington**	**NHL**	**79**	**42**	**38**	**80**	**112**	**6**	**2**	**5**	**7**	**12**
1989-90	**Washington**	**NHL**	**80**	**35**	**39**	**74**	**104**	**15**	**4**	**9**	**13**	**32**
	NHL Totals		**430**	**159**	**162**	**321**	**597**	**49**	**6**	**19**	**25**	**76**

Signed as free agent by **Boston**, July 6, 1983. Traded to **Edmonton** by **Boston** with Bill Ranford and future considerations for Andy Moog, March 8, 1988. Rights traded to **Washington** by **Edmonton** for Greg C. Adams, July 22, 1988. Traded to **St. Louis** by **Washington** for Peter Zezel and Mike Lalor, July 13, 1990.

COURTNALL, RUSSELL (RUSS)

Center/Right wing. Shoots right. 5'11", 183 lbs. Born, Duncan, B.C., June 2, 1965.
(Toronto's 1st choice, 7th overall, in 1983 Entry Draft).

			Regular Season					Playoffs				
Season	Club	Lea	GP	G	A	TP	PIM	GP	G	A	TP	PIM
1982-83	Victoria	WHL	60	36	61	97	33	12	11	7	18	6
1983-84	Cdn. Olympic	...	16	4	7	11	10	....	....	....	....	....
	Victoria	WHL	32	29	37	66	63	....	....	....	....	....
	Toronto	**NHL**	**14**	**3**	**9**	**12**	**6**	....	....	....	....	....
1984-85	**Toronto**	**NHL**	**69**	**12**	**10**	**22**	**44**	....	....	....	....	....
1985-86	**Toronto**	**NHL**	**73**	**22**	**38**	**60**	**52**	**10**	**3**	**6**	**9**	**8**
1986-87	**Toronto**	**NHL**	**79**	**29**	**44**	**73**	**90**	**13**	**3**	**4**	**7**	**11**
1987-88	**Toronto**	**NHL**	**65**	**23**	**26**	**49**	**47**	**6**	**2**	**1**	**3**	**0**
1988-89	**Toronto**	**NHL**	**9**	**1**	**1**	**2**	**4**	....	....	....	....	....
	Montreal	**NHL**	**64**	**22**	**17**	**39**	**15**	**21**	**8**	**5**	**13**	**18**
1989-90	**Montreal**	**NHL**	**80**	**27**	**32**	**59**	**27**	**11**	**5**	**1**	**6**	**10**
	NHL Totals		**453**	**139**	**177**	**316**	**285**	**61**	**21**	**17**	**38**	**47**

Traded to **Montreal** by **Toronto** for John Kordic and Montreal's sixth-round choice (Michael Doers) in 1989 Entry Draft, November 7, 1988.

COUTURIER, SYLVAIN (SIHL-vay koo-TOOR-ee-yah)

Center. Shoots right. 6'2", 205 lbs. Born, Greenfield Park, Que., April 23, 1968.
(Los Angeles' 3rd choice, 65th overall, in 1986 Entry Draft).

			Regular Season					Playoffs				
Season	Club	Lea	GP	G	A	TP	PIM	GP	G	A	TP	PIM
1985-86	Laval	QMJHL	68	21	37	58	64	14	1	7	8	28
1986-87	Laval	QMJHL	67	39	51	90	77	13	12	14	26	19
1987-88a	Laval	QMJHL	67	70	67	137	115	....	....	....	....	....
1988-89	**Los Angeles**	**NHL**	**16**	**1**	**3**	**4**	**2**	....	....	....	....	....
	New Haven	AHL	44	18	20	38	33	10	2	2	4	11
1989-90	New Haven	AHL	50	9	8	17	47	....	....	....	....	....
	NHL Totals		**16**	**1**	**3**	**4**	**2**	....	....	....	....	....

a QMJHL Third All-Star Team (1988)

COXE, CRAIG

Center. Shoots left. 6'4", 220 lbs. Born, Chula Vista, CA, January 21, 1964.
(Detroit's 4th choice, 66th overall, in 1982 Entry Draft).

			Regular Season					Playoffs				
Season	Club	Lea	GP	G	A	TP	PIM	GP	G	A	TP	PIM
1982-83	Belleville	OHL	64	14	27	41	102	4	1	2	3	2
1983-84	Belleville	OHL	45	17	28	45	90	3	2	0	2	4
1984-85	**Vancouver**	**NHL**	**9**	**0**	**0**	**0**	**49**	....	....	....	....	....
	Fredericton	AHL	62	8	7	15	242	4	2	1	3	16
1985-86	**Vancouver**	**NHL**	**57**	**3**	**5**	**8**	**176**	**3**	**0**	**0**	**0**	**2**
1986-87	**Vancouver**	**NHL**	**15**	**1**	**0**	**1**	**31**	....	....	....	....	....
	Fredericton	AHL	46	1	12	13	168	....	....	....	....	....
1987-88	**Vancouver**	**NHL**	**64**	**5**	**12**	**17**	**186**	....	....	....	....	....
	Calgary	**NHL**	**7**	**2**	**3**	**5**	**32**	**2**	**1**	**0**	**1**	**16**
1988-89	**St. Louis**	**NHL**	**41**	**0**	**7**	**7**	**127**	....	....	....	....	....
	Peoria	IHL	8	2	7	9	38	....	....	....	....	....
1989-90	**Vancouver**	**NHL**	**25**	**1**	**4**	**5**	**66**	....	....	....	....	....
	Milwaukee	IHL	5	0	5	5	4	....	....	....	....	....
	NHL Totals		**218**	**12**	**31**	**43**	**667**	**5**	**1**	**0**	**1**	**18**

Signed as a free agent by **Vancouver**, June 26, 1984. Traded to **Calgary** by **Vancouver** for Brian Bradley and Peter Bakovic, March 6, 1988. Traded to **St. Louis** by **Calgary** with Mike Bullard and Tim Corkery for Mark Hunter, Doug Giolmour, Steve Bozek and Michael Dark, September 6, 1988. Traded to **Chicago** by **St. Louis** for Rik Wilson, September 27, 1989. Claimed by **Vancouver** in NHL Waiver Draft, October 2, 1989.

CRAIG, MIKE

Right wing. Shoots right. 6', 180 lbs. Born London, Ont., June 6, 1971.
(Minnesota's 2nd choice, 28th overall, in 1989 Entry Draft).

			Regular Season					Playoffs				
Season	Club	Lea	GP	G	A	TP	PIM	GP	G	A	TP	PIM
1987-88	Oshawa	OHL	61	6	10	16	39	7	7	0	1	11
1988-89	Oshawa	OHL	63	36	36	72	34	6	3	1	4	6
1989-90	Oshawa	OHL	43	36	40	76	85	17	10	16	26	46

CRAVEN, MURRAY

Left wing. Shoots left. 6'3", 190 lbs. Born, Medicine Hat, Alta., July 20, 1964.
(Detroit's 1st choice, 17th overall, in 1982 Entry Draft).

			Regular Season					Playoffs				
Season	Club	Lea	GP	G	A	TP	PIM	GP	G	A	TP	PIM
1980-81	Medicine Hat	WHL	69	5	10	15	18	5	0	0	0	2
1981-82	Medicine Hat	WHL	72	35	46	81	49	....	....	....	....	....
1982-83	Medicine Hat	WHL	28	17	29	46	35	....	....	....	....	....
	Detroit	**NHL**	**31**	**4**	**7**	**11**	**6**	....	....	....	....	....
1983-84	**Detroit**	**NHL**	**15**	**0**	**4**	**4**	**6**	....	....	....	....	....
	Medicine Hat	WHL	48	38	56	94	53	4	5	3	8	4
1984-85	**Philadelphia**	**NHL**	**80**	**26**	**35**	**61**	**30**	**19**	**4**	**6**	**10**	**11**
1985-86	**Philadelphia**	**NHL**	**78**	**21**	**33**	**54**	**34**	**5**	**0**	**3**	**3**	**4**
1986-87	**Philadelphia**	**NHL**	**77**	**19**	**30**	**49**	**38**	**12**	**3**	**1**	**4**	**9**
1987-88	**Philadelphia**	**NHL**	**72**	**30**	**46**	**76**	**58**	**7**	**2**	**5**	**7**	**4**
1988-89	**Philadelphia**	**NHL**	**51**	**9**	**28**	**37**	**52**	**1**	**0**	**0**	**0**	**0**
1989-90	**Philadelphia**	**NHL**	**76**	**25**	**50**	**75**	**42**	....	....	....	....	....
	NHL Totals		**480**	**134**	**233**	**367**	**266**	**44**	**9**	**15**	**24**	**28**

Traded to **Philadelphia** by **Detroit** with Joe Paterson for Darryl Sittler, October 10, 1984.

CRAWFORD, LOUIS

Left wing. Shoots left. 6', 185 lbs. Born, Belleville, Ont., November 5, 1962.

			Regular Season					Playoffs				
Season	Club	Lea	GP	G	A	TP	PIM	GP	G	A	TP	PIM
1980-81	Kitchener	OHA	53	2	7	9	134	....	....	....	....	....
1981-82	Kitchener	OHL	64	11	17	28	243	15	3	4	7	71
1982-83	Rochester	AHL	64	5	11	16	142	13	1	1	2	7
1983-84	Rochester	AHL	76	7	6	13	234	17	2	4	6	87
1984-85	Rochester	AHL	70	8	7	15	213	1	0	0	0	10
1985-86	Nova Scotia	AHL	78	8	11	19	214	....	....	....	....	....
1986-87	Nova Scotia	AHL	35	3	4	7	48	....	....	....	....	....
1987-88	Nova Scotia	AHL	65	15	15	30	170	4	1	2	3	9
1988-89	Adirondack	AHL	74	23	23	46	179	9	0	6	6	32
1989-90	**Boston**	**NHL**	**7**	**0**	**0**	**0**	**20**	....	....	....	....	....
	Maine	AHL	62	15	13	28	162	....	....	....	....	....
	NHL Totals		**7**	**0**	**0**	**0**	**20**	....	....	....	....	....

Signed as free agent by **Buffalo**, August 23, 1984. Signed as a free agent by **Detroit**, August 11, 1988. Signed as a free agent by **Boston**, July 6, 1989.

CREIGHTON, ADAM (KRAY-ton)

Center. Shoots left. 6'5", 214 lbs. Born, Burlington, Ont., June 2, 1965.
(Buffalo's 3rd choice, 11th overall, in 1983 Entry Draft).

			Regular Season					Playoffs				
Season	Club	Lea	GP	G	A	TP	PIM	GP	G	A	TP	PIM
1981-82	Ottawa	OHL	60	15	27	42	73	17	7	1	8	40
1982-83	Ottawa	OHL	68	44	46	90	88	9	0	2	2	12
1983-84	**Buffalo**	**NHL**	**7**	**2**	**2**	**4**	**4**	....	....	....	....	....
	Ottawa	OHL	56	42	49	91	79	13	16	11	27	28
1984-85	**Buffalo**	**NHL**	**30**	**2**	**8**	**10**	**33**	....	....	....	....	....
	Rochester	NHL	6	5	3	8	2	5	2	1	3	20
	Ottawa	OHL	10	4	14	18	23	5	6	2	8	11
1985-86	**Buffalo**	**NHL**	**19**	**1**	**1**	**2**	**2**	....	....	....	....	....
	Rochester	AHL	32	17	21	38	27	....	....	....	....	....
1986-87	**Buffalo**	**NHL**	**56**	**18**	**22**	**40**	**26**	....	....	....	....	....
1987-88	**Buffalo**	**NHL**	**36**	**10**	**17**	**27**	**87**	....	....	....	....	....
1988-89	**Buffalo**	**NHL**	**24**	**7**	**10**	**17**	**44**	....	....	....	....	....
	Chicago	**NHL**	**43**	**15**	**14**	**29**	**92**	**15**	**5**	**6**	**11**	**44**
1989-90	**Chicago**	**NHL**	**80**	**34**	**36**	**70**	**224**	**20**	**3**	**6**	**9**	**59**
	NHL Totals		**295**	**89**	**110**	**199**	**512**	**35**	**8**	**12**	**20**	**103**

Traded to **Chicago** by **Buffalo** for Rick Vaive, December 26, 1988.

CRISTOFOLI, ED

Center. Shoots left. 6'2", 205 lbs. Born, Trail, B.C., May 14, 1967.
(Montreal's 9th choice, 142nd overall, in 1985 Entry Draft).

			Regular Season					Playoffs				
Season	Club	Lea	GP	G	A	TP	PIM	GP	G	A	TP	PIM
1985-86	U. of Denver	WCHA	46	10	9	19	32	....	....	....	....	....
1986-87	U. of Denver	WCHA	40	14	15	29	52	....	....	....	....	....
1987-88	U. of Denver	WCHA	38	12	27	39	64	....	....	....	....	....
1988-89	U. of Denver	WCHA	43	20	19	39	50	....	....	....	....	....
1989-90	**Montreal**	**NHL**	**9**	**0**	**1**	**1**	**4**	....	....	....	....	....
	Sherbrooke	AHL	57	16	19	35	31	12	2	4	6	14
	NHL Totals		**9**	**0**	**1**	**1**	**4**	....	....	....	....	....

CRONIN, SHAWN

Defense. Shoots left. 6'2", 210 lbs. Born, Flushing, MI, August 20, 1963.

			Regular Season					Playoffs				
Season	Club	Lea	GP	G	A	TP	PIM	GP	G	A	TP	PIM
1983-84	Ill-Chicago	CCHA	32	0	4	4	41	....	....	....	....	....
1984-85	Ill-Chicago	CCHA	31	2	6	8	52	....	....	....	....	....
1985-86	Ill-Chicago	CCHA	35	3	8	11	70	....	....	....	....	....
1986-87	Salt Lake	IHL	53	8	16	24	118	....	....	....	....	....
	Binghamton	AHL	12	0	1	1	60	10	0	0	0	41
1987-88	Binghamton	AHL	65	3	8	11	212	4	0	0	0	15
1988-89	**Washington**	**NHL**	**1**	**0**	**0**	**0**	**0**	....	....	....	....	....
	Baltimore	AHL	75	3	9	12	267	....	....	....	....	....
1989-90	**Winnipeg**	**NHL**	**61**	**0**	**4**	**4**	**243**	**5**	**0**	**0**	**0**	**7**
	NHL Totals		**62**	**0**	**4**	**4**	**243**	**5**	**0**	**0**	**0**	**7**

Signed as a free agent by **Hartford**, March, 1986. Signed as a free agent by **Philadelphia**, June 12, 1989. Traded to **Winnipeg** by **Philadelphia** for future considerations, July 21, 1989.

CROSSMAN, DOUGLAS (DOUG)

Defense. Shoots left. 6'2", 190 lbs. Born, Peterborough, Ont., June 30, 1960.
(Chicago's 6th choice, 112th overall, in 1979 Entry Draft).

			Regular Season					Playoffs				
Season	Club	Lea	GP	G	A	TP	PIM	GP	G	A	TP	PIM
1978-79	Ottawa	OHA	67	12	51	63	65	4	1	3	4	0
1979-80	Ottawa	OHA	66	20	96	116	48	11	7	6	13	19
1980-81	**Chicago**	**NHL**	**9**	**0**	**2**	**2**	**2**	....	....	....	....	....
	New Brunswick	AHL	70	13	43	56	90	13	5	6	11	36
1981-82	**Chicago**	**NHL**	**70**	**12**	**28**	**40**	**24**	**11**	**0**	**3**	**3**	**4**
1982-83	**Chicago**	**NHL**	**80**	**13**	**40**	**53**	**46**	**13**	**3**	**7**	**10**	**6**
1983-84	**Philadelphia**	**NHL**	**78**	**7**	**28**	**35**	**63**	**3**	**0**	**0**	**0**	**0**
1984-85	**Philadelphia**	**NHL**	**80**	**4**	**33**	**37**	**65**	**19**	**4**	**6**	**10**	**38**
1985-86	**Philadelphia**	**NHL**	**80**	**6**	**37**	**43**	**55**	**5**	**0**	**1**	**1**	**4**
1986-87	**Philadelphia**	**NHL**	**78**	**9**	**31**	**40**	**29**	**26**	**4**	**14**	**18**	**31**
1987-88	**Philadelphia**	**NHL**	**76**	**9**	**29**	**38**	**43**	**7**	**1**	**1**	**2**	**8**
1988-89	**Los Angeles**	**NHL**	**74**	**10**	**15**	**25**	**53**	**2**	**0**	**1**	**1**	**2**
	New Haven	AHL	3	0	0	0	0	....	....	....	....	....
1989-90	**NY Islanders**	**NHL**	**80**	**15**	**44**	**59**	**54**	**5**	**0**	**1**	**1**	**6**
	NHL Totals		**705**	**85**	**287**	**372**	**434**	**91**	**12**	**34**	**46**	**99**

Traded to **Philadelphia** by **Chicago** with Chicago's second round choice (Scott Mellanby) in the 1984 Entry Draft for **Behn Wilson**, June 8, 1983. Traded to **Los Angeles** by **Philadelphia** for Jay Wells, September 29, 1988. Traded to **NY Islanders** by **Los Angeles** to complete February 22, 1989, transaction in which Mark Fitzpatrick and Wayne McBean were traded to **NY Islanders** by **Los Angeles** for Kelly Hrudey, May 23, 1989.

CROWDER, KEITH SCOTT

Right wing. Shoots right. 6', 190 lbs. Born, Windsor, Ont., January 6, 1959.
(Boston's 4th choice, 57th overall, in 1979 Entry Draft).

			Regular Season					Playoffs				
Season	Club	Lea	GP	G	A	TP	PIM	GP	G	A	TP	PIM
1976-77	Peterborough	OHA	58	13	19	32	99	4	0	2	2	9
1977-78	Peterborough	OHA	58	30	30	60	139	14	3	5	8	21
1978-79	Peterborough	OHA	42	25	41	66	76	15	12	6	18	40
	Birmingham	WHA	5	1	0	1	17	....	....	....	....	....
1979-80	Binghamton	AHL	13	4	0	4	15	....	....	....	....	....
	Grand Rapids	IHL	20	10	13	23	22	....	....	....	....	....
1980-81	Springfield	AHL	26	12	18	30	34	....	....	....	....	....
	Boston	**NHL**	**47**	**13**	**12**	**25**	**172**	**3**	**2**	**0**	**2**	**9**
1981-82	**Boston**	**NHL**	**71**	**23**	**21**	**44**	**101**	**11**	**2**	**2**	**4**	**14**
1982-83	**Boston**	**NHL**	**74**	**35**	**39**	**74**	**105**	**17**	**1**	**6**	**7**	**54**
1983-84	**Boston**	**NHL**	**63**	**24**	**28**	**52**	**128**	**3**	**0**	**0**	**0**	**7**
1984-85	**Boston**	**NHL**	**79**	**32**	**38**	**70**	**142**	**4**	**3**	**2**	**5**	**19**
1985-86	**Boston**	**NHL**	**78**	**38**	**46**	**84**	**177**	**3**	**2**	**0**	**2**	**21**
1986-87	**Boston**	**NHL**	**58**	**22**	**30**	**52**	**106**	**4**	**0**	**1**	**1**	**4**
1987-88	**Boston**	**NHL**	**68**	**17**	**26**	**43**	**173**	**23**	**3**	**9**	**12**	**44**
1988-89	**Boston**	**NHL**	**69**	**15**	**18**	**33**	**147**	**10**	**0**	**2**	**2**	**37**
1989-90	**Los Angeles**	**NHL**	**55**	**4**	**13**	**17**	**93**	**7**	**1**	**0**	**1**	**9**
	NHL Totals		**662**	**223**	**271**	**494**	**1346**	**85**	**14**	**22**	**36**	**218**

Signed as a free agent by **Los Angeles**, June 28, 1989.

CROWDER, TROY

Right wing. Shoots right. 6'4", 215 lbs. Born, Sudbury, Ont., May 3, 1968.
(New Jersey's 6th choice, 108th overall, in 1986 Entry Draft).

			Regular Season					Playoffs				
Season	Club	Lea	GP	G	A	TP	PIM	GP	G	A	TP	PIM
1985-86	Hamilton	OHL	56	4	4	8	178	....	....	....	....	....
1986-87	Belleville	OHL	21	5	5	10	52	....	....	....	....	....
	North Bay	OHL	35	6	11	17	90	23	3	9	12	99
1987-88	**New Jersey**	**NHL**	....	....	....	....	....	**1**	**0**	**0**	**0**	**12**
	Utica	AHL	3	0	0	0	36	....	....	....	....	....
	North Bay		9	1	2	3	44	....	....	....	....	....
	Belleville	OHL	46	12	27	39	103	6	2	3	5	24
1988-89	Utica	AHL	62	6	4	10	152	2	0	0	0	25
1989-90	**New Jersey**	**NHL**	**10**	**0**	**0**	**0**	**23**	**2**	**0**	**0**	**0**	**10**
	Nashville	ECHL	3	0	0	0	15	....	....	....	....	....
	NHL Totals		**10**	**0**	**0**	**0**	**23**	**3**	**0**	**0**	**0**	**22**

CROWLEY, EDWARD

Defense. Shoots right. 6'2", 190 lbs. Born, Concord, MA, May 3, 1970.
(Toronto's 4th choice, 69th overall, in 1988 Entry Draft).

			Regular Season					Playoffs				
Season	Club	Lea	GP	G	A	TP	PIM	GP	G	A	TP	PIM
1987-88	Lawrence Aca.	HS	....	11	23	34	....	....	....	....	....	....
1988-89	U.S. Nat'l Jr.	....	7	1	1	2	0	....	....	....	....	....
	Lawrence Aca.	HS	....	12	24	36		....	....	....	....	....
1989-90	Boston College	H.E.	39	7	24	31	34	....	....	....	....	....

CROWLEY, JOE

Left wing. Shoots left. 6'2", 190 lbs. Born, Concord, MA, February 29, 1972.
(Edmonton's 3rd choice, 59th overall, in 1990 Entry Draft).

			Regular Season					Playoffs				
Season	Club	Lea	GP	G	A	TP	PIM	GP	G	A	TP	PIM
1988-89	Lawrence Aca.	HS	20	13	22	35	....	....	....	....	....	....
1989-90	Lawrence Aca.	HS	10	8	5	13	....	....	....	....	....	....

CRUICKSHANK, GORD

Center. Shoots right. 5'11", 185 lbs. Born, Toronto, Ont., May 4, 1965.
(Boston's 8th choice, 178th overall, in 1985 Entry Draft).

			Regular Season					Playoffs				
Season	Club	Lea	GP	G	A	TP	PIM	GP	G	A	TP	PIM
1984-85	Providence	H.E.	40	8	9	17	32	....	....	....	....	....
1985-86a	Providence	H.E.	38	34	18	52	80	....	....	....	....	....
1986-87a	Providence	H.E.	31	27	18	45	38	....	....	....	....	....
1987-88b	Providence	H.E.	36	29	16	45	31	....	....	....	....	....
	Maine	AHL	4	1	1	2	0	....	....	....	....	....
1988-89	Maine	AHL	DID NOT PLAY									
1989-90	Maine	AHL	24	9	8	17	16	....	....	....	....	....
	Johnstown	ECHL	5	3	4	7	2	....	....	....	....	....

a Hockey East Second All-Star Team (1986, 1987)
b NCAA East Second All-American Team (1988)

CULHANE, JIM

Defense. Shoots left. 6', 195 lbs. Born, Haileybury, Ont., March 13, 1965.
(Hartford's 6th choice, 214th overall, in 1984 Entry Draft).

			Regular Season					Playoffs				
Season	Club	Lea	GP	G	A	TP	PIM	GP	G	A	TP	PIM
1983-84	W. Michigan	CCHA	42	1	14	15	88	....	....	....	....	....
1984-85	W. Michigan	CCHA	37	2	8	10	84	....	....	....	....	....
1985-86	W. Michigan	CCHA	40	1	21	22	61	....	....	....	....	....
1986-87	W. Michigan	CCHA	43	9	24	33	163	....	....	....	....	....
1987-88	Binghamton	AHL	76	5	17	22	169	4	0	0	0	8
1988-89	Binghamton	AHL	72	6	11	17	200	....	....	....	....	....
1989-90	**Hartford**	**NHL**	**6**	**0**	**1**	**1**	**4**	....	....	....	....	....
	Binghamton	AHL	73	6	11	17	69	....	....	....	....	....
	NHL Totals		**6**	**0**	**1**	**1**	**4**	....	....	....	....	....

CULLEN, JOHN

Center. Shoots right. 5'10", 185 lbs. Born, Puslinch, Ont., August 2, 1964.
(Buffalo's 2nd choice, 10th overall, in 1986 Supplemental Draft).

			Regular Season					Playoffs				
Season	Club	Lea	GP	G	A	TP	PIM	GP	G	A	TP	PIM
1983-84a	Boston U.	ECAC	40	23	33	56	28	....	....	....	....	....
1984-85b	Boston U.	H.E.	41	27	32	59	46	....	....	....	....	....
1985-86bc	Boston U.	H.E.	43	25	49	74	54	....	....	....	....	....
1986-87d	Boston U.	H.E.	36	23	29	52	35	....	....	....	....	....
1987-88efgh	Flint	IHL	81	48	*109	*157	113	16	11	*15	26	16
1988-89	**Pittsburgh**	**NHL**	**79**	**12**	**37**	**49**	**112**	**11**	**3**	**6**	**9**	**28**
1989-90	**Pittsburgh**	**NHL**	**72**	**32**	**60**	**92**	**138**	....	....	....	....	....
	NHL Totals		**151**	**44**	**97**	**141**	**250**	**11**	**3**	**6**	**9**	**28**

a ECAC Rookie of the Year (1984)
b Hockey East First All-Star Team (1985, 1986)
c NCAA East Second All-American Team (1986)
d Hockey East Second All-Star Team (1987)
e IHL First All-Star Team (1988)
f Won James Gatschene Memorial Trophy (MVP-IHL) (1988)
g Shared Garry F. Longman Memorial Trophy (Top Rookie-IHL) with Ed Belfour (1988)
h Won Leo P. Lamoureux Memorial Trophy (Top Scorer-IHL) (1988)

Signed as a free agent by **Pittsburgh** June 21, 1988.

CUMMINS, JIM

Right wing. Shoots right. 6'2", 200 lbs. Born, Dearborn, MI, May 17, 1970.
(NY Rangers' 5th choice, 67th overall, in 1989 Entry Draft).

			Regular Season					Playoffs				
Season	Club	Lea	GP	G	A	TP	PIM	GP	G	A	TP	PIM
1988-89	Michigan State	CCHA	30	3	8	11	98	....	....	....	....	....
1989-90	Michigan State	CCHA	41	8	7	15	94	....	....	....	....	....

CUNNEYWORTH, RANDY WILLIAM

Left wing. Shoots left. 6', 190 lbs. Born, Etobicoke, Ont., May 10, 1961.
(Buffalo's 9th choice, 167th overall, in 1980 Entry Draft).

			Regular Season					Playoffs				
Season	Club	Lea	GP	G	A	TP	PIM	GP	G	A	TP	PIM
1979-80	Ottawa	OHA	63	16	25	41	145	11	0	1	1	13
1980-81	**Buffalo**	**NHL**	**1**	**0**	**0**	**0**	**2**	....	....	....	....	....
	Rochester	AHL	1	0	1	1	2	....	....	....	....	....
	Ottawa	OHA	67	54	74	128	240	15	5	8	13	35
1981-82	**Buffalo**	**NHL**	**20**	**2**	**4**	**6**	**47**	....	....	....	....	....
	Rochester	AHL	57	12	15	27	86	9	4	0	4	30
1982-83	Rochester	AHL	78	23	33	56	111	16	4	4	8	35
1983-84	Rochester	AHL	54	18	17	35	85	17	5	5	10	55
1984-85	Rochester	AHL	72	30	38	68	148	5	2	1	3	16
1985-86	**Pittsburgh**	**NHL**	**75**	**15**	**30**	**45**	**74**	....	....	....	....	....
1986-87	**Pittsburgh**	**NHL**	**79**	**26**	**27**	**53**	**142**	....	....	....	....	....
1987-88	**Pittsburgh**	**NHL**	**71**	**35**	**39**	**74**	**141**	....	....	....	....	....
1988-89	**Pittsburgh**	**NHL**	**70**	**25**	**19**	**44**	**156**	**11**	**3**	**5**	**8**	**26**
1989-90	**Winnipeg**	**NHL**	**28**	**5**	**6**	**11**	**34**	....	....	....	....	....
	Hartford	**NHL**	**43**	**9**	**9**	**18**	**41**	**4**	**0**	**0**	**0**	**2**
	NHL Totals		**387**	**117**	**134**	**251**	**637**	**15**	**3**	**5**	**8**	**28**

Traded to **Pittsburgh** by **Buffalo** with Mike Moller for Pat Hughes, October 4, 1985. Traded to **Winnipeg** by **Pittsburgh** with Rick Tabaracci and Dave McLlwain for Jim Kyte, Andrew McBain and Randy Gilhen, June 17, 1989. Traded to **Hartford** by **Winnipeg** for Paul MacDermid, December 13, 1989.

CURRAN, BRIAN

Defense. Shoots left. 6'5", 215 lbs. Born, Toronto, Ont., November 5, 1963.
(Boston's 2nd choice, 22nd overall, in 1982 Entry Draft).

			Regular Season					Playoffs				
Season	Club	Lea	GP	G	A	TP	PIM	GP	G	A	TP	PIM
1980-81	Portland	WHL	59	2	28	30	275	7	0	1	1	13
1981-82	Portland	WHL	51	2	16	18	132	14	1	7	8	63
1982-83	Portland	WHL	56	1	30	31	187	14	1	3	4	57
1983-84	Hershey	AHL	23	0	2	2	94	....	....	....	....	....
	Boston	**NHL**	**16**	**1**	**1**	**2**	**57**	**3**	**0**	**0**	**0**	**7**
1984-85	**Boston**	**NHL**	**56**	**0**	**1**	**1**	**158**	....	....	....	....	....
	Hershey	AHL	4	0	0	0	19	....	....	....	....	....
1985-86	**Boston**	**NHL**	**43**	**2**	**5**	**7**	**192**	**2**	**0**	**0**	**0**	**4**
1986-87	**NY Islanders**	**NHL**	**68**	**0**	**10**	**10**	**356**	**8**	**0**	**0**	**0**	**51**
1987-88	**NY Islanders**	**NHL**	**22**	**0**	**1**	**1**	**68**	....	....	....	....	....
	Springfield	AHL	8	1	0	1	43	....	....	....	....	....
	Toronto	**NHL**	**7**	**0**	**1**	**1**	**19**	**6**	**0**	**0**	**0**	**41**
1988-89	**Toronto**	**NHL**	**47**	**1**	**4**	**5**	**185**	....	....	....	....	....
1989-90	**Toronto**	**NHL**	**72**	**2**	**9**	**11**	**301**	**5**	**0**	**1**	**1**	**19**
	NHL Totals		**331**	**6**	**32**	**38**	**1336**	**24**	**0**	**1**	**1**	**122**

Signed as a free agent by **NY Islanders**, August 29, 1987. Traded to **Toronto** by **NY Islanders** for Toronto's sixth round choice (Pavel Gross) in 1988 Entry Draft, March 8, 1988.

CURRIE, DAN

Left wing. Shoots left. 6'2", 198 lbs. Born, Burlington, Ont., March 15, 1968.
(Edmonton's 4th choice, 84th overall, in 1986 Entry Draft).

			Regular Season					Playoffs				
Season	Club	Lea	GP	G	A	TP	PIM	GP	G	A	TP	PIM
1985-86	S.S. Marie	OHL	66	21	24	45	37	....	....	....	....	....
1986-87	S.S. Marie	OHL	66	31	52	83	53	4	2	1	3	2
1987-88	Nova Scotia	AHL	3	4	2	6	0	5	4	3	7	0
	S.S. Marie	OHL	57	50	59	109	53	6	3	9	12	4
1988-89	Cape Breton	AHL	77	29	36	65	29	....	....	....	....	....
1989-90	Cape Breton	AHL	77	36	40	76	28	....	....	....	....	....

DAGENAIS, MIKE

Defense. Shoots left. 6'3", 200 lbs. Born, Gloucester, Ont., July 22, 1969.
(Chicago's 4th choice, 60th overall, in 1987 Entry Draft).

			Regular Season					Playoffs				
Season	Club	Lea	GP	G	A	TP	PIM	GP	G	A	TP	PIM
1985-86	Peterborough	OHL	45	1	3	4	40	....	....	....	....	....
1986-87	Peterborough	OHL	56	1	17	18	66	12	4	1	5	20
1987-88	Peterborough	OHL	66	11	23	34	125	12	1	1	2	31
1988-89	Peterborough	OHL	62	14	23	37	122	13	3	3	6	12
1989-90	Peterborough	OHL	44	14	26	40	74	12	4	1	5	18

DAHL, KEVIN

Defense. Shoots right. 5'11", 190 lbs. Born, Regina, Sask., December 30, 1968.
(Montreal's 12th choice, 230th overall, in 1988 Entry Draft).

			Regular Season					Playoffs				
Season	Club	Lea	GP	G	A	TP	PIM	GP	G	A	TP	PIM
1987-88	Bowling Green	CCHA	44	2	23	25	78	....	....	....	....	....
1988-89	Bowling Green	CCHA	46	9	26	35	51	....	....	....	....	....
1989-90	Bowling Green	CCHA	43	8	22	30	74	....	....	....	....	....

DAHLEN, ULF (DAH lin)

Left/Right wing. Shoots left. 6'2", 195 lbs. Born, Ostersund, Sweden, January 12, 1967.
(NY Rangers' 1st choice, 7th overall, in 1985 Entry Draft).

			Regular Season					Playoffs				
Season	Club	Lea	GP	G	A	TP	PIM	GP	G	A	TP	PIM
1983-84	Ostersund	Swe.	36	15	11	26	10	....	....	....	....	....
1984-85	Ostersund	Swe.	36	33	26	59	20	....	....	....	....	....
1985-86	Bjorkloven	Swe.	21	4	3	7	8	....	....	....	....	....
1986-87	Bjorkloven	Swe.	31	9	12	21	20	6	6	2	8	4
1987-88	**NY Rangers**	**NHL**	**70**	**29**	**23**	**52**	**26**	....	....	....	....	....
	Colorado	IHL	2	2	2	4	0	....	....	....	....	....
1988-89	**NY Rangers**	**NHL**	**56**	**24**	**19**	**43**	**50**	**4**	**0**	**0**	**0**	**0**
1989-90	**NY Rangers**	**NHL**	**63**	**18**	**18**	**36**	**30**	....	....	....	....	....
	Minnesota	**NHL**	**13**	**2**	**4**	**6**	**0**	**7**	**1**	**4**	**5**	**2**
	NHL Totals		**202**	**73**	**64**	**137**	**106**	**11**	**1**	**4**	**5**	**2**

Traded to **Minnesota** by **NY Rangers** with Los Angeles' fourth round choice (Cal McGowan) – previously acquired by NY Rangers – in 1990 Entry Draft and future considerations, March 6, 1990.

DAHLQUIST, CHRIS

Defense. Shoots left. 6'1", 190 lbs. Born, Fridley, MN, December 14, 1962.

			Regular Season					Playoffs				
Season	Club	Lea	GP	G	A	TP	PIM	GP	G	A	TP	PIM
1981-82	Lake Superior	CCHA	39	4	10	14	62	....	....	....	....	....
1982-83	Lake Superior	CCHA	35	0	12	12	63	....	....	....	....	....
1983-84	Lake Superior	CCHA	40	4	19	23	76	....	....	....	....	....
1984-85	Lake Superior	CCHA	32	4	10	14	18	....	....	....	....	....
1985-86	Baltimore	AHL	65	4	21	25	64	....	....	....	....	....
	Pittsburgh	**NHL**	**5**	**1**	**2**	**3**	**2**	....	....	....	....	....
1986-87	**Pittsburgh**	**NHL**	**19**	**0**	**1**	**1**	**20**	....	....	....	....	....
	Baltimore	AHL	51	1	16	17	50	....	....	....	....	....
1987-88	**Pittsburgh**	**NHL**	**44**	**3**	**6**	**9**	**69**	....	....	....	....	....
1988-89	**Pittsburgh**	**NHL**	**43**	**1**	**5**	**6**	**42**	**2**	**0**	**0**	**0**	**0**
	Muskegon	IHL	10	3	6	9	14	....	....	....	....	....
1989-90	**Pittsburgh**	**NHL**	**62**	**4**	**10**	**14**	**56**	....	....	....	....	....
	Muskegon	IHL	6	1	1	2	8	....	....	....	....	....
	NHL Totals		**173**	**9**	**24**	**33**	**189**	**2**	**0**	**0**	**0**	**0**

Signed as a free agent by **Pittsburgh**, May 7, 1985.

DAIGNEAULT, JEAN-JACQUES (DAYN-yoh)

Defense. Shoots left. 5'11", 185 lbs. Born, Montreal, Que., October 12, 1965.
(Vancouver's 1st choice, 10th overall, in 1984 Entry Draft).

			Regular Season					Playoffs				
Season	Club	Lea	GP	G	A	TP	PIM	GP	G	A	TP	PIM
1981-82	Laval	QMJHL	64	4	25	29	41	18	1	3	4	2
1982-83ab	Longueuil	QMJHL	70	26	58	84	58	15	4	11	15	35
1983-84	Cdn. Olympic	....	62	6	15	21	40	....	....	....	....	....
	Longueuil	QMJHL	10	2	11	13	6	14	3	13	16	30
1984-85	**Vancouver**	**NHL**	**67**	**4**	**23**	**27**	**69**	....	....	....	....	....
1985-86	**Vancouver**	**NHL**	**64**	**5**	**23**	**28**	**45**	**3**	**0**	**2**	**2**	**0**
1986-87	**Philadelphia**	**NHL**	**77**	**6**	**16**	**22**	**56**	**9**	**1**	**0**	**1**	**0**
1987-88	**Philadelphia**	**NHL**	**28**	**2**	**2**	**4**	**12**	....	....	....	....	....
	Hershey	AHL	10	1	5	6	8	....	....	....	....	....
1988-89	Hershey	AHL	12	0	10	10	13	....	....	....	....	....
	Sherbrooke	AHL	63	10	33	43	48	6	1	3	4	2
1989-90	**Montreal**	**NHL**	**36**	**2**	**10**	**12**	**14**	**9**	**0**	**0**	**0**	**2**
	Sherbrooke	AHL	28	8	19	27	18	....	....	....	....	....
	NHL Totals		**272**	**19**	**74**	**93**	**196**	**21**	**1**	**2**	**3**	**2**

a QMJHL First All-Star Team (1983)
b Named QMJHL's Top Defenseman (1983)

Traded to **Philadelphia** by **Vancouver** with Vancouver's second-round choice (Kent Hawley) in 1986 Entry Draft for Dave Richter, Rich Sutter and Vancouver's third-round choice (Don Gibson) — acquired earlier — in 1986 Entry Draft, June 6, 1986. Traded to **Montreal** by **Philadelphia** for Scott Sandelin, November 7, 1988.

DALLMAN, ROD

Left wing. Shoots left. 5'11", 185 lbs. Born, Quesnal, B.C., January 26, 1967.
(NY Islanders' 8th choice, 118th overall, in 1985 Entry Draft).

			Regular Season					Playoffs				
Season	Club	Lea	GP	G	A	TP	PIM	GP	G	A	TP	PIM
1984-85	Prince Albert	WHL	40	8	11	19	133	12	3	4	7	51
1985-86	Prince Albert	WHL	59	20	21	41	198	....	....	....	....	....
1986-87	Prince Albert	WHL	47	13	21	34	240	5	0	1	1	32
1987-88	**NY Islanders**	**NHL**	**3**	**1**	**0**	**1**	**6**	....	....	....	....	....
	Springfield	AHL	59	9	17	26	355	....	....	....	....	....
	Peoria	IHL	8	3	4	7	18	7	0	2	2	65
1988-89	**NY Islanders**	**NHL**	**1**	**0**	**0**	**0**	**15**	....	....	....	....	....
	Springfield	AHL	67	12	12	24	360	....	....	....	....	....
1989-90	**NY Islanders**	**NHL**	....	....	....	....	....	**1**	**0**	**1**	**1**	**0**
	Springfield	AHL	43	10	20	30	129	15	5	5	10	59
	NHL Totals		**4**	**1**	**0**	**1**	**21**	**1**	**0**	**1**	**1**	**0**

Signed as a free agent by **Philadelphia**, July 31, 1990.

DAM, TREVOR

Right wing. Shoots right. 5'10", 210 lbs. Born, Scarborough, Ont., April 20, 1970.
(Chicago's 3rd choice, 50th overall, in 1988 Entry Draft).

			Regular Season					Playoffs				
Season	Club	Lea	GP	G	A	TP	PIM	GP	G	A	TP	PIM
1986-87	London	OHL	64	6	17	23	88	....	....	....	....	....
1987-88	London	OHL	66	25	38	63	169	12	0	3	3	19
1988-89	London	OHL	66	33	59	92	111	21	9	11	20	39
1989-90	London	OHL	56	20	54	74	91	6	2	5	7	15

DAMPHOUSSE, VINCENT (DAM-fooz)

Left wing. Shoots left. 6'1", 190 lbs. Born, Montreal, Que., December 17, 1967.
(Toronto's 1st choice, 6th overall, in 1986 Entry Draft).

			Regular Season					Playoffs				
Season	Club	Lea	GP	G	A	TP	PIM	GP	G	A	TP	PIM
1984-85	Laval	QMJHL	68	35	68	103	62	....	....	....	....	....
1985-86a	Laval	QMJHL	69	45	110	155	70	14	9	27	36	12
1986-87	**Toronto**	**NHL**	**80**	**21**	**25**	**46**	**26**	**12**	**1**	**5**	**6**	**8**
1987-88	**Toronto**	**NHL**	**75**	**12**	**36**	**48**	**40**	**6**	**0**	**1**	**1**	**10**
1988-89	**Toronto**	**NHL**	**80**	**26**	**42**	**68**	**75**	....	....	....	....	....
1989-90	**Toronto**	**NHL**	**80**	**33**	**61**	**94**	**56**	**5**	**0**	**2**	**2**	**2**
	NHL Totals		**315**	**92**	**164**	**256**	**197**	**23**	**1**	**8**	**9**	**20**

a QMJHL Second All-Star Team (1986)

DANEYKO, KENNETH (KEN) (DAN-ee-koh)

Defense. Shoots left. 6', 210 lbs. Born, Windsor, Ont., April 17, 1964.
(New Jersey's 2nd choice, 18th overall, in 1982 Entry Draft).

			Regular Season					Playoffs				
Season	Club	Lea	GP	G	A	TP	PIM	GP	G	A	TP	PIM
1980-81	Spokane	WHL	62	6	13	19	40	4	0	0	0	6
1981-82	Spokane	WHL	26	1	11	12	147	....	....	....	....	....
	Seattle	WHL	38	1	22	23	151	14	1	9	10	49
1982-83	Seattle	WHL	69	17	43	60	150	4	1	3	4	14
1983-84	**New Jersey**	**NHL**	**11**	**1**	**4**	**5**	**17**	....	....	....	....	....
	Kamloops	WHL	19	6	28	34	52	17	4	9	13	28
1984-85	**New Jersey**	**NHL**	**1**	**0**	**0**	**0**	**10**	....	....	....	....	....
	Maine	AHL	80	4	9	13	206	11	1	3	4	36
1985-86	**New Jersey**	**NHL**	**44**	**0**	**10**	**10**	**100**	....	....	....	....	....
	Maine	AHL	21	3	2	5	75	....	....	....	....	....
1986-87	**New Jersey**	**NHL**	**79**	**2**	**12**	**14**	**183**	....	....	....	....	....
1987-88	**New Jersey**	**NHL**	**80**	**5**	**7**	**12**	**239**	**20**	**1**	**6**	**7**	**83**
1988-89	**New Jersey**	**NHL**	**80**	**5**	**5**	**10**	**283**	....	....	....	....	....
1989-90	**New Jersey**	**NHL**	**74**	**6**	**15**	**21**	**216**	**6**	**2**	**0**	**2**	**21**
	NHL Totals		**369**	**19**	**53**	**72**	**1048**	**26**	**3**	**6**	**9**	**104**

DANIELS, JEFF

Left wing. Shoots left. 6'1", 195 lbs. Born, Oshawa, Ont., June 24, 1968.
(Pittsburgh's 6th choice, 109th overall, in 1986 Entry Draft).

			Regular Season					Playoffs				
Season	Club	Lea	GP	G	A	TP	PIM	GP	G	A	TP	PIM
1985-86	Oshawa	OHL	62	13	19	32	23	6	0	1	1	0
1986-87	Oshawa	OHL	54	14	9	23	22	15	3	2	5	5
1987-88	Oshawa	OHL	64	29	39	68	59	4	2	3	5	0
1988-89	Muskegon	IHL	58	21	21	42	58	11	3	5	8	11
1989-90	Muskegon	IHL	80	30	47	77	39	6	1	1	2	7

DANIELS, KIMBI

Center. Shoots right. 5'11", 175 lbs. Born, Brandon, Man., January 19, 1972.
(Philadelphia's 5th choice, 44th overall, in 1990 Entry Draft).

			Regular Season					Playoffs				
Season	Club	Lea	GP	G	A	TP	PIM	GP	G	A	TP	PIM
1988-89	Swift Current	WHL	68	30	31	61	48	12	6	6	12	12
1989-90	Swift Current	WHL	69	43	51	94	84	4	1	3	4	10

DANIELS, SCOTT

Left wing. Shoots left. 6'2", 205 lbs. Born, Prince Albert, Sask., September 19, 1969.
(Hartford's 6th choice, 136th overall, in 1989 Entry Draft).

			Regular Season					Playoffs				
Season	Club	Lea	GP	G	A	TP	PIM	GP	G	A	TP	PIM
1986-87	Kamloops	WHL	43	6	4	10	68	....	....	....	....	....
	N. Westminster	WHL	19	4	7	11	30	....	....	....	....	....
1987-88	N. Westminster	WHL	37	6	11	17	157	....	....	....	....	....
	Regina	WHL	19	2	3	5	83	....	....	....	....	....
1988-89	Regina	WHL	64	21	26	47	241	....	....	....	....	....
1989-90	Regina	WHL	52	28	31	59	171	....	....	....	....	....

DAOUST, DANIEL (DAN) (dow-OO)

Center. Shoots left. 5'11", 170 lbs. Born, Montreal, Que., February 29, 1960.

			Regular Season					Playoffs				
Season	Club	Lea	GP	G	A	TP	PIM	GP	G	A	TP	PIM
1978-79	Cornwall	QJHL	72	42	55	97	85	7	2	4	6	29
1979-80	Cornwall	QJHL	70	40	62	102	82	18	5	9	14	36
1980-81	Nova Scotia	AHL	80	38	60	98	106	6	1	3	4	10
1981-82	Nova Scotia	AHL	61	25	40	65	75	9	5	2	7	11
1982-83a	**Montreal**	**NHL**	**4**	**0**	**1**	**1**	**4**	....	....	....	....	....
	Toronto	**NHL**	**48**	**18**	**33**	**51**	**31**	....	....	....	....	....
1983-84	**Toronto**	**NHL**	**78**	**18**	**56**	**74**	**88**	....	....	....	....	....
1984-85	**Toronto**	**NHL**	**79**	**17**	**37**	**54**	**98**	....	....	....	....	....
1985-86	**Toronto**	**NHL**	**80**	**7**	**13**	**20**	**88**	**10**	**2**	**2**	**4**	**19**
1986-87	**Toronto**	**NHL**	**33**	**4**	**3**	**7**	**35**	**13**	**5**	**2**	**7**	**42**
	Newmarket	AHL	1	0	0	0	4	....	....	....	....	....
1987-88	**Toronto**	**NHL**	**67**	**9**	**8**	**17**	**57**	**4**	**0**	**0**	**0**	**2**
1988-89	**Toronto**	**NHL**	**68**	**7**	**5**	**12**	**54**	....	....	....	....	....
1989-90	**Toronto**	**NHL**	**65**	**7**	**11**	**18**	**89**	**5**	**0**	**1**	**1**	**20**
	NHL Totals		**522**	**87**	**167**	**254**	**544**	**32**	**7**	**5**	**12**	**83**

a NHL All-Rookie Team (1983)

Signed as free agent by **Montreal**, March 9, 1981. Traded to **Toronto** by **Montreal** for Toronto's third round choice (Ken Hodge — later transferred to Minnesota) in the 1984 Entry Draft, December 17, 1982.

DARVEAU, GUY

Defense. Shoots left. 6'1", 205 lbs. Born, Montreal, Que., April 7, 1968.
(Calgary's 10th choice, 210th overall, in 1988 Entry Draft).

			Regular Season					Playoffs				
Season	Club	Lea	GP	G	A	TP	PIM	GP	G	A	TP	PIM
1986-87	Longueuil	QMJHL	64	9	24	33	175	15	1	7	8	23
1987-88	Victoriaville	QMJHL	57	19	16	35	274	5	0	2	2	17
1988-89	Verdun	QMJHL	20	1	10	11	40	....	....	....	....	....
1989-90	Sherbrooke	AHL	38	2	2	4	120	2	0	0	0	2

Signed as a free agent by **Montreal**, October 2, 1989.

DAVIDSON, LEE

Center. Shoots left. 5'10", 165 lbs. Born, Winnipeg, Man., June 30, 1968.
(Washington's 9th choice, 166th overall, in 1986 Entry Draft).

			Regular Season					Playoffs				
Season	Club	Lea	GP	G	A	TP	PIM	GP	G	A	TP	PIM
1986-87	North Dakota	WCHA	41	16	12	28	65	....	....	....	....	....
1987-88	North Dakota	WCHA	40	22	24	46	74	....	....	....	....	....
1988-89	North Dakota	WCHA	41	16	37	53	60	....	....	....	....	....
1989-90ab	North Dakota	WCHA	45	26	*49	75	0	....	....	....	....	....

a WCHA Second All-Star Team (1990)
b NCAA West Second All-American Team (1990)

DAVIES, CLARK

Defense. Shoots left. 6', 185 lbs. Born, Yorkton, Sask., June 20, 1967.
(Buffalo's 1st choice, 18th overall, in 1988 Supplemental Draft).

			Regular Season					Playoffs				
Season	Club	Lea	GP	G	A	TP	PIM	GP	G	A	TP	PIM
1986-87	Ferris State	CCHA	42	5	20	25	42	....	....	....	....	....
1987-88	Ferris State	CCHA	40	4	15	19	65	....	....	....	....	....
1988-89	Ferris State	CCHA	32	3	10	13	59	....	....	....	....	....
1989-90	Ferris State	CCHA	36	4	9	13	38	....	....	....	....	....

DAVYDOV, EVGENY

Left wing. Shoots left. 6'1", 185 lbs. Born, Chelyabinsk, Soviet Union, May 27, 1967.
(Winnipeg's 14th choice, 235th overall, in 1989 Entry Draft).

			Regular Season					Playoffs				
Season	Club	Lea	GP	G	A	TP	PIM	GP	G	A	TP	PIM
1984-85	Chelyabinsk	USSR	5	1	0	1	2	....	....	....	....	....
1985-86	Chelyabinsk	USSR	39	11	5	16	22	....	....	....	....	....
1986-87	CSKA	USSR	32	11	2	13	8	....	....	....	....	....
1987-88	CSKA	USSR	44	16	7	23	18	....	....	....	....	....
1988-89	CSKA	USSR	35	9	7	16	4	....	....	....	....	....
1989-90	CSKA	USSR	44	17	6	23	16	....	....	....	....	....

DAY, JOSEPH (JOE)

Left wing. Shoots left. 5'11", 185 lbs. Born, Chicago, IL, May 11, 1968.
(Hartford's 8th choice, 186th overall, in 1987 Entry Draft).

			Regular Season					Playoffs				
Season	Club	Lea	GP	G	A	TP	PIM	GP	G	A	TP	PIM
1986-87	St. Lawrence	ECAC	33	9	11	20	25	....	....	....	....	....
1987-88	St. Lawrence	ECAC	30	21	16	37	36	....	....	....	....	....
1988-89	St. Lawrence	ECAC	36	21	27	48	44	....	....	....	....	....
1989-90a	St. Lawrence	ECAC	32	19	26	45	30	....	....	....	....	....

a ECAC Second All-Star Team (1990)

DEAN, KEVIN

Defense. Shoots left. 6'1", 195 lbs. Born, Madison, WI, April 1, 1969.
(New Jersey's 4th choice, 86th overall, in 1987 Entry Draft).

			Regular Season					Playoffs				
Season	Club	Lea	GP	G	A	TP	PIM	GP	G	A	TP	PIM
1987-88	N. Hampshire	H.E.	27	1	6	7	34	....	....	....	....	....
1988-89	N. Hampshire	H.E.	34	1	12	13	28	....	....	....	....	....
1989-90	N. Hampshire	H.E.	39	2	6	8	42	....	....	....	....	....

DEASLEY, BRYAN

Left wing. Shoots left. 6'3", 205 lbs. Born, Toronto, Ont., November 26, 1968.
(Calgary's 1st choice, 19th overall, in 1987 Entry Draft).

			Regular Season					Playoffs				
Season	Club	Lea	GP	G	A	TP	PIM	GP	G	A	TP	PIM
1986-87	U. of Michigan	CCHA	38	13	11	24	74	....	....	....	....	....
1987-88	U. of Michigan	CCHA	27	18	4	22	38	....	....	....	....	....
1988-89	Cdn. National	....	54	19	19	38	32	....	....	....	....	....
	Salt Lake	IHL	....	....	....	....	....	7	3	2	5	25
1989-90	Salt Lake	IHL	71	16	11	27	46	....	....	....	....	....

DeBLOIS, LUCIEN   (DEHB-loh-wah)

Right wing. Shoots right. 5'11", 200 lbs.   Born, Joliette, Que., June 21, 1957.
(NY Rangers' 1st choice, 8th overall, in 1977 Amateur Draft).

				Regular Season					Playoffs			
Season	Club	Lea	GP	G	A	TP	PIM	GP	G	A	TP	PIM
1975-76	Sorel	QJHL	70	56	55	111	112	5	1	1	2	32
1976-77	Sorel	QJHL	72	56	78	134	131	....	....	....	....	....
1977-78	NY Rangers	NHL	71	22	8	30	27	3	0	0	0	2
1978-79	New Haven	AHL	7	4	6	10	6	....	....	....	....	....
	NY Rangers	NHL	62	11	17	28	26	9	2	0	2	4
1979-80	NY Rangers	NHL	6	3	1	4	7	....	....	....	....	....
	Colorado	NHL	70	24	19	43	36	....	....	....	....	....
1980-81	Colorado	NHL	74	26	16	42	78	....	....	....	....	....
1981-82	Winnipeg	NHL	65	25	27	52	87	4	2	1	3	4
1982-83	Winnipeg	NHL	79	27	27	54	69	3	0	0	0	5
1983-84	Winnipeg	NHL	80	34	45	79	50	3	0	1	1	4
1984-85	Montreal	NHL	51	12	11	23	20	8	2	4	6	4
1985-86	Montreal	NHL	61	14	17	31	48	11	0	0	0	7
1986-87	NY Rangers	NHL	40	3	8	11	27	2	0	0	0	2
1987-88	NY Rangers	NHL	74	9	21	30	103	....	....	....	....	....
1988-89	NY Rangers	NHL	73	9	24	33	107	4	0	0	0	4
1989-90	Quebec	NHL	70	9	8	17	45	....	....	....	....	....
	NHL Totals		**876**	**228**	**249**	**477**	**730**	**47**	**6**	**6**	**12**	**36**

Traded to **Colorado** by **NY Rangers** with Pat Hickey, Mike McEwen, Dean Turner and future consideration (Bobby Crawford) for Barry Beck, November 2, 1979. Traded to **Winnipeg** by **Colorado** for Brent Ashton and Winnipeg's third-round choice (Dave Kasper) in the 1982 Entry Draft, July 15, 1981. Traded to **Montreal** by **Winnipeg** for Perry Turnbull, June 13, 1984. Signed as a free agent by **NY Rangers**, September 8, 1986. Signed as a free agent by **Quebec**, August 2, 1989.

DEBOER, PETER

Center/right wing. Shoots right. 6'1", 190 lbs.   Born, Dunnville, Ont., June 13, 1968.
(Toronto's 11th choice, 237th overall, in 1988 Entry Draft).

				Regular Season					Playoffs			
Season	Club	Lea	GP	G	A	TP	PIM	GP	G	A	TP	PIM
1987-88	Windsor	OHL	54	23	18	41	41	12	4	4	8	14
1988-89	Windsor	OHL	65	45	46	91	80	4	2	3	5	0
	Milwaukee	IHL	2	0	1	1	0	1	0	2	2	2
1989-90	Milwaukee	IHL	67	21	19	40	16	....	....	....	....	....

Traded to **Vancouver** by **Toronto** for Paul Lawless, February 27, 1989.

DEBRUSK, LOUIE   (dah-BRUHSK)

Left wing. Shoots left. 6'1", 200 lbs.   Born, Cambridge, Ont., March 19, 1971.
(NY Rangers' 4th choice, 49th overall, in 1989 Entry Draft).

				Regular Season					Playoffs			
Season	Club	Lea	GP	G	A	TP	PIM	GP	G	A	TP	PIM
1988-89	London	OHL	59	11	11	22	149	19	1	1	2	43
1989-90	London	OHL	61	21	19	40	198	6	2	2	4	24

de CARLE, MIKE

Left wing. Shoots left. 6', 200 lbs.   Born, Covina, CA, August 20, 1966.
(Buffalo's 2nd choice, 6th overall, in 1987 Supplemental Draft).

				Regular Season					Playoffs			
Season	Club	Lea	GP	G	A	TP	PIM	GP	G	A	TP	PIM
1985-86	Lake Superior	CCHA	36	12	21	33	40	....	....	....	....	....
1986-87	Lake Superior	CCHA	38	34	18	52	122	....	....	....	....	....
1987-88ab	Lake Superior	CCHA	43	27	39	66	83	....	....	....	....	....
1988-89	Lake Superior	CCHA	38	20	24	44	76	....	....	....	....	....
1989-90	Phoenix	IHL	24	5	4	9	44	....	....	....	....	....
	Fort Wayne	IHL	12	4	5	9	7	5	2	6	8	15

a NCAA All-Tournament Team (1988)
b CCHA Second All-Star Team (1988)

DEFREITAS, RICHARD (RICH)

Defense. Shoots left. 6'2", 195 lbs.   Born, Manchester, NH, January 28, 1969.
(Washington's 5th choice, 120th overall, in 1987 Entry Draft).

				Regular Season					Playoffs			
Season	Club	Lea	GP	G	A	TP	PIM	GP	G	A	TP	PIM
1988-89	Harvard	ECAC	5	0	2	2	6	....	....	....	....	....
1989-90	Harvard	ECAC	28	0	1	1	18	....	....	....	....	....

DEGRAY, DALE EDWARD

Defense. Shoots right. 6', 200 lbs.   Born, Oshawa, Ont., September 1, 1963.
(Calgary's 7th choice, 162nd overall, in 1981 Entry Draft).

				Regular Season					Playoffs			
Season	Club	Lea	GP	G	A	TP	PIM	GP	G	A	TP	PIM
1980-81	Oshawa	OHA	61	11	10	21	93	8	1	1	2	19
1981-82	Oshawa	OHL	66	11	23	34	162	12	3	4	7	49
1982-83	Oshawa	OHL	69	20	30	50	149	17	7	7	14	36
1983-84	Colorado	CHL	67	16	14	30	67	6	1	1	2	2
1984-85a	Moncton	AHL	77	24	37	61	63	....	....	....	....	....
1985-86	**Calgary**	NHL	1	0	0	0	0	....	....	....	....	....
	Moncton	AHL	76	10	31	41	128	6	0	1	1	0
1986-87	**Calgary**	NHL	27	6	7	13	29	....	....	....	....	....
	Moncton	AHL	45	10	22	32	57	5	2	1	3	19
1987-88	**Toronto**	NHL	56	6	18	24	63	5	0	1	1	16
	Newmarket	AHL	8	2	10	12	8	....	....	....	....	....
1988-89	**Los Angeles**	NHL	63	6	22	28	97	8	1	2	3	12
1989-90	New Haven	AHL	16	2	10	12	38	....	....	....	....	....
	Buffalo	NHL	6	0	0	0	6	....	....	....	....	....
	Rochester	AHL	50	6	25	31	118	17	5	6	11	59
	NHL Totals		**153**	**18**	**47**	**65**	**195**	**13**	**1**	**3**	**4**	**28**

a AHL Second All-Star Team (1985)
Traded to **Toronto** by **Calgary** for Toronto's fifth round choice (Scott Matusovich) in 1988 Entry Draft, September 17, 1987. Claimed by **Los Angeles** in NHL Waiver Draft, October 3, 1988. Traded to **Buffalo** by **Los Angeles** with future considerations for Bob Halkidis and future considerations, November 24, 1989.

DELAY, MICHAEL

Defense. Shoots left. 6', 190 lbs.   Born, Boston, MA, August 31, 1969.
(Toronto's 8th choice, 174th overall, in 1988 Entry Draft).

				Regular Season					Playoffs			
Season	Club	Lea	GP	G	A	TP	PIM	GP	G	A	TP	PIM
1988-89	Boston College	H.E.	1	1	0	1	0	....	....	....	....	....
1989-90	Boston College	H.E.	7	0	0	0	0	....	....	....	....	....

DELORME, GILBERT   (duh-LOHRM)

Defense. Shoots right. 6'1", 205 lbs.   Born, Boucherville, Que., November 25, 1962.
(Montreal's 2nd choice, 18th overall, in 1981 Entry Draft).

				Regular Season					Playoffs			
Season	Club	Lea	GP	G	A	TP	PIM	GP	G	A	TP	PIM
1979-80	Chicoutimi	QJHL	71	25	86	111	68	12	2	10	12	26
1980-81	Chicoutimi	QJHL	70	27	79	106	77	12	10	12	22	16
1981-82	**Montreal**	NHL	60	3	8	11	55	....	....	....	....	....
1982-83	**Montreal**	NHL	78	12	21	33	89	3	0	0	0	2
1983-84	**Montreal**	NHL	27	2	7	9	8	....	....	....	....	....
	St. Louis	NHL	44	0	5	5	41	11	1	3	4	11
1984-85	**St. Louis**	NHL	74	2	12	14	53	3	0	0	0	0
1985-86	**Quebec**	NHL	64	2	18	20	51	2	0	0	0	5
1986-87	**Quebec**	NHL	19	2	0	2	14	....	....	....	....	....
	Detroit	NHL	24	2	3	5	33	16	0	2	2	14
1987-88	**Detroit**	NHL	55	2	8	10	81	15	0	3	3	22
1988-89	**Detroit**	NHL	42	1	3	4	51	6	0	1	1	2
1989-90	**Pittsburgh**	NHL	54	3	7	10	44	....	....	....	....	....
	NHL Totals		**541**	**31**	**92**	**123**	**520**	**56**	**1**	**9**	**10**	**56**

Traded to **St. Louis** by **Montreal** with Greg Paslawski and Doug Wickenheiser for Perry Turnbull, December 21, 1983. Traded to **Quebec** by **St. Louis** for Bruce Bell, October 2, 1985. Traded to **Detroit** by **Quebec** with Brent Ashton and Mark Kumpel for Basil McRae, John Ogrodnick and Doug Shedden, January 17, 1987. Signed as a free agent by **Pittsburgh**, June 28, 1989.

DePALMA, LARRY

Left wing. Shoots left. 6', 195 lbs.   Born, Trenton, MI, October 27, 1965.

				Regular Season					Playoffs			
Season	Club	Lea	GP	G	A	TP	PIM	GP	G	A	TP	PIM
1984-85	N. Westminster	WHL	65	14	16	30	87	10	1	1	2	25
1985-86	Saskatoon	WHL	65	61	51	112	232	13	7	9	16	58
	Minnesota	NHL	1	0	0	0	0	....	....	....	....	....
1986-87	**Minnesota**	NHL	56	9	6	15	219	....	....	....	....	....
	Springfield	AHL	9	2	2	4	82	....	....	....	....	....
1987-88	**Minnesota**	NHL	7	1	1	2	15	....	....	....	....	....
	Baltimore	AHL	16	8	10	18	121	....	....	....	....	....
	Kalamazoo	IHL	22	6	11	17	215	....	....	....	....	....
1988-89	**Minnesota**	NHL	43	5	7	12	102	2	0	0	0	6
1989-90	Kalamazoo	IHL	36	7	14	21	218	4	1	1	2	32
	NHL Totals		**107**	**15**	**14**	**29**	**336**	**2**	**0**	**0**	**0**	**6**

Signed as a free agent by **Minnesota**, May 12, 1986.

DePOURCQ, JOHN

Center. Shoots left. 5'9", 180 lbs.   Born, Penticton, B.C., February 6, 1968.
(Pittsburgh's 1st choice, 21st overall, in 1989 Supplemental Draft).

				Regular Season					Playoffs			
Season	Club	Lea	GP	G	A	TP	PIM	GP	G	A	TP	PIM
1987-88	Ferris State	CCHA	40	26	27	53	22	....	....	....	....	....
1988-89	Ferris State	CCHA	23	9	19	28	4	....	....	....	....	....
1989-90	Ferris State	CCHA	38	22	35	57	12	....	....	....	....	....

DERKATCH, DALE

Center. Shoots right. 5'6", 170 lbs.   Born, Preeceville, Sask., October 17, 1964.
(Edmonton's 6th choice, 140th overall, in 1983 Entry Draft).

				Regular Season					Playoffs			
Season	Club	Lea	GP	G	A	TP	PIM	GP	G	A	TP	PIM
1981-82	Regina	WHL	71	62	80	142	92	19	11	23	34	38
1982-83a	Regina	WHL	67	*84	95	*179	62	....	....	....	....	....
1983-84	Regina	WHL	62	72	87	159	92	23	12	*41	*53	54
1984-85	Regina	WHL	4	4	7	11	0	7	2	5	7	10
1985-86	Asiago	Italy	28	41	59	100	18	8	10	16	26	12
1986-87	Ilves	Fin.	44	24	31	55	57	....	....	....	....	....
1987-88	Ilves	Fin.	41	28	24	52	24	....	....	....	....	....
1988-89	Ilves	Fin.	44	36	30	66	49	5	2	1	3	4
1989-90	Munich	W. Ger.	28	27	31	58	30	....	....	....	....	....

a WHL First All-Star Team (1983)

DESCHAMPS, MARC

Defense. Shoots right. 6'3", 210 lbs.   Born, Kapuskasing, Ont., September 29, 1970.
(Montreal's 6th choice, 104th overall, in 1989 Entry Draft).

				Regular Season					Playoffs			
Season	Club	Lea	GP	G	A	TP	PIM	GP	G	A	TP	PIM
1988-89	Cornell	ECAC	26	0	7	7	26	....	....	....	....	....
1989-90	Cornell	ECAC	13	0	2	2	10	....	....	....	....	....

Traded to **Washington** by **Montreal** for Alain Cote, June 22, 1990.

DESJARDINS, ERIC   (day-jar-DAN)

Defense. Shoots right. 6'1", 200 lbs.   Born, Rouyn, Que., June 14, 1969.
(Montreal's 3rd choice, 38th overall, in 1987 Entry Draft).

				Regular Season					Playoffs			
Season	Club	Lea	GP	G	A	TP	PIM	GP	G	A	TP	PIM
1986-87a	Granby	QMJHL	66	14	24	38	178	8	3	2	5	10
1987-88	Sherbrooke	AHL	3	0	0	0	6	4	0	2	2	2
b	Granby	QMJHL	62	18	49	67	138	5	0	3	3	10
1988-89	**Montreal**	NHL	36	2	12	14	26	14	1	1	2	6
1989-90	**Montreal**	NHL	55	3	13	16	51	6	0	0	0	10
	NHL Totals		**91**	**5**	**25**	**30**	**77**	**20**	**1**	**1**	**2**	**16**

a QMJHL Second All-Star Team (1987)
b QMJHL First All-Star Team (1988)

DESJARDINS, MARTIN (day-jar-DAN)

Center. Shoots left. 5'11", 179 lbs. Born, Ste-Rose, Que., January 28, 1967.
(Montreal's 5th choice, 75th overall, in 1985 Entry Draft).

			Regular Season					Playoffs				
Season	Club	Lea	GP	G	A	TP	PIM	GP	G	A	TP	PIM
1984-85	Trois Rivieres	QMJHL	66	29	34	63	76	7	4	6	10	6
1985-86	Trois Rivieres	QMJHL	71	49	69	118	103	4	2	4	6	4
1986-87	Trois Rivieres	QMJHL	52	32	52	84	77	....	....	....	....	....
	Longueuil	QMJHL	17	7	10	17	12	19	8	10	18	18
1987-88	Sherbrooke	AHL	75	34	36	70	117	5	1	1	2	8
1988-89	Sherbrooke	AHL	70	17	27	44	104	6	2	7	9	21
1989-90	**Montreal**	**NHL**	**8**	**0**	**2**	**2**	**2**	....	....	....	....	....
	Sherbrooke	AHL	65	21	26	47	72	12	4	*13	17	28
	NHL Totals		**8**	**0**	**2**	**2**	**2**	....	....	....	....	....

DESJARDINS, NORMAN

Right wing. Shoots right. 5'10", 180 lbs. Born, Montreal, Que., March 25, 1968.

			Regular Season					Playoffs				
Season	Club	Lea	GP	G	A	TP	PIM	GP	G	A	TP	PIM
1986-87	Granby	QMJHL	52	19	22	41	61	....	....	....	....	....
	Verdun	QMJHL	14	3	5	8	45	....	....	....	....	....
1987-88	Verdun	QMJHL	69	31	44	75	95	....	....	....	....	....
1988-89	Longueuil	QMJHL	63	26	61	87	72	....	....	....	....	....
1989-90	Sherbrooke	AHL	58	13	19	32	91	12	4	3	7	15

Signed as a free agent by **Montreal**, October 2, 1989.

DESMOND, NED

Defense. Shoots left. 6'3", 205 lbs. Born, New York, NY, February 18, 1966.
(St. Louis' 3rd choice, 54th overall, in 1985 Entry Draft).

			Regular Season					Playoffs				
Season	Club	Lea	GP	G	A	TP	PIM	GP	G	A	TP	PIM
1985-86	Dartmouth	ECAC	23	4	12	16	4	....	....	....	....	....
1986-87	Dartmouth	ECAC	24	4	9	13	28	....	....	....	....	....
1987-88	Dartmouth	ECAC	DID NOT PLAY — INJURED									
1988-89	Dartmouth	ECAC	17	0	4	4	10	....	....	....	....	....
	Peoria	IHL	9	0	0	0	17	....	....	....	....	....
1989-90	New Haven	AHL	1	0	0	0	0	....	....	....	....	....

DEVEREAUX, JOHN

Center. Shoots right. 6', 175 lbs. Born, Scituate, MA, June 8, 1965.
(Hartford's 4th choice, 173rd overall, in 1984 Entry Draft).

			Regular Season					Playoffs				
Season	Club	Lea	GP	G	A	TP	PIM	GP	G	A	TP	PIM
1984-85	Boston College	H.E.	19	3	3	6	6	....	....	....	....	....
1985-86	Boston College	H.E.	41	8	6	14	24	....	....	....	....	....
1986-87	Boston College	H.E.	39	14	20	34	16	....	....	....	....	....
1987-88	Boston College	H.E.	34	14	24	38	48	....	....	....	....	....
1988-89	Flint	IHL	11	3	1	4	11	....	....	....	....	....
1989-90	Winston-Salem	ECHL	58	22	48	70	110	....	....	....	....	....

DIDUCK, GERALD

Defense. Shoots right. 6'2", 207 lbs. Born, Edmonton, Alta., April 6, 1965.
(NY Islanders' 2nd choice, 16th overall, in 1983 Entry Draft).

			Regular Season					Playoffs				
Season	Club	Lea	GP	G	A	TP	PIM	GP	G	A	TP	PIM
1981-82	Lethbridge	WHL	71	1	15	16	81	12	0	3	3	27
1982-83	Lethbridge	WHL	67	8	16	24	151	20	3	12	15	49
1983-84	Lethbridge	WHL	65	10	24	34	133	5	1	4	5	27
	Indianapolis	IHL	....	....	....	....	....	10	1	6	7	19
1984-85	**NY Islanders**	**NHL**	**65**	**2**	**8**	**10**	**80**	....	....	....	....	....
1985-86	**NY Islanders**	**NHL**	**10**	**1**	**2**	**3**	**2**	....	....	....	....	....
	Springfield	AHL	61	6	14	20	173	....	....	....	....	....
1986-87	**NY Islanders**	**NHL**	**30**	**2**	**3**	**5**	**67**	**14**	**0**	**1**	**1**	**35**
	Springfield	AHL	45	6	8	14	120	....	....	....	....	....
1987-88	**NY Islanders**	**NHL**	**68**	**7**	**12**	**19**	**113**	**6**	**1**	**0**	**1**	**42**
1988-89	**NY Islanders**	**NHL**	**65**	**11**	**21**	**32**	**155**	....	....	....	....	....
1989-90	**NY Islanders**	**NHL**	**76**	**3**	**17**	**20**	**163**	**5**	**0**	**0**	**0**	**12**
	NHL Totals		**314**	**26**	**63**	**89**	**580**	**25**	**1**	**1**	**2**	**89**

DIMAIO, ROBERT (ROB) (duh-MIGH-oh)

Center. Shoots right. 5'8", 175 lbs. Born, Calgary, Alta., February 19, 1968.
(NY Islanders' 6th choice, 118th overall, in 1987 Entry Draft).

			Regular Season					Playoffs				
Season	Club	Lea	GP	G	A	TP	PIM	GP	G	A	TP	PIM
1986-87	Medicine Hat	WHL	70	27	43	70	130	20	7	11	18	46
1987-88	Medicine Hat	WHL	54	47	43	90	120	14	12	19	*31	59
1988-89	**NY Islanders**	**NHL**	**16**	**1**	**0**	**1**	**30**	....	....	....	....	....
	Springfield	AHL	40	13	18	31	67	....	....	....	....	....
1989-90	**NY Islanders**	**NHL**	**7**	**0**	**0**	**0**	**2**	**1**	**1**	**0**	**1**	**4**
	Springfield	AHL	54	25	27	52	69	16	4	7	11	45
	NHL Totals		**23**	**1**	**0**	**1**	**32**	**1**	**1**	**0**	**1**	**4**

DiMUZIO, FRANK

Left wing. Shoots right. 6', 195 lbs. Born, Toronto, Ont., August 12, 1967.
(Washington's 13th choice, 250th overall, in 1985 Entry Draft).

			Regular Season					Playoffs				
Season	Club	Lea	GP	G	A	TP	PIM	GP	G	A	TP	PIM
1984-85	Belleville	OHL	68	28	22	50	40	12	4	2	6	8
1985-86	Ottawa	OHL	63	29	26	55	105	....	....	....	....	....
1986-87a	Ottawa	OHL	61	*59	30	89	57	7	5	1	6	21
1987-88	Ottawa	OHL	48	51	44	95	96	16	9	11	20	34
1988-89	Baltimore	AHL	33	5	3	8	30	....	....	....	....	....
1989-90	Fiemme	Italy	28	13	8	21	21	10	8	4	12	6

a OHL Third All-Star Team (1987)

DINEEN, GORDON (GORD)

Defense. Shoots right. 6', 195 lbs. Born, Quebec City, Que., September 21, 1962.
(NY Islanders' 2nd choice, 42nd overall, in 1981 Entry Draft).

			Regular Season					Playoffs				
Season	Club	Lea	GP	G	A	TP	PIM	GP	G	A	TP	PIM
1980-81	S. S. Marie	OHA	68	4	26	30	158	19	1	7	8	58
1981-82	S. S. Marie	OHL	68	9	45	54	185	13	1	2	3	52
1982-83	**NY Islanders**	**NHL**	**2**	**0**	**0**	**0**	**4**	....	....	....	....	....
abc	Indianapolis	CHL	73	10	47	57	78	13	2	10	12	29
1983-84	Indianapolis	CHL	26	4	13	17	63	....	....	....	....	....
	NY Islanders	**NHL**	**43**	**1**	**11**	**12**	**32**	**9**	**1**	**1**	**2**	**28**
1984-85	**NY Islanders**	**NHL**	**48**	**1**	**12**	**13**	**89**	**10**	**0**	**0**	**0**	**26**
	Springfield	AHL	25	1	8	9	46	....	....	....	....	....
1985-86	**NY Islanders**	**NHL**	**57**	**1**	**8**	**9**	**81**	**3**	**0**	**0**	**0**	**2**
	Springfield	AHL	11	2	3	5	20	....	....	....	....	....
1986-87	**NY Islanders**	**NHL**	**71**	**4**	**10**	**14**	**110**	**7**	**0**	**4**	**4**	**4**
1987-88	**NY Islanders**	**NHL**	**57**	**4**	**12**	**16**	**62**	....	....	....	....	....
	Minnesota	**NHL**	**13**	**1**	**1**	**2**	**21**	....	....	....	....	....
1988-89	**Minnesota**	**NHL**	**2**	**0**	**1**	**1**	**2**	....	....	....	....	....
	Kalamazoo	IHL	25	2	6	8	49	....	....	....	....	....
	Pittsburgh	**NHL**	**38**	**1**	**2**	**3**	**42**	**11**	**0**	**2**	**2**	**8**
1989-90	**Pittsburgh**	**NHL**	**69**	**1**	**8**	**9**	**125**	....	....	....	....	....
	NHL Totals		**400**	**14**	**65**	**79**	**568**	**40**	**1**	**7**	**8**	**68**

a CHL First All-Star Team (1983)
b Won Bob Gassoff Trophy (CHL's Most Improved Defenseman) (1983)
c Won Bobby Orr Trophy (CHL's Top Defenseman) (1983)

Traded to **Minnesota** by **NY Islanders** for Chris Pryor and future considerations, March 8, 1988. Traded to **Pittsburgh** by **Minnesota** with Scott Bjugstad for Ville Siren and Steve Gotaas, December 17, 1988.

DINEEN, KEVIN

Right wing. Shoots right. 5'11", 195 lbs. Born, Quebec City, Que., October 28, 1963.
(Hartford's 3rd choice, 56th overall, in 1982 Entry Draft).

			Regular Season					Playoffs				
Season	Club	Lea	GP	G	A	TP	PIM	GP	G	A	TP	PIM
1981-82	U. of Denver	WCHA	26	10	10	20	70	....	....	....	....	....
1982-83	U. of Denver	WCHA	36	16	13	29	108	....	....	....	....	....
1983-84	Cdn. Olympic	...	52	5	11	16	2	....	....	....	....	....
1984-85	**Hartford**	**NHL**	**57**	**25**	**16**	**41**	**120**	....	....	....	....	....
	Binghamton	AHL	25	15	8	23	41	....	....	....	....	....
1985-86	**Hartford**	**NHL**	**57**	**33**	**35**	**68**	**124**	**10**	**6**	**7**	**13**	**18**
1986-87	**Hartford**	**NHL**	**78**	**40**	**39**	**79**	**110**	**6**	**2**	**1**	**3**	**31**
1987-88	**Hartford**	**NHL**	**74**	**25**	**25**	**50**	**217**	**6**	**4**	**4**	**8**	**8**
1988-89	**Hartford**	**NHL**	**79**	**45**	**44**	**89**	**167**	**4**	**1**	**0**	**1**	**10**
1989-90	**Hartford**	**NHL**	**67**	**25**	**41**	**66**	**164**	**6**	**3**	**2**	**5**	**18**
	NHL Totals		**412**	**193**	**200**	**393**	**902**	**32**	**16**	**14**	**30**	**85**

Played in NHL All-Star Game (1988, 1989)

DINEEN, PETER KEVIN

Defense. Shoots right. 5'11", 190 lbs. Born, Kingston, Ont., November 19, 1960.
(Philadelphia's 9th choice, 189th overall, in 1980 Entry Draft).

			Regular Season					Playoffs				
Season	Club	Lea	GP	G	A	TP	PIM	GP	G	A	TP	PIM
1977-78	Seattle	WHL	....	....	....	....	....	2	0	0	0	0
1978-79	Kingston	OHA	60	7	14	21	70	11	2	6	8	28
1979-80	Kingston	OHA	32	4	10	14	54	3	0	0	0	13
1980-81	Maine	AHL	41	6	7	13	100	16	1	2	3	82
1981-82	Maine	AHL	71	6	14	20	156	3	0	0	0	2
1982-83	Maine	AHL	2	0	0	0	0	....	....	....	....	....
	Moncton	AHL	57	0	10	10	76	....	....	....	....	....
1983-84	Moncton	AHL	63	0	10	10	120	....	....	....	....	....
	Hershey	AHL	12	0	1	1	32	....	....	....	....	....
1984-85	Hershey	AHL	79	4	19	23	144	....	....	....	....	....
1985-86	Binghamton	AHL	11	0	1	1	35	....	....	....	....	....
	Moncton	AHL	55	5	13	18	136	9	1	0	1	9
1986-87	**Los Angeles**	**NHL**	**11**	**0**	**2**	**2**	**8**	....	....	....	....	....
	New Haven	AHL	59	2	17	19	140	7	0	1	1	27
1987-88	Adirondack	AHL	76	8	26	34	137	11	0	2	2	20
1988-89	Adirondack	AHL	32	2	12	14	61	17	2	5	7	22
1989-90	**Detroit**	**NHL**	**2**	**0**	**0**	**0**	**5**	....	....	....	....	....
	Adirondack	AHL	27	3	6	9	28	6	0	1	1	10
	NHL Totals		**13**	**0**	**2**	**2**	**13**	....	....	....	....	....

Traded to **Edmonton** by **Philadelphia** for Bob Hoffmeyer, October 22, 1982. Signed as a free agent by **Boston**, July 16, 1984. Signed as a free agent by Los Angeles, July 30, 1986.

DIRK, ROBERT

Defense. Shoots left. 6'4", 205 lbs. Born, Regina, Sask., August 20, 1966.
(St. Louis' 4th choice, 53rd overall, in 1984 Entry Draft).

			Regular Season					Playoffs				
Season	Club	Lea	GP	G	A	TP	PIM	GP	G	A	TP	PIM
1982-83	Regina	WHL	1	0	0	0	0	....	....	....	....	....
1983-84	Regina	WHL	62	2	10	12	64	23	1	12	13	24
1984-85	Regina	WHL	69	10	34	44	97	8	0	0	0	4
1985-86	Regina	WHL	72	19	60	79	140	10	3	5	8	8
1986-87	Peoria	IHL	76	5	17	22	155	....	....	....	....	....
1987-88	**St. Louis**	**NHL**	**7**	**0**	**1**	**1**	**16**	**6**	**0**	**1**	**1**	**2**
	Peoria	IHL	54	4	21	25	126	....	....	....	....	....
1988-89	**St. Louis**	**NHL**	**9**	**0**	**1**	**1**	**11**	....	....	....	....	....
	Peoria	IHL	22	0	2	2	54	....	....	....	....	....
1989-90	**St. Louis**	**NHL**	**37**	**1**	**1**	**2**	**128**	**3**	**0**	**0**	**0**	**0**
	Peoria	IHL	24	1	2	3	79	....	....	....	....	....
	NHL Totals		**53**	**1**	**3**	**4**	**155**	**9**	**0**	**1**	**1**	**2**

DI VITA, DAVID

Defense. Shoots left. 6'2", 205 lbs. Born, St. Clair Shores, MI, February 3, 1969.
(Buffalo's 6th choice, 106th overall, in 1988 Entry Draft).

			Regular Season					Playoffs				
Season	Club	Lea	GP	G	A	TP	PIM	GP	G	A	TP	PIM
1987-88	Lake Superior	CCHA	26	1	0	1	20	....	....	....	....	....
1988-89	Lake Superior	CCHA	25	1	4	5	28	....	....	....	....	....
1989-90	Lake Superior	CCHA	46	4	12	16	58	....	....	....	....	....

DJOOS, PER

Defense. Shoots left. 5'11", 170 lbs.   Born, Mora, Sweden, May 11, 1968.
(Detroit's 7th choice, 127th overall, in 1986 Entry Draft).

			Regular Season					Playoffs			
Season	Club	Lea	GP	G	A	TP	PIM	GP	G	A	TP	PIM
1986-87	Brynas	Swe.	23	1	2	3	16	....	....	..	..	..
1987-88	Brynas	Swe.	34	4	11	15	18	....	....	..	..	..
1988-89	Brynas	Swe.	40	1	17	18	44	....	....	..	..	..
1989-90	Brynas	Swe.	37	5	13	18	34	5	1	3	4	6

DOBBIN, BRIAN

Right wing. Shoots right. 5'11", 205 lbs.   Born, Petrolia, Ont., August 18, 1966.
(Philadelphia's 6th choice, 100th overall, in 1984 Entry Draft).

			Regular Season					Playoffs			
Season	Club	Lea	GP	G	A	TP	PIM	GP	G	A	TP	PIM
1983-84	London	OHL	70	30	40	70	70	....	....	..	..	..
1984-85	London	OHL	53	42	57	99	63	8	7	4	11	2
1985-86	London	OHL	59	38	55	93	113	5	2	1	3.	9
1986-87	**Philadelphia**	**NHL**	**12**	**2**	**1**	**3**	**14**	....	....	..	..	..
	Hershey	AHL	52	26	35	61	66	5	4	2	6	15
1987-88	**Philadelphia**	**NHL**	**21**	**3**	**5**	**8**	**6**	....	....	..	..	..
	Hershey	AHL	54	36	47	83	58	12	7	8	15	15
1988-89	**Philadelphia**	**NHL**	**14**	**0**	**1**	**1**	**8**	**2**	**0**	**0**	**0**	**17**
a	Hershey	AHL	59	43	48	91	61	11	7	6	13	12
1989-90	**Philadelphia**	**NHL**	**9**	**1**	**1**	**2**	**11**	....	....	..	..	..
b	Hershey	AHL	68	38	47	85	58	....	....	..	..	..
	NHL Totals		**56**	**6**	**8**	**14**	**39**	**2**	**0**	**0**	**0**	**17**

a AHL First All-Star Team (1989)
b AHL Second All-Star Team (1990)

DOERS, MICHAEL

Right wing. Shoots right. 6', 175 lbs.   Born, Madison, WI, June 17, 1971.
(Toronto's 7th choice, 125th overall, in 1989 Entry Draft).

			Regular Season					Playoffs			
Season	Club	Lea	GP	G	A	TP	PIM	GP	G	A	TP	PIM
1988-89	Northwood Prep	HS	28	19	24	43	....	....	....	..	..	..
1989-90	U. of Vermont	ECAC	30	2	11	13	26	....	....	..	..	..

DOLLAS, BOBBY

Defense. Shoots left. 6'2", 212 lbs.   Born, Montreal, Que., January 31, 1965.
(Winnipeg's 2nd choice, 14th overall, in 1983 Entry Draft).

			Regular Season					Playoffs			
Season	Club	Lea	GP	G	A	TP	PIM	GP	G	A	TP	PIM
1982-83a	Laval	QMJHL	63	16	45	61	144	11	5	5	10	23
1983-84	**Winnipeg**	**NHL**	**1**	**0**	**0**	**0**	**0**	....	....	..	..	..
	Laval	QMJHL	54	12	33	45	80	14	1	8	9	23
1984-85	**Winnipeg**	**NHL**	**9**	**0**	**0**	**0**	**0**	....	....	..	..	..
	Sherbrooke	AHL	8	1	3	4	4	17	3	6	9	17
1985-86	**Winnipeg**	**NHL**	**46**	**0**	**5**	**5**	**66**	**3**	**0**	**0**	**0**	**2**
	Sherbrooke	AHL	25	4	7	11	29	....	....	..	..	..
1986-87	Sherbrooke	AHL	75	6	18	24	87	16	2	4	6	13
1987-88	**Quebec**	**NHL**	**9**	**0**	**0**	**0**	**2**	....	....	..	..	..
	Moncton	AHL	26	4	10	14	20	....	....	..	..	..
	Fredericton	AHL	33	4	8	12	27	15	2	2	4	24
1988-89	**Quebec**	**NHL**	**16**	**0**	**3**	**3**	**16**	....	....	..	..	..
	Halifax	AHL	57	5	19	24	65	4	1	0	1	14
1989-90	Cdn. National	....	68	8	29	37	60	....	....	..	..	..
	NHL Totals		**81**	**0**	**8**	**8**	**84**	**3**	**0**	**0**	**0**	**2**

a QMJHL Second All-Star Team (1983).

Traded to **Quebec** by **Winnipeg** for Stu Kulak, December 17, 1987.

DOMI, TAHIR (TIE)

Right wing. Shoots right. 5'10", 200 lbs.   Born, Windsor, Ont., November 1, 1969.
(Toronto's 2nd choice, 27th overall, in 1988 Entry Draft).

			Regular Season					Playoffs			
Season	Club	Lea	GP	G	A	TP	PIM	GP	G	A	TP	PIM
1986-87	Peterborough	OHL	18	1	1	2	79	....	....	..	..	..
1987-88	Peterborough	OHL	60	22	21	43	292	12	3	9	12	24
1988-89	Peterborough	OHL	43	14	16	30	175	17	10	9	19	70
1989-90	**Toronto**	**NHL**	**2**	**0**	**0**	**0**	**42**	....	....	..	..	..
	Newmarket	AHL	57	14	11	25	285	....	....	..	..	..
	NHL Totals		**2**	**0**	**0**	**0**	**42**	....	....	..	..	..

Traded to **NY Rangers** by **Toronto** with Mark Laforest for Greg Johnston, June 28, 1990.

DONATELLI, CLARK

Left wing. Shoots left. 5'10", 190 lbs.   Born, Providence, RI, November 22, 1965.
(NY Rangers' 4th choice, 98th overall, in 1984 Entry Draft).

			Regular Season					Playoffs			
Season	Club	Lea	GP	G	A	TP	PIM	GP	G	A	TP	PIM
1984-85	Boston U.	H.E.	40	17	18	35	46	....	....	..	..	..
1985-86ab	Boston U.	H.E.	43	28	34	62	30	....	....	..	..	..
1986-87	Boston U.	H.E.	37	15	23	38	46	....	....	..	..	..
1987-88	U.S. National	....	50	11	27	38	26	....	....	..	..	..
	U.S. Olympic	....	6	2	1	3	5	....	....	..	..	..
1988-89			DID NOT PLAY									
1989-90	**Minnesota**	**NHL**	**25**	**3**	**3**	**6**	**17**	....	....	..	..	..
	Kalamazoo	IHL	27	8	9	17	47	4	0	2	2	12
	NHL Totals		**25**	**3**	**3**	**6**	**17**	....	....	..	..	..

a NCAA East Second All-American Team (1986)
b Hockey East Second All-Star Team (1986)

Traded to **Edmonton** by **NY Rangers** with Ville Kentala, Reijo Ruotsalainen and Jim Wiemer for Mike Golden, Don Jackson and Miloslav Horava, October 2, 1986. Signed as a free agent by **Minnesota**, June 20, 1989.

DONATO, TED

Center. Shoots left. 5'10", 170 lbs.   Born, Dedham, MA, April 28, 1968.
(Boston's 5th choice, 98th overall, in 1987 Entry Draft).

			Regular Season					Playoffs			
Season	Club	Lea	GP	G	A	TP	PIM	GP	G	A	TP	PIM
1987-88	Harvard	ECAC	28	12	14	26	24	....	....	..	..	..
1988-89	Harvard	ECAC	34	14	37	51	30	....	....	..	..	..
1989-90	Harvard	ECAC	16	5	6	11	34	....	....	..	..	..

DONNELLY, GORDON (GORD)

Right wing. Shoots right. 6'1", 202 lbs.   Born, Montreal, Que., April 5, 1962.
(St. Louis' 3rd choice, 62nd overall, in 1981 Entry Draft).

			Regular Season					Playoffs			
Season	Club	Lea	GP	G	A	TP	PIM	GP	G	A	TP	PIM
1980-81	Sherbrooke	QMJHL	67	15	23	38	252	14	1	2	3	35
1981-82	Sherbrooke	QMJHL	60	8	41	49	250	22	2	7	9	106
1982-83	Salt Lake	CHL	67	3	12	15	222	6	1	1	2	8
1983-84	**Quebec**	**NHL**	**38**	**0**	**5**	**5**	**60**	....	....	..	..	..
	Fredericton	AHL	30	2	3	5	146	7	1	1	2	43
1984-85	**Quebec**	**NHL**	**22**	**0**	**0**	**0**	**33**	....	....	..	..	..
	Fredericton	AHL	42	1	5	6	134	6	0	1	1	25
1985-86	**Quebec**	**NHL**	**36**	**2**	**2**	**4**	**85**	**1**	**0**	**0**	**0**	**0**
	Fredericton	AHL	38	3	5	8	103	5	0	0	0	33
1986-87	**Quebec**	**NHL**	**38**	**0**	**2**	**2**	**143**	**13**	**0**	**0**	**0**	**53**
1987-88	**Quebec**	**NHL**	**63**	**4**	**3**	**7**	**301**	....	....	..	..	..
1988-89	**Quebec**	**NHL**	**16**	**4**	**0**	**4**	**46**	....	....	..	..	..
	Winnipeg	**NHL**	**57**	**6**	**10**	**16**	**228**	....	....	..	..	..
1989-90	**Winnipeg**	**NHL**	**55**	**3**	**3**	**6**	**222**	**6**	**0**	**1**	**1**	**8**
	NHL Totals		**325**	**19**	**25**	**44**	**1118**	**20**	**0**	**1**	**1**	**61**

Rights transferred to **Quebec** by **St. Louis** with rights to Claude Julien when St. Louis signed Jacques Demers as coach, August 19, 1983. Traded to **Winnipeg** by **Quebec** for Mario Marois, December 6, 1988.

DONNELLY, MIKE

Left wing. Shoots left. 5'11", 185 lbs.   Born, Detroit, MI, October 10, 1963.

			Regular Season					Playoffs			
Season	Club	Lea	GP	G	A	TP	PIM	GP	G	A	TP	PIM
1982-83	Michigan State	CCHA	24	7	13	20	8	....	....	..	..	..
1983-84	Michigan State	CCHA	44	18	14	32	40	....	....	..	..	..
1984-85	Michigan State	CCHA	44	26	21	47	48	....	....	..	..	..
1985-86ab	Michigan State	CCHA	44	59	38	97	65	....	....	..	..	..
1986-87	**NY Rangers**	**NHL**	**5**	**1**	**1**	**2**	**0**	....	....	..	..	..
	New Haven	AHL	58	27	34	61	52	7	2	0	2	9
1987-88	**NY Rangers**	**NHL**	**17**	**2**	**2**	**4**	**8**	....	....	..	..	..
	Colorado	IHL	8	7	11	18	15	....	....	..	..	..
	Buffalo	**NHL**	**40**	**6**	**8**	**14**	**44**	....	....	..	..	..
1988-89	**Buffalo**	**NHL**	**22**	**4**	**6**	**10**	**10**	....	....	..	..	..
	Rochester	AHL	53	32	37	69	53	....	....	..	..	..
1989-90	**Buffalo**	**NHL**	**12**	**1**	**2**	**3**	**8**	....	....	..	..	..
	Rochester	AHL	68	43	55	98	71	16	*12	7	19	9
	NHL Totals		**96**	**14**	**19**	**33**	**70**	....	....	..	..	..

a CCHA First All-Star Team (1986)
b NCAA West First All-American Team (1986)

Signed as a free agent by **NY Rangers**, August 15, 1986. Traded to **Buffalo** by **NY Rangers** with Rangers' fifth round choice (Alexander Mogilny) in 1988 Entry Draft for Paul Cyr and Buffalo's tenth round choice (Eric Fenton) in 1988 Entry Draft, December 31, 1987.

DOOLEY, SEAN

Defense. Shoots left. 6'3", 215 lbs.   Born, Ipswich, MA, March 22, 1969.
(Buffalo's 8th choice, 148th overall, in 1987 Entry Draft).

			Regular Season					Playoffs			
Season	Club	Lea	GP	G	A	TP	PIM	GP	G	A	TP	PIM
1987-88	Merrimack	NCAA	3	0	0	0	0	....	....	..	..	..
1988-89	Merrimack	NCAA	19	2	8	10	10	....	....	..	..	..
1989-90	Merrimack	H.E.	22	1	2	3	31	....	....	..	..	..

DORE, DANIEL

Right wing. Shoots right. 6'3", 202 lbs.   Born, Ferme-Neuve, Que., April 9, 1970.
(Quebec's 2nd choice, 5th overall, in 1988 Entry Draft).

			Regular Season					Playoffs			
Season	Club	Lea	GP	G	A	TP	PIM	GP	G	A	TP	PIM
1986-87	Drummondville	QMJHL	68	23	41	64	229	8	0	1	1	18
1987-88	Drummondville	QMJHL	64	24	39	63	218	17	7	11	18	42
1988-89	Drummondville	QMJHL	62	33	58	91	236	4	2	3	5	14
1989-90	**Quebec**	**NHL**	**16**	**2**	**3**	**5**	**59**	....	....	..	..	..
	Chicoutimi	QMJHL	24	6	23	29	112	6	0	3	3	27
	NHL Totals		**16**	**2**	**3**	**5**	**59**	....	....	..	..	..

DORION, DAN

Center. Shoots right. 5'9", 180 lbs.   Born, Astoria, NY, March 2, 1963.
(New Jersey's 10th choice, 232nd overall, in 1982 Entry Draft).

			Regular Season					Playoffs			
Season	Club	Lea	GP	G	A	TP	PIM	GP	G	A	TP	PIM
1982-83	W. Michigan	CCHA	34	11	20	31	23	....	....	..	..	..
1983-84	W. Michigan	CCHA	42	41	50	91	42	....	....	..	..	..
1984-85	W. Michigan	CCHA	39	21	46	67	28	....	....	..	..	..
1985-86abc	W. Michigan	CCHA	42	42	62	104	48	....	....	..	..	..
	New Jersey	**NHL**	**3**	**1**	**1**	**2**	**0**	....	....	..	..	..
	Maine	AHL	....	....	....	....	....	5	2	2	4	0
1986-87	Maine	AHL	70	16	22	38	47	....	....	..	..	..
1987-88	**New Jersey**	**NHL**	**1**	**0**	**0**	**0**	**2**	....	....	..	..	..
	Utica	AHL	65	30	35	65	98	....	....	..	..	..
1988-89	Maine	AHL	16	2	3	5	13	....	....	..	..	..
	Utica	AHL	15	7	4	11	19	....	....	..	..	..
1989-90	Fiemme	Italy	29	37	32	69	66	1	1	0	1	0
	NHL Totals		**4**	**1**	**1**	**2**	**2**	....	....	..	..	..

a NCAA West First All-American Team (1986)
b CCHA First All-Star Team (1986)
c CCHA Player of the Year (1986)

Traded to **Boston** by **New Jersey** for Jean-Marc Lanthier, December 9, 1988.

DOUCET, WAYNE

Left wing. Shoots left. 6'2", 203 lbs. Born, Etobicoke, Ont., June 19, 1970.
(NY Islanders' 2nd choice, 29th overall, in 1988 Entry Draft).

			Regular Season					Playoffs				
Season	Club	Lea	GP	G	A	TP	PIM	GP	G	A	TP	PIM
1986-87	Sudbury	OHL	64	20	28	48	85	....	....	....	....	....
1987-88	Sudbury	OHL	23	9	4	13	53	....	....	....	....	....
	Hamilton	OHL	37	11	14	25	74	1	0	0	0	8
1988-89	Springfield	AHL	6	2	2	4	4	....	....	....	....	....
	North Bay	OHL	11	3	2	5	58	....	....	....	....	....
	Kingston	OHL	53	22	29	51	193	....	....	....	....	....
1989-90	Kingston	OHL	66	32	47	79	127	7	2	5	7	18

DOURIS, PETER

Right wing. Shoots right. 6'1", 195 lbs. Born, Toronto, Ont., February 19, 1966.
(Winnipeg's 1st choice, 30th overall, in 1984 Entry Draft).

			Regular Season					Playoffs				
Season	Club	Lea	GP	G	A	TP	PIM	GP	G	A	TP	PIM
1983-84	N. Hampshire	ECAC	37	19	15	34	14	....	....	....	....	....
1984-85	N. Hampshire	H.E.	42	27	24	51	34	....	....	....	....	....
1985-86	**Winnipeg**	**NHL**	**11**	**0**	**0**	**0**	**0**	....	....	....	....	....
	Cdn. Olympic	....	33	16	7	23	18	....	....	....	....	....
1986-87	**Winnipeg**	**NHL**	**6**	**0**	**0**	**0**	**0**	....	....	....	....	....
	Sherbrooke	AHL	62	14	28	42	24	17	7	*15	*22	16
1987-88	**Winnipeg**	**NHL**	**4**	**0**	**2**	**2**	**0**	**1**	**0**	**0**	**0**	**0**
	Moncton	AHL	73	42	37	79	53	....	....	....	....	....
1988-89	Peoria	IHL	81	28	41	69	32	4	1	2	3	0
1989-90	**Boston**	**NHL**	**36**	**5**	**6**	**11**	**15**	**8**	**0**	**1**	**1**	**8**
	Maine	AHL	38	17	20	37	14	....	....	....	....	....
	NHL Totals		**57**	**5**	**8**	**13**	**15**	**9**	**0**	**1**	**1**	**8**

Traded to **St. Louis** by **Winnipeg** for Kent Carlson and St. Louis' twelfth-round choice (Sergei Kharin) in 1989 Entry Draft and St. Louis' fourth-round choice (Scott Levins) in 1990 Entry Draft, September 29, 1988. Signed as a free agent by **Boston**, June 27, 1989.

DOWD, JAMES (JIM)

Right wing. Shoots right. 6'1", 185 lbs. Born, Brick, NJ, December 25, 1968.
(New Jersey's 7th choice, 149th overall, in 1987 Entry Draft).

			Regular Season					Playoffs				
Season	Club	Lea	GP	G	A	TP	PIM	GP	G	A	TP	PIM
1987-88	Lake Superior	CCHA	45	18	27	45	16	....	....	....	....	....
1988-89	Lake Superior	CCHA	46	24	35	59	40	....	....	....	....	....
1989-90ab	Lake Superior	CCHA	46	25	*67	92	30	....	....	....	....	....

a CCHA Second All-Star Team (1990)
b NCAA West Second All-American Team (1990)

DOYLE, SHANE

Defense. Shoots left. 6'1", 200 lbs. Born, Lindsay, Ont., April 26, 1967.
(Vancouver's 3rd choice, 46th overall, in 1985 Entry Draft).

			Regular Season					Playoffs				
Season	Club	Lea	GP	G	A	TP	PIM	GP	G	A	TP	PIM
1984-85	Belleville	OHL	59	2	26	28	129	11	1	3	4	11
1985-86	Cornwall	OHL	55	4	28	32	206	6	1	0	1	17
1986-87	Oshawa	OHL	46	9	13	22	168	23	4	4	8	115
1987-88	Utica	AHL	14	0	1	1	38	....	....	....	....	....
	Flint	IHL	13	1	1	2	81	....	....	....	....	....
	Oshawa	OHL	21	3	18	21	66	3	0	2	2	6
1988-89	Indianapolis	IHL	62	4	36	40	224	....	....	....	....	....
1989-90	Winston-Salem	ECHL	7	1	4	5	44	....	....	....	....	....

Rights traded to **New Jersey** by **Vancouver** for New Jersey's twelfth-round choice (Neil Eisenhut) in 1987 Entry Draft, June 1, 1987.

DOYON, MARIO

Defense. Shoots right. 6', 174 lbs. Born, Quebec City, Que., August 27, 1968.
(Chicago's 5th choice, 119th overall, in 1986 Entry Draft).

			Regular Season					Playoffs				
Season	Club	Lea	GP	G	A	TP	PIM	GP	G	A	TP	PIM
1985-86	Drummondville	QMJHL	71	5	14	19	129	23	5	4	9	32
1986-87	Drummondville	QMJHL	65	18	47	65	150	8	1	3	4	30
1987-88	Drummondville	QMJHL	68	23	54	77	233	17	3	14	17	46
1988-89	**Chicago**	**NHL**	**7**	**1**	**1**	**2**	**6**	....	....	....	....	....
	Saginaw	IHL	71	16	32	48	69	6	0	0	0	8
1989-90	**Quebec**	**NHL**	**9**	**2**	**3**	**5**	**6**	....	....	....	....	....
	Indianapolis	IHL	66	9	25	34	50	....	....	....	....	....
	Halifax	AHL	5	1	2	3	0	6	1	3	4	2
	NHL Totals		**16**	**3**	**4**	**7**	**12**	....	....	....	....	....

Traded to **Quebec** by **Chicago** with Everett Sanipass and Dan Vincelette for Greg Millen, Michel Goulet and Quebec's sixth round choice in 1991 Entry Draft, March 5, 1990.

DRAGON, JOE

Center. Shoots right. 5'10", 185 lbs. Born, Fort Smith, N.W.T., February 20, 1969.
(Pittsburgh's 1st choice, 5th overall, in 1990 Supplemental Draft).

			Regular Season					Playoffs				
Season	Club	Lea	GP	G	A	TP	PIM	GP	G	A	TP	PIM
1988-89	Cornell	ECAC	3	1	1	2	2	....	....	....	....	....
1989-90	Cornell	ECAC	29	15	24	39	26	....	....	....	....	....

DRAKE, DALLAS

Center. Shoots left. 6', 165 lbs. Born, Trail, B.C., February 4, 1969.
(Detroit's 6th choice, 116th overall, in 1989 Entry Draft).

			Regular Season					Playoffs				
Season	Club	Lea	GP	G	A	TP	PIM	GP	G	A	TP	PIM
1988-89	N. Michigan	WCHA	38	17	22	39	22	....	....	....	....	....
1989-90	N. Michigan	WCHA	46	13	24	37	42	....	....	....	....	....

DRAPER, KRIS

Center. Shoots left. 5'11", 190 lbs. Born, Toronto, Ont., May 24, 1971.
(Winnipeg's 4th choice, 62nd overall, in 1989 Entry Draft).

			Regular Season					Playoffs				
Season	Club	Lea	GP	G	A	TP	PIM	GP	G	A	TP	PIM
1988-89	Cdn. National	....	60	11	15	26	16	....	....	....	....	....
1989-90	Cdn. National	....	61	12	22	34	44	....	....	....	....	....

DRIVER, BRUCE

Defense. Shoots left. 6', 185 lbs. Born, Toronto, Ont., April 29, 1962.
(Colorado's 6th choice, 108th overall, in 1981 Entry Draft).

			Regular Season					Playoffs				
Season	Club	Lea	GP	G	A	TP	PIM	GP	G	A	TP	PIM
1980-81	U. Wisconsin	WCHA	42	5	15	20	42	....	....	....	....	....
1981-82ab	U. Wisconsin	WCHA	46	7	37	44	84	....	....	....	....	....
1982-83	U. Wisconsin	WCHA	49	19	42	61	100	....	....	....	....	....
1983-84	Cdn. Olympic	....	61	11	17	28	44	....	....	....	....	....
	New Jersey	**NHL**	**4**	**0**	**2**	**2**	**0**	....	....	....	....	....
	Maine	AHL	12	2	6	8	15	16	0	10	10	8
1984-85	**New Jersey**	**NHL**	**67**	**9**	**23**	**32**	**36**	....	....	....	....	....
1985-86	**New Jersey**	**NHL**	**40**	**3**	**15**	**18**	**32**	....	....	....	....	....
	Maine	AHL	15	4	7	11	16	....	....	....	....	....
1986-87	**New Jersey**	**NHL**	**74**	**6**	**28**	**34**	**36**	....	....	....	....	....
1987-88	**New Jersey**	**NHL**	**74**	**15**	**40**	**55**	**68**	**20**	**3**	**7**	**10**	**14**
1988-89	**New Jersey**	**NHL**	**27**	**1**	**15**	**16**	**24**	....	....	....	....	....
1989-90	**New Jersey**	**NHL**	**75**	**7**	**46**	**53**	**63**	**6**	**1**	**5**	**6**	**6**
	NHL Totals		**361**	**41**	**169**	**210**	**259**	**26**	**4**	**12**	**16**	**20**

a WCHA First All-Team (1982)
b NCAA All-Tournament Team (1982)

DRUCE, JOHN

Right wing. Shoots right. 6'2", 200 lbs. Born, Peterborough, Ont., February 23, 1966.
(Washington's 2nd choice, 40th overall, in 1985 Entry Draft).

			Regular Season					Playoffs				
Season	Club	Lea	GP	G	A	TP	PIM	GP	G	A	TP	PIM
1984-85	Peterborough	OHL	54	12	14	26	90	17	6	2	8	21
1985-86	Peterborough	OHL	49	22	24	46	84	16	0	5	5	34
1986-87	Binghamton	AHL	77	13	9	22	131	12	0	3	3	28
1987-88	Binghamton	AHL	68	32	29	61	82	1	0	0	0	0
1988-89	**Washington**	**NHL**	**48**	**8**	**7**	**15**	**62**	**1**	**0**	**0**	**0**	**0**
	Baltimore	AHL	16	2	11	13	10	....	....	....	....	....
1989-90	**Washington**	**NHL**	**45**	**8**	**3**	**11**	**52**	**15**	**14**	**3**	**17**	**23**
	Baltimore	AHL	26	15	16	31	38	....	....	....	....	....
	NHL Totals		**93**	**16**	**10**	**26**	**114**	**16**	**14**	**3**	**17**	**23**

DRULIA, STAN

Right wing. Shoots right. 5'10", 190 lbs. Born, Elmira, NY, January 5, 1968.
(Pittsburgh's 11th choice, 214th overall, in 1986 Entry Draft).

			Regular Season					Playoffs				
Season	Club	Lea	GP	G	A	TP	PIM	GP	G	A	TP	PIM
1985-86	Belleville	OHL	66	43	36	79	73	....	....	....	....	....
1986-87	Hamilton	OHL	55	27	51	78	26	....	....	....	....	....
1987-88a	Hamilton	OHL	65	52	69	121	44	14	8	16	24	12
1988-89	Maine	AHL	3	1	1	2	0	....	....	....	....	....
b	Niagara Falls	OHL	47	52	93	145	59	17	11	*26	37	18
1989-90	Phoenix	IHL	16	6	3	9	2	....	....	....	....	....
	Cape Breton	AHL	31	5	7	12	2	....	....	....	....	....

a OHL Third All-Star Team (1988)
b OHL First All-Star Team (1989)

DRURY, TED

Center. Shoots left. 6'1", 185 lbs. Born, Boston, MA, September 13, 1971.
(Calgary's 2nd choice, 42nd overall, in 1989 Entry Draft).

			Regular Season					Playoffs				
Season	Club	Lea	GP	G	A	TP	PIM	GP	G	A	TP	PIM
1988-89	Fairfield Prep	HS	....	35	31	66	....	....	....	....	....	....
1989-90	Harvard	ECAC	17	9	13	22	10	....	....	....	....	....

DUBERMAN, JUSTIN

Right wing. Shoots right. 6', 185 lbs. Born, New Haven, CT, March 23, 1970.
(Montreal's 11th choice, 230th overall, in 1989 Entry Draft).

			Regular Season					Playoffs				
Season	Club	Lea	GP	G	A	TP	PIM	GP	G	A	TP	PIM
1988-89	North Dakota	WCHA	33	3	1	4	30	....	....	....	....	....
1989-90	North Dakota	WCHA	42	10	9	19	50	....	....	....	....	....

DUBOIS, ERIC

Defense. Shoots right. 6', 195 lbs. Born, Montreal, Que., May 20, 1971.
(Quebec's 6th choice, 76th overall, in 1989 Entry Draft).

			Regular Season					Playoffs				
Season	Club	Lea	GP	G	A	TP	PIM	GP	G	A	TP	PIM
1987-88	Laval	QMJHL	69	8	32	40	132	14	1	7	8	12
1988-89	Laval	QMJHL	68	15	44	59	126	17	1	11	12	55
1989-90	Laval	QMJHL	66	9	36	45	153	13	3	8	11	29

DUCHESNE, GAETAN (doo SHAYN)

Left wing. Shoots left. 5'11", 197 lbs. Born, Quebec City, Que., July 11, 1962.
(Washington's 8th choice, 152nd overall, in 1981 Entry Draft).

			Regular Season					Playoffs				
Season	Club	Lea	GP	G	A	TP	PIM	GP	G	A	TP	PIM
1979-80	Quebec	QJHL	46	9	28	37	22	5	0	2	2	9
1980-81	Quebec	QJHL	72	27	45	72	63	7	1	4	5	6
1981-82	**Washington**	**NHL**	**74**	**9**	**14**	**23**	**46**	....	....	....	....	....
1982-83	Hershey	AHL	1	1	0	1	0	....	....	....	....	....
	Washington	**NHL**	**77**	**18**	**19**	**37**	**52**	**4**	**1**	**1**	**2**	**4**
1983-84	**Washington**	**NHL**	**79**	**17**	**19**	**36**	**29**	**8**	**2**	**1**	**3**	**2**
1984-85	**Washington**	**NHL**	**67**	**15**	**23**	**38**	**32**	**5**	**0**	**1**	**1**	**7**
1985-86	**Washington**	**NHL**	**80**	**11**	**28**	**39**	**39**	**9**	**4**	**3**	**7**	**12**
1986-87	**Washington**	**NHL**	**74**	**17**	**35**	**52**	**53**	**7**	**3**	**0**	**3**	**14**
1987-88	**Quebec**	**NHL**	**80**	**24**	**23**	**47**	**83**	....	....	....	....	....
1988-89	**Quebec**	**NHL**	**70**	**8**	**21**	**29**	**56**	....	....	....	....	....
1989-90	**Minnesota**	**NHL**	**72**	**12**	**8**	**20**	**33**	**7**	**0**	**0**	**0**	**6**
	NHL Totals		**673**	**131**	**190**	**321**	**423**	**40**	**10**	**6**	**16**	**45**

Traded to **Quebec** by **Washington** with Alan Haworth and Washington's first-round choice (Joe Sakic) in 1987 Entry Draft for Clint Malarchuk and Dale Hunter, June 13, 1987. Traded to **Minnesota** by **Quebec** for Kevin Kaminski, June 19, 1989.

DUCHESNE, STEVE

Defense. Shoots left. 5'11", 195 lbs. Born, Sept-Iles, Que., June 30, 1965.

			Regular Season					Playoffs				
Season	Club	Lea	GP	G	A	TP	PIM	GP	G	A	TP	PIM
1983-84	Drummondville	QMJHL	67	1	34	35	79	....	....	....	....	....
1984-85a	Drummondville	QMJHL	65	22	54	76	94	5	4	7	11	8
1985-86	New Haven	AHL	75	14	35	49	76	5	0	2	2	9
1986-87b	**Los Angeles**	**NHL**	**75**	**13**	**25**	**38**	**74**	**5**	**2**	**2**	**4**	**4**
1987-88	**Los Angeles**	**NHL**	**71**	**16**	**39**	**55**	**109**	**5**	**1**	**3**	**4**	**14**
1988-89	**Los Angeles**	**NHL**	**79**	**25**	**50**	**75**	**92**	**11**	**4**	**4**	**8**	**12**
1989-90	**Los Angeles**	**NHL**	**70**	**20**	**42**	**62**	**36**	**10**	**2**	**9**	**11**	**6**
	NHL Totals		**295**	**74**	**156**	**230**	**311**	**31**	**9**	**18**	**27**	**36**

a QMJHL First All-Star Team (1985)
b NHL All-Rookie Team (1987)

Played in NHL All-Star Game (1989, 1990)

Signed as a free agent by **Los Angeles,** October 1, 1984.

DUCOLON, TOBY

Right wing. Shoots right. 6', 195 lbs. Born, St. Albans, VT, June 18, 1966.
(St. Louis' 3rd choice, 50th overall, in 1984 Entry Draft).

			Regular Season					Playoffs				
Season	Club	Lea	GP	G	A	TP	PIM	GP	G	A	TP	PIM
1984-85	U. of Vermont	ECAC	24	7	4	11	14	....	....	....	....	....
1985-86	U. of Vermont	ECAC	30	10	6	16	48	....	....	....	....	....
1986-87	U. of Vermont	ECAC	32	9	11	20	42	....	....	....	....	....
1987-88	U. of Vermont	ECAC	34	21	18	39	62	....	....	....	....	....
1988-89	Peoria	IHL	73	17	33	50	58	4	0	0	0	9
1989-90	Peoria	IHL	62	11	14	25	22	3	0	0	0	12

DUFRESNE, DONALD (DOO-FRAYN)

Defense. Shoots left. 6'1", 206 lbs. Born, Rimouski, Que., April 10, 1967.
(Montreal's 8th choice, 117th overall, in 1985 Entry Draft).

			Regular Season					Playoffs				
Season	Club	Lea	GP	G	A	TP	PIM	GP	G	A	TP	PIM
1983-84	Trois Rivieres	QMJHL	67	7	12	19	97	....	....	....	....	....
1984-85	Trois Rivieres	QMJHL	65	5	30	35	112	7	1	3	4	12
1985-86a	Trois Rivieres	QMJHL	63	8	32	40	160	1	0	0	0	0
1986-87a	Trois Rivieres	QMJHL	51	5	21	26	79	....	....	....	....	....
	Longueuil	QMJHL	16	0	8	8	18	20	1	8	9	38
1987-88	Sherbrooke	AHL	47	1	8	9	107	6	1	0	1	34
1988-89	**Montreal**	**NHL**	**13**	**0**	**1**	**1**	**43**	**6**	**1**	**1**	**2**	**4**
	Sherbrooke	AHL	47	0	12	12	170	....	....	....	....	....
1989-90	**Montreal**	**NHL**	**18**	**0**	**4**	**4**	**23**	**10**	**0**	**1**	**1**	**18**
	Sherbrooke	AHL	38	2	11	13	104	....	....	....	....	....
	NHL Totals		**31**	**0**	**5**	**5**	**66**	**16**	**1**	**2**	**3**	**22**

a QMJHL Second All-Star Team (1986, 1987)

DUGUAY, RONALD (RON) (doo-GAY)

Center. Shoots right. 6'2", 210 lbs. Born, Sudbury, Ont., July 6, 1957.
(NY Rangers' 2nd choice, 13th overall, in 1977 Amateur Draft).

			Regular Season					Playoffs				
Season	Club	Lea	GP	G	A	TP	PIM	GP	G	A	TP	PIM
1975-76a	Sudbury	OHA	61	42	92	134	101	17	11	9	20	37
1976-77	Sudbury	OHA	61	43	66	109	109	6	4	3	7	5
1977-78	**NY Rangers**	**NHL**	**71**	**20**	**20**	**40**	**43**	**3**	**1**	**1**	**2**	**2**
1978-79	**NY Rangers**	**NHL**	**79**	**27**	**36**	**63**	**35**	**18**	**5**	**4**	**9**	**11**
1979-80	**NY Rangers**	**NHL**	**73**	**28**	**22**	**50**	**37**	**9**	**5**	**2**	**7**	**11**
1980-81	**NY Rangers**	**NHL**	**50**	**17**	**21**	**38**	**83**	**14**	**8**	**9**	**17**	**16**
1981-82	**NY Rangers**	**NHL**	**72**	**40**	**36**	**76**	**82**	**10**	**5**	**1**	**6**	**31**
1982-83	**NY Rangers**	**NHL**	**72**	**19**	**25**	**44**	**58**	**9**	**2**	**2**	**4**	**28**
1983-84	**Detroit**	**NHL**	**80**	**33**	**47**	**80**	**34**	**4**	**2**	**3**	**5**	**2**
1984-85	**Detroit**	**NHL**	**80**	**38**	**51**	**89**	**51**	**3**	**1**	**0**	**1**	**7**
1985-86	**Detroit**	**NHL**	**67**	**19**	**29**	**48**	**26**	....	....	....	....	....
	Pittsburgh	**NHL**	**13**	**6**	**7**	**13**	**6**	....	....	....	....	....
1986-87	**Pittsburgh**	**NHL**	**40**	**5**	**13**	**18**	**30**	....	....	....	....	....
	NY Rangers	**NHL**	**34**	**9**	**12**	**21**	**9**	**6**	**2**	**0**	**2**	**4**
1987-88	**NY Rangers**	**NHL**	**48**	**4**	**4**	**8**	**23**	....	....	....	....	....
	Colorado	IHL	2	0	0	0	0	....	....	....	....	....
	Los Angeles	**NHL**	**15**	**2**	**6**	**8**	**17**	**2**	**0**	**0**	**0**	**0**
1988-89	**Los Angeles**	**NHL**	**70**	**7**	**17**	**24**	**48**	**11**	**0**	**0**	**0**	**6**
1989-90	Mannheimer	W. Ger.	22	11	7	18	38	....	....	....	....	....
	NHL Totals		**864**	**274**	**346**	**620**	**582**	**89**	**31**	**22**	**53**	**118**

a OHA Third All-Star Team (1976)

Played in NHL All-Star Game (1982)

Traded to **Detroit** by **NY Rangers** with Eddie Mio and Eddie Johnstone for Willie Huber, Mark Osborne and Mike Blaisdell, June 13, 1983. Traded to **Pittsburgh** by **Detroit** for Doug Shedden, March 11, 1986. Traded to **NY Rangers** by **Pittsburgh** for Chris Kontos, January 21, 1987. Traded to **Los Angeles** by **NY Rangers** for Mark Hardy, February 23, 1988.

DUKOVAC, PAUL C.

Defense. Shoots right. 6'1", 180 lbs. Born, New Liskeard, Ont., January 18, 1969.
(Vancouver's 1st choice, 2nd overall, in 1990 Supplemental Draft).

			Regular Season					Playoffs				
Season	Club	Lea	GP	G	A	TP	PIM	GP	G	A	TP	PIM
1988-89	Cornell	ECAC	14	1	4	5	8	....	....	....	....	....
1989-90	Cornell	ECAC	29	1	8	9	34	....	....	....	....	....

DUNCAN, IAIN

Left wing. Shoots left. 6'1", 200 lbs. Born, Weston, Ont., August 4, 1963.
(Winnipeg's 8th choice, 139th overall, in 1983 Entry Draft).

			Regular Season					Playoffs				
Season	Club	Lea	GP	G	A	TP	PIM	GP	G	A	TP	PIM
1983-84	Bowling Green	CCHA	44	11	20	31	65	....	....	....	....	....
1984-85	Bowling Green	CCHA	37	9	21	30	105	....	....	....	....	....
1985-86	Bowling Green	CCHA	41	26	26	52	124	....	....	....	....	....
1986-87a	Bowling Green	CCHA	39	28	40	68	141	....	....	....	....	....
	Winnipeg	**NHL**	**6**	**1**	**2**	**3**	**0**	**7**	**0**	**2**	**2**	**6**
1987-88b	**Winnipeg**	**NHL**	**62**	**19**	**23**	**42**	**73**	**4**	**0**	**1**	**1**	**0**
	Moncton	AHL	8	1	3	4	26	....	....	....	....	....
1988-89	**Winnipeg**	**NHL**	**57**	**14**	**30**	**44**	**74**	....	....	....	....	....
1989-90	Moncton	AHL	49	16	25	41	81	....	....	....	....	....
	NHL Totals		**125**	**34**	**55**	**89**	**147**	**11**	**0**	**3**	**3**	**6**

a CCHA First All-Star Team (1987)
b NHL All-Rookie Team (1988)

DUNCANSON, CRAIG

Left wing. Shoots left. 6', 190 lbs. Born, Sudbury, Ont., March 17, 1967.
(Los Angeles' 1st choice, 9th overall, in 1985 Entry Draft).

			Regular Season					Playoffs				
Season	Club	Lea	GP	G	A	TP	PIM	GP	G	A	TP	PIM
1983-84	Sudbury	OHL	62	38	38	76	176	....	....	....	....	....
1984-85a	Sudbury	OHL	53	35	28	63	129	....	....	....	....	....
1985-86	**Los Angeles**	**NHL**	**2**	**0**	**1**	**1**	**0**	....	....	....	....	....
	Sudbury	OHL	21	12	17	29	55	....	....	....	....	....
	Cornwall	OHL	40	31	50	81	135	6	4	7	11	2
	New Haven	AHL	....	....	....	....	....	2	0	0	0	5
1986-87	**Los Angeles**	**NHL**	**2**	**0**	**0**	**0**	**24**	....	....	....	....	....
	Cornwall	OHL	52	22	45	67	88	5	4	3	7	20
1987-88	**Los Angeles**	**NHL**	**9**	**0**	**0**	**0**	**12**	....	....	....	....	....
	New Haven	AHL	57	15	25	40	170	....	....	....	....	....
1988-89	**Los Angeles**	**NHL**	**5**	**0**	**0**	**0**	**0**	....	....	....	....	....
	New Haven	AHL	69	25	39	64	200	17	4	8	12	60
1989-90	**Los Angeles**	**NHL**	**10**	**3**	**2**	**5**	**9**	....	....	....	....	....
	New Haven	AHL	51	17	30	47	152	....	....	....	....	....
	NHL Totals		**28**	**3**	**3**	**6**	**45**	....	....	....	....	....

a OHL Third All-Star Team (1985)

DUNDAS, ROCKY

Right wing. Shoots right. 6', 195 lbs. Born, Regina, Sask., January 30, 1967.
(Montreal's 4th choice, 47th overall, in 1985 Entry Draft).

			Regular Season					Playoffs				
Season	Club	Lea	GP	G	A	TP	PIM	GP	G	A	TP	PIM
1983-84	Kelowna	WHL	72	15	24	39	57	....	....	....	....	....
1984-85	Kelowna	WHL	71	32	44	76	117	6	1	1	2	14
1985-86	Spokane	WHL	71	31	70	101	160	9	2	5	7	28
1986-87	Spokane	WHL	19	13	17	30	69	....	....	....	....	....
	Medicine Hat	WHL	29	22	24	46	63	20	4	8	12	44
1987-88	Baltimore	AHL	9	0	1	1	46	....	....	....	....	....
	Sherbrooke	AHL	38	9	6	15	104	3	0	0	0	7
1988-89	Sherbrooke	AHL	63	12	29	41	212	2	2	0	2	8
1989-90	**Toronto**	**NHL**	**5**	**0**	**0**	**0**	**14**	....	....	....	....	....
	Newmarket	AHL	62	18	15	33	158	....	....	....	....	....
	NHL Totals		**5**	**0**	**0**	**0**	**14**	....	....	....	....	....

DUNN, RICHARD L. (RICHIE)

Defense. Shoots left. 6', 200 lbs. Born, Boston, MA, May 12, 1957.

			Regular Season					Playoffs				
Season	Club	Lea	GP	G	A	TP	PIM	GP	G	A	TP	PIM
1975-76	Kingston	OHA	61	7	18	25	62	....	....	....	....	....
1976-77	Windsor	OHA	65	5	21	26	98	9	0	5	5	4
1977-78	Hershey	AHL	54	7	22	29	17	....	....	....	....	....
	Buffalo	**NHL**	**25**	**0**	**3**	**3**	**16**	**1**	**0**	**0**	**0**	**2**
1978-79	**Buffalo**	**NHL**	**24**	**0**	**3**	**3**	**14**	....	....	....	....	....
	Hershey	AHL	34	5	18	23	10	4	0	1	1	4
1979-80	**Buffalo**	**NHL**	**80**	**7**	**31**	**38**	**61**	**14**	**2**	**8**	**10**	**8**
1980-81	**Buffalo**	**NHL**	**79**	**7**	**42**	**49**	**34**	**8**	**0**	**5**	**5**	**6**
1981-82	**Buffalo**	**NHL**	**72**	**7**	**19**	**26**	**73**	**4**	**0**	**1**	**1**	**0**
1982-83	**Calgary**	**NHL**	**80**	**3**	**11**	**14**	**47**	**9**	**1**	**1**	**2**	**8**
1983-84	**Hartford**	**NHL**	**63**	**5**	**20**	**25**	**30**	....	....	....	....	....
1984-85	**Hartford**	**NHL**	**13**	**1**	**4**	**5**	**2**	....	....	....	....	....
ab	Binghamton	AHL	64	9	39	48	43	8	2	2	4	8
1985-86	**Buffalo**	**NHL**	**29**	**4**	**5**	**9**	**25**	....	....	....	....	....
	Rochester	AHL	34	6	17	23	12	....	....	....	....	....
1986-87	**Buffalo**	**NHL**	**2**	**0**	**1**	**1**	**2**	....	....	....	....	....
b	Rochester	AHL	64	6	26	32	47	18	1	6	7	6
1987-88	**Buffalo**	**NHL**	**12**	**2**	**0**	**2**	**8**	....	....	....	....	....
c	Rochester	AHL	68	12	35	47	52	7	3	3	6	2
1988-89	**Buffalo**	**NHL**	**4**	**0**	**1**	**1**	**2**	....	....	....	....	....
	Rochester	AHL	69	9	35	44	81	....	....	....	....	....
1989-90	Rochester	AHL	41	7	7	14	34	7	0	4	4	4
	NHL Totals		**483**	**36**	**140**	**176**	**314**	**36**	**3**	**15**	**18**	**24**

a Won Eddie Shore Plaque (AHL Outstanding Defenseman 1985)
b AHL First All-Star Team (1985, 1987)
c AHL Second All-Star Team (1988)

Signed as free agent by **Buffalo**, October 3, 1977. Traded to **Calgary** by **Buffalo** with Don Edwards and Buffalo's second round choice (Richard Kromm) in 1982 Entry Draft for Calgary's first round choice (Paul Cyr) and second round choice (Jens Johansson) in the 1982 Entry Draft and Calgary's second round choice (John Tucker) in 1983 Entry Draft, June 9, 1982. In addition, the two clubs exchanged first round draft choices in 1983 — Buffalo claimed Normand Lacombe and Calgary selected Dan Quinn. Traded to **Hartford** by **Calgary** with Joel Quenneville for Mickey Volcan, July 5, 1983. Signed as a free agent by **Buffalo**, July 10, 1985.

DUPUIS, GUY

Defense. Shoots right. 6'2", 200 lbs. Born, Moncton, N.B., May 10, 1970.
(Detroit's 3rd choice, 47th overall, in 1988 Entry Draft).

				Regular Season					Playoffs			
Season	Club	Lea	GP	G	A	TP	PIM	GP	G	A	TP	PIM
1986-87	Hull	QMJHL	69	5	10	15	35	8	1	2	3	2
1987-88	Hull	QMJHL	69	14	34	48	72	19	3	8	11	29
1988-89a	Hull	QMJHL	70	15	56	71	89	9	3	3	6	8
1989-90	Hull	QMJHL	70	8	41	49	96	11	1	3	4	8

a QMJHL Second All-Star Team (1989)

DUUS, JESPER

Defense. Shoots right. 5'11", 175 lbs. Born, Rodovre, Denmark, November 24, 1967.
(Edmonton's 12th choice, 241st overall, in 1987 Entry Draft).

				Regular Season					Playoffs			
Season	Club	Lea	GP	G	A	TP	PIM	GP	G	A	TP	PIM
1985-86	Rodovre	Den.	24	3	5	8	28	6	1	2	3	4
1986-87	Rodovre	Den.	24	6	14	20	14	6	1	3	4	6
1987-88	Farjestad	Swe.	26	2	5	7	8	....	....	....	....	....
1988-89	Farjestad	Swe.	36	4	4	8	10	....	....	....	....	....
1989-90	Farjestad	Swe.	41	4	9	13	28	10	1	0	1	4

DUVAL, MURRAY

Defense. Shoots left. 6'1", 195 lbs. Born, Thompson, Man., January 22, 1970.
(New York Rangers' 2nd choice, 26th overall, in 1988 Entry Draft).

				Regular Season					Playoffs			
Season	Club	Lea	GP	G	A	TP	PIM	GP	G	A	TP	PIM
1986-87	Spokane	WHL	27	2	6	8	21	....	....	....	....	....
1987-88	Spokane	WHL	70	26	37	63	104	15	5	2	7	22
1988-89	Tri-Cities	WHL	71	14	28	42	144	....	....	....	....	....
1989-90	Tri-Cities	WHL	7	4	4	8	10	....	....	....	....	....
	Kamloops	WHL	56	14	36	50	94	17	8	7	15	29

DYER, DEAN

Center. Shoots right. 6'3", 195 lbs. Born, Sherwood Park, Alta., April 11, 1969.
(Hartford's 3rd choice, 74th overall, in 1988 Entry Draft).

				Regular Season					Playoffs			
Season	Club	Lea	GP	G	A	TP	PIM	GP	G	A	TP	PIM
1987-88	Lake Superior	CCHA	45	6	16	22	38	....	....	....	....	....
1988-89	Lake Superior	CCHA	41	4	11	15	52	....	....	....	....	....
1989-90	Lake Superior	CCHA	9	0	2	2	8	....	....	....	....	....

DYKHUIS, KARL

Defense. Shoots left. 6'3", 185 lbs. Born, Sept-Iles, Que., July 8, 1972.
(Chicago's 1st choice, 16th overall, in 1990 Entry Draft).

				Regular Season					Playoffs			
Season	Club	Lea	GP	G	A	TP	PIM	GP	G	A	TP	PIM
1988-89	Hull	QMJHL	63	2	29	31	59	9	1	9	10	6
1989-90a	Hull	QMJHL	69	10	46	56	119	11	2	5	7	2

a QMJHL First All-Star Team (1990)

DYKSTRA, STEVEN

Defense. Shoots left. 6'2", 210 lbs. Born, Edmonton, Alta., December 1, 1962.

				Regular Season					Playoffs			
Season	Club	Lea	GP	G	A	TP	PIM	GP	G	A	TP	PIM
1981-82	Seattle	WHL	57	8	26	34	139	10	3	1	4	42
1982-83	Rochester	AHL	70	2	16	18	100	15	0	5	5	27
1983-84	Rochester	AHL	63	3	19	22	141	6	0	0	0	46
1984-85	Flint	IHL	15	1	7	8	36	....	....	....	....	....
	Rochester	AHL	51	9	23	32	113	2	0	1	1	10
1985-86	**Buffalo**	**NHL**	**64**	**4**	**21**	**25**	**108**	....	....	....	....	....
1986-87	**Buffalo**	**NHL**	**37**	**0**	**1**	**1**	**179**	....	....	....	....	....
	Rochester	AHL	18	0	0	0	77	....	....	....	....	....
1987-88	**Buffalo**	**NHL**	**27**	**1**	**1**	**2**	**91**	....	....	....	....	....
	Rochester	AHL	7	0	1	1	33	....	....	....	....	....
	Edmonton	**NHL**	**15**	**2**	**3**	**5**	**39**	....	....	....	....	....
1988-89	**Pittsburgh**	**NHL**	**65**	**1**	**6**	**7**	**126**	**1**	**0**	**0**	**0**	**2**
1989-90	**Hartford**	**NHL**	**9**	**0**	**0**	**0**	**2**	....	....	....	....	....
	Binghamton	AHL	53	5	17	22	55	....	....	....	....	....
	Maine	AHL	16	0	4	4	20	....	....	....	....	....
	NHL Totals		**217**	**8**	**32**	**40**	**545**	**1**	**0**	**0**	**0**	**2**

Signed as a free agent by **Buffalo**, December 10, 1982. Traded to **Edmonton** by **Buffalo** with Buffalo's seventh round choice (David Payne) in 1989 Entry Draft for Scott Metcalfe and Edmonton's ninth round choice (Donald Audette) in 1989 Entry Draft, February 11, 1988. Claimed by **Pittsburgh** in NHL Waiver Draft, October 3, 1988. Signed as a free agent by **Hartford**, October 9, 1989. Traded to **Boston** by **Hartford** for Jeff Sirkka, March 3, 1990.

DZIEDZIC, JOE

Left wing. Shoots left. 6'3", 200 lbs. Born, Minneapolis, MN, December 18, 1971.
(Pittsburgh's 2nd choice, 61st overall, in 1990 Entry Draft).

				Regular Season					Playoffs			
Season	Club	Lea	GP	G	A	TP	PIM	GP	G	A	TP	PIM
1989-90	Edison	HS	17	29	19	48	....	....	....	....	....	....

EAGLES, MICHAEL (MIKE)

Center. Shoots left. 5'10", 180 lbs. Born, Sussex, N.B., March 7, 1963.
(Quebec's 5th choice, 116th overall, in 1981 Entry Draft).

				Regular Season					Playoffs			
Season	Club	Lea	GP	G	A	TP	PIM	GP	G	A	TP	PIM
1980-81	Kitchener	OHA	56	11	27	38	64	18	4	2	6	36
1981-82	Kitchener	OHL	62	26	40	66	148	15	3	11	14	27
1982-83	**Quebec**	**NHL**	**2**	**0**	**0**	**0**	**2**	....	....	....	....	....
	Kitchener	OHL	58	26	36	62	133	12	5	7	12	27
1983-84	Fredericton	AHL	68	13	29	42	85	4	0	0	0	5
1984-85	Fredericton	AHL	36	4	20	24	80	3	0	0	0	2
1985-86	**Quebec**	**NHL**	**73**	**11**	**12**	**23**	**49**	**3**	**0**	**0**	**0**	**2**
1986-87	**Quebec**	**NHL**	**73**	**13**	**19**	**32**	**55**	**4**	**1**	**0**	**1**	**10**
1987-88	**Quebec**	**NHL**	**76**	**10**	**10**	**20**	**74**	....	....	....	....	....
1988-89	**Chicago**	**NHL**	**47**	**5**	**11**	**16**	**44**	....	....	....	....	....
1989-90	**Chicago**	**NHL**	**23**	**1**	**2**	**3**	**34**	....	....	....	....	....
	Indianapolis	IHL	24	11	13	24	47	13	*10	10	20	34
	NHL Totals		**294**	**40**	**54**	**94**	**258**	**7**	**1**	**0**	**1**	**12**

Traded to **Chicago** by **Quebec** for Bob Mason, July 5, 1988.

EAKINS, DALLAS

Defense. Shoots left. 6'2", 195 lbs. Born, Dade City, FL, February 27, 1967.
(Washington's 11th choice, 208th overall, in 1985 Entry Draft).

				Regular Season					Playoffs			
Season	Club	Lea	GP	G	A	TP	PIM	GP	G	A	TP	PIM
1984-85	Peterborough	OHL	48	0	8	8	96	7	0	0	0	18
1985-86	Peterborough	OHL	60	6	16	22	134	16	0	1	1	30
1986-87	Peterborough	OHL	54	3	11	14	145	12	1	4	5	37
1987-88	Peterborough	OHL	64	11	27	38	129	12	3	12	15	16
1988-89	Baltimore	AHL	62	0	10	10	139	....	....	....	....	....
1989-90	Moncton	AHL	75	2	11	13	189	....	....	....	....	....

EASTWOOD, MICHAEL

Center. Shoots right. 6'2", 190 lbs. Born, Ottawa, Ont., July 1, 1967.
(Toronto's 5th choice, 91st overall, in 1987 Entry Draft).

				Regular Season					Playoffs			
Season	Club	Lea	GP	G	A	TP	PIM	GP	G	A	TP	PIM
1987-88	W. Michigan	CCHA	42	5	8	13	14	....	....	....	....	....
1988-89	W. Michigan	CCHA	40	10	13	23	87	....	....	....	....	....
1989-90	W. Michigan	CCHA	40	25	27	52	36	....	....	....	....	....

EAVES, MURRAY

Center. Shoots right. 5'10", 185 lbs. Born, Calgary, Alta., May 10, 1960.
(Winnipeg's 3rd choice, 44th overall, in 1980 Entry Draft).

				Regular Season					Playoffs			
Season	Club	Lea	GP	G	A	TP	PIM	GP	G	A	TP	PIM
1978-79	U. of Michigan	WCHA	23	12	22	34	14	....	....	....	....	....
1979-80	U. of Michigan	WCHA	33	36	49	85	34	....	....	....	....	....
1980-81	**Winnipeg**	**NHL**	**12**	**1**	**2**	**3**	**5**	....	....	....	....	....
	Tulsa	CHL	59	24	34	58	59	8	5	5	10	13
1981-82	**Winnipeg**	**NHL**	**2**	**0**	**0**	**0**	**0**	....	....	....	....	....
	Tulsa	CHL	68	30	49	79	33	3	0	2	2	0
1982-83	**Winnipeg**	**NHL**	**26**	**2**	**7**	**9**	**2**	....	....	....	....	....
	Sherbrooke	AHL	40	25	34	59	16	....	....	....	....	....
1983-84	Sherbrooke	AHL	78	47	68	115	40	....	....	....	....	....
	Winnipeg	**NHL**	**2**	**0**	**0**	**0**	**0**	**2**	**0**	**0**	**0**	**2**
1984-85	**Winnipeg**	**NHL**	**3**	**0**	**3**	**3**	**0**	**2**	**0**	**1**	**1**	**0**
	Sherbrooke	AHL	47	26	42	68	28	15	5	13	18	35
1985-86	**Winnipeg**	**NHL**	**4**	**1**	**0**	**1**	**0**	....	....	....	....	....
	Sherbrooke	AHL	68	22	51	73	26	....	....	....	....	....
1986-87	Nova Scotia	AHL	76	26	38	64	46	4	1	1	2	2
1987-88	**Detroit**	**NHL**	**7**	**0**	**1**	**1**	**2**	....	....	....	....	....
	Adirondack	AHL	65	39	54	93	65	11	3	*11	14	8
1988-89ab	Adirondack	AHL	80	46	*72	118	11	16	*13	12	25	10
1989-90	**Detroit**	**NHL**	**1**	**0**	**0**	**0**	**0**	....	....	....	....	....
b	Adirondack	AHL	78	40	49	89	35	6	2	3	5	2
	NHL Totals		**57**	**4**	**13**	**17**	**9**	**4**	**0**	**1**	**1**	**2**

a AHL Second All-Star Team (1989)
b Won Fred Hunt Award (Sportsmanship-AHL) (1989, 1990)

Traded to **Edmonton** by **Winnipeg** for future considerations, July 3, 1986. Signed as a free agent by **Detroit**, July 12, 1987.

EDLUND, PAR

Right wing. Shoots right. 5'11", 180 lbs. Born, Sweden, April 9, 1967.
(Los Angeles' 3rd choice, 30th overall, in 1985 Entry Draft).

				Regular Season					Playoffs			
Season	Club	Lea	GP	G	A	TP	PIM	GP	G	A	TP	PIM
1986-87	Bjorkloven	Swe.	4	0	0	0	0	....	....	....	....	....
1987-88	Bjorkloven	Swe.	37	6	4	10	14	7	1	0	1	2
1988-89	Bjorkloven	Swe.	18	9	10	19	....	....	....	....	....	....
1989-90	Bjorkloven	Swe.	18	13	9	22	0	....	....	....	....	....

EGELAND, TRACY

Left wing. Shoots right. 6'1", 180 lbs. Born, Lethbridge, Alta., August 20, 1970.
(Chicago's 5th choice, 132nd overall, in 1989 Entry Draft).

				Regular Season					Playoffs			
Season	Club	Lea	GP	G	A	TP	PIM	GP	G	A	TP	PIM
1988-89	Prince Albert	WHL	66	28	22	50	88	4	0	1	1	13
1989-90	Prince Albert	WHL	61	39	26	65	160	13	7	10	17	26

EISENHUT, NEIL

Center. Shoots left. 6'1", 190 lbs. Born, Oliver, B.C., January 9, 1967.
(Vancouver's 11th choice, 238th overall, in 1987 Entry Draft).

				Regular Season					Playoffs			
Season	Club	Lea	GP	G	A	TP	PIM	GP	G	A	TP	PIM
1987-88	North Dakota	WCHA	42	12	20	32	14	....	....	....	....	....
1988-89	North Dakota	WCHA	41	22	16	38	20	....	....	....	....	....
1989-90	North Dakota	WCHA	45	22	32	54	46	....	....	....	....	....

EKLUND, PER-ERIK (PELLE)

Center. Shoots left. 5'10", 175 lbs. Born, Stockholm, Sweden, March 22, 1963.
(Philadelphia's 8th choice, 167th overall, in 1983 Entry Draft).

			Regular Season					Playoffs				
Season	Club	Lea	GP	G	A	TP	PIM	GP	G	A	TP	PIM
1981-82	AIK	Swe.	23	2	3	5	2	....	....	....	....	....
1982-83	AIK	Swe.	34	13	17	30	14	3	1	4	5	2
1983-84	AIK	Swe.	35	9	18	27	24	6	6	7	13	2
1984-85	AIK	Swe.	35	16	33	49	10	....	....	....	....	....
1985-86	**Philadelphia**	**NHL**	**70**	**15**	**51**	**66**	**12**	**5**	**0**	**2**	**2**	**0**
1986-87	**Philadelphia**	**NHL**	**72**	**14**	**41**	**55**	**2**	**26**	**7**	**20**	**27**	**2**
1987-88	**Philadelphia**	**NHL**	**71**	**10**	**32**	**42**	**12**	**7**	**0**	**3**	**3**	**0**
1988-89	**Philadelphia**	**NHL**	**79**	**18**	**51**	**69**	**23**	**19**	**3**	**8**	**11**	**2**
1989-90	**Philadelphia**	**NHL**	**70**	**23**	**39**	**62**	**16**	....	....	....	....	....
	NHL Totals		**362**	**80**	**214**	**294**	**65**	**57**	**10**	**33**	**43**	**4**

ELIK, TODD

Center. Shoots left. 6'2", 190 lbs. Born, Brampton, Ont., April 15, 1966.

			Regular Season					Playoffs				
Season	Club	Lea	GP	G	A	TP	PIM	GP	G	A	TP	PIM
1984-85	Kingston	OHL	34	14	11	25	6	....	....	....	....	....
	North Bay	OHL	23	4	6	10	2	4	2	0	2	0
1985-86	North Bay	OHL	40	12	34	46	20	10	7	6	13	0
1986-87	U. of Regina	CWUAA	27	26	34	60	137	....	....	....	....	....
1987-88	Colorado	IHL	81	44	56	100	83	12	8	12	20	9
1988-89	New Haven	AHL	43	11	25	36	31	17	10	12	22	44
	Denver	IHL	28	20	15	35	22	....	....	....	....	....
1989-90	**Los Angeles**	**NHL**	**48**	**10**	**23**	**33**	**4**	**10**	**3**	**9**	**12**	**10**
	New Haven	AHL	32	20	23	43	42	....	....	....	....	....
	NHL Totals		**48**	**10**	**23**	**33**	**4**	**10**	**3**	**9**	**12**	**10**

Signed as a free agent by **NY Rangers**, February 26, 1988. Traded to **Los Angeles** by **NY Rangers** with Igor Liba, Michael Boyce and future considerations for Dean Kennedy and Denis Larocque, December 12, 1988.

ELLETT, DAVID

Defense. Shoots left. 6'1", 200 lbs. Born, Cleveland, OH, March 30, 1964.
(Winnipeg's 4th choice, 75th overall, in 1982 Entry Draft).

			Regular Season					Playoffs				
Season	Club	Lea	GP	G	A	TP	PIM	GP	G	A	TP	PIM
1982-83	Bowling Green	CCHA	40	4	13	17	34	....	....	....	....	....
1983-84ab	Bowling Green	CCHA	43	15	39	54	96	....	....	....	....	....
1984-85	**Winnipeg**	**NHL**	**80**	**11**	**27**	**38**	**85**	**8**	**1**	**5**	**6**	**4**
1985-86	**Winnipeg**	**NHL**	**80**	**15**	**31**	**46**	**96**	**3**	**0**	**1**	**1**	**0**
1986-87	**Winnipeg**	**NHL**	**78**	**13**	**31**	**44**	**53**	**10**	**0**	**8**	**8**	**2**
1987-88	**Winnipeg**	**NHL**	**68**	**13**	**45**	**58**	**106**	**5**	**1**	**2**	**3**	**10**
1988-89	**Winnipeg**	**NHL**	**75**	**22**	**34**	**56**	**62**	....	....	....	....	....
1989-90	**Winnipeg**	**NHL**	**77**	**17**	**29**	**46**	**96**	**7**	**2**	**0**	**2**	**6**
	NHL Totals		**458**	**91**	**197**	**288**	**498**	**33**	**4**	**16**	**20**	**22**

a CCHA Second All-Star Team (1984).
b Named to NCAA All-Tournament Team (1984).

Played in NHL All-Star Game (1989)

ELYNUIK, PAT

Right wing. Shoots right. 6', 185 lbs. Born, Foam Lake, Sask., October 30, 1967.
(Winnipeg's 1st choice, 7th over all, in 1986 Entry Draft).

			Regular Season					Playoffs				
Season	Club	Lea	GP	G	A	TP	PIM	GP	G	A	TP	PIM
1984-85	Prince Albert	WHL	70	23	20	43	54	13	9	3	12	7
1985-86a	Prince Albert	WHL	68	53	53	106	62	20	7	9	16	17
1986-87a	Prince Albert	WHL	64	51	62	113	40	8	5	5	10	12
1987-88	**Winnipeg**	**NHL**	**13**	**1**	**3**	**4**	**12**	....	....	....	....	....
	Moncton	AHL	30	11	18	29	35	....	....	....	....	....
1988-89	**Winnipeg**	**NHL**	**56**	**26**	**25**	**51**	**29**	....	....	....	....	....
	Moncton	AHL	7	8	2	10	2	....	....	....	....	....
1989-90	**Winnipeg**	**NHL**	**80**	**32**	**42**	**74**	**83**	**7**	**2**	**4**	**6**	**2**
	NHL Totals		**149**	**59**	**70**	**129**	**124**	**7**	**2**	**4**	**6**	**2**

a WHL East All-Star Team (1986, 1987).

EMERSON, NELSON

Center. Shoots right. 5'11", 165 lbs. Born, Hamilton, Ont., August 17, 1967.
(St. Louis' 2nd choice, 44th overall, in 1985 Entry Draft).

			Regular Season					Playoffs				
Season	Club	Lea	GP	G	A	TP	PIM	GP	G	A	TP	PIM
1986-87a	Bowling Green	CCHA	45	26	35	61	28	....	....	....	....	....
1987-88bc	Bowling Green	CCHA	45	34	49	83	54	....	....	....	....	....
1988-89d	Bowling Green	CCHA	44	22	46	68	46	....	....	....	....	....
1989-90ce	Bowling Green	CCHA	44	30	52	82	42	....	....	....	....	....

a CCHA Freshman of the Year (1987)
b NCAA West Second All-American Team (1988)
c CCHA First All-Star Team (1988, 1990)
d CCHA Second All-Star Team (1989)
e NCAA West First All-American Team (1990)

EMMA, DAVID

Center. Shoots left. 5'11", 180 lbs. Born, Cranston, RI, January 14, 1969.
(New Jersey's 6th choice, 110th overall, in 1989 Entry Draft).

			Regular Season					Playoffs				
Season	Club	Lea	GP	G	A	TP	PIM	GP	G	A	TP	PIM
1988-89	Boston College	H.E.	36	20	31	51	36	....	....	....	....	....
1989-90ab	Boston College	H.E.	42	38	34	*72	46	....	....	....	....	....

a Hockey East First All-Star Team (1990)
b NCAA East First All-American Team (1990)

ENDEAN, CRAIG

Left wing. Shoots left. 5'11", 170 lbs. Born, Kamloops, B.C., April 13, 1968.
(Winnipeg's 5th choice, 92nd overall, in 1986 Entry Draft).

			Regular Season					Playoffs				
Season	Club	Lea	GP	G	A	TP	PIM	GP	G	A	TP	PIM
1985-86	Seattle	WHL	70	58	70	128	34	5	5	1	6	0
1986-87	Regina	WHL	76	69	77	146	34	3	5	0	5	4
	Winnipeg	**NHL**	**2**	**0**	**1**	**1**	**0**	....	....	....	....	....
1987-88a	Regina	WHL	69	50	86	136	50	4	4	9	13	8
1988-89	Moncton	AHL	18	3	9	12	16	....	....	....	....	....
	Fort Wayne	IHL	34	10	18	28	0	10	4	7	11	6
1989-90	Fort Wayne	IHL	20	2	11	13	8	....	....	....	....	....
	Adirondack	AHL	7	3	3	6	4	....	....	....	....	....
	NHL Totals		**2**	**0**	**1**	**1**	**0**	....	....	....	....	....

a WHL East All-Star Team (1988)

ENEBAK, JAKE

Left wing. Shoots left. 6'2", 200 lbs. Born, Northfield, MN, December 10, 1968.
(Quebec's 8th choice, 156th overall, in 1987 Entry Draft).

			Regular Season					Playoffs				
Season	Club	Lea	GP	G	A	TP	PIM	GP	G	A	TP	PIM
1987-88	U. Minnesota	WCHA	9	1	1	2	15	....	....	....	....	....
1988-89	U. Minnesota	WCHA	15	1	2	3	26	....	....	....	....	....
1989-90	U. Minnesota	WCHA	20	0	3	3	26	....	....	....	....	....

ENGEVIK, GLEN

Right wing. Shoots right. 6'1", 205 lbs. Born, Surrey, B.C., October 13, 1965.
(New Jersey's 1st choice, 3rd overall, in 1986 Supplemental Draft).

			Regular Season					Playoffs				
Season	Club	Lea	GP	G	A	TP	PIM	GP	G	A	TP	PIM
1986-87	U. of Denver	WCHA	40	10	8	18	32	....	....	....	....	....
1987-88	U. of Denver	WCHA	38	13	7	20	18	....	....	....	....	....
1988-89	U. of Denver	WCHA	42	12	12	24	33	....	....	....	....	....
1989-90	Nashville	ECHL	53	45	39	84	74	5	3	2	5	27

ENNIS, JIM

Defense. Shoots left. 6', 200 lbs. Born, Sherwood Park, Edmonton, Alta., July 10, 1967.
(Edmonton's 6th choice, 126th overall, in 1986 Entry Draft).

			Regular Season					Playoffs				
Season	Club	Lea	GP	G	A	TP	PIM	GP	G	A	TP	PIM
1985-86	Boston U.	H.E.	40	1	4	5	22	....	....	....	....	....
1986-87	Boston U.	H.E.	26	3	4	7	27	....	....	....	....	....
1987-88	**Edmonton**	**NHL**	**5**	**1**	**0**	**1**	**10**	....	....	....	....	....
	Nova Scotia	AHL	59	8	12	20	102	5	0	1	1	16
1988-89	Cape Breton	AHL	67	3	15	18	94	....	....	....	....	....
1989-90	Binghamton	AHL	69	3	12	15	61	....	....	....	....	....
	NHL Totals		**5**	**1**	**0**	**1**	**10**	....	....	....	....	....

Traded to **Hartford** by **Edmonton** for Norm MacIver, October 10, 1989.

ERICKSON, MICHAEL

Defense. Shoots left. 5'11", 175 lbs. Born, Worcester, MA, March 11, 1969.
(NY Islanders' 11th choice, 223rd overall, in 1987 Entry Draft).

			Regular Season					Playoffs				
Season	Club	Lea	GP	G	A	TP	PIM	GP	G	A	TP	PIM
1987-88	U. of Lowell	H.E.	31	2	4	6	22	....	....	....	....	....
1988-89	U. of Lowell	H.E.	33	4	2	6	50	....	....	....	....	....
1989-90	U. of Lowell	H.E.	32	1	3	4	42	....	....	....	....	....

ERIKSSON, NIKLAS

Center. 5'11", 180 lbs. Born, Leksand, Sweden, February 17, 1969.
(Philadelphia's 4th choice, 117th overall, in 1989 Entry Draft).

			Regular Season					Playoffs				
Season	Club	Lea	GP	G	A	TP	PIM	GP	G	A	TP	PIM
1988-89	Leksands	Swe.	33	18	12	30	22	....	....	....	....	....
1989-90	Leksands	Swe.	40	18	16	34	16	3	0	2	2	2

ERIKSSON, PATRIK

Center. Shoots left. 5'11", 175 lbs. Born, Gavle, Sweden, March 13, 1969.
(Winnipeg's 2nd choice, 37th overall, in 1987 Entry Draft).

			Regular Season					Playoffs				
Season	Club	Lea	GP	G	A	TP	PIM	GP	G	A	TP	PIM
1986-87	Brynas	Swe.	25	10	5	15	8	....	....	....	....	....
1987-88	Brynas	Swe.	35	14	9	23	6	....	....	....	....	....
1988-89	Brynas	Swe.	33	6	10	16	14	....	....	....	....	....
1989-90	Brynas	Swe.	40	16	17	33	18	5	3	2	3	4

ERIKSSON, PETER (KESSLER)

Left wing. Shoots right. 6'4", 224 lbs. Born, Kramfors, Sweden, July 12, 1965.
(Edmonton's 4th choice, 64th overall, in 1987 Entry Draft).

			Regular Season					Playoffs				
Season	Club	Lea	GP	G	A	TP	PIM	GP	G	A	TP	PIM
1985-86	HV-71	Swe.	30	7	8	15	18	1	0	0	0	0
1986-87	HV-71	Swe.	36	14	5	19	16	....	....	....	....	....
1987-88	HV-71	Swe.	37	14	9	23	20	2	1	0	1	0
1988-89	HV-71	Swe.	40	10	27	37	48	....	....	....	....	....
1989-90	**Edmonton**	**NHL**	**20**	**3**	**3**	**6**	**24**	....	....	....	....	....
	Cape Breton	AHL	21	5	12	17	36	5	2	2	4	2
	NHL Totals		**20**	**3**	**3**	**6**	**24**	....	....	....	....	....

ERIKSSON, TOMAZ

Left wing. Shoots left. 6', 195 lbs. Born, Stockholm, Sweden, March 23, 1967.
(Philadelphia's 4th choice, 83rd overall, in 1987 Entry Draft).

			Regular Season					Playoffs				
Season	Club	Lea	GP	G	A	TP	PIM	GP	G	A	TP	PIM
1986-87	Djurgarden	Swe.	20	7	4	11	14	2	2	0	2	0
1987-88	Djurgarden	Swe.	26	4	5	9	16	....	....	....	....	....
1988-89	Djurgarden	Swe.	38	6	13	19	50	....	....	....	....	....
1989-90	Djurgarden	Swe.	39	11	12	23	106	....	....	....	....	....

ERIXON, JAN

Right wing. Shoots left. 6', 190 lbs. Born, Skelleftea, Sweden, July 8, 1962.
(NY Rangers' 2nd choice, 30th overall, in 1981 Entry Draft).

			Regular Season					Playoffs				
Season	Club	Lea	GP	G	A	TP	PIM	GP	G	A	TP	PIM
1979-80	Skelleftea	...	15	1	0	1	2	....	....	....	....	....
1980-81	Skelleftea	...	32	6	6	12	4	3	1	0	1	0
1981-82	Skelleftea	...	30	7	7	14	26	....	....	....	....	....
1982-83	Skelleftea	...	36	10	19	29	32	....	....	....	....	....
1983-84	**NY Rangers**	**NHL**	**75**	**5**	**25**	**30**	**16**	**5**	**2**	**0**	**2**	**4**
1984-85	**NY Rangers**	**NHL**	**66**	**7**	**22**	**29**	**33**	**2**	**0**	**0**	**0**	**2**
1985-86	**NY Rangers**	**NHL**	**31**	**2**	**17**	**19**	**4**	**12**	**0**	**1**	**1**	**4**
1986-87	**NY Rangers**	**NHL**	**68**	**8**	**18**	**26**	**24**	**6**	**1**	**0**	**1**	**0**
1987-88	**NY Rangers**	**NHL**	**70**	**7**	**19**	**26**	**33**	....	....	....	....	....
1988-89	**NY Rangers**	**NHL**	**44**	**4**	**11**	**15**	**27**	**4**	**0**	**1**	**1**	**2**
1989-90	**NY Rangers**	**NHL**	**58**	**4**	**9**	**13**	**8**	**10**	**1**	**0**	**1**	**2**
	NHL Totals		**412**	**37**	**121**	**158**	**145**	**39**	**4**	**2**	**6**	**14**

ERREY, BOB (AIRY)

Left wing. Shoots left. 5'10", 180 lbs. Born, Montreal, Que., September 21, 1964.
(Pittsburgh's 1st choice, 15th overall, in 1983 Entry Draft).

			Regular Season					Playoffs				
Season	Club	Lea	GP	G	A	TP	PIM	GP	G	A	TP	PIM
1981-82	Peterborough	OHL	68	29	31	60	39	9	3	1	4	9
1982-83a	Peterborough	OHL	67	53	47	100	74	4	1	3	4	7
1983-84	**Pittsburgh**	**NHL**	**65**	**9**	**13**	**22**	**29**	....	....	....	....	....
1984-85	**Pittsburgh**	**NHL**	**16**	**0**	**2**	**2**	**7**	....	....	....	....	....
	Baltimore	AHL	59	17	24	41	14	8	3	4	7	11
1985-86	**Pittsburgh**	**NHL**	**37**	**11**	**6**	**17**	**8**	....	....	....	....	....
	Baltimore	AHL	18	8	7	15	28	....	....	....	....	....
1986-87	**Pittsburgh**	**NHL**	**72**	**16**	**18**	**34**	**46**	....	....	....	....	....
1987-88	**Pittsburgh**	**NHL**	**17**	**3**	**6**	**9**	**18**	....	....	....	....	....
1988-89	**Pittsburgh**	**NHL**	**76**	**26**	**32**	**58**	**124**	**11**	**1**	**2**	**3**	**12**
1989-90	**Pittsburgh**	**NHL**	**78**	**20**	**19**	**39**	**109**	....	....	....	....	....
	NHL Totals		**361**	**85**	**96**	**181**	**257**	**11**	**1**	**2**	**3**	**12**

a OHL First All-Star Team (1983)

ESAU, LEONARD

Defense. Shoots right. 6'3", 190 lbs. Born, Meadow Lake, Sask., June 3, 1968.
(Toronto's 5th choice, 86th overall, in 1988 Entry Draft).

			Regular Season					Playoffs				
Season	Club	Lea	GP	G	A	TP	PIM	GP	G	A	TP	PIM
1988-89	St. Cloud	NCAA	35	12	27	39	69	....	....	....	....	....
1989-90	St. Cloud	NCAA	29	8	11	19	83	....	....	....	....	....

ESPE, DAVID

Defense. Shoots left. 6', 185 lbs. Born, St. Paul, MN, November 3, 1966.
(Quebec's 5th choice, 78th overall, in 1985 Entry Draft).

			Regular Season					Playoffs				
Season	Club	Lea	GP	G	A	TP	PIM	GP	G	A	TP	PIM
1985-86	U. Minnesota	WCHA	27	0	6	6	18	....	....	....	....	....
1986-87	U. Minnesota	WCHA	45	4	8	12	28	....	....	....	....	....
1987-88	U. Minnesota	WCHA	43	4	10	14	68	....	....	....	....	....
1988-89			DID NOT PLAY									
1989-90	Halifax	AHL	48	2	16	18	26	1	0	0	0	4

EVANS, DOUG

Left wing. Shoots left. 5'9", 170 lbs. Born, Peterborough, Ont., June 2, 1963.

			Regular Season					Playoffs				
Season	Club	Lea	GP	G	A	TP	PIM	GP	G	A	TP	PIM
1981-82	Peterborough	OHL	56	17	49	66	176	9	0	2	2	41
1982-83	Peterborough	OHL	65	31	55	86	165	4	0	3	3	23
1983-84	Peterborough	OHL	61	45	79	124	98	8	4	12	16	26
1984-85	Peoria	IHL	81	36	61	97	189	20	18	14	32	*88
1985-86a	Peoria	IHL	60	46	51	97	179	10	4	6	10	32
	St. Louis	**NHL**	**13**	**1**	**0**	**1**	**2**	....	....	....	....	....
1986-87	**St. Louis**	**NHL**	**53**	**3**	**13**	**16**	**91**	**5**	**0**	**0**	**0**	**10**
	Peoria	IHL	18	10	15	25	39	....	....	....	....	....
1987-88	**St. Louis**	**NHL**	**41**	**5**	**7**	**12**	**49**	**2**	**0**	**0**	**0**	**0**
	Peoria	IHL	11	4	16	20	64	....	....	....	....	....
1988-89	**St. Louis**	**NHL**	**53**	**7**	**12**	**19**	**81**	**7**	**1**	**2**	**3**	**16**
1989-90	**St. Louis**	**NHL**	**3**	**0**	**0**	**0**	**0**	....	....	....	....	....
	Winnipeg	**NHL**	**27**	**10**	**8**	**18**	**33**	**7**	**2**	**2**	**4**	**10**
	Peoria	IHL	42	19	28	47	128	....	....	....	....	....
	NHL Totals		**190**	**26**	**40**	**66**	**256**	**21**	**3**	**4**	**7**	**36**

a IHL First All-Star Team (1986)

Signed as a free agent by **St. Louis**, June 10, 1985. Traded to **Winnipeg** by **St. Louis** for Ron Wilson, January 22, 1990.

EVANS, DOUGLAS B.

Defense. Shoots right. 6', 200 lbs. Born, San Jose, CA, July 12, 1971.
(Winnipeg's 9th choice, 131st overall, in 1989 Entry Draft).

			Regular Season					Playoffs				
Season	Club	Lea	GP	G	A	TP	PIM	GP	G	A	TP	PIM
1988-89	U. of Michigan	CCHA	38	0	8	8	41	....	....	....	....	....
1989-90	U. of Michigan	CCHA	31	2	3	5	24	....	....	....	....	....

EVANS, KEVIN ROBERT

Left wing. Shoots left. 5'9", 185 lbs. Born, Peterborough, Ont., July 10, 1965.

			Regular Season					Playoffs				
Season	Club	Lea	GP	G	A	TP	PIM	GP	G	A	TP	PIM
1986-87	Kalamazoo	IHL	73	19	31	50	648	....	....	....	....	....
1987-88	Kalamazoo	IHL	54	9	28	37	404	5	1	1	2	46
1988-89	Kalamazoo	IHL	50	22	34	56	326	....	....	....	....	....
1989-90	Kalamazoo	IHL	76	30	54	84	346	....	....	....	....	....

Signed as a free agent by **Minnesota**, August 8, 1988.

EVANS, SHAWN

Defense. Shoots left. 6'3", 195 lbs. Born, Kingston, Ont., September 7, 1965.
(New Jersey's 2nd choice, 24th overall, in 1983 Entry Draft).

			Regular Season					Playoffs				
Season	Club	Lea	GP	G	A	TP	PIM	GP	G	A	TP	PIM
1982-83	Peterborough	OHL	58	7	41	48	116	4	2	0	2	12
1983-84a	Peterborough	OHL	67	21	88	109	116	8	1	16	17	8
1984-85b	Peterborough	OHL	66	16	83	99	78	16	6	18	24	6
1985-86	**St. Louis**	**NHL**	**7**	**0**	**0**	**0**	**2**	....	....	....	....	....
	Peoria	IHL	55	8	26	34	36	....	....	....	....	....
1986-87	Nova Scotia	AHL	55	7	28	35	29	5	0	4	4	6
1987-88	Nova Scotia	AHL	79	8	62	70	109	5	1	1	2	40
1988-89	Springfield	AHL	68	9	50	59	125	....	....	....	....	....
1989-90	**NY Islanders**	**NHL**	**2**	**1**	**0**	**1**	**0**	....	....	....	....	....
	Springfield	AHL	63	6	35	41	102	18	6	11	17	35
	NHL Totals		**9**	**1**	**0**	**1**	**2**	....	....	....	....	....

a OHL Second All-Star Team (1984)
b OHL Third All-Star Team (1985)

Traded to **St. Louis** by **New Jersey** with New Jersey's fifth-round choice (Michael Wolak) in 1986 Entry Draft for Mark Johnson, September 19, 1985. Traded to **Edmonton** by **St. Louis** for Todd Ewen, October 15, 1986. Signed as a free agent by **NY Islanders**, June 20, 1988.

EVASON, DEAN

Center. Shoots right. 5'10", 180 lbs. Born, Flin Flon, Man., August 22, 1964.
(Washington's 3rd choice, 89th overall, in 1982 Entry Draft).

			Regular Season					Playoffs				
Season	Club	Lea	GP	G	A	TP	PIM	GP	G	A	TP	PIM
1980-81	Spokane	WHL	3	1	1	2	0	....	....	....	....	....
1981-82	Spokane	WHL	26	8	14	22	65	....	....	....	....	....
	Kamloops	WHL	44	21	55	76	47	4	2	1	3	0
1982-83	Kamloops	WHL	70	71	93	164	102	7	5	7	12	18
1983-84	**Washington**	**NHL**	**2**	**0**	**0**	**0**	**2**	....	....	....	....	....
a	Kamloops	WHL	57	49	88	137	89	17	*21	20	41	33
1984-85	**Washington**	**NHL**	**15**	**3**	**4**	**7**	**2**	....	....	....	....	....
	Hartford	**NHL**	**2**	**0**	**0**	**0**	**0**	....	....	....	....	....
	Binghamton	AHL	65	27	49	76	38	8	3	5	8	9
1985-86	**Hartford**	**NHL**	**55**	**20**	**28**	**48**	**65**	**10**	**1**	**4**	**5**	**10**
	Binghamton	AHL	26	9	17	26	29	....	....	....	....	....
1986-87	**Hartford**	**NHL**	**80**	**22**	**37**	**59**	**67**	**5**	**3**	**2**	**5**	**35**
1987-88	**Hartford**	**NHL**	**77**	**10**	**18**	**28**	**115**	**6**	**1**	**1**	**2**	**2**
1988-89	**Hartford**	**NHL**	**67**	**11**	**17**	**28**	**60**	**4**	**1**	**2**	**3**	**10**
1989-90	**Hartford**	**NHL**	**78**	**18**	**25**	**43**	**138**	**7**	**2**	**2**	**4**	**22**
	NHL Totals		**376**	**84**	**129**	**213**	**449**	**32**	**8**	**11**	**19**	**79**

a WHL First All-Star Team, West Division (1984)

Traded to **Hartford** by **Washington** with Peter Sidorkiewicz for David Jensen, March 12, 1985.

EVO, MATTHEW (MATT)

Left wing. Shoots left. 6', 185 lbs. Born, Royal Oak, MI, December 31, 1968.
(Vancouver's 12th choice, 234th overall, in 1987 Entry Draft).

			Regular Season					Playoffs				
Season	Club	Lea	GP	G	A	TP	PIM	GP	G	A	TP	PIM
1987-88	Ferris State	CCHA	40	7	8	15	46	....	....	....	....	....
1988-89	Ferris State	CCHA	26	3	4	7	38	....	....	....	....	....
1989-90	Ferris State	CCHA	15	2	0	2	22	....	....	....	....	....

EWEN, DEAN

Left wing. Shoots left. 6'1", 185 lbs. Born, St. Albert, Alta., February 28, 1969.
(NY Islanders' 3rd choice, 55th overall, in 1987 Entry Draft).

			Regular Season					Playoffs				
Season	Club	Lea	GP	G	A	TP	PIM	GP	G	A	TP	PIM
1985-86	N. Westminster	WHL	61	7	15	22	154	....	....	....	....	....
1986-87	N. Westminster	WHL	9	2	3	5	28	....	....	....	....	....
	Spokane	WHL	57	6	11	17	208	5	1	0	1	39
1987-88	Spokane	WHL	49	12	12	24	302	15	1	3	4	49
1988-89	Springfield	AHL	6	0	0	0	26	....	....	....	....	....
	Seattle	WHL	61	22	30	52	*307	....	....	....	....	....
1989-90	Springfield	AHL	34	0	7	7	194	....	....	....	....	....

EWEN, TODD

Right wing. Shoots right. 6'2", 220 lbs. Born, Saskatoon, Sask., March 22, 1966.
(Edmonton's 9th choice, 168th overall, in 1984 Entry Draft).

			Regular Season					Playoffs				
Season	Club	Lea	GP	G	A	TP	PIM	GP	G	A	TP	PIM
1982-83	Kamloops	WHL	3	0	0	0	2	2	0	0	0	0
1983-84	N. Westminster	WHL	68	11	13	24	176	7	2	1	3	15
1984-85	N. Westminster	WHL	56	11	20	31	304	10	1	8	9	60
1985-86	N. Westminster	WHL	60	28	24	52	289	....	....	....	....	....
	Maine	AHL	....	....	....	....	....	3	0	0	0	7
1986-87	**St. Louis**	**NHL**	**23**	**2**	**0**	**2**	**84**	**4**	**0**	**0**	**0**	**23**
	Peoria	IHL	16	3	3	6	110	....	....	....	....	....
1987-88	**St. Louis**	**NHL**	**64**	**4**	**2**	**6**	**227**	**6**	**0**	**0**	**0**	**21**
1988-89	**St. Louis**	**NHL**	**34**	**4**	**5**	**9**	**171**	**2**	**0**	**0**	**0**	**21**
1989-90	**St. Louis**	**NHL**	**3**	**0**	**0**	**0**	**11**	....	....	....	....	....
	Montreal	**NHL**	**41**	**4**	**6**	**10**	**158**	**10**	**0**	**0**	**0**	**4**
	Peoria	IHL	2	0	0	0	12	....	....	....	....	....
	NHL Totals		**165**	**14**	**13**	**27**	**651**	**22**	**0**	**0**	**0**	**69**

Traded to **St. Louis** by **Edmonton** for Shawn Evans, October 15, 1986. Traded to **Montreal** by **St. Louis** for future considerations, December 12, 1989.

FABIAN, SEAN

Defense. Shoots left. 6'1", 200 lbs. Born, Minneapolis, MN, May 11, 1969.
(Vancouver's 4th choice, 87th overall, in 1987 Entry Draft).

			Regular Season					Playoffs				
Season	Club	Lea	GP	G	A	TP	PIM	GP	G	A	TP	PIM
1987-88	U. Minnesota	WCHA	10	0	1	1	11	....	....	....	....	....
1988-89	U. Minnesota	WCHA	DID NOT PLAY									
1989-90	U. Minnesota	WCHA	40	0	10	10	74	....	....	....	....	....

FAIRFIELD, TONY

Right wing. Shoots right. 6'2", 205 lbs. Born, Edmonton, Alta., July 2, 1967.
(Edmonton's 7th choice, 167th overall, in 1985 Entry Draft).

			Regular Season					Playoffs				
Season	Club	Lea	GP	G	A	TP	PIM	GP	G	A	TP	PIM
1986-87	U. of Calgary	CWUAA	26	8	2	10	46	....	....	....	....	....
1987-88	U. of Calgary	CWUAA	21	1	5	6	49	....	....	....	....	....
1988-89	U. of Calgary	CWUAA	12	2	2	4	22	....	....	....	....	....
1989-90	U. of Calgary	CWUAA	23	5	7	12	49	....	....	....	....	....

FARRELL, SCOTT

Defense. Shoots left. 5'11", 190 lbs. Born, Richmond, B.C., April 15, 1970.
(Pittsburgh's 12th choice, 226th overall, in 1989 Entry Draft).

			Regular Season					Playoffs				
Season	Club	Lea	GP	G	A	TP	PIM	GP	G	A	TP	PIM
1985-86	N.Westminster	WHL	4	1	0	1	9	....	....	....	....	....
1986-87	N.Westminster	WHL	67	4	8	12	47	....	....	....	....	....
1987-88	Spokane	WHL	62	1	16	17	198	15	2	4	6	42
1988-89	Spokane	WHL	67	10	32	42	221	....	....	....	....	....
1989-90	Spokane	WHL	10	3	5	8	34	....	....	....	....	....
	Lethbridge	WHL	4	1	1	2	22	....	....	....	....	....
	Tri-Cities	WHL	35	3	10	13	84	7	0	1	1	4

FAUST, ANDRE

Center. Shoots left. 6'1", 180 lbs. Born, Joliette, Que., October 7, 1969.
(New Jersey's 8th choice, 173rd overall, in 1989 Entry Draft).

			Regular Season					Playoffs				
Season	Club	Lea	GP	G	A	TP	PIM	GP	G	A	TP	PIM
1988-89	Princeton	ECAC	26	18	16	34	34	....	....	....	....	....
1989-90a	Princeton	ECAC	22	9	28	37	20	....	....	....	....	....

a ECAC Second All-Star Team (1990)

FEATHERSTONE, GLEN

Defense. Shoots left. 6'4", 216 lbs. Born, Toronto, Ont., July 8, 1968.
(St. Louis' 4th choice, 73rd overall, in 1986 Entry Draft).

			Regular Season					Playoffs				
Season	Club	Lea	GP	G	A	TP	PIM	GP	G	A	TP	PIM
1985-86	Windsor	OHL	49	0	6	6	135	14	1	1	2	23
1986-87	Windsor	OHL	47	6	11	17	154	14	2	6	8	19
1987-88	Windsor	OHL	53	7	27	34	201	12	6	9	15	47
1988-89	St. Louis	NHL	18	0	2	2	22	6	0	0	0	0
	Peoria	IHL	37	5	19	24	97	....	....	....	....	....
1989-90	St. Louis	NHL	58	0	12	12	145	12	0	2	2	47
	NHL Totals		76	0	14	14	167	18	0	2	2	47

FEDERKO, BERNARD ALLAN (BERNIE)

Center. Shoots left. 6', 190 lbs. Born, Foam Lake, Sask., May 12, 1956.
(St. Louis' 1st choice, 7th overall, in 1976 Amateur Draft).

			Regular Season					Playoffs				
Season	Club	Lea	GP	G	A	TP	PIM	GP	G	A	TP	PIM
1973-74	Saskatoon	WHL	68	22	28	50	19	6	0	0	0	2
1974-75	Saskatoon	WHL	66	39	68	107	30	17	*15	7	22	8
1975-76ab	Saskatoon	WHL	72	72	*115	*187	108	20	18	*27	*45	8
1976-77	Kansas City	CHL	42	30	39	69	41	....	....	....	....	....
	St. Louis	NHL	31	14	9	23	15	4	1	1	2	2
1977-78	St. Louis	NHL	72	17	24	41	27	....	....	....	....	....
1978-79	St. Louis	NHL	74	31	64	95	14	....	....	....	....	....
1979-80	St. Louis	NHL	79	38	56	94	24	3	1	0	1	2
1980-81	St. Louis	NHL	78	31	73	104	47	11	8	10	18	2
1981-82	St. Louis	NHL	74	30	62	92	70	10	3	15	18	10
1982-83	St. Louis	NHL	75	24	60	84	24	4	2	3	5	0
1983-84	St. Louis	NHL	79	41	66	107	43	11	4	4	8	10
1984-85	St. Louis	NHL	76	30	73	103	27	3	0	2	2	4
1985-86	St. Louis	NHL	80	34	68	102	34	19	7	14	*21	17
1986-87	St. Louis	NHL	64	20	52	72	32	6	3	3	6	18
1987-88	St. Louis	NHL	79	20	69	89	52	10	2	6	8	18
1988-89	St. Louis	NHL	66	22	45	67	54	10	4	8	12	0
1989-90	Detroit	NHL	73	17	40	57	24	....	....	....	....	....
	NHL Totals		1000	369	761	1130	487	91	35	66	101	83

a WHL First All-Star Team (1976)
b Named WHL's Most Valuable Player (1976)

Played in NHL All-Star Game (1980, 1981)

Traded to **Detroit** by **St. Louis** with Tony McKegney for Adam Oates and Paul MacLean, June 15, 1989.

FEDOROV, SERGEI

Center. 6'1", 190 lbs. Born, Moscow, Soviet Union, December 13, 1969.
(Detroit's 4th choice, 74th overall, in 1989 Entry Draft).

			Regular Season					Playoffs				
Season	Club	Lea	GP	G	A	TP	PIM	GP	G	A	TP	PIM
1988-89	CSKA	USSR	44	4	8	12	35	....	....	....	....	....
1989-90	CSKA	USSR	48	19	10	29	20	....	....	....	....	....

FEDYK, BRENT (FEH-dihk)

Right wing. Shoots right. 6' 195 lbs. Born, Yorkton, Sask., March 8, 1967.
(Detroit's 1st choice, 8th overall, in 1985 Entry Draft).

			Regular Season					Playoffs				
Season	Club	Lea	GP	G	A	TP	PIM	GP	G	A	TP	PIM
1983-84	Regina	WHL	63	15	28	43	30	23	8	7	15	6
1984-85	Regina	WHL	66	35	35	70	48	8	5	4	9	0
1985-86	Regina	WHL	50	43	34	77	47	5	0	1	1	0
1986-87	Regina	WHL	12	9	6	15	9	....	....	....	....	....
	Seattle	WHL	13	5	11	16	9	....	....	....	....	....
	Portland	WHL	11	5	4	9	6	14	5	6	11	0
1987-88	Detroit	NHL	2	0	1	1	2	....	....	....	....	....
	Adirondack	AHL	34	9	11	20	22	5	0	2	2	6
1988-89	Detroit	NHL	5	2	0	2	0	....	....	....	....	....
	Adirondack	AHL	66	40	28	68	33	15	7	8	15	23
1989-90	Detroit	NHL	27	1	4	5	24	....	....	....	....	....
	Adirondack	AHL	33	14	15	29	24	6	2	1	3	4
	NHL Totals		34	3	5	8	26	....	....	....	....	....

FELIX, CHRIS

Defense. Shoots right. 5'10", 191 lbs. Born, Bramalea, Ont., May 27, 1964.

			Regular Season					Playoffs				
Season	Club	Lea	GP	G	A	TP	PIM	GP	G	A	TP	PIM
1982-83	S.S. Marie	OHL	68	16	57	73	39	16	2	12	14	10
1983-84	S.S. Marie	OHL	70	32	61	93	75	16	3	20	23	16
1984-85	S.S. Marie	OHL	66	29	72	101	89	16	7	*21	28	20
1985-86	Cdn. Olympic	....	73	7	33	40	33	....	....	....	....	....
1986-87	Cdn. Olympic	....	78	14	38	52	36	....	....	....	....	....
1987-88	Cdn. National	....	62	6	25	31	66	....	....	....	....	....
	Cdn. Olympic	....	6	1	2	3	2	....	....	....	....	....
	Fort Wayne	IHL	19	5	17	22	24	6	4	4	8	0
	Washington	NHL	....	....	....	....	....	1	0	0	0	0
1988-89	Washington	NHL	21	0	8	8	8	1	0	1	1	0
	Baltimore	AHL	50	8	29	37	44	....	....	....	....	....
1989-90	Washington	NHL	6	1	0	1	2	....	....	....	....	....
	Baltimore	AHL	73	19	42	61	115	12	0	11	11	18
	NHL Totals		27	1	8	9	10	2	0	1	1	0

Signed as a free agent by **Washington**, March 1, 1987.

FELSNER, DENNY

Left wing. Shoots left. 6', 180 lbs. Born, Warren, MI, April 29, 1970.
(St. Louis' 3rd choice, 55th overall, in 1989 Entry Draft).

			Regular Season					Playoffs				
Season	Club	Lea	GP	G	A	TP	PIM	GP	G	A	TP	PIM
1988-89	U. of Michigan	CCHA	39	30	19	49	22	....	....	....	....	....
1989-90	U. of Michigan	CCHA	33	27	16	43	24	....	....	....	....	....

FENTON, ERIC

Center. Shoots right. 6'2", 190 lbs. Born, Troy, NY, July 17, 1969.
(NY Rangers' 10th choice, 202nd overall, in 1988 Entry Draft).

			Regular Season					Playoffs				
Season	Club	Lea	GP	G	A	TP	PIM	GP	G	A	TP	PIM
1987-88	Yarmouth Aca.	HS	25	37	33	70	....	....	....	....	....	....
1988-89	U. of Maine	H.E.	DID NOT PLAY									
1989-90	U. of Maine	H.E.	7	2	2	4	2	....	....	....	....	....

FENTON, PAUL JOHN

Left wing. Shoots left. 5'11", 180 lbs. Born, Springfield, MA, December 22, 1959.

			Regular Season					Playoffs				
Season	Club	Lea	GP	G	A	TP	PIM	GP	G	A	TP	PIM
1979-80	Boston U.	ECAC	24	8	17	25	14	....	....	....	....	....
1980-81	Boston U.	ECAC	5	3	2	5	0	....	....	....	....	....
1981-82	Boston U.	ECAC	28	20	13	33	20	....	....	....	....	....
1982-83a	Peoria	IHL	82	60	51	111	53	....	....	....	....	....
	Colorado	CHL	1	0	1	1	0	3	2	0	2	2
1983-84	Binghamton	AHL	78	41	24	65	67	....	....	....	....	....
1984-85	Hartford	NHL	33	7	5	12	10	....	....	....	....	....
	Binghamton	AHL	45	26	21	47	18	....	....	....	....	....
1985-86	Hartford	NHL	1	0	0	0	0	....	....	....	....	....
b	Binghamton	AHL	75	53	35	88	87	6	2	0	2	2
1986-87	NY Rangers	NHL	8	0	0	0	2	....	....	....	....	....
c	New Haven	AHL	70	37	38	75	45	7	6	4	10	6
1987-88	Los Angeles	NHL	71	20	23	43	46	5	2	1	3	2
	New Haven	AHL	5	11	5	16	9	....	....	....	....	....
1988-89	Los Angeles	NHL	21	2	3	5	6	....	....	....	....	....
	Winnipeg	NHL	59	14	9	23	33	....	....	....	....	....
1989-90	Winnipeg	NHL	80	32	18	50	40	7	2	0	2	23
	NHL Totals		273	75	58	133	137	12	4	1	5	25

a IHL First All-Star Team (1983)
b AHL First All-Star Team (1986)
c AHL Second All-Star Team (1987)

Signed as free agent by **Hartford**, October 6, 1983. Claimed by **Los Angeles** in NHL Waiver Draft, October 5, 1987. Traded to **Winnipeg** by **Los Angeles** for Gilles Hamel, November 25, 1988.

FENYVES, DAVID (FEHN-vehs)

Defense. Shoots left. 5'11", 195 lbs. Born, Dunnville, Ont., April 29, 1960.

			Regular Season					Playoffs				
Season	Club	Lea	GP	G	A	TP	PIM	GP	G	A	TP	PIM
1978-79	Peterborough	OHA	66	2	23	25	122	19	0	5	5	18
1979-80a	Peterborough	OHA	66	9	36	45	92	14	0	3	3	14
1980-81	Rochester	AHL	77	6	16	22	146	....	....	....	....	....
1981-82	Rochester	AHL	73	3	14	17	68	5	0	1	1	4
1982-83	Rochester	AHL	51	2	19	21	45	....	....	....	....	....
	Buffalo	NHL	24	0	8	8	14	4	0	0	0	0
1983-84	Buffalo	NHL	10	0	4	4	9	2	0	0	0	7
	Rochester	AHL	70	3	16	19	55	16	1	4	5	22
1984-85	Buffalo	NHL	60	1	8	9	27	5	0	0	0	2
	Rochester	AHL	9	0	3	3	8	....	....	....	....	....
1985-86	Buffalo	NHL	47	0	7	7	37	....	....	....	....	....
1986-87	Buffalo	NHL	7	1	0	1	0	....	....	....	....	....
bc	Rochester	AHL	71	6	16	22	57	18	3	12	15	10
1987-88	Philadelphia	NHL	5	0	0	0	0	....	....	....	....	....
de	Hershey	AHL	75	11	40	51	47	12	1	8	9	10
1988-89	Philadelphia	NHL	1	0	1	1	0	....	....	....	....	....
de	Hershey	AHL	79	15	51	66	41	12	2	6	8	6
1989-90	Philadelphia	NHL	12	0	0	0	4	....	....	....	....	....
	Hershey	AHL	66	6	37	43	57	....	....	....	....	....
	NHL Totals		166	2	28	30	91	11	0	0	0	9

a OHA Second All-Star Team (1980)
b AHL Second All-Star Team (1987)
c Named AHL Playoff MVP (1987)
d AHL First All-Star Team, (1988, 1989)
e Won Eddie Shore Plaque (Outstanding Defenseman-AHL) (1988, 1989)

Signed as free agent by **Buffalo**, October 31, 1979. Claimed by **Philadelphia** in NHL Waiver Draft, October 5, 1987.

FERGUS, THOMAS JOSEPH (TOM)

Center. Shoots left. 6'3", 210 lbs. Born, Chicago, IL, June 16, 1962.
(Boston's 2nd choice, 60th overall, in 1980 Entry Draft).

			Regular Season					Playoffs				
Season	Club	Lea	GP	G	A	TP	PIM	GP	G	A	TP	PIM
1979-80	Peterborough	OHA	63	8	6	14	14	14	1	5	6	6
1980-81	Peterborough	OHA	63	43	45	88	33	5	1	4	5	2
1981-82	**Boston**	**NHL**	**61**	**15**	**24**	**39**	**12**	**6**	**3**	**0**	**3**	**0**
1982-83	**Boston**	**NHL**	**80**	**28**	**35**	**63**	**39**	**15**	**2**	**2**	**4**	**15**
1983-84	**Boston**	**NHL**	**69**	**25**	**36**	**61**	**12**	**3**	**2**	**0**	**2**	**9**
1984-85	**Boston**	**NHL**	**79**	**30**	**43**	**73**	**75**	**5**	**0**	**0**	**0**	**4**
1985-86	**Toronto**	**NHL**	**78**	**31**	**42**	**73**	**64**	**10**	**5**	**7**	**12**	**6**
1986-87	**Toronto**	**NHL**	**57**	**21**	**28**	**49**	**57**	**2**	**0**	**1**	**1**	**2**
	Newmarket	AHL	1	0	1	1	0	....	....	....	....	....
1987-88	**Toronto**	**NHL**	**63**	**19**	**31**	**50**	**81**	**6**	**2**	**3**	**5**	**2**
1988-89	**Toronto**	**NHL**	**80**	**22**	**45**	**67**	**48**	**....**	**....**	**....**	**....**	**....**
1989-90	**Toronto**	**NHL**	**54**	**19**	**26**	**45**	**62**	**5**	**2**	**1**	**3**	**4**
	NHL Totals		**621**	**210**	**310**	**520**	**450**	**52**	**16**	**14**	**30**	**42**

Traded to **Toronto** by **Boston** for Bill Derlago, October 11, 1985.

FERGUSON, CRAIG

Center. Shoots left. 6', 180 lbs. Born, Castro Valley, CA, April 8, 1970.
(Montreal's 7th choice, 146th overall, in 1989 Entry Draft).

			Regular Season					Playoffs				
Season	Club	Lea	GP	G	A	TP	PIM	GP	G	A	TP	PIM
1988-89	Yale	ECAC	24	11	6	17	20	....	....	....	....	....
1989-90	Yale	ECAC	35	6	15	21	38	....	....	....	....	....

FERGUSON, JOHN Jr.

Left wing. Shoots left. 6', 192 lbs. Born, Winnipeg, Man., July 7, 1967.
(Montreal's 15th choice, 247th overall, in 1985 Entry Draft).

			Regular Season					Playoffs				
Season	Club	Lea	GP	G	A	TP	PIM	GP	G	A	TP	PIM
1985-86	Providence	H.E.	18	1	2	3	2	....	....	....	....	....
1986-87	Providence	H.E.	23	0	0	0	6	....	....	....	....	....
1987-88	Providence	H.E.	34	0	5	5	31	....	....	....	....	....
1988-89	Providence	H.E.	40	14	15	29	61	....	....	....	....	....
1989-90	Sherbrooke	AHL	17	4	3	7	8	2	0	0	0	2
	Peoria	IHL	18	1	8	9	14	3	0	0	0	2

FERNER, MARK

Defense. Shoots left. 6', 193 lbs. Born, Regina, Sask., September 5, 1965.
(Buffalo's 12th choice, 194th overall, in 1983 Entry Draft).

			Regular Season					Playoffs				
Season	Club	Lea	GP	G	A	TP	PIM	GP	G	A	TP	PIM
1982-83	Kamloops	WHL	69	6	15	21	81	7	0	0	0	7
1983-84	Kamloops	WHL	72	9	30	39	169	14	1	8	9	20
1984-85a	Kamloops	WHL	69	15	39	54	91	15	4	9	13	21
1985-86	Rochester	AHL	63	3	14	17	87	....	....	....	....	....
1986-87	**Buffalo**	**NHL**	**13**	**0**	**3**	**3**	**9**	**....**	**....**	**....**	**....**	**....**
	Rochester	AHL	54	0	12	12	157	....	....	....	....	....
1987-88	Rochester	AHL	69	1	25	26	165	7	1	4	5	31
1988-89	**Buffalo**	**NHL**	**2**	**0**	**0**	**0**	**2**	**....**	**....**	**....**	**....**	**....**
	Rochester	AHL	55	0	18	18	97	....	....	....	....	....
1989-90	**Washington**	**NHL**	**2**	**0**	**0**	**0**	**0**	**....**	**....**	**....**	**....**	**....**
	Baltimore	AHL	74	7	28	35	76	11	1	2	3	21
	NHL Totals		**17**	**0**	**3**	**3**	**11**	**....**	**....**	**....**	**....**	**....**

a WHL First All-Star Team, West Division (1985)

Traded to **Washington** by **Buffalo** for Scott McCrory, June 1, 1989.

FERNHOLZ, JAMES (JIM)

Right wing. Shoots right. 6'2", 200 lbs. Born, Minneapolis, MN, March 16, 1969.
(Winnipeg's 9th choice, 184th overall, in 1987 Entry Draft).

			Regular Season					Playoffs				
Season	Club	Lea	GP	G	A	TP	PIM	GP	G	A	TP	PIM
1987-88	U. of Vermont	ECAC	23	3	5	8	12	....	....	....	....	....
1988-89	U. of Vermont	ECAC	28	3	11	14	16	....	....	....	....	....
1989-90	U. of Vermont	ECAC	31	3	6	9	22	....	....	....	....	....

FERRARO, RAY

Center. Shoots left. 5'10", 185 lbs. Born, Trail, B.C., August 23, 1964.
(Hartford's 5th choice, 88th overall, in 1982 Entry Draft).

			Regular Season					Playoffs				
Season	Club	Lea	GP	G	A	TP	PIM	GP	G	A	TP	PIM
1982-83	Portland	WHL	50	41	49	90	39	14	14	10	24	13
1983-84a	Brandon	WHL	72	*108	84	*192	84	11	13	15	28	20
1984-85	**Hartford**	**NHL**	**44**	**11**	**17**	**28**	**40**	**....**	**....**	**....**	**....**	**....**
	Binghamton	AHL	37	20	13	33	29	....	....	....	....	....
1985-86	**Hartford**	**NHL**	**76**	**30**	**47**	**77**	**57**	**10**	**3**	**6**	**9**	**4**
1986-87	**Hartford**	**NHL**	**80**	**27**	**32**	**59**	**42**	**6**	**1**	**1**	**2**	**8**
1987-88	**Hartford**	**NHL**	**68**	**21**	**29**	**50**	**81**	**6**	**1**	**1**	**2**	**6**
1988-89	**Hartford**	**NHL**	**80**	**41**	**35**	**76**	**86**	**4**	**2**	**0**	**2**	**4**
1989-90	**Hartford**	**NHL**	**79**	**25**	**29**	**54**	**109**	**7**	**0**	**3**	**3**	**2**
	NHL Totals		**427**	**155**	**189**	**344**	**415**	**33**	**7**	**11**	**18**	**24**

a WHL First All-Star Team (1984)

FERREIRA, BRIAN

Right wing. Shoots right. 6', 175 lbs. Born, Falmouth, MA, January 2, 1968.
(Boston's 7th choice, 160th overall, in 1986 Entry Draft).

			Regular Season					Playoffs				
Season	Club	Lea	GP	G	A	TP	PIM	GP	G	A	TP	PIM
1986-87	RPI	ECAC	30	17	15	32	22	....	....	....	....	....
1987-88	RPI	ECAC	32	18	19	37	48	....	....	....	....	....
1988-89	RPI	ECAC	15	3	13	16	28	....	....	....	....	....
1989-90	RPI	ECAC	34	10	35	45	36	....	....	....	....	....

FETISOV, VIACHESLAV (SLAVA) (feh-TEE-sahf)

Defense. Shoots left. 6'1", 220 lbs. Born, Moscow, Soviet Union, May 20, 1958.
(New Jersey's 6th choice, 150th overall, in 1983 Entry Draft).

			Regular Season					Playoffs				
Season	Club	Lea	GP	G	A	TP	PIM	GP	G	A	TP	PIM
1976-77	CSKA	USSR	28	3	4	7	14	....	....	....	....	....
1977-78a	CSKA	USSR	35	9	18	27	46	....	....	....	....	....
1978-79	CSKA	USSR	29	10	19	29	40	....	....	....	....	....
1979-80a	CSKA	USSR	37	10	14	24	46	....	....	....	....	....
1980-81	CSKA	USSR	48	13	16	29	44	....	....	....	....	....
1981-82ac	CSKA	USSR	46	15	26	41	20	....	....	....	....	....
1982-83a	CSKA	USSR	43	6	17	23	46	....	....	....	....	....
1983-84abd	CSKA	USSR	44	19	30	49	38	....	....	....	....	....
1984-85a	CSKA	USSR	20	13	12	25	6	....	....	....	....	....
1985-86abc	CSKA	USSR	40	15	19	34	12	....	....	....	....	....
1986-87ab	CSKA	USSR	39	13	20	33	18	....	....	....	....	....
1987-88a	CSKA	USSR	46	18	17	35	26	....	....	....	....	....
1988-89	CSKA	USSR	23	9	8	17	18	....	....	....	....	....
1989-90	**New Jersey**	**NHL**	**72**	**8**	**34**	**42**	**52**	**6**	**0**	**2**	**2**	**10**
	NHL Totals		**72**	**8**	**34**	**42**	**52**	**6**	**0**	**2**	**2**	**10**

a Soviet National League All-Star Team (1978, 1980, 1982-88)
b Pravda Trophy-Top Scoring Defenseman (1984, 1986-88)
c Soviet Player of the Year (1982, 1986)
d Gold Stick Award-Europe's Top Player (1984)

FINLEY, JEFF

Defense. Shoots left. 6'2", 185 lbs. Born, Edmonton, Alta., April 14, 1967.
(NY Islanders' 4th choice, 55th overall, in 1985 Entry Draft).

			Regular Season					Playoffs				
Season	Club	Lea	GP	G	A	TP	PIM	GP	G	A	TP	PIM
1983-84	Portland	WHL	5	0	0	0	5	5	0	1	1	4
1984-85	Portland	WHL	69	6	44	50	57	6	1	2	3	2
1985-86	Portland	WHL	70	11	59	70	83	15	1	7	8	16
1986-87	Portland	WHL	72	13	53	66	113	20	1	*21	22	27
1987-88	**NY Islanders**	**NHL**	**10**	**0**	**5**	**5**	**15**	**1**	**0**	**0**	**0**	**2**
	Springfield	AHL	52	5	18	23	50	....	....	....	....	....
1988-89	**NY Islanders**	**NHL**	**4**	**0**	**0**	**0**	**6**	**....**	**....**	**....**	**....**	**....**
	Springfield	AHL	65	3	16	19	55	....	....	....	....	....
1989-90	**NY Islanders**	**NHL**	**11**	**0**	**1**	**1**	**0**	**5**	**0**	**2**	**2**	**2**
	Springfield	AHL	57	1	15	16	41	13	1	4	5	23
	NHL Totals		**25**	**0**	**6**	**6**	**21**	**6**	**0**	**2**	**2**	**4**

FINN, STEVEN

Defense. Shoots left. 6', 198 lbs. Born, Laval, Que., August 20, 1966.
(Quebec's 3rd choice, 57th overall, in 1984 Entry Draft).

			Regular Season					Playoffs				
Season	Club	Lea	GP	G	A	TP	PIM	GP	G	A	TP	PIM
1982-83	Laval	QMJHL	69	7	30	37	108	6	0	2	2	6
1983-84	Laval	QMJHL	68	7	39	46	159	14	1	6	7	27
1984-85a	Laval	QMJHL	61	20	33	53	169	....	....	....	....	....
	Fredericton	AHL	4	0	0	0	14	6	1	1	2	4
1985-86	**Quebec**	**NHL**	**17**	**0**	**1**	**1**	**28**	**....**	**....**	**....**	**....**	**....**
	Laval	QMJHL	29	4	15	19	111	14	6	16	22	57
1986-87	**Quebec**	**NHL**	**36**	**2**	**5**	**7**	**40**	**13**	**0**	**2**	**2**	**29**
	Fredericton	AHL	38	7	19	26	73	....	....	....	....	....
1987-88	**Quebec**	**NHL**	**75**	**3**	**7**	**10**	**198**	**....**	**....**	**....**	**....**	**....**
1988-89	**Quebec**	**NHL**	**77**	**2**	**6**	**8**	**235**	**....**	**....**	**....**	**....**	**....**
1989-90	**Quebec**	**NHL**	**64**	**3**	**9**	**12**	**208**	**....**	**....**	**....**	**....**	**....**
	NHL Totals		**269**	**10**	**28**	**38**	**709**	**13**	**0**	**2**	**2**	**29**

a QMJHL Second All-Star Team (1985).

FIORENTINO, PETER

Defense. Shoots right. 6'1", 200 lbs. Born, Niagara Falls, Ont., December 22, 1968.
(NY Rangers' 11th choice, 215th overall, in 1988 Entry Draft).

			Regular Season					Playoffs				
Season	Club	Lea	GP	G	A	TP	PIM	GP	G	A	TP	PIM
1987-88	S.S. Marie	OHL	65	5	27	32	252	6	2	2	4	21
1988-89	S.S. Marie	OHL	55	5	24	29	220	....	....	....	....	....
	Denver	IHL	10	0	0	0	39	4	0	0	0	24
1989-90	Flint	IHL	64	2	7	9	302	....	....	....	....	....

FISHER, CRAIG

Center. Shoots left. 6'3", 185 lbs. Born, Oshawa, Ont., June 30, 1970.
(Philadelphia's 3rd choice, 56th overall, in 1988 Entry Draft).

			Regular Season					Playoffs				
Season	Club	Lea	GP	G	A	TP	PIM	GP	G	A	TP	PIM
1988-89	Miami-Ohio	CCHA	37	22	20	42	37	....	....	....	....	....
1989-90a	Miami-Ohio	CCHA	39	37	29	66	38	....	....	....	....	....
	Philadelphia	**NHL**	**2**	**0**	**0**	**0**	**0**	**....**	**....**	**....**	**....**	**....**
	NHL Totals		**2**	**0**	**0**	**0**	**0**	**....**	**....**	**....**	**....**	**....**

a CCHA First All-Star Team (1990)

FITZGERALD, SEAN

Left wing. Shoots left. 6'1", 210 lbs. Born, W. Seneca, NY, January 12, 1967.
(Los Angeles' 1st choice, 12th overall, in 1988 Supplemental Draft).

			Regular Season					Playoffs				
Season	Club	Lea	GP	G	A	TP	PIM	GP	G	A	TP	PIM
1987-88	Oswego State	NCAA	30	40	36	76		....	....	....	....	....
1988-89	Oswego State	NCAA	30	51	26	77	38	....	....	....	....	....
1989-90	New Haven	AHL	1	0	0	0	0	....	....	....	....	....

FITZGERALD, TOM

Center. Shoots right. 6'1", 195 lbs. Born, Melrose, MA, August 28, 1968.
(NY Islanders' 1st choice, 17th overall, in 1986 Entry Draft).

			Regular Season					Playoffs				
Season	Club	Lea	GP	G	A	TP	PIM	GP	G	A	TP	PIM
1986-87	Providence	H.E.	27	8	14	22	22	....	....	....	....	....
1987-88	Providence	H.E.	36	19	15	34	50	....	....	....	....	....
1988-89	**NY Islanders**	**NHL**	**23**	**3**	**5**	**8**	**10**	....	....	....	....	....
	Springfield	AHL	61	24	18	42	43	....	....	....	....	....
1989-90	**NY Islanders**	**NHL**	**19**	**2**	**5**	**7**	**4**	**4**	**1**	**0**	**1**	**4**
	Springfield	AHL	53	30	23	53	32	14	2	9	11	13
	NHL Totals		**42**	**5**	**10**	**15**	**14**	**4**	**1**	**0**	**1**	**4**

FITZPATRICK, ROSS

Center. Shoots left. 6', 190 lbs. Born, Penticton, B.C., October 7, 1960.
(Philadelphia's 7th choice, 147th overall, in 1980 Entry Draft).

			Regular Season					Playoffs				
Season	Club	Lea	GP	G	A	TP	PIM	GP	G	A	TP	PIM
1978-79	W. Michigan	CCHA	35	16	21	37	31	....	....	....	....	....
1979-80	W. Michigan	CCHA	34	26	33	59	22	....	....	....	....	....
1980-81a	W. Michigan	CCHA	36	28	43	71	22	....	....	....	....	....
1981-82	W. Michigan	CCHA	33	30	28	58	34	....	....	....	....	....
1982-83	**Philadelphia**	**NHL**	**1**	**0**	**0**	**0**	**0**	....	....	....	....	....
	Maine	AHL	66	29	28	57	32	12	5	1	6	12
1983-84	**Philadelphia**	**NHL**	**12**	**4**	**2**	**6**	**0**	....	....	....	....	....
	Springfield	AHL	45	33	30	63	28	4	3	2	5	2
1984-85	**Philadelphia**	**NHL**	**5**	**1**	**0**	**1**	**0**	....	....	....	....	....
	Hershey	AHL	35	26	15	41	8	....	....	....	....	....
1985-86	**Philadelphia**	**NHL**	**2**	**0**	**0**	**0**	**0**	....	....	....	....	....
b	Hershey	AHL	77	50	47	97	28	17	9	7	16	10
1986-87	Hershey	AHL	66	45	40	85	34	5	1	4	5	10
1987-88	Hershey	AHL	35	14	17	31	12	12	*11	4	15	8
1988-89	Hershey	AHL	11	6	9	15	4	9	2	2	4	4
1989-90b	Hershey	AHL	74	45	*58	103	26	....	....	....	....	....
	NHL Totals		**20**	**5**	**2**	**7**	**0**	....	....	....	....	....

a CCHA First All-Star Team (1981)
b AHL Second All-Star Team (1986, 1990)

FLAHERTY, JEFF

Right wing. Shoots right. 6'3", 210 lbs. Born, Boston, MA, July 16, 1968.
(Boston's 8th choice, 181st overall, in 1986 Entry Draft).

			Regular Season					Playoffs				
Season	Club	Lea	GP	G	A	TP	PIM	GP	G	A	TP	PIM
1986-87	U. of Lowell	H.E.	28	4	5	9	37	....	....	....	....	....
1987-88	U. of Lowell	H.E.	34	27	12	39	126	....	....	....	....	....
1988-89	U. of Lowell	H.E.	22	12	11	23	77	....	....	....	....	....
1989-90	U. of Lowell	H.E.	18	5	5	10	58	....	....	....	....	....

FLANAGAN, JOSEPH

Center. Shoots right. 6', 180 lbs. Born, Arlington, MA, March 5, 1969.
(Los Angeles' 13th choice, 238th overall, in 1988 Entry Draft).

			Regular Season					Playoffs				
Season	Club	Lea	GP	G	A	TP	PIM	GP	G	A	TP	PIM
1988-89	N. Hampshire	H.E.	23	11	34	45	4	....	....	....	....	....
1989-90	N. Hampshire	H.E.	34	12	24	36	6	....	....	....	....	....

FLANAGAN, PAUL

Defense. Shoots left. 6'2", 205 lbs. Born, Acton, MA, May 17, 1969.
(Buffalo's 7th choice, 127th overall, in 1987 Entry Draft).

			Regular Season					Playoffs				
Season	Club	Lea	GP	G	A	TP	PIM	GP	G	A	TP	PIM
1988-89	Northeastern	H.E.	25	1	4	5	....	....	....	....	....	....
1989-90	Northeastern	H.E.	30	0	1	1	32	....	....	....	....	....

FLATLEY, PATRICK (FLAT-lee)

Right wing. Shoots right. 6'2", 197 lbs. Born, Toronto, Ont., October 3, 1963.
(NY Islanders' 1st choice, 21st overall, in 1982 Entry Draft).

			Regular Season					Playoffs				
Season	Club	Lea	GP	G	A	TP	PIM	GP	G	A	TP	PIM
1981-82	U. Wisconsin	WCHA	17	10	9	19	40	....	....	....	....	....
1982-83ab	U. Wisconsin	WCHA	26	17	24	41	48	....	....	....	....	....
1983-84	Cdn. Olympic	....	57	33	17	50	136	....	....	....	....	....
	NY Islanders	**NHL**	**16**	**2**	**7**	**9**	**6**	**21**	**9**	**6**	**15**	**14**
1984-85	**NY Islanders**	**NHL**	**78**	**20**	**31**	**51**	**106**	**4**	**1**	**0**	**1**	**6**
1985-86	**NY Islanders**	**NHL**	**73**	**18**	**34**	**52**	**66**	**3**	**0**	**0**	**0**	**21**
1986-87	**NY Islanders**	**NHL**	**63**	**16**	**35**	**51**	**81**	**11**	**3**	**2**	**5**	**6**
1987-88	**NY Islanders**	**NHL**	**40**	**9**	**15**	**24**	**28**	....	....	....	....	....
1988-89	**NY Islanders**	**NHL**	**41**	**10**	**15**	**25**	**31**	....	....	....	....	....
	Springfield	AHL	2	1	1	2	2	....	....	....	....	....
1989-90	**NY Islanders**	**NHL**	**62**	**17**	**32**	**49**	**101**	**5**	**3**	**0**	**3**	**2**
	NHL Totals		**373**	**92**	**169**	**261**	**419**	**44**	**16**	**8**	**24**	**49**

a WCHA First All-Star Team (1983)
b Named to NCAA All-Tournament Team (1983)

FLETCHER, STEVEN

Left wing. Shoots left. 6'3", 205 lbs. Born, Montreal, Que., March 31, 1962.
(Calgary's 11th choice, 202nd overall, in 1980 Entry Draft).

			Regular Season					Playoffs				
Season	Club	Lea	GP	G	A	TP	PIM	GP	G	A	TP	PIM
1981-82	Hull	QMJHL	60	4	20	24	230	....	....	....	....	....
1982-83	Sherbrooke	AHL	36	0	1	1	119	....	....	....	....	....
	Fort Wayne	IHL	34	1	9	10	115	....	....	....	....	....
1983-84	Sherbrooke	AHL	77	3	7	10	208	....	....	....	....	....
1984-85	Sherbrooke	AHL	50	2	4	6	192	13	0	0	0	48
1985-86	Sherbrooke	AHL	64	2	12	14	293	....	....	....	....	....
1986-87	Sherbrooke	AHL	70	15	11	26	261	17	5	5	10	*82
1987-88	**Montreal**	**NHL**	....	....	....	....	....	**1**	**0**	**0**	**0**	**5**
	Sherbrooke	AHL	76	8	21	29	338	6	2	1	3	28
1988-89	**Winnipeg**	**NHL**	**3**	**0**	**0**	**0**	**5**	....	....	....	....	....
	Halifax	AHL	29	5	8	13	91	....	....	....	....	....
	Moncton	AHL	23	1	1	2	89	....	....	....	....	....
1989-90	Hershey	AHL	28	1	1	2	132	....	....	....	....	....
	NHL Totals		**3**	**0**	**0**	**0**	**5**	**1**	**0**	**0**	**0**	**5**

Signed as a free agent by **Montreal**, August 21, 1984. Traded to **Philadelphia** by **Winnipeg** for future considerations, December 12, 1988.

FLEURY, THEOREN

Center. Shoots right. 5'6", 160 lbs. Born, Oxbow, Sask., June 29, 1968.
(Calgary's 9th choice, 166th overall, in 1987 Entry Draft).

			Regular Season					Playoffs				
Season	Club	Lea	GP	G	A	TP	PIM	GP	G	A	TP	PIM
1986-87	Moose Jaw	WHL	66	61	68	129	110	9	7	9	16	34
1987-88	Moose Jaw	WHL	65	68	92	*160	235	....	....	....	....	....
	Salt Lake	IHL	2	3	4	7	7	8	11	5	16	16
1988-89	**Calgary**	**NHL**	**36**	**14**	**20**	**34**	**46**	**22**	**5**	**6**	**11**	**24**
	Salt Lake	IHL	40	37	37	74	81	....	....	....	....	....
1989-90	**Calgary**	**NHL**	**80**	**31**	**35**	**66**	**157**	**6**	**2**	**3**	**5**	**10**
	NHL Totals		**116**	**45**	**55**	**100**	**203**	**28**	**7**	**9**	**16**	**34**

FLICHEL, TODD (FLIH-kehl)

Defense. Shoots right. 6'3", 195 lbs. Born, Osgoode, Ont., September 14, 1964.
(Winnipeg's 10th choice, 169th overall, in 1983 Entry Draft).

			Regular Season					Playoffs				
Season	Club	Lea	GP	G	A	TP	PIM	GP	G	A	TP	PIM
1983-84	Bowling Green	CCHA	44	1	3	4	12	....	....	....	....	....
1984-85	Bowling Green	CCHA	42	5	7	12	62	....	....	....	....	....
1985-86	Bowling Green	CCHA	42	3	10	13	84	....	....	....	....	....
1986-87	Bowling Green	CCHA	42	4	15	19	77	....	....	....	....	....
1987-88	**Winnipeg**	**NHL**	**2**	**0**	**0**	**0**	**2**	....	....	....	....	....
	Moncton	AHL	65	5	12	17	102	....	....	....	....	....
1988-89	**Winnipeg**	**NHL**	**1**	**0**	**0**	**0**	**0**	....	....	....	....	....
	Moncton	AHL	74	2	29	31	81	10	1	4	5	25
1989-90	**Winnipeg**	**NHL**	**3**	**0**	**1**	**1**	**2**	....	....	....	....	....
	Moncton	AHL	65	7	14	21	74	....	....	....	....	....
	NHL Totals		**6**	**0**	**1**	**1**	**4**	....	....	....	....	....

FLOCKHART, RONALD (RON)

Center. Shoots left. 5'11", 185 lbs. Born, Smithers, B.C., October 10, 1960.

			Regular Season					Playoffs				
Season	Club	Lea	GP	G	A	TP	PIM	GP	G	A	TP	PIM
1979-80	Regina	WHL	65	54	76	130	63	17	11	23	34	18
1980-81	Maine	AHL	59	33	33	66	26	....	....	....	....	....
	Philadelphia	**NHL**	**14**	**3**	**7**	**10**	**11**	**3**	**1**	**0**	**1**	**2**
1981-82	**Philadelphia**	**NHL**	**72**	**33**	**39**	**72**	**44**	**4**	**0**	**1**	**1**	**2**
1982-83	**Philadelphia**	**NHL**	**73**	**29**	**31**	**60**	**49**	**2**	**1**	**1**	**2**	**2**
1983-84	**Philadelphia**	**NHL**	**8**	**0**	**3**	**3**	**4**	....	....	....	....	....
	Pittsburgh	**NHL**	**68**	**27**	**18**	**45**	**40**	....	....	....	....	....
1984-85	**Pittsburgh**	**NHL**	**12**	**0**	**5**	**5**	**4**	....	....	....	....	....
	Montreal	**NHL**	**42**	**10**	**12**	**22**	**14**	**2**	**1**	**1**	**2**	**2**
1985-86	**St. Louis**	**NHL**	**79**	**22**	**45**	**67**	**26**	**8**	**1**	**3**	**4**	**6**
1986-87	**St. Louis**	**NHL**	**60**	**16**	**19**	**35**	**12**	....	....	....	....	....
1987-88	**St. Louis**	**NHL**	**21**	**5**	**4**	**9**	**4**	....	....	....	....	....
1988-89	**Boston**	**NHL**	**4**	**0**	**0**	**0**	**0**	....	....	....	....	....
	Maine	AHL	9	5	6	11	0	....	....	....	....	....
	Peoria	IHL	2	0	2	2	2	....	....	....	....	....
1989-90	Bologna	Italy	36	48	85	133	15	9	5	9	14	0
	NHL Totals		**453**	**145**	**183**	**328**	**208**	**19**	**4**	**6**	**10**	**14**

Signed as free agent by **Philadelphia**, July 2, 1980. Traded to **Pittsburgh** by **Philadelphia** with Andy Brickley, Mark Taylor and Philadelphia's first round (Roger Belanger) and third round (Mike Stevens - later transferred to Vancouver) choices in 1984 Entry Draft for Rich Sutter and Pittsburgh's second round (Greg Smyth) and third round (David McLay) choices in 1984 Entry Draft, October 23, 1983. Traded to **Montreal** by **Pittsburgh** for John Chabot, November 9, 1984. Traded to **St. Louis** by **Montreal** for Perry Ganchar, August 26, 1985. Traded to **Boston** by **St. Louis** for future considerations, February 13, 1989.

FLOYD, LARRY DAVID

Center. Shoots left. 5'8", 180 lbs. Born, Peterborough, Ont., May 1, 1961.

			Regular Season					Playoffs				
Season	Club	Lea	GP	G	A	TP	PIM	GP	G	A	TP	PIM
1979-80	Peterborough	OHA	66	21	37	58	54	14	6	9	15	10
1980-81	Peterborough	OHA	44	26	37	63	43	5	2	2	4	0
1981-82	Peterborough	OHL	39	32	37	69	26	9	9	6	15	20
	Rochester	AHL	1	0	2	2	0	7	1	1	2	0
1982-83	**New Jersey**	**NHL**	**5**	**1**	**0**	**1**	**2**	....	....	....	....	....
a	Wichita	CHL	75	40	43	83	16	....	....	....	....	....
1983-84	**New Jersey**	**NHL**	**7**	**1**	**3**	**4**	**7**	....	....	....	....	....
	Maine	AHL	74	37	49	86	40	16	9	8	17	4
1984-85	Maine	AHL	72	30	51	81	24	3	0	1	1	2
1985-86	Maine	AHL	80	29	58	87	25	5	3	3	6	0
1986-87	Maine	AHL	77	30	44	74	50	....	....	....	....	....
1987-88	Utica	AHL	28	21	21	42	14	....	....	....	....	....
1988-89	Cape Breton	AHL	70	16	33	49	40	....	....	....	....	....
1989-90	Phoenix	IHL	76	39	40	79	50	....	....	....	....	....
	NHL Totals		**12**	**2**	**3**	**5**	**9**	....	....	....	....	....

a Won Ken McKenzie Trophy (CHL's Rookie of the Year) (1983)
Signed as free agent by **New Jersey**, September 16, 1982.

FOGARTY, BRYAN

Defense. Shoots left. 6'2", 198 lbs. Born, Brantford, Ont., June 11, 1969.
(Quebec's 1st choice, 9th overall, in 1987 Entry Draft).

			Regular Season					Playoffs				
Season	Club	Lea	GP	G	A	TP	PIM	GP	G	A	TP	PIM
1985-86	Kingston	OHL	47	2	19	21	14	10	1	3	4	4
1986-87a	Kingston	OHL	56	20	50	70	46	12	2	3	5	5
1987-88	Kingston	OHL	48	11	36	47	50	....	....	....	....	....
1988-89abc	Niagara Falls	OHL	60	47	*108	*155	88	17	10	22	32	36
1989-90	**Quebec**	**NHL**	**45**	**4**	**10**	**14**	**31**	....	....	....	....	....
	Halifax	AHL	22	5	14	19	6	6	2	4	6	0
	NHL Totals		**45**	**4**	**10**	**14**	**31**	....	....	....	....	....

a OHL First All-Star Team (1987, 1989)
b OHL Player of the Year (1989)
c Canadian Major Junior Player of the Year (1989)

FOLIGNO, MIKE ANTHONY (foh-LEE-noh)

Right wing. Shoots right. 6'2", 195 lbs. Born, Sudbury, Ont., January 29, 1959.
(Detroit's 1st choice, 3rd overall, in 1979 Entry Draft).

			Regular Season					Playoffs				
Season	Club	Lea	GP	G	A	TP	PIM	GP	G	A	TP	PIM
1977-78	Sudbury	OHA	67	47	39	86	112	....	....	....	....	....
1978-79a	Sudbury	OHA	68	65	85	*150	98	10	5	5	10	14
1979-80	**Detroit**	**NHL**	**80**	**36**	**35**	**71**	**109**	....	....	....	....	....
1980-81	**Detroit**	**NHL**	**80**	**28**	**35**	**63**	**210**	....	....	....	....	....
1981-82	**Detroit**	**NHL**	**26**	**13**	**13**	**26**	**28**	....	....	....	....	....
	Buffalo	**NHL**	**56**	**20**	**31**	**51**	**149**	**4**	**2**	**0**	**2**	**9**
1982-83	**Buffalo**	**NHL**	**66**	**22**	**25**	**47**	**135**	**10**	**2**	**3**	**5**	**39**
1983-84	**Buffalo**	**NHL**	**70**	**32**	**31**	**63**	**151**	**3**	**2**	**1**	**3**	**19**
1984-85	**Buffalo**	**NHL**	**77**	**27**	**29**	**56**	**154**	**5**	**1**	**3**	**4**	**12**
1985-86	**Buffalo**	**NHL**	**79**	**41**	**39**	**80**	**168**	....	....	....	....	....
1986-87	**Buffalo**	**NHL**	**75**	**30**	**29**	**59**	**176**	....	....	....	....	....
1987-88	**Buffalo**	**NHL**	**74**	**29**	**28**	**57**	**220**	**6**	**3**	**2**	**5**	**31**
1988-89	**Buffalo**	**NHL**	**75**	**27**	**22**	**49**	**156**	**5**	**3**	**1**	**4**	**21**
1989-90	**Buffalo**	**NHL**	**61**	**15**	**25**	**40**	**99**	**6**	**0**	**1**	**1**	**12**
	NHL Totals		**819**	**320**	**342**	**662**	**1755**	**39**	**13**	**11**	**24**	**143**

a OHL First All-Star Team (1979)

Traded to **Buffalo** by **Detroit** with Dale McCourt and Brent Peterson for Danny Gare, Jim Schoenfeld and Derek Smith, December 2, 1981.

FOOTE, ADAM

Defense. Shoots right. 6'1", 180 lbs. Born, Toronto, Ont., July 10, 1971.
(Quebec's 2nd choice, 22nd overall, in 1989 Entry Draft).

			Regular Season					Playoffs				
Season	Club	Lea	GP	G	A	TP	PIM	GP	G	A	TP	PIM
1988-89	S.S. Marie	OHL	66	7	32	39	120	....	....	....	....	....
1989-90	S.S. Marie	OHL	61	12	43	55	199	....	....	....	....	....

FORSLUND, THOMAS

Right wing. Shoots left. 6', 185 lbs. Born, Falund, Sweden, November 24, 1968.
(Calgary's 4th choice, 85th overall, in 1988 Entry Draft).

			Regular Season					Playoffs				
Season	Club	Lea	GP	G	A	TP	PIM	GP	G	A	TP	PIM
1986-87	Leksand	Swe.	23	3	5	8	....	....	....	....	....	
1987-88	Leksand	Swe.	37	9	10	19	....	....	....	....	....	
1988-89	Leksand	Swe.	39	14	16	30	56	....	....	....	....	....
1989-90	Leksand	Swe.	38	14	21	35	48	3	0	1	1	2

FORTIER, MARC

Center. Shoots right. 6', 192 lbs. Born, Windsor, Que., February 26, 1966.

			Regular Season					Playoffs				
Season	Club	Lea	GP	G	A	TP	PIM	GP	G	A	TP	PIM
1983-84	Chicoutimi	QMJHL	67	16	30	46	51	....	....	....	....	....
1984-85	Chicoutimi	QMJHL	68	35	63	98	114	14	8	4	12	16
1985-86	Chicoutimi	QMJHL	71	47	86	133	49	9	2	14	16	12
1986-87	Chicoutimi	QMJHL	65	66	135	201	39	19	11	40	51	20
1987-88	**Quebec**	**NHL**	**27**	**4**	**10**	**14**	**12**	....	....	....	....	....
	Fredericton	AHL	50	26	36	62	48	....	....	....	....	....
1988-89	**Quebec**	**NHL**	**57**	**20**	**19**	**39**	**45**	....	....	....	....	....
	Halifax	AHL	16	11	11	22	14	....	....	....	....	....
1989-90	**Quebec**	**NHL**	**59**	**13**	**17**	**30**	**28**	....	....	....	....	....
	Halifax	AHL	15	5	6	11	6	....	....	....	....	....
	NHL Totals		**143**	**37**	**46**	**83**	**85**	....	....	....	....	....

Signed as a free agent by **Quebec**, February 3, 1987.

FOSTER, COREY

Defense. Shoots left. 6'3", 200 lbs. Born, Ottawa, Ont., October 27, 1969.
(New Jersey's 1st choice, 12th overall, in 1988 Entry Draft).

			Regular Season					Playoffs				
Season	Club	Lea	GP	G	A	TP	PIM	GP	G	A	TP	PIM
1986-87	Peterborough	OHL	30	3	4	7	4	1	0	0	0	0
1987-88	Peterborough	OHL	66	13	31	44	58	11	5	9	14	13
1988-89	**New Jersey**	**NHL**	**2**	**0**	**0**	**0**	**0**	....	....	....	....	....
a	Peterborough	OHL	55	14	42	56	42	17	1	17	18	12
1989-90	Cape Breton	AHL	54	7	17	24	32	1	0	0	0	0
	NHL Totals		**2**	**0**	**0**	**0**	**0**	....	....	....	....	....

a OHL Third All-Star Team (1989)

Traded to **Edmonton** by **New Jersey** for Edmonton's first-round choice (Jason Millar) in 1989 Entry Draft, June 17, 1989.

FOSTER, STEPHEN

Defense. Shoots right. 6'3", 210 lbs. Born, Brockton, MA, March 21, 1971.
(Boston's 6th choice, 122nd overall, in 1989 Entry Draft).

			Regular Season					Playoffs				
Season	Club	Lea	GP	G	A	TP	PIM	GP	G	A	TP	PIM
1989-90	Catholic Mem.	HS	19	5	10	15	....	....	....	....	....	....
1989-90	Boston U.	H.E.	28	0	8	8	26	....	....	....	....	....

FOTIU, NICHOLAS EVLAMPIOS (NICK) (foh-TEE-oo)

Left wing. Shoots left. 6'2", 210 lbs. Born, Staten Island, NY, May 25, 1952.

			Regular Season					Playoffs				
Season	Club	Lea	GP	G	A	TP	PIM	GP	G	A	TP	PIM
1973-74	Cape Cod	NAHL	72	12	24	36	371	....	....	....	....	....
1974-75	Cape Cod	NAHL	5	2	1	3	13	....	....	....	....	....
	New England	WHA	61	2	2	4	144	4	2	0	2	27
1975-76	Cape Cod	NAHL	6	2	1	3	15	....	....	....	....	....
	New England	WHA	49	3	2	5	94	16	3	2	5	57
1976-77	**NY Rangers**	**NHL**	**70**	**4**	**8**	**12**	**174**	....	....	....	....	....
1977-78	New Haven	AHL	5	1	1	2	9	....	....	....	....	....
	NY Rangers	**NHL**	**59**	**2**	**7**	**9**	**105**	**3**	**0**	**0**	**0**	**5**
1978-79	**NY Rangers**	**NHL**	**71**	**3**	**5**	**8**	**190**	**4**	**0**	**0**	**0**	**6**
1979-80	**Hartford**	**NHL**	**74**	**10**	**8**	**18**	**107**	**3**	**0**	**0**	**0**	**6**
1980-81	**Hartford**	**NHL**	**42**	**4**	**3**	**7**	**79**	....	....	....	....	....
	NY Rangers	**NHL**	**27**	**5**	**6**	**11**	**91**	**2**	**0**	**0**	**0**	**4**
1981-82	**NY Rangers**	**NHL**	**70**	**8**	**10**	**18**	**151**	**10**	**0**	**2**	**2**	**6**
1982-83	**NY Rangers**	**NHL**	**72**	**8**	**13**	**21**	**90**	**5**	**0**	**1**	**1**	**6**
1983-84	**NY Rangers**	**NHL**	**40**	**7**	**6**	**13**	**115**	....	....	....	....	....
1984-85	**NY Rangers**	**NHL**	**46**	**4**	**7**	**11**	**54**	....	....	....	....	....
1985-86	New Haven	AHL	9	4	2	6	21	....	....	....	....	....
	Calgary	**NHL**	**9**	**0**	**1**	**1**	**21**	**11**	**0**	**1**	**1**	**34**
1986-87	**Calgary**	**NHL**	**42**	**5**	**3**	**8**	**145**	....	....	....	....	....
1987-88	**Philadelphia**	**NHL**	**23**	**0**	**0**	**0**	**40**	....	....	....	....	....
1988-89	**Edmonton**	**NHL**	**1**	**0**	**0**	**0**	**0**	....	....	....	....	....
1989-90	New Haven	AHL	31	0	3	3	40	....	....	....	....	....
	NHL Totals		**646**	**60**	**77**	**137**	**1362**	**38**	**0**	**4**	**4**	**67**

Signed as free agent by **NY Rangers**, July 23, 1976. Claimed by **Hartford** from **NY Rangers** in Expansion Draft, June 13, 1979. Traded to **NY Rangers** by **Hartford** for Rangers' fifth round choice (Bill Maguire) in 1981 Entry Draft, January 15, 1981. Traded to **Calgary** by **NY Rangers** for Calgary's sixth-round choice in 1987 Entry Draft, March 11, 1986. Signed as a free agent by **Philadelphia**, October 30, 1987.

FOWLER, ROB

Defense. Shoots left. 6'1", 195 lbs. Born, Tewksbury, MA, July 9, 1965.
(Winnipeg's 1st choice, 21st overall, in 1987 Supplemental Draft).

			Regular Season					Playoffs				
Season	Club	Lea	GP	G	A	TP	PIM	GP	G	A	TP	PIM
1984-85	Merrimack	NCAA	32	8	19	27	42	....	....	....	....	....
1985-86	Merrimack	NCAA	32	3	20	23	50	....	....	....	....	....
1986-87a	Merrimack	NCAA	35	2	25	27	49	....	....	....	....	....
1987-88	Moncton	AHL	68	2	11	13	51	....	....	....	....	....
1988-89	Fort Wayne	IHL	67	9	12	21	62	9	1	0	1	8
1989-90	Fort Wayne	IHL	59	8	14	22	75	5	0	2	2	19

a NCAA Division III First All-Star Team (1987)

FOX, JAMES CHARLES (JIMMY)

Right wing. Shoots right. 5'8", 185 lbs. Born, Coniston, Ont., May 18, 1960.
(Los Angeles' 2nd choice, 10th overall, in 1980 Entry Draft).

			Regular Season					Playoffs				
Season	Club	Lea	GP	G	A	TP	PIM	GP	G	A	TP	PIM
1978-79	Ottawa	OHA	53	37	66	103	4	4	2	1	3	2
1979-80ab	Ottawa	OHA	52	65	*101	*166	30	11	6	14	20	2
1980-81	**Los Angeles**	**NHL**	**71**	**18**	**25**	**43**	**8**	**4**	**0**	**1**	**1**	**0**
1981-82	**Los Angeles**	**NHL**	**77**	**30**	**38**	**68**	**23**	**9**	**1**	**4**	**5**	**0**
1982-83	**Los Angeles**	**NHL**	**77**	**28**	**40**	**68**	**8**	....	....	....	....	....
1983-84	**Los Angeles**	**NHL**	**80**	**30**	**42**	**72**	**26**	....	....	....	....	....
1984-85	**Los Angeles**	**NHL**	**79**	**30**	**53**	**83**	**10**	**3**	**0**	**1**	**1**	**0**
1985-86	**Los Angeles**	**NHL**	**39**	**14**	**17**	**31**	**2**	....	....	....	....	....
1986-87	**Los Angeles**	**NHL**	**76**	**19**	**42**	**61**	**48**	**5**	**3**	**2**	**5**	**0**
1987-88	**Los Angeles**	**NHL**	**68**	**16**	**35**	**51**	**18**	**1**	**0**	**0**	**0**	**0**
1988-89	**Los Angeles**	**NHL**	DID NOT PLAY - INJURED									
1989-90	**Los Angeles**	**NHL**	**11**	**1**	**1**	**2**	**0**	....	....	....	....	....
	NHL Totals		**578**	**186**	**293**	**479**	**143**	**22**	**4**	**8**	**12**	**0**

a OHA First All-Star Team (1980)
b Named OHA Most Valuable Player (1980)

FRANCESCHETTI, LOU (FRAN-sihs-KEH-tee)

Left wing. Shoots left. 6', 190 lbs. Born, Toronto, Ont., March 28, 1958.
(Washington's 8th choice, 71st overall, in 1978 Amateur Draft).

			Regular Season					Playoffs				
Season	Club	Lea	GP	G	A	TP	PIM	GP	G	A	TP	PIM
1976-77	Niagara Falls	OHA	61	23	30	53	80	....	....	....	....	....
1977-78	Niagara Falls	OHA	62	40	50	90	46	....	....	....	....	....
1978-79	Saginaw	IHL	2	1	1	2	0	....	....	....	....	....
	Port Huron	IHL	76	45	58	103	131	....	....	....	....	....
1979-80	Port Huron	IHL	15	3	8	11	31	....	....	....	....	....
	Hershey	AHL	65	27	29	56	58	14	6	9	15	32
1980-81	Hershey	AHL	79	32	36	68	173	10	3	7	10	30
1981-82	Hershey	AHL	50	22	33	55	89	....	....	....	....	....
	Washington	**NHL**	**30**	**2**	**10**	**12**	**23**	....	....	....	....	....
1982-83	Hershey	AHL	80	31	44	75	176	5	1	2	3	16
1983-84	Hershey	AHL	73	26	34	60	130	....	....	....	....	....
	Washington	**NHL**	**2**	**0**	**0**	**0**	**0**	**3**	**0**	**0**	**0**	**8**
1984-85	**Washington**	**NHL**	**22**	**4**	**7**	**11**	**45**	**5**	**1**	**1**	**2**	**15**
	Binghamton	AHL	52	29	43	72	75	....	....	....	....	....
1985-86	**Washington**	**NHL**	**76**	**7**	**14**	**21**	**131**	**8**	**0**	**0**	**0**	**15**
1986-87	**Washington**	**NHL**	**75**	**12**	**9**	**21**	**127**	**7**	**0**	**0**	**0**	**23**
1987-88	**Washington**	**NHL**	**59**	**4**	**8**	**12**	**113**	**4**	**0**	**0**	**0**	**14**
	Binghamton	AHL	6	2	4	6	4	....	....	....	....	....
1988-89	**Washington**	**NHL**	**63**	**7**	**10**	**17**	**123**	**6**	**1**	**0**	**1**	**8**
	Baltimore	AHL	10	8	7	15	30	....	....	....	....	....
1989-90	**Toronto**	**NHL**	**80**	**21**	**15**	**36**	**127**	**5**	**0**	**1**	**1**	**26**
	NHL Totals		**407**	**57**	**73**	**130**	**689**	**38**	**2**	**2**	**4**	**109**

Traded to **Toronto** by **Washington** for Toronto's fifth round choice (Mark Ouimet) in 1990 Entry Draft, June 29, 1989.

FRANCIS, RONALD (RON)

Center. Shoots left. 6'2", 200 lbs. Born, Sault Ste. Marie, Ont., March 1, 1963.
(Hartford's 1st choice, 4th overall, in 1981 Entry Draft).

			Regular Season					Playoffs				
Season	Club	Lea	GP	G	A	TP	PIM	GP	G	A	TP	PIM
1980-81	S. S. Marie	OHA	64	26	43	69	33	19	7	8	15	34
1981-82	S. S. Marie	OHL	25	18	30	48	46	....	....	....	....	....
	Hartford	NHL	59	25	43	68	51	....	....	....	....	....
1982-83	Hartford	NHL	79	31	59	90	60	....	....	....	....	....
1983-84	Hartford	NHL	72	23	60	83	45	....	....	....	....	....
1984-85	Hartford	NHL	80	24	57	81	66	....	....	....	....	....
1985-86	Hartford	NHL	53	24	53	77	24	10	1	2	3	4
1986-87	Hartford	NHL	75	30	63	93	45	6	2	2	4	6
1987-88	Hartford	NHL	80	25	50	75	87	6	2	5	7	2
1988-89	Hartford	NHL	69	29	48	77	36	4	0	2	2	0
1989-90	Hartford	NHL	80	32	69	101	73	7	3	3	6	8
	NHL Totals		647	243	502	745	487	33	8	14	22	20

Played in NHL All-Star Game (1983, 1985, 1990)

FRANTTI, GORDON

Left wing. Shoots left. 6'5", 235 lbs. Born, Laurium, MI, July 17, 1970.
(Philadelphia's 7th choice, 119th overall, in 1988 Entry Draft).

			Regular Season					Playoffs				
Season	Club	Lea	GP	G	A	TP	PIM	GP	G	A	TP	PIM
1988-89	West.Michigan	NAJHL	29	28	19	47	....	....	....	....	....	....
1989-90	W. Michigan	CCHA	30	7	4	11	16	....	....	....	....	....

FRANZOSA, DAVID

Left wing. Shoots left. 5'11", 175 lbs. Born, Reading, MA, November 20, 1970.
(Boston's 11th choice, 227th overall, in 1989 Entry Draft)

			Regular Season					Playoffs				
Season	Club	Lea	GP	G	A	TP	PIM	GP	G	A	TP	PIM
1988-89	Boston College	H.E.	16	2	1	3	0	....	....	....	....	....
1989-90	Boston College	H.E.	42	8	20	28	20	....	....	....	....	....

FRASER, CURT M.

Left wing. Shoots left. 6'1" 200 lbs. Born, Cincinnati, OH, January 12, 1958.
(Vancouver's 2nd choice, 22nd overall, in 1978 Amateur Draft).

			Regular Season					Playoffs				
Season	Club	Lea	GP	G	A	TP	PIM	GP	G	A	TP	PIM
1976-77	Victoria	WHL	60	34	41	75	82	4	4	2	6	4
1977-78	Victoria	WHL	66	48	44	92	256	13	10	7	17	28
1978-79	Vancouver	NHL	78	16	19	35	116	3	0	2	2	6
1979-80	Vancouver	NHL	78	17	25	42	143	4	0	0	0	2
1980-81	Vancouver	NHL	77	25	24	49	118	3	1	0	1	2
1981-82	Vancouver	NHL	79	28	39	67	175	17	3	7	10	98
1982-83	Vancouver	NHL	36	6	7	13	99	....	....	....	....	....
	Chicago	NHL	38	6	13	19	77	13	4	4	8	18
1983-84	Chicago	NHL	29	5	12	17	28	5	0	0	0	14
1984-85	Chicago	NHL	73	25	25	50	109	15	6	3	9	36
1985-86	Chicago	NHL	61	29	39	68	84	3	0	1	1	12
1986-87	Chicago	NHL	75	25	25	50	182	2	1	1	2	10
1987-88	Chicago	NHL	27	4	6	10	57	....	....	....	....	....
	Minnesota	NHL	10	1	1	2	20	....	....	....	....	....
1988-89	Minnesota	NHL	35	5	5	10	76	....	....	....	....	....
1989-90	Minnesota	NHL	8	1	0	1	22	....	....	....	....	....
	NHL Totals		704	193	240	433	1306	65	15	18	33	198

Traded to **Chicago** by **Vancouver** for Tony Tanti, January 6, 1983. Traded to **Minnesota** by **Chicago** for Dirk Graham, January 4, 1988.

FRASER, IAIN

Center. Shoots left. 5'10", 175 lbs. Born, Scarborough, Ont., August 10, 1969.
(NY Islanders' 12th choice, 233rd overall, in 1989 Entry Draft).

			Regular Season					Playoffs				
Season	Club	Lea	GP	G	A	TP	PIM	GP	G	A	TP	PIM
1986-87	Oshawa	OHL	5	1	2	3	0	....	....	....	....	....
1987-88	Oshawa	OHL	16	4	4	8	22	6	2	3	5	2
1988-89	Oshawa	OHL	62	33	57	90	87	6	2	8	10	12
1989-90a	Oshawa	OHL	56	40	65	105	75	17	10	*22	32	8

a Memorial Cup All-Star Team, Tournament MVP (1990)

FRAWLEY, WILLIAM DANIEL (DAN)

Right wing. Shoots right. 6'1", 190 lbs. Born, Sturgeon Falls, Ont., June 2, 1962.
(Chicago's 15th choice, 204th overall, in 1980 Entry Draft).

			Regular Season					Playoffs				
Season	Club	Lea	GP	G	A	TP	PIM	GP	G	A	TP	PIM
1979-80	Sudbury	OHA	63	21	26	47	67	8	0	1	1	2
1980-81	Cornwall	QMJHL	28	10	14	28	76	18	5	12	17	37
1981-82	Cornwall	OHL	64	27	50	77	239	5	3	8	11	19
1982-83	Springfield	AHL	80	30	27	57	107	....	....	....	....	....
1983-84	Chicago	NHL	3	0	0	0	0	....	....	....	....	....
	Springfield	AHL	69	22	34	56	137	4	0	1	1	12
1984-85	Chicago	NHL	30	4	3	7	64	1	0	0	0	0
	Milwaukee	IHL	26	11	12	23	125	....	....	....	....	....
1985-86	Pittsburgh	NHL	69	10	11	21	174	....	....	....	....	....
1986-87	Pittsburgh	NHL	78	14	14	28	218	....	....	....	....	....
1987-88	Pittsburgh	NHL	47	6	8	14	152	....	....	....	....	....
1988-89	Pittsburgh	NHL	46	3	4	7	66	....	....	....	....	....
	Muskegon	IHL	24	12	16	28	35	14	6	4	10	31
1989-90	Muskegon	IHL	82	31	47	78	165	15	9	12	21	51
	NHL Totals		273	37	40	77	674	1	0	0	0	0

Claimed by **Pittsburgh** from **Chicago** in NHL Waiver Draft, October 7, 1985.

FREER, MARK (FRIHR)

Center. Shoots left. 5'10", 180 lbs. Born, Peterborough, Ont., July 14, 1968.

			Regular Season					Playoffs				
Season	Club	Lea	GP	G	A	TP	PIM	GP	G	A	TP	PIM
1985-86	Peterborough	OHL	65	16	28	44	24	14	3	4	7	13
1986-87	Philadelphia	NHL	1	0	1	1	0	....	....	....	....	....
	Peterborough	OHL	65	39	43	82	44	12	2	6	8	5
1987-88	Philadelphia	NHL	1	0	0	0	0	....	....	....	....	....
	Peterborough	OHL	63	38	70	108	63	12	5	12	17	4
1988-89	Philadelphia	NHL	5	0	1	1	0	....	....	....	....	....
	Hershey	AHL	75	30	49	79	77	12	4	6	10	2
1989-90	Philadelphia	NHL	2	0	0	0	0	....	....	....	....	....
	Hershey	AHL	65	28	36	64	31	....	....	....	....	....
	NHL Totals		9	0	2	2	0	....	....	....	....	....

Signed as a free agent by **Philadelphia**, October 7, 1986.

FRENETTE, DEREK

Left wing. Shoots left. 6'1", 175 lbs. Born, Montreal, Que., July 13, 1971.
(St. Louis' 6th choice, 124th overall, in 1989 Entry Draft).

			Regular Season					Playoffs				
Season	Club	Lea	GP	G	A	TP	PIM	GP	G	A	TP	PIM
1988-89	Ferris State	CCHA	25	3	4	7	17	....	....	....	....	....
1989-90	Ferris State	CCHA	28	1	4	5	48	....	....	....	....	....

FRYCER, MIROSLAV (FREE-chuhr)

Right wing. Shoots left. 6', 200 lbs. Born, Ostrava, Czechoslovakia, September 27, 1959.

			Regular Season					Playoffs				
Season	Club	Lea	GP	G	A	TP	PIM	GP	G	A	TP	PIM
1979-80	Vitkovice	Czech	44	31	15	46	....	....	....	....	....	....
1980-81	Vitkovice	Czech	34	33	24	57	....	....	....	....	....	....
1981-82	Fredericton	AHL	11	9	5	14	16	....	....	....	....	....
	Quebec	NHL	49	20	17	37	47	....	....	....	....	....
	Toronto	NHL	10	4	6	10	31	....	....	....	....	....
1982-83	Toronto	NHL	67	25	30	55	90	4	2	5	7	0
1983-84	Toronto	NHL	47	10	16	26	55	....	....	....	....	....
1984-85	Toronto	NHL	65	25	30	55	55	....	....	....	....	....
1985-86	Toronto	NHL	73	32	43	75	74	10	1	3	4	10
1986-87	Toronto	NHL	29	7	8	15	28	....	....	....	....	....
1987-88	Toronto	NHL	38	12	20	32	41	3	0	0	0	6
1988-89	Detroit	NHL	23	7	8	15	47	....	....	....	....	....
	Edmonton	NHL	14	5	5	10	18	....	....	....	....	....
1989-90	Freiburg	W. Ger.	11	4	13	17	18	....	....	....	....	....
	NHL Totals		415	147	183	330	486	17	3	8	11	16

Played in NHL All-Star Game (1985)

Signed as free agent by **Quebec**, April 21, 1980. Traded to **Toronto** by **Quebec** with Quebec's seventh round choice (Jeff Triano) in 1982 Entry Draft for Wilf Paiement, March 9, 1982. Traded to **Detroit** by **Toronto** for Darren Veitch, June 10, 1988. Traded to **Edmonton** by **Detroit** for Edmonton's tenth-round choice (Rick Judson) in the 1989 Entry Draft, January 3, 1989.

GAETZ, LINK (GAYTZ)

Defense. Shoots left. 6'2", 210 lbs. Born, Vancouver, B.C., October 2, 1968.
(Minnesota's 2nd choice, 40th overall, in 1988 Entry Draft).

			Regular Season					Playoffs				
Season	Club	Lea	GP	G	A	TP	PIM	GP	G	A	TP	PIM
1986-87	N. Westminster	WHL	44	2	7	9	52	....	....	....	....	....
1987-88	Spokane	WHL	59	9	20	29	313	10	2	2	4	70
1988-89	Minnesota	NHL	12	0	2	2	53	....	....	....	....	....
	Kalamazoo	IHL	37	3	4	7	192	5	0	0	0	56
1989-90	Minnesota	NHL	5	0	0	0	33	....	....	....	....	....
	Kalamazoo	IHL	61	5	16	21	318	9	2	2	4	59
	NHL Totals		17	0	2	2	86	....	....	....	....	....

GAGE, JOSEPH WILLIAM (JODY)

Right wing. Shoots right. 6', 190 lbs. Born, Toronto, Ont., November 29, 1959.
(Detroit's 2nd choice, 45th overall, in 1979 Entry Draft).

			Regular Season					Playoffs				
Season	Club	Lea	GP	G	A	TP	PIM	GP	G	A	TP	PIM
1977-78	Hamilton	OHA	32	15	18	33	19	....	....	....	....	....
	Kitchener	OHA	36	17	27	44	21	9	4	3	7	4
1978-79	Kitchener	OHA	58	46	43	89	40	10	1	2	3	6
1979-80	Adirondack	AHL	63	25	21	46	15	5	2	1	3	0
1980-81	Detroit	NHL	16	2	2	4	22	....	....	....	....	....
	Adirondack	AHL	59	17	31	48	44	17	9	6	15	12
1981-82	Adirondack	AHL	47	21	20	41	21	....	....	....	....	....
	Detroit	NHL	31	9	10	19	2	....	....	....	....	....
1982-83	Adirondack	AHL	65	23	30	53	33	6	1	5	6	8
1983-84	Detroit	NHL	3	0	0	0	0	....	....	....	....	....
	Adirondack	AHL	73	40	32	72	32	6	3	4	7	2
1984-85	Adirondack	AHL	78	27	33	60	55	....	....	....	....	....
1985-86	Buffalo	NHL	7	3	2	5	0	....	....	....	....	....
a	Rochester	AHL	73	42	57	99	56	....	....	....	....	....
1986-87	Rochester	AHL	70	26	39	65	60	17	*14	5	19	24
1987-88	Buffalo	NHL	2	0	0	0	0	....	....	....	....	....
ab	Rochester	AHL	76	*60	44	104	46	5	2	5	7	10
1988-89	Rochester	AHL	65	31	38	69	60	....	....	....	....	....
1989-90	Rochester	AHL	75	45	38	83	42	17	4	6	10	12
	NHL Totals		59	14	14	28	24	....	....	....	....	....

a AHL First All-Star Team (1986, 1988)
b Won Les Cunningham Trophy (MVP-AHL) (1988)

Signed as a free agent by **Buffalo**, July 31, 1985

GAGNE, PAUL

Left wing. Shoots left. 5' 10", 180 lbs. Born, Iroquois Falls, Ont., February 6, 1962.
(Colorado's 1st choice, 19th overall, in 1980 Entry Draft).

			Regular Season					Playoffs				
Season	Club	Lea	GP	G	A	TP	PIM	GP	G	A	TP	PIM
1978-79	Windsor	OHA	87	24	18	42	64	7	1	1	2	2
1979-80a	Windsor	OHA	65	48	53	101	87	13	7	8	15	19
1980-81	**Colorado**	**NHL**	**61**	**25**	**16**	**41**	**12**	....	....	....	....	....
1981-82	**Colorado**	**NHL**	**59**	**10**	**12**	**22**	**17**	....	....	....	....	....
1982-83	**New Jersey**	**NHL**	**63**	**14**	**15**	**29**	**13**	....	....	....	....	....
	Wichita	CHL	16	1	9	10	9	....	....	....	....	....
1983-84	**New Jersey**	**NHL**	**66**	**14**	**18**	**32**	**33**	....	....	....	....	....
1984-85	**New Jersey**	**NHL**	**79**	**24**	**19**	**43**	**28**	....	....	....	....	....
1985-86	**New Jersey**	**NHL**	**47**	**19**	**19**	**38**	**14**	....	....	....	....	....
1986-87			DID NOT PLAY — INJURED					....	....	....	....	....
1987-88			DID NOT PLAY — INJURED					....	....	....	....	....
1988-89	**Toronto**	**NHL**	**16**	**3**	**2**	**5**	**6**	....	....	....	....	....
	Newmarket	AHL	56	33	41	74	29	5	4	4	8	5
1989-90	**NY Islanders**	**NHL**	**9**	**1**	**0**	**1**	**4**	....	....	....	....	....
	Newmarket	AHL	28	13	14	27	11	....	....	....	....	....
	Springfield	AHL	36	18	29	47	6	13	10	6	16	2
	NHL Totals		**400**	**110**	**101**	**211**	**127**	....	....	....	....	....

a OHA Second All-Star Team (1980)

Signed as a free agent by **Toronto**, July 28, 1988. Traded to **NY Islanders** by **Toronto** with Jack Capuano and Derek Laxdal for Mike Stevens and Gilles Thibaudeau, December 20, 1989.

GAGNE, SIMON

Right wing. Shoots right. 6'4", 200 lbs. Born, Montreal, Que., September 29, 1968.
(NY Rangers' 3rd choice, 46th overall, in 1987 Entry Draft).

			Regular Season					Playoffs				
Season	Club	Lea	GP	G	A	TP	PIM	GP	G	A	TP	PIM
1985-86	Laval	QMJHL	71	15	16	31	150	14	2	5	7	37
1986-87	Laval	QMJHL	66	19	35	54	90	15	9	11	20	12
1987-88	Drummondville	QMJHL	68	17	43	60	197	17	3	6	9	94
1988-89	Denver	IHL	69	7	18	25	78	4	1	0	1	7
1989-90	Moncton	AHL	28	4	5	9	27	....	....	....	....	....

GAGNER, DAVE

Center. Shoots left. 5'10", 185 lbs. Born, Chatham, Ont., December 11, 1964.
(NY Rangers' 1st choice, 12th overall, in 1983 Entry Draft).

			Regular Season					Playoffs				
Season	Club	Lea	GP	G	A	TP	PIM	GP	G	A	TP	PIM
1981-82	Brantford	OHL	68	30	46	76	31	11	3	6	9	6
1982-83a	Brantford	OHL	70	55	66	121	57	8	5	5	10	4
1983-84	Cdn. Olympic	...	50	19	18	37	26	....	....	....	....	....
	Brantford	OHL	12	7	13	20	4	6	0	4	4	6
1984-85	**NY Rangers**	**NHL**	**38**	**6**	**6**	**12**	**16**	....	....	....	....	....
	New Haven	AHL	38	13	20	33	23	....	....	....	....	....
1985-86	**NY Rangers**	**NHL**	**32**	**4**	**6**	**10**	**19**	....	....	....	....	....
	New Haven	AHL	16	10	11	21	11	4	1	2	3	2
1986-87	**NY Rangers**	**NHL**	**10**	**1**	**4**	**5**	**12**	....	....	....	....	....
	New Haven	AHL	56	22	41	63	50	7	1	5	6	18
1987-88	**Minnesota**	**NHL**	**51**	**8**	**11**	**19**	**55**	....	....	....	....	....
	Kalamazoo	IHL	14	16	10	26	26	....	....	....	....	....
1988-89	**Minnesota**	**NHL**	**75**	**35**	**43**	**78**	**104**	....	....	....	....	....
	Kalamazoo	IHL	1	0	1	1	4	....	....	....	....	....
1989-90	**Minnesota**	**NHL**	**79**	**40**	**38**	**78**	**54**	**7**	**2**	**3**	**5**	**16**
	NHL Totals		**285**	**94**	**108**	**202**	**260**	**7**	**2**	**3**	**5**	**16**

a OHL Second All-Star Team (1983)

Traded to **Minnesota** by **NY Rangers** with Jay Caulfield for Jari Gronstrand and Paul Boutilier, October 8, 1987.

GALL, WILLIAM (BILL)

Right wing. Shoots right. 6'2", 175 lbs. Born, Bryn Mawr, PA, May 14, 1968.
(Philadelphia's 5th choice, 104th overall, in 1987 Entry Draft).

			Regular Season					Playoffs				
Season	Club	Lea	GP	G	A	TP	PIM	GP	G	A	TP	PIM
1987-88	RIT	NCAA	23	8	8	16	4	....	....	....	....	....
1988-89	RIT	NCAA	37	8	19	27	46	....	....	....	....	....
1989-90	RIT	NCAA	27	9	21	30	30	....	....	....	....	....

GALLANT, GERARD (guh-LAHNT)

Left wing. Shoots left. 5'10", 185 lbs. Born, Summerside, P.E.I., September 2, 1963.
(Detroit's 4th choice, 107th overall, in 1981 Entry Draft).

			Regular Season					Playoffs				
Season	Club	Lea	GP	G	A	TP	PIM	GP	G	A	TP	PIM
1980-81	Sherbrooke	QMJHL	68	41	59	100	265	14	6	13	19	46
1981-82	Sherbrooke	QMJHL	58	34	58	92	260	22	14	24	38	84
1982-83	St. Jean	QMJHL	33	28	25	53	139	....	....	....	....	....
	Verdun	QMJHL	29	26	49	75	105	15	14	19	33	84
1983-84	Adirondack	AHL	77	31	33	64	195	7	1	3	4	34
1984-85	**Detroit**	**NHL**	**32**	**6**	**12**	**18**	**66**	**3**	**0**	**0**	**0**	**11**
	Adirondack	AHL	46	18	29	47	131	....	....	....	....	....
1985-86	**Detroit**	**NHL**	**52**	**20**	**19**	**39**	**106**	....	....	....	....	....
1986-87	**Detroit**	**NHL**	**80**	**38**	**34**	**72**	**216**	**16**	**8**	**6**	**14**	**43**
1987-88	**Detroit**	**NHL**	**73**	**34**	**39**	**73**	**242**	**16**	**6**	**9**	**15**	**55**
1988-89a	**Detroit**	**NHL**	**76**	**39**	**54**	**93**	**230**	**6**	**1**	**2**	**3**	**40**
1989-90	**Detroit**	**NHL**	**69**	**36**	**44**	**80**	**254**	....	....	....	....	....
	NHL Totals		**382**	**173**	**202**	**375**	**1114**	**41**	**15**	**17**	**32**	**149**

a NHL Second All-Star Team (1989)

GALLEY, GARRY

Defense. Shoots left. 6', 190 lbs. Born, Ottawa, Ont., April 16, 1963.
(Los Angeles' 4th choice, 100th overall, in 1983 Entry Draft).

			Regular Season					Playoffs				
Season	Club	Lea	GP	G	A	TP	PIM	GP	G	A	TP	PIM
1981-82	Bowling Green	CCHA	42	3	36	39	48	....	....	....	....	....
1982-83	Bowling Green	CCHA	40	17	29	46	40	....	....	....	....	....
1983-84ab	Bowling Green	CCHA	44	15	52	67	61	....	....	....	....	....
1984-85	**Los Angeles**	**NHL**	**78**	**8**	**30**	**38**	**82**	**3**	**1**	**0**	**1**	**2**
1985-86	**Los Angeles**	**NHL**	**49**	**9**	**13**	**22**	**46**	....	....	....	....	....
	New Haven	AHL	4	2	6	8	6	....	....	....	....	....
1986-87	**Los Angeles**	**NHL**	**30**	**5**	**11**	**16**	**57**	....	....	....	....	....
	Washington	**NHL**	**18**	**1**	**10**	**11**	**10**	**2**	**0**	**0**	**0**	**0**
1987-88	**Washington**	**NHL**	**58**	**7**	**23**	**30**	**44**	**13**	**2**	**4**	**6**	**13**
1988-89	**Boston**	**NHL**	**78**	**8**	**21**	**29**	**80**	**9**	**0**	**1**	**1**	**33**
1989-90	**Boston**	**NHL**	**71**	**8**	**27**	**35**	**75**	**21**	**3**	**3**	**6**	**34**
	NHL Totals		**382**	**46**	**135**	**181**	**394**	**48**	**6**	**8**	**14**	**92**

a CCHA First All-Star Team (1984)
b NCAA All-American (1984)

Traded to **Washington** by **Los Angeles** for Al Jensen, February 14, 1987. Signed as a free agent by **Boston**, July 8, 1988.

GALLOWAY, KYLE

Defense. Shoots left. 5'11", 170 lbs. Born, Winnipeg, Man., November 10, 1969.
(Winnipeg's 12th choice, 241st overall, in 1988 Entry Draft).

			Regular Season					Playoffs				
Season	Club	Lea	GP	G	A	TP	PIM	GP	G	A	TP	PIM
1988-89	U. Manitoba	CWUAA	8	0	1	1	6	....	....	....	....	....
1989-90	U. Manitoba	CWUAA	38	6	14	20	38	....	....	....	....	....

GANCHAR, PERRY

Right wing. Shoots right. 5'9", 180 lbs. Born, Saskatoon, Sask., October 28, 1963.
(St. Louis' 3rd choice, 113th overall, in 1982 Entry Draft).

			Regular Season					Playoffs				
Season	Club	Lea	GP	G	A	TP	PIM	GP	G	A	TP	PIM
1979-80	Saskatoon	WHL	27	9	14	23	60	....	....	....	....	....
1980-81	Saskatoon	WHL	72	26	53	79	117	....	....	....	....	....
1981-82	Saskatoon	WHL	53	38	52	90	82	5	3	3	6	17
1982-83	Saskatoon	WHL	68	68	48	116	105	6	1	4	5	24
	Salt Lake	CHL	....	....	....	....	....	1	0	1	1	0
1983-84	Montana	CHL	59	23	22	45	77	....	....	....	....	....
	St. Louis	**NHL**	**1**	**0**	**0**	**0**	**0**	**7**	**3**	**1**	**4**	**0**
1984-85	**St. Louis**	**NHL**	**7**	**0**	**2**	**2**	**0**	....	....	....	....	....
a	Peoria	IHL	63	41	29	70	114	20	4	11	15	49
1985-86	Sherbrooke	AHL	75	25	29	54	42	....	....	....	....	....
1986-87	Sherbrooke	AHL	68	22	29	51	64	17	9	8	17	37
1987-88	**Montreal**	**NHL**	**1**	**1**	**0**	**1**	**0**	....	....	....	....	....
	Sherbrooke	AHL	28	12	18	30	61	....	....	....	....	....
	Pittsburgh	**NHL**	**30**	**2**	**5**	**7**	**36**	....	....	....	....	....
1988-89	**Pittsburgh**	**NHL**	**3**	**0**	**0**	**0**	**0**	....	....	....	....	....
	Muskegon	IHL	70	39	34	73	114	14	7	8	15	6
1989-90	Muskegon	IHL	79	40	45	85	111	14	3	5	8	27
	NHL Totals		**42**	**3**	**7**	**10**	**36**	**7**	**3**	**1**	**4**	**0**

a IHL Second All-Star Team (1985)

Traded to **Montreal** by **St. Louis** for Ron Flockhart, August 26, 1985. Traded to **Pittsburgh** by **Montreal** for future considerations, December 17, 1987.

GARBUTT, MURRAY

Center. Shoots left. 6'1", 205 lbs. Born, Hanna, Alta., July 29, 1971.
(Minnesota's 3rd choice, 60th overall, in 1989 Entry Draft).

			Regular Season					Playoffs				
Season	Club	Lea	GP	G	A	TP	PIM	GP	G	A	TP	PIM
1987-88	Medicine Hat	WHL	9	2	1	3	15	16	0	1	1	15
1988-89	Medicine Hat	WHL	64	14	24	38	145	3	1	0	1	6
1989-90	Medicine Hat	WHL	72	38	27	65	221	3	1	0	1	21

GARDNER, JOEL

Center. Shoots left. 6', 175 lbs. Born, Petrolia, Ont., September 16, 1967.
(Boston's 10th choice, 244th overall, in 1986 Entry Draft).

			Regular Season					Playoffs				
Season	Club	Lea	GP	G	A	TP	PIM	GP	G	A	TP	PIM
1986-87	Colgate	ECAC	31	10	20	30	20	....	....	....	....	....
1987-88	Colgate	ECAC	31	14	32	46	24	....	....	....	....	....
1988-89	Colgate	ECAC	30	21	25	46	38	....	....	....	....	....
1989-90abc	Colgate	ECAC	38	26	36	62	62	....	....	....	....	....

a ECAC First All-Star Team (1990)
b NCAA East Second All-American Team (1990)
c NCAA All-Tournament Team (1990)

GARPENLOV, JOHAN

Left wing. Shoots left. 5'11", 185 lbs. Born, Stockholm, Sweden, March 21, 1968.
(Detroit's 5th choice, 85th overall, in 1986 Entry Draft).

			Regular Season					Playoffs				
Season	Club	Lea	GP	G	A	TP	PIM	GP	G	A	TP	PIM
1986-87	Djurgarden	Swe.	29	5	8	13	20	....	....	....	....	....
1987-88	Djurgarden	Swe.	30	7	10	17	12	....	....	....	....	....
1988-89	Djurgarden	Swe.	36	12	19	31	20	....	....	....	....	....
1989-90	Djurgarden	Swe.	39	20	13	33	35	....	....	....	....	....

GARTNER, MICHAEL ALFRED (MIKE)

Right wing. Shoots right. 6', 190 lbs. Born, Ottawa, Ont., October 29, 1959.
(Washington's 1st choice, 4th overall, in 1979 Entry Draft).

			Regular Season					Playoffs				
Season	Club	Lea	GP	G	A	TP	PIM	GP	G	A	TP	PIM
1976-77	Niagara Falls	OHA	62	33	42	75	125	....	....	....	....	....
1977-78a	Niagara Falls	OHA	64	41	49	90	56	....	....	....	....	....
1978-79	Cincinnati	WHA	78	27	25	52	123	3	0	2	2	2
1979-80	**Washington**	**NHL**	77	36	32	68	66	....	....	....	....	....
1980-81	**Washington**	**NHL**	80	48	46	94	100	....	....	....	....	....
1981-82	**Washington**	**NHL**	80	35	45	80	121	....	....	....	....	....
1982-83	**Washington**	**NHL**	73	38	38	76	54	4	0	0	0	4
1983-84	**Washington**	**NHL**	80	40	45	85	90	8	3	7	10	16
1984-85	**Washington**	**NHL**	80	50	52	102	71	5	4	3	7	9
1985-86	**Washington**	**NHL**	74	35	40	75	63	9	2	10	12	4
1986-87	**Washington**	**NHL**	78	41	32	73	61	7	4	3	7	14
1987-88	**Washington**	**NHL**	80	48	33	81	73	14	3	4	7	14
1988-89	**Washington**	**NHL**	56	26	29	55	71	....	....	....	....	....
	Minnesota	**NHL**	13	7	7	14	2	5	0	0	0	6
1989-90	**Minnesota**	**NHL**	67	34	36	70	32	....	....	....	....	....
	NY Rangers	**NHL**	12	11	5	16	6	10	5	3	8	12
	NHL Totals		**850**	**449**	**440**	**889**	**810**	**62**	**21**	**30**	**51**	**79**

a OHA First All-Star Team (1978)

Played in NHL All-Star Game (1980, 1985, 1986, 1988, 1990)

Traded to **Minnesota** by **Washington** with Larry Murphy for Dino Ciccarelli and Bob Rouse, March 7, 1989. Traded to **NY Rangers** by **Minnesota** for Ulf Dahlen, Los Angeles' fourth round choice (Cal McGowan) – previously acquired by NY Rangers – in 1990 Entry Draft and future considerations, March 6, 1990.

GAUDREAU, ROBERT

Right wing. Shoots right. 5'11", 185 lbs. Born, Lincoln, RI, January 20, 1970.
(Pittsburgh's 8th choice, 172nd overall, in 1988 Entry Draft).

			Regular Season					Playoffs				
Season	Club	Lea	GP	G	A	TP	PIM	GP	G	A	TP	PIM
1988-89a	Providence	H.E.	42	28	29	57	32	....	....	....	....	....
1989-90	Providence	H.E.	32	20	18	38	12	....	....	....	....	....

a Co-winner Hockey East Rookie of the Year (1989)

Rights traded to **Minnesota** by **Pittsburgh** for Richard Zemlak, November 1, 1988.

GAUME, DALLAS (GAHM)

Center. Shoots left. 5'10", 185 lbs. Born, Innisfal, Alta., August 27, 1963.

			Regular Season					Playoffs				
Season	Club	Lea	GP	G	A	TP	PIM	GP	G	A	TP	PIM
1982-83	Denver	WCHA	37	19	47	66	12	....	....	....	....	....
1983-84	Denver	WCHA	32	12	25	37	22	....	....	....	....	....
1984-85	Denver	WCHA	39	15	48	63	28	....	....	....	....	....
1985-86	Denver	WCHA	47	32	67	99	18	....	....	....	....	....
1986-87	Binghamton	AHL	77	18	39	57	31	12	1	1	2	7
1987-88	Binghamton	AHL	63	24	49	73	39	4	1	2	3	0
1988-89	**Hartford**	**NHL**	4	1	1	2	0	....	....	....	....	....
	Binghamton	AHL	57	23	43	66	16	....	....	....	....	....
1989-90	Binghamton	AHL	76	26	39	65	43	....	....	....	....	....
	NHL Totals		**4**	**1**	**1**	**2**	**0**	....	....	....	....	....

Signed as a free agent by **Hartford**, July 10, 1986.

GAUTHIER, DANIEL

Left wing. Shoots left. 6'1", 180 lbs. Born, Charlemagne, Que., May 17, 1970.
(Pittsburgh's 3rd choice, 62nd overall, in 1988 Entry Draft).

			Regular Season					Playoffs				
Season	Club	Lea	GP	G	A	TP	PIM	GP	G	A	TP	PIM
1986-87	Longueuil	QMJHL	64	23	22	45	23	18	4	5	9	15
1987-88	Victoriaville	QMJHL	66	43	47	90	53	5	2	1	3	0
1988-89	Victoriaville	QMJHL	64	41	75	116	84	16	12	17	29	30
1989-90	Victoriaville	QMJHL	62	45	69	114	32	16	8	*19	27	16

GAUTHIER, LUC

Defense. Shoots right. 5'9", 205 lbs. Born, Longueuil, Que., April 19, 1964.
Last amateur club: Longueuil Chevaliers (QMJHL).

			Regular Season					Playoffs				
Season	Club	Lea	GP	G	A	TP	PIM	GP	G	A	TP	PIM
1984-85	Longueuil	QMJHL	60	13	47	60	111	....	....	....	....	....
1985-86	Saginaw	IHL	66	9	29	38	160	....	....	....	....	....
1986-87	Sherbrooke	AHL	78	5	17	22	8	17	2	4	6	31
1987-88	Sherbrooke	AHL	61	4	10	14	105	6	0	0	0	18
1988-89	Sherbrooke	AHL	77	8	20	28	178	6	0	0	0	10
1989-90	Sherbrooke	AHL	79	3	23	26	139	12	0	4	4	35

Signed as a free agent by **Montreal**, October 7, 1986.

GAUVIN, STEPHANE

Left wing. Shoots left. 6'0", 175 lbs. Born, Vancouver, B.C., April 16, 1970.
(Winnipeg's 9th choice, 172nd overall, in 1989 Entry Draft).

			Regular Season					Playoffs				
Season	Club	Lea	GP	G	A	TP	PIM	GP	G	A	TP	PIM
1988-89	Cornell	ECAC	30	2	5	7	24	....	....	....	....	....
1989-90	Cornell	ECAC	29	2	2	4	34	....	....	....	....	....

GAVIN, ROBERT (STEWART)

Left wing. Shoots left. 6', 185 lbs. Born, Ottawa, Ont., March 15, 1960.
(Toronto's 4th choice, 74th overall, in 1980 Entry Draft).

			Regular Season					Playoffs				
Season	Club	Lea	GP	G	A	TP	PIM	GP	G	A	TP	PIM
1978-79	Toronto	OHA	61	24	25	49	83	3	1	0	1	0
1979-80	Toronto	OHA	68	27	30	57	52	4	1	1	2	2
1980-81	**Toronto**	**NHL**	14	1	2	3	13	....	....	....	....	....
	New Brunswick	AHL	46	7	12	19	42	13	1	0	1	2
1981-82	**Toronto**	**NHL**	38	5	6	11	29	....	....	....	....	....
1982-83	St. Catharines	AHL	6	2	4	6	17	....	....	....	....	....
	Toronto	**NHL**	63	6	5	11	44	4	0	0	0	0
1983-84	**Toronto**	**NHL**	80	10	22	32	90	....	....	....	....	....
1984-85	**Toronto**	**NHL**	73	12	13	25	38	....	....	....	....	....
1985-86	**Hartford**	**NHL**	76	26	29	55	51	10	4	1	5	13
1986-87	**Hartford**	**NHL**	79	20	21	41	28	6	2	4	6	10
1987-88	**Hartford**	**NHL**	56	11	10	21	59	6	2	2	4	4
1988-89	**Minnesota**	**NHL**	73	8	18	26	34	5	3	1	4	10
1989-90	**Minnesota**	**NHL**	80	12	13	25	76	7	0	2	2	12
	NHL Totals		**632**	**111**	**139**	**250**	**462**	**38**	**11**	**10**	**21**	**49**

Traded to **Hartford** by **Toronto** for Chris Kotsopoulos, October 7, 1985. Claimed by **Minnesota** in NHL Waiver Draft, October 3, 1988.

GAWLICKI, JEFF

Left wing. Shoots left. 6'2", 200 lbs. Born, Edmonton, Alta., April 15, 1968.
(Los Angeles' 7th choice, 174th overall, in 1987 Entry Draft).

			Regular Season					Playoffs				
Season	Club	Lea	GP	G	A	TP	PIM	GP	G	A	TP	PIM
1986-87	N. Michigan	WCHA	37	7	2	9	61	....	....	....	....	....
1987-88	N. Michigan	WCHA	30	2	3	5	64	....	....	....	....	....
1988-89	N. Michigan	WCHA	45	16	11	27	99	....	....	....	....	....
1989-90	N. Michigan	WCHA	36	3	2	5	67	....	....	....	....	....

GEARY, DEREK

Right wing. Shoots right. 6'3", 180 lbs. Born, Gloucester, MA, February 2, 1970.
(Boston's 5th choice, 123rd overall, in 1988 Entry Draft).

			Regular Season					Playoffs				
Season	Club	Lea	GP	G	A	TP	PIM	GP	G	A	TP	PIM
1987-88	Gloucester	HS	....	26	24	50	....	....	....	....	....	....
1988-89	Andover Aca.	HS	3	1	2	3	0	....	....	....	....	....
1989-90	Boston U.	H.E.	DID NOT PLAY									

GEIST, WILLIAM

Defense. Shoots right. 6'4", 190 lbs. Born, St. Paul, MN, February 9, 1969.
(Montreal's 10th choice, 164th overall, in 1987 Entry Draft).

			Regular Season					Playoffs				
Season	Club	Lea	GP	G	A	TP	PIM	GP	G	A	TP	PIM
1986-87	St. Paul	HS	21	7	14	21	....	....	....	....	....	....
1987-88	Choate	HS	28	11	16	27	31	....	....	....	....	....
1988-89			DID NOT PLAY									
1989-90	Dartmouth	ECAC	15	1	1	2	12	....	....	....	....	....

GELINAS, MARTIN

Left wing. Shoots left. 5'11", 195 lbs. Born, Shawinigan, Que., June 5, 1970.
(Los Angeles' 1st choice, 7th overall, in 1988 Entry Draft).

			Regular Season					Playoffs				
Season	Club	Lea	GP	G	A	TP	PIM	GP	G	A	TP	PIM
1987-88	Hull	QMJHL	65	63	68	131	74	17	15	18	33	32
1988-89	**Edmonton**	**NHL**	6	1	2	3	0	....	....	....	....	....
	Hull	QMJHL	41	38	39	77	31	9	5	4	9	14
1989-90	**Edmonton**	**NHL**	46	17	8	25	30	20	2	3	5	6
	NHL Totals		**52**	**18**	**10**	**28**	**30**	**20**	**2**	**3**	**5**	**6**

Traded to **Edmonton** by **Los Angeles** with Jimmy Carson and Los Angeles' first round choices in 1989, (acquired by New Jersey, June 17, 1989. New Jersey selected Jason Miller), 1991 and 1993 Entry Drafts and cash for Wayne Gretzky, Mike Krushelnyski and Marty McSorley, August 9, 1988.

GERMAIN, ERIC

Defense. Shoots left. 6'1", 195 lbs. Born, Quebec City, Que., June 26, 1966.

			Regular Season					Playoffs				
Season	Club	Lea	GP	G	A	TP	PIM	GP	G	A	TP	PIM
1983-84	St. Jean	QMJHL	57	2	15	17	60	4	1	0	1	6
1984-85	St. Jean	QMJHL	66	10	31	41	243	5	4	0	4	14
1985-86	St. Jean	QMJHL	66	5	38	43	183	10	0	6	6	56
1986-87	Flint	IHL	21	0	2	2	23	....	....	....	....	....
	Fredericton	AHL	44	2	8	10	28	....	....	....	....	....
1987-88	**Los Angeles**	**NHL**	4	0	1	1	13	1	0	0	0	4
	New Haven	AHL	69	0	10	10	0	....	....	....	....	....
1988-89	New Haven	AHL	55	0	9	9	93	17	0	3	3	23
1989-90	New Haven	AHL	59	3	12	15	112	....	....	....	....	....
	NHL Totals		**4**	**0**	**1**	**1**	**13**	**1**	**0**	**0**	**0**	**4**

Signed as a free agent by **Los Angeles**, July 1, 1986.

GERNANDER, KEN

Left wing. Shoots left. 5'10", 175 lbs. Born, Coleraine, MN, June 30, 1969.
(Winnipeg's 4th choice, 96th overall, in 1987 Entry Draft).

			Regular Season					Playoffs				
Season	Club	Lea	GP	G	A	TP	PIM	GP	G	A	TP	PIM
1987-88	U. Minnesota	WCHA	44	14	14	28	14	....	....	....	....	....
1988-89	U. Minnesota	WCHA	44	9	11	20	2	....	....	....	....	....
1989-90	U. Minnesota	WCHA	44	32	17	49	24	....	....	....	....	....

GERVAIS, VICTOR

Center. Shoots left. 5'9", 170 lbs. Born, Prince George, B.C., March 13, 1969.
(Washington's 8th choice, 187th overall, in 1989 Entry Draft).

			Regular Season					Playoffs				
Season	Club	Lea	GP	G	A	TP	PIM	GP	G	A	TP	PIM
1986-87	Seattle	WHL	66	13	30	43	58	....	....	....	....	....
1987-88	Seattle	WHL	69	30	46	76	134	....	....	....	....	....
1988-89	Seattle	WHL	72	54	65	119	158	....	....	....	....	....
1989-90	Baltimore	AHL	....	....	....	....	....	3	0	0	0	0
	Seattle	WHL	69	64	96	160	180	13	8	9	17	30

GIACIN, JIM

Left wing. Shoots left. 6'1", 195 lbs. Born, St. Louis, MO, January 6, 1971.
(Los Angeles' 8th choice, 182nd overall, in 1989 Entry Draft).

			Regular Season					Playoffs				
Season	Club	Lea	GP	G	A	TP	PIM	GP	G	A	TP	PIM
1988-89	Culver Aca.	HS	31	29	30	59	46	....	....	....	....	....
1989-90	St. Lawrence	ECAC	28	4	2	6	32	....	....	....	....	....

GIBSON, DON

Defense. Shoots right. 6'1", 210 lbs. Born, Deloraine, Man., December 29, 1967.
(Vancouver's 2nd choice, 49th overall, in 1986 Entry Draft).

			Regular Season					Playoffs				
Season	Club	Lea	GP	G	A	TP	PIM	GP	G	A	TP	PIM
1986-87	Michigan State	CCHA	43	3	3	6	74	....	....	....	....	....
1987-88	Michigan State	CCHA	43	7	12	19	118	....	....	....	....	....
1988-89	Michigan State	CCHA	39	7	10	17	107	....	....	....	....	....
1989-90a	Michigan State	CCHA	44	5	22	27	167	....	....	....	....	....

a CCHA Second All-Star Team (1990)

GIFFIN, LEE

Right wing. Shoots right. 5'11", 200 lbs. Born, Chatham, Ont., April 1, 1967.
(Pittsburgh's 2nd choice, 23rd overall, in 1985 Entry Draft)

			Regular Season					Playoffs				
Season	Club	Lea	GP	G	A	TP	PIM	GP	G	A	TP	PIM
1983-84	Oshawa	OHL	70	23	27	50	88	7	1	4	5	12
1984-85	Oshawa	OHL	62	36	42	78	78	5	1	2	3	2
1985-86	Oshawa	OHL	54	29	37	66	28	6	0	5	5	8
1986-87	**Pittsburgh**	**NHL**	**8**	**1**	**1**	**2**	**0**	....	....	....	....	....
a	Oshawa	OHL	48	31	69	100	46	23	*17	19	36	14
1987-88	**Pittsburgh**	**NHL**	**19**	**0**	**2**	**2**	**9**	....	....	....	....	....
	Muskegon	IHL	48	26	37	63	61	6	1	3	4	2
1988-89	Muskegon	IHL	63	30	44	74	93	12	5	7	12	8
1989-90	Flint	IHL	73	30	44	74	68	4	1	2	3	0
	NHL Totals		**27**	**1**	**3**	**4**	**9**	....	....	....	....	....

a OHL First All-Star Team (1987)

Traded to **NY Rangers** by **Pittsburgh** for future considerations, September 14, 1989.

GILBERT, GREGORY SCOTT (GREG)

Left wing. Shoots left. 6'1", 192 lbs. Born, Mississauga, Ont., January 22, 1962.
(NY Islanders' 5th choice, 80th overall, in 1980 Entry Draft).

			Regular Season					Playoffs				
Season	Club	Lea	GP	G	A	TP	PIM	GP	G	A	TP	PIM
1980-81	Toronto	OHA	64	30	37	67	73	5	2	6	8	16
1981-82 a	Toronto	OHL	65	41	67	108	119	10	4	12	16	23
	NY Islanders	**NHL**	**1**	**1**	**0**	**1**	**0**	**4**	**1**	**1**	**2**	**2**
1982-83	Indianapolis	CHL	24	11	16	27	23	....	....	....	....	....
	NY Islanders	**NHL**	**45**	**8**	**11**	**19**	**30**	**10**	**1**	**0**	**1**	**14**
1983-84	**NY Islanders**	**NHL**	**79**	**31**	**35**	**66**	**59**	**21**	**5**	**7**	**12**	**39**
1984-85	**NY Islanders**	**NHL**	**58**	**13**	**25**	**38**	**36**	....	....	....	....	....
1985-86	**NY Islanders**	**NHL**	**60**	**9**	**19**	**28**	**82**	**2**	**0**	**0**	**0**	**9**
	Springfield	AHL	2	0	0	0	2	....	....	....	....	....
1986-87	**NY Islanders**	**NHL**	**51**	**6**	**7**	**13**	**26**	**10**	**2**	**2**	**4**	**6**
1987-88	**NY Islanders**	**NHL**	**76**	**17**	**28**	**45**	**46**	**4**	**0**	**0**	**0**	**6**
1988-89	**NY Islanders**	**NHL**	**55**	**8**	**13**	**21**	**45**	....	....	....	....	....
	Chicago	**NHL**	**4**	**0**	**0**	**0**	**0**	**15**	**1**	**5**	**6**	**20**
1989-90	**Chicago**	**NHL**	**70**	**12**	**25**	**37**	**54**	**19**	**5**	**8**	**13**	**34**
	NHL Totals		**499**	**105**	**163**	**268**	**378**	**85**	**15**	**23**	**38**	**130**

a OHL Third All-Star Team (1982)

Traded to **Chicago** by **NY Islanders** for Chicago's fifth-round choice (Steve Young) in 1989 Entry Draft, March 7, 1989.

GILCHRIST, BRENT

Center. Shoots left. 5'11", 181 lbs. Born, Moose Jaw, Sask., April 3, 1967.
(Montreal's 6th choice, 79th overall, in 1985 Entry Draft).

			Regular Season					Playoffs				
Season	Club	Lea	GP	G	A	TP	PIM	GP	G	A	TP	PIM
1983-84	Kelowna	WHL	69	16	11	27	16	....	....	....	....	....
1984-85	Kelowna	WHL	51	35	38	73	58	6	5	2	7	8
1985-86	Spokane	WHL	52	45	45	90	57	9	6	7	13	19
1986-87	Spokane	WHL	46	45	55	100	71	5	2	7	9	6
	Sherbrooke	AHL	....	....	....	....	....	10	2	7	9	2
1987-88	Sherbrooke	AHL	77	26	48	74	83	6	1	3	4	6
1988-89	**Montreal**	**NHL**	**49**	**8**	**16**	**24**	**16**	**9**	**1**	**1**	**2**	**10**
	Sherbrooke	AHL	7	6	5	11	7	....	....	....	....	....
1989-90	**Montreal**	**NHL**	**57**	**9**	**15**	**24**	**28**	**8**	**2**	**0**	**2**	**2**
	NHL Totals		**106**	**17**	**31**	**48**	**24**	**17**	**3**	**1**	**4**	**12**

GILES, CURT (JIGHLS)

Defense. Shoots left. 5'8", 175 lbs. Born, The Pas, Man., November 30, 1958.
(Minnesota's 4th choice, 54th overall, in 1978 Amateur Draft).

			Regular Season					Playoffs				
Season	Club	Lea	GP	G	A	TP	PIM	GP	G	A	TP	PIM
1977-78	Minn.-Duluth	WCHA	34	11	36	47	62	....	....	....	....	....
1978-79	Minn.-Duluth	WCHA	30	3	38	41	38	....	....	....	....	....
1979-80	Oklahoma City	CHL	42	4	24	28	35	....	....	....	....	....
	Minnesota	**NHL**	**37**	**2**	**7**	**9**	**31**	**12**	**2**	**4**	**6**	**10**
1980-81	**Minnesota**	**NHL**	**67**	**5**	**22**	**27**	**56**	**19**	**1**	**4**	**5**	**14**
1981-82	**Minnesota**	**NHL**	**74**	**3**	**12**	**15**	**87**	**4**	**0**	**0**	**0**	**2**
1982-83	**Minnesota**	**NHL**	**76**	**2**	**21**	**23**	**70**	**5**	**0**	**2**	**2**	**6**
1983-84	**Minnesota**	**NHL**	**70**	**6**	**22**	**28**	**59**	**16**	**1**	**3**	**4**	**25**
1984-85	**Minnesota**	**NHL**	**77**	**5**	**25**	**30**	**49**	**9**	**0**	**0**	**0**	**17**
1985-86	**Minnesota**	**NHL**	**69**	**6**	**21**	**27**	**30**	**5**	**0**	**1**	**1**	**10**
1986-87	**Minnesota**	**NHL**	**11**	**0**	**3**	**3**	**4**	....	....	....	....	....
	NY Rangers	**NHL**	**61**	**2**	**17**	**19**	**50**	**5**	**0**	**0**	**0**	**6**
1987-88	**NY Rangers**	**NHL**	**13**	**0**	**0**	**0**	**10**	....	....	....	....	....
	Minnesota	**NHL**	**59**	**1**	**12**	**13**	**66**	....	....	....	....	....
1988-89	**Minnesota**	**NHL**	**76**	**5**	**10**	**15**	**77**	**5**	**0**	**0**	**0**	**4**
1989-90	**Minnesota**	**NHL**	**74**	**1**	**2**	**3**	**48**	**7**	**0**	**1**	**1**	**6**
	NHL Totals		**764**	**38**	**174**	**212**	**637**	**87**	**4**	**15**	**19**	**100**

Traded to **NY Rangers** by **Minnesota** with Tony McKegney and Minnesota's second-round choice (Troy Mallette) in 1988 Entry Draft for Bob Brooke and NY Rangers' rights to Minnesota's fourth-round choice in (Jeffery Stolp) 1988 Entry Draft previously acquired by NY Rangers in Mark Pavelich deal, November 13, 1986. Traded to **Minnesota** by **NY Rangers** for Byron Lomow and future considerations, November 20, 1987.

GILHEN, RANDY

Center. Shoots left. 5'10", 190 lbs. Born, Zweibrucken, West Germany, June 13, 1963.
(Hartford's 6th choice, 109th overall, in 1982 Entry Draft).

			Regular Season					Playoffs				
Season	Club	Lea	GP	G	A	TP	PIM	GP	G	A	TP	PIM
1980-81	Saskatoon	WHL	68	10	5	15	154	....	....	....	....	....
1981-82	Saskatoon	WHL	25	15	9	24	45	....	....	....	....	....
	Winnipeg	WHL	36	26	28	54	42	....	....	....	....	....
1982-83	**Hartford**	**NHL**	**2**	**0**	**1**	**1**	**0**	....	....	....	....	....
	Winnipeg	WHL	71	57	44	101	84	3	2	2	4	0
1983-84	Binghamton	AHL	73	8	12	20	72	....	....	....	....	....
1984-85	Salt Lake	IHL	57	20	20	40	28	....	....	....	....	....
	Binghamton	AHL	18	3	3	6	9	8	4	1	5	16
1985-86	Fort Wayne	IHL	82	44	40	84	48	15	10	8	18	6
1986-87	**Winnipeg**	**NHL**	**2**	**0**	**0**	**0**	**0**	....	....	....	....	....
	Sherbrooke	AHL	75	36	29	65	44	17	7	13	20	10
1987-88	**Winnipeg**	**NHL**	**13**	**3**	**2**	**5**	**15**	**4**	**1**	**0**	**1**	**10**
	Moncton	AHL	68	40	47	87	51	....	....	....	....	....
1988-89	**Winnipeg**	**NHL**	**64**	**5**	**3**	**8**	**38**	....	....	....	....	....
1989-90	**Pittsburgh**	**NHL**	**61**	**5**	**11**	**16**	**54**	....	....	....	....	....
	NHL Totals		**142**	**13**	**17**	**30**	**107**	**4**	**1**	**0**	**1**	**10**

Traded to **Pittsburgh** by **Winnipeg** with Jim Kyte and Andrew McBain for Randy Cunnyworth, Rick Tabaracci and Dave McLlwain, June 17, 1989.

GILL, TODD

Defense. Shoots left. 6'1", 185 lbs. Born, Brockville, Ont., November 9, 1965.
(Toronto's 2nd choice, 25th overall, in 1984 Entry Draft).

			Regular Season					Playoffs				
Season	Club	Lea	GP	G	A	TP	PIM	GP	G	A	TP	PIM
1982-83	Windsor	OHL	70	12	24	36	108	3	0	0	0	11
1983-84	Windsor	OHL	68	9	48	57	184	3	1	1	2	10
1984-85	**Toronto**	**NHL**	**10**	**1**	**0**	**1**	**13**	....	....	....	....	....
a	Windsor	OHL	53	17	40	57	148	4	0	1	1	14
1985-86	**Toronto**	**NHL**	**15**	**1**	**2**	**3**	**28**	**1**	**0**	**0**	**0**	**0**
	St. Catharines	AHL	58	8	25	33	90	10	1	6	7	17
1986-87	**Toronto**	**NHL**	**61**	**4**	**27**	**31**	**92**	**13**	**2**	**2**	**4**	**42**
	Newmarket	AHL	11	1	8	9	33	....	....	....	....	....
1987-88	**Toronto**	**NHL**	**65**	**8**	**17**	**25**	**131**	**6**	**1**	**3**	**4**	**20**
	Newmarket	AHL	2	0	1	1	2	....	....	....	....	....
1988-89	**Toronto**	**NHL**	**59**	**11**	**14**	**25**	**72**	....	....	....	....	....
1989-90	**Toronto**	**NHL**	**48**	**1**	**14**	**15**	**92**	**5**	**0**	**3**	**3**	**16**
	NHL Totals		**258**	**26**	**74**	**100**	**428**	**25**	**3**	**8**	**11**	**78**

a OHL Third All-Star Team (1985)

GILLIS, PAUL

Center. Shoots left. 5'11", 198 lbs. Born, Toronto, Ont., December 31, 1963.
(Quebec's 2nd choice, 34th overall, in 1982 Entry Draft).

			Regular Season					Playoffs				
Season	Club	Lea	GP	G	A	TP	PIM	GP	G	A	TP	PIM
1980-81	Niagara Falls	OHA	59	14	19	33	165	....	....	....	....	....
1981-82	Niagara Falls	OHL	65	27	62	89	247	5	1	5	6	26
1982-83	**Quebec**	**NHL**	**7**	**0**	**2**	**2**	**2**	....	....	....	....	....
	North Bay	OHL	61	34	52	86	151	6	1	3	4	26
1983-84	Fredericton	AHL	18	7	8	15	47	....	....	....	....	....
	Quebec	**NHL**	**57**	**8**	**9**	**17**	**59**	**1**	**0**	**0**	**0**	**2**
1984-85	**Quebec**	**NHL**	**77**	**14**	**28**	**42**	**168**	**18**	**1**	**7**	**8**	**73**
1985-86	**Quebec**	**NHL**	**80**	**19**	**24**	**43**	**203**	**3**	**0**	**2**	**2**	**14**
1986-87	**Quebec**	**NHL**	**76**	**13**	**26**	**39**	**267**	**13**	**2**	**4**	**6**	**65**
1987-88	**Quebec**	**NHL**	**80**	**7**	**10**	**17**	**164**	....	....	....	....	....
1988-89	**Quebec**	**NHL**	**79**	**15**	**25**	**40**	**163**	....	....	....	....	....
1989-90	**Quebec**	**NHL**	**71**	**8**	**14**	**22**	**234**	....	....	....	....	....
	NHL Totals		**527**	**84**	**138**	**222**	**1260**	**35**	**3**	**13**	**16**	**154**

GILMOUR, DOUGLAS (DOUG)

Center. Shoots left. 5'11", 170 lbs. Born, Kingston, Ont., June 25, 1963.
(St. Louis' 4th choice, 134th overall, in 1982 Entry Draft).

			Regular Season					Playoffs				
Season	Club	Lea	GP	G	A	TP	PIM	GP	G	A	TP	PIM
1981-82	Cornwall	OHL	67	46	73	119	42	5	6	9	15	2
1982-83ab	Cornwall	OHL	68	70	*107	*177	62	8	8	10	18	16
1983-84	**St. Louis**	**NHL**	**80**	**25**	**28**	**53**	**57**	**11**	**2**	**9**	**11**	**10**
1984-85	**St. Louis**	**NHL**	**78**	**21**	**36**	**57**	**49**	**3**	**1**	**1**	**2**	**2**
1985-86	**St. Louis**	**NHL**	**74**	**25**	**28**	**53**	**41**	**19**	**9**	**12**	***21**	**25**
1986-87	**St. Louis**	**NHL**	**80**	**42**	**63**	**105**	**58**	**6**	**2**	**2**	**4**	**16**
1987-88	**St. Louis**	**NHL**	**72**	**36**	**50**	**86**	**59**	**10**	**3**	**14**	**17**	**18**
1988-89	**Calgary**	**NHL**	**72**	**26**	**59**	**85**	**44**	**22**	**11**	**11**	**22**	**20**
1989-90	**Calgary**	**NHL**	**78**	**24**	**67**	**91**	**54**	**6**	**3**	**1**	**4**	**8**
	NHL Totals		**534**	**199**	**331**	**530**	**362**	**79**	**31**	**50**	**81**	**99**

a OHL First All-Star Team (1983)
b Named OHL's Most Outstanding Player (1983)

Traded to **Calgary** by **St. Louis** with Mark Hunter, Steve Bozek and Michael Dark for Mike Bullard, Craig Coxe and Tim Corkery, September 6, 1988.

GINGRAS, GASTON REGINALD (JING-rah)

Defense. Shoots left. 6', 190 lbs. Born, Temiscamingue, Que., February 13, 1959.
(Montreal's 1st choice, 27th overall, in 1979 Entry Draft).

			Regular Season					Playoffs				
Season	Club	Lea	GP	G	A	TP	PIM	GP	G	A	TP	PIM
1976-77	Kitchener	OHA	59	13	62	75	134	3	0	1	1	6
1977-78	Kitchener	OHA	32	13	24	37	31	....	....	....	....	....
	Hamilton	OHA	29	11	19	30	37	15	3	11	14	13
1978-79	Birmingham	WHA	60	13	21	34	35	....	....	....	....	....
1979-80	Nova Scotia	AHL	30	11	27	38	17	....	....	....	....	....
	Montreal	**NHL**	**34**	**3**	**7**	**10**	**18**	**10**	**1**	**6**	**7**	**8**
1980-81	**Montreal**	**NHL**	**55**	**5**	**16**	**21**	**22**	**1**	**1**	**0**	**1**	**0**
1981-82	**Montreal**	**NHL**	**34**	**6**	**18**	**24**	**28**	**5**	**0**	**1**	**1**	**0**
1982-83	**Montreal**	**NHL**	**22**	**1**	**8**	**9**	**8**	....	....	....	....	....
	Toronto	**NHL**	**45**	**10**	**18**	**28**	**10**	**3**	**1**	**2**	**3**	**2**
1983-84	**Toronto**	**NHL**	**59**	**7**	**20**	**27**	**16**	....	....	....	....	....
1984-85	**Toronto**	**NHL**	**5**	**0**	**2**	**2**	**0**	....	....	....	....	....
	St. Catharines	AHL	36	7	12	19	13	....	....	....	....	....
	Sherbrooke	AHL	21	3	14	17	6	17	5	4	9	4
1985-86	**Montreal**	**NHL**	**34**	**8**	**18**	**26**	**12**	**11**	**2**	**3**	**5**	**4**
	Sherbrooke	AHL	42	11	20	31	14	....	....	....	....	....
1986-87	**Montreal**	**NHL**	**66**	**11**	**34**	**45**	**21**	**5**	**0**	**2**	**2**	**0**
1987-88	**Montreal**	**NHL**	**2**	**0**	**1**	**1**	**2**	....	....	....	....	....
	St. Louis	**NHL**	**68**	**7**	**22**	**29**	**18**	**10**	**1**	**3**	**4**	**4**
1988-89	**St. Louis**	**NHL**	**52**	**3**	**10**	**13**	**6**	**7**	**0**	**1**	**1**	**2**
1989-90	Biel	Switz.	36	17	20	37	....	....	....	....	....	....
	NHL Totals		**476**	**61**	**174**	**235**	**161**	**52**	**6**	**18**	**24**	**20**

Traded to **Toronto** by **Montreal** for Toronto's second round choice in either 1985 or 1986 Entry Draft, December 17, 1982. Traded to **Montreal** by **Toronto** for Larry Landon, February 14, 1985. Traded to **St. Louis** by **Montreal** for Larry Trader and future considerations, October 13, 1987.

GLASGOW, ROBERT

Right wing. Shoots right. 6', 205 lbs. Born, Edmonton, Alta., April 22, 1968.
(Hartford's 8th choice, 179th overall, in 1986 Entry Draft).

			Regular Season					Playoffs				
Season	Club	Lea	GP	G	A	TP	PIM	GP	G	A	TP	PIM
1986-87	U. Alberta	CWUAA	24	5	4	9	8	....	....	....	....	....
1987-88	U. Alberta	CWUAA	47	21	14	35	24	....	....	....	....	....
1988-89	U. Alberta	CWUAA	38	17	29	46	14	....	....	....	....	....
1989-90	U. Alberta	CWUAA	26	13	13	26	18	....	....	....	....	....

GLENNON, MATTHEW (MATT)

Left wing. Shoots left. 6', 185 lbs. Born, Hull, MA, September 20, 1968.
(Boston's 6th choice, 119th overall, in 1987 Entry Draft).

			Regular Season					Playoffs				
Season	Club	Lea	GP	G	A	TP	PIM	GP	G	A	TP	PIM
1987-88	Boston College	H.E.	16	3	3	6	16	....	....	....	....	....
1988-89	Boston College	H.E.	16	1	6	7	4	....	....	....	....	....
1989-90	Boston College	H.E.	31	7	11	18	16	....	....	....	....	....

GLOVER, MICHAEL

Right wing. Shoots right. 5'11", 200 lbs. Born, Ottawa, Ont., July 23, 1968.
(Edmonton's 8th choice, 145th overall, in 1988 Entry Draft).

			Regular Season					Playoffs				
Season	Club	Lea	GP	G	A	TP	PIM	GP	G	A	TP	PIM
1985-86	S.S. Marie	OHL	61	14	19	33	133	....	....	....	....	....
1986-87	S.S. Marie	OHL	57	26	22	48	107	4	1	0	1	15
1987-88	S.S. Marie	OHL	63	41	42	83	130	6	3	3	6	14
1988-89	Cape Breton	AHL	61	9	11	20	156	....	....	....	....	....
1989-90	Phoenix	IHL	1	0	0	0	4	....	....	....	....	....

GLYNN, BRIAN

Defense. Shoots left. 6'4", 215 lbs. Born, Iserlohn, West Germany, November 23, 1967.
(Calgary's 2nd choice, 37th overall, in 1986 Entry Draft).

			Regular Season					Playoffs				
Season	Club	Lea	GP	G	A	TP	PIM	GP	G	A	TP	PIM
1984-85	Saskatoon	WHL	12	1	0	1	2	3	0	0	0	0
1985-86	Saskatoon	WHL	66	7	25	32	131	13	0	3	3	30
1986-87	Saskatoon	WHL	44	2	26	28	163	11	1	3	4	19
1987-88	**Calgary**	**NHL**	**67**	**5**	**14**	**19**	**87**	**1**	**0**	**0**	**0**	**0**
1988-89	**Calgary**	**NHL**	**9**	**0**	**1**	**1**	**19**	....	....	....	....	....
	Salt Lake	IHL	31	3	10	13	105	14	3	7	10	31
1989-90	**Calgary**	**NHL**	**1**	**0**	**0**	**0**	**0**	....	....	....	....	....
ab	Salt Lake	IHL	80	17	44	61	164	....	....	....	....	....
	NHL Totals		**77**	**5**	**15**	**20**	**106**	**1**	**0**	**0**	**0**	**0**

a IHL First All-Star Team (1990)
b Won Governors' Trophy (Outstanding Defenseman-IHL) (1990)

GOBER, MICHAEL

Left wing. Shoots right. 6'1", 195 lbs. Born, St. Louis, MO, April 10, 1967.
(Detroit's 8th choice, 137th overall, in 1987 Entry Draft).

			Regular Season					Playoffs				
Season	Club	Lea	GP	G	A	TP	PIM	GP	G	A	TP	PIM
1987-88	Trois-Rivieres	QMJHL	19	5	10	15	96	....	....	....	....	....
1988-89	Adirondack	AHL	41	15	7	22	55	2	0	0	0	4
1989-90	Adirondack	AHL	44	14	12	26	85	....	....	....	....	....

GOERTZ, DAVE

Defense. Shoots right. 5'11", 210 lbs. Born, Edmonton, Alta., March 28, 1965.
(Pittsburgh's 10th choice, 223rd overall, in 1983 Entry Draft).

			Regular Season					Playoffs				
Season	Club	Lea	GP	G	A	TP	PIM	GP	G	A	TP	PIM
1981-82	Regina	WHL	67	5	19	24	181	19	1	2	3	61
1982-83	Regina	WHL	69	4	22	26	132	5	0	2	2	9
1983-84	Prince Albert	WHL	60	13	47	60	111	5	2	3	5	0
	Baltimore	AHL	1	0	0	0	2	6	0	0	0	0
1984-85	Prince Albert	WHL	48	3	48	51	62	13	4	14	18	29
1985-86	Baltimore	AHL	74	1	15	16	76	....	....	....	....	....
1986-87	Baltimore	AHL	16	0	3	3	8	....	....	....	....	....
	Muskegon	IHL	44	3	17	20	44	15	0	4	4	14
1987-88	**Pittsburgh**	**NHL**	**2**	**0**	**0**	**0**	**2**	....	....	....	....	....
	Muskegon	IHL	73	8	36	44	87	6	0	4	4	14
1988-89	Muskegon	IHL	74	1	32	33	102	14	0	4	4	10
1989-90	Muskegon	IHL	51	3	18	21	64	....	....	....	....	....
	NHL Totals		**2**	**0**	**0**	**0**	**2**	....	....	....	....	....

GOLDEN, MIKE

Center. Shoots right. 6'1", 190 lbs. Born, Boston, MA, June 14, 1965.
(Edmonton's 2nd choice, 40th overall, in 1983 Entry Draft).

			Regular Season					Playoffs				
Season	Club	Lea	GP	G	A	TP	PIM	GP	G	A	TP	PIM
1985-86	U. of Maine	H.E.	24	3	16	29	10	....	....	....	....	....
1986-87	U. of Maine	H.E.	36	19	23	42	37	....	....	....	....	....
1987-88ab	U. of Maine	H.E.	44	31	44	75	46	....	....	....	....	....
1988-89	Denver	IHL	36	12	10	22	21	3	3	1	4	0
1989-90	Flint	IHL	68	13	33	46	30	4	0	0	0	2

a NCAA East Second All-American Team (1988)
b Hockey East Second All-Star Team (1988)

Traded to **NY Rangers** by **Edmonton** with Miloslav Horava and Don Jackson for Reijo Ruotsalainen, Ville Kentala, Clark Donatelli and Jim Wiemer, October 2, 1986.

GOMOLYAKOV, SERGEI

Center. Shoots left. 6'1", 205 lbs. Born, Chelyabinsk, Soviet Union, January 19, 1970.
(Calgary's 10th choice, 189th overall, in 1989 Entry Draft).

			Regular Season					Playoffs				
Season	Club	Lea	GP	G	A	TP	PIM	GP	G	A	TP	PIM
1988-89	Chelyabinsk	USSR	24	8	4	12	10	....	....	....	....	....
1989-90			DID NOT PLAY									

GOODALL, GLEN

Center. Shoots right. 5'8", 170 lbs. Born, Fort Nelson, B.C., January 22, 1970.
(Detroit's 9th choice, 206th overall, in 1988 Entry Draft).

			Regular Season					Playoffs				
Season	Club	Lea	GP	G	A	TP	PIM	GP	G	A	TP	PIM
1984-85	Seattle	WHL	59	5	21	26	6	....	....	....	....	....
1985-86	Seattle	WHL	65	13	28	41	53	4	1	1	2	0
1986-87	Seattle	WHL	68	63	49	112	64	....	....	....	....	....
1987-88	Seattle	WHL	70	53	64	117	88	....	....	....	....	....
1988-89	Seattle	WHL	70	52	62	114	58	....	....	....	....	....
	Flint	IHL	9	5	4	9	4	....	....	....	....	....
1989-90ab	Seattle	WHL	67	76	87	163	83	10	7	7	14	2

a WHL West Second All-Star Team (1990)
b WHL Player of the Year (1990)

GORMAN, SEAN

Defense. Shoots left. 6'3", 180 lbs. Born, Cambridge, MA, February 1, 1969.
(Boston's 12th choice, 245th overall, in 1987 Entry Draft).

			Regular Season					Playoffs				
Season	Club	Lea	GP	G	A	TP	PIM	GP	G	A	TP	PIM
1987-88	Princeton	ECAC	28	0	3	3	6	....	....	....	....	....
1988-89	Princeton	ECAC	17	0	2	2	20	....	....	....	....	....
1989-90	Princeton	ECAC	27	2	4	6	8	....	....	....	....	....

GOSSELIN, GUY

Defense. Shoots right. 5'11", 190 lbs. Born, Rochester, MN, January 6, 1964.
(Winnipeg's 6th choice, 159th overall, in 1982 Entry Draft).

			Regular Season					Playoffs				
Season	Club	Lea	GP	G	A	TP	PIM	GP	G	A	TP	PIM
1982-83	Minn.-Duluth	WCHA	4	0	0	0	0	....	....	....	....	....
1983-84	Minn.-Duluth	WCHA	37	3	3	6	26	....	....	....	....	....
1984-85	Minn.-Duluth	WCHA	47	3	7	10	25	....	....	....	....	....
1985-86	Minn.-Duluth	WCHA	39	2	16	18	53	....	....	....	....	....
1986-87a	Minn.-Duluth	WCHA	33	7	8	15	66	....	....	....	....	....
1987-88	**Winnipeg**	**NHL**	**5**	**0**	**0**	**0**	**6**	....	....	....	....	....
	U.S. National	....	50	3	19	22	82	....	....	....	....	....
	U.S. Olympic	....	6	0	3	3	2	....	....	....	....	....
1988-89	Moncton	AHL	58	2	8	10	56	10	1	1	2	2
1989-90	Moncton	AHL	70	2	10	12	37	....	....	....	....	....
	NHL Totals		**5**	**0**	**0**	**0**	**6**	....	....	....	....	....

a WCHA Second All-Star Team (1987)

GOTAAS, STEVE (GAH-tihs)

Center. Shoots right. 5' 9", 170 lbs. Born, Camrose, Alta., May 10, 1967.
(Pittsburgh's 4th choice, 86th overall, in 1985 Entry Draft).

			Regular Season					Playoffs				
Season	Club	Lea	GP	G	A	TP	PIM	GP	G	A	TP	PIM
1983-84	Prince Albert	WHL	65	10	22	32	47	5	0	1	1	0
1984-85	Prince Albert	WHL	72	32	41	73	66	13	3	6	9	17
1985-86	Prince Albert	WHL	61	40	61	101	31	....	....	....	....	....
1986-87	Prince Albert	WHL	68	53	55	108	94	8	5	6	11	16
1987-88	**Pittsburgh**	**NHL**	**36**	**5**	**6**	**11**	**45**	....	....	....	....	....
	Muskegon	IHL	34	16	22	38	4	....	....	....	....	....
1988-89	**Minnesota**	**NHL**	**12**	**1**	**3**	**4**	**6**	**3**	**0**	**1**	**1**	**5**
	Muskegon	IHL	19	9	16	25	34	....	....	....	....	....
	Kalamazoo	IHL	30	24	22	46	12	5	2	3	5	2
1989-90	Kalamazoo	IHL	1	1	0	1	0	2	0	0	0	2
	NHL Totals		**48**	**6**	**9**	**15**	**51**	**3**	**0**	**1**	**1**	**5**

Traded to **Minnesota** by **Pittsburgh** with Ville Siren for Gord Dineen and Scott Bjugstad, December 17, 1988.

GOTZIAMAN, CHRIS

Right wing. Shoots right. 6'2", 190 lbs. Born, Roseau, MN, November 29, 1971.
(New Jersey's 3rd choice, 29th overall, in 1990 Entry Draft).

			Regular Season					Playoffs				
Season	Club	Lea	GP	G	A	TP	PIM	GP	G	A	TP	PIM
1988-89	Roseau	HS	25	13	18	31	....	....	....	....	....	....
1989-90	Roseau	HS	28	34	31	65	....	....	....	....	....	....

GOULD, ROBERT (BOBBY)

Right wing. Shoots right. 6', 195 lbs. Born, Petrolia, Ont., September 2, 1957.
(Atlanta's 7th choice, 118th overall, in 1977 Amateur Draft).

			Regular Season					Playoffs				
Season	Club	Lea	GP	G	A	TP	PIM	GP	G	A	TP	PIM
1978-79a	N. Hampshire	ECAC	25	24	17	41	....	....	....	....	....	....
	Tulsa	CHL	5	2	0	2	4	....	....	....	....	....
1979-80	**Atlanta**	**NHL**	**1**	**0**	**0**	**0**	**0**	....	....	....	....	....
	Birmingham	CHL	79	27	33	60	73	4	2	4	6	0
1980-81	Birmingham	CHL	58	25	25	50	43	....	....	....	....	....
	Fort Worth	CHL	18	8	6	14	6	5	5	2	7	10
	Calgary	**NHL**	**3**	**0**	**0**	**0**	**0**	**11**	**3**	**1**	**4**	**4**
1981-82	Oklahoma City	CHL	1	0	1	1	0	....	....	....	....	....
	Calgary	**NHL**	**16**	**3**	**0**	**3**	**4**	....	....	....	....	....
	Washington	**NHL**	**60**	**18**	**13**	**31**	**69**	....	....	....	....	....
1982-83	**Washington**	**NHL**	**80**	**22**	**18**	**40**	**43**	**4**	**5**	**0**	**5**	**4**
1983-84	**Washington**	**NHL**	**78**	**21**	**19**	**40**	**74**	**5**	**0**	**2**	**2**	**4**
1984-85	**Washington**	**NHL**	**78**	**14**	**19**	**33**	**69**	**5**	**0**	**1**	**1**	**2**
1985-86	**Washington**	**NHL**	**79**	**19**	**19**	**38**	**26**	**9**	**4**	**3**	**7**	**11**
1986-87	**Washington**	**NHL**	**78**	**23**	**27**	**50**	**74**	**7**	**0**	**3**	**3**	**8**
1987-88	**Washington**	**NHL**	**72**	**12**	**14**	**26**	**56**	**14**	**3**	**1**	**4**	**21**
1988-89	**Washington**	**NHL**	**75**	**5**	**13**	**18**	**65**	**6**	**0**	**2**	**2**	**0**
1989-90	**Boston**	**NHL**	**77**	**8**	**17**	**25**	**92**	**17**	**0**	**0**	**0**	**4**
	NHL Totals		**697**	**145**	**159**	**304**	**572**	**78**	**15**	**13**	**28**	**58**

a ECAC Second All-Star Team (1979)

Traded to **Washington** by **Calgary** with Randy Holt for Pat Ribble and Washington's second round choice (Todd Francis — later transferred to Montreal in Doug Risebrough deal) in 1983 Entry Draft, November 25, 1981. Traded to **Boston** by **Washington** for Alain Cote, September 28, 1989.

GOULET, MICHEL (goo-LAY)

Left wing. Shoots left. 6'1", 195 lbs. Born, Peribonka, Que., April 21, 1960.
(Quebec's 1st choice, 20th overall, in 1979 Entry Draft).

			Regular Season					Playoffs				
Season	Club	Lea	GP	G	A	TP	PIM	GP	G	A	TP	PIM
1976-77	Quebec	QJHL	37	17	18	35	9	14	3	8	11	19
1977-78	Quebec	QJHL	72	73	62	135	109	1	0	1	1	0
1978-79	Birmingham	WHA	78	28	30	58	65	....	....	....	....	....
1979-80	**Quebec**	**NHL**	**77**	**22**	**32**	**54**	**48**	....	....	....	....	....
1980-81	**Quebec**	**NHL**	**76**	**32**	**39**	**71**	**45**	**4**	**3**	**4**	**7**	**7**
1981-82	**Quebec**	**NHL**	**80**	**42**	**42**	**84**	**48**	**16**	**8**	**5**	**13**	**6**
1982-83a	**Quebec**	**NHL**	**80**	**57**	**48**	**105**	**51**	**4**	**0**	**0**	**0**	**6**
1983-84b	**Quebec**	**NHL**	**75**	**56**	**65**	**121**	**76**	**9**	**2**	**4**	**6**	**17**
1984-85	**Quebec**	**NHL**	**69**	**55**	**40**	**95**	**55**	**17**	**11**	**10**	**21**	**17**
1985-86b	**Quebec**	**NHL**	**75**	**53**	**51**	**104**	**64**	**3**	**1**	**2**	**3**	**10**
1986-87b	**Quebec**	**NHL**	**75**	**49**	**47**	**96**	**61**	**13**	**9**	**5**	**14**	**35**
1987-88a	**Quebec**	**NHL**	**80**	**48**	**58**	**106**	**56**	....	....	....	....	....
1988-89	**Quebec**	**NHL**	**69**	**26**	**38**	**64**	**67**	....	....	....	....	....
1989-90	**Quebec**	**NHL**	**57**	**16**	**29**	**45**	**42**	....	....	....	....	....
	Chicago	**NHL**	**8**	**4**	**1**	**5**	**9**	**14**	**2**	**4**	**6**	**6**
	NHL Totals		**821**	**460**	**490**	**950**	**622**	**80**	**36**	**34**	**70**	**104**

a NHL Second All-Star Team (1983, 1988)
b NHL First All-Star Team (1984, 1986, 1987)

Played in NHL All-Star Game (1983-86, 1988)

Traded to **Chicago** by **Quebec** with Greg Millen and Quebec's sixth round choice in 1991 Entry Draft for Mario Doyon, Everett Sanipass and Dan Vincelette, March 5, 1990.

GOVEDARIS, CHRIS

Left wing. Shoots left. 6', 200 lbs. Born, Toronto, Ont., February 2, 1970.
(Hartford's 1st choice, 11th overall, in 1988 Entry Draft).

			Regular Season					Playoffs				
Season	Club	Lea	GP	G	A	TP	PIM	GP	G	A	TP	PIM
1986-87	Toronto	OHL	64	36	28	64	148	....	....	....	....	....
1987-88	Toronto	OHL	62	42	38	80	118	4	2	1	3	10
1988-89	Toronto	OHL	49	41	38	79	117	6	2	3	5	0
1989-90	**Hartford**	**NHL**	**12**	**0**	**1**	**1**	**6**	**2**	**0**	**0**	**0**	**2**
	Binghamton	AHL	14	3	3	6	4	....	....	....	....	....
	Hamilton	OHL	23	11	21	32	53	....	....	....	....	....
	NHL Totals		**12**	**0**	**1**	**1**	**6**	**2**	**0**	**0**	**0**	**2**

GRAHAM, DIRK MILTON

Right wing. Shoots right. 5'11", 190 lbs. Born, Regina, Sask., July 29, 1959.
(Vancouver's 5th choice, 89th overall, in 1979 Entry Draft).

			Regular Season					Playoffs				
Season	Club	Lea	GP	G	A	TP	PIM	GP	G	A	TP	PIM
1975-76	Regina	WHL	2	0	0	0	0	6	1	1	2	5
1976-77	Regina	WHL	65	37	28	65	66	....	....	....	....	....
1977-78	Regina	WHL	72	29	61	110	87	13	15	19	34	37
1978-79	Regina	WHL	71	48	60	108	252	....	....	....	....	....
1979-80	Dallas	CHL	62	17	15	32	96	....	....	....	....	....
1980-81	Fort Wayne	IHL	6	1	2	3	12	....	....	....	....	....
a	Toledo	IHL	61	40	45	85	88	....	....	....	....	....
1981-82	Toledo	IHL	72	49	56	105	68	13	10	11	*21	8
1982-83b	Toledo	IHL	78	70	55	125	88	11	13	7	*20	30
1983-84	**Minnesota**	**NHL**	**6**	**1**	**1**	**2**	**0**	**1**	**0**	**0**	**0**	**2**
c	Salt Lake	CHL	57	37	57	94	72	5	3	8	11	2
1984-85	**Minnesota**	**NHL**	**36**	**12**	**11**	**23**	**23**	**9**	**0**	**4**	**4**	**7**
	Springfield	AHL	37	20	28	48	41	....	....	....	....	....
1985-86	**Minnesota**	**NHL**	**80**	**22**	**33**	**55**	**87**	**5**	**3**	**1**	**4**	**2**
1986-87	**Minnesota**	**NHL**	**76**	**25**	**29**	**54**	**142**	....	....	....	....	....
1987-88	**Minnesota**	**NHL**	**28**	**7**	**5**	**12**	**39**	....	....	....	....	....
	Chicago	**NHL**	**42**	**17**	**19**	**36**	**32**	**4**	**1**	**2**	**3**	**4**
1988-89	**Chicago**	**NHL**	**80**	**33**	**45**	**78**	**89**	**16**	**2**	**4**	**6**	**38**
1989-90	**Chicago**	**NHL**	**73**	**22**	**32**	**54**	**102**	**5**	**1**	**5**	**6**	**2**
	NHL Totals		**421**	**139**	**175**	**314**	**514**	**40**	**7**	**16**	**23**	**55**

a IHL Second All-Star Team (1981)
b IHL First All-Star Team (1983)
c CHL First All-Star Team (1984)

Signed as free agent by **Minnesota**, August 17, 1983. Traded to **Chicago** by **Minnesota** for Curt Fraser, January 4, 1988.

GRANATO, TONY

Left wing. Shoots right. 5'10", 185 lbs. Born, Downers Grove, IL, July 25, 1964.
(NY Rangers' 5th choice, 120th overall, in 1982 Entry Draft).

			Regular Season					Playoffs				
Season	Club	Lea	GP	G	A	TP	PIM	GP	G	A	TP	PIM
1983-84	U. Wisconsin	WCHA	35	14	17	31	48	....	....	....	....	....
1984-85	U. Wisconsin	WCHA	42	33	34	67	94	....	....	....	....	....
1985-86	U. Wisconsin	WCHA	33	25	24	49	36	....	....	....	....	....
1986-87ab	U. Wisconsin	WCHA	42	28	45	73	64	....	....	....	....	....
1987-88	U.S. National	....	49	40	31	71	55	....	....	....	....	....
	U.S. Olympic	....	6	1	7	8	4	....	....	....	....	....
	Colorado	IHL	22	13	14	27	36	8	9	4	13	16
1988-89c	**NY Rangers**	**NHL**	**78**	**36**	**27**	**63**	**140**	**4**	**1**	**1**	**2**	**21**
1989-90	**NY Rangers**	**NHL**	**37**	**7**	**18**	**25**	**77**	....	....	....	....	....
	Los Angeles	**NHL**	**19**	**5**	**6**	**11**	**45**	**10**	**5**	**4**	**9**	**12**
	NHL Totals		**134**	**48**	**51**	**99**	**262**	**14**	**6**	**5**	**11**	**33**

a WCHA Second All-Star Team (1987)
b NCAA West Second All-American Team (1987)
c NHL All-Rookie Team (1989)

Traded to **Los Angeles** by **NY Rangers** with Tomas Sandstrom for Bernie Nicholls, January 20, 1990.

GRANT, KEVIN

Defense. Shoots right. 6'3", 210 lbs. Born, Toronto, Ont., January 9, 1969.
(Calgary's 3rd choice, 40th overall, in 1987 Entry Draft).

			Regular Season					Playoffs				
Season	Club	Lea	GP	G	A	TP	PIM	GP	G	A	TP	PIM
1985-86	Kitchener	OHL	63	2	15	17	204	5	0	1	1	11
1986-87	Kitchener	OHL	52	5	18	23	125	4	0	1	1	16
1987-88	Kitchener	OHL	48	3	20	23	138	4	0	1	1	4
1988-89	Salt Lake	IHL	3	0	1	1	5	3	0	0	0	12
	Sudbury	OHL	60	9	41	50	186	....	....	....	....	....
1989-90	Salt Lake	IHL	78	7	17	24	117	11	0	2	2	22

GRATTON, DAN

Center. Shoots left. 6', 185 lbs. Born, Brantford, Ont., December 7, 1966.
(Los Angeles' 2nd choice, 10th overall, in 1985 Entry Draft)

			Regular Season					Playoffs				
Season	Club	Lea	GP	G	A	TP	PIM	GP	G	A	TP	PIM
1983-84	Oshawa	OHL	65	40	34	74	55	7	2	5	7	15
1984-85	Oshawa	OHL	56	24	48	72	67	5	3	3	6	0
1985-86	Oshawa	OHL	10	3	5	8	15	....	....	....	....	....
	Ottawa	OHL	25	18	18	36	19	....	....	....	....	....
	Belleville	OHL	20	12	14	26	11	21	*20	9	29	16
1986-87	New Haven	AHL	49	6	10	16	45	2	0	0	0	0
1987-88	**Los Angeles**	**NHL**	**7**	**1**	**0**	**1**	**5**	....	....	....	....	....
	New Haven	AHL	57	18	28	46	77	....	....	....	....	....
1988-89	New Haven	AHL	29	5	13	18	41	....	....	....	....	....
	Flint	IHL	20	5	9	14	8	....	....	....	....	....
1989-90	Cdn. National	....	68	29	37	66	40	....	....	....	....	....
	NHL Totals		**7**	**1**	**0**	**1**	**5**	....	....	....	....	....

GRAVES, ADAM

Center. Shoots left. 5'11", 200 lbs. Born, Toronto, Ont., April 12, 1968.
(Detroit's 2nd choice, 22nd overall, in 1986 Entry Draft).

			Regular Season					Playoffs				
Season	Club	Lea	GP	G	A	TP	PIM	GP	G	A	TP	PIM
1985-86	Windsor	OHL	62	27	37	64	35	16	5	11	16	10
1986-87	Windsor	OHL	66	45	55	100	70	14	9	8	17	32
	Adirondack	AHL	....	....	....	....	....	5	0	1	1	0
1987-88	**Detroit**	**NHL**	**9**	**0**	**1**	**1**	**8**	....	....	....	....	....
	Windsor	OHL	37	28	32	60	107	12	14	18	*32	16
1988-89	**Detroit**	**NHL**	**56**	**7**	**5**	**12**	**60**	**5**	**0**	**0**	**0**	**4**
	Adirondack	AHL	14	10	11	21	28	14	11	7	18	17
1989-90	**Detroit**	**NHL**	**13**	**0**	**1**	**1**	**13**	....	....	....	....	....
	Edmonton	**NHL**	**63**	**9**	**12**	**21**	**123**	**22**	**5**	**6**	**11**	**17**
	NHL Totals		**141**	**16**	**19**	**35**	**204**	**27**	**5**	**6**	**11**	**21**

Traded to **Edmonton** by **Detroit** with Petr Klima, Joe Murphy and Jeff Sharples for Jimmy Carson, Kevin McClelland and Edmonton's fifth round choice in 1991 Entry Draft, November 2, 1989.

GRAVES, STEVE

Left wing. Shoots left. 5'10", 175 lbs.   Born, Trenton, Ont., April 7, 1964.
(Edmonton's 2nd choice, 41st overall, in 1982 Entry Draft).

			Regular Season					Playoffs				
Season	Club	Lea	GP	G	A	TP	PIM	GP	G	A	TP	PIM
1981-82	S. S. Marie	OHL	66	12	15	27	49	13	8	5	13	14
1982-83	S. S. Marie	OHL	60	21	20	41	48	5	0	0	0	4
1983-84	**Edmonton**	**NHL**	**2**	**0**	**0**	**0**	**0**	....	....	....	....	....
a	S. S. Marie	OHL	67	41	48	89	47	16	6	8	14	8
1984-85	Nova Scotia	AHL	80	17	15	32	20	6	0	1	1	4
1985-86	Nova Scotia	AHL	78	19	18	37	22	....	....	....	....	....
1986-87	**Edmonton**	**NHL**	**12**	**2**	**0**	**2**	**0**	....	....	....	....	....
	Nova Scotia	AHL	59	18	10	28	22	5	1	1	2	2
1987-88	**Edmonton**	**NHL**	**21**	**3**	**4**	**7**	**10**	....	....	....	....	....
	Nova Scotia	AHL	11	6	2	8	4	....	....	....	....	....
1988-89	Cdn. National	....	3	5	1	6	2	....	....	....	....	....
	TPS	Fin.	43	16	12	28	48	10	2	8	10	12
1989-90	Cdn. National	....	53	24	19	43	50	....	....	....	....	....
	NHL Totals		**35**	**5**	**4**	**9**	**10**					

a OHL Third All-Star Team (1984)

GREEN, MARK

Center. Shoots right. 6'4", 200 lbs.   Born, Watertown, NY, December 26, 1967.
(Winnipeg's 8th choice, 176th overall, in 1986 Entry Draft).

			Regular Season					Playoffs				
Season	Club	Lea	GP	G	A	TP	PIM	GP	G	A	TP	PIM
1987-88	Clarkson	ECAC	18	3	6	9	18	....	....	....	....	....
1988-89	Clarkson	ECAC	30	16	11	27	42	....	....	....	....	....
1989-90	Clarkson	ECAC	32	18	17	35	42	....	....	....	....	....

GREEN, RICHARD DOUGLAS (RICK)

Defense. Shoots left. 6'3", 220 lbs.   Born, Belleville, Ont., February 20, 1956.
(Washington's 1st choice and 1st overall in 1976 Amateur Draft).

			Regular Season					Playoffs				
Season	Club	Lea	GP	G	A	TP	PIM	GP	G	A	TP	PIM
1974-75	London	OHA	65	8	45	53	68	....	....	....	....	....
1975-76ab	London	OHA	61	13	47	60	69	5	1	0	1	4
1976-77	**Washington**	**NHL**	**45**	**3**	**12**	**15**	**16**	....	....	....	....	....
1977-78	**Washington**	**NHL**	**60**	**5**	**14**	**19**	**67**	....	....	....	....	....
1978-79	**Washington**	**NHL**	**71**	**8**	**33**	**41**	**62**	....	....	....	....	....
1979-80	**Washington**	**NHL**	**71**	**4**	**20**	**24**	**52**	....	....	....	....	....
1980-81	**Washington**	**NHL**	**65**	**8**	**23**	**31**	**91**	....	....	....	....	....
1981-82	**Washington**	**NHL**	**65**	**3**	**25**	**28**	**93**	....	....	....	....	....
1982-83	**Montreal**	**NHL**	**66**	**2**	**24**	**26**	**58**	**3**	**0**	**0**	**0**	**2**
1983-84	**Montreal**	**NHL**	**7**	**0**	**1**	**1**	**7**	**15**	**1**	**2**	**3**	**33**
1984-85	**Montreal**	**NHL**	**77**	**1**	**18**	**19**	**30**	**12**	**0**	**3**	**3**	**14**
1985-86	**Montreal**	**NHL**	**46**	**3**	**2**	**5**	**20**	**18**	**1**	**4**	**5**	**8**
1986-87	**Montreal**	**NHL**	**72**	**1**	**9**	**10**	**10**	**17**	**0**	**4**	**4**	**8**
1987-88	**Montreal**	**NHL**	**59**	**2**	**11**	**13**	**33**	**11**	**0**	**2**	**2**	**2**
1988-89	**Montreal**	**NHL**	**72**	**1**	**14**	**15**	**25**	**21**	**1**	**1**	**2**	**6**
1989-90	Meran	Italy	9	2	6	8	2	10	3	6	9	4
	NHL Totals		**776**	**41**	**206**	**247**	**564**	**97**	**3**	**16**	**19**	**73**

a OHA First All-Star Team (1976)
b OHA Outstanding Defenseman (1976)

Traded to **Montreal** by **Washington** with Ryan Walter for Brian Engblom, Rod Langway, Doug Jarvis and Craig Laughlin, September 9, 1982. Traded to **Detroit** by **Montreal** for Edmonton's fifth round choice – previously acquired by Detroit – in 1991 Entry Draft, June 15, 1990.

GREEN, TRAVIS

Center. Shoots right. 6', 195 lbs.   Born, Creston, B.C., December 20, 1970.
(NY Islanders' 2nd choice, 23rd overall, in 1989 Entry Draft).

			Regular Season					Playoffs				
Season	Club	Lea	GP	G	A	TP	PIM	GP	G	A	TP	PIM
1986-87	Spokane	WHL	64	8	17	25	27	3	0	0	0	0
1987-88	Spokane	WHL	72	33	54	87	42	15	10	10	20	13
1988-89	Spokane	WHL	75	51	51	102	79	....	....	....	....	....
1989-90	Spokane	WHL	50	45	44	89	80	....	....	....	....	....
	Medicine Hat	WHL	25	15	24	39	19	3	0	0	0	2

GREENLAW, JEFF

Left wing. Shoots left. 6'2", 230 lbs.   Born, Toronto, Ont., February 28, 1968.
(Washington's 1st choice, 19th overall, in 1986 Entry Draft).

			Regular Season					Playoffs				
Season	Club	Lea	GP	G	A	TP	PIM	GP	G	A	TP	PIM
1985-86	Cdn. Olympic	....	57	3	16	19	81	....	....	....	....	....
1986-87	**Washington**	**NHL**	**22**	**0**	**3**	**3**	**44**	....	....	....	....	....
	Binghamton	AHL	4	0	2	2	0	....	....	....	....	....
1987-88	**Washington**	**NHL**	...	...	...	...	...	**1**	**0**	**0**	**0**	**19**
	Binghamton	AHL	56	8	7	15	142	1	0	0	0	2
1988-89	Baltimore	AHL	55	12	15	27	115	....	....	....	....	....
1989-90	Baltimore	AHL	10	3	2	5	26	7	1	0	1	13
	NHL Totals		**22**	**0**	**3**	**3**	**44**	**1**	**0**	**0**	**0**	**19**

GREGG, RANDALL JOHN (RANDY)

Defense. Shoots left. 6'4", 215 lbs.   Born, Edmonton, Alta., February 19, 1956.

			Regular Season					Playoffs				
Season	Club	Lea	GP	G	A	TP	PIM	GP	G	A	TP	PIM
1977-78	U. of Alberta	CWUAA	24	7	23	30	37	....	....	....	....	....
1978-79a	U. of Alberta	CWUAA	24	5	16	21	47	....	....	....	....	....
1979-80	Cdn. National	...	56	7	17	24	36	....	....	....	....	....
	Cdn. Olympic	...	6	1	1	2	2	....	....	....	....	....
1980-81	Kokuda	Japan	35	12	18	30	30	....	....	....	....	....
1981-82	Kokuda	Japan	36	12	20	32	25	....	....	....	....	....
	Edmonton	**NHL**	....	....	....	....	....	**4**	**0**	**0**	**0**	**0**
1982-83	**Edmonton**	**NHL**	**80**	**6**	**22**	**28**	**54**	**16**	**2**	**4**	**6**	**13**
1983-84	**Edmonton**	**NHL**	**80**	**13**	**27**	**40**	**56**	**19**	**3**	**7**	**10**	**21**
1984-85	**Edmonton**	**NHL**	**57**	**3**	**20**	**23**	**32**	**17**	**0**	**6**	**6**	**12**
1985-86	**Edmonton**	**NHL**	**64**	**2**	**26**	**28**	**47**	**10**	**1**	**0**	**1**	**12**
1986-87	**Edmonton**	**NHL**	**52**	**8**	**16**	**24**	**42**	**18**	**3**	**6**	**9**	**17**
1987-88	**Edmonton**	**NHL**	**15**	**1**	**2**	**3**	**8**	**19**	**1**	**8**	**9**	**24**
	Cdn. National	...	37	2	6	8	37	....	....	....	....	....
	Cdn. Olympic	....	8	1	2	3	8	....	....	....	....	....
1988-89	**Edmonton**	**NHL**	**57**	**3**	**15**	**18**	**28**	**7**	**1**	**0**	**1**	**4**
1989-90	**Edmonton**	**NHL**	**48**	**4**	**20**	**24**	**42**	**20**	**2**	**6**	**8**	**16**
	NHL Totals		**453**	**40**	**148**	**188**	**309**	**130**	**13**	**37**	**50**	**119**

a CIAU Player of the Year (1979)
Signed as a free agent by **Edmonton**, October 18, 1982.

GREIG, MARK

Right wing. Shoots right. 5'11", 190 lbs.   Born, High River, Alta., January 25, 1970.
(Hartford's 1st choice, 15th overall, in 1990 Entry Draft).

			Regular Season					Playoffs				
Season	Club	Lea	GP	G	A	TP	PIM	GP	G	A	TP	PIM
1988-89	Lethbridge	WHL	71	36	72	108	113	8	5	5	10	16
1989-90a	Lethbridge	WHL	65	55	80	135	149	18	11	21	32	35

a WHL East First All-Star Team (1990)

GRESCHNER, RONALD JOHN (RON)   (GRESH-nur)

Defense. Shoots left. 6'2", 205 lbs.   Born, Goodsoil, Sask., December 22, 1954.
(NY Rangers' 2nd choice, 32nd overall, in 1974 Amateur Draft).

			Regular Season					Playoffs				
Season	Club	Lea	GP	G	A	TP	PIM	GP	G	A	TP	PIM
1972-73	N. Westminster	WHL	68	22	47	69	169	5	2	4	6	19
1973-74a	N. Westminster	WHL	67	33	70	103	170	11	5	6	11	18
1974-75	Providence	AHL	7	5	6	11	10	....	....	....	....	....
	NY Rangers	**NHL**	**70**	**8**	**37**	**45**	**93**	**3**	**0**	**1**	**1**	**2**
1975-76	**NY Rangers**	**NHL**	**77**	**6**	**21**	**27**	**93**	....	....	....	....	....
1976-77	**NY Rangers**	**NHL**	**80**	**11**	**36**	**47**	**89**	....	....	....	....	....
1977-78	**NY Rangers**	**NHL**	**78**	**24**	**48**	**72**	**100**	**3**	**0**	**0**	**0**	**2**
1978-79	**NY Rangers**	**NHL**	**60**	**17**	**36**	**53**	**66**	**18**	**7**	**5**	**12**	**16**
1979-80	**NY Rangers**	**NHL**	**76**	**21**	**37**	**58**	**103**	**9**	**0**	**6**	**6**	**10**
1980-81	**NY Rangers**	**NHL**	**74**	**27**	**41**	**68**	**112**	**14**	**4**	**8**	**12**	**17**
1981-82	**NY Rangers**	**NHL**	**29**	**5**	**11**	**16**	**16**	....	....	....	....	....
1982-83	**NY Rangers**	**NHL**	**10**	**3**	**5**	**8**	**0**	**8**	**2**	**2**	**4**	**12**
1983-84	**NY Rangers**	**NHL**	**77**	**12**	**44**	**56**	**117**	**2**	**1**	**0**	**1**	**2**
1984-85	**NY Rangers**	**NHL**	**48**	**16**	**29**	**45**	**42**	**2**	**0**	**3**	**3**	**12**
1985-86	**NY Rangers**	**NHL**	**78**	**20**	**28**	**48**	**104**	**5**	**3**	**1**	**4**	**11**
1986-87	**NY Rangers**	**NHL**	**61**	**6**	**34**	**40**	**62**	**6**	**0**	**5**	**5**	**0**
1987-88	**NY Rangers**	**NHL**	**51**	**1**	**5**	**6**	**82**	....	....	....	....	....
1988-89	**NY Rangers**	**NHL**	**58**	**1**	**10**	**11**	**94**	**4**	**0**	**1**	**1**	**6**
1989-90	**NY Rangers**	**NHL**	**55**	**1**	**9**	**10**	**53**	**10**	**0**	**0**	**0**	**16**
	NHL Totals		**982**	**179**	**431**	**610**	**1226**	**84**	**17**	**32**	**49**	**106**

a WHL First All-Star Team (1974)
Played in NHL All-Star Game (1980)

GRETZKY, WAYNE (GRETZ-kee)

Center. Shoots left. 6', 175 lbs. Born, Brantford, Ont., January 26, 1961.

			Regular Season					Playoffs				
Season	Club	Lea	GP	G	A	TP	PIM	GP	G	A	TP	PIM
1976-77	Peterborough	OHA	3	0	3	3	0	....	....	....	....	....
1977-78ab	S. S. Marie	OHA	64	70	112	182	14	13	6	20	26	0
1978-79	Indianapolis	WHA	8	3	3	6	0	....	....	....	....	....
cd	Edmonton	WHA	72	43	61	104	19	13	*10	10	*20	2
1979-80efg	Edmonton	NHL	79	51	*86	*137	21	3	2	1	3	0
1980-81 ehijk	Edmonton	NHL	80	55	*109	*164	28	9	7	14	21	4
1981-82 ehijklmq	Edmonton	NHL	80	*92	*120	*212	26	5	5	7	12	8
1982-83 ehijmnoq	Edmonton	NHL	80	*71	*125	*196	59	16	12	*26	*38	4
1983-84 ehimq	Edmonton	NHL	74	*87	*118	*205	39	19	13	*22	*35	12
1984-85 ehijmnopqr	Edmonton	NHL	80	*73	*135	*208	52	18	17	*30	*47	4
1985-86 ehijkr	Edmonton	NHL	80	52	*163	*215	46	10	8	11	19	2
1986-87 ehimqr	Edmonton	NHL	79	*62	*121	*183	28	21	5	*29	*34	6
1987-88gnp	Edmonton	NHL	64	40	*109	149	24	19	12	*31	*43	16
1988-89egs	Los Angeles	NHL	78	54	*114	168	26	11	5	17	22	0
1989-90gi	Los Angeles	NHL	73	40	*102	*142	42	7	3	7	10	0
	NHL Totals		**847**	**677**	***1302**	***1979**	**391**	**138**	**89**	**195**	**284**	**56**

a OHA Second All-Star Team (1978)
b Named OHA's Rookie of the Year (1978)
c WHA Second All-Star Team (1979)
d Named WHA's Rookie of the Year (1979)
e Won Hart Trophy (1980, 1981, 1982, 1983, 1984, 1985, 1986, 1987, 1989)
f Won Lady Byng Trophy (1980)
g NHL Second All-Star Team (1980, 1988, 1989, 1990)
h NHL First All-Star Team (1981, 1982, 1983, 1984, 1985, 1986, 1987)
i Won Art Ross Trophy (1981, 1982, 1983, 1984, 1985, 1986, 1987, 1990)
j NHL record for assists in regular season (1981, 1982, 1983, 1985, 1986)
k NHL record for points in regular season (1981, 1982, 1986)
l NHL record for goals in regular season (1982)
m Won Lester B. Pearson Award (1982, 1983, 1984, 1985, 1987)
n NHL record for assists in one playoff year (1983, 1985, 1988)
o NHL record for points in one playoff year (1983, 1985)
p Won Conn Smythe Trophy (1985, 1988)
q NHL Plus/Minus Leader (1982, 1983, 1984, 1985, 1987)
r Selected Chrysler-Dodge/NHL Performer of the Year (1985, 1986, 1987)
s Won Dodge Performance of the Year Award (1989)

Played in NHL All-Star Game (1980-1986, 1988-90)

Reclaimed by **Edmonton** as an under-age junior prior to Expansion Draft, June 9, 1979. Claimed as priority selection by **Edmonton**, June 9, 1979. Traded to **Los Angeles** by **Edmonton** with Mike Krushelnyski and Marty McSorley for Jimmy Carson, Martin Gelinas, Los Angeles' first round choices in 1989 (acquired by **New Jersey**, June 17, 1989. **New Jersey** selected Jason Miller), 1991 and 1993 Entry Drafts and cash, August 9, 1988.

GREYERBIEHL, JASON

Left wing. Shoots left. 6', 175 lbs. Born, Bramalea, Ont., March 24, 1970.
(Chicago's 7th choice, 174th overall, in 1989 Entry Draft).

			Regular Season					Playoffs				
Season	Club	Lea	GP	G	A	TP	PIM	GP	G	A	TP	PIM
1988-89	Colgate	ECAC	31	6	9	15	15	....	....	....	....	....
1989-90	Colgate	ECAC	38	12	20	32	20	....	....	....	....	....

GRIEVE, BRENT

Left wing. Shoots left. 6'1", 200 lbs. Born, Oshawa, Ont., May 9, 1969.
(NY Islanders' 4th choice, 65th overall, in 1989 Entry Draft).

			Regular Season					Playoffs				
Season	Club	Lea	GP	G	A	TP	PIM	GP	G	A	TP	PIM
1986-87	Oshawa	OHL	60	9	19	28	102	24	3	8	11	22
1987-88	Oshawa	OHL	55	19	20	39	122	7	0	1	1	8
1988-89	Oshawa	OHL	49	34	33	67	105	6	4	3	7	4
1989-90	Oshawa	OHL	62	46	47	93	125	17	10	10	20	26

GRIMSON, STU

Left wing. Shoots left. 6'5", 220 lbs. Born, Kamloops, B.C., May 20, 1965.
(Calgary's 8th choice, 143rd overall, in 1985 Entry Draft).

			Regular Season					Playoffs				
Season	Club	Lea	GP	G	A	TP	PIM	GP	G	A	TP	PIM
1982-83	Regina	WHL	48	0	1	1	105	5	0	0	0	14
1983-84	Regina	WHL	63	8	8	16	131	21	0	1	1	29
1984-85	Regina	WHL	71	24	32	56	248	8	1	2	3	14
1985-86	U. Manitoba	CWUAA	12	7	4	11	113	3	1	1	2	20
1986-87	U. Manitoba	CWUAA	29	8	8	16	67	14	4	2	6	28
1987-88	Salt Lake	IHL	38	9	5	14	268	....	....	....	....	....
1988-89	**Calgary**	**NHL**	1	0	0	0	5	....	....	....	....	....
	Salt Lake	IHL	72	9	18	27	397	14	2	3	5	86
1989-90	**Calgary**	**NHL**	3	0	0	0	17	....	....	....	....	....
	Salt Lake	IHL	62	8	8	16	319	4	0	0	0	8
	NHL Totals		**4**	**0**	**0**	**0**	**22**					

GRONSTRAND, JARI

Defense. Shoots left. 6'3", 195 lbs. Born, Tampere, Finland, November 14, 1962.
(Minnesota's 8th choice, 96th overall, in 1986 Entry Draft).

			Regular Season					Playoffs				
Season	Club	Lea	GP	G	A	TP	PIM	GP	G	A	TP	PIM
1982-83	Tappara	Fin.	35	2	2	4	18	.8	0	0	0	4
1983-84	Tappara	Fin.	32	2	4	6	14	9	0	2	2	4
1984-85	Tappara	Fin.	36	1	9	10	27	....	....	....	....	....
1985-86	Tappara	Fin.	36	9	5	14	26	8	1	2	3	4
1986-87	**Minnesota**	**NHL**	47	1	6	7	27	....	....	....	....	....
1987-88	**NY Rangers**	**NHL**	62	3	11	14	63	....	....	....	....	....
	Colorado	IHL	3	1	3	4	0	....	....	....	....	....
1988-89	**Quebec**	**NHL**	25	1	3	4	14	....	....	....	....	....
	Halifax	AHL	8	0	1	1	5	....	....	....	....	....
1989-90	**Quebec**	**NHL**	7	0	1	1	2	....	....	....	....	....
	Halifax	AHL	2	0	0	0	0	....	....	....	....	....
	NY Islanders	**NHL**	41	3	4	7	27	3	0	0	0	4
	Springfield	AHL	1	0	1	1	0	....	....	....	....	....
	NHL Totals		**182**	**8**	**25**	**33**	**133**	**3**	**0**	**0**	**0**	**4**

Traded to **NY Rangers** by Minnesota with Paul Boutilier for Jay Caufield and Dave Gagne, October 8, 1987. Traded to **Quebec** by **NY Rangers** with Bruce Bell, Walt Poddubny and NY Rangers' fourth round choice (Eric Dubois) in 1989 Entry Draft for Jason Lafreniere and Normand Rochefort, August 1, 1988.

GROSS, PAVEL

Right wing. Shoots right. 6'3", 195 lbs. Born, Ustin Ogroh, Czechoslovakia, May 11, 1968.
(NY Islanders' 7th choice, 111th overall, in 1988 Entry Draft).

			Regular Season					Playoffs				
Season	Club	Lea	GP	G	A	TP	PIM	GP	G	A	TP	PIM
1987-88	Sparta Praha	Czech	24	3	4	7	0	....	....	....	....	....
1988-89	Sparta Praha	Czech	27	12	13	25		....	....	....	....	....
1989-90	Sparta Praha	Czech	36	10	9	19		....	....	....	....	....

GRUHL, SCOTT KENNETH (GROOL)

Left wing. Shoots left. 5'11", 185 lbs. Born, Port Colborne, Ont., September 13, 1959.

			Regular Season					Playoffs				
Season	Club	Lea	GP	G	A	TP	PIM	GP	G	A	TP	PIM
1978-79	Sudbury	OHA	68	35	49	94	78	10	5	7	12	15
1979-80	Binghamton	AHL	4	1	0	1	0	....	....	....	....	....
a	Saginaw	IHL	75	53	40	93	100	7	2	6	8	16
1980-81	Houston	CHL	4	0	0	0	0	....	....	....	....	....
	Saginaw	IHL	77	56	34	90	87	13	*11	8	*19	12
1981-82	**Los Angeles**	**NHL**	7	2	1	3	2	....	....	....	....	....
	New Haven	AHL	73	28	41	69	107	4	0	4	4	2
1982-83	**Los Angeles**	**NHL**	7	0	2	2	4	....	....	....	....	....
	New Haven	AHL	68	25	38	63	114	12	3	3	6	22
1983-84b	Muskegon	IHL	56	40	56	96	46	....	....	....	....	....
1984-85bc	Muskegon	IHL	82	62	64	126	102	17	7	16	23	16
1985-86a	Muskegon	IHL	82	*59	50	109	178	14	7	*13	20	22
1986-87	Muskegon	IHL	67	34	39	73	157	15	5	7	12	54
1987-88	**Pittsburgh**	**NHL**	6	1	0	1	0	....	....	....	....	....
	Muskegon	IHL	55	28	47	75	115	6	5	1	6	12
1988-89	Muskegon	IHL	79	37	55	92	163	14	8	11	19	37
1989-90	Muskegon	IHL	80	41	51	92	206	15	8	6	14	26
	NHL Totals		**20**	**3**	**3**	**6**	**6**	....	....	....	....	....

a IHL Second All-Star Team (1980, 1986)
b IHL First All-Star Team (1984, 1985)
c Won James Gatschene Memorial Trophy (MVP-IHL) (1985)
Signed as a free agent by **Los Angeles**, October 11, 1979. Signed as a free agent by **Pittsburgh**, December 14, 1987.

GUAY, FRANCOIS

Center. Shoots left. 6', 190 lbs. Born, Gatineau, Que., June 8, 1968.
(Buffalo's 9th choice, 152nd overall, in 1986 Entry Draft).

			Regular Season					Playoffs				
Season	Club	Lea	GP	G	A	TP	PIM	GP	G	A	TP	PIM
1985-86	Laval	QMJHL	71	19	55	74	46	14	5	6	11	15
1986-87	Laval	QMJHL	63	52	77	129	67	14	5	13	18	18
1987-88	Laval	QMJHL	66	60	84	144	142	14	10	15	25	10
1988-89	Rochester	AHL	45	6	20	26	34	....	....	....	....	....
1989-90	**Buffalo**	**NHL**	1	0	0	0	0	....	....	....	....	....
	Rochester	AHL	69	28	35	63	39	16	4	8	12	12
	NHL Totals		**1**	**0**	**0**	**0**	**0**	....	....	....	....	....

GUAY, PAUL   (GAY)

Right wing. Shoots right. 5'11", 185 lbs.   Born, Providence, RI, September 2, 1963.
(Minnesota's 9th choice, 118th overall, in 1981 Entry Draft).

			Regular Season						Playoffs			
Season	Club	Lea	GP	G	A	TP	PIM	GP	G	A	TP	PIM
1981-82	Providence	ECAC	33	23	17	40	38	.....	....	....	....	....
1982-83a	Providence	ECAC	42	34	31	65	83	.....	....	....	....	....
1983-84	U.S. National	...	62	20	18	38	44	.....	....	....	....	....
	U.S. Olympic	...	6	1	0	1	8	.....	....	....	....	....
	Philadelphia	NHL	14	2	6	8	14	3	0	0	0	4
1984-85	**Philadelphia**	NHL	2	0	1	1	0	.....	....	....	....	....
	Hershey	AHL	74	23	30	53	123	.....	....	....	....	....
1985-86	**Los Angeles**	NHL	23	3	3	6	18	.....	....	....	....	....
	New Haven	AHL	57	15	36	51	101	5	3	0	3	11
1986-87	New Haven	AHL	6	1	3	4	11	.....	....	....	....	....
	Los Angeles	NHL	35	2	5	7	16	2	0	0	0	0
1987-88	**Los Angeles**	NHL	33	4	4	8	40	4	0	1	1	8
	New Haven	AHL	42	21	26	47	53	.....	....	....	....	....
1988-89	**Los Angeles**	NHL	2	0	0	0	2	.....	....	....	....	....
	New Haven	AHL	4	4	6	10	20	.....	....	....	....	....
	Boston	NHL	5	0	2	2	0	.....	....	....	....	....
	Maine	AHL	61	15	29	44	77	.....	....	....	....	....
1989-90	Utica	AHL	75	25	30	55	103	5	2	2	4	13
	NHL Totals		114	11	21	32	90	9	0	1	1	12

a ECAC Second All-Star Team (1983)
Rights traded to **Philadelphia** by **Minnesota** with Minnesota's third round choice in 1985 Entry Draft for Paul Holmgren, February 23, 1984. Traded to **Los Angeles** by **Philadelphia** with Philadelphia's fourth-round choice (Sylvain Couturier) in 1986 Entry Draft for Steve Seguin and Los Angeles' second-round choice (Jukka Seppo) in 1986 Entry Draft, October 11, 1985. Traded to **Boston** by **Los Angeles** for the rights to Dave Pasin, November 3, 1988. Signed as a free agent by **New Jersey**, August 14, 1989. Signed as a free agent by **NY Islanders**, August 13, 1990.

GUDEN, DAVE

Left wing. Shoots left. 6'1", 180 lbs.   Born, Brighton, MA, April 26, 1968.
(Los Angeles' 4th choice, 86th overall, in 1986 Entry Draft).

			Regular Season						Playoffs			
Season	Club	Lea	GP	G	A	TP	PIM	GP	G	A	TP	PIM
1986-87	Providence	H.E.	33	4	2	6	22	.....	....	....	....	....
1987-88	Providence	H.E.	34	1	5	6	8	.....	....	....	....	....
1988-89	Providence	H.E.	31	2	6	8	14	.....	....	....	....	....
1989-90	Providence	H.E.	27	4	0	4	28	.....	....	....	....	....

GUERARD, STEPHANE

Defense. Shoots left. 6'2", 198 lbs.   Born, St. Elizabeth, Que., April 12, 1968.
(Quebec's 3rd choice, 41st overall, in 1986 Entry Draft).

			Regular Season						Playoffs			
Season	Club	Lea	GP	G	A	TP	PIM	GP	G	A	TP	PIM
1985-86	Shawinigan	QMJHL	59	4	18	22	167	3	1	1	2	0
1986-87	Shawinigan	QMJHL	31	5	16	21	57	12	2	9	11	36
1987-88	**Quebec**	NHL	30	0	0	0	34	.....	....	....	....	....
1988-89	Halifax	AHL	37	1	9	10	140	4	0	0	0	8
1989-90	**Quebec**	NHL	4	0	0	0	6	.....	....	....	....	....
	Halifax	AHL	1	0	0	0	5	.....	....	....	....	....
	NHL Totals		34	0	0	0	40	.....	....	....	....	....

GUERIN, BILL   (GAIR-ihn)

Right wing. Shoots right. 6'2", 190 lbs.   Born, Wilbraham, MA, November 9, 1970.
(New Jersey's 1st choice, 5th overall, in 1989 Entry Draft).

			Regular Season						Playoffs			
Season	Club	Lea	GP	G	A	TP	PIM	GP	G	A	TP	PIM
1987-88	Springfield	USHL	38	31	44	75	146	.....	....	....	....	....
1988-89	Springfield	USHL	31	32	35	67	90	.....	....	....	....	....
1989-90	Boston College	H.E.	39	14	11	25	54	.....	....	....	....	....

GUIDOTTI, VINCE

Left wing. Shoots left. 6', 180 lbs.   Born, Sacramento, CA, April 29, 1967.
(St. Louis' 9th choice, 201st overall, in 1985 Entry Draft).

			Regular Season						Playoffs			
Season	Club	Lea	GP	G	A	TP	PIM	GP	G	A	TP	PIM
1985-86	U. of Maine	H.E.	16	0	0	0	8	.....	....	....	....	....
1986-87	U. of Maine	H.E.	39	1	3	4	40	.....	....	....	....	....
1987-88	U. of Maine	H.E.	44	7	19	26	69	.....	....	....	....	....
1988-89	U. of Maine	H.E.	42	7	23	30	76	.....	....	....	....	....
1989-90	Maine	AHL	2	0	0	0	0	.....	....	....	....	....
	Johnstown	ECHL	46	5	17	22	61	.....	....	....	....	....

GUILLET, ROBERT

Right wing. Shoots right. 5'11", 189 lbs.   Born, Montreal, Que., February 22, 1972.
(Montreal's 4th choice, 60th overall, in 1990 Entry Draft).

			Regular Season						Playoffs			
Season	Club	Lea	GP	G	A	TP	PIM	GP	G	A	TP	PIM
1989-90a	Longueuil	QMJHL	69	32	40	72	132	7	2	1	3	16

a QMJHL Third All-Star Team (1990)

GUSAROV, ALEXEI

Defense. Shoots left. 6'2", 170 lbs.   Born, Leningrad, Soviet Union, July 8, 1964.
(Quebec's 11th choice, 213th overall, in 1988 Entry Draft).

			Regular Season						Playoffs			
Season	Club	Lea	GP	G	A	TP	PIM	GP	G	A	TP	PIM
1981-82	Leningrad	USSR	20	1	2	3	16	.....	....	....	....	....
1982-83	Leningrad	USSR	42	2	1	3	32	.....	....	....	....	....
1983-84	Leningrad	USSR	43	2	3	5	32	.....	....	....	....	....
1984-85	CSKA	USSR	36	3	2	5	26	.....	....	....	....	....
1985-86	CSKA	USSR	40	3	5	8	30	.....	....	....	....	....
1986-87	CSKA	USSR	38	4	7	11	24	.....	....	....	....	....
1987-88	CSKA	USSR	39	3	2	5	28	.....	....	....	....	....
1988-89	CSKA	USSR	42	5	4	9	37	.....	....	....	....	....
1989-90	CSKA	USSR	42	4	7	11	42	.....	....	....	....	....

GUSTAFSSON, BENGT-AKE   (GUS-tuhf-suhn)

Center. Shoots left. 6', 200 lbs.   Born, Karlskoga, Sweden, March 23, 1958.
(Washington's 7th choice, 55th overall, in 1978 Amateur Draft).

			Regular Season						Playoffs			
Season	Club	Lea	GP	G	A	TP	PIM	GP	G	A	TP	PIM
1977-78	Farjestad	Swe.	32	15	10	25	10	.....	....	....	....	....
1978-79	Farjestad	Swe.	32	13	12	25	10	3	2	0	2	4
	Edmonton	WHA	.....	....	....	....	....	2	1	2	3	0
1979-80	**Washington**	NHL	80	22	38	60	17	.....	....	....	....	....
1980-81	**Washington**	NHL	72	21	34	55	26	.....	....	....	....	....
1981-82	**Washington**	NHL	70	26	34	60	40	.....	....	....	....	....
1982-83	**Washington**	NHL	67	22	42	64	16	4	0	1	1	4
1983-84	**Washington**	NHL	69	32	43	75	16	5	2	3	5	0
1984-85	**Washington**	NHL	51	14	29	43	8	5	1	3	4	0
1985-86	**Washington**	NHL	70	23	52	75	26	.....	....	....	....	....
1986-87	Bofors IK	Swe. 2	28	16	26	42	22	.....	....	....	....	....
	Swe. National	...	10	3	8	11	....	.....	....	....	....	....
1987-88	**Washington**	NHL	78	18	36	54	29	14	4	9	13	6
1988-89	**Washington**	NHL	72	18	51	69	18	4	2	3	5	6
1989-90	Farjestad	Swe.	37	22	24	46	14	.....	....	....	....	....
	NHL Totals		629	196	359	555	196	32	9	19	28	16

Reclaimed by **Washington** from **Edmonton** prior to Expansion Draft, June 9, 1979.

GUY, KEVAN

Defense. Shoots right. 6'3", 202 lbs.   Born, Edmonton, Alta., July 16, 1965.
(Calgary's 5th choice, 71st overall, in 1983 Entry Draft).

			Regular Season						Playoffs			
Season	Club	Lea	GP	G	A	TP	PIM	GP	G	A	TP	PIM
1982-83	Medicine Hat	WHL	69	7	20	27	89	5	0	3	3	16
1983-84	Medicine Hat	WHL	72	15	42	57	117	14	3	4	7	14
1984-85	Medicine Hat	WHL	31	7	17	24	46	10	1	2	3	2
1985-86	Moncton	AHL	73	4	20	24	56	10	0	2	2	6
1986-87	Moncton	AHL	46	2	10	12	38	.....	....	....	....	....
	Calgary	NHL	24	0	4	4	19	4	0	1	1	23
1987-88	**Calgary**	NHL	11	0	3	3	8	.....	....	....	....	....
	Salt Lake	IHL	61	6	30	36	51	19	1	6	7	26
1988-89	**Vancouver**	NHL	45	2	2	4	34	1	0	0	0	0
1989-90	**Vancouver**	NHL	30	2	5	7	32	.....	....	....	....	....
	Milwaukee	IHL	29	2	11	13	33	.....	....	....	....	....
	NHL Totals		110	4	14	18	93	5	0	1	1	23

Traded to **Vancouver** by **Calgary** with Brian Bradley and Peter Bakovic for Craig Coxe, March 6, 1988.

HAANPAA, ARI

Right wing. Shoots left. 6'1", 185 lbs.   Born, Nokia, Finland, November 28, 1965.
(NY Islanders' 5th choice, 83rd overall, in 1984 Entry Draft).

			Regular Season						Playoffs			
Season	Club	Lea	GP	G	A	TP	PIM	GP	G	A	TP	PIM
1983-84	Ilves	Fin.	27	0	1	1	8	2	0	0	0	2
1984-85	Ilves	Fin.	13	5	0	5	2	9	3	1	4	0
1985-86	Springfield	AHL	20	3	1	4	13	.....	....	....	....	....
	NY Islanders	NHL	18	0	7	7	20	.....	....	....	....	....
1986-87	**NY Islanders**	NHL	41	6	4	10	17	6	0	0	0	10
1987-88	**NY Islanders**	NHL	1	0	0	0	0	.....	....	....	....	....
	Springfield	AHL	61	14	19	33	34	.....	....	....	....	....
1988-89	Lukko	Fin.	42	28	19	47	36	.....	....	....	....	....
1989-90	Lukko	Fin.	24	17	9	26	59	.....	....	....	....	....
	NHL Totals		60	6	11	17	37	6	0	0	0	10

HAAPAKOSKI, MIKKO

Defense. Shoots right. 5'10", 180 lbs.   Born, Oulu, Finland, January 19, 1967.
(Detroit's 10th choice, 179th overall, in 1987 Entry Draft).

			Regular Season						Playoffs			
Season	Club	Lea	GP	G	A	TP	PIM	GP	G	A	TP	PIM
1985-86	Karpat	Fin.	17	0	4	4	0	5	1	0	1	6
1986-87	Karpat	Fin.	41	13	15	28	18	9	1	1	2	4
1987-88	Karpat	Fin.	43	7	7	14	40	.....	....	....	....	....
1988-89	Karpat	Fin.	40	7	18	25	20	5	1	1	2	2
1989-90	T.P.S.	Fin.	44	4	10	14	14	9	0	1	1	16

HAAS, DAVID

Left wing. Shoots left. 6'2", 197 lbs.   Born, Toronto, Ont., June 23, 1968.
(Edmonton's 5th choice, 105th overall, in 1986 Entry Draft).

			Regular Season						Playoffs			
Season	Club	Lea	GP	G	A	TP	PIM	GP	G	A	TP	PIM
1985-86	London	OHL	62	4	13	17	91	5	0	1	1	0
1986-87	London	OHL	5	1	0	1	5	.....	....	....	....	....
	Kitchener	OHL	4	0	1	1	4	.....	....	....	....	....
	Belleville	OHL	55	10	13	23	86	6	3	0	3	13
1987-88a	Windsor	OHL	63	60	47	107	246	11	9	11	20	50
1988-89	Cape Breton	AHL	61	9	9	18	325	.....	....	....	....	....
1989-90	Cape Breton	AHL	53	6	12	18	230	4	2	2	4	15

a OHL Second All-Star Team (1988)

HABSCHEID, MARC JOSEPH (HAB-shide)

Center. Shoots right. 6', 185 lbs. Born, Swift Current, Sask., March 1, 1963.
(Edmonton's 6th choice, 113th overall, in 1981 Entry Draft).

			Regular Season					Playoffs				
Season	Club	Lea	GP	G	A	TP	PIM	GP	G	A	TP	PIM
1980-81	Saskatoon	WHL	72	34	63	97	50	....	....	....	....	....
1981-82	**Edmonton**	**NHL**	**7**	**1**	**3**	**4**	**2**	....	....	....	....	....
a	Saskatoon	WHL	55	64	87	151	74	5	3	4	7	4
	Wichita	CHL	....	....	....	....	....	3	0	0	0	0
1982-83	Kamloops	WHL	6	7	16	23	8	....	....	....	....	....
	Edmonton	**NHL**	**32**	**3**	**10**	**13**	**14**	....	....	....	....	....
1983-84	**Edmonton**	**NHL**	**9**	**1**	**0**	**1**	**6**	....	....	....	....	....
	Moncton	AHL	71	19	37	56	32	....	....	....	....	....
1984-85	**Edmonton**	**NHL**	**26**	**5**	**3**	**8**	**4**	....	....	....	....	....
	Nova Scotia	AHL	48	29	29	58	65	6	4	3	7	9
1985-86	**Minnesota**	**NHL**	**6**	**2**	**3**	**5**	**0**	**2**	**0**	**0**	**0**	**0**
	Springfield	AHL	41	18	32	50	21	....	....	....	....	....
1986-87	**Minnesota**	**NHL**	**15**	**2**	**0**	**2**	**2**	....	....	....	....	....
	Cdn. Olympic	....	51	29	32	61	70	....	....	....	....	....
1987-88	**Minnesota**	**NHL**	**16**	**4**	**11**	**15**	**6**	....	....	....	....	....
	Cdn. National	....	61	19	34	53	42	....	....	....	....	....
	Cdn. Olympic	....	8	5	3	8	6	....	....	....	....	....
1988-89	**Minnesota**	**NHL**	**76**	**23**	**31**	**54**	**40**	**5**	**1**	**3**	**4**	**13**
1989-90	**Detroit**	**NHL**	**66**	**15**	**11**	**26**	**33**	....	....	....	....	....
	NHL Totals		**253**	**56**	**72**	**128**	**107**	**7**	**1**	**3**	**4**	**13**

a WHL Second All-Star Team (1982)

Traded to **Minnesota** by **Edmonton** with Don Barber and Emanuel Viveiros for Gord Sherven and Don Biggs, December 20, 1985. Signed as a free agent by **Detroit**, June 9, 1989.

HAGEN, GREG

Right wing. Shoots right. 5'11", 175 lbs. Born, St. Paul, MN, July 10, 1971.
(Pittsburgh's 11th choice, 205th overall, in 1989 Entry Draft).

			Regular Season					Playoffs				
Season	Club	Lea	GP	G	A	TP	PIM	GP	G	A	TP	PIM
1987-88	Hill-Murray	HS	26	25	18	43	....	....	....	....	....	....
1988-89	Hill-Murray	HS	25	28	32	60	....	....	....	....	....	....
1989-90			DID NOT PLAY									

HAJDU, RICHARD (HI-doo)

Left wing. Shoots left. 6', 185 lbs. Born, Victoria, B.C., May 10, 1965.
(Buffalo's 5th choice, 34th overall, in 1983 Entry Draft).

			Regular Season					Playoffs				
Season	Club	Lea	GP	G	A	TP	PIM	GP	G	A	TP	PIM
1981-82	Kamloops	WHL	64	19	21	40	50	4	0	0	0	0
1982-83	Kamloops	WHL	70	22	36	58	101	5	0	0	0	4
1983-84	Victoria	WHL	42	17	10	27	106	....	....	....	....	....
1984-85	Victoria	WHL	24	12	16	28	33	....	....	....	....	....
	Rochester	AHL	2	0	2	2	0	....	....	....	....	....
1985-86	**Buffalo**	**NHL**	**3**	**0**	**0**	**0**	**4**	....	....	....	....	....
	Rochester	AHL	54	10	27	37	95	....	....	....	....	....
1986-87	**Buffalo**	**NHL**	**2**	**0**	**0**	**0**	**0**	....	....	....	....	....
	Rochester	AHL	58	7	15	22	90	11	1	1	2	9
1987-88	Rochester	AHL	37	7	11	18	24	1	0	0	0	0
	Flint	IHL	17	4	6	10	30	....	....	....	....	....
1988-89	Cdn. National	....	50	14	11	25	22	....	....	....	....	....
1989-90	Cdn. National	....	42	6	10	16	8	....	....	....	....	....
	NHL Totals		**5**	**0**	**0**	**0**	**4**	....	....	....	....	....

HALKIDIS, BOB (hal-KEE-dihs)

Defense. Shoots left. 5'11", 200 lbs. Born, Toronto, Ont., March 5, 1966.
(Buffalo's 4th choice, 81st overall, in 1984 Entry Draft).

			Regular Season					Playoffs				
Season	Club	Lea	GP	G	A	TP	PIM	GP	G	A	TP	PIM
1983-84	London	OHL	51	9	22	31	123	8	0	2	2	27
1984-85	**Buffalo**	**NHL**	....	....	....	....	....	**4**	**0**	**0**	**0**	**19**
ab	London	OHL	62	14	50	64	154	8	3	6	9	22
1985-86	**Buffalo**	**NHL**	**37**	**1**	**9**	**10**	**115**	....	....	....	....	....
1986-87	**Buffalo**	**NHL**	**6**	**1**	**1**	**2**	**19**	....	....	....	....	....
	Rochester	AHL	59	1	8	9	144	8	0	0	0	43
1987-88	**Buffalo**	**NHL**	**30**	**0**	**3**	**3**	**115**	**4**	**0**	**0**	**0**	**22**
	Rochester	AHL	15	2	5	7	50	....	....	....	....	....
1988-89	**Buffalo**	**NHL**	**16**	**0**	**1**	**1**	**66**	....	....	....	....	....
	Rochester	AHL	16	0	6	6	64	....	....	....	....	....
1989-90	**Los Angeles**	**NHL**	**20**	**0**	**4**	**4**	**56**	....	....	....	....	....
	Rochester	AHL	18	1	13	14	70	....	....	....	....	....
	New Haven	AHL	30	3	17	20	67	....	....	....	....	....
	NHL Totals		**109**	**2**	**18**	**20**	**371**	**8**	**0**	**0**	**0**	**41**

a Named Outstanding Defenseman in OHL (1985)
b OHL First All-Star Team (1985)

Traded to **Los Angeles** by **Buffalo** with future considerations for Dale DeGray and future considerations, November 24, 1989.

HALL, DEAN

Center. Shoots left. 6'1", 175 lbs. Born, Winnipeg, Man., January 14, 1968.
(Boston's 4th choice, 76th overall, in 1986 Entry Draft).

			Regular Season					Playoffs				
Season	Club	Lea	GP	G	A	TP	PIM	GP	G	A	TP	PIM
1986-87	N. Michigan	WCHA	20	4	5	9	16	....	....	....	....	....
1987-88	N. Michigan	WCHA	31	5	6	11	22	....	....	....	....	....
1988-89	N. Michigan	WCHA	2	0	0	0	0	....	....	....	....	....
	Seattle	WHL	33	18	19	37	8	....	....	....	....	....
1989-90	Johnstown	ECHL	38	11	22	33	27	....	....	....	....	....

HALL, TAYLOR

Left wing. Shoots left. 5'11", 180 lbs. Born, Regina, Sask., February 20, 1964.
(Vancouver's 4th choice, 116th overall, in 1982 Entry Draft).

			Regular Season					Playoffs				
Season	Club	Lea	GP	G	A	TP	PIM	GP	G	A	TP	PIM
1981-82	Regina	WHL	48	14	15	29	43	11	2	3	5	14
1982-83	Regina	WHL	72	37	57	94	78	5	0	3	3	12
1983-84	**Vancouver**	**NHL**	**4**	**1**	**0**	**1**	**0**	....	....	....	....	....
a	Regina	WHL	69	63	79	142	42	23	*21	20	41	26
1984-85	**Vancouver**	**NHL**	**7**	**1**	**4**	**5**	**19**	....	....	....	....	....
1985-86	**Vancouver**	**NHL**	**19**	**5**	**5**	**10**	**6**	....	....	....	....	....
	Fredericton	AHL	45	21	14	35	28	1	0	0	0	0
1986-87	**Vancouver**	**NHL**	**4**	**0**	**0**	**0**	**0**	....	....	....	....	....
	Fredericton	AHL	36	21	20	41	23	....	....	....	....	....
1987-88	**Boston**	**NHL**	**7**	**0**	**0**	**0**	**4**	....	....	....	....	....
	Maine	AHL	71	33	41	74	58	10	1	4	5	21
1988-89	Maine	AHL	8	0	1	1	7	....	....	....	....	....
	Newmarket	AHL	9	5	5	10	14	....	....	....	....	....
1989-90	New Haven	AHL	51	14	23	37	10	....	....	....	....	....
	NHL Totals		**41**	**7**	**9**	**16**	**29**	....	....	....	....	....

a WHL First All-Star Team, East Division (1984)

HALLER, KEVIN

Defense. Shoots left. 6'2", 183 lbs. Born, Trochu, Alta., December 5, 1970.
(Buffalo's 1st choice, 14th overall, in 1989 Entry Draft).

			Regular Season					Playoffs				
Season	Club	Lea	GP	G	A	TP	PIM	GP	G	A	TP	PIM
1988-89	Regina	WHL	72	10	31	41	99	....	....	....	....	....
1989-90	**Buffalo**	**NHL**	**2**	**0**	**0**	**0**	**0**	....	....	....	....	....
a	Regina	WHL	58	16	37	53	93	11	2	9	11	16
	NHL Totals		**2**	**0**	**0**	**0**	**0**	....	....	....	....	....

a WHL East First All-Star Team (1990)

HAMALAINEN, ERIK

Defense. Shoots left. 6'1", 190 lbs. Born, Rauma, Finland, April 20, 1965.
(Detroit's 10th choice, 197th overall, in 1985 Entry Draft).

			Regular Season					Playoffs				
Season	Club	Lea	GP	G	A	TP	PIM	GP	G	A	TP	PIM
1985-86	Lukko	Fin.	31	13	6	19	32	....	....	....	....	....
1986-87	Lukko	Fin.	44	8	8	16	49	....	....	....	....	....
1987-88	Lukko	Fin.	44	8	4	12	52	8	0	3	3	2
1988-89	KalPa	Fin.	43	7	4	11	14	2	0	0	0	2
1989-90	KalPa	Fin.	44	9	20	29	32	....	....	....	....	....

HAMMOND, KEN

Defense. Shoots left. 6'1", 190 lbs. Born, Port Credit, Ont., August 22, 1963.
(Los Angeles' 8th choice, 152nd overall, in 1983 Entry Draft).

			Regular Season					Playoffs				
Season	Club	Lea	GP	G	A	TP	PIM	GP	G	A	TP	PIM
1982-83	RPI	ECAC	28	17	26	43	8	....	....	....	....	....
1983-84	RPI	ECAC	34	5	11	16	72	....	....	....	....	....
1984-85	**Los Angeles**	**NHL**	**3**	**1**	**0**	**1**	**0**	**3**	**0**	**0**	**0**	**4**
ab	RPI	ECAC	38	11	28	39	90	....	....	....	....	....
1985-86	**Los Angeles**	**NHL**	**3**	**0**	**1**	**1**	**2**	....	....	....	....	....
	New Haven	AHL	67	4	12	16	96	4	0	0	0	7
1986-87	**Los Angeles**	**NHL**	**10**	**0**	**2**	**2**	**11**	....	....	....	....	....
	New Haven	AHL	66	1	15	16	76	6	0	1	1	21
1987-88	**Los Angeles**	**NHL**	**46**	**7**	**9**	**16**	**69**	**2**	**0**	**0**	**0**	**4**
	New Haven	AHL	26	3	8	11	27	....	....	....	....	....
1988-89	**Edmonton**	**NHL**	**5**	**0**	**1**	**1**	**8**	....	....	....	....	....
	NY Rangers	**NHL**	**3**	**0**	**0**	**0**	**0**	....	....	....	....	....
	Denver	IHL	38	5	18	23	24	....	....	....	....	....
	Toronto	**NHL**	**14**	**0**	**2**	**2**	**12**	....	....	....	....	....
1989-90	Newmarket	AHL	75	9	45	54	106	....	....	....	....	....
	NHL Totals		**84**	**8**	**15**	**23**	**102**	**5**	**0**	**0**	**0**	**8**

a ECAC First All-Star Team (1985)
b Named to NCAA All-American Team (1985)

Claimed by **Edmonton** in NHL Waiver Draft, October 3, 1988. Claimed by **NY Rangers** on waivers from **Edmonton**, November 1, 1988. Traded to **Toronto** by **NY Rangers** for Chris McRae, February 21, 1989.

HANDY, RONALD (RON)

Left wing. Shoots left. 5'11", 175 lbs. Born, Toronto, Ont., January 15, 1963.
(NY Islanders' 3rd choice, 57th overall, in 1981 Entry Draft).

			Regular Season					Playoffs				
Season	Club	Lea	GP	G	A	TP	PIM	GP	G	A	TP	PIM
1980-81	S. S. Marie	OHA	66	43	43	86	45	18	3	5	8	25
1981-82	S. S. Marie	OHL	20	15	10	25	20	....	....	....	....	....
	Kingston	OHL	44	35	38	73	23	4	1	1	2	16
1982-83	Kingston	OHL	67	52	96	148	64	....	....	....	....	....
	Indianapolis	CHL	9	2	7	9	0	10	3	8	11	18
1983-84a	Indianapolis	CHL	66	29	46	75	40	10	2	5	7	0
1984-85	**NY Islanders**	**NHL**	**10**	**0**	**2**	**2**	**0**	....	....	....	....	....
b	Springfield	AHL	69	29	35	64	38	3	2	2	4	0
1985-86	Springfield	AHL	79	31	30	61	66	....	....	....	....	....
1986-87	Indianapolis	IHL	82	*55	80	135	57	6	4	3	7	2
1987-88	**St. Louis**	**NHL**	**4**	**0**	**1**	**1**	**0**	....	....	....	....	....
b	Peoria	IHL	78	53	63	116	61	7	2	3	5	4
1988-89	Peoria	IHL	81	43	57	100	24	....	....	....	....	....
1989-90	Peoria	IHL	82	36	39	75	52	5	3	1	4	0
	NHL Totals		**14**	**0**	**3**	**3**	**0**	....	....	....	....	....

a CHL Second All-Star Team (1984)
b IHL Second All-Star Team (1985, 1988)

HANKINSON, BEN

Center. Shoots right. 6'2", 180 lbs.   Born, Edina, MN, January 5, 1969.
(New Jersey's 5th choice, 107th overall, in 1987 Entry Draft).

				Regular Season					Playoffs			
Season	Club	Lea	GP	G	A	TP	PIM	GP	G	A	TP	PIM
1987-88	U. Minnesota	WCHA	24	4	7	11	36	....	....	....	....	....
1988-89	U. Minnesota	WCHA	43	7	11	18	115	....	....	....	....	....
1989-90a	U. Minnesota	WCHA	46	25	41	66	34	....	....	....	....	....

a WCHA First All-Star Team (1990)

HANKINSON, PETER

Right wing. Shoots right. 5'9", 170 lbs.   Born, Edina, MN, November 24, 1967.
(Winnipeg's 1st choice, 4th overall, in 1989 Supplemental Draft).

				Regular Season					Playoffs			
Season	Club	Lea	GP	G	A	TP	PIM	GP	G	A	TP	PIM
1986-87	U. Minnesota	WCHA	43	16	12	28	10	....	....	....	....	....
1987-88	U. Minnesota	WCHA	39	25	20	45	32	....	....	....	....	....
1988-89	U. Minnesota	WCHA	48	16	27	43	42	....	....	....	....	....
1989-90	U. Minnesota	WCHA	45	19	12	31	116	....	....	....	....	....

HANLEY, TIMOTHY

Right wing. Shoots right. 6', 200 lbs.   Born, Greenfield, MN, October 10, 1964.
(Los Angeles' 7th choice, 129th overall, in 1984 Entry Draft).

				Regular Season					Playoffs			
Season	Club	Lea	GP	G	A	TP	PIM	GP	G	A	TP	PIM
1984-85	N. Hampshire	H.E.	42	22	18	40	21	....	....	....	....	....
1985-86	N. Hampshire	H.E.	29	9	13	22	22	....	....	....	....	....
1986-87	N. Hampshire	H.E.	37	11	23	34	34	....	....	....	....	....
1987-88	N. Hampshire	H.E.	30	13	17	30	38	....	....	....	....	....
1988-89	Maine	AHL	4	0	0	0	0	....	....	....	....	....
	Springfield	AHL	33	13	15	28	10	....	....	....	....	....
	New Haven	AHL	1	0	0	0	5	....	....	....	....	....
1989-90	Springfield	AHL	9	2	0	2	22	....	....	....	....	....

HANNAN, DAVID (DAVE)

Center. Shoots left. 5'10", 185 lbs.   Born, Sudbury, Ont., November 26, 1961.
(Pittsburgh's 9th choice, 196th overall, in 1981 Entry Draft).

				Regular Season					Playoffs			
Season	Club	Lea	GP	G	A	TP	PIM	GP	G	A	TP	PIM
1979-80	S.S. Marie	OHA	28	11	10	21	31	....	....	....	....	....
	Brantford	OHA	25	5	10	15	26	....	....	....	....	....
1980-81	Brantford	OHA	56	46	35	81	155	6	2	4	6	20
1981-82	**Pittsburgh**	NHL	1	0	0	0	0	....	....	....	....	....
	Erie	AHL	76	33	37	70	129	....	....	....	....	....
1982-83	**Pittsburgh**	NHL	74	11	22	33	127	....	....	....	....	....
	Baltimore	AHL	5	2	2	4	13	....	....	....	....	....
1983-84	**Pittsburgh**	NHL	24	2	3	5	33	....	....	....	....	....
	Baltimore	AHL	47	18	24	42	98	10	2	6	8	27
1984-85	**Pittsburgh**	NHL	30	6	7	13	43	....	....	....	....	....
	Baltimore	AHL	49	20	25	45	91	....	....	....	....	....
1985-86	**Pittsburgh**	NHL	75	17	18	35	91	....	....	....	....	....
1986-87	**Pittsburgh**	NHL	58	10	15	25	56	....	....	....	....	....
1987-88	**Pittsburgh**	NHL	21	4	3	7	23	....	....	....	....	....
	Edmonton	NHL	51	9	11	20	43	12	1	1	2	8
1988-89	**Pittsburgh**	NHL	72	10	20	30	157	8	0	1	1	4
1989-90	**Toronto**	NHL	39	6	9	15	55	3	1	0	1	4
	NHL Totals		445	75	108	183	628	23	2	2	4	16

Traded to **Edmonton** by **Pittsburgh** with Craig Simpson, Moe Mantha and Chris Joseph for Paul Coffey, Dave Hunter and Wayne Van Dorp, November 24, 1987. Claimed by **Pittsburgh** in NHL Waiver Draft, October 3, 1988. Claimed by **Toronto** in NHL Waiver Draft, October 2, 1989.

HANUS, TIM

Left wing. Shoots left. 6'1", 185 lbs.   Born, Minneapolis, MN, May 12, 1969.
(Quebec's 7th choice, 135th overall, in 1987 Entry Draft).

				Regular Season					Playoffs			
Season	Club	Lea	GP	G	A	TP	PIM	GP	G	A	TP	PIM
1988-89	St. Cloud	NCAA	33	13	22	35	31	....	....	....	....	....
1989-90	St. Cloud	NCAA	34	22	24	46	54	....	....	....	....	....

HARDING, JEFF

Right wing. Shoots right. 6'3", 220 lbs.   Born, Toronto, Ont., April 6, 1969.
(Philadelphia's 2nd choice, 30th overall, in 1987 Entry Draft).

				Regular Season					Playoffs			
Season	Club	Lea	GP	G	A	TP	PIM	GP	G	A	TP	PIM
1987-88	Michigan State	CCHA	43	17	10	27	129	....	....	....	....	....
1988-89	**Philadelphia**	NHL	6	0	0	0	29	....	....	....	....	....
	Hershey	AHL	34	13	5	18	64	8	1	1	2	33
1989-90	**Philadelphia**	NHL	9	0	0	0	18	....	....	....	....	....
	Hershey	AHL	6	0	2	2	2	....	....	....	....	....
	NHL Totals		15	0	0	0	47	....	....	....	....	....

HARDY, MARK LEA

Defense. Shoots left. 5'11", 195 lbs.   Born, Semaden, Switzerland, February 1, 1959.
(Los Angeles' 3rd choice, 30th overall, in 1979 Entry Draft).

				Regular Season					Playoffs			
Season	Club	Lea	GP	G	A	TP	PIM	GP	G	A	TP	PIM
1977-78	Montreal	QJHL	72	25	57	82	150	13	3	10	13	22
1978-79	Montreal	QJHL	67	18	52	70	117	11	5	8	13	40
1979-80	Binghamton	AHL	56	3	13	16	32	....	....	....	....	....
	Los Angeles	NHL	15	0	1	1	10	4	1	1	2	9
1980-81	**Los Angeles**	NHL	77	5	20	25	77	4	1	2	3	4
1981-82	**Los Angeles**	NHL	77	6	39	45	130	10	1	2	3	9
1982-83	**Los Angeles**	NHL	74	5	34	39	101	....	....	....	....	....
1983-84	**Los Angeles**	NHL	79	8	41	49	122	....	....	....	....	....
1984-85	**Los Angeles**	NHL	78	14	39	53	97	3	0	1	1	2
1985-86	**Los Angeles**	NHL	55	6	21	27	71	....	....	....	....	....
1986-87	**Los Angeles**	NHL	73	3	27	30	120	5	1	2	3	10
1987-88	**Los Angeles**	NHL	61	6	22	28	99	....	....	....	....	....
	NY Rangers	NHL	19	2	2	4	31	....	....	....	....	....
1988-89	**Minnesota**	NHL	15	2	4	6	26	....	....	....	....	....
	NY Rangers	NHL	45	2	12	14	45	4	0	1	1	31
1989-90	**NY Rangers**	NHL	54	0	15	15	94	3	0	1	1	2
	NHL Totals		722	59	277	336	1023	33	4	10	14	67

Traded to **NY Rangers** by **Los Angeles** for Ron Duguay, February 23, 1988. Traded to **Minnesota** by **NY Rangers** for future considerations (Louie Debrusk) June 13, 1988. Traded to **NY Rangers** by **Minnesota** for Larry Bernard and NY Rangers fifth-round choice (Rhys Hollyman) in 1989 Entry Draft, December 9, 1988.

HARKINS, TODD

Right wing. Shoots right. 6'3", 210 lbs.   Born, Cleveland, OH, October 8, 1968.
(Calgary's 2nd choice, 42nd overall, in 1988 Entry Draft).

				Regular Season					Playoffs			
Season	Club	Lea	GP	G	A	TP	PIM	GP	G	A	TP	PIM
1987-88	Miami-Ohio	CCHA	34	9	7	16	133	....	....	....	....	....
1988-89	Miami-Ohio	CCHA	36	8	7	15	77	....	....	....	....	....
1989-90	Miami-Ohio	CCHA	40	27	17	44	78	....	....	....	....	....

HARLOCK, DAVID

Defense. Shoots left. 6'2", 195 lbs.   Born, Toronto, Ont., March 16, 1971.
(New Jersey's 2nd choice, 24th overall, in 1990 Entry Draft).

				Regular Season					Playoffs			
Season	Club	Lea	GP	G	A	TP	PIM	GP	G	A	TP	PIM
1988-89	St. Michael's	Jr. B	25	4	16	20	34	27	3	12	15	14
1989-90	U. of Michigan	CCHA	42	2	13	15	44	....	....	....	....	....

HARLOW, SCOTT

Left wing. Shoots left. 6'1", 185 lbs.   Born, East Bridgewater, MA, October 11, 1963.
(Montreal's 6th choice, 61st overall, in 1982 Entry Draft).

				Regular Season					Playoffs			
Season	Club	Lea	GP	G	A	TP	PIM	GP	G	A	TP	PIM
1982-83	Boston College	ECAC	24	6	19	25	19	....	....	....	....	....
1983-84	Boston College	ECAC	39	27	20	47	17	....	....	....	....	....
1984-85a	Boston College	ECAC	44	34	38	72	45	....	....	....	....	....
1985-86bcd	Boston College	H.E.	42	38	41	79	48	....	....	....	....	....
1986-87	Sherbrooke	AHL	66	22	26	48	6	15	5	6	11	6
1987-88	Sherbrooke	AHL	18	6	12	18	8	....	....	....	....	....
	St. Louis	NHL	1	0	1	1	0	....	....	....	....	....
	Baltimore	AHL	29	24	27	51	21	....	....	....	....	....
	Peoria	IHL	39	30	25	55	46	....	....	....	....	....
1988-89	Peoria	IHL	45	16	26	42	22	....	....	....	....	....
	Maine	AHL	30	16	17	33	8	....	....	....	....	....
1989-90	Maine	AHL	80	31	32	63	68	....	....	....	....	....
	NHL Totals		1	0	1	1	0	....	....	....	....	....

a Hockey East Second All-Star Team
b NCAA East First All-American Team (1986)
c Hockey East First All-Star Team (1986)
d Hockey East Player of the Year (1986)

Traded to **St. Louis** by **Montreal** for future considerations, January 21, 1988. Traded to **Boston** by **St. Louis** for Phil DeGaetano, February 3, 1989.

HARRIS, TIM

Right wing. Shoots right. 6'2", 190 lbs.   Born, Uxbridge, Ont., October 16, 1967.
(Calgary's 4th choice, 70th overall, in 1987 Entry Draft).

				Regular Season					Playoffs			
Season	Club	Lea	GP	G	A	TP	PIM	GP	G	A	TP	PIM
1985-86	Pickering	OPJHL	34	13	25	38	91	....	....	....	....	....
1986-87	Pickering	OPJHL	36	20	36	56	142	....	....	....	....	....
1987-88	Lake Superior	CCHA	43	8	10	18	79	....	....	....	....	....
1988-89	Lake Superior	CCHA	29	1	5	6	78	....	....	....	....	....
1989-90	Lake Superior	CCHA	39	6	17	23	71	....	....	....	....	....

HARTJE, TODD

Center. Shoots left. 6'1", 180 lbs.   Born, Anoka, MN, February 27, 1968.
(Winnipeg's 7th choice, 142nd overall, in 1987 Entry Draft).

				Regular Season					Playoffs			
Season	Club	Lea	GP	G	A	TP	PIM	GP	G	A	TP	PIM
1986-87	Harvard	ECAC	32	3	9	12	36	....	....	....	....	....
1987-88	Harvard	ECAC	32	5	17	22	40	....	....	....	....	....
1988-89	Harvard	ECAC	33	4	17	21	40	....	....	....	....	....
1989-90	Harvard	ECAC	28	6	10	16	29	....	....	....	....	....

HARTMAN, MIKE

Left wing. Shoots left. 6', 198 lbs. Born, Detroit, MI, February 7, 1967.
(Buffalo's 8th choice, 131st overall, in 1986 Entry Draft).

			Regular Season					Playoffs				
Season	Club	Lea	GP	G	A	TP	PIM	GP	G	A	TP	PIM
1985-86	Belleville	OHL	4	2	1	3	5	....	....	....	....	....
	North Bay	OHL	53	19	16	35	205	10	2	4	6	34
1986-87	**Buffalo**	**NHL**	**17**	**3**	**3**	**6**	**69**	....	....	....	....	....
	North Bay	OHL	32	15	24	39	144	19	7	8	15	88
1987-88	**Buffalo**	**NHL**	**18**	**3**	**1**	**4**	**90**	**6**	**0**	**0**	**0**	**35**
	Rochester	AHL	57	13	14	27	283	4	1	0	1	22
1988-89	**Buffalo**	**NHL**	**70**	**8**	**9**	**17**	**316**	**5**	**0**	**0**	**0**	**34**
1989-90	**Buffalo**	**NHL**	**60**	**11**	**10**	**21**	**211**	**6**	**0**	**0**	**0**	**18**
	NHL Totals		**165**	**25**	**23**	**48**	**686**	**17**	**0**	**0**	**0**	**87**

HARWELL, JOE

Defense. Shoots right. 6'3", 195 lbs. Born, Minneapolis, MN, November 21, 1968.
(Winnipeg's 8th choice, 121st overall, in 1987 Entry Draft).

			Regular Season					Playoffs				
Season	Club	Lea	GP	G	A	TP	PIM	GP	G	A	TP	PIM
1989-90	U. Wisconsin	WCHA	10	0	0	0	2	....	....	....	....	....

HATCHER, DERIAN

Defense. Shoots left. 6'5", 205 lbs. Born, Sterling Heights, MI, June 4, 1972.
(Minnesota's 1st choice, 8th overall, in 1990 Entry Draft).

			Regular Season					Playoffs				
Season	Club	Lea	GP	G	A	TP	PIM	GP	G	A	TP	PIM
1988-89	Detroit	NAJHL	51	19	35	54	100	....	....	....	....	....
1989-90	North Bay	OHL	64	14	38	52	81	5	2	3	5	8

HATCHER, KEVIN

Defense. Shoots right. 6'4", 225 lbs. Born, Detroit, MI, September 9, 1966.
(Washington's 1st choice, 17th overall, in 1984 Entry Draft).

			Regular Season					Playoffs				
Season	Club	Lea	GP	G	A	TP	PIM	GP	G	A	TP	PIM
1983-84	North Bay	OHL	67	10	39	49	61	4	2	2	4	11
1984-85	**Washington**	**NHL**	**2**	**1**	**0**	**1**	**0**	**1**	**0**	**0**	**0**	**0**
a	North Bay	OHL	58	26	37	63	75	8	3	8	11	9
1985-86	**Washington**	**NHL**	**79**	**9**	**10**	**19**	**119**	**9**	**1**	**1**	**2**	**19**
1986-87	**Washington**	**NHL**	**78**	**8**	**16**	**24**	**144**	**7**	**1**	**0**	**1**	**20**
1987-88	**Washington**	**NHL**	**71**	**14**	**27**	**41**	**137**	**14**	**5**	**7**	**12**	**55**
1988-89	**Washington**	**NHL**	**62**	**13**	**27**	**40**	**101**	**6**	**1**	**4**	**5**	**20**
1989-90	**Washington**	**NHL**	**80**	**13**	**41**	**54**	**102**	**11**	**0**	**8**	**8**	**32**
	NHL Totals		**372**	**58**	**121**	**179**	**603**	**48**	**8**	**20**	**28**	**146**

a OHL Second All-Star Team (1985)

Played in NHL All-Star Game (1990)

HAUER, BRETT

Defense. Shoots right. 6'2", 180 lbs. Born, Edina, MN, July 11, 1971.
(Vancouver's 3rd choice, 71st overall, in 1989 Entry Draft).

			Regular Season					Playoffs				
Season	Club	Lea	GP	G	A	TP	PIM	GP	G	A	TP	PIM
1988-89	Richfield	HS	24	8	15	23	70	....	....	....	....	....
1989-90	Minn.-Duluth	WCHA	37	2	6	8	44	....	....	....	....	....

HAWERCHUK, DALE (HOW-uhr-CHUHK)

Center. Shoots left. 5'11", 185 lbs. Born, Toronto, Ont., April 4, 1963.
(Winnipeg's 1st choice and 1st overall in 1981 Entry Draft).

			Regular Season					Playoffs				
Season	Club	Lea	GP	G	A	TP	PIM	GP	G	A	TP	PIM
1979-80	Cornwall	QJHL	72	37	66	103	21	18	20	25	45	0
1980-81abc	Cornwall	QJHL	72	81	102	183	69	19	15	20	35	8
1981-82d	**Winnipeg**	**NHL**	**80**	**45**	**58**	**103**	**47**	**4**	**1**	**7**	**8**	**5**
1982-83	**Winnipeg**	**NHL**	**79**	**40**	**51**	**91**	**31**	**3**	**1**	**4**	**5**	**8**
1983-84	**Winnipeg**	**NHL**	**80**	**37**	**65**	**102**	**73**	**3**	**1**	**1**	**2**	**0**
1984-85e	**Winnipeg**	**NHL**	**80**	**53**	**77**	**130**	**74**	**3**	**2**	**1**	**3**	**4**
1985-86	**Winnipeg**	**NHL**	**80**	**46**	**59**	**105**	**44**	**3**	**0**	**3**	**3**	**0**
1986-87	**Winnipeg**	**NHL**	**80**	**47**	**53**	**100**	**52**	**10**	**5**	**8**	**13**	**4**
1987-88	**Winnipeg**	**NHL**	**80**	**44**	**77**	**121**	**59**	**5**	**3**	**4**	**7**	**16**
1988-89	**Winnipeg**	**NHL**	**75**	**41**	**55**	**96**	**28**	....	....	....	....	....
1989-90	**Winnipeg**	**NHL**	**79**	**26**	**55**	**81**	**70**	**7**	**3**	**5**	**8**	**2**
	NHL Totals		**713**	**379**	**550**	**929**	**478**	**38**	**16**	**33**	**49**	**39**

a QMJHL First All-Star Team (1981)
b QMJHL Player of the Year (1981)
c Canadian Major Junior Player of the Year (1981)
d Won Calder Memorial Trophy (1982)
e NHL Second All-Star Team (1985)

Played in NHL All-Star Game (1982, 1985, 1986, 1988)

Traded to **Buffalo** by **Winnipeg** with Winnipeg's first round choice (Brad May) in 1990 Entry Draft and future considerations for Phil Housley, Scott Arniel, Jeff Parker and Buffalo's first round choice (Keith Tkachuk) in 1990 Entry Draft, June 16, 1990.

HAWGOOD, GREG

Left wing/Defense. Shoots left. 5'8", 175 lbs. Born, Edmonton, Alta., August 10, 1968.
(Boston's 9th choice, 202nd overall, in 1986 Entry Draft).

			Regular Season					Playoffs				
Season	Club	Lea	GP	G	A	TP	PIM	GP	G	A	TP	PIM
1985-86	Kamloops	WHL	71	34	85	119	86	16	9	22	31	16
1986-87a	Kamloops	WHL	61	30	93	123	139	....	....	....	....	....
1987-88	**Boston**	**NHL**	**1**	**0**	**0**	**0**	**0**	**3**	**1**	**0**	**1**	**0**
a	Kamloops	WHL	63	48	85	133	142	16	10	16	26	33
1988-89	**Boston**	**NHL**	**56**	**16**	**24**	**40**	**84**	**10**	**0**	**2**	**2**	**2**
	Maine	AHL	21	2	9	11	41	....	....	....	....	....
1989-90	**Boston**	**NHL**	**77**	**11**	**27**	**38**	**76**	**15**	**1**	**3**	**4**	**12**
	NHL Totals		**134**	**27**	**51**	**78**	**160**	**28**	**2**	**5**	**7**	**16**

a WHL West All-Star Team (1986, 1987, 1988)

HAWKINS, TODD

Right wing. Shoots right. 6'1", 195 lbs. Born, Kingston, Ont., August 2, 1966.
(Vancouver's 10th choice, 217th overall, in 1986 Entry Draft).

			Regular Season					Playoffs				
Season	Club	Lea	GP	G	A	TP	PIM	GP	G	A	TP	PIM
1984-85	Belleville	OHL	58	7	16	23	117	12	1	0	1	10
1985-86	Belleville	OHL	60	14	13	27	172	24	9	7	16	60
1986-87	Belleville	OHL	60	47	40	87	187	6	3	5	8	16
1987-88	Flint	IHL	50	13	13	26	337	16	3	5	8	*174
	Fredericton	AHL	2	0	4	4	11	....	....	....	....	....
1988-89	**Vancouver**	**NHL**	**4**	**0**	**0**	**0**	**9**	....	....	....	....	....
	Milwaukee	IHL	63	12	14	26	307	9	1	0	1	33
1989-90	**Vancouver**	**NHL**	**4**	**0**	**0**	**0**	**6**	....	....	....	....	....
	Milwaukee	IHL	61	23	17	40	273	5	4	1	5	19
	NHL Totals		**8**	**0**	**0**	**0**	**15**	....	....	....	....	....

HAWLEY, KENT

Center. Shoots left. 6'4", 215 lbs. Born, Kingston, Ont., February 20, 1968.
(Philadelphia's 3rd choice, 28th overall, in 1986 Entry Draft).

			Regular Season					Playoffs				
Season	Club	Lea	GP	G	A	TP	PIM	GP	G	A	TP	PIM
1985-86	Ottawa	OHL	64	21	30	51	96	....	....	....	....	....
1986-87	Ottawa	OHL	64	29	53	82	86	11	0	5	5	43
1987-88	Ottawa	OHL	55	29	48	77	84	16	7	6	13	20
1988-89	Hershey	AHL	54	9	17	26	47	....	....	....	....	....
1989-90	Hershey	AHL	24	6	4	10	28	....	....	....	....	....
	Hampton-Roads	ECHL	13	5	6	11	12	5	2	3	5	17

HAWORTH, ALAN JOSEPH GORDON (HAW-worth)

Center. Shoots right. 5'10", 190 lbs. Born, Drummondville, Que., September 1, 1960.
(Buffalo's 6th choice, 95th overall, in 1979 Entry Draft).

			Regular Season					Playoffs				
Season	Club	Lea	GP	G	A	TP	PIM	GP	G	A	TP	PIM
1976-77	Chicoutimi	QJHL	68	11	18	29	15	....	....	....	....	....
1977-78	Chicoutimi	QJHL	59	17	33	50	40	....	....	....	....	....
1978-79	Sherbrooke	QJHL	70	50	70	120	63	12	6	10	16	8
1979-80	Sherbrooke	QJHL	45	28	36	64	50	15	11	16	27	4
1980-81	Rochester	AHL	21	14	18	32	19	....	....	....	....	....
	Buffalo	**NHL**	**49**	**16**	**20**	**36**	**34**	**7**	**4**	**4**	**8**	**2**
1981-82	Rochester	AHL	14	5	12	17	10	....	....	....	....	....
	Buffalo	**NHL**	**57**	**21**	**18**	**39**	**30**	**3**	**0**	**1**	**1**	**2**
1982-83	**Washington**	**NHL**	**74**	**23**	**27**	**50**	**34**	**4**	**0**	**0**	**0**	**2**
1983-84	**Washington**	**NHL**	**75**	**24**	**31**	**55**	**52**	**8**	**3**	**2**	**5**	**4**
1984-85	**Washington**	**NHL**	**76**	**23**	**26**	**49**	**48**	**5**	**1**	**0**	**1**	**0**
1985-86	**Washington**	**NHL**	**71**	**34**	**39**	**73**	**72**	**9**	**4**	**6**	**10**	**11**
1986-87	**Washington**	**NHL**	**50**	**25**	**16**	**41**	**43**	**6**	**0**	**3**	**3**	**7**
1987-88	**Quebec**	**NHL**	**72**	**23**	**34**	**57**	**112**	....	....	....	....	....
1988-89	Bern	Switz.	36	24	29	53	....	....	....	....	....	....
1989-90	Bern	Switz.	36	31	30	61	....	....	....	....	....	....
	NHL Totals		**524**	**189**	**211**	**400**	**425**	**42**	**12**	**16**	**28**	**0**

Traded to **Washington** by **Buffalo** with Buffalo's third round choice (Milan Novy) in 1982 Entry Draft for Washington's second round choice (Mike Anderson) and fourth round choice (Timo Jutila) in 1982 Entry Draft, June 9, 1982. Traded to **Quebec** by **Washington** with Gaetan Duchesne and Washington's first-round choice (Joe Sakic) in 1987 Entry Draft for Clint Malarchuk and Dale Hunter, June 13, 1987.

HAYES, MATTHEW

Defense. Shoots left. 6'2", 180 lbs. Born, North Andover, MA, November 7, 1969.
(St. Louis' 7th choice, 135th overall, in 1988 Entry Draft).

			Regular Season					Playoffs				
Season	Club	Lea	GP	G	A	TP	PIM	GP	G	A	TP	PIM
1988-89	U. of Lowell	H.E.	30	0	4	4	30	....	....	....	....	....
1989-90	U. of Lowell	H.E.	14	0	1	1	10	....	....	....	....	....

HAYWARD, RICK

Defense. Shoots left. 6', 180 lbs. Born, Toledo, OH, February 25, 1966.
(Montreal's 9th choice, 162nd overall, in 1986 Entry Draft).

			Regular Season					Playoffs				
Season	Club	Lea	GP	G	A	TP	PIM	GP	G	A	TP	PIM
1985-86	Hull	QMJHL	59	3	40	43	354	15	2	11	13	98
1986-87	Sherbrooke	AHL	46	2	3	5	153	3	0	1	1	15
1987-88	Saginaw	IHL	24	3	4	7	129	....	....	....	....	....
	Salt Lake	IHL	17	1	3	4	124	13	0	1	1	120
1988-89	Salt Lake	IHL	72	4	20	24	313	10	4	3	7	42
1989-90	Salt Lake	IHL	58	5	13	18	419	....	....	....	....	....

Traded to **Calgary** by **Montreal** for Martin Nicoletti, February 20, 1988.

HEAPHY, SHAWN

Center. Shoots left. 5'8", 170 lbs. Born, Sudbury, Ont., January 27, 1968.
(Calgary's 1st choice, 26th overall, in 1989 Supplemental Draft).

			Regular Season					Playoffs				
Season	Club	Lea	GP	G	A	TP	PIM	GP	G	A	TP	PIM
1987-88	Michigan State	CCHA	44	19	24	43	48	....	....	....	....	....
1988-89	Michigan State	CCHA	47	26	17	43	80	....	....	....	....	....
1989-90	Michigan State	CCHA	45	28	31	59	54	....	....	....	....	....

HEDICAN, BRET

Left wing. Shoots left. 6'2", 188 lbs. Born, St. Paul, MN., August 10, 1970.
(St. Louis' 10th choice, 198th overall, in 1988 Entry Draft).

			Regular Season					Playoffs				
Season	Club	Lea	GP	G	A	TP	PIM	GP	G	A	TP	PIM
1988-89	St. Cloud	NCAA	28	5	3	8	28	....	....	....	....	....
1989-90	St. Cloud	NCAA	36	4	17	21	37	....	....	....	....	....

HEDLUND, TOMMY

Defense. Shoots left. 6', 185 lbs. Born, Stockholm, Sweden, February 9, 1967.
(NY Islanders' 5th choice, 89th overall, in 1985 Entry Draft).

			Regular Season					Playoffs				
Season	Club	Lea	GP	G	A	TP	PIM	GP	G	A	TP	PIM
1988-89	AIK	Swe.	30	3	4	7	28	....	....	....	....	....
1989-90	AIK	Swe.	17	1	3	4	20	2	0	0	0	12

HEED, JONAS

Defense. Shoots left. 6', 175 lbs. Born, Sodertalje, Sweden, January 3, 1967.
(Chicago's 6th choice, 116th overall, in 1985 Entry Draft).

			Regular Season					Playoffs				
Season	Club	Lea	GP	G	A	TP	PIM	GP	G	A	TP	PIM
1984-85	Sodertalje	Swe.	8	0	0	0	0	....	....	....	....	....
1985-86	Sodertalje	Swe.	17	3	2	5	6	....	....	....	....	....
1986-87	Sodertalje	Swe.	24	0	3	3	12	2	0	0	0	0
1987-88	Sodertalje	Swe.	26	1	4	5	12	....	....	....	....	....
1988-89	Sodertalje	Swe.	38	4	9	13	22	....	....	....	....	....
1989-90	Sodertalje	Swe.	36	7	4	11	28	2	0	0	0	0

HEINZE, STEPHEN

Center. Shoots right. 5'11", 180 lbs. Born, Lawrence, MA, January 30, 1970.
(Boston's 2nd choice, 60th overall, in 1988 Entry Draft).

			Regular Season					Playoffs				
Season	Club	Lea	GP	G	A	TP	PIM	GP	G	A	TP	PIM
1988-89	Boston College	H.E.	36	26	23	49	26	....	....	....	....	....
1989-90ab	Boston College	H.E.	40	27	36	63	41	....	....	....	....	....

a Hockey East First All-Star Team (1990)
b NCAA East First All-American Team (1990)

HEJNA, TONY

Left wing. Shoots left. 6', 190 lbs. Born, Buffalo, NY, January 8, 1968.
(St. Louis' 3rd choice, 52nd overall, in 1986 Entry Draft).

			Regular Season					Playoffs				
Season	Club	Lea	GP	G	A	TP	PIM	GP	G	A	TP	PIM
1986-87	RPI	ECAC	31	12	18	30	18	....	....	....	....	....
1987-88	RPI	ECAC	32	17	19	36	48	....	....	....	....	....
1988-89	RPI	ECAC	29	12	9	21	14	....	....	....	....	....
1989-90	RPI	ECAC	26	20	16	36	22	....	....	....	....	....

HELBER, MICHAEL

Center. Shoots right. 5'11", 175 lbs. Born, Ann Arbor, MI, June 23, 1970.
(Winnipeg's 11th choice, 178th overall, in 1988 Entry Draft).

			Regular Season					Playoffs				
Season	Club	Lea	GP	G	A	TP	PIM	GP	G	A	TP	PIM
1988-89	U. of Michigan	CCHA	35	8	10	18	15	....	....	....	....	....
1989-90	U. of Michigan	CCHA	20	3	2	5	8	....	....	....	....	....

HELGESON, JON

Left wing. Shoots left. 6'4", 210 lbs. Born, Roseau, MN, August 15, 1968.
(Vancouver's 6th choice, 133rd overall, in 1986 Entry Draft).

			Regular Season					Playoffs				
Season	Club	Lea	GP	G	A	TP	PIM	GP	G	A	TP	PIM
1987-88	U. Wisconsin	WCHA	5	0	2	2	2	....	....	....	....	....
1988-89	U. Wisconsin	WCHA	36	7	1	8	28	....	....	....	....	....
1989-90	U. Wisconsin	WCHA	18	2	2	4	12	....	....	....	....	....

HENRY, DALE

Left wing. Shoots left. 6', 205 lbs. Born, Prince Albert, Sask., September 24, 1964.
(New York Islanders' 10th choice, 163rd overall, in 1983 Entry Draft).

			Regular Season					Playoffs				
Season	Club	Lea	GP	G	A	TP	PIM	GP	G	A	TP	PIM
1981-82	Saskatoon	WHL	32	5	4	9	50	5	0	0	0	0
1982-83	Saskatoon	WHL	63	21	19	40	213	3	0	0	0	12
1983-84	Saskatoon	WHL	71	41	36	77	162	....	....	....	....	....
1984-85	**NY Islanders**	**NHL**	**16**	**2**	**1**	**3**	**19**	....	....	....	....	....
	Springfield	AHL	67	11	20	31	133	4	0	0	0	13
1985-86	**NY Islanders**	**NHL**	**7**	**1**	**3**	**4**	**15**	....	....	....	....	....
	Springfield	AHL	64	14	26	40	162	....	....	....	....	....
1986-87	**NY Islanders**	**NHL**	**19**	**3**	**3**	**6**	**46**	**8**	**0**	**0**	**0**	**2**
	Springfield	AHL	23	9	14	23	49	....	....	....	....	....
1987-88	**NY Islanders**	**NHL**	**48**	**5**	**15**	**20**	**115**	**6**	**1**	**0**	**1**	**17**
	Springfield	AHL	24	9	12	21	103	....	....	....	....	....
1988-89	**NY Islanders**	**NHL**	**22**	**2**	**2**	**4**	**66**	....	....	....	....	....
	Springfield	AHL	50	13	21	34	83	....	....	....	....	....
1989-90	**NY Islanders**	**NHL**	**20**	**0**	**2**	**2**	**2**	....	....	....	....	....
	Springfield	AHL	43	17	14	31	68	18	3	5	8	33
	NHL Totals		**132**	**13**	**26**	**39**	**263**	**14**	**1**	**0**	**1**	**19**

HENTGES, MATHEW

Defense. Shoots left. 6'5", 200 lbs. Born, St. Paul, MN, December 19, 1969.
(Chicago's 9th choice, 176th overall, in 1988 Entry Draft).

			Regular Season					Playoffs				
Season	Club	Lea	GP	G	A	TP	PIM	GP	G	A	TP	PIM
1988-89	Merrimack	NCAA	33	0	16	16	22	....	....	....	....	....
1989-90	Merrimack	H.E.	33	1	2	3	40	....	....	....	....	....

HEPPLE, ALAN

Defense. Shoots right. 5'9", 200 lbs. Born, Blaydon-on-Tyne, England, August 16, 1963.
(New Jersey's 9th choice, 169th overall, in 1982 Entry Draft).

			Regular Season					Playoffs				
Season	Club	Lea	GP	G	A	TP	PIM	GP	G	A	TP	PIM
1980-81	Ottawa	OHL	64	3	13	16	110	6	0	1	1	2
1981-82	Ottawa	OHL	66	6	22	28	160	17	2	10	12	84
1982-83	Ottawa	OHL	64	10	26	36	168	9	2	1	3	24
1983-84	**New Jersey**	**NHL**	**1**	**0**	**0**	**0**	**7**	....	....	....	....	....
	Maine	AHL	64	4	23	27	117	....	....	....	....	....
1984-85	**New Jersey**	**NHL**	**1**	**0**	**0**	**0**	**0**	....	....	....	....	....
	Maine	AHL	80	7	17	24	125	11	0	3	3	30
1985-86	**New Jersey**	**NHL**	**1**	**0**	**0**	**0**	**0**	....	....	....	....	....
	Maine	AHL	69	4	21	25	104	5	0	0	0	11
1986-87	Maine	AHL	74	6	19	25	137	....	....	....	....	....
1987-88	Utica	AHL	78	3	16	19	213	....	....	....	....	....
1988-89	Newmarket	AHL	72	5	29	34	122	5	0	1	1	23
1989-90	Newmarket	AHL	72	6	20	26	90	....	....	....	....	....
	NHL Totals		**3**	**0**	**0**	**0**	**7**	....	....	....	....	....

Signed as a free agent by **Toronto**, June 24, 1988.

HERNIMAN, STEVE

Defense. Shoots left. 6'4", 210 lbs. Born, Windsor, Ont., June 9, 1968.
(Vancouver's 5th choice, 112th overall, in 1986 Entry Draft).

			Regular Season					Playoffs				
Season	Club	Lea	GP	G	A	TP	PIM	GP	G	A	TP	PIM
1985-86	Cornwall	OHL	55	3	12	15	128	6	0	0	0	2
1986-87	Cornwall	OHL	64	2	8	10	121	3	0	0	0	0
1987-88	Cornwall	OHL	5	1	0	1	8	....	....	....	....	....
	S.S. Marie	OHL	52	3	14	17	111	6	0	1	1	18
1988-89	Kitchener	OHL	61	3	16	19	112	5	0	0	0	4
1989-90	Milwaukee	IHL	15	0	0	0	102	....	....	....	....	....

HEROUX, YVES (ay-ROO, EEV)

Right wing. Shoots right. 5'11", 185 lbs. Born, Terrebonne, Que., April 27, 1965.
(Quebec's 1st choice, 32nd overall, in 1983 Entry Draft).

			Regular Season					Playoffs				
Season	Club	Lea	GP	G	A	TP	PIM	GP	G	A	TP	PIM
1982-83	Chicoutimi	QMJHL	70	41	40	81	44	5	0	4	4	8
1983-84	Chicoutimi	QMJHL	56	28	25	53	67	....	....	....	....	....
	Fredericton	AHL	4	0	0	0	0	....	....	....	....	....
1984-85	Chicoutimi	QMJHL	66	42	54	96	123	14	5	8	13	16
1985-86	Fredericton	AHL	31	12	10	22	42	2	0	1	1	7
	Muskegon	IHL	42	14	8	22	41	....	....	....	....	....
1986-87	**Quebec**	**NHL**	**1**	**0**	**0**	**0**	**0**	....	....	....	....	....
	Fredericton	AHL	37	8	6	14	13	....	....	....	....	....
	Muskegon	IHL	25	6	8	14	31	2	0	0	0	0
1987-88	Baltimore	AHL	5	0	2	2	2	....	....	....	....	....
1988-89	Flint	IHL	82	43	42	85	98	....	....	....	....	....
1989-90	Flint	IHL	14	3	2	5	42	5	2	2	4	0
	NHL Totals		**1**	**0**	**0**	**0**	**0**	....	....	....	....	....

HERTER, JASON

Defense. Shoots right. 6'1", 182 lbs. Born, Hafford, Sask., October 2, 1970.
(Vancouver's 1st choice, 8th overall, in 1989 Entry Draft).

			Regular Season					Playoffs				
Season	Club	Lea	GP	G	A	TP	PIM	GP	G	A	TP	PIM
1988-89	North Dakota	WCHA	41	8	24	32	62	....	....	....	....	....
1989-90a	North Dakota	WCHA	38	11	39	50	40	....	....	....	....	....

a WCHA Second All-Star Team (1990)

HERVEY, MATT

Defense. Shoots right. 5'11", 205 lbs. Born, Whittier, CA, May 16, 1966.

			Regular Season					Playoffs				
Season	Club	Lea	GP	G	A	TP	PIM	GP	G	A	TP	PIM
1987-88	Moncton	AHL	69	9	20	29	265	....	....	....	....	....
1988-89	**Winnipeg**	**NHL**	**2**	**0**	**0**	**0**	**4**	....	....	....	....	....
	Moncton	AHL	73	8	28	36	295	10	1	2	3	42
1989-90	Moncton	AHL	47	3	13	16	168	....	....	....	....	....
	NHL Totals		**2**	**0**	**0**	**0**	**4**	....	....	....	....	....

Signed as a free agent by **Winnipeg**, September 27, 1988.

HEWARD, JAMIE

Right wing. Shoots right. 6'2", 185 lbs. Born, Regina, Sask., March 30, 1971.
(Pittsburgh's 1st choice, 16th overall, in 1989 Entry Draft).

			Regular Season					Playoffs				
Season	Club	Lea	GP	G	A	TP	PIM	GP	G	A	TP	PIM
1987-88	Regina	WHL	68	10	17	27	17	4	1	1	2	2
1988-89	Regina	WHL	52	31	28	59	29	....	....	....	....	....
1989-90	Regina	WHL	72	14	44	58	42	11	2	2	4	10

HILDITCH, TODD

Defense. Shoots right. 6'1", 200 lbs. Born, Vancouver, B.C., March 13, 1968.
(Washington's 9th choice, 144th overall, in 1988 Entry Draft).

			Regular Season					Playoffs				
Season	Club	Lea	GP	G	A	TP	PIM	GP	G	A	TP	PIM
1988-89	RPI	ECAC	29	1	1	2	56	....	....	....	....	....
1989-90	RPI	ECAC	33	1	3	4	48	....	....	....	....	....

HILL, SEAN

Defense. Shoots right. 6', 185 lbs. Born, Duluth, MN, February 14, 1970.
(Montreal's 9th choice, 167th overall, in 1988 Entry Draft).

			Regular Season					Playoffs				
Season	Club	Lea	GP	G	A	TP	PIM	GP	G	A	TP	PIM
1988-89	U. Wisconsin	WCHA	45	2	23	25	69	....	....	....	....	....
1989-90a	U. Wisconsin	WCHA	42	14	39	53	78	....	....	....	....	....

a WCHA Second All-Star Team (1990)

HILLER, JIM

Right wing. Shoots right. 6'1", 190 lbs. Born, St. Paul, MN, November 29, 1970.
(Los Angeles' 10th choice, 207th overall, in 1989 Entry Draft).

			Regular Season					Playoffs				
Season	Club	Lea	GP	G	A	TP	PIM	GP	G	A	TP	PIM
1988-89	Edina	HS	25	16	24	40	0	....	....	....	....	....
1989-90	N. Michigan	WCHA	39	23	33	56	52	....	....	....	....	....

HILLIER, RANDY GEORGE (HIHL-yuhr)

Defense. Shoots right. 6'1", 185 lbs. Born, Toronto, Ont., March 30, 1960.
(Boston's 4th choice, 102nd overall, in 1980 Entry Draft).

			Regular Season					Playoffs				
Season	**Club**	**Lea**	**GP**	**G**	**A**	**TP**	**PIM**	**GP**	**G**	**A**	**TP**	**PIM**
1978-79	Sudbury	OHA	61	8	25	33	173	10	2	5	7	21
1979-80	Sudbury	OHA	60	16	49	65	143	9	3	6	9	14
1980-81	Springfield	AHL	64	3	17	20	105	6	0	2	2	36
1981-82	Erie	AHL	35	6	13	19	52	....	....	....	....	....
	Boston	**NHL**	**25**	**0**	**8**	**8**	**29**	**8**	**0**	**1**	**1**	**16**
1982-83	**Boston**	**NHL**	**70**	**0**	**10**	**10**	**99**	**3**	**0**	**0**	**0**	**4**
1983-84	**Boston**	**NHL**	**69**	**3**	**12**	**15**	**125**	....	....	....	....	....
1984-85	**Pittsburgh**	**NHL**	**45**	**2**	**19**	**21**	**56**	....	....	....	....	....
1985-86	**Pittsburgh**	**NHL**	**28**	**0**	**3**	**3**	**53**	....	....	....	....	....
	Baltimore	AHL	8	0	5	5	14	....	....	....	....	....
1986-87	**Pittsburgh**	**NHL**	**55**	**4**	**8**	**12**	**97**	....	....	....	....	....
1987-88	**Pittsburgh**	**NHL**	**55**	**1**	**12**	**13**	**144**	....	....	....	....	....
1988-89	**Pittsburgh**	**NHL**	**68**	**1**	**23**	**24**	**141**	**9**	**0**	**1**	**1**	**49**
1989-90	**Pittsburgh**	**NHL**	**61**	**3**	**12**	**15**	**71**	....	....	....	....	....
	NHL Totals		**476**	**14**	**107**	**121**	**815**	**20**	**0**	**2**	**2**	**69**

Traded to **Pittsburgh** by **Boston** for Pittsburgh's fourth round choice in 1985 Entry Draft (later traded to Quebec), October 15, 1984.

HIRTH, MARK

Center. Shoots left. 6'2", 175 lbs. Born, Ann Arbor, MI, January 7, 1969.
(Hartford's 8th choice, 179th overall, in 1988 Entry Draft).

			Regular Season					Playoffs				
Season	**Club**	**Lea**	**GP**	**G**	**A**	**TP**	**PIM**	**GP**	**G**	**A**	**TP**	**PIM**
1987-88	Michigan State	CCHA	10	0	2	2	0	....	....	....	....	....
1988-89	Michigan State	CCHA	40	6	1	7	8	....	....	....	....	....
1989-90	Michigan State	CCHA	5	1	1	2	4	....	....	....	....	....

HOARD, BRIAN

Defense. Shoots right. 6'4", 195 lbs. Born, Oshawa, Ont., March 10, 1968.
(Toronto's 12th choice, 237th overall, in 1986 Entry Draft).

			Regular Season					Playoffs				
Season	**Club**	**Lea**	**GP**	**G**	**A**	**TP**	**PIM**	**GP**	**G**	**A**	**TP**	**PIM**
1985-86	Hamilton	OHL	34	2	2	4	69	....	....	....	....	....
1986-87	Hamilton	OHL	1	0	1	1	0	....	....	....	....	....
	Belleville	OHL	9	0	0	0	31	....	....	....	....	....
	S.S. Marie	OHL	44	4	8	12	137	4	0	0	0	2
1987-88	S.S. Marie	OHL	59	1	12	13	187	4	1	0	1	18
1988-89	Newmarket	AHL	54	2	5	7	208	2	0	0	0	12
1989-90	Newmarket	AHL	40	2	4	6	46	....	....	....	....	....

HOBSON, DOUG

Defense. Shoots left. 6', 186 lbs. Born, Prince Albert, Sask., April 9, 1968.
(Pittsburgh's 7th choice, 130th overall, in 1986 Entry Draft).

			Regular Season					Playoffs				
Season	**Club**	**Lea**	**GP**	**G**	**A**	**TP**	**PIM**	**GP**	**G**	**A**	**TP**	**PIM**
1985-86	Prince Albert	WHL	66	2	17	19	70	20	1	2	3	31
1986-87	Prince Albert	WHL	69	3	20	23	83	8	2	3	5	12
1987-88	Prince Albert	WHL	69	9	26	35	96	10	1	5	6	17
1988-89	Muskegon	IHL	62	5	17	22	82	1	0	1	1	11
1989-90	Muskegon	IHL	9	0	1	1	4	....	....	....	....	....

HODGE, KENNETH JR. (KEN)

Center. Shoots left. 6'1", 200 lbs. Born, Windsor, Ont., April 13, 1966.
(Minnesota's 2nd choice, 46th overall, in 1984 Entry Draft).

			Regular Season					Playoffs				
Season	**Club**	**Lea**	**GP**	**G**	**A**	**TP**	**PIM**	**GP**	**G**	**A**	**TP**	**PIM**
1984-85	Boston College	H.E.	41	20	44	64	28	....	....	....	....	....
1985-86	Boston College	H.E.	21	11	17	28	16	....	....	....	....	....
1986-87	Boston College	H.E.	37	29	33	62	30	....	....	....	....	....
1987-88	Kalamazoo	IHL	70	15	35	50	24	....	....	....	....	....
1988-89	**Minnesota**	**NHL**	**5**	**1**	**1**	**2**	**0**	....	....	....	....	....
	Kalamazoo	IHL	72	26	45	71	34	6	1	5	6	16
1989-90	Kalamazoo	IHL	68	33	53	86	19	....	....	....	....	....
	NHL Totals		**5**	**1**	**1**	**2**	**0**	....	....	....	....	....

HODGSON, DANIEL (DAN)

Center. Shoots right. 5'10", 175 lbs. Born, Fort Vermillion, Alta., August 29, 1965.
(Toronto's 4th choice, 83rd overall, in 1983 Entry Draft).

			Regular Season					Playoffs				
Season	**Club**	**Lea**	**GP**	**G**	**A**	**TP**	**PIM**	**GP**	**G**	**A**	**TP**	**PIM**
1982-83a	Prince Albert	WHL	72	56	74	130	66	....	....	....	....	....
1983-84b	Prince Albert	WHL	66	62	*119	181	65	5	5	3	0	7
1984-85cde	Prince Albert	WHL	64	70	*112	182	86	13	10	*26	*36	32
1985-86	**Toronto**	**NHL**	**40**	**13**	**12**	**25**	**12**	....	....	....	....	....
	St. Catharines	AHL	22	13	16	29	15	13	3	9	12	14
1986-87	Newmarket	AHL	20	7	12	19	16	....	....	....	....	....
	Vancouver	**NHL**	**43**	**9**	**13**	**22**	**25**	....	....	....	....	....
1987-88	**Vancouver**	**NHL**	**8**	**3**	**7**	**10**	**2**	....	....	....	....	....
	Fredericton	AHL	13	8	18	26	16	....	....	....	....	....
1988-89	**Vancouver**	**NHL**	**23**	**4**	**13**	**17**	**25**	....	....	....	....	....
	Milwaukee	IHL	47	27	55	82	47	11	6	7	13	10
1989-90	Gotteron	Switz.	36	17	22	39	....	....	....	....	....	....
	NHL Totals		**114**	**29**	**45**	**74**	**64**	....	....	....	....	....

a WHL Rookie of the Year (1983)
b WHL Second Team All-Star (1984)
c WHL First Team All-Star (1985)
d Named WHL Player of the Year (1985)
e Canadian Major Junior Player of the Year (1985)

Traded to **Vancouver** by **Toronto** with Jim Benning for Rick Lanz, December 2, 1986.

HOFFORD, JAMES (JIM)

Defense. Shoots right. 6', 190 lbs. Born, Sudbury, Ont., October 4, 1964.
(Buffalo's 8th choice, 114th overall, in 1983 Entry Draft).

			Regular Season					Playoffs				
Season	**Club**	**Lea**	**GP**	**G**	**A**	**TP**	**PIM**	**GP**	**G**	**A**	**TP**	**PIM**
1982-83	Windsor	OHL	63	8	20	28	173	3	0	1	1	15
1983-84	Windsor	OHL	1	0	0	0	2	....	....	....	....	....
1984-85	Rochester	AHL	71	2	13	15	166	5	0	0	0	16
1985-86	**Buffalo**	**NHL**	**5**	**0**	**0**	**0**	**5**	....	....	....	....	....
	Rochester	AHL	40	2	7	9	148	....	....	....	....	....
1986-87	**Buffalo**	**NHL**	**12**	**0**	**0**	**0**	**40**	....	....	....	....	....
	Rochester	AHL	54	1	8	9	204	13	1	0	1	57
1987-88	Rochester	AHL	69	3	15	18	322	7	0	0	0	28
1988-89	**Los Angeles**	**NHL**	**1**	**0**	**0**	**0**	**2**	....	....	....	....	....
	Rochester	AHL	34	1	9	10	139	....	....	....	....	....
1989-90	Rochester	AHL	52	1	9	10	233	17	1	1	2	56
	NHL Totals		**18**	**0**	**0**	**0**	**47**	....	....	....	....	....

Claimed by **Los Angeles** in NHL Waiver Draft, October 3, 1988. Claimed on waivers by **Buffalo**, October 19, 1988.

HOGUE, BENOIT (HOHG)

Center. Shoots left. 5'10", 190 lbs. Born, Repentigny, Que., October 28, 1966.
(Buffalo's 2nd choice, 35th overall, in 1985 Entry Draft).

			Regular Season					Playoffs				
Season	**Club**	**Lea**	**GP**	**G**	**A**	**TP**	**PIM**	**GP**	**G**	**A**	**TP**	**PIM**
1983-84	St. Jean	QMJHL	59	14	11	25	42	....	....	....	....	....
1984-85	St. Jean	QMJHL	63	46	44	90	92	....	....	....	....	....
1985-86	St. Jean	QMJHL	65	54	54	108	115	9	6	4	10	26
1986-87	Rochester	AHL	52	14	20	34	52	12	5	4	9	8
1987-88	**Buffalo**	**NHL**	**3**	**1**	**1**	**2**	**0**	....	....	....	....	....
	Rochester	AHL	62	24	31	55	141	7	6	1	7	46
1988-89	**Buffalo**	**NHL**	**69**	**14**	**30**	**44**	**120**	**5**	**0**	**0**	**0**	**17**
1989-90	**Buffalo**	**NHL**	**45**	**11**	**7**	**18**	**79**	**3**	**0**	**0**	**0**	**10**
	NHL Totals		**117**	**26**	**38**	**64**	**199**	**8**	**0**	**0**	**0**	**27**

HOHENBERGER, HERBERT

Defense. Shoots left. Born, Villach, Austria, February 8, 1969.

			Regular Season					Playoffs				
Season	**Club**	**Lea**	**GP**	**G**	**A**	**TP**	**PIM**	**GP**	**G**	**A**	**TP**	**PIM**
1986-87	Hull	QMJHL	68	20	23	43	105	8	3	3	6	12
1987-88	Hull	QMJHL	60	21	39	60	94	19	5	11	16	34
1988-89	Villach	Aus.	40	20	23	43	120	6	4	3	7	20
1989-90	Hull	QMJHL	65	16	50	66	125	11	3	7	10	10
	Sherbrooke	AHL	....	....	....	....	....	4	1	0	1	6

Signed as a free agent by **Montreal**, June 18, 1990.

HOLDEN, PAUL

Defense. Shoots left. 6'3", 210 lbs. Born, Kitchener, Ont., March 15, 1970.
(Los Angeles' 2nd choice, 28th overall, in 1988 Entry Draft).

			Regular Season					Playoffs				
Season	**Club**	**Lea**	**GP**	**G**	**A**	**TP**	**PIM**	**GP**	**G**	**A**	**TP**	**PIM**
1987-88	London	OHL	65	8	12	20	87	12	1	1	2	10
1988-89	London	OHL	54	11	21	32	90	20	1	3	4	17
1989-90a	London	OHL	61	11	31	42	78	6	1	1	2	7

a OHL Second All-Star Team (1990)

HOLIK, ROBERT

Center. Shoots right. 6'1", 185 lbs. Born, Jihlava, Czechoslovakia, January 1, 1971.
(Hartford's 1st choice, 10th overall, in 1989 Entry Draft).

			Regular Season					Playoffs				
Season	**Club**	**Lea**	**GP**	**G**	**A**	**TP**	**PIM**	**GP**	**G**	**A**	**TP**	**PIM**
1987-88	Dukla Jihlava	Czech.	31	5	9	14	....	....	....	....	....	....
1988-89	Dukla Jihlava	Czech.	24	7	10	17	....	....	....	....	....	....
1989-90	Dukla Jihlava	Czech	42	15	26	41		....	....	....	....	....

HOLLAND, DENNIS

Center. Shoots left. 5'10", 165 lbs. Born, Vernon, B.C., January 30, 1969.
(Detroit's 4th choice, 52nd overall, in 1987 Entry Draft).

			Regular Season					Playoffs				
Season	**Club**	**Lea**	**GP**	**G**	**A**	**TP**	**PIM**	**GP**	**G**	**A**	**TP**	**PIM**
1986-87a	Portland	WHL	51	43	62	105	40	20	7	14	21	20
1987-88b	Portland	WHL	67	58	86	144	115	....	....	....	....	....
1988-89bc	Portland	WHL	69	*82	85	*167	120	19	15	*22	*37	18
1989-90	Adirondack	AHL	78	19	34	53	53	6	1	1	2	10

a WHL Rookie of the Year (1987)
b WHL West All Star Team (1988, 1989)
c WHL Player of the Year (1989)

HOLLETT, STEVE

Center. Shoots left. 6'1", 200 lbs. Born, St. John's, Nfld., June 12, 1967.
(Washington's 10th choice, 187th overall, in 1985 Entry Draft).

			Regular Season					Playoffs				
Season	**Club**	**Lea**	**GP**	**G**	**A**	**TP**	**PIM**	**GP**	**G**	**A**	**TP**	**PIM**
1984-85	S. S. Marie	OHL	60	12	17	29	25	16	3	4	7	11
1985-86	S. S. Marie	OHL	63	31	34	65	81	....	....	....	....	....
1986-87	S. S. Marie	OHL	65	35	41	76	63	4	0	1	1	7
1987-88	Fort Wayne	IHL	76	42	32	74	56	5	0	2	2	2
1988-89	Fort Wayne	IHL	79	27	21	48	39	10	2	2	4	4
1989-90	Baltimore	AHL	43	4	10	14	18	18	0	0	0	0

HOLLYMAN, RHYS

Defense. Shoots right. 6'3", 210 lbs. Born, Toronto, Ont., January 30, 1970.
(Minnesota's 7th choice, 97th overall, in 1989 Entry Draft).

			Regular Season					Playoffs				
Season	**Club**	**Lea**	**GP**	**G**	**A**	**TP**	**PIM**	**GP**	**G**	**A**	**TP**	**PIM**
1988-89	Miami-Ohio	CCHA	33	8	5	13	60	....	....	....	....	....
1989-90	Miami-Ohio	CCHA	37	2	8	10	54	....	....	....	....	....

HOLMES, MARK

Center. Shoots right. 6'2", 200 lbs. Born, Kingston, Jamaica, June 7, 1964.

			Regular Season					Playoffs				
Season	Club	Lea	GP	G	A	TP	PIM	GP	G	A	TP	PIM
1984-85	Colgate	ECAC	20	3	5	8	12	....	....	....	....	....
1985-86	Colgate	ECAC	30	11	5	16	20	....	....	....	....	....
1986-87	Colgate	ECAC	31	12	14	26	45	....	....	....	....	....
1987-88	Colgate	ECAC	32	11	13	24	28	....	....	....	....	....
1988-89	Salt Lake	IHL	52	6	12	18	46	4	0	2	2	7
1989-90	Salt Lake	IHL	52	3	12	15	27	9	2	3	5	2

Signed as a free agent by **Calgary**, May 1, 1988.

HOLOIEN, DEAN

Defense. Shoots right. 6', 195 lbs. Born, Melford, Sask., April 18, 1969.
(Washington's 7th choice, 166th overall, in 1989 Entry Draft).

			Regular Season					Playoffs				
Season	Club	Lea	GP	G	A	TP	PIM	GP	G	A	TP	PIM
1986-87	Saskatoon	WHL	7	1	1	2	13	7	0	1	1	8
1987-88	Saskatoon	WHL	72	7	34	41	68	9	1	1	2	8
1988-89	Saskatoon	WHL	59	22	30	52	78	8	3	4	7	7
1989-90	Saskatoon	WHL	70	43	49	92	121	10	6	11	17	11

HOOVER, RON

Center. Shoots left. 6'1", 185 lbs. Born, Oakville, Ont., October 28, 1966.
(Hartford's 7th choice, 158th overall, in 1986 Entry Draft).

			Regular Season					Playoffs				
Season	Club	Lea	GP	G	A	TP	PIM	GP	G	A	TP	PIM
1985-86	W. Michigan	CCHA	43	10	23	33	36	....	....	....	....	....
1986-87	W. Michigan	CCHA	34	7	10	17	22	....	....	....	....	....
1987-88a	W. Michigan	CCHA	42	39	23	62	40	....	....	....	....	....
1988-89	W. Michigan	CCHA	42	32	27	59	66	....	....	....	....	....
1989-90	**Boston**	**NHL**	**2**	**0**	**0**	**0**	**0**	....	....	....	....	....
	Maine	AHL	75	28	26	54	57	....	....	....	....	....
	NHL Totals		**2**	**0**	**0**	**0**	**0**	....	....	....	....	....

a CCHA Second All-Star Team (1988)

HOPKINS, DEAN ROBERT

Right wing. Shoots right. 6'1", 210 lbs. Born, Cobourg, Ont., June 6, 1959.
(Los Angeles' 2nd choice, 29th overall, in 1979 Entry Draft).

			Regular Season					Playoffs				
Season	Club	Lea	GP	G	A	TP	PIM	GP	G	A	TP	PIM
1977-78	London	OHA	67	19	34	53	70	11	1	5	6	24
1978-79	London	OHA	65	37	55	92	149	7	6	0	6	27
1979-80	**Los Angeles**	**NHL**	**60**	**8**	**6**	**14**	**39**	**4**	**0**	**1**	**1**	**5**
1980-81	**Los Angeles**	**NHL**	**67**	**8**	**18**	**26**	**118**	**4**	**1**	**0**	**1**	**9**
1981-82	**Los Angeles**	**NHL**	**41**	**2**	**13**	**15**	**102**	**10**	**0**	**4**	**4**	**15**
1982-83	**Los Angeles**	**NHL**	**49**	**5**	**12**	**17**	**43**	....	....	....	....	....
	New Haven	AHL	20	9	8	17	58	....	....	....	....	....
1983-84	New Haven	AHL	79	35	47	82	162	....	....	....	....	....
1984-85	New Haven	AHL	20	7	10	17	38	....	....	....	....	....
	Nova Scotia	AHL	49	13	17	30	93	6	1	2	3	20
1985-86	**Edmonton**	**NHL**	**1**	**0**	**0**	**0**	**0**	....	....	....	....	....
	Nova Scotia	AHL	60	23	32	55	131	....	....	....	....	....
1986-87	Nova Scotia	AHL	59	20	25	45	84	1	0	0	0	5
1987-88	Nova Scotia	AHL	44	20	22	42	122	5	2	5	7	16
1988-89	**Quebec**	**NHL**	**5**	**0**	**2**	**2**	**4**	....	....	....	....	....
	Halifax	AHL	53	18	31	49	116	3	0	1	1	6
1989-90	Halifax	AHL	54	23	32	55	167	6	1	4	5	8
	NHL Totals		**223**	**23**	**51**	**74**	**306**	**18**	**1**	**5**	**6**	**29**

Traded to **Edmonton** by **Los Angeles** for cash, November 27, 1984. Traded to **Los Angeles** by **Edmonton** for future considerations, May 31, 1985. Signed as a free agent by **Edmonton**, September 27, 1985. Signed as a free agent by **Quebec**, July 15, 1988.

HORACEK, TONY (HOHR-uh-chehk)

Left wing. Shoots left. 6'3", 225 lbs. Born, Vancouver, B.C., February 3, 1967.
(Philadelphia's 8th choice, 147th overall, in 1985 Entry Draft).

			Regular Season					Playoffs				
Season	Club	Lea	GP	G	A	TP	PIM	GP	G	A	TP	PIM
1984-85	Kelowna	WHL	67	9	18	27	114	6	0	1	1	11
1985-86	Spokane	WHL	64	19	28	47	129	9	4	5	9	29
1986-87	Hershey	AHL	1	0	0	0	0	1	0	0	0	0
	Spokane	WHL	64	23	37	60	177	5	1	3	4	18
1987-88	Hershey	AHL	1	0	0	0	0	....	....	....	....	....
	Spokane	WHL	24	17	23	40	63	....	....	....	....	....
	Kamloops	WHL	26	14	17	31	51	18	6	4	10	73
1988-89	Hershey	AHL	10	0	0	0	38	....	....	....	....	....
	Indianapolis	IHL	43	11	13	24	138	....	....	....	....	....
1989-90	**Philadelphia**	**NHL**	**48**	**5**	**5**	**10**	**117**	....	....	....	....	....
	Hershey	AHL	12	0	5	5	25	....	....	....	....	....
	NHL Totals		**48**	**5**	**5**	**10**	**117**	....	....	....	....	....

HORAVA, MILOSLAV (HOHR-shuh-vuh)

Defense. Shoots left. 6'1", 197 lbs. Born, Kladno, Czechoslovakia, August 14, 1961.
(Edmonton's 8th choice, 176th overall, in 1981 Entry Draft).

			Regular Season					Playoffs				
Season	Club	Lea	GP	G	A	TP	PIM	GP	G	A	TP	PIM
1986-87	Boldi Kladno	Czech.	38	17	26	43	....	....	....	....	....	....
1987-88	Boldi Kladno	Czech.	29	7	11	18	....	....	....	....	....	....
1988-89	Boldi Kladno	Czech.	37	10	15	25	....	....	....	....	....	....
	NY Rangers	**NHL**	**6**	**0**	**1**	**1**	**0**	....	....	....	....	....
1989-90	**NY Rangers**	**NHL**	**45**	**4**	**10**	**14**	**26**	**2**	**0**	**1**	**1**	**0**
	NHL Totals		**51**	**4**	**11**	**15**	**26**	**2**	**0**	**1**	**1**	**0**

Traded to **NY Rangers** by **Edmonton** with Don Jackson, Mike Golden and future considerations for Reijo Ruotsalainen, Ville Kentala, Clark Donatelli and Jim Wiemer, October 23, 1986.

HOSTAK, MARTIN

Center. Shoots left. 6'3", 192 lbs. Born, Hradec Kralove, Czech., November 11, 1967.
(Philadelphia's 3rd choice, 62nd overall, in 1987 Entry Draft).

			Regular Season					Playoffs				
Season	Club	Lea	GP	G	A	TP	PIM	GP	G	A	TP	PIM
1986-87	Sparta Praha	Czech.	34	6	2	8	....	....	....	....	....	....
1987-88	Sparta Praha	Czech	26	8	9	17	....	....	....	....	....	....
1988-89	Sparta Praha	Czech.	35	11	15	26	....	....	....	....	....	....
1989-90	Sparta Praha	Czech	55	31	34	65	....	....	....	....	....	....

HOTHAM, GREGORY (GREG) (HOTH-am)

Defense. Shoots right. 5'11", 185 lbs. Born, London, Ont., March 7, 1956.
(Toronto's 5th choice, 84th overall, in 1976 Amateur Draft).

			Regular Season					Playoffs				
Season	Club	Lea	GP	G	A	TP	PIM	GP	G	A	TP	PIM
1974-75	Kingston	OHA	31	1	14	15	49	8	5	4	9	0
1975-76	Kingston	OHA	49	10	32	42	72	7	1	2	3	10
1976-77	Saginaw	IHL	60	4	33	37	100	....	....	....	....	....
1977-78	Saginaw	IHL	80	13	59	72	56	....	....	....	....	....
	Dallas	CHL	....	....	....	....	....	5	0	2	2	7
1978-79	New Brunswick	AHL	76	9	27	36	86	5	0	2	2	6
1979-80	**Toronto**	**NHL**	**46**	**3**	**10**	**13**	**10**	....	....	....	....	....
	New Brunswick	AHL	21	1	6	7	10	17	2	8	10	26
1980-81	**Toronto**	**NHL**	**11**	**1**	**1**	**2**	**11**	....	....	....	....	....
	New Brunswick	AHL	68	8	48	56	80	11	1	6	7	16
1981-82	**Toronto**	**NHL**	**3**	**0**	**0**	**0**	**0**	....	....	....	....	....
	Cincinnati	CHL	46	10	33	43	94	....	....	....	....	....
	Pittsburgh	**NHL**	**25**	**4**	**6**	**10**	**16**	**5**	**0**	**3**	**3**	**6**
1982-83	**Pittsburgh**	**NHL**	**58**	**2**	**30**	**32**	**39**	....	....	....	....	....
1983-84	**Pittsburgh**	**NHL**	**76**	**5**	**25**	**30**	**59**	....	....	....	....	....
1984-85	**Pittsburgh**	**NHL**	**11**	**0**	**2**	**2**	**4**	....	....	....	....	....
	Baltimore	AHL	44	4	27	31	43	15	4	4	8	34
1985-86	Baltimore	AHL	78	2	26	28	94	....	....	....	....	....
1986-87	Newmarket	AHL	51	4	9	13	60	....	....	....	....	....
1987-88	Newmarket	AHL	78	12	27	39	102	....	....	....	....	....
1988-89	Newmarket	AHL	73	9	42	51	62	5	1	4	5	0
1989-90	Newmarket	AHL	24	0	8	8	31	....	....	....	....	....
	NHL Totals		**230**	**15**	**74**	**89**	**139**	**5**	**0**	**3**	**3**	**6**

Traded to **Pittsburgh** by **Toronto** for Pittsburgh's sixth round choice (Craig Kales) in 1982 Entry Draft, February 3, 1982. Signed as a free agent by **Toronto**, July 3, 1986.

HOUDA, DOUG (HOO-duh)

Defense. Shoots right. 6'2", 200 lbs. Born, Blairmore, Alta., June 3, 1966.
(Detroit's 2nd choice, 28th overall, in 1984 Entry Draft).

			Regular Season					Playoffs				
Season	Club	Lea	GP	G	A	TP	PIM	GP	G	A	TP	PIM
1982-83	Calgary	WHL	71	5	23	28	99	16	1	3	4	44
1983-84	Calgary	WHL	69	6	30	36	195	4	0	0	0	7
1984-85a	Calgary	WHL	65	20	54	74	182	8	3	4	7	29
1985-86	**Detroit**	**NHL**	**6**	**0**	**0**	**0**	**4**	....	....	....	....	....
	Calgary	WHL	16	4	10	14	60	....	....	....	....	....
	Medicine Hat	WHL	35	9	23	32	80	25	4	19	23	64
1986-87	Adirondack	AHL	77	6	23	29	142	11	1	8	9	50
1987-88	**Detroit**	**NHL**	**11**	**1**	**1**	**2**	**10**	....	....	....	....	....
b	Adirondack	AHL	71	10	32	42	169	11	0	3	3	44
1988-89	**Detroit**	**NHL**	**57**	**2**	**11**	**13**	**67**	**6**	**0**	**1**	**1**	**0**
	Adirondack	AHL	7	0	3	3	8	....	....	....	....	....
1989-90	**Detroit**	**NHL**	**73**	**2**	**9**	**11**	**127**	....	....	....	....	....
	NHL Totals		**147**	**5**	**21**	**26**	**208**	**6**	**0**	**1**	**1**	**0**

a WHL Second All-Star Team, East Division (1985)
b AHL First All-Star Team (1988)

HOUGH, MIKE (HUHF)

Left wing. Shoots left. 6'1", 192 lbs. Born, Montreal, Que., February 6, 1963.
(Quebec's 7th choice, 181st overall, in 1982 Entry Draft).

			Regular Season					Playoffs				
Season	Club	Lea	GP	G	A	TP	PIM	GP	G	A	TP	PIM
1981-82	Kitchener	OHL	58	14	14	28	172	14	4	1	5	16
1982-83	Kitchener	OHL	61	17	27	44	156	12	5	4	9	30
1983-84	Fredericton	AHL	69	11	16	27	142	1	0	0	0	7
1984-85	Fredericton	AHL	76	21	27	48	49	6	1	1	2	2
1985-86	Fredericton	AHL	74	21	33	54	68	6	0	3	3	8
1986-87	Fredericton	AHL	10	1	3	4	20	....	....	....	....	....
	Quebec	**NHL**	**56**	**6**	**8**	**14**	**79**	**9**	**0**	**3**	**3**	**26**
1987-88	**Quebec**	**NHL**	**17**	**3**	**2**	**5**	**2**	....	....	....	....	....
	Fredericton	AHL	46	16	25	41	133	15	4	8	12	55
1988-89	**Quebec**	**NHL**	**46**	**9**	**10**	**19**	**39**	....	....	....	....	....
	Halifax	AHL	22	11	10	21	87	....	....	....	....	....
1989-90	**Quebec**	**NHL**	**43**	**13**	**13**	**26**	**84**	....	....	....	....	....
	NHL Totals		**162**	**31**	**33**	**64**	**204**	**9**	**0**	**3**	**3**	**26**

HOULDER, BILL

Defense. Shoots left. 6'3", 210 lbs. Born, Thunder Bay, Ont., March 11, 1967.
(Washington's 4th choice, 82nd overall, in 1985 Entry Draft).

			Regular Season					Playoffs				
Season	Club	Lea	GP	G	A	TP	PIM	GP	G	A	TP	PIM
1984-85	North Bay	OHL	66	4	20	24	37	8	0	0	0	2
1985-86	North Bay	OHL	59	5	30	35	97	10	1	6	7	12
1986-87a	North Bay	OHL	62	17	51	68	68	22	4	19	23	20
1987-88	**Washington**	**NHL**	**30**	**1**	**2**	**3**	**10**	....	....	....	....	....
	Fort Wayne	IHL	43	10	14	24	32	....	....	....	....	....
1988-89	**Washington**	**NHL**	**8**	**0**	**3**	**3**	**4**	....	....	....	....	....
	Baltimore	AHL	65	10	36	46	50	....	....	....	....	....
1989-90	**Washington**	**NHL**	**41**	**1**	**11**	**12**	**28**	....	....	....	....	....
	Baltimore	AHL	26	3	7	10	12	7	0	2	2	2
	NHL Totals		**79**	**2**	**16**	**18**	**42**	....	....	....	....	....

a OHL Third All-Star Team (1987)

HOUSE, KEN

Center. Shoots left. 6'1", 175 lbs.   Born, Scarborough, Ont., November 3, 1969.
(Washington's 12th choice, 250th overall, in 1989 Entry Draft).

			Regular Season					Playoffs				
Season	Club	Lea	GP	G	A	TP	PIM	GP	G	A	TP	PIM
1988-89	Miami-Ohio	CCHA	38	19	14	33	18	....	....	....	....	....
1989-90	Miami-Ohio	CCHA	37	10	5	15	32	....	....	....	....	....

HOUSLEY, PHIL   (HOWZ-lee)

Defense. Shoots left. 5'10", 185 lbs.   Born, St. Paul, MN, March 9, 1964.
(Buffalo's 1st choice, 6th overall, in 1982 Entry Draft).

			Regular Season					Playoffs				
Season	Club	Lea	GP	G	A	TP	PIM	GP	G	A	TP	PIM
1981-82	South St. Paul	HS	22	31	34	65	18	....	....	....	....	....
1982-83a	Buffalo	NHL	77	19	47	66	39	10	3	4	7	2
1983-84	Buffalo	NHL	75	31	46	77	33	3	0	0	0	6
1984-85	Buffalo	NHL	73	16	53	69	28	5	3	2	5	2
1985-86	Buffalo	NHL	79	15	47	62	54	....	....	....	....	....
1986-87	Buffalo	NHL	78	21	46	67	57	....	....	....	....	....
1987-88	Buffalo	NHL	74	29	37	66	96	6	2	4	6	6
1988-89	Buffalo	NHL	72	26	44	70	47	5	1	3	4	2
1989-90	Buffalo	NHL	80	21	60	81	32	6	1	4	5	4
	NHL Totals		608	178	380	558	386	35	10	17	27	22

a NHL All-Rookie Team (1983)

Played in NHL All-Star Game (1984, 1989, 1990)

Traded to **Winnipeg** by **Buffalo** with Scott Arniel, Jeff Parker and Buffalo's first round choice (Keith Tkachuk) in 1990 Entry Draft for Dale Hawerchuk, Winnipeg's first round choice (Brad May) in 1990 Entry Draft and future considerations, June 16, 1990.

HOWARD, SHAWN

Center. Shoots left. 6', 180 lbs.   Born, Anchorage, AK, March 20, 1968.
(NY Islanders' 9th choice, 181st overall, in 1987 Entry Draft).

			Regular Season					Playoffs				
Season	Club	Lea	GP	G	A	TP	PIM	GP	G	A	TP	PIM
1987-88	Minn.-Duluth	WCHA	37	13	8	21	42	....	....	....	....	....
1988-89	Minn.-Duluth	WCHA	39	7	9	16	31	....	....	....	....	....
1989-90	Minn.-Duluth	WCHA	40	19	19	38	58	....	....	....	....	....

HOWE, MARK STEVEN

Defence. Shoots left. 5'11", 185 lbs.   Born, Detroit, Mich., May 28, 1955.
(Boston's 2nd choice, 25th overall, in 1974 Amateur Draft).

			Regular Season					Playoffs				
Season	Club	Lea	GP	G	A	TP	PIM	GP	G	A	TP	PIM
1972-73	Toronto	OHA	60	38	66	104	27	....	....	....	....	....
1973-74ab	Houston	WHA	76	38	41	79	20	14	9	10	19	4
1974-75	Houston	WHA	74	36	40	76	30	13	*10	12	*22	0
1975-76	Houston	WHA	72	39	37	76	38	17	6	10	16	18
1976-77a	Houston	WHA	57	23	52	75	46	10	4	10	14	2
1977-78	New England	WHA	70	30	61	91	32	14	8	7	15	18
1978-79c	New England	WHA	77	42	65	107	32	6	4	2	6	6
1979-80	Hartford	NHL	74	24	56	80	20	3	1	2	3	2
1980-81	Hartford	NHL	63	19	46	65	54	....	....	....	....	....
1981-82	Hartford	NHL	76	8	45	53	18	....	....	....	....	....
1982-83d	Philadelphia	NHL	76	20	47	67	18	3	0	2	2	4
1983-84	Philadelphia	NHL	71	19	34	53	44	3	0	0	0	2
1984-85	Philadelphia	NHL	73	18	39	57	31	19	3	8	11	6
1985-86de	Philadelphia	NHL	77	24	58	82	36	5	0	4	4	0
1986-87d	Philadelphia	NHL	69	15	43	58	37	26	2	10	12	4
1987-88	Philadelphia	NHL	75	19	43	62	62	7	3	6	9	4
1988-89	Philadelphia	NHL	52	9	29	38	45	19	0	15	15	10
1989-90	Philadelphia	NHL	40	7	21	28	24	....	....	....	....	....
	NHL Totals		746	182	461	643	389	85	9	47	56	32

a WHA Second All-Star Team (1974, 1977)
b Named WHA's Rookie of the Year (1974)
c WHA First All-Star Team (1979)
d NHL First All-Star Team (1983, 1986, 1987)
e NHL Plus/Minus Leader (1986)

Played in NHL All-Star Game (1981, 1983, 1986, 1988)

Reclaimed by **Boston** from **Hartford** prior to Expansion Draft, June 9, 1979. Claimed as priority selection by **Hartford**, June 9, 1979. Traded to **Philadelphia** by **Hartford** with Hartford's third round choice (Derrick Smith) in 1983 Entry Draft for Ken Linseman, Greg Adams and Philadelphia's first (David Jensen) and third round choices (Leif Karlsson) in the 1983 Entry Draft, August 19, 1982.

HRBEK, PETR

Right wing. Shoots right. 5'11", 180 lbs.   Born, Prague, Czechoslovakia, April 3, 1969.
(Detroit's 3rd choice, 59th overall, in 1988 Entry Draft).

			Regular Season					Playoffs				
Season	Club	Lea	GP	G	A	TP	PIM	GP	G	A	TP	PIM
1986-87	Sparta Praha	Czech.	11	2	0	2	....	....	....	....	....	....
1987-88	Sparta Praha	Czech.	31	13	9	22	....	....	....	....	....	....
1988-89	Sparta Praha	Czech.	41	10	13	23	....	....	....	....	....	....
1989-90	Dukla Jihlava	Czech.	32	12	7	19	....	....	....	....	....	....

HRDINA, JIRI   (huhr-DEE-nuh)

Left wing. Shoots left. 6', 190 lbs.   Born, Mlada Boleslav, Czech., January 5, 1958.
(Calgary's 8th choice, 159th overall, in 1984 Entry Draft).

			Regular Season					Playoffs				
Season	Club	Lea	GP	G	A	TP	PIM	GP	G	A	TP	PIM
1985-86	Sparta Praha	Czech.	44	18	19	37	30	....	....	....	....	....
1986-87	Sparta Praha	Czech.	31	18	18	36	24	....	....	....	....	....
1987-88	Sparta Praha	Czech.	22	7	15	22	0	....	....	....	....	....
	Czech Olympic	....	8	2	5	7	4	....	....	....	....	....
	Calgary	NHL	9	2	5	7	2	1	0	0	0	0
1988-89	Calgary	NHL	70	22	32	54	26	4	0	0	0	0
1989-90	Calgary	NHL	64	12	18	30	31	6	0	1	1	2
	NHL Totals		143	36	55	91	59	11	0	1	1	2

HRISTICH, DMITRI

Left wing. Shoots right. 6'2", 190 lbs.   Born, Kiev, Soviet Union, July 2, 1969.
(Washington's 6th choice, 120th overall, in 1988 Entry Draft).

			Regular Season					Playoffs				
Season	Club	Lea	GP	G	A	TP	PIM	GP	G	A	TP	PIM
1987-88	Sokol Kiev	USSR	37	9	1	10	18	....	....	....	....	....
1988-89	Sokol Kiev	USSR	42	17	8	25	15	....	....	....	....	....
1989-90	Sokol Kiev	USSR	47	14	22	36	22	....	....	....	....	....

HRKAC, ANTHONY (TONY)   (HUHR-kuhz)

Center. Shoots left. 5'11", 175 lbs.   Born, Thunder Bay, Ont., July 7, 1966.
(St. Louis' 2nd choice, 32nd overall, in 1984 Entry Draft).

			Regular Season					Playoffs				
Season	Club	Lea	GP	G	A	TP	PIM	GP	G	A	TP	PIM
1984-85	North Dakota	WCHA	36	18	36	54	16	....	....	....	....	....
1985-86	Cdn. Olympic		62	19	30	49	36	....	....	....	....	....
1986-87abcd	North Dakota	WCHA	48	46	79	125	48	....	....	....	....	....
	St. Louis	NHL	....	....	....	....	....	3	0	0	0	0
1987-88	St. Louis	NHL	67	11	37	48	22	10	6	1	7	4
1988-89	St. Louis	NHL	70	17	28	45	8	4	1	1	2	0
1989-90	St. Louis	NHL	28	5	12	17	8	....	....	....	....	....
	Quebec	NHL	22	4	8	12	2	....	....	....	....	....
	Halifax	AHL	20	12	21	33	4	6	5	9	14	4
	NHL Totals		187	37	85	122	40	14	7	2	9	4

a WCHA First All-Star Team, Player of the Year (1987)
b NCAA West First All-American Team (1987)
c NCAA All-Tournament Team, Tournament MVP (1987)
d Winner of the 1987 Hobey Baker Memorial Trophy (Top U.S. Collegiate Player) (1987)

Traded to **Quebec** by **St. Louis** with Greg Millen for Jeff Brown, December 13, 1989.

HRSTKA, MARTIN

Left wing. Shoots left. 6', 180 lbs.   Born, Brno, Czechoslovakia, January 26, 1967.
(Vancouver's 6th choice, 109th overall, in 1985 Entry Draft).

			Regular Season					Playoffs				
Season	Club	Lea	GP	G	A	TP	PIM	GP	G	A	TP	PIM
1986-87	Dukla Trencin	Czech.	26	2	4	6	....	....	....	....	....	....
1987-88	Dukla Trencin	Czech.	22	5	6	11	....	....	....	....	....	....
1988-89	Dukla Trencin	Czech.	25	4	9	13	....	....	....	....	....	....
1989-90	Dukla Trencin	Czech.	39	8	7	15	....	....	....	....	....	....

HUBER, PHIL

Left wing. Shoots left. 5'10", 195 lbs.   Born. Calgary, Alta., January 10, 1969.
(NY Islanders' 8th choice, 149th overall, in 1989 Entry Draft).

			Regular Season					Playoffs				
Season	Club	Lea	GP	G	A	TP	PIM	GP	G	A	TP	PIM
1987-88	Kamloops	WHL	63	19	30	49	54	18	3	9	12	23
1988-89	Kamloops	WHL	72	54	68	122	103	16	18	13	31	48
1989-90a	Kamloops	WHL	72	63	89	152	176	17	12	11	23	44

a WHL West First All-Star Team (1990)

HUDDY, CHARLES WILLIAM (CHARLIE)

Defense. Shoots left. 6', 210 lbs.   Born, Oshawa, Ont., June 2, 1959.

			Regular Season					Playoffs				
Season	Club	Lea	GP	G	A	TP	PIM	GP	G	A	TP	PIM
1977-78	Oshawa	OHA	59	17	18	35	81	6	2	1	3	10
1978-79	Oshawa	OHA	64	20	38	58	108	5	3	4	7	12
1979-80	Houston	CHL	79	14	34	48	46	6	1	0	1	2
1980-81	Edmonton	NHL	12	2	5	7	6	....	....	....	....	....
	Wichita	CHL	47	8	36	44	71	17	3	11	14	10
1981-82	Wichita	CHL	32	7	19	26	51	....	....	....	....	....
	Edmonton	NHL	41	4	11	15	46	5	1	2	3	14
1982-83a	Edmonton	NHL	76	20	37	57	58	15	1	6	7	10
1983-84	Edmonton	NHL	75	8	34	42	43	12	1	9	10	8
1984-85	Edmonton	NHL	80	7	44	51	46	18	3	17	20	17
1985-86	Edmonton	NHL	76	6	35	41	55	7	0	2	2	0
1986-87	Edmonton	NHL	58	4	15	19	35	21	1	7	8	21
1987-88	Edmonton	NHL	77	13	28	41	71	13	4	5	9	10
1988-89	Edmonton	NHL	76	11	33	44	52	7	2	0	2	4
1989-90	Edmonton	NHL	70	1	23	24	56	22	0	6	6	11
	NHL Totals		641	76	265	341	468	120	13	54	67	95

a NHL Plus/Minus Leader (1983)

Signed as a free agent by **Edmonton**, September 14, 1979.

HUDSON, MIKE

Left wing. Shoots left. 6'1", 185 lbs.   Born, Guelph, Ont., February 6, 1967.
(Chicago's 6th choice, 140th overall, in 1986 Entry Draft).

			Regular Season					Playoffs				
Season	Club	Lea	GP	G	A	TP	PIM	GP	G	A	TP	PIM
1984-85	Hamilton	OHL	50	10	12	22	13	....	....	....	....	....
1985-86	Hamilton	OHL	7	3	2	5	4	....	....	....	....	....
	Sudbury	OHL	59	35	42	77	20	4	2	5	7	7
1986-87	Sudbury	OHL	63	40	57	97	18	....	....	....	....	....
1987-88	Saginaw	IHL	75	18	30	48	44	10	2	3	5	20
1988-89	Chicago	NHL	41	7	16	23	20	10	1	2	3	18
	Saginaw	IHL	30	15	17	32	10	....	....	....	....	....
1989-90	Chicago	NHL	49	9	12	21	56	4	0	0	0	2
	NHL Totals		90	16	28	44	76	14	1	2	3	20

HUFFMAN, KERRY

Defense. Shoots left. 6'2", 207 lbs. Born, Peterborough, Ont., January 3, 1968.
(Philadelphia's 1st choice, 20th overall, in 1986 Entry Draft).

			Regular Season					Playoffs				
Season	Club	Lea	GP	G	A	TP	PIM	GP	G	A	TP	PIM
1985-86	Guelph	OHL	56	3	24	27	35	20	1	10	11	10
1986-87	**Philadelphia**	**NHL**	**9**	**0**	**0**	**0**	**2**	....	....	....	....	....
	Hershey	AHL	3	0	1	1	0	4	0	0	0	0
a	Guelph	OHL	44	4	31	35	20	5	0	2	2	8
1987-88	**Philadelphia**	**NHL**	**52**	**6**	**17**	**23**	**34**	**2**	**0**	**0**	**0**	**0**
1988-89	**Philadelphia**	**NHL**	**29**	**0**	**11**	**11**	**31**	....	....	....	....	....
	Hershey	AHL	29	2	13	15	16	....	....	....	....	....
1989-90	**Philadelphia**	**NHL**	**43**	**1**	**12**	**13**	**34**	....	....	....	....	....
	NHL Totals		**133**	**7**	**40**	**47**	**101**	**2**	**0**	**0**	**0**	**0**

a OHL First All-Star Team (1987)

HUGHES, BRENT ALLEN

Left wing. Shoots left. 5'11", 185 lbs. Born, New Westminster, B.C., April 5, 1966.

			Regular Season					Playoffs				
Season	Club	Lea	GP	G	A	TP	PIM	GP	G	A	TP	PIM
1983-84	N. Westminster	WHL	67	21	18	39	133	9	2	2	4	27
1984-85	N. Westminster	WHL	64	25	32	57	135	11	2	1	3	37
1985-86	N. Westminster	WHL	71	28	52	80	180	....	....	....	....	....
1986-87	N. Westminster	WHL	8	5	4	9	22	....	....	....	....	....
	Victoria	WHL	61	38	61	99	146	5	4	1	5	8
1987-88	Moncton	AHL	73	13	19	32	206	....	....	....	....	....
1988-89	**Winnipeg**	**NHL**	**28**	**3**	**2**	**5**	**82**	....	....	....	....	....
	Moncton	AHL	54	34	34	68	286	10	9	4	13	40
1989-90	**Winnipeg**	**NHL**	**11**	**1**	**2**	**3**	**33**	....	....	....	....	....
	Moncton	AHL	65	31	29	60	277	....	....	....	....	....
	NHL Totals		**39**	**4**	**4**	**8**	**115**	....	....	....	....	....

Signed as a free agent by **Winnipeg**, June 13, 1988.

HUGHES, RYAN

Center. Shoots right. 6'1", 180 lbs. Born, Montreal, Que., January 17, 1972.
(Quebec's 2nd choice, 22nd overall, in 1990 Entry Draft).

			Regular Season					Playoffs				
Season	Club	Lea	GP	G	A	TP	PIM	GP	G	A	TP	PIM
1989-90	Cornell	ECAC	27	7	16	23	35	....	....	....	....	....

HULL, BRETT

Right wing. Shoots right. 5'11", 195 lbs. Born, Belleville, Ont., August 9, 1964.
(Calgary's 6th choice, 117th overall, in 1984 Entry Draft).

			Regular Season					Playoffs				
Season	Club	Lea	GP	G	A	TP	PIM	GP	G	A	TP	PIM
1984-85	Minn.-Duluth	WCHA	48	32	28	60	24	....	....	....	....	....
1985-86a	Minn.-Duluth	WCHA	42	52	32	84	46	....	....	....	....	....
	Calgary	**NHL**	....	....	....	....	....	**2**	**0**	**0**	**0**	**0**
1986-87	**Calgary**	**NHL**	**5**	**1**	**0**	**1**	**0**	**4**	**2**	**1**	**3**	**0**
bc	Moncton	AHL	67	50	42	92	16	3	2	2	4	2
1987-88	**Calgary**	**NHL**	**52**	**26**	**24**	**50**	**12**	....	....	....	....	....
	St. Louis	**NHL**	**13**	**6**	**8**	**14**	**4**	**10**	**7**	**2**	**9**	**4**
1988-89	**St. Louis**	**NHL**	**78**	**41**	**43**	**84**	**33**	**10**	**5**	**5**	**10**	**6**
1989-90def	**St. Louis**	**NHL**	**80**	***72**	**41**	**113**	**24**	**12**	**13**	**8**	**21**	**17**
	NHL Totals		**228**	**146**	**116**	**262**	**73**	**38**	**27**	**16**	**43**	**27**

a WCHA First All-Star Team (1986)
b AHL First All-Star Team (1987)
c Won Dudley "Red" Garrett Memorial Trophy (AHL's Top Rookie) (1987)
d NHL First All-Star Team (1990)
e Won Lady Byng Trophy (1990)
f Won Dodge Ram Tough Award (1990)

Played in NHL All-Star Game (1989, 1990)

Traded to **St. Louis** by **Calgary** with Steve Bozek for Rob Ramage and Rick Wamsley, March 7, 1988.

HULL, JODY

Right wing. Shoots right. 6'2", 200 lbs. Born, Cambridge, Ont., February 2, 1969.
(Hartford's 1st choice, 18th overall, in 1987 Entry Draft).

			Regular Season					Playoffs				
Season	Club	Lea	GP	G	A	TP	PIM	GP	G	A	TP	PIM
1985-86	Peterborough	OHL	61	20	22	42	29	16	1	5	6	4
1986-87	Peterborough	OHL	49	18	34	52	22	12	4	9	13	14
1987-88a	Peterborough	OHL	60	50	44	94	33	12	10	8	18	8
1988-89	**Hartford**	**NHL**	**60**	**16**	**18**	**34**	**10**	**1**	**0**	**0**	**0**	**2**
1989-90	**Hartford**	**NHL**	**38**	**7**	**10**	**17**	**21**	....	....	....	....	....
	Binghamton	AHL	21	7	10	17	6	....	....	....	....	....
	NHL Totals		**98**	**23**	**28**	**51**	**31**	**1**	**0**	**0**	**0**	**2**

a OHL Second All-Star Team (1988)

Traded to **NY Rangers** by **Hartford** for Carey Wilson and future considerations, July 9, 1990.

HULST, KENT

Center. Shoots left. 6', 180 lbs. Born, St. Thomas, Ont., April 8, 1968.
(Toronto's 4th choice, 69th overall, in 1986 Entry Draft).

			Regular Season					Playoffs				
Season	Club	Lea	GP	G	A	TP	PIM	GP	G	A	TP	PIM
1985-86	Belleville	OHL	43	6	17	23	20	....	....	....	....	....
	Windsor	OHL	17	6	10	16	9	....	....	....	....	....
1986-87	Windsor	OHL	37	18	20	38	49	....	....	....	....	....
	Belleville	OHL	27	13	10	23	17	6	1	1	2	0
1987-88	Belleville	OHL	66	42	43	85	48	6	3	1	4	7
1988-89	Belleville	OHL	45	21	41	62	43	....	....	....	....	....
	Flint	IHL	7	0	1	1	4	....	....	....	....	....
	Newmarket	AHL	....	....	....	....	....	2	1	1	2	2
1989-90	Newmarket	AHL	80	26	34	60	29	....	....	....	....	....

HUNT, BRIAN

Center. Shoots left. 6', 200 lbs. Born, Richmond Hill, Ont., February 12, 1969.
(Winnipeg's 4th choice, 73rd overall, in 1988 Entry Draft).

			Regular Season					Playoffs				
Season	Club	Lea	GP	G	A	TP	PIM	GP	G	A	TP	PIM
1986-87	Oshawa	OHL	61	13	22	35	22	26	5	10	15	13
1987-88	Oshawa	OHL	65	39	56	95	21	7	1	3	4	4
1988-89	Oshawa	OHL	63	30	56	86	36	6	2	2	4	0
1989-90	Moncton	AHL	43	4	11	15	19	....	....	....	....	....

HUNT, CURTIS

Defense. Shoots left. 6', 195 lbs. Born, North Battleford, Sask., January 28, 1967.
(Vancouver's 9th choice, 172nd overall, in 1985 Entry Draft).

			Regular Season					Playoffs				
Season	Club	Lea	GP	G	A	TP	PIM	GP	G	A	TP	PIM
1984-85	Prince Albert	WHL	64	2	13	15	61	13	0	3	3	24
1985-86	Prince Albert	WHL	72	5	29	34	108	18	2	8	10	28
1986-87	Prince Albert	WHL	47	6	31	37	101	8	1	3	4	4
1987-88	Flint	IHL	76	4	17	21	181	2	0	0	0	16
	Fredericton	AHL	1	0	0	0	2	....	....	....	....	....
1988-89	Milwaukee	IHL	65	3	17	20	226	11	1	2	3	43
1989-90	Milwaukee	IHL	69	8	25	33	237	3	0	1	1	4

HUNTER, DALE ROBERT

Center. Shoots left. 5'10", 198 lbs. Born, Petrolia, Ont., July 31, 1960.
(Quebec's 2nd choice, 41st overall, in 1979 Entry Draft).

			Regular Season					Playoffs				
Season	Club	Lea	GP	G	A	TP	PIM	GP	G	A	TP	PIM
1978-79	Sudbury	OHA	59	42	68	110	188	10	4	12	16	47
1979-80	Sudbury	OHA	61	34	51	85	189	9	6	9	15	45
1980-81	**Quebec**	**NHL**	**80**	**19**	**44**	**63**	**226**	**5**	**4**	**2**	**6**	**34**
1981-82	**Quebec**	**NHL**	**80**	**22**	**50**	**72**	**272**	**16**	**3**	**7**	**10**	**52**
1982-83	**Quebec**	**NHL**	**80**	**17**	**46**	**63**	**206**	**4**	**2**	**1**	**3**	**24**
1983-84	**Quebec**	**NHL**	**77**	**24**	**55**	**79**	**232**	**9**	**2**	**3**	**5**	**41**
1984-85	**Quebec**	**NHL**	**80**	**20**	**52**	**72**	**209**	**17**	**4**	**6**	**10**	***97**
1985-86	**Quebec**	**NHL**	**80**	**28**	**42**	**70**	**265**	**3**	**0**	**0**	**0**	**15**
1986-87	**Quebec**	**NHL**	**46**	**10**	**29**	**39**	**135**	**13**	**1**	**7**	**8**	**56**
1987-88	**Washington**	**NHL**	**79**	**22**	**37**	**59**	**240**	**14**	**7**	**5**	**12**	**98**
1988-89	**Washington**	**NHL**	**80**	**20**	**37**	**57**	**219**	**6**	**0**	**4**	**4**	**29**
1989-90	**Washington**	**NHL**	**80**	**23**	**39**	**62**	**233**	**15**	**4**	**8**	**12**	**61**
	NHL Totals		**762**	**205**	**431**	**636**	**2237**	**102**	**27**	**43**	**70**	**507**

Traded to **Washington** by **Quebec** with Clint Malarchuk for Gaetan Duchesne, Alan Haworth, and Washington's first-round choice (Joe Sakic) in 1987 Entry Draft, June 13, 1987.

HUNTER, MARK

Right wing. Shoots right. 6', 205 lbs. Born, Petrolia, Ont., November 12, 1962.
(Montreal's 1st choice, 7th overall, in 1981 Entry Draft).

			Regular Season					Playoffs				
Season	Club	Lea	GP	G	A	TP	PIM	GP	G	A	TP	PIM
1979-80	Brantford	OHA	66	34	56	90	171	11	2	8	10	27
1980-81	Brantford	OHA	53	39	40	79	157	6	3	3	6	27
1981-82	**Montreal**	**NHL**	**71**	**18**	**11**	**29**	**143**	**5**	**0**	**0**	**0**	**20**
1982-83	**Montreal**	**NHL**	**31**	**8**	**8**	**16**	**73**	....	....	....	....	....
1983-84	**Montreal**	**NHL**	**22**	**6**	**4**	**10**	**42**	**14**	**2**	**1**	**3**	**69**
1984-85	**Montreal**	**NHL**	**72**	**21**	**12**	**33**	**123**	**11**	**0**	**3**	**3**	**13**
1985-86	**St. Louis**	**NHL**	**78**	**44**	**30**	**74**	**171**	**19**	**7**	**7**	**14**	**48**
1986-87	**St. Louis**	**NHL**	**74**	**36**	**33**	**69**	**167**	**5**	**0**	**3**	**3**	**10**
1987-88	**St. Louis**	**NHL**	**66**	**32**	**31**	**63**	**136**	**5**	**2**	**3**	**5**	**24**
1988-89	**Calgary**	**NHL**	**66**	**22**	**8**	**30**	**194**	**10**	**2**	**2**	**4**	**23**
1989-90	**Calgary**	**NHL**	**10**	**2**	**3**	**5**	**39**	....	....	....	....	....
	NHL Totals		**490**	**189**	**140**	**329**	**1088**	**69**	**13**	**19**	**32**	**207**

Played in NHL All-Star Game (1986)

Traded to **St. Louis** by **Montreal** with Michael Dark and Montreal's second (Herb Raglan); third (Nelson Emerson); fifth (Dan Brooks); and sixth (Rick Burchill) round choices in 1985 Entry Draft, for St. Louis' first (Jose Charbonneau); second (Todd Richard); fourth (Martin Desjardins); fifth (Tom Sagissor); and sixth (Don Dufresne) round choices in 1985 Entry Draft, June 15, 1985. Traded to **Calgary** by **St. Louis** with Doug Gilmour, Steve Bozek and Michael Dark for Mike Bullard, Craig Coxe and Tim Corkery, September 6, 1988.

HUNTER, TIMOTHY ROBERT (TIM)

Right wing. Shoots right. 6'2", 202 lbs. Born, Calgary, Alta., September 10, 1960.
(Atlanta's 4th choice, 54th overall, in 1979 Entry Draft).

			Regular Season					Playoffs				
Season	Club	Lea	GP	G	A	TP	PIM	GP	G	A	TP	PIM
1979-80	Seattle	WHL	72	14	53	67	311	12	1	2	3	41
1980-81	Birmingham	CHL	58	3	5	8	*236	....	....	....	....	....
	Nova Scotia	AHL	17	0	0	0	62	6	0	1	1	45
1981-82	**Calgary**	**NHL**	**2**	**0**	**0**	**0**	**9**	....	....	....	....	....
	Oklahoma City	CHL	55	4	12	16	222	....	....	....	....	....
1982-83	Colorado	CHL	46	5	12	17	225	....	....	....	....	....
	Calgary	**NHL**	**16**	**1**	**0**	**1**	**54**	**9**	**1**	**0**	**1**	***70**
1983-84	**Calgary**	**NHL**	**43**	**4**	**4**	**8**	**130**	**7**	**0**	**0**	**0**	**21**
1984-85	**Calgary**	**NHL**	**71**	**11**	**11**	**22**	**259**	**4**	**0**	**0**	**0**	**24**
1985-86	**Calgary**	**NHL**	**66**	**8**	**7**	**15**	**291**	**19**	**0**	**3**	**3**	**108**
1986-87	**Calgary**	**NHL**	**73**	**6**	**15**	**21**	***361**	**6**	**0**	**0**	**0**	**51**
1987-88	**Calgary**	**NHL**	**68**	**8**	**5**	**13**	**337**	**9**	**4**	**0**	**4**	**32**
1988-89	**Calgary**	**NHL**	**75**	**3**	**9**	**12**	***375**	**19**	**0**	**4**	**4**	**32**
1989-90	**Calgary**	**NHL**	**67**	**2**	**3**	**5**	**279**	**6**	**0**	**0**	**0**	**4**
	NHL Totals		**481**	**43**	**54**	**97**	**2095**	**79**	**5**	**7**	**12**	**342**

HURD, KELLY

Right wing. Shoots right. 5'11", 185 lbs. Born, Castlegar, B.C., May 13, 1968.
(Detroit's 6th choice, 143rd overall, in 1988 Entry Draft).

			Regular Season					Playoffs				
Season	Club	Lea	GP	G	A	TP	PIM	GP	G	A	TP	PIM
1987-88	Michigan Tech	WCHA	41	18	22	40	34	....	....	....	....	....
1988-89	Michigan Tech	WCHA	42	18	14	32	36	....	....	....	....	....
1989-90	Michigan Tech	WCHA	37	12	13	25	50	....	....	....	....	....

HURLBUT, MICHAEL

Defense. Shoots left. 6'2", 200 lbs.   Born, Massena, NY, July 10, 1966.
(NY Rangers' 1st choice, 5th overall, in 1988 Supplemental Draft).

				Regular Season					Playoffs			
Season	Club	Lea	GP	G	A	TP	PIM	GP	G	A	TP	PIM
1985-86	St. Lawrence	ECAC	25	2	10	12	40	.....	....	....	....	....
1986-87	St. Lawrence	ECAC	35	8	15	23	44	.....	....	....	....	....
1987-88	St. Lawrence	ECAC	38	6	12	18	18	.....	....	....	....	....
1988-89a	St. Lawrence	ECAC	36	8	25	33	30	.....	....	....	....	....
	Denver	IHL	8	0	2	2	13	4	1	2	3	2
1989-90	Flint	IHL	74	3	34	37	38	3	0	1	1	2

a ECAC First All-Star Team (1989)

HUSCROFT, JAMIE

Right wing. Shoots left. 6'2", 200 lbs.   Born, Lister, B.C., January 9, 1967.
(New Jersey's 9th choice, 171st overall, in 1985 Entry Draft).

				Regular Season					Playoffs			
Season	Club	Lea	GP	G	A	TP	PIM	GP	G	A	TP	PIM
1983-84	Seattle	WHL	63	0	12	12	77	5	0	0	0	15
1984-85	Seattle	WHL	69	3	13	16	273	.....	....	....	....	....
1985-86	Seattle	WHL	66	6	20	26	394	5	0	1	1	18
1986-87	Seattle	WHL	21	1	18	19	99	.....	....	....	....	....
	Medicine Hat	WHL	35	4	21	25	170	20	0	3	3	*125
1987-88	Utica	AHL	71	5	7	12	316	.....	....	....	....	....
	Flint	IHL	3	1	0	1	2	16	0	1	1	110
1988-89	New Jersey	NHL	15	0	2	2	51	.....	....	....	....	....
	Utica	AHL	41	2	10	12	215	5	0	0	0	40
1989-90	New Jersey	NHL	42	2	3	5	149	5	0	0	0	16
	Utica	AHL	22	3	6	9	122	.....	....	....	....	....
	NHL Totals		57	2	5	7	200	5	0	0	0	16

HUSS, ANDERS

Center. Shoots right. 5'11", 185 lbs.   Born, Garle, Sweden, April 6, 1964.
(Washington's 8th choice, 225th overall, in 1983 Entry Draft).

				Regular Season					Playoffs			
Season	Club	Lea	GP	G	A	TP	PIM	GP	G	A	TP	PIM
1985-86	Brynas	Swe.	36	20	7	27	36	3	0	0	0	0
1986-87	Brynas	Swe.	33	12	13	25	40	.....	....	....	....	....
1987-88	Brynas	Swe.	40	14	12	26	28	.....	....	....	....	....
1988-89	Brynas	Swe.	40	22	17	39	26	.....	....	....	....	....
1989-90	Brynas	Swe.	36	19	18	37	32	5	3	2	5	0

HYNES, GORD

Defense. Shoots left. 6'1", 170 lbs.   Born, Montreal, Que., July 22, 1966.
(Boston's 5th choice, 115th overall, in 1985 Entry Draft).

				Regular Season					Playoffs			
Season	Club	Lea	GP	G	A	TP	PIM	GP	G	A	TP	PIM
1983-84	Medicine Hat	WHL	72	5	14	19	39	14	0	0	0	0
1984-85	Medicine Hat	WHL	70	18	45	63	61	10	6	9	15	17
1985-86	Medicine Hat	WHL	58	22	39	61	45	25	8	15	23	32
1986-87	Moncton	AHL	69	2	19	21	21	4	0	0	0	2
1987-88	Maine	AHL	69	5	30	35	65	7	1	3	4	4
1988-89	Cdn. National	....	61	8	38	46	44	.....	....	....	....	....
1989-90	Cdn. National	....	12	3	1	4	4	.....	....	....	....	....
	Varese	Italy	29	13	36	49	16	3	3	3	6	0

IAFRATE, AL   (IGH-uh-FRAY-tee)

Defense. Shoots left. 6'3", 215 lbs.   Born, Dearborn, Mich., March 21, 1966.
(Toronto's 1st choice, 4th overall, in 1984 Entry Draft).

				Regular Season					Playoffs			
Season	Club	Lea	GP	G	A	TP	PIM	GP	G	A	TP	PIM
1983-84	U.S. National	....	55	4	17	21	26	.....	....	....	....	....
	U.S. Olympic	....	6	0	0	0	2	.....	....	....	....	....
	Belleville	OHL	10	2	4	6	2	3	0	1	1	5
1984-85	Toronto	NHL	68	5	16	21	51	.....	....	....	....	....
1985-86	Toronto	NHL	65	8	25	33	40	10	0	3	3	4
1986-87	Toronto	NHL	80	9	21	30	55	13	1	3	4	11
1987-88	Toronto	NHL	77	22	30	52	80	6	3	4	7	6
1988-89	Toronto	NHL	65	13	20	33	72	.....	....	....	....	....
1989-90	Toronto	NHL	75	21	42	63	135	.....	....	....	....	....
	NHL Totals		430	78	154	232	433	29	4	10	14	21

Played in NHL All-Star Game (1988, 1990)

IHNACAK, MIROSLAV   (IH-nuh-chehk)

Left wing. Shoots left. 5'11", 175 lbs.   Born, Poprad, Czechoslovakia, November 19, 1962.
(Toronto's 12th choice, 171st overall, in 1982 Entry Draft).

				Regular Season			PIM		Playoffs			PIM
Season	Club	Lea	GP	G	A	TP		GP	G	A	TP	
1984-85	Kocise	Czech.	43	35	31	66	68	.....	....	....	....	....
1985-86	Kocise	Czech	21	16	16	32	....	.....	....	....	....	....
	Toronto	NHL	21	2	4	6	27	.....	....	....	....	....
	St. Catharines	AHL	13	4	4	8	2	13	8	3	11	10
1986-87	Toronto	NHL	34	6	5	11	12	1	0	0	0	0
	Newmarket	AHL	32	11	17	28	6	.....	....	....	....	....
1987-88	Newmarket	AHL	51	11	17	28	24	.....	....	....	....	....
1988-89	Detroit	NHL	1	0	0	0	0	.....	....	....	....	....
	Adirondack	AHL	62	34	37	71	32	13	4	3	7	16
1989-90	Halifax	AHL	57	33	37	70	43	5	1	4	5	6
	NHL Totals		56	8	9	17	39	1	0	0	0	0

Signed as a free agent by **Detroit**, November 18, 1988.

IHNACAK, PETER   (IH-nuh-chehk)

Center. Shoots right. 5'11", 180 lbs.   Born, Poprad, Czechoslovakia, May 3, 1957.
(Toronto's 3rd choice, 25th overall, in 1982 Entry Draft).

				Regular Season					Playoffs			
Season	Club	Lea	GP	G	A	TP	PIM	GP	G	A	TP	PIM
1979-80	Sparta Praha	Czech	44	22	12	34	....	.....	....	....	....	....
1980-81	Sparta Praha	Czech	44	23	22	45	....	.....	....	....	....	....
1981-82	Sparta Praha	Czech	39	16	22	38	30	.....	....	....	....	....
1982-83	Toronto	NHL	80	28	38	66	44	.....	....	....	....	....
1983-84	Toronto	NHL	47	10	13	23	24	.....	....	....	....	....
1984-85	Toronto	NHL	70	22	22	44	24	.....	....	....	....	....
1985-86	Toronto	NHL	63	18	27	45	16	10	2	3	5	12
1986-87	Newmarket	AHL	8	2	6	8	0	.....	....	....	....	....
	Toronto	NHL	58	12	27	39	16	13	2	4	6	9
1987-88	Toronto	NHL	68	10	20	30	41	5	0	3	3	4
1988-89	Toronto	NHL	26	2	16	18	10	.....	....	....	....	....
	Newmarket	AHL	38	14	16	30	8	.....	....	....	....	....
1989-90	Toronto	NHL	5	0	2	2	0	.....	....	....	....	....
	Newmarket	AHL	72	26	47	73	40	.....	....	....	....	....
	NHL Totals		417	102	165	267	175	28	4	10	14	25

ILJINA, TIMO

Center. Shoots left. 5'11", 175 lbs.   Born, Oulu, Finland, June 6, 1966.
(Washington's 6th choice, 143rd overall, in 1984 Entry Draft).

				Regular Season					Playoffs			
Season	Club	Lea	GP	G	A	TP	PIM	GP	G	A	TP	PIM
1986-87	Karpat	Fin.	28	5	4	9	8	3	0	0	0	0
1987-88	Karpat	Fin.	44	17	15	32	14	.....	....	....	....	....
1988-89	Karpat	Fin.	43	8	22	30	20	.....	....	....	....	....
1989-90	JOKP	Fin.	44	2	19	21	23	.....	....	....	....	....

INGMAN, JAN

Left wing. Shoots left. 6'2", 190 lbs.   Born, Grums, Sweden, November 25, 1961.
(Montreal's 3rd choice, 19th overall, in 1981 Entry Draft).

				Regular Season					Playoffs			
Season	Club	Lea	GP	G	A	TP	PIM	GP	G	A	TP	PIM
1985-86	Farjestad	Swe.	33	19	12	31	20	7	4	1	5	4
1986-87	Farjestad	Swe.	28	9	11	20	14	.....	....	....	....	....
1987-88	Farjestad	Swe.	28	6	7	13	14	9	5	3	8	2
1988-89	Farjestad	Swe.	32	15	19	34	24	2	1	1	2	6
1989-90	Farjestad	Swe.	32	15	13	28	16	10	5	3	8	2

Rights traded to **Winnipeg** by **Montreal** with Steve Penney for Brian Hayward, August 19, 1986.

ISSEL, KIM   (IH-sehl)

Right wing. Shoots right. 6'4", 200 lbs.   Born, Regina, Sask., September 25, 1967.
(Edmonton's 1st choice, 21st overall, in 1986 Entry Draft).

				Regular Season					Playoffs			
Season	Club	Lea	GP	G	A	TP	PIM	GP	G	A	TP	PIM
1985-86	Prince Albert	WHL	68	29	39	68	41	19	6	7	13	6
1986-87	Prince Albert	WHL	70	31	44	75	55	6	1	2	3	17
1987-88	Nova Scotia	AHL	68	2	25	27	31	2	1	0	1	10
1988-89	Edmonton	NHL	4	0	0	0	0	.....	....	....	....	....
	Cape Breton	AHL	65	34	28	62	4	.....	....	....	....	....
1989-90	Cape Breton	AHL	62	36	32	68	46	6	1	3	4	10
	NHL Totals		4	0	0	0	0	.....	....	....	....	....

JABLONSKI, JEFF

Left wing. Shoots left. 6', 185 lbs.   Born, Toledo, OH, June 20, 1967.
(NY Islanders' 11th choice, 185th overall, in 1986 Entry Draft).

				Regular Season					Playoffs			
Season	Club	Lea	GP	G	A	TP	PIM	GP	G	A	TP	PIM
1986-87	Lake Superior	CCHA	40	17	10	27	42	.....	....	....	....	....
1987-88	Lake Superior	CCHA	46	13	12	25	54	.....	....	....	....	....
1988-89	Lake Superior	CCHA	45	11	12	23	48	.....	....	....	....	....
1989-90	Lake Superior	CCHA	46	38	33	71	82	.....	....	....	....	....

JACKSON, DANE

Right wing. Shoots right. 6'1", 190 lbs.   Born, Winnipeg, Man., May 17, 1970.
(Vancouver's 3rd choice, 44th overall, in 1988 Entry Draft).

				Regular Season					Playoffs			
Season	Club	Lea	GP	G	A	TP	PIM	GP	G	A	TP	PIM
1988-89	North Dakota	WCHA	30	4	5	9	33	.....	....	....	....	....
1989-90	North Dakota	WCHA	44	15	11	26	56	.....	....	....	....	....

JACKSON, JAMES KENNETH (JIM)

Right wing. Shoots right. 5'8", 185 lbs.   Born, Oshawa, Ont., February 1, 1960.

				Regular Season					Playoffs			
Season	Club	Lea	GP	G	A	TP	PIM	GP	G	A	TP	PIM
1976-77	Oshawa	OHA	65	13	40	53	26	.....	....	....	....	....
1977-78	Oshawa	OHA	68	33	47	80	60	6	2	2	4	26
1978-79	Niagara Falls	OHA	62	26	39	65	73	20	6	9	15	16
1979-80	Niagara Falls	OHA	66	29	57	86	55	10	7	8	15	8
1980-81	Richmond	EHL	58	17	43	60	42	10	1	0	1	4
1981-82	Muskegon	IHL	82	24	51	75	72	.....	....	....	....	....
1982-83	Colorado	CHL	30	10	16	26	4	.....	....	....	....	....
	Calgary	NHL	48	8	12	20	7	8	2	1	3	2
1983-84	Colorado	CHL	25	5	27	32	4	.....	....	....	....	....
	Calgary	NHL	49	6	14	20	13	6	1	1	2	4
1984-85	Calgary	NHL	10	1	4	5	0	.....	....	....	....	....
	Moncton	CHL	24	2	5	7	6	.....	....	....	....	....
1985-86	Rochester	AHL	65	16	32	48	10	.....	....	....	....	....
1986-87	Rochester	AHL	71	19	38	57	48	16	5	4	9	6
1987-88	Buffalo	NHL	5	2	0	2	0	.....	....	....	....	....
	Rochester	AHL	74	23	48	71	23	7	2	6	8	4
1988-89	Rochester	AHL	73	19	50	69	14	.....	....	....	....	....
1989-90	Rochester	AHL	77	16	37	53	14	9	1	5	6	4
	NHL Totals		112	17	30	47	20	14	3	2	5	6

Signed as free agent by **Calgary**, October 8, 1982. Signed as a free agent by **Buffalo**, September 26, 1985.

JACKSON, JEFF

Left wing. Shoots left. 6'1", 195 lbs. Born, Dresden, Ont., April 24, 1965.
(Toronto's 2nd choice, 28th overall, in 1983 Entry Draft).

			Regular Season					Playoffs				
Season	Club	Lea	GP	G	A	TP	PIM	GP	G	A	TP	PIM
1982-83	Brantford	OHL	64	18	25	43	63	8	1	1	2	27
1983-84	Brantford	OHL	58	27	42	69	78	2	0	1	1	0
1984-85	**Toronto**	**NHL**	**17**	**0**	**1**	**1**	**24**	....	....	....	....	....
	Hamilton	OHL	20	13	14	27	51	17	8	12	20	26
1985-86	**Toronto**	**NHL**	**5**	**1**	**2**	**3**	**2**	....	....	....	....	....
	St. Catharines	AHL	74	17	28	45	122	13	5	2	7	30
1986-87	**Toronto**	**NHL**	**55**	**8**	**7**	**15**	**64**	....	....	....	....	....
	Newmarket	AHL	7	3	6	9	13	....	....	....	....	....
	NY Rangers	**NHL**	**9**	**5**	**1**	**6**	**15**	**6**	**1**	**1**	**2**	**16**
1987-88	**Quebec**	**NHL**	**68**	**9**	**18**	**27**	**103**	....	....	....	....	....
1988-89	**Quebec**	**NHL**	**33**	**4**	**6**	**10**	**28**	....	....	....	....	....
1989-90	**Quebec**	**NHL**	**65**	**8**	**12**	**20**	**71**	....	....	....	....	....
	NHL Totals		**252**	**35**	**47**	**82**	**307**	**6**	**1**	**1**	**2**	**16**

Traded to **NY Rangers** by **Toronto** with Toronto's third-round choice (Rob Zamuner) in 1989 Entry Draft for Mark Osborne, March 5, 1987. Traded to **Quebec** by **NY Rangers** with Terry Carkner for John Ogrodnick and David Shaw, September, 30, 1987.

JACKSON, MICHAEL

Right wing. Shoots right. 6', 190 lbs. Born, Mississauga, Ont., February 4, 1969.
(Toronto's 12th choice, 213th overall, in 1989 Entry Draft).

			Regular Season					Playoffs				
Season	Club	Lea	GP	G	A	TP	PIM	GP	G	A	TP	PIM
1988-89	Toronto	OHL	55	16	51	67	180	6	2	6	8	2
1989-90	Cornwall	OHL	41	23	42	65	100	6	2	4	6	33

JAGR, JAROMIR

Left wing. Shoots left. 6'2", 200 lbs. Born, Kladno, Czechoslovakia, February 15, 1972.
(Pittsburgh's 1st choice, 5th overall, in 1990 Entry Draft).

			Regular Season					Playoffs				
Season	Club	Lea	GP	G	A	TP	PIM	GP	G	A	TP	PIM
1988-89	Kladno	Czech.	39	8	10	18	....	....	....	....	....	....
1989-90	Kladno	Czech.	51	30	30	60	....	....	....	....	....	....

JANNEY, CRAIG

Center. Shoots left. 6'1", 190 lbs. Born, Hartford, CT, September 26, 1967.
(Boston's 1st choice, 13th overall, in 1986 Entry Draft).

			Regular Season					Playoffs				
Season	Club	Lea	GP	G	A	TP	PIM	GP	G	A	TP	PIM
1985-86	Boston College	H.E.	34	13	14	27	8	....	....	....	....	....
1986-87ab	Boston College	H.E.	37	26	55	81	6	....	....	....	....	....
1987-88	**Boston**	**NHL**	**15**	**7**	**9**	**16**	**0**	**23**	**6**	**10**	**16**	**11**
	U.S. National	....	52	26	44	70	6	....	....	....	....	....
	U.S. Olympic	....	5	3	1	4	2	....	....	....	....	....
1988-89	**Boston**	**NHL**	**62**	**16**	**46**	**62**	**12**	**10**	**4**	**9**	**13**	**21**
1989-90	**Boston**	**NHL**	**55**	**24**	**38**	**62**	**4**	**18**	**3**	**19**	**22**	**2**
	NHL Totals		**132**	**47**	**93**	**140**	**16**	**51**	**13**	**38**	**51**	**34**

a Hockey East First All-Star Team (1987)
b NCAA East First All-American Team (1987)

JANSSENS, MARK

Center. Shoots left. 6'3", 200 lbs. Born, Surrey, B.C., May 19, 1968.
(NY Rangers' 4th choice, 72nd overall, in 1986 Entry Draft).

			Regular Season					Playoffs				
Season	Club	Lea	GP	G	A	TP	PIM	GP	G	A	TP	PIM
1985-86	Regina	WHL	71	25	38	63	146	9	0	2	2	17
1986-87	Regina	WHL	68	24	38	62	209	3	0	1	1	14
1987-88	**NY Rangers**	**NHL**	**1**	**0**	**0**	**0**	**0**	....	....	....	....	....
	Colorado	IHL	6	2	2	4	24	12	3	2	5	20
	Regina	WHL	71	39	51	90	202	4	3	4	7	6
1988-89	**NY Rangers**	**NHL**	**5**	**0**	**0**	**0**	**0**	....	....	....	....	....
	Denver	IHL	38	19	19	38	104	4	3	0	3	18
1989-90	**NY Rangers**	**NHL**	**80**	**5**	**8**	**13**	**161**	**9**	**2**	**1**	**3**	**10**
	NHL Totals		**86**	**5**	**8**	**13**	**161**	**9**	**2**	**1**	**3**	**10**

JAQUES, STEVE

Defense. Shoots right. 5'11", 180 lbs. Born, Burnaby, B.C., February 21, 1969.
(Los Angeles' 11th choice, 228th overall, in 1989 Entry Draft).

			Regular Season					Playoffs				
Season	Club	Lea	GP	G	A	TP	PIM	GP	G	A	TP	PIM
1987-88	N. Westminster	WHL	69	15	31	46	336	5	0	4	4	31
1988-89	Tri-Cities	WHL	61	18	34	52	233	2	0	0	0	9
1989-90a	Tri-Cities	WHL	64	20	64	84	185	6	1	2	3	55

a WHL West Second All-Star Team (1990)

JARVENPAA, HANNU

Right wing. Shoots left. 6', 193 lbs. Born, Ii, Finland, May 19, 1963.
(Winnipeg's 4th choice, 71st overall, in 1986 Entry Draft).

			Regular Season					Playoffs				
Season	Club	Lea	GP	G	A	TP	PIM	GP	G	A	TP	PIM
1984-85	Karpat	Fin.	34	12	12	24	45	7	2	2	4	2
1985-86	Karpat	Fin.	36	26	9	35	48	5	5	2	7	12
1986-87	**Winnipeg**	**NHL**	**20**	**1**	**8**	**9**	**8**	....	....	....	....	....
1987-88	**Winnipeg**	**NHL**	**41**	**6**	**11**	**17**	**34**	....	....	....	....	....
	Moncton	AHL	5	3	1	4	2	....	....	....	....	....
1988-89	**Winnipeg**	**NHL**	**53**	**4**	**7**	**11**	**41**	....	....	....	....	....
	Moncton	AHL	4	1	0	1	0	....	....	....	....	....
1989-90	Lukko	Fin.	38	12	15	27	48	....	....	....	....	....
	NHL Totals		**114**	**11**	**26**	**37**	**83**	....	....	....	....	....

JARVI, IIRO

Right wing. Shoots left. 6'1", 198 lbs. Born, Helsinki, Finland, March 23, 1965.
(Quebec's 3rd choice, 54th overall, in 1983 Entry Draft).

			Regular Season					Playoffs				
Season	Club	Lea	GP	G	A	TP	PIM	GP	G	A	TP	PIM
1985-86	IFK Helsinki	Fin.	29	7	6	13	19	10	4	6	10	2
1986-87	IFK Helsinki	Fin.	43	23	30	53	82	5	1	5	6	9
1987-88	IFK Helsinki	Fin.	44	21	20	41	68	5	2	1	3	7
1988-89	**Quebec**	**NHL**	**75**	**11**	**30**	**41**	**40**	....	....	....	....	....
1989-90	**Quebec**	**NHL**	**41**	**7**	**13**	**20**	**18**	....	....	....	....	....
	Halifax	AHL	26	4	13	17	4	....	....	....	....	....
	NHL Totals		**116**	**18**	**43**	**61**	**58**	....	....	....	....	....

JARVIS, WESLEY HERBERT (WES)

Center. Shoots left. 5'11", 185 lbs. Born, Toronto, Ont., May 30, 1958.
(Washington's 18th choice, 213th overall, in 1978 Amateur Draft).

			Regular Season					Playoffs				
Season	Club	Lea	GP	G	A	TP	PIM	GP	G	A	TP	PIM
1976-77	Sudbury	OHA	65	36	60	96	24	6	3	2	5	7
1977-78	Sudbury	OHA	21	7	16	23	16	....	....	....	....	....
	Windsor	OHA	44	27	51	78	37	6	0	2	2	0
1978-79	Port Huron	IHL	73	44	65	109	39	7	4	4	8	2
1979-80	**Washington**	**NHL**	**63**	**11**	**15**	**26**	**8**	....	....	....	....	....
	Hershey	AHL	16	6	14	20	4	....	....	....	....	....
1980-81	**Washington**	**NHL**	**55**	**9**	**14**	**23**	**30**	....	....	....	....	....
	Hershey	AHL	24	15	25	40	39	10	3	13	16	2
1981-82	**Washington**	**NHL**	**26**	**1**	**12**	**13**	**18**	....	....	....	....	....
	Hershey	AHL	56	31	61	92	44	5	3	4	7	4
1982-83	**Minnesota**	**NHL**	**3**	**0**	**0**	**0**	**2**	....	....	....	....	....
	Birmingham	CHL	75	40	*68	*108	36	13	8	8	16	4
1983-84	**Los Angeles**	**NHL**	**61**	**9**	**13**	**22**	**36**	....	....	....	....	....
1984-85	**Toronto**	**NHL**	**26**	**0**	**1**	**1**	**2**	....	....	....	....	....
	St. Catharines	AHL	52	29	44	73	22	....	....	....	....	....
1985-86	**Toronto**	**NHL**	**2**	**1**	**0**	**1**	**2**	....	....	....	....	....
	St. Catharines	AHL	74	36	60	96	38	13	5	8	13	12
1986-87	**Toronto**	**NHL**	....	....	....	....	....	**2**	**0**	**0**	**0**	**2**
	Newmarket	AHL	70	28	50	78	32	....	....	....	....	....
1987-88	**Toronto**	**NHL**	**1**	**0**	**0**	**0**	**0**	....	....	....	....	....
	Newmarket	AHL	79	25	59	84	48	....	....	....	....	....
1988-89	Newmarket	AHL	52	22	31	53	38	5	2	4	6	4
1989-90	Newmarket	AHL	36	13	22	35	18	....	....	....	....	....
	NHL Totals		**237**	**31**	**55**	**86**	**98**	**2**	**0**	**0**	**0**	**2**

Traded to **Minnesota** by **Washington** with Rollie Boutin for Robbie Moore and Minnesota's eleventh round choice (Anders Huss) in the 1983 Entry Draft, August 4, 1982. Signed as free agent by **Los Angeles**, August 10, 1983. Signed as a free agent by **Toronto**, October 2, 1984.

JENNINGS, GRANT

Defense. Shoots left. 6'4", 220 lbs. Born, Hudson Bay, Sask., May 5, 1965.

			Regular Season					Playoffs				
Season	Club	Lea	GP	G	A	TP	PIM	GP	G	A	TP	PIM
1983-84	Saskatoon	WHL	64	5	13	18	102	....	....	....	....	....
1984-85	Saskatoon	WHL	47	10	24	34	134	2	1	0	1	2
1985-86	Binghamton	AHL	51	0	4	4	109	....	....	....	....	....
1986-87	Fort Wayne	IHL	3	0	0	0	0	....	....	....	....	....
	Binghamton	AHL	47	1	5	6	125	13	0	2	2	17
1987-88	**Washington**	**NHL**	....	....	....	....	....	**1**	**0**	**0**	**0**	**0**
	Binghamton	AHL	56	2	12	14	195	3	1	0	1	15
1988-89	**Hartford**	**NHL**	**55**	**3**	**10**	**13**	**159**	**4**	**1**	**0**	**1**	**17**
	Binghamton	AHL	2	0	0	0	2	....	....	....	....	....
1989-90	**Hartford**	**NHL**	**64**	**3**	**6**	**9**	**171**	**7**	**0**	**0**	**0**	**13**
	NHL Totals		**119**	**6**	**16**	**22**	**330**	**12**	**1**	**0**	**1**	**30**

Signed as a free agent by **Washington**, June 25, 1985. Traded to **Hartford** by **Washington** with Ed Kastelic for Mike Millar and Neil Sheehy, July 6, 1988.

JENSEN, CHRIS

Right wing. Shoots right. 5'11", 180 lbs. Born, Fort St. John, B.C., October 28, 1963.
(NY Rangers' 4th choice, 78th overall, in 1982 Entry Draft).

			Regular Season					Playoffs				
Season	Club	Lea	GP	G	A	TP	PIM	GP	G	A	TP	PIM
1982-83	North Dakota	WCHA	13	3	3	6	28	....	....	....	....	....
1983-84	North Dakota	WCHA	44	24	25	49	100	....	....	....	....	....
1984-85	North Dakota	WCHA	40	25	27	52	80	....	....	....	....	....
1985-86	North Dakota	WCHA	34	25	40	65	53	....	....	....	....	....
	NY Rangers	**NHL**	**9**	**1**	**3**	**4**	**0**	....	....	....	....	....
1986-87	**NY Rangers**	**NHL**	**37**	**6**	**7**	**13**	**21**	....	....	....	....	....
	New Haven	AHL	14	4	9	13	41	....	....	....	....	....
1987-88	**NY Rangers**	**NHL**	**7**	**0**	**1**	**1**	**2**	....	....	....	....	....
	Colorado	IHL	43	10	23	33	68	10	3	7	10	8
1988-89	Hershey	AHL	45	27	31	58	66	10	4	5	9	29
1989-90	**Philadelphia**	**NHL**	**1**	**0**	**0**	**0**	**0**	....	....	....	....	....
	Hershey	AHL	43	16	26	42	101	....	....	....	....	....
	NHL Totals		**54**	**7**	**11**	**18**	**23**	....	....	....	....	....

Traded to **Philadelphia** by **NY Rangers** for Michael Boyce, September 28, 1988.

JENSEN, DAVID A.

Center. Shoots left. 6'1", 195 lbs.   Born, Newton, MA, August 19, 1965.
(Hartford's 2nd choice, 20th overall, in 1983 Entry Draft).

			Regular Season					Playoffs				
Season	Club	Lea	GP	G	A	TP	PIM	GP	G	A	TP	PIM
1983-84	U.S. National	....	61	22	56	78	6	....	....	....	....	....
	U.S. Olympic	....	6	2	7	9	0	....	....	....	....	....
1984-85	**Hartford**	**NHL**	13	0	4	4	6	....	....	....	....	....
	Binghamton	AHL	40	8	9	17	2	....	....	....	....	....
1985-86	**Washington**	**NHL**	5	1	0	1	0	4	0	0	0	0
	Binghamton	AHL	41	17	14	31	4	4	2	4	6	0
1986-87	**Washington**	**NHL**	46	8	8	16	12	7	0	0	0	2
	Binghamton	AHL	6	2	5	7	0	....	....	....	....	....
1987-88	**Washington**	**NHL**	5	0	1	1	4	....	....	....	....	....
	Binghamton	AHL	9	5	2	7	2	....	....	....	....	....
	Fort Wayne	IHL	32	10	13	23	8	5	1	1	2	0
1988-89	Maine	AHL	18	12	8	20	2	....	....	....	....	....
1989-90	Maine	AHL	4	0	2	2	0	....	....	....	....	....
	NHL Totals		69	9	13	22	22	11	0	0	0	2

Traded to **Washington** by **Hartford** for Dean Evason and Peter Sidorkiewicz, March 12, 1985. Signed as a free agent by **Boston**, August 1, 1988.

JERRARD, PAUL

Right wing. Shoots right. 6'1", 185 lbs.   Born, Winnipeg, Man., April 30, 1965.
(NY Rangers' 10th choice, 173rd overall, in 1983 Entry Draft).

			Regular Season					Playoffs				
Season	Club	Lea	GP	G	A	TP	PIM	GP	G	A	TP	PIM
1983-84	Lake Superior	CCHA	40	8	18	26	48	....	....	....	....	....
1984-85	Lake Superior	CCHA	43	9	25	34	61	....	....	....	....	....
1985-86	Lake Superior	CCHA	38	13	11	24	34	....	....	....	....	....
1986-87	Lake Superior	CCHA	35	10	19	29	56	....	....	....	....	....
1987-88	Colorado	IHL	77	20	28	48	182	11	2	4	6	40
1988-89	**Minnesota**	**NHL**	5	0	0	0	4	....	....	....	....	....
	Denver	IHL	2	1	1	2	21	....	....	....	....	....
	Kalamazoo	IHL	68	15	25	40	195	6	2	1	3	37
1989-90	Kalamazoo	IHL	60	9	18	27	134	7	1	1	2	11
	NHL Totals		5	0	0	0	4					

Traded to **Minnesota** by **N.Y. Rangers** with Mark Tinordi, the rights to Bret Barnett and Mike Sullivan, and Los Angeles' third-round choice (Murray Garbutt) in 1989 Entry Draft – acquired March 10, 1987 by Minnesota – for Brian Lawton, Igor Liba and the rights to Eric Bennett, October 11, 1988.

JIRANEK, MARTIN

Center. Shoots left. 5'11", 170 lbs.   Born, Bashaw, Ont., October 3, 1969.
(Washington's 1st choice, 14th overall, in 1990 Supplemental Draft).

			Regular Season					Playoffs				
Season	Club	Lea	GP	G	A	TP	PIM	GP	G	A	TP	PIM
1988-89	Bowling Green	CCHA	41	9	18	27	36	....	....	....	....	....
1989-90	Bowling Green	CCHA	41	13	21	34	38	....	....	....	....	....

JOBE, TREVOR

Left wing. Shoots left. 6'1", 190 lbs.   Born, Lethbridge, Alta., May 14, 1967.
(Toronto's 7th choice, 133rd overall, in 1987 Entry Draft).

			Regular Season					Playoffs				
Season	Club	Lea	GP	G	A	TP	PIM	GP	G	A	TP	PIM
1984-85	Calgary	WHL	66	5	19	24	23	8	0	0	0	0
1985-86	Calgary	WHL	7	0	2	2	2	....	....	....	....	....
	Lethbridge	WHL	5	1	0	1	0	....	....	....	....	....
	Spokane	WHL	11	1	4	5	0	....	....	....	....	....
1986-87	Moose Jaw	WHL	58	54	33	87	53	9	4	2	6	4
1987-88	Moose Jaw	WHL	36	36	35	71	63	....	....	....	....	....
	Prince Albert	WHL	36	33	28	61	48	9	6	6	12	41
1988-89	Newmarket	AHL	75	23	24	47	90	5	0	1	1	12
1989-90	Newmarket	AHL	1	0	1	1	2	....	....	....	....	....
	Hampton-Roads	ECHL	51	48	23	71	143	5	5	5	10	30

JOHANNSON, CALLE   (yo-HAHN-suhn)

Defense. Shoots left. 5'11", 205 lbs.   Born, Goteborg, Sweden, February 14, 1967.
(Buffalo's 1st choice, 14th overall, in 1985 Entry Draft).

			Regular Season					Playoffs				
Season	Club	Lea	GP	G	A	TP	PIM	GP	G	A	TP	PIM
1983-84	V. Frolunda	Swe.	28	4	4	8	10	....	....	....	....	....
1984-85	V. Frolunda	Swe. 2	25	8	13	21	16	6	1	2	3	4
1985-86	Bjorkloven	Swe.	17	1	2	3	4	....	....	....	....	....
1986-87	Bjorkloven	Swe.	30	2	13	15	20	6	1	3	4	6
1987-88a	**Buffalo**	**NHL**	71	4	38	42	37	6	0	1	1	0
1988-89	**Buffalo**	**NHL**	47	2	11	13	33	....	....	....	....	....
	Washington	**NHL**	12	1	7	8	4	6	1	2	3	0
1989-90	**Washington**	**NHL**	70	8	31	39	25	15	1	6	7	4
	NHL Totals		200	15	87	102	99	27	2	9	11	4

a Named to NHL All-Rookie Team (1988)

Traded to **Washington** by **Buffalo** with Buffalo's second-round choice (Byron Dafoe) in 1989 Entry Draft for Clint Malarchuk, Grant Ledyard and Washington's sixth-round choice in 1991 Entry Draft, March 7, 1989.

JOHANSSON, JAMES (JIM)

Right wing. Shoots left. 6'2", 200 lbs.   Born, Rochester, MN, March 10, 1964.

			Regular Season					Playoffs				
Season	Club	Lea	GP	G	A	TP	PIM	GP	G	A	TP	PIM
1986-87	Landsberg	W.Ger.	57	46	56	102	90	....	....	....	....	....
1987-88	U.S. National	....	47	16	14	30	64	....	....	....	....	....
	U.S. Olympic	....	4	0	1	1	4	....	....	....	....	....
	Salt Lake	IHL	18	14	7	21	50	19	8	*15	23	55
1988-89	Salt Lake	IHL	82	35	40	75	87	13	2	5	7	13
1989-90	Salt Lake	IHL	82	22	41	63	74	14	1	4	5	6

Signed as a free agent by **Calgary**, February 25, 1988.

JOHANSSON, ROGER

Defense. Shoots left. 6'4", 190 lbs.   Born, Ljungby, Sweden, April 17, 1967.
(Calgary's 5th choice, 80th overall, in 1985 Entry Draft).

			Regular Season					Playoffs				
Season	Club	Lea	GP	G	A	TP	PIM	GP	G	A	TP	PIM
1986-87	Farjestad	Swe.	31	6	11	17	20	7	1	1	2	8
1987-88	Farjestad	Swe.	24	3	11	14	20	....	....	....	....	....
1988-89	Farjestad	Swe.	40	5	15	20	36	....	....	....	....	....
1989-90	**Calgary**	**NHL**	35	0	5	5	48	....	....	....	....	....
	NHL Totals		35	0	5	5	48					

JOHNSON, CHAD

Center. Shoots left. 6', 175 lbs.   Born, Grand Forks, ND, January 10, 1970.
(New Jersey's 7th choice, 117th overall, in 1988 Entry Draft).

			Regular Season					Playoffs				
Season	Club	Lea	GP	G	A	TP	PIM	GP	G	A	TP	PIM
1987-88	Rochester	USHL	36	15	26	41	43	....	....	....	....	....
1988-89	Rochester	USHL	34	14	24	38	59	4	1	2	3	2
1989-90	Minot	SJHL	54	33	43	76	89	....	....	....	....	....

JOHNSON, CRAIG

Center. Shoots left. 6'1", 180 lbs.   Born, St. Paul, MN, March 18, 1972.
(St. Louis' 1st choice, 33rd overall, in 1990 Entry Draft).

			Regular Season					Playoffs				
Season	Club	Lea	GP	G	A	TP	PIM	GP	G	A	TP	PIM
1988-89	Hill-Murray	HS	24	22	30	52	....	....	....	....	....	....
1989-90	Hill-Murray	HS	23	15	36	51	....	....	....	....	....	....

JOHNSON, GREG

Center. Shoots left. 5'11", 180 lbs.   Born, Thunder Bay, Ont., March 16, 1971.
(Philadelphia's 1st choice, 33rd overall, in 1989 Entry Draft).

			Regular Season					Playoffs				
Season	Club	Lea	GP	G	A	TP	PIM	GP	G	A	TP	PIM
1988-89abc	Thunder Bay	USHL	47	32	64	96	4	12	5	13	18	....
1989-90	North Dakota	WCHA	44	17	38	55	11	....	....	....	....	....

a Canadian Junior A Player of the Year (1989)
b USHL First All-Star Team (1989)
c Centennial Cup First All-Star Team (1989)

JOHNSON, JIM

Defense. Shoots left. 6'1", 190 lbs.   Born, New Hope, MN, August 9, 1962.

			Regular Season					Playoffs				
Season	Club	Lea	GP	G	A	TP	PIM	GP	G	A	TP	PIM
1981-82	Minn.-Duluth	WCHA	40	0	10	10	62	....	....	....	....	....
1982-83	Minn.-Duluth	WCHA	44	3	18	21	118	....	....	....	....	....
1983-84	Minn.-Duluth	WCHA	43	3	13	16	116	....	....	....	....	....
1984-85	Minn.-Duluth	WCHA	47	7	29	36	49	....	....	....	....	....
1985-86	**Pittsburgh**	**NHL**	80	3	26	29	115	....	....	....	....	....
1986-87	**Pittsburgh**	**NHL**	80	5	25	30	116	....	....	....	....	....
1987-88	**Pittsburgh**	**NHL**	55	1	12	13	87	....	....	....	....	....
1988-89	**Pittsburgh**	**NHL**	76	2	14	16	163	11	0	5	5	44
1989-90	**Pittsburgh**	**NHL**	75	3	13	16	154	....	....	....	....	....
	NHL Totals		366	14	90	104	635	11	0	5	5	44

Signed as a free agent by **Pittsburgh**, June 9, 1985.

JOHNSON, MARK

Center. Shoots left. 5'9", 170 lbs.   Born, Madison, WI, September 22, 1957.
(Pittsburgh's 3rd choice, 66th overall, in 1977 Amateur Draft).

			Regular Season					Playoffs				
Season	Club	Lea	GP	G	A	TP	PIM	GP	G	A	TP	PIM
1977-78a	U. Wisconsin	WCHA	42	*48	38	86	24	....	....	....	....	....
1978-79ab	U. Wisconsin	WCHA	40	*41	49	*90	34	....	....	....	....	....
1979-80	U.S. National	...	53	33	48	81	25	....	....	....	....	....
	U.S. Olympic	...	7	5	6	11	6	....	....	....	....	....
	Pittsburgh	**NHL**	17	3	5	8	4	5	2	2	4	0
1980-81	**Pittsburgh**	**NHL**	73	10	23	33	50	5	2	1	3	6
1981-82	**Pittsburgh**	**NHL**	46	10	11	21	30	....	....	....	....	....
	Minnesota	**NHL**	10	2	2	4	10	4	2	0	2	0
1982-83	**Hartford**	**NHL**	73	31	38	69	28	....	....	....	....	....
1983-84	**Hartford**	**NHL**	79	35	52	87	27	....	....	....	....	....
1984-85	**Hartford**	**NHL**	49	19	28	47	21	....	....	....	....	....
	St. Louis	**NHL**	17	4	6	10	2	3	0	1	1	0
1985-86	**New Jersey**	**NHL**	80	21	41	62	16	....	....	....	....	....
1986-87	**New Jersey**	**NHL**	68	25	26	51	22	....	....	....	....	....
1987-88	**New Jersey**	**NHL**	54	14	19	33	14	18	10	8	18	4
1988-89	**New Jersey**	**NHL**	40	13	25	38	24	....	....	....	....	....
1989-90	**New Jersey**	**NHL**	63	16	29	45	12	2	0	0	0	0
	NHL Totals		669	203	305	508	260	37	16	12	28	10

a WCHA First All-Star Team (1978, 1979)
b WCHA Player of the Year (1979)
Played in NHL All-Star Game (1984)

Traded to **Minnesota** by **Pittsburgh** for Minnesota's second round choice (Tim Hrynewich) in 1982 Entry Draft, March 2, 1982. Traded to **Hartford** by **Minnesota** with Kent-Erik Andersson for Jordy Douglas and Hartford's fifth round choice (Jiri Poner) in the 1984 Entry Draft, October 1, 1982. Traded to **St. Louis** by **Hartford** with Greg Millen for Mike Liut and Jorgen Pettersson, February 21, 1985. Traded to **New Jersey** by **St. Louis** for Shawn Evans and New Jersey's fifth-round choice (Michael Wolak) in 1986 Entry Draft, September 19, 1985.

JOHNSON, ROSS

Center. Shoots right. 5'11", 180 lbs.   Born, Green Bay, WI, August 5, 1967.
(Minnesota's 6th choice, 153rd overall, in 1985 Entry Draft).

			Regular Season					Playoffs				
Season	Club	Lea	GP	G	A	TP	PIM	GP	G	A	TP	PIM
1988-89	North Dakota	WCHA	19	5	7	12	6	....	....	....	....	....
1989-90	North Dakota	WCHA	43	6	9	15	22	....	....	....	....	....

JOHNSON, STEVE

Right wing. Shoots right. 6′, 190 lbs.   Born, Grand Forks, ND, March 3, 1966.
(Vancouver's 1st choice, 3rd overall, in 1987 Supplemental Draft).

			Regular Season					Playoffs			
Season	Club	Lea	GP	G	A	TP	PIM	GP	G	A	TP	PIM
1984-85	North Dakota	WCHA	41	18	16	34	10	....	....	....	....	....
1985-86	North Dakota	WCHA	38	31	28	59	40	....	....	....	....	....
1986-87	North Dakota	WCHA	48	26	44	70	38	....	....	....	....	....
1987-88ab	North Dakota	WCHA	42	34	*51	*85	28	....	....	....	....	....
1988-89	Milwaukee	IHL	64	18	34	52	37	2	0	0	0	0
1989-90	Milwaukee	IHL	5	0	2	2	0	....	....	....	....	....
	Phoenix	IHL	65	21	49	70	31	....	....	....	....	....

a WCHA First All-Star Team (1988)
b NCAA West First All-American Team (1988)

JOHNSTON, GREG

Right wing. Shoots right. 6′1″, 190 lbs.   Born, Barrie, Ont., January 14, 1965.
(Boston's 2nd choice, 42nd overall, in 1983 Entry Draft).

			Regular Season					Playoffs			
Season	Club	Lea	GP	G	A	TP	PIM	GP	G	A	TP	PIM
1982-83	Toronto	OHL	58	18	19	37	58	4	1	0	1	4
1983-84	**Boston**	**NHL**	15	2	1	3	2	....	....	....	....	....
	Toronto	OHL	57	38	35	73	67	9	4	2	6	13
1984-85	**Boston**	**NHL**	6	0	0	0	0	....	....	....	....	....
	Hershey	AHL	3	1	0	1	0	....	....	....	....	....
	Toronto	OHL	42	22	28	50	55	5	1	3	4	4
1985-86	**Boston**	**NHL**	20	0	2	2	0	....	....	....	....	....
	Moncton	AHL	60	19	26	45	56	10	4	6	10	4
1986-87	**Boston**	**NHL**	76	12	15	27	79	4	0	0	0	0
1987-88	**Boston**	**NHL**	....	....	....	....	....	3	0	1	1	2
	Maine	AHL	75	21	32	53	106	10	6	4	10	23
1988-89	**Boston**	**NHL**	57	11	10	21	32	10	1	0	1	6
	Maine	AHL	15	5	7	12	31	....	....	....	....	....
1989-90	**Boston**	**NHL**	9	1	1	2	6	5	1	0	1	4
	Maine	AHL	52	16	26	42	45	....	....	....	....	....
	NHL Totals		**183**	**26**	**29**	**55**	**119**	**22**	**2**	**1**	**3**	**12**

Traded to **NY Rangers** by **Boston** with future considerations for Chris Nilan, June 28, 1990.
Traded to **Toronto** by **NY Rangers** for Tie Domi and Mark Laforest, June 28, 1990.

JONES, BRAD

Left wing. Shoots left. 6′, 195 lbs.   Born, Sterling Heights, MI, June 26, 1965.
(Winnipeg's 7th choice, 156th overall, in 1984 Entry Draft).

			Regular Season					Playoffs			
Season	Club	Lea	GP	G	A	TP	PIM	GP	G	A	TP	PIM
1983-84	U. of Michigan	CCHA	37	8	26	34	32	....	....	....	....	....
1984-85	U. of Michigan	CCHA	34	21	27	48	66	....	....	....	....	....
1985-86a	U. of Michigan	CCHA	36	28	39	67	40	....	....	....	....	....
1986-87bc	U. of Michigan	CCHA	40	32	46	78	64	....	....	....	....	....
	Winnipeg	**NHL**	4	1	0	1	0	....	....	....	....	....
1987-88	**Winnipeg**	**NHL**	19	2	5	7	15	1	0	0	0	0
	U.S. National	....	50	27	23	50	59	....	....	....	....	....
1988-89	**Winnipeg**	**NHL**	22	6	5	11	6	....	....	....	....	....
	Moncton	AHL	44	20	19	39	62	7	0	1	1	22
1989-90	**Winnipeg**	**NHL**	2	0	0	0	0	....	....	....	....	....
	Moncton	AHL	15	5	6	11	47	....	....	....	....	....
	New Haven	AHL	36	8	11	19	71	....	....	....	....	....
	NHL Totals		**47**	**9**	**10**	**19**	**21**	**1**	**0**	**0**	**0**	**0**

a CCHA Second All-Star Team (1986)
b CCHA First All-Star Team (1987)
c NCAA West Second All-American Team (1987)

Traded to **Los Angeles** by **Winnipeg** for Phil Sykes, December 1, 1989.

JONES, CASEY

Center. Shoots left. 5′11″, 170 lbs.   Born, Temiscaming, Que., May 30, 1968.
(Boston's 10th choice, 230th overall, in 1987 Entry Draft).

			Regular Season					Playoffs			
Season	Club	Lea	GP	G	A	TP	PIM	GP	G	A	TP	PIM
1986-87	Cornell	ECAC	27	6	12	18	38	....	....	....	....	....
1987-88	Cornell	ECAC	27	10	22	32	26	....	....	....	....	....
1988-89	Cornell	ECAC	29	8	27	35	22	....	....	....	....	....
1989-90	Cornell	ECAC	27	6	*21	27	22	....	....	....	....	....

JONES, KEITH

Right wing. Shoots right. 6′2″, 190 lbs.   Born, Brantford, Ont., November 8, 1968.
(Washington's 7th choice, 141st overall, in 1988 Entry Draft).

			Regular Season					Playoffs			
Season	Club	Lea	GP	G	A	TP	PIM	GP	G	A	TP	PIM
1988-89	W. Michigan	CCHA	37	9	12	21	51	....	....	....	....	....
1989-90	W. Michigan	CCHA	40	19	18	37	82	....	....	....	....	....

JONSSON, STEFAN

Defense. Shoots left. 6′2″, 190 lbs.   Born, Sodertalje, Sweden, June 13, 1965.
(Calgary's 11th choice, 222nd overall, in 1984 Entry Draft).

			Regular Season					Playoffs			
Season	Club	Lea	GP	G	A	TP	PIM	GP	G	A	TP	PIM
1987-88	Sodertalje	Swe.	36	4	6	10	24	2	0	0	0	8
1988-89	Sodertalje	Swe.	37	4	2	6	44	....	....	....	....	....
1989-90	Sodertalje	Swe.	37	5	10	15	62	2	0	1	1	0

JONSSON, TOMAS   (YAHN-suhn)

Defense. Shoots left. 5′10″, 185 lbs.   Born, Falun, Sweden, April 12, 1960.
(NY Islanders' 2nd choice, 25th overall, in 1979 Entry Draft).

			Regular Season					Playoffs			
Season	Club	Lea	GP	G	A	TP	PIM	GP	G	A	TP	PIM
1978-79	MoDo AIK	Swe.	34	11	10	21	77	5	1	2	3	13
	Swe. National	....	15	2	3	5	16	....	....	....	....	....
1979-80	MoDo AIK	Swe.	36	3	12	15	42	....	....	....	....	....
	Swe. National	....	18	2	4	6	24	....	....	....	....	....
1980-81	MoDo AIK	Swe.	35	8	12	20	58	....	....	....	....	....
	Swe. National	....	19	0	2	2	2	....	....	....	....	....
1981-82	**NY Islanders**	**NHL**	70	9	25	34	51	10	0	2	2	21
1982-83	**NY Islanders**	**NHL**	72	13	35	48	50	20	2	10	12	18
1983-84	**NY Islanders**	**NHL**	72	11	36	47	54	21	3	5	8	22
1984-85	**NY Islanders**	**NHL**	69	16	34	50	58	7	1	2	3	10
1985-86	**NY Islanders**	**NHL**	77	14	30	44	62	3	0	1	1	4
1986-87	**NY Islanders**	**NHL**	47	6	25	31	36	10	1	4	5	6
1987-88	**NY Islanders**	**NHL**	72	6	41	47	115	5	2	2	4	10
1988-89	**NY Islanders**	**NHL**	53	9	23	32	34	....	....	....	....	....
	Edmonton	**NHL**	20	1	10	11	22	4	2	0	2	6
1989-90	Leksands	Swe.	40	11	15	26	54	3	1	1	2	4
	NHL Totals		**552**	**85**	**259**	**344**	**482**	**80**	**11**	**26**	**37**	**97**

Traded to **Edmonton** by **NY Islanders** for future considerations, February 15, 1989.

JOSEPH, ANTHONY

Right wing. Shoots right. 6′4″, 220 lbs.   Born, Cornwall, Ont., March 1, 1969.
(Winnipeg's 5th choice, 94th overall, in 1988 Entry Draft).

			Regular Season					Playoffs			
Season	Club	Lea	GP	G	A	TP	PIM	GP	G	A	TP	PIM
1987-88	Oshawa	OHL	49	9	18	27	126	7	0	0	0	9
1988-89	**Winnipeg**	**NHL**	2	1	0	1	0	....	....	....	....	....
	Oshawa	OHL	52	20	16	36	105	6	4	2	6	22
1989-90	Moncton	AHL	61	9	9	18	74	....	....	....	....	....
	NHL Totals		**2**	**1**	**0**	**1**	**0**	....	....	....	....	....

JOSEPH, CHRIS

Defense. Shoots right. 6′2″, 210 lbs.   Born, Burnaby, B.C., September 10, 1969.
(Pittsburgh's 1st choice, 5th overall, in 1987 Entry Draft).

			Regular Season					Playoffs			
Season	Club	Lea	GP	G	A	TP	PIM	GP	G	A	TP	PIM
1985-86	Seattle	WHL	72	4	8	12	50	5	0	3	3	12
1986-87	Seattle	WHL	67	13	45	58	155	....	....	....	....	....
1987-88	Seattle	WHL	23	5	14	19	49	....	....	....	....	....
	Pittsburgh	**NHL**	17	0	4	4	12	....	....	....	....	....
	Edmonton	**NHL**	7	0	4	4	6	....	....	....	....	....
	Nova Scotia	AHL	8	0	2	2	8	4	0	0	0	9
1988-89	**Edmonton**	**NHL**	44	4	5	9	54	....	....	....	....	....
	Cape Breton	AHL	5	1	1	2	18	....	....	....	....	....
1989-90	Cape Breton	AHL	61	10	20	30	69	6	2	1	3	4
	NHL Totals		**68**	**4**	**13**	**17**	**72**	....	....	....	....	....

Traded to **Edmonton** by **Pittsburgh** with Craig Simpson, Dave Hannan and Moe Mantha for Paul Coffey, Dave Hunter, and Wayne Van Dorp, November 24, 1987.

JOSEPH, FABIAN

Center. Shoots left. 5′8″, 165 lbs.   Born, Sydney, N.S., December 5, 1965.
(Toronto's 5th choice, 109th overall, in 1984 Entry Draft).

			Regular Season					Playoffs			
Season	Club	Lea	GP	G	A	TP	PIM	GP	G	A	TP	PIM
1982-83	Victoria	WHL	69	42	48	90	50	12	4	7	11	9
1983-84	Victoria	WHL	72	52	75	127	27	....	....	....	....	....
1984-85	Toronto	OHL	60	32	43	75	16	5	2	4	6	14
1985-86	Cdn. Olympic	....	71	26	18	44	51	....	....	....	....	....
1986-87	Cdn. Olympic	....	74	15	30	45	26	....	....	....	....	....
1987-88	Nova Scotia	AHL	77	31	39	70	20	5	0	3	3	8
1988-89	Cape Breton	AHL	70	32	34	66	30	....	....	....	....	....
1989-90	Cape Breton	AHL	77	33	53	86	46	6	0	3	3	4

JOYCE, ROBERT THOMAS (BOB)

Left wing. Shoots left. 6′1″, 195 lbs.   Born, St. John, N.B., July 11, 1966.
(Boston's 4th choice, 82nd overall, in 1984 Entry Draft).

			Regular Season					Playoffs			
Season	Club	Lea	GP	G	A	TP	PIM	GP	G	A	TP	PIM
1984-85	North Dakota	WCHA	41	18	16	34	10	....	....	....	....	....
1985-86	North Dakota	WCHA	38	31	28	59	40	....	....	....	....	....
1986-87abc	North Dakota	WCHA	48	52	37	89	42	....	....	....	....	....
1987-88	**Boston**	**NHL**	15	7	5	12	10	23	8	6	14	18
	Cdn. National	....	46	12	10	22	28	....	....	....	....	....
	Cdn. Olympic	....	4	1	0	1	0	....	....	....	....	....
1988-89	**Boston**	**NHL**	77	18	31	49	46	9	5	2	7	2
1989-90	**Boston**	**NHL**	23	1	2	3	22	....	....	....	....	....
	Washington	**NHL**	24	5	8	13	4	14	2	1	3	9
	NHL Totals		**139**	**31**	**46**	**77**	**82**	**46**	**15**	**9**	**24**	**29**

a WCHA First All-Star Team (1987)
b NCAA West First All-American Team (1987)
c Named to NCAA All-Tournament Team (1987)

Traded to **Washington** by **Boston** for Dave Christian, December 13, 1989.

JUDSON, RICK

Left wing. Shoots left. 5′11″, 180 lbs.   Born, Toledo, OH, August 13, 1969.
(Detroit's 11th choice, 204th overall, in 1989 Entry Draft).

			Regular Season					Playoffs			
Season	Club	Lea	GP	G	A	TP	PIM	GP	G	A	TP	PIM
1988-89	Ill.-Chicago	CCHA	42	14	20	34	20	....	....	....	....	....
1989-90	Ill.-Chicago	CCHA	38	19	22	41	18	....	....	....	....	....

JUHLIN, PATRIK

Left wing. Shoots left. 6'0", 185 lbs.   Born, Huddinge, Sweden, April 24, 1970.
(Philadelphia's 2nd choice, 34th overall, in 1989 Entry Draft).

			Regular Season					Playoffs				
Season	Club	Lea	GP	G	A	TP	PIM	GP	G	A	TP	PIM
1987-88	Vasteras	Swe.	28	25	10	35	....					
1988-89	Vasteras	Swe.	30	29	13	42	....					
1989-90	Vasteras	Swe.	35	10	13	23	18	2	0	0	0	0

JULIEN, CLAUDE

Defense. Shoots right. 6', 198 lbs.   Born, Blind River, Ont., April 23, 1960.

			Regular Season					Playoffs				
Season	Club	Lea	GP	G	A	TP	PIM	GP	G	A	TP	PIM
1979-80	Windsor	OHA	68	14	37	51	148	16	5	11	16	23
1980-81	Windsor	OHA	3	1	1	2	21	....				
	Port Huron	IHL	77	15	40	55	153	4	1	1	2	4
1981-82	Salt Lake	CHL	70	4	18	22	134	5	1	4	5	0
1982-83	Salt Lake	CHL	76	14	47	61	176	6	3	3	6	16
1983-84	Milwaukee	IHL	5	0	3	3	2	....				
	Fredericton	AHL	57	7	22	29	58	7	0	4	4	6
1984-85	**Quebec**	**NHL**	**1**	**0**	**0**	**0**	**0**	....				
	Fredericton	AHL	77	6	28	34	97	6	2	4	6	13
1985-86	**Quebec**	**NHL**	**13**	**0**	**1**	**1**	**25**	....				
	Fredericton	AHL	49	3	18	21	74	6	1	4	5	19
1986-87	Fredericton	AHL	17	1	6	7	22	....				
	France	....	36	15	50	65	....					
1987-88	Baltimore	AHL	30	6	14	20	22	....				
	Fredericton	AHL	35	1	14	15	52	13	1	3	4	30
1988-89a	Halifax	AHL	79	8	52	60	72	4	0	2	2	4
1989-90	Halifax	AHL	77	6	37	43	65	4	0	1	1	7
	NHL Totals		**14**	**0**	**1**	**1**	**25**	....				

a AHL Second All-Star Team (1989)

Signed as free agent by **St. Louis**, September 28, 1981. Rights transfered to **Quebec** by St. Louis with rights to Gord Donnelly when St. Louis signed Jacques Demers as coach, August 19, 1983.

JUNEAU, JOSEPH

Center. Shoots right. 6'0", 175 lbs.   Born, Pont-Rouge, Que., January 5, 1968.
(Boston's 3rd choice, 81st overall, in 1988 Entry Draft).

			Regular Season					Playoffs				
Season	Club	Lea	GP	G	A	TP	PIM	GP	G	A	TP	PIM
1987-88	RPI	ECAC	31	16	29	45	18	....				
1988-89	RPI	ECAC	30	12	23	35	40	....				
1989-90a	RPI	ECAC	34	18	*52	*70	31	....				

a NCAA East First All-American Team (1990)

KACHOWSKI, MARK EDWARD

Left wing. Shoots left. 5'10", 195 lbs.   Born, Edmonton, Alta., February 20, 1965.

			Regular Season					Playoffs				
Season	Club	Lea	GP	G	A	TP	PIM	GP	G	A	TP	PIM
1983-84	Kamloops	WHL	57	6	9	15	156	....				
1984-85	Kamloops	WHL	68	22	15	37	185	....				
1985-86	Kamloops	WHL	61	21	31	52	182	....				
1986-87	Flint	IHL	75	18	13	31	273	6	1	1	2	21
1987-88	**Pittsburgh**	**NHL**	**38**	**5**	**3**	**8**	**126**	....				
	Muskegon	IHL	25	3	6	9	72	5	0	2	2	11
1988-89	**Pittsburgh**	**NHL**	**12**	**1**	**1**	**2**	**43**	....				
	Muskegon	IHL	57	8	8	16	167	8	1	2	3	17
1989-90	**Pittsburgh**	**NHL**	**14**	**0**	**1**	**1**	**40**	....				
	Muskegon	IHL	61	23	8	31	129	12	2	4	6	21
	NHL Totals		**64**	**6**	**5**	**11**	**209**	....				

Signed as a free agent by **Pittsburgh**, August 31, 1987.

KADLEC, ARNOLD

Defense. Shoots left. 6'1", 200 lbs.   Born, Most, Czechoslovakia, January 8, 1959.
(Minnesota's 10th choice, 206th overall, in 1982 Entry Draft).

			Regular Season					Playoffs				
Season	Club	Lea	GP	G	A	TP	PIM	GP	G	A	TP	PIM
1986-87	CHZ Litvinov	Czech.	32	9	16	25		....				
1987-88	CHZ Litvinov	Czech.	29	0	13	13		....				
1988-89	CHZ Litvinov	Czech.	34	11	11	22		....				
1989-90	Lukko	Fin	29	4	11	15	36	....				

KADLEC, DRAHOMIR

Defense. Shoots left. 5'11", 200 lbs.   Born, Pribram, Czechoslovakia, November 29, 1965.
(Philadelphia's 13th choice, 245th overall, in 1988 Entry Draft).

			Regular Season					Playoffs				
Season	Club	Lea	GP	G	A	TP	PIM	GP	G	A	TP	PIM
1987-88	Dukla Jihlava	Czech.	29	3	7	10		....				
1988-89	Poldi Kladno	Czech.		7	14	21		....				
1989-90	Poldi Kladno	Czech.	49	8	21	29		....				

KAESE, TRENT   (KAY-see)

Right wing. Shoots right. 5'11", 225 lbs.   Born, Nanaimo, B.C., September 9, 1967.
(Buffalo's 8th choice, 161st overall, in 1985 Entry Draft).

			Regular Season					Playoffs				
Season	Club	Lea	GP	G	A	TP	PIM	GP	G	A	TP	PIM
1983-84	Lethbridge	WHL	64	6	6	12	33	1	0	0	0	0
1984-85	Lethbridge	WHL	67	20	18	38	107	4	0	1	1	7
1985-86	Lethbridge	WHL	67	24	41	65	67	10	5	3	8	8
1986-87	Swift Current	WHL	2	1	0	1	4	....				
	Calgary	WHL	68	30	24	54	117	....				
	Flint	IHL	1	0	0	0	0	6	4	1	5	9
1987-88	Rochester	AHL	37	6	11	17	32	3	1	2	3	2
	Flint	IHL	43	11	26	37	58	12	6	6	12	21
1988-89	**Buffalo**	**NHL**	**1**	**0**	**0**	**0**	**0**	....				
	Rochester	AHL	45	9	11	20	68	....				
	Flint	IHL	9	2	3	5	61	....				
1989-90	Phoenix	IHL	2	0	1	1	2	....				
	Winston-Salem	ECHL	57	56	51	107	110	8	5	1	6	18
	NHL Totals		**1**	**0**	**0**	**0**	**0**	....				

KAISER, KEVIN

Left wing. Shoots left. 6', 185 lbs.   Born, Winnipeg, Man., July 26, 1970.
(Quebec's 7th choice, 85th overall, in 1989 Entry Draft).

			Regular Season					Playoffs				
Season	Club	Lea	GP	G	A	TP	PIM	GP	G	A	TP	PIM
1988-89	Minn.-Duluth	WCHA	40	2	5	7	26	....				
1989-90	Minn.-Duluth	WCHA	39	9	11	20	24	....				

KAMENSKY, VALERI

Right wing. Shoots right. 6'0", 170 lbs.   Born, Voskresensk, Soviet Union, April 18, 1966.
(Quebec's 8th choice, 129th overall, in 1988 Entry Draft).

			Regular Season					Playoffs				
Season	Club	Lea	GP	G	A	TP	PIM	GP	G	A	TP	PIM
1982-83	Khimik	USSR	5	0	0	0	0	....				
1983-84	Khimik	USSR	20	2	2	4	6	....				
1984-85	Khimik	USSR	45	9	3	12	24	....				
1985-86	CSKA	USSR	40	15	9	24	8	....				
1986-87	CSKA	USSR	37	13	8	21	16	....				
1987-88	CSKA	USSR	51	26	20	46	40	....				
1988-89	CSKA	USSR	40	18	10	28	30	....				
1989-90	CSKA	USSR	45	19	18	37	38	....				

KAMES, VLADIMIR

Center. Shoots left. 5'11", 170 lbs.   Born, Czechoslovakia, September 23, 1965.
(New Jersey's 8th choice, 149th overall, in 1989 Entry Draft).

			Regular Season					Playoffs				
Season	Club	Lea	GP	G	A	TP	PIM	GP	G	A	TP	PIM
1988-89	Kladno	Czech.	34	11	22	33	28	....				
1989-90	Kladno	Czech.	42	17	27	44	....					

KAMINSKI, KEVIN

Center. Shoots left. 5'9", 170 lbs.   Born, Churchbridge, Sask., March 13, 1969.
(Minnesota's 3rd choice, 48th overall, in 1987 Entry Draft).

			Regular Season					Playoffs				
Season	Club	Lea	GP	G	A	TP	PIM	GP	G	A	TP	PIM
1986-87	Saskatoon	WHL	67	26	44	70	325	11	5	6	11	45
1987-88	Saskatoon	WHL	55	38	61	99	247	10	5	7	12	37
1988-89	**Minnesota**	**NHL**	**1**	**0**	**0**	**0**	**0**	....				
	Saskatoon	WHL	52	25	43	68	199	8	4	9	13	25
1989-90	**Quebec**	**NHL**	**1**	**0**	**0**	**0**	**0**	....				
	Halifax	AHL	19	3	4	7	128	2	0	0	0	5
	NHL Totals		**2**	**0**	**0**	**0**	**0**	....				

Traded to **Quebec** by **Minnesota** for Gaetan Duchesne, June 19, 1989.

KAMPERSAL, JEFFREY

Defense. Shoots right. 6'2", 190 lbs.   Born, Beverly, MA, January 27, 1970.
(NY Islanders' 12th choice, 205th overall, in 1988 Entry Draft).

			Regular Season					Playoffs				
Season	Club	Lea	GP	G	A	TP	PIM	GP	G	A	TP	PIM
1988-89	Princeton	ECAC	26	0	3	3	32	....				
1989-90	Princeton	ECAC	27	3	7	10	26	....				

KANE, SHAUN

Defense. Shoots left. 6'2", 180 lbs.   Born, Holyoke, MA, February 24, 1970.
(Minnesota's 3rd choice, 43rd overall, in 1988 Entry Draft).

			Regular Season					Playoffs				
Season	Club	Lea	GP	G	A	TP	PIM	GP	G	A	TP	PIM
1988-89	Providence	H.E.	37	2	9	11	54	....				
1989-90	Providence	H.E.	31	9	8	17	46	....				

KARALIS, TOM   (kuh-RAL-ihz)

Defense. Shoots left. 6'1", 205 lbs.   Born, Montreal, Que., May 24, 1964.

			Regular Season					Playoffs				
Season	Club	Lea	GP	G	A	TP	PIM	GP	G	A	TP	PIM
1981-82	Shawinigan	QMJHL	42	0	5	5	107	14	2	8	10	29
1982-83	Drummondville	QMJHL	64	6	11	17	218	....				
1983-84	Drummondville	QMJHL	67	16	37	53	316	10	2	6	8	28
1984-85	Drummondville	QMJHL	64	21	59	80	184	9	0	7	7	12
1985-86	Fredericton	AHL	51	4	8	12	106	....				
	Muskegon	IHL	21	5	8	13	81	11	1	3	4	32
1986-87	Fredericton	AHL	37	0	3	3	64	....				
	Muskegon	IHL	28	3	9	12	94	15	2	12	14	28
1987-88	Baltimore	AHL	17	0	2	2	87	....				
	Flint	IHL	65	5	26	31	268	2	0	0	0	2
1988-89	New Haven	AHL	11	2	3	5	8	....				
	Flint	IHL	38	1	6	7	170	....				
	Indianapolis	IHL	26	0	8	8	132	....				
1989-90	New Haven	AHL	2	0	0	0	0	....				
	Phoenix	IHL	17	1	3	4	35	....				
	Peoria	IHL	48	2	8	10	182	5	0	2	2	48

Signed as a free agent by **Quebec**, June 6, 1985.

KARJALAINEN, KYOSTI

Left wing. Shoots left. 6'1", 185 lbs.   Born, Gavle, Sweden, June 19, 1967.
(Los Angeles' 6th choice, 132nd overall, in 1987 Entry Draft).

			Regular Season					Playoffs				
Season	Club	Lea	GP	G	A	TP	PIM	GP	G	A	TP	PIM
1986-87	Brynas	Swe.	11	3	2	5	0	....				
1987-88	Brynas	Swe.	20	2	1	3	10	....				
1988-89	Brynas	Swe.	39	20	17	37	16	....				
1989-90	Brynas	Swe.	38	17	15	32	16	5	0	3	3	0

KARLSSON, LARS

Left wing. Shoots left. 5'10", 175 lbs.   Born, Karlstad, Sweden, August 18, 1966.
(Detroit's 7th choice, 152nd overall, in 1984 Entry Draft).

			Regular Season					Playoffs				
Season	Club	Lea	GP	G	A	TP	PIM	GP	G	A	TP	PIM
1986-87	Bjorkloven	Swe.	35	10	24	34	18	....				
1987-88	Farjestad	Swe.	39	6	13	19	42	....				
1988-89	Farjestad	Swe.	40	9	9	18	32	2	0	1	1	6
1989-90	Farjestad	Swe.	27	8	5	13	12	10	3	2	5	8

KASATONOV, ALEXEI

Defense. Shoots left. 6'1", 215 lbs. Born, Leningrad, Soviet Union, October 14, 1959.
(New Jersey's 9th choice, 213th overall, in 1983 Entry Draft).

			Regular Season					Playoffs				
Season	Club	Lea	GP	G	A	TP	PIM	GP	G	A	TP	PIM
1976-77	Leningrad	USSR	7	0	0	0	0	....	....	....	....	....
1977-78	Leningrad	USSR	35	4	7	11	15	....	....	....	....	....
1978-79	CSKA	USSR	40	5	14	19	30	....	....	....	....	....
1979-80a	CSKA	USSR	37	5	8	13	26	....	....	....	....	....
1980-81a	CSKA	USSR	47	10	12	22	38	....	....	....	....	....
1981-82a	CSKA	USSR	46	12	27	39	45	....	....	....	....	....
1982-83a	CSKA	USSR	44	12	19	31	37	....	....	....	....	....
1983-84a	CSKA	USSR	39	12	24	36	20	....	....	....	....	....
1984-85a	CSKA	USSR	40	18	18	36	26	....	....	....	....	....
1985-86a	CSKA	USSR	40	6	17	23	27	....	....	....	....	....
1986-87a	CSKA	USSR	40	13	17	30	16	....	....	....	....	....
1987-88a	CSKA	USSR	43	8	12	20	8	....	....	....	....	....
1988-89	CSKA	USSR	41	8	14	22	8	....	....	....	....	....
1989-90	CSKA	USSR	30	6	7	13	16	....	....	....	....	....
	New Jersey	**NHL**	**39**	**6**	**15**	**21**	**16**	**6**	**0**	**3**	**3**	**14**
	Utica	AHL	3	0	2	2	7	....	....	....	....	....
	NHL Totals		**39**	**6**	**15**	**21**	**16**	**6**	**0**	**3**	**3**	**14**

a Soviet National League All-Star Team (1980-88)

KASPER, STEPHEN NEIL (STEVE)

Center. Shoots left. 5'8", 170 lbs. Born, Montreal, Que., September 28, 1961.
(Boston's 3rd choice, 81st overall, in 1980 Entry Draft).

			Regular Season					Playoffs				
Season	Club	Lea	GP	G	A	TP	PIM	GP	G	A	TP	PIM
1978-79	Verdun	QJHL	67	37	67	104	53	11	7	6	13	22
1979-80	Sorel	QJHL	70	57	65	122	117	....	....	....	....	....
1980-81	**Boston**	**NHL**	**76**	**21**	**35**	**56**	**94**	**3**	**0**	**1**	**1**	**0**
1981-82a	**Boston**	**NHL**	**73**	**20**	**31**	**51**	**72**	**11**	**3**	**6**	**9**	**22**
1982-83	**Boston**	**NHL**	**24**	**2**	**6**	**8**	**24**	**12**	**2**	**1**	**3**	**10**
1983-84	**Boston**	**NHL**	**27**	**3**	**11**	**14**	**19**	**3**	**0**	**0**	**0**	**7**
1984-85	**Boston**	**NHL**	**77**	**16**	**24**	**40**	**33**	**5**	**1**	**0**	**1**	**9**
1985-86	**Boston**	**NHL**	**80**	**17**	**23**	**40**	**73**	**3**	**1**	**0**	**1**	**4**
1986-87	**Boston**	**NHL**	**79**	**20**	**30**	**50**	**51**	**3**	**0**	**2**	**2**	**0**
1987-88	**Boston**	**NHL**	**79**	**26**	**44**	**70**	**35**	**23**	**7**	**6**	**13**	**10**
1988-89	**Boston**	**NHL**	**49**	**10**	**16**	**26**	**49**	....	....	....	....	....
	Los Angeles	**NHL**	**29**	**9**	**15**	**24**	**14**	**11**	**1**	**5**	**6**	**10**
1989-90	**Los Angeles**	**NHL**	**77**	**17**	**28**	**45**	**27**	**10**	**1**	**1**	**2**	**2**
	NHL Totals		**670**	**161**	**263**	**424**	**491**	**84**	**16**	**22**	**38**	**74**

a Won Frank J. Selke Trophy (1982)

Traded to **Los Angeles** by **Boston** for Bobby Carpenter, January 23, 1989.

KASTELIC, EDWARD (ED) (KAS-tuh-lihk)

Right wing. Shoots right. 6'4", 215 lbs. Born, Toronto, Ont., January 29, 1964.
(Washington's 4th choice, 110th overall, in 1982 Entry Draft).

			Regular Season					Playoffs				
Season	Club	Lea	GP	G	A	TP	PIM	GP	G	A	TP	PIM
1981-82	London	OHL	68	5	18	23	63	4	0	1	1	4
1982-83	London	OHL	68	12	11	23	96	3	0	0	0	5
1983-84	London	OHL	68	17	16	33	218	8	0	2	2	41
1984-85	Moncton	AHL	62	5	11	16	187	....	....	....	....	....
	Binghamton	AHL	4	0	0	0	7	....	....	....	....	....
	Fort Wayne	IHL	5	1	0	1	37	....	....	....	....	....
1985-86	**Washington**	**NHL**	**15**	**0**	**0**	**0**	**73**	....	....	....	....	....
	Binghamton	AHL	23	7	9	16	76	....	....	....	....	....
1986-87	Binghamton	AHL	48	17	11	28	124	....	....	....	....	....
	Washington	**NHL**	**23**	**1**	**1**	**2**	**83**	**5**	**1**	**0**	**1**	**13**
1987-88	**Washington**	**NHL**	**35**	**1**	**0**	**1**	**78**	**1**	**0**	**0**	**0**	**19**
	Binghamton	AHL	6	4	1	5	6	....	....	....	....	....
1988-89	**Hartford**	**NHL**	**10**	**0**	**2**	**2**	**15**	....	....	....	....	....
	Binghamton	AHL	35	9	6	15	124	....	....	....	....	....
1989-90	**Hartford**	**NHL**	**67**	**6**	**2**	**8**	**198**	**2**	**0**	**0**	**0**	**0**
	NHL Totals		**150**	**8**	**5**	**13**	**447**	**8**	**1**	**0**	**1**	**32**

Traded to **Hartford** by **Washington** with Grant Jennings for Mike Millar and Neil Sheehy, July 6, 1988.

KAUTONEN, VELI-PEKKA

Defense. Shoots right. 6'2", 195 lbs. Born, Helsinki, Finland, May 9, 1970.
(Calgary's 3rd choice, 50th overall, in 1989 Entry Draft).

			Regular Season					Playoffs				
Season	Club	Lea	GP	G	A	TP	PIM	GP	G	A	TP	PIM
1987-88	IFK	Fin.	35	9	11	20	....	....	....	....	....	....
1988-89	IFK	Fin.	36	4	5	9	....	....	....	....	....	....
1989-90	IFK	Fin.	36	2	1	3	10	2	0	0	0	0

KEANE, MIKE

Right wing. Shoots right. 5'10", 178 lbs. Born, Winnipeg, Man., May 29, 1967.

			Regular Season					Playoffs				
Season	Club	Lea	GP	G	A	TP	PIM	GP	G	A	TP	PIM
1984-85	Moose Jaw	WHL	65	17	26	43	141	....	....	....	....	....
1985-86	Moose Jaw	WHL	67	34	49	83	162	13	6	8	14	9
1986-87	Moose Jaw	WHL	53	25	45	70	107	9	3	9	12	11
	Sherbrooke	AHL	....	....	....	....	....	9	2	2	4	16
1987-88	Sherbrooke	AHL	78	25	43	68	70	6	1	1	2	18
1988-89	**Montreal**	**NHL**	**69**	**16**	**19**	**35**	**69**	**21**	**4**	**3**	**7**	**17**
1989-90	**Montreal**	**NHL**	**74**	**9**	**15**	**24**	**78**	**11**	**0**	**1**	**1**	**8**
	NHL Totals		**143**	**25**	**34**	**59**	**147**	**32**	**4**	**4**	**8**	**25**

Signed as a free agent by **Montreal**, September 25, 1985.

KEARNEY, FRANCIS (TOBY)

Left wing. Shoots left. 6'2", 185 lbs. Born, Newburyport, MA, September 2, 1970.
(Calgary's 5th choice, 105th overall, in 1989 Entry Draft).

			Regular Season					Playoffs				
Season	Club	Lea	GP	G	A	TP	PIM	GP	G	A	TP	PIM
1988-89	Belmont Hill	HS	....	15	17	32	....	....	....	....	....	....
1989-90	U. of Vermont	ECAC	25	2	3	5	24	....	....	....	....	....

KECZMER, DAN

Defense. Shoots left. 6'1", 175 lbs. Born, Mt. Clemens, MI, May 25, 1968.
(Minnesota's 11th choice, 201st overall, in 1986 Entry Draft).

			Regular Season					Playoffs				
Season	Club	Lea	GP	G	A	TP	PIM	GP	G	A	TP	PIM
1986-87	Lake Superior	CCHA	38	3	5	8	26	....	....	....	....	....
1987-88	Lake Superior	CCHA	41	2	15	17	34	....	....	....	....	....
1988-89	Lake Superior	CCHA	46	3	26	29	68	....	....	....	....	....
1989-90a	Lake Superior	CCHA	43	13	23	36	48	....	....	....	....	....

a CCHA Second All-Star Team (1990)

KEKALAINEN, JARMO (kee kuh LAY nehn, YAHR moh)

Left wing. Shoots right. 6', 190 lbs. Born, Kuopio, Finland, July 3, 1966.

			Regular Season					Playoffs				
Season	Club	Lea	GP	G	A	TP	PIM	GP	G	A	TP	PIM
1987-88	Clarkson	ECAC	32	7	11	18	38	....	....	....	....	....
1988-89	Clarkson	ECAC	31	19	25	44	47	....	....	....	....	....
1989-90	**Boston**	**NHL**	**11**	**2**	**2**	**4**	**8**	....	....	....	....	....
	Maine	AHL	18	5	11	16	6	....	....	....	....	....
	NHL Totals		**11**	**2**	**2**	**4**	**8**	....	....	....	....	....

Signed as free agent by **Boston**, May 3, 1989.

KELFER, MICHAEL (MIKE)

Center. Shoots right. 5'10", 180 lbs. Born, Peabody, MA, January 2, 1967.
(Minnesota's 5th choice, 132nd overall, in 1985 Entry Draft).

			Regular Season					Playoffs				
Season	Club	Lea	GP	G	A	TP	PIM	GP	G	A	TP	PIM
1985-86	Boston U.	H.E.	39	13	14	27	40	....	....	....	....	....
1986-87	Boston U.	H.E.	33	21	19	40	20	....	....	....	....	....
1987-88a	Boston U.	H.E.	36	36	27	63	33	....	....	....	....	....
1988-89a	Boston U.	H.E.	33	23	29	52	22	....	....	....	....	....
1989-90	Springfield	AHL	57	24	18	42	10	....	....	....	....	....

a Hockey East Second All-Star Team (1988, 1989)

Traded to **NY Islanders** by **Minnesota** to complete March 7, 1989 deal for Reed Larson, May 12, 1989.

KELLOGG, BOB

Defense. Shoots left. 6'4", 200 lbs. Born, Springfield, MA, February 16, 1971.
(Chicago's 3rd choice, 48th overall, in 1989 Entry Draft).

			Regular Season					Playoffs				
Season	Club	Lea	GP	G	A	TP	PIM	GP	G	A	TP	PIM
1987-88	Springfield	USHL	....	15	35	50	....	....	....	....	....	....
1988-89	Springfield	USHL	....	13	34	47	....	....	....	....	....	....
1989-90	Northeastern	H.E.	36	3	12	15	30	....	....	....	....	....

KELLY, PAUL

Right wing. Shoots left. 6', 190 lbs. Born, Hamilton, Ont., April 17, 1967.
(Los Angeles' 9th choice, 191st overall, in 1986 Entry Draft).

			Regular Season					Playoffs				
Season	Club	Lea	GP	G	A	TP	PIM	GP	G	A	TP	PIM
1985-86	Guelph	OHL	59	26	32	58	95	20	10	7	17	19
1986-87	Guelph	OHL	61	27	48	75	67	5	2	4	6	0
1987-88	New Haven	AHL	60	14	25	39	23	....	....	....	....	....
1988-89	New Haven	AHL	12	4	5	9	22	....	....	....	....	....
	Utica	AHL	34	6	8	14	25	3	0	0	0	6
	Flint	IHL	4	0	1	1	0	....	....	....	....	....

KENNEDY, EDWARD (DEAN)

Defense. Shoots right. 6'2", 190 lbs. Born, Redver, Sask., January 18, 1963.
(Los Angeles' 2nd choice, 39th overall, in 1981 Entry Draft).

			Regular Season					Playoffs				
Season	Club	Lea	GP	G	A	TP	PIM	GP	G	A	TP	PIM
1980-81	Brandon	WHL	71	3	29	32	157	5	0	2	2	7
1981-82	Brandon	WHL	49	5	38	43	103	....	....	....	....	....
1982-83	Brandon	WHL	14	2	15	17	22	....	....	....	....	....
	Los Angeles	**NHL**	**55**	**0**	**12**	**12**	**97**	....	....	....	....	....
	Saskatoon	WHL	....	....	....	....	....	4	0	3	3	0
1983-84	**Los Angeles**	**NHL**	**37**	**1**	**5**	**6**	**50**	....	....	....	....	....
	New Haven	AHL	26	1	7	8	23	....	....	....	....	....
1984-85	New Haven	AHL	76	3	14	17	104	....	....	....	....	....
1985-86	**Los Angeles**	**NHL**	**78**	**2**	**10**	**12**	**132**	....	....	....	....	....
1986-87	**Los Angeles**	**NHL**	**66**	**6**	**14**	**20**	**91**	**5**	**0**	**2**	**2**	**10**
1987-88	**Los Angeles**	**NHL**	**58**	**1**	**11**	**12**	**158**	**4**	**0**	**1**	**1**	**10**
1988-89	**NY Rangers**	**NHL**	**16**	**0**	**1**	**1**	**40**	....	....	....	....	....
	Los Angeles	**NHL**	**51**	**3**	**10**	**13**	**63**	**11**	**0**	**2**	**2**	**8**
1989-90	**Buffalo**	**NHL**	**80**	**2**	**12**	**14**	**53**	**6**	**1**	**1**	**2**	**12**
	NHL Totals		**441**	**15**	**75**	**90**	**684**	**26**	**1**	**6**	**7**	**40**

Traded to **NY Rangers** by **Los Angeles** with Denis Larocque for Igor Liba, Michael Boyce, Todd Elik and future considerations, December 12, 1988. Traded to **Los Angeles** by **NY Rangers** for Los Angeles' fourth-round choice – later traded to Minnesota (Cal McGowan) – in 1990 Entry Draft, February 3, 1989. Traded to **Buffalo** by **Los Angeles** for Buffalo's fourth round choice in 1991 Entry Draft, October 4, 1989.

KENNEDY, SHELDON

Right wing. Shoots right. 5'11", 180 lbs. Born, Brandon, Man., June 15, 1969.
(Detroit's 5th choice, 80th overall, in 1988 Entry Draft).

			Regular Season					Playoffs				
Season	Club	Lea	GP	G	A	TP	PIM	GP	G	A	TP	PIM
1986-87	Swift Current	WHL	49	23	41	64	43	4	0	3	3	4
1987-88	Swift Current	WHL	59	53	64	117	45	10	8	9	17	12
1988-89	Swift Current	WHL	51	58	48	106	92	12	9	15	24	22
1989-90	**Detroit**	**NHL**	**20**	**2**	**7**	**9**	**10**	....	....	....	....	....
	Adirondack	AHL	26	11	15	26	35	....	....	....	....	....
	NHL Totals		**20**	**2**	**7**	**9**	**10**	....	....	....	....	....

KENNHOLT, KENNETH

Defense. Shoots left. 6'2", 195 lbs. Born, Djurgarden, Sweden, January 13, 1965.
(Calgary's 13th choice, 252nd overall, in 1989 Entry Draft).

			Regular Season					Playoffs				
Season	Club	Lea	GP	G	A	TP	PIM	GP	G	A	TP	PIM
1988-89	Djurgarden	Swe.	34	6	10	16	30	....	....	....	....	....
1989-90	Djurgarden	Swe.	38	7	10	17	30	7	2	2	4	2

KENTALA, VILLE

Left wing. Shoots left. 6'2", 180 lbs. Born, Alajarvi, Finland, February 21, 1966.
(NY Rangers' 8th choice, 182nd overall, in 1984 Entry Draft).

			Regular Season					Playoffs				
Season	Club	Lea	GP	G	A	TP	PIM	GP	G	A	TP	PIM
1984-85	IFK Helsinki	Fin. Jr.	26	18	10	28	34	4	2	3	5	4
1986-87	Karhukissat	Fin. 2	37	19	16	35	28	....	....	....	....	....
1986-87	Boston U.	H.E.	35	4	11	15	24	....	....	....	....	....
1987-88	Boston U.	H.E.	32	16	19	35	34	....	....	....	....	....
1988-89	Boston U.	H.E.	34	5	7	12	46	....	....	....	....	....
1989-90	Helsinki	Fin.	43	5	4	9	6	2	0	0	0	0

Traded to **Edmonton** by **NY Rangers** with Reijo Ruotsalainen, Clark Donatelli and Jim Wiemer for Don Jackson, Mike Golden, Miloslav Horava and future considerations, October 23, 1986.

KERR, ALAN

Right wing. Shoots right. 5'11", 195 lbs. Born, Hazelton, B.C., March 28, 1964.
(NY Islanders' 4th choice, 84th overall, in 1982 Entry Draft).

			Regular Season					Playoffs				
Season	Club	Lea	GP	G	A	TP	PIM	GP	G	A	TP	PIM
1981-82	Seattle	WHL	68	15	18	33	107	10	6	6	12	32
1982-83	Seattle	WHL	71	38	53	91	183	4	2	3	5	0
1983-84a	Seattle	WHL	66	46	66	112	141	5	1	4	5	12
1984-85	**NY Islanders**	**NHL**	**19**	**3**	**1**	**4**	**24**	**4**	**1**	**0**	**1**	**4**
	Springfield	AHL	62	32	27	59	140	4	1	2	3	2
1985-86	**NY Islanders**	**NHL**	**7**	**0**	**1**	**1**	**16**	**1**	**0**	**0**	**0**	**0**
	Springfield	AHL	71	35	36	71	127	....	....	....	....	....
1986-87	**NY Islanders**	**NHL**	**72**	**7**	**10**	**17**	**175**	**14**	**1**	**4**	**5**	**25**
1987-88	**NY Islanders**	**NHL**	**80**	**24**	**34**	**58**	**198**	**6**	**1**	**0**	**1**	**14**
1988-89	**NY Islanders**	**NHL**	**71**	**20**	**18**	**38**	**144**	....	....	....	....	....
1989-90	**NY Islanders**	**NHL**	**75**	**15**	**21**	**36**	**129**	**4**	**0**	**0**	**0**	**10**
	NHL Totals		**324**	**69**	**85**	**154**	**686**	**29**	**3**	**4**	**7**	**53**

a WHL First All-Star Team, West Division (1984)

KERR, KEVIN

Right wing. Shoots right. 5'10", 190 lbs. Born, North Bay, Ont., September 18, 1967.
(Buffalo's 4th choice, 56th overall, in 1986 Entry Draft).

			Regular Season					Playoffs				
Season	Club	Lea	GP	G	A	TP	PIM	GP	G	A	TP	PIM
1985-86	Windsor	OHL	59	21	51	72	266	16	6	8	14	55
1986-87	Windsor	OHL	63	27	41	68	264	14	3	8	11	45
1987-88	Rochester	AHL	72	18	11	29	352	5	1	3	4	42
1988-89	Rochester	AHL	66	20	18	38	306	....	....	....	....	....
1989-90	Rochester	AHL	8	0	1	1	22	....	....	....	....	....
	Phoenix	IHL	6	0	0	0	25	....	....	....	....	....
	Fort Wayne	IHL	43	11	16	27	219	5	0	1	1	3

KERR, TIM

Center/Right wing. Shoots right. 6'3", 230 lbs. Born, Windsor, Ont., January 5, 1960.

			Regular Season					Playoffs				
Season	Club	Lea	GP	G	A	TP	PIM	GP	G	A	TP	PIM
1978-79	Kingston	OHA	57	17	25	42	27	6	1	1	2	2
1979-80	Kingston	OHA	63	40	33	73	39	3	0	1	1	16
	Maine	AHL	7	2	4	6	2	....	....	....	....	....
1980-81	**Philadelphia**	**NHL**	**68**	**22**	**23**	**45**	**84**	**10**	**1**	**3**	**4**	**2**
1981-82	**Philadelphia**	**NHL**	**61**	**21**	**30**	**51**	**138**	**4**	**0**	**2**	**2**	**2**
1982-83	**Philadelphia**	**NHL**	**24**	**11**	**8**	**19**	**6**	**2**	**2**	**0**	**2**	**0**
1983-84	**Philadelphia**	**NHL**	**79**	**54**	**39**	**93**	**29**	**3**	**0**	**0**	**0**	**0**
1984-85	**Philadelphia**	**NHL**	**74**	**54**	**44**	**98**	**57**	**12**	**10**	**4**	**14**	**13**
1985-86	**Philadelphia**	**NHL**	**76**	**58**	**26**	**84**	**79**	**5**	**3**	**3**	**6**	**8**
1986-87a	**Philadelphia**	**NHL**	**75**	**58**	**37**	**95**	**57**	**12**	**8**	**5**	**13**	**2**
1987-88	**Philadelphia**	**NHL**	**8**	**3**	**2**	**5**	**12**	**6**	**1**	**3**	**4**	**4**
1988-89b	**Philadelphia**	**NHL**	**69**	**48**	**40**	**88**	**73**	**19**	**14**	**11**	**25**	**27**
1989-90	**Philadelphia**	**NHL**	**40**	**24**	**24**	**48**	**34**	....	....	....	....	....
	NHL Totals		**574**	**353**	**273**	**626**	**569**	**73**	**39**	**31**	**70**	**58**

a NHL Second All-Star Team (1987)
b Won Bill Masterton Award (1989)

Played in NHL All-Star Game (1984-86)

Signed as free agent by **Philadelphia**, October 25, 1979.

KESKINEN, ESA

Center. Shoots right. 5'9", 185 lbs. Born, Tampere, Finland, February 2, 1965.
(Calgary's 6th choice, 101st overall, in 1985 Entry Draft).

			Regular Season					Playoffs				
Season	Club	Lea	GP	G	A	TP	PIM	GP	G	A	TP	PIM
1986-87	TPS	Fin.	46	25	36	61	4	5	1	1	2	0
1987-88	TPS	Fin.	44	14	55	69	14	....	....	....	....	....
1988-89	Lukko	Fin.	41	24	46	70	12	....	....	....	....	....
1989-90	Lukko	Fin.	44	25	26	51	16	....	....	....	....	....

KHARIN, SERGEI

Right wing. Shoots right. 5'8", 165 lbs. Born, Odintsovo, Soviet Union, February 20, 1963.
(Winnipeg's 15th choice, 240th overall, in 1989 Entry Draft).

			Regular Season					Playoffs				
Season	Club	Lea	GP	G	A	TP	PIM	GP	G	A	TP	PIM
1980-81	Soviet Wings	USSR	2	0	0	0	0	....	....	....	....	....
1981-82	Soviet Wings	USSR	34	4	3	7	10	....	....	....	....	....
1982-83	Soviet Wings	USSR	49	5	5	10	20	....	....	....	....	....
1983-84	Soviet Wings	USSR	33	5	3	8	18	....	....	....	....	....
1984-85	Soviet Wings	USSR	34	12	8	20	6	....	....	....	....	....
1985-86	Soviet Wings	USSR	38	15	14	29	19	....	....	....	....	....
1986-87	Soviet Wings	USSR	40	16	11	27	14	....	....	....	....	....
1987-88	Soviet Wings	USSR	45	17	13	30	20	....	....	....	....	....
1988-89	Soviet Wings	USSR	44	15	9	24	14	....	....	....	....	....
1989-90	Soviet Wings	USSR	47	12	5	17	28	....	....	....	....	....

KHOMUTOV, ANDREI

Right wing. Shoots left. 5'9", 180 lbs. Born, Yaroslavl, Soviet Union, April 21, 1961.
(Quebec's 12th choice, 190th overall, in 1989 Entry Draft).

			Regular Season					Playoffs				
Season	Club	Lea	GP	G	A	TP	PIM	GP	G	A	TP	PIM
1979-80	CSKA	USSR	4	0	0	0	0	....	....	....	....	....
1980-81	CSKA	USSR	43	23	18	41	4	....	....	....	....	....
1981-82	CSKA	USSR	44	17	13	30	12	....	....	....	....	....
1982-83	CSKA	USSR	44	21	17	38	6	....	....	....	....	....
1983-84	CSKA	USSR	39	17	8	25	14	....	....	....	....	....
1984-85	CSKA	USSR	37	21	13	34	18	....	....	....	....	....
1985-86	CSKA	USSR	38	14	15	29	10	....	....	....	....	....
1986-87	CSKA	USSR	33	15	18	33	22	....	....	....	....	....
1987-88	CSKA	USSR	48	29	14	43	22	....	....	....	....	....
1988-89	CSKA	USSR	44	19	16	35	14	....	....	....	....	....
1989-90a	CSKA	USSR	47	21	14	35	12	....	....	....	....	....

a Soviet Player of the Year (1990)

KIDD, IAN

Defense. Shoots right. 5'11", 195 lbs. Born, Gresham, OR, May 11, 1964.

			Regular Season					Playoffs				
Season	Club	Lea	GP	G	A	TP	PIM	GP	G	A	TP	PIM
1985-86	North Dakota	WCHA	37	6	16	22	65	....	....	....	....	....
1986-87	North Dakota	WCHA	47	13	47	60	58	....	....	....	....	....
1987-88	**Vancouver**	**NHL**	**19**	**4**	**7**	**11**	**25**	....	....	....	....	....
	Fredericton	AHL	53	1	21	22	70	12	0	4	4	22
1988-89	**Vancouver**	**NHL**	**1**	**0**	**0**	**0**	**0**	....	....	....	....	....
	Milwaukee	IHL	76	13	40	53	124	4	0	2	2	7
1989-90	Milwaukee	IHL	65	11	36	47	86	....	....	....	....	....
	NHL Totals		**20**	**4**	**7**	**11**	**25**	....	....	....	....	....

Signed as a free agent by **Vancouver**, July 30, 1987.

KIENE, CHRIS (KEEN)

Defense. Shoots left. 6'5", 220 lbs. Born, So. Windsor, CT, March 6, 1966.
(New Jersey's 12th choice, 231st overall, in 1984 Entry Draft).

			Regular Season					Playoffs				
Season	Club	Lea	GP	G	A	TP	PIM	GP	G	A	TP	PIM
1987-88	Merrimack	NCAA	40	6	34	40	72	....	....	....	....	....
1988-89	Merrimack	NCAA	32	3	25	28	76	....	....	....	....	....
1989-90	Utica	AHL	67	5	17	22	60	1	0	0	0	2

KILSTROM, MATS

Defense. Shoots right. 6'2", 198 lbs. Born, Ludvika, Sweden, January 3, 1964.
(Calgary's 8th choice, 118th overall, in 1982 Entry Draft).

			Regular Season					Playoffs				
Season	Club	Lea	GP	G	A	TP	PIM	GP	G	A	TP	PIM
1981-82	Sodertalje	Swe.	25	2	3	5	20	....	....	....	....	....
1982-83	Sodertalje	Swe.	17	5	0	5	35	11	1	3	4	12
1983-84	Sodertalje	Swe.	25	4	3	7	25	3	1	0	1	0
1984-85	Brynas	Swe.	35	4	9	13	14	....	....	....	....	....
1985-86	Brynas	Swe.	35	3	8	11	48	3	1	0	1	4
1986-87	Sodertalje	Swe.	32	2	4	6	28	....	....	....	....	....
1987-88	Sodertalje	Swe.	37	5	7	12	36	2	0	2	2	0
1988-89	Sodertalje	Swe.	39	3	19	22	45	....	....	....	....	....
1989-90	Sodertalje	Swe.	37	7	16	23	26	2	0	1	1	5

KIMBLE, DARIN

Right wing. Shoots right. 6'2", 205 lbs. Born, Lucky Lake, Sask., November 22, 1968.
(Quebec's 5th choice, 66th overall, in 1988 Entry Draft).

			Regular Season					Playoffs				
Season	Club	Lea	GP	G	A	TP	PIM	GP	G	A	TP	PIM
1986-87	Prince Albert	WHL	68	17	13	30	190	....	....	....	....	....
1987-88	Prince Albert	WHL	67	35	36	71	307	10	3	2	5	4
1988-89	**Quebec**	**NHL**	**26**	**3**	**1**	**4**	**149**	....	....	....	....	....
	Halifax	AHL	39	8	6	14	188	....	....	....	....	....
1989-90	**Quebec**	**NHL**	**44**	**5**	**5**	**10**	**185**	....	....	....	....	....
	Halifax	AHL	18	6	6	12	37	6	1	1	2	61
	NHL Totals		**70**	**8**	**6**	**14**	**334**	....	....	....	....	....

KING, DEREK

Left wing. Shoots left. 6'1", 203 lbs.   Born, Hamilton, Ont., February 11, 1967.
(NY Islanders' 2nd choice, 13th overall, in 1985 Entry Draft).

			Regular Season					Playoffs				
Season	Club	Lea	GP	G	A	TP	PIM	GP	G	A	TP	PIM
1984-85a	S.S. Marie	OHL	63	35	38	73	106	16	3	13	16	11
1985-86	S.S. Marie	OHL	25	12	17	29	33	....	....	....	....	....
	Oshawa	OHL	19	8	13	21	15	6	3	2	5	13
1986-87	**NY Islanders**	**NHL**	2	0	0	0	0	....	....	....	....	....
b	Oshawa	OHL	57	53	53	106	74	17	14	10	24	40
1987-88	**NY Islanders**	**NHL**	55	12	24	36	30	5	0	2	2	2
	Springfield	AHL	10	7	6	13	6	....	....	....	....	....
1988-89	**NY Islanders**	**NHL**	60	14	29	43	14	....	....	....	....	....
	Springfield	AHL	4	4	0	4	0	....	....	....	....	....
1989-90	**NY Islanders**	**NHL**	46	13	27	40	20	4	0	0	0	4
	Springfield	AHL	21	11	12	23	33	....	....	....	....	....
	NHL Totals		**163**	**39**	**80**	**119**	**64**	**9**	**0**	**2**	**2**	**6**

a OHL Rookie of the Year (1985)
b OHL First All-Star Team (1987)

KING, KRIS

Left wing. Shoots left. 5'10". 190 lbs.   Born, Bracebridge, Ont., February 18, 1966.
(Washington's 4th choice, 80th overall, in 1984 Entry Draft).

			Regular Season					Playoffs				
Season	Club	Lea	GP	G	A	TP	PIM	GP	G	A	TP	PIM
1983-84	Peterborough	OHL	62	13	18	31	168	8	3	3	6	14
1984-85	Peterborough	OHL	61	18	35	53	222	16	2	8	10	28
1985-86	Peterborough	OHL	58	19	40	59	254	8	4	0	4	21
1986-87	Binghamton	AHL	7	0	0	0	18	....	....	....	....	....
	Peterborough	OHL	46	23	33	56	160	12	5	8	13	41
1987-88	**Detroit**	**NHL**	3	1	0	1	2	....	....	....	....	....
	Adirondack	AHL	76	21	32	53	337	10	4	4	8	53
1988-89	**Detroit**	**NHL**	55	2	3	5	168	2	0	0	0	2
1989-90	**NY Rangers**	**NHL**	68	6	7	13	286	10	0	1	1	38
	NHL Totals		**126**	**9**	**10**	**19**	**456**	**12**	**0**	**1**	**1**	**40**

Signed as a free agent by **Detroit**, March 23, 1987. Traded to **NY Rangers** by **Detroit** for Chris McRae and Detroit's fifth round choice (Tony Burns) in 1990 Entry Draft which was previously acquired by NY Rangers, September 7, 1989.

KIRTON, DOUG

Right wing. Shoots right. 6'2", 190 lbs.   Born, Penetanguishene, Ont., March 21, 1966.
(New Jersey's 12th choice, 236th overall, in 1986 Entry Draft).

			Regular Season					Playoffs				
Season	Club	Lea	GP	G	A	TP	PIM	GP	G	A	TP	PIM
1986-87	Colorado	WCHA	38	10	10	20	42	....	....	....	....	....
1987-88	Colorado	WCHA	31	11	17	28	42	....	....	....	....	....
1988-89	Colorado	WCHA	38	8	16	24	33	....	....	....	....	....
1989-90	Colorado	WCHA	37	19	21	40	47	....	....	....	....	....

KISIO, KELLY

Center. Shoots right. 5'9", 170 lbs.   Born, Peace River, Alta., September 18, 1959.

			Regular Season					Playoffs				
Season	Club	Lea	GP	G	A	TP	PIM	GP	G	A	TP	PIM
1978-79	Calgary	WHL	70	60	61	121	73	....	....	....	....	....
1979-80	Calgary	WHL	71	65	73	138	64	....	....	....	....	....
1980-81	Adirondack	AHL	41	10	14	24	43	....	....	....	....	....
	Kalamazoo	IHL	31	27	16	43	48	8	7	7	14	13
1981-82	Dallas	CHL	78	*62	39	101	59	16	*12	*17	*29	38
1982-83	Davos	Swit.	35	40	33	73	....	....	....	....	....	....
	Detroit	**NHL**	15	4	3	7	0	....	....	....	....	....
1983-84	**Detroit**	**NHL**	70	23	37	60	34	4	1	0	1	4
1984-85	**Detroit**	**NHL**	75	20	41	61	56	3	0	2	2	2
1985-86	**Detroit**	**NHL**	76	21	48	69	85	....	....	....	....	....
1986-87	**NY Rangers**	**NHL**	70	24	40	64	73	4	0	1	1	2
1987-88	**NY Rangers**	**NHL**	77	23	55	78	88	....	....	....	....	....
1988-89	**NY Rangers**	**NHL**	70	26	36	62	91	4	0	0	0	9
1989-90	**NY Rangers**	**NHL**	68	22	44	66	105	10	2	8	10	8
	NHL Totals		**521**	**163**	**304**	**467**	**532**	**25**	**3**	**11**	**14**	**25**

Signed as a free agent by **Detroit**, May 2, 1983. Traded to **NY Rangers** by **Detroit** with Lane Lambert and Jim Leavins for Glen Hanlon and New York's third-round choices in 1987 (Dennis Holland) and 1988 Entry Drafts, July 29, 1986.

KIVELA, TEPPO

Center. Shoots left. 5'11", 180 lbs.   Born, Espoo, Finland, November 8, 1969.
(Minnesota's 5th choice, 88th overall, in 1987 Entry Draft).

			Regular Season					Playoffs				
Season	Club	Lea	GP	G	A	TP	PIM	GP	G	A	TP	PIM
1986-87	HPK	Fin.	41	26	38	64	64	6	4	7	11	4
1987-88	HPK	Fin.	36	31	39	70	20	....	....	....	....	....
1988-89	HPK	Fin.	39	20	38	58	54	....	....	....	....	....
1989-90	HPK	Fin.	44	27	34	61	44	....	....	....	....	....

KJELLBERG, PATRIK

Left wing. Shoots left. 6'2", 196 lbs.   Born, Falun, Sweden, June 17, 1969.
(Montreal's 4th choice, 83rd overall, in 1988 Entry Draft).

			Regular Season					Playoffs				
Season	Club	Lea	GP	G	A	TP	PIM	GP	G	A	TP	PIM
1986-87	Falun	Swe.	27	11	13	24	14	....	....	....	....	....
1987-88	Falun	Swe.	29	15	10	25	18	....	....	....	....	....
1988-89	AIK	Swe.	25	7	9	16	8	....	....	....	....	....
1989-90	AIK	Swe.	33	8	16	24	6	3	1	0	1	0

KLATT, TRENT

Center. Shoots right. 6'1", 210 lbs.   Born, Robbinsdale, MN, January 30, 1971.
(Washington's 5th choice, 82nd overall, in 1989 Entry Draft).

			Regular Season					Playoffs				
Season	Club	Lea	GP	G	A	TP	PIM	GP	G	A	TP	PIM
1988-89	Osseo	HS	22	24	39	63	....	....	....	....	....	....
1989-90	U. Minnesota	WCHA	38	22	14	36	16	....	....	....	....	....

KLEINENDORST, SCOT   (KLIGH-nuhn-DOHRST)

Defense. Shoots left. 6'3", 215 lbs.   Born, Grand Rapids, MN, January 16, 1960.
(NY Rangers' 5th choice, 98th overall, in 1980 Entry Draft).

			Regular Season					Playoffs				
Season	Club	Lea	GP	G	A	TP	PIM	GP	G	A	TP	PIM
1978-79	Providence	ECAC	25	4	4	8	27	....	....	....	....	....
1979-80a	Providence	ECAC	30	1	12	13	38	....	....	....	....	....
1980-81	Providence	ECAC	32	3	31	34	75	....	....	....	....	....
1981-82	Providence	ECAC	33	11	27	38	85	....	....	....	....	....
	Springfield	AHL	5	0	4	4	11	....	....	....	....	....
1982-83	Tulsa	CHL	10	0	7	7	2	....	....	....	....	....
	NY Rangers	**NHL**	30	2	9	11	8	6	0	2	2	2
1983-84	**NY Rangers**	**NHL**	23	0	2	2	35	....	....	....	....	....
	Tulsa	CHL	10	4	5	9	4	....	....	....	....	....
1984-85	**Hartford**	**NHL**	35	1	8	9	69	....	....	....	....	....
	Binghamton	AHL	30	3	7	10	42	....	....	....	....	....
1985-86	**Hartford**	**NHL**	41	2	7	9	62	10	0	1	1	18
1986-87	**Hartford**	**NHL**	66	3	9	12	130	4	1	3	4	20
1987-88	**Hartford**	**NHL**	44	3	6	9	86	3	1	1	2	0
1988-89	**Hartford**	**NHL**	24	0	1	1	36	....	....	....	....	....
	Binghamton	AHL	4	0	1	1	19	....	....	....	....	....
	Washington	**NHL**	3	0	1	1	10	....	....	....	....	....
1989-90	**Washington**	**NHL**	15	1	3	4	16	3	0	0	0	0
	Baltimore	AHL	2	2	0	2	6	....	....	....	....	....
	NHL Totals		**281**	**12**	**46**	**58**	**452**	**26**	**2**	**7**	**9**	**40**

a ECAC Second All-Star Team (1980)

Traded to **Hartford** by **NY Rangers** for Blaine Stoughton, February 27, 1984. Traded to **Washington** by **Hartford** for Jim Thomson, March 6, 1989.

KLIMA, PETR   (KLEE-muh)

Left wing. Shoots right. 6', 190 lbs.   Born, Chomulov, Czech., December 23, 1964.
(Detroit's 5th choice, 88th overall, in 1983 Entry Draft).

			Regular Season					Playoffs				
Season	Club	Lea	GP	G	A	TP	PIM	GP	G	A	TP	PIM
1982-83	Czech. Jrs.	....	44	19	17	36	74	....	....	....	....	....
1983-84	Dukla Jihlava	Czech.	41	20	16	36	46	....	....	....	....	....
	Czech. Jrs.	....	7	6	5	11	NA	....	....	....	....	....
1984-85	Dukla Jihlava	Czech.	35	23	22	45	NA	....	....	....	....	....
	Czech. Nat'l	....	5	2	1	3	0	....	....	....	....	....
1985-86	**Detroit**	**NHL**	74	32	24	56	16	....	....	....	....	....
1986-87	**Detroit**	**NHL**	77	30	23	53	42	13	1	2	3	4
1987-88	**Detroit**	**NHL**	78	37	25	62	46	12	10	8	18	10
1988-89	**Detroit**	**NHL**	51	25	16	41	44	6	2	4	6	19
	Adirondack	AHL	5	5	1	6	4	....	....	....	....	....
1989-90	**Detroit**	**NHL**	13	5	5	10	6	....	....	....	....	....
	Edmonton	**NHL**	63	25	28	53	66	21	5	0	5	8
	NHL Totals		**356**	**154**	**121**	**275**	**220**	**52**	**18**	**14**	**32**	**41**

Traded to **Edmonton** by **Detroit** with Joe Murphy, Adam Graves and Jeff Sharples for Jimmy Carson, Kevin McClelland and Edmonton's fifth round choice in 1991 Entry Draft, November 2, 1989.

KLUZAK, GORDON (GORD)   (KLOO-zak)

Defense. Shoots left. 6'4", 215 lbs.   Born, Climax, Sask., March 4, 1964.
(Boston's 1st choice, 1st overall, in 1982 Entry Draft).

			Regular Season					Playoffs				
Season	Club	Lea	GP	G	A	TP	PIM	GP	G	A	TP	PIM
1980-81	Billings	WHL	68	4	34	38	160	5	0	1	1	4
1981-82a	Billings	WHL	38	9	24	33	110	....	....	....	....	....
1982-83	**Boston**	**NHL**	70	1	6	7	105	17	1	4	5	54
1983-84	**Boston**	**NHL**	80	10	27	37	135	3	0	0	0	0
1984-85			DID NOT PLAY — INJURED									
1985-86	**Boston**	**NHL**	70	8	31	39	155	3	1	1	2	16
1986-87			DID NOT PLAY — INJURED									
1987-88	**Boston**	**NHL**	66	6	31	37	135	23	4	8	12	59
1988-89	**Boston**	**NHL**	3	0	1	1	2	....	....	....	....	....
1989-90b	**Boston**	**NHL**	8	0	2	2	11	....	....	....	....	....
	NHL Totals		**297**	**25**	**98**	**123**	**543**	**46**	**6**	**13**	**19**	**129**

a WHL Second All-Star Team (1982)
b Won Bill Masterton Award (1990)

KOCUR, JOEY   (KOH-suhr)

Right wing. Shoots right. 6', 195 lbs.   Born, Kelvington, Sask., December 21, 1964.
(Detroit's 6th choice, 88th overall, in 1983 Entry Draft).

			Regular Season					Playoffs				
Season	Club	Lea	GP	G	A	TP	PIM	GP	G	A	TP	PIM
1982-83	Saskatoon	WHL	62	23	17	40	289	6	2	3	5	25
1983-84	Saskatoon	WHL	69	40	41	81	258	....	....	....	....	....
	Adirondack	AHL	....	....	....	....	....	5	0	0	0	20
1984-85	**Detroit**	**NHL**	17	1	0	1	64	3	1	0	1	5
	Adirondack	AHL	47	12	7	19	171	....	....	....	....	....
1985-86	**Detroit**	**NHL**	59	9	6	15	*377	....	....	....	....	....
	Adirondack	AHL	9	6	2	8	34	....	....	....	....	....
1986-87	**Detroit**	**NHL**	77	9	9	18	276	16	2	3	5	71
1987-88	**Detroit**	**NHL**	63	7	7	14	263	10	0	1	1	13
1988-89	**Detroit**	**NHL**	60	9	9	18	213	3	0	1	1	6
1989-90	**Detroit**	**NHL**	71	16	20	36	268	....	....	....	....	....
	NHL Totals		**347**	**51**	**51**	**102**	**1461**	**32**	**3**	**5**	**8**	**95**

KOCUR, KORY

Right wing. Shoots right. 5'11", 190 lbs.   Born, Kelvington, Sask., March 6, 1969.
(Detroit's 1st choice, 17th overall, in 1988 Entry Draft).

			Regular Season					Playoffs				
Season	Club	Lea	GP	G	A	TP	PIM	GP	G	A	TP	PIM
1986-87	Saskatoon	WHL	62	13	17	30	98	4	0	0	0	7
1987-88	Saskatoon	WHL	69	34	37	71	95	10	5	4	9	18
1988-89	Saskatoon	WHL	66	45	57	102	111	8	7	11	18	15
1989-90	Adirondack	AHL	79	18	37	55	36	6	1	2	3	2

KOLNIK, LUBOMIR

Right wing. Shoots left. 5'11", 180 lbs. Born, Czechoslovakia, January 23, 1969.
(New Jersey's 9th choice, 116th overall, in 1990 Entry Draft).

			Regular Season					Playoffs				
Season	Club	Lea	GP	G	A	TP	PIM	GP	G	A	TP	PIM
1989-90	Dukla Trencin	Czech.	53	37	25	62	....	....	....	....	....	....

KOLSTAD, DEAN

Defense. Shoots left. 6'6", 210 lbs. Born, Edmonton, Alta., June 16, 1968.
(Minnesota's 3rd choice, 33rd overall, in 1986 Entry Draft).

			Regular Season					Playoffs				
Season	Club	Lea	GP	G	A	TP	PIM	GP	G	A	TP	PIM
1985-86	N. Westminster	WHL	16	0	5	5	19	....	....	....	....	....
	Prince Albert	WHL	54	2	15	17	80	20	5	3	8	26
1986-87	Prince Albert	WHL	72	17	37	54	112	8	1	5	6	8
1987-88	Prince Albert	WHL	72	14	37	51	121	10	0	9	9	20
1988-89	**Minnesota**	**NHL**	**25**	**1**	**5**	**6**	**42**	....	....	....	....	....
	Kalamazoo	IHL	51	10	23	33	91	6	1	0	1	23
1989-90a	Kalamazoo	IHL	77	10	40	50	172	10	3	4	7	14
	NHL Totals		**25**	**1**	**5**	**6**	**42**	....	....	....	....	....

a IHL Second All-Star Team (1990)

KONROYD, STEPHEN MARK (STEVE) (KON-royd)

Defense. Shoots left. 6'1", 195 lbs. Born, Scarborough, Ont., February 10, 1961.
(Atlanta's 4th choice, 39th overall, in 1980 Entry Draft).

			Regular Season					Playoffs				
Season	Club	Lea	GP	G	A	TP	PIM	GP	G	A	TP	PIM
1979-80	Oshawa	OHA	62	11	23	34	133	7	0	2	2	14
1980-81	**Calgary**	**NHL**	**4**	**0**	**0**	**0**	**4**	....	....	....	....	....
a	Oshawa	OHA	59	19	47	68	232	11	3	11	14	35
1981-82	Oklahoma City	CHL	14	2	3	5	15	....	....	....	....	....
	Calgary	**NHL**	**63**	**3**	**14**	**17**	**78**	**3**	**0**	**0**	**0**	**12**
1982-83	**Calgary**	**NHL**	**79**	**4**	**13**	**17**	**73**	**9**	**2**	**1**	**3**	**18**
1983-84	**Calgary**	**NHL**	**80**	**1**	**13**	**14**	**94**	**8**	**1**	**2**	**3**	**8**
1984-85	**Calgary**	**NHL**	**64**	**3**	**23**	**26**	**73**	**4**	**1**	**4**	**5**	**2**
1985-86	**Calgary**	**NHL**	**59**	**7**	**20**	**27**	**64**	....	....	....	....	....
	NY Islanders	**NHL**	**14**	**0**	**5**	**5**	**16**	**3**	**0**	**0**	**0**	**6**
1986-87	**NY Islanders**	**NHL**	**72**	**5**	**16**	**21**	**70**	**14**	**1**	**4**	**5**	**10**
1987-88	**NY Islanders**	**NHL**	**62**	**2**	**15**	**17**	**99**	**6**	**1**	**0**	**1**	**4**
1988-89	**NY Islanders**	**NHL**	**21**	**1**	**5**	**6**	**2**	....	....	....	....	....
	Chicago	**NHL**	**57**	**5**	**7**	**12**	**40**	**16**	**2**	**0**	**2**	**10**
1989-90	**Chicago**	**NHL**	**75**	**3**	**14**	**17**	**34**	**20**	**1**	**3**	**4**	**19**
	NHL Totals		**650**	**34**	**145**	**179**	**647**	**83**	**9**	**14**	**23**	**89**

a OHA Second All-Star Team (1981)

Traded to **NY Islanders** by **Calgary** with Richard Kromm for John Tonelli, March 11, 1986. Traded to **Chicago** by **NY Islanders** with Bob Bassen for Marc Bergevin and Gary Nylund, November 25, 1988.

KONSTANTINOV, VLADIMIR

Defense. 5'11", 180 lbs. Born, Murmansk, Soviet Union, March 19, 1967.
(Detroit's 12th choice, 221st overall, in 1989 Entry Draft).

			Regular Season					Playoffs				
Season	Club	Lea	GP	G	A	TP	PIM	GP	G	A	TP	PIM
1984-85	CSKA	USSR	40	1	4	5	10	....	....	....	....	....
1985-86	CSKA	USSR	26	4	3	7	12	....	....	....	....	....
1986-87	CSKA	USSR	35	2	2	4	19	....	....	....	....	....
1987-88	CSKA	USSR	50	3	6	9	32	....	....	....	....	....
1988-89	CSKA	USSR	37	7	8	15	20	....	....	....	....	....
1989-90	CSKA	USSR	47	14	13	27	44	....	....	....	....	....

KONTOS, CHRISTOPHER (CHRIS) (KONN-tohs)

Left wing. Shoots left. 6'1", 195 lbs. Born, Toronto, Ont., December 10, 1963.
(NY Rangers' 1st choice, 15th overall, in 1982 Entry Draft).

			Regular Season					Playoffs				
Season	Club	Lea	GP	G	A	TP	PIM	GP	G	A	TP	PIM
1980-81	Sudbury	OHA	57	17	27	44	36	....	....	....	....	....
1981-82	Sudbury	OHL	12	6	6	12	18	....	....	....	....	....
	Toronto	OHL	59	36	56	92	68	10	7	9	16	2
1982-83	Toronto	OHL	28	21	33	54	23	....	....	....	....	....
	NY Rangers	**NHL**	**44**	**8**	**7**	**15**	**33**	....	....	....	....	....
1983-84	**NY Rangers**	**NHL**	**6**	**0**	**1**	**1**	**8**	....	....	....	....	....
	Tulsa	CHL	21	5	13	18	8	....	....	....	....	....
1984-85	**NY Rangers**	**NHL**	**28**	**4**	**8**	**12**	**24**	....	....	....	....	....
	New Haven	AHL	48	19	24	43	30	....	....	....	....	....
1985-86	Ilves	Fin.	36	16	15	31	30	....	....	....	....	....
	New Haven	AHL	21	8	15	23	12	5	4	2	6	4
1986-87	**Pittsburgh**	**NHL**	**31**	**8**	**9**	**17**	**6**	....	....	....	....	....
	New Haven	AHL	36	14	17	31	29	....	....	....	....	....
1987-88	**Pittsburgh**	**NHL**	**36**	**1**	**7**	**8**	**12**	....	....	....	....	....
	Muskegon	IHL	10	3	6	9	8	....	....	....	....	....
	Los Angeles	**NHL**	**6**	**2**	**10**	**12**	**2**	**4**	**1**	**0**	**1**	**4**
	New Haven	AHL	16	8	16	24	4	....	....	....	....	....
1988-89	Ilves	Fin.	36	16	15	31	30	....	....	....	....	....
	Los Angeles	**NHL**	**7**	**2**	**1**	**3**	**2**	**11**	**9**	**0**	**9**	**8**
1989-90	**Los Angeles**	**NHL**	**6**	**2**	**2**	**4**	**4**	**5**	**1**	**0**	**1**	**0**
	New Haven	AHL	42	10	20	30	25	....	....	....	....	....
	NHL Totals		**164**	**27**	**45**	**72**	**91**	**20**	**11**	**0**	**11**	**12**

Traded to **Pittsburgh** by **NY Rangers** for Ron Duguay, January 21, 1987. Traded to **Los Angeles** by **Pittsburgh** with Pittsburgh's sixth round choice in 1988 Entry Draft (Micah Alvazoff) for Bryan Erickson, February 5, 1988.

KORDIC, JOHN

Right wing. Shoots right. 6'2", 210 lbs. Born, Edmonton, Alta., March 22, 1965.
(Montreal's 6th choice, 80th overall, in 1984 Entry Draft).

			Regular Season					Playoffs				
Season	Club	Lea	GP	G	A	TP	PIM	GP	G	A	TP	PIM
1982-83	Portland	WHL	72	3	22	25	235	14	1	6	7	30
1983-84	Portland	WHL	67	9	50	59	232	14	0	13	13	56
1984-85a	Seattle	WHL	46	17	36	53	154	....	....	....	....	....
	Portland	WHL	25	6	22	28	73	....	....	....	....	....
	Sherbrooke	AHL	4	0	0	0	4	4	0	0	0	11
1985-86	**Montreal**	**NHL**	**5**	**0**	**1**	**1**	**12**	**18**	**0**	**0**	**0**	**53**
	Sherbrooke	AHL	68	3	14	17	238	....	....	....	....	....
1986-87	**Montreal**	**NHL**	**44**	**5**	**3**	**8**	**151**	**11**	**2**	**0**	**2**	**19**
	Sherbrooke	AHL	10	4	4	8	49	....	....	....	....	....
1987-88	**Montreal**	**NHL**	**60**	**2**	**6**	**8**	**159**	**7**	**2**	**2**	**4**	**26**
1988-89	**Montreal**	**NHL**	**6**	**0**	**0**	**0**	**13**	....	....	....	....	....
	Toronto	**NHL**	**46**	**1**	**2**	**3**	**185**	....	....	....	....	....
1989-90	**Toronto**	**NHL**	**55**	**9**	**4**	**13**	**252**	**5**	**0**	**1**	**1**	**33**
	NHL Totals		**216**	**17**	**16**	**33**	**772**	**41**	**4**	**3**	**7**	**131**

a WHL Second All-Star Team, West Division (1985).

Traded to **Toronto** by **Montreal** with Montreal's sixth-round choice (Michael Doers) in 1989 Entry Draft for Russ Courtnall, November 7, 1988.

KORN, JAMES A. (JIM)

Left wing. Shoots left. 6'4", 220 lbs. Born, Hopkins, MN, July 28, 1957.
(Detroit's 4th choice, 73rd overall, in 1977 Amateur Draft).

			Regular Season					Playoffs				
Season	Club	Lea	GP	G	A	TP	PIM	GP	G	A	TP	PIM
1977-78	Providence	ECAC	33	7	14	21	47	....	....	....	....	....
1978-79	Providence	ECAC	27	5	19	24	72	....	....	....	....	....
1979-80	**Detroit**	**NHL**	**63**	**5**	**13**	**18**	**108**	....	....	....	....	....
	Adirondack	AHL	14	2	7	9	40	....	....	....	....	....
1980-81	Adirondack	AHL	9	3	7	10	53	....	....	....	....	....
	Detroit	**NHL**	**63**	**5**	**15**	**20**	**246**	....	....	....	....	....
1981-82	**Detroit**	**NHL**	**59**	**1**	**7**	**8**	**104**	....	....	....	....	....
	Toronto	**NHL**	**11**	**1**	**3**	**4**	**44**	....	....	....	....	....
1982-83	**Toronto**	**NHL**	**80**	**8**	**21**	**29**	**236**	**3**	**0**	**0**	**0**	**26**
1983-84	**Toronto**	**NHL**	**65**	**12**	**14**	**26**	**257**	....	....	....	....	....
1984-85	**Toronto**	**NHL**	**41**	**5**	**5**	**10**	**171**	....	....	....	....	....
1985-86			DID NOT PLAY									
1986-87	**Buffalo**	**NHL**	**52**	**4**	**10**	**14**	**158**	....	....	....	....	....
1987-88	**New Jersey**	**NHL**	**52**	**8**	**13**	**21**	**140**	**9**	**0**	**2**	**2**	**71**
1988-89	**New Jersey**	**NHL**	**65**	**15**	**16**	**31**	**212**	....	....	....	....	....
1989-90	**New Jersey**	**NHL**	**37**	**2**	**3**	**5**	**99**	....	....	....	....	....
	Calgary	**NHL**	**9**	**0**	**2**	**2**	**26**	**4**	**1**	**0**	**1**	**12**
	NHL Totals		**597**	**66**	**122**	**188**	**1801**	**16**	**1**	**2**	**3**	**109**

Traded to **Toronto** by **Detroit** for Toronto's fourth round choice (Craig Coxe) in 1982 Entry Draft and Toronto's fifth round choice (Joey Kocur) in 1983 Entry Draft, March 8, 1982. Traded to **Calgary** by **Toronto** for Terry Johnson. Traded to **Buffalo** by **Calgary** for Brian Engblom, October 3, 1986. Traded to **New Jersey** by **Buffalo** for Jan Ludwig, May 22, 1987. Traded to **Calgary** by **New Jersey** for Calgary's fifth round choice (Peter Kuchyna) in 1990 Entry Draft, March 6, 1990.

KOROL, DAVID

Defense. Shoots right. 6'1", 185 lbs. Born, Winnipeg, Man., March 1, 1965.
(Detroit's 4th choice, 70th overall, in 1983 Entry Draft).

			Regular Season					Playoffs				
Season	Club	Lea	GP	G	A	TP	PIM	GP	G	A	TP	PIM
1981-82	Winnipeg	WHL	64	4	22	26	55	....	....	....	....	....
1982-83	Winnipeg	WHL	72	14	32	57	90	3	0	1	1	0
1983-84	Winnipeg	WHL	57	15	48	63	49	....	....	....	....	....
	Adirondack	AHL	2	0	4	4	0	3	0	0	0	0
1984-85	Regina	WHL	48	4	30	34	61	3	0	0	0	0
1985-86	Adirondack	AHL	74	3	9	12	56	3	0	1	1	4
1986-87	Adirondack	AHL	48	1	4	5	67	11	2	2	4	21
1987-88	Adirondack	AHL	53	2	17	19	61	10	0	4	4	7
1988-89	Adirondack	AHL	73	3	24	27	57	17	1	2	3	8
1989-90	Phoenix	IHL	62	1	12	13	45	....	....	....	....	....

KOSTICHKIN, PAVEL

Center. Shoots left. 6'2", 200 lbs. Born, Moscow, Soviet Union, November 9, 1968.
(Winnipeg's 12th choice, 199th overall, in 1988 Entry Draft).

			Regular Season					Playoffs				
Season	Club	Lea	GP	G	A	TP	PIM	GP	G	A	TP	PIM
1985-86	CSKA	USSR	16	5	4	9	12	....	....	....	....	....
1986-87	CSKA	USSR	13	0	3	3	4	....	....	....	....	....
1987-88	CSKA	USSR	40	8	0	8	20	....	....	....	....	....
1988-89	CSKA	USSR	31	4	2	6	16	....	....	....	....	....
1989-90	CSKA	USSR	25	3	4	7	14	....	....	....	....	....

KOSTYNSKI, DOUGLAS (DOUG) (kah-STIN-skee)

Center. Shoots right. 6'1", 170 lbs. Born, Castlegar, B.C., February 23, 1963.
(Boston's 9th choice, 186th overall, in 1982 Entry Draft).

			Regular Season					Playoffs				
Season	Club	Lea	GP	G	A	TP	PIM	GP	G	A	TP	PIM
1979-80	N. Westminster	WHL	11	1	4	5	12	....	....	....	....	....
1980-81	N. Westminster	WHL	64	18	40	58	51	....	....	....	....	....
1981-82	Kamloops	WHL	53	39	42	81	57	3	1	0	1	0
1982-83	Kamloops	WHL	75	57	59	116	55	7	2	7	9	6
1983-84	**Boston**	**NHL**	**9**	**3**	**1**	**4**	**2**	....	....	....	....	....
	Hershey	AHL	67	13	27	40	8	....	....	....	....	....
1984-85	**Boston**	**NHL**	**6**	**0**	**0**	**0**	**2**	....	....	....	....	....
	Hershey	AHL	55	17	27	44	26	....	....	....	....	....
1985-86	Moncton	AHL	72	18	36	54	24	8	3	1	4	9
1986-87	Moncton	AHL	74	21	45	66	22	6	2	1	3	0
1987-88	Adirondack	AHL	10	3	3	6	10	1	0	0	0	2
1988-89	SaiPa	Fin.	44	20	32	52	16	....	....	....	....	....
1989-90	SaiPa	Fin.	38	13	18	31	34	....	....	....	....	....
	NHL Totals		**15**	**3**	**1**	**4**	**4**	....	....	....	....	....

KOTSOPOULOS, CHRISTOPHER (CHRIS) (kaht-SAH-puh-luhz)

Defense. Shoots right. 6'3", 215 lbs. Born, Scarborough, Ont., November 27, 1958.

			Regular Season					Playoffs				
Season	Club	Lea	GP	G	A	TP	PIM	GP	G	A	TP	PIM
1978-79	Toledo	IHL	62	6	22	28	153	6	1	7	8	48
1979-80	New Haven	AHL	75	7	27	34	149	10	4	5	9	28
1980-81	**NY Rangers**	**NHL**	**54**	**4**	**12**	**16**	**153**	**14**	**0**	**3**	**3**	**63**
1981-82	**Hartford**	**NHL**	**68**	**13**	**20**	**33**	**147**	....	....	....	....	....
1982-83	**Hartford**	**NHL**	**68**	**6**	**24**	**30**	**125**	....	....	....	....	....
1983-84	**Hartford**	**NHL**	**72**	**5**	**13**	**18**	**118**	....	....	....	....	....
1984-85	**Hartford**	**NHL**	**33**	**5**	**3**	**8**	**53**	....	....	....	....	....
1985-86	**Toronto**	**NHL**	**61**	**6**	**11**	**17**	**83**	**10**	**1**	**0**	**1**	**14**
1986-87	**Toronto**	**NHL**	**43**	**2**	**10**	**12**	**75**	**7**	**0**	**0**	**0**	**14**
1987-88	**Toronto**	**NHL**	**21**	**2**	**2**	**4**	**19**	....	....	....	....	....
1988-89	**Toronto**	**NHL**	**57**	**1**	**14**	**15**	**44**	....	....	....	....	....
1989-90	**Detroit**	**NHL**	**2**	**0**	**0**	**0**	**10**	....	....	....	....	....
	Adirondack	AHL	24	2	4	6	4	4	0	0	0	2
	NHL Totals		**479**	**44**	**109**	**153**	**827**	**31**	**1**	**3**	**4**	**91**

Signed as a free agent by **NY Rangers**, July 10, 1980. Traded to **Hartford** by **NY Rangers** with Gerry McDonald and Doug Sulliman for Mike Rogers and future considerations, October 2, 1981. Traded to **Toronto** by **Hartford** for Stewart Gavin, October 7, 1985. Signed as a free agent by **Detroit**, June 23, 1989.

KOZAK, MICHAEL

Right wing. Shoots right. 6'2", 195 lbs. Born, Toronto, Ont., March 14, 1969.
(Chicago's 9th choice, 216th overall, in 1989 Entry Draft).

			Regular Season					Playoffs				
Season	Club	Lea	GP	G	A	TP	PIM	GP	G	A	TP	PIM
1987-88	Clarkson	ECAC	21	3	2	5	....	....	....	....	....	....
1988-89	Clarkson	ECAC	25	10	9	19	20	....	....	....	....	....
1989-90	Clarkson	ECAC	32	8	14	22	38	....	....	....	....	....

KRAMER, TED

Right wing. Shoots right. 6', 190 lbs. Born, Findlay, OH, October 29, 1969.
(Los Angeles 7th choice, 144th overall, in 1989 Entry Draft).

			Regular Season					Playoffs				
Season	Club	Lea	GP	G	A	TP	PIM	GP	G	A	TP	PIM
1988-89	U. of Michigan	CCHA	37	16	14	30	70	....	....	....	....	....
1989-90	U. of Michigan	CCHA	42	21	24	45	111	....	....	....	....	....

KRAUSS, ROBERT

Defense. Shoots left. 6'2", 210 lbs. Born, Grand Prairie, Alta., October 28, 1969.
(Washington's 5th choice, 78th overall, in 1988 Entry Draft).

			Regular Season					Playoffs				
Season	Club	Lea	GP	G	A	TP	PIM	GP	G	A	TP	PIM
1986-87	Calgary	WHL	70	3	17	20	130	....	....	....	....	....
1987-88	Lethbridge	WHL	69	6	21	27	245	....	....	....	....	....
1988-89	Tri-Cities	WHL	66	4	23	27	257	7	1	2	3	19
1989-90	Tri-Cities	WHL	33	5	19	24	107	....	....	....	....	....

KRAYER, ED

Left wing. Shoots left. 6'1", 175 lbs. Born, Acton, MA, June 6, 1967.
(New Jersey's 8th choice, 150th overall, in 1985 Entry Draft).

			Regular Season					Playoffs				
Season	Club	Lea	GP	G	A	TP	PIM	GP	G	A	TP	PIM
1985-86	Harvard	ECAC	34	9	22	31	4	....	....	....	....	....
1986-87	Harvard	ECAC	14	2	9	11	4	....	....	....	....	....
1987-88	Harvard	ECAC	DID NOT PLAY — INJURED									
1988-89	Harvard	ECAC	34	12	14	26	4	....	....	....	....	....
1989-90	Nashville	ECHL	55	7	25	32	23	4	0	2	2	2

Rights traded to **Los Angeles** by **New Jersey** for future considerations, August 31, 1989.

KRENTZ, DALE

Left wing. Shoots left. 5'11", 190 lbs. Born, Steinbach, Man., December 19, 1961.

			Regular Season					Playoffs				
Season	Club	Lea	GP	G	A	TP	PIM	GP	G	A	TP	PIM
1982-83	Michigan State	CCHA	42	11	24	35	50	....	....	....	....	....
1983-84	Michigan State	CCHA	44	12	20	32	34	....	....	....	....	....
1984-85	Michigan State	CCHA	44	24	30	54	26	....	....	....	....	....
1985-86	Adirondack	AHL	79	19	27	46	27	13	2	6	8	9
1986-87	**Detroit**	**NHL**	**8**	**0**	**0**	**0**	**0**	....	....	....	....	....
	Adirondack	AHL	71	32	39	71	68	11	3	4	7	10
1987-88	**Detroit**	**NHL**	**6**	**2**	**0**	**2**	**5**	**2**	**0**	**0**	**0**	**0**
a	Adirondack	AHL	67	39	43	82	65	8	*11	4	15	8
1988-89	**Detroit**	**NHL**	**16**	**3**	**3**	**6**	**4**	....	....	....	....	....
	Adirondack	AHL	36	21	20	41	30	....	....	....	....	....
1989-90	Adirondack	AHL	74	38	50	88	36	6	2	3	5	11
	NHL Totals		**30**	**5**	**3**	**8**	**9**	**2**	**0**	**0**	**0**	**0**

a AHL Second All-Star Team (1988)

Signed as a free agent by **Detroit**, June 5, 1985.

KRIVOKHIZA, YURI

Defense. Shoots left. 6'2", 191 lbs. Born, Minsk, Soviet Union, May 30, 1968.
(Montreal's 11th choice, 209th overall, in 1988 Entry Draft).

			Regular Season					Playoffs				
Season	Club	Lea	GP	G	A	TP	PIM	GP	G	A	TP	PIM
1988-89	Dynamo Minsk	USSR	25	2	7	9	22	....	....	....	....	....
1989-90	Dynamo Minsk	USSR	47	4	2	6	48	....	....	....	....	....

KROMM, RICHARD GORDON (RICH)

Left wing. Shoots left. 5'11", 190 lbs. Born, Trail, B.C., March 29, I964.
(Calgary's 2nd choice, 37th overall, in 1982 Entry Draft).

			Regular Season					Playoffs				
Season	Club	Lea	GP	G	A	TP	PIM	GP	G	A	TP	PIM
1981-82	Portland	WHL	60	16	38	54	30	14	0	3	3	17
1982-83	Portland	WHL	72	35	68	103	64	14	7	13	20	12
1983-84	Portland	WHL	10	10	4	14	13	....	....	....	....	....
	Calgary	**NHL**	**53**	**11**	**12**	**23**	**27**	**11**	**1**	**1**	**2**	**9**
1984-85	**Calgary**	**NHL**	**73**	**20**	**32**	**52**	**32**	**3**	**0**	**1**	**1**	**4**
1985-86	**Calgary**	**NHL**	**63**	**12**	**17**	**29**	**31**	....	....	....	....	....
	NY Islanders	**NHL**	**14**	**7**	**7**	**14**	**4**	**3**	**0**	**1**	**1**	**0**
1986-87	**NY Islanders**	**NHL**	**70**	**12**	**17**	**29**	**20**	**14**	**1**	**3**	**4**	**4**
1987-88	**NY Islanders**	**NHL**	**71**	**5**	**10**	**15**	**20**	**5**	**0**	**0**	**0**	**5**
1988-89	**NY Islanders**	**NHL**	**20**	**1**	**6**	**7**	**4**	....	....	....	....	....
	Springfield	AHL	48	21	26	47	15	....	....	....	....	....
1989-90	Springfield	AHL	9	3	4	7	4	16	1	5	6	4
	NHL Totals		**364**	**68**	**101**	**169**	**138**	**36**	**2**	**6**	**8**	**22**

Traded to **NY Islanders** by **Calgary** with Steve Konroyd for John Tonelli, March 11, 1986.

KRON, ROBERT

Right wing/Center. Shoots right. 5'10", 174 lbs. Born, Brno Czech., February 27, 1967.
(Vancouver's 5th choice, 88th overall, in 1985 Entry Draft).

			Regular Season					Playoffs				
Season	Club	Lea	GP	G	A	TP	PIM	GP	G	A	TP	PIM
1986-87	Zetor Brno	Czech.	28	14	11	25	....	....	....	....	....	....
1987-88	Zetor Brno	Czech.	32	12	6	18	....	....	....	....	....	....
1988-89	Zetor Brno	Czech.	43	28	19	47	....	....	....	....	....	....
1989-90	Zetor Brno	Czech.	39	22	22	44	....	....	....	....	....	....

KRUMPSCHMID, NORM

Center. Shoots left. 5'11", 190 lbs. Born, Sudbury, Ont., December 13, 1969.
(Vancouver's 2nd choice, 7th overall, in 1990 Supplemental Draft).

			Regular Season					Playoffs				
Season	Club	Lea	GP	G	A	TP	PIM	GP	G	A	TP	PIM
1988-89	Ferris State	CCHA	35	5	7	12	40	....	....	....	....	....
1989-90	Ferris State	CCHA	36	6	14	20	22	....	....	....	....	....

KRUPP, UWE (OO-VAY KROOP)

Defense. Shoots right. 6'6", 235 lbs. Born, Cologne, West Germany, June 24, 1965.
(Buffalo's 13th choice, 214th overall, in 1983 Entry Draft).

			Regular Season					Playoffs				
Season	Club	Lea	GP	G	A	TP	PIM	GP	G	A	TP	PIM
1983-84	KEC	W. Ger.	40	0	4	4	22	....	....	....	....	....
1984-85	KEC	W. Ger.	39	11	8	19	36	....	....	....	....	....
1985-86	KEC	W. Ger.	45	10	21	31	83	....	....	....	....	....
1986-87	**Buffalo**	**NHL**	**26**	**1**	**4**	**5**	**23**	....	....	....	....	....
	Rochester	AHL	42	3	19	22	50	17	1	11	12	16
1987-88	**Buffalo**	**NHL**	**75**	**2**	**9**	**11**	**151**	**6**	**0**	**0**	**0**	**15**
1988-89	**Buffalo**	**NHL**	**70**	**5**	**13**	**18**	**55**	**5**	**0**	**1**	**1**	**4**
1989-90	**Buffalo**	**NHL**	**74**	**3**	**20**	**23**	**85**	**6**	**0**	**0**	**0**	**4**
	NHL Totals		**245**	**11**	**46**	**57**	**314**	**17**	**0**	**1**	**1**	**23**

KRUPPKE, GORD (KRUP-kee)

Defense. Shoots right. 6'1", 200 lbs. Born, Slave Lake, Alta., April 2, 1969.
(Detroit's 2nd choice, 32nd overall, in 1987 Entry Draft).

			Regular Season					Playoffs				
Season	Club	Lea	GP	G	A	TP	PIM	GP	G	A	TP	PIM
1985-87	Prince Albert	WHL	62	1	8	9	81	20	4	4	8	22
1986-87	Prince Albert	WHL	49	2	10	12	129	8	0	0	0	9
1987-88	Prince Albert	WHL	54	8	8	16	113	10	0	0	0	46
1988-89	Prince Albert	WHL	62	6	26	32	254	3	0	0	0	11
1989-90	Adirondack	AHL	59	2	12	14	103	....	....	....	....	....

KRUSHELNYSKI, MICHAEL (MIKE) (KROO-shuhl-NIH-skee)

Center. Shoots left. 6'2", 200 lbs. Born, Montreal, Que., April 27, 1960.
(Boston's 7th choice, 120th overall, in 1979 Entry Draft).

			Regular Season					Playoffs				
Season	Club	Lea	GP	G	A	TP	PIM	GP	G	A	TP	PIM
1978-79	Montreal	QJHL	46	15	29	44	42	11	3	4	7	8
1979-80	Montreal	QJHL	72	39	60	99	78	6	2	3	5	2
1980-81	Springfield	AHL	80	25	28	53	47	7	1	1	2	29
1981-82	Erie	AHL	62	31	52	83	44	....	....	....	....	....
	Boston	**NHL**	**17**	**3**	**3**	**6**	**2**	**1**	**0**	**0**	**0**	**2**
1982-83	**Boston**	**NHL**	**79**	**23**	**42**	**65**	**43**	**17**	**8**	**6**	**14**	**12**
1983-84	**Boston**	**NHL**	**66**	**25**	**20**	**45**	**55**	**2**	**0**	**0**	**0**	**0**
1984-85	**Edmonton**	**NHL**	**80**	**43**	**45**	**88**	**60**	**18**	**5**	**8**	**13**	**22**
1985-86	**Edmonton**	**NHL**	**54**	**16**	**24**	**40**	**22**	**10**	**4**	**5**	**9**	**16**
1986-87	**Edmonton**	**NHL**	**80**	**16**	**35**	**51**	**67**	**21**	**3**	**4**	**7**	**18**
1987-88	**Edmonton**	**NHL**	**76**	**20**	**27**	**47**	**64**	**19**	**4**	**6**	**10**	**12**
1988-89	**Los Angeles**	**NHL**	**78**	**26**	**36**	**62**	**110**	**11**	**1**	**4**	**5**	**4**
1989-90	**Los Angeles**	**NHL**	**63**	**16**	**25**	**41**	**50**	**10**	**1**	**3**	**4**	**12**
	NHL Totals		**593**	**188**	**257**	**445**	**473**	**109**	**26**	**36**	**62**	**98**

Played in NHL All-Star Game (1985)

Traded to **Edmonton** by **Boston** for Ken Linseman, June 21, 1984. Traded to **Los Angeles** by **Edmonton** with Wayne Gretzky and Marty McSorley for Jimmy Carson, Martin Gelinas, Los Angeles' first round choices in 1989 (acquired by New Jersey, June 17, 1989. New Jersey selected Jason Miller), 1991 and 1993 Entry Drafts and cash, August 9, 1988.

KRUTOV, VLADIMIR

Left wing. Shoots left. 5'9", 195 lbs. Born, Moscow, Soviet Union, June 1, 1960.
(Vancouver's 11th choice, 238th overall, in 1986 Entry Draft).

			Regular Season					Playoffs				
Season	**Club**	**Lea**	**GP**	**G**	**A**	**TP**	**PIM**	**GP**	**G**	**A**	**TP**	**PIM**
1977-78	CSKA	USSR	1	0	0	0	0	....	....	....	....	....
1978-79	CSKA	USSR	25	8	3	11	6	....	....	....	....	....
1979-80	CSKA	USSR	40	30	12	42	16	....	....	....	....	....
1980-81	CSKA	USSR	47	25	15	40	20	....	....	....	....	....
1981-82a	CSKA	USSR	46	37	29	66	30	....	....	....	....	....
1982-83a	CSKA	USSR	44	32	21	53	34	....	....	....	....	....
1983-84a	CSKA	USSR	44	37	20	57	20	....	....	....	....	....
1984-85a	CSKA	USSR	40	23	30	53	26	....	....	....	....	....
1985-86a	CSKA	USSR	40	31	17	48	10	....	....	....	....	....
1986-87a	CSKA	USSR	39	26	24	50	16	....	....	....	....	....
1987-88a	CSKA	USSR	38	19	23	42	20	....	....	....	....	....
1988-89	CSKA	USSR	35	20	21	41	12	....	....	....	....	....
1989-90	**Vancouver**	**NHL**	**61**	**11**	**23**	**34**	**20**	....	....	....	....	....
	NHL Totals		**61**	**11**	**23**	**34**	**20**	....	....	....	....	....

a Soviet National League All-Star (1982-88)

KRYGIER, TODD (KREE-guhr)

Left wing. Shoots left. 5'11", 180 lbs. Born, Northville, MI, October 12, 1965.
(Hartford's 1st choice, 16th overall, in 1988 Supplemental Draft).

			Regular Season					Playoffs				
Season	**Club**	**Lea**	**GP**	**G**	**A**	**TP**	**PIM**	**GP**	**G**	**A**	**TP**	**PIM**
1987-88	U. Connecticut	NCAA	27	32	39	71	28	....	....	....	....	....
	New Haven	AHL	13	1	5	6	34	....	....	....	....	....
1988-89	Binghamton	AHL	76	26	42	68	77	....	....	....	....	....
1989-90	**Hartford**	**NHL**	**58**	**18**	**12**	**30**	**52**	**7**	**2**	**1**	**3**	**4**
	Binghamton	AHL	12	1	9	10	16	....	....	....	....	....
	NHL Totals		**58**	**18**	**12**	**30**	**52**	**7**	**2**	**1**	**3**	**4**

KRYS, MARK

Defense. Shoots right. 6', 185 lbs. Born, Timmins, Ont., May 29, 1969.
(Boston's 6th choice, 123rd overall, in 1988 Entry Draft).

			Regular Season					Playoffs				
Season	**Club**	**Lea**	**GP**	**G**	**A**	**TP**	**PIM**	**GP**	**G**	**A**	**TP**	**PIM**
1987-88	Boston U.	H.E.	34	0	6	6	40	....	....	....	....	....
1988-89	Boston U.	H.E.	35	0	7	7	54	....	....	....	....	....
1989-90	Boston U.	H.E.	30	0	4	4	34	....	....	....	....	....

KUCERA, FRANTISEK

Defense. Shoots right. 6'2", 205 lbs. Born, Prague, Czechoslovakia, February 3, 1968.
(Chicago's 3rd choice, 77th overall, in 1986 Entry Draft).

			Regular Season					Playoffs				
Season	**Club**	**Lea**	**GP**	**G**	**A**	**TP**	**PIM**	**GP**	**G**	**A**	**TP**	**PIM**
1986-87	Sparta Praha	Czech.	33	7	2	9	....	....	....	....	....	....
1987-88	Sparta Praha	Czech.	34	4	2	6	....	....	....	....	....	....
1988-89	Jihlava	Czech.	45	10	9	19	....	....	....	....	....	....
1989-90	Dukla Jihlava	Czech	43	9	10	19	....	....	....	....	....	....

KUCHYNA, PETER

Defense. Shoots right. 6'2", 180 lbs. Born, Czechoslovakia, January 14, 1970.
(New Jersey's 5th choice, 104th overall, in 1990 Entry Draft).

			Regular Season					Playoffs				
Season	**Club**	**Lea**	**GP**	**G**	**A**	**TP**	**PIM**	**GP**	**G**	**A**	**TP**	**PIM**
1989-90	Dukla Jihlava	Czech.	32	2	2	4	....	....	....	....	....	....

KUDELSKI, BOB

Right wing. Shoots right. 6'1", 200 lbs. Born, Feeding Hills, MA, March 3, 1964.
(Los Angeles' 1st choice, 2nd overall, in 1986 Supplemental Draft).

			Regular Season					Playoffs				
Season	**Club**	**Lea**	**GP**	**G**	**A**	**TP**	**PIM**	**GP**	**G**	**A**	**TP**	**PIM**
1983-84	Yale	ECAC	21	14	12	26	12	....	....	....	....	....
1984-85	Yale	ECAC	32	21	23	44	38	....	....	....	....	....
1985-86	Yale	ECAC	31	18	23	41	48	....	....	....	....	....
1986-87a	Yale	ECAC	30	25	22	47	34	....	....	....	....	....
1987-88	**Los Angeles**	**NHL**	**26**	**0**	**1**	**1**	**8**	....	....	....	....	....
	New Haven	AHL	50	15	19	34	41	....	....	....	....	....
1988-89	**Los Angeles**	**NHL**	**14**	**1**	**3**	**4**	**17**	....	....	....	....	....
	New Haven	AHL	60	32	19	51	43	17	8	5	13	12
1989-90	**Los Angeles**	**NHL**	**62**	**23**	**13**	**36**	**49**	**8**	**1**	**2**	**3**	**2**
	NHL Totals		**102**	**24**	**17**	**41**	**74**	**8**	**1**	**2**	**3**	**2**

a ECAC First All-Star Team (1987)

KULAK, STUART (STU)

Right wing. Shoots right. 5'10", 180 lbs. Born, Edmonton, Alta., March 10, 1963.
(Vancouver's 5th choice, 115th overall, in 1981 Entry Draft).

			Regular Season					Playoffs				
Season	**Club**	**Lea**	**GP**	**G**	**A**	**TP**	**PIM**	**GP**	**G**	**A**	**TP**	**PIM**
1979-80	Sherwood Park	AJHL	53	30	23	53	111	....	....	....	....	....
	Victoria	WHL	3	0	0	0	0	....	....	....	....	....
1980-81	Victoria	WHL	72	23	24	47	44	15	3	5	8	19
1981-82	Victoria	WHL	71	38	50	88	92	4	1	2	3	43
1982-83	**Vancouver**	**NHL**	**4**	**1**	**1**	**2**	**0**	....	....	....	....	....
	Victoria	WHL	50	29	33	62	130	10	10	9	19	29
1983-84	Fredericton	AHL	52	12	16	28	55	5	0	0	0	59
1984-85			DID NOT PLAY — INJURED									
1985-86	Fredericton	AHL	3	1	0	1	0	6	2	1	3	0
	Kalamazoo	IHL	30	14	8	22	38	2	2	0	2	0
1986-87	**Vancouver**	**NHL**	**28**	**1**	**1**	**2**	**37**	....	....	....	....	....
	Edmonton	**NHL**	**23**	**3**	**1**	**4**	**41**	....	....	....	....	....
	NY Rangers	**NHL**	**3**	**0**	**0**	**0**	**0**	**3**	**0**	**0**	**0**	**2**
1987-88	**Quebec**	**NHL**	**14**	**1**	**1**	**2**	**28**	....	....	....	....	....
	Moncton	AHL	37	9	12	21	58	....	....	....	....	....
1988-89	**Winnipeg**	**NHL**	**18**	**2**	**0**	**2**	**24**	....	....	....	....	....
	Moncton	AHL	51	30	29	59	98	10	5	6	11	16
1989-90	Moncton	AHL	36	14	23	37	72	....	....	....	....	....
	NHL Totals		**90**	**8**	**4**	**12**	**130**	**3**	**0**	**0**	**0**	**2**

Sold to **Edmonton** by **Vancouver**, December 11, 1986. Acquired by **NY Rangers** from **Edmonton** to complete Reijo Ruotsalanien trade, March 10, 1987. Claimed by **Quebec** in NHL Waiver Draft, October 5, 1987. Traded to **Winnipeg** by **Quebec** for Bob Dollas, December 17, 1987.

KULONEN, TIMO

Defense. Shoots right. 6'4", 210 lbs. Born, Forssa, Finland, November 1, 1967.
(Minnesota's 7th choice, 130th overall, in 1987 Entry Draft).

			Regular Season					Playoffs				
Season	**Club**	**Lea**	**GP**	**G**	**A**	**TP**	**PIM**	**GP**	**G**	**A**	**TP**	**PIM**
1986-87	KalPa	Fin.	39	2	8	10	20	....	....	....	....	....
1987-88	KalPa	Fin.	44	7	15	22	32	....	....	....	....	....
1988-89	Kalpa	Fin.	40	9	16	25	18	2	0	1	1	0
1989-90	Kalpa	Fin.	44	5	20	25	34	6	0	0	0	

KUMMU, AL

Defense. Shoots right. 6'4", 195 lbs. Born, Kitchener, Ont., January 21, 1969.
(Philadelphia's 8th choice, 201st overall, in 1989 Entry Draft).

			Regular Season					Playoffs				
Season	**Club**	**Lea**	**GP**	**G**	**A**	**TP**	**PIM**	**GP**	**G**	**A**	**TP**	**PIM**
1988-89	Humboldt	SJHL	35	7	22	29	115	....	....	....	....	....
1989-90	RPI	ECAC	33	9	13	22	50	....	....	....	....	....

KUMMU, RYAN

Defense. Shoots left. 6'3", 205 lbs. Born, Kitchener, Ont., June 5, 1967.
(Washington's 11th choice, 246th overall, in 1987 Entry Draft).

			Regular Season					Playoffs				
Season	**Club**	**Lea**	**GP**	**G**	**A**	**TP**	**PIM**	**GP**	**G**	**A**	**TP**	**PIM**
1986-87	RPI	ECAC	28	0	2	2	32	....	....	....	....	....
1987-88	RPI	ECAC	29	5	10	15	40	....	....	....	....	....
1988-89	RPI	ECAC	29	2	5	7	28	....	....	....	....	....
1989-90	Maine	AHL	8	0	0	0	11	....	....	....	....	....
	Erie	ECHL	45	5	30	35	71	7	0	8	8	10

KUMPEL, MARK

Right wing. Shoots right. 6', 190 lbs. Born, Wakefield, MA, March 7, 1961.
(Quebec's 4th choice, 108th overall, in 1980 Entry Draft).

			Regular Season					Playoffs				
Season	**Club**	**Lea**	**GP**	**G**	**A**	**TP**	**PIM**	**GP**	**G**	**A**	**TP**	**PIM**
1979-80	U. of Lowell	ECAC	30	18	18	36	12	....	....	....	....	....
1980-81	U. of Lowell	ECAC	1	2	0	2	0	....	....	....	....	....
1981-82	U. of Lowell	ECAC	35	17	13	30	23	....	....	....	....	....
1982-83	U. of Lowell	ECAC	7	8	5	13	0	....	....	....	....	....
	U.S. National	...	30	14	18	32	6	....	....	....	....	....
1983-84	U.S. National	...	61	14	19	33	19	....	....	....	....	....
	U.S. Olympic	...	6	1	0	1	2	....	....	....	....	....
	Fredericton	AHL	16	1	1	2	5	3	0	0	0	15
1984-85	**Quebec**	**NHL**	**42**	**8**	**7**	**15**	**26**	**18**	**3**	**4**	**7**	**4**
	Fredericton	AHL	18	9	6	15	17	....	....	....	....	....
1985-86	**Quebec**	**NHL**	**47**	**10**	**12**	**22**	**17**	**2**	**1**	**0**	**1**	**0**
	Fredericton	AHL	7	4	2	6	4	....	....	....	....	....
1986-87	**Quebec**	**NHL**	**40**	**1**	**8**	**9**	**16**	....	....	....	....	....
	Detroit	**NHL**	**5**	**0**	**1**	**1**	**0**	**8**	**0**	**0**	**0**	**4**
	Adirondack	AHL	7	2	3	5	0	1	1	0	1	0
1987-88	**Detroit**	**NHL**	**13**	**0**	**2**	**2**	**4**	....	....	....	....	....
	Adirondack	AHL	4	5	0	5	2	....	....	....	....	....
	Winnipeg	**NHL**	**32**	**4**	**4**	**8**	**19**	**4**	**0**	**0**	**0**	**4**
1988-89	Moncton	AHL	53	22	23	45	25	10	3	4	7	0
1989-90	**Winnipeg**	**NHL**	**56**	**8**	**9**	**17**	**21**	**7**	**2**	**0**	**2**	**2**
	NHL Totals		**235**	**31**	**43**	**74**	**103**	**39**	**6**	**4**	**10**	**14**

Traded to **Detroit** by **Quebec** with Brent Ashton and Gilbert Delorme for Basil McRae, John Ogrodnick and Doug Shedden, January 17, 1987. Traded to **Winnipeg** by **Detroit** for Jim Nill, January 11, 1988.

KURRI, JARI (KUHR-ree, YAH-ree)

Right wing. Shoots right. 6'1", 195 lbs. Born, Helsinki, Finland, May 18, 1960.
(Edmonton's 3rd choice, 69th overall, in 1980 Entry Draft).

			Regular Season					Playoffs				
Season	Club	Lea	GP	G	A	TP	PIM	GP	G	A	TP	PIM
1977-78	Jokerit	Fin.	29	2	9	11	12	....	....	....	....	....
1978-79	Jokerit	Fin.	33	16	14	30	12	....	....	....	....	....
1979-80	Jokerit	Fin.	33	23	16	39	22	6	7	2	9	13
1980-81	**Edmonton**	**NHL**	**75**	**32**	**43**	**75**	**40**	**9**	**5**	**7**	**12**	**4**
1981-82	**Edmonton**	**NHL**	**71**	**32**	**54**	**86**	**32**	**5**	**2**	**5**	**7**	**10**
1982-83	**Edmonton**	**NHL**	**80**	**45**	**59**	**104**	**22**	**16**	**8**	**15**	**23**	**8**
1983-84a	**Edmonton**	**NHL**	**64**	**52**	**61**	**113**	**14**	**19**	***14**	**14**	**28**	**13**
1984-85bc	**Edmonton**	**NHL**	**73**	**71**	**64**	**135**	**30**	**18**	***19**	**12**	**31**	**6**
1985-86a	**Edmonton**	**NHL**	**78**	***68**	**63**	**131**	**22**	**10**	**2**	**10**	**12**	**4**
1986-87c	**Edmonton**	**NHL**	**79**	**54**	**54**	**108**	**41**	**21**	***15**	**10**	**25**	**20**
1987-88	**Edmonton**	**NHL**	**80**	**43**	**53**	**96**	**30**	**19**	***14**	**17**	**31**	**12**
1988-89d	**Edmonton**	**NHL**	**76**	**44**	**58**	**102**	**69**	**7**	**3**	**5**	**8**	**6**
1989-90	**Edmonton**	**NHL**	**78**	**33**	**60**	**93**	**48**	**22**	**10**	**15**	**25**	**18**
	NHL Totals		**754**	**474**	**569**	**1043**	**348**	**146**	***92**	**110**	**202**	**101**

a NHL Second All-Star Team (1984, 1986)
b Won Lady Byng Memorial Trophy (1985)
c NHL First All-Star Team (1985, 1987)
d NHL Second All-Star Team (1989)

Played in NHL All-Star Game (1983, 1985, 1986, 1988-90)

KURVERS, TOM

Defense. Shoots left. 6', 205 lbs. Born, Minneapolis, MN, September 14, 1962.
(Montreal's 10th choice, 145th overall, in 1981 Entry Draft).

			Regular Season					Playoffs				
Season	Club	Lea	GP	G	A	TP	PIM	GP	G	A	TP	PIM
1980-81	Minn.-Duluth	WCHA	39	6	24	30	48	....	....	....	....	....
1981-82	Minn.-Duluth	WCHA	37	11	31	42	18	....	....	....	....	....
1982-83	Minn.-Duluth	WCHA	26	4	23	27	24	....	....	....	....	....
1983-84ab	Minn.-Duluth	WCHA	43	18	58	76	46	....	....	....	....	....
1984-85	**Montreal**	**NHL**	**75**	**10**	**35**	**45**	**30**	**12**	**0**	**6**	**6**	**6**
1985-86	**Montreal**	**NHL**	**62**	**7**	**23**	**30**	**36**	....	....	....	....	....
1986-87	**Montreal**	**NHL**	**1**	**0**	**0**	**0**	**0**	....	....	....	....	....
	Buffalo	**NHL**	**55**	**6**	**17**	**23**	**22**	....	....	....	....	....
1987-88	**New Jersey**	**NHL**	**56**	**5**	**29**	**34**	**46**	**19**	**6**	**9**	**15**	**38**
1988-89	**New Jersey**	**NHL**	**74**	**16**	**50**	**66**	**38**	....	....	....	....	....
1989-90	**New Jersey**	**NHL**	**1**	**0**	**0**	**0**	**0**	....	....	....	....	....
	Toronto	**NHL**	**70**	**15**	**37**	**52**	**29**	**5**	**0**	**3**	**3**	**4**
	NHL Totals		**394**	**59**	**191**	**250**	**201**	**36**	**6**	**18**	**24**	**48**

a WCHA First All-Star Team (1984)
b Won Hobey Baker Memorial Trophy (1984)

Traded to **Buffalo** by **Montreal** for Buffalo's second-round choice (Martin St. Amour) in 1988 Entry Draft, November 18, 1986. Traded to **New Jersey** by **Buffalo** for the rights to Detroit's third-round choice (Andrew MacVicar) in 1987 Entry Draft previously acquired by New Jersey in Mel Bridgman deal, June 13, 1987. Traded to **Toronto** by **New Jersey** for Toronto's first round choice in 1991 Entry Draft, October 16, 1989.

KURZAWSKI, MARK

Defense. Shoots right. 6'3", 200 lbs. Born, Chicago, IL, February 25, 1968.
(Chicago's 2nd choice, 35th overall, in 1986 Entry Draft).

			Regular Season					Playoffs				
Season	Club	Lea	GP	G	A	TP	PIM	GP	G	A	TP	PIM
1985-86	Windsor	OHL	66	11	25	36	66	16	3	5	8	23
1986-87	Windsor	OHL	65	5	23	28	98	14	3	4	7	38
1987-88	Windsor	OHL	62	8	13	21	150	12	1	2	3	8
1988-89	Saginaw	IHL	75	2	11	13	71	6	0	0	0	12
1989-90	Saginaw	IHL	10	0	0	0	8	....	....	....	....	....

KUSHNER, DALE

Left wing. Shoots left. 6'1", 205 lbs. Born, Terrace, B.C., June 13, 1966.

			Regular Season					Playoffs				
Season	Club	Lea	GP	G	A	TP	PIM	GP	G	A	TP	PIM
1984-85	Prince Albert	WHL	2	0	0	0	2	....	....	....	....	....
	Moose Jaw	WHL	17	5	2	7	23	....	....	....	....	....
	Medicine Hat	WHL	48	23	17	40	173	....	....	....	....	....
1985-86	Medicine Hat	WHL	66	25	19	44	218	10	3	3	6	18
1986-87	Medicine Hat	WHL	63	34	34	68	250	25	0	5	5	114
1987-88	Springfield	AHL	68	13	23	36	201	....	....	....	....	....
1988-89	Springfield	AHL	45	5	8	13	132	....	....	....	....	....
1989-90	**NY Islanders**	**NHL**	**2**	**0**	**0**	**0**	**2**	....	....	....	....	....
	Springfield	AHL	45	14	11	25	163	7	2	3	5	61
	NHL Totals		**2**	**0**	**0**	**0**	**2**	....	....	....	....	....

Signed as a free agent by **NY Islanders**, April 7, 1987. Signed as a free agent by **Philadelphia**, July 31, 1990.

KUWABARA, RYAN

Right wing. Shoots right. 6'1", 205 lbs. Born, Hamilton, Ont., March 23, 1972.
(Montreal's 2nd choice, 39th overall, in 1990 Entry Draft).

			Regular Season					Playoffs				
Season	Club	Lea	GP	G	A	TP	PIM	GP	G	A	TP	PIM
1988-89	Hamilton	Jr.B	39	13	23	36	118	....	....	....	....	....
1989-90	Ottawa	OHL	66	30	38	68	62	4	0	0	0	0

KYLLONEN, MARKKU (kill-OH-nen)

Left wing. Shoots left. 6'2", 200 lbs. Born, Joensuu, Finland, February 15, 1962.
(Winnipeg's 8th choice, 163rd overall, in 1987 Entry Draft).

			Regular Season					Playoffs				
Season	Club	Lea	GP	G	A	TP	PIM	GP	G	A	TP	PIM
1984-85	JoKP	Fin. 2	43	28	27	55	22	....	....	....	....	....
1985-86	JoKP	Fin. 2	34	12	12	24	14	....	....	....	....	....
1986-87	Karpat	Fin.	43	24	16	40	14	9	3	2	5	4
1987-88	Karpat	Fin.	43	8	24	32	32	....	....	....	....	....
1988-89	**Winnipeg**	**NHL**	**9**	**0**	**2**	**2**	**2**	....	....	....	....	....
	Moncton	AHL	60	14	20	34	16	5	1	0	1	0
1989-90	JOKP	Fin.	42	16	12	28	22	....	....	....	....	....
	NHL Totals		**9**	**0**	**2**	**2**	**2**	....	....	....	....	....

KYPREOS, NICHOLAS (NICK) (KIH-pree-ohz)

Left wing. Shoots left. 6', 195 lbs. Born, Toronto, Ont., June 4, 1966.

			Regular Season					Playoffs				
Season	Club	Lea	GP	G	A	TP	PIM	GP	G	A	TP	PIM
1983-84	North Bay	OHL	51	12	11	23	36	4	3	2	5	9
1984-85	North Bay	OHL	64	41	36	77	71	8	2	2	4	15
1985-86a	North Bay	OHL	64	62	35	97	112	....	....	....	....	....
1986-87	Hershey	AHL	10	0	1	1	4	....	....	....	....	....
b	North Bay	OHL	46	49	41	90	54	24	11	5	16	78
1987-88	Hershey	AHL	71	24	20	44	101	12	0	2	2	17
1988-89	Hershey	AHL	28	12	15	27	19	12	4	5	9	11
1989-90	**Washington**	**NHL**	**31**	**5**	**4**	**9**	**82**	**7**	**1**	**0**	**1**	**15**
	Baltimore	AHL	14	6	5	11	6	7	4	1	5	17
	NHL Totals		**31**	**5**	**4**	**9**	**82**	**7**	**1**	**0**	**1**	**15**

a OHL First All-Star Team (1986)
b OHL Second All-Star Team (1987)

Signed as a free agent by **Philadelphia**, September 30, 1984. Claimed by **Washington** in NHL Waiver Draft, October 2, 1989.

KYTE, JAMES (JIM) (KITE)

Defense. Shoots left. 6'5", 220 lbs. Born, Ottawa, Ont., March 21, 1964.
(Winnipeg's 1st choice, 12th overall, in 1982 Entry Draft).

			Regular Season					Playoffs				
Season	Club	Lea	GP	G	A	TP	PIM	GP	G	A	TP	PIM
1981-82	Cornwall	OHL	52	4	13	17	148	5	0	0	0	10
1982-83	**Winnipeg**	**NHL**	**2**	**0**	**0**	**0**	**0**	....	....	....	....	....
	Cornwall	OHL	65	6	30	36	195	8	0	2	2	24
1983-84	**Winnipeg**	**NHL**	**58**	**1**	**2**	**3**	**55**	**3**	**0**	**0**	**0**	**11**
1984-85	**Winnipeg**	**NHL**	**71**	**0**	**3**	**3**	**111**	**8**	**0**	**0**	**0**	**14**
1985-86	**Winnipeg**	**NHL**	**71**	**1**	**3**	**4**	**126**	**3**	**0**	**0**	**0**	**12**
1986-87	**Winnipeg**	**NHL**	**72**	**5**	**5**	**10**	**162**	**10**	**0**	**4**	**4**	**36**
1987-88	**Winnipeg**	**NHL**	**51**	**1**	**3**	**4**	**128**	....	....	....	....	....
1988-89	**Winnipeg**	**NHL**	**74**	**3**	**9**	**12**	**190**	....	....	....	....	....
1989-90	**Pittsburgh**	**NHL**	**56**	**3**	**1**	**4**	**125**	....	....	....	....	....
	NHL Totals		**455**	**14**	**26**	**40**	**897**	**24**	**0**	**4**	**4**	**73**

Traded to **Pittsburgh** by **Winnipeg** with Andrew McBain and Randy Gilhen for Randy Cunnyworth, Rick Tabaracci and Dave McLlwain, June 17, 1989.

LACKTEN, KURT

Right wing. Shoots right. 6', 177 lbs. Born, Kamsack, Sask., May 20, 1967.
(NY Islanders' 9th choice, 139th overall, in 1985 Entry Draft).

			Regular Season					Playoffs				
Season	Club	Lea	GP	G	A	TP	PIM	GP	G	A	TP	PIM
1984-85	Moose Jaw	WHL	66	18	13	31	141	....	....	....	....	....
1985-86	Calgary	WHL	61	5	20	25	112	....	....	....	....	....
1986-87	Swift Current	WHL	65	20	20	40	97	3	0	1	1	4
1987-88	Springfield	AHL	37	1	4	5	64	....	....	....	....	....
	Peoria	IHL	19	0	5	5	20	....	....	....	....	....
1988-89	Indianapolis	IHL	9	1	2	3	11	....	....	....	....	....
1989-90	Virginia	ECHL	8	0	4	4	7	....	....	....	....	....

LACOMBE, NORMAND

Right wing. Shoots right. 6', 205 lbs. Born, Pierrefonds, Que., October 18, 1964.
(Buffalo's 2nd choice, 10th overall, in 1983 Entry Draft).

			Regular Season					Playoffs				
Season	Club	Lea	GP	G	A	TP	PIM	GP	G	A	TP	PIM
1981-82	N. Hampshire	ECAC	35	18	16	34	38	....	....	....	....	....
1982-83	N. Hampshire	ECAC	35	18	25	43	48	....	....	....	....	....
1983-84	Rochester	AHL	44	10	16	26	45	....	....	....	....	....
1984-85	**Buffalo**	**NHL**	**30**	**2**	**4**	**6**	**25**	....	....	....	....	....
	Rochester	AHL	33	13	16	29	33	5	3	1	4	4
1985-86	**Buffalo**	**NHL**	**25**	**6**	**7**	**13**	**13**	....	....	....	....	....
	Rochester	AHL	32	10	13	23	56	....	....	....	....	....
1986-87	**Buffalo**	**NHL**	**39**	**4**	**7**	**11**	**8**	....	....	....	....	....
	Rochester	AHL	13	6	5	11	4	....	....	....	....	....
	Edmonton	**NHL**	**1**	**0**	**0**	**0**	**2**	....	....	....	....	....
	Nova Scotia	AHL	10	3	5	8	4	5	1	1	2	6
1987-88	**Edmonton**	**NHL**	**53**	**8**	**9**	**17**	**36**	**19**	**3**	**0**	**3**	**28**
1988-89	**Edmonton**	**NHL**	**64**	**17**	**11**	**28**	**57**	**7**	**2**	**1**	**3**	**21**
1989-90	**Edmonton**	**NHL**	**15**	**5**	**2**	**7**	**21**	....	....	....	....	....
	Philadelphia	**NHL**	**18**	**0**	**2**	**2**	**28**	....	....	....	....	....
	NHL Totals		**245**	**42**	**42**	**84**	**190**	**26**	**5**	**1**	**6**	**49**

Traded to **Edmonton** by **Buffalo** with Wayne Van Dorp and future considerations for Lee Fogolin and Mark Napier, March 6, 1987. Traded to **Philadelphia** by **Edmonton** for future considerations, January 5, 1990.

LACOUTURE, BILL

Right wing. Shoots right. 6'2", 190 lbs. Born, Framingham, MA, May 28, 1968.
(Chicago's 11th choice, 218th overall, in 1987 Entry Draft).

			Regular Season					Playoffs				
Season	Club	Lea	GP	G	A	TP	PIM	GP	G	A	TP	PIM
1987-88	N. Hampshire	H.E.	13	1	3	4	2	....	....	....	....	....
1988-89	N. Hampshire	H.E.	20	0	1	1	2	....	....	....	....	....
1989-90	N. Hampshire	H.E.	2	0	0	0	0	....	....	....	....	....

LACOUTURE, DAVID

Right wing. Shoots right. 6'3", 205 lbs. Born, Framingham, MA, December 30, 1969.
(St. Louis' 5th choice, 105th overall, in 1988 Entry Draft).

			Regular Season					Playoffs				
Season	Club	Lea	GP	G	A	TP	PIM	GP	G	A	TP	PIM
1988-89	Halifax Lions	Jr.A	16	10	15	25	48	....	....	....	....	....
1989-90	U. of Maine	H.E.	9	0	2	2	6	....	....	....	....	....

LACROIX, DANIEL

Left wing. Shoots left. 6'2", 185 lbs.   Born, Montreal, Que., March 11, 1969.
(NY Rangers' 2nd choice, 31st overall, in 1987 Entry Draft).

			Regular Season					Playoffs				
Season	Club	Lea	GP	G	A	TP	PIM	GP	G	A	TP	PIM
1986-87	Granby	QMJHL	54	9	16	25	311	8	1	2	3	22
1987-88	Granby	QMJHL	58	24	50	74	468	5	0	4	4	12
1988-89	Granby	QMJHL	70	45	49	94	320	4	1	1	2	57
	Denver	IHL	2	0	1	1	0	2	0	1	1	0
1989-90	Flint	IHL	61	12	16	28	128	4	2	0	2	24

LADOUCEUR, RANDY

(LAD-uh-SOOR)

Defense. Shoots left. 6'2", 220 lbs.   Born, Brockville, Ont., June 30, 1960.

			Regular Season					Playoffs				
Season	Club	Lea	GP	G	A	TP	PIM	GP	G	A	TP	PIM
1978-79	Brantford	OHA	64	3	17	20	141	....	....	....	....	....
1979-80	Brantford	OHA	37	6	15	21	125	8	0	5	5	18
1980-81	Kalamazoo	IHL	80	7	30	37	52	8	1	3	4	10
1981-82	Adirondack	AHL	78	4	28	32	78	5	1	1	2	6
1982-83	Detroit	NHL	27	0	4	4	16	....	....	....	....	....
	Adirondack	AHL	48	11	21	32	54	....	....	....	....	....
1983-84	Adirondack	AHL	11	3	5	8	12	....	....	....	....	....
	Detroit	NHL	71	3	17	20	58	4	1	0	1	6
1984-85	Detroit	NHL	80	3	27	30	108	3	1	0	1	0
1985-86	Detroit	NHL	78	5	13	18	196	....	....	....	....	....
1986-87	Detroit	NHL	34	3	6	9	70	....	....	....	....	....
	Hartford	NHL	36	2	3	5	51	6	0	2	2	12
1987-88	Hartford	NHL	67	1	7	8	91	6	1	1	2	4
1988-89	Hartford	NHL	75	2	5	7	95	1	0	0	0	10
1989-90	Hartford	NHL	71	3	12	15	126	7	1	0	1	10
	NHL Totals		539	22	94	116	811	27	4	3	7	42

Signed as a free agent by **Detroit**, November 1, 1979. Traded to **Hartford** by **Detroit** for Dave Barr, January 12, 1987.

LAFAYETTE, JUSTIN

Left wing. Shoots left. 6'6", 200 lbs.   Born, Vancouver, B.C., January 23, 1970.
(Chicago's 6th choice, 113th overall, in 1988 Entry Draft).

			Regular Season					Playoffs				
Season	Club	Lea	GP	G	A	TP	PIM	GP	G	A	TP	PIM
1987-88	Ferris State	CCHA	34	1	2	3	20	....	....	....	....	....
1988-89	Ferris State	CCHA	36	3	4	7	59	....	....	....	....	....
1989-90	Ferris State	CCHA	34	4	5	9	38	....	....	....	....	....

LAFLEUR, GUY DAMIEN

Right wing. Shoots right. 6', 185 lbs.   Born, Thurso, Que., September 20, 1951.
(Montreal's 1st choice and 1st overall in 1971 Amateur Draft)

			Regular Season					Playoffs				
Season	Club	Lea	GP	G	A	TP	PIM	GP	G	A	TP	PIM
1969-70	Quebec	QJHL	56	*103	67	170	89	15	*25	18	*43	24
1970-71	Quebec	QJHL	62	*130	79	*209	135	14	*22	*21	*43	24
1971-72	Montreal	NHL	73	29	35	64	48	6	1	4	5	2
1972-73	Montreal	NHL	69	28	27	55	51	17	3	5	8	9
1973-74	Montreal	NHL	73	21	35	56	29	6	0	1	1	4
1974-75a	Montreal	NHL	70	53	66	119	37	11	*12	7	19	15
1975-76ab	Montreal	NHL	80	56	69	*125	36	13	7	10	17	2
1976-77abcde	Montreal	NHL	80	56	*80	*135	20	14	9	*17	26	6
1977-78abdf	Montreal	NHL	78	60*	72	*132	26	15	*10	11	*21	16
1978-79a	Montreal	NHL	80	52	77	129	28	16	10	*13	*23	0
1979-80a	Montreal	NHL	74	50	75	125	12	3	3	1	4	0
1980-81	Montreal	NHL	51	27	*43	70	29	3	0	1	1	2
1981-82	Montreal	NHL	66	27	57	84	24	5	2	1	3	4
1982-83	Montreal	NHL	68	27	49	76	12	3	0	2	2	2
1983-84	Montreal	NHL	80	30	40	70	19	12	0	3	3	5
1984-85	Montreal	NHL	19	2	3	5	10	....	....	....	....	....
1985-86			DID NOT PLAY									
1986-87			DID NOT PLAY									
1987-88g			DID NOT PLAY									
1988-89	NY Rangers	NHL	67	18	27	45	12	4	1	0	1	0
1989-90	Quebec	NHL	39	12	22	34	4	....	....	....	....	....
	NHL Totals		1067	548	777	1325	397	128	58	76	134	67

a NHL First All-Star Team (1975, 1976, 1979, 1980)
b Won Art Ross Trophy (1976, 1977, 1978)
c Won Lester B. Pearson Award (1977)
d Won Hart Trophy (1977, 1978)
e Won Conn Smythe Trophy (1977)
f NHL Plus/Minus Leader (1978)
g Inducted into Hockey Hall of Fame (1988)
Signed as a free agent by **NY Rangers**, September 26, 1988. Signed as a free agent by, **Quebec**, July 14, 1989. **NY Rangers** received **Quebec's** fifth round choice (Sergei Zubov) in 1990 Entry Draft as compensation, June 16, 1990.

LaFONTAINE, PAT

Center. Shoots right. 5'10", 177 lbs.   Born, St. Louis, MO, February 22, 1965.
(NY Islanders' 1st choice, 3rd overall, in 1983 Entry Draft).

			Regular Season					Playoffs				
Season	Club	Lea	GP	G	A	TP	PIM	GP	G	A	TP	PIM
1982-83abcd	Verdun	QMJHL	70	*104	*130	*234	10	15	11	*24	*35	4
1983-84	U.S. National	...	58	56	55	111	22					
	U.S. Olympic	...	6	5	5	10	0					
	NY Islanders	NHL	15	13	6	19	6	16	3	6	9	8
1984-85	NY Islanders	NHL	67	19	35	54	32	9	1	2	3	4
1985-86	NY Islanders	NHL	65	30	23	53	43	3	1	0	1	0
1986-87	NY Islanders	NHL	80	38	32	70	70	14	5	7	12	10
1987-88	NY Islanders	NHL	75	47	45	92	52	6	4	5	9	8
1988-89	NY Islanders	NHL	79	45	43	88	26	....	....	....	....	....
1989-90e	NY Islanders	NHL	74	54	51	105	38	2	0	1	1	0
	NHL Totals		455	246	235	481	267	50	14	21	35	30

a QMJHL First All-Star Team (1983).
b QMJHL Most Valuable Player (1983).
c QMJHL Most Valuable Player in Playoffs (1983).
d Canadian Major Junior Player of the Year (1983).
e Won Dodge Performer of the Year Award (1990)
Played in NHL All-Star Game (1988-90)

LAFORGE, MARC

Defense. Shoots left. 6'2", 200 lbs.   Born, Sudbury, Ont., January 3, 1968.
(Hartford's 2nd choice, 32nd overall, in 1986 Entry Draft).

			Regular Season					Playoffs				
Season	Club	Lea	GP	G	A	TP	PIM	GP	G	A	TP	PIM
1985-86	Kingston	OHL	60	1	13	14	248	10	0	1	1	30
1986-87	Binghamton	AHL	....	....	....	....	....	4	0	0	0	7
	Kingston	OHL	53	2	10	12	224	12	1	0	1	79
1987-88	Sudbury	OHL	14	0	2	2	68	....	....	....	....	....
1988-89	Binghamton	AHL	38	2	2	4	179	....	....	....	....	....
	Indianapolis	IHL	14	0	2	2	138	....	....	....	....	....
1989-90	Hartford	NHL	9	0	0	0	43	....	....	....	....	....
	Binghamton	AHL	25	2	6	8	111	....	....	....	....	....
	Cape Breton	AHL	3	0	1	1	24	3	0	0	0	27
	NHL Totals		9	0	0	0	43					

Traded to **Edmonton** by **Hartford** for the rights to Cam Brauer, March 6, 1990.

LAFRENIERE, JASON

(LAH-frehn-YAIR)

Center. Shoots right. 5'11", 195 lbs.   Born, St. Catharines, Ont., December 6, 1966.
(Quebec's 2nd choice, 36th overall, in 1985 Entry Draft).

			Regular Season					Playoffs				
Season	Club	Lea	GP	G	A	TP	PIM	GP	G	A	TP	PIM
1983-84	Brantford	OHL	70	24	57	81	4	6	2	4	6	2
1984-85	Hamilton	OHL	59	26	69	95	10	17	12	16	28	0
1985-86a	Hamilton	OHL	14	12	10	22	2	....	....	....	....	....
a	Belleville	OHL	48	37	73	110	2	23	10	*22	*32	6
1986-87	Quebec	NHL	56	13	15	28	8	12	1	5	6	2
	Fredericton	AHL	11	3	11	14	0	....	....	....	....	....
1987-88	Quebec	NHL	40	10	19	29	4	....	....	....	....	....
	Fredericton	AHL	32	12	19	31	38	....	....	....	....	....
1988-89	NY Rangers	NHL	38	8	16	24	6	3	0	0	0	17
	Denver	IHL	24	10	19	29	17	....	....	....	....	....
1989-90	Flint	IHL	41	9	25	34	34	....	....	....	....	....
	Phoenix	IHL	14	4	9	13	0	....	....	....	....	....
	NHL Totals		134	31	50	81	18	15	1	5	6	19

a OHL First All-Star Team (1986)
Traded to **NY Rangers** by **Quebec** with Normand Rochefort for Bruce Bell, Jari Gronstrand, Walt Poddubny and NY Rangers' fourth round choice (Eric Dubois) in 1989 Entry Draft, August 1, 1988.

LAIDLAW, THOMAS (TOM)

Defense. Shoots left. 6'2", 215 lbs.   Born, Brampton, Ont., April 15, 1958.
(NY Rangers' 7th choice, 93rd overall, in 1978 Amateur Draft).

			Regular Season					Playoffs				
Season	Club	Lea	GP	G	A	TP	PIM	GP	G	A	TP	PIM
1978-79a	N. Michigan	CCHA	29	10	20	30	137	....	....	....	....	....
1979-80ab	N. Michigan	CCHA	39	8	30	38	83	....	....	....	....	....
	New Haven	AHL	1	0	0	0	0	10	1	6	7	27
1980-81	NY Rangers	NHL	80	6	23	29	100	14	1	4	5	18
1981-82	NY Rangers	NHL	79	3	18	21	104	10	0	3	3	14
1982-83	NY Rangers	NHL	80	0	10	10	75	9	1	1	2	10
1983-84	NY Rangers	NHL	79	3	15	18	62	5	0	0	0	8
1984-85	NY Rangers	NHL	61	1	11	12	52	3	0	2	2	4
1985-86	NY Rangers	NHL	68	6	12	18	103	7	0	2	2	12
1986-87	NY Rangers	NHL	63	1	10	11	65	....	....	....	....	....
	Los Angeles	NHL	11	0	3	3	4	5	0	0	0	2
1987-88	Los Angeles	NHL	57	1	12	13	47	5	0	2	2	4
1988-89	Los Angeles	NHL	70	3	17	20	63	11	2	3	5	6
1989-90	Los Angeles	NHL	57	1	8	9	42	....	....	....	....	....
	NHL Totals		705	25	139	164	717	69	4	17	21	78

a CCHA First All-Star Team (1979, 1980)
b NCAA All-Tournament Team (1980)
Traded to **Los Angeles** by **NY Rangers** with Bob Carpenter for Jeff Crossman, Marcel Dionne and Los Angeles' third-round choice (Draft choice acquired by Minnesota, June 17, 1989 October 12, 1988. Minnesota selected Murray Garbut.) in 1989 Entry Draft, March 10, 1987.

LAKSO, BOB

Left wing. Shoots left. 5'11", 180 lbs. Born, Baltimore, MD, April 13, 1962.
(Minnesota's 9th choice, 184th overall, in 1980 Entry Draft).

			Regular Season					Playoffs				
Season	Club	Lea	GP	G	A	TP	PIM	GP	G	A	TP	PIM
1980-81	Minn.-Duluth	WCHA	25	5	3	8	2	....	....	....	....	....
1981-82	Minn.-Duluth	WCHA	22	8	10	18	6	....	....	....	....	....
1982-83	Minn.-Duluth	WCHA	26	11	17	28	4	....	....	....	....	....
1983-84	Minn.-Duluth	WCHA	26	20	18	38	8	....	....	....	....	....
1984-85	Springfield	AHL	8	2	1	3	0	....	....	....	....	....
	Indianapolis	IHL	76	26	32	58	4	6	3	2	5	2
1985-86	Springfield	AHL	17	3	6	9	2	....	....	....	....	....
	Indianapolis	IHL	58	41	35	76	4	5	4	2	6	0
1986-87	Indianapolis	IHL	79	39	55	94	6	6	2	2	4	0
1987-88	Milwaukee	IHL	80	43	28	71	10	....	....	....	....	....
1988-89	Indianapolis	IHL	82	38	34	72	10	....	....	....	....	....
1989-90a	Indianapolis	IHL	82	42	58	100	6	5	3	3	6	0

a Won Iron Man Award (hardest worker-IHL) (1990)

LALA, JIRI

Right wing/Center. Shoots right. 5'10", 181 lbs. Born, Tabor, Czech., August 21, 1959.
(Quebec's 4th choice, 76th overall, in 1982 Entry Draft).

			Regular Season					Playoffs				
Season	Club	Lea	GP	G	A	TP	PIM	GP	G	A	TP	PIM
1986-87	Budejovice	Czech.	31	14	17	31	....	....	....	....	....	....
1987-88	Budejovice	Czech.	28	20	28	48	....	....	....	....	....	....
1988-89	Budejovice	Czech.	45	27	39	66	....	....	....	....	....	....
1989-90	Frankfurt	W. Ger.	35	36	39	75	12	....	....	....	....	....

LALONDE, TODD

Left wing. Shoots left. 6', 190 lbs. Born, Garson, Ont., August 4, 1969.
(Boston's 3rd choice, 56th overall, in 1987 Entry Draft).

			Regular Season					Playoffs				
Season	Club	Lea	GP	G	A	TP	PIM	GP	G	A	TP	PIM
1985-86	Sudbury	OHL	57	17	30	47	43	4	0	1	1	8
1986-87	Sudbury	OHL	29	5	11	16	71	....	....	....	....	....
1987-88	Sudbury	OHL	59	27	43	70	79	....	....	....	....	....
1988-89	Sudbury	OHL	52	32	44	76	57	....	....	....	....	....
1989-90	Maine	AHL	5	2	0	2	6	....	....	....	....	....
	Johnstown	ECHL	1	1	0	1	2	....	....	....	....	....

LALOR, MIKE

Defense. Shoots left. 6', 200 lbs. Born, Buffalo, NY, March 8, 1963.

			Regular Season					Playoffs				
Season	Club	Lea	GP	G	A	TP	PIM	GP	G	A	TP	PIM
1981-82	Brantford	OHL	64	3	13	16	114	11	0	6	6	11
1982-83	Brantford	OHL	65	10	30	40	113	8	1	3	4	20
1983-84	Nova Scotia	AHL	67	5	11	16	80	12	0	2	2	13
1984-85	Sherbrooke	AHL	79	9	23	32	114	17	3	5	8	36
1985-86	**Montreal**	**NHL**	**62**	**3**	**5**	**8**	**56**	**17**	**1**	**2**	**3**	**29**
1986-87	**Montreal**	**NHL**	**57**	**0**	**10**	**10**	**47**	**13**	**2**	**1**	**3**	**29**
1987-88	**Montreal**	**NHL**	**66**	**1**	**10**	**11**	**113**	**11**	**0**	**0**	**0**	**11**
1988-89	**Montreal**	**NHL**	**12**	**1**	**4**	**5**	**15**	....	....	....	....	....
	St. Louis	**NHL**	**36**	**1**	**14**	**15**	**54**	**10**	**1**	**1**	**2**	**14**
1989-90	**St. Louis**	**NHL**	**78**	**0**	**16**	**16**	**81**	**12**	**0**	**2**	**2**	**31**
	NHL Totals		**311**	**6**	**59**	**65**	**366**	**63**	**4**	**6**	**10**	**114**

Signed as a free agent by **Montreal**, September, 1983. Traded to **St. Louis** by **Montreal** for the option (exercised by Montreal) to switch first-round picks in 1990 Entry Draft and St. Louis' third-round choice in the 1991 Entry Draft, January 16, 1989. Traded to **Washington** by **St. Louis** with Peter Zezel for Geoff Courtnall, July 13, 1990.

LAMB, JEFF

Center. Shoots left. 5'11", 170 lbs. Born, Waterloo, IA, July 14, 1964.
(Pittsburgh's 1st choice, 4th overall, in 1986 Supplemental Draft).

			Regular Season					Playoffs				
Season	Club	Lea	GP	G	A	TP	PIM	GP	G	A	TP	PIM
1983-84	Denver	WCHA	15	0	2	2	8	....	....	....	....	....
1984-85	Denver	WCHA	39	14	25	39	62	....	....	....	....	....
1985-86	Denver	WCHA	45	23	31	54	75	....	....	....	....	....
1986-87	Denver	WCHA	40	10	24	34	58	....	....	....	....	....
1987-88	Maine	AHL	57	7	12	19	96	2	0	0	0	0
1988-89	Maine	AHL	58	11	15	26	64	....	....	....	....	....
1989-90	Phoenix	IHL	78	20	33	53	152	....	....	....	....	....

LAMB, MARK

Center. Shoots left. 5'9", 180 lbs. Born, Ponteix, Sask., August 3, 1964.
(Calgary's 5th choice, 72nd overall, in 1982 Entry Draft).

			Regular Season					Playoffs				
Season	Club	Lea	GP	G	A	TP	PIM	GP	G	A	TP	PIM
1981-82	Billings	WHL	72	45	56	101	46	5	4	6	10	4
1982-83	Nanaimo	WHL	30	14	37	51	16	....	....	....	....	....
	Medicine Hat	WHL	46	22	43	65	33	5	3	2	5	4
	Colorado	CHL	....	....	....	....	....	6	0	2	2	0
1983-84a	Medicine Hat	WHL	72	59	77	136	30	14	12	11	23	6
1984-85	Moncton	AHL	80	23	49	72	53	....	....	....	....	....
1985-86	**Calgary**	**NHL**	**1**	**0**	**0**	**0**	**0**	....	....	....	....	....
	Moncton	AHL	79	26	50	76	51	10	2	6	8	17
1986-87	**Detroit**	**NHL**	**22**	**2**	**1**	**3**	**8**	**11**	**0**	**0**	**0**	**11**
	Adirondack	AHL	49	14	36	50	45	....	....	....	....	....
1987-88	**Edmonton**	**NHL**	**2**	**0**	**0**	**0**	**0**	....	....	....	....	....
	Nova Scotia	AHL	69	27	61	88	45	5	0	5	5	6
1988-89	**Edmonton**	**NHL**	**20**	**2**	**8**	**10**	**14**	**6**	**0**	**2**	**2**	**8**
	Cape Breton	AHL	54	33	49	82	29	....	....	....	....	....
1989-90	**Edmonton**	**NHL**	**58**	**12**	**16**	**28**	**42**	**22**	**6**	**11**	**17**	**2**
	NHL Totals		**103**	**16**	**25**	**41**	**64**	**39**	**6**	**13**	**19**	**21**

a WHL First All-Star Team, East Division (1984)

Claimed by **Edmonton** in NHL Waiver Draft, October 5, 1987.

LAMBERT, DAN

Defense. Shoots left. 5'8", 175 lbs. Born, St. Boniface, Man., January 12, 1970.
(Quebec's 8th choice, 106th overall, in 1989 Entry Draft).

			Regular Season					Playoffs				
Season	Club	Lea	GP	G	A	TP	PIM	GP	G	A	TP	PIM
1986-87	Swift Current	WHL	68	13	53	66	95	4	1	1	2	9
1987-88	Swift Current	WHL	69	20	63	83	120	10	2	10	12	45
1988-89ab	Swift Current	WHL	57	25	77	102	158	12	9	19	28	12
1989-90a	Swift Current	WHL	50	17	51	68	119	4	2	3	5	12

a WHL East First All-Star Team (1989, 1990)
b WHL Best Defenseman (1989)

LAMBERT, LANE (LAM-buhrt)

Right wing. Shoots right. 6', 185 lbs. Born, Melfort, Sask., November 18, 1964.
(Detroit's 2nd choice, 25th overall, in 1983 Entry Draft).

			Regular Season					Playoffs				
Season	Club	Lea	GP	G	A	TP	PIM	GP	G	A	TP	PIM
1981-82	Saskatoon	WHL	72	45	69	114	111	5	1	1	2	25
1982-83a	Saskatoon	WHL	64	59	60	119	126	6	4	3	7	7
1983-84	**Detroit**	**NHL**	**73**	**20**	**15**	**35**	**115**	**4**	**0**	**0**	**0**	**10**
1984-85	**Detroit**	**NHL**	**69**	**14**	**11**	**25**	**104**	....	....	....	....	....
1985-86	**Detroit**	**NHL**	**34**	**2**	**3**	**5**	**130**	....	....	....	....	....
	Adirondack	AHL	45	16	25	41	69	16	5	5	10	9
1986-87	**NY Rangers**	**NHL**	**18**	**2**	**2**	**4**	**33**	....	....	....	....	....
	New Haven	AHL	11	3	3	6	19	....	....	....	....	....
	Quebec	**NHL**	**15**	**5**	**6**	**11**	**18**	**13**	**2**	**4**	**6**	**30**
1987-88	**Quebec**	**NHL**	**61**	**13**	**28**	**41**	**98**	....	....	....	....	....
1988-89	**Quebec**	**NHL**	**13**	**2**	**2**	**4**	**23**	....	....	....	....	....
	Halifax	AHL	59	25	35	60	162	4	0	2	2	2
1989-90	Cdn. National		54	28	36	64	48	....	....	....	....	....
	NHL Totals		**283**	**58**	**67**	**125**	**521**	**17**	**2**	**4**	**6**	**40**

a WHL Second All-Star Team (1983)

Traded to **NY Rangers** by **Detroit** with Kelly Kisio and Jim Leavins for Glen Hanlon and New York's third round choices in 1987 (Dennis Holland) and 1988 (Guy Dupuis) Entry Drafts, July 29, 1986. Traded to **Quebec** by **NY Rangers** for Pat Price, March 5, 1987.

LAMMENS, HANK

Defense. Shoots left. 6'2", 210 lbs. Born, Brockville, Ont., February 21, 1966.
(NY Islanders' 10th choice, 160th overall, in 1985 Entry Draft).

			Regular Season					Playoffs				
Season	Club	Lea	GP	G	A	TP	PIM	GP	G	A	TP	PIM
1984-85	St. Lawrence	ECAC	21	17	9	26	16	....	....	....	....	....
1985-86	St. Lawrence	ECAC	30	3	14	17	60	....	....	....	....	....
1986-87ab	St. Lawrence	ECAC	35	6	13	19	92	....	....	....	....	....
1987-88a	St. Lawrence	ECAC	32	3	6	9	64	....	....	....	....	....
1988-89	Springfield	AHL	69	1	13	14	55	....	....	....	....	....
1989-90	Springfield	AHL	43	0	6	6	27	7	0	0	0	14

a ECAC Second All-Star Team (1987, 1988)
b NCAA East Second All-American Team (1987)

a OHL Third All-Star Team (1982)
b Won Dudley "Red" Garrett Memorial Trophy (AHL's Rookie of the Year) (1983)
c AHL Second All-Star Team (1983)

LANGILLE, DEREK

Defense. Shoots left. 6', 185 lbs. Born, Toronto, Ont., June 25, 1969.
(Toronto's 9th choice, 150th overall, in 1989 Entry Draft).

			Regular Season					Playoffs				
Season	Club	Lea	GP	G	A	TP	PIM	GP	G	A	TP	PIM
1986-87	Belleville	OHL	42	0	2	2	27	6	0	0	0	0
1987-88	Belleville	OHL	36	3	7	10	45	....	....	....	....	....
	Kingston	OHL	32	4	7	11	66	....	....	....	....	....
1988-89	North Bay	OHL	60	20	38	58	128	12	1	6	7	22
1989-90	Newmarket	AHL	64	5	12	17	75	....	....	....	....	....

LANGWAY, ROD CORRY

Defense. Shoots left. 6'4", 224 lbs. Born, Formosa, Taiwan, May 3, 1957.
(Montreal's 3rd choice, 36th overall, in 1977 Amateur Draft).

			Regular Season					Playoffs				
Season	Club	Lea	GP	G	A	TP	PIM	GP	G	A	TP	PIM
1976-77	N. Hampshire	ECAC	34	10	43	53	52	....	....	....	....	....
1977-78	Hampton	AHL	30	6	16	22	50	....	....	....	....	....
	Birmingham	WHA	52	3	18	21	52	4	0	0	0	9
1978-79	Nova Scotia	AHL	18	6	13	19	29	....	....	....	....	....
	Montreal	**NHL**	**45**	**3**	**4**	**7**	**30**	**8**	**0**	**0**	**0**	**16**
1979-80	**Montreal**	**NHL**	**77**	**7**	**29**	**36**	**81**	**10**	**3**	**3**	**6**	**2**
1980-81	**Montreal**	**NHL**	**80**	**11**	**34**	**45**	**120**	**3**	**0**	**0**	**0**	**6**
1981-82	**Montreal**	**NHL**	**66**	**5**	**34**	**39**	**116**	**5**	**0**	**3**	**3**	**18**
1982-83ab	**Washington**	**NHL**	**80**	**3**	**29**	**32**	**75**	**4**	**0**	**0**	**0**	**0**
1983-84ab	**Washington**	**NHL**	**80**	**9**	**24**	**33**	**61**	**8**	**0**	**5**	**5**	**7**
1984-85c	**Washington**	**NHL**	**79**	**4**	**22**	**26**	**54**	**5**	**0**	**1**	**1**	**6**
1985-86	**Washington**	**NHL**	**71**	**1**	**17**	**18**	**61**	**9**	**1**	**2**	**3**	**6**
1986-87	**Washington**	**NHL**	**78**	**2**	**25**	**27**	**53**	**7**	**0**	**1**	**1**	**2**
1987-88	**Washington**	**NHL**	**63**	**3**	**13**	**16**	**28**	**6**	**0**	**0**	**0**	**8**
1988-89	**Washington**	**NHL**	**76**	**2**	**19**	**21**	**65**	**6**	**0**	**0**	**0**	**6**
1989-90	**Washington**	**NHL**	**58**	**0**	**8**	**8**	**39**	**15**	**1**	**4**	**5**	**12**
	NHL Totals		**853**	**50**	**258**	**308**	**783**	**86**	**5**	**19**	**24**	**88**

a Won James Norris Memorial Trophy (1983, 1984)
b NHL First All-Star Team (1983, 1984)
c NHL Second All-Star Team (1985)

Played in NHL All-Star Game (1981-86)

Claimed by **Montreal** as fill in Expansion Draft, June 13, 1979. Traded to **Washington** by **Montreal** with Doug Jarvis, Craig Laughlin and Brian Engblom for Ryan Walter and Rick Green, September 9, 1982.

LANIEL, MARC

Defense. Shoots left. 6'1", 190 lbs. Born, Oshawa, Ont., January 16, 1968.
(New Jersey's 4th choice, 62nd overall, in 1986 Entry Draft).

			Regular Season					Playoffs				
Season	Club	Lea	GP	G	A	TP	PIM	GP	G	A	TP	PIM
1985-86	Oshawa	OHL	66	9	25	34	27	6	2	3	5	6
1986-87	Oshawa	OHL	63	14	31	45	42	26	3	13	16	20
1987-88	Utica	AHL	2	0	0	0	0	....	....	....	....	....
a	Oshawa	OHL	41	8	32	40	56	7	2	2	4	4
1988-89	Utica	AHL	80	6	28	34	43	5	0	1	1	2
1989-90	Utica	AHL	20	0	0	0	25	....	....	....	....	....

a OHL Third All-Star Team (1988)

LANTHIER, JEAN-MARC

(LAN-tee-yay)

Right wing. Shoots right. 6'2", 195 lbs. Born, Montreal, Que., March 27, 1963.
(Vancouver's 2nd choice, 52nd overall, in 1981 Entry Draft).

			Regular Season					Playoffs				
Season	Club	Lea	GP	G	A	TP	PIM	GP	G	A	TP	PIM
1980-81	Quebec	QMJHL	37	13	32	45	18	....	....	....	....	....
	Sorel	QMJHL	35	6	33	39	29	7	1	4	5	4
1981-82	Laval	QMJHL	60	44	34	78	48	18	8	11	19	8
1982-83	Laval	QMJHL	69	39	71	110	54	12	6	17	23	8
1983-84	Vancouver	NHL	11	2	1	3	2	....	....	....	....	....
	Fredericton	AHL	60	25	17	42	29	7	4	6	10	0
1984-85	Vancouver	NHL	27	6	4	10	13	....	....	....	....	....
	Fredericton	AHL	38	8	5	13	15	....	....	....	....	....
1985-86	Vancouver	NHL	62	7	10	17	12	....	....	....	....	....
	Fredericton	AHL	7	5	5	10	2	....	....	....	....	....
1986-87	Fredericton	AHL	78	15	38	53	24	....	....	....	....	....
1987-88	Vancouver	NHL	5	1	1	2	2	....	....	....	....	....
	Fredericton	AHL	74	35	71	106	37	15	3	8	11	14
1988-89	Maine	AHL	24	7	16	23	16	....	....	....	....	....
	Utica	AHL	55	23	26	49	22	3	3	0	3	2
1989-90	Utica	AHL	50	13	19	32	32	4	1	1	2	2
	NHL Totals		**105**	**16**	**16**	**32**	**29**	....	....	....	....	....

Traded to **New Jersey** by **Boston** for Dan Dorion, December 9, 1988.

LANZ, RICK ROMAN

Defense. Shoots right. 6'2", 195 lbs. Born, Karlouyvary, Czech., September 16, 1961.
(Vancouver's 1st choice, 7th overall, in 1980 Entry Draft).

			Regular Season					Playoffs				
Season	Club	Lea	GP	G	A	TP	PIM	GP	G	A	TP	PIM
1978-79	Oshawa	OHA	65	12	47	59	88	5	1	3	4	14
1979-80a	Oshawa	OHA	52	18	38	56	51	7	2	3	5	6
1980-81	Vancouver	NHL	76	7	22	29	40	3	0	0	0	4
1981-82	Vancouver	NHL	39	3	11	14	48	....	....	....	....	....
1982-83	Vancouver	NHL	74	10	38	48	46	4	2	1	3	0
1983-84	Vancouver	NHL	79	18	39	57	45	4	0	4	4	2
1984-85	Vancouver	NHL	57	2	17	19	69	....	....	....	....	....
1985-86	Vancouver	NHL	75	15	38	53	73	3	0	0	0	0
1986-87	Vancouver	NHL	17	1	6	7	10	....	....	....	....	....
	Toronto	NHL	44	2	19	21	32	13	1	3	4	27
1987-88	Toronto	NHL	75	6	22	28	65	1	0	0	0	2
1988-89	Toronto	NHL	32	1	9	10	18	....	....	....	....	....
1989-90	Ambri	Switz.	36	4	14	18	....	....	....	....	....	....
	NHL Totals		**568**	**65**	**221**	**286**	**446**	**28**	**3**	**8**	**11**	**35**

a OHA Third All-Star Team (1980).
Traded to **Toronto** by **Vancouver** for Jim Benning and Dan Hodgson, December 2, 1986.
Signed as a free agent by **Chicago**, August 13, 1990.

LAPERRIERE, DANIEL

Defense. Shoots left. 6'1", 180 lbs., Born, Laval, Que., March 28, 1969.
(St. Louis' 4th choice, 93rd overall, in 1989 Entry Draft).

			Regular Season					Playoffs				
Season	Club	Lea	GP	G	A	TP	PIM	GP	G	A	TP	PIM
1988-89	St. Lawrence	ECAC	28	0	7	7	10	....	....	....	....	....
1989-90	St. Lawrence	ECAC	31	6	19	25	16	....	....	....	....	....

LAPPIN, PETER

Right wing. Shoots right. 5'11", 185 lbs. Born, St. Charles, IL., December 31, 1965.
(Calgary's 1st choice, 24th overall, in 1987 Supplemental Draft).

			Regular Season					Playoffs				
Season	Club	Lea	GP	G	A	TP	PIM	GP	G	A	TP	PIM
1984-85	St. Lawrence	ECAC	32	10	12	22	22	....	....	....	....	....
1985-86	St. Lawrence	ECAC	30	20	26	46	64	....	....	....	....	....
1986-87ab	St. Lawrence	ECAC	35	34	24	58	32	....	....	....	....	....
1987-88cdef	St. Lawrence	ECAC	30	16	36	52	26	....	....	....	....	....
g	Salt Lake	IHL	3	1	1	2	0	17	*16	12	*28	11
1988-89	Salt Lake	IHL	81	48	42	90	50	14	*9	9	18	4
1989-90	**Minnesota**	**NHL**	6	0	0	0	2	....	....	....	....	....
h	Kalamazoo	IHL	74	45	35	80	42	8	5	2	7	4
	NHL Totals		**6**	**0**	**0**	**0**	**2**	....	....	....	....	....

a NCAA East Second All-American Team (1987)
b ECAC Second All-Star Team (1987)
c NCAA East First All-American Team (1988)
d NCAA All-Tournament Team (1988)
e ECAC Player of the Year (1988)
f ECAC First All-Star Team (1988)
g IHL Playoff MVP (1988)
h IHL Second All-Star Team (1990)

Traded to **Minnesota** by **Calgary** for Minnesota's second round choice in 1990 Entry Draft which was later transferred to New Jersey (Chris Gotziaman), September 5, 1989.

LAPRADE, DOUGLAS

Right wing. Shoots right. 6', 185 lbs. Born, Port Arthur, Ont., October 9, 1968.
(Los Angeles' 12th choice, 217th overall, in 1988 Entry Draft).

			Regular Season					Playoffs				
Season	Club	Lea	GP	G	A	TP	PIM	GP	G	A	TP	PIM
1987-88	Lake Superior	CCHA	30	4	2	6	30	....	....	....	....	....
1988-89	Lake Superior	CCHA	45	4	6	10	48	....	....	....	....	....
1989-90	Lake Superior	CCHA	42	4	3	7	51	....	....	....	....	....

LARIONOV, IGOR

Center. Shoots left. 5'9", 165 lbs. Born, Voskresensk, Soviet Union, December 3, 1960.
(Vancouver's 11th choice, 214th overall, in 1988 Entry Draft).

			Regular Season					Playoffs				
Season	Club	Lea	GP	G	A	TP	PIM	GP	G	A	TP	PIM
1977-78	Voskresensk	USSR	6	3	0	3	4	....	....	....	....	....
1978-79	Voskresensk	USSR	32	3	4	7	12	....	....	....	....	....
1979-80	Voskresensk	USSR	42	11	7	18	24	....	....	....	....	....
1980-81	Voskresensk	USSR	43	22	23	45	36	....	....	....	....	....
1981-82	CSKA	USSR	46	31	22	53	6	....	....	....	....	....
1982-83a	CSKA	USSR	44	20	19	39	20	....	....	....	....	....
1983-84	CSKA	USSR	43	15	26	41	30	....	....	....	....	....
1984-85	CSKA	USSR	40	18	28	46	20	....	....	....	....	....
1985-86a	CSKA	USSR	40	21	31	52	33	....	....	....	....	....
1986-87a	CSKA	USSR	39	20	26	46	34	....	....	....	....	....
1987-88ab	CSKA	USSR	51	25	32	57	54	....	....	....	....	....
1988-89	CSKA	USSR	31	15	12	27	22	....	....	....	....	....
1989-90	**Vancouver**	**NHL**	74	17	27	44	20	....	....	....	....	....
	NHL Totals		**74**	**17**	**27**	**44**	**20**	....	....	....	....	....

a Soviet National League All-Star (1983, 1985-88)
b Soviet Player of the Year (1988)

LARKIN, JAMES

Right wing. Shoots right. 6', 180 lbs. Born, Wallingford, VT, April 4, 1970.
(Los Angeles' 10th choice, 175th overall, in 1988 Entry Draft).

			Regular Season					Playoffs				
Season	Club	Lea	GP	G	A	TP	PIM	GP	G	A	TP	PIM
1988-89	U. of Vermont	ECAC	34	16	19	35	8	....	....	....	....	....
1989-90	U. of Vermont	ECAC	28	20	15	35	14	....	....	....	....	....

LARMER, STEVE DONALD

Right wing. Shoots left. 5'10", 185 lbs. Born, Peterborough, Ont., June 16, 1961.
(Chicago's 11th choice, 120th overall, in 1980 Entry Draft).

			Regular Season					Playoffs				
Season	Club	Lea	GP	G	A	TP	PIM	GP	G	A	TP	PIM
1979-80	Niagara Falls	OHA	67	45	69	114	71	10	5	9	14	15
1980-81	**Chicago**	**NHL**	4	0	1	1	0	....	....	....	....	....
a	Niagara Falls	OHA	61	55	78	133	73	12	13	8	21	24
1981-82	**Chicago**	**NHL**	3	0	0	0	0	....	....	....	....	....
b	New Brunswick	AHL	74	38	44	82	46	15	6	6	12	0
1982-83cd	**Chicago**	**NHL**	80	43	47	90	28	11	5	7	12	8
1983-84	**Chicago**	**NHL**	80	35	40	75	34	5	2	2	4	7
1984-85	**Chicago**	**NHL**	80	46	40	86	16	15	9	13	22	14
1985-86	**Chicago**	**NHL**	80	31	45	76	47	3	0	3	3	4
1986-87	**Chicago**	**NHL**	80	28	56	84	22	4	0	0	0	2
1987-88	**Chicago**	**NHL**	80	41	48	89	42	5	1	6	7	0
1988-89	**Chicago**	**NHL**	80	43	44	87	54	16	8	9	17	22
1989-90	**Chicago**	**NHL**	80	31	59	90	40	20	7	15	22	2
	NHL Totals		**647**	**298**	**380**	**678**	**283**	**79**	**32**	**55**	**87**	**59**

a OHA Second All-Star Team (1981)
b AHL Second All-Star Team (1982)
c Won Calder Trophy (1983)
d NHL All-Rookie Team (1983)
Played in NHL All-Star Game (1990)

LAROCQUE, DENIS

(lah-RAHK)

Defense. Shoots left. 6'1", 195 lbs. Born, Hawkesbury, Ont., October 5, 1967.
(Los Angeles' 2nd choice, 44th overall, in 1986 Entry Draft).

			Regular Season					Playoffs				
Season	Club	Lea	GP	G	A	TP	PIM	GP	G	A	TP	PIM
1984-85	Guelph	OHL	62	1	15	16	67	....	....	....	....	....
1985-86	Guelph	OHL	66	2	17	19	144	....	....	....	....	....
1986-87	Guelph	OHL	45	4	10	14	82	5	0	2	2	9
1987-88	**Los Angeles**	**NHL**	8	0	1	1	18	....	....	....	....	....
	New Haven	AHL	58	4	10	14	154	....	....	....	....	....
1988-89	New Haven	AHL	15	2	2	4	51	....	....	....	....	....
	Denver	IHL	30	2	8	10	39	4	0	2	2	10
1989-90	Cape Breton	AHL	26	2	4	6	39	6	0	1	1	2
	NHL Totals		**8**	**0**	**1**	**1**	**18**	....	....	....	....	....

Traded to **NY Rangers** by **Los Angeles** with Dean Kennedy for Igor Liba, Michael Boyce, Todd Elik and future considerations, December 12, 1988.

LAROSE, GUY

Center. Shoots left. 5'9", 175 lbs. Born, Hull, Que., August 31, 1967.
(Buffalo's 11th choice, 224th overall, in 1985 Entry Draft).

			Regular Season					Playoffs				
Season	Club	Lea	GP	G	A	TP	PIM	GP	G	A	TP	PIM
1984-85	Guelph	OHL	58	30	30	60	63	....	....	....	....	....
1985-86	Guelph	OHL	37	12	36	48	55	....	....	....	....	....
	Ottawa	OHL	28	19	25	44	63	....	....	....	....	....
1986-87	Ottawa	OHL	66	28	49	77	77	11	2	8	10	27
1987-88	Moncton	AHL	77	22	31	53	127	....	....	....	....	....
1988-89	**Winnipeg**	**NHL**	3	0	1	1	6	....	....	....	....	....
	Moncton	AHL	72	32	27	59	176	10	4	4	8	37
1989-90	Moncton	AHL	79	44	26	70	232	....	....	....	....	....
	NHL Totals		**3**	**0**	**1**	**1**	**6**	....	....	....	....	....

Signed as a free agent by **Winnipeg**, July 16, 1987.

LAROUCHE, STEVE

Center. Shoots right. 5'11", 165 lbs. Born, Rouyn, Que., April 14, 1971.
(Montreal's 3rd choice, 41st overall, in 1989 Entry Draft).

			Regular Season					Playoffs				
Season	Club	Lea	GP	G	A	TP	PIM	GP	G	A	TP	PIM
1987-88	Trois-Rivieres	QMJHL	66	11	29	40	25	....	....	....	....	....
1988-89	Trois-Rivieres	QMJHL	70	51	102	153	53	4	4	2	6	6
1989-90a	Trois-Rivieres	QMJHL	60	55	90	145	40	7	3	5	8	8

a QMJHL Second All-Star Team (1990)

LARSON, JON

Defense. Shoots left. 6'1", 190 lbs.   Born, Roseau, MN, April 12, 1971.
(NY Islanders' 7th choice, 128th overall, in 1989 Entry Draft).

			Regular Season					Playoffs				
Season	Club	Lea	GP	G	A	TP	PIM	GP	G	A	TP	PIM
1988-89	Roseau	HS	23	7	23	30	....	....	....	....	....	....
1989-90	North Dakota	WCHA	18	0	1	1	10	....	....	....	....	....

LARSON, JOSEPH

Center. Shoots left. 6'1", 165 lbs.   Born, Minnetonka, MN, August 17, 1970.
(Winnipeg's 12th choice, 193rd overall, in 1989 Entry Draft).

			Regular Season					Playoffs				
Season	Club	Lea	GP	G	A	TP	PIM	GP	G	A	TP	PIM
1988-89	Minnetonka	HS	24	15	19	34	....	....	....	....	....	....
1989-90	St. Cloud St.	NCAA	5	0	1	1	6	....	....	....	....	....

LARSON, REED DAVID

Defense. Shoots right. 6', 195 lbs.   Born, Minneapolis, MN, July 30, 1956.
(Detroit's 2nd choice, 22nd overall, in 1976 Amateur Draft).

			Regular Season					Playoffs				
Season	Club	Lea	GP	G	A	TP	PIM	GP	G	A	TP	PIM
1975-76	U. Minnesota	WCHA	42	13	29	42	94	....	....	....	....	....
1976-77	U. Minnesota	WCHA	21	10	15	25	30	....	....	....	....	....
	Detroit	NHL	14	0	1	1	23	....	....	....	....	....
1977-78	Detroit	NHL	75	19	41	60	95	7	0	2	2	4
1978-79	Detroit	NHL	79	18	49	67	169	....	....	....	....	....
1979-80	Detroit	NHL	80	22	44	66	101	....	....	....	....	....
1980-81	Detroit	NHL	78	27	31	58	153	....	....	....	....	....
1981-82	Detroit	NHL	80	21	39	60	112	....	....	....	....	....
1982-83	Detroit	NHL	80	22	52	74	104	....	....	....	....	....
1983-84	Detroit	NHL	78	23	39	62	122	4	2	0	2	21
1984-85	Detroit	NHL	77	17	45	62	139	3	1	2	3	20
1985-86	Detroit	NHL	67	19	41	60	109	....	....	....	....	....
	Boston	NHL	13	3	4	7	8	3	1	0	1	6
1986-87	Boston	NHL	66	12	24	36	95	4	0	2	2	2
1987-88	Boston	NHL	62	10	24	34	93	8	0	1	1	6
	Maine	AHL	2	2	0	2	4	....	....	....	....	....
1988-89	Edmonton	NHL	10	2	7	9	15	....	....	....	....	....
	NY Islanders	NHL	33	7	13	20	35	....	....	....	....	....
	Minnesota	NHL	11	0	9	9	18	3	0	0	0	4
1989-90	Alleghe/Sile	Italy	34	17	32	49	49	9	7	18	25	2
	Buffalo	NHL	1	0	0	0	0	....	....	....	....	....
	NHL Totals		904	222	463	685	1391	32	4	7	11	63

Played in NHL All-Star Game (1978, 1980, 1981)

Traded to **Boston** by **Detroit** for Mike O'Connell, March 10, 1986. Traded to **NY Islanders** by **Edmonton** for future considerations, December 6, 1988. Traded to **Minnesota** by **NY Islanders** for future considerations (Mike Kelfer), March 7, 1989. Signed as a free agent by **Buffalo**, March 6, 1990.

LARSSON, PETER

Center. Shoots left. 5'9", 180 lbs.   Born, Sodertalje, Sweden, April 9, 1968.
(New Jersey's 10th choice, 236th overall, in 1989 Entry Draft).

			Regular Season					Playoffs				
Season	Club	Lea	GP	G	A	TP	PIM	GP	G	A	TP	PIM
1985-86	Sodertalje	Swe.	10	0	1	1	2	....	....	....	....	....
1986-87	Sodertalje	Swe.	26	3	4	7	8	....	....	....	....	....
1987-88	Sodertalje	Swe.	34	14	15	29	22	....	....	....	....	....
1988-89	Sodertalje	Swe.	40	20	17	37	26	....	....	....	....	....
1989-90	Sodertalje	Swe.	33	13	14	27	28	2	2	0	2	2

LARTER, TYLER

Center. Shoots left. 5'10", 185 lbs.   Born, Charlottetown, P.E.I., March 12, 1968.
(Washington's 3rd choice, 78th overall, in 1987 Entry Draft).

			Regular Season					Playoffs				
Season	Club	Lea	GP	G	A	TP	PIM	GP	G	A	TP	PIM
1985-86	S.S. Marie	OHL	60	15	40	55	137	....	....	....	....	....
1986-87	S.S. Marie	OHL	59	34	59	93	122	4	0	2	2	8
1987-88	S.S. Marie	OHL	65	44	65	109	155	4	3	9	12	8
1988-89	Baltimore	AHL	71	9	19	28	189	....	....	....	....	....
1989-90	Washington	NHL	1	0	0	0	0	....	....	....	....	....
	Baltimore	AHL	79	31	36	67	104	12	5	6	11	57
	NHL Totals		1	0	0	0	0	....	....	....	....	....

LATAL, JIRI

Defense. Shoots left. 6'1", 190 lbs.   Born, Olomouc, Czechoslovakia, February 2, 1967.
(Toronto's 6th choice, 106th overall, in 1985 Entry Draft).

			Regular Season					Playoffs				
Season	Club	Lea	GP	G	A	TP	PIM	GP	G	A	TP	PIM
1984-85	Sparta Praha	Czech.	26	2	2	4	10	....	....	....	....	....
1985-86	Sparta Praha	Czech.	27	3	2	5	....	....	....	....	....	....
1986-87	Sparta Praha	Czech.	9	1	0	2	....	....	....	....	....	....
1987-88	Dukla Trencin	Czech.	43	8	12	20	27	....	....	....	....	....
1988-89	Dukla Trencin	Czech.	45	6	17	23	....	....	....	....	....	....
1989-90	Philadelphia	NHL	32	6	13	19	6	....	....	....	....	....
	Hershey	AHL	22	10	18	28	10	....	....	....	....	....
	NHL Totals		32	6	13	19	6	....	....	....	....	....

Traded to **Philadelphia** by **Toronto** for Philadelphia's seventh round choice in 1991 Entry Draft, August 22, 1989.

LATOS, JAMES   (LA-toz)

Right wing. Shoots right. 6'1", 200 lbs.   Born, Wakaw, Sask., January 4, 1966.

			Regular Season					Playoffs				
Season	Club	Lea	GP	G	A	TP	PIM	GP	G	A	TP	PIM
1986-87	Portland	WHL	69	27	18	45	210	20	5	3	8	56
1987-88	Colorado	IHL	38	11	12	23	98	....	....	....	....	....
1988-89	NY Rangers	NHL	1	0	0	0	0	....	....	....	....	....
	Denver	IHL	37	7	5	12	157	4	0	0	0	17
1989-90	Denver	IHL	71	12	15	27	244	4	0	0	0	0
	NHL Totals		1	0	0	0	0	....	....	....	....	....

Signed as a free agent by **NY Rangers**, June 5, 1987.

LATTA, DAVID   (LA-tuh)

Left wing. Shoots left. 6'1", 190 lbs.   Born, Thunder Bay, Ont., January 3, 1967.
(Quebec's 1st choice, 15th overall, in 1985 Entry Draft).

			Regular Season					Playoffs				
Season	Club	Lea	GP	G	A	TP	PIM	GP	G	A	TP	PIM
1983-84	Kitchener	OHL	66	17	26	43	54	16	3	6	9	9
1984-85	Kitchener	OHL	52	38	27	65	26	4	2	4	6	4
1985-86	Quebec	NHL	1	0	0	0	0	....	....	....	....	....
	Fredericton	AHL	3	1	0	1	0	5	0	3	3	0
	Kitchener	OHL	55	36	34	70	60	5	7	1	8	15
1986-87a	Kitchener	OHL	50	32	46	78	46	4	0	3	3	2
1987-88	Quebec	NHL	10	0	0	0	0	....	....	....	....	....
	Fredericton	AHL	34	11	21	32	28	15	9	4	13	24
1988-89	Quebec	NHL	24	4	8	12	4	....	....	....	....	....
	Halifax	AHL	42	20	26	46	36	4	0	2	2	2
1989-90	Halifax	AHL	34	11	5	16	45	....	....	....	....	....
	NHL Totals		35	4	8	12	4	....	....	....	....	....

a OHL Third All-Star Team (1987)

LAUER, BRAD   (LAU-er)

Left wing. Shoots left. 6', 195 lbs.   Born, Humboldt, Sask., October 27, 1966.
(NY Islanders' 3rd choice, 34th overall, in 1985 Entry Draft).

			Regular Season					Playoffs				
Season	Club	Lea	GP	G	A	TP	PIM	GP	G	A	TP	PIM
1983-84	Regina	WHL	60	5	7	12	51	16	0	1	1	24
1984-85	Regina	WHL	72	33	46	79	57	8	6	6	12	9
1985-86	Regina	WHL	57	36	38	74	69	10	4	5	9	2
1986-87	NY Islanders	NHL	61	7	14	21	65	6	2	0	2	4
1987-88	NY Islanders	NHL	69	17	18	35	67	5	3	1	4	4
1988-89	NY Islanders	NHL	14	3	2	5	2	....	....	....	....	....
	Springfield	AHL	8	1	5	6	0	....	....	....	....	....
1989-90	NY Islanders	NHL	63	6	18	24	19	4	0	2	2	10
	Springfield	AHL	7	4	2	6	0	....	....	....	....	....
	NHL Totals		207	33	52	85	153	15	5	3	8	18

LAUS, PAUL

Defense. Shoots right. 6'1", 200 lbs.   Born, Beamsville, Ont., September 26, 1970.
(Pittsburgh's 2nd choice, 37th overall, in 1989 Entry Draft).

			Regular Season					Playoffs				
Season	Club	Lea	GP	G	A	TP	PIM	GP	G	A	TP	PIM
1987-88	Hamilton	OHL	56	1	9	10	171	14	0	0	0	28
1988-89	Niagara Falls	OHL	49	1	10	11	225	15	0	5	5	56
1989-90	Niagara Falls	OHL	60	13	35	48	231	16	6	16	22	71

LAVIOLETTE, PETER   (LAH-vee-oh-LEHT)

Defense. Shoots left. 6'2", 190 lbs.   Born, Franklin, MA, July 12, 1964.

			Regular Season					Playoffs				
Season	Club	Lea	GP	G	A	TP	PIM	GP	G	A	TP	PIM
1987-88	U.S. National	....	54	4	20	24	82	....	....	....	....	....
	U.S. Olympic	....	5	0	2	2	4	....	....	....	....	....
	Colorado	IHL	19	2	5	7	27	9	3	5	8	7
1988-89	NY Rangers	NHL	12	0	0	0	6	....	....	....	....	....
	Denver	IHL	57	6	19	25	120	3	0	0	0	4
1989-90	Flint	IHL	62	6	18	24	82	4	0	0	0	4
	NHL Totals		12	0	0	0	6	....	....	....	....	....

Signed as a free agent by **NY Rangers**, August 12, 1987.

LAVISH, JAMES

Right wing. Shoots right. 5'11", 175 lbs.   Born, Albany, NY, October 13, 1970.
(Boston's 9th choice, 185th overall, in 1989 Entry Draft).

			Regular Season					Playoffs				
Season	Club	Lea	GP	G	A	TP	PIM	GP	G	A	TP	PIM
1988-89	Deerfield Aca.	HS	....	16	18	34	....	....	....	....	....	....
1989-90	Yale	ECAC	27	6	11	17	40	....	....	....	....	....

LAVOIE, DOMINIC

Defense. Shoots right. 6'2", 200 lbs.   Born, Montreal, Que., November 21, 1967.

			Regular Season					Playoffs				
Season	Club	Lea	GP	G	A	TP	PIM	GP	G	A	TP	PIM
1985-86	St. Jean	QMJHL	70	12	37	49	99	10	2	3	5	20
1986-87	St. Jean	QMJHL	64	12	42	54	97	8	2	7	9	2
1987-88	Peoria	IHL	65	7	26	33	54	7	2	2	4	8
1988-89	St. Louis	NHL	1	0	0	0	0	....	....	....	....	....
	Peoria	IHL	69	11	31	42	98	4	0	0	0	4
1989-90	St. Louis	NHL	13	1	1	2	16	....	....	....	....	....
	Peoria	IHL	58	19	23	42	32	5	2	2	4	16
	NHL Totals		14	1	1	2	16	....	....	....	....	....

Signed as a free agent by **St. Louis**, September 22, 1986.

LAWLESS, PAUL

Left wing. Shoots left. 6', 185 lbs.   Born, Scarborough, Ont., July 2, 1964.
(Hartford's 1st choice, 14th overall, in 1982 Entry Draft).

			Regular Season					Playoffs				
Season	Club	Lea	GP	G	A	TP	PIM	GP	G	A	TP	PIM
1981-82	Windsor	OHL	68	24	25	49	47	9	1	1	2	4
1982-83	Windsor	OHL	33	15	20	35	25	....	....	....	....	....
	Hartford	**NHL**	47	6	9	15	4	....	....	....	....	....
1983-84	**Hartford**	**NHL**	6	0	3	3	0	....	....	....	....	....
a	Windsor	OHL	55	31	49	80	26	2	0	1	1	0
1984-85	Binghamton	AHL	8	1	1	2	0	....	....	....	....	....
	Salt Lake	IHL	72	49	48	97	14	7	5	3	8	20
1985-86	**Hartford**	**NHL**	64	17	21	38	20	1	0	0	0	0
1986-87	**Hartford**	**NHL**	60	22	32	54	14	2	0	2	2	2
1987-88	**Hartford**	**NHL**	28	4	5	9	16	....	....	....	....	....
	Philadelphia	**NHL**	8	0	5	5	0	....	....	....	....	....
	Vancouver	**NHL**	13	0	1	1	0	....	....	....	....	....
1988-89	**Toronto**	**NHL**	7	0	0	0	0	....	....	....	....	....
	Milwaukee	IHL	53	30	35	65	58	....	....	....	....	....
1989-90	Newmarket	AHL	3	1	0	1	0	....	....	....	....	....
	NHL Totals		233	49	76	125	54	3	0	2	2	2

a OHL Second All-Star Team (1984)

Traded to **Philadelphia** by **Hartford** for Lindsay Carson, January 22, 1988. Traded to **Vancouver** by **Philadelphia** with Vancouver's fifth round draft choice (acquired March 7, 1989 by Edmonton, who selected Peter White) in 1989 Entry Draft — acquired earlier by Philadelphia — for Willie Huber, March 1, 1988. Traded to **Toronto** by **Vancouver** for the rights to Peter Deboer, February 27, 1989.

LAWTON, BRIAN

Left wing. Shoots left. 6', 190 lbs.   Born, New Brunswick, NJ, June 29, 1965.
(Minnesota's 1st choice and 1st overall in 1983 Entry Draft).

			Regular Season					Playoffs				
Season	Club	Lea	GP	G	A	TP	PIM	GP	G	A	TP	PIM
1981-82	Mt. St. Charles	HS	26	45	43	88		....	....	....	....	....
1982-83	Mt. St. Charles	HS	23	40	43	83	....	....	....	....	....	....
1983-84	**Minnesota**	**NHL**	58	10	21	31	33	5	0	0	0	10
1984-85	**Minnesota**	**NHL**	40	5	6	11	24	....	....	....	....	....
	Springfield	AHL	42	14	28	42	37	4	1	1	2	2
1985-86	**Minnesota**	**NHL**	65	18	17	35	36	3	0	1	1	2
1986-87	**Minnesota**	**NHL**	66	21	23	44	86	....	....	....	....	....
1987-88	**Minnesota**	**NHL**	74	17	24	41	71	....	....	....	....	....
1988-89	**NY Rangers**	**NHL**	30	7	10	17	39	....	....	....	....	....
	Hartford	**NHL**	35	10	16	26	28	3	1	0	1	0
1989-90	**Hartford**	**NHL**	13	2	1	3	6	....	....	....	....	....
	Quebec	**NHL**	14	5	6	11	10	....	....	....	....	....
	Boston	**NHL**	8	0	0	0	14	....	....	....	....	....
	Maine	AHL	5	0	0	0	14	....	....	....	....	....
	NHL Totals		403	95	124	219	347	11	1	1	2	12

Traded to **NY Rangers** by **Minnesota** with Igor Liba, and the rights to Eric Bennett for Paul Jerrard and Mark Tinordi, the rights to Bret Barnett and Mike Sullivan, and Los Angeles' third-round choice (Murray Garbutt) in 1989 Entry Draft — acquired March 10, 1987 by Minnesota — October 11, 1988. Traded to **Hartford** by **NY Rangers** with Norm MacIver and Don Maloney for Carey Wilson and Hartford's fifth-round choice (Lubos Rob) in 1990 Entry Draft, December 26, 1988. Claimed on waivers by **Quebec** from **Hartford**, December 1, 1989. Signed as a free agent by **Boston**, February 7, 1990. Signed as a free agent by **Los Angeles**, July 27, 1990.

LAXDAL, DEREK

Right wing. Shoots right. 6'1", 178 lbs.   Born, St. Boniface, Man., February 21, 1966.
(Toronto's 7th choice, 151st overall, in 1984 Entry Draft).

			Regular Season					Playoffs				
Season	Club	Lea	GP	G	A	TP	PIM	GP	G	A	TP	PIM
1982-83	Portland	WHL	39	4	9	13	27	14	0	2	2	2
1983-84	Brandon	WHL	70	23	20	43	86	12	0	4	4	10
1984-85	**Toronto**	**NHL**	3	0	0	0	6	....	....	....	....	....
	Brandon	WHL	69	61	41	102	74	....	....	....	....	....
	St. Catharines	AHL	5	3	2	5	2	....	....	....	....	....
1985-86	Brandon	WHL	42	34	35	69	62	....	....	....	....	....
	N. Westminster	WHL	18	9	6	15	14	....	....	....	....	....
	St. Catharines	AHL	7	0	1	1	15	12	1	1	2	24
1986-87	**Toronto**	**NHL**	2	0	0	0	7	....	....	....	....	....
	Newmarket	AHL	78	24	20	44	69	....	....	....	....	....
1987-88	**Toronto**	**NHL**	5	0	0	0	6	....	....	....	....	....
	Newmarket	AHL	67	18	25	43	81	....	....	....	....	....
1988-89	**Toronto**	**NHL**	41	9	6	15	65	....	....	....	....	....
	Newmarket	AHL	34	22	22	44	53	2	0	2	2	5
1989-90	**NY Islanders**	**NHL**	12	3	1	4	6	1	0	2	2	2
	Newmarket	AHL	23	7	8	15	52	....	....	....	....	....
	Springfield	AHL	28	13	12	25	42	13	8	6	14	47
	NHL Totals		63	12	7	19	90	1	0	2	2	2

Traded to **NY Islanders** by **Toronto** with Jack Capuano and Paul Gagne for Mike Stevens and Gilles Thibaudeau, December 20, 1989.

LAYLIN, CORY

Left wing. Shoots left. 5'9", 160 lbs.   Born, St. Cloud, MN, January 24, 1970.
(Pittsburgh's 10th choice, 214th overall, in 1988 Entry Draft).

			Regular Season					Playoffs				
Season	Club	Lea	GP	G	A	TP	PIM	GP	G	A	TP	PIM
1988-89	U. Minnesota	WCHA	47	14	10	24	24	....	....	....	....	....
1989-90	U. Minnesota	WCHA	39	13	14	27	31	....	....	....	....	....

LEACH, JAMIE

Right wing. Shoots right. 6'1", 195 lbs.   Born, Winnipeg, Man., August 25, 1969.
(Pittsburgh's 3rd choice, 47th overall, in 1987 Entry Draft).

			Regular Season					Playoffs				
Season	Club	Lea	GP	G	A	TP	PIM	GP	G	A	TP	PIM
1985-86	N. Westminster	WHL	58	8	7	15	20	....	....	....	....	....
1986-87	Hamilton	OHL	64	12	19	31	67	....	....	....	....	....
1987-88	Hamilton	OHL	64	24	19	43	79	14	6	7	13	12
1988-89a	Niagara Falls	OHL	58	45	62	107	47	17	9	11	20	25
1989-90	**Pittsburgh**	**NHL**	10	0	3	3	0	....	....	....	....	....
	Muskegon	IHL	72	22	36	58	39	15	9	4	13	14
	NHL Totals		10	0	3	3	0	....	....	....	....	....

a OHL Third All-Star Team (1989)

LEACH, STEPHEN

Right Wing. Shoots right. 5'11", 180 lbs.   Born, Cambridge, MA, January 16, 1966.
(Washington's 2nd choice, 34th overall, in 1984 Entry Draft).

			Regular Season					Playoffs				
Season	Club	Lea	GP	G	A	TP	PIM	GP	G	A	TP	PIM
1984-85	N. Hampshire	H.E.	41	12	25	37	53	....	....	....	....	....
1985-86	**Washington**	**NHL**	11	1	1	2	2	6	0	1	1	0
	N. Hampshire	H.E.	25	22	6	28	30	....	....	....	....	....
1986-87	**Washington**	**NHL**	15	1	0	1	6	....	....	....	....	....
	Binghamton	AHL	54	18	21	39	39	13	3	1	4	6
1987-88	**Washington**	**NHL**	8	1	1	2	17	9	2	1	3	0
	U.S. National	....	49	26	20	46	30	....	....	....	....	....
	U.S. Olympic	....	6	1	2	3	0	....	....	....	....	....
1988-89	**Washington**	**NHL**	74	11	19	30	94	6	1	0	1	12
1989-90	**Washington**	**NHL**	70	18	14	32	104	14	2	2	4	8
	NHL Totals		178	32	35	67	223	35	5	4	9	20

LEAHY, GREG

Center. Shoots left. 6'3", 185 lbs.   Born, North Bay, Ont., February 19, 1970.
(NY Rangers' 8th choice, 139th overall, in 1989 Entry Draft).

			Regular Season					Playoffs				
Season	Club	Lea	GP	G	A	TP	PIM	GP	G	A	TP	PIM
1986-87	Calgary	WHL	64	6	16	22	170	....	....	....	....	....
1987-88	Lethbridge	WHL	56	18	24	42	161	....	....	....	....	....
1988-89	Portland	WHL	66	28	49	77	128	19	16	13	29	33
1989-90	Portland	WHL	50	20	43	63	131	....	....	....	....	....

LEAVINS, JIM
(LEH vihns)

Defense. Shoots left. 5'11", 185 lbs.   Born, Dinsmore, Sask., July 28, 1960.

			Regular Season					Playoffs				
Season	Club	Lea	GP	G	A	TP	PIM	GP	G	A	TP	PIM
1981-82	Denver	WCHA	41	8	34	42	56	....	....	....	....	....
1982-83	Denver	WCHA	33	16	24	40	20	....	....	....	....	....
1983-84	Denver	WCHA	39	13	26	39	38	....	....	....	....	....
1984-85	Fort Wayne	IHL	76	5	20	25	57	13	3	8	11	10
1985-86	Adirondack	AHL	36	4	21	25	19	....	....	....	....	....
	Detroit	**NHL**	37	2	11	13	26	....	....	....	....	....
1986-87	**NY Rangers**	**NHL**	4	0	1	1	4	....	....	....	....	....
	New Haven	AHL	54	7	21	28	16	7	0	4	4	2
1987-88	New Haven	AHL	11	2	5	7	8	....	....	....	....	....
a	Salt Lake	IHL	68	12	45	57	45	16	5	5	10	8
1988-89	Salt Lake	IHL	25	8	13	21	14	14	2	11	13	6
	Kookoo	Fin.	42	12	11	23	39	....	....	....	....	....
1989-90	Salt Lake	IHL	11	0	6	6	2	....	....	....	....	....
	Kookoo	Fin.	44	7	24	31	36	....	....	....	....	....
	NHL Totals		41	2	12	14	30	....	....	....	....	....

a IHL Second All-Star Team (1988)

Signed as a free agent by **Detroit**, November 9, 1985. Traded to **NY Rangers** by **Detroit** with Kelly Kisio and Lane Lambert for Glen Hanlon and **New York's** third-round choices in 1987 (Dennis Holland) and 1988 Entry Drafts, July 29, 1986. Traded to **Calgary** by **NY Rangers** for Don Mercier, November 6, 1987.

LEBEAU, BENOIT
(luh-BOH)

Left wing. Shoots left. 6'1", 190 lbs.   Born, Montreal, Que., June 4, 1968.
(Winnipeg's 6th choice, 101st overall, in 1988 Entry Draft).

			Regular Season					Playoffs				
Season	Club	Lea	GP	G	A	TP	PIM	GP	G	A	TP	PIM
1987-88	Merrimack	NCAA	40	35	38	73	52	....	....	....	....	....
1988-89	Merrimack	NCAA	32	18	20	38	46	....	....	....	....	....
1989-90	Merrimack	H.E.	32	9	6	15	46	....	....	....	....	....

LEBEAU, PATRICK

Left wing. Shoots left. 5'10", 170 lbs.   Born, St. Jerome, Que., March 17, 1970.
(Montreal's 8th choice, 167th overall, in 1989 Entry Draft).

			Regular Season					Playoffs				
Season	Club	Lea	GP	G	A	TP	PIM	GP	G	A	TP	PIM
1986-87	Shawinigan	QMJHL	66	26	52	78	90	13	2	6	8	17
1987-88	Shawinigan	QMJHL	53	43	56	99	116	11	3	9	12	16
1988-89	St. Jean	QMJHL	49	43	70	113	71	4	4	3	7	6
1989-90a	Victoriaville	QMJHL	72	68	*106	*174	109	16	7	15	22	12

a QMJHL First All-Star Team (1990)

LEBEAU, STEPHAN
(leh-BOH)

Center. Shoots right. 5'10", 172 lbs.   Born, St. Jerome, Que., February 28, 1968.

			Regular Season					Playoffs				
Season	Club	Lea	GP	G	A	TP	PIM	GP	G	A	TP	PIM
1984-85	Shawinigan	QMJHL	66	41	38	79	18	9	4	5	9	4
1985-86	Shawinigan	QMJHL	72	69	77	146	22	5	4	2	6	4
1986-87a	Shawinigan	QMJHL	65	77	90	167	60	14	9	20	29	20
1987-88a	Shawinigan	QMJHL	67	*94	94	188	66	11	17	9	26	10
	Sherbrooke	AHL	...	...	...	...	...	1	0	1	1	0
1988-89	**Montreal**	**NHL**	1	0	1	1	2	....	....	....	....	....
bcde	Sherbrooke	AHL	78	*70	64	*134	47	6	1	4	5	8
1989-90	**Montreal**	**NHL**	57	15	20	35	11	2	3	0	3	0
	NHL Totals		58	15	21	36	13	2	3	0	3	0

a QMJHL Second All-Star Team (1987, 1988)
b AHL First All-Star Team (1989)
c Won Dudley "Red" Garrett Memorial Trophy (Top Rookie-AHL) (1989)
d Won John B. Sollenberger Trophy (Top Scorer-AHL) 1989)
e Won Les Cunningham Trophy (MVP-AHL) (1989)

Signed as a free agent by **Montreal**, September 27, 1986.

LeBLANC, JEAN GLENN

Left wing. Shoots left. 6'1", 195 lbs. Born, Campbellton, N.B., January 21, 1964.

			Regular Season					Playoffs				
Season	Club	Lea	GP	G	A	TP	PIM	GP	G	A	TP	PIM
1983-84	Hull	QMJHL	69	39	35	74	32	....	....	....	....	....
1984-85	New Brunswick	AUAA	24	25	34	59	32	....	....	....	....	....
1985-86a	New Brunswick	AUAA	24	38	28	66	35	....	....	....	....	....
1986-87	**Vancouver**	**NHL**	**2**	**1**	**0**	**1**	**0**	....	....	....	....	....
	Fredericton	AHL	75	40	30	70	27	....	....	....	....	....
1987-88	**Vancouver**	**NHL**	**41**	**12**	**10**	**22**	**18**	....	....	....	....	....
	Fredericton	AHL	35	26	25	51	54	15	6	7	13	34
1988-89	**Edmonton**	**NHL**	**2**	**1**	**0**	**1**	**0**	**1**	**0**	**0**	**0**	**0**
	Cape Breton	AHL	3	4	0	4	0	....	....	....	....	....
	Milwaukee	IHL	61	39	31	70	42	....	....	....	....	....
1989-90	Cape Breton	AHL	77	*54	34	88	50	6	4	0	4	4
	NHL Totals		**45**	**14**	**10**	**24**	**18**	**1**	**0**	**0**	**0**	**0**

a Canadian University Player of the Year (1986)

Signed as a free agent by **Vancouver**, April 12, 1986. Traded to **Edmonton** by **Vancouver** with Vancouver's fifth-round choice (Peter White) in 1989 Entry Draft for Doug Smith and Gregory C. Adams, March 7, 1989.

LeBRUN, SEAN

Left wing. Shoots left. 6'2", 200 lbs. Born, Prince George, B.C., May 2, 1969.
(New York Islanders' 3rd choice, 37th overall, in 1988 Entry Draft).

			Regular Season					Playoffs				
Season	Club	Lea	GP	G	A	TP	PIM	GP	G	A	TP	PIM
1986-87	Spokane	WHL	6	2	5	7	9	....	....	....	....	....
	N. Westminster	WHL	55	21	32	53	47	....	....	....	....	....
1987-88a	N. Westminster	WHL	72	36	53	89	59	5	1	3	4	2
1988-89	Tri-Cities	WHL	71	52	73	125	92	5	0	4	4	13
1989-90	Springfield	AHL	63	9	33	42	20	....	....	....	....	....

a WHL West Division Second All-Star Team (1988)

LeCLAIR, JOHN

Center. Shoots left. 6'1", 185 lbs. Born, St. Albans, VT, July 5, 1969.
(Montreal's 2nd choice, 33rd overall, in 1987 Entry Draft).

			Regular Season					Playoffs				
Season	Club	Lea	GP	G	A	TP	PIM	GP	G	A	TP	PIM
1987-88	U. of Vermont	ECAC	31	12	22	34	62	....	....	....	....	....
1988-89	U. of Vermont	ECAC	18	9	12	21	40	....	....	....	....	....
1989-90	U. of Vermont	ECAC	10	10	6	16	38	....	....	....	....	....

LEDYARD, GRANT

Defense. Shoots left. 6'2", 200 lbs. Born, Winnipeg, Man., November 19, 1961.

			Regular Season					Playoffs				
Season	Club	Lea	GP	G	A	TP	PIM	GP	G	A	TP	PIM
1980-81	Saskatoon	WHL	71	9	28	37	148	....	....	....	....	....
1981-82	Fort Garry	MJHL	63	25	45	70	150	....	....	....	....	....
1982-83	Tulsa	CHL	80	13	29	42	115	....	....	....	....	....
1983-84a	Tulsa	CHL	58	9	17	26	71	9	5	4	9	10
1984-85	**NY Rangers**	**NHL**	**42**	**8**	**12**	**20**	**53**	**3**	**0**	**2**	**2**	**4**
	New Haven	AHL	36	6	20	26	18	....	....	....	....	....
1985-86	**NY Rangers**	**NHL**	**27**	**2**	**9**	**11**	**20**	....	....	....	....	....
	Los Angeles	**NHL**	**52**	**7**	**18**	**25**	**78**	....	....	....	....	....
1986-87	**Los Angeles**	**NHL**	**67**	**14**	**23**	**37**	**93**	**5**	**0**	**0**	**0**	**10**
1987-88	**Los Angeles**	**NHL**	**23**	**1**	**7**	**8**	**52**	....	....	....	....	....
	New Haven	AHL	3	2	1	3	4	....	....	....	....	....
	Washington	**NHL**	**21**	**4**	**3**	**7**	**14**	**14**	**1**	**0**	**1**	**30**
1988-89	**Washington**	**NHL**	**61**	**3**	**11**	**14**	**43**	....	....	....	....	....
	Buffalo	**NHL**	**13**	**1**	**5**	**6**	**8**	**5**	**1**	**2**	**3**	**2**
1989-90	**Buffalo**	**NHL**	**67**	**2**	**13**	**15**	**37**	....	....	....	....	....
	NHL Totals		**373**	**42**	**101**	**143**	**398**	**27**	**2**	**4**	**6**	**46**

a Won Bob Gassoff Trophy (CHL's Most Improved Defenseman) (1984)

Signed as a free agent by **NY Rangers**, July 7, 1982. Traded to **Los Angeles** by **NY Rangers** with Roland Melanson for Los Angeles' fourth-round choice in 1987 Entry Draft (Michael Sullivan) and Brian MacLellan, December 7, 1985. Traded to **Washington** by **Los Angeles** for Craig Laughlin, February 9, 1988. Traded to **Buffalo** by **Washington** with Clint Malarchuk and Washington's sixth-round choice in 1991 Entry Draft for Calle Johansson and Buffalo's second-round choice (Byron Dafoe) in 1989 Entry Draft, March 7, 1989.

LEEMAN, GARY

Right wing. Shoots right. 5'11", 180 lbs. Born, Toronto, Ont., February 19, 1964.
(Toronto's 2nd choice, 24th overall, in 1982 Entry Draft).

			Regular Season					Playoffs				
Season	Club	Lea	GP	G	A	TP	PIM	GP	G	A	TP	PIM
1981-82	Regina	WHL	72	19	41	60	112	3	2	2	4	0
1982-83ab	Regina	WHL	63	24	62	86	88	5	1	5	6	4
	Toronto	**NHL**	....	....	....	....	....	**2**	**0**	**0**	**0**	**0**
1983-84	**Toronto**	**NHL**	**52**	**4**	**8**	**12**	**31**	....	....	....	....	....
1984-85	**Toronto**	**NHL**	**53**	**5**	**26**	**31**	**72**	....	....	....	....	....
	St. Catharines	AHL	7	2	2	4	11	....	....	....	....	....
1985-86	**Toronto**	**NHL**	**53**	**9**	**23**	**32**	**20**	**10**	**2**	**10**	**12**	**2**
	St. Catharines	AHL	25	15	13	28	6	....	....	....	....	....
1986-87	**Toronto**	**NHL**	**80**	**21**	**31**	**52**	**66**	**5**	**0**	**1**	**1**	**14**
1987-88	**Toronto**	**NHL**	**80**	**30**	**31**	**61**	**62**	**2**	**2**	**0**	**2**	**2**
1988-89	**Toronto**	**NHL**	**61**	**32**	**43**	**75**	**66**	....	....	....	....	....
1989-90	**Toronto**	**NHL**	**80**	**51**	**44**	**95**	**63**	**5**	**3**	**3**	**6**	**16**
	NHL Totals		**459**	**152**	**206**	**358**	**380**	**24**	**7**	**14**	**21**	**34**

a WHL First All-Star Team (1983)
b Named WHL's Top Defenseman (1983)

Played in NHL All-Star Game (1989)

LEETCH, BRIAN

Defense. Shoots left. 5'11", 170 lbs. Born, Corpus Christi, TX, March 3, 1968.
(NY Rangers' 1st choice, 9th overall, in 1986 Entry Draft).

			Regular Season					Playoffs				
Season	Club	Lea	GP	G	A	TP	PIM	GP	G	A	TP	PIM
1986-87abcd	Boston College	H.E.	37	9	38	47	10	....	....	....	....	....
1987-88	**NY Rangers**	**NHL**	**17**	**2**	**12**	**14**	**0**	....	....	....	....	....
	U.S. National	....	50	13	61	74	38	....	....	....	....	....
	U.S. Olympic	....	6	1	5	6	4	....	....	....	....	....
1988-89ef	**NY Rangers**	**NHL**	**68**	**23**	**48**	**71**	**50**	**4**	**3**	**2**	**5**	**2**
1989-90	**NY Rangers**	**NHL**	**72**	**11**	**45**	**56**	**26**	....	....	....	....	....
	NHL Totals		**157**	**36**	**105**	**141**	**76**	**4**	**3**	**2**	**5**	**2**

a Hockey East Player of the Year (1987)
b Hockey East Rookie of the Year (1987)
c Hockey East First All-Star Team (1987)
d NCAA East First All-American Team (1987)
e NHL All-Rookie Team (1989)
f Won Calder Memorial Trophy (1989)

Played in NHL All-Star Game (1990)

LEFEBVRE, SYLVAIN

Defense. Shoots left. 6'2", 204 lbs. Born, Richmond, Que., October 14, 1967.

			Regular Season					Playoffs				
Season	Club	Lea	GP	G	A	TP	PIM	GP	G	A	TP	PIM
1984-85	Laval	QMJHL	66	7	5	12	31	....	....	....	....	....
1985-86	Laval	QMJHL	71	8	17	25	48	14	1	0	1	25
1986-87	Laval	QMJHL	70	10	36	46	44	15	1	6	7	12
1987-88	Sherbrooke	AHL	79	3	24	27	73	6	2	3	5	4
1988-89a	Sherbrooke	AHL	77	15	32	47	119	6	1	3	4	4
1989-90	**Montreal**	**NHL**	**68**	**3**	**10**	**13**	**61**	**6**	**0**	**0**	**0**	**2**
	NHL Totals		**68**	**3**	**10**	**13**	**61**	**6**	**0**	**0**	**0**	**2**

a AHL Second All-Star Team (1989)

Signed as a free agent by **Montreal**, September 24, 1986.

LEGAULT, ALEXANDRE

Defense. Shoots right. 6'1", 205 lbs. Born, Chicoutimi, Que., December 27, 1971.
(Edmonton's 2nd choice, 38th overall, in 1990 Entry Draft).

			Regular Season					Playoffs				
Season	Club	Lea	GP	G	A	TP	PIM	GP	G	A	TP	PIM
1988-89	Notre Dame	SJHL	64	9	31	40	....	....	....	....	....	....
1989-90	Boston U.	H.E.	43	9	21	30	54	....	....	....	....	....

LEHMANN, TOMMY

Center. Shoots left. 6'1", 185 lbs. Born, Solna, Sweden, February 3, 1964.
(Boston's 11th choice, 228th overall, in 1982 Entry Draft).

			Regular Season					Playoffs				
Season	Club	Lea	GP	G	A	TP	PIM	GP	G	A	TP	PIM
1982-83	AIK	Swe.	28	1	5	6	2	3	0	0	0	0
1983-84	AIK	Swe.	23	4	5	9	6	6	2	2	4	0
1984-85	AIK	Swe.	34	13	13	26	6	....	....	....	....	....
1985-86	AIK	Swe.	35	11	13	24	12	....	....	....	....	....
1986-87	AIK	Swe.	31	25	15	40	12	....	....	....	....	....
1987-88	**Boston**	**NHL**	**9**	**1**	**3**	**4**	**6**	....	....	....	....	....
	Maine	AHL	11	3	5	8	2	....	....	....	....	....
1988-89	**Boston**	**NHL**	**26**	**4**	**2**	**6**	**10**	....	....	....	....	....
	Maine	AHL	26	1	13	14	12	....	....	....	....	....
1989-90	**Edmonton**	**NHL**	**1**	**0**	**0**	**0**	**0**	....	....	....	....	....
	Cape Breton	AHL	19	6	11	17	7	6	2	2	4	2
	AIK	Swe.	22	7	9	16	12	3	1	1	2	0
	NHL Totals		**36**	**5**	**5**	**10**	**16**	....	....	....	....	....

Traded to **Edmonton** by **Boston** for Edmonton's third-round choice (Wes Walz) in 1989 Entry Draft, June 17, 1989.

LEITER, KEN

Defense. Shoots left. 6'1", 195 lbs. Born, Detroit, MI, April 19, 1961.
(NY Islanders' 6th choice, 101st overall, in 1980 Entry Draft).

			Regular Season					Playoffs				
Season	Club	Lea	GP	G	A	TP	PIM	GP	G	A	TP	PIM
1979-80	Michigan State	CCHA	38	0	10	10	96	....	....	....	....	....
1980-81	Michigan State	CCHA	31	2	13	15	48	....	....	....	....	....
1981-82	Michigan State	CCHA	31	7	13	20	50	....	....	....	....	....
1982-83	Michigan State	CCHA	40	3	24	27	50	....	....	....	....	....
1983-84	Indianapolis	CHL	68	10	26	36	46	10	3	4	7	0
1984-85	**NY Islanders**	**NHL**	**5**	**0**	**2**	**2**	**2**	....	....	....	....	....
	Springfield	AHL	39	3	12	15	12	4	0	3	3	2
1985-86	**NY Islanders**	**NHL**	**9**	**1**	**1**	**2**	**6**	....	....	....	....	....
	Springfield	AHL	68	7	27	34	51	....	....	....	....	....
1986-87	**NY Islanders**	**NHL**	**74**	**9**	**20**	**29**	**30**	**11**	**0**	**5**	**5**	**6**
1987-88	**NY Islanders**	**NHL**	**51**	**4**	**13**	**17**	**24**	**4**	**0**	**1**	**1**	**2**
	Springfield	AHL	2	0	4	4	0	....	....	....	....	....
1988-89			DID NOT PLAY									
1989-90	**Minnesota**	**NHL**	**4**	**0**	**0**	**0**	**0**	....	....	....	....	....
	Kalamazoo	IHL	4	1	1	2	0	....	....	....	....	....
	NHL Totals		**143**	**14**	**36**	**50**	**62**	**15**	**0**	**6**	**6**	**8**

Claimed by **Minnesota** from **NY Islanders** in NHL Waiver Draft, October 2, 1989.

LEMARQUE, ERIC

Right wing. Shoots right. 5'10", 185 lbs. Born, Canoga Park, CA, July 1, 1969.
(Boston's 11th choice, 224th overall, in 1987 Entry Draft).

			Regular Season					Playoffs				
Season	Club	Lea	GP	G	A	TP	PIM	GP	G	A	TP	PIM
1986-87	N. Michigan	WCHA	38	5	12	17	49	....	....	....	....	....
1987-88	N. Michigan	WCHA	39	8	22	30	54	....	....	....	....	....
1988-89	N. Michigan	WCHA	43	20	17	37	40	....	....	....	....	....
1989-90	N. Michigan	WCHA	40	17	32	49	45	....	....	....	....	....

LEMIEUX, CLAUDE (lehm-YOO)

Right wing. Shoots right. 6'1", 213 lbs. Born, Buckingham, Que., July 16, 1965.
(Montreal's 2nd choice, 26th overall, in 1983 Entry Draft).

			Regular Season					Playoffs				
Season	Club	Lea	GP	G	A	TP	PIM	GP	G	A	TP	PIM
1982-83	Trois Rivieres	QMJHL	62	28	38	66	187	4	1	0	1	30
1983-84	Montreal	NHL	8	1	1	2	12	....	....	....	....	....
	Verdun	QMJHL	51	41	45	86	225	9	8	12	20	63
	Nova Scotia	AHL	....	....	....	....	....	2	1	0	1	0
1984-85	Montreal	NHL	1	0	1	1	7	....	....	....	....	....
ab	Verdun	QMJHL	52	58	66	124	152	14	23	17	40	38
1985-86	Montreal	NHL	10	1	2	3	22	20	10	6	16	68
	Sherbrooke	AHL	58	21	32	53	145	....	....	....	....	....
1986-87	Montreal	NHL	76	27	26	53	156	17	4	9	13	41
1987-88	Montreal	NHL	78	31	30	61	137	11	3	2	5	20
1988-89	Montreal	NHL	69	29	22	51	136	18	4	3	7	58
1989-90	Montreal	NHL	39	8	10	18	106	11	1	3	4	38
	NHL Totals		281	97	92	189	576	77	22	23	45	225

a Named Most Valuable Player in QMJHL Playoffs (1985).
b QMJHL First All-Star Team (1985).

LEMIEUX, JOCELYN (lehm-YOO)

Left wing. Shoots left. 5'10", 200 lbs. Born, Mont Laurier, Que., November 18, 1967.
(St. Louis' 1st choice, 10th overall, in 1986 Entry Draft).

			Regular Season					Playoffs				
Season	Club	Lea	GP	G	A	TP	PIM	GP	G	A	TP	PIM
1984-85	Laval	QMJHL	68	13	19	32	92	....	....	....	....	....
1985-86a	Laval	QMJHL	71	57	68	125	131	14	9	15	24	37
1986-87	St. Louis	NHL	53	10	8	18	94	5	0	1	1	6
1987-88	St. Louis	NHL	23	1	0	1	42	5	0	0	0	15
	Peoria	IHL	8	0	5	5	35	....	....	....	....	....
1988-89	Montreal	NHL	1	0	1	1	0	....	....	....	....	....
	Sherbrooke	AHL	73	25	28	53	134	4	3	1	4	6
1989-90	Montreal	NHL	34	4	2	6	61	....	....	....	....	....
	Chicago	NHL	39	10	11	21	47	18	1	8	9	28
	NHL Totals		150	25	22	47	244	28	1	9	10	49

a QMJHL First All-Star Team (1986).

Traded to **Montreal** by **St. Louis** with Darrell May and St. Louis' second round choice (Patrice Brisebois) in the 1989 Entry Draft for Sergio Momesso and Vincent Riendeau, August 9, 1988. Traded to **Chicago** by **Montreal** for Chicago's third round choice (Charles Poulin) in 1990 Entry Draft, January 5, 1990.

LEMIEUX, MARIO (lehm-YOO)

Center. Shoots right. 6'4", 210 lbs. Born, Montreal, Que., October 5, 1965.
(Pittsburgh's 1st choice and 1st overall in 1984 Entry Draft).

			Regular Season					Playoffs				
Season	Club	Lea	GP	G	A	TP	PIM	GP	G	A	TP	PIM
1981-82	Laval	QMJHL	64	30	66	96	22	18	5	9	14	31
1982-83a	Laval	QMJHL	66	84	100	184	76	12	14	18	32	18
1983-84bcd	Laval	QMJHL	70	*133	*149	*282	92	14	*29	*23	*52	29
1984-85ef	Pittsburgh	NHL	73	43	57	100	54	....	....	....	....	....
1985-86gh	Pittsburgh	NHL	79	48	93	141	43	....	....	....	....	....
1986-87g	Pittsburgh	NHL	63	54	53	107	57	....	....	....	....	....
1987-88 hijklm	Pittsburgh	NHL	77	*70	98	*168	92	....	....	....	....	....
1988-89jkmn	Pittsburgh	NHL	76	*85	*114	*199	100	11	12	7	19	16
1989-90	Pittsburgh	NHL	59	45	78	123	78	....	....	....	....	....
	NHL Totals		427	345	493	838	424	11	12	7	19	16

a QMJHL Second All-Star Team (1983)
b QMJHL First All-Star Team (1984)
c QMJHL Most Valuable Player (1984)
d Canadian Major Junior Player of the Year (1984)
e Won Calder Memorial Trophy (1985)
f NHL All-Rookie Team (1985)
g NHL Second All-Star Team (1986, 1987)
h Won Lester B. Pearson Award (1986, 1988)
i Won Hart Trophy (1988)
j Won Art Ross Trophy (1988, 1989)
k NHL First All-Star Team (1988, 1989)
l Won Dodge Performance of the Year Award (1988)
m Won Dodge Ram Tough Award (1989)
n Won Dodge Performer of the Year Award (1988, 1989)

Played in NHL All-Star Game (1985, 1986, 1988-90)

LENARDON, TIM

Center/Left wing. Shoots left. 6'2", 185 lbs. Born, Trail, B.C., May 11, 1962.

			Regular Season					Playoffs				
Season	Club	Lea	GP	G	A	TP	PIM	GP	G	A	TP	PIM
1983-84	Brandon U.	CWUAA	24	22	21	43	....	....	....	....	....	....
1984-85	Brandon U.	CWUAA	24	21	39	60	....	....	....	....	....	....
1985-86a	Brandon U.	CWUAA	26	26	40	66	33	....	....	....	....	....
1986-87	New Jersey	NHL	7	1	1	2	0	....	....	....	....	....
	Maine	AHL	61	28	35	63	30	....	....	....	....	....
1987-88	Utica	AHL	79	38	53	91	72	....	....	....	....	....
1988-89	Utica	AHL	63	28	27	55	48	....	....	....	....	....
	Milwaukee	IHL	15	6	5	11	27	10	2	3	5	25
1989-90	Vancouver	NHL	8	1	0	1	4	....	....	....	....	....
	Milwaukee	IHL	66	32	36	68	134	6	1	1	2	4
	NHL Totals		15	2	1	3	4	....	....	....	....	....

a Canadian University Player of the Year (1986).

Signed as a free agent by **New Jersey**, August 6, 1986. Traded to **Vancouver** by **New Jersey** for Claude Vilgrain, March 7, 1989.

LEROUX, FRANCOIS

Defense. Shoots left. 6'6", 225 lbs. Born, Ste. Adele, Que., April 18, 1970.
(Edmonton's 1st choice, 19th overall, in 1988 Entry Draft).

			Regular Season					Playoffs				
Season	Club	Lea	GP	G	A	TP	PIM	GP	G	A	TP	PIM
1987-88	St. Jean	QMJHL	58	3	8	11	143	7	2	0	2	21
1988-89	St. Jean	QMJHL	57	8	34	42	185	....	....	....	....	....
	Edmonton	NHL	2	0	0	0	0	....	....	....	....	....
1989-90	Edmonton	NHL	3	0	1	1	0	....	....	....	....	....
	Victoriaville	QMJHL	54	4	33	37	169	....	....	....	....	....
	NHL Totals		5	0	1	1	0	....	....	....	....	....

LESCHYSHYN, CURTIS

Defense. Shoots left. 6'1", 205 lbs. Born, Thompson, Man., September 21, 1969.
(Quebec's 1st choice, 3rd overall, in 1988 Entry Draft).

			Regular Season					Playoffs				
Season	Club	Lea	GP	G	A	TP	PIM	GP	G	A	TP	PIM
1986-87	Saskatoon	WHL	70	14	26	40	107	11	1	5	6	14
1987-88	Saskatoon	WHL	56	14	41	55	86	10	2	5	7	16
1988-89	Quebec	NHL	71	4	9	13	71	....	....	....	....	....
1989-90	Quebec	NHL	68	2	6	8	44	....	....	....	....	....
	NHL Totals		139	6	15	21	115	....	....	....	....	....

LESSARD, RICK

Defense. Shoots left. 6'2", 200 lbs. Born, Timmins, Ont., January 9, 1968.
(Calgary's 6th choice, 142nd overall, in 1986 Entry Draft).

			Regular Season					Playoffs				
Season	Club	Lea	GP	G	A	TP	PIM	GP	G	A	TP	PIM
1985-86	Ottawa	OHL	64	1	20	21	231	....	....	....	....	....
1986-87	Ottawa	OHL	66	5	36	41	188	11	1	7	8	30
1987-88	Ottawa	OHL	58	5	34	39	210	16	1	0	1	31
1988-89	Calgary	NHL	6	0	1	1	2	....	....	....	....	....
a	Salt Lake	IHL	76	10	42	52	239	14	1	6	7	35
1989-90	Salt Lake	IHL	66	3	18	21	169	10	1	2	3	64
	NHL Totals		6	0	1	1	2	....	....	....	....	....

a IHL First All-Star Team (1989)

LIBA, IGOR

Right wing. Shoots right. 6', 192 lbs. Born, Presov, Czechoslovakia, November 4, 1960.
(Calgary's 7th choice, 91st overall, in 1983 Entry Draft).

			Regular Season					Playoffs				
Season	Club	Lea	GP	G	A	TP	PIM	GP	G	A	TP	PIM
1986-87	VSZ Kosice	Czech.	39	14	26	40	....	....	....	....	....	....
1987-88	VSZ Kosice	Czech.	31	13	16	29	....	....	....	....	....	....
1988-89	NY Rangers	NHL	10	2	5	7	15	....	....	....	....	....
	Los Angeles	NHL	27	5	13	18	21	2	0	0	0	2
1989-90	VSZ Kosice	Czech	44	17	20	37	....	....	....	....	....	....
	NHL Totals		37	7	18	25	36	2	0	0	0	2

Traded to **Minnesota** by **Calgary** for Minnesota's fifth round draft choice in 1988 Entry Draft (Thomas Forslund), May 20, 1988. Traded to **NY Rangers** by **Minnesota** with Brian Lawton and the rights to Eric Bennett for Paul Jerrard and Mark Tinordi, the rights to Bret Barnett and Mike Sullivan, and Los Angeles' third-round choice (Murray Garbutt) in 1989 Entry Draft — acquired March 10, 1987 by Minnesota — October 11, 1988. Traded to **Los Angeles** by **NY Rangers** with Michael Boyce, Todd Elik and future considerations for Dean Kennedy and Denis Larocque, December 12, 1988.

LIDSTER, DOUG

Defense. Shoots right. 6'1", 200 lbs. Born, Kamloops, B.C., October 18, 1960.
(Vancouver's 6th choice, 133rd overall, in 1980 Entry Draft).

			Regular Season					Playoffs				
Season	Club	Lea	GP	G	A	TP	PIM	GP	G	A	TP	PIM
1977-78	Seattle	WHL	2	0	0	0	0	....	....	....	....	....
1979-80	Colorado	WCHA	39	18	25	43	52	....	....	....	....	....
1980-81	Colorado	WCHA	36	10	30	40	54	....	....	....	....	....
1981-82	Colorado	WCHA	36	13	22	35	32	....	....	....	....	....
1982-83	Colorado	WCHA	34	15	41	56	30	....	....	....	....	....
1983-84	Cdn. Olympic	...	59	6	20	26	28	....	....	....	....	....
	Vancouver	NHL	8	0	0	0	4	2	0	1	1	0
1984-85	Vancouver	NHL	78	6	24	30	55	....	....	....	....	....
1985-86	Vancouver	NHL	78	12	16	28	56	3	0	1	1	2
1986-87	Vancouver	NHL	80	12	51	63	40	....	....	....	....	....
1987-88	Vancouver	NHL	64	4	32	36	105	....	....	....	....	....
1988-89	Vancouver	NHL	63	5	17	22	78	7	1	1	2	9
1989-90	Vancouver	NHL	80	8	28	36	36	....	....	....	....	....
	NHL Totals		451	47	168	215	374	12	1	3	4	11

LIDSTROM, NIKLAS

Defense. Shoots left. 6'1", 180 lbs. Born, Vasteras, Sweden, April 28, 1970.
(Detroit's 3rd choice, 53rd overall, in 1989 Entry Draft).

			Regular Season					Playoffs				
Season	Club	Lea	GP	G	A	TP	PIM	GP	G	A	TP	PIM
1988-89	Vasteras	Swe.	19	0	2	2	4	....	....	....	....	....
1989-90	Vasteras	Swe.	39	8	8	16	14	2	0	1	1	2

LILLIE, SHAWN

Left wing. Shoots left. 6', 180 lbs. Born, Sault Ste. Marie, Ont., August 13, 1967.
(Pittsburgh's 2nd choice, 9th overall, in 1988 Supplemental Draft).

			Regular Season					Playoffs				
Season	Club	Lea	GP	G	A	TP	PIM	GP	G	A	TP	PIM
1986-87	Colgate	ECAC	30	11	10	21	4	....	....	....	....	....
1987-88	Colgate	ECAC	32	12	22	34	12	....	....	....	....	....
1988-89	Colgate	ECAC	31	16	38	54	12	....	....	....	....	....
1989-90	Colgate	ECAC	38	17	22	39	32	....	....	....	....	....

LINDBERG, CHRIS

Center. Shoots left. 6'1", 185 lbs. Born, Fort Frances, Ont., April 16, 1967.

			Regular Season					Playoffs				
Season	Club	Lea	GP	G	A	TP	PIM	GP	G	A	TP	PIM
1987-88	Minn.-Duluth	WCHA	35	12	10	22	36	....	....	....	....	....
1988-89	Minn.-Duluth	WCHA	36	15	18	33	51	....	....	....	....	....
1989-90	Binghamton	AHL	32	4	4	8	36	....	....	....	....	....

Signed as a free agent by **Hartford**, March 17, 1989.

LINDEN, TREVOR

Center/Right wing. Shoots right. 6'4", 205 lbs. Born, Medicine Hat, Alta., April 11, 1970.
(Vancouver's 1st choice, 2nd overall, in 1988 Entry Draft).

			Regular Season					Playoffs				
Season	Club	Lea	GP	G	A	TP	PIM	GP	G	A	TP	PIM
1986-87	Medicine Hat	WHL	72	14	22	36	59	20	5	4	9	17
1987-88	Medicine Hat	WHL	67	46	64	110	76	16	*13	12	25	19
1988-89a	**Vancouver**	**NHL**	**80**	**30**	**29**	**59**	**41**	**7**	**3**	**4**	**7**	**8**
1989-90	**Vancouver**	**NHL**	**73**	**21**	**30**	**51**	**43**	....	....	....	....	....
	NHL Totals		**153**	**51**	**59**	**110**	**84**	**7**	**3**	**4**	**7**	**8**

a NHL All-Rookie Team (1989)

LINDHOLM, MIKAEL

Center. Shoots left. 6'1", 195 lbs. Born, Brynas, Sweden, December 19, 1964.
(Los Angeles' 10th choice, 237th overall, in 1987 Entry Draft).

			Regular Season					Playoffs				
Season	Club	Lea	GP	G	A	TP	PIM	GP	G	A	TP	PIM
1986-87	Brynas	Swe.	36	8	9	17	46	....	....	....	....	....
1987-88	Brynas	Swe.	38	9	8	17	56	....	....	....	....	....
1988-89	Brynas	Swe.	40	9	17	26	98	....	....	....	....	....
1989-90	**Los Angeles**	**NHL**	**18**	**2**	**2**	**4**	**2**	....	....	....	....	....
	New Haven	AHL	28	4	6	10	24	....	....	....	....	....
	NHL Totals		**18**	**2**	**2**	**4**	**2**	....	....	....	....	....

LINDMAN, MIKAEL

Defense. Shoots left. 6'0", 185 lbs. Born, Bolsaf, Sweden, May 15, 1967.
(Detroit's 12th choice, 239th overall, in 1985 Entry Draft).

			Regular Season					Playoffs				
Season	Club	Lea	GP	G	A	TP	PIM	GP	G	A	TP	PIM
1988-89	Skelleftea	Swe.	38	7	7	14	20	....	....	....	....	....
1989-90	Skelleftea	Swe.	28	2	5	7	8	5	0	0	0	0

LINK, ANTHONY (TONY)

Defense. Shoots right. 6'2", 205 lbs. Born, Anchorage, AK, April 3, 1969.
(Philadelphia's 6th choice, 125th overall, in 1987 Entry Draft).

			Regular Season					Playoffs				
Season	Club	Lea	GP	G	A	TP	PIM	GP	G	A	TP	PIM
1988-89	U. of Maine	H.E.	22	0	3	3	12	....	....	....	....	....
1989-90	U. of Maine	H.E.	15	0	3	3	6	....	....	....	....	....

LINSEMAN, KEN (LIHNS-muhn)

Center. Shoots left. 5'11", 180 lbs. Born, Kingston, Ont., August 11, 1958.
(Philadelphia's 2nd choice, 7th overall, in 1978 Amateur Draft).

			Regular Season					Playoffs				
Season	Club	Lea	GP	G	A	TP	PIM	GP	G	A	TP	PIM
1975-76	Kingston	OHA	65	61	51	112	92	7	5	0	5	18
1976-77a	Kingston	OHA	63	53	74	127	210	10	9	12	21	54
1977-78	Birmingham	WHA	71	38	38	76	126	5	2	2	4	15
1978-79	Maine	AHL	38	17	22	39	106	....	....	....	....	....
	Philadelphia	**NHL**	**30**	**5**	**20**	**25**	**23**	**8**	**2**	**6**	**8**	**22**
1979-80	**Philadelphia**	**NHL**	**80**	**22**	**57**	**79**	**107**	**17**	**4**	***18**	**22**	**40**
1980-81	**Philadelphia**	**NHL**	**51**	**17**	**30**	**47**	**150**	**12**	**4**	**16**	**20**	**67**
1981-82	**Philadelphia**	**NHL**	**79**	**24**	**68**	**92**	**275**	**4**	**1**	**2**	**3**	**6**
1982-83	**Edmonton**	**NHL**	**72**	**33**	**42**	**75**	**181**	**16**	**6**	**8**	**14**	**22**
1983-84	**Edmonton**	**NHL**	**72**	**18**	**49**	**67**	**119**	**19**	**10**	**4**	**14**	**65**
1984-85	**Boston**	**NHL**	**74**	**25**	**49**	**74**	**126**	**5**	**4**	**6**	**10**	**8**
1985-86	**Boston**	**NHL**	**64**	**23**	**58**	**81**	**97**	**3**	**0**	**1**	**1**	**17**
1986-87	**Boston**	**NHL**	**64**	**15**	**34**	**49**	**126**	**4**	**1**	**1**	**2**	**22**
1987-88	**Boston**	**NHL**	**77**	**29**	**45**	**74**	**167**	**23**	**11**	**14**	**25**	**56**
1988-89	**Boston**	**NHL**	**78**	**27**	**45**	**72**	**164**	....	....	....	....	....
1989-90	**Boston**	**NHL**	**32**	**6**	**16**	**22**	**66**	....	....	....	....	....
	Philadelphia	**NHL**	**29**	**5**	**9**	**14**	**30**	....	....	....	....	....
	NHL Totals		**802**	**249**	**522**	**771**	**1631**	**111**	**43**	**76**	**119**	**325**

a OHA Second All-Star Team (1977).

Traded to **Hartford** by **Philadelphia** with Greg Adams and Philadelphia's first (David Jensen) and third round choices (Leif Karlsson) in 1983 Entry Draft for Mark Howe and Hartford's third round choice (Derrick Smith) in the 1983 Entry Draft, August 19, 1982. Traded to **Edmonton** by **Hartford** with Don Nachbaur for Risto Siltanen and Brent Loney, August 19, 1982. Traded to **Boston** by **Edmonton** for Mike Krushelnyski, June 21, 1984. Traded to **Philadelphia** by **Boston** for Dave Poulin, January 16, 1990.

LOACH, LONNIE

Left wing. Shoots left. 5'10", 180 lbs. Born, New Liskeard, Ont., April 14, 1968.
(Chicago's 4th choice, 98th overall, in 1986 Entry Draft).

			Regular Season					Playoffs				
Season	Club	Lea	GP	G	A	TP	PIM	GP	G	A	TP	PIM
1985-86a	Guelph	OHL	65	41	42	83	63	20	7	8	15	16
1986-87	Guelph	OHL	56	31	24	55	42	5	2	1	3	2
1987-88	Guelph	OHL	66	43	49	92	75	....	....	....	....	....
1988-89	Flint	IHL	41	22	26	48	30	....	....	....	....	....
	Saginaw	IHL	32	7	6	13	27	....	....	....	....	....
1989-90	Indianapolis	IHL	3	0	0	0	0	....	....	....	....	....
	Fort Wayne	IHL	54	15	33	48	40	5	4	2	6	15

a OHL Rookie of the Year (1986).

LOEWEN, DARCY

Left wing. Shoots left. 5'10", 185 lbs. Born, Calgary, Alta., February 26, 1969.
(Buffalo's 2nd choice, 55th overall, in 1988 Entry Draft).

			Regular Season					Playoffs				
Season	Club	Lea	GP	G	A	TP	PIM	GP	G	A	TP	PIM
1986-87	Spokane	WHL	68	15	25	40	129	5	0	0	0	16
1987-88	Spokane	WHL	72	30	44	74	231	15	7	5	12	54
1988-89	Spokane	WHL	60	31	27	58	194	....	....	....	....	....
	Cdn. National	....	2	0	0	0	0	....	....	....	....	....
1989-90	**Buffalo**	**NHL**	**4**	**0**	**0**	**0**	**4**	....	....	....	....	....
	Rochester	AHL	50	7	11	18	193	5	1	0	1	6
	NHL Totals		**4**	**0**	**0**	**0**	**4**	....	....	....	....	....

LOGAN, ROBERT

Right wing. Shoots left. 6', 190 lbs. Born, Montreal, Que., February 22, 1964.
(Buffalo's 8th choice, 100th overall, in 1982 Entry Draft).

			Regular Season					Playoffs				
Season	Club	Lea	GP	G	A	TP	PIM	GP	G	A	TP	PIM
1982-83	Yale	ECAC	28	13	12	25	8	....	....	....	....	....
1983-84	Yale	ECAC	22	9	13	22	25	....	....	....	....	....
1984-85	Yale	ECAC	32	19	12	31	18	....	....	....	....	....
1985-86a	Yale	ECAC	27	19	21	40	22	....	....	....	....	....
1986-87	**Buffalo**	**NHL**	**22**	**7**	**3**	**10**	**0**	....	....	....	....	....
	Rochester	AHL	56	30	14	44	27	18	5	10	15	4
1987-88	**Buffalo**	**NHL**	**16**	**3**	**2**	**5**	**0**	....	....	....	....	....
	Rochester	AHL	45	23	15	38	35	....	....	....	....	....
1988-89	**Los Angeles**	**NHL**	**4**	**0**	**0**	**0**	**0**	....	....	....	....	....
	New Haven	AHL	66	21	32	53	27	13	2	3	5	9
	Rochester	AHL	5	2	2	4	2	....	....	....	....	....
1989-90	New Haven	AHL	11	2	4	6	4	....	....	....	....	....
	NHL Totals		**42**	**10**	**5**	**15**	**0**	....	....	....	....	....

a ECAC Second All-Star Team (1986).

Traded to **Los Angeles** by **Buffalo** with Buffalo's ninth-round choice (Jim Glacin) in 1989 Entry Draft for Larry Playfair, October 21, 1988.

LOISELLE, CLAUDE (LWAH-ZEHL)

Center. Shoots left. 5'11", 195 lbs. Born, Ottawa, Ont., May 29, 1963.
(Detroit's 1st choice, 23rd overall, in 1981 Entry Draft).

			Regular Season					Playoffs				
Season	Club	Lea	GP	G	A	TP	PIM	GP	G	A	TP	PIM
1980-81	Windsor	OHA	68	38	56	94	103	11	3	3	6	40
1981-82	**Detroit**	**NHL**	**4**	**1**	**0**	**1**	**2**	....	....	....	....	....
	Windsor	OHL	68	36	73	109	192	9	2	10	12	42
1982-83	**Detroit**	**NHL**	**18**	**2**	**0**	**2**	**15**	....	....	....	....	....
	Adirondack	AHL	6	1	7	8	0	6	2	4	6	0
1983-84	**Detroit**	**NHL**	**28**	**4**	**6**	**10**	**32**	....	....	....	....	....
	Adirondack	AHL	29	13	16	29	59	....	....	....	....	....
1984-85	**Detroit**	**NHL**	**30**	**8**	**1**	**9**	**45**	**3**	**0**	**2**	**2**	**0**
	Adirondack	AHL	47	22	29	51	24	....	....	....	....	....
1985-86	**Detroit**	**NHL**	**48**	**7**	**15**	**22**	**142**	....	....	....	....	....
	Adirondack	AHL	21	15	11	26	32	16	5	10	15	38
1986-87	**New Jersey**	**NHL**	**75**	**16**	**24**	**40**	**137**	....	....	....	....	....
1987-88	**New Jersey**	**NHL**	**68**	**17**	**18**	**35**	**121**	**20**	**4**	**6**	**10**	**50**
1988-89	**New Jersey**	**NHL**	**74**	**7**	**14**	**21**	**209**	....	....	....	....	....
1989-90	**Quebec**	**NHL**	**72**	**11**	**14**	**25**	**104**	....	....	....	....	....
	NHL Totals		**417**	**73**	**92**	**165**	**807**	**20**	**4**	**8**	**12**	**50**

Traded to **New Jersey** by **Detroit** for Tim Higgins, June 25, 1986. Traded to **Quebec** by **New Jersey** with Joe Cirella and New Jersey's eighth round choice (Alexander Karpovtsev) in 1990 Entry Draft for Walt Poddubny and Quebec's fourth round choice (Mike Bodnarchuk) in 1990 Entry Draft, June 17, 1989.

LOMOW, BYRON

Center. Shoots right. 5'11", 180 lbs. Born, Sherwood Park, Alta., April 27, 1965.

			Regular Season					Playoffs				
Season	Club	Lea	GP	G	A	TP	PIM	GP	G	A	TP	PIM
1982-83	Brandon	OHA	62	19	26	45	21	....	....	....	....	....
1983-84	Brandon	WHL	71	44	57	101	44	12	1	5	6	16
1984-85	Brandon	WHL	71	42	70	112	90	....	....	....	....	....
1985-86	Brandon	WHL	72	52	67	119	77	....	....	....	....	....
	Indianapolis	IHL	9	8	3	11	10	5	2	11	3	2
1986-87	Indianapolis	IHL	81	28	43	71	225	6	3	5	8	21
1987-88	Baltimore	AHL	71	14	26	40	77	....	....	....	....	....
	Colorado	IHL	10	2	10	12	7	....	....	....	....	....
1988-89	Fort Wayne	IHL	81	22	35	57	207	11	3	3	6	68
1989-90	Fort Wayne	IHL	79	29	24	53	230	5	3	2	5	25

Signed as a free agent by **Minnesota**, April 21, 1986. Traded to **NY Rangers** by **Minnesota** with future considerations for Curt Giles, November 20, 1987.

LONEY, TROY

Left wing. Shoots left. 6'3", 210 lbs. Born, Bow Island, Alta., September 21, 1963.
(Pittsburgh's 3rd choice, 52nd overall, in 1982 Entry Draft).

			Regular Season					Playoffs				
Season	Club	Lea	GP	G	A	TP	PIM	GP	G	A	TP	PIM
1980-81	Lethbridge	WHL	71	18	13	31	100	9	2	2	5	14
1981-82	Lethbridge	WHL	71	26	33	59	152	12	3	3	6	10
1982-83	Lethbridge	WHL	72	33	34	67	156	20	10	7	17	43
1983-84	**Pittsburgh**	**NHL**	**13**	**0**	**0**	**0**	**9**	....	....	....	....	....
	Baltimore	AHL	63	18	13	31	147	10	0	2	2	19
1984-85	**Pittsburgh**	**NHL**	**46**	**10**	**8**	**18**	**59**	....	....	....	....	....
	Baltimore	AHL	15	4	2	6	25	....	....	....	....	....
1985-86	**Pittsburgh**	**NHL**	**47**	**3**	**9**	**12**	**95**	....	....	....	....	....
	Baltimore	AHL	33	12	11	23	84	....	....	....	....	....
1986-87	**Pittsburgh**	**NHL**	**23**	**8**	**7**	**15**	**22**	....	....	....	....	....
	Baltimore	AHL	40	13	14	27	134	....	....	....	....	....
1987-88	**Pittsburgh**	**NHL**	**65**	**5**	**13**	**18**	**151**	....	....	....	....	....
1988-89	**Pittsburgh**	**NHL**	**69**	**10**	**6**	**16**	**165**	**11**	**1**	**3**	**4**	**24**
1989-90	**Pittsburgh**	**NHL**	**67**	**11**	**16**	**27**	**168**	....	....	....	....	....
	NHL Totals		**330**	**47**	**59**	**106**	**669**	**11**	**1**	**3**	**4**	**24**

LONGO, CHRIS

Right wing. Shoots right. 5'11", 180 lbs. Born, Belleville, Ont., January 5, 1972.
(Washington's 3rd choice, 51st overall, in 1990 Entry Draft).

			Regular Season					Playoffs				
Season	Club	Lea	GP	G	A	TP	PIM	GP	G	A	TP	PIM
1988-89	Kingston	Jr.B	40	28	29	57	54	....				
1989-90a	Peterborough	OHL	66	33	41	74	48	11	2	3	5	14

a OHL Rookie of the Year (1990)

LOOB, HAKAN
(LOOB, HOH-kuhn)

Right wing. Shoots right. 5'9", 180 lbs. Born, Visby, Sweden, July 3, 1960.
(Calgary's 10th choice, 181st overall, in 1980 Entry Draft).

			Regular Season					Playoffs				
Season	Club	Lea	GP	G	A	TP	PIM	GP	G	A	TP	PIM
1979-80	Farjestad	Swe.	36	15	4	19	20	....				
1980-81	Farjestad	Swe.	36	23	6	29	14	7	5	3	8	6
	Swe. National	...	6	0	1	1	0	....				
1981-82	Farjestad	Swe.	36	26	15	41	28	2	1	0	1	0
	Swe. National	...	21	8	3	11	8	....				
1982-83	Farjestad	Swe.	36	42	34	76	29	8	10	4	14	6
	Swe. National	...	11	2	2	4	8	....				
1983-84a	Calgary	NHL	77	30	25	55	22	11	2	3	5	2
1984-85	Calgary	NHL	78	37	35	72	14	4	3	3	6	0
1985-86	Calgary	NHL	68	31	36	67	36	22	4	10	14	6
1986-87	Calgary	NHL	68	18	26	44	26	5	1	2	3	0
1987-88b	Calgary	NHL	80	50	56	106	47	9	8	1	9	4
1988-89	Calgary	NHL	79	27	58	85	44	22	8	9	17	4
1989-90	Farjestad	Swe.	40	22	31	53	24	10	9	4	13	2
	NHL Totals		450	193	236	429	189	73	26	28	54	16

a NHL All-Rookie Team (1984)
b NHL First All-Star Team (1988)

LORENTZ, DAVID

Left wing. Shoots left. 5'9", 180 lbs. Born, Kitchener, Ont., March 16, 1969.
(Washington's 6th choice, 145th overall, in 1989 Entry Draft).

			Regular Season					Playoffs				
Season	Club	Lea	GP	G	A	TP	PIM	GP	G	A	TP	PIM
1987-88	Peterborough	OHL	65	8	25	33	78	12	3	4	7	0
1988-89	Peterborough	OHL	65	18	38	56	47	17	2	8	10	16
1989-90	Peterborough	OHL	57	22	31	53	55	12	3	2	5	8

LOVSIN, KEN

Defense. Shoots right. 6'2", 185 lbs. Born, Peace River, Alta., December 3, 1966.
(Hartford's 1st choice, 22nd overall, in 1987 Supplemental Draft).

			Regular Season					Playoffs				
Season	Club	Lea	GP	G	A	TP	PIM	GP	G	A	TP	PIM
1986-87	Saskatchewan	CWUAA	28	3	13	16	14	....				
1987-88	Saskatchewan	CWUAA	28	14	24	38	20	....				
1988-89	Cdn. National	....	59	0	10	10	59	....				
1989-90	Cdn. National	....	66	7	15	22	80	....				

Signed as a free agent by **Washington**, July 3, 1990.

LOWE, KEVIN HUGH
(LOH)

Defense. Shoots left. 6'2", 195 lbs. Born, Lachute, Que., April 15, 1959.
(Edmonton's 1st choice, 21st overall, in 1979 Entry Draft).

			Regular Season					Playoffs				
Season	Club	Lea	GP	G	A	TP	PIM	GP	G	A	TP	PIM
1977-78	Quebec	QJHL	64	13	52	65	86	4	1	2	3	6
1978-79a	Quebec	QJHL	68	26	60	86	120	6	1	7	8	36
1979-80	Edmonton	NHL	64	2	19	21	70	3	0	1	1	0
1980-81	Edmonton	NHL	79	10	24	34	94	9	0	2	2	11
1981-82	Edmonton	NHL	80	9	31	40	63	5	0	3	3	0
1982-83	Edmonton	NHL	80	6	34	40	43	16	1	8	9	10
1983-84	Edmonton	NHL	80	4	42	46	59	19	3	7	10	16
1984-85	Edmonton	NHL	80	4	21	25	104	16	0	5	5	8
1985-86	Edmonton	NHL	74	2	16	18	90	10	1	3	4	15
1986-87	Edmonton	NHL	77	8	29	37	94	21	2	4	6	22
1987-88	Edmonton	NHL	70	9	15	24	89	19	0	2	2	26
1988-89	Edmonton	NHL	76	7	18	25	98	7	1	2	3	4
1989-90bc	Edmonton	NHL	78	7	26	33	140	20	0	2	2	10
	NHL Totals		838	68	275	343	944	145	8	39	47	122

a QMJHL Second All-Star Team (1979)
b Won Bud Man of the Year Award (1990)
c Won King Clancy Memorial Trophy (1990)
Played in NHL All-Star Game (1984-86, 1988-90)

LOWRY, DAVE

Left wing. Shoots left. 6'1", 191 lbs. Born, Sudbury, Ont., January 14, 1965.
(Vancouver's 6th choice, 110th overall, in 1983 Entry Draft).

			Regular Season					Playoffs				
Season	Club	Lea	GP	G	A	TP	PIM	GP	G	A	TP	PIM
1982-83	London	OHL	42	11	16	27	48	3	0	0	0	14
1983-84	London	OHL	66	29	47	76	125	8	6	6	12	41
1984-85a	London	OHL	61	60	60	120	94	8	6	5	11	10
1985-86	Vancouver	NHL	73	10	8	18	143	3	0	0	0	0
1986-87	Vancouver	NHL	70	8	10	18	176	....				
1987-88	Vancouver	NHL	22	1	3	4	38	....				
	Fredericton	AHL	46	18	27	45	59	14	7	3	10	72
1988-89	St. Louis	NHL	21	3	3	6	11	10	0	5	5	4
	Peoria	IHL	58	31	35	66	45	....				
1989-90	St. Louis	NHL	78	19	6	25	75	12	2	1	3	39
	NHL Totals		264	41	30	71	443	25	2	6	8	43

a OHL First All-Star Team (1985)
Traded to **St. Louis** by **Vancouver** for Ernie Vargas, September 29, 1988.

LUBINA, LADISLAV

Left wing. Shoots left. 5'11", 182 lbs. Born, Dvur Kralove, Czech., February 11, 1967.
(Minnesota's 9th choice, 216th overall, in 1985 Entry Draft).

			Regular Season					Playoffs				
Season	Club	Lea	GP	G	A	TP	PIM	GP	G	A	TP	PIM
1986-87	Dukla Jihlava	Czech.	34	9	7	16	....					
1987-88	Dukla Jihlava	Czech.	34	12	9	21	....					
1988-89	Dukla Jihlava	Czech.	44	22	16	38	....					
1989-90	Dukla Jihlava	Czech	44	19	15	34	....					

LUDWIG, CRAIG LEE

Defense. Shoots left. 6'3", 222 lbs. Born, Rinelander, WI, March 15, 1961.
(Montreal's 5th choice, 61st overall, in 1980 Entry Draft).

			Regular Season					Playoffs				
Season	Club	Lea	GP	G	A	TP	PIM	GP	G	A	TP	PIM
1979-80	North Dakota	WCHA	33	1	8	9	32	....				
1980-81	North Dakota	WCHA	34	4	8	12	48	....				
1981-82	North Dakota	WCHA	37	4	17	21	42	....				
1982-83	Montreal	NHL	80	0	25	25	59	3	0	0	0	2
1983-84	Montreal	NHL	80	7	18	25	52	15	0	3	3	23
1984-85	Montreal	NHL	72	5	14	19	90	12	0	2	2	6
1985-86	Montreal	NHL	69	2	4	6	63	20	0	1	1	48
1986-87	Montreal	NHL	75	4	12	16	105	17	2	3	5	30
1987-88	Montreal	NHL	74	4	10	14	69	11	1	1	2	6
1988-89	Montreal	NHL	74	3	13	16	73	21	0	2	2	24
1989-90	Montreal	NHL	73	1	15	16	108	11	0	1	1	16
	NHL Totals		597	26	111	137	619	110	3	13	16	155

LUDZIK, STEVE

Center. Shoots left. 5'11", 185 lbs. Born, Toronto, Ont., April 3, 1962.
(Chicago's 3rd choice, 28th overall, in 1980 Entry Draft).

			Regular Season					Playoffs				
Season	Club	Lea	GP	G	A	TP	PIM	GP	G	A	TP	PIM
1979-80	Niagara Falls	OHA	67	43	76	119	102	10	6	6	12	16
1980-81	Niagara Falls	OHA	58	50	92	142	108	12	5	9	14	40
1981-82	Chicago	NHL	8	2	1	3	2	....				
	New Brunswick	AHL	73	21	41	62	142	15	3	7	10	6
1982-83	Chicago	NHL	66	6	19	25	63	13	3	5	8	20
1983-84	Chicago	NHL	80	9	20	29	73	4	0	1	1	9
1984-85	Chicago	NHL	79	11	20	31	86	15	1	1	2	16
1985-86	Chicago	NHL	49	6	5	11	21	3	0	0	0	12
1986-87	Chicago	NHL	52	5	12	17	34	4	0	0	0	0
1987-88	Chicago	NHL	73	6	15	21	40	5	0	1	1	13
1988-89	Chicago	NHL	6	1	0	1	8	....				
	Saginaw	IHL	65	21	57	78	129	6	0	1	1	17
1989-90	Buffalo	NHL	11	0	1	1	6	....				
	Rochester	AHL	54	25	29	54	71	16	5	6	11	57
	NHL Totals		424	46	93	139	333	44	4	8	12	70

LUIK, JAAN

Defense. Shoots left. 6'1", 210 lbs. Born, Scarborough, Ont., January 15, 1970.
(St. Louis' 4th choice, 72nd overall, in 1988 Entry Draft).

			Regular Season					Playoffs				
Season	Club	Lea	GP	G	A	TP	PIM	GP	G	A	TP	PIM
1987-88	Miami-Ohio	CCHA	35	2	5	7	93	....				
1988-89	Miami-Ohio	CCHA	33	1	8	9	43	....				
1989-90	Miami-Ohio	CCHA	35	1	11	12	64	....				

LUIK, SCOTT

Right wing. Shoots left. 6'1", 210 lbs. Born, Scarborough, Ont., January 15, 1970.
(New Jersey's 4th choice, 65th overall, in 1988 Entry Draft).

			Regular Season					Playoffs				
Season	Club	Lea	GP	G	A	TP	PIM	GP	G	A	TP	PIM
1987-88	Miami-Ohio	CCHA	34	4	10	14	47	....				
1988-89	Miami-Ohio	CCHA	36	13	13	26	92	....				
1989-90	Miami-Ohio	CCHA	16	4	7	11	32	....				
	Oshawa	OHL	34	15	14	29	20	17	4	5	9	20

LUMME, JYRKI

Defense. Shoots left. 6'1", 190 lbs. Born, Tampere, Finland, July 16, 1966.
(Montreal's 3rd choice, 57th overall, in 1986 Entry Draft).

			Regular Season					Playoffs				
Season	Club	Lea	GP	G	A	TP	PIM	GP	G	A	TP	PIM
1984-85	KooVee	Fin. 3	30	6	4	10	44	....				
1985-86	Ilves	Fin.	31	1	4	5	4	....				
1986-87	Ilves	Fin.	43	12	12	24	52	4	0	1	2	..
1987-88	Ilves	Fin.	43	8	22	30	75	....				
1988-89	Montreal	NHL	21	1	3	4	10	....				
	Sherbrooke	AHL	26	4	11	15	10	6	1	3	4	4
1989-90	Montreal	NHL	54	1	19	20	41	....				
	Vancouver	NHL	11	3	7	10	8	....				
	NHL Totals		86	5	29	34	59	....				

Traded to **Vancouver** by **Montreal** for St. Louis' second round choice in 1991 Entry Draft (previously acquired by Vancouver), March 6, 1990.

LUONGO, CHRISTOPHER (CHRIS)

Defense. Shoots right. 6', 180 lbs. Born, Detroit, MI, March 17, 1967.
(Detroit's 5th choice, 92nd overall, in 1985 Entry Draft).

			Regular Season					Playoffs				
Season	Club	Lea	GP	G	A	TP	PIM	GP	G	A	TP	PIM
1985-86	Michigan State	CCHA	38	1	5	6	29	....				
1986-87a	Michigan State	CCHA	27	4	16	20	38	....				
1987-88	Michigan State	CCHA	45	3	15	18	49	....				
1988-89b	Michigan State	CCHA	47	4	21	25	42	....				
1989-90	Adirondack	AHL	53	9	14	23	37	3	0	0	0	0

a Named to NCAA All-Tournament Team (1987)
b CCHA Second All-Star Team (1989)

LYONS, COREY

Right wing. Shoots left. 5'10", 185 lbs.   Born, Calgary, Alta., June 13, 1970.
(Calgary's 4th choice, 63rd overall, in 1989 Entry Draft).

			Regular Season					Playoffs			
Season	Club	Lea	GP	G	A	TP	PIM	GP	G	A	TP	PIM
1987-88	Lethbridge	WHL	2	0	0	0	0	....	....	....	....	....
1988-89	Lethbridge	WHL	71	53	59	112	36	8	4	9	13	7
1989-90	Lethbridge	WHL	72	63	79	142	26	19	11	15	26	4
	Salt Lake	IHL	...	....	....	....	....	1	0	0	0	0

MacARTHUR, KENNETH

Defense. Shoots left. 6'1", 185 lbs.   Born, Rossland, B.C., March 15, 1968.
(Minnesota's 5th choice, 148th overall, in 1988 Entry Draft).

			Regular Season					Playoffs			
Season	Club	Lea	GP	G	A	TP	PIM	GP	G	A	TP	PIM
1987-88	U. of Denver	WCHA	38	6	16	22	69	....	....	....	....	....
1988-89	U. of Denver	WCHA	42	11	19	30	77	....	....	....	....	....
1989-90	U. of Denver	WCHA	38	12	29	41	96	....	....	....	....	....
	Cdn. National	.....	13	2	1	3	14	....	....	....	....	....

MacDERMID, PAUL

Right wing. Shoots right. 6'1", 205 lbs.   Born, Chesley, Ont., April 14, 1963.
(Hartford's 2nd choice, 61st overall, in 1981 Entry Draft).

			Regular Season					Playoffs			
Season	Club	Lea	GP	G	A	TP	PIM	GP	G	A	TP	PIM
1980-81	Windsor	OHA	68	15	17	32	106	....	....	....	....	....
1981-82	**Hartford**	**NHL**	3	1	0	1	2	....	....	....	....	....
	Windsor	OHL	65	26	45	71	179	9	6	4	10	17
1982-83	**Hartford**	**NHL**	7	0	0	0	2	....	....	....	....	....
	Windsor	OHL	42	35	45	80	9	....	....	....	....	....
1983-84	**Hartford**	**NHL**	3	0	1	1	0	....	....	....	....	....
	Binghamton	AHL	70	31	30	61	130	....	....	....	....	....
1984-85	**Hartford**	**NHL**	31	4	7	11	29	....	....	....	....	....
	Binghamton	AHL	48	9	31	40	87	....	....	....	....	....
1985-86	**Hartford**	**NHL**	74	13	10	23	160	10	2	1	3	20
1986-87	**Hartford**	**NHL**	72	7	11	18	202	6	2	1	3	34
1987-88	**Hartford**	**NHL**	80	20	15	35	139	6	0	5	5	14
1988-89	**Hartford**	**NHL**	74	17	27	44	141	4	1	1	2	16
1989-90	**Hartford**	**NHL**	29	6	12	18	69	....	....	....	....	....
	Winnipeg	**NHL**	44	7	10	17	100	7	0	2	2	8
	NHL Totals		417	75	93	168	844	33	5	10	15	92

Traded to **Winnipeg** by **Hartford** for Randy Cunneyworth, December 13, 1989.

MacDONALD, BRUCE

Defense. Shoots left. 6'1", 195 lbs.   Born, Plaistow, NH, December 16, 1967.
(Philadelphia's 9th choice, 188th overall, in 1989 Entry Draft).

			Regular Season					Playoffs			
Season	Club	Lea	GP	G	A	TP	PIM	GP	G	A	TP	PIM
1987-88	N. Hampshire	H.E.	12	0	1	1	8	....	....	....	....	....
1988-89	N. Hampshire	H.E.	21	1	3	4	8	....	....	....	....	....
1989-90	N. Hampshire	H.E.	35	2	3	5	16	....	....	....	....	....

MacDONALD, DARIN

Left wing. Shoots left. 6', 180 lbs.   Born, Calgary, Alta., January 30, 1970.
(Edmonton's 12th choice, 229th overall, in 1988 Entry Draft).

			Regular Season					Playoffs			
Season	Club	Lea	GP	G	A	TP	PIM	GP	G	A	TP	PIM
1987-88	Boston U.	H.E.	12	2	1	3	0	....	....	....	....	....
1988-89	Boston U.	H.E.	35	6	6	12	10	....	....	....	....	....
1989-90	Boston U.	H.E.	38	4	3	7	29	....	....	....	....	....

MacDONALD, DOUG

Center. Shoots left. 6', 190 lbs.   Born, Port Moody, B.C., February 8, 1969.
(Buffalo's 3rd choice, 77th overall, in 1989 Entry Draft).

			Regular Season					Playoffs			
Season	Club	Lea	GP	G	A	TP	PIM	GP	G	A	TP	PIM
1988-89	U. Wisconsin	WCHA	44	23	25	48	50	....	....	....	....	....
1989-90	U. Wisconsin	WCHA	44	16	35	51	52	....	....	....	....	....

MacDOUGALL, WILLIAM HENRY

Center. Shoots right. 6', 185 lbs.   Born, Mississauga, Ont., August 10, 1966.

			Regular Season					Playoffs			
Season	Club	Lea	GP	G	A	TP	PIM	GP	G	A	TP	PIM
1989-90	Adirondack	AHL	11	10	7	17	4	....	....	....	....	....
abc	Erie	ECHL	57	80	68	148	226	....	....	....	....	....

a Named ECHL Most Valuable Player
b Named ECHL Rookie-of-the-Year
c ECHL First Team All-Star

Signed as a free agent by **Detroit**, December 8, 1989.

MacFARLANE, SHANE

Center. Shoots left. 5'10", 161 lbs.   Born, Warroad, MN, September 4, 1968.
(Buffalo's 1st choice, 24th overall, in 1990 Supplemental Draft).

			Regular Season					Playoffs			
Season	Club	Lea	GP	G	A	TP	PIM	GP	G	A	TP	PIM
1987-88	North Dakota	WCHA	27	0	1	1	8	....	....	....	....	....
1988-89	North Dakota	WCHA	30	1	4	5	8	....	....	....	....	....
1989-90	North Dakota	WCHA	22	3	2	5	10	....	....	....	....	....

MacINNIS, ALLAN

Defense. Shoots right. 6'2", 196 lbs.   Born, Inverness, N.S., July 11, 1963.
(Calgary's 1st choice, 15th overall, in 1981 Entry Draft).

			Regular Season					Playoffs			
Season	Club	Lea	GP	G	A	TP	PIM	GP	G	A	TP	PIM
1980-81	Kitchener	OHA	47	11	28	39	59	18	4	12	16	20
1981-82	**Calgary**	**NHL**	2	0	0	0	0	....	....	....	....	....
a	Kitchener	OHL	59	25	50	75	145	15	5	10	15	44
1982-83	**Calgary**	**NHL**	14	1	3	4	9	....	....	....	....	....
a	Kitchener	OHL	51	38	46	84	67	8	3	8	11	9
1983-84	Colorado	CHL	19	5	14	19	22	....	....	....	....	....
	Calgary	**NHL**	51	11	34	45	42	11	2	12	14	13
1984-85	**Calgary**	**NHL**	67	14	52	66	75	4	1	2	3	8
1985-86	**Calgary**	**NHL**	77	11	57	68	76	21	4	*15	19	30
1986-87b	**Calgary**	**NHL**	79	20	56	76	97	4	1	0	1	0
1987-88	**Calgary**	**NHL**	80	25	58	83	114	7	3	6	9	18
1988-89bc	**Calgary**	**NHL**	79	16	58	74	126	22	7	*24	*31	46
1989-90d	**Calgary**	**NHL**	79	28	62	90	82	6	2	3	5	8
	NHL Totals		528	126	380	506	621	75	20	62	82	123

a OHL First All-Star Team (1982, 1983)
b NHL Second All-Star Team (1987, 1989)
c Won Conn Smythe Trophy (1989)
d NHL First All-Star Team (1990)

Played in NHL All-Star Game (1985, 1988, 1990)

MacIVER, NORM

Defense. Shoots left. 5'11", 180 lbs.   Born, Thunder Bay, Ont., September 1, 1964.

			Regular Season					Playoffs			
Season	Club	Lea	GP	G	A	TP	PIM	GP	G	A	TP	PIM
1982-83	Minn.-Duluth	WCHA	45	1	26	27	40	6	0	2	2	2
1983-84a	Minn.-Duluth	WCHA	31	13	28	41	28	8	1	10	11	8
1984-85bc	Minn.-Duluth	WCHA	47	14	47	61	63	10	3	3	6	6
1985-86bc	Minn.-Duluth	WCHA	42	11	51	62	36	4	2	3	5	2
1986-87	**NY Rangers**	**NHL**	3	0	1	1	0	....	....	....	....	....
	New Haven	AHL	71	6	30	36	73	7	0	0	0	9
1987-88	**NY Rangers**	**NHL**	37	9	15	24	14	....	....	....	....	....
	Colorado	IHL	27	6	20	26	22	....	....	....	....	....
1988-89	**NY Rangers**	**NHL**	26	0	10	10	14	....	....	....	....	....
	Hartford	**NHL**	37	1	22	23	24	1	0	0	0	2
	Binghamton	AHL	2	0	0	0	0	....	....	....	....	....
1989-90	**Edmonton**	**NHL**	1	0	0	0	0	....	....	....	....	....
	Cape Breton	AHL	68	13	37	50	55	6	0	7	7	10
	NHL Totals		104	10	48	58	52	....	....	....	....	....

a WCHA Second All-Star Team (1984)
b WCHA First All-Star Team (1985, 1986)
c NCAA West First All-Star Team (1985, 1986)

Signed as a free agent by **NY Rangers**, September 8, 1986. Traded to **Hartford** by **NY Rangers** with Brian Lawton and Don Maloney for Carey Wilson and Hartford's fifth-round choice (Lubos Rob) in 1990 Entry Draft, December 26, 1988. Traded to **Edmonton** by **Hartford** for Jim Ennis, October 10, 1989.

MACKEY, DAVID

Left wing. Shoots left. 6'4", 200 lbs.   Born, Richmond, B.C., July 24, 1966.
(Chicago's 12th choice, 224th overall, in 1984 Entry Draft).

			Regular Season					Playoffs			
Season	Club	Lea	GP	G	A	TP	PIM	GP	G	A	TP	PIM
1982-83	Victoria	WHL	69	16	16	32	53	12	11	1	2	4
1983-84	Victoria	WHL	69	15	15	30	97	....	....	....	....	....
1984-85	Victoria	WHL	16	5	6	11	45	....	....	....	....	....
	Portland	WHL	56	28	32	60	122	6	2	1	3	13
1985-86	Kamloops	WHL	9	3	4	7	13	....	....	....	....	....
	Medicine Hat	WHL	60	25	32	57	167	25	6	3	9	72
1986-87	Saginaw	IHL	81	26	49	75	173	10	5	6	11	22
1987-88	**Chicago**	**NHL**	23	1	3	4	71	....	....	....	....	....
	Saginaw	IHL	62	29	22	51	211	10	3	7	10	44
1988-89	**Chicago**	**NHL**	23	1	2	3	78	....	....	....	....	....
	Saginaw	IHL	57	22	23	45	223	....	....	....	....	....
1989-90	**Minnesota**	**NHL**	16	2	0	2	28	....	....	....	....	....
	NHL Totals		62	4	5	9	177	....	....	....	....	....

Claimed by **Minnesota** in NHL Waiver Draft, October 2, 1989.

MacLEAN, JOHN

Right wing. Shoots right. 6', 200 lbs.   Born, Oshawa, Ont., November 20, 1964.
(New Jersey's 1st choice, 6th overall, in 1983 Entry Draft).

			Regular Season					Playoffs			
Season	Club	Lea	GP	G	A	TP	PIM	GP	G	A	TP	PIM
1981-82	Oshawa	OHL	67	17	22	39	197	12	3	6	9	63
1982-83	Oshawa	OHL	66	47	51	98	138	17	*18	20	*38	35
1983-84	**New Jersey**	**NHL**	23	1	0	1	10	....	....	....	....	....
	Oshawa	OHL	30	23	36	59	58	7	2	5	7	18
1984-85	**New Jersey**	**NHL**	61	13	20	33	44	....	....	....	....	....
1985-86	**New Jersey**	**NHL**	74	21	36	57	112	....	....	....	....	....
1986-87	**New Jersey**	**NHL**	80	31	36	67	120	....	....	....	....	....
1987-88	**New Jersey**	**NHL**	76	23	16	39	147	20	7	11	18	60
1988-89	**New Jersey**	**NHL**	74	42	45	87	127	....	....	....	....	....
1989-90	**New Jersey**	**NHL**	80	41	38	79	80	6	4	1	5	12
	NHL Totals		468	172	191	363	640	26	11	12	23	72

Played in NHL All-Star Game (1989)

MacLEAN, PAUL (muh KLAYN)

Right wing. Shoots right. 6', 190 lbs. Born, Grostenquin, France, March 9, 1958.
(St. Louis' 6th choice, 109th overall, in 1978 Amateur Draft).

			Regular Season					Playoffs				
Season	Club	Lea	GP	G	A	TP	PIM	GP	G	A	TP	PIM
1977-78	Hull	QJHL	66	38	33	71	125	....	....	....	....	....
1978-79	Dalhousie	AUAA	....	....	....	....	....	....	....	....	....	....
1979-80	Cdn. National	...	50	21	11	32	90	....	....	....	....	....
	Cdn. Olympic	...	6	2	3	5	6	....	....	....	....	....
1980-81	**St. Louis**	**NHL**	**1**	**0**	**0**	**0**	**0**	....	....	....	....	....
	Salt Lake	CHL	80	36	42	78	160	17	11	5	16	47
1981-82	**Winnipeg**	**NHL**	**74**	**36**	**25**	**61**	**106**	**4**	**3**	**2**	**5**	**20**
1982-83	**Winnipeg**	**NHL**	**80**	**32**	**44**	**76**	**121**	**3**	**1**	**2**	**3**	**6**
1983-84	**Winnipeg**	**NHL**	**76**	**40**	**31**	**71**	**155**	**3**	**1**	**0**	**1**	**0**
1984-85	**Winnipeg**	**NHL**	**79**	**41**	**60**	**101**	**119**	**8**	**3**	**4**	**7**	**4**
1985-86	**Winnipeg**	**NHL**	**69**	**27**	**29**	**56**	**74**	**2**	**1**	**0**	**1**	**7**
1986-87	**Winnipeg**	**NHL**	**72**	**32**	**42**	**74**	**75**	**10**	**5**	**2**	**7**	**16**
1987-88	**Winnipeg**	**NHL**	**77**	**40**	**39**	**79**	**76**	**5**	**2**	**0**	**2**	**23**
1988-89	**Detroit**	**NHL**	**76**	**36**	**35**	**71**	**118**	**5**	**1**	**1**	**2**	**8**
1989-90	**St. Louis**	**NHL**	**78**	**34**	**33**	**67**	**100**	**12**	**4**	**3**	**7**	**20**
	NHL Totals		**682**	**318**	**338**	**656**	**944**	**52**	**21**	**14**	**35**	**104**

Played in NHL All-Star Game (1985)

Traded to **Winnipeg** by **St. Louis** with Bryan Maxwell and Ed Staniowski for Scott Campbell and John Markell, July 3, 1981. Traded to **Detroit** by **Winnipeg** for Brent Ashton, June 13, 1988. Traded to **St. Louis** by **Detroit** with Adam Oates for Bernie Federko and Tony McKegney, June 15, 1989.

MacLEAN, TERRY

Center. Shoots left. 6'1", 180 lbs. Born, Montreal, Que., January 14, 1968.
(St. Louis' 11th choice, 220th overall, in 1986 Entry Draft).

			Regular Season					Playoffs				
Season	Club	Lea	GP	G	A	TP	PIM	GP	G	A	TP	PIM
1985-86	Longueuil	QMJHL	70	36	45	81	18	....	....	....	....	....
1986-87	Trois-Rivieres	QMJHL	69	41	76	117	20	....	....	....	....	....
1987-88	Trois-Rivieres	QMJHL	69	52	91	143	44	....	....	....	....	....
	Peoria	IHL	5	0	1	1	0	....	....	....	....	....
1988-89	Peoria	IHL	73	18	30	48	46	3	1	2	3	2
1989-90	Peoria	IHL	67	9	32	41	15	4	0	0	0	0

MacLELLAN, BRIAN

Left wing. Shoots left. 6'3", 215 lbs. Born, Guelph, Ont., October 27, 1958.

			Regular Season					Playoffs				
Season	Club	Lea	GP	G	A	TP	PIM	GP	G	A	TP	PIM
1980-81	Bowling Green	CCHA	37	11	14	25	96	....	....	....	....	....
1981-82	Bowling Green	CCHA	41	11	21	32	109	....	....	....	....	....
1982-83	**Los Angeles**	**NHL**	**8**	**0**	**3**	**3**	**7**	....	....	....	....	....
	New Haven	AHL	71	11	15	26	40	12	5	3	8	4
1983-84	New Haven	AHL	2	0	2	2	0	....	....	....	....	....
	Los Angeles	**NHL**	**72**	**25**	**29**	**54**	**45**	....	....	....	....	....
1984-85	**Los Angeles**	**NHL**	**80**	**31**	**54**	**85**	**53**	**3**	**0**	**1**	**1**	**0**
1985-86	**Los Angeles**	**NHL**	**27**	**5**	**8**	**13**	**19**	....	....	....	....	....
	NY Rangers	**NHL**	**51**	**11**	**21**	**32**	**47**	**16**	**2**	**4**	**6**	**15**
1986-87	**Minnesota**	**NHL**	**76**	**32**	**31**	**63**	**69**	....	....	....	....	....
1987-88	**Minnesota**	**NHL**	**75**	**16**	**32**	**48**	**74**	....	....	....	....	....
1988-89	**Minnesota**	**NHL**	**60**	**16**	**23**	**39**	**104**	....	....	....	....	....
	Calgary	**NHL**	**12**	**2**	**3**	**5**	**14**	**21**	**3**	**2**	**5**	**19**
1989-90	**Calgary**	**NHL**	**65**	**20**	**18**	**38**	**26**	**6**	**0**	**2**	**2**	**8**
	NHL Totals		**526**	**158**	**222**	**380**	**458**	**46**	**5**	**9**	**14**	**42**

Signed as a free agent by **Los Angeles**, May 12, 1982. Traded to **NY Rangers** by **Los Angeles** with Los Angeles' fourth-round draft choice in 1987 (Michael Sullivan) for Roland Melanson and Grant Ledyard, December 9, 1985. Traded to **Minnesota** by **NY Rangers** for Minnesota's third-round choice (Simon Gagne) in 1987 Entry Draft, September 8, 1986. Traded to **Calgary** by **Minnesota** with Minnesota's fourth-round choice (Robert Reichel) in 1989 Entry Draft for Shane Churla and Perry Berezan, March 4, 1989.

MacLEOD, PAT

Defense. Shoots left. 5'11", 190 lbs. Born, Melfort, Sask., June 15, 1969.
(Minnesota's 5th choice, 87th overall, in 1987 Entry Draft).

			Regular Season					Playoffs				
Season	Club	Lea	GP	G	A	TP	PIM	GP	G	A	TP	PIM
1987-88	Kamloops	WHL	50	13	33	46	27	18	2	7	9	6
1988-89	Kamloops	WHL	37	11	34	45	14	15	7	18	25	24
1989-90	Kalamazoo	IHL	82	9	38	47	27	10	1	6	7	2

MACOUN, JAMIE (muh-KOW-uhn)

Defense. Shoots left. 6'2", 197 lbs. Born, Newmarket, Ont., August 7, 1961.

			Regular Season					Playoffs				
Season	Club	Lea	GP	G	A	TP	PIM	GP	G	A	TP	PIM
1980-81	Ohio State	CCHA	38	9	20	29	83	....	....	....	....	....
1981-82	Ohio State	CCHA	25	2	18	20	89	....	....	....	....	....
1982-83	Ohio State	CCHA	19	6	21	27	54	....	....	....	....	....
	Calgary	**NHL**	**22**	**1**	**4**	**5**	**25**	**9**	**0**	**2**	**2**	**8**
1983-84a	**Calgary**	**NHL**	**72**	**9**	**23**	**32**	**97**	**11**	**1**	**0**	**1**	**0**
1984-85	**Calgary**	**NHL**	**70**	**9**	**30**	**39**	**67**	**4**	**1**	**0**	**1**	**4**
1985-86	**Calgary**	**NHL**	**77**	**11**	**21**	**32**	**81**	**22**	**1**	**6**	**7**	**23**
1986-87	**Calgary**	**NHL**	**79**	**7**	**33**	**40**	**111**	**3**	**0**	**1**	**1**	**8**
1987-88	**Calgary**	**NHL**	DID NOT PLAY — INJURED									
1988-89	**Calgary**	**NHL**	**72**	**8**	**19**	**27**	**76**	**22**	**3**	**6**	**9**	**30**
1989-90	**Calgary**	**NHL**	**78**	**8**	**27**	**35**	**70**	**6**	**0**	**3**	**3**	**10**
	NHL Totals		**470**	**53**	**157**	**210**	**527**	**77**	**6**	**18**	**24**	**83**

a NHL All-Rookie Team (1984).

Signed as free agent by **Calgary**, January 30, 1983.

MacTAVISH, CRAIG

Center. Shoots left. 6'1", 195 lbs. Born, London, Ont., August 15, 1958.
(Boston's 9th choice, 153rd overall, in 1978 Entry Draft).

			Regular Season					Playoffs				
Season	Club	Lea	GP	G	A	TP	PIM	GP	G	A	TP	PIM
1979-80	**Boston**	**NHL**	**46**	**11**	**17**	**28**	**8**	**10**	**2**	**3**	**5**	**7**
	Binghamton	AHL	34	17	15	32	29	....	....	....	....	....
1980-81	Boston	NHL	24	3	5	8	13	....	....	....	....	....
	Springfield	AHL	53	19	24	43	81	7	5	4	9	8
1981-82	**Boston**	**NHL**	**2**	**0**	**1**	**1**	**0**	....	....	....	....	....
	Erie	AHL	72	23	32	55	37	....	....	....	....	....
1982-83	**Boston**	**NHL**	**75**	**10**	**20**	**30**	**18**	**17**	**3**	**1**	**4**	**18**
1983-84	**Boston**	**NHL**	**70**	**20**	**23**	**43**	**35**	**1**	**0**	**0**	**0**	**0**
1984-85			DID NOT PLAY									
1985-86	**Edmonton**	**NHL**	**74**	**23**	**24**	**47**	**70**	**10**	**4**	**4**	**8**	**11**
1986-87	**Edmonton**	**NHL**	**79**	**20**	**19**	**39**	**55**	**21**	**1**	**9**	**10**	**16**
1987-88	**Edmonton**	**NHL**	**80**	**15**	**17**	**32**	**47**	**19**	**0**	**1**	**1**	**31**
1988-89	**Edmonton**	**NHL**	**80**	**21**	**31**	**52**	**55**	**7**	**0**	**1**	**1**	**8**
1989-90	**Edmonton**	**NHL**	**80**	**21**	**22**	**43**	**89**	**22**	**2**	**6**	**8**	**29**
	NHL Totals		**610**	**144**	**179**	**323**	**390**	**107**	**12**	**25**	**37**	**120**

Signed as a free agent by **Edmonton**, February 1, 1985.

MacVICAR, ANDREW

Left wing. Shoots left. 6'1", 210 lbs. Born, Dartmouth, N. S., March 12, 1969.
(Buffalo's 3rd choice, 53rd overall, in 1987 Entry Draft).

			Regular Season					Playoffs				
Season	Club	Lea	GP	G	A	TP	PIM	GP	G	A	TP	PIM
1986-87	Peterborough	OHL	64	6	13	19	33	11	2	1	3	7
1987-88	Peterborough	OHL	62	30	51	81	45	12	2	10	12	8
1988-89	Peterborough	OHL	66	25	29	54	56	17	5	6	11	30
1989-90	Sudbury	OHL	41	12	16	28	47	7	2	5	7	18

MADILL, JEFF

Right wing. Shoots left. 5'11", 195 lbs. Born, Oshawa, Ont., June 21, 1965.
(New Jersey's 2nd choice, 7th overall, in 1987 Supplemental Draft).

			Regular Season					Playoffs				
Season	Club	Lea	GP	G	A	TP	PIM	GP	G	A	TP	PIM
1984-85	Ohio State	CCHA	12	5	6	11	18	....	....	....	....	....
1985-86	Ohio State	CCHA	41	32	25	57	65	....	....	....	....	....
1986-87	Ohio State	CCHA	43	38	32	70	139	....	....	....	....	....
1987-88	Utica	AHL	58	18	15	33	127	....	....	....	....	....
1988-89	Utica	AHL	69	23	25	48	225	4	1	0	1	35
1989-90	Utica	AHL	74	43	26	69	233	4	1	2	3	33

MAGUIRE, KEVIN

Right Wing. Shoots right. 6'2", 200 lbs. Born, Toronto, Ont., January 5, 1963.

			Regular Season					Playoffs				
Season	Club	Lea	GP	G	A	TP	PIM	GP	G	A	TP	PIM
1984-85	St. Catharines	AHL	76	10	15	25	112	....	....	....	....	....
1985-86	St. Catharines	AHL	61	6	9	15	161	1	0	0	0	0
1986-87	**Toronto**	**NHL**	**17**	**0**	**0**	**0**	**74**	**1**	**0**	**0**	**0**	**0**
	Newmarket	AHL	51	4	2	6	131	....	....	....	....	....
1987-88	**Buffalo**	**NHL**	**46**	**4**	**6**	**10**	**162**	**5**	**0**	**0**	**0**	**50**
1988-89	**Buffalo**	**NHL**	**60**	**8**	**10**	**18**	**241**	**5**	**0**	**0**	**0**	**36**
1989-90	**Buffalo**	**NHL**	**61**	**6**	**9**	**15**	**115**	....	....	....	....	....
	Philadelphia	**NHL**	**5**	**1**	**0**	**1**	**6**	....	....	....	....	....
	NHL Totals		**189**	**19**	**25**	**44**	**598**	**11**	**0**	**0**	**0**	**86**

Signed as a free agent by **Toronto**, October 10, 1984. Claimed by **Buffalo** in NHL Waiver Draft, October, 5, 1987. Traded to **Philadelphia** by **Buffalo** with Buffalo's second round choice (Mikael Renberg) in 1990 Entry Draft for Jay Wells and Philadelphia's fourth round choice in 1991 Entry Draft, March 5, 1990. Traded to **Toronto** by **Philadelphia** with Philadelphia's eighth round choice in 1991 Entry Draft for Toronto's third round choice (Al Kinisky) in 1990 Entry Draft, June 16, 1990.

MAHER, JIM

Defense. Shoots left. 6'1", 210 lbs. Born, Warren, MI, June 30, 1970.
(Los Angeles' 2nd choice, 81st overall, in 1989 Entry Draft).

			Regular Season					Playoffs				
Season	Club	Lea	GP	G	A	TP	PIM	GP	G	A	TP	PIM
1988-89	Ill.-Chicago	CCHA	31	1	5	6	40	....	....	....	....	....
1989-90	Ill.-Chicago	CCHA	38	4	12	16	64	....	....	....	....	....

MAHONEY, SCOTT

Right wing. Shoots right. 5'10", 190 lbs. Born, Peterborough, Ont., April 19, 1969.
(Calgary's 4th choice, 61st overall, in 1987 Entry Draft).

			Regular Season					Playoffs				
Season	Club	Lea	GP	G	A	TP	PIM	GP	G	A	TP	PIM
1985-86	Peterborough	OHL	31	18	39	57	65	....	....	....	....	....
1986-87	Oshawa	OHL	54	13	9	22	161	22	4	1	5	117
1987-88	Oshawa	OHL	60	10	21	31	272	7	2	4	6	27
1988-89	Oshawa	OHL	56	14	22	36	207	6	1	4	5	18
1989-90	Sudbury	OHL	54	13	22	35	151	7	3	1	4	12

MAILHOT, JACQUES

Left wing. Shoots left. 6'2", 210 lbs. Born, Shawinigan, Que., December 5, 1961.

			Regular Season					Playoffs				
Season	Club	Lea	GP	G	A	TP	PIM	GP	G	A	TP	PIM
1987-88	Baltimore	AHL	15	2	0	2	167	....	....	....	....	....
	Fredericton	AHL	28	2	6	8	137	8	0	0	0	18
1988-89	**Quebec**	**NHL**	**5**	**0**	**0**	**0**	**33**	....	....	....	....	....
	Halifax	AHL	35	4	1	5	259	1	0	0	0	5
1989-90	Moncton	AHL	6	0	0	0	20	....	....	....	....	....
	Cape Breton	AHL	6	0	1	1	12	....	....	....	....	....
	Hampton-Roads	ECHL	5	0	2	2	62	....	....	....	....	....
	NHL Totals		**5**	**0**	**0**	**0**	**33**	....	....	....	....	....

Signed as a free agent by **Quebec**, August 15, 1988.

MAILLET, CLAUDE

Defense. Shoots right. 6'2", 200 lbs. Born, Memramcook, N.B., May 22, 1969.
(Chicago's 1st choice, 21st overall, in 1990 Supplemental Draft).

			Regular Season					Playoffs				
Season	Club	Lea	GP	G	A	TP	PIM	GP	G	A	TP	PIM
1988-89	Merrimack	NCAA	30	1	27	28	30	....	....	....	....	....
1989-90	Merrimack	H.E.	32	8	15	23	55	....	....	....	....	....

MAJOR, BRUCE

Center. Shoots left. 6'3", 180 lbs. Born, Vernon, B.C., January 3, 1967.
(Quebec's 6th choice, 99th overall, in 1985 Entry Draft).

			Regular Season					Playoffs				
Season	Club	Lea	GP	G	A	TP	PIM	GP	G	A	TP	PIM
1985-86	U. of Maine	H.E.	38	14	14	28	39	....	....	....	....	....
1986-87	U. of Maine	H.E.	37	14	10	24	12	....	....	....	....	....
1987-88	U. of Maine	H.E.	26	0	5	5	14	....	....	....	....	....
1988-89	U. of Maine	H.E.	42	13	11	24	22	....	....	....	....	....
1989-90	Halifax	AHL	32	5	6	11	23	....	....	....	....	....
	Greensboro	ECHL	12	4	3	7	6	10	2	2	4	12

MAJOR, MARK

Left wing. Shoots left. 6'4", 205 lbs. Born, Toronto, Ont., March 20, 1970.
(Pittsburgh's 2nd choice, 25th overall, in 1988 Entry Draft).

			Regular Season					Playoffs				
Season	Club	Lea	GP	G	A	TP	PIM	GP	G	A	TP	PIM
1987-88	North Bay	OHL	57	16	17	33	272	4	0	2	2	8
1988-89	North Bay	OHL	11	3	2	5	58	....	....	....	....	....
	Kingston	OHL	53	22	29	51	193	....	....	....	....	....
1989-90	Kingston	OHL	62	29	32	61	168	6	3	3	6	12

MAKAROV, SERGEI (muh-KAH-rahf)

Right wing. Shoots left. 5'11", 185 lbs. Born, Chelyabinsk, Soviet Union, June 19, 1958.
(Calgary's 14th choice, 231st overall, in 1983 Entry Draft).

			Regular Season					Playoffs				
Season	Club	Lea	GP	G	A	TP	PIM	GP	G	A	TP	PIM
1976-77	Chelyabinsk	USSR	11	1	0	1	4	....	....	....	....	....
1977-78	Chelyabinsk	USSR	36	18	13	31	10	....	....	....	....	....
1978-79a	CSKA	USSR	44	18	21	39	12	....	....	....	....	....
1979-80abc	CSKA	USSR	44	29	39	68	16	....	....	....	....	....
1980-81ab	CSKA	USSR	49	42	37	79	22	....	....	....	....	....
1981-82ab	CSKA	USSR	46	32	43	75	18	....	....	....	....	....
1982-83a	CSKA	USSR	30	25	17	42	6	....	....	....	....	....
1983-84ab	CSKA	USSR	44	36	37	73	28	....	....	....	....	....
1984-85abc	CSKA	USSR	40	26	39	65	28	....	....	....	....	....
1985-86ab	CSKA	USSR	40	30	32	62	28	....	....	....	....	....
1986-87abc	CSKA	USSR	40	21	32	53	26	....	....	....	....	....
1987-88ab	CSKA	USSR	51	23	45	68	50	....	....	....	....	....
1988-89	CSKA	USSR	44	21	33	54	42	....	....	....	....	....
1989-90de	**Calgary**	**NHL**	**80**	**24**	**62**	**86**	**55**	**6**	**0**	**6**	**6**	**0**
	NHL Totals		**80**	**24**	**62**	**86**	**55**	**6**	**0**	**6**	**6**	**0**

a Soviet National League All-Star (1979-88)
b Izvestia trophy-leading scorer (1980-82, 1984-88)
c Soviet Player of the Year (1980, 1985, 1987)
d NHL All-Rookie Team (1990)
e Won Calder Memorial Trophy (1990)

MAKELA, MIKKO (MAK-uh-luh, MEE-koh)

Left wing. Shoots left. 6'2", 193 lbs. Born, Tampere, Finland, February 28, 1965.
(NY Islanders' 5th choice, 66th overall, in 1983 Entry Draft).

			Regular Season					Playoffs				
Season	Club	Lea	GP	G	A	TP	PIM	GP	G	A	TP	PIM
1983-84	Ilves	Fin.	35	17	11	28	26	2	0	1	1	0
1984-85a	Ilves	Fin.	36	34	25	59	24	9	4	7	11	10
1985-86	**NY Islanders**	**NHL**	**58**	**16**	**20**	**36**	**28**	....	....	....	....	....
	Springfield	AHL	2	1	1	2	0	....	....	..	....	....
1986-87	**NY Islanders**	**NHL**	**80**	**24**	**33**	**57**	**24**	**11**	**2**	**4**	**6**	**8**
1987-88	**NY Islanders**	**NHL**	**73**	**36**	**40**	**76**	**22**	**6**	**1**	**4**	**5**	**6**
1988-89	**NY Islanders**	**NHL**	**76**	**17**	**28**	**45**	**22**	....	....	....	....	....
1989-90	**NY Islanders**	**NHL**	**20**	**2**	**3**	**5**	**2**	....	....	....	....	....
	Los Angeles	**NHL**	**45**	**7**	**14**	**21**	**16**	....	....	....	....	....
	NHL Totals		**352**	**102**	**138**	**240**	**114**	**17**	**3**	**8**	**11**	**14**

a Finnish League First All-Star Team (1985)

Traded to **Los Angeles** by **NY Islanders** for Ken Baumgartner and Hubie McDonough, November 29, 1989.

MALAKHOV, VLADIMIR

Defense. 6'3", 195 lbs. Born, Sverdlovsk, Soviet Union, August 30, 1968.
(NY Islanders' 10th choice, 191st overall, in 1989 Entry Draft).

			Regular Season					Playoffs				
Season	Club	Lea	GP	G	A	TP	PIM	GP	G	A	TP	PIM
1986-87	Spartak Moscow	USSR	22	0	1	1	12	....	....	....	....	....
1987-88	Spartak Moscow	USSR	28	2	2	4	26	....	....	....	....	....
1988-89	Spartak Moscow	USSR	34	6	2	8	16	....	....	....	....	....
1989-90	Spartak Moscow	USSR	48	2	10	12	32	....	....	....	....	....

MALEY, DAVID

Left wing. Shoots left. 6'2", 205 lbs. Born, Beaver Dam, WI, April 24, 1963.
(Montreal's 4th choice, 33rd overall, in 1982 Entry Draft).

			Regular Season					Playoffs				
Season	Club	Lea	GP	G	A	TP	PIM	GP	G	A	TP	PIM
1982-83	U. Wisconsin	WCHA	47	17	23	40	24	....	....	....	....	....
1983-84	U. Wisconsin	WCHA	38	10	28	38	56	....	....	....	....	....
1984-85	U. Wisconsin	WCHA	38	19	9	28	86	....	....	....	....	....
1985-86	U. Wisconsin	WCHA	42	20	40	60	135	....	....	....	....	....
	Montreal	**NHL**	**3**	**0**	**0**	**0**	**0**	**7**	**1**	**3**	**4**	**2**
1986-87	**Montreal**	**NHL**	**48**	**6**	**12**	**18**	**55**	....	...	...	....	....
	Sherbrooke	AHL	11	1	5	6	25	12	7	7	14	10
1987-88	**New Jersey**	**NHL**	**44**	**4**	**2**	**6**	**65**	**20**	**3**	**1**	**4**	**80**
	Utica	AHL	9	5	3	8	40	....	....	....	....	....
1988-89	**New Jersey**	**NHL**	**68**	**5**	**6**	**11**	**249**	....	....	....	....	....
1989-90	**New Jersey**	**NHL**	**67**	**8**	**17**	**25**	**160**	**6**	**0**	**0**	**0**	**25**
	NHL Totals		**230**	**23**	**37**	**60**	**529**	**33**	**4**	**4**	**8**	**107**

Traded to **New Jersey** by **Montreal** for New Jersey's third-round choice (Mathieu Schneider) in 1987 Entry Draft, June 13, 1987.

MALLETTE, TROY

Left wing. Shoots left. 6'2", 190 lbs. Born, Sudbury, Ont., February 25, 1970.
(New York Rangers' 1st choice, 22nd overall, in 1988 Entry Draft).

			Regular Season					Playoffs				
Season	Club	Lea	GP	G	A	TP	PIM	GP	G	A	TP	PIM
1986-87	S.S. Marie	OHL	65	20	25	45	157	4	0	2	2	12
1987-88	S.S. Marie	OHL	62	18	30	48	186	6	1	3	4	12
1988-89	S.S. Marie	OHL	64	39	37	76	172	0	0	0	0	0
1989-90	**NY Rangers**	**NHL**	**79**	**13**	**16**	**29**	**105**	**10**	**2**	**2**	**4**	**81**
	NHL Totals		**79**	**13**	**16**	**29**	**105**	**10**	**2**	**2**	**4**	**81**

MALLGRAVE, MATTHEW

Right wing. Shoots right. 6', 180 lbs. Born, Washington, D.C., May 3, 1970.
(Toronto's 6th choice, 132nd overall, in 1988 Entry Draft).

			Regular Season					Playoffs				
Season	Club	Lea	GP	G	A	TP	PIM	GP	G	A	TP	PIM
1988-89	St. Paul's	HS	....	24	14	38	....	....	....	....	....	....
1989-90	Harvard	ECAC	26	3	3	6	33	....	....	....	....	....

MALONEY, DONALD MICHAEL (DON) (ma-LOAN-ee)

Left wing. Shoots left. 6'1", 190 lbs. Born, Lindsay, Ont., September 5, 1958.
(NY Rangers' 1st choice, 26th overall, in 1978 Amateur Draft).

			Regular Season					Playoffs				
Season	Club	Lea	GP	G	A	TP	PIM	GP	G	A	TP	PIM
1976-77	Kitchener	OHA	38	22	34	56	126	....	....	....	....	....
1977-78	Kitchener	OHA	62	30	74	104	143	9	4	9	13	40
1978-79	New Haven	AHL	38	18	26	44	62	....	....	....	....	....
	NY Rangers	**NHL**	**28**	**9**	**17**	**26**	**39**	**18**	**7**	***13**	**20**	**19**
1979-80	**NY Rangers**	**NHL**	**79**	**25**	**48**	**73**	**97**	**9**	**0**	**4**	**4**	**10**
1980-81	**NY Rangers**	**NHL**	**61**	**29**	**23**	**52**	**99**	**13**	**1**	**6**	**7**	**13**
1981-82	**NY Rangers**	**NHL**	**54**	**22**	**36**	**58**	**73**	**10**	**5**	**5**	**10**	**10**
1982-83	**NY Rangers**	**NHL**	**78**	**29**	**40**	**69**	**88**	**5**	**0**	**1**	**1**	**0**
1983-84	**NY Rangers**	**NHL**	**79**	**24**	**42**	**66**	**62**	**5**	**1**	**4**	**5**	**0**
1984-85	**NY Rangers**	**NHL**	**37**	**11**	**16**	**27**	**32**	**3**	**4**	**0**	**4**	**2**
1985-86	**NY Rangers**	**NHL**	**68**	**11**	**17**	**28**	**56**	**16**	**2**	**1**	**3**	**31**
1986-87	**NY Rangers**	**NHL**	**72**	**19**	**38**	**57**	**117**	**6**	**2**	**1**	**3**	**6**
1987-88	**NY Rangers**	**NHL**	**66**	**12**	**21**	**33**	**60**	....	....	....	....	....
1988-89	**NY Rangers**	**NHL**	**31**	**4**	**9**	**13**	**16**	....	....	....	....	....
	Hartford	**NHL**	**21**	**3**	**11**	**14**	**23**	**4**	**0**	**0**	**0**	**8**
1989-90	**NY Islanders**	**NHL**	**79**	**16**	**27**	**43**	**47**	**5**	**0**	**0**	**0**	**2**
	NHL Totals		**753**	**214**	**345**	**559**	**809**	**94**	**22**	**35**	**57**	**101**

Played in NHL All-Star Game (1983, 1984)

Traded to **Hartford** by **NY Rangers** with Brian Lawton and Norm MacIver for Carey Wilson and Hartford's fifth-round choice (Lubos Rob) in 1990 Entry Draft, December 26, 1988. Signed as a free agent by **NY Islanders**, August 25, 1989.

MALTAIS, STEVE (MAHL-tayz)

Left wing. Shoots left. 6'2", 210 lbs. Born, Arvida, Que., January 25, 1969.
(Washington's 2nd choice, 57th overall, in 1987 Entry Draft).

			Regular Season					Playoffs				
Season	Club	Lea	GP	G	A	TP	PIM	GP	G	A	TP	PIM
1986-87	Cornwall	OHL	65	32	12	44	29	5	0	0	0	2
1987-88	Cornwall	OHL	59	39	46	85	30	11	9	6	15	33
1988-89	Cornwall	OHL	58	53	70	123	67	18	14	16	30	16
	Fort Wayne	IHL	....	....	....	....	....	4	2	1	3	0
1989-90	**Washington**	**NHL**	**8**	**0**	**0**	**0**	**2**	**1**	**0**	**0**	**0**	**0**
	Baltimore	AHL	67	29	37	66	54	12	6	10	16	6
	NHL Totals		**8**	**0**	**0**	**0**	**2**	**1**	**0**	**0**	**0**	**0**

MANDERVILLE, KENT

Left wing. Shoots left. 6'3", 200 lbs. Born, Edmonton, Alta., April 12, 1971.
(Calgary's 1st choice, 24th overall, in 1989 Entry Draft).

			Regular Season					Playoffs				
Season	Club	Lea	GP	G	A	TP	PIM	GP	G	A	TP	PIM
1988-89	Notre Dame	SJHL	58	39	36	75	165	....	....	....	....	....
1989-90a	Cornell	ECAC	26	11	15	26	28	....	....	....	....	....

a ECAC Rookie of the Year (1990)

MANSON, DAVE

Defense. Shoots left. 6'2", 190 lbs. Born, Prince Albert, Sask., January 27, 1967.
(Chicago's 1st choice, 11th overall, in 1985 Entry Draft).

			Regular Season					Playoffs				
Season	Club	Lea	GP	G	A	TP	PIM	GP	G	A	TP	PIM
1983-84	Prince Albert	WHL	70	2	7	9	233	5	0	0	0	4
1984-85	Prince Albert	WHL	72	8	30	38	247	13	1	0	1	34
1985-86	Prince Albert	WHL	70	14	34	48	177	20	1	8	9	63
1986-87	**Chicago**	**NHL**	**63**	**1**	**8**	**9**	**146**	**3**	**0**	**0**	**0**	**10**
1987-88	**Chicago**	**NHL**	**54**	**1**	**6**	**7**	**185**	**5**	**0**	**0**	**0**	**27**
	Saginaw	IHL	6	0	3	3	37	....	....	....	....	....
1988-89	**Chicago**	**NHL**	**79**	**18**	**36**	**54**	**352**	**16**	**0**	**8**	**8**	**84**
1989-90	**Chicago**	**NHL**	**59**	**5**	**23**	**28**	**301**	**20**	**2**	**4**	**6**	**46**
	NHL Totals		**255**	**25**	**73**	**98**	**984**	**44**	**2**	**12**	**14**	**167**

Played in NHL All-Star Game (1989)

MANTHA, MAURICE WILLIAM (MOE) (MAN-tha)

Defense. Shoots right. 6'2", 210 lbs. Born, Lakewood, OH, January 21, 1961.
(Winnipeg's 2nd choice, 23rd overall, in 1980 Entry Draft).

			Regular Season					Playoffs				
Season	Club	Lea	GP	G	A	TP	PIM	GP	G	A	TP	PIM
1978-79	Toronto	OHA	68	10	38	48	57	4	0	2	2	11
1979-80	Toronto	OHA	58	8	38	46	86	....	....	....	....	....
1980-81	**Winnipeg**	**NHL**	**58**	**2**	**23**	**25**	**35**	....	....	....	....	....
1981-82	Tulsa	CHL	33	8	15	23	56	....	....	....	....	....
	Winnipeg	**NHL**	**25**	**0**	**12**	**12**	**28**	**4**	**1**	**3**	**4**	**16**
1982-83	Sherbrooke	AHL	13	1	4	5	13	....	....	....	....	....
	Winnipeg	**NHL**	**21**	**2**	**7**	**9**	**6**	**2**	**2**	**2**	**4**	**0**
1983-84	Sherbrooke	AHL	7	1	1	2	10	....	....	....	....	....
	Winnipeg	**NHL**	**72**	**16**	**38**	**54**	**67**	**3**	**1**	**0**	**1**	**0**
1984-85	**Pittsburgh**	**NHL**	**71**	**11**	**40**	**51**	**54**	....	....	....	....	....
1985-86	**Pittsburgh**	**NHL**	**78**	**15**	**52**	**67**	**102**	....	....	....	....	....
1986-87	**Pittsburgh**	**NHL**	**62**	**9**	**31**	**40**	**44**	....	....	....	....	....
1987-88	**Pittsburgh**	**NHL**	**21**	**2**	**8**	**10**	**23**	....	....	....	....	....
	Edmonton	**NHL**	**25**	**0**	**6**	**6**	**26**	....	....	....	....	....
	Minnesota	**NHL**	**30**	**9**	**13**	**22**	**4**	....	....	....	....	....
1988-89	**Minnesota**	**NHL**	**16**	**1**	**6**	**7**	**10**	....	....	....	....	....
	Philadelphia	**NHL**	**30**	**3**	**8**	**11**	**33**	**1**	**0**	**0**	**0**	**0**
1989-90	**Winnipeg**	**NHL**	**73**	**2**	**26**	**28**	**28**	**7**	**1**	**5**	**6**	**2**
	NHL Totals		**582**	**72**	**270**	**342**	**460**	**17**	**5**	**10**	**15**	**18**

Traded to **Pittsburgh** by **Winnipeg**, May 1, 1984 to complete deal of March 6, 1984 when Pittsburgh traded Randy Carlyle to Winnipeg. Traded to **Edmonton** by **Pittsburgh** with Craig Simpson, Dave Hannan, and Chris Joseph for Paul Coffey, Dave Hunter, and Wayne Van Dorp, November 24, 1987. Traded to **Minnesota** by **Edmonton** for Keith Acton, January 22, 1988. Traded to **Philadelphia** by **Minnesota** for Toronto's fifth-round choice (Pat MacLeod) in 1989 Entry Draft, December 8, 1988. Claimed by **Winnipeg** in NHL Waiver Draft, October 2, 1989.

MARCHMENT, BRYAN

Defense. Shoots left. 6'1", 198 lbs. Born, West Hill-Scarborough, Ont., May 1, 1969.
(Winnipeg's 1st choice, 16th overall, in 1987 Entry Draft).

			Regular Season					Playoffs				
Season	Club	Lea	GP	G	A	TP	PIM	GP	G	A	TP	PIM
1985-86	Belleville	OHL	57	5	15	20	225	21	0	7	7	83
1986-87	Belleville	OHL	52	6	38	44	238	6	0	4	4	17
1987-88	Belleville	OHL	56	7	51	58	200	6	1	3	4	19
1988-89	**Winnipeg**	**NHL**	**2**	**0**	**0**	**0**	**2**	....	....	....	....	....
a	Belleville	OHL	43	14	36	50	118	5	0	1	1	12
1989-90	**Winnipeg**	**NHL**	**7**	**0**	**2**	**2**	**28**	....	....	....	....	....
	Moncton	AHL	56	4	19	23	217	....	....	....	....	....
	NHL Totals		**9**	**0**	**2**	**2**	**30**	....	....	....	....	....

a OHL Second All-Star Team (1989)

MARCIANO, LANCE

Defense. Shoots right. 6'2", 200 lbs. Born, Mt. Vernon, NY, December 12, 1969.
(NY Rangers' 11th choice, 220th overall, in 1987 Entry Draft).

			Regular Season					Playoffs				
Season	Club	Lea	GP	G	A	TP	PIM	GP	G	A	TP	PIM
1987-88	Yale	ECAC	18	0	2	2	16	....	....	....	....	....
1988-89	Yale	ECAC	24	1	0	1	26	....	....	....	....	....
1989-90	Yale	ECAC	27	0	9	9	34	....	....	....	....	....

MARCINYSHYN, DAVID (MAIR-sih-NIH-shuhn)

Defense. Shoots left. 6'3", 210 lbs. Born, Edmonton, Alta., February 4, 1967.

			Regular Season					Playoffs				
Season	Club	Lea	GP	G	A	TP	PIM	GP	G	A	TP	PIM
1985-86	Kamloops	WHL	57	2	7	9	111	16	1	3	4	12
1986-87	Kamloops	WHL	68	5	27	32	106	13	0	3	3	35
1987-88	Utica	AHL	73	2	7	9	179	....	....	....	....	....
	Flint	IHL	3	0	0	0	4	16	0	2	2	31
1988-89	Utica	AHL	74	4	14	18	101	5	0	0	0	13
1989-90	Utica	AHL	74	6	18	24	164	5	0	2	2	21

Signed as a free agent by **New Jersey**, September 26, 1986.

MARKOVICH, MICHAEL

Defense. Shoots left. 6'3", 200 lbs. Born, Grand Forks, ND, April 25, 1969.
(Pittsburgh's 6th choice, 121st overall, in 1989 Entry Draft).

			Regular Season					Playoffs				
Season	Club	Lea	GP	G	A	TP	PIM	GP	G	A	TP	PIM
1987-88	Rochester	USHL	48	13	41	54	38	....	....	....	....	....
1988-89	U. of Denver	WCHA	30	2	12	14	24	....	....	....	....	....
1989-90	U. of Denver	WCHA	42	4	17	21	34	....	....	....	....	....

MARKWART, NEVIN

Left wing. Shoots left. 5'10", 180 lbs. Born, Toronto, Ont., December 9, 1964.
(Boston's 1st choice, 21st overall, in 1983 Entry Draft).

			Regular Season					Playoffs				
Season	Club	Lea	GP	G	A	TP	PIM	GP	G	A	TP	PIM
1981-82	Regina	WHL	25	2	12	14	56	20	2	2	4	82
1982-83	Regina	WHL	43	27	39	66	91	1	0	0	0	0
1983-84	**Boston**	**NHL**	**70**	**14**	**16**	**30**	**121**	....	....	....	....	....
1984-85	**Boston**	**NHL**	**26**	**0**	**4**	**4**	**36**	**1**	**0**	**0**	**0**	**0**
	Hershey	AHL	38	13	18	31	79	....	....	....	....	....
1985-86	**Boston**	**NHL**	**65**	**7**	**15**	**22**	**207**	....	....	....	....	....
1986-87	**Boston**	**NHL**	**64**	**10**	**9**	**19**	**225**	**4**	**0**	**0**	**0**	**9**
	Moncton	AHL	3	3	3	6	11	....	....	....	....	....
1987-88	**Boston**	**NHL**	**25**	**1**	**12**	**13**	**85**	**2**	**0**	**0**	**0**	**2**
1988-89	Maine	AHL	1	0	1	1	0	....	....	....	....	....
1989-90	**Boston**	**NHL**	**8**	**1**	**2**	**3**	**15**	....	....	....	....	....
	NHL Totals		**258**	**33**	**58**	**91**	**689**	**7**	**0**	**0**	**0**	**11**

MAROIS, DANIEL

Right wing. Shoots right. 6'1", 190 lbs. Born, Montreal, Que., October 3, 1968.
(Toronto's 2nd choice, 28th overall, in 1987 Entry Draft).

			Regular Season					Playoffs				
Season	Club	Lea	GP	G	A	TP	PIM	GP	G	A	TP	PIM
1985-86	Verdun	QMJHL	58	42	35	77	110	5	4	2	6	6
1986-87	Chicoutimi	QMJHL	40	22	26	48	143	16	7	14	21	25
1987-88	Verdun	QMJHL	67	52	36	88	153	....	....	....	....	....
	Newmarket	AHL	8	4	4	8	4	....	....	....	....	....
	Toronto	**NHL**	....	....	....	....	....	**3**	**1**	**0**	**1**	**0**
1988-89	**Toronto**	**NHL**	**76**	**31**	**23**	**54**	**76**	....	....	....	....	....
1989-90	**Toronto**	**NHL**	**68**	**39**	**37**	**76**	**82**	**5**	**2**	**2**	**4**	**12**
	NHL Totals		**144**	**70**	**60**	**130**	**158**	**8**	**3**	**2**	**5**	**12**

MAROIS, MARIO (MAIR-wah)

Defense. Shoots right. 5'11", 190 lbs. Born, Ancienne Lorette, Que., December 15, 1957.
(NY Rangers' 5th choice, 62nd overall, in 1977 Amateur Draft).

			Regular Season					Playoffs				
Season	Club	Lea	GP	G	A	TP	PIM	GP	G	A	TP	PIM
1975-76	Quebec	QJHL	67	11	42	53	270	15	2	3	5	86
1976-77	Quebec	QJHL	72	17	67	84	239	14	1	17	18	75
1977-78	**NY Rangers**	**NHL**	**8**	**1**	**1**	**2**	**15**	**1**	**0**	**0**	**0**	**5**
	New Haven	AHL	52	8	23	31	147	12	5	3	8	31
1978-79	**NY Rangers**	**NHL**	**71**	**5**	**26**	**31**	**153**	**18**	**0**	**6**	**6**	**29**
1979-80	**NY Rangers**	**NHL**	**79**	**8**	**23**	**31**	**142**	**9**	**0**	**2**	**2**	**8**
1980-81	**NY Rangers**	**NHL**	**8**	**1**	**2**	**3**	**46**	....	....	....	....	....
	Vancouver	**NHL**	**50**	**4**	**12**	**16**	**115**	....	....	....	....	....
	Quebec	**NHL**	**11**	**0**	**7**	**7**	**20**	**5**	**0**	**1**	**1**	**6**
1981-82	**Quebec**	**NHL**	**71**	**11**	**32**	**43**	**161**	**13**	**1**	**2**	**3**	**44**
1982-83	**Quebec**	**NHL**	**36**	**2**	**12**	**14**	**108**	....	....	....	....	....
1983-84	**Quebec**	**NHL**	**80**	**13**	**36**	**49**	**151**	**9**	**1**	**4**	**5**	**6**
1984-85	**Quebec**	**NHL**	**76**	**6**	**37**	**43**	**91**	**18**	**0**	**8**	**8**	**12**
1985-86	**Quebec**	**NHL**	**20**	**1**	**12**	**13**	**42**	....	....	....	....	....
	Winnipeg	**NHL**	**56**	**4**	**28**	**32**	**110**	**3**	**1**	**4**	**5**	**6**
1986-87	**Winnipeg**	**NHL**	**79**	**4**	**40**	**44**	**106**	**10**	**1**	**3**	**4**	**23**
1987-88	**Winnipeg**	**NHL**	**79**	**7**	**44**	**51**	**111**	**5**	**0**	**4**	**4**	**6**
1988-89	**Winnipeg**	**NHL**	**7**	**1**	**1**	**2**	**17**	....	....	....	....	....
	Quebec	**NHL**	**42**	**2**	**11**	**13**	**101**	....	....	....	....	....
1989-90	**Quebec**	**NHL**	**67**	**3**	**15**	**18**	**104**	....	....	....	....	....
	NHL Totals		**840**	**73**	**339**	**412**	**1593**	**91**	**4**	**34**	**38**	**145**

Traded to **Vancouver** by **NY Rangers** with Jim Mayer for Jere Gillis and Jeff Bandura, November 11, 1980. Traded to **Quebec** by **Vancouver** for Garry Lariviere, March 10, 1981. Traded to **Winnipeg** by **Quebec** for Robert Picard, November 27, 1985. Traded to **Quebec** by **Winnipeg** for Gord Donnelly, December 6, 1988.

MARQUETTE, DALE

Left wing. Shoots left. 5'11", 190 lbs. Born, Prince George, B.C., March 8, 1968.
(Chicago's 10th choice, 197th overall, in 1987 Entry Draft).

			Regular Season					Playoffs				
Season	Club	Lea	GP	G	A	TP	PIM	GP	G	A	TP	PIM
1984-85	Lethbridge	WHL	50	4	4	8	46	2	0	1	1	0
1985-86	Lethbridge	WHL	64	12	14	26	83	10	4	3	7	12
1986-87	Brandon	WHL	68	41	29	70	59	....	....	....	....	....
1987-88	Brandon	WHL	62	51	52	103	48	....	....	....	....	....
	Saginaw	IHL	....	....	....	....	....	3	1	0	1	2
1988-89	Saginaw	IHL	46	11	8	19	35	6	1	1	2	2
1989-90	Indianapolis	IHL	32	3	3	6	13	....	....	....	....	....

MARSH, CHARLES BRADLEY (BRAD)

Defense. Shoots left. 6'3", 220 lbs. Born, London, Ont., March 31, 1958.
(Atlanta's 1st choice, 11th overall, in 1978 Amateur Draft).

			Regular Season					Playoffs				
Season	Club	Lea	GP	G	A	TP	PIM	GP	G	A	TP	PIM
1976-77a	London	OHA	63	7	33	40	121	20	3	5	8	47
1977-78b	London	OHA	62	8	55	63	192	11	2	10	12	21
1978-79	**Atlanta**	**NHL**	**80**	**0**	**19**	**19**	**101**	**2**	**0**	**0**	**0**	**17**
1979-80	**Atlanta**	**NHL**	**80**	**2**	**9**	**11**	**119**	**4**	**0**	**1**	**1**	**2**
1980-81	**Calgary**	**NHL**	**80**	**1**	**12**	**13**	**87**	**16**	**0**	**5**	**5**	**8**
1981-82	**Calgary**	**NHL**	**17**	**0**	**1**	**1**	**10**	....	....	....	....	....
	Philadelphia	**NHL**	**66**	**2**	**22**	**24**	**106**	**4**	**0**	**0**	**0**	**2**
1982-83	**Philadelphia**	**NHL**	**68**	**2**	**11**	**13**	**52**	**2**	**0**	**1**	**1**	**0**
1983-84	**Philadelphia**	**NHL**	**77**	**3**	**14**	**17**	**83**	**3**	**1**	**1**	**2**	**2**
1984-85	**Philadelphia**	**NHL**	**77**	**2**	**18**	**20**	**91**	**19**	**0**	**6**	**6**	**65**
1985-86	**Philadelphia**	**NHL**	**79**	**0**	**13**	**13**	**123**	**5**	**0**	**0**	**0**	**2**
1986-87	**Philadelphia**	**NHL**	**77**	**2**	**9**	**11**	**124**	**26**	**3**	**4**	**7**	**16**
1987-88	**Philadelphia**	**NHL**	**70**	**3**	**9**	**12**	**57**	**7**	**1**	**0**	**1**	**8**
1988-89	**Toronto**	**NHL**	**80**	**1**	**15**	**16**	**79**	....	....	....	....	....
1989-90	**Toronto**	**NHL**	**79**	**1**	**13**	**14**	**95**	**5**	**1**	**0**	**1**	**2**
	NHL Totals		**930**	**19**	**165**	**184**	**1127**	**93**	**6**	**18**	**24**	**124**

a OHA Third All-Star Team (1977)
b OHA First All-Star Team (1978)

Claimed by **Atlanta** as fill in Expansion Draft, June 13, 1979. Traded to **Philadelphia** by **Calgary** for Mel Bridgman, November 11, 1981. Claimed by **Toronto** in NHL Waiver Draft, October 3, 1988.

MARSHALL, CHRIS

Left wing. Shoots left. 5'10", 170 lbs. Born, Quincy, MA, December 12, 1968.
(Buffalo's 6th choice, 106th overall, in 1987 Entry Draft).

			Regular Season					Playoffs				
Season	Club	Lea	GP	G	A	TP	PIM	GP	G	A	TP	PIM
1987-88	Michigan State	CCHA	29	0	2	2	27	....	....	....	....	....
1988-89	Michigan State	CCHA	7	0	1	1	11	....	....	....	....	....
1989-90	Michigan State	CCHA	17	0	1	1	40	....	....	....	....	....

MARSHALL, JASON

Defense. Shoots right. 6'2", 185 lbs. Born, Cranbrook, B.C., February 22, 1971.
(St. Louis' 1st choice, 9th overall, in 1989 Entry Draft).

			Regular Season					Playoffs				
Season	Club	Lea	GP	G	A	TP	PIM	GP	G	A	TP	PIM
1988-89	Vernon	BCJHL	48	10	30	40	195	....	....	....	....	....
1989-90	Cdn. National	....	72	1	11	12	57	....	....	....	....	....

MARTIN, DONALD

Left wing. Shoots left. 6', 200 lbs. Born, London, Ont., March 29, 1968.
(Edmonton's 6th choice, 103rd overall, in 1988 Entry Draft).

			Regular Season					Playoffs				
Season	Club	Lea	GP	G	A	TP	PIM	GP	G	A	TP	PIM
1985-86	North Bay	OHL	7	0	0	0	21	....	....	....	....	....
	London	OHL	55	7	6	13	112	5	1	0	1	14
1986-87	London	OHL	63	19	38	57	127	....	....	....	....	....
1987-88	London	OHL	57	30	32	62	190	11	6	8	14	50
1988-89	Cape Breton	AHL	3	0	0	0	2	....	....	....	....	....
	Fort Wayne	IHL	40	11	5	16	123	....	....	....	....	....
1989-90	Phoenix	IHL	8	1	0	1	10	....	....	....	....	....

MARTIN, MATT

Defense. Shoots left. 6'3", 190 lbs. Born, Hamden, CT, April 30, 1971.
(Toronto's 4th choice, 66th overall, in 1989 Entry Draft).

			Regular Season					Playoffs				
Season	Club	Lea	GP	G	A	TP	PIM	GP	G	A	TP	PIM
1988-89	Avon Old Farms	HS	....	9	23	32	....	....	....	....	....	....
1989-90	U. of Maine	H.E.	DID NOT PLAY									

MARTIN, TOM

Left wing. Shoots left. 6'2", 200 lbs. Born, Kelowna, B.C., May 11, 1964.
(Winnipeg's 2nd choice, 74th overall, in 1982 Entry Draft).

			Regular Season					Playoffs				
Season	Club	Lea	GP	G	A	TP	PIM	GP	G	A	TP	PIM
1982-83	U. of Denver	WCHA	37	8	18	26	128	....	....	....	....	....
1983-84	Victoria	WHL	60	30	45	75	261	....	....	....	....	....
	Sherbrooke	AHL	5	0	0	0	16	....	....	....	....	....
1984-85	**Winnipeg**	**NHL**	**8**	**1**	**0**	**1**	**42**	**3**	**0**	**0**	**0**	**2**
	Sherbrooke	AHL	58	4	15	19	212	12	1	1	2	72
1985-86	**Winnipeg**	**NHL**	**5**	**0**	**0**	**0**	**0**	....	....	....	....	....
	Sherbrooke	AHL	69	11	18	29	227	....	....	....	....	....
1986-87	**Winnipeg**	**NHL**	**11**	**1**	**0**	**1**	**49**	....	....	....	....	....
	Adirondack	AHL	18	5	6	11	57	....	....	....	....	....
1987-88	**Hartford**	**NHL**	**5**	**1**	**2**	**3**	**14**	....	....	....	....	....
a	Binghamton	AHL	71	28	61	89	344	3	0	0	0	18
1988-89	**Minnesota**	**NHL**	**4**	**1**	**1**	**2**	**4**	....	....	....	....	....
	Hartford	**NHL**	**38**	**7**	**6**	**13**	**113**	**1**	**0**	**0**	**0**	**4**
1989-90	**Hartford**	**NHL**	**21**	**1**	**2**	**3**	**27**	....	....	....	....	....
	Binghamton	AHL	24	4	10	14	113	....	....	....	....	....
	NHL Totals		**92**	**12**	**11**	**23**	**249**	**4**	**0**	**0**	**0**	**6**

a AHL First All-Star Team (1988)

Signed as a free agent by **Hartford**, July 29, 1987. Claimed by **Minnesota** in NHL Waiver Draft, October 3, 1988. Claimed by **Hartford** on waivers from **Minnesota**, December 1988.

MARTINI, DARCY

Defense. Shoots left. 6'4", 220 lbs. Born, Castlegar, B.C., January 30, 1969.
(Edmonton's 8th choice, 162nd overall, in 1989 Entry Draft).

			Regular Season					Playoffs				
Season	Club	Lea	GP	G	A	TP	PIM	GP	G	A	TP	PIM
1988-89	Michigan Tech	WCHA	35	1	2	3	103	....	....	....	....	....
1989-90	Michigan Tech	WCHA	36	3	6	9	151	....	....	....	....	....

MARTINSON, STEVEN

Left wing. Shoots left. 6'1", 205 lbs. Born, Minnetonka, MN, June 21, 1959.

			Regular Season					Playoffs				
Season	Club	Lea	GP	G	A	TP	PIM	GP	G	A	TP	PIM
1982-83	Toledo	IHL	32	9	10	19	111	....	....	....	....	....
	Birmingham	CHL	43	4	5	9	184	13	1	2	3	*80
1983-84	Tulsa	CHL	42	3	6	9	240	6	0	0	0	43
1984-85	Toledo	IHL	54	4	10	14	300	2	0	0	0	21
1985-86	Hershey	AHL	69	3	6	9	*432	3	0	0	0	56
1986-87	Hershey	AHL	17	0	3	3	85	....	....	....	....	....
	Adirondack	AHL	14	1	1	2	78	11	2	0	2	108
1987-88	**Detroit**	**NHL**	**10**	**1**	**1**	**2**	**84**	....	....	....	....	....
	Adirondack	AHL	32	6	8	14	146	6	1	2	3	66
1988-89	**Montreal**	**NHL**	**25**	**1**	**0**	**1**	**87**	**1**	**0**	**0**	**0**	**10**
	Sherbrooke	AHL	10	5	7	12	61	....	....	....	....	....
1989-90	**Montreal**	**NHL**	**13**	**0**	**0**	**0**	**64**	....	....	....	....	....
	Sherbrooke	AHL	37	6	20	26	113	....	....	....	....	....
	NHL Totals		**48**	**2**	**1**	**3**	**235**	**1**	**0**	**0**	**0**	**10**

Signed as a free agent by **Philadelphia**, September 30, 1985. Signed as a free agent by **Detroit**, October 3, 1987. Signed as a free agent by **Montreal**, August 2, 1988.

MARTTILA, JUKKA

Defense. Shoots left. 6', 185 lbs. Born, Tampere, Finland, April 15, 1968.
(Winnipeg's 9th choice, 136th overall, in 1988 Entry Draft).

			Regular Season					Playoffs				
Season	Club	Lea	GP	G	A	TP	PIM	GP	G	A	TP	PIM
1986-87	Tappara	Fin.	33	4	1	5	18	....	....	....	....	....
1987-88	Tappara	Fin.	39	5	7	12	16	....	....	....	....	....
1988-89	Tappara	Fin.	43	11	20	31	32	....	....	....	....	....
1989-90	Tappara	Fin.	44	12	14	26	14	7	2	2	4	4

MARVIN, DAVID

Defense. Shoots right. 6'1", 180 lbs. Born, Warroad, MN, March 10, 1968.
(St. Louis' 10th choice, 201st overall, in 1987 Entry Draft).

			Regular Season					Playoffs				
Season	Club	Lea	GP	G	A	TP	PIM	GP	G	A	TP	PIM
1987-88	North Dakota	WCHA	35	4	17	21	12	....	....	....	....	....
1988-89	North Dakota	WCHA	38	4	6	10	24	....	....	....	....	....
1989-90	North Dakota	WCHA	45	3	23	26	70	....	....	....	....	....

MASKARINEC, MARTIN

Defense. Shoots left. 6'1", 185 lbs. Born, Prague, Czechoslovakia, February 3, 1969.
(Los Angeles' 9th choice, 186th overall, in 1989 Entry Draft).

			Regular Season					Playoffs				
Season	Club	Lea	GP	G	A	TP	PIM	GP	G	A	TP	PIM
1988-89	Sparta Praha	Czech.	31	3	1	4	....	....	....	....	....	....
1989-90	Sparta Praha	Czech.	46	3	11	14	....	....	....	....	....	....

MATHIESON, JIM

Defense. Shoots left. 6'1", 210 lbs. Born, Kindersley, Sask., January 24, 1970.
(Washington's 3rd choice, 59th overall, in 1989 Entry Draft).

			Regular Season					Playoffs				
Season	Club	Lea	GP	G	A	TP	PIM	GP	G	A	TP	PIM
1986-87	Regina	WHL	40	0	9	9	40	3	0	1	1	2
1987-88	Regina	WHL	72	3	12	15	115	4	0	2	2	4
1988-89	Regina	WHL	62	5	22	27	151	....	....	....	....	....
1989-90	**Washington**	**NHL**	**2**	**0**	**0**	**0**	**4**	....	....	....	....	....
	Regina	WHL	67	1	26	27	158	11	0	7	7	16
	Baltimore	AHL	....	....	....	....	....	3	0	0	0	4
	NHL Totals		**2**	**0**	**0**	**0**	**4**	....	....	....	....	....

MATIKAINEN, PETRI

Defense. Shoots left. 6', 185 lbs. Born, Savonlinna, Finland, January 7, 1967.
(Buffalo's 7th choice, 140th overall, in 1985 Entry Draft).

			Regular Season					Playoffs				
Season	Club	Lea	GP	G	A	TP	PIM	GP	G	A	TP	PIM
1984-85	SapKo	Fin.	24	0	4	4	34	....	....	....	....	....
1985-86	Oshawa	OHL	53	14	42	56	27	....	....	....	....	....
1986-87	Oshawa	OHL	50	8	34	42	53	21	2	12	14	36
1987-88	Tappara	Fin.	41	5	1	6	58	1	0	2	2	4
1988-89	Tappara	Fin.	44	4	13	17	32	8	0	0	0	10
1989-90	Tappara	Fin.	44	6	8	14	34	....	....	....	....	....

MATILAINEN, ARI

Right wing. Shoots right. 6'2", 195 lbs. Born, Finland, January 22, 1966.
(Minnesota's 7th choice, 190th overall, in 1988 Entry Draft).

			Regular Season					Playoffs				
Season	Club	Lea	GP	G	A	TP	PIM	GP	G	A	TP	PIM
1987-88	Assat Pori	Fin.	44	15	23	38	40	....	....	....	....	....
1988-89	Karpat	Fin.	36	11	10	21	28	....	....	....	....	....
1989-90	Tappara	Fin.	28	8	7	15	30	7	1	4	5	22

MATTEAU, STEPHANE (mah-TOH)

Left wing. Shoots left. 6'3", 195 lbs. Born, Rouyn-Noranda, Que., September 2, 1969.
(Calgary's 2nd choice, 25th overall, in 1987 Entry Draft).

			Regular Season					Playoffs				
Season	Club	Lea	GP	G	A	TP	PIM	GP	G	A	TP	PIM
1985-86	Hull	QMJHL	60	6	8	14	19	4	0	0	0	0
1986-87	Hull	QMJHL	69	27	48	75	113	8	3	7	10	8
1987-88	Hull	QMJHL	57	17	40	57	179	18	5	14	19	94
1988-89	Hull	QMJHL	59	44	45	89	202	9	8	6	14	30
	Salt Lake	IHL	....	....	....	....	....	9	0	4	4	13
1989-90	Salt Lake	IHL	81	23	35	58	130	10	6	3	9	38

MATULIK, IVAN (muh-TOO-lihk)

Right wing. Shoots left. 6'1", 200 lbs. Born, Nitra, Czechoslovakia, June 17, 1968.
(Edmonton's 7th choice, 147th overall, in 1986 Entry Draft).

			Regular Season					Playoffs				
Season	Club	Lea	GP	G	A	TP	PIM	GP	G	A	TP	PIM
1986-87	Bratislava	Czech.	25	1	3	4	....	....	....	....	....	....
1987-88	Nova Scotia	AHL	46	13	10	23	29	....	....	....	....	....
1988-89	Cape Breton	AHL	1	0	0	0	0	....	....	....	....	....
1989-90	Cape Breton	AHL	32	2	6	8	44	....	....	....	....	....
	Phoenix	IHL	29	3	5	8	46	....	....	....	....	....

MATUSOVICH, SCOTT

Defense. Shoots left. 6'2", 205 lbs. Born, Southbury, CT, October 31, 1969.
(Calgary's 5th choice, 90th overall, in 1988 Entry Draft).

			Regular Season					Playoffs				
Season	Club	Lea	GP	G	A	TP	PIM	GP	G	A	TP	PIM
1988-89	Yale	ECAC	25	3	11	14	40	....	....	....	....	....
1989-90	Yale	ECAC	28	1	15	16	55	....	....	....	....	....

MAY, ALAN

Right wing. Shoots right. 6'1", 200 lbs. Born, Barrhead, Alta., January 14, 1965.

			Regular Season					Playoffs				
Season	Club	Lea	GP	G	A	TP	PIM	GP	G	A	TP	PIM
1985-86	Medicine Hat	WHL	6	1	0	1	25	....	....	....	....	....
	N. Westminster	WHL	32	8	9	17	81	....	....	....	....	....
1986-87	Springfield	AHL	4	0	2	2	11	....	....	....	....	....
	Carolina	ACHL	42	23	14	37	310	5	2	2	4	57
1987-88	**Boston**	**NHL**	**3**	**0**	**0**	**0**	**15**	....	....	....	....	....
	Maine	AHL	61	14	11	25	257	....	....	....	....	....
	Nova Scotia	AHL	13	4	1	5	54	4	0	0	0	51
1988-89	**Edmonton**	**NHL**	**3**	**1**	**0**	**1**	**7**	....	....	....	....	....
	Cape Breton	AHL	50	12	13	25	214	....	....	....	....	....
	New Haven	AHL	12	2	8	10	99	16	6	3	9	*105
1989-90	**Washington**	**NHL**	**77**	**7**	**10**	**17**	**339**	**15**	**0**	**0**	**0**	**37**
	NHL Totals		**83**	**8**	**10**	**18**	**361**	**15**	**0**	**0**	**0**	**37**

Signed as a free agent by **Boston**, October 30, 1987. Traded to **Edmonton** by **Boston** for Moe Lemay, March 8, 1988. Traded to **Los Angeles** by **Edmonton** with Jim Wiemer for Brian Wilks and John English, March 7, 1989. Traded to **Washington** by **Los Angeles** for Washington's fifth-round choice (Thomas Newman) in 1989 Entry Draft, June 17, 1989.

MAY, ANDY

Center. Shoots left. 6'2", 185 lbs. Born, Orangeville, Ont., May 2, 1968.
(St. Louis' 7th choice, 136th overall, in 1986 Entry Draft).

			Regular Season					Playoffs				
Season	Club	Lea	GP	G	A	TP	PIM	GP	G	A	TP	PIM
1986-87	Northeastern	H.E.	26	5	5	10	17	....	....	....	....	....
1987-88	Northeastern	H.E.	17	2	5	7	10	....	....	....	....	....
1988-89	Northeastern	H.E.	30	12	14	26	43	....	....	....	....	....
1989-90	Northeastern	H.E.	35	13	15	28	35	....	....	....	....	....

MAY, BRAD

Left wing. Shoots left. 6', 200 lbs. Born, Toronto, Ont., November 29, 1971.
(Buffalo's 1st choice, 14th overall, in 1990 Entry Draft).

			Regular Season					Playoffs				
Season	Club	Lea	GP	G	A	TP	PIM	GP	G	A	TP	PIM
1988-89	Niagara Falls	OHL	65	8	14	22	304	17	0	1	1	55
1989-90a	Niagara Falls	OHL	61	32	58	90	223	16	9	13	22	64

a OHL Second All-Star Team (1990)

MAYER, DEREK

Defense. Shoots right. 6', 185 lbs. Born, Rossland, B.C., May 21, 1967.
(Detroit's 3rd choice, 43rd overall, in 1986 Entry Draft).

			Regular Season					Playoffs				
Season	Club	Lea	GP	G	A	TP	PIM	GP	G	A	TP	PIM
1985-86	Denver	WCHA	44	2	7	9	42	....	....	....	....	....
1986-87	Denver	WCHA	38	5	17	22	87	....	....	....	....	....
1987-88	Denver	WCHA	34	5	16	21	82	....	....	....	....	....
1988-89	Cdn. National	....	58	3	13	16	81	....	....	....	....	....
1989-90	Adirondack	AHL	62	4	26	30	56	5	0	6	6	4

MAZUR, JAY

Center/Right wing. Shoots right. 6'2", 205 lbs. Born, Hamilton, Ont., January 22, 1965.
(Vancouver's 12th choice, 230th overall, in 1983 Entry Draft).

			Regular Season					Playoffs				
Season	Club	Lea	GP	G	A	TP	PIM	GP	G	A	TP	PIM
1983-84	Maine	H.E.	34	14	9	23	14	....	....	....	....	....
1984-85	Maine	H.E.	31	0	6	6	20	....	....	....	....	....
1985-86	Maine	H.E.	5	7	12	18	....	....	....	....	....	
1986-87	Maine	H.E.	39	16	10	26	61	....	....	....	....	....
1987-88	Flint	IHL	39	17	11	28	28	....	....	....	....	
	Fredericton	AHL	31	14	6	20	28	15	4	2	6	38
1988-89	**Vancouver**	**NHL**	**1**	**0**	**0**	**0**	**0**	....	....	....	....	....
	Milwaukee	IHL	73	33	31	64	86	11	6	5	11	2
1989-90	**Vancouver**	**NHL**	**5**	**0**	**0**	**0**	**4**	....	....	....	....	....
	Milwaukee	IHL	70	20	27	47	63	6	3	0	3	6
	NHL Totals		**6**	**0**	**0**	**0**	**4**	....	....	....	....	....

McBAIN, ANDREW

Right wing. Shoots right. 6'1", 205 lbs. Born, Scarborough, Ont., January 18, 1965.
(Winnipeg's 1st choice, 8th overall, in 1983 Entry Draft).

			Regular Season					Playoffs				
Season	Club	Lea	GP	G	A	TP	PIM	GP	G	A	TP	PIM
1981-82	Niagara Falls	OHL	68	19	25	44	35	5	0	3	3	4
1982-83a	North Bay	OHL	67	33	87	120	61	8	2	6	8	17
1983-84	**Winnipeg**	**NHL**	**78**	**11**	**19**	**30**	**37**	**3**	**2**	**0**	**2**	**0**
1984-85	**Winnipeg**	**NHL**	**77**	**7**	**15**	**22**	**45**	**7**	**1**	**0**	**1**	**0**
1985-86	**Winnipeg**	**NHL**	**28**	**3**	**3**	**6**	**17**	....	....	....	....	....
1986-87	**Winnipeg**	**NHL**	**71**	**11**	**21**	**32**	**106**	**9**	**0**	**2**	**2**	**10**
1987-88	**Winnipeg**	**NHL**	**74**	**32**	**31**	**63**	**145**	**5**	**2**	**5**	**7**	**29**
1988-89	**Winnipeg**	**NHL**	**80**	**37**	**40**	**77**	**71**	....	....	....	....	....
1989-90	**Pittsburgh**	**NHL**	**41**	**5**	**9**	**14**	**51**	....	....	....	....	....
	Vancouver	**NHL**	**26**	**4**	**5**	**9**	**22**	....	....	....	....	....
	NHL Totals		**475**	**110**	**143**	**253**	**494**	**24**	**5**	**7**	**12**	**39**

a OHL Second All-Star Team (1983).

Traded to **Pittsburgh** by **Winnipeg** with Jim Kyte and Randy Gilhen for Randy Cunnyworth, Rick Tabaracci and Dave McLlwain, June 17, 1989. Traded to **Vancouver** by **Pittsburgh** with Dave Capuano and Dan Quinn for Rod Buskas, Barry Pederson and Tony Tanti, January 8, 1990.

McBEAN, WAYNE

Defense. Shoots left. 6'2", 190 lbs. Born, Calgary, Alta., February 21, 1969.
(Los Angeles' 1st choice, 4th overall, in 1987 Entry Draft).

			Regular Season					Playoffs				
Season	Club	Lea	GP	G	A	TP	PIM	GP	G	A	TP	PIM
1985-86	Medicine Hat	WHL	67	1	14	15	73	25	1	5	6	36
1986-87a	Medicine Hat	WHL	71	12	41	53	163	20	2	8	10	40
1987-88	**Los Angeles**	**NHL**	**27**	**0**	**1**	**1**	**26**	....	....	....	....	....
	Medicine Hat	WHL	30	15	30	45	48	16	6	17	23	50
1988-89	**Los Angeles**	**NHL**	**33**	**0**	**5**	**5**	**23**	....	....	....	....	....
	New Haven	AHL	7	1	1	2	2	....	....	....	....	....
	NY Islanders	**NHL**	**19**	**0**	**1**	**1**	**12**	....	....	....	....	....
1989-90	**NY Islanders**	**NHL**	**5**	**0**	**1**	**1**	**2**	**2**	**1**	**1**	**2**	**2**
	Springfield	AHL	58	6	33	39	48	17	4	11	15	31
	NHL Totals		**84**	**0**	**8**	**8**	**63**	**2**	**1**	**1**	**2**	**2**

a WHL East All-Star Team (1987)

Traded to **NY Islanders** by **Los Angeles** with Mark Fitzpatrick and future considerations (Doug Crossman acquired May 23, 1989) for Kelly Hrudey, February 22, 1989.

McBRIDE, DARYN

Center. Shoots right. 5'9", 180 lbs. Born, Ft. Saskatchewan, Alta., March 29, 1968.
(Pittsburgh's 10th choice, 194th overall, in 1987 Entry Draft).

			Regular Season					Playoffs				
Season	Club	Lea	GP	G	A	TP	PIM	GP	G	A	TP	PIM
1986-87	U. of Denver	WCHA	38	19	13	32	54	....	....	....	....	....
1987-88a	U. of Denver	WCHA	39	30	28	58	122	....	....	....	....	....
1988-89b	U. of Denver	WCHA	42	19	32	51	74	....	....	....	....	....
	Can. National	....	15	3	7	10	6	....	....	....	....	....
1989-90	Cdn. National	...	51	15	32	47	49	....	....	....	....	....

a WCHA Second All-Star Team (1988)
b WCHA First All-Star Team (1989)

McCAUGHEY, BRAD

Right wing. Shoots right. 6'2", 195 lbs. Born, Ann Arbor, MI, June 10, 1966.
(Montreal's 10th choice, 158th overall, in 1984 Entry Draft).

			Regular Season					Playoffs				
Season	Club	Lea	GP	G	A	TP	PIM	GP	G	A	TP	PIM
1984-85	U. of Michigan	CCHA	35	16	11	27	49	....	....	....	....	....
1985-86	U. of Michigan	CCHA	32	24	26	50	51	....	....	....	....	....
1986-87	U. of Michigan	CCHA	38	26	23	49	53	....	....	....	....	....
1987-88	U. of Michigan	CCHA	33	20	14	34	36	....	....	....	....	....
1988-89	Sherbrooke	AHL	1	1	0	1	0	....	....	....	....	....
	Peoria	IHL	71	30	38	68	14	4	2	2	4	0
1989-90	Springfield	AHL	7	3	2	5	0	....	....	....	....	....
	Peoria	IHL	23	8	6	14	2	....	....	....	....	....

McCLELLAND, KEVIN WILLIAM

Right wing. Shoots right. 6'2", 205 lbs. Born, Oshawa, Ont., July 4, 1962.
(Hartford's 4th choice, 71st overall, in 1980 Entry Draft).

			Regular Season					Playoffs				
Season	Club	Lea	GP	G	A	TP	PIM	GP	G	A	TP	PIM
1980-81	Niagara Falls	OHA	68	36	72	108	186	12	8	13	21	42
1981-82	Niagara Falls	OHL	46	36	47	83	184	....	....	....	....	....
	Pittsburgh	**NHL**	**10**	**1**	**4**	**5**	**4**	**5**	**1**	**1**	**2**	**5**
1982-83	**Pittsburgh**	**NHL**	**38**	**5**	**4**	**9**	**73**	....	....	....	....	....
1983-84	Baltimore	AHL	3	1	1	2	0	....	....	....	....	....
	Pittsburgh	**NHL**	**24**	**2**	**4**	**6**	**62**	....	....	....	....	....
	Edmonton	**NHL**	**52**	**8**	**20**	**28**	**127**	**18**	**4**	**6**	**10**	**42**
1984-85	**Edmonton**	**NHL**	**62**	**8**	**15**	**23**	**205**	**18**	**1**	**3**	**4**	**75**
1985-86	**Edmonton**	**NHL**	**79**	**11**	**25**	**36**	**266**	**10**	**1**	**0**	**1**	**32**
1986-87	**Edmonton**	**NHL**	**72**	**12**	**13**	**25**	**238**	**21**	**2**	**3**	**5**	**43**
1987-88	**Edmonton**	**NHL**	**74**	**10**	**6**	**16**	**281**	**19**	**2**	**3**	**5**	**68**
1988-89	**Edmonton**	**NHL**	**79**	**6**	**14**	**20**	**161**	**7**	**0**	**2**	**2**	**16**
1989-90	**Edmonton**	**NHL**	**10**	**1**	**1**	**2**	**13**	....	....	....	....	....
	Detroit	**NHL**	**61**	**4**	**5**	**9**	**183**	....	....	....	....	....
	NHL Totals		**561**	**68**	**111**	**179**	**1613**	**98**	**11**	**18**	**29**	**281**

Traded to **Pittsburgh** by **Hartford** with Pat Boutette as compensation for Hartford's signing of free agent goaltender Greg Millen, June 29, 1981. Traded to **Edmonton** by **Pittsburgh** with Pittsburgh's sixth round choice (Emanuel Viveiros) in 1984 Entry Draft for Tom Roulston, December 5, 1983. Traded to **Detroit** by **Edmonton** with Jimmy Carson and Edmonton's fifth round choice in 1991 Entry Draft for Petr Klima, Joe Murphy, Adam Graves and Jeff Sharples, November 2, 1989.

McCORMACK, BRIAN

Defense. Shoots right. 5'10", 170 lbs. Born, Bloomington, MN, November 11, 1969.
(Detroit's 7th choice, 164th overall, in 1988 Entry Draft).

			Regular Season					Playoffs				
Season	Club	Lea	GP	G	A	TP	PIM	GP	G	A	TP	PIM
1988-89	Harvard	ECAC	31	0	8	8	16	....	....	....	....	....
1989-90	Harvard	ECAC	27	2	3	5	36	....	....	....	....	....

McCORMACK, SCOTT

Defense. Shoots right. 6'1", 185 lbs. Born, Minneapolis, MN, September 25, 1967.
(New Jersey's 9th choice, 171st overall, in 1986 Entry Draft).

			Regular Season					Playoffs				
Season	Club	Lea	GP	G	A	TP	PIM	GP	G	A	TP	PIM
1986-87	Harvard	ECAC	10	1	1	2	0	....	....	....	....	....
1987-88	Harvard	ECAC	31	1	3	4	14	....	....	....	....	....
1988-89	Harvard	ECAC	19	1	8	9	10	....	....	....	....	....
1989-90	Harvard	ECAC	24	1	4	5	36	....	....	....	....	....

McCORMICK, MICHAEL

Left wing. Shoots left. 6'2", 220 lbs. Born, St. Boniface, Man., May 14, 1968.
(Chicago's 6th choice, 113th overall, in 1987 Entry Draft).

			Regular Season					Playoffs				
Season	Club	Lea	GP	G	A	TP	PIM	GP	G	A	TP	PIM
1987-88	North Dakota	WCHA	41	4	0	4	28	....	....	....	....	....
1988-89	North Dakota	WCHA	29	1	4	5	22	....	....	....	....	....
1989-90	North Dakota	WCHA	2	0	1	1	4	....	....	....	....	....

McCOSH, SHAWN

Center. Shoots right. 6', 180 lbs. Born, Oshawa, Ont., June 5, 1969.
(Detroit's 5th choice, 95th overall, in 1989 Entry Draft).

			Regular Season					Playoffs				
Season	Club	Lea	GP	G	A	TP	PIM	GP	G	A	TP	PIM
1986-87	Hamilton	OHL	50	11	17	28	49	6	1	0	1	2
1987-88	Hamilton	OHL	64	17	36	53	96	14	6	8	14	14
1988-89	Niagara Falls	OHL	56	41	62	103	75	14	4	13	17	23
1989-90	Hamilton	OHL	48	30	38	68	89	....	....	....	....	....

McCRADY, SCOTT

Defense. Shoots right. 6'1", 195 lbs. Born, Calgary, Alta., October 30, 1968.
(Minnesota's 2nd choice, 35th overall, in 1987 Entry Draft).

			Regular Season					Playoffs				
Season	Club	Lea	GP	G	A	TP	PIM	GP	G	A	TP	PIM
1985-86	Medicine Hat	WHL	65	8	25	33	114	25	0	7	7	67
1986-87	Medicine Hat	WHL	70	10	66	76	157	20	2	*21	23	30
1987-88a	Medicine Hat	WHL	65	7	70	77	132	16	2	17	19	34
1988-89	Kalamazoo	IHL	73	8	29	37	169	6	0	4	4	24
1989-90	Kalamazoo	IHL	3	0	0	0	11	4	0	0	0	19

a WHL East All-Star Team (1988)

Signed as a free agent by **Calgary**, August, 1990.

McCRIMMON, BYRON (BRAD)

Defense. Shoots left. 5'11", 197 lbs. Born, Dodsland, Sask., March 29, 1959.
(Boston's 2nd choice, 15th overall, in 1979 Entry Draft).

			Regular Season					Playoffs				
Season	Club	Lea	GP	G	A	TP	PIM	GP	G	A	TP	PIM
1977-78ab	Brandon	WHL	65	19	78	97	245	8	2	11	13	20
1978-79a	Brandon	WHL	66	24	74	98	139	22	9	19	28	34
1979-80	**Boston**	**NHL**	**72**	**5**	**11**	**16**	**94**	**10**	**1**	**1**	**2**	**28**
1980-81	**Boston**	**NHL**	**78**	**11**	**18**	**29**	**148**	**3**	**0**	**1**	**1**	**2**
1981-82	**Boston**	**NHL**	**78**	**1**	**8**	**9**	**83**	**2**	**0**	**0**	**0**	**2**
1982-83	**Philadelphia**	**NHL**	**79**	**4**	**21**	**25**	**61**	**3**	**0**	**0**	**0**	**4**
1983-84	**Philadelphia**	**NHL**	**71**	**0**	**24**	**24**	**76**	**1**	**0**	**0**	**0**	**4**
1984-85	**Philadelphia**	**NHL**	**66**	**8**	**35**	**43**	**81**	**11**	**2**	**1**	**3**	**15**
1985-86	**Philadelphia**	**NHL**	**80**	**13**	**43**	**56**	**85**	**5**	**2**	**0**	**2**	**2**
1986-87	**Philadelphia**	**NHL**	**71**	**10**	**29**	**39**	**52**	**26**	**3**	**5**	**8**	**30**
1987-88cd	**Calgary**	**NHL**	**80**	**7**	**35**	**42**	**98**	**9**	**2**	**3**	**5**	**22**
1988-89	**Calgary**	**NHL**	**72**	**5**	**17**	**22**	**96**	**22**	**0**	**3**	**3**	**30**
1989-90	**Calgary**	**NHL**	**79**	**4**	**15**	**19**	**78**	**6**	**0**	**2**	**2**	**8**
	NHL Totals		**826**	**68**	**256**	**324**	**952**	**98**	**10**	**16**	**26**	**147**

a WHL First All-Star Team (1978, 1979)
b Named WHL's Top Defenseman (1978)
c NHL Second All-Star Team (1988)
d NHL Plus/Minus Leader (1988)

Played in NHL All-Star Game (1988)

Traded to **Philadelphia** by **Boston** for Pete Peeters, June 9, 1982. Traded to **Calgary** by **Philadelphia** for Calgary's third round pick in 1988 Entry Draft (Dominic Roussel) and first round pick — acquired March 6, 1988 by Toronto — in 1989 Entry Draft, August 26, 1987. Toronto acquired Calgary's first round pick in 1989 Entry Draft from Philadelphia in deal for Ken Wregget, March 6, 1988. Toronto selected Steve Bancroft. Traded to **Detroit** by **Calgary** for Detroit's second round choice - later traded to New Jersey (David Harlock) - in 1990 Entry Draft, June 15, 1990.

McCRORY, SCOTT

Center. Shoots right. 5'10", 185 lbs. Born, Sudbury, Ont., February 27, 1967.
(Washington's 13th choice, 250th overall, in 1986 Entry Draft).

			Regular Season					Playoffs				
Season	Club	Lea	GP	G	A	TP	PIM	GP	G	A	TP	PIM
1985-86	Oshawa	OHL	66	52	80	132	40	6	5	8	13	0
1986-87ab	Oshawa	OHL	66	51	*99	*150	35	24	15	*22	*37	20
1987-88	Binghamton	AHL	72	18	33	51	29	4	0	1	1	2
1988-89	Baltimore	AHL	80	38	51	89	25	....	....	....	....	....
1989-90	Rochester	AHL	51	14	41	55	46	13	3	6	9	2

a OHL Player of the Year (1987)
b OHL First Team All-Star (1987)

Traded to **Buffalo** by **Washington** for Mark Ferner, June 1, 1989.

McDONOUGH, HUBIE

Center. Shoots left 5'9", 180 lbs. Born, Manchester, NH, July 8, 1963.

			Regular Season					Playoffs				
Season	Club	Lea	GP	G	A	TP	PIM	GP	G	A	TP	PIM
1986-87	Flint	IHL	82	27	52	79	59	6	3	2	5	0
1987-88	New Haven	AHL	78	30	29	59	43	....	....	....	....	....
1988-89	**Los Angeles**	**NHL**	**4**	**0**	**1**	**1**	**0**	....	....	....	....	....
	New Haven	AHL	74	37	55	92	41	17	10	*21	*31	6
1989-90	**Los Angeles**	**NHL**	**22**	**3**	**4**	**7**	**10**	....	....	....	....	....
	NY Islanders	**NHL**	**54**	**18**	**11**	**29**	**26**	**5**	**1**	**0**	**1**	**4**
	NHL Totals		**80**	**21**	**16**	**37**	**36**	**5**	**1**	**0**	**1**	**4**

Signed as a free agent by **Los Angeles**, April 18, 1988. Traded to **NY Islanders** by **Los Angeles** with Ken Baumgartner for Mikko Makela, November 29, 1989.

McEACHERN, SHAWN

Center. Shoots left. 6'0", 170 lbs. Born, Waltham, MA, February 28, 1969.
(Pittsburgh's 6th choice, 110th overall, in 1987 Entry Draft).

			Regular Season					Playoffs				
Season	Club	Lea	GP	G	A	TP	PIM	GP	G	A	TP	PIM
1988-89	Boston U.	H.E.	36	20	28	48	32	....	....	....	....	....
1989-90a	Boston U.	H.E.	43	25	31	56	78	....	....	....	....	....

a Hockey East Second All-Star Team (1990)

McGILL, ROBERT PAUL (BOB)

Defense. Shoot right. 6', 190 lbs. Born, Edmonton, Alta., April 27, 1962.
(Toronto's 2nd choice, 26th overall, in 1980 Entry Draft).

			Regular Season					Playoffs				
Season	Club	Lea	GP	G	A	TP	PIM	GP	G	A	TP	PIM
1979-80	Victoria	WHL	70	3	18	21	230	15	0	5	5	64
1980-81	Victoria	WHL	66	5	36	41	295	11	1	5	6	67
1981-82	**Toronto**	**NHL**	**68**	**1**	**10**	**11**	**263**	....	....	....	....	....
1982-83	**Toronto**	**NHL**	**30**	**0**	**0**	**0**	**146**	....	....	....	....	....
	St. Catharines	AHL	32	2	5	7	95	....	....	....	....	....
1983-84	**Toronto**	**NHL**	**11**	**0**	**2**	**2**	**51**	....	....	....	....	....
	St. Catharines	AHL	55	1	15	16	217	6	0	0	0	26
1984-85	**Toronto**	**NHL**	**72**	**0**	**5**	**5**	**250**	....	....	....	....	....
1985-86	**Toronto**	**NHL**	**61**	**1**	**4**	**5**	**141**	**9**	**0**	**0**	**0**	**35**
1986-87	**Toronto**	**NHL**	**56**	**1**	**4**	**5**	**103**	**3**	**0**	**0**	**0**	**0**
1987-88	**Chicago**	**NHL**	**67**	**4**	**7**	**11**	**131**	**3**	**0**	**0**	**0**	**2**
1988-89	**Chicago**	**NHL**	**68**	**0**	**4**	**4**	**155**	**16**	**0**	**0**	**0**	**33**
1989-90	**Chicago**	**NHL**	**69**	**2**	**10**	**12**	**204**	**5**	**0**	**0**	**0**	**2**
	NHL Totals		**502**	**9**	**46**	**55**	**1444**	**36**	**0**	**0**	**0**	**72**

Traded to **Chicago** by **Toronto** with Steve Thomas and Rick Vaive for Al Secord and Ed Olczyk, September 3, 1987.

McGILL, RYAN

Defense. Shoots right. 6'2", 195 lbs. Born, Sherwood Park, Alta., February 28, 1969.
(Chicago's 2nd choice, 29th overall, in 1987 Entry Draft).

			Regular Season					Playoffs				
Season	Club	Lea	GP	G	A	TP	PIM	GP	G	A	TP	PIM
1985-86	Lethbridge	WHL	64	5	10	15	171	10	0	1	1	9
1986-87	Swift Current	WHL	72	12	36	48	226	4	1	0	1	9
1987-88	Medicine Hat	WHL	67	5	30	35	224	15	7	3	10	47
1988-89	Saginaw	IHL	8	2	0	2	12	6	0	0	0	42
	Medicine Hat	WHL	57	26	45	71	172	3	0	2	2	15
1989-90	Indianapolis	IHL	77	11	17	28	215	14	2	2	4	29

McHUGH, MICHAEL (MIKE)

Left wing. Shoots left. 5'10", 190 lbs. Born, Bowdoin, ME, August 16, 1965.
(Minnesota's 1st choice, 1st overall, in 1988 Supplemental Draft).

			Regular Season					Playoffs				
Season	Club	Lea	GP	G	A	TP	PIM	GP	G	A	TP	PIM
1984-85	U. of Maine	H.E.	25	9	8	17	9	....	....	....	....	....
1985-86	U. of Maine	H.E.	38	9	10	19	24	....	....	....	....	....
1986-87	U. of Maine	H.E.	42	21	29	50	40	....	....	....	....	....
1987-88	U. of Maine	H.E.	44	29	37	66	90	....	....	....	....	....
1988-89	**Minnesota**	**NHL**	**3**	**0**	**0**	**0**	**2**	....	....	....	....	....
	Kalamazoo	IHL	70	17	29	46	89	6	3	1	4	17
1989-90	**Minnesota**	**NHL**	**3**	**0**	**0**	**0**	**0**	....	....	....	....	....
	Kalamazoo	IHL	73	14	17	31	96	10	0	6	6	16
	NHL Totals		**6**	**0**	**0**	**0**	**2**	....	....	....	....	....

McINNIS, MARTY

Center. Shoots right. 5'10", 165 lbs. Born, Hingman, MA, June 2, 1970.
(NY Islanders' 10th choice, 163rd overall, in 1988 Entry Draft).

			Regular Season					Playoffs				
Season	Club	Lea	GP	G	A	TP	PIM	GP	G	A	TP	PIM
1988-89	Boston College	H.E.	39	13	19	32	8	....	....	....	....	....
1989-90	Boston College	H.E.	41	24	29	53	43	....	....	....	....	....

McINTYRE, JOHN

Center. Shoots left. 6'1", 175 lbs. Born, Ravenswood, Ont., April 29, 1969.
(Toronto's 3rd choice, 49th overall, in 1987 Entry Draft).

			Regular Season					Playoffs				
Season	Club	Lea	GP	G	A	TP	PIM	GP	G	A	TP	PIM
1985-86	Guelph	OHL	30	4	6	10	25	20	1	5	6	31
1986-87	Guelph	OHL	47	8	22	30	95	....	....	....	....	....
1987-88	Guelph	OHL	39	24	18	42	109	....	....	....	....	....
1988-89	Newmarket	AHL	3	0	2	2	7	5	1	1	2	20
	Guelph	OHL	52	30	26	56	129	7	5	4	9	25
1989-90	**Toronto**	**NHL**	**59**	**5**	**12**	**17**	**117**	**2**	**0**	**0**	**0**	**2**
	Newmarket	AHL	6	2	2	4	12	....	....	....	....	....
	NHL Totals		**59**	**5**	**12**	**17**	**117**	**2**	**0**	**0**	**0**	**2**

McKAY, RANDY

Right wing. Shoots right. 6'1", 185 lbs. Born, Montreal, Que., January 25, 1967.
(Detroit's 6th choice, 113th overall, in 1985 Entry Draft).

			Regular Season					Playoffs				
Season	Club	Lea	GP	G	A	TP	PIM	GP	G	A	TP	PIM
1984-85	Michigan Tech	WCHA	25	4	5	9	32	....	....	....	....	....
1985-86	Michigan Tech	WCHA	40	12	22	34	46	....	....	....	....	....
1986-87	Michigan Tech	WCHA	39	5	11	16	46	....	....	....	....	....
1987-88	Michigan Tech	WCHA	41	17	24	41	70	....	....	....	....	....
	Adirondack	AHL	10	0	3	3	12	6	0	4	4	0
1988-89	**Detroit**	**NHL**	**3**	**0**	**0**	**0**	**0**	**2**	**0**	**0**	**0**	**2**
	Adirondack	AHL	58	29	34	63	170	14	4	7	11	60
1989-90	**Detroit**	**NHL**	**33**	**3**	**6**	**9**	**51**	....	....	....	....	....
	Adirondack	AHL	36	16	23	39	99	6	3	0	3	35
	NHL Totals		**36**	**3**	**6**	**9**	**51**	**2**	**0**	**0**	**0**	**2**

McKEGNEY, ANTHONY SYIIYD (TONY) (ma-KEG-nee)

Left wing. Shoots left. 6'1", 200 lbs. Born, Montreal, Que., February 15, 1958.
(Buffalo's 2nd choice, 32nd overall, in 1978 Amateur Draft).

			Regular Season					Playoffs				
Season	Club	Lea	GP	G	A	TP	PIM	GP	G	A	TP	PIM
1976-77a	Kingston	OHA	66	58	77	135	30	14	13	10	23	14
1977-78b	Kingston	OHA	55	43	49	92	19	5	3	3	6	0
1978-79	Hershey	AHL	24	21	18	39	4	1	0	0	0	0
	Buffalo	NHL	52	8	14	22	10	2	0	1	1	0
1979-80	Buffalo	NHL	80	23	29	52	24	14	3	4	7	2
1980-81	Buffalo	NHL	80	37	32	69	24	8	5	3	8	2
1981-82	Buffalo	NHL	73	23	29	52	41	4	0	0	0	2
1982-83	Buffalo	NHL	78	36	37	73	18	10	3	1	4	4
1983-84	Quebec	NHL	75	24	27	51	23	7	0	0	0	0
1984-85	Quebec	NHL	30	12	9	21	12	....	....	....	....	....
	Minnesota	NHL	27	11	13	24	4	9	8	6	14	0
1985-86	Minnesota	NHL	70	15	25	40	48	5	2	1	3	22
1986-87	Minnesota	NHL	11	2	3	5	16	....	....	....	....	....
	NY Rangers	NHL	64	29	17	46	56	6	0	0	0	12
1987-88	St. Louis	NHL	80	40	38	78	82	9	3	6	9	8
1988-89	St. Louis	NHL	71	25	17	42	58	3	0	1	1	0
1989-90	Detroit	NHL	14	2	1	3	8	....	....	....	....	....
	Quebec	NHL	48	16	11	27	45	....	....	....	....	....
	NHL Totals		853	303	302	605	469	77	24	23	47	52

a OHA First All-Star Team (1977).
b OHA Second All-Star Team (1978).

Traded to **Quebec** by **Buffalo** with Andre Savard, J.F. Sauve and Buffalo's third round choice (Iirvo Jarvi) in 1983 Entry Draft for Real Cloutier and Quebec's first round choice (Adam Creighton) in 1983 Entry Draft, June 8, 1983. Traded to **Minnesota** by **Quebec** with Bo Berglund for Brent Ashton and Brad Maxwell, December 14, 1984. Traded to **NY Rangers** by **Minnesota** with Curt Giles and Minnesota's second-round (Troy Mallette) choice in 1988 Entry Draft for Bob Brooke and NY Rangers' rights to Minnesota's fourth-round choice (Jeffery Stolp) in 1988 Entry Draft previously acquired by NY Rangers in Mark Pavelich deal, November 13, 1986. Traded to **St. Louis** by **NY Rangers** with Rob Whistle for Bruce Bell and future considerations, May 28, 1987. Traded to **Detroit** by **St. Louis**, with Bernie Federko for Adam Oates and Paul MacLean, June 15, 1989. Traded to **Quebec** by **Detroit** for Robert Picard and Greg C. Adams, December 4, 1989.

McKENNA, SEAN MICHAEL

Right wing. Shoots right. 6', 190 lbs. Born, Asbestos, Que., March 7, 1962.
(Buffalo's 3rd choice, 56th overall, in 1980 Entry Draft).

			Regular Season					Playoffs				
Season	Club	Lea	GP	G	A	TP	PIM	GP	G	A	TP	PIM
1980-81a	Sherbrooke	QJHL	71	57	47	104	122	14	9	9	18	12
1981-82	Buffalo	NHL	3	0	1	1	2	....	....	....	....	....
bc	Sherbrooke	QJHL	59	57	33	90	29	22	26	18	44	28
1982-83	Buffalo	NHL	46	10	14	24	4	....	....	....	....	....
	Rochester	AHL	26	16	10	26	14	16	*14	8	22	18
1983-84	Buffalo	NHL	78	20	10	30	45	3	1	0	1	2
1984-85	Buffalo	NHL	65	20	16	36	41	5	0	1	1	0
1985-86	Buffalo	NHL	45	6	12	18	28	....	....	....	....	....
	Los Angeles	NHL	30	4	0	4	7	....	....	....	....	....
1986-87	Los Angeles	NHL	69	14	19	33	10	5	0	1	1	0
1987-88	Los Angeles	NHL	30	3	2	5	12	....	....	....	....	....
	Toronto	NHL	40	5	5	10	12	2	0	0	0	0
1988-89	Toronto	NHL	3	0	1	1	0	....	....	....	....	....
	Newmarket	AHL	61	14	27	41	35	5	1	1	2	4
1989-90	Toronto	NHL	5	0	0	0	20	....	....	....	....	....
	Newmarket	AHL	73	17	17	34	30	....	....	....	....	....
	NHL Totals		414	82	80	162	181	15	1	2	3	2

a QMJHL First All-Star Team (1981)
b QMJHL Second All-Star Team (1982)
c Named Most Valuable Player, 1982 Memorial Cup

Traded to **Los Angeles** by **Buffalo** with Larry Playfair and Ken Baumgartner for Brian Engblom and Doug Smith, January 30, 1986. Traded to **Toronto** by **Los Angeles** for Mike Allison, December 14, 1987.

McKENZIE, JIM

Left wing. Shoots left. 6'3", 205 lbs. Born, Gull Lake, Sask., November 3, 1969.
(Hartford's 3rd choice, 73rd overall, in 1989 Entry Draft).

			Regular Season					Playoffs				
Season	Club	Lea	GP	G	A	TP	PIM	GP	G	A	TP	PIM
1985-86	Moose Jaw	WHL	3	0	2	2	0	....	....	....	....	....
1986-87	Moose Jaw	WHL	65	5	3	8	125	9	0	0	0	7
1987-88	Moose Jaw	WHL	62	1	17	18	134	....	....	....	....	....
1988-89	Victoria	WHL	67	15	27	42	176	8	1	4	5	30
1989-90	Hartford	NHL	5	0	0	0	4	....	....	....	....	....
	Binghamton	AHL	56	4	12	16	149	....	....	....	....	....
	NHL Totals		5	0	0	0	4	....	....	....	....	....

McLAUGHLIN, MICHAEL

Left wing. Shoots right. 6'1", 175 lbs. Born, Longmeadow, MA, March 29, 1970.
(Buffalo's 7th choice, 118th overall, in 1988 Entry Draft).

			Regular Season					Playoffs				
Season	Club	Lea	GP	G	A	TP	PIM	GP	G	A	TP	PIM
1988-89	U. of Vermont	ECAC	32	5	6	11	12	....	....	....	....	....
1989-90	U. of Vermont	ECAC	29	11	12	23	37	....	....	....	....	....

McLENNAN, DONALD (DON)

Defense. Shoots left. 6'3", 210 lbs. Born, Winnipeg, Man., October 4, 1968.
(Winnipeg's 3rd choice, 79th overall, in 1987 Entry Draft).

			Regular Season					Playoffs				
Season	Club	Lea	GP	G	A	TP	PIM	GP	G	A	TP	PIM
1986-87	U. of Denver	WCHA	35	2	2	4	38	....	....	....	....	....
1987-88	U. of Denver	WCHA	29	0	3	3	24	....	....	....	....	....
1988-89	U. of Denver	WCHA	26	1	3	4	28	....	....	....	....	....
1989-90	U. of Denver	WCHA	42	0	6	6	41	....	....	....	....	....

McLLWAIN, DAVE (MA-kuhl-WAYN)

Center. Shoots left. 6', 190 lbs. Born, Seaforth, Ont., June 9, 1967.
(Pittsburgh's 9th choice, 172nd overall, in 1986 Entry Draft).

			Regular Season					Playoffs				
Season	Club	Lea	GP	G	A	TP	PIM	GP	G	A	TP	PIM
1985-86	Kitchener	OHL	13	7	7	14	12	....	....	....	....	....
	North Bay	OHL	51	30	28	58	25	10	4	4	8	2
1986-87a	North Bay	OHL	60	46	73	119	35	24	7	18	25	40
1987-88	Pittsburgh	NHL	66	11	8	19	40	....	....	....	....	....
	Muskegon	IHL	9	4	6	10	23	6	2	3	5	8
1988-89	Pittsburgh	NHL	24	1	2	3	4	3	0	1	1	0
	Muskegon	IHL	46	37	35	72	51	7	8	2	10	6
1989-90	Winnipeg	NHL	80	25	26	51	60	7	0	1	1	2
	NHL Totals		170	37	36	73	104	10	0	2	2	2

a OHL Second Team All-Star (1987)

Traded to **Winnipeg** by **Pittsburgh** with Randy Cunnyworth and Rick Tabaracci for Jim Kyte, Andrew McBain and Randy Gilhen, June 17, 1989.

McNEIL, MICHAEL

Center. Shoots left. 6'1", 175 lbs. Born, Winona, MN, July 22, 1966.
(St. Louis' 1st choice, 14th overall, in 1988 Supplemental Draft).

			Regular Season					Playoffs				
Season	Club	Lea	GP	G	A	TP	PIM	GP	G	A	TP	PIM
1984-85	Notre Dame	NCAA	28	16	26	42	12	....	....	....	....	....
1985-86	Notre Dame	NCAA	34	18	29	47	32	....	....	....	....	....
1986-87	Notre Dame	NCAA	30	21	16	37	24	....	....	....	....	....
1987-88	Notre Dame	NCAA	32	28	44	72	12	....	....	....	....	....
1988-89	Moncton	AHL	1	0	0	0	0	....	....	....	....	....
	Fort Wayne	IHL	75	27	35	62	12	11	1	5	6	2
1989-90a	Indianapolis	IHL	74	17	24	41	10	14	6	4	10	21

a Won N.R. Poile Trophy (Playoff MVP–IHL) (1990)

McPHEE, MICHAEL JOSEPH (MIKE)

Left wing. Shoots left. 6'1", 203 lbs. Born, Sydney, N.S., July 14, 1960.
(Montreal's 8th choice, 124th overall, in 1980 Entry Draft).

			Regular Season					Playoffs				
Season	Club	Lea	GP	G	A	TP	PIM	GP	G	A	TP	PIM
1980-81	RPI	ECAC	29	28	18	46	22	....	....	....	....	....
1981-82	RPI	ECAC	6	0	3	3	4	....	....	....	....	....
1982-83	Nova Scotia	AHL	42	10	15	25	29	7	1	1	2	14
1983-84	Montreal	NHL	14	5	2	7	41	15	1	0	1	31
	Nova Scotia	AHL	67	22	33	55	101	....	....	....	....	....
1984-85	Montreal	NHL	70	17	22	39	120	12	4	1	5	32
1985-86	Montreal	NHL	70	19	21	40	69	20	3	4	7	45
1986-87	Montreal	NHL	79	18	21	39	58	17	7	2	9	13
1987-88	Montreal	NHL	77	23	20	43	53	11	4	3	7	8
1988-89	Montreal	NHL	73	19	22	41	74	20	4	7	11	30
1989-90	Montreal	NHL	56	23	18	41	47	9	1	1	2	16
	NHL Totals		439	124	126	250	462	104	24	18	42	175

Played in NHL All-Star Game (1989)

McPHERSON, DARWIN

Defense. Shoots left. 6'1", 195 lbs. Born, Flin Flon, Man., May 16, 1968.
(Boston's 4th choice, 67th overall, in 1987 Entry Draft).

			Regular Season					Playoffs				
Season	Club	Lea	GP	G	A	TP	PIM	GP	G	A	TP	PIM
1984-85	Brandon	WHL	39	2	0	2	36	....	....	....	....	....
1985-86	N. Westminster	WHL	63	2	8	10	149	....	....	....	....	....
1986-87	N. Westminster	WHL	65	10	22	32	242	....	....	....	....	....
1987-88	N. Westminster	WHL	47	1	17	18	192	5	0	0	0	16
1988-89	Saskatoon	WHL	59	4	13	17	256	8	0	1	1	27
1989-90	Peoria	IHL	18	1	0	1	94	....	....	....	....	....

Signed as a free agent by **St. Louis**, August 4, 1989.

McRAE, BASIL PAUL

Left wing. Shoots left. 6'2", 205 lbs. Born, Beaverton, Ont., January 5, 1961.
(Quebec's 3rd choice, 87th overall, in 1980 Entry Draft).

			Regular Season					Playoffs				
Season	Club	Lea	GP	G	A	TP	PIM	GP	G	A	TP	PIM
1979-80	London	OHA	67	24	36	60	116	5	0	0	0	18
1980-81	London	OHA	65	29	23	52	266	....	....	....	....	....
1981-82	Fredericton	AHL	47	11	15	26	175	....	....	....	....	....
	Quebec	NHL	20	4	3	7	69	9	1	0	1	34
1982-83	Quebec	NHL	22	1	1	2	59	....	....	....	....	....
	Fredericton	AHL	53	22	19	41	146	12	1	5	6	75
1983-84	Toronto	NHL	3	0	0	0	19	....	....	....	....	....
	St. Catharines	AHL	78	14	25	39	187	6	0	0	0	40
1984-85	Toronto	NHL	1	0	0	0	0	....	....	....	....	....
	St. Catharines	AHL	72	30	25	55	186	....	....	....	....	....
1985-86	Detroit	NHL	4	0	0	0	5	....	....	....	....	....
	Adirondack	AHL	69	22	30	52	259	17	5	4	9	101
1986-87	Detroit	NHL	36	2	2	4	193	....	....	....	....	....
	Quebec	NHL	33	9	5	14	149	13	3	1	4	*99
1987-88	Minnesota	NHL	80	5	11	16	382	....	....	....	....	....
1988-89	Minnesota	NHL	78	12	19	31	365	5	0	0	0	58
1989-90	Minnesota	NHL	66	9	17	26	*351	7	1	0	1	24
	NHL Totals		343	42	58	100	1592	34	5	1	6	215

Traded to **Toronto** by **Quebec** for Richard Turmol, August 12, 1983. Signed as a free agent by **Detroit**, July 17, 1985. Traded to **Quebec** by **Detroit** with John Ogrodnick and Doug Shedden for Brent Ashton, Gilbert Delorme and Mark Kumpel, January 17, 1987. Signed as a free agent by **Minnesota**, June 29, 1987.

McRAE, CHRIS

Left wing. Shoots left. 6', 180 lbs. Born, Newmarket, Ont., August 26, 1965.

			Regular Season					Playoffs				
Season	Club	Lea	GP	G	A	TP	PIM	GP	G	A	TP	PIM
1983-84	Belleville	OHL	9	0	0	0	19	....	....	....	....	....
	Sudbury	OHL	53	14	31	45	120	....	....	....	....	....
1984-85	Sudbury	OHL	6	0	2	2	10	....	....	....	....	....
	Oshawa	OHL	43	8	7	15	118	5	0	1	1	2
	St. Catharines	AHL	6	4	3	7	24	....	....	....	....	....
1985-86	St. Catharines	AHL	59	1	1	2	233	11	0	1	1	65
1986-87	Newmarket	AHL	51	3	6	9	193	....	....	....	....	....
1987-88	**Toronto**	**NHL**	**11**	**0**	**0**	**0**	**65**	....	....	....	....	....
	Newmarket	AHL	34	7	6	13	165	....	....	....	....	....
1988-89	**Toronto**	**NHL**	**3**	**0**	**0**	**0**	**12**	....	....	....	....	....
	Newmarket	AHL	18	3	1	4	85	....	....	....	....	....
	Denver	IHL	23	1	4	5	121	2	0	0	0	20
1989-90	**Detroit**	**NHL**	**7**	**1**	**0**	**1**	**45**	....	....	....	....	....
	Adirondack	AHL	46	9	10	19	290	....	....	....	....	....
	NHL Totals		**21**	**1**	**0**	**1**	**122**	....	....	....	....	....

Signed as a free agent by **Toronto**, October 16, 1985. Traded to **NY Rangers** by **Toronto** for Ken Hammond, February 21, 1989. Traded to **Detroit** by **NY Rangers** with Detroit's fifth round choice (Tony Burns) in 1990 Entry Draft which was previously acquired by NY Rangers for Kris King, September 7, 1989.

McRAE, KEN

Center. Shoots right. 6'1", 195 lbs. Born, Winchester, Ont., April 23, 1968.
(Quebec's 1st choice, 18th overall, in 1986 Entry Draft).

			Regular Season					Playoffs				
Season	Club	Lea	GP	G	A	TP	PIM	GP	G	A	TP	PIM
1985-86	Sudbury	OHL	66	25	49	74	127	4	2	1	3	12
1986-87	Sudbury	OHL	21	12	15	27	40	....	....	....	....	....
	Hamilton	OHL	20	7	12	19	25	7	1	1	2	12
1987-88	**Quebec**	**NHL**	**1**	**0**	**0**	**0**	**0**	....	....	....	....	....
	Hamilton	OHL	62	30	55	85	158	14	13	9	22	35
	Fredericton	AHL	....	....	....	....	....	3	0	0	0	8
1988-89	**Quebec**	**NHL**	**37**	**6**	**11**	**17**	**68**	....	....	....	....	....
	Halifax	AHL	41	20	21	41	87	....	....	....	....	....
1989-90	**Quebec**	**NHL**	**66**	**7**	**8**	**15**	**191**	....	....	....	....	....
	NHL Totals		**104**	**13**	**19**	**32**	**259**	....	....	....	....	....

McREYNOLDS, BRIAN

Center. Shoots left. 6'1", 180 lbs. Born, Penetanguishene, Ont., January 5, 1965.
(NY Rangers' 6th choice, 112th overall, in 1985 Entry Draft).

			Regular Season					Playoffs				
Season	Club	Lea	GP	G	A	TP	PIM	GP	G	A	TP	PIM
1985-86	Michigan State	CCHA	45	14	24	38	78	....	....	....	....	....
1986-87	Michigan State	CCHA	45	16	24	40	68	....	....	....	....	....
1987-88	Michigan State	CCHA	43	10	24	34	50	....	....	....	....	....
1988-89	Cdn. National	....	58	5	25	30	59	....	....	....	....	....
1989-90	**Winnipeg**	**NHL**	**9**	**0**	**2**	**2**	**4**	....	....	....	....	....
	Moncton	AHL	72	18	41	59	87	....	....	....	....	....
	NHL Totals		**9**	**0**	**2**	**2**	**4**	....	....	....	....	....

Signed as a free agent by **Winnipeg**, June 20, 1989. Traded to **NY Rangers** by **Winnipeg** for Simon Wheeldon, July 9, 1990.

McSORLEY, MARTIN J. (MARTY)

Defense/Right wing. Shoots right. 6'1", 220 lbs. Born, Hamilton, Ont., May 18, 1963.

			Regular Season					Playoffs				
Season	Club	Lea	GP	G	A	TP	PIM	GP	G	A	TP	PIM
1981-82	Belleville	OHL	58	6	13	19	234	....	....	....	....	....
1982-83	Belleville	OHL	70	10	41	51	183	4	0	0	0	7
	Baltimore	AHL	2	0	0	0	22	....	....	....	....	....
1983-84	**Pittsburgh**	**NHL**	**72**	**2**	**7**	**9**	**224**	....	....	....	....	....
1984-85	**Pittsburgh**	**NHL**	**15**	**0**	**0**	**0**	**15**	....	....	....	....	....
	Baltimore	AHL	58	6	24	30	154	14	0	7	7	47
1985-86	**Edmonton**	**NHL**	**59**	**11**	**12**	**23**	**265**	**8**	**0**	**2**	**2**	**50**
	Nova Scotia	AHL	9	2	4	6	34	....	....	....	....	....
1986-87	**Edmonton**	**NHL**	**41**	**2**	**4**	**6**	**159**	**21**	**4**	**3**	**7**	**65**
	Nova Scotia	AHL	7	2	2	4	48	....	....	....	....	....
1987-88	**Edmonton**	**NHL**	**60**	**9**	**17**	**26**	**223**	**16**	**0**	**3**	**3**	**67**
1988-89	**Los Angeles**	**NHL**	**66**	**10**	**17**	**27**	**350**	**11**	**0**	**2**	**2**	**33**
1989-90	**Los Angeles**	**NHL**	**75**	**15**	**21**	**36**	**322**	**10**	**1**	**3**	**4**	**18**
	NHL Totals		**388**	**49**	**78**	**127**	**1558**	**66**	**5**	**13**	**18**	**233**

Signed as free agent by **Pittsburgh**, July 30, 1982. Traded to **Edmonton** by **Pittsburgh** with Tim Hrynewich for Gilles Meloche, September, 12, 1985. Traded to **Los Angeles** by **Edmonton** with Wayne Gretzky and Mike Krushelnyski for Jimmy Carson, Martin Gelinas, Los Angeles' first round choices in 1989 (acquired by New Jersey, June 17, 1989. New Jersey selected Jason Miller), 1991 and 1993 Entry Drafts and cash, August 9, 1988.

McSWEEN, DON

Defense; Shoots left. 5'10", 195 lbs. Born, Detroit, MI, June 9, 1964.
(Buffalo's 10th choice, 154th overall, in 1983 Entry Draft).

			Regular Season					Playoffs				
Season	Club	Lea	GP	G	A	TP	PIM	GP	G	A	TP	PIM
1983-84	Michigan State	CCHA	46	10	26	36	30	....	....	....	....	....
1984-85	Michigan State	CCHA	44	2	23	25	52	....	....	....	....	....
1985-86a	Michigan State	CCHA	45	9	29	38	18	....	....	....	....	....
1986-87abc	Michigan State	CCHA	45	7	23	30	34	....	....	....	....	....
1987-88	**Buffalo**	**NHL**	**5**	**0**	**1**	**1**	**6**	....	....	....	....	....
	Rochester	AHL	63	9	29	38	108	6	0	1	1	15
1988-89	Rochester	AHL	66	7	22	29	45	....	....	....	....	....
1989-90	**Buffalo**	**NHL**	**4**	**0**	**0**	**0**	**6**	....	....	....	....	....
d	Rochester	AHL	70	16	43	59	43	17	3	10	13	12
	NHL Totals		**9**	**0**	**1**	**1**	**12**	....	....	....	....	....

a CCHA First All-Star Team (1986, 1987)
b NCAA West Second All-American Team (1987)
c Named to NCAA All-Tournament Team (1987)
d AHL First All-Star Team (1990)

MEAGHER, RICHARD (RICK) (muh-HAHR)

Center. Shoots left. 5'8", 175 lbs. Born, Belleville, Ont., November 2, 1953.

			Regular Season					Playoffs				
Season	Club	Lea	GP	G	A	TP	PIM	GP	G	A	TP	PIM
1975-76	Boston U.	ECAC	28	12	25	37	22	....	....	....	....	....
1976-77	Boston U.	ECAC	34	34	46	80	42	....	....	....	....	....
1977-78	Nova Scotia	AHL	57	20	27	47	33	11	5	3	8	11
1978-79	Nova Scotia	AHL	79	35	46	81	57	10	1	6	7	11
1979-80	**Montreal**	**NHL**	**2**	**0**	**0**	**0**	**0**	....	....	....	....	....
	Nova Scotia	AHL	64	32	44	76	53	6	3	4	7	2
1980-81	**Hartford**	**NHL**	**27**	**7**	**10**	**17**	**19**	....	....	....	....	....
	Binghamton	AHL	50	23	35	58	54	....	....	....	....	....
1981-82	**Hartford**	**NHL**	**65**	**24**	**19**	**43**	**51**	....	....	....	....	....
1982-83	**Hartford**	**NHL**	**4**	**0**	**0**	**0**	**0**	....	....	....	....	....
	New Jersey	**NHL**	**57**	**15**	**14**	**29**	**11**	....	....	....	....	....
1983-84	**New Jersey**	**NHL**	**52**	**14**	**14**	**28**	**16**	....	....	....	....	....
	Maine	AHL	10	6	4	10	2	....	....	....	....	....
1984-85	**New Jersey**	**NHL**	**71**	**11**	**20**	**31**	**22**	....	....	....	....	....
1985-86	**St. Louis**	**NHL**	**79**	**11**	**19**	**30**	**28**	**19**	**4**	**4**	**8**	**12**
1986-87	**St. Louis**	**NHL**	**80**	**18**	**21**	**39**	**54**	**6**	**0**	**0**	**0**	**11**
1987-88	**St. Louis**	**NHL**	**76**	**18**	**16**	**34**	**76**	**10**	**0**	**0**	**0**	**8**
1988-89	**St. Louis**	**NHL**	**78**	**15**	**14**	**29**	**53**	**10**	**3**	**2**	**5**	**6**
1989-90a	**St. Louis**	**NHL**	**76**	**8**	**17**	**25**	**47**	**8**	**1**	**0**	**1**	**2**
	NHL Totals		**667**	**141**	**164**	**305**	**377**	**53**	**8**	**6**	**14**	**39**

a Won Frank J. Selke Trophy (1990)

Signed as a free agent by **Montreal**, June 27, 1977. Traded to **Hartford** by **Montreal** with Montreal's third round (Paul MacDermid) and fifth round (Dan Bourbonnais) choices in 1981 Entry Draft for Hartford's third round (Dieter Hegen) and fifth round (Steve Rooney) choices in 1981 Entry Draft, June 5, 1980. Traded to **New Jersey** by **Hartford** with the rights to Garry Howatt for Merlin Malinowski and the rights to Scott Fusco, October 15, 1982. Traded to **St. Louis** by **New Jersey** with New Jersey's 12th round choice (Bill Butler) in 1986 Entry Draft for Perry Anderson, August 29, 1985.

MEARS, GLEN

Defense. Shoots right. 6'3", 215 lbs. Born, Anchorage, AK, July 14, 1972.
(Calgary's 5th choice, 62nd overall, in 1990 Entry Draft).

			Regular Season					Playoffs				
Season	Club	Lea	GP	G	A	TP	PIM	GP	G	A	TP	PIM
1989-90	Rochester	USHL	46	5	20	25	95	....	....	....	....	....

MEASURES, ALLAN

Defense. Shoots left. 5'11", 165 lbs. Born, Barrhead, Alta., May 8, 1965.
(Vancouver's 9th choice, 170th overall, in 1983 Entry Draft).

			Regular Season					Playoffs				
Season	Club	Lea	GP	G	A	TP	PIM	GP	G	A	TP	PIM
1982-83	Calgary	WHL	63	5	23	28	43	16	0	5	5	12
1983-84	Calgary	WHL	69	17	36	53	96	4	3	4	7	0
1984-85	Calgary	WHL	65	25	58	83	84	8	2	4	6	11
1985-86	Calgary	WHL	46	23	34	57	50	....	....	....	....	....
1986-87	Fredericton	AHL	29	3	8	11	12	....	....	....	....	....
	Kalamazoo	IHL	37	11	15	26	26	5	1	1	2	0
1987-88	Lukko	Fin.	44	3	13	16	72	....	....	....	....	....
1988-89	Lukko	Fin.	43	3	26	29	46	....	....	....	....	....
1989-90	Lukko	Fin.	40	10	10	20	36	....	....	....	....	....

MELLANBY, SCOTT

Right wing. Shoots right. 6'1", 210 lbs. Born, Montreal, Que., June 11, 1966.
(Philadelphia's 2nd choice, 27th overall, in 1984 Entry Draft).

			Regular Season					Playoffs				
Season	Club	Lea	GP	G	A	TP	PIM	GP	G	A	TP	PIM
1984-85	U. Wisconsin	WCHA	40	14	24	38	60	....	....	....	....	....
1985-86	U. Wisconsin	WCHA	32	21	23	44	89	....	....	....	....	....
	Philadelphia	**NHL**	**2**	**0**	**0**	**0**	**0**	....	....	....	....	....
1986-87	**Philadelphia**	**NHL**	**71**	**11**	**21**	**32**	**94**	**24**	**5**	**5**	**10**	**46**
1987-88	**Philadelphia**	**NHL**	**75**	**25**	**26**	**51**	**185**	**7**	**0**	**1**	**1**	**16**
1988-89	**Philadelphia**	**NHL**	**76**	**21**	**29**	**50**	**183**	**19**	**4**	**5**	**9**	**28**
1989-90	**Philadelphia**	**NHL**	**57**	**6**	**17**	**23**	**77**	....	....	....	....	....
	NHL Totals		**281**	**63**	**93**	**156**	**539**	**50**	**9**	**11**	**20**	**90**

MELNYK, DOUGLAS

Defense. Shoots left. 5'10", 185 lbs. Born, London, Ont., August 9, 1967.
(NY Islanders' 1st choice, 21st overall, in 1988 Supplemental Draft).

			Regular Season					Playoffs				
Season	Club	Lea	GP	G	A	TP	PIM	GP	G	A	TP	PIM
1986-87	W. Michigan	CCHA	43	2	7	9	40	....	....	....	....	....
1987-88	W. Michigan	CCHA	42	2	16	18	22	....	....	....	....	....
1988-89	W. Michigan	CCHA	30	2	4	6	28	....	....	....	....	....
1989-90	W. Michigan	CCHA	33	2	10	12	26	....	....	....	....	....

MELNYK, LARRY JOSEPH (MEHL-nihk)

Defense. Shoots left. 6', 195 lbs. Born, Saskatoon, Sask., February 21, 1960.
(Boston's 5th choice, 78th overall, in 1979 Entry Draft).

			Regular Season					Playoffs				
Season	Club	Lea	GP	G	A	TP	PIM	GP	G	A	TP	PIM
1978-79	N. Westminster	WHL	71	7	33	40	142	8	1	4	5	14
1979-80	N. Westminster	WHL	67	13	38	51	236	....	....	....	....	....
1980-81	**Boston**	**NHL**	**26**	**0**	**4**	**4**	**39**	....	....	....	....	....
	Springfield	AHL	47	1	10	11	109	1	0	0	0	0
1981-82	Erie	AHL	10	0	3	3	36	....	....	....	....	....
	Boston	**NHL**	**48**	**0**	**8**	**8**	**84**	**11**	**0**	**3**	**3**	**40**
1982-83	Baltimore	AHL	72	2	24	26	215	....	....	....	....	....
	Boston	**NHL**	**1**	**0**	**0**	**0**	**0**	**11**	**0**	**0**	**0**	**9**
1983-84	Hershey	AHL	50	0	18	18	156	....	....	....	....	....
	Moncton	AHL	14	0	3	3	17	....	....	....	....	....
	Edmonton	**NHL**	....	....	....	....	....	**6**	**0**	**1**	**1**	**0**
1984-85	**Edmonton**	**NHL**	**28**	**0**	**11**	**11**	**25**	**12**	**1**	**3**	**4**	**26**
	Nova Scotia	AHL	37	2	10	12	97	....	....	....	....	....
1985-86	**Edmonton**	**NHL**	**6**	**2**	**3**	**5**	**11**	....	....	....	....	....
	Nova Scotia	AHL	19	2	8	10	72	....	....	....	....	....
	NY Rangers	**NHL**	**46**	**1**	**8**	**9**	**65**	**16**	**1**	**2**	**3**	**46**
1986-87	**NY Rangers**	**NHL**	**73**	**3**	**12**	**15**	**182**	**6**	**0**	**0**	**0**	**4**
1987-88	**NY Rangers**	**NHL**	**14**	**0**	**1**	**1**	**34**	....	....	....	....	....
	Vancouver	**NHL**	**49**	**2**	**3**	**5**	**73**	....	....	....	....	....
1988-89	**Vancouver**	**NHL**	**74**	**3**	**11**	**14**	**82**	**4**	**0**	**0**	**0**	**2**
1989-90	**Vancouver**	**NHL**	**67**	**0**	**2**	**2**	**91**	....	....	....	....	....
	NHL Totals		**432**	**11**	**63**	**74**	**686**	**66**	**2**	**9**	**11**	**127**

Traded to **Edmonton** by **Boston** for John Blum, March 6, 1984. Traded to **NY Rangers** by **Edmonton** with Todd Strueby for Mike Rogers, December 20, 1985. Traded to **Vancouver** by **NY Rangers** with Willie Huber for Michel Petit, November 4, 1987.

MELROSE, KEVAN

Defense. Shoots left. 5'10", 200 lbs. Born, Calgary, Alta., March 28, 1966.
(Calgary's 7th choice, 138th overall in 1984 Entry Draft).

			Regular Season					Playoffs				
Season	Club	Lea	GP	G	A	TP	PIM	GP	G	A	TP	PIM
1986-87	Cdn. Olympic		8	1	0	1	4					
	Red Deer	AJHL	29	15	15	30	171	19	8	16	24	60
1987-88	Harvard	ECAC	31	4	6	10	50	....	....	....	....	....
1988-89	Harvard	ECAC	32	2	13	15	126	....	....	....	....	....
1989-90	Harvard	ECAC	16	1	6	7	124	....	....	....	....	....

MENDEL, ROBERT (ROB)

Defense. Shoots left. 6'1", 195 lbs. Born, Los Angeles, CA, September 19, 1968.
(Quebec's 5th choice, 93rd overall, in 1987 Entry Draft).

			Regular Season					Playoffs				
Season	Club	Lea	GP	G	A	TP	PIM	GP	G	A	TP	PIM
1986-87	U. Wisconsin	WCHA	42	1	7	8	26	....	....	....	....	....
1987-88	U. Wisconsin	WCHA	40	0	7	7	22	....	....	....	....	....
1988-89	U. Wisconsin	WCHA	44	1	14	15	37	....	....	....	....	....
1989-90	U. Wisconsin	WCHA	44	1	13	14	30	....	....	....	....	....

MERKLER, KEITH

Left wing. Shoots left. 6'2", 205 lbs. Born, Syosset, NY, April 23, 1971.
(Toronto's 8th choice, 129th overall, in 1989 Entry Draft).

			Regular Season					Playoffs				
Season	Club	Lea	GP	G	A	TP	PIM	GP	G	A	TP	PIM
1988-89	Portledge	HS	43	35	30	65	....	....	....	....	....	....
1989-90	Princeton	ECAC	8	0	0	0	4	....	....	....	....	....

MERKOSKY, GLENN (muhr-KAH-skee)

Center. Shoots left. 5'10", 175 lbs. Born, Edmonton, Alta., April 8, 1960.

			Regular Season					Playoffs				
Season	Club	Lea	GP	G	A	TP	PIM	GP	G	A	TP	PIM
1979-80	Calgary	WHL	72	49	40	89	95	7	4	6	10	14
1980-81	Binghamton	AHL	80	26	35	61	61	5	0	2	2	2
1981-82	**Hartford**	**NHL**	**7**	**0**	**0**	**0**	**2**	....	....	....	....	....
	Binghamton	AHL	72	29	40	69	83	10	0	2	2	2
1982-83	**New Jersey**	**NHL**	**34**	**4**	**10**	**14**	**20**	....	....	....	....	....
	Wichita	CHL	45	26	23	49	15	....	....	....	....	....
1983-84	**New Jersey**	**NHL**	**5**	**1**	**0**	**1**	**0**	....	....	....	....	....
	Maine	AHL	75	28	28	56	56	17	11	10	21	20
1984-85a	Maine	AHL	80	38	38	76	19	11	2	3	5	13
1985-86	**Detroit**	**NHL**	**17**	**0**	**2**	**2**	**0**	....	....	....	....	....
	Adirondack	AHL	59	24	33	57	22	17	5	7	12	15
1986-87bc	Adirondack	AHL	77	*54	31	85	66	11	6	8	14	7
1987-88	Adirondack	AHL	66	34	42	76	34	11	4	6	10	4
1988-89	Adirondack	AHL	76	31	46	77	13	17	8	11	19	10
1989-90	**Detroit**	**NHL**	**3**	**0**	**0**	**0**	**0**	....	....	....	....	....
	Adirondack	AHL	75	33	31	64	29	6	2	1	3	6
	NHL Totals		**66**	**5**	**12**	**17**	**22**	....	....	....	....	....

a AHL Second All-Star Team (1985)
b AHL First All-Star Team (1987)
c Won Fred T. Hunt Memorial Trophy (Sportsmanship-AHL 1987)

Signed as a free agent by **Hartford**, August 10, 1980. Signed as a free agent by **New Jersey**, September 14, 1982. Signed as a free agent by **Detroit,** July 15, 1985.

MERSCH, MIKE

Defense. Shoots left. 6'1", 210 lbs. Born, Skokie, IL, September 29, 1964.

			Regular Season					Playoffs				
Season	Club	Lea	GP	G	A	TP	PIM	GP	G	A	TP	PIM
1983-84	Ill.-Chicago	CCHA	29	0	5	5	18	....	....	....	....	....
1984-85	Ill.-Chicago	CCHA	35	1	14	15	36	....	....	....	....	....
1985-86	Ill.-Chicago	CCHA	36	4	19	23	30	....	....	....	....	....
1986-87	Salt Lake	IHL	43	3	12	15	101	17	0	10	10	14
1987-88	Salt Lake	IHL	1	0	0	0	2	....	....	....	....	....
	Flint	IHL	58	1	14	15	118	16	3	4	7	18
1988-89	New Haven	AHL	1	0	0	0	4	....	....	....	....	....
	Flint	IHL	55	5	20	25	101	....	....	....	....	....
	Muskegon	IHL	16	0	2	2	26	13	0	6	6	38
1989-90	Muskegon	IHL	82	10	38	48	161	15	1	4	5	41

Signed as a free agent by **Calgary**, April 22, 1986. Signed as a free agent by **Pittsburgh**, August 3, 1989.

MESSIER, MARK DOUGLAS (MEHZ-yay)

Center. Shoots left. 6'1", 210 lbs. Born, Edmonton, Alta., January 18, 1961.
(Edmonton's 2nd choice, 48th overall, in 1979 Entry Draft).

			Regular Season					Playoffs				
Season	Club	Lea	GP	G	A	TP	PIM	GP	G	A	TP	PIM
1977-78	Portland	WHL	....	....	....	....	....	7	4	1	5.	2
1978-79	Indianapolis	WHA	5	0	0	0	0	....	....	....	....	....
	Cincinnati	WHA	47	1	10	11	58	....	....	....	....	....
1979-80	**Edmonton**	**NHL**	**75**	**12**	**21**	**33**	**120**	**3**	**1**	**2**	**3**	**2**
	Houston	CHL	4	0	3	3	4	....	....	....	....	....
1980-81	**Edmonton**	**NHL**	**72**	**23**	**40**	**63**	**102**	**9**	**2**	**5**	**7**	**13**
1981-82a	**Edmonton**	**NHL**	**78**	**50**	**38**	**88**	**119**	**5**	**1**	**2**	**3**	**8**
1982-83a	**Edmonton**	**NHL**	**77**	**48**	**58**	**106**	**72**	**15**	**15**	**6**	**21**	**14**
1983-84bc	**Edmonton**	**NHL**	**73**	**37**	**64**	**101**	**165**	**19**	**8**	**18**	**26**	**19**
1984-85	**Edmonton**	**NHL**	**55**	**23**	**31**	**54**	**57**	**18**	**12**	**13**	**25**	**12**
1985-86	**Edmonton**	**NHL**	**63**	**35**	**49**	**84**	**68**	**10**	**4**	**6**	**10**	**18**
1986-87	**Edmonton**	**NHL**	**77**	**37**	**70**	**107**	**73**	**21**	**12**	**16**	**28**	**16**
1987-88	**Edmonton**	**NHL**	**77**	**37**	**74**	**111**	**103**	**19**	**11**	**23**	**34**	**29**
1988-89	**Edmonton**	**NHL**	**72**	**33**	**61**	**94**	**130**	**7**	**1**	**11**	**12**	**8**
1989-90ade	**Edmonton**	**NHL**	**79**	**45**	**84**	**129**	**79**	**22**	**9**	***22**	**31**	**20**
	NHL Totals		**798**	**380**	**590**	**970**	**1088**	**148**	**76**	**124**	**200**	**159**

a NHL First All-Star Team (1982, 1983, 1990)
b NHL Second All-Star Team (1984)
c Won Conn Smythe Trophy (1984)
d Won Hart Trophy (1990)
e Won Lester B. Pearson Award (1990)

Played in NHL All-Star Game (1982-86, 1988-90)

MESSIER, MITCH

Right wing. Shoots right. 6'2", 205 lbs. Born, Regina, Sask., August 21, 1965.
(Minnesota's 4th choice, 56th overall, in 1983 Entry Draft).

			Regular Season					Playoffs				
Season	Club	Lea	GP	G	A	TP	PIM	GP	G	A	TP	PIM
1983-84	Michigan State	CCHA	37	6	15	21	22	....	....	....	....	....
1984-85	Michigan State	CCHA	42	12	21	33	46	....	....	....	....	....
1985-86	Michigan State	CCHA	38	24	40	64	36	....	....	....	....	....
1986-87ab	Michigan State	CCHA	45	44	48	92	89	....	....	....	....	....
1987-88	**Minnesota**	**NHL**	**13**	**0**	**1**	**1**	**11**	....	....	....	....	....
	Kalamazoo	IHL	69	29	37	66	42	4	2	1	3	0
1988-89	**Minnesota**	**NHL**	**3**	**0**	**1**	**1**	**0**	....	....	....	....	....
	Kalamazoo	IHL	67	34	46	80	71	6	4	3	7	0
1989-90	**Minnesota**	**NHL**	**2**	**0**	**0**	**0**	**0**	....	....	....	....	....
	Kalamazoo	IHL	65	26	58	84	56	8	4	3	7	25
	NHL Totals		**18**	**0**	**2**	**2**	**11**	....	....	....	....	....

a CCHA First All-Star Team (1987)
b NCAA West First All-American Team (1987)

METCALFE, SCOTT

Left wing. Shoots left. 6', 200 lbs. Born, Toronto, Ont., January 6, 1967.
(Edmonton's 1st choice, 20th overall, in 1985 Entry Draft).

			Regular Season					Playoffs				
Season	Club	Lea	GP	G	A	TP	PIM	GP	G	A	TP	PIM
1983-84	Kingston	OHL	68	25	49	74	154	....	....	....	....	....
1984-85	Kingston	OHL	58	27	33	60	100	....	....	....	....	....
1985-86	Kingston	OHL	66	36	43	79	213	10	3	6	9	21
1986-87	Kingston	OHL	39	15	45	60	14	....	....	....	....	....
	Windsor	OHL	18	10	12	22	52	13	5	5	10	27
1987-88	**Edmonton**	**NHL**	**2**	**0**	**0**	**0**	**0**	....	....	....	....	....
	Nova Scotia	AHL	43	9	19	28	87	....	....	....	....	....
	Buffalo	**NHL**	**1**	**0**	**1**	**1**	**0**	....	....	....	....	....
	Rochester	AHL	22	2	13	15	56	7	1	3	4	24
1988-89	**Buffalo**	**NHL**	**9**	**1**	**1**	**2**	**13**	....	....	....	....	....
	Rochester	AHL	60	20	31	51	241	....	....	....	....	....
1989-90	**Buffalo**	**NHL**	**7**	**0**	**0**	**0**	**5**	....	....	....	....	....
	Rochester	AHL	43	12	17	29	93	2	0	1	1	0
	NHL Totals		**19**	**1**	**2**	**3**	**18**	....	....	....	....	....

Traded to **Buffalo** by **Edmonton** with Edmonton's ninth round choice (Donald Audette) in 1989 Entry Draft for Steve Dykstra and Buffalo's seventh round choice (David Payne) in 1989 Entry Draft, February 11, 1988.

MEWS, HAROLD RANDALL (HARRY)

Center. Shoots left. 5'10", 175 lbs. Born, Nepean, Ont., February 9, 1967.
(Washington's 1st choice, 20th overall, in 1988 Supplemental Draft).

			Regular Season					Playoffs				
Season	Club	Lea	GP	G	A	TP	PIM	GP	G	A	TP	PIM
1986-87	Northeastern	H.E.	29	10	15	25	70	....	....	....	....	....
1987-88	Northeastern	H.E.	37	16	23	39	82	....	....	....	....	....
1988-89a	Northeastern	H.E.	31	18	24	42	103	....	....	....	....	....
1989-90a	Northeastern	H.E.	36	20	*39	59	82	....	....	....	....	....

a Hockey East Second All-Star Team (1989, 1990)

MICHAYLUK, DAVID (DAVE) (muh-KIGH-luhk)

Right wing. Shoots left. 5'10", 180 lbs. Born, Wakaw, Sask., May 18, 1962.
(Philadelphia's 5th choice, 65th overall, in 1981 Entry Draft).

			Regular Season					Playoffs				
Season	Club	Lea	GP	G	A	TP	PIM	GP	G	A	TP	PIM
1980-81	Regina	WHL	72	62	71	133	39	11	5	12	17	8
1981-82	**Philadelphia**	**NHL**	**1**	**0**	**0**	**0**	**0**	....	....	....	....	....
a	Regina	WHL	72	62	111	172	128	12	16	24	*40	23
1982-83	**Philadelphia**	**NHL**	**13**	**2**	**6**	**8**	**8**	....	....	....	....	....
	Maine	AHL	69	32	40	72	16	8	0	2	2	0
1983-84	Springfield	AHL	79	18	44	62	37	4	0	0	0	2
1984-85	Hershey	AHL	3	0	2	2	2	....	....	....	....	....
b	Kalamazoo	IHL	82	*66	33	99	49	11	7	7	14	0
1985-86	Nova Scotia	AHL	3	0	1	1	0	....	....	....	....	....
	Muskegon	IHL	77	52	52	104	73	14	6	9	15	12
1986-87c	Muskegon	IHL	82	47	53	100	29	15	2	14	16	8
1987-88c	Muskegon	IHL	81	*56	81	137	46	6	2	0	2	18
1988-89cdef	Muskegon	IHL	80	50	72	*122	84	13	*9	12	*21	24
1989-90c	Muskegon	IHL	79	*51	51	102	80	15	8	*14	22	10
	NHL Totals		**14**	**2**	**6**	**8**	**8**	....	....	....	....	....

a WHL Second All-Star Team (1982)
b IHL Second All-Star Team (1985)
c IHL First All-Star Team (1987, 1988, 1989, 1990)
d IHL Playoff MVP (1989)
e Won James Gatschene Memorial Trophy (MVP-IHL) (1989)
f Won Leo P. Lamoureux Memorial Trophy (Top Scorer-IHL) (1989)

Signed as a free agent by **Pittsburgh**, May 24, 1989.

MICK, TROY

Left wing. Shoots left. 5'11", 180 lbs. Born, Burnaby, B.C., March 30, 1969.
(Pittsburgh's 6th choice, 130th overall, in 1988 Entry Draft).

			Regular Season					Playoffs				
Season	Club	Lea	GP	G	A	TP	PIM	GP	G	A	TP	PIM
1986-87	Portland	WHL	57	30	33	63	60	20	8	2	10	40
1987-88a	Portland	WHL	72	63	84	147	78	....	....	....	....	....
1988-89	Portland	WHL	66	49	*87	136	70	19	15	19	34	17
1989-90b	Regina	WHL	66	60	53	113	67	....	....	....	....	....

a WHL West All-Star Team (1988)
b WHL East First All-Star Team (1990)

MIDDENDORF, MAX

Right wing. Shoots right. 6'4", 210 lbs. Born, Syracuse, NY, August 18, 1967.
(Quebec's 3rd choice, 57th overall, in 1985 Entry Draft).

			Regular Season					Playoffs				
Season	Club	Lea	GP	G	A	TP	PIM	GP	G	A	TP	PIM
1984-85	Sudbury	OHL	63	16	28	44	106	....	....	....	....	....
1985-86	Sudbury	OHL	61	40	42	82	71	4	4	2	6	11
1986-87	**Quebec**	**NHL**	**6**	**1**	**4**	**5**	**4**	....	....	....	....	....
	Sudbury	OHL	31	31	29	60	7	....	....	....	....	....
	Kitchener	OHL	17	7	15	22	6	4	2	5	7	5
1987-88	**Quebec**	**NHL**	**1**	**0**	**0**	**0**	**0**	....	....	....	....	....
	Fredericton	AHL	38	11	13	24	57	12	4	4	8	18
1988-89	Halifax	AHL	72	41	39	80	85	4	1	2	3	6
1989-90	**Quebec**	**NHL**	**3**	**0**	**0**	**0**	**0**	....	....	....	....	....
	Halifax	AHL	48	20	17	37	60	....	....	....	....	....
	NHL Totals		**10**	**1**	**4**	**5**	**4**	....	....	....	....	....

MIEHM, KEVIN (MEE-yuhm)

Centre. Shoots left. 6'2", 190 lbs. Born, Kitchener, Ont., September 10, 1969.
(St. Louis' 2nd choice, 54th overall, in 1987 Entry Draft).

			Regular Season					Playoffs				
Season	Club	Lea	GP	G	A	TP	PIM	GP	G	A	TP	PIM
1986-87	Oshawa	OHL	61	12	27	39	19	26	1	8	9	12
1987-88	Oshawa	OHL	52	16	36	52	30	7	2	5	7	0
1988-89a	Oshawa	OHL	63	43	79	122	19	6	6	6	12	0
	Peoria	IHL	3	1	1	2	0	4	0	2	2	0
1989-90	Peoria	IHL	76	23	38	61	20	3	0	0	0	4

a OHL Third All-Star Team (1989)

MILLAR, MIKE (MILLER)

Right wing. Shoots left. 5'10", 170 lbs. Born, St. Catharines, Ont., April 28, 1965.
(Hartford's 2nd choice, 110th overall, in 1984 Entry Draft).

			Regular Season					Playoffs				
Season	Club	Lea	GP	G	A	TP	PIM	GP	G	A	TP	PIM
1982-83	Brantford	OHL	53	20	29	49	10	8	0	5	5	2
1983-84	Brantford	OHL	69	50	45	95	48	6	4	0	4	2
1984-85	Hamilton	OHL	63	*66	60	126	54	17	9	10	19	14
1985-86	Cdn. Olympic	...	69	50	38	88	74	....	....	....	....	....
1986-87	**Hartford**	**NHL**	**10**	**2**	**2**	**4**	**0**	....	....	....	....	....
	Binghamton	AHL	61	45	32	77	38	13	7	4	11	27
1987-88	**Hartford**	**NHL**	**28**	**7**	**7**	**14**	**6**	....	....	....	....	....
	Binghamton	AHL	31	32	17	49	42	....	....	....	....	....
1988-89	**Washington**	**NHL**	**18**	**6**	**3**	**9**	**4**	....	....	....	....	....
a	Baltimore	AHL	53	47	35	82	58	....	....	....	....	....
1989-90	**Boston**	**NHL**	**15**	**1**	**4**	**5**	**0**	....	....	....	....	....
	Maine	AHL	60	40	33	73	77	....	....	....	....	....
	NHL Totals		**71**	**16**	**16**	**32**	**10**	....	....	....	....	....

a AHL Second All-Star Team (1989)

Traded to **Washington** by **Hartford** with Neil Sheehy for Grant Jennings and Ed Kastelic, July 6, 1988. Traded to **Boston** by **Washington** for Alfie Turcotte, October 2, 1989. Signed as a free agent by **Toronto**, July 19, 1990.

MILLEN, COREY

Center. Shoots right. 5'7", 165 lbs. Born, Cloquet, MN, April 29, 1964.
(NY Rangers' 3rd choice, 57th overall, in 1982 Entry Draft).

			Regular Season					Playoffs				
Season	Club	Lea	GP	G	A	TP	PIM	GP	G	A	TP	PIM
1982-83	U. Minnesota	WCHA	21	14	15	29	18	....	....	....	....	....
1983-84	U.S. Olympic	...	45	15	11	26	10	....	....	....	....	....
1984-85	U. Minnesota	WCHA	38	28	36	64	60	....	....	....	....	....
1985-86ab	U. Minnesota	WCHA	48	41	42	83	64	....	....	....	....	....
1986-87bc	U. Minnesota	WCHA	42	36	29	65	62	....	....	....	....	....
1987-88	U.S. National	....	47	41	43	84	26	....	....	....	....	....
	U.S. Olympic	....	6	6	5	11	4	....	....	....	....	....
1988-89	Ambri	Switz.	36	32	29	61	....	6	4	3	7	....
1989-90	**NY Rangers**	**NHL**	**4**	**0**	**0**	**0**	**2**	....	....	....	....	....
	NHL Totals		**4**	**0**	**0**	**0**	**2**	....	....	....	....	....

a NCAA West Second All-American Team (1986)
b WCHA Second All-Star Team (1986, 1987)
c Named to NCAA All-Tournament Team (1987)

MILLER, AARON

Defense. Shoots right. 6'3", 175 lbs. Born, Buffalo, NY, August 11, 1971.
(NY Rangers' 6th choice, 88th overall, in 1989 Entry Draft).

			Regular Season					Playoffs				
Season	Club	Lea	GP	G	A	TP	PIM	GP	G	A	TP	PIM
1988-89	Niagara	Jr.A	59	24	38	62	60	....	....	....	....	....
1989-90	U. of Vermont	ECAC	31	1	15	16	24	....	....	....	....	....

MILLER, BRAD

Defense. Shoots left. 6'4", 220 lbs. Born, Edmonton, Alta., July 23, 1969.
(Buffalo's 2nd choice, 22nd overall, in 1987 Entry Draft).

			Regular Season					Playoffs				
Season	Club	Lea	GP	G	A	TP	PIM	GP	G	A	TP	PIM
1985-86	Regina	WHL	71	2	14	16	99	10	1	1	2	4
1986-87	Regina	WHL	67	10	38	48	154	3	0	0	0	6
1987-88	Rochester	AHL	3	0	0	0	4	2	0	0	0	2
	Regina	WHL	61	9	34	43	148	4	1	1	2	12
1988-89	**Buffalo**	**NHL**	**7**	**0**	**0**	**0**	**6**	....	....	....	....	....
	Regina	WHL	34	8	18	26	95	....	....	....	....	....
	Rochester	AHL	3	0	0	0	4	....	....	....	....	....
1989-90	**Buffalo**	**NHL**	**1**	**0**	**0**	**0**	**0**	....	....	....	....	....
	Rochester	AHL	60	2	10	12	273	8	1	0	1	52
	NHL Totals		**8**	**0**	**0**	**0**	**6**	....	....	....	....	....

MILLER, JASON

Center. Shoots left. 6'1", 180 lbs. Born, Edmonton, Alta., March 1, 1971.
(New Jersey's 2nd choice, 18th overall, in 1989 Entry Draft).

			Regular Season					Playoffs				
Season	Club	Lea	GP	G	A	TP	PIM	GP	G	A	TP	PIM
1987-88	Medicine Hat	WHL	71	11	18	29	28	15	0	1	1	2
1988-89	Medicine Hat	WHL	72	51	55	106	44	3	1	2	3	2
1989-90	Medicine Hat	WHL	66	43	56	99	40	3	3	2	5	0

MILLER, JAY

Left wing. Shoots left. 6'2", 210 lbs. Born, Wellesley, MA, July 16, 1960.
(Quebec's 2nd choice, 66th overall, in 1980 Entry Draft).

			Regular Season					Playoffs				
Season	Club	Lea	GP	G	A	TP	PIM	GP	G	A	TP	PIM
1981-82	N. Hampshire	ECAC	24	6	4	10	34	....	....	....	....	....
1982-83	N. Hampshire	ECAC	28	6	4	10	28	....	....	....	....	....
1983-84	Toledo	IHL	2	0	0	0	2	....	....	....	....	....
	Maine	AHL	15	1	1	2	27	....	....	....	....	....
1984-85	Muskegon	IHL	56	5	29	34	177	17	1	1	2	56
1985-86	Moncton	AHL	18	4	6	10	113	....	....	....	....	....
	Boston	**NHL**	**46**	**3**	**0**	**3**	**178**	**2**	**0**	**0**	**0**	**17**
1986-87	**Boston**	**NHL**	**55**	**1**	**4**	**5**	**208**	....	....	....	....	....
1987-88	**Boston**	**NHL**	**78**	**7**	**12**	**19**	**304**	**12**	**0**	**0**	**0**	**124**
1988-89	**Boston**	**NHL**	**37**	**2**	**4**	**6**	**168**	....	....	....	....	....
	Los Angeles	**NHL**	**29**	**5**	**3**	**8**	**133**	**11**	**0**	**1**	**1**	**63**
1989-90	**Los Angeles**	**NHL**	**68**	**10**	**2**	**12**	**224**	**10**	**1**	**1**	**2**	**10**
	NHL Totals		**313**	**28**	**25**	**53**	**1215**	**35**	**1**	**2**	**3**	**214**

Signed as a free agent by **Boston**, October 1, 1985. Traded to **Los Angeles** by **Boston** for future considerations, January 22, 1989.

MILLER, KEITH

Left wing. Shoots left. 6'2", 215 lbs. Born, Toronto, Ont., March 18, 1967.
(Quebec's 10th choice, 165th overall, in 1986 Entry Draft).

			Regular Season					Playoffs				
Season	Club	Lea	GP	G	A	TP	PIM	GP	G	A	TP	PIM
1985-86	Guelph	OHL	61	32	17	49	30	20	8	16	24	6
1986-87	Guelph	OHL	66	50	31	81	44	5	6	2	8	0
1987-88	Baltimore	AHL	21	6	5	11	12	....	....	....	....	....
1988-89	Halifax	AHL	12	6	3	9	6	....	....	....	....	....
	Fort Wayne	IHL	54	35	25	60	13	10	4	3	7	9
1989-90	Fort Wayne	IHL	51	26	19	45	10	....	....	....	....	....

MILLER, KELLY

Right wing. Shoots left. 5'11", 195 lbs. Born, Lansing, MI, March 3, 1963.
(NY Rangers' 9th choice, 183rd overall, in 1982 Entry Draft).

			Regular Season					Playoffs				
Season	Club	Lea	GP	G	A	TP	PIM	GP	G	A	TP	PIM
1981-82	Michigan State	CCHA	38	11	18	29	17	....	....	....	....	....
1982-83	Michigan State	CCHA	36	16	19	35	12	....	....	....	....	....
1983-84	Michigan State	CCHA	46	28	21	49	12	....	....	....	....	....
1984-85ab	Michigan State	CCHA	43	27	23	50	21	....	....	....	....	....
	NY Rangers	**NHL**	**5**	**0**	**2**	**2**	**2**	**3**	**0**	**0**	**0**	**2**
1985-86	**NY Rangers**	**NHL**	**74**	**13**	**20**	**33**	**52**	**16**	**3**	**4**	**7**	**4**
1986-87	**NY Rangers**	**NHL**	**38**	**6**	**14**	**20**	**22**	....	....	....	....	....
	Washington	**NHL**	**39**	**10**	**12**	**22**	**26**	**7**	**2**	**2**	**4**	**0**
1987-88	**Washington**	**NHL**	**80**	**9**	**23**	**32**	**35**	**14**	**4**	**4**	**8**	**10**
1988-89	**Washington**	**NHL**	**78**	**19**	**21**	**40**	**45**	**6**	**1**	**0**	**1**	**2**
1989-90	**Washington**	**NHL**	**80**	**18**	**22**	**40**	**49**	**15**	**3**	**5**	**8**	**23**
	NHL Totals		**394**	**75**	**114**	**189**	**231**	**61**	**13**	**15**	**28**	**41**

a CCHA First All-Star Team (1985)
b Named to NCAA All-American Team (1985)

Traded to **Washington** by **NY Rangers** with Bob Crawford and Mike Ridley for Bob Carpenter and, Washington's second-round choice (Jason Prosofsky) in 1989 Entry Draft, January 1, 1987.

MILLER, KEVIN

Center. Shoots right. 5'9", 170 lbs. Born, Lansing, MI, August 9, 1965.
(NY Rangers' 10th choice, 202nd overall, in 1984 Entry Draft).

			Regular Season					Playoffs				
Season	Club	Lea	GP	G	A	TP	PIM	GP	G	A	TP	PIM
1984-85	Michigan State	CCHA	44	11	29	40	84	....	....	....	....	....
1985-86	Michigan State	CCHA	45	19	52	71	112	....	....	....	....	....
1986-87	Michigan State	CCHA	42	25	56	81	63	....	....	....	....	....
1987-88	U.S. National	....	48	31	32	63	33	....	....	....	....	....
	U.S. Olympic		5	1	3	4	4	....	....	....	....	....
	Michigan State	CCHA	9	6	3	9	18	....	....	....	....	....
1988-89	**NY Rangers**	**NHL**	**24**	**3**	**5**	**8**	**2**	....	....	....	....	....
	Denver	IHL	55	29	47	76	19	4	2	1	3	2
1989-90	**NY Rangers**	**NHL**	**16**	**0**	**5**	**5**	**2**	....	....	....	....	....
	Flint	IHL	48	19	23	42	41	....	....	....	....	....
	NHL Totals		**40**	**3**	**10**	**13**	**4**	....	....	....	....	....

MILLER, KIP

Center. Shoots left. 5'10", 160 lbs. Born, Lansing, MI, June 11, 1969.
(Quebec's 4th choice, 72nd overall, in 1987 Entry Draft).

			Regular Season					Playoffs				
Season	Club	Lea	GP	G	A	TP	PIM	GP	G	A	TP	PIM
1986-87	Michigan State	CCHA	41	20	19	39	92	....	....	....	....	....
1987-88	Michigan State	CCHA	39	16	25	41	51	....	....	....	....	....
1988-89ab	Michigan State	CCHA	47	32	45	77	94	....	....	....	....	....
1989-90abcd	Michigan State	CCHA	45	48	*53	*101	60	....	....	....	....	....

a CCHA First All-Star Team (1989, 1990)
b NCAA West First All-American Team (1989, 1990)
c CCHA Player of the Year (1990)
d Won Hobey Baker Memorial Award (Top U.S. Collegiate Player) (1990)

MILLER, KRIS

Defense. Shoots left. 6', 185 lbs. Born, Bemidji, MN, March 30, 1969.
(Montreal's 6th choice, 80th overall, in 1987 Entry Draft).

			Regular Season					Playoffs				
Season	Club	Lea	GP	G	A	TP	PIM	GP	G	A	TP	PIM
1987-88	Minn.-Duluth	WCHA	32	1	6	7	30	....	....	....	....	....
1988-89	Minn.-Duluth	WCHA	39	2	10	12	37	....	....	....	....	....
1989-90	Minn.-Duluth	WCHA	39	2	11	13	59	....	....	....	....	....

MINER, JOHN

Defense. Shoots right. 5'10", 180 lbs. Born, Moose Jaw, Sask., August 28, 1965.
(Edmonton's 10th choice, 229th overall, in 1983 Entry Draft).

			Regular Season					Playoffs				
Season	Club	Lea	GP	G	A	TP	PIM	GP	G	A	TP	PIM
1982-83	Regina	WHL	71	11	23	34	126	5	1	1	2	20
1983-84	Regina	WHL	70	27	42	69	132	23	9	25	34	54
1984-85	Regina	WHL	66	30	54	84	128	8	4	10	14	12
1985-86	Nova Scotia	AHL	79	10	33	43	90	....	....	....	....	....
1986-87	Nova Scotia	AHL	45	5	28	33	38	5	0	3	3	4
1987-88	**Edmonton**	**NHL**	**14**	**2**	**3**	**5**	**16**	....	....	....	....	....
	Nova Scotia	AHL	61	8	26	34	61	....	....	....	....	....
1988-89	New Haven	AHL	7	2	3	5	4	17	3	12	15	40
1989-90	Lausanne	Switz.	36	10	32	51	....	....	....	....	....	....
	New Haven	AHL	7	1	6	7	2	....	....	....	....	....
	NHL Totals		**14**	**2**	**3**	**5**	**16**	....	....	....	....	....

Traded to **Los Angeles** by **Edmonton** for Craig Redmond, August 10, 1988

MITCHELL, ROY

Defense. Shoots right. 6'1", 200 lbs. Born, Edmonton, Alta., March 14, 1969.
(Montreal's 9th choice, 188th overall, in 1989 Entry Draft).

			Regular Season					Playoffs				
Season	Club	Lea	GP	G	A	TP	PIM	GP	G	A	TP	PIM
1986-87	Portland	WHL	68	7	32	39	103	20	0	3	3	23
1987-88	Portland	WHL	72	5	42	47	219	....	....	....	....	....
1988-89	Portland	WHL	72	9	34	43	177	19	1	8	9	38
1989-90	Sherbrooke	AHL	77	5	12	17	98	12	0	2	2	31

MITROVIC, SAVO

Right wing. Shoots right. 5'11", 190 lbs. Born, Toronto, Ont., April 2, 1969.
(Pittsburgh's 2nd choice, 10th overall, in 1990 Supplemental Draft).

			Regular Season					Playoffs				
Season	Club	Lea	GP	G	A	TP	PIM	GP	G	A	TP	PIM
1988-89	N. Hampshire	H.E.	34	2	8	10	22	....	....	....	....	....
1989-90	N. Hampshire	H.E.	37	30	21	51	40	....	....	....	....	....

MODANO, MICHAEL (MIKE)

Center. Shoots left. 6'3", 190 lbs. Born, Detroit, MI, June 7, 1970.
(Minnesota's 1st choice, 1st overall, in 1988 Entry Draft).

			Regular Season					Playoffs				
Season	Club	Lea	GP	G	A	TP	PIM	GP	G	A	TP	PIM
1986-87	Prince Albert	WHL	70	32	30	62	96	8	1	4	5	4
1987-88	Prince Albert	WHL	65	47	80	127	80	9	7	11	18	18
1988-89a	Prince Albert	WHL	41	39	66	105	74	....	....	....	....	....
	Minnesota	**NHL**	....	....	....	....	....	**2**	**0**	**0**	**0**	**0**
1989-90b	**Minnesota**	**NHL**	**80**	**29**	**46**	**75**	**63**	**7**	**1**	**1**	**2**	**12**
	NHL Totals		**80**	**29**	**46**	**75**	**63**	**9**	**1**	**1**	**2**	**12**

a WHL East All-Star Team (1989)
b NHL All-Rookie Team (1990)

MODRY, JAROSLAV

Defense. Shoots left. 6'2", 195 lbs. Born, Budejovice, Czechoslovakia, February 27, 1971.
(New Jersey's 11th choice, 179th overall, in 1990 Entry Draft).

			Regular Season					Playoffs				
Season	Club	Lea	GP	G	A	TP	PIM	GP	G	A	TP	PIM
1988-89	Budejovice	Czech.	28	0	1	1	....	....	....	....	....	....
1989-90	Budejovice	Czech.	41	2	2	4	....	....	....	....	....	....

MOES, MICHAEL

Center. Shoots left. 5'11", 185 lbs. Born, Burlington, Ont., March 30, 1967.
(Toronto's 2nd choice, 6th overall, in 1989 Supplemental Draft).

			Regular Season					Playoffs				
Season	Club	Lea	GP	G	A	TP	PIM	GP	G	A	TP	PIM
1986-87	U. of Michigan	CCHA	39	11	15	26	16	....	....	....	....	....
1987-88	U. of Michigan	CCHA	40	5	27	32	23	....	....	....	....	....
1988-89	U. of Michigan	CCHA	41	14	24	38	22	....	....	....	....	....
1989-90	U. of Michigan	CCHA	42	19	29	48	10	....	....	....	....	....
	Newmarket	AHL	8	2	1	3	2	....	....	....	....	....

MOGER, SANDY

Right wing. Shoots right. 6'2", 190 lbs. Born, 100 Mile House, B.C., March 21, 1969.
(Vancouver's 7th choice, 176th overall, in 1989 Entry Draft).

			Regular Season					Playoffs				
Season	Club	Lea	GP	G	A	TP	PIM	GP	G	A	TP	PIM
1988-89	Lake Superior	CCHA	21	3	5	8	26	....	....	....	....	....
1989-90	Lake Superior	CCHA	46	17	15	32	76	....	....	....	....	....

MOGILNY, ALEXANDER (moh-GIHL-nee)

Left wing. Shoots left. 5'11", 195 lbs. Born, Khabarousk, Soviet Union, February 18, 1969.
(Buffalo's 4th choice, 89th overall, in 1988 Entry Draft).

			Regular Season					Playoffs				
Season	Club	Lea	GP	G	A	TP	PIM	GP	G	A	TP	PIM
1986-87	CSKA	USSR	28	15	1	16	4	....	....	....	....	....
1987-88	CSKA	USSR	29	12	8	20	14	....	....	....	....	....
1988-89	CSKA	USSR	31	11	11	22	24	....	....	....	....	....
1989-90	**Buffalo**	**NHL**	**65**	**15**	**28**	**43**	**16**	**4**	**0**	**1**	**1**	**2**
	NHL Totals		**65**	**15**	**28**	**43**	**16**	**4**	**0**	**1**	**1**	**2**

MOKOSAK, CARL (MOH-ka-sak)

Left wing. Shoots left. 6'1", 180 lbs. Born, Fort Saskatchewan, Alta., September 22, 1962.

			Regular Season					Playoffs				
Season	Club	Lea	GP	G	A	TP	PIM	GP	G	A	TP	PIM
1979-80	Brandon	WHL	61	12	21	33	226	11	0	4	4	66
1980-81	Brandon	WHL	70	28	44	72	363	5	1	3	4	12
1981-82	**Calgary**	**NHL**	**1**	**0**	**1**	**1**	**0**	....	....	....	....	....
	Brandon	WHL	69	46	61	107	363	4	0	1	1	11
	Oklahoma City	CHL	2	1	1	2	2	4	1	1	2	0
1982-83	**Calgary**	**NHL**	**41**	**7**	**6**	**13**	**87**	....	....	....	....	....
	Colorado	CHL	28	10	12	22	106	5	1	0	1	12
1983-84	New Haven	AHL	80	18	21	39	206	....	....	....	....	....
1984-85	**Los Angeles**	**NHL**	**30**	**4**	**8**	**12**	**43**	....	....	....	....	....
	New Haven	AHL	11	6	6	12	26	....	....	....	....	....
1985-86	**Philadelphia**	**NHL**	**1**	**0**	**0**	**0**	**5**	....	....	....	....	....
	Hershey	AHL	79	30	42	72	312	16	0	4	4	111
1986-87	**Pittsburgh**	**NHL**	**3**	**0**	**0**	**0**	**4**	....	....	....	....	....
	Baltimore	AHL	67	23	27	50	228	....	....	....	....	....
1987-88	Muskegon	IHL	81	29	37	66	308	6	3	2	5	60
1988-89	**Boston**	**NHL**	**7**	**0**	**0**	**0**	**31**	**1**	**0**	**0**	**0**	**0**
	Maine	AHL	53	20	18	38	337	....	....	....	....	....
1989-90	Fort Wayne	IHL	55	12	21	33	315	....	....	....	....	....
	Phoenix	IHL	15	6	6	12	48	....	....	....	....	....
	NHL Totals		**83**	**11**	**15**	**26**	**170**	**1**	**0**	**0**	**0**	**0**

Signed as free agent by **Calgary**, July 21, 1981. Traded to **Los Angeles** by **Calgary** with Kevin LaVallee for Steve Bozek, June 20, 1983. Signed as a free agent by **Philadelphia**, July 23, 1985. Signed as a free agent by **Pittsburgh**, July 23, 1986.

MOKOSAK, JOHN (MOH-ka-sak)

Defense. Shoots left. 5'11", 200 lbs. Born, Edmonton, Alta., September 7, 1963.
(Hartford's 6th choice, 130th overall, in 1981 Entry Draft).

			Regular Season					Playoffs				
Season	Club	Lea	GP	G	A	TP	PIM	GP	G	A	TP	PIM
1980-81	Victoria	WHL	71	2	18	20	59	15	0	3	3	53
1981-82	Victoria	WHL	69	6	45	51	102	4	1	1	2	0
1982-83	Victoria	WHL	70	10	33	43	102	12	0	0	0	8
1983-84	Binghamton	AHL	79	3	21	24	80	....	....	....	....	....
1984-85	Binghamton	AHL	54	1	13	14	109	7	0	0	0	12
	Salt Lake	IHL	22	1	10	11	41	....	....	....	....	....
1985-86	Binghamton	AHL	64	0	9	9	196	6	0	0	0	6
1986-87	Binghamton	AHL	72	2	15	17	187	9	0	2	2	42
1987-88	Springfield	AHL	77	1	16	17	178	....	....	....	....	....
1988-89	**Detroit**	**NHL**	**8**	**0**	**1**	**1**	**14**	....	....	....	....	....
	Adirondack	AHL	65	4	31	35	195	17	0	5	5	49
1989-90	**Detroit**	**NHL**	**33**	**0**	**1**	**1**	**82**	....	....	....	....	....
	Adirondack	AHL	29	2	6	8	80	6	1	3	4	13
	NHL Totals		**41**	**0**	**2**	**2**	**96**	....	....	....	....	....

Signed as a free agent by **Detroit**, August 29, 1988.

MOLLER, MICHAEL JOHN (MIKE) (MOH-luhr)

Right wing. Shoots right. 6', 194 lbs. Born, Calgary, Alta., June 16, 1962.
(Buffalo's 2nd choice, 41st overall, in 1980 Entry Draft).

			Regular Season					Playoffs				
Season	Club	Lea	GP	G	A	TP	PIM	GP	G	A	TP	PIM
1979-80	Lethbridge	WHL	72	30	41	71	55	4	0	6	6	0
1980-81a	Lethbridge	WHL	70	39	69	108	71	9	6	10	16	12
	Buffalo	**NHL**	**5**	**2**	**2**	**4**	**0**	**3**	**0**	**1**	**1**	**0**
1981-82	**Buffalo**	**NHL**	**9**	**0**	**0**	**0**	**0**	....	....	....	....	....
a	Lethbridge	WHL	49	41	81	122	38	12	5	12	17	9
1982-83	**Buffalo**	**NHL**	**49**	**6**	**12**	**18**	**14**	....	....	....	....	....
	Rochester	AHL	10	1	6	7	2	11	2	4	6	4
1983-84	**Buffalo**	**NHL**	**59**	**5**	**11**	**16**	**27**	....	....	....	....	....
1984-85	**Buffalo**	**NHL**	**5**	**0**	**2**	**2**	**0**	....	....	....	....	....
	Rochester	AHL	73	19	46	65	27	5	1	1	2	0
1985-86	**Edmonton**	**NHL**	**1**	**0**	**0**	**0**	**0**	....	....	....	....	....
	Nova Scotia	AHL	62	16	15	31	24	....	....	....	....	....
1986-87	**Edmonton**	**NHL**	**6**	**2**	**1**	**3**	**0**	....	....	....	....	....
	Nova Scotia	AHL	70	14	33	47	28	1	0	0	0	0
1987-88	Nova Scotia	AHL	60	12	31	43	14	5	3	0	3	0
1988-89	Cdn. National	....	58	18	16	34	18	....	....	....	....	....
1989-90	Binghamton	AHL	12	1	2	3	6	....	....	....	....	....
	NHL Totals		**134**	**15**	**28**	**43**	**41**	**3**	**0**	**1**	**1**	**0**

a WHL First All-Star Team (1981, 1982)

Traded to **Pittsburgh** by **Buffalo** with Randy Cunneyworth for Pat Hughes, October 4, 1985. Traded to **Edmonton** by **Pittsburgh** for Pat Hughes, October 4, 1985.

MOLLER, RANDY

Defense. Shoots right. 6'2", 207 lbs. Born, Red Deer, Alta., August 23, 1963.
(Quebec's 1st choice, 11th overall, in 1981 Entry Draft).

			Regular Season					Playoffs				
Season	Club	Lea	GP	G	A	TP	PIM	GP	G	A	TP	PIM
1980-81	Lethbridge	WHL	46	4	21	25	176	9	0	4	4	24
1981-82	**Quebec**	**NHL**	....	....	....	....	....	**1**	**0**	**0**	**0**	**0**
a	Lethbridge	WHL	60	20	55	75	249	12	4	6	10	65
1982-83	**Quebec**	**NHL**	**75**	**2**	**12**	**14**	**145**	**4**	**1**	**0**	**1**	**4**
1983-84	**Quebec**	**NHL**	**74**	**4**	**14**	**18**	**147**	**9**	**1**	**0**	**1**	**45**
1984-85	**Quebec**	**NHL**	**79**	**7**	**22**	**29**	**120**	**18**	**2**	**2**	**4**	**40**
1985-86	**Quebec**	**NHL**	**69**	**5**	**18**	**23**	**141**	**3**	**0**	**0**	**0**	**26**
1986-87	**Quebec**	**NHL**	**71**	**5**	**9**	**14**	**144**	**13**	**1**	**4**	**5**	**23**
1987-88	**Quebec**	**NHL**	**66**	**3**	**22**	**25**	**169**	....	....	....	....	....
1988-89	**Quebec**	**NHL**	**74**	**7**	**22**	**29**	**136**	....	....	....	....	....
1989-90	**NY Rangers**	**NHL**	**60**	**1**	**12**	**13**	**139**	**10**	**1**	**6**	**7**	**32**
	NHL Totals		**568**	**34**	**131**	**165**	**1141**	**58**	**6**	**12**	**18**	**170**

a WHL Second All-Star Team (1982)

Traded to **NY Rangers** by **Quebec** for Michel Petit, October 5, 1989.

MOLLOY, MITCHELL DENNIS (MITCH)

Left wing. Shoots left. 6'3", 210 lbs. Born, Red Lake, Ont., October 10, 1966.

			Regular Season					Playoffs				
Season	Club	Lea	GP	G	A	TP	PIM	GP	G	A	TP	PIM
1988-89	Maine	AHL	47	1	8	9	177	....	....	....	....	....
1989-90	**Buffalo**	**NHL**	**2**	**0**	**0**	**0**	**10**	....	....	....	....	....
	Rochester	AHL	15	1	1	2	43	....	....	....	....	....
	Johnstown	ECHL	18	10	10	20	102	....	....	....	....	....
	NHL Totals		**2**	**0**	**0**	**0**	**10**	....	....	....	....	....

Signed as a free agent by **Buffalo**, February, 1990.

MOMESSO, SERGIO

Left wing. Shoots left. 6'3", 200 lbs. Born, Montreal, Que., September 4, 1965.
(Montreal's 3rd choice, 27th overall, in 1983 Entry Draft).

			Regular Season					Playoffs				
Season	Club	Lea	GP	G	A	TP	PIM	GP	G	A	TP	PIM
1982-83	Shawinigan	QMJHL	70	27	42	69	93	10	5	4	9	55
1983-84	**Montreal**	**NHL**	**1**	**0**	**0**	**0**	**0**	....	....	....	....	....
	Shawinigan	QMJHL	68	42	88	130	235	6	4	4	8	13
	Nova Scotia	AHL	....	....	....	....	....	8	0	2	2	4
1984-85a	Shawinigan	QMJHL	64	56	90	146	216	8	7	8	15	17
1985-86	**Montreal**	**NHL**	**24**	**8**	**7**	**15**	**46**	....	....	....	....	....
1986-87	**Montreal**	**NHL**	**59**	**14**	**17**	**31**	**96**	**11**	**1**	**3**	**4**	**31**
	Sherbrooke	AHL	6	1	6	7	10	....	....	....	....	....
1987-88	**Montreal**	**NHL**	**53**	**7**	**14**	**21**	**101**	**6**	**0**	**2**	**2**	**16**
1988-89	**St. Louis**	**NHL**	**53**	**9**	**17**	**26**	**139**	**10**	**2**	**5**	**7**	**24**
1989-90	**St. Louis**	**NHL**	**79**	**24**	**32**	**56**	**199**	**12**	**3**	**2**	**5**	**63**
	NHL Totals		**269**	**62**	**87**	**149**	**581**	**39**	**6**	**12**	**18**	**134**

a QMJHL First All-Star Team (1985)

Traded to **St. Louis** by **Montreal** with Vincent Riendeau for Jocelyn Lemieux, Darrell May and St. Louis' second round choice (Patrice Brisebois) in the 1989 Entry Draft, August 9, 1988.

MONGEAU, MICHEL

Center. Shoots left. 5'9", 180 lbs. Born, Montreal, Que., February 9, 1965.

			Regular Season					Playoffs				
Season	Club	Lea	GP	G	A	TP	PIM	GP	G	A	TP	PIM
1986-87	Saginaw	IHL	76	42	53	95	34	10	3	6	9	6
1987-88	France	....	30	31	21	52	....	....	....	....	....	....
1988-89	Flint	IHL	82	41	76	117	57	....	....	....	....	....
1989-90	**St. Louis**	**NHL**	**7**	**1**	**5**	**6**	**2**	**2**	**0**	**1**	**1**	**0**
abc	Peoria	IHL	73	39	*78	*117	53	5	3	4	7	6
	NHL Totals		**7**	**1**	**5**	**6**	**2**	**2**	**0**	**1**	**1**	**0**

a IHL First All-Star Team (1990)
b Won James Gatschene Memorial Trophy (MVP-IHL) (1990)
c Won Leo P. Lamoureux Memorial Trophy (Top Scorer-IHL) (1990)

Signed as a free agent by **St. Louis**, August 21, 1989.

MONTANARI, MARK

Center. Shoots left. 5'9", 185 lbs. Born, Toronto, Ont., June 3, 1969.
(Boston's 5th choice, 101st overall, in 1989 Entry Draft).

			Regular Season					Playoffs				
Season	Club	Lea	GP	G	A	TP	PIM	GP	G	A	TP	PIM
1987-88	Kitchener	OHL	63	25	31	56	146	4	1	1	2	10
1988-89	Kitchener	OHL	64	33	69	102	172	5	2	2	4	13
1989-90	Kitchener	OHL	33	15	36	51	71	16	9	16	25	54

MORE, JAYSON

Defense. Shoots right. 6'1", 190 lbs. Born, Souris, Man., January 12, 1969.
(NY Rangers' 1st choice, 10th overall, in 1987 Entry Draft).

			Regular Season					Playoffs				
Season	Club	Lea	GP	G	A	TP	PIM	GP	G	A	TP	PIM
1984-85	Lethbridge	WHL	71	3	9	12	101	4	1	0	1	7
1985-86	Lethbridge	WHL	61	7	18	25	155	9	0	2	2	36
1986-87	Brandon	WHL	21	4	6	10	62	....	....	....	....	....
	N. Westminster	WHL	43	4	23	27	155	....	....	....	....	....
1987-88a	N. Westminster	WHL	70	13	47	60	270	5	0	2	2	26
1988-89	**NY Rangers**	**NHL**	**1**	**0**	**0**	**0**	**0**	....	....	....	....	....
	Denver	IHL	62	7	15	22	138	3	0	1	1	26
1989-90	Flint	IHL	9	1	5	6	41	....	....	....	....	....
	Minnesota	**NHL**	**5**	**0**	**0**	**0**	**16**	....	....	....	....	....
	Kalamazoo	IHL	64	9	25	34	316	10	0	3	3	13
	NHL Totals		**6**	**0**	**0**	**0**	**16**	....	....	....	....	....

a WHL All-Star Team (1988)

Traded to **Minnesota** by **NY Rangers** for Dave Archibald, November 1, 1989.

MORIN, STEPHANE (mohr-AY)

Center. Shoots left. 6', 175 lbs. Born, Montreal, Que., March 27, 1969.
(Quebec's 3rd choice, 43rd overall, in 1989 Entry Draft).

			Regular Season					Playoffs				
Season	Club	Lea	GP	G	A	TP	PIM	GP	G	A	TP	PIM
1987-88	Chicoutimi	QMJHL	68	38	45	83	18	6	3	8	11	2
1988-89ab	Chicoutimi	QMJHL	70	77	*109	*186	71	....	....	....	....	....
1989-90	**Quebec**	**NHL**	**6**	**0**	**2**	**2**	**2**	....	....	....	....	....
	Halifax	AHL	65	28	32	60	60	6	3	4	7	6
	NHL Totals		**6**	**0**	**2**	**2**	**2**	....	....	....	....	....

a QMJHL First All-Star Team (1989)
b QMJHL Player of the Year (1989)

MORRIS, JON

Center. Shoots right. 6', 175 lbs. Born, Lowell, MA, May 6, 1966.
(New Jersey's 5th choice, 86th overall, in 1984 Entry Draft).

			Regular Season					Playoffs				
Season	Club	Lea	GP	G	A	TP	PIM	GP	G	A	TP	PIM
1984-85	Lowell	H.E.	42	29	31	60	16	....	....	....	....	....
1985-86	Lowell	H.E.	39	25	31	56	52	....	....	....	....	....
1986-87ab	Lowell	H.E.	35	28	33	61	48	....	....	....	....	....
1987-88	Lowell	H.E.	37	15	39	54	39	....	....	....	....	....
1988-89	**New Jersey**	**NHL**	**4**	**0**	**2**	**2**	**0**	....	....	....	....	....
1989-90	**New Jersey**	**NHL**	**20**	**6**	**7**	**13**	**8**	**6**	**1**	**3**	**4**	**23**
	Utica	AHL	49	27	37	64	6	....	....	....	....	....
	NHL Totals		**24**	**6**	**9**	**15**	**8**	**6**	**1**	**3**	**4**	**23**

a Hockey East First All-Star Team (1987)
b NCAA East Second All-American Team (1987)

MORROW, SCOTT

Left wing. Shoots left. 6'1", 180 lbs. Born, Chicago, IL, June 18, 1969.
(Hartford's 4th choice, 95th overall, in 1988 Entry Draft).

			Regular Season					Playoffs				
Season	Club	Lea	GP	G	A	TP	PIM	GP	G	A	TP	PIM
1988-89	N. Hampshire	H.E.	19	6	7	13	14	....	....	....	....	....
1989-90	N. Hampshire	H.E.	29	10	11	21	35	....	....	....	....	....

MORROW, STEVEN

Defense. Shoots left. 6'2", 210 lbs. Born, Plano, TX, April 3, 1968.
(Philadelphia's 10th choice, 209th overall, in 1987 Entry Draft).

			Regular Season					Playoffs				
Season	Club	Lea	GP	G	A	TP	PIM	GP	G	A	TP	PIM
1988-89	N. Hampshire	H.E.	30	0	0	0	28	....	....	....	....	....
1989-90	N. Hampshire	H.E.	35	2	7	9	40	....	....	....	....	....

MORTON, DEAN

Defense. Shoots right. 6'1", 195 lbs. Born, Peterborough, Ont., February 27, 1968.
(Detroit's 8th choice, 148th overall, in 1986 Entry Draft).

			Regular Season					Playoffs				
Season	Club	Lea	GP	G	A	TP	PIM	GP	G	A	TP	PIM
1985-86	Oshawa	OHL	63	5	6	11	117	5	0	0	0	9
1986-87	Oshawa	OHL	62	1	11	12	165	23	3	6	9	112
1987-88	Oshawa	OHL	57	6	19	25	187	7	0	0	0	18
1988-89	Adirondack	AHL	66	2	15	17	186	8	0	1	1	13
1989-90	**Detroit**	**NHL**	**1**	**1**	**0**	**1**	**2**	....	....	....	....	....
	Adirondack	AHL	75	1	15	16	183	6	0	0	0	30
	NHL Totals		**1**	**1**	**0**	**1**	**2**	....	....	....	....	....

MOYLAN, DAVE

Defense. Shoots left. 6'1", 195 lbs. Born, Tillsonburg, Ont., August 13, 1967.
(Buffalo's 4th choice, 77th overall, in 1985 Entry Draft).

			Regular Season					Playoffs				
Season	Club	Lea	GP	G	A	TP	PIM	GP	G	A	TP	PIM
1984-85	Sudbury	OHL	66	1	15	16	108	....	....	....	....	....
1985-86	Sudbury	OHL	52	10	25	35	87	4	0	0	0	15
1986-87	Sudbury	OHL	13	5	6	11	41	....	....	....	....	....
	Kitchener	OHL	38	1	7	8	57	3	2	0	2	11
1987-88	Baltimore	AHL	20	4	5	9	35	....	....	....	....	....
	Rochester	AHL	26	0	0	0	2	....	....	....	....	....
	Flint	IHL	9	0	2	2	10	....	....	....	....	....
1988-89	Rochester	AHL	20	0	2	2	15	....	....	....	....	....
	Jokerit	Fin.	15	4	4	8	38	5	0	0	0	2
1989-90	Jokerit	Fin.	42	3	8	11	107	....	....	....	....	....

MULLEN, BRIAN

Left wing. Shoots left. 5'10", 180 lbs. Born, New York, NY, March 16, 1962.
(Winnipeg's 7th choice, 128th overall, in 1980 Entry Draft).

			Regular Season					Playoffs				
Season	Club	Lea	GP	G	A	TP	PIM	GP	G	A	TP	PIM
1980-81	U. Wisconsin	WCHA	38	11	13	24	28	....	....	....	....	....
1981-82	U. Wisconsin	WCHA	33	20	17	37	10	....	....	....	....	....
1982-83	**Winnipeg**	**NHL**	**80**	**24**	**26**	**50**	**14**	**3**	**1**	**0**	**1**	**0**
1983-84	**Winnipeg**	**NHL**	**75**	**21**	**41**	**62**	**28**	**3**	**0**	**3**	**3**	**6**
1984-85	**Winnipeg**	**NHL**	**69**	**32**	**39**	**71**	**32**	**8**	**1**	**2**	**3**	**4**
1985-86	**Winnipeg**	**NHL**	**79**	**28**	**34**	**62**	**38**	**3**	**1**	**2**	**3**	**6**
1986-87	**Winnipeg**	**NHL**	**69**	**19**	**32**	**51**	**20**	**9**	**4**	**2**	**6**	**0**
1987-88	**NY Rangers**	**NHL**	**74**	**25**	**29**	**54**	**42**	....	....	....	....	....
1988-89	**NY Rangers**	**NHL**	**78**	**29**	**35**	**64**	**60**	**3**	**0**	**1**	**1**	**4**
1989-90	**NY Rangers**	**NHL**	**76**	**27**	**41**	**68**	**42**	**10**	**2**	**2**	**4**	**8**
	NHL Totals		**600**	**205**	**277**	**482**	**276**	**39**	**9**	**12**	**21**	**28**

Played in NHL All-Star Game (1989)

Traded to **NY Rangers** by **Winnipeg** with Winnipeg's tenth-round draft choice (Brett Barnett) in 1987 Entry Draft for NY Rangers' fifth-round choice in 1988 Entry Draft (Benoit Lebeau) – acquired earlier by NY Rangers – and NY Rangers' third round choice – later traded to St. Louis (Denny Felsner) – in 1989 Entry Draft, June 8, 1987.

MULLEN, JOE

Right wing. Shoots right. 5'9", 180 lbs. Born, New York, NY, February 26, 1957.

			Regular Season					Playoffs				
Season	Club	Lea	GP	G	A	TP	PIM	GP	G	A	TP	PIM
1977-78a	Boston College	ECAC	34	34	34	68	12	....	....	....	....	....
1978-79a	Boston College	ECAC	25	32	24	56	8	....	....	....	....	....
1979-80bc	Salt Lake	CHL	75	40	32	72	21	13	*9	11	20	0
	St. Louis	**NHL**	....	....	....	....	....	**1**	**0**	**0**	**0**	**0**
1980-81de	Salt Lake	CHL	80	59	58	*117	8	17	11	9	20	0
1981-82	Salt Lake	CHL	27	21	27	48	12	....	....	....	....	....
	St. Louis	**NHL**	**45**	**25**	**34**	**59**	**4**	**10**	**7**	**11**	**18**	**4**
1982-83	**St. Louis**	**NHL**	**49**	**17**	**30**	**47**	**6**	....	....	....	....	....
1983-84	**St. Louis**	**NHL**	**80**	**41**	**44**	**85**	**19**	**6**	**2**	**0**	**2**	**0**
1984-85	**St. Louis**	**NHL**	**79**	**40**	**52**	**92**	**6**	**3**	**0**	**0**	**0**	**0**
1985-86	**St. Louis**	**NHL**	**48**	**28**	**24**	**52**	**10**	....	....	....	....	....
	Calgary	**NHL**	**29**	**16**	**22**	**38**	**11**	**21**	***12**	**7**	**19**	**4**
1986-87f	**Calgary**	**NHL**	**79**	**47**	**40**	**87**	**14**	**6**	**2**	**1**	**3**	**0**
1987-88	**Calgary**	**NHL**	**80**	**40**	**44**	**84**	**30**	**7**	**2**	**4**	**6**	**10**
1988-89fgh	**Calgary**	**NHL**	**79**	**51**	**59**	**110**	**16**	**21**	***16**	**8**	**24**	**4**
1989-90	**Calgary**	**NHL**	**78**	**36**	**33**	**69**	**24**	**6**	**3**	**0**	**3**	**0**
	NHL Totals		**646**	**341**	**382**	**723**	**140**	**81**	**44**	**31**	**75**	**22**

a ECAC First All-Star Team (1978, 1979)
b CHL Second All-Star Team (1980)
c Won Ken McKenzie Trophy (CHL's Top Rookie) (1980)
d CHL First All-Star Team (1981)
e Won Tommy Ivan Trophy (CHL's Most Valuable Player) (1981)
f Won Lady Byng Trophy (1987, 1989)
g NHL First All-Star Team (1989)
h NHL Plus/Minus Leader (1989)

Played in NHL All-Star Game (1989, 1990)

Signed as a free agent by **St. Louis,** August 16, 1979. Traded to **Calgary** by **St. Louis** with Terry Johnson and Rik Wilson for Ed Beers, Charles Bourgeois and Gino Cavallini, February 1, 1986. Traded to **Pittsburgh** by **Calgary** for Pittsburgh's second round choice (Nicolas Perreault) in 1990 Entry Draft, June 16, 1990.

MULLER, KIRK

Center. Shoots left. 6', 205 lbs. Born, Kingston, Ont., February 8, 1966.
(New Jersey's 1st choice, 2nd overall, in 1984 Entry Draft).

			Regular Season					Playoffs				
Season	Club	Lea	GP	G	A	TP	PIM	GP	G	A	TP	PIM
1981-82	Kingston	OHL	67	12	39	51	27	4	5	1	6	4
1982-83ab	Guelph	OHL	66	52	60	112	41	....	....	....	....	....
1983-84b	Cdn. Olympic	...	21	4	3	7	6	....	....	....	....	....
	Guelph	OHL	49	31	63	94	27	....	....	....	....	....
1984-85	**New Jersey**	**NHL**	**80**	**17**	**37**	**54**	**69**	....	....	....	....	....
1985-86	**New Jersey**	**NHL**	**77**	**25**	**41**	**66**	**45**	....	....	....	....	....
1986-87	**New Jersey**	**NHL**	**79**	**26**	**50**	**76**	**75**	....	....	....	....	....
1987-88	**New Jersey**	**NHL**	**80**	**37**	**57**	**94**	**114**	**20**	**4**	**8**	**12**	**37**
1988-89	**New Jersey**	**NHL**	**80**	**31**	**43**	**74**	**119**	....	....	....	....	....
1989-90	**New Jersey**	**NHL**	**80**	**30**	**56**	**86**	**74**	**6**	**1**	**3**	**4**	**11**
	NHL Totals		**476**	**166**	**284**	**450**	**496**	**26**	**5**	**11**	**16**	**48**

a OHL's Most Gentlemanly Player (1983)
b OHL Third All-Star Team (1983, 1984)

Played in NHL All-Star Game (1985, 1986, 1988, 1990)

MULVENNA, GLENN

Center. Shoots left. 5'11", 185 lbs. Born, Calgary, Alta., February 18, 1967.

			Regular Season					Playoffs				
Season	Club	Lea	GP	G	A	TP	PIM	GP	G	A	TP	PIM
1986-87	N. Westminster	WHL	53	24	44	68	43	....	....	....	....	....
	Kamloops	WHL	18	13	8	21	18	13	4	6	10	10
1987-88	Kamloops	WHL	38	21	38	59	35	....	....	....	....	....
1988-89	Flint	IHL	32	9	14	23	12	....	....	....	....	....
	Muskegon	IHL	11	3	2	5	0	....	....	....	....	....
1989-90	Muskegon	IHL	52	14	21	35	17	1	2	5	7	0
	Fort Wayne	IHL	6	2	5	7	2	....	....	....	....	....

Signed as a free agent by **Pittsburgh**, December 3, 1987.

MUNI, CRAIG DOUGLAS (MYEW-nee)

Defense. Shoots left. 6'3", 200 lbs. Born, Toronto, Ont., July 19, 1962.
(Toronto's 1st choice, 25th overall, in 1980 Entry Draft).

			Regular Season					Playoffs				
Season	Club	Lea	GP	G	A	TP	PIM	GP	G	A	TP	PIM
1980-81	Kingston	OHA	38	2	14	16	65	....	....	....	....	....
	Windsor	OHA	25	5	11	16	41	11	1	4	5	14
	New Brunswick	AHL	....	....	....	....	....	2	0	1	1	10
1981-82	**Toronto**	**NHL**	**3**	**0**	**0**	**0**	**2**	....	....	....	....	....
	Windsor	OHL	49	5	32	37	92	9	2	3	5	16
	Cincinnati	CHL	....	....	....	....	....	3	0	2	2	2
1982-83	**Toronto**	**NHL**	**2**	**0**	**1**	**1**	**0**	....	....	....	....	....
	St. Catharines	AHL	64	6	32	38	52	....	....	....	....	....
1983-84	St. Catharines	AHL	64	4	16	20	79	7	0	1	1	0
1984-85	**Toronto**	**NHL**	**8**	**0**	**0**	**0**	**0**	....	....	....	....	....
	St. Catharines	AHL	68	7	17	24	54	....	....	....	....	....
1985-86	**Toronto**	**NHL**	**6**	**0**	**1**	**1**	**4**	....	....	....	....	....
	St. Catharines	AHL	73	3	34	37	91	13	0	5	5	16
1986-87	**Edmonton**	**NHL**	**79**	**7**	**22**	**29**	**85**	**14**	**0**	**2**	**2**	**17**
1987-88	**Edmonton**	**NHL**	**72**	**4**	**15**	**19**	**77**	**19**	**0**	**4**	**4**	**31**
1988-89	**Edmonton**	**NHL**	**69**	**5**	**13**	**18**	**71**	**7**	**0**	**3**	**3**	**8**
1989-90	**Edmonton**	**NHL**	**71**	**5**	**12**	**17**	**81**	**22**	**0**	**3**	**3**	**16**
	NHL Totals		**310**	**21**	**64**	**85**	**320**	**62**	**0**	**12**	**12**	**72**

Signed as a free agent by **Edmonton,** August 18, 1986. Sold to **Buffalo** by **Edmonton**, October 2, 1986. Traded to **Pittsburgh** by **Buffalo** for future considerations, October 3, 1986. Acquired by **Edmonton** from **Pittsburgh** to complete earlier trade for Gilles Meloche, October 6, 1986.

MURANO, ERIC

Center. Shoots right. 6', 190 lbs. Born, Montreal, Que., May 4, 1967.
(Vancouver's 4th choice, 91st overall, in 1986 Entry Draft).

			Regular Season					Playoffs				
Season	Club	Lea	GP	G	A	TP	PIM	GP	G	A	TP	PIM
1986-87	U. of Denver	WCHA	31	5	7	12	12	....	....	....	....	....
1987-88	U. of Denver	WCHA	37	8	13	21	26	....	....	....	....	....
1988-89	U. of Denver	WCHA	42	13	16	29	52	....	....	....	....	....
1989-90a	U. of Denver	WCHA	42	33	35	68	52	....	....	....	....	....

a WCHA Second All-Star Team (1990)

MURPHY, DANIEL

Defense. Shoots left. 6'1", 185 lbs. Born, Needham, MA, May 13, 1970.
(Boston's 5th choice, 102nd overall, in 1988 Entry Draft).

			Regular Season					Playoffs				
Season	Club	Lea	GP	G	A	TP	PIM	GP	G	A	TP	PIM
1988-89	St. Sebastien	HS	....	11	22	33	....	....	....	....	....	....
1989-90	U. of Maine	H.E.	42	1	9	10	26	....	....	....	....	....

MURPHY, GORDON

Defense. Shoots right. 6'3", 200 lbs. Born, Willowdale, Ont., February 23, 1967.
(Philadelphia's 10th choice, 189th overall, in 1985 Entry Draft).

			Regular Season					Playoffs				
Season	Club	Lea	GP	G	A	TP	PIM	GP	G	A	TP	PIM
1984-85	Oshawa	OHL	59	3	12	15	25	....	....	....	....	....
1985-86	Oshawa	OHL	64	7	15	22	56	6	1	1	2	6
1986-87	Oshawa	OHL	56	7	30	37	95	24	6	16	22	22
1987-88	Hershey	AHL	62	8	20	28	44	12	0	8	8	12
1988-89	**Philadelphia**	**NHL**	**75**	**4**	**31**	**35**	**68**	**19**	**2**	**7**	**9**	**13**
1989-90	**Philadelphia**	**NHL**	**75**	**14**	**27**	**41**	**95**	....	....	....	....	....
	NHL Totals		**150**	**18**	**58**	**76**	**163**	**19**	**2**	**7**	**9**	**13**

MURPHY, JOE

Left wing. Shoots left. 6'1", 190 lbs. Born, London, Ont., October 16, 1967.
(Detroit's 1st choice, 1st overall, in 1986 Entry Draft).

			Regular Season					Playoffs				
Season	Club	Lea	GP	G	A	TP	PIM	GP	G	A	TP	PIM
1985-86	Cdn. Olympic	...	8	3	3	6	2	....	....	....	....	....
a	Michigan State	CCHA	35	24	37	61	50	....	....	....	....	....
1986-87	**Detroit**	**NHL**	**5**	**0**	**1**	**1**	**2**	....	....	....	....	....
	Adirondack	AHL	71	21	38	59	61	10	2	1	3	33
1987-88	**Detroit**	**NHL**	**50**	**10**	**9**	**19**	**37**	**8**	**0**	**1**	**1**	**6**
	Adirondack	AHL	6	5	6	11	4	....	....	....	....	....
1988-89	**Detroit**	**NHL**	**26**	**1**	**7**	**8**	**28**	....	....	....	....	....
	Adirondack	AHL	47	31	35	66	66	16	6	11	17	17
1989-90	**Detroit**	**NHL**	**9**	**3**	**1**	**4**	**4**	....	....	....	....	....
	Edmonton	**NHL**	**62**	**7**	**18**	**25**	**56**	**22**	**6**	**8**	**14**	**16**
	NHL Totals		**152**	**21**	**36**	**57**	**127**	**30**	**6**	**9**	**15**	**22**

a CCHA Rookie of the Year (1986)

Traded to **Edmonton** by **Detroit** with Petr Klima, Adam Graves and Jeff Sharples for Jimmy Carson, Kevin McClelland and Edmonton's fifth round choice in 1991 Entry Draft, November 2, 1989.

MURPHY, LAWRENCE THOMAS (LARRY)

Defense. Shoots right. 6'1", 210 lbs. Born, Scarborough, Ont., March 8, 1961.
(Los Angeles' 1st choice, 4th overall, in 1980 Entry Draft).

			Regular Season					Playoffs				
Season	Club	Lea	GP	G	A	TP	PIM	GP	G	A	TP	PIM
1978-79	Peterborough	OHA	66	6	21	27	82	19	1	9	10	42
1979-80a	Peterborough	OHA	68	21	68	89	88	14	4	13	17	20
1980-81	Los Angeles	NHL	80	16	60	76	79	4	3	0	3	2
1981-82	Los Angeles	NHL	79	22	44	66	95	10	2	8	10	12
1982-83	Los Angeles	NHL	77	14	48	62	81	....	....	....	....	....
1983-84	Los Angeles	NHL	6	0	3	3	0	....	....	....	....	....
	Washington	NHL	72	13	33	46	50	8	0	3	3	6
1984-85	Washington	NHL	79	13	42	55	51	5	2	3	5	0
1985-86	Washington	NHL	78	21	44	65	50	9	1	5	6	6
1986-87b	Washington	NHL	80	23	58	81	39	7	2	2	4	6
1987-88	Washington	NHL	79	8	53	61	72	13	4	4	8	33
1988-89	Washington	NHL	65	7	29	36	70	....	....	....	....	....
	Minnesota	NHL	13	4	6	10	12	5	0	2	2	8
1989-90	Minnesota	NHL	77	10	58	68	44	7	1	2	3	31
	NHL Totals		785	151	478	629	643	68	15	29	44	104

a OHA First All-Star Team (1980)
b NHL Second All-Star Team (1987)

Traded to **Washington** by **Los Angeles** for Ken Houston and Brian Engblom, October 18, 1983. Traded to **Minnesota** by **Washington** with Mike Gartner for Dino Ciccarelli and Bob Rouse, March 7, 1989.

MURPHY, ROB

Center. Shoots left. 6'3", 200 lbs. Born, Hull, Que., April 7, 1968.
(Vancouver's 1st choice, 24th overall, in 1987 Entry Draft).

			Regular Season					Playoffs				
Season	Club	Lea	GP	G	A	TP	PIM	GP	G	A	TP	PIM
1986-87	Laval	QMJHL	70	35	54	89	86	14	3	4	7	15
1987-88	Vancouver	NHL	5	0	0	0	2	....	....	....	....	....
	Laval	QMJHL	26	11	25	36	82	....	....	....	....	....
	Drummondville	QMJHL	33	16	28	44	41	17	4	15	19	45
1988-89	Vancouver	NHL	8	0	1	1	2	....	....	....	....	....
	Milwaukee	IHL	8	4	2	6	4	11	3	5	8	34
	Drummondville	QMJHL	26	13	25	38	16	4	1	3	4	20
1989-90	Vancouver	NHL	12	1	1	2	0	....	....	....	....	....
a	Milwaukee	IHL	64	24	47	71	87	6	2	6	8	12
	NHL Totals		25	1	2	3	4	....	....	....	....	....

a Won Garry F. Longman Memorial Trophy (Top Rookie-IHL) (1990)

MURRAY, PAT

Left wing. Shoots left. 6'2", 185 lbs. Born, Stratford, Ont., August 20, 1969.
(Philadelphia's 2nd choice, 35th overall, in 1988 Entry Draft).

			Regular Season					Playoffs				
Season	Club	Lea	GP	G	A	TP	PIM	GP	G	A	TP	PIM
1987-88	Michigan State	CCHA	42	14	21	35	26	....	....	....	....	....
1988-89	Michigan State	CCHA	46	21	41	62	65	....	....	....	....	....
1989-90a	Michigan State	CCHA	45	24	60	84	36	....	....	....	....	....

a CCHA Second All-Star Team (1990)

MURRAY, ROB

Center. Shoots right. 6'1", 185 lbs. Born, Toronto, Ont., April 4, 1967.
(Washington's 3rd choice, 61st overall, in 1985 Entry Draft).

			Regular Season					Playoffs				
Season	Club	Lea	GP	G	A	TP	PIM	GP	G	A	TP	PIM
1984-85	Peterborough	OHL	63	12	9	21	155	17	2	7	9	45
1985-86	Peterborough	OHL	52	14	18	32	125	16	1	2	3	50
1986-87	Peterborough	OHL	62	17	37	54	204	3	1	4	5	8
1987-88	Fort Wayne	IHL	80	12	21	33	139	6	0	2	2	16
1988-89	Baltimore	AHL	80	11	23	34	235	....	....	....	....	....
1989-90	Washington	NHL	41	2	7	9	58	9	0	0	0	18
	Baltimore	AHL	23	5	4	9	63	....	....	....	....	....
	NHL Totals		41	2	7	9	58	9	0	0	0	18

MURRAY, ROBERT FREDERICK (BOB)

Defense. Shoots right. 5'10", 185 lbs. Born, Kingston, Ont., November 26, 1954.
(Chicago's 3rd choice, 52nd overall, in 1974 Amateur Draft).

			Regular Season					Playoffs				
Season	Club	Lea	GP	G	A	TP	PIM	GP	G	A	TP	PIM
1972-73	Cornwall	QJHL	32	9	26	35	34	12	1	21	22	43
1973-74	Cornwall	QJHL	63	23	76	99	88	5	0	6	6	6
1974-75	Dallas	CHL	75	14	43	57	130	10	2	6	8	13
1975-76	Chicago	NHL	64	1	2	3	44	....	....	....	....	....
1976-77	Chicago	NHL	77	10	11	21	71	2	0	1	1	2
1977-78	Chicago	NHL	70	14	17	31	41	4	1	4	5	2
1978-79	Chicago	NHL	79	19	32	51	38	4	1	0	1	6
1979-80	Chicago	NHL	74	16	34	50	60	7	2	4	6	6
1980-81	Chicago	NHL	77	13	47	60	93	3	0	0	0	2
1981-82	Chicago	NHL	45	8	22	30	48	15	1	6	7	16
1982-83	Chicago	NHL	79	7	32	39	73	13	2	3	5	10
1983-84	Chicago	NHL	78	11	37	48	78	5	3	1	4	6
1984-85	Chicago	NHL	80	5	38	43	56	15	3	6	9	20
1985-86	Chicago	NHL	80	9	29	38	75	3	0	2	2	0
1986-87	Chicago	NHL	79	6	38	44	80	4	1	0	1	4
1987-88	Chicago	NHL	62	6	20	26	44	5	1	3	4	2
1988-89	Chicago	NHL	15	2	4	6	27	16	2	3	5	22
	Saginaw	IHL	18	3	7	10	14	....	....	....	....	....
1989-90	Chicago	NHL	49	5	19	24	45	16	2	4	6	8
	NHL Totals		1008	132	382	514	873	112	19	37	56	106

Played in NHL All-Star Game (1981, 1983)

MURRAY, TROY NORMAN

Center. Shoots right. 6'1", 195 lbs. Born, Calgary, Alta., July 31, 1962.
(Chicago's 6th choice, 57th overall, in 1980 Entry Draft).

			Regular Season					Playoffs				
Season	Club	Lea	GP	G	A	TP	PIM	GP	G	A	TP	PIM
1980-81ab	North Dakota	WCHA	38	33	45	78	28	....	....	....	....	....
1981-82b	North Dakota	WCHA	26	13	17	30	62	....	....	....	....	....
	Chicago	NHL	1	0	0	0	0	7	1	0	1	5
1982-83	Chicago	NHL	54	8	8	16	27	2	0	0	0	0
1983-84	Chicago	NHL	61	15	15	30	45	5	1	0	1	7
1984-85	Chicago	NHL	80	26	40	66	82	15	5	14	19	24
1985-86c	Chicago	NHL	80	45	54	99	94	2	0	0	0	2
1986-87	Chicago	NHL	77	28	43	71	59	4	0	0	0	5
1987-88	Chicago	NHL	79	22	36	58	96	5	1	0	1	8
1988-89	Chicago	NHL	79	21	30	51	113	16	3	6	9	25
1989-90	Chicago	NHL	68	17	38	55	86	20	4	4	8	2
	NHL Totals		579	182	264	446	602	76	15	24	39	78

a WCHA Rookie of the Year (1981)
b WCHA Second All-Star Team (1981, 1982)
c Won Frank J. Selke Memorial Trophy (1986).

MURZYN, DANA (MUR-zihn)

Defense. Shoots left. 6'2", 200 lbs. Born, Calgary, Alta., December 9, 1966.
(Hartford's 1st choice, 5th overall, in 1985 Entry Draft).

			Regular Season					Playoffs				
Season	Club	Lea	GP	G	A	TP	PIM	GP	G	A	TP	PIM
1983-84	Calgary	WHL	65	11	20	31	135	2	0	0	0	10
1984-85a	Calgary	WHL	72	32	60	92	233	8	1	11	12	16
1985-86b	Hartford	NHL	78	3	23	26	125	4	0	0	0	10
1986-87	Hartford	NHL	74	9	19	28	95	6	2	1	3	29
1987-88	Hartford	NHL	33	1	6	7	45	....	....	....	....	....
	Calgary	NHL	41	6	5	11	94	5	2	0	2	13
1988-89	Calgary	NHL	63	3	19	22	142	21	0	3	3	20
1989-90	Calgary	NHL	78	7	13	20	140	6	2	2	4	2
	NHL Totals		367	29	85	114	641	42	6	6	12	74

a WHL First All-Star Team, East Division (1985).
b NHL All-Rookie Team (1986)

Traded to **Calgary** by **Hartford** with Shane Churla for Neil Sheehy, Carey Wilson and the rights to Lane MacDonald, January 3, 1988.

MUSIL, FRANTISEK (moo-SIHL)

Defense. Shoots left. 6'3", 215 lbs. Born, Vysoke Myto, Czech., December 17, 1964.
(Minnesota's 3rd choice, 38th overall, in 1983 Entry Draft).

			Regular Season					Playoffs				
Season	Club	Lea	GP	G	A	TP	PIM	GP	G	A	TP	PIM
1985-86	Dukla-Jihlava	Czech.	35	3	7	10	42	....	....	....	....	....
1986-87	Minnesota	NHL	72	2	9	11	148	....	....	....	....	....
1987-88	Minnesota	NHL	80	9	8	17	213	....	....	....	....	....
1988-89	Minnesota	NHL	55	1	19	20	54	5	1	1	2	4
1989-90	Minnesota	NHL	56	2	8	10	109	4	0	0	0	14
	NHL Totals		263	14	44	58	524	9	1	1	2	18

NACHBAUR, DONALD KENNETH (DON) (NAHK-bow-uhr)

Center. Shoots left. 6'2", 195 lbs. Born, Kitimat, B.C., January 30, 1959.
(Hartford's 3rd choice, 60th overall, in 1979 Entry Draft).

			Regular Season					Playoffs				
Season	Club	Lea	GP	G	A	TP	PIM	GP	G	A	TP	PIM
1977-78	Billings	WHL	68	23	27	50	128	20	*18	7	25	37
1978-79	Billings	WHL	69	44	52	96	175	8	2	3	5	10
1979-80	Springfield	AHL	70	12	17	29	119	....	....	....	....	....
1980-81	Hartford	NHL	77	16	17	33	139	....	....	....	....	....
1981-82	Hartford	NHL	77	5	21	26	117	....	....	....	....	....
1982-83	Moncton	AHL	70	33	32	65	125	....	....	....	....	....
	Edmonton	NHL	4	0	0	0	17	2	0	0	0	7
1983-84	New Haven	AHL	70	33	32	65	194	....	....	....	....	....
1984-85	Hershey	AHL	7	2	3	5	21	....	....	....	....	....
1985-86	Philadelphia	NHL	5	1	1	2	7	....	....	....	....	....
	Hershey	AHL	74	23	24	47	301	18	5	4	9	70
1986-87	Philadelphia	NHL	23	0	2	2	87	7	1	1	2	15
	Hershey	AHL	57	18	17	35	274	5	0	3	3	47
1987-88	Philadelphia	NHL	20	0	4	4	61	2	0	0	0	2
	Hershey	AHL	42	19	21	40	174	8	4	3	7	47
1988-89	Philadelphia	NHL	15	1	0	1	37	....	....	....	....	....
	Hershey	AHL	49	24	31	55	172	12	0	5	5	58
1989-90	Philadelphia	NHL	2	0	1	1	0	....	....	....	....	....
	Hershey	AHL	30	10	9	19	72	....	....	....	....	....
	NHL Totals		223	23	46	69	465	11	1	1	2	24

Traded to **Edmonton** by **Hartford** with Ken Linseman for Risto Siltanen and the rights to Brent Loney, August 19, 1982. Claimed by **Los Angeles** from **Edmonton** in NHL Waiver Draft, October 3, 1983. Signed as a free agent by **Philadelphia**, October 4, 1984.

NANNE, MARTY

Right wing. Shoots right. 6', 180 lbs. Born, Edina, MN, July 21, 1967.
(Chicago's 7th choice, 161st overall, in 1986 Entry Draft).

			Regular Season					Playoffs				
Season	Club	Lea	GP	G	A	TP	PIM	GP	G	A	TP	PIM
1985-86	U. Minnesota	WCHA	19	5	5	10	29	....	....	....	....	....
1986-87	U. Minnesota	WCHA	31	3	4	7	41	....	....	....	....	....
1987-88	U. Minnesota	WCHA	17	1	3	4	16	....	....	....	....	....
1988-89	Saginaw	IHL	36	4	10	14	47	....	....	....	....	....
1989-90	Indianapolis	IHL	50	3	3	6	36	....	....	....	....	....

NAPIER, ROBERT MARK (NAY-pyeer) (MARK)

Right wing. Shoots left. 5'10", 185 lbs.   Born, Toronto, Ont., January 28, 1957.
(Montreal's 1st choice, 10th overall, in 1977 Amateur Draft).

			Regular Season					Playoffs				
Season	Club	Lea	GP	G	A	TP	PIM	GP	G	A	TP	PIM
1973-74	Toronto	OHA	70	47	46	93	63	....	....	....	....	....
1974-75a	Toronto	OHA	61	66	64	130	106	23	*24	24	*48	13
1975-76b	Toronto	WHA	78	43	50	93	20	....	....	....	....	....
1976-77	Birmingham	WHA	80	60	36	96	24	....	....	....	....	....
1977-78	Birmingham	WHA	79	33	32	65	9	5	0	2	2	14
1978-79	**Montreal**	**NHL**	54	11	20	31	11	12	3	2	5	2
1979-80	**Montreal**	**NHL**	76	16	33	49	7	10	2	6	8	0
1980-81	**Montreal**	**NHL**	79	35	36	71	24	3	0	0	0	2
1981-82	**Montreal**	**NHL**	80	40	41	81	14	5	3	2	5	0
1982-83	**Montreal**	**NHL**	73	40	27	67	6	3	0	0	0	0
1983-84	**Montreal**	**NHL**	5	3	2	5	0	....	....	....	....	....
	Minnesota	**NHL**	58	13	28	41	17	12	3	2	5	0
1984-85	**Minnesota**	**NHL**	39	10	18	28	2	....	....	....	....	....
	Edmonton	**NHL**	33	9	26	35	19	18	5	5	10	7
1985-86	**Edmonton**	**NHL**	80	24	32	56	14	10	1	4	5	0
1986-87	**Edmonton**	**NHL**	62	8	13	21	2	....	....	....	....	....
	Buffalo	**NHL**	15	5	5	10	0	....	....	....	....	....
1987-88	**Buffalo**	**NHL**	47	10	8	18	8	6	0	3	3	0
1988-89	**Buffalo**	**NHL**	66	11	17	28	33	3	1	0	1	0
1989-90	Bologna	Italy	36	68	72	140	6	6	8	6	14	2
	NHL Totals		767	235	306	541	157	82	18	24	42	11

a OHA First All-Star Team (1975)
b Named WHA Rookie of the Year (1976)
Traded to **Minnesota** by **Montreal** with Keith Acton and Toronto's third round choice (Ken Hodge) — Montreal's property via earlier deal — for Bobby Smith, October 28, 1983. Traded to **Edmonton** by **Minnesota** for Gord Sherven and Terry Martin, January 24, 1985. Traded to **Buffalo** by **Edmonton** with Lee Fogolin for Normand Lacombe, Wayne Van Dorp and future considerations, March 6, 1987.

NAPIERALA, JEFF

Right wing. Shoots right. 6'1", 195 lbs.   Born, Muskegon, MI, February 27, 1968.
(Vancouver's 1st choice, 3rd overall, in 1989 Supplemental Draft).

			Regular Season					Playoffs				
Season	Club	Lea	GP	G	A	TP	PIM	GP	G	A	TP	PIM
1987-88	Lake Superior	CCHA	7	0	0	0	0	....	....	....	....	....
1988-89	Lake Superior	CCHA	43	17	9	26	22	....	....	....	....	....
1989-90	Lake Superior	CCHA	44	33	26	59	32	....	....	....	....	....

NASLUND, MATS (NAZZ-luhnd)

Left wing. Shoots left. 5'7", 160 lbs.   Born, Timra, Sweden, October 31, 1959.
(Montreal's 2nd choice, 37th overall, in 1979 Entry Draft).

			Regular Season					Playoffs				
Season	Club	Lea	GP	G	A	TP	PIM	GP	G	A	TP	PIM
1977-78	Timra Swe.	Swe.	35	13	6	19	14	....	....	....	....	....
1978-79	Brynas IF	Swe.	36	12	12	24	19	....	....	....	....	....
	Swe. National	...	13	8	3	11	12	....	....	....	....	....
1979-80	Brynas IF	Swe.	36	18	19	37	34	7	2	2	4	4
	Swe. Olympic	...	7	3	7	10	6	....	....	....	....	....
	Swe. National	...	21	3	11	14	10	....	....	....	....	....
1980-81	Brynas IF	Swe.	36	17	*25	*42	34	....	....	....	....	....
	Swe. National	...	25	4	6	10	20	....	....	....	....	....
1981-82	Brynas IF	Swe.	36	24	18	42	16	....	....	....	....	....
	Swe. National	...	24	6	9	15	40	....	....	....	....	....
1982-83a	**Montreal**	**NHL**	74	26	45	71	10	3	1	0	1	0
1983-84	**Montreal**	**NHL**	77	29	35	64	4	15	6	8	14	4
1984-85	**Montreal**	**NHL**	80	42	37	79	14	12	7	4	11	6
1985-86b	**Montreal**	**NHL**	80	43	67	110	16	20	8	11	19	4
1986-87	**Montreal**	**NHL**	79	25	55	80	16	17	7	15	22	11
1987-88c	**Montreal**	**NHL**	78	24	59	83	14	6	0	7	7	2
1988-89	**Montreal**	**NHL**	77	33	51	84	14	21	4	11	15	6
1989-90	**Montreal**	**NHL**	72	21	20	41	19	3	1	1	2	0
	NHL Totals		617	243	369	612	107	97	34	57	91	33

a Named to NHL All-Rookie Team (1983)
b NHL Second All-Star Team (1986)
c Won Lady Byng Memorial Trophy (1988)
Played in NHL All-Star Game (1984, 1986, 1988)

NATTRESS, ERIC (RIC)

Defense. Shoots right. 6'2", 210 lbs.   Born, Hamilton, Ont., May 25, 1962.
(Montreal's 2nd choice, 27th overall, in 1980 Entry Draft).

			Regular Season					Playoffs				
Season	Club	Lea	GP	G	A	TP	PIM	GP	G	A	TP	PIM
1979-80	Brantford	OHA	65	3	21	24	94	11	1	6	7	38
1980-81	Brantford	OHA	51	8	34	42	106	6	1	4	5	19
1981-82	Brantford	OHL	59	11	50	61	126	11	3	7	10	17
	Nova Scotia	AHL	....	....	....	....	....	5	0	1	1	7
1982-83	Nova Scotia	AHL	9	0	4	4	16	....	....	....	....	....
	Montreal	**NHL**	40	1	3	4	19	3	0	0	0	10
1983-84	**Montreal**	**NHL**	34	0	12	12	15	....	....	....	....	....
1984-85	**Montreal**	**NHL**	5	0	1	1	2	2	0	0	0	2
	Sherbrooke	AHL	72	8	40	48	37	16	4	13	17	20
1985-86	**St. Louis**	**NHL**	78	4	20	24	52	18	1	4	5	24
1986-87	**St. Louis**	**NHL**	73	6	22	28	24	6	0	0	0	2
1987-88	**Calgary**	**NHL**	63	2	13	15	37	6	1	3	4	0
1988-89	**Calgary**	**NHL**	38	1	8	9	47	19	0	3	3	20
1989-90	**Calgary**	**NHL**	49	1	14	15	26	6	2	0	2	0
	NHL Totals		380	15	93	108	222	60	4	10	14	58

Rights sold to **St. Louis** by **Montreal**, October 7, 1985. Traded to **Calgary** by **St. Louis** for Calgary's fourth-round choice (Andy Rymsha) in 1987 Entry Draft and fifth-round choice (Dave Lacouture) in 1988 Entry Draft, June 13, 1987.

NAUSS, DARREN

Right wing. Shoots right. 5'11", 180 lbs.   Born, Vancouver, B.C., March 19, 1967.
(Quebec's 11th choice, 198th overall, in 1987 Entry Draft).

			Regular Season					Playoffs				
Season	Club	Lea	GP	G	A	TP	PIM	GP	G	A	TP	PIM
1987-88	Minn.-Duluth	WCHA	41	8	13	21	24	....	....	....	....	....
1988-89	Minn.-Duluth	WCHA	40	10	4	14	40	....	....	....	....	....
1989-90	Minn.-Duluth	WCHA	37	21	17	38	24	....	....	....	....	....

NEDVED, PETR

Center. Shoots left. 6'3", 180 lbs.   Born, Liberec, Czechoslovakia, December 9, 1971.
(Vancouver's 1st choice, 2nd overall, in 1990 Entry Draft).

			Regular Season					Playoffs				
Season	Club	Lea	GP	G	A	TP	PIM	GP	G	A	TP	PIM
1988-89	Litvinov	Czech.	20	32	19	51	12	....	....	....	....	....
1989-90a	Seattle	WHL	71	65	80	145	80	11	4	9	13	2

a WHL and CHL Rookie of the Year

NEEDHAM, MICHAEL

Right wing. Shoots right. 5'10", 200 lbs.   Born, Calgary, Alta., April 4, 1970.
(Pittsburgh's 7th choice, 126th overall, in 1989 Entry Draft).

			Regular Season					Playoffs				
Season	Club	Lea	GP	G	A	TP	PIM	GP	G	A	TP	PIM
1986-87	Kamloops	WHL	3	1	2	3	0	11	2	1	3	5
1987-88	Kamloops	WHL	64	31	33	64	93	5	0	1	1	5
1988-89	Kamloops	WHL	49	24	27	51	55	16	2	9	11	13
1989-90a	Kamloops	WHL	60	59	66	125	75	17	11	13	24	10

a WHL West First All-Star Team (1990)

NEELY, CAM

Right wing. Shoots right. 6'1", 210 lbs.   Born, Comox, B.C., June 6, 1965.
(Vancouver's 1st choice, 9th overall, in 1983 Entry Draft).

			Regular Season					Playoffs				
Season	Club	Lea	GP	G	A	TP	PIM	GP	G	A	TP	PIM
1982-82	Portland	WHL	72	56	64	120	130	14	9	11	20	17
1983-84	Portland	WHL	19	8	18	26	29	....	....	....	....	....
	Vancouver	**NHL**	56	16	15	31	57	4	2	0	2	2
1984-85	**Vancouver**	**NHL**	72	21	18	39	137	....	....	....	....	....
1985-86	**Vancouver**	**NHL**	73	14	20	34	126	3	0	0	0	6
1986-87	**Boston**	**NHL**	75	36	36	72	143	4	5	1	6	8
1987-88a	**Boston**	**NHL**	69	42	27	69	175	23	9	8	17	51
1988-89	**Boston**	**NHL**	74	37	38	75	190	10	7	2	9	8
1989-90a	**Boston**	**NHL**	76	55	37	92	117	21	12	16	28	51
	NHL Totals		495	221	191	412	945	65	35	27	62	126

a NHL Second All-Star Team (1988, 1990)
Played in NHL All-Star Game (1988-90)
Traded to **Boston** by **Vancouver** with Vancouver's first-round choice in 1987 Entry Draft (Glen Wesley) for Barry Pederson, June 6, 1986.

NELSON, CHRISTOPHER

Defense. Shoots right. 6'2", 190 lbs.   Born, Philadelphia, PA, February 12, 1969.
(New Jersey's 6th choice, 96th overall, in 1988 Entry Draft).

			Regular Season					Playoffs				
Season	Club	Lea	GP	G	A	TP	PIM	GP	G	A	TP	PIM
1988-89	U. Wisconsin	WCHA	21	1	4	5	24	....	....	....	....	....
1989-90	U. Wisconsin	WCHA	34	1	3	4	38	....	....	....	....	....

NELSON, TODD

Defense. Shoots left. 6', 200 lbs.   Born, Prince Albert, Sask., May 15, 1969.
(Pittsburgh's 4th choice, 79th overall, in 1989 Entry Draft).

			Regular Season					Playoffs				
Season	Club	Lea	GP	G	A	TP	PIM	GP	G	A	TP	PIM
1985-86	Prince Albert	WHL	4	0	0	0	0	....	....	....	....	....
1986-87	Prince Albert	WHL	35	1	6	7	10	4	0	0	0	0
1987-88	Prince Albert	WHL	72	3	21	24	59	10	3	2	5	4
1988-89a	Prince Albert	WHL	72	14	45	59	72	4	1	3	4	4
1989-90a	Prince Albert	WHL	69	13	42	55	88	14	3	12	15	12

a WHL East Second All-Star Team (1989, 1990)

NEMETH, STEVE

Center. Shoots left. 5'8", 170 lbs.   Born, Calgary, Alta., February 11, 1967.
(NY Rangers' 10th choice, 196th overall, in 1985 Entry Draft).

			Regular Season					Playoffs				
Season	Club	Lea	GP	G	A	TP	PIM	GP	G	A	TP	PIM
1902-83	Lethbridge	WHL	2	0	1	1	0	....	....	....	....	....
1983-84	Lethbridge	WHL	68	22	20	42	33	5	1	1	2	2
1984-85	Lethbridge	WHL	67	39	55	94	39	4	2	3	5	13
1985-86	Lethbridge	WHL	70	42	69	111	47	10	5	5	10	6
1986-87	Kamloops	WHL	10	10	4	14	0	13	11	9	20	12
	Cdn. Olympic	....	43	14	7	21	12	....	....	....	....	....
1987-88	**NY Rangers**	**NHL**	12	2	0	2	2	....	....	....	....	....
	Colorado	IHL	57	13	24	37	28	10	2	1	3	8
1988-89	Cdn. National	....	26	6	10	16	10	....	....	....	....	....
	Denver	IHL	11	5	2	7	8	....	....	....	....	....
1989-90	Cdn. National	....	73	24	42	66	40	....	....	....	....	....
	NHL Totals		12	2	0	2	2	....	....	....	....	....

NESICH, JIM

Right wing. Shoots right. 5'11", 183 lbs.   Born, Dearborn, MI, February 22, 1966.
(Montreal's 8th choice, 116th overall, in 1984 Entry Draft).

			Regular Season					Playoffs				
Season	Club	Lea	GP	G	A	TP	PIM	GP	G	A	TP	PIM
1983-84	Verdun	QMJHL	70	22	24	46	35	10	11	5	16	2
1984-85	Verdun	QMJHL	65	19	33	52	72	14	1	6	7	25
1985-86	Verdun	QMJHL	71	26	55	81	114	5	0	0	0	8
	Sherbrooke	AHL	4	0	1	1	0	....	....	....	....	....
1986-87	Verdun	QMJHL	62	20	50	70	133	....	....	....	....	....
1987-88	Sherbrooke	AHL	53	4	10	14	51	4	1	2	3	20
1988-89	Sherbrooke	AHL	74	12	34	46	112	6	1	2	3	10
1989-90	Sherbrooke	AHL	62	21	31	52	79	12	2	*13	15	18

NEUFELD, RAY MATTHEW (NEW-feld)

Right wing. Shoots right. 6'3", 210 lbs. Born, St. Boniface, Man. April 15, 1959.
(Hartford's 4th choice, 81st overall, in 1979 Entry Draft).

			Regular Season					Playoffs				
Season	Club	Lea	GP	G	A	TP	PIM	GP	G	A	TP	PIM
1977-78	Flin Flon	WHL	72	23	46	69	224	15	4	4	8	39
1978-79	Edmonton	WHL	57	54	48	102	138	8	5	1	6	2
1979-80	**Hartford**	**NHL**	**8**	**1**	**0**	**1**	**0**	**2**	**1**	**0**	**1**	**0**
	Springfield	AHL	73	23	29	52	51	....	....	....	....	....
1980-81	**Hartford**	**NHL**	**52**	**5**	**10**	**15**	**44**	....	....	....	....	....
	Binghamton	AHL	25	7	7	14	43	6	2	0	2	0
1981-82	**Hartford**	**NHL**	**19**	**4**	**3**	**7**	**4**	....	....	....	....	....
	Binghamton	AHL	61	28	31	59	81	15	*9	8	17	10
1982-83	**Hartford**	**NHL**	**80**	**26**	**31**	**57**	**86**	....	....	....	....	....
1983-84	**Hartford**	**NHL**	**80**	**27**	**42**	**69**	**97**	....	....	....	....	....
1984-85	**Hartford**	**NHL**	**76**	**27**	**35**	**62**	**129**	....	....	....	....	....
1985-86	**Hartford**	**NHL**	**16**	**5**	**10**	**15**	**40**	....	....	....	....	....
	Winnipeg	**NHL**	**60**	**20**	**28**	**48**	**62**	**3**	**2**	**0**	**2**	**10**
1986-87	**Winnipeg**	**NHL**	**80**	**18**	**18**	**36**	**105**	**8**	**1**	**1**	**2**	**30**
1987-88	**Winnipeg**	**NHL**	**78**	**18**	**18**	**36**	**169**	**5**	**2**	**2**	**4**	**6**
1988-89	**Winnipeg**	**NHL**	**31**	**5**	**2**	**7**	**52**	....	....	....	....	....
	Boston	**NHL**	**14**	**1**	**3**	**4**	**28**	**10**	**2**	**3**	**5**	**9**
1989-90	**Boston**	**NHL**	**1**	**0**	**0**	**0**	**0**	....	....	....	....	....
	Maine	AHL	76	27	29	56	117	....	....	....	....	....
	NHL Totals		**595**	**157**	**200**	**357**	**816**	**28**	**8**	**6**	**14**	**55**

Traded to **Winnipeg** by **Hartford** for Dave Babych, November 21, 1985. Traded to **Boston** by **Winnipeg** for Moe Lemay, December 30, 1988.

NEURURER, PHILLIP

Defense. Shoots left. 6'2", 195 lbs. Born, Robbinsdale, MA, March 21, 1970.
(NY Islanders' 13th choice, 226th overall, in 1988 Entry Draft).

			Regular Season					Playoffs				
Season	Club	Lea	GP	G	A	TP	PIM	GP	G	A	TP	PIM
1988-89	N. Michigan	WCHA	23	0	1	1	12	....	....	....	....	....
1989-90	N. Michigan	WCHA	27	1	5	6	28	....	....	....	....	....

NEVERS, TOM

Center. Shoots left. 6'1", 170 lbs. Born, Edina, MN, September 13, 1971.
(Pittsburgh's 5th choice, 100th overall, in 1989 Entry Draft).

			Regular Season					Playoffs				
Season	Club	Lea	GP	G	A	TP	PIM	GP	G	A	TP	PIM
1987-88	Edina	HS	26	19	12	31	....					
1988-89	Edina	HS	21	19	18	37	....					
1989-90	Edina	HS	23	21	25	46	....					

NEZIOL, THOMAS (TOM)

Left wing. Shoots left. 6'1", 190 lbs. Born, Burlington, Ont., August 7, 1967.
(New Jersey's 6th choice, 128th overall, in 1987 Entry Draft).

			Regular Season					Playoffs				
Season	Club	Lea	GP	G	A	TP	PIM	GP	G	A	TP	PIM
1986-87	Miami-Ohio	CCHA	39	11	18	29	80	....	....	....	....	....
1987-88	Miami-Ohio	CCHA	34	13	13	26	52	....	....	....	....	....
1988-89	Miami-Ohio	CCHA	12	5	4	9	14	....	....	....	....	....
1989-90	Miami-Ohio	CCHA	31	11	4	15	14	....	....	....	....	....

NICHOLLS, BERNIE IRVINE (NICK-els)

Center. Shoots right. 6', 185 lbs. Born, Haliburton, Ont., June 24, 1961.
(Los Angeles' 6th choice, 73rd overall, in 1980 Entry Draft).

			Regular Season					Playoffs				
Season	Club	Lea	GP	G	A	TP	PIM	GP	G	A	TP	PIM
1979-80	Kingston	OHA	68	36	43	79	85	3	1	0	1	10
1980-81	Kingston	OHA	65	63	89	152	109	14	8	10	18	17
1981-82	New Haven	AHL	55	41	30	71	31	....	....	....	....	....
	Los Angeles	**NHL**	**22**	**14**	**18**	**32**	**27**	**10**	**4**	**0**	**4**	**23**
1982-83	**Los Angeles**	**NHL**	**71**	**28**	**22**	**50**	**124**	....	....	....	....	....
1983-84	**Los Angeles**	**NHL**	**78**	**41**	**54**	**95**	**83**	....	....	....	....	....
1984-85	**Los Angeles**	**NHL**	**80**	**46**	**54**	**100**	**76**	**3**	**1**	**1**	**2**	**9**
1985-86	**Los Angeles**	**NHL**	**80**	**36**	**61**	**97**	**78**	....	....	....	....	....
1986-87	**Los Angeles**	**NHL**	**80**	**33**	**48**	**81**	**101**	**5**	**2**	**5**	**7**	**6**
1987-88	**Los Angeles**	**NHL**	**65**	**32**	**46**	**78**	**114**	**5**	**2**	**6**	**8**	**11**
1988-89a	**Los Angeles**	**NHL**	**79**	**70**	**80**	**150**	**96**	**11**	**7**	**9**	**16**	**12**
1989-90	**Los Angeles**	**NHL**	**47**	**27**	**48**	**75**	**66**	....	....	....	....	....
	NY Rangers	**NHL**	**32**	**12**	**25**	**37**	**20**	**10**	**7**	**5**	**12**	**16**
	NHL Totals		**634**	**339**	**456**	**795**	**785**	**44**	**23**	**26**	**49**	**77**

a NHL Second All-Star Team (1989)

Played in NHL All-Star Game (1984, 1989, 1990)

Traded to **NY Rangers** by **Los Angeles** for Tomas Sandstrom and Tony Granato, January 20, 1990.

NIEMAN, THOMAS

Right wing. Shoots right. 6'0", 185 lbs. Born, Winnetka, IL, January 22, 1970.
(Buffalo's 11th choice, 223rd overall, in 1988 Entry Draft).

			Regular Season					Playoffs				
Season	Club	Lea	GP	G	A	TP	PIM	GP	G	A	TP	PIM
1988-89	Dartmouth	ECAC	26	7	11	18	38	....	....	....	....	....
1989-90	Dartmouth	ECAC	26	6	3	9	16	....	....	....	....	....

NIEUWENDYK, JOE (NOO-ihn-DIGHK)

Center. Shoots left. 6'1", 195 lbs. Born, Oshawa, Ont., September 10, 1966.
(Calgary's 2nd choice, 27th overall, in 1985 Entry Draft).

			Regular Season					Playoffs				
Season	Club	Lea	GP	G	A	TP	PIM	GP	G	A	TP	PIM
1984-85a	Cornell	ECAC	23	18	21	39	20	....	....	....	....	....
1985-86bc	Cornell	ECAC	21	21	21	42	45	....	....	....	....	....
1986-87bcd	Cornell	ECAC	23	26	26	52	26	....	....	....	....	....
	Calgary	**NHL**	**9**	**5**	**1**	**6**	**0**	**6**	**2**	**2**	**4**	**0**
1987-88efg	**Calgary**	**NHL**	**75**	**51**	**41**	**92**	**23**	**8**	**3**	**4**	**7**	**2**
1988-89	**Calgary**	**NHL**	**77**	**51**	**31**	**82**	**40**	**22**	**10**	**4**	**14**	**10**
1989-90	**Calgary**	**NHL**	**79**	**45**	**50**	**95**	**40**	**6**	**4**	**6**	**10**	**4**
	NHL Totals		**240**	**152**	**123**	**275**	**89**	**42**	**19**	**16**	**35**	**16**

a ECAC Rookie of the Year (1985).
b NCAA East First All-American Team (1986, 1987)
c ECAC First All-Star Team (1986, 1987)
d ECAC Player of the Year (1987)
e Won Calder Memorial Trophy (1988)
f NHL All-Rookie Team (1988)
g Won Dodge Ram Tough Award (1988)

Played in NHL All-Star Game (1988-90)

NIKOLIC, ALEX

Left wing. Shoots left. 6'2", 205 lbs. Born, Sudbury, Ont., January 3, 1970.
(Calgary's 8th choice, 147th overall, in 1989 Entry Draft).

			Regular Season					Playoffs				
Season	Club	Lea	GP	G	A	TP	PIM	GP	G	A	TP	PIM
1988-89	Cornell	ECAC	13	0	3	3	31	....	....	....	....	....
1989-90	Cornell	ECAC	28	6	9	15	54	....	....	....	....	....

NILAN, CHRISTOPHER JOHN (CHRIS) (NIGH-luhn)

Right wing. Shoots right. 6', 205 lbs. Born, Boston, MA, February 9, 1958.
(Montreal's 21st choice, 231st overall, in 1978 Amateur Draft).

			Regular Season					Playoffs				
Season	Club	Lea	GP	G	A	TP	PIM	GP	G	A	TP	PIM
1978-79	Northeastern	ECAC	32	9	17	26	....	....	....	....	....	....
1979-80	Nova Scotia	AHL	49	15	10	25	*304	....	....	....	....	....
	Montreal	**NHL**	**15**	**0**	**2**	**2**	**50**	**5**	**0**	**0**	**0**	**2**
1980-81	**Montreal**	**NHL**	**57**	**7**	**8**	**15**	**262**	**2**	**0**	**0**	**0**	**0**
1981-82	**Montreal**	**NHL**	**49**	**7**	**4**	**11**	**204**	**5**	**1**	**1**	**2**	**22**
1982-83	**Montreal**	**NHL**	**66**	**6**	**8**	**14**	**213**	**3**	**0**	**0**	**0**	**5**
1983-84	**Montreal**	**NHL**	**76**	**16**	**10**	**26**	***338**	**15**	**1**	**0**	**1**	***81**
1984-85	**Montreal**	**NHL**	**77**	**21**	**16**	**37**	***358**	**12**	**2**	**1**	**3**	**81**
1985-86	**Montreal**	**NHL**	**72**	**19**	**15**	**34**	**274**	**18**	**1**	**2**	**3**	***141**
1986-87	**Montreal**	**NHL**	**44**	**4**	**16**	**20**	**266**	**17**	**3**	**0**	**3**	**75**
1987-88	**Montreal**	**NHL**	**50**	**7**	**5**	**12**	**209**	....	....	....	....	....
	NY Rangers	**NHL**	**22**	**3**	**5**	**8**	**96**	....	....	....	....	....
1988-89	**NY Rangers**	**NHL**	**38**	**7**	**7**	**14**	**177**	**4**	**0**	**1**	**1**	**38**
1989-90	**NY Rangers**	**NHL**	**25**	**1**	**2**	**3**	**59**	**4**	**0**	**1**	**1**	**19**
	NHL Totals		**591**	**98**	**98**	**196**	**2506**	**85**	**8**	**6**	**14**	**464**

Traded to **NY Rangers** by **Montreal** for a switch of first round choices in 1989 Entry Draft, January 27, 1988. Traded to **Boston** by **NY Rangers** for Greg Johnston and future considerations, June 28, 1990.

NILL, JAMES EDWARD (JIM)

Right wing. Shoots right. 6', 185 lbs. Born, Hanna, Alta., April 11, 1958.
(St. Louis' 4th choice, 89th overall, in 1978 Amateur Draft).

			Regular Season					Playoffs				
Season	Club	Lea	GP	G	A	TP	PIM	GP	G	A	TP	PIM
1975-76	Medicine Hat	WHL	62	5	11	16	69	9	1	1	2	20
1976-77	Medicine Hat	WHL	71	23	24	47	140	4	2	2	4	4
1977-78	Medicine Hat	WHL	72	47	46	93	252	12	8	7	15	37
1978-79	U. of Calgary	CWUAA	20	9	8	17	42	....	....	....	....	....
1979-80	Cdn. National	...	45	13	19	32	54	....	....	....	....	....
	Cdn. Olympic	...	6	1	2	3	4	....	....	....	....	....
1980-81	Salt Lake	CHL	79	28	34	62	222	16	9	8	17	38
1981-82	**St. Louis**	**NHL**	**61**	**9**	**12**	**21**	**127**	....	....	....	....	....
	Vancouver	**NHL**	**8**	**1**	**2**	**3**	**5**	**16**	**4**	**3**	**7**	**67**
1982-83	**Vancouver**	**NHL**	**65**	**7**	**15**	**22**	**136**	**4**	**0**	**0**	**0**	**6**
1983-84	**Vancouver**	**NHL**	**51**	**9**	**6**	**15**	**78**	....	....	....	....	....
	Boston	**NHL**	**27**	**3**	**2**	**5**	**81**	**3**	**0**	**0**	**0**	**4**
1984-85	**Boston**	**NHL**	**49**	**1**	**9**	**10**	**62**	....	....	....	....	....
	Winnipeg	**NHL**	**20**	**8**	**8**	**16**	**38**	**8**	**0**	**1**	**1**	**28**
1985-86	**Winnipeg**	**NHL**	**61**	**6**	**8**	**14**	**75**	**3**	**0**	**0**	**0**	**4**
1986-87	**Winnipeg**	**NHL**	**36**	**3**	**4**	**7**	**52**	**3**	**0**	**0**	**0**	**7**
1987-88	**Winnipeg**	**NHL**	**24**	**0**	**1**	**1**	**44**	....	....	....	....	....
	Moncton	AHL	3	0	0	0	6	....	....	....	....	....
	Detroit	**NHL**	**36**	**3**	**11**	**14**	**55**	**16**	**6**	**1**	**7**	**62**
1988-89	**Detroit**	**NHL**	**71**	**8**	**7**	**15**	**83**	**6**	**0**	**0**	**0**	**25**
1989-90	**Detroit**	**NHL**	**15**	**0**	**2**	**2**	**18**	....	....	....	....	....
	Adirondack	AHL	20	10	8	18	24	....	....	....	....	....
	NHL Totals		**524**	**58**	**87**	**145**	**854**	**59**	**10**	**5**	**15**	**203**

Traded to **Vancouver** by **St. Louis** with Tony Currie, Rick Heinz and St. Louis' fourth round choice (Shawn Kilroy) in 1982 Entry Draft for Glen Hanlon, March 9, 1982. Traded to **Boston** by **Vancouver** for Peter McNab, February 3, 1984. Traded to **Winnipeg** by **Boston** for Morris Lukowich, February 14, 1985. Traded to **Detroit** by **Winnipeg** for Mark Kumpel, January 11, 1988.

NILSSON, STEFAN

Center. Shoots right. 5'11", 170 lbs. Born, Lulea, Sweden, April 5, 1968.
(Washington's 7th choice, 124th overall, in 1986 Entry Draft).

			Regular Season					Playoffs				
Season	Club	Lea	GP	G	A	TP	PIM	GP	G	A	TP	PIM
1985-86	Lulea	Swe.	4	0	0	0	0	....	....	....	....	....
1986-87	Lulea	Swe.	23	3	9	12	14	....	....	....	....	....
1987-88	Lulea	Swe.	31	10	10	20	24	....	....	....	....	....
1988-89	Lulea	Swe.	40	9	22	31	24	....	....	....	....	....
1989-90	Lulea	Swe.	38	11	26	37	32	5	0	0	0	4

NOLAN, OWEN

Right wing. Shoots right. 6'1", 195 lbs. Born, Belfast, Northern Ireland, February 12, 1972
(Quebec's 1st choice, 1st overall, in 1990 Entry Draft).

			Regular Season					Playoffs				
Season	Club	Lea	GP	G	A	TP	PIM	GP	G	A	TP	PIM
1988-89a	Cornwall	OHL	62	34	25	59	213	18	5	11	16	41
1989-90b	Cornwall	OHL	58	51	59	110	240	6	7	5	12	26

a OHL Rookie of the Year (1989)
b OHL First All-Star Team (1990)

NOONAN, BRIAN

Right wing. Shoots right. 6'1", 180 lbs. Born, Boston, MA, May 29, 1965.
(Chicago's 10th choice, 179th overall, in 1983 Entry Draft).

			Regular Season					Playoffs				
Season	Club	Lea	GP	G	A	TP	PIM	GP	G	A	TP	PIM
1984-85	N. Westminster	WHL	72	50	66	116	76	11	8	7	15	4
1985-86	Nova Scotia	AHL	2	0	0	0	0	....	....	....	....	....
	Saginaw	IHL	76	39	39	78	69	11	6	3	9	6
1986-87	Nova Scotia	AHL	70	25	26	51	30	5	3	1	4	4
1987-88	**Chicago**	**NHL**	**77**	**10**	**20**	**30**	**44**	**3**	**0**	**0**	**0**	**4**
1988-89	**Chicago**	**NHL**	**45**	**4**	**12**	**16**	**28**	**1**	**0**	**0**	**0**	**0**
	Saginaw	IHL	19	18	13	31	36	1	0	0	0	0
1989-90	**Chicago**	**NHL**	**8**	**0**	**2**	**2**	**6**	....	....	....	....	....
a	Indianapolis	IHL	56	40	36	76	85	....	....	....	....	....
	NHL Totals		**130**	**14**	**34**	**48**	**78**	**4**	**0**	**0**	**0**	**4**

a IHL Second All-Star Team (1990)

NORDMARK, ROBERT

Defense. Shoots right. 6'1", 200 lbs. Born, Kalix, Sweden, August 20, 1962.
(St. Louis' 3rd choice, 59th overall, in 1987 Entry Draft).

			Regular Season					Playoffs				
Season	Club	Lea	GP	G	A	TP	PIM	GP	G	A	TP	PIM
1984-85	Lulea	Swe.	33	3	9	12	30	....	....	....	....	....
1985-86	Lulea	Swe.	35	9	15	24	48	....	....	....	....	....
1986-87	Lulea	Swe.	32	7	8	15	46	3	0	3	3	4
1987-88	**St. Louis**	**NHL**	**67**	**3**	**18**	**21**	**60**	....	....	....	....	....
1988-89	**Vancouver**	**NHL**	**80**	**6**	**35**	**41**	**97**	**7**	**3**	**2**	**5**	**8**
1989-90	**Vancouver**	**NHL**	**44**	**2**	**11**	**13**	**34**	....	....	....	....	....
	NHL Totals		**191**	**11**	**64**	**75**	**191**	**7**	**3**	**2**	**5**	**8**

Traded to **Vancouver** by **St. Louis** for Dave Richter and Vancouver's second-round choice in 1990 Entry Draft, September 6, 1988.

NORTON, CHRIS

Defense. Shoots right. 6'2", 200 lbs. Born, Oakville, Ont., April 11, 1965.
(Winnipeg's 11th choice, 228th overall, in 1985 Entry Draft).

			Regular Season					Playoffs				
Season	Club	Lea	GP	G	A	TP	PIM	GP	G	A	TP	PIM
1984-85	Cornell	ECAC	29	4	19	23	34	....	....	....	....	....
1985-86a	Cornell	ECAC	21	8	15	23	56	....	....	....	....	....
1986-87	Cornell	ECAC	24	10	21	31	79	....	....	....	....	....
1987-88a	Cornell	ECAC	27	9	25	34	53	....	....	....	....	....
1988-89	Moncton	AHL	60	1	21	22	49	10	3	2	5	15
1989-90	Moncton	AHL	62	9	20	29	49	....	....	....	....	....

a ECAC Second All-Star Team (1986, 1988).

NORTON, D'ARCY

Left wing. Shoots left. 6'1", 180 lbs. Born, Camrose, Alta., May 2, 1967.
(Minnesota's 6th choice, 109th overall, in 1987 Entry Draft).

			Regular Season					Playoffs				
Season	Club	Lea	GP	G	A	TP	PIM	GP	G	A	TP	PIM
1984-85	Lethbridge	WHL	50	4	11	15	49	4	0	0	0	21
1985-86	Lethbridge	WHL	69	19	25	44	69	10	2	7	9	10
1986-87	Kamloops	WHL	71	45	57	102	66	13	7	9	16	15
1987-88	Kamloops	WHL	68	64	43	107	82	18	9	13	22	20
1988-89	Kalamazoo	IHL	75	39	38	77	79	6	2	3	5	15
1989-90	Kalamazoo	IHL	66	22	25	47	55	....	....	....	....	....

NORTON, JEFF

Defense. Shoots left. 6'2", 195 lbs. Born, Acton, MA, November 25, 1965.
(NY Islanders' 3rd choice, 62nd overall, in 1984 Entry Draft).

			Regular Season					Playoffs				
Season	Club	Lea	GP	G	A	TP	PIM	GP	G	A	TP	PIM
1984-85	U. of Michigan	CCHA	37	8	16	24	103	....	....	....	....	....
1985-86	U. of Michigan	CCHA	37	15	30	45	99	....	....	....	....	....
1986-87a	U. of Michigan	CCHA	39	12	36	48	92	....	....	....	....	....
1987-88	**NY Islanders**	**NHL**	**15**	**1**	**6**	**7**	**14**	**3**	**0**	**2**	**2**	**13**
	U.S. National		54	7	22	29	52	....	....	....	....	....
	U.S. Olympic	....	6	0	4	4	4	....	....	....	....	....
1988-89	**NY Islanders**	**NHL**	**69**	**1**	**30**	**31**	**74**	....	....	....	....	....
1989-90	**NY Islanders**	**NHL**	**60**	**4**	**49**	**53**	**65**	**4**	**1**	**3**	**4**	**17**
	NHL Totals		**144**	**6**	**85**	**91**	**153**	**4**	**1**	**3**	**4**	**17**

a CCHA Second All-Star Team (1987)

OATES, ADAM

Center. Shoots right. 5'11", 190 lbs. Born, Weston, Ont., August 27, 1962.

			Regular Season					Playoffs				
Season	Club	Lea	GP	G	A	TP	PIM	GP	G	A	TP	PIM
1982-83	RPI	ECAC	22	9	33	42	8	....	....	....	....	....
1983-84	RPI	ECAC	38	26	57	83	15	....	....	....	....	....
1984-85ab	RPI	ECAC	38	31	60	91	29	....	....	....	....	....
1985-86	**Detroit**	**NHL**	**38**	**9**	**11**	**20**	**10**	....	....	....	....	....
	Adirondack	AHL	34	18	28	46	4	17	7	14	21	4
1986-87	**Detroit**	**NHL**	**76**	**15**	**32**	**47**	**21**	**16**	**4**	**7**	**11**	**6**
1987-88	**Detroit**	**NHL**	**63**	**14**	**40**	**54**	**20**	**16**	**8**	**12**	**20**	**6**
1988-89	**Detroit**	**NHL**	**69**	**16**	**62**	**78**	**14**	**6**	**0**	**8**	**8**	**2**
1989-90	**St. Louis**	**NHL**	**80**	**23**	**79**	**102**	**30**	**12**	**2**	**12**	**14**	**4**
	NHL Totals		**326**	**77**	**224**	**301**	**95**	**50**	**14**	**39**	**53**	**18**

a ECAC First All-Star Team (1985)
b Named to NCAA All-American Team (1985)

Signed as a free agent by **Detroit,** June 28, 1985. Traded to **St. Louis** by **Detroit** with Paul MacLean for Bernie Federko and Tony McKegney, June 15, 1989.

NORWOOD, LEE CHARLES

Defense. Shoots left. 6'1", 198 lbs. Born, Oakland, CA, February 2, 1960.
(Quebec's 3rd choice, 62nd overall, in 1979 Entry Draft).

			Regular Season					Playoffs				
Season	Club	Lea	GP	G	A	TP	PIM	GP	G	A	TP	PIM
1978-79	Oshawa	OHA	61	23	38	61	171	5	2	2	4	17
1979-80	Oshawa	OHA	60	13	39	52	143	6	2	7	9	15
1980-81	Hershey	AHL	52	11	32	43	78	8	0	4	4	14
	Quebec	**NHL**	**11**	**1**	**1**	**2**	**9**	**3**	**0**	**0**	**0**	**2**
1981-82	**Quebec**	**NHL**	**2**	**0**	**0**	**0**	**2**	....	....	....	....	....
	Fredericton	AHL	29	6	13	19	74	....	....	....	....	....
	Washington	**NHL**	**26**	**7**	**10**	**17**	**125**	....	....	....	....	....
1982-83	**Washington**	**NHL**	**8**	**0**	**1**	**1**	**14**	....	....	....	....	....
	Hershey	AHL	67	12	36	48	90	5	0	1	1	2
1983-84	St. Catharines	AHL	75	13	46	59	91	7	0	5	5	31
1984-85ab	Peoria	IHL	80	17	60	77	229	18	1	11	12	62
1985-86	**St. Louis**	**NHL**	**71**	**5**	**24**	**29**	**134**	**19**	**2**	**7**	**9**	**64**
1986-87	**Detroit**	**NHL**	**57**	**6**	**21**	**27**	**163**	**16**	**1**	**6**	**7**	**31**
	Adirondack	AHL	3	0	3	3	0	....	....	....	....	....
1987-88	**Detroit**	**NHL**	**51**	**9**	**22**	**31**	**131**	**16**	**2**	**6**	**8**	**40**
1988-89	**Detroit**	**NHL**	**66**	**10**	**32**	**42**	**100**	**6**	**1**	**2**	**3**	**16**
1989-90	**Detroit**	**NHL**	**64**	**8**	**14**	**22**	**95**	....	....	....	....	....
	NHL Totals		**356**	**46**	**125**	**171**	**773**	**60**	**6**	**21**	**27**	**153**

a Won Governors' Trophy (IHL's Top Defenseman) 1985
b IHL First All-Star Team (1985)

Traded to **Washington** by **Quebec** for Tim Tookey and Washington's seventh round choice (Daniel Poudrier) in 1982 Entry Draft, February 1, 1982. Traded to **Toronto** by **Washington** for Dave Shand, October 6, 1983. Signed as a free agent by **St. Louis**, August 13, 1985. Traded to **Detroit** by **St. Louis** for Larry Trader, August 7, 1986.

NUMMINEN, TEPPO (NOO-mih-nehn)

Defense. Shoots right. 6'1", 175 lbs. Born, Tampere, Finland, July 3, 1968.
(Winnipeg's 2nd choice, 29th overall, in 1986 Entry Draft).

			Regular Season					Playoffs				
Season	Club	Lea	GP	G	A	TP	PIM	GP	G	A	TP	PIM
1985-86	Tappara	Fin.	31	2	4	6	6	8	0	0	0	0
1986-87	Tappara	Fin.	44	9	9	18	16	9	4	1	5	4
1987-88	Tappara	Fin.	40	10	10	20	29	10	6	6	12	6
1988-89	**Winnipeg**	**NHL**	**69**	**1**	**14**	**15**	**36**	....	....	....	....	....
1989-90	**Winnipeg**	**NHL**	**79**	**11**	**32**	**43**	**20**	**7**	**1**	**2**	**3**	**10**
	NHL Totals		**148**	**12**	**46**	**58**	**56**	**7**	**1**	**2**	**3**	**10**

NYLUND, GARY (NIGH-lund)

Defense. Shoots left. 6'4", 210 lbs. Born, Surrey, B.C., October 28, 1963.
(Toronto's 1st choice, 3rd overall, in 1982 Entry Draft).

			Regular Season					Playoffs				
Season	Club	Lea	GP	G	A	TP	PIM	GP	G	A	TP	PIM
1979-80	Portland	WHL	72	5	21	26	59	8	0	1	1	2
1980-81a	Portland	WHL	70	6	40	46	186	9	1	7	8	17
1981-82bc	Portland	WHL	65	7	59	66	267	15	3	16	19	74
1982-83	**Toronto**	**NHL**	**16**	**0**	**3**	**3**	**16**	....	....	....	....	....
1983-84	**Toronto**	**NHL**	**47**	**2**	**14**	**16**	**103**	....	....	....	....	....
1984-85	**Toronto**	**NHL**	**76**	**3**	**17**	**20**	**99**	....	....	....	....	....
1985-86	**Toronto**	**NHL**	**79**	**2**	**16**	**18**	**180**	**10**	**0**	**2**	**2**	**25**
1986-87	**Chicago**	**NHL**	**80**	**7**	**20**	**27**	**190**	**4**	**0**	**2**	**2**	**11**
1987-88	**Chicago**	**NHL**	**76**	**4**	**15**	**19**	**208**	**5**	**0**	**0**	**0**	**10**
1988-89	**Chicago**	**NHL**	**23**	**3**	**2**	**5**	**63**	....	....	....	....	....
	NY Islanders	**NHL**	**46**	**4**	**8**	**12**	**74**	....	....	....	....	....
1989-90	**NY Islanders**	**NHL**	**64**	**4**	**21**	**25**	**144**	**5**	**0**	**2**	**2**	**17**
	NHL Totals		**507**	**29**	**116**	**145**	**1077**	**24**	**0**	**6**	**6**	**63**

a WHL Second All-Star Team (1981)
b WHL First All-Star Team (1982)
c Named WHL's Top Defenseman (1982)

Signed as a free agent by **Chicago**, August 27, 1986. Traded to **NY Islanders** by **Chicago** with Marc Bergevin for Steve Konroyd and Bob Bassen, November 25, 1988.

O'BRIEN, DAVID

Right wing. Shoots right. 6'1", 180 lbs. Born, Brighton, MA, September 13, 1966.
(St. Louis' 13th choice, 241st overall, in 1986 Entry Draft).

			Regular Season					Playoffs				
Season	Club	Lea	GP	G	A	TP	PIM	GP	G	A	TP	PIM
1985-86	Northeastern	H.E.	39	23	16	39	18	....	....	....	....	....
1986-87	Northeastern	H.E.	35	16	24	40	12	....	....	....	....	....
1987-88a	Northeastern	H.E.	37	18	29	47	18	....	....	....	....	....
1988-89	Binghamton	AHL	53	3	12	15	11	....	....	....	....	....
1989-90	Peoria	AHL	57	9	14	23	21	1	0	0	0	0

a Hockey East First All-Star Team (1988)

O'CONNELL, MICHAEL THOMAS (MIKE)

Defense. Shoots right. 5'9", 180 lbs. Born, Chicago, IL, November 25, 1955.
(Chicago's 3rd choice, 43rd overall, in 1975 Amateur Draft).

			Regular Season					Playoffs				
Season	Club	Lea	GP	G	A	TP	PIM	GP	G	A	TP	PIM
1973-74	Kingston	OHA	70	16	43	59	81	....	....	....	....	....
1974-75a	Kingston	OHA	50	18	55	73	47	8	1	3	4	8
1975-76	Dallas	CHL	70	6	37	43	50	10	2	*8	10	8
1976-77	Dallas	CHL	63	15	53	68	30	5	1	4	5	0
1977-78	Chicago	NHL	6	1	1	2	2	....	....	....	....	....
	Dallas	CHL	62	6	45	51	75	13	1	*11	12	8
1978-79	Chicago	NHL	48	4	22	26	20	4	0	0	0	4
	New Brunswick	AHL	35	5	19	24	19	....	....	....	....	....
1979-80	Chicago	NHL	78	8	22	30	52	7	0	1	1	0
1980-81	Chicago	NHL	34	5	16	21	32	....	....	....	....	....
	Boston	NHL	48	10	22	32	42	3	1	3	4	2
1981-82	Boston	NHL	80	5	34	39	75	11	2	2	4	20
1982-83	Boston	NHL	80	14	39	53	42	17	3	5	8	12
1983-84	Boston	NHL	75	18	42	60	42	3	0	0	0	0
1984-85	Boston	NHL	78	15	40	55	64	5	1	5	6	0
1985-86	Boston	NHL	63	8	21	29	47	....	....	....	....	....
	Detroit	NHL	13	1	7	8	16	....	....	....	....	....
1986-87	Detroit	NHL	77	5	26	31	70	16	1	4	5	14
1987-88	Detroit	NHL	48	6	13	19	38	10	0	4	4	8
1988-89	Detroit	NHL	66	1	15	16	41	6	0	0	0	4
1989-90	Detroit	NHL	66	4	14	18	22	....	....	....	....	....
	NHL Totals		860	105	334	439	605	82	8	24	32	64

a OHA First All-Star Team (1975).
Played in NHL All-Star Game (1984)
Traded to **Boston** by **Chicago** for Al Secord, December 18, 1980. Traded to **Detroit** by **Boston** for Reed Larson, March 10, 1986.

O'CONNOR, MYLES

Defense. Shoots left. 5'11", 165 lbs. Born, Calgary, Alta., April 2, 1967.
(New Jersey's 4th choice, 45th overall, in 1985 Entry Draft).

			Regular Season					Playoffs				
Season	Club	Lea	GP	G	A	TP	PIM	GP	G	A	TP	PIM
1985-86	U. of Michigan	CCHA	37	6	19	25	73	....	....	....	....	....
1986-87	U. of Michigan	CCHA	39	15	39	54	111	....	....	....	....	....
1987-88	U. of Michigan	CCHA	40	9	25	34	78	....	....	....	....	....
1988-89ab	U. of Michigan	CCHA	40	3	31	34	91	....	....	....	....	....
	Utica	AHL	1	0	0	0	0	....	....	....	....	....
1989-90	Utica	AHL	76	14	33	47	124	5	1	2	3	26

a CCHA First All-Star Team (1989)
b NCAA West First All-American Team (1989)

ODELEIN, LYLE (Ah-duh-LEEN)

Center. Shoots left. 5'10", 206 lbs. Born, Quill Lake, Sask., July 21, 1968.
(Montreal's 8th choice, 141st overall, in 1986 Entry Draft).

			Regular Season					Playoffs				
Season	Club	Lea	GP	G	A	TP	PIM	GP	G	A	TP	PIM
1985-86	Moose Jaw	WHL	67	9	37	46	117	13	1	6	7	34
1986-87	Moose Jaw	WHL	59	9	50	59	70	9	2	5	7	26
1987-88	Moose Jaw	WHL	63	15	43	58	166	....	....	....	....	....
1988-89	Sherbrooke	AHL	33	3	4	7	120	3	0	2	2	5
	Peoria	IHL	36	2	8	10	116	....	....	....	....	....
1989-90	Montreal	NHL	8	0	2	2	33	....	....	....	....	....
	Sherbrooke	AHL	68	7	24	31	265	12	6	5	11	79
	NHL Totals		8	0	2	2	33	....	....	....	....	....

ODELEIN, SELMAR (AH-duh-LEEN)

Defense. Shoots right. 6', 205 lbs. Born, Quill Lake, Sask., April 11, 1966.
(Edmonton's 1st choice, 21st overall, in 1984 Entry Draft).

			Regular Season					Playoffs				
Season	Club	Lea	GP	G	A	TP	PIM	GP	G	A	TP	PIM
1983-84	Regina	WHL	71	9	42	51	45	23	4	11	15	45
1984-85	Regina	WHL	64	24	35	59	121	8	2	2	4	13
1985-86	Edmonton	NHL	4	0	0	0	0	....	....	....	....	....
	Regina	WHL	36	13	28	41	57	8	5	2	7	24
1986-87	Nova Scotia	AHL	2	0	1	1	2	....	....	....	....	....
1987-88	Edmonton	NHL	12	0	2	2	33	....	....	....	....	....
	Nova Scotia	AHL	43	9	14	23	75	5	0	1	1	31
1988-89	Edmonton	NHL	2	0	0	0	2	....	....	....	....	....
	Cape Breton	AHL	63	8	21	29	150	....	....	....	....	....
1989-90	Cdn. National	....	72	7	29	36	69	....	....	....	....	....
	NHL Totals		18	0	2	2	35	....	....	....	....	....

O'DWYER, BILL

Center. Shoots left. 6', 190 lbs. Born, South Boston, MA, January 25, 1960.
(Los Angeles' 10th choice, 157th overall, in 1980 Entry Draft).

			Regular Season					Playoffs				
Season	Club	Lea	GP	G	A	TP	PIM	GP	G	A	TP	PIM
1978-79	Boston College	ECAC	30	9	30	39	14	....	....	....	....	....
1979-80	Boston College	ECAC	33	20	22	42	22	....	....	....	....	....
1980-81	Boston College	ECAC	31	20	20	40	6	....	....	....	....	....
1981-82	Boston College	ECAC	30	15	26	41	10	....	....	....	....	....
1982-83	New Haven	AHL	77	24	23	47	29	11	3	4	7	9
1983-84	Los Angeles	NHL	5	0	0	0	0	....	....	....	....	....
	New Haven	AHL	58	15	42	57	39	....	....	....	....	....
1984-85	Los Angeles	NHL	13	1	0	1	15	....	....	....	....	....
	New Haven	AHL	46	19	24	43	27	....	....	....	....	....
1985-86	New Haven	AHL	41	10	15	25	41	5	0	1	1	2
1986-87	New Haven	AHL	65	22	42	64	74	3	0	0	0	14
1987-88	Boston	NHL	77	7	10	17	83	9	0	0	0	0
1988-89	Boston	NHL	19	1	2	3	8	....	....	....	....	....
1989-90	Boston	NHL	6	0	1	1	7	1	0	0	0	2
	Maine	AHL	71	26	45	71	56	....	....	....	....	....
	NHL Totals		120	9	13	22	113	10	0	0	0	2

Signed as a free agent by **NY Rangers**, July 13, 1985. Signed as a free agent by **Boston**, August 13, 1987. Signed as a free agent by **Los Angeles**, July 11, 1990.

OGRODNICK, JOHN ALEXANDER (oh-GRAHD-nik)

Left wing. Shoots left. 6', 205 lbs. Born, Ottawa, Ont., June 20, 1959.
(Detroit's 4th choice, 66th overall, in 1979 Entry Draft).

			Regular Season					Playoffs				
Season	Club	Lea	GP	G	A	TP	PIM	GP	G	A	TP	PIM
1977-78a	N. Westminster	WHL	72	59	29	88	47	21	14	7	21	14
1978-79	N. Westminster	WHL	72	48	36	84	38	6	2	0	2	4
1979-80	Detroit	NHL	41	8	24	32	8	....	....	....	....	....
	Adirondack	AHL	39	13	20	33	21	....	....	....	....	....
1980-81	Detroit	NHL	80	35	35	70	14	....	....	....	....	....
1981-82	Detroit	NHL	80	28	26	54	28	....	....	....	....	....
1982-83	Detroit	NHL	80	41	44	85	30	....	....	....	....	....
1983-84	Detroit	NHL	64	42	36	78	14	4	0	0	0	0
1984-85b	Detroit	NHL	79	55	50	105	30	3	1	1	2	0
1985-86	Detroit	NHL	76	38	32	70	18	....	....	....	....	....
1986-87	Detroit	NHL	39	12	28	40	6	....	....	....	....	....
	Quebec	NHL	32	11	16	27	4	13	9	4	13	6
1987-88	NY Rangers	NHL	64	22	32	54	16	....	....	....	....	....
1988-89	NY Rangers	NHL	60	13	29	42	14	3	2	0	2	0
	Denver	IHL	3	2	0	2	0	....	....	....	....	....
1989-90	NY Rangers	NHL	80	43	31	74	44	10	6	3	9	0
	NHL Totals		775	348	383	731	226	33	18	8	26	6

a Shared WHL Rookie of the Year Award with Keith Brown (Portland) (1978)
b NHL First All-Star Team (1985)
Played in NHL All-Star Game (1981, 1982, 1984-86)
Traded to **Quebec** by **Detroit** with Basil McRae and Doug Shedden for Brent Ashton, Gilbert Delorme and Mark Kumpel, January 17, 1987. Traded to **NY Rangers** by **Quebec** with David Shaw for Jeff Jackson and Terry Carkner, September 30, 1987.

OHMAN, ROGER

Defense. Shoots left. 6'2", 205 lbs. Born, Stockholm, Sweden, June 5, 1967.
(Winnipeg's 2nd choice, 39th overall, in 1985 Entry Draft).

			Regular Season					Playoffs				
Season	Club	Lea	GP	G	A	TP	PIM	GP	G	A	TP	PIM
1986-87	V. Frolunda	Swe.	26	4	10	14	16	2	0	1	1	0
1987-88	Moncton	AHL	67	11	17	28	38	....	....	....	....	....
1988-89	AIK	Swe.	36	11	8	19	20	....	....	....	....	....
1989-90	AIK	Swe.	39	8	17	25	22	3	0	0	0	0

OJANEN, JANNE (OY-uh-nehn YAHN-ee)

Center. Shoots left. 6'2", 185 lbs. Born, Tampere, Finland, April 9, 1968.
(New Jersey's 3rd choice, 45th overall, in 1986 Entry Draft).

			Regular Season					Playoffs				
Season	Club	Lea	GP	G	A	TP	PIM	GP	G	A	TP	PIM
1985-86	Tappara	Fin. Jr.	14	5	17	22	14	5	2	3	5	8
	Tappara	Fin.	3	0	0	0	2	....	....	....	....	....
1986-87	Tappara	Fin.	40	18	13	31	16	9	4	6	10	2
1987-88	Tappara	Fin.	44	21	31	52	30	10	4	4	8	12
1988-89	New Jersey	NHL	3	0	1	1	2	....	....	....	....	....
	Utica	AHL	72	23	37	60	10	5	0	3	3	0
1989-90	New Jersey	NHL	64	17	13	30	12	....	....	....	....	....
	NHL Totals		67	17	14	31	14	....	....	....	....	....

OKSYUTA, ROMAN

Right wing. Shoots left. 6'4", 215 lbs. Born, Voskresensk, Soviet Union, August 21, 1970.
(NY Rangers' 11th choice, 202nd overall, in 1989 Entry Draft).

			Regular Season					Playoffs				
Season	Club	Lea	GP	G	A	TP	PIM	GP	G	A	TP	PIM
1987-88	Voskresensk	USSR	11	1	0	1	4	....	....	....	....	....
1988-89	Voskresensk	USSR	34	13	3	16	14	....	....	....	....	....
1989-90	Voskresensk	USSR	37	13	6	19	16	....	....	....	....	....

OLAUSSON, FREDRIK

Defense. Shoots right. 6'2", 200 lbs. Born, Vaxsjo, Sweden, October 5, 1966.
(Winnipeg's 4th choice, 81st overall, in 1985 Entry Draft).

			Regular Season					Playoffs				
Season	Club	Lea	GP	G	A	TP	PIM	GP	G	A	TP	PIM
1984-85	Farjestad	Swe.	29	5	12	17	22	3	1	0	1	0
1985-86	Farjestad	Swe.	33	4	12	16	22	8	3	2	5	6
1986-87	Winnipeg	NHL	72	7	29	36	24	10	2	3	5	4
1987-88	Winnipeg	NHL	38	5	10	15	18	5	1	1	2	0
1988-89	Winnipeg	NHL	75	15	47	62	32	....	....	....	....	....
1989-90	Winnipeg	NHL	77	9	46	55	32	7	0	2	2	2
	NHL Totals		262	36	132	168	106	22	3	6	9	6

OLCZYK, ED (OHL-chehk)

Center. Shoots left. 6'1", 200 lbs. Born, Chicago, IL, August 16, 1966.
(Chicago's 1st choice, 3rd overall, in 1984 Entry Draft).

			Regular Season					Playoffs				
Season	Club	Lea	GP	G	A	TP	PIM	GP	G	A	TP	PIM
1983-84	U.S. Olympic	...	62	21	47	68	36	....	....	....	....	....
1984-85	Chicago	NHL	70	20	30	50	67	15	6	5	11	11
1985-86	Chicago	NHL	79	29	50	79	47	3	0	0	0	0
1986-87	Chicago	NHL	79	16	35	51	119	4	1	1	2	4
1987-88	Toronto	NHL	80	42	33	75	55	6	5	4	9	2
1988-89	Toronto	NHL	80	38	52	90	75	....	....	....	....	....
1989-90	Toronto	NHL	79	32	56	88	78	5	1	2	3	14
	NHL Totals		467	177	256	433	441	33	13	12	25	31

Traded to **Toronto** by **Chicago** with Al Secord for Rick Vaive, Steve Thomas and Bob McGill, September 3, 1987.

O'LEARY, RYAN

Center. Shoots left. 6'1", 205 lbs. Born, Duluth, MN, June 8, 1971.
(Calgary's 6th choice, 84th overall, in 1989 Entry Draft).

			Regular Season					Playoffs				
Season	Club	Lea	GP	G	A	TP	PIM	GP	G	A	TP	PIM
1988-89	Hermantown	HS	23	29	20	49	....	....	....	....	....	....
1989-90	Denver U.	WCHA	39	4	6	10	30	....	....	....	....	....

OLIMB, LAWRENCE

Defense. Shoots left. 5'10", 155 lbs. Born, Warroad, MN, August 11, 1969.
(Minnesota's 10th choice, 193rd overall, in 1987 Entry Draft).

			Regular Season					Playoffs				
Season	Club	Lea	GP	G	A	TP	PIM	GP	G	A	TP	PIM
1988-89	U. Minnesota	WCHA	47	10	29	39	50	....	....	....	....	....
1989-90	U. Minnesota	WCHA	46	6	36	42	44	....	....	....	....	....

OLIVER, DON

Right wing. Shoots left. 5'11", 175 lbs. Born, London, Ont., November 9, 1969.
(Detroit's 2nd choice, 8th overall, in 1990 Supplemental Draft).

			Regular Season					Playoffs				
Season	Club	Lea	GP	G	A	TP	PIM	GP	G	A	TP	PIM
1987-88	Ohio State	CCHA	34	5	13	18	81	....	....	....	....	....
1988-89	Ohio State	CCHA	39	15	14	29	29	....	....	....	....	....
1989-90	Ohio State	CCHA	40	19	26	45	27	....	....	....	....	....

OLSEN, DARRYL

Defense. Shoots left. 6', 180 lbs. Born, Calgary, Alta., October 7, 1966.
(Calgary's 10th choice, 185th overall in 1985 Entry Draft).

			Regular Season					Playoffs				
Season	Club	Lea	GP	G	A	TP	PIM	GP	G	A	TP	PIM
1985-86	N. Michigan	WCHA	37	5	20	25	46	....	....	....	....	....
1986-87	N. Michigan	WCHA	37	5	20	25	96	....	....	....	....	....
1987-88	N. Michigan	WCHA	35	11	20	31	59	....	....	....	....	....
1988-89	Cdn. National	....	3	1	0	1	4	....	....	....	....	....
ab	N. Michigan	WCHA	45	16	26	42	88	....	....	....	....	....
1989-90	Salt Lake	IHL	72	16	50	66	90	11	3	6	9	2

a NCAA West Second All-American Team (1989)
b WCHA First All-Star Team (1989)

O'REAR, HAYDEN

Defense. Shoots left. 6'1", 185 lbs. Born, Fairbanks, AK, October 8, 1970.
(Vancouver's 9th choice, 218th overall, in 1990 Entry Draft).

			Regular Season					Playoffs				
Season	Club	Lea	GP	G	A	TP	PIM	GP	G	A	TP	PIM
1989-90	Alaska-Anch.	NCAA	23	0	2	2	38	....	....	....	....	....

OSBORNE, KEITH

Right wing. Shoots right. 6'1", 180 lbs. Born, Toronto, Ont., April 2, 1969.
(St. Louis' 1st choice, 12th overall, in 1987 Entry Draft).

			Regular Season					Playoffs				
Season	Club	Lea	GP	G	A	TP	PIM	GP	G	A	TP	PIM
1986-87	North Bay	OHL	61	34	55	89	31	24	11	11	22	25
1987-88	North Bay	OHL	30	14	22	36	20	4	1	5	6	8
1988-89	North Bay	OHL	15	11	15	26	12	....	....	....	....	....
	Niagara Falls	OHL	50	34	49	83	45	17	12	12	25	36
1989-90	**St. Louis**	**NHL**	**5**	**0**	**2**	**2**	**8**	....	....	....	....	....
	Peoria	IHL	56	23	24	47	58	....	....	....	....	....
	NHL Totals		**5**	**0**	**2**	**2**	**8**	....	....	....	....	....

OSBORNE, MARK ANATOLE (AWS-born)

Left wing. Shoots left. 6'2", 205 lbs. Born, Toronto, Ont., August 13, 1961.
(Detroit's 2nd choice, 46th overall, in 1980 Entry Draft).

			Regular Season					Playoffs				
Season	Club	Lea	GP	G	A	TP	PIM	GP	G	A	TP	PIM
1979-80	Niagara Falls	OHA	52	10	33	43	104	10	2	1	3	23
1980-81	Niagara Falls	OHA	54	39	41	80	140	12	11	10	21	20
	Adirondack	AHL	....	....	....	....	....	13	2	3	5	2
1981-82	**Detroit**	**NHL**	**80**	**26**	**41**	**67**	**61**	....	....	....	....	....
1982-83	**Detroit**	**NHL**	**80**	**19**	**24**	**43**	**83**	....	....	....	....	....
1983-84	**NY Rangers**	**NHL**	**73**	**23**	**28**	**51**	**88**	**5**	**0**	**1**	**1**	**7**
1984-85	**NY Rangers**	**NHL**	**23**	**4**	**4**	**8**	**33**	**3**	**0**	**0**	**0**	**4**
1985-86	**NY Rangers**	**NHL**	**62**	**16**	**24**	**40**	**80**	**15**	**2**	**3**	**5**	**26**
1986-87	**NY Rangers**	**NHL**	**58**	**17**	**15**	**32**	**101**	....	....	....	....	....
	Toronto	**NHL**	**16**	**5**	**10**	**15**	**12**	**9**	**1**	**3**	**4**	**6**
1987-88	**Toronto**	**NHL**	**79**	**23**	**37**	**60**	**102**	**6**	**1**	**3**	**4**	**16**
1988-89	**Toronto**	**NHL**	**75**	**16**	**30**	**46**	**112**	....	....	....	....	....
1989-90	**Toronto**	**NHL**	**78**	**23**	**50**	**73**	**91**	**5**	**2**	**3**	**5**	**12**
	NHL Totals		**624**	**172**	**263**	**435**	**763**	**43**	**6**	**13**	**19**	**71**

Traded to **NY Rangers** by **Detroit** with Willie Huber and Mike Blaisdell for Ron Duguay, Eddie Mio and Eddie Johnstone, June 13, 1983. Traded to **Toronto** by **NY Rangers** for Jeff Jackson and Toronto's third-round choice (Rod Zamuner) in 1989 Entry Draft, March 5, 1987.

OSIECKI, MARK

Defense. Shoots right. 6'2", 200 lbs. Born, St. Paul, MN, July 23, 1968.
(Calgary's 10th choice, 187th overall, in 1987 Entry Draft).

			Regular Season					Playoffs				
Season	Club	Lea	GP	G	A	TP	PIM	GP	G	A	TP	PIM
1986-87	U. Wisconsin	WCHA	8	0	1	1	4	....	....	....	....	....
1987-88	U. Wisconsin	WCHA	18	0	1	1	22	....	....	....	....	....
1988-89	U. Wisconsin	WCHA	44	1	3	4	56	....	....	....	....	....
1989-90a	U. Wisconsin	WCHA	46	5	38	43	78	....	....	....	....	....

a NCAA All-Tournament Team (1990)

O'SULLIVAN, KEVIN

Defense. Shoots left. 6', 180 lbs. Born, Dorchester, MA, November 13, 1970.
(NY Islanders' 7th choice, 99th overall, in 1989 Entry Draft).

			Regular Season					Playoffs				
Season	Club	Lea	GP	G	A	TP	PIM	GP	G	A	TP	PIM
1988-89	Catholic Mem.	HS	....	8	20	28	....	....	....	....	....	....
1989-90	Boston U.	H.E.	43	0	6	6	42	....	....	....	....	....

OTTO, JOEL STUART

Center. Shoots right. 6'4", 220 lbs. Born, Elk River, MN, October 29, 1961.

			Regular Season					Playoffs				
Season	Club	Lea	GP	G	A	TP	PIM	GP	G	A	TP	PIM
1980-81	Bemidji State	NCAA	23	5	11	16	10	....	....	....	....	....
1981-82	Bemidji State	NCAA	31	19	33	52	24	....	....	....	....	....
1982-83	Bemidji State	NCAA	37	33	28	61	68	....	....	....	....	....
1983-84	Bemidji State	NCAA	31	32	43	75	32	....	....	....	....	....
1984-85	**Calgary**	**NHL**	**17**	**4**	**8**	**12**	**30**	**3**	**2**	**1**	**3**	**10**
	Moncton	AHL	56	27	36	63	89	....	....	....	....	....
1985-86	**Calgary**	**NHL**	**79**	**25**	**34**	**59**	**188**	**22**	**5**	**10**	**15**	**80**
1986-87	**Calgary**	**NHL**	**68**	**19**	**31**	**50**	**185**	**2**	**0**	**2**	**2**	**6**
1987-88	**Calgary**	**NHL**	**62**	**13**	**39**	**52**	**194**	**9**	**3**	**2**	**5**	**26**
1988-89	**Calgary**	**NHL**	**72**	**23**	**30**	**53**	**213**	**22**	**6**	**13**	**19**	**46**
1989-90	**Calgary**	**NHL**	**75**	**13**	**20**	**33**	**116**	**6**	**2**	**2**	**4**	**2**
	NHL Totals		**373**	**97**	**162**	**259**	**926**	**64**	**18**	**30**	**48**	**170**

Signed as a free agent by **Calgary**, September 11, 1984.

PADDOCK, GORDON

Defense. Shoots right. 6', 180 lbs. Born, Hamiota, Man., February 15, 1964.
(NY Islanders' 9th choice, 189th overall, in 1982 Entry Draft).

			Regular Season					Playoffs				
Season	Club	Lea	GP	G	A	TP	PIM	GP	G	A	TP	PIM
1981-82	Saskatoon	WHL	59	8	21	29	232	3	0	0	0	17
1982-83	Saskatoon	WHL	67	4	25	29	158	6	0	2	2	16
1983-84	Brandon	WHL	72	14	37	51	151	12	1	5	6	23
1984-85	Springfield	AHL	12	0	2	2	24	3	0	0	0	6
	Indianapolis	IHL	65	10	21	31	92	7	2	1	3	23
1985-86	Springfield	AHL	20	1	1	2	52	....	....	....	....	....
	Indianapolis	IHL	11	1	1	2	11	....	....	....	....	....
	Muskegon	IHL	47	1	20	21	87	....	....	....	....	....
1986-87	Springfield	AHL	78	6	11	17	127	....	....	....	....	....
1987-88	Springfield	AHL	74	8	26	34	127	....	....	....	....	....
1988-89	Hershey	AHL	75	6	36	42	105	12	0	1	1	17
1989-90	Hershey	AHL	65	4	19	23	60	....	....	....	....	....

Signed as a free agent by **Philadelphia**, August 29, 1988.

PAEK, JIM (PAYK)

Defense. Shoots left. 6'1", 200 lbs. Born, Seoul, Korea, April 7, 1967.
(Pittsburgh's 9th choice, 170th overall, in 1985 Entry Draft).

			Regular Season					Playoffs				
Season	Club	Lea	GP	G	A	TP	PIM	GP	G	A	TP	PIM
1984-85	Oshawa	OHL	54	2	13	15	57	5	1	0	1	9
1985-86	Oshawa	OHL	64	5	21	26	122	6	0	1	1	9
1986-87	Oshawa	OHL	57	5	17	22	75	26	1	14	15	43
1987-88	Muskegon	IHL	82	7	52	59	141	6	0	0	0	29
1988-89	Muskegon	IHL	80	3	54	57	96	14	1	10	11	24
1989-90	Muskegon	IHL	81	9	41	50	115	....	....	....	....	....

PALUCH, SCOTT

Defense. Shoots left. 6'3", 185 lbs. Born, Chicago, IL, March 9, 1966.
(St. Louis' 7th choice, 92nd overall, in 1984 Entry Draft).

			Regular Season					Playoffs				
Season	Club	Lea	GP	G	A	TP	PIM	GP	G	A	TP	PIM
1984-85	Bowling Green	CCHA	42	11	25	36	64	....	....	....	....	....
1985-86	Bowling Green	CCHA	34	10	11	21	44	....	....	....	....	....
1986-87	Bowling Green	CCHA	45	13	38	51	88	....	....	....	....	....
1987-88bc	Bowling Green	CCHA	44	14	47	61	88	....	....	....	....	....
1988-89	Peoria	IHL	81	10	39	49	92	4	1	1	2	31
1989-90	Peoria	IHL	79	10	28	38	59	....	....	....	....	....

a NCAA West First All-American Team (1988)
b CCHA First All-Star Team (1988)

PANCOE, DONALD

Defense. Shoots left. 6'1", 200 lbs. Born, St. George, Ont., February 23, 1969.
(Pittsburgh's 9th choice, 193rd overall, in 1988 Entry Draft).

			Regular Season					Playoffs				
Season	Club	Lea	GP	G	A	TP	PIM	GP	G	A	TP	PIM
1986-87	Hamilton	OHL	44	4	8	12	120	9	0	1	1	24
1987-88	Hamilton	OHL	60	2	12	14	144	14	0	1	1	55
1988-89	Niagara Falls	OHL	54	1	17	18	167	15	0	2	2	38
1989-90	Niagara Falls	OHL	61	2	16	18	114	....	....	....	....	....

PANEK, CHRISTOPHER (CHRIS)

Defense. Shoots left. 6'2", 205 lbs. Born, Buffalo, NY, October 13, 1966.
(Los Angeles' 1st choice, 11th overall, in 1987 Supplemental Draft).

			Regular Season					Playoffs				
Season	Club	Lea	GP	G	A	TP	PIM	GP	G	A	TP	PIM
1987-88	Plattsburgh	NCAA	33	11	26	37	84	....	....	....	....	....
1988-89	New Haven	AHL	41	4	18	22	13	....	....	....	....	....
	Flint	IHL	8	2	1	3	9	....	....	....	....	....
1989-90	New Haven	AHL	21	1	5	6	7	....	....	....	....	....

PARDOSKI, RYAN

Left wing. Shoots left. 6'1", 165 lbs. Born, Calgary, Alta., August 19, 1968.
(New Jersey's 8th choice, 150th overall, in 1986 Entry Draft).

			Regular Season					Playoffs				
Season	Club	Lea	GP	G	A	TP	PIM	GP	G	A	TP	PIM
1986-87	U. of Michigan	CCHA	39	4	9	13	26	....	....	....	....	....
1987-88	U. of Michigan	CCHA	31	4	9	13	36	....	....	....	....	....
1988-89	U. of Michigan	CCHA	38	11	3	14	36	....	....	....	....	....
1989-90	U. of Michigan	CCHA	33	4	5	9	16	....	....	....	....	....

PARENT, RUSSELL

Defense. Shoots left. 5'9", 180 lbs. Born, Winnipeg, Man., May 6, 1968.
(NY Rangers' 11th choice, 219th overall, in 1986 Entry Draft).

			Regular Season					Playoffs				
Season	Club	Lea	GP	G	A	TP	PIM	GP	G	A	TP	PIM
1986-87	North Dakota	WCHA	47	2	17	19	50	....	....	....	....	....
1987-88	North Dakota	WCHA	30	4	20	24	38	....	....	....	....	....
1988-89a	North Dakota	WCHA	40	9	28	37	51	....	....	....	....	....
1989-90	North Dakota	WCHA	45	9	50	59	88	....	....	....	....	....

a WCHA Second All-Star Team (1989)

PARKER, JEFF

Right wing. Shoots right. 6'3", 205 lbs. Born, St. Paul, MN, September 7, 1964.
(Buffalo's 9th choice, 111th overalll, in 1982 Entry Draft).

			Regular Season					Playoffs				
Season	Club	Lea	GP	G	A	TP	PIM	GP	G	A	TP	PIM
1983-84	Michigan State	CCHA	44	8	13	21	82	....	....	....	....	....
1984-85	Michigan State	CCHA	42	10	12	22	89	....	....	....	....	....
1985-86	Michigan State	CCHA	41	15	20	35	88	....	....	....	....	....
1986-87	**Buffalo**	**NHL**	**15**	**3**	**3**	**6**	**7**	....	....	....	....	....
	Rochester	AHL	54	14	8	22	75	14	1	3	4	19
1987-88	**Buffalo**	**NHL**	**4**	**0**	**2**	**2**	**2**	....	....	....	....	....
	Rochester	AHL	34	13	31	44	69	2	1	1	2	0
1988-89	**Buffalo**	**NHL**	**57**	**9**	**9**	**18**	**82**	**5**	**0**	**0**	**0**	**26**
	Rochester	AHL	6	2	4	6	9	....	....	....	....	....
1989-90	**Buffalo**	**NHL**	**61**	**4**	**5**	**9**	**70**	....	....	....	....	....
	NHL Totals		**137**	**16**	**19**	**35**	**161**	**5**	**0**	**0**	**0**	**26**

Traded to **Winnipeg** by **Buffalo** with Phil Housley, Scott Arniel and Buffalo's first round choice (Keith Tkachuk) in 1990 Entry Draft for Dale Hawerchuk, Winnipeg's first round choice (Brad May) in 1990 Entry Draft and future considerations, June 16, 1990.

PARKER, JOHN

Center. Shoots right. 6'1", 180 lbs. Born, St. Paul, MN, March 5, 1968.
(Calgary's 5th choice, 121st overall, in 1986 Entry Draft).

			Regular Season					Playoffs				
Season	Club	Lea	GP	G	A	TP	PIM	GP	G	A	TP	PIM
1986-87	U. Wisconsin	WCHA	8	0	1	1	4	....	....	....	....	....
1987-88	U. Wisconsin	WCHA	4	0	0	0	6	....	....	....	....	....
1988-89	U. Wisconsin	WCHA	20	1	7	8	16	....	....	....	....	....
1989-90	U. Wisconsin	WCHA	35	11	9	20	22	....	....	....	....	....

PASCUCCI, RONALD

Defense. Shoots left. 6'1", 180 lbs. Born, North Andover, MA, June 9, 1970.
(Washington's 14th choice, 246th overall, in 1988 Entry Draft).

			Regular Season					Playoffs				
Season	Club	Lea	GP	G	A	TP	PIM	GP	G	A	TP	PIM
1988-89	Belmont Hills	HS	....	9	20	29	....	....	....	....	....	....
1989-90	Boston College	H.E.	37	0	6	6	12	....	....	....	....	....

PASEK, DUSAN (PAH-shehk, do-SHAHN)

Center. Shoots left. 6'1", 200 lbs. Born, Bratislava, Czechoslovakia, September 7, 1960.
(Minnesota's 4th choice, 81st overall, in 1982 Entry Draft).

			Regular Season					Playoffs				
Season	Club	Lea	GP	G	A	TP	PIM	GP	G	A	TP	PIM
1986-87	Bratislava	Czech.	32	18	27	45	....	....	....	....	....	....
1987-88	Bratislava	Czech.	28	13	10	23	....	....	....	....	....	....
1988-89	**Minnesota**	**NHL**	**48**	**4**	**10**	**14**	**30**	**2**	**1**	**0**	**1**	**0**
1989-90	Kalamazoo	IHL	20	10	14	24	16	....	....	....	....	....
	NHL Totals		**48**	**4**	**10**	**14**	**30**	**2**	**1**	**0**	**1**	**0**

PASIN, DAVE (puh-SEEN)

Right wing. Shoots right. 6'1", 205 lbs. Born, Edmonton, Alta., July 8, 1966.
(Boston's 1st choice, 19th overall, in 1984 Entry Draft).

			Regular Season					Playoffs				
Season	Club	Lea	GP	G	A	TP	PIM	GP	G	A	TP	PIM
1982-83	Prince Albert	WHL	62	40	42	82	48	....	....	....	....	....
1983-84	Prince Albert	WHL	71	68	54	122	68	5	1	4	5	0
1984-85a	Prince Albert	WHL	65	64	52	116	88	10	10	11	21	10
1985-86	**Boston**	**NHL**	**71**	**18**	**19**	**37**	**50**	**3**	**0**	**1**	**1**	**0**
1986-87	Moncton	AHL	66	27	25	52	47	6	1	1	2	14
1987-88	Maine	AHL	30	8	14	22	39	8	4	3	7	13
1988-89	Maine	AHL	11	2	5	7	6	....	....	....	....	....
	Los Angeles	**NHL**	**5**	**0**	**0**	**0**	**0**	....	....	....	....	....
	New Haven	AHL	48	25	23	48	42	17	8	8	16	47
1989-90	New Haven	AHL	7	7	4	11	14	....	....	....	....	....
	Springfield	AHL	11	2	3	5	2	3	1	2	3	2
	NHL Totals		**76**	**18**	**19**	**37**	**50**	**3**	**0**	**1**	**1**	**0**

a WHL Second All-Star Team, East Division (1985).

Rights traded to **Los Angeles** by **Boston** for Paul Guay, November 3, 1988. Claimed on waivers by **NY Islanders** from **Los Angeles**, March 6, 1990.

PASLAWSKI, GREGORY STEPHEN (GREG) (pas-LAW-skee)

Right wing. Shoots right. 5'11", 190 lbs. Born, Kindersley, Sask., August 25, 1961.

			Regular Season					Playoffs				
Season	Club	Lea	GP	G	A	TP	PIM	GP	G	A	TP	PIM
1981-82	Nova Scotia	AHL	43	15	11	26	31	....	....	....	....	....
1982-83	Nova Scotia	AHL	75	46	42	88	32	6	1	3	4	8
1983-84	**Montreal**	**NHL**	**26**	**1**	**4**	**5**	**4**	....	....	....	....	....
	St. Louis	**NHL**	**34**	**8**	**6**	**14**	**17**	**9**	**1**	**0**	**1**	**2**
1984-85	**St. Louis**	**NHL**	**72**	**22**	**20**	**42**	**21**	**3**	**0**	**0**	**0**	**2**
1985-86	**St. Louis**	**NHL**	**56**	**22**	**11**	**33**	**18**	**17**	**10**	**7**	**17**	**13**
1986-87	**St. Louis**	**NHL**	**76**	**29**	**35**	**64**	**27**	**6**	**1**	**1**	**2**	**4**
1987-88	**St. Louis**	**NHL**	**17**	**2**	**1**	**3**	**4**	**3**	**1**	**1**	**2**	**2**
1988-89	**St. Louis**	**NHL**	**75**	**26**	**26**	**52**	**18**	**9**	**2**	**1**	**3**	**2**
1989-90	**Winnipeg**	**NHL**	**71**	**18**	**30**	**48**	**14**	**7**	**1**	**3**	**4**	**0**
	NHL Totals		**427**	**128**	**133**	**261**	**123**	**54**	**16**	**13**	**29**	**25**

Signed as free agent by **Montreal**, October 5, 1981. Traded to **St. Louis** by **Montreal** with Gilbert Delorme and Doug Wickenheiser for Perry Turnbull, December 21, 1983. Traded to **Winnipeg** by **St. Louis** with St. Louis' third round choice (Kris Draper) in 1989 Entry Draft for Winnipeg's third round choice (Denny Felsner) in 1989 Entry Draft and second round choice in 1991 Entry Draft, June 17, 1989.

PASMA, ROD

Defense. Shoots left. 6'4", 205 lbs. Born, Hespeler, Ont., February 26, 1972.
(Washington's 2nd choice, 30th overall, in 1990 Entry Draft).

			Regular Season					Playoffs				
Season	Club	Lea	GP	G	A	TP	PIM	GP	G	A	TP	PIM
1988-89	Georgetown	Jr.B	37	4	14	18	58	....	....	....	....	....
1989-90	Cornwall	OHL	64	3	16	19	142	6	0	2	2	15

PATERSON, JOSEPH (JOE)

Left wing. Shoots left. 6'2", 205 lbs. Born, Toronto, Ont., June 25, 1960.
(Detroit's 5th choice, 87th overall, in 1979 Entry Draft).

			Regular Season					Playoffs				
Season	Club	Lea	GP	G	A	TP	PIM	GP	G	A	TP	PIM
1978-79	London	OHA	59	22	19	41	158	7	2	3	5	13
1979-80	London	OHA	62	21	50	71	156	....	....	....	....	....
	Kalamazoo	IHL	4	1	2	3	2	3	2	1	3	11
1980-81	**Detroit**	**NHL**	**38**	**2**	**5**	**7**	**53**	....	....	....	....	....
	Adirondack	AHL	39	9	16	25	68	....	....	....	....	....
1981-82	**Detroit**	**NHL**	**3**	**0**	**0**	**0**	**0**	....	....	....	....	....
	Adirondack	AHL	74	22	28	50	132	5	1	4	5	6
1982-83	**Detroit**	**NHL**	**33**	**2**	**1**	**3**	**14**	....	....	....	....	....
	Adirondack	AHL	36	11	10	21	85	6	1	2	3	21
1983-84	**Detroit**	**NHL**	**41**	**2**	**5**	**7**	**148**	**3**	**0**	**0**	**0**	**7**
	Adirondack	AHL	20	10	15	25	43	....	....	....	....	....
1984-85	**Philadelphia**	**NHL**	**6**	**0**	**0**	**0**	**31**	**17**	**3**	**4**	**7**	**70**
	Hershey	AHL	67	26	27	53	173	....	....	....	....	....
1985-86	**Philadelphia**	**NHL**	**5**	**0**	**0**	**0**	**12**	....	....	....	....	....
	Hershey	AHL	20	5	10	15	68	....	....	....	....	....
	Los Angeles	**NHL**	**47**	**9**	**18**	**27**	**153**	....	....	....	....	....
1986-87	**Los Angeles**	**NHL**	**45**	**2**	**1**	**3**	**158**	**2**	**0**	**0**	**0**	**0**
1987-88	**Los Angeles**	**NHL**	**32**	**1**	**3**	**4**	**113**	....	....	....	....	....
	NY Rangers	**NHL**	**21**	**1**	**3**	**4**	**63**	....	....	....	....	....
1988-89	**NY Rangers**	**NHL**	**20**	**0**	**1**	**1**	**84**	....	....	....	....	....
	Denver	IHL	9	5	4	9	31	....	....	....	....	....
1989-90	Flint	IHL	69	21	26	47	198	4	0	1	1	2
	NHL Totals		**291**	**19**	**37**	**56**	**829**	**22**	**3**	**4**	**7**	**77**

Traded to **Philadelphia** by **Detroit** with Murray Craven for Darryl Sittler, October 19, 1984. Traded to **Los Angeles** by **Philadelphia** for Philadelphia's fourth-round choice (Mark Bar) — acquired earlier — in 1986 Entry Draft, December 18, 1985. Traded to **NY Rangers** by **Los Angeles** for Gordon Walker and Mike Siltala, January 21, 1988.

PATRICK, JAMES

Defense. Shoots right. 6'2", 195 lbs. Born, Winnipeg, Man., June 14, 1963.
(NY Rangers' 1st choice, 9th overall, in 1981 Entry Draft).

			Regular Season					Playoffs				
Season	Club	Lea	GP	G	A	TP	PIM	GP	G	A	TP	PIM
1981-82cde	North Dakota	WCHA	42	5	24	29	26	....	....	....	....	....
1982-83fg	North Dakota	WCHA	36	12	36	48	29	....	....	....	....	....
1983-84	Cdn. Olympic	....	63	7	24	31	52	....	....	....	....	....
	NY Rangers	**NHL**	**12**	**1**	**7**	**8**	**2**	**5**	**0**	**3**	**3**	**2**
1984-85	**NY Rangers**	**NHL**	**75**	**8**	**28**	**36**	**71**	**3**	**0**	**0**	**0**	**4**
1985-86	**NY Rangers**	**NHL**	**75**	**14**	**29**	**43**	**88**	**16**	**1**	**5**	**6**	**34**
1986-87	**NY Rangers**	**NHL**	**78**	**10**	**45**	**55**	**62**	**6**	**1**	**2**	**3**	**2**
1987-88	**NY Rangers**	**NHL**	**70**	**17**	**45**	**62**	**52**	....	....	....	....	....
1988-89	**NY Rangers**	**NHL**	**68**	**11**	**36**	**47**	**41**	**4**	**0**	**1**	**1**	**2**
1989-90	**NY Rangers**	**NHL**	**73**	**14**	**43**	**57**	**50**	**10**	**3**	**8**	**11**	**0**
	NHL Totals		**451**	**75**	**233**	**308**	**366**	**44**	**5**	**19**	**24**	**44**

a Most Valuable Player, 1981 Centennial Cup Tournament.
b First All-Star Team, 1981 Centennial Cup Tournament.
c WCHA Rookie of the Year (1982)
d WCHA Second All-Star Team (1982)
e Named to NCAA All-Tournament Team (1982)
f WCHA First All-Star Team (1983)
g NCAA All American (West) (1983)

PATTERSON, COLIN

Left wing. Shoots right. 6'2", 195 lbs. Born, Rexdale, Ont., May 11, 1960.

			Regular Season					Playoffs				
Season	Club	Lea	GP	G	A	TP	PIM	GP	G	A	TP	PIM
1980-81	Clarkson	ECAC	34	20	31	51	8	....	....	....	....	....
1981-82	Clarkson	ECAC	34	21	31	52	32	....	....	....	....	....
1982-83	Clarkson	ECAC	31	23	29	52	30	....	....	....	....	....
	Colorado	CHL	7	1	1	2	0	3	0	0	0	15
1983-84	**Calgary**	**NHL**	**56**	**13**	**14**	**27**	**15**	**11**	**1**	**1**	**2**	**6**
	Colorado	CHL	6	2	3	5	9	....	....	....	....	....
1984-85	**Calgary**	**NHL**	**57**	**22**	**21**	**43**	**5**	**4**	**0**	**0**	**0**	**5**
1985-86	**Calgary**	**NHL**	**61**	**14**	**13**	**27**	**22**	**19**	**6**	**3**	**9**	**10**
1986-87	**Calgary**	**NHL**	**68**	**13**	**13**	**26**	**41**	**6**	**0**	**2**	**2**	**2**
1987-88	**Calgary**	**NHL**	**39**	**7**	**11**	**18**	**28**	**9**	**1**	**0**	**1**	**8**
1988-89	**Calgary**	**NHL**	**74**	**14**	**24**	**38**	**56**	**22**	**3**	**10**	**13**	**24**
1989-90	**Calgary**	**NHL**	**61**	**5**	**3**	**8**	**20**	....	....	....	....	....
	NHL Totals		**416**	**88**	**99**	**187**	**187**	**71**	**11**	**16**	**27**	**55**

Signed as a free agent by **Calgary** March 24, 1983.

PAVLAS, PETR

Defense. Shoots left. 5'10", 170 lbs. Born, Olomouc, Czechoslovakia, February 4, 1968.
(Washington's 10th choice, 183rd overall, in 1988 Entry Draft).

			Regular Season					Playoffs				
Season	Club	Lea	GP	G	A	TP	PIM	GP	G	A	TP	PIM
1987-88	Dukla Trencin	Czech.	20	4	7	11	....	....	....	....	....	....
1988-89	Dukla Trencin	Czech.	31	14	15	29	....	....	....	....	....	....
1989-90	Gottwaldov	Czech	51	13	15	28	....	....	....	....	....	....

PAYNE, DAVIS

Left wing. Shoots left. 6'1", 190 lbs. Born, King City, Ont., October 24, 1970.
(Edmonton's 6th choice, 140th overall, in 1989 Entry Draft).

			Regular Season					Playoffs				
Season	Club	Lea	GP	G	A	TP	PIM	GP	G	A	TP	PIM
1988-89	Michigan Tech	WCHA	33	5	3	8	39	....	....	....	....	....
1989-90	Michigan Tech	WCHA	36	11	10	21	81	....	....	....	....	....

PAYNTER, KENT

Defense. Shoots left. 6', 185 lbs. Born, Summerside, PEI, April 17, 1965.
(Chicago's 9th choice, 159th overall, in 1983 Entry Draft).

			Regular Season					Playoffs				
Season	Club	Lea	GP	G	A	TP	PIM	GP	G	A	TP	PIM
1982-83	Kitchener	OHL	65	4	11	15	97	12	1	0	1	20
1983-84	Kitchener	OHL	65	9	27	36	94	16	4	9	13	18
1984-85	Kitchener	OHL	58	7	28	35	93	4	2	1	3	4
1985-86	Nova Scotia	AHL	23	1	2	3	36	....	....	....	....	....
	Saginaw	IHL	4	0	1	1	2	....	....	....	....	....
1986-87	Nova Scotia	AHL	66	2	6	8	57	2	0	0	0	0
1987-88	**Chicago**	**NHL**	**2**	**0**	**0**	**0**	**2**	....	....	....	....	....
	Saginaw	IHL	74	8	20	28	141	10	0	1	1	30
1988-89	**Chicago**	**NHL**	**1**	**0**	**0**	**0**	**2**	....	....	....	....	....
	Saginaw	IHL	69	12	14	26	148	6	2	2	4	17
1989-90	**Washington**	**NHL**	**13**	**1**	**2**	**3**	**18**	**3**	**0**	**0**	**0**	**10**
	Baltimore	AHL	60	7	20	27	110	11	5	6	1	34
	NHL Totals		**16**	**1**	**2**	**3**	**22**	**3**	**0**	**0**	**0**	**10**

Signed as a free agent by **Washington**, August 21, 1989.

PEARSON, ROB

Right wing. Shoots right. 6'1", 175 lbs. Born, Oshawa, Ont., August 3, 1971.
(Toronto's 2nd choice, 12th overall, in 1989 Entry Draft).

			Regular Season					Playoffs				
Season	Club	Lea	GP	G	A	TP	PIM	GP	G	A	TP	PIM
1988-89	Belleville	OHL	26	8	12	20	51	....	....	....	....	....
1989-90	Belleville	OHL	58	48	40	88	174	11	5	5	10	26

PEARSON, SCOTT

Left wing. Shoots left. 6'1", 205 lbs. Born, Cornwall, Ont., December 19, 1969.
(Toronto's 1st choice, 6th overall, in 1988 Entry Draft).

			Regular Season					Playoffs				
Season	Club	Lea	GP	G	A	TP	PIM	GP	G	A	TP	PIM
1986-87	Kingston	OHL	62	30	24	54	101	9	3	3	6	42
1987-88	Kingston	OHL	46	26	32	58	117	....	....	....	....	....
1988-89	**Toronto**	**NHL**	**9**	**0**	**1**	**1**	**2**	....	....	....	....	....
	Kingston	OHL	13	9	8	17	34	....	....	....	....	....
	Niagara Falls	OHL	32	26	34	60	90	17	14	10	24	53
1989-90	**Toronto**	**NHL**	**41**	**5**	**10**	**15**	**90**	**2**	**2**	**0**	**2**	**10**
	Newmarket	AHL	18	12	11	23	64	....	....	....	....	....
	NHL Totals		**50**	**5**	**11**	**16**	**92**	**2**	**2**	**0**	**2**	**10**

PEDERSEN, ALLEN

Defense. Shoots left. 6'4", 205 lbs. Born, Edmonton, Alta., January 13, 1965.
(Boston's 5th choice, 105th overall, in 1983 Entry Draft).

			Regular Season					Playoffs				
Season	Club	Lea	GP	G	A	TP	PIM	GP	G	A	TP	PIM
1982-83	Medicine Hat	WHL	63	3	10	13	49	5	0	0	0	7
1983-84	Medicine Hat	WHL	44	0	11	11	47	14	0	2	2	24
1984-85	Medicine Hat	WHL	72	6	16	22	66	10	0	0	0	9
1985-86	Moncton	AHL	59	1	8	9	39	3	0	0	0	0
1986-87	**Boston**	**NHL**	**79**	**1**	**11**	**12**	**71**	**4**	**0**	**0**	**0**	**4**
1987-88	**Boston**	**NHL**	**78**	**0**	**6**	**6**	**90**	**21**	**0**	**0**	**0**	**34**
1988-89	**Boston**	**NHL**	**51**	**0**	**6**	**6**	**69**	**10**	**0**	**0**	**0**	**2**
1989-90	**Boston**	**NHL**	**68**	**1**	**2**	**3**	**71**	**21**	**0**	**0**	**0**	**41**
	NHL Totals		**276**	**2**	**25**	**27**	**301**	**56**	**0**	**0**	**0**	**81**

PEDERSON, BARRY ALAN (PEE-duhr-suhn)

Center. Shoots right. 5'11", 185 lbs. Born, Big River, Sask., March 13, 1961.
(Boston's 1st choice, 18th overall, in 1980 Entry Draft).

			Regular Season					Playoffs				
Season	Club	Lea	GP	G	A	TP	PIM	GP	G	A	TP	PIM
1978-79	Victoria	WHL	72	31	53	84	41	....	....	....	....	....
1979-80	Victoria	WHL	72	52	88	140	50	16	13	14	27	31
1980-81a	Victoria	WHL	55	65	82	147	65	15	15	21	36	10
	Boston	**NHL**	**9**	**1**	**4**	**5**	**6**	....	....	....	....	....
1981-82	**Boston**	**NHL**	**80**	**44**	**48**	**92**	**53**	**11**	**7**	**11**	**18**	**2**
1982-83	**Boston**	**NHL**	**77**	**46**	**61**	**107**	**47**	**17**	**14**	**18**	**32**	**21**
1983-84	**Boston**	**NHL**	**80**	**39**	**77**	**116**	**64**	**3**	**0**	**1**	**1**	**2**
1984-85	**Boston**	**NHL**	**22**	**4**	**8**	**12**	**10**	....	....	....	....	....
1985-86	**Boston**	**NHL**	**79**	**29**	**47**	**76**	**60**	**3**	**1**	**0**	**1**	**0**
1986-87	**Vancouver**	**NHL**	**79**	**24**	**52**	**76**	**50**	....	....	....	....	....
1987-88	**Vancouver**	**NHL**	**76**	**19**	**52**	**71**	**92**	....	....	....	....	....
1988-89	**Vancouver**	**NHL**	**62**	**15**	**26**	**41**	**22**	....	....	....	....	....
1989-90	**Vancouver**	**NHL**	**16**	**2**	**7**	**9**	**10**	....	....	....	....	....
	Pittsburgh	**NHL**	**38**	**4**	**18**	**22**	**29**	....	....	....	....	....
	NHL Totals		**618**	**227**	**400**	**627**	**443**	**34**	**22**	**30**	**52**	**25**

a WHL First All-Star Team (1981)

Played in NHL All-Star Game (1983, 1984)

Traded to **Vancouver** by **Boston** for Cam Neely and Vancouver's first-round choice in 1987 Entry Draft (Glen Wesley), June 6, 1986. Traded to **Pittsburgh** by **Vancouver** with Rod Buskas and Tony Tanti for Dave Capuano, Andrew McBain and Dan Quinn, January 8, 1990.

PEDERSON, MARK

Left wing. Shoots left. 6'2", 196 lbs. Born, Prelate, Sask., January 14, 1968.
(Montreal's 1st choice, 15th overall, in 1986 Entry Draft).

			Regular Season					Playoffs				
Season	Club	Lea	GP	G	A	TP	PIM	GP	G	A	TP	PIM
1984-85	Medicine Hat	WHL	71	42	40	82	63	10	3	2	5	0
1985-86	Medicine Hat	WHL	72	46	60	106	46	25	12	6	18	25
1986-87a	Medicine Hat	WHL	69	56	46	102	58	20	*19	7	26	14
1987-88	Medicine Hat	WHL	62	53	58	111	55	16	*13	6	19	16
1988-89	Sherbrooke	AHL	75	43	38	81	53	6	7	5	12	4
1989-90	**Montreal**	**NHL**	**9**	**0**	**2**	**2**	**2**	**2**	**0**	**0**	**0**	**0**
b	Sherbrooke	AHL	72	53	42	95	60	11	10	8	18	19
	NHL Totals		**9**	**0**	**2**	**2**	**2**	**2**	**0**	**0**	**0**	**0**

a WHL East All-Star Team (1987)
b AHL First All-Star Team (1990)

PEDERSON, THOMAS

Defense. Shoots right. 5'9", 165 lbs. Born, Bloomington, MN, January 1, 1970.
(Minnesota's 12th choice, 217th overall, in 1989 Entry Draft).

			Regular Season					Playoffs				
Season	Club	Lea	GP	G	A	TP	PIM	GP	G	A	TP	PIM
1988-89	U. Minnesota	WCHA	36	4	20	24	40	....	....	....	....	....
1989-90	U. Minnesota	WCHA	43	8	30	38	58	....	....	....	....	....

PELLERIN, SCOTT

Left wing. Shoots left. 5'10", 180 lbs. Born, Shediac, N.B., January 9, 1970.
(New Jersey's 4th choice, 47th overall, in 1989 Entry Draft).

			Regular Season					Playoffs				
Season	Club	Lea	GP	G	A	TP	PIM	GP	G	A	TP	PIM
1988-89a	U. of Maine	H.E.	45	29	33	62	92	....	....	....	....	....
1989-90	U. of Maine	H.E.	42	22	34	56	68	....	....	....	....	....

a Co-winner Hockey East Rookie of the Year (1989)

PELTOLA, PEKKA

Right wing. Shoots right. 5'11" 185 lbs. Born, Helsinki, Finland, June 24, 1965.
(Winnipeg's 8th choice, 130th overall, in 1989 Entry Draft).

			Regular Season					Playoffs				
Season	Club	Lea	GP	G	A	TP	PIM	GP	G	A	TP	PIM
1988-89	HPK	Fin.	43	28	30	58	62	....	....	....	....	....
1989-90	HPK	Fin.	45	25	24	49	42	....	....	....	....	....

PELTOMAA, TIMO

Right wing. Shoots right. 6'1", 185 lbs. Born, Toijala, Finland, July 26, 1968.
(Los Angeles' 9th choice, 154th overall, in 1988 Entry Draft).

			Regular Season					Playoffs				
Season	Club	Lea	GP	G	A	TP	PIM	GP	G	A	TP	PIM
1987-88	Ilves	Fin.	20	0	1	1	32	....	....	....	....	....
1988-89	Ilves	Fin.	23	4	0	4	16	....	....	....	....	....
1989-90	Ilves	Fin.	43	7	3	10	28	....	....	....	....	....

PELUSO, MIKE

Defense. Shoots left. 6'4", 200 lbs. Born, Hibbing, MN, November 8, 1965.
(New Jersey's 10th choice, 190th overall, in 1984 Entry Draft).

			Regular Season					Playoffs				
Season	Club	Lea	GP	G	A	TP	PIM	GP	G	A	TP	PIM
1985-86	Alaska-Anch.	NCAA	32	2	11	13	59	....	....	....	....	....
1986-87	Alaska-Anch.	NCAA	30	5	21	26	68	....	....	....	....	....
1987-88	Alaska-Anch.	NCAA	35	4	33	37	76	....	....	....	....	....
1988-89	Alaska-Anch.	NCAA	33	10	27	37	75	....	....	....	....	....
1989-90	**Chicago**	**NHL**	**2**	**0**	**0**	**0**	**0**	....	....	....	....	....
	Indianapolis	IHL	75	7	10	17	279	14	0	1	1	58
	NHL Totals		**2**	**0**	**0**	**0**	**0**	....	....	....	....	....

Signed as a free agent by **Chicago**, September 7, 1989.

PENNEY, JACKSON

Center. Shoots left. 5'10", 180 lbs. Born, Edmonton, Alta., February 5, 1969.
(Boston's 4th choice, 80th overall, in 1989 Entry Draft).

			Regular Season					Playoffs				
Season	Club	Lea	GP	G	A	TP	PIM	GP	G	A	TP	PIM
1987-88	Victoria	WHL	53	22	36	58	31	8	3	2	5	14
1988-89a	Victoria	WHL	63	41	49	90	78	8	6	3	9	12
1989-90	Victoria	WHL	3	0	1	1	4	....	....	....	....	....
b	Prince Albert	WHL	55	53	32	85	91	12	11	4	15	28

a WHL East First All-Star Team (1989)
b WHL East Second All-Star Team (1990)

PEPLINSKI, JAMES DESMOND (JIM) (peh-PLINS-kee)

Right wing. Shoots right. 6'3", 209 lbs. Born, Renfrew, Ont., October 24, 1960.
(Atlanta's 5th choice, 75th overall, in 1979 Entry Draft).

			Regular Season					Playoffs				
Season	Club	Lea	GP	G	A	TP	PIM	GP	G	A	TP	PIM
1978-79	Toronto	OHA	66	23	32	55	88	3	0	1	1	0
1979-80	Toronto	OHA	67	35	66	101	89	4	1	2	3	15
1980-81	**Calgary**	**NHL**	**80**	**13**	**25**	**38**	**108**	**16**	**2**	**3**	**5**	**41**
1981-82	**Calgary**	**NHL**	**74**	**30**	**37**	**67**	**115**	**3**	**1**	**0**	**1**	**13**
1982-83	**Calgary**	**NHL**	**80**	**15**	**26**	**41**	**134**	**8**	**1**	**1**	**2**	**45**
1983-84	**Calgary**	**NHL**	**74**	**11**	**22**	**33**	**114**	**11**	**3**	**4**	**7**	**21**
1984-85	**Calgary**	**NHL**	**80**	**16**	**29**	**45**	**111**	**4**	**1**	**3**	**4**	**11**
1985-86	**Calgary**	**NHL**	**77**	**24**	**35**	**59**	**214**	**22**	**5**	**9**	**14**	**107**
1986-87	**Calgary**	**NHL**	**80**	**18**	**32**	**50**	**181**	**6**	**1**	**0**	**1**	**24**
1987-88	**Calgary**	**NHL**	**75**	**20**	**31**	**51**	**234**	**9**	**0**	**5**	**5**	**45**
	Cdn. Olympic	....	7	0	1	1	6	....	....	....	....	....
1988-89	**Calgary**	**NHL**	**79**	**13**	**25**	**38**	**241**	**20**	**1**	**6**	**7**	**75**
1989-90	**Calgary**	**NHL**	**6**	**1**	**0**	**1**	**4**	....	....	....	....	....
	NHL Totals		**705**	**161**	**262**	**423**	**1456**	**99**	**15**	**31**	**46**	**382**

PERGOLA, DAVID

Right wing. Shoots right. 6'1", 185 lbs. Born, Waltham, MA, March 4, 1969.
(Buffalo's 5th choice, 85th overall, in 1987 Entry Draft).

			Regular Season					Playoffs				
Season	Club	Lea	GP	G	A	TP	PIM	GP	G	A	TP	PIM
1987-88	Boston College	H.E.	33	5	7	12	22	....	....	....	....	....
1988-89	Boston College	H.E.	39	12	9	21	16	....	....	....	....	....
1989-90	Boston College	H.E.	39	6	4	10	22	....	....	....	....	....

PERREAULT, NICOLAS P.

Defense. Shoots left. 6'3", 200 lbs. Born, Loretteville, Que., April 24, 1972.
(Calgary's 2nd choice, 26th overall, in 1990 Entry Draft).

			Regular Season					Playoffs				
Season	Club	Lea	GP	G	A	TP	PIM	GP	G	A	TP	PIM
1989-90	Hawkesbury	COJHL	46	22	34	56	188	....	....	....	....	....

PERSSON, JOAKIM

Left wing. Shoots left. 5'8", 165 lbs. Born, Gavle, Sweden, May 15, 1966.
(Chicago's 10th choice, 195th overall, in 1984 Entry Draft).

			Regular Season					Playoffs				
Season	Club	Lea	GP	G	A	TP	PIM	GP	G	A	TP	PIM
1985-86	Stromsbro	Swe.	35	8	8	13	2	2	0	0	0	0
1986-87	Brynas	Swe.	34	9	8	17	10	....	....	....	....	....
1987-88	Stromsbro	Swe.	37	10	11	21	12	....	....	....	....	....
1988-89	Brynas	Swe.	39	7	10	17	22	....	....	....	....	....
1989-90	Brynas	Swe.	39	12	8	20	8	5	1	2	3	8

PERSSON, LARS RICKARD

Defense. Shoots left. 6'2", 205 lbs. Born, Ostersund, Sweden, August 24, 1969.
(New Jersey's 2nd choice, 23rd overall, in 1987 Entry Draft).

			Regular Season					Playoffs				
Season	Club	Lea	GP	G	A	TP	PIM	GP	G	A	TP	PIM
1987-88	Leksand	Swe.	21	2	0	2	8	....	....	....	....	....
1988-89	Leksand	Swe.	33	2	4	6	28	....	....	....	....	....
1989-90	Leksand	Swe.	40	9	10	19	56	....	....	....	....	....

PESKLEWIS, MATT

Left wing. Shoots left. 6'2", 185 lbs. Born, Edmonton, Alta., May 21, 1968.
(Boston's 4th choice, 97th overall, in 1986 Entry Draft).

			Regular Season					Playoffs				
Season	Club	Lea	GP	G	A	TP	PIM	GP	G	A	TP	PIM
1986-87	Boston U.	H.E.	24	0	2	2	28	....	....	....	....	....
1987-88	Boston U.	H.E.	28	0	11	11	54	....	....	....	....	....
1988-89	Boston U.	H.E.	12	2	7	9	31	....	....	....	....	....
1989-90	Boston U.	H.E.	DID NOT PLAY — INJURED									

PETERSON, BRETT

Defense. Shoots right. 6'2", 195 lbs. Born, St. Paul, MN, February 1, 1969.
(Calgary's 9th choice, 189th overall, in 1988 Entry Draft).

			Regular Season					Playoffs				
Season	Club	Lea	GP	G	A	TP	PIM	GP	G	A	TP	PIM
1988-89	U. of Denver	WCHA	19	0	3	3	4	....	....	....	....	....
1989-90	U. of Denver	WCHA	34	3	6	9	23	....	....	....	....	....

PETIT, MICHEL (puh-TEE)

Defense. Shoots right. 6'1", 205 lbs. Born, St. Malo, Que., February 12, 1964.
(Vancouver's 1st choice, 11th overall, in 1982 Entry Draft).

			Regular Season					Playoffs				
Season	Club	Lea	GP	G	A	TP	PIM	GP	G	A	TP	PIM
1981-82a	Sherbrooke	QMJHL	63	10	39	49	106	22	5	20	25	24
1982-83	**Vancouver**	**NHL**	**2**	**0**	**0**	**0**	**0**	....	....	....	....	....
a	St. Jean	QMJHL	62	19	67	86	196	3	0	0	0	35
1983-84	Cdn. Olympic	....	19	3	10	13	58	....	....	....	....	....
	Vancouver	**NHL**	**44**	**6**	**9**	**15**	**53**	**1**	**0**	**0**	**0**	**0**
1984-85	**Vancouver**	**NHL**	**69**	**5**	**26**	**31**	**127**	....	....	....	....	....
1985-86	**Vancouver**	**NHL**	**32**	**1**	**6**	**7**	**27**	....	....	....	....	....
	Fredericton	AHL	25	0	13	13	79	....	....	....	....	....
1986-87	**Vancouver**	**NHL**	**69**	**12**	**13**	**25**	**131**	....	....	....	....	....
1987-88	**Vancouver**	**NHL**	**10**	**0**	**3**	**3**	**35**	....	....	....	....	....
	NY Rangers	**NHL**	**64**	**9**	**24**	**33**	**223**	....	....	....	....	....
1988-89	**NY Rangers**	**NHL**	**69**	**8**	**25**	**33**	**154**	**4**	**0**	**2**	**2**	**27**
1989-90	**Quebec**	**NHL**	**63**	**12**	**24**	**36**	**215**	....	....	....	....	....
	NHL Totals		**422**	**53**	**130**	**183**	**965**	**5**	**0**	**2**	**2**	**27**

a QMJHL First All-Star Team (1982, 1983)

Traded to **NY Rangers** by **Vancouver** for Willie Huber and Larry Melnyk, November 4, 1987. Traded to **Quebec** by **NY Rangers** for Randy Moller, October 5, 1989.

PHILLIPS, GUY

Right wing. Shoots right. 6', 180 lbs. Born, Brooks, Alta., February 13, 1966.

			Regular Season					Playoffs				
Season	Club	Lea	GP	G	A	TP	PIM	GP	G	A	TP	PIM
1984-85	Medicine Hat	WHL	67	16	18	34	46	6	3	3	6	4
1985-86	Medicine Hat	WHL	72	38	55	93	66	25	10	13	23	7
1986-87	Medicine Hat	WHL	44	27	32	59	36	20	10	12	22	16
1987-88	Saginaw	IHL	73	16	30	46	14	8	2	1	3	0
1988-89	Saginaw	IHL	62	20	17	37	31	5	0	0	0	0
1989-90	Saginaw	IHL	33	4	4	8	24	2	0	0	0	0

Signed as a free agent by **Chicago**, December 30, 1987.

PICARD, MICHEL

Left wing. Shoots left. 5'11", 190 lbs. Born, Beauport, Que., November 7, 1969.
(Hartford's 8th choice, 178th overall, in 1989 Entry Draft).

			Regular Season					Playoffs				
Season	Club	Lea	GP	G	A	TP	PIM	GP	G	A	TP	PIM
1986-87	Trois-Rivieres	QMJHL	66	33	35	68	53	....	....	....	....	....
1987-88	Trois-Rivieres	QMJHL	69	40	55	95	71	....	....	....	....	....
1988-89	Trois-Rivieres	QMJHL	66	59	81	140	170	4	1	3	4	2
1989-90	Binghamton	AHL	67	16	24	40	98	....	....	....	....	....

PICARD, ROBERT RENE JOSEPH (PEE-car, roh-BEAR)

Defense. Shoots left. 6'2", 207 lbs. Born, Montreal, Que., May 25, 1957.
(Washington's 1st choice, 3rd overall, in 1977 Amateur Draft).

			Regular Season					Playoffs				
Season	Club	Lea	GP	G	A	TP	PIM	GP	G	A	TP	PIM
1975-76a	Montreal	QJHL	72	14	67	81	282	6	2	9	11	25
1976-77bc	Montreal	QJHL	70	32	60	92	267	13	2	10	12	20
1977-78	**Washington**	**NHL**	**75**	**10**	**27**	**37**	**101**	....	....	....	....	....
1978-79	**Washington**	**NHL**	**77**	**21**	**44**	**65**	**85**	....	....	....	....	....
1979-80	**Washington**	**NHL**	**78**	**11**	**43**	**54**	**122**	....	....	....	....	....
1980-81	**Toronto**	**NHL**	**59**	**6**	**19**	**25**	**68**	....	....	....	....	....
	Montreal	**NHL**	**8**	**2**	**2**	**4**	**6**	**1**	**0**	**0**	**0**	**0**
1981-82	**Montreal**	**NHL**	**62**	**2**	**26**	**28**	**106**	**5**	**1**	**1**	**2**	**7**
1982-83	**Montreal**	**NHL**	**64**	**7**	**31**	**38**	**60**	**3**	**0**	**0**	**0**	**0**
1983-84	**Montreal**	**NHL**	**7**	**0**	**2**	**2**	**0**	....	....	....	....	....
	Winnipeg	**NHL**	**62**	**6**	**16**	**22**	**34**	**3**	**0**	**0**	**0**	**12**
1984-85	**Winnipeg**	**NHL**	**78**	**12**	**22**	**34**	**107**	**8**	**2**	**2**	**4**	**8**
1985-86	**Winnipeg**	**NHL**	**20**	**2**	**5**	**7**	**17**	....	....	....	....	....
	Quebec	**NHL**	**48**	**7**	**27**	**34**	**36**	**3**	**0**	**2**	**2**	**2**
1986-87	**Quebec**	**NHL**	**78**	**8**	**20**	**28**	**71**	**13**	**2**	**10**	**12**	**10**
1987-88	**Quebec**	**NHL**	**65**	**3**	**13**	**16**	**103**	....	....	....	....	....
1988-89	**Quebec**	**NHL**	**74**	**7**	**14**	**21**	**61**	....	....	....	....	....
1989-90	**Quebec**	**NHL**	**24**	**0**	**5**	**5**	**28**	....	....	....	....	....
	Detroit	**NHL**	**20**	**0**	**3**	**3**	**20**	....	....	....	....	....
	NHL Totals		**899**	**104**	**319**	**423**	**1025**	**36**	**5**	**15**	**20**	**39**

a QJHL Second All-Star Team (1976)
b QJHL First All-Star Team (1977)
c Named QJHL's Top Defenseman (1977)

Played in NHL All-Star Game (1980, 1981)

Traded to **Toronto** by **Washington** with Tim Coulis and Washington's second round choice (Bob McGill) in 1980 Entry Draft for Mike Palmateer and Toronto's third round choice (Torrie Robertson) in 1980 Entry Draft, June 11, 1980. Traded to **Montreal** by **Toronto** for Michel Larocque, March 10, 1981. Traded to **Winnipeg** by **Montreal** for Winnipeg's third round choice (Patrick Roy) in 1984 Entry Draft, November 4, 1983. Traded to **Quebec** by **Winnipeg** for Mario Marois, November 27, 1985. Traded to **Detroit** by **Quebec** with Greg C. Adams for Tony McKegney, December 4, 1989.

PICHETTE, DAVE (pee-SHETT)

Defense. Shoots left. 6'3", 190 lbs. Born, Grand Falls, Nfld., February 4, 1960.

			Regular Season					Playoffs				
Season	Club	Lea	GP	G	A	TP	PIM	GP	G	A	TP	PIM
1978-79	Quebec	QJHL	57	10	16	26	134	6	1	1	2	35
1979-80	Quebec	QJHL	56	8	19	27	129	5	1	3	4	8
1980-81	Hershey	AHL	20	2	3	5	37	....	....	....	....	....
	Quebec	**NHL**	**46**	**4**	**16**	**20**	**62**	**1**	**0**	**0**	**0**	**14**
1981-82	**Quebec**	**NHL**	**67**	**7**	**30**	**37**	**152**	**16**	**2**	**4**	**6**	**22**
1982-83	**Quebec**	**NHL**	**53**	**3**	**21**	**24**	**49**	**2**	**0**	**1**	**1**	**0**
	Fredericton	AHL	16	3	11	14	14	....	....	....	....	....
1983-84	**Quebec**	**NHL**	**23**	**2**	**7**	**9**	**12**	....	....	....	....	....
	Fredericton	AHL	10	2	1	3	13	....	....	....	....	....
	St. Louis	**NHL**	**23**	**0**	**11**	**11**	**6**	**9**	**1**	**2**	**3**	**18**
1984-85	**New Jersey**	**NHL**	**71**	**17**	**40**	**57**	**41**	....	....	....	....	....
1985-86	**New Jersey**	**NHL**	**33**	**7**	**12**	**19**	**22**	....	....	....	....	....
	Maine	AHL	25	4	15	19	28	....	....	....	....	....
1986-87	Maine	AHL	61	6	16	22	69	....	....	....	....	....
1987-88	**NY Rangers**	**NHL**	**6**	**1**	**3**	**4**	**4**	....	....	....	....	....
	New Haven	AHL	46	10	21	31	37	....	....	....	....	....
1988-89	Cape Breton	AHL	39	5	21	26	20	....	....	....	....	....
1989-90	Halifax	AHL	58	3	18	21	65	....	....	....	....	....
	NHL Totals		**322**	**41**	**140**	**181**	**348**	**28**	**3**	**7**	**10**	**54**

Signed as free agent by **Quebec**, October 31, 1979. Traded to **St. Louis** by **Quebec** for Andre Dore, February 10, 1984. Claimed by **New Jersey** in NHL Waiver Draft, October 9, 1984.

PIIPARINEN, JARKKO

Left wing. Shoots left. 6'1", 185 lbs. Born, Lahti, Finland, April 18, 1966.
(New Jersey's 11th choice, 211th overall, in 1984 Entry Draft).

			Regular Season					Playoffs				
Season	Club	Lea	GP	G	A	TP	PIM	GP	G	A	TP	PIM
1988-89	Reipas	Fin.	18	5	9	14	22	....	....	....	....	....
1989-90	Reipas	Fin.	44	10	30	40	20	....	....	....	....	....

PILON, RICHARD

Defense. Shoots left. 6'", 202 lbs. Born, Saskatoon, Sask., April 30, 1968.
(NY Islanders' 9th choice, 143rd overall, in 1986 Entry Draft).

			Regular Season					Playoffs				
Season	Club	Lea	GP	G	A	TP	PIM	GP	G	A	TP	PIM
1986-87	Prince Albert	WHL	68	4	21	25	192	7	1	6	7	17
1987-88	Prince Albert	WHL	65	13	34	47	177	9	0	6	6	38
1988-89	**NY Islanders**	**NHL**	**62**	**0**	**14**	**14**	**242**	....	....	....	....	....
1989-90	**NY Islanders**	**NHL**	**14**	**0**	**2**	**2**	**31**	....	....	....	....	....
	NHL Totals		**76**	**0**	**16**	**16**	**273**	....	....	....	....	....

PION, RICHARD

Right wing. Shoots right. 5'10", 180 lbs. Born, Montreal, Que., July 20, 1965.

			Regular Season					Playoffs				
Season	Club	Lea	GP	G	A	TP	PIM	GP	G	A	TP	PIM
1985-86	Merrimack	NCAA	14	9	13	22	10	....	....	....	....	....
1986-87	Merrimack	NCAA	37	31	33	64	46	....	....	....	....	....
1987-88	Merrimack	NCAA	40	35	40	75	58	4	3	3	6	....
1988-89	Merrimack	NCAA	34	28	42	70	34	....	....	....	....	....
1989-90	Peoria	IHL	69	10	21	31	58	5	0	0	0	0

Signed as a free agent by **St. Louis**, August 21, 1989.

PITLICK, LANCE

Defense. Shoots right. 6', 185 lbs. Born, Minneapolis, MN, November 5, 1967.
(Minnesota's 10th choice, 180th overall, in 1986 Entry Draft).

			Regular Season					Playoffs				
Season	Club	Lea	GP	G	A	TP	PIM	GP	G	A	TP	PIM
1986-87	U. Minnesota	WCHA	45	0	9	9	88	....	....	....	....	....
1987-88	U. Minnesota	WCHA	38	3	9	12	76	....	....	....	....	....
1988-89	U. Minnesota	WCHA	47	4	9	13	95	....	....	....	....	....
1989-90	U. Minnesota	WCHA	14	3	2	5	26	....	....	....	....	....

PIVONKA, MICHAL

Center. Shoots left. 6'2", 200 lbs. Born, Kladno, Czechoslovakia, January 28, 1966.
(Washington's 3rd choice, 59th overall, in 1984 Entry Draft).

			Regular Season					Playoffs				
Season	Club	Lea	GP	G	A	TP	PIM	GP	G	A	TP	PIM
1985-86	Dukla-Jihlava	Czech.			UNAVAILABLE							
1986-87	**Washington**	**NHL**	**73**	**18**	**25**	**43**	**41**	**7**	**1**	**1**	**2**	**2**
1987-88	**Washington**	**NHL**	**71**	**11**	**23**	**34**	**28**	**14**	**4**	**9**	**13**	**4**
1988-89	**Washington**	**NHL**	**52**	**8**	**19**	**27**	**30**	**6**	**3**	**1**	**4**	**10**
	Baltimore	AHL	31	12	24	36	19	....	....	....	....	....
1989-90	**Washington**	**NHL**	**77**	**25**	**39**	**64**	**54**	**11**	**0**	**2**	**2**	**6**
	NHL Totals		**273**	**62**	**106**	**168**	**153**	**38**	**8**	**13**	**21**	**22**

PLANTE, DAN

Right wing. Shoots right. 5'11", 190 lbs. Born, St. Louis, MO, October 5, 1971.
(NY Islanders' 3rd choice, 48th overall, in 1990 Entry Draft).

			Regular Season					Playoffs				
Season	Club	Lea	GP	G	A	TP	PIM	GP	G	A	TP	PIM
1988-89	Edina	HS	27	10	26	36	....	....	....	....	....	....
1989-90	Edina	HS	24	8	18	26	....	....	....	....	....	....

PLANTE, DEREK

Center. Shoots left. 5'11", 160 lbs. Born, Duluth, MN, January 17, 1971.
(Buffalo's 7th choice, 161st overall, in 1989 Entry Draft).

			Regular Season					Playoffs				
Season	Club	Lea	GP	G	A	TP	PIM	GP	G	A	TP	PIM
1988-89	Cloquet	HS	24	30	33	63	....	....	....	....	....	....
1989-90	Minn.-Duluth	WCHA	28	10	11	21	12	....	....	....	....	....

PLAVSIC, ADRIEN

Defense. Shoots left. 6'1", 190 lbs. Born, Montreal, Que., January 13, 1970.
(St. Louis' 2nd choice, 30th overall, in 1988 Entry Draft).

			Regular Season					Playoffs				
Season	Club	Lea	GP	G	A	TP	PIM	GP	G	A	TP	PIM
1987-88	N. Hampshire	H.E.	30	5	6	11	45	....	....	....	....	....
1988-89	Cdn. National	....	62	5	10	15	25	....	....	....	....	....
1989-90	**St. Louis**	**NHL**	**4**	**0**	**1**	**1**	**2**	....	....	....	....	....
	Peoria	IHL	51	7	14	21	87	....	....	....	....	....
	Vancouver	**NHL**	**11**	**3**	**2**	**5**	**8**	....	....	....	....	....
	Milwaukee	IHL	3	1	2	3	14	6	1	3	4	6
	NHL Totals		**15**	**3**	**3**	**6**	**10**	....	....	....	....	....

Traded to **Vancouver** by **St. Louis** with Montreal's first round choice (Shawn Antoski) – previously acquired by St. Louis – in 1990 Entry Draft and St. Louis' second round choice in 1991 Entry Draft for Rich Sutter, Harold Snepsts and St. Louis' second round choice (Craig Johnson) – previously acquired by Vancouver – in 1990 Entry Draft, March 6, 1990.

PLAYFAIR, JAMES (JIM)

Defense. Shoots left. 6'4", 200 lbs. Born, Fort St. James, B.C., May 22, 1964.
(Edmonton's 1st choice, 20th overall, in 1982 Entry Draft).

			Regular Season					Playoffs				
Season	Club	Lea	GP	G	A	TP	PIM	GP	G	A	TP	PIM
1981-82	Portland	WHL	70	4	13	17	121	15	1	2	3	21
1982-83	Portland	WHL	63	8	27	35	218	14	0	5	5	16
1983-84	**Edmonton**	**NHL**	**2**	**1**	**1**	**2**	**2**	....	....	....	....	....
	Portland	WHL	16	5	6	11	38	....	....	....	....	....
	Calgary	WHL	60	11	15	26	134	4	0	1	1	2
1984-85	Nova Scotia	AHL	41	0	4	4	107	....	....	....	....	....
1985-86	Nova Scotia	AHL	73	2	12	14	160	....	....	....	....	....
1986-87	Nova Scotia	AHL	60	1	21	22	82	....	....	....	....	....
1987-88	**Chicago**	**NHL**	**12**	**1**	**3**	**4**	**21**	....	....	....	....	....
	Saginaw	IHL	50	5	21	26	133	....	....	....	....	....
1988-89	**Chicago**	**NHL**	**7**	**0**	**0**	**0**	**28**	....	....	....	....	....
	Saginaw	IHL	23	3	6	9	73	6	0	2	2	20
1989-90	Saginaw	IHL	67	7	24	31	137	14	1	5	6	24
	NHL Totals		**21**	**2**	**4**	**6**	**51**	....	....	....	....	....

Signed as a free agent by **Chicago**, July 31, 1987.

PLAYFAIR, LARRY WILLIAM

Defense. Shoots left. 6'4", 205 lbs. Born, Fort St. James, B.C., June 23, 1958.
(Buffalo's 1st choice, 13th overall, in 1978 Amateur Draft).

			Regular Season					Playoffs				
Season	Club	Lea	GP	G	A	TP	PIM	GP	G	A	TP	PIM
1976-77	Portland	WHL	65	2	17	19	199	8	0	0	0	4
1977-78a	Portland	WHL	71	13	19	32	402	8	0	2	2	58
1978-79	**Buffalo**	**NHL**	**26**	**0**	**3**	**3**	**60**	....	....	....	....	....
	Hershey	AHL	45	0	12	12	148	....	....	....	....	....
1979-80	**Buffalo**	**NHL**	**79**	**2**	**10**	**12**	**145**	**14**	**0**	**2**	**2**	**29**
1980-81	**Buffalo**	**NHL**	**75**	**3**	**9**	**12**	**169**	**8**	**0**	**0**	**0**	**26**
1981-82	**Buffalo**	**NHL**	**77**	**6**	**10**	**16**	**258**	**4**	**0**	**0**	**0**	**22**
1982-83	**Buffalo**	**NHL**	**79**	**4**	**13**	**17**	**180**	**5**	**0**	**1**	**1**	**11**
1983-84	**Buffalo**	**NHL**	**76**	**5**	**11**	**16**	**211**	**3**	**0**	**0**	**0**	**0**
1984-85	**Buffalo**	**NHL**	**72**	**3**	**14**	**17**	**157**	**5**	**0**	**3**	**3**	**9**
1985-86	**Buffalo**	**NHL**	**47**	**1**	**2**	**3**	**100**	....	....	....	....	....
	Los Angeles	**NHL**	**14**	**0**	**1**	**1**	**26**	....	....	....	....	....
1986-87	**Los Angeles**	**NHL**	**37**	**2**	**7**	**9**	**181**	....	....	....	....	....
1987-88	**Los Angeles**	**NHL**	**54**	**0**	**7**	**7**	**197**	**3**	**0**	**0**	**0**	**14**
1988-89	**Los Angeles**	**NHL**	**6**	**0**	**3**	**3**	**16**	....	....	....	....	....
	Buffalo	**NHL**	**42**	**0**	**3**	**3**	**110**	**1**	**0**	**0**	**0**	**0**
1989-90	**Buffalo**	**NHL**	**4**	**0**	**1**	**1**	**2**	....	....	....	....	....
	NHL Totals		**688**	**26**	**94**	**120**	**1812**	**43**	**0**	**6**	**6**	**111**

a WHL First All-Star Team (1978)

Traded to **Los Angeles** by **Buffalo** with Sean McKenna and Ken Baumgartner for Brian Engblom and Doug Smith, January 30, 1986. Traded to **Buffalo** by **Los Angeles** for Bob Logan and Buffalo's ninth-round choice (Jim Glacin) in 1989 Entry Draft, October 21, 1988

POCHIPINSKI, TREVOR

Defense. Shoots right. 6'2", 190 lbs. Born, Prince Albert, Sask., July 8, 1968.
(Los Angeles' 9th choice, 170th overall, in 1986 Entry Draft).

			Regular Season					Playoffs				
Season	Club	Lea	GP	G	A	TP	PIM	GP	G	A	TP	PIM
1987-88	Colorado	WCHA	37	2	6	8	91	....	....	....	....	....
1988-89	Colorado	WCHA	40	4	10	14	74	....	....	....	....	....
1989-90	Colorado	WCHA	40	5	13	18	54	....	....	....	....	....

PODDUBNY, WALTER MICHAEL (WALT) (puh-DUHB-nee)

Center. Shoots left. 6'1", 210 lbs. Born, Thunder Bay, Ont., February 14, 1960.
(Edmonton's 4th choice, 90th overall, in 1980 Entry Draft).

			Regular Season					Playoffs				
Season	Club	Lea	GP	G	A	TP	PIM	GP	G	A	TP	PIM
1979-80	Kitchener	OHA	19	3	9	12	35	....	....	....	....	....
	Kingston	OHA	43	30	17	47	36	3	0	2	2	0
1980-81	Milwaukee	IHL	5	4	2	6	4	....	....	....	....	....
	Wichita	CHL	70	21	29	50	207	11	1	6	7	26
1981-82	**Edmonton**	**NHL**	**4**	**0**	**0**	**0**	**0**	....	....	....	....	....
	Wichita	CHL	60	35	46	81	79	....	....	....	....	....
	Toronto	**NHL**	**11**	**3**	**4**	**7**	**8**	....	....	....	....	....
1982-83	**Toronto**	**NHL**	**72**	**28**	**31**	**59**	**71**	**4**	**3**	**1**	**4**	**0**
1983-84	**Toronto**	**NHL**	**38**	**11**	**14**	**25**	**48**	....	....	....	....	....
1984-85	**Toronto**	**NHL**	**32**	**5**	**15**	**20**	**26**	....	....	....	....	....
	St. Catharines	AHL	8	5	7	12	10	....	....	....	....	....
1985-86	**Toronto**	**NHL**	**33**	**12**	**22**	**34**	**25**	**9**	**4**	**1**	**5**	**4**
	St. Catharines	AHL	37	28	27	55	52	....	....	....	....	....
1986-87	**NY Rangers**	**NHL**	**75**	**40**	**47**	**87**	**49**	**6**	**0**	**0**	**0**	**8**
1987-88	**NY Rangers**	**NHL**	**77**	**38**	**50**	**88**	**76**	....	....	....	....	....
1988-89	**Quebec**	**NHL**	**72**	**38**	**37**	**75**	**107**	....	....	....	....	....
1989-90	**New Jersey**	**NHL**	**33**	**4**	**10**	**14**	**28**	....	....	....	....	....
	Utica	AHL	2	1	2	3	0	....	....	....	....	....
	NHL Totals		**447**	**179**	**230**	**409**	**438**	**19**	**7**	**2**	**9**	**12**

Played in NHL All-Star Game (1989)

Traded to **Toronto** by **Edmonton** with Phil Drouilliard for Laurie Boschman, March 28, 1982. Traded to **NY Rangers** by **Toronto** for Mike Allison, August 18, 1986. Traded to **Quebec** by **NY Rangers** with Bruce Bell, Jari Gronstrand and NY Rangers' fourth round choice (Eric Dubois) in 1989 Entry Draft for Jason Lafreniere and Normand Rochefort, August 1, 1988. Traded to **New Jersey** by **Quebec** with Quebec's fourth round choice (Mike Bodnarchuk) in 1990 Entry Draft for Joe Cirella, Claude Loiselle and New Jersey's eighth round choice (Alexander Karpovtsev) in 1990 Entry Draft, June 17, 1989.

PODEIN, SHJON

Center. Shoots left. 6'2", 200 lbs. Born, Rochester, MN, March 5, 1968.
(Edmonton's 9th choice, 166th overall, in 1988 Entry Draft).

			Regular Season					Playoffs				
Season	Club	Lea	GP	G	A	TP	PIM	GP	G	A	TP	PIM
1987-88	Minn.-Duluth	WCHA	30	4	4	8	48	....	....	....	....	....
1988-89	Minn. Duluth	WCHA	36	7	5	12	46	....	....	....	....	....
1989-90	Minn.-Duluth	WCHA	35	21	18	39	36	....	....	....	....	....

PODIAK, BRADLEY

Center. Shoots left. 6'1", 190 lbs. Born, Plymouth, MN., March 26, 1971.
(Winnipeg's 13th choice, 214th overall, in 1989 Entry Draft).

			Regular Season					Playoffs				
Season	Club	Lea	GP	G	A	TP	PIM	GP	G	A	TP	PIM
1988-89	Wayzata	HS	24	20	29	49		....	....	....	....	....
1989-90	U. of Denver	WCHA	40	4	1	5	33	....	....	....	....	....

PODLOSKI, RAY

Center. Shoots left. 6'2", 210 lbs. Born, Edmonton, Alta., January 5, 1966.
(Boston's 2nd choice, 40th overall, in 1984 Entry Draft).

			Regular Season					Playoffs				
Season	Club	Lea	GP	G	A	TP	PIM	GP	G	A	TP	PIM
1983-84	Portland	WHL	66	46	50	96	44	14	8	14	22	14
1984-85	Portland	WHL	67	63	75	138	41	6	3	1	4	7
1985-86	Portland	WHL	66	59	75	134	68	7	1	9	10	8
1986-87	Moncton	AHL	70	23	27	50	12	3	0	0	0	15
1987-88	Maine	AHL	36	12	20	32	12	5	1	2	3	19
1988-89	**Boston**	**NHL**	**8**	**0**	**1**	**1**	**22**	....	....	....	....	....
	Maine	AHL	71	20	34	54	70	....	....	....	....	....
1989-90	Cdn. National	....	58	18	16	34	38	....	....	....	....	....
	NHL Totals		**8**	**0**	**1**	**1**	**2**	....	....	....	....	....

POESCHEK, RUDY (POH-shehk)

Right wing. Shoots right. 6'2", 210 lbs. Born, Terrace, B.C., September 29, 1966.
(NY Rangers' 12th choice, 238th overall, in 1985 Entry Draft).

			Regular Season					Playoffs				
Season	Club	Lea	GP	G	A	TP	PIM	GP	G	A	TP	PIM
1983-84	Kamloops	WHL	47	3	9	12	93	8	0	2	2	7
1984-85	Kamloops	WHL	34	6	7	13	100	15	0	3	3	56
1985-86	Kamloops	WHL	32	3	13	16	92	16	3	7	10	40
1986-87	Kamloops	WHL	54	13	18	31	153	15	2	4	6	37
1987-88	**NY Rangers**	**NHL**	**1**	**0**	**0**	**0**	**2**	....	....	....	....	....
	Colorado	IHL	82	7	31	38	210	12	2	2	4	31
1988-89	**NY Rangers**	**NHL**	**52**	**0**	**2**	**2**	**199**	....	....	....	....	....
	Colorado	IHL	2	0	0	0	6	....	....	....	....	....
1989-90	**NY Rangers**	**NHL**	**15**	**0**	**0**	**0**	**55**	....	....	....	....	....
	Flint	IHL	38	8	13	21	109	....	....	....	....	....
	NHL Totals		**68**	**0**	**2**	**2**	**256**	....	....	....	....	....

POHL, MICHAEL

Center. Shoots left. 6'2", 185 lbs. Born, Rosenheim, West Germany, January 25, 1968.
(New Jersey's 14th choice, 243rd overall, in 1988 Entry Draft).

			Regular Season					Playoffs				
Season	Club	Lea	GP	G	A	TP	PIM	GP	G	A	TP	PIM
1987-88	Rosenheim	W. Ger.	44	7	9	16	32	....	....	....	....	....
1988-89	Rosenheim	W. Ger.	44	8	14	22	38	....	....	....	....	....
1989-90	Rosenheim	W. Ger.	38	10	11	21	28	....	....	....	....	....

POLILLO, PAUL

Center. Shoots left. 5'11", 175 lbs. Born, Brantford, Ont., April 24, 1967.
(Pittsburgh's 1st choice, 4th overall, in 1988 Supplemental Draft).

			Regular Season					Playoffs				
Season	Club	Lea	GP	G	A	TP	PIM	GP	G	A	TP	PIM
1986-87	W. Michigan	CCHA	42	18	48	66	35	....	....	....	....	....
1987-88a	W. Michigan	CCHA	42	25	60	85	34	....	....	....	....	....
1988-89	W. Michigan	CCHA	41	20	46	66	32	....	....	....	....	....
1989-90	W. Michigan	CCHA	40	19	35	54	34	....	....	....	....	....

a CCHA First All-Star Team (1988)

POPOVIC, PETER

Defense. Shoots right. 6'5", 210 lbs. Born, Koping, Sweden, February 10, 1968.
(Montreal's 5th choice, 93rd overall, in 1988 Entry Draft).

			Regular Season					Playoffs				
Season	Club	Lea	GP	G	A	TP	PIM	GP	G	A	TP	PIM
1986-87	Vasteras	Swe.	24	1	2	3	10	....	....	....	....	....
1987-88	Vasteras	Swe.	28	3	17	20	....	....	....	....	....	....
1988-89	Vasteras	Swe.	44	3	8	11	68	....	....	....	....	....
1989-90	Vasteras	Swe.	30	2	10	12	24	2	0	1	1	2

PORTER, DAVID

Left wing. Shoots left. 6'1", 170 lbs. Born, Milford, MI, June 2, 1967.
(NY Rangers' 10th choice, 199th overall, in 1987 Entry Draft).

			Regular Season					Playoffs				
Season	Club	Lea	GP	G	A	TP	PIM	GP	G	A	TP	PIM
1986-87	N. Michigan	WCHA	39	10	12	22	20	....	....	....	....	....
1987-88	N. Michigan	WCHA	38	9	19	28	16	....	....	....	....	....
1988-89	N. Michigan	WCHA	31	5	9	14	16	....	....	....	....	....
1989-90	N. Michigan	WCHA	37	5	9	14	38	....	....	....	....	....

POSMA, MIKE

Defense. Shoots right. 6'1", 195 lbs. Born, Utica, NY, December 16, 1967.
(St. Louis' 2nd choice, 31st overall, in 1986 Entry Draft).

			Regular Season					Playoffs				
Season	Club	Lea	GP	G	A	TP	PIM	GP	G	A	TP	PIM
1986-87	W. Michigan	CCHA	35	12	31	43	42	....	....	....	....	....
1987-88a	W. Michigan	CCHA	42	16	38	54	30	....	....	....	....	....
1988-89	W. Michigan	CCHA	43	7	34	41	58	....	....	....	....	....
1989-90	W. Michigan	CCHA	39	8	28	36	28	....	....	....	....	....

a CCHA Second All-Star Team (1988)

POTVIN, MARC

Right wing. Shoots right. 6'1", 195 lbs. Born, Kitchener, Ont., January 29, 1967.
(Detroit's 9th choice, 169th overall, in 1986 Entry Draft).

			Regular Season					Playoffs				
Season	Club	Lea	GP	G	A	TP	PIM	GP	G	A	TP	PIM
1986-87	Bowling Green	CCHA	43	5	15	20	74	....	....	....	....	....
1987-88	Bowling Green	CCHA	45	15	21	36	80	....	....	....	....	....
1988-89	Bowling Green	CCHA	46	23	12	35	63	....	....	....	....	....
1989-90	Bowling Green	CCHA	40	19	17	36	72	....	....	....	....	....
	Adirondack	AHL	5	2	1	3	9	4	0	1	1	23

POULIN, CHARLES

Center. Shoots left. 6', 170 lbs. Born, St. Jean, Que., July 27, 1972.
(Montreal's 3rd choice, 58th overall, in 1990 Entry Draft).

			Regular Season					Playoffs				
Season	Club	Lea	GP	G	A	TP	PIM	GP	G	A	TP	PIM
1989-90a	St. Hyacinthe	QMJHL	65	39	45	84	132	11	5	8	13	47

a QMJHL Third All-Star Team (1990)

POULIN, DAVID JAMES (DAVE) (POO-lihn)

Center. Shoots left. 5'11", 190 lbs. Born, Timmins, Ont., December 17, 1958.

			Regular Season					Playoffs				
Season	Club	Lea	GP	G	A	TP	PIM	GP	G	A	TP	PIM
1978-79	Notre Dame	WCHA	37	28	31	59	32	....	....	....	....	....
1979-80	Notre Dame	WCHA	24	19	24	43	46	....	....	....	....	....
1980-81	Notre Dame	WCHA	35	13	22	35	53	....	....	....	....	....
1981-82a	Notre Dame	CCHA	39	29	30	59	44	....	....	....	....	....
1982-83	Rogle	Swe.	32	35	27	62	64	....	....	....	....	....
	Maine	AHL	16	7	9	16	2	....	....	....	....	....
	Philadelphia	**NHL**	**2**	**2**	**0**	**2**	**2**	**3**	**1**	**3**	**4**	**9**
1983-84	**Philadelphia**	**NHL**	**73**	**31**	**45**	**76**	**47**	**3**	**0**	**0**	**0**	**2**
1984-85	**Philadelphia**	**NHL**	**73**	**30**	**44**	**74**	**59**	**11**	**3**	**5**	**8**	**6**
1985-86	**Philadelphia**	**NHL**	**79**	**27**	**42**	**69**	**49**	**5**	**2**	**0**	**2**	**2**
1986-87b	**Philadelphia**	**NHL**	**75**	**25**	**45**	**70**	**53**	**15**	**3**	**3**	**6**	**14**
1987-88	**Philadelphia**	**NHL**	**68**	**19**	**32**	**51**	**32**	**7**	**2**	**6**	**8**	**4**
1988-89	**Philadelphia**	**NHL**	**69**	**18**	**17**	**35**	**49**	**19**	**6**	**5**	**11**	**16**
1989-90	**Philadelphia**	**NHL**	**28**	**9**	**8**	**17**	**12**	....	....	....	....	....
	Boston	**NHL**	**32**	**6**	**19**	**25**	**12**	**18**	**8**	**5**	**13**	**8**
	NHL Totals		**499**	**167**	**252**	**419**	**315**	**81**	**25**	**27**	**52**	**61**

a CCHA Second All-Star Team (1982).
b Won Frank J. Selke Trophy (1987).
Played in NHL All-Star Game (1986, 1988)

Signed as free agent by **Philadelphia**, March 8, 1983. Traded to **Boston** by **Philadelphia** for Ken Linseman, January 16, 1990.

PRAJSLER, PETR (PRAYS-luhr)

Defense. Shoots left. 6'3", 200 lbs. Born, Hradec Kralove, Czech., September 21, 1965.
(Los Angeles' 5th choice, 93rd overall, in 1985 Entry Draft).

			Regular Season					Playoffs				
Season	Club	Lea	GP	G	A	TP	PIM	GP	G	A	TP	PIM
1986-87	Pardubice	Czech.	41	3	4	7	....	....	....	....	....	....
1987-88	**Los Angeles**	**NHL**	**7**	**0**	**0**	**0**	**2**	....	....	....	....	....
	New Haven	AHL	41	3	8	11	58	....	....	....	....	....
1988-89	**Los Angeles**	**NHL**	**2**	**0**	**3**	**3**	**0**	**1**	**0**	**0**	**0**	**0**
	New Haven	AHL	43	4	6	10	96	16	3	3	6	34
1989-90	**Los Angeles**	**NHL**	**34**	**3**	**7**	**10**	**47**	**3**	**0**	**0**	**0**	**0**
	New Haven	AHL	6	1	7	8	2	....	....	....	....	....
	NHL Totals		**43**	**3**	**10**	**13**	**49**	**4**	**0**	**0**	**0**	**0**

PRATT, JONATHAN

Center. Shoots left. 6'1", 180 lbs. Born, Danvers, MA, September 25, 1970.
(Minnesota's 9th choice, 154th overall, in 1989 Entry Draft).

			Regular Season					Playoffs				
Season	Club	Lea	GP	G	A	TP	PIM	GP	G	A	TP	PIM
1988-89	Pingree	HS	27	37	30	67	65	....	....	....	....	....
1989-90	Boston U.	H.E.	DID NOT PLAY									

PRAZNIK, JODY

Defense. Shoots right. 6'2", 195 lbs. Born, Winnipeg, Man., June 28, 1969.
(Detroit's 8th choice, 185th overall, in 1988 Entry Draft).

			Regular Season					Playoffs				
Season	Club	Lea	GP	G	A	TP	PIM	GP	G	A	TP	PIM
1987-88	Colorado	WCHA	37	5	10	15	46	....	....	....	....	....
1988-89	Saskatoon	WHL	28	2	9	11	28	8	0	2	2	2
1989-90	Hampton-Roads	ECHL	55	7	35	42	40	....	....	....	....	....

PRESLEY, WAYNE

Right wing. Shoots right. 5'11", 170 lbs. Born, Dearborn, MI, March 23, 1965.
(Chicago's 2nd choice, 39th overall, in 1983 Entry Draft).

			Regular Season					Playoffs				
Season	Club	Lea	GP	G	A	TP	PIM	GP	G	A	TP	PIM
1982-83	Kitchener	OHL	70	39	48	87	99	12	1	4	5	9
1983-84a	Kitchener	OHL	70	63	76	139	156	16	12	16	28	38
1984-85	**Chicago**	**NHL**	**3**	**0**	**1**	**1**	**0**	....	....	....	....	....
	Kitchener	OHL	31	25	21	46	77	....	....	....	....	....
	S.S. Marie	OHL	11	5	9	14	14	16	13	9	22	13
1985-86	**Chicago**	**NHL**	**38**	**7**	**8**	**15**	**38**	**3**	**0**	**0**	**0**	**0**
	Nova Scotia	AHL	29	6	9	15	22	....	....	....	....	....
1986-87	**Chicago**	**NHL**	**80**	**32**	**29**	**61**	**114**	**4**	**1**	**0**	**1**	**9**
1987-88	**Chicago**	**NHL**	**42**	**12**	**10**	**22**	**52**	**5**	**0**	**0**	**0**	**4**
1988-89	**Chicago**	**NHL**	**72**	**21**	**19**	**40**	**100**	**14**	**7**	**5**	**12**	**18**
1989-90	**Chicago**	**NHL**	**49**	**6**	**7**	**13**	**69**	**19**	**9**	**6**	**15**	**29**
	NHL Totals		**284**	**78**	**74**	**152**	**373**	**45**	**17**	**11**	**28**	**60**

a OHL First All-Star Team (1984)

PRIAKIN, SERGEI

Right wing. Shoots left. 6'3", 210 lbs. Born, Moscow, Soviet Union, December 7, 1963.
(Calgary's 12th choice, 252nd overall, in 1988 Entry Draft).

			Regular Season					Playoffs				
Season	Club	Lea	GP	G	A	TP	PIM	GP	G	A	TP	PIM
1987-88	Soviet Wings	USSR	44	10	15	25	16	....	....	....	....	....
1988-89	Soviet Wings	USSR	44	11	15	26	23	....	....	....	....	....
	Calgary	**NHL**	**2**	**0**	**0**	**0**	**2**	**1**	**0**	**0**	**0**	**0**
1989-90	**Calgary**	**NHL**	**20**	**2**	**2**	**4**	**0**	....	....	....	....	....
	Salt Lake	IHL	3	1	0	1	0	....	....	....	....	....
	NHL Totals		**22**	**2**	**2**	**4**	**2**	**1**	**0**	**0**	**0**	**0**

PRIESTLAY, KEN

Center. Shoots left. 5'10", 190 lbs. Born, Richmond, B.C., August 24, 1967.
(Buffalo's 5th choice, 98th overall, in 1985 Entry Draft).

			Regular Season					Playoffs				
Season	Club	Lea	GP	G	A	TP	PIM	GP	G	A	TP	PIM
1983-84	Victoria	WHL	55	10	18	28	31	....	....	....	....	....
1984-85	Victoria	WHL	50	25	37	62	48	....	....	....	....	....
1985-86	Victoria	WHL	72	73	72	145	45	....	....	....	....	....
	Rochester	AHL	4	0	2	2	0	....	....	....	....	....
1986-87	**Buffalo**	**NHL**	**34**	**11**	**6**	**17**	**8**	....	....	....	....	....
	Victoria	WHL	33	43	39	82	37	....	....	....	....	....
	Rochester	AHL	....	....	....	....	....	8	3	2	5	4
1987-88	**Buffalo**	**NHL**	**33**	**5**	**12**	**17**	**35**	**6**	**0**	**0**	**0**	**11**
	Rochester	AHL	43	27	24	51	47	....	....	....	....	....
1988-89	**Buffalo**	**NHL**	**15**	**2**	**0**	**2**	**2**	**3**	**0**	**0**	**0**	**2**
	Rochester	AHL	64	56	37	93	60	....	....	....	....	....
1989-90	**Buffalo**	**NHL**	**35**	**7**	**7**	**14**	**14**	**5**	**0**	**0**	**0**	**8**
	Rochester	AHL	40	19	39	58	46	....	....	....	....	....
	NHL Totals		**117**	**25**	**25**	**50**	**59**	**14**	**0**	**0**	**0**	**21**

PRIMEAU, KEITH

Center. Shoots left. 6'4", 220 lbs. Born, Toronto, Ont., November 24, 1971.
(Detroit's 1st choice, 3rd overall, in 1990 Entry Draft).

			Regular Season					Playoffs				
Season	Club	Lea	GP	G	A	TP	PIM	GP	G	A	TP	PIM
1988-89	Niagara Falls	OHL	48	20	35	55	56	17	9	16	25	12
1989-90a	Niagara Falls	OHL	65	*57	70	*127	97	16	*16	17	*33	49

a OHL Second All-Star Team (1990)

PROBERT, BOB (PROH buhrt)

Left wing. Shoots left. 6'3", 215 lbs. Born, Windsor, Ont., June 5, 1965.
(Detroit's 3rd choice, 46th overall, in 1983 Entry Draft).

			Regular Season					Playoffs				
Season	Club	Lea	GP	G	A	TP	PIM	GP	G	A	TP	PIM
1982-83	Brantford	OHL	51	12	16	28	133	8	2	2	4	23
1983-84	Brantford	OHL	65	35	38	73	189	6	0	3	3	16
1984-85	S.S. Marie	OHL	44	20	52	72	172	....	....	....	....	....
	Hamilton	OHL	4	0	1	1	21	....	....	....	....	....
1985-86	**Detroit**	**NHL**	**44**	**8**	**13**	**21**	**186**	....	....	....	....	....
	Adirondack	AHL	32	12	15	27	152	10	2	3	5	68
1986-87	**Detroit**	**NHL**	**63**	**13**	**11**	**24**	**221**	**16**	**3**	**4**	**7**	**63**
	Adirondack	AHL	7	1	4	5	15	....	....	....	....	....
1987-88	**Detroit**	**NHL**	**74**	**29**	**33**	**62**	***398**	**16**	**8**	**13**	**21**	**51**
1988-89	**Detroit**	**NHL**	**25**	**4**	**2**	**6**	**106**	....	....	....	....	....
1989-90	**Detroit**	**NHL**	**4**	**3**	**0**	**3**	**21**	....	....	....	....	....
	NHL Totals		**210**	**57**	**59**	**116**	**932**	**32**	**11**	**17**	**28**	**114**

Played in NHL All-Star Game (1988)

PROPP, BRIAN PHILIP

Left wing. Shoots left. 5'10", 195 lbs. Born, Lanigan, Sask., February 15, 1959.
(Philadelphia's 1st choice, 14th overall, in 1979 Entry Draft).

			Regular Season					Playoffs				
Season	Club	Lea	GP	G	A	TP	PIM	GP	G	A	TP	PIM
1976-77	Brandon	WHL	72	55	80	135	47	16	*14	12	26	5
1977-78a	Brandon	WHL	70	70	*112	*182	200	8	7	6	13	12
1978-79ab	Brandon	WHL	71	*94	*100	*194	127	22	15	23	*38	40
1979-80	Philadelphia	NHL	80	34	41	75	54	19	5	10	15	29
1980-81	Philadelphia	NHL	79	26	40	66	110	12	6	6	12	32
1981-82	Philadelphia	NHL	80	44	47	91	117	4	2	2	4	4
1982-83	Philadelphia	NHL	80	40	42	82	72	3	1	2	3	8
1983-84	Philadelphia	NHL	79	39	53	92	37	3	0	1	1	6
1984-85	Philadelphia	NHL	76	43	53	96	43	19	8	10	18	6
1985-86	Philadelphia	NHL	72	40	57	97	47	5	0	2	2	4
1986-87	Philadelphia	NHL	53	31	36	67	45	26	12	16	28	10
1987-88	Philadelphia	NHL	74	27	49	76	76	7	4	2	6	8
1988-89	Philadelphia	NHL	77	32	46	78	37	18	14	9	23	14
1989-90	Philadelphia	NHL	40	13	15	28	31	....	....	....	....	....
	Boston	NHL	14	3	9	12	10	20	4	9	13	2
	NHL Totals		804	372	488	860	679	136	56	69	125	123

a WHL First All-Star Team (1978, 1979)
b WHL Player of the Year (1979)

Played in NHL All-Star Game (1980, 1982, 1984, 1986, 1990)

Traded to **Boston** by **Philadelphia** for Boston's second round choice (Terran Sandwith) in 1990 Entry Draft, March 2, 1990. Signed as a free agent by **Minnesota**, July 25, 1990.

PROSOFSKY, JASON

Right wing. Shoots right. 6'4", 220 lbs. Born, Medicine Hat, Alta., May 4, 1971.
(NY Rangers' 2nd choice, 40th overall, in 1989 Entry Draft).

			Regular Season					Playoffs				
Season	Club	Lea	GP	G	A	TP	PIM	GP	G	A	TP	PIM
1987-88	Medicine Hat	WHL	47	6	1	7	94	14	0	0	0	20
1988-89	Medicine Hat	WHL	67	7	16	23	170	3	1	0	1	6
1989-90	Medicine Hat	WHL	71	12	13	25	153	3	0	0	0	8

PRYOR, CHRIS

Defense. Shoots right. 6', 200 lbs. Born, St. Paul, MN, January 23, 1961.

			Regular Season					Playoffs				
Season	Club	Lea	GP	G	A	TP	PIM	GP	G	A	TP	PIM
1979-80	N. Hampshire	ECAC	27	9	13	22	27	....	....	....	....	....
1980-81	N. Hampshire	ECAC	33	10	27	37	36	....	....	....	....	....
1981-82	N. Hampshire	ECAC	35	3	16	19	36	....	....	....	....	....
1982-83	N. Hampshire	ECAC	34	4	9	13	23	....	....	....	....	....
1983-84	Salt Lake	CHL	72	7	21	28	215	5	1	2	3	11
1984-85	Minnesota	NHL	4	0	0	0	16	....	....	....	....	....
	Springfield	AHL	77	3	21	24	158	....	....	....	....	....
1985-86	Minnesota	NHL	7	0	1	1	0	....	....	....	....	....
	Springfield	AHL	55	4	16	20	104	....	....	....	....	....
1986-87	Minnesota	NHL	50	1	3	4	49	....	....	....	....	....
	Springfield	AHL	5	0	2	2	17	....	....	....	....	....
1987-88	Minnesota	NHL	3	0	0	0	6	....	....	....	....	....
	NY Islanders	NHL	1	0	0	0	2	....	....	....	....	....
	Kalamazoo	IHL	56	4	16	20	171	....	....	....	....	....
1988-89	NY Islanders	NHL	7	0	0	0	25	....	....	....	....	....
	Springfield	AHL	54	3	6	9	205	....	....	....	....	....
1989-90	NY Islanders	NHL	10	0	0	0	24	....	....	....	....	....
	Springfield	AHL	60	3	7	10	105	18	1	3	4	12
	NHL Totals		82	1	4	5	122	....	....	....	....	....

Signed as a free agent by **Minnesota**, January 10, 1985. Traded to **NY Islanders** by **Minnesota** with future considerations for Gord Dineen, March 8, 1988.

PULLOLA, TOMMI

Center. Shoots left. 6'5", 200 lbs. Born, Vasa, Finland, May 18, 1971.
(Chicago's 4th choice, 111th overall, in 1989 Entry Draft).

			Regular Season					Playoffs				
Season	Club	Lea	GP	G	A	TP	PIM	GP	G	A	TP	PIM
1988-89	Sport	Fin.	40	11	13	24		....	....	....	....	....
1989-90	Lukko	Fin.	40	7	9	16	8	....	....	....	....	....

PURVES, JOHN

Right wing. Shoots right. 6'1", 201 lbs. Born, Toronto, Ont., February 12, 1968.
(Washington's 6th choice, 103rd overall, in 1986 Entry Draft).

			Regular Season					Playoffs				
Season	Club	Lea	GP	G	A	TP	PIM	GP	G	A	TP	PIM
1985-86	Belleville	OHL	16	3	9	12	6	....	....	....	....	....
	Hamilton	OHL	36	13	28	41	36	....	....	....	....	....
1986-87	Hamilton	OHL	28	12	11	23	37	9	2	0	2	12
1987-88	Hamilton	OHL	64	39	44	83	65	14	7	18	25	4
1988-89a	Niagara Falls	OHL	5	5	11	16	2	....	....	....	....	....
	North Bay	OHL	42	34	52	86	38	12	14	12	26	16
1989-90	Baltimore	AHL	75	29	35	64	12	9	5	7	12	4

a OHL Second All-Star Team (1989)

QUENNEVILLE, JOEL NORMAN (KWEHN vihl)

Defense. Shoots left. 6'1", 200 lbs. Born, Windsor, Ont., September 15, 1958.
(Toronto's 1st choice, 21st overall, in 1978 Amateur Draft).

			Regular Season					Playoffs				
Season	Club	Lea	GP	G	A	TP	PIM	GP	G	A	TP	PIM
1975-76	Windsor	OHA	66	15	33	48	61	....	....	....	....	....
1976-77	Windsor	OHA	65	19	59	78	169	9	6	5	11	112
1977-78a	Windsor	OHA	66	27	76	103	114	6	2	3	5	17
1978-79	New Brunswick	AHL	16	1	10	11	10	....	....	....	....	....
	Toronto	NHL	61	2	9	11	60	6	0	1	1	4
1979-80	Toronto	NHL	32	1	4	5	24	....	....	....	....	....
	Colorado	NHL	35	5	7	12	26	....	....	....	....	....
1980-81	Colorado	NHL	71	10	24	34	86	....	....	....	....	....
1981-82	Colorado	NHL	64	5	10	15	55	....	....	....	....	....
1982-83	New Jersey	NHL	74	5	12	17	46	....	....	....	....	....
1983-84	Hartford	NHL	80	5	8	13	95	....	....	....	....	....
1984-85	Hartford	NHL	79	6	16	22	96	....	....	....	....	....
1985-86	Hartford	NHL	71	5	20	25	83	10	0	2	2	12
1986-87	Hartford	NHL	37	3	7	10	24	6	0	0	0	0
1987-88	Hartford	NHL	77	1	8	9	44	6	0	2	2	2
1988-89	Hartford	NHL	69	4	7	11	32	4	0	3	3	4
1989-90	Hartford	NHL	44	1	4	5	34	....	....	....	....	....
	NHL Totals		794	53	136	189	705	26	0	8	8	22

a OHA Second All-Star Team (1978)

Traded to **Colorado** by **Toronto** with Lanny McDonald for Pat Hickey and Wilf Paiement, December 29, 1979. Traded to **Calgary** by **New Jersey** with Steve Tambellini for Phil Russell and Mel Bridgman, June 20, 1983. Traded to **Hartford** by **Calgary** with Richie Dunn for Mickey Volcan, July 5, 1983.

QUINN, DAN

Center. Shoots left. 5'10", 175 lbs. Born, Ottawa, Ont., June 1, 1965.
(Calgary's 1st choice, 13th overall, in 1983 Entry Draft).

			Regular Season					Playoffs				
Season	Club	Lea	GP	G	A	TP	PIM	GP	G	A	TP	PIM
1981-82	Belleville	OHL	67	19	32	51	41	....	....	....	....	....
1982-83	Belleville	OHL	70	59	88	147	27	4	2	6	8	2
1983-84	Belleville	OHL	24	23	36	59	12	....	....	....	....	....
	Calgary	NHL	54	19	33	52	20	8	3	5	8	4
1984-85	Calgary	NHL	74	20	38	58	22	3	0	0	0	0
1985-86	Calgary	NHL	78	30	42	72	44	18	8	7	15	10
1986-87	Calgary	NHL	16	3	6	9	14	....	....	....	....	....
	Pittsburgh	NHL	64	28	43	71	40	....	....	....	....	....
1987-88	Pittsburgh	NHL	70	40	39	79	50	....	....	....	....	....
1988-89	Pittsburgh	NHL	79	34	60	94	102	11	6	3	9	10
1989-90	Pittsburgh	NHL	41	9	20	29	22	....	....	....	....	....
	Vancouver	NHL	37	16	18	34	27	....	....	....	....	....
	NHL Totals		513	199	299	498	341	40	17	15	32	24

Traded to **Pittsburgh** by **Calgary** for Mike Bullard, November 12, 1986. Traded to **Vancouver** by **Pittsburgh** with Dave Capuano and Andrew McBain for Rod Buskas, Barry Pederson and Tony Tanti, January 8, 1990.

QUINN, JOE

Right wing. Shoots right. 5'11", 185 lbs. Born, Calgary, Alta., February 10, 1967.
(Hartford's 5th choice, 116th overall, in 1986 Entry Draft).

			Regular Season					Playoffs				
Season	Club	Lea	GP	G	A	TP	PIM	GP	G	A	TP	PIM
1986-87	Bowling Green	CCHA	39	4	13	17	22	....	....	....	....	....
1987-88	Bowling Green	CCHA	39	14	13	27	24	....	....	....	....	....
1988-89	Cdn. National	....	4	0	1	1	2	....	....	....	....	....
	Bowling Green	CCHA	47	21	20	41	36	....	....	....	....	....
1989-90	Bowling Green	CCHA	42	11	18	29	43	....	....	....	....	....

QUINNEY, KEN (KWIH-nee)

Right wing. Shoots right. 5'10", 186 lbs. Born, New Westminster, B.C., May 23, 1965.
(Quebec's 9th choice, 204th overall, in 1984 Entry Draft).

			Regular Season					Playoffs				
Season	Club	Lea	GP	G	A	TP	PIM	GP	G	A	TP	PIM
1981-82	Calgary	WHL	63	11	17	28	55	2	0	0	0	15
1982-83	Calgary	WHL	71	26	25	51	71	16	6	1	7	46
1983-84	Calgary	WHL	71	64	54	118	38	4	5	2	7	0
1984-85a	Calgary	WHL	56	47	67	114	65	7	6	4	10	15
1985-86	Fredericton	AHL	61	11	26	37	34	6	2	2	4	9
1986-87	Quebec	NHL	25	2	7	9	16	....	....	....	....	....
	Fredericton	AHL	48	14	27	41	20	....	....	....	....	....
1987-88	Quebec	NHL	15	2	2	4	5	....	....	....	....	....
b	Fredericton	AHL	58	37	39	76	39	13	3	5	8	35
1988-89	Halifax	AHL	72	41	49	90	65	4	3	0	3	0
1989-90	Halifax	AHL	44	9	16	25	63	2	0	0	0	2
	NHL Totals		40	4	9	13	21	....	....	....	....	....

a WHL First All-Star Team, East Division (1985)
b Won Tim Horton Award (Most Three-Star Points-AHL) (1988)

QUINTAL, STEPHANE (KIHN-TAHL)

Defense. Shoots right. 6'3", 215 lbs. Born, Boucherville, Que., October 22, 1968.
(Boston's 2nd choice, 14th overall, in 1987 Entry Draft).

			Regular Season					Playoffs				
Season	Club	Lea	GP	G	A	TP	PIM	GP	G	A	TP	PIM
1985-86	Granby	QMJHL	67	2	17	19	144	....	....	....	....	....
1986-87a	Granby	QMJHL	67	13	41	54	178	8	0	9	9	10
1987-88	Hull	QMJHL	38	13	23	36	138	19	7	12	19	30
1988-89	Boston	NHL	26	0	1	1	29	....	....	....	....	....
	Maine	AHL	16	4	10	14	28	....	....	....	....	....
1989-90	Boston	NHL	38	2	2	4	22	....	....	....	....	....
	Maine	AHL	37	4	16	20	27	....	....	....	....	....
	NHL Totals		64	2	3	5	51	....	....	....	....	....

a QMJHL First All-Star Team (1987)

QUINTIN, JEAN-FRANCOIS

Center. Shoots left. 6'1", 180 lbs. Born, St. Jean, Que., May 28, 1969.
(Minnesota's 4th choice, 75th overall, in 1989 Entry Draft).

			Regular Season					Playoffs				
Season	Club	Lea	GP	G	A	TP	PIM	GP	G	A	TP	PIM
1987-88	Shawinigan	QMJHL	70	28	70	98	143	11	5	8	13	26
1988-89	Shawinigan	QMJHL	69	52	100	152	105	10	9	15	24	16
1989-90	Kalamazoo	IHL	68	20	18	38	38	10	8	4	12	14

RACINE, YVES

Defense. Shoots left. 6', 185 lbs. Born, Matane, Que., February 7, 1969.
(Detroit's 1st choice, 11th overall, in 1987 Entry Draft).

			Regular Season					Playoffs				
Season	Club	Lea	GP	G	A	TP	PIM	GP	G	A	TP	PIM
1986-87	Longueuil	QMJHL	70	7	43	50	50	20	3	11	14	14
1987-88	Adirondack	AHL	....	....	....	....	....	9	4	2	6	2
a	Victoriaville	QMJHL	69	10	84	94	150	5	0	0	0	13
1988-89a	Victoriaville	QMJHL	63	23	85	108	95	16	3	*30	*33	41
	Adirondack	AHL	....	....	....	....	....	2	1	1	2	0
1989-90	**Detroit**	**NHL**	**28**	**4**	**9**	**13**	**23**	....	....	....	....	....
	Adirondack	AHL	46	8	27	35	31	....	....	....	....	....
	NHL Totals		**28**	**4**	**9**	**13**	**23**	....	....	....	....	....

a QMJHL First-All Star Team (1988, 1989)

RAGLAN, HERB

Right wing. Shoots right. 6', 205 lbs. Born, Peterborough, Ont., August 5, 1967.
(St. Louis' 1st choice, 37th overall, in 1985 Entry Draft).

			Regular Season					Playoffs				
Season	Club	Lea	GP	G	A	TP	PIM	GP	G	A	TP	PIM
1984-85	Peterborough	OHL	58	20	22	42	166	....	....	....	....	....
1985-86	**St. Louis**	**NHL**	**7**	**0**	**0**	**0**	**5**	**10**	**1**	**1**	**2**	**24**
	Kingston	OHL	28	10	9	19	88	10	5	2	7	30
1986-87	**St. Louis**	**NHL**	**62**	**6**	**10**	**16**	**159**	**4**	**0**	**0**	**0**	**2**
1987-88	**St. Louis**	**NHL**	**73**	**10**	**15**	**25**	**190**	**10**	**1**	**3**	**4**	**11**
1988-89	**St. Louis**	**NHL**	**50**	**7**	**10**	**17**	**144**	**8**	**1**	**2**	**3**	**13**
1989-90	**St. Louis**	**NHL**	**11**	**0**	**1**	**1**	**21**	....	....	....	....	....
	NHL Totals		**203**	**23**	**36**	**59**	**519**	**32**	**3**	**6**	**9**	**50**

RAHN, NOEL

Center. Shoots left. 6', 155 lbs. Born, Edina, MN, February 6, 1971.
(Quebec's 14th choice, 232nd overall, in 1989 Entry Draft).

			Regular Season					Playoffs				
Season	Club	Lea	GP	G	A	TP	PIM	GP	G	A	TP	PIM
1988-89	Edina	HS	24	21	16	37	....	....	....	....	....	....
1989-90	U. Wisconsin	WCHA	4	0	0	0	0	....	....	....	....	....

RAMAGE, GEORGE (ROB) (RAM-ihj)

Defense. Shoots right. 6'2", 195 lbs. Born, Byron, Ont., January 11, 1959.
(Colorado's 1st choice and 1st overall 1979 Entry Draft).

			Regular Season					Playoffs				
Season	Club	Lea	GP	G	A	TP	PIM	GP	G	A	TP	PIM
1975-76	London	OHA	65	12	31	43	113	5	0	1	1	11
1976-77a	London	OHA	65	15	58	73	177	20	3	11	14	55
1977-78b	London	OHA	59	17	48	65	162	11	4	5	9	29
1978-79	Birmingham	WHA	80	12	36	48	165	....	....	....	....	....
1979-80	**Colorado**	**NHL**	**75**	**8**	**20**	**28**	**135**	....	....	....	....	....
1980-81	**Colorado**	**NHL**	**79**	**20**	**42**	**62**	**193**	....	....	....	....	....
1981-82	**Colorado**	**NHL**	**80**	**13**	**29**	**42**	**201**	....	....	....	....	....
1982-83	**St. Louis**	**NHL**	**78**	**16**	**35**	**51**	**193**	**4**	**0**	**3**	**3**	**22**
1983-84	**St. Louis**	**NHL**	**80**	**15**	**45**	**60**	**121**	**11**	**1**	**8**	**9**	**32**
1984-85	**St. Louis**	**NHL**	**80**	**7**	**31**	**38**	**178**	**3**	**1**	**3**	**4**	**6**
1985-86	**St. Louis**	**NHL**	**77**	**10**	**56**	**66**	**171**	**19**	**1**	**10**	**11**	**66**
1986-87	**St. Louis**	**NHL**	**59**	**11**	**28**	**39**	**108**	**6**	**2**	**2**	**4**	**21**
1987-88	**St. Louis**	**NHL**	**67**	**8**	**34**	**42**	**127**	....	....	....	....	....
	Calgary	**NHL**	**12**	**1**	**6**	**7**	**37**	**9**	**1**	**3**	**4**	**21**
1988-89	**Calgary**	**NHL**	**68**	**3**	**13**	**16**	**156**	**20**	**1**	**11**	**12**	**26**
1989-90	**Toronto**	**NHL**	**80**	**8**	**41**	**49**	**202**	**5**	**1**	**2**	**3**	**20**
	NHL Totals		**835**	**120**	**380**	**500**	**1822**	**77**	**8**	**42**	**50**	**214**

a OHA Third All-Star Team (1977)
b OHA First All-Star Team (1978)

Played in NHL All-Star Game (1981, 1984, 1986, 1988)

Traded to **St. Louis** by **New Jersey** for St. Louis' first round choice (Rocky Trottier) in 1982 Entry Draft and first round choice (John MacLean) in 1983 Entry Draft, June 9, 1982. Traded to **Calgary** by **St. Louis** with Rick Wamsley for Brett Hull and Steve Bozek, March 7, 1988. Traded to **Toronto** by **Calgary** for Toronto's second-round choice (Kent Manderville) in 1989 Entry Draft, June 16, 1989.

RAMSEY, MICHAEL ALLEN (MIKE)

Defense. Shoots left. 6'3", 195 lbs. Born, Minneapolis, MN, December 3, 1960.
(Buffalo's 1st choice, 11th overall, in 1979 Entry Draft).

			Regular Season					Playoffs				
Season	Club	Lea	GP	G	A	TP	PIM	GP	G	A	TP	PIM
1978-79	U. Minnesota	WCHA	26	6	11	17	30	....	....	....	....	....
1979-80	U.S. National	...	56	11	22	33	55	....	....	....	....	....
	U.S. Olympic	...	7	0	2	2	8	....	....	....	....	....
	Buffalo	**NHL**	**13**	**1**	**6**	**7**	**6**	**13**	**1**	**2**	**3**	**12**
1980-81	**Buffalo**	**NHL**	**72**	**3**	**14**	**17**	**56**	**8**	**0**	**3**	**3**	**20**
1981-82	**Buffalo**	**NHL**	**80**	**7**	**23**	**30**	**56**	**4**	**1**	**1**	**2**	**14**
1982-83	**Buffalo**	**NHL**	**77**	**8**	**30**	**38**	**55**	**10**	**4**	**4**	**8**	**15**
1983-84	**Buffalo**	**NHL**	**72**	**9**	**22**	**31**	**82**	**3**	**0**	**1**	**1**	**6**
1984-85	**Buffalo**	**NHL**	**79**	**8**	**22**	**30**	**102**	**5**	**0**	**1**	**1**	**23**
1985-86	**Buffalo**	**NHL**	**76**	**7**	**21**	**28**	**117**	....	....	....	....	....
1986-87	**Buffalo**	**NHL**	**80**	**8**	**31**	**39**	**109**	....	....	....	....	....
1987-88	**Buffalo**	**NHL**	**63**	**5**	**16**	**21**	**77**	**6**	**0**	**3**	**3**	**29**
1988-89	**Buffalo**	**NHL**	**56**	**2**	**14**	**16**	**84**	**5**	**1**	**0**	**1**	**11**
1989-90	**Buffalo**	**NHL**	**73**	**4**	**21**	**25**	**47**	**6**	**0**	**1**	**1**	**8**
	NHL Totals		**741**	**62**	**220**	**282**	**791**	**60**	**7**	**16**	**23**	**138**

Played in NHL All-Star Game (1982, 1983, 1985, 1986)

RANHEIM, PAUL

Left wing. Shoots right. 6', 195 lbs. Born, St. Louis, MO, January 25, 1966.
(Calgary's 3rd choice, 38th overall, in 1984 Entry Draft).

			Regular Season					Playoffs				
Season	Club	Lea	GP	G	A	TP	PIM	GP	G	A	TP	PIM
1984-85	U. Wisconsin	WCHA	42	11	11	22	40	....	....	....	....	....
1985-86	U. Wisconsin	WCHA	33	17	17	34	34	....	....	....	....	....
1986-87a	U. Wisconsin	WCHA	42	24	35	59	54	....	....	....	....	....
1987-88bc	U. Wisconsin	WCHA	44	36	26	62	63	....	....	....	....	....
1988-89	**Calgary**	**NHL**	**5**	**0**	**0**	**0**	**0**	....	....	....	....	....
def	Salt Lake	IHL	75	*68	29	97	16	14	5	5	10	8
1989-90	**Calgary**	**NHL**	**80**	**26**	**28**	**54**	**23**	**6**	**1**	**3**	**4**	**2**
	NHL Totals		**85**	**26**	**28**	**54**	**23**	**6**	**1**	**3**	**4**	**2**

a WCHA Second All-Star Team (1987)
b NCAA West First All-American Team (1988)
c WCHA First All-Star Team (1988)
d IHL Second All-Star Team (1989)
e Won Garry F. Longman Memorial Trophy (Top Rookie-IHL) (1989)
f Won Ken McKenzie Trophy (Outstanding U.S.-born Rookie-IHL) (1989)

RATHBONE, JASON

Right wing. Shoots right. 6'0", 175 lbs. Born, Brookline, MA, April 13, 1970.
(NY Islanders' 8th choice, 121st overall, in 1988 Entry Draft).

			Regular Season					Playoffs				
Season	Club	Lea	GP	G	A	TP	PIM	GP	G	A	TP	PIM
1988-89	Boston College	H.E.	21	0	3	3	10	....	....	....	....	....
1989-90	Boston College	H.E.	37	4	7	11	20	....	....	....	....	....

RATUSHNY, DAN

Defense. Shoots right. 6'1", 185 lbs. Born, Nepean, Ont., October 29, 1970.
(Winnipeg's 2nd choice, 25th overall, in 1989 Entry Draft).

			Regular Season					Playoffs				
Season	Club	Lea	GP	G	A	TP	PIM	GP	G	A	TP	PIM
1988-89	Cornell	ECAC	28	2	13	15	50	....	....	....	....	....
1989-90ab	Cornell	ECAC	26	5	14	19	54	....	....	....	....	....

a ECAC First All-Star Team (1990)
b NCAA East Second All-American Team (1990)

RAY, ROBERT

Left wing. Shoots left. 6'0", 210 lbs. Born, Belleville, Ont., June 8, 1968.
(Buffalo's 5th choice, 97th overall, in 1988 Entry Draft).

			Regular Season					Playoffs				
Season	Club	Lea	GP	G	A	TP	PIM	GP	G	A	TP	PIM
1985-86	Cornwall	OHL	53	6	13	19	253	6	0	0	0	26
1986-87	Cornwall	OHL	46	17	20	37	158	5	1	1	2	16
1987-88	Cornwall	OHL	61	11	41	52	179	11	2	3	5	33
1988-89	Rochester	AHL	74	11	18	29	*446	....	....	....	....	....
1989-90	**Buffalo**	**NHL**	**27**	**2**	**1**	**3**	**99**	....	....	....	....	....
	Rochester	AHL	43	2	13	15	335	17	1	3	4	115
	NHL Totals		**27**	**2**	**1**	**3**	**99**	....	....	....	....	....

RECCHI, MARK

Right wing. Shoots left. 5'10", 185 lbs. Born, Kamloops, B.C., February 1, 1968.
(Pittsburgh's 4th choice, 67th overall, in 1988 Entry Draft).

			Regular Season					Playoffs				
Season	Club	Lea	GP	G	A	TP	PIM	GP	G	A	TP	PIM
1985-86	N. Westminster	WHL	72	21	40	61	55	....	....	....	....	....
1986-87	Kamloops	WHL	40	26	50	76	63	13	3	16	19	17
1987-88a	Kamloops	WHL	62	61	*93	154	75	17	10	*21	*31	18
1988-89	**Pittsburgh**	**NHL**	**15**	**1**	**1**	**2**	**0**	....	....	....	....	....
b	Muskegon	IHL	63	50	49	99	86	14	7	*14	*21	28
1989-90	**Pittsburgh**	**NHL**	**74**	**30**	**37**	**67**	**44**	....	....	....	....	....
	NHL Totals		**89**	**31**	**38**	**69**	**44**	....	....	....	....	....

a WHL West All-Star Team (1988)
b IHL Second All-Star Team (1989)

REED, JACE

Defense. Shoots left. 6'3", 210 lbs. Born, Grand Rapids, MN, March 22, 1971.
(NY Islanders' 5th choice, 86th overall, in 1989 Entry Draft).

			Regular Season					Playoffs				
Season	Club	Lea	GP	G	A	TP	PIM	GP	G	A	TP	PIM
1988-89	Grand Rapids	HS	25	4	17	21	10	....	....	....	....	....
1989-90	North Dakota	WCHA	10	0	0	0	0	....	....	....	....	....

REEKIE, JOE

Defense. Shoots left. 6'3", 215 lbs. Born, Petawawa, Ont., February 22, 1965.
(Buffalo's 6th choice, 119th overall, in 1985 Entry Draft).

			Regular Season					Playoffs				
Season	Club	Lea	GP	G	A	TP	PIM	GP	G	A	TP	PIM
1982-83	North Bay	OHL	59	2	9	11	49	8	0	1	1	11
1983-84	North Bay	OHL	9	1	0	1	18	....	....	....	....	....
	Cornwall	OHL	53	6	27	33	166	3	0	0	0	4
1984-85	Cornwall	OHL	65	19	63	82	134	9	4	13	17	18
1985-86	Rochester	AHL	77	3	25	28	178	....	....	....	....	....
	Buffalo	**NHL**	**3**	**0**	**0**	**0**	**14**	....	....	....	....	....
1986-87	**Buffalo**	**NHL**	**56**	**1**	**8**	**9**	**82**	....	....	....	....	....
	Rochester	AHL	22	0	6	6	52	....	....	....	....	....
1987-88	**Buffalo**	**NHL**	**30**	**1**	**4**	**5**	**68**	**2**	**0**	**0**	**0**	**4**
1988-89	**Buffalo**	**NHL**	**15**	**1**	**3**	**4**	**26**	....	....	....	....	....
	Rochester	AHL	21	1	2	3	56	....	....	....	....	....
1989-90	**NY Islanders**	**NHL**	**31**	**1**	**8**	**9**	**43**	....	....	....	....	....
	Springfield	AHL	15	1	4	5	24	....	....	....	....	....
	NHL Totals		**135**	**4**	**23**	**27**	**233**	**2**	**0**	**0**	**0**	**4**

Traded to **NY Islanders** by **Buffalo** for NY Islanders' sixth round choice (Bill Pye) in 1989 Entry Draft, June 17, 1989.

REICHEL, ROBERT

Center. Shoots left. 5'10", 170 lbs. Born, Most, Czechoslovakia, June 25, 1971.
(Calgary's 5th choice, 70th overall, in 1989 Entry Draft).

			Regular Season					Playoffs				
Season	Club	Lea	GP	G	A	TP	PIM	GP	G	A	TP	PIM
1988-89	Litvinov	Czech.	....	20	31	51	....	....	....	....	....	....
1989-90	Litvinov	Czech.	52	49	34	83	....	....	....	....	....	....

REID, DAVID

Left wing. Shoots left. 6', 210 lbs. Born, Toronto, Ont., May 15, 1964.
(Boston's 4th choice, 60th overall, in 1982 Entry Draft).

			Regular Season					Playoffs				
Season	Club	Lea	GP	G	A	TP	PIM	GP	G	A	TP	PIM
1981-82	Peterborough	OHL	68	10	32	42	41	9	2	3	5	11
1982-83	Peterborough	OHL	70	23	34	57	33	4	3	1	4	0
1983-84	**Boston**	**NHL**	**8**	**1**	**0**	**1**	**2**	....	....	....	....	....
	Peterborough	OHL	60	33	64	97	12	....	....	....	....	....
1984-85	**Boston**	**NHL**	**35**	**14**	**13**	**27**	**27**	**5**	**1**	**0**	**1**	**0**
	Hershey	AHL	43	10	14	24	6	....	....	....	....	....
1985-86	**Boston**	**NHL**	**37**	**10**	**10**	**20**	**10**	....	....	....	....	....
	Moncton	AHL	26	14	18	32	4	....	....	....	....	....
1986-87	**Boston**	**NHL**	**12**	**3**	**3**	**6**	**0**	**2**	**0**	**0**	**0**	**0**
	Moncton	AHL	40	12	22	34	23	5	0	1	1	0
1987-88	**Boston**	**NHL**	**3**	**0**	**0**	**0**	**0**	....	....	....	....	....
	Maine	AHL	63	21	37	58	40	10	6	7	13	0
1988-89	**Toronto**	**NHL**	**77**	**9**	**21**	**30**	**22**	....	....	....	....	....
1989-90	**Toronto**	**NHL**	**70**	**9**	**19**	**28**	**9**	**3**	**0**	**0**	**0**	**0**
	NHL Totals		**242**	**46**	**66**	**112**	**70**	**10**	**1**	**0**	**1**	**0**

Signed as a free agent by **Toronto**, June 23, 1988.

REIERSON, DAVID (DAVE)

Defense. Shoots right. 6', 185 lbs. Born, Bashaw, Alta., August 30, 1964.
(Calgary's 1st choice, 29th overall, in 1982 Entry Draft).

			Regular Season					Playoffs				
Season	Club	Lea	GP	G	A	TP	PIM	GP	G	A	TP	PIM
1982-83	Michigan Tech	CCHA	38	2	14	16	52	....	....	....	....	....
1983-84	Michigan Tech	CCHA	38	4	15	19	63	....	....	....	....	....
1984-85	Michigan Tech	CCHA	36	5	27	32	76	....	....	....	....	....
1985-86	Michigan Tech	WCHA	39	7	16	23	51	....	....	....	....	....
1986-87	Moncton	AHL	....	....	....	....	....	6	0	1	1	12
	Cdn. Olympic	....	61	1	17	18	36	....	....	....	....	....
1987-88	Salt Lake	IHL	48	10	19	29	42	16	2	14	16	30
	Cdn. Olympic	....	32	2	8	10	18	....	....	....	....	....
1988-89	**Calgary**	**NHL**	**2**	**0**	**0**	**0**	**2**	....	....	....	....	....
	Salt Lake	IHL	76	7	46	53	70	13	1	8	9	12
1989-90	Tappara	Fin.	32	7	5	12	28	7	0	2	2	12
	NHL Totals		**2**	**0**	**0**	**0**	**2**	....	....	....	....	....

REINHART, PAUL (RINE-hart)

Defense. Shoots left. 5'11", 200 lbs. Born, Kitchener, Ont., January 6, 1960.
(Atlanta's 1st choice, 12th overall, in 1979 Entry Draft).

			Regular Season					Playoffs				
Season	Club	Lea	GP	G	A	TP	PIM	GP	G	A	TP	PIM
1975-76	Kitchener	OHA	53	6	33	39	42	8	1	2	3	4
1976-77	Kitchener	OHA	51	4	14	18	16	3	0	2	2	4
1977-78	Kitchener	OHA	47	17	28	45	15	9	4	6	10	29
1978-79	Kitchener	OHA	66	51	78	129	57	10	3	10	13	16
1979-80	**Atlanta**	**NHL**	**79**	**9**	**38**	**47**	**31**	....	....	....	....	....
1980-81	**Calgary**	**NHL**	**74**	**18**	**49**	**67**	**52**	**16**	**1**	**14**	**15**	**16**
1981-82	**Calgary**	**NHL**	**62**	**13**	**48**	**61**	**17**	**3**	**0**	**1**	**1**	**2**
1982-83	**Calgary**	**NHL**	**78**	**17**	**58**	**75**	**28**	**9**	**6**	**3**	**9**	**2**
1983-84	**Calgary**	**NHL**	**27**	**6**	**15**	**21**	**10**	**11**	**6**	**11**	**17**	**2**
1984-85	**Calgary**	**NHL**	**75**	**23**	**46**	**69**	**18**	**4**	**1**	**1**	**2**	**0**
1985-86	**Calgary**	**NHL**	**32**	**8**	**25**	**33**	**15**	**21**	**5**	**13**	**18**	**4**
1986-87	**Calgary**	**NHL**	**76**	**15**	**53**	**68**	**22**	**4**	**0**	**1**	**1**	**6**
1987-88	**Calgary**	**NHL**	**14**	**0**	**4**	**4**	**10**	**8**	**2**	**7**	**9**	**6**
1988-89	**Vancouver**	**NHL**	**64**	**7**	**50**	**57**	**44**	**7**	**2**	**3**	**5**	**4**
1989-90	**Vancouver**	**NHL**	**67**	**17**	**40**	**57**	**30**	....	....	....	....	....
	NHL Totals		**648**	**133**	**426**	**559**	**277**	**83**	**23**	**54**	**77**	**42**

Played in NHL All-Star Game (1985, 1989)

Traded to **Vancouver** by **Calgary** with Steve Bozek for Vancouver's third round choice (Veli-Pekka Kautonen) in 1989 Entry Draft, September 6, 1988.

REISMAN, ERIC

Defense. Shoots left. 6'2", 220 lbs. Born, New York, NY, May 19, 1968.
(Boston's 8th choice, 228th overall, in 1988 Entry Draft).

			Regular Season					Playoffs				
Season	Club	Lea	GP	G	A	TP	PIM	GP	G	A	TP	PIM
1987-88	Ohio State	CCHA	29	0	3	3	45	....	....	....	....	....
1988-89	Ohio State	CCHA	38	4	6	10	56	....	....	....	....	....
1989-90	Ohio State	CCHA	39	1	2	3	91	....	....	....	....	....

RENBERG, MIKAEL

Left wing. Shoots left. 6'2", 185 lbs. Born, Pitea, Sweden, May 5, 1972.
(Philadelphia's 3rd choice, 40th overall, in 1990 Entry Draft).

			Regular Season					Playoffs				
Season	Club	Lea	GP	G	A	TP	PIM	GP	G	A	TP	PIM
1988-89	Pitea	Swe.	12	6	3	9	....	....	....	....	....	....
1989-90	Pitea	Swe.	29	15	19	34	....	....	....	....	....	....

RENDALL, BRUCE

Left wing. Shoots left. 6'1", 190 lbs. Born, Thunder Bay, Ont., April 18, 1967.
(Philadelphia's 2nd choice, 42nd overall, in 1985 Entry Draft).

			Regular Season					Playoffs				
Season	Club	Lea	GP	G	A	TP	PIM	GP	G	A	TP	PIM
1985-86	Michigan State	CCHA	45	14	18	32	68	....	....	....	....	....
1986-87	Michigan State	CCHA	44	11	14	25	113	....	....	....	....	....
1987-88	Michigan State	CCHA	39	10	2	12	70	....	....	....	....	....
1988-89	Hershey	AHL	37	7	8	15	12	....	....	....	....	....
	Indianapolis	IHL	15	2	2	4	9	....	....	....	....	....
1989-90	Hershey	AHL	9	2	1	3	4	....	....	....	....	....

REVENBERG, JAMES

Right wing. Shoots right. 5'11", 190 lbs. Born, Windsor, Ont., July 23, 1969.
(Vancouver's 5th choice, 134th overall, in 1989 Entry Draft).

			Regular Season					Playoffs				
Season	Club	Lea	GP	G	A	TP	PIM	GP	G	A	TP	PIM
1987-88	Windsor	OHL	66	1	6	7	206	12	0	0	0	41
1988-89	Windsor	OHL	58	9	15	24	292	3	2	0	2	32
1989-90	Milwaukee	IHL	56	1	6	7	314	4	0	0	0	45

REYNOLDS, BOBBY

Left wing. Shoots left. 5'11", 175 lbs. Born, Flint, MI, July 14, 1967.
(Toronto's 10th choice, 190th overall, in 1985 Entry Draft).

			Regular Season					Playoffs				
Season	Club	Lea	GP	G	A	TP	PIM	GP	G	A	TP	PIM
1985-86	Michigan State	CCHA	45	9	10	19	26	....	....	....	....	....
1986-87	Michigan State	CCHA	40	20	13	33	40	....	....	....	....	....
1987-88a	Michigan State	CCHA	46	42	25	67	52	....	....	....	....	....
1988-89ab	Michigan State	CCHA	47	36	41	77	78	....	....	....	....	....
1989-90	**Toronto**	**NHL**	**7**	**1**	**1**	**2**	**0**	....	....	....	....	....
	Newmarket	AHL	66	22	28	50	55	....	....	....	....	....
	NHL Totals		**7**	**1**	**1**	**2**	**0**	....	....	....	....	....

a CCHA Second All-Star Team (1988, 1989)
b NCAA West First All-American Team (1989)

RICARD, ERIC

Defense. Shoots left. 6'4", 220 lbs. Born, St. Cesaire, Que., February 16, 1969.
(Los Angeles' 3rd choice, 102nd overall, in 1989 Entry Draft).

			Regular Season					Playoffs				
Season	Club	Lea	GP	G	A	TP	PIM	GP	G	A	TP	PIM
1988-89	Granby	QMJHL	68	5	31	36	213	4	1	1	2	21
1989-90	New Haven	AHL	28	1	1	2	55	....	....	....	....	....

RICCI, MIKE

Center. Shoots left. 6"1", 190 lbs. Born, Scarborough, Ont., November 27, 1971.
(Philadelphia's 1st choice, 4th overall, in 1990 Entry Draft).

			Regular Season					Playoffs				
Season	Club	Lea	GP	G	A	TP	PIM	GP	G	A	TP	PIM
1988-89a	Peterborough	OHL	60	54	52	106	43	17	19	16	35	18
1989-90bcd	Peterborough	OHL	60	52	64	116	39	12	5	7	12	26

a OHL Second All-Star Team (1989)
b Canadian Major Junior Player of the Year (1990)
c OHL First All-Star Team (1990)
d OHL Player of the Year (1990)

RICE, STEVEN

Right wing. Shoots right. 6', 210 lbs. Born, Kitchener, Ont., May 26, 1971.
(NY Rangers' 1st choice, 20th overall, in 1989 Entry Draft).

			Regular Season					Playoffs				
Season	Club	Lea	GP	G	A	TP	PIM	GP	G	A	TP	PIM
1987-88	Kitchener	OHL	59	11	14	25	43	4	0	1	1	0
1988-89	Kitchener	OHL	64	36	30	66	42	5	2	1	3	8
1989-90ab	Kitchener	OHL	58	39	37	76	102	16	4	8	12	24

a OHL Third All-Star Team (1990)
b Memorial Cup All-Star Team (1990)

RICHARD, JEAN-MARC

Defense. Shoots left. 5'11", 178 lbs. Born, St. Raymond, Que., October 8, 1966.

			Regular Season					Playoffs				
Season	Club	Lea	GP	G	A	TP	PIM	GP	G	A	TP	PIM
1985-86a	Chicoutimi	QMJHL	72	20	87	107	111	9	3	5	8	14
1986-87a	Chicoutimi	QMJHL	67	21	81	102	105	16	6	25	31	28
1987-88	**Quebec**	**NHL**	**4**	**2**	**1**	**3**	**2**	....	....	....	....	....
	Fredericton	AHL	68	14	42	56	52	7	2	1	3	4
1988-89	Halifax	AHL	57	8	25	33	38	4	1	0	1	4
1989-90	**Quebec**	**NHL**	**1**	**0**	**0**	**0**	**0**	....	....	....	....	....
	Halifax	AHL	40	1	24	25	38	....	....	....	....	....
	NHL Totals		**5**	**2**	**1**	**3**	**2**	....	....	....	....	....

a QMJHL First All-Star Team (1986, 1987)

Signed as a free agent by **Quebec**, April 13, 1987.

RICHARD, MICHAEL (MIKE)

Center. Shoots left. 5'10", 194 lbs. Born, Scarborough, Ont., July 9, 1966.

			Regular Season					Playoffs				
Season	Club	Lea	GP	G	A	TP	PIM	GP	G	A	TP	PIM
1983-84	Toronto	OHL	66	19	17	36	12	9	2	1	3	0
1984-85	Toronto	OHL	66	31	41	72	15	5	0	0	0	11
1985-86	Toronto	OHL	63	32	48	80	28	4	1	1	2	2
1986-87	Toronto	OHL	66	57	50	107	38	....	....	....	....	....
1987-88a	Binghamton	AHL	72	46	48	94	23	4	0	3	3	4
	Washington	**NHL**	**4**	**0**	**0**	**0**	**0**	....	....	....	....	....
1988-89	Baltimore	AHL	80	44	63	107	51	....	....	....	....	....
1989-90	**Washington**	**NHL**	**3**	**0**	**2**	**2**	**0**	....	....	....	....	....
b	Baltimore	AHL	53	41	42	83	14	11	4	*13	17	6
	NHL Totals		**7**	**0**	**2**	**2**	**0**	....	....	....	....	....

a Won Dudley "Red" Garrett Memorial Trophy (Top Rookie - AHL) (1988).
b AHL Second All-Star Team (1990)

Signed as a free agent by **Washington**, October 9, 1987.

RICHARDS, TODD

Defense. Shoots right. 6', 194 lbs. Born, Robindale, MN, October, 20, 1966.
(Montreal's 3rd choice, 33rd overall, in 1985 Entry Draft).

			Regular Season					Playoffs				
Season	**Club**	**Lea**	**GP**	**G**	**A**	**TP**	**PIM**	**GP**	**G**	**A**	**TP**	**PIM**
1985-86	U. Minnesota	WCHA	38	6	23	29	38	....	....	....	....	....
1986-87	U. Minnesota	WCHA	49	8	43	51	70	....	....	....	....	....
1987-88a	U. Minnesota	WCHA	34	10	30	40	26	....	....	....	....	....
1988-89abc	U. Minnesota	WCHA	46	6	32	38	60	....	....	....	....	....
1989-90	Sherbrooke	AHL	71	6	18	24	73	5	1	2	3	6

a WCHA Second All-Star Team (1988, 1989)
b NCAA West Second All-American Team (1989)
c NCAA All-Tournament Team (1989)

RICHARDS, TRAVIS

Defense. Shoots left. 6', 180 lbs. Born, Robbinsdale, MN, March 22, 1970.
(Minnesota's 6th choice, 169th overall, in 1988 Entry Draft).

			Regular Season					Playoffs				
Season	**Club**	**Lea**	**GP**	**G**	**A**	**TP**	**PIM**	**GP**	**G**	**A**	**TP**	**PIM**
1987-88	Armstrong	HS	24	14	14	28	....	....	....	....	....	....
1988-89	U. Minnesota	WCHA	DID NOT PLAY									
1989-90	U. Minnesota	WCHA	45	4	24	28	38	....	....	....	....	....

RICHARDSON, LUKE

Defense. Shoots left. 6'4", 210 lbs. Born, Ottawa, Ont., March 26, 1969.
(Toronto's 1st choice, 7th overall, in 1987 Entry Draft).

			Regular Season					Playoffs				
Season	**Club**	**Lea**	**GP**	**G**	**A**	**TP**	**PIM**	**GP**	**G**	**A**	**TP**	**PIM**
1985-86	Peterborough	OHL	63	6	18	24	57	16	2	1	3	50
1986-87	Peterborough	OHL	59	13	32	45	70	12	0	5	5	24
1987-88	**Toronto**	**NHL**	**78**	**4**	**6**	**10**	**90**	**2**	**0**	**0**	**0**	**0**
1988-89	**Toronto**	**NHL**	**55**	**2**	**7**	**9**	**106**	....	....	....	....	....
1989-90	**Toronto**	**NHL**	**67**	**4**	**14**	**18**	**122**	**5**	**0**	**0**	**0**	**22**
	NHL Totals		**200**	**10**	**27**	**37**	**318**	**7**	**0**	**0**	**0**	**22**

RICHER, STEPHANE J. G. (REE-shay)

Defense. Shoots right. 5'11", 190 lbs. Born, Hull, Que., April 23, 1966.

			Regular Season					Playoffs				
Season	**Club**	**Lea**	**GP**	**G**	**A**	**TP**	**PIM**	**GP**	**G**	**A**	**TP**	**PIM**
1986-87	Hull	QMJHL	33	6	22	28	74	8	3	4	7	17
1987-88	Baltimore	AHL	22	0	3	3	6	....	....	....	....	....
	Sherbrooke	AHL	41	4	7	11	46	5	1	0	1	10
1988-89	Sherbrooke	AHL	70	7	26	33	158	6	1	2	3	18
1989-90	Sherbrooke	AHL	60	10	12	22	85	12	4	9	13	16

Signed as a free agent by **Montreal**, January 9, 1988. Signed as a free agent by **Los Angeles**, July 11, 1990.

RICHER, STEPHANE J. J. (REE-shay)

Right wing. Shoots right. 6'2", 200 lbs. Born, Ripon, Que., June 7, 1966.
(Montreal's 3rd choice, 29th overall, in 1984 Entry Draft).

			Regular Season					Playoffs				
Season	**Club**	**Lea**	**GP**	**G**	**A**	**TP**	**PIM**	**GP**	**G**	**A**	**TP**	**PIM**
1983-84	Granby	QMJHL	67	39	37	76	58	3	1	1	2	4
1984-85	**Montreal**	**NHL**	**1**	**0**	**0**	**0**	**0**	....	....	....	....	....
	Sherbrooke	AHL	....	....	....	....	....	9	6	3	9	10
	Granby	QMJHL	30	30	27	57	31	....	....	....	....	....
a	Chicoutimi	QMJHL	27	31	32	63	40	12	13	13	26	25
1985-86	**Montreal**	**NHL**	**65**	**21**	**16**	**37**	**50**	**16**	**4**	**1**	**5**	**23**
1986-87	**Montreal**	**NHL**	**57**	**20**	**19**	**39**	**80**	**5**	**3**	**2**	**5**	**0**
	Sherbrooke	AHL	12	10	4	14	11	....	....	....	....	....
1987-88	**Montreal**	**NHL**	**72**	**50**	**28**	**78**	**72**	**8**	**7**	**5**	**12**	**6**
1988-89	**Montreal**	**NHL**	**68**	**25**	**35**	**60**	**61**	**21**	**6**	**5**	**11**	**14**
1989-90	**Montreal**	**NHL**	**75**	**51**	**40**	**91**	**46**	**9**	**7**	**3**	**10**	**2**
	NHL Totals		**338**	**167**	**138**	**305**	**309**	**59**	**27**	**16**	**43**	**45**

a QMJHL Second All-Star Team (1985)

Played in NHL All-Star Game (1990)

RICHISON, GRANT DAVID

Defense. Shoots left. 6'2", 205 lbs. Born, Detroit, MI, May 5, 1967.

			Regular Season					Playoffs				
Season	**Club**	**Lea**	**GP**	**G**	**A**	**TP**	**PIM**	**GP**	**G**	**A**	**TP**	**PIM**
1988-89	U. of Calgary	CWUAA	16	2	12	14	59	....	....	....	....	....
1989-90	Moncton	AHL	50	2	10	12	28	....	....	....	....	....

Signed as a free agent by **Winnipeg**, October 18, 1989.

RICHMOND, STEVE

Defense. Shoots left. 6'1", 205 lbs. Born, Chicago, IL, December 11, 1959.

			Regular Season					Playoffs				
Season	**Club**	**Lea**	**GP**	**G**	**A**	**TP**	**PIM**	**GP**	**G**	**A**	**TP**	**PIM**
1978-79	U. of Michigan	CCHA	34	2	5	7	38	....	....	....	....	....
1979-80	U. of Michigan	CCHA	38	10	19	29	26	....	....	....	....	....
1980-81	U. of Michigan	CCHA	39	22	32	54	56	....	....	....	....	....
1981-82a	U. of Michigan	CCHA	38	6	30	36	68	....	....	....	....	....
1982-83	Tulsa	CHL	68	5	13	18	187	....	....	....	....	....
1983-84	Tulsa	CHL	38	1	17	18	114	....	....	....	....	....
	NY Rangers	**NHL**	**26**	**2**	**5**	**7**	**110**	**4**	**0**	**0**	**0**	**12**
1984-85	**NY Rangers**	**NHL**	**34**	**0**	**5**	**5**	**90**	....	....	....	....	....
	New Haven	AHL	37	3	10	13	122	....	....	....	....	....
1985-86	**NY Rangers**	**NHL**	**17**	**0**	**2**	**2**	**63**	....	....	....	....	....
	New Haven	AHL	11	2	6	8	32	....	....	....	....	....
	Detroit	**NHL**	**29**	**1**	**2**	**3**	**82**	....	....	....	....	....
	Adirondack	AHL	20	1	7	8	23	17	2	9	11	34
1986-87	**New Jersey**	**NHL**	**44**	**1**	**7**	**8**	**143**	....	....	....	....	....
1987-88	Utica	AHL	79	6	27	33	141	....	....	....	....	....
1988-89	**Los Angeles**	**NHL**	**9**	**0**	**2**	**2**	**26**	....	....	....	....	....
	New Haven	AHL	49	6	35	41	114	17	3	10	13	84
1989-90	Flint	IHL	10	1	3	4	19	4	0	1	1	16
	NHL Totals		**159**	**4**	**23**	**27**	**514**	**4**	**0**	**0**	**0**	**12**

a CCHA Second All-Star Team (1982)

Signed as a free agent by **NY Rangers**, June 22, 1982. Traded to **Detroit** by **NY Rangers** for Mike McEwen, December 26, 1985. Traded to **New Jersey** by **Detroit** for Sam St. Laurent, August 18, 1986.

RICHTER, BARRY

Defense. Shoots left. 6'2", 185 lbs. Born, Madison, WI, September 11, 1970.
(Hartford's 2nd choice, 32nd overall, in 1989 Entry Draft).

			Regular Season					Playoffs				
Season	**Club**	**Lea**	**GP**	**G**	**A**	**TP**	**PIM**	**GP**	**G**	**A**	**TP**	**PIM**
1988-89	Culver Aca.	HS	19	21	29	50	16	....	....	....	....	....
1989-90	U. Wisconsin	WCHA	42	13	23	36	36	....	....	....	....	....

RICHTER, DAVE (RIHK-tuhr)

Defense. Shoots right. 6'5", 220 lbs. Born, St. Boniface, Man., April 8, 1960.
(Minnesota's 10th choice, 205th overall, in 1980 Entry Draft).

			Regular Season					Playoffs				
Season	**Club**	**Lea**	**GP**	**G**	**A**	**TP**	**PIM**	**GP**	**G**	**A**	**TP**	**PIM**
1980-81	U. of Michigan	WCHA	36	2	13	15	56	....	....	....	....	....
1981-82	U. of Michigan	WCHA	36	9	12	21	78	....	....	....	....	....
	Nashville	CHL	2	0	1	1	0	....	....	....	....	....
	Minnesota	**NHL**	**3**	**0**	**0**	**0**	**11**	....	....	....	....	....
1982-83	**Minnesota**	**NHL**	**6**	**0**	**0**	**0**	**4**	....	....	....	....	....
	Birmingham	CHL	69	6	17	23	211	13	3	1	4	36
1983-84	Salt Lake	CHL	10	1	4	5	39	....	....	....	....	....
	Minnesota	**NHL**	**42**	**2**	**3**	**5**	**132**	**8**	**0**	**0**	**0**	**20**
1984-85	**Minnesota**	**NHL**	**55**	**2**	**8**	**10**	**221**	**9**	**1**	**0**	**1**	**39**
	Springfield	AHL	3	0	0	0	2	....	....	....	....	....
1985-86	**Minnesota**	**NHL**	**14**	**0**	**3**	**3**	**29**	....	....	....	....	....
	Philadelphia	**NHL**	**50**	**0**	**2**	**2**	**138**	**5**	**0**	**0**	**0**	**21**
1986-87	**Vancouver**	**NHL**	**78**	**2**	**15**	**17**	**172**	....	....	....	....	....
1987-88	**Vancouver**	**NHL**	**49**	**2**	**4**	**6**	**224**	....	....	....	....	....
1988-89	**St. Louis**	**NHL**	**66**	**1**	**5**	**6**	**99**	....	....	....	....	....
1989-90	**St. Louis**	**NHL**	**2**	**0**	**0**	**0**	**0**	....	....	....	....	....
	Peoria	IHL	9	1	4	5	30	....	....	....	....	....
	Phoenix	IHL	20	0	5	5	49	....	....	....	....	....
	NHL Totals		**365**	**9**	**40**	**49**	**1030**	**22**	**1**	**0**	**1**	**80**

Traded to **Philadelphia** by **Minnesota** with Bo Berglund for Ed Hospodar and Todd Bergen, November 29, 1985. Traded to **Vancouver** by **Philadelphia** with Rich Sutter and Vancouver's third-round choice (Don Gibson) — acquired earlier — in 1986 Entry Draft fror J.J. Daigneault and Vancouver's second-round choice (Kent Hawley) in 1986 Entry Draft, June 6, 1986. Traded to **St. Louis** by **Vancouver** with Vancouver's second-round choice in 1990 Entry Draft for Robert Nordmark, September 6, 1988.

RIDLEY, MIKE

Center. Shoots left. 6'1", 200 lbs. Born, Winnipeg, Man., July 8, 1963.

			Regular Season					Playoffs				
Season	**Club**	**Lea**	**GP**	**G**	**A**	**TP**	**PIM**	**GP**	**G**	**A**	**TP**	**PIM**
1983-84a	U. of Manitoba	GPAC	46	39	41	80	...	....	....	....	....	....
1984-85b	U. of Manitoba	GPAC	30	29	38	67	48	....	....	....	....	....
1985-86c	**NY Rangers**	**NHL**	**80**	**22**	**43**	**65**	**69**	**16**	**6**	**8**	**14**	**26**
1986-87	**NY Rangers**	**NHL**	**38**	**16**	**20**	**36**	**20**	....	....	....	....	....
	Washington	**NHL**	**40**	**15**	**19**	**34**	**20**	**7**	**2**	**1**	**3**	**6**
1987-88	**Washington**	**NHL**	**70**	**28**	**31**	**59**	**22**	**14**	**6**	**5**	**11**	**10**
1988-89	**Washington**	**NHL**	**80**	**41**	**48**	**89**	**49**	**6**	**0**	**5**	**5**	**2**
1989-90	**Washington**	**NHL**	**74**	**30**	**43**	**73**	**27**	**14**	**3**	**4**	**7**	**8**
	NHL Totals		**382**	**152**	**204**	**356**	**207**	**57**	**17**	**23**	**40**	**52**

a Canadian University Player of the Year; CIAU All-Canadian, GPAC MVP and First All-Star Team (1984)
b CIAU All-Canadian, GPAC First All-Star Team (1985)
c NHL All-Rookie Team (1986)

Played in NHL All-Star Game (1989)

Signed as a free agent by **NY Rangers**, September 26, 1985. Traded to **Washington** by **NY Rangers** with Bob Crawford and Kelly Miller for Bob Carpenter and, Washington's second-round choice (Jason Prosofsky) in 1989 Entry Draft, January 1, 1987.

RIIHIJARVI, HEIKKI

Defense. Shoots right. 6'5", 180 lbs. Born, Salla, Finland, April 6, 1966.
(Edmonton's 8th choice, 147th overall, in 1984 Entry Draft).

			Regular Season					Playoffs				
Season	**Club**	**Lea**	**GP**	**G**	**A**	**TP**	**PIM**	**GP**	**G**	**A**	**TP**	**PIM**
1985-86	TPS	Fin. Jr.	25	6	8	14	12	....	....	....	....	....
1986-87	Karpat	Fin.	36	4	4	8	10	....	....	....	....	....
1987-88	Karpat	Fin.	21	0	5	5	0	....	....	....	....	....
1988-89	Karpat	Fin.	43	8	11	19	14	5	0	2	2	4
1989-90	Jokerit	Fin.	44	3	10	13	16	....	....	....	....	....

ROBBINS, MATTHEW

Center. Shoots right. 5'10", 150 lbs. Born, Lowell, MA, March 11, 1970.
(NY Islanders' 9th choice, 170th overall, in 1989 Entry Draft).

			Regular Season					Playoffs				
Season	Club	Lea	GP	G	A	TP	PIM	GP	G	A	TP	PIM
1989-90	U. of Lowell	H.E.	14	2	8	10	4	....	....	....	....	....

ROBERGE, MARIO

Left wing. Shoots left. 5'11", 185 lbs. Born, Quebec City, Que., January 23, 1964.

			Regular Season					Playoffs				
Season	Club	Lea	GP	G	A	TP	PIM	GP	G	A	TP	PIM
1988-89	Sherbrooke	AHL	58	4	9	13	249	6	0	2	2	8
1989-90	Sherbrooke	AHL	73	13	27	40	247	12	5	2	7	53

Signed as a free agent by **Montreal**, October 5, 1988.

ROBERGE, SERGE

Right wing. Shoots right. 6'1", 195 lbs. Born, Quebec City, Que., March 31, 1965.

			Regular Season					Playoffs				
Season	Club	Lea	GP	G	A	TP	PIM	GP	G	A	TP	PIM
1984-85	Drummondville	QMJHL	45	8	19	27	299	....	....	....	....	....
1985-86			DID NOT PLAY									
1986-87	Virginia	ACHL	47	9	15	24	346	....	....	....	....	....
1987-88	Sherbrooke	AHL	30	0	1	1	130	5	0	0	0	21
1988-89	Sherbrooke	AHL	65	5	7	12	352	6	0	1	1	10
1989-90	Sherbrooke	AHL	66	8	5	13	343	12	2	0	2	44

Signed as a free agent by **Montreal**, January 25, 1988.

ROBERTS, ALEX

Defense. Shoots left. 6'1", 185 lbs. Born, Bloomfield Hills, MI, January 11, 1968.
(Chicago's 1st choice, 11th overall, in 1989 Supplemental Draft).

			Regular Season					Playoffs				
Season	Club	Lea	GP	G	A	TP	PIM	GP	G	A	TP	PIM
1986-87	U. of Michigan	CCHA	37	1	7	8	117	....	....	....	....	....
1987-88	U. of Michigan	CCHA	39	4	9	13	77	....	....	....	....	....
1988-89	U. of Michigan	CCHA	41	5	19	24	116	....	....	....	....	....
1989-90	U. of Michigan	CCHA	41	14	21	35	105	....	....	....	....	....

ROBERTS, DAVID

Left wing. Shoots left. 6', 180 lbs. Born, Alameda, CA, May 28, 1970.
(St. Louis' 5th choice, 114th overall, in 1989 Entry Draft).

			Regular Season					Playoffs				
Season	Club	Lea	GP	G	A	TP	PIM	GP	G	A	TP	PIM
1988-89	Avon Old Farms	HS	....	28	48	76	....	....	....	....	....	....
1989-90a	U. of Michigan	CCHA	42	21	32	53	46	....	....	....	....	....

a CCHA Rookie of the Year (1990)

ROBERTS, GARY

Left wing. Shoots left. 6'1", 190 lbs. Born, North York, Ont., May 23, 1966.
(Calgary's 1st choice, 12th overall, in 1984 Entry Draft).

			Regular Season					Playoffs				
Season	Club	Lea	GP	G	A	TP	PIM	GP	G	A	TP	PIM
1982-83	Ottawa	OHL	53	12	8	20	83	5	1	0	1	19
1983-84	Ottawa	OHL	48	27	30	57	144	13	10	7	17	62
1984-85	Moncton	AHL	7	4	2	6	7	....	....	....	....	....
a	Ottawa	OHL	59	44	62	106	186	5	2	8	10	10
1985-86a	Ottawa	OHL	24	26	25	51	83	....	....	....	....	....
a	Guelph	OHL	23	18	15	33	65	20	18	13	31	43
1986-87	**Calgary**	**NHL**	**32**	**5**	**10**	**15**	**85**	**2**	**0**	**0**	**0**	**4**
	Moncton	AHL	38	20	18	38	72	....	....	....	....	....
1987-88	**Calgary**	**NHL**	**74**	**13**	**15**	**28**	**282**	**9**	**2**	**3**	**5**	**29**
1988-89	**Calgary**	**NHL**	**71**	**22**	**16**	**38**	**250**	**22**	**5**	**7**	**12**	**57**
1989-90	**Calgary**	**NHL**	**78**	**39**	**33**	**72**	**222**	**6**	**2**	**5**	**7**	**41**
	NHL Totals		**255**	**79**	**74**	**153**	**839**	**39**	**9**	**15**	**24**	**131**

a OHL Second All-Star Team (1985, 1986)

ROBERTS, GORDON (GORDIE)

Defense. Shoots left. 6'1", 195 lbs. Born, Detroit, MI, October 2, 1957.
(Montreal's 7th choice, 54th overall, in 1977 Amateur Draft).

			Regular Season					Playoffs				
Season	Club	Lea	GP	G	A	TP	PIM	GP	G	A	TP	PIM
1974-75	Victoria	WHL	53	19	45	64	145	12	1	9	10	42
1975-76	New England	WHA	77	3	19	22	102	17	2	9	11	36
1976-77	New England	WHA	77	13	33	46	169	5	2	2	4	6
1977-78	New England	WHA	78	15	46	61	118	14	0	5	5	29
1978-79	New England	WHA	79	11	46	57	113	10	0	4	4	10
1979-80	**Hartford**	**NHL**	**80**	**8**	**28**	**36**	**89**	**3**	**1**	**1**	**2**	**2**
1980-81	**Hartford**	**NHL**	**27**	**2**	**11**	**13**	**81**	....	....	....	....	....
	Minnesota	**NHL**	**50**	**6**	**31**	**37**	**94**	**19**	**1**	**5**	**6**	**17**
1981-82	**Minnesota**	**NHL**	**79**	**4**	**30**	**34**	**119**	**4**	**0**	**3**	**3**	**27**
1982-83	**Minnesota**	**NHL**	**80**	**3**	**41**	**44**	**103**	**9**	**1**	**5**	**6**	**14**
1983-84	**Minnesota**	**NHL**	**77**	**8**	**45**	**53**	**132**	**15**	**3**	**7**	**10**	**23**
1984-85	**Minnesota**	**NHL**	**78**	**6**	**36**	**42**	**112**	**9**	**1**	**6**	**7**	**6**
1985-86	**Minnesota**	**NHL**	**76**	**2**	**21**	**23**	**101**	**5**	**0**	**4**	**4**	**8**
1986-87	**Minnesota**	**NHL**	**67**	**3**	**10**	**13**	**68**	....	....	....	....	....
1987-88	**Minnesota**	**NHL**	**48**	**1**	**10**	**11**	**103**	....	....	....	....	....
	Philadelphia	**NHL**	**11**	**1**	**2**	**3**	**15**	....	....	....	....	....
	St. Louis	**NHL**	**11**	**1**	**3**	**4**	**25**	**10**	**1**	**2**	**3**	**33**
1988-89	**St. Louis**	**NHL**	**77**	**2**	**24**	**26**	**90**	**10**	**1**	**7**	**8**	**8**
1989-90	**St. Louis**	**NHL**	**75**	**3**	**14**	**17**	**140**	**10**	**0**	**2**	**2**	**26**
	NHL Totals		**836**	**50**	**306**	**356**	**1272**	**94**	**9**	**42**	**51**	**164**

Claimed by **Hartford** from **Montreal** in 1979 Expansion Draft, June 22, 1979. Traded to **Minnesota** by **Hartford** for Mike Fidler, December 16, 1980. Traded to **Philadelphia** by **Minnesota** for future considerations, February 8, 1988. Traded to **St. Louis** by **Philadelphia** for future considerations, March 8, 1988.

ROBERTS, TIMOTHY

Center. Shoots left. 6'2", 180 lbs. Born, Boston, MA, March 6, 1969.
(Buffalo's 9th choice, 153rd overall, in 1987 Entry Draft).

			Regular Season					Playoffs				
Season	Club	Lea	GP	G	A	TP	PIM	GP	G	A	TP	PIM
1987-88	RPI	ECAC	28	5	9	14	40	....	....	....	....	....
1988-89	RPI	ECAC	27	4	11	15	50	....	....	....	....	....
1989-90	RPI	ECAC	26	2	10	12	31	....	....	....	....	....

ROBERTSON, TORRIE ANDREW

Left wing. Shoots left. 5'11", 200 lbs. Born, Victoria, B.C., August 2, 1961.
(Washington's 3rd choice, 55th overall, in 1980 Entry Draft).

			Regular Season					Playoffs				
Season	Club	Lea	GP	G	A	TP	PIM	GP	G	A	TP	PIM
1978-79	Victoria	WHL	69	18	23	41	141	15	1	2	3	29
1979-80	Victoria	WHL	72	23	24	47	298	17	5	7	12	117
1980-81	**Washington**	**NHL**	**3**	**0**	**0**	**0**	**0**	....	....	....	....	....
	Victoria	WHL	59	45	66	111	274	15	10	13	23	55
1981-82	Hershey	AHL	21	5	3	8	60	....	....	....	....	....
	Washington	**NHL**	**54**	**8**	**13**	**21**	**204**	....	....	....	....	....
1982-83	**Washington**	**NHL**	**5**	**2**	**0**	**2**	**4**	....	....	....	....	....
	Hershey	AHL	69	21	33	54	187	5	1	2	3	8
1983-84	**Hartford**	**NHL**	**66**	**7**	**13**	**20**	**198**	....	....	....	....	....
1984-85	**Hartford**	**NHL**	**74**	**11**	**30**	**41**	**337**	....	....	....	....	....
1985-86	**Hartford**	**NHL**	**76**	**13**	**24**	**37**	**358**	**10**	**1**	**0**	**1**	**67**
1986-87	**Hartford**	**NHL**	**20**	**1**	**0**	**1**	**98**	....	....	....	....	....
1987-88	**Hartford**	**NHL**	**63**	**2**	**8**	**10**	**293**	**6**	**0**	**1**	**1**	**6**
1988-89	**Hartford**	**NHL**	**27**	**2**	**4**	**6**	**84**	....	....	....	....	....
	Detroit	**NHL**	**12**	**2**	**2**	**4**	**63**	**6**	**1**	**0**	**1**	**17**
1989-90	**Detroit**	**NHL**	**42**	**1**	**5**	**6**	**112**	....	....	....	....	....
	Adirondack	IHL	27	3	13	16	47	6	1	1	2	33
	NHL Totals		**442**	**49**	**99**	**148**	**1751**	**22**	**2**	**1**	**3**	**90**

Traded to **Hartford** by **Washington** for Greg Adams, October 3, 1983. Traded to **Detroit** by **Hartford** for Jim Pavese, March 7, 1989.

ROBINSON, DOUGLAS SCOTT

Right wing. Shoots left. 6'2", 180 lbs. Born, 100 Mile House, B.C., March 29, 1964.

			Regular Season					Playoffs				
Season	Club	Lea	GP	G	A	TP	PIM	GP	G	A	TP	PIM
1982-83	Seattle	WHL	63	14	13	27	151	4	3	0	3	9
1983-84	Seattle	WHL	44	17	18	35	105	5	0	1	1	25
1984-85	Seattle	WHL	64	44	53	97	106	....	....	....	....	....
1985-86	U. of Calgary	CWUAA	18	3	9	12	61	....	....	....	....	....
1986-87	U. of Calgary	CWUAA	19	12	14	26	95	....	....	....	....	....
1987-88	U. of Calgary	CWUAA	21	14	14	28	64	....	....	....	....	....
1988-89	Kalamazoo	IHL	49	14	17	31	129	....	....	....	....	....
1989-90	**Minnesota**	**NHL**	**1**	**0**	**0**	**0**	**2**	....	....	....	....	....
	Kalamazoo	IHL	48	13	12	25	97	10	4	7	11	21
	NHL Totals		**1**	**0**	**0**	**0**	**2**	....	....	....	....	....

Signed as a free agent by **Minnesota**, September 27, 1988.

ROBINSON, LARRY CLARK

Defense. Shoots left. 6'4", 225 lbs. Born, Winchester, Ont., June 2, 1951.
(Montreal's 4th choice, 20th overall, in 1971 Amateur Draft).

			Regular Season					Playoffs				
Season	Club	Lea	GP	G	A	TP	PIM	GP	G	A	TP	PIM
1969-70	Brockville	OHA	40	22	29	51	74	....	....	....	....	....
1970-71	Kitchener	OHA	61	12	39	51	65	....	....	....	....	....
1971-72	Nova Scotia	AHL	74	10	14	24	54	15	2	10	12	31
1972-73	Nova Scotia	AHL	38	6	33	39	33	....	....	....	....	....
	Montreal	**NHL**	**36**	**2**	**4**	**6**	**20**	**11**	**1**	**4**	**5**	**9**
1973-74	**Montreal**	**NHL**	**78**	**6**	**20**	**26**	**66**	**6**	**0**	**1**	**1**	**26**
1974-75	**Montreal**	**NHL**	**80**	**14**	**47**	**61**	**76**	**11**	**0**	**4**	**4**	**27**
1975-76	**Montreal**	**NHL**	**80**	**10**	**30**	**40**	**59**	**13**	**3**	**3**	**6**	**10**
1976-77abc	**Montreal**	**NHL**	**77**	**19**	**66**	**85**	**45**	**14**	**2**	**10**	**12**	**12**
1977-78de	**Montreal**	**NHL**	**80**	**13**	**52**	**65**	**39**	**15**	**4**	***17**	***21**	**6**
1978-79b	**Montreal**	**NHL**	**67**	**16**	**45**	**61**	**33**	**16**	**6**	**9**	**15**	**8**
1979-80ab	**Montreal**	**NHL**	**72**	**14**	**61**	**75**	**39**	**10**	**0**	**4**	**4**	**2**
1980-81e	**Montreal**	**NHL**	**65**	**12**	**38**	**50**	**37**	**3**	**0**	**1**	**1**	**2**
1981-82	**Montreal**	**NHL**	**71**	**12**	**47**	**59**	**41**	**5**	**0**	**1**	**1**	**8**
1982-83	**Montreal**	**NHL**	**71**	**14**	**49**	**63**	**33**	**3**	**0**	**0**	**0**	**2**
1983-84	**Montreal**	**NHL**	**74**	**9**	**34**	**43**	**39**	**15**	**0**	**5**	**5**	**22**
1984-85	**Montreal**	**NHL**	**76**	**14**	**33**	**47**	**44**	**12**	**3**	**8**	**11**	**8**
1985-86e	**Montreal**	**NHL**	**78**	**19**	**63**	**82**	**39**	**20**	**0**	**13**	**13**	**22**
1986-87	**Montreal**	**NHL**	**70**	**13**	**37**	**50**	**44**	**17**	**3**	**17**	**20**	**6**
1987-88	**Montreal**	**NHL**	**53**	**6**	**34**	**40**	**30**	**11**	**1**	**4**	**5**	**4**
1988-89	**Montreal**	**NHL**	**74**	**4**	**26**	**30**	**22**	**21**	**2**	**8**	**10**	**12**
1989-90	**Los Angeles**	**NHL**	**64**	**7**	**32**	**39**	**34**	**10**	**2**	**3**	**5**	**10**
	NHL Totals		**1266**	**204**	**718**	**922**	**740**	**213**	**27**	**112**	**139**	**196**

a Won James Norris Memorial Trophy (1977, 1980)
b NHL First All-Star Team (1977, 1979, 1980)
c NHL Plus/Minus Leader (1977)
d Won Conn Smythe Trophy (1978)
e NHL Second All-Star Team (1978, 1981, 1986)

Played in NHL All-Star Game (1974, 1976-78, 1980, 1982, 1986, 1988, 1989)

Signed as a free agent by **Los Angeles**, July 26, 1989.

ROBINSON, ROBERT

Defense. Shoots left. 6'3", 210 lbs. Born, St. Catharines, Ont., April 19, 1967.
(St. Louis' 6th choice, 117th overall, in 1987 Entry Draft).

			Regular Season					Playoffs				
Season	Club	Lea	GP	G	A	TP	PIM	GP	G	A	TP	PIM
1985-86	Miami-Ohio	CCHA	38	1	9	10	24	....	....	....	....	....
1986-87	Miami-Ohio	CCHA	33	3	5	8	32	....	....	....	....	....
1987-88	Miami-Ohio	CCHA	35	1	3	4	56	....	....	....	....	....
1988-89	Miami-Ohio	CCHA	30	3	4	7	42	....	....	....	....	....
	Peoria	IHL	11	2	0	2	6	....	....	....	....	....
1989-90	Peoria	IHL	60	2	11	13	72	5	0	1	1	10

ROBISON, JEFF

Defense. Shoots left. 6'1", 175 lbs. Born, Wrentham, MA, June 3, 1970.
(Los Angeles' 5th choice, 91st overall, in 1988 Entry Draft).

			Regular Season					Playoffs				
Season	Club	Lea	GP	G	A	TP	PIM	GP	G	A	TP	PIM
1988-89	Providence	H.E.	41	0	5	5	36	....	....	....	....	....
1989-90	Providence	H.E.	35	2	8	10	16	....	....	....	....	....

ROBITAILLE, LUC (ROH-buh-tigh)

Left wing. Shoots left. 6'1", 190 lbs. Born, Montreal, Que., February 17, 1966.
(Los Angeles' 9th choice, 171st overall, in 1984 Entry Draft).

			Regular Season					Playoffs				
Season	Club	Lea	GP	G	A	TP	PIM	GP	G	A	TP	PIM
1983-84	Hull	QMJHL	70	32	53	85	48	....	....	....	....	....
1984-85a	Hull	QMJHL	64	55	94	149	115	5	4	2	6	27
1985-86bcd	Hull	QMJHL	63	68	123	191	91	15	17	27	44	28
1986-87ef	**Los Angeles**	**NHL**	**79**	**45**	**39**	**84**	**28**	**5**	**1**	**4**	**5**	**2**
1987-88g	**Los Angeles**	**NHL**	**80**	**53**	**58**	**111**	**82**	**5**	**2**	**5**	**7**	**18**
1988-89g	**Los Angeles**	**NHL**	**78**	**46**	**52**	**98**	**65**	**11**	**2**	**6**	**8**	**10**
1989-90g	**Los Angeles**	**NHL**	**80**	**52**	**49**	**101**	**38**	**10**	**5**	**5**	**10**	**10**
	NHL Totals		**317**	**196**	**198**	**394**	**213**	**31**	**10**	**20**	**30**	**40**

a QMJHL Second All-Star Team (1985)
b QMJHL First All-Star Team (1986)
c QMJHL Player of the Year (1986)
d Canadian Major Junior Player of the Year (1986)
e Won Calder Memorial Trophy (1987)
f NHL Second All-Star Team (1987)
g NHL First All-Star Team (1988, 1989, 1990)

Played in NHL All-Star Game (1988-90)

ROBITAILLE, MARTIN

Center. Shoots right. 5'10", 165 lbs. Born, St. Romuale, Que., March 17, 1969.
(Toronto's 1st choice, 15th overall, in 1990 Supplemental Draft).

			Regular Season					Playoffs				
Season	Club	Lea	GP	G	A	TP	PIM	GP	G	A	TP	PIM
1988-89	U. of Maine	H.E.	45	17	31	48	10	....	....	....	....	....
1989-90	U. of Maine	H.E.	46	24	28	52	24	....	....	....	....	....

ROCHEFORT, NORMAND (ROHSH-fohr)

Defense. Shoots left. 6'1", 211 lbs. Born, Trois Rivieres, Que., January 28, 1961.
(Quebec's 1st choice, 24th overall, in 1980 Entry Draft).

			Regular Season					Playoffs				
Season	Club	Lea	GP	G	A	TP	PIM	GP	G	A	TP	PIM
1978-79	Trois Rivieres	QJHL	72	17	57	74	30	13	3	11	14	17
1979-80	Trois Rivieres	QJHL	20	5	25	30	22	....	....	....	....	....
a	Quebec	QJHL	52	8	39	47	68	5	1	3	4	8
1980-81	Quebec	QJHL	9	2	6	8	14	....	....	....	....	....
	Quebec	**NHL**	**56**	**3**	**7**	**10**	**51**	**5**	**0**	**0**	**0**	**4**
1981-82	**Quebec**	**NHL**	**72**	**4**	**14**	**18**	**115**	**16**	**0**	**2**	**2**	**10**
1982-83	**Quebec**	**NHL**	**62**	**6**	**17**	**23**	**40**	**1**	**0**	**0**	**0**	**2**
1983-84	**Quebec**	**NHL**	**75**	**2**	**22**	**24**	**47**	**6**	**1**	**0**	**1**	**6**
1984-85	**Quebec**	**NHL**	**73**	**3**	**21**	**24**	**74**	**18**	**2**	**1**	**3**	**8**
1985-86	**Quebec**	**NHL**	**26**	**5**	**4**	**9**	**30**	....	....	....	....	....
1986-87	**Quebec**	**NHL**	**70**	**6**	**9**	**15**	**46**	**13**	**2**	**1**	**3**	**26**
1987-88	**Quebec**	**NHL**	**46**	**3**	**10**	**13**	**49**	....	....	....	....	....
1988-89	**NY Rangers**	**NHL**	**11**	**1**	**5**	**6**	**18**	....	....	....	....	....
1989-90	**NY Rangers**	**NHL**	**31**	**3**	**1**	**4**	**24**	**10**	**2**	**1**	**3**	**26**
	NHL Totals		**522**	**36**	**110**	**146**	**494**	**69**	**7**	**5**	**12**	**82**

a QMJHL Second All-Star Team (1980)

Traded to **NY Rangers** by **Quebec** with Jason Lafreniere for Bruce Bell, Jari Gronstrand, Walt Poddubny and NY Rangers' fourth round choice (Eric Dubois) in 1989 Entry Draft, August 1, 1988.

RODERICK, JOHN

Defense. Shoots left. 6'2", 190 lbs. Born, Cambridge, MA, February 25, 1971.
(St. Louis' 9th choice, 177th overall, in 1989 Entry Draft).

			Regular Season					Playoffs				
Season	Club	Lea	GP	G	A	TP	PIM	GP	G	A	TP	PIM
1989-90	St. Lawrence	ECAC	16	0	1	1	20	....	....	....	....	....

ROENICK, JEREMY (ROH-nihk)

Center. Shoots right. 5'11", 170 lbs. Born, Boston, MA, January 17, 1970.
(Chicago's 1st choice, 8th overall, in 1988 Entry Draft).

			Regular Season					Playoffs				
Season	Club	Lea	GP	G	A	TP	PIM	GP	G	A	TP	PIM
1987-88	Thayer Acad.	HS	24	34	50	84	....	....	....	....	....	....
1988-89	**Chicago**	**NHL**	**20**	**9**	**9**	**18**	**4**	**10**	**1**	**3**	**4**	**7**
a	Hull	QMJHL	28	34	36	70	14	....	....	....	....	....
	U.S. Jr. Nat'l.	....	11	8	8	16	0	....	....	....	....	....
1989-90	**Chicago**	**NHL**	**78**	**26**	**40**	**66**	**54**	**20**	**11**	**7**	**18**	**8**
	NHL Totals		**98**	**35**	**49**	**84**	**58**	**30**	**12**	**10**	**22**	**15**

a QMJHL Second All-Star Team (1989)

ROHLICEK, JEFF (ROHL-ih-chehk)

Center. Shoots left. 6', 180 lbs. Born, Park Ridge, IL, January 27, 1966.
(Vancouver's 2nd choice, 31st overall, in 1984 Entry Draft).

			Regular Season					Playoffs				
Season	Club	Lea	GP	G	A	TP	PIM	GP	G	A	TP	PIM
1983-84	Portland	WHL	71	44	53	97	22	14	13	8	21	10
1984-85a	Kelowna	WHL	65	39	52	91	26	6	3	6	9	2
	Portland	WHL	16	5	13	18	2	....	....	....	....	....
1985-86	Spokane	WHL	57	50	52	102	39	9	6	2	8	16
1986-87	Fredericton	AHL	70	19	37	56	22	....	....	....	....	....
1987-88	**Vancouver**	**NHL**	**7**	**0**	**0**	**0**	**4**	....	....	....	....	....
	Fredericton	AHL	65	26	31	57	50	....	....	....	....	....
1988-89	**Vancouver**	**NHL**	**2**	**0**	**0**	**0**	**4**	....	....	....	....	....
b	Milwaukee	IHL	78	47	63	110	106	11	6	6	12	8
1989-90	Springfield	AHL	12	1	2	3	4	7	3	2	5	6
	NHL Totals		**9**	**0**	**0**	**0**	**8**	....	....	....	....	....

a WHL Second All-Star Team, West Division (1985)
b IHL First All-Star Team (1989)

Traded to **NY Islanders** by **Vancouver** for Jack Capuano, March 6, 1990.

ROHLIK, STEVE

Left wing. Shoots left. 6', 180 lbs. Born, St. Paul, MN, May 15, 1968.
(Pittsburgh's 8th choice, 151st overall, in 1986 Entry Draft).

			Regular Season					Playoffs				
Season	Club	Lea	GP	G	A	TP	PIM	GP	G	A	TP	PIM
1986-87	U. Wisconsin	WCHA	31	3	0	3	34	....	....	....	....	....
1987-88	U. Wisconsin	WCHA	44	3	10	13	59	....	....	....	....	....
1988-89	U. Wisconsin	WCHA	45	11	14	25	44	....	....	....	....	....

ROHLIN, LEIF

Defense. Shoots left. 6'1", 196 lbs. Born, Vasteras, Sweden, February 26, 1968.
(Vancouver's 2nd choice, 33rd overall, in 1988 Entry Draft).

			Regular Season					Playoffs				
Season	Club	Lea	GP	G	A	TP	PIM	GP	G	A	TP	PIM
1987-88	Vasteras	Swe. 2	30	2	15	17	46	10	6	6	12	8
1988-89	Vasteras	Swe.	22	3	7	10	18	....	....	....	....	....
1989-90	Vasteras	Swe.	32	3	6	9	40	....	....	....	....	....

ROHLOFF, JON

Defense. Shoots right. 5'11", 200 lbs. Born, Mankato, MN, October 3, 1969.
(Boston's 7th choice, 186th overall, in 1988 Entry Draft).

			Regular Season					Playoffs				
Season	Club	Lea	GP	G	A	TP	PIM	GP	G	A	TP	PIM
1988-89	Minn.-Duluth	WCHA	9	1	2	3	44	....	....	....	....	....
1989-90	Minn.-Duluth	WCHA	5	0	1	1	6	....	....	....	....	....

ROLFE, DANIEL

Defense. Shoots left. 6'4", 200 lbs. Born, Inglewood, CA, December 25, 1967.
(St. Louis' 12th choice, 222nd overall, in 1987 Entry Draft).

			Regular Season					Playoffs				
Season	Club	Lea	GP	G	A	TP	PIM	GP	G	A	TP	PIM
1987-88	Ferris State	CCHA	13	1	1	2	36	....	....	....	....	....
1988-89	Ferris State	CCHA	28	0	2	2	54	....	....	....	....	....
1989-90	Ferris State	CCHA	31	0	6	6	48	....	....	....	....	....

ROMANIUK, RUSSELL

Left wing. Shoots left. 6', 185 lbs. Born, Winnipeg, Man., June 9, 1970.
(Winnipeg's 2nd choice, 31st overall, in 1988 Entry Draft).

			Regular Season					Playoffs				
Season	Club	Lea	GP	G	A	TP	PIM	GP	G	A	TP	PIM
1988-89	North Dakota	WCHA	39	17	14	31	32	....	....	....	....	....
	Cdn. National	....	3	1	0	1	0	....	....	....	....	....
1989-90	North Dakota	WCHA	45	36	15	51	54	....	....	....	....	....

RONAN, EDWARD (ED)

Right wing. Shoots right. 5'11", 170 lbs. Born, Quincy, MA, March 21, 1968.
(Montreal's 13th choice, 227th overall, in 1987 Entry Draft).

			Regular Season					Playoffs				
Season	Club	Lea	GP	G	A	TP	PIM	GP	G	A	TP	PIM
1987-88	Boston U.	H.E.	31	2	5	7	20	....	....	....	....	....
1988-89	Boston U.	H.E.	36	4	11	15	34	....	....	....	....	....
1989-90	Boston U.	H.E.	44	17	23	40	50	....	....	....	....	....

RONNING, CLIFF

Center. Shoots left. 5'8", 175 lbs. Born, Vancouver, B.C., October 1, 1965.
(St. Louis' 9th choice, 134th overall, in 1984 Entry Draft)

			Regular Season					Playoffs				
Season	Club	Lea	GP	G	A	TP	PIM	GP	G	A	TP	PIM
1983-84a	N. Westminster	WHL	71	69	67	136	10	9	8	13	21	10
1984-85bc	N. Westminster	WHL	70	*89	108	*197	20	11	10	14	24	4
1985-86	**St. Louis**	**NHL**	....	....	....	....	....	**5**	**1**	**1**	**2**	**2**
	Cdn. Olympic	...	71	55	63	118	53	....	....	....	....	....
1986-87	**St. Louis**	**NHL**	**42**	**11**	**14**	**25**	**6**	**4**	**0**	**1**	**1**	**0**
	Cdn. Olympic	....	26	16	16	32	12	....	....	....	....	....
1987-88	**St. Louis**	**NHL**	**26**	**5**	**8**	**13**	**12**	....	....	....	....	....
1988-89	**St. Louis**	**NHL**	**64**	**24**	**31**	**55**	**18**	**7**	**1**	**3**	**4**	**0**
	Peoria	IHL	12	11	20	31	8	....	....	....	....	....
1989-90	Asiago	Italy	36	67	49	116	25	6	7	12	19	4
	NHL Totals		**132**	**40**	**53**	**93**	**36**	**16**	**2**	**5**	**7**	**2**

a WHL Rookie of the Year (1984)
b WHL First All-Star Team (1985)
c WHL Most Valuable Player (1985)

ROONEY, LARRY

Defense. Shoots left. 5'11", 165 lbs. Born, Boston, MA, January 30, 1968.
(Buffalo's 6th choice, 89th overall, in 1986 Entry Draft).

			Regular Season					Playoffs				
Season	Club	Lea	GP	G	A	TP	PIM	GP	G	A	TP	PIM
1987-88	Providence	H.E.	33	1	9	10	34	....	....	....	....	....
1988-89	Providence	H.E	10	0	4	4	18	....	....	....	....	....
1989-90	Providence	H.E	33	7	12	19	34	....	....	....	....	....

ROONEY, STEVE

Left wing. Shoots left. 6'2", 205 lbs. Born, Canton, MA, June 28, 1962.
(Montreal's 8th choice, 88th overall, in 1981 Entry Draft)

			Regular Season					Playoffs				
Season	Club	Lea	GP	G	A	TP	PIM	GP	G	A	TP	PIM
1981-82	Providence	ECAC	31	7	10	17	41	....	....	....	....	....
1982-83	Providence	ECAC	42	10	20	30	31	....	....	....	....	....
1983-84	Providence	ECAC	33	11	16	27	46	....	....	....	....	....
1984-85	**Montreal**	**NHL**	**3**	**1**	**0**	**1**	**7**	**11**	**2**	**2**	**4**	**19**
	Providence	H.E.	31	7	10	17	41	....	....	....	....	....
1985-86	**Montreal**	**NHL**	**38**	**2**	**3**	**5**	**114**	**1**	**0**	**0**	**0**	**0**
1986-87	**Montreal**	**NHL**	**2**	**0**	**0**	**0**	**22**	....	....	....	....	....
	Sherbrooke	AHL	22	4	11	15	66	....	....	....	....	....
	Winnipeg	**NHL**	**30**	**2**	**3**	**5**	**57**	**8**	**0**	**0**	**0**	**34**
1987-88	**Winnipeg**	**NHL**	**56**	**7**	**6**	**13**	**217**	**5**	**1**	**0**	**1**	**33**
1988-89	**New Jersey**	**NHL**	**25**	**3**	**1**	**4**	**79**	....	....	....	....	....
1989-90	Utica	AHL	57	9	16	25	134	....	....	....	....	....
	NHL Totals		**154**	**15**	**13**	**28**	**496**	**25**	**3**	**2**	**5**	**86**

Traded to **Winnipeg** by **Montreal** for Winnipeg's third-round choice (Francois Gravel) in 1987 Entry Draft, January 8, 1987. Traded to **New Jersey** by **Winnipeg** with Winnipeg's third round choice (Brad Bombardir) in 1990 Entry Draft for Alain Chevrier and New Jersey's seventh round choice (Doug Evans) in 1989 Entry Draft, July 19, 1988.

ROOT, WILLIAM JOHN (BILL)

Defense. Shoots right. 6', 210 lbs. Born, Toronto, Ont., September 6, 1959.

			Regular Season					Playoffs				
Season	Club	Lea	GP	G	A	TP	PIM	GP	G	A	TP	PIM
1977-78	Niagara Falls	OHA	67	6	11	17	61	....	....	....	....	....
1978-79	Niagara Falls	OHA	67	4	31	35	119	20	4	7	11	42
1979-80	Nova Scotia	AHL	55	4	15	19	57	6	1	1	2	2
1980-81	Nova Scotia	AHL	63	3	12	15	76	6	0	1	1	2
1981-82	Nova Scotia	AHL	77	6	25	31	105	9	1	0	1	4
1982-83	**Montreal**	**NHL**	**46**	**2**	**3**	**5**	**24**	....	....	....	....	....
	Nova Scotia	AHL	24	0	7	7	29	....	....	....	....	....
1983-84	**Montreal**	**NHL**	**72**	**4**	**13**	**17**	**45**	....	....	....	....	....
1984-85	**Toronto**	**NHL**	**35**	**1**	**1**	**2**	**23**	....	....	....	....	....
	St. Catharines	AHL	28	5	9	14	10	....	....	....	....	....
1985-86	**Toronto**	**NHL**	**27**	**0**	**1**	**1**	**29**	**7**	**0**	**2**	**2**	**13**
	St. Catharines	AHL	14	7	4	11	11	....	....	....	....	....
1986-87	**Toronto**	**NHL**	**34**	**3**	**3**	**6**	**37**	**13**	**1**	**0**	**1**	**12**
	Newmarket	AHL	32	4	11	15	23	....	....	....	....	....
1987-88	**St. Louis**	**NHL**	**9**	**0**	**0**	**0**	**6**	....	....	....	....	....
	Philadelphia	**NHL**	**24**	**1**	**2**	**3**	**16**	**2**	**0**	**0**	**0**	**0**
1988-89	Newmarket	AHL	66	10	22	32	39	5	0	0	0	18
1989-90	Newmarket	AHL	47	8	7	15	20	....	....	....	....	....
	NHL Totals		**247**	**11**	**23**	**34**	**180**	**22**	**1**	**2**	**3**	**25**

Signed as free agent by **Montreal**, October 4, 1979. Traded to **Toronto** by **Montreal** for option of **Toronto**'s fourth round choice in 1985 or 1986 Entry Draft (choice was later traded back to **Toronto**), August 21, 1984. Traded to **Hartford** by **Toronto** for Dave Semenko, September 8, 1987. Claimed by **St. Louis** in NHL Waiver Draft, October 5, 1987. Claimed on waivers by **Philadelphia** form **St. Louis**, November 26, 1987. Traded to **Toronto** by **Philadelphia** for Mike Stothers, June 21, 1988.

ROSENBLATT, HOWARD DAVID

Defense. Shoots right. 6', 195 lbs. Born, Pawtucket, RI, January 3, 1969.
(Boston's 1st choice, 26th overall, in 1990 Supplemental Draft).

			Regular Season					Playoffs				
Season	Club	Lea	GP	G	A	TP	PIM	GP	G	A	TP	PIM
1987-88	Merrimack	NCAA	3	1	0	1	0	....	....	....	....	....
1988-89	Merrimack	NCAA	7	1	1	2	8	....	....	....	....	....
1989-90	Merrimack	H.E.	29	10	14	24	36	....	....	....	....	....

ROUPE, MAGNUS

Left wing. Shoots left. 6', 190 lbs. Born, Gislaved, Sweden, March 23, 1963.
(Philadelphia's 9th choice, 182nd overall, in 1982 Entry Draft).

			Regular Season					Playoffs				
Season	Club	Lea	GP	G	A	TP	PIM	GP	G	A	TP	PIM
1981-82	Farjestad	Swe.	24	5	3	8	8	2	0	0	0	0
1982-83	Farjestad	Swe.	29	7	4	11	16	6	1	1	2	8
1983-84	Farjestad	Swe.	36	2	3	5	38	....	....	....	....	....
1984-85	Farjestad	Swe.	31	9	6	15	16	3	1	0	1	0
1985-86	Farjestad	Swe.	35	11	10	21	38	8	3	2	5	18
1986-87	Farjestad	Swe.	31	11	6	17	64	7	0	2	2	10
1987-88	**Philadelphia**	**NHL**	**33**	**2**	**4**	**6**	**32**	....	....	....	....	....
	Hershey	AHL	23	6	16	22	10	11	3	4	7	31
1988-89	**Philadelphia**	**NHL**	**7**	**1**	**1**	**2**	**10**	....	....	....	....	....
	Hershey	AHL	12	2	6	8	17	....	....	....	....	....
	Farjestad	Swe.	18	9	4	13	58	2	0	1	1	6
1989-90	Farjestad	Swe.	39	19	17	36	64	9	1	2	3	14
	NHL Totals		**40**	**3**	**5**	**8**	**42**	....	....	....	....	....

ROUSE, ROBERT (BOB)

Defense. Shoots right. 6'1", 210 lbs. Born, Surrey, B.C., June 18, 1964.
(Minnesota's 3rd choice, 80th overall, in 1982 Entry Draft).

			Regular Season					Playoffs				
Season	Club	Lea	GP	G	A	TP	PIM	GP	G	A	TP	PIM
1980-81	Billings	WHL	70	0	13	13	116	5	0	0	0	2
1981-82	Billings	WHL	71	7	22	29	209	5	0	2	2	10
1982-83	Nanaimo	WHL	29	7	20	27	86	....	....	....	....	....
	Lethbridge	WHL	42	8	30	38	82	20	2	13	15	55
1983-84	**Minnesota**	**NHL**	**1**	**0**	**0**	**0**	**0**	....	....	....	....	....
a	Lethbridge	WHL	71	18	42	60	101	5	0	1	1	28
1984-85	**Minnesota**	**NHL**	**63**	**2**	**9**	**11**	**113**	....	....	....	....	....
	Springfield	AHL	8	0	3	3	6	....	....	....	....	....
1985-86	**Minnesota**	**NHL**	**75**	**1**	**14**	**15**	**151**	**3**	**0**	**0**	**0**	**0**
1986-87	**Minnesota**	**NHL**	**72**	**2**	**10**	**12**	**179**	....	....	....	....	....
1987-88	**Minnesota**	**NHL**	**74**	**0**	**12**	**12**	**168**	....	....	....	....	....
1988-89	**Minnesota**	**NHL**	**66**	**4**	**13**	**17**	**124**	....	....	....	....	....
	Washington	**NHL**	**13**	**0**	**2**	**2**	**36**	**6**	**2**	**0**	**2**	**4**
1989-90	**Washington**	**NHL**	**70**	**4**	**16**	**20**	**123**	**15**	**2**	**3**	**5**	**47**
	NHL Totals		**434**	**13**	**76**	**89**	**894**	**24**	**4**	**3**	**7**	**53**

a WHL First All-Star Team, East Division (1984)
Traded to **Washington** by **Minnesota** with Dino Ciccarelli for Mike Gartner and Larry Murphy, March 7, 1989.

ROUSSEAU, MARC

Defense. Shoots left. 6', 185 lbs. Born, N. Vancouver, B.C., May 17, 1968.
(Hartford's 4th choice, 102nd overall, in 1987 Entry Draft).

			Regular Season					Playoffs				
Season	Club	Lea	GP	G	A	TP	PIM	GP	G	A	TP	PIM
1986-87	U. of Denver	WCHA	39	3	18	21	70	....	....	....	....	....
1987-88	U. of Denver	WCHA	38	6	22	28	92	....	....	....	....	....
1988-89	U. of Denver	WCHA	43	10	18	28	68	....	....	....	....	....
1989-90	U. of Denver	WCHA	42	6	26	32	62	....	....	....	....	....

ROUTHIER, JEAN-MARC

Right wing. Shoots right. 6'2", 190 lbs. Born, Quebec, Que., February 2, 1968.
(Quebec's 2nd choice, 39th overall, in 1986 Entry Draft).

			Regular Season					Playoffs				
Season	Club	Lea	GP	G	A	TP	PIM	GP	G	A	TP	PIM
1985-86	Hull	QMJHL	71	18	16	34	111	15	3	6	9	27
1986-87	Hull	QMJHL	59	17	18	35	98	....	....	....	....	....
1987-88	Victoriaville	QMJHL	57	16	28	44	267	2	0	0	0	5
1988-89	Halifax	AHL	52	13	13	26	189	4	1	1	2	16
1989-90	**Quebec**	**NHL**	**8**	**0**	**0**	**0**	**9**	....	....	....	....	....
	Halifax	AHL	17	4	8	12	29	....	....	....	....	....
	NHL Totals		**8**	**0**	**0**	**0**	**9**	....	....	....	....	....

RUCHTY, MATTHEW

Left wing. Shoots left. 6'1", 210 lbs. Born, Kitchener, Ont., November 27, 1969.
(New Jersey's 4th choice, 65th overall, in 1988 Entry Draft).

			Regular Season					Playoffs				
Season	Club	Lea	GP	G	A	TP	PIM	GP	G	A	TP	PIM
1987-88	Bowling Green	CCHA	41	6	15	21	78	....	....	....	....	....
1988-89	Bowling Green	CCHA	43	11	21	32	110	....	....	....	....	....
1989-90	Bowling Green	CCHA	42	28	21	49	135	....	....	....	....	....

RUCINSKI, MIKE

Center. Shoots left. 5'11", 190 lbs. Born, Wheeling, IL, December 12, 1963.

			Regular Season					Playoffs				
Season	Club	Lea	GP	G	A	TP	PIM	GP	G	A	TP	PIM
1983-84	Ill.-Chicago	CCHA	33	17	26	43	12	....	....	....	....	....
1984-85	Ill.-Chicago	CCHA	40	29	32	61	28	....	....	....	....	....
1985-86	Ill.-Chicago	CCHA	37	16	31	47	18	....	....	....	....	....
1986-87	Moncton	AHL	42	5	9	14	14	....	....	....	....	....
	Salt Lake	IHL	29	16	25	41	19	17	9	*18	*27	28
1987-88	Saginaw	IHL	44	19	31	50	32	10	1	9	10	10
	Chicago	**NHL**	....	....	....	....	....	**2**	**0**	**0**	**0**	**0**
1988-89	**Chicago**	**NHL**	**1**	**0**	**0**	**0**	**0**	....	....	....	....	....
	Saginaw	IHL	81	35	72	107	40	6	2	4	6	14
1989-90	Indianapolis	IHL	80	28	41	69	27	13	3	8	11	8
	NHL Totals		**1**	**0**	**0**	**0**	**0**	**2**	**0**	**0**	**0**	**0**

Signed as a free agent by **Calgary**, August 10, 1986. Signed as a free agent by **Chicago**, July 8, 1987.

RUFF, LINDY CAMERON

Defense/Left wing. Shoots left. 6'2", 200 lbs. Born, Warburg, Alta., February 17, 1960.
(Buffalo's 2nd choice, 32nd overall, in 1979 Entry Draft).

			Regular Season					Playoffs				
Season	Club	Lea	GP	G	A	TP	PIM	GP	G	A	TP	PIM
1977-78	Lethbridge	WHL	66	9	24	33	219	8	2	8	10	4
1978-79	Lethbridge	WHL	24	9	18	27	108	6	0	1	1	0
1979-80	**Buffalo**	**NHL**	**63**	**5**	**14**	**19**	**38**	**8**	**1**	**1**	**2**	**19**
1980-81	**Buffalo**	**NHL**	**65**	**8**	**18**	**26**	**121**	**6**	**3**	**1**	**4**	**23**
1981-82	**Buffalo**	**NHL**	**79**	**16**	**32**	**48**	**194**	**4**	**0**	**0**	**0**	**28**
1982-83	**Buffalo**	**NHL**	**60**	**12**	**17**	**29**	**130**	**10**	**4**	**2**	**6**	**47**
1983-84	**Buffalo**	**NHL**	**58**	**14**	**31**	**45**	**101**	**3**	**1**	**0**	**1**	**9**
1984-85	**Buffalo**	**NHL**	**39**	**13**	**11**	**24**	**45**	**5**	**2**	**4**	**6**	**15**
1985-86	**Buffalo**	**NHL**	**54**	**20**	**12**	**32**	**158**	....	....	....	....	....
1986-87	**Buffalo**	**NHL**	**50**	**6**	**14**	**20**	**74**	....	....	....	....	....
1987-88	**Buffalo**	**NHL**	**77**	**2**	**23**	**25**	**179**	**6**	**0**	**2**	**2**	**23**
1988-89	**Buffalo**	**NHL**	**63**	**6**	**11**	**17**	**86**	....	....	....	....	....
	NY Rangers	**NHL**	**13**	**0**	**5**	**5**	**31**	**2**	**0**	**0**	**0**	**17**
1989-90	**NY Rangers**	**NHL**	**56**	**3**	**6**	**9**	**80**	**8**	**0**	**3**	**3**	**12**
	NHL Totals		**677**	**105**	**194**	**299**	**1237**	**52**	**11**	**13**	**24**	**193**

Traded to **NY Rangers** by **Buffalo** for NY Rangers' fifth-round choice (Richard Smehlik) in 1990 Entry Draft, March 7, 1989.

RUMBLE, DARREN

Defense. Shoots left. 6'1", 200 lbs. Born, Barrie, Ont., January 23, 1969.
(Philadelphia's 1st choice, 20th overall, in 1987 Entry Draft).

			Regular Season					Playoffs				
Season	Club	Lea	GP	G	A	TP	PIM	GP	G	A	TP	PIM
1986-87	Kitchener	OHL	64	11	32	43	44	4	0	1	1	9
1987-88	Kitchener	OHL	55	15	50	65	64	....	....	....	....	....
1988-89	Kitchener	OHL	46	11	28	39	25	5	1	0	1	2
1989-90	Kitchener	OHL	57	2	13	15	51	....	....	....	....	....

RUOHO, DANIEL

Defense. Shoots left. 6'3", 220 lbs. Born, Madison, WI, June 22, 1970.
(Buffalo's 9th choice, 160th overall, in 1988 Entry Draft).

			Regular Season					Playoffs				
Season	Club	Lea	GP	G	A	TP	PIM	GP	G	A	TP	PIM
1989-90	N. Michigan	WCHA	18	2	4	6	26	....	....	....	....	....

RUOTSALAINEN, REIJO (ROOTS-a-LAY-nen)

Defense. Shoots right. 5'8", 170 lbs. Born, Oulu, Finland, April 1, 1960.
(NY Rangers' 5th choice, 119th overall, in 1980 Entry Draft).

			Regular Season					Playoffs				
Season	Club	Lea	GP	G	A	TP	PIM	GP	G	A	TP	PIM
1977-78	Karpat	Fin.	30	9	14	23	4	....	....	....	....	....
1978-79	Karpat	Fin.	36	14	8	22	47	....	....	....	....	....
1979-80a	Karpat	Fin.	30	15	13	28	31	6	5	2	7	0
1980-81a	Karpat	Fin.	36	28	23	51	28	12	7	4	11	6
1981-82	**NY Rangers**	**NHL**	**78**	**18**	**38**	**56**	**27**	**10**	**4**	**5**	**9**	**2**
1982-83	**NY Rangers**	**NHL**	**77**	**16**	**53**	**69**	**22**	**9**	**4**	**2**	**6**	**6**
1983-84	**NY Rangers**	**NHL**	**74**	**20**	**39**	**59**	**26**	**5**	**1**	**1**	**2**	**2**
1984-85	**NY Rangers**	**NHL**	**80**	**28**	**45**	**73**	**32**	**3**	**2**	**0**	**2**	**6**
1985-86	**NY Rangers**	**NHL**	**80**	**17**	**42**	**59**	**47**	**16**	**0**	**8**	**8**	**6**
1986-87	**Edmonton**	**NHL**	**16**	**5**	**8**	**13**	**6**	**21**	**2**	**5**	**7**	**10**
	Bern	Switz.	36	26	28	54	....	....	....	....	....	....
1987-88	HV71	Swe.	39	10	22	32	26	....	....	....	....	....
1988-89	Bern	Switz.	36	17	30	47	....	9	4	7	11	....
1989-90	**New Jersey**	**NHL**	**31**	**2**	**5**	**7**	**14**	....	....	....	....	....
	Edmonton	**NHL**	**10**	**1**	**7**	**8**	**6**	**22**	**2**	**11**	**13**	**12**
	NHL Totals		**446**	**107**	**237**	**344**	**180**	**86**	**15**	**32**	**47**	**44**

a Named to Finnish League All-Star Team (1980, 1981)

Played in NHL All-Star Game (1986)

Traded to **Edmonton** by **NY Rangers** with Clark Donatelli, Ville Kentala and Jim Wiemer for Mike Golden, Don Jackson and Miloslav Horava, October 2, 1986. Claimed by **New Jersey** in NHL Waiver Draft, October 5, 1987. Traded to **Edmonton** by **New Jersey** for Jeff Sharples, March 6, 1990.

RUSNAK, DARIUS

Center. Shoots right. 6'1", 190 lbs. Born, Ruzomberok, Czechoslovakia, September 4, 1968.
(Philadelphia's 11th choice, 230th overall, in 1987 Entry Draft).

			Regular Season					Playoffs				
Season	Club	Lea	GP	G	A	TP	PIM	GP	G	A	TP	PIM
1986-87	Bratislava	Czech.	32	15	13	28	....	....	....	....	....	....
1987-88	Dukla Jihlava	Czech.	31	14	23	37	....	....	....	....	....	....
1988-89	Bratislava	Czech.	31	16	15	31	....	....	....	....	....	....
1989-90	KalPa	Fin.	44	29	24	53	77	1	0	1	1	0

RUSSELL, CAM

Defense. Shoots left. 6'4", 175 lbs. Born, Halifax, N.S., January 12, 1969.
(Chicago's 3rd choice, 50th overall, in 1987 Entry Draft).

			Regular Season					Playoffs				
Season	Club	Lea	GP	G	A	TP	PIM	GP	G	A	TP	PIM
1985-86	Hull	QMJHL	56	3	4	7	24	15	0	2	2	4
1986-87	Hull	QMJHL	66	3	16	19	119	8	0	1	1	16
1987-88a	Hull	QMJHL	53	9	18	27	141	19	2	5	7	39
1988-89	Hull	QMJHL	66	8	32	40	109	9	2	6	8	6
1989-90	**Chicago**	**NHL**	**19**	**0**	**1**	**1**	**27**	**1**	**0**	**0**	**0**	**0**
	Indianapolis	IHL	46	3	15	18	114	9	0	1	1	24
	NHL Totals		**19**	**0**	**1**	**1**	**27**	**1**	**0**	**0**	**0**	**0**

a QMJHL Third All-Star Team (1988)

RUSSELL, KERRY

Right wing. Shoots right. 5'11", 165 lbs. Born, Kamloops, B.C., June 23, 1969.
(Hartford's 6th choice, 137th overall, in 1988 Entry Draft).

			Regular Season					Playoffs				
Season	Club	Lea	GP	G	A	TP	PIM	GP	G	A	TP	PIM
1987-88	Michigan State	CCHA	46	16	23	39	50	....	....	....	....	....
1988-89	Michigan State	CCHA	46	5	23	28	50	....	....	....	....	....
1989-90	Michigan State	CCHA	45	15	12	27	62	....	....	....	....	....

RUTHERFORD, PAUL

Center. Shoots left. 6', 190 lbs. Born, Sudbury, Ont., January 1, 1969.
(NY Islanders' 6th choice, 100th overall, in 1988 Entry Draft).

			Regular Season					Playoffs				
Season	Club	Lea	GP	G	A	TP	PIM	GP	G	A	TP	PIM
1987-88	Ohio State	CCHA	40	18	23	41	40	....	....	....	....	....
1988-89	Ohio State	CCHA	39	16	27	43	52	....	....	....	....	....
1989-90	Ohio State	CCHA	40	15	16	31	40	....	....	....	....	....

SABOL, SHAUN

Defense. Shoots left. 6'3", 230 lbs. Born, Minneapolis, MN, July 13, 1966.
(Philadelphia's 9th choice, 209th overall, in 1986 Entry Draft).

			Regular Season					Playoffs				
Season	Club	Lea	GP	G	A	TP	PIM	GP	G	A	TP	PIM
1986-87	U. Wisconsin	WCHA	40	7	16	23	98	....	....	....	....	....
1987-88	U. Wisconsin	WCHA	8	4	3	7	10	....	....	....	....	....
	Hershey	AHL	51	1	9	10	66	2	0	0	0	5
1988-89	Hershey	AHL	58	7	11	18	134	12	0	2	2	35
1989-90	**Philadelphia**	**NHL**	**2**	**0**	**0**	**0**	**0**	....	....	....	....	....
	Hershey	AHL	46	6	16	22	49	....	....	....	....	....
	NHL Totals		**2**	**0**	**0**	**0**	**0**	....	....	....	....	....

RUUTTU, CHRISTIAN (ROO-TOO)

Center. Shoots left. 5'11", 194 lbs. Born, Lappeenranta, Finland, February 20, 1964.
(Buffalo's 9th choice, 134th overall, in 1983 Entry Draft).

			Regular Season					Playoffs				
Season	Club	Lea	GP	G	A	TP	PIM	GP	G	A	TP	PIM
1982-83	Assat Pori	Fin.	36	15	18	33	34	....	....	....	....	....
1983-84	Assat Pori	Fin.	37	18	42	60	72	9	2	5	7	12
1984-85	Assat Pori	Fin.	32	14	32	46	34	8	1	6	7	8
1985-86	IFK Helsinki	Fin.	36	16	38	54	47	10	3	6	9	8
1986-87	**Buffalo**	**NHL**	**76**	**22**	**43**	**65**	**62**	....	....	....	....	....
1987-88	**Buffalo**	**NHL**	**73**	**26**	**45**	**71**	**85**	**6**	**2**	**5**	**7**	**4**
1988-89	**Buffalo**	**NHL**	**67**	**14**	**46**	**60**	**98**	**2**	**0**	**0**	**0**	**2**
1989-90	**Buffalo**	**NHL**	**75**	**19**	**41**	**60**	**66**	**6**	**0**	**0**	**0**	**4**
	NHL Totals		**291**	**81**	**175**	**256**	**311**	**14**	**2**	**5**	**7**	**10**

Played in NHL All-Star Game (1988)

RUZICKA, VLADIMIR

Center. Shoots left. 6'3", 212 lbs. Born, Most, Czechoslovakia, June 6, 1963.
(Toronto's 5th choice, 73rd overall, in 1982 Entry Draft).

			Regular Season					Playoffs				
Season	Club	Lea	GP	G	A	TP	PIM	GP	G	A	TP	PIM
1986-87	CHZ Litvinov	Czech.	32	24	15	39	....	....	....	....	....	....
1987-88	Dukla Trencin	Czech.	34	32	21	53	....	....	....	....	....	....
1988-89	Dukla Trencin	Czech.	45	46	38	84	....	....	....	....	....	....
1989-90	**Edmonton**	**NHL**	**25**	**11**	**6**	**17**	**10**	....	....	....	....	....
	Litvinov	Czech	32	21	23	44	....	....	....	....	....	....
	NHL Totals		**25**	**11**	**6**	**17**	**10**	....	....	....	....	....

Traded to **Edmonton** by **Toronto** for Edmonton's fourth round choice (Greg Walters) in 1990 Entry Draft, December 21, 1989.

RYCHEL, WARREN (RIGH-chuhl)

Left wing. Shoots left. 6', 190 lbs. Born, Tecumseh, Ont., May 12, 1967.

			Regular Season					Playoffs				
Season	Club	Lea	GP	G	A	TP	PIM	GP	G	A	TP	PIM
1985-86	Ottawa	OHL	67	25	23	48	173	....	....	....	....	....
1986-87	Kitchener	OHL	49	16	12	28	96	4	0	0	0	9
1987-88	Peoria	IHL	7	2	1	3	7	....	....	....	....	....
	Saginaw	IHL	51	2	7	9	113	1	0	0	0	0
1988-89	**Chicago**	**NHL**	**2**	**0**	**0**	**0**	**17**	....	....	....	....	....
	Saginaw	IHL	50	15	14	29	226	6	0	0	0	51
1989-90	Indianapolis	IHL	77	23	16	39	374	14	1	3	4	64
	NHL Totals		**2**	**0**	**0**	**0**	**17**	....	....	....	....	....

Signed as a free agent by **Chicago**, September 19, 1986.

RYDMARK, DANIEL

Center/Wing. Shoots left. 5'10", 165 lbs. Born, Vasteras, Sweden, February 23, 1970.
(Los Angeles' 5th choice, 123rd overall, in 1989 Entry Draft).

			Regular Season					Playoffs				
Season	Club	Lea	GP	G	A	TP	PIM	GP	G	A	TP	PIM
1989-90	Farjestads	Swe.	35	9	12	21	20	5	0	0	0	4

RYMSHA, ANDREW (ANDY)

Defense. Shoots left. 6'3", 210 lbs. Born, St. Catharines, Ont., December 10, 1968.
(St. Louis' 5th choice, 82nd overall, in 1987 Entry Draft).

			Regular Season					Playoffs				
Season	Club	Lea	GP	G	A	TP	PIM	GP	G	A	TP	PIM
1986-87	W. Michigan	CCHA	41	7	12	19	60	....	....	....	....	....
1987-88	W. Michigan	CCHA	42	5	6	11	114	....	....	....	....	....
1988-89	W. Michigan	WCHA	35	3	4	7	139	....	....	....	....	....
1989-90	W. Michigan	WCHA	37	1	10	11	108	....	....	....	....	....

SABOURIN, KEN

Defense. Shoots left. 6'3", 205 lbs. Born, Scarborough, Ont. April 28, 1966.
(Calgary's 2nd choice, 33rd overall, in 1984 Entry Draft).

			Regular Season					Playoffs				
Season	Club	Lea	GP	G	A	TP	PIM	GP	G	A	TP	PIM
1982-83	S.S. Marie	OHL	58	0	8	8	90	10	0	0	0	14
1983-84	S.S. Marie	OHL	63	7	14	21	157	9	0	1	1	25
1984-85	S.S. Marie	OHL	63	5	19	24	139	16	1	4	5	10
1985-86	Moncton	AHL	3	0	0	0	0	6	0	1	1	2
	S.S. Marie	OHL	25	1	5	6	77	....	....	....	....	....
	Cornwall	OHL	37	3	12	15	94	6	1	2	3	6
1986-87	Moncton	AHL	75	1	10	11	166	6	0	1	1	27
1987-88	Salt Lake	IHL	71	2	8	10	186	16	1	6	7	57
1988-89	**Calgary**	**NHL**	**6**	**0**	**1**	**1**	**26**	**1**	**0**	**0**	**0**	**0**
	Salt Lake	IHL	74	2	18	20	197	11	0	1	1	26
1989-90	**Calgary**	**NHL**	**5**	**0**	**0**	**0**	**10**	....	....	....	....	....
	Salt Lake	IHL	76	5	19	24	336	11	0	2	2	40
	NHL Totals		**11**	**0**	**1**	**1**	**36**	**1**	**0**	**0**	**0**	**0**

SACCO, DAVID

Defense. Shoots right. 5'10", 190 lbs. Born, Medford, MA, July 31, 1970.
(Toronto's 9th choice, 195th overall, in 1988 Entry Draft).

			Regular Season					Playoffs				
Season	Club	Lea	GP	G	A	TP	PIM	GP	G	A	TP	PIM
1987-88	Boston U.	H.E.	34	16	20	36	40	....	....	....	....	....
1988-89	Boston U.	H.E.	35	14	29	43	40	....	....	....	....	....
1989-90	Boston U.	H.E.	3	0	4	4	2	....	....	....	....	....

SACCO, JOSEPH (JOE)

Left wing. Shoots right. 6'2", 190 lbs. Born, Medford, MA, February 4, 1969.
(Toronto's 4th choice, 71st overall, in 1987 Entry Draft).

			Regular Season					Playoffs				
Season	Club	Lea	GP	G	A	TP	PIM	GP	G	A	TP	PIM
1987-88	Boston U.	H.E.	34	16	20	36	40	....	....	....	....	....
1988-89	Boston U.	H.E.	33	21	19	40	66	....	....	....	....	....
1989-90	Boston U.	H.E.	44	28	24	52	70	....	....	....	....	....

SAGISSOR, THOMAS (TOM)

Right wing. Shoots left. 5'11", 202 lbs. Born, Hastings, MN, September 12, 1967.
(Montreal's 7th choice, 96th overall, in 1985 Entry Draft).

			Regular Season					Playoffs				
Season	Club	Lea	GP	G	A	TP	PIM	GP	G	A	TP	PIM
1986-87	U. Wisconsin	WCHA	41	1	4	5	32	....	....	....	....	....
1987-88	U. Wisconsin	WCHA	38	4	5	9	65					
1988-89	U. Wisconsin	WCHA	40	7	11	18	119	....	....	....	....	....
1989-90	U. Wisconsin	WCHA	43	19	28	47	122	....	....	....	....	....

ST. AMOUR, MARTIN

Left wing. Shoots left. 6'3", 195 lbs. Born, Montreal, Que., January 30, 1970.
(Montreal's 2nd choice, 34th overall, in 1988 Entry Draft).

			Regular Season					Playoffs				
Season	Club	Lea	GP	G	A	TP	PIM	GP	G	A	TP	PIM
1987-88	Verdun	QMJHL	61	20	50	70	111	....	....	....	....	....
1988-89	Verdun	QMJHL	28	19	17	36	87	....	....	....	....	....
	Trois-Rivieres	QMJHL	26	8	21	29	69	4	1	2	3	0
1989-90	Trois-Rivieres	QMJHL	60	57	79	136	162	7	7	9	16	19
	Sherbrooke	AHL	....	....	....	....	....	1	0	0	0	0

ST. CYR, JEFF

Defense. Shoots right. 6'3", 195 lbs. Born, New Liskeard, Ont., February 16, 1967.
(Hartford's 5th choice, 123rd overall, in 1987 Entry Draft).

			Regular Season					Playoffs				
Season	Club	Lea	GP	G	A	TP	PIM	GP	G	A	TP	PIM
1986-87	Michigan Tech.	WCHA	38	0	2	2	82	....	....	....	....	....
1987-88	Michigan Tech.	WCHA	40	0	7	7	98	....	....	....	....	....
1988-89	Michigan Tech.	WCHA	41	0	7	7	79	....	....	....	....	....
1989-90	Michigan Tech.	WCHA	36	2	7	9	81	....	....	....	....	....

SAKIC, JOE

Center. Shoots left. 5'11", 185 lbs. Born, Burnaby, B.C., July 7, 1969.
(Quebec's 2nd choice, 15th overall, in 1987 Entry Draft).

			Regular Season					Playoffs				
Season	Club	Lea	GP	G	A	TP	PIM	GP	G	A	TP	PIM
1986-87ab	Swift Current	WHL	72	60	73	133	31	4	0	1	1	0
1987-88acd	Swift Current	WHL	64	*78	82	*160	64	10	11	13	24	12
1988-89	Quebec	NHL	70	23	39	62	24	....	....	....	....	....
1989-90	Quebec	NHL	80	39	63	102	27	....	....	....	....	....
	NHL Totals		150	62	102	164	51	....	....	....	....	....

a WHL Player of the Year (1987, 1988)
b WHL Rookie of the Year (1987)
c Canadian Major Junior Player of the Year (1988)
d WHL East All-Star Team (1988)

Played in NHL All-Star Game (1990)

SALLE, JOHAN

Defense. Shoots left. 6'1", 185 lbs. Born, Orebro, Sweden, February 21, 1967.
(Philadelphia's 9th choice, 161st overall, in 1988 Entry Draft).

			Regular Season					Playoffs				
Season	Club	Lea	GP	G	A	TP	PIM	GP	G	A	TP	PIM
1987-88	Malmo	Swe.	36	9	4	13	48	....	....	....	....	....
1988-89	Malmo	Swe.	18	6	10	16	32	....	....	....	....	....
1989-90	Malmo	Swe.	32	12	16	28	98	....	....	....	....	....

SALMING, ANDERS BORJE (SAHL-mihng, BOHR-yuh)

Defense. Shoots left. 6'1", 185 lbs. Born, Kiruna, Sweden, April 17, 1951.

			Regular Season					Playoffs				
Season	Club	Lea	GP	G	A	TP	PIM	GP	G	A	TP	PIM
1970-71	Brynas	Swe.	27	2	6	8	22	....	....	....	....	....
1971-72	Brynas	Swe.	28	1	5	6	50	....	....	....	....	....
1972-73	Brynas	Swe.	26	5	4	9	34	....	....	....	....	....
1973-74	Toronto	NHL	76	5	34	39	48	4	0	1	1	4
1974-75a	Toronto	NHL	60	12	25	37	34	7	0	4	4	6
1975-76a	Toronto	NHL	78	16	41	57	70	10	3	4	7	9
1976-77b	Toronto	NHL	76	12	66	78	46	9	3	6	9	6
1977-78a	Toronto	NHL	80	16	60	76	70	6	2	2	4	6
1978-79a	Toronto	NHL	78	17	56	73	76	6	0	1	1	8
1979-80a	Toronto	NHL	74	19	52	71	94	3	1	1	2	2
1980-81	Toronto	NHL	72	5	61	66	154	3	0	2	2	4
1981-82	Toronto	NHL	69	12	44	56	170	....	....	....	....	....
1982-83	Toronto	NHL	69	7	38	45	104	4	1	4	5	10
1983-84	Toronto	NHL	68	5	38	43	92	....	....	....	....	....
1984-85	Toronto	NHL	73	6	33	39	76	....	....	....	....	....
1985-86	Toronto	NHL	41	7	15	22	48	10	1	6	7	14
1986-87	Toronto	NHL	56	4	16	20	42	13	0	3	3	14
1987-88	Toronto	NHL	66	2	24	26	82	6	1	3	4	8
1988-89	Toronto	NHL	63	3	17	20	86	....	....	....	....	....
1989-90	Detroit	NHL	49	2	17	19	52	....	....	....	....	....
	NHL Totals		1148	150	637	787	1344	81	12	37	49	91

a NHL Second All-Star Team (1975, 1976, 1978, 1979, 1980)
b NHL First All-Star Team (1977)

Played in NHL All-Star Game (1976-78)

Signed as free agent by **Toronto**, May 12, 1973. Signed as a free agent by **Detroit**, June 12, 1989.

SALO, VESA

Defense. Shoots left. 6'3", 200 lbs. Born, Rauma, Finland, April 17, 1965.
(NY Rangers' 3rd choice, 49th overall, in 1983 Entry Draft).

			Regular Season					Playoffs				
Season	Club	Lea	GP	G	A	TP	PIM	GP	G	A	TP	PIM
1986-87	Lukko	Fin.	44	4	22	26	34	....	....	....	....	....
1987-88	Ilves	Fin.	43	8	15	23	42	4	0	1	1	4
1988-89	Tappara	Fin.	42	7	14	21	46	8	0	2	2	8
1989-90	Tappara	Fin.	35	2	12	14	22	7	0	2	2	4

SAMUELSSON, KJELL (SHELL)

Defense. Shoots right. 6'6", 235 lbs. Born, Tyngsryd, Sweden, October 18, 1958.
(NY Rangers' 5th choice, 119th overall, in 1984 Entry Draft).

			Regular Season					Playoffs				
Season	Club	Lea	GP	G	A	TP	PIM	GP	G	A	TP	PIM
1982-83	Tyngsryd	Swe. 2	32	11	6	17	57	....	....	....	....	....
1983-84	Leksand	Swe.	36	6	6	12	59	....	....	....	....	....
1984-85	Leksand	Swe.	35	9	5	14	34	....	....	....	....	....
1985-86	New Haven	AHL	56	6	21	27	87	3	0	0	0	10
	NY Rangers	NHL	9	0	0	0	10	9	0	1	1	8
1986-87	NY Rangers	NHL	30	2	6	8	50	....	....	....	....	....
	Philadelphia	NHL	46	1	6	7	86	26	0	4	4	25
1987-88	Philadelphia	NHL	74	6	24	30	184	7	2	5	7	23
1988-89	Philadelphia	NHL	69	3	14	17	140	19	1	3	4	24
1989-90	Philadelphia	NHL	66	5	17	22	91	....	....	....	....	....
	NHL Totals		294	17	67	84	561	61	3	13	16	80

Played in NHL All-Star Game (1988)

Traded to **Philadelphia** by **NY Rangers** with NY Rangers' second-round choice (Patrik Juhlin) in 1989 Entry Draft for Bob Froese, December 18, 1986.

SAMUELSSON, MORGAN

Left wing. Shoots left. 5'9", 165 lbs. Born, Boden, Sweden, April 6, 1968.
(Quebec's 7th choice, 123rd overall, in 1986 Entry Draft).

			Regular Season					Playoffs				
Season	Club	Lea	GP	G	A	TP	PIM	GP	G	A	TP	PIM
1988-89	Lulea	Swe.	36	14	19	33	14	....	....	....	....	....
1989-90	Lulea	Swe.	29	4	10	14	30	5	1	0	1	4

SAMUELSSON, ULF

Defense. Shoots left. 6'1", 195 lbs. Born, Fagersta, Sweden, March 26, 1964.
(Hartford's 4th choice, 67th overall, in 1982 Entry Draft).

			Regular Season					Playoffs				
Season	Club	Lea	GP	G	A	TP	PIM	GP	G	A	TP	PIM
1981-82	Leksand	Swe.	31	3	1	4	40	....	....	....	....	....
1982-83	Leksand	Swe.	33	9	6	15	72	....	....	....	....	....
1983-84	Leksand	Swe.	36	5	11	16	53	....	....	....	....	....
1984-85	Hartford	NHL	41	2	6	8	83	....	....	....	....	....
	Binghamton	AHL	36	5	11	16	92	....	....	....	....	....
1985-86	Hartford	NHL	80	5	19	24	174	10	1	2	3	38
1986-87	Hartford	NHL	78	2	31	33	162	5	0	1	1	41
1987-88	Hartford	NHL	76	8	33	41	159	5	0	0	0	8
1988-89	Hartford	NHL	71	9	26	35	181	4	0	2	2	4
1989-90	Hartford	NHL	55	2	11	13	177	7	1	0	1	2
	NHL Totals		401	28	126	154	936	31	2	5	7	93

SANDELIN, SCOTT

Defense. Shoots right. 6', 200 lbs. Born, Hibbing, MN, August 8, 1964.
(Montreal's 5th choice, 48th overall, in 1982 Entry Draft).

			Regular Season					Playoffs				
Season	Club	Lea	GP	G	A	TP	PIM	GP	G	A	TP	PIM
1982-83	North Dakota	WCHA	21	0	4	4	10	....	....	....	....	....
1983-84	North Dakota	WCHA	41	4	23	27	24	....	....	....	....	....
1984-85	North Dakota	WCHA	38	4	17	21	30	....	....	....	....	....
1985-86ab	North Dakota	WCHA	40	7	31	38	38	....	....	....	....	....
	Sherbrooke	AHL	6	0	2	2	2	....	....	....	....	....
1986-87	Montreal	NHL	1	0	0	0	0	....	....	....	....	....
	Sherbrooke	AHL	74	7	22	29	35	16	2	4	6	2
1987-88	Montreal	NHL	8	0	1	1	2	....	....	....	....	....
	Sherbrooke	AHL	58	8	14	22	35	4	0	2	2	0
1988-89	Sherbrooke	AHL	12	0	9	9	8	....	....	....	....	....
	Hershey	AHL	39	6	9	15	38	8	2	1	3	4
1989-90	Hershey	AHL	70	4	27	31	38	....	....	....	....	....
	NHL Totals		9	0	1	1	2	....	....	....	....	....

a NCAA West Second All-Star Team (1986)
b WCHA First All-Star Team (1986).

Traded to **Philadelphia** by **Montreal** for the rights to J.J. Daigneault, November 7, 1988.

SANDERSON, GEOFF

Center. Shoots left. 6', 185 lbs. Born, Hay River, N.W.T, February 1, 1972.
(Hartford's 2nd choice, 36th overall, in 1990 Entry Draft).

			Regular Season					Playoffs				
Season	Club	Lea	GP	G	A	TP	PIM	GP	G	A	TP	PIM
1988-89	Swift Current	WHL	58	17	11	28	16	12	3	5	8	6
1989-90	Swift Current	WHL	70	32	62	94	56	4	1	4	5	8

SANDLAK, JIM

Right wing. Shoots right. 6'4", 219 lbs. Born, Kitchener, Ont., December 12, 1966.
(Vancouver's 1st choice, 4th overall, in 1985 Entry Draft)

			Regular Season					Playoffs				
Season	Club	Lea	GP	G	A	TP	PIM	GP	G	A	TP	PIM
1983-84	London	OHL	68	23	18	41	143	8	1	11	12	13
1984-85a	London	OHL	58	40	24	64	128	8	3	2	5	14
1985-86	Vancouver	NHL	23	1	3	4	10	3	0	1	1	0
	London	OHL	16	8	14	22	38	5	2	3	5	24
1986-87b	Vancouver	NHL	78	15	21	36	66	....	....	....	....	....
1987-88	Vancouver	NHL	49	16	15	31	81	....	....	....	....	....
	Fredericton	AHL	24	10	15	25	47	....	....	....	....	....
1988-89	Vancouver	NHL	72	20	20	40	99	6	1	1	2	2
1989-90	Vancouver	NHL	70	15	8	23	104	....	....	....	....	....
	NHL Totals		292	67	67	134	360	9	1	2	3	2

a OHL Third All-Star Team (1985)
b NHL All-Rookie Team (1987)

SANDSTROM, TOMAS

Right wing. Shoots left. 6'2", 200 lbs. Born, Jakobstad, Finland, September 4, 1964.
(NY Rangers' 2nd choice, 36th overall, in 1982 Entry Draft).

			Regular Season					Playoffs				
Season	Club	Lea	GP	G	A	TP	PIM	GP	G	A	TP	PIM
1983-84	Brynas	Swe.	34	19	16	29	81	....	....	....	....	....
1982-83	Brynas	Swe.	36	22	14	36	36	....	....	....	....	....
1983-84	Brynas	Swe.	43	20	10	30	81	....	....	....	....	....
1984-85a	NY Rangers	NHL	74	29	29	58	51	3	0	2	2	0
1985-86	NY Rangers	NHL	73	25	29	54	109	16	4	6	10	20
1986-87	NY Rangers	NHL	64	40	34	74	60	6	1	2	3	20
1987-88	NY Rangers	NHL	69	28	40	68	95	....	....	....	....	....
1988-89	NY Rangers	NHL	79	32	56	88	148	4	3	2	5	12
1989-90	NY Rangers	NHL	48	19	19	38	100	....	....	....	....	....
	Los Angeles	NHL	28	13	20	33	28	10	5	4	9	19
	NHL Totals		435	186	227	413	591	39	13	16	29	71

a NHL All-Rookie Team (1985)

Played in NHL All-Star Game (1988)

Traded to **Los Angeles** by **NY Rangers** with Tony Granato for Bernie Nicholls, January 20, 1990.

SANDSTROM, ULF

Right wing. Shoots right. 5'10", 180 lbs. Born, Harnosand, Sweden, April 24, 1967.
(Chicago's 5th choice, 92nd overall, in 1987 Entry Draft).

			Regular Season					Playoffs				
Season	Club	Lea	GP	G	A	TP	PIM	GP	G	A	TP	PIM
1986-87	MoDo	Swe.	25	2	4	6	14	6	3	0	3	0
1987-88	MoDo	Swe.	38	26	9	35	12	....	....	....	....	....
1988-89	MoDo	Swe.	39	19	14	33	16	....	....	....	....	....
1989-90	MoDo	Swe.	18	6	4	10	2	....	....	....	....	....

SANDWITH, TERRAN

Defense. Shoots left. 6'4", 210 lbs. Born, Edmonton, Alta., April 17, 1972.
(Philadelphia's 4th choice, 42nd overall, in 1990 Entry Draft).

			Regular Season					Playoffs				
Season	Club	Lea	GP	G	A	TP	PIM	GP	G	A	TP	PIM
1988-89	Tri-Cities	WHL	31	0	0	0	29	6	0	0	0	4
1989-90	Tri-Cities	WHL	70	4	14	18	92	7	0	2	2	14

SANGSTER, ROBERT (ROB)

Left wing. Shoots left. 5'11", 190 lbs. Born, Kitchener, Ont., May 2, 1969.
(Vancouver's 6th choice, 155th overall, in 1989 Entry Draft).

			Regular Season					Playoffs				
Season	Club	Lea	GP	G	A	TP	PIM	GP	G	A	TP	PIM
1987-88	Kitchener	OHL	58	2	7	9	196	4	0	1	1	12
1988-89	Kitchener	OHL	64	10	25	35	337	5	1	0	1	12
1989-90	Ottawa	OHL	45	8	24	32	251	1	0	0	0	7

SANIPASS, EVERETT

Left wing. Shoots left. 6'2", 204 lbs. Born, Big Cove, N.B., February 13, 1968.
(Chicago's 1st choice, 14th overall, in 1986 Entry Draft).

			Regular Season					Playoffs				
Season	Club	Lea	GP	G	A	TP	PIM	GP	G	A	TP	PIM
1985-86	Verdun	QMJHL	67	23	66	89	320	5	0	2	2	16
1986-87	Chicago	NHL	7	1	3	4	2	....	....	....	....	....
a	Granby	QMJHL	35	34	48	82	220	8	6	4	10	48
1987-88	Chicago	NHL	57	8	12	20	126	2	2	0	2	2
1988-89	Chicago	NHL	50	6	9	15	164	3	0	0	0	2
	Saginaw	IHL	23	9	12	21	76	....	....	....	....	....
1989-90	Chicago	NHL	12	2	2	4	17	....	....	....	....	....
	Quebec	NHL	9	3	3	6	8	....	....	....	....	....
	Indianapolis	IHL	33	15	13	28	121	....	....	....	....	....
	NHL Totals		135	20	29	49	317	5	2	0	2	4

a QMJHL First All-Star Team (1987)

Traded to **Quebec** by **Chicago** with Mario Doyon and Dan Vincelette for Greg Millen, Michel Goulet and Quebec's sixth round choice in 1991 Entry Draft, March 5, 1990.

SAPERGIA, BRENT (suh-PUHR-juh)

Right wing. Shoots right. 5'10", 195 lbs. Born, Moose Jaw, Sask. November 16, 1962.

			Regular Season					Playoffs				
Season	Club	Lea	GP	G	A	TP	PIM	GP	G	A	TP	PIM
1984-85a	Salt Lake	IHL	76	47	47	94	36	7	2	7	9	15
1985-86b	Salt Lake	IHL	80	58	65	123	127	1	0	1	1	2
1986-87	KalPa	Fin.	33	25	13	38	117	....	....	....	....	....
	New Haven	AHL	2	0	1	1	0	....	....	....	....	....
1987-88	Salt Lake	IHL	22	10	6	16	22	9	0	1	1	9
1988-89	Indianapolis	IHL	52	43	33	76	246	....	....	....	....	....
1989-90	Phoenix	IHL	43	19	13	32	159	....	....	....	....	....

a IHL Second All-Star Team (1985)
b IHL First All-Star Team (1986)

Signed as a free agent by **NY Rangers**, March 6, 1987. Signed as a free agent by **New Jersey**, September 1, 1989.

SATARDALEN, JEFF

Right wing. Shoots right. 6'1", 180 lbs. Born, Superior, WI, July 8, 1969.
(NY Islanders' 8th choice, 160th overall, in 1987 Entry Draft).

			Regular Season					Playoffs				
Season	Club	Lea	GP	G	A	TP	PIM	GP	G	A	TP	PIM
1988-89	St. Cloud	NCAA	35	17	19	36	22	....	....	....	....	....
1989-90	St. Cloud	NCAA	38	24	33	57	34	....	....	....	....	....

SAUMIER, RAYMOND

Right wing. Shoots right. 6', 195 lbs. Born, Hull, Que., February 27, 1969.
(Hartford's 7th choice, 157th overall, in 1989 Entry Draft).

			Regular Season					Playoffs				
Season	Club	Lea	GP	G	A	TP	PIM	GP	G	A	TP	PIM
1986-87	Laval	QMJHL	57	13	37	50	301	13	1	2	3	76
1987-88	Trois-Rivieres	QMJHL	62	30	58	88	356	....	....	....	....	....
1988-89	Trois-Rivieres	QMJHL	65	30	62	92	307	....	....	....	....	....
1989-90	Binghamton	AHL	56	9	11	20	171	....	....	....	....	....

SAUNDERS, MATTHEW

Left wing. Shoots left. 6', 180 lbs. Born, Ottawa, Ont., July 17, 1970.
(Chicago's 8th choice, 195th overall, in 1989 Entry Draft).

			Regular Season					Playoffs				
Season	Club	Lea	GP	G	A	TP	PIM	GP	G	A	TP	PIM
1988-89	Northeastern	H.E	26	8	9	17	14	....	....	....	....	....
1989-90	Northeastern	H.E	35	19	21	40	51	....	....	....	....	....

SAVAGE, JOEL

Right wing. Shoots right. 5'11", 205 lbs. Born, Surrey, B.C., December 25, 1969.
(Buffalo's 1st choice, 13th overall, in 1988 Entry Draft).

			Regular Season					Playoffs				
Season	Club	Lea	GP	G	A	TP	PIM	GP	G	A	TP	PIM
1986-87	Victoria	WHL	68	14	13	27	48	5	2	0	2	0
1987-88	Victoria	WHL	69	37	32	69	73	....	....	....	....	....
1988-89	Victoria	WHL	60	17	30	47	95	6	1	1	2	8
1989-90	Rochester	AHL	43	6	7	13	39	5	0	1	1	4

SAVAGE, REGINALD (REGGIE)

Center. Shoots left. 5'10", 180 lbs. Born, Montreal, Que., May 1, 1970.
(Washington's 1st choice, 15th overall, in 1988 Entry Draft).

			Regular Season					Playoffs				
Season	Club	Lea	GP	G	A	TP	PIM	GP	G	A	TP	PIM
1987-88	Victoriaville	QMJHL	68	68	54	122	77	5	2	3	5	8
1988-89	Victoriaville	QMJHL	54	58	55	113	178	16	15	13	28	52
1989-90	Victoriaville	QMJHL	63	51	43	94	79	16	13	10	23	40

SAVARD, DENIS JOSEPH (sa-VARH, den-NY)

Center. Shoots right. 5'10", 175 lbs. Born, Pointe Gatineau, Que., February 4, 1961.
(Chicago's 1st choice, 3rd overall, in 1980 Entry Draft).

			Regular Season					Playoffs				
Season	Club	Lea	GP	G	A	TP	PIM	GP	G	A	TP	PIM
1978-79	Montreal	QJHL	70	46	*112	158	88	11	5	6	11	46
1979-80ab	Montreal	QJHL	72	63	118	181	93	10	7	16	23	8
1980-81	Chicago	NHL	76	28	47	75	47	3	0	0	0	0
1981-82	Chicago	NHL	80	32	87	119	82	15	11	7	18	52
1982-83c	Chicago	NHL	78	35	86	121	99	13	8	9	17	22
1983-84	Chicago	NHL	75	37	57	94	71	5	1	3	4	9
1984-85	Chicago	NHL	79	38	67	105	56	15	9	20	29	20
1985-86	Chicago	NHL	80	47	69	116	111	3	4	1	5	6
1986-87	Chicago	NHL	70	40	50	90	108	4	1	0	1	12
1987-88	Chicago	NHL	80	44	87	131	95	5	4	3	7	17
1988-89	Chicago	NHL	58	23	59	82	110	16	8	11	19	10
1989-90	Chicago	NHL	60	27	53	80	56	20	7	15	22	41
	NHL Totals		736	351	662	1013	835	99	53	69	122	189

a QMJHL First All-Star Team (1980).
b Named QMJHL's Most Valuable Player (1980).
c NHL Second All-Star Team (1983).

Played in NHL All-Star Game (1982-84, 1986, 1988)

Traded to **Montreal** by **Chicago** for Chris Chelios and Montreal's second round choice in 1991 Entry Draft, June 29, 1990.

SAWYER, DAN

Defense. Shoots left. 6'1", 210 lbs. Born, Denville, NJ, October 28, 1970.
(Calgary's 11th choice, 210th overall, in 1989 Entry Draft).

			Regular Season					Playoffs				
Season	Club	Lea	GP	G	A	TP	PIM	GP	G	A	TP	PIM
1988-89	Ramapo	US Jr.	....	19	25	44	....	....	....	....	....	....
1989-90	Notre Dame	SJHL	33	12	10	22	68	....	....	....	....	....

SCHAFHAUSER, PATRICK

Defense. Shoots left. 6'1", 195 lbs. Born, St. Paul, MN, July 27, 1971.
(Pittsburgh's 8th choice, 142nd overall, in 1989 Entry Draft).

			Regular Season					Playoffs				
Season	Club	Lea	GP	G	A	TP	PIM	GP	G	A	TP	PIM
1988-89	Hill-Murray	HS	25	2	29	31	....	....	....	....	....	....
1989-90	Boston College	H.E.	39	1	6	7	30	....	....	....	....	....

SCHEIFELE, STEVE

Right wing. Shoots right. 6', 195 lbs. Born, Alexandria, VA, April 18, 1968.
(Philadelphia's 5th choice, 125th overall, in 1986 Entry Draft).

			Regular Season					Playoffs				
Season	Club	Lea	GP	G	A	TP	PIM	GP	G	A	TP	PIM
1986-87	Boston College	H.E.	38	13	13	26	28	....	....	....	....	....
1987-88	Boston College	H.E.	30	11	16	27	22	....	....	....	....	....
1988-89	Boston College	H.E.	40	24	14	38	30	....	....	....	....	....
1989-90	Boston College	H.E.	12	7	0	7	2	....	....	....	....	....

SCHENA, ROB

Defense. Shoots left. 6'1", 190 lbs. Born, Saugas, MA, February 5, 1967.
(Detroit's 9th choice, 176th overall, in 1985 Entry Draft).

			Regular Season					Playoffs				
Season	Club	Lea	GP	G	A	TP	PIM	GP	G	A	TP	PIM
1986-87	RPI	ECAC	30	1	9	10	32	....	....	....	....	....
1987-88	RPI	ECAC	30	5	9	14	56	....	....	....	....	....
1988-89	RPI	ECAC	32	7	5	12	64	....	....	....	....	....
	Adirondack	AHL	9	1	1	2	2	....	....	....	....	....
1989-90	Adirondack	AHL	43	5	8	13	36	....	....	....	....	....

SCHLEGEL, BRAD

Defense. Shoots right. 5'10", 180 lbs. Born, Kitchener, Ont., July 22, 1968.
(Washington's 8th choice, 144th overall, in 1988 Entry Draft).

			Regular Season					Playoffs				
Season	Club	Lea	GP	G	A	TP	PIM	GP	G	A	TP	PIM
1986-87	London	OHL	65	4	23	27	24	....	....	....	....	....
1987-88a	London	OHL	66	13	63	76	49	12	8	17	25	6
1988-89	Cdn. National	....	60	2	22	24	30	....	....	....	....	....
1989-90	Cdn. National	....	72	7	25	32	44	....	....	....	....	....

a OHL Second All-Star Team (1988)

SCHMALZBAUER, TONY

Defense. Shoots left. 6'2", 225 lbs. Born, New Brighton, MN, April 23, 1968.
(NY Islanders' 6th choice, 122nd overall, in 1986 Entry Draft).

				Regular Season					Playoffs			
Season	Club	Lea	GP	G	A	TP	PIM	GP	G	A	TP	PIM
1986-87	St. Cloud	NCAA	33	4	4	8	27	.....	.....	.....	.....	.....
1987-88	St. Cloud	NCAA	37	3	6	9	62	.....	.....	.....	.....	.....
1988-89	St. Cloud	NCAA	34	0	1	1	68	.....	.....	.....	.....	.....
1989-90	St. Cloud	NCAA	35	4	2	6	76	.....	.....	.....	.....	.....

SCHNEIDER, MATHIEU

Defense. Shoots left. 5'11", 189 lbs. Born, Woonsockett, RI, June 12, 1969.
(Montreal's 4th choice, 44th overall, in 1987 Entry Draft).

				Regular Season					Playoffs			
Season	Club	Lea	GP	G	A	TP	PIM	GP	G	A	TP	PIM
1986-87	Cornwall	OHL	63	7	29	36	75	5	0	0	0	22
1987-88	**Montreal**	**NHL**	4	0	0	0	2	.....	.....	.....	.....	.....
	Sherbrooke	AHL	.....	.....	.....	.....	.....	3	0	3	3	12
a	Cornwall	OHL	48	21	40	61	83	11	2	6	8	14
1988-89	Cornwall	OHL	59	16	57	73	96	18	7	20	27	30
1989-90	**Montreal**	**NHL**	44	7	14	21	25	9	1	3	4	31
	Sherbrooke	AHL	28	6	13	19	20					
	NHL Totals		**48**	**7**	**14**	**21**	**27**	**9**	**1**	**3**	**4**	**31**

a OHL First All-Star Team (1988)

SCHNEIDER, SCOTT

Center. Shoots right. 6'1", 175 lbs. Born, Rochester, MN, May 18, 1965.
(Winnipeg's 4th choice, 93rd overall, in 1984 Entry Draft).

				Regular Season					Playoffs			
Season	Club	Lea	GP	G	A	TP	PIM	GP	G	A	TP	PIM
1983-84	Colorado	WCHA	35	19	14	33	24	.....	.....	.....	.....	.....
1984-85	Colorado	WCHA	33	16	13	29	60	.....	.....	.....	.....	.....
1985-86	Colorado	WCHA	40	16	22	38	32	.....	.....	.....	.....	.....
1986-87	Colorado	WCHA	42	21	22	43	36	.....	.....	.....	.....	.....
1987-88	Moncton	AHL	68	12	23	35	28	.....	.....	.....	.....	.....
1988-89	Moncton	AHL	64	29	36	65	51	6	2	6	8	4
1989-90	Moncton	AHL	61	17	23	40	57	.....	.....	.....	.....	.....

SCISSONS, SCOTT

Center. Shoots left. 6'1", 200 lbs. Born, Saskatoon, Sask., October 29, 1971.
(NY Islanders' 1st choice, 6th overall, in 1990 Entry Draft).

				Regular Season					Playoffs			
Season	Club	Lea	GP	G	A	TP	PIM	GP	G	A	TP	PIM
1988-89	Saskatoon	WHL	71	30	56	86	65	7	0	4	4	16
1989-90	Saskatoon	WHL	61	40	47	87	81	10	3	8	11	6

SCOTT, KEVIN

Center. Shoots left. 5'10", 170 lbs. Born, Vernon, B.C., November 3, 1967.
(Detroit's 9th choice, 158th overall, in 1987 Entry Draft).

				Regular Season					Playoffs			
Season	Club	Lea	GP	G	A	TP	PIM	GP	G	A	TP	PIM
1987-88	N. Michigan	WCHA	36	9	12	21	42	.....	.....	.....	.....	.....
1988-89	N. Michigan	WCHA	40	11	14	25	36	.....	.....	.....	.....	.....
1989-90	N. Michigan	WCHA	34	20	14	34	46	.....	.....	.....	.....	.....

SCREMIN, CLAUDIO

Defense. Shoots right. 6'2", 205 lbs. Born, Burnaby, B.C., May 28, 1968.
(Washington's 12th choice, 204th overall, in 1988 Entry Draft).

				Regular Season					Playoffs			
Season	Club	Lea	GP	G	A	TP	PIM	GP	G	A	TP	PIM
1986-87	U. of Maine	H.E.	15	0	1	1	2	.....	.....	.....	.....	.....
1987-88	U. of Maine	H.E.	44	6	18	24	22	.....	.....	.....	.....	.....
1988-89	U. of Maine	H.E.	45	5	24	29	42	.....	.....	.....	.....	.....
1989-90	U. of Maine	H.E.	45	4	26	30	14	.....	.....	.....	.....	.....

Traded to **Minnesota** by **Washington** for Don Beaupre, November 1, 1988.

SEARS, SVERRE

Defense. Shoots left. 6'2", 185 lbs. Born, Boston, MA, October 17, 1970.
(Philadelphia's 6th choice, 159th overall, in 1989 Entry Draft).

				Regular Season					Playoffs			
Season	Club	Lea	GP	G	A	TP	PIM	GP	G	A	TP	PIM
1988-89	Belmont Hill	HS	23	5	19	24	34	.....	.....	.....	.....	.....
1989-90	Princeton	ECAC	3	0	1	1	14	.....	.....	.....	.....	.....

SECORD, ALAN WILLIAM (AL)　　　　　(SEE-cord)

Left wing. Shoots left. 6'1", 205 lbs. Born, Sudbury, Ont., March 3, 1958.
(Boston's 1st choice, 16th overall, in 1978 Amateur Draft).

				Regular Season					Playoffs			
Season	Club	Lea	GP	G	A	TP	PIM	GP	G	A	TP	PIM
1976-77	St. Catharines	OHA	57	32	34	66	343	14	4	3	7	46
1977-78	Hamilton	OHA	59	28	22	50	185	20	8	11	19	71
1978-79	Rochester	AHL	4	4	2	6	40	.....	.....	.....	.....	.....
	Boston	**NHL**	71	16	7	23	125	4	0	0	0	4
1979-80	**Boston**	**NHL**	77	23	16	39	170	10	0	3	3	65
1980-81	Springfield	AHL	8	3	5	8	21	.....	.....	.....	.....	.....
	Boston	**NHL**	18	0	3	3	42	.....	.....	.....	.....	.....
	Chicago	**NHL**	41	13	9	22	145	3	4	0	4	14
1981-82	Chicago	NHL	80	44	31	75	303	15	2	5	7	61
1982-83	Chicago	NHL	80	54	32	86	180	12	4	7	11	66
1983-84	Chicago	NHL	14	4	4	8	77	5	3	4	7	28
1984-85	Chicago	NHL	51	15	11	26	193	15	7	9	16	42
1985-86	Chicago	NHL	80	40	36	76	201	2	0	2	2	26
1986-87	Chicago	NHL	77	29	29	58	196	4	0	0	0	21
1987-88	Toronto	NHL	74	15	27	42	221	6	1	0	1	16
1988-89	Toronto	NHL	40	5	10	15	71	.....	.....	.....	.....	.....
	Philadelphia	NHL	20	1	0	1	38	14	0	4	4	31
1989-90	Chicago	NHL	43	14	7	21	131	12	0	0	0	8
	NHL Totals		**766**	**273**	**222**	**495**	**2093**	**102**	**21**	**34**	**55**	**382**

Played in NHL All-Star Game (1982, 1983)

Traded to **Chicago** by **Boston** for Mike O'Connell, December 18, 1980. Traded to **Toronto** by **Chicago** with Ed Olczyk for Rick Vaive, Steve Thomas and Bob McGill, September 3, 1987. Traded to **Philadelphia** by **Toronto** for Philadelphia's fifth-round choice (Keith Carney) in 1989 Entry Draft, February 7, 1989. Signed as a free agent by **Chicago**, August 7, 1989.

SEFTEL, STEVE

Left wing. Shoots left. 6'2", 200 lbs. Born, Kitchener, Ont., May 14, 1968.
(Washington's 2nd choice, 40th overall, in 1986 Entry Draft).

				Regular Season					Playoffs			
Season	Club	Lea	GP	G	A	TP	PIM	GP	G	A	TP	PIM
1985-86	Kingston	OHL	42	11	16	27	53	.....	.....	.....	.....	.....
1986-87	Kingston	OHL	54	21	43	64	55	12	1	4	5	9
1987-88	Binghamton	AHL	3	0	0	0	2	.....	.....	.....	.....	.....
	Kingston	OHL	66	32	43	75	51	.....	.....	.....	.....	.....
1988-89	Binghamton	AHL	58	12	15	27	70	.....	.....	.....	.....	.....
1989-90	Baltimore	AHL	74	10	19	29	52	12	4	3	7	10

SEJBA, JIRI

Left wing. Shoots left. 5'10", 185 lbs. Born, Pardubice, Czech., July 22, 1962.
(Buffalo's 9th choice, 182nd overall, in 1985 Entry Draft).

				Regular Season					Playoffs			
Season	Club	Lea	GP	G	A	TP	PIM	GP	G	A	TP	PIM
1986-87	Pardubice	Czech.	34	23	11	34	.....	.....	.....	.....	.....	.....
1987-88	Pardubice	Czech.	23	10	15	25	.....	.....	.....	.....	.....	.....
1988-89	Pardubice	Czech.	44	38	21	59	68	.....	.....	.....	.....	.....
1989-90	Pardubice	Czech	26	11	14	25	.....	.....	.....	.....	.....	.....

SELANNE, TEEMU

Right wing. Shoots right. 6', 180 lbs. Born, Helsinki, Finland, March 7, 1970.
(Winnipeg's 1st choice, 10th overall, in 1988 Entry Draft).

				Regular Season					Playoffs			
Season	Club	Lea	GP	G	A	TP	PIM	GP	G	A	TP	PIM
1987-88	Jokerit	Fin. Jr.	33	43	23	66	18	5	4	3	7	2
	Jokerit	Fin. 2	5	1	1	2	0	.....	.....	.....	.....	.....
1988-89	Jokerit	Fin.	34	35	33	68	12	5	7	3	10	4
1989-90	Jokerit	Fin.	11	4	8	12	0	.....	.....	.....	.....	.....

SEMAK, ALEXANDER

Center. Shoots left. 5'9", 190 lbs. Born, Ufa, Soviet Union, February 11, 1968.
(New Jersey's 12th choice, 207th overall, in 1988 Entry Draft).

				Regular Season					Playoffs			
Season	Club	Lea	GP	G	A	TP	PIM	GP	G	A	TP	PIM
1987-88	Moscow D'amo	USSR	47	21	14	35	40	.....	.....	.....	.....	.....
1988-89	Moscow D'amo	USSR	44	18	10	28	22	.....	.....	.....	.....	.....
1989-90	Moscow D'amo	USSR	43	23	11	34	33	.....	.....	.....	.....	.....

SEMCHUK, THOMAS (BRANDY)

Right wing. Shoots right. 6'1", 185 lbs. Born, Calgary, Alta., September 22, 1971.
(Los Angeles' 2nd choice, 28th overall, in 1990 Entry Draft)

				Regular Season					Playoffs			
Season	Club	Lea	GP	G	A	TP	PIM	GP	G	A	TP	PIM
1988-89	Cdn. National	....	42	11	11	22	60	.....	.....	.....	.....	.....
1989-90	Cdn. National	....	55	10	15	25	40	.....	.....	.....	.....	.....

SEMENOV, ANATOLI

Center. 6'2", 190 lbs. Born, Moscow, Soviet Union, March 5, 1962.
(Edmonton's 5th choice, 120th overall, in 1989 Entry Draft).

				Regular Season					Playoffs			
Season	Club	Lea	GP	G	A	TP	PIM	GP	G	A	TP	PIM
1979-80	Moscow D'amo	USSR	8	3	0	3	2	.....	.....	.....	.....	.....
1980-81	Moscow D'amo	USSR	47	18	14	32	18	.....	.....	.....	.....	.....
1981-82	Moscow D'amo	USSR	44	12	14	26	28	.....	.....	.....	.....	.....
1982-83	Moscow D'amo	USSR	44	22	18	40	26	.....	.....	.....	.....	.....
1983-84	Moscow D'amo	USSR	19	10	5	15	14	.....	.....	.....	.....	.....
1984-85	Moscow D'amo	USSR	30	17	12	19	32	.....	.....	.....	.....	.....
1985-86	Moscow D'amo	USSR	32	18	17	35	19	.....	.....	.....	.....	.....
1986-87	Moscow D'amo	USSR	40	15	29	44	32	.....	.....	.....	.....	.....
1987-88	Moscow D'amo	USSR	32	17	8	25	22	.....	.....	.....	.....	.....
1988-89	Moscow D'amo	USSR	31	9	12	21	24	.....	.....	.....	.....	.....
1989-90	Moscow D'amo	USSR	48	13	20	33	16	.....	.....	.....	.....	.....
	Edmonton	**NHL**	.....	.....	.....	.....	.....	2	0	0	0	0
	NHL Totals		.....	.....	.....	.....	.....	**2**	**0**	**0**	**0**	**0**

SENTNER, PETER G.

Defense. Shoots left. 6'1", 180 lbs. Born, Swampscott, MA, June 13, 1969.
(Los Angeles' 1st choice, 12th overall, in 1990 Supplemental Draft).

			Regular Season					Playoffs				
Season	Club	Lea	GP	G	A	TP	PIM	GP	G	A	TP	PIM
1987-88	U. of Lowell	ECAC	21	0	0	0	14	....	....	....	....	....
1988-89	U. of Lowell	ECAC	34	6	20	26	46	....	....	....	....	....
1989-90	U. of Lowell	ECAC	25	1	6	7	6	....	....	....	....	....

SEPPO, JUKKA PEKKA

Center/left wing. Shoots left. 6'2", 190 lbs. Born, Vaasa, Finland, January 22, 1968.
(Philadelphia's 2nd choice, 23rd overall, in 1986 Entry Draft).

			Regular Season					Playoffs				
Season	Club	Lea	GP	G	A	TP	PIM	GP	G	A	TP	PIM
1987-88	Vaasa Sport	Fin.	42	28	37	65	78	....	....	....	....	....
1988-89	IFK Helsinki	Fin.	35	7	13	20	28	....	....	....	....	....
1989-90	IFK Helsinki	Fin.	39	15	27	42	50	....	....	....	....	....

SEROWIK, JEFF

Defense. Shoots right. 6', 190 lbs. Born, Manchester, NH, October 1, 1967.
(Toronto's 5th choice, 85th overall, in 1985 Entry Draft).

			Regular Season					Playoffs				
Season	Club	Lea	GP	G	A	TP	PIM	GP	G	A	TP	PIM
1986-87	Providence	H.E.	33	3	8	11	22	....	....	....	....	....
1987-88	Providence	H.E.	33	3	9	12	44	....	....	....	....	....
1988-89	Providence	H.E.	35	3	14	17	48	....	....	....	....	....
1989-90a	Providence	H.E.	35	6	19	25	34	....	....	....	....	....

a Hockey East Second All-Star Team (1990)

SEVCIK, JAROSLAV (SEHV-chihk, YAR-o-slav)

Left wing. Shoots right. 5'9", 170 lbs. Born, Brno, Czechoslovakia, May 15, 1965.
(Quebec's 9th choice, 177th overall, in 1987 Entry Draft).

			Regular Season					Playoffs				
Season	Club	Lea	GP	G	A	TP	PIM	GP	G	A	TP	PIM
1986-87	Zetor Brno	Czech.	34	12	5	17	....	....	....	....	....	....
1987-88	Fredericton	AHL	32	9	7	16	6	....	....	....	....	....
1988-89	Halifax	AHL	78	17	41	58	17	4	1	1	2	2
1989-90	Quebec	NHL	13	0	2	2	2	....	....	....	....	....
	Halifax	AHL	50	17	17	34	36	3	0	1	1	0
	NHL Totals		13	0	2	2	2	....	....	....	....	....

SEVERYN, BRENT

Left wing. Shoots left. 6'2", 210 lbs. Born, Vegreville, Alta., February 22, 1966.

			Regular Season					Playoffs				
Season	Club	Lea	GP	G	A	TP	PIM	GP	G	A	TP	PIM
1987-88	U. of Alberta	CWUAA	46	21	29	50	178	....	....	....	....	....
1988-89	Halifax	AHL	47	2	12	14	141	....	....	....	....	....
1989-90	Quebec	NHL	35	0	2	2	42	....	....	....	....	....
	Halifax	AHL	43	6	9	15	105	6	1	2	3	49
	NHL Totals		35	0	2	2	42	....	....	....	....	....

Signed as a free agent by **Quebec**, July 15, 1988.

SEVIGNY, PIERRE

Left wing. Shoots left. 5'11", 180 lbs. Born, Trois-Rivieres, Que., September 8, 1971.
(Montreal's 4th choice, 51st overall, in 1989 Entry Draft).

			Regular Season					Playoffs				
Season	Club	Lea	GP	G	A	TP	PIM	GP	G	A	TP	PIM
1988-89	Verdun	QMJHL	67	27	43	70	88	....	....	....	....	....
1989-90	St-Hyacinthe	QMJHL	67	47	72	119	205	12	8	8	16	42

SEXSMITH, DEAN

Center. Shoots left. 6'1", 190 lbs. Born, Virden, Man., May 13, 1968.
(NY Islanders' 5th choice, 101st overall, in 1986 Entry Draft).

			Regular Season					Playoffs				
Season	Club	Lea	GP	G	A	TP	PIM	GP	G	A	TP	PIM
1985-86	Brandon	WHL	65	13	23	36	34	....	....	....	....	....
1986-87	Seattle	WHL	65	14	24	38	46	....	....	....	....	....
1987-88	Seattle	WHL	16	10	9	19	10	....	....	....	....	....
	Saskatoon	WHL	58	15	26	41	37	10	0	3	3	0
1988-89	Spokane	WHL	59	26	36	62	71	....	....	....	....	....
1989-90	Brandon	CWUAA	26	15	20	35	97	....	....	....	....	....

SHANAHAN, BRENDAN

Center/Right wing. Shoots right. 6'3", 210 lbs. Born, Mimico, Ont., January 23, 1969.
(New Jersey's 1st choice, 2nd overall, in 1987 Entry Draft).

			Regular Season					Playoffs				
Season	Club	Lea	GP	G	A	TP	PIM	GP	G	A	TP	PIM
1985-86	London	OHL	59	28	34	62	70	5	5	5	10	5
1986-87	London	OHL	56	39	53	92	92	....	....	....	....	....
1987-88	New Jersey	NHL	65	7	19	26	131	12	2	1	3	44
1988-89	New Jersey	NHL	68	22	28	50	115	....	....	....	....	....
1989-90	New Jersey	NHL	73	30	42	72	137	6	3	3	6	20
	NHL Totals		206	59	89	148	383	18	5	4	9	64

SHANK, DANIEL

Right wing. Shoots right. 5'10", 190 lbs. Born, Montreal, Que., May 12, 1967.

			Regular Season					Playoffs				
Season	Club	Lea	GP	G	A	TP	PIM	GP	G	A	TP	PIM
1986-87	Hull	QMJHL	46	26	43	69	325	....	....	....	....	....
1987-88	Hull	QMJHL	42	23	34	57	274	5	3	2	5	16
1988-89	Adirondack	AHL	42	5	20	25	113	17	11	8	19	102
1989-90	Detroit	NHL	57	11	13	24	143	....	....	....	....	....
	Adirondack	AHL	14	8	8	16	36	....	....	....	....	....
	NHL Totals		57	11	13	24	143	....	....	....	....	....

Signed as a free agent by **Detroit**, May 26, 1989.

SHANNON, DARRIN

Left wing. Shoots left. 6'2", 200 lbs. Born, Barrie, Ont., December 8, 1969.
(Pittsburgh's 1st choice, 4th overall, in 1988 Entry Draft).

			Regular Season					Playoffs				
Season	Club	Lea	GP	G	A	TP	PIM	GP	G	A	TP	PIM
1986-87	Windsor	OHL	60	16	67	83	116	14	4	6	10	8
1987-88	Windsor	OHL	43	33	41	74	49	12	6	12	18	9
1988-89	Windsor	OHL	54	33	48	81	47	4	1	6	7	2
	Buffalo	NHL	3	0	0	0	0	2	0	0	0	0
1989-90	Buffalo	NHL	17	2	7	9	4	6	0	1	1	4
	Rochester	AHL	50	20	23	43	25	9	4	1	5	2
	NHL Totals		20	2	7	9	4	8	0	1	1	4

Traded to **Buffalo** by **Pittsburgh** with Doug Bodger for Tom Barrasso and Buffalo's third-round choice (Joe Dziedzic) in 1990 Entry Draft, November 12, 1988.

SHANNON, DARRYL

Defense. Shoots left. 6'2", 190 lbs. Born, Barrie, Ont., June 21, 1968.
(Toronto's 2nd choice, 36th overall, in 1986 Entry Draft).

			Regular Season					Playoffs				
Season	Club	Lea	GP	G	A	TP	PIM	GP	G	A	TP	PIM
1985-86	Windsor	OHL	57	6	21	27	52	16	5	6	11	22
1986-87a	Windsor	OHL	64	23	27	50	83	14	4	8	12	18
1987-88b	Windsor	OHL	60	16	67	83	116	12	3	8	11	17
1988-89	Toronto	NHL	14	1	3	4	6	....	....	....	....	....
	Newmarket	AHL	61	5	24	29	37	5	0	3	3	10
1989-90	Toronto	NHL	10	0	1	1	12	....	....	....	....	....
	Newmarket	AHL	47	4	15	19	58	....	....	....	....	....
	NHL Totals		24	1	4	5	18	....	....	....	....	....

a OHL Second All-Star Team
b OHL First All-Star Team (1988)

SHARPLES, JEFF

Defense. Shoots left. 6'1", 195 lbs. Born, Terrace, B.C., July 28, 1967.
(Detroit's 2nd choice, 29th overall, in 1985 Entry Draft)

			Regular Season					Playoffs				
Season	Club	Lea	GP	G	A	TP	PIM	GP	G	A	TP	PIM
1983-84	Kelowna	WHL	72	9	24	33	51	....	....	....	....	....
1984-85a	Kelowna	WHL	72	12	41	53	90	6	0	1	1	6
1985-86	Spokane	WHL	3	0	0	0	4					
	Portland	WHL	19	2	6	8	44	15	2	6	8	6
1986-87	Detroit	NHL	3	0	1	1	2	2	0	0	0	2
	Portland	WHL	44	25	35	60	92	20	7	15	22	23
1987-88	Detroit	NHL	56	10	25	35	42	4	0	3	3	4
	Adirondack	AHL	4	2	1	3	4					
1988-89	Detroit	NHL	46	4	9	13	26	1	0	0	0	0
	Adirondack	AHL	10	0	4	4	8	....	....	....	....	....
1989-90	Adirondack	AHL	9	2	5	7	6	....	....	....	....	....
1989-90	Cape Breton	AHL	38	4	13	17	28	....	....	....	....	....
	Utica	AHL	13	2	5	7	19	5	1	2	3	15
	NHL Totals		105	14	35	49	70	7	0	3	3	6

a WHL Second All-Star Team, West Division (1985)

Traded to **Edmonton** by **Detroit** with Petr Klima, Joe Murphy and Adam Graves for Jimmy Carson, Kevin McClelland and Edmonton's fifth round choice in 1991 Entry Draft, November 2, 1989. Traded to **New Jersey** by **Edmonton** for Reijo Ruotsalainen, March 6, 1990.

SHAUNESSY, SCOTT

Defense/Left wing. Shoots left. 6'4", 220 lbs. Born, Newport, RI, January 22, 1964.
(Quebec's 9th choice, 192nd overall, in 1983 Entry Draft).

			Regular Season					Playoffs				
Season	Club	Lea	GP	G	A	TP	PIM	GP	G	A	TP	PIM
1983-84	Boston U.	ECAC	40	6	22	28	48	....	....	....	....	....
1984-85a	Boston U.	H.E.	42	7	15	22	87	....	....	....	....	....
1985-86b	Boston U.	H.E.	38	6	13	19	31	....	....	....	....	....
1986-87	Quebec	NHL	3	0	0	0	7	....	....	....	....	....
	Boston U.	H.E.	32	2	13	15	71	....	....	....	....	....
1987-88	Fredericton	AHL	60	0	9	9	257	1	0	0	0	2
1988-89	Quebec	NHL	4	0	0	0	16	....	....	....	....	....
	Halifax	AHL	41	3	10	13	106	....	....	....	....	....
1989-90	Halifax	AHL	26	3	5	8	107	....	....	....	....	....
	Fort Wayne	IHL	45	3	9	12	267	5	0	1	1	31
	NHL Totals		7	0	0	0	23					

a Hockey East Second All-Star Team (1985)
b Hockey East First All-Star Team (1986)

SHAW, BRAD

Defense. Shoots right. 5'11", 170 lbs. Born, Cambridge, Ont., April 28, 1964.
(Detroit's 5th choice, 86th overall, in 1982 Entry Draft).

			Regular Season					Playoffs				
Season	Club	Lea	GP	G	A	TP	PIM	GP	G	A	TP	PIM
1981-82	Ottawa	OHL	68	13	59	72	24	15	1	13	14	4
1982-83	Ottawa	OHL	63	12	66	78	24	9	2	9	11	4
1983-84a	Ottawa	OHL	68	11	71	82	75	13	2	*27	29	9
1984-85	Binghamton	AHL	24	1	10	11	4	8	1	8	9	6
	Salt Lake	IHL	44	3	29	32	25	....	....	....	....	....
1985-86	Hartford	NHL	8	0	2	2	4	....	....	....	....	....
	Binghamton	AHL	64	10	44	54	33	5	0	2	2	6
1986-87	Hartford	NHL	2	0	0	0	0	....	....	....	....	....
bc	Binghamton	AHL	77	9	30	39	43	12	1	8	9	2
1987-88	Hartford	NHL	1	0	0	0	0	....	....	....	....	....
b	Binghamton	AHL	73	12	50	62	50	4	0	5	5	4
1988-89	Cdn. National	....	4	1	0	1	2	....	....	....	....	....
	Hartford	NHL	3	1	0	1	0	3	1	0	1	0
1989-90d	Hartford	NHL	64	3	32	35	30	7	2	5	7	0
	NHL Totals		78	4	34	38	34	10	3	5	8	0

a OHL First All-Star Team (1984)
b AHL First All-Star Team (1987, 1988)
c Won Eddie Shore Plaque (AHL Outstanding Defenseman) (1987)
d NHL All-Rookie Team (1990)

Rights traded to **Hartford** by **Detroit** for Hartford's eighth round choice (Urban Nordin) in 1984 Entry Draft, May 29, 1984.

SHAW, DAVID

Defense. Shoots right. 6'1", 190 lbs. Born, St. Thomas, Ont., May 25, 1964.
(Quebec's 1st choice, 13th overall, in 1982 Entry Draft).

			Regular Season					Playoffs				
Season	Club	Lea	GP	G	A	TP	PIM	GP	G	A	TP	PIM
1981-82	Kitchener	OHL	68	6	25	31	94	15	2	2	4	51
1982-83	**Quebec**	**NHL**	**2**	**0**	**0**	**0**	**0**	....	....	....	....	....
	Kitchener	OHL	57	18	56	74	78	12	2	10	12	18
1983-84	**Quebec**	**NHL**	**3**	**0**	**0**	**0**	**0**	....	....	....	....	....
a	Kitchener	OHL	58	14	34	48	73	16	4	9	13	12
1984-85	**Quebec**	**NHL**	**14**	**0**	**0**	**0**	**11**	....	....	....	....	....
	Fredericton	AHL	48	7	6	13	73	2	0	0	0	7
1985-86	**Quebec**	**NHL**	**73**	**7**	**19**	**26**	**78**	....	....	....	....	....
1986-87	**Quebec**	**NHL**	**75**	**0**	**19**	**19**	**69**	....	....	....	....	....
1987-88	**NY Rangers**	**NHL**	**68**	**7**	**25**	**32**	**100**	....	....	....	....	....
1988-89	**NY Rangers**	**NHL**	**63**	**6**	**11**	**17**	**88**	**4**	**0**	**2**	**2**	**30**
1989-90	**NY Rangers**	**NHL**	**22**	**2**	**10**	**12**	**22**	....	....	....	....	....
	NHL Totals		**320**	**22**	**84**	**106**	**368**	**4**	**0**	**2**	**2**	**30**

a OHL First All-Star Team (1984).

Traded to **NY Rangers** by **Quebec** with John Ogrodnick for Jeff Jackson and Terry Carkner, September 30, 1987.

SHEDDEN, DOUGLAS ARTHUR (DOUG)

Right wing. Shoots right. 6', 185 lbs. Born, Wallaceburg, Ont., April 29, 1961.
(Pittsburgh's 5th choice, 93rd overall, in 1980 Entry Draft).

			Regular Season					Playoffs				
Season	Club	Lea	GP	G	A	TP	PIM	GP	G	A	TP	PIM
1979-80	Kitchener	OHA	16	10	16	26	26	....	....	....	....	....
	S. S. Marie	OHA	45	30	44	74	59	....	....	....	....	....
1980-81	S. S. Marie	OHA	66	51	72	123	114	19	16	22	38	10
1981-82	Erie	AHL	17	4	6	10	14	....	....	....	....	....
	Pittsburgh	**NHL**	**38**	**10**	**15**	**25**	**12**	....	....	....	....	....
1982-83	**Pittsburgh**	**NHL**	**80**	**24**	**43**	**67**	**54**	....	....	....	....	....
1983-84	**Pittsburgh**	**NHL**	**67**	**22**	**35**	**57**	**20**	....	....	....	....	....
1984-85	**Pittsburgh**	**NHL**	**80**	**35**	**32**	**67**	**30**	....	....	....	....	....
1985-86	**Pittsburgh**	**NHL**	**67**	**32**	**34**	**66**	**32**	....	....	....	....	....
	Detroit	**NHL**	**11**	**2**	**3**	**5**	**2**	....	....	....	....	....
1986-87	**Detroit**	**NHL**	**33**	**6**	**12**	**18**	**6**	....	....	....	....	....
	Adirondack	AHL	5	2	2	4	4	....	....	....	....	....
	Quebec	**NHL**	**16**	**0**	**2**	**2**	**8**	....	....	....	....	....
	Fredericton	AHL	15	12	6	18	0	....	....	....	....	....
1987-88	Baltimore	AHL	80	37	51	88	32	....	....	....	....	....
1988-89	**Toronto**	**NHL**	**1**	**0**	**0**	**0**	**2**	....	....	....	....	....
	Newmarket	AHL	29	14	26	40	6	....	....	....	....	....
1989-90	Newmarket	AHL	47	26	33	59	12	....	....	....	....	....
	NHL Totals		**393**	**131**	**176**	**307**	**166**	....	....	....	....	....

Traded to **Detroit** by **Pittsburgh** for Ron Duguay, March 11, 1986. Traded to **Quebec** by **Detroit** with Basil McRae and John Ogrodnick for Brent Ashton, Gilbert Delorme and Mark Kumpel, January 17, 1987. Signed as a free agent by **Toronto**, August 4, 1988.

SHEEHY, NEIL

Defense. Shoots right. 6'2", 210 lbs. Born, International Falls, MN, February 9, 1960.

			Regular Season					Playoffs				
Season	Club	Lea	GP	G	A	TP	PIM	GP	G	A	TP	PIM
1979-80	Harvard	ECAC	13	0	0	0	10	....	....	....	....	....
1980-81	Harvard	ECAC	26	4	8	12	22	....	....	....	....	....
1981-82	Harvard	ECAC	30	7	11	18	46	....	....	....	....	....
1982-83	Harvard	ECAC	34	5	13	18	48	....	....	....	....	....
1983-84	**Calgary**	**NHL**	**1**	**1**	**0**	**1**	**2**	**4**	**0**	**0**	**0**	**4**
	Colorado	CHL	74	5	18	23	151	....	....	....	....	....
1984-85	**Calgary**	**NHL**	**31**	**3**	**4**	**7**	**109**	....	....	....	....	....
	Moncton	AHL	34	6	9	15	101	....	....	....	....	....
1985-86	**Calgary**	**NHL**	**65**	**2**	**16**	**18**	**271**	**22**	**0**	**2**	**2**	**79**
	Moncton	AHL	4	1	1	2	21	....	....	....	....	....
1986-87	**Calgary**	**NHL**	**54**	**4**	**6**	**10**	**151**	**6**	**0**	**0**	**0**	**21**
1987-88	**Calgary**	**NHL**	**36**	**2**	**6**	**8**	**73**	....	....	....	....	....
	Hartford	**NHL**	**26**	**1**	**4**	**5**	**116**	**1**	**0**	**0**	**0**	**7**
1988-89	**Washington**	**NHL**	**72**	**3**	**4**	**7**	**179**	**6**	**0**	**0**	**0**	**19**
1989-90	**Washington**	**NHL**	**59**	**1**	**5**	**6**	**291**	**13**	**0**	**1**	**1**	**92**
	NHL Totals		**344**	**17**	**45**	**62**	**1192**	**52**	**0**	**3**	**3**	**222**

Signed as free agent by **Calgary**, August 16, 1983. Traded to **Hartford** by **Calgary** with Carey Wilson and the rights to Lane MacDonald for Dana Murzyn and Shane Churla, January 3, 1988. Traded to **Washington** by **Hartford** with Mike Millar for Grant Jennings and Ed Kastelic, July 6, 1988.

SHEPPARD, RAY

Right wing. Shoots right. 6'1", 180 lbs. Born, Pembroke, Ont., May 27, 1966.
(Buffalo's 3rd choice, 60th overall, in 1984 Entry Draft).

			Regular Season					Playoffs				
Season	Club	Lea	GP	G	A	TP	PIM	GP	G	A	TP	PIM
1983-84	Cornwall	OHL	68	44	36	80	69	....	....	....	....	....
1984-85	Cornwall	OHL	49	25	33	58	51	9	2	12	14	4
1985-86ab	Cornwall	OHL	63	*81	61	*142	25	6	7	4	11	0
1986-87	Rochester	AHL	55	18	13	31	11	15	12	3	15	2
1987-88c	**Buffalo**	**NHL**	**74**	**38**	**27**	**65**	**14**	**6**	**1**	**1**	**2**	**2**
1988-89	**Buffalo**	**NHL**	**67**	**22**	**21**	**43**	**15**	**1**	**0**	**1**	**1**	**0**
1989-90	**Buffalo**	**NHL**	**18**	**4**	**2**	**6**	**0**	....	....	....	....	....
	Rochester	AHL	5	3	5	8	2	17	8	7	15	9
	NHL Totals		**159**	**64**	**50**	**114**	**29**	**7**	**1**	**2**	**3**	**2**

a OHL Player of the Year (1986)
b OHL First All-Star Team (1986)
c NHL All-Rookie Team (1988)

Traded to **NY Rangers** by **Buffalo** for cash and future considerations, July 9, 1990.

SHIELDS, DAVID (DAVE)

Center. Shoots right. 5'9", 175 lbs. Born, Calgary, Alta., April 24, 1967.
(Minnesota's 12th choice, 235th overall, in 1987 Entry Draft).

			Regular Season					Playoffs				
Season	Club	Lea	GP	G	A	TP	PIM	GP	G	A	TP	PIM
1986-87	U. of Denver	WCHA	40	18	30	48	8	....	....	....	....	....
1987-88	U. of Denver	WCHA	21	10	7	17	2	....	....	....	....	....
1988-89	U. of Denver	WCHA	43	12	28	40	12	....	....	....	....	....
1989-90ab	U. of Denver	WCHA	42	31	43	74	24	....	....	....	....	....

a WCHA First All-Star Team (1990)
b NCAA West Second All-American Team (1990)

SHOEBOTTOM, BRUCE

Defense, Shoots left. 6'2", 200 lbs. Born, Windsor, Ont., August 20, 1965.
(Los Angeles' 1st choice, 47th overall, in 1983 Entry Draft).

			Regular Season					Playoffs				
Season	Club	Lea	GP	G	A	TP	PIM	GP	G	A	TP	PIM
1982-83	Peterborough	OHL	34	2	10	12	106	....	....	....	....	....
1983-84	Peterborough	OHL	16	0	5	5	73	....	....	....	....	....
1984-85	Perterborough	OHL	60	2	15	17	143	17	0	4	4	26
1985-86	New Haven	AHL	6	2	0	2	12	....	....	....	....	....
	Binghamton	AHL	62	7	5	12	249	....	....	....	....	....
1986-87	Fort Wayne	IHL	75	2	10	12	309	10	0	0	0	31
1987-88	**Boston**	**NHL**	**3**	**0**	**1**	**1**	**0**	**4**	**1**	**0**	**1**	**42**
	Maine	AHL	70	2	12	14	338	....	....	....	....	....
1988-89	**Boston**	**NHL**	**29**	**1**	**3**	**4**	**44**	**10**	**0**	**2**	**2**	**35**
	Maine	AHL	44	0	8	8	265	....	....	....	....	....
1989-90	**Boston**	**NHL**	**2**	**0**	**0**	**0**	**4**	....	....	....	....	....
1989-90	Maine	AHL	66	3	11	14	228	....	....	....	....	....
	NHL Totals		**34**	**1**	**4**	**5**	**48**	**14**	**1**	**2**	**3**	**77**

Traded to **Washington** by **Los Angeles** for Bryan Erickson, October 31, 1985. Signed as a free agent by **Boston**, July 20, 1987.

SHUCHUK, GARY

Right wing. Shoots right. 5'10", 185 lbs. Born, Edmonton, Alta., February 17, 1967.
(Detroit's 1st choice, 22nd overall, in 1988 Supplemental Draft).

			Regular Season					Playoffs				
Season	Club	Lea	GP	G	A	TP	PIM	GP	G	A	TP	PIM
1986-87	U. Wisconsin	WCHA	42	19	11	30	72	....	....	....	....	....
1987-88	U. Wisconsin	WCHA	44	7	22	29	70	....	....	....	....	....
1988-89	U. Wisconsin	WCHA	46	18	19	37	102	....	....	....	....	....
1989-90abc	U. Wisconsin	WCHA	45	*41	39	*80	70	....	....	....	....	....

a WCHA First All-Star Team (1990)
b WCHA Player of the Year (1990)
c NCAA West First All-American Team (1990)

SHUDRA, RON

Defense. Shoots left. 6'2", 192 lbs. Born, Winnipeg, Man., November 28, 1967.
(Edmonton's 3rd choice, 63rd overall, in 1986 Entry Draft).

			Regular Season					Playoffs				
Season	Club	Lea	GP	G	A	TP	PIM	GP	G	A	TP	PIM
1985-86a	Kamloops	WHL	72	10	40	50	81	16	1	11	12	11
1986-87	Kamloops	WHL	71	49	70	119	68	11	7	3	10	10
1987-88	**Edmonton**	**NHL**	**10**	**0**	**5**	**5**	**6**	....	....	....	....	....
	Nova Scotia	AHL	49	7	15	22	21	....	....	....	....	....
1988-89	Cape Breton	AHL	5	0	0	0	0	....	....	....	....	....
	Denver	IHL	64	11	14	25	44	2	0	0	0	0
1989-90	Fort Wayne	IHL	67	11	16	27	48	2	0	0	0	0
	NHL Totals		**10**	**0**	**5**	**5**	**6**	....	....	....	....	....

a WHL Rookie of the Year (1986)

Traded to **NY Rangers** by **Edmonton** for Jeff Crossman, October 27, 1988.

SHUTE, DAVID

Center. Shoots left. 5'11", 185 lbs. Born, Carlisle, PA, February 10, 1971.
(Pittsburgh's 9th choice, 163rd overall, in 1989 Entry Draft).

			Regular Season					Playoffs				
Season	Club	Lea	GP	G	A	TP	PIM	GP	G	A	TP	PIM
1988-89	Victoria	WHL	69	5	11	16	26	8	0	1	1	10
1989-90	Victoria	WHL	14	4	5	9	25	....	....	....	....	....
	Medicine Hat	WHL	48	13	15	28	56	....	....	....	....	....

SIDOROV, ANDREI

Right wing. Shoots right. 5'10", 185 lbs. Born, Soviet Union, May 15, 1969.
(Washington's 10th choice, 229th overall, in 1989 Entry Draft).

			Regular Season					Playoffs				
Season	Club	Lea	GP	G	A	TP	PIM	GP	G	A	TP	PIM
1989-90	Dynamo Harkov	USSR	29	6	5	11	14	....	....	....	....	....

SILLINGER, MIKE

Center. Shoots right. 5'10", 190 lbs. Born, Regina, Sask., June 29, 1971.
(Detroit's 1st choice, 11th overall, in 1989 Entry Draft).

			Regular Season					Playoffs				
Season	Club	Lea	GP	G	A	TP	PIM	GP	G	A	TP	PIM
1987-88	Regina	WHL	67	18	25	43	17	4	2	2	4	0
1988-89	Regina	WHL	72	53	78	131	52	....	....	....	....	....
1989-90a	Regina	WHL	70	57	72	129	41	11	12	10	22	2
	Adirondack	AHL	....	....	....	....	....	1	0	0	0	0

a WHL East Second All-Star Team (1990)

SIM, TREVOR

Center. Shoots right. 6'2", 192 lbs. Born, Calgary, Alta., June 9, 1970.
(Edmonton's 2nd choice, 53rd overall, in 1988 Entry Draft).

			Regular Season					Playoffs				
Season	Club	Lea	GP	G	A	TP	PIM	GP	G	A	TP	PIM
1987-88	Seattle	WHL	67	17	18	35	87	....	....	....	....	....
1988-89	Swift Current	WHL	63	20	27	47	117	11	10	6	16	20
1989-90	**Edmonton**	**NHL**	**3**	**0**	**1**	**1**	**2**	....	....	....	....	....
	Swift Current	WHL	6	3	2	5	21	....	....	....	....	....
	Kamloops	WHL	43	27	35	62	53	17	3	13	16	28
	NHL Totals		**3**	**0**	**1**	**1**	**2**	....	....	....	....	....

SIMARD, MARTIN

Right wing. Shoots right. 6'3", 215 lbs. Born, Montreal, Que., June 25, 1966.

			Regular Season					Playoffs				
Season	Club	Lea	GP	G	A	TP	PIM	GP	G	A	TP	PIM
1984-85	Granby	QMJHL	58	22	31	53	78	8	3	7	10	21
1985-86	Granby	QMJHL	54	32	28	69	129	....	....	....	....	....
	Hull	QMJHL	14	8	8	16	55	14	8	19	27	19
1986-87	Granby	QMJHL	41	30	47	77	105	8	3	7	10	21
1987-88	Salt Lake	IHL	82	8	23	31	281	19	6	3	9	100
1988-89	Salt Lake	IHL	71	13	15	28	221	14	4	0	4	45
1989-90	Salt Lake	IHL	59	22	23	45	151	11	5	8	13	12

Signed as a free agent by **Calgary**, May 19, 1987.

SIMON, CHRIS

Left wing. Shoots left. 6'3", 220 lbs. Born, Wawa, Ont., January 30, 1972.
(Philadelphia's 2nd choice, 25th overall, in 1990 Entry Draft).

			Regular Season					Playoffs				
Season	Club	Lea	GP	G	A	TP	PIM	GP	G	A	TP	PIM
1988-89	Ottawa	OHL	36	4	2	6	31	....	....	....	....	....
1989-90	Ottawa	OHL	57	36	38	74	146	3	2	1	3	4

SIMON, JASON

Left wing. Shoots left. 6'1", 190 lbs. Born, Sarnia, Ont., March 21, 1969.
(New Jersey's 9th choice, 215th overall, in 1989 Entry Draft).

			Regular Season					Playoffs				
Season	Club	Lea	GP	G	A	TP	PIM	GP	G	A	TP	PIM
1986-87	London	OHL	33	1	2	3	33	....	....	....	....	....
	Sudbury	OHL	26	2	3	5	50	....	....	....	....	....
1987-88	Sudbury	OHL	26	5	7	12	35	....	....	....	....	....
	Hamilton	OHL	29	5	13	18	124	11	0	2	2	15
1988-89	Windsor	OHL	62	23	39	62	193	4	1	4	5	13
1989-90	Utica	AHL	16	3	4	7	28	2	0	0	0	12

SIMPSON, CRAIG

Center. Shoots right. 6'2", 195 lbs. Born, London, Ont., February 15, 1967.
(Pittsburgh's 1st choice, 2nd overall, in 1985 Entry Draft)

			Regular Season					Playoffs				
Season	Club	Lea	GP	G	A	TP	PIM	GP	G	A	TP	PIM
1983-84	Michigan State	CCHA	46	14	43	57	38	....	....	....	....	....
1984-85ab	Michigan State	CCHA	42	31	53	84	33	....	....	....	....	....
1985-86	**Pittsburgh**	**NHL**	**76**	**11**	**17**	**28**	**49**	....	....	....	....	....
1986-87	**Pittsburgh**	**NHL**	**72**	**26**	**25**	**51**	**57**	....	....	....	....	....
1987-88	**Pittsburgh**	**NHL**	**21**	**13**	**13**	**26**	**34**	....	....	....	....	....
	Edmonton	**NHL**	**59**	**43**	**21**	**64**	**43**	**19**	**13**	**6**	**19**	**26**
1988-89	**Edmonton**	**NHL**	**66**	**35**	**41**	**76**	**80**	**7**	**2**	**0**	**2**	**10**
1989-90	**Edmonton**	**NHL**	**80**	**29**	**32**	**61**	**180**	**22**	***16**	**15**	***31**	**8**
	NHL Totals		**374**	**157**	**149**	**306**	**443**	**48**	**31**	**21**	**52**	**44**

a CCHA First All-Star Team (1985)
b NCAA All-American (1985)

Traded to **Edmonton** by **Pittsburgh** with Dave Hannan, Moe Mantha and Chris Joseph for Paul Coffey, Dave Hunter and Wayne Van Dorp, November 24, 1987.

SIMPSON, GEOFF

Defense. Shoots right. 6'1", 180 lbs. Born, Victoria, B.C., March 6, 1969.
(Boston's 10th choice, 206th overall, in 1989 Entry Draft).

			Regular Season					Playoffs				
Season	Club	Lea	GP	G	A	TP	PIM	GP	G	A	TP	PIM
1988-89	Estevan	SJHL	63	20	53	73	57	....	....	....	....	....
1989-90	N. Michigan	WCHA	39	4	19	23	40	....	....	....	....	....

SIMPSON, REID

Left wing. Shoots left. 6'1", 210 lbs. Born, Flin Flon, Man., May 21, 1969.
(Philadelphia's 3rd choice, 72nd overall, in 1989 Entry Draft).

			Regular Season					Playoffs				
Season	Club	Lea	GP	G	A	TP	PIM	GP	G	A	TP	PIM
1987-88	Prince Albert	WHL	72	13	14	27	164	10	1	0	1	43
1988-89	Prince Albert	WHL	59	26	29	55	264	4	2	1	3	30
1989-90	Prince Albert	WHL	29	15	17	32	121	14	4	7	11	34

SINISALO, ILKKA (sin-i-SAL-oh)

Left wing. Shoots left. 6'1", 200 lbs. Born, Valeakoski, Finland, July 10, 1958.

			Regular Season					Playoffs				
Season	Club	Lea	GP	G	A	TP	PIM	GP	G	A	TP	PIM
1977-78	IFK	Fin.	36	9	3	12	18	....	....	....	....	....
1978-79	IFK	Fin.	30	6	4	10	16	6	0	5	5	25
1979-80	IFK	Fin.	35	16	9	25	16	7	1	3	4	12
1980-81	IFK	Fin.	36	27	17	44	14	6	5	3	8	4
1981-82	**Philadelphia**	**NHL**	**66**	**15**	**22**	**37**	**22**	**4**	**0**	**2**	**2**	**0**
1982-83	**Philadelphia**	**NHL**	**61**	**21**	**29**	**50**	**16**	**3**	**1**	**1**	**2**	**0**
1983-84	**Philadelphia**	**NHL**	**73**	**29**	**17**	**46**	**29**	**2**	**2**	**0**	**2**	**0**
1984-85	**Philadelphia**	**NHL**	**70**	**36**	**37**	**73**	**16**	**19**	**6**	**1**	**7**	**0**
1985-86	**Philadelphia**	**NHL**	**74**	**39**	**37**	**76**	**31**	**5**	**2**	**2**	**4**	**2**
1986-87	**Philadelphia**	**NHL**	**42**	**10**	**21**	**31**	**8**	**18**	**5**	**1**	**6**	**4**
1987-88	**Philadelphia**	**NHL**	**68**	**25**	**17**	**42**	**30**	**7**	**4**	**2**	**6**	**0**
1988-89	**Philadelphia**	**NHL**	**13**	**1**	**6**	**7**	**2**	**8**	**1**	**1**	**2**	**0**
1989-90	**Philadelphia**	**NHL**	**59**	**23**	**23**	**46**	**26**	....	....	....	....	....
	NHL Totals		**526**	**199**	**209**	**408**	**180**	**66**	**21**	**10**	**31**	**6**

Signed as free agent by **Philadelphia**, February 14, 1981. Signed as a free agent by **Minnesota**, July 3, 1990.

SIREN, VILLE

Defense. Shoots left. 6'1", 185 lbs. Born, Tampere, Finland, February 10, 1964.
(Hartford's 3rd choice, 23rd overall, in 1983 Entry Draft).

			Regular Season					Playoffs				
Season	Club	Lea	GP	G	A	TP	PIM	GP	G	A	TP	PIM
1982-83	Ilves	Fin.	29	3	2	5	42	8	1	3	4	8
1983-84	Ilves	Fin.	36	1	10	11	40	2	0	0	0	2
	Fin. Olympic	....	2	0	0	0	0	....	....	....	....	....
1984-85	Ilves	Fin	36	11	13	24	24	9	0	2	2	10
1985-86	**Pittsburgh**	**NHL**	**60**	**4**	**8**	**12**	**32**	....	....	....	....	....
1986-87	**Pittsburgh**	**NHL**	**69**	**5**	**17**	**22**	**50**	....	....	....	....	....
1987-88	**Pittsburgh**	**NHL**	**58**	**1**	**20**	**21**	**62**	....	....	....	....	....
1988-89	**Pittsburgh**	**NHL**	**12**	**1**	**0**	**1**	**14**	....	....	....	....	....
	Minnesota	**NHL**	**38**	**2**	**10**	**12**	**58**	**4**	**0**	**0**	**0**	**4**
1989-90	**Minnesota**	**NHL**	**53**	**1**	**13**	**14**	**60**	**3**	**0**	**0**	**0**	**2**
	NHL Totals		**290**	**14**	**68**	**82**	**276**	**7**	**0**	**0**	**0**	**6**

Traded to **Pittsburgh** by **Hartford** for Pat Boutette, November 16, 1984. Traded to **Minnesota** by **Pittsburgh** with Steve Gotaas for Gord Dineen and Scott Bjugstad, December 17, 1988.

SJODIN, TOMMY

Defense. Shoots right. 5'11", 180 lbs. Born, Sundsvall, Sweden, August 13, 1965.
(Minnesota's 10th choice, 237th overall, in 1985 Entry Draft).

			Regular Season					Playoffs				
Season	Club	Lea	GP	G	A	TP	PIM	GP	G	A	TP	PIM
1987-88	Brynas	Swe.	40	6	9	15	28	....	....	....	....	....
1988-89	Brynas	Swe.	40	8	11	19	54	....	....	....	....	....
1989-90	Brynas	Swe.	40	14	14	28	46	5	0	0	0	2

SJOGREN, THOMAS

Right wing. Shoots right. 5'9", 180 lbs. Born, Teg, Sweden, June 8, 1968.
(Washington's 7th choice, 162nd overall, in 1987 Entry Draft).

			Regular Season					Playoffs				
Season	Club	Lea	GP	G	A	TP	PIM	GP	G	A	TP	PIM
1987-88	V. Frolunda	Swe. 2	36	36	27	63	42	10	6	6	12	8
1988-89	Sodertalje	Swe.	40	23	19	42	22	....	....	....	....	....
1989-90	Sodertalje	Swe.	33	7	8	15	14	2	0	1	1	0

SKALDE, JARROD

Center. Shoots left. 6'0", 170 lbs. Born, Niagara Falls, Ont., February 26, 1971.
(New Jersey's 3rd choice, 26th overall, in 1989 Entry Draft).

			Regular Season					Playoffs				
Season	Club	Lea	GP	G	A	TP	PIM	GP	G	A	TP	PIM
1987-88	Oshawa	OHL	60	12	16	28	24	7	2	1	3	2
1988-89	Oshawa	OHL	65	38	38	76	36	6	1	5	6	2
1989-90	Oshawa	OHL	62	40	52	92	66	17	10	7	17	6

SKARDA, RANDY

Defense. Shoots right. 6'1", 195 lbs. Born, St. Paul, MN, May 5, 1968.
(St. Louis' 8th choice, 157th overall, in 1986 Entry Draft).

			Regular Season					Playoffs				
Season	Club	Lea	GP	G	A	TP	PIM	GP	G	A	TP	PIM
1986-87	U. Minnesota	WCHA	43	3	10	13	77	....	....	....	....	....
1987-88ab	U. Minnesota	WCHA	42	19	26	45	102	....	....	....	....	....
1988-89	U. Minnesota	WCHA	43	6	24	30	91	....	....	....	....	....
1989-90	**St. Louis**	**NHL**	**25**	**0**	**5**	**5**	**11**	....	....	....	....	....
	Peoria	IHL	38	7	17	24	40	4	0	0	0	0
	NHL Totals		**25**	**0**	**5**	**5**	**11**	....	....	....	....	....

a NCAA West Second All-American Team (1988)
b WCHA First All-Star Team (1988)

SKRIKO, PETRI

Left wing. Shoots left. 5'10", 175 lbs. Born, Lapeenranta, Finland, March 12, 1962.
(Vancouver's 7th choice, 157th overall, in 1981 Entry Draft)

			Regular Season					Playoffs				
Season	Club	Lea	GP	G	A	TP	PIM	GP	G	A	TP	PIM
1981-82	SaiPa	Fin.	33	19	27	46	24	....	....	....	....	....
1982-83	SaiPa	Fin.	36	23	12	35	12	....	....	....	....	....
1983-84	SaiPa	Fin.	32	25	26	51	13	....	....	....	....	....
	Fin. Olympic	....	7	1	1	2	0	....	....	....	....	....
1984-85	**Vancouver**	**NHL**	**72**	**21**	**14**	**35**	**10**	....	....	....	....	....
1985-86	**Vancouver**	**NHL**	**80**	**38**	**40**	**78**	**34**	**3**	**0**	**0**	**0**	**0**
1986-87	**Vancouver**	**NHL**	**76**	**33**	**41**	**74**	**44**	....	....	....	....	....
1987-88	**Vancouver**	**NHL**	**73**	**30**	**34**	**64**	**32**	....	....	....	....	....
1988-89	**Vancouver**	**NHL**	**74**	**30**	**36**	**66**	**57**	**7**	**1**	**5**	**6**	**0**
1989-90	**Vancouver**	**NHL**	**77**	**15**	**33**	**48**	**36**	....	....	....	....	....
	NHL Totals		**452**	**167**	**198**	**365**	**213**	**10**	**1**	**5**	**6**	**0**

SKRUDLAND, BRIAN (SKROOD-luhnd)

Center. Shoots left. 6', 196 lbs. Born, Peace River, Alta., July 31, 1963.

			Regular Season					Playoffs				
Season	Club	Lea	GP	G	A	TP	PIM	GP	G	A	TP	PIM
1980-81	Saskatoon	WHL	66	15	27	42	97	....	....	....	....	....
1981-82	Saskatoon	WHL	71	27	29	56	135	5	0	1	1	2
1982-83	Saskatoon	WHL	71	35	59	94	42	6	1	3	4	19
1983-84	Nova Scotia	AHL	56	13	12	25	55	12	2	8	10	14
1984-85	Sherbrooke	AHL	70	22	28	50	109	17	9	8	17	23
1985-86	**Montreal**	**NHL**	**65**	**9**	**13**	**22**	**57**	**20**	**2**	**4**	**6**	**76**
1986-87	**Montreal**	**NHL**	**79**	**11**	**17**	**28**	**107**	**14**	**1**	**5**	**6**	**29**
1987-88	**Montreal**	**NHL**	**79**	**12**	**24**	**36**	**112**	**11**	**1**	**5**	**6**	**24**
1988-89	**Montreal**	**NHL**	**71**	**12**	**29**	**41**	**84**	**21**	**3**	**7**	**10**	**40**
1989-90	**Montreal**	**NHL**	**59**	**11**	**31**	**42**	**56**	**11**	**3**	**5**	**8**	**30**
	NHL Totals		**353**	**55**	**114**	**169**	**416**	**77**	**10**	**26**	**36**	**199**

Signed as a free agent by **Montreal**, September 13, 1983.

SLANEY, JOHN

Defense. Shoots left. 6', 190 lbs. Born, St. John's, Nfld., February 7, 1972.
(Washington's 1st choice, 9th overall, in 1990 Entry Draft).

			Regular Season					Playoffs				
Season	Club	Lea	GP	G	A	TP	PIM	GP	G	A	TP	PIM
1988-89	Cornwall	OHL	66	16	43	59	23	18	8	16	24	10
1989-90a	Cornwall	OHL	64	38	59	97	68	6	0	8	8	11

a OHL First All-Star Team (1990)

SLANINA, PETER

Defense. Shoots right. 6'2", 185 lbs. Born, Czechoslovakia, December 16, 1959.
(Toronto's 11th choice, 233rd overall, in 1984 Entry Draft).

			Regular Season					Playoffs				
Season	Club	Lea	GP	G	A	TP	PIM	GP	G	A	TP	PIM
1986-87	VSZ Kosice	Czech.	33	11	7	18	....	....	....	....	....	....
1987-88	VSZ Kosice	Czech.	34	7	15	22	....	....	....	....	....	....
1988-89	VSZ Kosice	Czech.	42	12	24	36	....	....	....	....	....	....
1989-90	KalPa	Fin.	39	12	17	29	45	6	0	0	0	4

SLEGR, JIRI

Defense. Shoots left. 5'11", 185 lbs. Born, Litvinov, Czechoslovakia, May 30, 1971.
(Vancouver's 3rd choice, 23rd overall, in 1990 Entry Draft).

			Regular Season					Playoffs				
Season	Club	Lea	GP	G	A	TP	PIM	GP	G	A	TP	PIM
1988-89	Litvinov	Czech.	8	0	0	0	....	....	....	....	....	....
1989-90	Litvinov	Czech.	51	4	15	19	....	....	....	....	....	....

SMAIL, DOUGLAS (DOUG)

Left wing. Shoots left. 5'9", 175 lbs. Born, Moose Jaw, Sask., September 2, 1957.

			Regular Season					Playoffs				
Season	Club	Lea	GP	G	A	TP	PIM	GP	G	A	TP	PIM
1978-79	North Dakota	WCHA	35	24	34	58	46	....	....	....	....	....
1979-80ab	North Dakota	WCHA	40	43	44	87	70	....	....	....	....	....
1980-81	**Winnipeg**	**NHL**	**30**	**10**	**8**	**18**	**45**	....	....	....	....	....
1981-82	**Winnipeg**	**NHL**	**72**	**17**	**18**	**35**	**55**	**4**	**0**	**0**	**0**	**0**
1982-83	**Winnipeg**	**NHL**	**80**	**15**	**29**	**44**	**32**	**3**	**0**	**0**	**0**	**6**
1983-84	**Winnipeg**	**NHL**	**66**	**20**	**17**	**37**	**62**	**3**	**0**	**1**	**1**	**7**
1984-85	**Winnipeg**	**NHL**	**80**	**31**	**35**	**66**	**45**	**8**	**2**	**1**	**3**	**4**
1985-86	**Winnipeg**	**NHL**	**73**	**16**	**26**	**42**	**32**	**3**	**1**	**0**	**1**	**0**
1986-87	**Winnipeg**	**NHL**	**78**	**25**	**18**	**43**	**36**	**10**	**4**	**0**	**4**	**10**
1987-88	**Winnipeg**	**NHL**	**71**	**15**	**16**	**31**	**34**	**5**	**1**	**0**	**1**	**22**
1988-89	**Winnipeg**	**NHL**	**47**	**14**	**15**	**29**	**52**	....	....	....	....	....
1989-90	**Winnipeg**	**NHL**	**79**	**25**	**24**	**49**	**63**	**5**	**1**	**0**	**1**	**0**
	NHL Totals		**676**	**188**	**206**	**394**	**456**	**41**	**9**	**2**	**11**	**49**

a WCHA Second All-Star Team (1980).
b Most Valuable Player, NCAA Tournament (1980).
Played in NHL All-Star Game (1990)
Signed as free agent by **Winnipeg**, May 22, 1980.

SMART, JASON

Center. Shoots left. 6'4", 210 lbs. Born, Prince George, B.C., January 23, 1970.
(Pittsburgh's 13th choice, 247th overall, in 1989 Entry Draft).

			Regular Season					Playoffs				
Season	Club	Lea	GP	G	A	TP	PIM	GP	G	A	TP	PIM
1986-87	Prince Albert	WHL	57	9	22	31	62	8	3	3	6	8
1987-88	Prince Albert	WHL	72	16	29	45	77	10	1	2	3	11
1988-89	Prince Albert	WHL	12	1	3	4	31	....	....	....	....	....
	Saskatoon	WHL	36	6	17	23	33	8	1	6	7	16
1989-90	Saskatoon	WHL	66	27	48	75	187	10	1	5	6	19

SMITH, DARIN

Left wing. Shoots left. 6'2", 205 lbs. Born, Vineland Station, Ont., February 20, 1967.
(St. Louis' 4th choice, 75th overall, in 1987 Entry Draft).

			Regular Season					Playoffs				
Season	Club	Lea	GP	G	A	TP	PIM	GP	G	A	TP	PIM
1986-87	North Bay	OHL	59	22	25	47	142	23	3	8	11	84
1987-88	Peoria	IHL	81	21	23	44	144	7	1	2	3	16
1988-89	Peoria	IHL	62	13	17	30	127	4	1	0	1	7
1989-90	Peoria	IHL	76	16	13	29	147	....	....	....	....	....

SMITH, DENNIS

Defense. Shoots left. 5'11", 190 lbs. Born, Detroit, MI, July 27, 1964.

			Regular Season					Playoffs				
Season	Club	Lea	GP	G	A	TP	PIM	GP	G	A	TP	PIM
1981-82	Kingston	OHL	48	2	24	26	84	4	0	2	2	0
1982-83	Kingston	OHL	58	6	30	36	100	....	....	....	....	....
1983-84	Kingston	OHL	62	10	41	51	165	....	....	....	....	....
1984-85	Osby	Swe.	30	15	15	30	74	....	....	....	....	....
1985-86	Peoria	IHL	70	5	15	20	102	10	0	2	2	18
1986-87	Adirondack	AHL	64	4	24	28	120	6	0	0	0	8
1987-88	Adirondack	AHL	75	6	24	30	213	11	2	2	4	47
1988-89	Adirondack	AHL	75	5	35	40	176	17	1	6	7	47
1989-90	**Washington**	**NHL**	**4**	**0**	**0**	**0**	**0**	....	....	....	....	....
a	Baltimore	AHL	74	8	25	33	103	12	0	3	3	65
	NHL Totals		**4**	**0**	**0**	**0**	**0**	....	....	....	....	....

a AHL Second All-Star Team (1990)

Signed as a free agent by **Detroit**, December 2, 1986. Signed as a free agent by **Washington**, July 25, 1989.

SMITH, DERRICK

Left wing. Shoots left. 6'2", 215 lbs. Born, Scarborough, Ont., January 22, 1965.
(Philadelphia's 2nd choice, 44th overall, in 1983 Entry Draft).

			Regular Season					Playoffs				
Season	Club	Lea	GP	G	A	TP	PIM	GP	G	A	TP	PIM
1982-83	Peterborough	OHL	70	16	19	35	47	....	....	....	....	....
1983-84	Peterborough	OHL	70	30	36	66	31	8	4	4	8	7
1984-85	**Philadelphia**	**NHL**	**77**	**17**	**22**	**39**	**31**	**19**	**2**	**5**	**7**	**16**
1985-86	**Philadelphia**	**NHL**	**69**	**6**	**6**	**12**	**57**	**4**	**0**	**0**	**0**	**10**
1986-87	**Philadelphia**	**NHL**	**71**	**11**	**21**	**32**	**34**	**26**	**6**	**4**	**10**	**26**
1987-88	**Philadelphia**	**NHL**	**76**	**16**	**8**	**24**	**104**	**7**	**0**	**0**	**0**	**6**
1988-89	**Philadelphia**	**NHL**	**74**	**16**	**14**	**30**	**43**	**19**	**5**	**2**	**7**	**12**
1989-90	**Philadelphia**	**NHL**	**55**	**3**	**6**	**9**	**32**	....	....	....	....	....
	NHL Totals		**422**	**69**	**77**	**146**	**301**	**75**	**13**	**11**	**24**	**70**

SMITH, DOUGLAS ERIC (DOUG)

Center. Shoots right. 5'11", 186 lbs. Born, Ottawa, Ont., May 17, 1963.
(Los Angeles' 1st choice, 2nd overall, in 1981 Entry Draft).

			Regular Season					Playoffs				
Season	Club	Lea	GP	G	A	TP	PIM	GP	G	A	TP	PIM
1979-80	Ottawa	OHA	64	23	34	57	45	11	2	0	2	33
1980-81	Ottawa	OHA	54	45	56	101	61	7	5	6	11	13
1981-82	**Los Angeles**	**NHL**	**80**	**16**	**14**	**30**	**64**	**10**	**3**	**2**	**5**	**11**
1982-83	**Los Angeles**	**NHL**	**42**	**11**	**11**	**22**	**12**	....	....	....	....	....
1983-84	**Los Angeles**	**NHL**	**72**	**16**	**20**	**36**	**28**	....	....	....	....	....
1984-85	**Los Angeles**	**NHL**	**62**	**21**	**20**	**41**	**58**	**3**	**1**	**0**	**1**	**4**
1985-86	**Los Angeles**	**NHL**	**48**	**8**	**9**	**17**	**56**	....	....	....	....	....
	Buffalo	**NHL**	**30**	**10**	**11**	**21**	**73**	....	....	....	....	....
1986-87	**Buffalo**	**NHL**	**62**	**16**	**24**	**40**	**106**	....	....	....	....	....
	Rochester	AHL	15	5	6	11	35	....	....	....	....	....
1987-88	**Buffalo**	**NHL**	**70**	**9**	**19**	**28**	**117**	**1**	**0**	**0**	**0**	**0**
1988-89	**Edmonton**	**NHL**	**19**	**1**	**1**	**2**	**9**	....	....	....	....	....
	Cape Breton	AHL	24	11	11	22	69	....	....	....	....	....
	Vancouver	**NHL**	**10**	**3**	**4**	**7**	**4**	**4**	**0**	**0**	**0**	**6**
1989-90	**Vancouver**	**NHL**	**30**	**3**	**4**	**7**	**72**	....	....	....	....	....
1989-90	**Pittsburgh**	**NHL**	**10**	**1**	**1**	**2**	**25**	....	....	....	....	....
	NHL Totals		**535**	**115**	**138**	**253**	**624**	**18**	**4**	**2**	**6**	**21**

Traded to **Buffalo** by **Los Angeles** with Brian Engblom for Sean McKenna, Larry Playfair and Ken Baumgartner, January 30, 1986. Claimed by **Edmonton** in NHL Waiver Draft, October 3, 1988. Traded to **Vancouver** by **Edmonton** with Gregory C. Adams for Jean LeBlanc and Vancouver's fifth round choice (Peter White) in 1989 Entry Draft, March 7, 1989. Traded to **Pittsburgh** by **Vancouver** for cash, February 26, 1990.

SMITH, GEOFF

Defense. Shoots left. 6'3", 190 lbs. Born, Edmonton, Alta., March 7, 1969.
(Edmonton's 3rd choice, 63rd overall, in 1987 Entry Draft).

			Regular Season					Playoffs				
Season	Club	Lea	GP	G	A	TP	PIM	GP	G	A	TP	PIM
1987-88	North Dakota	WCHA	42	4	12	16	34	....	....	....	....	....
1988-89	North Dakota	WCHA	9	0	1	1	8	....	....	....	....	....
	Kamloops	WHL	32	4	31	35	29	6	1	3	4	12
1989-90a	**Edmonton**	**NHL**	**74**	**4**	**11**	**15**	**52**	**3**	**0**	**0**	**0**	**0**
	NHL Totals		**74**	**4**	**11**	**15**	**52**	**3**	**0**	**0**	**0**	**0**

a NHL All-Rookie Team (1990)

SMITH, JAMES STEPHEN (STEVE)

Defense. Shoots left. 6'4", 215 lbs. Born, Glasgow, Scotland, April 30, 1963.
(Edmonton's 5th choice, 111th overall, in 1981 Entry Draft).

			Regular Season					Playoffs				
Season	Club	Lea	GP	G	A	TP	PIM	GP	G	A	TP	PIM
1980-81	London	OHA	62	4	12	16	141	....	....	....	....	....
1981-82	London	OHL	58	10	36	46	207	4	1	2	3	13
1982-83	Moncton	AHL	2	0	0	0	0	....	....	....	....	....
	London	OHL	50	6	35	41	133	3	1	0	1	10
1983-84	Moncton	AHL	64	1	8	9	176	....	....	....	....	....
1984-85	**Edmonton**	**NHL**	**2**	**0**	**0**	**0**	**2**	....	....	....	....	....
	Nova Scotia	AHL	68	2	28	30	161	5	0	3	3	40
1985-86	**Edmonton**	**NHL**	**55**	**4**	**20**	**24**	**166**	**6**	**0**	**1**	**1**	**14**
	Nova Scotia	AHL	4	0	2	2	11	....	....	....	....	....
1986-87	**Edmonton**	**NHL**	**62**	**7**	**15**	**22**	**165**	**15**	**1**	**3**	**4**	**45**
1987-88	**Edmonton**	**NHL**	**79**	**12**	**43**	**55**	**286**	**19**	**1**	**11**	**12**	**55**
1988-89	**Edmonton**	**NHL**	**35**	**3**	**19**	**22**	**97**	**7**	**2**	**2**	**4**	**20**
1989-90	**Edmonton**	**NHL**	**75**	**7**	**34**	**41**	**171**	**22**	**5**	**10**	**15**	**37**
	NHL Totals		**308**	**33**	**131**	**164**	**887**	**69**	**9**	**27**	**36**	**171**

SMITH, NATHAN (NATE)

Defense. Shoots left. 6'1", 190 lbs. Born, Brunswick, ME, July 13, 1967.
(Calgary's 9th choice, 164th overall in 1985 Entry Draft).

			Regular Season					Playoffs				
Season	Club	Lea	GP	G	A	TP	PIM	GP	G	A	TP	PIM
1986-87	Princeton	ECAC	25	0	3	3	10	....	....	....	....	....
1987-88	Princeton	ECAC	27	0	6	6	6	....	....	....	....	....
1988-89	Princeton	ECAC	24	1	5	6	12	....	....	....	....	....
1989-90	Princeton	ECAC	23	2	3	5	8	....	....	....	....	....

SMITH, RANDY

Center. Shoots left. 6'4", 200 lbs. Born, Saskatoon, Sask., July 7, 1965.

			Regular Season					Playoffs				
Season	Club	Lea	GP	G	A	TP	PIM	GP	G	A	TP	PIM
1983-84	Saskatoon	WHL	69	19	21	40	53	....	....	....	....	....
1984-85	Saskatoon	WHL	71	34	51	85	26	8	4	3	7	0
1985-86	Saskatoon	WHL	70	60	86	146	44	9	4	9	13	4
	Minnesota	**NHL**	**1**	**0**	**0**	**0**	**0**	....	....	....	....	....
1986-87	**Minnesota**	**NHL**	**2**	**0**	**0**	**0**	**0**	....	....	....	....	....
	Springfield	AHL	75	20	44	64	24	....	....	....	....	....
1987-88	Kalamazoo	IHL	77	13	43	56	54	6	0	8	8	2
1988-89	Maine	AHL	33	9	16	25	34	....	....	....	....	....
	Kalamazoo	IHL	23	4	9	13	2	....	....	....	....	....
1989-90	Kalamazoo	IHL	8	1	2	3	12	....	....	....	....	....
	Salt Lake	IHL	30	5	6	11	10	3	0	0	0	0
	NHL Totals		**3**	**0**	**0**	**0**	**0**	....	....	....	....	....

Signed as a free agent by **Minnesota**, May 12, 1986.

SMITH, ROBERT DAVID (BOBBY)

Center. Shoots left. 6'4", 210 lbs. Born, North Sydney, N.S., February 12, 1958.
(Minnesota's 1st choice and 1st overall in 1978 Amateur Draft).

			Regular Season					Playoffs				
Season	Club	Lea	GP	G	A	TP	PIM	GP	G	A	TP	PIM
1976-77a	Ottawa	OHA	64	*65	70	135	52	19	16	16	32	29
1977-78bc	Ottawa	OHA	61	69	*123	*192	44	16	15	15	30	10
1978-79d	Minnesota	NHL	80	30	44	74	39	....	....	....	....	....
1979-80	Minnesota	NHL	61	27	56	83	24	15	1	13	14	9
1980-81	Minnesota	NHL	78	29	64	93	73	19	8	17	25	13
1981-82	Minnesota	NHL	80	43	71	114	82	4	2	4	6	5
1982-83	Minnesota	NHL	77	24	53	77	81	9	6	4	10	17
1983-84	Minnesota	NHL	10	3	6	9	9	....	....	....	....	....
	Montreal	NHL	70	26	37	63	62	15	2	7	9	8
1984-85	Montreal	NHL	65	16	40	56	59	12	5	6	11	30
1985-86	Montreal	NHL	79	31	55	86	55	20	7	8	15	22
1986-87	Montreal	NHL	80	28	47	75	72	17	9	9	18	19
1987-88	Montreal	NHL	78	27	66	93	78	11	3	4	7	8
1988-89	Montreal	NHL	80	32	51	83	69	21	11	8	19	46
1989-90	Montreal	NHL	53	12	14	26	35	11	1	4	5	6
	NHL Totals		891	328	604	932	738	154	55	84	139	183

a OHA Second All-Star Team (1977)
b OHA First All-Star Team (1978)
c Named Canadian Major Junior Player of the Year (1978)
d Won Calder Memorial Trophy (1979)

Played in NHL All-Star Game (1981, 1982, 1989)

Traded to **Montreal** by **Minnesota** for Keith Acton, Mark Napier and Toronto's third round choice (Ken Hodge) in 1984 Entry Draft — Montreal's property via earlier deal — October 28, 1983. Traded to **Minnesota** by **Montreal** for Minnesota's fourth round choice in the 1992 Entry Draft, August 7, 1990.

SMITH, SANDY

Right wing. Shoots right. 5'11", 185 lbs. Born, Brainerd, MN, October 23, 1967.
(Pittsburgh's 5th choice, 88th overall, in 1986 Entry Draft).

			Regular Season					Playoffs				
Season	Club	Lea	GP	G	A	TP	PIM	GP	G	A	TP	PIM
1986-87	Minn.-Duluth	WCHA	35	3	3	6	26	....	....	....	....	....
1987-88	Minn.-Duluth	WCHA	41	22	9	31	47	....	....	....	....	....
1988-89	Minn.-Duluth	WCHA	40	6	16	22	75	....	....	....	....	....
1989-90	Minn.-Duluth	WCHA	39	15	16	31	53	....	....	....	....	....
	Muskegon	IHL	3	1	0	1	0	....	....	....	....	....

SMITH, STEVE

Defense. Shoots left. 5'9", 195 lbs. Born, Trenton, Ont., April 4, 1963.
(Philadelphia's 1st choice, 16th overall, in 1981 Entry Draft).

			Regular Season					Playoffs				
Season	Club	Lea	GP	G	A	TP	PIM	GP	G	A	TP	PIM
1980-81a	S. S. Marie	OHA	61	3	37	40	143	19	0	6	6	60
1981-82	Philadelphia	NHL	8	0	1	1	0	....	....	....	....	....
b	S. S. Marie	OHL	50	7	20	27	179	12	0	2	2	23
1982-83b	S. S. Marie	OHL	55	11	33	44	139	16	0	8	8	28
1983-84	Springfield	AHL	70	4	25	29	77	4	0	0	0	0
1984-85	Philadelphia	NHL	2	0	0	0	7	....	....	....	....	....
	Hershey	AHL	65	10	20	30	83	....	....	....	....	....
1985-86	Philadelphia	NHL	2	0	0	0	2	....	....	....	....	....
	Hershey	AHL	49	1	11	12	96	16	2	4	6	43
1986-87	Philadelphia	NHL	2	0	0	0	6	....	....	....	....	....
	Hershey	AHL	66	11	26	37	191	5	0	2	2	8
1987-88	Philadelphia	NHL	1	0	0	0	0	....	....	....	....	....
	Hershey	AHL	66	10	19	29	132	12	2	10	12	35
1988-89	Buffalo	NHL	3	0	0	0	0	....	....	....	....	....
	Rochester	AHL	48	2	12	14	79	....	....	....	....	....
1989-90	Rochester	AHL	42	3	15	18	107	17	0	5	5	27
	NHL Totals		18	0	1	1	15	....	....	....	....	....

a OHA Second All-Star Team (1981).
b OHL Second All-Star Team (1982, 1983).

Claimed by **Buffalo** in NHL Waiver Draft, October 3, 1988.

SMITH, VERN

Defense. Shoots left. 6'1", 190 lbs. Born, Winnipeg, Man., May 30, 1964.
(NY Islanders' 2nd choice, 42nd overall, in 1982 Entry Draft).

			Regular Season					Playoffs				
Season	Club	Lea	GP	G	A	TP	PIM	GP	G	A	TP	PIM
1981-82	Lethbridge	WHL	72	5	38	43	73	12	0	2	2	8
1982-83	Lethbridge	WHL	30	2	10	12	54	....	....	....	....	....
	Nanaimo	WHL	42	6	21	27	62	....	....	....	....	....
1983-84	N. Westminster	WHL	69	13	44	57	94	9	6	6	12	12
1984-85	NY Islanders	NHL	1	0	0	0	0	....	....	....	....	....
	Springfield	AHL	76	6	20	26	115	4	0	2	2	9
1985-86	Springfield	AHL	55	3	11	14	83	....	....	....	....	....
1986-87	Springfield	AHL	41	1	10	11	58	....	....	....	....	....
1987-88	Springfield	AHL	64	5	22	27	78	....	....	....	....	....
1988-89	Springfield	AHL	80	3	26	29	121	....	....	....	....	....
1989-90	Phoenix	IHL	48	4	19	23	37	....	....	....	....	....
	NHL Totals		1	0	0	0	0	....	....	....	....	....

SMOLINSKI, BRYAN

Center. Shoots right. 6', 185 lbs. Born, Toledo, OH, December 27, 1971.
(Boston's 1st choice, 21st overall, in 1990 Entry Draft).

			Regular Season					Playoffs				
Season	Club	Lea	GP	G	A	TP	PIM	GP	G	A	TP	PIM
1988-89	Stratford	OPJHL	46	32	62	94	132	....	....	....	....	....
1989-90	Michigan St.	CCHA	35	9	13	22	34	....	....	....	....	....

SMYL, STANLEY PHILLIP (STAN) (SMEEL)

Right wing. Shoots right. 5'8", 190 lbs. Born, Glendon, Alta., January 28, 1958.
(Vancouver's 3rd choice, 40th overall, in 1978 Amateur Draft).

			Regular Season					Playoffs				
Season	Club	Lea	GP	G	A	TP	PIM	GP	G	A	TP	PIM
1975-76	N. Westminster	WHL	72	32	42	74	169	19	8	6	14	58
1976-77	N. Westminster	WHL	72	36	31	66	200	13	6	7	13	51
1977-78	N. Westminster	WHL	53	29	47	76	211	20	14	21	35	43
1978-79	Dallas	CHL	3	1	1	2	9	....	....	....	....	....
	Vancouver	NHL	62	14	24	38	89	2	1	1	2	0
1979-80	Vancouver	NHL	77	31	47	78	204	4	0	2	2	14
1980-81	Vancouver	NHL	80	25	38	63	171	3	1	2	3	0
1981-82	Vancouver	NHL	80	34	44	78	144	17	9	9	18	25
1982-83	Vancouver	NHL	74	38	50	88	114	4	3	2	5	12
1983-84	Vancouver	NHL	80	24	43	67	136	4	2	1	3	4
1984-85	Vancouver	NHL	80	27	37	64	100	....	....	....	....	....
1985-86	Vancouver	NHL	73	27	35	62	144	....	....	....	....	....
1986-87	Vancouver	NHL	66	20	23	43	84	....	....	....	....	....
1987-88	Vancouver	NHL	57	12	25	37	110	....	....	....	....	....
1988-89	Vancouver	NHL	75	7	18	25	102	7	0	0	0	9
1989-90	Vancouver	NHL	47	1	15	16	71	....	....	....	....	....
	NHL Totals		851	260	399	659	1469	41	16	17	33	64

SMYTH, GREG (SMIHTH)

Defense. Shoots right. 6'3", 212 lbs. Born, Oakville, Ont., April 23, 1966.
(Philadelphia's 1st choice, 22nd overall, in 1984 Entry Draft).

			Regular Season					Playoffs				
Season	Club	Lea	GP	G	A	TP	PIM	GP	G	A	TP	PIM
1983-84	London	OHL	64	4	21	25	252	6	1	0	1	24
1984-85	London	OHL	47	7	16	23	188	8	2	2	4	27
1985-86	Hershey	AHL	2	0	1	1	5	8	0	0	0	60
a	London	OHL	46	12	42	54	199	4	1	2	3	28
1986-87	Philadelphia	NHL	1	0	0	0	0	1	0	0	0	2
	Hershey	AHL	35	0	2	2	158	2	0	0	0	19
1987-88	Philadelphia	NHL	48	1	6	7	192	5	0	0	0	38
	Hershey	AHL	21	0	10	10	102	....	....	....	....	....
1988-89	Quebec	NHL	10	0	1	1	70	....	....	....	....	....
	Halifax	AHL	43	3	9	12	310	4	0	1	1	35
1989-90	Quebec	NHL	13	0	0	0	57	....	....	....	....	....
	Halifax	AHL	49	5	14	19	235	6	1	0	1	52
	NHL Totals		72	1	7	8	319	6	0	0	0	40

a OHL Second All-Star Team (1986).

Traded to **Quebec** by **Philadelphia** with Philadelphia's third round choice (John Tanner) in the 1989 Entry Draft for Terry Carkner, July 25, 1988.

SNEDDON, KEVIN

Defense. Shoots left. 5'11", 170 lbs. Born, St. Catharines, Ont., April 23, 1970.
(Los Angeles' 12th choice, 249th overall, in 1989 Entry Draft).

			Regular Season					Playoffs				
Season	Club	Lea	GP	G	A	TP	PIM	GP	G	A	TP	PIM
1988-89	Harvard	ECAC	24	0	5	5	16	....	....	....	....	....
1989-90	Harvard	ECAC	26	0	8	8	18	....	....	....	....	....

SNEPSTS, HAROLD JOHN (SNEHPS)

Defense. Shoots left. 6'3", 210 lbs. Born, Edmonton, Alta., October 24, 1954.
(Vancouver's 3rd choice, 59th overall, in 1974 Amateur Draft).

			Regular Season					Playoffs				
Season	Club	Lea	GP	G	A	TP	PIM	GP	G	A	TP	PIM
1972-73	Edmonton	WHL	68	2	24	26	155	11	0	1	1	54
1973-74	Edmonton	WHL	68	8	41	49	239	....	....	....	....	....
1974-75	Seattle	CHL	19	1	6	7	58	....	....	....	....	....
	Vancouver	NHL	27	1	2	3	30	....	....	....	....	....
1975-76	Vancouver	NHL	78	3	15	18	125	2	0	0	0	4
1976-77	Vancouver	NHL	79	4	18	22	149	....	....	....	....	....
1977-78	Vancouver	NHL	75	4	16	20	118	....	....	....	....	....
1978-79	Vancouver	NHL	76	7	24	31	130	3	0	0	0	0
1979-80	Vancouver	NHL	79	3	20	23	202	4	0	2	2	8
1980-81	Vancouver	NHL	76	3	16	19	212	3	0	0	0	8
1981-82	Vancouver	NHL	68	3	14	17	153	17	0	4	4	50
1982-83	Vancouver	NHL	46	2	8	10	80	4	1	1	2	8
1983-84	Vancouver	NHL	79	4	16	20	152	4	0	1	1	15
1984-85	Minnesota	NHL	71	0	7	7	232	9	0	0	0	24
1985-86	Detroit	NHL	35	0	6	6	75	....	....	....	....	....
1986-87	Detroit	NHL	54	1	13	14	129	11	0	2	2	18
1987-88	Detroit	NHL	31	1	4	5	67	10	0	0	0	40
	Adirondack	AHL	3	0	2	2	14	....	....	....	....	....
1988-89	Vancouver	NHL	59	0	8	8	69	7	0	1	1	6
1989-90	Vancouver	NHL	39	1	3	4	26	....	....	....	....	....
	St. Louis	NHL	7	0	1	1	10	11	0	3	3	38
	NHL Totals		979	37	191	228	1959	85	1	14	15	219

Played in NHL All-Star Game (1977, 1982)

Traded to **Minnesota** by **Vancouver** for Al MacAdam, June 21, 1984. Signed as a free agent by **Detroit**, July 31, 1985. Signed as a free agent by **Vancouver**, October 6, 1988. Traded to **St. Louis** by **Vancouver** with Rich Sutter and St. Louis' second round choice (Craig Johnson) – previously acquired by Vancouver – in 1990 Entry Draft for Adrien Plavsic, Montreal's first round choice (Shawn Antoski) – previously acquired by St. Louis – in 1990 Entry Draft and St. Louis' second round choice in 1991 Entry Draft, March 6, 1990.

SNUGGERUD, DAVE

Left wing. Shoots left. 6', 190 lbs. Born, Minnetonka, MN. June 20, 1966.
(Buffalo's 1st choice, 1st overall, in 1987 Supplemental Draft).

			Regular Season					Playoffs				
Season	Club	Lea	GP	G	A	TP	PIM	GP	G	A	TP	PIM
1985-86	U. Minnesota	WCHA	42	14	18	32	47	....	....	....	....	....
1986-87	U. Minnesota	WCHA	39	30	29	59	38	....	....	....	....	....
1987-88	U.S. National	....	51	14	21	35	26	....	....	....	....	....
	U.S. Olympic	....	6	3	2	5	4	....	....	....	....	....
1988-89ab	U. Minnesota	WCHA	45	29	20	49	39	....	....	....	....	....
1989-90	Buffalo	NHL	80	14	16	30	41	6	0	0	0	2
	NHL Totals		80	14	16	30	41	6	0	0	0	2

a WCHA Second All-Star Team (1989)
b NCAA West Second All-American Team (1989)

SOBERLAK, PETER (SOH-buhr-lak)

Left wing. Shoots left. 6'3", 205 lbs. Born, Kamloops, B.C., May 12, 1969.
(Edmonton's 1st choice, 21st overall, in 1987 Entry Draft).

			Regular Season					Playoffs				
Season	Club	Lea	GP	G	A	TP	PIM	GP	G	A	TP	PIM
1985-86	Kamloops	WHL	55	10	11	21	46	3	1	1	2	9
1986-87	Kamloops	WHL	16	2	7	9	26	....	....	....	....	....
	Swift Current	WHL	52	31	35	66	19	....	....	....	....	....
1987-88	Swift Current	WHL	67	43	56	99	47	10	5	7	12	14
1988-89	Swift Current	WHL	37	25	33	58	21	12	5	11	16	11
1989-90	Cape Breton	AHL	60	15	8	23	22	....	....	....	....	....

SOCHA, GARY

Center. Shoots left. 6'4", 185 lbs. Born, North Attleboro, MA, December 30, 1969.
(Calgary's 3rd choice, 84th overall, in 1988 Entry Draft).

			Regular Season					Playoffs				
Season	Club	Lea	GP	G	A	TP	PIM	GP	G	A	TP	PIM
1988-89	Tabor	HS	30	20	22	42	....	....	....	....	....	....
1989-90	Providence	H.E.	25	2	2	4	8	....	....	....	....	....

SOLLY, JIM

Center. Shoots left. 6'1", 180 lbs. Born, St. Catharines, Ont., March 19, 1970.
(Winnipeg's 10th choice, 151st overall, in 1989 Entry Draft).

			Regular Season					Playoffs				
Season	Club	Lea	GP	G	A	TP	PIM	GP	G	A	TP	PIM
1988-89	Bowling Green	CCHA	40	4	9	13	14	....	....	....	....	....
1989-90	Bowling Green	CCHA	44	9	11	20	14	....	....	....	....	....

SORENSEN, MARK

Defense. Shoots left. 6', 180 lbs. Born Newmarket, Ont. March 27, 1969.
(Washington's 11th choice, 192nd overall, in 1988 Entry Draft).

			Regular Season					Playoffs				
Season	Club	Lea	GP	G	A	TP	PIM	GP	G	A	TP	PIM
1987-88	U. of Michigan	CCHA	39	3	9	12	77	....	....	....	....	....
1988-89	U. of Michigan	CCHA	33	1	5	6	33	....	....	....	....	....
1989-90	U. of Michigan	CCHA	40	3	5	8	42	....	....	....	....	....

SOULES, JASON

Defense. Shoots left. 6'2", 212 lbs. Born, Hamilton, Ont., March 14, 1971.
(Edmonton's 1st choice, 15th overall, in 1989 Entry Draft).

			Regular Season					Playoffs				
Season	Club	Lea	GP	G	A	TP	PIM	GP	G	A	TP	PIM
1987-88	Hamilton	OHL	19	1	1	2	56	4	0	0	0	13
1988-89	Niagara Falls	OHL	57	3	8	11	187	....	....	....	....	....
1989-90	Hamilton	OHL	27	2	10	12	62	....	....	....	....	....

SPANGLER, KEN

Defense. Shoots right. 5'11", 190 lbs. Born, Edmonton, Alta., May 2, 1967.
(Toronto's 2nd choice, 22nd overall, in 1985 Entry Draft).

			Regular Season					Playoffs				
Season	Club	Lea	GP	G	A	TP	PIM	GP	G	A	TP	PIM
1983-84	Calgary	WHL	71	1	12	13	119	4	0	0	0	6
1984-85	Calgary	WHL	71	5	30	35	251	8	6	2	8	18
1985-86a	Calgary	WHL	66	19	36	55	237	....	....	....	....	....
	St. Catharines	AHL	7	0	0	0	16	2	0	0	0	15
1986-87	Calgary	WHL	49	12	24	36	185	....	....	....	....	....
1987-88	Newmarket	AHL	64	3	6	9	128	....	....	....	....	....
1988-89	Baltimore	AHL	12	0	3	3	33	....	....	....	....	....
	Flint	IHL	37	4	15	19	97	....	....	....	....	....
1989-90	Phoenix	IHL	58	3	16	19	156	....	....	....	....	....

a WHL East All-Star Team (1986)

SPEER, MICHAEL

Defense. Shoots left. 6'2", 200 lbs. Born, Toronto, Ont., March 26, 1971.
(Chicago's 2nd choice, 27th overall, in 1989 Entry Draft).

			Regular Season					Playoffs				
Season	Club	Lea	GP	G	A	TP	PIM	GP	G	A	TP	PIM
1987-88	Guelph	OHL	53	4	10	14	60	....	....	....	....	....
1988-89	Guelph	OHL	65	9	31	40	185	7	2	4	6	23
1989-90	Owen Sound	OHL	61	18	39	57	176	12	3	7	10	21

SPENRATH, GREG

Left wing. Shoots left. 6'1", 210 lbs. Born, Edmonton, Alta., September 27, 1969.
(NY Rangers' 9th choice, 160th overall, in 1989 Entry Draft).

			Regular Season					Playoffs				
Season	Club	Lea	GP	G	A	TP	PIM	GP	G	A	TP	PIM
1987-88	N.Westminster	WHL	72	18	24	42	210	5	0	4	4	16
1988-89	Tri-Cities	WHL	64	26	35	61	213	7	4	2	6	23
1989-90	Tri-Cities	WHL	67	36	32	68	256	7	1	0	1	15

SPROTT, JIM

Defense. Shoots left. 6'1", 200 lbs. Born, Oakville, Ont., April 11, 1969.
(Quebec's 3rd choice, 51st overall, in 1987 Entry Draft).

			Regular Season					Playoffs				
Season	Club	Lea	GP	G	A	TP	PIM	GP	G	A	TP	PIM
1986-87	London	OHL	66	8	30	38	153	....	....	....	....	....
1987-88	London	OHL	65	8	23	31	211	12	1	6	7	8
1988-89a	London	OHL	64	15	42	57	236	21	4	17	21	68
1989-90	Halifax	AHL	22	2	1	3	103	....	....	....	....	....

a OHL Second All-Star Team (1989)

SRSEN, TOMAS

Left wing. Shoots left. 5'11", 180 lbs. Born, Olomouc, Czechoslovakia, August 25, 1966.
(Edmonton's 7th choice, 147th overall, in 1987 Entry Draft).

			Regular Season					Playoffs				
Season	Club	Lea	GP	G	A	TP	PIM	GP	G	A	TP	PIM
1987-88	Zetor Brno	Czech.	34	14	5	19	....	....	....	....	....	....
1988-89	Zetor Brno	Czech.	42	19	11	30	....	....	....	....	....	....
1989-90	Zetor Brno	Czech	30	7	15	22	....	....	....	....	....	....

STANLEY, DARYL

Defense/Left wing. Shoots left. 6'2", 200 lbs. Born, Winnipeg, Man., December 2, 1962.

			Regular Season					Playoffs				
Season	Club	Lea	GP	G	A	TP	PIM	GP	G	A	TP	PIM
1980-81	N. Westminster	WHL	66	7	27	34	127	....	....	....	....	....
1981-82	Saskatoon	WHL	65	7	25	32	175	5	1	1	2	14
	Maine	AHL	....	....	....	....	....	2	0	2	2	2
1982-83	Maine	AHL	44	2	5	7	95	2	0	0	0	0
1983-84	Springfield	AHL	51	4	10	14	122	....	....	....	....	....
	Philadelphia	**NHL**	**23**	**1**	**4**	**5**	**71**	**3**	**0**	**0**	**0**	**19**
1984-85	Hershey	AHL	24	0	7	7	33	....	....	....	....	....
1985-86	**Philadelphia**	**NHL**	**33**	**0**	**2**	**2**	**69**	**1**	**0**	**0**	**0**	**2**
	Hershey	AHL	27	0	4	4	88	....	....	....	....	....
1986-87	**Philadelphia**	**NHL**	**33**	**1**	**2**	**3**	**76**	**13**	**0**	**0**	**0**	**9**
1987-88	**Vancouver**	**NHL**	**57**	**2**	**7**	**9**	**151**	....	....	....	....	....
1988-89	**Vancouver**	**NHL**	**20**	**3**	**1**	**4**	**14**	....	....	....	....	....
1989-90	**Vancouver**	**NHL**	**23**	**1**	**1**	**2**	**27**	....	....	....	....	....
	NHL Totals		**189**	**8**	**17**	**25**	**408**	**17**	**0**	**0**	**0**	**30**

Signed as a free agent by **Philadelphia**, October 9, 1981. Traded to **Vancouver** by **Philadelphia** with Darren Jensen for Wendell Young and Vancouver's third round choice (Kimbi Daniels) in the 1990 Entry Draft, August 31, 1987.

STANTON, PAUL

Defense. Shoots right. 6', 190 lbs. Born, Boston, MA, June 22, 1967.
(Pittsburgh's 8th choice, 149th overall, in 1985 Entry Draft).

			Regular Season					Playoffs				
Season	Club	Lea	GP	G	A	TP	PIM	GP	G	A	TP	PIM
1985-86	U. Wisconsin	WCHA	36	4	6	10	16	....	....	....	....	....
1986-87	U. Wisconsin	WCHA	41	5	17	22	70	....	....	....	....	....
1987-88ab	U. Wisconsin	WCHA	45	9	38	47	98	....	....	....	....	....
1988-89c	U. Wisconsin	WCHA	45	7	29	36	126	....	....	....	....	....
1989-90	Muskegon	IHL	77	5	27	32	61	15	2	4	6	21

a NCAA West First All-American Team (1988)
b WCHA Second All-Star Team (1988)
c WCHA First All-Star Team (1989)

STAPLETON, MIKE

Center. Shoots right. 5'10", 165 lbs. Born, Sarnia, Ont., May 5, 1966.
(Chicago's 7th choice, 132nd overall, in 1984 Entry Draft).

			Regular Season					Playoffs				
Season	Club	Lea	GP	G	A	TP	PIM	GP	G	A	TP	PIM
1983-84	Cornwall	OHL	70	24	45	69	94	3	1	2	3	4
1984-85	Cornwall	OHL	56	41	44	85	68	9	2	4	6	23
1985-86	Cornwall	OHL	56	39	64	103	74	6	2	3	5	2
1986-87	**Chicago**	**NHL**	**39**	**3**	**6**	**9**	**6**	**4**	**0**	**0**	**0**	**2**
	Cdn. Olympic	....	21	2	4	6	4	....	....	....	....	....
1987-88	**Chicago**	**NHL**	**53**	**2**	**9**	**11**	**59**	....	....	....	....	....
	Saginaw	IHL	31	11	19	30	52	10	5	6	11	10
1988-89	**Chicago**	**NHL**	**7**	**0**	**1**	**1**	**7**	....	....	....	....	....
	Saginaw	IHL	69	21	47	68	162	6	1	3	4	4
1989-90	Saginaw	IHL	16	5	10	15	6	13	9	10	19	38
	NHL Totals		**99**	**5**	**16**	**21**	**72**	**4**	**0**	**0**	**0**	**2**

STARIKOV, SERGEI

Defense. Shoots left. 5'10", 215 lbs. Born, Chelyabinsk, Soviet Union, December 4, 1958.
(New Jersey's 7th choice, 152nd overall, in 1989 Entry Draft).

			Regular Season					Playoffs				
Season	Club	Lea	GP	G	A	TP	PIM	GP	G	A	TP	PIM
1976-77	Chelyabinsk	USSR	35	2	4	6	28	....	....	....	....	....
1977-78	Chelyabinsk	USSR	36	3	5	8	26	....	....	....	....	....
1978-79	Chelyabinsk	USSR	44	6	8	14	34	....	....	....	....	....
1979-80	CSKA	USSR	39	10	8	18	14	....	....	....	....	....
1980-81	CSKA	USSR	49	4	8	12	26	....	....	....	....	....
1981-82	CSKA	USSR	40	1	4	5	14	....	....	....	....	....
1982-83	CSKA	USSR	44	6	14	20	14	....	....	....	....	....
1983-84	CSKA	USSR	44	11	7	18	20	....	....	....	....	....
1984-85	CSKA	USSR	40	3	10	13	12	....	....	....	....	....
1985-86	CSKA	USSR	37	3	2	5	6	....	....	....	....	....
1986-87	CSKA	USSR	34	4	2	6	8	....	....	....	....	....
1987-88	CSKA	USSR	38	2	11	13	12	....	....	....	....	....
1988-89	CSKA	USSR	30	3	3	6	4	....	....	....	....	....
1989-90	**New Jersey**	**NHL**	**16**	**0**	**1**	**1**	**8**	....	....	....	....	....
	Utica	AHL	43	8	11	19	14	4	0	3	3	0
	NHL Totals		**16**	**0**	**1**	**1**	**8**	....	....	....	....	....

STASTNY, ANTON (STAHST-nee)

Left wing. Shoots left. 6', 188 lbs. Born, Bratislava, Czechoslovakia, August 5, 1959.
(Quebec's 4th choice, 83rd overall, in 1979 Entry Draft).

			Regular Season					Playoffs				
Season	Club	Lea	GP	G	A	TP	PIM	GP	G	A	TP	PIM
1978-79	Slovan	Czech.	44	32	19	51	....	....	....	....	....	....
1979-80	Slovan	Czech.	40	30	30	60	....	....	....	....	....	....
	Czech. Olympic	....	6	4	4	8	2	....	....	....	....	....
1980-81	**Quebec**	**NHL**	**80**	**39**	**46**	**85**	**12**	**5**	**4**	**3**	**7**	**2**
1981-82	**Quebec**	**NHL**	**68**	**26**	**46**	**72**	**16**	**16**	**5**	**10**	**15**	**10**
1982-83	**Quebec**	**NHL**	**79**	**32**	**60**	**92**	**25**	**4**	**2**	**2**	**4**	**0**
1983-84	**Quebec**	**NHL**	**69**	**25**	**37**	**62**	**14**	**9**	**2**	**5**	**7**	**7**
1984-85	**Quebec**	**NHL**	**79**	**38**	**42**	**80**	**30**	**16**	**3**	**3**	**6**	**6**
1985-86	**Quebec**	**NHL**	**74**	**31**	**43**	**74**	**19**	**3**	**1**	**1**	**2**	**0**
1986-87	**Quebec**	**NHL**	**77**	**27**	**35**	**62**	**8**	**13**	**3**	**8**	**11**	**6**
1987-88	**Quebec**	**NHL**	**69**	**27**	**45**	**72**	**14**	....	....	....	....	....
1988-89	**Quebec**	**NHL**	**55**	**7**	**30**	**37**	**12**	....	....	....	....	....
	Halifax	AHL	16	9	5	14	4	....	....	....	....	....
1989-90	Gotteron	Switz.	36	25	22	47	....	....	....	....	....	....
	NHL Totals		**650**	**252**	**384**	**636**	**150**	**66**	**20**	**32**	**52**	**31**

STASTNY, PETER   (STAHST-nee)

Center. Shoots left. 6'1", 199 lbs.   Born, Bratislava, Czechoslovakia, September 18, 1956.

			Regular Season					Playoffs			
Season	Club	Lea	GP	G	A	TP	PIM	GP	G	A	TP	PIM
1978-79	Slovan	Czech.	44	32	23	55	....	....	....	....	....	....
1979-80a	Slovan	Czech.	40	30	30	60	....	....	....	....	....	....
	Czech. Olympic	....	16	7	7	14	6	....	....	....	....	....
1980-81bcd	Quebec	NHL	77	39	70	109	37	5	2	8	10	7
1981-82	Quebec	NHL	80	46	93	139	91	12	7	11	18	10
1982-83	Quebec	NHL	75	47	77	124	78	4	3	2	5	10
1983-84	Quebec	NHL	80	46	73	119	73	9	2	7	9	31
1984-85	Quebec	NHL	75	32	68	100	95	18	4	19	23	24
1985-86	Quebec	NHL	76	41	81	122	60	3	0	1	1	2
1986-87	Quebec	NHL	64	24	53	77	43	13	6	9	15	12
1987-88	Quebec	NHL	76	46	65	111	69	....	....	....	....	....
1988-89	Quebec	NHL	72	35	50	85	117	....	....	....	....	....
1989-90	Quebec	NHL	62	24	38	62	24	....	....	....	....	....
	New Jersey	NHL	12	5	6	11	16	6	3	2	5	2
	NHL Totals		**749**	**385**	**674**	**1059**	**703**	**70**	**27**	**59**	**86**	**98**

a Czechoslovakian League Player of the Year (1980)
b Won Calder Memorial Trophy (1981)
c NHL record for assists by a rookie (1981)
d NHL record for points by a rookie (1981)
Played in NHL All-Star Game (1981, 1982-84, 1986, 1988)
Signed as free agent by **Quebec**, August 26, 1980. Traded to **New Jersey** by **Quebec** for Craig Wolanin and future considerations (Randy Velischek), March 6, 1990.

STAUBER, PETE

Left wing. Shoots left. 5'11", 185 lbs. Born, Duluth, MN, May 10, 1966.

			Regular Season					Playoffs			
Season	Club	Lea	GP	G	A	TP	PIM	GP	G	A	TP	PIM
1986-87	Lake Superior	CCHA	40	22	13	35	80	....	....	....	....	....
1987-88	Lake Superior	CCHA	45	25	33	58	103	....	....	....	....	....
1988-89	Lake Superior	CCHA	46	25	13	38	115	....	....	....	....	....
1989-90	Lake Superior	CCHA	46	25	31	56	90	....	....	....	....	....

Signed as a free agent by **Detroit**, June 21, 1990.

STAVJANA, ANTONIN

Defense. Shoots right. 6', 190 lbs.   Born, Gottwaldov, Czechoslovakia, February 10, 1963.
(Calgary's 11th choice, 247th overall, in 1986 Entry Draft).

			Regular Season					Playoffs			
Season	Club	Lea	GP	G	A	TP	PIM	GP	G	A	TP	PIM
1986-87	Gottwaldov	Czech.	33	11	7	18	....	....	....	....	....	....
1987-88	Gottwaldov	Czech.	28	5	11	16	....	....	....	....	....	....
1988-89	Gottwaldov	Czech.	43	11	12	23	....	....	....	....	....	....
1989-90	Gottwaldov	Czech.	46	7	14	21	....	....	....	....	....	....

STEEN, THOMAS

Center. Shoots left. 5'10", 195 lbs.   Born, Tocksmark, Sweden, June 8, 1960.
(Winnipeg's 5th choice, 103rd overall, in 1979 Entry Draft).

			Regular Season					Playoffs			
Season	Club	Lea	GP	G	A	TP	PIM	GP	G	A	TP	PIM
1976-77	Leksand	Swe.	2	1	1	2	2	....	....	....	....	....
1977-78	Leksand	Swe.	35	5	6	11	30	....	....	....	....	....
1978-79	Leksand	Swe.	23	13	4	17	35	2	0	0	0	0
	Swe. National	....	2	0	0	0	0	....	....	....	....	....
1979-80	Leksand	Swe.	18	7	7	14	14	2	0	0	0	6
1980-81	Farjestad	Swe.	32	16	23	39	30	7	4	2	6	8
	Swe. National	....	19	2	5	7	12	....	....	....	....	....
1981-82	Winnipeg	NHL	73	15	29	44	42	4	0	4	4	2
1982-83	Winnipeg	NHL	75	26	33	59	60	3	0	2	2	0
1983-84	Winnipeg	NHL	78	20	45	65	69	3	0	1	1	9
1984-85	Winnipeg	NHL	79	30	54	84	80	8	2	3	5	17
1985-86	Winnipeg	NHL	78	17	47	64	76	3	1	1	2	4
1986-87	Winnipeg	NHL	75	17	33	50	59	10	3	4	7	8
1987-88	Winnipeg	NHL	76	16	38	54	53	5	1	5	6	2
1988-89	Winnipeg	NHL	80	27	61	88	80	....	....	....	....	....
1989-90	Winnipeg	NHL	53	18	48	66	35	7	2	5	7	16
	NHL Totals		**667**	**186**	**388**	**574**	**554**	**43**	**9**	**25**	**34**	**58**

STERN, RONALD (RONNIE)

Right wing. Shoots right. 6', 195 lbs.   Born, Ste. Agathe, Que., January 11, 1967.
(Vancouver's 3rd choice, 70th overall, in 1986 Entry Draft).

			Regular Season					Playoffs			
Season	Club	Lea	GP	G	A	TP	PIM	GP	G	A	TP	PIM
1984-85	Longueuil	QMJHL	67	6	14	20	176	....	....	....	....	....
1985-86	Longueuil	QMJHL	70	39	33	72	317	....	....	....	....	....
1986-87	Longueuil	QMJHL	56	32	39	71	266	19	11	9	20	55
1987-88	Vancouver	NHL	15	0	0	0	52	....	....	....	....	....
	Fredericton	AHL	2	1	0	1	4	....	....	....	....	....
	Flint	IHL	55	14	19	33	294	16	8	8	16	94
1988-89	Vancouver	NHL	17	1	0	1	49	3	0	1	1	17
	Milwaukee	IHL	45	19	23	42	280	5	1	0	1	11
1989-90	Vancouver	NHL	34	2	3	5	208	....	....	....	....	....
	Milwaukee	IHL	26	8	9	17	165	....	....	....	....	....
	NHL Totals		**66**	**3**	**3**	**6**	**309**	**3**	**0**	**1**	**1**	**17**

STEVENS, JOHN

Defense. Shoots left. 6'1", 195 lbs.   Born, Campleton, N.B., May 4, 1966.
(Philadelphia's 5th choice, 47th overall, in 1984 Entry Draft).

			Regular Season					Playoffs			
Season	Club	Lea	GP	G	A	TP	PIM	GP	G	A	TP	PIM
1983-84	Oshawa	OHL	70	1	10	11	71	7	0	1	1	6
1984-85	Oshawa	OHL	44	2	10	12	61	5	0	2	2	4
	Hershey	AHL	3	0	0	0	0	....	....	....	....	....
1985-86	Kalamazoo	IHL	6	0	1	1	8	6	0	3	3	9
	Oshawa	OHL	65	1	7	8	146	6	0	2	2	14
1986-87	Philadelphia	NHL	6	0	2	2	14	....	....	....	....	....
	Hershey	AHL	63	1	15	16	131	3	0	0	0	7
1987-88	Philadelphia	NHL	3	0	0	0	0	....	....	....	....	....
	Hershey	AHL	59	1	15	16	108	....	....	....	....	....
1988-89	Hershey	AHL	78	3	13	16	129	12	1	1	2	29
1989-90	Hershey	AHL	79	3	10	13	193	....	....	....	....	....
	NHL Totals		**9**	**0**	**2**	**2**	**14**					

STEVENS, KEVIN

Left wing. Shoots left. 6'3", 210 lbs.   Born, Brockton, MA, April 15, 1965.
(Los Angeles' 6th choice, 108th overall, in 1983 Entry Draft).

			Regular Season					Playoffs			
Season	Club	Lea	GP	G	A	TP	PIM	GP	G	A	TP	PIM
1983-84	Boston College	ECAC	37	6	14	20	36	....	....	....	....	....
1984-85	Boston College	H.E.	40	13	23	36	36	....	....	....	....	....
1985-86	Boston College	H.E.	42	17	27	44	56	....	....	....	....	....
1986-87ab	Boston College	H.E.	39	35	35	70	54	....	....	....	....	....
1987-88	Pittsburgh	NHL	16	5	2	7	8	....	....	....	....	....
	U.S. National	....	44	22	23	45	52	....	....	....	....	....
	U.S. Olympic	....	5	1	3	4	2	....	....	....	....	....
1988-89	Pittsburgh	NHL	24	12	3	15	19	11	3	7	10	16
	Muskegon	IHL	45	24	41	65	113	....	....	....	....	....
1989-90	Pittsburgh	NHL	76	29	41	70	171	....	....	....	....	....
	NHL Totals		**116**	**46**	**46**	**92**	**198**	**11**	**3**	**7**	**10**	**16**

a Hockey East First All-Star Team (1987)
b NCAA East Second All-American Team (1987)
Rights traded to **Pittsburgh** by **Los Angeles** for Anders Hakansson, September 9, 1983.

STEVENS, MIKE

Left wing. Shoots left. 5'11", 195 lbs.   Born, Kitchener, Ont., December 30, 1965.
(Vancouver's 5th choice, 58th overall, in 1984 Entry Draft).

			Regular Season					Playoffs			
Season	Club	Lea	GP	G	A	TP	PIM	GP	G	A	TP	PIM
1982-83	Kitchener	OHL	13	0	4	4	16	12	0	1	1	9
1983-84	Kitchener	OHL	66	19	21	40	109	16	10	7	17	40
1984-85	Vancouver	NHL	6	0	3	3	6	....	....	....	....	....
	Kitchener	OHL	37	17	18	35	121	4	1	1	2	8
1985-86	Fredericton	AHL	79	12	19	31	208	6	1	1	2	35
1986-87	Fredericton	AHL	71	7	18	25	258	....	....	....	....	....
1987-88	Boston	NHL	7	0	1	1	9	....	....	....	....	....
	Maine	AHL	63	30	25	55	265	7	1	2	3	37
1988-89	NY Islanders	NHL	9	1	0	1	14	....	....	....	....	....
	Springfield	AHL	42	17	13	30	120	....	....	....	....	....
1989-90	Springfield	AHL	28	12	10	22	75	....	....	....	....	....
	Toronto	NHL	1	0	0	0	0	....	....	....	....	....
	Newmarket	AHL	46	16	28	44	86	....	....	....	....	....
	NHL Totals		**23**	**1**	**4**	**5**	**29**					

Traded to **Boston** by **Vancouver** for cash, October 6, 1987. Signed as a free agent by **NY Islanders**, August 20, 1988. Traded to **Toronto** by **NY Islanders** with Gilles Thibaudeau for Jack Capuano, Paul Gagne and Derek Laxdal, December 20, 1989.

STEVENS, SCOTT

Defense. Shoots left. 6'1", 215 lbs.   Born, Kitchener, Ont., April 1, 1964.
(Washington's 1st choice, 5th overall, in 1982 Entry Draft).

			Regular Season					Playoffs			
Season	Club	Lea	GP	G	A	TP	PIM	GP	G	A	TP	PIM
1980-81	Kitchener	OPJHL	39	7	33	40	82	....	....	....	....	....
	Kitchener	OHA	1	0	0	0	0	....	....	....	....	....
1981-82	Kitchener	OHL	68	6	36	42	158	15	1	10	11	71
1982-83a	Washington	NHL	77	9	16	25	195	4	1	0	1	26
1983-84	Washington	NHL	78	13	32	45	201	8	1	8	9	21
1984-85	Washington	NHL	80	21	44	65	221	5	0	1	1	20
1985-86	Washington	NHL	73	15	38	53	165	9	3	8	11	12
1986-87	Washington	NHL	77	10	51	61	283	7	0	5	5	19
1987-88b	Washington	NHL	80	12	60	72	184	13	1	11	12	46
1988-89	Washington	NHL	80	7	61	68	225	6	1	4	5	11
1989-90	Washington	NHL	56	11	29	40	154	15	2	7	9	25
	NHL Totals		**601**	**98**	**331**	**429**	**1628**	**67**	**9**	**44**	**53**	**180**

a NHL All-Rookie Team (1983)
b NHL First All-Star Team (1988)
Played in NHL All-Star Game (1985, 1989)
Signed as a free agent by **St. Louis**, July 16, 1990.

STEVENSON, SHAYNE

Right wing. Shoots right. 6'1", 190 lbs.   Born, London, Ont., October 26, 1970.
(Boston's 1st choice, 17th overall, in 1989 Entry Draft).

			Regular Season					Playoffs			
Season	Club	Lea	GP	G	A	TP	PIM	GP	G	A	TP	PIM
1987-88	Kitchener	OHL	66	24	50	74	104	4	1	1	2	4
1988-89	Kitchener	OHL	56	25	50	75	86	5	2	3	5	4
1989-90	Kitchener	OHL	56	28	61	89	225	17	16	21	37	31

STEVENSON, TURNER

Right wing. Shoots right. 6'3", 200 lbs. Born, Port Alberni, B.C., May 18, 1972.
(Montreal's 1st choice, 12th overall, in 1990 Entry Draft).

			Regular Season					Playoffs			
Season	Club	Lea	GP	G	A	TP	PIM	GP	G	A	TP	PIM
1988-89	Seattle	WHL	69	15	12	27	84	....	....	....	....	....
1989-90	Seattle	WHL	62	29	32	61	276	13	3	2	5	35

STEWART, ALLAN

Left wing. Shoots left. 6', 195 lbs.   Born, Grande Centre, Alta., January 31, 1964.
(New Jersey's 9th choice, 213th overall, in 1983 Entry Draft).

			Regular Season					Playoffs				
Season	Club	Lea	GP	G	A	TP	PIM	GP	G	A	TP	PIM
1982-83	Prince Albert	WHL	70	25	34	59	272	....	....	....	....	....
1983-84	Prince Albert	WHL	67	44	39	83	216	5	1	2	3	29
	Maine	AHL	....	....	....	....	....	3	0	0	0	0
1984-85	Maine	AHL	75	8	11	19	241	11	1	2	3	58
1985-86	**New Jersey**	**NHL**	**4**	**0**	**0**	**0**	**21**	....	....	....	....	....
	Maine	AHL	58	7	12	19	181	....	....	....	....	....
1986-87	**New Jersey**	**NHL**	**7**	**1**	**0**	**1**	**26**	....	....	....	....	....
	Maine	AHL	74	14	24	38	143	....	....	....	....	....
1987-88	**New Jersey**	**NHL**	**1**	**0**	**0**	**0**	**0**	....	....	....	....	....
	Utica	AHL	49	8	17	25	129	....	....	....	....	....
1988-89	**New Jersey**	**NHL**	**6**	**0**	**2**	**2**	**15**	....	....	....	....	....
	Utica	AHL	72	9	23	32	110	5	1	0	1	4
1989-90	Utica	AHL						1	0	0	0	11
	NHL Totals		**18**	**1**	**2**	**3**	**62**	....	....	....	....	....

STEWART, CAMERON

Center. Shoots left. 5'11", 188 lbs. Born, Kitchener, Ont., September 18, 1971.
(Boston's 2nd choice, 63rd overall, in 1990 Entry Draft).

			Regular Season					Playoffs				
Season	Club	Lea	GP	G	A	TP	PIM	GP	G	A	TP	PIM
1988-89	Elmira	Jr.B	43	48	50	88	138	....	....	....	....	....
1989-90	Elmira	Jr.B	46	44	95	139	172	....	....	....	....	....

STEWART, MICHAEL

Defense. Shoots left. 6'2", 195 lbs. Born, Calgary, Alta., May 30, 1972.
(NY Rangers' 1st choice, 13th overall, in 1990 Entry Draft).

			Regular Season					Playoffs				
Season	Club	Lea	GP	G	A	TP	PIM	GP	G	A	TP	PIM
1989-90	Michigan St.	CCHA	40	2	6	8	39	....	....	....	....	....

STIENBURG, TREVOR

Right wing. Shoots right. 6'1", 200 lbs.   Born, Kingston, Ont., May 13, 1966.
(Quebec's 1st choice, 15th overall, in 1984 Entry Draft).

			Regular Season					Playoffs				
Season	Club	Lea	GP	G	A	TP	PIM	GP	G	A	TP	PIM
1983-84	Guelph	OHL	65	33	18	51	104	....	....	....	....	....
1984-85	Guelph	OHL	18	7	12	19	38	....	....	....	....	....
	London	OHL	22	9	11	20	45	8	1	3	4	22
1985-86	**Quebec**	**NHL**	**2**	**1**	**0**	**1**	**0**	**1**	**0**	**0**	**0**	**0**
	London	OHL	31	12	18	30	88	5	0	0	0	20
1986-87	**Quebec**	**NHL**	**6**	**1**	**0**	**1**	**12**	....	....	....	....	....
	Fredericton	AHL	48	14	12	26	123	....	....	....	....	....
1987-88	**Quebec**	**NHL**	**8**	**0**	**1**	**1**	**24**	....	....	....	....	....
	Fredericton	AHL	55	12	24	36	279	13	3	3	6	115
1988-89	**Quebec**	**NHL**	**55**	**6**	**3**	**9**	**125**	....	....	....	....	....
1989-90	Halifax	AHL	11	3	3	6	36	....	....	....	....	....
	NHL Totals		**71**	**8**	**4**	**12**	**161**	**1**	**0**	**0**	**0**	**0**

STOLK, DARREN

Defense. Shoots left. 6'4", 205 lbs.   Born, Taber, Alta., July 22, 1968.
(Pittsburgh's 11th choice, 235th overall, in 1988 Entry Draft).

			Regular Season					Playoffs				
Season	Club	Lea	GP	G	A	TP	PIM	GP	G	A	TP	PIM
1986-87	Brandon	WHL	71	3	9	12	60	....	....	....	....	....
1987-88	Lethbridge	WHL	60	3	10	13	79	....	....	....	....	....
1988-89	Medicine Hat	WHL	65	8	31	39	141	3	0	0	0	2
1989-90	Muskegon	IHL	65	3	3	6	59	6	1	0	1	2

STONE, DONALD

Center. Shoots left. 5'11", 165 lbs.   Born, Detroit, MI, May 6, 1969.
(Detroit's 11th choice, 248th overall, in 1988 Entry Draft).

			Regular Season					Playoffs				
Season	Club	Lea	GP	G	A	TP	PIM	GP	G	A	TP	PIM
1987-88	U. of Michigan	CCHA	38	18	19	37	22	....	....	....	....	....
1988-89	U. of Michigan	CCHA	40	24	17	41	19	....	....	....	....	....
1989-90	U. of Michigan	CCHA	42	20	24	44	12	....	....	....	....	....

STOTHERS, MICHAEL PATRICK (MIKE)

Defense. Shoots left. 6'4", 215 lbs.   Born, Toronto, Ont., February 22, 1962.
(Philadelphia's 1st choice, 21st overall, in 1980 Entry Draft).

			Regular Season					Playoffs				
Season	Club	Lea	GP	G	A	TP	PIM	GP	G	A	TP	PIM
1979-80	Kingston	OHA	66	4	23	27	137	....	....	....	....	....
1980-81	Kingston	OHA	65	4	22	26	237	14	0	3	3	27
1981-82	Kingston	OHL	61	1	20	21	203	4	0	1	1	8
	Maine	AHL	5	0	0	0	4	1	0	0	0	0
1982-83	Maine	AHL	80	2	16	18	139	12	0	0	0	21
1983-84	Maine	AHL	61	2	10	12	109	17	0	1	1	34
1984-85	**Philadelphia**	**NHL**	**1**	**0**	**0**	**0**	**0**	....	....	....	....	....
	Hershey	AHL	59	8	18	26	142	....	....	....	....	....
1985-86	**Philadelphia**	**NHL**	**6**	**0**	**1**	**1**	**6**	**3**	**0**	**0**	**0**	**4**
	Hershey	AHL	66	4	9	13	221	13	0	3	3	88
1986-87	**Philadelphia**	**NHL**	**2**	**0**	**0**	**0**	**4**	**2**	**0**	**0**	**0**	**7**
	Hershey	AHL	75	5	11	16	283	5	0	0	0	10
1987-88	**Philadelphia**	**NHL**	**3**	**0**	**0**	**0**	**13**	....	....	....	....	....
	Hershey	AHL	13	3	2	5	55	....	....	....	....	....
	Toronto	**NHL**	**18**	**0**	**1**	**1**	**42**	....	....	....	....	....
	Newmarket	AHL	38	1	9	10	69	....	....	....	....	....
1988-89	Hershey	AHL	76	4	11	15	262	9	0	2	2	29
1989-90	Hershey	AHL	56	1	6	7	170	....	....	....	....	....
	NHL Totals		**30**	**0**	**2**	**2**	**65**	**5**	**0**	**0**	**0**	**11**

Traded to **Toronto** by **Philadelphia** for future considerations, December 4, 1987. Traded to **Philadelphia** by **Toronto** for Bill Root, June 21, 1988.

STRAPON, MARK

Defense. Shoots left. 6'3", 205 lbs.   Born, Hayward, WI, July 15, 1969.
(Philadelphia's 7th choice, 146th overall, in 1987 Entry Draft).

			Regular Season					Playoffs				
Season	Club	Lea	GP	G	A	TP	PIM	GP	G	A	TP	PIM
1987-88	St. Paul	USHL	48	4	12	16	34	....	....	....	....	....
1988-89	St. Paul	USHL	38	16	29	45	81	....	....	....	....	....
1989-90	U. Wisconsin	WCHA	27	0	7	7	50	....	....	....	....	....

STREET, KEITH

Center. Shoots left. 6'1", 170 lbs.   Born, Moose Jaw, Sask., March 18, 1965.

			Regular Season					Playoffs				
Season	Club	Lea	GP	G	A	TP	PIM	GP	G	A	TP	PIM
1985-86	Alaska-Fair.	NCAA	25	12	18	30	14	....	....	....	....	....
1986-87	Alaska-Fair.	NCAA	35	19	25	44	20	....	....	....	....	....
1987-88	Alaska-Fair.	NCAA	31	37	46	83	30	....	....	....	....	....
1988-89	Milwaukee	IHL	40	10	11	21	22	....	....	....	....	....
1989-90	Milwaukee	IHL	55	5	13	18	25	....	....	....	....	....

Signed as a free agent by **Vancouver**, July 22, 1988.

SUCHANEK, RUDOLF

Defense. Shoots right. 6'3", 215 lbs.   Born, Ceske Budejovice, Czech., January 27, 1962.
(Calgary's 12th choice, 241st overall, in 1984 Entry Draft).

			Regular Season					Playoffs				
Season	Club	Lea	GP	G	A	TP	PIM	GP	G	A	TP	PIM
1987-88	Budejovice	Czech.	33	3	18	21	....	....	....	....	....	....
1988-89	Budejovice	Czech.	45	7	24	31	60	....	....	....	....	....
1989-90	Budejovice	Czech.	27	2	3	5	....	....	....	....	....	....

SUHY, ANDY

Defense. Shoots left. 6'1", 190 lbs.   Born, Detroit, MI, March 9, 1970.
(Detroit's 8th choice, 158th overall, in 1989 Entry Draft).

			Regular Season					Playoffs				
Season	Club	Lea	GP	G	A	TP	PIM	GP	G	A	TP	PIM
1988-89	W. Michigan	CCHA	42	0	4	4	74	....	....	....	....	....
1989-90	W. Michigan	CCHA	34	3	5	8	52	....	....	....	....	....

SULLIMAN, SIMON DOUGLAS (DOUG)

Right wing. Shoots left. 6'2", 210 lbs.   Born, Glace Bay, N.S., August 29, 1959.
(NY Rangers' 1st choice, 13th overall, in 1979 Entry Draft).

			Regular Season					Playoffs				
Season	Club	Lea	GP	G	A	TP	PIM	GP	G	A	TP	PIM
1977-78	Kitchener	OHA	68	50	39	89	87	9	5	7	12	24
1978-79	Kitchener	OHA	68	38	77	115	88	10	5	7	12	7
1979-80	**NY Rangers**	**NHL**	**31**	**4**	**7**	**11**	**2**	....	....	....	....	....
	New Haven	AHL	31	9	7	16	9	....	....	....	....	....
1980-81	New Haven	AHL	45	10	16	26	18	1	0	0	0	0
	NY Rangers	**NHL**	**32**	**4**	**1**	**5**	**32**	**3**	**1**	**0**	**1**	**0**
1981-82	**Hartford**	**NHL**	**77**	**29**	**40**	**69**	**39**	....	....	....	....	....
1982-83	**Hartford**	**NHL**	**77**	**22**	**19**	**41**	**14**	....	....	....	....	....
1983-84	**Hartford**	**NHL**	**67**	**6**	**13**	**19**	**20**	....	....	....	....	....
1984-85	**New Jersey**	**NHL**	**57**	**22**	**16**	**38**	**4**	....	....	....	....	....
1985-86	**New Jersey**	**NHL**	**73**	**21**	**22**	**43**	**20**	....	....	....	....	....
1986-87	**New Jersey**	**NHL**	**78**	**27**	**26**	**53**	**14**	....	....	....	....	....
1987-88	**New Jersey**	**NHL**	**59**	**16**	**14**	**30**	**22**	**9**	**0**	**3**	**3**	**2**
1988-89	**Philadelphia**	**NHL**	**52**	**6**	**6**	**12**	**8**	**4**	**0**	**0**	**0**	**0**
1989-90	**Philadelphia**	**NHL**	**28**	**3**	**4**	**7**	**0**	....	....	....	....	....
	NHL Totals		**631**	**160**	**168**	**328**	**175**	**16**	**1**	**3**	**4**	**2**

Traded to **Hartford** by **NY Rangers** with Chris Kotsopoulos and Gerry McDonald for Mike Rogers and NY Rangers' tenth round choice (Simo Saarinen) in 1982 Entry Draft, October 2, 1981. Signed as a free agent by **New Jersey**, July 11, 1984. Claimed by **Philadelphia** in NHL Waiver Draft, October 3, 1988.

SULLIVAN, BRIAN

Right wing. Shoots right. 6'4", 195 lbs.   Born, South Windsor, CT, April 23, 1969.
(New Jersey's 3rd choice, 65th overall, in 1987 Entry Draft).

			Regular Season					Playoffs				
Season	Club	Lea	GP	G	A	TP	PIM	GP	G	A	TP	PIM
1987-88	Northeastern	H.E.	37	20	12	32	18	....	....	....	....	....
1988-89	Northeastern	H.E.	34	13	14	27	65	....	....	....	....	....
1989-90	Northeastern	H.E.	34	24	21	45	54	....	....	....	....	....

SULLIVAN, KEVIN

Right wing. Shoots right. 6'2", 180 lbs.   Born, Hartford, CT, May 16, 1968.
(Hartford's 9th choice, 228th overall, in 1987 Entry Draft).

			Regular Season					Playoffs				
Season	Club	Lea	GP	G	A	TP	PIM	GP	G	A	TP	PIM
1986-87	Princeton	ECAC	25	1	0	1	10	....	....	....	....	....
1987-88	Princeton	ECAC	22	0	3	3	8	....	....	....	....	....
1988-89	Princeton	ECAC	26	7	7	14	58	....	....	....	....	....
1989-90	Princeton	ECAC	27	12	13	25	28	....	....	....	....	....

Traded to **Minnesota** by **Hartford** for Mike Berger, October 7, 1989.

SULLIVAN, MICHAEL

Center. Shoots left. 6'2", 185 lbs.   Born, Marshfield, MA, February 27, 1968.
(NY Rangers' 4th choice, 69th overall, in 1987 Entry Draft).

			Regular Season					Playoffs				
Season	Club	Lea	GP	G	A	TP	PIM	GP	G	A	TP	PIM
1986-87	Boston U.	H.E.	37	13	18	31	18	....	....	....	....	....
1987-88	Boston U.	H.E.	30	18	22	40	30	....	....	....	....	....
1988-89	Boston U.	H.E.	36	19	17	36	30	....	....	....	....	....
1989-90	Boston U.	H.E.	38	11	20	31	26	....	....	....	....	....

Rights traded to **Minnesota** by **NY Rangers** with Paul Jerrard, the rights to Bret Barnett, and Los Angeles' third-round choice (Murray Garbutt) in 1989 Entry Draft — acquired March 10, 1987 by Minnesota — for Brian Lawton, Igor Liba and the rights to Eric Bennett, October 11, 1988.

SUMMANEN, RAIMO (SOO-ma-nen, RYE-moh)

Left wing. Shoots left. 5'11", 185 lbs. Born, Jyvaskyla, Finland, March 2, 1962.
(Edmonton's 6th choice, 125th overall, in 1982 Entry Draft).

			Regular Season					Playoffs				
Season	**Club**	**Lea**	**GP**	**G**	**A**	**TP**	**PIM**	**GP**	**G**	**A**	**TP**	**PIM**
1981-82	Kiekkoreipas	Fin.	36	15	6	21	17	2	2	0	2	0
1982-83	Ilves	Fin.	36	45	15	60	36	8	7	3	10	2
1983-84	Ilves	Fin.	37	28	19	47	26	....	....	....	....	....
	Edmonton	**NHL**	**2**	**1**	**4**	**5**	**2**	**5**	**1**	**4**	**5**	**0**
1984-85	**Edmonton**	**NHL**	**9**	**0**	**4**	**4**	**0**	....	....	....	....	....
	Nova Scotia	AHL	66	20	33	53	2	5	1	2	3	0
1985-86	**Edmonton**	**NHL**	**73**	**19**	**18**	**37**	**16**	**5**	**1**	**1**	**2**	**0**
1986-87	**Edmonton**	**NHL**	**48**	**10**	**7**	**17**	**15**	....	....	....	....	....
	Vancouver	**NHL**	**10**	**4**	**4**	**8**	**0**	....	....	....	....	....
1987-88	**Vancouver**	**NHL**	**9**	**2**	**3**	**5**	**2**	....	....	....	....	....
	Fredericton	AHL	20	7	15	22	38	....	....	....	....	....
	Flint	IHL	7	1	1	2	0	....	....	....	....	....
1988-89	Ilves	Fin.	44	35	46	81	22	5	4	3	7	6
1989-90	Ilves	Fin.	40	39	31	70	42	9	3	4	7	8
	NHL Totals		**151**	**36**	**40**	**76**	**35**	**10**	**2**	**5**	**7**	**0**

Traded to **Vancouver** by **Edmonton** for Moe Lemay, March 10, 1987.

SUNDIN, MATS

Center/Right wing. Shoots right. 6'3", 185 lbs. Born, Sollentuna, Sweden, February 13, 1971.
(Quebec's 1st choice, 1st overall, in 1989 Entry Draft).

			Regular Season					Playoffs				
Season	**Club**	**Lea**	**GP**	**G**	**A**	**TP**	**PIM**	**GP**	**G**	**A**	**TP**	**PIM**
1988-89	Nacka	Swe.	25	10	8	18	18	....	....	....	....	....
1989-90	Djurgardens	Swe.	34	10	8	18	16	8	7	0	7	4

SUNDSTROM, PATRIK

Center/Right wing. Shoots left. 6', 195 lbs. Born, Skelleftea, Sweden, December 14, 1961.
(Vancouver's 8th choice, 175th overall, in 1980 Entry Draft).

			Regular Season					Playoffs				
Season	**Club**	**Lea**	**GP**	**G**	**A**	**TP**	**PIM**	**GP**	**G**	**A**	**TP**	**PIM**
1979-80	Bjorkloven	Swe.	26	5	7	12	20	3	1	0	1	4
1980-81	Bjorkloven	Swe.	36	10	18	28	30	3	1	0	1	4
	Swe. National	...	15	4	2	6	6	....	....	....	....	....
1981-82	Bjorkloven	Swe.	36	22	13	35	38	7	3	4	7	6
	Swe. National	...	36	17	7	24	24	....	....	....	....	....
1982-83	**Vancouver**	**NHL**	**74**	**23**	**23**	**46**	**30**	**4**	**0**	**0**	**0**	**2**
1983-84	**Vancouver**	**NHL**	**78**	**38**	**53**	**91**	**37**	**4**	**0**	**1**	**1**	**7**
1984-85	**Vancouver**	**NHL**	**71**	**25**	**43**	**68**	**46**	....	....	....	....	....
1985-86	**Vancouver**	**NHL**	**79**	**18**	**48**	**66**	**28**	**3**	**1**	**0**	**1**	**0**
1986-87	**Vancouver**	**NHL**	**72**	**29**	**42**	**71**	**40**	....	....	....	....	....
1987-88	**New Jersey**	**NHL**	**78**	**15**	**36**	**51**	**42**	**18**	**7**	**13**	**20**	**14**
1988-89	**New Jersey**	**NHL**	**65**	**28**	**41**	**69**	**36**	....	....	....	....	....
1989-90	**New Jersey**	**NHL**	**74**	**27**	**49**	**76**	**34**	**6**	**1**	**3**	**4**	**2**
	NHL Totals		**591**	**203**	**335**	**538**	**293**	**35**	**9**	**17**	**26**	**25**

Traded to **New Jersey** by **Vancouver** with Vancouver's fourth round choice (Matt Ruchty) in 1988 Entry Draft for Kirk McLean and Greg Adams, September 15, 1987.

SUNDSTROM, PETER

Left wing. Shoots left. 6', 180 lbs. Born, Skelleftea, Sweden, December 14, 1961.
(New York Rangers' 3rd choice, 50th overall, in 1981 Entry Draft).

			Regular Season					Playoffs				
Season	**Club**	**Lea**	**GP**	**G**	**A**	**TP**	**PIM**	**GP**	**G**	**A**	**TP**	**PIM**
1980-81	Bjorkloven	Swe.	29	7	2	9	8	....	....	....	....	....
1981-82	Bjorkloven	Swe.	35	10	14	24	18	7	2	1	3	0
1982-83	Bjorkloven	Swe.	33	14	11	25	3	2	0	2	0	4
1983-84	**NY Rangers**	**NHL**	**77**	**22**	**22**	**44**	**24**	**5**	**1**	**3**	**4**	**0**
1984-85	**NY Rangers**	**NHL**	**76**	**18**	**25**	**43**	**34**	**3**	**0**	**0**	**0**	**0**
1985-86	**NY Rangers**	**NHL**	**53**	**8**	**15**	**23**	**12**	**1**	**0**	**0**	**0**	**2**
	New Haven	AHL	8	3	6	9	4	....	....	....	....	....
1986-87	Bjorkloven	Swe.	36	22	16	38	44	6	2	5	7	8
1987-88	**Washington**	**NHL**	**76**	**8**	**17**	**25**	**34**	**14**	**2**	**0**	**2**	**6**
1988-89	**Washington**	**NHL**	**35**	**4**	**2**	**6**	**12**	....	....	....	....	....
1989-90	**New Jersey**	**NHL**	**21**	**1**	**2**	**3**	**4**	....	....	....	....	....
	Utica	AHL	31	11	18	29	6	5	4	1	5	0
	NHL Totals		**338**	**61**	**83**	**144**	**120**	**23**	**3**	**3**	**6**	**8**

Traded by **NY Rangers** to **Washington** for Washington's fifth round selection in the 1988 Entry Draft, August 27, 1987. Traded to **Washington** by **NY Rangers** for Washington's fifth round choice (Martin Bergeron) in 1988 Entry Draft, August 28, 1987. Traded to **New Jersey** by **Washington** for New Jersey's 10th round choice in 1991 Entry Draft, June 19, 1989.

SUTER, GARY

Defense. Shoots left. 6', 190 lbs. Born, Madison, WI, June 24, 1964.
(Calgary's 10th choice, 180th overall, in 1984 Entry Draft).

			Regular Season					Playoffs				
Season	**Club**	**Lea**	**GP**	**G**	**A**	**TP**	**PIM**	**GP**	**G**	**A**	**TP**	**PIM**
1983-84	U. Wisconsin	WCHA	35	4	18	22	32	....	....	....	....	....
1984-85	U. Wisconsin	WCHA	39	12	39	51	110	....	....	....	....	....
1985-86ab	**Calgary**	**NHL**	**80**	**18**	**50**	**68**	**141**	**10**	**2**	**8**	**10**	**8**
1986-87	**Calgary**	**NHL**	**68**	**9**	**40**	**49**	**70**	**6**	**0**	**3**	**3**	**10**
1987-88c	**Calgary**	**NHL**	**75**	**21**	**70**	**91**	**124**	**9**	**1**	**9**	**10**	**6**
1988-89	**Calgary**	**NHL**	**63**	**13**	**49**	**62**	**78**	**5**	**0**	**3**	**3**	**10**
1989-90	**Calgary**	**NHL**	**76**	**16**	**60**	**76**	**97**	**6**	**0**	**1**	**1**	**14**
	NHL Totals		**362**	**77**	**269**	**346**	**510**	**36**	**3**	**24**	**27**	**42**

a Won Calder Memorial Trophy (1986)
b NHL All-Rookie Team (1986)
c NHL Second All-Star Team (1988)

Played in NHL All-Star Game (1986, 1988, 1989)

SUTTER, BRENT COLIN (SUH-tuhr)

Center. Shoots right. 5'11", 180 lbs. Born, Viking, Alta., June 10, 1962.
(NY Islanders' 1st choice, 17th overall, in 1980 Entry Draft).

			Regular Season					Playoffs				
Season	**Club**	**Lea**	**GP**	**G**	**A**	**TP**	**PIM**	**GP**	**G**	**A**	**TP**	**PIM**
1979-80	Red Deer	AJHL	59	70	101	171	....	....	....	....	....	....
	Lethbridge	WHL	5	1	0	1	2	....	....	....	....	....
1980-81	**NY Islanders**	**NHL**	**3**	**2**	**2**	**4**	**0**	....	....	....	....	....
	Lethbridge	WHL	68	54	54	108	116	9	6	4	10	51
1981-82	Lethbridge	WHL	34	46	33	79	162	....	....	....	....	....
	NY Islanders	**NHL**	**43**	**21**	**22**	**43**	**114**	**19**	**2**	**6**	**8**	**36**
1982-83	**NY Islanders**	**NHL**	**80**	**21**	**19**	**40**	**128**	**20**	**10**	**11**	**21**	**26**
1983-84	**NY Islanders**	**NHL**	**69**	**34**	**15**	**49**	**69**	**20**	**4**	**10**	**14**	**18**
1984-85	**NY Islanders**	**NHL**	**72**	**42**	**60**	**102**	**51**	**10**	**3**	**3**	**6**	**14**
1985-86	**NY Islanders**	**NHL**	**61**	**24**	**31**	**55**	**74**	**3**	**0**	**1**	**1**	**2**
1986-87	**NY Islanders**	**NHL**	**69**	**27**	**36**	**63**	**73**	**5**	**1**	**0**	**1**	**4**
1987-88	**NY Islanders**	**NHL**	**70**	**29**	**31**	**60**	**55**	**6**	**2**	**1**	**3**	**18**
1988-89	**NY Islanders**	**NHL**	**77**	**29**	**34**	**63**	**77**	....	....	....	....	....
1989-90	**NY Islanders**	**NHL**	**67**	**33**	**35**	**68**	**65**	**5**	**2**	**3**	**5**	**2**
	NHL Totals		**611**	**262**	**285**	**547**	**706**	**88**	**24**	**35**	**59**	**120**

Played in NHL All-Star Game (1985)

SUTTER, DUANE CALVIN (SUH-tuhr)

Right wing. Shoots right. 6'1", 185 lbs. Born, Viking, Alta., March 16, 1960.
(NY Islanders' 1st choice, 17th overall, in 1979 Entry Draft).

			Regular Season					Playoffs				
Season	**Club**	**Lea**	**GP**	**G**	**A**	**TP**	**PIM**	**GP**	**G**	**A**	**TP**	**PIM**
1976-77	Lethbridge	WHL	1	0	1	1	2	8	0	1	1	15
1977-78	Lethbridge	WHL	5	1	5	6	19	8	1	4	5	10
1978-79	Lethbridge	WHL	71	50	75	125	212	19	11	12	23	43
1979-80	Lethbridge	WHL	21	18	16	34	74	....	....	....	....	....
	NY Islanders	**NHL**	**56**	**15**	**9**	**24**	**55**	**21**	**3**	**7**	**10**	**74**
1980-81	**NY Islanders**	**NHL**	**23**	**7**	**11**	**18**	**26**	**12**	**3**	**1**	**4**	**10**
1981-82	**NY Islanders**	**NHL**	**77**	**18**	**35**	**53**	**100**	**19**	**5**	**5**	**10**	**57**
1982-83	**NY Islanders**	**NHL**	**75**	**13**	**19**	**32**	**118**	**20**	**9**	**12**	**21**	**43**
1983-84	**NY Islanders**	**NHL**	**78**	**17**	**23**	**40**	**94**	**21**	**1**	**3**	**4**	**48**
1984-85	**NY Islanders**	**NHL**	**78**	**17**	**24**	**41**	**174**	**10**	**0**	**2**	**2**	**47**
1985-86	**NY Islanders**	**NHL**	**80**	**20**	**33**	**53**	**157**	**3**	**0**	**0**	**0**	**16**
1986-87	**NY Islanders**	**NHL**	**80**	**14**	**17**	**31**	**169**	**14**	**1**	**0**	**1**	**26**
1987-88	**Chicago**	**NHL**	**37**	**7**	**9**	**16**	**70**	**5**	**0**	**0**	**0**	**21**
1988-89	**Chicago**	**NHL**	**75**	**7**	**9**	**16**	**214**	**16**	**3**	**1**	**4**	**15**
1989-90	**Chicago**	**NHL**	**72**	**4**	**14**	**18**	**156**	**20**	**1**	**1**	**2**	**48**
	NHL Totals		**731**	**139**	**203**	**342**	**1333**	**161**	**26**	**32**	**58**	**405**

Traded to **Chicago** by **NY Islanders** for Chicago's second round choice (Wayne Doucet) in 1988 Entry Draft, September 9, 1987.

SUTTER, RICHARD (RICH) (SUH-tuhr)

Right wing. Shoots right. 5'11", 165 lbs. Born, Viking, Alta., December 2, 1963.
(Pittsburgh's 1st choice, 10th overall, in 1982 Entry Draft).

			Regular Season					Playoffs				
Season	**Club**	**Lea**	**GP**	**G**	**A**	**TP**	**PIM**	**GP**	**G**	**A**	**TP**	**PIM**
1980-81	Lethbridge	WHL	72	23	18	41	255	9	3	1	4	35
1981-82	Lethbridge	WHL	57	38	31	69	263	12	3	3	6	55
1982-83	**Pittsburgh**	**NHL**	**4**	**0**	**0**	**0**	**0**	....	....	....	....	....
	Lethbridge	WHL	64	37	30	67	200	17	14	9	23	43
1983-84	Baltimore	AHL	2	0	1	1	0	....	....	....	....	....
	Pittsburgh	**NHL**	**5**	**0**	**0**	**0**	**0**	....	....	....	....	....
	Philadelphia	**NHL**	**70**	**16**	**12**	**28**	**93**	**3**	**0**	**0**	**0**	**15**
1984-85	**Philadelphia**	**NHL**	**56**	**6**	**10**	**16**	**89**	**11**	**3**	**0**	**3**	**10**
	Hershey	AHL	13	3	7	10	14	....	....	....	....	....
1985-86	**Philadelphia**	**NHL**	**78**	**14**	**25**	**39**	**199**	**5**	**2**	**0**	**2**	**19**
1986-87	**Vancouver**	**NHL**	**74**	**20**	**22**	**42**	**113**	....	....	....	....	....
1987-88	**Vancouver**	**NHL**	**80**	**15**	**15**	**30**	**165**	....	....	....	....	....
1988-89	**Vancouver**	**NHL**	**75**	**17**	**15**	**32**	**122**	**7**	**2**	**1**	**3**	**12**
1989-90	**Vancouver**	**NHL**	**62**	**9**	**9**	**18**	**133**	....	....	....	....	....
	St. Louis	**NHL**	**12**	**2**	**0**	**2**	**22**	**12**	**2**	**1**	**3**	**39**
	NHL Totals		**516**	**99**	**108**	**207**	**936**	**38**	**9**	**2**	**11**	**95**

Traded to **Philadelphia** by **Pittsburgh** with Pittsburgh's second round (Greg Smyth) and third round (David McLay) choices in 1984 Entry Draft for Andy Brickley, Mark Taylor, Ron Flockhart, Philadelphia's first round (Roger Belanger) and third round (Mike Stevens — later transferred to Vancouver) choices in 1984 Entry Draft, October 23, 1983. Traded to **Vancouver** by **Philadelphia**, with Dave Richter and Vancouver's third-round choice (Don Gibson) in 1986 Entry Draft — acquired earlier — for J.J. Daigneault and Vancouver's second-round choice (Kent Hawley) in 1986 Entry Draft, June 6, 1986. Traded to **St Louis** by **Vancouver** with Harold Snepsts and St. Louis' second round choice (Craig Johnson) – previously acquired by Vancouver – in 1990 Entry Draft for Adrien Plavsic, Montreal's first round choice (Shawn Antoski) – previously acquired by St. Louis – in 1990 Entry Draft and St. Louis' second round choice in 1991 Entry Draft, March 6, 1990.

SUTTER, RONALD (RON) (SUH-tuhr)

Center. Shoots right. 6', 185 lbs. Born, Viking, Alta., December 2, 1963.
(Philadelphia's 1st choice, 4th overall, in 1982 Entry Draft).

			Regular Season					Playoffs				
Season	**Club**	**Lea**	**GP**	**G**	**A**	**TP**	**PIM**	**GP**	**G**	**A**	**TP**	**PIM**
1980-81	Lethbridge	WHL	72	13	32	45	152	9	2	5	7	29
1981-82	Lethbridge	WHL	59	38	54	92	207	12	6	5	11	28
1982-83	**Philadelphia**	**NHL**	**10**	**1**	**1**	**2**	**9**	....	....	....	....	....
	Lethbridge	WHL	58	35	48	83	98	20	*22	*19	*41	45
1983-84	**Philadelphia**	**NHL**	**79**	**19**	**32**	**51**	**101**	**3**	**0**	**0**	**0**	**22**
1984-85	**Philadelphia**	**NHL**	**73**	**16**	**29**	**45**	**94**	**19**	**4**	**8**	**12**	**28**
1985-86	**Philadelphia**	**NHL**	**75**	**18**	**42**	**60**	**159**	**5**	**0**	**2**	**2**	**10**
1986-87	**Philadelphia**	**NHL**	**39**	**10**	**17**	**27**	**69**	**16**	**1**	**7**	**8**	**12**
1987-88	**Philadelphia**	**NHL**	**69**	**8**	**25**	**33**	**146**	**7**	**0**	**1**	**1**	**26**
1988-89	**Philadelphia**	**NHL**	**55**	**26**	**22**	**48**	**80**	**19**	**1**	**9**	**10**	**51**
1989-90	**Philadelphia**	**NHL**	**75**	**22**	**26**	**48**	**104**	....	....	....	....	....
	NHL Totals		**475**	**120**	**194**	**314**	**762**	**69**	**6**	**27**	**33**	**149**

SUTTON, BOYD

Center/Left wing. Shoots left. 5'10", 175 lbs. Born, Anchorage, AK, December 6, 1966.
(Buffalo's 10th choice, 203rd overall, in 1985 Entry Draft).

			Regular Season					Playoffs				
Season	Club	Lea	GP	G	A	TP	PIM	GP	G	A	TP	PIM
1985-86	Miami-Ohio	CCHA	33	8	13	21	24	....	....	....	....	....
1986-87	Miami-Ohio	CCHA	39	19	18	37	44	....	....	....	....	....
1987-88	Miami-Ohio	CCHA	37	17	16	33	34	....	....	....	....	....
1988-89	Miami-Ohio	CCHA	37	16	23	39	24	....	....	....	....	....
1989-90	Greensboro	ECHL	60	32	26	58	25	....	....	....	....	....

SUTTON, KENNETH

Defense. Shoots left. 6', 185 lbs. Born, Edmonton, Alta., May 11, 1969.
(Buffalo's 4th choice, 98th overall, in 1989 Entry Draft).

			Regular Season					Playoffs				
Season	Club	Lea	GP	G	A	TP	PIM	GP	G	A	TP	PIM
1988-89	Saskatoon	WHL	71	22	31	53	104	8	2	5	7	12
1989-90	Rochester	AHL	57	5	14	19	83	11	1	6	7	15

SVENSSON, MAGNUS

Defense. Shoots left. 5'11", 180 lbs. Born, Leksand, Sweden, March 1, 1963.
(Calgary's 13th choice, 250th overall, in 1987 Entry Draft).

			Regular Season					Playoffs				
Season	Club	Lea	GP	G	A	TP	PIM	GP	G	A	TP	PIM
1983-84	Leksand	Swe.	35	3	8	11	20	....	....	....	....	....
1984-85	Leksand	Swe.	35	8	7	15	22	....	....	....	....	....
1985-86	Leksand	Swe.	36	6	9	15	62	....	....	....	....	....
1986-87	Leksand	Swe.	33	8	16	24	42	....	....	....	....	....
1987-88	Leksand	Swe.	40	12	11	23	20	....	....	....	....	....
1988-89	Leksand	Swe.	39	15	22	37	40	10	3	5	8	8
1989-90	Leksand	Swe.	26	11	12	23	60	1	0	0	0	0

SVETLOV, SERGEI

Right wing. Shoots left. 6'1", 195 lbs. Born, Penza, Soviet Union, January 17, 1961.
(New Jersey's 10th choice, 180th overall, in 1988 Entry Draft).

			Regular Season					Playoffs				
Season	Club	Lea	GP	G	A	TP	PIM	GP	G	A	TP	PIM
1987-88	Moscow D'amo	USSR	35	12	18	30	14	....	....	....	....	....
1988-89	Moscow D'amo	USSR	31	12	10	22	21	....	....	....	....	....
1989-90	Moscow D'amo	USSR	15	3	4	7	8	....	....	....	....	....

SVITEK, VLADIMIR

Right wing. Shoots left. 6'2", 180 lbs. Born, Banska Bystrica, Czech., October 19, 1962.
(Philadelphia's 9th choice, 137th overall, in 1981 Entry Draft).

			Regular Season					Playoffs				
Season	Club	Lea	GP	G	A	TP	PIM	GP	G	A	TP	PIM
1986-87	VSZ Kosice	Czech.	22	4	8	12	....	....	....	....	....	....
1987-88	VSZ Kosice	Czech.	21	13	8	21	....	....	....	....	....	....
1988-89	VSZ Kosice	Czech.	45	13	24	37	....	....	....	....	....	....
1989-90	VSZ Kosice	Czech	50	16	27	43	....	....	....	....	....	....

SVOBODA, PETR (svah-BOH-duh)

Defense. Shoots left. 6'1", 170 lbs. Born, Most, Czechoslovakia, February 14, 1966.
(Montreal's 1st choice, 5th overall, in 1984 Entry Draft).

			Regular Season					Playoffs				
Season	Club	Lea	GP	G	A	TP	PIM	GP	G	A	TP	PIM
1983-84	Czech. Jrs.	....	40	15	21	36	14	....	....	....	....	....
1984-85	**Montreal**	**NHL**	**73**	**4**	**27**	**31**	**65**	**7**	**1**	**1**	**2**	**12**
1985-86	**Montreal**	**NHL**	**73**	**1**	**18**	**19**	**93**	**8**	**0**	**0**	**0**	**21**
1986-87	**Montreal**	**NHL**	**70**	**5**	**17**	**22**	**63**	**14**	**0**	**5**	**5**	**10**
1987-88	**Montreal**	**NHL**	**69**	**7**	**22**	**29**	**149**	**10**	**0**	**5**	**5**	**12**
1988-89	**Montreal**	**NHL**	**71**	**8**	**37**	**45**	**147**	**21**	**1**	**11**	**12**	**16**
1989-90	**Montreal**	**NHL**	**60**	**5**	**31**	**36**	**98**	**10**	**0**	**5**	**5**	**7**
	NHL Totals		**416**	**30**	**152**	**182**	**615**	**70**	**2**	**27**	**29**	**78**

SWEENEY, DON

Defense. Shoots left. 5'11", 170 lbs. Born, St. Stephen, N.B., August 17, 1966.
(Boston's 8th choice, 166th overall, in 1984 Entry Draft).

			Regular Season					Playoffs				
Season	Club	Lea	GP	G	A	TP	PIM	GP	G	A	TP	PIM
1984-85	Harvard	ECAC	29	3	7	10	30	....	....	....	....	....
1985-86	Harvard	ECAC	31	4	5	9	12	....	....	....	....	....
1986-87	Harvard	ECAC	34	7	4	11	22	....	....	....	....	....
1987-88ab	Harvard	ECAC	30	6	23	29	37	....	....	....	....	....
	Maine	AHL	....	....	....	....	....	6	1	3	4	0
1988-89	**Boston**	**NHL**	**36**	**3**	**5**	**8**	**20**	....	....	....	....	....
	Maine	AHL	42	8	17	25	24	....	....	....	....	....
1989-90	**Boston**	**NHL**	**58**	**3**	**5**	**8**	**58**	**21**	**1**	**5**	**6**	**18**
	Maine	AHL	11	0	8	8	8	....	....	....	....	....
	NHL Totals		**94**	**6**	**10**	**16**	**78**	**21**	**1**	**5**	**6**	**18**

a NCAA East All-American Team (1988)
b ECAC First All-Star Team (1988)

SWEENEY, ROBERT (BOB)

Right wing. Shoots right. 6'3", 200 lbs. Born, Concord, MA, January 25, 1964.
(Boston's 6th choice, 123rd overall, in 1982 Entry Draft).

			Regular Season					Playoffs				
Season	Club	Lea	GP	G	A	TP	PIM	GP	G	A	TP	PIM
1982-83	Boston College	ECAC	30	17	11	28	10	....	....	....	....	....
1983-84	Boston College	ECAC	23	14	7	21	10	....	....	....	....	....
1984-85a	Boston College	ECAC	44	32	32	64	43	....	....	....	....	....
1985-86	Boston College	H.E.	41	15	24	39	52	....	....	....	....	....
1986-87	**Boston**	**NHL**	**14**	**2**	**4**	**6**	**21**	**3**	**0**	**0**	**0**	**0**
	Moncton	AHL	58	29	26	55	81	4	0	2	2	13
1987-88	**Boston**	**NHL**	**80**	**22**	**23**	**45**	**73**	**23**	**6**	**8**	**14**	**66**
1988-89	**Boston**	**NHL**	**75**	**14**	**14**	**28**	**99**	**10**	**2**	**4**	**6**	**19**
1989-90	**Boston**	**NHL**	**70**	**22**	**24**	**46**	**93**	**20**	**0**	**2**	**2**	**30**
	NHL Totals		**239**	**60**	**65**	**125**	**286**	**56**	**8**	**14**	**22**	**115**

a ECAC Second Team All-Star (1985)

SWEENEY, TIM

Left wing. Shoots left. 5'11", 180 lbs. Born, Boston. MA, April 12, 1967.
(Calgary's 7th choice, 122nd overall, in 1985 Entry Draft).

			Regular Season					Playoffs				
Season	Club	Lea	GP	G	A	TP	PIM	GP	G	A	TP	PIM
1985-86	Boston College	H.E.	32	8	4	12	8	....	....	....	....	....
1986-87	Boston College	H.E.	38	31	18	49	28	....	....	....	....	....
1987-88	Boston College	H.E.	18	9	11	20	18	....	....	....	....	....
1988-89ab	Boston College	H.E.	39	29	44	73	26	....	....	....	....	....
1989-90cd	Salt Lake	IHL	81	46	51	97	32	11	5	4	9	4

a Hockey East First All-Star Team (1989)
b NCAA East Second All-American Team (1989)
c IHL Second All-Star Team (1990)
d Won Ken McKenzie Trophy (Outstanding U.S.-born rookie—IHL) (1990)

SYDOR, DARYL (CEE-der)

Defense. Shoots left. 6'0", 205 lbs. Born, Edmonton, Alta., May 13, 1972.
(Los Angeles' 1st choice, 7th overall, in 1990 Entry Draft).

			Regular Season					Playoffs				
Season	Club	Lea	GP	G	A	TP	PIM	GP	G	A	TP	PIM
1988-89	Kamloops	WHL	65	12	14	26	86	15	1	4	5	19
1989-90a	Kamloops	WHL	67	29	66	95	129	17	2	9	11	28

a WHL West First All-Star Team (1990)

SYKES, PHIL

Left wing. Shoots left. 6', 185 lbs. Born, Dawson Creek, B.C., May 18, 1959.

			Regular Season					Playoffs				
Season	Club	Lea	GP	G	A	TP	PIM	GP	G	A	TP	PIM
1979-80	North Dakota	WCHA	37	22	27	49	34	....	....	....	....	....
1980-81	North Dakota	WCHA	38	28	34	62	22	....	....	....	....	....
1981-82abc	North Dakota	WCHA	37	22	27	49	34	....	....	....	....	....
1982-83	**Los Angeles**	**NHL**	**7**	**2**	**0**	**2**	**2**	....	....	....	....	....
	New Haven	AHL	71	19	26	45	111	12	2	2	4	21
1983-84	**Los Angeles**	**NHL**	**3**	**0**	**0**	**0**	**2**	....	....	....	....	....
	New Haven	AHL	77	29	37	66	101	....	....	....	....	....
1984-85	**Los Angeles**	**NHL**	**79**	**17**	**15**	**32**	**38**	**3**	**0**	**1**	**1**	**4**
1985-86	**Los Angeles**	**NHL**	**76**	**20**	**24**	**44**	**97**	....	....	....	....	....
1986-87	**Los Angeles**	**NHL**	**58**	**6**	**15**	**21**	**133**	**5**	**0**	**1**	**1**	**8**
1987-88	**Los Angeles**	**NHL**	**40**	**9**	**12**	**21**	**82**	**4**	**0**	**0**	**0**	**0**
1988-89	**Los Angeles**	**NHL**	**23**	**0**	**1**	**1**	**8**	**3**	**0**	**0**	**0**	**8**
	New Haven	AHL	34	9	17	26	23	....	....	....	....	....
1989-90	**Winnipeg**	**NHL**	**48**	**9**	**6**	**15**	**26**	**4**	**0**	**0**	**0**	**0**
	New Haven	AHL	25	3	12	15	32	....	....	....	....	....
	Moncton	AHL	5	0	1	1	20	....	....	....	....	....
	NHL Totals		**334**	**63**	**73**	**136**	**388**	**19**	**0**	**2**	**2**	**20**

a WCHA First All-Star Team (1982)
b Named WCHA Player of the Year (1982)
c Named Most Valuable Player, NCAA Tournament (1982)

Signed as a free agent by **Los Angeles**, April 5, 1982. Traded to **Winnipeg** by **Los Angeles** for Brad Jones, December 1, 1989.

TAGLIANETTI, PETER

Defense. Shoots left. 6'2", 195 lbs. Born, Framingham, MA, August 15, 1963.
(Winnipeg's 4th choice, 43rd overall, in 1983 Entry Draft).

			Regular Season					Playoffs				
Season	Club	Lea	GP	G	A	TP	PIM	GP	G	A	TP	PIM
1981-82	Providence	ECAC	2	0	0	0	2	....	....	....	....	....
1982-83	Providence	ECAC	43	4	17	21	68	....	....	....	....	....
1983-84	Providence	ECAC	30	4	25	29	68	....	....	....	....	....
1984-85	**Winnipeg**	**NHL**	**1**	**0**	**0**	**0**	**0**	**1**	**0**	**0**	**0**	**0**
a	Providence	H.E.	35	6	18	24	32	....	....	....	....	....
1985-86	**Winnipeg**	**NHL**	**18**	**0**	**0**	**0**	**48**	**3**	**0**	**0**	**0**	**2**
	Sherbrooke	AHL	24	1	18	9	75	....	....	....	....	....
1986-87	**Winnipeg**	**NHL**	**3**	**0**	**0**	**0**	**12**	....	....	....	....	....
	Sherbrooke	AHL	54	5	14	19	104	10	2	5	7	25
1987-88	**Winnipeg**	**NHL**	**70**	**6**	**17**	**23**	**182**	**5**	**1**	**1**	**2**	**12**
1988-89	**Winnipeg**	**NHL**	**66**	**1**	**14**	**15**	**226**	....	....	....	....	....
1989-90	**Winnipeg**	**NHL**	**49**	**3**	**6**	**9**	**136**	**5**	**0**	**0**	**0**	**6**
	Moncton	AHL	3	0	2	2	2	....	....	....	....	....
	NHL Totals		**207**	**10**	**37**	**47**	**604**	**14**	**1**	**1**	**2**	**20**

a Hockey East First All-Star Team (1985).

TANCILL, CHRIS

Center. Shoots right. 5'10", 185 lbs. Born, Livonia, MI, February 7, 1968.
(Hartford's 1st choice, 15th overall, in 1989 Supplemental Draft).

			Regular Season					Playoffs				
Season	Club	Lea	GP	G	A	TP	PIM	GP	G	A	TP	PIM
1986-87	U. Wisconsin	WCHA	40	9	23	32	26	....	....	....	....	....
1987-88	U. Wisconsin	WCHA	44	13	14	27	48	....	....	....	....	....
1988-89	U. Wisconsin	WCHA	44	20	23	43	50	....	....	....	....	....
1989-90a	U. Wisconsin	WCHA	45	39	32	71	44	....	....	....	....	....

a NCAA All-Tournament Team, Tournament MVP (1990)

TANTI, TONY (TAN-tee)

Right wing. Shoots left. 5'9", 190 lbs. Born, Toronto, Ont., September 7, 1963.
(Chicago's 1st choice, 12th overall, in 1981 Entry Draft).

			Regular Season					Playoffs				
Season	Club	Lea	GP	G	A	TP	PIM	GP	G	A	TP	PIM
1980-81a	Oshawa	OHA	67	81	69	150	197	11	7	8	15	41
1981-82	Chicago	NHL	2	0	0	0	0	....	....	....	....	....
b	Oshawa	OHL	57	62	64	126	138	12	14	12	26	15
1982-83	Oshawa	OHL	30	34	28	62	35	....	....	....	....	....
	Chicago	NHL	1	1	0	1	0	....	....	....	....	....
	Vancouver	NHL	39	8	8	16	16	4	0	1	1	0
1983-84	Vancouver	NHL	79	45	41	86	50	4	1	2	3	0
1984-85	Vancouver	NHL	68	39	20	59	45	....	....	....	....	....
1985-86	Vancouver	NHL	77	39	33	72	85	3	0	1	1	11
1986-87	Vancouver	NHL	77	41	38	79	84	....	....	....	....	....
1987-88	Vancouver	NHL	73	40	37	77	90	....	....	....	....	....
1988-89	Vancouver	NHL	77	24	25	49	69	7	0	5	5	4
1989-90	Vancouver	NHL	41	14	18	32	50	....	....	....	....	....
	Pittsburgh	NHL	37	14	18	32	22	....	....	....	....	....
	NHL Totals		571	265	238	503	511	18	1	9	10	15

a OHA First All-Star Team (1981)
b OHL Second All-Star Team (1982)

Played in NHL All-Star Game (1986)

Traded to **Vancouver** by **Chicago** for Curt Fraser, January 6, 1983. Traded to **Pittsburgh** by **Vancouver** with Rod Buskas and Barry Pederson for Dave Capuano, Andrew McBain and Dan Quinn, January 8, 1990.

TARDIF, PATRICE

Center. Shoots left. 6'2", 175 lbs. Born, Thetford Mines, Que., October 30, 1970.
(St. Louis' 2nd choice, 54th overall, in 1990 Entry Draft).

			Regular Season					Playoffs				
Season	Club	Lea	GP	G	A	TP	PIM	GP	G	A	TP	PIM
1989-90	Lennoxville	CEGEP	27	58	36	94	36	....	....	....	....	....

TARRANT, JERRY

Defense. Shoots left. 6'2", 190 lbs. Born, Burlington, VT, April 3, 1966.
(Calgary's 1st choice, 26th overall, in 1988 Supplemental Draft).

			Regular Season					Playoffs				
Season	Club	Lea	GP	G	A	TP	PIM	GP	G	A	TP	PIM
1985-86	U. of Vermont	ECAC	23	0	4	4	22	....	....	....	....	....
1986-87	U. of Vermont	ECAC	32	3	9	12	34	....	....	....	....	....
1987-88	U. of Vermont	ECAC	31	2	8	10	28	....	....	....	....	....
1988-89	U. of Vermont	ECAC	34	3	19	22	54	....	....	....	....	....
1989-90	Flint	IHL	23	0	0	0	27	....	....	....	....	....
	Salt Lake	IHL	8	0	0	0	12	....	....	....	....	....

TATARINOV, MIKHAIL

Defense. 5'10", 195 lbs. Born, Penza, Soviet Union, July 16, 1966.
(Washington's 10th choice, 225th overall, in 1984 Entry Draft).

			Regular Season					Playoffs				
Season	Club	Lea	GP	G	A	TP	PIM	GP	G	A	TP	PIM
1983-84	Sokol Kiev	USSR	38	7	3	10	46	....	....	....	....	....
1984-85	Sokol Kiev	USSR	34	3	6	9	54	....	....	....	....	....
1985-86	Sokol Kiev	USSR	37	7	5	12	41	....	....	....	....	....
1986-87	Moscow D'amo	USSR	40	10	8	18	43	....	....	....	....	....
1987-88	Moscow D'amo	USSR	30	2	2	4	8	....	....	....	....	....
1988-89	Moscow D'amo	USSR	4	1	0	1	2	....	....	....	....	....
1989-90	Moscow D'amo	USSR	44	11	10	21	34	....	....	....	....	....

TAYLOR, CHRIS

Center. Shoots left. 6', 185 lbs. Born, Stratford, Ont., March 6, 1972.
(NY Islanders' 2nd choice, 27th overall, in 1990 Entry Draft).

			Regular Season					Playoffs				
Season	Club	Lea	GP	G	A	TP	PIM	GP	G	A	TP	PIM
1988-89	London	OHL	62	7	16	23	52	15	0	2	2	15
1989-90	London	OHL	66	45	60	105	60	6	3	2	5	6

TAYLOR, DAVID ANDREW (DAVE)

Right wing. Shoots right. 6', 200 lbs. Born, Levack, Ont., December 4, 1955.
(Los Angeles' 14th choice, 210th overall, in 1975 Amateur Draft).

			Regular Season					Playoffs				
Season	Club	Lea	GP	G	A	TP	PIM	GP	G	A	TP	PIM
1976-77	Clarkson	ECAC	34	41	67	108	....	....	....	....	....	....
	Fort Worth	CHL	7	2	4	6	6	....	....	....	....	....
1977-78	Los Angeles	NHL	64	22	21	43	47	2	0	0	0	5
1978-79	Los Angeles	NHL	78	43	48	91	124	2	0	0	0	2
1979-80	Los Angeles	NHL	61	37	53	90	72	4	2	1	3	4
1980-81a	Los Angeles	NHL	72	47	65	112	130	4	2	2	4	10
1981-82	Los Angeles	NHL	78	39	67	106	130	10	4	6	10	20
1982-83	Los Angeles	NHL	46	21	37	58	76	....	....	....	....	....
1983-84	Los Angeles	NHL	63	20	49	69	91	....	....	....	....	....
1984-85	Los Angeles	NHL	79	41	51	92	132	3	2	2	4	8
1985-86	Los Angeles	NHL	76	33	38	71	110	....	....	....	....	....
1986-87	Los Angeles	NHL	67	18	44	62	84	5	2	3	5	6
1987-88	Los Angeles	NHL	68	26	41	67	129	5	3	3	6	6
1988-89	Los Angeles	NHL	70	26	37	63	80	11	1	5	6	19
1989-90	Los Angeles	NHL	58	15	26	41	96	6	4	4	8	2
	NHL Totals		880	388	577	965	1301	52	20	26	46	82

a NHL Second All-Star Team (1981)

Played in NHL All-Star Game (1981, 1982, 1986)

TAYLOR, RANDY

Defense. Shoots right. 6'2", 195 lbs. Born, Cornwall, Ont., July 30, 1965.
(Pittsburgh's 2nd choice, 9th overall, in 1986 Supplemental Draft).

			Regular Season					Playoffs				
Season	Club	Lea	GP	G	A	TP	PIM	GP	G	A	TP	PIM
1983-84	Harvard	ECAC	23	0	3	3	4	....	....	....	....	....
1984-85	Harvard	ECAC	30	6	30	36	12	....	....	....	....	....
1985-86a	Harvard	ECAC	33	5	20	25	30	....	....	....	....	....
1986-87b	Harvard	ECAC	34	3	35	38	30	....	....	....	....	....
1987-88	Peoria	IHL	27	1	7	8	22	7	0	1	1	8
	Muskegon	IHL	37	0	14	14	14	....	....	....	....	....
1988-89	Flint	IHL	31	2	6	8	11	....	....	....	....	....
	Indianapolis	IHL	44	2	15	17	31	....	....	....	....	....
1989-90	Muskegon	IHL	63	2	22	24	29	15	0	5	5	8

a ECAC Second All-Star Team (1986)
b ECAC First All-Star Team (1987)

TAYLOR, TIM

Center. Shoots left. 5'11", 170 lbs. Born, Stratford, Ont., February 6, 1969.
(Washington's 2nd choice, 36th overall, in 1988 Entry Draft).

			Regular Season					Playoffs				
Season	Club	Lea	GP	G	A	TP	PIM	GP	G	A	TP	PIM
1986-87	London	OHL	34	7	9	16	11	....	....	....	....	....
1987-88	London	OHL	64	46	50	96	66	12	9	9	18	26
1988-89	London	OHL	61	34	80	114	93	21	*21	25	*46	58
1989-90	Baltimore	AHL	79	31	36	67	124	9	2	2	4	13

TEPPER, STEPHEN

Right wing. Shoots right. 6'4", 220 lbs. Born, Westboro, MA, March 10, 1969.
(Chicago's 7th choice, 134th overall, in 1987 Entry Draft).

			Regular Season					Playoffs				
Season	Club	Lea	GP	G	A	TP	PIM	GP	G	A	TP	PIM
1988-89	U. of Maine	H.E.	26	3	9	12	32	....	....	....	....	....
1989-90	U. of Maine	H.E.	41	10	6	16	68	....	....	....	....	....

THAYER, CHRIS

Center. Shoots right. 6'2", 190 lbs. Born, Exeter, NH, November 9, 1967.
(Chicago's 10th choice, 224th overall, in 1986 Entry Draft).

			Regular Season					Playoffs				
Season	Club	Lea	GP	G	A	TP	PIM	GP	G	A	TP	PIM
1986-87	Kent	HS	22	15	22	37	0	....	....	....	....	....
1987-88	N. Hampshire	H.E.	18	0	0	0	8	....	....	....	....	....
1988-89	N. Hampshire	H.E.	DID NOT PLAY									
1989-90	N. Hampshire	H.E.	DID NOT PLAY									

THELVEN, MICHAEL (TEHL-vihn)

Defense. Shoots right. 5'11", 185 lbs. Born, Stockholm, Sweden, January 7, 1961.
(Boston's 8th choice, 186th overall, in 1980 Entry Draft).

			Regular Season					Playoffs				
Season	Club	Lea	GP	G	A	TP	PIM	GP	G	A	TP	PIM
1978-79	Djurgarden	Swe.	10	0	1	1	8	....	....	....	....	....
1980-81	Djurgarden	Swe.	28	2	4	6	38	....	....	....	....	....
1981-82	Djurgarden	Swe.	34	5	3	8	53	6	2	1	3	2
1982-83	Djurgarden	Swe.	30	3	14	17	50	7	1	2	3	12
1983-84	Djurgarden	Swe.	27	6	8	14	51	5	1	1	2	6
1984-85	Djurgarden	Swe.	33	8	13	21	54	8	0	2	2	2
1985-86	Boston	NHL	60	6	20	26	48	3	0	0	0	0
1986-87	Boston	NHL	34	5	15	20	18	....	....	....	....	....
1987-88	Boston	NHL	67	6	25	31	57	21	3	3	6	26
1988-89	Boston	NHL	40	3	18	21	71	10	1	7	8	8
1989-90	Boston	NHL	6	0	2	2	23	....	....	....	....	....
	NHL Totals		207	20	80	100	217	34	4	10	14	34

THIBAUDEAU, GILLES (TIB-ah-doh)

Left wing. Shoots left. 5'10", 165 lbs. Born, Montreal, Que., March 4, 1963.

			Regular Season					Playoffs				
Season	Club	Lea	GP	G	A	TP	PIM	GP	G	A	TP	PIM
1983-84	St. Antoine	Jr. B	38	63	77	140	146	....	....	....	....	....
1984-85	Sherbrooke	AHL	7	2	4	6	0	....	....	....	....	....
a	Flint	IHL	71	52	45	97	81	....	....	....	....	....
1985-86	Sherbrooke	AHL	61	15	23	38	20	....	....	....	....	....
1986-87	Montreal	NHL	9	1	3	4	0	....	....	....	....	....
	Sherbrooke	AHL	62	27	40	67	26	....	....	....	....	....
1987-88	Montreal	NHL	17	5	6	11	0	8	3	3	6	2
	Sherbrooke	AHL	59	39	57	96	45	....	....	....	....	....
1988-89	Montreal	NHL	32	6	6	12	6	....	....	....	....	....
1989-90	NY Islanders	NHL	20	4	4	8	17	....	....	....	....	....
	Springfield	AHL	6	5	8	13	0	....	....	....	....	....
	Toronto	NHL	21	7	11	18	13	....	....	....	....	....
	Newmarket	AHL	10	7	13	20	4	....	....	....	....	....
	NHL Totals		99	23	30	53	36	8	3	3	6	2

a IHL Second All-Star Team (1985)

Signed as a free agent by **Montreal**, October 9, 1984. Traded to **Toronto** by **NY Islanders** with Mike Stevens for Jack Capuano, Paul Gagne and Derek Laxdal, December 20, 1989.

THOMAS, JOHN (SCOTT)

Right wing. Shoots right. 6'2", 195 lbs. Born, Buffalo, NY, January 18, 1970.
(Buffalo's 2nd choice, 56th overall, in 1989 Entry Draft).

			Regular Season					Playoffs				
Season	Club	Lea	GP	G	A	TP	PIM	GP	G	A	TP	PIM
1988-89	Nichols	HS	....	38	52	90	....	....	....	....	....	....
1989-90	Clarkson	ECAC	34	19	13	32	95	....	....	....	....	....

THOMAS, STEVE

Left wing. Shoots left. 5'10", 180 lbs.   Born, Stockport, England, July 15, 1963.

			Regular Season					Playoffs				
Season	Club	Lea	GP	G	A	TP	PIM	GP	G	A	TP	PIM
1983-84	Toronto	OHL	70	51	54	105	77	....	....	....	....	....
1984-85	**Toronto**	**NHL**	18	1	1	2	2	....	....	....	....	....
ab	St. Catharines	AHL	64	42	48	90	56	....	....	....	....	....
1985-86	**Toronto**	**NHL**	65	20	37	57	36	10	6	8	14	9
	St. Catharines	AHL	19	18	14	32	35	....	....	....	....	....
1986-87	**Toronto**	**NHL**	78	35	27	62	114	13	2	3	5	13
1987-88	**Chicago**	**NHL**	30	13	13	26	40	3	1	2	3	6
1988-89	**Chicago**	**NHL**	45	21	19	40	69	12	3	5	8	10
1989-90	**Chicago**	**NHL**	76	40	30	70	91	20	7	6	13	33
	NHL Totals		312	130	127	257	352	58	19	24	43	71

a Won AHL Rookie of the Year (1985)
b AHL First All-Star Team (1985)
Signed as a free agent by **Toronto**, May 12, 1984. Traded to **Chicago** by **Toronto** with Rick Vaive and Bob McGill for Al Secord and Ed Olczyk, September 3, 1987.

THOMLINSON, DAVE

Left wing. Shoots left. 6'1", 185 lbs.   Born, Edmonton, Alta., October 22, 1966.
(Toronto's 3rd choice, 43rd overall, in 1985 Entry Draft).

			Regular Season					Playoffs				
Season	Club	Lea	GP	G	A	TP	PIM	GP	G	A	TP	PIM
1984-85	Brandon	WHL	26	13	14	27	70	....	....	....	....	....
1985-86	Brandon	WHL	53	25	20	45	116	....	....	....	....	....
1986-87	Brandon	WHL	2	0	1	1	9	....	....	....	....	....
	Moose Jaw	WHL	70	44	36	80	117	9	7	3	10	19
1987-88	Peoria	IHL	74	27	30	57	56	7	4	3	7	11
1988-89	Peoria	IHL	64	27	29	56	154	3	0	1	1	8
1989-90	**St. Louis**	**NHL**	19	1	2	3	12	....	....	....	....	....
	Peoria	IHL	59	27	40	67	87	5	1	1	2	15
	NHL Totals		19	1	2	3	12	....	....	....	....	....

Signed as a free agent by **St. Louis**, June 4, 1987.

THOMPSON, BRENT

Defense. Shoots left. 6'2", 175 lbs.   Born, Calgary, Alta., January 9, 1971.
(Los Angeles' 1st choice, 39th overall, in 1989 Entry Draft).

			Regular Season					Playoffs				
Season	Club	Lea	GP	G	A	TP	PIM	GP	G	A	TP	PIM
1988-89	Medicine Hat	WHL	72	3	10	13	160	3	0	0	0	2
1989-90	Medicine Hat	WHL	68	10	35	45	167	3	0	1	1	14

THOMSON, JIM

Right wing. Shoots right. 6'1", 205 lbs.   Born, Edmonton, Alta., December 30, 1965.
(Washington's 9th choice, 185th overall, in 1984 Entry Draft).

			Regular Season					Playoffs				
Season	Club	Lea	GP	G	A	TP	PIM	GP	G	A	TP	PIM
1983-84	Toronto	OHL	60	10	18	28	68	9	1	0	1	26
1984-85	Toronto	OHL	63	23	28	51	122	5	3	1	4	25
	Binghamton	AHL	4	0	0	0	2	....	....	....	....	....
1985-86	Binghamton	AHL	59	15	9	24	195	....	....	....	....	....
1986-87	**Washington**	**NHL**	10	0	0	0	35	....	....	....	....	....
	Binghamton	AHL	57	13	10	23	360	10	0	1	1	40
1987-88	Binghamton	AHL	25	8	9	17	64	4	1	2	3	7
1988-89	**Washington**	**NHL**	14	2	0	2	53	....	....	....	....	....
	Hartford	**NHL**	5	0	0	0	14	....	....	....	....	....
	Baltimore	AHL	41	25	16	41	129	....	....	....	....	....
1989-90	**New Jersey**	**NHL**	3	0	0	0	31	....	....	....	....	....
	Binghamton	AHL	8	1	2	3	30	....	....	....	....	....
	Utica	AHL	60	20	23	43	124	4	1	0	1	19
	NHL Totals		32	2	0	2	133	....	....	....	....	....

Traded to **Hartford** by **Washington** for Scot Kleinendorst, March 6, 1989. Traded to **New Jersey** by **Hartford** for Chris Cichocki, October 31, 1989.

THORNTON, SCOTT

Center. Shoots left. 6'2", 200 lbs.   Born, London, Ont., January 9, 1971.
(Toronto's 1st choice, 3rd overall, in 1989 Entry Draft).

			Regular Season					Playoffs				
Season	Club	Lea	GP	G	A	TP	PIM	GP	G	A	TP	PIM
1987-88	Belleville	OHL	62	11	19	30	54	6	0	1	1	2
1988-89	Belleville	OHL	59	28	34	62	103	5	1	1	2	6
1989-90	Belleville	OHL	47	21	28	49	91	11	2	10	12	15

THYER, MARIO

Center. Shoots left. 5'11", 170 lbs. Born, Montreal, Que., September 29, 1966.

			Regular Season					Playoffs				
Season	Club	Lea	GP	G	A	TP	PIM	GP	G	A	TP	PIM
1987-88	U. of Maine	H.E.	44	24	42	66	4	....	....	....	....	....
1988-89	U. of Maine	H.E.	9	9	7	16	0	....	....	....	....	....
1989-90	**Minnesota**	**NHL**	5	0	0	0	0	1	0	0	0	2
	Kalamazoo	IHL	68	19	42	61	12	10	2	6	8	4
	NHL Totals		5	0	0	0	0	1	0	0	0	2

Signed as a free agent by **Minnesota**, July 12, 1989.

TICHY, MILAN

Defense. Shoots left. 6'3", 195 lbs. Born, Czechoslovakia, September 22, 1969.
(Chicago's 6th choice, 153rd overall, in 1989 Entry Draft).

			Regular Season					Playoffs				
Season	Club	Lea	GP	G	A	TP	PIM	GP	G	A	TP	PIM
1988-89	Skoda Plzen	Czech.	36	1	12	13	44	....	....	....	....	....
1989-90	Dukla Trencin	Czech.	51	14	8	22	....	....	....	....	....	....

TIKKANEN, ESA   (TEE-kuh-nehn)

Left wing. Shoots left. 6'1", 200 lbs.   Born, Helsinki, Finland, January 25, 1965.
(Edmonton's 4th choice, 82nd overall, in 1983 Entry Draft).

			Regular Season					Playoffs				
Season	Club	Lea	GP	G	A	TP	PIM	GP	G	A	TP	PIM
1981-82	Regina	WHL	2	0	0	0	0	....	....	....	....	....
1982-83	IFK	Fin. Jr.	30	34	31	65	104	4	4	3	7	10
	IFK	Fin.	....	....	....	....	....	1	0	0	0	2
1983-84	IFK	Fin. Jr.	6	5	9	14	13	4	4	3	7	8
	IFK	Fin.	36	19	11	30	30	2	0	0	0	0
1984-85	IFK	Fin.	36	21	33	54	42	....	....	....	....	....
	Edmonton	**NHL**	....	....	....	....	....	3	0	0	0	2
1985-86	**Edmonton**	**NHL**	35	7	6	13	28	8	3	2	5	7
	Nova Scotia	AHL	15	4	8	12	17	....	....	....	....	....
1986-87	**Edmonton**	**NHL**	76	34	44	78	120	21	7	2	9	22
1987-88	**Edmonton**	**NHL**	80	23	51	74	153	19	10	17	27	72
1988-89	**Edmonton**	**NHL**	67	31	47	78	92	7	1	3	4	12
1989-90	**Edmonton**	**NHL**	79	30	33	63	161	22	13	11	24	26
	NHL Totals		337	125	181	306	554	80	34	35	69	141

TILLEY, TOM

Defense. Shoots right. 6', 180 lbs.   Born, Trenton, Ont., March 28, 1965.
(St. Louis' 13th choice, 196th overall, in 1984 Entry Draft).

			Regular Season					Playoffs				
Season	Club	Lea	GP	G	A	TP	PIM	GP	G	A	TP	PIM
1984-85	Michigan State	CCHA	37	1	5	6	58	....	....	....	....	....
1985-86	Michigan State	CCHA	42	9	25	34	48	....	....	....	....	....
1986-87	Michigan State	CCHA	42	7	14	21	48	....	....	....	....	....
1987-88a	Michigan State	CCHA	46	8	18	26	44	....	....	....	....	....
1988-89	**St. Louis**	**NHL**	70	1	22	23	47	10	1	2	3	17
1989-90	**St. Louis**	**NHL**	34	0	5	5	6	....	....	....	....	....
	Peoria	IHL	22	1	8	9	13	....	....	....	....	....
	NHL Totals		104	1	27	28	53	10	1	2	3	17

a CCHA First All-Star Team (1988)

TINORDI, MARK

Defense. Shoots left. 6'4", 205 lbs.   Born, Red Deer, Alta., May 9, 1966.

			Regular Season					Playoffs				
Season	Club	Lea	GP	G	A	TP	PIM	GP	G	A	TP	PIM
1982-83	Lethbridge	WHL	64	0	4	4	50	20	1	1	2	6
1983-84	Lethbridge	WHL	72	5	14	19	53	5	0	1	1	7
1984-85	Lethbridge	WHL	58	10	15	25	134	4	0	2	2	12
1985-86	Lethbridge	WHL	58	8	30	38	139	8	1	3	4	15
1986-87	Calgary	WHL	61	29	37	66	148	....	....	....	....	....
	New Haven	AHL	2	0	0	0	2	2	0	0	0	0
1987-88	**NY Rangers**	**NHL**	24	1	2	3	50	....	....	....	....	....
	Colorado	IHL	41	8	19	27	150	11	1	5	6	31
1988-89	**Minnesota**	**NHL**	47	2	3	5	107	5	0	0	0	0
	Kalamazoo	IHL	10	0	0	0	35	....	....	....	....	....
1989-90	**Minnesota**	**NHL**	66	3	7	10	240	7	0	1	1	16
	NHL Totals		137	6	12	18	397	12	0	1	1	16

Signed as a free agent by **NY Rangers**, January 4, 1987.
Traded to **Minnesota** by **NY Rangers** with Paul Jerrard, the rights to Bret Barnett and Mike Sullivan, and Los Angeles' third-round choice (Murray Garbutt) in 1989 Entry Draft — acquired March 10, 1987 by Minnesota — for Brian Lawton, Igor Liba and the rights to Eric Bennett, October 11, 1988.

TIPPETT, DAVE   (TIP-it)

Left wing. Shoots left. 5'10", 180 lbs.   Born, Moosomin, Sask., August 25, 1961.

			Regular Season					Playoffs				
Season	Club	Lea	GP	G	A	TP	PIM	GP	G	A	TP	PIM
1981-82	North Dakota	WCHA	43	13	28	41	20	....	....	....	....	....
1982-83	North Dakota	WCHA	36	15	31	46	24	....	....	....	....	....
1983-84	Cdn. Olympic		66	14	19	33	24	....	....	....	....	....
	Hartford	**NHL**	17	4	2	6	2	....	....	....	....	....
1984-85	**Hartford**	**NHL**	80	7	12	19	12	....	....	....	....	....
1985-86	**Hartford**	**NHL**	80	14	20	34	18	10	2	2	4	4
1986-87	**Hartford**	**NHL**	80	9	22	31	42	6	0	2	2	4
1987-88	**Hartford**	**NHL**	80	16	21	37	32	6	0	0	0	2
1988-89	**Hartford**	**NHL**	80	17	24	41	45	4	0	1	1	0
1989-90	**Hartford**	**NHL**	66	8	19	27	32	7	1	3	4	2
	NHL Totals		483	75	120	195	183	33	3	8	11	12

Signed as free agent by **Hartford**, February 29, 1984.

TIRKKONEN, PEKKA

Center. Shoots left. 6'1", 195 lbs.   Born, Savonlinna, Finland, July 17, 1968.
(Boston's 2nd choice, 34th overall, in 1986 Entry Draft)

			Regular Season					Playoffs				
Season	Club	Lea	GP	G	A	TP	PIM	GP	G	A	TP	PIM
1987-88	T.P.S.	Fin.	44	11	12	23	4	....	....	....	....	....
1988-89	T.P.S.	Fin.	42	11	15	26	8	10	1	2	3	0
1989-90	T.P.S.	Fin.	41	17	11	28	0	9	3	4	7	0

TISDALE, TIMOTHY

Center. Shoots right. 6'1", 190 lbs.   Born, Shaunavon, Sask., May 28, 1968.
(Edmonton's 13th choice, 250th overall, in 1988 Entry Draft).

			Regular Season					Playoffs				
Season	Club	Lea	GP	G	A	TP	PIM	GP	G	A	TP	PIM
1987-88	Swift Current	WHL	32	11	15	26	45	....	....	....	....	....
1988-89	Swift Current	WHL	68	57	82	139	89	12	17	15	32	22
1989-90	Cape Breton	AHL	66	15	21	36	24	3	0	0	0	0

TKACHUK, GRANT **(kuh-CHUK)**

Left wing. Shoots left. 5'10", 180 lbs. Born, Lac La Biche, Alta., September 24, 1968.
(Buffalo's 9th choice, 169th overall, in 1987 Entry Draft).

			Regular Season					Playoffs				
Season	Club	Lea	GP	G	A	TP	PIM	GP	G	A	TP	PIM
1984-85	Saskatoon	WHL	71	8	16	24	55	3	0	1	1	2
1985-86	Saskatoon	WHL	52	18	27	45	82	12	1	3	4	15
1986-87	Saskatoon	WHL	71	46	36	82	108	11	4	3	7	12
1987-88a	Saskatoon	WHL	70	51	46	97	126	6	3	6	9	8
1988-89	Rochester	AHL	64	12	13	25	26	....	....	....	....	....
1989-90	Phoenix	IHL	72	17	23	40	66	....	....	....	....	....

a WHL East All-Star Team (1988)

TKACHUK, KEITH **(kuh-CHUK)**

Center. Shoots left. 6'2", 200 lbs. Born, Melrose, MA, March 28, 1972.
(Winnipeg's 1st choice, 19th overall, in 1990 Entry Draft)

			Regular Season					Playoffs				
Season	Club	Lea	GP	G	A	TP	PIM	GP	G	A	TP	PIM
1988-89	Malden Catholic	HS	21	30	16	46	....	....	....	....	....	....
1989-90	Malden Catholic	HS	6	12	14	26	....	....	....	....	....	....

TOCCHET, RICK **(TAHK-iht)**

Right wing. Shoots right. 6', 195 lbs. Born, Scarborough, Ont., April 9, 1964.
(Philadelphia's 5th choice, 121st overall, in 1983 Entry Draft).

			Regular Season					Playoffs				
Season	Club	Lea	GP	G	A	TP	PIM	GP	G	A	TP	PIM
1981-82	S. S. Marie	OHL	59	7	15	22	184	11	1	1	2	28
1982-83	S. S. Marie	OHL	66	32	34	66	146	16	4	13	17	67
1983-84	S. S. Marie	OHL	64	44	64	108	209	16	*22	14	*36	41
1984-85	**Philadelphia**	**NHL**	**75**	**14**	**25**	**39**	**181**	**19**	**3**	**4**	**7**	**72**
1985-86	**Philadelphia**	**NHL**	**69**	**14**	**21**	**35**	**284**	**5**	**1**	**2**	**3**	**26**
1986-87	**Philadelphia**	**NHL**	**69**	**21**	**26**	**47**	**288**	**26**	**11**	**10**	**21**	**72**
1987-88	**Philadelphia**	**NHL**	**65**	**31**	**33**	**64**	**301**	**5**	**1**	**4**	**5**	**55**
1988-89	**Philadelphia**	**NHL**	**66**	**45**	**36**	**81**	**183**	**16**	**6**	**6**	**12**	**69**
1989-90	**Philadelphia**	**NHL**	**75**	**37**	**59**	**96**	**196**	....	....	....	....	....
	NHL Totals		**419**	**162**	**200**	**362**	**1433**	**71**	**22**	**26**	**48**	**294**

Played in NHL All-Star Game (1989, 1990)

TODD, KEVIN

Center. Shoots left. 5'10", 180 lbs. Born, Winnipeg, Man., May 4, 1968.
(New Jersey's 7th choice, 129th overall, in 1986 Entry Draft).

			Regular Season					Playoffs				
Season	Club	Lea	GP	G	A	TP	PIM	GP	G	A	TP	PIM
1985-86	Prince Albert	WHL	55	14	25	39	19	20	7	6	13	29
1986-87	Prince Albert	WHL	71	39	46	85	92	8	2	5	7	17
1987-88	Prince Albert	WHL	72	49	72	121	83	10	8	11	19	27
1988-89	**New Jersey**	**NHL**	**1**	**0**	**0**	**0**	**0**	....	....	....	....	....
	Utica	AHL	78	26	45	71	62	4	2	0	2	6
1989-90	Utica	AHL	71	18	36	54	72	5	2	4	6	2
	NHL Totals		**1**	**0**	**0**	**0**	**0**	....	....	....	....	....

TOIVOLA, TERO

Left wing. Shoots left. 5'11", 155 lbs. Born, Tampere, Finland, July 22, 1968.
(Washington's 10th choice, 187th overall, in 1986 Entry Draft).

			Regular Season					Playoffs				
Season	Club	Lea	GP	G	A	TP	PIM	GP	G	A	TP	PIM
1987-88	Tappara	Fin.	31	6	8	14	18	7	0	1	1	12
1988-89	Tappara	Fin.	32	7	14	21	16	5	2	1	3	4
1989-90	KooKoo	Fin.	42	14	32	46	41	....	....	....	....	....

TOMBERLIN, JUSTIN

Center. Shoots left. 6', 190 lbs. Born, Grand Rapids, MN, November 15, 1970.
(Toronto's 11th choice, 192nd overall, in 1989 Entry Draft).

			Regular Season					Playoffs				
Season	Club	Lea	GP	G	A	TP	PIM	GP	G	A	TP	PIM
1988-89	Greenway	HS	24	32	18	50	0	....	....	....	....	....
1989-90	U. of Maine	H.E.	35	10	7	17	6	....	....	....	....	....

TOMLAK, MIKE

Left wing. Shoots left. 6'3", 205 lbs. Born, Thunder Bay, Ont., October 17, 1964.
(Toronto's 10th choice, 208th overall, in 1983 Entry Draft).

			Regular Season					Playoffs				
Season	Club	Lea	GP	G	A	TP	PIM	GP	G	A	TP	PIM
1987-88	Western Ont.	OUAA	39	24	52	76	....	....	....	....	....	....
1988-89	Western Ont.	OUAA	35	16	34	50	....	....	....	....	....	....
1989-90	**Hartford**	**NHL**	**70**	**7**	**14**	**21**	**48**	**7**	**0**	**1**	**1**	**2**
	NHL Totals		**70**	**7**	**14**	**21**	**48**	**7**	**0**	**1**	**1**	**2**

Signed as a free agent by **Hartford**, June, 1989.

TOMLINSON, DAVE

Center. Shoots left. 5'10", 185 lbs. Born, North Vancouver, B.C., May 8, 1969.
(Toronto's 1st choice, 3rd overall, in 1989 Supplemental Draft).

			Regular Season					Playoffs				
Season	Club	Lea	GP	G	A	TP	PIM	GP	G	A	TP	PIM
1987-88	Boston U.	H.E.	34	16	20	36	28	....	....	....	....	....
1988-89	Boston U.	H.E.	34	16	30	46	40	....	....	....	....	....
1989-90	Boston U.	H.E.	43	15	22	37	53	....	....	....	....	....

TONELLI, JOHN **(tah-NEL-ee)**

Left wing. Shoots left. 6'1", 200 lbs. Born, Milton, Ont., March 23, 1957.
(NY Islanders' 2nd choice, 33rd overall, in 1977 Amateur Draft).

			Regular Season					Playoffs				
Season	Club	Lea	GP	G	A	TP	PIM	GP	G	A	TP	PIM
1973-74	Toronto	OHA	69	18	37	55	62	....	....	....	....	....
1974-75a	Toronto	OHA	70	49	86	135	85	....	....	....	....	....
1975-76	Houston	WHA	79	17	14	31	66	17	7	7	14	18
1976-77	Houston	WHA	80	24	31	55	109	11	3	4	7	12
1977-78	Houston	WHA	65	23	41	64	103	6	1	3	4	8
1978-79	**NY Islanders**	**NHL**	**73**	**17**	**39**	**56**	**44**	**10**	**1**	**6**	**7**	**0**
1979-80	**NY Islanders**	**NHL**	**77**	**14**	**30**	**44**	**49**	**21**	**7**	**9**	**16**	**18**
1980-81	**NY Islanders**	**NHL**	**70**	**20**	**32**	**52**	**57**	**16**	**5**	**8**	**13**	**16**
1981-82b	**NY Islanders**	**NHL**	**80**	**35**	**58**	**93**	**57**	**19**	**6**	**10**	**16**	**18**
1982-83	**NY Islanders**	**NHL**	**76**	**31**	**40**	**71**	**55**	**20**	**7**	**11**	**18**	**20**
1983-84	**NY Islanders**	**NHL**	**73**	**27**	**40**	**67**	**66**	**17**	**1**	**3**	**4**	**31**
1984-85b	**NY Islanders**	**NHL**	**80**	**42**	**58**	**100**	**95**	**10**	**1**	**8**	**9**	**10**
1985-86	**NY Islanders**	**NHL**	**65**	**20**	**41**	**61**	**50**	....	....	....	....	....
	Calgary	**NHL**	**9**	**3**	**4**	**7**	**10**	**22**	**7**	**9**	**16**	**49**
1986-87	**Calgary**	**NHL**	**78**	**20**	**31**	**51**	**72**	**3**	**0**	**0**	**0**	**4**
1987-88	**Calgary**	**NHL**	**74**	**17**	**41**	**58**	**84**	**6**	**2**	**5**	**7**	**8**
1988-89	**Los Angeles**	**NHL**	**77**	**31**	**33**	**64**	**110**	**6**	**0**	**0**	**0**	**8**
1989-90	**Los Angeles**	**NHL**	**73**	**31**	**37**	**68**	**62**	**10**	**1**	**2**	**3**	**6**
	NHL Totals		**905**	**308**	**484**	**792**	**811**	**160**	**38**	**71**	**109**	**188**

a OHA First All-Star Team (1975)
b NHL Second Team All-Star (1982, 1985)

Played in NHL All-Star Game (1982, 1985)

Traded to **Calgary** by **NY Islanders** for Richard Kromm and Steve Konroyd, March 11, 1986. Signed as a free agent by **Los Angeles**, June 29, 1988.

TOOKEY, TIMOTHY RAYMOND (TIM)

Center. Shoots left. 5'11", 180 lbs. Born, Edmonton, Alta., August 29, 1960.
(Washington's 4th choice, 88th overall, in 1979 Entry Draft).

			Regular Season					Playoffs				
Season	Club	Lea	GP	G	A	TP	PIM	GP	G	A	TP	PIM
1977-78	Portland	WHL	72	16	15	31	55	8	2	2	4	5
1978-79	Portland	WHL	56	33	47	80	55	25	6	14	20	6
1979-80	Portland	WHL	70	58	83	141	55	8	2	5	7	4
1980-81	**Washington**	**NHL**	**29**	**10**	**13**	**23**	**18**	....	....	....	....	....
	Hershey	AHL	47	20	38	58	129	....	....	....	....	....
1981-82	**Washington**	**NHL**	**28**	**8**	**8**	**16**	**35**	....	....	....	....	....
	Hershey	AHL	14	4	9	13	10	....	....	....	....	....
	Fredericton	AHL	16	6	10	16	16	....	....	....	....	....
1982-83	**Quebec**	**NHL**	**12**	**1**	**6**	**7**	**4**	....	....	....	....	....
	Fredericton	AHL	53	24	43	67	24	9	5	4	9	0
1983-84	**Pittsburgh**	**NHL**	**8**	**0**	**2**	**2**	**2**	....	....	....	....	....
	Baltimore	AHL	58	16	28	44	25	8	1	1	2	2
1984-85	Baltimore	AHL	74	25	43	68	74	15	8	10	18	13
1985-86ab	Hershey	AHL	69	35	*62	97	66	18	*11	8	19	10
1986-87	**Philadelphia**	**NHL**	**2**	**0**	**0**	**0**	**0**	**10**	**1**	**3**	**4**	**2**
cde	Hershey	AHL	80	51	*73	*124	45	5	5	4	9	0
1987-88	**Los Angeles**	**NHL**	**20**	**1**	**6**	**7**	**8**	....	....	....	....	....
	New Haven	AHL	11	6	7	13	2	....	....	....	....	....
1988-89	**Los Angeles**	**NHL**	**7**	**2**	**1**	**3**	**4**	....	....	....	....	....
	New Haven	AHL	33	11	18	29	30	....	....	....	....	....
	Muskegon	IHL	18	7	14	21	7	8	2	9	11	4
1989-90	Hershey	AHL	42	18	22	40	28	....	....	....	....	....
	NHL Totals		**106**	**22**	**36**	**58**	**71**	**10**	**1**	**3**	**4**	**2**

a AHL Second All-Star Team (1986)
b AHL Playoff MVP (1986)
c AHL First All-Star Team (1987)
d Won Les Cunningham Plaque (MVP-AHL 1987)
e Won John B. Sollenberger Trophy (Top Scorer–AHL 1987)

Traded to **Quebec** by **Washington** with Washington's seventh round choice (Daniel Poudrier) in 1982 Entry Draft for Lee Norwood and Quebec's sixth round choice (Mats Kihlstron) —later transferred to Calgary— in 1982 Entry Draft, February 1, 1982. Signed as free agent by **Pittsburgh**, September 12, 1983. Signed as a free agent by **Philadelphia,** July 23, 1985. Claimed by **Los Angeles** in NHL Waiver Draft, October 5, 1987. Traded to **Pittsburgh** by **Los Angeles** for Patrick Mayer, March 7, 1989

TORKKI, JARI **(TOHR-kee)**

Left wing. Shoots left. 5'11", 165 lbs. Born, Rauma, Finland, August 11, 1965.
(Chicago's 6th choice, 115th overall, in 1983 Entry Draft).

			Regular Season					Playoffs				
Season	Club	Lea	GP	G	A	TP	PIM	GP	G	A	TP	PIM
1985-86	Lukko	Fin.	32	22	18	40	40	....	....	....	....	....
1986-87	Lukko	Fin.	44	27	8	35	42	....	....	....	....	....
1987-88	Lukko	Fin.	43	23	24	47	54	8	4	3	7	12
1988-89	**Chicago**	**NHL**	**4**	**1**	**0**	**1**	**0**	....	....	....	....	....
	Saginaw	IHL	72	30	42	72	22	6	2	1	3	4
1989-90	Indianapolis	IHL	66	25	29	54	50	11	5	2	7	8
	NHL Totals		**4**	**1**	**0**	**1**	**0**	....	....	....	....	....

TORREL, DOUGLAS

Center. Shoots right. 6'2", 175 lbs. Born, Hibbing, MN, April 29, 1969.
(Vancouver's 3rd choice, 66th overall, in 1987 Entry Draft).

			Regular Season					Playoffs				
Season	Club	Lea	GP	G	A	TP	PIM	GP	G	A	TP	PIM
1988-89	Minn.-Duluth	WCHA	40	4	6	10	36	....	....	....	....	....
1989-90	Minn.-Duluth	WCHA	39	11	11	22	48	....	....	....	....	....

TOUPAL, RADEK

Center. Shoots right. 5'11", 185 lbs. Born, Pisek, Czechoslovakia, August 18, 1966.
(Edmonton's 6th choice, 126th overall, in 1987 Entry Draft).

			Regular Season					Playoffs				
Season	Club	Lea	GP	G	A	TP	PIM	GP	G	A	TP	PIM
1982-83	Budejovice	Czech.	3	1	0	1	0	....	....	....	....	....
1983-84	Budejovice	Czech.	6	0	2	2	0	....	....	....	....	....
1984-85	Budejovice	Czech.	40	8	10	18	16	....	....	....	....	....
1985-86	Budejovice	Czech.	43	21	14	35	....	....	....	....	....	....
1986-87	Budejovice	Czech.	35	16	14	30	20	....	....	....	....	....
1987-88	Budejovice	Czech.	31	16	17	33	10	....	....	....	....	....
1988-89	Budejovice	Czech.	43	29	29	58	10	....	....	....	....	....
1989-90	Budejovice	Czech.	47	23	27	50	....	....	....	....	....	....

TOWNSHEND, GRAEME

Right wing. Shoots right. 6'2", 225 lbs. Born, Kingston, Jamaica, October 2, 1965.

			Regular Season					Playoffs				
Season	Club	Lea	GP	G	A	TP	PIM	GP	G	A	TP	PIM
1985-86	RPI	ECAC	29	1	7	8	52	....	....	....	....	....
1986-87	RPI	ECAC	29	6	1	7	50	....	....	....	....	....
1987-88	RPI	ECAC	32	6	14	20	64	....	....	....	....	....
1988-89	Maine	AHL	5	2	1	3	11	....	....	....	....	....
	RPI	ECAC	31	6	16	22	50	....	....	....	....	....
1989-90	**Boston**	**NHL**	**4**	**0**	**0**	**0**	**7**	....	....	....	....	....
	Maine	AHL	64	15	13	28	162	....	....	....	....	....
	NHL Totals		**4**	**0**	**0**	**0**	**7**	....	....	....	....	....

TRESL, LADISLAV

Center. Shoots left. 6'1", 170 lbs. Born, Brno, Czechoslovakia, July 30, 1961.
(Quebec's 10th choice, 183rd overall, in 1987 Entry Draft)

			Regular Season					Playoffs				
Season	Club	Lea	GP	G	A	TP	PIM	GP	G	A	TP	PIM
1986-87	Zetor Brno	Czech.	33	13	11	24	....	....	....	....	....	....
1987-88	Fredericton	AHL	30	6	16	22	16	....	....	....	....	....
1988-89	Halifax	AHL	67	24	35	59	28	4	0	1	1	4
1989-90	Halifax	AHL	66	35	39	74	64	6	3	2	5	6

TRETOWICZ, DAVID

Defense. Shoots left. 5'11", 190 lbs. Born, Liverpool, NY, March 15, 1969.
(Calgary's 11th choice, 231st overall, in 1988 Entry Draft).

			Regular Season					Playoffs				
Season	Club	Lea	GP	G	A	TP	PIM	GP	G	A	TP	PIM
1987-88	Clarkson	ECAC	35	8	14	22	28	....	....	....	....	....
1988-89	Clarkson	ECAC	32	6	17	23	22	....	....	....	....	....
1989-90a	Clarkson	ECAC	35	15	24	39	34	....	....	....	....	....

a ECAC Second All-Star Team (1990)

TROTTIER, BRYAN JOHN (TRAH-chay)

Center. Shoots left. 5'11", 195 lbs. Born, Val Marie, Sask., July 17, 1956.
(NY Islanders' 2nd choice, 22nd overall, in 1974 Amateur Draft).

			Regular Season					Playoffs				
Season	Club	Lea	GP	G	A	TP	PIM	GP	G	A	TP	PIM
1972-73	Swift Current	WHL	67	16	29	45	10	....	....	....	....	....
1973-74	Swift Current	WHL	68	41	71	112	76	13	7	8	15	8
1974-75ab	Lethbridge	WHL	67	46	*98	144	103	6	2	5	7	14
1975-76c	**NY Islanders**	**NHL**	**80**	**32**	**63**	**95**	**21**	**13**	**1**	**7**	**8**	**8**
1976-77	**NY Islanders**	**NHL**	**76**	**30**	**42**	**72**	**34**	**12**	**2**	**8**	**10**	**2**
1977-78d	**NY Islanders**	**NHL**	**77**	**46**	***77**	**123**	**46**	**7**	**0**	**3**	**3**	**4**
1978-79defg	**NY Islanders**	**NHL**	**76**	**47**	***87**	***134**	**50**	**10**	**2**	**4**	**6**	**13**
1979-80h	**NY Islanders**	**NHL**	**78**	**42**	**62**	**104**	**68**	**21**	***12**	**17**	***29**	**16**
1980-81	**NY Islanders**	**NHL**	**73**	**31**	**72**	**103**	**74**	***18**	**11**	***18**	**29**	**34**
1981-82i	**NY Islanders**	**NHL**	**80**	**50**	**79**	**129**	**88**	**19**	**6**	***23**	***29**	**40**
1982-83	**NY Islanders**	**NHL**	**80**	**34**	**55**	**89**	**68**	**17**	**8**	**12**	**20**	**18**
1983-84i	**NY Islanders**	**NHL**	**68**	**40**	**71**	**111**	**59**	**21**	**8**	**6**	**14**	**49**
1984-85	**NY Islanders**	**NHL**	**68**	**28**	**31**	**59**	**47**	**10**	**4**	**2**	**6**	**8**
1985-86	**NY Islanders**	**NHL**	**78**	**37**	**59**	**96**	**72**	**3**	**1**	**1**	**2**	**2**
1986-87	**NY Islanders**	**NHL**	**80**	**23**	**64**	**87**	**50**	**14**	**8**	**5**	**13**	**12**
1987-88j	**NY Islanders**	**NHL**	**77**	**30**	**52**	**82**	**48**	**6**	**0**	**0**	**0**	**10**
1988-89k	**NY Islanders**	**NHL**	**73**	**17**	**28**	**45**	**44**	....	....	....	....	....
1989-90	**NY Islanders**	**NHL**	**59**	**13**	**11**	**24**	**29**	**4**	**1**	**0**	**1**	**4**
	NHL Totals		**1123**	**500**	**853**	**1353**	**798**	**175**	**64**	**106**	**170**	**220**

a WHL Most Valuable Player (1975)
b WHL First All-Star Team (1975)
c Won Calder Memorial Trophy (1976)
d NHL First All-Star Team (1978, 1979)
e Won Art Ross Trophy (1979)
f Won Hart Trophy (1979)
g NHL Plus/Minus Leader (1979)
h Won Conn Smythe Trophy (1980)
i NHL Second All-Star Team (1982, 1984)
j Named Budweiser/NHL Man of the Year (1988)
k Won King Clancy Memorial Trophy (1989)

Played in NHL All-Star Game (1976, 1978, 1980, 1982, 1983, 1985, 1986)

Signed as a free agent by **Pittsburgh**, July 20, 1990.

TRUE, SOREN

Right wing. Shoots left. 6'0", 175 lbs. Born, Aarhus, Denmark, February 9, 1968.
(NY Rangers' 12th choice, 240th overall, in 1986 Entry Draft).

			Regular Season					Playoffs				
Season	Club	Lea	GP	G	A	TP	PIM	GP	G	A	TP	PIM
1988-89	Humboldt	SJHL	63	45	68	113	75	....	....	....	....	....
1989-90	Flint	IHL	54	15	17	32	49	4	0	1	1	2

TSUJIURA, STEVE (tah-JUR-a)

Center. Shoots left. 5'5", 155 lbs. Born, Goaldale, Alta., February 28, 1962.
(Philadelphia's 10th choice, 205th overall, in 1981 Entry Draft).

			Regular Season					Playoffs				
Season	Club	Lea	GP	G	A	TP	PIM	GP	G	A	TP	PIM
1978-79	Medicine Hat	WHL	62	24	45	69	14	....	....	....	....	....
1979-80	Medicine Hat	WHL	72	25	77	102	36	16	9	4	13	14
1980-81	Medicine Hat	WHL	72	55	84	139	60	5	4	4	8	0
1981-82	U. of Calgary	CWUAA	37	26	53	79	33	....	....	....	....	....
1982-83	Maine	AHL	78	15	51	66	46	14	3	4	7	8
1983-84	Springfield	AHL	78	24	56	80	27	4	4	3	7	2
1984-85	Maine	AHL	69	28	38	66	40	11	3	8	11	14
1985-86a	Maine	AHL	80	31	55	86	34	5	2	3	5	2
1986-87	Maine	AHL	80	24	41	65	73	....	....	....	....	....
1987-88	Utica	AHL	54	15	32	47	55	....	....	....	....	....
	Maine	AHL	12	2	8	10	10	10	2	4	6	24
1988-89	Maine	AHL	79	15	41	56	67	....	....	....	....	....
1989-90	Maine	AHL	8	2	4	6	10	....	....	....	....	....

a AHL Most Sportsmanlike Player of the Year (1986)

Signed as free agent by **New Jersey**, July 15, 1984. Traded to **Boston** by **New Jersey** for Boston's tenth round choice (Alexander Semak) in 1988 Entry Draft, March 8, 1988.

TUCKER, JOHN

Center. Shoots right. 6', 197 lbs. Born, Windsor, Ont., September 29, 1964.
(Buffalo's 4th choice, 31st overall, in 1983 Entry Draft).

			Regular Season					Playoffs				
Season	Club	Lea	GP	G	A	TP	PIM	GP	G	A	TP	PIM
1981-82	Kitchener	OHL	67	16	32	48	32	15	2	3	5	2
1982-83	Kitchener	OHL	70	60	80	140	33	11	5	9	14	10
1983-84ab	**Buffalo**	**NHL**	**21**	**12**	**4**	**16**	**4**	**3**	**1**	**0**	**1**	**0**
	Kitchener	OHL	39	40	60	100	25	12	12	18	30	8
1984-85	**Buffalo**	**NHL**	**64**	**22**	**27**	**49**	**21**	**5**	**1**	**5**	**6**	**0**
1985-86	**Buffalo**	**NHL**	**75**	**31**	**34**	**65**	**39**	....	....	....	....	....
1986-87	**Buffalo**	**NHL**	**54**	**17**	**34**	**51**	**21**	....	....	....	....	....
1987-88	**Buffalo**	**NHL**	**45**	**19**	**19**	**38**	**20**	**6**	**7**	**3**	**10**	**18**
1988-89	**Buffalo**	**NHL**	**60**	**13**	**31**	**44**	**31**	**3**	**0**	**3**	**3**	**0**
1989-90	**Buffalo**	**NHL**	**8**	**1**	**2**	**3**	**2**	....	....	....	....	....
	Washington	**NHL**	**38**	**9**	**19**	**28**	**10**	**12**	**1**	**7**	**8**	**4**
	NHL Totals		**365**	**124**	**170**	**294**	**148**	**29**	**10**	**18**	**28**	**22**

a OHL First All-Star Team (1984)
b OHL Player of the Year (1984)

Traded to **Washington** by **Buffalo** for future considerations, January 5, 1990. Traded to **Buffalo** by **Washington** for cash, July 3, 1990.

TUER, ALLAN (AL) (TOOR)

Defense. Shoots left. 6', 190 lbs. Born, North Battleford, Sask., July 19, 1963.
(Los Angeles' 8th choice, 186th overall, in 1981 Entry Draft).

			Regular Season					Playoffs				
Season	Club	Lea	GP	G	A	TP	PIM	GP	G	A	TP	PIM
1980-81	Regina	WHL	31	0	7	7	58	8	0	1	1	37
1981-82	Regina	WHL	63	2	18	20	*486	13	0	3	3	117
1982-83	Regina	WHL	71	3	27	30	229	5	0	0	0	37
1983-84	New Haven	AHL	78	0	20	20	195	....	....	....	....	....
1984-85	New Haven	AHL	56	0	7	7	241	....	....	....	....	....
1985-86	**Los Angeles**	**NHL**	**45**	**0**	**1**	**1**	**150**	....	....	....	....	....
	New Haven	AHL	8	1	0	1	53	....	....	....	....	....
1986-87	New Haven	AHL	69	1	14	15	273	5	0	1	1	48
1987-88	**Minnesota**	**NHL**	**6**	**1**	**0**	**1**	**29**	....	....	....	....	....
	Kalamazoo	IHL	68	2	15	17	303	7	0	0	0	34
1988-89	**Hartford**	**NHL**	**4**	**0**	**0**	**0**	**23**	....	....	....	....	....
	Binghamton	AHL	43	1	7	8	234	....	....	....	....	....
1989-90	**Hartford**	**NHL**	**2**	**0**	**0**	**0**	**6**	....	....	....	....	....
	Binghamton	AHL	58	3	7	10	56	....	....	....	....	....
	NHL Totals		**57**	**1**	**1**	**2**	**208**	....	....	....	....	....

Signed as a free agent by **Edmonton**, August 18, 1986. Claimed by **Minnesota** in NHL Waiver Draft, October 5, 1987. Signed as a free agent by **Hartford**, July 12, 1988.

TURCOTTE, ALFIE

Center. Shoots left. 5'9", 170 lbs. Born, Gary, IN, June 5, 1965.
(Montreal's 1st choice, 17th overall, in 1983 Entry Draft).

			Regular Season					Playoffs				
Season	Club	Lea	GP	G	A	TP	PIM	GP	G	A	TP	PIM
1982-83	Nanaimo	WHL	36	23	27	50	22	....	....	....	....	....
	Portland	WHL	39	26	51	77	26	14	14	18	32	9
1983-84	Portland	WHL	32	22	41	63	39	....	....	....	....	....
	Montreal	**NHL**	**30**	**7**	**7**	**14**	**10**	....	....	....	....	....
1984-85	**Montreal**	**NHL**	**53**	**8**	**16**	**24**	**35**	**5**	**0**	**0**	**0**	**0**
1985-86	**Montreal**	**NHL**	**2**	**0**	**0**	**0**	**2**	....	....	....	....	....
	Sherbrooke	AHL	75	29	36	65	60	....	....	....	....	....
1986-87	Nova Scotia	AHL	70	27	41	68	37	5	2	4	6	2
1987-88	**Winnipeg**	**NHL**	**3**	**0**	**0**	**0**	**0**	....	....	....	....	....
a	Baltimore	AHL	33	21	33	54	42	....	....	....	....	....
	Moncton	AHL	25	12	25	37	18	....	....	....	....	....
	Sherbrooke	AHL	8	3	8	11	4	....	....	....	....	....
1988-89	**Winnipeg**	**NHL**	**14**	**1**	**3**	**4**	**2**	....	....	....	....	....
	Moncton	AHL	54	27	39	66	74	10	3	9	12	17
1989-90	**Washington**	**NHL**	**4**	**0**	**2**	**2**	**0**	....	....	....	....	....
	Baltimore	AHL	65	26	40	66	42	12	7	9	16	14
	NHL Totals		**106**	**16**	**28**	**44**	**49**	**5**	**0**	**0**	**0**	**0**

a AHL Second All-Star team (1988)

Traded to **Edmonton** by **Montreal** for future considerations, June 25, 1986. Sold to **Montreal** by **Edmonton**, May 14, 1987. Traded to **Winnipeg** by **Montreal** for future considerations, January 14, 1988. Signed as a free agent by **Boston**, June 27, 1989. Traded to **Washington** by **Boston** for Mike Millar, October 2, 1989.

TURCOTTE, DARREN

Center. Shoots left. 6', 185 lbs. Born, Boston, MA, March 2, 1968.
(NY Rangers' 6th choice, 114th overall, in 1986 Entry Draft).

			Regular Season					Playoffs				
Season	Club	Lea	GP	G	A	TP	PIM	GP	G	A	TP	PIM
1985-86	North Bay	OHL	62	35	37	72	35	10	3	4	7	8
1986-87	North Bay	OHL	55	30	48	78	20	18	12	8	20	6
1987-88	Colorado	IHL	8	4	3	7	9	6	2	6	8	8
	North Bay	OHL	32	30	33	63	16	4	3	0	3	4
1988-89	**NY Rangers**	**NHL**	**20**	**7**	**3**	**10**	**4**	**1**	**0**	**0**	**0**	**0**
	Denver	IHL	40	21	28	49	32	....	....	....	....	....
1989-90	**NY Rangers**	**NHL**	**76**	**32**	**34**	**66**	**32**	**10**	**1**	**6**	**7**	**4**
	NHL Totals		**96**	**39**	**37**	**76**	**36**	**11**	**1**	**6**	**7**	**4**

TURGEON, PIERRE

Center. Shoots left. 6'1", 203 lbs. Born, Rouyn, Que., August 29, 1969.
(Buffalo's 1st choice, 1st overall, in 1987 Entry Draft).

			Regular Season					Playoffs				
Season	Club	Lea	GP	G	A	TP	PIM	GP	G	A	TP	PIM
1985-86	Granby	QMJHL	69	47	67	114	31	....	....	....	....	....
1986-87	Granby	QMJHL	58	69	85	154	8	7	9	6	15	15
1987-88	**Buffalo**	**NHL**	**76**	**14**	**28**	**42**	**34**	**6**	**4**	**3**	**7**	**4**
1988-89	**Buffalo**	**NHL**	**80**	**34**	**54**	**88**	**26**	**5**	**3**	**5**	**8**	**2**
1989-90	**Buffalo**	**NHL**	**80**	**40**	**66**	**106**	**29**	**6**	**2**	**4**	**6**	**2**
	NHL Totals		**236**	**88**	**148**	**236**	**89**	**17**	**9**	**12**	**21**	**8**

Played in NHL All-Star Game (1990)

TURGEON, SYLVAIN

Left wing. Shoots left. 6', 195 lbs.   Born, Noranda, Que., January 17, 1965.
(Hartford's 1st choice, 2nd overall, in 1983 Entry Draft).

				Regular Season					Playoffs			
Season	Club	Lea	GP	G	A	TP	PIM	GP	G	A	TP	PIM
1981-82	Hull	QMJHL	57	33	40	73	78	14	11	11	22	16
1982-83a	Hull	QMJHL	67	54	109	163	103	7	8	7	15	10
1983-84b	**Hartford**	**NHL**	76	40	32	72	55	....	....	....	....	....
1984-85	**Hartford**	**NHL**	64	31	31	62	67	....	....	....	....	....
1985-86	**Hartford**	**NHL**	76	45	34	79	88	9	2	3	5	4
1986-87	**Hartford**	**NHL**	41	23	13	36	45	6	1	2	3	4
1987-88	**Hartford**	**NHL**	71	23	26	49	71	6	0	0	0	4
1988-89	**Hartford**	**NHL**	42	16	14	30	40	4	0	2	2	4
1989-90	**New Jersey**	**NHL**	72	30	17	47	81	1	0	0	0	0
	NHL Totals		442	208	167	375	447	26	3	7	10	16

a QMJHL First All-Star Team (1983)
b NHL All-Rookie Team (1984)
Played in NHL All-Star Game (1986)
Traded to **New Jersey** by **Hartford** for Pat Verbeek, June 17, 1989.

TURNER, BRAD

Defense. Shoots right. 6'2", 190 lbs.   Born, Winnipeg, Man., May 25, 1968.
(Minnesota's 6th choice, 58th overall, in 1986 Entry Draft).

				Regular Season					Playoffs			
Season	Club	Lea	GP	G	A	TP	PIM	GP	G	A	TP	PIM
1986-87	U. of Michigan	CCHA	40	3	10	13	40	....	....	....	....	....
1987-88	U. of Michigan	CCHA	39	3	11	14	52	....	....	....	....	....
1988-89	U. of Michigan	CCHA	33	3	8	11	38	....	....	....	....	....
1989-90	U. of Michigan	CCHA	32	8	9	17	34	....	....	....	....	....

TUSTIAN, ROBERT

Right wing. Shoots right. 6'2", 220 lbs. Born, Hamilton, Ont., April 4, 1968.
(St. Louis' 1st choice, 14th overall, in 1989 Supplemental Draft).

				Regular Season					Playoffs			
Season	Club	Lea	GP	G	A	TP	PIM	GP	G	A	TP	PIM
1988-89	Michigan Tech	WCHA	37	0	3	3	51	....	....	....	....	....
1989-90	Michigan Tech	WCHA	37	6	9	15	74	....	....	....	....	....

TUTT, BRIAN

Defense. Shoots left. 6'1", 195 lbs.   Born, Small Well, Alta., June 9, 1962.
(Philadelphia's 6th choice, 126th overall, in 1980 Entry Draft).

				Regular Season					Playoffs			
Season	Club	Lea	GP	G	A	TP	PIM	GP	G	A	TP	PIM
1979-80	Calgary	WHL	2	0	0	2	2	4	0	1	1	6
1980-81	Calgary	WHL	72	10	41	51	111	22	3	11	14	30
1981-82	Calgary	WHL	40	2	16	18	85	9	2	2	4	22
1982-83	Maine	AHL	31	0	0	0	28	....	....	....	....	....
	Toledo	IHL	23	5	10	15	26	11	1	7	8	16
1983-84	Springfield	AHL	1	0	0	0	2	....	....	....	....	....
a	Toledo	IHL	82	7	44	51	79	13	0	6	6	16
1984-85	Hershey	AHL	3	0	0	0	8	....	....	....	....	....
a	Kalamazoo	IHL	80	8	45	53	62	11	2	4	6	19
1985-86	Kalamazoo	IHL	82	11	39	50	129	6	1	6	7	11
1986-87	Maine	AHL	41	6	15	21	19	....	....	....	....	....
	Kalamazoo	IHL	19	2	7	9	10	....	....	....	....	....
1987-88	New Haven	AHL	32	1	12	13	33	....	....	....	....	....
1988-89	Baltimore	AHL	6	1	5	6	6	....	....	....	....	....
	Cdn. National	....	63	0	19	19	87	....	....	....	....	....
1989-90	**Washington**	**NHL**	7	1	0	1	2	....	....	....	....	....
	Baltimore	AHL	67	2	13	15	80	9	1	0	1	4
	NHL Totals		7	1	0	1	2	....	....	....	....	....

a IHL Second All-Star Team (1984, 1985)
Signed as a free agent by **Washington**, July 25, 1989.

TUTTLE, STEVE

Right wing. Shoots right. 6'1", 180 lbs.   Born, Vancouver, B.C., January 5, 1966.
(St. Louis' 8th choice, 113th overall, in 1984 Entry Draft).

				Regular Season					Playoffs			
Season	Club	Lea	GP	G	A	TP	PIM	GP	G	A	TP	PIM
1984-85	U. Wisconsin	WCHA	28	3	4	7	0	....	....	....	....	....
1985-86	U. Wisconsin	WCHA	32	2	10	12	2	....	....	....	....	....
1986-87	U. Wisconsin	WCHA	42	31	21	52	14	....	....	....	....	....
1987-88ab	U. Wisconsin	WCHA	45	27	39	66	18	....	....	....	....	....
1988-89	**St. Louis**	**NHL**	53	13	12	25	6	6	1	2	3	0
1989-90	**St. Louis**	**NHL**	71	12	10	22	4	5	0	1	1	2
	NHL Totals		124	25	22	47	10	11	1	3	4	2

a NCAA West Second All-American Team (1988)
b WCHA Second All-Star Team (1988)

TWIST, ANTHONY

Defense. Shoots left. 6', 210 lbs.   Born, Sherwood Park, Alta., May 9, 1968.
(St. Louis' 9th choice, 177th overall, in 1988 Entry Draft).

				Regular Season					Playoffs			
Season	Club	Lea	GP	G	A	TP	PIM	GP	G	A	TP	PIM
1987-88	Saskatoon	WHL	55	1	8	9	226	10	1	1	2	6
1988-89	Peoria	IHL	67	3	8	11	312	....	....	....	....	....
1989-90	**St. Louis**	**NHL**	28	0	0	0	124	....	....	....	....	....
	Peoria	IHL	36	1	5	6	200	5	0	1	1	8
	NHL Totals		28	0	0	0	124	....	....	....	....	....

VAIVE, RICHARD CLAUDE (RICK)   (VIHV)

Right wing. Shoots right. 6', 200 lbs.   Born, Ottawa, Ont., May 14, 1959.
(Vancouver's 1st choice, 5th overall, in 1979 Entry Draft).

				Regular Season					Playoffs			
Season	Club	Lea	GP	G	A	TP	PIM	GP	G	A	TP	PIM
1976-77	Sherbrooke	QJHL	67	51	59	110	91	18	10	13	23	78
1977-78	Sherbrooke	QJHL	68	76	79	155	199	9	8	4	12	38
1978-79	Birmingham	WHA	75	26	33	59	*248	....	....	....	....	....
1979-80	**Vancouver**	**NHL**	47	13	8	21	111	....	....	....	....	....
	Toronto	NHL	22	9	7	16	77	3	1	0	1	11
1980-81	Toronto	NHL	75	33	29	62	229	3	1	0	1	4
1981-82	Toronto	NHL	77	54	35	89	157	....	....	....	....	....
1982-83	Toronto	NHL	78	51	28	79	105	4	2	5	7	6
1983-84	Toronto	NHL	76	52	41	93	114	....	....	....	....	....
1984-85	Toronto	NHL	72	35	33	68	112	....	....	....	....	....
1985-86	Toronto	NHL	61	33	31	64	85	9	6	2	8	9
1986-87	Toronto	NHL	73	32	34	66	61	13	4	2	6	23
1987-88	Chicago	NHL	76	43	26	69	108	5	6	2	8	38
1988-89	Chicago	NHL	30	12	13	25	60	....	....	....	....	....
	Buffalo	NHL	28	19	13	32	64	5	2	1	3	8
1989-90	**Buffalo**	**NHL**	70	29	19	48	74	6	4	2	6	6
	NHL Totals		785	415	317	732	1357	48	26	14	40	105

Played in NHL All-Star Game (1982-84)
Traded to **Toronto** by **Vancouver** with Bill Derlago for Dave Williams and Jerry Butler, February 18, 1980. Traded to **Chicago** by **Toronto** with Steve Thomas and Bob McGill for Al Secord and Ed Olczyk, September 3, 1987. Traded to **Buffalo** by **Chicago** for Adam Creighton, December 26, 1988.

VALIMONT, CARL

Defense. Shoots left. 6'1", 180 lbs.   Born, Southington, CT, March 1, 1966.
(Vancouver's 10th choice, 193rd overall, in 1985 Entry Draft).

				Regular Season					Playoffs			
Season	Club	Lea	GP	G	A	TP	PIM	GP	G	A	TP	PIM
1984-85	U. of Lowell	H.E.	40	4	11	15	24	....	....	....	....	....
1985-86	U. of Lowell	H.E.	26	1	9	10	12	....	....	....	....	....
1986-87	U. of Lowell	H.E.	36	8	9	17	36	....	....	....	....	....
1987-88a	U. of Lowell	H.E.	38	6	26	32	59	....	....	....	....	....
1988-89	Milwaukee	IHL	79	4	33	37	56	11	2	8	10	12
1989-90	Milwaukee	IHL	78	13	28	41	48	3	0	1	1	6

a Hockey East Second All-Star Team (1988)

VALK, GARRY

Right wing. Shoots right. 6'1", 190 lbs.   Born, Edmonton, Alta., November 27, 1967.
(Vancouver's 5th choice, 108th overall, in 1987 Entry Draft).

				Regular Season					Playoffs			
Season	Club	Lea	GP	G	A	TP	PIM	GP	G	A	TP	PIM
1987-88	North Dakota	WCHA	38	23	12	35	64	....	....	....	....	....
1988-89	North Dakota	WCHA	40	14	17	31	71	....	....	....	....	....
1989-90	North Dakota	WCHA	43	22	17	39	92	....	....	....	....	....

VALLIS, LINDSAY

Right wing. Shoots right. 6'2", 200 lbs.   Born, Winnipeg, Man., January 12, 1971.
(Montreal's 1st choice, 13th overall, in 1989 Entry Draft).

				Regular Season					Playoffs			
Season	Club	Lea	GP	G	A	TP	PIM	GP	G	A	TP	PIM
1987-88	Seattle	WHL	68	31	45	76	65	....	....	....	....	....
1988-89	Seattle	WHL	63	21	32	53	48	....	....	....	....	....
1989-90	Seattle	WHL	65	34	43	77	68	13	6	5	11	14

VALO, JOHN

Defense. Shoots left. 6', 210 lbs. Born, Warren, MI, April 12, 1970.
(St. Louis' 10th choice, 198th overall, in 1989 Entry Draft.)

				Regular Season					Playoffs			
Season	Club	Lea	GP	G	A	TP	PIM	GP	G	A	TP	PIM
1988-89	Detroit Comp.	NAJHL	26	4	6	10	42	....	....	....	....	....
1989-90	Hamilton	OHL	31	3	6	9	38	....	....	....	....	....

VAN ALLEN, SHAUN

Center. Shoots left. 6'1", 205 lbs.   Born, Shaunavon, Sask., August 29, 1967.
(Edmonton's 7th choice, 147th overall, in 1987 Entry Draft).

				Regular Season					Playoffs			
Season	Club	Lea	GP	G	A	TP	PIM	GP	G	A	TP	PIM
1985-86	Saskatoon	WHL	55	12	11	23	43	13	4	8	12	28
1986-87	Saskatoon	WHL	72	38	59	97	116	11	4	6	10	24
1987-88	Milwaukee	IHL	40	14	28	42	34	....	....	....	....	....
	Nova Scotia	AHL	19	4	10	14	17	4	1	1	2	4
1988-89	Cape Breton	AHL	76	32	42	74	81	....	....	....	....	....
1989-90	Cape Breton	AHL	61	25	44	69	83	4	0	2	2	8

VAN DORP, WAYNE

Left wing. Shoots left. 6'4", 225 lbs. Born, Vancouver, B.C., May 19, 1961.

			Regular Season					Playoffs				
Season	Club	Lea	GP	G	A	TP	PIM	GP	G	A	TP	PIM
1979-80	Seattle	WHL	68	8	13	21	195	12	3	1	4	33
1980-81	Seattle	WHL	63	22	30	52	242	5	1	0	1	10
1984-85	GIJS Groningen	Neth.	29	38	46	84	112	6	6	2	8	23
	Erie	ACHL	7	9	8	17	21	10	0	2	6	2
1985-86a	GIJS Groningen	Neth.	29	19	24	43	81	8	9	*12	21	6
1986-87	Rochester	AHL	47	7	3	10	192	....	....	....	....	....
	Nova Scotia	AHL	11	2	3	5	37	5	0	0	0	56
	Edmonton	**NHL**	**3**	**0**	**0**	**0**	**25**	**3**	**0**	**0**	**0**	**2**
1987-88	**Pittsburgh**	**NHL**	**25**	**1**	**3**	**4**	**75**	....	....	....	....	....
	Nova Scota	AHL	12	2	2	4	87	....	....	....	....	....
1988-89	Rochester	AHL	28	3	6	9	202	....	....	....	....	....
	Chicago	**NHL**	**8**	**0**	**0**	**0**	**23**	**16**	**0**	**1**	**1**	**17**
	Saginaw	IHL	11	4	3	7	60	....	....	....	....	....
1989-90	**Chicago**	**NHL**	**61**	**7**	**4**	**11**	**303**	**8**	**0**	**0**	**0**	**23**
	NHL Totals		**97**	**8**	**7**	**15**	**426**	**27**	**0**	**1**	**1**	**42**

a Named playoff MVP (1986)

Traded to **Edmonton** by **Buffalo** with Normand Lacombe and future considerations for Lee Fogolin and Mark Napier, March 6, 1987. Traded to **Pittsburgh** by **Edmonton** with Paul Coffey and Dave Hunter for Craig Simpson, Dave Hannan, Moe Mantha, and Chris Joseph, November 24, 1987. Traded to **Buffalo** by **Pittsburgh** for future considerations, September 30, 1988. Traded to **Chicago** by **Buffalo** for Chicago's seventh-round choice (Viktor Gordijuk) in 1990 Entry Draft, February 16, 1989.

VAN KESSEL, JOHN

Right wing. Shoots right. 6'4", 180 lbs. Born, Bridgewater, N.S., December 19, 1969.
(Los Angeles' 3rd choice, 49th overall, in 1988 Entry Draft).

			Regular Season					Playoffs				
Season	Club	Lea	GP	G	A	TP	PIM	GP	G	A	TP	PIM
1986-87	Belleville	OHL	61	1	10	11	58	....	....	....	....	....
1987-88	North Bay	OHL	50	13	16	29	214	4	1	1	2	16
1988-89	North Bay	OHL	50	7	13	20	218	11	2	4	6	31
1989-90	New Haven	AHL	6	1	1	2	9	....	....	....	....	....
	North Bay	OHL	40	7	21	28	127	5	0	3	3	16

VARY, JOHN

Defense. Shoots right. 6'2", 205 lbs. Born, Owen Sound, Ont., February 11, 1972.
(NY Rangers' 3rd choice, 55th overall, in 1990 Entry Draft).

			Regular Season					Playoffs				
Season	Club	Lea	GP	G	A	TP	PIM	GP	G	A	TP	PIM
1988-89	North Bay	OHL	45	2	7	9	38	3	0	0	0	0
1989-90	North Bay	OHL	59	7	39	46	79	5	0	2	2	8

VASKE, DENNIS

Defense. Shoots left. 6'2", 210 lbs. Born, Rockford, IL., October 11, 1967.
(NY Islanders' 2nd choice, 38th overall, in 1986 Entry Draft).

			Regular Season					Playoffs				
Season	Club	Lea	GP	G	A	TP	PIM	GP	G	A	TP	PIM
1986-87	Minn.-Duluth	WCHA	33	0	2	2	40	....	....	....	....	....
1987-88	Minn.-Duluth	WCHA	39	1	6	7	90	....	....	....	....	....
1988-89	Minn.-Duluth	WCHA	37	9	19	28	86	....	....	....	....	....
1989-90	Minn.-Duluth	WCHA	37	5	24	29	72	....	....	....	....	....

VEILLEUX, STEVE

Defense. Shoots right. 6', 190 lbs. Born, Lachenaie, Que., March 9, 1969.
(Vancouver's 2nd choice, 45th overall, in 1987 Entry Draft).

			Regular Season					Playoffs				
Season	Club	Lea	GP	G	A	TP	PIM	GP	G	A	TP	PIM
1985-86	Trois Rivieres	QMJHL	67	1	20	21	132	5	0	0	0	13
1986-87	Trois Rivieres	QMJHL	62	6	22	28	227	....	....	....	....	....
1987-88a	Trois Rivieres	QMJHL	63	7	25	32	150	....	....	....	....	....
1988-89a	Trois Rivieres	QMJHL	49	5	28	33	149	4	0	0	0	10
	Milwaukee	IHL	1	0	0	0	0	4	0	0	0	13
1989-90	Milwaukee	IHL	76	4	12	16	195	2	0	0	0	2

a QMJHL Second All-Star Team (1988, 1989)

VEITCH, DARREN WILLIAM (VEECH)

Defense. Shoots right. 6', 190 lbs. Born, Saskatoon, Sask., April 24, 1960.
(Washington's 1st choice, 5th overall, in 1980 Entry Draft).

			Regular Season					Playoffs				
Season	Club	Lea	GP	G	A	TP	PIM	GP	G	A	TP	PIM
1976-77	Regina	WHL	1	0	0	0	0	....	....	....	....	....
1977-78	Regina	WHL	71	13	32	45	135	9	0	2	2	4
1978-79	Regina	WHL	51	11	36	47	80	....	....	....	....	....
1979-80a	Regina	WHL	71	29	*93	122	118	18	13	18	31	13
1980-81	**Washington**	**NHL**	**59**	**4**	**21**	**25**	**46**	....	....	....	....	....
	Hershey	AHL	26	6	22	28	12	10	6	3	9	15
1981-82	Hershey	AHL	10	5	10	15	16	....	....	....	....	....
	Washington	**NHL**	**67**	**9**	**44**	**53**	**54**	....	....	....	....	....
1982-83	**Washington**	**NHL**	**10**	**0**	**8**	**8**	**0**	....	....	....	....	....
	Hershey	AHL	5	0	1	1	2	....	....	....	....	....
1983-84	Hershey	AHL	11	1	6	7	4	....	....	....	....	....
	Washington	**NHL**	**46**	**6**	**18**	**24**	**17**	**5**	**0**	**1**	**1**	**15**
1984-85	**Washington**	**NHL**	**75**	**3**	**18**	**21**	**37**	**5**	**0**	**1**	**1**	**4**
1985-86	**Washington**	**NHL**	**62**	**3**	**9**	**12**	**27**	....	....	....	....	....
	Detroit	**NHL**	**13**	**0**	**5**	**5**	**2**	....	....	....	....	....
1986-87	**Detroit**	**NHL**	**77**	**13**	**45**	**58**	**52**	**12**	**3**	**4**	**7**	**8**
1987-88	**Detroit**	**NHL**	**63**	**7**	**33**	**40**	**45**	**11**	**1**	**5**	**6**	**6**
1988-89	**Toronto**	**NHL**	**37**	**3**	**7**	**10**	**16**	....	....	....	....	....
	Newmarket	AHL	33	5	19	24	29	5	0	4	4	4
1989-90b	Newmarket	AHL	78	13	54	67	30	....	....	....	....	....
	NHL Totals		**509**	**48**	**208**	**256**	**296**	**33**	**4**	**11**	**15**	**33**

a WHL First All-Star Team (1980)
b AHL Second All-Star Team (1990)

Traded to **Detroit** by **Washington** for John Barrett and Greg Smith, March 10, 1986. Traded to **Toronto** by **Detroit** for Miroslav Frycer, June 10, 1988.

VELISCHEK, RANDY (VEHL-ih-shehk)

Defense. Shoots left. 6', 200 lbs. Born, Montreal, Que., February 10, 1962.
(Minnesota's 3rd choice, 53rd overall, in 1980 Entry Draft).

			Regular Season					Playoffs				
Season	Club	Lea	GP	G	A	TP	PIM	GP	G	A	TP	PIM
1979-80	Providence	ECAC	31	5	5	10	20	....	....	....	....	....
1980-81	Providence	ECAC	33	3	12	15	26	....	....	....	....	....
1981-82a	Providence	ECAC	33	1	14	15	38	....	....	....	....	....
1982-83bc	Providence	ECAC	41	18	34	52	50	....	....	....	....	....
	Minnesota	**NHL**	**3**	**0**	**0**	**0**	**2**	**9**	**0**	**0**	**0**	**0**
1983-84	Salt Lake	CHL	43	7	21	28	54	5	0	3	3	2
	Minnesota	**NHL**	**33**	**2**	**2**	**4**	**10**	**1**	**0**	**0**	**0**	**0**
1984-85	**Minnesota**	**NHL**	**52**	**4**	**9**	**13**	**26**	**9**	**2**	**3**	**5**	**8**
	Springfield	AHL	26	2	7	9	22	....	....	....	....	....
1985-86	**New Jersey**	**NHL**	**47**	**2**	**7**	**9**	**39**	....	....	....	....	....
	Maine	AHL	21	0	4	4	4	....	....	....	....	....
1986-87	**New Jersey**	**NHL**	**64**	**2**	**16**	**18**	**52**	....	....	....	....	....
1987-88	**New Jersey**	**NHL**	**51**	**3**	**9**	**12**	**66**	**19**	**0**	**2**	**2**	**20**
1988-89	**New Jersey**	**NHL**	**80**	**4**	**14**	**18**	**70**	....	....	....	....	....
1989-90	**New Jersey**	**NHL**	**62**	**0**	**6**	**6**	**72**	**6**	**0**	**0**	**0**	**4**
	NHL Totals		**392**	**17**	**63**	**80**	**337**	**44**	**2**	**5**	**7**	**32**

a ECAC Second All-Star Team (1982)
b ECAC First All-Star Team (1983)
c Named ECAC Player of the Year (1983)

Claimed by **New Jersey** from **Minnesota** in NHL Waiver Draft, October 7, 1985. Traded to **Quebec** by **New Jersey** as future considerations with Craig Wolanin to complete March 6, 1990 Peter Stastny deal, August 13, 1990.

VELLUCCI, MIKE

Defense. Shoots left. 6'1", 180 lbs. Born, Farmington, MI, August 11, 1966.
(Hartford's 3rd choice, 131st overall, in 1984 Entry Draft).

			Regular Season					Playoffs				
Season	Club	Lea	GP	G	A	TP	PIM	GP	G	A	TP	PIM
1983-84	Belleville	OHL	67	2	20	22	83	3	1	0	1	6
1984-85			DID NOT PLAY — INJURED									
1985-86	Belleville	OHL	64	11	32	43	154	24	2	5	7	45
1986-87	Salt Lake	IHL	60	5	30	35	94	....	....	....	....	....
1987-88	**Hartford**	**NHL**	**2**	**0**	**0**	**0**	**11**	....	....	....	....	....
	Binghamton	AHL	3	0	0	0	2	....	....	....	....	....
	Milwaukee	IHL	66	7	18	25	202	....	....	....	....	....
1988-89	Binghamton	AHL	37	9	9	18	59	....	....	....	....	....
	Indianapolis	IHL	12	1	2	3	43	....	....	....	....	....
1989-90	Erie	ECHL	22	7	20	27	57	....	....	....	....	....
	Winston-Salem	ECHL	10	2	7	9	21	....	....	....	....	....
	NHL Totals		**2**	**0**	**0**	**0**	**11**	....	....	....	....	....

VENKUS, CHRISTOPHER

Right wing. Shoots right. 5'11", 190 lbs. Born, Hinsdale, IL, April 14, 1969.
(Washington's 13th choice, 225th overall, in 1988 Entry Draft).

			Regular Season					Playoffs				
Season	Club	Lea	GP	G	A	TP	PIM	GP	G	A	TP	PIM
1987-88	W. Michigan	CCHA	42	8	9	17	76	....	....	....	....	....
1988-89	W. Michigan	CCHA	42	2	11	13	66	....	....	....	....	....
1989-90	W. Michigan	CCHA	DID NOT PLAY									

VENNE, STEPHANE

Defense. Shoots right. 6'3", 210 lbs. Born, Montreal, Que., April 29, 1969.
(Quebec's 6th choice, 87th overall, in 1988 Entry Draft).

			Regular Season					Playoffs				
Season	Club	Lea	GP	G	A	TP	PIM	GP	G	A	TP	PIM
1987-88	U. of Vermont	ECAC	29	9	12	21	52	....	....	....	....	....
1988-89	U. of Vermont	ECAC	19	4	5	9	35	....	....	....	....	....
1989-90	U. of Vermont	ECAC	31	6	9	15	62	....	....	....	....	....

VERBEEK, PATRICK (PAT) (vuhr-BEEK)

Right wing. Shoots right. 5'9", 190 lbs. Born, Sarnia, Ont., May 24, 1964.
(New Jersey's 3rd choice, 43rd overall, in 1982 Entry Draft).

			Regular Season					Playoffs				
Season	Club	Lea	GP	G	A	TP	PIM	GP	G	A	TP	PIM
1981-82	Sudbury	OHL	66	37	51	88	180	....	....	....	....	....
1982-83	Sudbury	OHL	61	40	67	107	184	....	....	....	....	....
	New Jersey	**NHL**	**6**	**3**	**2**	**5**	**8**	....	....	....	....	....
1983-84	**New Jersey**	**NHL**	**79**	**20**	**27**	**47**	**158**	....	....	....	....	....
1984-85	**New Jersey**	**NHL**	**78**	**15**	**18**	**33**	**162**	....	....	....	....	....
1985-86	**New Jersey**	**NHL**	**76**	**25**	**28**	**53**	**79**	....	....	....	....	....
1986-87	**New Jersey**	**NHL**	**74**	**35**	**24**	**59**	**120**	....	....	....	....	....
1987-88	**New Jersey**	**NHL**	**73**	**46**	**31**	**77**	**227**	**20**	**4**	**8**	**12**	**51**
1988-89	**New Jersey**	**NHL**	**77**	**26**	**21**	**47**	**189**	....	....	....	....	....
1989-90	**Hartford**	**NHL**	**80**	**44**	**45**	**89**	**228**	**7**	**2**	**2**	**4**	**26**
	NHL Totals		**543**	**214**	**196**	**410**	**1171**	**27**	**6**	**10**	**16**	**77**

Traded to **Hartford** by **New Jersey** for Sylvain Turgeon, June 17, 1989.

VERMETTE, MARK

Right wing. Shoots right. 6'1", 203 lbs. Born, Cochenour, Ont., October 3, 1967.
(Quebec's 8th choice, 134th overall, in 1986 Entry Draft).

			Regular Season					Playoffs				
Season	Club	Lea	GP	G	A	TP	PIM	GP	G	A	TP	PIM
1985-86	Lake Superior	CCHA	32	1	4	5	7	....	....	....	....	....
1986-87	Lake Superior	CCHA	38	19	17	36	59	....	....	....	....	....
1987-88abc	Lake Superior	CCHA	46	*45	30	75	154	....	....	....	....	....
1988-89	**Quebec**	**NHL**	**12**	**0**	**4**	**4**	**7**	....	....	....	....	....
	Halifax	AHL	52	12	16	28	30	1	0	0	0	0
1989-90	**Quebec**	**NHL**	**11**	**1**	**5**	**6**	**8**	....	....	....	....	....
	Halifax	AHL	47	20	17	37	44	6	1	5	6	6
	NHL Totals		**23**	**1**	**9**	**10**	**15**	....	....	....	....	....

a NCAA West All-American Team (1988)
b CCHA Player of the Year (1988)
c CCHA First All-Star Team (1988)

VESEY, JIM

Center. Shoots right. 6'1", 200 lbs.. Born, Boston, MA, September 29, 1965.
(St. Louis' 11th choice, 155th overall, in 1984 Entry Draft).

			Regular Season					Playoffs				
Season	Club	Lea	GP	G	A	TP	PIM	GP	G	A	TP	PIM
1984-85	Merrimack	NCAA	33	19	11	30	28	....	....	....	....	....
1985-86	Merrimack	NCAA	32	29	32	61	67	....	....	....	....	....
1986-87	Merrimack	NCAA	35	22	36	58	57	....	....	....	....	....
1987-88	Merrimack	NCAA	33	33	50	83	....	....	....	....	....	....
1988-89	**St. Louis**	**NHL**	**5**	**1**	**1**	**2**	**7**	....	....	....	....	....
a	Peoria	IHL	76	47	46	93	137	4	1	2	3	6
1989-90	**St. Louis**	**NHL**	**6**	**0**	**1**	**1**	**0**	....	....	....	....	....
	Peoria	IHL	60	47	44	91	75	5	1	3	4	21
	NHL Totals		**11**	**1**	**2**	**3**	**7**	....	....	....	....	....

a IHL First All-Star Team (1989)

VIAL, DENNIS

Defense. Shoots left. 6'1", 190 lbs. Born, Sault Ste. Marie, Ont., April 10, 1969.
(NY Rangers' 5th choice, 110th overall, in 1988 Entry Draft).

			Regular Season					Playoffs				
Season	Club	Lea	GP	G	A	TP	PIM	GP	G	A	TP	PIM
1986-87	Hamilton	OHL	53	1	8	9	194	8	0	0	0	8
1987-88	Hamilton	OHL	52	3	17	20	229	13	2	2	4	49
1988-89	Niagara Falls	OHL	50	10	27	37	227	15	1	7	8	44
1989-90	Flint	IHL	79	6	29	35	351	4	0	0	0	10

VICHOREK, MARK (vuh-CHORE-ik)

Defense. Shoots right. 6'3", 200 lbs. Born, Moose Lake, MN, August 11, 1966.
(Philadelphia's 12th choice, 245th overall, in 1982 Entry Draft).

			Regular Season					Playoffs				
Season	Club	Lea	GP	G	A	TP	PIM	GP	G	A	TP	PIM
1982-83	Lake Superior	CCHA	36	2	13	15	24	....	....	....	....	....
1983-84	Lake Superior	CCHA	40	3	8	11	14	....	....	....	....	....
1984-85	Lake Superior	CCHA	44	4	11	15	36	....	....	....	....	....
1985-86	Lake Superior	CCHA	41	9	11	20	40	....	....	....	....	....
1986-87	Binghamton	AHL	64	1	12	13	63	....	....	....	....	....
	Salt Lake	IHL	16	1	0	1	32	17	0	8	8	23
1987-88	Binghamton	AHL	26	0	4	4	48	....	....	....	....	....
	Milwaukee	IHL	49	4	5	9	67	....	....	....	....	....
1988-89	New Haven	AHL	23	1	5	6	26	17	2	4	6	57
	Flint	IHL	44	4	9	13	47	....	....	....	....	....
1989-90	Phoenix	IHL	29	2	8	10	57	....	....	....	....	....
	Flint	IHL	31	2	4	6	30	5	0	1	1	19

VILGRAIN, CLAUDE

Right wing. Shoots right. 6'1", 195 lbs. Born, Port-au-Prince, Haiti, March 1, 1963.
(Detroit's 6th choice, 107th overall, in 1982 Entry Draft).

			Regular Season					Playoffs				
Season	Club	Lea	GP	G	A	TP	PIM	GP	G	A	TP	PIM
1983-84	U. of Moncton	AUAA	20	11	20	31	8	....	....	....	....	....
1984-85	U. of Moncton	AUAA	24	35	28	63	20	....	....	....	....	....
1985-86	U. of Moncton	AUAA	19	17	20	37	25	....	....	....	....	....
1986-87	Cdn. Olympic	....	78	28	42	70	38	....	....	....	....	....
1987-88	**Vancouver**	**NHL**	**6**	**1**	**1**	**2**	**0**	....	....	....	....	....
	Cdn. National	....	61	21	20	41	41	....	....	....	....	....
	Cdn. Olympic	....	6	0	0	0	0	....	....	....	....	....
1988-89	Utica	AHL	55	23	30	53	41	5	0	2	2	2
	Milwaukee	IHL	23	9	13	22	26	....	....	....	....	....
1989-90	**New Jersey**	**NHL**	**6**	**1**	**2**	**3**	**4**	**4**	**0**	**0**	**0**	**0**
	Utica	AHL	73	37	52	89	32	....	....	....	....	....
	NHL Totals		**12**	**2**	**3**	**5**	**4**	**4**	**0**	**0**	**0**	**0**

Signed as a free agent by **Vancouver**, June 18, 1987. Traded to **New Jersey** by **Vancouver** for Tim Lenardon, March 7, 1989.

VINCELETTE, DANIEL

Left wing. Shoots left. 6'1", 200 lbs. Born, Verdun, Que., August 1, 1967.
(Chicago's 3rd choice, 74th overall, in 1985 Entry Draft).

			Regular Season					Playoffs				
Season	Club	Lea	GP	G	A	TP	PIM	GP	G	A	TP	PIM
1984-85	Drummondville	QMJHL	64	11	24	35	124	12	0	1	1	11
1985-86	Drummondville	QMJHL	70	37	47	84	234	22	11	14	25	40
1986-87	Drummondville	QMJHL	50	34	35	69	288	8	6	5	11	17
	Chicago	**NHL**	....	....	....	....	....	**3**	**0**	**0**	**0**	**0**
1987-88	**Chicago**	**NHL**	**69**	**6**	**11**	**17**	**109**	**4**	**0**	**0**	**0**	**0**
1988-89	**Chicago**	**NHL**	**66**	**11**	**4**	**15**	**119**	**5**	**0**	**0**	**0**	**4**
	Saginaw	IHL	2	0	0	0	14	....	....	....	....	....
1989-90	**Chicago**	**NHL**	**2**	**0**	**0**	**0**	**4**	....	....	....	....	....
	Indianapolis	IHL	49	16	13	29	262	....	....	....	....	....
	Quebec	**NHL**	**11**	**0**	**1**	**1**	**25**	....	....	....	....	....
	NHL Totals		**148**	**17**	**16**	**33**	**257**	**12**	**0**	**0**	**0**	**4**

Traded to **Quebec** by **Chicago** with Mario Doyon and Everett Sanipass for Greg Millen, Michel Goulet and Quebec's sixth round choice in 1991 Entry Draft, March 5, 1990.

VIRTA, HANNU (VIR-ta, HAN-oo)

Defense. Shoots left. 6', 180 lbs. Born, Turku, Finland, March 22, 1963.
(Buffalo's 2nd choice, 38th overall, in 1981 Entry Draft).

			Regular Season					Playoffs				
Season	Club	Lea	GP	G	A	TP	PIM	GP	G	A	TP	PIM
1980-81a	T.P.S.	Fin.	1	0	1	1	0	4	0	1	1	4
1981-82b	T.P.S.	Fin.	36	5	12	17	6	7	1	1	2	2
	Buffalo	**NHL**	**3**	**0**	**1**	**1**	**4**	**4**	**0**	**1**	**1**	**0**
1982-83	**Buffalo**	**NHL**	**74**	**13**	**24**	**37**	**18**	**10**	**1**	**2**	**3**	**4**
1983-84	**Buffalo**	**NHL**	**70**	**6**	**30**	**36**	**12**	**3**	**0**	**0**	**0**	**2**
1984-85	**Buffalo**	**NHL**	**51**	**1**	**23**	**24**	**16**	....	....	....	....	....
1985-86	**Buffalo**	**NHL**	**47**	**5**	**23**	**28**	**16**	....	....	....	....	....
1986-87c	T.P.S.	Fin.	41	13	30	43	20	5	0	3	3	2
1987-88	T.P.S.	Fin.	44	10	28	38	20	....	....	....	....	....
1988-89	T.P.S.	Fin.	43	7	25	32	30	10	1	7	8	0
1989-90	T.P.S.	Fin.	41	7	19	26	14	9	0	6	6	10
	NHL Totals		**245**	**25**	**101**	**126**	**66**	**17**	**1**	**3**	**4**	**6**

a Named to All-Star Team, 1981 European Junior Championships
b Named Rookie of the Year in Finnish National League (1982)
c Finnish League First All-Star Team (1987)

VITOLINSH, HARIJS

Center. Shoots left. 6'2", 205 lbs. Born, Riga, Soviet Union, April 30, 1968.
(Montreal's 10th choice, 188th overall, in 1988 Entry Draft).

			Regular Season					Playoffs				
Season	Club	Lea	GP	G	A	TP	PIM	GP	G	A	TP	PIM
1987-88	Dynamo Riga	USSR	25	2	2	4	22	....	....	....	....	....
1988-89	Dynamo Riga	USSR	36	3	2	5	16	....	....	....	....	....
1989-90	Dynamo Riga	USSR	45	7	6	13	18	....	....	....	....	....

VIVEIROS, EMANUEL (VEE-VEH-ROHZ)

Defense. Shoots left. 6', 175 lbs. Born, St. Albert, Alta., January 8, 1966.
(Edmonton's 6th choice, 106th overall, in 1984 Entry Draft).

			Regular Season					Playoffs				
Season	Club	Lea	GP	G	A	TP	PIM	GP	G	A	TP	PIM
1982-83	Prince Albert	WHL	59	6	26	32	55	....	....	....	....	....
1983-84	Prince Albert	WHL	67	15	94	109	48	2	0	3	3	6
1984-85a	Prince Albert	WHL	68	17	71	88	94	13	2	9	11	14
1985-86	**Minnesota**	**NHL**	**4**	**0**	**1**	**1**	**0**	....	....	....	....	....
bc	Prince Albert	WHL	57	22	70	92	30	20	4	24	28	4
1986-87	**Minnesota**	**NHL**	**1**	**0**	**1**	**1**	**0**	....	....	....	....	....
	Springfield	AHL	76	7	35	42	38	....	....	....	....	....
1987-88	**Minnesota**	**NHL**	**24**	**1**	**9**	**10**	**6**	....	....	....	....	....
	Kalamazoo	IHL	57	15	48	63	41	....	....	....	....	....
1988-89	Kalamazoo	IHL	54	11	29	40	37	....	....	....	....	....
1989-90			DID NOT PLAY — INJURED									
	NHL Totals		**29**	**1**	**11**	**12**	**6**	....	....	....	....	....

a WHL Second All-Star Team, East Division (1985)
b WHL East All-Star Team (1986)
c WHL Player of the Year (1986)

Traded to **Minnesota** by **Edmonton** with Marc Habscheid, Don Barber for Gord Sherven and Don Biggs, December 20, 1985. Signed as a free agent by **Hartford**, February 9, 1990.

VLACH, ROSTISLAV

Center/left wing. Shoots left. 6', 170 lbs. Born, Gottwaldov, Czech., July 3, 1962.
(Los Angeles' 9th choice, 216th overall, in 1987 Entry Draft).

			Regular Season					Playoffs				
Season	Club	Lea	GP	G	A	TP	PIM	GP	G	A	TP	PIM
1987-88	Gottwaldov	Czech.	30	15	14	29	4	....	....	....	....	....
1988-89	Gottwaldov	Czech.	41	20	18	38	83	....	....	....	....	....
1989-90	Gottwaldov	Czech	51	16	24	40	....	....	....	....	....	....

VLK, PETER

Left wing. Shoots left. 6', 180 lbs. Born, Havlicek Brod, Czechoslovakia, January 7, 1964.
(NY Islanders' 5th choice, 97th overall, in 1987 Entry Draft).

			Regular Season					Playoffs				
Season	Club	Lea	GP	G	A	TP	PIM	GP	G	A	TP	PIM
1987-88	Dukla Jihlava	Czech.	18	6	3	9	....	....	....	....	....	....
1988-89	Dukla Jihlava	Czech.	33	11	8	19	66	....	....	....	....	....
1989-90	Dukla Jihlava	Czech	48	19	21	40	....	....	....	....	....	....

VOLEK, DAVID (VAH-lehk)

Left/Right wing. Shoots left. 6', 185 lbs. Born, Prague, Czechoslovakia, June 18, 1966.
(NY Islanders' 11th choice, 208th overall, in 1984 Entry Draft).

			Regular Season					Playoffs				
Season	Club	Lea	GP	G	A	TP	PIM	GP	G	A	TP	PIM
1986-87	Sparta Praha	Czech.	39	27	25	52	....	....	....	....	....	....
1987-88	Sparta Praha	Czech.	30	18	12	30	....	....	....	....	....	....
1988-89a	**NY Islanders**	**NHL**	**77**	**25**	**34**	**59**	**24**	....	....	....	....	....
1989-90	**NY Islanders**	**NHL**	**80**	**17**	**22**	**39**	**41**	**5**	**1**	**4**	**5**	**0**
	NHL Totals		**157**	**42**	**56**	**98**	**65**	**5**	**1**	**4**	**5**	**0**

a NHL All-Rookie Team (1989)

VOLHOFFER, TROY

Right wing. Shoots left. 5'11", 185 lbs. Born, Regina, Sask., February 9, 1966.

			Regular Season					Playoffs				
Season	Club	Lea	GP	G	A	TP	PIM	GP	G	A	TP	PIM
1983-84	Winnipeg	WHL	66	22	37	59	92	....	....	....	....	....
1984-85	Saskatoon	WHL	62	21	31	52	82	....	....	....	....	....
1985-86	Saskatoon	WHL	72	55	55	110	118	13	8	10	18	20
1986-87	Baltimore	AHL	67	11	25	36	90	....	....	....	....	....
1987-88	New Haven	AHL	18	2	6	8	30	....	....	....	....	....
	Muskegon	IHL	33	4	13	17	54	....	....	....	....	....
1988-89	Flint	IHL	63	6	23	29	186	....	....	....	....	....
	Muskegon	IHL	2	0	0	0	9	....	....	....	....	....
1989-90	Winston-Salem	ECHL	46	26	40	66	157	9	8	6	14	23

Signed as a free agent by **Pittsburgh**, December 9, 1986.

VON STEFENELLI, PHILIP

Defense. Shoots left. 6'1", 195 lbs. Born, Vancouver, B.C., April 10, 1969.
(Vancouver's 5th choice, 122nd overall, in 1988 Entry Draft).

			Regular Season					Playoffs				
Season	Club	Lea	GP	G	A	TP	PIM	GP	G	A	TP	PIM
1987-88	Boston U.	H.E.	34	3	13	16	38	....	....	....	....	....
1988-89	Boston U.	H.E.	33	2	6	8	34	....	....	....	....	....
1989-90	Boston U.	H.E.	44	8	20	28	40	....	....	....	....	....

VUKONICH, MICHAEL

Center. Shoots left. 6'1", 190 lbs. Born, Duluth, MN, May 11, 1968.
(Los Angeles' 4th choice, 90th overall, in 1987 Entry Draft).

			Regular Season					Playoffs				
Season	Club	Lea	GP	G	A	TP	PIM	GP	G	A	TP	PIM
1987-88	Harvard	ECAC	32	9	14	23	24	....	....	....	....	....
1988-89	Harvard	ECAC	27	11	8	19	12	....	....	....	....	....
1989-90a	Harvard	ECAC	27	22	29	51	18	....	....	....	....	....

a ECAC First All-Star Team (1990)

VUKOTA, MICK

Right wing. Shoots right. 6'2", 195 lbs. Born, Saskatoon, Sask., September 14, 1966.

			Regular Season					Playoffs				
Season	Club	Lea	GP	G	A	TP	PIM	GP	G	A	TP	PIM
1985-86	Spokane	WHL	64	19	14	33	369	9	6	4	10	68
1986-87	Spokane	WHL	61	25	28	53	*337	4	0	0	0	40
1987-88	Springfield	AHL	52	7	9	16	375	....	....	....	....	....
	NY Islanders	NHL	17	1	0	1	82	2	0	0	0	23
1988-89	NY Islanders	NHL	48	2	2	4	237	....	....	....	....	....
	Springfield	AHL	3	1	0	1	33	....	....	....	....	....
1989-90	NY Islanders	NHL	76	4	8	12	290	1	0	0	0	17
	NHL Totals		141	7	10	17	609	3	0	0	0	40

Signed as a free agent by **NY Islanders**, March 2, 1987.

VYAZMIKIN, IGOR

Right wing. Shoots right. 6'1", 190 lbs. Born, Moscow, Soviet Union, January 8, 1966.
(Edmonton's 13th choice, 252nd overall, in 1987 Entry Draft).

			Regular Season					Playoffs				
Season	Club	Lea	GP	G	A	TP	PIM	GP	G	A	TP	PIM
1983-84	CSKA	USSR	38	8	12	20	4	....	....	....	....	....
1984-85	CSKA	USSR	26	6	5	11	6	....	....	....	....	....
1985-86	CSKA	USSR	19	7	6	13	6	....	....	....	....	....
1986-87	CSKA	USSR	4	0	0	0	0	....	....	....	....	....
1987-88	CSKA	USSR	8	1	0	1	16	....	....	....	....	....
1988-89	CSKA	USSR	30	10	7	17	20	....	....	....	....	....
1989-90	Voskresensk	USSR	34	11	13	24	26	....	....	....	....	....

VYKOUKAL, JIRI

Defense. Shoots right. 5'11", 175 lbs. Born, Olomouc, Czechoslovakia, March 11, 1971.
(Washington's 9th choice, 208th overall, in 1989 Entry Draft).

			Regular Season					Playoffs				
Season	Club	Lea	GP	G	A	TP	PIM	GP	G	A	TP	PIM
1989-90	Sparta Praha	Czech.	47	5	12	17	....	....	....	....	....	....

WAHLSTEN, SAMI

Left wing. Shoots left. 6', 175 lbs. Born, Turku, Finland, November 25, 1967.
(Philadelphia's 6th choice, 146th overall, in 1988 Entry Draft).

			Regular Season					Playoffs				
Season	Club	Lea	GP	G	A	TP	PIM	GP	G	A	TP	PIM
1987-88	T.P.S.	Fin.	43	11	8	19	23	....	....	....	....	....
1988-89	Jokerit	Fin.	44	27	30	57	24	5	1	1	2	0
1989-90	Jokerit	Fin.	44	21	15	36	15	....	....	....	....	....

WALKER, GORD

Left wing. Shoots left. 6', 175 lbs. Born, Castlegar, B.C., August 12, 1965.
(New York Rangers' 3rd choice, 54th overall, in 1983 Entry Draft).

			Regular Season					Playoffs				
Season	Club	Lea	GP	G	A	TP	PIM	GP	G	A	TP	PIM
1982-83	Portland	WHL	66	24	30	54	95	14	5	8	13	12
1983-84	Portland	WHL	58	28	41	69	65	14	8	11	19	18
1984-85a	Kamloops	WHL	66	67	67	134	76	15	*13	14	27	34
1985-86	New Haven	AHL	46	11	28	39	66	....	....	....	....	....
1986-87	NY Rangers	NHL	1	1	0	1	4	....	....	....	....	....
	New Haven	AHL	59	24	20	44	58	7	3	2	5	0
1987-88	NY Rangers	NHL	18	1	4	5	17	....	....	....	....	....
	New Haven	AHL	14	10	9	19	17	....	....	....	....	....
	Colorado	IHL	16	4	9	13	4	....	....	....	....	....
1988-89	Los Angeles	NHL	11	1	0	1	2	....	....	....	....	....
	New Haven	AHL	60	21	25	46	50	17	7	8	15	23
1989-90	Los Angeles	NHL	1	0	0	0	0	....	....	....	....	....
1989-90	New Haven	AHL	24	14	7	21	8	....	....	....	....	....
	NHL Totals		31	3	4	7	23					

a WHL First All-Star Team (1985)

Traded to **Los Angeles** by NY Rangers with Mike Siltala for Joe Paterson, January 21, 1988.

WALLWORK, ROBERT

Center. Shoots left. 5'11", 180 lbs. Born, Boston, Mass., March, 15, 1968.
(Buffalo's 12th choice, 244th overall, in 1988 Entry Draft).

			Regular Season					Playoffs				
Season	Club	Lea	GP	G	A	TP	PIM	GP	G	A	TP	PIM
1987-88	Miami-Ohio	CCHA	36	6	24	30	59	....	....	....	....	....
1988-89	Miami-Ohio	CCHA	19	1	8	9	30	....	....	....	....	....
1989-90	Miami-Ohio	CCHA	40	12	30	42	60	....	....	....	....	....

WALSH, MIKE

Left wing. Shoots right. 6'2", 195 lbs. Born, New York, NY, April 3, 1962.

			Regular Season					Playoffs				
Season	Club	Lea	GP	G	A	TP	PIM	GP	G	A	TP	PIM
1980-81	Colgate	ECAC	35	10	15	25	62	....	....	....	....	....
1981-82	Colgate	ECAC	26	2	7	9	42	....	....	....	....	....
1982-83	Colgate	ECAC	24	9	14	23	36	....	....	....	....	....
1983-84	Colgate	ECAC	35	16	17	33	94	....	....	....	....	....
1984-85			DID NOT PLAY									
1985-86	Malmo	Swe.	42	52	27	79	....	....	....	....	....	....
1986-87	Springfield	AHL	67	20	26	46	32	....	....	....	....	....
1987-88	NY Islanders	NHL	1	0	0	0	0	....	....	....	....	....
	Springfield	AHL	77	27	23	50	48	....	....	....	....	....
1988-89	NY Islanders	NHL	13	2	0	2	4	....	....	....	....	....
	Springfield	AHL	68	31	34	65	73	....	....	....	....	....
1989-90	Springfield	AHL	69	34	20	54	43	8	2	2	4	10
	NHL Totals		14	2	0	2	4	....	....	....	....	....

Signed as a free agent by **NY Islanders**, August, 1986.

WALTER, BRET

Center. Shoots right. 6'1", 195 lbs. Born, Calgary, Alta., April 28, 1968.
(NY Rangers' 2nd choice, 51st overall, in 1986 Entry Draft).

			Regular Season					Playoffs				
Season	Club	Lea	GP	G	A	TP	PIM	GP	G	A	TP	PIM
1985-86	U. of Alberta	CWUAA	37	8	17	25	10	....	....	....	....	....
1986-87	U. of Alberta	CWUAA	43	17	17	34	24	....	....	....	....	....
	Cdn. Olympic		2	0	0	0	0	....	....	....	....	....
1987-88	U. of Alberta	CWUAA	21	7	10	17	18	....	....	....	....	....
1988-89	Denver	IHL	47	12	10	22	41	2	0	0	0	0
1989-90	Flint	IHL	6	1	1	2	4	....	....	....	....	....
	Fort Wayne	IHL	24	5	5	10	47	1	0	0	0	2

WALTER, RYAN WILLIAM

Center/Left wing. Shoots left. 6', 200 lbs. Born, New Westminster, B.C., April 23, 1958.
(Washington's 1st choice, 2nd overall, in 1978 Amateur Draft).

			Regular Season					Playoffs				
Season	Club	Lea	GP	G	A	TP	PIM	GP	G	A	TP	PIM
1974-75	Kamloops	WHL	9	8	4	12	2	2	1	1	2	2
1975-76	Kamloops	WHL	72	35	49	84	96	12	3	9	12	10
1976-77	Kamloops	WHL	71	41	58	99	100	5	1	3	4	11
1977-78abc	Seattle	WHL	62	54	71	125	148	....	....	....	....	....
1978-79	Washington	NHL	69	28	28	56	70	....	....	....	....	....
1979-80	Washington	NHL	80	24	42	66	106	....	....	....	....	....
1980-81	Washington	NHL	80	24	44	68	150	....	....	....	....	....
1981-82	Washington	NHL	78	38	49	87	142	....	....	....	....	....
1982-83	Montreal	NHL	80	29	46	75	40	3	0	0	0	11
1983-84	Montreal	NHL	73	20	29	49	83	15	2	1	3	4
1984-85	Montreal	NHL	72	19	19	38	59	12	2	7	9	13
1985-86	Montreal	NHL	69	15	34	49	45	5	0	1	1	2
1986-87	Montreal	NHL	76	23	23	46	34	17	7	12	19	10
1987-88	Montreal	NHL	61	13	23	36	39	11	2	4	6	6
1988-89	Montreal	NHL	78	14	17	31	48	21	3	5	8	6
1989-90	Montreal	NHL	70	8	16	24	59	11	0	2	2	0
	NHL Totals		886	255	370	625	875	95	16	32	48	52

a WHL Most Valuable Player (1978)
b WHL Player of the Year (1978)
c WHL First All-Star Team (1978)
Played in NHL All-Star Game (1983)

Traded to **Montreal** by **Washington** with Rick Green for Rod Langway, Brian Engblom, Doug Jarvis and Craig Laughlin, September 9, 1982.

WALZ, WES

Center. Shoots right. 5'10", 180 lbs.   Born, Calgary, Alta., May 15, 1970.
(Boston's 3rd choice, 57th overall, in 1989 Entry Draft).

			Regular Season					Playoffs				
Season	Club	Lea	GP	G	A	TP	PIM	GP	G	A	TP	PIM
1988-89a	Lethbridge	WHL	63	29	75	104	32	8	1	5	6	6
1989-90	**Boston**	**NHL**	**2**	**1**	**1**	**2**	**0**	....	....	....	....	....
b	Lethbridge	WHL	56	54	86	140	69	19	13	*24	*37	33
	NHL Totals		**2**	**1**	**1**	**2**	**0**	....	....	....	....	....

a WHL Rookie of the Year (1989)
b WHL East First All-Star Team (1990)

WARD, DIXON

Right wing. Shoots right. 6'0", 195 lbs.   Born, Leduc, Alta., September 23, 1968.
(Vancouver's 6th choice, 128th overall, in 1988 Entry Draft).

			Regular Season					Playoffs				
Season	Club	Lea	GP	G	A	TP	PIM	GP	G	A	TP	PIM
1988-89	North Dakota	WCHA	37	8	9	17	26	....	....	....	....	....
1989-90	North Dakota	WCHA	45	35	34	69	44	....	....	....	....	....

WARD, EDWARD

Right wing. Shoots right. 6'3", 190 lbs.   Born, Edmonton, Alta., November 10, 1969.
(Quebec's 7th choice, 108th overall, in 1988 Entry Draft).

			Regular Season					Playoffs				
Season	Club	Lea	GP	G	A	TP	PIM	GP	G	A	TP	PIM
1987-88	N. Michigan	WCHA	25	0	2	2	40	....	....	....	....	....
1988-89	N. Michigan	WCHA	42	5	15	20	36	....	....	....	....	....
1989-90	N. Michigan	WCHA	39	5	11	16	77	....	....	....	....	....

WARE, MICHAEL

Defense. Shoots right. 6'5", 205 lbs.   Born, York, Ont., March 22, 1967.
(Edmonton's 3rd choice, 62nd overall, in 1985 Entry Draft).

			Regular Season					Playoffs				
Season	Club	Lea	GP	G	A	TP	PIM	GP	G	A	TP	PIM
1984-85	Hamilton	OHL	57	4	14	18	225	12	0	1	1	29
1985-86	Hamilton	OHL	44	8	11	19	155	....	....	....	....	....
1986-87	Cornwall	OHL	50	5	19	24	173	5	0	1	1	10
1987-88	Nova Scotia	AHL	52	0	8	8	253	3	0	0	0	16
1988-89	**Edmonton**	**NHL**	**2**	**0**	**1**	**1**	**11**	....	....	....	....	....
	Cape Breton	AHL	48	1	11	12	317	....	....	....	....	....
1989-90	**Edmonton**	**NHL**	**3**	**0**	**0**	**0**	**4**	....	....	....	....	....
	Cape Breton	AHL	54	6	13	19	191	6	0	3	3	29
	NHL Totals		**5**	**0**	**1**	**1**	**15**	....	....	....	....	....

WATTERS, TIMOTHY J. (TIM)

Defense. Shoots left. 5'11", 180 lbs.   Born, Kamloops, B.C., July 25, 1959.
(Winnipeg's 6th choice, 124th overall, in 1979 Entry Draft).

			Regular Season					Playoffs				
Season	Club	Lea	GP	G	A	TP	PIM	GP	G	A	TP	PIM
1978-79	Michigan Tech	WCHA	38	6	21	27	48	....	....	....	....	....
1979-80	Cdn. National	....	56	8	21	29	43	....	....	....	....	....
	Cdn. Olympic	....	6	1	1	2	0	....	....	....	....	....
1980-81ab	Michigan Tech	WCHA	43	12	38	50	36	....	....	....	....	....
1981-82	Tulsa	CHL	5	1	2	3	0	....	....	....	....	....
	Winnipeg	**NHL**	**69**	**2**	**22**	**24**	**97**	**4**	**0**	**1**	**1**	**8**
1982-83	**Winnipeg**	**NHL**	**77**	**5**	**18**	**23**	**98**	**3**	**0**	**0**	**0**	**2**
1983-84	**Winnipeg**	**NHL**	**74**	**3**	**20**	**23**	**169**	**3**	**1**	**0**	**1**	**2**
1984-85	**Winnipeg**	**NHL**	**63**	**2**	**20**	**22**	**74**	**8**	**0**	**1**	**1**	**16**
1985-86	**Winnipeg**	**NHL**	**56**	**6**	**8**	**14**	**97**	....	....	....	....	....
1986-87	**Winnipeg**	**NHL**	**63**	**3**	**13**	**16**	**119**	**10**	**0**	**0**	**0**	**21**
1987-88	**Winnipeg**	**NHL**	**36**	**0**	**0**	**0**	**106**	**4**	**0**	**0**	**0**	**4**
	Cdn. National	....	8	0	1	1	2	....	....	....	....	....
	Cdn. Olympic	....	2	0	2	2	0	....	....	....	....	....
1988-89	**Los Angeles**	**NHL**	**76**	**3**	**18**	**21**	**168**	**11**	**0**	**1**	**1**	**6**
1989-90	**Los Angeles**	**NHL**	**62**	**1**	**10**	**11**	**92**	**4**	**0**	**0**	**0**	**6**
	NHL Totals		**576**	**25**	**129**	**154**	**1020**	**47**	**1**	**3**	**4**	**65**

a WCHA First All-Star Team (1981)
b Named to NCAA All-Tournament Team (1981)
Signed as a free agent by **Los Angeles**, June 27, 1988.

WAVER, JEFF

Defense. Shoots left. 5'11", 190 lbs.   Born, St. Boniface, Man., September 28, 1968.
(Pittsburgh's 5th choice, 89th overall, in 1987 Entry Draft).

			Regular Season					Playoffs				
Season	Club	Lea	GP	G	A	TP	PIM	GP	G	A	TP	PIM
1986-87	Hamilton	OHL	63	12	28	40	132	9	0	5	5	23
1987-88	Hamilton	OHL	64	27	34	61	134	14	6	7	13	24
1988-89a	Kingston	OHL	55	30	43	73	95	....	....	....	....	....
	Muskegon	IHL	3	0	1	1	0	1	0	0	0	0
1989-90	Virginia	ECHL	55	28	20	48	73	4	1	4	5	4
	Muskegon	IHL	4	0	2	2	2	....	....	....	....	....

a OHL Third All-Star Team (1989)

WEIGHT, DOUG

Center. Shoots left. 5'11", 185 lbs. Born, Warren, MI, January 21, 1971.
(NY Rangers' 2nd choice, 34th overall, in 1990 Entry Draft).

			Regular Season					Playoffs				
Season	Club	Lea	GP	G	A	TP	PIM	GP	G	A	TP	PIM
1988-89	Bloomfield	NAJHL	34	26	53	79	105	....	....	....	....	....
1989-90	Lake Superior	CCHA	46	21	48	69	44	....	....	....	....	....

WEINRICH, ERIC

(WIGHN-rick)

Defense. Shoots left. 6'1", 190 lbs.   Born, Roanoke, VA, December 19, 1966.
(New Jersey's 3rd choice, 32nd overall, in 1985 Entry Draft).

			Regular Season					Playoffs				
Season	Club	Lea	GP	G	A	TP	PIM	GP	G	A	TP	PIM
1985-86	U. of Maine	H.E.	34	0	15	15	26	....	....	....	....	....
1986-87ab	U. of Maine	H.E.	41	12	32	44	59	....	....	....	....	....
1987-88	U. of Maine	H.E.	8	4	7	11	22	....	....	....	....	....
	U.S. National	....	38	3	9	12	24	....	....	....	....	....
	U.S. Olympic	....	3	0	0	0	0	....	....	....	....	....
1988-89	**New Jersey**	**NHL**	**2**	**0**	**0**	**0**	**0**	....	....	....	....	....
	Utica	AHL	80	17	27	44	70	5	0	1	1	4
1989-90	**New Jersey**	**NHL**	**19**	**2**	**7**	**9**	**11**	**6**	**1**	**3**	**4**	**17**
cd	Utica	AHL	57	12	48	60	38	....	....	....	....	....
	NHL Totals		**21**	**2**	**7**	**9**	**11**	**6**	**1**	**3**	**4**	**17**

a Hockey East First All-Star Team (1987)
b NCAA East Second All-American Team (1987)
c AHL First All-Star Team (1990)
d Won Eddie Shore Plaque (Outstanding Defenseman-AHL) (1990)

WEISBROD, JOHN

Center. Shoots right. 6'1", 185 lbs.   Born, Syosset, NY, October 8, 1968.
(Minnesota's 4th choice, 73rd overall, in 1987 Entry Draft).

			Regular Season					Playoffs				
Season	Club	Lea	GP	G	A	TP	PIM	GP	G	A	TP	PIM
1987-88	Harvard	ECAC	22	8	11	19	16	....	....	....	....	....
1988-89	Harvard	ECAC	31	22	13	35	61	....	....	....	....	....
1989-90	Harvard	ECAC	27	11	21	32	62	....	....	....	....	....

WELLS, GORDON (JAY)

Defense. Shoots left. 6'1", 210 lbs.   Born, Paris, Ont., May 18, 1959.
(Los Angeles' 1st choice, 16th overall, in 1979 Entry Draft).

			Regular Season					Playoffs				
Season	Club	Lea	GP	G	A	TP	PIM	GP	G	A	TP	PIM
1977-78	Kingston	OHA	68	9	13	22	195	5	1	2	3	6
1978-79a	Kingston	OHA	48	6	21	27	100	11	2	7	9	29
1979-80	Binghamton	AHL	28	0	6	6	48	....	....	....	....	....
	Los Angeles	**NHL**	**43**	**0**	**0**	**0**	**113**	**4**	**0**	**0**	**0**	**11**
1980-81	**Los Angeles**	**NHL**	**72**	**5**	**13**	**18**	**155**	**4**	**0**	**0**	**0**	**27**
1981-82	**Los Angeles**	**NHL**	**60**	**1**	**8**	**9**	**145**	**10**	**1**	**3**	**4**	**41**
1982-83	**Los Angeles**	**NHL**	**69**	**3**	**12**	**15**	**167**	....	....	....	....	....
1983-84	**Los Angeles**	**NHL**	**69**	**3**	**18**	**21**	**141**	....	....	....	....	....
1984-85	**Los Angeles**	**NHL**	**77**	**2**	**9**	**11**	**185**	**3**	**0**	**1**	**1**	**0**
1985-86	**Los Angeles**	**NHL**	**79**	**11**	**31**	**42**	**226**	....	....	....	....	....
1986-87	**Los Angeles**	**NHL**	**77**	**7**	**29**	**36**	**155**	**5**	**1**	**2**	**3**	**10**
1987-88	**Los Angeles**	**NHL**	**58**	**2**	**23**	**25**	**159**	**5**	**1**	**2**	**3**	**21**
1988-89	**Philadelphia**	**NHL**	**67**	**2**	**19**	**21**	**184**	**18**	**0**	**2**	**2**	**51**
1989-90	**Philadelphia**	**NHL**	**59**	**3**	**16**	**19**	**129**	....	....	....	....	....
	Buffalo	**NHL**	**1**	**0**	**1**	**1**	**0**	**6**	**0**	**0**	**0**	**12**
	NHL Totals		**731**	**39**	**179**	**218**	**1759**	**55**	**3**	**10**	**13**	**173**

a OHA First All-Star Team (1979)
Traded to **Philadelphia** by **Los Angeles** for Doug Crossman, September 29, 1988. Traded to **Buffalo** by **Philadelphia** with Philadelphia's fourth round choice in 1991 Entry Draft for Kevin Maguire and Buffalo's second round choice (Mikael Renberg) in 1990 Entry Draft, March 5, 1990.

WENAAS, JEFF

(WEHN-as)

Center. Shoots left. 6', 200 lbs.   Born, Eastend, Sask., September 1, 1967.
(Calgary's 3rd choice, 38th overall, in 1985 Entry Draft).

			Regular Season					Playoffs				
Season	Club	Lea	GP	G	A	TP	PIM	GP	G	A	TP	PIM
1984-85	Medicine Hat	WHL	70	27	27	54	70	9	2	5	7	7
1985-86	Medicine Hat	WHL	65	20	26	46	57	25	7	10	17	20
1986-87	Medicine Hat	WHL	70	42	29	71	68	17	9	9	18	28
1987-88	Salt Lake	IHL	80	23	39	62	109	17	5	2	7	25
1988-89	Salt Lake	IHL	17	2	8	10	6	....	....	....	....	....
	Cdn. National	....	21	2	3	5	17	....	....	....	....	....
1989-90	Salt Lake	IHL	38	4	4	8	29	1	0	0	0	0

WERENKA, BRAD

Defense. Shoots left. 6'2", 205 lbs.   Born, Two Hills, Alta., February 12, 1969.
(Edmonton's 2nd choice, 42nd overall, in 1987 Entry Draft).

			Regular Season					Playoffs				
Season	Club	Lea	GP	G	A	TP	PIM	GP	G	A	TP	PIM
1986-87	N. Michigan	WCHA	30	4	4	8	35	....	....	....	....	....
1987-88	N. Michigan	WCHA	34	7	23	30	26	....	....	....	....	....
1988-89	N. Michigan	WCHA	28	7	13	20	16	....	....	....	....	....
1989-90	N. Michigan	WCHA	8	2	5	7	8	....	....	....	....	....

WERNESS, LANCE

Right wing. Shoots right. 6', 175 lbs.   Born, Burnsville, MN, March 28, 1969.
(Chicago's 9th choice, 176th overall, in 1987 Entry Draft).

			Regular Season					Playoffs				
Season	Club	Lea	GP	G	A	TP	PIM	GP	G	A	TP	PIM
1987-88	U. Minnesota	WCHA	27	8	5	13	20	....	....	....	....	....
1988-89	U. Minnesota	WCHA	13	2	4	6	12	....	....	....	....	....
1989-90	U. Minnesota	WCHA	2	0	1	1	2	....	....	....	....	....

WESLEY, GLEN

Defense. Shoots left. 6'1", 195 lbs. Born, Red Deer, Alta., October 2, 1968.
(Boston's 1st choice, 3rd overall, in 1987 Entry Draft).

			Regular Season					Playoffs				
Season	Club	Lea	GP	G	A	TP	PIM	GP	G	A	TP	PIM
1983-84	Portland	WHL	3	1	2	3	0	....	....	....	....	....
1984-85	Portland	WHL	67	16	52	68	76	6	1	6	7	8
1985-86a	Portland	WHL	69	16	75	91	96	15	3	11	14	29
1986-87a	Portland	WHL	63	16	46	62	72	20	8	18	26	27
1987-88b	**Boston**	**NHL**	**79**	**7**	**30**	**37**	**69**	**23**	**6**	**8**	**14**	**22**
1988-89	**Boston**	**NHL**	**77**	**19**	**35**	**54**	**61**	**10**	**0**	**2**	**2**	**4**
1989-90	**Boston**	**NHL**	**78**	**9**	**27**	**36**	**48**	**21**	**2**	**6**	**8**	**36**
	NHL Totals		**234**	**35**	**92**	**127**	**178**	**54**	**8**	**16**	**24**	**62**

a WHL West All-Star Team (1986, 1987)
b NHL All-Rookie Team (1988)

Played in NHL All-Star Game (1989)

WHEELDON, SIMON

Center. Shoots left. 5'11", 170 lbs. Born, Vancouver, B.C., August 30, 1966.
(Edmonton's 11th choice, 231st overall, in 1984 Entry Draft).

			Regular Season					Playoffs				
Season	Club	Lea	GP	G	A	TP	PIM	GP	G	A	TP	PIM
1983-84	Victoria	WHL	56	14	24	38	43	....	....	....	....	....
1984-85a	Victoria	WHL	67	50	76	126	78	....	....	....	....	....
	Nova Scotia	AHL	4	0	1	1	0	1	0	0	0	0
1985-86	Victoria	WHL	70	61	96	157	85	....	....	....	....	....
1986-87	Flint	IHL	41	17	53	70	20	....	....	....	....	....
	New Haven	AHL	38	11	28	39	39	5	0	0	0	6
1987-88	**NY Rangers**	**NHL**	**5**	**0**	**1**	**1**	**4**	....	....	....	....	....
b	Colorado	IHL	69	45	54	99	80	13	8	11	19	12
1988-89	**NY Rangers**	**NHL**	**6**	**0**	**1**	**1**	**2**	....	....	....	....	....
b	Denver	IHL	74	50	56	106	77	4	0	2	2	6
1989-90	Flint	IHL	76	34	49	83	61	4	1	2	3	2
	NHL Totals		**11**	**0**	**2**	**2**	**6**	....	....	....	....	....

a WHL Second All-Star Team, West Division (1985)
b IHL Second All-Star Team (1988, 1989)

Signed as a free agent by **NY Rangers**, September 8, 1986. Traded to **Winnipeg** by **NY Rangers** for Brian McReynolds, July 9, 1990.

WHITE, PETER

Left wing. Shoots left. 5'11", 200 lbs. Born, Montreal, Que., March 15, 1969.
(Edmonton's 4th choice, 92nd overall, in 1989 Entry Draft).

			Regular Season					Playoffs				
Season	Club	Lea	GP	G	A	TP	PIM	GP	G	A	TP	PIM
1988-89	Michigan State	CCHA	46	20	33	53	17	....	....	....	....	....
1989-90	Michigan State	CCHA	45	22	40	62	6	....	....	....	....	....

WHITE, ROBERT

Defense. Shoots right. 6'0", 185 lbs. Born, Brockville, Ont., March 9, 1968.
(Hartford's 10th choice, 221st overall, in 1988 Entry Draft).

			Regular Season					Playoffs				
Season	Club	Lea	GP	G	A	TP	PIM	GP	G	A	TP	PIM
1986-87	St. Lawrence	ECAC	30	2	9	11	52	....	....	....	....	....
1987-88	St. Lawrence	ECAC	31	4	16	20	29	....	....	....	....	....
1988-89	St. Lawrence	ECAC	35	5	19	24	64	....	....	....	....	....
1989-90	St. Lawrence	ECAC	32	2	15	17	96	....	....	....	....	....

WHITHAM, SHAWN

Defense. Shoots left. 5'11", 195 lbs. Born, Verdun, Que., March 13, 1967.
(Buffalo's 10th choice, 173rd overall, in 1986 Entry Draft).

			Regular Season					Playoffs				
Season	Club	Lea	GP	G	A	TP	PIM	GP	G	A	TP	PIM
1985-86	Providence	H.E.	38	10	14	24	91	....	....	....	....	....
1986-87	Providence	H.E.	31	9	11	20	57	....	....	....	....	....
1987-88	Providence	H.E.	29	8	17	25	71	....	....	....	....	....
1988-89	Rochester	AHL	46	4	15	19	75	....	....	....	....	....
	Flint	IHL	17	3	13	16	18	....	....	....	....	....
1989-90	Phoenix	IHL	3	0	0	0	2	....	....	....	....	....

WHITTEMORE, TODD

Forward. Shoots left. 6'1", 175 lbs. Born, Taunton, MA, June 20, 1967.
(Toronto's 9th choice, 169th overall, in 1985 Entry Draft).

			Regular Season					Playoffs				
Season	Club	Lea	GP	G	A	TP	PIM	GP	G	A	TP	PIM
1986-87	Providence	H.E.	29	1	4	5	12	....	....	....	....	....
1987-88	Providence	H.E.	34	5	10	15	30	....	....	....	....	....
1988-89	Providence	H.E.	29	7	1	8	28	....	....	....	....	....
1989-90	Providence	H.E.	16	4	2	6	30	....	....	....	....	....

WHYTE, SEAN

Center/Right wing. Shoots right. 6', 200 lbs. Born, Sudbury, Ont., May 4, 1970.
(Los Angeles' 7th choice, 165th overall, in 1989 Entry Draft).

			Regular Season					Playoffs				
Season	Club	Lea	GP	G	A	TP	PIM	GP	G	A	TP	PIM
1988-89	Guelph	OHL	53	20	44	64	57	....	....	....	....	....
1989-90	Owen Sound	OHL	54	23	30	53	90	3	0	1	1	10

WICKENHEISER, DOUGLAS PETER (DOUG) (WIHK ehn HIGH zuhr)

Center. Shoots left. 6'1", 200 lbs. Born, Regina, Sask., March 30, 1961.
(Montreal's 1st choice and 1st overall in 1980 Entry Draft).

			Regular Season					Playoffs				
Season	Club	Lea	GP	G	A	TP	PIM	GP	G	A	TP	PIM
1977-78	Regina	WHL	68	37	51	88	49	13	4	5	9	4
1978-79	Regina	WHL	68	32	62	94	141	....	....	....	....	....
1979-80abc	Regina	WHL	71	*89	81	*170	99	18	14	*26	*40	20
1980-81	**Montreal**	**NHL**	**41**	**7**	**8**	**15**	**20**	....	....	....	....	....
1981-82	**Montreal**	**NHL**	**56**	**12**	**23**	**35**	**43**	....	....	....	....	....
1982-83	**Montreal**	**NHL**	**78**	**25**	**30**	**55**	**49**	....	....	....	....	....
1983-84	**Montreal**	**NHL**	**27**	**5**	**5**	**10**	**6**	....	....	....	....	....
	St. Louis	**NHL**	**46**	**7**	**21**	**28**	**19**	**11**	**2**	**2**	**4**	**2**
1984-85	**St. Louis**	**NHL**	**68**	**23**	**20**	**43**	**36**	....	....	....	....	....
1985-86	**St. Louis**	**NHL**	**36**	**8**	**11**	**19**	**16**	**19**	**2**	**5**	**7**	**12**
1986-87	**St. Louis**	**NHL**	**80**	**13**	**15**	**28**	**37**	**6**	**0**	**0**	**0**	**2**
1987-88	**Vancouver**	**NHL**	**80**	**7**	**19**	**26**	**36**	....	....	....	....	....
1988-89	**NY Rangers**	**NHL**	**1**	**1**	**0**	**1**	**0**	....	....	....	....	....
	Flint	IHL	21	9	7	16	18	....	....	....	....	....
	Cdn. National	....	26	7	15	22	40	....	....	....	....	....
	Washington	**NHL**	**16**	**2**	**5**	**7**	**4**	**5**	**0**	**0**	**0**	**2**
	Baltimore	AHL	2	0	5	5	0	....	....	....	....	....
1989-90	**Washington**	**NHL**	**27**	**1**	**8**	**9**	**20**	....	....	....	....	....
	Baltimore	AHL	35	9	19	28	22	12	2	5	7	22
	NHL Totals		**556**	**111**	**165**	**276**	**286**	**41**	**4**	**7**	**11**	**18**

a WHL First All-Star Team (1980)
b WHL Most Valuable Player (1980)
c Named Canadian Major Junior Player of the Year (1980)

Traded to **St. Louis** by **Montreal** with Gilbert Delorme and Greg Paslawski for Perry Turnbull, December 21, 1983. Claimed by **Hartford** in NHL Waiver Draft, October 5, 1987. Claimed by **Vancouver** in NHL Waiver Draft, October 5, 1987. Signed as a free agent by **NY Rangers**, August 12, 1988. Signed as a free agent by **Washington**, February 28, 1989.

WIEBE, DANIEL

Right wing. Shoots left. 6'4", 190 lbs. Born, Manning, Alta., April 3, 1969.
(Quebec's 10th choice, 171st overall, in 1988 Entry Draft).

			Regular Season					Playoffs				
Season	Club	Lea	GP	G	A	TP	PIM	GP	G	A	TP	PIM
1987-88	U. of Alberta	CWUAA	25	6	4	10	....	....	....	....	....	....
1988-89	U. of Alberta	CWUAA	40	5	8	13	56	....	....	....	....	....
1989-90	U. of Alberta	CWUAA	17	6	2	8	40	....	....	....	....	....

WIEGAND, CHARLES

Center. Shoots left. 6'1", 175 lbs. Born, Burlington, VT, December 28, 1968.
(NY Rangers' 8th choice, 157th overall, in 1987 Entry Draft).

			Regular Season					Playoffs				
Season	Club	Lea	GP	G	A	TP	PIM	GP	G	A	TP	PIM
1988-89	Ferris State	CCHA	36	5	5	10	44	....	....	....	....	....
1989-90	Ferris State	CCHA	34	10	11	21	50	....	....	....	....	....

WIEMER, JAMES DUNCAN (JIM) (WEE-muhr)

Defense. Shoots left. 6'4", 208 lbs. Born, Sudbury, Ont., January 9, 1961.
(Buffalo's 5th choice, 83rd overall, in 1980 Entry Draft).

			Regular Season					Playoffs				
Season	Club	Lea	GP	G	A	TP	PIM	GP	G	A	TP	PIM
1978-79	Peterborough	OHA	61	15	12	27	50	18	4	4	8	15
1979-80	Peterborough	OHA	53	17	32	49	63	14	6	9	15	19
1980-81	Peterborough	OHA	65	41	54	95	102	5	1	2	3	15
1981-82	Rochester	AHL	74	19	26	45	57	9	0	4	4	2
1982-83	**Buffalo**	**NHL**	....	....	....	....	....	**1**	**0**	**0**	**0**	**0**
	Rochester	AHL	74	15	44	59	43	15	5	15	20	22
1983-84	**Buffalo**	**NHL**	**64**	**5**	**15**	**20**	**48**	....	....	....	....	....
	Rochester	AHL	12	4	11	15	11	18	3	13	16	20
1984-85	**Buffalo**	**NHL**	**10**	**3**	**2**	**5**	**4**	....	....	....	....	....
	Rochester	AHL	13	1	9	10	24	....	....	....	....	....
	NY Rangers	**NHL**	**22**	**4**	**3**	**7**	**30**	**1**	**0**	**0**	**0**	**0**
	New Haven	AHL	33	9	27	36	39	....	....	....	....	....
1985-86	**NY Rangers**	**NHL**	**7**	**3**	**0**	**3**	**2**	**8**	**1**	**0**	**1**	**6**
ab	New Haven	AHL	73	24	49	73	108	....	....	....	....	....
1986-87	New Haven	AHL	6	0	7	7	6	....	....	....	....	....
	Nova Scotia	AHL	59	9	25	34	72	5	0	4	4	2
1987-88	**Edmonton**	**NHL**	**12**	**1**	**2**	**3**	**15**	**2**	**0**	**0**	**0**	**2**
	Nova Scotia	AHL	57	11	32	43	99	5	1	1	2	14
1988-89	Cape Breton	AHL	51	12	29	41	80	....	....	....	....	....
	Los Angeles	**NHL**	**9**	**2**	**3**	**5**	**20**	**10**	**2**	**1**	**3**	**19**
	New Haven	AHL	3	1	1	2	2	7	2	3	5	2
1989-90	**Boston**	**NHL**	**61**	**5**	**14**	**19**	**63**	**8**	**0**	**1**	**1**	**4**
	Maine	AHL	6	3	4	7	27	....	....	....	....	....
	NHL Totals		**185**	**23**	**39**	**62**	**182**	**30**	**3**	**2**	**5**	**31**

a AHL First All-Star Team (1986)
b AHL Defenseman of the Year (1986)

Traded to **NY Rangers** by **Buffalo** with Steve Patrick for Dave Maloney and Chris Renaud, December 6, 1984. Traded to **Edmonton** by **NY Rangers** with Reijo Ruotsalainen, Clark Donatelli and Ville Kentala for Don Jackson, Mike Golden, Miloslav Horvava and future considerations, October 23, 1986. Traded to **Los Angeles** by **Edmonton** with Alan May for Brian Wilks and John English, March 7, 1989. Signed as a free agent by **Boston**, July 6, 1989.

WILDGOOSE, LYLE

Left wing. Shoots left. 6', 175 lbs. Born, Chelmsford, Ont., October 28, 1968.
(Calgary's 1st choice, 25th overall, in 1990 Supplemental Draft).

			Regular Season					Playoffs				
Season	Club	Lea	GP	G	A	TP	PIM	GP	G	A	TP	PIM
1987-88	Providence	H.E.	33	12	19	31	54	....	....	....	....	....
1988-89	Providence	H.E.	32	11	17	28	34	....	....	....	....	....
1989-90	Providence	H.E.	35	17	18	35	38	....	....	....	....	....

WILKIE, BOB

Defense. Shoots right. 6'2", 200 lbs. Born, Calgary, Alta., February 11, 1969.
(Detroit's 3rd choice, 41st overall, in 1987 Entry Draft).

			Regular Season					Playoffs				
Season	Club	Lea	GP	G	A	TP	PIM	GP	G	A	TP	PIM
1986-87	Swift Current	WHL	65	12	38	50	50	4	1	3	4	2
1987-88	Swift Current	WHL	67	12	68	80	124	10	4	12	16	8
1988-89	Swift Current	WHL	62	18	67	85	89	12	1	11	12	47
1989-90	Adirondack	AHL	58	5	33	38	64	6	1	4	5	2

WILKINSON, NEIL

Defense. Shoots right. 6'3", 180 lbs. Born, Selkirk, Man., August 16, 1967.
(Minnesota's 2nd choice, 30th overall, in 1986 Entry Draft).

			Regular Season					Playoffs				
Season	Club	Lea	GP	G	A	TP	PIM	GP	G	A	TP	PIM
1986-87	Michigan State	CCHA	19	3	4	7	18	....	....	....	....	....
1987-88	Medicine Hat	WHL	55	11	21	32	157	5	1	0	1	2
1988-89	Kalamazoo	IHL	39	5	15	20	96	....	....	....	....	....
1989-90	**Minnesota**	**NHL**	**36**	**0**	**5**	**5**	**100**	**7**	**0**	**2**	**2**	**11**
	Kalamazoo	IHL	20	6	7	13	62	....	....	....	....	....
	NHL Totals		**36**	**0**	**5**	**5**	**100**	**7**	**0**	**2**	**2**	**11**

WILKS, BRIAN

Center. Shoots right. 5'11", 175 lbs. Born, North York, Ont., February 27, 1966.
(Los Angeles' 2nd choice, 24th overall, in 1984 Entry Draft).

			Regular Season					Playoffs				
Season	Club	Lea	GP	G	A	TP	PIM	GP	G	A	TP	PIM
1982-83	Kitchener	OHL	69	6	17	23	25	1	0	0	0	0
1983-84	Kitchener	OHL	64	21	54	75	36	16	6	14	20	9
1984-85	**Los Angeles**	**NHL**	**2**	**0**	**0**	**0**	**0**	....	....	....	....	....
	Kitchener	OHL	58	30	63	93	52	4	2	4	6	2
1985-86	**Los Angeles**	**NHL**	**43**	**4**	**8**	**12**	**25**	....	....	....	....	....
1986-87	**Los Angeles**	**NHL**	**1**	**0**	**0**	**0**	**0**	....	....	....	....	....
	New Haven	AHL	43	16	20	36	23	7	1	3	4	7
1987-88	New Haven	AHL	18	4	8	12	26	....	....	....	....	....
1988-89	Cape Breton	AHL	12	4	11	15	27	....	....	....	....	....
	Los Angeles	**NHL**	**2**	**0**	**0**	**0**	**2**	....	....	....	....	....
	New Haven	AHL	44	15	19	34	48	....	....	....	....	....
1989-90	Cape Breton	AHL	53	13	20	33	85	....	....	....	....	....
	Muskegon	IHL	15	6	11	17	10	15	7	10	17	41
	NHL Totals		**48**	**4**	**8**	**12**	**27**	....	....	....	....	....

Traded to **Edmonton** by **Los Angeles** with John English for Jim Wiemer and Alan May, March 7, 1989. Traded to **Pittsburgh** by **Edmonton** for future considerations, March 6, 1990.

WILLIAMS, DAVID

Defense. Shoots right. 6'2", 195 lbs. Born, Plainfield, NJ, August 25, 1967.
(New Jersey's 12th choice, 234th overall, in 1985 Entry Draft).

			Regular Season					Playoffs				
Season	Club	Lea	GP	G	A	TP	PIM	GP	G	A	TP	PIM
1986-87	Dartmouth	ECAC	23	2	19	21	20	....	....	....	....	....
1987-88	Dartmouth	ECAC	25	8	14	22	30	....	....	....	....	....
1988-89ab	Dartmouth	ECAC	25	4	11	15	28	....	....	....	....	....
1989-90	Dartmouth	ECAC	26	3	12	15	32	....	....	....	....	....

a ECAC First All-Star Team (1989)
b NCAA East Second All-American Team (1989)

WILLIAMS, SEAN

Right wing. Shoots left. 6'1", 180 lbs. Born, Oshawa, Ont., January 28, 1968.
(Chicago's 11th choice, 245th overall, in 1986 Entry Draft).

			Regular Season					Playoffs				
Season	Club	Lea	GP	G	A	TP	PIM	GP	G	A	TP	PIM
1984-85	Oshawa	OHL	40	6	7	13	28	5	1	0	1	0
1985-86	Oshawa	OHL	55	15	23	38	23	6	2	3	5	4
1986-87	Oshawa	OHL	62	21	23	44	32	25	7	5	12	19
1987-88a	Oshawa	OHL	65	*58	65	123	38	7	3	3	6	6
1988-89	Saginaw	IHL	77	32	27	59	75	6	0	3	3	0
1989-90	Indianapolis	IHL	78	21	37	58	25	14	8	5	13	12

a OHL First All-Star Team (1988)

WILSON, CAREY

Center. Shoots right. 6'2", 205 lbs. Born, Winnipeg, Man., May 19, 1962.
(Chicago's 8th choice, 67th overall, in 1980 Entry Draft).

			Regular Season					Playoffs				
Season	Club	Lea	GP	G	A	TP	PIM	GP	G	A	TP	PIM
1979-80	Dartmouth	ECAC	31	16	22	38	20	....	....	....	....	....
1980-81	Dartmouth	ECAC	24	9	13	22	52	....	....	....	....	....
1981-82	Helsinki	Fin.	29	15	17	32	58	7	1	4	5	6
1982-83	Helsinki	Fin.	36	16	24	40	62	9	1	3	4	12
1983-84	Cdn. Olympic	...	56	19	24	43	34	....	....	....	....	....
	Calgary	**NHL**	**15**	**2**	**5**	**7**	**2**	**6**	**3**	**1**	**4**	**2**
1984-85	**Calgary**	**NHL**	**74**	**24**	**48**	**72**	**27**	**4**	**0**	**0**	**0**	**0**
1985-86	**Calgary**	**NHL**	**76**	**29**	**29**	**58**	**24**	**9**	**0**	**2**	**2**	**2**
1986-87	**Calgary**	**NHL**	**80**	**20**	**36**	**56**	**42**	**6**	**1**	**1**	**2**	**6**
1987-88	**Calgary**	**NHL**	**34**	**9**	**21**	**30**	**18**	....	....	....	....	....
	Hartford	**NHL**	**36**	**18**	**20**	**38**	**22**	**6**	**2**	**4**	**6**	**2**
1988-89	**Hartford**	**NHL**	**34**	**11**	**11**	**22**	**14**	....	....	....	....	....
	NY Rangers	**NHL**	**41**	**21**	**34**	**55**	**45**	**4**	**1**	**2**	**3**	**2**
1989-90	**NY Rangers**	**NHL**	**41**	**9**	**17**	**26**	**57**	**10**	**2**	**1**	**3**	**0**
	NHL Totals		**431**	**143**	**221**	**364**	**251**	**45**	**9**	**11**	**20**	**14**

Rights traded to **Calgary** by **Chicago** for Denis Cyr, November 8, 1982. Traded to **Hartford** by **Calgary** with Neil Sheehy and the rights to Lane MacDonald for Dana Murzyn and Shane Churla, January 3, 1988. Traded by **NY Rangers** by **Hartford** with Hartford's fifth-round choice (Lubos Rob) in 1990 Entry Draft for Brian Lawton, Norm MacIver and Don Maloney, December 26, 1988. Traded to **Hartford** by **NY Rangers** with future considerations for Jody Hull, July 9, 1990.

WILSON, DOUGLAS, JR. (DOUG)

Defense. Shoots left. 6'1", 185 lbs. Born, Ottawa, Ont., July 5, 1957.
(Chicago's 1st choice, 6th overall, in 1977 Amateur Draft).

			Regular Season					Playoffs				
Season	Club	Lea	GP	G	A	TP	PIM	GP	G	A	TP	PIM
1975-76	Ottawa	OHA	58	26	62	88	142	12	5	10	15	24
1976-77a	Ottawa	OHA	43	25	54	79	85	19	4	20	24	34
1977-78	**Chicago**	**NHL**	**77**	**14**	**20**	**34**	**72**	**4**	**0**	**0**	**0**	**0**
1978-79	**Chicago**	**NHL**	**56**	**5**	**21**	**26**	**37**	....	....	....	....	....
1979-80	**Chicago**	**NHL**	**73**	**12**	**49**	**61**	**70**	**7**	**2**	**8**	**10**	**6**
1980-81	**Chicago**	**NHL**	**76**	**12**	**39**	**51**	**80**	**3**	**0**	**3**	**3**	**2**
1981-82bc	**Chicago**	**NHL**	**76**	**39**	**46**	**85**	**54**	**15**	**3**	**10**	**13**	**32**
1982-83	**Chicago**	**NHL**	**74**	**18**	**51**	**69**	**58**	**13**	**4**	**11**	**15**	**12**
1983-84	**Chicago**	**NHL**	**66**	**13**	**45**	**58**	**64**	**5**	**0**	**3**	**3**	**2**
1984-85d	**Chicago**	**NHL**	**78**	**22**	**54**	**76**	**44**	**12**	**3**	**10**	**13**	**12**
1985-86	**Chicago**	**NHL**	**79**	**17**	**47**	**64**	**80**	**3**	**1**	**1**	**2**	**2**
1986-87	**Chicago**	**NHL**	**69**	**16**	**32**	**48**	**36**	**4**	**0**	**0**	**0**	**0**
1987-88	**Chicago**	**NHL**	**27**	**8**	**24**	**32**	**28**	....	....	....	....	....
1988-89	**Chicago**	**NHL**	**66**	**15**	**47**	**62**	**69**	**4**	**1**	**2**	**3**	**0**
1989-90d	**Chicago**	**NHL**	**70**	**23**	**50**	**73**	**40**	**20**	**3**	**12**	**15**	**18**
	NHL Totals		**887**	**214**	**525**	**739**	**732**	**90**	**17**	**60**	**77**	**86**

a OHA First All-Star Team (1977)
b Won James Norris Memorial Trophy (1982)
c NHL First All-Star Team (1982)
d NHL Second All-Star Team (1985, 1990)

Played in NHL All-Star Game (1982-86, 1990)

WILSON, MITCH

Center. Shoots right. 5'8", 190 lbs. Born, Kelowna, B.C., February 15, 1962.

			Regular Season					Playoffs				
Season	Club	Lea	GP	G	A	TP	PIM	GP	G	A	TP	PIM
1980-81	Seattle	WHL	64	8	23	31	253	5	3	0	3	31
1981-82	Seattle	WHL	60	18	17	35	436	10	3	7	10	55
1982-83	Wichita	CHL	55	4	6	10	186	....	....	....	....	....
1983-84	Maine	AHL	71	6	8	14	349	17	3	6	9	98
1984-85	**New Jersey**	**NHL**	**9**	**0**	**2**	**2**	**21**	....	....	....	....	....
	Maine	AHL	51	6	3	9	220	2	0	0	0	32
1985-86	Maine	AHL	64	4	3	7	217	3	0	0	0	2
1986-87	**Pittsburgh**	**NHL**	**17**	**2**	**1**	**3**	**83**	....	....	....	....	....
	Baltimore	AHL	58	8	9	17	*353	....	....	....	....	....
1987-88	Muskegon	IHL	68	27	25	52	400	5	1	0	1	23
1988-89	Muskegon	IHL	61	16	34	50	*382	11	4	5	9	*83
1989-90	Muskegon	IHL	63	13	24	37	283	15	1	4	5	97
	NHL Totals		**26**	**2**	**3**	**5**	**104**	....	....	....	....	....

Signed as a free agent by **New Jersey**, October 12, 1982. Signed as a free agent by **Pittsburgh**, July 24, 1986.

WILSON, RICHARD WILLIAM (RIK)

Defense. Shoots right. 6', 180 lbs. Born, Long Beach, CA, June 17, 1962.
(St. Louis' 1st choice, 12th overall, in 1980 Entry Draft).

			Regular Season					Playoffs				
Season	Club	Lea	GP	G	A	TP	PIM	GP	G	A	TP	PIM
1980-81a	Kingston	OHA	68	30	70	100	108	13	1	9	10	18
	Salt Lake	CHL	....	....	....	....	....	4	1	1	2	2
1981-82	Kingston	OHL	16	9	10	19	38	....	....	....	....	....
	St. Louis	**NHL**	**48**	**3**	**18**	**21**	**24**	**9**	**0**	**3**	**3**	**14**
1982-83	**St. Louis**	**NHL**	**56**	**3**	**11**	**14**	**50**	....	....	....	....	....
	Salt Lake	CHL	4	0	0	0	0	....	....	....	....	....
1983-84	Montana	CHL	6	0	3	3	2	....	....	....	....	....
	St. Louis	**NHL**	**48**	**7**	**11**	**18**	**53**	**11**	**0**	**0**	**0**	**9**
1984-85	**St. Louis**	**NHL**	**51**	**8**	**16**	**24**	**39**	**2**	**0**	**1**	**1**	**0**
1985-86	**St. Louis**	**NHL**	**32**	**0**	**4**	**4**	**48**	....	....	....	....	....
	Calgary	**NHL**	**2**	**0**	**0**	**0**	**0**	....	....	....	....	....
	Nova Scotia	AHL	13	4	5	9	11	....	....	....	....	....
	Moncton	AHL	8	3	3	6	2	....	....	....	....	....
1986-87	Nova Scotia	AHL	45	8	13	21	109	5	1	3	4	20
1987-88	**Chicago**	**NHL**	**14**	**4**	**5**	**9**	**6**	....	....	....	....	....
	Saginaw	IHL	33	4	5	9	105	....	....	....	....	....
1988-89	Villach	Aus.	45	17	43	60	110	....	....	....	....	....
1989-90	Peoria	IHL	15	1	4	5	34	....	....	....	....	....
	NHL Totals		**251**	**25**	**65**	**90**	**220**	**22**	**0**	**4**	**4**	**23**

a OHA First All-Star Team (1981)

Traded to **Calgary** by **St. Louis** with Joe Mullen and Terry Johnson for Ed Beers, Charles Bourgeois and Gino Cavallini, February 1, 1986. Traded to **Chicago** by **Calgary** for Tom McMurchy, March 11, 1986. Signed as a free agent by **St. Louis**, July 19, 1989. Traded to **St. Louis** by **Chicago** for Craig Coxe, September 27, 1989.

WILSON, RONALD LEE (RON)

Center. Shoots left. 5'9", 170 lbs.   Born, Toronto, Ont., May 13, 1956.
(Montreal's 15th choice, 133rd overall, in 1976 Amateur Draft).

			Regular Season					Playoffs				
Season	Club	Lea	GP	G	A	TP	PIM	GP	G	A	TP	PIM
1974-75	Toronto	OHA	16	6	12	18	6	23	9	17	26	6
1975-76	St. Catharines	OHA	64	37	62	99	44	4	1	6	7	7
1976-77	Nova Scotia	AHL	67	15	21	36	18	6	0	0	0	0
1977-78	Nova Scotia	AHL	59	15	25	40	17	11	4	4	8	9
1978-79	Nova Scotia	AHL	77	33	42	75	91	10	5	6	11	14
1979-80	**Winnipeg**	**NHL**	**79**	**21**	**36**	**57**	**28**	....	....	....	....	....
1980-81	**Winnipeg**	**NHL**	**77**	**18**	**33**	**51**	**55**	....	....	....	....	....
1981-82	**Winnipeg**	**NHL**	**39**	**3**	**13**	**16**	**49**	....	....	....	....	....
	Tulsa	CHL	41	20	38	58	22	3	1	0	1	2
1982-83	Sherbrooke	AHL	65	30	55	85	71	....	....	....	....	....
	Winnipeg	**NHL**	**12**	**6**	**3**	**9**	**4**	**3**	**2**	**2**	**4**	**2**
1983-84	**Winnipeg**	**NHL**	**51**	**3**	**12**	**15**	**12**	....	....	....	....	....
	Sherbrooke	AHL	22	10	30	40	16	....	....	....	....	....
1984-85	**Winnipeg**	**NHL**	**75**	**10**	**9**	**19**	**31**	**8**	**4**	**2**	**6**	**2**
1985-86	**Winnipeg**	**NHL**	**54**	**6**	**7**	**13**	**16**	**1**	**0**	**0**	**0**	**0**
	Sherbrooke	AHL	10	9	8	17	9	....	....	....	....	....
1986-87	**Winnipeg**	**NHL**	**80**	**3**	**13**	**16**	**13**	**10**	**1**	**2**	**3**	**0**
1987-88	**Winnipeg**	**NHL**	**69**	**5**	**8**	**13**	**28**	**1**	**0**	**0**	**0**	**2**
1988-89a	Moncton	AHL	80	31	61	92	110	8	1	4	5	20
1989-90	Moncton	AHL	47	16	37	53	39	....	....	....	....	....
	St. Louis	**NHL**	**33**	**3**	**17**	**20**	**23**	**12**	**3**	**5**	**8**	**18**
	NHL Totals		**569**	**78**	**151**	**229**	**259**	**35**	**10**	**11**	**21**	**24**

a AHL Second All-Star Team (1989)

Sold to **Winnipeg** by **Montreal**, October 4, 1979. Traded to **St. Louis** by **Winnipeg** for Doug Evans, January 22, 1990.

WILSON, ROSS

Right wing. Shoots right. 6'3", 195 lbs.   Born, Val Caron, Ont., June 26, 1969.
(Los Angeles' 3rd choice, 43rd overall, in 1987 Entry Draft).

			Regular Season					Playoffs				
Season	Club	Lea	GP	G	A	TP	PIM	GP	G	A	TP	PIM
1986-87	Peterborough	OHL	66	28	11	39	91	12	3	5	8	16
1987-88	Peterborough	OHL	66	29	30	59	114	12	2	9	11	15
1988-89	Peterborough	OHL	64	48	41	89	90	15	10	13	23	23
1989-90	New Haven	AHL	61	19	14	33	39	....	....	....	....	....

WINNES, CHRISTOPHER (CHRIS)

Right wing. Shoots right. 6', 170 lbs.   Born, Ridgefield, CT, February 12, 1968.
(Boston's 9th choice, 161st overall, in 1987 Entry Draft).

			Regular Season					Playoffs				
Season	Club	Lea	GP	G	A	TP	PIM	GP	G	A	TP	PIM
1987-88	N. Hampshire	H.E.	30	17	19	36	28	....	....	....	....	....
1988-89	N. Hampshire	H.E.	30	11	20	31	22	....	....	....	....	....
1989-90	N. Hampshire	H.E.	24	10	13	23	12	....	....	....	....	....

WITKOWSKI, BYRON

Left wing. Shoots left. 6'3", 195 lbs.   Born, Edenwold, Sask., November 20, 1969.
(Quebec's 13th choice, 211th overall, in 1989 Entry Draft).

			Regular Season					Playoffs				
Season	Club	Lea	GP	G	A	TP	PIM	GP	G	A	TP	PIM
1988-89	Nipawin	SJHL	64	52	38	90	169	....	....	....	....	....
1989-90	W. Michigan	CCHA	36	1	2	3	36	....	....	....	....	....

WOLAK, MICHAEL

Center. Shoots left. 5'10", 185 lbs.   Born, Utica, NY, April 29, 1968.
(St. Louis' 5th choice, 87th overall, in 1986 Entry Draft).

			Regular Season					Playoffs				
Season	Club	Lea	GP	G	A	TP	PIM	GP	G	A	TP	PIM
1985-86	Kitchener	OHL	62	24	44	68	48	5	0	9	9	2
1986-87	Kitchener	OHL	9	3	6	9	6	....	....	....	....	....
	Belleville	OHL	25	20	16	36	18	....	....	....	....	....
	Windsor	OHL	26	7	14	21	26	14	2	7	9	2
1987-88	Windsor	OHL	63	42	72	114	86	9	7	4	11	22
1988-89	Flint	IHL	2	0	1	1	4	....	....	....	....	....
	Windsor	OHL	35	19	38	57	56	4	5	4	9	4
	Peoria	IHL	8	2	4	6	16	1	0	0	0	0
1989-90	Peoria	IHL	50	7	16	23	31	....	....	....	....	....

WOLANIN, CHRISTOPHER

Defense. Shoots left. 6'2", 205 lbs.   Born, Detroit, MI, September 12, 1968.
(Vancouver's 10th choice, 212th overall, in 1988 Entry Draft).

			Regular Season					Playoffs				
Season	Club	Lea	GP	G	A	TP	PIM	GP	G	A	TP	PIM
1987-88	Ill-Chicago	CCHA	37	1	6	7	38	....	....	....	....	....
1988-89	Ill-Chicago	CCHA	30	1	9	10	33	....	....	....	....	....
1989-90	Ill-Chicago	CCHA	34	1	6	7	116	....	....	....	....	....

WOLANIN, CRAIG   (wuh-LAN-ihn)

Defense. Shoots left. 6'3", 205 lbs.   Born, Grosse Pointe, MI, July 27, 1967.
(New Jersey's 1st choice, 3rd overall, in 1985 Entry Draft).

			Regular Season					Playoffs				
Season	Club	Lea	GP	G	A	TP	PIM	GP	G	A	TP	PIM
1984-85	Kitchener	OHL	60	5	16	21	95	4	1	1	2	2
1985-86	**New Jersey**	**NHL**	**44**	**2**	**16**	**18**	**74**	....	....	....	....	....
1986-87	**New Jersey**	**NHL**	**68**	**4**	**6**	**10**	**109**	....	....	....	....	....
1987-88	**New Jersey**	**NHL**	**78**	**6**	**25**	**31**	**170**	**18**	**2**	**5**	**7**	**51**
1988-89	**New Jersey**	**NHL**	**56**	**3**	**8**	**11**	**69**	....	....	....	....	....
1989-90	**New Jersey**	**NHL**	**37**	**1**	**7**	**8**	**47**	....	....	....	....	....
	Utica	AHL	6	2	4	6	2	....	....	....	....	....
	Quebec	**NHL**	**13**	**0**	**3**	**3**	**10**	....	....	....	....	....
	NHL Totals		**296**	**16**	**65**	**81**	**479**	**18**	**2**	**5**	**7**	**51**

Traded to **Quebec** by **New Jersey** with future considerations (Randy Velischek) for Peter Stastny, March 6, 1990.

WOLF, GREGORY (GREGG)

Defense. Shoots left. 6'1", 200 lbs.   Born, Buffalo, NY, August 20, 1969.
(Hartford's 6th choice, 144th overall, in 1987 Entry Draft).

			Regular Season					Playoffs				
Season	Club	Lea	GP	G	A	TP	PIM	GP	G	A	TP	PIM
1987-88	Colgate	ECAC	32	0	7	7	66	....	....	....	....	....
1988-89	Colgate	ECAC	13	1	3	4	20	....	....	....	....	....
1989-90	Colgate	ECAC	38	1	0	1	58	....	....	....	....	....

WOOD, RANDY

Left wing. Shoots left. 6', 195 lbs.   Born, Princeton, NJ, October 12, 1963.

			Regular Season					Playoffs				
Season	Club	Lea	GP	G	A	TP	PIM	GP	G	A	TP	PIM
1983-84	Yale	ECAC	18	7	7	14	10	....	....	....	....	....
1984-85a	Yale	ECAC	32	25	28	53	23	....	....	....	....	....
1985-86bc	Yale	ECAC	31	25	30	55	26	....	....	....	....	....
1986-87	Springfield	AHL	75	23	24	47	57	....	....	....	....	....
	NY Islanders	**NHL**	**6**	**1**	**0**	**1**	**4**	**13**	**1**	**3**	**4**	**14**
1987-88	**NY Islanders**	**NHL**	**75**	**22**	**16**	**38**	**80**	**5**	**1**	**0**	**1**	**6**
	Springfield	AHL	1	0	1	1	0	....	....	....	....	....
1988-89	**NY Islanders**	**NHL**	**77**	**15**	**13**	**28**	**44**	....	....	....	....	....
	Springfield	AHL	1	1	1	2	0	....	....	....	....	....
1989-90	**NY Islanders**	**NHL**	**74**	**24**	**24**	**48**	**39**	**5**	**1**	**1**	**2**	**4**
	NHL Totals		**232**	**62**	**53**	**115**	**167**	**23**	**3**	**4**	**7**	**24**

a ECAC Second All-Star Team (1985)
b ECAC First All-Star Team (1986)
c NCAA East Second All-Star Team (1986)

Signed as a free agent by **NY Islanders**, September 17, 1986.

WOODCROFT, CRAIG

Left wing. Shoots left. 6'1", 185 lbs.   Born, Toronto, Ont., December 3, 1969.
(Chicago's 7th choice, 134th overall, in 1988 Entry Draft).

			Regular Season					Playoffs				
Season	Club	Lea	GP	G	A	TP	PIM	GP	G	A	TP	PIM
1987-88	Colgate	ECAC	29	7	10	17	28	....	....	....	....	....
1988-89	Colgate	ECAC	29	20	29	49	62	....	....	....	....	....
	Cdn. National	.....	2	0	0	0	4	....	....	....	....	....
1989-90	Colgate	ECAC	37	20	26	46	108	....	....	....	....	....

WOODLEY, DAN

Center. Shoots right. 5'11", 185 lbs.   Born, Oklahoma City, OK, December 29, 1967.
(Vancouver's 1st choice, 7th overall, in 1986 Entry Draft).

			Regular Season					Playoffs				
Season	Club	Lea	GP	G	A	TP	PIM	GP	G	A	TP	PIM
1984-85	Portland	WHL	63	21	36	57	108	1	0	0	0	0
1985-86	Portland	WHL	62	45	47	92	100	12	0	8	8	31
1986-87	Portland	WHL	47	30	50	80	81	19	*19	17	*36	52
1987-88	**Vancouver**	**NHL**	**5**	**2**	**0**	**2**	**17**	....	....	....	....	....
a	Flint	IHL	69	29	37	66	104	9	1	3	4	26
1988-89	Milwaukee	IHL	30	9	12	21	48	....	....	....	....	....
	Sherbrooke	AHL	30	9	16	25	69	4	1	6	7	5
1989-90	Sherbrooke	AHL	65	18	40	58	144	10	1	6	7	58
	NHL Totals		**5**	**2**	**0**	**2**	**17**					

a Won Ken McKenzie Trophy (American Rookie of the Year-IHL) (1988)

Traded to **Montreal** by **Vancouver** for Jose Charbonneau, January 25, 1989.

WOODS, ROBERT

Defense. Shoots left. 6', 170 lbs.   Born, Leroy, Sask., January 24, 1968.
(New Jersey's 11th choice, 201st overall, in 1988 Entry Draft).

			Regular Season					Playoffs				
Season	Club	Lea	GP	G	A	TP	PIM	GP	G	A	TP	PIM
1987-88	Brandon	WHL	72	21	56	77	84	4	1	5	6	9
1988-89	Brandon	WHL	68	26	50	76	100	....	....	....	....	....
	Utica	AHL	11	0	1	1	2	4	0	0	0	2
1989-90	Utica	AHL	58	2	12	14	30	5	0	0	0	6

WOODWARD, ROBERT

Left wing. Shoots left. 6'4", 220 lbs.   Born, Evanston, IL, January 15, 1971.
(Vancouver's 2nd choice, 29th overall, in 1989 Entry Draft).

			Regular Season					Playoffs				
Season	Club	Lea	GP	G	A	TP	PIM	GP	G	A	TP	PIM
1988-89	Deerfield	HS	29	46	71	117	12	....	....	....	....	....
1989-90	Michigan State	CCHA	37	17	9	26	8	....	....	....	....	....

WOOLLEY, JASON

Defense. Shoots left. 6'0", 185 lbs.   Born, Toronto, Ont., July 27, 1969.
(Washington's 4th choice, 61st overall, in 1989 Entry Draft).

			Regular Season					Playoffs				
Season	Club	Lea	GP	G	A	TP	PIM	GP	G	A	TP	PIM
1988-89	Michigan State	CCHA	47	12	25	37	26	....	....	....	....	....
1989-90	Michigan State	CCHA	45	10	38	48	26	....	....	....	....	....

YAKE, TERRY

Center. Shoots right. 5'11", 185 lbs.   Born, New Westminster, B.C., October 22, 1968.
(Hartford's 3rd choice, 81st overall, in 1987 Entry Draft).

			Regular Season					Playoffs				
Season	Club	Lea	GP	G	A	TP	PIM	GP	G	A	TP	PIM
1984-85	Brandon	WHL	11	1	1	2	0	....	....	....	....	....
1985-86	Brandon	WHL	72	26	26	52	49	....	....	....	....	....
1986-87	Brandon	WHL	71	44	58	102	64	....	....	....	....	....
1987-88	Brandon	WHL	72	55	85	140	59	3	4	2	6	7
1988-89	**Hartford**	**NHL**	**2**	**0**	**0**	**0**	**0**	....	....	....	....	....
	Binghamton	AHL	75	39	56	95	57	....	....	....	....	....
1989-90	**Hartford**	**NHL**	**2**	**0**	**1**	**1**	**0**	....	....	....	....	....
	Binghamton	AHL	77	13	42	55	37	....	....	....	....	....
	NHL Totals		**4**	**0**	**1**	**1**	**0**	....	....	....	....	....

YAREMCHUK, GARY
(yuh-RHEM-chuhk)

Center. Shoots left. 6', 185 lbs.   Born, Edmonton, Alta., August 15, 1961.
(Toronto's 2nd choice, 24th overall, in 1981 Entry Draft).

			Regular Season					Playoffs				
Season	Club	Lea	GP	G	A	TP	PIM	GP	G	A	TP	PIM
1979-80	Portland	WHL	41	21	34	55	23	6	1	4	5	2
1980-81	Portland	WHL	72	56	79	135	121	....	....	....	....	....
1981-82	**Toronto**	**NHL**	**18**	**0**	**3**	**3**	**10**	....	....	....	....	....
	Cincinnati	CHL	53	21	35	56	101	4	0	2	2	4
1982-83	**Toronto**	**NHL**	**3**	**0**	**0**	**0**	**2**	....	....	....	....	....
	St. Catharines	AHL	61	17	28	45	72	....	....	....	....	....
1983-84	**Toronto**	**NHL**	**1**	**0**	**0**	**0**	**0**	....	....	....	....	....
	St. Catharines	AHL	73	24	37	61	84	7	5	1	6	2
1984-85	**Toronto**	**NHL**	**12**	**1**	**1**	**2**	**16**	....	....	....	....	....
	St. Catharines	AHL	66	17	47	64	75	....	....	....	....	....
1985-86	Adirondack	AHL	60	12	32	44	90	1	1	0	1	0
1986-87	Jokerit	Fin.	20	7	21	28	116	....	....	....	....	....
1987-88	Karpat	Fin.	36	16	27	43	92	....	....	....	....	....
1988-89	KooKoo	Fin.	44	12	27	39	50	....	....	....	....	....
1989-90	KooKoo	Fin.	42	16	19	35	81	....	....	....	....	....
	NHL Totals		**34**	**1**	**4**	**5**	**28**	....	....	....	....	....

Signed as a free agent by **Detroit**, August 13, 1985.

YAREMCHUK, KEN
(yuh-REHM-chuhk)

Center. Shoots right. 5'11", 185 lbs.   Born, Edmonton, Alta., January 1, 1964.
(Chicago's 1st choice, 7th overall, in 1982 Entry Draft).

			Regular Season					Playoffs				
Season	Club	Lea	GP	G	A	TP	PIM	GP	G	A	TP	PIM
1980-81	Portland	WHL	72	35	72	107	105	9	2	8	10	24
1981-82a	Portland	WHL	72	58	99	157	181	15	10	21	31	12
1982-83b	Portland	WHL	66	51	*109	160	76	14	11	15	26	12
1983-84	**Chicago**	**NHL**	**47**	**6**	**7**	**13**	**19**	1	0	0	0	0
1984-85	**Chicago**	**NHL**	**63**	**10**	**16**	**26**	**16**	15	5	5	10	37
	Milwaukee	IHL	7	4	6	10	9	....	....	....	....	....
1985-86	**Chicago**	**NHL**	**78**	**14**	**20**	**34**	**43**	3	1	1	2	2
1986-87	**Toronto**	**NHL**	**20**	**3**	**8**	**11**	**16**	6	0	0	0	0
	Newmarket	AHL	14	2	4	6	21	....	....	....	....	....
1987-88	**Toronto**	**NHL**	**16**	**2**	**5**	**7**	**10**	6	0	2	2	10
	Cdn. National	....	38	15	18	33	63	....	....	....	....	....
	Cdn. Olympic	....	8	3	3	6	2	....	....	....	....	....
1988-89	**Toronto**	**NHL**	**11**	**1**	**0**	**1**	**2**	....	....	....	....	....
	Newmarket	AHL	55	25	33	58	145	5	7	7	14	12
1989-90	Asiago	Italy	34	37	76	113	32	6	5	6	11	8
	NHL Totals		**235**	**36**	**56**	**92**	**106**	**31**	**6**	**8**	**14**	**49**

a WHL First All-Star Team (1982)
b WHL Second All-Star Team (1983)
Acquired by **Toronto** from **Chicago** with Jerome Dupont and Chicago's fourth-round choice in 1987 Entry Draft (Joe Sacco) as compensation for signing of free agent Gary Nylund, September 6, 1986.

YASHIN, SERGEI

Left wing. Shoots left. 5'11", 200 lbs. Born, Penza, Soviet Union, March 6, 1962.
(Edmonton's 7th choice, 141st overall, in 1989 Entry Draft).

			Regular Season					Playoffs				
Season	Club	Lea	GP	G	A	TP	PIM	GP	G	A	TP	PIM
1979-80	Moscow D'amo	USSR	2	0	1	1	0	....	....	....	....	....
1980-81	Moscow D'amo	USSR	23	2	6	8	6	....	....	....	....	....
1981-82	Moscow D'amo	USSR	41	13	13	26	4	....	....	....	....	....
1982-83	Moscow D'amo	USSR	43	17	6	23	36	....	....	....	....	....
1983-84	Moscow D'amo	USSR	34	16	9	25	22	....	....	....	....	....
1984-85	Moscow D'amo	USSR	40	15	20	35	32	....	....	....	....	....
1985-86	Moscow D'amo	USSR	40	14	19	33	26	....	....	....	....	....
1986-87	Moscow D'amo	USSR	40	6	11	17	36	....	....	....	....	....
1987-88	Moscow D'amo	USSR	47	13	11	24	34	....	....	....	....	....
1988-89	Moscow D'amo	USSR	44	18	10	28	30	....	....	....	....	....
1989-90	Moscow D'amo	USSR	48	14	15	29	14	....	....	....	....	....

YAWNEY, TRENT

Defense. Shoots left. 6'3", 185 lbs.   Born, Hudson Bay, Sask., September 29, 1965.
(Chicago's 2nd choice, 45th overall, in 1984 Entry Draft).

			Regular Season					Playoffs				
Season	Club	Lea	GP	G	A	TP	PIM	GP	G	A	TP	PIM
1982-83	Saskatoon	WHL	59	6	31	37	44	6	0	2	2	0
1983-84	Saskatoon	WHL	73	13	46	59	81	....	....	....	....	....
1984-85	Saskatoon	WHL	72	16	51	67	158	3	1	6	7	7
1985-86	Cdn. Olympic	....	73	6	15	21	60	....	....	....	....	....
1986-87	Cdn. Olympic	....	51	4	15	19	37	....	....	....	....	....
1987-88	**Chicago**	**NHL**	**15**	**2**	**8**	**10**	**15**	5	0	4	4	8
	Cdn. National	....	60	4	12	16	81	....	....	....	....	....
	Cdn. Olympic	....	8	1	1	2	6	....	....	....	....	....
1988-89	**Chicago**	**NHL**	**69**	**5**	**19**	**24**	**116**	15	3	6	9	20
1989-90	**Chicago**	**NHL**	**70**	**5**	**15**	**20**	**82**	20	3	5	8	27
	NHL Totals		**154**	**12**	**42**	**54**	**213**	**40**	**6**	**15**	**21**	**55**

YOUNG, C.J.

Right wing. Shoots right. 5'10", 180 lbs. Born, Waban, MA, January 1, 1968.
(New Jersey's 1st choice, 5th overall, in 1989 Supplemental Draft).

			Regular Season					Playoffs				
Season	Club	Lea	GP	G	A	TP	PIM	GP	G	A	TP	PIM
1986-87	Harvard	ECAC	34	17	12	29	30	....	....	....	....	....
1987-88	Harvard	ECAC	28	13	16	29	40	....	....	....	....	....
1988-89a	Harvard	ECAC	36	20	31	51	36	....	....	....	....	....
1989-90bc	Harvard	ECAC	28	21	28	49	32	....	....	....	....	....

a ECAC Second All-Star Team (1989)
b ECAC First All-Star Team (1990)
c NCAA East Second All-American Team (1990)

YOUNG, SCOTT

Right wing. Shoots right. 6', 190 lbs.   Born, Clinton, MA, October 1, 1967.
(Hartford's 1st choice, 11th overall, in 1986 Entry Draft).

			Regular Season					Playoffs				
Season	Club	Lea	GP	G	A	TP	PIM	GP	G	A	TP	PIM
1985-86a	Boston U.	H.E.	38	16	13	29	31	....	....	....	....	....
1986-87	Boston U.	H.E.	33	15	21	36	24	....	....	....	....	....
1987-88	**Hartford**	**NHL**	**7**	**0**	**0**	**0**	**2**	4	1	0	1	0
	U.S. National	....	56	11	47	58	31	....	....	....	....	....
	U.S. Olympic	....	6	2	6	8	4	....	....	....	....	....
1988-89	**Hartford**	**NHL**	**76**	**19**	**40**	**59**	**27**	4	2	0	2	4
1989-90	**Hartford**	**NHL**	**80**	**24**	**40**	**64**	**47**	7	2	0	2	2
	NHL Totals		**163**	**43**	**80**	**123**	**76**	**15**	**5**	**0**	**5**	**6**

a Hockey East Rookie of the Year (1986)

YOUNG, SCOTT MELBOURNE

Defense. Shoots left. 6'1", 195 lbs. Born, Burlington, Ont., May 26, 1965.

			Regular Season					Playoffs				
Season	Club	Lea	GP	G	A	TP	PIM	GP	G	A	TP	PIM
1985-86	Colgate	ECAC	28	5	6	11	88	....	....	....	....	....
1986-87	Colgate	ECAC	33	13	15	28	113	....	....	....	....	....
1987-88	Colgate	ECAC	14	4	10	14	44	....	....	....	....	....
1988-89	Colgate	ECAC	31	15	22	37	150	....	....	....	....	....
1989-90	New Haven	AHL	58	7	11	18	62	....	....	....	....	....

Signed as a free agent by **Los Angeles**, March 28, 1989.

YSEBAERT, PAUL
(IGHS-BAHRT)

Center. Shoots left. 6'1", 185 lbs.   Born, Sarnia, Ont., May 15, 1966.
(New Jersey's 4th choice, 74th overall, in 1984 Entry Draft).

			Regular Season					Playoffs				
Season	Club	Lea	GP	G	A	TP	PIM	GP	G	A	TP	PIM
1984-85	Bowling Green	CCHA	42	23	32	55	54	....	....	....	....	....
1985-86a	Bowling Green	CCHA	42	23	45	68	50	....	....	....	....	....
1986-87a	Bowling Green	CCHA	45	27	58	85	44	....	....	....	....	....
	Cdn. Olympic	....	5	1	0	1	4	....	....	....	....	....
1987-88	Utica	AHL	78	30	49	79	60	....	....	....	....	....
1988-89	**New Jersey**	**NHL**	**5**	**0**	**4**	**4**	**0**	....	....	....	....	....
	Utica	AHL	56	36	44	80	22	5	0	1	1	4
1989-90	**New Jersey**	**NHL**	**5**	**1**	**2**	**3**	**0**	....	....	....	....	....
bcd	Utica	AHL	74	53	52	*105	61	5	2	4	6	0
	NHL Totals		**10**	**1**	**6**	**7**	**0**	....	....	....	....	....

a CCHA Second All-Star Team (1986, 1987)
b AHL First All-Star Team (1990)
c Won John B. Sollenberger Trophy (Top Scorer-AHL) (1990)
d Won Les Cunningham Trophy (MVP-AHL) (1990)

YUDIN, ALEXANDER

Defense. Shoots left. 6'1", 190 lbs. Born, Minsk, Soviet Union, April 1, 1969.
(Calgary's 12th choice, 231st overall, in 1989 Entry Draft).

			Regular Season					Playoffs				
Season	Club	Lea	GP	G	A	TP	PIM	GP	G	A	TP	PIM
1986-87	Dynamo Minsk	USSR	35	0	4	4	36	....	....	....	....	....
1987-88	Dynamo Minsk	USSR	33	2	7	9	28	....	....	....	....	....
1988-89	Moscow D'amo	USSR	20	2	1	3	27	....	....	....	....	....
1989-90	Moscow D'amo	USSR	36	4	5	9	36	....	....	....	....	....

YZERMAN, STEVE
(IGH-zuhr-muhn)

Center. Shoots right. 5'11", 185 lbs.   Born, Cranbrook, B.C., May 9, 1965.
(Detroit's 1st choice, 4th overall, in 1983 Entry Draft).

			Regular Season					Playoffs				
Season	Club	Lea	GP	G	A	TP	PIM	GP	G	A	TP	PIM
1981-82	Peterborough	OHL	58	21	43	64	65	6	0	1	1	16
1982-83	Peterborough	OHL	56	42	49	91	33	4	1	4	5	0
1983-84a	**Detroit**	**NHL**	**80**	**39**	**48**	**87**	**33**	4	3	3	6	0
1984-85	**Detroit**	**NHL**	**80**	**30**	**59**	**89**	**58**	3	2	1	3	2
1985-86	**Detroit**	**NHL**	**51**	**14**	**28**	**42**	**16**	....	....	....	....	....
1986-87	**Detroit**	**NHL**	**80**	**31**	**59**	**90**	**43**	16	5	13	18	8
1987-88	**Detroit**	**NHL**	**64**	**50**	**52**	**102**	**44**	3	1	3	4	6
1988-89b	**Detroit**	**NHL**	**80**	**65**	**90**	**155**	**61**	6	5	5	10	2
1989-90	**Detroit**	**NHL**	**79**	**62**	**65**	**127**	**79**	....	....	....	....	....
	NHL Totals		**514**	**291**	**401**	**692**	**334**	**32**	**16**	**25**	**41**	**18**

a NHL All-Rookie Team (1984)
b Won Lester B. Pearson Award (1989)
Played in NHL All-Star Game (1984, 1988-90)

ZALAPSKI, ZARLEY

Defense. Shoots left. 6'1", 210 lbs.   Born, Edmonton, Alta., April 22, 1968.
(Pittsburgh's 1st choice, 4th overall, in 1986 Entry Draft).

			Regular Season					Playoffs			
Season	Club	Lea	GP	G	A	TP	PIM	GP	G	A	TP	PIM
1985-86	Cdn. Olympic	....	59	22	37	59	56	....	....	....	....	....
1986-87	Cdn. Olympic	....	74	11	29	40	28	....	....	....	....	....
1987-88	**Pittsburgh**	**NHL**	15	3	8	11	7	....	....	....	....	....
	Cdn. National	....	47	3	13	16	32	....	....	....	....	....
	Cdn. Olympic	....	8	1	3	4	2	....	....	....	....	....
1988-89a	**Pittsburgh**	**NHL**	58	12	33	45	57	11	1	8	9	13
1989-90	**Pittsburgh**	**NHL**	51	6	25	31	37	....	....	....	....	....
	NHL Totals		124	21	66	87	101	11	1	8	9	13

a NHL All-Rookie Team (1989)

ZAMUNER, ROB

Center. Shoots left. 6'2", 200 lbs.   Born, Oakville, Ont., September 17, 1969.
(NY Rangers' 3rd choice, 45th overall, in 1989 Entry Draft).

			Regular Season					Playoffs			
Season	Club	Lea	GP	G	A	TP	PIM	GP	G	A	TP	PIM
1987-88	Guelph	OHL	58	20	41	61	18	....	....	....	....	....
1988-89a	Guelph	OHL	66	46	65	111	38	7	5	5	10	9
1989-90	Flint	IHL	77	44	35	79	32	4	1	0	1	6

a OHL Third All-Star Team (1989)

ZAVISHA, BRAD

Left wing. Shoots left. 6'2", 195 lbs. Born, Hines Creek, Alta., January 4, 1972.
(Quebec's 3rd choice, 43rd overall, in 1990 Entry Draft).

			Regular Season					Playoffs			
Season	Club	Lea	GP	G	A	TP	PIM	GP	G	A	TP	PIM
1988-89	Seattle	WHL	52	8	13	21	43	....	....	....	....	....
1989-90	Seattle	WHL	69	22	38	60	124	13	1	6	7	16

ZELEPUKHIN, VALERI

Right wing. Shoots left. 5'11", 180 lbs. Born, Voskresensk, Soviet Union, September 17, 1968.
(New Jersey's 13th choice, 221st overall, in 1990 Entry Draft).

			Regular Season					Playoffs			
Season	Club	Lea	GP	G	A	TP	PIM	GP	G	A	TP	PIM
1984-85	Voskresensk	USSR	5	0	0	0	2	....	....	....	....	....
1985-86	Voskresensk	USSR	33	2	2	4	10	....	....	....	....	....
1986-87	Voskresensk	USSR	19	1	0	1	4	....	....	....	....	....
1987-88	SKA Kalanin	USSR	18	18	6	24		....	....	....	....	....
	CSKA	USSR	19	3	1	4	8	....	....	....	....	....
1988-89	CSKA	USSR	17	2	3	5	2	....	....	....	....	....
1989-90	Voskresensk	USSR	46	17	14	31	28	....	....	....	....	....

ZEMLAK, RICHARD ANDREW

Right wing. Shoots right. 6'2", 190 lbs.   Born, Wynard, Sask., March 3, 1963.
(St. Louis' 9th choice, 209th overall, in 1981 Entry Draft).

			Regular Season					Playoffs			
Season	Club	Lea	GP	G	A	TP	PIM	GP	G	A	TP	PIM
1980-81	Spokane	WHL	72	19	19	38	132	4	1	1	2	6
1981-82	Spokane	WHL	26	9	20	29	113	....	....	....	....	....
	Winnipeg	WHL	2	1	2	3	0	....	....	....	....	....
	Medicine Hat	WHL	41	11	20	31	70	....	....	....	....	....
	Salt Lake	CHL	6	0	0	0	2	1	0	0	0	0
1982-83	Medicine Hat	WHL	51	20	17	37	119	....	....	....	....	....
	Nanaimo	WHL	18	2	8	10	50	....	....	....	....	....
1983-84	Montana	CHL	14	2	2	4	17	....	....	....	....	....
	Toledo	IHL	45	8	19	27	101	....	....	....	....	....
1984-85	Muskegon	IHL	64	19	18	37	223	17	5	4	9	68
	Fredericton	AHL	16	3	4	7	59	....	....	....	....	....
1985-86	Fredericton	AHL	58	6	5	11	305	3	0	0	0	49
	Muskegon	IHL	3	1	2	3	36	....	....	....	....	....
1986-87	**Quebec**	**NHL**	20	0	2	2	47	....	....	....	....	....
	Fredericton	AHL	29	9	6	15	201	....	....	....	....	....
1987-88	**Minnesota**	**NHL**	54	1	4	5	307	....	....	....	....	....
1988-89	**Minnesota**	**NHL**	3	0	0	0	13	....	....	....	....	....
	Kalamazoo	IHL	2	1	3	4	22	....	....	....	....	....
	Pittsburgh	**NHL**	31	0	0	0	135	1	0	0	0	10
	Muskegon	IHL	18	5	4	9	55	8	1	1	2	35
1989-90	**Pittsburgh**	**NHL**	19	1	5	6	43	....	....	....	....	....
	Muskegon	IHL	61	17	39	56	263	14	3	4	7	105
	NHL Totals		127	2	11	13	545	1	0	0	0	10

Rights sold to **Quebec** by **St. Louis** with rights to Dan Wood and Roger Hagglund, June 22, 1984. Claimed by **Minnesota** in NHL Waiver Draft, October 5, 1987. Traded to **Pittsburgh** by **Minnesota** for the rights to Rob Gaudreau, November 1, 1988.

ZETTLER, ROB

Defense. Shoots left. 6'3", 190 lbs.   Born, Sept Iles, Que., March 8, 1968.
(Minnesota's 5th choice, 55th overall, in 1986 Entry Draft).

			Regular Season					Playoffs			
Season	Club	Lea	GP	G	A	TP	PIM	GP	G	A	TP	PIM
1985-86	S.S. Marie	OHL	57	5	23	28	92	....	....	....	....	....
1986-87	S.S. Marie	OHL	64	13	22	35	89	4	0	0	0	0
1986-87	S.S. Marie	OHL	64	13	22	35	89	4	0	0	0	0
1987-88	Kalamazoo	IHL	2	0	1	1	0	7	0	2	2	2
	S.S. Marie	OHL	64	7	41	48	77	6	2	2	4	9
1988-89	**Minnesota**	**NHL**	2	0	0	0	0	....	....	....	....	....
	Kalamazoo	IHL	80	5	21	26	79	6	0	1	1	26
1989-90	**Minnesota**	**NHL**	31	0	8	8	45	....	....	....	....	....
	Kalamazoo	IHL	41	6	10	16	64	....	....	....	....	....
	NHL Totals		33	0	8	8	45	....	....	....	....	....

ZEZEL, PETER   (ZEH-zuhl)

Center. Shoots left. 5'9", 200 lbs.   Born, Toronto, Ont., April 22, 1965.
(Philadelphia's 1st choice, 41st overall, in 1983 Entry Draft).

			Regular Season					Playoffs			
Season	Club	Lea	GP	G	A	TP	PIM	GP	G	A	TP	PIM
1982-83	Toronto	OHL	66	35	39	74	28	4	2	4	6	0
1983-84	Toronto	OHL	68	47	86	133	31	9	7	5	12	4
1984-85	**Philadelphia**	**NHL**	65	15	46	61	26	19	1	8	9	28
1985-86	**Philadelphia**	**NHL**	79	17	37	54	76	5	3	1	4	4
1986-87	**Philadelphia**	**NHL**	71	33	39	72	71	25	3	10	13	10
1987-88	**Philadelphia**	**NHL**	69	22	35	57	42	7	3	2	5	7
1988-89	**Philadelphia**	**NHL**	26	4	13	17	15	....	....	....	....	....
	St. Louis	**NHL**	52	17	36	53	27	10	6	6	12	4
1989-90	**St. Louis**	**NHL**	73	25	47	72	30	12	1	7	8	4
	NHL Totals		435	133	253	386	287	78	17	34	51	57

Traded to **St. Louis** by **Philadelphia** for Mike Bullard, November 29, 1988. Traded to **Washington** by **St. Louis** with Mike Lalor for Geoff Courtnall, July 13, 1990.

ZMOLEK, DOUG

Defense. Shoots left. 6'1", 195 lbs.   Born, Rochester, MN, November 3, 1970.
(Minnesota's 1st choice, 7th overall, in 1989 Entry Draft).

			Regular Season					Playoffs			
Season	Club	Lea	GP	G	A	TP	PIM	GP	G	A	TP	PIM
1988-89	John Marshall	HS	29	17	41	58	....	....	....	....	....	....
1989-90	U. Minnesota	WCHA	40	1	10	11	52	....	....	....	....	....

ZOMBO, RICHARD (RICK)

Defense. Shoots right. 6'1", 195 lbs.   Born, Des Plaines, IL., May 8, 1963.
(Detroit's 6th choice, 149th overall, in 1981 Entry Draft).

			Regular Season					Playoffs			
Season	Club	Lea	GP	G	A	TP	PIM	GP	G	A	TP	PIM
1983-84	North Dakota	WCHA	34	7	24	31	40	....	....	....	....	....
1984-85	**Detroit**	**NHL**	1	0	0	0	0	....	....	....	....	....
	Adirondack	AHL	56	3	32	35	70	....	....	....	....	....
1985-86	**Detroit**	**NHL**	14	0	1	1	16	....	....	....	....	....
	Adirondack	AHL	69	7	34	41	94	17	0	4	4	40
1986-87	**Detroit**	**NHL**	44	1	4	5	59	7	0	1	1	9
	Adirondack	AHL	25	0	6	6	22	....	....	....	....	....
1987-88	**Detroit**	**NHL**	62	3	14	17	96	16	0	6	6	55
1988-89	**Detroit**	**NHL**	75	1	20	21	106	6	0	1	1	16
1989-90	**Detroit**	**NHL**	77	5	20	25	95	....	....	....	....	....
	NHL Totals		273	10	59	69	372	29	0	8	8	80

ZUBOV, SERGEI

Defense. Shoots left. 6', 185 lbs. Born, Moscow, Soviet Union, July 22, 1970.
(NY Rangers' 5th choice, 85th overall, in 1990 Entry Draft).

			Regular Season					Playoffs			
Season	Club	Lea	GP	G	A	TP	PIM	GP	G	A	TP	PIM
1988-89	CSKA	USSR	29	1	4	5	10	....	....	....	....	....
1989-90	CSKA	USSR	48	6	2	8	16	....	....	....	....	....

ZYGULSKI, SCOTT

Defense. Shoots right. 6'1", 190 lbs. Born, South Bend, IN, April 11, 1970.
(Detroit's 7th choice, 137th overall, in 1989 Entry Draft).

			Regular Season					Playoffs			
Season	Club	Lea	GP	G	A	TP	PIM	GP	G	A	TP	PIM
1988-89	Culver Aca.	HS	29	11	16	27	16	....	....	....	....	....
1989-90	Boston College	H.E.	14	0	1	1	6	....	....	....	....	....

Marcel Dionne is a notable addition to this year's Retired NHL Player Index. Selected second overall in the 1971 Amateur Draft, his 18-season NHL career began in Detroit. He moved to Los Angeles in 1975-76, and became the Kings' offensive superstar, recording six 50-goal seasons. Traded to the Rangers in March of 1987, he played parts of three seasons in New York. He is the NHL's second-leading career goal scorer with 731 and third-leading point-scorer with 1,771.

Retired NHL Player Index

Abbreviations: Teams/Cities: — **Atl.** – Atlanta, **Bos.** – Boston; **Buf.** – Buffalo; **Cal.** – California; **Cgy.** – Calgary; **Chi.** – Chicago; **Cle.** – Cleveland; **Col.** – Colorado; **Det.** – Detroit; **Edm.** – Edmonton; **Ham.** – Hamilton; **Hfd.** – Hartford; **L.A.** – Los Angeles; **Min.** – Minnesota; **Mtl.** – Montreal; **Mtl.M.** – Montreal Maroons; **Mtl.W.** – Montreal Wanderers; **N.J.** – New Jersey; **NY** – New York; **NYA** – NY Americans; **NYI** – New York Islanders; **NYR** – New York Rangers; **Oak.** – Oakland; **Ott.** – Ottawa; **Phi.** – Philadelphia; **Pit.** – Pittsburgh; **Que.** – Quebec; **St.L.** – St. Louis; **Tor.** – Toronto; **Van.** – Vancouver; **Wpg.** – Winnipeg; **Wsh.** – Washington.

Total seasons are rounded off to the nearest full season. **A** – assists; **G** – goals; **GP** – games played; **PIM** – penalties in minutes; **TP** – total points. Assists not recorded during 1917-18 season.

Name	NHL Teams	NHL Seasons	Regular Schedule GP	G	A	TP	PIM	Playoffs GP	G	A	TP	PIM	First NHL Season	Last NHL Season
A														
Abbott, Reg	Mtl.	1	3	0	0	0	0	....	....	....	....	....	1952-53	1952-53
Abel, Gerry	Det.	1	1	0	0	0	0	....	....	....	....	....	1966-67	1966-67
Abel, Sid	Det., Chi.	14	613	189	283	472	376	96	28	30	58	77	1938-39	1953-54
Abel, Clarence	NYR, Chi.	8	332	18	18	36	359	38	1	1	2	56	1926-27	1933-34
Abgrall, Dennis	L.A.	1	13	0	2	2	4	....	....	....	....	....	1975-76	1975-76
Abrahamsson, Thommy	Hfd.	1	32	6	11	17	16	....	....	....	....	....	1980-81	1980-81
Achtymichuk, Gene	Mtl., Det.	4	32	3	5	8	2	....	....	....	....	....	1951-52	1958-59
Acomb, Doug	Tor.	1	2	0	1	1	0	....	....	....	....	....	1969-70	1969-70
Adam, Douglas	NYR	1	4	0	1	1	0	....	....	....	....	....	1949-50	1949-50
Adam, Russ	Tor.	1	8	1	2	3	11	....	....	....	....	....	1982-83	1982-83
Adams, Jack J.	Tor., Ott.	7	173	82	29	111	292	12	3	0	3	9	1917-18	1926-27
Adams, Jack	Mtl.	1	42	6	12	18	11	3	0	0	0	0	1940-41	1940-41
Adams, Stewart	Chi., Tor.	4	106	9	26	35	60	11	3	3	6	14	1929-30	1932-33
Adduono, Rick	Bos., Atl.	2	4	0	0	0	2	....	....	....	....	....	1975-76	1979-80
Affleck, Bruce	St.L., Van., NYI	7	280	14	66	80	86	8	0	0	0	0	1974-75	1983-84
Ahern, Fred	Cal., Cle., Col.	4	146	31	30	61	130	2	0	1	1	2	1974-75	1977-78
Ahlin	Chi.	1	1	0	0	0	0	....	....	....	....	....	1937-38	1937-38
Ahrens, Chris	Min.	6	52	0	3	3	84	1	0	0	0	0	1972-73	1977-78
Ailsby, Lloyd	NYR	1	3	0	0	0	2	....	....	....	....	....	1951-52	1951-52
Albright, Clint	NYR	1	59	14	5	19	19	....	....	....	....	....	1948-49	1948-49
Aldcorn, Gary	Tor., Det., Bos.	5	226	41	56	97	78	6	1	2	3	4	1956-57	1960-61
Alexander, Claire	Tor., Van.	4	155	18	47	65	36	16	2	4	6	4	1974-75	1977-78
Alexandre, Art	Mtl.	2	11	0	2	2	8	4	0	0	0	0	1931-32	1932-33
Allen, George	NYR, Chi., Mtl.	8	339	82	115	197	179	41	9	10	19	32	1938-39	1946-47
Allen, Jeff	Cle.	1	4	0	0	0	2	....	....	....	....	....	1977-78	1977-78
Allen, Keith	Det.	2	28	0	4	4	8	5	0	0	0	0	1953-54	1954-55
Allen, Viv	NYA	1	6	0	1	1	0	....	....	....	....	....	1940-41	1940-41
Alley, Steve	Hfd.	2	15	3	3	6	11	3	0	1	1	0	1979-80	1980-81
Allison, Dave	Mtl.	1	3	0	0	0	12	....	....	....	....	....	1983-84	1983-84
Allison, Ray	Hfd., Phi.	7	238	64	93	157	223	12	2	3	5	20	1979-80	1986-87
Allum, Bill	NYR	1	1	0	1	1	0	....	....	....	....	....	1940-41	1940-41
Amadio, Dave	Det., L.A.	3	125	5	11	16	163	16	1	2	3	18	1957-58	1968-69
Amodeo, Mike	Wpg.	1	19	0	0	0	2	....	....	....	....	....	1979-80	1979-80
Anderson, Bill	Bos.	1	....	....	....	....	....	1	0	0	0	0	1942-43	1942-43
Anderson, Dale	Det.	1	13	0	0	0	6	2	0	0	0	0	1956-57	1956-57
Anderson, Doug	Mtl.	1	....	....	....	....	....	2	0	0	0	0	1952-53	1952-53
Anderson, Earl	Det., Bos.	3	109	19	19	38	22	5	0	1	1	0	1974-75	1976-77
Anderson, Jim	L.A.	2	7	1	2	3	2	4	0	0	0	2	1967-68	1968-69
Anderson, Murray	Wsh.	1	40	0	1	1	68	....	....	....	....	....	1974-75	1974-75
Anderson, Ron C.	Det., L.A., St.L., Buf.	5	251	28	30	58	146	5	0	0	0	4	1967-68	1971-72
Anderson, Ron H.	Wsh.	1	28	9	7	16	8	....	....	....	....	....	1974-75	1974-75
Anderson, Russ	Pit., Hfd., L.A.	10	519	22	99	121	1086	10	0	3	3	28	1976-77	1984-85
Anderson, Tom	Det., NYA	8	319	62	127	189	190	16	2	7	9	62	1934-35	1941-42
Andersson Kent-Erik	Min., NYR	7	456	72	103	175	78	50	4	11	15	4	1977-78	1983-84
Andersson, Peter	Wsh., Que.	3	172	10	41	51	80	7	0	2	2	2	1983-84	1985-86
Andrascik, Steve	NYR	1	....	....	....	....	....	1	0	0	0	0	1971-72	1971-72
Andrea, Paul	NYR, Pit., Cal., Buf.	4	150	31	49	80	10	....	....	....	....	....	1965-66	1970-71
Andrews, Lloyd	Tor.	4	53	8	5	13	10	7	2	0	2	5	1921-22	1924-25
Andruff, Ron	Mtl., Col.,	5	153	19	36	55	54	2	0	0	0	0	1974-75	1978-79
Angotti, Lou	NYR, Chi., Phi., Pit., St.L.	10	653	103	186	289	228	65	8	8	16	17	1964-65	1973-74
Anholt, Darrel	Chi.	1	1	0	0	0	0	....	....	....	....	....	1983-84	1983-84
Anslow, Bert	NYR	1	2	0	0	0	0	....	....	....	....	....	1947-48	1947-48
Antonovich, Mike	Min., Hfd., N.J.	5	87	10	15	25	37	....	....	....	....	....	1975-76	1983-84
Apps, Syl (Jr.)	NYR, Pit., L.A.	10	727	183	423	606	311	23	5	5	10	23	1970-71	1979-80
Apps, Syl (Sr.)	Tor.	10	423	201	231	432	56	69	25	28	53	16	1936-37	1947-48
Arbour, Al	Det., Chi., Tor., St.L.	11	626	12	58	70	617	86	1	8	9	92	1953-54	1970-71
Arbour, Amos	Mtl., Ham., Tor.	6	109	51	13	64	66	....	....	....	....	....	1918-19	1923-24
Arbour, Jack	Det., Tor.	2	47	5	1	6	56	....	....	....	....	....	1926-27	1928-29
Arbour, John	Bos., Pit., Van., St.L.	5	106	1	9	10	149	5	0	0	0	0	1965-66	1971-72
Arbour, Ty	Pit., Chi.	5	207	28	28	56	112	11	2	0	2	6	1926-27	1930-31
Archambault, Michel	Chi.	1	3	0	0	0	0	....	....	....	....	....	1976-77	1976-77
Archibald, Jim	Min.	3	16	1	2	3	45	....	....	....	....	....	1984-85	1986-87
Areshenkoff, Ronald	Edm.	1	4	0	0	0	0	....	....	....	....	....	1979-80	1979-80
Armstrong, Bob	Bos.	12	542	13	86	99	671	42	1	7	8	28	1950-51	1961-62
Armstrong, George	Tor.	21	1187	296	417	713	721	110	26	34	60	52	1949-50	1970-71
Armstrong, Murray	Tor., NYA, Det.,	8	270	67	121	188	72	30	4	6	10	2	1937-38	1945-46
Armstrong, Red	Tor.	1	7	1	1	2	2	....	....	....	....	....	1962-63	1962-63
Arnason, Chuck	Mtl., Atl., Pit., K.C., Col., Cle., Min., Wsh.	8	401	109	90	199	122	9	2	4	0	4	1071-72	1978-79
Arthur, Fred	Hfd., Phi.	3	80	1	8	9	49	4	0	0	0	2	1980-81	1982-83
Arundel, John	Tor.	1	3	0	0	0	0	....	....	....	....	....	1949-50	1949-50
Ashbee, Barry	Bos., Phi.	5	284	15	70	85	291	17	0	4	4	22	1965-66	1973-74
Ashby, Don	Tor., Col., Edm.	6	188	40	56	96	40	12	1	0	1	4	1075-76	1980-81
Ashworth, Frank	Chi.	1	18	5	4	9	2	....	....	....	....	....	1946-47	1946-47
Asmundson, Oscar	NYR, Det., St.L., NYA, Mtl.	5	112	11	23	34	30	9	0	2	2	4	1932-33	1937-38
Atanas, Walt	NYR	1	49	13	8	21	40	....	....	....	....	....	1944-45	1944-45
Atkinson, Steve	Bos., Buf., Wsh.	6	302	60	51	111	104	1	0	0	0	0	1968-69	1974-75
Attwell, Bob	Col.	2	22	1	5	6	0	....	....	....	....	....	1979-80	1980-81
Attwell, Ron	St.L., NYR	1	21	1	7	8	8	....	....	....	....	....	1967-68	1967-68
Aubin, Norm	Tor.	2	69	18	13	31	30	1	0	0	0	0	1981-82	1982-83
Aubry, Pierre	Que., Det.	5	202	24	26	50	133	20	1	1	2	32	1980-81	1984-85
Aubuchon, Ossie	Bos., NYR	2	50	19	12	31	4	6	1	0	1	0	1942-43	1943-44
Auge, Les	Col.	1	6	0	3	3	4	....	....	....	....	....	1980-81	1980-81
Aurie, Larry	Det.	12	489	147	129	276	279	24	6	9	15	10	1927-28	1938-39
Awrey, Don	Bos., St.L., Mtl., Pit., NYR, Col.	16	979	31	158	189	1065	71	0	18	18	150	1963-64	1978-79
Ayres, Vern	NYA, Mtl.W., St.L., NYR	6	211	6	14	20	350	....	....	....	....	....	1930-31	1935-36
B														
Babando, Pete	Bos., Det., Chi., NYR	6	351	86	73	159	194	17	3	3	6	6	1947-48	1952-53
Babin, Mitch	St.L.	1	8	0	0	0	0	....	....	....	....	....	1975-76	1975-76
Baby, John	Cle., Min.	2	26	2	8	10	26	....	....	....	....	....	1977-78	1978-79
Babych, Wayne	St.L., Pit., Que., Hfd.	9	519	192	246	438	498	41	7	9	16	25	1978-79	1986-87
Backman, Mike	NYR	3	18	1	6	7	18	10	2	2	4	2	1981-82	1983-84
Backor, Peter	Tor.	1	36	4	5	9	6	....	....	....	....	....	1944-45	1944-45
Backstrom, Ralph	Mtl., L.A., Chi.	17	1032	278	361	639	386	116	27	32	59	68	1956-57	1972-73
Bailey, Ace (I.)	Tor.	8	314	111	82	193	472	20	3	4	7	12	1926-27	1933-34
Bailey, Ace (G.)	Bos., Det., St.L., Wsh.	10	568	107	171	278	633	15	2	4	6	28	1968-69	1977-78
Bailey, Bob	Tor., Det., Chi.	5	150	15	21	36	207	15	0	4	4	22	1953-54	1957-58
Bailey, Reid	Phi., Tor., Hfd.	4	40	1	3	4	105	16	0	2	2	25	1980-81	1983-84
Baird, Ken	Cal.	1	10	0	2	2	15	....	....	....	....	....	1971-72	1971-72
Baker, Bill	Mtl., Col., St.L., NYR	3	143	7	25	32	175	6	0	0	0	0	1980-81	1982-83
Baldwin, Doug	Tor., Det., Chi.	3	24	0	1	1	8	....	....	....	....	....	1945-46	1947-48
Balfour, Earl	Tor., Chi.,	7	288	30	22	52	78	26	0	3	3	4	1951-52	1960-61

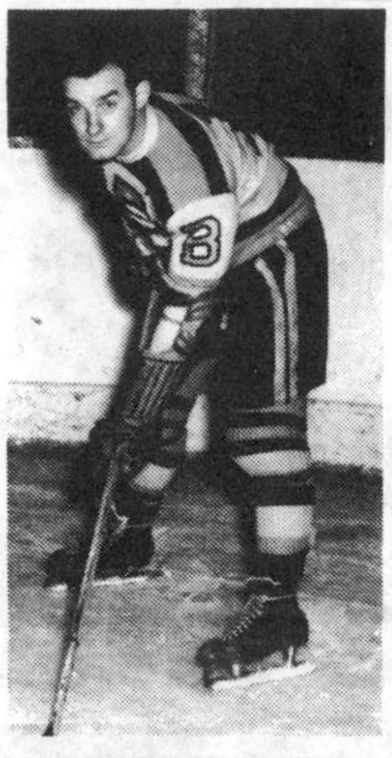

Ossie Aubuchon

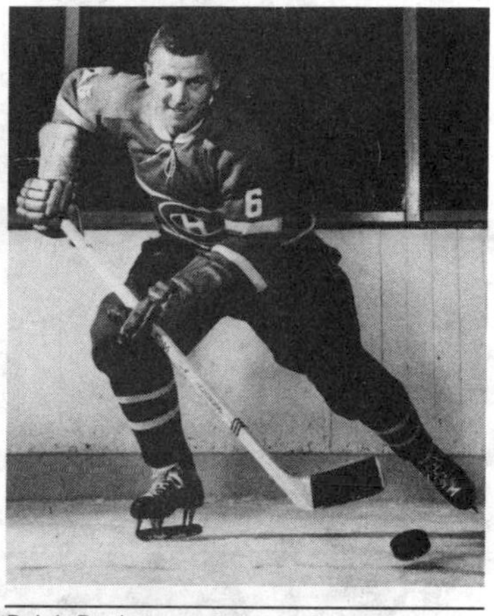

Ralph Backstrom

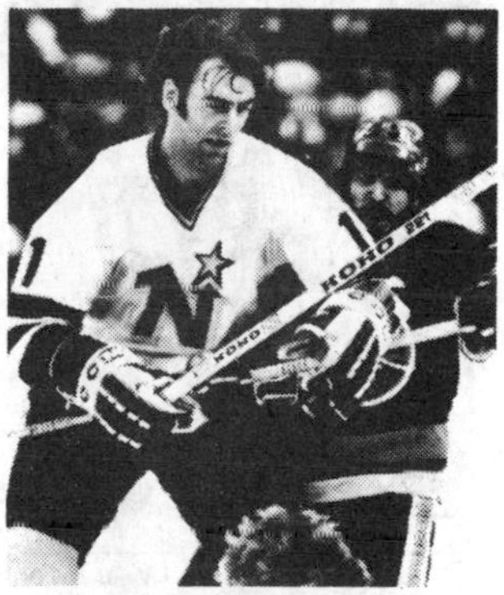

Harvey Bennett

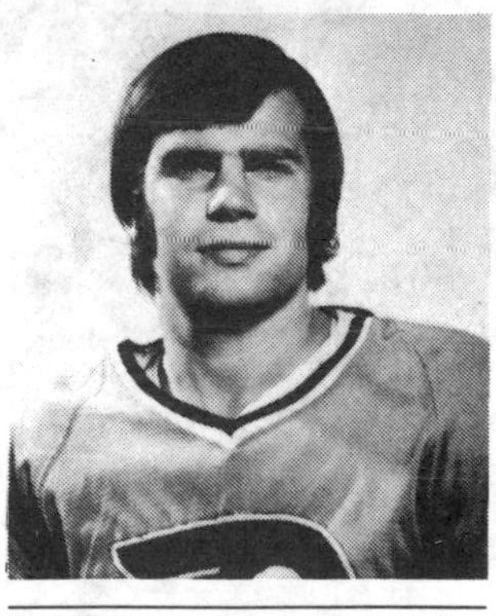

Tom Bladon

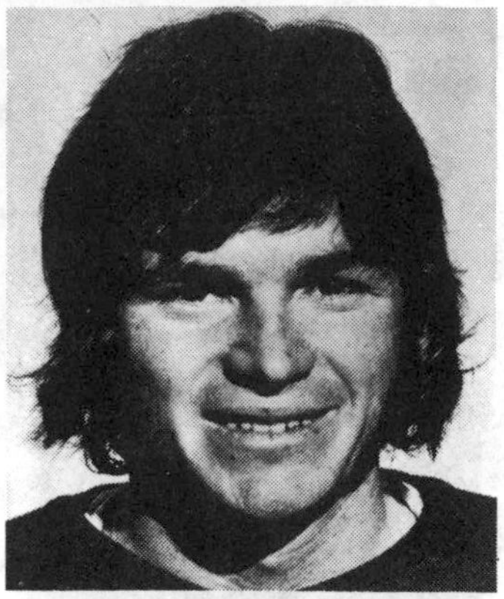
Mike Bloom

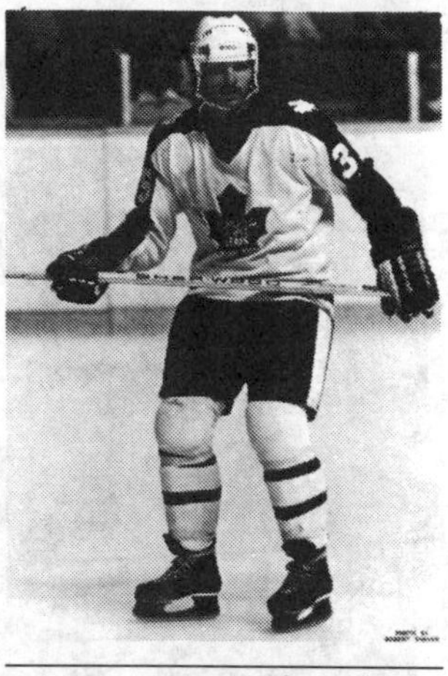
Serge Boisvert

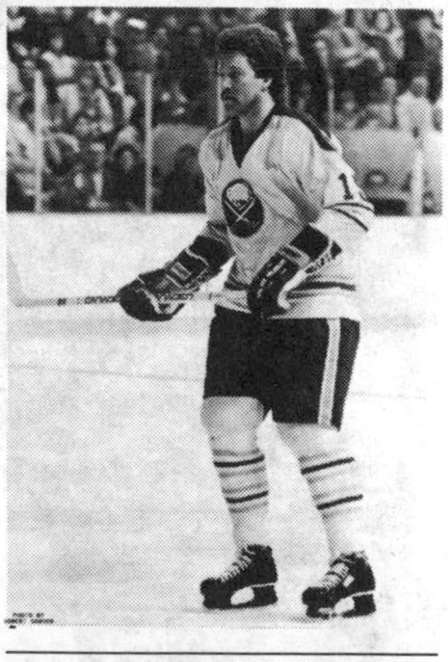
Mike Boland

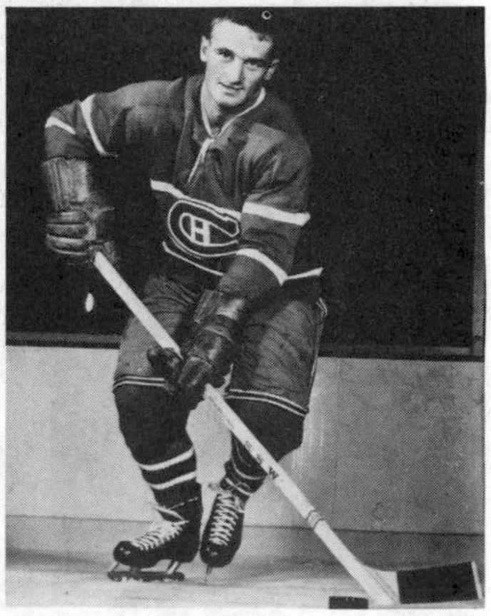
Marcel Bonin

Name	NHL Teams	NHL Seasons	Regular Schedule GP	G	A	TP	PIM	Playoffs GP	G	A	TP	PIM	First NHL Season	Last NHL Season
Balfour, Murray	Mtl., Chi., Bos.	8	306	67	90	157	391	40	9	10	19	45	1956-57	1964-65
Ball, Terry	Phi., Buf.	4	74	7	19	26	26	....	....	....	....	....	1967-68	1971-72
Balon, Dave	NYR, Mtl., Min., Van.	14	775	192	222	414	607	78	14	21	35	109	1959-60	1972-73
Baltimore, Byron	Edm.	1	2	0	0	0	4	....	....	....	....	....	1979-80	1979-80
Baluik, Stanley	Bos.	1	7	0	0	0	2	....	....	....	....	....	1959-60	1959-60
Bandura, Jeff	NYR	1	2	0	1	1	0	....	....	....	....	....	1980-81	1980-81
Barbe, Andy	Tor.	1	1	0	0	0	2	....	....	....	....	....	1950-51	1950-51
Barber, Bill	Phi.	12	903	420	463	883	623	129	53	55	108	109	1972-73	1984-85
Barilko, Bill	Tor.	5	252	26	36	62	456	47	5	7	12	104	1946-47	1950-51
Barkley, Doug	Chi., Det.	6	253	24	80	104	382	30	0	9	9	63	1957-58	1965-66
Barlow, Bob	Min.	2	77	16	17	33	10	6	2	2	4	6	1969-70	1970-71
Barnes, Blair	L.A.	1	1	0	0	0	0	....	....	....	....	....	1982-83	1982-83
Barnes, Norm	Phi., Hfd.	5	156	6	38	44	178	12	0	0	0	8	1976-77	1981-82
Brennan, Dan	L.A.	2	8	0	1	1	9	....	....	....	....	....	1983-84	1985-86
Baron, Normand	Mtl., St.L.	2	27	2	0	2	51	3	0	0	0	22	1983-84	1985-86
Barrett, Fred	Min., L.A.	13	745	25	123	148	67	44	0	2	2	60	1970-71	1983-84
Barrett, John	Det., Wsh., Min.	8	488	20	77	97	644	16	2	2	4	50	1980-81	1987-88
Barrie, Doug	Pit., Buf., L.A.	3	158	10	42	52	268	....	....	....	....	....	1968-69	1971-72
Barry, Ed	Bos.	1	19	1	3	4	2	....	....	....	....	....	1946-47	1946-47
Barry, Marty	NYA, Bos., Det., Mtl.	12	509	195	192	387	205	43	15	18	33	34	1927-28	1939-40
Barry, Ray	Bos.	1	18	1	2	3	6	....	....	....	....	....	1951-52	1951-52
Bartel, Robin	Cgy., Van.	2	41	0	1	1	14	6	0	0	0	16	1985-86	1986-87
Bartlett, Jim	Mtl., NYR, Bos.	5	191	34	23	57	273	2	0	0	0	0	1954-55	1960-61
Barton, Cliff	Pit., Phi., NYR	3	85	10	9	19	22	....	....	....	....	....	1929-30	1939-40
Bathe, Frank	Det., Phi.,	9	224	3	28	31	542	27	1	3	4	42	1974-75	1983-84
Bathgate, Andy	NYR, Tor., Det., Pit.	17	1069	349	624	973	624	54	21	14	35	76	1952-53	1970-71
Bathgate, Frank	NYR	1	2	0	0	0	2	....	....	....	....	....	1952-53	1952-53
Bauer, Bobby	Bos.	10	327	123	137	260	36	48	11	8	19	6	1935-36	1951-52
Baumgartner, Mike	K.C.	1	17	0	0	0	0	....	....	....	....	....	1974-75	1974-75
Baun, Bob	Tor., Oak., Det.	17	964	37	187	224	1493	96	3	12	15	171	1956-57	1972-73
Baxter, Paul	Que., Pit., Cgy.	8	472	48	121	169	1564	40	0	5	5	162	1979-80	1986-87
Beadle, Sandy	Wpg.	1	6	1	0	1	2	....	....	....	....	....	1980-81	1980-81
Beaton, Frank	NYR	2	25	1	1	2	43	....	....	....	....	....	1978-79	1979-80
Beattie, Red	Bos., Det., NYA	9	335	62	85	147	137	22	4	2	6	6	1930-31	1938-39
Beaudin, Norm	St.L., Min.	2	25	1	2	3	4	....	....	....	....	....	1967-68	1970-71
Beaudoin, Serge	Atl.	1	3	0	0	0	0	....	....	....	....	....	1979-80	1979-80
Beaudoin, Yves	Wsh.	3	11	0	0	0	5	....	....	....	....	....	1985-86	1987-88
Beckett, Bob	Bos.	4	68	7	6	13	18	....	....	....	....	....	1956-57	1963-64
Bedard, James	Chi.	2	22	1	1	2	8	....	....	....	....	....	1949-50	1950-51
Bednarski, John	NYR, Edm.	4	100	2	18	20	114	1	0	0	0	0	1974-75	1979-80
Beers, Eddy	Cgy., St.L.	5	250	94	116	210	256	41	7	10	17	47	1981-82	1985-86
Behling, Dick	Det.	2	5	1	0	1	2	....	....	....	....	....	1940-41	1942-43
Beisler, Frank	NYA	2	2	0	0	0	0	....	....	....	....	....	1936-37	1939-40
Belanger, Alain	Tor.	1	9	0	1	1	6	....	....	....	....	....	1977-78	1977-78
Belanger, Roger	Pit.	1	44	3	5	8	32	....	....	....	....	....	1984-85	1984-85
Belisle, Danny	NYR	1	4	2	0	2	0	....	....	....	....	....	1960-61	1960-61
Beliveau, Jean	Mtl.	20	1125	507	712	1219	1029	162	79	97	176	211	1950-51	1970-71
Bell, Billy	Mtl.W, Mtl., Ott.	6	61	3	1	4	4	9	0	0	0	0	1917-18	1923-24
Bell, Harry	NYR	1	1	0	1	1	0	....	....	....	....	....	1946-47	1946-47
Bell, Joe	NYR	2	62	8	9	17	18	....	....	....	....	....	1942-43	1946-47
Belland, Neil	Van., Pit.	6	109	13	32	45	54	21	2	9	11	23	1981-82	1986-87
Bellefeuille, Pete	Tor., Det.	4	92	26	4	30	58	....	....	....	....	....	1925-26	1929-30
Bellemer, Andy	Mtl.M.	1	15	0	0	0	0	....	....	....	....	....	1932-33	1932-33
Bend, Lin	NYR	1	8	3	1	4	2	....	....	....	....	....	1942-43	1942-43
Bennett, Bill	Bos., Hfd.	2	31	4	7	11	65	....	....	....	....	....	1978-79	1979-80
Bennett, Curt	St.L., NYR, Atl.	10	580	152	182	334	347	21	1	1	2	57	1970-71	1979-80
Bennett, Frank	Det.	1	7	0	1	1	2	....	....	....	....	....	1943-44	1943-44
Bennett, Harvey	Pit., Wsh., Phi., Min., St.L.	5	268	44	46	90	340	4	0	0	0	2	1974-75	1978-79
Bennett, Max	Mtl.	1	1	0	0	0	0	....	....	....	....	....	1935-36	1935-36
Benoit, Joe	Mtl.	5	185	75	69	144	94	11	6	3	9	11	1940-41	1946-47
Benson, Bill	NYA	2	67	11	25	36	35	....	....	....	....	....	1940-41	1941-42
Benson, Bobby	Bos.	1	8	0	1	1	4	....	....	....	....	....	1924-25	1924-25
Bentley, Doug	Chi., NYR	13	566	219	324	543	217	23	9	8	17	8	1939-40	1953-54
Bentley, Max	Chi., Tor., NYR	12	646	245	299	544	179	52	18	27	45	14	1940-41	1953-54
Bentley, Reggie	Chi.	1	11	1	2	3	2	....	....	....	....	....	1942-43	1942-43
Berenson, Red	Mtl., NYR, St.L., Det.	17	987	261	397	658	305	85	23	14	37	49	1961-62	1977-78
Bergdinon, Fred	Bos.	1	2	0	0	0	0	....	....	....	....	....	1925-26	1925-26
Bergen, Todd	Phi.	1	14	11	5	16	4	17	4	9	13	8	1984-85	1984-85
Bergeron, Michel	Det., NYI, Wsh.	5	229	80	58	138	165	....	....	....	....	....	1974-75	1978-79
Bergeron, Yves	Pit.	2	3	0	0	0	0	....	....	....	....	....	1974-75	1976-77
Berglund, Bo	Que., Min., Phi.	3	130	28	39	67	40	9	2	0	2	6	1983-84	1985-86
Bergloff, Bob	Min.	1	2	0	0	0	5	....	....	....	....	....	1982-83	1982-83
Bergman, Gary	Det., Min., K.C.	12	838	68	299	367	1249	21	0	5	5	20	1964-65	1975-76
Bergman, Thommie	Det.	6	246	21	44	65	243	7	0	2	2	2	1972-73	1979-80
Berlinquette, Louis	Mtl., Mtl.M., Pit.	8	193	44	29	73	111	16	1	1	2	0	1917-18	1925-26
Bernier, Serge	Phi., L.A., Que.	7	302	78	119	197	234	5	1	1	2	0	1968-69	1980-81
Berry, Bob	Mtl., L.A.	8	541	159	191	350	344	26	2	6	8	6	1968-69	1976-77
Berry, Doug	Col.	2	121	10	33	43	25	....	....	....	....	....	1979-80	1980-81
Berry, Fred	Det.	1	3	0	0	0	0	....	....	....	....	....	1976-77	1976-77
Besler, Phil	Bos., Chi., Det.	2	30	1	4	5	18	....	....	....	....	....	1935-36	1938-39
Bessone, Pete	Det.	1	6	0	1	1	6	....	....	....	....	....	1937-38	1937-38
Bethel, John	Wpg.	1	17	0	2	2	4	....	....	....	....	....	1979-80	1979-80
Bettio, Sam	Bos.	1	44	9	12	21	32	....	....	....	....	....	1949-50	1949-50
Beverley, Nick	Bos., Pit., NYR, Min., L.A., Col.	11	502	18	94	112	156	7	0	1	1	0	1966-67	1979-80
Bialowas, Dwight	Atl., Min.	4	164	11	46	57	46	....	....	....	....	....	1973-74	1976-77
Bianchin, Wayne	Pit., Edm.	7	276	68	41	109	137	3	0	1	1	6	1973-74	1979-80
Bidner, Todd	Wsh.	1	12	2	1	3	7	....	....	....	....	....	1981-82	1981-82
Biggs, Don	Min.	1	1	0	0	0	0	....	....	....	....	....	1984-85	1984-85
Bignell, Larry	Pit.	2	20	0	3	3	2	3	0	0	0	2	1973-74	1974-75
Bilodeau, Gilles	Que.	1	9	0	1	1	25	....	....	....	....	....	1979-80	1979-80
Bionda, Jack	Tor., Bos.	4	93	3	9	12	113	11	0	1	1	14	1955-56	1958-59
Black, Stephen	Det., Chi.	2	113	11	20	31	77	13	0	0	0	13	1949-50	1950-51
Blackburn, Bob	NYR., Pit.	3	135	8	12	20	105	6	0	0	0	4	1968-69	1970-71
Blackburn, Don	Bos., Phi., NYR, NYI, Min.	6	185	23	44	67	87	12	3	0	3	10	1962-63	1972-73
Blade, Hank	Chi.	2	24	2	3	5	2	....	....	....	....	....	1946-47	1947-48
Bladon, Tom	Phi., Pit., Edm., Wpg., Det.	9	610	73	197	270	392	86	8	29	37	70	1972-73	1980-81
Blaine, Gary	Mtl.	1	1	0	0	0	0	....	....	....	....	....	1954-55	1954-55
Blair, Andy	Tor., Chi.	9	402	74	86	160	323	38	6	6	12	32	1928-29	1936-37
Blair, Chuck	Tor.	2	3	0	0	0	0	....	....	....	....	....	1948-49	1950-51
Blair, George	Tor.	1	2	0	0	0	0	....	....	....	....	....	1950-51	1950-51
Blake, Mickey	St.L., Bos., Tor.	2	16	1	1	2	4	....	....	....	....	....	1934-35	1935-36
Blake, Toe	Mtl.M., Mtl.	15	578	235	292	527	272	57	25	37	62	23	1932-33	1947-48
Blight, Rick	Van., L.A.	7	326	96	125	221	170	5	0	5	5	2	1975-76	1982-83
Blinco, Russ	Mtl.M, Chi.	6	268	59	66	125	24	19	3	3	6	4	1933-34	1938-39
Block, Ken	Van.	1	1	0	0	0	0	....	....	....	....	....	1970-71	1970-71
Blomqvist, Timo	Wsh., N.J.	5	243	4	53	57	293	13	0	0	0	24	1981-82	1986-87
Bloom, Mike	Wsh., Det.	3	201	30	47	77	215	....	....	....	....	....	1974-75	1976-77
Boddy, Gregg	Van.	5	273	23	44	67	263	3	0	0	0	0	1971-72	1975-76
Bodnar, Gus	Tor., Chi., Bos.	12	667	142	254	396	207	32	4	3	7	10	1943-44	1954-55
Boehm, Ron	Oak.	1	16	2	1	3	10	....	....	....	....	....	1967-68	1967-68
Boesch, Garth	Tor.	4	197	9	28	37	205	34	2	5	7	18	1946-47	1949-50
Boh, Rick	Min.	1	8	2	1	3	4	....	....	....	....	....	1987-88	1987-88
Boileau, Marc	Det.	1	54	5	6	11	8	....	....	....	....	....	1961-62	1961-62
Boileau, Rene	NYA	1	7	0	0	0	0	....	....	....	....	....	1925-26	1925-26
Boimistruck, Fred	Tor.	2	83	4	14	18	45	....	....	....	....	....	1981-82	1982-83
Boisvert, Serge	Tor., Mtl.	5	46	5	7	12	8	23	3	7	10	4	1982-83	1987-88
Boivin, Leo	Tor., Bos., Det., Pit., Min.	19	1150	72	250	322	1192	54	3	10	13	59	1951-52	1969-70
Boland, Mike A.	Phi.	1	2	0	0	0	0	....	....	....	....	....	1974-75	1974-75
Boland, Mike J.	K.C., Buf.	2	23	1	2	3	29	3	1	0	1	2	1974-75	1978-79
Boldirev, Ivan	Bos., Cal., Chi., Atl., Van., Det.	15	1052	361	505	866	507	48	13	20	33	14	1970-71	1984-85
Bolduc, Danny	Det., Cgy.	3	102	22	19	41	33	1	0	0	0	0	1978-79	1983-84
Bolduc, Michel	Que.	2	10	0	0	0	6	....	....	....	....	....	1981-82	1982-83
Boll, Buzz	Tor., NYA, Bos.	11	436	133	130	263	148	29	7	3	10	13	1933-34	1943-44
Bolonchuk, Larry	Van., Wsh.	4	74	3	9	12	97	....	....	....	....	....	1972-73	1977-78

			Regular Schedule					Playoffs					First	Last
Name	NHL Teams	NHL Seasons	GP	G	A	TP	PIM	GP	G	A	TP	PIM	First NHL Season	Last NHL Season
Bolton, Hughie	Tor.	8	235	10	51	61	221	17	0	5	5	14	1949-50	1956-57
Bonar, Dan	L.A.	3	170	25	39	64	208	14	3	4	7	22	1980-81	1982-83
Bonin, Marcel	Det., Bos., Mtl.	9	454	97	175	272	336	50	11	14	25	51	1952-53	1961-62
Boo, Jim	Min.	1	6	0	0	0	22	....	....	....	....	....	1977-78	1977-78
Boone, Buddy	Bos.	2	34	5	3	8	28	22	2	1	3	25	1956-57	1957-58
Boothman, George	Tor.	2	58	17	19	36	18	5	2	1	3	2	1942-43	1943-44
Bordeleau, Chris.	Mtl., St.L., Chi.,	4	205	38	65	103	82	19	4	7	11	17	1968-69	1971-72
Bordeleau, J. P.	Chi.	10	519	97	126	223	143	48	3	6	9	12	1969-70	1979-80
Bordeleau, Paulin	Van.	3	183	33	56	89	47	5	2	1	3	0	1973-74	1975-76
Borotsik, Jack	St.L.	1	1	0	0	0	0	....	....	....	....	....	1974-75	1974-75
Bossy, Mike	NYI	10	752	573	553	1126	210	129	85	75	160	38	1977-78	1986-87
Bostrom, Helge	Chi.	4	96	3	3	6	58	13	0	0	0	16	1929-30	1932-33
Botell, Mark	Phi.	1	32	4	10	14	31	....	....	....	....	....	1981-82	1981-82
Botting, Cam	Atl.	1	2	0	1	1	0	....	....	....	....	....	1975-76	1975-76
Boucha, Henry	Det., Min., K.C., Col.	6	247	53	49	102	157	....	....	....	....	....	1971-72	1976-77
Bouchard, Emile (Butch)	Mtl.	15	785	49	144	193	863	113	11	21	32	121	1941-42	1955-56
Bouchard, Dick	NYR	1	1	0	0	0	0	....	....	....	....	....	1954-55	1954-55
Bouchard, Edmond	Mtl., Ham., NYA, Pit.	8	223	19	20	39	105	....	....	....	....	....	1921-22	1928-29
Bouchard, Pierre	Mtl., Wsh.	12	595	24	82	106	433	76	3	10	13	56	1970-71	1981-82
Boucher, Billy	Mtl., Bos., NYA	7	213	93	35	128	391	21	9	3	12	35	1921-22	1927-28
Boucher, Frank	Ott., NYR	14	557	161	262	423	118	56	16	18	34	12	1921-22	1943-44
Boucher, George	Ott., Mtl.M, Chi.	15	457	122	62	184	712	44	11	4	15	84	1917-18	1931-32
Boucher, Robert	Mtl.	1	12	0	0	0	0	....	....	....	....	....	1923-24	1923-24
Boudrias, Andre	Mtl., Min., Chi., St.L., Van.	12	662	151	340	491	218	34	6	10	16	12	1963-64	1975-76
Boughner, Barry	Oak., Cal.	2	20	0	0	0	11	....	....	....	....	....	1969-70	1970-71
Bourbonnais, Dan	Hfd.	2	59	3	25	28	11	....	....	....	....	....	1981-82	1983-84
Bourbonnais, Rick	St.L.	3	71	9	15	24	29	4	0	1	1	0	1975-76	1977-78
Bourcier, Conrad	Mtl.	1	6	0	0	0	0	....	....	....	....	....	1935-36	1935-36
Bourcier, Jean	Mtl.	1	9	0	1	1	0	....	....	....	....	....	1935-36	1935-36
Bourgeault, Leo	Tor. NYR, Ott., Mtl.	8	307	24	20	44	269	24	1	1	2	18	1926-27	1934-35
Bourgeois, Charlie	Cgy., St.L., Hfd.	7	290	16	54	70	788	40	2	3	5	194	1981-82	1987-88
Bourne, Bob	NYI, L.A.	14	964	258	324	582	605	139	40	56	96	108	1974-75	1987-88
Boutette, Pat	Tor., Hfd., Pit.	10	756	171	282	453	1354	46	10	14	24	109	1975-76	1984-85
Bowcher, Clarence	NYA	2	47	2	2	4	110	....	....	....	....	....	1926-27	1927-28
Bowman, Kirk	Chi.	3	88	11	17	28	19	7	1	0	1	0	1976-77	1978-79
Bowman, Ralph	Ott., St.L., Det.	7	274	8	17	25	260	22	2	2	4	6	1933-34	1939-40
Bownass, Jack	Mtl., NYR	4	80	3	8	11	58	....	....	....	....	....	1957-58	1961-62
Bowness, Rick	Atl., Det., St. L, Wpg.	7	173	18	37	55	191	5	0	0	0	2	1975-76	1981-82
Boyd, Bill	NYR, NYA	4	138	15	7	22	72	9	0	0	0	2	1926-27	1929-30
Boyd, Irwin	Bos., Det.	4	97	18	19	37	51	15	0	1	1	4	1931-32	1943-44
Boyd, Randy	Pit., Chi., NYI, Van.	8	257	20	67	87	328	13	0	2	2	26	1981-82	1988-89
Boyer, Wally	Tor., Chi., Oak. Pit.	7	365	54	105	159	163	15	1	3	4	0	1965-66	1971-72
Brackenborough, John	Bos.	1	7	0	0	0	0	....	....	....	....	....	1925-26	1925-26
Brackenbury, Curt	Que., Edm., St.L.	4	141	9	17	26	226	2	0	0	0	0	1979-80	1982-83
Bradley, Barton	Bos.	1	1	0	0	0	0	....	....	....	....	....	1949-50	1949-50
Bradley, Lyle	Cal. Cle.	2	6	1	0	1	2	....	....	....	....	....	1973-74	1976-77
Bragnalo, Rick	Wsh.	4	145	15	35	50	46	....	....	....	....	....	1975-76	1978-79
Brannigan, Andy	NYA	2	26	1	2	3	31	....	....	....	....	....	1940-41	1941-42
Brasar, Per-Olov	Min., Van.	5	348	64	142	206	33	13	1	2	3	0	1977-78	1981-82
Brayshaw, Russ	Chi.	1	43	5	9	14	24	....	....	....	....	....	1944-45	1944-45
Breitenbach, Ken	Buf.	3	68	1	13	14	49	8	0	1	1	4	1975-76	1978-79
Brennan, Doug	NYR	3	123	9	7	16	152	16	1	0	1	21	1931-32	1933-34
Brennan, Tom	Bos.	2	22	2	2	4	2	....	....	....	....	....	1943-44	1944-45
Brenneman, John	Chi., NYR, Tor., Det., Oak.	5	152	21	19	40	46	....	....	....	....	....	1964-65	1968-69
Bretto, Joe	Chi.	1	3	0	0	0	4	....	....	....	....	....	1944-45	1944-45
Brewer, Carl	Tor., Det., St.L.	12	604	25	198	223	1037	72	3	17	20	140	1957-58	1979-80
Briden, Archie	Det., Pit.	2	72	9	5	14	56	....	....	....	....	....	1926-27	1929-30
Bridgman, Mel	Phi., Cgy., N.J., Det., Van.	14	977	252	449	701	1625	125	28	39	67	298	1975-76	1988-89
Briere, Michel	Pit.	1	76	12	32	44	20	10	5	3	8	17	1969-70	1969-70
Brindley, Doug	Tor.	1	3	0	0	0	0	....	....	....	....	....	1970-71	1970-71
Brink, Milt	Chi.	1	5	0	0	0	0	....	....	....	....	....	1936-37	1936-37
Brisson, Gerry	Mtl.	1	4	0	2	2	4	....	....	....	....	....	1962-63	1962-63
Britz, Greg	Tor., Hfd.	3	8	0	0	0	4	....	....	....	....	....	1983-84	1986-87
Broadbent, Harry	Ott. Mt.M, NYA	11	302	122	45	167	553	41	13	3	16	69	1918-19	1928-29
Broden, Connie	Mtl.	3	6	2	1	3	2	7	0	1	1	0	1955-56	1957-58
Brooks, Gord	St.L., Wsh.	3	70	7	18	25	37	....	....	....	....	....	1971-72	1974-75
Brophy, Bernie	Mtl.M, Det.	3	62	4	4	8	25	2	0	0	0	2	1925-26	1929-30
Brossart, Willie	Phi., Tor., Wsh.	6	129	1	14	15	88	1	0	0	0	0	1970-71	1975-76
Brown, Adam	Det. Chi. Bos.	10	391	104	113	217	358	26	2	14	6	14	1941-42	1951-52
Brown, Arnie	Tor. NYR, Det., NYI, Atl.	12	681	44	141	185	738	22	0	6	6	23	1961-62	1973-74
Brown, Connie	Det.	5	91	15	24	39	12	14	2	3	5	0	1938-39	1942-43
Brown, Fred	Mtl.M	1	19	1	0	1	0	9	0	0	0	0	1927-28	1927-28
Brown, George	Mtl.	3	79	6	22	28	34	7	0	0	0	2	1936-37	1938-39
Brown, Gerry	Det.	2	23	4	5	9	2	12	2	1	3	4	1941-42	1945-46
Brown, Harold	NYR	1	13	2	1	3	2	....	....	....	....	....	1945-46	1945-46
Brown, Jim	L.A.	1	3	0	1	1	5	....	....	....	....	....	1982-83	1982-83
Brown, Larry	NYR, Det., Phi., L.A.	9	455	7	53	60	180	35	0	4	4	10	1969-70	1977-78
Brown, Stan	NYR, Det.	2	48	8	2	10	18	2	0	0	0	0	1926-27	1927-28
Brown, Wayne	Bos.	1	....	....	....	....	....	4	0	0	0	2	1953-54	1953-54
Browne, Cecil	Chi.	1	13	2	0	2	4	....	....	....	....	....	1927-28	1927-28
Brownschidle, Jack	St.L., Hfd.	9	494	39	162	201	151	26	0	5	5	18	1977-78	1985-86
Brownschidle, Jeff	Hfd.	2	7	0	1	1	2	....	....	....	....	....	1981-82	1982-83
Brubaker, Jeff	Hfd., Mtl., Cgy., Tor., Edm., NYR, Det.	8	178	16	9	25	512	2	0	0	0	27	1979-80	1988-89
Bruce, Gordie	Bos.	3	28	4	9	13	13	7	2	3	5	4	1940-41	1945-46
Bruce, Morley	Ott.	4	72	8	1	9	27	12	0	0	0	3	1917-18	1921-22
Bruneteau, Eddie	Det.	7	180	40	42	82	35	26	7	6	13	0	1940-41	1948-49
Bruneteau, Mud	Det.	11	411	139	138	277	80	77	23	14	37	22	1935-36	1945-46
Brydge, Bill	Tor., Det., NYA	9	368	26	52	78	506	2	0	0	0	4	1926-27	1935-36
Brydson, Glenn	Mtl.M, St.L., NYR, Chi.	8	299	56	79	135	203	11	0	0	0	8	1930-31	1937-38
Brydson, Gord	Tor.	1	8	2	0	2	8	....	....	....	....	....	1929-30	1929-30
Bubla, Jiri	Van.	5	256	17	101	118	202	6	0	0	0	7	1981-82	1985-86
Buchanan, Al	Tor.	2	4	0	1	1	2	....	....	....	....	....	1948-49	1949-50
Buchanan, Bucky	NYR	1	2	0	0	0	0	....	....	....	....	....	1948-49	1948-49
Buchanan, Mike	Chi.	1	1	0	0	0	0	....	....	....	....	....	1951-52	1951-52
Buchanan, Ron	Bos., St.L.	2	5	0	0	0	0	....	....	....	....	....	1966-67	1969-70
Bucyk, John	Det., Bos.,	23	1540	556	813	1369	497	124	41	64	103	42	1955-56	1977-78
Buhr, Doug	K.C.	1	6	0	2	2	4	....	....	....	....	....	1974-75	1974-75
Bukovich, Tony	Det.	2	44	7	3	10	6	6	0	1	1	0	1943-44	1944-45
Buller, Hy	Det., NYR	5	188	22	58	80	215	....	....	....	....	....	1943-44	1953-54
Bulley, Ted	Chi., Wsh., Pit.	8	414	101	113	214	704	29	5	5	10	24	1976-77	1983-84
Burch, Billy	Ham., NYA, Bos., Chi.	11	390	137	53	190	251	2	0	0	0	0	1922-23	1932-33
Burchell, Fred	Mtl.	2	4	0	0	0	2	....	....	....	....	....	1950-51	1953-54
Burdon, Glen	K.C.	1	11	0	2	2	0	....	....	....	....	....	1974-75	1974-75
Burega, Bill	Bos.	1	4	0	1	1	4	....	....	....	....	....	1955-56	1955-56
Burke, Eddie	Bos., NYA	4	106	29	20	49	55	....	....	....	....	....	1931-32	1934-35
Burke, Marty	Mtl., Pit., Ott., Chi.	11	494	19	47	66	560	31	2	4	6	44	1927-28	1937-38
Burmeister, Roy	NYA	3	67	4	3	7	2	....	....	....	....	....	1929-30	1931-32
Burnett, Kelly	NYR	1	3	1	0	1	0	....	....	....	....	....	1952-53	1952-53
Burns, Bobby	Chi.	3	20	1	0	1	8	....	....	....	....	....	1927-28	1929-30
Burns, Charlie	Det., Bos., Oak., Pit., Min.	11	749	106	198	304	252	31	5	4	9	4	1958-59	1972-73
Burns, Gary	NYR	2	11	2	2	4	18	5	0	0	0	6	1980-81	1981-82
Burns, Norm	NYR	1	11	0	4	4	2	....	....	....	....	....	1941-42	1941-42
Burns, Robin	Pit., K.C.	5	190	31	38	69	139	....	....	....	....	....	1970-71	1975-76
Burrows, Dave	Pit., Tor.	10	724	29	135	164	377	29	1	5	6	25	1971-72	1980-81
Burry, Bert	Ott.	1	4	0	0	0	0	....	....	....	....	....	1932-33	1932-33
Burton, Cummy	Det.	3	43	0	2	2	21	3	0	0	0	0	1955-56	1958-59
Burton, Nelson	Wsh.	2	8	1	0	1	21	....	....	....	....	....	1977-78	1978-79
Bush, Eddie	Det.	2	27	4	6	10	50	12	1	6	7	23	1938-39	1941-42
Busniuk, Mike	Phi.	2	143	3	23	26	297	25	2	5	7	34	1979-80	1980-81
Busniuk, Ron	Buf.	2	6	0	3	3	4	....	....	....	....	....	1972-73	1973-74
Buswell, Walt	Det., Mtl.	8	368	10	40	50	164	24	2	1	3	10	1932-33	1939-40
Butler, Dick	Chi.	1	7	2	0	2	0	....	....	....	....	....	1947-48	1947-48
Butler, Jerry	Tor., Van., Wpg., NYR, St.L.	11	641	99	120	219	515	48	3	3	6	79	1972-73	1982-83
Butters, Bill	Min.	2	72	1	4	5	77	....	....	....	....	....	1977-78	1978-79

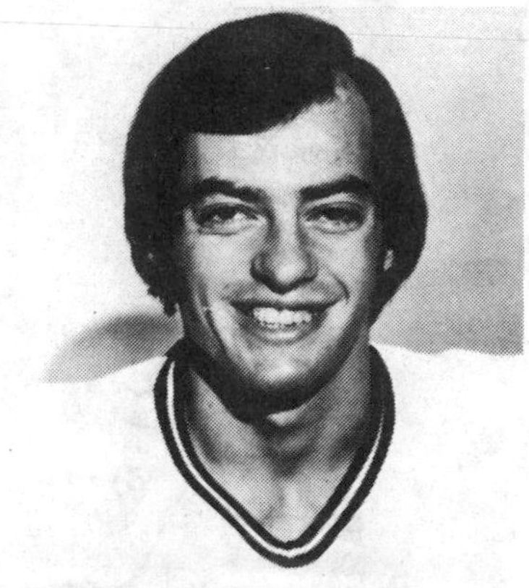

Paulin Bordeleau

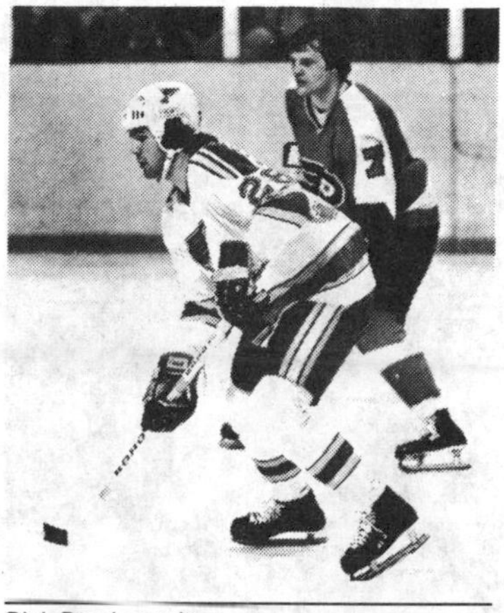

Rick Bourbonnais

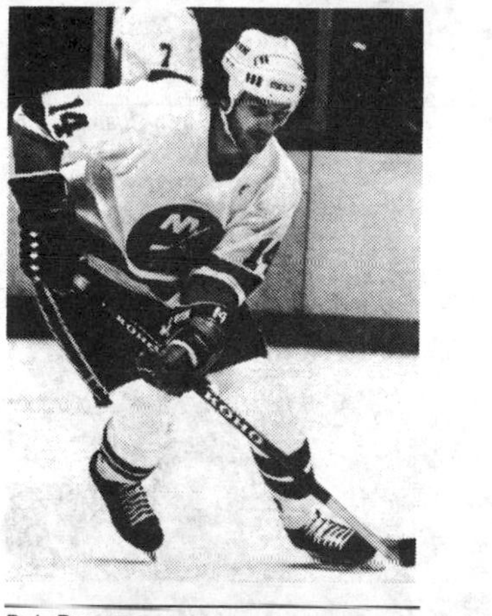

Bob Bourne

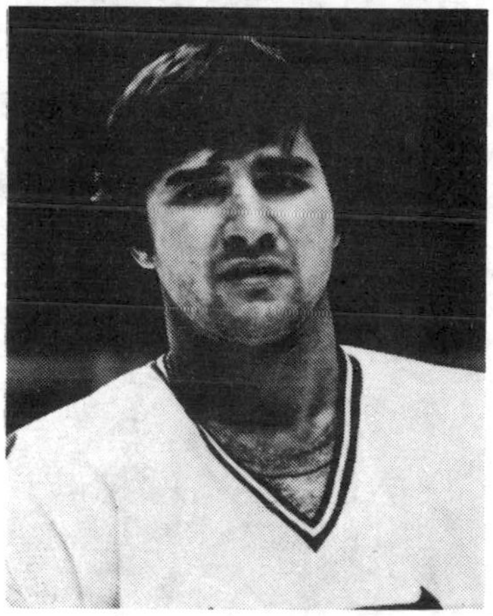

Pat Boutette

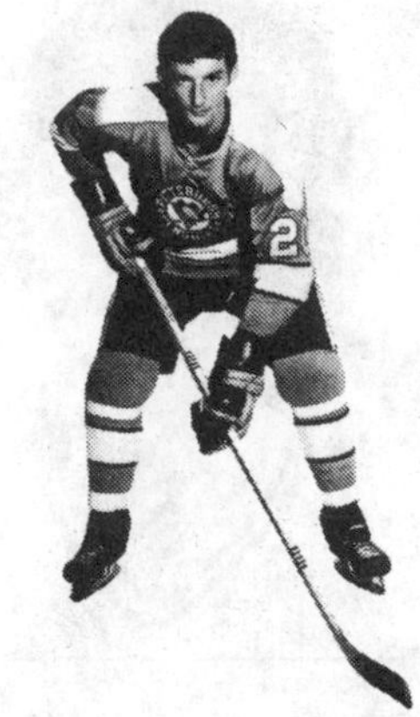

Dave Burrows

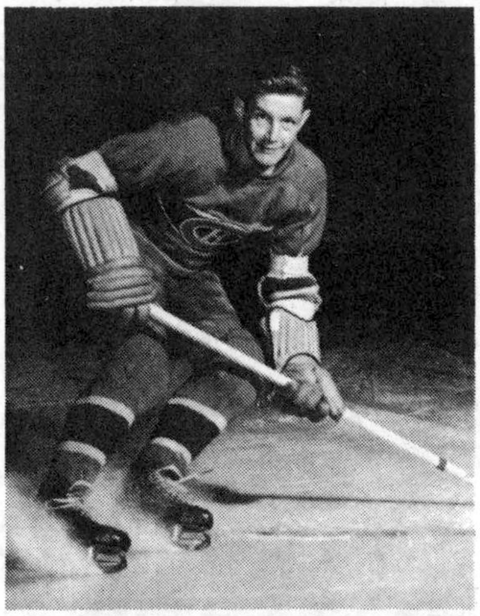

Murph Chamberlain

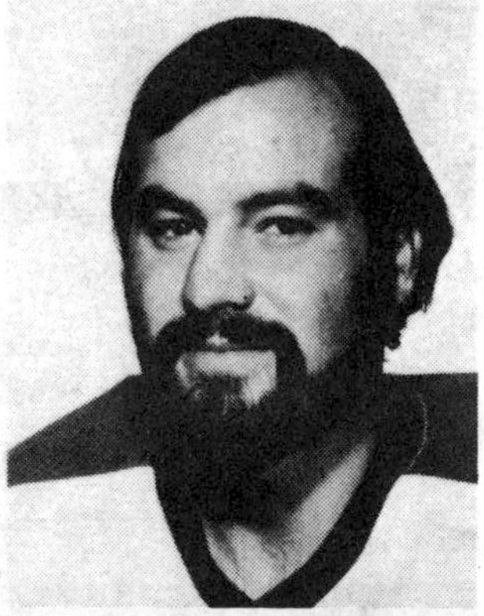

Rick Chartraw

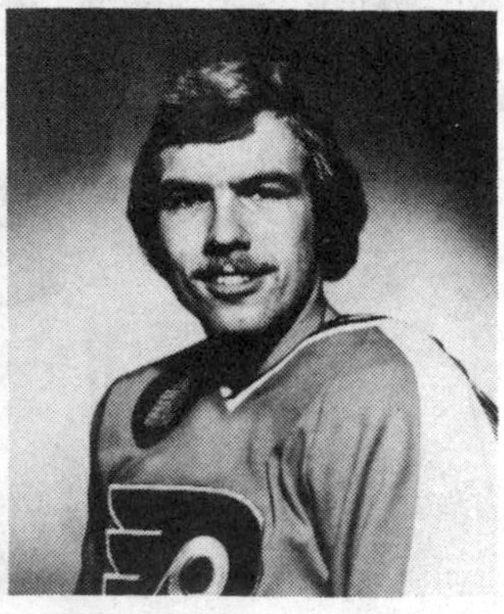

Bill Clement

Name	NHL Teams	NHL Seasons	Regular Schedule					Playoffs					Last NHL Season	Last Pro Season
			GP	G	A	TP	PIM	GP	G	A	TP	PIM		
Buttrey, Gord	Chi.	1	10	0	0	0	0	10	0	0	0	0	1943-44	1943-44
Buynak, Gordon	St. L	1	4	0	0	0	2	....	....	....	....	....	1974-75	1974-75
Byers, Gord	Bos.	1	1	0	1	1	0	....	....	....	....	....	1949-50	1949-50
Byers, Jerry	Min., Atl, NYR	4	43	3	4	7	10	....	....	....	....	....	1972-73	1977-78
Byers, Mike	Tor., Phi., Buf., L.A.	4	166	42	34	76	39	4	0	1	1	0	1967-68	1971-72

C

Name	NHL Teams	NHL Seasons	GP	G	A	TP	PIM	GP	G	A	TP	PIM	Last NHL Season	Last Pro Season
Caffery, Jack	Tor., Bos.	3	57	3	2	5	22	10	1	0	1	4	1954-55	1957-58
Caffery, Terry	Chi., Min.	2	14	0	0	0	0	1	0	0	0	0	1969-70	1970-71
Cahan, Larry	Tor., NYR, Oak., L.A.	13	665	38	92	130	700	29	1	1	2	38	1954-55	1970-71
Cahill, Chuck	Bos.	2	32	0	1	1	4	....	....	....	....	....	1925-26	1926-27
Cain, Herbert	Mtl.M, Mtl., Bos.	13	571	206	194	400	178	64	16	13	29	13	1933-34	1945-46
Cain, Jim	Mtl.M, Tor.	2	61	4	0	4	35	....	....	....	....	....	1924-25	1925-26
Cairns, Don	K.C., Col.	2	9	0	1	1	2	....	....	....	....	....	1975-76	1976-77
Calder, Eric	Wsh.	2	2	0	0	0	0	....	....	....	....	....	1981-82	1982-83
Calladine, Norm	Bos.	3	63	19	29	48	8	....	....	....	....	....	1942-43	1944-45
Callander, Drew	Phi., Van.	4	39	6	2	8	7	....	....	....	....	....	1976-77	1979-80
Callighen, Brett	Edm.	3	160	56	89	145	132	14	4	6	10	8	1979-80	1981-82
Callighen, Patsy	NYR	1	36	0	0	0	32	9	0	0	0	0	1927-28	1927-28
Camazzola, James	Chi.	2	3	0	0	0	0	....	....	....	....	....	1983-84	1986-87
Camazzola, Tony	Wsh.	1	3	0	0	0	4	....	....	....	....	....	1981-82	1981-82
Cameron, Al	Det., Wpg.	6	282	11	44	55	356	7	0	1	1	2	1975-76	1980-81
Cameron, Scotty	NYR	1	35	8	11	19	0	....	....	....	....	....	1942-43	1942-43
Cameron, Billy	Mtl., NYA	2	39	0	0	0	2	6	0	0	0	0	1923-24	1925-26
Cameron, Craig	Det., St.L., Min., NYI	9	552	87	65	152	202	27	3	1	4	17	1966-67	1975-76
Cameron, Dave	Col., N.J.	3	168	25	28	53	238	....	....	....	....	....	1981-82	1983-84
Cameron, Harry	Tor., Ott., Mtl.	6	127	90	37	117	120	20	7	3	10	29	1917-18	1922-23
Campbell, Bryan	L.A., Chi.	5	260	35	71	106	74	22	3	4	7	2	1967-68	1971-72
Campbell, Colin	Pit., Col., Edm., Van., Det.	11	636	25	103	128	1292	45	4	10	14	181	1974-75	1984-85
Campbell, Dave	Mtl.	1	3	0	0	0	0	....	....	....	....	....	1920-21	1920-21
Campbell, Don	Chi.	1	17	1	3	4	8	....	....	....	....	....	1943-44	1943-44
Campbell, Scott	Wpg., St.L.	3	80	4	21	25	243	....	....	....	....	....	1979-80	1981-82
Campbell, Spiff	Ott., NYA	3	77	5	1	6	12	2	0	0	0	0	1923-24	1925-26
Campbell, Wade	Wpg., Bos.	6	213	9	27	36	305	10	0	0	0	20	1982-83	1987-88
Campeau, Tod	Mtl.	3	42	5	9	14	16	1	0	0	0	0	1943-44	1948-49
Campedelli, Dom	Mtl.	1	2	0	0	0	0	....	....	....	....	....	1985-86	1985-86
Carbol, Leo	Chi.	1	6	0	1	1	4	....	....	....	....	....	1942-43	1942-43
Cardin, Claude	St.L.	1	1	0	0	0	0	....	....	....	....	....	1967-68	1967-68
Cardwell, Steve	Pit.	3	53	9	11	20	35	4	0	0	0	2	1970-71	1972-73
Carey, George	Que, Ham., Tor.	5	72	22	8	30	14	....	....	....	....	....	1919-20	1923-24
Carleton, Wayne	Tor., Bos., Cal.	7	278	55	73	128	172	18	2	4	6	14	1965-66	1971-72
Carlin, Brian	L.A.	1	5	1	0	1	0	....	....	....	....	....	1971-72	1971-72
Carlson, Jack	Min., St.L.	6	236	30	15	45	417	25	1	2	3	72	1978-79	1986-87
Carlson, Kent	Mtl., St.L., Wsh.	5	113	7	11	18	148	8	0	0	0	13	1983-84	1988-89
Carlson, Steve	L.A.	1	52	9	12	21	23	4	1	1	2	7	1979-80	1979-80
Caron, Alain	Oak., Mtl.	2	60	9	13	22	18	....	....	....	....	....	1967-68	1968-69
Carpenter, Eddie	Que, Ham.	2	44	10	4	14	23	....	....	....	....	....	1919-20	1920-21
Carr, Al	Tor.	1	5	0	1	1	4	....	....	....	....	....	1943-44	1943-44
Carr, Gene	St.L., NYR, L.A., Pit., Atl.	8	465	79	136	215	365	35	5	8	13	66	1971-72	1978-79
Carr, Lorne	NYR, NYA, Tor.	13	580	194	222	416	132	53	10	9	19	13	1933-34	1945-46
Carriere, Larry	Buf. Atl, Van., L.A., Tor.	7	366	16	74	90	463	27	0	3	3	42	1972-73	1979-80
Carrigan, Gene	NYR, StL, Det.	3	37	2	1	3	13	4	0	0	0	0	1930-31	1934-35
Carroll, Billy	NYI, Edm., Det.	7	322	30	54	84	113	71	6	12	18	18	1980-81	1986-87
Carroll, George	Mtl.M, Bos.	1	15	0	0	0	9	....	....	....	....	....	1924-25	1924-25
Carroll, Greg	Wsh., Det., Hfd.	2	131	20	34	54	44	....	....	....	....	....	1978-79	1979-80
Carruthers, Dwight	Det. Phi.	2	2	0	0	0	0	....	....	....	....	....	1965-66	1967-68
Carse, Bill	NYR, Chi.	4	124	28	43	71	38	16	3	2	5	0	1938-39	1941-42
Carse, Bob	Chi., Mtl.	5	167	32	55	87	52	10	0	2	2	2	1939-40	1947-48
Carson, Bill	Tor., Bos.	4	159	54	24	78	156	11	3	0	3	14	1926-27	1929-30
Carson, Frank	Mtl.M., NYA, Det.	7	248	42	48	90	166	22	0	2	2	9	1925-26	1933-34
Carson, Gerry	Mtl., NYR, Mtl.M.	6	261	12	11	23	205	22	0	0	0	12	1928-29	1936-37
Carson, Lindsay	Phi., Hfd.	7	373	66	80	146	524	49	4	10	14	56	1981-82	1987-88
Carter, Billy	Mtl., Bos.	3	16	0	0	0	6	....	....	....	....	....	1957-58	1961-62
Carter, Lyle	Cal.	1	15	0	0	0	2	....	....	....	....	....	1971-72	1971-72
Carter, Ron	Edm.	1	2	0	0	0	0	....	....	....	....	....	1979-80	1979-80
Carveth, Joe	Det., Bos., Mtl.	11	504	150	189	339	81	69	21	16	37	28	1940-41	1950-51
Cashman, Wayne	Bos.	17	1027	277	516	793	1041	145	31	57	88	250	1964-65	1982-83
Cassidy, Tom	Pit.	1	26	3	4	7	15	....	....	....	....	....	1977-78	1977-78
Cassolato, Tony	Wsh.	3	23	1	6	7	4	....	....	....	....	....	1979-80	1981-82
Ceresino, Ray	Tor.	1	12	1	1	2	2	....	....	....	....	....	1948-49	1948-49
Cernik, Frantisek	Det.	1	49	5	4	9	13	....	....	....	....	....	1984-85	1984-85
Chad John	Chi.	3	80	15	22	37	29	10	0	1	1	2	1939-40	1945-46
Chalmers, Bill	NYR	1	1	0	0	0	0	....	....	....	....	....	1953-54	1953-54
Chalupa, Milan	Det.	1	14	0	5	5	6	....	....	....	....	....	1984-85	1984-85
Chamberlain, Murph	Tor., Mtl., NYA, Bos.	12	510	100	175	275	769	66	14	17	31	96	1937-38	1948-49
Champagne, Andre	Tor.	1	2	0	0	0	0	....	....	....	....	....	1962-63	1962-63
Chapman, Art	Bos., NYA	10	438	62	174	236	140	25	1	5	6	9	1930-31	1939-40
Chapman, Blair	Pit., St.L.	7	402	106	125	231	158	25	4	6	10	15	1976-77	1982-83
Charlebois, Bob	Min.	1	7	1	0	1	0	....	....	....	....	....	1967-68	1967-68
Charron, Guy	Mtl., Det., K.C., Wsh.	12	734	221	309	530	146	....	....	....	....	....	1969-70	1980-81
Chartier, Dave	Wpg.	1	1	0	0	0	0	....	....	....	....	....	1980-81	1980-81
Chartraw, Rick	Mtl., L.A., NYR, Edm.	10	420	28	64	92	399	75	7	9	16	80	1974-75	1983-84
Check, Lude	Det., Chi.	2	27	6	2	8	4	....	....	....	....	....	1943-44	1944-45
Chernoff, Mike	Min.	1	1	0	0	0	0	....	....	....	....	....	1968-69	1968-69
Cherry, Dick	Bos., Phi.	3	145	12	10	22	45	4	1	0	1	4	1956-57	1969-70
Cherry, Don	Bos.	1	....	....	....	....	....	1	0	0	0	0	1954-55	1954-55
Chevrefils, Real	Bos., Det.	8	387	104	97	201	185	30	5	4	9	20	1951-52	1958-59
Chicoine, Dan	Cle. Min.	3	31	1	2	3	12	1	0	0	0	0	1977-78	1979-80
Chinnick, Rick	Min.	2	4	0	2	2	0	....	....	....	....	....	1973-74	1974-75
Chipperfield, Ron	Edm., Que.,	2	83	22	24	46	34	....	....	....	....	....	1979-80	1980-81
Chisholm, Art	Bos.	1	3	0	0	0	0	....	....	....	....	....	1960-61	1960-61
Chisholm, Colin	Min.	1	1	0	0	0	0	....	....	....	....	....	1986-87	1986-87
Chisholm, Lex	Tor.	2	54	10	8	18	19	3	1	0	1	0	1939-40	1940-41
Chorney, Marc	Pit. L.A.	4	210	8	27	35	209	7	0	1	1	2	1980-81	1983-84
Chouinard, Gene	Ott.	1	8	0	0	0	0	....	....	....	....	....	1927-28	1927-28
Chouinard, Guy	Atl, Cgy., St.L.	10	578	205	370	575	120	46	9	28	37	12	1974-75	1983-84
Christie, Mike	Cal., Cle., Col., Van.	7	412	15	101	116	550	2	0	0	0	0	1974-75	1980-81
Christoff, Steve	Min. Cgy., L.A.	5	248	77	64	141	108	35	16	12	28	25	1979-80	1983-84
Chrystal, Bob	NYR	2	132	11	14	25	112	....	....	....	....	....	1953-54	1954-55
Church, Jack	Tor., NYA., Bos.	6	145	5	22	27	164	25	1	1	2	18	1938-39	1945-46
Ciesla, Hank	Chi., NYR	4	269	26	51	77	87	6	0	2	2	0	1955-56	1958-59
Clackson, Kim	Pit., Que.	2	106	0	8	8	370	8	0	0	0	70	1979-80	1980-81
Clancy, Francis (King)	Ott., Tor.	16	592	137	143	280	904	61	9	8	17	92	1921-22	1936-37
Clancy, Terry	Oak., Tor.	4	93	6	6	12	39	....	....	....	....	....	1967-68	1972-73
Clapper, Dit	Bos.	20	833	228	246	474	462	86	13	17	30	50	1927-28	1946-47
Clark, Andy	Bos.	1	5	0	0	0	0	....	....	....	....	....	1927-28	1927-28
Clark, Dan	NYR	1	4	0	1	1	6	....	....	....	....	....	1978-79	1978-79
Clark, Dean	Edm.	1	1	0	0	0	0	....	....	....	....	....	1983-84	1983-84
Clark, Gordie	Bos.	2	8	0	1	1	0	1	0	0	0	0	1974-75	1975-76
Clarke, Bobby	Phi.	15	1144	358	852	1210	1453	136	42	77	119	152	1969-70	1983-84
Cleghorn, Odie	Mtl., Pit.	10	180	95	29	124	147	23	9	2	11	2	1918-19	1927-28
Cleghorn, Sprague	Ott. Tor. Mtl., Bos.	10	256	84	39	123	489	37	7	8	15	48	1918-19	1927-28
Clement, Bill	Phi., Wsh., Atl., Cgy.	11	719	148	208	356	383	50	5	3	8	26	1971-72	1981-82
Cline, Bruce	NYR	1	30	2	3	5	10	....	....	....	....	....	1956-57	1956-57
Clippingdale, Steve	L.A., Wsh.	2	19	1	2	3	9	1	0	0	0	0	1976-77	1979-80
Cloutier, Real	Que. Buf.	6	317	146	198	344	119	25	7	5	12	20	1979-80	1984-85
Cloutier, Rejean	Det.	2	5	0	2	2	2	....	....	....	....	....	1979-80	1981-82
Cloutier, Roland	Det., Que.	3	34	8	9	17	2	....	....	....	....	....	1977-78	1979-80
Clune, Wally	Mtl.	1	5	0	0	0	6	....	....	....	....	....	1955-56	1955-56
Coalter, Gary	Cal., K.C.	2	34	2	4	6	2	....	....	....	....	....	1973-74	1974-75
Coates, Steve	Det.	1	5	1	0	1	24	....	....	....	....	....	1976-77	1976-77
Cochrane, Glen	Phi., Van., Chi., Edm.	10	411	17	72	89	1556	18	1	1	2	31	1978-79	1988-89
Coflin, Hughie	Chi.	1	31	0	3	3	33	....	....	....	....	....	1950-51	1950-51
Colley, Tom	Min.	1	1	0	0	0	2	....	....	....	....	....	1974-75	1974-75

			Regular Schedule					Playoffs					First	Last
Name	NHL Teams	NHL Seasons	GP	G	A	TP	PIM	GP	G	A	TP	PIM	NHL Season	NHL Season
Collings, Norm	Mtl.	1	1	0	1	1	0	....	....	....	....	....	1934-35	1934-35
Collins, Bill	Min., Mtl., Det., St. L, NYR, Phi., Wsh.	11	768	157	154	311	415	18	3	5	8	12	1967-68	1977-78
Collins, Gary	Tor.	1	....	....	....	....	....	2	0	0	0	0	1958-59	1958-59
Collyard, Bob	St.L.	1	10	1	3	4	4	....	....	....	....	....	1973-74	1973-74
Colville, Mac	NYR	9	353	71	104	175	132	40	9	10	19	14	1935-36	1946-47
Colville, Neil	NYR	12	464	99	166	265	213	46	7	19	26	33	1935-36	1948-49
Colwill, Les	NYR	1	69	7	6	13	16	....	....	....	....	....	1958-59	1958-59
Comeau, Rey	Mtl., Atl, Col.	9	564	98	141	239	175	9	2	1	3	8	1971-72	1979-80
Conacher, Brian	Tor., Det.	5	154	28	28	56	84	12	3	2	5	21	1961-62	1971-72
Conacher, Charlie	Tor., Det., NYA	12	460	225	173	398	516	49	17	18	35	53	1929-30	1940-41
Conacher, Jim	Det., Chi., NYR	8	328	85	117	202	91	19	5	2	7	4	1945-46	1952-53
Conacher, Lionel	Pit., NYA, Mtl.M., Chi.	12	500	80	105	185	882	35	2	2	4	34	1925-26	1936-37
Conacher, Pete	Chi., NYR, Tor.	6	229	47	39	86	57	7	0	0	0	0	1951-52	1957-58
Conacher, Roy	Bos., Det., Chi.	11	490	226	200	426	90	42	15	15	30	14	1938-39	1951-52
Conn, Hugh	NYA	2	96	9	28	37	22	....	....	....	....	....	1933-34	1934-35
Connelly, Wayne	Mtl., Bos., Min., Det., St. L, Van.	10	543	133	174	307	156	24	11	7	18	4	1960-61	1971-72
Connolly, Bert	NYR, Chi.	3	87	13	15	28	37	14	1	0	1	0	1934-35	1937-38
Connor, Cam	Mtl., Edm., NYR	5	89	9	22	31	256	20	5	0	5	6	1978-79	1982-83
Connor, Harry	Bos., NYA, Ott.	4	134	16	5	21	139	10	0	0	0	2	1927-28	1930-31
Connors, Bobby	NYA, Det.	3	78	17	10	27	110	2	0	0	0	10	1926-27	1929-30
Contini, Joe	Col., Min.	3	68	17	21	38	34	2	0	0	0	0	1977-78	1980-81
Convey, Eddie	NYR	3	36	1	1	2	33	....	....	....	....	....	1930-31	1932-33
Cook, Bill	NYR	11	452	223	132	355	386	46	13	12	25	66	1926-27	1936-37
Cook, Bob	Van., Det., NYI, Min.	4	72	13	9	22	22	....	....	....	....	....	1970-71	1974-75
Cook, Bud	Bos., Ott., St.L.	3	51	5	4	9	22	....	....	....	....	....	1931-32	1934-35
Cook, Bun	NYR, Bos.	11	473	158	144	302	427	46	15	3	18	57	1926-27	1936-37
Cook, Lloyd	Bos.	1	4	1	0	1	0	....	....	....	....	....	1924-25	1924-25
Cook, Tom	Chi., Mtl.M.	8	311	72	89	161	169	24	2	4	6	17	1929-30	1937-38
Cooper, Carson	Bos., Mtl., Det.	8	278	110	57	167	111	4	0	0	0	2	1924-25	1931-32
Cooper, Ed	Col.	2	49	8	7	15	46	....	....	....	....	....	1980-81	1981-82
Cooper, Hal	NYR	1	8	0	0	0	2	....	....	....	....	....	1944-45	1944-45
Cooper, Joe	NYR, Chi.	11	420	30	66	96	442	32	3	5	8	6	1935-36	1946-47
Copp, Bob	Tor.	2	40	3	9	12	26	....	....	....	....	....	1942-43	1950-51
Corbeau, Bert	Mtl.. Ham., Tor.,	10	257	65	33	98	589	14	2	0	2	10	1917-18	1926-27
Corbett, Michael	L.A.	1	....	....	....	....	....	2	0	1	1	2	1967-68	1967-68
Corcoran, Norm	Bos., Det., Chi.	4	29	1	3	4	21	4	0	0	0	6	1949-50	1955-56
Cormier, Roger	Mtl.	1	0	0	0	0	0	....	....	....	....	....	1925-26	1925-26
Corrigan, Charlie	Tor., NYA	2	19	2	2	4	2	....	....	....	....	....	1937-38	1940-41
Corrigan, Mike	L.A., Van., Pit.	10	594	152	195	347	698	17	2	3	5	20	1967-68	1977-78
Corriveau, Andre	Mtl.	1	3	0	1	1	0	....	....	....	....	....	1953-54	1953-54
Cory, Ross	Wpg.	2	51	2	10	12	41	....	....	....	....	....	1979-80	1980-81
Cossete, Jacques	Pit.	3	64	8	6	14	29	3	0	1	1	4	1975-76	1978-79
Costello, Les	Tor.	3	15	2	3	5	11	6	2	2	4	2	1947-48	1949-50
Costello, Murray	Chi., Bos., Det.	4	162	13	19	32	54	5	0	0	0	2	1953-54	1956-57
Costello, Rich	Tor.	2	12	2	2	4	2	....	....	....	....	....	1983-84	1985-86
Cotch, Charlie	Ham.	1	11	1	0	1	0	....	....	....	....	....	1924-25	1924-25
Cote, Alain	Que.	10	696	103	190	293	383	67	9	15	24	44	1979-80	1988-89
Cote, Ray	Edm.	3	15	0	0	0	4	14	3	2	5	0	1982-83	1984-85
Cotton, Baldy	Pit., Tor., NYA	12	500	101	103	204	419	43	4	9	13	46	1925-26	1936-37
Coughlin, Jack	Tor., Que, Mtl., Ham.	3	19	2	0	2	0	....	....	....	....	....	1917-18	1920-21
Coulis, Tim	Wsh., Min.	4	47	4	5	9	138	3	1	0	1	2	1979-80	1985-86
Coulson, D'arcy	Phi.	1	28	0	0	0	103	....	....	....	....	....	1930-31	1930-31
Coulter, Art	Chi., NYR	11	465	30	82	112	563	49	4	5	9	61	1931-32	1941-42
Coulter, Neal	NYI	3	26	5	5	10	11	1	0	0	0	0	1985-86	1987-88
Coulter, Tommy	Chi.	1	2	0	0	0	0	....	....	....	....	....	1933-34	1933-34
Cournoyer, Yvan	Mtl.	16	968	428	435	863	255	147	64	63	127	47	1963-64	1978-79
Courteau, Yves	Cgy., Hfd.	3	22	2	5	7	4	1	0	0	0	0	1984-85	1986-87
Couture, Billy	Mtl., Ham., Bos.	10	239	33	18	51	350	32	2	0	2	42	1917-18	1926-27
Couture, Gerry	Det., Mtl., Chi.,	10	385	86	70	156	89	45	9	7	16	4	1944-45	1953-54
Couture, Rosie	Chi., Mtl.	8	304	48	56	104	184	23	1	5	6	15	1928-29	1935-36
Cowan, Tommy	Phi.	1	1	0	0	0	0	....	....	....	....	....	1930-31	1930-31
Cowick, Bruce	Phi., Wsh., St.L.	3	70	5	6	11	43	8	0	0	0	9	1973-74	1975-76
Cowley, Bill	St.L., Bos.	13	549	195	353	548	174	64	13	33	46	22	1934-35	1946-47
Cox, Danny	Tor., Ott., Det., NYR, St.L.	9	329	47	49	96	110	10	0	1	1	6	1926-27	1934-35
Crashley, Bart	Det., K.C., L.A.	6	140	7	36	43	50	....	....	....	....	....	1965-66	1975-76
Crawford, Bob	St.L., Hfd., NYR, Wsh.	7	246	71	71	142	72	11	0	1	1	8	1979-80	1986-87
Crawford, Bobby	Col., Det.	2	16	1	3	4	6	....	....	....	....	....	1980-81	1982-83
Crawford, John	Bos.	13	547	38	140	178	202	66	4	13	17	36	1937-38	1949-50
Crawford, Marc	Van.	6	176	19	31	50	229	20	1	2	3	44	1981-82	1986-87
Crawford, Rusty	Ott., Tor.,	2	38	10	3	13	51	2	2	1	3	0	1917-18	1918-19
Creighton, Dave	Bos., Chi., Tor., NYR	12	615	140	174	314	223	51	11	13	24	20	1948-49	1959-60
Creighton, Jimmy	Det.,	1	11	1	0	1	2	....	....	....	....	....	1930-31	1930-31
Cressman, Dave	Min.	2	85	6	8	14	37	....	....	....	....	....	1974-75	1975-76
Cressman, Glen	Mtl.	1	4	0	0	0	2	....	....	....	....	....	1956-57	1956-57
Crisp, Terry	Bos., St.L., Phi., NYI	11	536	67	134	201	135	110	15	28	43	40	1965-66	1976-77
Croghen, Maurice	Mtl.M.	1	16	0	0	0	4	....	....	....	....	....	1937-38	1937-38
Crombeen, Mike	Cle., St.L., Hfd.	8	475	55	68	123	218	27	6	2	8	32	1977-78	1984-85
Crossett, Stan	Phi.,	1	21	0	0	0	10	....	....	....	....	....	1930-31	1930-31
Croteau, Gary	L.A., Det., Cal., K.C., Col.	12	684	144	175	319	143	11	3	2	5	8	1968-69	1979-80
Crowder, Bruce	Bos., Pit.	4	243	47	51	98	156	31	8	4	12	41	1981-82	1984-85
Crozier, Joe	Tor.,	1	5	0	3	3	2	....	....	....	....	....	1959-60	1959-60
Crutchfield, Nels	Mtl.	1	41	5	5	10	20	2	0	1	1	22	1934-35	1934-35
Cullen, Barry	Tor., Det.	5	219	32	52	84	111	6	0	0	0	2	1955-56	1959-60
Cullen, Brian	Tor., NYR	7	326	56	100	156	92	19	3	0	3	2	1954-55	1960-61
Cullen, Ray	NYR, Det., Min., Van.	6	313	92	123	215	120	20	3	10	13	2	1965-66	1970-71
Cummins, Barry	Cal.	1	36	1	2	3	39	....	....	....	....	....	1973-74	1973-74
Cunningham, Bob	NYR	2	4	0	1	1	0	....	....	....	....	....	1960-61	1961-62
Cunningham, Jim	Phi.	1	1	0	0	0	4	....	....	....	....	....	1977-78	1977-78
Cunningham, Les	NYA, Chi.	2	60	7	19	26	21	1	0	0	0	2	1936-37	1939-40
Cupolo, Bill	Bos.	1	47	11	13	24	10	7	1	2	3	0	1944-45	1944-45
Currie, Glen	Wsh., L.A.	8	326	39	79	118	100	12	1	3	4	4	1979-80	1987-88
Currie, Hugh	Mtl.	1	1	0	0	0	0	....	....	....	....	....	1950-51	1950-51
Currie, Tony	St.L., Hfd., Van.	8	290	92	119	211	83	16	4	12	16	14	1977-78	1984-85
Curry, Floyd	Mtl.	11	601	105	99	204	147	91	23	17	40	38	1947-48	1957-58
Curtale, Tony	Cgy.	1	2	0	0	0	0	....	....	....	....	....	1980-81	1980-81
Curtis, Paul	Mtl., L.A., St.L.	4	185	3	34	37	151	5	0	0	0	2	1969-70	1972-73
Cushenan, Ian	Chi., Mtl., NYR, Det.	5	129	3	11	14	134	....	....	....	....	....	1956-57	1963-64
Cusson, Jean	Oak.	1	2	0	0	0	0	....	....	....	....	....	1967-68	1967-68
Cyr, Denis	Cgy., Chi., St.L.	6	193	41	43	84	36	4	0	0	0	0	1980-81	1985-86
Cyr, Paul	Buf., NYR	7	383	89	124	213	497	18	3	6	9	21	1982-83	1988-89

D

Dahlin, Kjell	Mtl.	3	166	57	59	116	10	35	6	11	17	6	1985-86	1987-88
Dahlstrom, Cully	Chi.	8	342	88	118	206	58	29	6	8	14	4	1937-38	1944-45
Daigle, Alain	Chi.	6	389	56	50	106	122	17	0	1	1	0	1974-75	1979-80
Dailey, Bob	Van., Phi.	9	561	94	231	325	814	63	12	34	46	106	1973-74	1981-82
Daley, Frank	Det.	1	5	0	0	0	0	2	0	0	0	0	1928-29	1928-29
Daley, Pat	Wpg.	2	12	1	0	1	13	....	....	....	....	....	1979-80	1980-81
Dalgarno, Brad	NYI	4	95	14	18	32	144	5	0	1	1	19	1985-86	1988-89
Dallman, Marty	Tor.	2	6	0	1	1	0	....	....	....	....	....	1987-88	1988-89
Dame, Bunny	Mtl.	1	34	2	5	7	4	....	....	....	....	....	1941-42	1941-42
Damore, Hank	NYR	1	4	1	0	1	2	....	....	....	....	....	1943-44	1943-44
Dark, Michael	St.L.	2	43	5	6	11	14	....	....	....	....	....	1986-87	1987-88
Darragh, Harry	Pit., Phi., Bos., Tor.	8	308	68	49	117	50	16	1	3	4	4	1925-26	1932-33
Darragh, Jack	Ott.	6	120	68	21	89	84	21	14	2	16	7	1917-18	1923-24
David, Richard	Que.	3	31	4	4	8	10	1	0	0	0	0	1979-80	1982-83
Davidson, Bob	Tor.,	12	491	94	160	254	398	82	5	17	22	79	1934-35	1945-46
Davidson, Gord	NYR	2	51	3	6	9	8	....	....	....	....	....	1942-43	1943-44
Davie, Bob	Bos.	3	41	0	1	1	25	....	....	....	....	....	1933-34	1935-36
Davies, Ken	NYR	1	....	....	....	....	....	1	0	0	0	0	1947-48	1947-48
Davis, Bob	Det.	1	3	0	0	0	0	....	....	....	....	....	1932-33	1932-33
Davis, Kim	Pit., Tor.	4	36	5	7	12	12	4	0	0	0	0	1977-78	1980-81
Davis, Lorne	Mtl., Chi., Det., Bos.	6	95	8	12	20	20	18	3	1	4	10	1951-52	1959-60

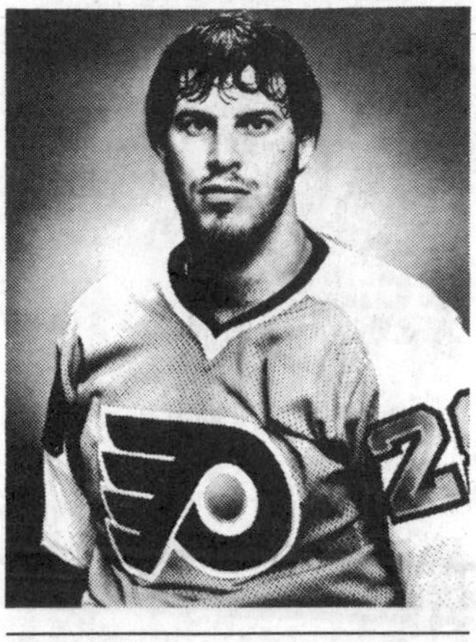

Glen Cochrane

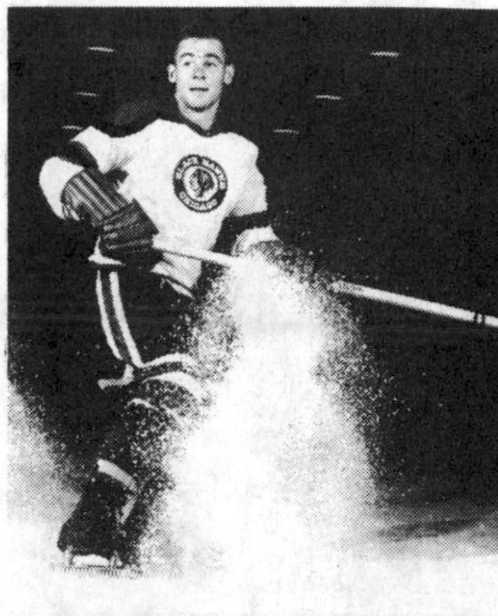

Pete Conacher

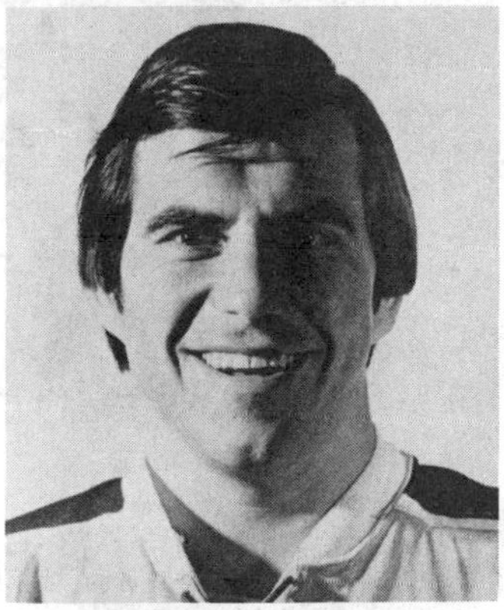

Gary Croteau

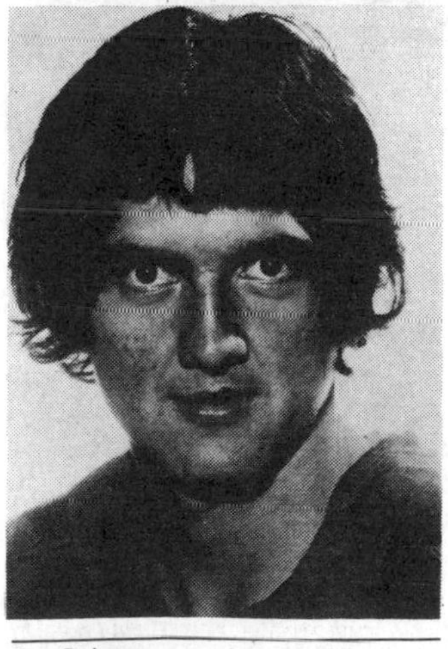

Ron Delorme

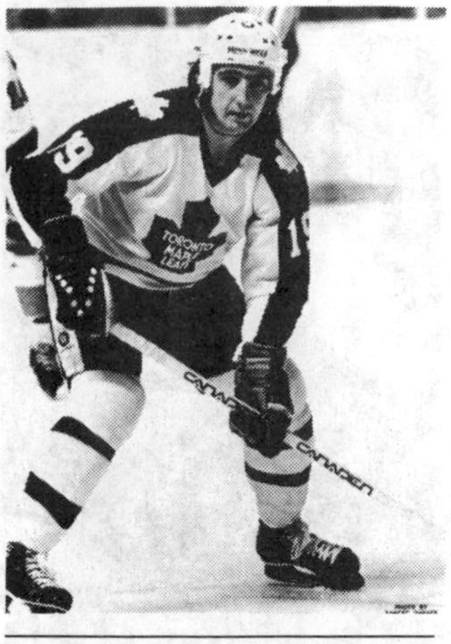
Bil Derlago

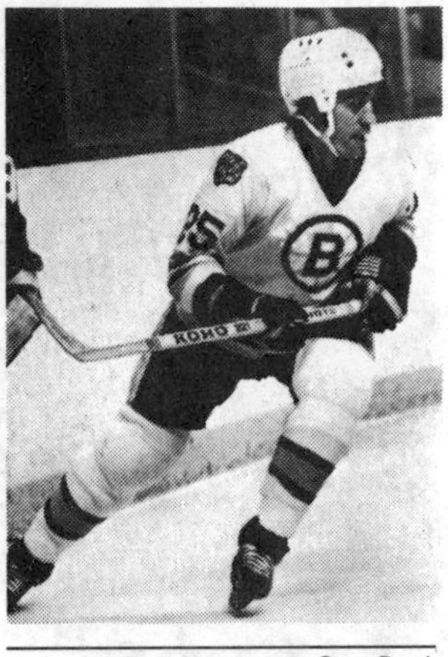
Gary Doak

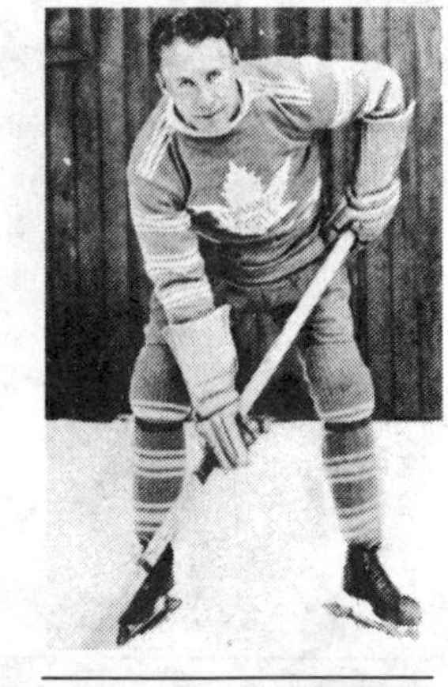
Ken Doraty

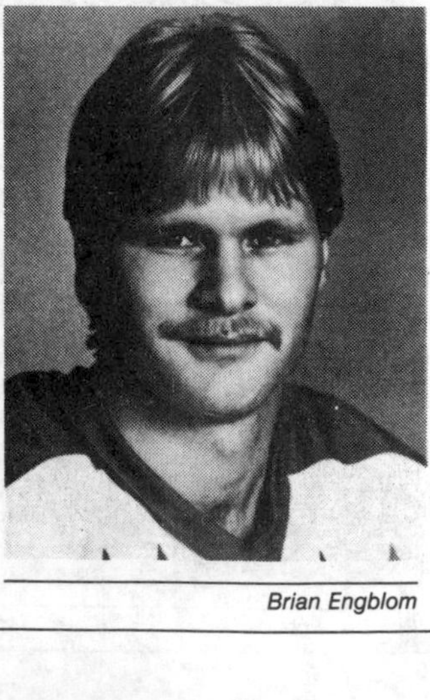
Brian Engblom

			Regular Schedule					Playoffs					Last	Last
Name	NHL Teams	NHL Seasons	GP	G	A	TP	PIM	GP	G	A	TP	PIM	NHL Season	Pro Season
Davis, Mal	Det., Buf.	5	100	31	22	53	34	7	1	0	1	0	1980-81	1985-86
Davison, Murray	Bos.	1	1	0	0	0	0	....	....	....	....	....	1965-66	1965-66
Dawes, Robert	Tor., Mtl.	4	32	2	7	4	6	10	0	0	0	2	1946-47	1950-51
Day, Hap	Tor., NYA	14	581	86	116	202	596	53	4	7	11	56	1924-25	1937-38
Dea, Billy	Chi., NYR, Det., Pit.	8	397	67	54	121	44	11	2	0	2	6	1953-54	1970-71
Deacon, Don	Det.	3	30	6	4	10	6	2	2	1	3	0	1936-37	1939-40
Deadmarsh, Butch	Buf., ATL, K.C.	5	137	12	5	17	155	4	0	0	0	17	1970-71	1974-75
Dean, Barry	Col., Phi.	3	165	25	56	81	146	....	....	....	....	....	1976-77	1978-79
Debenedet, Nelson	Det., Pit.	2	46	10	4	14	13	....	....	....	....	....	1973-74	1974-75
Debol, David	Hfd.	2	92	26	26	52	4	3	0	0	0	0	1979-80	1980-81
Defazio, Dean	Pit.	1	22	0	2	2	28	....	....	....	....	....	1983-84	1983-84
Delmonte, Armand	Bos.	1	1	0	0	0	0	....	....	....	....	....	1945-46	1945-46
Delorme, Ron	Col., Van.	9	524	83	83	166	667	25	1	2	3	59	1976-77	1984-85
Delory, Valentine	NYR	1	0	0	0	0	0	....	....	....	....	....	1948-49	1948-49
Delparte, Guy	Col.	1	48	1	8	9	18	....	....	....	....	....	1976-77	1976-77
Delvecchio, Alex	Det.	24	1549	456	825	1281	383	121	35	69	104	29	1950-51	1973-74
DeMarco, Ab	Chi., Tor., Bos., NYR	7	209	72	93	165	53	11	3	0	3	2	1938-39	1946-47
DeMarco, Albert	NYR, St.L., Pit., Van., L.A., Bos.	9	344	44	80	124	75	25	1	2	3	17	1969-70	1978-79
DeMeres, Tony	Mtl., NYR	6	83	20	22	42	23	3	0	0	0	0	1937-38	1943-44
Denis, Johnny	NYR	2	10	0	2	2	2	....	....	....	....	....	1946-47	1949-50
Denis, Lulu	Mtl.	2	3	0	1	1	0	....	....	....	....	....	1949-50	1950-51
Denneny, Corbett	Tor., Ham., Chi.	9	175	99	29	128	130	15	7	4	11	6	1917-18	1927-28
Denneny, Cy	Ott., Bos.	12	326	250	69	319	176	37	18	3	21	31	1917-18	1928-29
Dennis, Norm	St.L.	4	12	3	0	3	11	5	0	0	0	2	1968-69	1971-72
Denoird, Gerry	Tor.	1	15	0	0	0	0	....	....	....	....	....	1922-23	1922-23
Derlago, Bill	Van., Bos., Wpg., Que., Tor.	9	555	189	227	416	247	13	5	0	5	8	1978-79	1986-87
Desaulniers, Gerard	Mtl.	3	8	0	2	2	4	....	....	....	....	....	1950-51	1953-54
Desilets, Joffre	Mtl., Chi.	5	192	37	45	82	57	7	1	0	1	7	1935-36	1939-40
Desjardins, Vic	Chi., NYR	2	87	6	15	21	27	16	0	0	0	0	1930-31	1931-32
Deslauriers, Jacques	Mtl.	1	2	0	0	0	0	....	....	....	....	....	1955-56	1955-56
Devine, Kevin	NYI	1	2	0	1	1	8	....	....	....	....	....	1982-83	1982-83
Dewar, Tom	NYR	1	9	0	2	2	4	....	....	....	....	....	1943-44	1943-44
Dewsbury, Al	Det., Chi.	9	347	30	78	108	365	14	1	5	6	60	1946-47	1955-56
Deziel, Michel	Buf.	1	....	....	....	....	....	1	0	0	0	0	1974-75	1974-75
Dheere, Marcel	Mtl.	1	11	1	2	3	2	5	0	0	0	6	1942-43	1942-43
Diachuk, Edward	Det.	1	12	0	0	0	19	....	....	....	....	....	1960-61	1960-61
Dick, Harry	Chi.	1	12	0	1	1	12	....	....	....	....	....	1946-47	1946-47
Dickens, Ernie	Tor., Chi.	6	278	12	44	56	48	13	0	0	0	4	1941-42	1950-51
Dickenson, Herb	NYR	2	48	18	17	35	10	....	....	....	....	....	1951-52	1952-53
Dietrich, Don	Chi., N.J.	2	28	0	7	7	10	....	....	....	....	....	1983-84	1985-86
Dill, Bob	NYR	2	76	15	15	30	135	....	....	....	....	....	1943-44	1944-45
Dillabough, Bob	Det., Bos., Pit., Oak.	7	283	32	54	86	76	17	3	0	3	0	1961-62	1969-70
Dillon, Cecil	NYR, Det.	10	453	167	131	298	105	43	14	9	23	14	1930-31	1939-40
Dillon, Gary	Col.	1	13	1	1	2	29	....	....	....	....	....	1980-81	1980-81
Dillon, Wayne	NYR, Wpg.	4	229	43	66	109	60	3	0	1	1	0	1975-76	1979-80
Dineen, Bill	Det., Chi.	5	323	51	44	95	122	37	1	1	2	18	1953-54	1957-58
Dineen, Gary	Min.	1	4	0	1	1	0	....	....	....	....	....	1968-69	1968-69
Dinsmore, Chuck	Mtl.M	4	100	6	2	8	44	12	1	0	1	6	1924-25	1929-30
Dionne, Marcel	Det., L.A., NYR	18	1348	731	1040	1771	600	49	21	24	45	17	1971-72	1988-89
Doak, Gary	Det., Bos., Van., NYR	16	789	23	107	130	908	78	2	4	6	121	1965-66	1980-81
Dobson, Jim	Min., Col.	3	11	0	0	0	6	....	....	....	....	....	1979-80	1981-82
Doherty, Fred	Mtl.	1	3	0	0	0	0	....	....	....	....	....	1918-19	1918-19
Donaldson, Gary	Chi.	1	1	0	0	0	0	....	....	....	....	....	1973-74	1973-74
Donnelly, Babe	Mtl.M.	1	34	0	1	1	14	2	0	0	0	0	1926-27	1926-27
Donnelly, Dave	Bos., Chi., Edm.	5	137	15	24	39	150	5	0	0	0	0	1983-84	1987-88
Doran, Red (l.)	Det.	1	24	3	2	5	10	....	....	....	....	....	1946-47	1946-47
Doran, Red (J.)	NYA., Det., Mtl.	5	98	5	10	15	110	3	0	0	0	0	1933-34	1939-40
Doraty, Ken	Chi., Tor., Det.	5	103	15	26	41	24	15	7	2	9	2	1926-27	1937-38
Dore, Andre	NYR, St.L., Que.	7	257	14	81	95	261	23	1	2	3	32	1978-79	1984-85
Dorey, Jim	Tor., NYR	4	232	25	74	99	553	11	0	2	2	40	1968-69	1971-72
Dornhoefer, Gary	Bos., Phi.	14	787	214	328	542	1291	80	17	19	36	203	1963-64	1977-78
Dorohoy, Eddie	Mtl.	1	16	0	0	0	6	....	....	....	....	....	1948-49	1948-49
Douglas, Jordy	Hfd., Min., Wpg.	6	268	76	62	138	160	6	0	0	0	4	1979-80	1984-85
Douglas, Kent	Tor., Oak., Det.	7	428	33	115	148	631	19	1	3	4	33	1962-63	1968-69
Douglas, Les	Det.	4	52	6	12	18	8	10	3	2	5	0	1940-41	1946-47
Downie, Dave	Tor.	1	11	0	1	1	2	....	....	....	....	....	1932-33	1932-33
Draper, Bruce	Tor.	1	1	0	0	0	0	....	....	....	....	....	1962-63	1962-63
Drillon, Gordie	Tor., Mtl.	7	311	155	139	294	56	50	26	15	41	10	1936-37	1942-43
Driscoll, Pete	Edm.	2	60	3	8	11	97	3	0	0	0	0	1979-80	1980-81
Drolet, Rene	Phi., Det.	2	2	0	0	0	0	....	....	....	....	....	1971-72	1974-75
Drouillard, Clarence	Det.	1	10	0	1	1	0	....	....	....	....	....	1937-38	1937-38
Drouin, Jude	Mtl., Min., NYI, Wpg.	12	666	151	305	456	346	72	27	41	68	33	1968-69	1980-81
Drouin, Polly	Mtl.	6	173	27	57	84	80	5	0	1	1	5	1935-36	1940-41
Drummond, John	NYR	1	2	0	0	0	0	....	....	....	....	....	1944-45	1944-45
Drury, Herb	Pit., Phi.	6	213	24	13	37	203	4	1	1	2	0	1925-26	1930-31
Dube, Gilles	Mtl.., Det.	2	12	1	2	3	2	2	0	0	0	0	1949-50	1953-54
Dube, Norm	K.C.	2	57	8	10	18	54	....	....	....	....	....	1974-75	1975-76
Dudley, Rick	Buf., Wpg.	6	309	75	99	174	292	25	7	2	9	69	1972-73	1980-81
Duff, Dick	Tor., NYR, Mtl., L.A., Buf.	18	1030	283	289	572	743	114	30	49	79	78	1954-55	1971-72
Dufour, Luc	Bos., Que., St.L.	3	167	23	21	44	199	18	1	0	1	32	1982-83	1984-85
Dufour, Marc	NYR, L.A.	3	14	1	0	1	2	....	....	....	....	....	1963-64	1968-69
Duggan, Jack	Ott.	1	27	0	0	0	0	2	0	0	0	0	1925-26	1925-26
Duggan, Ken	Min.	1	1	0	0	0	0	....	....	....	....	....	1987-88	1987-88
Duguid, Lorne	Mtl.M, Det., Bos.	6	135	9	15	24	57	2	0	0	0	4	1931-32	1936-37
Dumart, Woodie	Bos.	16	771	211	218	429	99	82	12	15	27	23	1935-36	1953-54
Dunbar, Dale	Van., Bos.	2	2	0	0	0	2	....	....	....	....	....	1985-86	1988-89
Duncan, Art	Det., Tor.	5	156	18	16	34	225	5	0	0	0	4	1926-27	1930-31
Dunlap, Frank	Tor.	1	15	0	1	1	2	....	....	....	....	....	1943-44	1943-44
Dunlop, Blake	Min., Phi., St.L., Det.	11	550	130	274	404	172	40	4	10	14	18	1973-74	1983-84
Dunn, Dave	Van., Tor.	3	184	14	41	55	313	10	1	1	2	41	1973-74	1975-76
Dupere, Denis	Tor., Wsh., St.L., K.C., Col.	8	421	80	99	179	66	16	1	0	1	0	1970-71	1977-78
Dupont, Andre	NYR, St.L., Phi., Que.	13	810	59	185	244	1986	140	14	18	32	352	1970-71	1982-83
Dupont, Jerome	Chi., Tor.	6	214	7	29	36	468	20	0	2	2	56	1981-82	1986-87
Dupont, Norm	Mtl., Wpg., Hfd.	5	256	55	85	140	52	13	4	2	6	0	1979-80	1983-84
Durbano, Steve	St.L., Pit., K.C., Col.	6	220	13	60	73	1127	5	0	2	2	8	1972-73	1978-79
Duris, Vitezslav	Tor.	2	89	3	20	23	62	3	0	1	1	2	1980-81	1982-83
Dussault, Norm	Mtl.	4	206	31	62	93	47	7	3	1	4	0	1947-48	1950-51
Dutkowski, Duke	Chi., NYA, NYR	5	200	16	30	46	172	6	0	0	0	6	1926-27	1933-34
Dutton, Red	Mtl.M, NYA	10	449	29	67	96	871	18	1	0	1	33	1926-27	1935-36
Dvorak, Miroslav	Phi.	3	193	11	74	85	51	18	0	2	2	6	1982-83	1984-85
Dwyer, Mike	Col., Cgy.	4	31	2	6	8	25	1	1	0	1	0	1978-79	1981-82
Dyck, Henry	NYR	1	1	0	0	0	0	....	....	....	....	....	1943-44	1943-44
Dye, Babe	Tor., Ham., Chi., NYA	11	271	200	41	241	200	15	11	2	13	11	1919-20	1930-31
Dyte, John	Chi.	1	27	1	0	1	31	....	....	....	....	....	1943-44	1943-44

E

Eakin, Bruce	Cgy., Det.	4	13	2	2	4	4	....	....	....	....	....	1981-82	1985-86
Eatough, Jeff	Buf.	1	1	0	0	0	0	....	....	....	....	....	1981-82	1981-82
Eaves, Mike	Min., Cgy.	8	324	83	143	226	80	43	7	10	17	14	1978-79	1985-86
Ecclestone, Tim	St.L., Det., Tor., Atl.	11	692	126	233	359	346	48	6	11	17	76	1967-68	1977-78
Edberg, Rolf	Wsh.	3	184	45	58	103	24	....	....	....	....	....	1978-79	1980-81
Eddolls, Frank	Mtl., NYR	8	317	23	43	66	114	31	0	2	2	10	1944-45	1951-52
Edestrand, Darryl	St.L., Phi., Pit., Bos., L.A.	10	455	34	90	124	404	42	3	9	12	57	1967-68	1978-79
Edmundson, Garry	Mtl., Tor.	3	43	4	6	10	49	11	0	1	1	8	1951-52	1960-61
Edur, Tom	Col., Pit	2	158	17	70	87	67	....	....	....	....	....	1976-77	1977-78
Egan, Pat	NYA, Det., Bos., NYR	11	554	77	153	230	776	44	9	4	13	44	1939-40	1950-51
Egers, Jack	NYR, St.L., Wsh.	7	284	64	69	133	154	32	5	6	11	32	1969-70	1975-76
Ehman, Gerry	Bos., Det., Tor., Oak, Cal.	9	429	96	118	214	100	41	10	10	20	12	1957-58	1970-71
Eldebrink, Anders	Van., Que.	2	55	3	11	14	29	14	0	0	0	0	1981-82	1982-83
Elik, Boris	Det.	1	3	0	0	0	0	....	....	....	....	....	1962-63	1962-63
Elliot, Fred	Ott.	1	43	2	0	2	6	....	....	....	....	....	1928-29	1928-29
Ellis, Ron	Tor.	16	1034	332	308	640	207	70	18	8	26	20	1963-64	1980-81
Eloranta, Kari	Cgy., St.L.	5	267	13	103	116	155	26	1	7	8	19	1981-82	1986-87

Name	NHL Teams	NHL Seasons	Regular Schedule GP	G	A	TP	PIM	Playoffs GP	G	A	TP	PIM	First NHL Season	Last NHL Season
Emberg, Eddie	Mtl.	1	....	....	....	....	....	2	1	0	1	0	1944-45	1944-45
Emms, Hap	Mtl.M, NYA, Det., Bos.	10	320	37	53	90	311	14	0	0	0	12	1926-27	1937-38
Engblom, Brian	Mtl., Wsh., L.A., Buf., Cgy.	11	659	29	177	206	599	48	3	9	12	43	1976-77	1986-87
Engele, Jerry	Min.	3	100	2	13	15	162	2	0	1	1	0	1975-76	1977-78
English, John	L.A.	1	3	1	3	4	4	1	0	0	0	0	1987-88	1987-88
Erickson, Aut	Bos., Chi., Oak., Tor.	7	227	7	84	31	182	7	0	0	0	2	1959-60	1969-70
Erickson, Bryan	Wsh., L.A., Pit.	5	278	74	102	176	121	11	3	4	7	7	1983-84	1987-88
Erickson, Grant	Bos., Min.	2	6	1	0	1	4	....	....	....	....	....	1968-69	1969-70
Eriksson, Rolie	Min., Van.	3	193	48	95	143	26	2	1	0	1	0	1976-77	1978-79
Eriksson, Thomas	Phi.	5	208	22	76	98	107	19	0	3	3	6	1980-81	1985-86
Esposito, Phi.	Chi., Bos., NYR	18	1282	717	873	1590	910	130	61	76	137	137	1963-64	1980-81
Evans, Chris	Tor., Buf., St.L., Det., K.C.	5	241	19	42	61	143	12	1	1	2	8	1969-70	1974-75
Evans, Daryl	L.A., Wsh., Tor.	6	113	22	30	52	25	11	5	8	13	12	1981-82	1986-87
Evans, Jack	NYR, Chi.	14	752	19	80	99	989	56	2	2	4	97	1948-49	1962-63
Evans, John	Phi.	3	103	14	25	39	34	1	0	0	0	0	1978-79	1982-83
Evans, Paul	Tor.	2	11	1	1	2	21	2	0	0	0	0	1976-77	1977-78
Evans, Stewart	Det., Mtl., Mtl.M	8	367	28	49	77	425	26	0	0	0	20	1930-31	1938-39
Ezinicki, Bill	Tor., Bos., NYR	9	368	79	105	184	713	40	5	8	13	87	1944-45	1954-55
F														
Fahey, Trevor	NYR	1	1	0	0	0	0	....	....	....	....	....	1964-65	1964-65
Fairbairn, Bill	NYR, Min. St.L.	11	658	162	261	423	173	54	13	22	35	42	1968-69	1978-79
Falkenberg, Bob	Det.	5	54	1	5	6	26	....	....	....	....	....	1966-67	1971-72
Farrant, Walt	Chi.	1	1	0	0	0	0	....	....	....	....	....	1943-44	1943-44
Farrish, Dave	NYR, Que, Tor.	7	430	17	110	127	440	14	0	2	2	24	1976-77	1983-84
Fashoway, Gordie	Chi.	1	13	3	2	5	14	....	....	....	....	....	1950-51	1950-51
Faubert, Mario	Pit.	7	231	21	90	111	292	10	2	2	4	6	1974-75	1981-82
Faulkner, Alex	Tor., Det.	3	101	15	17	32	15	12	5	0	5	2	1961-62	1963-64
Fauss, Ted	Tor.	2	28	0	2	2	15	....	....	....	....	....	1986-87	1987-88
Feamster, Dave	Chi.	4	169	13	24	37	155	33	3	5	8	61	1981-82	1984-85
Featherstone, Tony	Oak., Cal., Min.	3	130	17	21	38	65	2	0	0	0	0	1969-70	1973-74
Feltrin, Tony	Pit., NYR	4	48	3	3	6	65	....	....	....	....	....	1980-81	1985-86
Ferguson	Chi.	1	1	0	0	0	0	....	....	....	....	....	1939-40	1939-40
Ferguson, George	Tor., Pit, Min	12	797	160	238	398	431	86	14	23	37	44	1972-73	1983-84
Ferguson, John	Mtl.	8	500	145	158	303	1214	85	20	18	38	260	1963-64	1970-71
Ferguson, Lorne	Bos., Det., Chi.	8	422	82	80	162	193	31	6	3	9	24	1949-50	1958-59
Ferguson, Norm	Oak., Cal.	4	279	73	66	139	72	10	1	4	5	7	1968-69	1971-72
Ferner, Mark	Buf.	1	13	0	3	3	9	....	....	....	....	....	1986-87	1986-87
Fidler, Mike	Cle., Min, Hfd., Chi.	7	271	84	97	181	124	....	....	....	....	....	1976-77	1982-83
Field, Wilf	NYA, Mtl., Chi.	6	218	17	25	42	151	3	0	0	0	0	1936-37	1944-45
Fielder, Guyle	Det., Chi.	4	36	0	0	0	2	6	0	0	0	2	1950-51	1957-58
Fillion, Bob	Mtl.	7	327	37	61	98	84	33	7	4	11	10	1943-44	1949-50
Fillion, Marcel	Bos.	1	1	0	0	0	0	....	....	....	....	....	1944-45	1944-45
Filmore, Tommy	Det., NYA, Bos.	4	116	15	12	27	33	....	....	....	....	....	1930-31	1933-34
Finkbeiner, Lloyd	NYA	1	1	0	0	0	0	....	....	....	....	....	1940-41	1940-41
Finney, Sid	Chi.	3	59	10	7	17	4	7	0	0	0	2	1951-52	1953-54
Finnigan, Ed	Bos.	1	3	0	0	0	0	....	....	....	....	....	1935-36	1935-36
Finnigan, Frank	Ott., Tor., St.L.	14	555	115	88	203	405	39	6	9	15	22	1923-24	1936-37
Fischer, Ron	Buf.	2	18	0	7	7	6	....	....	....	....	....	1981-82	1982-83
Fisher, Alvin	Tor.	1	9	1	0	1	4	....	....	....	....	....	1924-25	1924-25
Fisher, Dunc	NYR, Bos., Det.	7	275	45	70	115	10	21	4	4	8	14	1947-48	1958-59
Fisher, Joe	Det.	4	66	8	12	20	13	15	2	1	3	6	1939-40	1942-43
Fitchner, Bob	Que	2	78	12	20	32	59	3	0	0	0	10	1979-80	1980-81
Fitzpatrick, Sandy	NYR, Min.	2	22	3	6	9	8	12	0	0	0	0	1061-65	1967-68
Flaman, Fern	Bos., Tor.	17	910	34	174	208	1370	63	4	8	12	93	1944-45	1960-61
Fleming, Reggie	Mtl., Chi., Bos., NYR, Phi., Buf.	12	749	108	132	240	1468	50	3	6	9	106	1959-60	1970-71
Flesch	Ham.	1	1	0	0	0	0	....	....	....	....	....	1920-21	1920-21
Flesch, John	Min, Pit, Col.	4	124	18	23	41	117	....	....	....	....	....	1974-75	1979-80
Flett, Bill	L.A., Phi., Tor., Atl, Edm.	11	689	202	215	417	501	52	7	16	23	42	1967-68	1979-80
Flockhart, Rob	Van., Min	5	55	2	5	7	14	1	1	0	1	2	1976-77	1980-81
Floyd, Larry	N.J.	2	12	2	3	5	9	....	....	....	....	....	1982-83	1983-84
Fogolin, Lee	Buf., Edm.	13	924	44	195	239	1318	108	5	19	24	173	1974-75	1986-87
Fogolin, Lidio (Lee)	Det., Chi.	9	427	10	48	58	575	28	0	2	2	30	1947-48	1955-56
Folco, Peter	Van.	1	2	0	0	0	0	....	....	....	....	....	1973-74	1973-74
Foley, Gerry	Tor., NYR, L.A.	4	142	9	14	23	99	9	0	1	1	2	1954-55	1968-69
Foley, Rick	Chi., Phi., Det.	3	67	11	26	37	180	4	0	1	1	4	1970-71	1973-74
Folk, Bill	Det.	2	12	0	0	0	4	....	....	....	....	....	1951-52	1952-53
Fontaine, Len	Det.	2	46	8	11	19	10	....	....	....	....	....	1972-73	1973-74
Fontas, Jon	Min.	2	2	0	0	0	0	....	....	....	....	....	1979-80	1980-81
Fonteyne, Val	Det., NYR, Pit.	13	820	75	154	229	26	59	3	10	13	8	1959-60	1971-72
Fontinato, Louie	NYR, Mtl.	9	535	26	78	104	1247	21	0	2	2	42	1954-55	1962-63
Forbes, Dave	Bos., Wsh.	6	363	64	64	128	341	45	1	4	5	13	1973-74	1978-79
Forbes, Mike	Bos., Edm.	3	50	1	11	12	41	....	....	....	....	....	1977-78	1981-82
Forey, Connie	St.L.	1	4	0	0	0	2	....	....	....	....	....	1973-74	1973-74
Forsey, Jack	Tor.	1	19	7	9	16	10	3	0	1	1	0	1942-43	1942-43
Forslund, Gus	Ott.	1	48	4	9	13	2	....	....	....	....	....	1932-33	1932-33
Forsyth, Alex	Wsh.	1	1	0	0	0	0	....	....	....	....	....	1976-77	1976-77
Fortier, Charles	Mtl.	1	1	0	0	0	0	....	....	....	....	....	1923-24	1923-24
Fortier, Dave	Tor., NYI, Van.	4	205	8	21	29	335	20	0	2	2	33	1972-73	1976-77
Fortin, Ray	St.L.	3	92	2	6	8	33	6	0	0	0	8	1967-68	1969-70
Foster, Dwight	Bos., Col., N.J., Det.	10	541	111	163	274	420	35	5	12	17	4	1977-78	1986-87
Foster, Herb	NYR	2	5	1	0	1	5	....	....	....	....	....	1940-41	1947-48
Foster, Harry	NYR, Bos., Det.	4	83	3	2	5	32	....	....	....	....	....	1929-31	1934-35
Fowler, Jimmy	Tor.	3	135	18	29	47	39	18	0	3	3	2	1936-37	1938-39
Fowler, Tom	Chi.	1	24	0	1	1	18	....	....	....	....	....	1946-47	1946-47
Fox, Greg	Atl, Chi., Pit.	8	494	14	92	106	637	44	1	9	10	67	1977-78	1984-85
Foyston, Frank	Det.	2	64	17	7	24	32	....	....	....	....	....	1926-27	1927-28
Frampton, Bob	Mtl.	1	2	0	0	0	0	3	0	0	0	0	1949-50	1949-50
Francis, Bobby	Det.	1	14	2	0	2	0	....	....	....	....	....	1982-83	1982-83
Fraser, Archie	NYR	1	3	0	1	1	0	....	....	....	....	....	1943-44	1943-44
Fraser, Gord	Chi., Det., Mtl., Pit., Phi.	5	144	24	12	36	224	2	1	0	1	6	1926-27	1930-31
Fraser, Harry	Chi.	1	21	5	4	9	0	....	....	....	....	....	1944-45	1944-45
Fraser, Jack	Ham.	1	1	0	0	0	0	....	....	....	....	....	1923-24	1923-24
Frederickson, Frank	Det., Bos., Pit.	5	165	39	34	73	206	10	2	5	7	26	1926-27	1930-31
Frew, Irv	Mtl.M, St.L., Mtl.	3	95	2	5	7	146	4	0	0	0	6	1933-34	1935-36
Friday, Tim	Det.	1	23	0	3	3	6	....	....	....	....	....	1985-86	1985-86
Fridgen, Dan	Hfd.	2	13	2	3	5	2	....	....	....	....	....	1981-82	1982-83
Friest, Ron	Min.	3	64	7	7	14	191	6	1	0	1	7	1980-81	1982-83
Frig, Len	Chi., Cal., Cle., St.L.	7	311	13	51	64	479	14	2	1	3	0	1972-73	1979-80
Frost, Harry	Bos.	1	3	0	0	0	0	1	0	0	0	0	1938-39	1938-39
Fryday, Bob	Mtl.	2	5	1	0	1	0	....	....	....	....	....	1949-50	1951-52
Ftorek, Robbie	Det., Que, NYR	8	334	77	150	227	262	19	9	6	15	28	1972-73	1984-85
Fullan, Lawrence	Wsh.	1	4	1	0	1	0	....	....	....	....	....	1974-75	1974-75
Fusco, Mark	Hfd.	2	80	3	12	15	42	....	....	....	....	....	1983-84	1984-85
G														
Gadsby, Bill	Chi., NYR, Det.	20	1248	130	437	567	1539	67	4	23	27	92	1946-47	1965-66
Gagne, Art	Mtl., Bos., Ott., Det.	6	228	67	33	100	257	11	2	1	3	20	1926-27	1931-32
Gagne, Pierre	Bos.	1	2	0	0	0	0	....	....	....	....	....	1959-60	1959-60
Gagnon, Germaine	Mtl., NYI, Chi., K.C.	5	259	40	101	141	72	49	2	3	5	2	1971-72	1975-76
Gagnon, Johnny	Mtl., Bos., NYA	10	454	120	141	261	295	32	12	12	24	37	1930-31	1939-40
Gainey, Bob	Mtl.	16	1160	239	262	501	585	182	25	48	73	151	1973-74	1988-89
Gainor, Dutch	Bos., NYR, Ott., Mtl.M	7	243	51	56	107	129	25	2	1	3	14	1927-28	1934-35
Galarneau, Michel	Hfd.	3	78	7	10	17	34	....	....	....	....	....	1980-81	1982-83
Galbraith, Percy	Bos., Ott.	8	347	29	31	60	223	31	4	7	11	24	1926-27	1933-34
Gallagher, John	Mtl.M, Det., NYA	7	204	14	19	33	153	22	2	3	5	27	1930-31	1938-39
Gallimore, Jamie	Min.	1	2	0	0	0	0	....	....	....	....	....	1977-78	1977-78
Gallinger, Don	Bos.	5	222	65	88	153	89	23	5	5	10	19	1942-43	1947-48
Gamble, Dick	Mtl., Chi., Tor.	8	195	41	41	82	66	14	1	2	3	4	1950-51	1966-67
Gambucci, Gary	Min.	2	51	2	7	9	9	....	....	....	....	....	1971-72	1973-74
Gans, Dave	L.A.	2	6	0	0	0	2	....	....	....	....	....	1982-83	1985-86

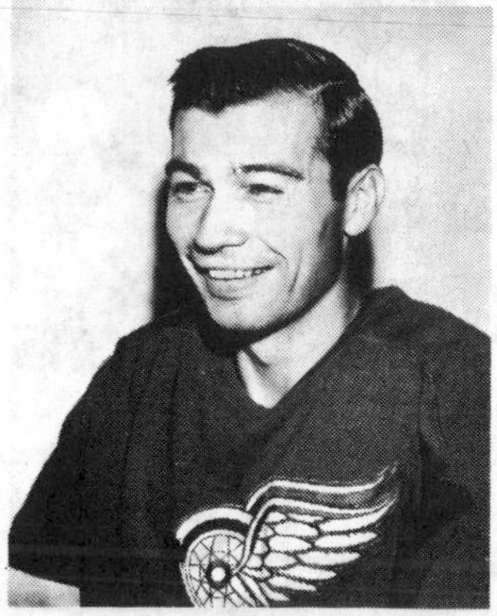
Guyle Fielder

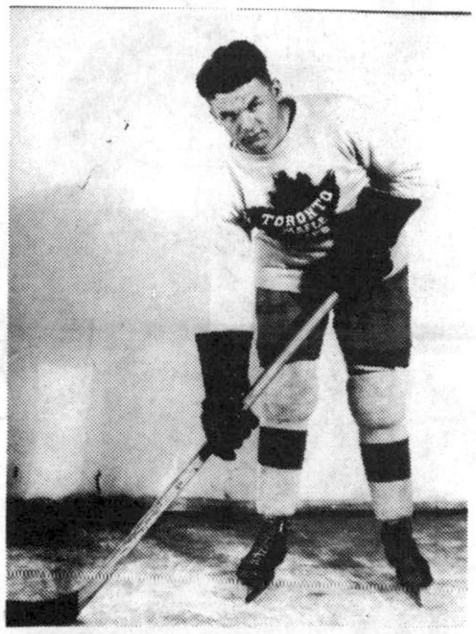
Frank Finnigan

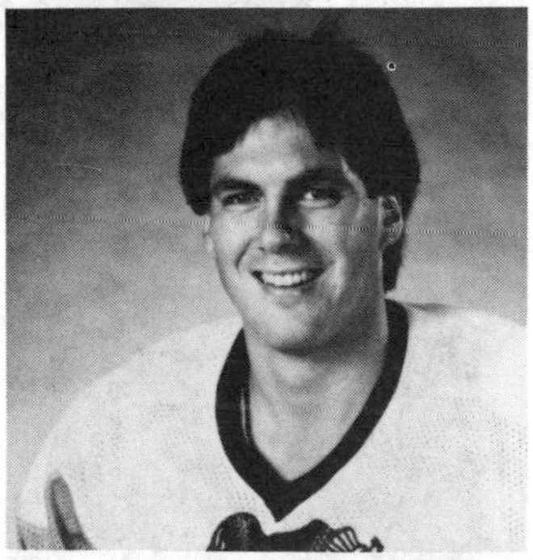
Dan Frawley

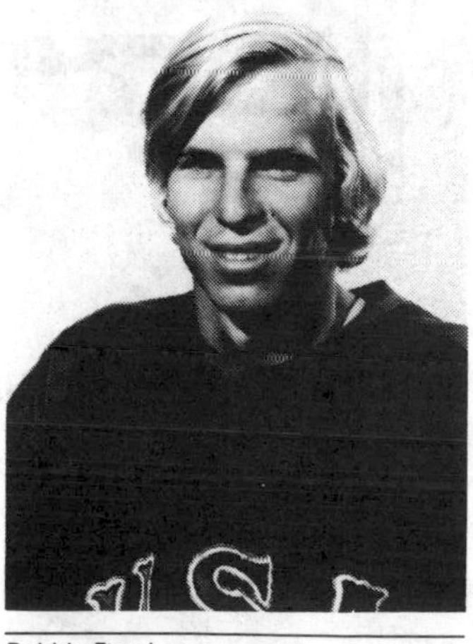
Robbie Ftorek

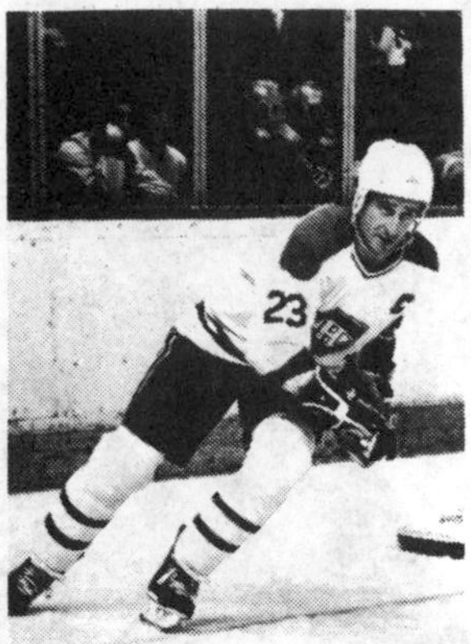

Bob Gainey

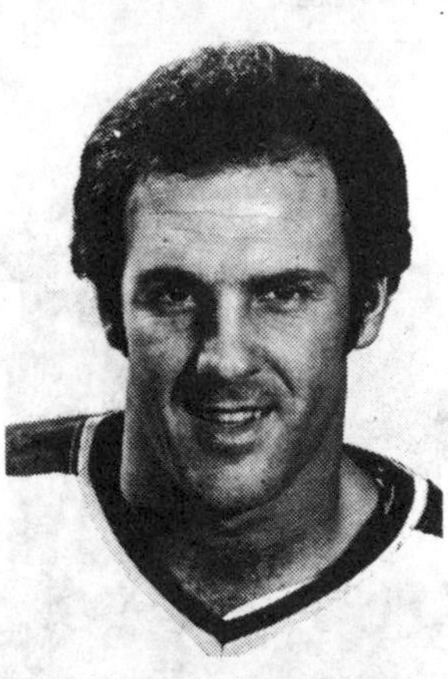

Gary Gambucci

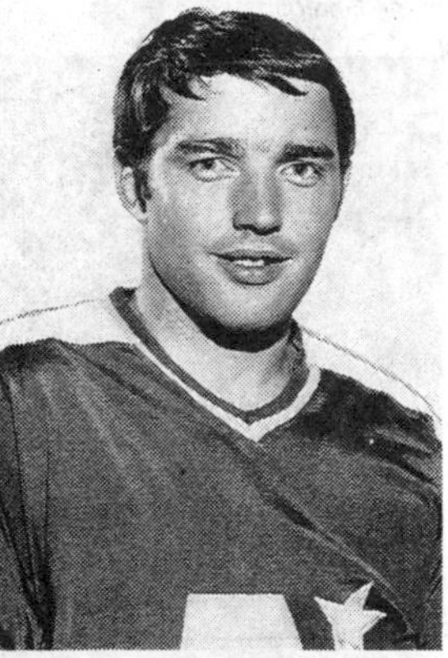

Danny Grant

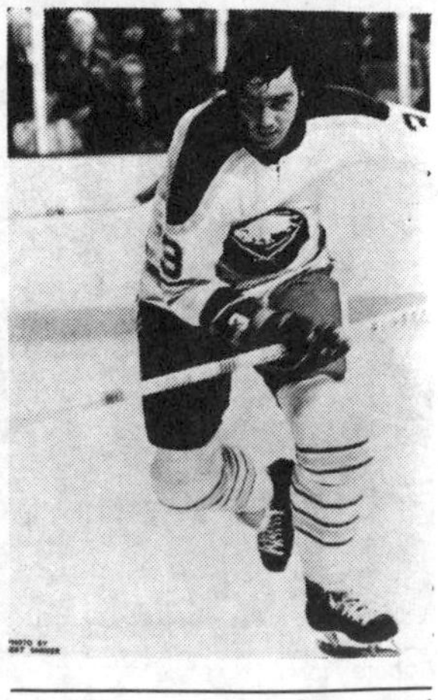

Jocelyn Guevremont

Name	NHL Teams	NHL Seasons	Regular Schedule					Playoffs					First NHL Season	Last NHL Season
			GP	G	A	TP	PIM	GP	G	A	TP	PIM		
Gardiner, Herb	Mtl., Chi.	3	101	10	9	19	52	7	0	1	1	14	1926-27	1928-29
Gardner, Bill	Chi., Hfd.	9	380	73	115	188	68	45	3	8	11	17	1980-81	1988-89
Gardner, Cal	NYR, Tor., Chi., Bos.	12	696	154	238	392	517	61	7	10	17	20	1945-46	1956-57
Gardner, Dave	Mtl., St.L., Cal., Cle., Phi.	7	350	75	115	190	41	....	....	....	....	....	1972-73	1979-80
Gardner, Paul	Col., Tor., Pit., Wsh., Buf.	7	447	201	201	402	207	16	2	6	8	14	1976-77	1985-86
Gare, Danny	Buf., Det., Edm.	13	827	354	331	685	1285	64	25	21	46	195	1974-75	1986-87
Gariepy, Ray	Bos., Tor.	2	36	1	6	7	43	....	....	....	....	....	1953-54	1955-56
Garland, Scott	Tor., L.A.	3	91	13	24	37	115	7	1	2	3	35	1975-76	1978-79
Garner, Bob	Pit.	1	1	0	0	0	0	....	....	....	....	....	1982-83	1982-83
Garrett, Red	NYR	1	23	1	1	2	18	....	....	....	....	....	1942-43	1942-43
Gassoff, Bob	St.L.	4	245	11	47	58	866	9	0	1	1	16	1973-74	1976-77
Gassoff, Brad	Van.	4	122	19	17	36	163	3	0	0	0	0	1975-76	1978-79
Gatzos, Steve	Pit.	4	89	15	20	35	83	1	0	0	0	0	1981-82	1984-85
Gaudreault, Armand	Bos.	1	44	15	9	24	27	7	0	2	2	8	1944-45	1944-45
Gaudreault, Leo	Mtl.	3	67	8	4	12	30	....	....	....	....	....	1927-28	1932-33
Gaulin, Jean-Marc	Que.	4	26	4	3	7	8	1	0	0	0	0	1982-83	1985-86
Gauthier, Art	Mtl.	1	13	0	0	0	0	1	0	0	0	0	1926-27	1926-27
Gauthier, Fern	NYR, Mtl., Det.	6	229	46	50	96	35	22	5	1	6	7	1943-44	1948-49
Gauthier, Jean	Mtl., Phi., Bos.	10	166	6	29	35	150	14	1	3	4	22	1960-61	1969-70
Gauvreau, Jocelyn	Mtl.	1	2	0	0	0	0	....	....	....	....	....	1983-84	1983-84
Geale, Bob	Pit.	1	1	0	0	0	2	....	....	....	....	....	1984-85	1984-85
Gee, George	Chi., Det.	9	551	135	183	318	345	41	6	13	19	32	1945-46	1953-54
Geldart, Gary	Min.	1	4	0	0	0	5	....	....	....	....	....	1970-71	1970-71
Gendron, Jean-Guy	NYR, Mtl., Bos., Phi.	14	863	182	201	383	701	42	7	4	11	47	1955-56	1971-72
Geoffrion, Bernie	Mtl., NYR	16	883	393	429	822	689	132	58	60	118	88	1950-51	1967-68
Geoffrion, Danny	Mtl., Wpg., Que.	3	111	20	32	52	99	2	0	0	0	7	1979-80	1981-82
Geran, Gerry	Mtl.W., Bos.	2	37	5	1	6	6	....	....	....	....	....	1917-18	1925-26
Gerard, Eddie	Ott.	6	128	50	30	80	99	26	7	3	10	51	1917-18	1922-23
Getliffe, Ray	Bos., Mtl.	10	393	136	137	273	280	45	9	10	19	30	1935-36	1944-45
Giallonardo, Mario	Col.	2	23	0	3	3	6	....	....	....	....	....	1979-80	1980-81
Gibbs, Barry	Bos., Min., Atl., St.L., L.A.	13	797	58	224	282	945	36	4	2	6	67	1967-68	1979-80
Gibson, Doug	Bos., Wsh.	3	63	9	19	28	0	1	0	0	0	0	1973-74	1977-78
Gibson, John	L.A., Wpg.	3	48	0	2	2	120	....	....	....	....	....	1980-81	1983-84
Giesebrecht, Gus	Det.	4	135	27	51	78	13	17	2	3	5	0	1938-39	1941-42
Gilbert, Ed	K.C., Pit.	3	166	21	31	52	22	....	....	....	....	....	1974-75	1976-77
Gilbert, Jean	Bos.	2	9	0	0	0	4	....	....	....	....	....	1962-63	1964-65
Gilbert, Rod	NYR	18	1065	406	615	1021	508	79	34	33	67	43	1960-61	1977-78
Gilbertson, Stan	Wsh., Pit., Cal., St.L.	6	428	85	89	174	148	3	1	1	2	2	1971-72	1976-77
Gillen, Don	Phi., Hfd.	2	35	2	4	6	22	....	....	....	....	....	1979-80	1981-82
Gillie, Ferrand	Det.	1	1	0	0	0	0	....	....	....	....	....	1928-29	1928-29
Gillies, Clark	NYI, Buf.	14	958	319	378	697	1023	164	47	47	94	287	1974-75	1987-88
Gillis, Jere	Que., Buf., Phi., Van., NYR	9	386	78	95	173	230	19	4	7	11	9	1977-78	1986-87
Gillis, Mike	Col., Bos.	6	246	33	43	76	186	27	2	5	7	10	1978-79	1983-84
Girard, Bob	Wsh., Cal., Cle.	5	305	45	69	114	140	....	....	....	....	....	1975-76	1979-80
Girard, Kenny	Tor.	3	7	0	1	1	2	....	....	....	....	....	1956-57	1959-60
Giroux, Art	Det., Mtl., Bos.	3	54	6	4	10	14	2	0	0	0	0	1932-33	1935-36
Giroux, Larry	Det., Hfd., St.L., K.C.	7	274	15	74	89	333	5	0	0	0	4	1973-74	1979-80
Giroux, Pierre	L.A.	1	6	1	0	1	17	....	....	....	....	....	1982-83	1982-83
Gladney, Bob	L.A., Pit.	2	14	1	5	6	4	....	....	....	....	....	1982-83	1983-84
Gladu, Jean	Bos.	1	40	6	14	20	2	7	2	2	4	0	1944-45	1944-45
Glennie, Brian	Tor., L.A.	10	572	14	100	114	621	32	0	1	1	66	1969-70	1978-79
Gloeckner, Lorry	Det.	1	13	0	2	2	6	....	....	....	....	....	1978-79	1978-79
Gloor, Dan	Van.	1	2	0	0	0	0	....	....	....	....	....	1973-74	1973-74
Glover, Fred	Det., Chi.	4	92	13	11	24	62	3	0	0	0	0	1948-49	1952-53
Glover, Howie	Chi., Det., NYR, Mtl.	5	144	29	17	46	101	11	1	2	3	2	1958-59	1968-69
Godden, Ernie	Tor.	1	5	1	1	2	6	....	....	....	....	....	1981-82	1981-82
Godfrey, Warren	Bos., Det.	16	786	32	125	157	752	52	1	4	5	42	1952-53	1967-68
Godin, Eddy	Wsh.	2	27	3	6	9	12	....	....	....	....	....	1977-78	1978-79
Godin, Sammy	Ott., Mtl.	3	83	4	3	7	36	....	....	....	....	....	1927-28	1933-34
Goegan, Peter	Det., NYR, Min.	11	383	19	67	86	365	33	1	3	4	61	1957-58	1967-68
Goldham, Bob	Tor., Chi., Det.	12	650	28	143	171	400	66	3	14	17	53	1941-42	1955-56
Goldsworthy, Bill	Bos., Min., NYR	14	771	283	258	541	793	40	18	19	37	30	1964-65	1977-78
Goldsworthy, Leroy	NYR, Det., Chi., Mtl., Bos., NYA	9	337	66	57	123	79	22	1	0	1	4	1929-30	1938-39
Goldup, Glenn	Mtl., L.A.	9	291	52	67	119	303	16	4	3	7	22	1973-74	1981-82
Goldup, Hank	Tor., NYR	6	181	57	76	133	95	26	5	1	6	6	1939-40	1945-46
Gooden, Bill	NYR	2	53	9	11	20	15	....	....	....	....	....	1942-43	1943-44
Goodenough, Larry	Phi., Van.	6	242	22	77	99	179	22	3	15	18	10	1974-75	1979-80
Goodfellow, Ebbie	Det.	14	554	134	190	324	516	45	8	8	16	65	1929-30	1942-43
Gordon, Fred	Det., Bos.	2	77	8	7	15	68	1	0	0	0	0	1926-27	1927-28
Gordon, Jackie	NYR	3	36	3	10	13	0	9	1	1	2	7	1948-49	1950-51
Gorence, Tom	Phi., Edm.	6	303	58	53	111	89	37	9	6	15	47	1978-79	1983-84
Goring, Butch	L.A., NYI, Bos.	16	1107	375	513	888	102	134	38	50	88	32	1969-70	1984-85
Gorman, Dave	Atl.	1	3	0	0	0	0	....	....	....	....	....	1979-80	1979-80
Gorman, Ed	Ott., Tor.	4	111	14	5	19	108	8	0	0	0	2	1924-25	1927-28
Gosselin, Benoit	NYR	1	7	0	0	0	33	....	....	....	....	....	1977-78	1977-78
Gottselig, Johnny	Chi.	16	589	177	195	372	225	43	13	13	26	20	1928-29	1944-45
Gould, John	Buf., Van., Atl.	9	504	131	138	269	113	14	3	2	5	4	1971-72	1979-80
Gould, Larry	Van.	1	2	0	0	0	0	....	....	....	....	....	1973-74	1973-74
Goupille, Red	Mtl.	8	222	12	28	40	256	8	2	0	2	6	1935-36	1942-43
Goyer, Gerry	Chi.	1	40	1	2	3	4	3	0	0	0	2	1967-68	1967-68
Goyette, Phil	Mtl., NYR, St.L., Buf.	16	941	207	467	674	131	94	17	29	46	26	1956-57	1971-72
Graboski, Tony	Mtl.	3	66	6	10	16	18	2	0	0	0	0	1940-41	1942-43
Gracie, Bob	Tor., Bos., NYA, Mtl., Mtl.M., Chi.	9	378	82	109	191	207	33	4	7	11	4	1930-31	1938-39
Gradin, Thomas	Van., Bos.	9	677	209	384	593	298	42	17	25	42	20	1978-79	1986-87
Graham, Leth	Ott., Ham.	6	26	3	0	3	0	1	0	0	0	0	1920-21	1925-26
Graham, Pat	Pit., Tor.	3	103	11	17	28	136	4	0	0	0	2	1981-82	1983-84
Graham, Rod	Bos.	1	14	2	1	3	7	....	....	....	....	....	1974-75	1974-75
Graham, Ted	Chi., Mtl.M., Det., St.L., Bos., NYA	9	343	14	25	39	300	23	3	1	4	34	1927-28	1936-37
Grant, Danny	Mtl., Det., Min., L.A.	13	736	263	273	536	239	43	10	14	24	19	1965-66	1978-79
Gratton, Norm	NYR, Atl., Buf., Min.	5	201	39	44	83	64	6	0	1	1	2	1971-72	1975-76
Gravelle, Leo	Mtl., Det.	5	223	44	34	78	42	17	4	1	5	2	1946-47	1950-51
Graves, Hilliard	Cal., Atl., Van., Wpg.	9	556	118	163	281	209	2	0	0	0	0	1970-71	1979-80
Gray, Alex	NYR, Tor.	2	50	7	0	7	30	13	1	0	1	0	1927-28	1928-29
Gray, Terry	Bos., Mtl., L.A., St.L.	6	147	26	28	54	64	35	5	5	10	22	1961-62	1970-71
Green	Det.	1	2	0	0	0	0	....	....	....	....	....	1928-29	1928-29
Green, Red	Ham., NYA, Bos., Det.	6	195	59	13	72	261	....	....	....	....	....	1923-24	1928-29
Green, Ted	Bos.	11	620	48	206	254	1029	31	4	8	12	54	1960-61	1971-72
Green, Wilf	Ham., NYA	4	103	33	8	41	151	....	....	....	....	....	1923-24	1926-27
Greig, Bruce	Cal.	2	9	0	1	1	46	....	....	....	....	....	1973-74	1974-75
Grenier, Lucien	Mtl., L.A.	4	151	14	14	28	18	2	0	0	0	0	1968-69	1971-72
Grenier, Richard	NYI	1	10	1	1	2	2	....	....	....	....	....	1972-73	1972-73
Grigor, George	Chi.	1	2	1	0	1	0	1	0	0	0	0	1943-44	1943-44
Grisdale, John	Tor., Van.	6	250	4	39	43	346	10	0	1	1	15	1972-73	1978-79
Gronsdahl, Lloyd	Bos.	1	10	1	2	3	0	....	....	....	....	....	1941-42	1941-42
Gross, Llyod	Tor., NYA, Bos., Det.	3	62	11	5	16	20	1	0	0	0	0	1926-27	1934-35
Grosso, Don	Det., Chi., Bos.	9	334	86	116	202	90	50	14	12	26	46	1938-39	1946-47
Grosvenar, Len	Ott., NYA, Mtl.	6	147	9	11	20	78	4	0	0	0	2	1927-28	1932-33
Groulx, Wayne	Que.	1	1	0	0	0	0	....	....	....	....	....	1984-85	1984-85
Gruen, Danny	Det., Col.	3	49	9	13	22	19	....	....	....	....	....	1972-73	1976-77
Gryp, Bob	Bos., Wsh.	3	74	11	13	24	33	....	....	....	....	....	1973-74	1975-76
Guevremont, Jocelyn	Van., Buf., NYR	9	571	84	223	307	319	40	4	17	21	18	1971-72	1979-80
Guidolin, Aldo	NYR	4	182	9	15	24	117	....	....	....	....	....	1952-53	1955-56
Guidolin, Bep	Bos., Det., Chi.	9	519	107	171	278	606	24	5	7	12	35	1942-43	1951-52
Guindon, Bobby	Wpg.	1	6	0	1	1	0	....	....	....	....	....	1979-80	1979-80
Gustavsson, Peter	Col.	1	2	0	0	0	0	....	....	....	....	....	1981-82	1981-82

H

Hachborn, Len	Phi., L.A.	3	102	20	39	59	29	7	0	3	3	7	1983-84	1985-86
Haddon, Llyod	Det.	1	8	0	0	0	2	1	0	0	0	0	1959-60	1959-60
Hadfield, Vic	NYR, Pit.	16	1002	323	389	712	1154	73	27	21	48	117	1961-62	1976-77
Haggarty, Jim	Mtl.	1	5	1	1	2	0	3	2	1	3	0	1941-42	1941-42
Hagglund, Roger	Que.	1	3	0	0	0	0	....	....	....	....	....	1984-85	1984-85
Hagman, Matti	Bos., Edm.	4	237	56	89	145	36	20	5	2	7	6	1976-77	1981-82

Name	NHL Teams	NHL Seasons	Regular Schedule					Playoffs					First NHL Season	Last NHL Season
			GP	G	A	TP	PIM	GP	G	A	TP	PIM		
Haidy, Adam	Det.	1	....	....	....	....	....	1	0	0	0	0	1949-50	1949-50
Hajt, Bill	Buf.	14	854	42	202	244	433	80	2	16	18	70	1973-74	1986-87
Hakansson, Anders	Min., Pit., L.A.	5	330	52	46	98	141	6	0	0	0	2	1981-82	1985-86
Halderson, Slim	Det., Tor.	1	44	3	2	5	65	....	....	....	....	....	1926-27	1926-27
Hale, Larry	Phi.	4	196	5	37	42	90	8	0	0	0	12	1968-69	1971-72
Haley, Len	Det.	2	30	2	2	4	14	6	1	3	4	6	1959-60	1960-61
Hall, Bob	NYA	1	8	0	0	0	0	....	....	....	....	....	1925-26	1925-26
Hall, Del	Cal.	3	9	2	0	2	2	....	....	....	....	....	1971-72	1973-74
Hall, Joe	Mtl.	2	37	15	1	16	85	12	0	2	2	0	1917-18	1918-19
Hall, Murray	Chi., Det., Min., Van.	9	164	35	48	83	46	6	0	0	0	0	1961-62	1971-72
Hall, Wayne	NYR	1	4	0	0	0	0	....	....	....	....	....	1960-61	1960-61
Halliday, Milt	Ott.	3	67	1	0	1	6	6	0	0	0	0	1926-27	1928-29
Hallin, Mats	NYI, Min.	5	152	17	14	31	193	15	1	0	1	13	1982-83	1986-87
Halward, Doug	Bos., L.A., Van., Det., Edm.	14	653	69	224	293	774	47	7	10	17	113	1975-76	1988-89
Hamel, Gilles	Buf., Wpg., L.A.	9	519	127	147	274	276	27	4	5	9	10	1980-81	1988-89
Hamel, Herb	Tor.	1	2	0	0	0	14	....	....	....	....	....	1930-31	1930-31
Hamel, Jean	St.L., Det., Que., Mtl.	12	699	26	95	121	766	33	0	2	2	44	1972-73	1983-84
Hamill, Red	Bos., Chi.	12	442	128	94	222	160	13	1	2	3	12	1937-38	1950-51
Hamilton, Al	NYR, Buf., Edm.	7	257	10	78	88	258	7	0	0	0	2	1965-66	1979-80
Hamilton, Chuck	Mtl., St.L.	2	4	0	2	2	2	....	....	....	....	....	1961-62	1972-73
Hamilton, Jack	Tor.	3	138	31	48	79	76	11	2	1	3	0	1942-43	1945-46
Hamilton, Jim	Pit.	8	95	14	18	32	28	6	3	0	3	0	1977-78	1984-85
Hamilton, Reg	Tor., Chi.	12	387	18	71	89	412	64	6	6	12	54	1935-36	1946-47
Hammarstrom, Inge	Tor., St.L.	6	427	116	123	239	86	13	2	3	5	4	1973-74	1978-79
Hampson, Gord	Cgy.	1	4	0	0	0	5	....	....	....	....	....	1982-83	1982-83
Hampson, Ted	Tor., NYR, Det., Oak., Cal., Min.	12	676	108	245	353	94	35	7	10	17	2	1959-60	1971-72
Hampton, Rick	Cal., Cle., L.A.	6	337	59	113	172	147	2	0	0	0	0	1974-75	1979-80
Hamway, Mark	NYI	3	53	5	13	18	9	1	0	0	0	0	1984-85	1986-87
Hangsleben, Al	Hfd., Wsh., L.A.	3	185	21	48	69	396	....	....	....	....	....	1979-80	1981-82
Hanna, John	NYR, Mtl., Phi.	5	198	6	26	32	206	....	....	....	....	....	1958-59	1967-68
Hannigan, Gord	Tor.	4	161	29	31	60	117	9	2	0	2	8	1952-53	1955-56
Hannigan, Pat	Tor., NYR, Phi.	5	182	30	39	69	116	11	1	2	3	11	1959-60	1968-69
Hannigan, Ray	Tor.	1	3	0	0	0	2	....	....	....	....	....	1948-49	1948-49
Hansen, Ritchie	NYI, St.L.	4	20	2	8	10	6	....	....	....	....	....	1976-77	1981-82
Hanson, Dave	Det., Min.	2	33	1	1	2	65	....	....	....	....	....	1978-79	1979-80
Hanson, Emil	Det.	1	7	0	0	0	6	....	....	....	....	....	1932-33	1932-33
Hanson, Keith	Cgy.	1	25	0	2	2	77	....	....	....	....	....	1983-84	1983-84
Hanson, Ossie	Chi.	1	7	0	0	0	0	....	....	....	....	....	1937-38	1937-38
Harbaruk, Nick	Pit., St.L.	5	364	45	75	120	273	14	3	1	4	20	1969-70	1973-74
Hardy, Joe	Oak., Cal.	2	63	9	14	23	51	4	0	0	0	0	1969-70	1970-71
Hargreaves, Jim	Van.	2	66	1	7	8	105	....	....	....	....	....	1970-71	1972-73
Harmon, Glen	Mtl.	9	452	50	96	146	334	53	5	10	15	37	1942-43	1950-51
Harms, John	Chi.	2	44	5	5	10	21	3	3	0	3	2	1943-44	1944-45
Harnott, Happy	Bos.	1	6	0	0	0	6	....	....	....	....	....	1933-34	1933-34
Harper, Terry	Mtl., L.A., Det., St.L., Col.	19	1066	35	221	256	1362	112	4	13	17	140	1962-63	1980-81
Harrer, Tim	Cgy.	1	3	0	0	0	2	....	....	....	....	....	1982-83	1982-83
Harrington, Hago	Bos., Mtl.	3	72	9	3	12	15	4	1	0	1	2	1925-26	1932-33
Harris, Billy	Tor., Oak., Cal., Pit.	12	769	126	219	345	205	62	8	10	18	30	1955-56	1968-69
Harris, Billy	NYI, L.A., Tor.	12	897	231	327	558	394	71	19	19	38	48	1972-73	1983-84
Harris, Duke	Min., Tor.	1	26	1	4	5	4	....	....	....	....	....	1967-68	1967-68
Harris, Hugh	Buf.	1	60	12	26	38	17	3	0	0	0	0	1972-73	1972-73
Harris, Ron	Det., Oak., Atl., NYR	12	476	20	91	111	484	28	4	3	7	33	1962-63	1975-76
Harris, Smokey	Bos.	2	40	5	5	10	28	2	0	0	0	0	1924-25	1930-31
Harris, Tod	Mtl., Min., Det., St.L., Phi.	12	788	30	168	198	1000	100	1	22	23	230	1963-64	1974-75
Harrison, Ed	Bos., NYR	4	194	27	24	51	53	9	1	0	1	2	1947-48	1950-51
Harrison, Jim	Bos., Tor., Chi., Edm.	8	324	67	86	153	435	13	1	1	2	43	1968-69	1979-80
Hart, Gerry	Det., NYI, Que., St.L.	15	730	29	150	179	1240	78	3	12	15	175	1968-69	1982-83
Hart, Gizzy	Det., Mtl.	3	100	6	8	14	12	8	0	1	1	0	1926-27	1932-33
Hartsburg, Craig	Min.	10	570	98	315	413	818	61	15	27	42	70	1979-80	1988-89
Harvey, Doug	Mtl., NYR, Det., St.L.	20	1113	88	452	540	1216	137	8	64	72	152	1947-48	1968-69
Harvey, Fred	Min., Atl., K.C., Det.	7	407	90	118	208	131	14	0	2	2	8	1970-71	1976-77
Harvey, Hugh	K.C.	2	18	1	1	2	4	....	....	....	....	....	1974-75	1975-76
Hassard, Bob	Tor., Chi.	5	126	9	28	37	22	....	....	....	....	....	1949-50	1954-55
Hatoum, Ed	Det., Van.	3	47	3	6	9	25	....	....	....	....	....	1968-69	1970-71
Haworth, Alan	Buf., Wsh., Que.	8	524	189	211	400	425	42	12	16	28	28	1980-81	1987-88
Haworth, Gord	NYR	1	2	0	1	1	0	....	....	....	....	....	1952-53	1952-53
Hawryliw, Neil	NYI	1	1	0	0	0	0	....	....	....	....	....	1981-82	1981-82
Hay, Billy	Chi.	8	506	113	273	386	244	67	15	21	36	62	1959-60	1966-67
Hay, George	Chi., Det.	7	242	74	60	134	84	8	2	3	5	14	1926-27	1933-34
Hay, Jim	Det.	3	75	1	5	6	22	9	1	0	1	2	1952-53	1954-55
Hayek, Peter	Min.	1	1	0	0	0	0	....	....	....	....	....	1981-82	1981-82
Hayes, Chris	Bos.	1	....	....	....	....	....	1	0	0	0	0	1971-72	1971-72
Haynes, Paul	Mtl.M., Bos., Mtl.	11	390	61	134	195	164	25	2	8	10	13	1930-31	1940-41
Hazlett, Steve	Van.	1	1	0	0	0	0	....	....	....	....	....	1979-80	1979-80
Head, Galen	Det.	1	1	0	0	0	0	....	....	....	....	....	1967-68	1967-68
Headley, Fern	Bos., Mtl.	1	27	1	1	2	6	5	0	0	0	0	1924-25	1924-25
Healey, Dick	Det.	1	1	0	0	0	2	....	....	....	....	....	1960-61	1960-61
Heaslip, Mark	NYR, L.A.	3	117	10	19	29	110	5	0	0	0	2	1976-77	1978-79
Heath, Randy	NYR	2	13	2	4	6	15	....	....	....	....	....	1984-85	1985-86
Hebenton, Andy	NYR, Bos.	9	630	189	202	391	83	22	6	5	11	8	1955-56	1963-64
Hedberg, Anders	NYR	7	465	172	225	397	144	58	22	24	46	31	1978-79	1984-85
Heffernan, Frank	Tor.	1	17	0	0	0	4	....	....	....	....	....	1919-20	1919-20
Heffernan, Gerry	Mtl.	3	83	33	35	68	27	11	3	3	6	8	1941-42	1943-44
Heidt, Mike	L.A.	1	6	0	1	1	7	....	....	....	....	....	1983-84	1983-84
Heindl, Bill	Min., NYR	3	18	2	1	3	0	....	....	....	....	....	1970-71	1972-73
Heinrich, Lionel	Bos.	1	35	1	1	2	33	....	....	....	....	....	1955-56	1955-56
Heiskala, Earl	Phi.	3	127	13	11	24	294	....	....	....	....	....	1968-69	1970-71
Helander, Peter	L.A.	1	7	0	1	1	0	....	....	....	....	....	1982-83	1982-83
Heller, Ott.	NYR	15	647	55	176	231	465	61	6	8	14	61	1931-32	1945-46
Helman, Harry	Ott.	3	42	1	0	1	7	5	0	0	0	0	1922-23	1924-25
Helminen, Raimo	NYR, Min., NYI	3	117	13	46	59	16	2	0	0	0	0	1985-86	1988-89
Hemmerling, Tony	NYA	2	24	3	3	6	4	....	....	....	....	....	1935-36	1936-37
Henderson, Archie	Wsh., Min., Hfd.	3	23	3	1	4	92	....	....	....	....	....	1980-81	1982-83
Henderson, Murray	Bos.	8	405	24	62	86	305	41	2	3	5	23	1944-45	1951-52
Henderson, Paul	Det., Tor., Atl.	13	707	236	241	477	304	56	11	14	25	28	1962-63	1979-80
Hendrickson, John	Det.	3	5	0	0	0	4	....	....	....	....	....	1957-58	1961-62
Henning, Lorne	NYI	9	544	73	111	184	102	81	7	7	14	8	1972-73	1980-81
Henry, Camille	NYR, Chi., St.L.	14	727	279	249	528	88	47	6	12	18	7	1953-54	1969-70
Hepple, Alan	N.J.	3	3	0	0	0	7	....	....	....	....	....	1983-84	1985-86
Herberts, Jimmy	Bos., Tor., Det.	6	206	83	29	112	250	9	3	0	3	35	1924-25	1929-30
Herchenratter, Art	Det.	1	10	1	2	3	2	....	....	....	....	....	1940-41	1940-41
Hergerts, Fred	NYA	2	19	2	4	6	2	....	....	....	....	....	1934-35	1935-36
Hergesheimer, Philip	Chi., Bos.	4	125	21	41	62	19	7	0	0	0	2	1939-40	1942-43
Hergesheimer, Wally	NYR, Chi.	7	351	114	85	199	106	5	1	0	1	0	1951-52	1958-59
Heron, Red	Tor., NYA, Mtl.	4	106	21	19	40	38	16	2	2	4	55	1938-39	1941-42
Hess, Bob	St.L., Buf., Hfd.	8	329	27	95	122	178	4	1	1	2	2	1974-75	1983-84
Heximer, Orville	NYR, Bos., NYA	3	85	13	7	20	28	5	0	0	0	2	1929-30	1934-35
Hextall, Bryan Sr.	NYR	11	447	188	175	363	221	37	8	9	17	19	1936-37	1947-48
Hextall, Bryan Jr.	NYR, Pit., Atl., Det., Min.	8	549	99	161	260	738	18	0	4	4	59	1962-63	1975-76
Hextall, Dennis	NYR, L.A., Cal., Min., Det., Wsh.	13	681	153	350	503	1398	22	3	3	6	45	1968-69	1979-80
Heyliger, Vic	Chi.	2	34	2	3	5	2	....	....	....	....	....	1937-38	1943-44
Hicke, Bill	Mtl., NYR, Oak.	14	729	168	234	402	395	42	3	10	13	41	1958-59	1971-72
Hicke, Ernie	Cal., Atl., NYI, Min., L.A.	8	520	132	140	272	407	2	1	0	1	0	1970-71	1977-78
Hickey, Greg	NYR	1	1	0	0	0	0	....	....	....	....	....	1977-78	1977-78
Hickey, Pat	NYR, Col., Tor., Que., St.L.	10	646	192	212	404	351	55	5	11	16	37	1975-76	1984-85
Hicks, Doug	Min., Chi., Edm., Wsh.	9	561	37	131	168	442	....	....	....	....	....	1974-75	1982-83
Hicks, Glenn	Det.	2	108	6	12	18	127	....	....	....	....	....	1979-80	1980-81
Hicks, Hal	Mtl.M., Det.	3	110	7	2	9	72	....	....	....	....	....	1928-29	1930-31
Hicks, Wayne	Chi., Bos., Mtl., Phi., Pit.	5	115	13	23	36	22	2	0	1	1	2	1959-60	1967-68
Hidi, Andre	Wsh.	2	7	2	1	3	9	2	0	0	0	0	1983-84	1984-85
Hiemer, Ullie	N.J.	3	143	19	54	73	176	....	....	....	....	....	1984-85	1986-87
Higgins, Paul	Tor.	2	25	0	0	0	152	1	0	0	0	0	1981-82	1982-83
Higgins, Tim	Chi., N.J., Det.	11	706	154	198	352	719	65	5	8	13	77	1978-79	1988-89
Hildebrand, Ike	NYR, Chi.	2	41	7	11	18	16	....	....	....	....	....	1953-54	1954-55

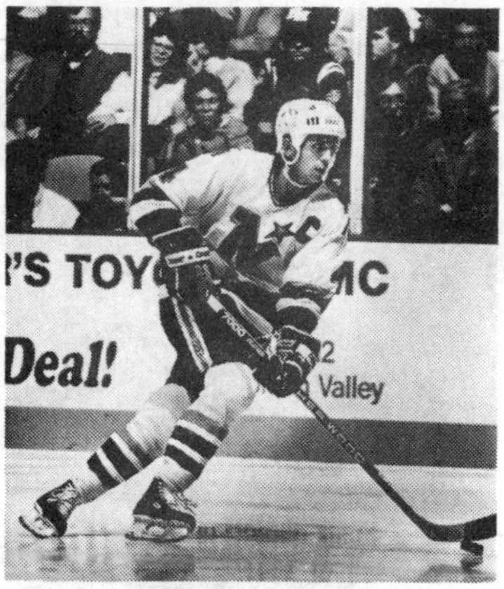

Craig Hartsburg

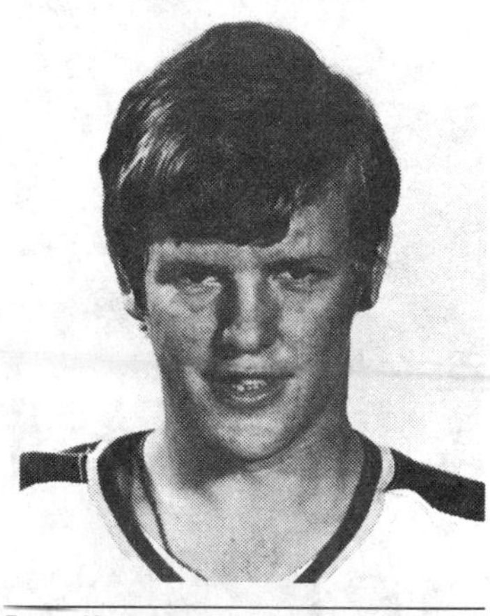
Buster Harvey

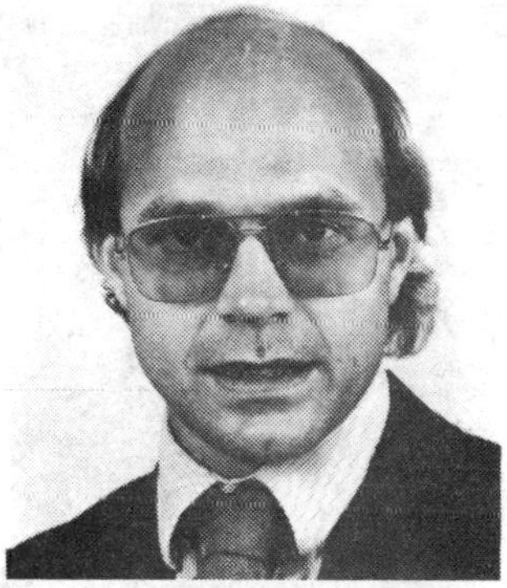
Lorne Henning

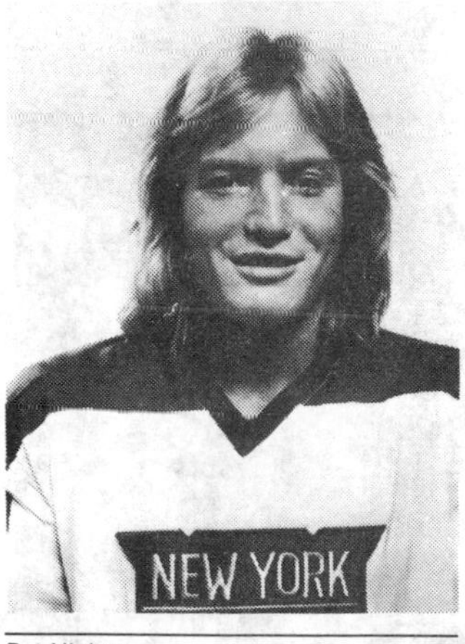

Pat Hickey

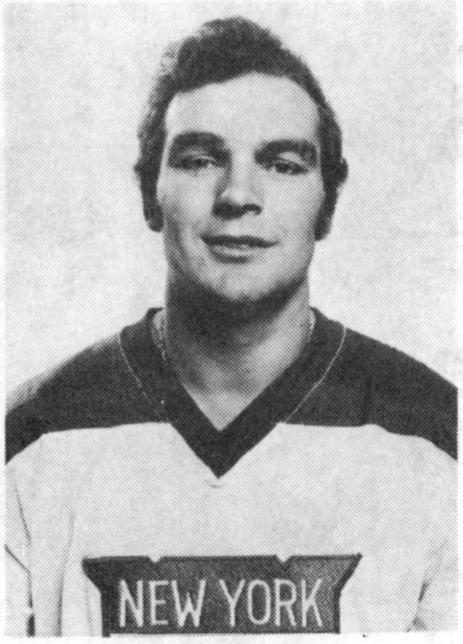

Ken Hodge

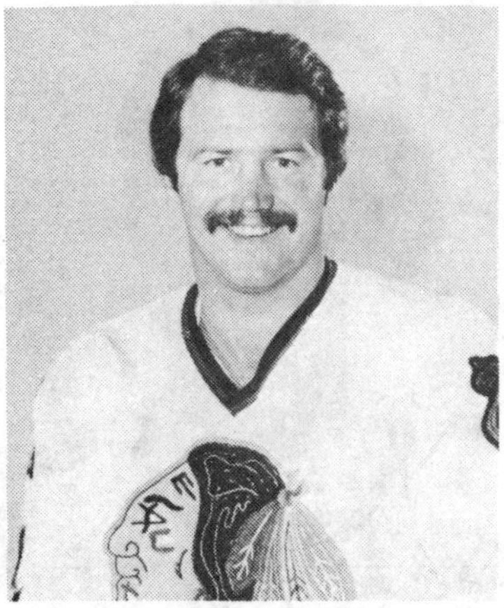

Randy Holt

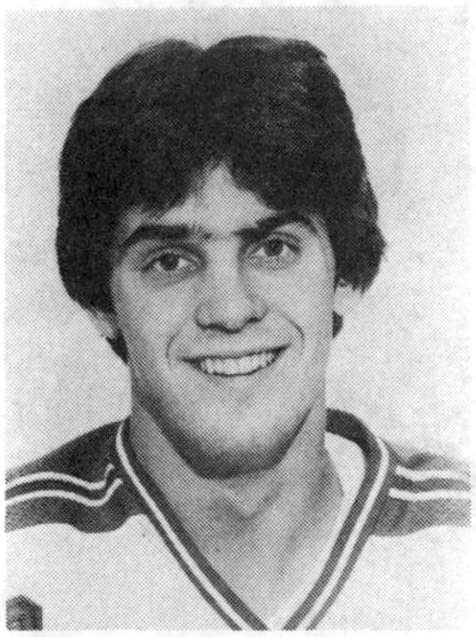

Ed Hospodar

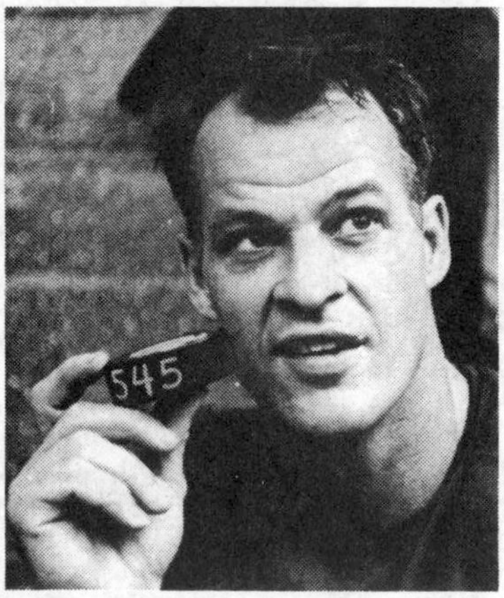

Gordie Howe

Name	NHL Teams	NHL Seasons	Regular Schedule GP	G	A	TP	PIM	Playoffs GP	G	A	TP	PIM	First NHL Season	Last NHL Season
Hill, Al	Phi.	8	221	40	55	95	227	51	8	11	19	43	1976-77	1987-88
Hill, Brian	Hfd.	1	19	1	1	2	4	....	....	....	....	....	1979-80	1979-80
Hill, Mel	Bos., NYA, Tor.	9	323	89	109	198	128	43	12	7	19	18	1937-38	1945-46
Hiller, Dutch	NYR, Det., Bos., Mtl.	9	385	91	113	204	163	48	9	8	17	21	1937-38	1945-46
Hillman, Floyd	Bos.	1	6	0	0	0	10	....	....	....	....	....	1956-57	1956-57
Hillman, Larry		19790	36	196	232	579	74	2	9	11	30	19 5	1972-73	
	Det., Bos., Tor., Min., Mtl., Phi., L.A., Buf.											4- 55		
Hillman, Wayne	Chi., NYR, Min., Phi.	13	691	18	86	104	534	28	0	3	3	19	1960-61	1972-73
Hilworth, John	Det.	3	57	1	1	2	89	....	....	....	....	....	1977-78	1979-80
Himes, Normie	NYA	9	402	106	113	219	127	2	0	0	0	0	1926-27	1934-35
Hindmarch, Dave	Cgy.	4	99	21	17	38	25	10	0	0	0	6	1980-81	1983-84
Hinse, Andre	Tor.	1	4	0	0	0	0	....	....	....	....	....	1967-68	1967-68
Hinton, Dan	Chi.	1	14	0	0	0	16	....	....	....	....	....	1976-77	1976-77
Hirsch, Tom	Min.	3	31	1	7	8	30	12	0	0	0	6	1983-84	1987-88
Hirschfeld, Bert	Mtl.	2	33	1	4	5	2	5	1	0	1	0	1949-50	1950-51
Hislop, Jamie	Que., Cgy.	5	345	75	103	178	86	28	3	2	5	11	1979-80	1983-84
Hitchman, Lionel	Ott., Bos.	12	413	28	33	61	523	40	4	1	5	77	1922-23	1933-34
Hlinka, Ivan	Van.	2	137	42	81	123	28	16	3	10	13	8	1981-82	1982-83
Hodge, Ken	Chi., Bos., NYR	13	881	328	472	800	779	97	34	47	81	120	1965-66	1977-78
Hodgson, Rick	Hfd.	1	6	0	0	0	6	1	0	0	0	0	1979-80	1979-80
Hodgson, Ted	Bos.	1	4	0	0	0	0	....	....	....	....	....	1966-67	1966-67
Hoekstra, Cecil	Mtl.	1	4	0	0	0	0	....	....	....	....	....	1959-60	1959-60
Hoekstra, Ed	Phi.	1	70	15	21	36	6	7	0	1	1	0	1967-68	1967-68
Hoene, Phi.	L.A.	3	37	2	4	6	22	....	....	....	....	....	1972-73	1974-75
Hoffinger, Vic	Chi.	2	28	0	1	1	30	....	....	....	....	....	1927-28	1928-29
Hoffman, Mike	Hfd.	3	9	1	3	4	2	....	....	....	....	....	1982-83	1985-86
Hoffmeyer, Bob	Chi., Phi., N.J.	6	198	14	52	66	325	3	0	1	1	25	1977-78	1984-85
Hogaboam, Bill	Atl., Det., Min.	8	332	80	109	189	100	2	0	0	0	0	1972-73	1979-80
Hoganson, Dale	L.A., Mtl., Que.	7	343	13	77	90	186	11	0	3	3	12	1969-70	1981-82
Holbrook, Terry	Min.	2	43	3	6	9	4	6	0	0	0	0	1972-73	1973-74
Holland, Jerry	NYR	2	37	8	4	12	6	....	....	....	....	....	1974-75	1975-76
Hollett, Frank	Tor., Ott., Bos., Det.	13	565	132	181	313	378	79	8	26	34	38	1933-34	1945-46
Hollingworth, Gord	Chi., Det.	4	163	4	14	18	201	3	0	0	0	2	1954-55	1957-58
Holmes, Bill	Mtl., NYA.	2	51	6	4	10	35	....	....	....	....	....	1925-26	1929-30
Holmes, Chuck	Det.	2	23	1	3	4	10	....	....	....	....	....	1958-59	1961-62
Holmes, Lou	Chi.	2	59	1	4	5	6	2	0	0	0	2	1931-32	1932-33
Holmes, Warren	L.A.	3	45	8	18	26	7	....	....	....	....	....	1981-82	1983-84
Holmgren, Paul	Phi., Min.	10	527	144	179	323	1684	82	19	32	51	195	1975-76	1984-85
Holota, John	Det.	2	15	2	0	2	0	....	....	....	....	....	1942-43	1945-46
Holloway, Bruce	Van.	1	2	0	0	0	0	....	....	....	....	....	1984-85	1984-85
Holst, Greg	NYR	3	11	0	0	0	0	....	....	....	....	....	1975-76	1977-78
Holt, Gary	Cal., Clev., St.L.	5	101	13	11	24	183	....	....	....	....	....	1973-74	1977-78
Holt, Randy	Chi., Clev., Van., L.A., Cgy., Wsh., Phi.	10	395	4	37	41	1438	21	2	3	5	83	1974-75	1983-84
Holway, Albert	Tor., Mtl.M., Pit.	5	117	7	2	9	48	8	0	0	0	2	1923-24	1928-29
Homenuke, Ron	Van.	1	1	0	0	0	0	....	....	....	....	....	1972-73	1972-73
Hopkins, Dean	L.A., Edm.	5	218	23	49	72	302	18	1	5	6	29	1979-80	1985-86
Hopkins, Larry	Tor., Wpg.	4	60	13	16	29	26	6	0	0	0	2	1977-78	1982-83
Horbul, Doug	K.C.	1	4	1	0	1	2	....	....	....	....	....	1974-75	1974-75
Hordy, Mike	NYI	2	11	0	0	0	7	....	....	....	....	....	1978-79	1979-80
Horeck, Pete	Chi., Det., Bos.	8	426	106	118	224	340	34	6	8	14	43	1944-45	1951-52
Horne, George	Mtl.M, Tor.	3	54	9	3	12	34	4	0	0	0	4	1925-26	1928-29
Horner, Red	Tor.	12	490	42	110	152	1264	71	7	10	17	166	1928-29	1939-40
Hornung, Larry	St.L.	2	48	2	9	11	10	11	0	2	2	2	1970-71	1971-72
Horton, Tim	Tor., NYR, Buf., Pit.	24	1446	115	403	518	1611	126	11	39	50	183	1949-50	1973-74
Horvath, Bronco	NYR, Mtl., Bos., Chi., Tor., Min.	9	434	141	185	326	319	36	12	9	21	18	1955-56	1967-68
Hospodar, Ed	NYR, Hfd., Phi., Min., Buf.	9	450	17	51	68	1314	44	4	1	5	206	1979-80	1987-88
Houck, Paul	Min.	3	16	1	2	3	2	....	....	....	....	....	1985-86	1987-88
Houde, Claude	K.C.	2	59	3	6	9	40	....	....	....	....	....	1974-75	1975-76
Houle, Rejean	Mtl.	11	635	161	247	408	395	90	14	34	48	66	1969-70	1982-83
Houston, Ken	Atl., Cgy., Wsh., L.A.	9	570	161	167	328	624	35	10	9	19	66	1975-76	1983-84
Howard, Frank	Tor.	1	2	0	0	0	0	....	....	....	....	....	1936-37	1936-37
Howatt, Garry	NYI, Hfd., N.J.	12	720	112	156	268	1836	87	12	14	26	289	1972-73	1983-84
Howe, Gordie	Det., Hfd.	26	1767	801	1049	1850	1685	157	68	92	160	220	1946-47	1979-80
Howe, Marty	Hfd., Bos.	6	197	2	29	31	99	15	1	2	3	9	1979-80	1984-85
Howe, Syd	Ott., Phi., Tor., St.L., Det.	17	691	237	291	528	214	70	17	27	44	10	1929-30	1945-46
Howe, Vic	NYR	3	33	3	4	7	10	....	....	....	....	....	1950-51	1954-55
Howell, Harry	NYR, Oak., L.A.	21	1411	94	324	418	1298	38	3	3	6	32	1952-53	1972-73
Howell, Ron	NYR	2	4	0	0	0	4	....	....	....	....	....	1954-55	1955-56
Howse, Don	L.A.	1	33	2	5	7	6	2	0	0	0	0	1979-80	1979-80
Howson, Scott	NYI	2	18	5	3	8	4	....	....	....	....	....	1984-85	1985-86
Hoyda, Dave	Phi., Wpg.	4	132	6	17	23	299	12	0	0	0	17	1977-78	1980-81
Hrechkosy, Dave	Cal., St.L.	4	140	42	24	66	41	3	1	0	1	2	1973-74	1976-77
Hrycuik, Jim	Wsh.	1	21	5	5	10	12	....	....	....	....	....	1974-75	1974-75
Hrymnak, Steve	Chi., Det.	2	18	2	1	3	4	2	0	0	0	0	1951-52	1952-53
Hrynewich, Tim	Pit.	2	55	6	8	14	82	....	....	....	....	....	1982-83	1983-84
Huard, Rolly	Tor.	1	1	1	0	1	0	....	....	....	....	....	1930-31	1930-31
Huber, Willie	Det., NYR, Van., Phi.	10	655	104	217	321	950	33	5	5	10	35	1978-79	1987-88
Hubick, Greg	Tor., Van.	2	77	6	9	15	10	....	....	....	....	....	1975-76	1979-80
Huck, Fran	Mtl., St.L.	3	94	24	30	54	38	11	3	4	7	2	1969-70	1972-73
Hucul, Fred	Chi., St.L.	5	164	11	30	41	113	6	1	0	1	10	1950-51	1967-68
Hudson, Dave	NYI, K.C., Col.	6	409	59	124	183	89	2	1	1	2	0	1972-73	1977-78
Hudson, Lex	Pit.	1	2	0	0	0	0	2	0	0	0	0	1978-79	1978-79
Hudson, Ron	Det.	2	34	5	2	7	2	....	....	....	....	....	1937-38	1939-40
Huggins, Al	Mtl.M	1	20	1	1	2	2	....	....	....	....	....	1930-31	1930-31
Hughes, Al	NYA	2	60	6	8	14	22	....	....	....	....	....	1930-31	1931-32
Hughes, Brent	L.A., Phi., St.L., Det., K.C.	8	435	15	117	132	440	22	1	3	4	53	1967-68	1974-75
Hughes, Frank	Cal.	1	5	0	0	0	0	....	....	....	....	....	1971-72	1971-72
Hughes, Howie	L.A.	3	168	25	32	57	30	14	2	0	2	2	1967-68	1969-70
Hughes, Jack	Col.	2	46	2	5	7	104	....	....	....	....	....	1980-81	1981-82
Hughes, John	Van., Edm., NYR	3	70	2	14	16	211	7	0	1	1	16	1979-80	1980-81
Hughes, Pat	Mtl., Pit., Edm., Buf., St.L., Hfd.	10	573	130	128	258	653	71	8	25	33	77	1977-78	1986-87
Hughes, Rusty	Det.	1	40	0	1	1	48	....	....	....	....	....	1929-30	1929-30
Hull, Bobby	Chi., Wpg., Hfd.	16	1063	610	560	1170	640	119	62	67	129	102	1957-58	1979-80
Hull, Dennis	Chi., Det.	14	959	303	351	654	261	104	33	34	67	30	1964-65	1977-78
Hunt, Fred	NYA, NYR	2	59	15	14	29	6	....	....	....	....	....	1940-41	1944-45
Hunter, Dave	Edm., Pit., Wpg.	10	746	133	190	323	918	105	16	24	40	211	1979-80	1988-89
Huras, Larry	NYR	1	1	0	0	0	0	....	....	....	....	....	1976-77	1976-77
Hurlburt, Bob	Van.	1	1	0	0	0	2	....	....	....	....	....	1974-75	1974-75
Hurley, Paul	Bos.	1	1	0	1	1	0	....	....	....	....	....	1968-69	1968-69
Hurst, Ron	Tor.	2	64	9	7	16	7	3	0	2	2	4	1955-56	1956-57
Huston, Ron	Cal.	2	79	15	31	46	8	....	....	....	....	....	1973-74	1974-75
Hutchinson, Ronald	NYR	1	9	0	0	0	0	....	....	....	....	....	1960-61	1960-61
Hutchison, Dave	L.A., Tor., Chi., N.J.	10	584	19	97	116	1550	48	2	12	14	149	1974-75	1983-84
Hutton, William	Bos., Ott., Phi.	2	64	3	2	5	8	2	0	0	0	0	1929-30	1930-31
Hyland, Harry	Mtl.W, Ott.	1	16	14	0	14	0	....	....	....	....	....	1917-18	1917-18
Hynes, Dave	Bos.	2	22	4	0	4	2	....	....	....	....	....	1973-74	1974-75

I

Name	NHL Teams	NHL Seasons	Regular Schedule GP	G	A	TP	PIM	Playoffs GP	G	A	TP	PIM	First NHL Season	Last NHL Season
Imlach, Brent	Tor.	2	3	0	0	0	2	....	....	....	....	....	1965-66	1966-67
Ingarfield, Earl	NYR, Pit., Oak., Cal.	13	746	179	226	405	239	21	9	8	17	10	1958-59	1970-71
Ingarfield, Earl Jr.	Atl., Cgy., Det.	2	39	4	4	8	22	2	0	1	1	0	1979-80	1980-81
Inglis, Bill	L.A., Buf.	3	36	1	3	4	4	11	1	2	3	4	1967-68	1970-71
Ingoldsby, Johnny	Tor.	2	29	5	1	6	15	....	....	....	....	....	1942-43	1943-44
Ingram, Frank	Bos., Chi.	4	102	24	16	40	69	11	0	1	1	2	1924-25	1931-32
Ingram, Ron	Chi., Det., NYR	4	114	5	15	20	81	2	0	0	0	0	1956-57	1964-65
Irvin, Dick	Chi.	3	94	29	23	52	76	2	2	0	2	4	1926-27	1928-29
Irvine, Ted	Bos., L.A., NYR, St.L.	11	724	154	177	331	657	83	16	24	40	115	1963-64	1976-77
Irwin, Ivan	Mtl., NYR	5	155	2	27	29	214	5	0	0	0	8	1952-53	1957-58
Isaksson, Ulf	L.A.	1	50	7	15	22	10	....	....	....	....	....	1982-83	1982-83

Name	NHL Teams	NHL Seasons	Regular Schedule					Playoffs					First NHL Season	Last NHL Season
			GP	G	A	TP	PIM	GP	G	A	TP	PIM		
J														
Jackson, Art	Tor., Bos., NYA.	11	466	116	175	291	144	51	8	12	20	27	1934-35	1944-45
Jackson, Harvey	Bos.	15	636	241	234	475	437	71	18	12	30	53	1929-30	1943-44
Jackson, Don	Min., Edm., NYR	10	311	16	52	68	640	53	4	5	9	147	1977-78	1986-87
Jackson, Hal	Chi., Det.	8	222	17	34	51	208	31	1	2	3	33	1936-37	1946-47
Jackson, John	Chi.	1	48	2	5	7	38	....	....	....	....	....	1946-47	1946-47
Jackson, Lloyd	NYA	1	14	1	1	2	0	....	....	....	....	....	1936-37	1936-37
Jackson, Stan	Tor., Bos., Ott.	5	84	9	4	13	74	....	....	....	....	....	1921-22	1926-27
Jackson, Walt	NYA	3	82	16	11	27	18	....	....	....	....	....	1932-33	1934-35
Jacobs, Paul	Tor.	1	1	0	0	0	0	....	....	....	....	....	1918-19	1918-19
Jacobs, Tim	Cal.	1	46	0	10	10	35	....	....	....	....	....	1975-76	1975-76
Jalo, Risto	Edm.	1	3	0	3	3	0	....	....	....	....	....	1985-86	1985-86
Jalonen, Kari	Cgy., Edm.	2	37	9	6	15	4	5	1	0	1	0	1982-83	1983-84
James, Gerry	Tor.	5	149	14	26	40	257	15	1	0	1	8	1954-55	1959-60
James, Val	Buf., Tor.	2	11	0	0	0	30	....	....	....	....	....	1981-82	1986-87
Jamieson, Jim	NYR	1	1	0	1	1	0	....	....	....	....	....	1943-44	1943-44
Jankowski, Lou	Det., Chi.	4	127	19	18	37	15	1	0	0	0	0	1950-51	1954-55
Jarrett, Doug	Chi., NYR	13	775	38	182	220	631	99	7	16	23	82	1964-65	1976-77
Jarrett, Gary	Tor., Det., Oak., Cal.	7	341	72	92	164	131	11	3	1	4	9	1960-61	1971-72
Jarry, Pierre	NYR, Tor., Det., Min.	7	344	88	117	205	142	5	0	1	1	0	1971-72	1977-78
Jarvis, Doug	Mtl., Wsh., Hfd.	13	964	139	264	403	263	105	14	27	41	42	1975-76	1987-88
Jarvis, Jim	Pit., Phi., Tor.	3	108	17	15	32	62	....	....	....	....	....	1929-30	1936-37
Javanainen, Arto	Pit.	1	14	4	1	5	2	....	....	....	....	....	1984-85	1984-85
Jeffrey, Larry	Det., Tor., NYR	8	368	39	62	101	293	38	4	10	14	42	1961-62	1968-69
Jenkins, Dean	L.A.	1	5	0	0	0	2	....	....	....	....	....	1983-84	1983-84
Jenkins, Roger	Tor., Chi., Mtl., Bos., Mtl.M., NYA	8	328	15	39	54	279	25	1	7	8	12	1930-31	1938-39
Jennings, Bill	Det., Bos.	5	108	32	33	65	45	20	4	4	8	6	1940-41	1944-45
Jensen, David H.	Min.	3	18	0	2	2	11	....	....	....	....	....	1983-84	1985-86
Jensen, Steve	Min., L.A.	7	439	113	107	220	318	12	0	3	3	9	1975-76	1981-82
Jeremiah, Ed	NYA, Bos.	1	15	0	1	1	0	....	....	....	....	....	1931-32	1931-32
Jerwa, Frank	Bos., St.L.	4	91	11	16	27	53	....	....	....	....	....	1931-32	1934-35
Jerwa, Joe	NYR, Bos., NYA	7	233	29	58	87	315	17	2	3	5	20	1930-31	1938-39
Jirik, Jaroslav	St.L.	1	3	0	0	0	0	....	....	....	....	....	1969-70	1969-70
Joanette, Rosario	Mtl.	1	2	0	1	1	4	....	....	....	....	....	1944-45	1944-45
Jodzio, Rick	Col., Clev.	1	70	2	8	10	71	....	....	....	....	....	1977-78	1977-78
Johannesen, Glenn	NYI	1	2	0	0	0	0	....	....	....	....	....	1985-86	1985-86
Johansen, Trevor	Tor., Col., L.A.	5	286	11	46	57	282	13	0	3	3	21	1977-78	1981-82
Johansson, Bjorn	Clev.	2	15	1	1	2	10	....	....	....	....	....	1976-77	1977-78
Johannson, John	N.J.	1	5	0	0	0	0	....	....	....	....	....	1983-84	1983-84
Johns, Don	NYR, Mtl., Min.	6	153	2	21	23	76	....	....	....	....	....	1960-61	1967-68
Johnson, Al	Mtl., Det.	4	105	21	28	49	30	11	2	2	4	6	1956-57	1962-63
Johnson, Brian	Det.	1	3	0	0	0	5	....	....	....	....	....	1983-84	1983-84
Johnson, Ivan	NYR, NYA	12	435	38	48	86	808	60	5	2	7	161	1926-27	1937-38
Johnson, Danny	Tor., Van., Det.	3	121	18	19	37	24	....	....	....	....	....	1969-70	1971-72
Johnson, Earl	Det.	1	1	0	0	0	0	....	....	....	....	....	1953-54	1953-54
Johnson, Jim	NYR, Phi., L.A.	8	302	75	111	186	73	7	0	2	2	2	1964-65	1971-72
Johnson, Norm	Bos., Chi.	3	61	5	20	25	41	14	4	0	4	6	1957-58	1959-60
Johnson, Terry	Que., St.L., Cgy., Tor.	9	285	3	24	27	580	38	0	4	4	118	1979-80	1987-88
Johnson, Tom	Mtl., Bos.	17	978	51	213	264	960	111	8	15	23	109	1947-48	1964-65
Johnson, Virgil	Chi.	3	75	2	9	11	27	19	0	3	3	4	1937-38	1944-45
Johnson, William	Tor.	1	1	0	0	0	0	....	....	....	....	....	1949-50	1949-50
Johnston, Bernie	Hfd.	2	57	12	24	36	44	3	0	1	1	0	1979-80	1980-81
Johnston, George	Chi.	4	58	20	12	32	2	....	....	....	....	....	1941-42	1946-47
Johnston, Jay	Wsh.	2	8	0	0	0	13	....	....	....	....	....	1980-81	1981-82
Johnston, Joey	Min., Cal., Chi.	6	332	85	106	191	320	....	....	....	....	....	1968-69	1975-76
Johnston, Larry	L.A., Det., K.C., Col.	7	320	9	64	73	580	....	....	....	....	....	1967-68	1976-77
Johnston, Marshall	Min., Cal.	7	251	14	52	66	58	6	0	0	0	2	1967-68	1973-74
Johnston, Randy	NYI	1	4	0	0	0	4	....	....	....	....	....	1979-80	1979-80
Johnstone, Eddie	NYR, Det.	10	426	122	136	258	375	55	13	10	23	83	1975-76	1986-87
Johnstone, Ross	Tor.	2	42	5	4	9	14	3	0	0	0	0	1943-44	1944-45
Jollat, Aurel	Mtl.	16	654	270	190	460	757	54	14	19	33	89	1922-23	1937-38
Joliat, Bobby	Mtl.	1	1	0	0	0	0	....	....	....	....	....	1924-25	1924-25
Joly, Greg	Wsh., Det.	9	365	21	76	97	250	5	0	0	0	8	1974-75	1982-83
Joly, Yvan	Mtl.	3	2	0	0	0	0	10	0	0	0	0	1979-80	1982-83
Jonathon, Stan	Bos., Pit.	8	411	91	110	201	751	63	8	4	12	137	1975-76	1982-83
Jones, Bob	NYR	1	2	0	0	0	0	....	....	....	....	....	1968-69	1968-69
Jones, Buck	Det., Tor.	4	50	2	2	4	36	12	0	1	1	18	1938-39	1942-43
Jones, Jim	Cal.	1	2	0	0	0	0	....	....	....	....	....	1971-72	1971-72
Jones, Jimmy	Tor.	3	148	13	18	31	68	19	1	5	6	11	1977-78	1979-80
Jones, Ron	Bos., Pit., Wsh.	5	54	1	4	5	31	....	....	....	....	....	1971-72	1975-76
Joyal, Eddie	Det., Tor., L.A., Phi.	9	466	128	134	262	103	50	11	8	19	18	1962-63	1971-72
Juckes, Bing	NYR	2	16	2	1	3	6	....	....	....	....	....	1947-48	1949-50
Jutila, Timo	Buf.	1	10	1	5	6	13	....	....	....	....	....	1984-85	1984-85
Juzda, Bill	NYR, Tor.	9	393	14	54	68	398	42	0	3	3	46	1940-41	1951-52
K														
Kabel, Bob	NYR	2	48	5	13	18	34	....	....	....	....	....	1959-60	1960-61
Kachur, Ed	Chi.	2	96	10	14	24	35	....	....	....	....	....	1956-57	1957-58
Kaiser, Vern	Mtl.	1	50	7	5	12	33	2	0	0	0	0	1950-51	1950-51
Kalbfleish, Walter	Ott., St.L., NYA, Bos.	4	36	0	4	4	32	5	0	0	0	2	1933-34	1936-37
Kaleta, Alex	Chi., NYR	7	387	92	121	213	190	17	1	6	7	2	1941-42	1950-51
Kallur, Anders	NYI	6	383	101	110	211	149	78	12	23	35	32	1979-80	1984-85
Kaminsky, Max	Ott., St.L., Bos., Mtl.M.	4	130	22	34	56	38	4	0	0	0	0	1933-34	1936-37
Kampman, Bingo	Tor.	5	189	14	30	44	287	47	1	4	5	38	1937-38	1941-42
Kane, Frank	Det.	1	2	0	0	0	0	....	....	....	....	....	1943-44	1943-44
Kannegiesser, Gord	St.L.	2	23	0	1	1	15	....	....	....	....	....	1967-68	1971-72
Kannegiesser, Sheldon	Pit., NYR, L.A., Van.	8	366	14	67	81	202	18	0	2	2	10	1970-71	1977-78
Karlander, Al	Det.	4	212	36	56	92	70	4	0	1	1	0	1969-70	1972-73
Kaszycki, Mike	NYI, Wsh., Tor.	5	226	42	80	122	108	19	2	6	8	10	1977-78	1982-83
Kea, Ed	Atl., St.L.	10	583	30	145	175	508	32	2	4	6	39	1973-74	1982-83
Kearns, Dennis	Van.	10	677	31	290	321	386	11	1	2	3	8	1971-72	1980-81
Keating, Jack	NYA	2	35	5	5	10	17	....	....	....	....	....	1931-32	1932-33
Keating, John	Det.	2	11	2	1	3	4	....	....	....	....	....	1938-39	1939-40
Keating, Mike	NYR	1	1	0	0	0	0	....	....	....	....	....	1977-78	1977-78
Keats, Duke	Det., Chi.	3	80	3	19	49	113	....	....	....	....	....	1926-27	1928-29
Keeling, Butch	Tor., NYR	12	528	157	63	220	331	47	11	11	22	32	1926-27	1937-38
Keenan, Larry	Tor., St.L., Buf., Phi.	6	233	38	64	102	28	46	15	16	31	12	1961-62	1971-72
Kehoe, Rick	Tor., Pit.	14	906	371	396	767	120	39	4	17	21	4	1971-72	1984-85
Keller, Ralph	NYR	1	3	1	0	1	6	....	....	....	....	....	1962-63	1962-63
Kellgren, Christer	Col.	1	5	0	0	0	0	....	....	....	....	....	1981-82	1981-82
Kelly, Bob	St.L., Pit., Chi.	6	425	87	109	196	687	23	6	3	9	40	1973-74	1978-79
Kelly, Bob	Phi., Wsh.	12	837	154	208	362	1454	101	9	14	23	172	1970-71	1981-82
Kelly, Dave	Det.	1	16	2	0	2	4	....	....	....	....	....	1976-77	1976-77
Kelly, John Paul	L.A.	7	400	54	70	124	366	18	1	1	2	41	1979-80	1985-86
Kelly, Reg	Tor., Chi., NYA	8	289	74	53	127	105	39	7	6	13	10	1934-35	1941-42
Kelly, Pete	St.L., Det., NYA	7	180	21	38	59	68	19	3	1	4	8	1934-35	1941-42
Kelly, Red	Det., Tor.	20	1316	281	542	823	327	164	33	59	92	51	1947-48	1966-67
Kemp, Kevin	Hfd.	1	3	0	0	0	4	....	....	....	....	....	1980-81	1980-81
Kemp, Stan	Tor.	1	1	0	0	0	2	....	....	....	....	....	1948-49	1948-49
Kendall, William	Chi., Tor.	5	132	16	10	26	28	5	0	0	0	0	1933-34	1937-38
Kennedy, Forbes	Chi., Det., Bos., Phi., Tor.	11	603	70	108	178	988	12	2	4	6	64	1956-57	1968-69
Kennedy, Ted	Tor.	14	696	231	329	560	432	78	29	31	60	32	1942-43	1956-57
Kenny, Eddie	NYR, Chi.	2	11	0	0	0	18	....	....	....	....	....	1930-31	1934-35
Keon, Dave	Tor., Hfd.	18	1296	396	590	986	117	92	32	36	68	6	1960-61	1981-82
Kerr, Reg	Cle., Chi., Edm.	6	263	66	94	160	169	7	1	0	1	7	1977-78	1983-84
Kessell, Rick	Pit., Cal.	5	135	4	24	28	6	....	....	....	....	....	1969-70	1973-74
Ketola, Veli-Pekka	Col.	1	44	9	5	14	4	....	....	....	....	....	1981-82	1981-82
Ketter, Kerry	Atl.	1	41	0	2	2	58	....	....	....	....	....	1972-73	1972-73
Kiessling, Udo	Min.	1	1	0	0	0	2	....	....	....	....	....	1981-82	1981-82
Kilrea, Brian	Det., L.A.	2	26	3	5	8	12	....	....	....	....	....	1957-58	1967-68

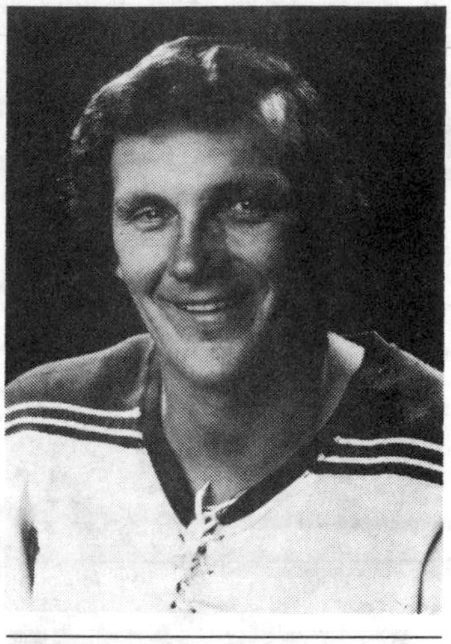

Ted Irvine

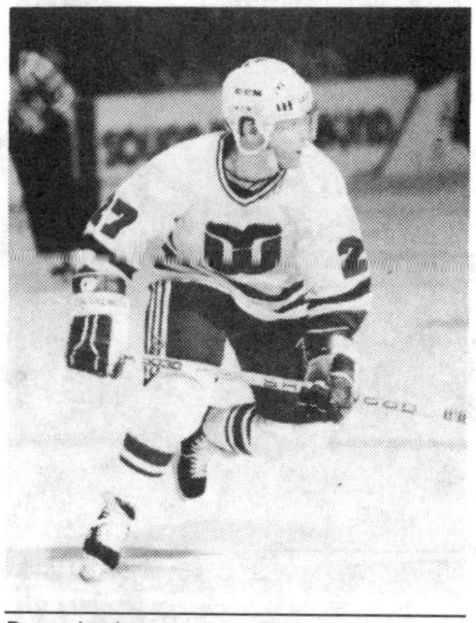

Doug Jarvis

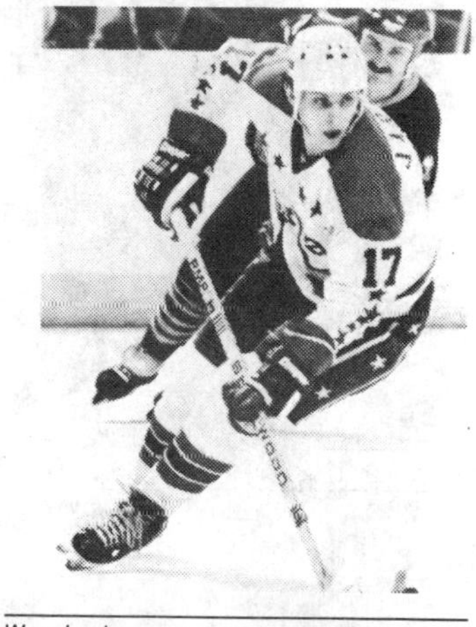

Wes Jarvis

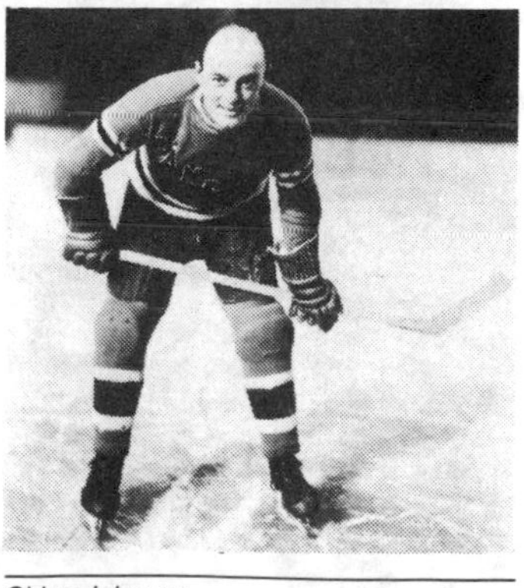

Ching Johnson

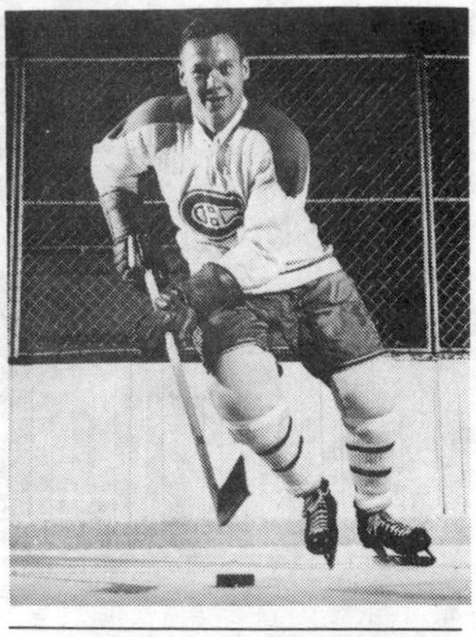

Tom Johnson

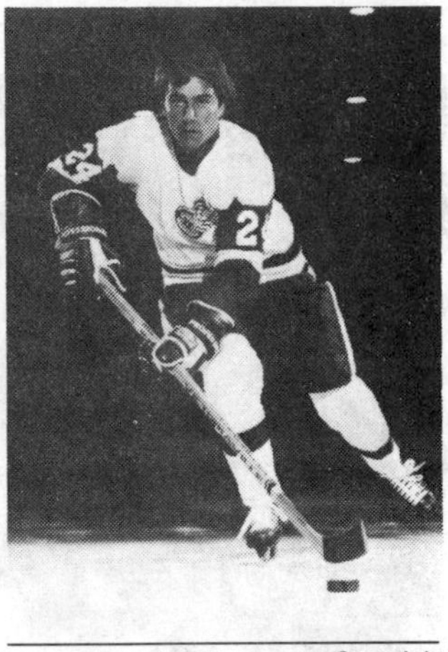

Greg Joly

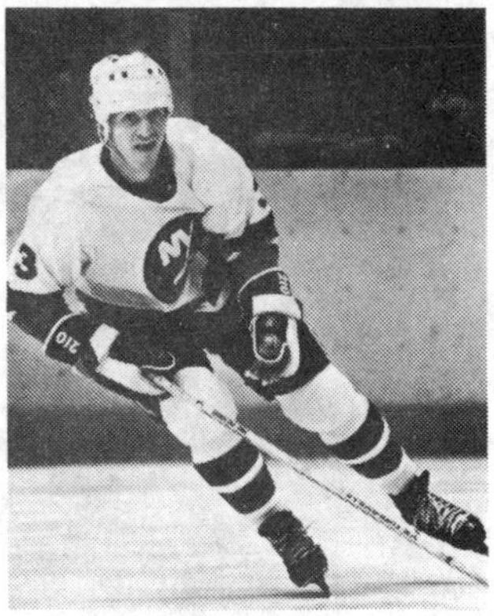

Tomas Jonsson

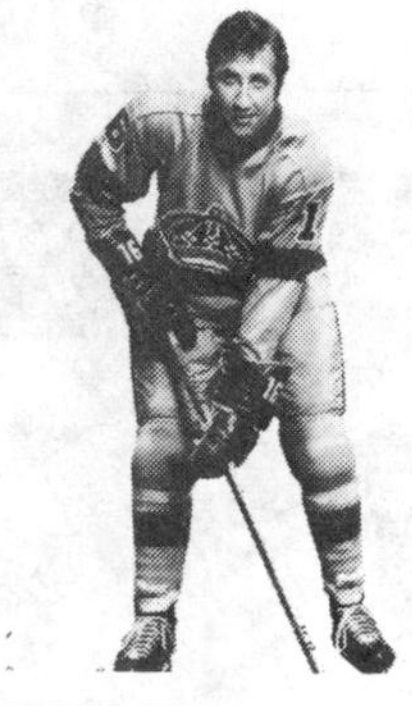

Eddie Joyal

Name	NHL Teams	NHL Seasons	Regular Schedule					Playoffs					First NHL Season	Last NHL Season
			GP	G	A	TP	PIM	GP	G	A	TP	PIM		
Kilrea, Hec	Ott., Det., Tor.	15	633	167	129	296	438	48	8	7	15	18	1925-26	1939-40
Kilrea, Ken	Det.	5	88	16	23	39	8	10	2	2	4	4	1938-39	1943-44
Kilrea, Wally	Ott., Phi., NYA, Mtl.M., Det.	9	315	35	58	93	87	25	2	4	6	6	1929-30	1937-38
Kindrachuk, Orest	Phi., Pit., Wsh.	10	508	118	261	379	648	76	20	20	40	53	1972-73	1981-82
King, Frank	Mtl.	1	10	1	0	1	2	....	....	....	....	....	1950-51	1950-51
King, Wayne	Cal.	3	73	5	18	23	34	....	....	....	....	....	1973-74	1975-76
Kinsella, Brian	Wsh.	2	10	0	1	1	0	....	....	....	....	....	1975-76	1976-77
Kinsella, Ray	Ott.	1	14	0	0	0	0	....	....	....	....	....	1930-31	1930-31
Kirk, Bobby	NYR	1	39	4	8	12	14	....	....	....	....	....	1937-38	1937-38
Kirkpatrick, Bob	NYR	1	49	12	12	24	6	....	....	....	....	....	1942-43	1942-43
Kirton, Mark	Tor., Det., Van.	6	266	57	56	113	121	4	1	2	3	7	1979-80	1984-85
Kitchen, Bill	Mtl., Tor.	4	41	1	4	5	40	3	0	1	1	0	1981-82	1984-85
Kitchen, Hobie	Mtl.M., Det.	2	47	5	4	9	58	....	....	....	....	....	1925-26	1926-27
Kitchen, Mike	Col., N.J.	8	474	12	62	74	370	2	0	0	0	2	1976-77	1983-84
Klassen, Ralph	Cal., Clev., Col., St.L.	9	497	52	93	145	120	26	4	2	6	12	1975-76	1983-84
Klein, Jim	Bos., NYA	8	169	30	24	54	68	5	0	0	0	2	1928-29	1937-38
Klingbeil, Ike	Chi.	1	5	1	2	3	2	....	....	....	....	....	1936-37	1936-37
Klukay, Joe	Tor., Bos.	11	566	109	127	236	189	71	13	10	23	23	1942-43	1955-56
Knibbs, Bill	Bos.	1	53	7	10	17	4	....	....	....	....	....	1964-65	1964-65
Knott, Nick	NYA	1	14	3	1	4	9	....	....	....	....	....	1941-42	1941-42
Knox, Paul	Tor.	1	1	0	0	0	0	....	....	....	....	....	1954-55	1954-55
Komadoski, Neil	L.A., St.L.	8	502	16	76	92	632	23	0	2	2	47	1972-73	1979-80
Konik, George	Pit.	1	52	7	8	15	26	....	....	....	....	....	1967-68	1967-68
Kopak, Russ	Bos.	1	24	7	9	16	0	....	....	....	....	....	1943-44	1943-44
Korab, Jerry	Chi., Van., Buf., L.A.	15	975	114	341	455	1629	93	8	18	26	201	1970-71	1984-85
Korney, Mike	Det., NYR	4	77	9	10	19	59	....	....	....	....	....	1973-74	1978-79
Koroll, Cliff	Chi.	11	814	208	254	462	376	85	19	29	48	67	1969-70	1979-80
Kortko, Roger	NYI	2	79	7	17	24	28	10	0	3	3	17	1984-85	1985-86
Kostynski, Doug	Bos.	2	15	3	1	4	4	....	....	....	....	....	1983-84	1984-85
Kotanen, Dick	Det., NYR	2	2	0	1	1	0	....	....	....	....	....	1948-49	1950-51
Kowal, Joe	Buf.	2	22	0	5	5	13	2	0	0	0	0	1976-77	1977-78
Kozak, Don	L.A., Van.	7	437	96	86	182	480	29	7	2	9	69	1972-73	1978-79
Kozak, Les	Tor.	1	12	1	0	1	2	....	....	....	....	....	1961-62	1961-62
Kraftcheck, Stephen	Bos., NYR, Tor.	4	157	11	18	29	83	6	0	0	0	7	1950-51	1958-59
Krake, Skip	Bos., L.A., Buf.	7	249	23	40	63	182	10	1	0	1	17	1963-64	1970-71
Krol, Joe	NYR, NYA	3	26	10	4	14	8	....	....	....	....	....	1936-37	1941-42
Krook, Kevin	Col.	1	3	0	0	0	2	....	....	....	....	....	1978-79	1978-79
Krulicki, Jim	NYR, Det.	1	41	0	3	3	6	....	....	....	....	....	1970-71	1970-71
Kryskow, Dave	Chi., Wsh., Det., Atl.	4	231	33	56	89	174	12	2	0	2	4	1972-73	1975-76
Kryznowski, Edward	Bos., Chi.	5	237	15	22	37	65	18	0	1	1	4	1948-49	1952-53
Kuhn, Gord	NYA	1	12	1	1	2	4	....	....	....	....	....	1932-33	1932-33
Kukulowicz, Adolph	NYR	2	4	1	0	1	0	....	....	....	....	....	1952-53	1953-54
Kullman, Arnie	Bos.	2	13	0	1	1	11	....	....	....	....	....	1947-48	1949-50
Kullman, Eddie	NYR	6	343	56	70	126	298	6	1	0	1	2	1947-48	1953-54
Kuntz, Alan	NYR	2	45	10	12	22	12	6	1	0	1	2	1941-42	1945-46
Kuntz, Murray	St.L.	1	7	1	2	3	0	....	....	....	....	....	1974-75	1974-75
Kurtenbach, Orland	NYR, Bos., Tor., Van.	13	639	119	213	332	628	19	2	4	6	70	1960-61	1973-74
Kuryluk, Mervin	Chi.	1	....	....	....	....	....	2	0	0	0	0	1961-62	1961-62
Kuzyk, Ken	Clev.	2	41	5	9	14	8	....	....	....	....	....	1976-77	1977-78
Kwong, Larry	NYR	1	1	0	0	0	0	....	....	....	....	....	1947-48	1947-48
Kyle, Bill	NYR	2	3	0	3	3	0	....	....	....	....	....	1949-50	1950-51
Kyle, Gus	NYR, Bos.	3	203	6	20	26	362	14	1	2	3	34	1949-50	1951-52

L

Name	NHL Teams	NHL Seasons	Regular Schedule					Playoffs					First NHL Season	Last NHL Season
			GP	G	A	TP	PIM	GP	G	A	TP	PIM		
Labadie, Mike	NYR	1	3	0	0	0	0	....	....	....	....	....	1952-53	1952-53
Labatte, Neil	St.L.	2	26	0	2	2	19	....	....	....	....	....	1978-79	1981-82
L'abbe, Moe	Chi.	1	5	0	1	1	0	....	....	....	....	....	1972-73	1972-73
Labine, Leo	Bos., Det.	11	643	128	193	321	730	60	11	12	23	82	1951-52	1961-62
Labossierre, Gord	NYR, L.A., Min.	6	215	44	62	106	75	10	2	3	5	28	1963-64	1971-72
Labovitch, Max	NYR	1	5	0	0	0	4	....	....	....	....	....	1943-44	1943-44
Labraaten, Dan	Det., Cgy.	4	268	71	73	144	47	5	1	0	1	4	1978-79	1981-82
Labre, Yvon	Pit., Wsh.	9	317	14	87	101	788	....	....	....	....	....	1970-71	1980-81
Labrie, Guy	Bos., NYR	2	42	4	9	13	16	....	....	....	....	....	1943-44	1944-45
Lach, Elmer	Mtl.	14	664	215	408	623	478	76	19	45	64	36	1940-41	1953-54
Lachance, Earl	Mtl.	1	1	0	0	0	0	....	....	....	....	....	1926-27	1926-27
Lachance, Michel	Col.	1	21	0	4	4	22	....	....	....	....	....	1978-79	1978-79
Lacombe, Francois	Oak., Buf., Que.	4	78	2	17	19	54	3	1	0	1	0	1968-69	1979-80
Lacroix, Andre	Phi., Chi., Hfd.	6	325	79	119	198	44	16	2	5	7	0	1967-68	1979-80
Lacroix, Pierre	Que., Hfd.	4	274	24	108	132	197	8	0	2	2	10	1979-80	1982-83
Lafleur, Rene	Mtl.	1	0	0	0	0	0	....	....	....	....	....	1924-25	1924-25
Laforce, Ernie	Mtl.	1	0	0	0	0	0	....	....	....	....	....	1942-43	1942-43
LaForest, Bob	L.A.	1	5	1	0	1	2	....	....	....	....	....	1983-84	1983-84
Laforge, Claude	Mtl., Det., Phi.	8	192	24	33	57	82	5	1	2	3	15	1957-58	1968-69
Laframboise, Pete	Cal., Wsh., Pit.	4	227	33	55	88	70	9	1	0	1	0	1971-72	1974-75
Lafrance, Adie	Mtl.	1	3	0	0	0	2	2	0	0	0	0	1933-34	1933-34
Lafrance, Leo	Mtl., Chi.	2	33	2	0	2	6	....	....	....	....	....	1926-27	1927-28
Lafreniere, Roger	Det., St.L.	2	13	0	0	0	4	....	....	....	....	....	1962-63	1972-73
Lagace, Jean-Guy	Pit., Buf., K.C.	6	187	9	39	48	251	....	....	....	....	....	1968-69	1975-76
Lagace, Michel	Pit.	1	17	0	1	1	14	....	....	....	....	....	1968-69	1968-69
Laird, Robbie	Min.	1	1	0	0	0	0	....	....	....	....	....	1979-80	1979-80
Lajeunesse, Serge	Det., Phi.	5	103	1	4	5	103	7	1	2	3	4	1970-71	1974-75
Lalande, Hec	Chi., Det.	4	151	21	39	60	120	....	....	....	....	....	1953-54	1957-58
Lalonde, Bobby	Van., Atl., Bos., Cgy.	11	641	124	210	334	298	16	4	2	6	6	1971-72	1981-82
Lalonde, Edouard	Mtl., NYA	6	99	124	27	151	122	12	22	1	23	0	1917-18	1926-27
Lalonde, Ron	Pit., Wsh.	7	397	45	78	123	106	....	....	....	....	....	1972-73	1978-79
Lamb, Joe	Mtl.M., Ott., NYA, Bos., Mtl., St.L., Det.	11	444	108	101	209	601	18	1	1	2	51	1927-28	1937-38
Lambert, Yvon	Mtl., Buf.	10	683	206	273	479	340	90	27	22	49	67	1972-73	1981-82
Lamby, Dick	St.L.	3	22	0	5	5	22	....	....	....	....	....	1978-79	1980-81
Lamirande, Jean-Paul	NYR, Mtl.	4	49	5	5	10	26	8	0	0	0	4	1946-47	1954-55
Lamoureux, Leo	Mtl.	6	235	19	79	98	145	28	1	6	7	16	1941-42	1946-47
Lamoureux, Mitch	Pit., Phi.	3	73	11	9	20	59	....	....	....	....	....	1983-84	1987-88
Lampman, Mike	St.L., Van., Wsh.	4	96	17	20	37	34	....	....	....	....	....	1972-73	1976-77
Lancien, Jack	NYR	4	63	1	5	6	35	6	0	1	1	2	1946-47	1950-51
Landon, Larry	Mtl., Tor.	2	9	0	0	0	2	....	....	....	....	....	1983-84	1984-85
Lane, Gord	Wsh., NYI	10	539	19	94	113	1228	75	3	14	17	214	1975-76	1984-85
Lane, Myles	NYR, Bos.	3	60	4	1	5	41	10	0	0	0	0	1928-29	1933-34
Langdon, Steve	Bos.	3	7	0	1	1	2	4	0	0	0	2	1974-75	1977-78
Langelle, Pete	Tor.	4	137	22	51	73	11	41	5	9	14	4	1938-39	1941-42
Langevin, Chris	Buf.	2	22	3	1	4	22	....	....	....	....	....	1983-84	1985-86
Langevin, Dave	NYI, Min., L.A.	8	513	12	107	119	530	87	2	15	17	106	1979-80	1986-87
Langlais, Alain	Min.	2	25	4	4	8	10	....	....	....	....	....	1973-74	1974-75
Langlois, Al	Mtl., NYR, Det., Bos.	9	448	21	91	112	488	53	1	5	6	60	1957-58	1965-66
Langlois, Charlie	Ham., NYA., Pit., Mtl.	4	151	22	3	25	201	2	0	0	0	0	1924-25	1927-28
Lanyon, Ted	Pit.	1	5	0	0	0	4	....	....	....	....	....	1967-68	1967-68
Laperriere, Jacques	Mtl.	12	691	40	242	282	674	88	9	22	31	101	1962-63	1973-74
Lapointe, Guy	Mtl., St.L., Bos.	16	884	171	451	622	893	123	26	44	70	138	1968-69	1983-84
Lapointe, Rick	Det., Phi., St.L., Que., L.A.	11	664	44	176	220	831	46	2	7	9	64	1975-76	1985-86
Laprade, Edgar	NYR	10	501	108	172	280	42	18	4	9	13	4	1945-46	1954-55
LaPrairie, Ben	Chi.	1	7	0	0	0	0	....	....	....	....	....	1936-37	1936-37
Lariviere, Garry	Que., Edm.	4	219	6	57	63	167	14	0	5	5	8	1979-80	1982-83
Larmer, Jeff	Col., N.J., Chi.	5	158	37	51	88	57	5	1	0	1	2	1981-82	1985-86
Larochelle, Wildor	Mtl., Chi.	12	474	92	74	166	211	34	6	4	10	24	1925-26	1936-37
Larose, Charles	Bos.	1	6	0	0	0	0	....	....	....	....	....	1925-26	1925-26
Larose, Claude	Mtl., Min., St.L.	16	943	226	257	483	887	97	14	18	32	143	1962-63	1977-78
Larose, Claude	NYR	2	25	4	7	11	2	2	0	0	0	0	1979-80	1981-82
Larouche, Pierre	Pit., Mtl., Hfd., NYR	14	812	395	427	822	237	64	20	34	54	16	1974-75	1987-88
Larson, Norman	NYA., NYR	3	89	25	18	43	12	....	....	....	....	....	1940-41	1946-47
Latreille, Phil	NYR	1	4	0	0	0	2	....	....	....	....	....	1960-61	1960-61
Lauder, Marty	Bos.	1	3	0	0	0	2	....	....	....	....	....	1927-28	1927-28
Lauen, Mike	Wpg.	1	3	0	1	1	0	....	....	....	....	....	1983-84	1983-84
Laughlin, Craig	Mtl., Wsh., L.A., Tor.	8	549	136	205	341	364	33	6	6	12	20	1981-82	1988-89
Laughton, Mike	Oak., Cal.	4	189	39	48	87	101	11	2	4	6	0	1967-68	1970-71

			Regular Schedule					Playoffs					First	Last
Name	NHL Teams	NHL Seasons	GP	G	A	TP	PIM	GP	G	A	TP	PIM	NHL Season	NHL Season
Laurence, Red	Atl., St.L.	2	79	15	22	37	14	....	....	....	....	....	1978-79	1979-80
LaVallee, Kevin	Cgy., L.A., St.L., Pit.	7	366	110	125	235	85	32	5	8	13	24	1980-81	1986-87
Lavarre, Mark	Chi.	3	78	9	16	25	58	1	0	0	0	2	1985-86	1987-88
Lavender, Brian	St.L., NYI, Det., Cal.	4	184	16	26	42	174	3	0	0	0	2	1971-72	1974-75
Laviolette, Jack	Mtl.	1	18	2	0	2	0	2	0	0	0	0	1917-18	1917-18
Lawson, Danny	Det., Min., Buf.	5	219	28	29	57	61	16	0	1	1	2	1967-68	1971-72
Laycoe, Hal	NYR, Mtl., Bos.	11	531	25	77	102	292	40	2	5	7	39	1945-46	1955-56
Leach, Larry	Bos.	3	126	13	29	42	91	7	1	1	2	8	1958-59	1961-62
Leach, Reggie	Bos., Cal., Phi., Det.	13	934	381	285	666	387	94	47	22	69	22	1970-71	1982-83
Leavins, Jim	Det., NYR	2	41	2	12	14	30	....	....	....	....	....	1985-86	1986-87
LeBlanc, Fern	Det.	3	34	5	6	11	0	....	....	....	....	....	1976-77	1978-79
LeBlanc, J.P.	Chi., Det.	5	153	14	30	44	87	2	0	0	0	0	1968-69	1978-79
LeBrun, Al	NYR	2	6	0	2	2	4	....	....	....	....	....	1960-61	1965-66
Lecaine, Bill	Pit.	1	4	0	0	0	0	....	....	....	....	....	1968-69	1968-69
Leclair, Jackie	Mtl.,	3	160	20	40	60	56	20	6	0	7	6	1954-55	1956-57
Leclerc, Rene	Det.	2	87	10	11	21	105	....	....	....	....	....	1968-69	1970-71
Lecuyer, Doug	Chi., Wpg., Pit.	4	126	11	31	42	178	7	4	0	4	15	1978-79	1982-83
Ledingham, Walt	Chi., NYI	3	15	0	2	2	4	....	....	....	....	....	1972-73	1976-77
LeDuc, Albert	Mtl., Ott., NYR	10	383	57	35	92	614	31	5	6	11	32	1925-26	1934-35
LeDuc, Rich	Bos., Que.	4	130	28	38	66	55	5	0	0	0	9	1972-73	1980-81
Lee, Bobby	Mtl.	1	1	0	0	0	0	....	....	....	....	....	1942-43	1942-43
Lee, Edward	Que.	1	2	0	0	0	5	....	....	....	....	....	1984-85	1984-85
Lee, Peter	Pit.	6	431	114	131	245	257	19	0	8	8	4	1977-78	1982-83
Lefley, Bryan	N.Y.I., K.C., Col.	5	228	7	29	36	101	2	0	0	0	0	1972-73	1977-78
Lefley, Chuck	Mtl., St.L.	9	407	128	164	292	137	29	5	8	13	10	1970-71	1980-81
Leger, Roger	NYR, Mtl.	5	187	18	53	71	71	20	0	7	7	14	1943-44	1949-50
Legge, Barry	Que., Wpg.	3	107	1	11	12	144	....	....	....	....	....	1979-80	1981-82
Legge, Randy	NYR	1	12	0	2	2	2	....	....	....	....	....	1972-73	1972-73
Lehto, Petteri	Pit.	1	6	0	0	0	4	....	....	....	....	....	1984-85	1984-85
Lehtonen, Antero	Wsh.	1	65	9	12	21	14	....	....	....	....	....	1979-80	1979-80
Lehvonen, Henri	K.C.	1	4	0	0	0	0	....	....	....	....	....	1974-75	1974-75
Leier, Edward	Chi.	2	16	2	1	3	2	....	....	....	....	....	1949-50	1950-51
Leinonen, Mikko	NYR, Wsh.	4	162	31	78	109	71	20	2	11	13	28	1981-82	1984-85
Leiter, Bobby	Bos., Pit., Atl.	10	447	98	126	224	144	8	3	0	3	2	1962-63	1975-76
Lemaire, Jacques	Mtl.	12	853	366	469	835	217	145	61	78	139	63	1967-68	1978-79
Lemay, Moe	Van., Edm., Bos., Wpg.	8	317	72	94	166	442	28	6	3	9	55	1981-82	1988-89
Lemelin, Roger	K.C.	2	19	0	1	1	6	....	....	....	....	....	1974-75	1975-76
Lemieux, Alain	St.L., Que., Pit.	6	119	28	44	72	38	19	4	6	10	0	1981-82	1986-87
Lemieux, Bob	Oak.	1	19	0	1	1	12	....	....	....	....	....	1967-68	1967-68
Lemieux, Jacques	L.A.	2	91	11	32	43	76	1	0	0	0	0	1967-68	1968-69
Lemieux, Jean	L.A., Atl., Wsh.	6	204	23	63	86	39	3	1	1	2	0	1969-70	1977-78
Lemieux, Real	Det., L.A., NYR, Buf.	8	456	51	104	155	262	18	2	4	6	10	1966-67	1973-74
Lemieux, Richard	Van., St.L., K.C., Atl.	5	274	39	82	121	132	2	0	0	0	0	1971-72	1975-76
Lepine, Hec	Mtl.	1	33	5	2	7	2	....	....	....	....	....	1925-26	1925-26
Lepine, Pit	Mtl.	13	526	143	98	241	392	41	7	5	12	26	1925-26	1937-38
Leroux, Gaston	Mtl.	1	2	0	0	0	0	....	....	....	....	....	1935-36	1935-36
Lesieur, Art	Mtl., Chi.	4	100	4	2	6	50	14	0	0	0	4	1928-29	1935-36
Lesuk, Bill	Bos., Phi., L.A., Wsh., Wpg.	8	388	44	63	107	368	9	1	0	1	12	1968-69	1979-80
Leswick, Jack	Chi.	1	47	1	7	8	16	....	....	....	....	....	1933-34	1933-34
Leswick, Peter	NYA, Bos.	2	3	1	0	1	0	....	....	....	....	....	1936-37	1944-45
Leswick, Tony	NYR, Det., Chi.	12	740	165	159	324	900	59	13	10	23	91	1945-46	1957-58
Levandoski, Joseph	NYR	1	8	1	1	2	0	....	....	....	....	....	1946-47	1946-47
Leveille, Norm	Bos.	2	75	17	25	42	49	....	....	....	....	....	1981-82	1982-83
Lever, Don	Van., Atl., Cgy., Col., N.J., Buf.	15	1020	313	367	680	593	30	7	10	17	26	1972-73	1986-87
Levie, Craig	Wpg., Min., Van., St.L.	6	183	22	53	75	177	16	2	3	5	32	1981-82	1986-87
Levinsky, Alex	Tor., Chi., NYR	9	367	23	56	79	287	34	2	1	3	2	1930-31	1938-39
Levo, Tapio	Col., N.J.,	2	107	16	53	69	36	....	....	....	....	....	1981-82	1982-83
Lewicki, Danny	Tor., NYR, Chi.	9	461	105	135	240	177	28	0	4	4	8	1950-51	1958-59
Lewis, Bob	NYR	1	8	0	0	0	0	....	....	....	....	....	1975-76	1975-76
Lewis, Dave	NYI, L.A., N.J., Det.	15	1008	36	187	223	953	91	1	20	21	143	1973-74	1987-88
Lewis, Douglas	Mtl..	1	3	0	0	0	0	....	....	....	....	....	1946-47	1946-47
Lewis, Herbie	Det.	11	483	148	161	309	248	38	13	10	23	6	1928-29	1938-39
Ley, Rick	Tor., Hfd.	6	310	12	72	84	528	14	0	2	2	20	1968-69	1980-81
Libett, Nick	Det., K.C., Pit.	14	982	237	268	505	472	16	6	2	8	2	1967-68	1980-81
Licari, Anthony	Det.	1	9	0	1	1	0	....	....	....	....	....	1946-47	1946-47
Liddington, Bob	Tor.	1	11	0	1	1	2	....	....	....	....	....	1970-71	1970-71
Lindgren, Lars	Van., Min.	6	394	25	113	138	325	40	5	6	11	20	1978-79	1983-84
Lindsay, Ted	Det., Chi.	17	1068	379	472	851	1808	133	47	49	96	194	1944-45	1964-65
Lindstrom, Willy	Wpg., Edm., Pit.	8	582	161	162	323	200	57	14	18	32	24	1979-80	1986-87
Liscombe, Carl	Det.	9	383	137	140	277	133	59	22	19	41	20	1937-38	1945-46
Litzenberger, Ed	Mtl., Chi., Det., Tor.	12	618	178	238	416	283	40	5	13	18	34	1952-53	1963-64
Locas, Jacques	Mtl..	2	59	7	8	15	66	....	....	....	....	....	1947-48	1948-49
Lochead, Bill	NYR, Det., Col.	6	330	69	62	131	180	7	3	0	3	6	1974-75	1979-80
Locking, Norm	Chi.	2	48	2	6	8	26	1	0	0	0	0	1934-35	1935-36
Lofthouse, Mark	Wsh., Det.	6	181	42	38	80	73	....	....	....	....	....	1977-78	1982-83
Logan, Dave	Chi., Van.	6	218	5	29	34	470	12	0	0	0	10	1975-76	1980-81
Long, Barry	L.A., Det., Wpg.	5	280	11	68	79	250	5	0	1	1	18	1972-73	1981-82
Long, Stanley	Mtl..	1	....	....	....	....	....	3	0	0	0	0	1951-52	1951-52
Lonsberry, Ross	Phi., Pit., Bos., L.A.	15	968	256	310	566	806	100	21	25	46	87	1966-67	1980-81
Loob, Peter	Que.	1	8	1	2	3	0	....	....	....	....	....	1984-85	1984-85
Lorentz, Jim	NYR, Buf., Bos., St.L.	10	659	161	238	399	208	54	12	10	22	30	1968-69	1977-78
Lorimer, Bob	NYI, Col., N.J.	10	529	22	90	112	431	49	3	10	13	83	1976-77	1985-86
Lorraine, Rod	Mtl..	6	179	28	39	67	30	11	0	3	3	0	1935-36	1941-42
Loughlin, Clem	Det., Chi.	3	101	8	6	14	77	....	....	....	....	....	1926-27	1928-29
Loughlin, Wilf	Tor.	1	14	0	0	0	2	....	....	....	....	....	1923-24	1923-24
Lowdermilk, Dwayne	Wsh.	1	2	0	1	1	2	....	....	....	....	....	1980-81	1980-81
Lowe, Darren	Pit.	1	8	1	2	3	0	....	....	....	....	....	1983-84	1983-84
Lowe, Norm	NYR	2	4	1	1	2	0	....	....	....	....	....	1948-49	1949-50
Lowe, Ross	Bos., Mtl..	3	77	6	8	14	82	2	0	0	0	0	1949-50	1951-52
Lowery, Fred	Mtl.M., Pit.	2	54	1	0	1	10	2	0	0	0	6	1924-25	1925-26
Lowrey, Eddie	Ott., Ham.	3	24	2	0	2	3	....	....	....	....	....	1917-18	1920-21
Lowrey, Gerry	Chi., Ott., Tor., Phi., Pit.	6	209	48	48	96	148	2	1	0	1	2	1927-28	1932-33
Lucas, Danny	Phi.	1	6	1	0	1	0	....	....	....	....	....	1978-79	1978-79
Lucas, Dave	Det.	1	1	0	0	0	0	....	....	....	....	....	1962-63	1962-63
Luce, Don	NYR, Det., Buf., L.A., Tor.	13	894	225	329	554	364	71	17	22	39	52	1969-70	1981-82
Ludvig, Jan	N.J., Buf.	7	314	54	87	141	418	....	....	....	....	....	1982-83	1988-89
Lukowich, Bernie	Pit., St.L.	2	79	13	15	28	34	2	0	0	0	0	1973-74	1974-75
Lukowich, Morris	Wpg., Bos., L.A.	8	582	199	219	418	584	11	0	2	2	24	1979-80	1986-87
Luksa, Charlie	Hfd.	1	8	0	1	1	4	....	....	....	....	....	1979-80	1979-80
Lumley, Dave	Mtl., Edm., Hfd.	9	437	98	160	258	680	61	6	8	14	131	1978-79	1986-87
Lund, Pentti	NYR, Bos.	7	259	44	55	99	40	18	7	5	12	0	1946-47	1952-53
Lundberg, Brian	Pit.	1	1	0	0	0	2	....	....	....	....	....	1982-83	1982-83
Lunde, Len	Min., Van., Det., Chi.	8	321	39	83	122	75	20	3	2	5	2	1958-59	1970-71
Lundholm, Bengt	Wpg.	5	275	48	95	143	72	14	3	4	7	14	1981-82	1985-86
Lundrigan, Joe	Tor., Wsh.	2	52	2	8	10	22	....	....	....	....	....	1972-73	1974-75
Lundstrom, Tord	Det.	1	11	1	1	2	0	....	....	....	....	....	1973-74	1973-74
Lundy, Pat	Det. Chi.	5	150	37	32	69	31	9	1	1	2	2	1945-46	1950-51
Lupien, Gilles	Mtl., Pit., Hfd.	5	226	5	25	30	416	25	0	0	0	21	1977-78	1981-82
Lupul, Gary	Van.	7	293	70	75	145	243	25	4	7	11	11	1979-80	1985-86
Lyle, George	Det., Hfd.	4	99	24	38	62	51	....	....	....	....	....	1979-80	1982-83
Lynch, Jack	Pit., Det., Wsh.	7	382	24	106	130	336	....	....	....	....	....	1972-73	1978-79
Lynn, Vic	Det., Mtl., Tor., Bos., Chi.	10	326	49	76	125	274	47	7	10	17	46	1943-44	1953-54
Lyon, Steve	Pit.	1	3	0	0	0	2	....	....	....	....	....	1976-77	1976-77
Lyons, Ron	Bos., Phi.	1	36	2	4	6	29	5	0	0	0	0	1930-31	1930-31
Lysiak, Tom	Atl., Chi.	13	919	292	551	843	567	78	25	38	63	49	1973-74	1985-86

M

MacAdam, Al	Phi., Cal., Cle., Min., Van.	12	864	240	351	591	509	64	20	24	44	21	1973-74	1984-85
MacDonald, Blair	Edm., Van.	4	219	91	100	191	65	11	0	6	6	2	1979-80	1982-83
MacDonald, Brett	Van.	1	1	0	0	0	0	....	....	....	....	....	1987-88	1987-88
MacDonald, Kilby	NYR	4	151	36	34	70	47	15	1	2	3	4	1939-40	1944-45
MacDonald, Lowell	Det., L.A., Pit.	13	506	180	210	390	92	30	11	11	22	12	1961-62	1977-78

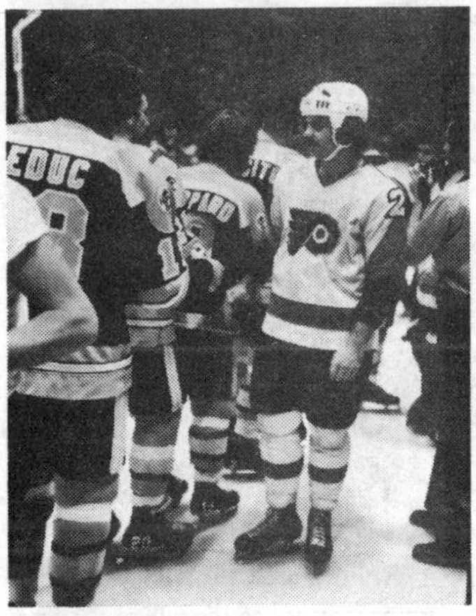

Orest Kindrachuk

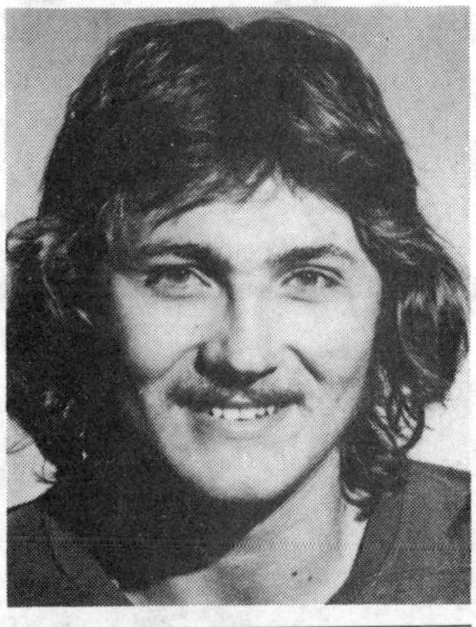

Mike Korney

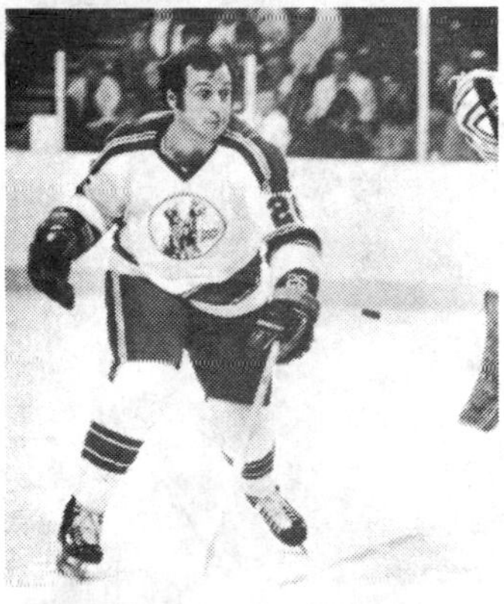

Jean-Guy Lagace

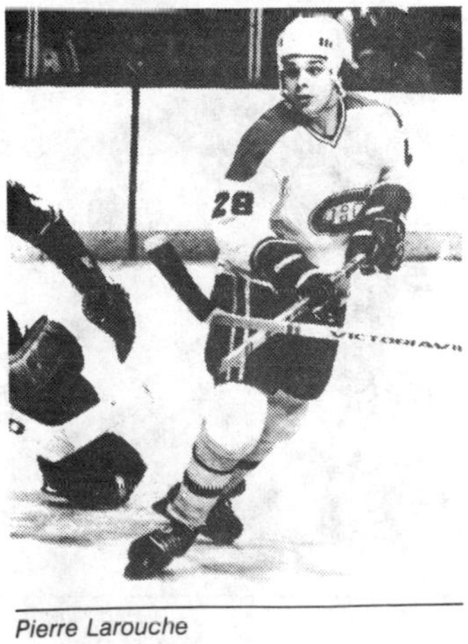

Pierre Larouche

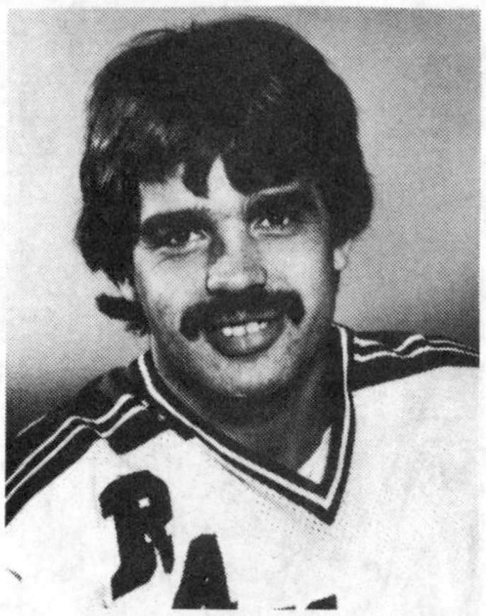

Mikko Leinonen

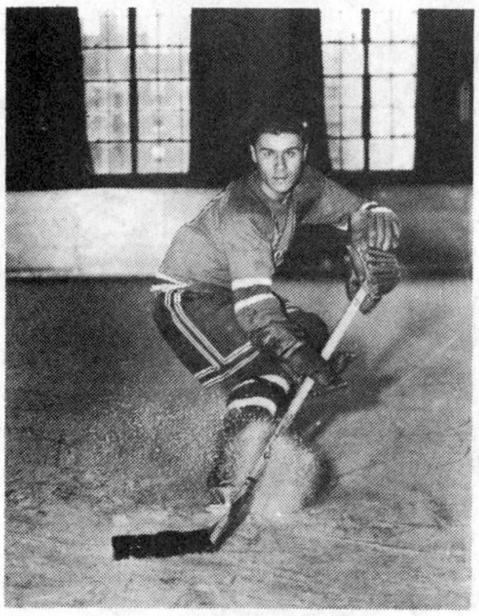

Tony Leswick

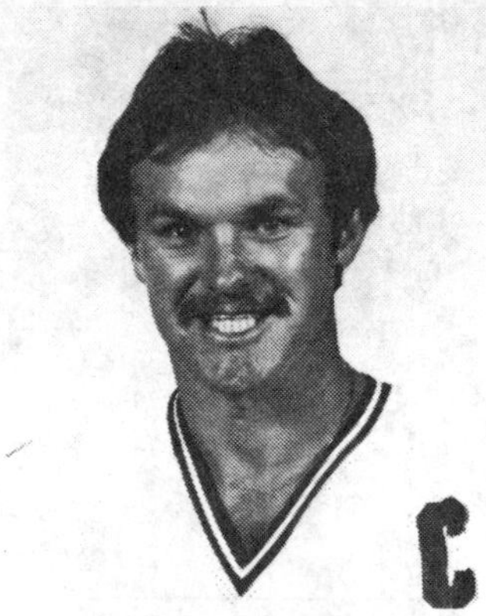

Rick Ley

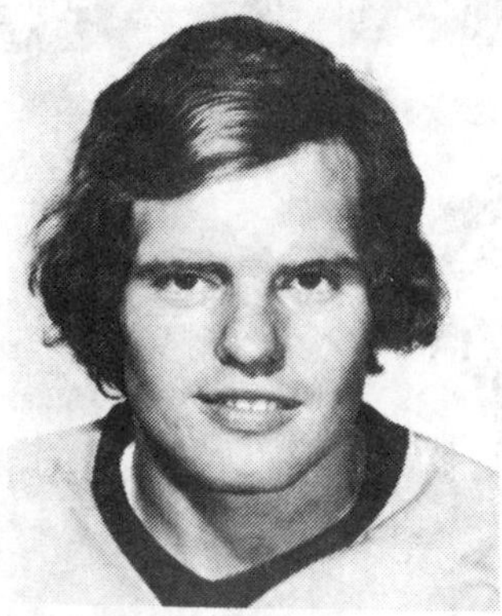

Barry Long

Name	NHL Teams	NHL Seasons	Regular Schedule					Playoffs					First NHL Season	Last NHL Season
			GP	G	A	TP	PIM	GP	G	A	TP	PIM		
MacDonald, Parker	Tor., NYR, Det., Bos., Min.	14	676	144	179	323	253	75	14	14	28	20	1952-53	1968-69
MacDougall, Kim	Min.	1	1	0	0	0	0	....	....	....	....	....	1974-75	1974-75
MacEachern, Shane	St.L.	1	1	0	0	0	0	....	....	....	....	....	1987-88	1987-88
Macey, Hubert	NYR, Mtl.	3	30	6	9	15	0	8	0	0	0	0	1941-42	1946-47
MacGregor, Bruce	Det., NYR	14	893	213	257	470	217	107	19	28	47	44	1960-61	1973-74
MacGregor, Randy	Hfd.	1	2	1	1	2	2	....	....	....	....	....	1981-82	1981-82
MacGuigan, Garth	NYI	1	2	0	0	0	0	....	....	....	....	....	1979-80	1979-80
MacIntosh, Ian	NYR	1	4	0	0	0	4	....	....	....	....	....	1952-53	1952-53
MacIver, Don	Wpg.	1	6	0	0	0	2	....	....	....	....	....	1979-80	1979-80
MacKasey, Blair	Tor.	1	1	0	0	0	2	....	....	....	....	....	1976-77	1976-77
MacKay, Calum	Det., Mtl.	8	237	50	55	105	214	38	5	13	18	20	1946-47	1954-55
Mackay, Dave	Chi.	1	29	3	0	3	26	5	0	1	1	2	1940-41	1940-41
MacKay, Mickey	Chi., Pit., Bos.	4	151	44	19	63	79	11	0	0	0	6	1926-27	1929-30
MacKay, Murdo	Mtl.	3	19	0	3	3	0	15	1	2	3	0	1945-46	1947-48
Mackell, Fleming	Tor., Bos.	13	665	149	220	369	562	80	22	41	63	75	1947-48	1959-60
MacKenzie, Barry	Min.	1	6	0	1	1	6	....	....	....	....	....	1968-69	1968-69
MacKenzie, Bill	Chi., Mtl.(M),Mtl., NYR	7	266	15	14	29	133	19	1	1	2	11	1932-33	1939-40
MacKey, Reggie	NYR	1	34	0	0	0	16	1	0	0	0	0	1926-27	1926-27
Mackie, Howie	Det.	2	20	1	0	1	4	8	0	0	0	0	1936-37	1937-38
MacKinnon, Paul	Wsh.	5	147	5	23	28	91	....	....	....	....	....	1979-80	1983-84
MacLeish, Rick	Phi., Hfd., Pit., Det.	14	846	349	410	759	434	114	54	53	107	38	1970-71	1983-84
MacMillan, Billy	Tor., Atl., NYI	7	446	74	77	151	184	53	6	6	12	40	1970-71	1976-77
MacMillan, Bob	NYR, St.L., Atl., Cgy., Col., N.J., Chi.	11	753	228	349	577	260	31	8	11	19	16	1974-75	1984-85
MacMillan, John	Tor., Det.	5	104	5	10	15	32	12	0	1	1	2	1960-61	1964-65
MacNeil, Al	Tor., Mtl., Chi., NYR, Pit.	11	524	17	75	92	617	37	0	4	4	67	1955-56	1967-68
MacNeil, Bernie	St.L.	1	4	0	0	0	0	....	....	....	....	....	1973-74	1973-74
Macoun, Jamie	Cgy.	5	320	37	111	148	381	49	3	9	12	43	1982-83	1986-87
MacPherson, Bud	Mtl.	7	259	5	33	38	233	29	0	3	3	21	1948-49	1956-57
MacSweyn, Ralph	Phi.	5	47	0	5	5	10	8	0	0	0	6	1967-68	1971-72
Madigan, Connie	St.L.	1	20	0	3	3	25	5	0	0	0	4	1972-73	1972-73
Magee, Dean	Min.	1	7	0	0	0	4	....	....	....	....	....	1977-78	1977-78
Maggs, Daryl	Chi., Cal., Tor.	3	135	14	19	33	54	4	0	0	0	0	1971-72	1979-80
Magnan, Marc	Tor.	1	4	0	1	1	5	....	....	....	....	....	1982-83	1982-83
Magnuson, Keith	Chi.	11	589	14	125	139	1442	68	3	9	12	164	1969-70	1979-80
Mahaffy, John	Mtl., NYR	3	37	11	25	36	4	1	0	1	1	0	1942-43	1944-45
Mahovlich, Frank	Tor., Det., Mtl.	18	1181	533	570	1103	1056	137	51	67	118	163	1956-57	1973-74
Mahovlich, Pete	Det., Mtl., Pit.	16	884	288	485	773	916	88	30	42	72	134	1965-66	1980-81
Mailley, Frank	Mtl.	1	1	0	0	0	0	....	....	....	....	....	1942-43	1942-43
Mair, Jim	Phi., NYI, Van.	5	76	4	15	19	49	3	1	2	3	4	1970-71	1974-75
Majeau, Fern	Mtl.	2	56	22	24	466	43	1	0	0	0	0	1943-44	1944-45
Maki, Chico	Chi.	15	841	143	292	435	345	113	17	36	53	43	1960-61	1975-76
Maki, Wayne	Chi., St.L., Van.	6	246	57	79	136	184	2	1	0	1	2	1967-68	1972-73
Makkonen, Karl	Edm.	1	9	2	2	4	0	....	....	....	....	....	1979-80	1979-80
Malinowski, Merlin	Col., N.J., Hfd.	5	282	54	111	165	121	....	....	....	....	....	1978-79	1982-83
Malone, Cliff	Mtl.	1	3	0	0	0	0	....	....	....	....	....	1951-52	1951-52
Malone, Greg	Pit., Hfd., Que.	11	704	191	310	501	661	20	3	5	8	32	1976-77	1986-87
Malone, Joe	Mtl., Que., Ham.	7	125	146	21	167	23	9	5	0	5	0	1917-18	1923-24
Maloney, Dan	Chi., L.A., Det., Tor.	11	737	192	259	451	1489	40	4	7	11	35	1970-71	1981-82
Maloney, Dave	NYR, Buf.	11	657	71	246	317	1154	49	7	17	24	91	1974-75	1984-85
Maloney, Phi.	Bos., Tor., Chi.	5	158	28	43	71	16	6	0	0	0	0	1949-50	1959-60
Maluta, Ray	Bos.	2	25	2	3	5	6	2	0	0	0	0	1975-76	1976-77
Manastersky, Tom	Mtl.	1	6	0	0	0	11	....	....	....	....	....	1950-51	1950-51
Mancuso, Gus	Mtl., NYR	4	42	7	9	16	17	....	....	....	....	....	1937-38	1942-43
Mandich, Dan	Min.	4	111	5	11	16	303	7	0	0	0	2	1982-83	1985-86
Manery, Kris	Van., Wpg., Clev., Min.	4	250	63	64	127	91	....	....	....	....	....	1977-78	1980-81
Manery, Randy	L.A., Det., Atl.	10	582	50	206	256	415	13	0	2	2	12	1970-71	1979-80
Mann, Jack	NYR	2	9	3	4	7	0	....	....	....	....	....	1943-44	1944-45
Mann, Jimmy	Wpg., Que., Pit.	8	293	10	20	30	895	22	0	0	0	89	1979-80	1987-88
Mann, Ken	Det.	1	1	0	0	0	0	....	....	....	....	....	1975-76	1975-76
Mann, Norm	Tor.	2	31	0	3	3	4	1	0	0	0	0	1938-39	1940-41
Manners, Rennison	Pit., Phi.	2	37	3	2	5	14	....	....	....	....	....	1929-30	1930-31
Manno, Bob	Van., Tor., Det.	8	371	41	131	172	274	17	2	4	6	12	1976-77	1984-85
Manson, Ray	Bos., NYR	2	2	0	1	1	0	....	....	....	....	....	1947-48	1948-49
Mantha, Georges	Mtl..	13	498	89	102	181	148	36	6	2	8	16	1928-29	1940-41
Mantha, Sylvio	Mtl., Bos.	14	543	63	72	135	667	46	5	4	9	66	1923-24	1936-37
Maracle, Buddy	NYR	1	11	1	3	4	4	4	0	0	0	0	1930-31	1930-31
Marcetta, Milan	Tor., Min.	3	54	7	15	22	10	17	7	7	14	4	1966-67	1968-69
March, Mush	Chi.	17	758	153	233	386	523	48	12	15	27	41	1928-29	1944-45
Marchinko, Brian	Tor., NYI	4	47	2	6	8	0	....	....	....	....	....	1970-71	1973-74
Marcon, Lou	Det.	3	70	0	4	4	42	....	....	....	....	....	1958-59	1962-63
Marcotte, Don	Bos.	15	868	230	254	484	317	132	34	27	61	81	1965-66	1981-82
Marini, Hector	NYI, N.J.	5	154	27	46	73	246	10	3	6	9	14	1978-79	1983-84
Mario, Frank	Bos.	2	53	9	19	28	24	....	....	....	....	....	1941-42	1944-45
Mariucci, John	Chi.	5	223	11	34	45	308	8	0	3	3	26	1940-41	1947-48
Mark, Gordon	N.J.	2	55	3	7	10	109	....	....	....	....	....	1986-87	1987-88
Markell, John	Wpg.	2	52	11	10	21	36	....	....	....	....	....	1979-80	1980-81
Marker, Gus	Det., Mtl.M., Tor., NYA	10	336	64	69	133	136	45	6	8	14	36	1932-33	1941-42
Markham, Ray	NYR	1	14	1	1	2	21	7	1	0	1	24	1979-80	1979-80
Markle, Jack	Tor.	1	8	0	1	1	0	....	....	....	....	....	1935-36	1935-36
Marks, Jack	Mtl.W, Tor., Que.	2	7	0	0	0	4	....	....	....	....	....	1917-18	1919-20
Marks, John	Chi.	10	657	112	163	275	330	57	5	9	14	60	1972-73	1981-82
Marotte, Gilles	Bos., Chi., L.A., NYR, St.L.	12	808	56	265	321	872	29	3	3	6	26	1965-66	1976-77
Marquess, Mark	Bos.	1	27	5	4	9	27	4	0	0	0	0	1946-47	1946-47
Marsh, Gary	Det., Tor.	2	7	1	3	4	4	....	....	....	....	....	1967-68	1968-69
Marsh, Peter	Wpg., Chi.	5	279	48	71	119	224	26	1	5	6	33	1979-80	1983-84
Marshall, Bert	Det., Oak., Cal., NYR, NYI	14	868	17	181	198	926	72	4	22	26	99	1965-66	1978-79
Marshall, Don	Mtl., NYR, Buf., Tor.	19	1176	265	324	589	127	94	8	15	23	14	1951-52	1971-72
Marshall, Paul	Pit., Tor., Hfd.	4	95	15	18	33	17	1	0	0	0	0	1979-80	1982-83
Marshall, Willie	Tor.	4	33	1	15	16	2	....	....	....	....	....	1952-53	1958-59
Marson, Mike	Wsh., L.A.	6	196	24	24	48	233	....	....	....	....	....	1974-75	1979-80
Martin, Clare	Bos., Det., Chi., NYR	6	237	12	28	40	78	22	0	2	2	6	1941-42	1951-52
Martin, Frank	Bos., Chi.	6	282	11	46	57	122	10	0	1	1	2	1952-53	1957-58
Martin, Grant	Van., Wsh.	4	44	0	4	4	55	1	1	0	1	2	1983-84	1986-87
Martin, Jack	Tor.	1	1	0	0	0	0	....	....	....	....	....	1960-61	1960-61
Martin, Pit	Det., Bos., Chi., Van.	17	1101	324	485	809	609	100	27	31	58	56	1961-62	1978-79
Martin, Rick	Buf., L.A.	11	685	384	317	701	477	63	24	29	53	74	1971-72	1981-82
Martin, Ron	NYA	2	94	13	16	29	36	....	....	....	....	....	1932-33	1933-34
Martin, Terry	Buf., Que., Tor., Edm., Min.	10	479	104	101	205	202	21	4	2	6	26	1975-76	1984-85
Martin, Tom	Tor.	1	3	1	0	1	0	....	....	....	....	....	1967-68	1967-68
Martineau, Don	Atl., Min., Det.	4	90	6	10	16	63	....	....	....	....	....	1973-74	1976-77
Maruk, Dennis	Cal., Clev., Min., Wsh.	14	888	356	522	878	761	34	14	22	36	26	1975-76	1988-89
Masnick, Paul	Mtl., Chi., Tor.	6	232	18	41	59	139	33	4	5	9	27	1950-51	1957-58
Mason, Charley	NYR, NYA, Det., Chi.	4	95	7	18	25	44	4	0	1	1	0	1934-35	1938-39
Massecar, George	NYA	3	100	12	11	23	46	....	....	....	....	....	1929-30	1931-32
Masters, Jamie	St.L.	3	33	1	13	14	2	2	0	0	0	0	1975-76	1978-79
Masterton, Bill	Min.	1	38	4	8	12	4	....	....	....	....	....	1967-68	1967-68
Mathers, Frank	Tor.	3	23	1	3	4	4	....	....	....	....	....	1948-49	1951-52
Mathiasen, Dwight	Pit.	3	33	1	7	8	18	....	....	....	....	....	1985-86	1987-88
Matte, Joe	Tor., Ham., Bos., Mtl.	4	64	18	14	32	43	....	....	....	....	....	1919-20	1925-26
Matte, Joe	Chi.	1	12	0	1	1	0	....	....	....	....	....	1942-43	1942-43
Matte, Roland	Det.	1	12	0	1	1	0	....	....	....	....	....	1929-30	1929-30
Mattiussi, Dick	Pit., Oak., Cal.	4	200	8	31	39	124	8	0	1	1	6	1967-68	1970-71
Matz, Johnny	Mtl.	1	30	3	2	5	0	5	0	0	0	2	1924-25	1924-25
Maxner, Wayne	Bos.	2	62	8	9	17	48	....	....	....	....	....	1964-65	1965-66
Maxwell, Brad	Min., Que., Tor., Van., NYR	10	612	98	270	368	1270	79	12	49	61	178	1977-78	1986-87
Maxwell, Bryan	Min., St.L., Wpg., Pit.	8	331	18	77	95	745	15	1	1	2	86	1977-78	1984-85
Maxwell, Kevin	Min., Col., N.J.	3	66	6	15	21	61	16	3	4	7	24	1980-81	1983-84
Maxwell, Wally	Tor.	1	2	0	0	0	0	....	....	....	....	....	1952-53	1952-53
Mayer, Jim	NYR	1	4	0	0	0	0	....	....	....	....	....	1979-80	1979-80
Mayer, Pat	Pit.	1	1	0	0	0	4	....	....	....	....	....	1987-88	1987-88
Mayer, Shep	Tor.	1	12	1	2	3	4	....	....	....	....	....	1942-43	1942-43
Mazur, Eddie	Mtl., Chi.	6	107	8	20	28	120	25	4	5	9	22	1950-51	1956-57
McAdam, Gary	Buf., Pit., Det., Cal., Wsh., N.J., Tor.	11	534	96	132	228	243	30	6	5	11	16	1975-76	1985-86
McAdam, Sam	NYR	1	5	0	0	0	0	....	....	....	....	....	1930-31	1930-31
McAndrew, Hazen	NYA	1	7	0	1	1	6	....	....	....	....	....	1941-42	1941-42

Name	NHL Teams	NHL Seasons	Regular Schedule GP	G	A	TP	PIM	Playoffs GP	G	A	TP	PIM	First NHL Season	Last NHL Season
McAneeley, Ted	Cal.	3	158	8	35	43	141	....	....	....	....	....	1972-73	1974-75
McAtee, Jud	Det.	3	46	15	13	28	6	14	2	1	3	0	1942-43	1944-45
McAtee, Norm	Bos.	1	13	0	1	1	0	....	....	....	....	....	1946-47	1946-47
McAvoy, George	Mtl.	1	....	....	....	....	....	4	0	0	0	0	1954-55	1954-55
McBride, Cliff	Mtl.M., Tor.	2	2	0	0	0	0	....	....	....	....	....	1928-29	1929-30
McBurney, Jim	Chi.	1	1	0	1	1	0	....	....	....	....	....	1952-53	1952-53
McCabe, Stan	Det., Mtl.M.	4	78	9	4	13	49	....	....	....	....	....	1929-30	1933-34
McCaffrey, Bert	Tor., Pit., Mtl.	7	260	42	30	72	202	8	2	1	3	12	1924-25	1930-31
McCahill, John	Col.	1	1	0	0	0	0	....	....	....	....	....	1977-78	1977-78
McCaig, Douglas	Det., Chi.	7	263	8	21	29	255	17	0	1	1	8	1941-42	1950-51
McCallum, Dunc	NYR, Pit.	5	187	14	35	49	230	10	1	2	3	12	1965-66	1970-71
McCalmon, Eddie	Chi., Phi.	2	39	5	0	5	14	....	....	....	....	....	1927-28	1930-31
McCann, Rick	Det.	6	43	1	4	5	6	....	....	....	....	....	1967-68	1974-75
McCarthy, Dan	NYR	1	5	4	0	4	4	....	....	....	....	....	1980-81	1980-81
McCarthy, Kevin	Phi., Van., Pit.	10	537	67	191	258	527	21	2	3	5	20	1977-78	1986-87
McCarthy, Tom	Det., Bos.	4	60	8	9	17	8	....	....	....	....	....	1956-57	1960-61
McCarthy, Tom	Que., Ham.	2	34	19	3	22	10	....	....	....	....	....	1919-20	1920-21
McCarthy, Tom	Min., Bos.	9	460	178	221	399	330	68	12	26	38	67	1979-80	1987-88
McCartney, Walt	Mtl.	1	2	0	0	0	0	....	....	....	....	....	1932-33	1932-33
McCaskill, Ted	Min.	1	4	0	2	2	0	....	....	....	....	....	1967-68	1967-68
McClanahan, Rob	Buf., Hfd., NYR	5	224	38	63	101	126	34	4	12	16	31	1979-80	1983-84
McCord, Bob	Bos., Det., Min., St.L.	7	316	58	68	126	262	14	2	5	7	10	1963-64	1972-73
McCord, Dennis	Van.	1	3	0	0	0	0	....	....	....	....	....	1973-74	1973-74
McCormack, John	Tor., Mtl., Chi.	8	311	25	49	74	35	22	1	1	2	0	1947-48	1954-55
McCourt, Dale	Det., Buf., Tor.	7	532	194	284	478	124	21	9	7	16	6	1977-78	1983-84
McCreary, Bill E.	NYR, Det., Mtl., St.L.	10	309	53	62	115	108	48	6	16	22	14	1953-54	1970-71
McCreary, Bill	Tor.	1	12	1	0	1	4	....	....	....	....	....	1980-81	1980-81
McCreary, Keith	Mtl., Pit., Atl.	10	532	131	112	243	294	16	0	4	4	6	1961-62	1974-75
McCreedy, Johnny	Tor.	2	64	17	12	29	25	21	4	3	7	16	1941-42	1944-45
McCrimmon, Jim	St.L.	1	2	0	0	0	0	....	....	....	....	....	1974-75	1974-75
McCulley, Bob	Mtl.	1	1	0	0	0	0	....	....	....	....	....	1934-35	1934-35
McCurry, Duke	Pit.	4	148	21	11	32	119	4	0	2	2	4	1925-26	1928-29
McCutcheon, Brian	Det.	3	37	3	1	4	7	....	....	....	....	....	1974-75	1976-77
McCutheon, Darwin	Tor.	1	1	0	0	0	0	....	....	....	....	....	1981-82	1981-82
McDill, Jeff	Chi.	1	1	0	0	0	0	....	....	....	....	....	1976-77	1976-77
McDonagh, Bill	NYR	1	4	0	0	0	2	....	....	....	....	....	1949-50	1949-50
McDonald, Ab	Mtl., Chi., Bos., Det., Pit., St.L.	15	762	182	248	430	200	84	21	29	50	42	1957-58	1971-72
McDonald, Brian	Chi., Buf.	2	12	0	0	0	29	8	0	0	0	2	1967-68	1970-71
McDonald, Bucko	Det., Tor., NYR	11	448	35	88	123	206	63	6	1	7	24	1934-35	1944-45
McDonald, Butch	Det., Chi.	2	66	8	20	28	2	5	0	2	2	10	1939-40	1944-45
McDonald, Gerry	Hfd.	1	3	0	0	0	0	....	....	....	....	....	1981-82	1981-82
McDonald, Jack	Mtl.W, Mtl., Que., Tor.	5	73	27	11	38	13	12	2	0	2	0	1917-18	1921-22
McDonald, John	NYR	1	43	10	9	19	6	....	....	....	....	....	1943-44	1943-44
McDonald, Lanny	Tor., Col., Cgy.	16	1111	500	506	1006	899	117	44	40	84	120	1973-74	1988-89
McDonald, Robert	NYR	1	1	0	0	0	0	....	....	....	....	....	1943-44	1943-44
McDonald, Terry	K.C.	1	8	0	1	1	6	....	....	....	....	....	1975-76	1975-76
McDonnell, Joe	Van., Pit.	3	50	2	10	12	34	....	....	....	....	....	1981-82	1985-86
McDonnell, Moylan	Ham.	1	20	1	1	2	0	....	....	....	....	....	1920-21	1920-21
McDonough, Al	L.A., Pit., Atl., Det.	5	237	73	88	161	73	8	0	1	1	2	1970-71	1977-78
McDougal, Mike	NYR, Hfd.	4	61	8	10	18	43	....	....	....	....	....	1978-79	1982-83
McElmury, Jim	Min., K.C., Col.	5	180	14	47	61	49	....	....	....	....	....	1972-73	1977-78
McEwen, Mike	NYR, Col., NYI, L.A., Wsh., Det., Hfd.	12	716	108	296	404	460	78	12	36	48	48	1976-77	1987-88
McFadden, Jim	Det., Chi.	7	412	100	126	226	89	49	10	9	19	30	1947-48	1953-54
McFadyen, Don	Chi.	4	179	12	33	45	77	12	2	2	4	5	1932-33	1935-36
McFall, Dan	Wpg.	2	9	0	1	1	0	....	....	....	....	....	1984-85	1985-86
McFarland, George	Chi.	1	2	0	0	0	0	....	....	....	....	....	1926-27	1926-27
McGeough, Jim	Wsh., Pit.	4	57	7	10	17	32	....	....	....	....	....	1981-82	1980-07
McGibbon, John	Mtl.	1	1	0	0	0	2	....	....	....	....	....	1942-43	1942-43
McGill, Jack	Mtl.	3	134	27	10	37	71	3	2	0	2	0	1934-35	1936-37
McGill, Jack G.	Bos.	4	97	23	36	59	42	27	7	4	11	17	1941-42	1946-47
McGregor, Sandy	NYR	1	2	0	0	0	2	....	....	....	....	....	1963-64	1963-64
McGuire, Mickey	Pit.	2	36	3	0	3	6	....	....	....	....	....	1926-27	1927-28
McIlhargey, Jack	Phi., Van., Hfd.	8	393	11	36	47	1102	27	0	3	3	68	1974-75	1981-82
McInenly, Bert	Det., NYA, Ott., Bos.	6	166	19	15	34	144	4	0	0	0	2	1930-31	1935-36
McIntosh, Bruce	Min.	1	2	0	0	0	0	....	....	....	....	....	1972-73	1972-73
McIntosh, Paul	Buf.	2	48	0	0	2	66	2	0	0	0	7	1974-75	1975-76
McIntyre. Jack	Bos.. Chi.. Det.	11	499	109	102	211	173	29	7	6	13	4	1949-50	1959-60
McIntyre, Larry	Tor.	2	41	0	3	3	26	....	....	....	....	....	1969-70	1972-73
McKay, Doug	Det.	1	....	....	....	....	....	1	0	0	0	0	1949-50	1949-50
McKay, Ray	Chi., Buf., Cal.	6	140	2	16	18	102	1	0	0	0	0	1968-69	1973-74
McKechnie, Walt	Min., Cal., Bos., Det., Wsh., Clev., Tor., Col.	16	955	214	392	606	469	15	7	5	12	9	1967-68	1982-83
McKegney, Ian	Chi.	1	3	0	0	0	2	....	....	....	....	....	1976-77	1976-77
McKell, Jack	Ott.	2	42	4	1	5	42	9	0	0	0	0	1919-20	1920-21
McKendry, Alex	NYI, Cgy.	4	46	3	6	9	21	6	2	2	4	0	1977-78	1980-81
McKenney, Don	Bos., NYR, Tor., Det., St.L.	13	798	237	345	582	211	58	18	29	47	10	1954-55	1967-68
McKenny, Jim	Tor., Min.	14	604	82	247	329	294	37	7	9	16	10	1965-66	1978-79
McKenzie, Brian	Pit.	1	6	1	1	2	4	....	....	....	....	....	1971-72	1971-72
McKenzie, John	Chi., Det., NYR, Bos.	12	691	206	268	474	917	69	15	32	47	133	1958-59	1971-72
McKinnon, Alex	Ham., NYA, Chi.	5	194	19	10	29	235	....	....	....	....	....	1924-25	1928-29
McKinnon, Bob	Chi.	1	2	0	0	0	0	....	....	....	....	....	1928-29	1928-29
McKinnon, John	Mtl., Pit., Phi.	6	218	28	11	39	224	2	0	0	0	4	1925-26	1930-31
McLean, Don	Wsh.	1	9	0	0	0	6	....	....	....	....	....	1975-76	1975-76
McLean, Fred	Que., Ham.	2	9	0	0	0	2	....	....	....	....	....	1919-20	1920-21
McLean, Jack	Tor.	3	67	14	24	38	76	13	2	2	4	8	1942-43	1944-45
McLellan, John	Tor.	1	2	0	0	0	0	....	....	....	....	....	1951-52	1951-52
McLellan, Scott	Bos.	1	2	0	0	0	0	....	....	....	....	....	1982-83	1982-83
McLellan, Todd	NYI	1	5	1	1	2	0	....	....	....	....	....	1987-88	1987-88
McLenahan, Roly	Det.	1	9	2	1	3	10	2	0	0	0	0	1945-46	1945-46
McLeod, Al	Det.	1	26	2	2	4	24	....	....	....	....	....	1973-74	1973-74
McLeod, Jackie	NYR	5	106	14	23	37	12	7	0	0	0	0	1949-50	1954-55
McMahon, Mike	NYR, Min., Chi., Det., Pit., Buf.	8	224	15	68	83	171	14	3	7	10	4	1963-64	1971-72
McMahon, Mike C.	Mtl., Bos	3	57	7	18	25	102	13	1	2	3	30	1942-43	1945-46
McManama, Bob	Pit.	3	99	11	25	36	28	8	0	1	1	6	1973-74	1975-76
McManus, Sammy	Mtl.M., Bos.	2	26	0	1	1	8	1	0	0	0	0	1934-35	1936-37
McMurchy, Tom	Chi., Edm.	4	55	8	4	12	65	....	....	....	....	....	1983-84	1987-88
McNab, Max	Det.	4	128	16	19	35	24	25	1	0	1	4	1947-48	1950-51
McNab, Peter	Buf., Bos., Van., N.J.	14	954	363	450	813	179	107	40	42	82	20	1973-74	1986-87
McNabney, Sid	Mtl.	1	....	....	....	....	....	5	0	1	1	2	1950-51	1950-51
McNamara, Howard	Mtl.	1	11	1	0	1	2	....	....	....	....	....	1919-20	1919-20
McNaughton, George	Que.	1	1	0	0	0	0	....	....	....	....	....	1919-20	1919-20
McNeill, Billy	Det.	6	257	21	46	67	142	4	1	1	2	4	1956-57	1963-64
McNeill, Stu	Det.	3	10	1	1	2	2	....	....	....	....	....	1957-58	1959-60
McPhee, George	NYR, N.J.	7	115	24	25	49	257	29	5	3	8	69	1982-83	1988-89
McReavy, Pat	Bos., Det.	4	55	5	10	15	4	20	3	3	6	9	1938-39	1941-42
McSheffrey, Bryan	Van., Buf.	3	90	13	7	20	44	....	....	....	....	....	1972-73	1974-75
McTaggart, Jim	Wsh.	2	71	3	10	13	205	....	....	....	....	....	1980-81	1981-82
McTavish, Gordon	St.L., Wpg.	2	11	1	3	4	2	....	....	....	....	....	1978-79	1979-80
McVeigh, Charley	Chi., NYA	9	397	84	88	172	138	4	0	0	0	2	1926-27	1934-35
McVicar, Jack	Mtl.M.	2	88	2	4	6	63	2	0	0	0	2	1930-31	1931-32
Meehan, Gerry	Tor., Phi., Buf., Van., Atl., Wsh.	10	670	180	243	423	111	10	0	1	1	0	1968-69	1978-79
Meeke, Brent	Cal., Clev.	5	75	9	22	31	8	....	....	....	....	....	1972-73	1976-77
Meeker, Howie	Tor.	8	346	83	102	185	329	42	6	9	15	50	1946-47	1953-54
Meeker, Mike	Pit.	1	4	0	0	0	5	....	....	....	....	....	1978-79	1978-79
Meeking, Harry	Tor., Det., Bos.	3	63	18	3	21	42	14	4	2	6	0	1917-18	1926-27
Meger, Paul	Mtl.	6	212	39	52	91	112	35	3	8	11	16	1949-50	1954-55
Meighan, Ron	Min., Pit.	2	48	3	7	10	18	....	....	....	....	....	1981-82	1982-83
Meissner, Barrie	Min.	2	6	0	1	1	4	....	....	....	....	....	1967-68	1968-69
Meissner, Dick	Bos., NYR	5	171	11	15	26	37	....	....	....	....	....	1959-60	1964-65
Melametsa, Anssi	Wpg.	1	27	0	3	3	2	....	....	....	....	....	1985-86	1985-86
Melin, Roger	Min.	2	3	0	0	0	0	....	....	....	....	....	1980-81	1981-82
Mellor, Tom	Det.	2	26	2	4	6	25	....	....	....	....	....	1973-74	1974-75
Melnyk, Gerry	Det., Chi., St.L.	6	269	39	77	116	34	53	6	6	12	6	1955-56	1967-68
Melrose, Barry	Wpg., Tor., Det.	6	300	10	23	33	728	7	0	2	2	38	1979-80	1985-86
Menard, Hillary	Chi.	1	1	0	0	0	0	....	....	....	....	....	1953-54	1953-54

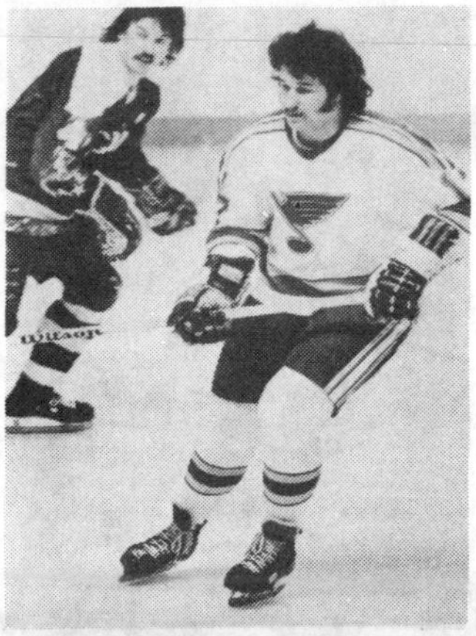
Bernie Lukowich

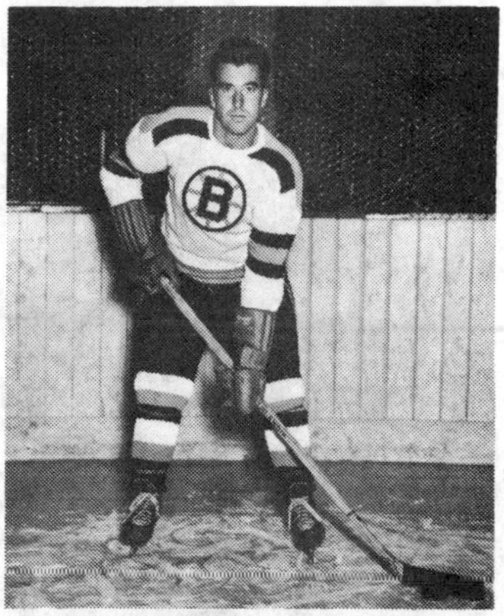
Phil Maloney

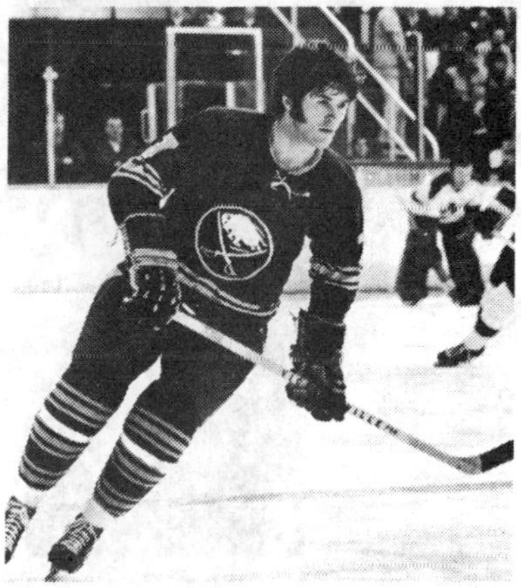
Rick Martin

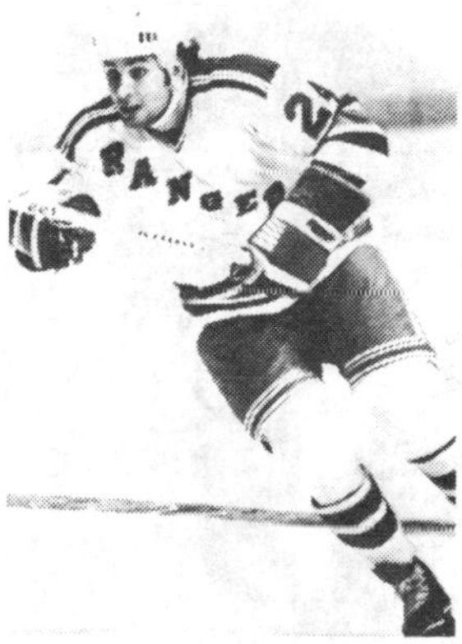
Warren Miller

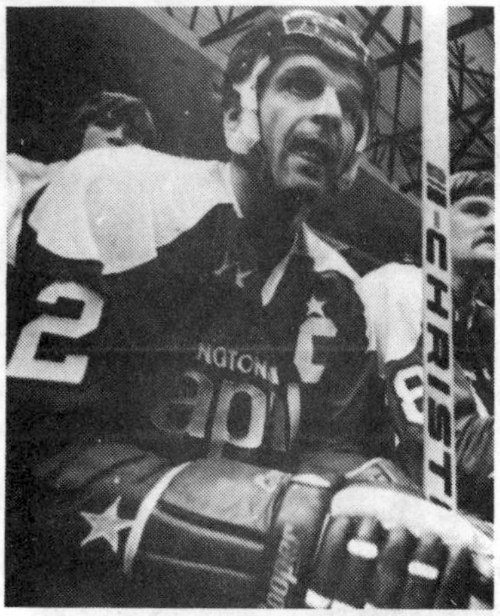

Doug Mohns

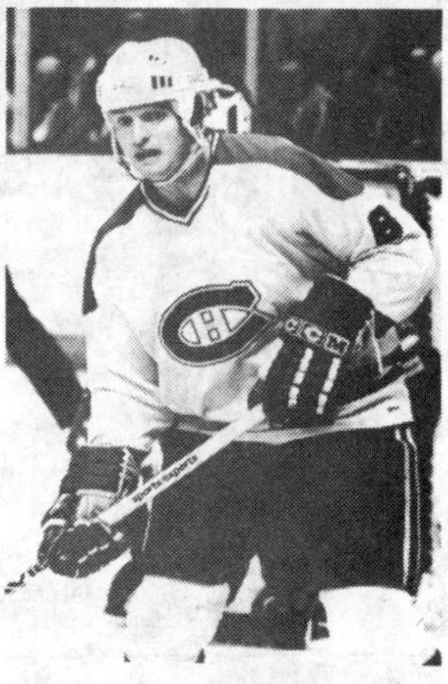

Pierre Mondou

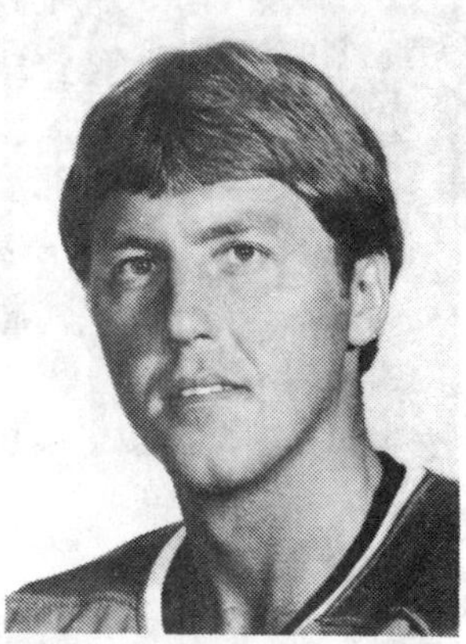

Lew Morrison

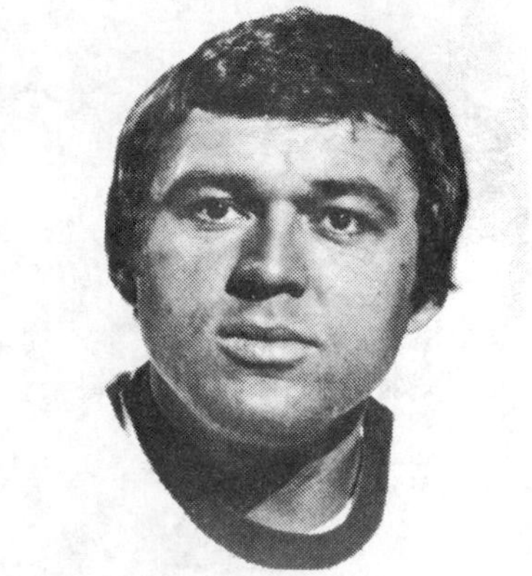

Vaclav Nedomansky

			Regular Schedule					Playoffs						
Name	NHL Teams	NHL Seasons	GP	G	A	TP	PIM	GP	G	A	TP	PIM	First NHL Season	Last NHL Season
Menard, Howie	Det., L.A., Chi., Oak.	4	151	23	42	65	87	19	3	7	10	36	1963-64	1969-70
Mercredi, Vic	Atl.	1	2	0	0	0	0	....	....	....	....	....	1974-75	1974-75
Meredith, Greg	Cgy.	2	38	6	4	10	8	5	3	1	4	4	1980-81	1982-83
Merkosky, Glenn	Hfd., N.J., Det.	4	63	5	12	17	22	....	....	....	....	....	1981-82	1985-86
Meronek, Bill	Mtl.	2	19	5	8	13	0	1	0	0	0	0	1939-40	1942-43
Merrick, Wayne	St.L., Cal., Clev., NYI	12	774	191	265	456	303	102	19	30	49	30	1972-73	1983-84
Merrill, Horace	Ott.	2	11	0	0	0	0	....	....	....	....	....	1917-18	1919-20
Messier, Paul	Col.	1	9	0	0	0	4	....	....	....	....	....	1978-79	1978-79
Metz, Don	Tor.	8	172	20	35	55	42	47	7	8	15	10	1939-40	1948-49
Metz, Nick	Tor.	12	518	131	119	250	149	76	19	20	39	31	1934-35	1947-48
Michaluk, Art	Chi.	1	5	0	0	0	0	....	....	....	....	....	1947-48	1947-48
Michaluk, John	Chi.	1	1	0	0	0	0	....	....	....	....	....	1950-51	1950-51
Michayluk, Dave	Phi.	2	14	2	6	8	8	....	....	....	....	....	1981-82	1982-83
Micheletti, Joe	St.L., Col.	3	158	11	60	71	114	11	1	11	12	10	1979-80	1981-82
Micheletii, Pat	Min.	1	12	2	0	2	8	....	....	....	....	....	1987-88	1987-88
Mickey, Larry	Chi., NYR., Tor., Mtl., L.A., Phi., Buf.	11	292	39	53	92	160	9	1	0	1	10	1964-65	1974-75
Mickoski, Nick	NYR, Chi., Det., Bos.	13	703	158	184	342	319	18	1	6	7	6	1947-48	1959-60
Middleton, Rick	NYR, Bos.	14	1005	448	540	988	157	114	45	55	100	19	1974-75	1987-88
Migay, Rudy	Tor.	10	418	59	92	151	293	15	1	0	1	20	1949-50	1959-60
Mikita, Stan	Chi.	22	1394	541	926	1467	1270	155	59	91	150	169	1958-59	1979-80
Mikkelson, Bill	L.A., N.Y.I., Wsh.	4	147	4	18	22	105	....	....	....	....	....	1971-72	1976-77
Mikol, Jim	Tor., NYR	2	34	1	4	5	8	....	....	....	....	....	1962-63	1964-65
Milbury, Mike	Bos.	12	754	49	189	238	1552	86	4	24	28	219	1975-76	1986-87
Milks, Hib	Pit., Phi., NYR, Ott.	8	314	87	41	128	179	10	0	0	0	2	1925-26	1932-33
Millar, Hugh	Det.	1	4	0	0	0	0	1	0	0	0	0	1946-47	1946-47
Miller, Bill	Mtl.M., Mtl.	3	95	7	3	10	16	12	0	0	0	0	1934-35	1936-37
Miller, Bob	Bos., Col., L.A.	6	404	75	119	294	220	36	4	7	11	27	1977-78	1984-85
Miller, Earl	Chi., Tor.	5	116	19	14	33	124	10	1	0	1	6	1927-28	1931-32
Miller, Jack	Chi.	2	17	0	0	0	4	....	....	....	....	....	1949-50	1950-51
Miller, Paul	Col.	1	3	0	3	3	0	....	....	....	....	....	1981-82	1981-82
Miller, Perry	Det.	4	217	10	51	61	387	....	....	....	....	....	1977-78	1980-81
Miller, Tom	Det., NYI	4	118	16	25	41	34	....	....	....	....	....	1970-71	1974-75
Miller, Warren	NYR, Hfd.	4	262	40	50	90	137	6	1	0	1	0	1979-80	1982-83
Minor, Gerry	Van.	5	140	11	21	32	173	12	1	3	4	25	1979-80	1983-84
Miszuk, John	Det., Chi., Phi., Min.	6	237	7	39	46	232	19	0	3	3	19	1963-64	1969-70
Mitchell, Bill	Det.	1	1	0	0	0	0	....	....	....	....	....	1963-64	1963-64
Mitchell, Herb	Bos.	2	53	6	0	6	38	....	....	....	....	....	1924-25	1925-26
Mitchell, Red	Chi.	3	83	4	5	9	67	....	....	....	....	....	1941-42	1944-45
Moe, Billy	NYR	5	261	11	42	53	163	1	0	0	0	0	1944-45	1948-49
Moffat, Lyle	Tor., Wpg.	3	97	12	16	28	51	....	....	....	....	....	1972-73	1979-80
Moffat, Ron	Det.	3	36	1	1	2	8	7	0	0	0	0	1932-33	1934-35
Moher, Mike	N.J.	1	9	0	1	1	28	....	....	....	....	....	1982-83	1982-83
Mohns, Doug	Bos., Chi., Min., Atl., Wsh.	22	1390	248	462	710	1250	94	14	36	50	122	1953-54	1974-75
Mohns, Lloyd	NYR	1	1	0	0	0	0	....	....	....	....	....	1943-44	1943-44
Molin, Lars	Van.	3	172	33	65	98	37	19	2	9	11	7	1981-82	1983-84
Molyneaux, Larry	NYR	2	45	0	1	1	20	3	0	0	0	8	1937-38	1938-39
Monahan, Garry	Mtl., Det., L.A., Tor., Van.	12	748	116	169	285	484	22	3	1	4	13	1967-68	1978-79
Monahan, Hartland	Cal., NYR, Wsh., Pit., L.A., St.L.	7	334	61	80	141	163	6	0	0	0	4	1973-74	1980-81
Mondou, Armand	Mtl.	12	385	47	71	118	99	35	3	5	8	12	1928-29	1939-40
Mondou, Pierre	Mtl.	9	548	194	262	456	179	69	17	28	45	26	1976-77	1984-85
Mongrain, Bob	Buf., L.A.	6	83	13	14	27	14	11	1	2	3	2	1979-80	1985-86
Monteith, Hank	Det.	3	77	5	12	17	6	4	0	0	0	0	1968-69	1970-71
Moore, Dickie	Mtl., Tor., St.L.	14	719	261	347	608	652	135	46	64	110	122	1951-52	1967-68
Moran, Amby	Mtl., Chi.	2	35	1	1	2	24	....	....	....	....	....	1926-27	1927-28
Morenz, Howie	Mtl., Chi., NYR	14	550	273	197	470	563	47	21	11	32	68	1923-24	1936-37
Moretto, Angelo	Clev.	1	5	1	2	3	2	....	....	....	....	....	1976-77	1976-77
Morin, Pete	Mtl.	1	31	10	12	22	7	1	0	0	0	0	1941-42	1941-42
Morris, Bernie	Bos.	1	6	2	0	2	0	....	....	....	....	....	1924-25	1924-25
Morris, Elwyn	Tor., NYR	4	135	13	29	42	58	18	4	2	6	16	1943-44	1948-49
Morrison, Dave	L.A., Van.	4	39	3	3	6	4	....	....	....	....	....	1980-81	1984-85
Morrison, Don	Det., Chi.	3	112	18	28	46	12	3	0	1	1	0	1947-48	1950-51
Morrison, Doug	Bos.	4	23	7	3	10	15	....	....	....	....	....	1979-80	1984-85
Morrison, Gary	Phi.	3	43	1	15	16	70	5	0	1	1	2	1979-80	1981-82
Morrison, George	St.L.	2	115	17	21	38	13	3	0	0	0	0	1970-71	1971-72
Morrison, Jim	Bos., Tor., Det., NYR, Pit.	12	704	40	160	200	542	36	0	12	12	38	1951-52	1970-71
Morrison, John	NYA	1	18	0	0	0	0	....	....	....	....	....	1925-26	1925-26
Morrison, Kevin	Col.	1	41	4	11	15	23	....	....	....	....	....	1979-80	1979-80
Morrison, Lew	Phi., Atl., Wsh., Pit.	9	564	39	52	91	107	17	0	0	0	2	1969-70	1977-78
Morrison, Mark	NYR	2	10	1	1	2	0	....	....	....	....	....	1981-82	1983-84
Morrison, Roderick	Det.	1	34	8	7	15	4	3	0	0	0	0	1947-48	1947-48
Morrow, Ken	NYI	10	550	17	88	105	309	127	11	22	33	97	1979-80	1988-89
Mortson, Gus	Tor., Chi., Det.	13	797	46	152	198	1380	54	5	8	13	68	1946-47	1958-59
Mosdell, Kenny	NYA, Mtl., Chi.	16	693	141	168	309	475	79	16	13	29	48	1941-42	1958-59
Mosienko, Bill	Chi.	14	711	258	282	540	117	22	10	4	14	15	1941-42	1954-55
Mott, Morris	Cal.	3	199	18	32	50	49	....	....	....	....	....	1972-73	1974-75
Motter, Alex	Bos., Det.	8	267	39	64	103	135	40	3	9	12	41	1934-35	1942-43
Moxey, Jim	Cal., Clev., L.A.	3	127	22	27	49	59	....	....	....	....	....	1974-75	1976-77
Mulhern, Richard	Atl., L.A., Tor., Wpg.	6	303	27	93	120	217	7	0	3	3	5	1975-76	1980-81
Muloin, Wayne	Det., Oak., Cal., Min.	3	147	3	21	24	93	11	0	0	0	2	1963-64	1970-71
Mulvey, Grant	Chi., N.J.	10	586	149	135	284	816	42	10	5	15	70	1974-75	1983-84
Mulvey, Paul	Wsh., Pit., L.A.	4	225	30	51	81	613	....	....	....	....	....	1978-79	1981-82
Mummery, Harry	Tor., Que., Mtl., Ham.	6	106	33	13	46	161	7	1	4	5	0	1917-18	1922-23
Munro, Dunc	Mtl.	8	239	28	18	46	170	25	3	2	5	24	1924-25	1931-32
Munro, Gerry	Mtl., Tor.	2	33	1	0	1	22	....	....	....	....	....	1924-25	1925-26
Murdoch, Bob L.	Cal., Clev., St.L.	4	260	72	85	157	127	....	....	....	....	....	1975-76	1978-79
Murdoch, Bob J.	Mtl., L.A., Atl., Cgy.	12	757	60	218	278	764	69	4	18	22	92	1970-71	1981-82
Murdoch, Don	NYR, Edm., Det.	6	320	121	117	238	155	24	10	8	18	16	1976-77	1981-82
Murdoch, Murray	NYR	11	507	84	108	192	197	55	9	12	21	28	1926-27	1936-37
Murphy, Brian	Det.	1	1	0	0	0	0	....	....	....	....	....	1974-75	1974-75
Murphy, Mike	St.L. NYR, L.A.	12	831	238	318	556	514	66	13	23	36	54	1971-72	1982-83
Murphy, Ron	NYR, Chi., Det., Bos.	18	889	205	274	479	460	53	7	8	15	26	1952-53	1969-70
Murray, Allan	NYA	7	277	5	9	14	163	14	0	0	0	8	1933-34	1939-40
Murray, Bob J.	Atl., Van.	4	194	6	16	22	98	9	1	1	2	15	1973-74	1976-77
Murray, Jim	L.A.	1	30	0	2	2	14	....	....	....	....	....	1967-68	1967-68
Murray, Ken	Tor., N.Y.I., Det., K.C.	5	106	1	10	11	135	....	....	....	....	....	1969-70	1975-76
Murray, Leo	Mtl.	1	6	0	0	0	2	....	....	....	....	....	1932-33	1932-33
Murray, Mike	Phi.	1	1	0	0	0	0	....	....	....	....	....	1987-88	1987-88
Murray, Randy	Tor.	1	3	0	0	0	2	....	....	....	....	....	1969-70	1969-70
Murray, Terry	Cal., Phi., Det., Wsh.	8	302	4	76	80	199	18	2	2	4	10	1972-73	1981-82
Myers, Hap	Buf.	1	13	0	0	0	6	....	....	....	....	....	1970-71	1970-71
Myles, Vic	NYR	1	45	6	9	15	57	....	....	....	....	....	1942-43	1942-43

N

Nahrgang, Jim	Det.	3	57	5	12	17	34	....	....	....	....	....	1974-75	1976-77
Nanne, Lou	Min.	11	635	68	157	225	356	32	4	10	14	9	1967-68	1977-78
Nantais. Richard	Min.	3	63	5	4	9	79	....	....	....	....	....	1974-75	1976-77
Nattrass, Ralph	Chi.	4	223	18	38	56	308	....	....	....	....	....	1946-47	1949-50
Natyshak, Mike	Que.	1	4	0	0	0	0	....	....	....	....	....	1987-88	1987-88
Nechaev, Victor	L.A.	1	3	1	0	1	0	....	....	....	....	....	1982-83	1982-83
Nedomansky, Vaclav	Det., NYR, St.L.	6	421	122	156	278	88	7	3	5	8	0	1977-78	1982-83
Neely, Bob	Tor., Col.	5	283	39	59	98	266	26	5	7	12	15	1973-74	1977-78
Neilsen, Jim	NYR, Cal., Clev.	16	1023	69	299	368	904	65	1	17	18	61	1962-63	1977-78
Nelson, Gordie	Tor.	1	3	0	0	0	11	....	....	....	....	....	1969-70	1969-70
Nesterenko, Eric	Tor., Chi.	21	1219	250	324	574	1273	124	13	24	37	127	1951-52	1971-72
Nethery, Lance	NYR, Edm.	2	41	11	14	25	14	14	5	3	8	9	1980-81	1981-82
Neville, Mike	Tor., NYA	4	62	6	3	9	14	2	0	0	0	0	1917-18	1930-31
Nevin, Bob	Tor., NYR, Min., L.A.	18	1128	307	419	726	211	84	16	18	34	24	1957-58	1975-76
Newberry, John	Mtl., Hfd.	4	22	0	4	4	6	2	0	0	0	0	1982-83	1985-86
Newell, Rick	Det.	2	7	0	0	0	0	....	....	....	....	....	1972-73	1973-74
Newman, Dan	NYR, Mtl., Edm.	4	126	17	24	41	63	3	0	0	0	4	1976-77	1979-80
Newman, John	Det.	1	8	1	1	2	0	....	....	....	....	....	1930-31	1930-31
Nicholson, Al	Bos.	2	19	0	1	1	4	....	....	....	....	....	1955-56	1956-57

Name	NHL Teams	NHL Seasons	Regular Schedule GP	G	A	TP	PIM	Playoffs GP	G	A	TP	PIM	First NHL Season	Last NHL Season
Nicholson, Edward	Det.	1	1	0	0	0	0	....	....	....	....	....	1947-48	1947-48
Nicholson, Graeme	Bos., Col., NYR	3	52	2	7	9	60	....	....	....	....	....	1978-79	1982-83
Nicholson, John	Chi.	1	2	1	0	1	0	....	....	....	....	....	1937-38	1937-38
Nicholson, Neil	Oak., N.Y.I.	4	39	3	1	4	23	2	0	0	0	0	1969-70	1977-78
Nicholson, Paul	Wsh.	3	62	4	8	12	18	....	....	....	....	....	1974-75	1976-77
Niekamp, Jim	Det.	2	29	0	2	2	27	....	....	....	....	....	1970-71	1971-72
Nienhuis, Kraig	Bos.	3	87	20	16	36	39	2	0	0	0	14	1985-86	1987-88
Nighbor, Frank	Ott., Tor.	13	348	135	61	196	255	36	11	9	20	27	1917-18	1929-30
Nigro, Frank	Tor.	2	68	8	18	26	39	3	0	0	0	2	1982-83	1983-84
Nilsson, Kent	Atl., Cgy., Min., Edm.	8	547	263	422	685	116	59	11	41	52	14	1979-80	1986-87
Nilsson, Ulf	NYR	4	170	57	112	169	85	25	8	14	22	27	1978-79	1982-83
Nistico, Lou	Col.	1	3	0	0	0	0	....	....	....	....	....	1977-78	1977-78
Noble, Reg	Tor., Mtl.M., Det.	16	526	167	79	246	807	32	4	5	9	39	1917-18	1932-33
Noel, Claude	Wsh.	1	7	0	0	0	0	....	....	....	....	....	1979-80	1979-80
Nolan, Pat	Tor.	1	2	0	0	0	0	....	....	....	....	....	1921-22	1921-22
Nolan, Ted	Det., Pit.	3	78	6	16	22	105	....	....	....	....	....	1981-82	1985-86
Nolet, Simon	Phi., K.C., Pit., Col.	10	562	150	182	332	187	34	6	3	9	8	1967-68	1976-77
Noris, Joe	Pit., St.L., Buf.	3	55	2	5	7	22	....	....	....	....	....	1971-72	1973-74
Norrish, Rod	Min.	2	21	3	3	6	2	....	....	....	....	....	1973-74	1974-75
Northcott, Baldy	Mtl.M., Chi.	11	446	133	112	245	273	31	8	5	13	14	1928-29	1938-39
Norwich, Craig	Wpg., St.L., Col.	2	104	17	58	75	60	....	....	....	....	....	1979-80	1980-81
Novy, Milan	Wsh.	1	73	18	30	48	16	2	0	0	0	0	1982-83	1982-83
Nowak, Hank	Pit., Det., Bos.	4	180	26	29	55	161	13	1	0	1	8	1973-74	1976-77
Nykoluk, Mike	Tor.	1	32	3	1	4	20	....	....	....	....	....	1956-57	1956-57
Nyrop, Bill	Mtl., Min.	4	207	12	51	63	101	35	1	7	8	22	1975-76	1981-82
Nystrom, Bob	NYI	14	900	235	278	513	1248	157	39	44	83	236	1972-73	1985-86

O

Name	NHL Teams	NHL Seasons	Regular Schedule GP	G	A	TP	PIM	Playoffs GP	G	A	TP	PIM	First NHL Season	Last NHL Season
Oatman, Russell	Det., Mtl.M., NYR	3	124	20	9	29	100	17	1	0	1	18	1926-27	1928-29
O'Brien, Dennis	Min., Col., Clev., Bos.	10	592	31	91	122	1017	34	1	2	3	101	1970-71	1979-80
O'Brien, Obie	Bos.	1	2	0	0	0	0	....	....	....	....	....	1955-56	1955-56
O'Callahan, Jack	Chi., N.J.	7	389	27	104	131	541	32	4	11	15	41	1982-83	1988-89
O'Connor, Buddy	Mtl., NYR	10	509	140	257	397	34	53	15	21	36	6	1941-42	1950-51
Oddleifson, Chris	Bos., Van.	9	524	95	191	286	464	14	1	6	7	8	1972-73	1980-81
O'Donnell, Fred	Bos.	2	115	15	11	26	98	5	0	1	1	5	1972-73	1973-74
O'Donoghue, Don	Oak., Cal.	3	125	18	17	35	35	3	0	0	0	0	1969-70	1971-72
Odrowski, Gerry	Det., Oak., St.L.	6	299	12	19	31	111	30	0	1	1	16	1960-61	1971-72
O'Flaherty, Gerry	Tor., Van., Atl.	8	438	99	95	194	168	7	2	2	4	6	1971-72	1978-79
O'Flaherty, John	NYA	2	21	5	1	6	0	....	....	....	....	....	1940-41	1941-42
Ogilvie, Brian	Chi., St.L.	6	90	15	21	36	29	....	....	....	....	....	1972-73	1978-79
O'Grady, George	Mtl.M.	1	4	0	0	0	0	....	....	....	....	....	1917-18	1917-18
Okerlund, Todd	NYI	1	4	0	0	0	2	....	....	....	....	....	1987-88	1987-88
Oliver, Harry	Bos., NYA	11	473	127	85	212	147	35	10	6	16	22	1926-27	1936-37
Oliver, Murray	Det., Bos., Tor., Min.	17	1127	274	454	728	319	35	9	16	25	10	1957-58	1974-75
Olmstead, Bert	Chi., Mtl., Tor.	14	848	181	421	602	884	115	16	42	58	101	1948-49	1961-62
Olson, Dennis	Det.	1	4	0	0	0	0	....	....	....	....	....	1957-58	1957-58
O'Neil, Paul	Van., Bos.	2	6	0	0	0	0	....	....	....	....	....	1973-74	1975-76
O'Neill, Jim	Bos., Mtl.	6	165	6	30	36	109	11	1	1	2	13	1933-34	1941-42
O'Neill, Tom	Tor.	2	66	10	12	22	53	4	0	0	0	6	1943-44	1944-45
O'Regan, Tom	Pit.	3	60	5	12	17	10	....	....	....	....	....	1983-84	1985-86
Orban, Bill	Chi., Min.	3	114	8	15	23	67	3	0	0	0	0	1967-68	1969-70
O'Ree, Willie	Bos.	2	45	4	10	14	26	....	....	....	....	....	1957-58	1960-61
O'Reilly, Terry	Bos.	14	891	204	402	606	2095	108	25	42	67	335	1971-72	1984-85
Orlando, Gaetano	Buf.	3	98	18	26	44	51	5	0	4	4	14	1984-85	1986-87
Orlando, Jimmy	Det.	6	200	7	24	31	375	36	0	9	9	105	1936-37	1942-43
Orleski, Dave	Mtl.	2	2	0	0	0	0	....	....	....	....	....	1980-81	1981-82
Orr, Bobby	Bos., Chi.	12	657	270	645	915	953	74	26	66	92	107	1966-67	1978-79
Osburn, Randy	Tor., Phi.	2	27	0	2	2	0	....	....	....	....	....	1972-73	1974-75
O'Shea, Danny	Min., Chi., St.L.	5	369	64	115	179	265	39	3	7	10	62	1968-69	1972-73
O'Shea, Kevin	Buf., St.L.	3	134	13	18	31	85	12	2	1	3	10	1970-71	1972-73
Ouelette, Eddie	Chi.	1	43	3	2	5	11	1	0	0	0	0	1935-36	1935-36
Ouelette, Gerry	Bos.	1	34	5	4	9	0	....	....	....	....	....	1960-61	1960-61
Owchar, Dennis	Pit., Col.	6	288	30	85	115	200	10	1	1	2	8	1974-75	1979-80
Owen, George	Bos.	5	192	44	33	77	151	21	2	5	7	25	1928-29	1932-33

P

Name	NHL Teams	NHL Seasons	Regular Schedule GP	G	A	TP	PIM	Playoffs GP	G	A	TP	PIM	First NHL Season	Last NHL Season
Pachal, Clayton	Bos., Col.	3	35	2	3	5	95	....	....	....	....	....	1976-77	1978-79
Paddock, John	Wsh., Phi., Que.	5	87	8	14	22	86	5	2	0	2	0	1975-76	1982-83
Paiement, Rosaire	Phi., Van.	5	190	48	52	100	343	3	3	0	3	0	1967-68	1971-72
Paiement, Wilf	K.C., Col., Tor., Que., NYR, Buf., Pit.	14	946	356	458	814	1757	69	18	17	35	185	1974-75	1987-88
Palangio, Peter	Mtl., Det., Chi.	5	71	13	10	23	28	7	0	0	0	0	1926-27	1937-38
Palazzari, Aldo	Bos., NYR	1	35	8	3	11	4	....	....	....	....	....	1943-44	1943-44
Palazzari, Doug	St.L.	4	108	18	20	38	23	2	0	0	0	0	1974-75	1978-79
Palmer, Brad	Min., Bos.	3	168	32	38	70	58	29	9	5	14	16	1980-81	1982-83
Palmer, Rob R.	L.A., N.J.	7	320	9	101	110	115	8	1	2	3	6	1977-78	1983-84
Palmer, Rob H.	Chi.	3	16	0	3	3	2	....	....	....	....	....	1973-74	1975-76
Panagabko, Ed	Bos.	2	29	0	3	3	38	....	....	....	....	....	1955-56	1956-57
Papike, Joe	Chi.	3	21	3	3	6	4	5	0	2	2	0	1940-41	1944-45
Pappin, Jim	Tor., Chi., Cal., Clev.	14	767	278	295	573	667	92	33	34	67	101	1963-64	1976-77
Paradise, Bob	Min., Atl., Pit., Wsh.	8	368	8	54	62	393	12	0	1	1	19	1971-72	1978-79
Pargeter, George	Mtl.	1	4	0	0	0	0	....	....	....	....	....	1946-47	1946-47
Parise, J.P.	Bos., Tor., Min., NYI, Clev.	14	890	238	356	594	706	86	27	31	58	87	1965-66	1978-79
Parizeau, Michel	St.L., Phi.	1	58	3	14	17	18	....	....	....	....	....	1971-72	1971-72
Park, Brad	NYR, Bos., Det.	17	1113	213	683	896	1429	161	35	90	125	217	1968-69	1984-85
Parkes, Ernie	Mtl.M.	1	17	0	0	0	2	....	....	....	....	....	1924-25	1924-25
Parsons, George	Tor.	3	64	12	13	25	17	7	3	2	5	11	1936-37	1938-39
Paterson, Mark	Hfd.	4	29	3	3	6	33	....	....	....	....	....	1982-83	1985-86
Paterson, Rick	Chi.	9	430	50	43	93	136	61	7	10	17	51	1978-79	1986-87
Patey, Doug	Wsh.	3	45	4	2	6	8	....	....	....	....	....	1976-77	1978-79
Patey, Larry	Cal., St.L., NYR	12	717	153	163	316	631	40	8	10	18	57	1973-74	1984-85
Patrick, Craig	Cal., St.L., K.C., Min., Wsh.	8	401	72	91	163	61	2	0	1	1	0	1971-72	1978-79
Patrick, Glenn	St.L., Cal., Clev.	3	38	2	3	5	72	....	....	....	....	....	1973-74	1976-77
Patrick, Lester	NYR	1	1	0	0	0	2	....	....	....	....	....	1926-27	1926-27
Patrick, Lynn	NYR	10	455	145	190	335	270	44	10	6	16	22	1934-35	1945-46
Patrick, Muzz	NYR	5	166	5	26	31	133	25	4	0	4	34	1937-38	1945-46
Patrick, Steve	Buf., NYR, Que.	6	250	40	68	108	242	12	0	1	1	12	1980-81	1985-86
Patterson, Dennis	K.C., Phi.	3	138	6	22	28	67	....	....	....	....	....	1974-75	1979-80
Patterson, George	Bos., Det., St.L., Tor., Mtl., NYA	9	289	51	27	78	221	3	0	0	0	2	1926-27	1934-35
Paul, Butch	Det.	1	3	0	0	0	0	....	....	....	....	....	1964-65	1964-65
Paulus, Rollie	Mtl.	1	33	0	0	0	0	....	....	....	....	....	1925-26	1925-26
Pavelich, Mark	NYR, Min.	6	353	137	191	328	336	23	7	17	24	14	1981-82	1986-87
Pavelich, Marty	Det.	10	634	93	159	252	454	91	13	15	28	74	1947-48	1956-57
Pavese, Jim	St.L., NYR, Det., Hfd.	8	328	13	44	57	689	34	0	6	6	81	1981-82	1988-89
Payer, Evariste	Mtl.	1	1	0	0	0	0	....	....	....	....	....	1917-18	1917-18
Payne, Steve	Min.	10	613	228	238	466	435	71	35	35	70	60	1978-79	1987-88
Pearson, Mel	NYR, Pit.	5	38	2	6	8	25	....	....	....	....	....	1949-50	1967-68
Peer, Bert	Det.	1	1	0	0	0	0	....	....	....	....	....	1939-40	1939-40
Peirson, Johnny	Bos.	11	545	153	173	326	315	49	9	17	26	26	1946-47	1957-58
Pelensky, Perry	Chi.	1	4	0	0	0	5	....	....	....	....	....	1983-84	1983-84
Pelletier, Roger	Phi.	1	1	0	0	0	0	....	....	....	....	....	1967-68	1967-68
Peloffy, Andre	Wsh.	1	9	0	0	0	2	....	....	....	....	....	1974-75	1974-75
Pelyk, Mike	Tor.	9	441	26	88	114	566	40	0	3	3	41	1967-68	1977-78
Pennington, Cliff	Mtl., Bos.	3	101	17	42	59	6	....	....	....	....	....	1960-61	1962-63
Perlini, Fred	Tor.	2	8	2	3	5	0	....	....	....	....	....	1981-82	1983-84
Perreault, Fern	NYR	2	3	0	0	0	0	....	....	....	....	....	1947-48	1949-50
Perreault, Gilbert	Buf.	17	1191	512	814	1326	500	90	33	70	103	44	1970-71	1986-87
Perry, Brian	Oak., Buf.	3	96	16	29	45	24	8	1	1	2	4	1968-69	1970-71
Persson, Stefan	NYI	9	622	52	317	369	574	102	7	50	57	69	1977-78	1985-86
Pesut, George	Cal.	2	92	3	22	25	130	....	....	....	....	....	1974-75	1975-76
Peters, Frank	NYR	1	43	0	0	0	59	4	0	0	0	2	1930-31	1930-31
Peters, Garry	Mtl., NYR, Phi., Bos.	8	331	34	34	68	261	9	2	2	4	31	1964-65	1971-72

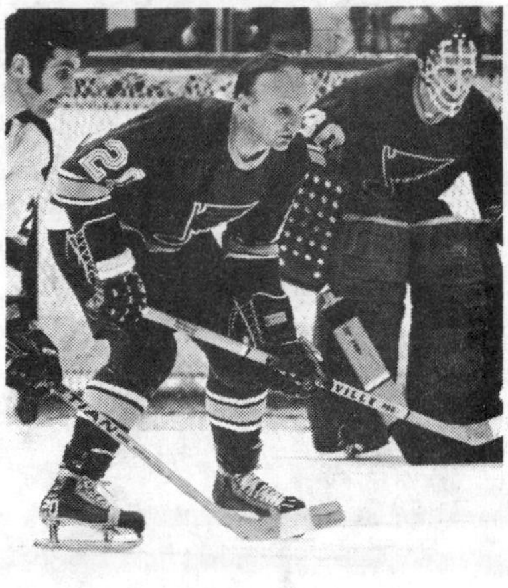
Gerry Odrowski

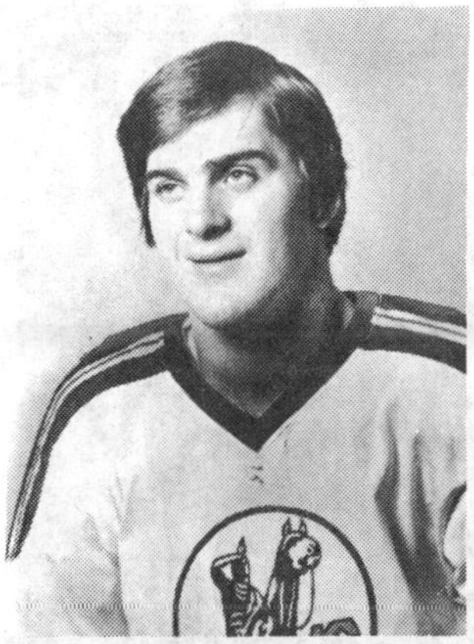
Wilf Paiement

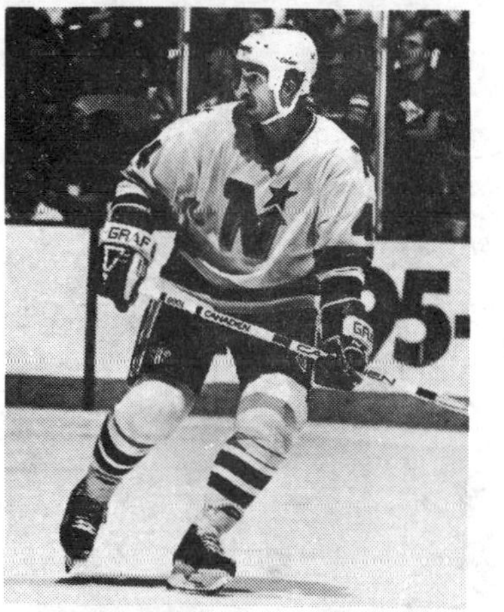
Steve Payne

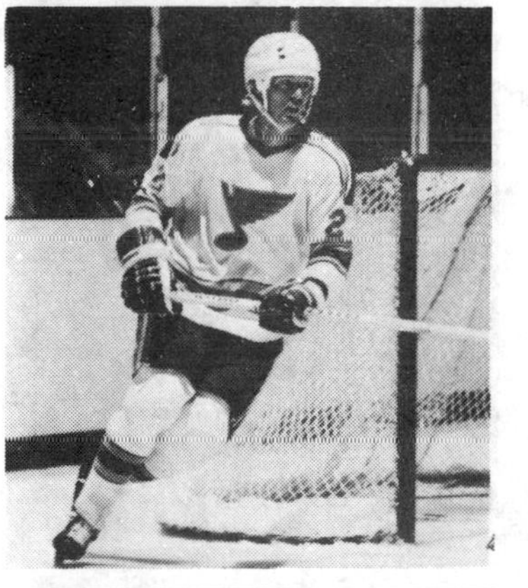
Jorgen Pettersson

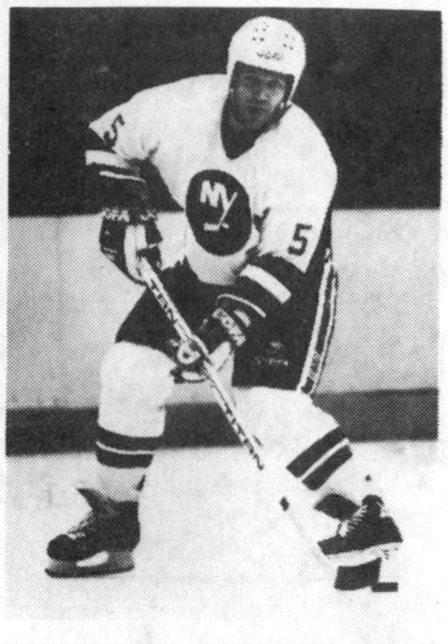

Denis Potvin

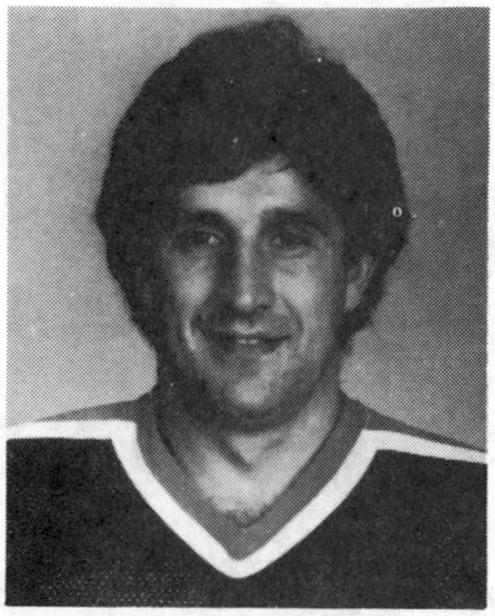

Jaroslav Pouzar

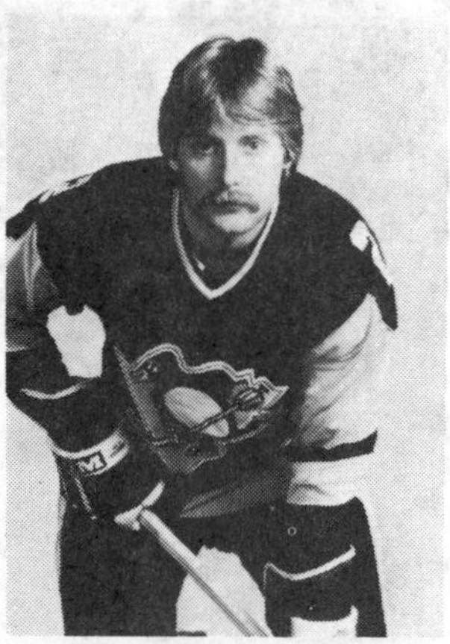

Pat Price

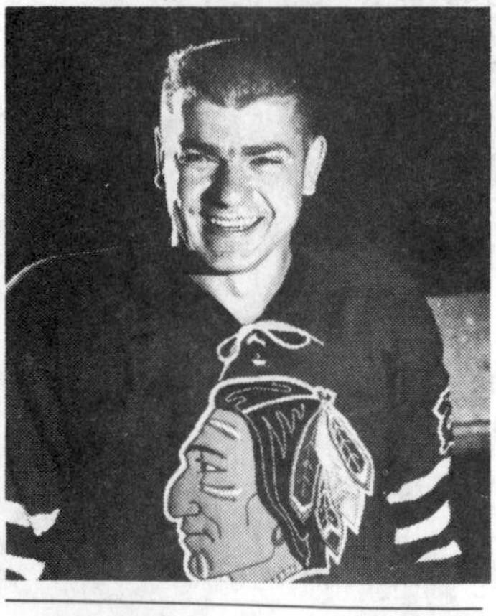

Metro Prystai

Name	NHL Teams	NHL Seasons	Regular Schedule GP	G	A	TP	PIM	Playoffs GP	G	A	TP	PIM	First NHL Season	Last NHL Season
Peters, Jim	Det., Chi., Mtl., Bos.	9	574	125	150	275	186	60	5	9	14	22	1945-46	1953-54
Peters, Jimmy	Det., L.A.	9	309	37	36	73	48	11	0	2	2	2	1964-65	1974-75
Peters, Steve	Col.	1	2	0	1	1	0	....	....	....	....	....	1979-80	1979-80
Peterson, Brent	Det., Buf., Van., Hfd.	10	620	72	141	213	484	31	4	4	8	65	1979-80	1988-89
Pettersson, Jorgen	St.L., Hfd., Wsh.	6	435	174	192	366	117	44	15	12	27	4	1980-81	1985-86
Pettinger, Eric	Ott., Bos., Tor.	3	97	7	12	19	83	4	1	0	1	8	1928-29	1930-31
Pettinger, Gord	Det., NYR, Bos.	8	292	42	74	116	77	49	4	5	9	11	1932-33	1939-40
Phair, Lyle	L.A.	3	48	6	7	13	12	1	0	0	0	0	1985-86	1987-88
Phillipoff, Harold	Atl., Chi.,	3	141	26	57	83	267	6	0	2	2	9	1977-78	1979-80
Phillips, Bat	Mtl.M.	1	27	1	1	2	6	4	0	0	0	2	1929-30	1929-30
Phillips, Bill	Mtl.M., NYA.	8	302	52	31	83	232	28	6	2	8	19	1925-26	1932-33
Phillips, Charlie	Mtl.	1	17	0	0	0	6	....	....	....	....	....	1942-43	1942-43
Picard, Noel	Atl., Mtl., St.L.	7	335	12	63	75	616	50	2	11	13	167	1964-65	1972-73
Picard, Roger	St.L.	1	15	2	2	4	21	....	....	....	....	....	1967-68	1967-68
Picketts, Hal	NYA.	1	48	3	1	4	32	....	....	....	....	....	1933-34	1933-34
Pidhirny, Harry	Bos.	1	2	0	0	0	0	....	....	....	....	....	1957-58	1957-58
Pierce, Randy	Col., N.J., Hfd.	8	277	62	76	138	223	2	0	0	0	0	1977-78	1984-85
Pike, Alf	NYR	6	234	42	77	119	145	21	4	2	6	12	1939-40	1946-47
Pilote, Pierre	Chi., Tor.	14	890	80	418	498	1251	86	8	53	61	102	1955-56	1968-69
Pinder, Gerry	Chi., Cal.	3	223	55	69	124	135	17	0	4	4	6	1969-70	1971-72
Pirus, Alex	Min., Det.	4	159	30	28	58	94	2	0	1	1	2	1976-77	1979-80
Pitre, Didier	Mtl.	6	127	64	17	81	50	14	2	2	4	0	1917-18	1922-23
Plager, Barclay	St.L.	10	614	44	187	231	1115	68	3	20	23	182	1967-68	1976-77
Plager, Bob	NYR, St.L.	14	644	20	126	146	802	74	2	17	19	195	1964-65	1977-78
Plager, William	Min., St.L., Atl.	9	263	4	34	38	292	31	0	2	2	26	1967-68	1975-76
Plamondon, Gerry	Mtl.	5	74	7	13	20	10	11	5	2	7	2	1945-46	1950-51
Plante, Cam	Tor.	1	2	0	0	0	0	....	....	....	....	....	1984-85	1984-85
Plante, Pierre	NYR, Que., Phi., St.L., Chi.	9	599	125	172	297	599	33	2	6	8	51	1971-72	1979-80
Plantery, Mark	Wpg.	1	25	1	5	6	14	....	....	....	....	....	1980-81	1980-81
Plaxton, Hugh	Mtl.M.	1	15	1	2	3	4	....	....	....	....	....	1932-33	1932-33
Pleau, Larry	Mtl.	3	94	9	15	24	27	4	0	0	0	0	1969-70	1971-72
Plett, Willi	Atl., Cgy., Min., Bos.	13	834	222	215	437	2572	83	24	22	46	466	1975-76	1987-88
Plumb, Rob	Det.	1	7	2	1	3	0	....	....	....	....	....	1977-78	1977-78
Plumb, Ron	Hfd.	1	26	3	4	7	14	....	....	....	....	....	1979-80	1979-80
Pocza, Harvie	Wsh.	2	3	0	0	0	0	....	....	....	....	....	1979-80	1981-82
Podolsky, Nels	Det.	1	1	0	0	0	0	7	0	0	0	4	1948-49	1948-49
Poeta, Anthony	Chi.	1	1	0	0	0	0	....	....	....	....	....	1951-52	1951-52
Poile, Bud	NYR, Bos., Det., Tor., Chi.,	7	311	107	122	229	91	23	4	4	8	8	1942-43	1949-50
Poile, Don	Det.	2	66	7	9	16	12	4	0	0	0	0	1954-55	1957-58
Poirer, Gordie	Mtl.	1	10	0	1	1	0	....	....	....	....	....	1939-40	1939-40
Polanic, Tom	Min.	2	19	0	2	2	53	5	1	1	2	4	1969-70	1970-71
Polich, John	NYR	2	3	0	1	1	0	....	....	....	....	....	1939-40	1940-41
Polich, Mike	Mtl., Min.	5	226	24	29	53	57	23	2	1	3	2	1976-77	1980-81
Polis, Greg	Pit., St.L., NYR, Wsh.	10	615	174	169	343	391	7	0	2	2	6	1970-71	1979-80
Poliziani, Daniel	Bos.	1	1	0	0	0	0	3	0	0	0	0	1958-59	1958-59
Polonich, Dennis	Det.	8	390	59	82	141	1242	7	1	0	1	19	1974-75	1982-83
Pooley, Poul	Wpg.	2	15	0	3	3	0	....	....	....	....	....	1984-85	1985-86
Popein, Larry	NYR, Oak.	8	449	80	141	221	162	16	1	4	5	6	1954-55	1967-68
Popiel, Paul	Bos., L.A., Det., Van., Edm.	7	224	13	41	54	210	4	1	0	1	4	1965-66	1979-80
Portland, Jack	Chi., Mtl., Bos.	10	381	15	56	71	323	33	1	3	4	25	1933-34	1942-43
Porvari, Jukka	Col., N.J.	2	39	3	9	12	4	....	....	....	....	....	1981-82	1982-83
Posa, Victor	Chi.	1	2	0	0	0	2	....	....	....	....	....	1985-86	1985-86
Posavad, Mike	St.L.	2	8	0	0	0	0	....	....	....	....	....	1985-86	1986-87
Potvin, Denis	NYI	15	1060	310	742	1052	1356	185	56	108	164	253	1973-74	1987-88
Potvin, Jean	L.A., Min., Phi., NYI, Cle.	11	613	63	224	287	478	39	2	9	11	17	1970-71	1980-81
Poudrier, Daniel	Que.	1	25	1	5	6	10	....	....	....	....	....	1985-86	1987-88
Poulin, Dan	Min., Phi.	2	5	3	1	4	4	....	....	....	....	....	1981-82	1982-83
Pouzar, Jaroslav	Edm.	4	186	34	48	82	136	29	6	4	10	16	1982-83	1986-87
Powell, Ray	Chi.	1	31	7	15	22	2	....	....	....	....	....	1950-51	1950-51
Powis, Geoff	Chi.	1	2	0	0	0	0	....	....	....	....	....	1967-68	1967-68
Powis, Lynn	Chi., K.C.	2	130	19	33	52	25	1	0	0	0	0	1973-74	1974-75
Pratt, Babe	Bos., NYR, Tor.	12	517	83	209	292	473	63	12	17	29	90	1935-36	1946-47
Pratt, Jack	Bos.	2	37	2	0	2	42	4	0	0	0	0	1930-31	1931-32
Pratt, Kelly	Pit.	1	22	0	6	6	15	....	....	....	....	....	1974-75	1974-75
Pratt, Tracy	Van., Col., Buf., Pit. Tor., Oak.	10	580	17	97	114	1026	25	0	1	1	62	1967-68	1976-77
Prentice, Dean	Pit., Min., Det., NYR, Bos.	22	1378	391	469	860	484	54	13	17	30	38	1952-53	1973-74
Prentice, Eric	Tor.	1	5	0	0	0	4	....	....	....	....	....	1943-44	1943-44
Preston, Rich	Chi., N.J.	8	580	127	164	291	348	47	4	18	22	56	1979-80	1986-87
Preston, Yves	Phi.	2	28	7	3	10	4	....	....	....	....	....	1978-79	1980-81
Price, Bob	Ott.	1	1	0	0	0	0	....	....	....	....	....	1919-20	1919-20
Price, Jack	Chi.	3	57	4	6	10	24	4	0	0	0	0	1951-52	1953-54
Price, Noel	Pit., L.A., Det., Tor., NYR, Mtl., Atl.	14	499	14	114	128	333	12	0	1	1	8	1957-58	1975-76
Price, Pat	NYI, Edm., Pit., Que., NYR, Min.	13	726	43	218	261	1456	74	2	10	12	195	1975-76	1987-88
Price, Tom	Cal., Clev., Pit.	5	29	0	2	2	12	....	....	....	....	....	1974-75	1978-79
Primeau, Joe	Tor.	9	310	66	177	243	111	38	5	18	23	12	1927-28	1935-36
Primeau, Kevin	Van.	1	2	0	0	0	4	....	....	....	....	....	1980-81	1980-81
Pringle, Ellie	NYA	1	6	0	0	0	0	....	....	....	....	....	1930-31	1930-31
Prodgers, Goldie	Tor., Ham.	6	110	63	22	85	33	....	....	....	....	....	1919-20	1924-25
Pronovost, Andre	Det., Min., Mtl., Bos.	10	556	94	104	198	408	70	11	11	22	58	1956-57	1967-68
Pronovost, Jean	Wsh., Pit., Atl.	14	998	391	383	774	413	35	11	9	20	14	1968-69	1981-82
Pronovost, Marcel	Det., Tor.	21	1206	88	257	345	851	134	8	23	31	104	1950-51	1969-70
Provost, Claude	Mtl.	15	1005	254	335	589	469	126	25	38	63	86	1955-56	1969-70
Prystai, Metro	Chi., Det.	11	674	151	179	330	231	43	12	14	26	8	1947-48	1957-58
Pudas, Al	Tor.	1	3	0	0	0	0	....	....	....	....	....	1926-27	1926-27
Pulford, Bob	Tor., L.A.	16	1079	281	362	643	792	89	25	26	51	126	1956-57	1971-72
Pulkkinen, Dave	NYI	1	2	0	0	0	0	....	....	....	....	....	1972-73	1972-73
Purpur, Cliff	Det., Chi., St.L.	5	144	26	34	60	46	16	1	2	3	4	1934-35	1944-45
Pusie, Jean	Mtl., NYR, Bos.	5	61	1	4	5	28	7	0	0	0	0	1930-31	1935-36
Pyatt, Nelson	Det., Wsh., Col.	7	296	71	63	134	67	....	....	....	....	....	1973-74	1979-80

Q

Name	NHL Teams	NHL Seasons	Regular Schedule GP	G	A	TP	PIM	Playoffs GP	G	A	TP	PIM	First NHL Season	Last NHL Season
Quackenbush, Bill	Det., Bos.	14	774	62	222	284	95	79	2	19	21	8	1942-43	1955-56
Quackenbush, Max	Bos., Chi.,	2	61	4	7	11	30	6	0	0	0	4	1950-51	1951-52
Quenneville, Leo	NYR	1	25	0	3	3	10	3	0	0	0	0	1929-30	1929-30
Quilty, John	Mtl., Bos.	4	125	36	34	70	81	13	3	5	8	9	1940-41	1947-48
Quinn, Pat	Tor., Van., Atl.	9	606	18	113	131	950	11	0	1	1	21	1968-69	1976-77

R

Name	NHL Teams	NHL Seasons	Regular Schedule GP	G	A	TP	PIM	Playoffs GP	G	A	TP	PIM	First NHL Season	Last NHL Season
Radley, Yip	NYA, Mtl.M.	2	18	0	1	1	13	....	....	....	....	....	1930-31	1936-37
Raglan, Clare	Det., Chi.	3	100	4	9	13	52	3	0	0	0	0	1950-51	1952-53
Raleigh, Don	NYR	10	535	101	219	320	96	18	6	5	11	6	1943-44	1955-56
Ramsay, Beattie	Tor.,	1	43	0	2	2	10	....	....	....	....	....	1927-28	1927-28
Ramsay, Craig	Buf.	14	1070	252	420	672	201	89	17	31	48	27	1971-72	1984-85
Ramsay, Wayne	Buf.	1	2	0	0	0	0	....	....	....	....	....	1977-78	1977-78
Ramsey, Les	Chi.	1	11	2	2	4	2	....	....	....	....	....	1944-45	1944-45
Randall, Ken	Tor., Ham., NYA	10	217	67	28	95	360	13	3	1	4	19	1917-18	1926-27
Ranieri, George	Bos.	1	2	0	0	0	0	....	....	....	....	....	1956-57	1956-57
Ratelle, Jean	NYR, Bos.	21	1281	491	776	1267	276	123	32	66	98	24	1960-61	1980-81
Rathwell, John	Bos.	1	1	0	0	0	0	....	....	....	....	....	1974-75	1974-75
Rausse, Errol	Wsh.	3	31	7	3	10	0	....	....	....	....	....	1979-80	1981-82
Rautakallio, Pekka	Atl., Cgy.	3	235	33	121	154	122	23	2	5	7	8	1979-80	1981-82
Ravlich, Matt	Bos., Chi., Det., L.A.	9	410	12	78	90	364	24	1	5	6	16	1962-63	1972-73
Raymond, Armand	Mtl.	2	22	0	2	2	10	....	....	....	....	....	1937-38	1939-40
Raymond, Paul	Mtl.	4	76	2	3	5	6	5	0	0	0	2	1932-33	1937-38
Read, Mel	NYR	1	1	0	0	0	0	....	....	....	....	....	1946-47	1946-47
Reardon, Ken	Mtl.	7	341	26	96	122	604	31	2	5	7	62	1940-41	1949-50
Reardon, Terry	Bos., Mtl.	7	193	47	53	100	73	30	8	10	18	12	1938-39	1946-47
Reaume, Marc	Tor., Det., Mtl., Van.	9	344	8	43	51	273	21	0	2	2	8	1954-55	1970-71
Reay, Billy	Det., Mtl.	10	479	105	162	267	202	63	13	16	29	43	1943-44	1952-53
Redahl, Gord	Bos.	1	18	0	1	1	2	....	....	....	....	....	1958-59	1958-59
Redding, George	Bos.	2	35	3	2	5	10	....	....	....	....	....	1924-25	1925-26

			Regular Schedule					Playoffs						
Name	NHL Teams	NHL Seasons	GP	G	A	TP	PIM	GP	G	A	TP	PIM	First NHL Season	Last NHL Season
Redmond, Craig	L.A., Edm.	5	191	16	68	84	134	3	1	0	1	2	1984-85	1988-89
Redmond, Dick	Min., Cal., Chi., St.L., Atl., Bos.	13	771	133	312	445	504	66	9	22	31	27	1969-70	1981-82
Redmond, Mickey	Mtl., Det.	9	538	233	195	428	219	16	2	3	5	2	1967-68	1975-76
Reeds, Mark	St.L., Hfd.	8	365	45	114	159	135	53	8	9	17	23	1981-82	1988-89
Regan, Bill	NYR, NYA	3	67	3	2	5	67	8	0	0	0	2	1929-30	1932-33
Regan, Larry	Bos., Tor.,	5	280	41	95	136	71	42	7	14	21	18	1956-57	1960-61
Regier, Darcy	Clev., NYI	3	26	0	2	2	35	....	....	....	....	....	1977-78	1983-84
Reibel, Earl	Det., Chi., Bos.	6	409	84	161	245	75	39	6	14	20	4	1953-54	1958-59
Reid, Dave	Tor.	3	7	0	0	0	0	....	....	....	....	....	1952-53	1955-56
Reid, Gerry	Det.	1	....	....	....	....	....	2	0	0	0	2	1948-49	1948-49
Reid, Gordie	NYA	1	1	0	0	0	2	....	....	....	....	....	1936-37	1936-37
Reid, Reg	Tor.	2	40	2	0	2	4	2	0	0	0	0	1924-25	1925-26
Reid, Tom	Chi., Min.	11	701	17	113	130	654	42	1	13	14	49	1967-68	1977-78
Reigle, Ed	Bos.	1	17	0	2	2	25	....	....	....	....	....	1950-51	1950-51
Reinikka, Ollie	NYR	1	16	0	0	0	0	....	....	....	....	....	1926-27	1926-27
Reise, Leo Jr.	Chi., Det., NYR	9	494	28	81	109	399	52	8	5	13	68	1945-46	1953-54
Reise, Leo Sr.	Ham., NYA, NYR	8	199	36	29	65	177	6	0	0	0	16	1920-21	1929-30
Renaud, Mark	Hfd., Buf.	5	152	6	50	56	86	....	....	....	....	....	1979-80	1983-84
Ribble, Pat	Atl., Chi., Tor., Wsh., Cgy.	8	349	19	60	79	365	8	0	1	1	12	1975-76	1982-83
Richard, Henri	Mtl.	20	1256	358	688	1046	928	180	49	80	129	181	1955-56	1974-75
Richard, Jacques	Alt., Buf., Que.	10	556	160	187	347	307	35	5	5	10	34	1972-73	1982-83
Richard, Maurice	Mtl.	18	978	544	421	965	1285	133	82	44	126	188	1942-43	1959-60
Richardson, Dave	NYR, Chi., Det.	4	45	3	2	5	27	....	....	....	....	....	1963-64	1967-68
Richardson, Glen	Van.	1	24	3	6	9	19	....	....	....	....	....	1975-76	1975-76
Richardson, Ken	St.L.	3	49	8	13	21	16	....	....	....	....	....	1974-75	1978-79
Richer, Bob	Buf.	1	3	0	0	0	0	....	....	....	....	....	1972-73	1972-73
Riley, Bill	Wsh., Wpg.	5	139	31	30	61	320	....	....	....	....	....	1974-75	1979-80
Riley, Jack	Det., Mtl., Bos.,	4	104	10	22	32	8	4	0	3	3	0	1932-33	1935-36
Riley, Jim	Det.	1	17	0	2	2	14	....	....	....	....	....	1926-27	1926-27
Riopellie, Howard	Mtl.	3	169	27	16	43	73	8	1	1	2	2	1947-48	1949-50
Rioux, Gerry	Wpg.	1	8	0	0	0	6	....	....	....	....	....	1979-80	1979-80
Rioux, Pierre	Cgy.	1	14	1	2	3	4	....	....	....	....	....	1982-83	1982-83
Ripley, Vic	Chi., Bos., NYR, St.L.	7	278	51	49	100	173	20	4	1	5	10	1928-29	1934-35
Risebrough, Doug	Mtl., Cgy.	14	740	185	286	471	1542	124	21	37	58	238	1974-75	1986-87
Rissling, Gary	Wsh., Pit.	7	221	23	30	53	1008	5	0	1	1	4	1978-79	1984-85
Ritchie, Bob	Phi., Det.	2	29	8	4	12	10	....	....	....	....	....	1976-77	1977-78
Ritchie, Dave	Mtl.W, Ott., Tor., Que., Mtl.	6	54	15	3	18	27	1	0	0	0	0	1917-18	1925-26
Ritson, Alex	NYR	1	1	0	0	0	0	....	....	....	....	....	1944-45	1944-45
Rittinger, Alan	Bos.	1	19	3	7	10	0	....	....	....	....	....	1943-44	1943-44
Rivard, Bob	Pit.	1	27	5	12	17	4	....	....	....	....	....	1967-68	1967-68
Rivers, Gus	Mtl.	3	88	4	5	9	12	16	2	0	2	2	1929-30	1931-32
Rivers, Wayne	Det., Bos., St.L., NYR	7	108	15	30	45	94	....	....	....	....	....	1961-62	1968-69
Rizzuto, Garth	Van.	1	37	3	4	7	16	....	....	....	....	....	1970-71	1970-71
Roach, Mickey	Tor., Ham., NYA	8	209	75	27	102	41	....	....	....	....	....	1919-20	1926-27
Robert, Claude	Mtl.	1	23	1	0	1	9	....	....	....	....	....	1950-51	1950-51
Robert, Rene	Tor., Pit., Buf., Col.	12	744	284	418	702	597	50	22	19	41	73	1970-71	1981-82
Robert, Sammy	Ott.	1	1	0	0	0	0	....	....	....	....	....	1917-18	1917-18
Roberto, Phil	Mtl., St.L., Det., K.C., Col., Clev.	8	385	75	106	181	464	31	9	8	17	69	1969-70	1976-77
Roberts, Doug	Det., Dak., Cal., Bos.	10	419	43	104	147	342	16	2	3	5	46	1965-66	1974-75
Roberts, Jim	Mtl., St.L.	15	1006	126	194	320	621	153	20	16	36	160	1963-64	1977-78
Roberts, Jimmy	Min.	3	106	17	23	40	33	2	0	0	0	0	1976-77	1978-79
Robertson, Fred	Tor., Det.,	2	34	1	0	1	35	7	0	0	0	0	1931-32	1933-34
Robertson, Geordie	Buf.	1	5	1	2	3	7	....	....	....	....	....	1982-83	1982-83
Robertson, George	Mtl.	2	31	2	5	7	6	....	....	....	....	....	1947-48	1948-49
Robidoux, Florent	Chi	3	52	7	4	11	75	....	....	....	....	....	1980-81	1983-84
Robinson, Doug	Chi., NYR, L.A.	7	239	44	67	111	34	11	4	3	7	0	1963-64	1970-71
Robinson, Earl	Mtl.M., Chi., Mtl.	11	418	83	98	181	133	25	5	4	9	0	1928-29	1939-40
Robinson, Moe	Mtl.	1	1	0	0	0	0	....	....	....	....	....	1979-80	1979-80
Robitaille, Mike	NYR, Det., Buf., Van.	8	382	23	105	128	280	13	0	1	1	4	1969-70	1976-77
Roche, Michel	Mtl.M., Ott., St.L., Mtl., Det.	4	112	20	18	38	44	....	....	....	....	....	1930-31	1934-35
Roche, Earl	Mtl.M., Bos., Ott., St.L., Det.	4	146	25	27	52	48	2	0	0	0	0	1930-31	1934-35
Roche, Ernest	Mtl.	1	4	0	0	0	2	....	....	....	....	....	1950-51	1950-51
Rochefort, Dave	Det.	1	1	0	0	0	0	....	....	....	....	....	1966-67	1966-67
Rochefort, Leon	NYR, Mtl., Phi., L.A., Det., Atl., Van.	15	617	121	147	268	93	39	4	4	8	16	1960-61	1975-76
Rockburn, Harvey	Det., Ott.	3	94	4	2	6	254	....	....	....	....	....	1929-30	1932-33
Rodden, Eddie	Chi., Tor., Bos., NYR	4	98	6	14	20	152	2	0	1	1	0	1926-27	1930-31
Rogers, Alfred	Min.	2	14	2	4	6	0	....	....	....	....	....	1973-74	1974-75
Rogers, Mike	Hfd., NYR, Edm.	7	484	202	317	519	184	17	1	13	14	6	1979-80	1985-86
Rolfe, Dale	Bos., L.A., Det., NYR	9	509	25	125	150	556	71	5	24	29	89	1959-60	1974-75
Romanchych, Larry	Chi., Atl	6	298	68	97	165	102	7	2	2	4	4	1970-71	1976-77
Rombough, Doug	Buf., NYI, Min.	4	150	24	27	51	80	....	....	....	....	....	1972-73	1975-76
Romnes, Doc	Chi., Tor., NYA	10	359	67	137	204	42	43	7	18	25	4	1930-31	1939-40
Ronan, Skene	Ott.	1	11	0	0	0	0	....	....	....	....	....	1918-19	1918-19
Ronson, Len	NYR, Oak.	2	18	2	1	3	10	....	....	....	....	....	1960-61	1968-69
Ronty, Paul	Bos., NYR, Mtl.	8	488	101	211	312	103	21	1	7	8	6	1947-48	1954-55
Ross, Art	Mtl.W	1	3	1	0	1	0	....	....	....	....	....	1917-18	1917-18
Ross, Jim	NYR	2	62	2	11	13	29	....	....	....	....	....	1951-52	1952-53
Rossignol, Roland	Det., Mtl.	3	14	3	5	8	6	1	0	0	0	2	1943-44	1945-46
Rota, Darcy	Chi., Atl., Van.	11	794	256	239	495	973	60	14	7	21	147	1973-74	1983-84
Rota, Randy	Mtl., L.A., K.C., Col.	5	212	38	39	77	60	5	0	1	1	0	1972-73	1976-77
Rothschild, Sam	Mtl.M., NYA	4	99	8	6	14	24	10	0	0	0	0	1924-25	1927-28
Roulston, Rolly	Det.	3	24	0	6	6	10	....	....	....	....	....	1935-36	1937-38
Roulston, Tom	Edm., Pit.	6	195	47	49	96	74	21	2	2	4	2	1980-81	1985-86
Rousseau, Bobby	Mtl., Min., NYR	15	942	245	458	703	359	128	27	57	84	69	1960-61	1974-75
Rousseau, Guy	Mtl.	2	4	0	1	1	0	....	....	....	....	....	1954-55	1956-57
Rousseau, Roland	Mtl.	1	2	0	0	0	0	....	....	....	....	....	1952-53	1952-53
Rowe, Bobby	Bos.	1	4	1	0	1	0	....	....	....	....	....	1924-25	1924-25
Rowe, Mike	Pit.	3	11	0	0	0	11	....	....	....	....	....	1984-85	1986-87
Rowe, Ron	NYR	1	5	1	0	1	0	....	....	....	....	....	1947-48	1947-48
Rowe, Tom	Wsh., Hfd., Det.	7	357	85	100	185	615	3	2	0	2	0	1976-77	1982-83
Roy, Stephane	Min.	1	12	1	0	1	0	....	....	....	....	....	1987-88	1987-88
Rozzini, Gino	Bos.	1	31	5	10	15	20	6	1	2	3	6	1944-45	1944-45
Ruelle, Bernard	Det.	1	2	1	0	1	0	....	....	....	....	....	1943-44	1943-44
Ruhnke, Kent	Bos.	1	2	0	1	1	0	....	....	....	....	....	1975-76	1975-76
Rundqvist, Thomas	Mtl.	1	2	0	1	1	0	....	....	....	....	....	1984-85	1984-85
Runge, Paul	Bos., Mtl.M., Mtl.	7	143	18	22	40	57	7	0	0	0	6	1930-31	1937-38
Ruotsalinen, Reijo	NYR, Edm.	6	405	104	225	329	160	64	13	21	34	32	1981-82	1986-87
Rupp, Duane	NYR, Tor., Min., Pit.	10	374	24	93	117	220	10	2	2	4	8	1962-63	1972-73
Ruskowski, Terry	Chi., L.A., Pit., Min.	10	630	113	313	426	1354	21	1	6	7	86	1979-80	1988-89
Russell, Churchill	NYR	3	90	20	16	36	12	....	....	....	....	....	1945-46	1947-48
Russell, Phil	Chi., Atl., Cgy., N.J., Buf.	15	1016	99	325	424	2038	73	4	22	26	202	1972-73	1986-87

S

Saarinen, Simo	NYR	1	8	0	0	0	0	....	....	....	....	....	1984-85	1984-85
Sabourin, Bob	Tor.	1	1	0	0	0	2	....	....	....	....	....	1951-52	1951-52
Sabourin, Gary	St.L., Tor., Cal., Clev.	10	627	169	188	357	397	62	19	11	30	58	1967-68	1976-77
Sacharuk, Larry	NYR, St.L.	5	151	29	33	62	42	2	1	1	2	2	1972-73	1976-77
Saganiuk, Rocky	Tor., Pit.	6	259	57	65	122	201	6	1	0	1	15	1978-79	1983-84
St. Laurent, Andre	NYI, Det., L.A., Pit.	11	644	129	187	316	749	59	8	12	20	48	1973-74	1983-84
St. Laurent, Dollard	Mtl., Chi.	12	652	29	133	162	496	92	2	22	24	87	1950-51	1961-62
St. Marseille, Frank	St.L., L.A.	10	707	140	285	425	242	88	20	25	45	18	1967-68	1976-77
St. Sauveur, Claude	Atl.	1	79	24	24	48	23	2	0	0	0	0	1975-76	1975-76
Saleski, Don	Phi., Col.	9	543	128	125	253	629	82	13	17	30	131	1971-72	1979-80
Salovaara, John	Det.	2	90	2	13	15	70	....	....	....	....	....	1974-75	1975-76
Salvian, Dave	NYI	1	....	0	1	1	2	1	0	1	1	2	1976-77	1976-77
Samis, Phi.	Tor.	2	2	0	0	0	0	5	0	1	1	2	1947-48	1949-50
Sampson, Gary	Wsh.	4	105	13	22	35	25	12	1	0	1	0	1983-84	1986-87
Sanderson, Derek	Bos., NYR, St.L., Van., Pit.	13	598	202	250	452	911	56	18	12	30	187	1965-66	1977-78
Sandford, Ed	Bos., Det., Chi.	9	502	106	145	251	355	42	12	11	24	27	1947-48	1955-56
Sands, Charlie	Tor., Bos., Mtl., NYR	12	432	99	109	208	58	44	6	6	12	4	1932-33	1943-44
Sargent, Gary	L.A., Min.	8	402	61	161	222	273	20	5	7	12	8	1975-76	1982-83
Sarner, Craig	Bos.	1	7	0	0	0	0	....	....	....	....	....	1974-75	1974-75
Sarrazin, Dick	Phi.	3	100	20	35	55	22	4	0	0	0	0	1968-69	1971-72

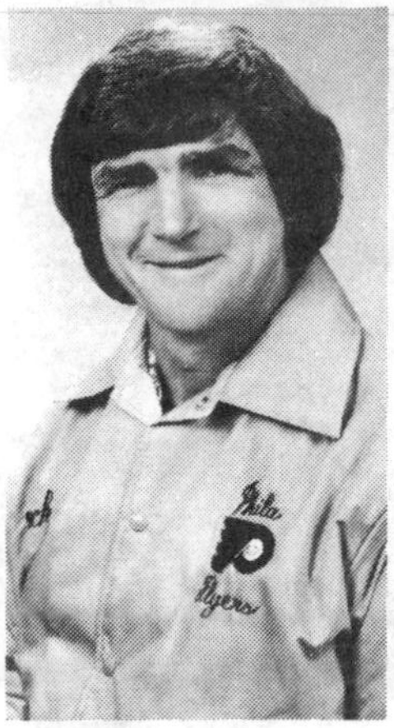

Pat Quinn

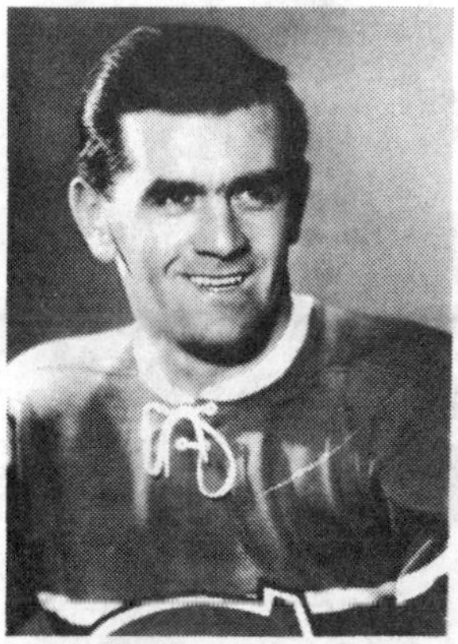

Maurice Richard

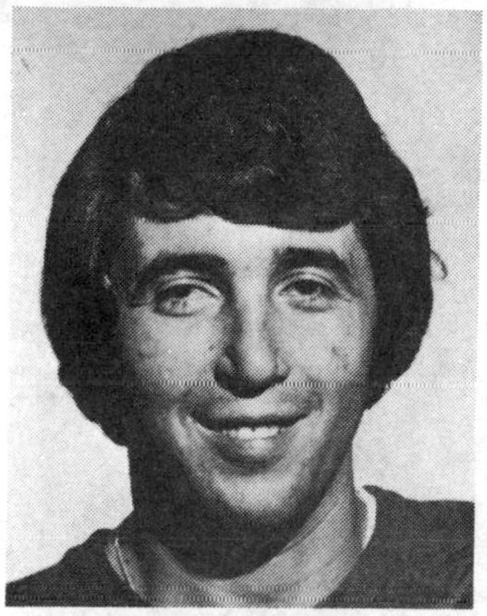

Phil Roberto

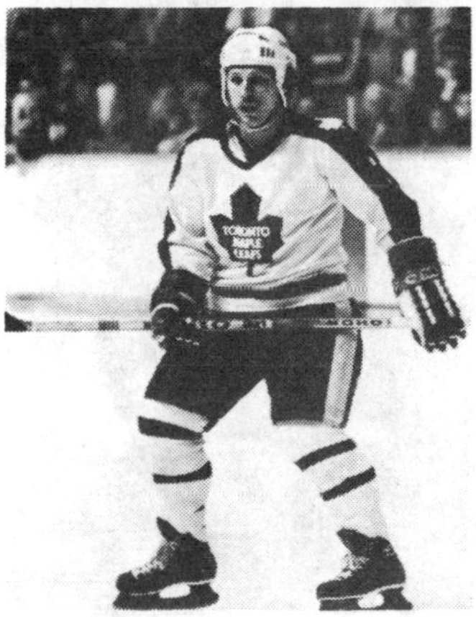

Rocky Saganiuk

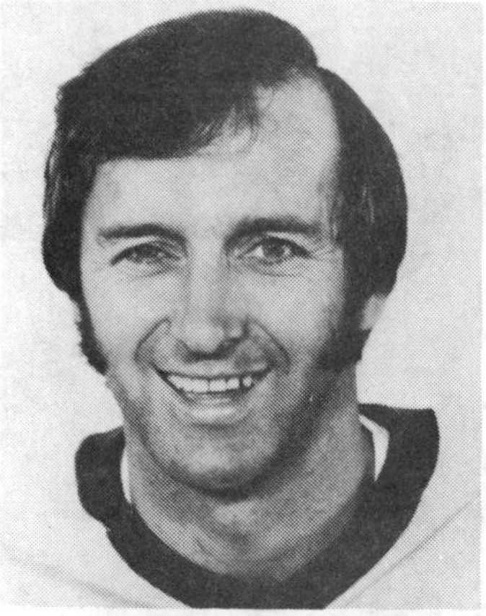
Frank St. Marseille

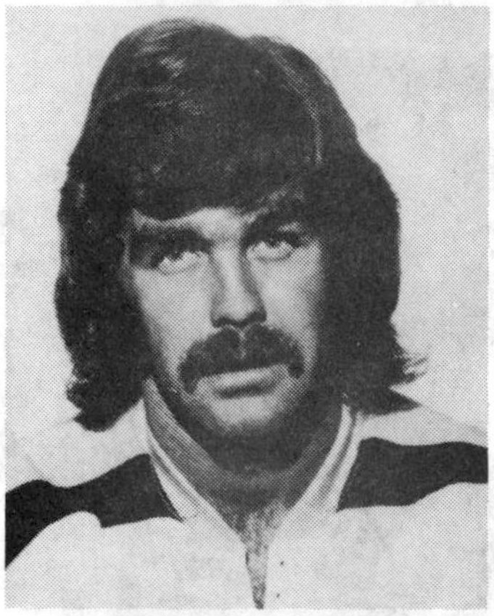
Derek Sanderson

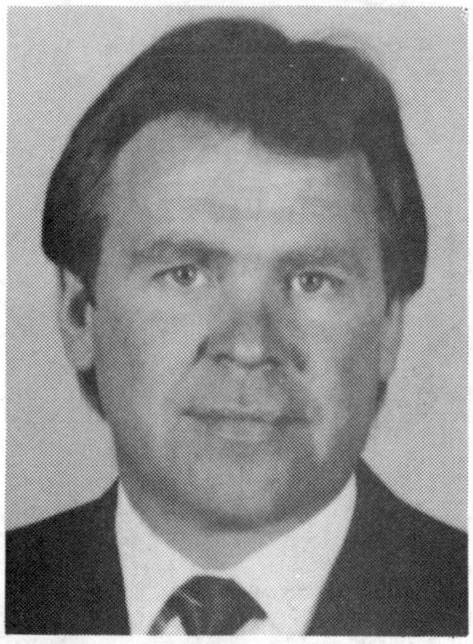
Glen Sather

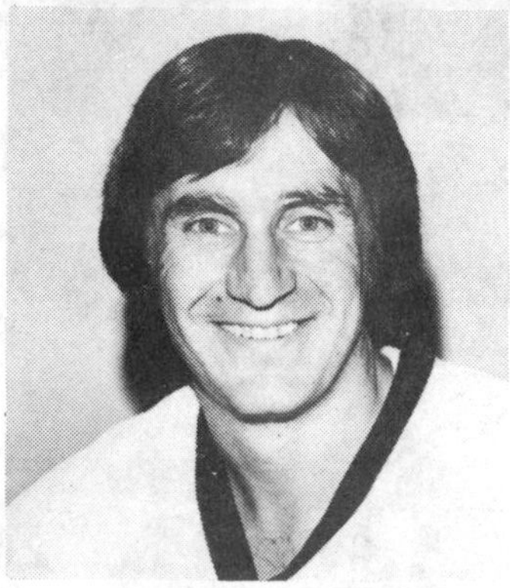
Bobby Schmautz

			Regular Schedule					Playoffs					First	Last
Name	NHL Teams	NHL Seasons	GP	G	A	TP	PIM	GP	G	A	TP	PIM	NHL Season	NHL Season
Saskamoose, Fred	Chi.	1	11	0	0	0	6	....	....	....	....	....	1953-54	1953-54
Sasser, Grant	Pit.	1	3	0	0	0	0	....	....	....	....	....	1983-84	1983-84
Sather, Glen	Bos., Pit., NYR, St.L., Mtl., Min.	10	658	80	113	193	724	72	1	5	6	86	1966-67	1975-76
Saunders, Bernie	Que.	2	10	0	1	1	8	....	....	....	....	....	1979-80	1980-81
Saunders, Bud	Ott.	1	19	1	3	4	4	....	....	....	....	....	1933-34	1933-34
Saunders, David	Van.	1	56	7	13	20	10	....	....	....	....	....	1987-88	1987-88
Sauve, Jenn F.	Buf., Que.	7	290	65	138	203	117	36	9	12	21	10	1980-81	1986-87
Savage, Tony	Bos., Mtl.	1	49	1	5	6	6	2	0	0	0	0	1934-35	1934-35
Savard, Andre	Bos., Buf., Que.	12	790	211	271	482	411	85	13	18	31	77	1973-74	1984-85
Savard, Jean	Chi., Hfd.	3	43	7	12	19	29	....	....	....	....	....	1977-78	1979-80
Savard, Serge	Mtl., Wpg.	17	1040	106	333	439	592	130	19	49	68	88	1966-67	1982-83
Scamurra, Peter	Wsh.	4	132	8	25	33	59	....	....	....	....	....	1975-76	1979-80
Sceviour, Darin	Chi.	1	1	0	0	0	0	....	....	....	....	....	1986-87	1986-87
Schaeffer, Butch	Chi.,	1	5	0	0	0	6	....	....	....	....	....	1936-37	1936-37
Schamehorn, Kevin	Det., L.A.	3	10	0	0	0	17	....	....	....	....	....	1976-77	1980-81
Schella, John	Van.	2	115	2	18	20	224	....	....	....	....	....	1970-71	1971-72
Scherza, Chuck	Bos., NYR	2	56	6	6	12	35	....	....	....	....	....	1943-44	1944-45
Schinkel, Ken	NYR, Pit.	12	636	127	198	325	163	19	7	2	9	4	1959-60	1972-73
Schliebener, Andy	Van.	3	84	2	11	13	74	6	0	0	0	0	1981-82	1984-85
Schmautz, Bobby	Chi., Bos., Edm., Col., Van.	13	764	271	286	557	988	73	28	33	61	92	1967-68	1980-81
Schmautz, Cliff	Buf., Phi.	1	56	13	19	32	33	....	....	....	....	....	1970-71	1970-71
Schmidt, Clarence	Bos.,	1	7	1	0	1	2	....	....	....	....	....	1943-44	1943-44
Schmidt, Jackie	Bos.	1	45	6	7	13	6	5	0	0	0	0	1942-43	1942-43
Schmidt, Joseph	Bos.	1	2	0	0	0	0	....	....	....	....	....	1943-44	1943-44
Schmidt, Milt	Bos.	16	778	229	346	575	466	86	24	25	49	60	1936-37	1954-55
Schmidt, Norm	Pit.	4	125	23	33	56	73	....	....	....	....	....	1983-84	1987-88
Schnarr, Werner	Bos.	2	25	0	0	0	0	....	....	....	....	....	1924-25	1925-26
Schock, Danny	Bos., Phi.	2	20	1	2	3	0	1	0	0	0	0	1969-70	1970-71
Schock, Ron	Bos., St.L., Pit., Buf.	15	909	166	351	517	260	55	4	16	20	29	1963-64	1977-78
Schoenfeld, Jim	Buf., Det., Bos.	13	719	51	204	255	1132	75	3	13	16	151	1972-73	1984-85
Schofield, Dwight	Det., Mtl., St.L., Wsh., Pit., Wpg.	7	211	8	22	30	631	9	0	0	0	55	1976-77	1987-88
Schreiber, Wally	Min.	2	41	8	10	18	12	....	....	....	....	....	1987-88	1988-89
Schriner, Sweeny	NYA, Tor.	11	484	206	204	410	148	60	18	11	29	54	1934-35	1945-46
Schultz, Dave	Phi., L.A., Pit., Buf.	9	535	79	121	200	2294	73	8	12	20	412	1971-72	1979-80
Schurman, Maynard	Hfd.	1	7	0	0	0	0	....	....	....	....	....	1979-80	1979-80
Schutt, Rod	Mtl., Pit., Tor.	8	286	77	92	169	177	22	8	6	14	26	1977-78	1985-86
Sclisizzi, Enio	Det., Chi.	6	81	12	11	23	26	13	0	0	0	6	1946-47	1952-53
Scott, Ganton	Tor., Ham., Mtl.M.	3	53	1	1	2	0	....	....	....	....	....	1922-23	1924-25
Scott, Laurie	NYA, NYR	2	62	6	3	9	28	....	....	....	....	....	1926-27	1927-28
Scruton, Howard	L.A.	1	4	0	4	4	9	....	....	....	....	....	1982-83	1982-83
Seabrooke, Glen	Phi.	3	19	1	6	7	4	....	....	....	....	....	1986-87	1988-89
Sedlbauer, Ron	Van., Chi., Tor.	7	430	143	86	229	210	19	1	3	4	27	1974-75	1980-81
Seguin, Dan	Min., Van.	2	37	2	6	8	50	....	....	....	....	....	1970-71	1973-74
Seguin, Steve	L.A.	1	5	0	0	0	9	....	....	....	....	....	1984-85	1984-85
Seibert, Earl	NYR, Chi., Det.	15	652	187	276	768	66	11	8	9	19	66	1931-32	1945-46
Seiling, Ric	Buf., Det.	10	738	179	208	387	573	62	14	14	28	36	1977-78	1986-87
Seiling, Rod	Tor., NYR, Wsh., St.L., Atl.	17	979	62	269	331	603	77	4	8	12	55	1962-63	1978-79
Selby, Brit	Tor., Phi., St.L.	8	350	55	62	117	163	16	1	1	2	8	1964-65	1971-72
Self, Steve	Wsh.	1	3	0	0	0	0	....	....	....	....	....	1976-77	1976-77
Selwood, Brad	Tor., L.A.	3	163	7	40	47	153	6	0	0	0	4	1970-71	1979-80
Semenko, Dave	Edm., Hfd., Tor.	9	575	65	88	153	1175	73	6	6	12	208	1979-80	1987-88
Senick, George	NYR	1	13	2	3	5	8	....	....	....	....	....	1952-53	1952-53
Seppa, Jyrki	Wpg.	1	13	0	2	2	6	....	....	....	....	....	1983-84	1983-84
Serafini, Ron	Cal.	1	2	0	0	0	2	....	....	....	....	....	1973-74	1973-74
Servinis, George	Min.	1	5	0	0	0	0	....	....	....	....	....	1987-88	1987-88
Shack, Eddie	NYR, Tor., Bos., L.A., Buf., Pit.	17	1047	239	226	465	1437	74	6	7	13	151	1958-59	1974-75
Shack, Joe	NYR	2	70	23	13	36	20	....	....	....	....	....	1942-43	1944-45
Shakes, Paul	Cal.	1	21	0	4	4	12	....	....	....	....	....	1973-74	1973-74
Shanahan, Sean	Mtl., Col., Bos.	3	40	1	3	4	47	....	....	....	....	....	1975-76	1977-78
Shand, Dave	Atl., Tor., Wsh.	8	421	19	84	103	544	26	1	2	3	83	1976-77	1984-85
Shannon, Charles	NYA	1	4	0	0	0	2	....	....	....	....	....	1939-40	1939-40
Shannon, Gerry	Ott., St.L., Bos., Mtl.M.	5	183	23	29	52	121	9	0	1	1	2	1933-34	1937-38
Sharpley, Glen	Min., Chi.	6	389	117	161	278	199	27	7	11	18	24	1976-77	1981-82
Shaunessy, Scott	Que.	1	3	0	0	0	7	....	....	....	....	....	1986-87	1986-87
Shay, Norman	Bos., Tor.	2	53	5	2	7	34	....	....	....	....	....	1924-25	1925-26
Shea, Pat	Chi.	1	14	0	1	1	0	....	....	....	....	....	1931-32	1931-32
Sheehan, Bobby	Mtl., Cal., Chi., Det., NYR, Col., L.A.	9	310	48	63	111	50	25	4	3	7	8	1969-70	1981-82
Sheehy, Tim	Det., Hfd.	2	27	2	1	3	0	....	....	....	....	....	1977-78	1979-80
Shelton, Doug	Chi.	1	5	0	1	1	0	....	....	....	....	....	1967-68	1967-68
Sheppard, Frank	Det.	1	8	1	1	2	0	....	....	....	....	....	1927-28	1927-28
Sheppard, Gregg	Bos., Pit.	10	657	205	293	498	243	92	32	40	72	31	1972-73	1981-82
Sheppard, Johnny	Det., NYA, Bos., Chi.	8	311	68	58	126	224	10	0	0	0	0	1926-27	1933-34
Sherf, John	Det.	5	19	0	0	0	8	8	0	1	1	2	1935-36	1943-44
Shero, Fred	NYR	3	145	6	14	20	137	13	0	2	2	8	1947-48	1949-50
Sherritt, Gordon	Det.	1	8	0	0	0	12	....	....	....	....	....	1943-44	1943-44
Sherven, Gord	Edm., Min., Hfd.	5	97	13	22	35	33	3	0	0	0	0	1983-84	1987-88
Shewchuck, Jack	Bos.	6	187	9	19	28	160	20	0	1	1	19	1938-39	1944-45
Shibicky, Alex	NYR	8	317	110	91	201	161	40	12	12	24	12	1935-36	1945-46
Shields, Al	Ott., Phi., NYA, Mtl.M., Bos.	11	460	39	49	88	637	17	0	1	1	14	1927-28	1937-38
Shill, Bill	Bos.	3	79	21	13	34	18	7	1	2	3	2	1942-43	1946-47
Shill, Jack	Tor., Bos., NYA, Chi.	6	163	15	20	35	70	27	1	6	7	13	1933-34	1938-39
Shinske, Rick	Clev., St.L.	3	63	5	16	21	10	....	....	....	....	....	1976-77	1978-79
Shires, Jim	Det., St.L., Pit.	3	56	3	6	9	32	....	....	....	....	....	1970-71	1972-73
Shmyr, Paul	Chi., Cal., Min., Hfd.	7	343	13	72	85	528	34	3	3	6	44	1968-69	1981-82
Shore, Eddie	Bos., NYA	14	553	105	179	284	1047	55	6	13	19	187	1926-27	1939-40
Shore, Hamby	Ott.	1	18	3	0	3	0	....	....	....	....	....	1917-18	1917-18
Shores, Aubry	Phi.	1	1	0	0	0	0	....	....	....	....	....	1930-31	1930-31
Short, Steve	L.A., Det.	2	6	0	0	0	2	....	....	....	....	....	1977-78	1978-79
Shutt, Steve	Mtl., L.A.	13	930	424	393	817	410	99	50	48	98	65	1972-73	1984-85
Siebert, Babe	Mtl.M., NYR, Bos., Mtl.	14	593	140	156	296	982	54	8	7	15	62	1925-26	1938-39
Silk, Dave	NYR, Bos., Wpg., Det.	7	249	54	59	113	271	13	2	4	6	13	1979-80	1985-86
Siltala, Mike	Wsh., NYR	3	7	1	0	1	2	....	....	....	....	....	1981-82	1987-88
Siltanen, Risto	Edm., Hfd., Que.	8	562	90	265	355	266	32	6	12	18	30	1979-80	1986-87
Simonetti, Frank	Bos.	4	115	5	8	13	76	12	0	1	1	8	1984-85	1987-88
Simmer, Charlie	Cal., Cle., L.A., Bos., Pit.	14	712	342	369	711	544	24	9	9	18	32	1974-75	1987-88
Simmons, Al	Cal., Bos.	3	11	0	1	1	21	1	0	0	0	0	1971-72	1975-76
Simon, Cully	Det., Chi.	3	130	4	11	15	121	14	0	1	1	6	1942-43	1944-45
Simon, Thain	Det.	1	3	0	0	0	0	....	....	....	....	....	1946-47	1946-47
Simpson, Bobby	Atl., St.L., Pit.	5	175	35	29	64	98	6	0	1	1	2	1976-77	1982-83
Simpson, Cliff	Det.	2	6	0	1	1	0	2	0	0	0	0	1946-47	1947-48
Simpson, Joe	NYA	6	228	21	19	40	156	2	0	0	0	0	1925-26	1930-31
Sims, Al	Bos., Hfd., L.A.	10	475	49	116	165	286	41	0	2	2	14	1973-74	1982-83
Sinclair, Reg	NYR, Det.	3	208	49	43	92	139	3	1	0	1	0	1950-51	1952-53
Singbush, Alex	Mtl.	1	32	0	5	5	15	3	0	0	0	4	1940-41	1940-41
Sirois, Bob	Phi., Wsh.	6	286	92	120	212	42	....	....	....	....	....	1974-75	1979-80
Sittler, Darryl	Tor., Phi., Det.	15	1096	484	637	1121	948	76	29	45	74	137	1970-71	1984-85
Sjoberg, Lars-Erik	Wpg.	1	79	7	27	34	48	....	....	....	....	....	1979-80	1979-80
Skaare, Bjorne	Det.	1	1	0	0	0	0	....	....	....	....	....	1978-79	1978-79
Skilton, Raymie	Mtl.W	1	1	1	0	1	0	....	....	....	....	....	1917-18	1917-18
Skinner, Alf	Tor., Bos., Mtl.M., Pit.	4	70	26	4	30	56	7	8	1	9	0	1917-18	1925-26
Skinner, Larry	Col.	4	47	10	12	22	8	2	0	0	0	0	1976-77	1979-80
Skov, Glen	Det., Chi., Mtl.	12	650	106	136	242	413	53	7	7	14	48	1949-50	1960-61
Sleaver, John	Chi.	2	24	2	0	2	6	....	....	....	....	....	1953-54	1956-57
Sleigher, Louis	Que., Bos.	6	194	46	53	99	146	17	1	1	2	64	1979-80	1985-86
Sloan, Tod	Tor., Chi.	13	745	220	262	482	781	47	9	12	21	47	1947-48	1960-61
Slobodzian, Peter	NYA	1	41	3	2	5	54	....	....	....	....	....	1940-41	1940-41
Slowinski, Eddie	NYR	6	291	58	74	132	63	16	2	6	8	6	1947-48	1952-53
Sly, Darryl	Tor., Min., Van.	4	79	1	2	3	20	....	....	....	....	....	1965-66	1970-71
Smart, Alec	Mtl.	1	8	2	5	7	0	....	....	....	....	....	1942-43	1942-43
Smedsmo, Dale	Tor.	1	4	0	0	0	0	....	....	....	....	....	1972-73	1972-73
Smillie, Don	Bos.	1	12	2	2	4	4	....	....	....	....	....	1933-34	1933-34
Smith, Alex	Ott., Det., Bos., NYA	11	443	41	50	91	643	19	0	2	2	40	1924-25	1934-35
Smith, Arthur	Tor., Ott.	4	137	15	10	25	249	4	1	1	2	8	1927-28	1930-31
Smith, Barry	Bos., Col.	3	114	7	7	14	10	....	....	....	....	....	1975-76	1980-81

Name	NHL Teams	NHL Seasons	Regular Schedule GP	G	A	TP	PIM	Playoffs GP	G	A	TP	PIM	First NHL Season	Last NHL Season
Smith, Brad	Van., Atl., Cgy., Det., Tor.	9	222	28	34	62	591	20	3	3	6	49	1978-79	1986-87
Smith, Brian D.	L.A., Min.	2	67	10	10	20	33	7	0	0	0	0	1967-68	1968-69
Smith, Brian S.	Det.	3	61	2	8	10	12	5	0	0	0	0	1957-58	1960-61
Smith, Carl	Det.	1	7	1	1	2	2	....	....	....	....	....	1943-44	1943-44
Smith, Clint	NYR, Chi.	11	483	161	236	397	24	44	10	14	24	2	1936-37	1946-47
Smith, Dallas	Bos., NYR	16	890	55	252	307	959	86	3	29	32	128	1959-60	1977-78
Smith, Dalton	NYA, Det.	2	11	1	2	3	0	....	....	....	....	....	1936-37	1943-44
Smith, Derek	Buf., Det.	8	335	78	116	194	60	30	9	14	23	13	1975-76	1982-83
Smith, Des	Mtl.M., Mtl., Chi., Bos.	5	195	22	25	47	236	25	1	4	5	18	1937-38	1941-42
Smith, Don	Mtl.	1	10	1	0	1	4	....	....	....	....	....	1919-20	1919-20
Smith, Don A.	NYR	1	11	1	1	2	0	1	0	0	0	0	1949-50	1949-50
Smith, Floyd	Bos., NYR, Det., Tor., Buf.	13	616	129	178	307	207	48	12	11	23	16	1954-55	1971-72
Smith, George	Tor.	1	9	0	0	0	0	....	....	....	....	....	1921-22	1921-22
Smith, Glen	Chi.	1	2	0	0	0	0	....	....	....	....	....	1950-51	1950-51
Smith, Glenn	Tor.	1	9	0	0	0	0	....	....	....	....	....	1922-23	1922-23
Smith, Gord	Wsh., Wpg.	6	299	9	30	39	284	....	....	....	....	....	1974-75	1979-80
Smith, Greg	Cal., Clev., Min., Det., Wsh.	13	829	56	232	288	1110	63	4	7	11	106	1975-76	1987-88
Smith, Hooley	Ott., Mtl.M., Bos., NYA	17	715	200	215	415	1013	54	11	8	19	109	1924-25	1940-41
Smith, Kenny	Bos.	7	331	78	93	171	49	30	8	13	21	6	1944-45	1950-51
Smith, Randy	Min.	2	3	0	0	0	0	....	....	....	....	....	1985-86	1986-87
Smith, Rick	Bos., Cal., St.L., Det., Wsh.	11	687	52	167	219	560	78	3	23	26	73	1968-69	1980-81
Smith, Roger	Pit., Phi.	6	210	20	4	24	172	4	3	0	3	0	1925-26	1930-31
Smith, Ron	NYI	1	11	1	1	2	14	....	....	....	....	....	1972-73	1972-73
Smith, Sid	Tor.	12	601	186	183	369	94	44	17	10	27	2	1946-47	1957-58
Smith, Stan	NYR	2	9	2	1	3	0	....	....	....	....	....	1939-40	1940-41
Smith, Stu E.	Mtl.	2	17	2	4	6	2	....	....	....	....	....	1940-41	1941-42
Smith, Stu G.	Hfd.	4	77	2	10	12	95	....	....	....	....	....	1979-80	1982-83
Smith, Tommy	Que.	1	10	0	0	0	9	....	....	....	....	....	1919-20	1919-20
Smith, Wayne	Chi.	1	2	1	1	2	2	1	0	0	0	0	1966-67	1966-67
Smith, Vern	NYI	1	1	0	0	0	0	....	....	....	....	....	1984-85	1984-85
Smrke, John	St.L., Que.	3	103	11	17	28	33	....	....	....	....	....	1977-78	1979-80
Smrke, Stan	Mtl.	2	9	0	3	3	0	....	....	....	....	....	1956-57	1957-58
Smylie, Rod	Tor., Ott.	6	76	4	1	5	10	9	1	2	3	2	1920-21	1925-26
Snell, Ron	Pit.	2	7	3	2	5	6	....	....	....	....	....	1968-69	1969-70
Snell, Ted	Pit., K.C., Det.	2	104	7	18	25	22	....	....	....	....	....	1973-74	1974-75
Snow, Sandy	Det.	1	3	0	0	0	2	....	....	....	....	....	1968-69	1968-69
Sobchuk, Denis	Det., Que.	2	35	5	6	11	2	....	....	....	....	....	1979-80	1982-83
Sobchuk, Gene	Van.	1	1	0	0	0	0	....	....	....	....	....	1973-74	1973-74
Solheim, Ken	Chi., Min., Det., Edm.	5	135	19	20	39	34	3	1	1	2	2	1980-81	1985-86
Solinger, Bob	Tor., Det.	5	99	10	11	21	19	....	....	....	....	....	1951-52	1959-60
Somers, Art	Chi., NYR	6	222	33	56	89	189	30	1	5	6	20	1929-30	1934-35
Sommer, Roy	Edm.	1	3	1	0	1	7	....	....	....	....	....	1980-81	1980-81
Songin, Tom	Bos.	3	43	5	5	10	22	....	....	....	....	....	1978-79	1980-81
Sonmor, Glen	NYR	2	28	2	0	2	21	....	....	....	....	....	1953-54	1954-55
Sorrell, John	Det., NYA	11	490	127	119	246	100	42	12	15	27	10	1930-31	1940-41
Sparrow, Emory	Bos.	1	6	0	0	0	4	....	....	....	....	....	1924-25	1924-25
Speck, Fred	Det., Van.	3	28	1	2	3	2	....	....	....	....	....	1968-69	1971-72
Speer, Bill	Pit., Bos.	4	130	5	20	25	79	8	1	0	1	4	1967-68	1970-71
Speers, Ted	Det.	1	4	1	1	2	0	....	....	....	....	....	1985-86	1985-86
Spencer, Brian	Tor., NYI, Buf., Pit.	10	553	80	143	223	634	37	1	5	6	29	1969-70	1978-79
Spencer, Irv	NYR, Bos., Det.	8	230	12	38	50	127	16	0	0	0	8	1959-60	1967-68
Speyer, Chris	Tor., NYA	3	14	0	0	0	0	....	....	....	....	....	1923-24	1933-34
Spring, Don	Wpg.	4	259	1	52	55	80	6	0	0	0	10	1980-81	1983-84
Spring, Frank	Bos., St.L., Cal., Clev.	5	61	14	20	34	12	....	....	....	....	....	1969-70	1976-77
Spring, Jesse	Ham., Pit., Tor., NYA	6	137	11	2	13	62	2	0	2	2	2	1923-24	1929-30
Spruce, Andy	Van., Col.	3	172	31	42	73	111	2	0	2	2	2	1976-77	1978-79
Stackhouse, Ron	Cal., Det., Pit.	12	889	87	372	459	824	32	5	8	13	38	1970-71	1981-82
Stackhouse, Ted	Tor.	1	12	0	0	0	2	5	0	0	0	0	1921-22	1921-22
Stahan, Butch	Mtl.	1	....	....	....	....	....	3	0	1	1	2	1944-45	1944-45
Staley, Al	NYR	1	1	0	1	1	0	....	....	....	....	....	1948-49	1948-49
Stamler, Lorne	L.A., Tor., Wpg.	4	116	14	11	25	16	....	....	....	....	....	1976-77	1979-80
Standing, George	Min.	1	2	0	0	0	0	....	....	....	....	....	1967-68	1967-68
Stanfield, Fred	Chi., Bos., Min., Buf.	14	914	211	405	616	134	106	21	35	56	10	1964-65	1977-78
Stanfield, Jack	Chi.	1	....	....	....	....	....	1	0	0	0	0	1965-66	1965-66
Stanfield, Jim	L.A.	3	7	0	1	1	0	....	....	....	....	....	1969-70	1971-72
Stankiewicz, Edward	Det.	2	6	0	0	0	2	....	....	....	....	....	1953-54	1955-56
Stankiewicz, Myron	St.L., Phi.	1	35	0	7	7	36	1	0	0	0	0	1968-69	1968-69
Stanley, Allan	NYR, Chi., Bos., Tor., Phi.	21	1244	100	333	433	792	109	7	36	43	80	1948-49	1968-69
Stanley, Barney	Chi.	1	1	0	0	0	0	....	....	....	....	....	1927-28	1927-28
Stanowski, Wally	Tor., NYR	10	428	23	88	111	160	60	3	14	17	13	1939-40	1950-51
Stapleton, Brian	Wsh.	1	1	0	0	0	0	....	....	....	....	....	1975-76	1975-76
Stapleton, Pat	Bos., Chi.	10	635	43	294	337	353	65	10	39	49	38	1961-62	1972-73
Starr, Harold	Ott., Mtl.M., Mtl., NYR	7	203	6	5	11	186	17	1	0	1	2	1929-30	1935-36
Starr, Wilf	NYA, Det.	4	89	8	6	14	25	7	0	2	2	2	1932-33	1935-36
Stasiuk, Vic	Chi., Det., Bos.	14	745	183	254	437	669	69	16	18	34	40	1949-50	1962-63
Stastny, Marian	Que., Tor.	5	322	121	173	294	110	32	5	17	22	7	1981-82	1985-86
Staszak, Ray	Det.	1	4	0	1	1	7	....	....	....	....	....	1985-86	1985-86
Steele, Frank	Det.	1	1	0	0	0	0	....	....	....	....	....	1930-31	1930-31
Steen, Anders	Wpg.	1	42	5	11	16	22	....	....	....	....	....	1980-81	1980-81
Stefaniw, Morris	Atl.	1	13	1	1	2	2	....	....	....	....	....	1972-73	1972-73
Stefanski, Bud	NYR	1	1	0	0	0	0	....	....	....	....	....	1977-78	1977-78
Stemkowski, Pete	Tor., Det., NYR, L.A.	15	967	206	349	555	866	83	25	29	54	136	1963-64	1977-78
Stenlund, Vern	Clev.	1	4	0	0	0	0	....	....	....	....	....	1976-77	1976-77
Stephens, Phil	Mtl.W, Mtl.	2	8	1	0	1	0	....	....	....	....	....	1917-18	1921-22
Stephenson, Bob	Hfd., Tor.	1	18	2	3	5	4	....	....	....	....	....	1979-80	1979-80
Sterner, Ulf	NYR	1	4	0	0	0	0	....	....	....	....	....	1964-65	1964-65
Stevens, Paul	Bos.	1	17	0	0	0	0	....	....	....	....	....	1925-26	1925-26
Stewart, Bill	Buf., St.L., Tor., Min.	8	261	7	64	71	424	13	1	3	4	11	1977-78	1985-86
Stewart, Blair	Det., Wsh., Que.	7	229	34	44	78	326	....	....	....	....	....	1973-74	1979-80
Stewart, Gaye	Tor., Chi., Det., NYR, Mtl.	11	502	185	159	344	274	25	2	9	11	16	1941-42	1953-54
Stewart, Jack	Det., Chi.	12	565	31	84	115	765	80	5	14	19	143	1938-39	1951-52
Stewart, John	Pit., Atl., Cal., Que.	6	260	58	60	118	158	4	0	0	0	10	1970-71	1979-80
Stewart, Ken	Chi.	1	6	1	1	2	2	....	....	....	....	....	1941-42	1941-42
Stewart, Nels	Mtl.M., Bos., NYA	15	651	324	191	515	953	54	15	13	28	61	1925-26	1939-40
Stewart, Paul	Que.	1	21	2	0	2	74	....	....	....	....	....	1979-80	1979-80
Stewart, Ralph	Van., NYI	7	252	57	73	130	28	19	4	4	8	2	1970-71	1977-78
Stewart, Robert	Bos., Cal., Clev., St.L., Pit.	9	510	27	101	128	809	5	1	1	2	2	1971-72	1979-80
Stewart, Ron	Tor., Bos., St.L., NYR, Van., NYI	21	1353	276	253	529	560	119	14	21	35	60	1952-53	1972-73
Stewart, Ryan	Wpg.	1	3	1	0	1	0	....	....	....	....	....	1985-86	1985-86
Stiles, Tony	Cgy.	1	30	2	7	9	20	....	....	....	....	....	1983-84	1983-84
Stoddard, Jack	NYR	2	80	16	15	31	31	....	....	....	....	....	1951-52	1952-53
Stoltz, Roland	Wsh.	1	14	2	2	4	14	....	....	....	....	....	1981-82	1981-82
Stone, Steve	Van.	1	2	0	0	0	0	....	....	....	....	....	1973-74	1973-74
Stoughton, Blaine	Pit., Tor., Hfd., NYR	8	526	258	191	449	204	8	4	2	6	2	1973-74	1983-84
Stoyanovich, Steve	Hfd.	1	23	3	5	8	11	....	....	....	....	....	1983-84	1983-84
Strain, Neil	NYR	1	52	11	13	24	12	....	....	....	....	....	1952-53	1952-53
Strate, Gord	Det.	3	61	0	0	0	34	....	....	....	....	....	1956-57	1958-59
Stratton, Art	NYR, Det., Chi., Pit., Phi.	4	95	18	33	51	24	5	0	0	0	0	1959-60	1967-68
Strobel, Art	NYR	1	7	0	0	0	0	....	....	....	....	....	1943-44	1943-44
Strong, Ken	Tor.	3	15	2	2	4	6	....	....	....	....	....	1982-83	1984-85
Strueby, Todd	Edm.	3	5	0	1	1	2	....	....	....	....	....	1981-82	1983-84
Stuart, Billy	Tor., Bos.	7	193	30	17	47	145	17	1	0	1	12	1920-21	1926-27
Stumpf, Robert	St.L., Pit.	1	10	1	1	2	20	....	....	....	....	....	1974-75	1974-75
Sturgeon, Peter	Col.	2	6	0	1	1	2	....	....	....	....	....	1979-80	1980-81
Suikkanen, Kai	Buf.	2	2	0	0	0	0	....	....	....	....	....	1981-82	1982-83
Sullivan, Barry	Det.	1	1	0	0	0	0	....	....	....	....	....	1947-48	1947-48
Sullivan, Bob	Hfd.	1	62	18	19	37	18	....	....	....	....	....	1982-83	1982-83
Sullivan, Frank	Tor., Chi.	4	8	0	0	0	2	....	....	....	....	....	1949-50	1955-56
Sullivan, Peter	Wpg.	2	126	28	54	82	40	....	....	....	....	....	1979-80	1980-81
Sullivan, Red	Bos., Chi., NYR	11	557	107	239	346	441	18	1	2	3	7	1949-50	1960-61
Summerhill, Bill	Mtl., NYA	3	72	14	17	31	70	3	0	0	0	2	1938-39	1941-42
Suomi, Al	Chi.	1	5	0	0	0	0	....	....	....	....	....	1936-37	1936-37
Sutherland, Bill	Mtl., Phi., Tor., St.L., Det.	6	250	70	58	128	99	14	2	4	6	0	1962-63	1971-72
Sutherland, Ron	Bos.	1	2	0	0	0	0	....	....	....	....	....	1931-32	1931-32

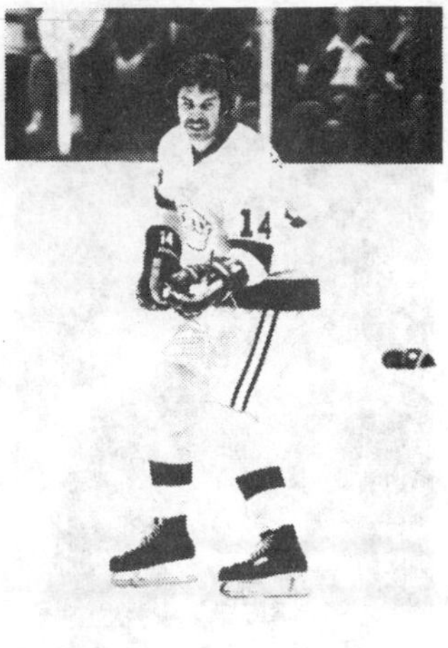

Dave Schultz

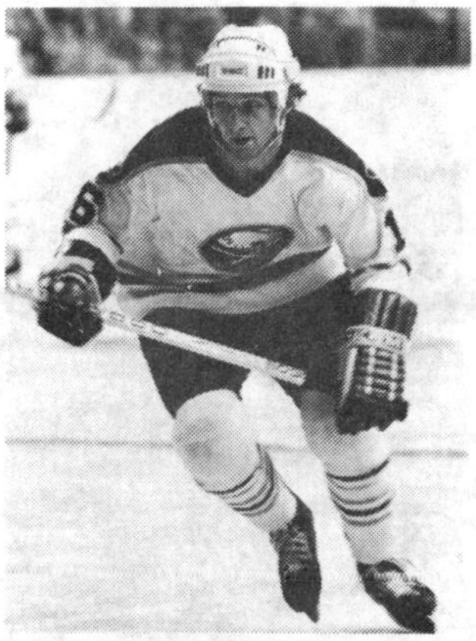

Ric Seiling

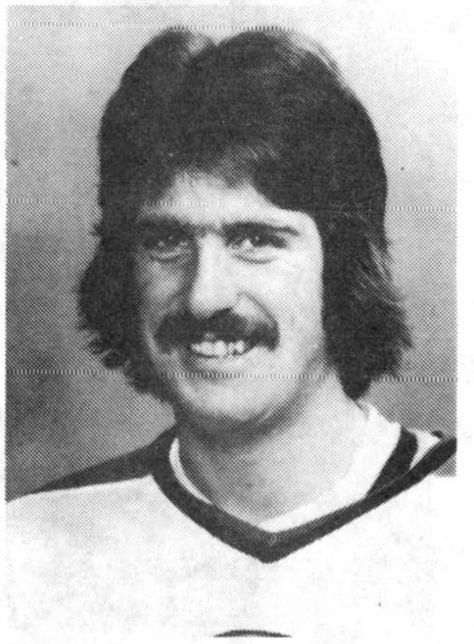

Charlie Simmer

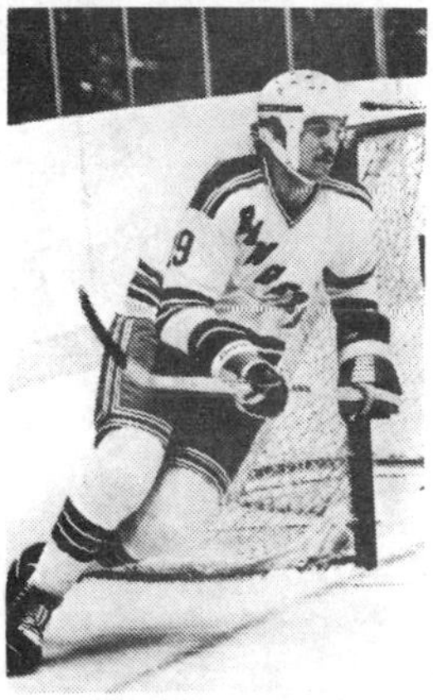

Dean Talafous

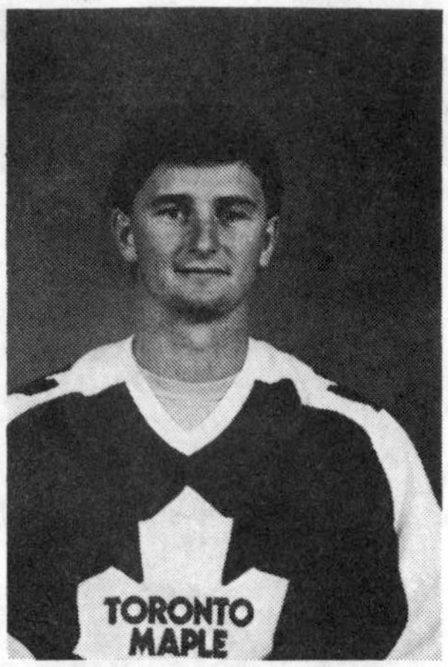

Greg Terrion

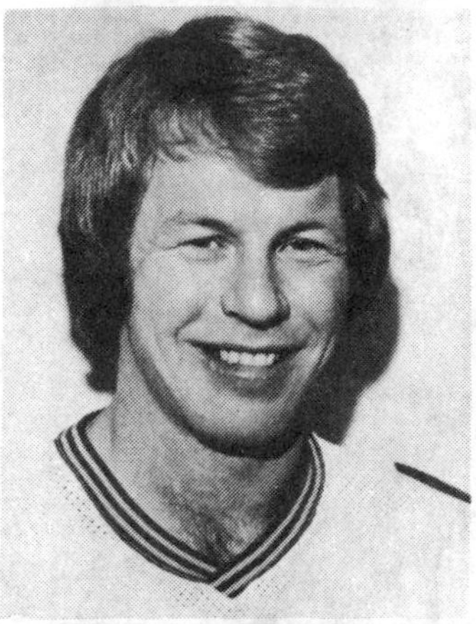

John Van Boxmeer

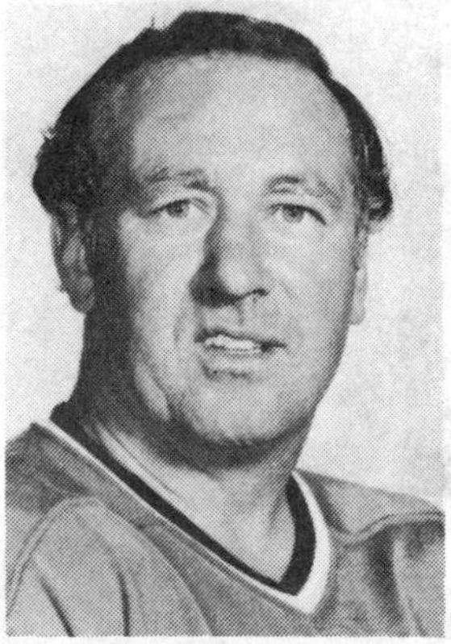

Ed Van Impe

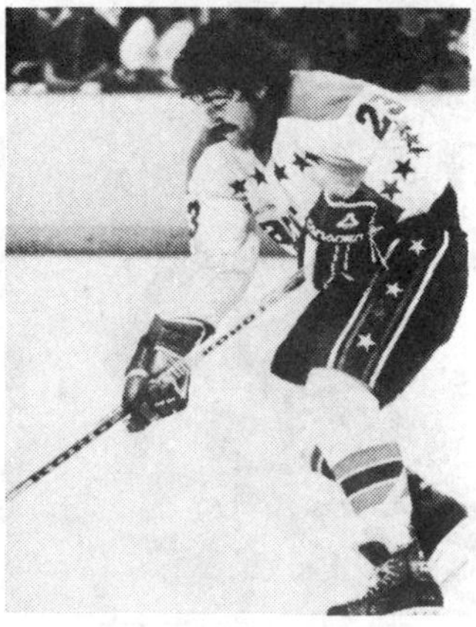

Dennis Ververgaert

Name	NHL Teams	NHL Seasons	Regular Schedule GP	G	A	TP	PIM	Playoffs GP	G	A	TP	PIM	First NHL Season	Last NHL Season
Sutter, Brian	St.L.	12	779	303	333	636	1786	65	21	21	42	249	1976-77	1987-88
Sutter, Darryl	Chi.	8	406	161	118	279	288	51	24	19	43	26	1979-80	1986-87
Suzor, Mark	Phi., Col.	2	64	4	16	20	60	....	....	....	....	....	1976-77	1977-78
Svensson, Leif	Wsh.	2	121	6	40	46	49	....	....	....	....	....	1978-79	1979-80
Swain, Garry	Pit.	1	9	1	1	2	0	....	....	....	....	....	1968-69	1968-69
Swarbrick, George	Oak., Pit., Phi.	4	132	17	25	42	173	....	....	....	....	....	1967-68	1970-71
Sweeny, Bill	NYR	1	4	1	0	1	0	....	....	....	....	....	1959-60	1959-60
Sykes, Bob	Tor.	1	2	0	0	0	0	....	....	....	....	....	1974-75	1974-75
Szura, Joe	Oak.	2	90	10	15	25	30	7	2	3	5	2	1967-68	1968-69

T

Name	NHL Teams	NHL Seasons	Regular Schedule GP	G	A	TP	PIM	Playoffs GP	G	A	TP	PIM	First NHL Season	Last NHL Season
Taft, John	Det.	1	15	0	2	2	4	....	....	....	....	....	1978-79	1978-79
Talafous, Dean	Atl., Min., NYR	8	497	104	154	258	163	21	4	7	11	11	1974-75	1981-82
Talakoski, Ron	NYR	2	9	0	1	1	33	....	....	....	....	....	1986-87	1987-88
Talbot, Jean-Guy	Mtl., Min., Det., St.L., Buf.	17	1056	43	242	285	1006	150	4	26	30	142	1954-55	1970-71
Tallon, Dale	Van., Chi., Pit.	10	642	98	238	336	568	33	2	10	12	45	1970-71	1979-80
Tambellini, Steve	NYI, Col., N.J., Cgy., Van.	10	553	160	150	310	105	2	0	1	1	0	1978-79	1987-88
Tanguay, Chris	Que.	1	2	0	0	0	0	....	....	....	....	....	1981-82	1981-82
Tannahill, Don	Van.	2	111	30	33	63	25	....	....	....	....	....	1972-73	1973-74
Tardif, Marc	Mtl., Que.	8	517	194	207	401	443	62	13	15	28	75	1969-70	1982-83
Taylor, Billy	Tor., Det., Bos., NYR	7	323	87	180	267	120	33	6	18	24	13	1939-40	1947-48
Taylor, Billy	NYR	1	2	0	0	0	0	....	....	....	....	....	1964-65	1964-65
Taylor, Bob	Bos.	1	8	0	0	0	6	....	....	....	....	....	1929-30	1929-30
Taylor, Ted	NYR, Det., Min., Van.	6	166	23	35	58	181	....	....	....	....	....	1964-65	1971-72
Taylor, Harry	Tor., Chi.	3	66	5	10	15	30	1	0	0	0	0	1946-47	1951-52
Taylor, Mark	Phi., Pit., Wsh.	5	209	42	68	110	73	6	0	0	0	0	1981-82	1985-86
Taylor, Ralph	Chi., NYR	3	99	4	1	5	169	4	0	0	0	10	1927-28	1929-30
Teal, Jeff	Mtl.	1	6	0	1	1	0	....	....	....	....	....	1984-85	1984-85
Teal, Skip	Bos.	1	1	0	0	0	0	....	....	....	....	....	1954-55	1954-55
Teal, Victor	NYI	1	1	0	0	0	0	....	....	....	....	....	1973-74	1973-74
Tebbutt, Greg	Que., Pit.	2	26	0	3	3	35	....	....	....	....	....	1979-80	1983-84
Terbenche, Paul	Chi., Buf.	5	189	5	26	31	28	12	0	0	0	0	1967-68	1973-74
Terrion, Greg	L.A., Tor.	8	556	93	150	243	339	35	2	9	11	41	1980-81	1987-88
Terry, Bill	Min.	1	5	0	0	0	0	....	....	....	....	....	1987-88	1987-88
Tessier, Orval	Mtl., Bos.	3	59	5	7	12	6	....	....	....	....	....	1954-55	1960-61
Thatchell, Spence	NYR	1	1	0	0	0	0	....	....	....	....	....	1942-43	1942-43
Theberge, Greg	Wsh.	5	153	15	63	78	73	4	0	1	1	0	1979-80	1983-84
Therrien, Gaston	Que.	3	22	0	8	8	12	9	0	1	1	4	1980-81	1982-83
Thelin, Mats	Bos.	3	163	8	19	27	107	5	0	0	0	6	1984-85	1986-87
Thibeault, Laurence	Det., Mtl.	2	5	0	2	2	0	....	....	....	....	....	1944-45	1945-46
Thiffault, Leo	Min.	1	....	....	....	....	....	5	0	0	0	0	1967-68	1967-68
Thomas, Cy	Chi., Tor.	1	14	2	2	4	12	....	....	....	....	....	1947-48	1947-48
Thomas, Reg	Que.	1	39	9	7	16	6	....	....	....	....	....	1979-80	1979-80
Thompson, Cliff	Bos.	2	13	0	1	1	2	....	....	....	....	....	1941-42	1948-49
Thompson, Errol	Tor., Det., Pit.	10	599	208	185	393	184	34	7	5	12	11	1970-71	1980-81
Thompson, Kenneth	Mtl.W	1	1	0	0	0	0	....	....	....	....	....	1917-18	1917-18
Thompson, Paul	NYR, Chi.	13	586	153	179	332	336	48	11	11	22	54	1926-27	1938-39
Thoms, Bill	Tor., Chi., Bos.	13	549	135	206	341	176	44	6	10	16	6	1932-33	1944-45
Thomson, Bill	Det., Chi.	2	10	2	2	4	0	2	0	0	0	0	1938-39	1943-44
Thomson, Floyd	St.L.	8	411	56	97	153	341	10	0	2	2	6	1971-72	1979-80
Thomson, Jack	NYA	3	15	1	1	2	0	2	0	0	0	0	1938-39	1940-41
Thomson, Jimmy	Tor., Chi.	13	787	19	215	234	920	63	2	13	15	135	1945-46	1957-58
Thomson, Rhys	Mtl., Tor.	2	25	0	2	2	38	....	....	....	....	....	1939-40	1942-43
Thornbury, Tom	Pit.	1	14	1	8	9	16	....	....	....	....	....	1983-84	1983-84
Thorsteinson, Joe	NYA	1	4	0	0	0	0	....	....	....	....	....	1932-33	1932-33
Thurier, Fred	NYA, NYR	3	80	25	27	52	18	....	....	....	....	....	1940-41	1944-45
Thurlby, Tom	Oak.	1	20	1	2	3	4	....	....	....	....	....	1967-68	1967-68
Tidey, Alex	Buf., Edm.	3	9	0	0	0	8	2	0	0	0	0	1976-77	1979-80
Timgren, Ray	Tor., Chi.	6	251	14	44	58	70	30	3	9	12	6	1948-49	1954-55
Titanic, Morris	Buf.	2	19	0	0	0	0	....	....	....	....	....	1974-75	1975-76
Tkaczuk, Walt	NYR	14	945	227	451	678	556	93	19	32	51	119	1967-68	1980-81
Toal, Mike	Edm.	1	3	0	0	0	0	....	....	....	....	....	1979-80	1979-80
Tomalty, Glenn	Wpg.	1	1	0	0	0	0	....	....	....	....	....	1979-80	1979-80
Tomlinson, Kirk	Min.	1	1	0	0	0	0	....	....	....	....	....	1987-88	1987-88
Toomey, Sean	Min.	1	1	0	0	0	0	....	....	....	....	....	1986-87	1986-87
Toppazzini, Jerry	Bos., Chi., Det.	12	783	163	244	407	436	40	13	9	22	13	1952-53	1963-64
Toppazzini, Zellio	Bos., NYR, Chi.	5	123	21	22	43	49	2	0	0	0	0	1948-49	1956-57
Touhey, Bill	Mtl.M., Ott., Bos.	7	280	65	40	105	107	2	1	0	1	0	1927-28	1933-34
Toupin, Jaques	Chi.	1	8	1	2	3	0	4	0	0	0	0	1943-44	1943-44
Townsend, Art	Chi.	1	5	0	0	0	0	....	....	....	....	....	1926-27	1926-27
Trader, Larry	Det., St.L., Mtl.	4	91	5	13	18	74	3	0	0	0	0	1982-83	1987-88
Trainor, Wes	NYR	1	17	1	2	3	6	....	....	....	....	....	1948-49	1948-49
Trapp, Bobby	Chi.	2	82	4	4	8	129	2	0	0	0	4	1926-27	1927-28
Trapp, Doug	Buf.	1	2	0	0	0	0	....	....	....	....	....	1986-87	1986-87
Traub, Percy	Chi., Det.	3	130	3	3	6	214	4	0	0	0	6	1926-27	1928-29
Tredway, Brock	L.A.	1	....	....	....	....	....	1	0	0	0	0	1981-82	1981-82
Tremblay, Brent	Wsh.	2	10	1	0	1	6	....	....	....	....	....	1978-79	1979-80
Tremblay, Gilles	Mtl.	9	509	168	162	330	161	48	9	14	23	4	1960-61	1968-69
Tremblay, J.C.	Mtl.	13	794	57	306	363	204	108	14	51	65	58	1959-60	1971-72
Tremblay, Marcel	Mtl.	1	10	0	2	2	0	....	....	....	....	....	1938-39	1938-39
Tremblay, Mario	Mtl.	12	852	258	326	584	1043	100	20	29	49	187	1974-75	1985-86
Tremblay, Nels	Mtl.	2	3	0	1	1	0	2	0	0	0	0	1944-45	1945-46
Trimper, Tim	Chi., Wpg., Min.	6	190	30	36	66	153	2	0	0	0	2	1979-80	1984-85
Trottier, Dave	Mtl.M., Det.	11	446	121	113	234	508	31	4	3	7	41	1928-29	1938-39
Trottier, Guy	NYR, Tor.	3	115	28	17	45	37	9	1	0	1	16	1968-69	1971-72
Trottier, Rocky	N.J.	2	38	6	4	10	2	....	....	....	....	....	1983-84	1984-85
Trudel, Louis	Chi., Mtl.	8	306	49	69	118	122	24	1	3	4	6	1933-34	1940-41
Trudell, Rene	NYR	3	129	24	28	52	72	5	0	0	0	2	1945-46	1947-48
Tudin, Connie	Mtl.	1	4	0	1	1	4	....	....	....	....	....	1941-42	1941-42
Tudor, Rob	Van., St.L.	3	28	4	4	8	19	3	0	0	0	0	1978-79	1982-83
Turlick, Gord	Bos.	1	2	0	0	0	2	....	....	....	....	....	1959-60	1959-60
Turnbull, Ian	Tor., L.A., Pit.	10	628	123	317	440	753	55	13	32	45	94	1973-74	1982-83
Turnbull, Perry	St.L., Mtl., Wpg.	9	608	188	163	351	1245	34	6	7	13	86	1979-80	1987-88
Turnbull, Randy	Cgy.	1	1	0	0	0	2	....	....	....	....	....	1981-82	1981-82
Turner, Bob	Mtl., Chi.	8	478	19	51	70	307	68	1	4	5	44	1955-56	1962-63
Turner, Dean	NYR, Col., L.A.	4	35	1	0	1	59	....	....	....	....	....	1978-79	1982-83
Tustin, Norman	NYR	1	18	2	4	6	0	....	....	....	....	....	1941-42	1941-42
Tuten, Audley	Chi.	2	39	4	8	12	48	....	....	....	....	....	1941-42	1942-43

UV

Name	NHL Teams	NHL Seasons	Regular Schedule GP	G	A	TP	PIM	Playoffs GP	G	A	TP	PIM	First NHL Season	Last NHL Season
Ubriaco, Gene	Pit., Oak., Chi.	3	177	39	35	74	50	11	2	0	2	4	1967-68	1969-70
Ullman, Norm	Det., Tor.	20	1410	490	739	1229	712	106	30	53	83	67	1955-56	1974-75
Unger, Garry	Tor., Det., St.L., Atl., L.A., Edm.	16	1105	413	391	804	1075	52	12	18	30	105	1967-68	1982-83
Vadnais, Carol	Mtl., Oak., Cal., Bos., NYR, N.J.	17	1087	169	418	587	1813	106	10	40	50	185	1966-67	1982-83
Vail, Eric	Atl, Cgy., Det.	9	591	216	260	476	281	20	5	6	11	6	1973-74	1981-82
Vail, Melville	NYR	2	50	4	1	5	18	10	0	0	0	2	1928-29	1929-30
Valentine, Chris	Wsh.	3	105	43	52	95	127	2	0	0	0	4	1981-82	1983-84
Valiquette, Jack	Tor., Col.	7	350	84	134	218	79	23	3	6	9	4	1974-75	1980-81
Van Boxmeer, John	Mtl., Col., Buf., Que.	11	588	84	274	358	465	38	5	15	20	37	1973-74	1983-84
Van Impe, Ed	Chi., Phi., Pit.	11	700	27	126	153	1025	66	1	12	13	131	1966-67	1976-77
Vasko, Elmer	Chi., Min.	13	786	34	166	200	719	78	2	7	9	73	1956-57	1969-70
Vasko, Rick	Det.	3	31	3	7	10	29	....	....	....	....	....	1977-78	1980-81
Vautour, Yvon	NYI, Col., N.J., Que.	6	204	26	33	59	401	....	....	....	....	....	1979-80	1984-85
Vaydik, Greg	Chi.	1	5	0	0	0	0	....	....	....	....	....	1976-77	1976-77
Venasky, Vic	L.A.	7	430	61	101	162	66	21	1	5	6	12	1972-73	1978-79
Veneruzzo, Gary	St.L.	2	7	1	1	2	0	9	0	2	2	2	1967-68	1971-72
Verret, Claude	Buf.	2	14	2	5	7	2	....	....	....	....	....	1983-84	1984-85
Verstraete, Leigh	Tor.	3	8	0	1	1	14	....	....	....	....	....	1982-83	1987-88
Ververgaert, Dennis	Van., Phi., Wsh.	8	583	176	216	392	247	8	1	2	3	6	1973-74	1980-81
Veysey, Sid	Van.	1	1	0	0	0	0	....	....	....	....	....	1977-78	1977-78
Vickers, Steve	NYR	10	698	246	340	586	330	68	24	25	49	58	1972-73	1981-82
Vigneault, Alain	St.L.	2	42	2	5	7	82	4	0	1	1	26	1981-82	1982-83

Name	NHL Teams	NHL Seasons	Regular Schedule					Playoffs					First NHL Season	Last NHL Season
			GP	G	A	TP	PIM	GP	G	A	TP	PIM		
Vipond, Pete	Cal.	1	3	0	0	0	0	....	....	....	....	....	1972-73	1972-73
Vokes, Ed	Chi.	1	5	0	0	0	0	....	....	....	....	....	1930-31	1930-31
Volcan, Mickey	Hfd., Cgy.	4	162	8	33	41	146	....	....	....	....	....	1980-81	1983-84
Volmar, Doug	Det., L.A.	4	62	13	8	21	26	2	1	0	1	0	1969-70	1972-73
Voss, Carl	Tor., NYR, Det., Ott., St.L., Mtl.M., NYA, Chi.	8	261	34	70	104	50	24	5	3	8	0	1926-27	1937-38

W

Name	NHL Teams	NHL Seasons	GP	G	A	TP	PIM	GP	G	A	TP	PIM	First NHL Season	Last NHL Season
Waddell, Don	L.A.	1	1	0	0	0	0	....	....	....	....	....	1980-81	1980-81
Waite, Frank	NYR	1	17	1	3	4	4	....	....	....	....	....	1930-31	1930-31
Walker, Howard	Wsh., Cal.	3	83	2	13	15	133	....	....	....	....	....	1980-81	1982-83
Walker, Jack	Det.	2	80	5	8	13	18	....	....	....	....	....	1926-27	1927-28
Walker, Kurt	Tor.	3	71	4	5	9	152	16	0	0	0	34	1975-76	1977-78
Walker, Russ	L.A.	2	17	1	0	1	41	....	....	....	....	....	1976-77	1977-78
Wall, Bob	Det., L.A., St.L.	8	322	30	55	85	155	22	0	3	3	2	1964-65	1971-72
Wallin, Peter	NYR	2	52	3	14	17	14	14	2	6	8	6	1980-81	1981-82
Walsh, Jim	Buf.	1	4	0	1	1	4	....	....	....	....	....	1981-82	1981-82
Walton, Bobby	Mtl.	1	4	0	0	0	0	....	....	....	....	....	1943-44	1943-44
Walton, Mike	Tor., Bos., Van., Chi., St.L.	12	588	201	247	448	357	47	14	10	24	45	1965-66	1978-79
Wappel, Gord	Atl., Cgy.	3	20	1	1	2	10	2	0	0	0	4	1979-80	1981-82
Ward, Don	Chi., Bos.	2	34	0	1	1	160	....	....	....	....	....	1957-58	1959-60
Ward, Jimmy	Mtl.M., Mtl.	12	532	147	127	274	455	31	4	4	8	18	1927-28	1938-39
Ward, Joe	Col.	1	4	0	0	0	2	....	....	....	....	....	1980-81	1980-81
Ward, Ron	Tor., Van.,	2	89	2	5	7	6	....	....	....	....	....	1969-70	1971-72
Wares, Eddie	NYR, Det., Chi.	9	291	60	102	162	161	45	5	7	12	34	1936-37	1946-47
Warner, Bob	Tor.	2	10	1	1	2	4	4	0	0	0	0	1975-76	1976-77
Warner, Jim	Hfd.	1	32	0	3	3	10	....	....	....	....	....	1979-80	1979-80
Warwick, Bill	NYR	2	14	3	3	6	16	....	....	....	....	....	1942-43	1943-44
Warwick, Grant	NYR, Bos., Mtl.	9	395	147	142	289	220	16	2	4	6	6	1941-42	1949-50
Wasnie, Nick	Chi., Mtl., NYA, Ott., St.L.	7	248	57	34	91	176	14	6	3	9	20	1927-28	1934-35
Watson, Bill	Chi.	4	115	23	36	59	12	6	0	2	2	0	1985-86	1988-89
Watson, Bryan	Mtl., Oak., Pit., Det., St.L., Wsh.	16	878	17	135	152	2212	32	2	0	2	70	1963-64	1978-79
Watson, Dave	Col.	2	18	0	1	1	10	....	....	....	....	....	1979-80	1980-81
Watson, Harry	NYA, Det., Tor., Chi.	14	805	236	207	443	150	62	16	9	25	27	1941-42	1956-57
Watson, Jim	Det., Buf.	7	221	4	19	23	345	....	....	....	....	....	1963-64	1971-72
Watson, Jimmy	Phi.	10	613	38	148	186	492	101	5	34	39	89	1972-73	1981-82
Watson, Joe	Bos., Phi., Col.	14	835	38	178	216	447	84	3	12	15	82	1964-65	1978-79
Watson, Phil	NYR, Mtl.	13	590	144	265	409	532	45	10	25	35	67	1935-36	1947-48
Watts, Brian	Det.	1	4	0	0	0	0	....	....	....	....	....	1975-76	1975-76
Webster, Aubrey	Phi., Mtl.M.	2	5	0	0	0	0	....	....	....	....	....	1930-31	1934-35
Webster, Don	Tor.	1	27	7	6	13	28	5	0	0	0	12	1943-44	1943-44
Webster, John	NYR	1	14	0	0	0	4	....	....	....	....	....	1949-50	1949-50
Webster, Tom	Bos., Det., Cal.	5	102	33	42	75	61	1	0	0	0	0	1968-69	1979-80
Weiland, Cooney	Bos., Ott., Det.	11	508	173	160	333	147	45	12	10	22	12	1928-29	1938-39
Weir, Stan	Cal., Tor., Edm., Col., Det.	10	642	139	207	346	183	37	6	5	11	4	1972-73	1982-83
Weir, Wally	Que., Hfd., Pit.	6	320	21	45	66	625	23	0	1	1	96	1979-80	1984-85
Wellington, Duke	Que.	1	1	0	0	0	0	....	....	....	....	....	1919-20	1919-20
Wensink, John	Bos., Que., Col., N.J., St.L.	8	403	70	68	138	840	43	2	6	8	86	1973-74	1982-83
Wentworth, Cy	Chi., Mtl.M., Mtl.	13	578	39	68	107	355	35	5	6	11	22	1927-28	1939-40
Wesley, Blake	Phi., Hfd., Que., Tor.	7	298	18	46	64	486	19	2	2	4	30	1979-80	1985-86
Westfall, Ed	Bos., NYI	18	1227	231	394	625	544	95	22	37	59	41	1961-62	1978-79
Wharram, Kenny	Chi.	14	766	252	281	533	222	80	16	27	43	38	1951-52	1968-69
Wharton, Len	NYR	1	1	0	0	0	0	....	....	....	....	....	1944-45	1944-45
Wheldon, Donald	St.L.	1	2	0	0	0	0	....	....	....	....	....	1974-75	1974-75
Whelton, Bill	Wpg.	1	2	0	0	0	0	....	....	....	....	....	1980-81	1980-81
Whistle, Rob	NYR, St.L.	2	51	7	5	12	16	4	0	0	0	2	1985-86	1987-88
White, Bill	L.A., Chi.	9	604	50	215	265	495	91	7	32	39	76	1967-68	1975-76
White, Moe	Mtl.	1	4	0	1	1	2	....	....	....	....	....	1945-46	1945-46
White, Sherman	NYR	2	4	0	2	2	0	....	....	....	....	....	1946-47	1949-50
White, Tex	Pit., NYA, Phi.	6	203	33	12	45	141	4	0	0	0	2	1925-26	1930-31
White, Tony	Wsh., Min.	5	164	37	28	65	104	....	....	....	....	....	1974-75	1979-80
Whitelaw, Bob	Det.	2	32	0	2	2	2	8	0	0	0	0	1940-41	1941-42
Whitlock, Bob	Min.	1	1	0	0	0	0	....	....	....	....	....	1969-70	1969-70
Widing, Juha	NYR, L.A., Clev.	8	575	144	226	370	208	8	1	2	3	2	1969-70	1976-77
Wiebe, Art	Chi.	11	411	14	27	41	209	31	1	3	4	8	1932-33	1943-44
Wilcox, Archie	Mtl.M., Bos., St.L.	6	212	8	14	22	158	12	1	0	1	10	1929-30	1934-35
Wilcox, Barry	Van.	2	33	3	2	5	15	....	....	....	....	....	1972-73	1974-75
Wilder, Arch	Det.	1	18	0	2	2	2	....	....	....	....	....	1940-41	1940-41
Wiley, Jim	Pit., Van.	5	63	4	10	14	8	....	....	....	....	....	1972-73	1976-77
Wilkins, Barry	Bos., Van., Pit.	9	418	27	125	152	663	6	0	1	1	4	1966-67	1975-76
Wilkinson, John	Bos.	1	9	0	0	0	3	....	....	....	....	....	1943-44	1943-44
Willard, Rod	Tor.	1	1	0	0	0	0	....	....	....	....	....	1982-83	1982-83
Williams, Burr	Det., St.L., Bos.	3	19	0	1	1	28	2	0	0	0	8	1933-34	1936-37
Williams, Dave	Tor., Van., Det., L.A., Hfd.	14	962	241	272	513	3966	83	12	23	35	455	1974-75	1987-88
Williams, Fred	Det.	1	44	2	5	7	10	....	....	....	....	....	1976-77	1976-77
Williams, Gord	Phi.	2	2	0	0	0	2	....	....	....	....	....	1981-82	1982-83
Williams, Tom	Bos., Min., Cal., Wsh.	13	663	161	269	430	177	10	2	5	7	2	1961-62	1975-76
Williams, Tommy	NYR, L.A.	8	397	115	138	253	73	29	8	7	15	4	1971-72	1978-79
Williams, Warren	St.L., Cal.	3	108	14	35	49	131	....	....	....	....	....	1973-74	1975-76
Willson, Don	Mtl.	2	22	2	7	9	0	3	0	0	0	0	1937-38	1938-39
Wilson, Behn	Phi., Chi.	9	601	98	260	358	1480	67	12	29	41	190	1978-79	1987-88
Wilson, Bert	NYR, L.A., St.L., Cgy.	8	478	37	44	81	646	21	0	2	2	42	1973-74	1980-81
Wilson, Bob	Chi.	1	1	0	0	0	0	....	....	....	....	....	1953-54	1953-54
Wilson, Cully	Tor., Mtl., Ham., Chi.	5	125	60	23	83	232	2	1	0	1	6	1919-20	1926-27
Wilson, Gord	Bos.	1	....	....	....	....	....	2	0	0	0	0	1954-55	1954-55
Wilson, Hub	NYA	1	2	0	0	0	0	....	....	....	....	....	1931-32	1931-32
Wilson, Jerry	Mtl.	1	3	0	0	0	2	....	....	....	....	....	1956-57	1956-57
Wilson, Johnny	Det., Chi., Tor., NYR	13	688	161	171	332	190	66	14	13	27	11	1949-50	1961-62
Wilson, Larry	Det., Chi.	6	152	21	48	69	75	4	0	0	0	0	1949-50	1955-56
Wilson, Murray	Mtl., L.A.	7	386	94	95	189	162	53	5	14	19	32	1972-73	1978-79
Wilson, Rick	Mtl., St.L., Det.	4	239	6	26	32	105	3	0	0	0	0	1973-74	1976-77
Wilson, Roger	Chi.	1	7	0	2	2	6	....	....	....	....	....	1974-75	1974-75
Wilson, Ron	Tor., Min.	7	177	26	67	93	68	20	4	13	17	8	1977-78	1987-88
Wilson, Wally	Bos.	1	53	11	8	19	18	1	0	0	0	0	1947-48	1947-48
Wing, Murray	Det.	1	1	0	1	1	0	....	....	....	....	....	1973-74	1973-74
Wiseman, Eddie	Det., NYA, Bos.	10	454	115	164	279	137	45	10	10	20	16	1932-33	1941-42
Wiste, Jim	Chi., Van.	3	52	1	10	11	8	....	....	....	....	....	1968-69	1970-71
Witherspoon, Jim	L.A.	1	2	0	0	0	0	....	....	....	....	....	1975-76	1975-76
Witiuk, Steve	Chi.	1	33	3	8	11	14	....	....	....	....	....	1951-52	1951-52
Woit, Benny	Det., Chi.	7	334	7	26	33	170	41	2	6	8	18	1950-51	1956-57
Wojciechowski, Steven	Det.	2	54	19	20	39	17	6	0	1	1	0	1944-45	1946-47
Wolf, Bennett	Pit.	3	30	0	1	1	133	....	....	....	....	....	1980-81	1982-83
Wong, Mike	Det.	1	22	1	1	2	12	....	....	....	....	....	1975-76	1975-76
Wood, Robert	NYR	1	1	0	0	0	0	....	....	....	....	....	1950-51	1950-51
Woods, Paul	Det.	7	501	72	124	196	276	7	0	5	5	4	1977-78	1983-84
Woytowich, Bob	Bos., Min., Pit., L.A.	8	503	32	126	158	352	24	1	3	4	20	1964-65	1971-72
Wright, John	Van., St.L., K.C.	3	127	16	36	52	67	....	....	....	....	....	1972-73	1974-75
Wright, Keith	Phi.	1	1	0	0	0	0	....	....	....	....	....	1967-68	1967-68
Wright, Larry	Phi., Cal., Det.	5	106	4	8	12	19	....	....	....	....	....	1971-72	1977-78
Wycherley, Ralph	NYA	2	28	4	7	11	6	....	....	....	....	....	1940-41	1941-42
Wylie, Duane	Chi.	2	14	3	3	6	2	....	....	....	....	....	1974-75	1976-77
Wylie, William	NYR	1	1	0	0	0	0	....	....	....	....	....	1950-51	1950-51
Wyrozub, Randy	Buf.	4	100	8	10	18	10	....	....	....	....	....	1970-71	1973-74

YZ

Name	NHL Teams	NHL Seasons	GP	G	A	TP	PIM	GP	G	A	TP	PIM	First NHL Season	Last NHL Season
Yackel, Ken	Bos.	1	6	0	0	0	2	2	0	0	0	0	1958-59	1958-59
Yaremchuk, Gary	Tor.	4	34	1	4	5	28	....	....	....	....	....	1981-82	1984-85
Yates, Ross	Hfd.	1	7	1	1	2	4	....	....	....	....	....	1983-84	1983-84
Young, Brian	Chi.	1	8	0	2	2	6	....	....	....	....	....	1980-81	1980-81
Young, Douglas	Mtl., Det.	10	391	35	45	80	303	28	1	5	6	16	1931-32	1940-41
Young, Howie	Det., Chi., Van.	8	336	12	62	74	851	19	2	4	6	46	1960-61	1970-71
Young, Tim	Min., Wpg., Phi.	10	620	195	341	536	438	36	7	24	31	27	1975-76	1984-85

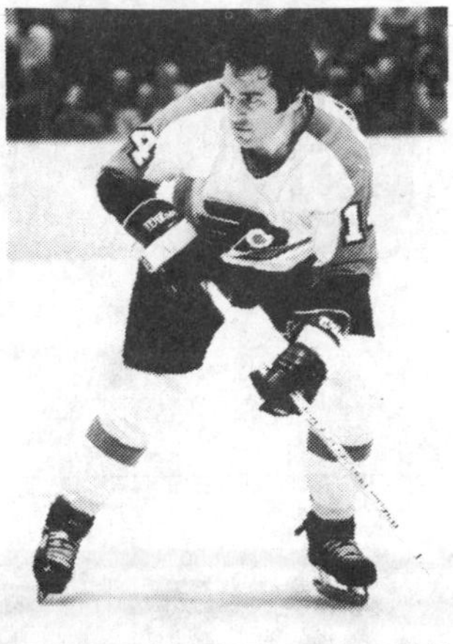

Joe Watson

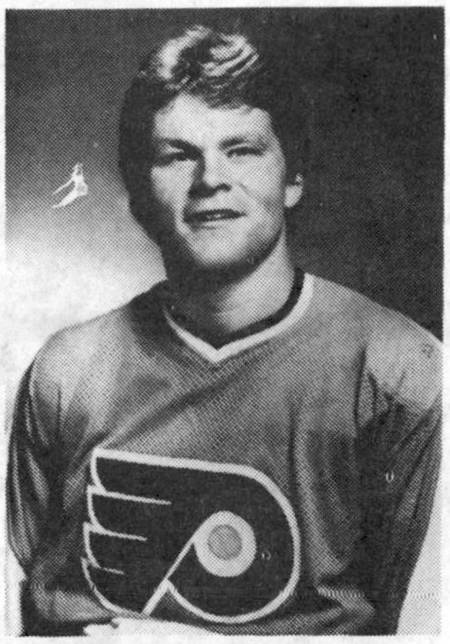

Behn Wilson

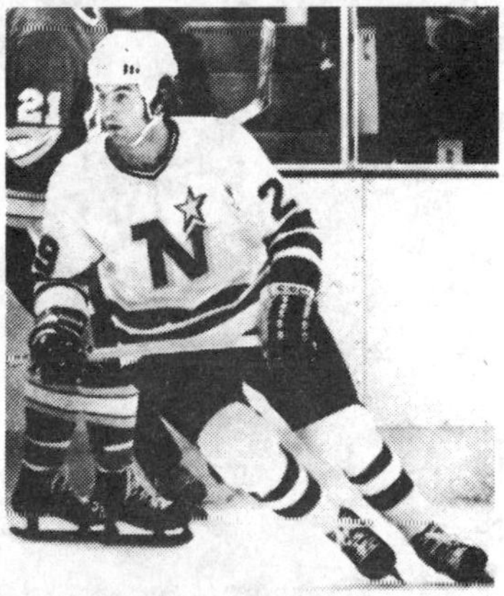

Tom Younghans

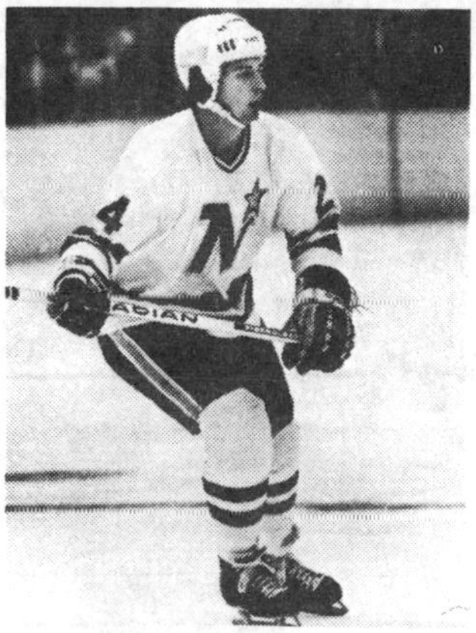

Ron Zanussi

Name	NHL Teams	NHL Seasons	Regular Schedule					Playoffs					First NHL Season	Last NHL Season
			GP	G	A	TP	PIM	GP	G	A	TP	PIM		
Young, Warren	Min., Pit., Det.	7	236	72	77	149	472	....	....	....	....	....	1981-82	1987-88
Younghans, Tom	Min., NYR	6	429	44	41	85	373	24	2	1	3	21	1976-77	1981-82
Zabroski, Marty	Chi.	1	1	0	0	0	0	....	....	....	....	....	1944-45	1944-45
Zaharko, Miles	Atl., Chi.	4	129	5	32	37	84	3	0	0	0	0	1977-78	1981-82
Zaine, Rod	Pit., Buf.	2	61	10	6	16	25	....	....	....	....	....	1970-71	1971-72
Zanussi, Joe	NYR, Bos., St.L.	3	87	1	13	14	46	4	0	1	1	2	1974-75	1976-77
Zanussi, Ron	Min., Tor.	5	299	52	83	135	373	17	0	4	4	17	1977-78	1981-82
Zeidel, Larry	Det., Chi., Phi.	5	158	3	16	19	198	12	0	1	1	12	1951-52	1968-69
Zeniuk, Ed	Det.	1	2	0	0	0	0	....	....	....	....	....	1954-55	1954-55
Zetterstrom, Lars	Van.	1	14	0	1	1	2	....	....	....	....	....	1978-79	1978-79
Zuke, Mike	St.L., Hfd.	8	455	86	196	282	220	26	6	6	12	12	1978-79	1985-86
Zunich, Ruby	Det.	1	2	0	0	0	2	....	....	....	....	....	1943-44	1943-44

Curtis Joseph of the St. Louis Blues.

1990-91 Goaltender Register

Note: The 1990-91 Goaltender Register lists every goaltender who appeared in an NHL game in the 1989-90 season, every goaltender drafted in the first two rounds of the 1989 and 1990 Entry Drafts and other goaltenders on NHL Reserve Lists.

Trades and roster changes are current as of August 15, 1990.

To calculate a goaltender's goals-against-per-game average **(Avg)**, divide goals against **(GA)** by minutes played **(Mins)** and multiply this result by **60**.

Abbreviations: A list of league names can be found at the beginning of the Player Register. **Avg** – goals against per game average; **GA** – goals against; **GP** – games played; **L** – losses; **Lea** – league; **SO** – shutouts; **T** – ties; **W** – wins.

Player Register begins on page 207.

ANDERSON, DEAN

Goaltender. Catches left. 5'10", 175 lbs. Born, Oshawa, Ont., July 14, 1966.
(Toronto's 1st choice, 11th overall, in 1988 Supplemental Draft).

			Regular Season								Playoffs						
Season	Club	Lea	GP	W	L	T	Mins	GA	SO	Avg	GP	W	L	Mins	GA	SO	Avg
1984-85	U. Wisconsin	WCHA	36	21	13	0	2072	148	0	4.29	....	....	....	....	....	....	....
1985-86	U. Wisconsin	WCHA	20	13	6	0	1128	80	0	4.25	....	....	....	....	....	....	....
1986-87	U. Wisconsin	WCHA	9	4	2	0	409	27	0	3.96	....	....	....	....	....	....	....
1987-88a	U. Wisconsin	WCHA	45	30	13	2	2718	148	2	3.27	....	....	....	....	....	....	....
1988-89	Newmarket	AHL	2	0	1	0	38	4	0	6.32	1	0	1	30	1	0	2.00
	Flint	IHL	16	1	12	0	770	82	1	6.39	....	....	....	....	....	....	....
1989-90	Knoxville	ECHL	17	6	8	3	997	73	0	4.39	....	....	....	....	....	....	....

a WCHA Second All-Star Team (1988)

BARRASSO, TOM (buh-RAH-soh)

Goaltender. Catches right. 6'3", 207 lbs. Born, Boston, MA, March 31, 1965.
(Buffalo's 1st choice, 5th overall, in 1983 Entry Draft).

			Regular Season								Playoffs						
Season	Club	Lea	GP	W	L	T	Mins	GA	SO	Avg	GP	W	L	Mins	GA	SO	Avg
1982-83	Acton-Boxboro	Mass.	23	....	....	....	1035	17	10	0.73	....	....	....	....	....	....	....
1983-84abcd	**Buffalo**	**NHL**	**42**	**26**	**12**	**3**	**2475**	**117**	**2**	**2.84**	**3**	**0**	**2**	**139**	**8**	**0**	**3.45**
1984-85ef	**Buffalo**	**NHL**	**54**	**25**	**18**	**10**	**3248**	**144**	***5**	***2.66**	**5**	**2**	**3**	**300**	**22**	**0**	**4.40**
	Rochester	AHL	5	3	1	1	267	6	1	1.35	....	....	....	....	....	....	....
1985-86	**Buffalo**	**NHL**	**60**	**29**	**24**	**5**	**3561**	**214**	**2**	**3.61**	....	....	....	....	....	....	....
1986-87	**Buffalo**	**NHL**	**46**	**17**	**23**	**2**	**2501**	**152**	**2**	**3.65**	....	....	....	....	....	....	....
1987-88	**Buffalo**	**NHL**	**54**	**25**	**18**	**8**	**3133**	**173**	**2**	**3.31**	**4**	**1**	**3**	**224**	**16**	**0**	**4.29**
1988-89	**Buffalo**	**NHL**	**10**	**2**	**7**	**0**	**545**	**45**	**0**	**4.95**	....	....	....	....	....	....	....
	Pittsburgh	**NHL**	**44**	**18**	**15**	**7**	**2406**	**162**	**0**	**4.04**	**11**	**7**	**4**	**631**	**40**	**0**	**3.80**
1989-90	**Pittsburgh**	**NHL**	**24**	**7**	**12**	**3**	**1294**	**101**	**0**	**4.68**	....	....	....	....	....	....	....
	NHL Totals		**334**	**149**	**129**	**38**	**19163**	**1108**	**13**	**3.47**	**23**	**10**	**12**	**1294**	**86**	**0**	**3.99**

a NHL First All-Star Team (1984)
b Won Vezina Trophy (1984)
c Won Calder Memorial Trophy (1984)
d NHL All-Rookie Team (1984)
e NHL Second All-Star Team (1985)
f Shared William Jennings Trophy with Bob Sauve (1985)

Played in NHL All-Star Game (1985)

Traded to **Pittsburgh** by **Buffalo** with Buffalo's third-round choice (Joe Dziedzic) in 1990 Entry Draft for Doug Bodger and Darrin Shannon, November 12, 1988.

BEAUPRE, DONALD WILLIAM (DON) (boh-PRAY)

Goaltender. Catches left. 5'9", 165 lbs. Born, Waterloo, Ont., September 19, 1961.
(Minnesota's 2nd choice, 37th overall, in 1980 Entry Draft).

			Regular Season								Playoffs						
Season	Club	Lea	GP	W	L	T	Mins	GA	SO	Avg	GP	W	L	Mins	GA	SO	Avg
1978-79	Sudbury	OHA	54	....	....	....	3248	200	2	4.70	10	....	....	600	44	0	4.20
1979-80a	Sudbury	OHA	59	28	29	2	3447	248	0	4.32	9	5	4	552	38	0	4.13
1980-81	**Minnesota**	**NHL**	**44**	**18**	**14**	**11**	**2585**	**138**	**0**	**3.20**	**6**	**4**	**2**	**360**	**26**	**0**	**4.33**
1981-82	Nashville	CHL	5	2	3	0	299	25	0	5.02	....	....	....	....	....	....	....
	Minnesota	**NHL**	**29**	**11**	**8**	**9**	**1634**	**101**	**0**	**3.71**	**2**	**0**	**1**	**60**	**4**	**0**	**4.00**
1982-83	Birmingham	CHL	10	8	2	0	599	31	0	3.11	....	....	....	....	....	....	....
	Minnesota	**NHL**	**36**	**19**	**10**	**5**	**2011**	**120**	**0**	**3.58**	**4**	**2**	**2**	**245**	**20**	**0**	**4.90**
1983-84	Salt Lake	CHL	7	2	5	0	419	30	0	4.30	....	....	....	....	....	....	....
	Minnesota	**NHL**	**33**	**16**	**13**	**2**	**1791**	**123**	**0**	**4.12**	**13**	**6**	**7**	**782**	**40**	**1**	**3.07**
1984-85	**Minnesota**	**NHL**	**31**	**10**	**17**	**3**	**1770**	**109**	**1**	**3.69**	**4**	**1**	**1**	**184**	**12**	**0**	**3.91**
1985-86	**Minnesota**	**NHL**	**52**	**25**	**20**	**6**	**3073**	**182**	**1**	**3.55**	**5**	**2**	**3**	**300**	**17**	**0**	**3.40**
1986-87	**Minnesota**	**NHL**	**47**	**17**	**20**	**6**	**2622**	**174**	**1**	**3.98**	....	....	....	....	....	....	....
1987-88	**Minnesota**	**NHL**	**43**	**10**	**22**	**3**	**2288**	**161**	**0**	**4.22**	....	....	....	....	....	....	....
1988-89	**Minnesota**	**NHL**	**1**	**0**	**1**	**0**	**59**	**3**	**0**	**3.05**	....	....	....	....	....	....	....
	Kalamazoo	IHL	3	1	2	0	179	9	1	3.02	....	....	....	....	....	....	....
	Washington	**NHL**	**11**	**5**	**4**	**0**	**578**	**28**	**1**	**2.91**	....	....	....	....	....	....	....
	Baltimore	AHL	30	14	12	2	1715	102	0	3.57	....	....	....	....	....	....	....
1989-90	**Washington**	**NHL**	**48**	**23**	**18**	**5**	**2793**	**150**	**2**	**3.22**	**8**	**4**	**3**	**401**	**18**	**0**	**2.69**
	NHL Totals		**375**	**154**	**147**	**50**	**21204**	**1289**	**6**	**3.65**	**42**	**19**	**18**	**2332**	**137**	**1**	**3.52**

a OHA First All-Star Team (1980)

Played in NHL All-Star Game (1981)

Traded to **Washington** by **Minnesota** for rights to Claudio Scremin, November 1, 1988.

BEAUREGARD, STEPHANE

Goaltender. Catches right. 5'11", 185 lbs. Born, Cowansville, Que., January 10, 1968.
(Winnipeg's 3rd choice, 52nd overall, in 1988 Entry Draft).

			Regular Season								Playoffs						
Season	Club	Lea	GP	W	L	T	Mins	GA	SO	Avg	GP	W	L	Mins	GA	SO	Avg
1986-87	St. Jean	QMJHL	13	6	7	0	785	58	0	4.43	5	1	3	260	26	0	6.00
1987-88a	St. Jean	QMJHL	66	38	20	3	3766	229	2	3.65	7	3	4	423	34	0	4.82
1988-89	Moncton	AHL	15	4	8	2	824	62	0	4.51	....	....	....	....	....	....	....
	Fort Wayne	IHL	16	9	5	0	830	43	0	3.10	9	4	4	484	21	*1	*2.60
1989-90	**Winnipeg**	**NHL**	**19**	**7**	**8**	**3**	**1079**	**59**	**0**	**3.28**	**4**	**1**	**3**	**238**	**12**	**0**	**3.03**
	Fort Wayne	IHL	33	20	8	3	1949	115	0	3.54	....	....	....	....	....	....	....
	NHL Totals		**19**	**7**	**8**	**3**	**1079**	**59**	**0**	**3.28**	**4**	**1**	**3**	**238**	**12**	**0**	**3.03**

a QMJHL First All-Star Team (1988)

BELFOUR, ED

Goaltender. Catches left. 6', 175 lbs. Born, Carmen, Man., April 21, 1965.

			Regular Season								Playoffs						
Season	Club	Lea	GP	W	L	T	Mins	GA	SO	Avg	GP	W	L	Mins	GA	SO	Avg
1986-87a	North Dakota	WCHA	34	29	4	0	2049	81	3	2.43	....	....	....	....	....	....	....
1987-88bc	Saginaw	IHL	61	32	25	0	*3446	183	3	3.19	9	4	5	561	33	0	3.53
1988-89	**Chicago**	**NHL**	**23**	**4**	**12**	**3**	**1148**	**74**	**0**	**3.87**	....	....	....	....	....	....	....
	Saginaw	IHL	29	12	10	0	1760	92	0	3.10	5	2	3	298	14	0	2.82
1989-90	Cdn. National	....	33	13	12	6	1808	93	0	3.08	....	....	....	....	....	....	....
	Chicago	**NHL**	....	....	....	....	....	....	....	....	**9**	**4**	**2**	**409**	**17**	**0**	**2.49**
	NHL Totals		**23**	**4**	**12**	**3**	**1148**	**74**	**0**	**3.87**	**9**	**4**	**2**	**409**	**17**	**0**	**2.49**

a WCHA First All-Star Team (1987)
b IHL First All-Star Team (1988)
c Shared Garry F. Longman Memorial Trophy (Top Rookie - IHL) (1988)

Signed as a free agent by **Chicago**, September 25, 1987.

BERGERON, JEAN-CLAUDE

Goaltender. Catches left. 6'2", 192 lbs. Born, Hauterive, Que., October 14, 1968.
(Montreal's 6th choice, 104th overall, in 1988 Entry Draft).

			Regular Season								Playoffs						
Season	Club	Lea	GP	W	L	T	Mins	GA	SO	Avg	GP	W	L	Mins	GA	SO	Avg
1987-88	Verdun	QMJHL	49	13	31	3	2715	265	0	5.86	....	....	....	....	....	....	....
1988-89	Verdun	QMJHL	44	8	34	1	2417	199	0	4.94	....	....	....	....	....	....	....
	Sherbrooke	AHL	5	4	1	0	302	18	0	3.58	....	....	....	....	....	....	....
1989-90abc	Sherbrooke	AHL	40	21	8	7	2254	103	2	*2.74	9	6	2	497	28	0	3.38

a AHL First All-Star Team (1990)
b Shared Harry "Hap" Holmes Trophy (fewest goals-against-AHL) with Andre Racicot (1990)
c Won Baz Bastien Award (Top Goaltender-AHL) (1990)

BERNHARDT, TIMOTHY JOHN (TIM) (burn-HEART)

Goaltender. Catches left. 5'9", 160 lbs. Born, Sarnia, Ont., January 17, 1958.
(Atlanta's 2nd choice, 47th overall, in 1978 Amateur Draft).

			Regular Season								Playoffs						
Season	Club	Lea	GP	W	L	T	Mins	GA	SO	Avg	GP	W	L	Mins	GA	SO	Avg
1976-77a	Cornwall	QJHL	44	....	....	....	2497	151	0	3.63	12	....	....	720	47	0	3.92
1977-78a	Cornwall	QJHL	54	....	....	....	3165	179	2	3.39	9	....	....	540	27	2	3.00
1978-79	Tulsa	CHL	46	....	....	....	2705	191	0	4.24	....	....	....	....	....	....	....
1979-80	Birmingham	CHL	34	15	16	1	1933	122	1	3.79	3	....	....	160	17	0	6.38
1980-81	Birmingham	CHL	29	11	13	2	1598	106	1	3.98	....	....	....	....	....	....	....
1981-82	Oklahoma City	CHL	10	1	8	0	526	45	0	5.13	....	....	....	....	....	....	....
	Rochester	AHL	29	15	10	.2	1586	95	0	3.59	9	4	3	527	29	0	3.30
1982-83	**Calgary**	**NHL**	**6**	**0**	**5**	**0**	**280**	**21**	**0**	**4.50**	....	....	....	....	....	....	....
	Colorado	CHL	34	19	11	1	1896	122	0	3.86	5	2	3	304	19	0	3.75
1983-84	St. Catharines	AHL	42	25	13	4	2461	154	0	3.75	5	2	3	288	17	0	3.54
1984-85	**Toronto**	**NHL**	**37**	**13**	**19**	**4**	**2182**	**136**	**0**	**3.74**	....	....	....	....	....	....	....
	St. Catharines	AHL	14	5	7	2	801	55	0	412	....	....	....	....	....	....	....
1985-86	**Toronto**	**NHL**	**23**	**4**	**12**	**3**	**1266**	**107**	**0**	**5.07**	....	....	....	....	....	....	....
	St.Catharines	AHL	14	6	4	2	776	38	1	2.94	3	0	3	140	12	0	5.14
1986-87	**Toronto**	**NHL**	**1**	**0**	**0**	**0**	**20**	**3**	**0**	**9.00**	....	....	....	....	....	....	....
	Newmarket	AHL	31	6	17	0	1705	117	1	4.12	....	....	....	....	....	....	....
1987-88	Newmarket	AHL	49	22	19	4	2704	166	0	3.68	....	....	....	....	....	....	....
1988-89	Newmarket	AHL	37	17	16	2	2004	145	1	4.34	....	....	....	....	....	....	....
1989-90	Newmarket	AHL	14	4	7	1	755	51	0	4.71	....	....	....	....	....	....	....
	NHL Totals		**67**	**17**	**36**	**2**	**3748**	**267**	**0**	**4.27**	....	....	....	....	....	....	....

a QMJHL First All-Star Team (1977, 1978)

Signed as a free agent by **Toronto,** December 5, 1984.

BERTHIAUME, DANIEL (bair-TYOHM)

Goaltender. Catches left. 5'9", 150 lbs. Born, Longueuil, Que., January 26, 1966.
(Winnipeg's 3rd choice, 60th overall, in 1985 Entry Draft).

			Regular Season								Playoffs						
Season	Club	Lea	GP	W	L	T	Mins	GA	SO	Avg	GP	W	L	Mins	GA	SO	Avg
1984-85	Chicoutimi	QMJHL	59	40	11	2	2177	149	0	4.11	14	8	6	770	51	0	3.97
1985-86	Chicoutimi	QMJHL	66	34	29	3	3718	286	1	4.62	9	4	5	580	36	0	3.72
	Winnipeg	**NHL**	....	....	....	....	....	....	....	....	**1**	**0**	**1**	**68**	**4**	**0**	**3.53**
1986-87	**Winnipeg**	**NHL**	**31**	**18**	**7**	**3**	**1758**	**93**	**1**	**3.17**	**8**	**4**	**4**	**439**	**21**	**0**	**2.07**
	Sherbrooke	AHL	7	4	3	0	420	23	0	3.29	....	....	....	....	....	....	....
1987-88	**Winnipeg**	**NHL**	**56**	**22**	**19**	**7**	**3010**	**176**	**2**	**3.51**	**5**	**1**	**4**	**300**	**25**	**0**	**5.00**
1988-89	**Winnipeg**	**NHL**	**9**	**0**	**8**	**0**	**443**	**44**	**0**	**5.96**	....	....	....	....	....	....	....
	Moncton	AHL	21	6	9	2	1083	76	0	4.21	3	1	2	180	11	0	3.67
1989-90	**Winnipeg**	**NHL**	**24**	**10**	**11**	**3**	**1387**	**86**	**1**	**3.72**	....	....	....	....	....	....	....
	Minnesota	**NHL**	**5**	**1**	**3**	**0**	**240**	**14**	**0**	**3.50**	....	....	....	....	....	....	....
	NHL Totals		**125**	**51**	**48**	**13**	**6838**	**413**	**4**	**3.62**	**14**	**5**	**9**	**807**	**50**	**0**	**3.72**

Traded to **Minnesota** by **Winnipeg** for future considerations, January 22, 1990.

BESTER, ALLAN J.

Goaltender. Catches left. 5'7", 150 lbs. Born, Hamilton, Ont., March 26, 1964.
(Toronto's 3rd choice, 48th overall, in 1983 Entry Draft).

			Regular Season								Playoffs						
Season	Club	Lea	GP	W	L	T	Mins	GA	SO	Avg	GP	W	L	Mins	GA	SO	Avg
1981-82	Brantford	OHL	19	4	11	0	970	68	0	4.21	....	....	....	....	....	....	....
1982-83a	Brantford	OHL	56	29	21	3	3210	188	0	3.51	8	3	3	480	20	*1	*2.50
1983-84	Toronto	NHL	32	11	16	4	1848	134	0	4.35	....	....	....	....	....	....	....
	Brantford	OHL	23	12	9	1	1271	71	1	3.35	1	0	1	60	5	0	5.00
1984-85	Toronto	NHL	15	3	9	1	767	54	1	4.22	....	....	....	....	....	....	....
	St. Catharines	AHL	30	9	18	1	1669	133	0	4.78	....	....	....	....	....	....	....
1985-86	Toronto	NHL	1	0	0	0	20	2	0	6.00	....	....	....	....	....	....	....
	St.Catharines	AHL	50	23	23	3	2855	173	1	3.64	11	7	3	637	27	0	2.54
1986-87	Toronto	NHL	36	10	14	3	1808	110	2	3.65	1	0	0	39	1	0	1.54
	Newmarket	AHL	3	1	0	0	190	6	0	1.89	....	....	....	....	....	....	....
1987-88	Toronto	NHL	30	8	12	5	1607	102	2	3.81	5	2	3	253	21	0	4.98
1988-89	Toronto	NHL	43	17	20	3	2460	156	2	3.80	....	....	....	....	....	....	....
1989-90	Toronto	NHL	42	20	16	0	2506	165	0	4.49	4	0	3	196	14	0	4.29
	Newmarket	AHL	5	2	1	1	264	18	0	4.09	....	....	....	....	....	....	....
	NHL Totals		199	69	85	16	11016	723	7	3.94	10	2	6	488	36	0	4.42

a OHL First All-Star Team (1983)

BILLINGTON, CRAIG

Goaltender. Catches left. 5'10", 170 lbs. Born, London, Ont., September 11, 1966.
(New Jersey's 2nd choice, 23rd overall, in 1984 Entry Draft).

			Regular Season								Playoffs						
Season	Club	Lea	GP	W	L	T	Mins	GA	SO	Avg	GP	W	L	Mins	GA	SO	Avg
1983-84	Belleville	OHL	44	20	19	0	2335	162	1	4.16	1	0	0	30	3	0	6.00
1984-85a	Belleville	OHL	47	26	19	0	2544	180	1	4.25	14	7	5	761	47	1	3.71
1985-86	New Jersey	NHL	18	4	9	1	901	77	0	5.13	....	....	....	....	....	....	....
	Belleville	OHL	3	2	1	0	180	11	0	3.67	20	9	6	1133	68	0	3.60
1986-87	New Jersey	NHL	22	4	13	2	1114	89	0	4.79	....	....	....	....	....	....	....
	Maine	AHL	20	9	8	2	1151	70	0	3.65	....	....	....	....	....	....	....
1987-88	Utica	AHL	*59	22	27	8	*3404	208	1	3.67	....	....	....	....	....	....	....
1988-89	New Jersey	NHL	3	1	1	0	140	11	0	4.71	....	....	....	....	....	....	....
	Utica	AHL	41	17	18	6	2432	150	2	3.70	4	1	3	220	18	0	4.91
1989-90	Utica	AHL	38	20	13	1	2087	138	0	3.97	....	....	....	....	....	....	....
	NHL Totals		43	9	23	3	2155	177	0	4.93	....	....	....	....	....	....	....

a OHL First All-Star Team (1985)

BLUE, JOHN

Goaltender. Catches left. 5'10", 185 lbs. Born, Huntington Beach, CA, February 19, 1966.
(Winnipeg's 9th choice, 197th overall, in 1986 Entry Draft).

			Regular Season								Playoffs						
Season	Club	Lea	GP	W	L	T	Mins	GA	SO	Avg	GP	W	L	Mins	GA	SO	Avg
1984-85	U. Minnesota	WCHA	34	23	10	0	1964	111	2	3.39	...	...	...	...	...	...	...
1985-86a	U. Minnesota	WCHA	29	20	6	0	1588	80	2	3.02	...	...	...	...	...	...	...
1986-87	U. Minnesota	WCHA	33	21	9	1	1889	99	3	3.14	...	...	...	...	...	...	...
1987-88	Kalamazoo	IHL	15	3	8	4	847	65		4.60	1	0	1	40	6		9.00
	U.S. National	....	13	3	4	1	588	33	0	3.37	....	....	....	....	....	....	....
1988-89	Kalamazoo	IHL	17	8	6	0	970	69	0	4.27	....	....	....	....	....	....	....
1989-90	Phoenix	IHL	19	5	10	3	986	92	0	5.65	....	....	....	....	....	....	....
	Knoxville	ECHL	19	6	10	1	1000	85	0	5.15	....	....	....	....	....	....	....

a WCHA First All-Star Team (1986)

Traded to **Minnesota** by **Winnipeg** for Winnipeg's seventh round choice in 1988 Entry Draft (Markus Akerblom), March 7, 1988.

BRADLEY, JOHN

Goaltender. Catches left. 6', 165 lbs. Born, Pawtucket, RI, February 6, 1968.
(Buffalo's 4th choice, 84th overall, in 1987 Entry Draft).

			Regular Season								Playoffs						
Season	Club	Lea	GP	W	L	T	Mins	GA	SO	Avg	GP	W	L	Mins	GA	SO	Avg
1987-88	Boston U.	H.E.	9	4	4	0	528	40	0	4.53	....	....	....	....	....	....	....
1988-89	Boston U.	H.E.	11	5	4	1	584	53	0	5.45	....	....	....	....	....	....	....
1989-90	Boston U.	H.E.	7	2	3	1	377	20	1	3.18	....	....	....	....	....	....	....

BRODEUR, MARTIN

Goaltender. Catches left. 6', 190 lbs. Born, Montreal, Que., May 6, 1972.
(New Jersey's 1st choice, 20th overall, in 1990 Entry Draft).

			Regular Season								Playoffs						
Season	Club	Lea	GP	W	L	T	Mins	GA	SO	Avg	GP	W	L	Mins	GA	SO	Avg
1989-90a	St. Hyacinthe	QMJHL	42	23	13	2	2333	166	0	4.01	12	5	7	678	46	0	4.07

a QMJHL Third All-Star Team (1990)

BROWER, SCOTT

Goaltender. Catches left. 6', 185 lbs. Born, Viking, Alta., September 26, 1964.
(NY Rangers' 12th choice, 243rd overall, in 1984 Entry Draft).

			Regular Season								Playoffs						
Season	Club	Lea	GP	W	L	T	Mins	GA	SO	Avg	GP	W	L	Mins	GA	SO	Avg
1984-85	North Dakota	WCHA	31	15	12	2	1808	99	0	3.28	....	....	....	....	....	....	....
1985-86	North Dakota	WCHA	20	11	6	0	1096	67	0	3.47	....	....	....	....	....	....	....
1986-87	North Dakota	WCHA	15	11	4	0	803	44	0	3.29	....	....	....	....	....	....	....
1987-88	North Dakota	WCHA	23	10	12	0	1450	88	1	3.64	....	....	....	....	....	....	....
1988-89	Flint	IHL	5	1	2	0	235	22	0	5.62	....	....	....	....	....	....	....
	Denver	IHL	20	3	5	0	938	82	0	5.25	1	0	0	31	1	0	1.94
1989-90	Flint	IHL	21	7	7	3	1078	80	0	4.45	....	....	....	....	....	....	....
	Phoenix	IHL	1	0	1	0	20	1	0	3.00	....	....	....	....	....	....	....
	Erie	ECHL	5	2	2	0	243	20	0	4.93	....	....	....	....	....	....	....

BRUNETTA, MARIO

Goaltender. Catches right. 6'3", 180 lbs. Born, Quebec City, Que., January 25, 1967.
(Quebec's 9th choice, 162nd overall, in 1985 Entry Draft).

			Regular Season								Playoffs						
Season	Club	Lea	GP	W	L	T	Mins	GA	SO	Avg	GP	W	L	Mins	GA	SO	Avg
1984-85	Quebec	QMJHL	45	20	21	1	2255	192	0	5.11	2	0	2	120	13	0	6.50
1985-86	Laval	QMJHL	63	30	25	1	3383	279	0	4.95	14	9	5	834	60	0	4.32
1986-87	Laval	QMJHL	59	27	25	4	3469	261	1	4.51	14	8	6	820	63	0	4.61
1987-88	Quebec	NHL	29	10	12	1	1550	96	0	3.72	....	....	....	....	....	....	....
	Fredericton	AHL	5	4	1	0	300	24	0	4.80	....	....	....	....	....	....	....
1988-89	Quebec	NHL	5	1	3	0	226	19	0	5.04	....	....	....	....	....	....	....
	Halifax	AHL	36	14	14	5	1898	124	0	3.92	3	0	2	142	12	0	5.07
1989-90	Quebec	NHL	6	1	2	0	191	13	0	4.08	....	....	....	....	....	....	....
	Halifax	AHL	24	8	14	2	1444	99	0	4.11	....	....	....	....	....	....	....
	NHL Totals		40	12	16	1	1967	128	0	3.90	....	....	....	....	....	....	....

BURCHILL, RICH

Goaltender. Catches right. 6', 180 lbs. Born, Boston, MA, January 3, 1967.
(St. Louis' 5th choice, 121st overall, in 1985 Entry Draft).

			Regular Season								Playoffs						
Season	Club	Lea	GP	W	L	T	Mins	GA	SO	Avg	GP	W	L	Mins	GA	SO	Avg
1987-88	Northeastern	H.E.	6	3	2	0	323	22	0	4.08	....	....	....	....	....	....	....
1988-89	Northeastern	H.E.	30	16	12	2	1815	118	0	3.90	....	....	....	....	....	....	....
1989-90	Johnstown	ECHL	32	16	13	1	1704	130	0	4.57	....	....	....	....	....	....	....

BURKE, SEAN

Goaltender. Catches left. 6'4", 210 lbs. Born, Windsor, Ont., January 29, 1967.
(New Jersey's 2nd choice, 24th overall, in 1985 Entry Draft).

			Regular Season								Playoffs						
Season	Club	Lea	GP	W	L	T	Mins	GA	SO	Avg	GP	W	L	Mins	GA	SO	Avg
1984-85	Toronto	OHL	49	25	21	3	2987	211	0	4.24	5	1	3	266	25	0	5.64
1985-86	Toronto	OHL	47	16	27	3	2840	233	0	4.92	4	0	4	238	24	0	6.05
1986-87	Cdn. Olympic	....	42	27	13	2	2550	130	0	3.05	....	....	....	....	....	....	....
1987-88	New Jersey	NHL	13	10	1	0	689	35	1	3.05	17	9	8	1001	57	*1	3.42
	Cdn. National	....	37	19	9	2	1962	92	1	2.81	....	....	....	....	....	....	....
	Cdn. Olympic	....	4	1	2	1	238	12	0	3.02	....	....	....	....	....	....	....
1988-89	New Jersey	NHL	62	22	31	9	3590	230	3	3.84	....	....	....	....	....	....	....
1989-90	New Jersey	NHL	52	22	22	6	2914	175	0	3.60	2	0	2	125	8	0	3.84
	NHL Totals		127	54	54	15	7193	440	4	3.67	19	9	10	1126	65	0	3.46

Played in NHL All-Star Game (1989)

CAPRICE, FRANK (kuh-PREEZ)

Goaltender. Catches left. 5'9", 150 lbs. Born, Hamilton, Ont., May 2, 1962.
(Vancouver's 8th choice, 178th overall, in 1981 Entry Draft).

			Regular Season								Playoffs						
Season	Club	Lea	GP	W	L	T	Mins	GA	SO	Avg	GP	W	L	Mins	GA	SO	Avg
1979-80	London	OHA	18	3	7	3	919	74	1	4.84	3	1	1	94	10	0	6.38
1980-81	London	OHA	42	11	26	0	2171	190	0	5.25	....	....	....	....	....	....	....
1981-82a	London	OHL	45	24	17	2	2614	196	0	4.50	4	1	3	240	18	0	4.50
	Dallas	CHL	3	0	3	0	178	19	0	6.40	....	....	....	....	....	....	....
1982-83	Vancouver	NHL	1	0	0	0	20	3	0	9.09	....	....	....	....	....	....	....
	Fredericton	AHL	14	5	8	1	819	50	0	3.67	....	....	....	....	....	....	....
1983-84	Vancouver	NHL	19	8	2	2	1098	62	1	3.39	....	....	....	....	....	....	....
	Fredericton	AHL	18	11	5	2	1089	49	2	2.70	....	....	....	....	....	....	....
1984-85	Vancouver	NHL	28	8	14	3	1523	122	0	4.81	....	....	....	....	....	....	....
1985-86	Vancouver	NHL	7	0	3	2	308	28	0	5.46	....	....	....	....	....	....	....
	Fredericton	AHL	26	12	11	2	1526	109	0	4.29	6	2	4	333	22	0	3.96
1986-87	Vancouver	NHL	25	8	11	2	1390	89	0	3.84	....	....	....	....	....	....	....
	Fredericton	AHL	12	5	5	0	686	47	0	4.11	....	....	....	....	....	....	....
1987-88	Vancouver	NHL	22	7	10	2	1250	87	0	4.18	....	....	....	....	....	....	....
1988-89	Milwaukee	IHL	39	24	12	0	2204	143	2	3.89	2	0	1	91	5	0	3.30
1989-90	Maine	AHL	10	2	6	1	550	46	0	5.02	....	....	....	....	....	....	....
	Milwaukee	IHL	20	8	6	3	1098	78	0	4.26	3	0	2	142	10	0	4.23
	NHL Totals		102	31	40	11	5589	391	1	4.20	....	....	....	....	....	....	....

a OHL Third All-Star Team (1982).

Traded to **Boston** by **Vancouver** for Boston's twelfth-round choice (Jan Bergman) in 1989 Entry Draft, June 17, 1989.

CASEY, JON

Goaltender. Catches right. 5'9", 155 lbs. Born, Grand Rapids, MN, August 29, 1962.

			Regular Season								Playoffs						
Season	Club	Lea	GP	W	L	T	Mins	GA	SO	Avg	GP	W	L	Mins	GA	SO	Avg
1980-81	North Dakota	WCHA	5	3	1	0	300	19	0	3.80	....	....	....	....	....	....	....
1981-82	North Dakota	WCHA	18	15	3	0	1038	48	1	2.77	....	....	....	....	....	....	....
1982-83	North Dakota	WCHA	17	9	6	2	1020	42	0	2.51	....	....	....	....	....	....	....
1983-84	North Dakota	WCHA	37	25	10	2	2180	115	2	3.13	....	....	....	....	....	....	....
	Minnesota	NHL	2	1	0	0	84	6	0	4.29	....	....	....	....	....	....	....
1984-85ab	Baltimore	AHL	46	30	11	4	2646	116	*4	*2.63	*13	8	3	689	38	0	3.31
1985-86	Minnesota	NHL	26	11	11	1	1402	91	0	3.89	....	....	....	....	....	....	....
	Springfield	AHL	9	4	3	1	464	30	0	3.88	....	....	....	....	....	....	....
1986-87	Springfield	AHL	13	1	8	0	770	56	0	4.36	....	....	....	....	....	....	....
	Indianapolis	IHL	31	14	15	0	1794	133	0	4.45	....	....	....	....	....	....	....
1987-88	Minnesota	NHL	14	1	7	4	663	41	0	3.71	....	....	....	....	....	....	....
	Kalamazoo	IHL	42	24	13	5	2541	154		3.64	7	3	3	382	26		4.08
1988-89	Minnesota	NHL	55	18	17	12	2961	151	1	3.06	4	1	3	211	16	0	4.55
1989-90	Minnesota	NHL	61	31	22	4	3407	183	3	3.22	7	3	4	415	21	1	3.04
	NHL Totals		158	62	57	21	8517	472	4	3.33	11	4	7	626	37	1	3.55

a Won Baz Bastien Trophy (AHL Most Valuable Goaltender) (1985)
b AHL First All-Star Team (1985)

Signed as a free agent by **Minnesota**, April 1, 1984.

CASHMAN, SCOTT

Goaltender. Catches left. 6'2", 175 lbs. Born, Ottawa, Ont., September 20, 1969.
(Minnesota's 8th choice, 112th overall, in 1989 Entry Draft).

			Regular Season								Playoffs						
Season	Club	Lea	GP	W	L	T	Mins	GA	SO	Avg	GP	W	L	Mins	GA	SO	Avg
1988-89	Kanata	COJHL	43	....	....	....	2395	138	0	3.46	....	....	....	....	....	....	....
1989-90ab	Boston U.	H.E.	*39	*23	14	1	*2277	122	*2	3.27	....	....	....	....	....	....	....

a Hockey East Rookie of the Year (1990)
b Hockey East Second All-Star Team (1990)

CHABOT, FREDERIC

Goaltender. Catches right. 5'11", 177 lbs. Born, Hebertville, Que., February 12, 1968.
(New Jersey's 10th choice, 192nd overall, in 1986 Entry Draft).

			Regular Season								Playoffs						
Season	Club	Lea	GP	W	L	T	Mins	GA	SO	Avg	GP	W	L	Mins	GA	SO	Avg
1986-87	Drummondville	QMJHL	62	31	29	0	3508	293	1	5.01	8	2	6	481	40	0	4.99
1987-88	Drummondville	QMJHL	58	27	24	4	3276	237	1	4.34	16	10	6	1019	56	*1	*3.30
1988-89a	Prince Albert	WHL	54	21	29	0	2957	202	2	4.10	4	1	1	199	16	0	4.82
1989-90	Sherbrooke	AHL	2	1	1	0	119	8	0	4.03	....	....	....	....	....	....	....
	Fort Wayne	IHL	23	6	13	3	1208	87	1	4.32	....	....	....	....	....	....	....

a WHL East All-Star Team (1989)

Signed as a free agent by **Montreal**, January 16, 1990.

CHEVELDAE, TIM (SHE-vehl-day)

Goaltender. Catches left. 5'11", 175 lbs. Born, Melville, Sask., February 15, 1968.
(Detroit's 4th choice, 64th overall, in 1986 Entry Draft).

			Regular Season								Playoffs						
Season	Club	Lea	GP	W	L	T	Mins	GA	SO	Avg	GP	W	L	Mins	GA	SO	Avg
1985-86	Saskatoon	WHL	36	21	10	3	2030	165	0	4.88	8	6	2	480	29	0	3.63
1986-87	Saskatoon	WHL	33	20	11	0	1909	133	2	4.18	5	4	1	308	20	0	3.90
1987-88a	Saskatoon	WHL	66	44	19	3	3798	235	1	3.71	6	4	2	364	27	0	4.45
1988-89	**Detroit**	**NHL**	**2**	**0**	**2**	**0**	**122**	**9**	**0**	**4.43**	....	....	....	....	....	....	....
	Adirondack	AHL	30	20	8	0	1694	98	1	3.47	2	1	0	99	9	0	5.45
1989-90	**Detroit**	**NHL**	**28**	**10**	**9**	**8**	**1600**	**101**	**0**	**3.79**	....	....	....	....	....	....	....
	Adirondack	AHL	31	17	8	6	1848	116	0	3.77	....	....	....	....	....	....	....
	NHL Totals		**30**	**10**	**11**	**8**	**1722**	**110**	**0**	**3.83**	....	....	....	....	....	....	....

a WHL East All-Star Team (1988)

CHEVRIER, ALAIN

Goaltender. Catches left. 5'8", 180 lbs. Born, Cornwall Ont., April 23, 1961.

			Regular Season								Playoffs						
Season	Club	Lea	GP	W	L	T	Mins	GA	SO	Avg	GP	W	L	Mins	GA	SO	Avg
1982-83	Miami-Ohio	CCHA	33	15	16	1	1894	125	0	3.96	....	....	....	....	....	....	....
1983-84	Miami-Ohio	CCHA	32	9	19	1	1509	123	0	4.89	....	....	....	....	....	....	....
1984-85	Fort Wayne	IHL	56	26	21	7	3219	194	0	3.62	9	5	4	556	28	0	3.02
1985-86	**New Jersey**	**NHL**	**37**	**11**	**18**	**2**	**1862**	**143**	**0**	**4.61**	....	....	....	....	....	....	....
1986-87	**New Jersey**	**NHL**	**58**	**24**	**26**	**2**	**3153**	**227**	**0**	**4.32**	....	....	....	....	....	....	....
1987-88	**New Jersey**	**NHL**	**45**	**18**	**19**	**3**	**2354**	**148**	**1**	**3.77**	....	....	....	....	....	....	....
1988-89	**Winnipeg**	**NHL**	**22**	**8**	**8**	**2**	**1092**	**78**	**1**	**4.29**	....	....	....	....	....	....	....
	Chicago	**NHL**	**27**	**13**	**11**	**2**	**1573**	**92**	**0**	**3.51**	**16**	**9**	**7**	**1013**	**44**	**0**	**2.61**
1989-90	**Chicago**	**NHL**	**39**	**16**	**14**	**3**	**1894**	**132**	**0**	**4.18**	....	....	....	....	....	....	....
	Pittsburgh	**NHL**	**3**	**1**	**2**	**0**	**166**	**14**	**0**	**5.06**	....	....	....	....	....	....	....
	NHL Totals		**231**	**91**	**98**	**14**	**12094**	**834**	**2**	**4.14**	**16**	**9**	**7**	**1013**	**44**	**0**	**2.61**

Signed as a free agent by **New Jersey**, May 31, 1985. Traded to **Winnipeg** by **New Jersey** with New Jersey's seventh round (Doug Evans) choice in 1989 Entry Draft for Steve Rooney and **Winnipeg's** third round choice (Brad Bombardir) in 1990 Entry Draft, July 19, 1988. Traded to **Chicago** by **Winnipeg** for Chicago's fourth-round choice (Allain Roy) in 1989 Entry Draft, January 19, 1989. Traded to **Pittsburgh** by **Chicago** for future considerations, March 6, 1990. Signed as a free agent by **Detroit**, July 5, 1990.

CLIFFORD, CHRIS

Goaltender. Catches left. 5'9", 165 lbs. Born, Kingston, Ont., May 26, 1966.
(Chicago's 6th choice, 111th overall, in 1984 Entry Draft).

			Regular Season								Playoffs						
Season	Club	Lea	GP	W	L	T	Mins	GA	SO	Avg	GP	W	L	Mins	GA	SO	Avg
1983-84	Kingston	OHL	50	16	28	0	2808	229	2	4.89	....	....	....	....	....	....	....
1984-85	Kingston	OHL	52	15	34	0	2768	241	0	5.22	....	....	....	....	....	....	....
	Chicago	**NHL**	**1**	**0**	**0**	**0**	**20**	**0**	**0**	**0.00**	....	....	....	....	....	....	....
1985-86	Kingston	OHL	50	26	21	3	2988	178	1	3.57	10	5	5	564	31	1	3.30
1986-87	Kingston	OHL	44	18	25	0	2596	191	1	4.41	12	6	6	730	42	0	3.45
1987-88	Saginaw	IHL	22	9	7	2	1146	80		4.19	....	....	....	....	....	....	....
1988-89	**Chicago**	**NHL**	**1**	**0**	**0**	**0**	**4**	**0**	**0**	**0.00**	....	....	....	....	....	....	....
	Saginaw	IHL	7	4	2	0	321	23	0	4.30	....	....	....	....	....	....	....
1989-90	Muskegon	IHL	23	17	4	1	1352	77	0	3.42	6	3	3	360	24	0	4.01
	Virginia	ECHL	10	7	1	0	547	16	0	1.75	....	....	....	....	....	....	....
	NHL Totals		**2**	**0**	**0**	**0**	**24**	**0**	**0**	**0.00**	....	....	....	....	....	....	....

CLOUTIER, JACQUES (clootz-YAY)

Goaltender. Catches left. 5'7", 167 lbs. Born, Noranda, Que., January 3, 1960.
(Buffalo's 4th choice, 55th overall, in 1979 Entry Draft).

			Regular Season								Playoffs						
Season	Club	Lea	GP	W	L	T	Mins	GA	SO	Avg	GP	W	L	Mins	GA	SO	Avg
1977-78	Trois Rivieres	QJHL	71	....	....	....	4134	240	*4	3.48	13	....	....	779	40	1	3.08
1978-79a	Trois Rivieres	QJHL	72	....	....	....	4168	218	*3	*3.14	13	....	....	780	36	0	*2.77
1979-80	Trois Rivieres	QJHL	55	27	20	7	3222	231	2	4.30	7	3	4	420	33	0	4.71
1980-81	Rochester	AHL	*61	27	27	6	*3478	209	1	3.61	....	....	....	....	....	....	....
1981-82	Rochester	AHL	23	14	7	2	1366	64	0	2.81	....	....	....	....	....	....	....
	Buffalo	**NHL**	**7**	**5**	**1**	**0**	**311**	**13**	**0**	**2.51**	....	....	....	....	....	....	....
1982-83	**Buffalo**	**NHL**	**25**	**10**	**7**	**6**	**1390**	**81**	**0**	**3.50**	....	....	....	....	....	....	....
	Rochester	AHL	13	7	3	1	634	42	0	3.97	16	12	4	992	47	0	2.84
1983-84	Rochester	AHL	*51	26	22	1	*2841	172	1	3.63	*18	9	9	*1145	68	0	3.56
1984-85	**Buffalo**	**NHL**	**1**	**0**	**0**	**1**	**65**	**4**	**0**	**3.69**	....	....	....	....	....		
	Rochester	AHL	14	10	2	1	803	36	0	2.69	....	....	....	....	....	....	....
1985-86	**Buffalo**	**NHL**	**15**	**5**	**9**	**1**	**872**	**49**	**1**	**3.37**	....	....	....	....	....	....	....
	Rochester	AHL	14	10	2	2	835	38	1	2.73	....	....	....	....	....	....	....
1986-87	**Buffalo**	**NHL**	**40**	**11**	**19**	**5**	**2167**	**137**	**0**	**3.79**	....	....	....	....	....	....	....
1987-88	**Buffalo**	**NHL**	**20**	**4**	**8**	**2**	**851**	**67**	**0**	**4.72**	....	....	....	....	....	....	....
1988-89	**Buffalo**	**NHL**	**36**	**15**	**14**	**0**	**1786**	**108**	**0**	**3.63**	**4**	**1**	**3**	**238**	**10**	**1**	**2.52**
	Rochester	AHL	11	2	7	0	527	41	0	4.67	....	....	....	....	....	....	....
1989-90	**Chicago**	**NHL**	**43**	**18**	**15**	**2**	**2178**	**112**	**2**	**3.09**	**4**	**0**	**2**	**175**	**8**	**0**	**2.74**
	NHL Totals		**187**	**68**	**73**	**17**	**9620**	**571**	**1**	**3.56**	**8**	**1**	**5**	**413**	**18**	**1**	**2.62**

a QMJHL First All-Star Team (1979)

Traded to **Chicago** by **Buffalo** for future considerations, September 28, 1989.

COLE, THOMAS

Goaltender. Catches left. 6', 185 lbs. Born, Woburn, MA, February 18, 1969.
(Edmonton's 10th choice, 187th overall, in 1989 Entry Draft).

			Regular Season								Playoffs						
Season	Club	Lea	GP	W	L	T	Mins	GA	SO	Avg	GP	W	L	Mins	GA	SO	Avg
1988-89	Northeastern	H.E.	6	2	4	0	319	30	0	5.64	....	....	....	....	....	....	....
1989-90	Northeastern	H.E.	25	10	12	2	1412	106	0	4.51	....	....	....	....	....	....	....

CONNELL, PAUL

Goaltender. Catches left. 5'8", 160 lbs. Born, Cranston, RI, March 19, 1967.
(Philadelphia's 1st choice, 19th overall, in 1988 Supplemental Draft).

			Regular Season								Playoffs						
Season	Club	Lea	GP	W	L	T	Mins	GA	SO	Avg	GP	W	L	Mins	GA	SO	Avg
1986-87	Bowling Green	CCHA	7	4	1	0	324	23	0	4.26	....	....	....	....	....	....	....
1987-88	Bowling Green	CCHA	39	27	10	2	2322	155	0	4.00	....	....	....	....	....	....	....
1988-89	Bowling Green	CCHA	41	21	16	3	2439	140	0	3.44	....	....	....	....	....	....	....
1989-90	Bowling Green	CCHA	18	8	6	0	943	79	0	5.03	....	....	....	....	....	....	....

COWLEY, WAYNE

Goaltender. Catches left. 6'0", 185 lbs. Born, Scarborough, Ont., December 4, 1964.

			Regular Season								Playoffs						
Season	Club	Lea	GP	W	L	T	Mins	GA	SO	Avg	GP	W	L	Mins	GA	SO	Avg
1985-86	Colgate	ECAC	7	2	2	0	313	23	1	4.42	....	....	....	....	....	....	....
1986-87	Colgate	ECAC	31	21	8	1	1805	106	0	3.52	....	....	....	....	....	....	....
1987-88	Colgate	ECAC	20	11	7	1	1162	58	1	2.99	....	....	....	....	....	....	....
1988-89	Salt Lake	IHL	29	17	7	1	1423	94	0	3.96	2	1	0	69	6	0	5.22
1989-90	Salt Lake	IHL	36	15	12	5	2009	124	1	3.70	....	....	....	....	....	....	....

Signed as a free agent by **Calgary**, May 1, 1988.

CROZIER, JIM

Goaltender. Catches left. 5'9", 160 lbs. Born, North Bay, Ont., February 9, 1968.
(Hartford's 1st choice, 20th overall, in 1990 Supplemental Draft).

			Regular Season								Playoffs						
Season	Club	Lea	GP	W	L	T	Mins	GA	SO	Avg	GP	W	L	Mins	GA	SO	Avg
1987-88	Cornell	ECAC	3	2	1	0	180	11	0	3.67	....	....	....	....	....	....	....
1988-89	Cornell	ECAC	5	1	0	0	127	2	0	0.94	....	....	....	....	....	....	....
1989-90	Cornell	ECAC	16	6	7	2	866	38	0	*2.63	....	....	....	....	....	....	....

DAFOE, BYRON

Goaltender. Catches left. 5'11", 175 lbs. Born, Duncan, B.C., February 25, 1971.
(Washington's 2nd choice, 35th overall, in 1989 Entry Draft).

			Regular Season								Playoffs						
Season	Club	Lea	GP	W	L	T	Mins	GA	SO	Avg	GP	W	L	Mins	GA	SO	Avg
1988-89	Portland	WHL	59	29	24	3	3279	291	1	5.32	*18	10	8	*1091	81	*1	4.45
1989-90	Portland	WHL	40	14	21	3	2265	193	0	5.11	....	....	....	....	....	....	....

D'ALESSIO, CORRIE

Goaltender. Catches left. 5'11", 155 lbs. Born, Cornwall, Ont., September 9, 1969.
(Vancouver's 4th choice, 107th overall, in 1988 Entry Draft).

			Regular Season								Playoffs						
Season	Club	Lea	GP	W	L	T	Mins	GA	SO	Avg	GP	W	L	Mins	GA	SO	Avg
1987-88a	Cornell	ECAC	25	17	8	0	1457	67	0	2.76	....	....	....	....	....	....	....
1988-89	Cornell	ECAC	29	15	13	1	1684	96	1	3.42	....	....	....	....	....	....	....
1989-90	Cornell	ECAC	16	6	7	2	887	50	0	3.38	....	....	....	....	....	....	....

a ECAC All-Rookie Team (1988)

D'AMOUR, MARC (dah-MOHR)

Goaltender. Catches left. 5'10", 195 lbs. Born, Sudbury, Ont., April 29, 1961.

			Regular Season								Playoffs						
Season	Club	Lea	GP	W	L	T	Mins	GA	SO	Avg	GP	W	L	Mins	GA	SO	Avg
1979-80	S. S. Marie	OHA	33	16	15	0	1429	117	0	4.91	....	....	....	....	....	....	....
1980-81	S. S. Marie	OHA	16	7	1	1	653	38	0	3.49	14	5	4	683	41	0	3.60
1981-82a	S. S. Marie	OHL	41	28	12	1	3284	130	1	*3.27	10	3	2	504	30	0	3.57
1982-83	Colorado	CHL	42	16	21	2	2373	153	1	3.87	1	....	....	59	4	0	4.08
1983-84	Colorado	CHL	36	18	12	1	1917	131	0	4.10	1	0	0	20	0	0	0.00
1984-85	Moncton	AHL	37	18	14	2	2051	115	0	3.36	....	....	....	....	....	....	....
	Salt Lake	IHL	12	7	2	2	694	33	0	2.85	....	....	....	....	....	....	....
1985-86	**Calgary**	**NHL**	**15**	**2**	**4**	**2**	**560**	**32**	**0**	**3.43**	....	....	....	....	....	....	....
	Moncton	AHL	21	6	9	3	1129	72	0	3.83	5	1	4	296	20	0	4.05
1986-87	Binghamton	AHL	8	5	3	0	461	30	0	3.90	....	....	....	....	....	....	....
	Salt Lake	IHL	10	3	6	0	523	37	0	4.24	....	....	....	....	....	....	....
	Can. Olympic	....	1	0	0	0	30	4	0	8.00	....	....	....	....	....	....	....
1987-88	Salt Lake	IHL	*62	26	19	5	3245	177	0	3.27	*19	*12	7	*1123	67		3.58
1988-89	**Philadelphia**	**NHL**	**1**	**0**	**0**	**0**	**19**	**0**	**0**	**0.00**	....	....	....	....	....	....	....
	Hershey	AHL	39	19	13	3	2174	127	0	3.51	....	....	....	....	....	....	....
	Indianapolis	IHL	6	2	3	0	324	20	0	3.70	....	....	....	....	....	....	....
1989-90	Hershey	AHL	43	15	20	6	2505	148	2	3.54	....	....	....	....	....	....	....
	NHL Totals		**16**	**2**	**4**	**2**	**579**	**32**	**0**	**3.32**	....	....	....	....	....	....	....

a OHL First All-Star Team (1982)

Signed as free agent by **Calgary**, June 7, 1982. Signed as a free agent by **Philadelphia**, September 30, 1988.

DELGUIDICE, MATT

Goaltender. Catches right. 5'9", 170 lbs. Born, West Haven, CT, March 5, 1967.
(Boston's 4th choice, 77th overall, in 1987 Entry Draft).

			Regular Season								Playoffs						
Season	Club	Lea	GP	W	L	T	Mins	GA	SO	Avg	GP	W	L	Mins	GA	SO	Avg
1987-88					DID NOT PLAY												
1988-89	U. of Maine	H.E.	20	16	4	0	1090	57	1	*3.14	....	....	....	....	....	....	....
1989-90	U. of Maine	H.E.	23	16	4	0	1257	68	0	3.25	....	....	....	....	....	....	....

DELIANIEDIS, DANIEL JAMES (DAN) (duh-lan-dis)

Goaltender. Catches left. 5'9", 185 lbs. Born, Worcester, MA, July 3, 1964.

			Regular Season								Playoffs						
Season	Club	Lea	GP	W	L	T	Mins	GA	SO	Avg	GP	W	L	Mins	GA	SO	Avg
1982-83	Colgate	ECAC	6	3	0	1	221	14	0	3.80	....	....	....	....	....	....	....
1983-84	Colgate	ECAC	6	2	2	0	260	28	0	6.46	....	....	....	....	....	....	....
1984-85	Colgate	ECAC	5	1	0	0	160	10	0	3.76	....	....	....	....	....	....	....
1985-86	Colgate	ECAC	26	13	12	1	1470	110	0	4.49	....	....	....	....	....	....	....
1986-87a	Mohawk Valley	ACHL	35	....	....	....	1943	161	0	4.97	12	7	5	714	43	0	3.61
1987-88	Utica	AHL	22	7	7	3	1048	73	0	4.18	....	....	....	....	....	....	....
1988-89	Utica	AHL	3	0	1	0	94	8	0	5.11	....	....	....	....	....	....	....
1989-90	Nashville	ECHL	5	1	2	1	264	18	0	4.09	....	....	....	....	....	....	....

a ACHL Second All-Star Team (1987)

Signed as a free agent by **New Jersey**, October 20, 1987.

DEPINTO, DAVID

Goaltender. Catches left. 5'7", 165 lbs. Born, Elk Grove, IL, March 2, 1967.
(Quebec's 1st choice, 1st overall, in 1989 Supplemental Draft).

			Regular Season								Playoffs						
Season	Club	Lea	GP	W	L	T	Mins	GA	SO	Avg	GP	W	L	Mins	GA	SO	Avg
1986-87	Ill.-Chicago	CCHA	17	9	7	0	955	64	0	4.02	...	...	...	...	...	...	...
1987-88	Ill.-Chicago	CCHA	20	9	8	1	1083	76	0	4.21	...	...	...	...	...	...	...
1988-89	Ill.-Chicago	CCHA	38	21	12	4	2266	137	0	3.63	...	...	...	...	...	...	...
1989-90	Ill.-Chicago	CCHA	32	9	21	1	1812	158	0	5.23	...	...	...	...	...	...	...

DERKSEN, DUANE

Goaltender. Catches left. 6'1", 180 lbs. Born, St. Boniface, Man., July 7, 1968.
(Washington's 4th choice, 57th overall, in 1988 Entry Draft).

			Regular Season								Playoffs						
Season	Club	Lea	GP	W	L	T	Mins	GA	SO	Avg	GP	W	L	Mins	GA	SO	Avg
1988-89	U. Wisconsin	WCHA	11	4	5	0	561	37	1	3.96	...	...	...	...	...	...	...
1989-90ab	U. Wisconsin	WCHA	*41	*31	8	1	*2345	133	*2	*3.40	...	...	...	...	...	...	...

a WCHA Second All-Star Team (1990)
b NCAA All-Tournament Team, Tournament Top Goaltender (1990).

DONEGHY, MICHAEL

Goaltender. Catches left. 6', 165 lbs. Born, Boston, MA, July 28, 1970.
(Chicago's 10th choice, 237th overall, in 1989 Entry Draft).

			Regular Season								Playoffs						
Season	Club	Lea	GP	W	L	T	Mins	GA	SO	Avg	GP	W	L	Mins	GA	SO	Avg
1988-89	Catholic Mem.	HS	24	...	...	...	1080	30	9	1.25	...	...	...	...	...	...	...
1989-90	Merrimack	H.E.	9	3	5	0	424	36	1	5.09	...	...	...	...	...	...	...

DRAPER, TOM

Goaltender. Catches left. 5'11", 180 lbs. Born, Outremont, Que., November 20, 1966.
(Winnipeg's 8th choice, 165th overall, in 1985 Entry Draft).

			Regular Season								Playoffs						
Season	Club	Lea	GP	W	L	T	Mins	GA	SO	Avg	GP	W	L	Mins	GA	SO	Avg
1983-84	U. of Vermont	ECAC	20	8	12	0	1205	82	0	4.08	...	...	...	...	...	...	...
1984-85	U. of Vermont	ECAC	24	5	17	0	1316	90	0	4.11	...	...	...	...	...	...	...
1985-86	U. of Vermont	ECAC	29	15	12	1	1697	87	1	3.08	...	...	...	...	...	...	...
1986-87a	U. of Vermont	ECAC	29	16	13	0	1662	96	2	3.47	...	...	...	...	...	...	...
1987-88	Tappara	Fin.	28	16	3	9	1619	87	0	3.22	...	...	...	...	...	...	...
1988-89	**Winnipeg**	**NHL**	**2**	**1**	**1**	**0**	**120**	**12**	**0**	**6.00**	...	...	...	...	...	...	...
b	Moncton	AHL	*54	27	17	5	*2962	171	2	3.46	7	5	2	419	24	0	3.44
1989-90	**Winnipeg**	**NHL**	**6**	**2**	**4**	**0**	**359**	**26**	**0**	**4.35**	...	...	...	...	...	...	...
	Moncton	AHL	51	20	24	3	2844	167	1	3.52	...	...	...	...	...	...	...
	NHL Totals		**8**	**3**	**5**	**0**	**479**	**38**	**0**	**4.75**	...	...	...	...	...	...	...

a ECAC First All-Star Team (1987).
b AHL Second All-Star Team (1989)

DUNHAM, CHRIS

Goaltender. Catches left. 6'2", 170 lbs. Born, Johnson City, NY, June 1, 1972.
(New Jersey's 4th choice, 53rd overall, in 1990 Entry Draft).

			Regular Season								Playoffs						
Season	Club	Lea	GP	W	L	T	Mins	GA	SO	Avg	GP	W	L	Mins	GA	SO	Avg
1989-90	Canterbury	HS	32	...	...	...	1558	68	3	1.96	...	...	...	...	...	...	...

DYCK, LARRY

Goaltender. Catches left. 5'11", 180 lbs. Born, Winkler, Man., December 15, 1965.

			Regular Season								Playoffs						
Season	Club	Lea	GP	W	L	T	Mins	GA	SO	Avg	GP	W	L	Mins	GA	SO	Avg
1988-89	Kalamazoo	IHL	42	17	20	2	2308	168	0	4.37	...	...	...	...	...	...	...
1989-90	Kalamazoo	IHL	36	20	12	0	1959	116	0	3.55	7	2	3	353	22	0	3.74
	Knoxville	ECHL	3	1	1	1	184	12	0	3.91	...	...	...	...	...	...	...

Signed as a free agent by **Minnesota**, November 10, 1988.

ERICKSON, CHAD

Goaltender. Catches right. 5'9", 175 lbs. Born, Minneapolis, MN, August 21, 1970.
(New Jersey's 8th choice, 138th overall, in 1988 Entry Draft).

			Regular Season								Playoffs						
Season	Club	Lea	GP	W	L	T	Mins	GA	SO	Avg	GP	W	L	Mins	GA	SO	Avg
1988-89	Minn.-Duluth	WCHA	15	5	7	1	821	49	0	3.58	...	...	...	...	...	...	...
1989-90ab	Minn.-Duluth	WCHA	39	19	19	1	2301	141	0	3.68	...	...	...	...	...	...	...

a WCHA Second All-Star Team (1990)
b NCAA West First All-American Team (1990)

ESSENSA, BOB (EH-sehn-sah)

Goaltender. Catches left. 6', 160 lbs. Born, Toronto, Ont., January 14, 1965.
(Winnipeg's 5th choice, 71st overall, in 1983 Entry Draft).

			Regular Season								Playoffs						
Season	Club	Lea	GP	W	L	T	Mins	GA	SO	Avg	GP	W	L	Mins	GA	SO	Avg
1983-84	Michigan State	CCHA	17	11	4	0	946	44	2	2.79	...	...	...	...	...	...	...
1984-85	Michigan State	CCHA	18	15	2	0	1059	29	2	1.64	...	...	...	...	...	...	...
1985-86a	Michigan State	CCHA	23	17	4	1	1333	74	1	3.33	...	...	...	...	...	...	...
1986-87	Michigan State	CCHA	25	19	3	1	1383	64	2	2.78	...	...	...	...	...	...	...
1987-88	Moncton	AHL	27	7	11	1	1287	100	1	4.66	...	...	...	...	...	...	...
1988-89	**Winnipeg**	**NHL**	**20**	**6**	**8**	**3**	**1102**	**68**	**1**	**3.70**	...	...	...	...	...	...	...
	Fort Wayne	IHL	22	14	7	0	1287	70	0	3.26	...	...	...	...	...	...	...
1989-90b	**Winnipeg**	**NHL**	**36**	**18**	**9**	**5**	**2035**	**107**	**1**	**3.15**	**4**	**2**	**1**	**206**	**12**	**0**	**3.50**
	Moncton	AHL	6	3	3	0	358	15	0	2.51	...	...	...	...	...	...	...
	NHL Totals		**56**	**24**	**17**	**8**	**3137**	**175**	**2**	**3.35**	**4**	**2**	**1**	**206**	**12**	**0**	**3.50**

a CCHA Second All-Star Team (1986)
b NHL All-Rookie Team (1990)

EXELBY, RANDY

Goaltender. Catches left. 5'9", 170 lbs. Born, Toronto, Ont., August 13, 1965.
(Montreal's 1st choice, 20th overall, in 1986 Supplemental Draft).

			Regular Season								Playoffs						
Season	Club	Lea	GP	W	L	T	Mins	GA	SO	Avg	GP	W	L	Mins	GA	SO	Avg
1983-84	Lake Superior	CCHA	21	6	10	0	905	75	0	4.97	...	...	...	...	...	...	...
1984-85	Lake Superior	CCHA	36	22	11	1	1999	112	0	3.36	...	...	...	...	...	...	...
1985-86	Lake Superior	CCHA	28	14	11	1	1625	98	0	3.61	...	...	...	...	...	...	...
1987-87	Lake Superior	CCHA	28	12	9	1	1357	91	0	4.02	...	...	...	...	...	...	...
1987-88	Sherbrooke	AHL	19	7	10	0	1050	49	0	2.80	4	2	2	212	13	0	3.68
1988-89	**Montreal**	**NHL**	**1**	**0**	**0**	**0**	**3**	**0**	**0**	**0.00**	...	...	...	...	...	...	...
abc	Sherbrooke	AHL	52	*31	13	6	2935	146	*6	*2.98	6	1	4	329	24	0	4.38
1989-90	**Edmonton**	**NHL**	**1**	**0**	**1**	**0**	**60**	**5**	**0**	**5.00**	...	...	...	...	...	...	...
	Phoenix	IHL	41	11	18	5	2146	163	0	4.56	...	...	...	...	...	...	...
	NHL Totals		**2**	**0**	**1**	**0**	**63**	**5**	**0**	**4.76**	...	...	...	...	...	...	...

a AHL First All-Star Team (1989)
b Shared Harry "Hap Holmes Trophy (fewest goals-against-AHL) with Francois Gravel (1989)
c Won Baz Bastien Award (Top Goaltender-AHL) (1989)

Traded to **Edmonton** by **Montreal** for future considerations, October 2, 1989.

FANNING, TODD

Goaltender. Catches left. 5'11", 175 lbs. Born, Winnipeg, Man., February 12, 1968.
(Vancouver's 6th choice, 129th overall, in 1987 Entry Draft).

			Regular Season								Playoffs						
Season	Club	Lea	GP	W	L	T	Mins	GA	SO	Avg	GP	W	L	Mins	GA	SO	Avg
1986-87	Ohio State	CCHA	24	11	10	0	1276	97	0	4.56	...	...	...	...	...	...	...
1987-88	Ohio State	CCHA	28	8	11	3	1290	102	0	4.84	...	...	...	...	...	...	...
1988-89	Ohio State	CCHA	33	9	19	4	1894	154	0	4.88	...	...	...	...	...	...	...
1989-90	Ohio State	CCHA	24	5	11	0	1293	113	0	5.24	...	...	...	...	...	...	...

FELICIO, MARC

Goaltender. Catches left. 5'7", 170 lbs. Born, Woonsockett, RI, December 1, 1968.
(Minnesota's 11th choice, 214th overall, in 1987 Entry Draft).

			Regular Season								Playoffs						
Season	Club	Lea	GP	W	L	T	Mins	GA	SO	Avg	GP	W	L	Mins	GA	SO	Avg
1987-88	Ferris State	CCHA	18	4	9	0	806	74	0	5.50	...	...	...	...	...	...	...
1988-89	Ferris State	CCHA	19	6	9	1	1045	85	0	4.88	...	...	...	...	...	...	...
1989-90	Ferris State	CCHA	17	2	7	0	738	59	0	4.81	...	...	...	...	...	...	...

FISET, STEPHANE

Goaltender. Catches left. 6', 175 lbs. Born, Montreal, Que., June 17, 1970.
(Quebec's 3rd choice, 24th overall, in 1988 Entry Draft).

			Regular Season								Playoffs						
Season	Club	Lea	GP	W	L	T	Mins	GA	SO	Avg	GP	W	L	Mins	GA	SO	Avg
1987-88	Victoriaville	QMJHL	40	15	17	4	2221	146	1	3.94	2	0	2	163	10	0	3.68
1988-89a	Victoriaville	QMJHL	43	25	14	0	2401	138	1	*3.45	12	*9	2	711	33	0	*2.78
1989-90	**Quebec**	**NHL**	**6**	**0**	**5**	**1**	**342**	**34**	**0**	**5.96**	...	...	...	...	...	...	...
	Victoriaville	QMJHL	24	14	6	3	1383	63	1	*2.73	*14	7	6	*790	49	0	3.72
	NHL Totals		**6**	**0**	**5**	**1**	**342**	**34**	**0**	**5.96**	...	...	...	...	...	...	...

a QMJHL First All-Star Team (1989)

FITZPATRICK, MARK

Goaltender. Catches right. 6'2", 190 lbs. Born, Toronto, Ont., November 13, 1968.
(Los Angeles' 2nd choice, 27th overall, in 1987 Entry Draft).

			Regular Season								Playoffs						
Season	Club	Lea	GP	W	L	T	Mins	GA	SO	Avg	GP	W	L	Mins	GA	SO	Avg
1985-86	Medicine Hat	WHL	41	26	6	1	2074	99	1	2.86	19	12	5	986	58	0	3.53
1986-87	Medicine Hat	WHL	50	31	11	4	2844	159	4	3.35	20	12	8	1224	71	1	3.48
1987-88	Medicine Hat	WHL	63	36	15	6	3600	194	2	3.23	16	12	4	959	52	*1	*3.25
1988-89	**Los Angeles**	**NHL**	**17**	**6**	**7**	**3**	**957**	**64**	**0**	**4.01**	...	...	...	...	...	...	...
	New Haven	AHL	18	10	5	1	980	54	1	3.31	...	...	...	...	...	...	...
	NY Islanders	**NHL**	**11**	**3**	**5**	**2**	**627**	**41**	**0**	**3.92**	...	...	...	...	...	...	...
1989-90	**NY Islanders**	**NHL**	**47**	**19**	**19**	**5**	**2653**	**150**	**3**	**3.39**	**4**	**0**	**2**	**152**	**13**	**0**	**5.13**
	NHL Totals		**75**	**28**	**31**	**10**	**4237**	**255**	**3**	**3.61**	**4**	**0**	**2**	**152**	**13**	**0**	**5.13**

Traded to **NY Islanders** by **Los Angeles** with Wayne McBean and future considerations (Doug Crossman, acquired May 23, 1989) for Kelly Hrudey, February 22, 1989.

FLETCHER, JOHN

Goaltender. Catches right. 5'7", 165 lbs. Born, Holden, MA, October 14, 1967.
(Vancouver's 9th choice, 192nd overall, in 1987 Entry Draft).

			Regular Season								Playoffs						
Season	Club	Lea	GP	W	L	T	Mins	GA	SO	Avg	GP	W	L	Mins	GA	SO	Avg
1986-87a	Clarkson	ECAC	23	11	8	1	1240	62	4	2.99	...	...	...	...	...	...	...
1987-88bc	Clarkson	ECAC	33	16	11	3	1820	97	1	3.19	...	...	...	...	...	...	...
1988-89	Clarkson	ECAC	23	9	8	2	1146	79	0	4.13	...	...	...	...	...	...	...
1989-90	Clarkson	ECAC	34	20	11	3	1900	89	0	3.13	...	...	...	...	...	...	...

a ECAC Rookie of the Year (1987)
b ECAC First All-Star Team (1988)
c NCAA East Second All-American Team (1988)

FORD, BRIAN

Goaltender. Catches left. 5'10", 170 lbs. Born, Edmonton, Alta., September 22, 1961.

			Regular Season								Playoffs						
Season	Club	Lea	GP	W	L	T	Mins	GA	SO	Avg	GP	W	L	Mins	GA	SO	Avg
1980-81	Billings	WHL	44	14	26	0	2435	204	0	5.03	3	...	...	143	15	0	4.66
1981-82	Billings	WHL	53	19	26	1	2791	256	0	5.50	5	...	...	226	26	0	5.86
1982-83	Carolina	ACHL	4	...	...	...	203	7	0	2.07	...	...	...	...	...	...	...
	Fredericton	AHL	27	14	7	2	1443	84	0	*3.49	1	0	0	11	1	0	5.56
1983-84	**Quebec**	**NHL**	**3**	**1**	**1**	**0**	**123**	**13**	**0**	**6.34**	...	...	...	...	...	...	...
a	Fredericton	AHL	36	17	17	1	2132	105	2	*2.96	4	1	3	223	18	0	4.84
1984-85	**Pittsburgh**	**NHL**	**8**	**2**	**6**	**0**	**457**	**48**	**0**	**6.30**	...	...	...	...	...	...	...
	Baltimore	AHL	6	3	3	0	363	21	0	3.47	...	...	...	...	...	...	...
	Muskegon	IHL	22	17	5	0	1321	59	1	2.68	...	...	...	...	...	...	...
1985-86	Baltimore	AHL	39	12	20	4	2230	136	1	3.66	...	...	...	...	...	...	...
	Muskegon	IHL	9	4	4	0	513	33	0	3.06	*13	*12	1	*793	41	0	3.10
1986-87	Baltimore	AHL	32	10	11	0	1541	99	0	3.85	...	...	...	...	...	...	...
1987-88	Springfield	AHL	35	12	15	4	1898	118	0	3.73	...	...	...	...	...	...	...
1988-89	Rochester	AHL	19	12	4	1	1075	60	2	3.35	...	...	...	...	...	...	...
1989-90	Rochester	AHL	19	7	6	4	1076	69	0	3.85	...	...	...	...	...	...	...
	NHL Totals		**11**	**3**	**7**	**0**	**580**	**61**	**0**	**6.31**	...	...	...	...	...	...	...

a Won Harry (Hap) Holmes Memorial Trophy (AHL's leading goaltender) (1984)

Signed as a free agent by **Quebec**, August 1, 1982. Traded to **Pittsburgh** by **Quebec** for Tom Thornbury, December 6, 1984.

FOSTER, NORM

Goaltender. Catches left. 5'9", 175 lbs. Born, Vancouver, B.C., February 10, 1965.
(Boston's 11th choice, 222nd overall, in 1983 Entry Draft).

			Regular Season								Playoffs						
Season	Club	Lea	GP	W	L	T	Mins	GA	SO	Avg	GP	W	L	Mins	GA	SO	Avg
1984-85	Michigan State	CCHA	26	22	4	0	1531	67	0	2.63	....	....	....	....	....	....	....
1985-86	Michigan State	CCHA	24	17	5	1	1414	87	0	3.69	....	....	....	....	....	....	....
1986-87	Michigan State	CCHA	24	14	7	1	1383	90	1	3.90	....	....	....	....	....	....	....
1987-88	Milwaukee	IHL	38	10	22	1	2001	170	0	5.10	....	....	....	....	....	....	....
1988-89	Maine	AHL	47	16	17	6	2411	156	1	3.88	....	....	....	....	....	....	....
1989-90	Maine	AHL	*64	23	28	10	*3664	217	3	3.55	....	....	....	....	....	....	....

FOURNIER, ROB

Goaltender. Catches left. 6', 190 lbs. Born, Sudbury, Ont., April 8, 1969.
(St. Louis' 3rd choice, 51st overall, in 1988 Entry Draft).

			Regular Season								Playoffs						
Season	Club	Lea	GP	W	L	T	Mins	GA	SO	Avg	GP	W	L	Mins	GA	SO	Avg
1986-87	North Bay	OHL	25	13	6	1	1281	72	2	3.37	....	....	....	....	....	....	....
1987-88a	North Bay	OHL	61	30	23	5	3601	210	1	3.50	4	0	4	255	21	0	4.94
1988-89	North Bay	OHL	9	0	7	1	582	99	0	10.20	....	....	....	....	....	....	....
	Niagara Falls	OHL	32	11	5	0	1293	104	0	4.83	7	0	3	154	20	0	7.79
1989-90	Niagara Falls	OHL	1	0	1	0	60	7	0	7.00	....	....	....	....	....	....	....
	North Bay	OHL	24	8	13	2	1344	93	0	4.15	....	....	....	....	....	....	....

a OHL Second All-Star Team (1988)

FRANCIS, MICHAEL

Goaltender. Catches left. 6', 165 lbs. Born, Braintree, MA, November 19, 1969.
(St. Louis' 12th choice, 240th overall, in 1988 Entry Draft).

			Regular Season								Playoffs						
Season	Club	Lea	GP	W	L	T	Mins	GA	SO	Avg	GP	W	L	Mins	GA	SO	Avg
1987-88	Harvard	ECAC	10	6	3	0	580	25	0	2.59	....	....	....	....	....	....	....
1988-89	Harvard	ECAC	3	2	0	0	140	2	0	0.86	....	....	....	....	....	....	....
1989-90	Harvard	ECAC	3	1	1	0	143	9	0	3.78	....	....	....	....	....	....	....

FROESE, ROBERT GLENN (BOB) (FROHZ)

Goaltender. Catches left. 5'11", 180 lbs. Born, St. Catharines, Ont., June 30, 1958.
(St. Louis' 11th choice, 160th overall, in 1978 Amateur Draft).

			Regular Season								Playoffs						
Season	Club	Lea	GP	W	L	T	Mins	GA	SO	Avg	GP	W	L	Mins	GA	SO	Avg
1975-76	St. Catharines	OHA	39	....	....	....	1976	193	0	5.83	4	....	....	240	20	0	5.00
1976-77	Niagara Falls	OHA	39	....	....	....	2063	162	2	4.68	....	....	....	....	....	....	....
1977-78	Niagara Falls	OHA	52	....	....	....	3128	249	0	4.71	3	....	....	236	17	0	4.36
1978-79	Saginaw	IHL	21	....	....	....	1050	58	0	3.31	....	....	....	....	....	....	....
	Milwaukee	IHL	14	....	....	....	715	42	1	3.52	7	....	....	334	23	0	4.14
1979-80	Maine	AHL	1	0	1	0	60	5	0	5.00	....	....	....	....	....	....	....
	Saginaw	IHL	52	....	....	....	2827	178	0	3.78	4	....	....	213	13	0	3.66
1980-81	Saginaw	IHL	43	....	....	....	2298	114	3	2.98	*13	....	....	*806	29	*2	*2.16
1981-82	Maine	AHL	33	16	11	4	1900	104	2	3.28	....	....	....	....	....	....	....
1982-83	Maine	AHL	33	18	11	3	1966	110	2	3.36	....	....	....	....	....	....	....
	Philadelphia	**NHL**	**25**	**17**	**4**	**2**	**1407**	**59**	**4**	**2.52**	....	....	....	....	....	....	....
1983-84	**Philadelphia**	**NHL**	**48**	**28**	**13**	**7**	**2863**	**150**	**2**	**3.14**	**3**	**0**	**2**	**154**	**11**	**0**	**4.28**
1984-85	**Philadelphia**	**NHL**	**17**	**13**	**2**	**0**	**923**	**37**	**1**	**2.41**	**4**	**0**	**1**	**146**	**11**	**0**	**4.52**
	Hershey	AHL	4	1	2	1	245	15	0	3.67	....	....	....	....	....	....	....
1985-86ab	**Philadelphia**	**NHL**	**51**	***31**	**10**	**3**	**2728**	**116**	***5**	***2.55**	**5**	**2**	**3**	**293**	**15**	**0**	**3.07**
1986-87	**Philadelphia**	**NHL**	**3**	**3**	**0**	**0**	**180**	**8**	**0**	**2.67**	....	....	....	....	....	....	....
	NY Rangers	**NHL**	**28**	**14**	**11**	**0**	**1474**	**92**	**0**	**3.74**	**4**	**1**	**1**	**165**	**10**	**0**	**3.84**
1987-88	**NY Rangers**	**NHL**	**25**	**8**	**11**	**3**	**1443**	**85**	**0**	**3.53**	....	....	....	....	....	....	....
1988-89	**NY Rangers**	**NHL**	**30**	**9**	**14**	**4**	**1621**	**102**	**1**	**3.78**	**2**	**0**	**2**	**72**	**8**	**0**	**6.67**
1989-90	**NY Rangers**	**NHL**	**15**	**5**	**7**	**1**	**812**	**45**	**0**	**3.33**	....	....	....	....	....	....	....
	NHL Totals		**242**	**128**	**72**	**23**	**13451**	**694**	**13**	**3.10**	**18**	**3**	**9**	**830**	**55**	**0**	**3.98**

a NHL Second All-Star Team (1986)
b Shared William Jennings Trophy with Darren Jensen (1986)

Played in NHL All-Star Game (1986)

Signed as a free agent by **Philadelphia**, June 18, 1981. Traded to **NY Rangers** by **Philadelphia** for Kjell Samuelsson and NY Rangers' second round choice (Patrik Juhlin) in 1989 Entry Draft, December 18, 1986.

FUHR, GRANT (FYOOR)

Goaltender. Catches right. 5'10", 186 lbs. Born, Spruce Grove, Alta., September 28, 1962.
(Edmonton's 1st choice, 8th overall, in 1981 Entry Draft).

			Regular Season								Playoffs						
Season	Club	Lea	GP	W	L	T	Mins	GA	SO	Avg	GP	W	L	Mins	GA	SO	Avg
1979-80ab	Victoria	WHL	43	30	12	0	2488	130	2	3.14	8	5	3	465	22	0	2.84
1980-81a	Victoria	WHL	59	48	9	1	3448	160	*4	*2.78	15	12	3	899	45	*1	*3.00
1981-82c	**Edmonton**	**NHL**	**48**	**28**	**5**	**14**	**2847**	**157**	**0**	**3.31**	**5**	**2**	**3**	**309**	**26**	**0**	**5.05**
1982-83	Moncton	AHL	10	4	5	1	604	40	0	3.98	....	....	....	....	....	....	....
	Edmonton	**NHL**	**32**	**13**	**12**	**5**	**1803**	**129**	**0**	**4.29**	**1**	**0**	**0**	**11**	**0**	**0**	**0.00**
1983-84	**Edmonton**	**NHL**	**45**	**30**	**10**	**4**	**2625**	**171**	**1**	**3.91**	**16**	**11**	**4**	**883**	**44**	**1**	**2.99**
1984-85	**Edmonton**	**NHL**	**46**	**26**	**8**	**7**	**2559**	**165**	**1**	**3.87**	***18**	***15**	**3**	**1064**	**55**	**0**	**3.10**
1985-86	**Edmonton**	**NHL**	**40**	**29**	**8**	**0**	**2184**	**143**	**0**	**3.93**	**9**	**5**	**4**	**541**	**28**	**0**	**3.11**
1986-87	**Edmonton**	**NHL**	**44**	**22**	**13**	**3**	**2388**	**137**	**0**	**3.44**	**19**	**14**	**5**	**1148**	**47**	**0**	**2.46**
1987-88de	**Edmonton**	**NHL**	***75**	***40**	**24**	**9**	***4304**	**246**	***4**	**3.43**	***19**	***16**	**2**	***1136**	**55**	**0**	**2.90**
1988-89	**Edmonton**	**NHL**	**59**	**23**	**26**	**6**	**3341**	**213**	**1**	**3.83**	**7**	**3**	**4**	**417**	**24**	**1**	**3.45**
1989-90	**Edmonton**	**NHL**	**21**	**9**	**7**	**3**	**1081**	**70**	**1**	**3.89**	....	....	....	....	....	....	....
	Cape Breton	AHL	2	2	0	0	120	6	0	3.01	....	....	....	....	....	....	....
	NHL Totals		**410**	**220**	**113**	**51**	**23132**	**1431**	**8**	**3.71**	**94**	**66**	**25**	**5509**	**279**	**2**	**3.04**

a WHL First All-Star Team (1980, 1981)
b WHL Rookie of the Year (1980)
c NHL Second All-Star Team (1982)
d NHL First All-Star Team (1988)
e Won Vezina Trophy (1988)

Played in NHL All-Star Game (1982, 1984-86, 1988-89)

FURLAN, FRANK

Goaltender. Catches left. 5'9", 174 lbs. Born, Nanaimo, B.C., March 8, 1968.
(Winnipeg's 7th choice, 155th overall, in 1986 Entry Draft).

			Regular Season								Playoffs						
Season	Club	Lea	GP	W	L	T	Mins	GA	SO	Avg	GP	W	L	Mins	GA	SO	Avg
1986-87	Michigan Tech	WCHA	11	1	10	0	623	66	0	6.36	...	...	...	...	...	...	...
1987-88	Michigan Tech	WCHA	16	4	10	0	864	87	0	6.04	....	....	....	....	....	....	....
1988-89	Tri-Cities	WHL	46	17	23	3	2662	191	1	4.31	3	0	1	67	7	0	6.27
1989-90	Moncton	AHL	2	0	0	0	29	7	0	14.48	....	....	....	....	....	....	....
	Fort Wayne	IHL	1	0	1	0	40	6	0	9.00	....	....	....	....	....	....	....
	Hampton-Roads	ECHL	7	5	1	0	380	24	0	3.78	....	....	....	....	....	....	....

GALUPPO, SANDY

Goaltender. Catches left. 5'10", 160 lbs. Born, Farmingdale, NY, October 4, 1969.
(Edmonton's 1st choice, 22nd overall, in 1990 Supplemental Draft).

			Regular Season								Playoffs						
Season	Club	Lea	GP	W	L	T	Mins	GA	SO	Avg	GP	W	L	Mins	GA	SO	Avg
1987-88	Boston College	H.E.	8	2	2	1	341	30	0	5.28	....	....	....	....	....	....	....
1988-89	Boston College	H.E.	12	6	3	0	525	28	0	3.20	....	....	....	....	....	....	....
1989-90	Boston College	H.E.	22	11	9	1	1235	73	0	3.55	....	....	....	....	....	....	....

GAMBLE, TROY

Goaltender. Catches left. 5'11", 190 lbs. Born, New Glasgow, N.S., April 7, 1967.
(Vancouver's 2nd choice, 25th overall, in 1985 Entry Draft).

			Regular Season								Playoffs						
Season	Club	Lea	GP	W	L	T	Mins	GA	SO	Avg	GP	W	L	Mins	GA	SO	Avg
1984-85a	Medicine Hat	WHL	37	27	6	2	2095	100	3	2.86	2	1	1	120	9	0	4.50
1985-86	Medicine Hat	WHL	45	28	11	0	2264	142	0	3.76	11	5	4	530	31	0	3.51
1986-87	**Vancouver**	**NHL**	**1**	**0**	**1**	**0**	**60**	**4**	**0**	**4.00**	....	....	....	....	....	....	....
	Spokane	WHL	38	17	17	1	2155	163	0	4.54	5	0	5	298	35	0	7.05
	Medicine Hat	WHL	11	7	3	0	646	46	0	4.27	....	....	....	....	....	....	....
1987-88b	Spokane	WHL	67	36	26	1	3824	235	0	3.69	15	7	8	875	56	1	3.84
1988-89	**Vancouver**	**NHL**	**5**	**2**	**3**	**0**	**302**	**12**	**0**	**2.38**	....	....	....	....	....	....	....
	Milwaukee	IHL	42	23	9	0	2198	138	0	3.77	11	5	5	640	35	0	3.28
1989-90	Milwaukee	IHL	*56	22	21	4	2779	160	2	4.21	....	....	....	....	....	....	....
	NHL Totals		**6**	**2**	**4**	**0**	**362**	**16**	**0**	**2.65**	....	....	....	....	....	....	....

a WHL First All-Star Team, East Division (1985)
b WHL First All-Star Team, West Division (1988)

GILMOUR, DARRYL

Goaltender. Catches left. 6', 171 lbs. Born, Winnipeg, Man., February 13, 1967.
(Philadelphia's 3rd choice, 48th overall, in 1985 Entry Draft).

			Regular Season								Playoffs						
Season	Club	Lea	GP	W	L	T	Mins	GA	SO	Avg	GP	W	L	Mins	GA	SO	Avg
1984-85	Moose Jaw	WHL	58	15	35	0	3004	297	0	5.93	....	....	....	....	....	....	....
1985-86a	Moose Jaw	WHL	62	19	34	3	3482	276	1	4.76	9	4	4	490	48	0	5.88
1986-87	Moose Jaw	WHL	31	14	13	2	1776	123	2	4.16	....	....	....	....	....	....	....
	Portland	WHL	24	15	7	1	1460	111	0	4.56	19	12	7	1167	83	1	4.27
1987-88	Hershey	AHL	25	14	7	0	1273	78	1	3.68	....	....	....	....	....	....	....
1988-89	Hershey	AHL	38	16	14	5	2093	144	0	4.13	....	....	....	....	....	....	....
1989-90	New Haven	AHL	23	10	11	2	1356	85	0	3.76	....	....	....	....	....	....	....
	Nashville	ECHL	10	6	3	0	529	43	0	4.87	....	....	....	....	....	....	....

a WHL First All-Star Team, East Division (1986).

GILMORE, MIKE

Goaltender. Catches left. 5'10", 175 lbs. Born, Detroit, MI, March 11, 1968.
(NY Rangers' 1st choice, 18th overall, in 1990 Supplemental Draft).

			Regular Season								Playoffs						
Season	Club	Lea	GP	W	L	T	Mins	GA	SO	Avg	GP	W	L	Mins	GA	SO	Avg
1988-89	Michigan State	CCHA	3	1	0	0	74	5	0	4.04	....	....	....	....	....	....	....
1989-90	Michigan State	CCHA	12	9	1	0	638	29	0	2.73	....	....	....	....	....	....	....

GORDON, SCOTT

Goaltender. Catches left. 5'10", 175 lbs. Born, Brockton, MA, February 6, 1963.

			Regular Season								Playoffs						
Season	Club	Lea	GP	W	L	T	Mins	GA	SO	Avg	GP	W	L	Mins	GA	SO	Avg
1982-83	Boston College	ECAC	9	3	3	0	371	15	0	2.43	...	...	...	...	...	...	...
1983-84	Boston College	ECAC	35	21	13	0	2034	127	1	3.75	...	...	...	...	...	...	...
1984-85	Boston College	H.E.	36	23	11	2	2179	131	1	3.61	...	...	...	...	...	...	...
1985-86a	Boston College	H.E.	32	17	8	1	1852	112	2	3.63	...	...	...	...	...	...	...
1986-87	Fredericton	AHL	32	9	12	2	1616	120	0	4.46	...	...	...	...	...	...	...
1987-88	Baltimore	AHL	34	7	17	3	1638	145	0	5.31	....	....	....	....	....	....	....
1988-89	Halifax	AHL	2	0	2	0	116	10	0	5.17	....	....	....	....	....	....	....
1989-90	**Quebec**	**NHL**	**10**	**2**	**8**	**0**	**597**	**53**	**0**	**5.33**	....	....	....	....	....	....	....
	Halifax	AHL	48	28	16	3	2851	158	0	3.33	6	2	4	340	28	0	4.94
	NHL Totals		**10**	**2**	**8**	**0**	**597**	**53**	**0**	**5.33**	....	....	....	....	....	....	....

a Hockey East First All-Star Team (1986)

Signed as a free agent by **Quebec**, October 2, 1986.

GOSSELIN, MARIO

Goaltender. Catches left. 5'8", 165 lbs. Born, Thetford Mines, Que., June 15, 1963.
(Quebec's 3rd choice, 55th overall, in 1982 Entry Draft).

			Regular Season								Playoffs						
Season	Club	Lea	GP	W	L	T	Mins	GA	SO	Avg	GP	W	L	Mins	GA	SO	Avg
1980-81	Shawinigan	QMJHL	21	4	9	0	907	75	0	4.96	1	0	0	20	2	0	6.00
1981-82a	Shawinigan	QMJHL	60	....	....	....	3404	2496	0	4.05	14	....	....	788	58	0	4.42
1982-83	Shawinigan	QMJHL	46	32	9	1	2496	133	3	3.12	8	5	3	457	29	0	3.81
1983-84	Cdn. Olympic	...	36	....	....	....	2007	126	0	3.77	....	....	....	....	....	....	....
	Quebec	**NHL**	**3**	**2**	**0**	**0**	**148**	**3**	**1**	**1.21**	....	....	....	....	....	....	....
1984-85	**Quebec**	**NHL**	**35**	**19**	**10**	**3**	**1960**	**109**	**1**	**3.34**	**17**	**9**	**8**	**1059**	**54**	**0**	**3.06**
1985-86	**Quebec**	**NHL**	**31**	**14**	**14**	**1**	**1726**	**111**	**2**	**3.86**	**1**	**0**	**1**	**40**	**5**	**0**	**7.50**
	Fredericton	AHL	5	2	2	1	304	15	0	2.96	....	....	....	....	....	....	....
1986-87	**Quebec**	**NHL**	**30**	**13**	**11**	**1**	**1625**	**86**	**0**	**3.18**	**11**	**7**	**4**	**654**	**37**	**0**	**3.39**
1987-88	**Quebec**	**NHL**	**54**	**20**	**28**	**4**	**3002**	**189**	**2**	**3.78**	....	....	....	....	....	....	....
1988-89	**Quebec**	**NHL**	**39**	**11**	**19**	**3**	**2064**	**146**	**0**	**4.24**	....	....	....	....	....	....	....
	Halifax	AHL	3	3	0	0	183	9	0	2.95	....	....	....	....	....	....	....
1989-90	**Los Angeles**	**NHL**	**26**	**7**	**11**	**1**	**1226**	**79**	**0**	**3.87**	**3**	**0**	**2**	**63**	**3**	**0**	**2.90**
	NHL Totals		**218**	**86**	**93**	**13**	**11751**	**723**	**6**	**3.81**	**32**	**16**	**15**	**1815**	**99**	**0**	**3.27**

a QMJHL Second All-Star Team (1982)

Played in NHL All-Star Game (1986)

Signed as a free agent by **Los Angeles**, June 14, 1989.

GRAVEL, FRANCOIS (gruh-VEHL)

Goaltender. Catches right. 6'2", 185 lbs. Born, Ste. Foy, Que., October 21, 1968.
(Montreal's 5th choice, 58th overall, in 1987 Entry Draft).

			Regular Season								Playoffs						
Season	Club	Lea	GP	W	L	T	Mins	GA	SO	Avg	GP	W	L	Mins	GA	SO	Avg
1985-86	St. Jean	QMJHL	42	13	15	2	1827	151	0	4.96	5	3	2	307	38	0	7.42
1986-87	Shawinigan	QMJHL	40	18	17	5	2415	194	0	4.82	11	8	3	678	47	0	4.16
1987-88	Shawinigan	QMJHL	44	19	20	2	2499	200	1	4.80	8	4	4	488	39	0	4.80
1988-89a	Sherbrooke	AHL	33	12	10	3	1625	95	2	3.51	1	1	0	40	3	0	4.50
1989-90	Sherbrooke	AHL	12	4	3	3	545	38	0	4.18	....	....	....	....	....	....	....
	Halifax	AHL	2	0	1	1	125	10	0	4.79	....	....	....	....	....	....	....

a Shared Harry "Hap" Holmes Trophy (fewest goals-against-AHL) with Randy Exelby (1989)

GREENLAY, MIKE

Goaltender. Catches left. 6'3", 200 lbs. Born, Vitoria, Brazil, September 15, 1968.
(Edmonton's 9th choice, 189th overall, in 1986 Entry Draft).

			Regular Season								Playoffs						
Season	Club	Lea	GP	W	L	T	Mins	GA	SO	Avg	GP	W	L	Mins	GA	SO	Avg
1986-87	Lake Superior	CCHA	17	7	5	0	744	44	0	3.54	....	....	....	....	....	....	....
1987-88	Lake Superior	CCHA	19	10	3	3	1023	57	0	3.34	....	....	....	....	....	....	....
1988-89	Saskatoon	WHL	20	10	8	1	1128	86	0	4.57	6	2	0	174	16	0	5.52
	Lake Superior	CCHA	2	1	1	0	85	6	0	4.23	....	....	....	....	....	....	....
1989-90	**Edmonton**	**NHL**	**2**	**0**	**0**	**0**	**20**	**4**	**0**	**12.00**	....	....	....	....	....	....	....
	Cape Breton	AHL	46	19	18	5	2595	146	2	3.38	5	1	3	306	26	0	5.09
	NHL Totals		**2**	**0**	**0**	**0**	**20**	**4**	**0**	**12.00**	....	....	....	....	....	....	....

GREGORIO, MICHAEL

Goaltender. Catches left. 6'2", 180 lbs. Born, Reading, MA, August 17, 1969.
(Toronto's 10th choice, 216th overall, in 1988 Entry Draft).

			Regular Season								Playoffs						
Season	Club	Lea	GP	W	L	T	Mins	GA	SO	Avg	GP	W	L	Mins	GA	SO	Avg
1989-90	Kent State	NCAA	2	0	0	0	38	2	0	3.18	....	....	....	....	....	....	....

GUENETTE, STEVE (guh-NEHT)

Goaltender. Catches left. 5'10", 175 lbs. Born, Gloucester Ont., November 13, 1965.

			Regular Season								Playoffs						
Season	Club	Lea	GP	W	L	T	Mins	GA	SO	Avg	GP	W	L	Mins	GA	SO	Avg
1983-84	Guelph	OHL	38	9	18	2	1808	155	0	5.14	....	....	....	....	....	....	....
1984-85	Guelph	OHL	47	16	22	4	2593	200	1	4.63	....	....	....	....	....	....	....
1985-86a	Guelph	OHL	48	26	20	1	2908	165	*3	3.40	20	15	3	1167	54	1	2.77
1986-87	**Pittsburgh**	**NHL**	**2**	**0**	**2**	**0**	**113**	**8**	**0**	**4.25**	....	....	....	....	....	....	....
	Baltimore	AHL	54	21	23	0	3035	157	5	3.10	....	....	....	....	....	....	....
1987-88	**Pittsburgh**	**NHL**	**19**	**12**	**7**	**0**	**1092**	**61**	**1**	**3.35**	....	....	....	....	....	....	....
bc	Muskegon	IHL	33	23	4	5	1943	91	*4	*2.81	....	....	....	....	....	....	....
1988-89	**Pittsburgh**	**NHL**	**11**	**5**	**6**	**0**	**574**	**41**	**0**	**4.29**	....	....	....	....	....	....	....
	Muskegon	IHL	10	6	4	0	597	39	0	*3.92	....	....	....	....	....	....	....
c	Salt Lake	IHL	30	24	5	0	1810	82	2	*2.72	*13	*8	5	*782	44	0	3.38
1989-90	**Calgary**	**NHL**	**2**	**1**	**1**	**0**	**119**	**8**	**0**	**4.03**	....	....	....	....	....	....	....
	Salt Lake	IHL	47	22	21	4	2779	160	0	3.45	*10	4	4	545	35	*1	3.85
	NHL Totals		**34**	**18**	**16**	**0**	**1898**	**118**	**1**	**3.73**	....	....	....	....	....	....	....

a OHL Second All-Star Team (1986)
b Won James Norris Memorial Trophy (IHL Top Goaltender) (1988, 1989)
c IHL Second All-Star Team (1988, 1989)

Signed as a free agent by **Pittsburgh**, April 6, 1985. Traded to **Calgary** by **Pittsburgh** for Calgary's sixth-round choice (Mike Needham) in 1989 Entry Draft, January 9, 1989.

HACKETT, JEFF

Goaltender. Catches left. 6'1", 175 lbs. Born, London, Ont., June 1, 1968.
(NY Islanders's 2nd choice, 34th overall, in 1987 Entry Draft).

			Regular Season								Playoffs						
Season	Club	Lea	GP	W	L	T	Mins	GA	SO	Avg	GP	W	L	Mins	GA	SO	Avg
1986-87	Oshawa	OHL	31	18	9	2	1672	85	2	3.05	15	8	7	895	40	0	2.68
1987-88a	Oshawa	OHL	53	30	21	2	3165	205	0	3.89	7	3	4	438	31	0	4.25
1988-89	**NY Islanders**	**NHL**	**13**	**4**	**7**	**0**	**662**	**39**	**0**	**3.53**	....	....	....	....	....	....	....
	Springfield	AHL	29	12	14	2	1677	116	0	4.15	....	....	....	....	....	....	....
1989-90b	Springfield	AHL	54	24	25	3	3045	187	1	3.68	*17	*10	5	934	60	0	3.85
	NHL Totals		**13**	**4**	**7**	**0**	**662**	**39**	**0**	**3.53**	....	....	....	....	....	....	....

a OHL Third All-Star Team (1988)
b Won Jack Butterfield Trophy (Playoff MVP-AHL) (1990)

HANLON, GLEN

Goaltender. Catches right. 6', 185 lbs. Born, Brandon, Man., February 20, 1957.
(Vancouver's 3rd choice, 40th overall, in 1977 Amateur Draft).

			Regular Season								Playoffs						
Season	Club	Lea	GP	W	L	T	Mins	GA	SO	Avg	GP	W	L	Mins	GA	SO	Avg
1974-75	Brandon	WHL	43	....	....	....	2498	176	0	4.22	5	....	....	284	29	0	6.12
1975-76a	Brandon	WHL	64	....	....	....	3523	234	4	3.99	5	....	....	300	33	0	6.60
1976-77a	Brandon	WHL	65	....	....	....	3784	195	*4	*3.09	16	....	....	914	53	0	3.48
1977-78	**Vancouver**	**NHL**	**4**	**1**	**2**	**1**	**200**	**9**	**0**	**2.70**	....	....	....	....	....	....	....
bc	Tulsa	CHL	53	....	....	....	3123	160	*3	3.07	2	....	....	120	5	0	*2.50
1978-79	**Vancouver**	**NHL**	**31**	**12**	**13**	**5**	**1821**	**94**	**3**	**3.10**	....	....	....	....	....	....	....
1979-80	**Vancouver**	**NHL**	**57**	**17**	**29**	**10**	**3341**	**193**	**0**	**3.47**	**2**	**0**	**0**	**60**	**3**	**0**	**3.00**
1980-81	**Vancouver**	**NHL**	**17**	**5**	**8**	**0**	**798**	**59**	**1**	**4.44**	....	....	....	....	....	....	....
	Dallas	CHL	4	3	1	0	239	8	1	2.01	....	....	....	....	....	....	....
1981-82	**Vancouver**	**NHL**	**28**	**8**	**14**	**5**	**1610**	**106**	**1**	**3.95**	....	....	....	....	....	....	....
	St. Louis	**NHL**	**2**	**0**	**1**	**0**	**76**	**8**	**0**	**6.30**	**3**	**0**	**2**	**109**	**9**	**0**	**4.95**
1982-83	**St. Louis**	**NHL**	**14**	**3**	**8**	**1**	**671**	**50**	**0**	**4.47**	....	....	....	....	....	....	....
	NY Rangers	**NHL**	**21**	**9**	**10**	**1**	**1173**	**67**	**0**	**3.43**	**1**	**0**	**1**	**60**	**5**	**0**	**5.00**
1983-84	**NY Rangers**	**NHL**	**50**	**28**	**14**	**4**	**2837**	**166**	**1**	**3.51**	**5**	**2**	**3**	**308**	**13**	**1**	**2.53**
1984-85	**NY Rangers**	**NHL**	**44**	**14**	**20**	**7**	**2510**	**175**	**0**	**4.18**	**3**	**0**	**3**	**168**	**14**	**0**	**5.00**
1985-86	**NY Rangers**	**NHL**	**23**	**5**	**12**	**1**	**1170**	**65**	**0**	**3.33**	**3**	**0**	**0**	**75**	**6**	**0**	**4.80**
	Adirondack	AHL	10	5	4	1	605	33	0	3.27	....	....	....	....	....	....	....
	New Haven	AHL	5	3	2	0	279	22	0	4.73	....	....	....	....	....	....	....
1986-87	**Detroit**	**NHL**	**36**	**11**	**16**	**5**	**1963**	**104**	**1**	**3.18**	**8**	**5**	**2**	**467**	**13**	***2**	**1.67**
1987-88	**Detroit**	**NHL**	**47**	**22**	**17**	**5**	**2623**	**141**	***4**	**3.23**	**8**	**4**	**3**	**431**	**22**	***1**	**3.06**
1988-89	**Detroit**	**NHL**	**39**	**13**	**14**	**8**	**2092**	**124**	**1**	**3.56**	**2**	**0**	**1**	**78**	**7**	**0**	**5.38**
1989-90	**Detroit**	**NHL**	**45**	**15**	**18**	**5**	**2290**	**154**	**1**	**4.03**	....	....	....	....	....	....	....
	NHL Totals		**458**	**163**	**196**	**58**	**25175**	**1515**	**13**	**3.61**	**35**	**11**	**14**	**1756**	**92**	**4**	**3.14**

a WHL First All-Star Team (1976, 1977)
b CHL Rookie of the Year (1978)
c CHL First All-Star Team (1978)

Traded to **St. Louis** by **Vancouver** for Tony Currie, Jim Nill, Rick Heinz and St. Louis' fourth round choice (Shawn Kilroy) in 1982 Entry Draft, March 9, 1982. Traded to **NY Rangers** by **St. Louis** with Vaclav Nedomansky for Andre Dore, January 4, 1983. Traded to **Detroit** by **NY Rangers** with New York's third round choices in 1987 (Dennis Holland) and 1988 (Guy Dupuis) Entry Drafts for Kelly Kisio, Lane Lambert and Jim Leavins, July 29, 1986.

HANSCH, RANDY

Goaltender. Catches right. 5'11", 165 lbs. Born, Edmonton, Alta., February 8, 1966.
(Detroit's 5th choice, 112th overall, in 1984 Entry Draft).

			Regular Season								Playoffs						
Season	Club	Lea	GP	W	L	T	Mins	GA	SO	Avg	GP	W	L	Mins	GA	SO	Avg
1983-84	Victoria	WHL	36	12	19	0	1894	144	0	4.56	....	....	....	....	....	....	....
1984-85	Victoria	WHL	52	17	28	3	3021	260	0	5.16	....	....	....	....	....	....	....
1985-86	Kamloops	WHL	31	10	21	0	1821	172	0	5.67	14	11	2	820	36	1	2.63
1986-87	Kalamazoo	IHL	16	8	7	0	926	60	2	3.88	....	....	....	....	....	....	....
	Adirondack	AHL	10	6	4	0	544	36	0	3.97	10	5	4	579	34	0	3.52
1987-88			DID NOT PLAY-INJURED														
1988-89	Cdn. National	....	29	9	12	4	1489	96	0	3.86	....	....	....	....	....	....	....
1989-90	Hampton-Roads	ECHL	4	1	3	0	240	20	0	5.00	....	....	....	....	....	....	....

HARRIS, PETER

Goaltender. Catches left. 6'2", 210 lbs. Born, Haverhill, MA, April 22, 1968.
(NY Islanders' 8th choice, 164th overall, in 1986 Entry Draft).

			Regular Season								Playoffs						
Season	Club	Lea	GP	W	L	T	Mins	GA	SO	Avg	GP	W	L	Mins	GA	SO	Avg
1986-87	U. of Lowell	H.E.	6	1	2	1	279	22	0	4.73	....	....	....	....	....	....	....
1987-88	U. of Lowell	H.E.	DID NOT PLAY														
1988-89	U. of Lowell	H.E.	9	1	2	0	401	29	0	4.34	....	....	....	....	....	....	....
1989-90	U. of Lowell	H.E.	1	0	0	0	31	3	0	5.86	....	....	....	....	....	....	....

HARVEY, CHRIS

Goaltender. Catches left. 6'1", 180 lbs. Born, Cambridge, MA, December 8, 1967.
(Boston's 1st choice, 23rd overall, in 1988 Supplemental Draft).

			Regular Season								Playoffs						
Season	Club	Lea	GP	W	L	T	Mins	GA	SO	Avg	GP	W	L	Mins	GA	SO	Avg
1986-87	Brown	ECAC	22	9	13	0	1241	88	0	4.26	....	....	....	....	....	....	....
1987-88	Brown	ECAC	21	3	17	1	1235	104	0	5.05	....	....	....	....	....	....	....
1988-89	Brown	ECAC	23	1	22	0	1327	131	0	5.92	....	....	....	....	....	....	....
1989-90ab	Brown	ECAC	28	10	15	3	1646	107	0	3.90	....	....	....	....	....	....	....

a ECAC Second All-Star Team (1990)
b NCAA East Second All-American Team (1990)

HASEK, DOMINIK

Goaltender. Catches left. 6', 175 lbs. Born, Pardubice, Czechoslovakia, January 29, 1965.
(Chicago's 11th choice, 199th overall, in 1983 Entry Draft).

			Regular Season								Playoffs						
Season	Club	Lea	GP	W	L	T	Mins	GA	SO	Avg	GP	W	L	Mins	GA	SO	Avg
1981-82	Pardubice	Czech.	12	....	....	....	661	34	....	3.09	....	....	....	....	....	....	....
1982-83	Pardubice	Czech.	42	....	....	....	2358	105	....	2.67	....	....	....	....	....	....	....
1983-84	Pardubice	Czech.	40	....	....	....	2304	108	....	2.81	....	....	....	....	....	....	....
1984-85	Pardubice	Czech.	42	....	....	....	2419	131	....	3.25	....	....	....	....	....	....	....
1985-86a	Pardubice	Czech.	45	....	....	....	2689	138	....	3.08	....	....	....	....	....	....	....
1986-87ab	Pardubice	Czech.	43	....	....	....	2515	103	....	2.46	....	....	....	....	....	....	....
1987-88ac	Pardubice	Czech.	31	....	....	....	2265	98	....	2.60	....	....	....	....	....	....	....
1988-89abc	Pardubice	Czech.	42	....	....	....	2507	114	....	2.73	....	....	....	....	....	....	....
1989-90abc	Dukla Jihlava	Czech.	40	....	....	....	2251	80	....	2.13	....	....	....	....	....	....	....

a Czechoslovakian Goaltender-of-the-Year (1986, 1987, 1988, 1989, 1990).
b Czechoslovakian Player-of-the-Year (1987, 1989, 1990).
c Czechoslovakian First-Team All-Star (1988, 1989, 1990).

HAYWARD, BRIAN

Goaltender. Catches left. 5'10", 180 lbs. Born, Weston, Ont., June 25, 1960.

			Regular Season								Playoffs						
Season	Club	Lea	GP	W	L	T	Mins	GA	SO	Avg	GP	W	L	Mins	GA	SO	Avg
1978-79	Cornell	ECAC	25	18	6	0	1469	95	0	3.88	3	2	1	179	14	0	4.66
1979-80	Cornell	ECAC	12	2	7	0	508	52	0	6.02	....	....	....	....	....	....	....
1980-81	Cornell	ECAC	19	11	4	1	967	58	1	3.54	4	2	1	181	18	0	4.50
1981-82ab	Cornell	ECAC	22	11	10	1	1320	68	0	3.09	....	....	....	....	....	....	....
1982-83	Sherbrooke	AHL	22	6	11	3	1208	89	1	4.42	....	....	....	....	....	....	....
	Winnipeg	**NHL**	**24**	**10**	**12**	**2**	**1440**	**89**	**1**	**3.71**	**3**	**0**	**3**	**160**	**14**	**0**	**5.24**
1983-84	**Winnipeg**	**NHL**	**28**	**7**	**18**	**2**	**1530**	**124**	**0**	**4.86**	....	....	....	....	....	....	....
	Sherbrooke	AHL	15	4	8	0	781	69	0	5.30	....	....	....	....	....	....	....
1984-85	**Winnipeg**	**NHL**	**61**	**33**	**17**	**7**	**3436**	**220**	**0**	**3.84**	**6**	**2**	**4**	**309**	**23**	**0**	**4.47**
1985-86	**Winnipeg**	**NHL**	**52**	**13**	**28**	**5**	**2721**	**217**	**0**	**4.79**	**2**	**0**	**1**	**68**	**6**	**0**	**5.29**
	Sherbrooke	AHL	3	2	0	1	185	5	0	1.62	....	....	....	....	....	....	....
1986-87c	**Montreal**	**NHL**	**37**	**19**	**13**	**4**	**2178**	**102**	**1**	***2.81**	**13**	**6**	**5**	**708**	**32**	**0**	**2.71**
1987-88c	**Montreal**	**NHL**	**39**	**22**	**10**	**4**	**2247**	**107**	**2**	**2.86**	**4**	**2**	**2**	**230**	**9**	**0**	**2.35**
1988-89c	**Montreal**	**NHL**	**36**	**20**	**13**	**3**	**2091**	**101**	**1**	**2.90**	**2**	**1**	**1**	**124**	**7**	**0**	**3.39**
1989-90	**Montreal**	**NHL**	**29**	**10**	**12**	**6**	**1647**	**94**	**1**	**3.37**	**1**	**0**	**0**	**33**	**2**	**0**	**3.64**
	NHL Totals		**306**	**134**	**123**	**33**	**17290**	**1054**	**6**	**3.66**	**31**	**11**	**16**	**1632**	**93**	**0**	**3.42**

a ECAC First All-Star Team (1982)
b NCAA All-America Team (1982)
c Shared William Jennings Trophy with Patrick Roy (1987, 1988, 1989)

Signed as a free agent by **Winnipeg**, May 5, 1982. Traded to **Montreal** by **Winnipeg** for Steve Penney and the rights to Jan Ingman, August 19, 1986

HEALY, GLENN

Goaltender. Catches left. 5'10", 185 lbs. Born, Pickering, Ont., August 23, 1962.

			Regular Season								Playoffs						
Season	Club	Lea	GP	W	L	T	Mins	GA	SO	Avg	GP	W	L	Mins	GA	SO	Avg
1981-82	W. Michigan	CCHA	27	7	19	1	1569	116	0	4.44	....	....	....	....	....	....	....
1982-83	W. Michigan	CCHA	30	8	19	2	1732	116	0	4.01	....	....	....	....	....	....	....
1983-84	W. Michigan	CCHA	38	19	16	3	2241	146	0	3.90	....	....	....	....	....	....	....
1984-85	W. Michigan	CCHA	37	21	14	2	2171	118	0	3.26	....	....	....	....	....	....	....
1985-86	New Haven	AHL	43	21	15	4	2410	160	0	3.98	2	0	2	49	11	0	5.55
	Los Angeles	**NHL**	**1**	**0**	**0**	**0**	**51**	**6**	**0**	**7.06**	....	....	....	....	....	....	....
1986-87	New Haven	AHL	47	21	15	0	2828	173	1	3.67	7	3	4	427	19	0	2.67
1987-88	**Los Angeles**	**NHL**	**34**	**12**	**18**	**1**	**1869**	**135**	**1**	**4.33**	**4**	**1**	**3**	**240**	**20**	**0**	**5.00**
1988-89	**Los Angeles**	**NHL**	**48**	**25**	**19**	**2**	**2699**	**192**	**0**	**4.27**	**3**	**0**	**1**	**97**	**6**	**0**	**3.71**
1989-90	**NY Islanders**	**NHL**	**39**	**12**	**19**	**6**	**2197**	**128**	**2**	**3.50**	**4**	**1**	**2**	**166**	**9**	**0**	**3.25**
	NHL Totals		**122**	**49**	**56**	**9**	**6816**	**461**	**3**	**4.05**	**11**	**2**	**6**	**503**	**35**	**0**	**4.17**

Signed as a free agent by **Los Angeles**, June 13, 1985. Signed as a free agent by **NY Islanders**, August 16, 1989.

HEBERT, GUY (HEE-buhrt, GIGH)

Goaltender. Catches left. 5'8", 180 lbs. Born, Troy, NY, January 7, 1967.
(St. Louis' 8th choice, 159th overall, in 1987 Entry Draft).

			Regular Season								Playoffs						
Season	Club	Lea	GP	W	L	T	Mins	GA	SO	Avg	GP	W	L	Mins	GA	SO	Avg
1986-87	Hamilton Col.	NCAA	18	12	5	0	1070	40	0	2.19	....	....	....	....	....	....	....
1987-88	Hamilton Col.	NCAA	8	5	3	0	450	19	0	2.53	....	....	....	....	....	....	....
1988-89	Hamilton Col.	NCAA	25	18	7	0	1453	62	0	2.56	....	....	....	....	....	....	....
1989-90	Peoria	IHL	30	7	13	7	1706	124	1	4.36	2	0	1	76	5	0	3.95

HEINKE, MICHAEL

Goaltender. Catches left. 5'11", 165 lbs. Born, Denville, NY, January 11, 1971.
(New Jersey's 5th choice, 89th overall, in 1989 Entry Draft).

			Regular Season								Playoffs						
Season	Club	Lea	GP	W	L	T	Mins	GA	SO	Avg	GP	W	L	Mins	GA	SO	Avg
1988-89	Avon Old Farms	HS	23	....	....	....	1035	63	2	2.74	....	....	....	....	....	....	....
1989-90	Avon Old Farms	HS	23	....	....	....	1020	42	0	1.85	....	....	....	....	....	....	....

HEXTALL, RON

Goaltender. Catches left. 6'3", 192 lbs. Born, Winnipeg, Man., May 3, 1964.
(Philadelphia's 6th choice, 119th overall, in 1982 Entry Draft).

			Regular Season								Playoffs						
Season	Club	Lea	GP	W	L	T	Mins	GA	SO	Avg	GP	W	L	Mins	GA	SO	Avg
1981-82	Brandon	WHL	30	12	11	0	1398	133	0	5.71	3	0	2	103	16	0	9.32
1982-83	Brandon	WHL	44	13	30	0	2589	249	0	5.77							
1983-84	Brandon	WHL	46	29	13	2	2670	190	0	4.27	10	5	5	592	37	0	3.75
1984-85	Hershey	AHL	11	4	6	0	555	34	0	3.68							
	Kalamazoo	IHL	19	6	11	1	1103	80	0	4.35							
1985-86ab	Hershey	AHL	*53	30	19	2	*3061	174	*5	3.41	13	5	7	780	42	*1	3.23
1986-87cdef	**Philadelphia**	**NHL**	***66**	**37**	**21**	**6**	***3799**	**190**	**1**	**3.00**	***26**	**15**	**11**	***1540**	**71**	***2**	**2.77**
1987-88g	**Philadelphia**	**NHL**	**62**	**30**	**22**	**7**	**3561**	**208**	**0**	**3.50**	**7**	**2**	**4**	**379**	**30**	**0**	**4.75**
1988-89h	**Philadelphia**	**NHL**	***64**	**30**	**28**	**6**	***3756**	**202**	**0**	**3.23**	**15**	**8**	**7**	**886**	**49**	**0**	**3.32**
1989-90	**Philadelphia**	**NHL**	**8**	**4**	**2**	**1**	**419**	**29**	**0**	**4.15**							
	Hershey	AHL	1	1	0	0	49	3	0	3.67							
	NHL Totals		**200**	**101**	**73**	**20**	**11535**	**629**	**1**	**3.27**	**48**	**25**	**22**	**2805**	**150**	**2**	**3.21**

a AHL First All-Star Team (1986)
b AHL Rookie of the Year (1986)
c NHL First All-Star Team (1987)
d Won Vezina Trophy (1987)
e Won Conn Smythe Trophy (1987)
f NHL All-Rookie Team (1987)
g Scored a goal vs. Boston, December 8, 1987
h Scored a goal in playoffs vs. Washington, April 11, 1989

Played in NHL All-Star Game (1988)

HOFFORT, BRUCE

Goaltender. Catches left. 5'10", 185 lbs. Born, North Battleford, Sask., July 30, 1966.

			Regular Season								Playoffs						
Season	Club	Lea	GP	W	L	T	Mins	GA	SO	Avg	GP	W	L	Mins	GA	SO	Avg
1987-88ab	Lake Superior	CCHA	31	23	4	3	1787	79	2	2.65							
1988-89ac	Lake Superior	CCHA	44	27	10	5	2595	117	0	2.71							
1989-90	**Philadelphia**	**NHL**	**7**	**3**	**0**	**2**	**329**	**20**	**0**	**3.65**							
	Hershey	AHL	40	16	18	4	2284	139	1	3.65							
	NHL Totals		**7**	**3**	**0**	**2**	**329**	**20**	**0**	**3.65**							

a CCHA First All-Star Team (1988, 1989)
b NCAA All-Tournament Team (1988)
c CCHA Player of the Year (1989)

Signed as free agent by **Philadelphia**, June 30, 1989.

HRIVNAK, JIM

Goaltender. Catches left. 6'2", 185 lbs. Born, Montreal, Que., May 28, 1968.
(Edmonton's 4th choice, 61st overall, in 1986 Entry Draft).

			Regular Season								Playoffs						
Season	Club	Lea	GP	W	L	T	Mins	GA	SO	Avg	GP	W	L	Mins	GA	SO	Avg
1985-86	Merrimack	NCAA	21	12	8	0	1230	75	0	3.66							
1986-87	Merrimack	NCAA	34	27	7	0	1618	58	3	2.14							
1987-88	Merrimack	NCAA	37	31	6	0	2119	84	4	2.38							
1988-89	Baltimore	AHL	10	1	8	0	502	55	0	6.57							
1989-90	**Washington**	**NHL**	**11**	**5**	**5**	**0**	**609**	**36**	**0**	**3.55**							
a	Baltimore	AHL	47	24	19	2	2722	139	*4	3.06	6	4	2	360	19	0	3.17
	NHL Totals		**11**	**5**	**5**	**0**	**609**	**36**	**0**	**3.55**							

a AHL Second All-Star Team (1990)

HRUDEY, KELLY STEPHEN (ROO-dee)

Goaltender. Catches left. 5'10", 180 lbs. Born, Edmonton, Alta., January 13, 1961.
(NY Islanders' 2nd choice, 38th overall, in 1980 Entry Draft).

			Regular Season								Playoffs						
Season	Club	Lea	GP	W	L	T	Mins	GA	SO	Avg	GP	W	L	Mins	GA	SO	Avg
1978-79	Medicine Hat	WHL	57	12	34	7	3093	318	0	6.17							
1979-80	Medicine Hat	WHL	57	25	23	4	3049	212	1	4.17	13	6	6	638	48	0	4.51
1980-81a	Medicine Hat	WHL	55	32	19	1	3023	200	4	3.97	4			244	17	0	4.18
	Indianapolis	CHL									2			135	8	0	3.56
1981-82bc	Indianapolis	CHL	51	27	19	4	3033	149	1	*2.95	13	11	2	842	34	*1	*2.42
1982-83bcd	Indianapolis	CHL	47	*26	17	1	2744	139	2	3.04	10	*7	3	*637	28	0	*2.64
1983-84	Indianapolis	CHL	6	3	2	1	370	21	0	3.40							
	NY Islanders	**NHL**	**12**	**7**	**2**	**0**	**535**	**28**	**0**	**3.14**							
1984-85	**NY Islanders**	**NHL**	**41**	**19**	**17**	**3**	**2335**	**141**	**2**	**3.62**	**5**	**1**	**3**	**281**	**8**	**0**	**1.71**
1985-86	**NY Islanders**	**NHL**	**45**	**19**	**15**	**8**	**2563**	**137**	**1**	**3.21**	**2**	**0**	**2**	**120**	**6**	**0**	**3.00**
1986-87	**NY Islanders**	**NHL**	**46**	**21**	**15**	**7**	**2634**	**145**	**0**	**3.30**	**14**	**7**	**7**	**842**	**38**	**0**	**2.71**
1987-88	**NY Islanders**	**NHL**	**47**	**22**	**17**	**5**	**2751**	**153**	**3**	**3.34**	**6**	**2**	**4**	**381**	**23**	**0**	**3.62**
1988-89	**NY Islanders**	**NHL**	**50**	**18**	**24**	**3**	**2800**	**183**	**0**	**3.92**							
	Los Angeles	**NHL**	**16**	**10**	**4**	**2**	**974**	**47**	**1**	**2.90**	**10**	**4**	**6**	**566**	**35**	**0**	**3.71**
1989-90	**Los Angeles**	**NHL**	**52**	**22**	**21**	**6**	**2860**	**194**	**2**	**4.07**	**9**	**4**	**4**	**539**	**39**	**0**	**4.34**
	NHL Totals		**309**	**138**	**115**	**34**	**17452**	**1028**	**9**	**3.53**	**46**	**18**	**26**	**2729**	**149**	**0**	**3.28**

a WHL Second All-Star Team (1981)
b CHL First All-Star Team (1982, 1983)
c Shared Terry Sawchuk Trophy (CHL's Leading Goaltenders) with Rob Holland (1982, 1983)
d Won Tommy Ivan Trophy (CHL's Most Valuable Player) (1983)

Traded to **Los Angeles** by **NY Islanders** for Mark Fitzpatrick, Wayne McBean and future considerations (Doug Crossman, acquired May 23, 1989) February 22, 1989.

HUGHES, CHARLES

Goaltender. Catches right. 5'8", 165 lbs. Born, Quincy, MA, January 30, 1970.
(New Jersey's 13th choice, 222nd overall, in 1988 Entry Draft).

			Regular Season								Playoffs						
Season	Club	Lea	GP	W	L	T	Mins	GA	SO	Avg	GP	W	L	Mins	GA	SO	Avg
1988-89	Harvard	ECAC	17	15	1	0	990	46	1	2.79							
1989-90	Harvard	ECAC	11	5	5	1	669	43	0	3.86							

ING, PETER

Goaltender. Catches left. 6'2", 165 lbs. Born, Toronto, Ont., April 28, 1969.
(Toronto's 3rd choice, 48th overall, in 1988 Entry Draft).

			Regular Season								Playoffs						
Season	Club	Lea	GP	W	L	T	Mins	GA	SO	Avg	GP	W	L	Mins	GA	SO	Avg
1986-87	Windsor	OHL	28	13	11	3	1615	105	0	3.90	5	4	0	161	9	0	3.35
1987-88	Windsor	OHL	43	30	7	1	2422	125	2	3.10	3	2	0	225	7	0	1.87
1988-89	Windsor	OHL	19	7	7	3	1043	76	*1	4.37							
a	London	OHL	32	18	11	2	1848	104	*2	3.38	21	11	9	1093	82	0	4.50
1989-90	**Toronto**	**NHL**	**3**	**0**	**2**	**1**	**182**	**18**	**0**	**5.93**							
	Newmarket	AHL	48	16	19	12	2829	184	0	3.90							
	London	OHL	8	6	2	0	480	27	0	3.38							
	NHL Totals		**3**	**0**	**2**	**1**	**182**	**18**	**0**	**5.93**							

a OHL Third All-Star Team (1989)

IRBE, ARTUR

Goaltender. Catches left. 5'7", 180 lbs. Born, Riga, Soviet Union, February 2, 1967.
(Minnesota's 10th choice, 196th overall, in 1989 Entry Draft).

			Regular Season								Playoffs						
Season	Club	Lea	GP	W	L	T	Mins	GA	SO	Avg	GP	W	L	Mins	GA	SO	Avg
1986-87	Dynamo Riga	USSR	2				27	1	0	2.22							
1987-88a	Dynamo Riga	USSR	34				1870	84	0	2.69							
1988-89	Dynamo Riga	USSR	41				2460	117	0	2.85							
1989-90	Dynamo Riga	USSR	48				2880	116	0	2.42							

a Soviet National League Rookie-of-the-Year (1988)

JABLONSKI, PAT

Goaltender. Catches right. 6', 175 lbs. Born, Toledo, OH, June 20, 1967.
(St. Louis' 6th choice, 138th overall, in 1985 Entry Draft).

			Regular Season								Playoffs						
Season	Club	Lea	GP	W	L	T	Mins	GA	SO	Avg	GP	W	L	Mins	GA	SO	Avg
1985-86	Windsor	OHL	29	6	16	4	1600	119	1	4.46	6	0	3	263	20	0	4.56
1986-87	Windsor	OHL	41	22	14	2	2328	128	*3	3.30	12	8	4	710	38	0	3.21
1987-88	Peoria	IHL	5	2	2	1	285	17	0	3.58							
	Windsor	OHL	18	14	3	0	994	48	2	*2.90	9	*8	0	537	28	0	3.13
1988-89	Peoria	IHL	35	11	20	0	2051	163	1	4.77	3	0	2	130	13	0	6.00
1989-90	**St. Louis**	**NHL**	**4**	**0**	**3**	**0**	**280**	**17**	**0**	**4.90**							
	Peoria	IHL	36	14	17	4	2023	165	0	4.89	4	1	3	223	19	0	5.11
	NHL Totals		**4**	**0**	**3**	**0**	**280**	**17**	**0**	**4.90**							

JEFFREY, MIKE

Goaltender. Catches right. 6'3", 195 lbs. Born, Kamloops, B.C., April 6, 1965.
(Boston's 1st choice, 19th overall, in 1987 Supplemental Draft).

			Regular Season								Playoffs						
Season	Club	Lea	GP	W	L	T	Mins	GA	SO	Avg	GP	W	L	Mins	GA	SO	Avg
1984-85	N. Michigan	WCHA	12	7	3	0	573	44	0	4.61							
1985-86	N. Michigan	WCHA	15	5	6	0	743	58	0	4.69							
1986-87	N. Michigan	WCHA	28	13	12	1	1601	102	0	3.82							
1987-88	N. Michigan	WCHA	30	13	13	4	1801	107	0	3.56							
1988-89	Maine	AHL	44	16	22	2	2368	148	1	3.75							
1989-90	Maine	AHL	13	6	4	0	633	46	0	4.36							
	Johnstown	IHL	14	5	6	1	755	49	0	3.89							

JOSEPH, CURTIS

Goaltender. Catches left. 5'10", 182 lbs. Born, Keswick, Ont., April 29, 1967.

			Regular Season								Playoffs						
Season	Club	Lea	GP	W	L	T	Mins	GA	SO	Avg	GP	W	L	Mins	GA	SO	Avg
1988-89abc	U. Wisconsin	WCHA	38	21	11	5	2267	94	1	2.49							
1989-90	**St. Louis**	**NHL**	**15**	**9**	**5**	**1**	**852**	**48**	**0**	**3.38**	**6**	**4**	**1**	**327**	**18**	**0**	**3.30**
	Peoria	IHL	23	10	8	2	1241	80	0	3.87							
	NHL Totals		**15**	**9**	**5**	**1**	**852**	**48**	**0**	**3.38**	**6**	**4**	**1**	**327**	**18**	**0**	**3.30**

a WCHA First All-Star Team (1989)
b WCHA Player of the Year (1989)
c WCHA Rookie of the Year (1989)

Signed as a free agent by **St. Louis**, June 16, 1989.

KIDD, TREVOR

Goaltender. Catches left. 6'2", 176 lbs. Born, St. Boniface, Man., March 29, 1972.
(Calgary's 1st choice, 12th overall, in 1990 Entry Draft).

			Regular Season								Playoffs						
Season	Club	Lea	GP	W	L	T	Mins	GA	SO	Avg	GP	W	L	Mins	GA	SO	Avg
1988-89	Brandon	WHL	32				1509	102	0	4.06							
1989-90a	Brandon	WHL	*63	24	32	2	*3676	254	2	3.15							

a WHL East First All-Star Team (1990)

KING, SCOTT

Goaltender. Catches left. 6'1", 170 lbs. Born, Thunder Bay, Ont., June 25, 1967.
(Detroit's 10th choice, 190th overall, in 1986 Entry Draft).

			Regular Season								Playoffs						
Season	Club	Lea	GP	W	L	T	Mins	GA	SO	Avg	GP	W	L	Mins	GA	SO	Avg
1986-87	U. of Maine	H.E.	21	11	6	1	1111	58	0	3.13							
1987-88a	U. of Maine	H.E.	33	25	5	1	1761	91	0	3.10							
1988-89a	U. of Maine	H.E.	27	13	8	0	1394	83	0	3.57							
1989-90b	U. of Maine	H.E.	29	17	7	2	1526	67	1	2.63							

a Hockey East Second All-Star Team (1988, 1989)
b Hockey East First All-Star Team (1990).

KNICKLE, RICHARD (RICK)

Goaltender. Catches left. 5'10", 155 lbs. Born, Chatham, N.B., February 26, 1960.
(Buffalo's 7th choice, 116th overall, in 1979 Entry Draft).

			Regular Season								Playoffs						
Season	Club	Lea	GP	W	L	T	Mins	GA	SO	Avg	GP	W	L	Mins	GA	SO	Avg
1977-78	Brandon	WHL	49	34	5	7	2806	182	0	3.89	8	....	....	450	36	0	4.82
1978-79a	Brandon	WHL	38	26	3	8	2240	118	1	*3.16	16	12	3	886	41	*1	*2.78
1979-80	Brandon	WHL	33	11	14	1	1604	125	0	4.68	....	....	....	....	....	....	....
	Muskegon	IHL	16	....	....	....	829	52	0	3.76	3	....	....	156	17	0	6.54
1980-81b	Erie	EHL	43	....	....	....	2347	125	1	*3.20	8	....	....	446	14	0	*1.88
1981-82	Rochester	AHL	31	10	12	5	1753	108	1	3.70	3	0	2	125	7	0	3.37
1982-83	Flint	IHL	27	....	....	....	1638	92	2	3.37	3	....	....	193	10	0	3.11
	Rochester	AHL	4	....	....	....	143	11	0	4.64	....	....	....	....	....	....	....
1983-84c	Flint	IHL	60	32	21	5	3518	203	3	3.46	8	8	0	480	24	0	3.00
1984-85	Sherbrooke	AHL	14	7	6	0	780	53	0	4.08	....	....	....	....	....	....	....
	Flint	IHL	36	18	11	3	2018	115	2	3.42	7	3	4	401	27	0	4.04
1985-86	Saginaw	IHL	39	16	15	0	2235	135	2	3.62	3	2	1	193	12	0	3.73
1986-87	Saginaw	IHL	26	9	13	0	1413	113	0	4.80	5	1	4	329	21	0	3.83
1987-88	Flint	IHL	1	0	1	0	60	4		4.00	....	....	....	....	....	....	
	Peoria	IHL	13	2	8	1	705	58		4.94	6	3	3	294	20		4.08
1988-89de	Fort Wayne	IHL	47	22	16	0	2716	141	1	*3.11	4	1	2	173	15	0	5.20
1989-90	Flint	IHL	55	25	24	1	2998	210	1	4.20	2	0	2	101	13	0	7.72

a WHL First All-Star Team (1979)
b EHL First All-Star Team (1981)
c IHL Second All-Star Team (1984)
d IHL First All-Star Team (1989)
e Won James Norris Memorial Trophy (Top Goaltender-IHL) (1989)

Signed as a free agent by **Montreal,** February 8, 1985.

KOLZIG, OLAF

Goaltender. Catches left. 6'3", 205 lbs. Born, Johannesburg, South Africa, April 6, 1970.
(Washington's 1st choice, 19th overall, in 1989 Entry Draft).

			Regular Season								Playoffs						
Season	Club	Lea	GP	W	L	T	Mins	GA	SO	Avg	GP	W	L	Mins	GA	SO	Avg
1987-88	N. Westminster	WHL	15	6	5	0	650	48	1	4.43	3	....	....	149	11	0	4.43
1988-89	Tri-Cities	WHL	30	16	10	2	1671	97	1	*3.48	....	....	....	....	....	....	....
1989-90	**Washington**	**NHL**	**2**	**0**	**2**	**0**	**120**	**12**	**0**	**6.00**	....	....	....	....	....	....	....
	Tri-Cities	WHL	48	27	27	3	2504	250	1	4.38	6	4	0	318	27	0	5.09
	NHL Totals		**2**	**0**	**2**	**0**	**120**	**12**	**0**	**6.00**	....	....	....	....	....	....	....

KRAKE, PAUL

Goaltender. Catches left. 6', 175 lbs. Born, Lloydminster, Sask., March 25, 1969.
(Quebec's 10th choice, 148th overall, in 1989 Entry Draft).

			Regular Season								Playoffs						
Season	Club	Lea	GP	W	L	T	Mins	GA	SO	Avg	GP	W	L	Mins	GA	SO	Avg
1988-89	Alaska-Anch.	NCAA	19	....	....	....	1111	75	0	4.05	....	....	....	....	....	....	....
1989-90	Alaska-Anch.	NCAA	18	8	6	2	937	58	0	3.87	....	....	....	....	....	....	....

KRUESEL, JEFFREY

Goaltender. Catches right. 5'11", 180 lbs. Born, Rochester, MN, June 1, 1970.
(Los Angeles' 8th choice, 133rd overall, in 1988 Entry Draft).

			Regular Season								Playoffs						
Season	Club	Lea	GP	W	L	T	Mins	GA	SO	Avg	GP	W	L	Mins	GA	SO	Avg
1987-88	John Marshall	HS	19	....	....	....	855	31	4	1.67	....	....	....	....	....	....	....
1988-89	St. Cloud	NCAA	6	1	3	0	193	19	0	5.59	....	....	....	....	....	....	....

KUNTAR, LES

Goaltender. Catches left. 6'2", 194 lbs. Born, Buffalo, NY, July 28, 1969.
(Montreal's 8th choice, 122nd overall, in 1987 Entry Draft).

			Regular Season								Playoffs						
Season	Club	Lea	GP	W	L	T	Mins	GA	SO	Avg	GP	W	L	Mins	GA	SO	Avg
1987-88	St. Lawrence	ECAC	10	6	1	0	488	27	0	3.31	....	....	....	....	....	....	....
1988-89	St. Lawrence	ECAC	14	11	2	0	786	31	0	2.37	....	....	....	....	....	....	....
1989-90	St. Lawrence	ECAC	20	7	11	1	1136	80	0	4.23	....	....	....	....	....	....	....

LaFOREST, MARK ANDREW

Goaltender. Catches left. 5'11", 190 lbs. Born, Welland, Ont., July 10, 1962.

			Regular Season								Playoffs						
Season	Club	Lea	GP	W	L	T	Mins	GA	SO	Avg	GP	W	L	Mins	GA	SO	Avg
1981-82	Niagara Falls	OHL	24	10	13	1	1365	105	1	4.62	5	1	2	300	19	0	3.80
1982-83	North Bay	OHL	54	34	17	1	3140	195	0	3.73	8	4	4	474	31	0	3.92
1983-84	Adirondack	AHL	7	3	3	1	351	29	0	4.96	....	....	....	....	....	....	....
	Kalamazoo	IHL	13	4	5	2	718	48	1	4.01	....	....	....	....	....	....	....
1984-85	Adirondack	AHL	11	2	3	1	430	35	0	488	....	....	....	....	....	....	....
1985-86	**Detroit**	**NHL**	**28**	**4**	**21**	**0**	**1383**	**114**	**1**	**4.95**	....	....	....	....	....	....	....
	Adirondack	AHL	19	13	5	1	1142	57	0	2.99	*17	*12	5	*1075	58	0	3.24
1986-87	**Detroit**	**NHL**	**5**	**2**	**1**	**0**	**219**	**12**	**0**	**3.29**	....	....	....	....	....	....	....
a	Adirondack	AHL	37	23	8	0	2229	105	*3	2.83	....	....	....	....	....	....	....
1987-88	**Philadelphia**	**NHL**	**21**	**5**	**9**	**2**	**972**	**60**	**1**	**3.70**	**2**	**1**	**0**	**48**	**1**	**0**	**1.25**
	Hershey	AHL	5	2	1	2	309	13	0	2.52	....	....	....	....	....	....	....
1988-89	**Philadelphia**	**NHL**	**17**	**5**	**7**	**2**	**933**	**64**	**0**	**4.12**	....	....	....	....	....	....	....
	Hershey	AHL	3	2	0	0	185	9	0	2.92	12	7	5	744	27	1	2.18
1989-90	**Toronto**	**NHL**	**27**	**9**	**14**	**0**	**1343**	**87**	**0**	**3.89**	....	....	....	....	....	....	....
	Newmarket	AHL	10	6	4	0	604	33	1	3.28	....	....	....	....	....	....	....
	NHL Totals		**98**	**25**	**52**	**5**	**4850**	**337**	**2**	**4.17**	**2**	**1**	**0**	**48**	**1**	**0**	**1.25**

a Won Baz Bastien Trophy (AHL Most Valuable Goaltender) (1987)

Signed as free agent by **Detroit**, April 29, 1983. Traded to **Philadelphia** by **Detroit** for Philadelphia's second-round choice (Bob Wilkie) in 1987 Entry Draft, June 13, 1987. Traded to **Toronto** by **Philadelphia** for Toronto's sixth round choice in 1991 Entry Draft and its seventh round choice in 1991 Entry Draft (previously obtained from Philadelphia), September 8, 1989. Traded to **NY Rangers** by **Toronto** with Tie Domi for Greg Johnston, June 28, 1990.

LAGRAND, SCOTT

Goaltender. Catches left. 6'1", 170 lbs. Born, Potsdam, NY, February 11, 1970.
(Philadelphia's 5th choice, 77th overall, in 1988 Entry Draft).

			Regular Season								Playoffs						
Season	Club	Lea	GP	W	L	T	Mins	GA	SO	Avg	GP	W	L	Mins	GA	SO	Avg
1989-90	Boston College	H.E.	24	17	4	0	1268	57	0	2.70	....	....	....	....	....	....	....

LAURIN, STEVE

Goaltender. Catches left. 5'10", 150 lbs. Born, Barrie, Ont., December 2, 1967.
(Hartford's 10th choice, 249th overall, in 1987 Entry Draft).

			Regular Season								Playoffs						
Season	Club	Lea	GP	W	L	T	Mins	GA	SO	Avg	GP	W	L	Mins	GA	SO	Avg
1986-87	Dartmouth	ECAC	15	0	14	0	883	75	0	5.09	....	....	....	....	....	....	....
1987-88a	Dartmouth	ECAC	16	4	9	1	874	59	1	4.05	....	....	....	....	....	....	....
1988-89	Dartmouth	ECAC	13	2	9	1	747	57	0	4.57	....	....	....	....	....	....	....
1989-90	Dartmouth	ECAC	22	4	14	4	1366	100	0	4.32	....	....	....	....	....	....	....

a ECAC Second All-Star Team (1988)

LEHKONEN, TIMO

Goaltender. Catches left. 5'11", 170 lbs. Born, Helsinki, Finland, January 8, 1966.
(Chicago's 4th choice, 90th overall, in 1984 Entry Draft).

			Regular Season								Playoffs						
Season	Club	Lea	GP	W	L	T	Mins	GA	SO	Avg	GP	W	L	Mins	GA	SO	Avg
1988-89	TPS	Fin.	12	8	4	0	644	25	0	2.33	....	....	....	....	....	....	....
1989-90	HPK	Fin.	35	18	13	4	2032	123	0	3.63	....	....	....	....	....	....	....

LEMELIN, REJEAN (REGGIE) (LEHM-uh-lihn)

Goaltender. Catches left. 5'11", 170 lbs. Born, Quebec City, Que. November 19, 1954.
(Philadelphia's 6th choice, 125th overall, in 1974 Amateur Draft).

			Regular Season								Playoffs						
Season	Club	Lea	GP	W	L	T	Mins	GA	SO	Avg	GP	W	L	Mins	GA	SO	Avg
1972-73	Sherbrooke	QJHL	28	....	....	....	1681	146	0	5.21	2	....	....	120	12	0	6.00
1973-74	Sherbrooke	QJHL	35	....	....	....	2061	158	0	4.60	1	....	....	60	3	0	3.00
1974-75	Philadelphia	NAHL	43	....	....	....	2277	131	3	3.45	....	....	....	....	....	....	....
1975-76	Philadelphia	NAHL	29	....	....	....	1601	97	1	3.63	3	....	....	171	15	0	5.26
1976-77	Springfield	AHL	3	2	1	0	180	10	0	3.33	....	....	....	....	....	....	....
	Philadelphia	NAHL	51	26	19	1	2763	170	1	3.61	3	....	....	191	14	0	4.40
1977-78a	Philadelphia	AHL	60	31	21	7	3585	177	4	2.96	2	0	2	119	12	0	6.05
1978-79	Philadelphia	AHL	13	3	9	1	780	36	0	2.77	....	....	....	....	....	....	....
	Atlanta	**NHL**	**18**	**8**	**8**	**1**	**994**	**55**	**0**	**3.32**	**1**	**0**	**0**	**20**	**0**	**0**	**0.00**
1979-80	**Atlanta**	**NHL**	**3**	**0**	**2**	**0**	**150**	**15**	**0**	**6.00**	....	....	....	....	....	....	....
	Birmingham	CHL	38	13	21	2	2188	137	0	3.76	2	0	1	79	5	0	3.80
1980-81	Birmingham	CHL	13	3	8	2	757	56	0	4.44	....	....	....	....	....	....	....
	Calgary	**NHL**	**29**	**14**	**6**	**7**	**1629**	**88**	**2**	**3.24**	**6**	**3**	**3**	**366**	**22**	**0**	**3.61**
1981-82	**Calgary**	**NHL**	**34**	**10**	**5**	**6**	**1866**	**135**	**0**	**4.34**	....	....	....	....	....	....	....
1982-83	**Calgary**	**NHL**	**39**	**16**	**12**	**8**	**2211**	**133**	**0**	**3.61**	**7**	**3**	**3**	**327**	**27**	**0**	**4.95**
1983-84	**Calgary**	**NHL**	**51**	**21**	**12**	**9**	**2568**	**150**	**0**	**3.50**	**8**	**4**	**4**	**448**	**32**	**0**	**4.29**
1984-85	**Calgary**	**NHL**	**56**	**30**	**12**	**10**	**3176**	**183**	**1**	**3.46**	**4**	**1**	**3**	**248**	**15**	**1**	**3.63**
1985-86	**Calgary**	**NHL**	**60**	**29**	**24**	**4**	**3369**	**229**	**1**	**4.08**	**3**	**0**	**1**	**109**	**7**	**0**	**3.85**
1986-87	**Calgary**	**NHL**	**34**	**16**	**9**	**1**	**1735**	**94**	**2**	**3.25**	**2**	**0**	**1**	**101**	**6**	**0**	**3.56**
1987-88	**Boston**	**NHL**	**49**	**24**	**17**	**6**	**2828**	**138**	**3**	**2.93**	**17**	**11**	**6**	**1027**	**45**	***1**	***2.63**
1988-89	**Boston**	**NHL**	**40**	**19**	**15**	**6**	**2392**	**120**	**0**	**3.01**	**4**	**1**	**3**	**252**	**16**	**0**	**3.81**
1989-90b	**Boston**	**NHL**	**43**	**22**	**15**	**2**	**2310**	**108**	**2**	**2.81**	**3**	**0**	**1**	**135**	**13**	**0**	**5.78**
	NHL Totals		**456**	**209**	**137**	**60**	**25128**	**1448**	**11**	**3.46**	**55**	**23**	**25**	**3033**	**183**	**2**	**3.62**

a AHL First All-Star Team (1978)
b Shared William Jennings Trophy with Andy Moog (1990)

Played in NHL All-Star Game (1989)

Signed as free agent by **Atlanta**, August 17, 1978. Signed as a free agent by **Boston**, August 13, 1987.

LETOURNEAU, RAYMOND GEORGE (RAY)

Goaltender. Catches left. 5'11", 185 lbs. Born, Penacook, NH, January 14, 1969.
(Philadelphia's 2nd choice, 9th overall, in 1990 Supplemental Draft).

			Regular Season								Playoffs						
Season	Club	Lea	GP	W	L	T	Mins	GA	SO	Avg	GP	W	L	Mins	GA	SO	Avg
1987-88	Yale	ECAC	4	0	3	0	175	24	0	8.21	....	....	....	....	....	....	....
1988-89	Yale	ECAC	7	1	5	0	378	42	0	6.66	....	....	....	....	....	....	....
1989-90	Yale	ECAC	28	8	19	1	1631	125	0	4.59	....	....	....	....	....	....	....

LINDFORS, SAKARI

Goaltender. Catches left. 5'7", 150 lbs. Born, Helsinki, Finland, April 27, 1966.
(Quebec's 9th choice, 150th overall, in 1988 Entry Draft).

			Regular Season								Playoffs						
Season	Club	Lea	GP	W	L	T	Mins	GA	SO	Avg	GP	W	L	Mins	GA	SO	Avg
1988-89	IFK Helsinki	Fin.	24	11	11	2	1433	89	1	3.75	....	....	....	....	....	....	....
1989-90	IFK Helsinki	Fin.	42	23	15	4	2518	146	2	3.48	....	....	....	....	....	....	....

LITTMAN, DAVID

Goaltender. Catches left. 6', 172 lbs. Born, Cranston, RI, June 13, 1967.
(Buffalo's 12th choice, 211th overall, in 1987 Entry Draft).

			Regular Season								Playoffs						
Season	Club	Lea	GP	W	L	T	Mins	GA	SO	Avg	GP	W	L	Mins	GA	SO	Avg
1985-86	Boston College	H.E.	7	4	0	1	312	18	0	3.46	....	....	....	....	....	....	....
1986-87	Boston College	H.E.	21	15	5	0	1182	68	0	3.45	....	....	....	....	....	....	....
1987-88a	Boston College	H.E.	30	11	16	2	1726	116	0	4.03	....	....	....	....	....	....	....
1988-89bc	Boston College	H.E.	*32	19	9	4	*1945	107	0	3.30	....	....	....	....	....	....	....
1989-90	Rochester	AHL	14	5	6	1	681	37	0	3.26	....	....	....	....	....	....	....
	Phoenix	IHL	18	8	7	2	1047	64	0	3.67	....	....	....	....	....	....	....

a Hockey East Second All-Star Team (1988)
b Hockey East First All-Star Team (1989)
c NCAA East Second All-American Team (1989)

LIUT, MICHAEL (MIKE) (lee-OOT)

Goaltender. Catches left. 6'2", 195 lbs. Born, Weston, Ont., January 7, 1956.
(St. Louis' 5th choice, 56th overall, in 1976 Amateur Draft).

			Regular Season								Playoffs						
Season	**Club**	**Lea**	**GP**	**W**	**L**	**T**	**Mins**	**GA**	**SO**	**Avg**	**GP**	**W**	**L**	**Mins**	**GA**	**SO**	**Avg**
1973-74	Bowling Green	CCHA	24	10	12	0	1272	88	1	4.15	....	....	....	....	....	....	....
1974-75	Bowling Green	CCHA	20	12	6	1	1174	78	0	3.99	....	....	....	....	....	....	....
1975-76	Bowling Green	CCHA	21	13	5	0	1171	50	2	2.56	....	....	....	....	....	....	....
1976-77	Bowling Green	CCHA	24	18	4	0	1346	61	2	2.72	....	....	....	....	....	....	....
1977-78	Cincinnati	WHA	27	8	12	0	1215	86	0	4.25	....	....	....	....	....	....	....
1978-79	Cincinnati	WHA	54	23	27	4	3181	184	*3	3.47	3	1	2	179	12	0	4.02
1979-80	**St. Louis**	**NHL**	**64**	**32**	**23**	**9**	**3661**	**194**	**2**	**3.18**	**3**	**0**	**3**	**193**	**12**	**0**	**3.73**
1980-81ab	**St. Louis**	**NHL**	**61**	**33**	**14**	**13**	**3570**	**199**	**1**	**3.34**	**11**	**5**	**6**	**685**	**50**	**0**	**4.38**
1981-82	**St. Louis**	**NHL**	***64**	**28**	**28**	**7**	***3691**	**250**	**2**	**4.06**	**10**	**5**	**3**	**494**	**27**	**0**	**3.28**
1982-83	**St. Louis**	**NHL**	***68**	**21**	**27**	**13**	***3794**	**235**	**1**	**3.72**	**4**	**1**	**3**	**240**	**15**	**0**	**3.75**
1983-84	**St. Louis**	**NHL**	**58**	**25**	**29**	**4**	**3425**	**197**	**3**	**3.45**	**11**	**6**	**5**	**714**	**29**	**1**	**2.44**
1984-85	**St. Louis**	**NHL**	**32**	**12**	**12**	**6**	**1869**	**119**	**1**	**3.82**	....	....	....	....	....	....	....
	Hartford	**NHL**	**12**	**4**	**7**	**1**	**731**	**36**	**1**	**2.95**	....	....	....	....	....	....	....
1985-86	**Hartford**	**NHL**	**57**	**27**	**23**	**4**	**3282**	**198**	**2**	**3.62**	**8**	**5**	**2**	**441**	**14**	***1**	***1.90**
1986-87c	**Hartford**	**NHL**	**59**	**31**	**22**	**5**	**3476**	**187**	***4**	**3.23**	**6**	**2**	**4**	**332**	**25**	**0**	**4.52**
1987-88	**Hartford**	**NHL**	**60**	**25**	**28**	**5**	**3532**	**187**	**2**	**3.18**	**3**	**1**	**1**	**160**	**11**	**0**	**4.13**
1988-89	**Hartford**	**NHL**	**35**	**13**	**19**	**1**	**2006**	**142**	**1**	**4.25**	....	....	....	....	....	....	....
1989-90	**Hartford**	**NHL**	**29**	**15**	**12**	**1**	**1683**	**74**	***3**	***2.64**	....	....	....	....	....	....	....
	Washington	**NHL**	**8**	**4**	**4**	**0**	**478**	**17**	***1**	***2.13**	**9**	**4**	**4**	**507**	**28**	**0**	**3.31**
	NHL Totals		**607**	**270**	**248**	**69**	**35198**	**2035**	**24**	**3.47**	**65**	**29**	**31**	**3766**	**211**	**2**	**3.36**

a NHL First All-Star Team (1981)
b Won Lester B. Pearson Award (1981)
c NHL Second All-Star Team (1987)

Played in NHL All-Star Game (1981)

Reclaimed by **St. Louis** from Cincinnati (WHA) prior to Expansion Draft, June 9, 1979. Traded to **Hartford** by **St. Louis** with Jorgen Pettersson for Mark Johnson and Greg Millen, February 21, 1985. Traded to **Washington** by **Hartford** for Yvon Corriveau, March 6, 1990.

LOEWEN, JAMIE

Goaltender. Catches left. 5'10", 165 lbs. Born, N. Vancouver, B.C., September 23, 1968.
(Minnesota's 1st choice, 12th overall, in 1989 Supplemental Draft).

			Regular Season								Playoffs						
Season	**Club**	**Lea**	**GP**	**W**	**L**	**T**	**Mins**	**GA**	**SO**	**Avg**	**GP**	**W**	**L**	**Mins**	**GA**	**SO**	**Avg**
1988-89	Alaska-Fair.	NCAA	24	....	....	....	1501	84	0	3.48	....	....	....	....	....	....	....
1989-90	Alaska-Fair.	NCAA	17	5	12	0	1023	101	0	5.94	....	....	....	....	....	....	....

LORENZ, DANNY

Goaltender. Catches left. 5'10", 170 lbs. Born, Murrayville, BC, December 12, 1969.
(NY Islanders' 4th choice, 58th overall, in 1988 Entry Draft).

			Regular Season								Playoffs						
Season	**Club**	**Lea**	**GP**	**W**	**L**	**T**	**Mins**	**GA**	**SO**	**Avg**	**GP**	**W**	**L**	**Mins**	**GA**	**SO**	**Avg**
1986-87	Seattle	WHL	38	12	21	2	2103	199	0	5.68	....	....	....	....	....	....	....
1987-88	Seattle	WHL	62	20	37	2	3302	314	0	5.71	....	....	....	....	....	....	....
1988-89	Springfield	AHL	4	2	1	0	210	12	0	3.43	....	....	....	....	....	....	....
a	Seattle	WHL	*68	31	33	4	*4003	240	*3	3.60	....	....	....	....	....	....	....
1989-90a	Seattle	WHL	56	37	15	2	3226	221	0	4.11	13	6	7	751	40	0	3.21

a WHL West First All-Star Team (1989, 1990)

LUKOWSKI, BRIAN

Goaltender. Catches left. 5'9", 160 lbs. Born, Buffalo, NY, January 8, 1971.
(St. Louis' 11th choice, 219th overall, in 1989 Entry Draft).

			Regular Season								Playoffs						
Season	**Club**	**Lea**	**GP**	**W**	**L**	**T**	**Mins**	**GA**	**SO**	**Avg**	**GP**	**W**	**L**	**Mins**	**GA**	**SO**	**Avg**
1989-90	Lake Superior	CCHA	4	1	0	0	114	8	0	4.20	....	....	....	....	....	....	....

MALARCHUK, CLINT

Goaltender. Catches left. 6', 187 lbs. Born, Grande Prairie, Alta. May 1, 1961.
(Quebec's 3rd choice, 74th overall, in 1981 Entry Draft).

			Regular Season								Playoffs						
Season	**Club**	**Lea**	**GP**	**W**	**L**	**T**	**Mins**	**GA**	**SO**	**Avg**	**GP**	**W**	**L**	**Mins**	**GA**	**SO**	**Avg**
1979-80	Portland	WHL	37	21	10	0	1948	147	0	4.53	1	0	0	40	3	0	4.50
1980-81	Portland	WHL	38	28	8	0	2235	142	3	3.81	4	....	....	307	21	0	4.10
1981-82	**Quebec**	**NHL**	**2**	**0**	**1**	**1**	**120**	**14**	**0**	**7.00**	....	....	....	....	....	....	....
	Fredericton	AHL	51	15	34	2	2906	247	0	5.10	....	....	....	....	....	....	....
1982-83	Fredericton	AHL	25	....	....	....	1506	78	0	3.11	....	....	....	....	....	....	....
	Quebec	**NHL**	**15**	**8**	**5**	**2**	**900**	**71**	**0**	**4.73**	....	....	....	....	....	....	....
1983-84	Fredericton	AHL	11	5	5	1	663	40	0	3.62	....	....	....	....	....	....	....
	Quebec	**NHL**	**23**	**10**	**9**	**2**	**1215**	**80**	**0**	**3.95**	**1**	**0**	**0**	**0**	**0**	**0**	**0.00**
1984-85	Fredericton	AHL	*56	26	25	4	*3347	198	2	3.55	6	2	4	379	20	0	3.17
1985-86	**Quebec**	**NHL**	**46**	**26**	**12**	**4**	**2657**	**142**	**4**	**3.21**	**3**	**0**	**2**	**143**	**11**	**0**	**4.62**
1986-87	**Quebec**	**NHL**	**54**	**18**	**26**	**9**	**3092**	**175**	**1**	**3.40**	**3**	**0**	**2**	**140**	**8**	**0**	**3.43**
1987-88	**Washington**	**NHL**	**54**	**24**	**20**	**4**	**2926**	**154**	***4**	**3.16**	**4**	**0**	**2**	**193**	**15**	**0**	**4.66**
1988-89	**Washington**	**NHL**	**42**	**16**	**18**	**7**	**2428**	**141**	**1**	**3.48**	**1**	**0**	**1**	**59**	**5**	**0**	**5.08**
	Buffalo	**NHL**	**7**	**3**	**1**	**1**	**326**	**13**	**1**	**2.39**	....	....	....	....	....	....	....
1989-90	**Buffalo**	**NHL**	**29**	**14**	**11**	**2**	**1596**	**89**	**0**	**3.35**	....	....	....	....	....	....	....
	NHL Totals		**272**	**119**	**103**	**32**	**15260**	**879**	**11**	**3.46**	....	....	....	....	....	....	....

Traded to **Washington** by **Quebec** with Dale Hunter for Gaetan Duchesne, Alan Haworth, and Washington's first-round choice (Joe Sakic) in 1987 Entry Draft, June 13, 1987. Traded to **Buffalo** by **Washington** with Grant Ledyard and Washington's sixth-round choice in 1991 Entry Draft for Calle Johansson and Buffalo's second-round choice (Byron Dafoe) in 1989 Entry Draft, March 7, 1989.

MANELUK, GEORGE

Goaltender. Catches left. 5'11", 185 lbs. Born, Winnipeg, Man., July 25, 1967.
(NY Islanders' 4th choice, 76th overall, in 1987 Entry Draft).

			Regular Season								Playoffs						
Season	**Club**	**Lea**	**GP**	**W**	**L**	**T**	**Mins**	**GA**	**SO**	**Avg**	**GP**	**W**	**L**	**Mins**	**GA**	**SO**	**Avg**
1986-87	Brandon	WHL	58	16	35	4	3258	315	0	5.80	....	....	....	....	....	....	....
1987-88	Brandon	WHL	64	24	33	3	3651	297	0	4.88	4	1	3	271	22	0	4.87
	Springfield	AHL	2	0	1	1	125	9	0	4.32	....	....	....	....	....	....	....
	Peoria	IHL	3	1	2	0	148	14	0	5.68	1	0	1	60	5	0	5.00
1988-89	Springfield	AHL	24	7	13	0	1202	84	0	4.19	....	....	....	....	....	....	....
1989-90	Springfield	AHL	27	11	9	1	1382	94	1	4.08	....	....	....	....	....	....	....
	Winston-Salem	ECHL	3	2	0	0	140	11	0	4.71	....	....	....	....	....	....	....

MASON, BOB

Goaltender. Catches right. 6'1", 180 lbs. Born, International Falls, MN, April 22, 1961.

			Regular Season								Playoffs						
Season	**Club**	**Lea**	**GP**	**W**	**L**	**T**	**Mins**	**GA**	**SO**	**Avg**	**GP**	**W**	**L**	**Mins**	**GA**	**SO**	**Avg**
1981-82	Minn.-Duluth	WCHA	26	....	....	....	1401	115	0	4.45	....	....	....	....	....	....	....
1982-83	Minn.-Duluth	WCHA	43	....	....	....	2593	151	1	3.49	....	....	....	....	....	....	....
1983-84	U.S. National	...	33	....	....	....	1895	89	0	2.82	....	....	....	....	....	....	....
	U.S. Olympic	...	3	....	....	....	160	10	0	3.75	....	....	....	....	....	....	....
	Hershey	AHL	5	1	4	0	282	26	0	5.53	....	....	....	....	....	....	....
	Washington	**NHL**	**2**	**2**	**0**	**0**	**120**	**3**	**0**	**1.50**	....	....	....	....	....	....	....
1984-85	**Washington**	**NHL**	**12**	**8**	**2**	**1**	**661**	**31**	**1**	**2.81**	....	....	....	....	....	....	....
	Binghamton	AHL	20	10	6	1	1052	58	1	3.31	....	....	....	....	....	....	....
1985-86	**Washington**	**NHL**	**1**	**1**	**0**	**0**	**16**	**0**	**0**	**0.00**	....	....	....	....	....	....	....
	Binghamton	AHL	34	20	11	2	1940	126	0	3.90	3	1	1	124	9	0	4.35
1986-87	**Washington**	**NHL**	**45**	**20**	**18**	**5**	**2536**	**137**	**0**	**3.24**	**4**	**2**	**2**	**309**	**9**	**1**	**1.75**
	Binghamton	AHL	2	1	1	0	119	4	0	2.02	....	....	....	....	....	....	....
1987-88	**Chicago**	**NHL**	**41**	**13**	**18**	**8**	**2312**	**160**	**0**	**4.15**	**1**	**0**	**1**	**60**	**3**	**0**	**3.00**
1988-89	**Quebec**	**NHL**	**22**	**5**	**14**	**1**	**1168**	**92**	**0**	**4.73**	....	....	....	....	....	....	....
	Halifax	AHL	23	11	7	1	1278	73	1	3.43	2	0	2	97	9	0	5.57
1989-90	**Washington**	**NHL**	**16**	**4**	**9**	**1**	**822**	**48**	**0**	**3.50**	....	....	....	....	....	....	....
	Baltimore	AHL	13	9	2	2	770	44	0	3.43	6	2	4	373	20	0	3.22
	NHL Totals		**139**	**53**	**61**	**16**	**7635**	**471**	**1**	**3.70**	**5**	**2**	**3**	**369**	**12**	**1**	**1.95**

Signed as a free agent by **Washington**, February 21, 1984. Signed as a free agent by **Chicago**, June 12, 1987. Traded to **Quebec** by **Chicago** for Mike Eagles, July 5, 1988. Traded to **Washington** by **Quebec** for future considerations, June 17, 1989.

McKAY, ROSS LEE

Goaltender. Catches right. 5'11", 175 lbs. Born, Edmonton, Alta., March 3, 1964.

			Regular Season								Playoffs						
Season	**Club**	**Lea**	**GP**	**W**	**L**	**T**	**Mins**	**GA**	**SO**	**Avg**	**GP**	**W**	**L**	**Mins**	**GA**	**SO**	**Avg**
1988-89	Binghamton	AHL	19	5	9	2	938	81	1	5.18	....	....	....	....	....	....	....
	Indianapolis	IHL	5	1	3	0	187	18	0	5.78	....	....	....	....	....	....	....
1989-90	Binghamton	AHL	18	0	10	1	713	58	0	4.88	....	....	....	....	....	....	....
	Knoxville	ECHL	8	4	2	1	426	20	0	2.81	....	....	....	....	....	....	....

Signed as a free agent by **Hartford**, May 2, 1988.

McKICHAN, STEVE (muh-KEE-Kan)

Goaltender. Catches left. 5'11", 180 lbs. Born, Strathroy, Ont., May 29, 1967.
(Vancouver's 2nd choice, 7th overall, in 1988 Supplemental Draft).

			Regular Season								Playoffs						
Season	**Club**	**Lea**	**GP**	**W**	**L**	**T**	**Mins**	**GA**	**SO**	**Avg**	**GP**	**W**	**L**	**Mins**	**GA**	**SO**	**Avg**
1986-87	Miami-Ohio	CCHA	28	3	19	0	1351	130	0	5.77	....	....	....	....	....	....	....
1987-88	Miami-Ohio	CCHA	34	12	17	1	1767	140	1	4.75	....	....	....	....	....	....	....
1988-89	Miami-Ohio	CCHA	21	4	15	0	1014	85	0	5.02	....	....	....	....	....	....	....
1989-90	Virginia	ECHL	28	16	11	2	1445	97	0	4.02	....	....	....	....	....	....	....
	Milwaukee	IHL	1	1	0	0	40	2	0	3.00	....	....	....	....	....	....	....

McLEAN, KIRK

Goaltender. Catches left. 6', 185 lbs. Born, Willowdale, Ont., June 26, 1966.
(New Jersey's 6th choice, 107th overall, in 1984 Entry Draft).

			Regular Season								Playoffs						
Season	**Club**	**Lea**	**GP**	**W**	**L**	**T**	**Mins**	**GA**	**SO**	**Avg**	**GP**	**W**	**L**	**Mins**	**GA**	**SO**	**Avg**
1983-84	Oshawa	OHL	17	5	9	0	940	67	0	4.28	....	....	....	....	....	....	....
1984-85	Oshawa	OHL	47	23	17	2	2581	143	1	*3.32	5	1	3	271	21	0	4.65
1985-86	**New Jersey**	**NHL**	**2**	**1**	**1**	**0**	**111**	**11**	**0**	**5.95**	....	....	....	....	....	....	....
	Oshawa	OHL	51	24	21	2	2830	169	1	3.58	4	1	2	201	18	0	5.37
1986-87	**New Jersey**	**NHL**	**4**	**1**	**1**	**0**	**160**	**10**	**0**	**3.75**	....	....	....	....	....	....	....
	Maine	AHL	45	15	23	4	2606	140	1	3.22	....	....	....	....	....	....	....
1987-88	**Vancouver**	**NHL**	**41**	**11**	**27**	**3**	**2380**	**147**	**1**	**3.71**	....	....	....	....	....	....	....
1988-89	**Vancouver**	**NHL**	**42**	**20**	**17**	**3**	**2477**	**127**	**4**	**3.08**	**5**	**2**	**3**	**302**	**18**	**0**	**3.58**
1989-90	**Vancouver**	**NHL**	***63**	**21**	**30**	**10**	***3739**	**216**	**0**	**3.47**	....	....	....	....	....	....	....
	NHL Totals		**152**	**54**	**76**	**16**	**8867**	**511**	**5**	**3.46**	**5**	**2**	**3**	**302**	**18**	**0**	**3.58**

Played in NHL All-Star Game (1990)

Traded to **Vancouver** by **New Jersey** with Greg Adams for Patrik Sundstrom and Vancouver's fourth round choice (Matt Ruchty) in 1988 Entry Draft, September 15, 1987.

MELANSON, ROLAND JOSEPH (ROLLIE) (mel-AWN-son)

Goaltender. Catches left. 5'10", 180 lbs. Born, Moncton, N.B., June 28, 1960.
(NY Islanders' 4th choice, 59th overall, in 1979 Entry Draft).

			Regular Season								Playoffs						
Season	**Club**	**Lea**	**GP**	**W**	**L**	**T**	**Mins**	**GA**	**SO**	**Avg**	**GP**	**W**	**L**	**Mins**	**GA**	**SO**	**Avg**
1978-79a	Windsor	OHA	58	....	....	....	3468	258	1	4.41	7	....	....	392	31	0	4.75
1979-80	Windsor	OHA	22	11	8	0	1099	90	0	4.91	....	....	....	....	....	....	....
	Oshawa	OHA	38	26	12	0	2240	136	3	3.64	7	3	4	420	32	0	4.57
1980-81bc	Indianapolis	CHL	52	31	16	3	3056	131	2	*2.57	....	....	....	....	....	....	....
	NY Islanders	**NHL**	**11**	**8**	**1**	**1**	**620**	**32**	**0**	**3.10**	**3**	**1**	**0**	**92**	**6**	**0**	**3.91**
1981-82	**NY Islanders**	**NHL**	**36**	**22**	**7**	**6**	**2115**	**114**	**0**	**3.23**	**3**	**0**	**1**	**64**	**5**	**0**	**4.69**
1982-83de	**NY Islanders**	**NHL**	**44**	**24**	**12**	**5**	**2460**	**109**	**1**	**2.66**	**5**	**2**	**2**	**238**	**10**	**0**	**2.52**
1983-84	**NY Islanders**	**NHL**	**37**	**20**	**11**	**2**	**2019**	**110**	**0**	**3.27**	**6**	**0**	**1**	**87**	**5**	**0**	**3.45**
1984-85	**NY Islanders**	**NHL**	**8**	**3**	**3**	**0**	**425**	**35**	**0**	**4.94**	....	....	....	....	....	....	....
	Minnesota	**NHL**	**20**	**5**	**10**	**3**	**1142**	**70**	**0**	**4.10**	....	....	....	....	....	....	....
1985-86	**Minnesota**	**NHL**	**6**	**2**	**1**	**2**	**325**	**24**	**0**	**4.43**	....	....	....	....	....	....	....
	Los Angeles	**NHL**	**22**	**4**	**16**	**1**	**1246**	**87**	**0**	**4.19**	....	....	....	....	....	....	....
	New Haven	AHL	3	1	2	0	179	13	0	4.36	....	....	....	....	....	....	....
1986-87	**Los Angeles**	**NHL**	**46**	**18**	**21**	**6**	**2734**	**168**	**1**	**3.69**	**5**	**1**	**4**	**260**	**24**	**0**	**5.54**
1987-88	**Los Angeles**	**NHL**	**47**	**17**	**20**	**7**	**2676**	**195**	**2**	**4.37**	**1**	**0**	**1**	**60**	**9**	**0**	**9.00**
1988-89	**Los Angeles**	**NHL**	**4**	**1**	**1**	**0**	**178**	**19**	**0**	**6.40**	....	....	....	....	....	....	....
	New Haven	AHL	29	11	15	3	1734	106	1	3.67	*17	9	8	*1019	74	1	4.36
1989-90	Utica	AHL	48	24	19	3	2737	167	1	3.66	5	1	4	298	20	0	4.03
	NHL Totals		**281**	**124**	**103**	**33**	**15940**	**971**	**4**	**3.65**	**23**	**4**	**9**	**801**	**59**	**0**	**4.42**

a OHA Second All-Star Team (1979)
b CHL First All-Star Team (1981)
c Won Ken McKenzie Trophy (CHL's Rookie of the Year) (1981)
d Shared William Jennings Trophy with Billy Smith (1983)
e NHL Second All-Star Team (1983)

Traded to **Minnesota** by **NY Islanders** for Minnesota's first round choice in 1985 Entry draft (Brad Dalgarno), November 19, 1984. Traded to **NY Rangers** by **Minnesota** for New York's second round draft choice in 1986 (Neil Wilkinson) and fourth round choice in 1987 (John Weisbrod), December 9, 1985. Traded to **Los Angeles** by **NY Rangers** with Grant Ledyard for Brian MacLellan and Los Angeles' fourth round draft choice in 1987 (Michael Sullivan), December 9, 1985. Signed as a free agent by **New Jersey**, August 10, 1989.

MERTEN, MATT

Goaltender. Catches left. 6'3", 190 lbs. Born, Milford, MA, June 29, 1967.
(Vancouver's 8th choice, 175th overall, in 1986 Entry Draft).

			Regular Season								Playoffs						
Season	Club	Lea	GP	W	L	T	Mins	GA	SO	Avg	GP	W	L	Mins	GA	SO	Avg
1986-87	Providence	H.E.	24	6	14	2	1455	104	0	4.29	....	....	....	....	....	....	....
1987-88	Providence	H.E.	25	8	11	1	1328	100	0	4.52	....	....	....	....	....	....	....
1988-89	Providence	H.E.	20	7	8	1	1067	69	0	3.88	....	....	....	....	....	....	....
1989-90	Providence	H.E.	16	8	4	2	908	38	0	*2.51	....	....	....	....	....	....	....

MILLEN, GREG H.

Goaltender. Catches right. 5'9", 175 lbs. Born, Toronto, Ont., June 25, 1957.
(Pittsburgh's 4th choice, 102nd overall, in 1977 Amateur Draft).

			Regular Season								Playoffs						
Season	Club	Lea	GP	W	L	T	Mins	GA	SO	Avg	GP	W	L	Mins	GA	SO	Avg
1976-77	Peterborough	OHA	59	....	....	....	3457	244	0	4.23	4	....	....	240	23	0	5.75
1977-78	Kalamazoo	IHL	3	....	....	....	180	14	0	4.67	....	....	....	....	....	....	....
	S. S. Marie	OHA	25	....	....	....	1449	105	1	4.29	13	....	....	774	61	0	4.73
1978-79	**Pittsburgh**	**NHL**	**28**	**14**	**11**	**1**	**1532**	**86**	**2**	**3.37**	....	....	....	....	....	....	....
1979-80	**Pittsburgh**	**NHL**	**44**	**18**	**18**	**7**	**2586**	**157**	**2**	**3.64**	**5**	**2**	**3**	**300**	**21**	**0**	**4.20**
1980-81	**Pittsburgh**	**NHL**	**63**	**25**	**27**	**10**	**3721**	**258**	**0**	**4.16**	**5**	**2**	**3**	**325**	**19**	**0**	**3.51**
1981-82	**Hartford**	**NHL**	**55**	**11**	**30**	**12**	**3201**	**229**	**0**	**4.29**	....	....	....	....	....	....	....
1982-83	**Hartford**	**NHL**	**60**	**14**	**38**	**6**	**3520**	**282**	**1**	**4.81**	....	....	....	....	....	....	....
1983-84	**Hartford**	**NHL**	***60**	**21**	**30**	**9**	***3583**	**221**	**2**	**3.70**	....	....	....	....	....	....	....
1984-85	**Hartford**	**NHL**	**44**	**16**	**22**	**6**	**2659**	**187**	**1**	**4.22**	....	....	....	....	....	....	....
	St. Louis	**NHL**	**10**	**2**	**7**	**1**	**607**	**35**	**0**	**3.46**	**1**	**0**	**1**	**60**	**2**	**0**	**2.00**
1985-86	**St. Louis**	**NHL**	**36**	**14**	**16**	**6**	**2168**	**129**	**1**	**3.57**	**10**	**6**	**3**	**586**	**29**	**0**	**2.97**
1986-87	**St. Louis**	**NHL**	**42**	**15**	**18**	**9**	**2482**	**146**	**0**	**3.53**	**4**	**1**	**3**	**250**	**10**	**0**	**2.40**
1987-88	**St. Louis**	**NHL**	**48**	**21**	**19**	**7**	**2854**	**167**	**1**	**3.51**	**10**	**5**	**5**	**600**	**38**	**0**	**3.80**
1988-89	**St. Louis**	**NHL**	**52**	**22**	**20**	**7**	**3019**	**170**	***6**	**3.38**	**10**	**5**	**5**	**649**	**34**	**0**	**3.14**
1989-90	**St. Louis**	**NHL**	**21**	**11**	**7**	**3**	**1245**	**61**	**1**	**2.94**	....	....	....	....	....	....	....
	Quebec	**NHL**	**18**	**3**	**14**	**1**	**1080**	**95**	**0**	**5.28**	....	....	....	....	....	....	....
	Chicago	**NHL**	**10**	**5**	**4**	**1**	**575**	**32**	**0**	**3.34**	**14**	**6**	**6**	**613**	**40**	**0**	**3.92**
	NHL Totals		**591**	**212**	**281**	**86**	**34802**	**2255**	**17**	**3.89**	**59**	**27**	**29**	**3383**	**193**	**0**	**3.42**

Signed as free agent by **Hartford**, June 15, 1981. As compensation, **Pittsburgh** received Pat Boutette and the rights to Kevin McLelland, June 29, 1981. Traded to **St. Louis** by **Hartford** with Mark Johnson for Mike Liut and Jorgen Pettersson, February 21, 1985. Traded to **Quebec** by **St. Louis** with Tony Hrkac for Jeff Brown, December 13, 1989. Traded to **Chicago** by **Quebec** with Michel Goulet and Quebec's sixth round choice in 1991 Entry Draft for Mario Doyon, Everett Sanipass and Dan Vincelette, March 5, 1990.

MOOG, DONALD ANDREW (ANDY) (MOHG)

Goaltender. Catches left. 5'8", 170 lbs. Born, Penticton, B.C., February 18, 1960.
(Edmonton's 6th choice, 132nd overall, in 1980 Entry Draft).

			Regular Season								Playoffs						
Season	Club	Lea	GP	W	L	T	Mins	GA	SO	Avg	GP	W	L	Mins	GA	SO	Avg
1978-79	Billings	WHL	26	13	5	4	1306	90	4	4.13	5	1	3	229	21	0	5.50
1979-80a	Billings	WHL	46	23	14	1	2435	149	1	3.67	3	2	1	190	10	0	3.16
1980-81	**Edmonton**	**NHL**	**7**	**3**	**3**	**0**	**313**	**20**	**0**	**3.83**	**9**	**5**	**4**	**526**	**32**	**0**	**3.65**
	Wichita	CHL	29	14	13	1	1602	89	0	3.33	5	3	2	300	16	0	3.20
1981-82	**Edmonton**	**NHL**	**8**	**3**	**5**	**0**	**399**	**32**	**0**	**4.81**	....	....	....	....	....	....	....
b	Wichita	CHL	40	23	13	3	2391	119	1	2.99	7	3	4	434	23	0	3.18
1982-83	**Edmonton**	**NHL**	**50**	**33**	**8**	**7**	**2833**	**167**	**1**	**3.54**	**16**	**11**	**5**	**949**	**48**	**0**	**3.03**
1983-84	**Edmonton**	**NHL**	**38**	**27**	**8**	**1**	**2212**	**139**	**1**	**3.77**	**7**	**4**	**0**	**263**	**12**	**0**	**2.74**
1984-85	**Edmonton**	**NHL**	**39**	**22**	**9**	**3**	**2019**	**111**	**1**	**3.30**	**2**	**0**	**0**	**20**	**0**	**0**	**0.00**
1985-86	**Edmonton**	**NHL**	**47**	**27**	**9**	**7**	**2664**	**164**	**1**	**3.69**	**1**	**1**	**0**	**60**	**1**	**0**	**1.00**
1986-87	**Edmonton**	**NHL**	**46**	**28**	**11**	**3**	**2461**	**144**	**0**	**3.51**	**2**	**2**	**0**	**120**	**8**	**0**	**4.00**
1987-88	**Boston**	**NHL**	**6**	**4**	**2**	**0**	**360**	**17**	**1**	**2.83**	**7**	**1**	**4**	**354**	**25**	**0**	**4.24**
	Cdn. National	....	27	10	7	5	1438	86	0	3.58	....	....	....	....	....	....	....
	Cdn. Olympic	....	4	4	0	0	240	9		2.25	....	....	....	....	....	....	....
1988-89	**Boston**	**NHL**	**41**	**18**	**14**	**8**	**2482**	**133**	**1**	**3.22**	**6**	**4**	**2**	**359**	**14**	**0**	**2.34**
1989-90c	**Boston**	**NHL**	**46**	**24**	**10**	**7**	**2536**	**122**	**3**	**2.89**	**20**	**13**	**7**	**1195**	**44**	***2**	***2.21**
	NHL Totals		**328**	**189**	**79**	**36**	**18279**	**1049**	**9**	**3.44**	....	....	....	....	....	....	....

a WHL Second All-Star Team (1980)
b CHL Second All-Star Team (1982)
c Shared William Jennings Trophy with Rejean Lemelin (1990)

Played in NHL All-Star Game (1985, 1986)

Traded to **Boston** by **Edmonton** for Geoff Courtnall, Bill Ranford and future considerations, March 8, 1988.

MORSCHAUSER, GUS

Goaltender. Catches left. 5'9", 155 lbs. Born, Kitchener, Ont., March 26, 1969.
(Vancouver's 8th choice, 197th overall, in 1989 Entry Draft).

			Regular Season								Playoffs						
Season	Club	Lea	GP	W	L	T	Mins	GA	SO	Avg	GP	W	L	Mins	GA	SO	Avg
1988-89	Kitchener	OHL	41	....	....	....	2311	132	2	3.43	....	....	....	....	....	....	....
1989-90	Kitchener	OHL	6	2	2	1	345	141	0	3.83	....	....	....	....	....	....	....
	Hamilton	OHL	38	6	27	3	2110	184	0	5.23	....	....	....	....	....	....	....
	Milwaukee	IHL	3	1	1	0	119	12	0	6.05	....	....	....	....	....	....	....

MUZZATTI, JASON

Goaltender. Catches left. 6'1", 190 lbs. Born, Toronto, Ont., February 3, 1970.
(Calgary's 1st choice, 21st overall, in 1988 Entry Draft).

			Regular Season								Playoffs						
Season	Club	Lea	GP	W	L	T	Mins	GA	SO	Avg	GP	W	L	Mins	GA	SO	Avg
1987-88a	Michigan State	CCHA	33	19	9	3	1915	109	0	3.41	....	....	....	....	....	....	....
1988-89	Michigan State	CCHA	42	32	9	1	2515	127	3	*3.03	....	....	....	....	....	....	....
1989-90bc	Michigan State	CCHA	33	*24	6	0	1976	99	0	3.01	....	....	....	....	....	....	....

a CCHA Second All-Star Team (1988)
b CCHA First All-Star Team (1990)
c NCAA West Second All-American Team (1990)

MYLLYS, JARMO (YAR-meh MEE-luhz)

Goaltender. Catches right. 5'8", 150 lbs. Born, Sovanlinna, Finland, May 29, 1965.
(Minnesota's 9th choice, 172nd overall, in 1987 Entry Draft).

			Regular Season								Playoffs						
Season	Club	Lea	GP	W	L	T	Mins	GA	SO	Avg	GP	W	L	Mins	GA	SO	Avg
1987-88	Lukko	Fin.	43	....	....	....	2580	160	....	3.72	....	....	....	....	....	....	....
1988-89	**Minnesota**	**NHL**	**6**	**1**	**4**	**0**	**238**	**22**	**0**	**5.55**	....	....	....	....	....	....	....
	Kalamazoo	IHL	28	13	8	4	1523	93	0	3.66	6	2	4	419	22	0	3.15
1989-90	**Minnesota**	**NHL**	**4**	**0**	**3**	**0**	**156**	**16**	**0**	**6.15**	....	....	....	....	....	....	....
a	Kalamazoo	IHL	49	31	9	3	2715	159	1	3.51	5	4	0	258	11	0	2.56
	NHL Totals		**10**	**1**	**7**	**0**	**394**	**38**	**0**	**5.79**	....	....	....	....	....	....	....

a IHL Second All-Star Team (1990)

MYLNIKOV, SERGEI (MIHL-nih-Kahf)

Goaltender. Catches left. 5'10", 176 lbs. Born, Chelyabinsk, Soviet Union, October 6, 1958.
(Quebec's 9th choice, 127th overall, in 1989 Entry Draft).

			Regular Season								Playoffs						
Season	Club	Lea	GP	W	L	T	Mins	GA	SO	Avg	GP	W	L	Mins	GA	SO	Avg
1976-77	Chelyabinsk	USSR	2	....	....	....	120	2	....	1.00	....	....	....	....	....	....	....
1977-78	Chelyabinsk	USSR	22	....	....	....	1320	71	....	3.22	....	....	....	....	....	....	....
1978-79	Chelyabinsk	USSR	32	....	....	....	1862	90	....	2.90	....	....	....	....	....	....	....
1979-80	Chelyabinsk	USSR	17	....	....	....	1023	58	....	3.40	....	....	....	....	....	....	....
1980-81	Leningrad	USSR	40	....	....	....	2415	157	....	3.90	....	....	....	....	....	....	....
1981-82	Leningrad	USSR	42	....	....	....	2310	132	....	3.42	....	....	....	....	....	....	....
1982-83	Chelyabinsk	USSR	37	....	....	....	1954	124	....	3.80	....	....	....	....	....	....	....
1983-84	Chelyabinsk	USSR	37	....	....	....	2173	91	....	2.51	....	....	....	....	....	....	....
1984-85	Chelyabinsk	USSR	28	....	....	....	1360	74	....	3.26	....	....	....	....	....	....	....
1985-86	Chelyabinsk	USSR	37	....	....	....	2126	96	....	2.70	....	....	....	....	....	....	....
1986-87	Chelyabinsk	USSR	36	....	....	....	2059	103	....	3.00	....	....	....	....	....	....	....
1987-88	Chelyabinsk	USSR	28	....	....	....	1559	69	....	2.65	....	....	....	....	....	....	....
1988-89	Chelyabinsk	USSR	33	....	....	....	1980	85	....	2.58	....	....	....	....	....	....	....
1989-90	**Quebec**	**NHL**	**10**	**1**	**7**	**2**	**568**	**47**	**0**	**4.96**	....	....	....	....	....	....	....
	NHL Totals		**10**	**1**	**7**	**2**	**568**	**47**	**0**	**4.96**	....	....	....	....	....	....	....

NEWMAN, THOMAS

Goaltender. Catches left. 6'1", 190 lbs. Born, Golden Valley, MN, February 23, 1971.
(Los Angeles' 4th choice, 103rd overall, in 1989 Entry Draft).

			Regular Season								Playoffs						
Season	Club	Lea	GP	W	L	T	Mins	GA	SO	Avg	GP	W	L	Mins	GA	SO	Avg
1989-90	U. Minnesota	WCHA	35	19	13	2	1982	127	0	3.84	....	....	....	....	....	....	....

O'NEILL, MICHAEL (MIKE)

Goaltender. Catches left. 5'7", 160 lbs. Born, LaSalle, Que., November 3, 1967.
(Winnipeg's 1st choice, 15th overall, in 1988 Supplemental Draft).

			Regular Season								Playoffs						
Season	Club	Lea	GP	W	L	T	Mins	GA	SO	Avg	GP	W	L	Mins	GA	SO	Avg
1985-86	Yale	ECAC	6	3	1	0	389	17	0	3.53	....	....	....	....	....	....	....
1986-87a	Yale	ECAC	16	9	6	1	964	55	2	3.42	....	....	....	....	....	....	....
1987-88	Yale	ECAC	24	6	17	0	1385	101	0	4.37	....	....	....	....	....	....	....
1988-89ab	Yale	ECAC	25	10	14	1	1490	93	0	3.74	....	....	....	....	....	....	....
1989-90	Tappara	Fin.	41	23	13	5	2369	127	2	3.22	....	....	....	....	....	....	....

a ECAC First All-Star Team (1987, 1989)
b NCAA East First All-American Team (1989)

PANG, DARREN

Goaltender. Catches left. 5'5" 155 lbs. Born, Meaford, Ont. Feb. 17, 1964

			Regular Season								Playoffs						
Season	Club	Lea	GP	W	L	T	Mins	GA	SO	Avg	GP	W	L	Mins	GA	SO	Avg
1982-83	Belleville	OHL	12	....	....	....	570	44	0	4.63	....	....	....	....	....	....	....
	Ottawa	OHL	47	....	....	....	2729	166	1	3.65	9	5	4	510	33	0	3.88
1983-84	Ottawa	OHL	43	....	....	....	2318	117	2	*3.03	....	....	....	....	....	....	....
1984-85	Milwaukee	IHL	53	19	29	3	3129	226	0	4.33	....	....	....	....	....	....	....
	Chicago	**NHL**	**1**	**0**	**1**	**0**	**60**	**4**	**0**	**4.00**	....	....	....	....	....	....	....
1985-86	Saginaw	IHL	44	21	21	0	2638	148	2	3.37	8	3	5	492	32	0	3.90
1986-87	Nova Scotia	AHL	7	4	2	0	389	21	0	3.24	3	1	2	200	11	0	3.30
1986-87a	Saginaw	IHL	44	25	16	0	2500	151	0	3.62	....	....	....	....	....	....	....
1987-88b	**Chicago**	**NHL**	**45**	**17**	**23**	**1**	**2548**	**163**	**0**	**3.84**	**4**	**1**	**3**	**240**	**18**	**0**	**4.50**
1988-89	**Chicago**	**NHL**	**35**	**10**	**11**	**6**	**1644**	**120**	**0**	**4.38**	**2**	**0**	**0**	**10**	**0**	**0**	**0.00**
	Saginaw	IHL	2	1	0	0	89	6	0	4.04	....	....	....	....	....	....	....
1989-90	Indianapolis	IHL	7	4	1	2	401	17	1	2.54	4	3	1	253	12	0	2.85
	NHL Totals		**81**	**27**	**35**	**7**	**4252**	**287**	**0**	**4.05**	**6**	**1**	**3**	**250**	**18**	**0**	**4.32**

a IHL Second All-Star Team (1987)
b NHL All-Rookie Team (1988)

Signed as a free agent by **Chicago**, August 15, 1984.

PARSON, MIKE

Goaltender. Catches left. 6'0", 170 lbs. Born, Listowel, Ont., March 12, 1970.
(Boston's 2nd choice, 38th overall, in 1989 Entry Draft).

			Regular Season								Playoffs						
Season	Club	Lea	GP	W	L	T	Mins	GA	SO	Avg	GP	W	L	Mins	GA	SO	Avg
1987-88	Guelph	OHL	31	9	17	2	1703	135	0	4.76	....	....	....	....	....	....	....
1988-89	Guelph	OHL	*53	25	22	5	*3047	194	0	3.82	7	3	4	421	29	0	4.13
1989-90	Owen Sound	OHL	49	21	21	4	2750	207	1	4.52	12	5	7	722	61	0	4.24

PEETERS, PETER (PETE)

Goaltender. Catches left. 6'1", 195 lbs. Born, Edmonton, Alta., August 17, 1957.
(Philadelphia's 9th choice, 135th overall, in 1977 Amateur Draft).

			Regular Season								Playoffs						
Season	Club	Lea	GP	W	L	T	Mins	GA	SO	Avg	GP	W	L	Mins	GA	SO	Avg
1975-76	Medicine Hat	WHL	37	....	....	....	2074	147	0	4.25	....	....	....	....	....	....	....
1976-77	Medicine Hat	WHL	62	....	....	....	3423	232	1	4.07	4	....	....	204	17	0	5.00
1977-78	Milwaukee	IHL	32	....	....	....	1698	93	1	3.29	....	....	....	....	....	....	....
	Maine	AHL	17	....	....	....	855	40	1	2.80	11	....	....	562	25	*1	2.67
1978-79	**Philadelphia**	**NHL**	**5**	**1**	**2**	**1**	**280**	**16**	**0**	**3.43**	....	....	....	....	....	....	....
ab	Maine	AHL	35	25	6	3	2067	100	*2	*2.90	6	5	0	329	15	0	2.74
1979-80	**Philadelphia**	**NHL**	**40**	**29**	**5**	**5**	**2373**	**108**	**1**	**2.73**	**13**	**8**	**5**	**799**	**37**	**1**	**2.78**
1980-81	**Philadelphia**	**NHL**	**40**	**22**	**12**	**5**	**2333**	**115**	**2**	**2.96**	**3**	**2**	**1**	**180**	**12**	**0**	**4.00**
1981-82	**Philadelphia**	**NHL**	**44**	**23**	**18**	**3**	**2591**	**160**	**0**	**3.71**	**4**	**1**	**2**	**220**	**17**	**0**	**4.64**
1982-83cd	**Boston**	**NHL**	**62**	***40**	**11**	**9**	**3611**	**142**	***8**	***2.36**	**17**	**9**	**8**	***1024**	**61**	**1**	**3.57**
1983-84	**Boston**	**NHL**	**50**	**29**	**16**	**2**	**2868**	**151**	**0**	**3.16**	**3**	**0**	**3**	**180**	**10**	**0**	**3.33**
1984-85	**Boston**	**NHL**	**51**	**19**	**26**	**4**	**2975**	**172**	**1**	**3.47**	**1**	**0**	**1**	**60**	**4**	**0**	**4.00**
1985-86	**Boston**	**NHL**	**8**	**3**	**4**	**1**	**485**	**31**	**0**	**3.84**	....	....	....	....	....	....	....
	Washington	**NHL**	**34**	**19**	**11**	**3**	**2021**	**113**	**1**	**3.35**	**9**	**5**	**4**	**544**	**24**	**0**	**2.65**
1986-87	**Washington**	**NHL**	**37**	**17**	**11**	**4**	**2002**	**107**	**0**	**3.21**	**3**	**1**	**2**	**180**	**9**	**0**	**3.00**
	Binghamton	AHL	4	3	0	0	245	4	1	0.98	....	....	....	....	....	....	....
1987-88	**Washington**	**NHL**	**35**	**14**	**12**	**5**	**1896**	**88**	**2**	***2.78**	**12**	**7**	**5**	**654**	**34**	**0**	**3.12**
1988-89	**Washington**	**NHL**	**33**	**20**	**7**	**3**	**1854**	**88**	**4**	**2.85**	**6**	**2**	**4**	**359**	**24**	**0**	**4.01**
1989-90	**Philadelphia**	**NHL**	**24**	**1**	**13**	**5**	**1140**	**72**	**1**	**3.79**	....	....	....	....	....	....	....
	NHL Totals		**463**	**237**	**148**	**50**	**26429**	**1363**	**20**	**3.09**	**71**	**35**	**35**	**4200**	**232**	**2**	**3.31**

a AHL Second All-Star Team (1979)
b Shared Harry "Hap" Holmes Memorial Trophy (AHL's Leading Goaltenders) with Robbie Moore (1979)
c NHL First All-Star Team (1983)
d Won Vezina Trophy (1983)

Played in NHL All-Star Game (1980, 1981, 1983, 1984)

Traded to **Boston** by **Philadelphia** for Brad McCrimmon, June 9, 1982. Traded to **Washington** by **Boston** for Pat Riggin, November 14, 1985. Signed as a free agent by **Philadelphia,** June 17, 1989. Traded to **Winnipeg** by **Philadelphia** with Keith Acton for future considerations, September 28, 1989. Traded to **Philadelphia** by **Winnipeg** with Keith Acton for future considerations, October 3, 1989.

PERREAULT, JOCELYN

Goaltender. Catches right. 6'4", 210 lbs. Born, Montreal, Que., January 8, 1966.

			Regular Season								Playoffs						
Season	Club	Lea	GP	W	L	T	Mins	GA	SO	Avg	GP	W	L	Mins	GA	SO	Avg
1986-87	Sherbrooke	AHL	13	8	4	0	722	40	0	3.32	6	3	0	258	9	0	2.09
1987-88a	Sherbrooke	AHL	25	8	11	1	1244	77	0	3.71	1	0	0	30	2	0	4.00
1988-89	Hershey	AHL	8	3	3	1	394	22	0	3.35	....	....	....	....	....	....	....
	Indianapolis	IHL	5	0	3	0	214	22	0	6.17	....	....	....	....	....	....	....
1989-90	Greensboro	ECHL	6	3	3	0	294	24	0	4.89	....	....	....	....	....	....	....

a Shared Harry "Hap" Holmes Memorial Trophy (AHL Leading Goaltender) with Vincent Riendeau (1988)

Signed as a free agent by **Montreal**, September 30, 1986.

PERRY, ALAN

Goaltender. Catches right. 5'8", 155 lbs. Born, Providence, RI, August 30, 1966.
(St. Louis' 5th choice, 56th overall, in 1984 Entry Draft).

			Regular Season								Playoffs						
Season	Club	Lea	GP	W	L	T	Mins	GA	SO	Avg	GP	W	L	Mins	GA	SO	Avg
1984-85	Windsor	OHL	34	15	17	0	1905	135	1	4.25	2	0	2	120	14	0	7.00
1985-86	Windsor	OHL	42	*28	10	2	2424	131	*3	3.24	13	8	5	697	51	0	4.39
1986-87	Peoria	IHL	6	0	5	0	312	36	0	6.92	....	....	....	....	....	....	....
	Belleville	OHL	15	7	7	1	843	64	0	4.56	6	2	4	367	18	1	2.94
1987-88	Peoria	IHL	20	7	10	0	1069	77	2	4.32	2	0	1	68	6		5.29
1988-89	Indianapolis	IHL	47	14	22	0	2266	195	0	5.16	....	....	....	....	....	....	....
1989-90	Halifax	AHL	2	0	1	0	38	3	0	4.74	....	....	....	....	....	....	....

PIETRANGELO, FRANK (PEE-tuhr-AN-jehl-oh)

Goaltender. Catches left. 5'10", 182 lbs. Born, Niagara Falls, Ont., December 17, 1964.
(Pittsburgh's 4th choice, 63rd overall, in 1983 Entry Draft).

			Regular Season								Playoffs						
Season	Club	Lea	GP	W	L	T	Mins	GA	SO	Avg	GP	W	L	Mins	GA	SO	Avg
1982-83	U. Minnesota	WCHA	25	15	6	1	1348	80	1	3.55	....	....	....	....	....	....	....
1983-84	U. Minnesota	WCHA	20	13	7	0	1141	66	0	3.47	....	....	....	....	....	....	....
1984-85	U. Minnesota	WCHA	17	8	3	3	912	52	0	3.42	....	....	....	....	....	....	....
1985-86	U. Minnesota	WCHA	23	15	7	0	1284	76	0	3.55	....	....	....	....	....	....	....
1986-87	Muskegon	IHL	35	23	11	0	2090	119	2	3.42	15	10	4	923	46	0	2.99
1987-88	**Pittsburgh**	**NHL**	**21**	**9**	**11**	**0**	**1207**	**80**	**1**	**3.98**	....	....	....	....	....	....	....
	Muskegon	IHL	15	11	3	1	868	43		2.97	....	....	....	....	....	....	....
1988-89	**Pittsburgh**	**NHL**	**15**	**5**	**3**	**0**	**669**	**45**	**0**	**4.04**	....	....	....	....	....	....	....
	Muskegon	IHL	13	10	1	0	760	38	1	3.00	9	*8	1	566	29	0	3.07
1989-90	**Pittsburgh**	**NHL**	**21**	**8**	**6**	**2**	**1066**	**77**	**0**	**4.33**	....	....	....	....	....	....	....
	Muskegon	IHL	12	9	2	1	691	38	0	3.30	....	....	....	....	....	....	....
	NHL Totals		**57**	**22**	**20**	**4**	**2942**	**202**	**1**	**4.12**	....	....	....	....	....	....	....

POTVIN, FELIX

Goaltender. Catches left. 6'1", 180 lbs. Born, Anjou, Que., June 23, 1971.
(Toronto's 2nd choice, 31st overall, in 1990 Entry Draft).

			Regular Season								Playoffs						
Season	Club	Lea	GP	W	L	T	Mins	GA	SO	Avg	GP	W	L	Mins	GA	SO	Avg
1988-89	Chicoutimi	QMJHL	*65	25	31	1	*3489	271	*2	4.66	....	....	....	....	....	....	....
1989-90	Chicoutimi	QMJHL	*62	*31	26	2	*3478	231	*2	3.99	....	....	....	....	....	....	....

a QMJHL Second All-Star Team (1990)

PUPPA, DAREN (POO-puh)

Goaltender. Catches right. 6'3", 205 lbs. Born, Kirkland Lake, Ont., March 23, 1963.
(Buffalo's 7th choice, 76th overall, in 1983 Entry Draft).

			Regular Season								Playoffs						
Season	Club	Lea	GP	W	L	T	Mins	GA	SO	Avg	GP	W	L	Mins	GA	SO	Avg
1983-84	RPI	ECAC	32	24	6	0	....	....	....	2.94	....	....	....	....	....	....	....
1984-85	RPI	ECAC	32	31	1	0	1830	78	0	2.56	....	....	....	....	....	....	....
1985-86	**Buffalo**	**NHL**	**7**	**3**	**4**	**0**	**401**	**21**	**1**	**3.14**	....	....	....	....	....	....	....
	Rochester	AHL	20	8	11	0	1092	79	0	4.34	....	....	....	....	....	....	....
1986-87	**Buffalo**	**NHL**	**3**	**0**	**2**	**1**	**185**	**13**	**0**	**4.22**	....	....	....	....	....	....	....
1986-87a	Rochester	AHL	57	*33	14	0	3129	146	1	2.80	*16	*10	6	*944	48	*1	3.05
1987-88	**Buffalo**	**NHL**	**17**	**8**	**6**	**1**	**874**	**61**	**0**	**4.19**	**3**	**1**	**1**	**142**	**11**	**0**	**4.65**
	Rochester	AHL	26	14	8	2	1415	65	2	2.76	2	0	1	108	5	0	2.78
1988-89	**Buffalo**	**NHL**	**37**	**17**	**10**	**6**	**1908**	**107**	**1**	**3.36**	....	....	....	....	....	....	....
1989-90b	**Buffalo**	**NHL**	**56**	***31**	**16**	**6**	**3241**	**156**	**1**	**2.89**	**6**	**2**	**4**	**370**	**15**	**0**	**2.43**
	NHL Totals		**120**	**59**	**38**	**14**	**6609**	**358**	**3**	**3.25**	**9**	**3**	**5**	**512**	**26**	**0**	**3.05**

a AHL First All-Star Team (1987)
b NHL Second All-Star Team (1990)

Played in NHL All-Star Game (1990)

PYE, BILL

Goaltender. Shoots left. 5'9", 170 lbs. Born, Canton, MI, April 9, 1969.
(Buffalo's 5th choice, 107th overall, in 1989 Entry Draft).

			Regular Season								Playoffs						
Season	Club	Lea	GP	W	L	T	Mins	GA	SO	Avg	GP	W	L	Mins	GA	SO	Avg
1987-88	N. Michigan	WCHA	13	....	....	....	654	49	0	4.49	....	....	....	....	....	....	....
1988-89	N. Michigan	WCHA	43	26	15	2	2533	133	1	3.15	....	....	....	....	....	....	....
1989-90	N. Michigan	WCHA	36	20	14	1	2035	149	1	4.39	....	....	....	....	....	....	....

RACICOT, ANDRE

Goaltender. Catches left. 5'11", 165 lbs. Born, Rouyn, Que., June 9, 1969.
(Montreal's 5th choice, 83rd overall, in 1989 Entry Draft).

			Regular Season								Playoffs						
Season	Club	Lea	GP	W	L	T	Mins	GA	SO	Avg	GP	W	L	Mins	GA	SO	Avg
1986-87	Granby	QMJHL	3	1	2	0	180	19	0	6.33	....	....	....	....	....	....	....
1987-88	Granby	QMJHL	30	15	11	1	1547	105	1	4.07	5	1	4	298	23	0	4.63
1988-89a	Granby	QMJHL	54	22	24	3	2944	198	0	4.04	4	0	4	218	18	0	4.95
1989-90	**Montreal**	**NHL**	**1**	**0**	**0**	**0**	**13**	**3**	**0**	**13.85**	....	....	....	....	....	....	....
b	Sherbrooke	AHL	33	19	11	2	1948	97	1	2.99	5	0	4	227	18	0	4.76
	NHL Totals		**1**	**0**	**0**	**0**	**13**	**3**	**0**	**13.85**	....	....	....	....	....	....	....

a QMJHL Second All-Star Team (1989)
b Shared Harry "Hap" Holmes Trophy (fewest goals-against-AHL) with J.C. Bergeron (1990)

RACINE, BRUCE

Goaltender. Catches left. 6', 175 lbs. Born, Cornwall, Ont., August 9, 1966.
(Pittsburgh's 3rd choice, 58th overall, in 1985 Entry Draft).

			Regular Season								Playoffs						
Season	Club	Lea	GP	W	L	T	Mins	GA	SO	Avg	GP	W	L	Mins	GA	SO	Avg
1984-85	Northeastern	H.E.	26	11	14	1	1615	103	1	3.83	....	....	....	....	....	....	....
1985-86	Northeastern	H.E.	32	17	14	1	1920	147	0	4.56	....	....	....	....	....	....	....
1986-87ab	Northeastern	H.E.	33	12	18	3	1966	133	0	4.06	....	....	....	....	....	....	....
1987-88b	Northeastern	H.E.	30	15	11	4	1808	108	1	3.58	....	....	....	....	....	....	....
1988-89	Muskegon	IHL	51	*37	11	0	*3039	184	*3	3.63	5	4	1	300	15	0	3.00
1989-90	Muskegon	IHL	49	29	15	4	2911	182	1	3.75	....	....	....	....	....	....	....

a Hockey East First All-Star Team (1987)
b NCAA East First All-American Team (1987, 1988)

RANFORD, BILL

Goaltender. Catches left. 5'10", 170 lbs. Born, Brandon, Man., December 14, 1966.
(Boston's 2nd choice, 52nd overall, in 1985 Entry Draft).

			Regular Season								Playoffs						
Season	Club	Lea	GP	W	L	T	Mins	GA	SO	Avg	GP	W	L	Mins	GA	SO	Avg
1983-84	N. Westminster	WHL	27	10	14	0	1450	130	0	5.38	1	0	0	27	2	0	4.44
1984-85	N. Westminster	WHL	38	19	17	0	2034	142	0	4.19	7	2	3	309	26	0	5.05
1985-86	N. Westminster	WHL	53	17	29	1	2791	225	0	4.84	....	....	....	....	....	....	....
	Boston	**NHL**	**4**	**3**	**1**	**0**	**240**	**10**	**0**	**2.50**	**2**	**0**	**2**	**120**	**7**	**0**	**3.50**
1986-87	**Boston**	**NHL**	**41**	**16**	**20**	**2**	**2234**	**124**	**3**	**3.33**	**2**	**0**	**2**	**123**	**8**	**0**	**3.90**
	Moncton	AHL	3	3	0	0	180	6	0	2.00	....	....	....	....	....	....	....
1987-88	**Edmonton**	**NHL**	**6**	**3**	**0**	**2**	**325**	**16**	**0**	**2.95**	....	....	....	....	....	....	....
	Maine	AHL	51	27	16	6	2856	165	1	3.47	....	....	....	....	....	....	....
1988-89	**Edmonton**	**NHL**	**29**	**15**	**8**	**2**	**1509**	**88**	**1**	**3.50**	....	....	....	....	....	....	....
1989-90a	**Edmonton**	**NHL**	**56**	**24**	**16**	**9**	**3107**	**165**	**1**	**3.19**	***22**	***16**	**6**	***1401**	**59**	**0**	**2.53**
	NHL Totals		**136**	**61**	**45**	**15**	**7415**	**403**	**5**	**3.26**	**26**	**16**	**10**	**1644**	**74**	**0**	**2.70**

a Won Conn Smythe Trophy (1990)

Traded to **Edmonton** by **Boston** with Geoff Courtnall and future considerations for Andy Moog, March 8, 1988.

RAYMOND, ALAIN

Goaltender. Catches left. 5'10", 177 lbs. Born, Rimouski, Que., June 24, 1965.
(Washington's 11th choice, 224th overall, in 1983 Entry Draft).

			Regular Season								Playoffs						
Season	Club	Lea	GP	W	L	T	Mins	GA	SO	Avg	GP	W	L	Mins	GA	SO	Avg
1983-84	Trois Rivieres	QMJHL	53	18	25	0	2725	223	3	4.91	....	....	....	....	....	....	....
1984-85a	Trois Rivieres	QMJHL	58	29	26	1	3295	220	2	4.01	7	3	5	438	32	0	4.38
1985-86	Cdn. Olympic	....	46	25	18	3	2571	151	4	3.52	....	....	....	....	....	....	....
1986-87b	Fort Wayne	IHL	45	23	16	0	2433	134	1	*3.30	6	2	3	320	23	0	4.31
1987-88	**Washington**	**NHL**	**1**	**0**	**1**	**0**	**40**	**2**	**0**	**3.00**	....	....	....	....	....	....	....
	Fort Wayne	IHL	40	20	15	3	2271	142	2	3.75	2	0	1	67	7		6.27
1988-89	Baltimore	AHL	41	14	22	2	2301	162	0	4.22	....	....	....	....	....	....	....
1989-90	Baltimore	AHL	11	4	5	2	612	34	0	3.33	....	....	....	....	....	....	....
	Hampton-Roads	ECHL	31	17	12	1	2048	123	0	3.60	....	....	....	....	....	....	....
	NHL Totals		**1**	**0**	**1**	**0**	**40**	**2**	**0**	**3.00**	....	....	....	....	....	....	....

a QMJHL Second All-Star Team (1985)
b Shared James Norris Memorial Trophy (IHL's Top Goaltender) with Michel Dufour (1987)

REAUGH, DARYL (RAY)

Goaltender. Catches left. 6'4", 200 lbs. Born, Prince George, B.C., February 13, 1965.
(Edmonton's 2nd choice, 42nd overall, in 1984 Entry Draft).

			Regular Season								Playoffs						
Season	Club	Lea	GP	W	L	T	Mins	GA	SO	Avg	GP	W	L	Mins	GA	SO	Avg
1983-84	Kamloops	WHL	55	....	....	....	2748	199	1	4.34	17	....	....	972	57	0	3.52
1984-85	**Edmonton**	**NHL**	**1**	**0**	**1**	**0**	**60**	**5**	**0**	**5.00**	....	....	....	....	....	....	....
a	Kamloops	WHL	49	....	....	....	2749	170	2	3.71	14	....	....	787	56	0	4.27
1985-86	Nova Scotia	AHL	38	15	18	4	2205	156	0	4.24	....	....	....	....	....	....	....
1986-87	Nova Scotia	AHL	46	19	22	0	2637	163	1	3.71	2	0	2	120	13	0	6.50
1987-88	**Edmonton**	**NHL**	**6**	**1**	**1**	**0**	**176**	**14**	**0**	**4.77**	....	....	....	....	....	....	....
	Nova Scotia	AHL	8	2	5	0	443	33	0	4.47	....	....	....	....	....	....	....
	Milwaukee	IHL	9	0	8	0	493	44		5.35	....	....	....	....	....	....	....
1988-89	Cape Breton	AHL	13	3	10	0	778	72	0	5.55	....	....	....	....	....	....	....
1989-90	Binghamton	AHL	52	8	31	6	2375	192	0	4.21	....	....	....	....	....	....	....
	NHL Totals		**7**	**1**	**2**	**0**	**236**	**19**	**0**	**4.83**	....	....	....	....	....	....	....

a WHL First All-Star Team, West Division (1985)

REDDICK, ELDON

Goaltender. Catches left. 5'8", 170 lbs. Born, Halifax, N.S., October 6, 1964.

			Regular Season								Playoffs						
Season	Club	Lea	GP	W	L	T	Mins	GA	SO	Avg	GP	W	L	Mins	GA	SO	Avg
1982-83	Nanaimo	WHL	66	19	38	1	3549	383	0	6.46	....	....	....	....	....	....	....
1983-84	N. Westminster	WHL	50	24	22	2	2930	215	0	4.40	9	4	5	542	53	0	5.87
1984-85	Brandon	WHL	47	14	30	1	2585	243	0	5.64	....	....	....	....	....	....	....
1985-86	Fort Wayne	IHL	29	15	11	0	1674	86	*3	3.00	....	....	....	....	....	....	....
1986-87	**Winnipeg**	**NHL**	**48**	**21**	**21**	**4**	**2762**	**149**	**0**	**3.24**	**3**	**0**	**2**	**166**	**10**	**0**	**3.61**
1987-88	**Winnipeg**	**NHL**	**28**	**9**	**13**	**3**	**1487**	**102**	**0**	**4.12**	....	....	....	....	....	....	....
	Moncton	AHL	9	2	6	1	545	26	0	2.86	....	....	....	....	....	....	....
1988-89	**Winnipeg**	**NHL**	**41**	**11**	**17**	**7**	**2109**	**144**	**0**	**4.10**	....	....	....	....	....	....	....
1989-90	**Edmonton**	**NHL**	**11**	**5**	**4**	**2**	**604**	**31**	**0**	**3.08**	**1**	**0**	**0**	**2**	**0**	**0**	**0.00**
	Cape Breton	AHL	15	9	4	1	821	54	0	3.95	....	....	....	....	....	....	....
	Phoenix	IHL	3	2	1	0	185	7	0	2.27	....	....	....	....	....	....	....
	NHL Totals		**128**	**46**	**55**	**16**	**6962**	**426**	**0**	**3.67**	**4**	**0**	**2**	**168**	**10**	**0**	**3.57**

Signed as a free agent by **Winnipeg**, September 27, 1985. Traded to **Edmonton** by **Winnipeg** for future considerations, September 28, 1989.

REED, BRANDON

Goaltender. Catches left. 5'10", 170 lbs. Born, Lansing, MI, January 23, 1969.
(NY Islanders' 1st choice, 11th overall, in 1990 Supplemental Draft).

			Regular Season								Playoffs						
Season	Club	Lea	GP	W	L	T	Mins	GA	SO	Avg	GP	W	L	Mins	GA	SO	Avg
1987-88	Lake Superior	CCHA	1	0	0	0	20	3	0	9.00	....	....	....	....	....	....	....
1988-89	Lake Superior	CCHA	3	1	0	1	111	3	0	1.63	....	....	....	....	....	....	....
1989-90	Lake Superior	CCHA	19	11	3	2	975	61	0	3.76	....	....	....	....	....	....	....

REESE, JEFF

Goaltender. Catches left. 5'9", 170 lbs. Born, Brantford, Ont., March 24, 1966.
(Toronto's 3rd choice, 67th overall, in 1984 Entry Draft).

			Regular Season								Playoffs						
Season	Club	Lea	GP	W	L	T	Mins	GA	SO	Avg	GP	W	L	Mins	GA	SO	Avg
1983-84	London	OHL	43	18	19	0	2308	173		4.50	6	3	3	327	27	0	4.95
1984-85	London	OHL	50	31	15	1	2878	186	1	3.88	8	5	2	440	20	1	2.73
1985-86	London	OHL	57	25	26	3	3281	215	0	3.93	5	0	4	299	25	0	5.02
1986-87	Newmarket	AHL	50	11	29	0	2822	193	1	4.10	....	....	....	....	....	....	....
1987-88	**Toronto**	**NHL**	**5**	**1**	**2**	**1**	**249**	**17**	**0**	**4.10**	....	....	....	....	....	....	....
	Newmarket	AHL	28	10	14	3	1587	103	0	3.89	....	....	....	....	....	....	....
1988-89	**Toronto**	**NHL**	**10**	**2**	**6**	**1**	**486**	**40**	**0**	**4.94**	....	....	....	....	....	....	....
	Newmarket	AHL	37	17	14	3	2072	132	0	3.82	....	....	....	....	....	....	....
1989-90	**Toronto**	**NHL**	**21**	**9**	**6**	**3**	**1101**	**81**	**0**	**4.41**	**2**	**1**	**1**	**108**	**6**	**0**	**3.33**
	Newmarket	AHL	7	3	2	2	431	29	0	4.04	....	....	....	....	....	....	....
	NHL Totals		**36**	**12**	**14**	**5**	**1836**	**138**	**0**	**4.51**	**2**	**1**	**1**	**108**	**6**	**0**	**3.33**

REID, JOHN

Goaltender. Catches right. 5'11", 202 lbs. Born, Windsor, Ont., February 18, 1967.
(Chicago's 8th choice, 158th overall, in 1985 Entry Draft).

			Regular Season								Playoffs						
Season	Club	Lea	GP	W	L	T	Mins	GA	SO	Avg	GP	W	L	Mins	GA	SO	Avg
1984-85	Belleville	OHL	31	16	6	0	1443	92	0	3.83	2	1	0	79	4	0	3.04
1985-86	North Bay	OHL	47	28	14	2	2627	164	1	3.75	10	5	4	577	37	0	3.85
1986-87	North Bay	OHL	47	*33	12	1	2737	142	1	3.11	24	14	10	1496	92	0	3.69
1987-88	Colorado	IHL	32	15	14	1	1673	117	0	4.20	....	....	....	....	....	....	....
	Saginaw	IHL	5	3	1	0	260	11	0	2.54	1	0	1	58	5		5.17
1988-89	Indianapolis	IHL	5	2	2	0	244	16	0	3.93	....	....	....	....	....	....	....
	Saginaw	IHL	12	6	3	0	633	37	0	3.51	....	....	....	....	....	....	....
1989-90	Nashville	ECHL	36	18	17	3	2004	149	0	4.46	....	....	....	....	....	....	....

REIMER, MARK (RIGH-muhr)

Goaltender. Catches left. 5'11", 170 lbs. Born, Calgary, Alta., March 23, 1967.
(Detroit's 5th choice, 74th overall, in 1987 Entry Draft).

			Regular Season								Playoffs						
Season	Club	Lea	GP	W	L	T	Mins	GA	SO	Avg	GP	W	L	Mins	GA	SO	Avg
1984-85	Saskatoon	WHL	2	2	0	0	120	7	0	3.50	....	....	....	....	....	....	....
1985-86	Saskatoon	WHL	41	17	18	3	2362	192	0	4.88	5	....	....	300	25	0	5.00
1986-87	Saskatoon	WHL	42	24	15	2	2442	141	1	3.46	6	....	....	360	20	0	3.33
1987-88	Portland	WHL	38	13	23	2	2268	208	0	5.50	....	....	....	....	....	....	....
	Flint	IHL	5	0	3	0	169	22	0	7.86	....	....	....	....	....	....	....
	Adirondack	AHL	8	6	1	0	459	24	0	3.14	1	0	0	20	0	0	0.00
1988-89	Adirondack	AHL	18	5	6	3	900	64	0	4.27	....	....	....	....	....	....	....
	Flint	IHL	17	5	8	0	1022	83	0	4.87	....	....	....	....	....	....	....
1989-90	Adirondack	AHL	36	14	17	3	2092	131	0	3.76	....	....	....	....	....	....	....

REIN, KENTON (RIGHN)

Goaltender. Catches left. 5'11', 195 lbs. Born, Saskatoon, Sask., September 12, 1967.
(Buffalo's 11th choice, 194th overall, in 1986 Entry Draft).

			Regular Season								Playoffs						
Season	Club	Lea	GP	W	L	T	Mins	GA	SO	Avg	GP	W	L	Mins	GA	SO	Avg
1985-86	Prince Albert	WHL	23	18	3	0	1302	71	0	3.27	6	5	0	308	4	2	0.78
1986-87a	Prince Albert	WHL	51	29	18	3	2996	159	0	3.18	8	3	5	443	31	0	4.20
1987-88	Flint	IHL	1	0	1	0	20	3		9.00	....	....	....	....	....	....	....
1988-89	Rochester	AHL	15	5	6	2	676	39	2	3.46	....	....	....	....	....	....	....
	Flint	IHL	8	1	6	0	439	29	0	3.96	....	....	....	....	....	....	....
1989-90	Winston-Salem	ECHL	24	16	6	1	1353	88	0	3.90	....	....	....	....	....	....	....

a WHL First All-Star Team (1987)

REPP, CARL

Goaltender. Catches right. 6'1", 175 lbs. Born, Trail, B.C., June 10, 1966.
(Los Angeles' 1st choice, 23rd overall, in 1989 Supplemental Draft).

			Regular Season								Playoffs						
Season	Club	Lea	GP	W	L	T	Mins	GA	SO	Avg	GP	W	L	Mins	GA	SO	Avg
1988-89	UBC	CWUAA	28	13	14	1	1696	117	2	4.14	....	....	....	....	....	....	....
1989-90	New Haven	AHL	24	8	13	2	1393	98	0	4.22	....	....	....	....	....	....	....
	Phoenix	IHL	12	1	7	0	527	51	0	5.90	....	....	....	....	....	....	....

RHODES, DAMIAN

Goaltender. Catches left. 6', 165 lbs. Born, St. Paul, MN, May 28, 1969.
(Toronto's 6th choice, 112th overall, in 1987 Entry Draft).

			Regular Season								Playoffs						
Season	Club	Lea	GP	W	L	T	Mins	GA	SO	Avg	GP	W	L	Mins	GA	SO	Avg
1987-88	Michigan Tech	WCHA	29	16	10	1	1625	114	0	4.20	....	....	....	....	....	....	....
1988-89	Michigan Tech	WCHA	37	15	22	0	2216	163	0	4.41	....	....	....	....	....	....	....
1989-90	Michigan Tech	WCHA	25	6	17	0	1358	119	0	6.26	....	....	....	....	....	....	....

RICHARDS, MARK A.

Goaltender. Catches left. 5'7", 180 lbs. Born, Jamison, PA, June 24, 1969.
(Winnipeg's 1st choice, 19th overall, in 1990 Supplemental Draft).

			Regular Season								Playoffs						
Season	Club	Lea	GP	W	L	T	Mins	GA	SO	Avg	GP	W	L	Mins	GA	SO	Avg
1988-89	U. of Lowell	H.E.	18	1	12	1	918	83	0	5.42	....	....	....	....	....	....	....
1989-90	U. of Lowell	H.E.	32	11	19	2	1773	149	0	5.04	....	....	....	....	....	....	....

RICHTER, MIKE

Goaltender. Catches left. 5'11", 185 lbs. Born, Philadelphia, PA, September 22, 1966.
(NY Rangers' 2nd choice, 28th overall, in 1985 Entry Draft.)

			Regular Season								Playoffs						
Season	Club	Lea	GP	W	L	T	Mins	GA	SO	Avg	GP	W	L	Mins	GA	SO	Avg
1985-86a	U. Wisconsin	WCHA	24	14	9	0	1394	92	1	3.96	....	....	....	....	....	....	....
1986-87b	U. Wisconsin	WCHA	36	19	16	1	2136	126	0	3.54	....	....	....	....	....	....	....
1987-88	Colorado	IHL	22	16	5	0	1298	68	1	3.14	10	5	3	536	35		3.92
	U.S. National	....	29	17	7	2	1559	86	0	3.31	....	....	....	....	....	....	....
	U.S. Olympic	....	4	2	2	0	230	15	0	3.91	....	....	....	....	....	....	....
1988-89	Denver	IHL	*57	23	26	0	3031	217	1	4.30	4	0	4	210	21	0	6.00
	NY Rangers	**NHL**	....	....	....	....	....	....	....	....	**1**	**1**	**0**	**58**	**4**	**0**	**4.14**
1989-90	**NY Rangers**	**NHL**	**23**	**12**	**5**	**5**	**1320**	**66**	**0**	**3.00**	**6**	**3**	**2**	**330**	**19**	**0**	**3.45**
	Flint	IHL	13	7	4	2	782	49	0	3.76	....	....	....	....	....	....	....
	NHL Totals		**23**	**12**	**5**	**5**	**1320**	**66**	**0**	**3.00**	**7**	**3**	**3**	**388**	**23**	**0**	**3.55**

a WCHA Rookie of the Year (1986)
b WCHA Second All-Star Team (1987)

RIENDEAU, VINCENT (ree-EHN-doh)

Goaltender. Catches left. 5'10", 185 lbs. Born, St. Hyacinthe, Que., April 20, 1966.

			Regular Season								Playoffs						
Season	Club	Lea	GP	W	L	T	Mins	GA	SO	Avg	GP	W	L	Mins	GA	SO	Avg
1985-86a	Drummondville	QMJHL	57	33	20	3	3336	215	2	3.87	23	10	13	1271	106	1	5.00
1986-87b	Sherbrooke	AHL	41	25	14	0	2363	114	2	2.89	13	8	5	742	47	0	3.80
1987-88	**Montreal**	**NHL**	**1**	**0**	**0**	**0**	**36**	**5**	**0**	**8.33**	....	....	....	....	....	....	....
c	Sherbrooke	AHL	44	27	13	3	2521	112	*4	*2.67	2	0	2	127	7	0	3.31
1988-89	**St. Louis**	**NHL**	**32**	**11**	**15**	**5**	**1842**	**108**	**0**	**3.52**	....	....	....	....	....	....	....
1989-90	**St. Louis**	**NHL**	**43**	**17**	**19**	**5**	**2551**	**149**	**1**	**3.50**	**8**	**3**	**4**	**397**	**24**	**0**	**3.63**
	NHL Totals		**76**	**28**	**34**	**10**	**4429**	**262**	**1**	**3.55**	**8**	**3**	**4**	**397**	**24**	**0**	**3.63**

a QMJHL Second All-Star Team (1986)
b Won Harry "Hap" Holmes Memorial Trophy (AHL Leading Goaltender) (1987)
c Shared Harry "Hap" Holmes Memorial Trophy (AHL Leading Goaltender) with Jocelyn Perreault (1988)

Signed as a free agent by **Montreal**, October 9, 1985. Traded to **St. Louis** by **Montreal** with Sergio Momesso for Jocelyn Lemieux, Darrell May and St. Louis' second round choice (Patrice Brisebois) in 1989 Entry Draft, August 9, 1988.

ROMAINE, MARK

Goaltender. Catches left. 5'9", 160 lbs. Born, Sharon, MA, October 25, 1968.
(New Jersey's 2nd choice, 10th overall, in 1989 Supplemental Draft).

			Regular Season								Playoffs						
Season	Club	Lea	GP	W	L	T	Mins	GA	SO	Avg	GP	W	L	Mins	GA	SO	Avg
1986-87	Providence	H.E.	5	....	....	....	289	25	0	5.19	....	....	....	....	....	....	....
1987-88	Providence	H.E.	19	....	....	....	883	60	0	4.08	....	....	....	....	....	....	....
1988-89	Providence	H.E.	29	....	....	....	1536	95	1	3.71	....	....	....	....	....	....	....
1989-90	Providence	H.E.	19	12	5	1	1023	52	1	3.05	....	....	....	....	....	....	....

ROSATI, MICHAEL

Goaltender. Catches left. 5'10", 170 lbs. Born, Toronto, Ont., January 7, 1968.
(N Y Rangers' 6th choice, 131st overall, in 1988 Entry Draft).

			Regular Season								Playoffs						
Season	Club	Lea	GP	W	L	T	Mins	GA	SO	Avg	GP	W	L	Mins	GA	SO	Avg
1987-88	Hamilton	OHL	62	29	25	3	3468	233	1	4.03	14	8	6	833	66	0	4.75
1988-89	Niagara Falls	OHL	52	*28	15	2	2339	174	1	4.45	16	10	4	861	62	0	4.32
1989-90	Erie	ECHL	18	12	5	0	1056	73	0	4.14	....	....	....	....	....	....	....

ROUSSEL, DOMINIC (roo-SEHL)

Goaltender. Catches left. 6'1", 195 lbs. Born, Hull, Que., February 22, 1970.
(Philadelphia's 4th choice, 63rd overall, in 1988 Entry Draft).

			Regular Season								Playoffs						
Season	Club	Lea	GP	W	L	T	Mins	GA	SO	Avg	GP	W	L	Mins	GA	SO	Avg
1987-88	Trois Rivieres	QMJHL	51	18	25	4	2905	251	0	5.18	....	....	....	....	....	....	....
1988-89	Shawinigan	QMJHL	46	24	15	2	2555	171	0	4.02	10	6	4	638	36	0	3.39
1989-90	Shawinigan	QMJHL	37	20	14	1	1985	133	0	4.02	....	....	....	....	....	....	....

ROY, ALAIN

Goaltender. Catches left. 5'10", 170 lbs. Born, Campbellton, N.B., February 6, 1970.
(Winnipeg's 6th choice, 69th overall, in 1989 Entry Draft).

			Regular Season								Playoffs						
Season	Club	Lea	GP	W	L	T	Mins	GA	SO	Avg	GP	W	L	Mins	GA	SO	Avg
1988-89	Harvard	ECAC	16	14	2	0	952	40	0	2.46	....	....	....	....	....	....	....
1989-90	Harvard	ECAC	15	7	8	0	867	54	1	3.74	....	....	....	....	....	....	....

ROY, PATRICK (WAH)

Goaltender. Catches left. 6', 182 lbs. Born, Quebec City, Que., October 5, 1965.
(Montreal's 4th choice, 51st overall, in 1984 Entry Draft).

			Regular Season								Playoffs						
Season	**Club**	**Lea**	**GP**	**W**	**L**	**T**	**Mins**	**GA**	**SO**	**Avg**	**GP**	**W**	**L**	**Mins**	**GA**	**SO**	**Avg**
1982-83	Granby	QMJHL	54				2808	293	0	6.26							
1983-84	Granby	QMJHL	61	29	29	1	3585	265	0	4.44	4	0	4	244	22	0	5.41
1984-85	Granby	QMJHL	44	16	25	1	2463	228	0	5.55							
	Sherbrooke	AHL	1	1	0	0	60	4	0	4.00	12	10	3	*769	37	0	*2.89
	Montreal	**NHL**	**1**	**1**	**0**	**0**	**20**	**0**	**0**	**0.00**							
1985-86ab	**Montreal**	**NHL**	**47**	**23**	**18**	**3**	**2651**	**148**	**1**	**3.35**	**20**	***15**	**5**	**1218**	**39**	***1**	**1.92**
1986-87c	**Montreal**	**NHL**	**46**	**22**	**16**	**6**	**2686**	**131**	**1**	**2.93**	**6**	**4**	**2**	**330**	**22**	**0**	**4.00**
1987-88cd	**Montreal**	**NHL**	**45**	**23**	**12**	**9**	**2586**	**125**	**3**	**2.90**	**8**	**3**	**4**	**430**	**24**	**0**	**3.35**
1988-89cefg	**Montreal**	**NHL**	**48**	**33**	**5**	**6**	**2744**	**113**	**4**	***2.47**	**19**	**13**	**6**	**1206**	**42**	**2**	***2.09**
1989-90efg	**Montreal**	**NHL**	**54**	***31**	**16**	**5**	**3173**	**134**	**3**	***2.53**	**11**	**5**	**6**	**641**	**26**	**1**	**2.43**
	NHL Totals		**241**	**133**	**67**	**29**	**13860**	**651**	**12**	**2.82**	**64**	**40**	**23**	**3825**	**153**	**4**	**2.40**

a Won Conn Smythe Trophy (1986)
b NHL All-Rookie Team (1986)
c Shared William Jennings Trophy with Brian Hayward (1987, 1988, 1989)
d NHL Second All-Star Team (1988)
e Won Vezina Trophy (1989, 1990)
f NHL First All-Star Team (1989, 1990)
g Won Trico Goaltending Award (1989, 1990)

Played in NHL All-Star Game (1988, 1990)

ST. LAURENT, SAM (sa-luh-RAH)

Goaltender. Catches left. 5'10", 190 lbs. Born, Arvida, Que., February 16, 1959.

			Regular Season								Playoffs						
Season	**Club**	**Lea**	**GP**	**W**	**L**	**T**	**Mins**	**GA**	**SO**	**Avg**	**GP**	**W**	**L**	**Mins**	**GA**	**SO**	**Avg**
1977-78	Chicoutimi	QJHL	60				3251	351	0	6.46							
1978-79	Chicoutimi	QJHL	70				3806	290	0	4.57	1			47	8	0	10.21
1979-80	Maine	AHL	5	2	1	0	229	17	0	4.45							
	Toledo	IHL	38				2143	138	2	3.86	4			239	24	0	6.03
1980-81	Maine	AHL	7	3	3	0	363	28	0	4.63							
	Toledo	IHL	30				1614	113	1	4.20							
1981-82	Toledo	IHL	4				248	11	0	2.66							
	Maine	AHL	25	15	7	1	1396	76	0	3.27	4	1	3	240	18	0	4.50
1982-83	Maine	AHL	30				1739	109	0	3.76	*17			*1012	54	0	3.20
1983-84	Maine	AHL	38	14	18	4	2158	145	0	4.03	12	9	2	708	32	*1	*2.71
1984-85a	Maine	AHL	55	26	22	7	3245	168	4	3.11	10	5	5	656	45	0	4.12
1985-86	**New Jersey**	**NHL**	**4**	**2**	**1**	**0**	**188**	**13**	**1**	**4.15**							
	Maine	AHL	50	24	20	4	2862	161	1	3.38							
1986-87	**Detroit**	**NHL**	**6**	**1**	**2**	**2**	**342**	**16**	**0**	**2.81**							
	Adirondack	AHL	25	7	13	0	1397	98	1	4.21	3	0	2	105	10	0	5.71
1987-88	**Detroit**	**NHL**	**6**	**2**	**2**	**0**	**294**	**16**	**0**	**3.27**	**1**	**0**	**0**	**10**	**1**	**0**	**6.00**
	Adirondack	AHL	32	12	14	4	1826	104	2	3.42	1	0	1	59	6	0	6.10
1988-89	**Detroit**	**NHL**	**4**	**0**	**1**	**1**	**141**	**9**	**0**	**3.83**							
b	Adirondack	AHL	34	20	11	3	2054	113	0	3.30	16	*11	5	956	47	*2	*2.95
1989-90	**Detroit**	**NHL**	**14**	**2**	**6**	**1**	**607**	**38**	**0**	**3.76**							
	Adirondack	AHL	13	10	2	1	785	40	0	3.06							
	NHL Totals		**34**	**7**	**12**	**4**	**1572**	**92**	**1**	**3.51**	**1**	**0**	**0**	**10**	**1**	**0**	**6.00**

a AHL Second All-Star Team (1985)
b Won Jack Butterfield Trophy (Playoff MVP-AHL) (1989)

Signed as a free agent by **Philadelphia**, October 10, 1979. Traded to **Detroit** by **New Jersey** for Steve Richmond, August 18, 1986. Traded to **NY Rangers** by **Detroit** for cash, June 26, 1990.

SARJENT, GEOFF

Goaltender. Catches left. 5'9", 175 lbs. Born, Newmarket, Ont., November 30, 1969.
(St. Louis' 1st choice, 17th overall, in 1990 Supplemental Draft).

			Regular Season								Playoffs						
Season	**Club**	**Lea**	**GP**	**W**	**L**	**T**	**Mins**	**GA**	**SO**	**Avg**	**GP**	**W**	**L**	**Mins**	**GA**	**SO**	**Avg**
1988-89	Michigan Tech	WCHA	6	0	3	2	329	22	0	4.01							
1989-90	Michigan Tech	WCHA	19	4	13	0	1043	94	0	5.41							

SCHOEN, BRYAN

Goaltender. Catches left. 6'2", 180 lbs. Born, St. Paul, MN, September 9, 1970.
(Minnesota's 6th choice, 91st overall, in 1989 Entry Draft).

			Regular Season								Playoffs						
Season	**Club**	**Lea**	**GP**	**W**	**L**	**T**	**Mins**	**GA**	**SO**	**Avg**	**GP**	**W**	**L**	**Mins**	**GA**	**SO**	**Avg**
1988-89	Minnetonka	HS	17				765	23	0	1.35							
1989-90	U. of Denver	WCHA	18	8	9	0	1040	81	0	4.67							

SCOTT, RON

Goaltender. Catches left. 5'8", 155 lbs. Born, Guelph, Ont., July 21, 1960.

			Regular Season								Playoffs						
Season	**Club**	**Lea**	**GP**	**W**	**L**	**T**	**Mins**	**GA**	**SO**	**Avg**	**GP**	**W**	**L**	**Mins**	**GA**	**SO**	**Avg**
1980-81	Michigan State	WCHA	33	11	21	1	1899	123	2	3.89							
1981-82	Michigan State	CCHA	39	24	13	1	2298	109	2	2.85							
1982-83a	Michigan State	CCHA	40	29	9	1	2273	100	2	2.64							
1983-84	**NY Rangers**	**NHL**	**9**	**2**	**3**	**3**	**485**	**29**	**0**	**3.59**							
b	Tulsa	CHL	29	13	13	3	1717	109	0	3.81	5			280	20	0	4.28
1984-85	New Haven	AHL	36	13	18	4	2047	130	0	3.81							
1985-86	**NY Rangers**	**NHL**	**4**	**0**	**3**	**0**	**156**	**11**	**0**	**4.23**							
	New Haven	AHL	19	8	8	1	1069	66	1	3.70	2	1	1	143	8	0	3.36
1986-87	**NY Rangers**	**NHL**	**1**	**0**	**0**	**1**	**65**	**5**	**0**	**4.62**							
	New Haven	AHL	29	16	7	0	1744	107	2	3.68							
1987-88	**NY Rangers**	**NHL**	**2**	**1**	**1**	**0**	**90**	**6**	**0**	**4.00**							
	New Haven	AHL	17	8	7	1	963	49	0	3.05							
	Colorado	IHL	8	3	4	0	395	33	0	5.01	5	1	4	259	16		3.71
1988-89	Denver	IHL	18	7	11	0	990	79	0	4.79							
1989-90	**Los Angeles**	**NHL**	**12**	**5**	**6**	**0**	**654**	**40**	**0**	**3.67**	**1**	**0**	**0**	**32**	**4**	**0**	**7.50**
	New Haven	AHL	22	8	11	1	1224	79	1	3.87							
	NHL Totals		**28**	**8**	**13**	**4**	**1450**	**91**	**0**	**3.77**	**1**	**0**	**0**	**32**	**4**	**0**	**7.50**

a CCHA First All-Star Team (1983)
b Shared Terry Sawchuk Trophy (CHL's leading goaltenders) with John Vanbiesbrouck (1984)

Signed as a free agent by **NY Rangers**, May 25, 1983.

SHARPLES, WARREN

Goaltender. Catches left. 6', 190 lbs. Born, Calgary, Alta., March 1, 1968.
(Calgary's 8th choice, 184th overall, in 1986 Entry Draft).

			Regular Season								Playoffs						
Season	**Club**	**Lea**	**GP**	**W**	**L**	**T**	**Mins**	**GA**	**SO**	**Avg**	**GP**	**W**	**L**	**Mins**	**GA**	**SO**	**Avg**
1986-87	U. of Michigan	CCHA	32	12	16	1	1720	148	1	5.14							
1987-88	U. of Michigan	CCHA	33	18	15	0	1930	132	0	4.10							
1988-89	U. of Michigan	CCHA	33	17	11	2	1887	116	0	3.69							
1989-90	U. of Michigan	CCHA	*39	20	10	0	*2165	117	0	3.24							
	Salt Lake	IHL	3	0	3	0	178	13	0	4.38							

SIDORKIEWICZ, PETER (sih-DOHR-kuh-vihch)

Goaltender. Catches left. 5'9", 180 lbs. Born, Dabrown Bialostocka, Poland, June 29, 1963.
(Washington's 5th choice, 91st overall, in 1981 Entry Draft).

			Regular Season								Playoffs						
Season	**Club**	**Lea**	**GP**	**W**	**L**	**T**	**Mins**	**GA**	**SO**	**Avg**	**GP**	**W**	**L**	**Mins**	**GA**	**SO**	**Avg**
1980-81	Oshawa	OHA	7	3	3	0	308	24	0	4.68	5	2	2	266	20	0	4.52
1981-82	Oshawa	OHL	29	14	11	1	1553	123	*2	4.75	1	0	0	13	1	0	4.62
1982-83	Oshawa	OHL	60	36	20	3	3536	213	0	3.61	17	15	1	1020	60	0	3.53
1983-84a	Oshawa	OHL	52	28	21	1	2966	250	1	4.15	7	3	4	420	27	*1	3.86
1984-85	Binghamton	AHL	45	31	9	5	2691	137	3	3.05	8	4	4	481	31	0	3.87
	Fort Worth	IHL	10	4	4	2	590	43	0	4.37							
1985-86	Binghamton	AHL	49	21	22	3	2819	150	2	*3.19	4	1	3	235	12	0	3.06
1986-87b	Binghamton	AHL	57	23	16	0	3304	161	4	2.92	13	6	7	794	36	0	*2.72
1987-88	**Hartford**	**NHL**	**1**	**0**	**1**	**0**	**60**	**6**	**0**	**6.00**							
	Binghamton	AHL	42	19	17	3	2345	144	0	3.68	3	0	2	147	8	0	3.27
1988-89c	**Hartford**	**NHL**	**44**	**22**	**18**	**4**	**2635**	**133**	**4**	**3.03**	**2**	**0**	**2**	**124**	**8**	**0**	**3.87**
1989-90	**Hartford**	**NHL**	**46**	**19**	**19**	**7**	**2703**	**161**	**1**	**3.57**	**7**	**3**	**4**	**429**	**23**	**0**	**3.22**
	NHL Totals		**91**	**41**	**38**	**11**	**5398**	**300**	**5**	**3.33**	**9**	**3**	**6**	**553**	**31**	**0**	**3.36**

a OHL Third All-Star Team (1984).
b AHL Second All-Star Team (1987)
c NHL All-Rookie Team (1989)

Traded to **Hartford** by **Washington** with Dean Evason for David Jensen, March 12, 1985.

SIMPSON, SHAWN

Goaltender. Catches left. 5'11", 180 lbs. Born, Gloucester Ont., August 10, 1968.
(Washington's 3rd choice, 60th overall, in 1986 Entry Draft).

			Regular Season								Playoffs						
Season	**Club**	**Lea**	**GP**	**W**	**L**	**T**	**Mins**	**GA**	**SO**	**Avg**	**GP**	**W**	**L**	**Mins**	**GA**	**SO**	**Avg**
1985-86	S.S. Marie	OHL	42	10	26	1	2213	217	1	5.88							
1986-87a	S.S. Marie	OHL	46	20	22	2	2673	184	0	4.13	4	0	4	243	17	0	4.20
1987-88	S.S. Marie	OHL	57	26	29	1	3214	234	2	4.37	6	2	4	401	27	0	4.04
1988-89	Baltimore	AHL	1	0	1	0	60	7	0	7.00							
	Oshawa	OHL	33	18	10	3	1818	131	0	4.32	6	2	4	368	23	1	3.75
1989-90	Baltimore	AHL	15	6	4	1	733	45	0	3.68							

a OHL Second All-Star Team (1987)

SKORODENSKI, WARREN

Goaltender. Catches left. 6'1", 180 lbs. Born, Winnipeg, Man., March 22, 1960.

			Regular Season								Playoffs						
Season	**Club**	**Lea**	**GP**	**W**	**L**	**T**	**Mins**	**GA**	**SO**	**Avg**	**GP**	**W**	**L**	**Mins**	**GA**	**SO**	**Avg**
1977-78	Calgary	WHL	53	8	22	10	2460	213	1	5.20							
1978-79	Calgary	WHL	66	26	31	5	3595	309	1	5.16	15	7	8	884	61	0	4.14
1979-80	Calgary	WHL	66	39	23	2	3724	261	1	4.21	7	3	4	357	29	0	4.87
1980-81	New Brunswick	AHL	2	0	1	0	124	9	0	4.35							
	Flint	IHL	47				2602	189	2	4.36	6			301	18	0	3.58
1981-82	**Chicago**	**NHL**	**1**	**0**	**1**	**0**	**60**	**5**	**0**	**5.00**							
a	New Brunswick	AHL	28	16	8	4	1644	70	*3	*2.55	2	0	2	90	6	0	4.00
1982-83	Springfield	AHL	13				592	49	0	4.97							
	Birmingham	CHL	25	11	11	1	1450	81	1	3.35	5			195	19	0	5.85
1983-84	Sherbrooke	AHL	19	5	10	2	1048	88	0	5.04							
	Springfield	AHL	14	3	11	0	756	67	0	5.32	2	0	2	124	13	0	6.28
1984-85	**Chicago**	**NHL**	**27**	**11**	**9**	**3**	**1396**	**75**	**2**	**3.22**	**2**	**0**	**0**	**33**	**6**	**0**	**10.91**
1985-86	**Chicago**	**NHL**	**1**	**0**	**1**	**0**	**60**	**6**	**0**	**6.00**							
	Nova Scotia	AHL	32	11	14	2	1716	109	0	3.81							
1986-87	**Chicago**	**NHL**	**3**	**1**	**0**	**1**	**155**	**7**	**0**	**2.71**							
	Nova Scotia	AHL	32	10	15	0	1813	121	2	4.00							
	Saginaw	IHL	6	4	1	0	319	21	0	3.95	6	3	2	304	24	0	4.74
1987-88	**Edmonton**	**NHL**	**3**	**0**	**0**	**0**	**61**	**7**	**0**	**6.89**							
	Nova Scotia	AHL	46	25	15	5	2746	171	0	3.74	5	1	4	305	22	0	4.33
1988-89	Cape Breton	AHL	25	11	13	1	1497	111	0	4.45							
	Cdn. National	....	22	8	9	1	1160	82	0	4.24							
1989-90	Cdn. National	....	41	18	17	0	2182	140	0	3.85							
	NHL Totals		**35**	**12**	**11**	**4**	**1732**	**100**	**2**	**3.46**	**2**	**0**	**0**	**33**	**6**	**0**	**10.91**

a Shared Harry "Hap" Holmes Memorial Trophy with Bob Janecyk (1982)

Signed as a free agent by **Chicago**, August 12, 1979. Signed as a free agent by **Edmonton**, October 8, 1987.

SNOW, GARTH

Goaltender. Catches left. 6'3", 200 lbs. Born, Wrentham, MA, July 28, 1969.
(Quebec's 6th choice, 114th overall, in 1987 Entry Draft).

			Regular Season								Playoffs						
Season	**Club**	**Lea**	**GP**	**W**	**L**	**T**	**Mins**	**GA**	**SO**	**Avg**	**GP**	**W**	**L**	**Mins**	**GA**	**SO**	**Avg**
1988-89	U. of Maine	H.E.	5	2	2	0	241	14	1	3.49							
1989-90							DID NOT PLAY										

STAUBER, ROBB

Goaltender. Catches left. 5'10", 165 lbs. Born, Duluth, MN, November 25, 1967.
(Los Angeles' 5th choice, 107th overall, in 1986 Entry Draft).

			Regular Season								Playoffs						
Season	**Club**	**Lea**	**GP**	**W**	**L**	**T**	**Mins**	**GA**	**SO**	**Avg**	**GP**	**W**	**L**	**Mins**	**GA**	**SO**	**Avg**
1986-87	U. Minnesota	WCHA	20	13	5	0	1072	63	0	3.53							
1987-88abcd	U. Minnesota	WCHA	44	34	10	0	2621	119	5	2.72							
1988-89e	U. Minnesota	WCHA	34	26	8	0	2024	82	0	2.43							
1989-90	**Los Angeles**	**NHL**	**2**	**0**	**1**	**0**	**83**	**11**	**0**	**7.95**							
	New Haven	AHL	14	6	6	2	851	43	0	3.03							
	NHL Totals		**2**	**0**	**1**	**0**	**83**	**11**	**0**	**7.95**							

a Won Hobey Baker Memorial Award (Top U.S. Collegiate Player) (1988)
b NCAA West First All-American Team (1988)
c WCHA Player of the Year (1988)
d WCHA First All-Star Team (1988)
e WCHA Second All-Star Team (1989)

STEFAN, GREGORY STEVEN (GREG) (STEH-fihn)

Goaltender. Catches left. 5'11", 180 lbs. Born, Brantford, Ont., February 11, 1961.
(Detroit's 5th choice, 128th overall, in 1981 Entry Draft).

			Regular Season								Playoffs						
Season	Club	Lea	GP	W	L	T	Mins	GA	SO	Avg	GP	W	L	Mins	GA	SO	Avg
1979-80	Oshawa	OHA	17	8	6	0	897	58	0	3.88	....	....	....	....	....	....	....
1980-81	Oshawa	OHA	46	23	14	3	2407	174	0	4.34	6	2	3	298	20	0	4.02
1981-82	**Detroit**	**NHL**	**2**	**0**	**2**	**0**	**120**	**10**	**0**	**5.00**	....	....	....	....	....	....	....
	Adirondack	AHL	29	11	13	3	1571	99	2	3.78	1	0	0	20	0	0	0.00
1982-83	**Detroit**	**NHL**	**35**	**6**	**16**	**9**	**1847**	**139**	**0**	**4.52**	....	....	....	....	....	....	....
1983-84	**Detroit**	**NHL**	**50**	**19**	**22**	**2**	**2600**	**152**	**2**	**3.51**	**3**	**1**	**2**	**210**	**8**	**0**	**2.29**
1984-85	**Detroit**	**NHL**	**46**	**21**	**19**	**3**	**2635**	**190**	**0**	**4.33**	**3**	**0**	**3**	**138**	**17**	**0**	**7.39**
1985-86	**Detroit**	**NHL**	**37**	**10**	**20**	**5**	**2068**	**155**	**1**	**4.50**	....	....	....	....	....	....	....
1986-87	**Detroit**	**NHL**	**43**	**20**	**17**	**3**	**2351**	**135**	**1**	**3.45**	**9**	**4**	**5**	**508**	**24**	**0**	**2.83**
1987-88	**Detroit**	**NHL**	**33**	**17**	**9**	**5**	**1854**	**96**	**1**	**3.11**	**10**	**5**	**4**	**531**	**32**	**1**	**3.62**
1988-89	**Detroit**	**NHL**	**46**	**21**	**17**	**3**	**2499**	**167**	**0**	**4.01**	**5**	**2**	**3**	**294**	**18**	**0**	**3.67**
1989-90	**Detroit**	**NHL**	**7**	**1**	**5**	**0**	**359**	**24**	**0**	**4.01**	....	....	....	....	....	....	....
	Adirondack	AHL	3	1	0	1	128	7	0	3.28	....	....	....	....	....	....	....
	NHL Totals		**299**	**115**	**128**	**30**	**16333**	**1068**	**5**	**3.92**	**30**	**12**	**17**	**1681**	**99**	**1**	**3.53**

STOLP, JEFFREY

Goaltender. Catches left. 6'0", 170 lbs. Born, Hibbing, MN, June 20, 1970.
(Minnesota's 4th choice, 64th overall, in 1988 Entry Draft).

			Regular Season								Playoffs						
Season	Club	Lea	GP	W	L	T	Mins	GA	SO	Avg	GP	W	L	Mins	GA	SO	Avg
1988-89	U. Minnesota	WCHA	16	7	2	3	742	45	0	3.64	....	....	....	....	....	....	....
1989-90	U. Minnesota	WCHA	10	5	1	0	417	33	1	4.75	....	....	....	....	....	....	....

TABARACCI, RICHARD

Goaltender. Catches left. 5'10", 185 lbs. Born, Toronto, Ont., January 2, 1969.
(Pittsburgh's 2nd choice, 26th overall, in 1987 Entry Draft).

			Regular Season								Playoffs						
Season	Club	Lea	GP	W	L	T	Mins	GA	SO	Avg	GP	W	L	Mins	GA	SO	Avg
1986-87	Cornwall	OHL	59	23	32	3	3347	290	1	5.20	5	1	4	303	26	0	3.17
1987-88a	Cornwall	OHL	58	*33	18	6	3448	200	*3	3.48	11	5	6	642	37	0	3.46
	Muskegon	IHL	...	...	...	...	....	....	...	....	1	0	0	13	1	0	4.62
1988-89	**Pittsburgh**	**NHL**	**1**	**0**	**0**	**0**	**33**	**4**	**0**	**7.27**	....	....	....	....	....	....	....
b	Cornwall	OHL	47	18	18	4	2449	163	1	3.99	18	10	8	1080	65	*1	3.61
1989-90	Moncton	AHL	27	10	15	2	1580	107	0	4.06	....	....	....	....	....	....	....
	Fort Wayne	IHL	22	8	9	1	1064	73	0	4.12	3	1	2	159	19	0	7.17
	NHL Totals		**1**	**0**	**0**	**0**	**33**	**4**	**0**	**7.27**	....	....	....	....	....	....	....

a OHL First All-Star Team (1988)
b OHL Second All-Star Team (1989)

Traded to **Winnipeg** by **Pittsburgh** with Randy Cunnyworth and Dave McLlwain for Jim Kyte, Andrew McBain and Randy Gilhen, June 17, 1989.

TAKKO, KARI (TAH-koh)

Goaltender. Catches left. 6'2", 185 lbs. Born, Uusikaupunki, Finland, June 23, 1963.
(Minnesota's 5th choice, 97th overall, in 1984 Entry Draft).

			Regular Season								Playoffs						
Season	Club	Lea	GP	W	L	T	Mins	GA	SO	Avg	GP	W	L	Mins	GA	SO	Avg
1985-86	Springfield	AHL	43	18	19	3	2286	161	1	4.05	....	....	....	....	....	....	....
	Minnesota	**NHL**	**1**	**0**	**1**	**0**	**60**	**3**	**0**	**3.00**	....	....	....	....	....	....	....
1986-87	**Minnesota**	**NHL**	**38**	**13**	**18**	**4**	**2075**	**119**	**0**	**3.44**	....	....	....	....	....	....	....
	Springfield	AHL	5	3	2	0	300	16	1	3.20	....	....	....	....	....	....	....
1987-88	**Minnesota**	**NHL**	**37**	**8**	**19**	**6**	**1919**	**143**	**1**	**4.47**	....	....	....	....	....	....	....
1988-89	**Minnesota**	**NHL**	**32**	**8**	**15**	**4**	**1603**	**93**	**0**	**3.48**	**3**	**0**	**1**	**105**	**7**	**0**	**4.00**
1989-90	**Minnesota**	**NHL**	**21**	**4**	**12**	**0**	**1012**	**68**	**0**	**4.03**	**1**	**0**	**0**	**4**	**0**	**0**	**0.00**
	NHL Totals		**129**	**33**	**65**	**14**	**6669**	**426**	**1**	**3.83**	**4**	**0**	**1**	**109**	**7**	**0**	**3.85**

TANNER, JOHN

Goaltender. Catches left. 6'3", 182 lbs. Born, Cambridge, Ont., March 17, 1971.
(Quebec's 4th choice, 54th overall, in 1989 Entry Draft).

			Regular Season								Playoffs						
Season	Club	Lea	GP	W	L	T	Mins	GA	SO	Avg	GP	W	L	Mins	GA	SO	Avg
1987-88a	Peterborough	OHL	26	18	4	3	1532	88	0	3.45	2	....	....	98	3	0	1.84
1988-89	Peterborough	OHL	34	22	10	0	1923	107	2	*3.34	8	4	3	369	23	0	3.74
1989-90	**Quebec**	**NHL**	**1**	**0**	**1**	**0**	**60**	**3**	**0**	**3.00**	....	....	....	....	....	....	....
	Peterborough	OHL	18	6	8	2	1037	70	0	4.05	....	....	....	....	....	....	....
	London	OHL	19	12	5	1	1097	53	1	2.93	6	2	4	341	24	0	4.22
	NHL Totals		**1**	**0**	**1**	**0**	**60**	**3**	**0**	**3.00**	....	....	....	....	....	....	....

a Won Dave Pinkey Trophy (Top Team Goaltending OHL) shared with Todd Bojcun (1989)

TERRERI, CHRIS

Goaltender. Catches left. 5'9", 160 lbs. Born, Providence, RI, November 15, 1964.
(New Jersey's 3rd choice, 87th overall, in 1983 Entry Draft).

			Regular Season								Playoffs						
Season	Club	Lea	GP	W	L	T	Mins	GA	SO	Avg	GP	W	L	Mins	GA	SO	Avg
1982-83	Providence	ECAC	11	7	1	0	528	17	2	1.93	....	....	....	....	....	....	....
1983-84	Providence	ECAC	10	4	2	0	391	20	0	3.07	....	....	....	....	....	....	....
1984-85abc	Providence	H.E.	33	15	13	5	1956	116	1	3.35	....	....	....	....	....	....	....
1985-86	Providence	H.E.	22	6	16	0	1320	84	0	3.74	....	....	....	....	....	....	....
1986-87	**New Jersey**	**NHL**	**7**	**0**	**3**	**1**	**286**	**21**	**0**	**4.41**	....	....	....	....	....	....	....
	Maine	AHL	14	4	9	1	765	57	0	4.47	....	....	....	....	....	....	....
1987-88	Utica	AHL	7	5	1	0	399	18	0	2.71	....	....	....	....	....	....	....
	U.S. National	....	26	17	7	2	1430	81	0	3.40	....	....	....	....	....	....	....
	U.S. Olympic	....	3	1	1	0	128	14	0	6.56	....	....	....	....	....	....	....
1988-89	**New Jersey**	**NHL**	**8**	**0**	**4**	**2**	**402**	**18**	**0**	**2.69**	....	....	....	....	....	....	....
	Utica	AHL	39	20	15	3	2314	132	0	3.42	2	0	1	80	6	0	4.50
1989-90	**New Jersey**	**NHL**	**35**	**15**	**12**	**3**	**1931**	**110**	**0**	**3.42**	**4**	**2**	**2**	**238**	**13**	**0**	**3.28**
	NHL Totals		**50**	**15**	**19**	**6**	**2619**	**149**	**0**	**3.41**	**4**	**2**	**2**	**238**	**13**	**0**	**3.28**

a Hockey East All-Star Team
b Hockey East Player of the Year (1985)
c NCAA All-American Team (1985)

TUGNUTT, RON

Goaltender. Catches left. 5'11", 155 lbs. Born, Scarborough, Ont., October 22, 1967.
(Quebec's 4th choice, 81st overall, in 1986 Entry Draft).

			Regular Season								Playoffs						
Season	Club	Lea	GP	W	L	T	Mins	GA	SO	Avg	GP	W	L	Mins	GA	SO	Avg
1984-85	Peterborough	OHL	18	7	4	2	938	59	0	3.77	...	...	...	...	...	...	...
1985-86	Peterborough	OHL	26	18	7	0	1543	74	1	2.88	3	2	0	133	6	0	2.71
1986-87a	Peterborough	OHL	31	21	7	2	1891	88	2	*2.79	6	3	3	374	21	1	3.37
1987-88	**Quebec**	**NHL**	**6**	**2**	**3**	**0**	**284**	**16**	**0**	**3.38**	....	....	....	....	....	....	....
	Fredericton	AHL	34	20	9	4	1964	118	1	3.60	4	1	2	204	11	0	3.24
1988-89	**Quebec**	**NHL**	**26**	**10**	**10**	**3**	**1367**	**82**	**0**	**3.60**	....	....	....	....	....	....	....
	Halifax	AHL	24	14	7	2	1368	79	1	3.46	....	....	....	....	....	....	....
1989-90	**Quebec**	**NHL**	**35**	**5**	**24**	**3**	**1978**	**152**	**0**	**4.61**	....	....	....	....	....	....	....
	Halifax	AHL	6	1	5	0	366	23	0	3.77	....	....	....	....	....	....	....
	NHL Totals		**67**	**17**	**37**	**6**	**3629**	**250**	**0**	**4.13**	....	....	....	....	....	....	....

a OHL First All-Star Team (1987)

VANBIESBROUCK, JOHN (van-BEES-bruhk)

Goaltender. Catches left. 5'7", 175 lbs. Born, Detroit, MI, September 4, 1963.
(NY Rangers' 5th choice, 72nd overall, in 1981 Entry Draft).

			Regular Season								Playoffs						
Season	Club	Lea	GP	W	L	T	Mins	GA	SO	Avg	GP	W	L	Mins	GA	SO	Avg
1980-81a	S.S. Marie	OHA	56	31	16	1	2941	203	0	4.14	11	3	3	457	24	1	3.15
1981-82	**NY Rangers**	**NHL**	**1**	**1**	**0**	**0**	**60**	**1**	**0**	**1.00**	....	....	....	....	....	....	....
	S.S. Marie	OHL	31	12	12	2	1686	102	0	3.62	7	1	4	276	20	0	4.35
1982-83b	S.S. Marie	OHL	62	39	21	1	3471	209	0	3.61	16	7	6	944	56	*1	3.56
1983-84	**NY Rangers**	**NHL**	**3**	**2**	**1**	**0**	**180**	**10**	**0**	**3.33**	**1**	**0**	**0**	**1**	**0**	**0**	**0.00**
cde	Tulsa	CHL	37	20	13	2	2153	124	*3	3.46	4	4	0	240	10	0	*2.50
1984-85	**NY Rangers**	**NHL**	**42**	**12**	**24**	**3**	**2358**	**166**	**1**	**4.22**	**1**	**0**	**0**	**20**	**0**	**0**	**0.00**
1985-86fg	**NY Rangers**	**NHL**	**61**	***31**	**21**	**5**	**3326**	**184**	**3**	**3.32**	**16**	**8**	**8**	**899**	**49**	***1**	**3.27**
1986-87	**NY Rangers**	**NHL**	**50**	**18**	**20**	**5**	**2656**	**161**	**0**	**3.64**	**4**	**1**	**3**	**195**	**11**	**1**	**3.38**
1987-88	**NY Rangers**	**NHL**	**56**	**27**	**22**	**7**	**3319**	**187**	**2**	**3.38**	....	....	....	....	....	....	....
1988-89	**NY Rangers**	**NHL**	**56**	**28**	**21**	**4**	**3207**	**197**	**0**	**3.69**	**2**	**0**	**1**	**107**	**6**	**0**	**3.36**
1989-90	**NY Rangers**	**NHL**	**47**	**19**	**19**	**7**	**2734**	**154**	**1**	**3.38**	**6**	**2**	**3**	**298**	**15**	**0**	**3.02**
	NHL Totals		**316**	**138**	**128**	**31**	**17840**	**1060**	**7**	**3.57**	**30**	**11**	**15**	**1520**	**81**	**2**	**3.20**

a OHA Third All-Star Team (1981).
b OHL Second All-Star Team (1983).
c CHL First All-Star Team (1984)
d Shared Terry Sawchuk Trophy (CHL's leading goaltenders) with Ron Scott (1984)
e Shared Tommy Ivan Trophy (CHL's Most Valuable Player) with Bruce Affleck of Indianapolis (1984)
f Won Vezina Trophy (1986)
g NHL First All-Star Team (1986)

VERNON, MICHAEL (MIKE)

Goaltender. Catches left. 5'9", 170 lbs. Born, Calgary, Alta., February 24, 1963.
(Calgary's 2nd choice, 56th overall, in 1981 Entry Draft).

			Regular Season								Playoffs						
Season	Club	Lea	GP	W	L	T	Mins	GA	SO	Avg	GP	W	L	Mins	GA	SO	Avg
1980-81	Calgary	WHL	59	33	17	1	3154	198	1	3.77	22	....	....	1271	82	1	3.87
1981-82ab	Calgary	WHL	42	22	14	2	2329	143	3	3.68	9	....	....	527	30	0	3.42
	Oklahoma City	CHL	....	....	....	....	....	....	....	....	1	0	1	70	4	0	3.43
1982-83	**Calgary**	**NHL**	**2**	**0**	**2**	**0**	**100**	**11**	**0**	**6.59**	....	....	....	....	....	....	....
ab	Calgary	WHL	50	19	18	2	2856	155	3	3.26	16	9	7	925	60	0	3.89
1983-84	**Calgary**	**NHL**	**1**	**0**	**1**	**0**	**11**	**4**	**0**	**22.22**	....	....	....	....	....	....	....
c	Colorado	CHL	46	30	13	2	2648	148	1	*3.35	6	2	4	347	21	0	3.63
1984-85	Moncton	AHL	41	10	20	4	2050	134	0	3.92	....	....	....	....	....	....	....
1985-86	**Calgary**	**NHL**	**18**	**9**	**3**	**3**	**921**	**52**	**1**	**3.39**	***21**	**12**	***9**	**1229**	**60**	**0**	**2.93**
	Moncton	AHL	6	3	1	2	374	21	0	3.37	....	....	....	....	....	....	....
	Salt Lake	IHL	10	....	....	....	600	34	1	3.40	....	....	....	....	....	....	....
1986-87	**Calgary**	**NHL**	**54**	**30**	**21**	**1**	**2957**	**178**	**1**	**3.61**	**5**	**2**	**3**	**263**	**16**	**0**	**3.65**
1987-88	**Calgary**	**NHL**	**64**	**39**	**16**	**7**	**3565**	**210**	**1**	**3.53**	**9**	**4**	**4**	**515**	**34**	**0**	**3.96**
1988-89d	**Calgary**	**NHL**	**52**	***37**	**6**	**5**	**2938**	**130**	**0**	**2.65**	***22**	***16**	**5**	***1381**	**52**	***3**	**2.26**
1989-90	**Calgary**	**NHL**	**47**	**23**	**14**	**9**	**2795**	**146**	**0**	**3.13**	**6**	**2**	**3**	**342**	**19**	**0**	**3.33**
	NHL Totals		**238**	**138**	**63**	**21**	**13287**	**731**	**3**	**3.30**	**63**	**36**	**24**	**3730**	**181**	**0**	**2.91**

a WHL First All-Star Team (1982, 1983)
b WHL Most Valuable Player (1982, 1983)
c CHL Second All-Star Team (1984)
d NHL Second All-Star Team (1989)

Played in NHL All-Star Game (1988-90)

WAITE, JIMMY

Goaltender. Catches right. 6', 165 lbs. Born, Sherbrooke, Que., April 15, 1969.
(Chicago's 1st choice, 8th overall, in 1987 Entry Draft).

			Regular Season								Playoffs						
Season	Club	Lea	GP	W	L	T	Mins	GA	SO	Avg	GP	W	L	Mins	GA	SO	Avg
1986-87a	Chicoutimi	QMJHL	50	23	17	3	2569	209	2	4.48	11	4	6	576	54	1	5.63
1987-88	Chicoutimi	QMJHL	36	17	16	1	2000	150	0	4.50	4	1	2	222	17	0	4.59
1988-89	**Chicago**	**NHL**	**11**	**0**	**7**	**1**	**494**	**43**	**0**	**5.22**	....	....	....	....	....	....	....
	Saginaw	IHL	5	3	1	0	304	10	0	1.97	....	....	....	....	....	....	....
1989-90	**Chicago**	**NHL**	**4**	**2**	**0**	**0**	**183**	**14**	**0**	**4.59**	....	....	....	....	....	....	....
bc	Indianapolis	IHL	54	*34	14	5	*3207	135	*5	*2.53	*10	*9	1	*602	19	*1	*1.89
	NHL Totals		**15**	**2**	**7**	**1**	**677**	**57**	**0**	**5.05**	....	....	....	....	....	....	....

a QMJHL Second All-Star Team (1987)
b IHL First All-Star Team (1990)
c Won James Norris Memorial Trophy (Top Goaltender-IHL) (1990)

WAKALUK, DARCY (WAHK-uh-luhk)

Goaltender. Catches left. 5'11", 180 lbs. Born, Pincher Creek, Alta., March 14, 1966.
(Buffalo's 7th choice, 144th overall, in 1984 Entry Draft).

			Regular Season								Playoffs						
Season	Club	Lea	GP	W	L	T	Mins	GA	SO	Avg	GP	W	L	Mins	GA	SO	Avg
1983-84	Kelowna	WHL	31	....	....	....	1555	163	0	6.29	....	....	....	....	....	....	....
1984-85	Kelowna	WHL	54	19	30	4	3094	244	0	4.73	5	1	4	282	22	0	4.68
1985-86	Spokane	WHL	47	21	22	1	2562	224	1	5.25	7	3	4	419	37	0	5.30
1986-87	Rochester	AHL	11	2	2	0	545	26	0	2.86	5	2	0	141	11	0	4.68
1987-88	Rochester	AHL	55	27	16	3	2763	159	0	3.45	6	3	3	328	22	0	4.02
1988-89	**Buffalo**	**NHL**	**6**	**1**	**3**	**0**	**214**	**15**	**0**	**4.21**	....	....	....	....	....	....	....
	Rochester	AHL	33	11	14	0	1566	97	1	3.72	....	....	....	....	....	....	....
1989-90	Rochester	AHL	56	31	16	4	3095	173	2	3.35	*17	*10	6	*1001	50	0	*3.01
	NHL Totals		**6**	**1**	**3**	**0**	**214**	**15**	**0**	**4.21**	....	....	....	....	....	....	....

WAMSLEY, RICHARD (RICK) (WAHMS-lee)

Goaltender. Catches left. 5'11", 185 lbs. Born, Simcoe, Ont., May 25, 1959.
(Montreal's 5th choice, 58th overall, in 1979 Entry Draft).

			Regular Season								Playoffs						
Season	Club	Lea	GP	W	L	T	Mins	GA	SO	Avg	GP	W	L	Mins	GA	SO	Avg
1977-78	Hamilton	OHA	25	....	....	....	1495	74	2	2.97	....	....	....	....	....	....	....
1978-79	Brantford	OHA	24	....	....	....	1444	128	0	5.32	....	....	....	....	....	....	....
1979-80	Nova Scotia	AHL	40	19	16	2	2305	125	2	3.25	3	1	1	143	12	0	5.03
1980-81	**Montreal**	**NHL**	**5**	**3**	**0**	**1**	**253**	**8**	**1**	**1.90**	....	....	....	....	....	....	....
	Nova Scotia	AHL	43	17	19	3	2372	155	0	3.92	4	2	1	199	6	*1	1.81
1981-82a	**Montreal**	**NHL**	**38**	**23**	**7**	**7**	**2206**	**101**	**2**	**2.75**	**5**	**2**	**3**	**300**	**11**	**0**	***2.20**
1982-83	**Montreal**	**NHL**	**46**	**27**	**12**	**5**	**2583**	**151**	**0**	**3.51**	**3**	**0**	**3**	**152**	**7**	**0**	**2.77**
1983-84	**Montreal**	**NHL**	**42**	**19**	**17**	**3**	**2333**	**144**	**2**	**3.70**	**1**	**0**	**1**	**32**	**0**	**0**	**0.00**
1984-85	**St. Louis**	**NHL**	**40**	**23**	**12**	**5**	**2319**	**126**	**0**	**3.26**	**2**	**0**	**2**	**120**	**7**	**0**	**3.50**
1985-86	**St. Louis**	**NHL**	**42**	**22**	**16**	**3**	**2517**	**144**	**1**	**3.43**	**10**	**4**	**6**	**569**	**29**	**0**	**3.90**
1986-87	**St. Louis**	**NHL**	**41**	**17**	**15**	**6**	**2410**	**142**	**0**	**3.54**	**2**	**1**	**1**	**120**	**5**	**0**	**2.50**
1987-88	**St. Louis**	**NHL**	**31**	**13**	**16**	**1**	**1818**	**103**	**2**	**3.40**	....	....	....	....	....	....	....
	Calgary	**NHL**	**2**	**1**	**0**	**0**	**73**	**5**	**0**	**4.11**	**1**	**0**	**1**	**33**	**2**	**0**	**3.64**
1988-89	**Calgary**	**NHL**	**35**	**17**	**11**	**4**	**1927**	**95**	**2**	**2.96**	**1**	**0**	**1**	**20**	**2**	**0**	**6.00**
1989-90	**Calgary**	**NHL**	**36**	**18**	**8**	**6**	**1969**	**107**	**2**	**3.26**	**1**	**0**	**1**	**49**	**9**	**0**	**11.02**
	NHL Totals		**358**	**183**	**114**	**41**	**20408**	**1126**	**12**	**3.31**	**26**	**7**	**19**	**1395**	**72**	**0**	**3.09**

a Shared Williams Jennings Trophy with Denis Herron (1982)

Traded to **St. Louis** by **Montreal** with Hartford's second round choice (Brian Benning); — Montreal property via earlier deal — Montreal's second round choice (Tony Hrkac) and third round choice (Robert Dirk), all in the 1984 Entry Draft, for St. Louis' first (Shayne Corson) and second round (Stephane Richer) choices in the 1984 Entry Draft, June 9, 1984. Traded to **Calgary** by **St. Louis** with Rob Ramage for Brett Hull and Steve Bozek, March 7, 1988.

WEEKS, STEPHEN (STEVE)

Goaltender. Catches left. 5'11", 165 lbs. Born, Scarborough, Ont., June 30, 1958.
(NY Rangers' 12th choice, 176th overall, in 1978 Amateur Draft).

			Regular Season								Playoffs						
Season	Club	Lea	GP	W	L	T	Mins	GA	SO	Avg	GP	W	L	Mins	GA	SO	Avg
1977-78	N. Michigan	CCHA	19	....	....	....	1015	56	1	3.31	....	....	....	....	....	....	....
1978-79	N. Michigan	CCHA	25	....	....	....	1437	82	0	3.42	....	....	....	....	....	....	....
1979-80	N. Michigan	CCHA	36	29	6	1	2133	105	0	2.95	....	....	....	....	....	....	....
1980-81	New Haven	AHL	36	14	17	3	2065	142	1	4.04	....	....	....	....	....	....	....
	NY Rangers	**NHL**	**1**	**0**	**1**	**0**	**60**	**2**	**0**	**2.00**	**1**	**0**	**0**	**14**	**1**	**0**	**4.29**
1981-82	**NY Rangers**	**NHL**	**49**	**23**	**16**	**9**	**2852**	**179**	**1**	**3.77**	**4**	**1**	**2**	**127**	**9**	**0**	**4.25**
1982-83	**NY Rangers**	**NHL**	**18**	**9**	**5**	**3**	**1040**	**68**	**0**	**3.92**	....	....	....	....	....	....	....
	Tulsa	CHL	19	8	10	0	1116	60	0	3.23	....	....	....	....	....	....	....
1983-84	**NY Rangers**	**NHL**	**26**	**10**	**11**	**2**	**1361**	**90**	**0**	**3.97**	....	....	....	....	....	....	....
	Tulsa	CHL	3	3	0	0	180	7	0	2.33	....	....	....	....	....	....	....
1984-85	**Hartford**	**NHL**	**24**	**10**	**12**	**2**	**1457**	**93**	**2**	**3.82**	....	....	....	....	....	....	....
	Binghamton	AHL	5	5	0	0	303	13	0	2.57	....	....	....	....	....	....	....
1985-86	**Hartford**	**NHL**	**27**	**13**	**13**	**0**	**1544**	**99**	**1**	**3.85**	**3**	**1**	**2**	**169**	**8**	**0**	**2.84**
1986-87	**Hartford**	**NHL**	**25**	**12**	**8**	**2**	**1367**	**78**	**1**	**3.42**	**1**	**0**	**0**	**36**	**1**	**0**	**1.67**
1987-88	**Hartford**	**NHL**	**18**	**6**	**7**	**2**	**918**	**55**	**0**	**3.59**	....	....	....	....	....	....	....
	Vancouver	**NHL**	**9**	**4**	**3**	**2**	**550**	**31**	**0**	**3.38**	....	....	....	....	....	....	....
1988-89	**Vancouver**	**NHL**	**35**	**11**	**19**	**5**	**2056**	**102**	**0**	**2.98**	**3**	**1**	**1**	**140**	**8**	**0**	**3.43**
1989-90	**Vancouver**	**NHL**	**21**	**4**	**11**	**4**	**1142**	**79**	**0**	**4.15**	....	....	....	....	....	....	....
	NHL Totals		**253**	**102**	**106**	**33**	**14347**	**876**	**5**	**3.66**	**12**	**3**	**5**	**486**	**27**	**0**	**3.33**

Traded to **Vancouver** by **Hartford** for Richard Brodeur, March 8, 1988.

WHITMORE, KAY

Goaltender. Catches left. 5'11", 175 lbs. Born, Sudbury, Ont., April 10, 1967.
(Hartford's 2nd choice, 26th overall, in 1985 Entry Draft).

			Regular Season								Playoffs						
Season	Club	Lea	GP	W	L	T	Mins	GA	SO	Avg	GP	W	L	Mins	GA	SO	Avg
1983-84	Peterborough	OHL	29	17	8	0	1471	110	0	4.49	....	....	....	....	....	....	....
1984-85a	Peterborough	OHL	53	*35	16	2	3077	172	*2	3.35	17	10	4	1020	58	0	3.41
1985-86b	Peterborough	OHL	41	27	12	2	2467	114	*3	*2.77	14	8	5	837	40	0	2.87
1986-87	Peterborough	OHL	36	14	17	5	2159	118	1	3.28	7	3	3	366	17	1	2.79
1987-88	Binghamton	AHL	38	17	15	4	2137	121	*3	3.40	2	0	2	118	10	0	5.08
1988-89	**Hartford**	**NHL**	**3**	**2**	**1**	**0**	**180**	**10**	**0**	**3.33**	**2**	**0**	**2**	**135**	**10**	**0**	**4.44**
	Binghamton	AHL	*56	21	29	4	*3200	241	1	4.52	....	....	....	....	....	....	....
1989-90	**Hartford**	**NHL**	**9**	**4**	**2**	**1**	**442**	**26**	**0**	**3.53**	....	....	....	....	....	....	....
	Binghamton	AHL	24	3	19	2	1386	109	0	4.72	....	....	....	....	....	....	....
	NHL Totals		**12**	**6**	**4**	**2**	**622**	**36**	**0**	**3.47**	**2**	**0**	**2**	**135**	**10**	**0**	**4.44**

a OHL Third All-Star Team (1985)
b OHL First All-Star Team (1986)

WILLIAMS, MIKE

Goaltender. Catches left. 6', 185 lbs. Born, Woodhaven, MI, April 16, 1967.
(Quebec's 12th choice, 219th overall, in 1987 Entry Draft).

			Regular Season								Playoffs						
Season	Club	Lea	GP	W	L	T	Mins	GA	SO	Avg	GP	W	L	Mins	GA	SO	Avg
1986-87	Ferris State	CCHA	17	4	9	0	846	65	0	4.61	...	....	....	....	....	....	....
1987-88	Ferris State	CCHA	30	11	11	5	1671	122	0	4.38	...	....	....	....	....	....	....
1988-89	Ferris State	CCHA	25	6	13	5	1394	84	0	3.62	....	....	....	....	....	....	....
1989-90	Ferris State	CCHA	31	9	16	0	1697	138	0	4.88	....	....	....	....	....	....	....

WREGGET, KEN

Goaltender. Catches left. 6'1", 195 lbs. Born, Brandon, Man., March 25, 1964.
(Toronto's 4th choice, 45th overall, in 1982 Entry Draft).

			Regular Season								Playoffs						
Season	Club	Lea	GP	W	L	T	Mins	GA	SO	Avg	GP	W	L	Mins	GA	SO	Avg
1981-82	Lethbridge	WHL	36	19	12	0	1713	118	0	4.13	3	....	....	84	3	0	2.14
1982-83	Lethbridge	WHL	48	26	17	1	2696	157	0	3.49	20	14	5	1154	58	1	3.02
1983-84	**Toronto**	**NHL**	**3**	**1**	**1**	**1**	**165**	**14**	**0**	**5.09**	....	....	....	....	....	....	....
a	Lethbridge	WHL	53	32	20	0	3053	161	0	*3.16	4	1	3	210	18	0	5.14
1984-85	**Toronto**	**NHL**	**23**	**2**	**15**	**3**	**1278**	**103**	**0**	**4.84**	....	....	....	....	....	....	....
	St. Catharines	AHL	12	2	8	1	688	48	0	4.19	....	....	....	....	....	....	....
1985-86	**Toronto**	**NHL**	**30**	**9**	**13**	**4**	**1566**	**113**	**0**	**4.33**	**10**	**6**	**4**	**607**	**32**	***1**	**3.16**
	St. Catharines	AHL	18	8	9	0	1058	78	1	4.42	....	....	....	....	....	....	....
1986-87	**Toronto**	**NHL**	**56**	**22**	**28**	**3**	**3026**	**200**	**0**	**3.97**	**13**	**7**	**6**	**761**	**29**	**1**	**2.29**
1987-88	**Toronto**	**NHL**	**56**	**12**	**35**	**4**	**3000**	**222**	**2**	**4.44**	**2**	**0**	**1**	**108**	**11**	**0**	**6.11**
1988-89	**Toronto**	**NHL**	**32**	**9**	**20**	**2**	**1888**	**139**	**0**	**4.42**	....	....	....	....	....	....	....
	Philadelphia	**NHL**	**3**	**1**	**1**	**0**	**130**	**13**	**0**	**6.00**	**5**	**2**	**2**	**268**	**10**	**1**	**2.24**
1989-90	**Philadelphia**	**NHL**	**51**	**22**	**24**	**3**	**2961**	**169**	**0**	**3.42**	....	....	....	....	....	....	....
	NHL Totals		**254**	**78**	**137**	**20**	**14014**	**973**	**2**	**4.16**	**30**	**15**	**13**	**1744**	**82**	**3**	**2.82**

a WHL First All-Star Team, East Division (1984)

Traded to **Philadelphia** by **Toronto** for Philadelphia's first-round choice (Rob Pearson) and Calgary's first-round choice (Steve Bancroft) — acquired by Philadelphia in the Brad McCrimmon trade — in 1989 Entry Draft, March 6, 1989.

YOUNG, WENDELL

Goaltender. Catches left. 5'9", 185 lbs. Born, Halifax, N.S., August 1, 1963.
(Vancouver's 3rd choice, 73rd overall, in 1981 Entry Draft).

			Regular Season								Playoffs						
Season	Club	Lea	GP	W	L	T	Mins	GA	SO	Avg	GP	W	L	Mins	GA	SO	Avg
1980-81	Kitchener	OHA	42	19	15	0	2215	164	1	4.44	14	9	1	800	42	*1	3.15
1981-82	Kitchener	OHL	60	38	17	2	3470	195	1	3.37	15	12	1	900	35	*1	*2.33
1982-83a	Kitchener	OHL	61	41	19	0	3611	231	1	3.84	12	6	5	720	43	0	3.58
1983-84	Fredericton	AHL	11	7	3	0	569	39	1	4.11	....	....	....	....	....	....	....
	Milwaukee	IHL	6	....	....	....	339	17	0	3.01	....	....	....	....	....	....	....
	Salt Lake	CHL	20	11	6	0	1094	80	0	4.39	4	0	2	122	11	0	5.42
1984-85	Fredericton	AHL	22	7	11	3	1242	83	0	4.01	....	....	....	....	....	....	....
1985-86	**Vancouver**	**NHL**	**22**	**4**	**9**	**3**	**1023**	**61**	**0**	**3.58**	**1**	**0**	**1**	**60**	**5**	**0**	**5.00**
	Fredericton	AHL	24	12	8	4	1457	78	0	3.21	....	....	....	....	....	....	....
1986-87	**Vancouver**	**NHL**	**8**	**1**	**6**	**1**	**420**	**35**	**0**	**5.00**	....	....	....	....	....	....	....
	Fredericton	AHL	30	11	16	0	1676	118	0	4.22	....	....	....	....	....	....	....
1987-88bcd	**Philadelphia**	**NHL**	**6**	**3**	**2**	**0**	**320**	**20**	**0**	**3.75**	....	....	....	....	....	....	....
	Hershey	AHL	51	*33	15	1	2922	135	1	2.77	12	*12	0	*767	28	*1	*2.19
1988-89	**Pittsburgh**	**NHL**	**22**	**12**	**9**	**0**	**1150**	**92**	**0**	**4.80**	**1**	**0**	**0**	**39**	**1**	**0**	**1.54**
1989-90	**Pittsburgh**	**NHL**	**43**	**16**	**20**	**3**	**2318**	**161**	**1**	**4.17**	....	....	....	....	....	....	....
	NHL Totals		**101**	**36**	**46**	**7**	**5231**	**369**	**1**	**4.23**	**2**	**0**	**1**	**99**	**6**	**0**	**3.64**

a OHL Third All-Star Team (1983)
b AHL First All-Star Team (1988)
c Won Baz Bastien Award (AHL Most Valuable Goaltender) (1988)
d Won Jack Butterfield Trophy (AHL Playoff MVP) (1988)

Traded to **Philadelphia** by **Vancouver** with Vancouver's third round choice (Kimbi Daniels) in 1990 Entry Draft for Daryl Stanley, August 28, 1987. Traded to **Pittsburgh** by **Philadelphia** with Philadelphia's seventh-round choice (Mika Valila) in 1990 Entry Draft for Pittburgh's third-round choice (Chris Therien) in 1990 Entry Draft, September 1, 1988.

Yves Belanger

John Garrett

Cesare Maniago

Frank Brimsek

Gilles Gratton

Steve Penney

Gary Bromley

Goran Hogosta

Glenn Resch

Jiri Crha

Pete LoPresti

Mike Veisor

Retired NHL Goaltender Index

Abbreviations: Teams/Cities:—**Atl.**-Atlanta; **Bos.**-Boston; **Buf.**-Buffalo; **Cal.**-California; **Cgy.**-Calgary; **Chi.**-Chicago; **Cle.**-Cleveland; **Col.**-Colorado; **Det.**-Detroit; **Edm.**-Edmonton; **Ham.**-Hamilton; **Hfd.**-Hartford; **L.A.**-Los Angeles; **Min.**-Minnesota; **Mtl.**-Montreal; **Mtl. M.**-Montreal Maroons; **Mtl. W.**-Montreal Wanderers; **N.J.**-New Jersey; **NY**-New York; **NYA**-NY Americans; **NYI**-New York Islanders; **NYR**-New York Rangers; **Oak.**-Oakland; **Ott.**-Ottawa; **Phi.**-Philadelphia; **Pit.**-Pittsburgh; **Que.**-Quebec; **St. L.**-St. Louis; **Tor.**-Toronto; **Van.**-Vancouver; **Wpg.**-Winnipeg; **Wsh.**-Washington.

Avg – goals against per 60 minutes played; **GA** – goals against; **GP** – games played; **Mins** – minutes played; **SO** – shutouts.

			Regular Schedule								Playoffs									
Name	NHL Teams	NHL Seasons	GP	W	L	T	Mins	GA	SO	Avg	GP	W	L	T	Mins	GA	SO	Avg	First NHL Season	Last NHL Season
Abbott, George	Bos.	1	1	0	1	0	60	7	0	7.00	....	....	....	....	....	....	....	....	1943-44	1943-44
Adams, John	Bos., Wsh.	2	22	9	10	1	1180	85	1	4.32	....	....	....	....	....	....	....	....	1972-73	1974-75
Aiken, Don	Mtl.	1	1	0	1	0	34	6	0	10.59	....	....	....	....	....	....	....	....	1957-58	1957-58
Aitkenhead, Andy	NYR	3	106	47	43	16	6570	257	11	2.35	10	6	3	1	608	15	3	1.48	1932-33	1934-35
Almas, Red	Det., Chi.	3	3	0	2	1	180	13	0	4.33	5	1	3	....	263	13	0	2.97	1946-47	1952-53
Anderson, Lorne	NYR	1	3	1	2	0	180	18	0	6.00	....	....	....	....	....	....	....	....	1951-52	1951-52
Astrom, Hardy	NYR, Col.	3	83	17	44	12	4456	278	0	3.74	....	....	....	....	....	....	....	....	1977-78	1980-81
Baker, Steve	NYR	4	57	20	20	11	3081	190	3	3.70	14	7	7	....	826	55	0	4.00	1979-80	1982-83
Bannerman, Murray	Van., Chi.	8	289	116	125	33	16470	1051	8	3.83	40	20	18	....	2322	165	0	4.26	1977-78	1986-87
Baron, Marco	Bos., L.A., Edm.	6	86	34	39	9	4822	292	1	3.63	1	0	1	....	20	3	0	9.00	1979-80	1984-85
Bassen, Hank	Chi., Det., Pit.	9	157	47	66	31	8829	441	5	2.99	5	1	4	....	274	11	0	2.41	1954-55	1967-68
Bastien, Baz	Tor.	1	5	0	4	1	300	20	0	4.00	....	....	....	....	....	....	....	....	1945-46	1945-46
Bauman, Gary	Mtl., Min.	3	35	6	18	6	1718	102	0	3.56	....	....	....	....	....	....	....	....	1966-67	1968-69
Bedard, Jim	Wsh.	2	73	17	40	13	4232	278	1	3.94	....	....	....	....	....	....	....	....	1977-78	1978-79
Behrend, Marc	Wpg.	3	38	12	19	3	1991	164	1	4.94	7	1	3	....	312	19	0	3.65	1983-84	1985-86
Belanger, Yves	St.L., Atl., Bos.	6	78	27	36	6	4134	259	2	3.76	....	....	....	....	....	....	....	....	1974-75	1979-80
Belhumeur, Michel	Phi., Wsh.	3	65	9	36	7	3306	254	0	4.61	1	0	0	....	10	1	0	6.00	1972-73	1975-76
Bell, Gordie	Tor., NYR	2	8	3	5	0	480	31	0	3.88	2	1	1	....	120	9	0	4.50	1945-46	1955-56
Benedict, Clint	Ott., Mtl.M.	13	362	190	43	28	22321	863	57	2.32	48	25	18	4	2907	87	15	1.80	1917-18	1929-30
Bennett, Harvey	Bos.	1	24	10	12	2	1470	103	0	4.20	....	....	....	....	....	....	....	....	1944-45	1944-45
Beveridge, Bill	Det., Ott., St.L., Mtl.M., NYR	9	297	87	166	42	18375	879	18	2.87	5	2	3	....	300	11	0	2.20	1929-30	1942-43
Bibeault, Paul	Mtl., Tor., Bos., Chi.	7	214	68	82	21	12890	785	10	3.65	20	6	14	....	1237	71	2	3.44	1940-41	1946-47
Binette, Andre	Mtl.	1	1	1	0	0	60	4	0	4.00	....	....	....	....	....	....	....	....	1954-55	1954-55
Binkley, Les	Pit.	5	196	58	94	34	11046	575	11	3.12	7	5	2	....	428	15	0	2.10	1967-68	1971-72
Bittner, Richard	Bos.	1	1	0	0	1	60	3	0	3.00	....	....	....	....	....	....	....	....	1949-50	1949-50
Blake, Mike	L.A.	3	40	13	5	15	2117	150	0	4.25	....	....	....	....	....	....	....	....	1981-82	1983-84
Boisvert, Gilles	Det.	1	3	0	3	0	180	9	0	3.00	....	....	....	....	....	....	....	....	1959-60	1959-60
Bouchard, Dan	Atl., Cgy., Que., Wpg.	14	655	286	232	113	37919	2061	27	3.26	43	13	30	....	2549	147	1	3.46	1972-73	1985-86
Bourque, Claude	Mtl., Det.	2	62	16	38	8	3830	192	5	3.01	3	1	2	....	188	8	1	2.55	1938-39	1939-40
Boutin, Rollie	Wsh.	3	22	7	10	1	1137	75	0	3.96	....	....	....	....	....	....	....	....	1978-79	1980-81
Bouvrette, Lionel	NYR	1	1	0	1	0	60	6	0	6.00	....	....	....	....	....	....	....	....	1942-43	1942-43
Bower, Johnny	NYR, Tor.	15	552	251	196	90	32077	1347	37	2.52	74	34	35	....	4350	184	5	2.54	1953-54	1969-70
Brannigan, Andy	NYA	1	1	0	0	0	7	0	0	0.00	....	....	....	....	....	....	....	....	1940-41	1940-41
Brimsek, Frank	Bos., Chi.	10	514	252	182	80	31210	1404	40	2.70	68	32	36	....	4365	186	2	2.56	1938-39	1949-50
Broda, Turk	Tor.	14	629	302	224	101	38173	1609	62	2.53	101	58	42	1	6389	211	13	1.98	1936-37	1951-52
Broderick, Ken	Min., Bos.	3	27	11	12	1	1464	74	2	3.03	....	....	....	....	....	....	....	....	1969-70	1974-75
Broderick, Len	Mtl.	1	1	1	0	0	60	2	0	2.00	....	....	....	....	....	....	....	....	1957-58	1957-58
Brodeur, Richard	NYI, Van., Hfd.	9	385	131	176	62	21968	1410	6	3.85	33	13	20	....	2009	111	1	3.32	1979-80	1987-88
Bromley, Gary	Buf., Van.	6	136	54	44	28	7427	425	7	3.43	7	2	5	....	360	25	0	4.17	1973-74	1980-81
Brooks, Arthur	Tor.	1	4	2	1	0	220	23	0	5.75	....	....	....	....	....	....	....	....	1917-18	1917-18
Brooks, Ross	Bos.	3	54	37	7	6	3047	134	4	2.64	1	0	0	....	20	3	0	9.00	1972-73	1974-75
Brophy, Frank	Que.	1	21	3	18	0	1247	148	0	7.05	....	....	....	....	....	....	....	....	1919-20	1919-20
Brown, Andy	Det., Pit.	3	62	22	26	9	3373	213	1	3.79	....	....	....	....	....	....	....	....	1971-72	1973-74
Brown, Ken	Chi.	1	1	0	0	0	18	1	0	3.33	....	....	....	....	....	....	....	....	1970 71	1970-71
Bullock, Bruce	Van.	3	16	3	9	3	927	74	0	4.79	....	....	....	....	....	....	....	....	1972-73	1976-77
Buzinski, Steve	NYR	1	9	2	6	1	560	55	0	5.89	....	....	....	....	....	....	....	....	1942-43	1942-43
Caley, Don	St.L.	1	1	0	0	0	30	3	0	6.00	....	....	....	....	....	....	....	....	1967-68	1967-68
Caron, Jacques	L.A., St.L., Van.	5	72	24	29	11	3846	211	2	3.29	12	4	7	....	639	34	0	3.19	1967-68	1973-74
Carter, Lyle	Cal.	1	15	4	7	0	721	50	0	4.16	....	....	....	....	....	....	....	....	1971-72	1971-72
Chabot, Lorne	NYR, Tor., Mtl., Chi., Mtl.M., NYA	11	411	206	140	65	25309	861	73	2.04	37	13	17	6	2558	64	5	1.50	1926-27	1936-37
Chadwick, Ed	Tor., Bos.	6	184	57	92	35	10980	551	14	3.01	....	....	....	....	....	....	....	....	1955-56	1961-62
Champoux, Bob	Det., Cal.	2	17	2	11	3	923	80	0	5.20	1	0	0	....	55	4	0	4.36	1963-64	1973-74
Cheevers, Gerry	Tor., Bos.	13	418	230	94	74	24394	1175	26	2.89	88	47	35	....	5396	242	8	2.69	1961-62	1979-80
Clancy, Frank	Tor.	1	1	0	0	0	1	0	0	0.00	....	....	....	....	....	....	....	....	1931-32	1931-32
Cleghorn, Odie	Pit.	1	1	1	0	0	60	2	0	2.00	....	....	....	....	....	....	....	....	1925-26	1925-26
Colvin, Les	Bos.	1	1	0	1	0	60	4	0	4.00	....	....	....	....	....	....	....	....	1948-49	1948-49
Conacher, Charlie	Tor., Det.	13	3	0	0	0	9	0	0	0.00	....	....	....	....	....	....	....	....	1929-30	1940-41
Connell, Alex	Ott., Det., NYA, Mtl.M.	12	417	199	155	59	26030	830	81	1.91	21	9	5	7	1309	26	4	1.19	1924-25	1936-37
Corsi, Jim	Edm.	1	26	8	14	3	1366	83	0	3.65	....	....	....	....	....	....	....	....	1979-80	1979-80
Courteau, Maurice	Bos.	1	6	2	4	0	360	33	0	5.50	....	....	....	....	....	....	....	....	1943-44	1943-44
Cox, Abbie	Mtl.M., Det., NYA, Mtl.	3	5	1	1	2	263	11	0	2.51	....	....	....	....	....	....	....	....	1929-30	1935-36
Craig, Jim	Atl., Bos., Min.	3	30	11	10	7	1588	100	0	3.78	....	....	....	....	....	....	....	....	1979-80	1983-84
Crha, Jiri	Tor.	2	69	28	27	11	3942	261	0	3.97	5	0	4	....	186	21	0	6.77	1979-80	1980-81
Crozier, Roger	Det., Buf., Wsh.	14	518	206	197	74	28567	1446	30	3.04	31	14	15	....	1769	82	1	2.78	1963-64	1976-77
Cude, Wilf	Phi., Bos., Chi., Det., Mtl.	10	282	100	129	49	17486	796	24	2.73	19	7	11	1	1317	51	1	2.32	1930-31	1940-41
Cutts, Don	Edm.	1	6	1	2	1	269	16	0	3.57	....	....	....	....	....	....	....	....	1979-80	1979-80
Cyr, Claude	Mtl.	1	1	0	0	0	20	1	0	3.00	....	....	....	....	....	....	....	....	1958-59	1958-59
Dadswell, Doug	Cgy.	2	27	8	8	3	1346	99	0	4.41	....	....	....	....	....	....	....	....	1986-87	1987-88
Daley, Joe	Pit., Buf., Det.	4	105	34	44	19	5836	326	3	3.35	....	....	....	....	....	....	....	....	1968-69	1971-72
Damore, Nick	Bos.	1	1	0	1	0	60	3	0	3.00	....	....	....	....	....	....	....	....	1941-42	1941-42
D'Amour, Mark	Cgy.	1	15	2	4	2	560	32	0	3.43	....	....	....	....	....	....	....	....	1985-86	1985-86
Daskalakis, Cleon	Bos.	3	12	3	4	1	506	41	0	4.86	....	....	....	....	....	....	....	....	1984-85	1986-87
Davidson, John	St.L., NYR	10	301	123	124	39	17109	1004	7	3.52	31	16	14	....	1862	77	1	2.48	1973-74	1982-83
Decourcy, Robert	NYR	1	1	0	1	0	29	6	0	12.41	....	....	....	....	....	....	....	....	1947-48	1947-48
Defelice, Norman	Bos.	1	10	3	5	2	600	30	0	3.00	....	....	....	....	....	....	....	....	1956-57	1956-57
DeJordy, Denis	Chi., L.A., Mtl., Det.	11	316	124	127	51	17798	929	15	3.13	18	6	9	....	946	55	0	3.49	1962-63	1973-74
Desjardins, Gerry	L.A., Chi., NYI, Buf.	10	331	122	153	44	19014	1042	12	3.29	35	15	15	....	1874	108	0	3.46	1968-69	1977-78
Dickie, Bill	Chi.	1	1	1	0	0	60	3	0	3.00	....	....	....	....	....	....	....	....	1941-42	1941-42
Dion, Connie	Det.	2	38	23	11	4	2280	119	0	3.13	5	1	4	....	300	17	0	3.40	1943-44	1944-45
Dion, Michel	Que., Wpg., Pit.	6	227	60	118	32	12695	898	2	4.24	5	2	3	....	304	22	0	4.34	1979-80	1984-85
Dolson, Clarence	Det.	3	93	35	44	13	5820	192	16	1.98	2	0	2	....	120	7	0	3.50	1928-29	1930-31
Dowie, Bruce	Tor.	1	2	0	1	0	72	4	0	3.33	....	....	....	....	....	....	....	....	1983-84	1983-84
Dryden, Dave	NYR, Chi., Buf., Edm.	9	203	48	57	24	10424	555	9	3.19	3	0	2	....	133	9	0	4.06	1961-62	1979-80
Dryden, Ken	Mtl.	8	397	258	57	74	23352	870	46	2.24	112	80	32	....	6846	274	10	2.40	1970-71	1978-79
Dumas, Michel	Chi.	2	8	2	1	2	362	24	0	3.98	1	0	0	....	19	1	0	3.16	1974-75	1976-77
Dupuis, Bob	Edm.	1	1	0	1	0	60	4	0	4.00	....	....	....	....	....	....	....	....	1979-80	1979-80
Durnan, Bill	Mtl.	7	383	208	112	62	22945	901	34	2.36	45	27	18	....	2851	99	2	2.08	1943-44	1949-50
Dyck, Ed	Van.	3	49	8	28	5	2453	178	1	4.35	....	....	....	....	....	....	....	....	1971-72	1973-74
Edwards, Don	Buf., Cgy., Tor.	10	459	208	155	77	26181	1449	16	3.32	42	16	21	....	2302	132	1	3.44	1976-77	1985-86
Edwards, Gary	St.L., L.A., Clev., Min., Edm., Pit.	13	286	88	125	43	16002	973	10	3.65	11	5	4	....	537	34	0	3.80	1968-69	1981-82
Edwards, Marv	Pit., Tor., Cal.	4	61	15	34	7	3467	218	2	3.77	....	....	....	....	....	....	....	....	1968-69	1973-74
Edwards, Roy	Det., Pit.	7	236	92	88	38	13109	637	12	2.92	4	0	3	....	206	11	0	3.20	1967-68	1973-74
Eliot, Darren	L.A., Det., Buf.	5	89	25	41	12	4931	377	1	4.59	1	0	0		40	7	0	10.50	1984-85	1988-89
Ellacott, Ken	Van.	1	12	2	3	4	555	41	0	4.43	....	....	....	....	....	....	....	....	1982-83	1982-83
Esposito, Tony	Mtl., Chi.	16	886	423	307	151	52585	2563	76	2.92	99	45	53	....	6017	308	6	3.09	1968-69	1983-84
Evans, Claude	Mtl., Bos.	2	5	2	2	1	280	16	0	3.43	....	....	....	....	....	....	....	....	1954-55	1957-58
Farr, Rocky	Buf.	3	19	2	6	3	722	42	0	3.49	....	....	....	....	....	....	....	....	1972-73	1974-75
Favell, Doug	Phi., Tor., Col.	12	373	123	153	69	20771	1096	18	3.17	21	5	16	....	1270	66	1	3.12	1967-68	1978-79
Forbes, Jake	Tor., Ham., NYA, Phi.	13	210	84	114	11	12922	594	19	2.76	2	0	2	....	120	7	0	3.50	1919-20	1932-33

Name	NHL Teams	NHL Seasons	Regular Schedule								Playoffs								First NHL Season	Last NHL Season
			GP	W	L	T	Mins	GA	SO	Avg	GP	W	L	T	Mins	GA	SO	Avg		
Ford, Brian	Que., Pit.	2	11	3	7	0	580	61	0	6.31	....	....	....	....	....	....	....	....	1983-84	1984-85
Fowler, Hec	Bos.	1	7	1	6	0	420	43	0	6.14	....	....	....	....	....	....	....	....	1924-25	1924-25
Francis, Emile	Chi., NYR	6	95	31	52	11	5660	355	1	3.76	....	....	....	....	....	....	....	....	1946-47	1951-52
Franks, Jim	Det., NYR, Bos.	4	43	12	23	7	2580	185	1	4.30	1	0	1	....	30	2	0	4.00	1936-37	1943-44
Frederick, Ray	Chi.	1	5	0	4	1	300	22	0	4.40	....	....	....	....	....	....	....	....	1954-55	1954-55
Friesen, Karl	N.J.	1	4	0	2	1	130	16	0	7.38	....	....	....	....	....	....	....	....	1986-87	1986-87
Gamble, Bruce	NYR, Bos., Tor., Phi.	10	327	109	139	47	18442	992	22	3.23	5	0	4	....	206	25	0	7.28	1958-59	1971-72
Gardiner, Bert	NYR, Mtl., Chi., Bos.	6	144	49	68	27	8760	554	3	3.79	9	4	5	....	647	20	0	1.85	1935-36	1943-44
Gardiner, Chuck	Chi.	7	316	112	152	52	19687	664	42	2.02	21	12	6	3	1532	35	5	1.37	1927-28	1933-34
Gardner, George	Det., Van.	5	66	16	30	6	3313	207	0	3.75	....	....	....	....	....	....	....	....	1965-66	1971-72
Garrett, John	Hfd., Que., Van.	6	207	68	91	37	11763	837	1	4.27	9	4	3	....	461	33	0	4.30	1979-80	1984-85
Gatherum, Dave	Det.	1	3	2	0	1	180	3	1	1.00	....	....	....	....	....	....	....	....	1953-54	1953-54
Gauthier, Paul	Mtl.	1	1	0	0	1	70	2	0	1.71	....	....	....	....	....	....	....	....	1937-38	1937-38
Gelineau, Jack	Bos., Chi.	4	143	46	64	33	8580	447	7	3.13	4	2	2	....	260	7	1	1.62	1948-49	1953-54
Giacomin, Ed	NYR, Det.	13	610	289	206	97	35693	1675	54	2.82	65	29	35	....	3834	180	1	2.82	1965-66	1977-78
Gilbert, Gilles	Min., Bos., Det.	14	416	182	148	60	23677	1290	18	3.27	32	17	15	....	1919	97	3	3.03	1969-70	1982-83
Gill, Andre	Bos.	1	5	3	2	0	270	13	1	2.89	....	....	....	....	....	....	....	....	1967-68	1967-68
Goodman, Paul	Chi.	3	52	23	20	9	3240	117	6	2.17	3	0	3	....	187	10	0	3.21	1937-38	1940-41
Grahame, Ron	Bos., L.A., Que.	4	114	50	43	15	6472	409	5	3.79	4	2	1	....	202	7	0	2.08	1977-78	1980-81
Grant, Ben	Tor., NYA., Bos.	6	50	17	26	4	2990	188	4	3.77	....	....	....	....	....	....	....	....	1928-29	1943-44
Grant, Doug	Det., St.L.	7	77	27	34	8	4199	280	2	4.00	....	....	....	....	....	....	....	....	1973-74	1979-80
Gratton, Gilles	St.L., NYR	2	47	13	18	9	2299	154	0	4.02	....	....	....	....	....	....	....	....	1975-76	1976-77
Gray, Gerry	Det., NYI	2	8	1	5	1	440	35	0	4.77	....	....	....	....	....	....	....	....	1970-71	1972-73
Gray, Harrison	Det.	1	1	0	0	0	40	5	0	730	....	....	....	....	....	....	....	....	1963-64	1963-64
Hainsworth, George	Mtl., Tor.	11	465	246	145	74	29415	937	94	1.91	52	21	26	5	3486	112	8	1.93	1926-27	1936-37
Hall, Glenn	Det., Chi., St.L.	18	906	407	327	165	53484	2239	84	2.51	115	49	65	....	6899	321	6	2.79	1952-53	1970-71
Hamel, Pierre	Tor., Wpg.	4	69	13	41	7	3766	276	0	4.40	....	....	....	....	....	....	....	....	1974-75	1980-81
Harrison, Paul	Min., Tor., Pit., Buf.	7	109	28	53	8	5806	408	2	4.22	4	0	1	....	157	9	0	3.44	1975-76	1981-82
Head, Don	Bos.	1	38	9	26	3	2280	161	2	4.24	....	....	....	....	....	....	....	....	1961-62	1961-62
Hebert, Sammy	Tor., Ott.	2	4	1	3	0	200	19	0	5.70	....	....	....	....	....	....	....	....	1917-18	1923-24
Heinz, Rick	St.L., Van.	5	49	14	19	5	2356	159	2	4.05	1	0	0	....	8	1	0	7.50	1980-81	1984-85
Henderson, John	Bos.	2	46	15	15	15	2700	113	5	2.51	2	0	2	....	120	8	0	4.00	1954-55	1955-56
Henry, Gord	Bos.	4	3	1	2	0	180	5	1	1.67	5	0	4	....	283	21	0	4.45	1948-49	1952-53
Henry, Jim	NYR, Chi., Bos.	9	404	159	178	67	24240	1166	28	2.88	29	11	18	....	1741	81	2	2.79	1941-42	1954-55
Herron, Denis	Pit., K.C., Mtl.	14	462	146	203	76	25608	1579	10	3.70	15	5	10	....	901	50	0	3.33	1972-73	1985-86
Highton, Hec	Chi.	1	24	10	14	0	1440	108	0	4.50	....	....	....	....	....	....	....	....	1943-44	1943-44
Himes, Normie	NYA	2	2	0	0	1	79	3	0	2.28	....	....	....	....	....	....	....	....	1927-28	1928-29
Hodge, Charlie	Mtl., Oak., Van.	13	358	152	124	60	20593	927	24	2.70	16	6	8	....	803	32	2	2.39	1954-55	1970-71
Hoganson, Paul	Pit.	1	2	0	1	0	57	7	0	7.37	....	....	....	....	....	....	....	....	1970-71	1970-71
Hogosta, Goran	NYI, Que.	2	22	5	12	3	1208	83	1	4.12	....	....	....	....	....	....	....	....	1977-78	1979-80
Holden, Mark	Mtl., Wpg.	4	8	2	2	1	372	25	0	4.03	....	....	....	....	....	....	....	....	1981-82	1984-85
Holland, Ken	Hfd.	1	1	0	1	0	60	7	0	7.00	....	....	....	....	....	....	....	....	1980-81	1980-81
Holland, Robbie	Pit.	2	44	11	22	9	2513	171	1	4.06	....	....	....	....	....	....	....	....	1979-80	1980-81
Holmes, Harry	Tor., Det.	4	105	41	54	10	6510	264	17	2.43	7	4	3	....	420	26	0	3.71	1917-18	1927-28
Horner, Red	Tor.	1	1	0	0	0	1	1	0	60.00	....	....	....	....	....	....	....	....	1932-33	1932-33
Inness, Gary	Pit., Phi., Wsh.	7	162	58	61	27	8710	494	2	3.40	9	5	4	....	540	24	0	2.67	1973-74	1980-81
Ireland, Randy	Buf.	1	2	0	0	0	30	3	0	6.00	....	....	....	....	....	....	....	....	1978-79	1978-79
Irons, Robbie	St.L.	1	1	0	0	0	3	0	0	0.00	....	....	....	....	....	....	....	....	1968-69	1968-69
Ironstone, Joe	NYA, Tor.	2	2	1	1	0	110	3	0	1.64	....	....	....	....	....	....	....	....	1925-26	1927-28
Jackson, Doug	Chi.	1	6	2	3	1	360	42	0	7.00	....	....	....	....	....	....	....	....	1947-48	1947-48
Jackson, Percy	Bos., NYA, NYR	4	7	1	3	1	392	26	0	3.98	....	....	....	....	....	....	....	....	1931-32	1935-36
Janaszak, Steve	Min., Col.	2	3	0	1	1	160	15	0	5.63	....	....	....	....	....	....	....	....	1979-80	1981-82
Janecyk, Bob	Chi., L.A.	6	110	43	47	13	6250	432	2	4.15	3	0	3	....	184	10	0	3.26	1983-84	1988-89
Jenkins, Roger	NYA	1	1	0	1	0	30	7	0	14.00	....	....	....	....	....	....	....	....	1938-39	1938-39
Jensen, Al	Det., Wsh., L.A.	7	179	95	53	18	9974	557	8	3.35	12	5	5	....	598	32	0	3.21	1980-81	1986-87
Jensen, Darren	Phi.	2	30	15	10	1	1496	95	2	3.81	....	....	....	....	....	....	....	....	1984-85	1985-86
Johnson, Bob	St.L., Pit.	2	24	9	9	1	1059	66	0	3.74	....	....	....	....	....	....	....	....	1972-73	1974-75
Johnston, Eddie	Bos., Tor., St.L., Chi.	16	592	236	256	87	34209	1855	32	3.25	18	7	10	....	1023	57	1	3.34	1962-63	1977-78
Junkin, Joe	Bos.	1	1	0	0	0	8	0	0	0.00	....	....	....	....	....	....	....	....	1968-69	1968-69
Kaarela, Jari	Col.	1	5	2	2	0	220	22	0	6.00	....	....	....	....	....	....	....	....	1980-81	1980-81
Kampurri, Hannu	N.J.	1	13	1	10	1	645	54	0	5.02	....	....	....	....	....	....	....	....	1984-85	1984-85
Karakas, Mike	Chi., Mtl.	8	336	114	169	53	20616	1002	28	2.92	23	11	12	....	1434	72	3	3.01	1935-36	1945-46
Keans, Doug	L.A., Bos.	9	210	96	64	26	11388	666	4	3.51	9	2	6		432	34	0	4.72	1979-80	1987-88
Keenan, Don	Bos.	1	1	0	1	0	60	4	0	4.00	....	....	....	....	....	....	....	....	1958-59	1958-59
Kerr, Dave	Mtl.M., NYA, NYR	11	426	203	148	75	26519	960	51	2.17	40	18	19	3	2616	76	8	1.74	1930-31	1940-41
Kleisinger, Terry	NYR	1	4	0	2	0	191	14	0	4.40	....	....	....	....	....	....	....	....	1985-86	1985-86
Klymkiw, Julian	NYR	1	1	0	0	0	19	2	0	6.32	....	....	....	....	....	....	....	....	1958-59	1958-59
Kurt, Gary	Cal.	1	16	1	7	5	838	60	0	4.30	....	....	....	....	....	....	....	....	1971-72	1971-72
Lacroix, Al	Mtl.	1	5	1	4	0	280	16	0	3.20	....	....	....	....	....	....	....	....	1925-26	1925-26
LaFerriere, Rick	Col.	1	1	0	0	0	20	1	0	3.00	....	....	....	....	....	....	....	....	1981-82	1981-82
Larocque, Michel	Mtl., Tor., Phi., St.L.	11	312	160	89	45	17615	978	17	3.33	14	6	6	....	759	37	1	2.92	1973-74	1983-84
Laskowski, Gary	L.A.	2	59	19	27	5	2942	228	0	4.65	....	....	....	....	....	....	....	....	1982-83	1983-84
Laxton, Gord	Pit.	4	17	4	9	0	800	74	0	5.55	....	....	....	....	....	....	....	....	1975-76	1978-79
LeDuc, Albert	Mtl.	1	1	0	0	0	2	1	0	30.00	....	....	....	....	....	....	....	....	1931-32	1931-32
Legris, Claude	Det.	2	4	0	1	1	91	4	0	2.64	....	....	....	....	....	....	....	....	1980-81	1981-82
Lehman, Hugh	Chi.	2	48	20	24	4	3047	136	6	2.68	2	0	1	1	120	10	0	5.00	1926-27	1927-28
Lessard, Mario	L.A.	6	240	92	97	39	13529	843	9	3.74	20	6	12	....	1136	83	0	4.38	1978-79	1983-84
Levasseur, Louis	Min.	1	1	0	1	0	60	7	0	7.00	....	....	....	....	....	....	....	....	1979-80	1979-80
Levinsky, Alex	Tor.	1	1	0	0	0	1	1	0	60.00	....	....	....	....	....	....	....	....	1932-33	1932-33
Lindbergh, Pelle	Phi.	5	157	87	49	15	9151	503	7	3.30	23	12	10	....	1214	63	3	3.11	1981-82	1985-86
Lindsay, Bert	Mtl.W., Tor.	2	20	6	14	0	2219	118	0	3.19	....	....	....	....	....	....	....	....	1917-18	1918-19
Lockett, Ken	Van.	2	55	13	15	8	2348	131	2	3.35	1	0	1	...	60	6	0	6.00	1974-75	1975-76
Lockhart, Howie	Tor., Que., Ham., Bos.	5	57	17	39	0	3371	282	1	5.02	....	....	....	....	....	....	....	....	1919-20	1924-25
LoPresti, Pete	Min., Edm.	6	175	43	102	20	9858	668	5	4.07	2	0	2	....	77	6	0	4.68	1974-75	1980-81
LoPresti, Sam	Chi.	2	74	30	38	6	4530	236	4	3.13	8	3	5	....	530	17	1	1.92	1940-41	1941-42
Loustel, Ron	Wpg.	1	1	0	1	0	60	10	0	10.00	....	....	....	....	....	....	....	....	1980-81	1980-81
Low, Ron	Tor., Wsh., Det., Que., Edm., NJ	11	382	102	203	37	20502	1463	4	4.28	7	1	6	....	452	29	0	3.85	1972-73	1984-85
Lozinski, Larry	Det.	1	30	6	11	7	1459	105	0	4.32	....	....	....	....	....	....	....	....	1980-81	1980-81
Lumley, Harry	Det., NYR, Chi., Tor., Bos.	16	804	332	324	143	48107	2210	71	2.76	76	29	47	....	4759	199	7	2.51	1943-44	1959-60
MacKenzie, Shawn	N.J.	1	4	0	1	0	130	15	0	6.92	....	....	....	....	....	....	....	....	1982-83	1982-83
Maniago, Cesare	Tor., Mtl., NYR, Min., Van.	15	568	189	261	96	32570	1774	30	3.27	36	15	21	....	2245	100	3	2.67	1960-61	1977-78
Marios, Jean	Tor., Chi.	2	3	1	2	0	180	15	0	5.00	....	....	....	....	....	....	....	....	1943-44	1953-54
Martin, Seth	St.L.	1	30	8	10	7	1552	67	1	2.59	2	0	0	....	73	5	0	4.11	1967-68	1967-68
Mattson, Markus	Wpg., Min., L.A.	4	92	21	46	14	5007	343	6	4.11	....	....	....	....	....	....	....	....	1979-80	1983-84
May, Darrell	St.L.	2	6	1	5	0	364	31	0	5.11	....	....	....	....	....	....	....	....	1985-86	1987-88
Mayer, Gilles	Tor.	4	9	1	7	1	540	25	0	2.78	....	....	....	....	....	....	....	....	1949-50	1955-56
McAuley, Ken	NYR	2	96	17	64	15	5740	537	1	5.61	....	....	....	....	....	....	....	....	1943-44	1944-45
McCartan, Jack	NYR	2	12	3	7	2	680	43	1	3.79	....	....	....	....	....	....	....	....	1959-60	1960-61
McCool, Frank	Tor.	2	72	34	31	7	4320	242	4	3.36	13	8	5	....	807	30	4	2.23	1944-45	1945-46
McDuffe, Pete	St.L., NYR, K.C., Det.	5	57	11	36	6	3207	218	0	4.08	1	0	1	....	60	7	0	7.00	1971-72	1975-76
McGrattan, Tom	Det.	1	1	0	0	0	8	0	0	0.00	....	....	....	....	....	....	....	....	1947-48	1947-48
McKenzie, Bill	Det., K.C., Col.	6	91	18	49	13	4776	326	2	4.10	....	....	....	....	....	....	....	....	1973-74	1979-80
McLachlan, Murray	Tor.	1	2	0	1	0	25	4	0	9.60	....	....	....	....	....	....	....	....	1970-71	1970-71
McLelland, Dave	Van.	1	2	1	1	0	120	10	0	5.00	....	....	....	....	....	....	....	....	1972-73	1972-73
McLeod, Don	Det., Phi.	2	18	3	10	1	879	74	0	5.05	....	....	....	....	....	....	....	....	1970-71	1971-72
McLeod, Jim	St.L.	1	16	6	6	4	880	44	0	3.00	....	....	....	....	....	....	....	....	1971-72	1971-72
McNamara, Gerry	Tor.	2	7	2	2	1	323	15	0	2.79	....	....	....	....	....	....	....	....	1960-61	1969-70
McNeil, Gerry	Mtl.	7	276	119	105	52	16535	650	28	2.36	35	17	18	....	2284	72	5	1.89	1947-48	1956-57
McRae, Gord	Tor.	5	71	21	32	10	3799	221	1	3.49	8	2	5	....	454	22	0	2.91	1972-73	1977-78
Meloche, Gilles	Chi., Cal., Cle., Min., Pit.	18	788	270	351	131	45401	2756	20	3.64	45	21	19	....	2464	143	2	3.48	1970-71	1987-88
Micalef, Corrado	Det.	5	113	26	59	15	5794	409	2	4.24	3	0	0	....	49	8	0	9.80	1981-82	1985-86
Middlebrook, Lindsay	Wpg., Min., N.J., Edm.	4	37	3	23	6	1845	152	0	4.94	....	....	....	....	....	....	....	....	1979-80	1982-83
Millar, Joe	Bos.	1	6	1	3	2	360	25	0	4.17	....	....	....	....	....	....	....	....	1957-58	1957-58

Name	NHL Teams	NHL Seasons	Regular Schedule								Playoffs								First NHL Season	Last NHL Season
			GP	W	L	T	Mins	GA	SO	Avg	GP	W	L	T	Mins	GA	SO	Avg		
Miller, Joe	NYA, Pit., Phi.	4	130	24	90	16	7981	386	16	2.90	3	2	1	....	180	3	1	1.00	1927-28	1930-31
Mio, Eddie	Edm., NYR, Det.	7	192	83	85	31	12299	822	6	4.01	17	9	7	....	986	63	0	3.83	1979-80	1985-86
Mitchell, Ivan	Tor.	3	21	11	9	0	1232	93	0	4.53	....	....	....	....	....	....	....	....	1919-20	1921-22
Moffatt, Mike	Bos.	3	19	7	7	2	979	70	0	4.29	11	6	5	....	663	38	0	3.44	1981-82	1983-84
Moore, Alfie	NYA, Det., Chi.,	4	21	7	14	0	1290	81	1	3.77	3	1	2	....	180	7	0	2.33	1936-37	1939-40
Moore, Robbie	Phi., Wsh.	2	6	3	1	1	257	8	2	1.87	5	3	2	....	268	18	0	4.03	1978-79	1982-83
Morisette, Jean	Mtl.	1	1	0	1	0	36	4	0	6.67	....	....	....	....	....	....	....	....	1963-64	1963-64
Mowers, Johnny	Det.	4	152	65	55	25	9350	399	15	2.56	32	19	13	....	2000	85	2	2.55	1940-41	1946-47
Mrazek, Jerry	Phi.	1	1	0	0	0	6	1	0	10.00	....	....	....	....	....	....	....	....	1975-76	1975-76
Mummery, Harry	Que., Ham.	2	4	2	1	0	191	20	0	6.28	....	....	....	....	....	....	....	....	1919-20	1921-22
Murphy, Hal	Mtl.	1	1	1	0	0	60	4	0	4.00	....	....	....	....	....	....	....	....	1952-53	1952-53
Murray, Tom	Mtl.	1	1	0	1	0	60	4	0	4.00	....	....	....	....	....	....	....	....	1929-30	1929-30
Myre, Phil	Mtl., Atl., St.L., Phi., Col., Buf.	14	439	149	198	76	25220	1482	14	3.53	12	6	5	....	747	41	1	3.29	1969-70	1982-83
Newton, Cam	Pit.	2	16	4	7	1	814	51	0	3.76	....	....	....	....	....	....	....	....	1970-71	1972-73
Norris, Jack	Bos., Chi., L.A.	4	58	19	26	4	3119	202	2	3.89	....	....	....	....	....	....	....	....	1964-65	1970-71
Oleschuk, Bill	K.C., Col.	4	55	7	28	10	2835	188	1	3.98	....	....	....	....	....	....	....	....	1975-76	1979-80
Olesevich, Dan	NYR	1	1	0	0	1	40	2	0	3.00	....	....	....	....	....	....	....	....	1961-62	1961-62
Ouimet, Ted	St.L.	1	1	0	1	0	60	2	0	2.00	....	....	....	....	....	....	....	....	1968-69	1968-69
Pageau, Paul	L.A.	1	1	0	1	0	60	8	0	8.00	....	....	....	....	....	....	....	....	1980-81	1980-81
Paille, Marcel	NYR	7	107	33	52	21	6342	362	2	3.42	....	....	....	....	....	....	....	....	1957-58	1964-65
Palmateer, Mike	Tor., Wsh.	8	356	149	138	52	20131	1183	17	3.53	29	12	17	....	1765	89	2	3.03	1976-77	1983-84
Parent, Bernie	Bos., Tor., Phi.	13	608	270	197	121	35136	1493	55	2.55	71	38	33	....	4302	174	6	2.43	1965-66	1978-79
Parent, Bob	Tor.	2	3	0	2	0	160	15	0	5.63	....	....	....	....	....	....	....	....	1981-82	1982-83
Parro, Dave	Wsh.	4	77	21	36	10	4015	274	2	4.09	....	....	....	....	....	....	....	....	1980-81	1983-84
Patrick, Lester	NYR	....	....	....	....	....	....	....	....	....	1	1	0	0	46	1	0	1.30	1927-28	1927-28
Pelletier, Marcel	Chi., NYR	2	8	1	6	1	395	33	0	5.01	....	....	....	....	....	....	....	....	1950-51	1962-63
Penney, Steve	Mtl., Wpg.	5	91	35	38	12	5194	313	1	3.62	27	15	12	....	1604	72	4	2.69	1983-84	1987-88
Perreault, Robert	Mtl., Det., Bos.	3	31	8	16	6	1833	106	2	3.47	....	....	....	....	....	....	....	....	1955-56	1962-63
Pettie, Jim	Bos.	3	21	9	7	2	1157	71	1	3.68	....	....	....	....	....	....	....	....	1976-77	1978-79
Plante, Jacques	Mtl., NYR, St.L., Tor., Bos.	18	837	434	246	137	49553	1965	82	2.38	112	71	37	....	6651	241	15	2.17	1952-53	1972-73
Plasse, Michel	St.L., Mtl., K.C., Pit., Col., Que.	11	299	92	136	54	16760	1058	2	3.79	4	1	2	....	195	9	1	2.77	1970-71	1981-82
Plaxton, Hugh	Mtl.M.	1	1	0	1	0	59	5	0	5.08	....	....	....	....	....	....	....	....	1932-33	1932-33
Pronovost, Claude	Bos., Mtl.	2	3	1	1	0	120	7	1	3.50	....	....	....	....	....	....	....	....	1955-56	1958-59
Pusey, Chris	Det.	1	1	0	0	0	40	3	0	4.50	....	....	....	....	....	....	....	....	1985-86	1985-86
Rayner, Chuck	NYA, NYR	10	424	138	209	77	25491	1294	25	3.05	18	9	9	....	1134	46	1	2.43	1940-41	1952-53
Redquest, Greg	Pit.	1	1	0	0	0	13	3	0	13.85	....	....	....	....	....	....	....	....	1977-78	1977-78
Reece, Dave	Bos.	1	14	7	5	2	777	43	2	3.32	....	....	....	....	....	....	....	....	1975-76	1975-76
Resch, Glenn	NYI, Col., N.J., Phi.	14	571	231	224	82	32279	1761	26	3.27	41	17	17	....	2044	85	2	2.50	1973-74	1986-87
Rheaume, Herb	Mtl.	1	31	10	19	1	1889	92	0	2.97	....	....	....	....	....	....	....	....	1925-26	1925-26
Ricci, Nick	Pit.	4	19	7	12	0	1087	79	0	4.36	....	....	....	....	....	....	....	....	1979-80	1982-83
Richardson, Terry	Det., St.L.	5	20	3	11	0	906	85	0	5.63	....	....	....	....	....	....	....	....	1973-74	1978-79
Ridley, Curt	NYR, Van., Tor.	6	104	27	47	16	5498	355	1	3.87	2	0	2	....	120	8	0	4.00	1974-75	1980-81
Riggin, Denis	Det.	2	18	5	10	2	985	54	1	3.29	....	....	....	....	....	....	....	....	1959-60	1962-63
Riggin, Pat	Atl., Cgy., Wsh., Bos., Pit.	9	350	153	120	52	19872	1135	11	3.43	25	8	13	....	1336	72	0	3.23	1979-80	1987-88
Ring, Bob	Bos.	1	1	0	0	0	34	4	0	7.06	....	....	....	....	....	....	....	....	1965-66	1965-66
Rivard, Fern	Min.	4	55	9	20	7	2865	190	2	3.98	....	....	....	....	....	....	....	....	1968-69	1974-75
Roach, John	Tor., NYR, Det.	14	491	218	204	69	30423	1246	58	2.46	34	15	16	3	2206	69	8	1.88	1921-22	1934-35
Roberts, Moe	Bos., NYA, Chi.	4	10	2	5	0	506	31	0	3.68	....	....	....	....	....	....	....	....	1925-26	1951-52
Robertson, Earl	NYA, Det.	6	190	60	95	34	11820	575	16	2.92	15	6	7	....	995	29	2	1.75	1936-37	1941-42
Rollins, Al	Tor., Chi., NYR	9	430	138	205	84	25717	1196	28	2.79	13	6	7	....	755	30	0	2.38	1949-50	1950 60
Romano, Roberto	Pit., Bos.	5	125	45	64	7	7046	474	4	4.04	....	....	....	....	....	....	....	....	1982-83	1986-87
Rupp, Pat	Det.	1	1	0	1	0	60	4	0	4.00	....	....	....	....	....	....	....	....	1963-64	1963-64
Rutherford, Jim	Det., Pit., Tor., L.A.	13	457	150	227	59	25895	1576	14	3.65	8	2	5	....	440	28	0	3.82	1970-71	1982-83
Rutledge, Wayne	L.A.	3	82	22	30	5	4325	241	2	3.34	8	2	2	....	378	20	0	3.17	1967-68	1969-70
St.Croix, Rick	Phi., Tor.	8	129	49	54	18	7275	450	2	3.71	11	4	6	....	562	29	1	3.10	1977-78	1984-85
Sands, Charlie	Mtl.	1	1	0	0	0	25	5	0	12.00	....	....	....	....	....	....	....	....	1939-40	1939-40
Sands, Mike	Min.	2	6	0	5	0	302	26	0	5.17	....	....	....	....	....	....	....	....	1984-85	1986-87
Sauve, Bob	Buf., Det., Chi., N.J.	12	405	178	149	53	22991	1321	8	3.45	34	15	16		1850	95	4	3.08	1976-77	1987-88
Sawchuk, Terry	Det., Bos., Tor., L.A., NYR	21	971	435	337	188	57205	2401	103	2.52	106	54	48	....	6291	267	12	2.64	1949-50	1969-70
Schaefer, Joe	NYR	2	2	0	1	0	86	8	0	5.58	....	....	....	....	....	....	....	....	1959-60	1960-61
Sevigny, Richard	Mtl., Que.	8	176	90	44	20	9485	507	5	3.21	6	0	3	....	208	13	0	3.75	1979-80	1986-87
Shields, Al	NYA	1	2	0	0	0	41	9	0	13.17	....	....	....	....	....	....	....	....	1931-32	1931-32
Simmons, Don	Bos., Tor., NYR	11	247	100	104	39	14436	705	20	2.93	24	13	11	....	1436	64	3	2.67	1956-57	1968-69
Simmons, Gary	Cal., Clev., L.A.	4	107	30	57	15	6162	366	5	3.56	1	0	0	....	20	1	0	3.00	1974-75	1977-78
Skidmore, Paul	St.L.	1	2	1	1	0	120	6	0	3.00	....	....	....	....	....	....	....	....	1981-82	1981-82
Smith, Al	Tor., Pit., Det., Buf., Hfd., Col.	10	233	68	99	36	12752	735	10	3.46	6	1	4	....	317	21	0	3.97	1965-66	1980-81
Smith, Billy	L.A., NYI	18	680	305	233	105	38431	2031	22	3.17	132	88	36		7645	348	5	2.73	1971-72	1988-89
Smith, Gary	Tor., Oak., Cal., Chi., Van., Min., Wsh., Wpg.	14	532	152	237	67	29619	1675	26	3.39	20	5	13	....	1153	62	1	3.23	1965-66	1979-80
Smith, Norman	Mtl.M., Det.	8	199	81	83	35	12297	475	17	2.32	12	9	2	....	880	18	3	1.23	1931-32	1944-45
Sneddon, Bob	Cal.	1	5	0	2	0	225	21	0	5.60	....	....	....	....	....	....	....	....	1970-71	1970-71
Soetaert, Doug	NYR, Wpg., Mtl.	12	284	110	103	44	15583	1030	6	3.97	5	1	2	....	180	14	0	4.67	1975-76	1986-87
Spooner, Red	Pit.	1	1	0	1	0	60	6	0	6.00	....	....	....	....	....	....	....	....	1929-30	1929-30
Staniowski, Ed	St.L., Wpg., Hfd.	10	219	67	104	21	12075	818	2	4.06	8	1	6	....	428	28	0	3.92	1975-76	1984-85
Starr, Harold	Mtl.M.	1	1	0	0	0	3	0	0	0.00	....	....	....	....	....	....	....	....	1931-32	1931-32
Stein, Phil	Tor.	1	1	0	0	1	70	2	0	1.71	....	....	....	....	....	....	....	....	1939-40	1939-40
Stephenson, Wayne	St.L., Phi., Wsh.	10	328	146	93	46	18343	937	14	3.06	26	11	12	....	1522	79	2	3.11	1971-72	1980-81
Stevenson, Doug	NYR, Chi.	2	8	2	6	0	480	39	0	4.88	....	....	....	....	....	....	....	....	1944-45	1945-46
Stewart, Charles	Bos.	3	77	31	41	5	4737	194	10	2.46	....	....	....	....	....	....	....	....	1924-25	1926-27
Stewart, Jim	Bos.	1	1	0	1	0	20	5	0	15.00	....	....	....	....	....	....	....	....	1979-80	1979-80
Stuart, Herb	Det.	1	3	0	1	0	180	5	0	1.67	....	....	....	....	....	....	....	....	1926-27	1926-27
Sylvestri, Don	Bos.	1	3	0	0	2	102	6	0	3.53	....	....	....	....	....	....	....	....	1984-85	1984-85
Tataryn, Dave	NYR	1	2	1	1	0	80	10	0	7.50	....	....	....	....	....	....	....	....	1976-77	1976-77
Taylor, Bobby	Phi., Pit.	5	46	15	17	6	2268	155	0	4.10	....	....	....	....	....	....	....	....	1971-72	1975-70
Teno, Harvey	Det.	1	5	2	3	0	3.00	15	0	3.00	....	....	....	....	....	....	....	....	1938-39	1938-39
Thomas, Wayne	Mtl., Tor., NYR	8	243	103	93	34	13768	766	10	3.34	15	6	8	....	849	50	1	3.53	1972-73	1980-81
Thompson, Tiny	Bos., Det.	12	553	284	194	75	34174	1183	81	2.08	44	20	22	....	2970	93	7	1.88	1928-29	1939-40
Tremblay, Vince	Tor., Pit.	5	58	12	26	8	2785	223	1	4.80	....	....	....	....	....	....	....	....	1979-80	1983-84
Tucker, Ted	Cal.	1	5	1	1	1	177	10	0	3.39	....	....	....	....	....	....	....	....	1973-74	1973-74
Turner, Joe	Det.	1	1	0	0	1	60	3	0	3.00	....	....	....	....	....	....	....	....	1941-42	1941-42
Vachon, Rogatien	Mtl., L.A., Det., Bos.	16	795	355	291	115	46298	2310	51	2.99	48	23	23	....	2876	133	2	2.77	1966-67	1981-82
Veisor, Mike	Chi., Hfd., Wpg.	10	139	41	62	26	7806	532	5	4.09	4	0	2	....	180	15	0	5.00	1973-74	1983-84
Vezina, Georges	Mtl.	9	191	105	80	5	11564	633	13	3.28	26	19	6	....	1596	74	4	2.78	1917-18	1925-26
Villemure, Gilles	NYR, Chi.	10	205	98	65	27	11581	542	13	2.81	14	5	5	....	656	32	0	2.93	1963-64	1976-77
Wakely, Ernie	Mtl., St.L.	5	113	41	42	17	6344	290	8	2.79	10	2	6	....	509	37	1	4.36	1962-63	1971-72
Walsh, James	Mtl.M., NYA	7	108	48	43	16	6461	250	12	2.32	8	2	4	2	570	16	2	1.68	1926-27	1932-33
Watt, Jim	St.L.	1	1	0	0	0	20	2	0	6.00	....	....	....	....	....	....	....	....	1973-74	1973-74
Wetzel, Carl	Det., Min.	2	7	1	3	1	302	22	0	4.37	....	....	....	....	....	....	....	....	1964-65	1967-68
Wilson, Dunc	Phi., Van., Tor., NYR, Pit.	10	287	80	150	33	15851	988	8	3.74	....	....	....	....	....	....	....	....	1969-70	1978-79
Wilson, Lefty	Det., Tor., Bos.	3	3	0	0	1	85	1	0	0.71	....	....	....	....	....	....	....	....	1953-54	1957-58
Winkler, Hal	NYR, Bos.	2	75	35	26	14	4739	126	21	1.60	10	2	3	5	640	18	2	1.69	1926-27	1927-28
Wolfe, Bernie	Wsh.	4	120	20	61	21	6104	424	1	4.17	....	....	....	....	....	....	....	....	1975-76	1978-79
Woods, Alec	NYA	1	1	0	1	0	70	3	0	2.57	....	....	....	....	....	....	....	....	1936-37	1936-37
Worsley, Gump	NYR, Mtl., Min.	21	862	335	353	150	50232	2432	43	2.90	70	41	25	....	4081	192	5	2.82	1952-53	1973-74
Worters, Roy	Pit., NYA, Mtl.	12	484	171	233	68	30175	1143	66	2.27	11	3	6	2	690	24	3	2.09	1925-26	1936-37
Worthy, Chris	Oak., Cal.	3	26	5	10	4	1326	98	0	4.43	....	....	....	....	....	....	....	....	1968-69	1970-71
Young, Doug	Det.	1	1	0	0	0	21	1	0	2.86	....	....	....	....	....	....	....	....	1933-34	1933-34
Zanier, Mike	Edm.	1	3	1	1	1	185	12	0	3.89	....	....	....	....	....	....	....	....	1984-85	1984-85

Notes

Vancouver's Trevor Linden

CELEBRATE HOCKEY with NHL publications

Reserve your copy of next year's *NHL Official Guide & Record Book* and order the *NHL Rule Book & Schedule*

A NOTE ABOUT CANADA'S GOODS AND SERVICES TAX

The publisher regrets that all Canadian orders for the *1991-92 NHL Guide & Record Book* must include the new 7% federal goods and services tax. Orders for the 1990-91 edition or for the *NHL Rule Book* received before December 31, 1990 remain tax exempt. If you order in this tax exempt period, please remit $19.45 per copy for the *1990-91 NHL Guide & Record Book*; $5.50 per copy for the *NHL Rule Book*. These prices include postage and handling.

Notes

1989-90 Transactions

August, 1989

22 - **Jiri Latal** traded to Philadelphia by Toronto for Philadelphia's seventh round choice in 1991 Entry Draft.

31 - Rights to **Ed Krayer** traded to Los Angeles by New Jersey for future considerations.

September

1 - **Barry Beck** traded to Los Angeles by NY Rangers for NY Islanders' fourth round choice (**Jeff Nielson**) — previously acquired by Los Angeles — in 1990 Entry Draft.

5 - **Peter Lappin** traded to Minnesota by Calgary for Minnesota's second round choice in 1990 Entry Draft which was later transferred to New Jersey (**Chris Gotziaman**).

7 - **Kris King** traded to NY Rangers by Detroit for **Chris McCrae** and Detroit's fifth round choice (**Tony Burns**) in 1990 Entry Draft which was previously acquired by NY Rangers.

8 - **Mark LaForest** traded to Toronto by Philadelphia for Toronto's sixth round choice in 1991 Entry Draft and its seventh round choice in 1991 Entry Draft (previously obtained from Philadelphia).

14 - **Lee Giffen** traded to NY Rangers by Pittsburgh for future considerations.

27 - **Rik Wilson** traded to St. Louis by Chicago for **Craig Coxe**.

28 - **Eldon Reddick** traded to Edmonton by Winnipeg for future considerations.

- **Keith Acton** and **Pete Peeters** traded to Winnipeg by Philadelphia for future considerations.

- **Bob Gould** traded to Boston by Washington for **Alain Cote**.

- **Jacques Cloutier** traded to Chicago by Buffalo for future considerations.

October

2 - **Randy Exelby** traded to Edmonton by Montreal for future considerations.

- **Mike Millar** traded to Boston by Washington for **Alfie Turcotte**.

- **NHL Waiver Draft**

Player	Claimed by	From
Greg C. Adams	Quebec	Vancouver
Dave Hannan	Toronto	Pittsburgh
Moe Mantha	Winnipeg	Philadelphia
Kent Nilsson	New Jersey	Edmonton
David Mackey	Minnesota	Chicago
Craig Coxe	Vancouver	Chicago
Mikael Andersson	Hartford	Buffalo
Nick Kypreos	Washington	Philadelphia

3 - **Keith Acton** and **Pete Peeters** traded to Philadelphia by Winnipeg for future considerations.

4 - **Dean Kennedy** traded to Buffalo by Los Angeles for Buffalo's fourth round choice in 1991 Entry Draft.

5 - **Michel Petit** traded to Quebec by NY Rangers for **Randy Moller**.

7 - **Kevin Sullivan** traded to Minnesota by Hartford for **Mike Berger**.

10 - **Norm MacIver** traded to Edmonton by Hartford for **Jim Ennis**.

16 - **Tom Kurvers** traded to Toronto by New Jersey for Toronto's first round choice in 1991 Entry Draft.

24 - **Rod Buskas** traded to Vancouver by Pittsburgh for Vancouver's sixth round choice (**Ian Moran**) in 1990 Entry Draft.

31 - **Jim Thomson** traded to New Jersey by Hartford for **Chris Cichocki**.

November

1 - **Jayson More** traded to Minnesota by NY Rangers for **Dave Archibald**.

2 - **Petr Klima**, **Joe Murphy**, **Adam Graves** and **Jeff Sharples** traded to Edmonton by Detroit for **Jimmy Carson**, **Kevin McClelland** and Edmonton's fifth round choice in 1991 Entry Draft.

10 - **Brian Benning** traded to Los Angeles by St. Louis for Los Angeles' third round choice in 1991 Entry Draft.

24 - **Bob Halkidis** and future considerations traded to Los Angeles by Buffalo for **Dale DeGray** and future considerations.

29 - **Mikko Makela** traded to Los Angeles by NY Islanders for **Ken Baumgartner** and **Hubie McDonough**.

December

1 - **Phil Sykes** traded to Winnipeg by Los Angeles for **Brad Jones**.

4 - **Tony McKegney** traded to Quebec by Detroit for **Robert Picard** and **Greg C. Adams**.

12 - **Todd Ewen** traded to Montreal by St. Louis for future considerations.

13 - **Paul MacDermid** traded to Winnipeg by Hartford for **Randy Cunneyworth**.

- **Bob Joyce** traded to Washington by Boston for **Dave Christian**.

- **Tony Hrkac** and **Greg Millen** traded to Quebec by St. Louis for **Jeff Brown**.

20 - **Jack Capuano**, **Paul Gagne** and **Derek Laxdal** traded to NY Islanders by Toronto for **Mike Stevens** and **Gilles Thibaudeau**.

21 - **Vladimir Ruzicka** traded to Edmonton by Toronto for Edmonton's fourth round choice (**Greg Walters**) in 1990 Entry Draft, December 21, 1989.

January 1990

5 - **Jocelyn Lemieux** traded to Chicago by Montreal for Chicago's third round choice (**Charles Poulin**) in 1990 Entry Draft.

- **John Tucker** traded to Washington by Buffalo for future considerations.

- **Aaron Broten** traded to Minnesota by New Jersey for **Bob Brooke**.

- **Normand Lacombe** traded to Philadelphia by Edmonton for future considerations.

8 - **Dave Capuano**, **Andrew McBain** and **Dan Quinn** traded to Vancouver by Pittsburgh for **Rod Buskas**, **Barry Pederson** and **Tony Tanti**.

16 - **Ken Linseman** traded to Philadelphia by Boston for **Dave Poulin**.

18 - **Todd Charlesworth** traded to NY Rangers by Edmonton for future considerations.

20 - **Bernie Nicholls** traded to NY Rangers by Los Angeles for **Tomas Sandstrom** and **Tony Granato**.

22 - **Daniel Berthiaume** traded to Minnesota by Winnipeg for future considerations.

- **Ron Wilson** traded to St. Louis by Winnipeg for **Doug Evans**.

February

26 - **Doug Smith** traded to Pittsburgh by Vancouver for cash.

March

2 - **Brian Propp** traded to Boston by Philadelphia for Boston's second round choice (**Terran Sandwith**) in 1990 Entry Draft.

3 - **Steve Dykstra** traded to Boston by Hartford for **Jeff Sirkka**.

5 - **Greg Millen**, **Michel Goulet** and Quebec's sixth round choice in 1991 Entry Draft traded to Chicago by Quebec for **Mario Doyon**, **Everett Sanipass** and **Dan Vincelette**, March 5, 1990.

- **Kevin Maguire** traded to Philadelphia by Buffalo with Buffalo's second round choice (**Mikael Renberg**) in 1990 Entry Draft for **Jay Wells** and Philadelphia's fourth round choice in 1991 Entry Draft.

- **Mike Liut** traded to Washington by Hartford for **Yvon Corriveau**.

6 - **Adrien Plavsic**, Montreal's first round choice (**Shawn Antoski**) — previously acquired by St. Louis — in 1990 Entry Draft and St. Louis' second round choice in 1991 Entry Draft traded to Vancouver by St. Louis for **Rich Sutter**, **Harold Snepsts** and St. Louis' second round choice (**Craig Johnson**) — previously acquired by Vancouver — in 1990 Entry Draft.

- **Jim Korn** traded to Calgary by New Jersey for Calgary's fifth round choice (**Peter Kuchyna**) in 1990 Entry Draft.

- **Mike Gartner** traded to NY Rangers by Minnesota for **Ulf Dahlen** and Los Angeles' fourth round choice — previously acquired by NY Rangers (**Cal McGowan**) and future considerations.

- **Alain Chevrier** traded to Pittsburgh by Chicago for future considerations.

- **Jack Capuano** traded to Vancouver by NY Islanders for **Jeff Rohlicek**.

- **Jyrki Lumme** traded to Vancouver by Montreal for St. Louis' second round choice is 1991 Entry Draft (previously acquired by Vancouver).

- **Peter Stastny** traded to New Jersey by Quebec for **Craig Wolanin** and future considerations.

- **Jeff Sharples** traded to New Jersey by Edmonton for **Reijo Ruotsalainen**.

- **Brian Wilks** traded to Pittsburgh by Edmonton for future considerations.

- The rights to **Cam Brauer** traded to Hartford by Edmonton for **Marc Laforge**.

June

1 - **Rob Whistle** traded to St. Louis by Washington for St. Louis' eighth round choice (**Steve Martell**) in 1990 Entry Draft.

15 - NHL Supplemental Draft:

Quebec	**Mike McKee** (Princeton)
Vancouver	**Paul Dukovac** (Cornell)
Detroit	**Mike Casselman** (Clarkson)
Philadelphia	**Steve Beadle** (Michigan State)
Pittsburgh	**Joe Dragon** (Cornell)
Quebec	invalid claim
Vancouver	**Norm Krumpschmid** (Ferris State)
Detroit	**Don Oliver** (Ohio State)
Philadelphia	**Ray Letourneau** (Yale)
Pittsburgh	**Savo Mitrovic** (New Hampshire)
NY Islanders	**Brandon Reed** (Lake Superior)
Los Angeles	**Peter Sentner** (Lowell)
Minnesota	**Rod Houk** (U. of Regina)
Washington	**Martin Jiranek** (Bowling Green)
Toronto	**Martin Robitaille** (U. of Maine)
New Jersey	**Mike Haviland** (Elmira)
St. Louis	**Geoff Sarjeant** (Michigan Tech)
NY Rangers	**Mike Gilmore** (Michigan State)
Winnipeg	**Mark Richards** (Lowell)
Hartford	**Jim Crozier** (Cornell)
Chicago	**Claude Maillet** (Merrimack)
Edmonton	**Sandy Galupo** (Boston College)
Montreal	**Bruce Coles** (RPI)
Buffalo	**Shane McFarlane** (North Dakota)
Calgary	**Lyle Wildgoose** (Providence)
Boston	**Howard Rosenblatt** (Merrimack)

- **Rick Green** traded to Detroit by Montreal for Edmonton's fifth round choice — previously acquired by Detroit — in 1991 Entry Draft.

- **Brad McCrimmon** traded to Detroit from Calgary for Detroit's second round pick in the 1990 Entry Draft (later traded to New Jersey (**David Harlock**).

16 - **Dale Hawerchuk**, Winnipeg's first round choice (**Brad May**) in 1990 Entry Draft and future considerations traded to Buffalo by Winnipeg for **Phil Housley**, **Scott Arniel**, **Jeff Parker** and Buffalo's first round choice (**Keith Tkachuk**) in 1990 Entry Draft.

- **Kevin Maguire** and Philadelphia's eighth round choice in 1991 Entry Draft traded to Toronto by Philadelphia for Toronto's third round choice (**Al Kinisky**) in 1990 Entry Draft.

- **Joey Mullen** traded to Pittsburgh by Calgary for Pittsburgh's second round choice (**Nicolas Perreault**) in 1990 Entry Draft.

- NY Rangers received Quebec's fifth round choice (**Sergei Zubov**) in 1990 Entry Draft as compensation for Quebec's signing of **Guy Lafleur**.

- New Jersey's first and second round choices (picks **11** and **32**) in 1990 Entry Draft traded to Calgary for Calgary's first and two second round picks — previously acquired from Detroit and Minnesota — (picks **20**, **24** and **29**) in 1990 Entry Draft.

22 - **Marc Deschamps** traded to Washington by Montreal for **Alain Cote**.

26 - **Sam St. Laurent** traded to NY Rangers by Detroit for cash.

28 - **Chris Nilan** traded to Boston by NY Rangers for **Greg Johnston** and future considerations.

- **Greg Johnston** traded to Toronto by NY Rangers for **Tie Domi** and **Mark LaForest**.

29 - **Denis Savard** traded to Montreal by Chicago for **Chris Chelios** and Montreal's second round draft choice in 1991 Entry Draft.

July

3 - **John Tucker** traded to Buffalo by Washington for cash.

9 - **Jody Hull** traded to NY Rangers by Hartford for **Carey Wilson** and future considerations.

- **Ray Sheppard** traded to NY Rangers by Buffalo for cash and future considerations.

- **Simon Wheeldon** traded to Winnipeg by NY Rangers for **Brian McReynolds**.

16 - **Geoff Courtnall** traded to St. Louis by Washington for **Peter Zezel** and **Mike Lalor**.

August

7 - **Bobby Smith** traded to Minnesota by Montreal for Minnesota's fourth round choice in 1992 Entry Draft.

13 - **Randy Velischek** traded to Quebec by New Jersey to complete March 6, 1990 Peter Stastny–Craig Wolanin deal.

NHL Schedule 1990-91
continued from inside front cover

Game #	Visitor	Home
Thur. Nov. 29		
268	Edmonton	Boston
269	Hartford	Pittsburgh
270	Toronto	Vancouver
271	Detroit	Chicago
272	Los Angeles	St Louis
Fri. Nov. 30		
273	Montreal	Washington
274	NY Islanders	New Jersey
275	NY Rangers	Philadelphia
276	Minnesota	Winnipeg
Sat. Dec. 1		
277	NY Rangers	Boston
278	Edmonton	Hartford
279	Buffalo	Quebec
280	Calgary	Montreal
281	Washington	NY Islanders
282	New Jersey	St Louis
283	Pittsburgh	Minnesota
284	Toronto	Los Angeles
285	*Chicago	Detroit
Sun. Dec. 2		
286	Detroit	Buffalo
287	Calgary	Quebec
288	Edmonton	Philadelphia
289	St Louis	Chicago
290	Vancouver	Winnipeg
Mon. Dec. 3		
291	Hartford	Montreal
292	Pittsburgh	NY Rangers
293	New Jersey	Winnipeg
Tues. Dec. 4		
294	Boston	Detroit
295	Vancouver	NY Islanders
Wed. Dec. 5		
296	Montreal	Hartford
297	Quebec	Edmonton
298	NY Rangers	Calgary
299	Vancouver	New Jersey
300	Washington	Pittsburgh
301	Minnesota	Toronto
302	Winnipeg	Los Angeles
Thur. Dec. 6		
303	Montreal	Boston
304	Buffalo	Philadelphia
305	NY Islanders	Chicago
306	Toronto	Minnesota
Fri. Dec. 7		
307	Hartford	Buffalo
308	Quebec	Calgary
309	NY Rangers	Edmonton
310	New Jersey	Washington
311	Vancouver	Pittsburgh
312	St Louis	Detroit
Sat. Dec. 8		
313	Boston	Montreal
314	Pittsburgh	Hartford
315	Washington	New Jersey
316	Philadelphia	Minnesota
317	Chicago	Toronto
318	Detroit	St Louis
319	Winnipeg	Los Angeles
Sun. Dec. 9		
320	Boston	Buffalo
321	Philadelphia	Chicago
322	Calgary	Edmonton
Mon. Dec. 10		
323	Quebec	Vancouver
Tues. Dec. 11		
324	Buffalo	Detroit
325	New Jersey	NY Islanders
326	NY Rangers	Los Angeles
327	Philadelphia	Washington
328	Chicago	Pittsburgh
329	Winnipeg	St Louis
330	Calgary	Minnesota
Wed. Dec. 12		
331	Boston	Hartford
332	Montreal	Toronto
333	Vancouver	Edmonton
Thur. Dec. 13		
334	Hartford	Boston
335	Quebec	Detroit
336	NY Islanders	Philadelphia
337	New Jersey	Pittsburgh
338	Winnipeg	Chicago
339	Minnesota	St Louis
340	Calgary	Los Angeles
Fri. Dec. 14		
341	Pittsburgh	Buffalo
342	NY Rangers	Vancouver
Sat. Dec. 15		
343	New Jersey	Boston
344	Hartford	Washington
345	Montreal	Winnipeg
346	NY Islanders	Quebec
347	*Detroit	Philadelphia
348	St Louis	Toronto
349	*Chicago	Minnesota
350	Edmonton	Los Angeles
Sun. Dec. 16		
351	St Louis	Buffalo
352	Philadelphia	Winnipeg
353	Detroit	Pittsburgh
354	*Minnesota	Chicago
355	*Calgary	Vancouver
Mon. Dec. 17		
356	Washington	NY Rangers
Tues. Dec. 18		
357	Boston	New Jersey
358	Buffalo	Hartford
359	Montreal	Quebec
360	Toronto	NY Islanders
361	Philadelphia	Detroit
362	Winnipeg	Pittsburgh
363	Vancouver	Calgary
364	Los Angeles	Edmonton
Wed. Dec. 19		
365	Quebec	Montreal
366	Toronto	NY Rangers
367	Washington	Chicago
Thur. Dec. 20		
368	Buffalo	Boston
369	Hartford	NY Islanders
370	New Jersey	Philadelphia
371	Minnesota	Pittsburgh
372	Washington	St Louis
373	Winnipeg	Detroit
374	Los Angeles	Calgary
375	Edmonton	Vancouver
Sat. Dec. 22		
376	Minnesota	Boston
377	Philadelphia	Hartford
378	NY Rangers	Montreal
379	New Jersey	Quebec
380	Pittsburgh	NY Islanders
381	*Toronto	Washington
382	Detroit	Winnipeg
383	Chicago	St Louis
384	Edmonton	Calgary
385	Los Angeles	Vancouver
Sun. Dec. 23		
386	Boston	NY Rangers
387	Minnesota	Hartford
388	Quebec	Buffalo
389	Montreal	Philadelphia
390	NY Islanders	Pittsburgh
391	Toronto	New Jersey
392	Detroit	Chicago
393	Vancouver	Edmonton
Wed. Dec. 26		
394	Boston	Buffalo
395	Hartford	Quebec
396	Pittsburgh	Washington
397	St Louis	Chicago
398	Winnipeg	Minnesota
Thur. Dec. 27		
399	Montreal	Vancouver
400	NY Islanders	New Jersey
401	Philadelphia	Los Angeles
402	St Louis	Toronto
403	Calgary	Edmonton
Fri. Dec. 28		
404	Boston	Winnipeg
405	Chicago	Buffalo
406	NY Rangers	Washington
407	Detroit	Pittsburgh
408	Edmonton	Vancouver
Sat. Dec. 29		
409	Boston	Minnesota
410	Hartford	Calgary
411	Buffalo	New Jersey
412	Montreal	Los Angeles
413	Washington	Quebec
414	Chicago	NY Islanders
415	Philadelphia	St Louis
416	Pittsburgh	Toronto
Sun. Dec. 30		
417	Hartford	Edmonton
418	New Jersey	NY Rangers
Mon. Dec. 31		
419	Philadelphia	Buffalo
420	Montreal	Calgary
421	*Quebec	NY Islanders
422	St Louis	Pittsburgh
423	Chicago	Detroit
424	Los Angeles	Minnesota
425	Vancouver	Winnipeg
Tues. Jan. 1		
426	*New Jersey	Washington
Wed. Jan. 2		
427	Vancouver	Hartford
428	NY Islanders	Buffalo
429	Montreal	Edmonton
430	Los Angeles	NY Rangers
431	Minnesota	Detroit
432	Calgary	Winnipeg
Thur. Jan. 3		
433	Vancouver	Boston
434	Quebec	St Louis
435	Los Angeles	NY Islanders
436	NY Rangers	Pittsburgh
437	New Jersey	Chicago
438	Toronto	Minnesota
Fri. Jan. 4		
439	Winnipeg	Buffalo
440	Philadelphia	Washington
441	Detroit	Edmonton
Sat. Jan. 5		
442	Washington	Boston
443	Winnipeg	Hartford
444	Quebec	Montreal
445	Philadelphia	NY Islanders
446	NY Rangers	St Louis
447	*New Jersey	Pittsburgh
448	Los Angeles	Toronto
449	Detroit	Calgary
450	Vancouver	Minnesota
Sun. Jan. 6		
451	Pittsburgh	Montreal
452	Los Angeles	Chicago
Mon. Jan. 7		
453	Winnipeg	Boston
454	Philadelphia	NY Rangers
Tues. Jan. 8		
455	Boston	Quebec
456	Hartford	Los Angeles
457	Buffalo	Vancouver
458	Minnesota	NY Islanders
459	St Louis	New Jersey
460	Edmonton	Pittsburgh
461	Calgary	Toronto
Wed. Jan. 9		
462	NY Islanders	Montreal
463	St Louis	NY Rangers
464	Edmonton	Detroit
Thur. Jan. 10		
465	Quebec	Boston
466	Hartford	Vancouver
467	Buffalo	Los Angeles
468	Calgary	Pittsburgh
469	Toronto	Chicago
Fri. Jan. 11		
470	NY Rangers	Detroit
471	Calgary	Washington
472	Chicago	Winnipeg
Sat. Jan. 12		
473	Philadelphia	Boston
474	Hartford	Toronto
475	Buffalo	Minnesota
476	Washington	Montreal
477	St Louis	Quebec
478	Detroit	NY Islanders
479	*Edmonton	New Jersey
480	Vancouver	Los Angeles
Sun. Jan. 13		
481	Hartford	NY Rangers
482	St Louis	Montreal
483	NY Islanders	Quebec
484	Edmonton	Philadelphia
485	Minnesota	Chicago
486	Calgary	Winnipeg
Mon. Jan. 14		
487	Detroit	Boston
488	Buffalo	Toronto
489	Los Angeles	New Jersey
Tues. Jan. 15		
490	Boston	NY Islanders
491	Montreal	Minnesota
492	Edmonton	NY Rangers
493	Pittsburgh	Philadelphia
494	Washington	St Louis
495	Winnipeg	Calgary
Wed. Jan. 16		
496	Los Angeles	Hartford
497	Detroit	Buffalo
498	Chicago	New Jersey
499	Winnipeg	Vancouver
Thur. Jan. 17		
500	Los Angeles	Boston
501	Montreal	St Louis
502	Quebec	Philadelphia
503	Edmonton	NY Islanders
504	Chicago	NY Rangers
505	Pittsburgh	Toronto
506	Washington	Minnesota
Sat. Jan. 19		
All-Star Game at Chicago		
Mon. Jan. 21		
507	Minnesota	Winnipeg
Tues. Jan. 22		
508	Boston	Buffalo
509	Toronto	Quebec
510	NY Rangers	NY Islanders
511	New Jersey	Pittsburgh
512	Calgary	Philadelphia
513	Washington	Detroit
514	St Louis	Minnesota
515	Los Angeles	Edmonton
Wed. Jan. 23		
516	Calgary	Hartford
517	Toronto	Montreal
518	Edmonton	Vancouver
Thur. Jan. 24		
519	Hartford	Boston
520	Buffalo	Chicago
521	Quebec	New Jersey
522	Washington	Philadelphia
Fri. Jan. 25		
523	NY Islanders	Winnipeg
524	NY Rangers	Edmonton
525	Minnesota	Washington
526	St Louis	Detroit
527	Los Angeles	Vancouver
Sat. Jan. 26		
528	*Calgary	Boston
529	Philadelphia	Hartford
530	*Buffalo	Montreal
531	Pittsburgh	Quebec
532	Minnesota	New Jersey
533	Toronto	Chicago
534	Detroit	St Louis
535	Vancouver	Los Angeles
Sun. Jan. 27		
536	*Boston	Montreal
537	*Calgary	Buffalo
538	*NY Islanders	Washington
539	*Edmonton	Winnipeg
Mon. Jan. 28		
540	New Jersey	Detroit
541	Minnesota	Toronto
542	Chicago	Vancouver
Tues. Jan. 29		
543	NY Islanders	Hartford
544	Buffalo	St Louis
545	Winnipeg	Quebec
546	Washington	Pittsburgh
Wed. Jan. 30		
547	Winnipeg	Montreal
548	NY Rangers	Calgary
549	New Jersey	Los Angeles
550	Detroit	Minnesota
551	Vancouver	Edmonton
Thur. Jan. 31		
552	Montreal	Boston
553	Hartford	St Louis
554	Quebec	Buffalo
555	Washington	NY Islanders
556	NY Rangers	Vancouver
557	Pittsburgh	Philadelphia
Fri. Feb. 1		
558	Toronto	Detroit
559	Chicago	Edmonton
Sat. Feb. 2		
560	*Boston	Pittsburgh
561	*Hartford	Philadelphia
562	Montreal	NY Islanders
563	Minnesota	Quebec
564	New Jersey	St Louis
565	Winnipeg	Washington
566	Detroit	Toronto
567	Chicago	Calgary
568	Vancouver	Los Angeles